D0722655

HANDBOOK OF
CHILD PSYCHOLOGY

HANDBOOK OF CHILD PSYCHOLOGY

FIFTH EDITION

Volume 1:   Theoretical Models of Human Development

Editor-in-Chief

WILLIAM DAMON

Volume Editor

RICHARD M. LERNER

John Wiley & Sons, Inc.

New York • Chichester • Weinheim • Brisbane • Singapore • Toronto

Publisher: Jeffrey W. Brown

Editor: Kelly A. Franklin

Managing Editor: Maureen B. Drexel

Composition
and Management: Publications Development Company of Texas

This text is printed on acid-free paper.

Copyright © 1998 by John Wiley & Sons, Inc.

All rights reserved. Published simultaneously in Canada.

Reproduction or translation of any part of this work beyond
that permitted by Section 107 or 108 of the 1976 United
States Copyright Act without the permission of the copyright
owner is unlawful. Requests for permission or further
information should be addressed to the Permissions Department,
John Wiley & Sons, Inc.

This publication is designed to provide accurate and authoritative
information in regard to the subject matter covered. It is sold
with the understanding that the publisher is not engaged in
rendering professional services. If legal, accounting, medical,
psychological, or any other expert assistance is required, the
services of a competent professional person should be sought.

Library of Congress Cataloging-in-Publication Data:

Handbook of child psychology / William Damon, editor. — 5th ed.
      p.   cm.
    Includes bibliographical references and index.
    Contents: v. 1. Theoretical models of human development / Richard
M. Lerner, volume editor — v. 2. Cognition, perception, and
language / Deanna Kuhn and Robert Siegler, volume editors — v.
3. Social, emotional, and personality development / Nancy Eisenberg,
volume editor — v. 4. Child psychology in practice / Irving E.
Sigel and K. Ann Renninger, volume editors.
    ISBN 0-471-05527-1 (v. 1 : cloth : alk. paper). — ISBN
0-471-17893-4 (set : alk. paper)
    1. Child psychology. I. Damon, William, 1944–
BF721.H242   1997
155.4—dc21   96-49157

Printed in the United States of America

10 9 8 7 6 5 4 3 2 1

Editorial Advisory Board

Dr. Joseph Campos
University of California
Berkeley, California

Dr. Eileen Mavis Hetherington
University of Virginia
Charlottesville, Virginia

Dr. John F. Flavell
Stanford University
Stanford, California

Dr. Marshall M. Haith
University of Denver
Denver, Colorado

Dr. Paul Mussen
Berkeley, California

Contributors

Paul B. Baltes, Ph.D.
Max Planck Institute for Human Development
Berlin, Germany

Thomas Bidell, Ph.D.
Boston College School of Education
Chestnut Hill, Massachusetts

Jochen Brandtstädter, Ph.D.
Universität Trier
Trier, Germany

Urie Bronfenbrenner, Ph.D.
Human Development and Family Studies
Cornell University
Ithaca, New York

Robert B. Cairns, Ph.D.
Social Development Research Center
University of North Carolina
Chapel Hill, North Carolina

Mihaly Csikszentmihalyi, Ph.D.
Committee on Human Development
University of Chicago
Chicago, Illinois

Jack Demick, Ph.D.
Department of Psychology
Suffolk University
Boston, Massachusetts

Glen H. Elder, Jr., Ph.D.
Carolina Population Center
University of North Carolina
Chapel Hill, North Carolina

Kurt W. Fischer, Ph.D.
Department of Psychology
Harvard University
Cambridge, Massachusetts

Celia B. Fisher, Ph.D.
Department of Psychology
Fordham University
Bronx, New York

Howard E. Gardner, Ph.D.
Department of Psychology
Harvard University
Cambridge, Massachusetts

Jacqueline Goodnow, Ph.D.
School of Behavioural Sciences
Macquarie University
North Ryde, New South Wales, Australia

Gilbert Gottlieb, Ph.D.
Center for Developmental Science
University of North Carolina
Chapel Hill, North Carolina

Giyoo Hatano, Ph.D.
Department of Human Relations
Keio University
Tokyo, Japan

Jacquelyne Faye Jackson, Ph.D.
Institute of Human Development
University of California—Berkeley
Berkeley, California

Frank C. Keil, Ph.D.
Department of Psychology
Cornell University
Ithaca, New York

Richard M. Lerner, Ph.D.
Center for Child, Family, and Community Partnerships
Boston College
Chestnut Hill, Massachusetts

Robert LeVine, Ph.D.
Graduate School of Education
Harvard University
Cambridge, Massachusetts

Robert Lickliter, Ph.D.
Department of Psychology
VPI & State University
Blacksburg, Virginia

Ulman Lindenberger, Ph.D.
Max Planck Institute for Human Development
Berlin, Germany

David Magnusson, Ph.D.
Psykologiska Institutionen
Stockholms Universitet
Stockholm, Sweden

Hazel Markus, Ph.D.
Department of Psychology
Stanford University
Stanford, California

Peggy J. Miller, Ph.D.
Department of Speech Communication
University of Illinois
Urbana, Illinois

Pamela A. Morris, Ph.D.
Human Development and Family Studies
Cornell University
Ithaca, New York

Elissa L. Newport, Ph.D.
Department of Brain and Cognitive Sciences
University of Rochester
Rochester, New York

Willis F. Overton, Ph.D.
Department of Psychology
Temple University
Philadelphia, Pennsylvania

Kevin Rathunde, Ph.D.
Department of Family and Consumer Sciences
The University of Utah
Salt Lake City, Utah

Richard A. Shweder, Ph.D.
Committee on Human Development
University of Chicago
Chicago, Illinois

Linda B. Smith, Ph.D.
Department of Psychology
Indiana University
Bloomington, Indiana

Elizabeth S. Spelke, Ph.D.
Department of Brain and Cognitive Sciences
Massachusetts Institute of Technology
Cambridge, Massachusetts

Håkan Stattin, Ph.D.
Department of Social Sciences
University of Örebro
Örebro, Sweden

Ursula M. Staudinger, Ph.D.
Max Planck Institute for
    Human Development
Berlin, Germany

Esther Thelen, Ph.D.
Department of Psychology
Indiana University
Bloomington, Indiana

Jaan Valsiner, Ph.D.
Department of Psychology
Clark University
Worcester, Massachusetts

Francisco A. Villarruel, Ph.D.
Institute for Children, Youth, and Family
Michigan State University
East Lansing, Michigan

Douglas Wahlsten, Ph.D.
Department of Psychology
University of Alberta
Edmonton, Canada

Seymour Wapner, Ph.D.
School of Psychology
Clark University
Worcester, Massachusetts

Foreword

PAUL MUSSEN

This fifth edition of the *Handbook of Child Psychology* belongs to an invaluable scholarly tradition: the presentation, at approximately 15-year intervals, of a well-planned, comprehensive, authoritative account of the current state of the field. Successive editions of the *Handbook* (or *Manual*, as it was called in the first three editions) reflect the history of the study of human development over the past half-century.

The first two editions (the second, a moderately revised version of the first) reported the accomplishments of the field in an earlier era during which there were relatively few developmental psychologists. *Description* and *measurement of changes over time* were the principal goals of research and speculation. Very little attention was paid to explanation, theory, systems, or models.

The years immediately following World War II were a watershed for science, a period marked by an immensely powerful surge in interest and activity in all sciences, including psychology. The number of scientifically trained psychologists proliferated, and fields or subdivisions within the discipline became more clearly defined. A more modern form of developmental psychology began to take shape and became a major field that was linked to other areas of psychology and allied disciplines but had its own agendas of research and theory. Continuities with earlier work were evident in new investigations and conceptualizations of standard topics—that is, topics of enduring interest—such as language, intelligence, moral behavior, the nature–nurture controversy, and social influences on development. Not surprisingly, the new investigations surpassed the earlier ones in breadth, depth, and scientific sophistication.

Most significantly, the scope of the field was immeasurably extended to include numerous new topics; innovative, more adequate methods of investigation were devised, and *explanation*—and therefore theories about mechanisms and processes—was emphasized. And, for many reasons, the new generation of developmental psychologists—many of whom were trained in other areas such as social, experimental, and clinical psychology—were generally more productive than their predecessors.

Among the myriad factors that account for the many significant advances in the field are: a basic quest for knowledge, and the self-perpetuating nature of scientific endeavors—investigations that yield interesting, sometimes unexpected, findings prompt new questions (as well as modifications of theories) and, consequently, further research. In addition, and of equal importance, developmental psychologists are generally sensitive to social issues and technological changes that may have significant impacts on children's health and development. These concerns frequently are sources of novel investigations and theories, further expanding the boundaries of the field.

Because developmental psychology had been transformed since the end of World War II, the third (1970) edition of the *Manual,* which I edited, was inevitably vastly different from the first two. In addition to up-to-date chapters on topics of continued interest, it included several chapters on theory, psycholinguistics, aggression, attachment, behavior genetics, and creativity, all of which still stand as central issues.

Like most productive scientific disciplines, developmental psychology continues to progress ceaselessly, in profound and complex ways, and at an ever-increasing rate. In

1983, the fourth edition of the *Handbook* was published. It was twice the size of the third edition, and it encompassed standard topics (usually handled in more refined and penetrating ways) and many new, fruitful areas.

Like the years following World War II, the period since 1980 has been one of unprecedented growth, change, and specialization in developmental psychology. The many theoretical and empirical developments in the discipline generated the need for this new edition. It is virtually impossible to delineate the numerous factors affecting its structure and contents, but some of the most significant influences—only a small sample, hardly an exhaustive list—can be highlighted. For example, compelling evidence of the variety and complexity of the determinants of all parameters of psychological development (and the interactions among them) cast doubt on the explanatory power of major theories that conceptualized development in terms of very few dimensions. In widely accepted current approaches and models, development is viewed as the product of multiple variables operating at multiple levels. This orientation, most explicit in several chapters of Volume 1, is also apparent in many other sections in which person–context interactions are discussed. The multivariate approach also calls attention to the limitations on generalizations from research; conclusions derived from a study with a particular population and under specified conditions may not be valid for other groups or under other circumstances. As a consequence, many chapters in this new edition include in-depth discussions of patterns of development in ethnic minorities and in diverse familial and peer group contexts. Renewed vigorous and innovative research in critical psychological parameters such as temperament, character, and emotion, reflected in several chapters, has also been significantly influenced by the multivariable approach.

As the search for the processes underlying development continues, the need to involve significant advances in other scientific disciplines accelerates. Thus, the present edition has chapters that incorporate information from the cognitive sciences, information processing, neurology, and the cultural psychology of development. Moreover, the boundaries of the field have been substantially broadened and enhanced by recent empirical work and conceptualization about psychological development throughout the life span, as reflected in several chapters.

Fortunately, in recent years, professional practitioners and policy makers have recognized the actual and potential contributions of developmental psychology to the solution of critical social and educational problems—for example, problems of parenting, childrearing in nontraditional families, effective teaching, school drop-out, and violence in television programs. Because of this recognition and the notable advances in applied research, one of the volumes of this edition is devoted exclusively to child psychology in practice.

To assist him in the extraordinarily difficult and complicated task of selecting and organizing the most prominent and exciting areas of contemporary developmental psychology, William Damon, the general editor, chose six volume editors who are recognized leaders in the field and have considerable experience in editing journals and books. Next, outstanding experts were invited to contribute critical, integrated chapters on the theoretical and substantive accomplishments of their area of expertise.

As a consequence of these authors' impeccable scholarship, intuitive and informed insights, dedication, creativity, and painstaking work, the fifth edition of the *Handbook* fully achieves its purpose: the timely presentation of an accurate and comprehensive report of the current state of developmental psychology. Readers who compare these volumes with earlier editions will be impressed with how much our understanding of human development has been enhanced in recent years, how much more solid information is available, and how much deeper and more relevant conceptualizations in the field have become. But this indispensable publication is more than an encyclopedic report, for it is enriched by thoughtful perceptions of key issues and keen insights about where matters stand and what still needs to be done. It is an invaluable aid in mapping out the future directions of this vital and dynamic field. The editors and authors have done the field of developmental psychology a great service. Everyone who is seriously interested in human development is deeply indebted to them.

Preface to The Handbook of Child Psychology, Fifth Edition

WILLIAM DAMON

THE *HANDBOOK'S* BACK PAGES—AND OURS

Developmental questions may be asked about almost any human endeavor—even about the enterprise of asking developmental questions. We may ask: How has the field of developmental study developed? In a field that has been preoccupied by continuity and change, where are the continuities and where are the changes?

Many of the chapters of this fifth edition of the *Handbook of Child Psychology* address our field's growth and progress in connection with the particular topics that they examine, and the three historical chapters (by Cairns, by Overton, and by Valsiner) present a panoramic view of our profession. As general editor of the *Handbook's* fifth edition, I wish to add a further data point: the history of the *Handbook,* which stands as an indicator of the continuities and changes within our field. The *Handbook* has long and notable credentials as a beacon, organizer, and encyclopedia of developmental study. What does its history tell us about where we have been, what we have learned, and where we are going? What does it tell us about what has changed and what has remained the same in the questions that we ask, in the methods that we use, and in the theoretical ideas that we draw on in our quest to understand human development?

It is tempting to begin with a riddle: What fifth edition has six predecessors but just three prior namesakes? Given the context of the riddle, there is not much mystery to the answer, but the reasons for it will tell us something about the *Handbook* and its history.

Leonard Carmichael was President of Tufts University when he guided Wiley's first edition of the *Handbook.* The book (one volume at that time) was called the *Manual of Child Psychology,* in keeping with Carmichael's intention of producing an "advanced scientific manual to bridge the gap between the excellent and varied elementary textbooks in this field and the scientific periodical literature. . . ."[1]

The publication date was 1946, and Carmichael complained that "this book has been a difficult and expensive one to produce, especially under wartime conditions."[2] Nevertheless, the project was worth the effort. The *Manual* quickly became the bible of graduate training and scholarly work in the field, available virtually everywhere that children's development was studied. Eight years later, now head of the Smithsonian Institution as well as editor of the book's second edition, Carmichael wrote, in the preface: "The favorable reception that the first edition received not only in America but all over the world is indicative of the growing importance of the study of the phenomena of the growth and development of the child."[3]

The second edition had a long life; not until 1970 did Wiley bring out a third edition. Carmichael was retired by then, but he still had a keen interest in the book. At his insistence, his own name became part of the title of the third edition: *Carmichael's Manual of Child Psychology.* Paul Mussen took over as editor, and once again the project flourished. Now a two-volume set, the third edition swept across the social sciences, generating widespread interest in developmental psychology and its related disciplines. Rarely had a scholarly compendium become both so dominant in its own field and so familiar in related disciplines. The set became an essential source for graduate students and advanced scholars alike. Publishers referred to *Carmichael's Manual* as the standard against which other scientific handbooks were compared. The fourth edition, published in 1983, was redesignated by John Wiley & Sons as the *Handbook of Child Psychology.* By then, Carmichael had passed away. The set of books, now expanded to four volumes, became widely referred to in the field as "the Mussen handbook."

Words can have the power to reawaken dusty memories. When John Wiley & Sons replaced the title word *Manual* with *Handbook,* an important piece of scholarly history was inadvertently recalled. Wiley's fourth edition had a long-forgotten ancestor that was unknown to most of the new book's readers. The ancestor was called *A Handbook of Child Psychology,* and it preceded Wiley's own first edition by over 15 years. I quote here from two statements by Leonard Carmichael:

> Both as editor of the *Manual* and as the author of a special chapter, the writer is indebted . . . [for] extensive excerpts and the use of other materials previously published in the *Handbook of Child Psychology, Revised Edition.* . . .[4]

> Both the *Handbook of Child Psychology* and the *Handbook of Child Psychology, Revised Edition,* were edited by Dr. Carl Murchison. I wish to express here my profound appreciation for the pioneer work done by Dr. Murchison in producing these handbooks and other advanced books in psychology. The *Manual* owes much in spirit and content to the foresight and editorial skill of Dr. Murchison.[5]

The first quote comes from Carmichael's preface to the 1946 edition, the second from his preface to the 1954 edition. We shall never know why Carmichael waited until the 1954 edition to add the personal tribute to Carl Murchison. Perhaps a careless typist dropped the laudatory passage from a handwritten version of the 1946 preface, and its omission escaped Carmichael's notice. Perhaps eight years of further adult development increased Carmichael's generosity of spirit; or perhaps Murchison or his family complained. In any case, Carmichael from the start directly acknowledged the roots of his *Manual,* if not their author. Those roots are a revealing part of the *Handbook's* story— and of our own "back pages," as intellectual descendants of the early pioneers in the Murchison and Carmichael handbooks.

Carl Murchison was a scholar/impresario who edited *The Psychological Register;* founded and edited key psychological journals; wrote books on social psychology,

politics, and the criminal mind; and compiled an assortment of handbooks, psychology texts, autobiographies of renowned psychologists, and even a book on psychic beliefs (Sir Arthur Conan Doyle and Harry Houdini were among the contributors). Murchison's first *Handbook of Child Psychology* was published by a small university press in 1931, when the field itself was still in its childhood. Murchison wrote:

> Experimental psychology has had a much older scientific and academic status [than child psychology], but at the present time it is probable that much less money is being spent for pure research in the field of experimental psychology than is being spent in the field of child psychology. In spite of this obvious fact, many experimental psychologists continue to look upon the field of child psychology as a proper field of research for women and for men whose experimental masculinity is not of the maximum. This attitude of patronage is based almost entirely upon a blissful ignorance of what is going on in the tremendously virile field of child behavior.[6]

Murchison's masculine figures of speech, of course, are from another time; they might supply good material for a social history study of gender stereotyping. That aside, Murchison was prescient in the task that he undertook and the way that he went about it. At the time this passage was written, developmental psychology was known only in Europe and in a few American labs and universities. Nevertheless, Murchison predicted the field's impending ascent: "The time is not far distant, if it is not already here, when nearly all competent psychologists will recognize that one-half of the whole field of psychology is involved in the problem of how the infant becomes an adult psychologically."[7]

For his original 1931 *Handbook,* Murchison looked to Europe and to a handful of American centers (or "field stations") for child research (Iowa, Minnesota, University of California at Berkeley, Columbia, Stanford, Yale, Clark). Murchison's Europeans included a young epistemologist named Jean Piaget, who, in an essay on "Children's Philosophies," quoted from verbal interviews of 60 Genevan children between the ages of 4 and 12 years. Piaget's chapter would provide most American readers with their introduction to his initial research program on children's conceptions of the world. Another European, Charlotte Bühler, wrote a chapter on children's social behavior. In this chapter, which still reads freshly today, Bühler described intricate play and communication patterns among toddlers—patterns that developmental psychology would not rediscover until the late 1970s. Bühler also anticipated the critiques of Piaget that would appear during the sociolinguistics heyday of the 1970s: "Piaget, in his studies on children's talk and reasoning, emphasizes that their talk is much more egocentric than social . . . that children from three to seven years accompany all their manipulations with talk which actually is not so much intercourse as monologue . . . [but] the special relationship of the child to each of the different members of the household is distinctly reflected in the respective conversations."[8] Other Europeans included Anna Freud, who wrote on "The Psychoanalysis of the Child," and Kurt Lewin, who wrote on "Environmental Forces in Child Behavior and Development."

The Americans whom Murchison chose were equally distinguished. Arnold Gesell wrote a nativistic account of his twin studies—an enterprise that remains familiar to us today—and Louis Terman wrote a comprehensive account of everything known about the "gifted child." Harold Jones described the developmental effects of birth order, Mary Cover Jones wrote about children's emotions, Florence Goodenough wrote about children's drawings, and Dorothea McCarthy wrote about language development. Vernon Jones's chapter on "children's morals" focused on the growth of *character,* a notion that was to become lost to the field during the cognitive-developmental revolution, but has lately reemerged as a primary concern in the study of moral development.

Murchison's vision of child psychology left room for an examination of cultural differences as well. He included a young anthropologist named Margaret Mead, just back from her tours of Samoa and New Guinea. In this early essay, Mead wrote that her motivation in traveling to the South Seas was to discredit the view that Piaget, Levy-Bruhl, and other nascent structuralists had put forth concerning "animism" in young children's thinking. (Interestingly, about one-third of Piaget's chapter in the same volume was dedicated to showing how it takes Genevan children years to outgrow animism.) Mead reported some data that she called "amazing": "In not one of the 32,000 drawings (by young 'primitive' children) was there a single case of personalization of animals, material phenomena, or inanimate objects."[9] Mead parlayed these data into a tough-minded critique of Western psychology's ethnocentrism, making the point that animism and other beliefs are more likely to be culturally induced than intrinsic to

early cognitive development. This is hardly an unfamiliar theme in contemporary psychology. Mead also offered a research guide for developmental field workers in strange cultures, complete with methodological and practical advice, such as: translate questions into native linguistic categories; don't do controlled experiments; don't do studies that require knowing ages of subjects, which are usually unknowable; and live next door to the children whom you are studying.

Despite the imposing roster of authors that Murchison had assembled for the 1931 *Handbook of Child Psychology,* his achievement did not satisfy him for long. Barely two years later, Murchison put out a second edition, of which he wrote: "Within a period of slightly more than two years, this first revision bears scarcely any resemblance to the original *Handbook of Child Psychology.* This is due chiefly to the great expansion in the field during the past three years and partly to the improved insight of the editor."[10]

Murchison also saw fit to provide the following warning in his second edition: "There has been no attempt to simplify, condense, or to appeal to the immature mind. This volume is prepared specifically for the scholar, and its form is for his maximum convenience."[11] It is likely that sales of Murchison's first volume did not approach textbook levels. Perhaps he also received negative comments regarding its accessibility. For the record, though, despite Murchison's continued use of masculine phraseology, 10 of the 24 authors in the second edition were women.

Murchison exaggerated when he wrote that his second edition bore little resemblance to the first. Almost half of the chapters were virtually the same, with minor additions and updating. Moreover, some of the authors whose original chapters were dropped were asked to write about new topics. So, for example, Goodenough wrote about mental testing rather than about children's drawings, and Gesell wrote a more general statement of his maturational theory that went well beyond the twin studies.

But Murchison also made some abrupt changes. Anna Freud was dropped, auguring the marginalization of psychoanalysis within academic psychology. Leonard Carmichael made his first appearance, as author of a major chapter (by far, the longest in the book) on prenatal and perinatal growth. Three other physiologically oriented chapters were added as well: one on neonatal motor behavior, one on visual–manual functions during the first two years of life, and one on physiological "appetites" such as hunger, rest, and sex. Combined with the Goodenough and Gesell shifts in focus, these additions gave the 1933 *Handbook* more of a biological thrust, in keeping with Murchison's long-standing desire to display the hard-science backbone of the emerging field.

Leonard Carmichael took his 1946 *Manual* several steps further in the same direction. First, he appropriated five Murchison chapters on biological or experimental topics such as physiological growth, scientific methods, and mental testing. Second, he added three new biologically oriented chapters on animal infancy, on physical growth, and on motor and behavioral maturation (a *tour de force* by Myrtal McGraw that instantly made Gesell's chapter in the same volume obsolete). Third, he commissioned Wayne Dennis to write an adolescence chapter that focused exclusively on physiological changes associated with puberty. Fourth, Carmichael dropped Piaget and Bühler.

But five Murchison chapters on social and cultural influences in development were retained: two chapters on environmental forces on the child (by Kurt Lewin and by Harold Jones), Dorothea McCarthy's chapter on children's language, Vernon Jones's chapter on children's morality (now entitled "Character Development—An Objective Approach"), and Margaret Mead's chapter on "primitive" children (now enhanced by several spectacular photos of mothers and children from exotic cultures around the world). Carmichael stayed with three other psychologically oriented Murchison topics (emotional development, gifted children, and sex differences), but selected new authors to cover them.

Carmichael's 1954 revision—his second and final edition—was very close in structure and content to the 1946 *Manual.* Carmichael again retained the heart of Murchison's original vision, many of Murchison's original authors and chapter topics, and some of the same material that dated all the way back to the 1931 *Handbook.* Not surprisingly, the chapters that were closest to Carmichael's own interests got the most significant updating. As Murchison had tried to do, Carmichael leaned toward the biological and physiological whenever possible. He clearly favored experimental treatments of psychological processes. Yet Carmichael still kept the social, cultural, and psychological analyses by Lewin, Mead, McCarthy, Terman, Harold Jones, and Vernon Jones, and he even went so far as to add one new chapter on social development by Harold and Gladys Anderson and one new chapter on emotional development by Arthur Jersild.

The Murchison/Carmichael volumes make for fascinating reading, even today. The perennial themes of the field were there from the start: the nature–nurture debate; the generalizations of universalists opposed by the particularizations of contextualists; the alternating emphases on continuities and discontinuities during ontogenesis; and the standard categories of maturation, learning, locomotor activity, perception, cognition, language, emotion, conduct, morality, and culture—all separated for the sake of analysis, yet, as authors throughout each of the volumes acknowledged, all somehow inextricably joined in the dynamic mix of human development.

These things have not changed. Yet much in the early handbooks/manuals is now irrevocably dated. Long lists of children's dietary preferences, sleeping patterns, elimination habits, toys, and somatic types look quaint and pointless through today's lenses. The chapters on children's thought and language were done prior to the great contemporary breakthroughs in neurology and brain/behavior research, and they show it. The chapters on social and emotional development were ignorant of the processes of social influence and self-regulation that soon would be revealed through attribution research and other studies in social psychology. Terms such as *behavior genetics, social cognition, dynamic systems, information processing,* and *developmental psychopathology* were unknown. Even Mead's rendition of the "primitive child" stands as a weak straw in comparison to the wealth of cross-cultural knowledge available today.

Most tellingly, the assortments of odd facts and normative trends were tied together by very little theory throughout the Carmichael chapters. It was as if, in the exhilaration of discovery at the frontiers of a new field, all the facts looked interesting in and of themselves. That, of course, is what makes so much of the material seem odd and arbitrary. It is hard to know what to make of the lists of facts, where to place them, which ones were worth keeping track of and which ones are expendable. Not surprisingly, the bulk of the data presented in the Carmichael manuals seems not only outdated by today's standards but, worse, irrelevant.

By 1970, the importance of theory for understanding human development had become apparent. Looking back on Carmichael's last *Manual,* Paul Mussen wrote: "The 1954 edition of this *Manual* had only one theoretical chapter, and that was concerned with Lewinian theory which, so far as we can see, has not had a significant lasting impact on developmental psychology."[12] The intervening years had seen a turning away from the norm of psychological research once fondly referred to as "dust-bowl empiricism."

The Mussen 1970 handbook—or *Carmichael's Manual,* as it was still called—had an entirely new look. The two-volume set carried only one chapter from the earlier books—Carmichael's updated version of his own long chapter on the "Onset and Early Development of Behavior," which had made its appearance under a different title in Murchison's 1933 edition. Otherwise, as Mussen wrote in his preface, "It should be clear from the outset . . . that the present volumes are not, in any sense, a *revision* of the earlier editions; this is a completely new *Manual.*"[13]

And it was. In comparison to Carmichael's last edition 16 years earlier, the scope, variety, and theoretical depth of the Mussen volumes were astonishing. The field had blossomed, and the new *Manual* showcased many of the new bouquets that were being produced. The biological perspective was still strong, grounded by chapters on physical growth (by J. M. Tanner) and physiological development (by Dorothy Eichorn), and by Carmichael's revised chapter (now made more elegant by some excerpts from Greek philosophy and modern poetry). But two other cousins of biology also were represented, in an ethological chapter by Eckhard Hess, and a behavior genetics chapter by Gerald McClearn. These chapters were to define the major directions of biological research in the field for at least the next three decades.

As for theory, Mussen's *Handbook* was thoroughly permeated with it. Much of the theorizing was organized around the approaches that, in 1970, were known as the "three grand systems": (a) Piaget's cognitive-developmentalism, (b) psychoanalysis, and (c) learning theory. Piaget was given the most extensive treatment. He reappeared in the *Manual,* this time authoring a comprehensive (and some say, definitive) statement of his entire theory, which now bore little resemblance to his 1931/1933 sortings of children's intriguing verbal expressions. In addition, chapters by John Flavell, by David Berlyne, by Martin Hoffman, and by William Kessen, Marshall Haith, and Philip Salapatek, all gave major treatments to one or another aspect of Piaget's body of work. Other approaches were represented as well. Herbert and Ann Pick explicated Gibsonian theory in a chapter on sensation and perception, Jonas Langer

wrote a chapter on Werner's organismic theory, David McNeill wrote a Chomskian account of language development, and Robert LeVine wrote an early version of what was soon to become "culture theory."

With its increased emphasis on theory, the 1970 *Manual* explored in depth a matter that had been all but neglected in the *Manual's* previous versions: the mechanisms of change that could account for, to use Murchison's old phrase, "the problem of how the infant becomes an adult psychologically." In the process, old questions such as the relative importance of nature *versus* nurture were revisited, but with far more sophisticated conceptual and methodological tools.

Beyond theory building, the 1970 *Manual* addressed an array of new topics and featured new contributors: peer interaction (Willard Hartup), attachment (Eleanor Maccoby and John Masters), aggression (Seymour Feshback), individual differences (Jerome Kagan and Nathan Kogan), and creativity (Michael Wallach). All of these areas of interest are still very much with us at century's end.

If the 1970 *Manual* reflected a blossoming of the field's plantings, the 1983 *Handbook* reflected a field whose ground cover had spread beyond any boundaries that could have been previously anticipated. New growth had sprouted in literally dozens of separate locations. A French garden, with its overarching designs and tidy compartments, had turned into an English garden, a bit unruly but often glorious in its profusion. Mussen's two-volume *Carmichael's Manual* had now become the four-volume Mussen *Handbook,* with a page-count increase that came close to tripling the 1970 edition.

The grand old theories were breaking down. Piaget was still represented by his 1970 piece, but his influence was on the wane throughout the other chapters. Learning theory and psychoanalysis were scarcely mentioned. Yet the early theorizing had left its mark, in vestiges that were apparent in new approaches, and in the evident conceptual sophistication with which authors treated their material. No return to dust-bowl empiricism could be found anywhere in the set. Instead, a variety of classical and innovative ideas were coexisting: ethology, neurobiology, information processing, attribution theory, cultural approaches, communications theory, behavioral genetics, sensory-perception models, psycholinguistics, sociolinguistics, discontinuous stage theories, and continuous memory theories all took their places, with none quite on center stage. Research topics now ranged from children's play to brain lateralization, from children's family life to the influences of school, day care, and disadvantageous risk factors. There also was coverage of the burgeoning attempts to use developmental theory as a basis for clinical and educational interventions. The interventions usually were described at the end of chapters that had discussed the research relevant to the particular intervention efforts, rather than in whole chapters dedicated specifically to issues of practice.

This brings us to the present—the *Handbook's* fifth (but really seventh) edition. I will leave it to future reviewers to provide a summation of what we have done. The volume editors have offered introductory and/or concluding renditions of their own volumes. I will add to their efforts by stating here the overall intent of our design, and by commenting on some directions that our field has taken in the years from 1931 to 1998.

We approached this edition with the same purpose that Murchison, Carmichael, and Mussen before us had shared: "to provide," as Mussen wrote, "a comprehensive and accurate picture of the current state of knowledge—the major systematic thinking and research—in the most important research areas of the psychology of human development."[14] We assumed that the *Handbook* should be aimed "specifically for the scholar," as Murchison declared, and that it should have the character of an "advanced text," as Carmichael defined it. We expected, though, that our audience may be more interdisciplinary than the readerships of previous editions, given the greater tendency of today's scholars to cross back and forth among fields such as psychology, cognitive science, neurobiology, history, linguistics, sociology, anthropology, education, and psychiatry. We also believed that research-oriented practitioners should be included under the rubric of the "scholars" for whom this *Handbook* was intended. To that end, we devoted, for the first time, an entire volume to "child psychology in practice."

Beyond these very general intentions, we have let chapters in the *Handbook's* fifth edition take their own shape. We solicited the chapters from authors who were widely acknowledged to be among the leading experts in their areas of the field; although we know that, given an entirely open-ended selection process and budget, we would have invited a very large number of other leading researchers whom we did not have the space—and thus the privilege—

to include. With only two exceptions, every author whom we invited chose to accept the challenge.

Our directive to authors was simple: Convey your area of the field as you see it. From then on, the 112 authors took center stage—with, of course, much constructive feedback from reviewers and volume editors. But no one tried to impose a perspective, a preferred method of inquiry, or domain boundaries on any of the chapters. The authors freely expressed their views on what researchers in their areas attempt to accomplish, why they do so, how they go about it, what intellectual sources they draw on, what progress they have made, and what conclusions they have reached.

The result, in my opinion, is yet more glorious profusion, but perhaps contained a bit by some broad patterns that have emerged across our garden. Powerful theoretical models and approaches—not quite unified theories, such as the three grand systems—have begun once again to organize much of the field's research and practice. There is great variety in these models and approaches, and each is drawing together significant clusters of work. Some have been only recently formulated, and some are combinations or modifications of classic theories that still have staying power.

Among the formidable models and approaches that the reader will find in this *Handbook* are the dynamic system theories, the life-span and life-course approaches, cognitive science and neural models, the behavior genetics approach, person–context interaction theories, action theories, cultural psychology, ecological models, neo-Piagetian and neo-Vygotskian models. Although some of these models and approaches have been in the making for some time, my impression is that they are just now coming into their own, in that researchers now are drawing on them more directly, taking their implied assumptions and hypotheses seriously, using them with specificity and with full control, and exploiting all of their implications for practice. A glance at the contents listings for the *Handbook's* four volumes will reveal the staggering breadth of concerns addressed through use of these models and approaches.

The other pattern that emerges is a self-conscious reflection about the notion of development. The reflection is an earnest one, yet it has a more affirmative tone than similar discussions in recent years. We have just passed through a time when the very credibility of a developmental approach was itself thrown into question. The whole idea of progress and advance, implicit in the notion of development, seemed out of step with ideological principles of diversity and equality.

Some genuine intellectual benefits accrued from that critique: the field has come to better appreciate diverse developmental pathways. But, like many critique positions, it led to excesses that created, for some in the field of developmental study, a kind of crisis of faith. For some, it became questionable even to explore issues that lie at the heart of human development. Learning, growth, achievement, individual continuity and change, common beliefs and standards—all became suspect as subjects of investigation.

Fortunately, as the contents of this *Handbook* attest, such doubts are waning. As was probably inevitable, the field's center of gravity has returned to the study of development. After all, the story of growth during infancy, childhood, and adolescence is a developmental story of multi-faceted learning, of acquisitions of skills and knowledge, of waxing powers of attention and memory, of formations and transformations of character and personality, of increases in understanding of self and others, of advances in emotional and behavioral regulation, of progress in communicating and collaborating with others, and of a host of other achievements that are chronicled in this *Handbook*. Parents and teachers in every part of the world recognize and value such developmental achievements in their children, although they do not always know how to foster them. Neither do we in all cases. But the kinds of scientific understanding that the *Handbook's* authors explicate in their chapters—scientific understanding created by themselves as well as by fellow researchers in the field of developmental study—have brought us all several giant steps toward this goal.

NOTES

1. Carmichael, L. (Ed.). (1946). *Manual of child psychology.* New York: Wiley, p. viii.

2. Carmichael, L. (Ed.). (1946). *Manual of child psychology.* New York: Wiley, p. vi.

3. Carmichael, L. (Ed.). (1954). *Manual of child psychology: Second edition.* New York: Wiley, p. v.

4. Carmichael, L. (Ed.). (1946). *Manual of child psychology.* New York: Wiley, p. vi.

5. Carmichael, L. (Ed.). (1954). *Manual of child psychology: Second edition.* New York: Wiley, p. vii.

6. Murchison, C. (Ed.). (1931). *A handbook of child psychology.* Worcester, MA: Clark University Press, p. ix.

7. Murchison, C. (Ed.). (1931). *A handbook of child psychology.* Worcester, MA: Clark University Press, p. x.

8. Buhler, C. (1931). The social participation of infants and toddlers. In C. Murchison (Ed.), *A handbook of child psychology.* Worcester, MA: Clark University Press, p. 138.

9. Mead, M. (1931). The primitive child. In C. Murchison (Ed.), *A handbook of child psychology.* Worcester, MA: Clark University Press, p. 400.

10. Murchison, C. (Ed.). (1933). *A handbook of child psychology: Second edition (Revised).* Worcester, MA: Clark University Press, p. viii.

11. Murchison, C. (Ed.). (1933). *A handbook of child psychology: Second edition (Revised).* Worcester, MA: Clark University Press, p. viii.

12. Mussen, P. (Ed.). (1970). *Carmichael's manual of child psychology.* New York: Wiley, p. x.

13. Mussen, P. (Ed.). (1970). *Carmichael's manual of child psychology.* New York: Wiley, p. x.

14. Mussen, P. (Ed.). (1983). *Handbook of child psychology.* New York: Wiley, p. vii.

Acknowledgments

The fifth edition of the *Handbook* was truly a team effort. The six volume editors have my deepest gratitude for their countless hours of devoted work. No project editor has ever had a finer group of collaborators. I also thank Kelly Franklin, of John Wiley & Sons, Inc., for her inspired editorial efforts from the time of the project's inception. Without Kelly's persistence and good sense, publication in 1998 would not have been possible.

Many people contributed invaluable advice during one or another phase of the fifth edition's production. They are far too many to mention here, even if I had managed to keep systematic records of all conversations on the project's development. The final product has benefited greatly from the insights and feedback of all those who responded.

In particular, I note two giants of the field whose wise counsel and generosity remain prominent in my mind: Paul Mussen and Eleanor Maccoby.

In slightly altered form, my preface was published in *Human Development* (March–April, 1997). I am grateful to Barbara Rogoff for her editorial help in this process, and to Anne Gregory for her help in obtaining background materials. Josef and Marsy Mittlemann's support has been vital in facilitating this and other scholarly activities at the Brown University Center for the Study of Human Development. My assistant, Pat Balsofiore, deserves our unending gratitude for her valiant work in helping to organize this vast endeavor.

WILLIAM DAMON

Contents

CHAPTER 1

Theories of Human Development: Contemporary Perspectives

RICHARD M. LERNER

The editor of the third edition of this *Handbook of Child Psychology,* Paul Mussen, presaged what today is abundantly clear about the contemporary nature of theories of human development. Mussen (1970, p. vii) said that "the major contemporary empirical and theoretical emphases in the field of developmental psychology . . . seem to be on *explanations* of the psychological changes that occur, the mechanisms and processes accounting for growth and development." He thus alerted developmentalists to a burgeoning interest not in structure, function, or content per se, but in change, in the processes through which change occurs, and thus in the means through which structures transform and functions evolve over the course of human life.

Today, Mussen's vision has been crystallized. The cutting edge of contemporary developmental theory is represented by conceptions of process—how structures function and how functions are structured over time. Thus, as reflected in this volume, most contemporary theories of human development are not tied necessarily to a particular

content domain—although particular empirical issues or substantive foci (e.g., motor development, successful aging, wisdom, extraordinary cognitive achievements, language acquisition, the self, psychological complexity, or concept formation) may lend themselves readily as exemplary sample cases of the processes depicted in a given theory.

Furthermore, the chapters in this volume illustrate that the power of contemporary developmental theories lies in their ability not to be limited by (or, perhaps better, be confounded by an inextricable association with) a unidimensional portrayal of the developing person (e.g., the person seen from the vantage point of only cognitions, or emotions, or stimulus–response connections; see Piaget, 1970; Freud, 1949; and Bijou & Baer, 1961, respectively). Thus, in contemporary developmental theories, the person is not biologized, psychologized, or sociologized. Rather, the individual is "systemized"—that is, his or her development is embedded within an integrated matrix of variables derived from multiple levels of organization, and development is

1

conceptualized as deriving from the dynamic relations among the variables within this multitiered matrix.

The theories represented in this volume use the polarities that engaged developmental theory in the past (e.g., nature–nurture, individual–society, biology–culture; Lerner, 1976, 1986), but not to "split" depictions of developmental processes along conceptually implausible and empirically counterfactual lines (Gollin, 1981; Overton, this volume), or to force counterproductive choices between false opposites; rather, these issues are used to gain insight into the integrations that exist among the multiple levels of organization involved in human development.[1] These contemporary theories are certainly more complex than their one-sided predecessors; however, they are also more nuanced, more flexible, more balanced, and less susceptible to extravagant, or even absurd, claims (for instance, that "nature," split from "nurture," can shape the course of human development; that there is a gene for altruism, militarism, intelligence, and even television watching; or that when the social context is demonstrated to affect development, the influence can be reduced to a genetic one; e.g., Hamburger, 1957; Lorenz, 1966; Plomin, 1986; Plomin, Corley, DeFries, & Faulker, 1990; Rowe, 1994; Rushton, 1987, 1988).

These mechanistic and atomistic views of the past have been replaced by theoretical models that stress the dynamic synthesis of multiple levels of analysis, a perspective having its roots in systems theories of biological development (Cairns, this volume; Gottlieb, 1992; Kuo, 1930, 1967, 1976; Schneirla, 1956, 1957). In other words, development, understood as a property of systemic change in the multiple and integrated levels of organization (ranging from biology to culture and history) comprising human life and its ecology, or, in other words, a *developmental systems perspective,* is an overarching conceptual frame associated with contemporary theoretical models in the field of human development.

Accordingly, the power of contemporary theories lies in the multilevel and, hence, multidimensional design criteria they impose on concepts (and research) pertinent to any content area about, or dimension of, the person. As illustrated

---

[1] I am indebted to William Damon for suggesting the points raised in this paragraph.

by the above depiction of the multilevel, changing matrix representing the system involved in development, this power of a developmental systems perspective is constituted by four interrelated, and in fact "fused" (Tobach & Greenberg, 1984), assumptive components found in contemporary theories of human development: (a) change and relative plasticity; (b) relationism and the integration of levels of organization; (c) historical embeddedness and temporality; and (d) the limits of generalizability, diversity, and individual differences.

Although the four assumptive components frame contemporary theories of human development, each has a long and rich tradition in the history of the field (Cairns, this volume). For instance, Cairns describes James Mark Baldwin's (1897) interest in studying development-in-context, and thus in integrated, multilevel, and hence interdisciplinary scholarship. These interests were shared as well by Lightner Witmer, the founder in 1896 of the first psychological clinic in the United States (Cairns, this volume; Lerner, 1977). Cairns describes the conception of developmental processes—involving reciprocal interaction, bidirectionality, plasticity, and biobehavioral organization (all quite modern emphases)—as integral in the thinking of the founders of the field of human development. For instance, Wilhelm Stern (1914; see Kreppner, 1994) stressed the holism that is associated with a developmental systems perspective about these features of developmental processes. Other contributors to the foundations and early progress of the field of human development (e.g., John Dewey, 1916; Kurt Lewin, 1935, 1954; and John B. Watson, 1928) stressed the importance of linking child development research with application and child advocacy—a theme of very contemporary relevance (Zigler & Finn-Stevenson, 1992), and one to which I will return later.

Although, as noted, the concepts involved in each of the four thematic components of contemporary theories are interrelated, for purposes of explication I will treat each concept successively. The combined import of these four conceptual components has important implications for research and for application—for policies and programs—in human development. These implications, which will be presented after all of the dimensions have been discussed, allow the field of human development to contribute, through its theory-based research about the changing person–context system, good science and good service to the diverse constituencies interested in enhancing the world's human and social capital (Hamburg, 1992).

CHANGE AND RELATIVE PLASTICITY

Contemporary theories stress that the focus of developmental understanding must be on (systematic) change (chapters by Brandtstädter; Bronfenbrenner & Morris; Csikszentmihalyi & Rathunde; Fischer & Bidell; Gardner; Gottlieb, Wahlsten, & Lickliter; Magnusson & Stattin; Overton; Thelen & Smith; and Wapner & Demick, this volume; Ford & Lerner, 1992; Sameroff, 1983). This focus is required because of the belief that the potential for change exists across (a) the life span and (b) the multiple levels of organization comprising the ecology of human development (e.g., chapters by Baltes, Lindenberger, & Staudinger; Bronfenbrenner & Morris; Elder; and Shweder et al., this volume; Baltes, 1987). Although it is also assumed that systematic change is not limitless (e.g., it is constrained by both past developments and by contemporary ecological, or contextual, conditions), contemporary theories stress that *relative plasticity* exists across life (chapters by Baltes et al.; Brandtstädter; Keil; Overton; and Spelke & Newport, this volume; Lerner, 1984).

Relative plasticity has important implications for understanding the range of intraindividual variation that can exist over ontogeny (Fisher, Jackson, & Villarruel, this volume) and, in turn, for applying developmental science. For instance, the presence of relative plasticity legitimates a proactive search across the life span for characteristics of people and of their contexts that, together, can influence the design of policies and programs promoting positive development (Birkel, Lerner, & Smyer, 1989; Fisher & Lerner, 1994; Lerner & Hood, 1986). For example, the plasticity of intellectual development, which is a feature of a systems view of mental functioning (see the chapters by Fischer & Bidell; Gardner; and Keil, this volume), provides legitimation for educational policies and school- and community-based programs aimed at enhancing cognitive and social cognitive development (Dryfoos, 1994; Villarruel & Lerner, 1994); such implications for the design of policies and programs stand in marked contrast to those associated with mechanistic, genetic reductionistic theories that suggest that genetic inheritance constrains intellectual development among particular minority and/or low-income groups (Herrnstein, 1973; Herrnstein & Murray, 1994; Jensen, 1969, 1980; Rushton, 1987, 1988).

Features of Plasticity in Human Development

T. C. Schneirla (1956, 1957), the renowned comparative psychologist, emphasized that behavioral differences among species could best be identified through analysis of their respective ontogenies. He suggested that species could be differentiated along a "stereotypy–plasticity continuum," a theoretical metric comparing the level of capacity for systematic changes, for behavioral variability, or simply, for plasticity, attained over the course of animals' life spans. The location of a species closer to the plasticity end of the continuum was associated with the *eventual* development in ontogeny of more complex behavioral repertoires and, according to Hebb (1949, 1980), with higher ratios of brain association fibers to sensory fibers (i.e., with higher A/S ratios).

Both Schneirla and Hebb stressed, however, that species capable of higher levels of eventual plasticity spend a comparatively greater proportion of their ontogenies developing this capacity than do species whose final level of development is marked by lower levels of plasticity and, thus, greater degrees of behavioral stereotypes (see discussions of neoteny by Csikszentmihalyi & Rathunde, this volume; Gould, 1977; Lerner, 1984). The key point of the Schneirla/Hebb position is, then, that plasticity is a developmental phenomenon.

Schneirla and his colleagues (e.g., Tobach, 1981; Tobach & Schneirla, 1968) argued that development involved neither a separate additive nor even a simple interactive interrelation of hereditary and environmental influences. Rather, a dynamic interaction (Lerner, 1978, 1986), a "fusion" (1986; Tobach & Greenberg, 1984), or a systemic synthesis across the levels of organization incorporating hereditary and environmental influences (Ford & Lerner, 1992), characterized the process of development. In other words, a developmental systems (Ford & Lerner, 1992; Gottlieb, 1992) conception of developmental process—for instance, as found in theoretical perspectives such as "developmental contextualism" (Lerner, 1986, 1991, 1996)—has been associated with animal comparative and human developmental theory and research built on the tradition initiated by Schneirla.

From the perspective of this tradition, plasticity is a feature of an animal's functioning that occurs as a consequence of the history of dynamic interactions, or fusions, between the individual's organismic characteristics and the specific experiences it encounters over the course of its life. Within this view of the developmental character of plasticity, interspecies differences in plasticity arise in relation to differences among species in organismic characteristics as these characteristics influence *and are influenced by* the sorts of prototypical experiences they encounter in their "normative" ecological niche. Similarly, intraspecies, interindividual differences in plasticity arise in relation to differences among animals' organismic characteristics (e.g., their specific genotypes) as these characteristics influence and are influenced by their unique experiential history.

Accordingly, from the perspective articulated by Schneirla, Hebb, and others (e.g., Gottlieb, 1992; Lerner, 1984, 1991; Tobach, 1981; Tobach & Greenberg, 1984), the study of plasticity—whether directed to an analysis of inter- or intraspecies differences—always involves scrutiny of the history of dynamic organism-context interactions or, in more general terms, of the fused or systemic relations between nature and nurture. Thus, plasticity is not a product of nature (e.g., of genes in general or, more specifically, of a purported genetic program) or of nurture (e.g., a specific learning regimen, reinforcement program, or sequence of stimulation). Rather, the level of plasticity attained by an animal over the course of its life is an outcome of the *temporally changing and dynamic relation* of nature and nurture (Elder, this volume; Ford & Lerner, 1992; Lerner, 1984, 1991). Plasticity is, then, a feature of the process of development.

Other views of plasticity exist. For example, Brauth, Hall, and Dooling (1991) see plasticity as based on genetic programs that code for developmental processes but are themselves not involved in, or influenced by, development. Brauth et al.'s view is not dissimilar from that of Wilson (1975), who considered plasticity as being a fundamental outcome of a particular genetic complement or genetic structure (rather than, for instance, seeing genes themselves as plastic entities; Lerner, 1984). In the views of Brauth et al. or of Wilson, nurture (environment or experience) plays a secondary role in the chain of influences

eventuating in plasticity. Nurture facilitates or inhibits the unfolding of the genetic program, but it does not interact, or fuse, with the genes themselves. Nurture thus cannot influence the quality of the purported program.

This position is represented in the contention of Brauth et al. (1991) that "proximate causal sequences are the immediate cause–effect sequences by which information in the genotype is 'read out' during development in the presence of environmental stimuli" (p. 1); in their assertion of "the fact that the genetic program's code for developmental processes is contingent on appropriate environmental stimulation" (p. 3); and in their belief that "the course of the individual development [sic] is determined by a set of complex interactions between environmental stimuli and genetic programs. In terms of this conceptualization, individual variations arise from epigenetic processes whose courses are both constrained by and facilitated by genetic mechanisms (i.e., they are canalized)" (p. 164). Accordingly, the experience an animal encounters is in essence only the "releaser" of an "instinct to learn" (p. 2), of "innate predispositions" (p. 8), or of "innate preferences" (p. 8) caused by genetic programs that, in turn, "result from differential reproductive success of individuals carrying particular phenotypes (i.e., from natural selection)" (p. 3).

The distinctions between the Brauth et al. (1991) genetic program conception of plasticity and the developmental systems view of this feature of development are perhaps most pronounced in the treatment afforded the topic of epigenesis in the respective conceptions. Both conceptions hold that epigenesis is involved in the development across ontogeny of the set of (increasingly more complex) behaviors that characterizes the level of plasticity prototypic of a species or of an individual over the course of its life. However, within the former (genetic determinist) conception, epigenesis is construed as a program that unfolds over the course of life; although both "biological and environmental signals" (p. 3) are believed to release components of the epigenetic program, epigenesis is seen as a genetically controlled means for maintaining *continuity* in development.

To illustrate, in discussing what they regard as three fundamental questions in developmental psychobiology, Brauth et al. (1991) indicate that the first question is: "Is there *continuity* in development, i.e., what is the nature of the epigenetic programs unfolding at each phase of development?" (p. 3). As I noted above, Brauth et al. underscore their view that epigenesis is genetically determined by maintaining that behavioral variation arises from epigenetic processes that are constrained and facilitated by genetic mechanisms.

The view of epigenesis found within a developmental systems conception (e.g., see Gottlieb et al., this volume; Gottlieb, 1970, 1983, 1992; Lerner, 1984) is quite different. Descriptively, epigenesis refers to emergent—that is, qualitatively *discontinuous*—features of development (Lerner, 1986; Werner, 1957). In regard to the explanation of epigenetic phenomena, emphasis is placed on the dynamic interaction, or fusion, of levels of organization, which, as noted above, is an emphasis found throughout the tradition promoted by Schneirla (1956, 1957; see also Tobach, 1981; Tobach & Greenberg, 1984). To illustrate, Gottlieb (1992) offers a conception of epigenesis that stresses the bidirectionality of influences among the levels of organization involved in development. He indicates that individual development involves the emergence of new structural and functional properties and competencies at all levels of analysis (e.g., molecular, subcellular, cellular, organismic) of a developmental system, including the organism–environment relational level. These emergent characteristics derive from *horizontal* coactions involving intralevel relationships (e.g., gene–gene, cell–cell, tissue–tissue, or organism--organism) and from *vertical* coactions involving interlevel relationships (e.g., gene–cytoplasm, cell–tissue, or behavioral activity–nervous system). These horizontal and vertical coactions are reciprocal in that influences occur in any direction: from one "component" to another within a level; from lower-level to higher-level components; and/or from higher-level to lower-level components within the developmental system. From this perspective, the causes of development are the *relationships* among components, and not the components themselves (Gottlieb, 1992; Lerner, 1991).

For example, the emergence of menarche is a result of vertical coactions involving biology, culture, physical features of the ecology, and the socioeconomic resources (related, for instance, to available technology, nutrition, and medical care) of the society within which the young female is embedded. For instance, among youth of African ancestry living in Cuba, the median age of menarche is 12.4 years, whereas the median age of menarche for girls of corresponding ancestry living in Uganda, in South Africa, and in New Guinea is 13.4 years, 15.0 years, and 18.8 years, respectively (Katchadourian, 1977). These differences have been associated with variation in the nutritional and medical resources available to young girls in the nations studied; better nutrition and medical care are linked to a lower age of menarche. Similarly, differences in age of menarche within a nation are often seen when youth from urban areas are compared with those from poor rural areas; those from the urban settings have lower ages of menarche as a consequence of their advantaged socioeconomic situation. For example, in Romania, the average age of menarche is 13.5 years in towns and 14.6 in villages. Corresponding urban–rural differences have been found in nations of the former Soviet Union (where contrasts are 13.0 years and 14.3 years, respectively) and in India (where contrasts are 12.8 and 14.2 years, respectively) (Tanner, 1970, 1991). In Hong Kong, the average age of menarche of girls from rich, from average-income, and from poor families is 12.5 years, 12.8 years, and 13.3 years, respectively (Tanner, 1970, 1991).

The distinction between the developmental systems view of plasticity and the genetic determination/genetic program conception of this feature of development is clearly not just a matter of semantics or of emphasis. To the contrary, the distinction pertains to important logical and empirical issues. In regard to the logical issues, the linear and mechanistic view of the genetic determination/programming of plasticity is unfalsifiable. The genetic program that purportedly causes the plasticity of behavior is indexed only by the behavior involved in the manifestation of plasticity. The presence of the behavior is taken as evidence of the genetic program, and variation in the behavior is taken as an indication of the degree of "appropriate environmental stimulation" (Brauth et al., 1991, p. 3), and *not* as information pertinent to the assumption of the presence of a causal genetic program. Thus, although behavior is the only evidence used to index this viewpoint, there is no behavioral evidence that can lead to the rejection of the belief in the presence of a genetic program for plasticity.

In regard to the empirical issues, there is abundant evidence within the field of molecular genetics that the "fact" of a genetic program, as proposed by Brauth et al. (1991), is, in actuality, a counterfactual assertion. Indeed, molecular genetics provides evidence that the entire view of genetic activity represented by genetic determinists is mistaken.

For example, molecular geneticist Mae-Wan Ho (1984, p. 285) has indicated that:

Forever exorcised from our collective consciousness is any remaining illusion of development as a genetic programme involving the readout of the DNA "master" tape by the cellular "slave" machinery. On the contrary, it is the cellular machinery which imposes control over the genes. . . . The classical view of the ultraconservative genome—the unmoved mover of development—is completely turned around. Not only is there no master tape to be read out automatically, but the "tape" itself can get variously chopped, rearranged, transposed, and amplified in different cells at different times.

Similarly, molecular and cell biologist R. C. Strohman (1993, p. 150) notes that:

Many experimental biologists outside the biomedical–industrial complex are just now coming (back) to grips with the facts of epigenesis, with the profound mystery that developmental biology is, with the poverty of gene programs as an explanatory device, and with a crisis defined by the realization that an increasingly deficient theory of developmental genetics is the only theory currently available. The question remains: If biologists are starting to learn this lesson, will the psychologists be far behind?

Some psychologists have incorporated this "lesson" into their theory and research (e.g., Gottlieb, 1992; Tobach, 1981; Tobach & Greenberg, 1984), and, as a consequence, have reached conclusions about the systems nature of development in general, and of the processes involved in plasticity in particular. I have noted Gottlieb's earlier (1992) views in this regard, and I have pointed to developmental contextual theory as an instance of this systems perspective applied to an understanding of the nature of plasticity in human behavior and development (e.g., Lerner, 1984, 1991, 1995, 1996).

In essence, the "genetic program" view of plasticity represented by Brauth et al. (1991) and by other advocates of a genetic primacy perspective—for instance, behavior geneticists (Plomin, 1986; Plomin et al., 1990; Rowe, 1994) or human sociobiologists (Belsky, Steinberg, & Draper, 1991; Freedman, 1979; MacDonald, 1994; Rushton, 1987, 1988)—is quite distinct from the "developmental process/systems" view forwarded by, among others, Schneirla, Hebb, Tobach, Gottlieb, and Greenberg. Moreover, the genetic program view is not supported by the current literature in molecular genetics (Ho, 1984; Strohman, 1993a, 1993b). Indeed, as Gottlieb (1992) has observed:

"The ultimate aim of dissolving the nature–nurture dichotomy will be achieved only through the establishment of a fully developmental theory of the phenotype from gene to organism" (p. vii).

Implications of Plasticity for Continuity–Discontinuity in Development

Given such a potential for plasticity, a basic feature of the system of processes involved in human development is that both constancy and change—both continuity and discontinuity—may exist across life. The presence of—or better, the potentiality for—at least some plasticity means that the key way of casting the issue of continuity–discontinuity of development is not a matter of deciding what exists for a given process or function; instead, the issue should be cast in terms of determining the patterns of interactions among levels of the developmental system that may promote continuity and/or discontinuity for a particular process or function at a given point in ontogeny and/or history. The same process may exhibit either continuity or discontinuity with earlier life periods, and/or may exhibit some features of both continuity and discontinuity, depending on the particular dynamic interaction that exists among levels at a given point in time. Thus, neither continuity nor discontinuity is absolute. Both are probabilistically present features of change, and the actualization of either is dependent on prevailing developmental conditions within the organism as well as its context.

Simmons and Blyth (1987) and their colleagues illustrate the possibility of either continuity or discontinuity in females' self-esteem across early adolescence. Whether continuity or discontinuity in self-esteem occurs depends on the confluence of other organismic and contextual changes experienced by the females. For instance, discontinuity (in the direction of decrement) of self-esteem is most likely when the young adolescent female is experiencing simultaneously the organismic changes associated with menarche and the contextual alterations associated with the transition from elementary school to junior high school.

The developmental literature suggesting these ideas about plasticity and the relativity of continuity and discontinuity has, to a great extent, been associated with the life-span view of human development (chapters by Baltes et al. and Elder, this volume; Baltes, 1987; Brim & Kagan, 1980;

Elder, 1974; Featherman, 1983; Lerner, 1984, 1986). Within this perspective, the context for development is seen not merely as a simple stimulus environment, but rather as an "ecological environment . . . conceived topologically as a nested arrangement of concentric structures, each contained within the next" (Bronfenbrenner, 1979, p. 22; see also Bronfenbrenner & Morris, this volume) and including variables from biological, psychological, physical, and sociocultural levels, all changing interdependently across history (Riegel, 1975, 1976a, 1976b).

The life-span perspective is linked, then, to a concern with issues about the relations between evolution and ontogeny, about the role the developing person plays in his or her own development, about human plasticity, and therefore about life course continuity and discontinuity (Baltes, 1987; Lerner & Busch-Rossnagel, 1981; Scarr & McCartney, 1983; Tobach, 1981). These issues are linked by the idea that reciprocal relations (i.e., dynamic interactions; Lerner, 1978) between individuals and the multiple contexts within which they live characterize human development (Bronfenbrenner, 1979; see also Bronfenbrenner & Morris, this volume). In other words, all the issues raised by this perspective derive from a common appreciation of the basic role of the necessary link between an organism's development and its changing, multilevel context. The functional significance of this changing organism–context relation requires adoption of a developmental systems perspective—or, more specifically, of a probabilistic epigenetic conception (Gottlieb, 1970; Schneirla, 1957) or a developmental contextual view (Lerner, 1986, 1991, 1996)—of an individual's development.

RELATIONISM AND THE INTEGRATION OF LEVELS OF ORGANIZATION

Contemporary theories stress that the bases for change, and for both plasticity and constraints in development, lie in the relations that exist among the multiple levels of organization that comprise the substance of human life (see chapters in this volume by Baltes et al.; Brandtstädter; Bronfenbrenner & Morris; Cairns; Csikszentmihalyi & Rathunde; Elder; Fischer & Bidell; Fisher et al.; Gardner; Gottlieb et al.; Magnusson & Stattin; Overton; Shweder et al.; Thelen & Smith; Valsiner; and Wapner & Demick; see also Ford & Lerner, 1992; Schneirla, 1957; Tobach,

1981). These levels range from the inner biological, through the individual/psychological and the proximal social relational (e.g., involving dyads, peer groups, and nuclear families), to the sociocultural level (including key macro-institutions such as educational, public policy, governmental, and economic systems) and the natural and designed physical ecologies of human development (Bronfenbrenner, 1979; Bronfenbrenner & Morris, this volume; Riegel, 1975). These tiers are structurally and functionally integrated, thus requiring a systems view of the levels involved in human development (Ford & Lerner, 1992; Sameroff, 1983; Smith & Thelen, 1993; Thelen & Smith, 1994; Wapner, 1993). As noted earlier, developmental contextualism is one instance of such a viewpoint (Lerner, 1986, 1991, 1995, 1996).

Such a developmental systems perspective promotes a *relational* unit of analysis as a requisite for developmental analysis (see chapters in this volume by Brandtstädter; Bronfenbrenner & Morris; Csikszentmihalyi & Rathunde; Elder; Fisher et al.; Gottlieb et al.; Magnusson & Stattin; see also Lerner, 1991). Variables associated with any level of organization exist (are structured) in relation to variables from other levels; the qualitative and quantitative dimensions of the function of any variable are shaped as well by the relations that variable has with variables from other levels. Unilevel units of analysis (or the components of, or elements in, a relation) are not an adequate target of developmental analysis; rather, the relation itself—the interlevel linkage—should be the focus of such analysis (Fisher et al., this volume; Lerner, 1991; Riegel, 1975).

Relationism and integration have a clear implication for unilevel theories of development. At best, such theories are severely limited and inevitably provide a nonveridical depiction of development, due to their focus on what are essentially main effects embedded in higher-order interactions (e.g., see Walsten, 1990); at worst, such theories are neither valid nor useful. Accordingly, biogenic theories (e.g., genetic reductionistic conceptions such as behavioral genetics or sociobiology; Freedman, 1979; Plomin, 1986; Rowe, 1994; Wilson, 1975), psychogenic theories (e.g., behavioristic or functional analysis models; Baer, 1970, 1976; Bijou, 1976; Bijou & Baer, 1961, Skinner, 1938), or sociogenic theories (e.g., "social mold" conceptions of socialization; Homans, 1961; see Hartup, 1978, for a review) do not provide adequate theoretical frames for understanding human development).

Thus, neither nature theories nor nurture theories provide adequate conceptual frames for understanding human development (Hirsch, 1970; Lewontin, 1992). For instance, theories that stress critical periods of development (e.g., Ainsworth, Blehar, Waters, & Well, 1978; Bowlby, 1969; Erikson, 1959, 1968; Lorenz, 1965, 1966)—that is, periods of ontogeny constrained by biology (e.g., by genetics or by maturation)—are seen from the perspective of theories that stress relationism and integration as conceptually flawed (and empirically counterfactual).

Many nature–nurture interaction theories also fall short in this regard; they still treat variables of nature and nurture as separable entities, and they view their connection in manners analogous to the interaction term in an analysis of variance (e.g., Bijou, 1976; Erikson, 1959; Plomin, 1986; see also Gollin, 1981; Hebb, 1970; Walsten, 1990). The theories represented in this volume (a) move beyond the simplistic division of sources of development into nature-related and nurture-related variables or processes, and (b) see the multiple levels of organization that exist within the ecology of human development as part of an inextricably fused developmental system.

Relationism, Integration, and the Role of Timing in Human Development

Because of the mutual embeddedness of organism and context, a given organismic attribute will have different implications for developmental outcomes in the milieu of different contextual conditions; the organism attribute is given its functional meaning only by virtue of its relation to a specific context. If the context changes significantly, as it may over time, then the same organism attribute will have a different import for development. In turn, the same contextual condition will lead to alternative developments as different organisms interact with it.

To state this position in somewhat stronger terms, a given organismic attribute only has meaning for psychological development by virtue of its timing of interaction—that is, its relation to a particular set of time-bound, contextual conditions (Elder, this volume; Lerner, Jacobson, & Perkins, 1992). For example, the biological import of menarche per se, and its implications for changes in the young girl's sexual behaviors, will vary in relation to the time, within an individual's ontogeny, when menarche occurs. Menarche may have a detrimental influence on the

girl's resistance to engaging in problem behaviors (e.g., unsafe sex or delinquency) if it occurs at a time early in the girl's adolescence, and especially if, at this time, the girl is still thinking in "concrete operational" (Piaget, 1950, 1970) terms and is embedded in a social and/or school setting where older, postpubertal females and males are in attendance (e.g., Caspi, Lynam, Moffitt, & Silva, 1993; Stattin & Magnusson, 1990). If menarche occurs at a later time in the girl's life—for example, when she is in the "formal operational" (Piaget, 1950, 1970) period of cognitive development—such problem behaviors may be less likely to occur, especially if she has a social and/or school setting composed in the main of same-age males and females (Stattin & Magnusson, 1990).

The import of any set of contextual conditions for psychosocial behavior and development can only be understood by specifying the context's relation to the specific developmental features of the organisms within it. Reversing the above example of the import of the timing of menarche for problem behaviors, it is possible to argue that knowing the age status of the peer group during adolescence will not alone be sufficient for understanding the incidence of problem behaviors in adolescent girls; menarche status and timing, in interaction with the age constitution of the peer group, all need to be considered to attain such understanding.

This central role for the timing of organism–context interactions in the determination of the nature and outcomes of development is, of course, the probabilistic component of probabilistic epigenesis (Gottlieb, 1970, 1983, 1992; Gottlieb et al., this volume; Kuo, 1967, 1976; Scarr, 1982; Scarr & McCartney, 1983; Tobach, 1981). Accordingly, one must consider the meaning of such probabilism for the ways in which individuals can, through influencing their context, produce their own development (cf. Brandtstädter, this volume). More generally, one should consider how the probabilistic—that is, interindividually differentially timed—interactions between organismic characteristics and contextual variables form a process of developmental change involving an active, self-constructing, unique life course for each person. I will discuss these issues below, when I consider the role of biology and context in providing a basis of individual differences in human development. However, it is useful to consider first how the concepts of relationism and integration afford understanding of the role in human development of fusions among levels of analysis.

The Fusion of Levels in Human Development

Within a developmental systems perspective, no single level of organization is seen as the primary or the ultimate causal influence on behavior and development. Instead, a field, or a configural view of developmental causality, is maintained (Ford, 1987; Ford & Lerner, 1992; Overton, this volume), and variables from different levels (e.g., heredity and environment) are seen as coequal forces in the determination of behavior.

Indeed, the domains—heredity (genes) and environment—are seen to be completely integrated in life (Gollin, 1981). This fusion of heredity and environment—of nature and nurture—means that they are mutually permissive and mutually constraining in influencing behavior. Biology may "permit" more or less of a given behavior, and/or may promote one or another quite different behavior; what occurs depends on the environmental circumstances within which people exist and, more superordinately, on the timing of the interaction between these environmental circumstances and the biological characteristics of the people in the setting (Anastasi, 1958; Lehrman, 1953, 1970; Schneirla, 1956, 1957; Tobach & Schneirla, 1968).

To illustrate, in one set of circumstances, a girl may have genes that are associated with beginning her menstrual cycle quite early—say, at about 10 years of age; yet, as noted earlier, the nutritional and health care she receives will influence whether her cycle begins at this time, later, or perhaps even earlier (Katchadourian, 1977). The environment may "promote" more or less of a particular behavior, and/or may afford one or another characteristic, depending on the specific biological characteristics of the people living in the environment (Tanner, 1991). Excellent nutritional and health care may maximize the possible height of members of groups of people who are of hereditarily shorter stature than the average person (e.g., members of pygmy tribes); however, no known diet or medical intervention will increase the typically occurring height of members of this group to the levels found, say, in groups having hereditarily tall stature (Katchadourian, 1977).

Thus, genes and environment always constrain each other, but their mutual influence on each other means that these constraints are flexible, not absolute. The human genome constrains humans' ability to see through the skull of another person in order to inspect the brain for lesions or tumors; however, this same genome—by participating in the development of humans' cognitive system, ingenuity, and industriousness—contributes to an ability to peer into the brains of others through the invention and implementation of X-ray and CAT-scan machines.

The developmental systems perspective is consistent, then, with geneticist R. C. Lewontin's (1981) views about the issue of constraints:

It is trivially true that material conditions of one level constrain organization at higher levels in principle. But that is not the same as saying that such constraints are quantitatively nontrivial. Although every object in the universe has a gravitational interaction with every other object, no matter how distant, I do not, in fact, need to adjust my body's motion to the movement of individuals in the next room. The question is not whether the nature of the human genotype is relevant to social organization, but whether the former constrains the latter in a nontrivial way, or whether the two levels are effectively decoupled. It is the claim of vulgar sociobiology that some kinds of human social organization are either impossible, or that they can be maintained only at the expense of constant psychic and political stress, which will inevitably lead to undesirable side effects because the nature of the human genome dictates a "natural" social organization. Appeals to abstract dependencies (in principle) of one level or another do not speak to the concrete issue of whether society is genetically constrained in an important way . . . in fact, constraints at one level may be destroyed by higher level activity. No humans can fly by flapping their arms because of anatomical and physiological constraints that reflect the human genome. But humans do fly, by using machines that are the product of social organization and that could not exist without very complex social interaction and evolution. As another example, the memory capacity of a single individual is limited, but social organization, through written records and the complex institutions associated with them, makes all knowledge recoverable for each individual. Far from being constrained by lower-level limitations, culture transcends them and feeds back to lower levels to relieve the constraints. Social organization, and human culture in particular, are best understood as negating constraints rather than being limited by them. (p. 244)

In short, then, the fusion of heredity and environment, as conceived of within a perspective emphasizing developmental systems, means there is a resulting mutuality of influence between these two levels of organization; in addition, there is a mutuality of flexibility in the constraints they impose on behavior and development. This fusion means there is relative plasticity in human behavior and development. However, the range of behaviors that can occur in an individual's life is certainly not infinite or limitless (Lerner, 1984). Females cannot, as a group, begin their menstrual cycle (that is, experience menarche) at 5 years of age; and pygmies, as a group, cannot have an average adult height of 6 feet. However, the concept of relative plasticity means that the number of distinct characteristics any one individual could show is quite large, given the fusion of heredity and environment. Girls' menarche can begin, within normal limits, at anytime between the ninth and seventeenth years (Katchadourian, 1977; Tanner, 1991), the average height of any group of adults can vary widely, and the intelligence, personality, or motivation of people can show an enormous degree of variation (Plomin, 1986).

Given the character of relative plasticity, then, extensive variability exists among people because (a) genotypes and environments vary and (b) no two people in the world have the same fusion of genes and environments across their lives (Lerner, 1988; Lerner & Tubman, 1989). Even if two individuals have the same genotype [as is the case for monozygotic (MZ) twins] and experience the same array of people and events, any variation in the timing of these experiences could lead to differences between the pair. In other words, individual differences between people—in their genes, in their contexts, and in the timing of interrelation between genes and contexts—provide the bases of variability in human development (Elder, this volume).

Even MZ twins do not share the same environments across life. Environments differ in their physical, interpersonal, community, and cultural characteristics. Although identical twins have the same genotype, their respective genes are not likely to be fused with identical environments across their entire life spans. Each twin meets different people, may have different teachers, and may fall in love with and marry a different type of person. Even for identical twins, behavior and development will be different.

Simply stated, there are multiple levels of the environment or context of life, and differences exist within each level. For example, within the physical environment are differences in noise level, pollution, climate, and terrain. As discussed in more detail below, genotypes are at least equally variable, and they too exist in an intraorganism milieu that has potentially changing "physical environmental" characteristics—for example, involving the products of

cellular metabolism (Gottlieb, 1991). The fusion of these two sources of human behavior and development means that, in effect, each person is distinct. The magnitude of individual differences among people underscores the gross errors one makes when characterizing entire groups of people—racial, religious, or gender groups—as homogeneous and undifferentiated in significant ways.

In short, integrated interlevel changes comprise the process of developmental change within a developmental systems perspective. If the course of human development is the product of the processes involved in the "fusions" (or "dynamic interactions"; Lerner, 1978, 1979, 1984) among integrative levels, then the processes of development are more plastic than often previously believed (cf. Brim & Kagan, 1980).

HISTORICAL EMBEDDEDNESS AND TEMPORALITY

The relational units of analysis that are of concern in contemporary theories are understood as change units (see chapters by Brandtstädter; Bronfenbrenner & Morris; Magnusson & Stattin; and Thelen & Smith, this volume; Lerner, 1991). The change component of these units derives from the idea that all of the levels of organization involved in human development are embedded in history; that is, they are integrated with historical change (chapters by Baltes et al.; Cairns; Elder; Overton; Shweder et al.; and Valsiner, this volume; Elder, 1980; Elder, Modell, & Parke, 1993). Relationism and integration mean that no level of organization functions as a consequence of its own isolated activity (chapters by Brandtstädter; Gottlieb et al.; Thelen & Smith; and Wapner & Demick, this volume; Gottlieb, 1992; Tobach, 1981; Tobach & Schneirla, 1968). Each level functions as a consequence of its fusion (its structural integration) with other levels (Gottlieb et al., this volume; Tobach & Greenberg, 1984). History—change occurring over time—is incessant and continuous, and it is a level of organization that is fused with all other levels. This linkage means that change is a necessary, an inevitable, feature of variables from all levels of organization (chapters by Baltes et al.; Brandtstädter; Overton; and Wapner & Demick, this volume; Baltes, 1987; Lerner, 1984); in addition, this linkage means that the structure, as well as the function, of variables changes over time.

An illustration of the temporality of developmental change occurs in regard to secular trends in child and adolescent physical and physiological maturation (Garn, 1980; Katchadourian, 1977; Tanner, 1991). Since 1900, children of preschool age have been taller (an average of 1.0 centimeter) and heavier (an average of 0.5 kilogram) in each successive decade (Katchadourian, 1977). Changes in height and weight occurring during the adolescent growth spurt have involved gains of 2.5 centimeters and 2.5 kilograms, respectively (Falkner, 1972; Katchadourian, 1977). In addition, there has been a historical trend toward a younger average age of menarche. Among European samples of young girls, there was an average decrease of about four months in age, per decade, from about 1840 to about 1950 (Tanner, 1962, 1991). This rate seems to have slowed down, but has not stopped (Marshall & Tanner, 1986; Tanner, 1991). Within American samples, however, the trend toward a younger age of menarche seems to have stopped in about 1940. Since that time, the expected (mean) age of menarche among European and American samples has been 12.5 years. In Japan, a dramatic secular trend has been evidenced. From the immediate post-World War II years until about 1975, the average age of menarche accelerated by 11 months per decade (Marshall & Tanner, 1986). These temporal changes in the biological maturation of youth have been linked to historical improvements in health and nutrition in the respective nations, and variation has been associated with socioeconomic and technological changes in their societies. Biological structure and function and societal structure and function are linked systemically across history.

Indeed, at the biological level of organization, one prime set of such structural changes is subsumed under the concept of evolution (chapters by Cairns; Gardner; Gottlieb et al.; Keil; and Overton, this volume; Gould, 1977; Lewontin, 1981; Lewontin, Rose, & Kamin, 1984); of course, the concept of evolution can be applied also to functional changes (Darwin, 1872; Gottlieb, 1992). At more macro levels of organization, many of the historically linked changes in social and cultural institutions or products are evaluated in the context of discussions of the concept of progress (Nisbet, 1980).

The continuity of change that constitutes history can lead to both intraindividual (or, more generally, intralevel) continuity or discontinuity in development—depending on the rate, scope, and particular substantive component of the developmental system by which change is measured (chapters by Baltes et al., and Elder, this volume; Brim & Kagan, 1980; Lerner, 1986, 1988; Lerner & Tubman, 1989). Thus, continuity at one level of analysis may be coupled with discontinuity at another level; quantitative continuity or discontinuity may be coupled with qualitative continuity or discontinuity within and across levels; and continuity or discontinuity can exist in regard to both the processes involved in (or the "explanations" of) developmental change and in the features, depictions, or outcomes (i.e., the "descriptions") of these processes (Cairns & Hood, 1983; Lerner, 1986).

These patterns of within-person change pertinent to continuity and discontinuity can result in either constancy or variation in the rates at which different individuals develop in regard to a particular substantive domain of development. Thus, any pattern of intraindividual change can be combined with any instance of interindividual differences in within-person change (i.e., with any pattern of stability or instability; Lerner, 1986; Lerner & Tubman, 1989). In other words, continuity–discontinuity is a dimension of intraindividual change and is distinct from, and independent of, stability–instability—which involves between-person change, and is, therefore, a group (not an individual) concept (Baltes & Nesselroade, 1973; Lerner, 1976, 1986).

In sum, because historical change is continuous, temporality is infused in all levels of organization (Elder, this volume; Elder, Modell, & Parke, 1993). Accordingly, the temporality involved in contemporary theories of human development necessitates change-sensitive measures of structure and function *and* change-sensitive (i.e., longitudinal) designs (chapters by Bronfenbrenner & Morris; Fischer et al.; and Overton, this volume; Baltes, Reese, & Nesselroade, 1977; Brim & Kagan, 1980). The key question vis-à-vis temporality in such research is not whether change occurs, but whether the changes that do occur make a difference for a given developmental outcome (Lerner, Skinner, & Sorell, 1980).

Given that the study of these changes will involve appraisal of both quantitative and qualitative features of change, which may occur at multiple levels of organization, there is a need to use both quantitative and qualitative data collection and analysis methods—methods associated with the range of disciplines having specialized expertise at the multiple levels of organization at which either quantitative or qualitative change can occur (Shweder et al., this volume). In essence, then, the concepts of historical embeddedness and temporality indicate that, to address adequately the relational, integrated, embedded, and temporal changes involved in human life, a program of developmental research must involve multiple occasions, methods, levels, variables, and cohorts (Baltes, 1987; Lerner, 1986, 1991; Schaie & Strother, 1968).

Temporality, Basic Process, and Application in Human Development

A developmental systems perspective—and the implications it suggests for research, through concepts such as temporality—may seem descriptively cumbersome, inelegant (if not untestable) in regard to explanations of individual and group (e.g., family) behavior and development, and, as a consequence, of little use in the formulation of interventions (policies or programs) aimed at enhancing individual and social life. In response to such criticism, I would argue that, in the face of the profound historical changes in the lives of children and their families that have occurred across this century (e.g., see Elder et al., 1993; Hernandez, 1993), it would seem, at best, implausible to maintain that the nature of the human life course has been unaffected by this history. For example, it is not plausible to assert that: (a) the historical changes that have resulted in an average age of menarche of 12.5 years in America— that is, an age when girls, although they may be capable of sexual reproduction, typically do not have the cognitive or behavioral capacity to assume the responsibilities that may accrue from sexual relations—are not related to (b) historical increases in the United States in rates of engagement in high-risk sexual behaviors, teenage pregnancy, childbearing, and one-parent teenage families (Dryfoos, 1990; Hernandez, 1993; Lerner, 1995). Accordingly, it would seem necessary to adopt some sort of developmental systems perspective in order to incorporate the impact of such historical changes, and the contemporary diversity they have created, into the matrix of covariation considered in developmental explanations and the interventions that should, at least ideally, be derived from them (Lerner & Miller, 1993).

Yet, it would be traditional in developmental psychology to assert that the historical variation and contemporary diversity of human (individual and group) development were irrelevant for understanding *basic* processes. Indeed,

within developmental psychology, the conventional view of basic process, whether involving cognition, emotion, personality, or social behavior, is that it is a function generalizable across time and place. I believe, however, that data such as those presented by Elder et al. (1993) and Hernandez (1993)—which document the profound impact of historical change on individual and family life over the course of just the past two centuries—constitute a serious challenge to the ontological presuppositions that have grounded this view of basic process and of developmental psychology's theory and research about people's ontogenies.

Can learning, cognition, and emotional life—and the brain and neuroendocrine systems underlying these functions—be argued to occur invariantly in the context of the differing economic, nutritional, and medical resource environments, and the systems of work, school, and family relationships, that have occurred over the course of the past century and that, today, are involved in the diverse social contexts (e.g., families) of America and the world? Can developmental psychology, with a historical record of minimal attention to history (Elder et al., 1993), context (Bronfenbrenner, 1979), and diversity (Graham, 1992; Lerner, 1991), contend that the atemporal and acontextual study of the individual is an appropriate or adequate focus of its inquiry?

I believe the answer to both of these questions is "No," and, quite simply, the traditional view of basic process found in developmental psychology (i.e., the prototypic view for much of the past 50 to 60 years) cannot be defended in the face of the historical and contextual variation characterizing American individuals and families across the past century. Indeed, without adequate tests of, and evidence for, its presuppositions about the irrelevance of temporality, context, and diversity for its view of basic process, the field of developmental psychology fails in even an attempt to represent veridically the course of human life (Cairns, this volume).

By weaving historical change and contextual specificities into the matrix of causal covariation that shapes human developmental trajectories, I believe that a developmental systems perspective can reconstitute the core process of human development, from a reductionistic and individualistic process to a synthetic, or multilevel integrated, one. That is, a developmental systems perspective stresses temporality and relationality and the field, or configural, view of causality noted above (Ford & Lerner, 1992; Overton, this volume). Through the seemingly simple step of integrating historical change, contextual variation, and individual developmental change, a developmental systems perspective provides a paradigmatic departure from the psychogenic, biogenic, or reductionistic environmentalist models of causality that have undergirded the theories of child development that have been prevalent during most of the 20th century (Gottlieb, 1992; Lerner, 1986, 1991). These theories typify a reductionism and a contextual insensitivity that occur because developmental psychologists are traditionally focused on psychogenic views of the course of human development (Dannefer, 1984; Meyer, 1988).

Such a psychogenic, or exclusively individualistic perspective, has led numerous developmental psychologists, and perhaps especially those who study cognitive functioning, to take the a priori position that any phenomenon of individual behavior and development that interacts with the context is not a basic psychological process; this same orientation has resulted in the contention that information about temporal or interindividual variation is not relevant to the understanding of basic process. Accordingly, the several "revolutions" that have occurred over the past 150 years in the nature of the family context of American children's development (e.g., involving decreases in family size; changes in maternal and paternal employment patterns; a different set of structures—for instance, single-parent units—characterizing American families; and the spread of youth poverty; Hernandez, 1993) have not been seen by the psychogenicists populating developmental psychology as relevant to the nature or study of basic process.

However, the historical changes and contextual variation that characterize America's children and families challenge this position, not only by presenting ontologically revolutionary ideas to developmental psychologists, but as well by promoting epistemological revisions among those who have studied child development through unidisciplinary lenses. As noted by Cahan, Mechling, Sutton-Smith, and White (1993, p. 210), "if childhood is not everywhere and everyplace the same—and the anthropologists and social historians have been amply demonstrating to us that it is not—then the meaning and object of all forms of psychological research have to be reconsidered." Accordingly, a multiplicity of qualitative and quantitative methods—associated with the several disciplines that have demonstrated this temporal and relational specificity of child development—must be used to construct the knowledge of the multiple levels of organization that are involved in the system linking children and contexts (Shweder et al., this volume). Use of these methods in relation to contextually sensitive theory affords an empirically richer focus on classic issues in the study of personality (e.g., regarding individual differences) and of cognition (e.g., regarding learning) that have concerned developmental psychologists across the 20th century (e.g., see chapters in this volume by Cairns; Magnusson & Stattin; and Spelke & Newport).

In short, I believe that a developmental systems view of the historical and developmental ecology of individual and family life helps reduce the incidence of what Elder et al. (1993, p. 6) term the "blindness to social history and context" prevalent in much of psychology—and even sociology—a blindness that, to paraphrase Elder et al. (p. 7) has envisioned the child as embedded in the atemporal and acontextual realm of abstract developmental theory. This is, to say the least, a curious conceptual stance for a field seemingly focused on change.

THE LIMITS OF GENERALIZABILITY, DIVERSITY, AND INDIVIDUAL DIFFERENCES

The temporality of the changing relations among levels of organization means that changes that are seen within one historical period (or time of measurement), and/or with one set of instances of variables from the multiple levels of the ecology of human development, may not be seen at other points in time (chapters by Bronfenbrenner & Morris; Cairns; Elder; and Valsiner, this volume; Baltes et al., 1977; Bronfenbrenner, 1979). What is seen in one data set may be only an instance of what does or what could exist. Accordingly, contemporary theories focus on diversity—of people, of relations, of settings, and of times of measurement (chapters by Baltes et al.; Brandtstädter; Bronfenbrenner & Morris; Fischer & Bidell; Fisher et al.; Overton; and Wapner & Demick, this volume; Lerner, 1991, 1995, 1996).

Individual differences within and across all levels of organization are seen as having core, substantive significance in the understanding of human development (Baltes et al., this volume; Lerner, 1991, 1995, 1996). Diversity is the exemplary illustration of the presence of relative plasticity in human development (Fisher et al., this volume;

Lerner, 1984). Diversity is also the best existing evidence of the potential for change in the states and conditions of human life (Brim & Kagan, 1980).

Moreover, the individual structural and functional characteristics of a person constitute an important source of his or her development (chapters by Brandtstädter and by Csikszentmihalyi & Rathunde, this volume; Brandtstädter, 1985; Lerner, 1982; Lerner & Busch-Rossnagel, 1981). The individuality of each person promotes variation in the fusions he or she has with the levels of organization within which he or she is embedded. For instance, the distinct actions or physical features of a person promote differential actions (or reactions) in others toward him or her (Lerner, 1987). These differential actions, which constitute feedback to the person, shape, at least in part, further change in the person's characteristics of individuality (Lerner & Lerner, 1989; Schneirla, 1957).

For example, the changing match, congruence, or goodness-of-fit between the developmental characteristics of the person and of his or her context provides a basis for consonance or dissonance in the ecological milieu of the person. The dynamic nature of this interaction constitutes a source of variation in positive and negative outcomes of developmental change (chapters by Baltes et al., and by Fischer & Bidell, this volume; Chess & Thomas, 1984; Lerner & Lerner, 1983; Thomas & Chess, 1977; Thomas, Chess, Birch, Hertzig, & Korn, 1963).

Several studies of American adolescents report that pubertal maturation alters negatively the nature of the social interactions between youth and their parents; for example, at the height of pubertal change more conflict and greater emotional distance are seen (e.g., Hill, Holmbeck, Marlow, Green, & Lynch, 1985a, 1985b; Holmbeck & Hill, 1991; Steinberg, 1987, 1990; Steinberg & Hill, 1978). However, these findings have been derived in large part from research with homogeneous European American samples of adolescents and their families (Brooks-Gunn & Reiter, 1990). Accordingly, when diversity is introduced into the database used for understanding the links between pubertal change and adolescent–parent relationships, a much more complicated—and richer and more interesting—pattern is evident. Among samples of Latino (primarily, Mexican American) boys and their families, pubertal maturation brings adolescents *closer* to their parents (Molina & Chassin, 1996). Puberty among these Latino youths is associated with greater parental social support and less intergenerational conflict than is the case either for corre-

spondingly mature European American samples (where the completely opposite effect of puberty on family relations is seen) or for Latino youths prior to or after their maturation.

In essence, then, racial/ethnic, cultural, and developmental diversity must be understood systemically in order to appreciate the nature and variation that exist within and across time in human behavior and development. In other words, individual differences arise inevitably from the action of the developmental system; in turn, they move the system in manners that elaborate diversity further. It is useful to discuss in more detail the nature and import of individuality in human development.

Bases of Individual Differences in Human Development

The fusion of levels of organization—involving levels associated with the individual (e.g., his or her genetic inheritance) and with the context (e.g., the social and institutional world within which the person develops)—provides the field of relationships causing structural and functional development. Variations in the timing of the intermeshing of changes associated with one or more components of this field are, in turn, the cause of interindividual differences in structural and functional development (Elder, this volume; Lerner, et al., 1992). Such individual differences are promoted further by the fact that, across the life span, no two people have precisely the same elements in their "causal fields" (Ford & Lerner, 1992; Lerner, 1988; Lerner & Foch, 1987; Lerner & Tubman, 1989; Overton, this volume). Indeed, humans' genetic endowment provides a basis of the uniqueness of each human life and gives substance to the claim that all humans have an individually unique causal field of biology-context relations across their lives.

For example, estimates of the number of gene pairs in humans typically range between 10,000 and 100,000. If one considers how much genotype variability can be produced by the reshuffling process of meiosis (the division that forms the sex cells—sperm and ova) occurring with 100,000 gene pairs, then the potential for variability is so enormous that "it is next to impossible that there have ever been two individuals with the same combination of genes" (McClearn, 1981, p. 19).

Indeed, a conservative estimate is that there are over 7×10^{17} (or over 70 trillion) potential human genotypes. Geneticists have estimated that each human has the capacity to generate any one of $10^{3,000}$ different eggs or sperm; by comparison, their estimate of the number of sperm of all men who have ever lived is only 10^{24}. Thus, considering $10^{3,000}$ eggs possibly being generated by an individual woman and $10^{3,000}$ sperm possibly being generated by an individual man, the likelihood of anyone ever—in the past, present, or future—having the same genotype as anyone else (except when multiple identical births occur, of course) becomes dismissibly small (McClearn, 1981, p. 19).

A given human's genetic individuality may be seen to be even greater if we recognize that genetic does not mean congenital. The "total genome is not functioning at fertilization, or at birth, or at any other time of life" (McClearn, 1981, p. 26). Therefore, the expression of any individual human genotype is a developmental phenomenon, influenced in regard to the turning on and/or off of genes by the internal and the external components of the individual's history of genotype–environment fusions. McClearn (1981, p. 26) gives, as an illustration:

> the differential production of certain kinds of hemoglobin during various phases of development. For example, production of the beta chain accelerates at the time of birth and peaks after a few months, whereas production of the alpha chain rises prenatally and maintains a high level.

A still further indication of the possible variability among humans is the nature of genes' molecular structure: It is estimated that 6 billion nucleotide bases comprise the DNA of the human genome (McClearn, 1981). The vast number of these distinct chemicals provides an enormous "population" within which mutation (permanent alterations in genetic material) can occur.

This enormous genetic variability among humans is all the more striking because, in the determination of behavior, it is fused with environments that have at least equal variation (e.g., see Bronfenbrenner, 1979; Bronfenbrenner & Morris, this volume; Willems, 1973). As I noted earlier, not only do people have individually distinct genotypes, but no two people (including MZ twins) share the same historical array of events, contexts, and social encounters across their lives. As suggested by Lerner (1988; Lerner & Tubman, 1989), not only does each person have a "biological genotype" (to use a redundancy) but each person has, as well, a "social genotype" (to use an oxymoron). Across life, these two domains of individuality change interdependently, and this integration means that, in the determination of behavior and development, heredity and environment do not

function separately. In addition, they do not merely interact; *interaction* connotes two independent entities that merely multiply in their effects on behavior (Gollin, 1981; Tobach, 1981). *Fusion* implies a reciprocal relation between components of an intermeshed system. Such interactions are termed dynamic.

As Gottlieb (1991, p. 5) explains, the most significant feature of this dynamic, systems view "is the explicit recognition that the genes are an integral part of the system and that their activity (i.e., genetic expression) is affected by events at other levels of the system, including the environment of the organism." Genes must dynamically interact with the environment if they are to be involved in the development of any physical or behavioral characteristic of a person. In this regard, Gottlieb (1991, p. 24) indicates that "Genetic activity does not by itself produce finished traits such as blue eyes, arms, legs, or neurons. The problem of anatomical and physiological differentiation remains unsolved, but it is unanimously recognized as requiring influences above the strictly cellular level (i.e., cell-to-cell interactions, positional influences, and so forth). . . . Thus, the concept of the genetic determination of traits is truly outmoded."

In sum, the influence of genes depends thoroughly on where they exist in space (within the developing person) and in developmental time (i.e., when, in the life of the person, they coact with the environment). Accordingly, it is important to understand that dynamic interactions between biology (organism, genes, or heredity) and context (the multiple levels of the human development) provide a basis for the relative plasticity of behavior and development.

These dynamic interactions create, and promote a focus in developmental scholarship on, individual differences—of people and of settings—*and* on changes in both of these types of differences and in the relations between them (i.e., in person–context relations). Understanding and study of these temporal dimensions of dynamic interactions are critical not only for theoretical precision but also for advancing research and application in human development. This assertion leads to some concluding comments.

CONCLUSIONS AND IMPLICATIONS

I have argued that the major assumptive dimensions of contemporary theories of human development—systematic change and relative plasticity, relationism and integration, embeddedness and temporality, and generalizability limits and diversity—are very much intertwined facets of a common theoretical core. They form the corpus of a superordinate developmental systems view of human development (chapters by Bronfenbrenner & Morris; Fischer & Bidell; Gardner; Gottlieb et al.; Magnusson & Stattin; Thelen & Smith; and Wapner & Demick, this volume; Ford & Lerner, 1992). As is the case with the several defining features of the life-span developmental perspective, which—according to Baltes (1987)—need to be considered as an integrated whole, the assumptive dimensions of contemporary developmental theories need to be appreciated simultaneously. Such appreciation is required to understand the breadth, scope, and implications for research and application of this "family" of concepts involved in contemporary theories.

Implications for Research

A developmental systems perspective involves the study of active people providing a source, across the life span, of their individual developmental trajectories; this development occurs through the dynamic interactions people experience with the specific characteristics of the changing contexts within which they are embedded (Brandtstädter, this volume). This stress on the dynamic relation between the individual and his or her context results in the recognition that a synthesis of perspectives from multiple disciplines is needed to understand the multilevel (e.g., person, family, and community) integrations involved in human development. In addition, to understand the basic process of human development—the process of change involved in the relations between individuals and contexts—both descriptive and explanatory research must be conducted within the actual ecology of people's lives.

In the case of explanatory studies, such investigations, by their very nature, constitute intervention research. The role of the developmental researcher conducting explanatory research is to understand the ways in which variations in person–context relations account for the character of human developmental trajectories, life paths that are enacted in the "natural laboratory" of the "real world." Therefore, to gain understanding of how theoretically relevant variations in person–context relations may influence developmental trajectories, the researcher may introduce policies and/or programs as, if you will, "experimental manipulations" of the proximal and/or distal natural ecology; evaluations of the outcomes of such interventions become, then, a means to bring data to bear on theoretical issues pertinent to person–context relations and, more specifically, on the plasticity in human development that may exist, or that may be capitalized on, to enhance human life (Csikszentmihalyi & Rathunde, this volume; Lerner, 1984). In other words, a key theoretical issue for explanatory research in human development is the extent to which changes—in the multiple, fused levels of organization comprising human life—can alter the structure and/or function of behavior and development.

Life itself is, of course, an intervention. The accumulation of the specific roles and events a person experiences across the life span—involving normative age-graded events, normative history-graded events, and nonnormative events (Baltes et al., this volume; Baltes, Reese, & Lipsitt, 1980)—alters each person's developmental trajectory in a manner that would not have occurred had another set of roles and events been experienced. The interindividual differences in intraindividual change that exist as a consequence of these naturally occurring interventions attest to the magnitude of the systematic changes in structure and function—the plasticity—that characterize human life.

Explanatory research is necessary, however, to understand what variables, from what levels of organization, are involved in particular instances of plasticity that have been seen to exist. In addition, such research is necessary to determine what instances of plasticity may be created by science or society. In other words, explanatory research is needed to ascertain the extent of human plasticity or the limits of plasticity (Baltes, 1987; Baltes et al., this volume; Lerner, 1984). From a developmental systems perspective, the conduct of such research may lead the scientist to alter the natural ecology of the person or group he or she is studying. Such research may involve proximal and/or distal variations in the context of human development (Lerner & Ryff, 1978); in any case, these manipulations constitute theoretically guided alterations of the roles and events a person or group experiences at, or over, a portion of the life span.

These alterations are indeed, then, interventions—planned attempts to alter the system of person–context relations that constitute the basic process of change; they are conducted in order to ascertain the specific bases of, or to test the limits of, particular instances of human plasticity

(Baltes, 1987; Baltes & Baltes, 1980; Baltes et al., this volume). These interventions are a researcher's attempt to substitute designed person–context relations for naturally occurring ones in an effort to understand the process of changing person–context relations that provides the basis of human development. In short, basic research in human development is intervention research (Lerner et al., 1994).

Accordingly, the cutting edge of theory and research in human development lies in the application of the conceptual and methodological expertise of human development scientists to the natural ontogenetic laboratory of the real world. Multilevel—and hence, multivariate—and longitudinal research methods must be used by scholars from multiple disciplines to derive, from theoretical models of person–context relations, programs of "applied research"; these endeavors must involve the design, delivery, and evaluation of interventions aimed at enhancing—through scientist-introduced variation—the course of human development (Birkel, Lerner, & Smyer, 1989).

Relationism and contextualization have brought to the fore of scientific, intervention, and policy concerns some issues that are pertinent to the functional import of diverse instances of person–context interactions. Examples are studies of the effects of maternal employment, of marital disruption, or of single-parent families, on infant, child, and young adolescent development; the importance of quality day care, of variation in school structure and function, and of neighborhood resources and programs for the immediate and long-term development in children of healthy physical, psychological, and social characteristics; and the effects of peer group norms and behaviors, of risk behaviors, and of economic resources on the healthy development of children and youth.

As a result of greater study of the actual contexts within which children and parents live, behavioral and social scientists have shown increasing appreciation of the diversity of patterns of individual and family development that exist, and that comprise the range of human structural and functional characteristics. Such diversity—involving racial, ethnic, gender, national, and cultural variation—has, to the detriment of the knowledge base in human development, not been a prime concern of empirical analysis (Fisher et al., this volume; Hagen, Paul, Gibb, & Wolters, 1990).

Yet, for several reasons, this diversity must become a key focus of concern in the study of human development. Diversity of people and their settings means that one cannot assume that general rules of development either exist for, or apply in the same way to, all children and families (Fisher & Brennan, 1992; Fisher & Tryon, 1990; Lerner, 1988; Lerner & Tubman, 1989). This is not to say that general features of human development do not exist, or that descriptive research documenting such characteristics is not an important component of past, present, and future scholarship. However, the lawful individuality of human behavior and development means that one should not make a priori assumptions that characteristics identified in one group, or even in several groups, exist or function in the same way in another group. Moreover, even when common characteristics are identified in diverse groups, we cannot be certain that the individual or unique attributes of each group—even if they account for only a small proportion of the variance in the respective groups' functioning—are not of prime import for understanding the distinctive nature of the groups' development *or* for planning key components of policies or programs (i.e., for planning "services") designed for the groups.

A new research agenda is necessary—an agenda that focuses on diversity and context while at the same time attending to commonalities of individual development, family changes, and the mutual influences between the two. In other words, diversity should be placed at the fore of our research agenda. Then, with a knowledge of individuality, we can determine empirically the parameters of commonality, of interindividual generalizability. We should no longer make a priori assumptions about the existence of generic developmental laws or the primacy of such laws, even if they are found to exist, in providing the key information about the life of a given person or group.

Integrated multidisciplinary and developmental research devoted to the study of diversity and context must be moved to the fore of scholarly concern. In addition, however, scholars involved in such research must have at least two other concerns, deriving from the view that basic, explanatory research in human development is, in its essence, intervention research.

Implications for Policies and Programs

The integrative research promoted by a developmental systems view of human development should be synthesized with two other foci. Research in human development that is concerned with one or even a few instances of individual and contextual diversity cannot be assumed to be useful for understanding the life course of all people. Similarly, policies and programs derived from such research, or associated with it in the context of a researcher's tests of ideas pertinent to human plasticity, cannot hope to be applicable, or equally appropriate and useful, in all contexts or for all individuals. Therefore, developmental and individual differences-oriented policy development and program (intervention) design and delivery must be integrated fully with the new research base for which I am calling.

Because of the variation in settings within which people live, studying development in a standard (for example, a "controlled") environment does not provide information pertinent to the actual (ecologically valid) developing relations between individually distinct people and their specific contexts (for example, their particular families, schools, or communities). This point underscores the need to conduct research in real-world settings (Bronfenbrenner, 1974; Zigler & Finn-Stevenson, 1992) and highlights these ideas: (a) policies and programs constitute natural experiments, that is, planned interventions for people and institutions; and (b) the evaluation of such activities becomes a central focus in the developmental systems research agenda I have described (Cairns, this volume; Lerner, 1995; Lerner, Ostrom, & Freel, 1995; Ostrom, Lerner, & Freel, 1995).

In this view, policy and program endeavors do not constitute secondary work, or derivative applications, conducted after research evidence has been compiled. Quite to the contrary, policy development and implementation, and program design and delivery, become integral components of the present vision for research; the evaluation component of such policy and intervention work provides critical feedback about the adequacy of the conceptual frame from which this research agenda should derive (Zigler & Finn-Stevenson, 1992).

To be successful, this developmental, individual-differences, and contextual view of research, policy, and programs for human development requires more than collaboration across disciplines: Multiprofessional collaboration is essential. Colleagues in the research, policy, and intervention communities must plan and implement their activities in a synthesized manner in order to successfully develop and extend this vision. All components of this collaboration must be understood as equally valuable—indeed, as equally essential. The collaborative activities of colleagues in university outreach, in service design and

delivery, in policy development and analysis, and in academic research are vital to the success of this new agenda for science and service for children, youth, and their various contexts—their families, schools, and communities. Moreover, such collaborative activities must involve the communities within which such work is undertaken (Lerner & Miller, 1993; Lerner, Miller, & Ostrom, 1995; Miller & Lerner, 1994).

In other words, to enhance ecological validity, and to provide empowerment and increased capacity among the people we are trying both to understand and to serve with our synthetic research and intervention activities, we must work with the community to codefine the nature of our research and program design, and our delivery and evaluation endeavors. In short, we must find ways to apply our scientific expertise to collaborate with, and promote the life chances of, the people participating in our developmental scholarship. Such steps will provide needed vitality for the future progress of the field of human development.

Enhancing Applied Developmental Science across the Life Span

The future scholarly and societal significance of our field lies in application of developmental science, that is, in building a scientific enterprise that works to help envision, enact, and sustain effective policies and programs promoting the positive development of people across the life span (Zigler & Finn-Stevenson, 1992). Such a focus of the scholarship of our field is, on the one hand, a logical and—if judged by the above noted trends in the theoretical foci of our field—an inevitable outcome of the growth and progress we have experienced as a scientific community (Cairns, this volume; Zigler & Finn-Stevenson, 1992). On the other hand, the four key sets of conceptual themes involved in contemporary theories in our field lead us to embrace a focus (a) on ecologically embedded research, (b) on testing our notions of person–context relational systems, and (c) on relative plasticity, in order to appraise whether theoretically predicated changes in the nature and course of the relations children have with the proximal and distal features of their context can alter in salutary ways the trajectories of their development. In other words, the concepts of development embraced in our field lead us to test our theories through intervention/action research. Simply, I believe that within the field of scholarship about human development, basic research and applied research are synthetic, indivisible endeavors.

A developmental systems perspective leads us to recognize that, if we are to have an adequate and sufficient science of child development, we must integratively study individual and contextual levels of organization in a relational and temporal manner (Bronfenbrenner, 1974; Zigler & Finn-Stevenson, 1992). Anything less will not constitute adequate science. And if we are to serve America's children and families through our science, if we are to help develop successful policies and programs through our scholarly efforts, then we must accept nothing less than the integrative temporal and relational model of the child that is embodied in the developmental systems perspective forwarded in contemporary theories of human development.

Through its research, our field has an opportunity to serve both scholarship and the communities, families, and people of our world. By integrating policies and programs sensitive to the diversity of our communities and our people, by combining the assets of our scholarly and research traditions with the strengths of our people, we can improve on the often-cited idea of Kurt Lewin (1943), that there is nothing as practical as a good theory. We can, through the application of our science to serve our world's citizens, actualize the idea that there is nothing of greater value to society than a science devoted to using its scholarship to improve the life chances of all people.

REFERENCES

Ainsworth, M. D. S., Blehar, M. C., Waters, E., & Wall, S. (1978). *Patterns of attachment.* Hillsdale, NJ: Erlbaum.

Anastasi, A. (1958). Heredity, environment, and the question, "how?" *Psychological Review, 65,* 197–208.

Baer, D. M. (1970). An age-irrelevant concept of development. *Merrill-Palmer Quarterly of Behavior and Development, 16,* 238–245.

Baer, D. M. (1976). The organism as host. *Human Development, 19,* 87–98.

Baldwin, J. M. (1897). *Social and ethical interpretations in mental development: A case study in social psychology.* New York: Macmillan.

Baltes, P. B. (1987). Theoretical propositions of life-span developmental psychology: On the dynamics between growth and decline. *Developmental Psychology, 23,* 611–626.

Baltes, P. B., & Baltes, M. M. (1980). Plasticity and variability in psychological aging: Methodological and theoretical issues. In G. E. Gurski (Ed.), *Determining the effects of aging on the central nervous system* (pp. 41–66). Berlin: Schering.

Baltes, P. B., & Nesselroade, J. R. (1973). The developmental analysis of individual differences on multiple measures. In J. R. Nesselroade & H. W. Reese (Eds.), *Life-span developmental psychology: Introduction to research methodological issues* (pp. 219–251). New York: Academic Press.

Baltes, P. B., Reese, H. W., & Lipsitt, L. P. (1980). Life-span developmental psychology. *Annual Review of Psychology, 31,* 65–110.

Baltes, P. B., Reese, H. W., & Nesselroade, J. R. (1977). *Life-span developmental psychology: Introduction to research methods.* Monterey, CA: Brooks/Cole.

Belsky, J., Steinberg, L., & Draper, P. (1991). Childhood experience, interpersonal development, and reproductive strategy: An evolutionary theory of socialization. *Child Development, 62,* 647–670.

Bertalanffy, L., von (1933). *Modern theories of development.* London: Oxford University Press.

Bijou, S. W. (1976). *Child development: The basic stage of early childhood.* Englewood Cliffs, NJ: Prentice-Hall.

Bijou, S. W., & Baer, D. M. (Ed.). (1961). *Child development: A systematic and empirical theory.* New York: Appleton-Century-Crofts.

Birkel, R., Lerner, R. M., & Smyer, M. A. (1989). Applied developmental psychology as an implementation of a life-span view of human development. *Journal of Applied Developmental Psychology, 10,* 425–445.

Bowlby, J. (1969). *Attachment and loss: Vol. 1. Attachment.* New York: Basic Books.

Brandtstädter, J. (1985). Individual development in social action contexts: Problems of explanation. In J. R. Nesselroade & A. von Eye (Eds.), *Individual development and social change: Explanatory analysis* (pp. 243–264). New York: Academic Press.

Brauth, S. E., Hall, W. S., & Dooling, R. J. (Eds.). (1991). *Plasticity of development.* Cambridge, MA: MIT Press.

Brim, O. G., Jr., & Kagan, J. (Eds.). (1980). *Constancy and change in human development.* Cambridge, MA: Harvard University Press.

Bronfenbrenner, U. (1974). Developmental research, public policy, and the ecology of childhood. *Child Development, 45,* 1–5.

Bronfenbrenner, U. (1979). *The ecology of human development.* Cambridge, MA: Harvard University Press.

Brooks-Gunn, J., & Reiter, E. O. (1990). The role of pubertal processes in the early adolescent transition. In S. Feldman & G. Elliott (Eds.), *At the threshold: The developing adolescent* (pp. 16–53). Cambridge, MA: Harvard University Press.

Cahan, E., Mechling, J., Sutton-Smith, B., & White, S. H. (1993). The elusive historical child: Ways of knowing the child of history and psychology. In G. H. J. Elder, J. Modell, & R. D. Parke (Eds.), *Children in time and place: Developmental and historical insights* (pp. 192–223). New York: Cambridge University Press.

Cairns, R. B., & Hood, K. E. (1983). Continuity in social development: A comparative perspective on individual difference prediction. In P. B. Baltes & O. G. Brim, Jr. (Eds.), *Life-span development and behavior* (Vol. 5). New York: Academic Press.

Caspi, A., Lynam, D., Moffitt, E. E., & Silva, P. A. (1993). Unraveling girls' delinquency: Biological, dispositional, and contextual contributions to adolescent misbehavior. *Developmental Psychology, 29,* 19–30.

Chess, S., & Thomas, A. (1984). *The origins and evolution of behavior disorders: Infancy to early adult life.* New York: Brunner/Mazel.

Dannefer, D. (1984). Adult developmental and socialization theory: A paradigmatic reappraisal. *American Sociological Review, 49,* 100–116.

Darwin, C. (1872). *The expression of emotion in men and animals.* London: J. Murray.

Dewey, J. (1916). *Democracy and education: An introduction to the philosophy of education.* New York: Macmillan.

Dryfoos, J. G. (1990). *Adolescents at risk: Prevalence and prevention.* New York: Oxford University Press.

Dryfoos, J. G. (1994). *Full-service schools: A revolution in health and social services of children, youth and families.* San Francisco: Jossey-Bass.

Elder, G. H., Jr. (1974). *Children of the Great Depression: Social change in life experiences.* Chicago: University of Chicago Press.

Elder, G. H., Jr. (1980). Adolescence in historical perspective. In J. Adelson (Ed.), *Handbook of adolescent psychology* (pp. 3–46). New York: Wiley.

Elder, G. H., Jr., Modell, J., & Parke, R. D. (Eds.). (1993). *Children in time and place: Developmental and historical insights.* New York: Cambridge University Press.

Erikson, E. H. (1959). Identity and the life-cycle. *Psychological Issues, 1,* 18–164.

Erikson, E. H. (1968). *Identity, youth and crisis.* New York: Norton.

Falkner, F. (1972). Physical growth. In H. L. Bennett & A. H. Einhorn (Eds.), *Pediatrics.* New York: Appleton-Century-Crofts.

Featherman, D. L. (1983). Life-span perspectives in social science research. In P. B. Baltes & O. G. Brim, Jr. (Eds.), *Life-span development and behavior* (Vol. 5, pp. 1–57). New York: Academic Press.

Fisher, C. B., & Brennan, M. (1992). Application and ethics in developmental psychology. In D. L. Featherman, R. M. Lerner, & M. Perlmutter (Eds.), *Life-span development and behavior* (Vol. 11, pp. 189–219). Hillsdale, NJ: Erlbaum.

Fisher, C. B., & Lerner, R. M. (Eds.). (1994). *Applied developmental psychology.* New York: McGraw-Hill.

Fisher, C. B., & Tryon, W. W. (1990). Emerging ethical issues in an emerging field. In C. B. Fisher & W. W. Tryon (Eds.), *Ethics in applied developmental psychology: Emerging issues in an emerging field* (pp. 1–15). Norwood, NJ: ABLEX.

Ford, D. H. (1987). *Humans as self-constructing living systems.* Hillsdale, NJ: Erlbaum.

Ford, D. L., & Lerner, R. M. (1992). *Developmental systems theory: An integrative approach.* Newbury Park, CA: Sage.

Freedman, D. G. (1979). *Human sociobiology: A holistic approach.* New York: Free Press.

Freud, S. (1949). *Outline of psychoanalysis.* New York: Norton.

Garn, S. M. (1980). Continuities and change in maturational timing. In O. G. Brim, Jr. & J. Kagan (Eds.), *Constancy and change in human development* (pp. 113–162). Cambridge, MA: Harvard University Press.

Gollin, E. S. (1981). Development and plasticity. In E. S. Gollin (Ed.), *Developmental plasticity: Behavioral and biological aspects of variations in development* (pp. 231–251). New York: Academic Press.

Gottlieb, G. (1970). Conceptions of prenatal behavior. In R. Aronson, E. Tobach, D. S. Lehrman, & J. S. Rosenblatt (Eds.), *Development and evolution of behavior: Essays in memory of T. C. Schneirla* (pp. 111–137). San Francisco: Freeman.

Gottlieb, G. (1983). The psychobiological approach to developmental issues. In M. M. Haith & J. J. Campos (Eds.), *Handbook of child psychology: Infancy and biological bases* (Vol. 2, pp. 1–26). New York: Wiley.

Gottlieb, G. (1991). The experiential canalization of behavioral development: Theory. *Developmental Psychology, 27,* 4–13.

Gottlieb, G. (1992). *Individual development and evolution: The genesis of novel behavior.* New York: Oxford University Press.

Gould, S. J. (1977). *Ontogeny and phylogeny.* Cambridge, MA: Belknap Press of Harvard.

Graham, S. (1992). "Most of the subjects were white and middle class": Trends in published research on African Americans in selected APA journals, 1970–1989. *American Psychologist, 47,* 629–639.

Hagen, J. W., Paul, B., Gibb, S., & Wolters, C. (1990, March). Trends in research as reflected by publications in *Child Development: 1930–1989.* In *Biennial Meeting of the Society for Research on Adolescence,* Atlanta, GA.

Hamburg, D. A. (1992). *Today's children: Creating a future for a generation in crisis.* New York: Time Books.

Hamburger, V. (1957). The concept of development in biology. In D. B. Harris (Ed.), *The concept of development* (pp. 49–58). Minneapolis: University of Minnesota Press.

Hartup, W. W. (1978). Perspectives on child and family interaction: Past, present, and future. In R. M. Lerner & G. B. Spanier (Eds.), *Child influences on marital and family interaction: A life-span perspective* (pp. 23–45). New York: Academic Press.

Hebb, D. O. (1949). *The organization of behavior.* New York: Wiley.

Hebb, D. O. (1970). A return to Jensen and his social critics. *American Psychologist, 25,* 568.

Hebb, D. O. (1980). *Essay on mind.* Hillsdale, NJ: Erlbaum.

Hernandez, D. J. (1993). *America's children: Resources from family, government, and the economy.* New York: Russell-Sage Foundation.

Herrnstein, R. (1973). *IQ and the meritocracy.* Boston: Little, Brown.

Herrnstein, R., & Murray, C. (1994). *The bell curve.* New York: Free Press.

Hill, J. P., Holmbeck, G. N., Marlow, L., Green, T. M., & Lynch, M. E. (1985a). Menarcheal status and parent–child relations in families of seventh-grade girls. *Journal of Youth and Adolescence, 14,* 301–316.

Hill, J. P., Holmbeck, G. N., Marlow, L., Green, T. M., & Lynch, M. E. (1985b). Pubertal status and parent–child relations in families of seventh-grade boys. *Journal of Early Adolescence, 5,* 31–44.

Hirsch, J. (1970). Behavior-genetic analysis and its biosocial consequences. *Seminars in Psychiatry, 2,* 89–105.

Ho, M. -W. (1984). Environment and heredity in development and evolution. In M. -W. Ho & P. T. Saunders (Eds.), *Beyond neo-Darwinism: An introduction to the new evolutionary paradigm* (pp. 267–289). London: Academic Press.

Holmbeck, G. N., & Hill, J. P. (1991). Conflictive engagement, positive affect, and menarche in families with seventh-grade girls. *Child Development, 62,* 1030–1048.

Homans, G. C. (1961). *Social behavior: Its elementary forms.* New York: Harcourt, Brace, & World.

Jensen, A. R. (1969). How much can we boost IQ and scholastic achievement? *Harvard Educational Review, 39,* 1–123.

Jensen, A. R. (1980). *Bias in mental testing.* New York: Free Press.

Katchadourian, H. (1977). *The biology of adolescence.* San Francisco: Freeman.

Kreppner, K. (1994). William L. Stern: A neglected founder of developmental psychology. In R. D. Parke, P. A. Ornstein, J. J. Rieser, & C. Zahn-Waxler (Eds.), *A century of developmental psychology* (pp. 311–331). Washington, DC: American Psychological Association.

Kuo, Z.-Y. (1930). The genesis of the cat's response to the rat. *Journal of Comparative Psychology, 11,* 1–35.

Kuo, Z.-Y. (1967). *The dynamics of behavior development.* New York: Random House.

Kuo, Z.-Y. (1976). *The dynamics of behavior development: An epigenetic view.* New York: Plenum Press.

Lehrman, D. S. (1953). A critique of Konrad Lorenz's theory of instinctive behavior. *Quarterly Review of Biology, 28,* 337–363.

Lehrman, D. S. (1970). Semantic and conceptual issues in the nature–nurture problem. In L. R. Aronson, E. Tobach, & J. S. Rosenblatt (Eds.), *Development and evolution of behavior: Essays in memory of T. C. Schneirla* (pp. 17–52). San Francisco: Freeman.

Lerner, R. M. (1976). *Concepts and theories of human development.* Reading, MA: Addison-Wesley.

Lerner, R. M. (1977). Biographies of DeSanctis, S. (Vol. III, p. 96), Dewey, J. (Vol. IV, p. 94), Gesell, A. (Vol. V, p. 209), Goodenough, F. (Vol. V, p. 225), Locke, J. (Vol. VI, p. 443), Terman, L. M. (Vol. XI, p. 102), Werner, H. (Vol. XI, pp. 419–420), & Witmer, L. (Vol. XI, p. 425). In B. B. Wolman (Ed.), *International encyclopedia of neurology, psychiatry, psychoanalysis, and psychology.* New York: Van Nostrand-Reinhold.

Lerner, R. M. (1978). Nature, nurture, and dynamic interactionism. *Human Development, 21,* 1–20.

Lerner, R. M. (1979). The life-span view of human development: The sample case of aging. *Contemporary Psychology, 24,* 1008–1009.

Lerner, R. M. (1982). Children and adolescents as producers of their own development. *Developmental Review, 2,* 342–370.

Lerner, R. M. (1984). *On the nature of human plasticity.* New York: Cambridge University Press.

Lerner, R. M. (1986). *Concepts and theories of human development* (2nd ed.). New York: Random House.

Lerner, R. M. (1987). A life-span perspective for early adolescence. In R. M. Lerner & T. T. Foch (Eds.), *Biological–psychosocial interactions in early adolescence: A life-span perspective* (pp. 9–34). Hillsdale, NJ: Erlbaum.

Lerner, R. M. (1988). Personality development: A life-span perspective. In E. M. Hetherington, R. M. Lerner, & M. Perlmutter (Eds.), *Child development in life-span perspective* (pp. 21–46). Hillsdale, NJ: Erlbaum.

Lerner, R. M. (1991). Changing organism–context relations as the basic process of development: A developmental–contextual perspective. *Developmental Psychology, 27,* 27–32.

Lerner, R. M. (1995). *America's youth in crisis: Challenges and options for programs and policies.* Thousand Oaks, CA: Sage.

Lerner, R. M. (1996). Relative plasticity, integration, temporality, and diversity in human development: A developmental contextual perspective about theory, process, and method. *Developmental Psychology, 32,* 781–786.

Lerner, R. M., & Busch-Rossnagel, N. A. (Eds.). (1981). *Individuals as producers of their development: A life-span perspective.* New York: Academic Press.

Lerner, R. M., & Foch, T. T. (Eds.). (1987). *Biological–psychosocial interactions in early adolescence.* Hillsdale, NJ: Erlbaum.

Lerner, R. M., & Hood, K. E. (1986). Plasticity in development: Concepts and issues for intervention. *Journal of Applied Developmental Psychology, 7,* 139–152.

Lerner, R. M., Jacobson, L. P., & Perkins, D. F. (1992). Timing, process, and the diversity of developmental trajectories in human life: A developmental contextual perspective. In G. Turkewitz & D. Devenny (Eds.), *Developmental time and timing* (pp. 41–59). Hillsdale, NJ: Erlbaum.

Lerner, R. M., & Lerner, J. V. (1983). Temperament–intelligence reciprocities in early childhood: A contextual model. In M. Lewis (Ed.), *Origins of intelligence: Infancy and early childhood* (pp. 399–421). New York: Plenum Press.

Lerner, R. M., & Lerner, J. V. (1989). Organismic and social contextual bases of development: The sample case of early adolescence. In W. Damon (Ed.), *Child development today and tomorrow* (pp. 69–85). San Francisco: Jossey-Bass.

Lerner, R. M., & Miller, J. R. (1993). Integrating human development research and intervention for America's children: The Michigan State University model. *Journal of Applied Developmental Psychology, 14,* 347–364.

Lerner, R. M., Miller, J. R., Knott, J. H., Corey, K. E., Bynum, T. S., Hoopfer, L. C., McKinney, M. H., Abrams, L. A., Hula, R. C., & Terry, P. A. (1994). Integrating scholarship and outreach in human development research, policy, and service: A developmental contextual perspective. In D. L. Featherman, R. M. Lerner, & M. Perlmutter (Eds.), *Life-span development and behavior* (Vol. 12, pp. 249–273). Hillsdale, NJ: Erlbaum.

Lerner, R. M., Miller, J. R., & Ostrom, C. W. (1995, Spring). Integrative knowledge, accountability, access, and the American university of the twenty-first century: A family and consumer sciences vision of the future of higher education. *Kappa Omicron Nu FORUM, 8*(1), 11–27.

Lerner, R. M., Ostrom, C. W., & Freel, M. A. (1995). Promoting positive youth and community development through outreach scholarship: Comments on Zeldin and Peterson. *Journal of Adolescent Research, 10,* 486–502.

Lerner, R. M., & Ryff, C. D. (1978). Implementation of the life-span view of human development: The sample case of attachment. In P. B. Baltes (Ed.), *Life-span development and behavior* (Vol. 1, pp. 1–44). New York: Academic Press.

Lerner, R. M., Skinner, E. A., & Sorell, G. T. (1980). Methodological implications of contextual/dialectic theories of development. *Human Development, 23,* 225–235.

Lerner, R. M., & Tubman, J. (1989). Conceptual issues in studying continuity and discontinuity in personality development across life. *Journal of Personality, 57,* 343–373.

Lewin, K. (1935). *A dynamic theory of personality.* New York: McGraw-Hill.

Lewin, K. (1943). Psychology and the process of group living. *Journal of Social Psychology, 17,* 113–131.

Lewin, K. (1954). Behavior and development as a function of the total situation. In L. Carmichael (Ed.), *Manual of child psychology* (2nd ed.). New York: Wiley.

Lewontin, R. C. (1981). On constraints and adaptation. *Behavioral and Brain Sciences, 4,* 244–245.

Lewontin, R. C. (1992). Foreword. In R. M. Lerner (Ed.), *Final solutions: Biology, prejudice, and genocide* (pp. vii-viii). University Park: Penn State Press.

Lewontin, R. C., Rose, S., & Kamin, L. J. (1984). *Not in our genes: Biology, ideology, and human nature.* New York: Pantheon Press.

Lorenz, K. (1965). *Evolution and modification of behavior.* Chicago: University of Chicago Press.

Lorenz, K. (1966). *On aggression.* New York: Harcourt, Brace, & World.

MacDonald, K. (1994). *A people that shall dwell alone: Judaism as an evolutionary group strategy.* Westport, CT: Greenwood.

Marshall, W. A., & Tanner, J. M. (1986). Puberty. In F. Falkner & J. M. Tanner (Eds.), *Human growth* (2nd ed.) (Vol. 2, pp. 171–209). New York: Plenum Press.

McClearn, G. E. (1981). Evolution and genetic variability. In E. S. Gollin (Ed.), *Developmental plasticity: Behavioral and biological aspects of variations in development* (pp. 3–31). New York: Academic Press.

Meyer, J. W. (1988). The social construction of the psychology of childhood: Some contemporary processes. In E. M. Hetherington, R. M. Lerner, & M. Perlmutter (Eds.), *Child development in life-span perspective* (pp. 47–65). Hillsdale, NJ: Erlbaum.

Miller, J. R., & Lerner, R. M. (1994). Integrating research and outreach: Developmental contextualism and the human ecological perspective. *Home Economics Forum, 7,* 21–28.

Molina, B. S. G., & Chassin, L. (1996). The parent–adolescent relationship at puberty: Hispanic ethnicity and parent alcoholism as moderators. *Developmental Psychology, 32,* 675–686.

Mussen, P. H. (Ed.). (1970). *Carmichael's manual of child psychology* (3rd ed.). New York: Wiley.

Nisbet, R. A. (1980). *History of the idea of progress.* New York: Basic Books.

Ostrom, C. W., Lerner, R. M., & Freel, M. A. (1995). Building the capacity of youth and families through university-community collaborations: The development-in-context evaluation (DICE) model. *Journal of Adolescent Research, 10,* 427–448.

Piaget, J. (1950). *The psychology of intelligence.* New York: Harcourt Brace.

Piaget, J. (1970). Piaget's theory. In P. H. Mussen (Ed.), *Carmichael's manual of child psychology* (Vol. 1, pp. 703–732). New York: Wiley.

Plomin, R. (1986). *Development, genetics, and psychology.* Hillsdale, NJ: Erlbaum.

Plomin, R., Corley, R., DeFries, J. C., & Faulker, D. W. (1990). Individual differences in television viewing in early childhood: Nature as well as nurture. *Psychological Science, 1,* 371–377.

Riegel, K. F. (1975). Toward a dialectical theory of development. *Human Development, 18,* 50–64.

Riegel, K. F. (1976a). The dialectics of human development. *American Psychologist, 31,* 689–700.

Riegel, K. F. (1976b). From traits and equilibrium toward developmental dialectics. In W. J. Arnold & J. K. Cole (Eds.), *Nebraska Symposium on Motivation* (pp. 348–408). Lincoln: University of Nebraska.

Rowe, D. C. (1994). *The limits of family influence: Genes, experience, and behavior.* New York: Guilford Press.

Rushton, J. P. (1987). An evolutionary theory of health, longevity, and personality: Sociobiology and r/K reproductive strategies. *Psychological Reports, 60,* 539–549.

Rushton, J. P. (1988). Do r/K reproductive strategies apply to human differences? *Social Biology, 35,* 337–340.

Sameroff, A. J. (1983). Developmental systems: Contexts and evolution. In W. Kessen (Ed.), *Handbook of child psychology: Vol. 1. History, theory, and methods* (pp. 237–294). New York: Wiley.

Scarr, S. (1982). Development is internally guided, not determined. *Contemporary Psychology, 27,* 852–853.

Scarr, S., & McCartney, K. (1983). How people make their own environments: A theory of genotype–environment effects. *Child Development, 54,* 424–435.

Schaie, K. W., & Strother, C. R. (1968). A cross-sequential study of age changes in cognitive behavior. *Psychological Bulletin, 70,* 671–680.

Schneirla, T. C. (1956). Interrelationships of the innate and the acquired in instinctive behavior. In P. P. Grasse (Ed.), *L'instinct dans le comportement des animaux et de l'homme* (pp. 387–452). Paris: Masson et Cie.

Schneirla, T. C. (1957). The concept of development in comparative psychology. In D. B. Harris (Ed.), *The concept of development* (pp. 78–108). Minneapolis: University of Minnesota Press.

Simmons, R. G., & Blyth, D. A. (1987). *Moving into adolescence: The impact of pubertal change and school context.* Hawthorne, NJ: Aldine.

Skinner, B. F. (1938). *The behavior of organisms.* New York: Appleton.

Smith, L. B., & Thelen, E. (Eds.). (1993). *A dynamic systems approach to development: Applications.* Cambridge, MA: MIT Press.

Stattin, H., & Magnusson, D. (1990). *Pubertal maturation in female development.* Hillsdale, NJ: Erlbaum.

Steinberg, L. (1987). The impact of puberty on family relations: Effects of pubertal status and pubertal timing. *Developmental Psychology, 23,* 833–840.

Steinberg, L. (1990). Autonomy, conflict, and harmony in the family relationship. In S. S. Feldman & G. R. Elliott (Eds.), *At the threshold: The developing adolescent* (pp. 255–276). Cambridge, MA: Harvard University Press.

Steinberg, L., & Hill, J. (1978). Patterns of family interaction as a function of age, the onset of puberty, and formal thinking. *Developmental Psychology, 14,* 683–684.

Stern, W. (1914). *Psychologie der frühen Kindheit bis zum sechsten Lebensiahr.* Leipzig: Quelle & Meyer.

Strohman, R. C. (1993a). Organism and experience [Review of the book *Final solutions*]. *Journal of Applied Developmental Psychology, 14,* 147–151.

Strohman, R. C. (1993b). Book reviews. *Integrative Physiology and Behavioral Science, 28,* 99–110.

Tanner, J. M. (1962). *Growth at adolescence.* Springfield, IL: Thomas.

Tanner, J. M. (1970). Physical growth. In P. H. Mussen (Ed.), *Carmichael's manual of child psychology* (Vol. 1, pp. 77–155). New York: Wiley.

Tanner, J. M. (1991). Menarche, secular trend in age of. In R. M. Lerner, A. C. Petersen, & J. Brooks-Gunn (Eds.), *Encyclopedia of adolescence* (pp. 637–641). New York: Garland.

Thelen, E., & Smith, L. B. (1994). *A dynamic systems approach to the development of cognition and action.* Cambridge, MA: MIT Press.

Thomas, A., & Chess, S. (1977). *Temperament and development.* New York: Brunner/Mazel.

Thomas, A., Chess, S., Birch, H. G., Hertzig, M. E., & Korn, S. (1963). *Behavioral individuality in early childhood.* New York: New York University Press.

Tobach, E. (1981). Evolutionary aspects of the activity of the organism and its development. In R. M. Lerner & N. A. Busch-Rossnagel (Eds.), *Individuals as producers of their development: A life-span perspective* (pp. 37–68). New York: Academic Press.

Tobach, E., & Greenberg, G. (1984). The significance of T. C. Schneirla's contribution to the concept of levels of integration. In G. Greenberg & E. Tobach (Eds.), *Behavioral*

evolution and integrative levels (pp. 1–7). Hillsdale, NJ: Erlbaum.

Tobach, E., & Schneirla, T. C. (1968). The biopsychology of social behavior of animals. In R. E. Cooke & S. Levin (Eds.), *Biologic basis of pediatric practice* (pp. 68–82). New York: McGraw-Hill.

Villarruel, F. A., & Lerner, R. M. (Eds.). (1994, Spring). *Promoting community-based programs for socialization and learning.* San Francisco: Jossey-Bass.

Walsten, D. (1990). Insensitivity of the analysis of variance to heredity–environment interaction. *Behavioral and Brain Sciences, 13,* 109–120.

Wapner, S. (1993). Parental development: A holistic, developmental systems-oriented perspective. In J. Demick, K. Bursik, & R. DiBiase (Eds.), *Parental development* (pp. 3–37). Hillsdale, NJ: Erlbaum.

Watson, J. B. (1928). *Psychological care of infant and child.* New York: Norton.

Werner, H. (1957). The concept of development from a comparative and organismic point of view. In D. B. Harris (Ed.), *The concept of development* (pp. 125–148). Minneapolis: University of Minnesota Press.

Willems, E. P. (1973). Behavioral ecology and experimental analysis: Courtship is not enough. In J. R. Nesselroade & H. W. Reese (Eds.), *Life-span developmental psychology: Methodological issues.* New York: Academic Press.

Wilson, E. O. (1975). *Sociobiology: The new synthesis.* Cambridge, MA: Harvard University Press.

Zigler, E., & Finn-Stevenson, M. (1992). Applied developmental psychology. In M. H. Bornstein & M. E. Lamb (Eds.), *Developmental psychology: An advanced textbook* (3rd ed., pp. 677–729). Hillsdale, NJ: Erlbaum.

CHAPTER 2

The Making of Developmental Psychology

ROBERT B. CAIRNS

This chapter is an introduction to the ideas, people, and events that have guided scientific activity in developmental psychology over the past century. Its preparation has been facilitated by several recent publications on the history of developmental psychology. The views of the past held by active researchers are reflected in chapters of the edited volume, *A Century of Developmental Psychology* (Parke, Ornstein, Rieser, & Zahn-Waxler, 1994). The contributors are, with few exceptions, currently involved in contemporary research. Secondary commentaries can provide useful guides and interpretations, but there is no substitute for consulting original sources. To that end, a reprint series containing historically significant original articles and volumes has been prepared by Wozniak (e.g., 1993, 1997).

Other recent volumes include the contributions of professional historians and others who are not enmeshed in current empirical debates of the discipline (e.g., Broughton & Freeman-Moir, 1982; Elder, Modell, & Parke, 1993). In addition, the social relevance and the making of the discipline in American society have been told expertly by Sears (1975) and White (1995). Any single overview—including this one—can tell only part of the story.[1]

---

[1] This chapter owes much to two earlier chapters that I wrote on the history of developmental psychology (Cairns, 1983; Cairns & Ornstein, 1979), and I am deeply grateful to several people who contributed to the preparation of the earlier works: Peter A. Ornstein, Beverley D. Cairns, Robert R. Sears, William Kessen, Ronald W. Oppenheim, Alice Smuts, and Lloyd Borstlemann. In this version, I benefited from the careful reading of the entire manuscript by Robert Wozniak who offered invaluable insights, criticism, and corrections. In the final preparation of the manuscript, the staff of the Center for Developmental Science provided helpful assistance. I am particularly indebted to Philip R. Rodkin for his help. This chapter could not have been written without the multiple contributions of Beverley D. Cairns.

Adopting the convention used in the previous *Handbook of Child Psychology*, 20 years must lapse before a contribution or event qualifies as historical. Two decades constitute approximately one generation in the life of our science; therefore, 1976 is the endpoint for material in this revised chapter. This rule makes the task manageable and sharpens the focus on the events of the past.

DEVELOPMENT AND HISTORY

It is mildly ironic that an area committed to the study of the origins and development of behavior and consciousness traditionally has shown little interest in its own origins and development. In the great handbooks of the field, the first five (Carmichael, 1946, 1954; Murchison, 1931, 1933; Mussen, 1970) did not include historical overviews; in the 1983 edition of this volume, this state of affairs was changed when two chapters on history were included (Borstelmann, 1983; Cairns, 1983). The earlier reluctance to look to our past, though regrettable, is understandable. If substantive progress is to be made in new empirical research, it will be won by those who look ahead rather than backward. There are also institutional and economic limits on scholarship where journal space is precious, and historical reviews and comments are afforded low priority. The upshot is that contemporaneous research articles tend to bypass the work and insights of earlier investigators. This neglect of the past has been correlated with a more general tendency to give short shrift to competing findings, concepts, and interpretations. Such shortcomings in scholarship, if unchecked, can undermine real progress in the discipline.

Historical accounts are neither static nor immutable. As new information about the nature of developmental phenomena becomes available, perspectives on earlier events may shift in emphasis and interpretation. Similarly, as new findings and issues emerge, prior relevance can be reevaluated and viewed in a fresh light. The rediscovery of J. M. Baldwin's contributions is a case in point. With the increased interest in integrative concepts of cognitive, moral, and social development, it was perhaps inevitable that researchers should rediscover the intellectual foundation for developmental studies provided by Baldwin. A direct line of influence has been drawn between the concepts of J. M. Baldwin and those of Jean Piaget, L. S. Vygotsky,

H. Wallon, and L. Kohlberg (see Broughton & Freeman-Moir, 1982; Cairns, 1992; Valsiner & van der Veer, 1993). The construction of the intellectual history of a science is necessarily an ongoing enterprise.

One point of consensus is that developmental psychology has its own distinctive history, which is associated with but independent of the history of experimental or general psychology. The year 1979—one century after Wundt established a psychology laboratory at the University of Leipzig—was the centennial of scientific psychology (Hearst, 1979). The assignment involves a modest fiction, since even a casual reading of the literature of the day indicates that the enterprise of modern psychology was already well under way in 1879 in the laboratories of Helmholtz, Fechner, Weber, Lotze, James, and Galton (Littman, 1979).

Looking backward, it might seem inevitable that the study of behavioral development should have emerged as the focal problem for the new science of psychology. Several of the founders of the discipline approached the subject matter of psychology from a developmental perspective, and the genetic theme was influential in philosophical and biological thought in the late 19th century. Alfred Binet in France, William Preyer and William Stern in Germany, Herbert Spencer and George J. Romanes in England, and several American psychologists (from G. S. Hall and John Dewey to James Mark Baldwin and John B. Watson) agreed on the fundamental viewpoint of development, if little else. What is the fundamental viewpoint? Watson, who is often depicted as an opponent of the developmental approach, indicated that developmental methods require the continuous observation and analysis "of the stream of activity beginning when the egg is fertilized and ever becoming more complex as age increases" (1926, p. 33). For Watson, the developmental approach was:

> [the] fundamental point of view of the behaviorist—viz. that in order to understand man you have to understand the life history of his activities. It shows, too, most convincingly, that psychology is a natural science—a definite part of biology. (p. 34)

Nor was the kernel idea of development a new one for biological science or for psychology. It had guided the work and thinking of physiologist Karl von Baer (1828) and those who followed his early lead in the establishment of comparative embryology. It was also a basic theme in the earliest systematic statements of psychology (Reinert, 1979).

But not all of the founders of the new science subscribed to the developmental perspective or the assumption that psychology was a definite part of biology. Some of the most influential—including Wilhelm Wundt himself—had a different view. Noting the difficulties that one encounters in efforts to study young children in experimental settings, Wundt argued that "it is an error to hold, as is sometimes held, that the mental life of adults can never be fully understood except through the analysis of the child's mind. The exact opposite is the true position to take" (1907, p. 336).

Even the father of child psychology in America, G. Stanley Hall, relegated developmental concerns to minor league status in the new psychology. In the inaugural lectures at Johns Hopkins, Hall (1885) followed his mentor Wundt in holding that psychology could be divided into three areas: (a) experimental psychology, (b) historical psychology, and (c) the study of instinct. The study of children and adolescents was assigned to historical psychology, which included as well the study of primitive people and folk beliefs. Instinct psychology dealt with those processes and behaviors that were considered innate, thus encompassing much of what is today called comparative and evolutionary psychology. Of the three divisions, Hall considered experimental psychology to be the "more central and reduced to far more exact methods." These methods included the use of reaction time, psychophysical procedures, and introspection to examine the relations between sensation and perception. Historical and instinct psychology necessarily relied on observational and correlational methods, hence were seen as less likely to yield general and enduring principles. Hall's divisions were consistent with the proposals of numerous writers—Auguste Compte, John Stuart Mills, Wilhelm Wundt—who called for a second psychology to address aspects of human mind and behavior that were based in the culture (Cahan & White, 1992; Wundt, 1916). In Hall's account, the 2nd psychology was a second-class psychology.

The division between experimental and developmental psychology has proved to be remarkably durable—but that is getting ahead of the story. The main point is that developmental issues could have been nuclear concerns for the new science, but they were not. They have not even played a significant role in the history of experimental psychology (see Boring, 1929, 1950).

There is also consensus that the initiation of the scientific study of children represents the convergence of two forces, one social and the other scientific. The scientific background is the primary focus of this chapter, and our principal attention will be given to the intellectual and empirical foundations of the discipline.

But there were also social and political roots. Sears (1975) observed, in his classic chapter titled "Your Ancients Revisited," that:

> By the end of the [19th] century, there had developed a vaguely cohesive expertise within the professions of education and medicine, and the origins of social work as a helping profession were clearly visible. During the first two decades of the twentieth century, these professions began relevant research to improve their abilities, but their main influence on the future science was their rapidly expanding services for children in the schools, hospitals, clinics, and social agencies. This expansion continued after World War I, and it was in the next decade, the 1920s, that scientists from several non-professionally oriented ("pure science") disciplines began to join the researchers from the child-oriented professions to create what we now view as the scientific field of child development. But like the engineering sciences which evolved from physics and chemistry, child development is a product of social needs that had little to do with science qua science. . . . The field grew out of *relevance*. (p. 4, author's emphasis)

Whether it is viewed as a creation of social forces or as an inevitable outcome of open scientific inquiry, developmental psychology was established as a separate research discipline only within the past century. However, its scientific roots in biology extend back at least an additional 100 years. It was then that fundamental questions on the origin of life, species transmutation, and individual development began to generate empirical investigations.

BIOLOGICAL ROOTS: EMBRYOLOGY AND EVOLUTION

A strong case could be made that the early scientific roots of developmental psychology are to be found in embryology and evolutionary biology rather than in experimental psychophysics. Two core ideas in 19th-century biological thought directly shaped developmental psychology and require attention: (a) K. E. von Baer's developmental principle and (b) C. R. Darwin's evolutionary theory.

The Developmental Principle

Karl Ernst von Baer (1792–1876) ranks as one of the great original biologists of the 19th century, alongside Curvier, Lamarck, and Darwin (Hamburger, 1970). Born in Estonia, of German ancestry, he did his pivotal work on anatomical development at Würzburg and Königsberg. The pioneer of comparative embryology, von Baer discovered the human ovum and the notochord (the gelatinous, cylindrical cord in the embryo of vertebrates around which, in higher forms, the backbone and skull develop). More relevant to this chapter, von Baer generalized beyond his empirical work in embryology and anatomy to enunciate general principles on the fundamental nature of ontogenetic change (Baer, 1828–1837). He proposed that development proceeds, in successive stages, from the more general to the more specific, from relatively homogeneous states to increasingly differentiated hierarchically organized structures.

Although von Baer himself considered his developmental proposals to be revolutionary, they initially received only modest attention. After a bout of extreme fatigue, disappointment, and disillusionment, von Baer moved to Russia in 1834 and became librarian of the Academy of Science in St. Petersburg. Later, he was appointed leader of a Russian Arctic expedition where he conducted geographical, botanical, and biological research relevant to evolution and development. At the end of his career, he returned to Estonia, the country of his birth, and served as President of the University of Tartu.

Von Baer's developmental principles may seem commonplace to modern students; his general axioms are mentioned in introductory chapters of texts on biological and cognitive development. But when the ideas were first proposed, they challenged the then-dominant explanations for how development proceeds. Two views vied for prominence throughout most of the 19th century: (a) preformism and (b) epigenesis (Gould, 1977). Preformism held that developmental transformations were illusions because the essential characteristics of the individual had already formed at the beginning of ontogenesis. Only the size and relations of the parts to each other changed, and their essential properties were preset and predetermined. Although preformism is dismissed nowadays as drawings of a miniaturized adult in the womb, the concept of a homunculus is not essential to the model (Gould, 1977).

What was basic to preformism was the idea that development could bring about changes in the shape and relationships among organs, but development fails to bring out new or novel properties. Hence, stability and predictability from embryogenesis and infancy to adulthood was expected, if one's measurement tools were adequate. Absurd? Perhaps, except that the proposals do not appear entirely unreasonable if one considers parallels in modern genetic theory, where genes endure unchanged even though the organisms that they create do not. Moreover, particular alleles are assumed to be associated with the ontogeny of specific structural and behavioral characteristics. At another level, modern developmental researchers often assume that the primary traits and dispositions—such as attachment and aggression—develop and become stabilized during the interchanges of infancy and early childhood. These dispositions and the internalized models thus generated may be transformed over development into age-appropriate expression, but not in underlying type.

The other major 19th-century approach to development was epigenetic. Novelties were brought about through progressive transformations in development. But what determines the course of the transformations and, ultimately, the nature of the finished product? The earlier vitalistic answer—*entelechy,* the Aristotelian vital force—was no longer acceptable to most 19th-century epigeneticists. Among other problems, the teleological answer looked to be an admission of ignorance. But without developmental regulation and direction, what would prevent growth from occurring willy-nilly into diverse and monstrous forms? The concept of epigenesis-as-developmental-transformations could not stand alone. It required additional assumptions to account for the sequential properties of development and its orderly nature (Bertalanffy, 1933; Gould, 1977).

This theoretical void was filled in 19th-century biology by the recapitulation concept prominent in *Naturphilosophie,* a significant philosophical movement in Germany. Recapitulation bound together the two main forms of organic creation, ontogeny (individual development) and phylogeny (species development), into a single framework. In embryonic development, organisms are assumed to pass through the adult forms of all species that had been ancestral to them during evolution. Organisms in embryogenesis experience a fast-forward replay of evolutionary history. With this predictable and orderly progression, novel features may be added only in the terminal or mature phases of development. This concept, labeled the "biogenetic law" by Ernst Haeckel (1866), was enormously influential in 19th century biology. The recapitulation hypothesis also provided the biological metaphor for G. S. Hall's account of adolescence and S. Freud's original formulations of repression and psychosexual stages (Sulloway, 1979, pp. 198–204, 258–264).

In opposition to prominent biologists of his day, von Baer argued that recapitulation was based on faulty observations and romanticism rather than logic. In his own research, he found that organisms of related species were indeed highly similar in anatomy during their early stages of embryonic growth. However, contrary to the expectations of the recapitulation interpretation, species-typical differences appeared early in the course of development, not only in its final stages. Moreover, the organization at successive stages seemed to uniquely fit the organism for its current circumstances. It was not merely the mechanical repetition of earlier ancestral forms, as implied by the recapitulation model (de Beer, 1958). To sharpen the epigenetic account, von Baer (1828) offered four laws by which development could be described:

1. The general features of a large group of animals appear earlier in the embryo than the special features.
2. Less general characteristics are developed from the more general, and so forth, until finally the most specialized appear.
3. Each embryo of a given species, instead of passing through the stages of other animals, departs more and more from them.
4. Fundamentally, therefore, the embryo of a higher animal is never like a lower animal, but only like its embryo.

Von Baer held that development was a continuing process of differentiation and organization; hence, novelties could arise at each stage, not merely the terminal one. When this embryological principle was later applied to structures, actions, thoughts, and social behaviors (e.g., Piaget, 1951; Werner, 1948), it produced far-reaching consequences. The conclusion proposed in 1828 was that developmental processes demand rigorous study in their own right; they cannot be derived from analogies to evolution.

Although von Baer was recognized as a leading embryologist, his generalizations on the nature of development were not immediately accepted. They were inconsistent with broadly held beliefs in biology, and von Baer's rejection of the Darwinian account of evolution probably did not help matters. Despite compelling empirical and comparative evidence, for most of the 19th century von Baer's developmental generalizations fared poorly in open competition with the recapitulation proposal.

Von Baer's developmental ideas were not entirely ignored in his time, however. It was in Carpenter's (1854) influential physiological textbook that Herbert Spencer discovered von Baer's formulation of the developmental principle. Spencer (1886) wrote that von Baer's work represented "one of the most remarkable indications of embryology."

> It was in 1852 that I became acquainted with von Baer's expression of this general principle. The universality of law had ever been with me as a postulate, carrying with it a correlative belief, tacit if now avowed, in unity of method throughout Nature. This statement that every plant and animal, originally homogeneous, becomes gradually heterogeneous, set up a process of coordination among accumulated thoughts that were previously unorganized, or but partially organized. (p. 337)

Spencer's work, in turn, inspired the genetic epistemology of James Mark Baldwin and his successors, including Jean Piaget. Von Baer's other line of influence on psychology appears in animal behavior and comparative psychology through the work of Z.-Y. Kuo, T. C. Schneirla, and L. Carmichael in the 20th century. The modern dynamic systems model, transactional theory, developmental psychobiology, and developmental science have von Baer's principle of development as a kernel concept (e.g., see chapters by Lerner; Thelen & Smith; Wapner & Demick, this Volume). Moreover, time and timing are central in von Baer's formulation, consistent with modern concepts of critical periods in embryogenesis and sensitive periods in behavior development, and with the concepts of neoteny and heterochrony in behavioral evolution (Cairns, 1976; de Beer, 1958; Gottlieb, 1992; Gould, 1977).

There have been some major revisions, of course. The developmental principle identified a key feature of epigenesis—homogeneity giving way to heterogeneity through progressive differentiation, then integration into reorganized structures—but it did not solve the problem of how development is directed. In his writing, he remained vaguely teleological, a position that seemed consistent with *Naturphilosophie* but out of line with his rigorous experimental work and careful theoretical analysis. Leaving the directionality issue open-ended invited continued application of the recapitulation proposition. The puzzle of directionality in embryological development took almost 100 years to solve (Bertalanffy, 1933).

Evolution and Development

"To what extent and in what manner has the work of Charles Darwin influenced developmental psychology?" (Charlesworth, 1992, p. 5). In answering his question on Darwin's impact, Charlesworth concludes that the influence is much less direct and much weaker than has been traditionally accepted. He finds only few direct links to Darwinian propositions or to evolutionary theory in modern developmental psychology. This is regrettable because:

> ... Darwin's contribution and its current elaborations can enhance developmental research, whereas the latter can assist the former by putting its hypotheses to competent test. (p. 13)

It should be noted that Charlesworth's conclusion on the modest impact of evolutionary theory on developmental psychology is at variance with other judgments in the literature. For example, Kessen (1965) credited Darwin with dramatically changing our concept of children and childhood. This effect, according to Kessen (1965), was both direct (through Darwin's published observations of his infant son) and indirect (through the profound impact of evolutionary ideas on the developmental contributions of W. Preyer, J. M. Baldwin, G. S. Hall, and H. Taine). A similar conclusion is expressed by Wohlwill (1973), who tracks three lines of Darwinian influence on developmental thought through Baldwin, Preyer, and S. Freud.

The proposition regarding the impact of Darwin depends in large measure on how broadly or narrowly Darwin's influence is defined. As observed above, the study of individual development is rooted in embryology, not in evolution. In her overview of the history of embryology, Jane Oppenheimer (1959) observes that the methods and concepts of embryological science owe little to the concepts of evolutionary biology. Moreover, von Baer himself explicitly rejected the Darwinian construction of evolution.

The picture becomes blurred, however, with E. Haeckel's (1866) wedding of ontogenetic and evolutionary concepts in the recapitulation principle. Haeckel was an enormously influential advocate of Darwinian evolution in the second half of the 19th century, and his influence is strongly represented in Preyer (1888) and Hall (1904). Moreover, a direct

line can be drawn from Darwinian commentaries on the evolution of the emotions and intelligence to the work of comparative psychologists G. J. Romanes (1889) and C. L. Morgan (1896), and from these pivotal figures in the late 19th century to the foundation of modern comparative work on psychobiological integration and concepts of learning. The importance of evolutionary themes is told by Sigmund Freud himself (1957). It is also a core message in Sulloway's (1979) intellectual biography that was aptly titled, "Freud, Biologist of the Mind."

Those aspects of Darwin's evolutionary theory that have had only a modest influence on developmental psychology concern its strong implications for the heritability of behavior and the evolution of behavioral propensities. At least one modern model of sociobiology views ontogenetic variation as "developmental noise" (Wilson, 1975). This is because sociobiological emphasis is on (a) variations in structures of societies, not variations in individual life histories, and (b) the biological contributors to those variations in group structures, including the genetic determinants of aggressive behaviors, altruism, and cooperation. As in the logic of Wundt, immature expression of these phenomena in individuals is seen as ephemeral and individualistic; genetic and evolutionary forces may be viewed more clearly when they are aggregated across persons into societal structures (see Gottlieb, Wahlsten, & Lickliter, Ch. 5, this Volume).

In contrast, evolutionary concepts have had a major impact on research in comparative studies of development in animals from the mid-19th century to the present. In England, Douglas Spalding (1873) reported the remarkable effects of early experience in establishing filial preferences in newly hatched chicks. His experimental demonstrations seemed to confirm that phyletic and ontogenetic influences must operate in tandem, that the young animal was predisposed to form preferences during a period of high sensitivity shortly after hatching, and that the experiences that occurred then were especially effective in the rapid establishment of preferences.

George John Romanes, a young scientist who had the confidence of Darwin, was impressed by Spalding's demonstrations and, with him, emphasized the early formation and plasticity of behavior within the framework of its evolutionary foundation. More generally, Romanes's analysis of the stage-paced development of sexuality and cognition served as a basic text for the two most important theorists in developmental psychology, Sigmund Freud and James Mark Baldwin. *Mental Evolution in Man* (Romanes, 1889) was one of the most annotated books in Freud's library, and Sulloway (1979) suggests that it provided inspiration for Freud's later emphasis on the early appearance of infantile sexuality. In accord with recapitulation theory, Romanes had placed the onset of human sexuality at 7 weeks. J. M. Baldwin (1895), for his part, gives explicit credit to Romanes and Spencer as providing inspiration and direction to the work embodied in his *Mental Development in the Child and the Race*. It should also be observed that Romanes, whose aim was to clarify the evolution of the mind and consciousness, is also regarded as the father of comparative psychology (Gottlieb, 1979; Klopfer & Hailman, 1967).

Studies of behavioral development in nonhumans were also rapidly becoming a focal concern in North America. The Canadian physiologist, Wesley Mills, offered an especially clear statement of the need for developmental studies in a *Psychological Review* paper that appeared in 1899. In the article, Mills took E. L. Thorndike (1898) to task for his narrow view of how experimental analyses can contribute to understanding animal learning and intelligence.

For Mills, the notions of ecological validity and biological constraints on learning would not be unfamiliar ideas. What, then, would be the method that he could endorse as being likely to yield the secrets of social behavior and cognition? In a remarkable passage, Mills (1899) outlines a strategy that anticipates the importance of understanding development in context. He wrote:

> Were it possible to observe an animal, say a dog, from the moment of its birth onward continuously for one year, noting the precise conditions and all that happens under these conditions, the observer being unnoticed by the creature studied, we should, I believe be in possession of one of the most valuable contributions it is possible to make to comparative psychology. This would imply not one, but several persons giving up their whole time, day and night, by turns, to such a task. As yet, but very imperfect approaches have been made to anything of the kind; nevertheless, such as they have been, they are the most valuable contribution thus made, in the opinion of the present writer, and the more of such we have the better.
>
> If to such a study another were added, in which the effect of altering conditions from time to time with the special object of testing the results on an animal or animals similarly closely observed from birth onward, we should have another most valuable contribution to comparative psychology; but experiment on animals whose history is unknown must, in the nature of the case, be very much less valuable than in such an instance as that just proposed. (p. 273)

However convincing Mills's proposals may appear in retrospect, E. L. Thorndike completed the work, and experimental methods won the battle of the day and, for the most part, the war of the century. By the next generation, experimental studies of learning in animals and children were dominated by Thorndikian short-term, nondevelopmental experimental designs, at least in the United States. It should be noted, in Thorndike's defense, that the main point of his experimental laboratory work, first described in *Animal Intelligence* (1898, p. 1), was to clarify "the nature of the processes of association in the animal mind." It was, in effect, the study of animal consciousness and the role that representation plays in learning methods. Thorndike's statement of the "law of effect" proved to be enormously influential.

In summary, thoughtful investigators of development in nonhuman animals have been concerned with evolutionary and ontogenetic issues and how they are interrelated. The focus was reflected in the work of Romanes (1889), Morgan (1896), and Mills (1898) in the latter part of the 19th century, and in the work of Kuo (1930), Schneirla (1959), Tinbergen (1972), and Hinde (1966) in the mid-20th century. This dual concern, along with the research on animals and young humans that it has stimulated, has helped establish the conceptual and empirical foundations for a fresh developmental synthesis. Whether Darwinian thought has been influential for modern developmental psychology depends on which evolutionary ideas are evaluated and which aspects of developmental psychology are examined.

THE EMERGENCE OF DEVELOPMENTAL PSYCHOLOGY (1882–1912)

Developmental studies flourished *despite* the influence of traditional psychophysical laboratories rather than because of it. The study of behavioral and mental development was going full steam in the 1890s. By mid-decade, genetic or developmental psychology had its own scientific journals (*L'Année Psychologique*, 1894; *Pedagogical Seminary*, 1891, later to be renamed the *Journal of Genetic Psychology*), research institutes (Sorbonne, 1893; Clark University, 1890), influential textbooks (e.g., *The Mind of the Child*, 1982; *L'évolution intellectuelle et morale de l'enfant*, 1893; *Mental Development in the Child and the Race*, 1895), professional organizations (e.g., Child Study Section of the National Education Association, 1893; Société Libre pour l'Étude Psychologique de l'Enfant, 1899), and psychological clinic (University of Pennsylvania, 1896). As early as 1888, G. Stanley Hall was able to refer to the "nearly fourscore studies of young children printed by careful empirical and often thoroughly scientific observers" (Hall, 1888, p. xxiii). The field had advanced so far that it was christened with a name—Paidoskopie—to emphasize its newly won scientific independence (Compayré, 1893). Happily, the activity survived the name.

There is, however, no strong consensus on which year should serve as an anchor for developmental psychology's centennial. The problem is that the area is now sufficiently diverse so that one can point to several landmark dates, depending on which movement or which pioneer one wishes to commemorate. The founding of the child development research institute at Clark University and the establishment of the journal *Pedagogical Seminary*, by G. Stanley Hall, were clearly of signal importance for the area. But to celebrate Hall's contributions over those of Alfred Binet can hardly be justified. Binet, at almost the same time, was laying the foundations for modern experimental child psychology at the Sorbonne and establishing *L'Année Psychologique* as a prime source for developmental publications. Perhaps the dilemma may be eased by recognizing that these major advances were themselves beneficiaries of a zeitgeist that seems to have begun about 1880 and gained significant momentum with the publication of William Preyer's *The Mind of the Child* in 1882.[2]

---

[2] There is some ambiguity about the actual publication date of *The Mind of the Child*. In the preface to the second edition, Preyer tells us that "the first edition of this book appeared in October, 1881" (p. xvi). That seems straightforward enough, but the publication date of the original German work was 1882. The discrepancy apparently arose because of the lag between the time when the author signed off the Preface (in Jena, October 6, 1881) and the time the finished book was actually published. Similar ambiguity surrounds the traditional assignment of 1879 as the founding of Wundt's laboratory; it was an ongoing enterprise at the time, and William James claimed priority anyway.

The book has been called "the first work of modern psychology" (see Reinert, 1979), providing "the greatest stimulation for the development of modern ontogenetic psychology" (Munn, 1965).

Not everyone agrees with these high evaluations of Preyer's work or of its originality (see, for instance, Bühler, 1930; Kessen, 1965; and below). Nonetheless, Preyer's book served as a powerful catalyst for the further study of development in psychology and in biology, and 1882 seems to be a reasonable date for us to begin this story of the development of modern developmental psychology. In addition to Hall and Binet, two other persons—James Mark Baldwin and Sigmund Freud—contributed much to the molding of the area. The nature and extent of their contributions will be the main focus of this section.

Embryos and Infants

When *The Mind of the Child* was published, William T. Preyer (1841–1897) intended it to be only the first installment of a more comprehensive study of the nature of development. He completed the project four years later, with publication of *The Special Physiology of the Embryo* (Preyer, 1885). That these two contributions were not translated together and studied as a unit is a pity, for, in Preyer's mind, the issues to which they were addressed were mutually dependent and complementary. Preyer assumed that the methods and concepts applicable to embryological study could be applied with advantage to behavioral study, and that investigations of the one would support and complement investigations of the other. Why then two books? As Preyer (1882) explains it:

> I proposed to myself a number of years ago, the task of studying the child, both before birth and in the period immediately following, from the physiological point of view, with the object of arriving at an explanation of the origin of separate vital processes. It was soon apparent to me that a division of the work would be advantageous to its prosecution. For life in the embryo is so essentially different a thing from life beyond it, that a separation must make it easier both for the investigator to do his work and for the reader to follow the expositions of the results. I have, therefore, discussed by itself, life before birth, in the "Physiology of the Embryo." (p. ix)

Preyer completed work on both phases of the project, embryogenesis and postnatal development, in a significant number of species (including humans). It is almost true that his feat has yet to be matched by another single investigator.

What drew Preyer to the study of development in the first place? That question cannot be answered definitively, but we do know that he was trained in physiology in Germany and, with others of his generation, came under the spell of Ernst Haeckel's vision of the unity of science and the centrality of development in evolution and life. Preyer recognized that the scientific program of modern biology would be incomplete without a careful analysis of human development from conception through maturity, and that such a program would necessarily be interdisciplinary. As he put it, such prenatal and postnatal observations "are necessary, from the physiological, the psychological, the linguistic, and the pedagogic point of view, and nothing can supply their place" (1882, pp. 186–187). Beyond Preyer's appreciation that intellectual and scholarly breadth were required for the productive study of children, he established methodological standards for the enterprise. The procedures that he endorsed, and followed, belied the proposition that children, even immature and unborn ones, could not be studied objectively and with profit.

Preyer was not the first person to undertake detailed observations of his offspring for scientific purposes. A professor of Greek and philosophy at the University of Marburg, Dietrich Tiedemann (1748–1803), had earlier employed the method, and his 1787 monograph *Observations on the Development of Mental Capabilities in Children* (Murchison & Langer, 1927), seems to have been the first known published psychological diary of longitudinal development in children, according to Reinert (1979). In the hundred years between Tiedemann and Preyer, several studies appeared, some of which were sufficiently free of parental bias and distortion from other sources to be considered useful scientific contributions (Reinert, 1979, has an informative account of this work).

An article by Charles Darwin played an important role in stimulating further interest in the endeavor. In 1877, it appeared in the new psychological journal *Mind,* having been triggered by the appearance, two months earlier, of a translation of H. Taine's (1876) parallel observations in the immediately preceding issue. Darwin's article was based on 37-year-old notes he made during the first two years of one of his sons. Although inferior to the other reports in terms of systematicity of observation and depth of

reporting, Darwin's contribution served to legitimize the method and promoted research with children.

The methodological standards that Preyer established for himself are admirable, even by today's criteria. He reports that he "adhered strictly, without exception," to the following rules:

1. Only direct observations were cited by the investigator, and they were compared for accuracy with observations made by others.

2. All observations were recorded immediately and in detail, regardless of whether they seemed uninteresting or "meaningless articulations."

3. To the extent possible, observations were unobtrusive and "every artificial strain upon the child" was avoided.

4. "Every interruption of one's observation for more than a day demands the substitution of another observer, and, after taking up the work again, a verification of what has been perceived and noted down in the interval."

5. "Three times, at least, every day the same child is to be observed, and everything incidentally noticed is to be put upon paper, no less than that which is methodically ascertained with reference to definite questions" [*The Mind of the Child* (1882), Vol. 2, pp. 187–188].

In brief, most problems of observation and categorization were anticipated by Preyer, including those of reliability and observer agreement.

How Preyer chose to organize his findings is almost as interesting as his methods and findings. For Preyer, the mind of the child, like Gaul, can be divided into three parts: (a) Senses, (b) Will, and (c) Intellect. Because his knowledge about the comparative development of vision, hearing, taste, smell, touch, and temperature perception was surprisingly broad, many—but not all—of Preyer's (1882) generalizations on the "Development of Senses" were on target. A few of his statements were demonstrably wrong. For instance, he wrote "the normal human being at birth hears nothing" (p. 96). Preyer arrived at an opposite (and correct) set of conclusions on the capabilities of various nonhuman species to hear at birth. In light of the care and precision of most of the observations, it's puzzling that Preyer made such an elementary error. In retrospect, we may speculate that a primary flaw was theoretical rather than methodological. Preyer's conclusions on neonatal incompetence were colored by his general assumption that human beings were less mature at birth than were species ancestral to them (i.e., neoteny). This was not the first time, nor the last, that strongly held hypotheses about the nature of children led to erroneous conclusions, despite disconfirming empirical evidence.

The "Development of Will" provided an informative and informed analysis of the onset of such patterns as sitting, grabbing, pointing, standing, and other motoric acts. But Preyer was looking for more than a behavioral inventory: He hoped to find out how the pattern arose. For instance, "deliberate" pointing seemed to arise from the early action of abortive "seizing" or "grabbing," and only at about 9 months of age did "pointing" gain the capacity to signal to others the child's wants and needs. Among other things, he concludes: "The first deliberate intention-movements occur only after the close of the first three months" (p. 332). Preyer thus found, in the study of the development of movement patterns, reflexes, and other actions, a possible clue to the systematic analysis of the onset of intentionality.

The third part of *The Mind of the Child,* "Development of Intellect," includes the consideration of language comprehension and production as well as the development of social cognition, including the concept of the self. Preyer's discussion proceeds, with uncommonly good sense, from a description of the onset of landmarks of language development to an attempt to determine when the notion of "ego," or the self, develops. For Preyer, it occurs when the child can recognize "as belonging to him the parts of his body that he can feel and see" (p. 189). Whatever the other merits of that proposal, it permits Preyer to undertake a series of observations and mini-experiments on the matter. One section deals with the ability of children to respond to their reflections in a mirror; another, with the uses and misuses of personal pronouns by young children.

In addition to his study of infancy and early childhood, Preyer left another legacy to modern developmentalists, *The Special Physiology of the Embryo* (1885). To complete his analysis of the "origin of separate vital processes," Preyer conducted experiments and made observations on the embryos of invertebrates, amphibia, birds, and various mammals. Some of these observations—on the prenatal development of sensory and motor functions—have only recently been confirmed and extended using modern techniques. In line with recent interpretations of early development, Preyer concluded that (a) integrated, spontaneous motor activity was antecedent to the development of responsiveness to sensory stimulation, and (b) motor activity may provide the substrate for later mental, emotional, and linguistic performance. Because of his pioneering studies, he is acknowledged to be the father of behavioral embryology (Gottlieb, 1973).

Preyer has sometimes been depicted as the prototypic methodologist—careful, precise, compulsive, and pedestrian. On this score, Karl Bühler (1930) writes that *The Mind of the Child* was "a remarkable book full of interesting and conscientious observations, but poor in original ideas" (p. 27) and that "Preyer himself was no pioneer in psychology" (p. 27). Others have echoed the exact words, along with the sentiment that his book was more like a developmental psychophysiology than a developmental psychology" (Reinert, 1979).[3]

Has Preyer's empirical reputation outrun his theoretical contribution to developmental psychology? The answer depends in part on what aspects of theory one chooses to focus on. Preyer's main concern in preparing both *Mind of the Child* and *Special Physiology* was the clarification of a basic issue of development: the relations between ontogeny and phylogeny of behavior, and how these two processes influenced each other. His categorization of the dates of onset was *not* an end in itself, to develop a behavioral timetable. Rather, his aim was to establish the lawful sequence of development of sensory and cognitive systems so that meaningful generalizations could be drawn between species and among systems in development.

Hence, for Preyer (1882) one key theoretical issue was how to reconcile competing claims of the "nativists" and the "empiricists" in the origin and perfection of the "vital processes" of behavior and thought. As far as human vision (or other sensory processes) was concerned, he concluded that "my observations show that . . . *both parties*

---

[3] Did cultural stereotypes play a role in the evaluation of *The Mind of the Child?* For instance, Compayré (1893) called the book a "monument of German assiduousness." Mateer (1918) remarked (in the context of comparing Frenchman Peréz's "logical, brilliant style" with that of Preyer) that: "The French write brilliantly and convincingly but their technique is apt to be at fault. They seem to hit intuitively upon right premises and conclusions, although their data may be unconvincing or scanty. The German work is more stolid, more convincing in its facts but less inspiring in application" (pp. 24–24).

are right" (Vol. 1, p. 35, my emphasis). In a discussion that constitutes an early model for the developmental landscape of C. H. Waddington (1971), he speculates that "The brain comes into the world provided with a great number of impressions upon it. Some of these are quite obscure, some few are distinct" (Vol. 2, p. 211). Through experience, some of the pathways are obliterated, and others are deepened.

Lest Preyer be written off as a naïve nativist, it should be added that his position was closer to the bidirectional approach of modern developmental psychobiology than to the innate ideas of Immanuel Kant. Drawing on studies of the comparative anatomy of the brain as well as cross-species comparisons of behavior, he concluded (1882) that there is feedback between experience and normal structural development in the brain. He offered a foresightful statement of the bidirectional structure–function hypothesis, reaching the conclusion that "*The brain grows through its own activity*" (Vol. 2, p. 98, my emphasis). How then does the individual contribute to his or her own development? Preyer's answer was clearly speculative, but it followed the same line of reasoning that is reflected in the structure–function bidirectional proposals offered in the next century by developmental psychobiologists and modern neurobiologists. (See also chapters by Brandtstädter and by Gottlieb et al., in this Volume.)

The theoretical import of Preyer's behavioral timetable comes into focus when viewed in the context of Haeckel's biogenetic law. Its key assumption was that human maturation was *accelerated* with respect to ancestral species. That is, as noted earlier, in this concept humans are presumed to pass through the several stages of development more rapidly than the species from which they were derived, so that evolutionary "novelties" and distinctively human characteristics appear at maturity, not in infancy. To be tested, the view required precise information about the relative rates of maturation; hence the need for exactness in plotting the onset of particular behaviors. But Preyer was not a biogenetic apologist. He offered the compelling hypothesis that humans' maturation rate was retarded relative to ancestral species, an idea that ran counter to the accepted version of recapitulation. In other words, human beings should enjoy a longer (not shorter) period of immaturity than their closest phyletic relatives. Accordingly, in most "vital processes" and behavior, there should be relatively greater plasticity in development and opportunities for

learning for children than for nonhuman animals (Vol. 1, pp. 70–71). This is essentially an early statement of behavioral neoteny: that the relatively slower rate of maturation should be an advantage in making for an extended period of curiosity, flexibility, and adaptability in human beings (see also Fiske, 1883). Echoes of his theoretical interpretations can be found in modern studies of ontogenetic-phyletic relations (e.g., de Beer, 1958; Cairns, 1976; Mason, 1980) and the bidirectionality of structure–function relations (e.g., Gottlieb, 1976; Kuo, 1967).

Tracing the heritage that Preyer left for developmental study, we find that he set high standards for scientific observation of behavioral development. Though not unflawed, his observations were carefully recorded and sanely written. For those who followed him, Preyer embedded the study of children in the framework of biological science, and he demonstrated how interdisciplinary techniques could be employed. Beyond the methodological message, there was a theoretical one. Preyer was a man of his times, evolutionary in outlook and committed to the clarification of the relations between ontogeny and phylogeny, between nature and nurture. Surprisingly, he was perhaps as influential in embryology as in developmental psychology. Through his work, talented young men and women were recruited to experimental embryology (including Hans Spemann, who identified "critical periods" and "organizers" in embryological development). Perhaps most important, Preyer demonstrated, by his successful integration of experimental studies of human and nonhuman young, that the investigation of behavioral development could be as much a scientific enterprise as a social, humanistic movement. Happily, other colleagues in America and Europe understood the message.

Memory and Intelligence

In a recent article on the scientific contributions of Alfred Binet (1857–1911), Siegler (1992) observes: "It is ironic that Binet's contribution should be so strongly associated with reducing intelligence to a single number, the IQ score, when the recurring theme of his research was the remarkable diversity of intelligence" (p. 175). That is only one of the ironies in Binet's work and life. Another is that he was arguably the greatest French psychologist of his day; yet he was unable to obtain a professorship in France. Moreover, the intelligence test that he developed with Simon, which was intended to provide guides on how "to learn to learn," has been used over the past century as a basis for classifying children and adults into intellectual categories that are presumed to be constant over life.

Statements about historical priority and influence are delicate matters, but among non-French observers there is no serious debate over the claim that Alfred Binet was France's first significant experimental psychologist.[4] What makes his work of special importance for this chapter is that he was the premier early experimental child psychologist whose observations extended beyond the laboratory. The results have been far-reaching. Jenkins and Paterson (1961) observed, "Probably no psychological innovation has had more impact on the societies of the Western world than the development of the Binet–Simon scales" (p. 81). Given the influence of this procedure identified with Binet's name, it is understandable, yet regrettable, that his other contributions to developmental psychology have gained so little attention. As it turns out, it took experimental child psychology some 70 years to catch up with some of Binet's insights on cognition and the organization of memory.

Throughout his career, Binet was characterized by an independence of thought and action, starting with his introduction to psychology. It was his third choice in careers, after he had dropped out of law school and medical training (Wolf, 1973). In 1879/1880, Binet began independent reading in psychology at the Bibliothèque Nationale in Paris. Curiously, he selectively avoided experimental psychology (the Wundtian version) by reading little or no German, and he took no trips to Leipzig. Shortly after he began work in psychology, he published his first paper, a useful discussion of experiential contributions to the psychophysics of two-point tactile discrimination. For research training, Binet affiliated himself with the distinguished neurologist, Jean Martin Charcot, at the Salpêtrière (a noted Paris hospital). Over a period of seven years, Binet collaborated with Charcot and Charles Féré in studies of hypnotism and its expression in normal persons and in the patient population. Binet's introduction to "experimental methods" thus was some distance removed from the then-acceptable laboratory procedures. His apprenticeship in research led to some spectacular controversies, with young Binet in the middle of the fray. The problem was that certain phenomena reported by the Salpêtrière group defied credibility—for example, that the effects of hypnotic suggestion migrate from one side of the body to the other by virtue of electromagnetic influences (a very large magnet was used in demonstrations). Attempts to replicate the phenomena elsewhere proved unrewarding. As it turned out, the research procedures followed by Binet and Féré were remarkably casual, and they gave scant attention to the possible suggestibility of their subjects or of themselves (see Siegler, 1992).

An absurd idea? In light of our present knowledge about the brain and hypnotism, it was a thoroughly naïve proposition. But this is the stuff out of which discoveries are made. Féré shortly afterward (1888) became the first investigator to discover that emotional changes were correlated with electrical changes in the human body. Naïve or not, he is credited with discovering the resistance method of measurement and developing the first statement of arousal theory (Thompson & Robinson, 1979, p. 444).

While he was at the Salpêtrière, Binet's research skills were simultaneously being sharpened in the embryological laboratory of E. G. Balbiani. He became acquainted first-hand with the rigorous procedures of biological research and the then-current concepts of evolution, development, and genetics. This work culminated in 1894 with his being awarded a doctorate in natural science from the Sorbonne and his appointment as Director of the Laboratory of Physiological Psychology at the same institution. In that year, Binet also founded and edited *L'Année Psychologique*, coauthored two books (one dealing with the determinants of the extraordinary memory feats of chess masters and calculators; the other, a critical treatment of the methods and approaches of experimental psychology), and published 15 articles. Among the articles were studies of the psychology of aesthetics, suggestibility, the nervous system of invertebrates, perception in children, and studies on the development of memory. Only one year's work? No, because some of the studies had been ongoing over the previous two to three years; yes, because his publication list was just as impressive in 1895 as in 1894. This pattern was maintained until his death in 1911, except that, later in his

---

[4] But not France's first child psychologist. Peréz (1878) published his *The First Three Years of the Child* several years before Preyer's *The Mind of the Child* (1882). The two authors covered the same ground, but, as Reinert (1979) indicates, Peréz was generally considered to be the more imaginative and Preyer the more methodical.

career, he also wrote and supervised plays that were produced in Paris and London (Wolf, 1973).

Prolificacy can be embarrassing if one hasn't much to write about. That seems not to have been a problem for Binet, due in large measure to his "very open, curious, and searching" mind. Binet was so described when, prior to completing his doctorate, he was named laureate by the Moral and Political Academy of the Institute of France (Wolf, 1973). Although he began his research training in the library, he soon became committed to the task of expanding the empirical foundations of the area in ways that seemed novel if not heretical. He early rejected the conventional methods of experimental psychology (as it had been practiced in Leipzig and Baltimore) as being narrow and misleading. On introspective experiments, he wrote, in his *Introduction to Experimental Psychology:*

> Subjects go into a little room, respond by electrical signals, and leave without so much as a word to the experimenter. . . . With the three choices only—"equal," "greater," or "less"—they often seem to set up the results of the experiments in advance. Their aim is simplicity, but is only a factitious one, artificial, produced by the suppression of all troublesome complications. (Binet, Phillippe, Courtier, & Henri, 1894, pp. 28–30)

Nor was he impressed by the large-scale studies by G. S. Hall and his students, who used the questionnaire methodology. On the latter, Binet (1903) wrote:

> The Americans, who love to do things big, often publish experiments made on hundreds or even thousands of persons. They believe that the conclusive value of a study is proportional to the number of observations. That is a myth. (p. 299)

These hardly were the sorts of comments that would endear him to his American and German colleagues, and Howard C. Warren, one of the more generous reviewers, reciprocated by "confessing to a feeling of disappointment when it is considered what even a short book like this might have been" (Warren, 1894).

What Binet had to offer psychology was a pragmatic, multimethod, multipopulation approach to the problems of behavior. Instead of relying merely on introspection and psychophysiological experimentation, Binet thoroughly dissected behavioral phenomena. To explore memory, for instance, he varied the nature of the stimuli (memory for figures and for linguistic material; memory for meaningful sentences vs. individual words), the subjects tested (chess masters and superior "calculators" who performed on the stage; normal children and retarded children), measures employed (free recall, recognition, physiological measures of blood pressure and electrical activity), type of design (large group samples, individual analysis over long-term periods), and statistics employed. Through it all, Binet selected designs, procedures, and subjects with a purpose, not merely because they were available. To investigate imagination and creativity, he studied gifted playwrights and explored new techniques (inkblots, word association, and case history information).

Such methodological catholicism is not without pitfalls. He was open not only to new discoveries but to new sources of error. In his day, he received high praise and devastating criticism for his work, and both seemed earned. The early studies were vulnerable: Binet was in the process of learning a trade for which there were, as yet, no masters. He came out on the short end of a devastating exchange on the "magnetic" nature of hypnotism (Siegler, 1992), and there was equally justified criticism by H. S. Jennings (1898/1899) on Binet's interpretations of his studies on the psychic life of the lower beasts. S. Franz (1898), a student of J. M. Cattell, took him to task for the quality of his statistical presentation in a series of studies on the relation between cognition and physical measures in children. Florence Mateer (1918) doubtless had Binet in mind when she commented that "the French write brilliantly and convincingly but their technique is apt to be at fault" (p. 24). Such errors—and the attitudes they fed—unfortunately masked the fundamental brilliance of Binet's work. Though shy in personal demeanor, Binet as a scientist was not a timid man; he was outspoken, and his criticism of naïve generalizations and wrongheaded conceptualizations placed him at odds with beliefs held by then-dominant leaders of the discipline. He published what he believed, and seems to have judged the long-term gains to be worth the short-term costs to his career and influence.

Binet reported demonstrational studies of memory and perception that he had conducted with his two young daughters. The work was extended in succeeding years not only with his children (through adolescence) but with diverse subjects and areas of memory. Along with his collaborators, notably Victor Henri, the work was extended to persons who were extraordinarily talented or retarded.

Because Binet operated on the working assumption that the study of normal processes was the key to understanding special talents or deficits, his laboratory also made a major investment in the analysis of memory in normal children, adolescents, and adults. Binet was highly sensitive to the need for convergent analyses that intersect on a common problem. He argued in 1903 that "our psychology is not yet so advanced" that we can limit our analyses to information obtained in the laboratory; rather, complex intellectual functions are best understood in studies of persons "whom we know intimately, to relatives and friends."

Binet did not, however, disdain large-scale research designs; he simply believed that they were insufficient *in themselves* to tell the full story about the nature of memory processes. In collaboration with Henri, he conducted a remarkable series of studies on memory development that involved several hundred children.

In one of their analyses, Binet and Henri (1894) found that the children reconstructed material into chunks of information that were meaningful to them. It should be noted that this idea of active reorganization has now returned to occupy the attention of "modern" views of memory and recall (e.g., Paris, 1978). In the words of Binet and Henri, as translated by Thieman and Brewer (1978):

> The children have a tendency to replace a word from the spoken text when the word appears in a rather lofty style, with another word with which they are better acquainted, and which they encounter more often in their own conversation. Their act of memory is accompanied by an act of translation. (p. 256)

How Binet and his colleagues chose to follow up this experimental work is instructive. Noting that other researchers might do things differently, Binet embarked on an intensive study of "superior functions" in relatives (namely, his two adolescent daughters) and friends. Binet did not give up on experimental designs so much as he extended their boundaries by conducting experiments on persons whose histories and characteristics were known intimately to him. For Binet, the key to unlocking the secrets of intelligence involved not only mapping its outline in large-scale studies but also making a detailed tracing of its internal features in individual analysis. This movement back and forth—from a focus on individuals to a focus on large samples, then back to individuals—was a distinctive and deliberate research strategy.

Attention to two or three children, rather than to a single individual or to large samples, inevitably leads one to a focus on the differences among them. So it was with Binet. He was not the first psychologist, of course, to be curious about differences among persons and their assessment and explanation. Francis Galton (1883) had earlier used sensory discrimination tests to assess differences in basic abilities. The rationale for such tests was stated succinctly by Galton (1883): "The only information that reaches us concerning outward events appears to pass through the avenue of our senses; and the more perceptive the senses are of difference, the larger is the field upon which our judgment and intelligence can act" (p. 27).

In other words, modest differences at the level of sensation would be directly reflected in "complex" cognitive functioning, or would be multiplied. A similar rationale (and research strategy) was recommended by the American psychologist, James McKeen Cattell, in an article entitled "Mental Tests and Measurement" (1890). Specifically, Cattell proposed that mental measurement should employ several tests of "basic" sensory and motor abilities, including assessments of color discrimination, reaction time, and other standard psychophysical procedures. Other experimental psychologists—including Joseph Jastrow at Wisconsin, Hugo Munsterberg at Freiberg, and J. A. Gilbert at Yale and Iowa (1894, 1897)—concurred.

Characteristically, Binet and Henri (1895) took an approach that was radically different from that of their American and German colleagues. It was, however, wholly consistent with the conclusions they had arrived at in their earlier studies of memory development; namely, it was absurd to focus on elementary units of memory as opposed to a recall for ideas and meaning. Furthermore, from Binet's studies of individuals, it seemed clear that great differences could be observed among persons in terms of "higher" mental functions, including language skills, suggestibility, common-sense judgments, and imagination. Binet and Henri (1895) thus argued for a methodological strategy that was precisely opposite to that of Galton and Cattell:

> The higher and more complex a process is, the more it varies in individuals; sensations vary from one individual to another,

but less so than memory; memory of sensations varies less than memories of ideas, etc. The result is that if one wishes to study the differences between two individuals, it is necessary to begin with the most intellectual and complex processes, and it is only secondarily necessary to consider the simple and elementary processes . . . (Binet & Henri, 1895, p. 417).

Although "complex processes" are more difficult to measure than simple ones, less precision is required because individual differences in complex functions are much greater than in elementary ones. The more fundamental problem that Binet and Henri identified is that it is easier to separate the intellect into its parts than it is to put the elements together and create a functioning, competent whole. That is, the greatest challenges arise not in the initial assessment of sensory elements but in determining how they should be *combined* to predict intellectual performance. How should the components be appropriately weighted, and what is the nature of the process by which sensations are translated into cognitions? The solution that Binet and Henri offered was a wholly pragmatic one: Bypass the recombination problem and assess the complex functions directly. Given this simplifying solution, Binet and Henri outlined a programmatic approach to the assessment of individual differences that was completed 10 years later.

The child study movement in France directly contributed to the eventual development of workable mental tests. Soon after the formation of the *Société libre pour l'Étude psychologique de l'Enfant* (Society for the Psychological Study of the Child), Binet was invited to become a member and he shortly became a leading voice in its activities and publications. The *Société* not only prodded the Ministry of Public Instruction to think constructively about the needs of retarded children, but was also influential in having a commission appointed to set up special classes. Binet, as a leader of the Société, was appointed to the commission. It was not entirely coincidental, then, that he was invited to develop tests for identifying children who could benefit from special instruction, and the results of the work were reported in a series of articles in *L'Année Psychologique* in 1905 (Binet & Simon, 1905) and later extended (Binet 1908, 1911). Although the articles offered guidelines for assessment in each of three areas (medical, educational, psychological), their greatest attention was

given to psychological tests. The 30 tests of the 1905 scale followed the outline offered by Binet and Henri (1895) some 10 years earlier, except some procedures—including the suggested use of inkblots to study imagination—were omitted and new techniques were borrowed from other investigators—among them, Ebbinghaus's incomplete sentence technique (1897) and Jacobs's (1887) "memory for digits" test.

Although most of the basic concepts of intelligence test construction were reflected in the initial scale (e.g., multiple tests arranged in order of difficulty, various areas of competence tested, age standardization, and external validation), the refinement of the scale so it could be used productively with normal children required extensive further revision. The task was begun by Binet (1908, 1911) and completed by American developmental psychologists, notably Goddard (1911) and Terman (1916). Despite the magnitude of their achievement, Binet and Simon (1905) were fully aware of the limitations of the technique as well as its promise. They wrote in conclusion:

We have wished simply to show that it is possible to determine in a precise and truly scientific way the mental level of an intelligence, to compare this level with a normal level, and consequently to determine by how many years a child is retarded. Despite the inevitable errors of a first work, which is of a groping character, we believe that we have demonstrated this possibility. (p. 336)

They had indeed.

Binet eschewed identification as a theorist, even declining initially to offer a definition of intelligence, "a problem of fearful complexity." He added, in 1908:

Some psychologists affirm that intelligence can be measured; others declare that it is impossible to measure intelligence. But there are still others, better informed, who ignore these theoretical discussions and apply themselves to the actual solving of the problem. (p. 163)

Despite his disinclination to define intelligence, Binet was not hesitant to take a strong stand on the nature of intellectual functioning and its determinants. The design of the tests themselves reflects the assumption that the aim was to diagnose different levels of functioning, not to assess the child's "faculty" for thought. Consistent with this functional view of cognitive processing, Binet argued that one of the test's primary virtues would be to identify children who needed to "learn to learn." For Binet, intellectual adaptation reflected dynamic, ever-changing processes that underwent constant modification and reorganization. Hence his focus on the ways that these processes become organized over time, and their "plasticity and extendibility" (1909, pp. 127–128). On this score, he proposed a program of "mental orthopedics" that should be followed to enhance cognitive functioning. In *Les Idées modernes sur les Enfants* (1909), Binet specifically deplores the notion that "the intelligence of the individual is a fixed quantity" and protests the idea as "brutal pessimism" (p. 126). Ironically, exactly the opposite assumption fueled the enthusiasm of most American translators for the test, along with the conviction that this "fixed quantity" is hereditarily determined, and a child's "true score" can be identified within limits of sampling error.

How can we summarize Binet's primary contributions to understanding development? Beyond his specific insights on psychological phenomena, three fundamental advances may be attributed to this remarkable scientist. The first concerns the insight that the assessment of individual differences in higher-order cognition requires a molar rather than a molecular strategy. In retrospect, the idea seems to make a good deal of sense, but it was embraced by American psychology only after the research of Binet and Simon made the conclusion inescapable. After all, it seems intuitively obvious that precise, microanalytic experimental methods *should* be superior to molar, complex ones in predicting everyday behavior. The idea dies slowly, and it is alive and well today in the study of social development. As with cognition, recent molecular analyses of social interactions appear to fare less well in prediction and classification than do molar assessments of the same phenomena. Exactly why molar techniques have an advantage continues to be a matter of debate, and Binet's analysis may still be the key.

A second contribution is related to the first. For Binet, the "two sciences of psychology," described later by Cronbach (1957), were both essential. Binet pioneered both experimental child psychology and the study of individual differences. His stance on the matter is embodied in the methodological credo: "To observe and experiment, to experiment and observe, this is the only method that can obtain for us a particle of truth" (Binet, 1904, translated by Wolf, 1973, p. 293). As Binet saw it, problems inevitably arise when the two basic methodologies are divorced. If questions are raised that cannot be settled by experimentation, then they should be dismissed "since they are not susceptible to the sole criterion of certainty" that modern psychology can accept.

One other, more general legacy requires comment. Beyond the other pioneers in the field, Binet was one of the first to provide convincing evidence for the proposition that a *science* of human development was possible. He understood the complexity of the problem, but he persevered in the attempt to help developmental psychology "become a science of great social utility" (Binet, 1908). Binet demonstrated that an empirical science of behavioral development in humans was within grasp, if the investigator maintained a profound respect for the information yielded from the dual methods of observation and experimentation.

The New Psychology in America

In leading the organization of the new science of psychology in America, G. Stanley Hall (1844–1924) had no peer. In his long career, he proved to be an effective and durable advocate, writer, and spokesman for psychology and for children in America. The story of Hall's career has been expertly told by Ross (1972) and White (1992), with the latter providing fresh insights on Hall's role in science and social policy. Born in Massachusetts, Hall was a minister, professor of philosophy, experimental psychologist, child psychologist, educational psychologist, university president, and leader of the child study movement. He was also a premier figure in American psychology: the first professor of psychology in America (at Johns Hopkins, 1883) and the first president of the American Psychological Association (1891). As is the case with truly effective teachers, Hall had great enthusiasm and tolerance for ideas, and he was a master at conveying his enthusiasm to others. He had a large vision for psychology and its destiny in creating better persons and a more perfect society.

But how did he fare as a scientist and a theorist in the light of history? In the previous edition of the *Handbook*, this chapter concluded that Hall had a large influence on the growth and organization of the new psychology in America, and that he provided a foundation for the scientific study of children and adolescents. It was concluded that Hall's own research contributions were modest and his theoretical proposals were flawed by being too tightly woven to the informed beliefs of his day and too loosely linked to empirical data. The grand vision of the science that he offered had only modest substance. After spending several years carefully sifting the evidence, Sheldon White (1992) has arrived at a radically different conclusion regarding Hall's contributions. He observes:

> Recent writings usually picture Hall as a functionary and figurehead, condense his ideas into a few slogans, quote criticisms of his work by his often rivalrous peers, and effectively concede Hall his administrative trophies while ignoring most of what he had to say. (p. 33)

Some did listen to what Hall had to say, because, like Mark Hopkins, his mentor at Williams College, he was a masterful teacher (White, 1992). Lewis Terman, Arnold Gesell, and E. C. Sanford were strongly influenced by Hall in their graduate training at Clark University. John Dewey, James McKeen Cattell, and Joseph Jastrow took courses from Hall at Johns Hopkins. Others—including Earl Barnes, who initiated investigations of children at Leland Stanford Junior University in the 1890s—were attracted to Hall's method and perspectives through the child study movement (Goodwin, 1987; Zenderland, 1988). These scientists helped shape the face of 20th-century psychology in America.

Hall's introduction to developmental psychology occurred in 1880, when he returned to America from postdoctoral study in Europe with Wundt. He brought with him from Germany the "questionnaire method" to study "the contents of children's minds." The method was initially aimed at helping teachers learn what concepts children had available at the time that they entered school. The procedure involved asking children brief questions about their experiences and about the meaning of words—for example, "Have you ever seen a cow?" or "Where are your ribs?" The answers were scored right or wrong, and the percentage correct was used to describe groups of children, not individuals. Rural children were compared with city ones, boys with girls, Black children with White ones, and so on. The questionnaire method, at least in terms of the kind of questions asked, was a precursor of later general aptitude tests of general information and vocabulary. In Hall's core investigation, children just entering school in Boston were asked some 134 questions, such as those given above. Data collection was voluminous but haphazard; about half of the protocols from the 400 children tested had to be eliminated.

In commenting on this research, White (1992) writes:

> The questionnaire work was methodologically weak, to be sure, but the methodological regulations psychology subsequently put into place have probably been excessively restrictive. Hall's questionnaires asked people to give narrative accounts of children's behaviors in everyday situations, and this kind of approach is becoming more popular nowadays. (p. 33)

The point is well taken. Educators were impressed by Hall's vision of how scientific research had the potential to revolutionize educational practices (Hall, 1883, 1891). Zenderland (1988) suggests that the main impact of the child study movement on psychology was to pave the way for the acceptance of clinical psychology.

Hall's opportunity to shape the direction of psychology in America came when he was offered the first professorship in psychology in the United States, at Johns Hopkins University in 1884. He had been selected over C. S. Peirce and G. S. Morris—no modest competition. Peirce is viewed by many to be the preeminent American philosopher, and Morris was a "brilliant lecturer" (White, 1992). Following the general model established by Wundt at Leipzig, Hall set up a teaching laboratory at Hopkins and recruited to it several young persons who were later to play a formative role in the development of the science. In the first laboratory course, the students included John Dewey, James McKeen Cattell, Joseph Jastrow, and E. H. Hartwell. With the support and encouragement of Johns Hopkins president D. Gilman, Hall also established the first psychological journal in the United States, the *American Journal of Psychology*. On the basis of his success at Hopkins, Hall was offered in 1889 the opportunity of shaping a university himself by serving as first president of Clark University. Hall remained at Clark until his death in 1924, and established there a tradition of developmental study that remains strong today.

In the spirit of *Naturphilosophie*, Hall applied the biogenetic law to all aspects of human development. For Hall, the implications for the education, rearing, and religious instruction of children were manifold. He warned about the hazards of "unnatural" and "artificial" constraints on learning and early development, and expressed disdain for parents and teachers who attempt to instruct children rather than permitting their natures to unfold. According to Hall's view of recapitulation, behaviors, like morphological structures, follow an invariant course of development that has been determined by ancestral evolutionary progression. Interference with that natural process would be detrimental, and likely to bring about a stunting of growth or "developmental arrest."

Hall's biogenetic framework led him to a focus on the phenomena of adolescent development. In behavior, the fast-forward replay of ancestral psychological characteristics ended in adolescence, and the individual became free to superimpose distinctive and individual talents on the predetermined developmental sequence. Hence, it should be the stage of greatest plasticity and possibility for change. As Hall (1904) put it:

> While adolescence is the great revealer of the past of the race, its earlier stages must be ever surer and safer and the later possibilities ever greater and more prolonged, for it, and not maturity as now defined, is the only point of departure for the super anthropoid that man is to become. (Vol. 2, p. 94)

Hall's designation of adolescence as the time when the child begins a fresh set of tracks was optional. Other recapitulation theories propose that the adding on of unique features occurs in the early postnatal period, or even prenatally (see Gould, 1977, for an informed discussion of the matter). Convinced that the adolescent period was the nuclear one for the fulfillment of human potential, Hall (1904) prepared a two-volume compendium entitled *Adolescence: Its Psychology and Its Relations to Physiology, Anthropology, Sociology, Sex, Crime, Religion, and Education.* The book offered a broad sweep of citations from philosophical, physiological, anthropological, religious, and psychological sources. Where the data fell short, Hall offered speculative evolutionary and moralistic interpretations. The product was impressive in scope and uneven in logic and scientific rigor.

But it was often on target. Some of the insights and discussions appear remarkably modern in content if not in tone. On social cognition and developmental changes in attitudes, Hall (1904) wrote:

> Children's attitude toward punishment . . . tested by 2,536 children (ages 6–16) showed also a marked pubescent increase

in the sense of the need of the remedial function of punishment as distinct from the view of it as vindictive, or getting even, common in earlier years. There is also a marked increase in discriminating the kinds and degrees of offenses; in taking account of mitigating circumstances, the inconvenience caused others, the involuntary nature of the offense and the purpose of the culprit. All this continues to increase up to sixteen. (Vol. 2, pp. 394–395)

Similarly, in a discussion of moral reasoning, Hall (1904) concluded: "Thus with puberty comes a change of view-point from judging actions by results to judging by motives" (Vol. 2, p. 394). The statement was also based on empirical data using a reformed version of the questionnaire method. In this context, Hall cites Schallenberger's study (1894) on the development of moral judgments:

> From one thousand boys and one thousand girls of each age from six to sixteen who answered the question as to what should be done to a girl with a new box of paints who beautified the parlor chairs with them with a wish to please her mother, the following conclusion was drawn. Most of the younger children would whip the girl, but from fourteen on the number declines very rapidly. Few of the young children suggest explaining why it was wrong, while at twelve, 181, and at sixteen, 751 would explain. The motive of the younger children in punishment is revenge; with the older ones that of preventing a repetition of the act comes in; and higher and later comes the purpose of reform. With age comes also a marked distinction between the act and its motive and a sense of the girl's ignorance.[5] (Vol. 2, pp. 393–394)

Adolescence thus is "the stage when life pivots from an autocentric to an heterocentric basis" (Vol. 2, p. 301).

So far, so good, except Hall had the misfortune of discovering the biogenetic law at about the time that the new generation of biologists was discarding it. If evolution and recapitulation ranked high on Hall's psychological priori-

---

[5] Twenty-two thousand subjects? Not really. Schallenberger's (1894) article in the *Pedagogical Seminary* actually reported the responses of 3,434 girls and boys who were 6 to 16 years of age. The misinterpretation arose because Schallenberger transformed their responses to proportional scores, then multiplied by 1,000 to permit comparisons between age-sex groups. Nonetheless, a sample of 3,434 boys and girls is impressive in any era, especially before the invention of computers, electric calculators, and mechanical pencils.

ties, then morality and religion ran a close second. The linkages came about in ways that were not always immediately obvious, but seemed to represent his faith in the psychic "continuity throughout the universe" (Vol. 2, p. 208).

How does one evaluate Hall's contributions to developmental psychology? It is almost true to say that they were unique. Kessen (1965) provides a perceptive and succinct summary: "There have been diggers in the sand pile of child study since him, but in a sense, Hall has had no descendants—only heirs" (p. 151). More recently, White (1992) concluded that Hall made three significant contributions:

1. Hall provided a "first cooperative 'normal science' of child development" through his questionnaire program. The point is that the questionnaires, although limited as scientific instruments in the ways that Hall employed them, had great potential for describing children's lives in natural context.

2. Hall viewed social participation as a catalyst for internal organization, and thereby provided a "social-biological" conception of childhood.

3. Hall was guided by the need "to arrive at a scientific synthesis on the one side and practical recommendations on the other."

Related to the third point, one contribution should not be overlooked because it has potentially large implications for both developmental theory and intervention models. Hall focused on adolescence because he believed it was a period of great vulnerability and the time when novel actions and beliefs were established and consolidated, for good or for ill. In his view, infants and children were more or less buffered, a belief shared by his student Arnold Gesell (see below). Although Hall's reasoning about recapitulation was clearly off base, his intuitions about developmental plasticity in adolescence were inventive and provocative.

Hall also expanded the boundaries of the academic discipline and stimulated fresh approaches to it. Of special importance was his pivotal role in the organization and support of the activities of the child study movement in America, including the Child Study Section of the National Education Association.

In his scientific role, Hall was more an importer and translator of scientific methods and theories than he was a creator of them. In addition to the questionnaire method and the biogenetic law, Hall helped bring to America Wundtian experimental procedures and Preyer's volume on

The Mind of the Child (Hall wrote the foreword to the American translation). He also helped change the face of American psychology when, in 1909, he arranged a meeting between Sigmund Freud and his lieutenants (C. G. Jung, A. A. Brill, E. Jones, and S. Ferenczi) and the most prominent psychologists in North America. This meeting was held to commemorate the 20th anniversary of the founding of Clark University, and it is generally viewed as a key event in the acceptance of psychoanalysis in North America at a time when Freud felt ostracized by the European scientific establishment. In the same year, Clark University presented an honorary degree to William Stern, another significant pioneer in the establishment of developmental psychology. Throughout his career, Hall remained open to new and fresh approaches, and he promoted efforts to make psychology more useful and relevant to society.

In sum, Hall was a remarkable teacher and catalyst for the field. Some of the most significant areas of developmental study—mental testing, child study, early education, adolescence, life-span psychology, evolutionary influences on development—were stimulated or anticipated by Hall. Because of shortcomings in the methods he employed and the theory he endorsed, few investigators stepped forward to claim Hall as a scientific mentor. His reach exceeded his grasp in the plan to apply the principles of the new science to society. Psychology's principles were too modest, and society's problems were too large. Perhaps we should use a fresh accounting to judge Hall's contributions, one that takes into account the multiple facets of his influence on individuals, the discipline, and society. The audit would reveal that all of us who aspire to better the lot of children and adolescents can claim him as a mentor.

Making Developmental Theory

Nowadays, any account of the scientific study of cognitive and social development must take note of the singular contributions of James Mark Baldwin (1861–1932). His role as an intellectual leader of the emergent discipline is now well established. Baldwin's *Mental Development in the Child and the Race* (1895) was one of the first attempts to construct a genetic epistemology within the framework of the "new psychology" (Broughton & Freeman-Moir, 1982; Cairns & Ornstein, 1979; Mueller, 1976). The companion volume, *Social and Ethical Interpretations of Mental Development* (Baldwin, 1897), was the first systematic effort by a psychologist to use developmental ideas to bridge the gap between the study of social institutions (i.e., sociology) and the study of individual functioning (i.e., psychology).

Recent scholarship has compared Baldwin's proposals with those of Jean Piaget. In this regard, Wozniak (1982, p. 42) writes:

> Baldwin proposed a biosocial, genetic theory of intelligence, a theory of mind in the broadest sense, which was conceptually far ahead of his time. This theory contained within it, en germe, many of the most important concepts of the biological theory of intelligence and of the genetic epistemology which Piaget was to develop.

Other studies show direct lines of descent of key ideas and concepts expressed by Baldwin to those commonly associated with Piaget and Vygotsky (Broughton, 1981; Cahan, 1984; Valsiner & Van der Veer, 1988; Wozniak, 1982). But it would be a mistake to view Baldwin's thinking only through a Piagetian or Vygotskian lens. Baldwin's distinctive ideas on evolutionary epistemology, cross-generational transmission of developmental accommodations, the dynamics and social embeddedness of personality, and the dual genesis of cognition are sufficiently provocative to demand study in their own right.

Baldwin is less of a "shadowy figure" nowadays than he was just 14 years ago (Broughton & Freeman-Moir, 1982, p. 2). Baldwin was born in 1861 in Columbia, South Carolina, and died in 1934 in Paris. Following undergraduate training in philosophy and psychology, and a year of advanced study in Europe (including a semester in Leipzig with Wilhelm Wundt), Baldwin completed a doctorate at Princeton University in 1888. In the 4 years that he was on the faculty at the University of Toronto, he founded an experimental laboratory and began a research program on "infant psychology." The results of this work, which were published in the journal *Science* 100 years ago, dealt with the ontogeny of movement patterns, handedness, color vision, suggestibility, and research methodology (Baldwin, 1890, 1891, 1892, 1893). These findings provided the empirical basis for his first major work on mental development.

From the beginning, Baldwin was more a theoretical psychologist than an experimental one. He employed research findings to illustrate theoretical principles rather than to systematize empirical phenomena. Primary in Baldwin's thinking was the "conviction that no consistent view of mental development in the individual could possibly be reached without a doctrine of the race development[6] of consciousness—that is, the great problem of the evolution of mind" (Baldwin, 1895, p. vii). In this conviction, he followed the theoretical lead of Herbert Spencer in philosophy and George John Romanes in biology, and the empirical lead of Wilhelm Preyer and Alfred Binet. After this intensive but brief involvement with the experimental investigation of infants, Baldwin returned to issues of psychological and evolutionary theory, historical commentary, editorial activities, and philosophical construction and systemization. The study of development was no longer an empirical activity for him, but questions of psychological genesis remained at the core of his theoretical and philosophical speculations.

He was a key figure in the organization of psychology as a science, the establishment of three of its basic journals (*Psychological Review, Psychological Bulletin,* and *Psychological Abstracts*), and the founding of two major departments of psychology (at the University of Toronto and Princeton University) and the reestablishment of a third (at Johns Hopkins University). He served as one of the first presidents of the American Psychological Association when he was only 36 years of age. He won the highest honors available to psychologists in his day, including the Gold Medal of the Royal Academy of Denmark and the first honorary Doctorate of Science degree awarded by Oxford University. It is now generally acknowledged by those who have reviewed the record that Baldwin stands alongside William James, John Dewey, and C. S. Peirce as one of the primary intellectual forces involved in the founding of American psychology as a science.

Metaphysics and Development

In an excellent analysis of the structure of Baldwin's thought, Wozniak (1982) writes, "Baldwin had deep intellectual roots in the 'mental philosophy' tradition which dominated American higher education during the nineteenth century" (p. 13). Yet he early gained a respect for the emerging biological and behavioral sciences, and the

---

[6] *Race development* is one of the unconventional expressions employed by Baldwin. Race in this context refers to variations across the human species. In effect, cross-cultural studies of the development of cognition are required to complement studies of individual development in humans.

possibility that there might be a scientific explanation for the origin of knowledge and the perception of reality. At the outset of his career, Baldwin explicitly oriented his empirical and theoretical work toward a synthesis of metaphysics and psychological science (Wozniak, 1982, p. 14). In the early 1890s, he became convinced that genetic study must be the central theme for the synthesis of reason and reality.

Throughout the remainder of his career, "the great topic of development itself" (Baldwin, 1895, p. x) dominated his work and thinking. In his day, Baldwin expanded the application of genetic concepts in three emergent disciplines— psychology, evolutionary biology, and sociology—and in one established discipline—philosophy. Baldwin's own scientific life illustrates his view that cognitive development is not limited to childhood. As Wozniak (1982) observes:

> Baldwin was himself subject of a series of intellectual transformations. So great, in fact, are the differences in conceptual structure and content among his major books . . . that one wonders if perhaps there might not have been three Baldwins at work: a mental philosopher (roughly to 1889), an evolutionary psychologist (approximately 1889–1903), and an evolutionary epistemologist (1903–1915). (p. 14)

Although Wozniak's characterization of the marked intellectual transitions in Baldwin's career seems accurate, Baldwin appears to have moved beyond scientific psychology even before the turn of the century, coincident with his work on the *Dictionary of Philosophy and Psychology.* Given the scope and complexity of Baldwin's work, any brief summary is likely to be misleading. Shortcomings in the following account may be corrected by consulting more complete analyses that have recently become available, including Wozniak (1982), on the intellectual origins of genetic epistemology; Mueller (1976) and Valsiner and Van der Veer (1988), on the relations between psychology and sociology; and Cahan (1984), on the comparison of the genetic psychologies of Baldwin and Piaget. In addition, various chapters in the previous edition of the *Handbook of Child Psychology* (1983) attempt to place Baldwin's contributions into contemporary and historical context (Cairns, 1983; Harter, 1983; Sameroff, 1983). Then there are the voluminous writings of Baldwin himself, including 21 books and more than 100 articles. Baldwin's own thoughtful summary of his life's work is perhaps the best place to begin (Baldwin, 1930).

Mental Development and Social Ontogeny

The two works of Baldwin that have proved most stimulating to modern developmental psychologists are *Mental Development in the Child and the Race* (Baldwin, 1895), and *Social and Ethical Interpretations of Mental Development* (Baldwin, 1897). The earlier book presented Baldwin's attempt to formulate a "genetic epistemology." In individual development, a key mechanism for bringing about growth in the "cognitive scheme" is the "circular reaction." This invention of Baldwin's is linked to concepts of learning that appeared later and explained how experience could become internalized into habit through recurrent self-stimulation or imitation. A consideration of ontogenesis challenged the then-dominant idea that consciousness was "a fixed substance, with fixed attributes" (Baldwin, 1895, p. 2). He writes with respect to the static conceptions of traditional approaches:

> The genetic idea reverses all this. Instead of a fixed substance, we have the conception of a growing, developing activity. Functional psychology succeeds faculty psychology. Instead of beginning with the most elaborate exhibition of this growth and development, we shall find most instruction in the simplest activity that is at the same time the same activity. Development is a process of involution as well as of evolution, and the elements come to be hidden under the forms of complexity which they build up. . . . Now that this genetic conception has arrived, it is astonishing that it did not arrive sooner, and it is astonishing that the "new" psychology has hitherto made so little of it. (1895, p. 3)

In Baldwin's eyes, development proceeds from infancy to adulthood through stages, beginning with a reflexive or physiological stage, continuing through "sensorimotor" and "ideomotor" stages, and progressing to a stage of symbolic transformations (Baldwin, 1895). Only in the most advanced stage do "syllogistic forms come to have an independent or a priori force, and pure thought emerges— thought, that is, which thinks of anything or nothing. The subject of thought has fallen out, leaving the shell of form" (Baldwin, 1930, p. 23). From its earliest formulation, Baldwin's stage theory of mental development focused attention on process as much as on structure. Many of the terms that he employed—"accommodation," "assimilation," "imitation," "circular reaction"—are commonplace in today's textbooks, although it cannot be assumed that

Piagetian meanings are necessarily the same as Baldwinian ones.

Social and Ethical Interpretations in Mental Development: A Study in Social Psychology (Baldwin, 1897) appeared only 2 years later. This book is the first work by an American psychologist on social-cognitive development in childhood; it is also the first volume in English that includes "social psychology" in its title (Mueller, 1976). In this work, the cognitive-stage model is extended to issues of social development, social organization, and the origins of the self. Baldwin felt that the essential issues of social psychology had been neglected because of the void that existed between the concepts of psychology and sociology:

> And it is equally true, though it has never been adequately realized, that it is in genetic theory that social or collective psychology must find both its root and its ripe fruitage. We have no social psychology, because we have had no doctrine of the *socius*. We have had theories of the ego and the alter; but that they did not reveal the socius is just their condemnation. So the theorist of society and institutions has floundered in seas of metaphysics and biology, and no psychologist has brought him a life-preserver, nor even heard his cry for help. (1895, p. ix)

In social development, there is a "dialectic of personal growth" that progresses from an egocentric receptive stage to a subjective one and, eventually, to an empathic social stage. In Baldwin's scheme:

> The development of the child's personality could not go on at all without the modification of his sense of himself by suggestions from others. So he himself, at every stage, is really in part some one else, even in his own thought of himself. (1897, p. 30)

Consistent with his emphasis on developmental processes of the self rather than static structures, personality is not fixed by early experience or by genes. Accordingly, "personality remains after all a progressive, developing, never-to-be-exhausted thing" (Baldwin, 1897, p. 338). Actions are fluid, dynamic, and responsive to the immediate setting. In Baldwin's view:

> [The child's] wants are a function of the social situation as a whole. . . . His wants are not consistent. They are in every case the outcome of the social situation; and it is absurd to endeavor to express the entire body of his wants as a fixed quantity under such a term of description as "selfish," or "generous," or other, which has reference to one class only of the varied situations of his life. (1897, p. 31)

The self becomes progressively and inevitably accommodated to others and to the traditions of society. This "social heredity" is mediated through imitation and the operation of an internal circular reaction. From each relationship, there emerges a refined sense of oneself and of others. "The only thing that remains more or less stable is a growing sense of self which include both terms, the ego and the alter (Baldwin, 1897, p. 30).

Sociogenesis

One other primary developmental concern of Baldwin involves the relations between nature and nurture and the cross-generational transmission of modifications in individual development. In light of the metaphysical synthesis that guided Baldwin's thinking, it was entirely fitting for him to argue that the nature–nurture dichotomy falsely "supposes that these two agencies are opposed forces" and that it fails to entertain the possibility that "most of man's equipment is due to both causes working together" (Baldwin, 1895, p. 77). Evolutionary adaptations and developmental accommodations operate toward the same goals, although they are established over vastly different time intervals. Extending this analysis to the problem of how this synchrony is established and maintained, Baldwin wrote:

> It is clear that we are led to relatively distinct questions: questions which are now familiar to us when put in the terms covered by the words, "phylogenesis" and "ontogenesis." First, how has the development of organic life proceeded, showing constantly, as it does, forms of greater complexity and higher adaptation? This is the phylogenetic question . . . But the second question, the ontogenetic question, is of equal importance: the question, How does the individual organism manage to adjust itself better and better to its environment? . . . This latter problem is the most urgent, difficult, and neglected question of the new genetic psychology. (1895, pp. 180–181)

Beginning in his first developmental volume (Baldwin, 1895) and continuing through *Development and Evolution* (Baldwin, 1902), Baldwin expanded on his view of the cross-generational transmission of behavior tendencies through "organic selection." He proposed that "accommodations" that occur in the lifetime of the individual could be transmitted to the next generation in the form of "adaptations" of the species by means of the process that he labeled "organic selection" (Baldwin, 1895, p. 174). The essence of the idea was that ontogenetic accommodations can serve to direct the course of evolutionary change. How was it accomplished? On this matter, there remains debate on exactly what processes were implicated (e.g., Gottlieb, 1979, 1987; Piaget, 1978; Vonèche, 1982). Baldwin was clearly reaching for a developmental mechanism of directed selection that would supplement the Darwinian concept of natural selection, without invoking "the Lamarckian factor" (i.e., the inheritance of acquired characteristics). Over the years, Baldwin sharpened this concept (Baldwin, 1930). The proposal became known in biology as the "Baldwin effect" (Cairns, 1983; Gottlieb, 1979), despite Baldwin's large debt to the crisp logic of C. L. Morgan (1896, 1902).

Toward a Critical Evaluation

Since the modernity of Baldwin's theory has become acknowledged, it has seemed reasonable to evaluate its adequacy by modern standards. Certain shortcomings in coherence and expression appear in a cursory examination of his books; other problems demand the examination of the work of Baldwin's contemporaries. Doubtless the most important measure of his theory has to do with its effects on subsequent investigators, including those in the present generation.

Perhaps because of his openness to novel conceptions, Baldwin sometimes evolved the meaning of basic concepts in the theoretical models that he proposed. The relativity of his ideas to time and context renders any static description of his theory misleading. It also confounds comparisons that may be made with his contemporaries and apparent intellectual heirs, including Piaget and Vygotsky.

Baldwin's work illustrated another premise of his theoretical perspective—that an individual undergoes the "constant modification of his sense of himself by suggestions from others" (1897, p. 30). On this score, his early work in mental philosophy was heavily influenced by the metaphysical view of Scottish commonsense philosophy in general and the intuitional realism of James McCosh, his mentor at Princeton (Mueller, 1976; Wozniak, 1982). During the second period, his research laboratory owed much to the prior

work of Preyer, Binet, and Shinn. Similarly, his conceptions of "organic selection" seemed to have drawn much from the work of Morgan (1896) and Osborn (1896). In the work on genetic logic and precision of philosophical definition, Baldwin drew on contemporaries William James and C. S. Peirce in his conception of the task and its execution. Baldwin typically was generous in acknowledging these influences, and thereby highlighted his own distinctive insights and creativity.

Baldwin's writing style and organization were uneven. On some issues, as is illustrated by some quotes in this chapter, he was incisive, powerful, and challenging. He could also, however, be obtuse. William James, one of the few American psychologists who remained friendly with Baldwin, gently remarked, "This article (like much of its author's [Baldwin's] writing) is in places deficit in perspicuity" (James, 1894, p. 210). Other critics were less generous. James Sully, an important British experimentalist and a contemporary of Baldwin, began and ended a review of *Mental Development in the Child and the Race* with the following comments:

> This is a book which presents special difficulties to the reviewer. One looks on a biological work—for such Professor Baldwin's work seems to be quite as much as a psychological one—for arrangement, structure, organic form: in the present case one is struck almost at first glance by the apparent absence of these attributes. And the first impression is by no means dispelled as one begins to read. . . .
>
> To sum up my impression of Prof. Baldwin's book. It seems to me in many respects fresh and stimulating. On the other hand in what looks like an over-straining after originality apparent newness of conception often turns on closer examination to be but newness of phrasing. *When new ideas are put forward one misses for the most part an impartial and thorough-going confronting of theory with fact* (1896a, pp. 97, 102–103, my italics).

Unclarity was not limited to this first volume. In comparing Baldwin's discussions of social development with those of C. H. Cooley (1902), Sewney (1945, p. 84) indicated that "Cooley presented his views in a language that is lucid and readable, and free of the confusing and jumbled terminology that fills the writings of Baldwin." In an unpublished journal located by Mueller (1976, p. 250), Cooley himself allowed the following comments on Baldwin's style and motivation:

A great fault with strenuous writers like Baldwin is that in their eagerness to produce they do not allow time enough for their imaginations to grow naturally and thoroughly into the mastery of a subject. They force it, and so impair its spontaneity, its sanity and humanness. What they write may be stimulating, consecutive, attractive for a time, but it is not food to live on. A style like this Goethe calls mannerism or "*das manirierte.*" If you wish to produce anything of lasting value, you see to it that the subject matter, the truth, is the first interest of your mind, not your books, your essay, yourself as discoverer and communicator of truth. (quoted from Mueller, 1976, p. 250)

A modern reviewer, otherwise sympathetic to Baldwin, indicated that "there is much in Baldwin's work that is unfinished and confusing" (Broughton, 1981, p. 402). Examples of the unfinished business included theoretical discontinuities in Baldwin's social theory, and internal inconsistencies in the description of stages.

Baldwin's style may have been more than an inconvenience for readers. It permitted him to reform explanations and concepts so that one and the same term could take on fresh nuances or alternative meanings, depending on its context. Imprecision in presentation thereby promotes projection in interpretation. Perhaps this explains the considerable dispute as to what exactly was meant by Baldwin in his use of such terms as *organic selection, imitation,* and *genetic method.*

Baldwin tended to incorporate new ideas into his own developmental view, and he did not always appear to be sensitive to possible contradictions between the new and the old. Baldwin seems to have benefited greatly from Josiah Royce and William James in his concepts of the social self (Valsiner & Van der Veer, 1988). He also introduced some of the ideas of Osborn (1896) and Morgan (1896) in his revision of the concept of "organic selection." It was, however, a process of assimilation, not imitation. Most of the ideas were transformed when they became incorporated into a genetic framework. This long-term pattern of intellectual reformulation and reconstruction may account for why Baldwin invented new terms for old ideas and was particularly sensitive to the issue of intellectual priority and ownership. In his eyes, the concepts were new inventions. Priority and recognition were especially important for Baldwin, and this concern may help explain his haste to publish.

To illustrate, consider the concept of *organic selection.* The aim of the concept was clear from the beginning: to link the accommodations that occur in the life history of the individual to the adaptations that occur in the life history of the species. But the identification of the precise mechanisms has proved to be something of a projective test. This is due in part to the assimilation by Baldwin of the terms and logical argument outlined by C. Lloyd Morgan (1896). In a brief but brilliant essay on this matter, reprinted as an appendix in Baldwin's volume on *Development and Evolution,* Morgan (1902) refers to the collaboration of individual modification in development and adaptive variation in phylogenesis as *coincident variations.* The concept of coincident variation was incorporated into Baldwin's account of organic selection, but it was unclear when he accepted the important corollary that there were no direct connections between specific individual experiences in ontogeny and specific variations in phylogeny. Eventually, Baldwin did clarify the concept (Baldwin, 1930).

All this is to say that the contributions of Baldwin did not arise independently of the rich intellectual context in which he lived and drew inspiration. But he also inspired his colleagues. Consistent with his model of social-cognitive development, the influences were bidirectional. There is now ample evidence that a large number of investigators in four disciplines were challenged by Baldwin's proposals and conceptions on development. In his commitment to the concept of development and its systematic application, Baldwin was more persuasive, thoughtful, and persistent than any of his peers, including G. Stanley Hall. He envisioned a new *genetic science* (Baldwin, 1930).

Lawrence Kohlberg deserves credit—more than any other psychologist of the present generation—for having brought the attention of American psychologists to the theoretical contributions of Baldwin. Before Kohlberg's (1969) classic article on social cognition, there was scant recognition among modern developmental psychologists of the extent to which Baldwinian insights have persisted in the discipline. Kohlberg himself studied Baldwin's work independently in graduate school to establish a theoretical framework for his investigation of ethical and moral development. It is therefore fitting that the primary book on Baldwin's theory should be edited by two of Kohlberg's former students (Broughton & Freeman-Moir, 1982) and that Kohlberg's chapter in that volume contained some of its most noteworthy passages. His essay provides a succinct answer to the question: What are the real differences between Baldwin's and Piaget's theories? Kohlberg (1982) writes:

> In the end, the fundamental distinction between Baldwin's moral psychology and Piaget's is that Piaget's psychology has no self. Piaget starts with an ego knowing objects, but knowing them first egocentrically. Development is a progressive movement toward objectivity. In contrast, for Baldwin all experience is experience of a self, not just of a bodily and cognitive ego. This means first that central to the self is not cognition but will. Second, it means that from the start experience is *social* and reflective. The child's sense of self is a sense of will and capacity in the relation of self to others. The individual is fundamentally a potentially moral being, not because of social authority and rules (as Durkheim and Piaget thought) but because his ends, his will, his self is that of a shared social self. (pp. 311–312)

It is also an integrative self. Baldwin (1897) himself indicated: "In spite of the large place which I assign to Imitation in the social life, I should prefer to have my theory known as the 'Self' or the 'Self Thought' theory of social organization" (p. xviii).

Baldwin's theoretical work anticipated much of Piaget's theory of cognitive and moral development. Piaget's use of Baldwin's distinctive terms—from circular reaction and cognitive scheme to accommodation, assimilation, and sensorimotor—point to a direct line of intellectual descent. More importantly, as Cahan (1984, p. 128) has observed, "the goals, genetic approach, and epistemological assumptions underlying Piaget's inquiry into cognitive development found explicit statement around the turn of the century in Baldwin's work." The mediational linkages from Baldwin are readily identified. From 1912 to his death in 1934, Baldwin's primary residence was in Paris. His work was well regarded in French intellectual circles in general, and by Pierre Janet in particular. As Piaget wrote to Mueller (1976, p. 244):

> Unfortunately I did not know Baldwin personally, but his works had a great influence on me. Furthermore, Pierre Janet, whose courses I took in Paris, cited him constantly and had been equally very influenced by him. . . .

There is also a written record in the pattern of Piaget's citations of Baldwin. Curiously, these references appeared in works that were published very early (1926) or very late (1978) in Piaget's career.

It would be a mistake to infer that Piaget's theory was simply a revision of Baldwin's original. As Broughton (1981) and Cahan (1984) have observed, the differences are as great as the similarities. In addition to the insightful distinction made by Kohlberg, there is a large difference in the scientific styles of the two investigators that, in turn, gave rise to marked differences in the content of their approaches. Baldwin used the methods and analyses of experimental psychology to illustrate developmental theory. He learned early that the methods of experimental psychology were inadequate to evaluate the developmental theory that he was constructing. Given this dilemma, he chose to abandon the scientific issues and address the philosophical ones.

Piaget, on the other hand, was trained in biology rather than philosophy. As an empirical scientist, he employed observations to understand phenomena rather than merely demonstrate principles. Piaget was challenged to invent methods appropriate to the empirical issues he sought to comprehend. The clinical method of direct observation and the creation of developmentally appropriate tasks provided him with the tools for revising, extending, and evaluating his proposals. They also permitted others to assess the replicability of the phenomena and determine the adequacy of the theory. More important, the objective tracking of phenomena over time permitted Piaget and those who followed his lead to arrive at insights that were not self-evident to experimentalists or armchair observers. The insights, in turn, contributed to the vitality of Piaget's developmental model.

Despite the shortcomings in Baldwin's theoretical system and empirical work, his proposals have nonetheless exercised a large direct and indirect influence on developmental theorists in the 20th century. As Valsiner and Van der Veer (1988) document, there are direct connections between Baldwin's (1897) concepts of the development of the self in social context and George H. Mead's (1934) symbolic interactionism, on the one hand, and L. S. Vygotsky's (1962) propositions on the social-contextual origins of personality, on the other. Baldwin's work was the common denominator, since neither Mead nor Vygotsky referred to the other directly. The Valsiner and Van der Veer (1988) analysis is consistent with independent evidence that (a) Baldwin's work had a significant influence on C. H. Cooley as well as Mead, in formulations of symbolic interactionism; and (b) Baldwin's influence on Vygotsky was mediated primarily through Janet's writings. Valsiner and Van der Veer (1988) point out that the assimilation of Baldwin's influence was selective. On the one hand, Cooley (1902) and Mead (1934) tended to discard the developmental features of Baldwin's self theory. On the other hand, Vygotsky (1962) preserved both the ontogenetic focus and the social dynamics of Baldwin's system.

In addressing the issue of what lasting significance Baldwin's developmental concepts may have for the science, we first must ask why they vanished from psychology in the first place. The primary explanation was that Baldwin's theoretical formulations were out of line with the ideas and empirical trends that were to dominate the new American psychology of the early 20th century. The new psychology was to be dominated by models that either denied the importance of cognition or diminished the importance of development beyond infancy. Moreover, his developmental concepts of the mind and of social processes required research methods that were simply not available to the discipline. The further Baldwin went beyond the study of infancy, the more speculative and removed from data he became. But the fulfillment of his aim—the building of a science of development—demanded a continuing tension between a drive for system and a drive for evidence. As Quine (1981, p. 31) has observed:

> If either of these drives were unchecked by the other, it would issue in something unworthy of the name of scientific theory: in the one case a mere record of observations, and in the other a myth without foundation.

Baldwin lacked the cadre of colleagues and students to help him translate his developmental ideas into an empirical science. Without adequate methodologies, he became increasingly removed from the validation and correction of his ideas, and, like William James before him, became increasingly drawn to philosophy and away from the empirical issues of developmental psychology.

There were other factors that various writers have felt were important in limiting his influence: (a) his writing style failed to inspire confidence in the validity of his ideas; (b) he failed to produce students who might have continued his work (i.e., in the 5 years that he was at Johns Hopkins, no students completed the doctoral program in psychology); and (c) his severe embarrassment in a personal scandal that became public led to abrupt termination from his academic position at Johns Hopkins in 1909. After that incident, he spent little time in the United States, and his name seems to have been virtually blacklisted by the next generation of psychologists. Each of these events may have contributed to the regression and submersion of Baldwin's concepts in American psychology. Ironically, Baldwin's forced move to Paris may have facilitated the acceptance of his concepts. European psychologists tended to be more receptive to developmental concepts and methods than their American counterparts.

Beyond these contributing factors, the unfinished business in Baldwin's agenda was to create methods, techniques, and analyses that are appropriate for developmental study. Piaget and Vygotsky, who helped establish those methods and revised their concepts in the light of their results, had an enormous impact on modern developmental thinking. Recent methodological critiques have suggested that the systematic study of developmental processes requires not only different statistics, but also different research designs and different ways to organize empirical observations (Cairns, 1986; Valsiner, 1986; Wohlwill, 1973). Furthermore, it was explicit in Baldwin's proposals that the task of disentangling development-in-context was necessarily an interdisciplinary activity that extends beyond the traditional boundaries of psychology. Sully (1896a) was probably correct when he observed that Baldwin's *Mental Development in the Child and the Race* was as relevant to biology as it was to psychology. And Mueller (1976) was likely accurate when he noted that Baldwin's *Social and Ethical Interpretation of Mental Development* was as relevant to sociology as to psychology.

The broader point is that Baldwin may have failed in his larger goal even if he had written more precisely, recruited more students, and died of old age in Baltimore rather than Paris. He would have failed because he had envisioned a science different from any that could be accommodated by the new psychology. It appears that many of the obstacles that precluded the adoption of developmental concepts into the psychology of the 1890s remain in place in the 1990s.

What might we conclude about James Mark Baldwin? Beyond whatever shortcomings may have existed in his writing and teaching, and beyond whatever honors he coveted and disappointments he endured, he ultimately succeeded in reaching the part of the goal that was within his grasp. He had insight and vision to describe developmental ideas that continue to inspire and challenge after 100 years.

Developmental Psychopathology

Sigmund Freud (1856–1939) stood in curious relationship to the founding of developmental psychology. Unlike the other investigators covered in this section, Freud published no empirical research on behavioral development per se: He observed few children in a clinical setting, and none in a traditional experimental design. Yet psychoanalysis has emerged as one of the more important influences—if not the most important—for developmental psychology in the 20th century. Further, the early acceptance of psychoanalysis in the United States and elsewhere was due in part to the enthusiasm of G. Stanley Hall. As Freud himself described the emergence of the psychoanalytic movement:

> In 1909 Freud and Jung were invited to the United States by G. Stanley Hall to deliver a series of lectures on psychoanalysis at Clark University, Worcester, Mass. From that time forward interest in Europe grew rapidly; it showed itself, however, in a forcible rejection of the new teachings, characterized by an emotional colouring which sometimes bordered upon the unscientific. (1926/1973, vol. 18, p. 720)

Hall recognized a novel developmental idea when he saw one. His promotion of psychoanalysis occurred at a time when it was suffering rejection in Europe and obscurity in North America. Freud's (1910) lectures at Clark, published in Hall's *American Journal of Psychology,* remain one of the most lucid and succinct presentations of psychoanalysis by its founder.

Born in Moravia and raised in Vienna, Freud as a student showed the catholicity of interests that was to appear in his mature work. Though anatomy and physiology were his primary areas of concentration, he was greatly impressed by the work of Darwin and Haeckel, on the one hand, and by the ideas of British associationist John Stuart Mill, on the other. After completing medical studies, Freud engaged in neurobiological research for several years, initiating, among other things, a phyletic/ontogenetic analysis of the fetal brain and the mapping of sensory neural tracts. Freud's early physiological publications

were well received, and he achieved international recognition as a highly promising researcher and methodologist.

The mid-1880s constituted a turning point in his career when he decided to practice neurology, in part for economic considerations, according to Jones (1953). To further his training in this specialty, Freud won a fellowship to study in Paris with the renowned neurologist, J. M. Charcot. From 13 October 1885 until 28 February 1886, Freud thus worked in the facilities at the Salpêtrière and, presumably, shared some of the same interests as Alfred Binet. Apparently both young men were attracted by Charcot's demonstrations of the interrelations between physical symptoms and the mind, including the use of hypnotism in the remission of hysteric symptoms and in probing the "unconscious" mind. Binet, characteristically, was the first of the two to publish on issues of sexual perversions and their origins. In a remarkable yet almost forgotten paper entitled *"Le fétichisme dans l'amour,"* Binet (1887) described the ease with which sexual attractions and impulses could be associated with neutral objects, and the "abnormal" could be brought about by normal mechanisms of associative learning. In this paper in an early volume of the *Revue Philosophique,* Binet anticipated three of the major themes identified with psychoanalysis; namely, (a) the continuity between mechanisms that regulate normal and abnormal behaviors and emotions, (b) the significance of sexuality in psychopathology, and (c) the essential lawfulness of human behavior.

Returning to Vienna, Freud began his neurological practice, leading to a collaboration with Josef Breuer in the writing of *Studies in Hysteria* (1895/1936). When Freud substituted free association and dream analysis for hypnotism in reaching the unconscious, psychoanalysis was invented.

Might Binet's concepts of unconscious have contributed to the psychoanalytic movement? In a remarkable passage in Breuer and Freud (1895/1936), we find:

> The continuation of the hysterical symptoms which originated in the hypnoid state, during the normal state, agrees perfectly with our experiences concerning post-hypnotic suggestions. But this also implies that complexes of ideas incapable of consciousness co-exist with groups of ideas, which function consciously; that is to say, there is a *splitting of the psyche.* . . . It seems certain that this too can originate without hypnoidism from an abundance of rejected ideas which were repressed, but not suppressed from consciousness. *In*

this or that way here develops a sphere of psychic existence,
which is now ideationally impoverished and rudimentary, and
now more or less equal to the waking thoughts, for the cogni-
tion of which we are indebted above all to Binet and Janet.
(Breuer & Freud, 1936, p. 188, my emphasis)

One reason that the Binet-Janet-Freud linkage has been heretofore overlooked may be that A. A. Brill failed to include this section in his earlier English translation of *Studies in Hysteria* (i.e., before 1936). A mere oversight? Perhaps, but Sulloway (1979) proposes a less benign interpretation of selective recall and biased citations in psychoanalysis. He asks, "Why is the history of intellectual revolution so often the history of conscious and unconscious attempts by the participants to obscure the true nature and roots of their own revolutionary activity?" (p. 6). His answer is that there "generally exists a powerful underlying tension between the forward-looking orientation of the would-be discoverer and the backward-looking orientation of the historian" (p. 7). Innovation, novelty, and discovery are the stuff out of which new scientific movements are created. There is strong temptation to ignore or denigrate research and researchers who threaten the illusions of novelty or validity—despite a commitment of the scientist to balanced and thorough scholarship. Although psychoanalysis illustrates this temptation, it hardly constitutes a unique case in the past of developmental psychology.

As Freud (1926/1973) has pointed out, psychoanalysis "in the course of time came to have two meanings: (1) a particular method of treating nervous disorders and (2) the science of unconscious mental processes, which has also been appropriately described as 'depth psychology'" (p. 720). Psychoanalysis, the theory, involves strong assumptions about the development and evolution of personality that psychoanalysis, the method and therapy, does not. Why, then, did psychoanalysis-as-theory emerge as a developmental one?

One answer would be that it was demanded by the data. The roles of, say, infant sexuality and the primacy of early experiences would be seen as having been revealed by the use of psychoanalysis-as-method. A second possibility, not incompatible with the first, is that Freud may have been intellectually prepared to focus on the formative nature of ontogenetic events by virtue of his research training and experience in neurobiology. Recall that Freud had, in his physiological work, undertaken analyses of embryogenesis.

Finally, broader intellectual-scientific forces appear to have been at work. As Gould (1977) and others have noted, parallels to the then-contemporary evolutionary developmental assumptions seem to be liberally represented throughout psychoanalytic thought. That Freud should draw on biological approaches in the formulation of his theory of personality and psychopathology seems entirely reasonable, in light of his scientific training in the area.

Contrary to the view that Freud employed physics as the basic model for psychoanalysis, the theory seems more analogous to the biological thought of the day than to either "physical" or even "medical" models. Hence, certain psychoanalytic propositions appear to be immediately parallel to Darwinian–Haeckelian proposals on development and evolution. These include: (a) the never-ceasing intrapsychic struggle and competition among instincts for survival and expression; (b) the psychoanalytic focus on two immanent motivational forces that figure importantly in evolution-instincts that bring about reproduction (sexual, libido), and instincts that bring about selection and destruction (aggression, Thanatos); (c) the assumed preestablished progression of the stages of ontogenesis that parallel the stages of phylogenesis, hence the appearance of sexual expression in human infancy; and (d) the notion of developmental arrest or fixation, an idea introduced into recapitulation theory to account for fetal teratology, whereby "monsters" would be produced if the ancestral stages of phyletic evolution were not permitted to be sequentially produced in individual development.

Later, in *Moses and Monotheism* (1939), Freud makes his debt to the biogenetic law explicit. As we have already seen, the primary American psychological recapitulationist, G. Stanley Hall, recognized the fundamental harmony of his ideas on development and evolution with those of psychoanalysis.

The methodological legacy of psychoanalysis requires comment. Freud's main endeavor in life, according to Freud himself, was "to infer or to guess how the mental apparatus is constructed and what forces interplay and counteract it" (Jones, 1953, vol. 1, p. 45).

The inferences on development and infantile experiences were colored, in large measure, by statements and reconstructed memories of his adult neurotic patients. It was a narrow data base, hardly adequate to construct a theory of normal development. But Freud had an advantage that most other theorists of his day (and these days) did not have: he, like Binet, was permitted the opportunity to study complex processes in "persons whom we know intimately." Psychoanalysis thus evolved from the exhaustive observation of single individuals over a long-term period, including Freud's own self analysis. Theory construction and its evaluation thus proceeded on an idiographic basis, following a research strategy not unlike the method he found effective in his earlier physiological studies.

If the contributions of investigators who employed the idiographic method are any indication—Preyer, Binet, Baldwin, Lewin, Piaget—then the procedure seems not wholly without merits. But there are pitfalls. While Binet argued that it was necessary to work back and forth—verifying and testing one's hypotheses at both levels of analysis—Freud eventually expressed a disdain for systematic experimental work, and the validity of the results it produced. For instance, in response to what seemed to be the experimental demonstration of repression in the laboratory, Freud observed: "I cannot put much value on these confirmations because the wealth of reliable observations on which these assertions rest makes them independent of experimental verification" (cited in Shakow & Rapaport, 1964, p. 129). Freud had earlier held that the rejection of psychoanalytic teachings had been for "emotional" and "unscientific" reasons. Here the suggestion appears to be that they should be accepted on the same grounds. In time, the validity of psychoanalytic assertions came to be evaluated by dogma, not by data. That's a pity on two counts. First, the history of developmental research indicates that Freud was correct in holding that idiographic methods are no less "scientific" than are nomothetic ones, though the more enduring advances have occurred when the two methods have been coupled. Second, the scientific status of the entire area was compromised when it became permissible to denigrate the value of a conclusive empirical observation or experiment if it happened to be in conflict with a kernel hypothesis.

In any case, psychoanalysis has thrived for 100 years in science and society. Its direct impact upon the health and social sciences and literature cannot be overestimated. As a scientific orientation, the breadth of its roots in the evolutionary-developmental thought of Darwin and Haeckel, on the one hand, and the psychological associationism of J. S. Mills and British empiricism, on the other, made it especially susceptible to hybridization. For

example, psychoanalysis-as-theory was as readily married to the hypothetico-deductive behavioral model of C. Hull as it was to the ethological theory of K. Lorenz and N. Tinbergen. Both syntheses—social learning theory and attachment theory—have proved to be exceedingly influential in developmental research, a matter which we revisit.

One kernel assumption that has made psychoanalysis particularly attractive to developmentalists has been its focus on the very early years as formative and determinative. The events of infancy and early childhood are presumed to provide the foundation for adult personality and psychopathology. This broad assumption demands research on infancy and early childhood and on the events that occur in the familial relationships. Ironically, the assumption also implies that the events that occur later in ontogeny—during childhood and adolescence and early adulthood—are necessarily less plastic and malleable, hence less critical for understanding personality and psychopathology. Psychoanalysis is a developmental theory, up to a point. Hence, childhood is seen as the "latency" period, and adolescence is viewed as a period of activating the propensities and conflicts of the earliest years. The goal of much research in this tradition has been to demonstrate that there are strong continuities from infancy and the preschool period throughout childhood, adolescence, and early adulthood.

There is a formal similarity between psychoanalysis and most of its descendant theories—including Object Relations Theory and Attachment Theory—in that the principal dynamic processes of development are restricted to the earliest years. Once these personality dispositions and structures become established and fixed, other nondevelopmental processes come into play. Under very special circumstances, such as psychoanalytic therapy, later interventions are possible. As Fenichel (1945) observes, the transference relationship in psychoanalysis is seen as a reconstructive psychiatric intervention where the fixations and conflicts of infancy and childhood are relived and repaired.

The broader point is that psychoanalysis and its descendant models implicate developmental processes—reciprocal interaction, bidirectionality, behavioral plasticity, biobehavioral organization—only up to a critical point in ontogeny. In the usual case, this point is infancy or very early childhood. These developmental processes, then, become less active and less relevant, and the personality structures and dispositions that they produced govern the nature and quality of the individual's adaptations throughout the life course.

Other Trends in Science and Society

Child Clinics

Psychoanalysis clearly played the leading role in setting the agenda for future studies of developmental psychopathology, but other, nearly forgotten forces were operating to link psychology and society. One notable event, particularly relevant to child study, was the opening of the first psychological clinic in the United States. It was founded in 1896 at the University of Pennsylvania under the direction of Lightner Witmer, a former student of Wundt and Cattell.

The aim of Witmer's work was to assist in the diagnosis and treatment of children with school problems, and to apply the principles of the newly established science to everyday concerns. What were those principles? In Witmer's view, the study of children required a multidisciplinary approach, and from the beginning he brought together different professions, including social workers, physicians, and practicing psychologists. In the absence of a treatment model, he created one. Although the clinic was essentially a local Philadelphia operation, it grew and prospered under Witmer's leadership, and a journal, the *Psychological Clinic,* was founded to describe its activities. The concept of an applied psychology, as well as a clinical psychology, caught on, and one of the students from Witmer's group at Pennsylvania, Morris Viteles, led the way in the establishment of industrial psychology in America (Viteles, 1932).

Developmental Theory

From 1900 forward, when theoretical activity in developmental psychology was on the wane in the United States, it began to thrive in Europe. Following the impetus provided by Preyer, developmental work in German-speaking countries expanded, with the young William L. Stern (1871–1938) playing a leading role. Stern was instrumental in extending the theoretical and institutional foundations of the new science in Germany from the turn of the century through the early 1930s (Kreppner, 1992). In 1909, he was sufficiently prominent in the discipline that he was awarded an honorary degree from Clark University.

Kreppner (1992) has recently argued that Stern should be viewed as the peer of Preyer, Binet, Freud, Hall, and Baldwin as a pioneer in developmental psychology. Remembered in American psychology mostly for his proposal that the mental ages could be converted into an intellectual quotient (Petersen, 1925; Stern, 1911, 1914)—a transformation that was designed to equate intelligence scores across chronological ages—little systematic recognition has been given to his fundamental role in establishing three areas of psychology as scientific disciplines: (a) differential psychology, (b) personality psychology, and (c) developmental psychology. Stern's influence is seen in the ideas on development that he generated, in the institutions he created, and in the students whom he influenced, including Heinz Werner and Martha Muchow.

Although he completed his dissertation with Hermann Ebbinghaus, Stern saw early that the study of human development required a unified perspective (Kreppner, 1992). In this regard, Binet and Henri (1895) had earlier confronted the dualism between elementarism and holism in understanding children's cognitive functioning and problem solving. In the same spirit:

> [Stern criticized] the view that psychological elements are carriers of psychological forces . . . a person's actions are defined not by single elements but by the entire structure of environment, person, and person–environment interaction. Thus, a wholistic view was one of the fundamental bases from which Stern constructed his person-oriented theoretical framework. (Kreppner, 1994, p. 317)

Consistent with the dialectic philosophy, Stern described the tug-of-war between personal dispositions and environmental constraints in development. This brings up the issue of how plastic or malleable are actions in ontogeny. The individual is a complex unit that is not entirely determined by the forces within or the forces without. In this regard, Stern wrote:

> This is the fact of personal plasticity or malleability, a domain of intentional education or unintentional influences of the milieu. This domain is narrower than many empiricists might be aware of. For the person is not only a passive recipient of the environmental forces impinging on him, but he is also reacting to these forces. The way he shapes and keeps a kind of plasticity is not only a symptom of the conflict between activity and passivity, it is also a tool for overcoming

it: It is a mirror which is a weapon at the same time. (W. Stern, 1918, pp. 50–51, quoted from Kreppner, 1994, p. 318)

But it should be recalled that a dialectical systems perspective is not necessarily a developmental perspective. Stern's dual interest in development and individual differences presents a dilemma The inclusion of developmental change in any discussion of characteristics of the self—traits and types—adds fresh complications. The theoretical task is to resolve the tension between changing, adaptable features that promote fresh adaptations, and enduring, permanent features that provide for predictable individual differences. On this score, the proposal of the IQ ratio held age constant and focused on individual differences; it represented the differential assessment, nondevelopmental side of Stern's thinking. His students represented both features of Stern's thought, from the nondevelopmental representations of topographical theory (Lewin, 1935) to the thoroughly developmental concepts of mental development and symbolic transformation in Werner (1940).

His influence extended even beyond the boundaries of recent retrospectives. Through the work of Gordon Allport, Stern's ideas became prominently represented in the classic volume *Personality* (Allport, 1937). Stern's strong influence is seen in Allport's concepts of the holistic nature of personality organization and functioning, and idiographic and nomothetic models. In the study of individual differences, Stern literally wrote the book, authoring one of the first systematic texts on differential psychology (1911), a volume that is still admirable in its precision and clarity.

After establishing and directing the Psychological Institute at Hamburg University, Stern was expelled from Germany in 1933 by the Nazi regime. He came to the United States in 1934, was appointed in the Department of Psychology at Duke University, and died in Durham, North Carolina, in 1938. As in the case of J. M. Baldwin, his ideas have survived, but his name recognition temporarily lapsed.

Child Study

In France, developmental work progressed in brilliant leaps in education and became bogged down in the universities. Binet himself was rejected in his three attempts to secure an academic appointment as chairs became open at the Sorbonne and the Collége de France. He died without having been named to a professorship in France, despite his preeminent role in the establishment of psychology as an empirical science. Binet's founding of a laboratory for the experimental study of educational problems inspired E. Claparéde's establishment of the J. J. Rousseau Institute in Geneva.

In England, James Sully (1896b) and William Drummond (1907) produced influential textbooks on psychology and on development, although there was relatively little novel research being conducted on children (but see McDougall, 1906–1908). In this regard, Mateer (1918) observed that "on the whole English contributions to child study, in so far as it deals with the child of preschool age, have been imitative rather than original and very scanty in number" (p. 28). Additionally, the contributions of G. Stanley Hall were being brought back to Europe whence they had originated. The British Child Study Association, in England, and the Society for the Psychological Study of the Child, in France, were two of the more influential groups modeled after Hall's American association. Comparable developments were occurring in Italy, Russia, Denmark, and Portugal, but these events were relatively remote from the mainstream of ongoing developmental work and thinking. They soon were to become less remote with the importation by Mateer (1918) of classical conditioning methods for studying learning in infants and children.

From 1890 onward, North America joined Europe as a primary center for the scientific study of children. Millicent Shinn's "Notes on the Development of a Child" appeared in 1893 and led to a renewed interest in individual studies. At the time, her replication and extension of Preyer's method was considered to be a "masterpiece" (Mateer, 1918).

Development and Education

The work of Binet, Hall, and Stern has underscored the intimate linkage between basic developmental research and educational practice. These investigators became psychologists, however, and they focused on developmental phenomena in their research and their writings on education. It was a different course with John Dewey. Cahan (1994) notes in her review of Dewey's contributions to the science,

Education was Dewey's most enduring, comprehensive, and synthetic philosophical problem and the one for which he became best known. His interest in education "fused with and brought together what might otherwise have been separate interests—that in psychology and that in social institutions and social life." (Cahan, 1994, p. 146)

Influenced by the neo-Hegelianism of George S. Morris and W. T. Harris, on the one hand, and the pragmatism of C. S. Peirce and William James, on the other, Dewey evolved a distinctive view of education that focused on the social circumstances of the child. The dialectic between the child and the environments in which he or she lived and adapted was key to understanding the nature of development. In this framework, schools became the natural settings for the study of development.

Dewey held that the experiences of children in school could prepare them to develop those intellectual and moral virtues that would establish a better society (Dewey, 1916). How is this to be achieved? According to Dewey, the subject matter of education should not be imposed by the agenda of the adult but should be drawn from the child's immediate environment and from the child's current interests. The task then would be to begin with the child's needs and concerns, not the teacher's.

Sound familiar? These ideas were in the air in the early decades of the 20th century. The Baldwin–Piaget concepts of accommodation and assimilation were first cousins to the idea that there is a "constant reorganizing and restructuring of experience" (Dewey, 1916, p. 82). So are the views of Stern that "the way [the child] shapes and keeps a kind of plasticity is not only a symptom of the conflict between activity and passivity, it is also a tool for overcoming it." Vygotsky's "zone of proximal development" captures a similar concept. These interwoven ideas owe much to Hegelian idealism and the emergent, developmental assumptions with which it has been associated.

At the level of theory, Dewey created a framework for conceptualizing development and education rather than providing a tightly knit model to guide teaching practices. There are ambiguities, however, in how the transition is made from theory to practice. For example, the idea of a "restructuring of experience" does not provide prescriptive rules on how challenging the task must be, or how much assistance and drill the child should be given.

In a review of Dewey's work and thought, Cahan (1994) emphasized that Dewey considered education to be an opportunity for society to reformulate itself, and that "the school is cast as a lever for social change" (Cahan, 1994,

p. 163). This central theme was expressed early by Dewey (1899) in a lecture at the University of Chicago:

> The obvious fact is that our social life has undergone a thorough and radical change. If our education is to have any meaning for life, it must pass through an equally complete transformation. . . . The introduction of active occupations, of nature study, of elementary science, of art, of history; the relegation of the merely symbolic and formal to a secondary position; the change in the moral atmosphere, in the relation of pupils to teachers—of discipline; the introduction of more active, expressive, and self-directing factors—all these are not mere accidents, they are necessities of the larger social evolution. . . . To do this means to make each one of our schools an embryonic community life, active with types of occupations that reflect the life of the larger society, and permeated throughout with the spirit of art, history, and science. When the school introduces and trains each child of society into membership within such a little community, saturating him with the spirit of service, and providing him with instruments of effective self-direction, we shall have the deepest and best guarantee of a larger society which is worthy, lovely, and harmonious. (pp. 43–44)

Hence, educational theory "becomes political theory, and the education is inevitably cast into the struggle for social reform" (Cremin, 1964, p. 118). In Dewey's framework, there is an explicit fusion among the science of human development, educational applications, social reform, and morality. Viewed in historical perspective, Dewey's work and vision may be seen as yet another legacy of his former teacher at Johns Hopkins, G. Stanley Hall.

Themes of the Foundational Period

The emergence of modern developmental psychology in the late 19th and early 20th centuries was hardly a coherent, systematic enterprise. For instance, Dewey's broad philosophical view of development and the embryological concepts of von Baer and evolutionary constructs of Darwin seemed to live in different lands. Considered as a whole, developmental work and theory were diverse, vigorous, contentious, fresh, and, in many instances, brilliant. Despite the lack of unanimity in method and theory, certain themes seemed to capture the attention and guide the work of these early developmental investigators. Seven themes of general significance were:

1. The ontogeny of consciousness and intelligence.
2. Intentionality and the correspondence between thought and action.
3. The relations between evolution and development.
4. The nature–nurture debate.
5. The effects of early experience and when development ceases.
6. Moral development.
7. How the science may contribute to the society.

Knowledge and Consciousness

"Theory of the mind" concepts are hardly new for developmentalists. Indeed, for both comparative and developmental investigators, the origins of consciousness and the development of knowledge were the major empirical concerns in the formative period of the science. The main business of comparative psychology, in the view of Romanes (1884), was to investigate the continuity of consciousness and intelligence from animals to man. To establish the linkage, it was necessary to undertake studies of animal consciousness and of animals' apparent "intelligent" adaptations to the varied circumstances of life. Why continuity? For Romanes, continuity would demonstrate that human beings were on the same continuum as animals in the evolutionary scheme. Using information brought to him from varied and informal sources, Romanes collected anecdotes on how various beasts (dogs, chickens, spiders, cats) demonstrated high levels of intelligence in their adaptations, and transmitted this knowledge to descendants through Larmarckian mechanisms of hereditary transmission.

Here C. Lloyd Morgan entered the scene. Recall that Morgan's major contribution to developmental and evolutionary thought was his elegant refutation of the concept of hereditary transmission of acquired characteristics, a variation of which Baldwin labeled "organic selection" (Klopfer & Hailman, 1967; Morgan, 1896, 1902). The logic of his argument against Larmarckianism extended beyond psychology and beyond behavior.

Morgan was also instrumental in helping establish some limits on the projection of higher-order cognitive processes to lower organisms. Initially a skeptic about interpreting the mental status of nonhuman animals, he formulated a canon (or criterion) by which such attributions may be permissible. Now known as *Morgan's Canon,* it reads "In no case may we interpret an action as the outcome of the exercise of a higher psychical faculty, if it can be interpreted as the outcome of the exercise of one which stands lower in the psychological scale" (Morgan, 1894, p. 53). In its assumption that the "psychic facility" of nonhuman animals can be qualitatively different from those of human beings, Morgan's criterion helped put a break on the more blatant forms of 19th century anthropomorphism (see also Schneirla, 1966). As a byproduct, it invited a shift from a focus on animal consciousness to a focus on animal behavior, including analyses of the roles of biophysical and chemical processes within the organism and physical and social forces without.

The shift was nontrivial. By 1906, H. S. Jennings entitled his magnificent study of the activities of paramecia as "The *Behavior* of Lower Organisms." Earlier, Binet's work on infusoria and other lower beasts was labeled, "The *Psychic Life* of Micro-Organisms" (my emphases). Through Jennings and J. Loeb, the shift in focus paved the way for J. B. Watson's behaviorism (1914) and, ironically, the denial of consciousness. In the article, "How Lloyd Morgan's Canon Backfired," Costall (1993) proposes that "C. L. Morgan argued that the behavior of animals and humans could only be treated in intentionalist terms; his Canon was an attempt to stem anthropocentrism but has been consistently misunderstood" (p. 13; see also Wozniak, 1993). Whatever might have been Morgan's own intentions, he played a pivot role in extending accounts of behavioral development in animals and children beyond mentalism and anthropomorphism. This was a critical step if developmental research was to be promoted from the second class status that it had been assigned by Wundt (1907) and Hall (1885).

Questions on the origin of knowledge were also central for early developmentalists. Not only were child psychologists concerned with "the content of children's minds" (Hall, 1891), but with how the content got into the mind. Preyer gave primary attention to the establishment of the senses, language, and cognition, and Binet and Baldwin early focused on experimental studies of childhood perception, discrimination, and memory. Baldwin's (1895, 1915) developmental theory on the origins of knowledge arose in part from an admixture of the speculations of the post-Kantian and the evolutionary views of Herbert Spencer and G. J. Romanes on stages in consciousness and cognition.

At its root, however, were observations of infants that provided empirical substance to the ideas of reflexive, sensorimotor, and ideomotor adaptations. Baldwin's mature theory of "genetic epistemology" was, essentially, a theory of the mind. It was based for the most part on intuition and the framework that had been established by predecessors in philosophy and biology. It seems no mere coincidence that the dominant concern with cognition and intelligence gave rise to the most robust empirical tests and the most reliable experimental methods of the period.

The Relations between Thoughts and Actions

Although the problem of consciousness was the major theme, questions of the linkages between thoughts and actions lagged not far behind. At what point in ontogeny do "willful" acts arise, and what is the relationship among consciousness and intention and action at any stage of development? These related questions were explored by virtually all early developmental investigators, but, again, with different emphases and different conclusions. Binet and Freud, in part because of their experience with hypnotism and their exposure to the work of Charcot, were concerned with the role of unconscious processes in the direction and control of behavior, both normal and pathological. Binet's (1892) studies of alterations of personality dealt with the effects of unconscious forces, and Breuer and Freud (1895) made motivation and unconscious control the central theme of psychoanalytic theory. On this score, one of the more interesting observations from this period is the discovery of the linkage between Binet's and Freud's views of unconscious processes. Similarly, Baldwin (1897) considered how conscious acts, with practice and time, become unconscious, and how awareness and intentionality develop in step with cognitive development. Nonetheless, the study of "intentionality" posed formidable methodological problems that were not solved (although Preyer launched an early assault on the problem in his studies of infants).

Ontogeny and Phylogeny

How may development be defined: in terms of the ontogeny of individuals, or the ontogeny of the species? Developmental psychology was born in the wake of the biological revolution created by the formulation and widespread adoption of the Wallace–Darwin theory of species origins. The challenge to produce a similarly powerful theory of individual genesis was felt by biologists and psychologists alike. The initially popular candidates for such a general developmental theory were unfortunately limited.

Doubtless the most influential early developmental theory was the "biogenetic law." Virtually all early important developmental writers were recapitulationists of one sort or another. Adoption of the recapitulation perspective did not, however, preclude consideration of alternative or supplementary views. On this score, the delayed maturation hypothesis of Preyer and the Baldwin–Morgan–Osborne proposal on organic selection represented efforts to solve the puzzle of how development could contribute to evolution as well as the reverse.

The "biogenetic law" collapsed shortly after the turn of the century, when the cornerstone assumption of recapitulation was discredited in biology (Gould, 1977). Embryological studies indicated that morphological steps in development could not be simply accounted for in terms of ancestral analogs. Even in embryogenesis, morphology was adaptive to the special conditions that prevailed and, as von Baer had earlier argued, development was appropriately described in terms of early differentiation of structures in ways that became increasingly distinctive for the species. The idea that evolutionary modifications and developmental adaptations are mutually supportive has been repeatedly offered, from the proposals of Morgan and Baldwin to those of modern ethology and developmental psychobiology. To be sure, the recapitulation doctrine was wrongheaded, but the issues to which it was addressed remain fundamental for the science.

Nature and Nurture

A related but separable matter concerns the extent to which an individual's behavior and propensities reflect the operation of experiences as opposed to an inborn, heritable potential. The "nature–nurture" problem, as labeled by Galton (1871), continues to tantalize developmental theorists. Positions on this matter were as diverse then as they are now. Virtually all writers of this early period paid at least lip service to the proposal that it was not an "either–or" proposition but a question of how the two influences were fused in the course of development.

A variety of methods were employed for the study of "natural" influence on behavior. Preyer, for instance, assumed that the actions that develop in the absence of training must reflect the operation of innate factors in the infancy of an individual child. Galton, in a nomothetic approach, placed emphasis on the information to be obtained from pedigree studies, familial and twin comparisons, and selective breeding in animals. Along with Karl Pearson, he developed new statistical tools for the evaluation of covariation and correlation, and these fit neatly with the metric scale of intelligence. They also invited the partitioning of variance into heritable and environmental sources, a technique that also provided the foundation for modern quantitative behavioral genetics and a century of controversy.

When Does Development End?

All early developmentalists, by definition, assumed that experience played a role in the establishment and maintenance of basic systems of behavior, emotion, and cognition. There were radical differences among them regarding *when* they considered experience to be relevant, since timing made all of the difference in the world (see Elder, Ch. 16, this Volume). For G. Stanley Hall, individual experience played a major role in adolescence; early experience was virtually irrelevant because evolutionary forces laid the course for development up through adolescence. For Freud, it was just the opposite: infancy was key; he assumed very early development to be basic in laying the foundations for adult behavior. Beyond infancy and early childhood, the person resisted enduring changes (except under psychoanalytic treatment). For Preyer, it was embryogenesis. And for Baldwin, personality development was a continuing, never-to-be-exhausted process over the life course, so turning points could occur throughout ontogeny.

When the details of timing and plasticity of development were left unspecified, investigators could talk past each and share a happy illusion that they referred to the same issues and outcomes. A basic premise of psychoanalytic theory is the strong hierarchical assumption that very early experiences are foundational for the thoughts, actions, and relations that follow. Psychoanalytically oriented writers could be radical developmentalists, but only for one phase of the life course. Once the personality structures, motives, and "working models" become established, focus was given to the processes of maintenance, not those of establishment and change. On the other hand, investigators in a Baldwinian life-course perspective could look to events that occurred over ontogeny.

In the absence of longitudinal information on the behavioral adaptations of human beings, there was no adequate basis for selecting or rejecting these theoretical assumptions about the timing and functions of early experience. Although Mills (1898) called for systematic longitudinal study, it took a half-century before this method was systematically explored, and still another 90 years before it became a method of choice.

Morality and the Perfectibility of Humans

The concern with intentionality and willfulness can be viewed as part of a broader question of ethics: How can science help understand how human perfectibility may be achieved and imperfections avoided? This core issue was clearly pervasive in the moral psychologies of Tetens and Carus, and it was also a matter of no little import for Spencer, Hall, Baldwin, and several others of the era. A goal shared by many of them was to formulate a developmental science, which, in its highest application, would supplement—or supplant—religion.

By 1900, the key empirical finding—that stages existed in the "development of moral judgments"—had been established, in that older children gave greater weight to the motivation and intentions of a transgressor than did younger children. Similarly, striking age-developmental differences were obtained in the level of abstraction of the "moral judgments," and in the extent to which older children as opposed to younger (12–16 years vs. 6–10 years) took the point of view of the offender. These generalizations were drawn from voluminous questionnaire studies, based on the responses of thousands of children at each age level (e.g., Hall, 1904; Schallenberger, 1894). The methodology, but not the conclusions, was severely criticized at home and abroad. On matters of moral conduct, J. M. Baldwin's proposals adumbrated both Hartshorne and May on the specificity of moral conduct, and the proposals of Kohlberg on the development of the self and moral reasoning.

Social Applications

The application to the needs of society presented both opportunities and problems. To promote the application of "scientific" principles to rearing and educating children, child study movements arose in America, and similar efforts were initiated on the continent and in England. The problem was that scientific principles were in short supply. On this point, William James noted, in *Talks with Teachers* (1900), that "all the useful facts from that discipline could be held in the palm of one hand." Not everyone, including Binet and Hall, agreed with James. Then, as now, the temptation was great to go beyond commonsense beliefs in writing about children.

The ideas and claims of some early developmentalists had political ramifications as well. One of the outcomes was the establishment and rapid growth of the eugenics movement, with Francis Galton as its intellectual leader and the protection of superior genes as its goal in England. One byproduct of "Social Darwinism" was the importance attached to the newly devised metric scale of intelligence and the belief that it would permit rapid identification of innate, stable differences in talent. A movement in Germany, promoted by Haeckel (1901), carried a message of biological ethnic superiority and led to dark political goals.

There was also a very bright side to the application of developmental principles and ideas (see Sears, 1975). Persons concerned with the science tended to act as child advocates, lending their prestige to the passage of child labor laws, the revision of elementary and secondary school curricula, and the promulgation of child-centered rearing and control practices. The discipline may not have directly benefited from these efforts, but the welfare of children did. Then there was the enormous impact that John Dewey's concepts of human development had on teaching and schooling practices. The field moved ahead to consolidate its claim to be an empirical science as well as a progressive social movement.

In summary, the modern study of behavioral development had an auspicious beginning as a vigorous, multidisciplinary undertaking that was pregnant with new ideas, fresh approaches, and novel developmental methods. To the founders, the resolution of the basic problems of development seemed within grasp. Perhaps they were, but that early promise was not to be fulfilled, at least not for another half-century.

THE MIDDLE PERIOD (1913–1946): INSTITUTIONALIZATION AND EXPANSION

One-third of the 20th century, from 1913 to 1946, encompassed two world wars, an economic depression of unprecedented depth and duration, the rise to world power of two new political-economic systems, and unspeakable horrors of mass destruction and genocide. These events affected the course of all intellectual and scientific work

undertaken during the period, and developmental psychology was no exception.

Paradoxically, some of the events that had tragic worldwide consequences served to enrich and broaden the discipline. World War I brought attention to the advantages and potential of psychological assessment, particularly intelligence testing. It also sent the primary American developmental theorist, James Mark Baldwin, to France, where he enjoyed greater influence than he had had in his own country. World War II contributed toward the establishment of psychology as a profession as well as a science. The American prosperity enjoyed in the 1920s was directly translated into liberal support for the discipline by private foundations and state funds. Likewise, the depression of the 1930s and early 1940s effected a massive withdrawal of funds and, concomitantly, a drop in the level of research activity on developmental problems.

Nazi persecution in the 1930s brought to America a cadre of brilliant theorists from Europe. Some, including Kurt Lewin, Fritz Heider, and Heinz Werner, gained an opportunity to change the direction of modern social psychology and to keep alive the developmental concept. For others, including Karl Bühler and William Stern, the exodus was a tragedy wherein their talents and achievements were virtually unappreciated and ignored. And what directions might the study of social development have taken if Charlotte Bühler had been permitted to remain safe and free at her Institute in Vienna rather than becoming an adjunct faculty member in Los Angeles?

Beyond societal and political influences, there was much to be accomplished within the area. There was an immediate need to extend the methodological boundaries of the discipline in order to permit systematic investigation of the several issues claimed by its investigators and theorists. Hence, the formulation of ways to translate ideas into research operations remained a first task. Virtually all substantive issues required attention, from social, cognitive, and sensorimotor analyses to the study of language, moral development, and psychobiological changes. In the 1920s, with the widespread granting of funds that were specifically assigned to support studies of children, there was an explosive increase in empirical research.

In the establishment of its empirical foundations, the enterprise of child and developmental psychology became segregated into separate subareas, topics, and theories. No single model, not even behaviorism, was broad enough to encompass and provide direction for the activities of researchers. The fragmentation stimulated efforts to put the field back together again through the publication of handbooks (which served to summarize the diverse investigations) and the founding of development-centered journals and scientific societies. But in the absence of a compelling and coherent general theory of development, the subareas of developmental investigation and thought evolved along separate trajectories. The story of the main events and ideas of this period is perhaps best told by recounting the progress made in the several areas of inquiry—from mental testing and moral development to language and thought and developmental psychobiology. That will be the strategy adopted in this section, beginning with some comments on the institutionalization of American developmental psychology and ending with a brief review of some major theoretical ideas of this period.

Institutions and Development

The child study movement led by G. Stanley Hall in the 1880s and 1890s bore fruit some 20 years later. Child study associations had been established in one form or another in all regions of the country. Collectively, they formed a potent movement for child advocacy. In 1906, an Iowa housewife and mother, Cora Bussey Hillis, proposed that a research station be established for the study and improvement of child rearing (Sears, 1975). Her argument was simple but compelling: If research could improve corn and hogs, why could it not improve the rearing of children? The campaign to establish a Child Welfare Research Station at the University of Iowa was eventually successful. The Iowa unit was established in 1917 and its research–laboratory school opened in 1921.

The Iowa facility—along with a comparable research unit that opened shortly afterward at the Merrill-Palmer Institute in Detroit—became the model for child development institutes that were to spring up across the United States and Canada in the 1920s and 1930s. Because one of the main functions of the institutes was dissemination of information about children, various publications were established, ranging from university monograph series (at Iowa, Columbia, Minnesota, Toronto, and Berkeley) and journals (*Child Development, Child Development Monographs*) to handbooks (Murchison, 1931, 1933) and magazines (*Child Study, Parents Magazine*). Most of the institutes also awarded advanced degrees, thereby helping to create a new professional workforce. The graduates found placements in university teaching and research positions, as well as in a wide range of applied settings. An interdisciplinary organization, the Society for Research in Child Development, was established in 1930 to provide a forum and a framework for scientific contributors to the discipline (Frank, 1935).

The story of this "golden age" for the study of children in America has been told expertly by two of its participants (Sears, 1975; Senn, 1975), so only an overview is required here. New funds from diverse private and governmental sources were made available to researchers in child development. Among the more notable contributors were the individual sponsors of the Fels and Merrill-Palmer child study institutes, along with various special-mission projects (i.e., Terman's study of gifted children, by the Commonwealth Fund; the study of the effects of motion pictures on children, by the Payne Foundation; the causes of morality, by the Institute for Religious and Social Education).

But in terms of sheer impact on the field, the Laura Spelman Rockefeller Memorial (LSRM) must be acknowledged as having the greatest influence. Through LSRM funds, major centers for research were established at three universities (California, Columbia, Minnesota). Substantial support was awarded to the existing institutes at Yale and Iowa, and smaller-scale research centers were created at the University of Michigan and in Washington, D.C. Studies of personality and child development at Vassar, Sarah Lawrence, and Teachers College (Columbia) also shared in the Rockefeller support. And that's not all. Under the general direction of Lawrence Frank, the Rockefeller funds provided support for individual research projects (including C. Bühler's pioneering investigations) and made possible the establishment of the national Child Study Association (see *Child Study*, Vols. 1–3). Such liberal support for child study provided stimulation for ongoing work at Stanford, Harvard, Toronto, and Cornell. All in all, the effect was to confirm Binet's observation that Americans like to do things big.

To summarize in detail the specific activities and accomplishments of these institutes from 1920 to 1940 is beyond the scope of this review. At midstream, Goode-nough (1930b) provided an informative coverage of the work and accomplishments during a period of great activity. Each institute soon evolved its own "personality" in terms of methods employed and problems addressed. The issues that the institutes tackled should illustrate the point.

1. *Mental testing.* Virtually all of the institutes were committed, at some level, to clarifying the problems of intelligence assessment and how individual differences in test performance came about. By the late 1930s, studies at Iowa on the effects of enrichment on intelligence test performance had appeared, and longitudinal work on the stability and change of IQ had begun at Fels and Berkeley. Anderson (1939) at Minnesota offered a provocative theory of the continuity of intellectual functions, based on the extent to which early tests assessed functions that overlapped with those assessed in later tests. The faculty at Stanford, headed by Lewis Terman and Quinn McNemar, strongly contested any strong claims on the malleability of intelligence (Minton, 1984).

2. *Longitudinal study.* Most thoughtful developmental psychologists recognized the need for gaining adequate information about behavior and development over a significant portion of the life span. But the lack of resources inhibited such long-term, large-scale investigations of behavior and cognition. Here is where the institutes were invaluable. Two of the institutes—Berkeley and Fels—launched systematic longitudinal investigations. The work complemented the already initiated study by Terman at Stanford.

3. *Behavioral and emotional development.* The study of children's fears and how they arise was undertaken at Columbia, Johns Hopkins, Minnesota, California, and Washington University (St. Louis). This work, essentially an extension of the projects launched by Watson and his collaborators at Johns Hopkins (see below), dealt with the problems of how emotions arise in ontogeny and how fears are learned and unlearned (Jersild, Markey, & Jersild, 1933; M. Jones, 1931).

4. *Growth and physical maturation.* The early work of the Iowa group was concerned with the study of children's physical development, including the care and feeding of children (Baldwin & Stecher, 1924). Similarly, Arnold Gesell's institute at Yale led the way in establishing graphs of normal development for use in identifying instances of aberrant behavior or developmental disorders (see below). The Fels Institute early established a tradition for clarifying the relations between physical and behavioral development, leading to, among other things, significant advances in assessment and diagnosis of psychosomatic relations.

5. *Research methods.* John Anderson and Florence Goodenough at Minnesota, Dorothy S. Thomas at Columbia, and H. McM. Bott at Toronto recognized the need for more adequate observational research methods (see Anderson, 1931; Bott, 1934; Goodenough, 1929; Thomas, 1929). But the methodological work was not limited to observational techniques. Goodenough (1930a) continued to explore alternative and flexible methods for personality and intellectual assessment (including her Draw-a-Person test), and these workers led the way in ensuring that high levels of statistical sophistication would be employed in research design and analysis. Dorothy McCarthy at Minnesota and Jean Piaget at the J. J. Rousseau Institute began their influential studies of the origins of children's language and thought (see below).

This is a mere sampling of the major concerns and issues. Without detracting from the intellectual and scientific quality of the work completed, it should be noted that few major theorists were associated with the newly founded institutes. There were some notable exceptions to this generalization, including Jean Piaget at the Rousseau Institute and, in the 1940s, Kurt Lewin and Robert Sears at Iowa. For the most part, the institutes were devoted to the pragmatic problem that Mrs. Hollis had identified, "How can we improve the way that children are reared?" The area soon learned that it had neither methods nor theories adequate to the task. The institutes focused on devising more adequate methods, leaving the primary theoretical work to others.

Mental Testing

In the eyes of many developmentalists in the 1920s and 1930s, the major obstacle to establishing a credible science of child psychology was not theoretical so much as it was methodological. Given Binet's insights on and career-long devotion to the matter, it seems altogether fitting that he, along with his collaborators, engineered the most significant methodological advance of the first half-century of the science. Whatever may be the flaws and shortcomings of the Binet–Simon method of intellectual assessment, it provided the tool that was required for the precise study of children's development, and for the translation of cognitive events into quantifiable units. The test opened the door for comparisons of significant psychological dimensions across ontogeny, and for the analysis of individual differences among persons. It also provided a reliable method for addressing the major themes that had been identified in the first era of the field, including the problems of nature–nurture, early experience, continuity of consciousness, and the predictability of behavior and cognition.

Goodard (1911) deserves credit for having been the first to bring the Binet–Simon scale to America, but Lewis M. Terman and his colleagues at Stanford University were key in extending the use of intelligence tests in America and worldwide through their revision of the Binet–Simon scales. The Stanford–Binet individually-administered tests helped establish clinical psychology as a separate profession in clinics, schools, the military, and industry, fulfilling one of Binet's visions (Petersen, 1925).

Like other students of G. S. Hall who gravitated toward educational psychology, Terman's initial academic appointment at Stanford was in the School of Education. Formerly a school principal, Terman had a long-standing interest in the problems of individual differences in the classroom. He selected as his dissertation project the comparison of seven bright and seven dull boys on various measures (Terman, 1906). He had been acquainted with Binet's work since his research for his undergraduate thesis at Indiana University, and, given his background and the Barnes-associated tradition at Stanford for large-scale study, it seemed entirely in character that Terman should attempt an extensive standardization of the Binet–Simon scales (on some 1,000 California schoolchildren; Terman, 1916). Among other improvements to the scale, Terman adopted a suggestion by William Stern that any child's performance could be expressed in terms of an Intelligence Quotient (IQ). In his commitment to observation and standardization, Terman proved to be a worthy successor to Binet. The Americanized version of the test was an almost immediate success. The method was widely adopted and the essential idea was used to construct group tests to meet the needs of the military (in screening recruits for World War I) and the schools to sort out highly gifted or retarded children (Goodenough, 1954).

This is not the place to attempt a comprehensive account of the testing movement; useful histories of mental testing, through 1925, can be found in Peterson (1925) and Young (1924), and more recent accounts can be found in Goodenough (1954), Tuddenham (1962), and Carroll and Horn (1981). Three comments on mental testing and its relation to developmental psychology are in order, however.

First, the method paved the way for systematic comparisons across time, across persons, and across conditions. This was a necessary step toward the conduct of longitudinal studies of human behavior. It also provided the tool for comparing persons of different backgrounds, races, and environmental experiences, thereby permitting the researcher to address anew the problems of heredity and environmental influence. The study of the effects of early experience on IQ was explored by Sherman and Key (1932), by Wheeler (1942), and by the Iowa group led by Skeels and Wellman (Skeels, 1966; Skeels, Upgraff, Wellman, & Williams, 1938). In addition, the procedure was applied in ways not anticipated by its innovators. For instance, Kamin (1974) reported the tests were used as a screening device for immigrants to the United States—a practice that was hardly appropriate, given the diverse backgrounds of the persons being tested and the conditions of assessment. The device proved to be an exceedingly powerful tool for categorization and for differentiation of cognitive abilities.

The second comment concerns the relation of the testing movement to the rest of psychology, especially the rest of developmental psychology. Interest in the use of the procedure as a research device initially rode a wave of enthusiasm, followed by a period of neglect. When experimental studies of how performance on intelligence tests could be modified were conducted in the 1930s, it became clear that increments of one or more standard deviations (e.g., 10 to 20 IQ points) were not uncommon and could be brought about in a relatively brief period (4 to 16 weeks) (see Jones, 1954, for a review of this work). In addition, Sherman and Key (1932) demonstrated that a negative correlation was obtained between IQ and age among children living in culturally deprived Appalachia. Such findings raised questions about the environmental contributions to IQ scores, and much debate about the nature and meaning of the findings followed (see McNemar, 1940; Minton, 1984). A parallel controversy arose over the interpretation of twin data, and the implications of findings from the tests of monozygotics, dizygotics, and other types of siblings for the inheritance of intelligence. The issues subsided, without clear resolution, in the late 1930s, then came to the forefront again some 30 years later.

Third, the method of intelligence testing did not give rise to a coherent theory of the development of intelligence. The theoretical debates centered mostly around matters of test structure and statistical analysis (e.g., whether a single factor could account for the variance or whether two or multiple factors were required) and whether the results of the experimental tests were being properly interpreted. There was a significant gap between the emerging theories of cognition (following the model of Baldwin and Piaget) and the methods of assessment being employed. Neither Piaget nor Baldwin are mentioned in Goodenough's (1954) comprehensive chapter on "mental growth." The gap was not unprecedented: A parallel problem could be found between the methods of social interactional assessment and the theories of personality and social learning patterns (see below). But the test procedures proved their worth in education and in the marketplace, even though they could not be readily integrated into the existing body of psychological theory. Hence, the testing movement evolved and prospered outside the mainstream of developmental psychology (Dahlstrom, 1985).

Longitudinal Studies

According to Wesley Mills (1899), the discipline needed (a) longitudinal studies of individual organisms from birth to maturity, and (b) systematic experimental manipulations of the long-term conditions for development. Without that information, one could scarcely hope to achieve a firm grasp of the processes of development, whether nonhuman or human. Because the major hypotheses about development were concerned at their root with these processes, one would have thought that longitudinal studies would have been given the highest priority in the new discipline. They were not. Perhaps the practical difficulties in mounting life-span projects in humans seemed too formidable, or the investment and risks seemed too great. For whatever reasons, the information available about longitudinal development by the end of the first period of the area's history was either sketchy (e.g., Binet's study of his two daughters) or subjective and retrospective (e.g., psychoanalytic interviews). But, on this fragmentary information, the most

influential psychoanalytic and behavioristic theories of cognitive and personality development were formulated, and few data were available to assess their implications or correct their shortcomings.

One of the obstacles for longitudinal study—the need for measurement—seemed to be solved by the development of a reliable device for the metric assessment of cognitive abilities. That advance was sufficient for Lewis M. Terman, who perfected the instrument and pioneered the first large-scale longitudinal study of behavioral/cognitive characteristics in 1921. He selected 952 boys and girls in California, from 2 to 14 years of age, who achieved a test score of 140 IQ or above. This group comprised the brightest children (in terms of test performance) who could be found in a population of about a quarter-million (Terman, 1925). His initial aim seems to have been the planning of educational procedures for gifted children. As it turned out, the sample provided the core group for follow-up studies that continued through most of the 20th century. At several stages in childhood and early adulthood, these "gifted" children-cum-adults were reassessed, with the behavioral net widened to include personality characteristics, life accomplishments, and social adaptations. Later, their spouses and children were included in the study, and each group of subjects was followed through the 60th year of life (Sears, 1975). Despite shortcomings in the original design (e.g., absence of a matched nongifted control or comparison group), the data provide a rich yield of development through the life span. Overall, the work constitutes one of the major achievements of the science in its first century, incorporating the efforts of three of its most influential figures (Binet, Terman, & Sears).

Another factor that had inhibited longitudinal studies was the need for research institutes that would survive as long as their subjects. That problem was solved in the 1920s by formation of the several child research institutes across the United States. Soon afterward, longitudinal projects were initiated at Berkeley, Fels Institute, Minnesota, and Harvard. Initially, smaller short-term projects were undertaken to investigate particular issues. Mary Shirley (1931, 1933a, 1933b), for instance, completed a two-year-long investigation of the motor, emotional, and social development of infants. In contrast to the cross-sectional studies of Gesell, her longitudinal work permitted her to identify particular sequences in growth and change.

Experimental intervention studies of the sort that Mills (1899) had called for in animals were undertaken with children. Myrtle McGraw's (1935) work with Jimmy and Johnny, twins who were given different training experiences, is one of the better instances of the use of what Gesell called the "co-twin" control procedure. By providing "enrichment" experiences prior to the normal onset of basic motor functions, McGraw was able to demonstrate that experiences can facilitate the appearance and consolidation of climbing and other movement patterns. The "enriched" twin continued to show a modest advantage over the control twin, even though age and associated growth greatly diminished the apparent gains (see Bergenn, Dalton, & Lipsitt, 1994, for a more detailed account of McGraw and her contributions). Along with these well-known works, a large number of lesser-known investigations were addressed to the same issues, using short-term longitudinal interventions to influence intelligence test performance (e.g., Hilgard, 1933), and motor skills (e.g., Jersild, 1932).

These studies of longitudinal development were limited to children, at least in the initial stages. What about development beyond childhood? Since the early investigations of Quetelet, there had been few attempts to address directly the problems of developmental change during maturity. The exceptions are noteworthy because they provide part of the foundation for contemporary emphasis on the study of development over the entire life span of human experience. One of the first texts on aging was produced by G. Stanley Hall (1922), shortly before his death. Later in the same decade, Hollingsworth (1927) published a text on development over the whole life span, and some 12 years later, Pressey, Janney, and Kuhlen (1939) extended the coverage.

The database for these extensions to developmental issues over the life span was meager, at best. Surprisingly little research on behavioral development in adolescence was stimulated; perhaps Hall's major work gave the appearance that all of the important questions were already answered. One of the more interesting studies of this age group was reported by Bühler (1931), who analyzed the diaries of some 100 adolescents. In describing this work, Bühler writes:

> Intimate friendship is by all authors, considered as a characteristic of adolescence, not of childhood. The same is true of that love or devotion which one calls *hero-worship*. This is

also considered as a very characteristic feature of puberty. Charlotte Bühler studied, on the basis of adolescents' diaries, the distribution and types of hero-worship during puberty. Her collection of about one hundred authentic diaries contains contributions from different countries, different milieus, and different age groups. . . . There are German, Austrian, American, Czech, Swedish, and Hungarian diaries in this collection. Statistics show that the average age at which girls begin to write diaries is thirteen years and eight months, while the average age for boys is fourteen years and eleven months. In all of the girls' diaries either a "crush" or a flirtation plays a role, sometimes both. The period of the "crush" is from thirteen years and nine months to seventeen years. The boys' diaries show a larger variety of types of friendship. In the place of the "crush," a devoted admiration for a leader or for a girl, or often for an older woman, plays a role. (Bühler, 1931, p. 408)

Diaries provided an innovative substitute for prospective longitudinal data, providing an account of the adolescent's most intimate thoughts, concerns, hopes, and wishes. But it also had certain hazards, with the problems of selection paramount (e.g., who keeps a diary, what is selectively omitted or recorded). Because of its inherently private nature, the method has few safeguards against fraud. On this score, Sigmund Freud wrote a laudatory introduction to the published version of a diary that, upon critical examination, proved to be a fake. It is a modest irony that the young Cyril Burt (1920/1921) exposed the fraud. Some 50 years later, Kamin (1974) and others raised questions about biases and the accuracy of data in Burt's own work on twins reared apart. Despite the pitfalls, diaries continued to provide a potentially rich source of information about the beliefs, attitudes, and conflicts of adolescents.

Given the amount of time, effort, and funding required for these longitudinal studies, what could be said about their payoffs by midcentury? Were they worth the investment? The early returns indicated that the highest levels of predictability were obtained when the assessment procedures had previously established reliability and utility (i.e., intelligence and physiological measures). In social and personality characteristics, however, individual differences appeared to be demonstrably less stable over time. Because the longitudinal work was, for the most part, atheoretical, except for an implicit belief in the long-term stability of human characteristics, the early findings posed serious problems for interpretation. Were the methods and measures at fault, or was the theoretical framework itself to blame? It took research another half-century to answer this question.

Behaviorism and Learning

At about the time that World War I began in Europe, American psychology underwent an internal upheaval. John B. Watson (1878–1957) called behaviorism a "purely American production" (1914, p. ix). Its essential message—that the study of humans, animals, and children required the objective methods of natural science—was of fundamental importance, but it was hardly novel. Others close to Watson, including his mentors in behavioral biology (Jacques Loeb and H. S. Jennings) and his colleagues in psychology (e.g., K. Dunlap), had expressed similar ideas. But none had presented the argument with the persuasiveness and flair that Watson did in person and in print. As Watson put it:

> Psychology as the behaviorist views it is a purely objective experimental branch of natural science. Its theoretical goal is the prediction and control of behavior. Introspection forms no essential part of its methods, nor is the scientific value of its data dependent upon the readiness with which they lend themselves to interpretation in terms of consciousness. The behaviorist attempts to get a unitary scheme of animal response. He recognizes no dividing line between man and brute. The behavior of man, with all of its refinement and complexity, forms only a part of his total field of investigation. (1914, p. 1)

For Watson, there was an essential unity in animal and human psychology. The methodological differences that trifurcated the discipline for Hall and divided it for Wundt were not valid; the study of children, animals, and adult human beings could be reduced to the same behavioral, noncognitive techniques. Moreover, Watson called for a pragmatic psychology, one that could be applied in society and useful in everyday affairs. Watson liberalized psychology by holding, in effect, that the science could apply itself to any problem of life and behavior.

Watson was originally trained in comparative psychology and heavily influenced by biologist Jacques Loeb, who was "concerned with explaining animal behavior in terms of physiol-chemical influences and without the use of anthropomorphic, psychic, or mentalistic terms" (Jensen, 1962, p. x). His explanatory concept of "tropism"

was borrowed from studies of plants, where stimulus-directed movement occurs, say, toward sunlight. At the same time, another behavioral biologist, H. S. Jennings, agreed with Loeb on the need for objective analysis, but he also emphasized the "complexity and variability of behavior in lower organisms and the importance of internal factors as determinants of behavior" (Jensen, 1962, p. x). How Loeb—Watson's mentor at Chicago, and Jennings—Watson's senior colleague at Johns Hopkins—outlined many of the essential ideas of behaviorism is a fascinating story that has been brilliantly documented by D. D. Jensen (1962; see also Pauly, 1981).

Watson's contributions to development evolved through two stages: empirical and theoretical. Consider first his methodological and research contributions to developmental study. Consistent with his vision, Watson set about to demonstrate the relevance of purely behavioral procedures to the study of human behavior. He began his work with newborn infants and the analysis of the conditioning of emotional reactions (Watson & Morgan, 1917; Watson & Rayner, 1920). Watson was well prepared for the task; by mid-career, he had been recognized as one of America's leading researchers in comparative and physiological psychology (Buckley, 1979; Horowitz, 1992).

Why did Watson choose to work with infants? Given the methodological outline of behaviorism, would it not have been as appropriate to begin with adolescents or adults? Watson provided the answer himself in his "lifechart" of human activities, where he asserted that "to understand man," one must begin with the history of human behavior (1926). He saw personality as being shaped by learning experiences from birth onward. Innate reflexes and inherent emotions provided the substrate, and conditioning and learning mechanisms permitted the elaboration of emotions and behavior in development. Personality thus was the outcome of a hierarchical structure, and discrete learning experiences provided the essential building blocks. The conditioning of early emotions—love, fear, or rage—provided the foundation for all that followed. In his stress on emotions and early experience, Watson seems to have been influenced directly by Freud (as Watson suggested in 1936, in his autobiographical statement), as well as by other views of personality current in the day (including McDougall's, 1926, theory of sentiments). In any case, the study of emotional development in infancy became the focus for Watson's experimental and observational work from 1916 to 1920. Because of his work, Watson (along with E. L. Thorndike) was credited in an early *Handbook of Child Psychology* as having initiated experimental child psychology (Anderson, 1931, p. 3). Binet was overlooked again.

The infant work was conducted in the laboratories and newborn nursery at Johns Hopkins Hospital from 1916 through 1920; it was interrupted by Watson's service in World War I and terminated by his being fired from Hopkins in 1920. The series involved controlled observation of stimuli that elicit emotional reactions in infants (Watson & Morgan, 1917), a systematic attempt to catalogue the behavior responses present at birth and shortly afterward (Watson, 1926), and the experimental conditioning and manipulation of fear reactions (Watson & Rayner, 1920).

Although Watson's conditioning studies were only demonstrational and would hardly deserve publication on their methodological merit, they proved to be enormously influential. Following the lead of the more extensive and careful work of Florence Mateer (1918) and of the Russian investigator N. Krasnogorski, who first reported in 1909 the conditioning of salivation in children (see Krasnogorski, 1925; Munn, 1954; Valsiner, 1988). Watson boldly attacked the problem of the conditioning of emotions in infancy in the "case of Albert." What was impressive about this work was the finding that fear was conditioned and, once established, resisted extinction and readily generalized. As M. C. Jones (1931) pointed out, "conditioned emotional responses" differ from earlier demonstrations of reflexive conditioning in that there was one obvious discrepancy: "Whereas the conditioned reflex is extremely unstable, emotional responses are often acquired as the result of one traumatic experience and are pertinacious even in the absence of reinforcement" (p. 87). According to Watson, "guts can learn" (1928), and they seemed to have excellent memories. He wrote, "This proof of the conditioned origin of a fear response puts us on a natural science grounds in our study of emotional behavior. It yields an explanatory principle which will account for the enormous complexity in the emotional behavior of adults" (1928, p. 202). Conditioned emotional responses, whether in the form of the "CER" of B. F. Skinner and W. K. Estes (1944), the "two-factor theory of anxiety" of Solomon and Wynne (1953), or the "learned helplessness" concept of Maier, Seligman, and Solomon (1969), have continued to play a significant if enigmatic role in neobehavioral accounts of personality and development.

Although Watson himself completed no further scientific investigations, his experimental studies with infants were taken up by students and colleagues through the 1920s and early 1930s (see M. C. Jones, 1931). Mary Cover Jones (1924) explored the problem of the extinction of emotional reactions, demonstrating how experimentally produced fears could be "undone." H. E. Jones (1930) clarified the short-term stability of the response (not great after 2 months). Later, experimental psychologists investigated the possibility of neonatal (e.g., Marquis, 1931; Wickens & Wickens, 1940) and fetal (Spelt, 1938) conditioning, along with extensive studies of early motor learning. Watson's work also stimulated the development of observational methods to assess children's behaviors, on the one hand, and the establishment of the family of behavioristic theories of learning, on the other (e.g., Guthrie, 1935; Hull, 1943; Skinner, 1938; Tolman, 1932).

This brings us to Watson's theory of psychological development, which grew both more extreme and more expansive the further he became removed from data in time and space. As Watson's ideas on child development became elaborated, it seemed clear that he considered all emotions—not merely fear and rage—to be obstacles for adaptive behavior and a happy life. Among other things, he campaigned, in his influential best-seller, *Psychological Care of Infant and Child* (1928), against too much mother love. The child, he said, would become "honeycombed" with affection and, eventually, would be a social "invalid" wholly dependent on the attention and responses of others. Love, like fear, can make one sick to the stomach.

Despite such rhetoric, Watson's books carried a deadly serious message for the 1920s and 1930s. Science could lead to improved and efficient ways to rear children, and if mothers and children could be liberated from each other early in the child's life, the potential of both would be enhanced. This "modern" view of child rearing was predictably controversial, attracting both converts and devastating criticism. Along with his emotionally cool view of personality, Watson became increasingly extreme in his environmentalism. Although he was developmental in his approach, Watson downplayed the role of psychobiological factors in personality after birth, considering learning to be the key mechanism for the pacing and stabilizing of behavior development from birth to maturity. Biology was important, of course, but only as it established potential for learning. In the absence of evidence on the long-term effects of early experience or longitudinal studies of human development, Watson was skating on extremely thin ice. To his credit, he said so (1926, p. 10). But Watson was in no position to obtain corrective or confirming data; except for occasional part-time teaching at the New School, in New York, and a lecture series at Clark University, he had dropped out of academia and out of scientific research in 1920.

Watson nonetheless became a symbol for a scientific approach to child rearing during the 1920s and 1930s through his popular magazine articles (e.g., in *Harper's* and *Atlantic Monthly*). His views extended into education, pediatrics, psychiatry, and child study, where the stress on the acquisition of habits and avoidance of emotions became translated into prescriptions for behavioristic child rearing. A cursory review of these materials reveals virtually no empirical citations, except for references to the demonstrational studies that Watson conducted or loosely supervised. It should be noted, however, that Watson's advice for mothers to adopt a psychologically antiseptic approach toward their children had not been original with him. In physician Emmet Holt's *The Care and Feeding of Children,* a bestseller since its first edition in 1894, the same guidance had been given on the evils of kissing children ("Tuberculosis, diphtheria, syphilis, and many other grave diseases may be communicated in this way"; Holt, 1916, p. 174) or playing with babies ("They are made nervous and irritable"; Holt, 1916, p. 171). Watson didn't offer fresh guidance so much as new reasons. In the book promotion in 1928, Watson was described as "America's greatest child psychologist" (Buckley, 1989, Fig. 15).

What might have happened if Watson had remained involved in empirical research? We can only guess that his statements would have been more closely tied to facts rather than speculations, and that his views about child rearing would have become less idiosyncratic and less extreme (see Buckley, 1989). But, as we have indicated elsewhere, certain problems remained at the heart of his system (Cairns & Ornstein, 1979). Beyond the behavioristic model of an emotionless and mindless child, perhaps the most salient weakness in Watson's view was the assumption that development was a mechanistic process that could be reduced to fundamental units of learning. Seemingly all behavior was learned, from birth onward, and the earliest experiences were the most basic. This was a peculiar and unnecessary position for a behaviorist to take. Although Watson early claimed psychology was "a definite

part of biology," his view of development was nonbiological and nonorganismic. Learning is an essential process in development, but it is not the only process.

Experimental studies of learning in children did not begin and end with Watson. Another influential line of research followed the lead of E. L. Thorndike in studies of verbal learning and in the analysis of the "law of effect" and different reward and punishment contingencies (see Peterson, 1931, for a review of relevant studies). The work followed not only the laboratory analogues used by Thorndike (following Binet & Henri, 1895, and Ebbinghaus, 1897), but also within-classroom manipulations of the efficacy of different kinds of reward–punishment feedback (e.g., Hurlock, 1924). The studies of learning and memory were, for the most part, divorced from conditioning research in infants and animals, studies of mental testing, and investigations of language and thought. Areas of inquiry that might be seen as potentially fitting together to form a developmental view of cognition instead evolved separately, each toward its own distinctive methodology, concepts, and discipline affiliation. It would be another 50 years before serious attempts were made to bring them back together (see Carroll & Horn, 1981; Ornstein, 1978).

Maturation and Growth

While Watson served as the spokesman for behaviorism and environmentalism in child development, Arnold Gesell (1880–1961) was gaining stature as an advocate of the role of growth and maturation in behavior. Trained at Clark University in the early 1900s, Gesell absorbed G. S. Hall's vision of the significance of child study, the importance of biological controls in behavior, and the practical implications of child research, particularly for education. After earning his PhD degree, Gesell worked initially in schools and curriculum (as did most of the Clark graduates in developmental psychology in that period). He returned to complete an MD degree at Yale, then founded a child study laboratory in 1911, which permitted him to extend the tradition of W. Preyer and M. Shinn. Gesell (1931, 1933) early demonstrated himself to be an innovative and careful methodologist. He was one of the first to make extensive use of motion pictures in behavioral analysis and to explore the advantages of using twins as controls in experimental studies (i.e., one twin is subjected to the experimental manipulation, the other serves as a maturational control).

In 1928, Gesell published *Infancy and Human Growth,* a remarkable report on several years of study of the characteristics of infancy. According to Gesell, one of his aims was to provide "objective expression to the course, the pattern, and the rate of mental growth in normal and exceptional children" (p. viii). The other aim was theoretical, and the last section of the book takes on "the broad problem of heredity in relation to early mental growth and personality formation . . . and the significance of human infancy" (p. ix).

Gesell (1928) was characteristically thorough in dealing with both problems, and his normative tables and descriptions of how *Baby Two* (2 months old) differs from *Baby Three* and *Baby Nine* ring true to the contemporary reader. On basic characteristics of physical, motor, and perceptual development, children showed reasonably constant growth and age-differentiation. If the infants selected did not, as in a couple of instances, they may be substituted for by more "representative" ones. All in all, the business of establishing appropriate norms was seen as an essential part of his medical practice and the practical issues of diagnosis. As Gesell later described it:

> [The clinical practice] has always been conducted in close correlation with a systematic study of normal child development. One interest has reinforced the other. Observations of normal behavior threw light on maldevelopment; and the deviations of development in turn helped to expose what lay beneath a deceptive layer of "obviousness" in normal infancy. (Gesell & Amatruda, 1941, p. v)

Gesell and his associates established definitive norms for growth and behavioral change in the first five years of life, in a series of exhaustive and detailed reports (e.g., Gesell & Amatruda, 1941; Gesell & Thompson, 1934, 1938).

Few psychologists nowadays regard Gesell as a theorist. That is a pity, for his contributions might have provided a useful stabilizing influence during a period that became only nominally committed to "developmental" study. "Growth" was a key concept for Gesell. But what did he mean by growth? Horticultural terms have long been popular in describing children (a classic example being Froebel's coining of "kindergarten"). But Gesell was too astute to become trapped in a botanical analogue; he recognized human behavioral and mental growth as having distinctive properties of its own. He wrote:

> Mental growth is a constant process of transformation, of reconstruction. The past is not retained with the same completeness as in the tree. The past is sloughed as well as projected, it is displaced and even transmuted to a degree which the anatomy of the tree does not suggest. There are stages, and phases, and a perpetuating knitting together of what happens and happened. Mental growth is a process of constant incorporation, revision, reorganization, and progressive hierarchical inhibition. The reorganization is so pervading that the past almost loses its identity. (1928, p. 22)

What does this lead to? For Gesell, it led to a new perspective on the relations between heredity and environment. Similar to what Preyer had written some 50 years before, Gesell concluded:

> The supreme genetic law appears to be this: All present growth hinges on past growth. Growth is not a simple function neatly determined by X units of inheritance plus Y units of environment, but is a historical complex which reflects at every stage the past which it incorporates. In other words we are led astray by an artificial dualism of heredity and environment, if it blinds us to the fact that growth is a continuous self conditioning process, rather than a drama controlled, *ex machina,* by two forces. (1928, p. 357)

These are not the only similarities to the interpretations offered by earlier students of infant development. Recall Preyer's analysis of infancy, and the functions of the extended immaturity of children for the plasticity of behavior. The concept of neoteny was elegantly restated by Gesell, along with a fresh idea on the social responsiveness that is unique to humans:

> The preeminence of human infancy lies in the prolongation and deepening of plasticity. There is specific maturation of behavior patterns as in subhuman creatures; but this proceeds less rigidly and the total behavior complex is suspended in a state of greater formativeness. This increased modifiability is extremely sensitive to the social milieu and is constantly transforming the context of adaptive behavior. In the impersonal aspects of adaptive behavior of the nonlanguage type (general practical intelligence) there is a high degree of early correspondence between man and other primates. This correspondence may prove to be so consistent in some of its elements as to suggest evolutionary and even recapitulatory explanations. But transcending, pervading, and dynamically altering that strand of similarity is a generalized conditionability and

a responsiveness to other personalities, to which man is special heir. This pre-eminent sociality exists even through the
prelanguage period, long before the child has framed a single
word. Herein lies his humanity. (1928, p. 354)

As a rule, Gesell stood close to his data. When he ventured away, he was drawn irresistibly back to the facts that
had been meticulously collected and to his belief in the cu-
rative effects of maturation. He felt strongly that the understanding of the properties of growth qua growth would
be the key to unlocking the central dilemmas of psychology.
The same year that Watson offered his polemic on the role
of early stimulation in child rearing, Gesell offered the
counterposition on the invulnerability of the infant to experience. He wrote:

All things considered, the inevitableness and surety of maturation are the most impressive characteristics of early development. It is the hereditary ballast which conserves and
stabilizes the growth of each individual infant. It is indigenous in its impulsion; but we may well be grateful for this
degree of determinism. If it did not exist the infant would be
a victim of a flaccid malleability which is sometimes ro-
mantically ascribed to him. His mind, his spirit, his personality would fall a ready prey to disease, to starvation, to
malnutrition, and worst of all to misguided management. As
it is, the inborn tendency toward optimum development is so
inveterate that he benefits liberally from what is good in our
practice, and suffers less than he logically should from our
unenlightenment. Only if we give respect to this inner core
of inheritance can we respect the important individual differences which distinguish infants as well as men. (1928,
p. 378)

The infant is more robust than he appears, in that he is
buffered by psychobiological fail-safe systems and driven
by an "inborn tendency toward optimum development."
The message is a general one, issued by one who observed
the remarkable commonalities in infant growth as it progresses, inevitably, from the stage of the neonate to the
first year and beyond.

Does this inborn inertia apply to all features of infant
growth—to mental development as well as personality and
social development? On this matter, Gesell drew a distinction between the mechanisms that control cognitive and social growth. In the latter instance—social growth—the
essential determinants were the social matrix present in the

"web of life" and the "conditioned system of adaptation to
the whole human family." Sound Watsonian? Not really, for
Gesell is closer to the transactional views of James Mark
Baldwin than to the unidirectional ones of behaviorism and
its emphasis on the parental shaping of children. Gesell
wrote:

All children are thus, through correlation, adapted to their
parents and to each other. Even the maladjustments between
parent and child are adaptations in a psychobiological sense
and can only be comprehended if we view them as lawfully
conditioned modes of adaptation. Growth is again the key
concept. For better or for worse, children and their elders
must grow up with each other, which means in interrelation
one to the other. The roots of the growth of the infant's personality reach into other human beings. (1928, p. 375)

In effect, maturational changes demand interactional ones,
and the nature of the resolution reached between the child
and others at each stage is the stuff out of which personality is built. Gesell offers here the outline for a psychobiological theory of social development.

Where did the theory go? Not very far in Gesell's work,
for it remained in a bare outline form, with scant data to
back it up. Like Baldwin before him, Gesell did not have
the methods (or perhaps the desire) to continue to explore
the dynamic message implicit in this psychobiological view
of social interactions. That is doubly unfortunate, for his
views on social development were at least as reasonable and
no more speculative than those of Watson. If enunciated
more fully, they may have provided explicit guides for his
next-door colleagues in the Institute of Human Relations
when they set about to fabricate the first version of social
learning theory. Some 40 years later, the essential model
was explicated by Bell (1968) and Bell and Harper (1977),
using surprisingly similar models and metaphors.

In speaking of Gesell's legacy, Thelen and Adolph
(1992) comment on some of the paradoxes in Gesell's
work:

His devotion to maturation as the final cause was unwavering,
yet he acted as though the environment mattered, and his
work contains threads of real process. He believed in the individuality of the child but chose the dictates of the genes over
the whims of the environment. He wanted to liberate and
reassure parents but may only have added to the arsenal of
parental guilt. (p. 379).

The Middle Period (1913–1946): Institutionalization and Expansion **71**

In retrospect, Gesell's views may seem paradoxical only because we fail to respect the distinctions that he made. A key distinction is that social interactions of children are more likely than motor and sensory structures to be impacted by experience; hence, there is a "generalized conditionality and a responsiveness to other personalities, to which man is special heir." Gesell did not assume the primacy of early experience; rather, the infant is buffered because "the inborn tendency toward optimum development is so inveterate that he benefits liberally from what is good in our practice, and suffers less than he logically should from our unenlightenment." This is a powerful message, consistent with the earlier pronouncement from Hall on adolescence. At the least, it indicates that investigators should look beyond infancy for the formative effects of experience, particularly the effects in "responsiveness to other personalities."

Gesell was a pioneering investigator who understood the totality of the organism. He also understood that experiential factors must be considered in any systematic developmental account. Although he appreciated the multiple ways that environmental events could influence behavior, he declined to assign them priority in accounting for the development of basic motor, sensory, and emotional systems.

Other investigators recognized the role of age-related biological changes in the development of behavior, and their relations to the occurrence of basic changes in emotional, cognitive, and social patterns. For example, M. C. Jones (1931), in discussing the development of emotions, remarks that a wariness or fear of unfamiliar persons tends to emerge in the second half of the first year of life (from 20 weeks to 40 weeks; see Bayley, 1932, and Washburn, 1929). Jones notes that this phenomenon appears in the absence of any apparent pairing of the stranger with some external noxious stimulus; hence, it would not fit very well with the Watsonian view of the conditioned elaboration of fear or of love. Other developmental mechanisms must be at work.

Why, then, the relative popularity of experimental demonstrations of fear and its conditioning and extinction, as opposed to careful longitudinal studies of the development of the phenomena subsumed by fear? Jones's (1931) answer was insightful and doubtless correct: "Because training and practice are more readily subject to laboratory proof, we have at times minimized the importance of the less accessible intraorganismic factors" (p. 78).

The availability of funding and staffing for the major child development institutes permitted the support of significant studies of maturation and growth at Teachers College (Columbia), Berkeley, Iowa, Minnesota, and Fels Institute. Among the more notable studies was that of Mary Shirley at the University of Minnesota. To extend Gesell's cross-sectional observations, Shirley conducted a longitudinal investigation of motor, emotional, and personality development over the first two years of life with 25 infants, and published the results in a comprehensive three-volume work (Shirley, 1931, 1933a, 1933b). Similarly, the Shermans at Washington University (St. Louis), McGraw (1935) at Teachers College, and K. M. B. Bridges at Montreal completed useful studies of growth-related changes in infants and young children.

Social and Personality Development

In a review of studies of social behavior in children, Charlotte Bühler (1931) gave an American, Will S. Monroe, credit for having completed the first studies of "the social consciousness of children." Monroe's work, published in German (1899), reported a number of questionnaire studies dealing with various aspects of social development. For instance, children were asked what sort of "chum" they preferred, what kinds of moral qualities they found in friends, and what their attitudes were about punishment, responsibility, and discipline. Monroe's work was not, however, the first published set of studies on these matters. Earl Barnes of Stanford (who had been Monroe's teacher) had earlier edited a two-volume work (*Studies in Education;* 1896–1897, 1902–1903) that had covered the same ground, reporting a reasonably comprehensive set of questionnaire studies of social disposition. Margaret Schallenberger (1894), for instance, had been at Stanford and was a student of Barnes at the time she completed the report discussed above on age-related changes in the social judgments of children. In the 1890s, questionnaires were being circulated to teachers throughout the country, through the various state child study associations (in Illinois, South Carolina, Massachusetts), and literally thousands of children were being asked brief questions about their social attitudes, morals, and friendships. G. Stanley Hall from time to time would include questionnaires in the *Pedagogical Seminary,* and would ask readers to submit the results to him.

Because of the shortcomings in the method, ranging from haphazard sampling procedures to problems in nonstandard administration and scoring of questions, the questionnaire studies were hardly models of scientific research. Nonetheless, certain age-related phenomena were sufficiently robust to appear despite the methodological slippage. Hence the earlier cited conclusion by Schallenberger about the reliance of young children on concrete forms of punishment, with reasoning and empathy playing roles of increasing importance in early adolescence. These findings were given wide circulation in Hall's *Adolescence,* and provided the empirical substrate for some of the more useful sections of that work. In time, the criticisms took effect, and after about 10 to 15 years of questionnaire studies, the method was no longer a procedure of choice. As Bühler notes, "little was done in the decade after Monroe made this first start in the direction of developmental social psychology," and, she concludes, the studies failed because of "the lack of a systematic point of view" (1931, p. 392).

Following a hiatus in work on social development, another method was introduced for studying the social behavior of infants and children in the mid-1920s. It was essentially an extension of the "objective" or "behavioral" procedures that had been used in the investigation of individual infants and young animals. Almost simultaneously, reports of behavioral studies appeared in child study institutes in Vienna, New York (Columbia), Minnesota, and Toronto. Somewhat earlier, Jean Piaget had recorded the naturalistic verbal exchanges among young children (Piaget, 1926). Five of the first eight *Child Development Monographs* from Teachers College (Columbia) were concerned with the methods and outcomes obtained by the behavioral assessments of social patterns (Arrington, 1932; Barker, 1930; Beaver, 1930; Loomis, 1931; Thomas, 1929). Dorothy S. Thomas, who co-authored with sociologist W. I. Thomas *The Child in America* (1928), seems to have spearheaded this attempt to apply "the methodological scheme of *experimental sociology* to children." In addition to the work of Thomas and her colleagues, insightful methodological papers on the procedure were published by Goodenough (1929, 1930a) at Minnesota and Bott (1934) at Toronto. Charlotte Bühler (1927) should herself be credited with having pioneered the controlled experimental observations of infants, and she seems to have been the first investigator to have completed an "experimental study of children's social attitudes in the first and second year of life" (Bühler, 1931).

Observational studies from 1927 to 1937 generated almost as much enthusiasm as earlier questionnaire studies. They were based on the assumption that the stream of behavior could be classified into particular behavior units, and that these units could be submitted to the statistical analyses previously developed for the treatment of experimental and test data. Careful attention was given to the basic issues of observation, including observer agreement, code reliability, stability of measures, various facets of validity and generality, and statistical evaluation. The issues attacked by the method ranged from the mere descriptive and demographic—including size and sex composition of groups as a function of age (Parten, 1933) and nature of play activities (Challman, 1932)—to studies of the natural occurrence of aggression (e.g., Goodenough, 1931) and reciprocal patterns of interchange (Bott, 1934). By 1931, Bühler was able to cite some 173 articles, many of which dealt directly with the observation of children's social behavior patterns. In the following 5 to 10 years, an equal number of studies was reported, some of which are now recognized as having laid the foundation for work taken up again in the 1970s (e.g., Murphy, 1937). In terms of method, the reports were on a par with the current generation of observational analyses of social interchanges.

What theoretical ideas were associated with these behavioral methods and to what extent was there a "systematic" point of view? There was, as it turns out, as little theoretical guidance for this work as for the earlier questionnaire studies. The work was behavioral, but it was not concerned with developmental processes, either learning or psychobiological. J. M. Baldwin had virtually been forgotten (save for some exceptions, e.g., Piaget, 1926). Given D. S. Thomas's (1929) aims and background, it is mildly surprising that the procedures at Columbia were not more intimately linked to the sociological models of Cooley, Mead, and Baldwin. Perhaps that conceptual extension was part of the general scheme, but it failed to materialize in the work completed at Teachers College or at the other child institutes. As it turned out, the research focused on the immediate determinants of the actions and interactions of children, but scant information was gained about their relationship to how interactions are learned or modified, or what they mean for longer term personality development.

If there were any theoretical underpinnings for the research on interactions and social development, the model seems to have been drawn either from a belief in the importance of growth and maturation, or from a commitment to the enduring nature of personality types, as determined by genetic, constitutional, or early experience factors. In this regard, Bühler (1931) classified infants into three types, depending on their reactions to social stimulation. "These types were called the socially blind, the socially dependent, and the socially independent behavior" (1931, p. 411). Socially blind children don't pay much attention to the actions and reactions of other persons; instead they take toys, play, and move about without regard for the other child. The socially dependent child, on the other hand, is "deeply impressed by other's presence and activities; . . . he observes the effect of his behavior on the other and carefully watches the other's reactions." The socially independent child "is one who—though aware of the other's presence and responsive to his behavior—yet does not seem dependent on him, is neither intimidated nor inspired" (1931, p. 411). Bühler sees these dispositions as being independent of home and rearing conditions; hence, they are "primary" dispositions. Retests of the children (who were 6 to 18 months of age) suggested to Bühler that these types were relatively stable, but she adds the caveat that, "it remains to be seen, of course, whether these pioneer observations will be confirmed by other authors" (1931, p. 411).

In retrospect, the interactional studies were estranged from the issues being debated by the dominant theories of the day—psychoanalytic, learning, cognitive—and few seemed willing to attempt to bridge the theoretical or empirical gaps. As it turned out, the data did find a useful service in the practical areas of nursery school management and the training of young teachers. Because the findings were either ignored or deemed irrelevant by those concerned with major psychological theories of development, the method and its concerns passed from the scene, temporarily.

Moral Development

The perfectibility of humans and the establishment of a higher moral order had been a continuing concern for developmentalists. Although questionnaires on children's beliefs and attitudes toward transgressions and punishments were useful, they had obvious shortcomings as scientific instruments. In the 1920s and 1930s, work on these issues continued, but with a self-conscious appreciation of the limits of the techniques that were available. Nonetheless,

there were substantive issues to be addressed and real-life problems to be solved, and it seemed entirely reasonable to expect that the investigators of moral development would be ingenious enough to meet the challenge (see V. Jones, 1933). Out of this need arose three major advances in the study of moral development: (a) the use of short-term experimental manipulations in the assessment of honesty and prosocial behaviors; (b) the employment of observations of naturally occurring rule-making and moral judgments; and (c) the refinement of attitudinal questionnaires that might be employed in the assessment of particular experiences.

The demonstration of the utility of short-term experimental procedures with school-age children has an unusual background, at least in comparing what the sponsors had hoped to learn and what they actually got. Hugh Hartshorne was a professor in the School of Religion at the University of Southern California, and Mark May was a psychologist at Syracuse University when they were recruited to Columbia University by the Institute of Social and Religious Research to conduct a multiyear project on how Sunday schools, churches, and religious youth groups could better do their job. E. L. Thorndike was a guiding force in the initiation and interpretation of this research. If physical science could solve problems for the society, why could not behavioral science help solve some of the moral and ethical issues that had arisen?

The project was an ambitious one: to analyze the effects of various institutions of the society on moral behaviors, and to determine how the institutions could improve their performance. At the outset, Hartshorne and May recognized that they must solve the problem of the assessment of moral and ethical behaviors. Following a critique of then-available questionnaire and rating procedures, Hartshorne and May concluded that a fresh approach to the study of values and character was required. They wrote: "Although recognizing the importance of attitude and motive for both social welfare and individual character, as ordinarily understood, we realized that in any objective approach to ethical conduct we must begin with the *facts of conduct*" (1929, Vol. 3, pp. 361–362). Accordingly, the investigators developed a battery of tests and experimental settings designed to yield information about honesty, helpfulness and cooperation, inhibition, and persistence. The best known measures are the brief experimental assessments of deceit (permitting the misuse of answer sheets, peeping, and other forms of cheating, all of which were monitored in sly ways by the experimenter). They also devised various sociometric techniques, including a "Guess Who" procedure to assess peer reputation. The results of this work and the authors' interpretation on the relative specificity of moral conduct have been widely discussed. For our purposes, it is sufficient to note that this was one of the first studies to be conducted of short-term experimental manipulations of social behavior in school-age children. In addition, the authors offered a courageous theoretical statement on how ethical conduct is acquired (via Thorndikian learning principles). It was not exactly what the sponsoring agency had expected, or wanted. The Executive Secretary of the sponsoring Institute of Social and Religious Research wrote apologetically in the foreword:

> To lay minds this volume, at first glance, may seem overloaded with matter that has little to do with moral and religious education—a medley of tests and statistics and a paucity of clear directions as to building character. Such readers might profitably reflect that these preliminary processes are inevitable if character education is ever to emerge from guesswork into a science. Medical and surgical science had to follow a similar road to advance from magic and quackery. (Hartshorne & May, 1929, Vol. 2, p. v)

Hartshorne and May had concluded that traditional religious and moral instruction have little, if any, relationship to the results of experimental tests of honesty and service to others.

With questionnaire procedures generally in disfavor by the 1920s, the essential problem of how to quantify attitudes remained. L. L. Thurstone, a pioneering quantitative psychologist at the University of Chicago, was recruited by the Payne Foundation to determine the effects that moviegoing had on the social attitudes and prejudices of children. The assignment provided Thurstone the opportunity to develop a new technology for the assessment of moral/ethnic attitudes. In a series of studies, Thurstone and his colleague, R. C. Peterson (Peterson & Thurstone, 1933), introduced new methodologies for gauging the effects of specific motion pictures on attitudes toward national/ethnic groups. They used a pre- and posttest design, coupled with a 5-month follow-up test (post-posttest). Although these studies seem to be little known to contemporary writers, Thurstone himself (1952) considered them to be highly influential for his development of an attitude assessment methodology. Moreover, the work provided a

wholly convincing demonstration of the strong effects that certain films had in decreasing, or increasing, racial and religious prejudice. In some cases (such as the inflammatory *Birth of a Nation*), the unfavorable racial attitudes induced by viewing the film were detected 5 months later. This study was an admirable forerunner to the research of the 1960s and 1970s concerned with the effects of television (see also, Jones, 1933).

A major advance was pioneered by Jean Piaget in his assessments of moral reasoning (Piaget, 1932/1973). Piaget's clinical method—observing the actions of individual children and carefully recording their responses—permitted him to identify changes in the children's employment of rules and their origins. Although the procedure shared the self-report properties of questionnaires, his observations and direct inquiries permitted a more precise identification of the standards being invoked idiosyncratically by the children. Again, the impact of Piaget's reports seems to reflect in large measure the theoretical significance of his interpretations.

The Development of Language and Cognition

From 1924 onward, the problem of how language and thought develop attracted the attention of the brightest talents of the discipline. Some of them—including Jean Piaget and L. S. Vygotsky—were concerned with language as a vehicle for understanding how thought patterns develop in the child. Others focused on language as a phenomenon in itself, with attention given to the "amazingly rapid acquisition of an extremely complex system of symbolic habits by young children" (McCarthy, 1954).

The comprehensive review articles by Dorothy McCarthy that span this period provide an excellent overview of the era (McCarthy, 1931, 1933, 1946, 1954). At one time or another, virtually all major developmental investigators have been drawn to the study of language development, and so were some nondevelopmentalists as well. The intimate relationship that exists between language and thought was brought brilliantly to the attention of psychologists by Jean Piaget in a small book that he published to report the results of his new functional approach to the study of language development. Piaget's study of language breathed fresh life into one of the oldest questions of the area: How do thought, logic, and consciousness develop? Language was a mirror to the mind, for Piaget; it was to be used to reflect the nature and structure of the mental schemas that gave rise to verbal expressions. In this work, Piaget seems to have been explicitly guided by J. M. Baldwin's view that the young child proceeds in his thought to progressively discriminate himself from nonself. The major empirical marker for this shift in thinking was movement from egocentric speech to socialized speech. Piaget wrote:

> "Egocentric" functions are the more immature functions, and tend to dominate the verbal productions of children 3–7 years of age, and, to a lesser extent, children 7–12 years. In this form of speech, a child does not bother to know to whom he is speaking nor whether he is being listened to. He talks either for himself or for the pleasure of associating anyone who happens to be there with the activity of the moment. This talk is ego-centric, partly because the child speaks only about himself, but chiefly because he does not attempt to place himself at the point of view of his hearer. Anyone who happens to be there will serve as an audience. (1932/1952, p. 9)

Socialized speech, where the child "really exchanges his thoughts with others, either by telling his hearer something that will interest him and influence his actions, or by an actual interchange of ideas by argument or even by collaboration in pursuit of a common aim" (p. 9–10), does not emerge until about age 7 or 8, and the process is not complete until 11 or 12 years of age. Later in the same volume, Piaget linked egocentricism to the child's tendency to personalize thought:

> [Without the ability to "objectify" one's thinking,] the mind tends to project intentions into everything, or connect every thing together by means of relations not based on observation . . . the more the ego is made the centre of interests, the less will the mind be able to depersonalize its thought, and to get rid of the idea that in all things are intentions either favourable or hostile (animism, artificialism, etc.). . . . Egocentricism is therefore obedient to the self's good pleasure and not to the dictates of impersonal logic. It is also an indirect obstacle, because only the habits of discussion and social life will lead to the logical point of view, and ego-centricism is precisely what renders these habits impossible. (1932/1952, pp. 237–238)

In other words, Piaget shares with both Baldwin and Freud the assumption that the child's concept of reality and logic develops from contact with the external world, emerging from an amorphous sense of the self. It is not insignificant that, in the foreword to *The Language and Thought of the Child* (1932/1952), Piaget stated:

> I have also been deeply impressed by the social psychology of M. C. Blondel and Professor J. M. Baldwin. It will likewise be apparent how much I owe to psychoanalysis, which in my opinion has revolutionized the psychology of primitive thought. (pp. xx–xxi)

The method employed by Piaget and the concepts he embraced stimulated almost immediate worldwide attention and controversy. In McCarthy's thorough reviews of the empirical data that bore on this question (including her own), she (1931, 1933, 1946, 1954) traced the evolution of a huge literature on the matter. Strict interpretation of Piaget's categories suggested that, over a wide variety of populations and settings in which young children were observed, seldom did the proportion of egocentric remarks exceed 6% to 8%. Moreover, the negative evidence came not merely from studies of children in the United States; an equally convincing set of disconfirming investigations emerged from studies of Chinese (Kuo, 1937), Russians (Vygotsky & Luria, 1929), and Germans (Bühler, 1931). After identifying what was meant by the concept of egocentric as opposed to socialized speech, C. Bühler wrote:

> It is agreed, however, among other authors—e.g., William Stern and David and Rosa Katz—that this result is due to the special conditions of life in the "Maison des Petits" in Geneva, where Piaget's work was done. The Katzes (1927) emphasize, in opposition to Piaget, that even the special relationship of the child to each of the different members of the household is distinctly reflected in the respective conversations. This is surely true of all the dialogues they published. (Bühler, 1931, p. 400)

This was a key point for Bühler, who had just spent several years of her life demonstrating the quality and nature of the social patterns of children in infancy and early childhood. She had conclusively shown the truly "social" nature of their behaviors. Note that Bühler attributes the discrepant findings to the contextual–relational specificity of Piaget's initial observations. Piaget seemed to accept that explanation, at least for the time being. In the foreword to the second edition of *The Language and Thought of the Child* (1932), he wrote:

[Our] original enquiries dealt only with the language of children among themselves as observed in the very special scholastic conditions of Maison des Petits de L'Institut Rousseau. Now, Mlle. M. Muchow, M. D. Katz, Messrs. Galli and Maso, and M. A. Lora [Luria], after studying from the same point of view children with different scholastic environments in Germany, Spain, and Russia, and especially after studying children's conversations in their families, have reached results which, on certain points, differ considerably from ours. Thus, while the little pupils show in their conversations coefficients of ego-centricism more or less analogous to those we have observed, M. Katz's children, talking among themselves or with their parents, behave quite differently. (pp. xxiii–xxiv).

Another explanation, favored by McCarthy (1933, 1954), is that the problem resided in the ambiguity of the classification system employed by Piaget. For whatever reason, there were notably few confirmations of Piaget's assertion that young children were predominantly egocentric in their speech. The controversy extended into the 1970s (see, e.g., Garvey & Hogan, 1973; Mueller, 1972), along with replications of the earlier disconfirmation of Piaget's report.

The issue was significant for the area because it had implications for the understanding of virtually all psychological aspects of development, whether cognitive, linguistic, social, or moral. Beyond the issue of whether egocentric speech was 6% or 40% or 60%, there was agreement that this form of communication tended to decrease as a function of the child's age. Why? Piaget's answer, which seemed compatible with the earlier formulations of Baldwin and Freud, was that egocentric communication directly reflected young children's "personalized" mode of thinking, and that as children became more objective in their views of themselves and of reality, the transition to socialized speech occurred. Egocentric speech became dysfunctional and was discarded. A counterproposal by the Russian psychologist L. S. Vygotsky (1939) constituted a serious challenge to the Piagetian interpretation. The key to Vygotsky's proposal is that, at maturity, two speech systems exist: inner speech and socialized speech. For Vygotsky (1939):

The relation of thought to word is first of all not a thing, but a process; it is a proceeding from thought to word and, conversely, from word to thought . . . every thought moves, grows and develops, each fulfills a function and solves a given problem. This flow of thought occurs as an inner movement through a series of planes. The first step in the analysis of the relationship between thoughts and words is the investigation of the different phases and planes through which the thought passes before it is embodied in words. (p. 33)

Herein lies the need for a developmental investigation of speech functions, for it may provide us with an answer as to how thought and speech are interrelated. This investigation:

reveals, in the first place, two different planes in speech. There is an inner, meaningful semantic aspect of speech and there is the external, acoustic, phonic aspect. These two aspects although forming a true unity, have their own particular laws of movement. . . . A number of facts in the development of children's speech reveal the existence of independent movement in the phonic and the semantic aspects of speech. (1939, p. 33)

How does Vygotsky interpret the role of egocentric speech and how does his interpretation differ from Piaget's? Although egocentric speech has no apparent function of its own in Piaget's formulation—it merely reflects the child's egocentric thinking and is thereby doomed to disappear with the child's cognitive growth—it assumes great functional importance for Vygotsky. Egocentric speech constitutes, in effect, a developmental way station "a stage which precedes the development of inner speech" (1939, p. 38). It is a form of speech that aids in the young child's thought processes but, rather than waning in childhood and becoming dysfunctional, egocentric speech undergoes an evolution with "inner speech" and thought as its end product. Vygotsky (1939) wrote:

To consider the dropping of the coefficient of egocentric speech to zero as a symptom of decline of this speech would be like saying that the child stops to count at the moment when he ceases to use his fingers and starts to do the calculations in his mind. In reality, behind the symptoms of dissolution lies a progressive development, . . . the formation of a new speech form. (p. 40)

Vygotsky then took a significant step forward in the analysis of both speech functions and their relation to thought, by conducting some ingenious experiments on the nature of egocentric speech. He went beyond naturalistic observations to manipulate theoretically relevant dimensions. He determined, for instance, that the incidence of egocentric speech decreased sharply when children were placed in the company of others who could not possibly understand them—deaf and dumb children, or children speaking a foreign language. Vygotsky reports that the coefficient of egocentric speech "sank rapidly, reaching zero in the majority of cases and in the rest diminished eight times on the average." While these findings seem "paradoxical" for Piaget's view, they were consistent with the idea that "the true source of egocentric speech is the lack of differentiation of speech for oneself from speech for others; it can function only in connection with social speech" (1939, p. 41).

To summarize the rest of Vygotsky's argument and experimental work would take us beyond the limits of this overview (see McCarthy, 1954). The story did not end in the 1930s; many of the same concerns and proposals were to reappear in the 1960s and 1970s. Unfortunately, the brilliant Vygotsky—who was born the same year as Piaget—died in 1934 at the age of 38. His developmental views were brought forward to contemporary psychology by his colleague and collaborator, A. R. Luria.

The functional analysis of language development, while most intriguing on theoretical grounds, constituted only a portion of the total research effort devoted to language. Researchers focused, in addition, on developmental stages in language expression (e.g., prelinguistic utterances, phonetic development, the growth of vocabulary, changes in syntactic complexity as a function of age) and individual differences in language development and how they arise (through experience, schooling, early exposure, and so on). The literature on these matters was such that, by the end of this period, no child development text could be prepared without a significant section given to the report and summary of these findings. The mass of data seemed to outrun the ability of theorists to organize it in terms of meaningful models.

Developmental Psychobiology and Ethology

The Gesellian emphasis on growth and maturation was part of a broader attempt within developmental psychology and developmental biology to unlock the secrets of ontogeny (see McGraw, 1946). On this count, the understanding of the mechanisms of genetic transfer was significantly advanced by (a) the rediscovery of the work of Mendel, and (b) the revolutionary discoveries of the loci of units of chromosomal transmission. But these events raised a significant question for developmentalists. If all somatic cells have the same genetic code, how does differentiation occur in development and why do cells at maturity have distinctly different functions and properties? Where is the "master plan" for development, and how can particular cells be induced to perform their unique and special services for the organism?

Among the embryologists who addressed these issues, Hans Spemann (1938) provided a provocative suggestion following his discoveries that cellular tissues could be successfully transplanted from one area of presumptive growth to another. If the transplantation occurs at the appropriate time in development, tissues from the presumptive area of the neural plate of amphibia could be successfully transplanted to areas where limbs would arise. The tissue would then develop in accord with its surroundings, so that the tissue would take on the characteristics of skin or muscle, not of the brain. On the basis of these experiments, Spemann proposed that extranuclear or contextual forces served to "organize" the development of cellular materials in the course of ontogeny. Once organization occurred, during the period that was critical for the development of its form and function, then the effects would be irreversible or highly resistant to change (see Waddington, 1939).

Such demonstrations provided the substantive empirical examples for the formulation of a view on development that has come to be known as "organismic" theory or "system" theory of biological development (Bertalanffy, 1933). In its initial form, organismic theory was concerned with the question: What directs development? The answer, simply stated, is: The organism. Development is directed by the constraints inherent in the relationship among elements of the living system as they act on themselves and on each other. These elements can be cells, clusters of cells, or entire subsystems, such as those formed by hormonal processes. The kernel idea is that the several features of the organism, including its behavior, depend on the whole reciprocating system of which they form parts. The mutual regulation among components permits, among other things, possible feedback to the original source and self-regulation.

Organismic theory was compatible with the Darwinian perspective of evolution as a dynamic, adaptive process. Development is equally dynamic. It required only a modest conceptual leap to consider behavior as being an essential component of the organismic system, and its development could be understood only in terms of other biological and social features of the system. Hence the "system" in which the organism developed was not merely under the skin. Organization could be broadened to include feedback from other organisms and from the social network in which development occurred. Two developmental-comparative psychologists, T. C. Schneirla and Zing-Yang Kuo, led the way, in the early 1930s, for the application of the organismic perspective to the problems of behavioral ontogeny.

The problem that Schneirla tackled was how to unravel the complex social structure of army ants, who despite their lack of gray matter, were highly coordinated in virtually all phases of their adaptation. Wilson (1975) considers the species as a prototypic "truly social" one. How is the high level of social organization accomplished? Schneirla (1933) attacked the problem by undertaking a series of comprehensive field investigations in Panama and laboratory studies in his facilities at the American Museum of Natural History. He tested the assumption that colony organization does not arise from some single internal source; rather, the complex social system arises as an outcome of the interdependence of developmental events in the brood, workers, queen, and the contextual environmental constraints.

Schneirla identified the pattern of empirical relationships that provided elegant support for his developmental analysis of social organization. He discovered, for instance, that a primary trigger for migration and foraging raids in the colony was the heightened activity produced by the developing larvae. When the larvae emerged from the quiescent phase of development, their activity stimulated the rest of the colony to action, keying both foraging raids and migration. When the activity of the larval brood diminished as a consequence of growth-related changes, the raids ceased and the nomadic phase ended. The surplus food that then became available in the colony (due to decreased needs of the young) fattened the queen and served to trigger a new ovulatory cycle, thus recreating the conditions for reproduction. Looking backward on this work, Schneirla (1957) concluded: "The cyclic pattern thus is self-rearoused in a feedback fashion, the product of a reciprocal relationship between queen and colony functions, not of a timing mechanism endogenous to the queen."

Z.-Y. Kuo, a Chinese psychologist who completed his doctoral training with E. C. Tolman at Berkeley before returning to work in China, came to similar conclusions at about the same time. Kuo was originally motivated by J. B. Watson's claims about the malleability of behavior, given the control over the conditions of development. He went beyond Watson and collected relevant data. In a series of provocative studies, where he produced unique environments for the young animals to grow up in, Kuo demonstrated that key features of social patterns could be changed, and novel ones created. Cats, for instance, could be made to "love" rats, not kill them, if the kittens were raised together with rodents from infancy onward (Kuo, 1930, 1967). Beyond behavioral plasticity, Kuo addressed the fundamental problem of behavioral origins, and when and how novel behavior patterns arise in the course of ontogeny.

In his study of the origin of "instinctive" behaviors, such as pecking, vocalization, and movement patterns in birds, Kuo assumed that these characteristics arose in development because of necessary feedback relationships among central nervous system, physiological, and behavioral functions. Pushing the organismic proposal on the self-stimulative role of behavior to its limits, Kuo offered the proposal that the behavior of the embryo itself provided feedback that would help to direct its subsequent development. Preyer (1888) had earlier suggested the possibility of such feedback effects in development, but there were scant data relevant to the proposal.

The story of how Kuo explored these ideas can be found in a series of papers that he published during the 1930s, and a summary appears in his later volume on behavioral development (e.g., Kuo, 1930, 1939, 1967). He first had to solve the problem of how to keep embryos alive while viewing their development (he invented a way to produce a "window" by removing the external shell but keeping the embryo and the membranes surrounding it intact). Kuo was then able to plot, from the onset of development to hatching, the movement patterns in the egg, including the initial stages of heart activity, breathing, limb movement, and pecking. On the basis of these observations, he concluded that the activity of the organism itself was influential in determining the direction of development, including leg coordination and pecking. The initial report of these observations met initial skepticism (e.g., Carmichael, 1933), and for good reason. Some of Kuo's speculations have not been upheld because he did not give sufficient weight to the effects of spontaneous central nervous system innervation in producing cycles of activity and inactivity (Oppenheim,

1973). But his more general assumption that feedback functions can contribute to embryonic development has in some instances been strikingly confirmed. For example, inhibition of leg movement in the chick embryo has been found to be associated with ossification of the joints and difficulty in posthatching mobility (Drachman & Coulombre, 1962). Moreover, self-produced vocal calls by the embryo facilitate the development of posthatching species-typical preferences (Gottlieb, 1976).

As powerful as were Schneirla's and Kuo's demonstrations of the utility of a developmental approach to behavior, they had little immediate effect on child psychology (although Kuo's work was discussed at length by Carmichael, 1933, in the revised *Handbook of Child Psychology,* and Schneirla was a reviewer for the same volume). Not until the next generation was their essential message heard and understood in both comparative and developmental psychology.

Another psychobiological researcher had greater immediate success and visibility. Leonard Carmichael carried the psychological tradition of William Preyer into the 1930s. His *Handbook* chapters (Carmichael, 1933, 1946) provided a scholarly reminder of the unsolved problems of the relations between biological development and behavioral establishment. Carmichael also brought to the attention of child psychologists the impressive body of literature concerned with the analysis of early biological-behavioral development. The chapter by Myrtle McGraw (1946) provided an excellent critical overview of the basic issues of developmental psychobiology.

In Europe, the study of the "biology of behavior," or ethology, experienced a rebirth in Konrad Lorenz's article, *"Der Kumpan in der Umwelt des Vogels"* (1935; translated and published in English in 1937). In this paper, Lorenz reasserted the contribution of evolutionary forces in the determination of behavior, and reminded biologists and psychologists of the importance of early experience and its possible irreversibility. Building on the foundation laid at the turn of the 20th century by an American, C. O. Whitman, and a German, O. Heinroth, Lorenz offered a convincing argument for studying instinct and the evolutionary basis of behavior. Taking American behaviorists head on, Lorenz argued that the effects of experiences in the "critical period" could not be accounted for in then-available principles of learning and association. Specifically, he distinguished the phenomenon of imprinting (the establishment of filial preferences and species identification in

precocial birds) from "association learning" on four counts. Imprinting (a) occurred only during an early critical period, (b) was irreversible in later development, (c) was supraorganismic in its effects (not limited to the imprinted object but to the species of which the object was a member), and (d) took place prior to the developmental appearance of the response that was "conditioned" (e.g., sexual preferences were influenced, even though they were not present in infancy). Virtually no immediate notice was taken of ethological work by developmental psychologists; the gulf between disciplines, combined with World War II, delayed the introduction of these ideas into the mainstream of psychological and developmental thought.

Theoretical Trends of the Middle Period

What theoretical activity took place over this third of the 20th century? A great deal, for each of the major developmental models established in the previous period underwent revision, modification, and extension. Behaviorism was liberalized and enlivened by a marriage with psychoanalysis. Psychoanalysis itself was split into three recognizable subdivisions: (a) classical psychoanalysis (Munroe, 1955), (b) postpsychoanalytic theory, and (c) neopsychoanalytic theory. Similarly, the Baldwinian approach to cognitive and social development was partitioned and extended: (a) in the theory of mental development now associated with Jean Piaget, (b) in the symbolic interactionism movement in sociology, anthropology, and psychiatry, and (c) in Vygotsky's expansion of the proposal that "each child is part someone else, even in his own thought of himself."

Although Piaget and Vygotsky have been the most prominent representatives of the Baldwinian developmental tradition in America, Henri Wallon (1879–1962) became almost as prominent in Eastern Europe, Africa, South America, and, foremost, in France. But then, and now, he has received virtually no recognition from the English-speaking world. His student, René Zazzo (1984, p. 9) observes: "As a direct descendant of J. M. Baldwin and a precursor of the theoreticians of attachment, Wallon viewed the other person as basic and primary" (see also Wallon, 1984b). In brief, Wallon argued for a more integrative, more interactive, and more social view of the developing organism than did his contemporary and competitor, Jean Piaget (see Birns, pp. 59–65; Piaget, 1984; Wallon, 1984a).

Nor was behavioral Darwinism overlooked. The foundations for modern ethology had been laid by Whitman in America and Heinroth in Europe, and extended in the 1930s and 1940s by Lorenz and Tinbergen. The "organismic" approach affected theories in biology and psychology. Most immediately related to developmental concerns were the developmental psychobiological theory of Schneirla and Kuo and the cognitive-organismic principles of Stern, Lewin, and Werner. At first blush, it seemed as if Baldwin's vision that "every man have his theory" had been fulfilled.

Except for some intrafamilial squabbles, there were few direct confrontations or face-offs among the major theories—not so much out of mutual respect as because of selective inattention. As A. Baldwin (1967, 1980) has observed, developmental theories tended to talk past each other rather than at each other; they had different aims, were concerned with different issues, employed different methods, and were challenged by different findings. In due course, as the interests and concerns of the discipline shifted, each of the general orientations was to experience its day in the sun.

A few comments are in order on three major theoretical systems of the period that have not yet been singled out for attention: social learning theory, psychoanalysis and its derivatives, and Lewinian "field theory."

Social Neobehaviorism

The family of theories called "social learning" descended from a wedding of the general behavioral models of the 1930s and psychoanalytic ideas of personality. During the heyday of general behavioral systems, four models of learning emerged as especially influential: (a) the behavior system of Clark Hull (1943), (b) the contiguity learning model of E. R. Guthrie (1935), (c) the purposive behaviorism of E. C. Tolman (1932), and (d) the operant learning theory of B. F. Skinner (1938, 1953). Despite their differences in language and in basic assumptions about the nature of learning, the models shared the belief that the principles of learning were universal, transcending differences in species, age, and circumstances.

Beyond a faith in the universality of the basic principles of behavior, there was a need to specify the implications of these theories for distinctly human problems, including the acquisition of personality patterns and social dispositions. J. B. Watson led the way early in offering bold speculations about the learning and unlearning of fears and loves. The

challenge to the writers of the 1930s was to provide a more systematic, and yet equally convincing, case for the learning of significant human behaviors. To this end, a group of able young scientists at Yale University set about to put the study of personality processes on a solid empirical and behavioral basis (Maher & Maher, 1979). This group attempted to link certain concepts of psychoanalysis with assumptions drawn from the general behavioral theory of Clark Hull. The upshot was a remarkably influential set of concepts that was to dominate theoretical formulations in child psychology for the next several decades.

The first major collaborative effort was directed at the analysis of the controls of aggressive patterns, as viewed from a psychoanalytic-behavioral perspective. The product of this collaboration, a slim volume entitled *Frustration and Aggression,* appeared on the eve of World War II and gained immediate attention and influence (Dollard, Miller, Doob, Mowrer, & Sears, with others, 1939). Although the basic hypothesis that "aggression is always a consequence of frustration" (p. 27) was soon amended by the authors themselves (see Miller, Sears, Mowrer, Doob, & Dollard, 1941), the idea behind the work was enthusiastically endorsed. The associationistic assumptions of psychoanalysis were neatly melded with the stimulus–drive assumptions of Hullian theory.

The direct application of concepts of learning and imitation to children was soon made by Miller and Dollard (1941) in their book *Social Learning and Imitation.* This was not the first such extension; the Sears study of infant frustration (cited in Dollard, Miller, Doob, Mowrer, & Sears, 1939), and Mowrer's study of enuresis (1938) had already shown that social learning principles could be readily applied to problems of child development. After World War II, the full impact of the social learning perspective was to be felt by child psychology.

Psychoanalysis

By the 1930s, the enterprise of psychoanalysis had undergone multiple divisions and had exercised a significant impact on the study of behavioral development. The most obvious influence was direct, through the teachings of Sigmund Freud himself and those who remained faithful to the orthodox theory. But equally powerful influences were indirect, mediated through the theories of those who—like J. B. Watson, J. Piaget, and R. R. Sears—had been impressed by particular features of psychoanalytic theory. In between were the so-called "post-Freudians" (those who extended psychoanalytic theory within the constraints established by Freud himself) and "neo-Freudians" (those psychoanalysts who revolted by challenging certain inviolable assumptions, such as the emphasis on infantile sexuality and the primacy of early experience). These various themes have been expertly traced in discussions of psychoanalytic theory (e.g., Hall & Lindzey, 1957; Munroe, 1955). For our present purposes, some comments on the relation between psychoanalysis and the study of behavioral development are in order.

By the late 1930s, psychoanalysis appeared to many child psychologists to be the answer to their search for a unifying theory of development. One of the more influential writers on the matter was Freud's daughter, Anna Freud. Her view on the adequacy of the theory for understanding personality development—indeed, all features of development—was unambiguous and uncompromising. In the chapter that she prepared for the first edition of *A Handbook of Child Psychology,* Anna Freud (1931) wrote:

> Psychoanalysis does not permit itself to be ranged with other conceptions: it refuses to be put on an equal basis with them. The universal validity which psychoanalysis postulates for its theories makes impossible its limitation to any special sphere such as the conception of the neurotic child or even the sexual development of the child. Psychoanalysis goes beyond these boundaries, within which it might even have been granted the right of judgment, and encroaches upon domains which, as demonstrated by the table of contents of this book, other specialists consider their own. (p. 561)

Psychoanalysis would settle for nothing less than the whole pie of developmental psychology, and it came close to getting it in one form or another through the rest of the 20th century.

It seemed inevitable that empirically minded American psychologists would attempt to put some of the key propositions of the theory to experimental test—indeed, the enterprise attracted some of the best young scientists in psychology. What did they find? In summing up the then-available results of the experimental assessments of fixation, regression, projection, and other psychoanalytic mechanisms, Sears (1944) wrote:

> One is driven to the conclusion that experimental psychology has not yet made a major contribution to these problems.

. . . It seems doubtful whether the sheer testing of psychoanalytical theory is an appropriate task for experimental psychology. Instead of trying to ride on the tail of a kite that was never meant to carry such a load, experimentalists would probably be wise to get all the hunches, intuitions, and experience possible from psychoanalysis and then, for themselves, start the laborious task of constructing a systematic psychology of personality, but a system based on behavioral rather than experiential data. (p. 329)

All this is to say that the experimental testing of psychoanalytic proposals was not a profitable enterprise. Sears was to follow his own advice, as we shall see, and would pave the way for the modern generations of social learning theory.

Despite the equivocal returns on the scientific analysis of the theory, its influence gained, not faded, during the 1930s and 1940s. Virtually every major theoretical system concerned with human behavior—save those that dealt with purely physiological, motor, or sensory phenomena—was accommodated to psychoanalytic theory. Behaviorism (whether "radical" Watsonianism or conventional Hullian theory) and Piagetian cognitive theory alike were significantly influenced in that era, just as ethology and social learning theory were influenced in the present one. The immediate effects on child-rearing practices were as great, if not greater, than the earlier ones associated with Holt and Watson. With the publication of the first edition of Benjamin Spock's (1946) best-selling manual on infant care, the American public was encouraged to adopt practices not inconsistent with psychoanalytic training. The rapid growth of professional clinical psychology—World War II had demanded specialists in diagnosis and therapy—also underscored the need for a theory of assessment and treatment. The major tools available for the task included projective tests (typically based on psychoanalytic assumptions) and methods of psychotherapy (derived, directly or indirectly, from the psychoanalytic interview). Psychology as a profession and a science became increasingly indebted to psychoanalytic theory and practice.

But psychoanalysts themselves proved to be an intellectually heterogeneous lot, and the theory could hardly be viewed as a static, unchanging view of personality. Among the more prominent heretics were Carl Jung, Alfred Adler, Karen Horney, Eric Fromm, and Harry Stack Sullivan. They shared in common an emphasis on the interpersonal implications of dynamic theory, as these were expressed in the family system and in interpersonal exchanges of later childhood and maturity. With this focus on "object relations," there was a concomitant de-emphasis on the importance of infantile sexuality and the reversibility of very early experiences (see Munroe, 1955). Horney (1937) and Sullivan led the way in the neo-Freudian theory of interpersonal relations. In 1940, in a lengthy article in *Psychiatry*, Sullivan outlined a rapprochement between theories of symbolic interaction that had become associated with sociology and anthropology and a neoanalytic interpersonal theory of psychopathology. Sullivan's position was that the "self-dynamism" arises from "the recurrent interpersonal situations of life." Ideas about the self-dynamism (which is not an entity but a process) are derived from the interpersonal settings of life and depend, in large measure, on the "consensual validation" of the views of "significant others" with whom one interacts. Because of the continuing impact of the social system on one's behavior and one's thought of oneself, the development of personality is a continuing, ongoing process. Sullivan's views had a significant impact on subsequent sociological (Cottrell, 1942, 1969), psychiatric (Bateson, Jackson, Hayley, & Weakland, 1956; Jackson, 1968), and psychological models of social interaction.

Field Theory and Ecological Psychology

When Kurt Lewin immigrated to the United States in the early 1930s, he had already established himself as a distinguished child psychologist in Germany. American readers were first introduced to his powerful theory of "behavior and development as a function of the total situation" in two articles that appeared in English in 1931. In his classic theoretical paper, "Conflict between Aristotelian and Galileian Modes of Thought in Psychology" (1931a), Lewin offered an elegant defense for studying individual children in the actual, concrete, total situation of which they are a part. He argued that the dynamics of behavior—the study of the forces that exercise momentary control over the direction and form of actions—cannot be clarified by the use of standard statistical methods. Averages that are obtained by combining the results of large numbers of children in a "standard" environment are bound to obscure the precise dynamic controls of behavior, not clarify them. "An inference from the average to the concrete particular case is . . . impossible. The concepts of the average child and of the average situation are abstractions that have no utility whatever

for the investigation of dynamics" (Lewin, 1931b, p. 95). Lewin provided a rationale for the conclusion that had been arrived at intuitively by some of his most insightful predecessors (Preyer, Binet, Freud, and Piaget). The conclusion stood in sharp contrast to that arrived at by Galton and most American psychologists.

Lewin's ideas about method were consistent with his theoretical position on the contextual relativity of psychological experience and action. A key element in Lewin's theorizing was his emphasis on the *psychological* environment as opposed to the physical or objectively determined concrete environment. Lewin observed, "All these things and events are defined for the child partly by their 'appearance' but above all by their 'functional possibilities' (the *Wirkwelt* in v. Uexküll's sense)" (Lewin, 1931b, p. 100). In endorsing animal behaviorist J. von Uexküll's emphasis on the individual's reconstructed inner space (the *Umwelt* and the *Innenwelt*) as opposed to the objective mechanical forces of the external world (see Loeb, 1964), he captured an idea whose implications have yet to be fully realized. Lewin formulated his psychological field theory in keeping with the gestalt and system theoretic approaches. Although behavior is seen as a function of both the person and the environment, these two major variables "are mutually dependent upon each other. In other words, to understand or to predict behavior, the person and his environment have to be considered as *one* constellation of interdependent factors. We call the totality of these factors the life space *(LSp)* of that individual" (Lewin, 1954, p. 919). Lewin's theory was basically a model of action, to account for the directionality of behavior in terms of the forces present in a given psychological environment. But the effective forces belong neither to the person nor to the field alone; actions can be understood only in the totality of forces as they are merged to determine behavior.

In his work in the United States in the 1930s and 1940s, Lewin extended this theoretical model to diverse social and developmental phenomena, including the analysis of conflict, social influence, level of aspiration, and goal setting, as well as the effects of autocratic and democratic environments. Beyond their influence on specific research programs, Lewin's principles of behavior and development became incorporated into the discipline without being identified with his particular school of thought. For instance, his "field theory" demanded attention to the context in which behavior occurred and, particularly, the individual's personal response to that setting. The "environment" was not merely the physical and social context, but the child's perception of that setting. So one and the same "objective" environment may be perceived differently, according to the needs of the child and the forces that operate on him or her; conversely, seemingly identical responses may reflect the operation of quite different psychological forces. There is a contextual relativity to both stimuli and responses, and neither should be divorced from the social/environmental matrix in which each is embedded.

This overview does not permit an account of Lewin's developmental and social theory (excellent summaries may be found in Baldwin, 1967, and Estes, 1954). It should be noted that Lewin and the Lewinians pioneered in the study of conflict resolution (Lewin, 1935), level of aspiration (Lewin, Dembo, Festinger, & Sears, 1944), small group processes (Lewin, Lippitt, & White, 1939), and the effects of interruption and frustration (Barker, Dembo, & Lewin, 1941). One of Lewin's post-doctoral students, Roger Barker, carried the essential concepts of ecological psychology to the next generation (Barker, 1963, 1964, 1968; Barker & Wright, 1951). Urie Bronfenbrenner (1979) has been enormously influential in extending the essential ideas (Bronfenbrenner, 1979, 1993, 1995). Furthermore, other students inspired by Lewin virtually sculpted the face of modern social psychology. There was also an immediate and direct connection to developmental psychology. Marian Radke Yarrow, an eminent developmental psychologist, was Lewin's protégé at MIT, where she taught the graduate seminar on Lewinian theory to H. Kelley, J. Thibaut, and M. Deutsch, among others.

What did Lewinian theory not cover? Criticisms of field theory note that relatively little attention is given to the processes of enduring change—namely, those of learning. Although Lewin clearly acknowledges that "somatic" changes in the child can have a significant influence on the psychological environment, field theory gives only modest attention to how such developmental changes may be integrated with modifications in psychological forces. Hence, the model is exceedingly convincing as a descriptive model, but how it may be critically tested, modified, and falsified is less clear. Lewin's emphasis woke psychology from its behavioristic slumbers by pointing out that the context-free objective "stimulus" may be an illusion. The implications for methodology and theory, especially in the study of social development and social psychology, were enormous.

Comments on the Middle Period

It seems ironic that the most notable development in child psychology during this period was brought about initially by social and economic forces instead of scientific advances. Child research institutes were founded throughout the United states, and, once established, they became enormously influential in the science and remained so throughout the better part of the 20th century. Behind the foundations and the governmental–university agencies that provided the actual financial support for the institutes, there was a broad nationwide coalition of concerned teachers and parents who pressed for more attention, scientific and otherwise, to the needs of children. This was the same social/political "movement" that had been given early form and direction by G. Stanley Hall in the 1880s and 1890s. But the establishment of study centers did not a science make, and investigators were immediately challenged to develop more adequate procedures in virtually every sector of child research. Each area of study—intelligence, honesty, emotionality, language, thinking, perception, growth, predictability—presented its own problems of methodology and analysis, and each had to be solved in its own terms. The upshot was an inevitable fragmentation of developmental study.

What were the empirical advances in the period? To attempt to answer that question would be tantamount to compressing the information contained in the three compendia edited by C. Murchison (1931, 1933) and L. Carmichael (1946). Beyond the demonstration that almost all aspects of child behavior and cognition could be profitably studied by empirical procedures—something that had been promised but not demonstrated in the earlier period—we find substantive findings that perplexed the researchers themselves and seemed to defy integration with earlier concepts of the child. These phenomena included the specificity of honesty, the rapid conditionability of fear in infants, the egocentricism of children, the physical normality (or superiority) of bright children, and the modest predictability of behavior over time and space. Spectacular controversies were ignited by studies of early experience that purported to show that children's basic intellectual adaptations could be influenced by especially beneficial or neglectful early experiences. Perhaps more important for the science than controversy were the less dramatic yet critical advances in describing the "normal" (i.e., species-typical) course of sensorimotor, cognitive, and behavioral development.

Theoretical activity in this period proceeded at two "levels," specific and general. The empirical advances—methodological and substantive—produced information that demanded attention and integration. Hartshorne and May (1928) offered their "specificity" proposal on altruism and honesty; C. Bühler (1931), her account of three social "types" in infancy; F. Goodenough (1931), her explanation for the development of anger and quarrels; J. Anderson (1939), his hypothesis on the "overlap" in successive tests of infant competence; and so on. These data-based hypotheses constituted a necessary step between empirical studies of child behavior and the overarching theoretical conceptions that had stimulated the research in the first place.

On the second level, various attempts were made to establish a general integrative theory of development in order to fill the void left by the collapse of the recapitulation hypothesis. For every general developmental theory that vied for hegemony in the 1920s and 1930s, a straight line may be drawn backward to antecedent models of the 1880s and 1890s. The cognitive-developmental proposals of J. Piaget, L. S. Vygotsky, H. Wallon, and H. Werner were immediately linked to the concepts of J. M. Baldwin; the developmental psychobiology of Z-Y. Kuo, T. C. Schneirla, and L. von Bertalanffy followed the prior conceptual advances in animal behavior and experimental embryology; the maturational model of A. Gesell constituted in several respects an extension of the developmental views of W. Preyer; the scientific basis for Watsonian behaviorism was established by the prior work of Morgan, Loeb, and Jennings, among others; and the several versions of psychoanalysis each retained some central elements of the parent theory.

Despite obvious differences among the above models, they shared a family similarity in that they were, in a basic sense, developmental. Differences among them arose on assumptions about how developmental processes might be most adequately described and how behavioral phenomena might be most appropriately conceptualized. These assumptions, in turn, reflected which behavioral or cognitive phenomena were addressed by the theory, and in which species. Although psychoanalysis gained a clear edge in popular recognition and clinical applications, organismic models became quietly influential in the research of psychobiological and cognitive investigators. But none of the models achieved clear dominance, and the science could not claim as its own a unifying theory of behavioral development that might complement or extend the theory of biological evolution. Indeed, advances in identifying the contextual events that determined actions and learning raised questions on whether a general theory of behavioral development was possible.

THE MODERN ERA

Following a general depression in research activity during World War II, work on behavioral development began an upward slope in the postwar period and has only recently shown signs of leveling. A new "golden age" began for the discipline and it has surpassed those of the two previous eras (1895–1905 and 1925–1935). New techniques and approaches were introduced in rapid succession, stimulated in part by advances in electronic recording, coding, and computer analysis. The effective "life span" of research methods—from new projective procedures to questionnaires on authoritarianism or brief experimental procedures for studying learning—appeared to have been shortened from about 15 to about 10 years. Promising ideas—on test anxiety, social reinforcement satiation, impulsivity, and modeling—entered rapidly, dominated the area briefly, then faded away, often without a decent postmortem or obituary.

In large measure, the quickened pace of research activity and analysis could be attributed to great increases in federal support for empirical research and the opening of new teaching and research positions. A new institute established by the National Institutes of Health (NIH) was devoted to research on child health and human development, and other institutes accepted a developmental orientation to understanding problem behaviors (e.g., National Institute of Mental Health, National Institute of Drug Abuse). In addition, the U. S. Congress funded an unprecedented national program to provide poor and disadvantaged children with a "Head Start" prior to school entry. Two psychologists, Urie Bronfenbrenner and Edward Zigler, were instrumental in initiating the program and directing it through its early years. Other developmental psychologists were involved in the creation of television programs to enhance education and learning (e.g., *Sesame Street*). This period has been one of expansion, invention, and criticism, with new innovations and discoveries in virtually all areas of developmental research and application.

One of the more visible early theoretical trends in this period was the rise, domination, and passing of general learning theories. Until their grip began to fail in the early 1960s, behavioral models of learning were hegemonous in American psychology, and developmental psychology was no exception. To enter the theoretical mainstream, research in the several areas of child study, from language acquisition and cognitive learning to social behavior and child rearing, had to be couched in learning terms. Behaviors did not develop, they were acquired. Despite their austere and parsimonious construction, learning models appeared to be remarkably adaptable for developmental psychologists—but not adaptive enough. By the mid-1960s, the area began to rediscover the dynamic developmental models on which the field had been established. They appeared in quite different forms in studies of language and cognition, in investigations of basic motor and perceptual processes, and in longitudinal studies of social and personality development. The area also rediscovered the basic psychoanalytic assumption that the first relationships were critical for understanding psychopathology and the core features of personality.

Many of the ideas and problems that had been pursued over the first half of the 20th century came again to the forefront, from the study of growth patterns in motor and sensory development, in cognitive changes in thought and language, and in the effects of interactions on social and personality development.

This section of developmental history overlaps with contemporary events, including those covered in other chapters of this edition of the *Handbook*. The closer one comes to current trends, the more difficult it is to disentangle ephemeral interests from enduring changes. Hence we will stop short, leaving the final 20 years for those who survey the contemporary scene. To illustrate some of the shifts that have occurred, I comment briefly on the trends that were observed up through the mid-1970s in three domains: (a) social learning theory, (b) attachment theory, and (c) cognitive development.

Social Learning: Rise, Decline, and Reinvention

Contrary to general impressions, there is no single "social learning theory"; there are several. The plurality came about initially because there was only modest consensus on which principles of learning were universal. Over the past half-century, a number of social learning theories have evolved from the basic frameworks established by Skinner and the neo-Hullian theorists, each with its distinctive emphasis and adherents. It has been a complex and often misunderstood endeavor, and we comment here only on some of the historical highlights.

Rise

Robert R. Sears can be recognized as the person whose influence was pervasive in the introduction of the psychoanalytic learning synthesis to the study of children. One of the original members of the Yale group that created neo-Hullian social learning theory (Dollard et al., 1939; Miller et al., 1941), Sears was a pivotal influence for students and colleagues at the Iowa Child Welfare Research Station, Harvard University, and Stanford University. With his colleagues at these institutions, many of whom went on to develop influential revisions of social learning (including E. E. Maccoby, J. Whiting, V. Nowlis, J. Gewirtz, Richard Walters, A. Bandura, and Sears's wife, Pauline Snedden Sears), Sears was instrumental in bringing about major changes in the scope and concerns of developmental psychology.

In the first major publication to come from this group (Sears, Whiting, Nowlis, & Sears, 1953), "aggression" and "dependency" were seen as motives that were learned early in the life history of the child. How were they learned? The answer was not an easy one, at least not for Hullians, because the theory of conditioned drives had not been elaborated by Clark Hull (1951) and had been only vaguely outlined by Freud. Drawing from both of these views, Sears and his colleagues argued that these key social motives were acquired as a universal consequence of the early familial experiences of the child. Moreover, variations in the strength of the drives and in their expression were produced by differences in the quality of the parent–child relationship, as indexed by the rewards, punishments, and frustrations that occurred in the mother–child interaction. This social learning theory was extended to account for the development of gender role-typing (through internalization of parental values and self-reinforcement) and conscience (through nurturance and the withdrawal of love by the mother).

The semistructured interview technique was extensively employed to investigate parental attitudes, beliefs, and child-rearing practices. Large-scale studies were conducted by Sears and his colleagues in Iowa, Massachusetts, and California (Palo Alto). One aim was to replicate key findings at each of the three sites by using a common research technique. Employing lengthy in-depth interviews with parents as a primary research technique, these studies attempted to relate child-rearing practices with assessment of children's social behavior and personality patterns. The assessments of children capitalized on advances that had been made in observational methodology, and revised or developed child-appropriate "projective test" measures. Instead of using inkblots or semistructured pictures, the investigators used dolls and dollhouses to permit the preschool child to reconstruct the nuclear family (Bach, 1946). The interview and observational procedures provided the model for a wide range of cross-cultural and cross-age studies (e.g., Whiting & Whiting, 1975).

One of the great strengths of social learning theory and its practitioners was their openness to data, whether supportive or disconfirmatory. Hence, the original statement underwent revisions, both modest (e.g., Sears, Maccoby, & Levin, 1957; Sears, Rau, & Alpert, 1965) and major (e.g., Bandura & Walters, 1959; Whiting & Whiting, 1975), in attempts to extend it and correct its shortcomings.

Decline

What were the shortcomings? Some were identified by the investigators themselves in three large-scale studies of child rearing conducted in Iowa, Massachusetts, and California. When the results of the 20-year research effort were compiled and analyzed, the outcomes provided only modest support for the theory that had inspired the work. The problem was that there were few reliable correlates between variations in child-rearing practices and the children's social behavior and personality patterns.

Eleanor Maccoby, a key participant in this work, indicated that the problem lay as much in the theory as in the method. Looking backward after 35 years, Maccoby (1994) wrote:

[F]ew connections were found between parental child-rearing practices (as reported by parents in detailed interviews) and independent assessments of children's personality characteristics—so few, indeed, that virtually nothing was published relating the two sets of data. The major yield of the study was a book on child-rearing practices as seen from the perspective of mothers [Sears, Maccoby, & Levin, 1957]. This book was mainly descriptive and included only very limited tests of the theories that led to the study. Sears and colleagues later conducted a study with preschoolers focused specifically on the role of identification with the same-sex parent in producing

progress toward social maturity. They used a much expanded range of assessment techniques, including observations of parent–child interaction. The hypothesis that identification with parents was a primary mechanism mediating children's acquisition of a cluster of well-socialized attributes was, once again, not supported (see especially R. R. Sears, Rau, & Alpert, 1965, Table 40, p. 246). (p. 594)

Not all of the outcomes were negative, nor were all unreliable. But the overall pattern of the findings provided scant support for the ideas that had inspired the work in the first place. What was to blame—the theory or the methods employed to test it? The methods could be criticized, and so could the theory.

In an incisive and courageous evaluation published at the height of the social learning era, Marian Radke Yarrow and her colleagues wrote:

Childrearing research is a curious combination of loose methodology that is tightly interwoven with provocative hypotheses of developmental processes and relationships. The compelling legend of maternal influences on child behavior that has evolved does not have its roots in solid data, and its precise verification remains in many respects a subject for future research. The findings from the preceding analyses of data make it difficult to continue to be complacent about methodology, and difficult to continue to regard replication as a luxury. The child's day-to-day experiences contribute significantly to his behavior and development and are in many respects the essence of developmental theory. An exact understanding is important to science and society. In attempting to build on this knowledge, each researcher is a methodologist and as such has a responsibility for excellence. (Yarrow, Campbell, & Burton, 1968, p. 152)

Two noteworthy contributions by Sears and his colleagues require mention. In a presidential address to the American Psychological Association, Sears (1951) brought renewed attention to the theoretical concept of social interaction and the bidirectionality of familial relations. Although the research methods employed by the Sears group made it difficult to study interactional phenomena directly, these concepts figured importantly in the conceptions that were offered in each of Sears's major subsequent publications. They provided the impetus for renewed attention to the issues that had been initially raised by James Mark Baldwin, and were then represented in the work of psychiatrist H. S. Sullivan (1940, 1953) and sociologist Leonard Cottrell (1942).

The second contribution was the reintegration of child development research into the mainstream of psychology, a position that it had not held for most of the previous half-century. By linking the study of children to the then-current theoretical systems of psychology, the door was opened for a fresh generation of psychologists to enter the field. The gains were not without cost, however, in that much of the earlier developmental work was set aside or ignored by the new group. Traditional developmental studies, as embodied in the chapters of successive editions of the Carmichael *Manual,* were seen as irrelevant for the basic issues of social learning and social control. Instead of descriptions of developmental change, this generation of developmentalists was concerned with explanations of change in terms of the "new" concepts of social interchange, imitation, dyadic analysis, dependency, aggression, and conscience. Overlooked in the social learning revolution was the fact that each of these concepts had been familiar to the founding generation, and the phenomena to which the concepts refer had been extensively researched in the next generation.

Coming back to the evolution of social learning theories, we find that, in the early 1960s, the movement was split into two major divisions, each of which was in intellectual debt to the parental movement and to the reinforcement concepts of B. F. Skinner (1953). J. Gewirtz, S. Bijou, and D. Baer (Bijou & Baer, 1961; Gewirtz, 1961) followed Skinner's lead in applying the ideas and concepts of operant conditioning to analyses of behavior modification in normal and retarded children. But there were problems in negotiating the theoretical transition from pigeons to children. Just as the concept of "conditioned" or "learned motivation" had presented difficulties for the initial social learning theories, the notion of "conditioned" or "social reinforcement" proved to be an enigmatic concept for the operant revision (see Gewirtz & Baer, 1958; Parton & Ross, 1965).

Reinvention

The resurgence of social learning theory was led by Albert Bandura and Richard Walters (1963), who shifted the substantive and explanatory basis of the model. They argued that the wedding of learning concepts to psychoanalysis tended to short-change both models. Social learning should exploit learning mechanisms, including cognitive processes that govern imitation and reinforcement. In their work, "modeling" was seen as a primary mechanism for the acquisition of novel actions and, as such, a key to understanding socialization and transgenerational transmission. They had, in effect, reinstituted the construct of "imitation" to the nuclear role that it had played in J. M. Baldwin's formulation.

The next modification in social learning theory came shortly afterward, when Albert Bandura revitalized the theory and established it on a foundation of distinctively human, cognitive processes. The need for further revision arose when it became clear that the short-term studies of imitation and social learning of children were open to alternative, cognitive interpretations. For instance, examination of the determinants and outcomes of modeling (i.e., imitation) in children indicated that children did not behave in a fashion that was analogous to observation learning in animals. A similar phenomenon was observed in the effects of social reinforcement (i.e., verbal reward) with children. Marked variations in reinforcer effectiveness could be induced simply by instructions or other cognitive manipulations, leading to the interpretation that "social reinforcement" in children may more appropriately be viewed in terms of information transmission processes than primary reinforcement processes (see Paris & Cairns, 1972; Stevenson, 1965). Other "information" interpretations of punishment, dependency, and conscience appeared (e.g., Walters & Parke, 1964). A similar revision was made in the interpretation of imitation and modeling, for parallel reasons (Bandura, 1969). Patterson (1979) extended observational methods in inventive ways, hence paved the way for precise assessments of social learning hypotheses.

Along with Rotter (1954) and Mischel (1973), Bandura shifted the focus of social learning from preoccupation with psychoanalytic conflicts and anxieties to the positive, productive features of children. With the concepts of self-efficacy and self-regulation, he affirmed the distinctive qualities of human adaptation, and he shifted the focus of the orientation from human problems to human potential. But these are not opposed foci in Bandura's revision of social learning theory. On this score, Grusec (1994) observes:

> Bandura's interest in self-efficacy arose from his studies of the role of participant modeling in the treatment of phobic disorders. A striking feature of the outcomes of these studies was the extent to which individuals' perceptions of their own feeling of effectiveness determined how easily changes in

behavior and fear arousal were achieved and maintained. According to self-efficacy theory, people develop domain-specific beliefs about their own abilities and characteristics that guide their behavior by determining what they try to achieve and how much effort they put into their performance in that particular situation or domain. (p. 488)

In a century-long cycle, social cognition–learning reformulations came to embrace not only J. M. Baldwin's concept of imitation but also his concept of the self as a central organizing theme.

Some characteristics of behaviorist models have remained virtually unchanged in the several generations of social learning theories. Social learning researchers have maintained a curious stance toward the concept of development. From Watson onward, learning theories have been developmental in the sense that they have shared the "fundamental point" that humans' activities should be studied historically. Social learning views have been slow to consider processes of age-related shifts in development (Cairns, 1979; Grusec, 1994). The implicit assumption has persisted that the incremental changes in cognition and learning are sufficient to account for the major phenomena of social development, including their establishment, maintenance, and change.

Attachment: Discovery and Loss

With the rediscovery of imitation and modeling, students of social learning found fresh and robust phenomena to analyze, and a new generation of social learning models was born. So it was with mother–infant attachment. The systematic investigation of mother–infant attachment in studies of animal behavior, and subsequently in studies of humans, breathed new life into the psychoanalytic framework. According to an early definition by Ainsworth (1972), attachment refers to "an affectional tie or bond that one individual (person or animal) forms between himself and another specific individual" (p. 100).

The prototypic attachment is that which develops between mothers and infants. That a strong tie develops early in life is certainly no new revelation. However, the systematic study of attachment behavior in animals and humans began only in the post-World War II era. Scott (1962, 1963), and Harlow (1958) opened the door for the systematic study of this early affectional relationship with their

now classic studies of the young puppy and infant rhesus monkey. At about the same time, Bowlby (1958) and his former postdoctoral associates (Ainsworth, 1963; Schaffer & Emerson, 1964) offered influential statements on attachment in human infants.

The Phenomena of Attachment

Harry F. Harlow (1958) announced in his American Psychological Association presidential address the results of some dramatic findings on the importance of somatosensory contact in the formation of the bond of the infant monkey to inanimate "surrogate" mothers. According to the initial interpretation of these findings, tactile stimulation—or "contact comfort"—was a more powerful determinant than hunger in the infant's formation of a social attachment. Subsequent work by Harlow and others led to significant modifications in the initial interpretations—on the necessary and sufficient conditions for the development of mammalian attachments (e.g., Cairns, 1966); on the stability and plasticity of effects induced by early social experience (e.g., Mason & Kinney, 1974; Suomi & Harlow, 1972). Nonetheless, the image of "motherless monkeys" had a catalytic effect in stimulating studies of mother–infant relations and, more generally, investigations of the development of social interactions.

Given the critical role assigned to early experiences in most developmental theories, it is curious that so little systematic work had been conducted on mother–infant attachment before the modern era. It is especially surprising because the intense relationship established between infants and mothers is perhaps the most easily detected and robust social phenomenon observed across mammals. At about the time when infants begin to locomote independently, they become extremely distressed when removed involuntarily or separated from their mothers (or mother-surrogates). Reunion tends to produce an immediate cessation of distress (e.g., the young quit crying, screaming, or bleating). Infants in this age range also express heightened weariness or fear when confronted with strange persons and strange places—or even familiar persons in strange places. These phenomena can be demonstrated in virtually all mammalian species; human babies show intermediate levels of intensity.

The multiple dimensions of early-formed bonds were investigated in experimental and observational work with birds (i.e., imprinting) and mammals (i.e., attachment). By the mid-1960s, a comprehensive picture could be drawn of the conditions for the emergence and maintenance of, and for change in attachment relationships (Harlow, 1958; Rosenblatt & Lehrman, 1963; Scott, 1963). The findings permitted four empirical generalizations about the nature of mammalian attachment (Cairns, 1966):

1. At birth and in the immediate postnatal period, there is an elegant synchrony between the actions and physiological states of the mother and of the infant. Moreover, the actions of the infant serve to maintain the mother in a maternal condition and sculpt her physiology so that it supports the contemporaneous needs of the infant. A parallel feedback loop serves similar functions for the infant, and a reciprocal relationship becomes established between the actions and states of the infant and those of the mother (Rosenblatt & Lehrman, 1963). Biological needs and social actions become mutually supportive (Hofer, 1994). In effect, the actions and biological conditions of the infant and mother rapidly become organized around each other.

2. Proximity and mutual mother–infant engagement promote the establishment of a social attachment that persists in the absence of the psychobiological conditions that originally promoted the interaction. In most mammalian species, the bond is intense, and involuntary separation triggers disorganization, distress, and disruption in both the infant and the mother. The distress is so extreme that it can be assessed by a host of behavioral and biological assessments.

3. Intense social attachment can be established under diverse conditions (e.g., the absence of milk, the absence of contact comfort, and, paradoxically, the presence of intense punishment). The influence of these conditions depends, in large measure, on the contexts of reciprocal exchange. Moreover, attachment can develop in older as well as younger animals (maternal attachment is but one of the special conditions). Experimental studies have indicated that social attachment strength increases with interaction, time spent, and exclusivity of relationship.

4. Maturational changes trigger modifications in the nature and the quality of attachment; maturation of the young is synchronized with maternal behavioral and physiological changes that are consistent with the mother's preparation for the next generation of offspring. New attachments are formed typically within minutes and hours rather than weeks and months, possibly to balance the tension between conservation and survival (Cairns & Werboff, 1967; Mason & Kinney, 1974). In this regard, the adaptation had to be rapid in order for the vulnerable infant to live.

Attachment Theory

Studies of infant–mother attachment came in the wake of these systematic investigations, and they stimulated enormous scientific and public interest (Maccoby & Masters, 1970). Psychoanalyst John Bowlby began a series of seminars on these issues at the Tavistock Clinic in London in the 1950s, and expanded the series in the 1960s (Foss, 1961, 1965; see Bretherton & Waters, 1985). Two key research programs reported in these discussions were: (a) the observations of Schafer and Emerson (1964) on the age of onset of attachment and (b) Ainsworth's (1963) observational report of infant–mother attachment in Uganda. Schafer and Emerson (1964) discovered that human infants begin to exhibit discriminative attachment at about 8 to 9 lunar months after birth, and that these attachments were formed with respect to a wide range of persons who were intimately involved in the infants' caretaking.

John Bowlby first became known for his contributions to object relations theory and, specifically, the significance of early mother–infant bonds (i.e., Bowlby, 1946, 1952). Beginning in the early 1950s, he began informal interdisciplinary seminars that involved, along with others, the eminent ethologist Robert Hinde. One outcome of these discussions was a paper published in the *International Journal of Psychoanalysis* where Bowlby integrated concepts from object relations theory with evolutionary assumptions. He thereby generated a framework of attachment that fused psychoanalysis and ethology (Bowlby, 1958). In an important set of volumes, Bowlby described the implications of his "attachment theory" for understanding maternal–child anxiety, separation, and loss (1969, 1973).

In Bowlby's view of attachment, priority is given to the events that occur during the child's early years in the establishment of a relatively stable attachment system. Mother-infant separation is likely to produce enduring negative consequences. The nature of the attachment that is formed in early development gives rise to an internal representational model formed by the child. Moreover, the processes that give rise to an attachment involve intense mutual regulation and mutual organization between the mother and infant. Bowlby (1952) wrote:

If growth is to proceed smoothly, the tissues must be exposed to the influence of the appropriate organizer at critical periods. In the same way, if mental development is to proceed smoothly, it would appear to be necessary for the undifferentiated psyche to be exposed during certain critical periods to the influence of the psychic organizer—the mother. (p. 53)

Unlike ethological/animal behavior work, Bowlby's object relations/attachment theory has a distinctive focus on individual differences. In addition, its goal, like object relations theory, is to provide a comprehensive account of psychopathology. Like ethological assumptions, it emphasizes the formative effects of early experiences.

Any discussion of modern "Attachment Theory" must include Mary D. S. Ainsworth, Bowlby's long-term collaborator. Ainsworth conducted a pair of influential observational studies on mother–infant relations in Uganda (Ainsworth, 1967) and Baltimore (Ainsworth, Blehar, Waters, & Wall, 1978). One of the procedures to emerge from the later study was a controlled observation procedure labeled the "Strange Situation" (Ainsworth et al., 1978).[7] This assessment involved a series of very brief separations (i.e., 1 to 3 minutes), with special attention given to the quality of the reunions. The coding of a reunion provided a classification procedure by which children were diagnosed as securely attached (Type B) or insecurely attached (Types A and C), along with various subtypes (Ainsworth et al., 1978). A primary attraction of Attachment Theory is its presumption that these types are linked to the quality of later relationships and to psychopathology.

An extended discussion of Attachment Theory and its strengths and shortcomings is beyond the limits of this chapter and would catapult the account into the contemporary period. For the current state of affairs on this enormously influential theory, the modern developmental version of neopsychoanalysis, see Bretherton and Waters (1985) and Goldberg, Muir, and Kerr (1995).

Cognitive Re-Emergence

This era also saw the re-emergence of cognitive-developmental questions as a central focus for thinking and research. Stimulated by a national re-examination of

the educational process (e.g., Bruner, 1960), in part because of influential volumes on Piaget (Flavell, 1963; Hunt, 1961) and Vygotsky (Cole, 1978), and in part because of the fading vigor of social learning approaches, the problem of how mental development occurs became a dominant concern for developmental researchers. It is a re-emergence—rather than a revolution—because the issues of mind, consciousness, and mental development were central to the discipline at its founding.

Virtually all aspects of the field were touched by the fresh emphasis. Investigations of language development, thinking, sensation, and information processing in children flourished as they had in no earlier era. Even hard-core behavioristic models proved to be vulnerable to cognitive modifications, with the new directions on "mediational mechanisms" being provided by T. and H. Kendler (Kendler & Kendler, 1962) and M. Kuenne (1946). Information-processing approaches were challenged to build bridges to cognitive developmental studies and interpretations. Given the thrust of the movement, it seemed inevitable that the barriers between social development and cognitive development should be transcended, and that it should become once again permissible to refer to concepts of others and of one self (see Harter, 1983; Lewis & Brooks-Gunn, 1979). The recent history of this movement and the statement of the rapprochement among experimental–cognitive concepts, social cognition, and cognitive–developmental concepts are covered in other chapters of this *Handbook* (see, for example, chapters by Baltes et al.; Fischer & Bidell; Gardner; Keil; Overton; and Spelke & Newport, in this Volume).

Historical Themes and Contemporary Advances

One hundred years after it began, developmental research and theory continues to be diverse, vigorous, contentious, fresh, and in many instances, brilliant. In concluding this chapter, we recall the themes that were identified in the beginning, in order to take stock of the progress made and the pitfalls encountered in a century of scientific work.

Knowledge and Consciousness

Understanding the mind and how it develops and functions remains a major concern for developmentalists. Because of advances in technology, investigators who study the relations between brain processes and cognitive activity have achieved spectacular advances in identifying pathways and plasticity over time. And there is now compelling evidence

---

[7] The "Strange Situation" seems to have been modeled after the assessments of attachment employed with nonhuman mammals (see Scott, 1963).

to support Preyer's speculation that "the brain grows through its own activity." Yet, plenty of controversies remain, and certain basic issues continue to be controversial (e.g., is there an area in the brain devoted to language?) despite impressive advances in understanding and methodology. At least some of the matters that remain unresolved have less to do with how the brain is studied than with how our constructs of the mind are formulated and our measures are organized (Morrison & Ornstein, 1996; see the chapters by Gottlieb et al.; Magnusson & Stattin; Overton; and Valsiner, this Volume).

Thoughts and Actions

The self and its distinctive processes (e.g., self-concepts, self-efficacy, self-regulation) continue to be central for modern researchers. What was attributed to the "Will" in the 1890s is attributed to the self and its processes (motives, values, dispositions) in the 1990s. What has changed, however, are methods, measures, and the findings that they yield. The multilevel, multimeasure methodological procedures of the late 20th century have exposed some myths. One's own self-attributions are not necessarily the same as descriptions of the self by others, and the differences are systematically linked to the domains assessed, the contexts of assessment, and the meaning of the measures. The story of how the discrepancies between the self and others is now being addressed belongs, however, to today, not to the past. The current state of information on these matters is addressed elsewhere in this volume (see chapters by Baltes et al.; Brandstädter; Csikszentmihalyi & Rathunde; and Fisher et al, this Volume).

Ontogeny and Phylogeny

How may development be best defined: in terms of the ontogeny of individuals, the ontogeny of the species, or the ontogeny of both? This was one of the first issues in the systematic development of the science, and it has been one of the last to be reassessed in the present era. But it is now being addressed as a matter of how cross-generational transfer occurs, and how there may be turning points across generations as well as across ontogeny. According to a recent collaborative statement, "Developmental investigation focuses attention to the ontogenies of both embryos and ancestors, and to the process by which pathways may be repeated or redirected across successive generations" (Carolina Consortium on Human Development, 1996, p. 1). Intergenerational investigations may become a primary

methodology of the future as they become feasible and practical (see, for example, Bronfenbrenner & Morris, Ch. 17, and Elder, Ch. 16, this volume).

Nature and Nurture

After a century of controversy, the nature–nurture debate is still being contested both in public and in the laboratory (e.g., Herrnstein & Murray, 1994; Lehrman, 1953, 1970). Recall that J. M. Baldwin resolved the matter by observing that "most of man's equipment is due to both causes working together," and Preyer arrived at the same conclusion. Much of the contemporary work in quantitative behavior genetics on twins has been limited to documenting that there are indeed genetic influences on behavior. The field now promises to begin to address the question of how "both causes work together" at the level of biology, interactions, and social networks (see, for example, chapters by Gottlieb et al.; Lerner; Magnusson & Stattin; Overton; Thelen & Smith; and Wapner & Demick, this Volume).

When Does Development End?

Virtually all researchers in this discipline are developmentalists—including arch-maturationist Arnold Gesell. The naïve idea of strict preformism and unidirectional causation has been a strawman since the beginning of the science. But there remain radical differences among investigators in *when* they believe experiences to be extremely relevant, and when they consider them to be irrelevant. Early speculations on this issue were handicapped by a paucity of systematic normative and experimental information. In the absence of longitudinal information on the behavioral adaptations of human beings, there was no adequate basis for selecting or rejecting these theoretical assumptions about the timing and functions of early experience. Neurobehavioral, cognitive, and social developmental research in the modern era has begun to clarify the role of time and timing across several domains. This information is reviewed, for example, by Baltes et al., Ch. 18; Brandstädter, Ch. 14; Elder, Ch. 16; Gardner, Ch. 8; Keil, Ch. 7; Overton, Ch. 3; Spelke & Newport, Ch. 6; Thelen & Smith, Ch. 19; and Wapner & Demick, Ch. 13, this Volume.

Morality and the Perfectibility of Humans

Values and moral development continue to be important for the discipline, although the work has been handicapped by serious methodological challenges. With a few important exceptions, the conceptual framework for understanding the development of personal values has been given less attention than in the earlier eras. It seems likely that this domain will come to the forefront in the next era, given its centrality in understanding the human condition. Indeed, the new concern with the self and with self-organization in the social context prepares the way for an integrated view of morality. As Kohlberg insightfully observed, "An individual is fundamentally a potentially moral being, not because of social authority and rules (as Durkheim and Piaget thought) but because his ends, his will, his self is that of a shared social self" (Kohlberg, 1982, pp. 311–312). For a review of related contemporary issues, see chapters by Baltes et al.; Brandstädter; and Csikszentmihalyi & Rathunde, this Volume.

Social Applications

Applications continue to present large opportunities and large problems. Sears (1975) concluded that the discipline was created to be relevant. In this regard, White (1996) wrote:

> Child study of some sort has to be part and parcel of any social design for children. Though developmental psychology is not, in the traditional sense, a policy science it has nevertheless a significant role to play in the organization and management of systems of governance directed towards children and families. (p. 413)

As research has become increasingly more tied to specific social concerns and social needs, some have feared that the science would be compromised. That has not occurred. To the contrary, carefully evaluated social applications have help created a more robust, verifiable, and relevant science (Lerner, Ch. 1, this Volume). The successes and failures of, say, violence preventive interventions help clarify the strengths and limitations of theoretical analyses that gave rise to the interventions.

One other byproduct of social applications should be mentioned. The rapid growth of the discipline has created some unanticipated hazards for developmental study, not the least of which is the intense competition for publication space and research support. In one unfortunate outcome, closely knit research groups have formed tight theoretical and/or empirical coalitions that promote inclusion and practice exclusion. Under these conditions, dominant methodologies and ideas tend to monopolize resources while ignoring or distorting competing concepts and disconfirming evidence. Although these efforts tend to self-correct in the long term, they may create fragmentation and misunderstanding in the short term. In this regard, efforts to achieve effective applications often act as catalysts to bring ideas and findings to common ground and common standards.

Toward an Interdisciplinary Science

In June 1994, a Nobel Foundation symposium comprised of noted biologists and psychologists called for an integrated, unified framework for the study of development (Magnusson, 1996). No single source or single investigator can be credited, since it has become an interdisciplinary, international movement. In the history of the discipline, this is a singular event. Over the past 100 years, the insights and emphases of developmental investigators in Europe—from Binet and Stern to Lewin and Bühler—have often been on a different frequency than those in North America, and the reverse held as well. When exceptions occurred—early, with Baldwin, Piaget, Vygotsky, and Freud; and later, with Magnusson, Bronfenbrenner, Bandura, Bruner, and Bowlby—the entire discipline was revitalized.

The contemporary press toward better integrated models of development arose from multiple sources. These include social development and social ecology (e.g., Bronfenbrenner, 1995; Ford & Lerner, 1992), developmental psychobiology and ethology (Bateson, 1991; Gottlieb, 1992; Hinde, 1970; Hood, Greenberg, & Tobach, 1995), the dynamic systems approach (Smith & Thelen, 1993; Thelen & Smith, 1994), developmental psychopathology (e.g., Hay & Angold, 1993; Cicchetti & Cohen, 1994), cognitive development (Baltes & Baltes, 1990; van der Veer & Valsiner, 1991), and developmental science (Cairns, Elder, & Costello, 1996; Magnusson, 1996). Due in part to methodological advances in the study of development, basic perceptual and movement patterns gained fresh life and new direction. It appears that studies of social development, emotion, and cognition may be the greatest beneficiaries of the current drive toward a more integrated developmental framework.

Given the advances in theory—advances which were not possible until empirical data became available to sort out the developmental concepts—the field now seems on the threshold of becoming a true interdisciplinary science. The longitudinal studies initiated in the 1960s and 1970s in Stockholm by David Magnusson, in Finland by Lea Pulkinnen, and in England by Michael Rutter and David Farrington provided models for U.S. researchers in the 1980s and 1990s. Longitudinal research on children and adolescents has triggered a new revolution in methodology and findings, and it has helped the field regain the vitality enjoyed in early eras. The multilevel information is now being organized around individuals in the natural contexts of their lives. When wedded to concerns of origins and plasticity, this information becomes "the essence of developmental theory" (Yarrow et al., 1968).

REFERENCES

Ainsworth, M. D. S. (1963). The development of infant-mother interaction among the Ganda. In B. M. Foss (Ed.), *Determinants of infant behavior* (Vol. 2, pp. 67–104). New York: Wiley.

Ainsworth, M. D. S. (1967). *Infancy in Uganda: Infant care and the growth of love.* Baltimore: Johns Hopkins University Press.

Ainsworth, M. D. S. (1972). Attachment and dependency: A comparison. In J. L. Gewirtz (Ed.), *Attachment and dependency.* New York: Wiley.

Ainsworth, M. D. S., Blehar, M. C., Waters, E., & Wall, S. (1978). *Patterns of attachment: A psychological study of the Strange Situation.* Hillsdale, NJ: Erlbaum.

Allport, G. W. (1937). *Personality: A psychological interpretation.* New York: Holt.

Anderson, J. E. (1931). The methods of child psychology. In C. Murchison (Ed.), *A handbook of child psychology* (pp. 1–27). Worcester, MA: Clark University Press.

Anderson, J. E. (1939). The limitations of infant and preschool test in the measurement of intelligence. *Journal of Psychology, 8,* 351–379.

Arrington, R. E. (1932). *Interrelations in the behavior of young children* (Child Development Monographs No. 8). New York: Teachers College, Columbia University Press.

Bach, G. R. (1946). Father fantasies and father-typing in father-separated children. *Child Development, 17,* 63–80.

Baer, K. E. von. (1828–1837). *Über Entwickelungsgeschichte der Thiere: Beobachtung und Reflexion* (2 vols.). Königsberg: Bornträger.

Baldwin, A. (1980). *Theories of child development.* New York: Wiley. (Original work published 1967)

Baldwin, B. T., & Stecher, L. I. (1924). *The psychology of the preschool child.* New York: Appleton.

Baldwin, J. M. (1890). Origin of right- or left-handedness. *Science, 16,* 302–303.

Baldwin, J. M. (1891). Suggestion in infancy. *Science, 17,* 113–117.

Baldwin, J. M. (1892a). Infants' movements. *Science, 19,* 15–16.

Baldwin, J. M. (1892b). Origin of volition in childhood. *Science, 20,* 286–287.

Baldwin, J. M. (1893). Distance and color perception by infants. *Science, 21,* 231–232.

Baldwin, J. M. (1895). *Mental development in the child and the race: Methods and processes.* New York: Macmillan.

Baldwin, J. M. (1902). *Development and evolution.* New York: Macmillan.

Baldwin, J. M. (1906). *Social and ethical interpretations in mental development: A study in social psychology.* New York: Macmillan. (Original work published 1897)

Baldwin, J. M. (1915). *Genetic theory of reality, being the outcome of genetic logic, as issuing in the aesthetic theory of reality called pancalism.* New York: Putnam.

Baldwin, J. M. (1930). [Autobiography]. *A History of Psychology in Autobiography, 1,* 1–30.

Baltes, P. B. (1979). Life-span developmental psychology: Some converging observations on history and theory. In P. B. Baltes & O. G. Brim, Jr. (Eds.), *Life-span development and behavior* (Vol. 2, pp. 255–279). New York: Academic Press.

Baltes, P. B., & Baltes, M. M. (Eds.). (1990). *Successful aging: Perspectives from the behavioral sciences.* New York: Cambridge University Press.

Baltes, P. B., Reese, H. W., & Nesselroade, J. R. (1977). *Life-span developmental psychology: Introduction to research methods.* Monterey, CA: Brooks/Cole.

Bandura, A. (1969). *Principles of behavior modification.* New York: Holt, Rinehart and Winston.

Bandura, A., & Walters, R. H. (1959). *Adolescent aggression.* New York: Ronald Press.

Bandura, A., & Walters, R. H. (1963). *Social learning and personality development.* New York: Holt, Rinehart and Winston.

Barker, M. (1930). *A technique for studying the social-material activities of young children* (Child Development Monographs No. 3). New York: Columbia University Press.

Barker, R. G. (Ed.). (1963). *The stream of behavior: Explorations of its structure and content.* New York: Appleton-Century-Crofts.

Barker, R. G. (1964). *Big school, small school: High school size and student behavior.* Stanford, CA: Stanford University Press.

Barker, R. G. (1968). *Ecological psychology: Concepts and methods for studying the environment of human behavior.* Stanford, CA: Stanford University Press.

Barker, R. G., Dembo, T., & Lewin, K. (1941). Frustration and regression: An experiment with young children. *University of Iowa Studies in Child Welfare, 18*(No. 1).

Barnes, E. (1896–1897, 1902–1903). *Studies in education* (2 vols.). Philadelphia: Author.

Bateson, G., Jackson, D. D., Hayley, J., & Weakland, J. H. (1956). Toward a theory of schizophrenia. *Behavioral Science, 1,* 251–264.

Bateson, P. P. G. (Ed.). (1991). *The development and integration of behavior: Essays in honor of Robert Hinde.* New York: Cambridge University Press.

Bayley, N. (1932). A study of crying of infants during mental and physical tests. *Journal of Genetic Psychology, 40,* 306–329.

Beaver, A. P. (1930). *The initiation of social contacts by preschool children* (Child Development Monographs No. 7). New York: Columbia University Press.

Bell, R. Q. (1968). A reinterpretation of the direction of effects in studies of socialization. *Psychological Review, 75,* 81–95.

Bell, R. Q., & Harper, L. V. (1977). *Child effects on adults.* Hillsdale, NJ: Erlbaum.

Bergenn, V. W., Dalton, T. C., & Lipsitt, L. P. (1994). Myrtle B. McGraw: A growth scientist. In R. D. Parke, P. A. Ornstein, J. J. Rieser, & C. Zahn-Waxler (Eds.), *A century of developmental psychology* (pp. 389–423). Washington, DC: American Psychological Association.

Bertalanffy, L., von (1933). *Modern theories of development: An introduction to theoretical biology* (J. H. Woodger, Trans.). London: Oxford University Press.

Bijou, S. W., & Baer, D. M. (1961). *Child development.* New York: Appleton-Century-Crofts.

Binet, A. (1887). Le Fétichisme dans l'amour. *Revue Philosophique, 24,* 143–167, 252–274.

Binet, A. (1892). *Les Altérations de la personnalité.* Paris: Félix Alcan. (Transated into English in 1896)

Binet, A. (1903). *L'étude experimentale de l'intelligence.* Paris: Schleicher.

Binet, A. (1908). Le développement de l'intelligence chez enfants. *L'Année Psychologique, 14,* 1–94.

Binet, A. (1911). Nouvelles recherches sur la measure du niveau intellectuel chez les enfants d'ecole. *L'Année Psychologique, 17,* 145–201.

Binet, A. (1973). Nos commission de travail. In T. H. Wolfe (Ed.), *Alfred Binet.* Chicago: University of Chicago Press. (Original work published 1904)

Binet, A. (1978). *Les idées modernes sur les enfants.* Paris: Flammnarion. (Original work published 1909)

Binet, A., & Henri, V. (1894). La mémoire des phrases (mémoire des idées). *L'Année Psychologique, 1,* 24–59.

Binet, A., & Henri, V. (1895). La psychologie individuelle. *L'Année Psychologique, 2,* 411–465.

Binet, A., Phillippe, J., Courtier, J., & Henri, V. (1894). *Introduction à la psychologie expérimentale.* Paris: Alcan.

Binet, A., & Simon, T. (1905). Méthods nouvelles pour le diagnostic du niveau intellectuel des anormaux. *L'Année Psychologique, 11,* 191–244.

Birns, B. (1984). Piaget and Wallon: Two giants of unequal visibility. In G. Voyat (Ed.), *The world of Henri Wallon* (pp. 59–65). New York: Jason Aronson.

Boring, E. G. (1950). *A history of experimental psychology.* New York: Century. (Original work published 1929)

Borstlemann, L. J. (1983). Children before psychology: Ideas about children from antiquity to the late 1800s. In P. H. Mussen (Series Ed.) & W. Kessen (Vol. Ed.), *Handbook of child psychology* (4th ed., pp. 1–80). New York: Wiley.

Bott, H. McM. (1934). *Personality development in young children.* Toronto: University of Toronto Press.

Bowlby, J. (1946). *Forty-four juvenile thieves: Their characters and home backgrounds.* London: Bailliere, Tindall & Cox.

Bowlby, J. (1952). *Maternal care and mental health* (2nd ed.). Geneva: World Health Organization.

Bowlby, J. (1958). The nature of the child's tie to his mother. *International Journal of Psycho-Analysis, 39,* 350–373.

Bowlby, J. (1969). *Attachment and loss: Vol. 1. Attachment.* New York: Basic Books.

Bowlby, J. (1973). *Attachment and loss: Vol. 2. Separation: Anxiety and anger.* New York: Basic Books.

Bretherton, I., & Waters, E. (1985). *Growing points of attachment: Theory and research.* Chicago: University of Chicago Press.

Breuer, J., & Freud, S. (1936). *Studies in hysteria* (A. A. Brill, Trans.). New York: Nervous and Mental Disease. (Original work published 1895)

Bronfenbrenner, U. (1979). *The ecology of human development: Experiments by nature and design.* Cambridge, MA: Harvard University Press.

Bronfenbrenner, U. (1993). The ecology of cognitive development: Research models and fugitive findings. In R. H. Wozniak & K. W. Fischer (Eds.), *Development in context: Acting and thinking in specific environments* (pp. 3–44). Hillsdale, NJ: Erlbaum.

Bronfenbrenner, U. (1995). Developmental ecology through space and time: A future perspective. In P. Moen, G. H. Elder, Jr., & K. Lüscher (Eds.), *Examining lives in context: Perspectives on the ecology of human development* (pp. 619–647). Washington, DC: American Psychological Association.

Broughton, J. M. (1981). The genetic psychology of James Mark Baldwin. *American Psychologist, 36,* 396–407.

Broughton, J. M., & Freeman-Moir, D. J. (1982). *The cognitive developmental psychology of James Mark Baldwin: Current theory and research in genetic epistemology.* Norwood, NJ: ABLEX.

Bruce, D. (1986). Lashley's shift from bacteriology to neuropsychology, 1910–1917, and the influence of Jennings, Watson, and Franz. *Journal of the History of the Behavioral Sciences, 22,* 27–44.

Bruner, J. (1960). *The process of education.* Cambridge, MA: Harvard University Press.

Buckley, K. W. (1989). *Mechanical man: John Broadus Watson and the beginnings of behaviorism.* New York: Guilford Press.

Bühler, C. (1927). Die ersten sozialen Verhaltungsweisen des Kindes. In *Soziologische und psychologische Studien über das erste Lebensjahr.* Jena: Fischer.

Bühler, C. (1929). Personality types based on experiments with children. *Proceedings and Papers of the 9th International Congress of Psychology,* 100–112.

Bühler, C. (1931). The social behavior of the child. In C. Murchison (Ed.), *A handbook of child psychology* (pp. 374–416). Worcester, MA: Clark University Press.

Bühler, C. (1933). The social behavior of children. In C. Murchison (Ed.), *A handbook of child psychology* (2nd ed., pp. 392–431). Worcester, MA: Clark University Press.

Bühler, K. (1930). *The mental development of the child: A summary of modern psychology theory.* New York: Harcourt Brace.

Burt, C. (1920–1921). A young girl's diary. *British Journal of Psychology: Medical Section, 1,* 353–357.

Cahan, E. D. (1984). The genetic psychologies of James Mark Baldwin and Jean Piaget. *Developmental Psychology, 20,* 128–135.

Cahan, E. D. (1994). John Dewey and human development. In R. D. Parke, P. A. Ornstein, J. J. Rieser, & C. Zahn-Waxler (Eds.), *A century of developmental psychology* (pp. 145–167). Washington, DC: American Psychological Association.

Cahan, E. D., & White, S. H. (1992). Proposals for a second psychology. *American Psychologist, 47,* 224–235.

Cairns, R. B. (1966). Attachment behavior of mammals. *Psychological Review, 73,* 409–426.

Cairns, R. B. (1976). The ontogeny and phylogeny of social behavior. In M. E. Hahn & E. C. Simmel (Eds.), *Evolution and communicative behavior* (pp. 115–139). New York: Academic Press.

Cairns, R. B. (1979). *Social development: The origins and plasticity of social interchanges.* San Francisco: Freeman.

Cairns, R. B. (1983a). The emergence of developmental psychology. In P. H. Mussen (Series Ed.) & W. Kessen (Vol. Ed.), *Handbook of child psychology: Vol. 1. History, theory, and methods* (4th ed., pp. 41–102). New York: Wiley.

Cairns, R. B. (1983b). The genesis of genetic epistemology. *Journal of the History of the Behavioral Sciences, 19,* 260–263.

Cairns, R. B. (1986). Phenomena lost: Issues in the study of development. In J. Valsiner (Ed.), *The individual subject and scientific psychology* (pp. 97–112). New York: Plenum Press.

Cairns, R. B. (1992). The making of a developmental science: The contributions and intellectual heritage of James Mark Baldwin. *Developmental Psychology, 28,* 17–24.

Cairns, R. B., & Ornstein, P. A. (1979). Developmental psychology. In E. S. Hearst (Ed.), *The first century of experimental psychology* (pp. 459–510). Hillsdale, NJ: Erlbaum.

Cairns, R. B., & Werboff, J. (1967). Behavior development in the dog: An interspecific analysis. *Science, 158,* 1070–1072.

Carmichael, L. (1933). Origin and prenatal growth of behavior. In C. Murchison (Ed.), *A handbook of child psychology* (2nd ed., pp. 31–159). Worcester, MA: Clark University Press.

Carmichael, L. (Ed.). (1946). *Manual of child psychology.* New York: Wiley.

Carolina Consortium on Human Development. (1996). A collaborative statement. In R. B. Cairns, G. H. Elder, & E. J. Costello (Eds.), *Developmental science* (pp. 1–7). New York: Cambridge University Press.

Carpenter, W. B. (1854). *Principles of comparative physiology* (4th ed.). Philadelphia: Blanchard and Lea.

Carroll, J. B., & Horn, J. L. (1981). On the scientific basis of ability testing. *American Psychologist, 36,* 1012–1020.

Cattell, J. (1890). Mental tests and measurements. *Mind, 15,* 373–381.

Challman, R. C. (1932). Factors influencing friendships among preschool children. *Child Development, 3,* 146–158.

Charlesworth, W. R. (1992). Charles Darwin and developmental psychology: Past and present. *Developmental Psychology, 28,* 5–16.

Cicchetti, D., & Cohen, D. J. (Eds.). (1995). *Developmental psychopathology.* New York: Wiley.

Claparède, E. (1930). [Autobiography]. In C. Murchison (Ed.), *A history of psychology in autobiography* (Vol. 1, pp. 63–96). Worcester, MA: Clark University Press.

Cole, M. (Ed.). (1978). *Mind in society: The development of higher psychological processes.* Cambridge: Harvard University Press.

Compayré, G. (1893). *L'évolution intellectuelle et morale de l'enfant.* Paris: Hachette.

Cooley, C. H. (1902). *Human nature and the social order.* New York: Free Press.

Costall, A. (1993). How Lloyd Morgan's canon backfired. *Journal of the History of the Behavioral Sciences, 29,* 113–122.

Costello, E. J., & Angold, A. (1996). Developmental psychopathology. In R. B. Cairns, G. H. Elder, Jr., & E. J. Costello (Eds.), *Developmental science* (pp. 168–189). New York: Cambridge University Press.

Cottrell, L. S., Jr. (1942). The analysis of situational fields in social psychology. *American Sociological Review, 7,* 370–382.

Cottrell, L. S., Jr. (1969). Interpersonal interaction and the development of the self. In D. A. Goslin (Ed.), *Handbook of socialization theory and research* (pp. 543–579). Chicago: Rand McNally.

Cremin, L. A. (1964). *The transformation of the school: Progressivism in American education, 1876–1957.* New York: Vintage Books.

Cronbach, L. J. (1957). The two disciplines of scientific psychology. *American Psychologist, 12,* 671–784.

Dahlstrom, W. G. (1985). The development of psychological testing. In G. A. Kimble & K. Schlesinger (Eds.), *Topics in the history of psychology* (Vol. 2, pp. 63–113). New York: Wiley.

Darwin, C. (1877). Biographical sketch of an infant. *Mind, 2,* 285–294.

de Beer, G. (1958). *Embryos and ancestors* (3rd ed.). London: Oxford University Press.

Dewey, J. (1899). *The school and society.* Chicago: University of Chicago Press.

Dewey, J. (1916). *Democracy and education: An introduction to the philosophy of education.* New York: Macmillan.

Dollard, J., Miller, N. E., Doob, L. W., Mowrer, O. H., & Sears, R. R. (with Ford, C. S., Hovland, C. I., & Sollenberger, R. T.). (1939). *Frustration and aggression.* New Haven, CT: Yale University Press.

Drachman, D. B., & Coulombre, A. J. (1962). Experimental clubfoot and arthrogryposis multiplex congenita. *Lancet, 283,* 523–526.

Drummond, W. B. (1907). *An introduction to child study.* London: Arnold.

Ebbinghaus, H. (1897). Über eine neue Methode zur Prüfung geistiger Fähigkeiten und ihre Anwedung bei Schulkindern. *Zeitschrift für angewandte psychologie, 13,* 401–459.

Elder, G. H., Jr., Modell, J., & Parke, R. D. (Eds.). (1993). *Children in time and place: Developmental and historical insights.* New York: Cambridge University Press.

Estes, W. K. (1944). *An experimental study of punishment* (Psychological Monographs, 57, 3). Evanston, IL: American Psychological Association.

Estes, W. K. (1954). Kurt Lewin. In W. Estes, S. Koch, K. MacCorquodale, P. Meehl, C. Mueller, Jr., W. Schoenfeld, & W. Verplanck (Eds.), *Modern learning theory* (pp. 317–344). New York: Appleton-Century-Crofts.

Fenichel, O. (1945). *The psychoanalytic theory of neurosis.* New York: Norton.

Féré, C. (1888). Note sur les modifications de la résistance électrique sous l'influence des excitations sensorielles et des émotions. *Comptes Rendus de la Société de Biologie, 40,* 217–219.

Fiske, J. (1883). *Excursions of an evolutionist.* Boston: Houghton Mifflin.

Flavell, J. H. (1963). *The developmental psychology of Jean Piaget.* Princeton, NJ: Van Nostrand.

Ford, D. H., & Lerner, R. M. (1992). *Developmental systems theory: An integrative approach.* Newbury Park, CA: Sage.

Foss, B. M. (Ed.). (1961). *Determinants of infant behavior.* New York: Wiley.

Foss, B. M. (Ed.). (1965). *Determinants of infant behavior: II.* New York: Wiley.

Frank, L. (1935). The problem of child development. *Child Development, 6,* 7–18.

Franz, S. I. (1898). [Review of the book *L'Année Psychologique* Vol. 4]. *Psychological Review, 5,* 665.

Freud, A. (1931). Psychoanalysis of the child. In C. Murchison (Ed.), *A hand-book of child psychology* (pp. 555–567). Worcester, MA: Clark University Press.

Freud, S. (1910). The origin and development of psychoanalysis. *American Journal of Psychology, 21,* 181–218.

Freud, S. (1926/1973). Psychoanalysis: Fundamentals. In *Encyclopedia Britannica* (Vol. 18). Chicago: Encyclopedia Britannica.

Freud, S. (1939). *Moses and monotheism.* New York: Random House.

Freud, S. (1957). *A general selection from the works of Sigmund Freud.* New York: Liveright.

Galton, F. (1871). *Hereditary genius: An inquiry into its laws and consequences.* New York: Appleton.

Galton, F. (1883). *Inquiries into human faculty and its development*. London: Macmillan.

Garvey, C., & Hogan, R. (1973). Social speech and social interaction: Egocentrism revisited. *Child Development, 44,* 562–568.

Gesell, A. (1928). *Infancy and human growth*. New York: Macmillan.

Gesell, A. (1931). The developmental psychology of twins. In C. Murchison (Ed.), *A handbook of child psychology* (pp. 209–235). Worcester, MA: Clark University Press.

Gesell, A. (1933). Maturation and the patterning of behavior. In C. Murchison (Ed.), *A handbook of child psychology* (2nd ed., pp. 158–203). Worcester, MA: Clark University Press.

Gesell, A., & Amatruda, C. S. (1941). *Developmental diagnosis: Normal and abnormal child development*. New York: Hoeber.

Gesell, A., & Thompson, H. (1938). *The psychology of early growth*. New York: Macmillan.

Gesell, A., & Thompson, H. (with Amatruda, C. S.). (1934). *Infant behavior: Its genesis and growth*. New York: McGraw-Hill.

Gewirtz, J. L. (1961). A learning analysis of the effects of normal stimulation, privation, and deprivation on the acquisition of social motivation and attachment. In B. M. Foss (Ed.), *Determinants of infant behavior*. New York: Wiley.

Gewirtz, J. L., & Baer, D. (1958). The effect of brief social deprivation on behaviors for a social reinforcer. *Journal of Abnormal and Social Psychology, 56,* 49–56.

Gilbert, J. A. (1894). Researches on the mental and physical development of school children. *Studies of the Yale Psychology Laboratories, 2,* 40–100.

Gilbert, J. A. (1897). Researches upon school children and college students. *University of Iowa Studies: Studies in Psychology, 1,* 1–39.

Goddard, H. H. (1911). Two thousand normal children measured by the Binet measuring scale of intelligence. *Pedagogical Seminary, 18,* 232–259.

Goldberg, S., Muir, R., & Kerr, J. (Eds.). (1995). *Attachment theory: Social, developmental, and clinical perspectives*. Hillsdale, NJ: Analytic Press.

Goodenough, F. L. (1929). The emotional behavior of young children during mental tests. *Journal of Juvenile Research, 13,* 204–219.

Goodenough, F. L. (1930a). Interrelationships in the behavior of young children. *Child Development, 1,* 29–47.

Goodenough, F. L. (1930b). Work of child development research centers: A survey. *Child Study, 4,* 292–302.

Goodenough, F. L. (1931). *Anger in young children*. Minneapolis: University of Minnesota Press.

Goodenough, F. L. (1954). The measurement of mental growth in childhood. In L. Carmichael (Ed.), *Manual of child psychology* (2nd ed., pp. 459–491). New York: Wiley.

Goodwin, C. J. (1987). In Hall's shadow: Edmund Clark Sanford, 1859–1924. *Journal of the History of the Behavioral Sciences, 23,* 153–168.

Gottlieb, G. (1973). Dedication to W. Preyer, 1841–1897. In G. Gottlieb (Ed.), *Behavioral embryology* (pp. xv–xix). New York: Academic Press.

Gottlieb, G. (1976). The roles of experience in the development of behavior and the nervous system. In G. Gottlieb (Ed.), *Neural and behavioral specificity* (pp. 3–48). New York: Academic Press.

Gottlieb, G. (1979). Comparative psychology and ethology. In E. Hearst (Ed.), *The first century of experimental psychology* (pp. 147–173). Hillsdale, NJ: Erlbaum.

Gottlieb, G. (1987). The developmental basis for evolutionary change. *Journal of Comparative Psychology, 101,* 262–272.

Gottlieb, G. (1992). *Individual development and evolution: The genesis of novel behavior*. New York: Oxford University Press.

Gould, S. J. (1977). *Ontogeny and phylogeny*. Cambridge, MA: Harvard University Press.

Grusec, J. E. (1994). Social learning theory and developmental psychology: The legacies of Robert R. Sears and Albert Bandura. In R. D. Parke, P. A. Ornstein, J. J. Rieser, & C. Zahn-Waxler (Eds.), *A century of developmental psychology* (pp. 473–497). Washington, DC: American Psychological Association.

Guthrie, E. R. (1935). *The psychology of learning*. New York: Harper.

Haeckel, E. (1866). *Generelle Morphologie der Organismen* (2 vols.). Berlin: Georg Reimer.

Haeckel, E. (1901). *The riddle of the universe at the close of the nineteenth century*. London: Watts.

Hall, C. S., & Lindzey, G. (1957). *Theories of personality*. New York: Wiley.

Hall, G. S. (1883). The contents of children's minds. *Princeton Review, 2,* 249–272.

Hall, G. S. (1885). The new psychology. *Andover Review, 3,* 120–135, 239–248.

Hall, G. S. (1888–1889). Foreword. In W. Preyer (Ed.), *The mind of the child* (Vol. 1). New York: Appleton.

Hall, G. S. (1891). The contents of children's minds on entering school. *Pedagogical Seminary, 1,* 139–173.

Hall, G. S. (1904). *Adolescence: Its psychology and its relations to physiology, anthropology, sociology, sex, crime, religion, and education* (2 vols.). New York: Appleton.

Hall, G. S. (1922). *Senescence, the last half of life.* New York: Appleton.

Hamburger, V. (1970). Von Baer: Man of many talents. *Quarterly Review of Biology, 45,* 173–176.

Harlow, H. F. (1958). The nature of love. *American Psychologist, 13,* 673–685.

Harlow, H. F., & Zimmerman, R. R. (1959). Affectional responses in the infant monkey. *Science, 130,* 421–432.

Harter, S. (1983). Developmental perspectives on the self-system. In P. H. Mussen (Series Ed.) & M. Hetherington (Vol. Ed.), *Handbook of child psychology* (4th ed.) (Vol. 4, pp. 275–386). New York: Wiley.

Hartshorne, H., & May, M. S. (1928–1930). *Studies in the nature of character* (3 vols.). New York: Macmillan.

Hay, D. F., & Angold, A. (1993). Introduction: Precursors and causes in development and pathogenesis. In D. F. Hay & A. Angold (Eds.), *Precursors and causes in development and psychopathology* (pp. 1–22). Chichester, England: Wiley.

Hearst, E. (Ed.). (1979). *The first century of experimental psychology.* Hillsdale, NJ: Erlbaum.

Herrnstein, R. J., & Murray, C. (1994). *The bell curve: Intelligence and class structure in American life.* New York: Free Press.

Hilgard, J. (1933). The effect of early and delayed practice on memory and motor performances studied by the method of cotwin control. *Genetic Psychology Monographs, 14,* 493–567.

Hinde, R. A. (1966). *Animal behavior.* New York: McGraw-Hill.

Hinde, R. A. (1970). *Animal behavior: A synthesis of ethology and comparative psychology* (2nd ed.). New York: McGraw-Hill.

Hofer, M. A. (1994). Hidden regulators in attachment, separation, and loss. *Monographs of the Society for Research in Child Development, 59*(2/3, Serial No. 240).

Hollingworth, H. L. (1927). *Mental growth and decline: A survey of developmental psychology.* New York: Appleton.

Holt, L. E. (1916). *The care and feeding of children: A catechism for the use of mothers and children's nurses* (8th ed., Rev.). New York: Appleton. (Original work published 1894)

Hood, K. E., Greenberg, G., & Tobach, E. (Eds.). (1995). *Behavioral development: Concepts of approach/withdrawal and integrative levels.* New York: Garland.

Horney, K. (1937). *The neurotic personality of our time.* New York: Norton.

Horowitz, F. D. (1992). John B. Watson's legacy: Learning and environment. *Developmental Psychology, 28,* 360–367.

Hull, C. L. (1943). *Principles of behavior.* New York: Appleton-Century-Crofts.

Hull, C. L. (1951). *Essentials of behavior.* New Haven, CT: Yale University Press.

Hunt, J. McV. (1961). *Intelligence and experience.* New York: Ronald Press.

Hurlock, E. B. (1924). The value of praise and reproof as incentives for children. *Archives of Psychology, 11*(71).

Jackson, D. D. (Ed.). (1968). *Communication, family, and marriage.* Palo Alto, CA: Science & Behavior Books.

Jacobs, J. (1887). Experiments on "prehension." *Mind, 12,* 75–79.

James, W. (1890). *The principles of psychology* (Vol. 1). New York: Macmillan.

James, W. (1894). Review of "internal speech and song." *Psychological Review, 1,* 209–210.

James, W. (1900). *Talks to teachers on psychology: And to students on some of life's ideals.* New York: Holt.

Jenkins, J. J., & Paterson, D. G. (Eds.). (1961). *Studies in individual differences: The search for intelligence.* New York: Appleton-Century-Crofts.

Jennings, H. S. (1898–1899). The psychology of a protozoan. *American Journal of Psychology, 10,* 503–515.

Jennings, H. S. (1906). *Behavior of the lower organisms.* New York: Macmillan.

Jensen, D. D. (1962). Foreword to the reprinted edition. In H. S. Jennings, *Behavior of the lower organisms* (pp. ix–xvii). Bloomington: Indiana University Press.

Jersild, A. T. (1932). *Training and growth in the development of children: A study of the relative influence of learning and maturation* (Child Development Monographs No. 10). New York: Teachers College, Columbia University Press.

Jersild, A. T., Markey, F. V., & Jersild, C. L. (1933). *Children's fears, dreams, wishes, daydreams, likes, dislikes, pleasant and unpleasant memories: A study by the interview method of 400 children aged 5 to 12* (Child Development Monographs No. 12). New York: Teachers College, Columbia University Press.

Jones, E. (1953). *The life and work of Sigmund Freud* (Vol. 1). New York: Basic Books.

Jones, H. E. (1930). The galvanic skin reflex in infancy. *Child Development, 1,* 106–110.

Jones, H. E. (1954). The environment and mental development. In L. Carmichael (Ed.), *Manual of child psychology* (2nd ed.). New York: Wiley.

Jones, M. C. (1924). A laboratory study of fear: The case of Peter. *Pedagogical Seminary, 31,* 308–315.

Jones, M. C. (1931). The conditioning of children's emotions. In C. Murchison (Ed.), *A handbook of child psychology* (pp. 71–93). Worcester, MA: Clark University Press.

Jones, V. (1933). Children's morals. In C. Murchison (Ed.), *A handbook of child psychology* (2nd ed., pp. 486–533). Worcester, MA: Clark University Press.

Kagan, J., & Moss, H. A. (1962). *Birth to maturity, a study in psychological development.* New York: Wiley.

Kamin, L. J. (1974). *The science and politics of IQ.* Hillsdale, NJ: Erlbaum.

Katz, D., & Katz, R. (1927). *Gespräche mit Kindern: Untersuchungen zur Sozialpsychologie und Pädagogik.* Berlin: Springer.

Kendler, H. H., & Kendler, T. S. (1962). Vertical and horizontal processes in problem solving. *Psychological Review, 69,* 1–16.

Kessen, W. (1965). *The child.* New York: Wiley.

Klopfer, P. H., & Hailman, J. P. (1967). *An introduction to animal behavior: Ethology's first century.* Englewood Cliffs, NJ: Prentice-Hall.

Kohlberg, L. (1969). Stage and sequence: The cognitive-developmental approach to socialization. In D. A. Goslin (Ed.), *Handbook of socialization theory and research* (pp. 347–480). Chicago: Rand McNally.

Kohlberg, L. (1982). Moral development. In J. M. Broughton & D. J. Freeman-Moir (Eds.), *The cognitive developmental psychology of James Mark Baldwin: Current theory and research in genetic epistemology* (pp. 277–325). Norwood, NJ: ABLEX.

Krasnogorski, N. I. (1925). The conditioned reflex and children's neuroses. *American Journal of Diseases in Children, 30,* 753–768.

Kreppner, K. (1992). William L. Stern, 1871–1938: A neglected founder of developmental psychology. *Developmental Psychology, 28,* 539–547.

Kreppner, K. (1994). William L. Stern: A neglected founder of developmental psychology. In R. D. Parke, P. A. Ornstein, J. J. Rieser, & C. Zahn-Waxler (Eds.), *A century of developmental psychology* (pp. 311–331). Washington, DC: American Psychological Association.

Kuenne, M. R. (1946). Experimental investigation of the relation of language to transposition behavior in young children. *Journal of Experimental Psychology, 36,* 471–490.

Kuo, H. H. (1937). A study of the language development of Chinese children. *Chinese Journal of Psychology, 1,* 334–364.

Kuo, Z.-Y. (1930). The genesis of the cat's response to the rat. *Journal of Comparative Psychology, 11,* 1–35.

Kuo, Z.-Y. (1939). Studies in the physiology of the embryonic nervous system: IV. Development of acetylcholine in the chick embryo. *Journal of Neurophysiology, 2,* 488–493.

Kuo, Z.-Y. (1967). *The dynamics of behavioral development: An epigenetic view.* New York: Random House.

Lehrman, D. S. (1953). A critique of Konrad Lorenz's theory of instinctive behavior. *Quarterly Review of Biology, 28,* 337–363.

Lehrman, D. S. (1970). Semantic and conceptual issues in the nature–nurture problem. In L. R. Aronson, D. S. Lehrman, E. Tobach, & J. S. Rosenblatt (Eds.), *Development and evolution of behavior: Essays in memory of T. C. Schneirla* (pp. 17–52). San Francisco: Freeman.

Lewin, K. (1931a). Conflict between Aristotelian and Galileian modes of thought in psychology. *Journal of General Psychology, 5,* 141–177.

Lewin, K. (1931b). Environmental forces in child behavior and development. In C. Murchison (Ed.), *A handbook of child psychology* (2nd ed., pp. 590–625). Worcester, MA: Clark University Press.

Lewin, K. (1935). *A dynamic theory of personality.* New York: McGraw-Hill.

Lewin, K. (1954). Behavior and development as a function of the total situation. In L. Carmichael (Ed.), *Manual of child psychology* (2nd ed.). New York: Wiley.

Lewin, K., Dembo, T., Festinger, L., & Sears, P. (1944). Level of aspiration. In J. McV. Hunt (Ed.), *Handbook of personality and the behavior disorders* (Vol. 1, pp. 333–378). New York: Ronald Press.

Lewin, K., Lippitt, R., & White, R. (1939). Patterns of aggressive behavior in experimentally created "social climates." *Journal of Social Psychology, 10,* 271–299.

Lewis, M., & Brooks-Gunn, J. (1979). *Social cognition and the acquisition of self.* New York: Plenum Press.

Littman, R. A. (1979). Social and intellectual origins of experimental psychology. In E. Hearst (Ed.), *The first century of experimental psychology* (pp. 39–85). Hillsdale, NJ: Erlbaum.

Loeb, J. (1964). *The mechanistic conception of life.* Cambridge, MA: Harvard University Press. (Original work published 1912)

Loomis, A. M. (1931). *A technique for observing the social behavior of nursery school children* (Child Development Monographs No. 5). New York: Teachers College, Columbia University Press.

Lorenz, K. Z. (1935). Der Kumpan in der Umwelt das Vogels. *Journal of Ornithology, 83,* 137–213.

Lorenz, K. Z. (1937). The companion in the bird's world. *Auk, 54,* 245–273.

Maccoby, E. E. (1994). The role of parents in the socialization of children: An historical overview. In R. D. Parke, P. A. Ornstein, J. J. Rieser, & C. Zahn-Waxler (Eds.), *A century of developmental psychology* (pp. 589–615). Washington, DC: American Psychological Association.

Maccoby, E. E., & Masters, J. C. (1970). Attachment and dependency. In P. H. Mussen (Ed.), *Carmichael's manual of child psychology* (3rd ed.) (Vol. 2, pp. 73–157). New York: Wiley.

Magnusson, D. (1988). *Individual development in paths through life: Vol. 1. A longitudinal study.* Hillsdale, NJ: Erlbaum.

Magnusson, D. (1995). Individual development: A holistic integrated model. In P. Moen, G. H. Elder, Jr., & K. Luscher (Eds.), *Examining lives in context: Perspectives on the ecology of human development* (pp. 19–60). Washington, DC: American Psychological Association.

Magnusson, D. (Ed.). (1996). *The lifespan development of individuals: Behavioral, neurobiological, and psychosocial perspectives: A synthesis.* New York: Cambridge University Press.

Magnusson, D., & Bergman, L. R. (1990). A pattern approach to the study of pathways from childhood to adulthood. In L. N. Robins & M. Rutter (Eds.), *Straight and devious pathways from childhood to adulthood* (pp. 101–115). Cambridge, England: Cambridge University Press.

Maher, B. A., & Maher, W. B. (1979). Psychopathology. In E. Hearst (Ed.), *The first century of experimental psychology* (pp. 561–622). Hillsdale, NJ: Erlbaum.

Maier, S. F., Seligman, M. E. P., & Solomon, R. L. (1969). Pavlovian fear conditioning and learned helplessness. In R. Church & B. Campbell (Eds.), *Punishment and adversive behavior* (pp. 299–342). New York: Appleton-Century-Crofts.

Marquis, D. B. (1931). Can conditioned responses be established in the newborn infant? *Journal of Genetic Psychology, 39,* 479–492.

Mason, W. A. (1980). Social ontogeny. In P. Marler & J. G. Vandenbergh (Eds.), *Social behavior and communication.* New York: Plenum Press.

Mason, W. A., & Kinney, M. D. (1974). Redirection of filial attachments in rhesus monkeys: Dogs as mother surrogates. *Science, 183,* 1209–1211.

Mateer, F. (1918). *Child behavior: A critical and experimental study of young children by the method of conditioned reflexes.* Boston: Badger.

McCarthy, D. (1931). Language development. In C. Murchison (Ed.), *A handbook of child psychology* (pp. 278–315). Worcester, MA: Clark University Press.

McCarthy, D. (1933). Language development in children. In C. Murchison (Ed.), *A handbook of child psychology* (2nd ed., pp. 329–373). Worcester, MA: Clark University Press.

McCarthy, D. (1946). Language development in children. In L. Carmichael (Ed.), *Manual of child psychology* (pp. 476–581). New York: Wiley.

McCarthy, D. (1954). Language development in children. In L. Carmichael (Ed.), *Manual of child psychology* (2nd ed., pp. 492–630). New York: Wiley.

McDougall, W. (1906–1908). An investigation of the colour sense of two infants. *British Journal of Psychology, 2,* 338–352.

McDougall, W. (1926). *An introduction to social psychology* (Rev. ed.). Boston: Luce.

McGraw, M. (1935). *Growth: A study of Johnny and Jimmy.* New York: Appleton-Century-Crofts.

McGraw, M. B. (1946). Maturation of behavior. In L. Carmichael (Ed.), *Manual of child psychology* (pp. 332–369). New York: Wiley.

McNemar, Q. (1940). A critical examination of the University of Iowa studies of environmental influences upon the IQ. *Psychological Bulletin, 37,* 63–92.

Mead, G. H. (1934). *Mind, self and society.* Chicago: University of Chicago Press.

Miller, N. E., & Dollard, J. (1941). *Social learning and imitation.* New York: McGraw-Hill.

Miller, N. E., Sears, R. R., Mowrer, O. H., Doob, L. W., & Dollard, J. I. (1941). The frustration-aggression hypothesis. *Psychological Review, 48,* 337–342.

Mills, W. (1898). *The nature and development of animal intelligence.* London: Unwin.

Mills, W. (1899). The nature of animal intelligence and the methods of investigating it. *Psychological Review, 6,* 262–274.

Minton, H. L. (1984). The Iowa Child Welfare Research Station and the 1940 debate on intelligence: Carrying on the legacy of a concerned mother. *Journal of the History of the Behavioral Sciences, 20,* 160–176.

Mischel, W. (1973). Toward a cognitive social learning reconceptualization of personality. *Psychological Review, 80,* 252–283.

Monroe, W. S. (1899). *Die Entwicklung des sozialen Bewusstseins der Kinder.* Berlin: Reuther & Reichard.

Morgan, C. L. (1896). *Habit and instinct.* London: Edward Arnold.

Morgan, C. L. (1902). "New statement" from Professor Lloyd Morgan. In J. M. Baldwin (Ed.), *Development and evolution* (pp. 347–348). New York: Macmillan.

Morgan, C. L. (1903). *An introduction to comparative psychology.* London: W. Scott. (Original work published 1894)

Morrison, F. J., & Ornstein, P. A. (1996). Cognitive development. In R. B. Cairns, G. H. Elder, Jr., & E. J. Costello (Eds.), *Developmental science* (pp. 121–134). New York: Cambridge University Press.

Mowrer, O. H. (1938). Apparatus for the study and treatment of enuresis. *American Journal of Psychology, 51,* 163–168.

Mueller, E. (1972). The maintenance of verbal exchanges between young children. *Child Development, 43,* 930–938.

Mueller, R. H. (1976). A chapter in the history of the relationship between psychology and sociology in America: James Mark Baldwin. *Journal of the History of Behavioral Sciences, 12,* 240–253.

Munn, N. L. (1954). Learning in children. In L. Carmichael (Ed.), *Manual of child psychology* (2nd ed., pp. 374–458). New York: Wiley.

Munn, N. L. (1965). *The evolution and growth of human behavior* (2nd ed.). Boston: Houghton Mifflin.

Munroe, R. L. (1955). *Schools of psychoanalytic thought.* New York: Dryden Press.

Murchison, C. (Ed.). (1931). *A handbook of child psychology.* Worcester, MA: Clark University Press.

Murchison, C. (Ed.). (1933). *A handbook of child psychology* (2nd ed.). Worcester, MA: Clark University Press.

Murchison, C., & Langer, S. (1927). Tiedemann's observations on the development of the mental faculties of children. *Journal of Genetic Psychology, 34,* 205–230.

Murphy, L. B. (1937). *Social behavior and child personality: An exploratory study of some roots of sympathy.* New York: Columbia University Press.

Mussen, P. H. (Ed.). (1970). *Carmichael's manual of child psychology* (2 vols.). New York: Wiley.

Oppenheim, R. W. (1973). Prehatching and hatching behavior: Comparative and physiological consideration. In G. Gottlieb (Ed.), *Behavioral embryology* (pp. 163–244). New York: Academic Press.

Oppenheimer, J. M. (1959). Embryology and evolution: Nineteenth century hopes and twentieth century realities. *Quarterly Review of Biology, 34,* 271–277.

Ornstein, P. A. (Ed.). (1978). *Memory development in children.* Hillsdale, NJ: Erlbaum.

Osborn, H. F. (1896). Ontogenetic and phylogenetic variation. *Science, 4,* 786–789.

Paris, S. G. (1978). Coordination of means and goals in the development of mnemonic skills. In P. A. Ornstein (Ed.), *Memory development in children* (pp. 259–273). Hillsdale, NJ: Erlbaum.

Paris, S. G., & Cairns, R. B. (1972). An experimental and ethological investigation of social reinforcement in retarded children. *Child Development, 43,* 717–729.

Parke, R. D., Ornstein, P. A., Rieser, J. J., & Zahn-Waxler, C. (1994). The past is prologue: An overview of a century of developmental psychology. In R. D. Parke, P. A. Ornstein, J. J. Rieser, & C. Zahn-Waxler (Eds.), *A century of developmental psychology* (pp. 1–70). Washington, DC: American Psychological Association.

Parten, M. B. (1933). Social play among preschool children. *Journal of Abnormal and Social Psychology, 28,* 136–147.

Parton, D. A., & Ross, A. O. (1965). Social reinforcement of children's motor behavior: A review. *Psychological Bulletin, 64,* 65–73.

Patterson, G. R. (1979). A performance theory for coercive family interaction. In R. B. Cairns (Ed.), *The analysis of social interactions: Methods, issues, and illustrations* (pp. 119–162). Hillsdale, NJ: Erlbaum.

Pauly, P. J. (1981). The Loeb-Jennings debate and the science of animal behavior. *Journal of the History of the Behavioral Sciences, 17,* 504–515.

Peréz, B. (1878). *La psychologic de l'enfant: Les trois premières ann'ees* [The first three years of childhood] (A. M. Christie, Ed. & Trans.). Chicago: Marquis. (Original work published 1851)

Peterson, J. (1925). *Early conceptions and tests of intelligence.* Yonkers-on-Hudson, NY: World Book.

Peterson, J. (1931). Learning in children. In C. Murchison (Ed.), *A handbook of child psychology* (pp. 316–376). Worcester, MA: Clark University Press.

Peterson, R. C., & Thurstone, L. L., (1933). Motion pictures and the social attitudes of children. In W. W. Charters (Ed.), *Motion pictures and youth* (Pt. 3, pp. 1–75). New York: Macmillan.

Piaget, J. (1926). *The language and thought of the child.* New York: Harcourt Brace. (Original work published 1923)

Piaget, J. (1931). Children's philosophies. In C. Murchison (Ed.), *A handbook of child psychology* (pp. 377–391). Worcester, MA: Clark University Press.

Piaget, J. (1951). *Play, dreams, and imitation in childhood.* New York: Norton.

Piaget, J. (1952). [Autobiography]. *A History of Psychology in Autobiography, 4,* 237–256.

Piaget, J. (1973). *Le jugement moral chez l'enfant* (4th ed.). Paris: Presses Universitaires de France. (Original work published 1932)

Piaget, J. (1978). *Behavior and evolution.* New York: Pantheon Books.

Piaget, J. (1984). The role of imitation in the development of representational thought. In G. Voyat (Ed.), *The world of Henri Wallon* (pp. 105–114). New York: Jason Aronson.

Pressey, S. L., Janney, J. E., & Kuhlen, J. E. (1939). *Life: A psychological survey.* New York: Harper.

Preyer, W. (1885). *Specielle Physiologic des Embryo.* Untersuchungen über die Lebenserscheinungen vor der Geburt. Leipzig: Grieben.

Preyer, W. (1888–1889). The mind of the child (2 vols.). New York: Appleton. (Original work published 1882)

Quine, W. V. (1981). *Theories and things.* Cambridge, MA: Belknap Press.

Reinert, G. (1979). Prolegomena to a history of life-span developmental psychology. In P. B. Baltes & O. G. Brim (Eds.), *Life-span development and behavior* (Vol. 2, pp. 205–254). New York: Academic Press.

Romanes, G. J. (1884). *Mental evolution in animals.* New York: Appleton.

Romanes, G. J. (1889). *Mental evolution in man: Origin of human faculty.* New York: Appleton.

Rosenblatt, J. S., & Lehrman, D. S. (1963). Maternal behavior of the laboratory rat. In H. L. Rheingold (Ed.), *Maternal behavior in mammals.* New York: Wiley.

Ross, D. G. (1972). *Stanley Hall: The psychologist as prophet.* Chicago: University of Chicago Press.

Rotter, J. B. (1954). *Social learning and clinical psychology.* Englewood Cliffs, NJ: Prentice-Hall.

Sameroff, A. J. (1983). Developmental systems: Contexts and evolution. In P. H. Mussen (Series Ed.) & W. Kessen (Vol. Ed.), *Handbook of child psychology: Vol. 1. History, theory, and methods* (4th ed., pp. 237–294). New York: Wiley.

Schaffer, H. R., & Emerson, P. E. (1964). The development of social attachments in infancy. *Monographs of the Society for Research in Child Development, 29*(3, Whole No. 94).

Schallenberger, M. E. (1894). A study of children's rights, as seen by themselves. *Pedagogical Seminary, 3,* 87–96.

Schneider, W. H. (1992). After Binet: French intelligence testing, 1900–1950. *Journal of the History of the Behavioral Sciences, 28,* 111–132.

Schneirla, T. C. (1933). Studies on army ants in Panama. *Journal of Comparative Psychology, 15,* 267–299.

Schneirla, T. C. (1957). Theoretical consideration of cyclic processes in Doryline ants. *Proceedings of the American Philosophical Society, 101,* 106–133.

Schneirla, T. C. (1959). An evolutionary and developmental theory of biphasic processes underlying approach and withdrawal. In M. R. Jones (Ed.), *Nebraska Symposium on Motivation, 1958* (pp. 1–42). Lincoln: University of Nebraska Press.

Schneirla, T. C. (1966). Behavioral development and comparative psychology. *Quarterly Review of Biology, 41,* 283–302.

Schneirla, T. C. (1972). Levels in the psychological capacities of animals. In L. A. Aronson, E. Tobach, J. S. Rosenblatt, & D. S. Lehrman (Eds.), *Selected writings of T. C. Schneirla* (pp. 199–237). San Francisco: Freeman.

Scott, J. P. (1962). Critical periods in behavioral development. *Science, 138,* 949–958.

Scott, J. P. (1963). *The process of primary socialization in canine and human infants* (Monographs of the Society for Research in Child Development, 28, 1). Lafayette, IN: Child Development.

Sears, R. R. (1944). Experimental analysis of psychoanalytic phenomena. In J. McV. Hunt (Ed.), *Personality and the behavior disorders* (Vol. 1, pp. 306–332). New York: Ronald Press.

Sears, R. R. (1951). A theoretical framework for personality and social behavior. *American Psychologist, 6,* 476–483.

Sears, R. R. (1975). Your ancients revisited: A history of child development. In E. M. Hetherington (Ed.), *Review of child development research* (Vol. 5). Chicago: University of Chicago Press.

Sears, R. R., Maccoby, E. E., & Levin, H. (1957). *Patterns of child rearing.* Evanston, IL: Row-Peterson.

Sears, R. R., Rau, L., & Alpert, R. (1965). *Identification and child rearing.* Stanford, CA: Stanford University Press.

Sears, R. R., Whiting, J. W. M., Nowlis, V., & Sears, P. S. (1953). Some child-rearing antecedents of aggression and dependency in young children. *Genetic Psychology Monographs, 47,* 135–234.

Senn, M. J. E. (1975). Insights on the child development movement in the United States. *Monographs of the Society for Research in Child Development, 40*(Serial No. 161).

Sewney, V. D. (1945). *The social theory of James Mark Baldwin.* New York: King's Crown Press.

Shakow, D., & Rapaport, D. (1964). *The influence of Freud on American psychology.* New York: International Universities Press.

Sherman, M., & Key, C. B. (1932). The intelligence of isolated mountain children. *Child Development, 3,* 279–290.

Shinn, M. (1893–1899). Notes on the development of a child. *University of California Publications, 1.*

Shinn, M. (1900). *Biography of a baby.* Boston: Houghton Mifflin.

Shirley, M. M. (1931). *The first two years. A study of twenty-five babies: Vol. 1. Postural and locomotor development.* Minneapolis: University of Minnesota Press.

Shirley, M. M. (1933a). *The first two years. A study of twenty-five babies: Vol. 2. Intellectual development.* Minneapolis: University of Minnesota Press.

Shirley, M. M. (1933b). *The first two years. A study of twenty-five babies: Vol. 3. Personality manifestations.* Minneapolis: University of Minnesota Press.

Siegler, R. S. (1992). The other Alfred Binet. *Developmental Psychology, 28,* 179–190.

Sigismund, B. (1856). *Kind und Welt: Vatern, Muttern und Kinderfreuden gewidmet.* Braunschweig: Vieweg.

Skeels, H. M. (1966). Adult status of children with contrasting early life experiences. *Monographs of the Society for Research in Child Development, 31*(3, Whole No. 105).

Skeels, H. M., Updegraff, R., Wellman, B. L., & Williams, H. M. (1938). A study of environmental stimulation: An orphanage preschool project. *University of Iowa Studies in Child Welfare, 15*(No. 4).

Skinner, B. F. (1938). *The behavior of organisms: An experimental analysis.* New York: Appleton-Century-Crofts.

Skinner, B. F. (1953). *Science and human behavior.* New York: Macmillan.

Smith, L. B., & Thelen, E. (Eds.). (1993). *A dynamic systems approach to development: Applications.* Cambridge, MA: MIT Press.

Solomon, R. L., & Wynne, L. C. (1953). Traumatic avoidance learning: Acquisition in normal dogs. *Psychological Monographs, 67*(No. 354).

Spalding, D. A. (1873). Instinct: With original observations in young animals. *Macmillan's Magazine, 27,* 282–293.

Spelt, D. K. (1938). Conditioned responses in the human fetus *in utero. Psychological Bulletin, 35,* 712–713.

Spemann, H. (1938). *Embryonic development and induction.* New Haven, CT: Yale University Press.

Spencer, H. (1886). *A system of synthetic philosophy: Vol. 1. First principles* (4th ed.). New York: Appleton.

Spock, B. (1946). *The common sense book of baby and child care.* New York: Duell, Sloan and Pearce.

Stern, W. (1911). *Die differentielle Psychologic in ihren methodischen Grundlagen.* Leipzig: Barth.

Stern, W. (1914). *The psychological methods of testing intelligence* (F. M. Whipple, Trans.). Baltimore: Warwick & York.

Stern, W. (1918). *Grundgedanken der personalistischen Philosophie.* Berlin: Reuther & Reichard.

Stevenson, H. W. (1965). Social reinforcement with children. In L. P. Lipsitt & C. C. Spiker (Eds.), *Advances in child development and behavior* (Vol. 2, pp. 97–126). New York: Academic Press.

Sullivan, H. S. (1940). Some conceptions of modern psychiatry. *Psychiatry, 3,* 1–117.

Sullivan, H. S. (1953). *The interpersonal theory of psychiatry.* New York: Norton.

Sulloway, F. J. (1979). *Freud, biologist of the mind: Beyond the psychoanalytic legend.* New York: Basic Books.

Sully, J. (1896a). Review of "Mental development in the child and the race: Methods and processes." *Mind, 5,* 97–103.

Sully, J. (1896b). *Studies of childhood.* New York: Appleton.

Suomi, S. J., & Harlow, H. F. (1972). Social rehabilitation of isolate-reared monkeys. *Developmental Psychology, 6,* 487–496.

Taine, H. (1876). Note sur l'acquisition du langage chez les enfants et dans l'espèce humaine. *Revue Philosophique, 1,* 3–23.

Terman, L. M. (1906). Genius and stupidity. *Pedagogical Seminary, 13,* 307–313.

Terman, L. M. (1916). *The measurement of intelligence.* Boston: Houghton Mifflin.

Terman, L. M. (1925). *Genetic studies of genius: Vol. 1. Mental and physical traits of a thousand gifted children.* Stanford: Stanford University Press.

Thelen, E., & Adolph, K. E. (1992). Arnold L. Gesell: The paradox of nature and nurture. *Developmental Psychology, 28,* 368–380.

Thelen, E., & Adolph, K. E. (1994). Arnold L. Gesell: The paradox of nature and nurture. In R. D. Parke, P. A. Ornstein, J. J. Rieser, & C. Zahn-Waxler (Eds.), *A century of developmental psychology* (pp. 357–387). Washington, DC: American Psychological Association.

Thelen, E., & Smith, L. B. (Eds.). (1994). *A dynamic systems approach to the development of cognition and action.* Cambridge, MA: MIT Press.

Thieman, T. J., & Brewer, W. F. (1978). Alfred Binet on memory for ideas. *Genetic Psychology Monographs, 97,* 243–264.

Thomas, D. S. (1929). *Some new techniques for studying social behavior* (Child Development Monographs No. 1). New York: Teachers College, Columbia University Press.

Thomas, W. I., & Thomas, D. S. (1928). *The child in America: Behavior problems and programs.* New York: Knopf.

Thompson, R. F., & Robinson, D. N. (1979). Physiological psychology. In E. Hearst (Ed.), *The first century of experimental psychology* (pp. 407–454). Hillsdale, NJ: Erlbaum.

Thorndike, E. L. (1898). Animal intelligence: An experimental study of the associative processes in animals. *Psychological Monographs, 2*(Whole No. 8).

Thurstone, L. L. (1952). [Autobiography]. A *History of Psychology in Autobiography, 5,* 295–331.

Tiedemann, D. (1787). Beobachtungen über die Entwickelung der Seelenfähigkeiten bei Kindern. *Hessische Beiträge zur Gelehrsamkeit und Kunst, 2*(2/3, Whole No. 6/7).

Tinbergen, N. (1972). *The animal in its world; explorations of an ethologist, 1932–1972.* London: Allen & Unwin.

Tolman, E. C. (1932). *Purposive behavior in animals and men.* New York: Appleton-Century-Crofts.

Tucker, W. H. (1994). Fact and fiction in the discovery of Sir Cyril Burt's flaws. *Journal of the History of the Behavioral Sciences, 30,* 335–347.

Valsiner, J. (Ed.). (1986). *The individual in scientific psychology.* New York: Plenum Press.

Valsiner, J. (1988). *Developmental psychology in the Soviet Union.* Brighton, England: Harvester Press.

Valsiner, J., & Van der Veer, R. (1988). On the social nature of human cognition: An analysis of the shared intellectual roots of George Herbert Mead and Lev Vygotsky. *Journal for the Theory of Social Behavior, 18,* 117–135.

Valsiner, J., & Van der Veer, R. (1993). The encoding of distance: The concept of the zone of proximal development and its interpretations. In R. R. Cocking & K. A. Renninger (Eds.), *The development and meaning of psychological distance* (pp. 35–62). Hillsdale, NJ: Erlbaum.

Van der Veer, R., & Valsiner, J. (1991). *Understanding Vygotsky: A quest for synthesis.* Oxford, England: Blackwell.

Viteles, M. S. (1932). *Industrial psychology.* New York: Norton.

Vonèche, J. J. (1982). Evolution, development, and the growth of knowledge. In J. M. Broughton & D. J. Freeman-Moir (Eds.), *The cognitive developmental psychology of James Mark Baldwin: Current theory and research in genetic epistemology* (pp. 51–79). Norwood, NJ: ABLEX.

Vygotsky, L. S. (1939). Thought and speech. *Psychiatry, 2,* 29–54.

Vygotsky, L. S. (1962). *Thought and language.* Cambridge, MA: MIT Press.

Vygotsky, L. S., & Luria, A. R. (1929). The function and fate of egocentric speech. *Proceedings and Papers of the 9th International Congress of Psychology,* 464–465.

Waddington, C. H. (1939). *An introduction to modern genetics.* New York: Macmillan.

Waddington, C. H. (1971). Concepts of development. In E. Tobach, L. R. Aronson, & E. Shaw (Eds.), *The biopsychology of development* (pp. 17–23). New York: Academic Press.

Wallon, H. (1984a). Genetic psychology. In G. Voyat (Ed.), *The world of Henri Wallon* (pp. 15–32). New York: Jason Aronson.

Wallon, H. (1984b). The psychological and sociological study of the child. In G. Voyat (Ed.), *The world of Henri Wallon* (pp. 205–224). New York: Jason Aronson.

Walters, R. H., & Parke, R. D. (1964). Social motivation, dependency and susceptibility to social influence. In L. Berkowitz (Ed.), *Advances in experimental social psychology* (Vol. 1, pp. 232–276). New York: Academic Press.

Warren, H. C. (1894). Review of Binet's L'introduction à la psychologie expérimentale. *Psychological Review, 1,* 530–531.

Washburn, R. W. (1929). A study of the smiling and laughing of infants in the first year of life. *Genetic Psychology Monographs, 6,* 397–537.

Watson, J. B. (1914). *Behavior: An introduction to comparative psychology.* New York: Henry Holt.

Watson, J. B. (1924). *Psychology, from the standpoint of a behaviorist* (2nd ed.). Philadelphia: Lippincott.

Watson, J. B. (1926). What the nursery has to say about instincts. In C. Murchison (Ed.), *Psychologies of 1925* (pp. 1–35). Worcester, MA: Clark University Press.

Watson, J. B. (1928). *Psychological care of infant and child.* New York: Norton.

Watson, J. B. (1936). [Autobiography]. *History of Psychology in Autobiography, 3,* 271–281.

Watson, J. B., & Morgan, J. J. B. (1917). Emotional reactions and psychological experimentation. *American Journal of Psychology, 28,* 163–174.

Watson, J. B., & Rayner, R. A. (1920). Conditional emotional reactions. *Journal of Experimental Psychology, 3,* 1–14.

Werner, H. (1948). *Comparative psychology of mental development* (Rev. ed.). Chicago: Follett. (Original work published 1940)

Wheeler, L. R. (1942). A comparative study of East Tennessee mountain children. *Journal of Educational Psychology, 33,* 321–334.

White, S. H. (1992). G. Stanley Hall: From philosophy to developmental psychology. *Developmental Psychology, 28,* 25–34.

White, S. H. (1996). The relationship of developmental psychology to social policy. In E. F. Zigler, S. L. Kagan, & N. W. Hall (Eds.), *Children, families, and governments: Preparing for the twenty-first century* (pp. 409–426). New York: Cambridge University Press.

Whiting, B. B., & Whiting, J. W. M. (1975). *Children of six cultures: A psycho-cultural analysis.* Cambridge, MA: Harvard University Press.

Whitman, C. O. (1899). Animal behavior. In E. B. Wilson (Ed.), *Biological lectures from the Marine Biological Laboratory, Wood's Hole, MA, 1898.* Boston: Ginn.

Wickens, D. D., & Wickens, C. D. (1940). A study of conditioning in the neonate. *Journal of Experimental Psychology, 26,* 94–102.

Wilson, E. O. (1975). *Sociobiology: The new synthesis.* Cambridge, MA: Harvard University Press.

Wohlwill, J. (1973). *The study of behavioral development.* New York: Academic Press.

Wolf, T. H. (1973). *Alfred Binet.* Chicago: University of Chicago Press.

Wozniak, R. J. (1982). Metaphysics and science, reason and reality: The intellectual origins of genetic epistemology. In J. M. Broughton & D. J. Freeman-Moir (Eds.), *The cognitive developmental psychology of James Mark Baldwin: Current theory and research in genetic epistemology* (pp. 13–45). Norwood, NJ: ABLEX.

Wozniak, R. J. (Ed.). (1993). *The roots of behaviourism.* London: Routledge/Thoemmes Press.

Wozniak, R. J. (Ed.). (1995). *Mind, adaptation, and childhood.* London: Routledge/Thoemmes Press.

Wundt, W. (1907). *Outlines of psychology* (C. H. Judd, Trans.). New York: Stechert.

Wundt, W. (1916). *Elements of folk psychology: Outlines of a psychology history of the development of mankind.* New York: Macmillan.

Yarrow, M. R., Campbell, J. D., & Burton, R. V. (1968). *Child rearing: An inquiry into research and methods.* San Francisco: Jossey-Bass.

Young, K. (1924). The history of mental testing. *Pedagogical Seminary, 31,* 1–48.

Zazzo, R. (1984). Who is Henri Wallon? In G. Voyat (Ed.), *The world of Henri Wallon* (pp. 7–14). New York: Jason Aronson.

Zenderland, L. (1988). From psychological evangelism to clinical psychology: The child-study legacy. *Journal of the History of the Behavioral Sciences, 24,* 152–165.

CHAPTER 3

Developmental Psychology: Philosophy, Concepts, and Methodology

WILLIS F. OVERTON

The broad basic question I address in this chapter concerns the nature of contemporary developmental psychology and how it functions. We know that developmental psychology is a knowledge-building enterprise of some type, but it is important to begin inquiry with a question, rather than with a particular definitional answer. A definition tends to close, rather than open, some fundamental features of inquiry. Any specific definition of developmental psychology and its mission necessarily emerges out of some complex set of concepts. This set forms a platform, a context, or a conceptual base for the entire domain. The base, like the foundation of a building, gives form to the structure that arises from it. Design the foundation in one fashion, and the building that emerges has a particular shape and functions in a particular way. Construct the foundation differently, and a different building and alternative functions emerge. Fail to create a sound foundation, and risk the later collapse of the whole enterprise. When texts begin with the words "Development is . . ." or "Developmental psychology is . . . ," that definition points backward to the nature of the specific conceptual base and forward to the nature of the mission to be accomplished. In its forward-looking function, such a definition signals the empirical, methodological, and theoretical dimensions of the complete edifice.

In building a house, or a domain of knowledge, special differentiated skills are needed. One may, of course, be a

The writing of this chapter was partially supported by a research leave granted by Temple University.

master builder who possesses all the necessary skills for all phases of the construction process, but even in this case, there is a recognition of the functionally differentiated nature of groups of skills. In this functional differentiation, the empirical investigator is much like a building contractor who has characteristic skills in the pragmatics of manipulating materials that operate in the service of discovering the best possible fit, given the suggested design. Many a design has been modified and even discarded in the process of trying to actually build a house—or a domain of knowledge. The theorist is the architect, creating designs that suggest an order and an organization that are more or less expected to work for the contractor. Although designs get modified, few contractors would be without a design when working on any complex activity. Designs guide and give meaning to projects.

Along with the design and building functions and their associated skills, a third function and set of skills—those of the structural engineer—are of critical importance in building a house. The structural engineer ensures that the foundation will successfully carry the planned weight load. The structural engineer's skills lie in analyzing foundations and selecting, rejecting, and modifying foundations according to issues of internal coherence and the functions that the building will ultimately serve.

Structural engineering in the world of inquiry is the domain of philosophy. Philosophy's traditional function has been *conceptual clarification*—exploring conceptual foundations and ensuring that they can carry the intended load. The aim of this chapter is to examine and explore several diverse contexts that have constituted the source of our understanding of the nature and functioning of developmental psychology. We will see that these lead and have led to quite different knowledge edifices, and we will ask whether these alternative structures are all equally viable. Thus, this chapter is primarily a work of structural engineering. However, as already suggested, the functions of the three roles of knowledge building should never be, and, in fact, can never be isolated. As a consequence, foundations will be examined in the context of their implications for the concepts, theories, methodology, methods, and procedures of developmental psychology.

Before directly addressing fundamental presuppositions that carry the load and give shape to the domain of inquiry called developmental psychology, it is important at the beginning to try to remove an obstacle that could impede this project. For years, psychology in general—and developmental psychology, specifically—has taught students that structural engineering does not count. Psychologists in training have long been taught that philosophical issues do not count; and if philosophical issues do not count, why in the world should one proceed to examine the arguments presented in this chapter? Traditionally, students of psychology have been instructed that while conceptual *clarification* may be the province of philosophy, conceptual *application* is the province of psychology, and the two domains must be kept separate and distinct. More broadly, the claim has been that philosophy is the province of reason and its general form, reflection, and that psychology is a science and consequently limits itself to observation and experimentation.

This negating of the importance of examining fundamental presuppositions is often reinforced by a narrative of the 19th-century historical split when psychology broke away from philosophy to pursue its own observational and experimental aims. Another chapter in the same story tells of psychology's allegiance to a "scientific method" of observation, causation, and induction, and *only* observation, causation, and induction. The point of all of this instruction is to warn students to distrust and avoid reflective activities involved in conceptual clarification. This warning itself, however, derives from the basic *conceptual presupposition* that reason and reflection are mysterious and can only be clarified after sufficient empirical observations have been compiled. Morris R. Cohen, a philosopher, captured the spirit of this point of view as far back as 1931:

> Modernistic anti-rationalism is bent on minimizing the role of reason in science. . . . According to the currently fashionable view, it is of the very essence of scientific method to distrust all reason and to rely on the facts only. The motto, "Don't think; find out," often embodies this attitude. Scientific method is supposed to begin by banishing all preconceptions or anticipations of nature. In the first positive stage it simply collects facts; in the second, it classifies them; then it lets the facts themselves suggest a working hypothesis to explain them. (1931, p. 76)

Over the past 40 or so years, many powerful arguments have been mounted against this split between reason and observation and the subsequent denial of reflection. Some of these arguments will be discussed later in this chapter. Indeed, enough arguments have emerged that the attitude itself has often been declared dead, as, for example, in the frequently made claim that positivism is dead. And yet, like the mythical hydra, new forms of this split continue to appear and exert a contextual shaping effect. Sometimes the split is found in the disparagement of reason itself, as in some contemporary versions of what has been called "postmodern" thought. Sometimes the split is found in various explicit and implicit attacks against theory, as in a particular rhetoric that states that all theories must be induced directly from observations or be "data-based." Sometimes it is found in a dogmatic retort given to any reflective critique—"That's just philosophy." Often it is found in the celebration of the analytic over the synthetic, as when analytic methods are presented as the only acceptable tools for expanding our knowledge domain. Frequently it is found in valuing the instrumental over the expressive, as when behavior is understood *only* in the context of success or failure of adjustment to some external criteria, and *never* as an index or expression of an embodied self-organizing system that constitutes the person (see Overton, in press).

In whatever of these or other multiple forms it appears, the most significant point to emphasize is that the split between reason and observation, along with the subsequent disparagement of reason and reflection, is itself the direct consequence of a conceptual presupposition favoring a particular type of knowledge building. The presupposition operates as a specific foundation for building. It is not, in itself, a given in any self-evident or directly observational fashion. That is, it is simply *a specific claim* and, as with any claim or argument, reasons must be presented for the value of the claim. These reasons and the claim itself require reflection on and clarification of the conceptual foundation on which they rest before they can be rationally accepted as valid or invalid. It is just possible that the split between reason and observations is part of a very bad foundation for our discipline, but this cannot be decided without further exploring foundational issues.

THE CONCEPT OF DEVELOPMENT

We can start our exploration of the nature of developmental psychology and its mission by first focusing on development broadly and later discussing psychology. We begin with the one feature of development that receives universal agreement. Above all else, development is about *change*.

Whatever disagreements may arise—and they do arise very rapidly—change is our foremost concern and is therefore the focus of our inquiry. The recognition that change is fundamental immediately leads to the question of the characterization of change that should frame our understanding of development. One of the most popular characterizations of developmental change, at least among developmental psychologists, has been the idea that development is defined as "changes in observed behavior across age." This understanding is certainly a quick and ready pragmatic definition suitable to act as an operational guide to a series of empirical investigations. However, if this understanding were used to give a broad meaning to the domain of inquiry called development, some very significant problems would emerge.

First, consider the idea that change in this definition is linked to age. On any close examination, it becomes clear that although age may operate fairly well at an observational level of discourse, on a reflective level it fails to make any meaningful distinctions. Age has no unique qualities that differentiate it from time; age is simply one index of time. Further, there is nothing unique or novel about units of age–time, such as years, months, weeks, minutes, and so on. Should we then say that development is about changes that occur in time? But all change occurs "in" time, and we therefore come back to simply saying that development is about change. The implication here is that, to arrive at meaningful distinctions that can direct a broad area of inquiry, we will have to explore further the nature of change itself. Before doing this, however, we shall consider a second problematic outcome of defining development as "changes in observed behavior across age." This is the problem of the meaning of "change of observed behavior."

The Expressive-Constitutive Person and the Instrumental-Communicative Person

Behavior is clearly the observational focus of our empirical investigations—the dependent variable of our research efforts. The problem is whether "change in observed behavior" introduces the kind of reflective distinction needed to articulate a broad field of inquiry. Observed behavior, or *action,* more generally speaking—at any level from the neuronal to the molar—can reflect and has been thought of as reflecting both *expressive-constitutive* and *instrumental-communicative* functions. Expressive action reflects some fundamental organization or systems. For example, in human ontogenesis we sometimes speak of cognitive systems, affective systems, and motivational systems. Constitutive action refers to the creative function of human action; to the making of new behaviors, new intentions, new meanings. Instrumental action is understood as a means to attaining some outcome; it is the pragmatic dimension of action. Again, in human ontogenesis a cognition or thought may be the means to solve a problem; the emotion of crying may lead to acquiring a caregiver; or walking around may be instrumental in acquiring nourishment. Communicative action extends action into the domain of the intersubjective. As Taylor (1995) points out, the expressive-constitutive is the process whereby we come "to have the world we have," and the instrumental-communicative is the process whereby "we order the things in that world" (p. ix). Both expressive-constitutive and instrumental-communicative functions of action have been the focus of developmental investigations. However, confusions arise that impact on inquiry, unless the reflective distinction is made explicit.

Consider some examples from human ontogenesis that make either expressive-constitutive functions or instrumental-communicative functions the focus of inquiry. Investigations of the infant–caregiver attachment relationship measure the proximity-seeking action of the child. When considered as proximity seeking per se, the action has an instrumental character. Bowlby and his colleagues (1958), however, are primarily interested in this action as an expression of an underlying attachment organization; hence, their focus is on the expressive. Piagetian tasks such as the object permanence task or the conservation task, from an instrumental perspective, constitute successful or unsuccessful problem-solving activities. Piaget and his colleagues, however, focus on the tasks as expressions of particular types of cognitive organization. On the other hand, while students' grade point average may be understood as reflecting, in part, some intellectual organization, the focus of a number of social-cognitive investigations has been on the instrumental quality of this action as an adjustment to the social-cultural context. Similarly, walking can be examined from the point of view of its expression of a certain form of physical organization, but some investigators have focused on walking as instrumental to locomotion or reaching a goal. Emotions also may be explored as expressions of affective organization (e.g., Boesch, 1984; Sroufe, 1979) or as instrumental in attaining a particular

outcome (e.g., Campos, Campos, & Barrett, 1989). Finally, although language development may be investigated as a means of communicative functioning, it may be, and has been, alternatively examined as an expression of affective/cognitive organization (Bloom, 1993, Ch. 7, Volume 2).

From these and other examples, it becomes clear that any action can be understood from the perspective of either its expressive-constitutive or its instrumental-communicative functions. *Neither* the expressive-constitutive *nor* the instrumental-communicative functions are given to direct observation; *both* are reflective characterizations drawn and refined from commonsense understandings, and each may be a legitimate focus of inquiry. When, however, the distinction between expressive-constitutive and instrumental-communicative is not made explicit, "observed behavior" becomes ambiguous. This ambiguity fosters confusion about the specific aim of inquiry and allows implicit values to seep in, eventually splitting and contextualizing the field without benefit of critical examination. For example, consider what occurs when "observed behavior" is implicitly framed by historical behavioristic and positivistic values. Because behaviorism and positivism excluded the idea that "organization" or "system" could be fundamental to inquiry, "observed behavior" became implicitly identified with the instrumental-communicative and *only* the instrumental-communicative. This led to a belief that we, in fact, directly *see* instrumental-communicative action and that any other function must be indirect, inferred, or derived. Thus, in this scenario, a kind of implicit split was created between the expressive-constitutive and the instrumental-communicative—a split that resulted in suppression of the expressive-constitutive as a legitimate primary object of inquiry. At best, expressive-constitutive change became treated as epiphenomenal, as a feature to be explained by the fundamental instrumental-communicative change. The opposite scenario could be proposed as an alternative example: "Expressive" and "observed" behavior could be merged in an identification that resulted in the instrumental being devalued as an object of developmental inquiry.

Failure to make the expressive/instrumental distinction concerning "observed behavior" leads to a split where dichotomies compete with each other for the title of "legitimate" or "significant" or "meaningful" inquiry. The split, in turn, has a ripple effect that impacts on both theory and method. For example, to a significant degree, the classical battles between the Piagetians, Wernerians, and Eriksonians on the expressive-constitutive side and the Skinnerians,

Spence-Hull Learning Theorists, and Social Learning Theorists of the Dollard and Miller school on the instrumental-communicative side represented exactly this split. Each side, if not the principal figures themselves, classically assumed that its part constituted the whole. With respect to methods, the effects are more subtle, or at least less explored. For example, an examination of issues of validity and reliability illustrates that validity is central to expressive interests, and reliability is central to instrumental interests. The often-repeated Research Methods 101 lesson, which privileges reliability with the claim that reliability concerns must be the starting of measurement, is a story told by classical instrumentalists.

To explicitly assert the distinction between expressive-constitutive and instrumental-communicative functions of action is to make an assertion of inclusivity. The distinction recognizes that each function assumes a legitimate role in a unified whole of developmental inquiry and that the nature of inquiry is always relative to the goals of inquiry. The distinction suggests that there is a value to considering change in a relational context in which features that would be held to be dichotomous in an otherwise split context are represented as alternative lines of sight on the same object of inquiry. From this relational perspective, then, issues associated with ambiguities arising from contextualizing development as "changes in observed behavior" are reduced significantly by insisting on the substitution of the phrase "changes in expressive-constitutive and instrumental-communicative features of observed behavior." This substitution does not, however, resolve the problem of exactly what kinds of change should be called developmental. For this problem, further reflection on change itself is needed.

Transformational Change and Variational Change

If developmental inquiry is to be an inclusive discipline, it seems reasonable to approach the issue of "developmental change" from as broad a perspective as possible. From such a perspective, two identifiable types of change appear that offer themselves as candidates for inclusion under the concept "developmental":

1. *Transformational change* refers to change in form, pattern, or organization. This is morphological change. As forms change, novel forms result; consequently, transformational change involves the emergence of novelty.

As forms change, they become increasingly complex. This increased complexity is a complexity of pattern rather than a linear additive complexity of elements. In other words, transformational complexity is holistic in nature. The philosopher E. Nagel referred to this type of change when he claimed that the term "development" implies two fundamental features: (a) "the notion of a system, possessing a definite structure [i.e., organization] . . ."; and (b) "the notion of a set of sequential changes in the system yielding relatively permanent but novel increments not only in its structures [i.e., organization] but in its modes of operation as well" (1957, p. 17).

2. *Variational change* refers to the degree or extent that a change varies from an assumed standard. Variational change can be understood as quantitative in nature—an increase or decrease from the standard—or as qualitative in terms of specific differences among the variants. In either case, the complexity of variational change is often thought of as additive.

Embryological changes constitute some of the clearest and most concrete examples of transformational or morphological change (Edelman, 1992; Gottlieb, 1992). Through processes of differentiation and reintegration, movement occurs from the single-celled zygote to the highly organized functioning systems of the nine-month fetus. Some cognitive and social-emotional phenomena of human ontogenesis may also be thought of as reflecting transformational change. For example, action may undergo a sequence of transformations to become symbolic thought, and further transformations lead to a reflective symbolic thought exhibiting novel logical characteristics. Memory may reflect transformational changes moving from recognition memory to recall memory. The sense of self and identity (Ball & Chandler, 1989; Damon & Hart, 1988; Nucci, 1996) have been portrayed by some as moving through a sequence of transformations. Emotions have been understood as differentiations from an initial relatively global affective matrix (Lewis, 1993; Sroufe, 1979). Physical changes, such as changes in locomotion, have also been conceptualized as transformational changes (Thelen & Ulrich, 1991).

At any given level of form, there are quantitative and qualitative variants that constitute variational change. If thinking is understood as undergoing transformational change, then, at any given transformational level, variational changes are reflected in variants of thought (e.g., analytic styles and synthetic styles). If emotions are presented as undergoing transformational change, then, at any transformational level, variational change is reflected, for example, in differences in the degree of emotionality (more or less anxious, empathic, altruistic, and so on). If identity is thought of as undergoing transformational change, then, at any transformational level, there is variational change in the type of identity assumed (e.g., individualistic or communal). If memory undergoes transformational change, there is variational change in differences in memory capacity, memory style, and memory content.

Transformational change has been identified with normative issues such as changes typical of physical systems or changes typical of phyla, species, and individuals. The focus of interest here concerns sequences of universal forms whose movement defines a path or trajectory. Concepts of irreversibility, discontinuity (nonadditivity), sequence, and directionality are associated with transformational change. Variational change has been identified with differential issues across and within individuals and groups. Here, interest has focused on local individual and group differences that suggest a particularity and a to-and-fro movement of change. Concepts of reversibility, continuity, and cyclicity are associated with variational change. When change is considered in terms of both life forms and physical systems, transformational change is identified with what has been called the "Arrow of Time," and variational change is identified with the notion of the "Cycles of Time" (Overton, 1994a, 1994b; Valsiner, 1994).

Like changes in expressive-constitutive and instrumental-communicative action, transformational and variational changes are not distinctions of direct observation but characterizations reflectively drawn and refined from commonsense understandings. Water changes in form from gas to liquid to ice. The seasons cycle each year. A seedling grows into an oak tree, but the height and size of oak trees vary. A person changes in both form and function during growth from embryo to adult. As a reflective characterization, the transformational/variational distinction also parallels the expressive/instrumental in being open to alternative contextual interpretations. On the one hand, each type of change can be framed as an analytic distinction constructed within a relational matrix. This relational frame is one in which transformation and variation are represented as differing perspectives on the same object of inquiry—developmental change. The value of

this interpretation is that it offers the possibility of analytic distinctions made within a framework of inclusiveness. On the other hand, each type of change can be interpreted within the more typical split context. The split frame results in the view that analytic distinctions are true cuts of nature in which *either* transformational change *or* variational change represents "true" change, reflecting the "real" nature of the object of inquiry. As will be discussed in greater detail later in this chapter, the split context suffers from the fact that it demands exclusivity, which becomes masked as an analytic ideal.

When transformational/variational change, and changes in expressive-constitutive/instrumental-communicative action are cast into a relational matrix, they reflect alternative images of the totality of developmental change. The *expressive-constitutive/instrumental-communicative dimension articulates what it is that changes during development.* It is the *subject* and *subject's* action that becomes foreground along this line of sight. Piaget and Skinner, for example, each construct a radically different vision of the nature of the changing subject, but both focus on the subject. Piaget, himself, regards expressive and instrumental to each be essential features of what changes. "Schemes," and "operations" are identified as the source of the subject's expressive-constitutive action, while "procedures" are conceived as instrumental strategies designed to succeed in the actual world. For Skinner, on the other hand, the expressive is denied or marginalized, and "operants" represent the subject's instrumental adjustments to a changing environment. The *transformational/variational dimension articulates the quality of the change taking place.* Here, it is the *action* rather than the function of the action that becomes the foreground. Here actions that are expressive/instrumental in function, vary and transform. Later in the chapter, for example, the neo-Darwinian theory of evolutionary change will be discussed, as will systems theory. In these cases, the primary focus is on variational and transformational change of action while the expressive/instrumental functions of the action fade to the background.

Casting the dimensions of what changes, and the quality of change, as complementary points of view reveals that the dimension components can be recombined depending on the goal of inquiry. Thus, for example, it is possible to form a transformational/expressive-constitutive dimension. This focus highlights inquiry into the sequence of system changes—whether affective, emotional, physical, or cognitive system—which become reflected in sequential changes in cognitive/affective meanings that the subject projects onto its world. Similarly, the variational/instrumental-communicative dimension can be thought of as focusing inquiry on variational changes in action that result in procedures—again whether affective, emotional, physical, cognitive, and so on—which the subject employs in adjustment and adaptation.

These preliminary reflections on changes in expressive/instrumental action and transformational/variational change provide a base from which it is possible to suggest a relatively inclusive definition of development that moves beyond the ambiguities of "change in observed behavior across age" and more reasonably begins to carry the load of all of developmental inquiry. Development within this context is understood to refer to *formal (transformational) and functional (variational) changes in the expressive-constitutive and instrumental-communicative features of behavior.* Behavior is understood broadly as action in this definition, thus not limiting developmental inquiry to a specific field of investigation. Disciplines as diverse as history, anthropology, philosophy, sociology, evolutionary biology, neurobiology, and psychology, as well as natural science investigations of system changes, all become potential forms of developmental inquiry. Developmental change within this inclusive definition includes at least phylogenesis (i.e., the development of phyla, or evolutionary change); ontogenesis (i.e., the development of the individual); embryogenesis (i.e., the development of the embryo); microgenesis (i.e., development across short time scales, such as the development of an individual percept or individual memory); pathogenesis (i.e., the development of pathology); and orthogenesis (i.e., normal development). From this perspective, developmental inquiry necessarily becomes interdisciplinary and comparative in nature.

This inclusive relational definition of development is a starting point for further excursions both backward, into the fundamental context that frames the definition (and frames other basic features of developmental inquiry), and forward to conceptual, theoretical, and methodological consequences of understanding development in this fashion. For example, in looking forward to consequences of this understanding, light is cast on a significant but often obscured conceptual feature of some of the classical developmental controversies. Consider the following frequently debated questions: Is development universal (typical of most people, regardless of specific biological circumstances, culture, or social background) or particular (typical of only some people)? Is development directional (irreversible) or reversible? What changes in development: expressive organization or instrumental behaviors? Is development continuous (linear; capable of being represented additively) or discontinuous (nonlinear, i.e., emergent novel forms appear).

These and other questions represent controversies because, and only because, they cast the fundamental nature of development into a split frame of reference. The split is illustrated by the categorical either/or form of the questions. Within this split frame, all fundamental questions become "Which one?" Thus, as suggested earlier, this conceptual prejudice advances the argument that one or the other member of the pair necessarily constitutes the "real" feature of development, and the opposite member is only apparently real. Once framed in this split fashion, it is generally further assumed that some set of empirical investigations will ultimately record a definitive answer to the either/or question. The simple empirical observation that generations of empirical investigations have failed to resolve any of these issues demonstrates the inadequacy of this assumption. Nevertheless, the fundamental conceptual prejudice continues to hold the controversies in place as controversies. The move to defining development as transformational/variational and expressive/instrumental is a movement away from this prejudice. It is a step toward healing the either/or split by asserting the reality of both members of the bipolar relationship.

From this relational position, "Which one?" questions become inappropriate, and inquiry is directed toward exploring the nature of the functioning of each pole of the bipolar relationship and exploring the relationship between the poles. Thus, for example, from this relational position it is possible to assert with some confidence, on both rational and empirical grounds, that while the content of memory or memory strategies, as well as the content of thinking or thinking styles, is particular (variable change), recall memory and symbolic thought are typical acquisitions of all human ontogenesis (transformational change). Similarly, there would appear to be little doubt that a raised grade point average can be reversed (variable change), but this in no way denies that the movement from babbling to language may be more profitably understood as sequential and directional and, hence, irreversible (transformational change). Reflection, as well as commonsense observation, suggests that there is some coherence to behavior and that this coherence expresses meaning (expressive); yet, at the same time, there is little to deny that this activity functions in the context of a world that imposes demands on it (variable, instrumental). Reflection on several scientific disciplines, as well as commonsense observation, also suggests that in some arenas transformational novelty emerges, while in others changes are reasonably represented as additive (variational).

This conceptual illustration of the opening of developmental inquiry to a relational understanding without fundamental "Which one?" questions, or their surrogate, "How much?" (Anastasi, 1958) questions, has ripple effects that move out from conceptual issues themselves to implications for empirical methodology. The most general implication is that empirical inquiry in this context abandons the aim of broad-based debunking found in instrumentalist approaches to science (see the later discussion of methodology). When a relational methodological understanding emerges, questions such as whether stages exist (transformational change, discontinuity, sequence) or are absent (variational change, continuity) in cognitive/affective/social development simply disappear. In place of questions of this sort, inquiry that focuses on the transformational pole of change would, as a part of that type of inquiry, empirically examine the plausibility of various models of stage change. Inquiry focused on variational change would be explicitly recognized as irrelevant to stage issues as such, and relevant to issues such as the stability of individual differences across age, time, or stages. Further, this recognition of change-specific inquiry leads to a recognition of the importance of change-specific techniques of measurement. In this example, investigations whose central aim is to examine transformational (stage, sequence, discontinuity) features of change often call for the application of contemporary order-scaling techniques and correlational techniques to assess patterns, both synchronic and diachronic (see later discussion of methodology and, e.g., Bond & Bunting, 1995; Henning & Rudinger, 1985; Kingma & Van Den Bos, 1989). Studies of variational change (stability, continuity) and of tracing the trajectory of variational change (i.e., the developmental function) typically call for traditional correlational procedures and traditional experimental procedures (see later discussion of methodology, and, e.g., Appelbaum & McCall, 1983).

The major point is that casting our fundamental understanding of development into an inclusive relational frame has profound implications for the concepts and theories, as well as the methodology and methods, of developmental inquiry. The next section illustrates the critical nature of these implications by examining a complementary case in which a particular variety of developmental change (i.e., evolutionary change) was cast historically into a split frame and then generalized as a broad metatheoretical model for other areas of developmental investigation, including human ontogenesis. This case history will describe the problems associated with this split model interpretation and will explore a proposed remedy of moving our intellectual grounding to the kind of relational perspective just noted.

Following the description of a relational developmental metanarrative that will ground and sustain an inclusive understanding of development, there will be a section devoted to epistemological/ontological issues. There, a history of the metaphysical traditions that present the conceptual framework for split and relational approaches will be described, along with the implications for concepts and theories of development drawn from these traditions. Finally, these traditions will serve as background for a section exploring split and relational approaches to the methodology and methods of developmental psychology.

SPLIT AND RELATIONAL MODELS OF DEVELOPMENTAL CHANGE

Several points are to be kept in mind in considering this history of evolutionary interpretation. First, the interpretation to be described constitutes a split position because it severs variational change from transformational change and assigns a privileged status to variational change. In other words, this position makes variational change "the real" and asserts that the appearance of transformational change must be understood as variational change hidden in some disguise.

Second, the fragmentation that emerges from the split position does not simply frame descriptive categories of change; it extends into the explanation of change. The nature of explanation and the relationship of description and explanation will be discussed in a later section on methodology. Here, it is important to recognize that split positions assert the priority of individual elements over the relational whole. Consequently, split positions assign either/or explanatory values to the segregated individual elements. Traditionally, the elements are treated as "causes," and the two broad classes of elements used to explain change are "biological" causes or factors and "social-cultural" causes or factors. Thus, it is assumed within a split position that all change can be totally explained by one or the other, or by some *additive combination* of these two elementary foundational factors (Anastasi, 1958; Schneirla, 1956, 1957).

The split position is most obvious when framed as a classical "Which one?" question. Here the claim is made that any developmental outcome is fundamentally caused by biological factors or fundamentally caused by social-cultural factors. However, today, few would admit to such a bold posture, and the additive "compromise" would be suggested instead. This compromise comes in two types: (a) A quantitative type claims that a developmental outcome is caused to x extent by biological factors and to y extent by social-cultural factors. Note, however, that this claim is no different in form than the claim that development is caused either 100% by biological factors or 100% by social-cultural factors. Only the numbers have been changed; the split remains (see Anastasi, 1958; Lerner, 1986; Overton, 1973). (b) A qualitative type of additive compromise asserts that biological factors *a, b, c,* and social-cultural factors *d, e,* and *f* combine additively to yield a complete explanation of change. This is the solution most directly suggested by the evolutionary story to be described. But again, this compromise in no way changes the form of the argument; the split remains.

The explanatory categories generated by split positions stand in contrast to those generated by relational positions. As will be elaborated later, relational positions aim to heal the biological/social-cultural split both by offering categories that describe the biological and the social-cultural as alternative ways of viewing the same whole (see Gollin, 1981; Gottlieb, 1992; Lerner, 1986; Overton, 1973, 1994a; Tobach, 1981) and by suggesting that action constitutes a broad-based mechanism of development that itself differentiates into biological and social-cultural manifestations (Eckenesberger, 1989; Oppenheimer, 1991a, 1991b; Overton, 1994c).

The third and final point about the story of evolutionary change concerns the level of discourse at which the splits between transformational and variational change and between biological and social-cultural factors operate. Ear-

lier, the differentiation between the observational and the reflective was alluded to in the discussion of the relation between observation and reason in knowledge-building activity. Now, this differentiation needs to be refined to recognize several reflective levels (see Figure 3.1).

If "nature," "the real," or "the true" were the aim of knowledge building, then the *observational level of discourse* is talk about one's current understanding of nature. For example, I might see/understand/experience the change from childhood to adolescence as full of *Sturm und Drang*, as a smooth passage, or as some of both. Regardless of which characterization I select, and whether or not I generalize, this understanding is my observational level of dealing with the world, my commonsense level of understanding the nature of things. At one point historically, commonsense understanding about evolution or species change was that

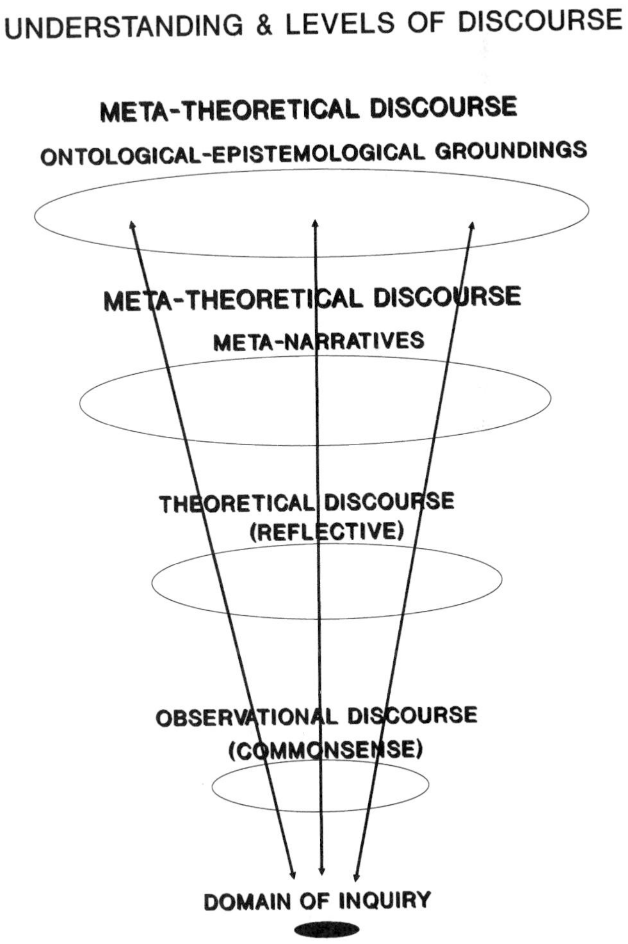

UNDERSTANDING & LEVELS OF DISCOURSE

Figure 3.1 Levels of discourse in understanding a domain of inquiry.

species were static and evolution did not occur. Today, our commonsense understanding is that evolution does occur.

Although the observational, commonsense, or folk understanding has a sense of immediacy and concreteness, we can and do focus our attention on this commonsense understanding and we do think about it. In so doing, we have moved to a reflective level of understanding where the first critical differentiation is that of the theoretical level of discourse. Here, thought is about organizing and assigning values to observational understandings. The *theoretical level of discourse* is talk about observational understanding, and this talk may itself range from informal hunches to highly refined theories about the nature of things, including human behavior and evolution. Thus, I may have a hunch that, despite other observations, the transition to adolescence is fundamentally one of crisis. At the same time, I may or may not support a Freudian or Eriksonian theory of the transition to adolescence. Similarly, I may have a hunch about how evolution works, and may or may not support some variety of Darwinian theory.

There is, however, a second differentiation of the reflective level that is critical for inquiry: the metatheoretical level of discourse. At this level, thought organizes the reflections of the theoretical level and assigns values to reflected thought. The *metatheoretical level of discourse* is talk about reflective understandings. This discourse may entail ontological values about the nature of things as well as epistemological values about our theory of how we know. This discourse may also entail casting the abstract features of theories onto a broader stage where they come to operate as models for domains far beyond their original scope. Consider an example concerning ontology (i.e., the nature of "the real"). At the metatheoretical level, I may find that my support for the Eriksonian theory of the transition to adolescence is informed by my understanding of change as entailing both transformation (discontinuity) and variation (continuity). In a similar fashion, I may find that my support for Darwinian theory is tempered by its exclusive reliance on an understanding of change involving only variation. But it is also the case that, at this metatheoretical level, Darwin's theory of species change can become generalized as a model of change across a broad spectrum of domains of inquiry (see Gould, 1993); just as, earlier, the Newtonian theory of matter became generalized as a model of all nature. In fact, this casting of a particular notion of evolution onto the metatheoretical stage, along with

implications for other domains, becomes the central focus of the story of evolution.

Given the several levels of discourse, where do the splits between transformational and variational change and between biological and social-cultural factors operate? For the investigator who functions within a split frame, the guiding *assumption* is that splits are fundamental cuts of nature. Consequently, observational, theoretical, and metatheoretical cuts are viewed simply as accurate reflections of nature, drawn inductively from nature. This is the fundamental and foundational *belief* of all "atomistic" understandings of the nature of things, including change. Nature comes in fundamentally isolated pieces, and only through the analytic decomposition of the whole do we arrive at "the real" individual units. On the other hand, the investigator who functions within a relational frame makes the explicit assumption that the story about splits of nature is one of a number of possible stories and not necessarily the most productive one for inquiry. This point of view asserts that the metatheoretical level of discourse is as fundamental as the observational level, and there is no understanding outside of some form of discourse. Hence, from the relational perspective, the belief that nature is composed of two different kinds of things—biological things and social-cultural things—is dictated as much by a metatheoretical story about nature, or what has also been called a metanarrative, as by any intuitions about nature itself.

This is the important message advanced by the relational position: If the consequences of a fundamentally split system are judged to inappropriately restrict inquiry, then we have the freedom to choose another metatheoretical story or metanarrative that more adequately suits the ends of inquiry. This view of freedom stands in contrast to the arguments of some contemporary post-modern writers such as Jean-François Lyotard (1984) and Richard Rorty (1982, 1993), who claim that freedom is found only in suppressing metanarratives. The relational perspective's counterargument to post-modernism is to note that the very idea of the value of the suppression of metanarratives entails a metanarrative.

The following, then, is a story told from a relational point of view about a split understanding of evolution. The evolutionary and the developmental biologist, the geneticist, and the paleontologist all function within the context of the dominant evolutionary metatheoretical narrative while engaging in discourse activities that construct, modify, and elaborate a theoretical story about the nature of phyla and species changes across history. A metatheoretical narrative or metanarrative is a generalized reading of a theoretical story. Theoretical stories are relatively open to revision, but metanarratives are further removed from the modification process and tend to maintain stability in the face of observational and theoretical challenge. Metanarratives act as broad frames, templates, or metaphors for conceptualizing several domains beyond the field of origin. When metanarratives become too removed from the modification process, they harden into dogma.

The Neo-Darwinian Split Metanarrative

The most influential contemporary understanding of the nature of evolutionary change is the metanarrative called the *neo-Darwinian synthesis,* also termed *the modern synthesis.* This story emerged in the 1940s based on a marriage of the evolutionary position of Darwin, called classical Darwinism, and the genetics of Mendel. There is some irony to the use of the term "modern"; the story is now some 50 years old. However, in evolutionary terms, 50 years is but a blink. It is well known that the core of the synthesis is the duality of *random variation* and *natural selection.* From the beginning, both for Mendel with respect to genetics, and for Darwin with evolution, there was a rigid separation (i.e., split) between the *internal* and the *external.* For evolutionists, the statement "Mutations are random with respect to their environment" meant that the processes that accounted for the variation between individuals were independent of the evolutionary process that selects individuals. For geneticists, the genotype constituted the internal state of the organism, and the phenotype constituted the outside or outward manifestation (see Figure 3.2).

Along with the split between inner and outer, the most important feature of the neo-Darwinian synthesis is that evolutionary *change* is defined in terms of variation in gene frequencies and *only* variation in gene frequencies. Thus, the metanarrative establishes that *change is understood as variation, not transformation.* Transformational change is essentially written out of the story and treated as epiphenomenal. Within the metanarrative, genes (or DNA, to be more precise) cause phenotypes by supplying "information," "instructions," or "programs." Genes themselves are

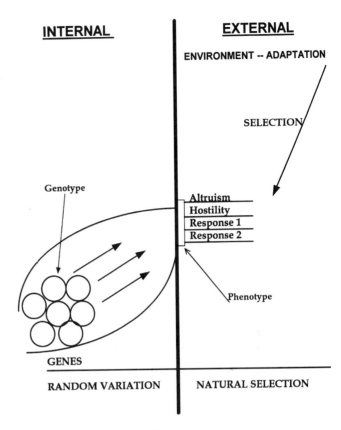

Figure 3.2   The neo-Darwinian metanarrative.

thought of as "packages" of independent causes, or "gene pools" that exert their influence in a one-way outward causal flow of direction. This independent causal aggregate and the transmission of causes from this aggregate then result in the outward manifestation called the phenotype.

This metanarrative has come to acquire a number of metaphors that support and enhance interpretations of split-off entities, fragments, aggregates, and linear unidirectional causality (Nijhout, 1990; Oyama, 1989). The "bean bag" concept of the genome as composed of independent packages is one such metaphor. The notion that "instructions are transmitted" is another. The very idea of "program," "blueprint," and "instructions" constitutes others.

The *internal* aggregate produces random variation, but the *external* natural selection determines the appearance of change. The *phenotype* constitutes the observed variability of the organism. The environment operates on this variability as an *independent causal agent* to select those characteristics that promote survival. Two points need emphasis about this dualistic (i.e., split internal and external) understanding of causes. First, we have here the prototype for biological causes (internal) and social-cultural causes (external) as split, independent forces. Causality remains linear (additive) and unidirectional in the split model. When we tell the inside story, there is no reciprocal causation; causes simply operate independently and in a single direction, from internal toward external. The outside story replicates this. Again, there is no reciprocal causation; but the direction is external toward internal.

The second point to note about the dualistic narrative of evolution as variation is the manner in which the concept of "adaptation" becomes formulated and established as a central feature of the external story (Gould & Vrba, 1981; Lewontin, 1994). In this story, adaptation means virtually the same thing as "adjustment." Both adaptation and adjustment refer to a *change designed to fit an independent context. Context* (i.e., social-cultural factors) selects those characteristics that best fit; hence the central notion of competition and survival of the fittest.

In summary, the evolutionary metanarrative described by the neo-Darwinian synthesis involves an *internal* aggregate gene pool that presents a package of solutions, and an *external* environment that presents various problems to be solved (see Lewontin, 1994). This "adaptationist" program splits subject (genes) and object (environment) into isolated bits of reality and assigns chance variation to the former and contingent selection to the latter. The overall process is entirely contingent. All elements—inside and outside—are fundamentally interchangeable, and any outcome could have been otherwise had other elements randomly appeared. At no point does any fundamental principle of organization enter the process; hence, all change is, in principle, reversible (Overton, 1994a).

This dualistic (i.e., split internal and external), variational, and contingent story of evolution has functioned on both the theoretical and the metatheoretical levels of discourse. For some investigators concerned directly with theoretical and empirical issues of evolution, it has been the theoretical frame within which their work proceeds. On the other hand, at the metatheoretical level, this story has functioned as a kind of overarching template or metaphor that shapes thinking about the nature of change in many diverse fields. Often, in the latter case, applications are drawn from the metanarrative in a nonreflective fashion; or without any recognition of the role being played by the

metanarrative. There are many possible applications of this split neo-Darwinian metanarrative to issues of developmental change. Those described below are selected to illustrate the breadth and depth to which this form of thinking has impacted on developmental issues, theory, concepts, and methodology.

The Neo-Darwinian Metanarrative: Developmental Applications

The first example of the effect of the split evolutionary metanarrative on developmental understanding is the famous/infamous nature–nurture issue. Although the neo-Darwinian narrative did not generate the nature–nurture controversy (that had more to do with the original great splitters, Galileo and Descartes, who will be discussed in a later section), it supports its continuance and limits "solutions" to attempts to put the nature pieces and nurture pieces back together. The controversy is supported by the neo-Darwinian radical rupture of the whole into an inside (gene, biology) story that comes to be called nature, and an outside (social-cultural, experience) story called nurture. Once this split is confirmed as ontologically real, then behaviors or characteristics (e.g., altruism, aggression, empathy, thinking, language) are explained as the causal outcome of one or the other, or some additive combination of the two. The controversy becomes the questions of "Which one?" fundamentally determines change, or "How much?" does each contribute to determining change, or "How?" does each contribute to determining change (Anastasi, 1958; Lerner, 1978; Overton, 1973).

The "solution" to the nature–nurture issue under this split metanarrative requires choosing among several strategies designed to deal with combining and/or suppressing *independent pieces.* One of these strategies is *biological determinism,* which treats the outside story as epiphenomenal, and argues that the fundamental causes of behavior are given by the inside story. For example, this strategy argues that the capacity for violence is given by the genes (the real cause) and social-cultural events simply trigger or do not trigger the underlying biological capacity. *Social determinism,* the mirror image of biological determinism, is the strategy of treating the inside story as epiphenomenal, while arguing that the outside story provides the fundamental causes of behavior. The claim here is that there is sufficient genetic variability for either violence or gentleness, and, therefore, social-cultural factors are the real cause of violent behavior. Both strategies usually decry the idea of dualism, but they deal with the dualism by suppressing the functional reality of one or the other sides of the neo-Darwinian narrative.

A third split nature–nurture strategy has been called "conventional interactionism" (Oyama, 1989; see also, Lerner, 1978; Overton, 1973). Dualism, although clearly a functional part of the scheme, is ignored in this strategy, and it is insisted that any characteristic is partially the effect of each factor. This strategy sometimes places the duality on a continuum and argues that various characteristics are more or less determined by one or the other factor (e.g., see Scarr, 1992). This is the quantitative additive compromise that was mentioned earlier with respect to split issues generally. In the fourth and final strategy, *bio/social interactionism,* dualism is *celebrated.* Generally, this approach makes claims that the *biological* sets the limits, or establishes "predispositions" or "constraints" for behavior, and the *social-cultural* determines behavioral expression. This is the qualitative additive compromise that was mentioned earlier with respect to split issues. This compromise is the most direct reflection of the neo-Darwinian metanarrative of the nature of change (e.g., see Karmiloff-Smith, 1991).

These four nature–nurture strategies do not exhaust the list of possible "solutions," nor are they necessarily individually mutually exclusive. Each tends at times to merge into another. However, neither the complexities of nature–nurture, nor even the details of alternative nonsplit solutions (see, e.g, Gottlieb, 1992, 1997; Lerner, 1992; Magnusson, 1995), are central here. Rather, the central point of emphasis here is that the whole class of traditional solution strategies emerges because and *only* because of the acceptance of a particular story about the nature of things. This is the story in which "nature" (genetics, biology) is identified with an ontologically real *inside* that is radically split from an ontologically real *outside* called "nurture" (experience, social-cultural). If this conceptual distinction was rejected as an ontological description of "the real" and accepted instead as alternative lines of sight on the same whole, the controversies themselves evaporate.

A second example of the use of the neo-Darwinian metanarrative as a template for understanding developmental phenomena emerges from the behaviorist literature. In this arena, several have noted (Oyama, 1989; Skinner, 1984; Smith, 1990) that Skinner's perspective represents a direct application of the neo-Darwinian story. Skinner's operants had to originate from somewhere, but Skinner's behavioristic outside story of the subject (instrumental as opposed to expressive function of behavior) never required an articulation or elaboration on these internal origins. All that was required was the output of the inside neo-Darwinian story, the random variation of a set of operant (instrumental) responses. Given this base, Skinner's outside story can and does focus on natural selection or "selection by consequences" as presenting "the real" functional variables in the development of behavior.

More central to contemporary developmental psychological interests than Skinner's position is the work of Belsky, Steinberg, and Draper (1991), who used the neo-Darwinian metaphor as a frame for a developmental theory of socialization. Their strategy for explaining socialization has been to wed a sociobiological approach to Bronfenbrenner's (1979) behavioral ecology. *Sociobiology* asserts the adaptationist strategic claim that natural selection favors behavioral strategies that increase fitness. Sociobiology also provides the authors with an inside story biologically grounded in "the modern view of evolution" (p. 663) (i.e., the 1940s "'modern' synthesis" or neo-Darwinian synthesis). *Behavioral ecology,* on the other hand, represents the outside story; the argument that behavior strategies are "contextually conditioned," shaped, or selected by the environment. "From sociobiology we take the maxim that natural selection tends to favor behavior that increases fitness. From *behavioral ecologists* we take the maxim that behavioral strategies that contribute to reproductive success are . . . contextually conditioned" (p. 648). And, "central to our theory is the notion drawn from modern evolutionary biology that humans . . . adjust their life histories in response to contextual conditions in a manner that will enhance reproductive fitness—or at least would have in the environment of evolutionary adaptation" (p. 663). Again, the issue is not to critique this approach from either a theoretical or an observational level of discourse. The point here is to recognize that this approach arises from a particular metanarrative, and the consequences of accepting this metanarrative are different from those that follow from accepting another metanarrative. In particular, this metanarrative fosters split theoretical and observational understandings of the nature of developmental change, and its explanation. The consequence of this split story is that only variability is allowed as fundamentally real developmental change, and explanation can occur only within the categories of biological causes and social-cultural causes.

The investigation of mechanisms of development constitutes another important contemporary example of the neo-Darwinian metanarrative of variational change and internal–external causes being applied as the conceptual contextualization of an important developmental psychological issue (see Hoppe-Graff, 1989; Sternberg, 1984, for a general discussion of developmental mechanisms). Siegler (1989; Siegler & Munakata, 1993) has presented a scheme that represents several hypothesized mechanisms of cognitive development as being analogous to several genes (see Buss, 1995, for a similar approach to psychological mechanisms). Each mechanism produces alternative types (random variation) and the environment selects (natural selection) these types according to fitness criteria (see Figure 3.3).

For Siegler, a mechanism of cognitive development is any "mental process that improves children's ability to process information" (1989, p. 353). This means that the

developmental outcome (effect) of any mechanism (cause) is improvement in stored knowledge. Improvement here refers either to increases in amount of knowledge stored, or to the effectiveness of the machinery that stores and accesses the knowledge. Thus, ultimately, development is defined in terms of stored knowledge. This in itself limits developmental change to variational change; there is no room here for transformational change as a fundamental type of change. To account for the change in stored knowledge, Siegler proposes five broadly conceived "mechanisms" of development: (a) synaptogenesis (a member of the broader class of neural mechanisms), (b) associative competition, (c) encoding, (d) analogy, and (e) strategy choice.

Each proposed developmental mechanism is understood as being analogous to an individual gene. Each is an internal packet with an outward flow of causality from genotype to phenotype. The strategy choice gene, to take one example of the five mechanisms (see Figure 3.3), causes variation in the phenotype. The result is variation in external behavior, as in learning strategy 1, strategy 2, strategy 3, and so on. As a specific analogy here, consider the idea of tail length in an animal. The human would have an innately prewired set of alternative strategies just as the rat would have a set of alternative genes for tail length (or technically, alleles at a particular locus). The rat might phenotypically appear with a possible tail length of 1, 2, or 3 inches, depending on whether it had allele 1, allele 2, or allele 3; and individual children might come with strategy 1, strategy 2, or strategy 3.

Having presented the inside story of variational and *only* variational change, the outside story then comes into play for Siegler. The alternative strategies are conceived as being in competition for survival. The environment selects (i.e., causes) the strategy that is to survive, and that strategy is the one that best facilitates the processing of information and, hence, the building of stored knowledge.

In summary, for Siegler, fast and effective knowledge acquisition defines human development and is explained by phenotypical behaviors, which are explained by underlying causal mechanism that are built into the system. Considering knowledge acquisition, the phenotypical behavior, and the underlying mechanism as a totality constitutes both a description and an explanation of development. Siegler and Munakata (1993) have said: "The centrality of variation and selection within . . . change mechanisms does not seem coincidental. Multiple competing entities seem essential

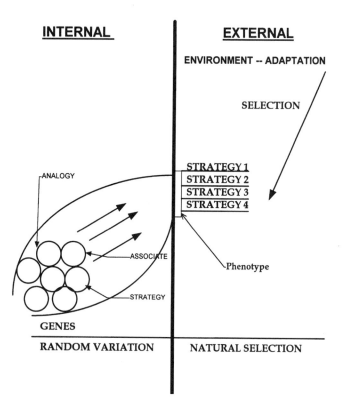

Figure 3.3 The neo-Darwinian metanarrative and mechanisms of development (variational change).

for adaptation to changing environments. Effective selection among the variants is essential . . . for producing progressively more successful performance. Achieving these functions of variation and selection may be essential for any developing system" (p. 3).

In passing, it is worth noting that Kuhn and her colleagues (Kuhn, Garcia-Mila, Zohar, & Andersen, 1995) have recently proposed a wide-ranging cognitive position concerning the development of scientific reasoning. Their position parallels Siegler's with respect to the exclusivity of variational change and adaptation. In their scheme, knowledge acquisition strategies, metacognitive competence, and metastrategic competence are presumed to be available in rudimentary forms in young children and constitute the elementary building blocks of scientific reasoning. These skills appear as intraindividual variability of behavior in problem solving, and development or change "appears as a gradual shift in the distribution of the use of a set of strategies of varying adequacy" (p. 9). White (1995), in commenting on this movement "toward an evolutionary epistemology of scientific reasoning" (p. 129), notes the striking similarity to the historical behavioral "scheme of trial-and-error learning proposed by Edward L. Thorndike (1898) at the turn of the century" (p. 134) and contrasts it with the Piagetian perspective that emphasizes the dialectic of transformational and variational change as codefining fundamental features of development (Overton, 1990):

> Instead of wide-sweeping structural changes in the logical engines available to the child, there are changes in cognitive *elements* that the child can call into play when confronted with a problematic situation. The changes are not wide sweeping. They are more local, particulate. Yet there is transfer. . . . The emergence of scientific reasoning depends on an orchestration of a number of cognitive *elements* that have to work together. *Change, as it occurs, is by no means irreversible.* (White, 1995, p. 135, emphasis added)

Before turning to a final example of an application of the neo-Darwinian metaphor as a template for understanding and explanation, it should again be pointed out that, in the examples already described, the type of change being identified as developmental is variational change and not transformational or morphological change. Siegler's proposed mechanisms of development, along with Kuhn's, Skinner's, and the sociobiology/behavioral ecology behavioral and

socialization approaches, all describe change in which no fundamental transformational novelty emerges. In each example, forms and the change of forms—such as changes in forms of thought from infancy to childhood and to adolescence; or changes in forms of personality organization; or changes in emotional organization from global affect to differentiated specific emotions—are simply excluded from discussion or treated as epiphenomenal. In each of the neo-Darwinian generalizations, inside causes (nature) provide a variational base of behaviors, and outside causes (nurture) winnow down and shape that variation. Variation and the winnowing and shaping process constitute the definition and explanation of development within this story. Transformational or morphological change has simply been written out of the fundamental story of development and treated as mere appearance.

A fourth and final example of the application of the neo-Darwinian split template concerns not a specific domain of developmental inquiry, but a particular type of philosophical thought most appropriately called *post-modern pragmatism,* a marriage of post-modern thinking and American pragmatism. This example is presented to illustrate both the breadth of metanarrative influence, and how various fields reinforce each other in a manner that superficially appears to be the product of independent analyses but, on closer inspection, actually reflects an adherence to identical categories of thought. Post-modern pragmatism currently influences the way some understand developmental change (see Chandler & Carpendale, 1994), and it is important to recognize the quality of this influence. The specific relevance of this example resides in the way the neo-Darwinian metanarrative is used to justify the explanatory categories of post-modern pragmatism and, subsequently, the way that various domains of developmental inquiry (e.g., developmental psychology) appeal to these explanatory categories to justify their own neo-Darwinian claims. This form of mutual reinforcement represents an interesting exercise in what has traditionally been viewed as vicious circular reasoning.

The contemporary work of the philosophical champion of post-modern pragmatism, Richard Rorty (1982, 1993), is a paradigmatic illustration of this circularity. Rorty begins from a post-modern position that can best be understood as a set of related attempts to define individual freedom in absolute terms, as the absence of all constraints. In this effort, post-modern thought attacks any ideas that might be suggestive of constraint and might, hence, limit the potential for absolute freedom. Included as denounced categories are "system," "unity," "totality," and "synthesis" (see Overton, 1994a, 1994b). Quite naturally, it follows from this perspective that metanarratives are to be denounced because they too offer a constraint—a rational constraint—on absolute individual freedom. In fact, from this post-modern perspective, all *rational* inquiry is a kind of constraint. This leaves the radical post-modernist in the same position as—and, in a fashion, reinforcing—the older positivist position that "the real" is given by observation and *only* observation (see later discussion on methodology, and Laudan, 1996). Within this frame, Rorty, following François Lyotard (1984), announces the death of metanarratives and consequently the death of traditional philosophical inquiry, understood as a *rational* exploration of epistemological (metanarratives about knowing) and ontological (metanarratives about the nature of the real) issues. This leaves Rorty's "epistemological behaviorism" and other similarly post-modern approaches in the peculiar position of having generated and employed a very powerful metanarrative whose fundamental tenet is the denial of metanarratives.

From this precarious base of the denial of all metanarratives, Rorty argues that philosophy continues to play a role in the inquiry process by limiting itself to analytic considerations of whatever seems to work best. This limiting of the inquiry playing field to what works best is the pragmatic theme of Rorty's post-modern pragmatism. But the question immediately arises as to how judgments can be made of what does, in fact, work best. The criteria for judging the bad and the best cannot emerge from some general principle because that would constitute a metanarrative, which is not permitted in the post-modern framework.

Rorty is not oblivious to this problem of needing some standard against which to judge good, better, and best. Were he not to address the issue—were he to say, for example, that there are no standards or norms—his own philosophical inquiry would sink back into the relativism, solipsism, and nihilism of Lyotard and other skeptical post-modern thinkers. Without standards, every thought and every observation becomes equal to any other thought or observation. Consequently, Rorty's own thoughts and observations would lose any special value. Rorty's solution is one that has historically appealed to pragmatists.

He invokes the Darwinian evolutionary categories as the standard against which judgments of merit will be made. The language of Darwinism "provides a useful [i.e., convenient] vocabulary in which to formulate the pragmatist position" (1993, p. 447). This means that what we have called the neo-Darwinian metanarrative is used by Rorty, but ostensibly not as a metanarrative. Instead, the neo-Darwinian position is supposedly a simple convenience of language that facilitates the description of the way things "really" are. Once introduced, however, this Darwinian language generates the very categories that will carry explanation. Exactly these Darwinian categories will define, by arbitrary definition, the way things "really" are, and the same categories will offer a preferred explanation for the way things are. Most importantly, they will do so in the context of a denial that reflective or interpretation considerations enter the process in any meaningful way.

A Rortyian pragmatist stance has the potential for exerting a significant influence on the way other fields understand developmental change. The perspective sends the strong message that the neo-Darwinian category system of "random variation and natural selection" is not a modifiable story, a metanarrative, but the *best* description of how things "really" are. This moves the metanarrative into the realm of dogma. It also reinforces a long-standing bias on the part of some, as described in the introduction to this chapter, to regard anything conceptual as suspect, and to regard anything that *claims* to be uninterpreted descriptions of pristine observations of nature as "scientific" (see later discussion on methodology). Rorty's form of pragmatism permits the categories of neo-Darwinism to frame our understanding and explanation of development, while claiming that categories exert no influence on our understanding and explanation of development.

The Neo-Darwinian Metanarrative: A Flawed Story of Change?

The several examples that have been presented demonstrate the current and potential influence of a split metanarrative—specifically, the neo-Darwinian metanarrative—on the understanding and explanation of developmental change. However, to this point, no argument has been put forth suggesting anything particularly problematic about this influence. Indeed, if the neo-Darwinian metanarrative of a radical split of inside from outside—of the random variation caused by inside and the natural selection caused by outside—is working successfully in a wide variety of domains, why not simply declare it a success and get on with the more directly empirical tasks of inquiry? The answer is that the acceptance of this metanarrative as defining developmental change is, in fact, highly problematic even within the specific domains of inquiry that are most directly affected by its influence. The fundamentals of the general problem are described by a rather embarrassing dilemma that results from this acceptance.

The dilemma is this: The neo-Darwinian evolutionary story is being used by psychology, philosophy, and other fields as a grand scheme for understanding developmental change. However, contemporary investigators of biological and evolutionary change themselves complain that this evolutionary story is badly flawed because it fails, in fact, to consider developmental change. That is, investigators who explore theoretical and empirical levels of biological and evolutionary phenomena criticize the neo-Darwinian narrative because it omits development. More specifically, say its critics, it omits the kind of developmental change defined as transformational change. Thus, if we accept the critiques of these investigators—including Daniel Brooks (1992; Brooks & Wiley, 1988), Gerald Edelman (1992), Scott Gilbert (1992), Brien Goodwin (1992), Stephen J. Gould (1993), Stuart Kauffman (1992, 1995), Richard Lewontin (1994), and Francisco Varela (Varela, Thompson, & Rosch, 1991)—it appears that developmental psychology is increasingly employing the generalization of a flawed, or at least incomplete, developmental scheme to define and explain development. This same criticism has been articulated within the psychological community by a variety of evolution-oriented investigators (see, e.g., Bateson, 1985; Gottlieb, 1992, and this Volume; Kuo, 1967; Lehrman, 1970; Schneirla, 1957, 1966; Tobach, 1981).

These contemporary scientists are not becoming anti-Darwinian nor are they becoming antievolutionary. They are simply articulating the need for modification and expansion of the neo-Darwinian story. Evolutionary biologists, developmental biologists, neurobiologists, geneticists, paleontologists, and psychologists speak in many different voices when they argue this point. However, they uniformly agree on the following: Regardless of the level of analysis one chooses to explore, concepts of *organization, system, structure, or form—as well as the transformation of organization, system, structure, or form—must enter into a*

revised evolutionary narrative in every bit as central a fashion as concepts of variation and selection enter the current narrative. That is, development—conceived as ordered changes in the form, organization, or structure of a system—must be directly integrated into the current narrative of variational change and selection.

Gilbert (1992), a developmental biologist, describes the origin of the exclusion of development (transformational change) from evolution. The problems of "how changes in development might lead to changes in evolution were eclipsed by the Modern Synthesis of the 1940s [the neo-Darwinian synthesis]. In this program, evolution meant changes in gene frequency, and these earlier problems were cast aside as being unimportant" (p. 473). Edelman (1992), a neurobiologist, goes on to articulate the dominant theme of most contemporary revisionist critics by arguing for the need to reintroduce the centrality of form and change of form (transformation) into an expanded neo-Darwinian narrative. "The part of Darwin's program that needs most to be completed . . . is concerned with how animal form, tissue structure, and tissue function could have arisen from ancestors—the problem of morphologic evolution" (p. 48). "Morphology—the shape of cells, tissues, organs, and finally the whole animal—is the largest single basis for behavior" (p. 49). "To accomplish it [completing Darwin's program] we need to show how development (embryology) is related to evolution. We need to know how genes affect form through development" (p. 51).

Along with the criticism that there is more to the story of evolution than variational changes in gene frequencies, the narrative revisionists argue against the interpretation of genes as independent split-off atomic entities, and they call for a recognition that "genomic regulatory networks underlying ontogeny, exhibit powerful 'self-organized' structural and dynamical properties" (Kauffman, 1992, p. 153). As a consequence of recognizing the genome itself as a self-organizing system (i.e., an active form-changing organization), there is a call to "invent a new theory of evolution which encompasses the marriage of selection and self-organization" (Kauffman, 1992, p. 153; see also Varela, Thompson, & Rosch, 1991).

Further, this group points out that evolutionary theory—as limited to random variation and natural selection—has become too sharply focused on the maintenance of diversity (i.e., focused on the reversible, and the cyclical) while ignoring the significance of the origin and developmental paths of diverse forms (i.e., the transformational, and the directional) (Brooks, 1992; Levin & Lewontin, 1985).

Finally, the revisionists argue that the concept of adaptation to a split-off environment, as described by the neo-Darwinian metanarrative of natural selection, severely limits understanding. They argue for a healing of the dualism of a split-off internal and external through a recognition that it is both the case that biological organisms construct their social-cultural world, and that the social-cultural world constructs biological organisms (Edelman, 1992; Lewontin, 1994).

Virtually all of the themes argued by contemporary evolutionary revisionists assert the need for an understanding that is relational in nature, an understanding where inside and outside, variation and transformation, biological and social-cultural as well as other fundamental splits are viewed as analytic distinctions, not ontological cuts in nature. This relational understanding yields distinctions that allow an investigator to stand at a particular line of sight and explore from that particular point of view without declaring that point of view to be "the real." An illustration of these themes in human ontogenesis is found in the contrast between the split-off adaptationist story found, for example, in Skinnerian theory and in the social learning theories discussed earlier, and the relational picture of adaptation found in the work of Jean Piaget. Like Skinner (1984) and social learning theories, Piaget (1952) introduces adaptation as a fundamental and central theoretical concept. However, unlike these neo-Darwinian theorists, Piaget's concept of adaptation is always understood as the complement of a second central theoretical concept, organization. As with the modern evolutionary revisionists, Piaget stresses time and time again that *organization* (the form) and *adaptation* (the function) are two poles of the same relational matrix, two aspects of the same whole. It is neither that organization will ultimately be reduced to adaptation, nor that organization provides the variation and adaptation the selection. Novel organization emerges from processes of adaptation, but adaptation operates under the constraints of current organization. Organization and change of organization (transformational change) become the focus when inquiry is directed toward issues of emergent novelty, sequence, and irreversibility. Adaptation becomes focal as inquiry is directed toward issues of activity, process, and variation. Structure and function are not independent, split-off, either/or solutions to problems; structure and function, organization and activity, and form and process are alternative perspectives on the same whole.

In summary, the neo-Darwinian "modern synthesis" is a split metanarrative that has consequences for developmental inquiry across a broad range of domains. As a narrative that speaks of variational change exclusively, it provides a conceptual context for, and reinforces, other narratives that would claim development is about variational change and *only* variational change, and that explanation is about biological causes and/or social-cultural causes. To the extent that revisionist criticisms of this story are accepted as valid, a remedy is needed, and this remedy is the move to a relational metanarrative that disavows an ontological distinction between inside and outside, biology and social-cultural, transformational and variational. The next section will sketch the outline of such a metanarrative and will suggest some of the implications of this story for the understanding and explanation of development.

The Relational Developmental Metanarrative

A new conceptual scheme is needed to deal with problems generated by the neo-Darwinian metanarrative. This new scheme must be inclusive and must admit both transformational and variational change as necessary features of understanding. This new scheme must broadly heal the Cartesian splits between inside and outside, subject and object, organization and adaptation, form and process, biological and social-cultural, nature and nurture. In other words, a conceptual scheme is needed that can support the inclusive definition of development presented earlier in this chapter: formal (transformational) and functional (variational) changes in the expressive-constitutive and instrumental-communicative features of action. One approach to accomplishing this task would be to build from the theory of self-organizing systems that has been playing a prominent heuristic role in biological, physical, sociological, and psychological domains of science (see Overton, 1975, 1994a, 1994b, for an overview within the psychological domain; Kauffman, 1992, 1995, for overviews within the biological and evolutionary domains; and Nicolis & Prigogine, 1989, for an overview within the physical domain; and Luhmann, 1995, for an overview within the sociological domain). Using the theory of self-organizing systems as a base, it is possible to abstract a coherent integrated metanarrative about evolutionary and other developmental change. This metanarrative conceptualizes organisms (including all variety of subjects such as the biological, the social-cultural, and the psychological, along with all variety of similarly defined objects) fundamentally in relational terms rather than as aggregates of independent and isolated pieces. Figure 3.4 graphically illustrates the outlines of such a relational conceptual scheme.

From the perspective of this relational scheme, the biological and social-cultural are no longer two independent pieces of nature, split off into an ontologically real inside and outside, as was the case with the neo-Darwinian metanarrative. In the relational scheme, the biological and the social-cultural are interpenetrating and interdependent emergent subsystems or fields. They emerge from a broader

self-organizing system characterized by holistic features identified with organized—as distinct from additive—complexity. This broad inclusive system can be termed the bio/social-cultural action matrix. Biology here is a differentiated dimension of the fundamental action system. Similarly, the social-cultural is not an independent piece, composed of atomic elements interacting in a "billiard ball" atomic universe. The social-cultural is a differentiated dimension of the general self-organizing action system. Indeed, if we think of the fundamental self-organizing system as a unified action matrix, then the organizations that we call "the organism," "the biological environment," and the "social-cultural environment" are all differentiations that emerge from the action of that broad system. All such subsystems (including the psychological subject) represent transformations generated by the action of the system, and consequently the scheme is both relational and developmental.

This relational-developmental metanarrative heals all fundamental splits in the same manner by recognizing that these (e.g., "inner and outer," "subject and object," "nature and nurture," "biological and social-cultural," "organization and adaptation," "structure and function," "variational and transformational change") are bipolar contrastive terms, or alternative moments in time, that represent alternative points of view on the same whole. They are *not descriptions* of independently appearing "natural" entities. They are fundamental relational bipolar concepts in the sense that the philosopher Hegel described the dialectic, and illustrated it with the example of master and slave as relational concepts. In the master–slave dialectic, it is impossible to define or understand the freedom of the master without reference to the constraints of slavery; and consequently impossible to define the constraints of slavery without reference to the freedom of the master. Neither freedom nor constraint can be understood in the absence of the other.

Inner and outer, subject and object, nature and nurture, biological and social, variation and transformation are relational concepts in exactly the sense that the hands in Escher's famous "Drawing Hands" (shown in Figure 3.5) are relational. It is senseless to ask: *Which* hand is doing the drawing and which hand is being drawn? A similarly meaningless question would be: *How much* is one or the other hand contributing to the drawing? Do the two hands contribute to the drawing and in some sense interact? Of course they interact, but not in an additive fashion such that

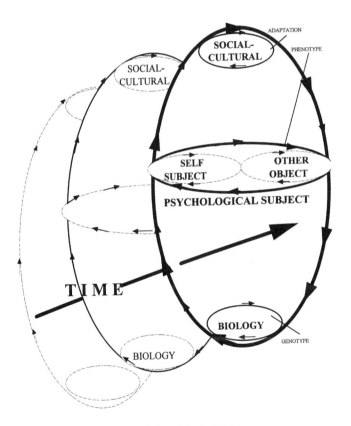

Bio/Social-Cultural Action Matrix

Figure 3.4 The relational developmental metanarrative and mechanism of development (variational and transformational change): the differentiation of dynamic subsystems through action (arrows).

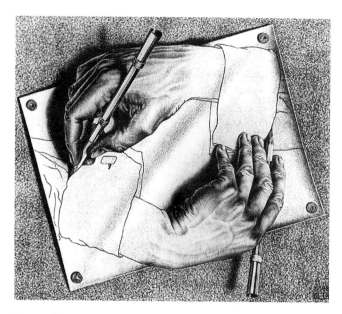

Figure 3.5   The relational developmental metanarrative in pictorial form: Escher's "drawing hands." © 1996 M. C. Escher/Cordon Art-Baarn-Holland. All rights reserved.

contributions to drawing and being drawn could be parceled out and ascribed to one or the other hand. In the split story—whether reference is made to the biological, the social-cultural, or the psychological—"interaction" has implied two disconnected, fragmented, individual pieces of nature that come into contact with each other to produce a third thing (see Lerner, 1978; Overton, 1973; see also Magnusson & Stattin, this Volume for an extended discussion of alternative forms of interaction). In the relational approach, there is interpenetration, interdefinition, fusion (Tobach & Greenberg, 1984), and, most broadly, relationship. Independent items represent an abstraction that may prove useful for certain analytic purposes, but such perspective-based abstractions in no way deny the underlying holism (see Gollin, 1981). The analytic and the synthetic are, themselves, two poles of a relational matrix, as are the notions of abstract and concrete.

Hegel referred to this relational flow of categories, where rigid either/or splits are healed, as the "identity of opposites." Left hand and right hand (see Figure 3.5)—like biological and social, or inner and outer, and so on (see Figure 3.4)—are identical as each defines and is defined by the other. Yet, at the same time, there is a left and there is a right. We can explore their oppositeness by

taking a particular point of view, a particular perspective, but the point of view is taken in the context of an understanding that there is an underlying identity. We can talk about what either hand is doing, from the perspective of that hand. This allows causal terms into the explanatory system, but the causal terms are always themselves defined by a point of view. Causal terms are always theory-laden, as Hanson (1958) demonstrated, and a specific theory is always a perspective. Causal terms are necessary for the kind of inquiry called scientific inquiry, but there is no necessary reason to proclaim that causal terms identify pristine pieces of nature; nor that causal terms are the only forms of scientific explanation (see the later discussion of methodology). That is a story told by the split metanarrative.

The relational-developmental metanarrative can be and is being applied as the context for understanding both evolution and all forms of developmental change. In these understandings, variational and transformational change constitute an identity of opposites. Individual variation is constrained by organization, and organized action leads to novel variation. Form constrains variational action, and variational action yields novel forms. Variational action is cyclical, but the cycles become form and the formed action continues to cycle. Thus, change moves in a spiraling directional fashion (see Figure 3.6). In the study of human ontogenesis, one approach may explore individual differences while another examines the organization and transformation of these differences as they move in the direction of broadly defined ends (see Emde, 1994; Overton 1994a, 1994b). Individual differences and universal transformations are alternative perspectives on the same whole of human ontogenesis when development is framed by this metanarrative.

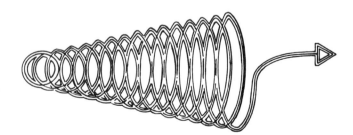

Figure 3.6   The relational developmental metanarrative: cycles of individual variation (cycles of time) spiral to form transformational directional change (arrow of time).

It should be evident that the application of this metanarrative, drawn from self-organizing systems to the understanding and explanation of development, simply eliminates nature–nurture as a meaningful problem. The action of the fundamental matrix (see Figure 3.4) leads to the emergence and differentiation of novel organization. One pole of the novel organization comes to be termed the biological field, and the other pole becomes termed the social-cultural field. From this novel organization, further action leads to the differentiation termed the "psychological subject" or "person." The action of the person (if that is our system of interest, or point of view), in turn, leads to the emergence of novel structures and novel functions. Hence, as Anastasi (1958) suggested almost 40 years ago, questions of which one causes development, or how much each contributes to development, simply fade to meaninglessness within this scheme. The relevant question becomes: *How,* in the course of active differentiation and novel reintegration, do the biological field, the social-cultural field, and the person, come to offer constraints and opportunities for development?

The relational developmental metanarrative does not ignore the need to articulate mechanisms of change. However, within this scheme, "mechanism" is not necessarily identified with an aggregate of causal devices. Within this metanarrative, "mechanism" refers to the *means* or *method* of change rather than foundational fragmented pieces of nature that produce effects called "change." In this relational systems approach, the broadly understood method, means, or mechanism of change (whether phylogenetic, ontogenetic, microgenetic, or other) is the *action of the system itself* (see Figure 3.4). When the point of view is the organism, the mechanism of change is the action of the organism as it engages progressively differentiated biological and social-cultural subsystems. Action as the mechanism of change is, of course, too broad and abstract for any specific theory, but here we speak in a metanarrative voice. Because theories drawn from this metanarrative are more precisely articulated, specific features of system action or processes become candidates as mechanisms of change (see Overton, 1994a, 1994b).

In the relational developmental metanarrative, adaptation and selection processes are not ignored. However, within this frame, selection is not adaptation to a split-off social-cultural or physical world. Adaptation and organization are bipolar relational concepts; adaptation necessarily operates in the context of a changing organization just as

organization necessarily occurs in the context of a changing social-cultural world. This relationship holds both for phylogenesis and for ontogenesis (Gariepy, 1995). Theories that propose to explain social and emotional, or cognitive ontogenesis within this framework need to consistently recognize that organisms construct the social-cultural environment to which they adapt. Adaptation is the language of the outward pole of this relationship. This voice is a necessary part of the whole; but organization is the language of the inward pole, and its voice is an equally necessary part of the same totality. Concepts that suggest the social-cultural world "molds" or "shapes" behavior, and the organization of behavior, or suggest that behavior is "adjusted in response to contextual conditions," are inappropriate because they belong to the vocabulary of the split metanarrative. Concepts suggesting that the social-cultural world provides "opportunities," "contexts," or "settings" for behavioral and organizational change belong to the vocabulary of the relational metanarrative.

EPISTEMOLOGICAL/ONTOLOGICAL ISSUES

In broad outline, this chapter has moved from an exclusive to an inclusive understanding of the nature of development, and has illustrated some of the consequences of each. The chapter has also sketched, in some metanarrative detail, an outline of the kind of conceptual scheme that supports an inclusive definition and leads to a unique program of developmental inquiry. In sketching this outline, it was suggested that the relational metanarrative can find its grounding in the theory of self-organizing systems. This is so, but it is only one side of the story. The other side is that the relational metanarrative also finds its grounding in certain higher-order metanarrative levels of discourse—that is, in the levels of ontological and epistemological discourse (see Figure 3.1). There is no contradiction in finding the grounding of a broad conceptual scheme both in a theoretical position and in a set of more general metaissues. Again, this is an instance of the identity of opposites, of Escher's Drawing Hands. Ontological-epistemological discourse is the one hand, and theoretical discourse is the other. In another frame of inquiry, theoretical discourse is one hand, and observational discourse is the other.

Grounding the relational metanarrative in both poles prevents regression to a split exclusivity. This is not a minor, nor an uncommon, problem. In essence, the process begins when the theoretical position that supports the metanarrative fails to achieve an explicit and coherent ontological-epistemological grounding. As a consequence, interpretation of key theoretical concepts begins to drift toward the prevailing popular, but implicit, ontological-epistemological frame. For example, a self-organizing systems theoretical approach entails relational categories of organization/process. However, the approach may drift toward a split characterization in which *either* organization *or* process is understood as constituting the foundational real, and its opposite is cast as mere appearance. As the drift progresses, other concepts of the seemingly novel theoretical position become assimilated to exclusive either/or categories. Then, because the metatheoretical narrative was grounded only in the theoretical, the metatheoretical narrative itself tends to become assimilated to the old exclusivity and so, for example, "relational" comes to be understood as an association of individual elements, and "complexity," as the addition of elements; and "real" change becomes identified with variability and *only* variability.

Thelen and Smith's (1994; see also this Volume, and Thelen & Ulrich, 1991) treatment of self-organizing or dynamic systems theory is one of a number of possible illustrations of this regressive process. Thelen and Smith present a careful articulation of the fundamental relational principles of a dynamic systems approach "which stress wholeness, self-organization, nonlinearity, developmental buffering or equifinality, and hierarchical levels of organization" (1994, p. xx). They also emphasize the centrality of action to systems theory for any account of developmental change. However, this legitimate focus with respect to action, process, and function becomes joined with a denial of structure or organization. It is here that the implicit split enters and frames further interpretation. Thelen and Smith cast structure, organization, and system itself as "appearances" to be explained by the split-off reality of process, "although behavior and development *appear* structured, there are no structures" (p. xix, emphasis added). The implicit reliance on a split ontological-epistemological position continues as the appearance of structure is asserted to itself arise out of a uniformity of elements, "when the elements of such complex systems cooperate, they give rise to behavior with a unitary character, and thus to the *illusion* of structure" (p. xix, emphasis

added). With the groundwork laid for a split or exclusive interpretation of self-organizing systems, it then becomes a short conceptual step to supporting the Darwinian split metanarrative in which variability and *only* variability constitutes "real" change: "We retain the classic Darwinian emphasis on variability as *the source* of new forms" (p. 145, emphasis added).

As this example suggests, it is just as necessary to ground fundamental concepts at the level of ontological/epistemological discourse as it is to ground them at the theoretical and observational levels. Only through such multiple groundings can developmental inquiry coherently operate within an inclusive framework, and not regress to exclusivity. This section will explore some of the central features of ontological/epistemological groundings both historically and from a contemporary perspective.

Metaphysics is the broad area of philosophical inquiry concerned with conceptual inquiry into the nature, origin, and structure of the world or "being." *Ontology* is the domain of metaphysics concerned with the question of what constitutes the "Real" (Putnam, 1987). *Epistemology* is about knowing, and its primary question concerns the validity of what and how we know. Understood relationally, epistemology is a narrative about how we know what is Real, and ontology is a narrative about the Real as we know it. Historically, each domain has offered sets of alternatives in answer to its fundamental question. The basic epistemological candidates for yielding valid knowledge have been *reason* and *observation*. In the ontological domain, *matter* and *form* have been primary candidates for the Real. When matter is interpreted as bits, or elements, or uniform pieces, and form is taken as pattern, structure, or organization, then *uniformity* and *organization,* as the surrogates of matter and form, enter as the candidates for what is the Real. A related set of candidates for the nature of the Real concerns the assumed activity status of matter and form. The Real may be assumed to be fundamentally *inactive and unchanging,* or it may be assumed to be fundamentally *active and changing.* Thus, it is possible to conceptualize (a) an inactive and unchanging matter—a Newtonian favorite; (b) an active and changing matter—a pre-Newtonian understanding, as well as Einstein's post-Newtonian understanding of the nature of the physical world; (c) an inactive and unchanging form—a position often attributed to Plato; and (d) an active and changing form—Leibniz's monadology, and Hegel's dialectic.

In discussing ontology and the Real, it cannot be too strongly emphasized, nor too often repeated, that there is a critical distinction between the use of the term "real" in everyday commonsense life and the ontological Real. No one argues that there is a lack of reality or realness in the experienced everyday world. This is commonsense realism. Commonsense realism accepts the material existence of a real, actual, or manifest world, and all ontological/epistemological perspectives treat people, and animals, and physical objects as having such a real existence. The ontological issue of the Real with a capital R (Putnam, 1987) is a very different issue. It concerns the idea of having a base or foundation from which everything else emerges. In this limited sense, the Real is defined as that which is not dependent on something else; that which cannot be reduced to something else.

If we were to engage in a split metanarrative, then matter and form would become a dichotomy. In this case, the assertion of *either* matter *or* form as the Real would designate the other as reducible Appearance. Asserting split matter to be the Real yields a *materialist ontology*. Within this ontological position, form, pattern, organization, and ideas are appearances that ultimately find their source or origin in the foundational Real (i.e., matter). For example, "system," within this split ontological frame, is simply the reflection of individual elements of matter such as neurons. Or, as a social example, "community" is merely the linear aggregate of individuals. Choosing split-off form as the foundational Real asserts an *idealist ontology*. Elements, individuals, and bits achieve an identity only in the context of the pattern or form that constitutes the Real. Within this ontological context, "system" is the foundational Real, and matter, such as neurons, a mere reflection of this Real. "Community" in this case would be foundational and "individuals" would be an expression of this form. When the narrative is split, as in these cases, the Real becomes an absolute foundation and this is referred to as *foundationalism* or a foundationalist position.

Plato and Aristotle and the Relational-Developmental Tradition

For Plato and Aristotle, there were no radical splits between ontology and epistemology, nor between the alternatives in each domain. Each took the problem of knowing as his focus, but reason and observation, and form and matter,

constituted a nonreducible matrix for understanding the world. Plato favored an epistemological emphasis on reason; Aristotle articulated more precisely the dialectical balance of reason and observation. Plato's point of view, or line of sight, began from the ontological significance of form or pattern described in his doctrine of Ideas. However, he admitted another line of sight: matter as a "formless, indefinite, substrate of things" (Stace, 1924). Aristotle emphasized the significance of the relational nature of form and matter. Form and matter were understood as dialectically related, as in Escher's Drawing Hands. Formless matter or matterless form were simply not possible. Aristotle maintained that only individual things exist, but "existence" did not imply a simple split-off matter. Existence implied matter in the context of the categories (forms) of space and time. Thus, existence was not the criterion of the Real; the relational form/matter constituted the Real. As Ross (1959) points out, " 'Matter' is not for Aristotle a certain kind of thing as we speak of matter in opposition to mind. It is a purely relative term—relative to form" (p. 76).

Plato and Aristotle also held a relational view of inactivity/fixity and activity/change. Plato is most widely known for his postulation of a realm of timeless forms (i.e., a realm of the unchanging). In modern times, this notion has cast Plato as the father of the search for "essences" of nature and, thus, what has been called *essentialism* (see Mayr, 1982). Conceived in this split fashion, the fixed forms of essentialism constitute the conceptual grounding for contemporary nativist positions that interpret "structure" and "organization" as fixed and unchanging. It is unlikely, however, that Plato intended this split interpretation (Cornford, 1937; Lovejoy, 1936; Nisbet, 1969). Plato himself specifically stated "that *only* the divine is changeless; that the world of man and society is an incessant process of development and of becoming" (Nisbet, 1969, p. 308).

Aristotle's relational understanding of the nature of *being* (static, fixed, inactive, unchanging) and *becoming* (active, changing) is expressed in his concepts of the "potentiality" and "actuality" of individual things. The actuality of an object of inquiry (i.e., what the object is at a given moment) points to its being. The passage from potentiality to actuality points to the becoming of the object (Ross, 1959, p. 176; Wartofsky, 1968). Coming into being (i.e., becoming) constituted Aristotle's conceptualization of developmental change and—as in the definition of development elaborated earlier in this chapter—he emphasized both the transformational and variational nature of change as critical relational features of becoming. Aristotle referred to transformational change as "generation and destruction," and he termed variational change "alteration" (Ross, 1959, pp. 101–102). Despite the centrality of development (i.e., becoming) to his system, it is often suggested that Aristotle's ideas promoted an understanding of nature as a hierarchical organization of unchanging forms that later became celebrated as the *scala naturae* or "The Great Chain of Being" (Lovejoy, 1936). The attribution of this nonevolutionary, and hence nondevelopmental, view of nature to Aristotle confuses his ontological/epistemological stance with the proposal of a single possible biological classificatory system (Lovejoy, 1936, p. 58). Aristotle was the champion of a logic of classification, but the other side of the story is that he also recognized the dangers and limitations of any specific system of classification. To characterize Aristotle as an antievolutionist who promotes a static conception of hierarchical forms (Mayr, 1982) misses the relational character of Aristotle's work.

Galileo and Descartes: Origins of the Split Tradition

It was in the Renaissance scientific work of Galileo, more than any other, that ontological and epistemological splitting (Putnam, 1987), or a "divide and conquer" strategy (Dennett, 1991; Hundert, 1995), began to be formally articulated. Looking back to Democritus and anticipating John Locke, Galileo argued that matter and only matter constituted the Real, and that all other perceptible qualities were only apparently real:

> The methodological precept "only the mechanical measurable properties of matter are of value in formulating scientific laws" became converted into the metaphysical statement "only the mechanical measurable properties of matter are *real*." And Galileo argued for the reality of these properties and the unreality of all others (colors, tastes, smells, etc.). . . . These latter properties he concluded were subjective illusions; only the former were objective, real. (Berlin, 1956, p. 47)

Thus, with Galileo, nature became split into Real nature—identified with matter—and hence, the later identification of "materialism," "naturalism," and "physicalism"—and Apparent nature identified with mind. Subject became split

from object, with the identification of subject as the apparently real and object as the really Real. There was also the anticipation of an epistemological splitting that became increasingly central in the 18th century. Galileo, while recognizing the necessity of both analysis and synthesis, argued a privileged position for analysis. In the 18th century, matter, elements, and analysis would come to constitute the bedrock foundation of knowledge, and mind, relations, and synthesis became secondary and derived phenomena:

> This analytic process, according to Galileo, is the presupposition of all exact knowledge of nature. The method of formulation of scientific concepts is both analytical and synthetic. It is only by splitting an apparently simple event into its elements and by reconstructing it from these that we can arrive at an understanding of it. (Cassirer, 1951, p. 10)

Galileo was a central figure in setting a framework for ontological and epistemological splitting, but the 17th-century philosophical work of Descartes firmly anchored and fleshed out this type of ontological–epistemological metanarrative (Prosch, 1964). In his *Meditations,* Descartes established the frame for all future foundationalisms (Bernstein, 1983). His well known method of doubt was designed to arrive at an absolute certain base for knowledge. For Descartes, this journey to certain knowledge led from doubting all things, to the one foundational thing that he argued could ultimately not be doubted—that he was doubting. To doubt was to think, and, thus emerged Descartes's "cogito ergo sum," (I think, therefore, I am). It was this elevation of the "I," the Subjective, to an absolute primacy that went beyond foundationalism itself and established what has become known as the *Cartesian split* of nature into the dichotomy of Subject (Ideas) and Object (Matter). The split constitutes the origin of ontological *dualism.* Subject and Object, mind and body, unextended substance (forms, ideas) and extended substance (matter) are cast as dichotomies according to which each member of a pair stands in a mutually exclusive relation to its opposing member.

Having literally invented dualism by splitting the Real into a Subject piece and an Object piece, Descartes—and all others who have since accepted the Cartesian categories—was faced with the problem of how to put the individual pieces back together again. If there is an absolute bedrock to nature and this bedrock is composed of individual elements, there must be a glue that can join the pieces into the appearance of wholeness. Descartes favored the solution called *interactionism*, a solution not unlike the interactionist positions described earlier with reference to nature and nurture.

In an important sense, the 18th century—called the Enlightenment—was a reaction against Descartes (Cassirer, 1951). In the context of a relational metanarrative (to be discussed later in this chapter), that goes back to Aristotle and Plato and forward from Leibniz to Hegel, the opposition was to both foundationalism and to the split dichotomization. However, the line of thought that was to be known as the English Enlightenment or British Empiricism, accepted both the context of foundationalism and splitting. This movement, founded in Newton's advances in the physical sciences and elaborated in the philosophical works of John Locke, Bishop George Berkeley, and David Hume, while operating within the Cartesian split categories (Searle, 1992) sought to suppress the subjective and constitute the objective as the Real. Dualism had split the universe into two dichotomous elements, and the 18th-century empiricist reaction was to pursue the advocacy of a *monism* according to which the two would be reduced to a single Real. However, the "one" continued to be based on a dichotomous choice according to which *either* ideas (idealism) *or* matter (materialism) must constitute an absolute bedrock Real. This solution, which continues to have a significant impact on contemporary inquiry, merely suppresses one of the terms of the split; it does not reject the split solution itself (Taylor, 1991). Searle (1992) captures the contemporary impact of the continuing split:

> Along with the Cartesian tradition we have inherited a vocabulary, and with the vocabulary a certain set of categories, within which we are historically conditioned to think about these problems. The vocabulary is not innocent, because implicit in the vocabulary are a surprising number of theoretical claims. . . . The vocabulary includes a series of apparent oppositions: "physical" versus "mental," "body" versus "mind," "materialism" versus "mentalism," "matter" versus "spirit." Implicit in these oppositions is the thesis that the same phenomenon under the same aspects cannot literally satisfy both terms. (p. 14)

The 18th-century English Enlightenment reaction against Descartes then was not an opposition to splitting. It was an opposition to Descartes's particular type of splitting, as well as to his epistemological stance. The Enlightenment was part of a continuing historical process struggling to move away from the repressive authority of the Church and the constraints of dogma in matters of knowing. Descartes's work typified these constraints. For Descartes, the subjective "I" that could not be doubted knew the world according to innate ideas, and these were the imprint of the divine workman—God. From this bedrock of divinely instilled universal innate ideas, the knowing of the particulars of the world entailed a process of *deduction* (i.e., the form of logical reasoning that moves from the universal to the particular). The English Enlightenment progression from Locke to Berkeley to Hume represents, in part, an attack on this form of rationalism that harkens back to Scholasticism and claims that a priori knowledge and reason constitute inherent characteristics of mind that can be employed to deduce the true nature of the world (Cassirer, 1951).

The modern period, or *Modernity*—which includes the Enlightenment—is defined both by a quest for absolute certainty of knowledge (Toulmin, 1990), and by an effort to expand individual freedom, especially freedom of thought. Building knowledge on rational and reasoned grounds, rather than on the grounds of authority and dogma, was understood as the key to each of these goals. However, for English Enlightenment philosophers and those who followed their lead, reason and rationality themselves became a part of split-off Appearance. Reason and observation, deduction and induction, the rational and the empirical came to be understood as Cartesian dichotomies; and the first member of each pair was identified as pointing to Appearance, while the second member was identified as pointing to the Real.

Descartes's rationalism became the ground for the fundamental epistemological split between reason and observation that, as discussed in the introduction of this chapter, continues to influence contemporary inquiry. The epistemological doctrines of *Rationalism*—claiming reason as foundational to knowing—and *Empiricism*—claiming that the senses and, hence, observation are foundational to knowing—are often traced back to Plato and Aristotle. However, for Plato and Aristotle, the tension between reason and the senses was a tension between modes of knowing, and not a dichotomous choice to answer a "Which one?" question. Only during the Enlightenment, and as a reaction against Descartes's rationalism, did empiricism ultimately become a philosophical doctrine asserting that knowledge derives *from observation and only from observation.*

Newton and the Objectivist Split Tradition

The thought of the English Enlightenment emerged from the background of the earlier advances of the physical sciences, particularly the work of Newton. Newton's major contribution had been the redefinition of the nature of matter in a way that conceived of all bodies as fundamentally inactive. Prior to Newton, matter was understood as inherently active. Matter had been conceived in terms of the relation of being (static, fixed) and becoming (active, changing). Newton, however, through his concept of inertia, split activity and matter and redefined matter as inactivity. For Newton, "'being' seemed to be simply the power, or 'force,' of inactivity, the passive power of remaining in motion in a straight line, unless acted upon by another force, and the passive power of remaining at rest unless and until acted upon by another force. 'Being' and (active) 'force' were thus separated" (Prosch, 1964, p. 52).

The redefinition of bodies as inert matter and the assumption of the atomicity of matter (i.e., bodies are ultimately composed of some elementary stuff that is uniform in nature and, in combination, yields the things of the world) were basic for Newton's formulation of his laws of motion. However, they were also ideas that a later generation generalized into a metaphysical worldview that identified the nature of the Real as fixed inert matter and *only* fixed inert matter. This worldview has been called the "billiard ball" notion of the universe, "the notion that basically everything . . . was made up of small, solid particles, in themselves inert, but always in motion and elasticity rebounding from each other, . . . and operating mechanically" (Prosch, 1964, p. 66).

The historical impact of this "billiard ball" or "clockwork" or "mechanistic" worldview on the understanding of development has been severalfold. First, the reduction of the subject to the object meant that the object approach was to be the only legitimate approach to understanding change. Given the split of the subject (spirit) from the object (matter), and given that the Real was understood to reside in the object, it was not possible to entertain the subject "point of view" as a legitimate perspective for developmental inquiry. In fact, there is no possibility of entertaining even the notion of "point of view" within this worldview, be-

cause, within a mechanistic ontological–epistemological stance, there is only the truth of object, or the falsity of error. Expressive/instrumental change (i.e., change conceptualized from the subject or person point of view) loses all fundamental legitimacy in this context. Further, instrumental change itself became legitimate only to the extent that it could be separated from the expressive and treated completely as object. When viewed with a Newtonian eye, later expressive/instrumental theories of human ontogenesis, including those of Werner, Piaget, and Erikson, as well as other psychodynamic theories (e.g., Mahler's, Sullivan's, Bowlby's, and Winnicott's) were viewed skeptically because they attempted to construct theories of change that were theories about the subject point of view. Skinner's instrumental theory became celebrated because it explicitly denied the value of the expressive and proposed that any expressive "possessing demon" could be reduced totally to the instrumental "complex repertoire of behavior" (Skinner, 1971).

Because fixity and uniformity constituted the Real, a second historical impact of the Newtonian tradition (Matson, 1964) was that change, other than random movement (a split-off notion of Aristotle's "alternation" or variational change), came necessarily to be treated as Appearance. Transformational change and its allied concepts of "sequence," "discontinuity," "emergence," "nonlinearity," "novelty," "direction," "irreversibility," and "organization" became problems, not solutions. These problems could not be solved until they were reduced to unchanging laws of the motion of the fixed and uniform smallest possible elements of matter—the atom (i.e., *atomism*). Whether the atoms of inquiry were the physical particles of the physicist; the genes and DNA of the later-day molecular biologist; the neurons of the neurophysiologist; the elements of consciousness of the early structuralist psychologists; the responses of the later behavioral psychologists; or the image or representational encodings of some contemporary cognitive psychologists, these were the bedrock elements that in linear combination with causal forces generated the appearance of transformational change (see the later discussion of methodology). Real change was represented by the metaphor of the "Cycle of Time," according to which Apparent transformational change is ultimately resolvable into contingently determined and totally reversible movement (Coveney & Highfield, 1990; Gould, 1987; Nisbet, 1969; Overton, 1994a; Valsiner, 1994).

The impact of the Newtonian mechanistic worldview was not limited to ontological issues. The epistemological legacy of this tradition also reflects the assumptions of inert matter and atomism. From the Reality of the split-off object there grew the doctrine of *Objectivism*—"scientific realism," or what the American philosopher Hilary Putnam (1990) has called the "God's eye view." According to this position, there is a mind-independent fixed Real, and this forms the essential absolute foundation for all knowing; hence the Newtonian foundationalism. If the flux of the manifest world constituted Appearance, then the task of knowing was the task of analysis down to the level of the Real mind-independent fixed base, and the detection of forces acting on these elements. Further, analysis and detection were to take the form of closer and closer observations until the laws of nature would stand forth, not as subjectively generated hypotheses, or suppositions drawn deductively from some higher-order premises ("*Hypotheses non fingo* [I make no hypotheses]," said Newton), but as "observed correlations" or "empirical generalizations" inductively generated from these same observations (Wartofsky, 1968, pp. 183–184). Thus, the epistemological legacy of Newtonian tradition was a thoroughgoing empiricism that was driven by the primacy of an *analytic ideal* of the complete *reductionism,* and a synthetic method of a mind-independent *induction* (i.e., the form of logical reasoning that moves, via generalization and *only* generalization, from the particular to the universal).

Locke and Hume, and Later Forms of the Objectivist Split Tradition

The ontological and epistemological implications of the mechanistic worldview were progressively worked out in philosophy by the line of British Empiricism. John Locke, accepting the split Cartesian categories, and following Galileo's lead, divided nature into "primary" and "secondary qualities." Primary qualities were features of Newtonian dead matter and constituted the Real. Secondary qualities were features of mind and constituted Appearance. Thus began an organized program of moving away from Descartes's focus on the Subject, not by denying the split of Subject and Object, but by accepting the split and claiming that Object and *only* Object constituted the Real. Locke's image of the mind of the child as a *tabula rasa* was part of this movement, as was his famous slogan that

became the rallying cry for future generations of empiricists: "There is nothing in the intellect which is not first in the senses." In this program, mind would ultimately disappear as Subject and reappear as Object (Matson, 1964); in the 20th century, even the objective mind would fade into objective behavior with the arrival of behaviorism.

Locke's move to the objective mind was incomplete. He eliminated Descartes's innate ideas, but he left the subject with the active power of reflection, comprised of the agent's actions of judging, willing, and comparing. Bishop George Berkeley, himself an idealist in matters of ontology, moved the epistemological program a step further by denying that reflection constituted an inherent activity of mind, and by redefining ideas as particularistic images. This redefinition further served to split the *universal* and the *individual.* It represents the introduction of *nominalism*—the doctrine that the particular constitutes the Real, and universals constitute Appearance. Reinforcing the ontology of elements and uniformity, the doctrine of nominalism continues the suppression of the legitimacy of form, organization, structure, and system. Not only are complex material bodies ultimately composed of *nothing but* uniform fixed elements, ideas too must have the same status. Complex ideas necessarily emerged out of elementary sense data according to the only mechanism ever available to the empiricist tradition, *associations.*

It was left to David Hume to arrive at the ultimate skepticism concerning the possibility of valid (i.e., universal and necessary) knowledge. He thus passed on a legacy that continues to consider "all" knowledge as "necessarily" nothing but particular and contingent bits of facts, or pure observations, that generalize inductively into broad complex principles and ideas. Berkeley had rejected Locke's central activity of mind, but he had not rejected the notion of mind as agent. Hume, following the empiricist doctrine that all knowledge comes through observation and *only* observation, destroyed mind as agent by posing the simple question of where in direct sensory experience we observe mind, self, soul, and personal identity. Because these cannot be "seen" in direct sensory experience, Hume concluded that they cannot be considered fundamental to inquiry; they are Appearances to be explained, they cannot do the explaining. The notion of "necessity" (i.e., the quality of "must") suffers the same fate because it too cannot be directly observed. In the famous Humean example, we may believe there is a necessary relation between a billiard ball that moves across the table, comes into contact with the second ball, and is followed by the second ball moving off. We may *say* that the first ball necessarily caused the second to move. However, all we "see" is a contingent series of events. We *see* no "necessity," nor do we *see* "universality," and in the Newtonian split world, only seeing counts. At the end of Hume's argument, all the complex or abstract ideas that had constituted categories of knowing—Space, Time, Substance, Order, Relations, Causality, Necessity—were nothing but particular images called "ideas," contingently gathered together according to principles of Association.

Hume represented the zenith of the Newtonian tradition with respect to knowledge, but Hume's skepticism about valid knowledge did not dampen the influence of Newtonian splitting on future generations. In the 19th century, the Utilitarian philosophy of Jeremy Bentham, passed down through James and John Stuart Mill, and Alexander Baine, sought to apply the Newtonian paradigm—not to knowing, but to the explanation of actions, values, morals, and politics (Halevy, 1955). The *experimental* psychologies of Wundt and Titchener grew from this ground, followed by the functionalist perspectives of Angell, Carr, Woodworth, and, ultimately, behaviorism and multiple forms of neobehaviorism, including learning theories and social learning theories of development.

In the 20th century, the Newtonian–Humean split tradition continued operating as a metanarrative for various domains of inquiry, including developmental inquiry. In philosophy, the tradition extended its influence in the articulation of Anglo-American analytic philosophy, which took what has been termed a "linguistic turn." Analytic philosophy was, in one sense, a general reaction against the dominance of metaphysical systems or worldviews, including the worldview that describes the Newtonian–Humean tradition. In another sense, analytic philosophy simply drove the Newtonian–Cartesian worldview underground, where it continued to exert a strong contextual influence as a metanarrative. As the name suggests, analytic philosophy has continued to maintain the Cartesian split categories, and, to the present day, in various surrogate forms, it pursues the analytic ideal of finding the "atoms," or absolute bedrock foundational elements of knowing (Rorty, 1979). The British line of this approach located its foundationalism in the analysis of "ordinary language." The American line—as will be more fully discussed in a later section on

methodology—pursued the same goal in the "neutral data language" and "observation sentences" of logical positivism, elaborated in the writings of Moritz Schlick, Roudolf Carnap, Gustav Bergmann, Herbert Feigl, Carl Hempel, A. J. Ayer, and the "earlier" Ludwig Wittgenstein (of the *Tractatus Logico-Philosophicus*).

At the end of the Anglo-American line of analytic philosophy, we are left with the continuing metanarrative impact of the Newtonian–Humean wing of the Cartesian split tradition about ontology and epistemology. This is a tradition of exclusivity. Subject is split off from object, form from matter, becoming from being, structure from function, reason (interpretation, theory) from observation, intellect from sense, necessity from contingency, deduction from induction, synthesis from analysis, universals from particulars, unity from diversity, and wholes from parts. There is no operation of Escher's Drawing Hands here. Each pair forms an exclusive either/or dichotomy, and the second member of each pair is asserted to constitute the nature of the Real.

Leibniz, Kant, Hegel, and the Relational Developmental Tradition

The work of the German Enlightenment is more ambiguous with respect to the heritage of Cartesian splitting and the construction of a relational epistemological–ontological grounding. On the one hand, this movement preserved, modified, and extended the relational approach found in Plato and Aristotle. On the other hand, especially in Kant's ontology, the Cartesian legacy of Subject divided against Object continued to subvert the relational epistemological–ontological ground. At the forefront of the German Enlightenment stands Leibniz's grand synthesis of a universal mathematics, and a metaphysics of individuality (Gadamer, 1993). For Leibniz, epistemology as the universal, the knowing of the Subject, was joined in a relational matrix with ontology, the particular, the being of the Object. Ernst Cassirer, a 20th-century philosopher, captures this fundamental relational quality of Leibniz's work when he asserts that "the central thought of Leibniz's philosophy is therefore to be looked for neither in the concept of individuality nor in that of universality. These concepts are explicable only in mutual relationship; they reflect one another" (1951, p. 33).

With ontology as the line of sight, Leibniz, a contemporary of Locke, refused to split off being from becoming.

Activity and ceaseless change were fundamental to the nature of the Real. In his concept of substance, Leibniz substituted a "pluralistic universe" in place of Descartes's dualism, or the materialist monism given by Locke. Leibniz's monad is the fundamental unit of this universe. The monad " 'is' only in so far as it is active, and its activity consists in a continuous transition from one new state to another as it produces these states out of itself in unceasing succession. . . . Never is one of these elements just like another; never can it be resolved into the same sum of purely static qualities" (Cassirer, 1951, p. 29). "In Leibniz's philosophy an inalienable prerogative is first gained for the individual entity. The individual no longer functions as a special case, as an example; it now expresses something essential in itself. . . . Every individual substance is not only a fragment of the universe, it is the universe itself seen from a particular viewpoint. And only the totality of these unique points of view gives us the truth of reality" (Cassirer, 1951, pp. 32–33).

From an epistemological line of sight, if substance is in "continuous transition from one state to another," then understanding entails the rational discovery of the rule of this transition and the laws according to which it occurs. This is Leibniz's rationalism. It differs significantly from Descartes's in that there is no return to God as the imprinter of these universal ideas, nor is reason split from observation. Universal ideas as rules and laws, and particular experiences as observations, are relational or correlational. Knowing may begin in observation, but observation proceeds in the context of some system, some idea, some form. Analysis is not suppressed in Leibniz's system; in fact, it occupies a significant place in his thought. However, analysis is not privileged over synthesis; all analysis implies a whole or synthetic aspect according to which the analysis proceeds. Cassirer points out that, for Leibniz, the "concept of the *whole* has gained a different and deeper significance. For the universal whole which is to be grasped can no longer be reduced to a mere sum of its parts. The new whole is organic, not mechanical; its nature does not consist in the sum of its parts but is presupposed by its parts and constitutes the condition of the possibility of their nature and being" (1951, p. 31).

The Leibnizian tradition is a relational tradition, and it emerged, as Cassirer suggests, from an organic understanding of the nature of events and the nature of knowing. Thus, it was within an emerging organic worldview that specific features of the relational ontological–epistemological ground came to be articulated. The significance of the legacy of the Leibnizian relational tradition for developmental inquiry—like the significance of the legacy of the Newtonian–Humean split tradition—is severalfold. First, it established a distinct rationale for the proposal that knowing necessarily proceeds from a "point of view" or line of sight. The importance of perspective or point of view is traceable to Plato (Kainz, 1988), but Leibniz gave it a central significance by embedding it in the relational context of parts to whole. Point of view here does not imply an unrestrained relativism as it sometimes seems to suggest in contemporary usage. A point of view within the Leibnizian tradition only becomes a point of view as it is embedded with other points of view within a broader context. For example, Subject and Object become points of view only within a broader organic unity that unites the two within a relational matrix. Without this unity, Subject and Object are simply isolated elements, and the application of the phrase "point of view" in such a case is quite meaningless.

In the post-modern era of contemporary Continental philosophy, point of view continues to exert a strong influence through the concept of a "horizon" of understanding or inquiry. The notion of horizon appears in the works of Nietzsche and Husserl, but it has been most fully developed in the hermeneutics of Hans-Georg Gadamer (1989). A *horizon* is the entire range of understanding that can be generated from a particular vantage point. Achieving a horizon entails placing something in the foreground, or what is termed the process of *foregrounding*, a methodological principle that is inherently relational in nature. Whatever is foregrounded must be foregrounded from something else. Consequently, foregrounding makes visible this other that is joined with it in a relational matrix. With respect to developmental inquiry, for example, to foreground the subject is to recognize the object; to foreground the expressive is to recognize the instrumental; to foreground the transformational is to recognize the variational. The reciprocity of horizons, or what is termed the *"fusion" of horizons*, ultimately constitutes truth in such a relational system. The situation here is similar to the familiar reversible figure of the vase/person, shown in Figure 3.7. From one vantage point, we foreground, and thus acquire, the horizon of two faces turned toward each other. The two faces then become a legitimate object of inquiry, moving toward a full achievement of this horizon. From another vantage point, a

Figure 3.7 Reversible figure: foregrounding and the fusion of horizons.

vase is foregrounded and a different horizon is acquired. Both horizons yield legitimate objects of study; yet both are parts of the one whole, and that whole constitutes the fusion of horizons.

Other developmental implications of the Leibnizian relational tradition follow from the principle that activity, change, and organization are as fundamental as stability, fixity, and uniformity. Activity–stability, change–fixity, and organization–uniformity compose the bipolarities, or relative moments, of the ontological–epistemological relational matrix. This became known as the principle of *Becoming* in philosophical and in developmental inquiry (Overton, 1991a). It contrasts directly with the Newtonian–Humean tradition of *Being,* where activity, change (other than random variation), and organization are treated as ultimately reducible Appearances.

The principle of Becoming, whose origins are traceable to the pre-Socratic works of Anaximander and Heraclitus (Wartofsky, 1968), takes, as its line of sight, activity, change, and organization as necessary and nonreducible features of the cosmos (Allport, 1955; Nisbet, 1969). In the 18th century, Becoming was generalized from Leibniz's ontology to an understanding of man, society, and nature.

In 1725, Giambattista Vico attacked the static view of human nature and proposed that changes of society are the reflection of the imminent and necessary development of the human mind. Kant, in his *General History of Nature and Theory of the Heavens* (1755), applied the notion of Becoming to the material world, and maintained that this world continuously evolves in a systematic and ordered fashion. And, from 1784 on, in a series of four volumes, Johann Gottfried Herder extended the idea of Becoming to include nature, living species, and human society alike (Toulmin & Goodfield, 1965).

In the late 18th and early 19th centuries, the most influential figure to advance the principle of Becoming was G. W. F. Hegel (1770–1831). For Hegel, history was a necessary dynamic process of growth, defined as expressive/transformational change. Most importantly for developmental inquiry, Hegel proposed that this growth is best characterized as being dialectical in nature. The essence of Hegel's *dialectic* is the notion of a process through which concepts or fundamental features of a system *differentiate* and move toward *integration*. Any initial concept or any basic feature of a system—called a "thesis" or an "affirmation"—contains implicit within itself an inherent contradiction that differentiates into a second concept or feature—the "antithesis" or "negation" of the thesis. As a consequence, even in the single unity of thesis there is the implicit relation of thesis/antithesis, just as in the unity of the single organic cell there is the implicit division into the unity of multiple cells. This points to the fundamental relational character of the dialectic. As thesis and antithesis undergo differentiation into a polarity of opposites, a potential space between them is generated, which becomes the ground for a new unity or integration—the "synthesis." Thus, a new relational matrix composed of three realms—thesis/antithesis/synthesis—is formed.

The integration that emerges from the differentiation, like all integrations, is incomplete. The synthesis represents a new thesis, and thus begins a new growth cycle of differentiation and integration. All integrations represent the part–whole relations of an organic holism, as well as the dynamic process of inherent activity and inherent change. Further, any given integration demonstrates the identity of opposites, discussed earlier. To illustrate, it is from notions like "inner," "biological," and "nature" (affirmations) that there arise notions like "outer," "social," and "nurture" (negations of the affirmations). In the synthesis of the affirmations and negations, it is recognized, for example, that nature and nurture are opposites; yet each defines and is defined by the other. Hence, although they are opposites, they are identical. This understanding of the dialectic provides further grounding for the relational developmental metanarrative.

It is particularly important to note that the dialectic suggests a grounding for understanding change as directional. In split understandings, there must always be a controversy over whether change is best characterized as *either* cyclical (variational) *or* directional (transformational). This is the age-old conflict, in all fields of change inquiry, of the "Cycle of Time" versus the "Arrow of Time." Within the dialectical context, this dichotomy is resolved through recognition that the polarities of thesis/antithesis constitute the cyclical dimension of change. However, such cycles are never closed, as they would be in a circle. When a circle is opened a bit, it does not return precisely to its starting point. As a consequence, with the continuation of activity, the open cycle forms a spiral (the synthesis or integration). With the repetition of spirals, a direction is formed (Overton 1994a, 1994b) (see Figure 3.6).

In the 19th century, the principle of Becoming was extended in the works of social theorists such as Comte, Marx, and Spencer, and in the writings of biologists such as Wolff, Goethe, and von Baer. Herbert Spencer (1820–1903) is particularly worth noting because he appears to have been the first to attempt to translate the dialectical feature of Becoming, from the status of an epistemological–ontological background framing principle, to that of a scientific principle (Nisbet, 1969). For Spencer, the necessary order of development was a process of differentiation whereby organisms and society advance from homogeneity of structure to heterogeneity of structure. James Mark Baldwin (1895, 1897) also deserves mention. Baldwin first formulated a developmental psychology specifically in terms of dialectical categories. As Broughton points out, "his [Baldwin's] . . . orientation came to be tempered with a Hegelian view of dialectical progress through qualitatively distinct levels of consciousness" (1981, p. 399) (see also Freeman-Moir, 1982).

In the 20th century, Heinz Werner (1957, 1958) drew his own theoretical approach from the dialectical feature of the principle of Becoming. In this context, he proposed the orthogenetic (normal development) principle as a universal explanatory principle, or law, of transformational change. The *orthogenetic principle* asserts that "whenever there is development it proceeds from an initial state of relative globality and lack of differentiation to a state of increasing differentiation, articulation, and hierarchic integration" (1957, p. 126). But Werner was not alone among 20th-century developmentalists in constructing metanarrative

and theoretical understandings framed by the dialectic of Becoming. Piaget, for example, draws from the same image in laying out the metatheoretical grounding for his *equilibration* explanation of human transformational development: "These global transformations . . . gradually denote a sort of law of evolution which can be phrased as follows: assimilation and accommodation proceed from a state of chaotic undifferentiation to a state of differentiation with correlative coordination" (Piaget, 1954, p. 352). Similarly, Vygotsky (1978) maintains that development is best characterized as "a complex dialectical process characterized by periodicity, unevenness in the development of different functions, metamorphosis or qualitative transformation of one form into another" (p. 73).

It is significant also that these three major developmentalists of the last half of the 20th century—Werner (Werner & Kaplan, 1963, p. 11), Piaget (Piaget & Garcia, 1991, p. 8), and Vygotsky (1978, p. 56)—all considered development to be change entailing a spirality that emerges from cycles and yields direction (see Figure 3.6). As Vygotsky noted specifically with respect to higher psychological functions, "Development, as often happens, proceeds here not in a circle but in a spiral, passing through the same point at each new revolution while advancing to a higher level" (p. 56).

Along with classical developmental theorists like Werner, Piaget, and Vygotsky, dynamic theorists, both from the British object-relations and the ego psychology schools have found the core dialectical Becoming notions of "activity," "differentiation," and "integration" central for understanding both normal and pathological human ontogenesis (Overton & Horowitz, 1991). W.R.D. Fairbairn (1952), the founder of British object-relations theory, based his opposition to Freud's developmental understanding on Freud's Newtonian splitting of activity (becoming) and structure (being). Fairbairn objected to the way Freud conceived the ego "as a structure without any energy in its own right, and the 'id' is conceived as a source of energy without structure" (p. 148). In place of this split, Fairbairn launched the object-relations movement with the relational idea that it is unproductive to split system and activity, or structure and energy. Consequently, "complex ego structures are better conceived to be the product of the differentiation of an original and single dynamic ego-structure present at the beginning" (p. 148). D. W. Winnicott expanded this position and went on to argue that the main trend in development (which he referred to as "maturation") "can be gathered into the various meanings of the word integration" (1965, p. 59). John Bowlby, also a central figure in the British object-relations group, continued this line of thought by citing the significance of both "hierarchical structure" and "integration" (1958, p. 364), and by describing the beginnings of life as a dynamic structure, which in the course of development becomes "elaborated, through processes of integration and learning" (p. 365). Most recently, several dynamically oriented American investigators, including Steven Mitchell (1988), Thomas Ogden (1986), and Arnold Modell (1993), have explicitly drawn their theoretical understandings of the developing person from a grounding in the images of dialectical Becoming.

Ego psychology, from its founding, has offered a vision of the person beginning development as a relatively undifferentiated activity matrix (Hartmann, 1958; Hartmann, Kris, & Loewenstein, 1946), and, through action, differentiating functions of mobility, perception, memory, intention, and thinking, which become integrated as the system, organization, or structure termed "ego." As Hartmann (1958) noted, "ego development is a differentiation" (p. 49) and "we are dealing here with the coexistence of differentiation and integration" (p. 53). Jacobson (1964), Mahler (1979), and Kernberg (1976) all ground their own work in this tradition, and each assumes an initial lack of differentiation—in both the intrapsychic and interpersonal realms—that moves toward increasing differentiation and integration. Mahler, in fact, ultimately converts this metanarrative representation into her theoretical concept of the "separation–individuation process." Erikson, in conceptualizing his "epigenetic" principle of ego development, grounds this in the notion of a "dynamic balance of opposites" that achieves an integration and moves toward further balanced opposites. "We must, for each of the major stages of development, propose two seemingly contrary dispositions, ... although vital involvement depends on their balance. The first two, in infancy, are a sense of trust and a sense of mistrust: their balance, we claim, helps create the basis for the most essential overall outlook on life, namely, hope" (Erikson, Erikson, & Kivnick, 1986, p. 33).

This discussion has focused on the historical impact of the Leibnizian–Hegelian tradition as it advanced and articulated the principle of Becoming. More broadly, the philosophical grounding of relational developmental tradition was progressively elaborated from Leibniz to Kant to Hegel, and Kant's own contribution simultaneously both advanced and retarded this process. Kant's line of sight was epistemological, and because knowing is a human action, his focus was on the human conditions necessary for knowledge. Hume, after splitting reason (mind) from observation, had come to argue that valid (universal and necessary) knowledge cannot be found in the observational world, which yields only the particular and the contingent. Kant agreed but, adopting a relational stance, he argued that that fact does not lead to the dismissal of valid knowledge. Rather, it simply demonstrates that if contingent knowledge is a feature of the observational world, then valid knowledge must be a feature of thought, of mind.

Arguing from the relational perspective, Kant maintained that both valid and contingent knowledge are essential aspects of human experience (i.e., both the universal and the particular, the necessary and the contingent are features of human experience). Consequently, the question was not—as assumed in Newtonian–Humean split tradition—whether it was possible to have valid knowledge. The central question became the conditions of mind that had to be assumed in order to produce the experienced valid knowledge. Kant began the description of these conditions with the presupposition that reason/thought/concepts form a relational matrix with observation/intuitions/perceptions. This affirmation of the Leibnizian relational tradition—itself often described as Kant's attempt to reconcile rationalism and empiricism—is nowhere better articulated than in his famous relational aphorism, "*Concepts without percepts are empty, percepts without concepts are blind* (Thoughts without contents are empty, intuitions without concepts are blind. . . . The understanding cannot see, the senses cannot think. By their union only can knowledge be produced)" (Kant, 1781/1966, p. 45).

From this overarching relational commitment, Kant presented a philosophical sketch of human cognition that further affirmed both the activity and organization features of the Becoming tradition. Kant's description of mind basically entailed three interrelated dynamic organizational components. Because Kant did not split structure and function, these dynamic organizations are sometimes examined from the structural perspective and are called faculties and forms. At other times, they are examined from the functional perspective and called powers or activities: First, sense data or content is transformed into a priori categories of space and time according to the *"forms of intuition"* or forms of perception. Second, perceptions become synthesized in terms of a priori *"categories of understanding"* (e.g., existence, reality, causality, necessity), which operate as a base-level rule system that orders percepts according to the very features that Hume had dismissed (e.g., necessity, causality, reality, existence). Third, the *"imaginative faculty"* characterizes the activity of mind as it functions to synthesize perceptions and categories into objects of knowledge; "There exists therefore in us an active power for the synthesis of the manifold which we call imagination. . . . This imagination is meant to change the manifold of intuition into an image" (1781/1966, p. 112).

In addition to these three basic components of mind, Kant described a faculty of "judgment." Judgment is the active process that *applies knowledge*—gained through intuition, understanding, and imagination—to the practical world. This scheme of the relation between knowledge per se, and the accessing and application of that knowledge, became the background for a later cognitive developmental distinction between the development of a cognitive competence, and the development of procedures for accessing and applying that competence (Chandler & Chapman, 1991; Overton, 1990, 1991d).

Kant and the Phenomena–Noumena Split

Although this sketch of human cognition is grounded in the relational, two additional features of Kant's position are inconsistent with the relational developmental tradition: (a) Kant's Cartesian split of phenomena and noumena, and (b) the fact that Kant considered the categories and forms of intuition to be fundamentally unchanging. *Noumena* were described as *"things-in-themselves,"* or objects and events independent of any representation of the object or event. *Phenomena* were described as representations of objects and events as they are known by the knower. For Kant, these spheres were split. The thing-in-itself was disconnected from knowing, and knowing was disconnected from the thing-in-itself. A direct consequence of this split is that the Subject (person) point of view became a privileged position, in the same way that the Newtonian–Humean tradition had made the Object point of view a privileged position.

One broad impact of this Kantian split for developmental inquiry is that it came to form the background logic for

the nativist side of the nature–nurture debate, just as the Newtonian–Humean split formed the background logic for the nurture side. This nativism, whether with respect to Chomskyian (1972) explanations of language (Hirsh-Pasek, Golinkoff, & Reeves, 1994; Jackendoff, 1994; Overton, 1994c), or with respect to the neonativism that is currently popular in the infant cognitive literature (e.g., Baillargeon, 1993; Karmiloff-Smith, 1991; Mandler, 1992; Spelke, 1991; Spelke, Breinlinger, & Jacobson, 1992; see also Spelke & Newport, this Volume), presents a picture of the human mind as a set of innate rules, untouched by history and culture—an inversion of the empiricist tradition, which presents a picture of history and culture, untouched by the human mind.

Hegel's Relational Developmental Reconciliation of Mind and Nature

Hegel resolved Kant's split and moved his static categories back into a more fully coherent relational developmental context. Hegel (1807, Introduction) began his work from the position that there could be no detached thing-in-itself, just as there could be no detached knowing-in-itself. Rather, the world of knowing and the world of actual objects operated within the same dialectical relational matrix as other fundamental categories. This is the meaning of his well-known relational aphorism, "What is reasonable [the known] is actual [the object] and what is actual is reasonable" (Hegel, 1830, p. 9). Like Kant and others who held this line of thought, Hegel took the subject or phenomenological point of view. However, for Hegel, the world of actual objects and events became a dialectical feature of this perspective.

In his *phenomenology* (i.e., the study experience) of mind (i.e., of the subject), Hegel distinguished two features or "moments" of consciousness: (a) the "moment of knowledge" (i.e., knowing, thinking, "notion") and (b) the "moment of truth" (i.e., the actual or "object"). At any point, these moments may not stand in a harmonious relationship, as when what one thinks to be the case (moment of knowledge) turns out to be in error with respect to the actual world (moment of truth). History here comes to play a central role, and knowledge becomes developmental. When there is a lack of correspondence of these two moments, then "consciousness must alter its knowledge to make it conform to the object" (1807, p. 54). Thus, while Kant maintained that knowing is action, but action that remains static in its form, Hegel held knowing to be action that transforms itself across time.

In Hegel, the Kantian stable and fixed features of mind became fluid and changing, or, as Hundert (1989) points out, Kant's metaphor of mind as "a steel filing cabinet" became replaced by a metaphor of organic growth. This metaphor of organic growth then assumes the position as background that sustains and promotes future thinking from a relational developmental perspective. The metaphor is evident in the relational concepts of "differentiation" and "integration" that emerge from the dialectic, and Hegel's description of the development of knowledge, presented in the first pages of his *Phenomenology,* stands as a prototype for the developmental organic vision:

> The bud disappears in the bursting-forth of the blossom, and one might say that the former is refuted by the latter; similarly, when the fruit appears, the blossom is shown up in its turn as a false manifestation of the plant, and the fruit now emerges as the truth instead. These forms are not just distinguished from one another, they also supplant one another as mutually incompatible. Yet at the same time their fluid nature makes them moments of an organic unity in which they not only do not conflict, but in which each is as necessary as the other; and this mutual necessity alone constitutes the life of the whole. (Hegel, 1807, p. 2)

The Hegelian image of growth according to active processes of system differentiation and integration contrasts sharply with the Kantian image of fixed, a priori given active systems. A number of contemporary domains of developmental inquiry reflect the legacy of these traditions. For example, the Kantian metaphor of mind as a fixed "steel filing cabinet" provides background support for contemporary approaches to developmental inquiry that offer the digital computer as their guiding model of the nature of mind. The computer image itself fixes an understanding of the nature of cognitive/affective processes, of change, and of persons. The reality that emerges from this metaphor portrays cognitive development either as a simple increase in representational content (Scholnick & Cookson, 1994), which this machine, through various linear causal mechanisms, "processes," or as an increase in the efficiency of the computational machinery itself (Siegler, 1989, 1996; Sternberg, 1984; Valsiner, 1991). In this picture, there is no room for the expressive/transformational

change found in the works of Hegelian-oriented investigators such as Piaget, Werner, Erikson, Bowlby, Mahler, and others.

The Kantian/Hegelian contrast also grounds and sustains an important debate in the domain of affective development among those who begin from a shared understanding that "emotions are not 'stimuli' or 'responses' but central, organizing features of personality and behavior" (Malatesta et al., 1989, p. 5). Moving from this shared "subject" or person point of view that takes expressive change as the domain of developmental inquiry, a Kantian group (e.g., Ekman, 1984; Izard, 1977; Izard & Malatesta, 1987) and a Hegelian group (e.g., Lewis, 1993; Sroufe, 1979) set off on different paths concerning how best to characterize the affective development of the child. The Kantians argue for the adequacy of models that describe the infant as having a number of "discrete" basic emotions innately available. The Hegelians argue that a more adequate description suggests that the infant begins her affective life—as well as her social and cognitive life—as a relatively undifferentiated action system that becomes differentiated and reintegrated through operating on the actual world. Malatesta et al. (1989) capture the psychological translation of the Hegelian framework with respect to Sroufe's work: "Affects begin as undifferentiated precursor states of distress and nondistress and differentiate into specific emotions only gradually. Differentiation occurs in a stage-like way as a function of major developmental reorganizations" (p. 11).

It is instructive to note how this debate between the Hegelian and Kantian positions about affective development contrasts with the legacy of the Newtonian–Humean tradition. Campos and his colleagues' recent work on emotional development is illustrative (Campos, Campos, & Barrett, 1989; Campos, Mumme, Kermoian, & Campos, 1994). Campos et al. (1989) set up a *dichotomy* between the Hegelian–Kantian expressive view of emotion ("emotion as a special subjective state," p. 394) as a structural position, and Campos's own instrumental definition ("emotional signal," p. 398) as a functional position. Having split structure from function, and the expressive from the instrumental, Campos et al. (1994) argue in favor of a shift to understanding emotions as instrumental-functional. This position is described as a "new functionalism" because it adds an "adaptive" (i.e., the signal feature) element, introduced by evolutionary theory (see Figure 3.2) and pragmatist philosophy, to the traditional antecedent–consequent causal schema of the "old" functionalism. Kagan's (1994) understanding of the nature of emotion, which he approaches from "a nonpragmatic, Baconian frame" (p. 8), represents the older Newtonian–Humean functionalism. In Kagan's case, expressive is again split off from instrumental but it is the cause–effect relation of "(1) a precipitating event in a context accompanied by (2) changes in motor behavior" (p. 9) that identifies this foundational understanding of the nature of emotions.

The fact that Campos offers "new functionalism" as a "new relational view" illustrates how the meanings of key concepts become defined by the broad epistemological/ontological frame in which they are embedded (Overton, 1991a). For Campos, "relational," in this "new functionalism," is defined exclusively as "organism and the environment" as seen from the Object point of view (i.e., the split-off adaptive element of Figure 3.2). In other words, the Subject point of view (i.e., the Kantian/Hegelian phenomenological perspective) is written out as relationally meaningless: "In the past, emotions were considered to be feeling states indexed by behavioral expressions; now, emotions are considered to be processes of establishing, maintaining, or disrupting the relation between the organism and the environment" (Campos et al., 1989, p. 394). Thus, as in other proposals, a split argument presses for the either/or solution rather than suggesting that the expressive-constitutive and the instrumental-communicative are complementary lines of sight on the broad domain of developmental inquiry.

The debate over the form of emotional development is paralleled by a debate about the nature of the relationship between cognitive and emotional development. This debate is also framed by split and relational positions.. The split positions assert that conceptual boundaries are cuts of nature. The relational developmental position understands them as moments of functioning. As Santostefano (1995) points out, "Cognition and emotion will remain segregated as long as investigators view the boundary as real and the domains as opposites, either independent of each other (e.g., Zajonc, Pietromonico, & Bargh, 1982), parallel and interacting with one another (e.g., Leventhal, 1982) or with one dominating the other (e.g., Izard, 1982; Mandler, 1982)" (p. 63).

The Hegelian focus is on transformational and expressive changes of the Subject (i.e., of mind) (Taylor, 1979, 1995). The movement toward harmony or the integration of the moment of knowledge and the moment of truth is a feature of the phenomenological point of view. However, this focus, which entails universal and necessary features of the form of change, does not exclude the natural world of the individual, or contingent events, or variational change. Mind and nature form the same relational matrix as other dialectically defined concepts.

Hegel termed the ideal goal, or the ultimate integration of the dialectic forms, the "Absolute" or "Absolute Idea"—a subjective notion, in point of view (Taylor, 1979). However, Hegel's aim was the reconciliation of all fundamental contradictions. His general principle of the "identity of opposites" meant that the necessary transformational features of mind imply, and are implied by, contingent variational features of nature, just as variational features of nature imply, and are implied by, transformational features of mind. As Charles Taylor (1979) points out, "Fundamental to Hegel's theory . . . was the principle of embodiment. Subjectivity was necessarily situated in life, in nature, and in a setting of social practices and institutions" (p. 164). Thus, the Hegelian Absolute does not imply a kind of teleological cause of development, claiming that development proceeds independently of natural and social-cultural conditions. In fact, "Hegel's writings provide us with multifaceted investigations of the various ways in which thought is conditioned by such things as nature (in his account of the psychological development of consciousness and the capacity for thought) and cultural history" (Stern, 1991, p. 30).

Phenomenological Constructivism and Realism

The Hegelian reconciliation of mind and nature established the conceptual base for a particular type of constructivism that is probably best referred to as phenomenological constructivism. *Constructivism* is broadly the position that the activity of mind necessarily participates in the construction of the *known* world. Constructivism is an epistemological position that affirms the necessity of the constitutive dimension of the person in *all* knowing. Constructivism is usually contrasted with *Realism* which is the epistemological claim that the world as known is a direct reflection of a mind-independent world. For the realist, perception of this world is direct, without the mediating activity of mind (see, for example, Gibson, 1966, 1979). *Phenomenological constructivism* is the position that thought constructs the world as known, but the known world is a co-actor in the process of construction. Following Hegel, there are alternative object worlds, and it is important to be explicit about whether inquiry is focusing on the subject's object world—in which case, inquiry explores phenomenological constructivism—or the physical-social-cultural object world—in which case, inquiry explores implications of the settings within which phenomenological constructivism occurs. Hilary Putnam clearly captures the sense of phenomenological constructivism: "My view is not a view in which the mind makes up the world. . . . If one must use metaphorical language, then let the metaphor be this: the mind and the world jointly make up the mind and the world" (1987, p. 1).

Phenomenological constructivism best characterizes Piaget's writings, as he suggests when he declares himself, "neither empiricist nor apriorist but rather constructivist or partisan of dialectic as a source of novelties" (1992, p. 215). Kesselring's (1981, 1985) analysis of the Hegelian character of Piaget's developmental understanding suggests a similar perspective on Piaget's constructivism. However, the contemporary psychodynamic theories that take an object-relations point of view present the most systematic elaboration of phenomenological constructivism. Psychodynamic theory has long distinguished between the phenomenological object and the environmental object (see, e.g., Balint, 1968; Ogden, 1986). This distinction is basic to Donald Winnicott's well-known paradox of the infant–mother relationship: The infant actively constructs the mother (phenomenological object), but the mother (environmental object) is coacting in this construction ("The baby creates the object, but the object was there waiting to be created"; Winnicott, 1971, p. 89).

Object-relations as a family of theories of human development, along with Erikson's ego theory and the cognitive/affective theories of Piaget and Werner, all focus their inquiry on the psychological development of the individual, the person. This development entails the initial differentiation of phenomenological Subject and Object from a relatively undifferentiated field of action. At the same time, from an Object point of view, there is an existing world of relatively permanent, differentiated objects—social, cultural, physical, and biological objects—as well as the individual as Object (see Figure 3.4). Phenomenological constructivist inquiry may take as "point of view" either the constructive process or the correlation between this process and social-cultural/biological objects. In other words, from the Hegelian perspective, theories of

intrapsychic development and theories of *interpersonal* development do not necessarily conflict. Winnicott's work (1965) is again illustrative as he moves between an inquiry focused on the intrapsychic differentiation of Subject/Object dynamic systems, and interpersonal issues of infant–mother interaction as these facilitate or impede the intrapsychic growth of the infant.

Winnicott's approach, and other object-relations approaches, illustrates an actual application of Hegelian principles to the resolution of the intrapsychic–interpersonal dichotomy. A similar potential resolution may be found in Piagetian and Vygotskyian approaches to development. The development of individual intrapsychic dynamic organizations has been the Piagetian focus of inquiry, but a good deal of Piaget's own investigations concerned the role of the interpersonal social-cultural context (Chapman, 1986; Kitchener, 1991; Piaget, 1995; Youniss & Damon, 1992). The social-cultural interpersonal process has been the Vygotskian focus; yet Vygotsky's writings demonstrate a significant interest in intrapsychic dynamic organizations of the person. Van der Veer and Valsiner (1994) argue that, in fact, it is inaccurate to depict Piaget and Vygotsky as irreconcilable opponents because Piaget and Vygotsky did not differ about the development of "personal-cognitive (and affective) structures" (p. 6), and there is an "actual closeness of the basic personalistic standpoints of both . . . [that] has gone without attention" (p. 6). As a consequence of both their reciprocal interests and their metanarrative closeness, Piaget and Vygotsky can reasonably be offered as alternative poles of a broadly unified approach to developmental inquiry: Piaget's intrapsychic inquiry functions in the context of the Vygotskian interpersonal action, and Vygotsky's interpersonal inquiry functions in the context of the Piagetian intrapsychic action.

The Marxist Split Tradition

This relational rapprochement between the intrapsychic and the interpersonal hinges on understanding Piaget and Vygotsky in the context of the Leibnizian–Hegelian relational developmental tradition. When Vygotsky is interpreted in the context of the writings of Karl Marx, a split understanding reappears. Marx was an early admirer of Hegel and an heir of the Leibnizian–Hegelian tradition. In this context, his work affirmed the centrality of both activity and the dialectic. However, and most importantly, Marx elevated the material world to an absolute privileged position as *the* source of thought. In this move, Marx reasserted a split tradition. Marx's *dialectical materialism* thus became another foundationalist position, similar to the Newtonian–Humean tradition in that both appeal to a mind-independent material world as the absolute bedrock of the Real. This commitment to a split-off absolute material given, as the Real, at times permits a convenient marriage between contemporary behavioral approaches to development and contemporary Marxist approaches (Reese, 1995). In both types of approaches, the intrapsychic cognitive/affective person is explained by material social-cultural factors, and *only* by these factors. In both approaches, instrumental (mediated) activity is privileged over expressive. In other words, in both behavioral and Marxist approaches, the person as expressive/transformational is necessarily treated as Appearance, and the material represented as instrumental/variable is necessarily treated as the Real.

Social and Biological Constructivism

The Marxist split tradition became the ground for a second type of constructivism, *social constructivism*. To understand social constructivism it must again be emphasized that, according to Marxism, the material world of instrumental-communicative social relations, and *only* this world, builds the categories of thought. Once thought is built in this fashion, the person projects these socially instilled categories back onto the world and, in this sense, constructs the known world. Hence, social constructivism is the constructing of the known world from an instrumental-communicative social relations foundation, and *only* from this foundation. This position was later elaborated by the pragmatist George Herbert Mead under the rubric of "social behaviorism" (Mead, 1934). Vygotsky, who was writing at about the same time as Mead, has come to be viewed as the father of the social constructivist movement—probably largely because Vygotsky's writings were initially "discovered and propagated by small groups of 'progressive' young Marxists who saw his work as providing, among other things, a foundation for a criticism of the prevailing tendency to attribute individual failure and success to genetic endowment" (Van der Veer & Valsiner, 1994, p. 5).

When Vygotsky is placed in a social constructivist framework, there is no rapprochement between him and Piaget—between the interpersonal and the intrapsychic. In fact, when Vygotsky is located in this frame, his work

becomes more closely aligned with the Gibsonian (Gibson, 1966, 1979) realist ecological position. In this context, the person's "intentions" become reduced to instrumental acts that change through a Darwinian-like selection process in accordance with the affordances of the environment for action (Reed, 1993; Rogoff, 1993).

Social constructivism, as a split position, tends to not even address phenomenological constructivism. Instead, social constructivism places itself in a dichotomous, either/or relationship with yet a third variety of constructivism, *biological constructivism*. Biological constructivism emerges from the Kantian split and involves the claim that the person cognitively/affectively constructs the world as known, but the biological genetic endowment determines the fundamental nature of the person. The contemporary work of Sandra Scarr (1992) nicely illustrates biological constructivism. Scarr maintains, on the one hand, that "reality" is constructed by experience, and thus, it is "not a property of a physical world" (p. 50). On the other hand, she asserts that "*genotypes drive experiences*. . . . In this model, parental genes determine their phenotypes, the child's genes determine his or her phenotype, and the child's environment is merely a reflection of the characteristics of both parents and child" (p. 54). A similar biological constructivism, but one that focuses more directly on cognitive development, is illustrated in the work of Karmiloff-Smith (1991). As suggested earlier, Karmiloff-Smith is among a group of contemporary neonativists (see Carey & Gelman, 1991) who claim that the basic foundations of mind (i.e., learning constraints) are prewired and that further development entails learning built on these constraints. In this context, Karmiloff-Smith argues for a reconciliation between nativism and constructivism based on acceptance of the notion that "a nativist stance is required for an account of the *initial* architecture of the mind" (p. 172), and recognition that this nativism "does not necessarily preclude a constructivist approach with respect to *subsequent* development" (p. 173). The biological and social constructivist confrontation, as it turns out, is yet another manifestation of the split nature–nurture dichotomy, and nature (nativist)–nurture (learning) reconciliations are manifestations of the split bio/social metanarrative described in Figure 3.2.

The Marxist split tradition continues to exert a strong contextual influence over both the interpretation of Vygotsky's approach and, more broadly, the interpretation of the relationship between the intrapsychic and the interpersonal.

The Marxist tradition has been elaborated, and these elaborations often function as the epistemological–ontological ground for conceptualizing the interpersonal and social-cultural features of development. Jurgen Habermas's "critical theory" represents the most carefully and fully articulated contemporary elaboration of the Marxist split tradition.

Habermas, Bakhtin, and the Marxist Split Tradition

In a negative sense, the core of Habermas's work is the denial of any possible centrality of the expressive-constitutive subject as a point of reference. As Thomas McCarthy points out, "the key to Habermas's approach is his rejection of the 'paradigm of consciousness' and its associated 'philosophy of the subject' in favor of the through-and-through intersubjectivist paradigm of 'communicative' action" (1993, p. x). Habermas himself considers this move to an exclusive privileging of the instrumental-communicative to be a "paradigm-change" that leaves behind any vestige of Cartesian "subjectivism" or the "metaphysics of subjectivity" (Habermas, 1993a, p. 296). From this position, Habermas analyzes favorably George Herbert Mead's "social behaviorism" (1991, 1992) as furthering the same paradigm shift, and he attacks "the moral point of view" taken by expressive-constitutive oriented developmental investigators such as Kohlberg, because here "issues of moral cognition take precedence over questions of practical orientation" (1993b, p. 121).

In a more positive vein, Habermas attempts to locate all the traditional dialectical tensions—between subject and object, self and other, reason and observation—*within* the domain of communication and social practice (McCarthy, 1991). If this conceptualization functioned as "a point of view," thereby allowing another point of view that located the same tensions in a complementary fashion within the expressive-constitutive subject, it would constitute a powerful perspective from which to explore the instrumental-communicative features of development. However, Habermas insists that the dialectical tensions *must be located in the instrumental-communicative realm, and only in the instrumental-communicative realm.* This insistence on exclusivity undercuts the potential of the position by perpetuating a split that ultimately unnecessarily constrains developmental inquiry.

M. M. Bakhtin represents a final figure of significance in the continuing elaboration of the Marxist tradition

Bakhtin's (1986) contribution is a conception of meaning and language that is thoroughly external to the expressive-constitutive subject (Kent, 1991). This account follows Habermas, and roots meaning and language totally in the field of intersubjective communicative interaction. Also, as in Habermas, the movement away from the expressive-constitutive subject as one source of meaning and language is viewed as an attack on Cartesian "subjectivism." According to Bakhtin, the utterance or "speech genre" that forms the fundamental unit of communicative interaction is *the* source of meaning and language. The utterance is the fundamental element of dialogue between individuals, and dialogue constitutes the instrumental action source of *all* meaning. Thus, following Habermas, the intrasubjective (i.e., intrapsychic) and intersubjective are split. Meaning necessarily becomes isolated in and *only* in intersubjective dialogue—the instrumental-communicative. In this split scheme, there is no room for the notion of language-as-system, found in the works of Saussure, Roman Jakobson, and Chomsky; there is no room for the notion that the child acquires language in order to express intentional states of meaning, found in the work of Bloom (1993, this *Handbook*, Volume 2); and there is no room for the general idea that meaning is as much a reflection of the internal mental states of the subject, as it is a reflection of the external social and physical world (Overton, 1994c). In a review of Bloom's work, Farrar (1996) illustrates the distinction between a Bakhtin-like functionalist view of language, and Bloom's own relational perspective:

> Many researchers view language from a functionalist orientation in which language is conceptualized as a tool or *instrument* that children learn as a way to accomplish different *communicative* goals. Bloom suggests that, although this is one of the functions that language can be used for (among others), such a characterization ignores the internal psychological dimension of language. When children use language as a tool, they are using it to *express* their intentions or their mental states. Consequently, she proposes that what is primary to children's ability to use and learn language is their ability to represent mental meanings in their acts of *expression and interpretation.* (p. 106, emphasis added)

Bakhtin's attack on Cartesian "subjectivism" is one of a long line of such critiques that includes those of John Dewey, Heidegger, Wittgenstein, Quine, Habermas, and Hans-Georg Gadamer (Bernstein, 1983; Kent, 1991). From a relational perspective, the appropriate focus of such critiques is the notion of the isolated individual cut off from history and culture. Cartesian "subjectivism" is itself a reflection of the Cartesian "split" (conversely, the "split" is a reflection of the "subjectivism"). If the person were not presented in atomistic isolation, then any focus on the subject as person would necessarily entail history and culture, just as any focus on the intersubjective, the mediational, the pragmatic, or the instrumental-communicative would necessarily entail the expressive, fully embodied subject (Overton, 1997a, 1997b). Only in a split tradition, whether it be the Humean split of Skinner, the Kantian split of Scarr and Chomsky, or the Marxist split of Habermas and Bakhtin, does one believe that *only* one *or* the other must constitute the ultimate Real. Searle (1992, 1995) characterizes the relational approach, which allows inquiry into changes of the expressive subject without engaging in Cartesian "subjectivism," as an acceptance of the irreducibility of a "first-person ontology." Objective (i.e., public, intersubjective, scientific) methods of inquiry (i.e., epistemological activities) can be applied to both Subject and Object, when both are granted the status of ontological reality. Inquiry is then expanded, not constrained.

Culture and Development

The Marxist split tradition has, in recent times, been an influential background for metanarratives about culture and development. Wertsch (1991) clearly highlights this in his "sociocultural" approach to development. He begins his broadly synthetic account by setting a contrast between developmental inquiry that focuses on "the universals of mental functioning" and his own focus on "sociocultural specifics." However, rather than continuing this contrast of the universal and the particular—the transcendent and the immanent—in a relational context, Wertsch explicitly establishes the Marxist ontological agenda, and casts Vygotsky and Luria solidly in this tradition.

> In pursuing a line of reasoning that reflected their concern with Marxist claims about the *primacy of social forces* [emphasis added], Vygotsky and his colleagues . . . contended that many of the design features of mediational means [instrumental activity] originated in social life. As stated by Luria (1981), "in order to explain the highly complex forms of human consciousness one must go beyond the human organism. One must seek the origins of conscious activity and 'categorical' behavior not in the recesses of the human brain or in the depths of the spirit, but in the external conditions of life. Above all, this means that one must seek these origins in

the external processes of social life, in the social and historical forms of human existence" (p. 25). (Wertsch, 1991, pp. 33–34)

The Marxist split tradition then becomes the bridge between Vygotsky and Bakhtin:

> Both Vygotsky and Bakhtin believed that human communicative practices give rise to mental functioning in the individual. . . . They were convinced that "the social dimension of consciousness is primary in time and in fact. The individual dimension of consciousness is derivative and secondary (Vygotsky, 1979, p. 30)." (Wertsch, 1991, p. 13)

However, in Wertsch's estimation, Vygotsky failed to sufficiently pursue the Marxist tradition, for, given that Vygotsky was "interested in formulating a Marxist psychology, he made precious little mention of broader historical, institutional, or cultural processes" (1991, p. 46). Consequently, Wertsch draws on Habermas's (1984) account of instrumental-communicative activity, and moves beyond Vygotsky to Bahktin's contribution, in order to pursue the general claim that "mediational means emerge in response to a wide range of social forces" (1991, p. 34).

Shweder's (1990) approach to culture and development is another contemporary illustration of the background influence of the Marxist split tradition (see also Cole, 1995, 1996; Miller, 1996; Rogoff, 1990, 1993). However, in proposing an outline for a "cultural psychology," Shweder follows a more Habermas-like strategy by locating the dialectic tension of subject and culture necessarily in the realm of the instrumental, thereby denying any reality to the fully embodied expressive subject. In Shweder's metanarrative, the universal, the transcendent, the ideal, the fixed, are explicitly denied any fundamental reality (1990, p. 25); thus, a dichotomy is established that privileges the particular, the immanent, the practical, the relative. As a result, when Shweder (e.g., Shweder & Sullivan, 1990) identifies the subject or person of his subject-culture inquiry, it explicitly is not, nor could it be, the universal or ideal subject found in some domains of cognitive/affective and personality research. Shweder explicitly excludes this subject and instead offers the "semiotic subject" characterized only by instrumental rationality and instrumental intentionality. In fact, the final result here is little different than a straightforward Skinnerian position. In the latter type of frame (Skinner, 1971), it is permissible to consider "higher mental processes" only to the extent that they are understood as being defined by a specific repertoire of instrumental responses correlated with specific stimuli. Similarly, for Shweder, "rationality" and "intentions" are defined as instrumental problem-solving behaviors that are correlated with cultural contexts.

When the Marxist tradition is the ground for developmental inquiry, as in these illustrative examples, activity is central—as action is central in the Leibnizian–Hegelian relational tradition. However, it is important to keep in focus the fact that activity, in the Marxist tradition, is necessarily restricted to the instrumental-communicative. When Rogoff (1993), for example, discusses cognition—or as Shweder discusses intentions, or Bakhtin discusses language and meaning—it becomes restrictively defined as "the active process of solving mental and other problems" (p. 124). The Leibnizian–Hegelian tradition accepts this instrumental action and expressive mental action as relational moments. But when Rogoff addresses the expressive, she first reframes it as a static formulation, and then rejects it disparagingly as "cognition as a collection of mental possessions" (p. 124). The result of splitting off the expressive subject is that Rogoff's own "relational" approach is restricted to a relation between the instrumental subject and cultural contexts. This she presents as an approach that permits the consideration of "individual thinking or cultural functioning as foreground without assuming that they are actually separate elements" (p. 124). This is correct, but the assumption of "separate elements" has already been made in the background, and the unwanted element of this assumption has already been suppressed.

The expressive-constitutive/instrumental-communicative Leibnizian–Hegelian tradition of the centrality of action is illustrated in a number of developmental "action theories" (see Oppenheimer, 1991a, for a review; Overton, in press). However, a particularly rich account is found in the work of E. E. Boesch (1991). As Eckensberger (1989) points out:

Boesch begins with the notion that any action and any goal has two dimensions or aspects: one . . . is *the instrumental aspect,* that an action is carried out instrumentally in order to reach a goal. For example, one takes a hammer to drive a nail into the wall. There is, however, a second aspect in any action, which Boesch calls the *subjective-functional aspect* [the expressive] Here, the driving of the nail may have the subjective-functional meaning that one feels proud of being

able to do so, one may also enjoy it, or it may even be related to feelings of rage. In any case, the action of nailing receives a meaning beyond its instrumental purpose. (p. 30)

From this base, Boesch (1980, 1991, 1992) and Eckensberger (1989, 1990, 1996) formulate the beginnings of a developmentally oriented cultural psychology that is more inclusive than those founded in the Marxist tradition. Boesch's system and Eckensberger's extension of the system draw from Piaget—whom Boesch calls the first action theorist; from Janet's dynamic theory; from psychodynamic theory; and from Kurt Lewin's field theory. Elaborating on the relational theme of expressive/instrumental action, Boesch and Eckensberger argue for a cultural psychology that aims at an integration of "cultural and individual change . . . individual and collective meaning systems . . . [and one that] should try to bridge the gap between objectivism and subjectivism" (Eckensberger, 1990). To this end, they establish a framework bound by two polar dimensions of developmental processes. One of these, Boesch calls the process of "primary structuration" which involves "the development of internal action schemes and the *objectivation of actions as culture*" (Eckensberger, 1989, p. 30). In this process, individual meaning systems develop and become expressively projected onto the cultural contexts. The other pole or "secondary structuration" entails collective cultural meaning systems providing historical changing contexts for the formation of individual meaning systems. Thus, as the title of one of Boesch's (1992) papers suggests, "Culture–Individual–Culture" forms the cycle of knowledge.

Inclusive relational developmental models of the individual and the culture are, of course, not limited to the European continent. Damon (1988, 1991; Damon & Hart, 1988), for example, presents the outline of just such an approach in his discussion of "two complementary developmental functions, . . . the social and the personality functions of social development" (1988, p. 3). Moving within the broader Leibnizian–Hegelian concepts of differentiation and integration, Damon presents the interpenetration of the two functions as an identity of opposites. The social function is an act of integration serving to "establish and maintain relations with other, to become an accepted member of society-at-large, to regulate one's behavior according to society's codes and standards" (p. 3). The personality function, on the other hand, is the function of individuation, an act of differentiation serving the formation of the individual's personal identity. It requires "distinguishing oneself from others, determining one's own unique direction in life, and finding within the social network a position uniquely tailored to one's own particular nature, needs, and aspirations" (p. 3). Turiel (this *Handbook,* Volume 3; Turiel & Wainryb, 1994) and Nucci (1996; Nucci & Lee, 1993; Nucci & Weber, 1995) and Killen (1996) detail similar approaches to the relation of person and culture in a series of theoretical and empirical explorations of the development of social and moral reasoning, and Tesson and Youniss (1995) describe a related perspective on individual psychological development, and contemporary microsociological theory. Erikson (1968), of course, was formulating exactly this type of relational developmental model when he described identity as "a process 'located' *in the core of the individual* and yet also *in the core of his communal culture*" (p. 22).

As Habermas and Bakhtin reflect contemporary philosophical elaborations of the Marxist tradition, Hans-Georg Gadamer (1976, 1989, 1993), in Europe, and Charles Taylor (1979, 1985, 1995), in North America, illustrate the contemporary form of the Leibnizian–Hegelian relational developmental philosophical tradition. Although both Gadamer and Taylor reject features of the Hegelian system (e.g., the idea of the attainment of absolute knowledge), each draws from and extends Hegel's notions of the relational and the developmental, and of the centrality of action as both expressive-constitutive and instrumental-communicative.

Gadamer, Taylor, and the Leibnizian–Hegelian Relational Developmental Tradition

Gadamer's "universal hermeneutics" or "philosophical hermeneutics" (as distinct from Habermas's "critical hermeneutics") presents the broader, more systematic approach of the two. *Hermeneutics* is about the interpretation of meaning. Its heritage goes back to a classical period when the hermeneutic task involved the discovery of the meaning of sacred texts. Schleiermacher made important formative contributions during the Romantic period. Vico and Droysen later added a historical dimension to the problem of interpretation, and Dilthey, in his *Critique of Historical Reason* at the turn of the 20th century, developed the method of *Verstehen* (understanding) as a methodology for the human sciences (Bleicher, 1980).

In the work of Gadamer, the heir of this tradition, hermeneutics includes a methodology (see the relational developmental methodology section of this chapter), but is broader than a methodology alone. Hermeneutics is a general philosophical position that seeks to answer the question: "How is understanding possible?" (Gadamer, 1989).

The Hermeneutic Circle: Ontogenetic Change, and the Scientific Logic of Retroduction

For hermeneutics, the *"hermeneutic circle"*—a reaffirmation of the Leibnizian–Hegelian holism of the unity of parts to a whole—constitutes the *fundamental background condition for all understanding.* Understanding moves forward from pre-understanding to understanding in a circular movement. The whole—whether it is a text that requires understanding, or some general phenomenon of inquiry, such as human development—is initially approached with the meanings, or "prejudices," that constitute common sense. These are the initial meanings of what hermeneutics terms the "pre-understanding." These anticipatory meanings—called "the horizon of a particular present" (Gadamer, 1989, p. 306)—are projected onto the phenomenon of inquiry. As a consequence, they form an early stage in understanding. However, the object of inquiry is not merely a figment of projection. The object of inquiry is itself an internally coherent whole; consequently, the object of inquiry reciprocally operates as a corrective source of further projections of meaning. Through this circle of projection and correction understanding advances, and the notion of an advance or progression is appropriate here because the hermeneutic circle is never a closed circle. The hermeneutic circle represents—following Hegel's dialectic—the open *cycle* whose action creates a continuing directional spirality to knowing (see Figure 3.6). "The circle is constantly expanding, since the concept of the whole is relative, and being integrated in ever larger contexts always affects the understanding of the individual part" (Gadamer, 1989, p. 190).

The hermeneutic circle forms the conceptual context for several features of developmental inquiry. When inquiry is focused on the nature of ontogenetic change, the hermeneutic circle becomes the conceptual context for the Piagetian theory of assimilation/accommodation, as the action mechanism of change. Assimilation constitutes the projection of expressive meanings (i.e., affects, perceptions, cognitions) onto a world being constituted. Accommodation constitutes the action of correction, as assimilation yields partial success/partial failure. Psychological development necessarily proceeds from some organization (sensorimotor, representational, reflective) that constitutes pre-understanding, and this is projected to constitute the world as experienced. But this projection meets the demands of a world with its own structure, and action corrects itself in anticipation of further projection.

When inquiry is focused on defining the scientific nature of developmental inquiry, then the hermeneutic circle articulates the relational scientific logic called "retroduction." As will be detailed in the later methodology section, split-off scientific methodologies have described the logic of science as being *either* deductive logic, *or* inductive logic, *or* some *additive* combination of the two. *Retroduction* is a logic that overcomes the dichotomy, and identifies "top-down" and "bottom-up" approaches as relational points of view. The logic of retroduction (sometimes also called "abduction") was originally described by the pragmatist philosopher Charles Sanders Pierce (1992; Hanson, 1958; Overton, 1991b). Along with a modified version called "inference to the best explanation" (Harman, 1965), retroduction identifies a scientific logic that requires the projection of *interpretations* (e.g., narratives, theories, models) as plausible explanations of the domain of study. Interpretations are not, however, fantasies. They are formulated, and corrected, in the light of all available background information (including both reasons and observations). Thus, the hermeneutic circle of projected interpretations and corrected understanding constitutes the relational logic of science which warrants the expansion of systematized empirical knowledge.

In claiming the hermeneutic circle as the core precondition for understanding, Gadamer follows Heidegger, who grounds the concept in the existential:

> Heidegger describes the circle in such a way that the understanding of the text remains permanently determined by the anticipatory movement of fore-understanding. . . . The circle, then, is not formal in nature. It is neither subjective nor objective, but describes understanding as the interplay of the movement of tradition and the movement of the interpreter. The anticipation of meaning that governs our understanding of a text is not an act of subjectivity, but proceeds from the commonality that binds us to the tradition. But this commonality is constantly being formed in our relation to tradition. Tradition is not simply a permanent precondition; rather, we

produce it ourselves inasmuch as we understand, participate in the evolution of tradition, and hence further determine it ourselves. Thus the circle of understanding is not a "methodological" circle, but describes an element of the ontological structure of understanding. (Gadamer, 1989, p. 293)

From the perspective of the hermeneutic circle, grounded existentially in this fashion, (a) epistemology and ontology are joined as relative moments in the whole of understanding, and (b) understanding is identified as both relational (the reciprocity of the interpreter and tradition) and variational/transformational (the oscillating movement of part and whole leads to changes in the form of the individual and the form of tradition).

The hermeneutic circle, as the precondition for understanding, owes an obvious debt to the Leibnizian–Hegelian holistic tradition. Gadamer acknowledges this debt and identifies himself as "an heir of Hegel." However, this kinship is defined most significantly when Gadamer articulates the specific conditions for understanding, for he endorses the Hegelian "dialectic of the universal and concrete as the summation of the whole of metaphysics . . . and along with this to realize that this has to be summed up ever anew" (Gadamer, 1993, p. 51).

The preservation and renewal of the dialectic of universal and concrete—the transcendental and the immanent—defines the core of Gadamer's approach and distinguishes his approach from that of Habermas. For Gadamer, *universal and concrete stand in a dialectic relationship;* an identity of opposites. Each is granted an ontological reality. Habermas, on the other hand, denies ontological reality to the universal, and thus splits the dialectic.

Existentially, Gadamer places the dialectic of the universal and the concrete in the medium of language. "Language is not an instrumental setup, a tool, that we apply, but the element in which we live and which we can never objectify to the extent that it ceases to surround us" (1993, p. 50). Language attains both a universal function in understanding and a concretization in communicative speech. When the understanding is foregrounded, "understanding is always interpretation" (1989, p. 307). From this perspective, language activity is the source of anticipatory meanings that form a part of the hermeneutic circle. "Let us remember . . . that understanding always includes an element of application and thus produces an ongoing process of concept formation" (p. 403).

When communication is foregrounded, the notion of *dialogue* becomes as central to Gadamer as it is to Habermas or Bakhtin. "Thus there emerged all at once and behind all methodology . . . and all epistemology the unity of dialogue and dialectic that related Hegel and Plato to one another" (Gadamer, 1993, p. 47). The action of dialogue or conversation constitutes the "structure of verbal understanding" and it is within dialogue, characterized as "a dialectic of question and answer" (Gadamer, 1989, p. 576), that Gadamer locates change of understanding. However, *dialogue is not limited to the interpersonal.* Dialogue can be between interpreter and other (i.e., interpersonal), between interpreter and self (i.e., intrapersonal, "which since Plato is the way we think of thinking," 1993, p. 57), or between interpreter and the object of inquiry (i.e., methodological dialogue; see "retroductive" logic in this section and in the section on methodology later in this chapter).

Gadamer maintains that all experience is defined by the active dialogue between expressive understanding and instrumental communication, but this position does not imply that linguistic meaning is foundational to other types of meaning. This is a particularly important point because of Habermas's (1980) claim that the nonlinguistic experience of work and the nonlinguistic experience of domination are arguments against Gadamer's claim to universality. On this point, Gadamer joins Ricoeur (1991), who asserts that the hermeneutic tradition, in fact, "shares with phenomenology the thesis of the derivative character of linguistic meaning" (p. 41). Gadamer (1989) says:

> Who denies that our specific human possibilities do not subsist solely in language? There is a prelinguistic experience of the world. . . . The language of gesture, facial expression, and movement binds us to each other. There are laughter and tears. . . . There is the world of science within which the exact, specialized languages of symbolism and mathematics provide sure foundations for the elaboration of theory, . . . I acknowledge that these phenomena demonstrate that behind all the relativities of language and convention there is something in common which is no longer language, but which looks to an ever-possible verbalization. (pp. 546–547)

When Gadamer specifically addresses the phenomenological point of view, he argues that while all experience shares this "lingual dimension" (i.e., a potential to verbalization), the starting point for understanding and interpretation is not language but the question of what is brought to

language. Gadamer argues that *play* phenomenologically constitutes the base form of experience that becomes transformed into structures, including linguistic structures. Play, as Gadamer defines it, is an orientation to the world exemplified in the *relatively* unstructured action of the preverbal child. In play, there is an acknowledgment of:

> The primacy of play over the consciousness of the player. . . . Play clearly represents an order in which the to-and-fro motion of play follows of itself. It is part of play that the movement is not only without goal or purpose but also without effort. It happens, as it were, by itself. (1989, pp. 104–105)

Thus, play, from the Subject point of view, is not instrumental. Play is expressive in character or what Gadamer calls "self-presentation":

> Play is really limited to presenting itself. . . . But self-presentation is a universal ontological characteristic of nature. We know today how inadequate are conceptions of biological purpose when it comes to an understanding the form of living things. So too it is an inadequate approach to ask what the life function and biological purpose of play is. First and foremost, play is self-presentation. (1989, p. 108)

Gadamer's ontological argument is that expressive alternating action (i.e., variational change) exhibited in the to-and-fro motion of play transforms itself into novel structure. This argument is echoed directly in Piaget's theoretical claim that the repeated action of assimilation to-and-fro opens accommodative action and leads to transformation into novel mental organization.

Charles Taylor's work, on the development of understanding and the development of self, closely parallels Gadamer's. He acknowledges the heritage: "My whole way of thinking on these issues [of understanding] has been much influenced by Gadamer (with some input, I have to admit, from Hegel as well)" (1995, p. 148). Understanding and self are formed in the activity of conversation (dialogue) for Taylor, as they are for Gadamer, Habermas, and Bakhtin. However, this formation, this development, is not encapsulated in the instrumental-communicative alone, as it is for Habermas and Bakhtin. Following Isaiah Berlin's analysis of the contribution of Herder to language and meaning, Taylor (1995) distinguishes between the expressive-constitutive dimension and the instrumental dimension of the person that has been discussed throughout this chapter.

As already described, the expressive-constitutive dimension refers to the creative features of human action or mental functioning—to the making of new behaviors, new intentions, new meanings. The instrumental, or instrumental-communicative, dimension is about the application of behaviors, intentions, and meanings to order the world and succeed in it. In the expressive-constitutive processes, we come "to have the world we have." In the instrumental processes, "we order the things in that world" (1995, p. ix). *Dialogue occurs between the expressive-constitutive person who creates the world, and the world that creates the person; not between a set of disembodied instrumentalities and a world that creates the instrumentalities.* Further, dialogue is not limited to the verbal. The nonverbal play discussed by Gadamer, the early rhythmic action of the infant (Sanders, 1975, 1989), and the sensorimotor transactions of infant and primary caregiver (Trevarthen, 1980) all constitute the dialogue.

Taylor, like Gadamer and Hegel, locates his inquiry in the horizon of phenomenology. His discussion of the dialogical nature of the self (i.e., the self formed in the dialogue of person and world), as well as the dialogical nature of understanding, centers on the expressive-constitutive dimension of the person, and he describes this person as the "subject of embodied agency, which has developed out of modern phenomenology as in the works of Heidegger and Merleau-Ponty" (Taylor, 1995, p. 21). For Merleau-Ponty (1962, 1963) and Taylor, embodiment has a double meaning. It refers to the body as physical structure, and the body as lived experience actively engaged with the world.

The Embodied Relational Person of Developmental Inquiry

Taylor's assertion of the centrality of the embodied subject is not, as he strongly emphasizes, a simple claim that various functions such as thinking, perception, and so on, depend empirically, or causally, on certain states of the body (e.g., not being able to see, if one's eyes are closed). *Embodiment* is the claim that our perception, thinking, and understanding, our "experiencing or living the world is essentially that of an agent with this particular kind of body" (1995, p. 62). Thus, the centrality of the concept of embodiment is not an empirical claim about causes, but an epistemological/ontological grounding. The embodied subject in the relational developmental tradition forms a bridge between the biological and the social-cultural, as discussed earlier in relation to Figure 3.4. Although the embodied subject, through one form of dialogue, creates and is created by the social-cultural world, so too the embodied subject, through another form of dialogue, creates and is created by the biological world. The biological, the psychological, and the social-cultural all emerge from a relatively undifferentiated action field.

The notion of the embodied/expressive/engaged subject provides Taylor with a context within which to critique views of thinking (and of mind, more broadly) that split off mind, or disengage mind from life. Thus, Taylor argues for the inadequacy of "representationalist" (see, e.g., Mandler, 1988, 1992; Spelke, 1991) information-processing, computer, or mind-as-a-camera approaches:

> [They] offer us the picture of agents who in perceiving the world take in "bits" of information from their surroundings, and then "process" them in some fashion, in order to emerge with the "picture" of the world they have; who then act on the basis of this picture to fulfill their goals, through a "calculus" of means and ends. (Taylor, 1995, p. 63)

Beyond critique, the notion of the *embodied/expressive/engaged subject* has recently come to frame converging alternatives to the *traditional representationalist disengaged conceptions of mind,* and the development of mind. These alternative phenomenological concepts of mind emerge from diverse interests of inquiry (i.e., interests located in the spheres of the biological, the person, the social-cultural), and they generally function under the rubric of *embodiment theory* or enactment theory (Mueller, Sokol, & Overton, in press; Overton, 1994a, 1994c, 1997a, 1997b).

Embodiment theory, in fact, moves the premise of the present discussion full circle. The premise of this section has been that the relational developmental metanarrative (see the discussion surrounding Figure 3.4) and the inclusive relational definition of development require a relational epistemological/ontological grounding. Embodiment theory illustrates—from the phenomenological line of sight—the type of theory and of theoretical inquiry that is generated by the Leibnizian–Hegelian tradition and relational developmental metanarrative.

Interrelated features of embodiment theory have been formulated by Bloom (1993), Edelman (1992), Johnson (1987), Lakoff (1987, 1994), Langer (1994), Maturana and

Varela (1988), Ogden (1986), Santostefano (1995), Varela, Thompson, and Rosch (1991), and Winnicott (1965) (see also Overton, 1994a, 1994c, 1997a, 1997b; Overton & Horowitz, 1991), among others. In each of these formulations, the embodied/expressive/engaged subject is central to the formation of mind, when mind is defined as the organization of all of the psychological functions of cognitive/affective understanding—wishing, willing, feeling, desiring, thinking, reasoning, languaging, perceiving, believing, remembering.

Edelman's (1992) work is illustrative with respect to the biological line of sight. Edelman begins from the fundamental argument—shared with Searle, Lakoff, Johnson, and others—that the mind and thought depend critically on the body and the brain. This position stands in opposition to current functionalist positions that present computer and representationalist models of the mind disengaged from the body. The position also stands in opposition to those split-culturalist positions that offer a similarly disengaged "cultural mind" or "group mind" (Gergen, 1994).

The mind is embodied. It is necessarily the case that certain dictates of the body must be followed by the mind. . . . Symbols do not get assigned meanings by formal means; instead it is assumed that symbolic structures are meaningful *to begin with.* This is so because categories are determined by bodily structure and by adaptive use as a result of evolution and behavior. (Edelman, 1992, p. 239)

From this base, Edelman (1992) argues that organic *morphology*—the *organization* of cells, tissues, and organisms—holds the biological key to behavior, development, and evolution. "The fundamental basis for all behavior and for the emergence of mind is animal and species morphology and how it functions" (p. 41). Therefore, the central question is how "animal *form* arises and *changes* during development" (p. 46, emphasis added). In turn, morphology of the brain, conceptualized as a *self-organizing system,* ensures that "natural selection" is not interpreted as an intrusion of the contingent causal factors described in the discussion surrounding Figure 3.2. For Edelman, the completion of Darwin's program demands the relational recognition that embodied behavior itself alters selection, as selection alters embodied behavior (see Figure 3.4).

When the line of sight becomes cognition, Varela, Thompson, and Rosch's (1991) approach is broadly illustrative. Like others who take the embodied approach to mind, they differentiate this approach from the disengaged split representationalist understanding of cognition, and they describe the split understanding as one whose:

Ontological and epistemological commitments are basically twofold: We assume that the world is pregiven, that its features can be specified prior to any cognitive activity. Then to explain the relation between this cognitive activity and a pregiven world, we hypothesize the existence of mental representations inside the cognitive system (whether these be images, symbols, or subsymbolic patterns of activity distributed across a network). (p. 135)

In place of this split understanding, Varela, Thompson, and Rosch develop their own position that all cognition emerges from embodied action:

Cognition depends upon the kinds of experience that come from having a body with various sensorimotor capacities, and . . . these individual sensorimotor capacities are themselves embedded in a more encompassing biological, psychological, and cultural context. (p. 176)

In turn, they recognize that the foremost proponent of exactly this embodied view was Jean Piaget, who argued throughout his writings that all cognition emerges from recurrent patterns of sensorimotor action defined by the cycle of assimilation and accommodation. In fact, no developmental investigator in the 20th century held a more consistent or more highly articulated view of the centrality of embodied activity than did Piaget (Overton, 1994a, 1994c).

Finally, when the line of sight is social-cultural, the earlier-discussed works of Boesch (1991), Eckensberger (1995, 1996), Damon (1988, 1991), Nucci (1996), Turiel (this *Handbook,* Volume 3; Turiel & Wainryb, 1994) and Killen (1996) all describe the embodied perspective. Eckensberger, for example, discusses culture as a "meaning-and-rule system which is a precondition for and, at the same time, a result of actions" (1996, p. 79). Similarly, Boesch describes culture as an "action field" closely related to Kurt Lewin's notion of "life space." From the cultural line of sight, the action field "embraces the totality of action opportunities and conditions a culture can offer its population" (1991, p. 32).

Pragmatism

A final epistemological/ontological tradition that requires a brief exploration to establish a grounding for an inclusive understanding of development is the American pragmatism of Pierce, James, and Dewey. Pragmatism's fundamental postulates cohere as a contextualist worldview (Pepper, 1942) that draws on many Leibnizian–Hegelian themes, including holism, action, change, and the dialectic. The focus of these themes, however, is located on the *instrumental* rather than the *expressive* pole of the relational dialectic. If Gadamer and Taylor (see also Ricoeur, 1991) can be said to represent the phenomenological perspective of the relational developmental philosophical grounding, then pragmatism, particularly the work of James and of Dewey, can be read as representing the instrumental perspective. In this sense, it is not accidental that Dewey's variety of pragmatism is titled "instrumentalism."

Putnam (1995) cites *holism* as one of the chief characteristics of James's philosophy. This holistic commitment leads to an "obvious if implicit rejection of many familiar dualisms: fact, value, and theory are all seen by James as interpenetrating and interdependent" (p. 7). In fact, James (1975) addresses virtually all of the traditional dichotomies of split-off traditions, and he, along with Dewey (1925), argues for a relational interpenetrating understanding of universal/particular, inner/outer, subject/object, theory/practice, monism/pluralism, and unity/diversity. However, although affirming the ontological reality of the dialectic of interpenetration, the stress and the focus of pragmatism are on the particular, the outer, the object, practice, pluralism, and diversity.

Epistemologically, pragmatism repudiates the foundationalism of an ultimate fixed object of knowledge, and insists on the connection of knowledge and action. Knowledge arises out of action, out of particular practices or *praxis*. In this respect, James and Dewey differ little from Habermas, Gadamer, Bahktin, and Taylor. Rather than specifically elaborating the notion of dialogue as the mediator of knowing (expressive and instrumental), the concept of experience carries this function in pragmatism. Experience manifests its relational dialectical character in being what James terms a "double-barrelled" (1912, p. 10) concept. "It recognizes in its primary integrity no division between act and material, subject and object, but contains them both in an unanalyzed totality" (Dewey, 1925,

pp. 10–11). *Experience* refers to *both* the action of the subject (i.e., the subject's embodied active exploration, active manipulation, and active observation of the object world), *and* the object world's active impingement on the subject. "It includes *what* men do and suffer, *what* they strive for . . . and endure, and also *how* men act and are acted upon" (p. 10). For purposes of empirical investigation, inquiry separates this integrity into two points of view and hence two different analytic meanings. However, the empirical question is not—as Wohlwill (1973a) once asked, concerning the place of experience in developmental psychology—whether experience is truly one or the other. The question is how each form of experience contributes to the understanding of human development.

Change and novelty are also basic to the pragmatists' position. However, the focus of change in pragmatism is on the variational rather than the transformational. Similarly, novelty is the new variant rather than the emergent level of organization found in transformational change. This focus is due, in part, to pragmatism's Darwinian evolutionary commitment ("Darwin opened our minds to the power of chance-happenings to bring forth fit results if only they have time to add themselves together," James, 1975, p. 57) along with the commitment to the joint relationship of the instrumental and adaptation.

Pragmatism's focus on variational change and variational novelty also follows from a preference for pluralism and diversity over unity (James, 1975, p. 79). In the discourse of pragmatism, and especially in James's writings, concepts of "unity," "order," "form," and "pattern" tend to be interpreted as denoting the fixed and unchanging, in the sense of an Absolute Transcendentalism (p. 280) or an essentialism. When this is the horizon of understanding, change necessarily becomes restricted to the sphere of diversity. If it is only in the sphere of diversity and pluralism that there is "some separation among things, . . . some free play of parts on one another, some real novelty or chance" (p. 78), then change must be restricted to this sphere. For pragmatism, it is in the sphere of pluralism and diversity that "the world is still in process of making" (p. 289).

The suggestion that pragmatism can be read as representing the instrumental perspective of the relational developmental philosophical grounding falters, given this type-restrictive identification of unity with the static and fixed, and of diversity with the active and changing. In the broad relational developmental tradition, activity and change are not split off and, thus, encapsulated. Unity and synonyms of unity—including "the universal," "the transcendent," "order," "system," "form," "pattern," "organization," and "structure"—have been understood throughout the Leibnizian–Hegelian tradition as ontologically active and changing. Further, as emphasized throughout this section, the Leibnizian–Hegelian tradition grants the same ontological reality to diversity and synonyms of diversity—including "the concrete," the "immanent," "disorder," "plurality," "content," and "function." From the expressive and transformational point of view within this tradition, structures function (act) and change, and self-organizing systems operate (act) and change. From the instrumental and variational point of view within this tradition, action is variational (diversity, plurality, and individual differences) and changing.

A related problem concerns the ambivalent posture that pragmatism takes toward the notion of order or unity. If implicit in the writing of the pragmatists, it is quite clear and explicit in Stephen Pepper's (1942) distillation of the presuppositions of the pragmatists that disorder or diversity is a fundamental category of pragmatism–contextualism. However, because pragmatism offers itself as not denying any category that has a practical value ("I call pragmatism a mediator and reconciler. . . . She has in fact no prejudices whatever," James, 1975, p. 43), it cannot deny order, unity, organization, pattern, or structure. Pragmatism does, however, approach these concepts from a certain distance and with a certain distrust. Most importantly, in some readings, pragmatism tends to interpret order or unity as an end to be attained, rather than as a legitimate ontological real. In this case, order is *treated,* if not directly conceptualized, as Appearance. Such a reading of pragmatism splits the dialectical relation between the transcendent and the immanent, unity and diversity, found in both Gadamer and Taylor. When this split occurs, pragmatism takes on the flattened character described earlier in the post-modern approach of Richard Rorty. As the philosopher Thomas McCarthy (1991) points out, "Rorty's epistemological behaviorism is a variant of the contextualism common to most postmodernist thinkers" (p. 20). It entails "a radically contextualist account [that] . . . amounts to flattening out our notions of reason and truth by removing any air of transcendence from them" (pp. 14–15).

Reading pragmatism–contextualism as Rorty's epistemological behaviorism, or as Mead's earlier pragmatic

social behaviorism, leads to a joining of pragmatism to the split Marxist and behavioral traditions, and, hence, to a denial of an ontological reality to the expressive/transformational subject. This reading establishes the bridge that has recently attracted both neo-Marxists and neobehaviorists to pragmatism. Illustrative of this joining, Reese argues that "dialectical materialism is a version of contextualism" (1993, p. 71) and "behavior analysis is consistent with contextualism" (1995, p. 2). Similarly, Morris (1988) has proclaimed and argued for "contextualism: the world view of behavior analysis" (p. 289), and Wertsch (1991) finds in Mead's pragmatism the tie to the Marxist side of Vygotsky. This reading has also grounded and sustained much of the "new functionalism" in developmental inquiry, which identifies developmental phenomena with adaptive instrumental behavior (e.g., see Cassidy, 1994, for this reading of psychological attachment, and Campos et al., 1994, for this reading of the nature of emotions).

This split reading of pragmatism is not necessarily canonical, however. Pepper (1979), in a work following his well-known *World Hypotheses,* acknowledges the significance of *integration* in contextualism. He argues relationally that the integration the pragmatist should stress "is an integration of conflicts" (p. 411), hence, a dialectical integration. He also warns the contextualist against the danger of an overemphasis on the contingent, the accidental, the variable. For Pepper, the contextualist has been "so impressed with evidences of historical change and cultural influences and the shifting contexts of value that he cannot easily bring himself to accept any degree of permanence" (p. 414). Pepper chides the constricted contextualist by arguing that "there is much more permanence in the world than the contextualist admits" (p. 414). Similarly, Hilary Putnam, who has elaborated an extensive contemporary relational reading of pragmatism, sometimes refers to this reading as "internal realism" and sometimes as "pragmatic realism" (1987, 1990, 1995). In either case, the "realism" is the commonsense realism discussed earlier—neither the realism of the mind (idealism), nor the realism of the world (materialism). The "internal" and "pragmatic" features of Putnam's system assert the position of a pragmatism that includes both the expressive and the instrumental.

Finally, pragmatism need not be read as a split tradition that suppresses order and change of form, as can be gleaned from the writings of Dewey (1934), one of the founders of pragmatism:

There is in nature . . . something more than mere flux and change. Form is arrived at whenever a stable, even though moving, equilibrium is reached. Changes interlock and sustain one another. Whenever there is this coherence there is endurance. Order is not imposed from without but is made out of the relations of harmonious interactions that energies bear to one another. Because it is active . . . order itself develops. It comes to include within its balanced movement a greater variety of changes. (p. 14)

If pragmatism is read as joining order to disorder, and joining activity and change to both structure and function, as this quote from Dewey and the work of Putnam and others suggest, then pragmatism enlarges the philosophical grounding of the relational developmental tradition, and it enlarges the field of developmental inquiry. Illustrations of the impact of this expanded grounding of pragmatism are found, for example, in Damon and Hart (1988), with respect to social development; in Nucci (1996), on moral development; and in the work of Varela, Thompson, and Rosch (1991) and Wapner and Demick (1990; and this Volume) for cognitive development. Piaget (1985)—considering the relation between his earlier investigations of operational knowing (expressive/transformational) and contemporary explorations of procedural knowing (instrumental/variational)—found in this new arena "a possible synthesis of genetic structuralism, the focus of all of our previous work, with the functionalism found in the work of J. Dewey and of E. Claparede" (p. 68).

The aim of this section has been to establish a broad epistemological/ontological grounding for an inclusive understanding of development as formal (transformational) and functional (variational) changes in the expressive-constitutive and instrumental-communicative features of behavior. This has been done by following the historical thread of the Leibnizian–Hegelian tradition and noting the locations where this thread splits off toward exclusivity. Ultimately, the illustrations given do not aim to categorize particular writings. Rather, they suggest the consequences that follow for the domain of developmental inquiry when a particular path is taken. In the concluding section, the epistemological–ontological grounding, the relational developmental metanarrative, and the inclusive concept of development become the interwoven context for a discussion of the nature of the scientific understanding and explanation of developmental phenomena. The section will center on issues of methodology, where methodology is understood broadly as metanarratives for empirical scientific inquiry (Asendorpf & Valsiner, 1992). Methods, in the narrow sense of specific techniques for designing, conducting, and evaluating empirical research, will be considered within the context of alternative methodologies. Some specific features of developmental methods can be found in surveys such as those by Achenbach (1978); Appelbaum and McCall (1983); Baltes, Reese, and Nesselroade (1977); Connell and Tanaka (1987); Henning and Rudinger (1985); Kingma and Van Den Bos (1989); Schroder, Edelstein, and Hoppe-Graff (1991); von Eye and Brandtstädter, (1989); and Wohlwill (1973b).

In an important sense, the discussion to the present point has constructed our developmental landscape and has populated it with certain types of people (expressive/instrumental) who change in certain ways (transformationally/variationally) and who act in a biological-social-cultural world that both creates them and is created by them. Now, the task is to inquire into how best to investigate the changing character of these persons and this world. This is the task of methodology.

METHODOLOGY: EXPLANATION AND UNDERSTANDING

Our focus to this point has been developmental inquiry as a broad-based knowledge-building activity. Now, we turn more specifically to developmental psychology as an empirical science. The historical dialogue has arrived at a common agreement that whatever else it may be, any empirical science is a human activity—an epistemological activity—with certain broad orientations and aims. The historical dialogue has further led to common agreement that the most general aim and orientation of empirical science is the establishment of a *systematic* body of knowledge that is tied to observational evidence (Lakatos, 1978a; Laudan, 1977; Nagel, 1979; Wartofsky, 1968). That is, any empirical science aims at building a *system* or an *organization* of knowledge that represents *patterns* of relationships among phenomena and processes of the experienced world. These patterns constitute explanations of the phenomena and processes under consideration. Further, to be properly empirical, the explanations must have implications that are *in some sense* open to observational/experimental assessment.

If science aims toward order, it begins in the flux and chaos of the everyday experience that is often termed *commonsense* (see the earlier discussion of the commonsense level of observation; see also Nagel, 1967, 1979; Overton, 1991b; Pepper, 1942; Wartofsky, 1968). As the philosopher Ernst Nagel has described it, "All scientific inquiry takes its departure from commonsense beliefs and distinctions, and eventually supports its findings by falling back on common sense" (1967, p. 6). This commonsense base is what Gadamer refers to as the "anticipatory meanings" of pre-understanding (see earlier discussion).

For the science of developmental psychology, this starting point includes activities that are commonly referred to as perceiving, thinking, feeling, relating, remembering, valuing, intending, playing, creating, languaging, comparing, reasoning, wishing, willing, judging, and so on. These activities, and the change of these activities, as understood on a commonsense level of experience or discourse (see Figure 3.1), constitute the problems of developmental psychology. They are problems because, although they represent the stability of practical everyday life, even the most meager reflection reveals that they appear inconsistent, contradictory, and muddled. Refined and critically reflective theories—including embodiment, cultural, biological, sociobiological, information processing, Piagetian, Gibsonian, Vygotskian, Eriksonian, Chomskyian and the rest—all represent attempts to explain (i.e., to bring order into) the contradictory, inconsistent, muddled features of these various domains of inquiry.

There is little disagreement among scientists, historians of science, and philosophers of science about where science begins—in common sense and the contradictions that show up when we begin to examine common sense—and where it leads—to refined theories and laws that explain. Science is a human knowledge-building activity designed to *bring order and organization into the flux of everyday experience.* Disagreement emerges only when the question is raised of exactly how, or by what route, science moves from common sense to refined knowledge. *This issue—the route from common sense to science—constitutes the methodology of science.* Historically, two routes have been proposed and traveled. One emerges from the Newtonian–Humean split epistemological–ontological tradition. Those who follow this route are directed to avoid interpretation and to carefully

walk the path of observation and *only* observation. On this path, reason enters *only* as an analytic heuristic—a tool for overcoming conflicts by generating ever more pristine observations, free from interpretation. The second route emerges from the Leibnizian–Hegelian relational tradition. Those who follow this route are directed toward a relational dialectical path on which interpretation and observation interpenetrate and form an identity of opposites, as exemplified by Escher's Drawing Hands. On this path, interpretation, reason (broadly considered), and observation become coequal partners in conflict resolution.

The following discussion will sketch the *evolution of methodology* from the early relational methodology of Aristotle to the split methodology of the Baconian–Newtonian tradition, and finally to a contemporary relational methodology that has been progressively defined in the work of N. R. Hanson, Ernst Cassirer, Mary Hesse, Thomas Kuhn, Stephen Toulmin, Imre Lakatos, Gerald Holton, Hans-Georg Gadamer, Hilary Putnam, Richard Bernstein, Paul Ricoeur, Larry Laudan, and Bruno Latour among others. This evolution of scientific methodologies is outlined in Table 3.1. In tracing this evolution, particular emphasis will be placed on positivism. Positivism is the specific 20th-century definition of the Baconian–Newtonian methodology, and positivism—and its legacy—has been the context for much of our past thinking about methods in developmental psychology. The impact of the legacy

Table 3.1   Scientific Methodologies

	Split Tradition: Bacon, Newton		Relational Tradition: Aristotle, Leibniz, Hegel
Positivism	Instrumentalism		Paradigms, Research Programs, Research Traditions
Laws Theories	Context of discovery: Metaphysics Metanarratives Models and theories		Metaphysics Metanarratives Models and theories
	Context of justification: Laws		Laws
Observation Experiment Assessment	Observation Experiment Assessment		Observation Experiment\Assessment

of positivism on specific developmental research methods, along with contemporary relational alternatives, will be described in the course of this discussion.

Aristotle's Relational Methodology: The Nature of Scientific Explanation

The history of the two routes from common sense to refined knowledge is traceable to Aristotle's relational position on explanation. Aristotle (Randall, 1960; Ross, 1959) proposed that the complete explanation of any phenomenon requires four interconnected types of explanation: (a) formal explanation, (b) final explanation, (c) material cause, and (d) efficient cause. The first two entail pattern, order, and morphological or structural explanation, and the last two entail causal or functional explanation. Here, as in other features of Aristotle's work, structure and function operate in a dialectical relation. The first pattern explanation, *formal explanation,* is an articulation of the form, structure, pattern, order, morphology, or organization of the action or activity of interest. The second pattern explanation, *final explanation,* is the articulation of the directional/sequential pattern or order of the action or activity. Aristotle did not present formal and final explanations as causes in the sense that a cause implies something productive, as in "Cause A produces the effect B." Formal and final explanation were presented as *principles of intelligibility* (Randall, 1960; Taylor, 1995). They give meaning to the action or activity of interest, in terms of both its present organization and the sequence of transformational changes that the active system undergoes.

Examples of formal explanation in contemporary biological and natural sciences include the structure of the atom, of DNA, of the solar system, and of the universe. Kinship structures, mental structures, mental organization, structures of language, ego and superego, schemes, operations, and cognitive structures are familiar formal pattern explanations drawn from the human sciences. The commonality among all these examples is that, from a postulated underlying action or activity (functioning), a formulation of the pattern of the action is inferred, and this pattern gives meaning to the phenomenon and, hence, makes it intelligible (Overton, 1975).

The classic example of final explanation drawn from the natural sciences is the Second Law of Thermodynamics. Described in its most intuitive and universal form, the

Second Law is the principle that all isolated systems—including the universe, the ideal isolated system—change in a direction toward maximally diffuse or random states measured by the quantity termed "entropy." This irreversible directionality stands as a fundamental explanation for processes that are as varied as the decay of cities and the expansion of the universe. It also provides the context for explanations of self-organization and self-organizing systems as phenomena that operate far from equilibrium (see Overton, 1991b, 1994a). Werner's orthogenetic principle, Piaget's equilibration process, Erikson's epigenetic principle, and Mahler's individuation–separation principle, all constitute final explanatory principles in contemporary developmental inquiry. Again, as with formal explanation, the commonality among all final explanations is the interpretative inference of order drawn from a postulated functional activity; a structure–function explanation.

Causal explanation within Aristotle's scheme was described in terms of two broad categories; *material cause* and *efficient cause.* Material cause refers to the substance that constitutes the phenomenon of inquiry. Contemporary examples in the human sciences include the various hereditary, physiological, and neurological aspects of the organism. Efficient cause describes that which "moves" the phenomenon. In the human sciences, efficient cause can include material causes as, for example, when it is suggested that a specific behavior is determined by biological causes. Efficient cause also has come to include the stimulus, the situation, the environment, the sociocultural context, and so on.

Baconian–Newtonian Split Methodology

Aristotle's system requires that the four explanations be interrelated. Formal and material entail explanation of the momentary state of the phenomenon under inquiry (Being), and final and efficient offer explanation of the change (Becoming) of the phenomenon. With the emergence in the 17th century of Francis Bacon's observational methods and, more generally, the split Newtonian worldview, formal explanation and final explanation were suppressed as legitimate explanations because they entail an explicitly interpretative dimension that goes beyond the Baconian observational ideal. Science increasingly became identified with, and defined by, the specification of a strictly observable causality. If pattern were to be the aim of science, pattern had to be redefined as conjunctions of observable causes and effects, not as organization or form. Newton's methodology—called *mechanical explanation* (Prosch, 1964)—became the prototype for the Baconian–Newtonian methodological route from common sense to critically refined scientific knowledge, and this continues to impact developmental psychology to the present day, in the form of the legacy of positivism.

Mechanical explanation is composed of three steps: (a) *reduction,* (b) *causation, and* (c) *induction* (see the earlier section, "Newton and the Objectivist Split Tradition"). *Reduction* is the method designed to drive out interpretations from the commonsense experience under investigation. Later joined to operationalism, the idea of this step is that commonsense observation is error-laden, and it is only through ever more careful observation that science can eliminate this error and ultimately arrive at the elementary stable bedrock unit that constitutes the level of "data" and the atom of inquiry. In psychology, this atom came to be the observable response. Reductionism is also termed "elementarism," the "analytic ideal," and "atomism." As discussed earlier, reductionism is itself an implication of the Newtonian–Humean epistemology of empiricism (i.e., knowledge derives from observation and *only* from observation) and its split-off ontology of realism–materialism (i.e., the universe as composed of inactive matter constitutes the ultimate Reality).

Following the reduction of the commonsense phenomenon of interest to the reliably stable observable atom of the data level, the second step of mechanical explanation involves finding the *material and efficient causes* that operates on the atom and produces change. Whether this is thought of as a causal force or—following Hume's later destruction of the idea of causality—as a correlation between antecedent and consequence, this step was to become the conceptual and methodological cornerstone of all later experimental understandings of development. If the phenomenon of interest is, in *Reality,* inherently fixed—or, like billiard balls, inherently inert but moving about in a random fashion—then the search for the cause of *Apparent* systematic change becomes critical. The searched-for antecedent cause was to become the *Independent Variable* of experimental method. The atom of inquiry became the *Dependent Variable.* When John Stuart Mill later added his several canons (rules) of eliminative induction (Copi, 1953)—proposed to facilitate observational choice among

several potential competing causes—the fundamental framework for all future *experimental designs* was set.

The third step of Newtonian mechanical explanation is the *induction* of laws or lawlike statements (e.g., hypotheses, theoretical propositions) from the observed regularity of antecedent cause and consequent effect. It is critical that the process is fundamentally inductive (i.e., deriving the universal from observable particulars by generalization and *only* generalization) because this reinforces the empiricist epistemological doctrine that knowledge ultimately must come through observation and *only* observation. In addition, an exclusively inductive approach supports the ontological position that universal propositions (laws, hypotheses, theories) derive only from particulars, which constitute the Real. Thus, the fundamental nature of induction ensures that all theorylike statements must be *empirical generalizations* drawn from pristine data relations. When, at a later period in this tradition, the *hypothetical–deductive method* was introduced, nothing essential was changed. Induction continued to constitute the foundational logic of science. Hypotheses that defined the hypothetical domain were understood to be strictly inductive generalizations, drawn from pristine data. Deductive logic—the deductive domain—was admitted for the sole purpose of drawing logical predictions from these induced hypotheses, thus returning to the level of data. A change to a relational understanding of the logic of science awaited a new methodology that could accommodate Pierce's (1992) retroductive logic. This logic, which, as suggested earlier, involves a dialectical understanding of the relationship between interpretation and observation, will be further elaborated in a later discussion.

Positivism

The Baconian–Newtonian methodological framework was established in the late 17th and the 18th century. In the middle of the 19th century, it began to be formalized into a general strategy designed to split and, thus, demarcate empirical science from nonscience. It was at this time that the Age of Metaphysics came to an end. The ending was defined by philosophy's turning away from imperialistic dogmatic applications of broad philosophical systems, and directing its reflections toward what were called the "positive" sciences. Auguste Comte, writing a history of philosophy at the time, coined the term "positivism" when he described a division of three ages of thought: an early theological age, a metaphysical age that was just passing, and an age of positive science (Gadamer, 1993; Schlick, 1991). The positive sciences were understood as those that located inquiry in the "given" or "positive." This positive sphere was identified as the sphere of "experience" rather than a sphere of the transcendental a priori. However, under the continuing influence of the "silent" metaphysics of the Newtonian–Humean tradition of empiricism and materialism, the "given" of experience became defined, not as commonsense observations or a commonsense level of discourse (see Figure 3.1), but as observations that had been purified (i.e., reduced) of all interpretative features (i.e., reduced to "data" or, more specifically, a type of data termed "sense data"). Thus, the positive sciences came to be those that were grounded in the Baconian–Newtonian methodology, and positivism came to consist of the rules that further codified that methodology (see Table 3.1).

Following Comte, positivism was articulated across the remainder of the 19th century and into the early 20th century by John Stuart Mill, Richard Avenarius, and Ernst Mach. In the 1920s and 1930s, positivism assumed a new posture in the philosophical work of the Vienna Circle, composed of such principal figures as Moritz Schlick, Rudolf Carnap, Herbert Feigl, Gustav Bergmann, Otto Neurath, Kurt Godel, and A. J. Ayer (see Smith, 1986, and the earlier discussion in this chapter). This "logical" positivism—which Schlick preferred to call "consistent empiricism" (1991, p. 54)—grew in the context of the legacy of the Newtonian–Humean tradition that was coming to be called analytic philosophy (see the earlier section, "Locke and Hume, and Later Forms of the Objectivist Split Tradition"). At this point, analytic philosophy was taking its "linguistic turn" away from traditional epistemological questions of how the Real is known, and replacing these with questions of what it means to make the language claim that the Real is known. In this context, logical positivism concerned itself not with knowing the Real but with the nature of statements that claim to know the Real (Schlick, 1991, p. 40).

Logical positivism focused on the reductionist and inductive features of Baconian–Newtonian methodology. These were presented as the descriptive features of science, and because they go hand in hand with (causal) explanation, science from a positivist point of view is often characterized as the *description and explanation of phenomena.* This

reductionistic focus ultimately led to the articulation of two complementary criteria for the demarcation of science from nonscience (Lakatos, 1978a; Overton, 1984). First, a proposition (e.g., a hypothesis, a theoretical statement, a law) was acceptable as scientifically meaningful if, and *only* if, it could be reduced to words whose meaning could be directly observed and pointed to. "The meaning of the word must ultimately be *shown,* it has to be *given.* This takes place through an act of pointing or showing" (Schlick, 1991, p. 40). The words "whose meaning could be directly observed" constituted a *neutral observation language*—completely objective, and free from subjective or mind-dependent interpretation. Thus, all theoretical language required reduction to pristine observations and a neutral observational language. Second, a statement was acceptable as scientifically meaningful if, and *only* if, it could be shown to be a strictly inductive generalization, drawn directly from the pristine observations. Thus, to be scientifically meaningful, any universal propositions (e.g., hypotheses, theories, laws) had to be demonstrably nothing more than summary statements of the pristine observations themselves (see Table 3.1).

Formal logic was introduced into the methodology of logical positivism as a purely interpretation free heuristic device for joining one inductive generalization to another to form a theory (i.e., a theory is understood within the context of positivism as a set of logical conjunctions of meaningful scientific statements), and—as described below—for explaining and predicting specific observations within a set of inductive theories or laws. For this reason, as suggested earlier, the position is often referred to as a *hypothetical (inductive)–deductive* approach. It was in this context that Carl Hempel (1942, 1967) introduced the "covering law model" of scientific explanation, which became the prototype of all later explanations formulated within positivism or within the legacy of positivism (e.g., Suppe, 1977). The covering law model of explanation became particularly important for developmental inquiry because it treated historical events as analogous to physical events in the sense that earlier events were considered the causal antecedents of later events (Ricoeur, 1984).

According to the covering law model, scientific explanation takes a deductive (i.e., formal) logical form; that is, particular events are explained when they are logically subsumed under a universal law or lawlike statement (i.e., a highly confirmed *inductive empirical generalization;* Ayer,

1970; Hempel, 1942). Assume, for example, that we had available an inductive universal law of socialization stating: "For any x, if x is a human child, then x increases in social competence when parents act responsively to the child's needs." This law becomes the major premise of the deductive argument. Next, the initial conditions of an experiment present antecedent conditions *(causal conditions)* of a minor premise: "This is a human child (or group of human children), and *the parents of this child (these children) have acted responsively.*" Finally, assume that the experiment yields the observed event or conclusion: "This child (group of children) increases in social competence." Major premise, minor premise, and conclusion in this example are consistent, and the observed event is said to be explained by the law that covers it. It should be noted, as Popper (1959) later did, that the actual logic of this proposal is faulty in that it entails an invalid argument form called the "fallacy of the affirmed consequence." Stated without the logical formality, this simply means that the observed event could have occurred for many reasons having nothing to do with the "law" itself. It should also be noted that if the observed event had been: "This child (group of children) *does not* increase in social competence" then that observation would have, indeed, constituted a valid logical refutation or falsification of the law itself (or of a theoretical proposition, or hypothesis, if these had been the major premise). In this latter example, major premise, minor premise, and conclusion comprise the valid deductive argument form *modus tollens,* (If p, then q; not q; therefore, not p). It was this distinction between the invalid "affirmed consequence" argument of the covering law model, and the valid argument of "modus tollens" that later became the base of Popper's (1959) contention that science proceeds by falsification rather than confirmation.

In the covering law model, as well as in Popper's later discussions, *cause, law, explanation, and prediction* are tightly interwoven. An event is explained when it is "covered" by a law or lawlike statement (i.e., a universal conditional) and when its antecedents are legitimately called its causes. Further, prediction is simply the inversion of the universal conditional (i.e., "If parents act responsively to the child's needs, then there is an increase in the child's social competence"). As a result of this close relation of explanation and prediction, the predictive value of a hypothesis becomes one criterion of the validity of an explanation.

Although logical positivism was formulated primarily within the natural sciences, its tenets were exported into behavioral science through Bridgman's (1927) "operationalism." The reductionism of positivism culminated in Ayer's (1946) "Principle of Verifiability." According to this principle, a statement is scientifically meaningful to the extent that, in principle, there is the possibility of direct experience (pristine observation) that will verify or falsify it. Bridgman's operationalism extended this principle by not only setting the criteria of scientific meaning, but also identifying the specific nature of this meaning. Thus, within operationalism, the meaning of a scientific concept resides in the application of the concept (i.e., in the definition of the concept in operational or applicatory terms). Among the classic examples of the principle of operationalism is the idea that the meaning of "intelligence" is given in the score received on an intelligence test, or that the meaning of "anxiety" is given in the score received on an anxiety test. It is important to recognize that operationalism was intended in the context of positivism's exclusivity—that is, in positivism's position that *all substantive features of theory* should be reducible to direct observations. As a consequence, *operationalism* is distinct from the notion that there is a need to *operationalize* specific key concepts of an experimental hypothesis. Rejection of operationalism does not imply rejection of the necessity of operationalizing key concepts, any more than the rejection of empiricism implies the rejection of empirical science.

Positivism and operationalism set the specific rules for the Baconian–Newtonian methodological path from common sense to critically refined scientific knowledge (see Table 3.1). According to these rules, all interpretation was to be split off and, hence, suppressed through the reduction of common sense to atomic facts. *Facts* were identified as the highly reliable pristine observations—phrased in the neutral observational language—that remained following the reduction of commonsense experience. Facts were *data*, and *truth* was defined as the *correspondence* of data to more general theoretical propositions. This reduction, supported by the broad Newtonian–Humean tradition, ensured that universals, organization, pattern, and order could not enter explanation as fundamental features. Explanatory laws, theories, and hypotheses—whether explicitly cast as causal relations, or described as contingent relations, probabilistic statistical relations, or the amount of variance of one (dependent) variable accounted for by another (independent) variable—all constituted inductions drawn from particular (i.e., nominal) pristine observations.

Logical positivism reached its zenith in the 1940s and 1950s, but ultimately both the friends and the foes of positivism recognized its failure as a broad demarcationist strategy. Upon this failure, the dialogue concerning methodology has continued. Positivism failed for many reasons:

1. It became clear, as demonstrated in the work of Quine (1953) and others (e.g., Lakatos, 1978a; Popper, 1959; Putnam, 1983), that rich theories are not reducible to a neutral observational language.

2. There was a demonstrated inadequacy of induction as the method for arriving at theoretical propositions (Hanson, 1958, 1970; Lakatos, 1978b; Popper, 1959).

3. It became evident that the covering law model was highly restricted in its application (Ricoeur, 1984) and faulty in its logic (Popper, 1959).

4. It was recognized that there are theories that warrant the attribution "scientific" despite the fact that they lead to no testable predictions (Putnam, 1983; Toulmin, 1961).

All of these failures can perhaps best be summarized by saying that, ultimately, positivism failed because its fundamental aim was the suppression of interpretation in science; that is, it failed because it assumed the posture of a foundationalist exclusivity.

Despite the widely recognized failure of positivism, its legacy has continued to exert a broad and deep influence on the science of developmental psychology. To a significant degree, developmental psychology grew up during the hegemony of positivism. It is, therefore, not surprising that the practitioners of developmental psychology both embraced its tenets and passed them on, often quietly and implicitly, to later generations of investigators as "the" *scientific method.* In a review of conceptual development, Case (this *Handbook,* Volume 2) describes a significant case history of this intergenerational influence of positivism as it formed the silent background within which the 1970 edition of this *Handbook* critiqued the Piagetian approach to development (Flavell, 1970). This critique, in turn, became the context for the 1983 *Handbook* review of conceptual development (Gelman & Baillergeon, 1983). This type of intergenerational transmission constitutes the legacy of positivism.

Faith in the tenets of positivism is, of course, supported and sustained by faith in one of the split epistemological–ontological groundings discussed earlier, as well as by faith in metanarratives supported by these groundings. The convergence and interpenetration of each of these supporting faiths tends to create an insulated system that treats dissenting voices as "nonscientific" and, hence, "irrelevant." It is often said that we become prisoners of method. From one point of view, this is true; however, it is also true that methods become prisoners of our metaphysics, including those metaphysics whose fundamental principle is that there is no metaphysics.

The Legacy of Positivism and Research Methods

The continuing impact of positivism on method is found today in each of the features of the general methodology: *reduction, causation, and induction.* Methodologically, reductionism and inductionism constitute an epistemological stance that prescribes a particular type of explanation for those who accept its mandate. Reduction and induction are, in fact, simply the inverse representations of the identical stance. Any reductionistic statement can be directly translated into a statement of induction, and vice versa. For example, to claim that an inferred construct (e.g., mental organization, system, scheme, trait) is scientifically valid if, and *only* if, it is reducible to some set of observations, is inductively reframed as the claim that such an inferred construct is valid if, and *only* if, it is inductively derived from those observations. Today, when some psychological disciplines describe a preference for "data-driven" (i.e., inductively arrived at) theories, this is the same epistemological preference that was expressed in earlier days for operationally defined theories containing no "surplus meaning."

The Legacy of Reductionism–Inductionism

Although reductionism–inductionism constitutes an epistemological belief (or beliefs), this stance fosters the ontological belief that the visible (or potentially visible) constitutes the ultimate Real. The combined impact of these self-reinforcing beliefs is that inquiry becomes focused exclusively on the visible (or potentially visible) as the sole legitimate arena for generating refined scientific knowledge. Broadly, this has encouraged support of three closely interrelated doctrines:

1. *Scientific realism* is the doctrine that the subject matter of scientific theories and research exists independently of our knowledge (see Overton, 1991b, and the earlier section, "Newton and the Objectivist Split Tradition").

2. *Physicalism* is the doctrine that all phenomena, including persons, can be completely described according to physical categories.

3. A particular brand of *naturalism* that follows from physicalism. This is the notion that persons are identical to other natural events and, thus, can be scientifically understood completely in terms of spatio-temporal laws (see Katz, 1990; Taylor, 1985).

It is instructive, for example, that Quine, who was most effective in destroying positivism's brand of reductionism, fostered a movement toward naturalizing the activity of knowing (see Putnam, 1983, for a critique). This, in fact, substituted one form of reductionism for another, and Quine's "naturalized epistemology" currently functions under the rubric "eliminative materialism," which promotes the position that the mental can and will ultimately be reduced to the neurophysiological (Churchland, 1995; Churchland, 1986).

In a more limited arena, the continuing faith in reduction to the visible fosters the attitude that developmental psychology advances only to the degree that it excludes interpretation and pursues ever more precise and detailed noninterpretative descriptive efforts. This faith has led some investigators to shun research directed by broad developmental theories in favor of efforts designed to get at what "children actually do." Examples are found in suggestions that argue "the priority of description in developmental psychology" (Sugarman, 1987a, p. 392) and in claims for the availability of methods that allow investigators "direct" access to developmental change (Siegler & Crowley, 1991). Suggestions and claims of this sort contrast sharply with a relational perspective's assertion that analysis–generalization (reduction–induction) split from interpretative context lacks meaning, and interpretation divorced from analysis–generalization lacks substance.

Task-analysis and *rule-assessment* techniques, offered as methods of choice by information-processing approaches (e.g., Kail & Bisanz, 1982), often illustrate the background belief that ever finer microanalyses will ultimately yield a bedrock neutral observation of the "actual" or a "direct" observation of development. A currently popular manifestation

of this approach is found in the application of the "microgenetic" method (e.g., Kuhn et al., 1995; Siegler, 1996). As originally coined by Heinz Werner (1956), *microgenesis* describes a comparative method designed to assess the form of development (transformational change) across a short temporal series. Thus, for example, the transformational change in the microgenesis of a single percept taking a few milliseconds could be compared with the ontogenesis of a concept taking several years.

The aim of the comparative method broadly, and microgenesis specifically, was to establish empirical evidence for general laws of transformational development (e.g., Werner's orthogenetic principle of increasing differentiation, articulation, and hierarchic integration of systems) by establishing the scope of contexts to which they could legitimately be said to apply. Contemporary information-processing usage, however, has abandoned the transformational and comparative features of the method. Instead, it describes microgenesis as a method of making observations across a brief temporal series, and it offers this method as "a direct means for studying cognitive development." In this latter usage, "development" is limited to instrumental/variational change, and the intensive "trial-by-trial analysis" of instrumental behavior is aimed at reducing ontogenetic *change* to visible *differences* that appear across learning trials. This contemporary reductionistic scheme of identifying development with differences across trials evokes White's (1995) comments on the striking similarity of this "new" method to Thorndike's turn-of-the-century behaviorist "scheme of trial-and-error learning."

The legacy of positivism's reductionist–inductivist attitude, reflected in methods directed toward an ever more exclusive reliance on finer and finer microanalytic techniques, finds a parallel illustration in the indiscriminate use of the technique of "task simplification." This technique entails simplifying the procedural details of a task (e.g., the task itself, the scoring criteria, the instructions), usually in an effort to more "directly" assess what the child "can actually do." Lourenco and Machado (1996) identify a number of examples of this technique that have been applied to tasks that Piaget created to assess the presence or absence of a theoretically defined expressive competence.

Issues of Validity.   A significant issue associated with *task simplification* is that it often operates to illegitimately reduce an expressive competence to an instrumental behavior. For example, Piaget's balance beam task (Inhelder & Piaget, 1958) was designed to assess the availability of a broad-based expressive logical competence that was taken to represent the transformation of an ontogenetically earlier, more narrowly defined, logical competence (Overton, 1990). However, Siegler's (1976) modifications of this task reduced it to a manifestation of local instrumental problem-solving behavior. Ultimately, this conversion itself became the ground for Siegler's tautological conclusion that "much of children's knowledge can profitably be characterized as rules for solving problems" (Siegler & Shipley, 1987, p. 103). Similarly, Piagetian tasks created to assess the infant's nascent expressive differentiation of subject and object (i.e., object permanence) have been reduced to tasks of instrumental habituation to partially occluded perceptual arrays (e.g., Baillargeon, 1987). This conversion, in turn, has become the ground for the inappropriately drawn conclusion that a score derived from the perceptual habituation task "provides strong evidence that Piaget (1952, 1954) underestimated the conceptual abilities of young infants" (Johnson & Aslin, 1995, p. 739).

The implications of the uncritical application of task simplification extend far beyond any particular theoretical approach (Liben, in press). This type of task simplification represents a broad failure of methodology to acknowledge the central role of what Messick (1995) has termed *"score validity"* (i.e., an integrated approach to the content, criterion, and construct validity as this set applies to any score) in the measurement of the expressive-constitutive and instrumental-communicative features of behavior, and in the measurement of formal (transformational) and functional (variational) changes in these features. Despite warnings by some that "a reliable test can be invalid, but a valid test cannot be unreliable" (Baltes et al., 1977, p. 70), a good deal of the developmental literature carries a split message implying that validity is derivative. The claim of this message is that, if consistent behavior (i.e., reliability) is observed in an appropriately controlled setting, then validity will follow naturally. Often, this message is more implicit than explicit. For example, Volume 1 of the 1983 edition of this *Handbook,* devoted largely to methods, shows no index references to content validity or criterion validity, and only two single-page references to construct validity. The two brief comments on construct validity appear in the chapter on assessment (Messick, 1983), leaving

the chapter on design and analysis (Appelbaum & McCall, 1983) devoted entirely to issues of reliability.

The general failure to systematically acknowledge the central significance of validity across the entire research process rests partly on yet another conceptual split. The empirical research process in developmental, as well as other areas of psychology, has often been rigidly dichotomized into separate domains of *experimental research* and *assessment research.* Illustrative is the presence, in Volume 1 of the 1983 edition of this *Handbook,* of one chapter on design and analysis and another chapter on assessment. As shaped by this dichotomy, the experimental (and quasi-experimental) arena is characterized as the domain of independent and dependent variables, where consistency of behavior (reliability) and appropriate controls (i.e., design) necessarily ensure the *validity of conclusions about cause-and-effect relations.* The foundational assumption here is that, if reliability and appropriate controls are established, validity becomes the natural outcome of the design process.

Within the dichotomy of experimental and assessment research, experimental design is not a vehicle for creating validity; it is a vehicle for reducing *threats* to an otherwise naturally occurring "statistical conclusion validity," "internal validity," and "external validity" (Cook & Campbell, 1979). In this context, the problem of the meaning of scores (i.e., score validity) is rarely discussed at all. When score validity is discussed, it is identified with the operational reduction of constructs so that "definitions are clear and in conformity with public understanding of the words being used" (Cook & Campbell, 1979, p. 60). Assessment research, on the other hand, is described within the experimental–assessment dichotomy as the investigation of inferred meaning. Assessment entails the exploration of latent variables (i.e., inferred dispositions, traits, states, mental organization, mental systems, and so on), as well as the exploration of changes and stabilities in these latent variables. In the assessment domain, formal tests are designed to tap the inferred systems according to test theory, and a central feature of the process is the establishment of the content, criterion, or construct validity of the test scores themselves (Anastasi, 1988). The result of the experimental–assessment dichotomy is that score validity becomes identified with assessment investigations—and perhaps with education and clinical concerns—and reliability/control/validity becomes identified with hypothesis testing and experimentation.

The developmental psychological implication of this dichotomy is that, to the degree that developmental psychology represents itself as an "experimental" discipline, score validity becomes merely a kind of extra or pre-experimental activity associated with the reduction or operationalization of concepts to the visible.

The distinction between experimental and assessment research can be useful and even necessary at times for analytically differentiating interrelated parts and associated specific research aims of the whole of the research process. For example, assessment is *often* directed at detecting expressive and transformational aspects of development; and experimentation is often directed at the instrumental and variational aspects. However, when treated as a dichotomy, the distinction fails to appreciate both the subtle complexity of the research process, and the fact that, in both arenas, *conclusions necessarily rest on the meaning of a score.* Because conclusions necessarily rest on score meaning, the content, criterion, and construct validity are no less central and necessary features of experimental investigations than of assessment investigations. Consider, for example, the field of attachment research. Does an aggregated set of behavioral scores, codified as a "secure" attachment, represent the assessment of a latent variable, or does it represent the dependent variable of a quasi-experiment involving the effect of an independent variable such as child care? The answer, of course, is that the set represents both, and either, given the aim of the research under consideration. But, regardless of the aim, it is critical to any conclusions that the scores must validly and demonstrably implicate attachment and not some other construct.

Messick (1995) has recently addressed the fragmentation issue in a proposal that begins by explicitly recognizing that the meaning of a score, or score validity, joins the domains of assessment and experimentation:

> Score is used generically in its broadest sense to mean any coding or summarization of observed consistencies or performance regularities on a test, questionnaire, observation procedure, or other assessment devices such as work samples, portfolios, and realistic problem simulations. This general usage subsumes qualitative as well as quantitative summaries. It applies, for example, to behavior protocols, to clinical appraisals, to computerized verbal score reports, and to behavioral or performance judgments or ratings.... Scores may also refer to functional consistencies and attributes of groups, situations or environments. (p. 742)

Following this centering of the broad issue of score validity, Messick points out that the standard concept of score validity has itself been a fragmented one in which content, criterion, and construct validity are treated as separate and substitutable types. In place of this fragmentation, Messick (1989, 1995) offers an integrated concept that interrelates these features "as fundamental aspects of a more *comprehensive theory of construct validation*" (1995, p. 741). Under this proposal, the explicit determination of score validity is a necessary and central feature of research investigations, regardless of whether the aims of the investigation are fundamentally experimentation, assessment, or some combination of the two.

The dichotomizing of experimentation and assessment partially explains the failure of developmental psychology to take seriously the central significance of score or unified construct validity. However, positivism's legacy concerning *interpretation* ultimately accounts for both the dichotomy itself and the failure. Assessment (broadly) and score meaning (more narrowly) require interpretation and reasoned arguments—theory, rhetoric, and reason—that go far beyond the notion of observed scores as pristine bits of neutral data. But the legacy of positivism is a background instruction to the investigator that interpretation, theory, and reasoned argument should, whenever possible, be banished from the research enterprise in favor of a reduction to the visible.

Messick emphasizes the *centrality of interpretation,* which lies at the root of a unified concept of score or construct validity. Following Chronbach (1988), Messick (1995) thus argues that "validity is an evaluation argument" (p. 747) that cannot be totally defined according to observed correlations generated in measurements of, for example, convergent, divergent, and criterion aspects of validity. Score meaning necessarily involves such observational evidence (see, e.g., Waters & Tinsley, 1985), but it equally involves theoretical rationales and persuasive interpretative arguments. Taking this message seriously with respect to our methods of scientific inquiry, however, requires a complete exorcism of the ghost of positivism's reduction to the visible, and a move to a relational perspective concerning interpretation and observation in the process of scientific activity.

Issues of Measurement. The legacy of positivism's reduction to and induction from the visible is not limited to data definition and collection methods. The legacy also frames attitudes and beliefs about *measurement and data-analytic techniques*. One consequence of this legacy is that statistical procedures sometimes come to be applied as if they were mechanical truth generators that can burrow beneath commonsense observations and yield an interpretation-free reality. Block (1995a) has written a critique of this attitude as it has formed the ground for a prominent contemporary approach to personality and personality development, called the "Big Five." The "Big Five" or "the five-factor approach" (e.g., Costa & McCrae, 1992) refers to a representation of personality structure as five orthogonal factors derived from the application of factor analysis to trait-name adjectives. The claim of interest both here and for Block is the assertion that these five factors: (a) Surgency, (b) Agreeableness, (c) Conscientiousness, (d) Emotional Stability versus Neuroticism, and (e) Openness to Experience—have emerged as (i.e., been induced from) pristine empirical observations or facts, free of theoretical interpretation, through the application of the technique of factor analysis. Thus, the assertion is made that the presence of these five, and *only* these five factors, constitutes "an empirical fact, like the fact that there are seven continents on earth or eight American presidents from Virginia" (McCrae & John, 1992, p. 194), while the five-factor "theoretical model . . . [is itself] rooted in factor analysis" (McCrae & Costa, 1989, p. 108).

Block's analysis of the five-factor approach hinges on his general opposition to the reductionist–inductivist belief that factor analysis permits "easy empiricism rather than tough theory to develop our scientific constructs" (1995a, p. 189). Quoting Cliff (1983) in a more general context, Block (1995a) points out that, for any factor analysis:

> There are typically an infinity of alternative sets of parameters [e.g., factor loadings] which are equally consistent with the data, many of which would lead to entirely different conclusions concerning the nature of the latent variables. (pp. 122–123)

> The method of factor analysis cannot choose among the infinity of possibilities. *The decision requires conceptual argument and empirical work*; one must return to the task of being a psychologist [emphasis added]. (p. 190)

Block's general critique is broad and complex but, with respect to the place of factor analysis, it ends with the suggestion that, although this is an extraordinarily useful

method (see Appelbaum & McCall, 1983, for a general introduction to developmental applications), factor analysis "by itself cannot be empowered to make paramount and controlling decisions regarding the concepts to be used in the field of personality" (p. 209). For Block, as for others who have moved beyond the creed of reductionism–inductionism, these decisions must be left to the dialectical of conceptual argument and empirical method.

The tenacity of the reductionist–inductivist attitude is illustrated in two replies to Block's article, written by several of the chief proponents of the factor-analytic-based five-factor approach (Costa & McCrae, 1995; Goldberg & Saucier, 1995). In their replies, rather than directly addressing Block's methodological concerns about the need for a conceptually "wider reflection," these authors locate their points of rebuttal *within* the framework of factor analysis itself, where, not surprisingly, they maintain a focus on issues of reliability and control. Thus, Block argues for a movement beyond the legacy of positivism to a dialectic between the conceptual and the observational, and the various five-factor proponents argue the split position that observation will, if reliably reproduced and properly controlled, yield the conceptual. As Block summarizes the discussion:

> Costa and McCrae and Goldberg and Saucier essentially ignore the many concerns I expressed regarding the method and practice of factor analysis and continue their adherence to factor analytic results as a sufficient basis for conceptual decision. I reject factor analysis as *the* way to choose or settle upon a set of fundamental constructs. . . . As an ancillary aid to theoretical thinking, sure, use the method; but as the sole or primary criterion I believe the method to be deficient. Factor analysis cannot be depended upon to provide conceptually clean and cogent constructs. (1995b, p. 227)

The broad concern with the impact of positivism's legacy on the use of data-analytic techniques has also been extensively discussed in the context of the growth and popularity of structural equation modeling (i.e., "causal" modeling) in the investigation of developmental change (Connell & Tanaka, 1987; Henning & Rudinger, 1985). Structural equation modeling is a particularly powerful multivariate technique that allows the test of hypotheses about presumed (causal) linkages among multiple variables employing either experimental or nonexperimental data. Some structural modeling methods (termed latent variable or LV methods) such as LISREL also allow the inclusion of hypotheses about measurement error and its impact on the relations among variables. A key feature of structural equation modeling is that it is designed to *test theoretical hypotheses* about linkages among variables. It is not designed to *uncover* "causal" relations, and a critical consequence of this feature is that the use of structural equation modeling necessitates a well-thought-out and explicitly a priori specified theoretical model. However, as Mulaik (1987) points out, the legacy of positivism leads some to treat structural equation modeling as an atheoretical data-searching procedure. In this case, investigators illegitimately take "correlational data obtained for a number of variables, specify a general model of proposed causal relations, and then fix and free parameters in trial-and-error fashion until they find a specific model that fits the data" (p. 19). Mulaik, along with several others (e.g., Connell, 1987; Martin, 1987), details a series of problems that arise from this atheoretical use of the technique. In this context, Martin cautions the readers of investigations employing structural equation modeling to focus their attention on the "clarity of the presentation of the theoretical framework that motivates the research. When method (rather than theory) becomes the major focal point of substantive research, the tail (as it has been said) wags the dog" (p. 36). Connell (1987), while enthusiastic about the possibility of the technique's operating as "a *conceptual* corrective, by forcing the researcher to . . . grapple with the big picture" also acknowledges the danger of its use as "a smokescreen for theoretically barren research" (p. 172). Connell notes his concern "that complicated methodological techniques such as SEM sometimes offer refuge to atheoretical investigations" (p. 168).

If positivism's legacy can promote the misuse of data-analytic techniques, it can also discourage the emergence and application of techniques. Connell (1987) has suggested that the methodological zeitgeist is a central feature of whether new data-analytic strategies will be readily employed. When the legacy of an earlier zeitgeist continues to privilege the observed over the inferred, then techniques designed to explore latent (i.e., inferred) variables both as momentary configurations and as sequences of changes become open to both misuse (e.g., treating the inferred as if it were an observed) and disuse. As an illustration concerning disuse, consider Appelbaum and McCall's chapter on developmental methods in the 1983 edition of this *Handbook*. The chapter focused exclusively on issues of functional (variational) changes in the instrumental features of observed behavior. Methods were subsumed under, and limited by, two fundamental tasks that the authors defined as the scientific mission of developmental psychology: (a) determining changes of the "developmental function" (i.e., "the average value of a dependent variable [observed behavior] plotted over age") and (b) specifying "the stability or lack of stability of individual differences in behavioral characteristics over developmental time and the interrelationships of attributes within or across time" (p. 443). The task of charting changes in developmental function was identified as primarily the province of "descriptive" and experimental methods involving classical univariate and multivariate statistical analyses, and the focus on individual differences was identified as the province of correlational analyses.

There is no quarrel with the significance of these classical data-analytic techniques for the tasks Appelbaum and McCall (1983) identify. However, if we move beyond the legacy of the reduction to the visible, it becomes clear that these developmental tasks, and their associated techniques, tell but half the story of developmental inquiry. Further, the half of the story that they tell is the portion that is most compatible with the legacy of positivism. If developmental inquiry is to fully escape the restrictive nature of positivism, then it must include the formal as well as the functional, the expressive as well as the instrumental. The inclusive tasks of developmental inquiry must encompass not only the developmental function, but also a determination of the *sequences* that constitute that function; and they must include, along with interindividual differences, the *organization* or structure of intraindividual activity patterns. In a word, the other half of the story is a focus on *pattern or order*, both as a momentary form or a dynamic self-organizing system that identifies the (expressive) person, and as sequences of forms (i.e., transformations) that, as a whole, constitute the trajectory of the developmental function. This focus on pattern/order is either lacking or is treated as a minor secondary interest, not only in Appelbaum and McCall, but in most classic treatments of developmental methods (e.g., Achenbach, 1978; Baltes et al., 1977; Wohlwill, 1973b).

Classical Test Theory (CTT) and Item Response Theory (IRT).   Over the past two decades, a family of data-analytic techniques, designed specifically to address problems of synchronic and diachronic pattern and order, has matured into a set of powerful tools for the exploration of the expressive (trait patterns, ability patterns), and transformational (sequential changes in trait patterns, ability patterns) features of development. These techniques have emerged out of Item Response Theory (IRT) scaling models, also known as latent trait theory and item characteristic curve (ICC) theory. Classical Test Theory (CTT) models estimate expressive characteristics simply as the observed score on a given test. This approach has a number of weaknesses. Especially with respect to developmental concerns, CTT is limited as there is no assumption of a relationship between a given expressive pattern, and the transformational sequence of that pattern. For example, CTT models can address the question of whether a person is low or high on a trait of "egocentrism," but it cannot facilitate assessment of whether several proposed forms of "egocentrism" constitute a unidimensional sequence, or where a person falls on such a scale. IRT models have been proposed to overcome such shortcomings (see Appelbaum, Burchinal, & Terry, 1989; Messick, 1983, for detailed comparisons of CTT and IRT models). A number of the new data-analytic techniques, surveyed initially by Bentler (1980) and later expanded by Henning and Rudinger (1985), are presented in Table 3.2. These are often termed "models for qualitative data." For the present purposes, it is better to consider them simply as synchronic and diachronic order techniques or procedures. This usage avoids yet another reductionistic prejudice, namely the prejudice that interval and ratio scale data represent the bedrock of nature to which ordinal and nominal data must ultimately yield.

A recent study (Overton & Mueller, 1996) that examined the expressive development of several types of class reasoning and propositional reasoning illustrates the value of pattern/order techniques. In this study, a Rasch model demonstrated that, in support of Piaget's developmental-transformational theory of reasoning, various class reasoning items and propositional reasoning items, constitute a single developmental dimension (reasoning) composed of hierarchically related transformed levels of reasoning (concrete reasoning, formal reasoning). The Rasch model is based on the premise that item difficulty and ability are the only two factors responsible for success or failure on any particular item. Item difficulty parameters are estimated according to the total number of persons who are scored correct on each item. Person ability parameters are estimated according to the total number of items each

Table 3.2 Synchronic and Diachronic Order Data-Analytic Techniques

Model	Source
I. Latent attribute models	
A. *Latent structure models*	Lazarsfeld & Henry (1968)
Latent class model	Goodman (1974)
Latent class with response-error	Dayton & MacReady (1980)
B. *Scalability models*	
Scalogram analysis	Guttman (1950)
Probabilistic scale analysis	Proctor (1970)
Multiple scale analysis	Mokken (1971)
Bi- and multiform scales	Goodman (1975)
Probabilistic validation	Dayton & MacReady (1976)
Order analysis	Krus (1976)
Scaling of order hypothesis	Davison (1979, 1980)
Probabilistic unfolding	Coombs & Smith (1973)
Quasi-independent model	Goodman (1975)
C. *Latent trait models*	
Rasch model	Rasch (1966); Fisher (1976)
Mokken model	Mokken (1971)
Normal ogive model	Lord & Novick (1968)
Two- & three-parameter logistic models	Birnbaum (1968)
Logistic change model	Fischer (1976)
D. *Factor analysis (FA) models*	
FA for dichotomous variables	Muthen (1978); Christoffersson (1975)
Monotonicity analysis	Bentler (1970)
II. Prediction models	
A. Dichotomous regression model	
Logit model	Grizzle, Starmer, & Koch (1969)
B. Structural equation models	
LISREL	Joreskog & Sorbom (1981)
Partial Least Squares (PLS)	Wold (1979)
C. Cross-classification with error models	
Prediction analysis	Hildebrand et al. (1977)
Ordinal pattern analysis	Throngate (1986)
Fitting cross-classification	Thomas (1977)
Matching model	Hubert (1979)
D. Multidimensional contingency table with Partial Least Squares	Wold & Bertholet (1983)
III. Multinomial response models	
A. Log-linear model	Goodman (1972); Bishop, Fienberg, & Holland (1975); Haberman (1979)
B. Analysis of correspondence	Linder & Berchtold (1982)
C. Dual scaling for categorical data	Nishisato (1980)

This classification, originally defined by Bentler (1980) and modified by Henning and Rudinger (1985), has been further elaborated and modified here.

person scores correctly. The model provides both a statistical test for unidimensionality, and information about item difficulty. Predictions about relative item difficulty (e.g., concrete reasoning vs. formal reasoning items) are statistically evaluated on the basis of item parameters and standard errors given by Rasch analysis, and items that measure the same level (e.g., concrete reasoning) cluster together, and do not overlap with items that measure a different level (e.g., formal reasoning). In a related study (Foltz, Overton, & Ricco, 1995), the investigators using a Rasch model, were able to demonstrate that all items of a purported test of expressive formal reasoning do, indeed, constitute a unidimensional scale.

Pattern/order techniques have grown in importance over the past decade. Perhaps this is a sign that positivism's methodological zeitgeist is, in fact, passing or, alternately, beginning to pass in some interaction with the increasing accessibility and relevance of the techniques to empirical investigations—two additional features suggested by Connell (1987) as factors influencing the use of new data-analytic techniques. Whatever the reason, there are now scattered, throughout the developmental literature, numerous illustrations of the application of these techniques (e.g., see Bentler, 1980; Bond & Bunting, 1995; Connell & Tanaka, 1987; Elliott, 1982; Henning & Rudinger, 1985; Kingma & Van Den Bos, 1989; Magnusson, 1995; McArdle, 1991; Schroder, 1992; Schroder, Edelstein, & Hoppe-Graff, 1991; Spada & Kluwe, 1980; Thorngate, 1992; von Eye, 1990; von Eye & Brandtstädter, 1989; von Eye, Kreppner, & Wessels, 1992; Wohlwill, 1991).

The Legacy of Causality

Reduction and induction, positivism's twin tools, were designed to drive out interpretation and leave only a bedrock of pristine mind-independent facts. Reduction operated to reach the bedrock where the exclusive essentials of scientific explanation—*material and efficient causes*—were to be found. Induction was to summarize the uncovered relations between these causes and their effects as hypotheses, theories, and laws. It matters little substantively that positivism, following Hume, actually eschewed the term "causes" and spoke instead of "associations and correlations" (Pearson, 1911) or "functional relations" (Schlick, 1959) between antecedents (causes, independent variables) and consequences (effects, dependent variables); nor does it matter substantively that there was a move away from a hard determinism of necessary and sufficient causes to probabilistic models. In these and other maneuvers—including renaming causes "risk factors" and "process variables"—the methodological/metaphysical frame of *cause as the sole legitimate explanatory/predictive construct* remained, as it continues to remain in place today in the legacy of positivism.

The legacy of encapsulating "science" into the categories of reduction–induction and causality is so pervasive and powerful that it is difficult, especially when operating in the context of day-to-day empirical investigations, to step back and recognize that there are, in fact, reasoned alternatives to this frame. Philosophical dialogue adds depth to the conversation, and facilitates the process of stepping back. In this case, philosophical dialogue reminds us that a relational alternative is available (see Table 3.1). The relational alternative to reduction–induction, as described earlier in connection with Gadamer's philosophy, is a methodological instantiation of the "hermeneutic circle." This relational alternative is the logic of retroduction (or "abduction") (Hanson, 1958; Overton, 1991b; Pierce, 1992). Retroduction, and its modified form—"inference to the best explanation" (Harman, 1965)—explicitly demands the construction of *interpretations* (e.g., narratives, theories, models) that, in light of all available background information (reasons and observations), *plausibly explain* (order) the phenomenon under study. Retroduction, thus, warrants that interpretation and observation are interpenetrating co-actors in the methodology of empirical science. From the relational alternative, empirical research—assessment and experimentation—entails testing the *plausibility* of such retroductively produced interpretations; quite a different story, with significantly different implications, than the story of the reductive–inductive testing of the *probabilities* of mind-independent empirical generalizations drawn directly from pristine "data."

The relational methodological alternative to the claim of causality is a reminder that, since the failure of positivism, (a) causality has not been uniformly accepted as the sole type of scientific explanation, for pattern explanation has come to be an equally viable and scientifically acceptable type of explanation (see, e.g., Bunge, 1963; Cartwright, 1995; Hanson, 1958; Kitcher, 1981; Laudan, 1996; Overton & Reese, 1981; Putnam, 1983; Toulmin, 1953); and (b) it has become recognized that causes are themselves never free of the interpretative frames that give them meaning as causes (see, e.g., Hanson, 1958; Holton, 1973; Kuhn, 1962, 1977; Lakatos, 1978a; Laudan, 1977; Overton & Reese, 1981; Putnam, 1983). What Hanson (1958) has said about Galileo's approach to the law of falling bodies, and about cause broadly, illustrates these facets of the relational alternative:

> He [Galileo] seeks not a descriptive formula; nor does he seek to predict observations of freely falling bodies. He already has a formula. . . . He seeks more: an *explanation* of these data. They must be intelligibly systematized. . . . He has no confidence in observations which cannot be explained theoretically. Galileo was not seeking the cause of the acceleration; that was Descartes' programme. Galileo wished only to understand. His law of constant acceleration (1632) is not a causal law. (p. 37)

> What we refer to as "causes" are theory-loaded from the beginning to end. They are not simple, tangible links in the chain of sense experience, but rather details in an intricate pattern of concepts. (p. 54)

> Causes certainly are connected with effects; but this is because our theories connect them, not because the world is held together by cosmic glue. (p. 64)

A relational methodological program, built on these alternatives as well as other features of the relational perspective, has increasingly come to supplant positivism's program in science-at-large (Hanson, 1958; Kuhn, 1962, 1977; Lakatos, 1978a, 1978b; Laudan, 1977, 1996). Despite this supplanting, and despite early warnings in the developmental literature about problems of exclusive reliance on causal explanations (Overton & Reese, 1981; Wohlwill, 1973b), along with discussions of methodological alternatives (e.g., Hopkins & Butterworth, 1990; Kitchener, 1983; Liben, 1987; Oppenheimer, 1991a; Overton, 1991b; Silvern, 1984), the positivist legacy of pristine mind-independent causes as the sole legitimate explanatory/predictive feature of method has continued to impact developmental psychology. Examples of this legacy are found in journal articles that argue "investigation of the possible causes of development ought to be a primary goal of developmental research" (Sugarman, 1987b), and in methods texts that proclaim that variables such as "mental constructs," "phases," "levels," and "stages" "do not *explain* anything" (Friedrich, 1972, p. 15). Examples can be found in claims that pattern fails as explanation because states

and sequences of patterns are "not tied to specific antecedent [causal] variables whose measurement procedures are well defined" (Brainerd, 1978, p. 180), and in assertions that laws of pattern change, such as Piaget's equilibration process, must themselves be explained by individual causal agents (e.g., Flavell, 1985, p. 290).

Description and Explanation, and Mechanisms of Development. Perhaps the most pervasive impact of positivism's causal legacy appears in the dichotomy between *description* and *explanation,* which is, in fact, merely a surrogate for the positivists' division of methodology into reduction (description) and causality (explanation). Substantively, the description–explanation dichotomy was fostered in contemporary developmental psychology by Flavell and Wohlwill's (1969) early distinction between two aspects of the developmental process: the formal and the functional. This distinction is related to the formal/functional distinction made in the present paper. However, for Flavell and Wohlwill, and especially for Flavell (1984), the distinction entailed a split in which the formal became the descriptive "what" of development (i.e., the "outputs" of development) and function became the explanatory "how" of development (i.e., the causal inputs, the "mechanisms") (Flavell & Wohlwill, 1969, pp. 67–68). Further, and most importantly for the present point, for Flavell (1984), the causal represented the exclusive foundational base of scientific explanation:

> Mechanisms are considered by many to be the more important half of the story. . . . Moreover, the mechanisms half appears to be the explanation half (the "how" versus the "what" of development), and explanation is the ultimate objective of any science. (p. 188)

In this scenario, there is obviously no room for pattern explanation. At best, pattern—whether the synchronic pattern of mental constructs or the diachronic pattern of sequences—becomes a description to be explained by causal mechanisms and *only* causal mechanisms. As a consequence, any pattern offered as explanation (e.g., the mental constructs and developmental laws offered by Werner, Erikson, and Piaget) is treated as description, and the only question left open is the accuracy of the description. This cascade of implications also offers a clue to a methodological issue that has long bothered Flavell and other cognitive investigators. The "diagnosis" issue (see Flavell, 1985, 1992; Flavell, Miller, & Miller, 1993) is the assessment question of how, given an interest in cognitive or cognitive/affective "entities," we can know that the child, in fact, "has" a particular entity of interest. For example, suppose we are interested in whether a child "has" a "theory of mind" according to which the child is able to make inferences about another's mental state. The problem is to avoid both a false positive (really has it, but is not assessed) and a false negative (doesn't have it, but is assessed) in diagnosing whether the child "has" a "theory of mind." Because—given the way the question has been framed—these mental "entities" are thought of as the "what" of development, solutions have been sought in classical descriptive methods of task simplification and the control of settings. However, as tasks becomes simplified, they are invariably successfully performed by more children at any age and by children at younger ages. Thus, the "it" is "found" at younger and younger ages (Flavell, 1992) with wider and wider characteristics. But, unless the "it" is found in everybody, this does little to solve the diagnosis problem because it merely increases the pool from which false negatives and false positives may emerge, and virtually ensures Flavell's conclusion that "the diagnosis problem in cognitive development has proved to be a formidable one" (1992, p. 999). The alternative nonpositivist relational solution here is to treat the "it" not as a descriptive entity, but as an interpreted pattern of action. Given that the "it" is a retroductively established pattern, the instantiation of this pattern in any given behavior becomes an issue of construct validity broadly considered, rather than an issue of task simplification and control (see Kingma & Van Den Bos, 1989, for an alternative nonpositivist solution).

Because it splits scientific activity into a dichotomy of description and explanation, the methodological legacy of positivism continues to identify *mechanisms of change* with classical causal entities. This interpretation of developmental, or transitional, mechanisms (Ribaupierre, 1989; Sternberg, 1984) was described earlier, in the context of metanarratives of development (see Figures 3.2 and 3.3). There, a suggestion was also made that can now be seen as a move beyond positivism. The suggestion was that "mechanism" not be limited in meaning to "cause" but be understood as the *method or means* of change. In this case, the *action of the system* itself constitutes the mechanism of

change, and hence explains development. Because system and action represent a relational unit, the explanation becomes a relational, structure/function explanation. It is, of course, also possible to think of activity as a cause (e.g., Hoppe-Graff, 1989), and on this basis it is possible to maintain positivism's legacy in the definition that cause equals explanation. However, this is a rather procrustean maneuver because the action of a system is not a necessary and sufficient condition of *some independent entity,* nor does it increase the probability of some independent entity. Rather, a pattern of action is the means (mechanism) by which the pattern of action itself changes, and this fails to fit any classical or contemporary definition of cause (e.g., Mulaik, 1987).

If the pattern of action of a system constitutes the fundamental explanation of the system's change, then structure/function represents two sides of a unified explanation; structural explanation reflects a focus on pattern, and functional explanation reflects a focus on activity. Taking Piaget's work as an example, the *functional* explanation of transformational change is given by the dialectical *actions* of assimilation and accommodation. However, it is the *system* that assimilates and accommodates. Consequently, the synchronic system patterns that identify mental constructs, and the diachronic patterns that identify sequences represent the *structural* side of explanation. For example, a mental construct such as "scheme" or "operation" identifies particular modes of pattern action, and these modes offer explanation. Thus, to claim retroductively that the child's thought can best be characterized by a pattern of action termed "concrete operation" is to present an explanation for a wide variety of behaviors, but it is not a causal explanation in the tradition of positivism. Similarly, Piaget's "equilibration process" (Piaget, 1983) is a retroductively established claim about developmental sequences (comprising the pattern action just described, and the transformation of this pattern action) in the domains of cognition and affect. This claim is that systems move from states of dynamic imbalance to states of dynamic balance, which result in the transformation (transition) of the system and the consequent emergence of novel systemic properties. This process is an explanation of transformational change—as are Werner's orthogenetic principle, which is consistent with Piaget's equilibration process but operates at a higher level of abstraction, and Erikson's epigenetic principle, which is also consistent with Piaget's explanation but is presented in a less detailed fashion (Overton, 1991a, 1991b; Overton & Reese, 1981).

The assertion that pattern explains, and that pattern is not merely a feature of split-off descriptive activity, requires a clear understanding of the interpretative method and the empirical character of the assessment of the interpretative method. Pattern is always an interpretative characterization, and it is arrived at retroductively. Pattern is never a thing "seen," regardless of whether the "seeing" is done with the human eye, the most advanced high-tech imaging techniques, or, as discussed earlier, some mechanical truth generator that claims to burrow beneath commonsense observations. Pattern is arrived at by a circular process, but the circle is not vicious; it is more akin to the hermeneutic circle that is open and comes to represent an expanding spiral (see the earlier section, "Gadamer and Taylor and the Leibnizian–Hegelian Relational Developmental Tradition"). Given some limited area of observation and a defined theoretical context, a pattern interpretation is drawn. The pattern explanation is then empirically assessed through its application to a wider observational arena. This critical step ensures that the circle will be open-ended (a spiral) and not vicious. It also leads to increasing the explanatory power of the pattern interpretation (Liben, 1987). The specific means of empirical assessment may occur in experimental contexts and in contexts described earlier with respect to evidential methods for pattern/order analyses (Table 3.2). In either type of context, the empirical evidence for the pattern explanation assesses the *plausibility* of the interpretation as a coherent, well-articulated, and powerful explanation.

Only the prejudice from the legacy of positivism isolates action patterns into a sealed-off sphere termed "description." There is no question that any theory provides the categories that order (i.e., describe) the world. Skinner ordered the world through categories of "stimulus," "response," and "reinforcement"; Werner, through "differentiation" and "integration"; and some contemporary theorists, through categories such as "representations," "production systems," and "semiotic subjects." The point is that, like Escher's Drawing Hands, these and other "descriptive" categories enter into explanation, as explanation enters into these descriptive categories.

Functionalism. This represents a final substantive example of the influence of positivism's causal legacy. A variety of historical meanings have been applied to the concept of functionalism (Overton, 1984, 1991d). However, its most prominent contemporary meaning entails a commitment to defining all psychological phenomena and states in terms of causes and effects. Thus, all mental states and sequences are ultimately viewed as decomposable into elements explained in terms of stimulus inputs and response outputs. Further, because functional relationships imply reversible causation (Cook & Campbell, 1979), stimuli that occur following a response can as readily be treated as causal as those that precede the response. This is illustrated in the earlier described metanarrative of neo-Darwinian development (see Figure 3.2). In this metanarrative, the phenotype can be considered the psychological state (i.e., the person, or some subsystem of the person). It is defined by both the antecedent material genetic causes, and the subsequent efficient causes identified as environmental selection. The earlier discussion of Kagan's (1994) "old" functionalism and of Campos's "new" functionalism with respect to emotions (Campos et al., 1994) further illustrates this explanatory doctrine. Kagan's definition of emotion is a functionalism that commits only to an antecedent cause ("a participating event in a context") and a consequent effect ("changes in motor behavior") as a definition of emotion. Campos, on the other hand, relies more on the relationship between the output and the "adaptive" (i.e., signal) feature of the causal environment.

Functionalism is a popular doctrine that has been applied to emotional development, social–emotional development (e.g., social learning theories; see Overton & Horowitz, 1991), and cognitive development (the neonativists discussed earlier all assume a functionalist position, as do most recent connectionist models of mind; see Elman, Bates, Johnson, Karmiloff-Smith, Parisi, & Plunkett, 1996). There has even been a serious attempt to redefine Piagetian theory in functionalist terms (Beilin, 1987). Common to all these efforts is the attempt to offer "descriptions" and "explanations" that exclude pattern, order, transformation, organization, and system, or to give these concepts functionalist (causal, "input-output") interpretations. This is, of course, the irony of the legacy of positivism—the degree to which interpretation defends the exclusivity of a position, whose fundamental claim is the nonscientific character of interpretation.

In each of the described examples of the legacy of positivism's causal exclusivity, the focus has been on substantive issues and their impact on methods. However, the same legacy is found in discussions of methods themselves. Thus, despite demurrals to the effect that description and explanation always go hand in hand, methods often become rigidly dichotomized into descriptive (cross-sectional and longitudinal) research designs that "address methods of properly identifying developmental change" (Baltes et al., 1977, p. 177), and explanatory designs that "are aimed at explaining developmental change in terms of time-related antecedents and mechanisms" (p. 176). Baltes et al. further illustrate this dichotomization in the following comments:

> The aims of developmental psychology include the pursuit of knowledge about the determinants and mechanisms that help us understand the how and why of development: What causes the change? This aspect of knowledge-building is often called explicative, explanatory, or analytic, because its goal is to find causal-type relationships and thus to go beyond descriptive predictions of the nature of behavioral development. (p. 4)

> The ideal of explanatory-analytic research is to demonstrate the cause of development. . . . In explanatory research, age-change functions or alternative developmental phenomena typically are seen as part of the dependent variable, . . . and researchers' efforts are aimed at finding the controlling variables and processes. (p. 177)

These comments demonstrate how methods and substantive argument can combine in a self-reinforcing closed circle to prolong the claim that variational change is the only ultimately legitimate developmental change, and cause is the only legitimate scientific explanation. Discussions of methods that take this approach either ignore methods that are relevant to expressive and transformational features of development, or stretch these methods to fit a causal bed. Thus, methods that focus on assessment, and pattern/order methods of data analysis are infrequently described in broad discussions of developmental methods (e.g., Appelbaum & McCall, 1983; Baltes et al., 1977). On the other hand, structural equation modeling often finds a place in these discussions merely because this method has received the dubious label "causal modeling" which, as Bentler (1980) points out, implies that the method is intended to be used "to explain, rather than describe, the data" (p. 83).

Toward a Contemporary Relational Methodology

Although the legacy of positivism continues to impact research methods, the failure of positivism was a signal that interpretation as a necessary and fundamental feature of science could no longer be suppressed. New research methods and new approaches to old research methods are currently being constructed on this recognition, and over the past 40 years a new relational methodology has been emerging. This methodology is transforming the split Baconian–Newtonian methodology, and in this transformation it is providing a rational base from which to evolve a system of empirical methods that is *both* more *coherent* and more *adaptive to the goals of science.*

Instrumentalism

The first halting step in the emergence of a contemporary relational methodology—one that again treats interpretation and observation as coequal dialectical defined partners in the knowledge-building activity called science—was the rise of *conventionalism* or *instrumentalism* (Kaplan, 1964; Lakatos, 1978a; Laudan, 1984; Overton, 1984; Pepper, 1942; Popper, 1959). Instrumentalism was another grand strategy designed to demarcate science from nonscience. It accepted the failure of reductive–inductive features of positivism and admitted the introduction of theoretical interpretation as an irreducible dimension of science (see Table 3.1). However, theories and models were treated as mere *convenient or instrumental heuristic devices* for making predictions. Thus, theories in instrumentalism were restricted to the same predictive function that formal deductive systems performed in positivism.

To introduce theories and models—even when restricted to functioning as kinds of calculating devices—instrumentalism dichotomized science into separate and unequal spheres: the *context of discovery* and the *context of justification* (see Table 3.1; Overton, 1984; Richenbach, 1938). The context of justification constitutes the sphere of Baconian–Newtonian reduction (to hard data understood as pristine observations)/causality (explanation)/induction (laws). For instrumentalism, this sphere continues to assert epistemological privilege, and it continues to function as the final and absolute privileged arbiter of truth. The context of discovery, on the other hand, consists of theoretical terms, theoretical entities, and models. For instrumentalism, the propositions of the context of discovery could be the product of the scientist's hunches, guesses, creative imagination, metaphysical presuppositions, or metanarratives. Their origins mattered little because the propositions of this sphere were restricted to the secondary function of merely guiding predictions. Lakatos (1978a) clearly articulated the asymmetry of the two domains which, in fact, left the whole Baconian–Newtonian methodology in place: "For the conventionalist . . . [theoretical] discoveries are primarily inventions of new and simpler pigeonhole systems" (p. 107). However, the "genuine progress of science . . . takes place [still, as with positivism] on the ground level of proven facts [i.e., pristine observations] and changes on the theoretical level are merely instrumental" (p. 106).

Functionalism Updated. Instrumentalism was a move, but only a partial move, toward a full integration of interpretation and observation. Instrumentalism, like positivism itself, continues to impact on developmental inquiry. The primary novelty of instrumentalism—theories and models treated solely as prediction devices—has had its greatest influence by providing an updated version of functionalism. From an instrumentalist position, any predictive device can be inserted between the input and output, the sole limiting factors being the simplicity of the device (i.e., parsimony in comparison with other devices) and the predictive power of the device. Thus, today, most computational, representationalist, and connectionist theories of mind are characterized by their commitment to instrumentalism and functionalism (see Overton, 1994c; Overton & Horowitz, 1991). An instructive contemporary illustration is found in connectionist and dynamic systems models discussed by Elman et al. (1996). In this arena, linear and nonlinear dynamic equations are written as inductive analytic descriptions of relations between sensory input and behavioral output, or rate of behavioral change. The equations are, thus, descriptive of the predictive device that operates between input and output. In dynamic systems theory, as framed by the functionalist narrative, this device is termed a "system." The generalized descriptions are understood functionally as the principles or "laws" that govern (unknown) causal agents that produce the output—"Dynamic equations are offered as a description of the laws governing a causal agent" (p. 179). Given that this implicates a causal understanding, the dynamic equations are claimed to constitute an "explanation" of the behavior or rate of behavioral change under investigation. Finally, an important goal of this activity is the production of laws that implicate the fewest number of causes possible, thus ensuring that the fundamental criterion of parsimony is met: *"One of our goals here is to illustrate how the number of causes or mechanisms required to*

explain complex patterns of change can be reduced within a connectionist framework. . . . For those who value parsimony and theoretical austerity, this should be viewed as an advance" (p. 174).

Instrumentalism with Falsification

Popper (1959) added a unique dimension to instrumentalism through the claim that theories and models should become acceptable in the body of science if, and *only* if, they specify observational results that, if found, would disprove or falsify a theory. In essence, Popper recognized that simplicity and predictive power were weak criteria for warranting a theory. Because, as described earlier, it is not *logically* possible to confirm or verify a theory, both simplicity and predictive power constitute a subjective element that Popper sought to eliminate by suggesting the criterion of falsification (Lakatos, 1978a; Overton, 1994c). Here, however, as in positivism and in instrumentalism itself, an interpretation-free observational foundation, and *only* an interpretation-free observational foundation, continued as the final privileged arbiter of the scientific.

Contemporary Relational Methodology

Instrumentalism opened the door for interpretation to reenter science but hesitated in allowing it to become a full partner in the scientific process of building a systematic body of knowledge. The movement to a dialectically defined full partnership of interpretation and observation required a radical move, one that would (a) abandon the foundationalism of an absolute mind-independent reality serving as a privileged judge of truth and science, and (b) free up the notion of scientific explanation that was fossilized by this foundationalism. In this radical move, the *coherence* of the knowledge system, as it evolves toward a fusion of horizons, would become as significant a criterion of truth as the correspondence of theoretical propositions and observations (see Laudan, 1996; Overton, 1991b); the overall logic of science would more closely resemble the retroductive process, discussed earlier in this chapter, than either the split-off inductive or split-off deductive logics; and pattern and cause would, as in Aristotle's early relational presentation, constitute the dialectical poles of scientific explanation (Overton 1991b, 1991c). In sum, this radical move defined the second path from common sense to highly refined knowledge—the path that emerged from the Leibnizian–Hegelian relational background in which interpretation and observation interpenetrate and form an identity of opposites (see Table 3.1).

Retroduction, Interpretation/Observation, and Pattern/Causal Explanation

The radical methodological step had its historical grounding in the evolution of this relational metaphysics, as described in an earlier section of this chapter. However, the impact of Hanson's (1958) work is usually credited as the significant methodological step, and this came to be elaborated, supplemented, and transformed by Toulmin (1953, 1961, 1990), Kuhn (1962, 1977), Holton (1973, 1993), Lakatos (1978a, 1978b), Laudan (1977, 1984, 1996), and Putnam (1983, 1987, 1990), among others. Hanson argued three basic points:

1. Captured in his famous phrase "All data are theory-laden" is the fundamental principle of the relational perspective: Interpretation and observation constitute an identity of opposites. Consequently, there can be no meaningful split between explanation and description, and no way of establishing a pristine mind-independent database from which to induce laws of nature. Laws, lawfulness, theoretical propositions, and hypotheses emerge from the coaction of theory and observation (Table 3.1; also, Toulmin, 1953).

2. Scientific explanation consists of conceptual patterns as well as causes (Toulmin, 1953, 1961). Hence, the postulation and analysis of pattern/order relations constitutes a legitimate and fundamental interest of scientific explanation.

3. Retroduction characterizes the logic of science. Paths from the particular to the universal, and from the universal to the particular, are each moments of retroduction or instantiations of the hermeneutic circle, and not isolated nor privileged competitors as "the" path to refined scientific knowledge.

Kuhn's contribution to the methodological move built on the fundamental principle of the relational tradition and expanded the interpretative domain. Following an earlier distinction made by Toulmin (1953, 1961), Kuhn (1962, 1977) argued that the interpretative focus in scientific research is not merely "theory" as a specific organization of explanatory statements about some phenomenon, but an organized set of presuppositions, attitudes, and beliefs called "paradigms"(see Table 3.1). Paradigms could be narrow in focus or as broad as a worldview (Overton, 1984). They function to give meaning to (i.e., make intelligible) and direct the research process. They operate as part of the warp and woof of the entire evolving knowledge system (see Table 3.1), not merely as instrumental heuristic devices of an isolated context of discovery. Holton (1973, 1993) expanded this analysis of the impact of conceptual presuppositions on scientific thought through a historical examination of what he termed "thematic" components of scientific activity.

Lakatos and Laudan—although disagreeing with Kuhn, and with each other, on a specific understanding of the nature of scientific *progress,* and also expressing concern about some potentially *relativistic* features of Kuhn's argument—each accepted the fundamental principle of the relational tradition, and further articulated the domain of Kuhn's paradigms (Overton, 1984). Lakatos (1978a) defined this domain as *the "scientific research program,"* and he described it as a stratified series of conceptual levels consisting of (a) a *hard core,* (b) a *positive heuristic,* and (c) a *belt of auxiliary hypotheses.*

The *hard core* constitutes the conceptual framework, composed of metaphysical and metanarrative propositions, that defines the ontology of the field of investigation (see Table 3.1). For example, as suggested earlier in this chapter and as illustrated by Lakatos, Cartesian metaphysics functioned as the hard core of a research program. Because research proceeded within the context of this metaphysical scaffolding, work on some areas that it defined as legitimate problem areas was encouraged, and work on others that were "meaningless" within the categories of this particular hard core was discouraged. The *positive heuristic* is the long-range research methodology of the research program. The hard core is relatively unchanging, but the positive heuristic, formulated within the categories of the hard core, exhibits greater flexibility for change. An example of the positive heuristic is the functionalism of the Cartesian or Baconian–Newtonian methodology, as contrasted with the structure/function approach of the Leibnizian–Hegelian tradition. The move within the Baconian–Newtonian methodology from a hard determinism of specific cause and effects to a functionalism is an illustration of the flexibility of the positive heuristic within a given hard core. The hard core and positive heuristic establish the frame within which a *family of theories* is generated. For example, as discussed earlier, Werner, Piaget, Erikson, Winnicott, Mahler, Bowlby, and embodiment theory constitute a family of theories that instantiate the Leibnizian–Hegelian hard core and the relational methodology. The *belt of auxiliary hypotheses* then consists of sets of empirical hypotheses that are embodied in the theories, and these come to constitute the empirically refutable component of the research tradition.

Laudan (1977, 1996) has few differences with Lakatos concerning the structure of the interpretative frame, but he terms this organization a "research tradition" (see Table 3.1) and captures its essential features as follows:

> *A research tradition is thus a set of ontological and methodological "do's" and "don'ts".* . . . Although it is vital to distinguish between the ontological and the methodological components of a research tradition, the two are often intimately related, and for a very natural reason: namely, that one's views about the appropriate *methods* of inquiry are generally compatible with one's views about the *objects* of inquiry. (1977, p. 80)

> Theories represent exemplifications of more fundamental views about the world, and the manner in which theories are modified and changed only makes sense when seen against the backdrop of those more fundamental commitments. I call the cluster of beliefs which constitute such fundamental views "research traditions." Generally, these consist of at least two components: (1) a set of beliefs about what sorts of entities and processes make up the domain of inquiry; and (2) a set of epistemic and methodological norms about how the domain is to be investigated, how the theories are to be tested, how data are to be collected, and the like. (1996, p. 83)

The broadly interpretative domain joins the empirical domain in the relational methodology through the question of how to gauge the advance of science. In positivism, the empirical measure was the inductive growth of highly confirmed (i.e., verified) observations as hypotheses, theories, and laws. In instrumentalism, the measure was similar but the empirical falsification of theories replaced verification as the vehicle of advancement. With the move toward a relational methodology, it became clear that rich theories cannot be falsified (Lakatos, 1978a; Quine, 1953; Toulmin, 1953; see also Overton, 1984, 1991b). As Lakatos noted, empirical hypotheses can be falsified, but

that falsification only *indirectly* implicates the theory from which the hypothesis was drawn.

Because of the failure of the doctrine of theory falsification, falsified empirical hypotheses came to be treated as empirical *anomalies,* which are judged as evidence that is relevant to a theory's plausibility. For Kuhn (1962), empirical anomalies simply add up until they trigger a kind of gestalt switch, at which point investigators begin to abandon current theories and paradigms. Lakatos (1978a) criticized Kuhn's solution on the basis of its being subjective. As an alternative, Lakatos proposed a more instrumental solution. He argued that, although anomalies must be explicitly noted as they occur, the primary feature of scientific progress is the research program's continuing ability to predict novel or unexpected phenomena with some degree of success, *and within the context of a rational, coherent, preplanned positive heuristic.* Only when the predictive ability of the program begins to falter can anomalies begin to weigh against the theory.

Laudan's (1977) contribution begins from a broadly pragmatic position that conceptualizes the advance of science as the solution of problems, rather than the making of observational discoveries. In this context, science pursues the aim of establishing order and organization by maximizing "the scope of solved empirical problems, while minimizing the scope of anomalous and conceptual problems" (p. 66). In articulating this position, Laudan argues that Lakatos's instrumental criterion of scientific progress is insufficient because it fails to weigh the degree to which different empirical anomalies pose an "epistemic threat" to a theory. Hence, Laudan insists, a *rational* criterion is needed for deciding the *weighing* of empirical anomalies as well as problems of conceptual coherence (e.g., logical inconsistencies, conceptual ambiguities). The research tradition presents just such a rational means.

This sketch of the evolution of the relational methodology from Hanson to Laudan charts the general outlines of the dialogue of this evolving story. However, this chronology captures neither the parallel and converging streams of thought that have supported the evolution, nor the crosscurrents of controversy that often seem to threaten a devolution. With respect to the former, two converging streams require at least a brief mention. The first of these is the neo-Kantian line, especially the Marburg School, represented particularly in the writings of Ernst Cassirer (e.g., 1923, 1960). This line of thought, throughout the period of positivism, sustained and elaborated the alternative relational view that, in the natural sciences, as in other arenas of human knowledge-building activity, thought and observation form an irreducible identity of opposites.

The second supporting stream of thought that has been central in the movement to a relational methodology is the growth of hermeneutics. As discussed earlier (see the section, "Gadamer and Taylor and the Leibnizian–Hegelian Relational Developmental Tradition"), hermeneutics focuses on the problem of interpretation. While hermeneutics has a long history, it was at the beginning of the 20th century that Dilthey developed the method of *Verstehen* (understanding) as a methodology for the social sciences. In Dilthey's scheme, understanding stood in opposition to explanation, for understanding proceeded through a consideration of contexts and patterns and not through a search for causes and effects. In one sense, then, hermeneutics and the methodology of understanding enhanced a split that was being created by positivism between the "interpretative" sciences and the natural sciences. On the other hand, work within hermeneutics provided a fertile ground for the further elaboration of the nature of meaning, pattern, and intelligibility against a time when positivism would play itself out and a relational methodology—as an integration of understanding and explanation—might emerge.

Today, particularly in the work of Gadamer (1989, 1993) and Ricoeur (1984, 1991), this promise of the contribution of hermeneutics—and a version of hermeneutics termed "narrative knowing"—to empirical science broadly is being realized. Gadamer's contribution was discussed earlier in this chapter; Ricoeur's contribution is found in his attempts to mend "the methodological dualism of explanation and understanding and to substitute a subtle dialectic for this clear-cut alternative" (1991, p. 126). In this dialectical mending, Ricoeur demonstrates, from an interpretative point of view, how Aristotle's causal explanations and pattern explanations "rather than constituting mutually exclusive poles, . . . [are] relative moments in a complex process" (1991, p. 126). This demonstration directly converges with and supplements the mending proposed from an empirical perspective by Hanson (1958), Kuhn (1962), and the other relational methodologists described above.

As a concluding note—both to this chapter and to this discussion of the evolution of the methodology and methods of the empirical scientific inquiry termed developmental psychology—it should be explicitly recognized that this historical movement, perhaps like any development, has not proceeded in a linear or unchallenged fashion. Like transformational development itself, which proceeds in variational cycles that partially loop back on themselves and then form spirals to advance again, always in the context of dialogical conflict, the movement to a relational methodology has also traced a spiraling configuration. Today, the greatest challenge to the continued development of the relational tradition broadly, and the relational methodology, comes from the threat of relativism. As Laudan (1996) has recently observed, the work of Hanson and others is often given a postpositivist or postmodernist twist, and translated into a relativistic stance. Simply put, the argument is: If there is no absolute, fixed, mind-independent Real, then "anything goes," and hence one interpretation or experience becomes as valid as another. This closing statement is not the place to discuss the inadequacies of this stance (Bernstein, 1983; Latour, 1993; Laudan, 1996; Overton, 1990, 1991b, 1991c, 1991d, 1994a, 1994b). However, as a concluding statement, it should be said that relativism, like absolutism—and like their respective twins, skepticism and dogmatism—become the "isms" that they are, and operate as split doctrines, only when the dialectic of reason and observation is collapsed into one, or the other, pole of a dichotomized experience. Relativism, like absolutism, can exist if, and *only* if, we choose to contextualize inquiry within Cartesian split categories. Then, and only then, is thought forced into *either* a relativism *or* an absolutism. To the extent that the dialectic is maintained and not collapsed, then the particular and the universal simply constitute two interpenetrating and coacting lines of sight of the whole that is called inquiry.

ACKNOWLEDGMENTS

I express my appreciation and thanks first to Ulrich Mueller for his research and editing assistance, but most of all for his being constantly available to thoughtfully discuss many of the issues that appear in this chapter. Thanks to too many students to mention by name, for critically examining the chapter and making suggestions. Special thanks to Jeremy Zonana for a most helpful and thorough copyediting. Thanks to a number of colleagues for making critical comments on earlier drafts: Robbie Case, Lutz

Eckensberger, David Palermo, Nora Newcombe, Hayne Reese, Helmut Reich, Marsha Weinraub, and Alexander von Eye. Finally, thanks to Richard Lerner for his editorial work, and for his support and most helpful suggestions throughout the project.

REFERENCES

Achenbach, T. M. (1978). *Research in developmental psychology: Concepts, strategies, methods.* New York: Free Press.

Allport, G. (1955). *Becoming.* New Haven, CT: Yale University Press.

Anastasi, A. (1958). Heredity, environment, and the question "how?" *Psychological Review, 65,* 197–208.

Anastasi, A. (1988). *Psychological testing* (6th ed.). New York: Macmillan.

Appelbaum, M. I., Burchinal, M. R., & Terry, R. A. (1989). Quantitative methods and the search for continuity. In M. H. Bornstein & N. A. Krasnegor (Eds.), *Stability and continuity in mental development* (pp. 251–272). Hillsdale, NJ: Erlbaum.

Appelbaum, M. I., & McCall, R. B. (1983). Design and analysis in developmental psychology. In W. Kessen (Ed.), *Handbook of child psychology* (Vol. 1, pp. 416–476). New York: Wiley.

Asendorpf, J. B., & Valsiner, J. (1992). Editors' introduction: Three dimensions of developmental perspectives. In J. B. Asendorpf & J. Valsiner (Eds.), *Stability and change in development: A study of methodological reasoning* (pp. ix–xxii). London: Sage.

Ayer, A. J. (1946). *Language, truth and logic* (2nd ed.). New York: Dover.

Ayer, A. J. (1970). What is a law of nature. In B. A. Brody (Ed.), *Readings in the philosophy of science* (pp. 39–54). Englewood Cliffs, NJ: Prentice-Hall.

Baillargeon, R. (1987). Object permanence in 3.5- and 4.5-month-old infants. *Developmental Psychology, 23,* 655–664.

Baillargeon, R. (1993). The object concept revisited: New directions in the investigation of infants' physical knowledge. In C. Granrud (Ed.), *Visual perception and cognition in infancy* (pp. 265–313). Hillsdale, NJ: Erlbaum.

Bakhtin, M. M. (1986). In C. Emerson & M. Holquist (Eds.), *Speech genres and other late essays* (V. W. McGee, Trans.). Austin: University of Texas Press.

Baldwin, J. M. (1895). *Mental development in the child and the race: Methods and process.* New York: Macmillan.

Baldwin, J. M. (1897). *Social and ethical interpretations in mental development: A study in social psychology.* New York: Macmillan.

Balint, M. (1968). *The basic fault.* London: Tavistock.

Ball, L., & Chandler, M. (1989). Identity formation in suicidal and nonsuicidal youth: The role of self-continuity. *Development and Psychopathology, 1,* 257–275.

Baltes, P. B., Reese, H. W., & Nesselroade, J. R. (1977). *Life-span developmental psychology: Introduction to research methods.* Monterey, CA: Brooks/Cole.

Bateson, P. (1985). Problems and possibilities in fusing developmental and evolutionary thought. In G. Butterworth, J. Rutkowska, & M. Scaife (Eds.), *Evolution and developmental psychology* (pp. 3–21). New York: St. Martin's Press.

Beilin, H. (1987). Current trends in cognitive development research: Towards a new synthesis. In B. Inhelder, D. de Caprona, & A. Cornu-Wells (Eds.), *Piaget today* (pp. 37–64). Hillsdale, NJ: Erlbaum.

Belsky, J., Steinberg, L., & Draper, P. (1991). Childhood experience, interpersonal development, and reproductive strategy: An evolutionary theory of socialization. *Child Development, 62,* 647–670.

Bentler, P. (1970). A comparison of monotonicity analysis with factor analysis. *Educational and Psychological Measurement, 30,* 241–250.

Bentler, P. (1980). The study of cognitive development through modeling with qualitative data. In R. H. Kluwe & H. Spada (Eds.), *Developmental models of thinking* (pp. 77–106). New York: Academic Press.

Berlin, I. (1956). *The age of enlightenment.* New York: Mentor Book.

Bernstein, R. J. (1983). *Beyond objectivism and relativism: Science, hermeneutics, and praxis.* Philadelphia: University of Pennsylvania Press.

Birnbaum, A. (1968). Some latent trait models and their use in inferring an examinee's ability. In F. M. Lord & M. R. Novick (Eds.), *Statistical theory of mental test scores* (pp. 62–73). Reading, MA: Addison-Wesley.

Bishop, Y. M. M., Fienberg, S. E., & Holland, P. W. (1975). *Discrete multivariate analysis: Theory and practice.* Cambridge, MA: MIT Press.

Bleicher, J. (1980). *Contemporary hermeneutics: Hermeneutics as method, philosophy and critique.* Boston: Routledge & Kegan Paul.

Block, J. (1995a). A contrarian view of the five-factor approach to personality description. *Psychological Bulletin, 117,* 187–215.

Block, J. (1995b). Going beyond the five factors given: Rejoinder to Costa and McCrae (1995) and Goldberg and Saucier (1995). *Psychological Bulletin, 117,* 226–229.

Bloom, L. (1993). *The transition from infancy to language: Acquiring the power of expression.* New York: Cambridge University Press.

Boesch, E. E. (1980). *Kultur and handlung.* Bern: Huber.

Boesch, E. E. (1984). The development of affective schemata. *Human Development, 27,* 173–182.

Boesch, E. E. (1991). *Symbolic action theory and cultural psychology.* Berlin, Germany: Springer-Verlag.

Boesch, E. E. (1992). Culture—individual—culture: The cycle of knowledge. In M. V. Cranach, W. Doise, & G. Mugny (Eds.), *Social representations and the solid bases of knowledge* (pp. 89–95). Lewiston, NY: Hogrefe & Huber.

Bond, T. G., & Bunting, E. (1995). Piaget and measurement: III. Reassessing the methode clinique. *Archives de Psychologie, 63,* 231–255.

Bowlby, J. (1958). The nature of the child's tie to his mother. *International Journal of Psychoanalysis, 39,* 350–373.

Brainerd, C. J. (1978). The stage question in cognitive developmental theory. *Behavioral and Brain Sciences, 2,* 173–213.

Bridgman, P. (1927). *The logic of modern physics.* New York: Macmillan.

Brooks, D. R. (1992). Incorporating origins into evolutionary theory. In F. J. Varela & J. Dupuy (Eds.), *Understanding origins: Contemporary views on the origin of life, mind and society: Boston studies in the philosophy of science* (Vol. 130, pp. 191–212). Boston: Kluwer.

Brooks, D. R., & Wiley, E. O. (1988). *Evolution as entropy: Toward a unified theory of biology* (2nd ed.). Chicago: University of Chicago Press.

Bronfenbrenner, U. (1979). *The ecology of human development.* Cambridge, MA: Harvard University Press.

Broughton, J. M. (1981). The genetic psychology of James Mark Baldwin. *American Psychologist, 36,* 396–407.

Bunge, M. (1963). *Causality.* New York: Meridan.

Buss, D. M. (1995). Evolutionary psychology: A new paradigm for psychological science. *Psychological Inquiry, 6,* 31–34.

Campos, J. J., Campos, R. G., & Barrett, K. C. (1989). Emergent themes in the study of emotional development and emotion regulation. *Developmental Psychology, 25,* 394–402.

Campos, J. J., Mumme, D. L., Kermoian, R., & Campos, R. G. (1994). A functionalist perspective on the nature of emotion. In N. A. Fox (Ed.), The development of emotion regulation: Biological and behavioral considerations. *Monographs of the Society for Research in Child Development, 59*(2/3, Serial No. 240), 284–303.

Carey, S., & Gelman, R. (Eds.). (1991). *The epigenesis of mind: Essays on biology and cognition.* Hillsdale, NJ: Erlbaum.

Cartwright, N. (1995). The reality of causes in a world of instrumental laws. In R. Boyd, P. Gasper, & J. D. Trout (Eds.), *The philosophy of science* (pp. 379–386). Cambridge, MA: MIT Press.

Case, R. (in press). The development of conceptual structure. In R. S. Siegler & D. Kuhn (Eds.), *Handbook of child psychology: Vol. 2. Cognition, perception and language* (5th ed.). New York: Wiley.

Cassidy, J. (1994). Emotion regulation: Influences of attachment relationships. In N. A. Fox (Ed.), The development of emotion regulation: Biological and behavioral considerations. *Monographs of the Society for Research in Child Development, 59*(2/3, Serial No. 240), 228–249.

Cassirer, E. (1923). *Substance and function and Einstein's theory of relativity.* Chicago: Open Court.

Cassirer, E. (1951). *The philosophy of the enlightenment.* Boston: Beacon Press.

Cassirer, E. (1960). *The logic of the humanities.* New Haven, CT: Yale University Press.

Chandler, M., & Carpendale, J. (1994). Concerning the rumored falling to earth of "time's arrow." *Psychological Inquiry, 5,* 245–248.

Chandler, M., & Chapman, M. (Eds.). (1991). *Criteria for competence: Controversies in the assessment of children's abilities.* Hillsdale, NJ: Erlbaum.

Chapman, M. (1986). The structure of exchange: Piaget's sociological theory. *Human Development, 29,* 181–194.

Christoffersson, A. (1976). Factor analysis of dichotomized variables. *Psychometrika, 40,* 5–32.

Chronbach, L. J. (1988). Five perspectives on validation argument. In H. Wainer & H. Braun (Eds.), *Test validity* (pp. 34–55). Hillsdale, NJ: Erlbaum.

Churchland, P. M. (1995). *The engine of reason, the seat of the soul: A philosophical journey into the brain.* Cambridge, MA: MIT Press.

Churchland, P. S. (1986). *Neurophilosophy.* Cambridge, MA: MIT Press.

Cliff, N. (1983). Some cautions concerning the application of causal modeling methods. *Multivariate Behavioral Research, 18,* 115–126.

Cohen, M. R. (1931). *Reason and nature: An essay on the meaning of scientific method.* New York: Harcourt, Brace.

Cole, M. (1995). Culture and cognitive development: From cross-cultural research to creating systems of cultural mediation. *Culture and Psychology, 1,* 25–54.

Cole, M. (1996). *Cultural psychology: A once and future discipline.* Cambridge, MA: Harvard University Press.

Connell, J. P. (1987). Structural equation modeling and the study of child development: A question of goodness of fit. *Child Development, 58,* 167–175.

Connell, J. P., & Tanaka, J. S. (Eds.). (1987). Special section on structural equation modeling. *Child Development, 58,* 1–175.

Cook, T. D., & Campbell, D. T. (1979). *Quasi-experimentation: Design and analysis for field settings.* Chicago: Rand McNally.

Coombs, C. H., & Smith, E. K. (1973). On the detection of structure in attitudes and developmental processes. *Psychological Review, 80,* 337–351.

Copi, I. M. (1953). *Introduction to logic.* New York: Macmillian.

Cornford, F. M. (1937). *Plato's cosmology.* London: Routledge & Kegan Paul.

Costa, P. T., Jr., & McCrae, R. R. (1992). The five-factor model of personality and its relevance to personality disorders. *Journal of Personality Disorders, 6,* 343–359.

Costa, P. T., Jr., & McCrae, R. R.(1995). Solid ground in the wetlands of personality: A reply to Block. *Psychological Bulletin, 117,* 216–220.

Coveney, P., & Highfield, R. (1990). *The arrow of time.* New York: Fawcett Columbia.

Cronbach, L. J. (1988). Five perspectives on validation argument. In H. Wainer & H. Braun (Eds.), *Test validity* (pp. 34–35). Hillsdale, NJ: Erlbaum.

Damon, W. (1988). Socialization and individuation. In G. Handel (Ed.), *Childhood socialization* (pp. 3–10). Hawthorne, NY: Aldine de Gruyter.

Damon, W. (1991). Problems of direction in socially shared cognition. In L. B. Resnick, J. M. Levine, & S. D. Teasley (Eds.), *Socially shared cognition* (pp. 384–397). Washington: American Psychological Association.

Damon, W., & Hart, D. (1988). *Self-understanding in childhood and adolescence.* New York: Cambridge University Press.

Davison, M. L. (1979). Testing a unidimensional, qualitative unfolding model for attitudinal or developmental data. *Psychometrika, 44,* 179–194.

Davison, M. L. (1980). A psychological scaling model for testing order hypotheses. *British Journal of Mathematical and Statistical Psychology, 33,* 123–141.

Dayton, C. M., & MacReady, G. B. (1976). A probabilistic model for validation of behavioral hierarchies. *Psychometrika, 41,* 189–204.

Dayton, C. M., & MacReady, G. B. (1980). A scaling model with response errors and intrinsically unscalable respondents. *Psychometrika, 45,* 343–356.

Dennett, D. (1991). *Consciousness explained.* Boston: Little, Brown.

Dewey, J. (1925). *Experience and nature.* La Salle, IL: Open Court Press.

Dewey, J. (1934). *Art as experience.* New York: Berkeley.

Eckensberger, L. H. (1989). A bridge between theory and practice, between general laws and contexts? *Psychology and Developing Societies, 1,* 21–35.

Eckensberger, L. H. (1990). On the necessity of the culture concept in psychology: A view from cross-cultural psychology. In F. J. R. van de Vijver & G. J. M. Hutschemaekers (Eds.), *The investigation of culture. Current issues in cultural psychology* (pp. 153–183). Tilburg, Germany: Tilburg University Press.

Eckensberger, L. H. (1995). Activity or action: Two different roads towards an integration of culture into psychology. *Culture and Psychology, 1,* 67–80.

Eckensberger, L. H. (1996). Agency, action and culture: Three basic concepts for psychology in general and for cross-cultural psychology in specific. In J. Pandey, D. Sinha, & D. P. S. Bhawuk (Eds.), *Asian contributions to cross-cultural psychology* (pp. 75–102). London: Sage.

Edelman, G. M. (1992). *Bright air, brilliant fire: On the matter of the mind.* New York: Basic Books.

Ekman, P. (1984). Expression and the nature of emotion. In K. Scherer & P. Ekman (Eds.), *Approaches to emotion* (pp. 329–343). Hillsdale, NJ: Erlbaum.

Elliott, C. (1982). The measurement characteristics of developmental tests. In S. Modgil & C. Modgil (Eds.), *Jean Piaget: Consensus and controversy* (pp. 241–255). New York: Holt, Rinehart and Winston.

Elman, J. L., Bates, E. A., Johnson, M. H., Karmiloff-Smith, A., Parisi, D., & Plunkett, K. (1996). *Rethinking innateness: A connectionist perspective on development.* Cambridge, MA: MIT Press.

Emde, R. N. (1994). Individuality, context, and the search for meaning. *Child Development, 64,* 719–737.

Erikson, E. H. (1968). *Identity youth and crisis.* New York: Norton.

Erikson, E. H., Erikson, J. M., & Kivnick, H. K. (1986). *Vital involvement in old age.* New York: Norton.

Fairbairn, W. R. D. (1952). *An object-relations theory of the personality.* New York: Basic Books.

Farrar, M. J. (1996). Learning to speak your mind [Review of the book *The transition from infancy to language: Acquiring the power of expression*]. *Contemporary Psychology, 41,* 106–108.

Fischer, G. H. (1976). Some probabilistic models for measuring change. In D. N. M. de Gruijter & L. J. T. van der Kamp (Eds.), *Advances in psychological and educational measurement* (pp. 96–110). New York: Wiley.

Flavell, J. H. (1970). Concept development. In P. H. Mussen (Ed.), *Carmichael's handbook of child development* (3rd ed., pp. 983–1060). New York: Wiley.

Flavell, J. H. (1984). Discussion. In R. J. Sternberg (Ed.), *Mechanisms of cognitive development* (pp. 187–209). New York: Freeman.

Flavell, J. H. (1985). *Cognitive development* (2nd ed.). Englewood Cliffs, NJ: Prentice-Hall.

Flavell, J. H. (1992). Cognitive development: Past, present, and future. *Developmental Psychology, 28,* 998–1005.

Flavell, J. H., Miller, P. H., & Miller, S. A. (1993). *Cognitive development* (3rd ed.). Englewood Cliffs, NJ: Prentice-Hall.

Flavell, J. H., & Wohlwill, J. F. (1969). Formal and functional aspects of cognitive development. In D. Elkind & J. H. Flavell (Eds.), *Studies in cognitive development: Essays in honor of Jean Piaget* (pp. 67–120). New York: Oxford University Press.

Foltz, C., Overton, W. F., & Ricco, R. B. (1995). Proof construction: Adolescent development from inductive problem-solving. *Journal of Experimental Child Psychology, 59,* 179–195.

Freeman-Moir, D. J. (1982). The origin of intelligence. In J. M. Broughton & D. J. Freeman-Moir (Eds.), *The cognitive developmental psychology of James Mark Baldwin: Current theory and research in genetic epistemology* (pp. 127–168). Norwood, NJ: ABLEX.

Friedrich, D. (1972). *A primer for developmental methodology.* Minneapolis, MN: Burgess.

Gadamer, H. G. (1976). *Hegel's dialectic: Five hermeneutic studies* (P. Christopher Smith, Trans.). New Haven, CT: Yale University Press.

Gadamer, H. G. (1989). *Truth and method* (2nd rev. ed.) (J. Weinsheimer & D. Marshall, Trans.). New York: Crossroad.

Gadamer, H. G. (1993). *Reason in the age of science.* Cambridge, MA: MIT Press.

Gariépy, J. (1995). The evolution of a developmental science: Early determinism, modern interactionism, and a new systemic approach. In R. Vasta (Ed.), *Annals of child development: A research annual* (Vol. 11, pp. 167–224). Bristol, PA: Jessica Kingsley.

Gelman, R., & Baillargeon, R. (1983). A review of some Piagetian concepts. In P. H. Mussen (Ed.), *Carmichael's handbook of child development* (4th ed., pp. 167–230). New York: Wiley.

Gergen, K. J. (1994). The communal creation of meaning. In W. F. Overton & D. S. Palermo (Eds.), *The nature and ontogenesis of meaning* (pp. 19–40). Hillsdale, NJ: Erlbaum.

Gibson, J. J. (1966). *The senses considered as perceptual systems.* Boston: Houghton-Mifflin.

Gibson, J. J. (1979). *The ecological approach to visual perception.* Boston: Houghton-Mifflin.

Gilbert, S. F. (1992). Cells in search of community: Critiques of Weismannism and selectable units in ontogeny. *Biology and Philosophy, 7,* 473–487.

Goldberg, L. R., & Saucier, G. (1995). So what do you propose we use instead? A reply to Block. *Psychological Bulletin, 117,* 21–225.

Goodman, L. A. (1972). A modified multiple regression approach to the analysis of dichotomous variables. *American Sociological Review, 37,* 28–46.

Goodman, L. A. (1974). Exploratory latent structure analysis using both identifiable and unidentifiable models. *Biometrika, 61,* 215–231.

Goodman, L. A. (1975). A new model for scaling response patterns: An application of the quasi-independence concept. *Journal of the American Statistical Association, 70,* 755–768.

Goodwin, B. C. (1985). The disappearance of the organism in Neo Darwinism. In G. Butterworth, J. Rutkowska, & M. Scaife (Eds.), *Evolution and developmental psychology* (pp. 45–66). New York: St. Martin's Press.

Goodwin, B. C. (1992). The evolution of generic forms. In F. J. Varela & J. Dupuy (Eds.), *Understanding origins: Contemporary views on the origin of life, mind and society. Boston studies in the philosophy of science* (Vol. 130, pp. 213–226). Boston: Kluwer.

Gollin, E. S. (1981). Development and plasticity. In E. S. Gollin (Ed.), *Developmental plasticity: Behavior and biological aspects of variations in development* (pp. 231–331). New York: Academic Press.

Gottlieb, G. (1992). *Individual development and evolution: The genesis of novel behavior.* New York: Oxford University Press.

Gottlieb, G. (1997). *Synthesizing nature–nurture.* Mahwah, NJ: Erlbaum.

Gould, S. J. (1986). Archetype and adaptation. *Natural History, 95*(10), 16–28.

Gould, S. J. (1987). *Time's arrow time's cycle: Myth and metaphor in the discovery of geological time.* Cambridge, MA: Harvard University Press.

Gould, S. J. (1993). *Eight little piggies: Reflections in natural history.* New York: Norton.

Gould, S. J., & Vrba, E. (1981). Exaptation: A missing term in the science of form. *Paleobiology, 8,* 4–15.

Graziano, W. G. (1995). Evolutionary psychology: Old music, but now on CDs? *Psychological Inquiry, 6,* 41–44.

Grizzle, J. E., Starmer, C. F., & Koch, G. G. (1969). Analysis of categorical data by linear models. *Biometrics, 25,* 489–504.

Guttman, L. (1950). The basis for scalogram analysis. In S. A. Stouffer, L. Guttman, E. A. Suchman, P. F. Lazarsfeld, S. Star, & J. A. Clausen (Eds.), *Measurement and prediction* (pp. 60–90). Princeton, NJ: Princeton University Press.

Haberman, S. J. (1979). *Analysis of qualitative data: Vol. 2. New developments.* New York: Academic Press.

Habermas, J. (1980). The hermeneutic claim to universality. In J. Bleicher (Ed.), *Contemporary hermeneutics: Hermeneutics as method, philosophy and critique* (pp. 181–211). Boston: Routledge & Kegan Paul.

Habermas, J. (1984). *The theory of communicative action: Vol. 1. Reason and the rationalization of society* (Thomas McCarthy, Trans.). Boston: Beacon Press.

Habermas, J. (1991). The paradigm shift in Mead. In M. Aboulafia (Ed.), *Philosophy, social theory, and the thought of George Herbert Mead* (pp. 138–168). Albany: State University of New York Press.

Habermas, J. (1992). *Postmetaphysical thinking: Philosophical essays* (William Mark Hohengarten, Trans.). Cambridge, MA: MIT Press.

Habermas, J. (1993a). *The philosophical discourse of modernity: Twelve lectures* (Frederick G. Lawrence, Trans.). Cambridge, MA: MIT Press.

Habermas, J. (1993b). *Justification and application: Remarks on discourse ethics* (Ciaran P. Cronin, Trans.). Cambridge, MA: MIT Press.

Halevy, E. (1955). *The growth of philosophic radicalism.* Boston: Beacon Press.

Hanson, N. R. (1958). *Patterns of discovery.* London and New York: Cambridge University Press.

Hanson, N. R. (1970). Is there a logic of scientific discovery? In B. A. Brody (Ed.), *Readings in the philosophy of science* (pp. 620–633). Englewood Cliffs, NJ: Prentice-Hall.

Harman, G. H. (1965). Inference to the best explanation. *Philosophical Review, 74,* 88–95.

Hartmann, H. (1958). *Ego psychology and the problem of adaptation.* New York: International Universities Press.

Hartmann, H., Kris, E., & Loewenstein, R. M. (1946). Comments on the formation of psychic structure. *Psychoanalytic Study of the Child, 2,* 11–38.

Hegel, G. W. F. (1807). *Phenomenology of spirit* (A. V. Miller, Trans.). New York: Oxford University Press.

Hegel, G. W. F. (1830). *Hegel's logic: Being part one of the encyclopedia of the philosophical sciences* (W. Wallace, Trans.). New York: Oxford University Press.

Hempel, C. G. (1942). The function of general laws in history. *The Journal of Philosophy, 39,* 35–48.

Hempel, C. G. (1967). Scientific explanation. In S. Morgenbesser (Ed.), *Philosophy of science today* (pp. 79–88). New York: Basic Books.

Henning, H. J., & Rudinger, G. (1985). Analysis of qualitative data in developmental psychology. In J. R. Nesselroade & A. Von Eye (Eds.), *Individual and social change: Explanatory analysis* (pp. 295–341). New York: Academic Press.

Hildebrand, D. K., Laing, J. D., & Rosenthal, H. (1977). *Prediction analysis of cross-classifications.* New York: Wiley

Hirsh-Pasek, K., Golinkoff, R. M., & Reeves, L. (1994). Constructivist explanations for language acquisition may be insufficient: The case for language-specific principles. In W. F. Overton & D. S. Palermo (Eds.), *The nature and ontogenesis of meaning* (pp. 237–254). Hillsdale, NJ: Erlbaum.

Holton, G. (1973). *Thematic origins of scientific thought: Kepler to Einstein.* Cambridge, MA: Harvard University Press.

Holton, G. (1993). *Science and anti-science.* Cambridge, MA: Harvard University Press.

Hopkins, B., & Butterworth, G. (1990). Concepts of causality in explanations of development. In G. Butterworth & P. Bryant (Eds.), *Causes of development: Interdisciplinary approaches* (pp. 3–32). Hillsdale, NJ: Erlbaum.

Hoppe-Graff, S. (1989). The study of transitions in development: Potentialities of the longitudinal approach. In A. Ribaupierre (Ed.), *Transition mechanisms in child development: The longitudinal perspective* (pp. 1–30). Cambridge, England: Cambridge University Press.

Hubert, L. J. (1979). Matching models in the analysis of cross-classification. *Psychometrika, 44,* 21–41.

Hundert, E. M. (1989). *Philosophy, psychiatry and neuroscience: Three approaches to the mind.* New York: Oxford University Press.

Hundert, E. M. (1995). *Lessons from an optical illusion: On nature and nurture, knowledge and values.* Cambridge, MA: Harvard University Press.

Inhelder, B., & Piaget, J. (1958). *The growth of logical thinking from childhood to adolescence.* New York: Wiley.

Izard, C. E. (1977). *Human emotions.* New York: Plenum Press.

Izard, C. E. (1982). Comments on emotions and cognition: Can there be a working relationship? In M. S. Clark & S. T. Fiske

(Eds.), *Affect and cognition* (pp. 229–242). Hillsdale, NJ: Erlbaum.

Izard, C. E., & Malatesta, C. W. (1987). Perspectives on emotional development: I. Differential emotions theory of early emotional development. In J. Osofksy (Ed.), *Handbook of infant development* (2nd ed., pp. 494–554). New York: Wiley.

Jackendoff, R. (1994). Word meanings and what it takes to learn them: Reflections on the Piaget-Chomsky debate. In W. F. Overton & D. S. Palermo (Eds.), *The nature and ontogenesis of meaning* (pp. 129–144). Hillsdale, NJ: Erlbaum.

Jacobson, E. (1964). *The self and the object world.* New York: International Universities Press.

James, W. (1912). *Essays in radical empiricism.* New York: Longmans, Green.

James, W. (1975). *Pragmatism and the meaning of truth.* Cambridge, MA: Harvard University Press.

Johnson, M. (1987). *The body in the mind.* Chicago: University of Chicago Press.

Johnson, S. P., & Aslin, R. N. (1995). Perception of object unity in 2-month-old infants. *Developmental Psychology, 31,* 739–745.

Joreskog, K. G., & Sorbom, D. (1982). *Lisrel v. Analysis of structural relationships by maximum likelihood and least squares methods* (Research Rep. No. 81-8). Uppsala: University of Uppsala.

Kagan, J. (1994). On the nature of emotion. In N. A. Fox (Ed.), The development of emotion regulation: Biological and behavioral considerations. *Monographs of the Society for Research in Child Development, 59*(2/3, Serial No. 240), 7–24.

Kail, R., & Bisanz, J. (1982). Cognitive development: An information-processing perspective. In R. Vasta (Ed.), *Strategies and techniques of child study* (pp. 209–243). New York: Academic Press.

Kainz, H. P. (1988). *Paradox, dialectic, and system: A contemporary reconstruction of the Hegelian problematic.* University Park: Pennsylvania State University Press.

Kant, I. (1966). *Critique of pure reason* (F. Max Muller, Trans.). New York: Anchor Books. (Original work published 1781)

Kaplan, A. (1964). *The conduct of inquiry: Methodology for behavioral science.* San Francisco: Chandler.

Karmiloff-Smith, A. (1991). Beyond modularity: Innate constraints and developmental change. In S. Carey & R. Gelman (Eds.), *The epigenesis of mind: Essays on biology and cognition* (pp. 171–197). Hillsdale, NJ: Erlbaum.

Katz, J. (1990). *The metaphysics of meaning.* Cambridge, MA: MIT Press.

Kauffman, S. (1992). Origin of order in evolution: Self-organization and selection. In F. J. Varela & J. Dupuy (Eds.),

Understanding origins: Contemporary views on the origin of life, mind and society. Boston studies in the philosophy of science (Vol. 130, pp. 153–181). Boston: Kluwer.

Kauffman, S. (1995). *At home in the universe: The search for the laws of self-organization and complexity.* New York: Oxford University Press.

Kent, T. (1991). Hermeneutics and genre: Bakhtin and the problem of communicative interaction. In D. R. Hiley, J. F. Bohman, & R. Shusterman (Eds.), *The interpretive turn: Philosophy, science, culture* (pp. 282–303). Ithaca, NY: Cornell University Press.

Kernberg, O. (1976). *Object relations theory and clinical psychoanalysis.* New York: Jason Aronson.

Kesselring, T. (1981). *Entwicklung und widerspruch. Ein vergleich zwischen Piaget's genetischer epistemologie und Hegel's dialektik.* Frankfurt am Main, Germany: Suhrkamp Verlag.

Kesselring, T. (1985). *Die produktivitaet der antinomie. Hegel's dialektik im lichte der genetischen erkenntnistheorie und der formalen logik.* Frankfurt am Main, Germany: Suhrkamp Verlag.

Killen, M. (1996). Justice and care. *Journal for a Just and Caring Education, 2,* 42–58.

Kingma, J., & Van Den Bos, K. P. (1989). Unidimensional scales: New methods to analyze the sequences in concept development. *Genetic, Social and General Psychological Monographs, 114,* 477–508.

Kitchener, R. F. (1983). Developmental explanations. *Review of Metaphysics, 36,* 791–817.

Kitchener, R. F. (1991). Jean Piaget: The unknown sociologist? *British Journal of Sociology, 42,* 421–442.

Kitcher, P. (1981). Explanatory unification. *Philosophy of Science, 48,* 507–531.

Kruz, D. J. (1976). *Order analysis of binary matrices.* Los Angeles: Theta Press.

Kuhn, D., Garcia-Mila, M., Zohar, A., & Andersen, C. (1995). Strategies of knowledge acquisition. *Monographs of the Society for Research in Child Development, 60*(4, Serial no. 245).

Kuhn, T. S. (1962). *The structure of scientific revolutions.* Chicago: University of Chicago Press.

Kuhn, T. S. (1977). *The essential tension.* Chicago: University of Chicago Press.

Kuo, Z. Y. (1967). *The dynamics of behavior development.* New York: Random House.

Lakatos, I. (1978a). *The methodology of scientific research programmes: Philosophical papers* (Vol. 1). New York: Cambridge University Press.

Lakatos, I. (1978b). *Mathematics, science and epistemology: Philosophical papers* (Vol. 2). New York: Cambridge University Press.

Lakoff, G. (1987). *Women, fire, and dangerous things. What categories reveal about the mind.* Chicago: University of Chicago Press.

Lakoff, G. (1994). What is a conceptual system? In W. Overton & D. Palermo (Eds.), *The nature and ontogenesis of meaning* (pp. 41–90). Hillsdale, NJ: Erlbaum.

Langer, J. (1994). From acting to understanding: The comparative development of meaning. In W. Overton & D. Palermo (Eds.), *The nature and ontogenesis of meaning* (pp. 191–214). Hillsdale, NJ: Erlbaum.

Latour, B. (1993). *We have never been modern.* Cambridge, MA: Harvard University Press.

Laudan, L. (1977). *Progress and its problems: Towards a theory of scientific growth.* Berkeley: University of California Press.

Laudan, L. (1984). *Science and values: The aims of science and their role in scientific debate.* Los Angeles: University of California Press.

Laudan, L. (1996). *Beyond positivism and relativism: Theory, method, and evidence.* Boulder, Co: Westview Press.

Lazarsfeld, P. F., & Henry, N. W. (1968). *Latent structure analysis.* Boston: Houghton Mifflin.

Lehrman, D. S. (1970). Semantic and conceptual issues in the nature–nurture problem. In L. R. Aronson, E. Tobach, D. S. Lehrman, & J. S. Rosenblatt (Eds.), *Development and evolution of behavior: Essays in memory of T. C. Schneirla* (pp. 17–52). San Francisco: Freeman.

Lerner, R. M. (1978). Nature, nurture, and dynamic interactionism. *Human Development, 21,* 1–20.

Lerner, R. M. (1986). *Concepts and theories of human development* (2nd ed.). New York: Random House.

Lerner, R. M. (1992). *"Final solutions": Biology, prejudice, and genocide.* University Park: Pennsylvania State Press.

Leventhal, H. (1982). The integration of emotion and cognition: A view from perceptual-motor theory of emotion. In M. S. Clark & S. T. Fiske (Eds.), *Affect and cognition* (pp. 121–156). Hillsdale, NJ: Erlbaum.

Levins, R., & Lewontin, R. (1985). *The dialectical biologist.* Cambridge, MA: Harvard University Press.

Lewis, M. (1993). The emergence of human emotions. In M. Lewis & J. Haviland (Eds.), *Handbook of emotions* (pp. 223–235). New York: Guilford Press.

Lewontin, R. C. (1994). *Inside and outside: Gene, environment and organism.* Worcester, MA: Clark University Press.

Liben, L. S. (1987). Information processing and Piagetian theory: Conflict or congruence? In L. S. Liben (Ed.), *Development and learning: Conflict or congruence?* (pp. 109–132). Hillsdale, NJ: Erlbaum.

Liben, L. S. (in press). Children's understanding of spatial representations of place. Mapping the methodological landscape. In N. Foreman & R. Gillet (Eds.), *A handbook of spatial paradigms and methodologies.* Hillsdale, NJ: Erlbaum.

Linder, A., & Berchtold, W. (1982). *Statistische methoden* (Vol. 3). Basel: Birkhauser.

Lord, F. M., & Novick, M. R. (Eds.). (1968). *Statistical theory of mental test scores.* Reading, MA: Addison-Wesley.

Lourenco, O., & Machado, A. (1996). In defense of Piaget's theory: A reply to 10 common criticisms. *Psychological Review, 103,* 143–164.

Lovejoy, A. O. (1936). *The great chain of being.* Cambridge, MA: Harvard University Press.

Luhman, N. (1995). *Social systems.* Stanford, CA: Stanford University Press.

Luria, A. R. (1981). In J. V. Wertsch (Ed.), *Language and cognition.* New York: Wiley.

Lyotard, J. (1984). *The postmodern condition: A report on knowledge.* Minneapolis: University of Minnesota Press.

Magnusson, D. (1995). Individual development: A holistic, integrated model. In P. Moen, G. H. Elder, & K. Luscher (Eds.), *Examining lives in context* (pp. 19–60). Washington, DC: American Psychological Association.

Mahler, M. (1979). *Selected papers of Margaret S. Mahler.* New York: Jason Aronson.

Malatesta, C. Z., Culver, C., Tesman, J. R., & Shepard, B. (1989). The development of emotion expression during the first two years of life. *Monographs of the Society for Research in Child Development, 54*(No. 219).

Mandler, G. (1982). The structure of value: Accounting for taste. In M. S. Clark & S. T. Fiske (Eds.), *Affect and cognition* (pp. 211–227). Hillsdale, NJ: Erlbaum.

Mandler, J. M. (1988). How to build a baby: On the development of an accessible representational system. *Cognitive Development, 3,* 113–136.

Mandler, J. M. (1992). How to build a baby: II. Conceptual primitives. *Psychological Review, 99,* 587–604.

Martin, J. A. (1987). Structural equation modeling: A guide for the perplexed. *Child Development, 58,* 33–37.

Marx, K. (1959). Theses on Feuerbach. In L. S. Feuer (Ed.), *Marx and Engels: Basic writings on politics and philosophy.* Garden City, NY: Doubleday.

Maturana, H. R., & Varela, F. J. (1988). *The tree of knowledge. The biological roots of human understanding.* Boston: Shambhala.

Matson, F. (1964). *The broken image.* New York: Braziller.

Mayr, E. (1982). *The growth of biological thought.* Cambridge, MA: Harvard University Press.

Mayr, E. (1988). *Toward a new philosophy of biology.* Cambridge, MA: Harvard University Press.

McArdle, J. J. (1991). Structural models of developmental theory in psychology. In P. van Geert & L. P. Mos (Eds.), *Annals of theoretical psychology* (Vol. 7, pp. 139–160). New York: Plenum Press.

McCarthy, T. (1991). *Ideals and illusions: On reconstruction and deconstruction in contemporary critical theory.* Cambridge, MA: MIT Press.

McCarthy, T. (1993). Introduction. In J. Habermas (Ed.) & Frederick G. Lawrence (Trans.), *The philosophical discourse of modernity* (pp. vii-xvii). Cambridge, MA: MIT Press.

McCrae, R. R., & John, O. P. (1992). An introduction to the five factor model and its applications. *Journal of Personality, 60,* 175–215.

McCrae, R. R., & Costa, P. T., Jr. (1989). Rotation to maximize the construct validity of factors in the NEO Personality Inventory. *Multivariate Behavioral Research, 24,* 107–124.

Mead, G. H. (1934). *Mind, self and society: From the standpoint of a social behaviorist.* Chicago: University of Chicago Press.

Merleau-Ponty, M. (1962). *Phenomenology of perception* (Colin Smith, Trans.). London: Routledge & Kegan Paul.

Merleau-Ponty, M. (1963). *The structure of behavior* (Alden Fisher, Trans.). Boston: Beacon Press.

Messick, S. (1983). Assessment of children. In W. Kessen (Ed.), *Handbook of child psychology* (Vol. 1, pp. 477–526). New York: Wiley.

Messick, S. (1989). Validity. In R. L. Linn (Ed.), *Educational measurement* (3rd ed., pp. 13–103). New York: Macmillan.

Messick, S. (1995). Validity of psychological assessment: Validation of inferences from persons' responses and performances as scientific inquiry into score meaning. *American Psychologist, 50,* 741–749.

Miller, J. G. (1996). Theoretical issues in cultural psychology. In J. W. Berry, Y. H. Poortinga, & J. Pandey (Eds.), *Handbook of cross-cultural psychology: Theory and method* (pp. 85–128). Boston: Allyn & Bacon.

Mitchell, S. A. (1988). *Relational concepts in psychoanalysis: An integration.* Cambridge, MA: Harvard University Press.

Modell, A. H. (1993). *The private self.* Cambridge, MA: Harvard University Press.

Mokken, R. J. (1971). *A theory and procedures of scale analysis.* The Hague: Mouton.

Morris, E. K. (1988). Contextualism: The world view of behavior analysis. *Journal of Experimental Child Psychology, 46,* 289–323.

Mueller, U., Sokol, B., & Overton, W. F. (in press). Reframing a constructivist model of the development of mental representation: The role of higher-order operations. *Developmental Review.*

Mulaik, S. A. (1987). Toward a conception of causality applicable to experimentation and causal modeling. *Child Development, 58,* 18–32.

Muthen, B. (1978). Contributions to factor analysis of dichotomous variables. *Psychometrika, 43,* 551–560.

Nagel, E. (1957). Determinism and development. In D. B. Harris (Ed.), *The concept of development* (pp. 15–24). Minneapolis: University of Minnesota Press.

Nagel, E. (1967). The nature and aim of science. In S. Morgenbesser (Ed.), *Philosophy of science today* (pp. 5–13). New York: Basic Books.

Nagel, E. (1979). *The structure of science* (2nd ed.). Cambridge, MA: Hackett.

Nicolis, G., & Prigogine, I. (1989). *Exploring complexity.* New York: Freeman.

Nijhout, H. F. (1990). Metaphors and the role of genes in development. *BioEssays, 12,* 441–446.

Nisbet, R. (1969). *Social change and history.* New York: Oxford University Press.

Nishisato, S. (1980). *Analysis of categorical data: Dual scaling and its application.* Toronto: University of Toronto Press.

Nucci, L. P. (1996). Morality and the personal sphere of action. In E. Reed, E. Turiel, & T. Brown (Eds.), *Values and knowledge* (pp. 41–60). Hillsdale, NJ: Erlbaum.

Nucci, L. P., & Lee, J. Y. (1993). Morality and personal autonomy. In G. Noam & T. Wren (Eds.), *The moral self* (pp. 123–148). Cambridge, MA: MIT Press.

Nucci, L. P., & Weber, E. K. (1995). Social interactions in the home and the development of young children's conceptions of the personal. *Child Development, 66,* 1438–1452.

Ogden, T. H. (1986). *The matrix of the mind: Object relations and the psychoanalytic dialogue.* Northvale, NJ: Jason Aronson.

Oppenheimer, L. (1991a). The concept of action: A historical perspective. In L. Oppenheimer & J. Valsiner (Eds.), *The origins of action: Interdisciplinary and international perspectives* (pp. 1–35). New York: Springer-Verlag.

Oppenheimer, L. (1991b). Determinants of action: An organismic and holistic approach. In L. Oppenheimer & J. Valsiner

(Eds.), *The origins of action: Interdisciplinary and international perspectives* (pp. 37–63). New York: Springer-Verlag.

Overton, W. F. (1973). On the assumptive base of the nature-nurture controversy: Additive versus interactive conceptions. *Human Development, 16,* 74–89.

Overton, W. F. (1975). General systems, structure and development. In K. F. Riegel & G. C. Rosenwald (Eds.), *Structure and transformation: Developmental and historical aspects* (pp. 61–81). New York: Wiley.

Overton, W. F. (1976). The active organism in structuralism. *Human Development, 19,* 71–86.

Overton, W. F. (1984). World views and their influence on psychological theory and research: Kuhn-Lakatos-Laudan. In H. W. Reese (Ed.), *Advances in child development and behavior* (Vol. 18, pp. 191–226). New York: Academic Press.

Overton, W. F. (1990). Competence and procedures: Constraints on the development of logical reasoning. In W. F. Overton (Ed.), *Reasoning, necessity, and logic: Developmental perspectives* (pp. 1–32). Hillsdale, NJ: Erlbaum.

Overton, W. F. (1991a). Historical and contemporary perspectives on developmental theory and research strategies. In R. Downs, L. Liben, & D. Palermo (Eds.), *Visions of aesthetics, the environment, and development: The legacy of Joachim Wohlwill* (pp. 263–311). Hillsdale, NJ: Erlbaum.

Overton, W. F. (1991b). The structure of developmental theory. In H. W. Reese (Ed.), *Advances in child development and behavior* (Vol. 23, pp. 1–37). New York: Academic Press.

Overton, W. F. (1991c). Metaphor, recursive systems, and paradox in science and developmental theory. In H. W. Reese (Ed.), *Advances in child development and behavior* (Vol. 23, pp. 59–71). New York: Academic Press.

Overton, W. F. (1991d). Competence, procedures and hardware: Conceptual and empirical considerations. In M. Chandler & M. Chapman (Eds.), *Criteria for competence: Controversies in the assessment of children's abilities* (pp. 19–42). Hillsdale, NJ: Erlbaum.

Overton, W. F. (1994a). The arrow of time and cycles of time: Concepts of change, cognition, and embodiment. *Psychological Inquiry, 5,* 215–237.

Overton, W. F. (1994b). Interpretationism, pragmatism, realism, and other ideologies. *Psychological Inquiry, 5,* 260–271.

Overton, W. F. (1994c). Contexts of meaning: The computational and the embodied mind. In W. F. Overton & D. S. Palermo (Eds.), *The nature and ontogenesis of meaning* (pp. 1–18). Hillsdale, NJ: Erlbaum.

Overton, W. F. (in press-a). Relational-developmental theory: A psychology perspective. In D. Gorlitz, H. J. Harloff,

J. Valsiner, & G. Mey (Eds.), *Children, cities and psychological theories: Developing relationships.* Berlin and New York: Aldine de Gruyter.

Overton, W. F. (in press-b). Beyond dichotomy: An embodied active agent for cultural psychology. *Culture and Psychology, 3.*

Overton, W. F., & Horowitz, H. (1991). Developmental psychopathology: Differentiations and integrations. In D. Cicchetti & S. Toth (Eds.), *Rochester Symposium on developmental psychopathology* (Vol. 3, pp. 1–41). Rochester, NY: University of Rochester Press.

Overton, W. F., & Mueller, U. (1996, September). *The development of negation—A Rasch modelling approach.* Paper presented at the meeting of The Growing Mind: Centennial of Jean Piaget's birth, Geneva, Switzerland.

Overton, W. F., & Reese, H. W. (1981). Conceptual prerequisites for an understanding of stability-change and continuity-discontinuity. *International Journal of Behavioral Development, 4,* 99–123.

Oyama, S. (1989). Ontogeny and the central dogma: Do we need the concept of genetic programming in order to have an evolutionary perspective? In M. R. Gunnar & E. Thelen (Eds.), *Systems and development: The Minnesota Symposia on child psychology* (Vol. 22, pp. 1–34). Hillsdale, NJ: Erlbaum.

Pearson, K. (1911). *The grammar of science* (Part 1, Physical). London: Adam & Charles Black.

Pepper, S. C. (1942). *World hypotheses.* Berkeley: University of California Press.

Pepper, S. C. (1979). Contextualistic criticism. In M. Rader (Ed.), *A modern book of esthetics: An anthology* (5th ed. pp. 404–416).

Piaget, J. (1952). *The origins of intelligence in children.* New York: Norton.

Piaget, J. (1954). *The construction of reality in the child.* New York: Basic Books.

Piaget, J. (1983). *Intelligence and affectivity: Their relationship during child development.* Palo Alto, CA: Annual Reviews.

Piaget, J. (1985). *The equilibration of cognitive structures.* Chicago: University of Chicago Press.

Piaget, J. (1992). *Morphisms and categories: Comparing and transforming.* Hillsdale, NJ: Erlbaum.

Piaget, J. (1995). *Sociological studies.* New York: Routledge.

Piaget, J., & Garcia, R. (1991). *Toward a logic of meanings.* Hillsdale, NJ: Erlbaum.

Pierce, C. S. (1992). *Reasoning and the logic of things: The Cambridge conference lectures of 1898.* Cambridge, MA: Harvard University Press.

Popper, K. (1959). *The logic of scientific discovery.* London: Hutchinson.

Proctor, H. H. (1970). A probabilistic formulation and statistical analysis of Guttman scaling. *Psychometrika, 35,* 73–78.

Prosch, H. (1964). *The genesis of twentieth century philosophy.* New York: Doubleday.

Putnam, H. (1983). *Realism and reason: Philosophical papers* (Vol. 3). New York: Cambridge University Press.

Putnam, H. (1987). *The many faces of realism.* Cambridge, England: Cambridge University Press.

Putnam, H. (1990). *Realism with a human face.* Cambridge, MA: Harvard University Press.

Putnam, H. (1995). *Pragmatism.* Cambridge, MA: Blackwell.

Quine, W. V. (1953). *From a logical point of view.* Cambridge, MA: Harvard University Press.

Randall, J. H. (1960). *Aristotle.* New York: Columbia University Press.

Rasch, G. (1966). An item analysis which takes individual differences into account. *British Journal of Mathematical and Statistical Psychology, 19,* 49–57.

Reed, E. S. (1993). The intention to use a specific affordance: A conceptual framework for psychology. In R. H. Wozniak & K. W. Fischer (Eds.), *Development in context: Acting and thinking in specific environments* (pp. 45–76). Hillsdale, NJ: Erlbaum.

Reese, H. W. (1993). Contextualism and dialectical materialism. In S. C. Hayes, L. J. Hayes, H. W. Reese, & T. R. Sarbin (Eds.), *Varieties of scientific contextualism* (pp. 71–105). Reno, NV: Context Press.

Reese, H. W. (1995). Soviet psychology and behavior analysis: Philosophical similarities and substantive differences. *Behavioral Development, 5,* 2–4.

Reichenbach, H. (1938). *Experience and prediction.* Chicago: University of Chicago Press.

Ribaupierre, A. (Ed.). (1989). *Transition mechanisms in child development: The longitudinal perspective* (pp. 1–30). Cambridge, England: Cambridge University Press.

Ricoeur, P. (1984). *Time and narrative* (Vol. 1) (K. McLaughlin & D. Pellauer, Trans.). Chicago: University of Chicago Press.

Ricoeur, P. (1991). *From text to action: II. Essays in hermeneutics* (K. Blamey & J. B. Thompson, Trans.). Evanston, IL: Northwestern University Press.

Rogoff, B. (1990). *Apprenticeship in thinking: Cognitive development in sociocultural activity.* New York: Oxford University Press.

Rogoff, B. (1993). Children's guided participation and participatory appropriation in sociocultural activity. In R. H. Wozniak & K. W. Fischer (Eds.), *Development in context: Acting and thinking in specific environments* (pp. 121–154). Hillsdale, NJ: Erlbaum.

Rorty, R. (1979). *Philosophy and the mirror of nature.* Princeton, NJ: Princeton University Press.

Rorty, R. (1982). *The consequences of pragmatism.* Minneapolis: University of Minnesota Press.

Rorty, R. (1993). Putnam and the relativist menace. *The Journal of Philosophy, 90,* 443–461.

Ross, W. D. (1959). *Aristotle.* Cleveland, OH: Meridian Books.

Sanders, L. W. (1975). Infant and caretaking environment: Investigation and conceptualization of adaptive behavior in a system of increasing complexity. In E. J. Anthony (Ed.), *Explorations in child psychiatry* (pp. 129–166). New York: Plenum Press.

Sanders, L. W. (1989). Investigation of the infant and its caregiving environment as a biological system. In S. I. Greenspan & G. H. Pollack (Eds.), *The course of life* (2nd ed., pp. 359–391). Madison, WI: International Universities Press.

Santostefano, S. (1995). Embodied meanings, cognition and emotion: Pondering how three are one. In D. Cicchetti & S. L. Toth (Eds.), *Rochester Symposium on developmental psychopathology: Vol. 6. Emotion, cognition and representation* (pp. 59–132). Rochester, NY: University of Rochester Press.

Scarr, S. (1992). Developmental theories for the 1990s: Development and individual differences. *Child Development, 63,* 1–19.

Schlick, M. (1959). Causality in everyday life and in recent science. In E. Sprague & P. W. Taylor (Eds.), *Knowledge and value* (pp. 193–210). New York: Harcourt, Brace.

Schlick, M. (1991). Positivism and realism. In R. Boyd, P. Gasper, & J. D. Trout (Eds.), *The philosophy of science* (pp. 37–55). Cambridge, MA: MIT Press.

Schneirla, T. C. (1956). Interrelationships of the innate and the acquired in instinctive behavior. In P. P. Grasse (Ed.), *L'instinct dans le comportement des animaux et de l'homme* (pp. 387–452). Paris: Mason et Cie.

Schneirla, T. C. (1957). The concept of development in comparative psychology. In D. B. Harris (Ed), *The concept of development* (pp. 78–108). Minneapolis: University of Minnesota Press.

Schneirla, T. C. (1966). Instinct and aggression. *Natural History, 75,* 16ff.

Scholnick, E. K., & Cookson, K. (1994). A developmental analysis of cognitive semantics: What is the role of metaphor in the construction of knowledge and reasoning? In W. F. Overton & D. S. Palermo (Eds.), *The nature and ontogenesis of meaning* (pp. 109–128). Hillsdale, NJ: Erlbaum.

Schroder, E. (1992). Modeling qualitative change in individual development. In J. B. Asendorpf & J. Valsiner (Eds.), *Stability and change in development: A study of methodological reasoning* (pp. 1–20). London: Sage.

Schroder, E., Edelstein, W., & Hoppe-Graff, S. (1991). Qualitative analyses of individual differences in intraindividual change: Examples from cognitive development. In D. Magnusson, L. Bergman, G. Rudinger, & S. B. Torestad (Eds.), *Problems and methods in longitudinal research: Stability and change* (pp. 166–189). Cambridge, England: Cambridge University Press.

Searle, J. (1992). *The rediscovery of the mind.* Cambridge, MA: MIT Press.

Searle, J. (1995, November). The mystery of consciousness. *The New York Review, 62*(17), 60–65.

Shweder, R. A. (1990). Cultural psychology—What is it? In J. W. Stigler, R. A. Shweder, & G. Herdt (Eds.), *Cultural psychology: Essays on comparative human development* (pp. 1–46). New York: Cambridge University Press.

Shweder, R. A., & Sullivan, M. A. (1990). *The semiotic subject of cultural psychology.* In L. Pervin (Ed.), *Handbook of personality: Theory and research* (pp. 399–416). New York: Guilford Press.

Siegler, R. S. (1976). Three aspects of cognitive development. *Cognitive Psychology, 8,* 481–520.

Siegler, R. S. (1989). Mechanisms of cognitive development. *Annual Review of Psychology, 40,* 353–379.

Siegler, R. S. (1996). *Emerging minds: The process of change in children's thinking.* New York: Oxford University Press.

Siegler, R. S., & Crowley, K. (1991). The microgenetic method: A direct means for studying cognitive development. *American Psychologist, 46,* 606–620.

Siegler, R. S., & Crowley, K. (1992). Microgenetic methods revisited. *American Psychologist, 47,* 1241–1243.

Siegler, R. S., & Shipley, C. (1987). The role of learning in children's strategy choices. In L. S. Liben (Ed.), *Development and learning: Conflict or congruence* (pp. 71–108). Hillsdale, NJ: Erlbaum.

Siegler, R. S., & Munakata, Y. (1993, Winter). Beyond the immaculate transition: Advances in the understanding of change. *SRCD Newsletter.*

Silvern, L. E. (1984). Emotional-behavioral disorders: A failure of system functions. In G. Gollin (Ed.), *Malformations of development: Biological and psychological sources and consequences* (pp. 95–152). New York: Academic Press.

Skinner, B. F. (1971). *Beyond freedom and dignity.* New York: Bantam Books.

Skinner, B. F. (1984). Selection by consequences. *Behavioral and Brain Sciences. 7,* 1–43.

Smith, L. D. (1986). *Behaviorism and logical positivism: A reassessment of the alliance.* Stanford, CA: Stanford University Press.

Smith, L. D. (1990). Metaphors of knowledge and behavior in the behaviorist tradition. In D. E. Leary (Ed.), *Metaphors in the history of psychology.* New York: Cambridge University Press.

Spada, H., & Kluwe, R. H. (1980). Two models of intellectual development and their reference to the theory of Piaget. In R. H. Kluwe & H. Spada (Eds.), *Developmental models of thinking* (pp. 1–31). New York: Academic Press.

Spelke, E. S. (1991). Physical knowledge in infancy: Reflections on Piaget's theory. In S. Carey & R. Gelman (Eds.), *The epigenesis of mind: Essays on biology and cognition* (pp. 133–170). Hillsdale, NJ: Erlbaum.

Spelke, E. S., Breinlinger, M. J., & Jacobson, K. (1992). Origins of knowledge. *Psychological Review, 99,* 605–632.

Stace, W. T. (1924). *The philosophy of Hegel.* New York: Dover.

Sroufe, L. A. (1979). Socioemotional development. In J. Osofsky (Ed.), *Handbook of infant development* (pp. 462–516). New York: Wiley.

Stern, D. S. (1991). Foundationalism, holism, or Hegel. *Journal of the British Society for Phenomenology, 22,* 21–32.

Sternberg, R. J. (Ed.). (1984). *Mechanisms of cognitive development.* New York: Freeman.

Sugarman, S. (1987a). The priority of description in developmental psychology. *International Journal of Behavioral Development, 10,* 391–414.

Sugarman, S. (1987b). Reply to Peter Bryant. *International Journal of Behavioral Development, 10,* 423–424.

Suppe, F. (Ed.). (1977). *The structure of scientific theories* (2nd ed.). Urbana: University of Illinois Press.

Taylor, C. (1979). *Hegel and modern society.* New York: Cambridge University Press.

Taylor, C. (1985). *Human agency and language: Philosophical papers* (Vol. 1). New York: Cambridge University Press.

Taylor, C. (1991). The dialogical self. In D. R. Hiley, J. F. Bohman, & R. Shusterman (Eds.), *The interpretive turn: Philosophy, science, culture* (pp. 304–314). Ithaca, NY: Cornell University Press.

Taylor, C. (1995). *Philosophical arguments.* Cambridge, MA: Harvard University Press.

Tesson, G., & Youniss, J. (1995). Micro-sociology and psychological development. *Sociological Studies of Children, 7,* 101–126.

Thelen, E., & Smith, L. B. (1994). *A dynamic systems approach to the development of cognition and action.* Cambridge, MA: MIT Press.

Thelen, E., & Ulrich, B. D. (1991). Hidden skills. *Monographs of the Society for Research in Child Development, 56*(1, Serial No. 223).

Thomas, H. (1977). Fitting cross-classification table data to models when observations are subject to classification error. *Psychometrika, 42,* 199–206.

Thorndike, E. L. (1898). Animal intelligence: An experimental study of the associative processes in animals. *Psychological Review, Monograph Supplements, 2*(Serial No. 8).

Thorngate, W. (1992). Evidential statistics and the analysis of developmental patterns. In J. B. Asendorpf & J. Valsiner (Eds.), *Stability and change in development: A study of methodological reasoning* (pp. 63–83). London: Sage.

Tobach, E. (1981). Evolutionary aspects of the activity of the organism and its development. In R. M. Lerner & N. A. Busch-Rosnagel (Eds.), *Individuals as producers of their development: A life-span perspective* (pp. 37–68). New York: Academic Press.

Tobach, E., & Greenberg, G. (1984). The significance of T. C. Schneirla's contribution to the concept of integration. In G. Greenberg & E. Tobach (Eds.), *Behavioral evolution and integrative levels* (pp. 1–7). Hillsdale, NJ: Erlbaum.

Toulmin, S. (1953). *The philosophy of science.* New York: Harper & Row.

Toulmin, S. (1961). *Foresight and understanding.* New York: Harper & Row.

Toulmin, S. (1990). *Cosmopolis: The hidden agenda of modernity.* Chicago: University of Chicago Press.

Toulmin, S., & Goodfield, J. (1965). *The discovery of time.* New York: Harper & Row.

Trevarthen, C. (1980). The foundations of intersubjectivity: Development of interpersonal and cooperative understanding in infants. In D. R. Olson (Ed.), *The social foundations of language and thought: Essays in honor of Jerome S. Bruner* (pp. 316–342). New York: Norton.

Turiel, E., & Wainryb, C. (1994). Social reasoning and the varieties of social experience in cultural contexts. In H. W. Reese (Ed.), *Advances in child development and behavior* (Vol. 25, pp. 289–326). New York: Academic Press.

Valsiner, J. (1991). Construction of the mental: From the "cognitive revolution" to the study of development. *Theory and Psychology, 4,* 477–494.

Valsiner, J. (1994). Irreversibility of time and the construction of historical developmental psychology. *Mind, Culture, and Activity, 1,* 25–42.

Van der Veer, R., & Valsiner, J. (1994). Reading Vygotsky: From fascination to construction. In R. Van der Veer & J. Valsiner (Eds.), *The Vygotsky reader* (pp. 1–7). Cambridge, MA: Blackwell.

Varela, F. J., Thompson, E., & Rosch, E. (1991). *The embodied mind: Cognitive science and human experience.* Cambridge, MA: MIT Press.

von Eye, A. (1990). *Introduction to configural frequency analysis: The search for types and antitypes in cross-classifications.* New York: Cambridge University Press.

von Eye, A., & Brandtstädter, J. (1989). Application of prediction analysis to cross-classifications of ordinal data. *Biometrical Journal, 30,* 651–665.

von Eye, A., Kreppner, K., & Wessels, H. (1992). Differential change in systems of categorical variables. In J. B. Asendorpf & J. Valsiner (Eds.), *Stability and change in development: A study of methodological reasoning* (pp. 21–53). London: Sage.

Vygotsky, L. S. (1978). *Mind in society: The development of higher psychological processes.* Cambridge, MA: Harvard University Press.

Vygotsky, L. S. (1979). Consciousness as a problem in the psychology of behavior. *Soviet Psychology, 17,* 3–35.

Wapner, S., & Demick, J. (1990). Development of experience and action: Levels of integration in human functioning. In G. Greenberg & E. Tobach (Eds.), *Theories of the evolution of knowing: The T. C. Schneirla conference series* (Vol. 4, pp. 47–67).

Wartofsky, M. (1968). *Conceptual foundations of scientific thought.* Toronto: Macmillan.

Waters, H. S., & Tinsley, V. S. (1985). Evaluating the discriminant and convergent validity of developmental constructs: Another look at the concept of egocentrism. *Psychological Bulletin,* 483–495.

Werner, H. (1956). Microgenesis and aphasia. *Journal of Abnormal and Social Psychology, 52,* 347–353.

Werner, H. (1957). The concept of development from a comparative and organismic point of view. In D. B. Harris (Ed.), *The concept of development: An issue in the study of human behavior* (pp. 125–148). Minneapolis: University of Minnesota Press.

Werner, H. (1958). *Comparative psychology of mental development.* New York: International Universities Press.

Werner, H., & Kaplan, B. (1963). *Symbol formation.* New York: Wiley.

Wertsch, J. V. (1991). *Voices of the mind: A sociocultural approach to mediated action.* Cambridge, MA: Harvard University Press.

White, S. (1995). Toward an evolutionary epistemology of scientific reasoning. *Monographs of the Society for Research in Child Development, 60*(4, Serial no. 245), 129–136.

Winnicott, D. W. (1965). *The maturational process and the facilitating environment.* New York: International Universities Press.

Winnicott, D. W. (1971). *Playing and reality.* New York: Basic Books.

Wohlwill, J. F. (1973a). The concept of experience: S or R? *Human Development, 16*, 90–107.

Wohlwill, J. F. (1973b). *The study of behavioral development.* New York: Academic Press.

Wohlwill, J. F. (1991). Relations between method and theory in developmental research: A partial-isomorphism view. In P. van Geert & L. P. Mos (Eds.), *Annals of theoretical psychology* (Vol. 7, pp. 91–138). New York: Plenum Press.

Wold, H. (1979). *Model constructions and evaluation when theoretical knowledge is scarce* (Cahier 79.06). Department of Econometrics, University of Geneva, Geneva, Switzerland.

Wold, H., & Bertholet, J. L. (1983). The PLS (partial least squares) approach to multidimensional contingency tables. *Metron, 41*, 105–126.

Youniss, J., & Damon, W. (1992). Social construction in Piaget's theory. In H. Beilin & P. B. Pufall (Eds.), *Piaget's theory: Prospects and possibilities* (pp. 267–286). Hillsdale, NJ: Erlbaum.

Zajonc, R. B., Pietromonaco, P., & Bargh, J. (1982). Independence and interaction of affect and cognition. In M. S. Clark & S. T. Fiske (Eds.), *Affect and cognition* (pp. 211–227). Hillsdale, NJ: Erlbaum.

CHAPTER 4

The Development of the Concept of Development: Historical and Epistemological Perspectives

JAAN VALSINER

THE CONCEPT OF DEVELOPMENT AS EXEMPLIFIED IN GENERAL MODELS

Child psychology today is surprisingly free of interest in building general models of human development. The discipline is filled with hyperactive efforts to accumulate data, but attempts to make sense of the data, in terms of models of basic developmental processes, are relatively rare. Contemporary child psychology seems to be proclaiming that general theory building is of no consequence—a standpoint

that may be considered damaging to the health of any science (Crick, 1988). In the past, general models of development emerged within the context of the history of developmental psychology. It may therefore be of use to consider how these models might help us to make sense of our current empirical efforts.

This chapter analyzes the underlying conceptual structure of selected models of development that have emerged during specific time periods in the history of developmental psychology. The three kinds of models that are analyzed are grouped according to their emphases: (a) differentiation, (b) equilibration, and (c) the teaching–learning processes. The criterion for selection has been the explicit effort of the creators and users of these models to account for the process of development—a complicated task throughout the history of the study of development and the creation of models. Nevertheless, the specific reasons for such complications may suggest varied ways in which these (and other

This chapter was written when the author was a Senior Fulbright Visiting Professor at the Universidade de Brasilia, Brazil, in 1995. The support of the Fulbright Foundation for the work in Brasilia is gratefully acknowledged. The manuscript was finished during a stay in Berlin, supported by the 1995 Research Prize awarded to the author by the Alexander-von-Humboldt Stiftung.

possible models) could be integrated into future developmental research practices.

Child Psychology and the Construction of Scientific Objectivity

Child psychologists work amid a multiplicity of empirical topics and partially formed concepts of development. This discrepancy between the theoretical and the empirical domains in child psychology leads to the dissociation of domains of particular and general knowledge (Shanahan, Valsiner, & Gottlieb, 1997), and these dissociated domains can easily vanish behind the myriad of topic- and context-specific empirical findings. The discipline can thus be faced with the loss of "the forest beyond the trees."

For various reasons, there is an increasing fragmentation of knowledge in child psychology. First, over recent decades, certain social norms for conducting empirical work have become dominant. These norms have distanced researchers from the phenomena (cf. Cairns, 1986) and have led to a relative alienation of inductively abstracted knowledge from the realities of human life. For example, the phenomenon of mother–infant mutual bonding may represent a relevant human relationship that is detectable across countries, times, and contexts. In contrast is the abstracted use of infants' (or mothers') attachment type (A, B, C, or other) as a *de facto* personality characteristic that predicts some future state of the children (or mothers). The basic question of attachment (as a relationship) is lost, and it is replaced by another question (of prediction), because the use of conventionalized methods and data-analytic strategies sets constraints for the research process.

Second, child psychology (like the rest of psychology) has become an intellectual "hostage" to the "empire of chance" (Gigerenzer, 1993). Beginning from the very real need to study different children and to chart out (empirically) the ranges of existing phenomena, the research practices have become dominated by canonical procedures of inductive inference that are coded into a socially constructed hybrid version of statistics and called "the scientific method" (Gigerenzer et al., 1989). The status of statistics as *one kind* of inductive logic of inference is not deniable, but its overgeneralization to the point of overtaking the whole of the scientific method constitutes a case of sociohistorical construction of psychology as science. Psychology's objectivity of knowledge is often equated with

the demonstrated use of large numbers of subjects (large N), "random sampling," "standardized methods," differences among averages (and the statistical significance of those differences), and the currently *en vogue* brand-name data-analytic packages. This characterization of received research practices may be somewhat caricaturistic, but it should bring home the interesting discrepancy between a belief in objectivity and the historically constructed nature of objective research (Daston, 1992).

Efforts to achieve objectivity through social definition of the scientific method are based on the inevitable uncertainty that social sciences face. In the phenomena these sciences study, deterministic and indeterministic moments coincide. Methodological systems borrowed from common sense (in the form of public accounting; see Porter, 1992) and from classical physics are fitted primarily for the deterministic facets of the issues under investigation. The indeterministic side then becomes covered by reliance on the probability notions. In its collective meaning systems, psychology has successfully fused two kinds of probability concepts—(a) frequentistic and (b) subjective (Bayesian)—while successfully avoiding the third possible option: probability as propensity. The prevalence of the frequentistic probability notion is in line with the primacy of inductive inference orientation. An accumulated frequency of some observed phenomenon becomes transformed into a probability estimate to characterize *expectations for the future*.

Such transformation creates a major problem for the study of development. In child psychology, the emergence of novelty—be it age-based growth, or the emergence of new psychological functions—is an axiomatic given. Thus, violation of frequentistic probabilities is central for making sense of development, because the future cannot be predicted from the past (except in extremely general terms). Hence, a borrowing of the hybrid of statistical method, as part of the takeover of all of psychology by the "empire of chance," leads to a state wherein child psychology tends to overlook the processes of development (Benigni & Valsiner, 1985).

Third, as a result of the prevalence of inductive empiricism as the ideal of science, much of child psychology entails empirical work that has been labeled *pseudo-empirical* (Smedslund, 1994, 1995). Researchers who create their hypotheses usually do not trace the sources of those hypotheses. Many commonsense ideas, encoded in the semantics of language terms that are used in setting the hypotheses, bring in implicit meanings. As Smedslund has explained:

> [P]sychological research tends to be pseudoempirical, that is, it tends to involve empirical studies of relationships which follow logically from the meanings of the concepts involved. An example would be studying whether all bachelors are really male and unmarried. (Smedslund, 1995, p. 196)

Because children are among the most nonneutral objects of investigation, child psychology may be particularly vulnerable to researchers' empirical efforts to demonstrate their underlying understandings of the issues. Societies set up certain expectations for the course of "normal" child development, and much of researchers' effort is dedicated to proving empirically that persons at the fringes of such norms (e.g., persons "at risk" for some negative outcome) are of some (special) kind. This pseudoempiricism can be countered by careful elucidation of theoretical assumptions and their linkage with research questions, thereby providing the investigator with new knowledge that cannot be derived from the meanings of the terms in current use.

This picture of how child psychology is delivered today is less than complimentary. There has been, on the one hand, a proliferation of empirical work, and, on the other, a theoretical loss of focus on the issues of development per se. Conceptual difficulties in making sense of development are inevitable in a growing science that faces a most difficult target phenomenon (its object itself is constantly changing). In the study of development, one must cope with its complexity, its dynamic change, and the lack of a universal terminology that would fit the study of its complexity (Van Geert, 1986, 1988). The major theoretical questions are: how might that complexity be conceptualized, and how might psychologists' mainly empirical interests be used productively for creating a general understanding of development?

The Root of the Problem: Specificity of Development

The ability to maintain a consistent developmental viewpoint in child (or adult) psychology is constrained by three fundamental obstacles:

1. The irreversible nature of development—due to the irreversibility of time (Bergson, 1911; Prigogine, 1973).

2. The complex—yet dynamic and often ill-defined—nature of the developing structure (organism, person, social network, community, etc.) and its equally dynamic and structured environment (Bronfenbrenner, 1979, 1989, 1993; Bronfenbrenner & Crouter, 1983; Bronfenbrenner & Morris, this Volume).

3. The multilevel nature of the developing system and of the environment (Gottlieb, 1992; Lerner, 1991).

None of these three features of psychological phenomena is obligatory for nondevelopmental areas of psychology. Traditions in nondevelopmental psychology can fail by not paying attention to both the irreversibility of time and the structure of the phenomena. A perspective in which psychological phenomena are reducible to their elementary constituents has been prominent in nondevelopmental psychology since its beginning.

Such axiomatic oversights—intellectual "shortcuts" of a kind—are not available to developmental researchers, at least not without the severe consequence of eliminating the actual study of development from developmental psychology. Hence, in developmental psychology, we face fundamental theoretical problems that seem irrelevant from the standpoint of a psychologist who has no interest in development.

Psychology, Development, and Modern Physics

Classical physics had no need for the irreversibility notion when applied to time. Only with the discoveries of indeterministic chemical reactions has the need for recognition of time as an irreversible entity entered into some domains of the physical sciences (Prigogine, 1973, 1980, 1987). This recognition of time leads to rethinking of what constitutes rational knowledge:

> We are no longer fascinated by a rationality which depicts the universe and knowledge as something on its way to being achieved. The future is no longer given; it is no longer implied in the present. This means the end of the classical ideal of omniscience. The world of processes in which we live and which is part of us can no longer be rejected as appearances or illusions determined by our mode of observation. (Prigogine, 1983, p. 78)

Contemporary thermodynamics, by making time-dependent irreversible processes the target of investigation, integrates physical and biological sciences (Prigogine, 1976, 1980) and encompasses developmental psychology (Prigogine, 1982). The ground is laid for the return of historicism to psychology—at least to developmental psychology.

However, the rediscovery of historicism is complicated by a specific feature of development—its novelty-producing nature. The theoretical schemes of the developmental sciences must accommodate the principal unpredictability of the actual courses of development. This is not a simple task for a discipline for which "prediction and control of behavior" has, for decades, been an accepted guarantee of its scientific status.

Irreversibility of Time and Development

The irreversible nature of developmental phenomena—bound to the irreversibility of time (Bergson, 1911)—renders most of the methodological axioms of nondevelopmental psychologies futile for the study of development. For instance, the assumption of *repetition* of the *same* phenomena over time—the axiom that allows the accumulation of derived data that are free from a time-bound character—is challenged by the irreversibility of developmental time. Even if it is possible to classify some observable phenomena into a similar class, and to detect such categorized phenomena over time, each subsequent specimen of the same category is not the same (but merely similar). As a result of this admission, summary indexes of categorized data lumped together over study periods eliminate the temporal (sequential) unfolding of the developing phenomenon (Valsiner, 1995a). This is a specific problem for the investigators of development—and no problem at all for nondevelopmental research practices. In the latter, detection of forms that have already emerged in development (rather than those currently in the process of emergence) is the desirable norm. What is being recorded is what already exists, and the question of how it came to exist is of no interest.

The irreversibility of development also sets limits on the verification of the discoveries over historical time. Thus, the same experiments (e.g., the replication of the Istomina's memory study—see Folds-Bennett, 1994; Schneider & Hasselhorn, 1994; Valsiner, 1994c) cannot be replicated in exactly the same way, given the nature of the conditions (social, economic, and other) under which the subjects live in different societies and historical periods.

Reconstructions of stable moments in psychological development amount to a reliance on *outcomes* of development (intermediate "steady states" in development), rather than on *processes*. This shift of focus from processes to outcomes has had a curious effect on the discourse of developmental psychologists. Their efforts are channeled toward construction of a multitude of "stage theories"—accounts of classification of phenomena into similar categories, distributed over ontogenetic time. We often speak of "Piaget's *stage* theory *of* development"—meaning that Piaget indeed described intermediate outcomes of development in terms of stages. What we overlook is Piaget's theory of the process of development, or of equilibration, which was oriented to explaining transformation from one stage to another.

Development as Construction of Novel Forms

Development can be defined as constructive transformation of form in irreversible time through the process of organism ↔ environment interchange. The notions of *form* (or structure), *construction,* and *transformation* are of key relevance in this axiomatic stage-setting for models of development. Each of these notions has been disputed frequently by opponents whose axioms are different. Thus, the basic "battle" between Continental-European gestalt (and *ganzheit*) psychology on the one hand, and Anglo-American associationism on the other, has framed much of the history of developmental psychology (see the chapter by Cairns in this Volume). This battle never ended—nor could it—because the difference between axiomatics (structure as such versus structure as reducible to elements) is in itself a matter of assumptions, not of truth. Likewise, the assumption that organisms construct their development—that is, the axiom of the active creation of novelty—is of an axiomatic nature.

This very general notion of development is well rooted in the history of developmental biology and psychology. Its origins are obviously in the *Naturphilosophie* of the 18th and 19th centuries and can be traced to Johann Wolfgang Goethe's ideas about biology. In a more recognizable heritage, Piaget's focus on constructive transformation of structures (Piaget, 1965, 1970, 1971)—an extension of developmental biology to the realm of psychological structures—centers on this systemic notion of development. Heinz Werner's theoretical stance—following Karl Ernst von Baer's embryology—also fits here (von Baer, 1828; Werner, 1957).

By the end of the 19th century, the focus on development was a widely recognized central topic in psychology, so its conceptualization was not foreign to well-known psychologists whose role in developmental psychology is usually overlooked. Wilhelm Wundt summarized the core of the idea in his *Völkerpsychologie* of 1900:

> [The] basic law of all mental development [is that] what follows always originates from what precedes and nevertheless appears opposed to it as a new creation . . . every stage of [this] development is already contained in the preceding and is, at the same time, a new phenomenon. (Wundt, 1973, p. 149)

The crucial unifying feature was the notion of *synthesis*—whether by way of structural reorganization that produces new quality in the aggregate (as in chemical synthesis or gestalt psychology), or by way of confronting and overcoming conflict in a case of dialectically united opposites. Along similar lines, George Herbert Mead was setting up his account of the social development of personal psychological processes (Cook, 1993; Joas, 1985). In that construction, Mead had to assume an open-system view on life (i.e., developmental) processes:

> Plants and animals . . . [in contrast with inanimate objects] present to science objects *whose essential characters are found not in that which undergoes transformation but in the process itself and in the forms which the object assumes within that process.* Since the process involves the interaction of animal or plant with surrounding objects, it is evident that the *process of life as really confers characters upon the environment as it does upon the plant or the animal.* (Mead, 1932, p. 34, emphasis added)

The emphasis on novelty construction in development stems from the basic assumption of the open-system nature of development (Ford & Lerner, 1992; Lerner, 1978, 1984; Valsiner, 1987). All biological, psychological, and social organisms exist and develop only because of their permanent exchange relations with their environments. Hence, models that explain processes of development are those that either imply their dynamic interchange or take it into account in direct ways. Developmental phenomena are

self-organizing systems, rather than ontological objects (Allen, 1981; Jantsch, 1980).

Selection of Developmental Models

The selection of models for closer historical and conceptual scrutiny was guided by the axiomatics outlined above. All three kinds of models—for differentiation, for equilibration, and for teaching–learning processes—recognize the emergence of novelty through active construction by the agent, are structuralistic in their basis (yet they allow for dynamics), and are historically rooted in developmental biology (rather than psychology) as well as in philosophies that have emerged on the basis of biological worldviews (Baldwin, 1906; Bergson, 1907; Sewertzoff, 1929).

DIFFERENTIATION MODELS

Any conceptual model of development that entails the core of a previous state of the developing organism (X) becoming transformed into a reorganized structure (X--Y), and/or becoming transformed from a more articulated (plural) systemic form to a singular one, can be considered to belong to the class of differentiation models. Theoretical discourse that utilizes the focus on *something becoming something else* has been called *genetic* or *cogenetic logic* (Baldwin, 1906; Herbst, 1995). Formalization of such developmental logic has been only in its infancy during the 20th century. Nevertheless, any differentiation model implies some (usually not explicated) form of logic of change in irreversible time.

We can elaborate the general nature of the differentiation models further. If the transformation of structure in the direction of greater systemic complexity (i.e., X → {X--Y} transformation) can be conveniently referred to as progression, then its reversal (i.e., transformation of {X--Y} → X) may be referred to as regression. The latter is included in the differentiation models. For the sake of completeness, we should speak of *differentiation and dedifferentiation* models, following the lead of Kurt Goldstein (1933, p. 437). It is important to reiterate that any process of dedifferentiation (often subsumed under the label "regression," which implies return to a previous state) is part of an *ongoing* process of development. Any "return" to a previous state is axiomatically ruled out by the irreversibility of time, which renders every new developmental state to be unique. However, states that can be viewed as *similar* to previous ones can be detected when we study the human life course. Development can be conceptualized graphically as a helix that is unfolding in irreversible time. At different parts of the curves of the helix, the new state can resemble a previous state. Yet a new state never repeats a preceding one.

Numerous examples of differentiation models have been used in various areas of child psychology. These models have emerged on the basis of biological (Sewertzoff, 1929; von Baer, 1828) and linguistic (a diachronic focus, *à la* Saussure; see Engler, 1968) research targets. In the studies on child language development, we can encounter descriptions of how children's recognition or production of phonemes or words is transformed in ontogeny. Stage models of cognitive development indicate differentiation of cognitive structures (Case, 1985; Fischer, 1980), and microgenetic analyses of children's mental operations reveal transformation of problem-solving strategies with age (Draguns, 1984; Inhelder et al., 1992; Siegler & Crowley, 1991). Despite their wide *de facto* usage, their general axiomatic formulations have been rare in developmental psychology. Perhaps that has led to the curious status of Heinz Werner's work, which is mentioned in connection with his axiomatization of the differentiation principle but is not used in empirical practice. As will be shown below, the history of differentiation models is far richer than the usual half-use of Werner's work.

Historical Overview of Differentiation Models

The image of differentiation—the growth of a structure over time—is a very easy thought model for any naturalist who looks at the growth processes in nature. The history of differentiation models can be traced back to the view of nature propagated by Goethe, and to the traditions of *Naturphilosophie*. From that background, the founder of embryology, Karl Ernst von Baer, fit the model with his observations of the ontogeny of organ systems (von Baer, 1828). The integrated nature of differentiated organ systems was a given for a natural scientist, and there was never a need to reiterate the truism that only the organized biological *system* (rather than its components) lives. The focus on differentiation was slighltly more complicated in the development of evolutionary thought (Gottlieb, 1992;

Gottlieb, Wahlsten, & Lickliter, this Volume; Oyama, 1985).

The Role of James Mark Baldwin

Baldwin's work has been seminal in various aspects of developmental psychology (see Cairns, 1992, and this Volume; Glickman, 1985; Valsiner, 1994a). His role in the elaboration of the differentiation models was equally profound because it took place in the context of his creation of the ideas of genetic logic—logic for development (Baldwin, 1906). This logic for development has to take into account the open-endedness of the developmental process: how novel forms may emerge at some junction, given a previously existing structure and its current relation with the environment (Baldwin, 1895, 1897). The organism is active within its environment—through a process of constant experimentation, of trying and trying again (engaging in "persistent imitation")—which leads to the differentiation of the environment and of the intrapsychological world.

Heterogeneity of Experiences.   Baldwin was one of the first developmentalists to understand the theoretical dangers of viewing the organism's environment in terms of its static features. The world of the developing person is variable, and that variability takes realistic forms, which entail social interaction:

> [The] child begins to learn in addition the fact that persons are in a measure individual in their treatment of him, and hence that individuality has elements of uncertainty or *irregularity* about it. This growing sense is very clear to one who watches an infant in its second half-year. Sometimes the mother gives a biscuit, but sometimes she does not. Sometimes the father smiles and tosses the child; sometimes he does not. And the child looks for signs of these varying moods and methods of treatment. Its new pains of disappointment arise directly on the basis of that former sense of regular personal presence upon which its expectancy went forth. (Baldwin, 1894, p. 277)

From such heterogeneity of the person's social environment, there follows a need for selective treatment of that heterogeneity by the person. The previously established "schema" (Baldwin, 1908, p. 184) allows the person to become selective as to the variety of presently actual environmental inputs. According to Baldwin (1898):

[The person] comes more and more to reflect the social judgment in his own systematic determination of knowledge; and there arises within himself a criterion of private sort which is in essential harmony with the social demand, because genetically considered it reflects it. The individual becomes a law unto himself, exercises his private judgment, fights his own battles for truth, shows the virtue of independence and the vice of obstinacy. But he has learned to do it by the selective control of his social environment, *and in this judgment he has just a sense of this social outcome.* (pp. 19–20)

The social nature of a person is expressed in his or her personal individuality, which becomes differentiated from its social roots and acquires relative autonomy. Mere slavish mirroring of the social world is rendered impossible by the heterogeneity of the latter. The need for "systematic determination" of the new knowledge is triggered by *internalized* selection mechanisms that operate within mental processes—cognitive schemas (Baldwin, 1898, p. 10). The notion of such schemas—not as representations of the world but as *preorganizers* of the person's encounters with the *future states* of the world—continued in the work of Frederick Bartlett (Rosa, 1993), Jean Piaget (Chapman, 1988, 1992), and Lev Vygotsky (Van der Veer & Valsiner, 1991). Thus, the relevance of presently emerging differentiated structures of thought or action was to provide a basis for future encounters with ever-unpredictable environments.

Differentiation of Thought and Action: Contributions of Pierre Janet

Perhaps the most central figure for the development of psychological thought in the first decades of the 20th century was the shy French psychiatrist Pierre Janet (Valsiner & Van der Veer, 1997, chapter 3; Van der Veer & Valsiner, 1988). Janet was the originator of the analysis of subconscious processes. His work was the basis for various kinds of activity theories that proliferated in the 20th century (Boesch, 1983, 1991; Leontiev, 1981).

Hierarchical Organization of Functions. Janet's main focus was on the demonstration of the differentiation and mutual integration of thinking and acting phenomena in the structure of personality (Janet, 1889, 1926, 1928). In the process of differentiation, some parts of the functional system establish their role as regulators over the others.

Different clinical cases provide evidence for this hierarchical control notion of the normal functioning of the mind, by way of pathological excesses that can be obtained by rather simple alteration of the control system. At one extreme is found the complete blocking of concrete action by thought processes (Janet, 1921). At the other extreme, one can find thought processes that automatically are triggered by perceptual experiences and lead to uncritical and unchecked execution of actions (Janet, 1925, p. 210).

The Role of Tensions in Differentiating Structure. The ways in which persons handle the differentiation and integration of their personality systems are highly variable. The concept of *psychological tension* is present at all levels of Janet's thought–action hierarchy (Sjövall, 1967, pp. 52–56). At the higher level of that hierarchy, the phenomena of personal will can be observed as the highest control mechanism. Thus, will is not a mystical entity that stands outside of the regular action-control hierarchy and acts in opposition to it; rather, it is the highest-level part of the hierarchical system, a part that emerges through development.

The process of differentiation is characterized by tension between parts of the previously differentiated structure. Because of this tension, psychological work is focused on these parts.

The patients who are ill-satisfied with their action watch themselves and by dint of observations, through anxiety about themselves, they fall into a sort of perpetual auto-analysis. They become psychologists; which is in its way a disease of the mind. (Janet, 1921, p. 152)

The crucial feature of handling such tensions is the *personal synthesis* of experiences of one's past, in the personal present, through the use of language (Meyerson, 1947). This focus relates Janet's differentiation focus with the equilibration models (described below). Similar emphases on processes of fusion versus differentiation can be found in the work of Henri Wallon (1942, 1945).

The "Orthogenetic Principle" of Heinz Werner

Heinz Werner's legacy in developmental psychology has been widely noted (e.g., Langer, 1970; Lerner, 1979, 1986), and its linkages with the history of the differentiation models is clear; yet, the implications of his theoretical contributions rarely appear in contemporary developmental research (for exceptions, see Brent, 1978, 1984; Kaplan, 1983; Langer, 1980, 1982, 1983, 1986, 1990; Wapner & Demick, this Volume). The marginalization of Werner's ideas in contemporary developmental psychology is a concrete example of how the discipline has been conceptually inconsistent. Werner's overall view on development constitutes the quintessence of developmental thought over the past century. Some argue that Werner himself created too grand a theoretical frame to which he tried to fit too wide an array of empirical evidence (see below), but this evaluation of Werner's work is not a sufficient reason to delegate his work to the exotic contexts of history (or of Clark University). In many different ways, contemporary developmental scientists necessarily arrive at another version of thought that emphasizes differentiation and hierarchical integration.

Historical Context: Werner's Intellectual Interdependency

Werner's interest in the process of the genesis of novelty was guided by his work in William Stern's Institute at the University of Hamburg in the 1920s. However, even earlier, his interest in the emergence of metaphoric speech (Werner, 1919, pp. 209–211) provided evidence for his consistent application of the differentiation notion to psychological functions. In the 1920s, the differentiation perspective as well as its methodological tools became established.

The Hamburg Context.   Werner was in the best possible place for his investigations—the University of Hamburg, where Stern's institute was an active center of developmental and ecological psychology. The simultaneous presence in Hamburg of the philosopher Ernst Cassirer, the theoretical biologist Johann Jakob von Uexküll (1928, 1957, 1980), and William Stern, made the university a center of intellectual advancement in multiple fields (Eyferth, 1976; Grossmann, 1986; Hardesty, 1976; Kreppner, 1992a). Contemporary environmental psychology owes much to the work of Marta Muchow (Muchow, 1931; Muchow & Muchow, 1935; Wohlwill, 1985), a scholar whose work emerged from that context. The young Gordon Allport visited there in 1923–1924, and took back to the United States the traditions of morphogenic

methodology in psychology, as well as the personological stance itself.

The Legacy of William Stern.   Aside from constituting much of Werner's intellectual environment in Hamburg, the legacy of William Stern for developmental thought models should be restored to its appropriate role. Stern's personalistic epistemology, developed decades before his administrative roles at Hamburg University and outlined in various publications (Stern, 1906, 1911, 1918, 1919), has been the foundation for efforts to understand differentiation processes both within persons' development, and in the development of persons as a population. The latter focus has placed Stern in the role of the founder of differential psychology (or, as it is now labeled, the "psychology of individual differences"). This label is inexact because it lumps together two kinds of "individual differences": (a) the *inter*individual differences between persons at the same moment in time (i.e., the usual preoccupation of nondevelopmental psychology), and *intra*individual differences within any person's conduct over time (and in changing contexts). Stern (1911, p. 18) made the latter distinction very clearly, and its value has been emphasized during later decades (Cox, Ornstein, & Valsiner, 1991; Lerner, 1986). It can be said that actual human development takes place within the realm of intraindividual differences—i.e., the person's flexible actions in relation to constantly changing environments. Interindividual differences may provide researchers with information about multiple trajectories of development, but do not provide access to information about the actual developmental processes.

Stern's real concerns about human psychological differentiation went far beyond the trivial idea that interindividual differences are important to study. Despite the eminent availability of Stern's theoretical work in English translations (Stern, 1938), and explanations of it by Stern himself (Stern, 1930) and by others (Allport, 1937; Eyferth, 1976; Grossmann, 1986; Hardesty, 1976; Kreppner, 1992a, 1992b; Lamiell, 1991; Werner, 1938), the basic theoretical notions of his personalistic worldview have remained foreign to contemporary psychology.

Contradictory Unity of Persons and Contexts within Time.   From the beginning of the development of his personalistic worldview, Stern emphasized the contradictory unity of persons and things (1906, p. 16). The person, a multifaceted, functioning whole *(unitas multiplex),* is spontaneously active relative to surrounding things; yet the organization of both the person and things has a structure that is constantly in the process of reorganization (by the goal-orientedness of the active person).

Stern's theoretical system is therefore process-oriented, as is reflected in his hierarchy and convergence principles (Stern, 1919, pp. 8–10). The person is constantly living through (experiencing) relations with the external world, which entail simultaneously separation *(Spaltung)* of, and tension *(Spannung)* between, different facets of the total wholeness of experience (Stern, 1935, p. 103). This process is very similar to Piaget's reliance on the unity of assimilation and accommodation, but Stern's personalism is stated in the context of the heterogeneous totality of person ↔ world relations, rather than in relation to information coming into the cognitive system.

Differentiation of Personal Worlds. Each person has a separate person-relevant—"personal"—world of his or her own making (Stern, 1935, p. 126). That world is constructed by two parallel processes in person ↔ world relations: (a) participation in the world (the *centrifugal direction*—spontaneous actions guided by the material nature of the world; Stern, 1938, p. 388), and (b) the world's impression on the person (the *centripetal direction*—reactions of the person to the demand characteristics of the world). The personal world differentiates itself from the surrounding world and serves as a further guide in development. Stern (1938) saw it leading to the emergence of novelty:

> However great the power exerted by the world to make the individual fall in with its trend, he nevertheless continues to be a "person" and can react to its influence only as a person, thereby modifying and deflecting its very tendency. And vice versa, however strikingly novel and penetrating the effect of the impress by which the genius of an artist, the founder of a religion, a statesman, puts a new face upon the world; since this modified world has no creative genius, it can absorb novelty only in a diluted, simplified form; and since it meanwhile follows its own laws and is subject to other influences, it perforce modifies all acquisitions. (p. 90)

Stern's personalistic theory was a basis for Werner's systematic and pervasive emphasis on the differentiation notion. Furthermore, Stern had an "old-fashioned" adamant insistence that goal-oriented and volitional processes should be considered by psychology as relevant phenomena.

Differentiation Processes in Language Use. Ernst Cassirer's classic three-volume synthesis, *The Philosophy of Symbolic Forms,* appeared in the 1920s (Cassirer, 1923, 1926, 1929). Of the trilogy, perhaps the last volume was of greatest importance for Werner's conceptualization of development as differentiation. Cassirer (1929/1957) made explicit the ever-dynamic and constructive role of language:

> Language does not flow along tranquilly in a ready-made bed; at every turn it must dig out its channel anew—and it is this living flow which at every step produces new and more highly developed forms. Herein lies its true and fundamental strength, but from the standpoint of the concept and of conceptual thought also its weakness. For the concept in the strict sense tends to set a goal for this surge and flow; it demands stability and unambiguousness. In its *being,* it seeks to transcend and negate everything that language must tolerate in its becoming. (p. 336)

Werner benefited from the philosophy of Cassirer and from other German researchers of the 1920s who were interested in the intricacies of language. For instance, his experimental task of discovery of word meanings (Werner, 1954) is based largely on the ideas of Hans Sperber (1923). The rich heritage of the neuropsychology of language functions, which was available in the 1920s, was demonstrably a rich source for the advancement of Werner's ideas (Werner, 1940a, 1956).

In Werner's own sphere of interest, the processes of sign-making in language—in both verbal and graphic forms—have been in a central place. The question of construction of meanings of words in the context of sentences, and changes in meanings, was a target of his investigations (Werner, 1930, 1931, 1954; Werner & Kaplan, 1963). Likewise, the emergence of structure in the flow of melodies (Werner, 1926, 1940b) was consistently in Werner's focus of interest. However, the basic principle of differentiation lay beneath all of his interests.

Werner's "Orthogenetic Principle" Reexamined

For English-language psychology, the received version of Werner's general view is in a passage from his presentation at the First Minnesota Symposium on Child Development in 1957. It is usually given as:

> Developmental psychology postulates one regulative principle of development; it is an orthogenetic principle which states that wherever development occurs it proceeds from a state of relative globality and lack of differentiation to a state of increasing differentiation, articulation, and hierarchical integration. (Werner, 1957, p. 126)

Elaborations of the Orthogenetic Principle. To understand Werner's intentions, his elaborations of his idea need to be considered. First, it is important to emphasize Werner's focus on the emergence of the polarity (differentiation) of the subject (of action) and its object:

> [I]ncreasing subject–object differentiation involves the corollary that the organism becomes increasingly less dominated by the immediate concrete situation; the person is less stimulus-bound and less impelled by his own alternative states. A consequence of this freedom is the clearer understanding of goals, the possibility of employing substitutive means and alternative ends. There is hence a greater capacity for delay and planned action. The person is better able to exercise choice and willfully rearrange a situation. In short, he can manipulate the environment rather than passively respond to the environment. This freedom from the domination of the immediate situation also permits a more accurate assessment of others. (Werner, 1957, p. 127)

This focus on increased person–environment differentiation reflects Baldwin's earlier argument that the best proof of sociogenetic origins of psychological functions was their autonomy from the immediate field of social demands (see above; also Brandtstädter, this Volume).

However, the orthogenetic law was not meant to be a unilinearity-prescribing principle at the level of concrete developmental phenomena. In actuality, Werner recognized the multilinearity of developmental trajectories (Werner, 1957, p. 137). Differentiation was viewed as including dedifferentiation as its complementary part. The process of hierarchical integration involves qualitative reorganization of the "lower" (i.e., previously established) levels of organization, when the higher levels emerge in their specificity:

> [D]evelopment . . . tends towards stabilization. Once a certain stable level of integration is reached, the possibility of further development must depend on whether or not the behavioral patterns have become so automatized that they

cannot take part in reorganization. . . . The individual, for instance, builds up sensorimotor schemata . . . these are the goal of early learning at first, but later on become instruments or apparatuses for handling the environment. Since no two situations in which an organism finds itself are alike, the usefulness of these schemata in adaptive behavior will depend on their stability as well as on their pliability (a paradoxical "stable flexibility").

> [If] one assumes that the emergence of higher levels of operations involves hierarchic integration, it follows that lower-level operations will have to be reorganized in terms of their functional nature so that they become subservient to higher functioning. A clear example of this is the change of the functional nature of imagery from a stage where images serve only memory, fantasy, and concrete conceptualization, to a stage where images have been transformed to schematic symbols of abstract concepts and thought. (Werner, 1957, pp. 139–140)

Werner's perspective on subject–object differentiation consistently led to the notion of psychological mediating devices emerging as human-made organizers of the mental and affective processes (e.g., his reference to the transformation of imagery to symbols). In this notion, there exists a clear parallel with Lev Vygotsky's emphasis on semiotic mediating devices (Van der Veer & Valsiner, 1991). In Werner's (1940a) terms, these mediating devices emerge in the differentiation process:

> Development from a lower to a higher type of action—in terms of differentiation—is marked by the appearance of circuitous approaches, that is, means of action, instruments of mediation. On the level of the most primitive action, object (stimulus) and subject (response) are not separated by the devices of mediation; that is, the interaction is *immediate*. Development in the mode of action is further determined by a growing specificity of the personal and subjective as against the objective aspect of the action involved. The growth and differentiation of the personal factor in action are demonstrated in the emergence of a specifically personal *motivation*. The growing recognition of a self-dependent objectivity is reflected in the development of *planful behavior*. (p. 191)

Werner's inclusion of motivation among the emerging set of mediating devices serves as an example of theoretical alleys in psychology that have been suggested and then forgotten. Persons as constructors of their own motivation—via construction of cultural meanings—allow ever-new forms of self-regulation to emerge in ontogeny, and innovation of cultural meaning systems (as well as differentiation of language forms—e.g., metaphoric devices) in human history.

Historical Misfits and Inconsistencies

An interesting question still remains for an investigator of the history of ideas. Why has Werner's developmental theorizing become marginalized into "mainstream" and "others" by the social forces that govern the differentiation of conceptual systems? Werner's own elaborations of his general ideas may be useful in this explanation. In the 1950s and 1960s, his direction of thought may have diverged from the one that became the mainstream in North American psychology, which at that time could feel itself dominant in the whole world.

Werner's position offered a differentiated, articulated, and hierarchically integrated system of epistemological activity among researchers. He was explicit about the *directiveness* of developmental processes (Werner, 1957, p. 126, footnote) at a time when most contemporary (and subsequent) developmental psychology was wary of introducing teleological notions into its core. Last (but not least), Werner's thinking entailed a clear distinction between "primitive" ("lower") and "civilized" ("higher") forms of thinking (e.g., Werner & Kaplan, 1956). This distinction was common in cognitive psychology of the 1920s and 1930s, and was not ideologized for its value-inclusiveness. Lev Vygotsky explicitly accepted that notion, and so did significant other contributors to the knowledge of development (e.g., Goldstein, 1971).

However, Werner's thinking was not immune to his intellectual context, as illustrated by his treatment of empirical evidence. Fundamental principles, like that of development as a differentiation process in general, emerge in science and become abstract general postulates. They are only illustrated by empirical evidence, not proven (or disproven). At the same time, empirical evidence plays a vital role in the build-up of lower-level abstract knowledge about specific issues that are of interest (for a similar view, see Branco & Valsiner, 1997; Kindermann & Valsiner, 1989; Valsiner, 1991b).

Thus, Werner and Kaplan (1956) held:

> It is the aim of developmental psychology to view the total behavior of all organisms in terms of similar developmental principles. It is our belief that such an approach is fruitful in *coordinating*, within a single descriptive framework,

psychological phenomena observed in phylogenesis, ontogenesis, psychopathology, ethnopsychology, etc., and linking these observations to the formulation and *systematic examination of experimentally testable hypotheses.* . . . [The orthogenetic principle] has the status of an heuristic "law." . . . Though itself not subject to empirical test, it is valuable to developmental psychologists in *directing inquiry* and in *determining the actual range of applicability* with regard to the behavior of organisms. (p. 866, emphasis added)

Much of the confusion surrounding Werner's ideas seems to be related to the focus of the phrase "coordinating . . . psychological phenomena" across (sub)disciplines of psychology, and to the question of what kinds of "experimentally testable hypotheses" the orthogenetic principle guides the researchers to construct. On both accounts, Werner himself can be observed to have been inconsistent. First, in his empirical data presentations, he moved freely among microgenetic, ontogenetic, pathogenetic, and historical-linguistic evidence (e.g., Werner, 1957, pp. 142–143, Figures 1–4), leaving the impression that these domains of developmental phenomena are the same from the viewpoint of the orthogenetic principle. The specificities of the domains often remained unmentioned, yet it would be particularly consistent with the orthogenetic principle if these domains themselves were hierarchically ordered, with each level having developed its own unique specificity.

The second confusion seems to stem from Werner's "keeping up with time" in his years of work in the United States during the 1950s and early 1960s. The whole discipline of psychology was, around that time, changing in the direction of canonizing empiricism as the epitome of science. Werner's own empirical credo had been explicitly that of the experimental study, the unfolding of psychological phenomena in time (e.g., his *microgenetic* experimental focus, in parallel with Friedrich Sander's methodology of *Aktualgenese;* see Sander, 1928, for an overview; see also Draguns, 1984). For Werner to remain consistent with his method and the orthogenetic principle, all hypotheses generated at that intellectual junction needed to be developmental—in the sense of positing that one or another course of differentiation or dedifferentiation was observable under specifically set experimental conditions. The hypotheses should have been about the actual *process of unfolding of structure* in development, rather than about the *outcomes* of such development. Previously, Werner himself had argued against the elimination of the processes from consideration (Werner, 1937). By the 1950s and 1960s, however, Werner was ready to allow outcomes-comparison hypotheses under the umbrella of his "heuristic law." For example:

> With regard to specific developmental hypotheses, one may formulate testable empirical propositions such as "Individuals under anxiety *manifest more* magical practices than non-anxious individuals," "Schizophrenics *manifest more* magical practices than "normals," "Individuals in preliterate societies *have more* magical practices than individuals in advanced technologies," etc. The determination of whether or not one is willing to accept these hypotheses as confirmed rests on empirical study. (Werner & Kaplan, 1956, p. 869, emphasis added)

The move from comparison within persons over time to comparison between persons while eliminating time (i.e., the use of the interindividual reference frame; Valsiner, 1987) is inconsistent with the orthogenetic principle. Undoubtedly, the hypotheses mentioned in the above quote—stating that differences of "more" (or "less") of some outcome characteristic exist within a certain group of subjects—are possible. Yet, their knowledge-constructing value belongs to the realm of nondevelopmental psychology. It can be argued that Werner's *laissez-faire* orientation to move between developmental levels is the core for this inconsistency. Similar inconsistencies have been found in other theoretical constructions as well (e.g., Branco, 1996—a reanalysis of Urie Bronfenbrenner's and Ulric Neisser's work). When the general social climate of a science guides scientists toward dissociation of the empirical work from its theoretical complement, eclecticism emerges.

Other Differentiation Models

The history of developmental ideas presents numerous examples of the utilization of differentiation models, even if the concept of differentiation is not always given a theoretically central focus. Both biological and social foci on development encompass such models with equal ease.

George Herbert Mead's Double Differentiation of Person and Society

Mead's work has been recently put into the perspective of his own intellectual environment (Cook, 1993; Joas, 1985). In an effort to overcome both the separation of the person and society and their intellectual fusion in pragmatist talk, Mead suggested a double-feedback-loop model of differentiation of *both* the person (in terms of different "me"-s, as well as the "generalized other"; see Dodds, Lawrence, & Valsiner, 1997; Valsiner & Van der Veer, 1998, chapter 6) and the social world (social institutions). The person, acting within an environment, changes it; and feedback from this process and outcome leads to the intrapsychological reconstruction of the self. The latter, in its turn, feeds into further actions on the environment, with a resulting change, and so on. The process of differentiation of the subject and object maintains the dynamic relation between them, yet the process is constantly undergoing change:

> [R]esponse to the social conduct of the self may be in the role of another—we present his arguments in imagination and do it with his intonations and gestures and even perhaps with his facial expression. In this way we play the roles of all our group; indeed, it is only so far as we do this that they become part of our social environment—to be aware of another self as a self implies that we have played his role or that of another with whose type we identify him for purposes of intercourse. The inner response to our reaction to others is therefore as varied as is our social environment. . . . (Mead, 1913, p. 377)

The inner and outer worlds of acting persons thus become differentiated in coordination, and transformation in one leads to some transformation in the other.

Lev Vygotsky's Dialectical Synthesis

The core of Vygotsky's work was the demonstration of the presence of construction of novelty in the process of living through experiences (Van der Veer & Valsiner, 1991, 1994, chapter 9; Vygotsky, 1925/1971). Development from his viewpoint entailed differentiation of psychological functions (from "lower" to "higher" kinds, distinguished by the semiotic mediation of volitional processes).

Vygotsky was aware of the need to rethink existing methods of psychology to allow for the study of the differentiation process. Hence, his "method of double stimulation" entails analysis of the process by which the subject constructs further differentiation of the stimulus field, given the goal orientation of a task (Valsiner, 1989a, chapter 3). The main reason for constructing such methodology was, for Vygotsky, the need to discover the moments when a person arrives at a dialectical synthesis—both within the line of actions (similar to Köhler's "insight"-based problem solving by apes) and between the lines of action and semiotic reflection. In the latter case, the current problem-solving situation can be restructured in terms of its meaning, which guides the person's relations with that situation. The capacity of humans to move from acting to speaking to contemplating, and to generalization of the meaning of general states of the *psyche* (e.g., the states of "depression" or "happiness"), constitutes a process of psychological differentiation wherein higher mental functions become integrated into the structure of all functions in a control role.

The "method of double stimulation" entails a number of radical ideas in reconstructing developmental psychology's experimental method. First, it is explicitly structuralistic; the subject is viewed as encountering the *whole field* of the experimental setting (and not merely the elements of it that are purposefully varied—the "independent variables"). Second, the subject is considered as the active agent who reconstructs that field by introducing into it the goal subfields ("stimulus-objects," in Vygotsky's terminology) and the means to reach those goals ("stimulus-means"). This functional differentiation of the experimental structured stimulus field into two kinds of relevant parts (goals and means), while leaving the rest of the field to constitute the background, is *guided* by the experimenter *but cannot be determined* by him or her. The experimenter gives the subject a task embedded within the field, but the subject can refuse to perform that task, and may turn it into another one. In other terms, the *psychological experiment is only partially controllable* by the experimenter.

The notion of "double stimulation" entails two differentiations: (a) between "stimulus-object" and "stimulus-means," and (b) between two kinds of means that can be used to organize the subject's conduct in the experimental field. The *action* means are created in the situation; the interpretation of the situation occurs on the basis of *semiotic* means that link the present situation with the subject's past experiences. Human subjects, through the use of language (widely understood as any semiotic system), constantly make their own meaning in any situation they experience—including that of a psychological experiment. This interpretational activity of the subject is not controllable by the experimenter, and it cannot be eliminated. Vygotsky's methodological idea was to turn that inevitably uncontrollable moment of human interpretation into the target of investigation—the equivalent of the "dependent variable" in his method is the microgenetic process by which the subject attempts to reach the goal, and the corresponding construction of meanings. The empirical bases of Vygotsky's ideas were gestalt psychological experimentation with primates, and Mikhail Basov's investigations of children's behavior.

Mikhail Basov's Differentiation Theory of Structural Forms

Basov's work has recently become available to a modern readership (Basov, 1991). Its origins are in the realm of gestalt psychology and its unification with developmental principles (Valsiner, 1988, chapter 5). Unlike Vygotsky, who remained largely nonspecific when the processes of dialectical synthesis were questioned, Basov tried to demonstrate the emergence of novel differentiated structures through the use of three increasingly complex forms (and the "transitional forms" between them) that are constructed in ontogeny (Basov, 1929, 1931).

1. The *temporal chain of acts* is a form wherein actions follow one another without specific connections in time. These are actions triggered by a given situation at a given time. Neither past experience nor expectations for the future are involved in this flow of context-specific behaving. An example of this form may be taken from the erratic sequence of activities of a toddler, who may toddle from one area to another and be involved with a sequence of separate activities, without linkages from one to another.

2. The *associatively determined process* is a structural form of behavior that operates on the basis of associations between the present state and past experiences. This differentiated structure entails continuity in time from past to present (e.g., contemporary modeling efforts of temporal processes through Markovian analyses, and other forms of time-series analyses, are axiomatically limited to detect this form of differentiation *à la* Basov). However, the differentiation of form here does not include any orientation toward the future; hence, it cannot be viewed as the ultimate result of differentiation.

3. The *apperceptively determined process* constitutes the unification of the linkages past → present and present → expected future. The expectations for the future—the apperceptive focus—provide the structure of action in any given moment of its focus. This is used to integrate selected associative ties with past experiences into the structure, which then is instrumental in bringing about *a* future.

Lewin's Topological Psychology

Lewin's dynamic view on human action and thinking has been a significant contributor to psychological ideas (Zeigarnik, 1981). His general methodological orientation radically transcended the associationistic worldview of most of psychology:

> Field theory is probably best characterized as a method: namely, a method of analyzing causal relations and of building scientific constructs. This method of analyzing causal relations can be expressed in the form of certain general statements about the nature of the conditions of change. (Lewin, 1943, p. 294)

The unity of the fields leads to explanations of change in terms of field structure and forces (Lewin, 1935, 1938, 1939), or gradients (Waddington, 1966, 1970). The effort Lewin undertook was to overcome the "Aristotelian models" in psychology (Lewin, 1931; Valsiner, 1984). Instead of letting an average or most frequently observed case represent the reality of psychological functions (this is what Lewin designated as the "Aristotelian model" of thought), he attempted to analyze the whole field structure of the active person. Emphasis on the field structure and its transformability was a productive way to accomplish this goal.

Even as its main focus was to describe the present state of the psychological functioning of the person (Lewin, 1935, 1936a, 1938), the developmental side of his field theory existed in efforts to explain the person's navigation within a field, and in microgenesis of the person's lifespace change. That navigation entails reconstruction of personal meanings, which lead to dramatic differences in the perspective on the same environment:

> In Mark Twain's *Life on the Mississippi,* the passengers on the boat enjoy the "scenery," but for the pilot the U-shape of the two hills, which a passenger admires, means a signal to turn sharply, and the beautiful waves in the middle of the river mean dangerous rocks. The psychological connection of these "stimuli" with actions has changed, and therefore the meaning has changed. (Lewin, 1942, p. 229)

Thus, the psychological field differentiates in terms of actions and in terms of reconstructed meanings of different aspects of the environment. This developmental facet of Lewin's topological system shows clear use of the differentiation model (Lewin, 1942). The person's psychological field structure during an entrance into a novel environment is undifferentiated; it becomes differentiated through the sequence of the person's actions while exploring the environment (Lewin, 1933, 1943). Empirical work that was guided by Lewin provided classic illustrations of a situation-transformation process (e.g., the "Zeigarnik Effect"—Zeigarnik, 1927). Zeigarnik and Lewin demonstrated the formative role of unfinished activity on the memory processes.

Lewin's general ideas on methodology matched these empirical practices. His focus on the experimental method in developmental psychology as targeting the *conditions* under which one or another *transformation of the field could be demonstrated* ("conditional-genetic analysis"; Lewin, 1927) opened the way to others for direct investigation of differentiation processes (e.g., Boesch, 1991; Bourdieu, 1973, 1985; Bronfenbrenner, 1979, this Volume; Valsiner, 1987).

Contemporary Approaches in Developmental Psychology

In different areas of developmental psychology today, one can observe continuities with, and elaboration of, different kinds of differentiation models. Ford and Lerner (1992) in their Developmental Systems Theory, demonstrate how the structure of life course emerges by differentiation (pp. 200–204). Their version of the differentiation model entails a focus on *heterarchy* (as opposed to hierarchy)—a differentiating structure where "influences" move not only from the top down, but also from the bottom up (Ford & Lerner, 1992, p. 114).

Fogel (1993), who is interested in the process of adult–infant communication, uses a differentiation model to investigate the emergence of relationships from the flow of interactive coregulation. The emergence of gestures from the flow of adult–infant interaction has been analyzed in depth by Lyra (1989; Lyra, Pantoja, & Cabral, 1991; Lyra & Rossetti-Ferreira, 1995; Lyra & Winegar, 1996). In addition to articulation and hierarchical integration, development entails the process of *abbreviation* of the differentiating phenomena, relative to their preceding states.

The importance of the presence of abbreviation—the loss of some aspects of the previously differentiated phenomenon—has been noted by researchers over many decades (Dewey, 1895, pp. 26–29). It has also been described as "fossilization of behavior" by Lev Vygotsky. The function of such abbreviation, where human semiotic construction is concerned, is to preserve the phenomena of the past as feed-forward markers in the present. "[One] of the main functions of symbols is to 'abbreviate' reality" (Lyra & Rossetti-Ferreira, 1995). Differentiation of the speech and action lines in ontogeny, and establishment of a relative autonomy between them, allows semiotic mediating devices to take over regulation of development in dynamic, flexible ways (Gupta & Valsiner, 1995). In the domain of social actions, children's construction of social roles in play (Oliveira, 1996; Oliveira & Rossetti-Ferreira, 1996), and adolescents' construction of personal secret meanings (Oliveira & Valsiner, 1997), demonstrate how the general principles of differentiation guide developing persons toward autonomy of the intrapsychological and interpersonal domains. Georg Simmel's (1906, 1908) notions of the emergence of secrecy as a cultural phenomenon fits the differentiation notion. At the opposite end of the personal/social separation continuum, the processes of coregulation of interaction give rise to differentiated systems of metacommunication (Fogel & Branco, 1997).

Contemporary work using differentiation models has received positive impetus from dynamic systems theory, and particularly from the potentials that experimental theoretical psychology (Van Geert, 1994) provides for its formal modeling efforts. As has been demonstrated by Van Geert (1991), relatively simple formal models can generate complex patterns of developmental trajectories. These demonstrations open new possibilities for constructing developmental theories that could move away from the impoverished bases of ordinary language-based descriptions (Van Geert, 1986, 1988) and toward formalizations that are adequate for the developmental phenomena of differentiation.

Summary: Differentiation as the Core of Development

The ideas of differentiation and integration have reemerged consistently in the history of developmental psychology. Nevertheless, these ideas have been used to capture the external picture of development as it unfolds over time. The internal (process) mechanisms of such differentiation are rarely made explicit. (Janet's "tension" notion, along with various efforts to consider "synthesis" in the differentiation process, have been steps in that direction.) In equilibration models, the issue of organization of the making of new differentiated states comes to the focus of attention.

EQUILIBRATION MODELS

The class of equilibration models includes any formal model that entails (a) an initial state of harmonious existence of a system; (b) emergence of some disruption in that state, due to perturbations in the organism–environment relation; and (c) time-dependent (as well as teleological) movement toward the restoration of the initial state of harmony. The teleological movement is the major constitutive criterion of the equilibration models because, in some versions, the outcome does not need to be accepted as actually restoring the "harmony," and the original "harmony" is not necessarily harmonious. Thus, dialectical perspectives that posit transition from one form of "contradiction" to another (new) one (Riegel, 1975, 1976), as well as all disequilibration models, fit under the general label used here. Likewise, the notion of equilibration/disequilibration is central for the focus on organization and disorganization within Developmental Systems Theory (Ford & Lerner, 1992, pp. 171–173).

Recent Origins of Equilibration Models

The prehistory of the equilibration models in recent Western theoretical thought goes back to Herbert Spencer, who viewed the existence of living organisms in terms of a system of movement towards an *average* equilibrium state (Spencer, 1864, paragraphs 170–176). This emphasis was merely a transition of the dominant role, attributed to the average, to the time-based change processes (Valsiner, 1984, 1986). Mere extensions of the average-affirming processes to cover those of development were a way to fit the latter into an organized frame of preservation of the predictability of change processes.

The creative period for the developmental ideas of the 19th century was the last decade, the 1890s (see Cairns, this Volume), during which numerous disputes on the nature of emotion (Baldwin, 1894; Dewey, 1894, 1895; Irons, 1895a, 1895b; James, 1884, 1890, 1894; Worcester, 1893) and the "reflex arc" (Dewey, 1896) led to emphasis on the *functional* and *dynamic* nature of developmental processes. The role of James Mark Baldwin in the elaboration of the general equilibration idea—through the notions of assimilation and accommodation—is particularly noteworthy as an intermediate step in the development of equilibration models, which were later used by Piaget. The elaboration of the equilibration model was evident in the thought of the philosopher-semiotician Charles Sanders Peirce.

Peirce's Idea of Development through Disequilibriae

Peirce's main focus on abductive inference—viewed as the "third way" to escape the confines of induction and deduction—led him to the need to make sense of development. The abductive "jump" beyond the "information given" meant capturing *history in the making.* Recognizing that the developmental process constantly undermines automatisms and habits in conduct (and borrowing from Baldwin in this), Peirce formulated in generic terms what in our time could be recognized as a law of development through disequilibration.

> [P]rotoplasm is in an excessively unstable condition; and *it is the characteristic of unstable equilibrium, that near that point excessively minute causes may produce startlingly large effects.* Here, then, the usual departures from regularity will be followed by others that are very great; and the large fortuitous departures from law so produced, will tend still further to break up the laws, supposing that these are of the nature of habits. Now, this breaking up of habit and renewed fortuitous spontaneity will, according to the law of mind, be accompanied by an intensification of feeling. The nerve-protoplasm is, without doubt, in the most unstable condition of any kind of matter; and consequently, there the resulting feeling is the most manifest. (Peirce, 1892, p. 18, emphasis added)

Peirce here undoubtedly antedated the current popular fascination with "chaos theory." He emphasized that, through the constant process of disequilibration, taking place in irreversible time, conditions are created for living organisms to construct new preadaptational forms. The notion of irreversibility of time is absorbed, slowly and painfully, into the theoretical models of the developmentalists of the 20th century via the philosophy of Henri Bergson.

The Role of Henri Bergson

Bergson's (1911) philosophy is widely acknowledged, but its substance is not well understood. Bergson borrowed greatly from the traditions of the "organic evolution" thought of the 1890s, which was the focus of discourse because of the efforts of Henry Osborn, James Mark Baldwin, and C. Lloyd Morgan.

Living Systems and Development

Bergson's emphasis on the contrast between living and nonliving objects was closely related to the nature versus science debates of the 1890s (Bergson, 1907, 1911). The notion of duration is the basis for his claim of a drastic difference between living systems and isolated physical objects. *Living systems are always in the process of becoming.* Bergson's criticism of the science of his time was directed at the unwarranted transfer of analytic ideas from the study of the inanimate world to that of natural systems. In the latter, the past (through selective memory) enters in functional ways into the construction of novelty in the present. The process of becoming is one of creative adaptation that goes beyond the immediate needs of the environment.

The Constructive Concept of Adaptation

A central concept in Bergson's developmental thought was the notion of *adaptation.* That concept—popular as it was (and is) in evolutionary and developmental discourses—can carry different meanings. First, it has been seen as a direct reaction to the conditions that are causing either "positive" change (by giving rise to new variations) or "negative" change (by eliminating misfitting emerged variations). Bergson disagreed with both of these meanings (on the basis of their mechanistic elaboration; Bergson, 1911, p. 63), and called for seeing adaptation in the process of the emergence of novel mechanisms in ways that are *coordinated with* context demands (but not "molded" or "shaped" by them). Thus, in psychological development, the psychological functions develop new organizational forms that make it possible for them to encounter new possible conditions in the future (as opposed to the idea of "fitting in" with the environmental demands of the present). The adaptations are organic (systemic) growths oriented toward a set of future possibilities (which, because they do not exist in the present, cannot be precisely defined). Nevertheless, these new forms canalize the further encounters of the organism with the environment, as described in Bergson's (1911) discussion of the canalizing involved in vision (pp. 105–108) and the role of concepts in canalizing conscious processes (pp. 305–308). Regarding creative adaptation, the organizational forms that emerge in adaptation go beyond "fitting with" the present state of the survival conditions; they set the basis for facing the challenges of possible future demands. Bergson's kind of adaptation is a prime example of the relevance of "goodness of misfit" in the process of development (Valsiner & Cairns, 1992).

It is not coincidental that the history of equilibration models is closely linked with that of developmental biology and philosophy, rather than psychology. At the turn of the 20th century, thinkers were eager to solve grand problems of the natural and human worlds, rather than worry about maintaining (or overcoming) disciplinary boundaries. Thus, Bergson's ideas were based on an integration of the biological, physical, and social topics of his time; Baldwin moved from observing his children to making contributions to evolutionary theory; and so on. Only later was there talk about a scientist being an "X" rather than a "Y" in one's formal identification. When a biology-minded Swiss youngster named Jean Piaget became involved, through a series of coincidences, in the study of human mental development, the questions of "Piaget as psychologist or biologist" were raised. It may suffice to emphasize that the general biological focus—together with the autonomous character of the author, led to Piaget's contributions to our understanding of development.

Piaget's Model

Piaget's constructivist perspective on the creation of personal and social knowledge emerged at the intersection of his psychodynamic orientation and psychometric study tasks. (An autobiographic retrospect is given in Piaget, 1952; also see Chapman, 1988.) Piaget followed the more general theoretical leads of Henri Bergson and James Mark Baldwin, as well as those of Pierre Janet (Amann-Gainotti, 1992; Amann-Gainotti & Ducret, 1992). Undoubtedly, his orientation was far more directly concentrated on the individual person as a constructor of knowledge, and largely overlooked the "social context."

Piaget looked at genetic epistemology from his dynamic structuralist perspective. He was ambiguous about the stance of this perspective in terms of evolutionary thought (Hooker, 1994). Piaget's structuralism was a continuation of the gestalt psychological thought, yet it posed as a "third alternative" to elementaristic empiricism and holistic philosophizing (Piaget, 1970a, 1971b, chapter 1). Thus, by *genetic epistemology,* Piaget had in mind "study of the way in which the subject constructs and organizes his knowledge during his historical development (ontogenetic and sociogenetic)" (Piaget, 1965, p. 31). The study of the

construction of knowledge allows for an understanding of the structure that is being constructed.

Structure and Function

A structure contains "certain unifying elements and connections, but these elements cannot be singled out or defined independently of the connections involved" (Piaget, 1971a, p. 139). Because the structures are dynamic, they function in the context of their wider structural ties:

> [F]unction is the action exerted by the functioning of a substructure on that of the total structure, whether the latter be itself a substructure containing the former or the structure of the entire organism. (p. 141)

Piaget's dynamic structuralism was aimed at capturing both the developmental process and the continuity (maintenance) of existing organizational forms. The latter aspect has led investigators (e.g., Fabricius, 1983) to trace the philosophical influences of Immanuel Kant in Piaget's thought, and the former aspect can be linked with Piaget's continuing concern with creativity in evolution and the philosophy of Henri Bergson (see Bergson, 1911; Chapman, 1988, 1992; Piaget, 1952). Given researchers' usual habit of viewing ideas in their static form, Piaget's version of structuralism has often been presented as something difficult to grasp (e.g., the notion of "schema") or inconsistent with the notion of construction. However, in appropriating Piaget's thinking, cognitive models are liable to perceptive error, and the unity of structure and its change is overlooked. Piaget explicitly stated that it is impossible to separate the organization and the adaptation of a structure; an organized system of knowledge is an open system and hence is interdependent with its environment.

Piaget's building of his theoretical system on the open-systemic nature of knowledge construction led him to address the issues of possibilities, impossibilities, and necessities (Piaget, 1986; Piaget & Voyat, 1979; Vuyk, 1981). The process of knowledge construction is dynamic—each possibility for structural transformation is an outcome of a previous transformation that has made it possible to move on to the next structural state. The basis for this dynamic restructuring process is the general property of autoregulation, which plays a role at all levels of organismic unity, from the most biological (the generation of proteins by interaction of the genome with the environment, see

Wahlsten & Gottlieb, 1997) to the most psychological and social (the cognitive construction of schemas).

Piaget's Equilibration Model: Progressing Equilibrium

The main developmental mechanism that emerged from Piaget's mostly empirical research (done quite slowly, over four decades, until 1957) is the notion of equilibration (Moessinger, 1978; Rowell, 1983). Piaget's equilibration encompasses progressing equilibration (*equilibration majorante*), a process that would not reach an equilibrium state. Hence, Piaget's notion of development is open-ended in its constructivity of new structures:

> We can observe a process (hence the term "equilibration") leading from certain states of equilibrium to others, qualitatively different, and passing through multiple "nonbalances" and reequilibrations. Thus the problems to be solved involve various forms of equilibrium, the reasons for nonbalance, and above all the causal mechanisms, or methods, of equilibrations and reequilibrations. It is especially important to stress from the very beginning the fact that, *in certain cases, the reequilibrations merely form returns to previous equilibriums;* however, those that are fundamental for development consist, on the contrary, in the formation not only of new equilibriums but also in general of better equilibriums. We can, therefore, speak of "increasing equilibrations," and raise the question of self-organization. (Piaget, 1977, pp. 3–4, emphasis added)

Piaget faced an uncertain equilibrium between the mindsets of classical logic and of the Bergsonian focus on irreversible duration. In the former, the thought processes were free of the irreversibility of time; hence, one could introduce concepts such as reversible operations, regression to previous equilibria, and so on. In contrast, within the Bergsonian mindset, phenomena that look like "regressions" are actually dedifferentiations of more complex previous structures that are now similar to, but not identical with, some previous states. It can be argued (Valsiner, 1987, pp. 52–58) that Piaget's theoretical construction was imbued by that tension all through his career, and it lead to inconsistencies in his various expressions of the notion of equilibration.

Piaget relied heavily on the notion of equilibration as a process that contains two part-processes: (a) assimilation and (b) accommodation. Assimilation entails the "integration of external elements into evolving or completed structures" (Piaget, 1970b, p. 706). Accommodation is defined by Piaget as "any modification of an assimilatory scheme or structure by the elements it assimilates" (p. 708). Piaget created these two part-processes of the progressing equilibration as mutually interdependent components of the same functional whole:

> [A]ssimilation and accommodation are not two separate functions but the two functional poles, set in opposition to each other, of any adaptation. So it is only by abstraction that one can speak of assimilation alone . . . but it must always be remembered that there can be no assimilation of anything into the organism or its functioning without a corresponding accommodation. . . . (Piaget, 1971a, p. 173)

Ironically, many psychologists' renderings of Piaget's equilibration notion have failed to recognize this mutuality of the two processes. Piaget himself perhaps fed the tendency to separate assimilation and accommodation, when he wrote about their relationships in terms of a "balance" or "ratio" (e.g., Piaget, 1970b, p. 708).

Post-Piagetian Models

Amid the variety of models of development that have been formulated after Piaget, the focus has remained on the description of levels (or stages), rather than on elaboration of the mechanisms through which the developing child advances from one state or stage to another. Fischer's skill theory (Fischer, 1980; Fischer & Ferrar, 1987, 1992; also see Fischer & Bidell, this Volume) makes an effort to conceptualize the transition through a focus on the unevenness of development at any time. On the basis of such unevenness, the progressing equilibration (or dialectical synthesis of novelty) can be easily put into theoretical use in the model. This was attempted by Pascual-Leone (1976), but without persistence and empirical precision. The careful analysis done by Robbie Case, in the domain of children's cognitive progression, provides precision to the transition between stages (Case, 1985, 1991; Case, Hayward, Lewis, & Hurst, 1988). The issue of plasticity remains a crucial unsolved problem for post-Piagetian models of development, because the mechanism of transition from state to state may include both orderly and disorderly forms, which are difficult to conceptualize in mechanistic terms (Lerner, 1990). Equilibration models necessarily have to deal with qualitative, directed, and progressive change

(Moshman, 1997), for which there exist relatively few formalized models.

Efforts to use the contemporary fascination with "neural network" modeling (Fischer, Bullock, Rotenberg, & Raya, 1993) have raised the question of explanatory mechanisms of cognitive development and have reverted the discipline to where it was when it was still connected with the neurological sciences (e.g., see Bekhterev, 1994). Bekhterev's ever-grandiose system of a hierarchy of associative reflexes was *de facto* the model of the contemporary "neural networks" that proliferate in today's computer-based models.

MODELS REFLECTING THE UNITY OF TEACHING AND LEARNING

Both of the kinds of models considered so far—those of differentiation and equilibration—have excluded the potential presence of some purposeful "social other" from the picture of development. As a result, the developing child is presented as if he or she faces the "objective" environment "out there" and learns solely from that experience something about the objective world.

However, the objective world of the child is *purposefully subjectified* by the actions of others. All the persons surrounding the child, all who participate in the care and upbringing of the child, have their own objectives in mind while organizing the environment within which the child is to experience relevant developmental events. Hence, it is important to analyze how the joint efforts of the learner and the teacher (or, the inexperienced and the more experienced) are organized. The processes involved are much more complex than those usually described by easy reference to "learning," as has been pointed out in numerous ways (Lerner, 1995; Voss & Valsiner, 1996).

What are the models of teaching and learning like? Given the social–relational complexity of the process of teaching and learning, the models considered here are less clearly defined than the differentiation and equilibration models described earlier. A major issue here is the multilevel nature of the simultaneous teaching–learning processes, which follows from the notion of differentiation (Lerner, 1979).

In their most general form, models of teaching and learning entail two asymmetrically related partners (persons, or social institutions), and the subdominant partner is assumed to be oriented toward further development by using the input from the dominant one. The particular kinds of relations between the two are the focus of teaching–learning models.

Theories of learning per se have proceeded far beyond the traditions of a build-up of associationistic connections, and have started to emphasize the dynamic relationships of the organism with the environment (Voss, 1996). In human learning processes, the unity of the subjective reflection and the object of mastery of novel capacities has led to synthesis of the traditionally separated "understanding" and "explaining" psychologies (Groeben, 1986). The traditional views on learning have come closer to the perspectives that emphasize its (human) parallel component process—instruction, or teaching. Hence, we can talk of the unified processes of teaching and learning, where the goal-directed intentions and actions of the teachers are negotiated through the actions and intentions of the learners. The resulting teaching–learning process is co-constructionist, and theoretical models emphasize the nature of the process. Not surprisingly, the notion of a "zone of proximal development," a metaphor used by Lev Vygotsky, has been borrowed in multiple versions.

The Zone of Proximal Development (ZPD)—Movement in Irreversible Time

The ZPD is usually defined as the difference between what a child can accomplish with guidance, and what he or she can achieve through individual effort and solo performance (i.e., the sociocentric definition); or, the process in which the child transcends his or her own present level of development through constructive play (Vygotsky, 1933/1966). In both cases, the concept is taken hostage by the realities of irreversible time (Valsiner & Van der Veer, 1993).

Irreversibility of time sets up very specific demands for the developing child. First, a person is always the agent in any ongoing interaction with the environment, and because other agents are only episodically involved, no "social other" can live the life of the individual developing child. The developing child's flow of experiencing is unique (as was emphasized by Bergson), and although that flow is constituted through social interaction, its psychological nature remains a personal and inevitably subjective "time-dependent egocentrism" of development. The role of the social other is not diminished in the course of human development, but the focus remains on the developing child, the only person who is knowledgeable about his or her own life experiences (Valsiner, 1989a).

Second, the personal experiencing process—a microgenesis of action within environment—sets up the *possible* conditions for the construction of the immediate next moment in one's personal experience. Out of those possibilities, the actual experience charts the actual next present moment (formerly, the nearest future moment). The synthesizing functions of the person's psychological system remain crucial; they accomplish learning *with or without* immediate social support (in the form of scaffolding, or teaching). Thus, the role of the social other in the learning process is simultaneously important and unimportant. The social other sets up the environments that are experienced by the developing person, but the presence of a social other in each and every encounter of the child with the environment is not necessary (nor is it possible). The developing child experiences both individual and socially guided encounters with the world as a singular person, integrated within self.

Historical Roots

The origin of the notion of the ZPD remains veiled in historical mystery. Contrary to Vygotsky's own claim that he borrowed the notion from Ernest Meumann and Dorothea McCarthy, traces of it have not been found in their work (see Van der Veer & Valsiner, 1991, for a detailed analysis of this historical mystery). However, metaphoric expressions very similar to the nature of the ZPD idea can be found elsewhere—for example, in this passage by Henri Bergson:

> [C]onsciousness is the light that plays around the zone of possible actions or potential activity [French: *activité virtuelle*] which surrounds the action really performed [French: *qui entoure l'action effectivement accompli*] by the living being. It signifies hesitation or choice. Where many equally possible actions are indicated without there being any real action (as in a deliberation that has not come to an end), consciousness is intense. Where the action performed is the only action possible (as in activity of the somnambulistic or more generally automatic kind), consciousness is reduced to nothing. Representation and knowledge exist none the less in the case if we find a whole series of systematized movements the last of which is already prefigured in the first, and if, besides, consciousness can flash out of them at the shock of an obstacle. From this point of view, *the consciousness of a living being*

> *may be defined as an arithmetical difference between potential [virtuelle] and real activity. It measures the interval between representation and action.* (Bergson, 1911, pp. 159–160; French original inserts from Bergson, 1945, pp. 154–155)

If we leave aside Bergson's occasional return to mechanistic concepts (i.e., of "arithmetical difference"), the rest of his conceptualization of the constructive nature of consciousness seems very modern. During the life course, the developing person constantly faces complex choice points where new actions (and their semiotic representations) need to be constructed. These constructions are nearest "neighbors" to the already existing actions. The person constantly moves beyond previously established states, to areas of acting and thinking that have not yet been actualized. This is the essence of the zone of proximal development, later used as a convenient metaphor by Vygotsky.

Epistemological Bases

The central question of teaching–learning models is: *How can one person be—and/or become—like another?* The very encounter of persons in teaching–learning contexts entails purposeful efforts of at least some of them (e.g., the teachers) to encourage the others (the students) to be like some ideal role/goal model. Yet any learner, while perhaps developing toward such a designated goal-state, retains his or her unique individuality. Persons can only act *as if* they were the other; in reality, they always remain themselves.

At the turn of the 20th century, the focus on human *as-if (als-ob)* type actions was systematically analyzed by Hans Vaihinger (1920). Development necessarily entails construction of an as-if (or, desired-state) image, which the developing person then strives for. The basic duality that guides human development is a constant process of construction of the contrast between the present state (as is) and the desired state (as if). This contrast requires that the constant empathic processes between the two states be relevant. The developing person has to feel his or her way into the set-up as-if state, and act in order to overcome this difference.

Similar issues were raised within the aesthetic theory of *Einfühlung* of Theodor Lipps (1903, 1923; Witasek, 1901). The question—How can an observer of an object of art experience feelings similar to those of the object's author or those of another observer?—was a relevant general question about human understanding (Wispé, 1987). On the basis of early childhood empathy, sophisticated versions of aesthetic experiencing can develop in ontogeny. The latter can be viewed as complex forms of coordination between the differentiated as-is ↔ as-if structures as those unfold in time. Vygotsky's focus on "dialectical synthesis" (1925/1971) and Baldwin's focus on aesthetic semblance (1911, 1915) were examples of theoretical constructions that elaborated that major issue.

Today, the question of an as-if type of existence is largely subsumed under the label of *intersubjectivity*. The basis for any construction of intersubjectivity is a set of fundamental axioms that are taken for granted in the social world:

> [F]irst, the existence of intelligent (endowed with consciousness) fellow-men and, second, the experienceability (in principle similar to mine) by my fellow-men of the objects in the life-world. . . . I know that "the same" Object must necessarily show different aspects to each of us. First, because the world in my reach cannot be identical with the world in your reach, etc.; because my here is your there; and because my zone of operation is not the same as yours. And, second, because my biographical situation with its relevance systems, hierarchies of plans, etc., is not yours and, consequently, the explications of the horizon of objects in my case and yours could take entirely different directions. . . . (Schütz & Luckmann, 1973, p. 59)

Two socially constructed idealizations are involved here: (a) *interchangeability of standpoints,* and (b) *congruence of relevance systems* (Schütz & Luckmann, 1973, p. 60). Any teaching–learning situation is at odds with this notion of intersubjectivity. The teacher's standpoint (role) is not interchangeable with that of the student, and the congruence of the relevance systems of the teacher with those of the learner need not be taken for granted. From that perspective, the ZPD is necessarily a concept in which the teacher and learner roles are interdependent and asymmetric. The teacher attempts to "keep" the learner within his or her "zone of operation" (as generated by the teaching goals), but the learner may attempt to renegotiate the limits of his or her zone. Focus on the process of negotiation is the crucial feature of co-constructionist approaches to human development (Valsiner, 1994b). Furthermore, the parallel teleology of the teaching–learning process, which is goal-directed in the acting of both teachers and learners, sets up novel demands for methodology (see below).

Methodological Repercussions

The ZPD concept faces the possible immediate futures of the developmental process in all their levels of relative indeterminacy. It entails efforts to reflect the *present* process of emergence of new psychological functions, which will become discernible *in the near future*. Thus, from the point of view of detection (or "measurement"—a word more often used by psychologists), the ZPD concept is necessarily ephemeral because it is impossible to detect (i.e., match with a model of established form) a form that is only presently in the process of becoming. Developmental psychology is in need of creating descriptive categories with open ends (e.g., "actual $x \rightarrow$ <followed by> possible y or z"). The set of possibilities at the next time step can be attached to the detection of an actual detected form. Thus, detecting a behavioral form of aggression in the actions of a 3-year-old (and accumulating instances of a similar kind over observation time) tells us nothing about the teaching–learning process going on at the given time. Exactly the same observed behavior can be recorded, together with its potential next aftermaths (e.g., "escalation of aggression," "turn to a friendly interchange," "escape from the field"), to provide us with a possible functional context of the detected single case of "aggressive behavior."

Teaching Experiments

The axiom of sociogenetic primacy—that psychological functions first emerge in the interpsychological sphere and subsequently become established in the intrapsychological one—has been used to support the use of teaching experiments. Efforts of intervention (teaching), whether they succeed or fail, are expected to allow access to the *emerging* psychological functions at the given present. A successful teaching of X is taken as proof that X was within the zone of proximal development at the time when the teaching effort started. Conversely, if the teaching effort fails, the opposite conclusion is likely: Whatever was taught was not (or not yet) within the ZPD (Valsiner & Van der Veer, 1993).

This inferential frame applied to teaching experiments is actually one of simple cause → effect, and it contradicts the open-system nature of human development. Such projection axiomatically eliminates the open-endedness (constructivity) of development. What is (and is not) projected into the ZPD depends on the success (or luck) of the microgenetic intervention, and on the process of encounter between the social other and the developing person (our target organism). A teaching experiment is merely a context in which one of the two teleological orientations (i.e., the goal of the teacher) is relatively fixed in its direction, while the other (the goal of the learner) is not (and cannot be) assumed to have similar directionality (Branco & Valsiner, 1992, 1996). Rather, the learner has a possibility to converge or diverge in matching his or her goal orientations with those of the teacher. The learner can likewise assume a neutral or noncooperative stance, thereby undermining the teaching efforts. As a result, it is not possible to "measure" the ZPD on the basis of the mere success or failure of a teaching experiment (i.e., on the basis of outcomes of the teaching efforts). Instead, a direct look at the process of joint construction of a teaching–learning event can give the investigator an insight into the learner's move beyond the present state of development.

Contemporary Teaching–Learning Models

Despite the theoretical complications of the ZPD concept (Valsiner & Van der Veer, 1993), different models that either borrow components of or use the term ZPD have been expanded in the pertinent literature over the past two decades. An analysis of major efforts of that kind reveals the contemporary state of our conceptual thought.

Participatory Appropriation

Rogoff has attempted to make sense of the teaching–learning processes through a focus on participatory observational learning in cultural contexts for activities (Rogoff, 1990, 1992, 1993; Rogoff & Lave, 1984). Rogoff is consistent in her emphasis on context-linkage of all developmental processes all of the time (Rogoff, 1990, 1993). She provides an explicit solution to the problem of the context— the *sociocultural activity,* which involves "active participation of people in socially constituted practices" (Rogoff, 1990, p. 14), acts in the role of the unit of analysis. Within that unit, persons are involved in interactive problem solving rather than in lengthy intrapersonal contemplations or "soul-searching." Rogoff's notion of *participatory appropriation* entails acceptance of transformation of cultural forms into novel states (both by persons and by groups): "[P]articipatory appropriation involves individuals changing through their own *adjustments* and *understanding* of

the sociocultural activity" (Rogoff, 1993, p. 141, emphasis added).

When studying situated activities, microgenetic (specific problem solving) and ontogenetic aspects of development become united in Rogoff's model. The active (but not always persistent) guidance by the social others of the developing person is complemented by the person's own constructive role in his or her own development. The child is always an *active* apprentice who participates in the socially guided activity settings. The metaphor of apprenticeship allows Rogoff to emphasize the active-but-subordinate role of the developing child in his or her ontogeny.

Rogoff's theory entails dynamically coordinated interdependence between guidance and apprenticeship. This interdependence makes it possible for her theory to overcome the individualistic ethos of most of the existing psychological theories, which omit systemic (i.e., coordination of parts of the system and its environment) and dynamic notions from their conceptual texture.

Cole's Model of ZOPED

Cole's emphasis on the unity of teaching and learning processes emerges from his studies of cultural tools (Cole, 1995; Newman, Griffin, & Cole, 1989; Scribner & Cole, 1981). His theoretical construction is based on "cultural practice theory" (Laboratory of Comparative Human Cognition, 1983; hereinafter, LCHC).

The problem of relationships between microgenetic (situationally emerging) and ontogenetic phenomena in human development occupies the central focus of cultural practice theory. Cole has been interested in the ways in which context *selection* (LCHC, 1983, pp. 332–333) and *creation* (Newman, Griffin, & Cole, 1989, p. 12) are socioculturally organized. Cole's consistent interest in the notion of a zone of proximal development is congruent with his claim that "a cultural practice theory takes cultural contexts, that is, socially assembled situations, not individual persons or abstract cultural dimensions as the unit of analysis" (LCHC, 1983, p. 334). The main mechanism by which culture and person are related is that of *mutual interweaving.* Cole (1992, p. 26) uses the metaphor of "intermingling of threads from two ropes"—those of biological "modules" and cultural contexts. This interweaving reflects a general process in which "the culture becomes individual and the individuals create their culture" (LCHC, 1983, p. 349)—or, in other terms, the culture and cognition are *mutually constituted.* The locus of the mutual constituting process is in the concrete activities that are carried out in everyday life. Leontiev's (1975, 1981) activity theory serves as an appropriate theoretical tool in that context (Cole, 1985; Newman, Griffin, & Cole, 1989). The emphasis on socially organized transfer between contexts leads Cole to emphasize on the concept of appropriation (Newman, Griffin, & Cole, 1989, pp. 62–65), along the lines emphasized by Leontiev. The culture provides a range of cultural mediating devices (tools or signs) to the developing child in specific activity contexts, and the child takes over (appropriates) those cultural means, reconstructing them in the process of activity.

Wertsch's Model of Teaching and Learning through Polyphony of "Voices in the Mind"

Wertsch's work derives from the Vygotskian semiotic mediation viewpoint (Wertsch, 1979, 1983, 1995) on the one hand, and the activity theoretic perspective (Leontiev, 1981) on the other (Wertsch, 1981). In his thinking about the zone of proximal development, Wertsch looked on the dynamic process of situation redefinition as the primary means by which persons involved in a joint activity context guide one another's development. The partners are constantly in some relationship of intersubjectivity (sharing a similar situation definition), which they transcend by the process of situation redefinition (Wertsch, 1984, pp. 7–13).

By the mid-1980s, Wertsch had turned to the integration of his semiotically mediated activity approach with the wider sociolinguistic context (Wertsch, 1985; Wertsch & Stone, 1985) that has been characterized by the dynamic worldview of Mikhail Bakhtin's (1981) literary theory. Wertsch's theoretical stance thus acquires a new layer. The activity framing remains in the background of Wertsch's accounts, but the new layer of the theory entails a focus on interpretable utterance. Wertsch takes over Bakhtin's emphasis on dialogicality and makes it work for his system. The multiplicity of "voices"—appropriated by the person from the sociocultural environment—leads to study of the complexity of messages (Wertsch, 1990, 1991, 1995). The result is a consistent return to the study of ambivalences embedded in communicative messages. Different "voices" can be seen in the utterances in ways that "interanimate" or dominate each other in the act of speaking in situated activity contexts. On the basis of

these contexts, macro-level psychological phenomena—like historical identity—emerge in the process of development (Penuel & Wertsch, 1995a).

New Voices in the Study of Teaching–Learning Processes

Aside from derivations from the Vygotskian teaching–learning parent model of ZPD, new efforts are underway to rethink the educational process and to expand the empirical applications of the products of such reconceptualization. Wertsch's version of the "voices" model has given rise to a productive research tradition involving the study of interaction in the classroom (Góes, 1994; Smolka, 1990, 1994; Smolka, Fontana, & Laplane, 1994; Wertsch & Smolka, 1993). This research demonstrates how different cultural voices become appropriated in ways that create novel meanings in specific contexts (Smolka, Góes, & Pino, 1996). The notion of "voices" is currently gaining both an empirical demonstration of its relevance in the teaching–learning process (Junefeldt, 1994; Mercado, 1994), and further theoretical elaboration (Pino, 1994).

In parallel with the expansion of the voices of the mind in the field of studies of child development, the proliferation of analysis of discourse foci in the social sciences has led to a reformulation of issues of teaching and learning in terms of *discursive learning* (Edwards & Mercer, 1989; Van Oers, 1996). In conjunction with the focus on teaching–learning as a human activity (Engeström, 1990; Moll, 1992; Veggetti, 1994), researchers increasingly direct their focus to the study of actual interaction processes in the classroom, in conjunction with the curricular tasks set up by the educational institutions (Colomina & Rochera, 1992; De Gispert & Colomina, 1994; Onrubia & Mayordomo, 1994; Segués & Onrubia, 1992). Coll and his colleagues (Coll & Onrubia, 1994; Coll, Colomina, Onrubia, & Rochera, 1992) have focused on two intertwined processes that are taking place in the area of teaching and learning: (a) *progressive cessation and transfer of control* (from the teacher to the student), and (b) *construction of a system of shared meanings.* The latter necessitates the study of dialogue between teachers and children in the classroom, and the utilization of units of analysis that preserve the complexity of the meaning negotiations *(didactic sequences).* The generic notion of ZPD is assumed to be made specific through the study of meaning negotiations as these are accessible in these didactic sequences.

Numerous efforts exist to provide concrete elaborations for the ZPD concept. Some (e.g., Calil, 1994; Ignjatovic-Savic, Kovac-Cerovac, Plut, & Pesikan, 1988; Moll, 1990; Portes, Smith, & Cuentas, 1994) attempt to measure differences between different posited "zones" of action; others try to clarify the relations of that concept with other close concepts (e.g., "scaffolding"—Rojas-Drummond & Rico, 1994; "situated cognitive representations"—Saada-Robert, 1994). Further extension of the ZPD model into the domain of semiotic mediation leads to relating of teaching–learning processes to the meaningfulness of everyday life contexts (Altman, 1993; Alvarez, 1994; Del Rio & Alvarez, 1992; Fuhrer, 1993; Fuhrer, Kaiser, & Hangartner, 1995).

Differentiation of Actions and Reflection

Pablo Del Rio (1990, 1994; Del Rio & Alvarez, 1995) has extended the ZPD model to include its cultural–psychological counterpart in the realm of "stream of consciousness"—the *zone of syncretic representation* (ZSR). This zone includes a set of frames and operators that are based on action, but, as part of their coming into existence, they start to provide meaning for future actions and life events. These concepts are represent-actions (Del Rio, 1994, p. 22)—syncretic complexes of action and representation—and Del Rio says of them:

> [They] articulate both the organism and the environment, the setting of the action and the representation, whether individually or shared, [and they] seem to point towards a reconceptualization of the context in which, more than being a simple setting for executing the products of the mind or for receiving information, it takes on the role of an essential part of the very scheme of individual and shared psychological activity. (p. 22)

The ZSR constitutes an "extracortical brain" of sociocultural nature. It can be studied through analysis of the semiotics of immediate everyday life environments (Del Rio & Alvarez, 1992, 1995). On the basis of their activity, human beings construct complex semiotic devices that are used to regulate their conduct. Thus, generalized and undefinable concepts such as "the Castillian soul" (Del Rio & Alvarez, 1995), or "historical identity" (Penuel & Wertsch,

1995b) emerge as meaning complexes that are worth careful investigation.

Del Rio's effort to link the human syncretic repertoire of cultural mediating devices parallels the German tradition of cultural psychology (Boesch, 1983, 1989, 1991), which concentrates on the construction of personal meanings *(fantasms)* at the intersection of acting and experiencing collective–cultural myths (stories) in society. A similar direction is emerging from the neo-Gibsonian constructivism of Reed (1993, 1995). The social focus on teaching–learning also permeates Bronfenbrenner's developmental ideas (Bronfenbrenner, 1979, 1989; this Volume; Bronfenbrenner & Crouter, 1983; Bronfenbrenner & Ceci, 1994). In turn, one of the recent efforts to build a novel methodological scheme following the work of Lev Vygotsky has been undertaken by Ratner (1991). Ratner's efforts are predicated on a need to treat the children's developmental environments from a systemic perspective, for which he creates a symbiotic relationship between Vygotsky and Bronfenbrenner.

Summary: Conceptualizing Teaching–Learning Processes

It has been interesting to analyze the complications that irreversibility of time produces for models of teaching and learning. Bergson's (1911) description of development indicates how states of being and processes of becoming are difficult to interrelate:

> That the child can become a youth, ripen to maturity and decline to old age, we understand when we consider that vital evolution is here the reality itself. Infancy, adolescence, maturity, old age, are mere views of the mind, *possible steps* imagined by us, from without, along the continuity of a progress. On the contrary, let childhood, adolescence, maturity and old age be given as integral parts of the evolution, they become *real stops,* and we can no longer conceive how evolution is possible, for rests placed beside rests will never be equivalent to a movement. How, with what is made, can we reconstitute what is being made? How, for instance, from childhood once posited as a *thing,* shall we pass to adolescence, when, by the hypothesis, childhood only is given. . . ? . . . all that we have to do, in fact, is to give up the cinematographical habits of our intellect. When we say "The child becomes a man," let us take care not to fathom too deeply the literal meaning of the expression, or we shall find that, when we posit the subject "child," the attribute "man" does not yet apply to it, and that, when we express the attribute "man," it

applies no more to the subject "child." The reality, which is the transition from childhood to manhood, has slipped between our fingers. . . . (pp. 339–340)

Bergson's views antedate the problems of modeling teaching–learning processes. Our common language prescribes description not of those processes—fuzzy and dynamic though they are—but of their intermediate relatively stable outcomes. Thus, we easily talk about the child "knowing X" at age W, and "knowing Y" at age W + 1. Such analysis reconstructs the process of learning *as if* it were similar to a film that owes its existence to a sequential projection of still-frames on the screen. In terms of the ZPD "talk" described above, any contrast of "actual" and "potential" states of development reflects that cinematographic image (which, for Bergson, was an obstacle to understanding the underlying process). Almost 100 years after Bergson, the criticism of such cinematographic images is still relevant for our theorizing about learning and development:

> A sequence of film frames is a finished, well-defined product, the effects of which are predetermined by the synchronization of the projection speed with the processing parameters of the human visual system. In contrast, phenomena of learning processes entail the active participation of the organism in its given state in the creation of the next stage. If we were to apply this notion to the film analogy, we would get a film in which (in the beginning of the projection onto the screen) it is not yet clear which frames may be projected next, and in which the previous and presently projected frames are probabilistically determining the nature of the next frames to come. If such a film were ever possible, it would amount to a highly uncertain experience for the viewer, who could not predict what the next experience would be like. Last (but not least), the simple physical system of static images projected in a time sequence would never fit as the model for open-systemic processes. (Voss & Valsiner, 1996, p. 330)

Different versions of the teaching–learning models described here have been conceptually stuck between the need to explicate the process of learning, on the one hand, and to describe a set of outcomes in time sequence, on the other. As long as those models have made use of the latter terminology (e.g., "At stage X, the child can learn Y if taught in way Z"), the actual process of how the teaching–learning takes place remains hidden from the focus of research. Our contemporary efforts to concentrate on the complexity of the actual interaction phenomena within the teaching–learning settings may provide a wealth of empirical evidence about the loose structuring and high dynamicity of the teaching–learning process. However, if there are no matching theoretical models of such processes, meaningfulness of the empirical data is not yet obvious.

INTERSECTIONS AMONG THE THREE KINDS OF MODELS

Development has been understood by the users of all three types of models described here as constructive transformation of form in irreversible time through the process of organism ↔ environment interchange. Development entails emergence of qualitatively new forms (i.e., it is a constructive process) that lead to new ways of interchange of the organism with its environment.

The three kinds of models intersect in a number of ways. Differentiation models—while focusing on the structural transformation of the system—often utilize equilibration terminology to explain how the transformation processes actually proceed. The teaching–learning models can add the social context to the differentiation–equilibration complex. Thus, Vygotsky's theoretical model of development (for which the ZPD concept was merely a metaphorical extension; Valsiner & Van der Veer, 1993) is a teaching–learning model that uses differentiation as well as disequilibration (i.e., dialectical synthesis emerging from disequilibriae) in its conceptual structure. Nevertheless, the main focus of attention for Vygotsky remained on the teaching–learning process (*obuchenie*). In a similar vein, Werner's primary emphasis on differentiation was not antithetical to the teaching–learning models' support of such differentiation.

A theoretical tradition that unifies the three models is that of Ernest Boesch (1983, 1991). Built explicitly along the lines of the field theory of Kurt Lewin and the equilibration notions of Jean Piaget, and in an attempt to give a semiotic account of the processes of human thinking, Boesch's model creates a system of cultural developmental psychology. It has been developed further by other members of the Saarbrücken Group of cultural psychology (Eckensberger, 1995; Krewer, 1992).

A feature that emerges from all of the models is *relevance*—the developing organism participates in its own development beyond merely "fitting in" with the environmental conditions. Instead, development includes construction of novel forms in anticipation of *possible future conditions* of organism ↔ environment interchanges. Surely such feed-forward orientation of development fits the irreversible nature of developmental time; yet it is exactly that feature that acts as the central complication for the construction of developmental methodology.

METHODOLOGICAL IMPLICATIONS

The major role of methodology in any science is in granting consistency between abstract and concrete—theoretical and empirical—facets of the research process, while keeping in close touch with the phenomena that are the object of investigation (Branco & Valsiner, 1997; Winegar & Valsiner, 1992). Developmental psychology has been in a severe methodological crisis during recent decades because, in most cases, its empirical enterprise and assumed theoretical stance have not been consistent with one another (Valsiner, 1997, chapter 3). The reasons for this crisis are clear if we return to the notion of development. In a definition similar to the one utilized earlier in this chapter, Ford and Lerner (1992) have outlined a systemic view on the issue:

> Individual human development involves *incremental and transformational processes* that, through a *flow of* interactions among current characteristics of the person and his or her current contexts, produces *a succession of* relatively enduring changes that *elaborate or increase* the diversity of the person's structural and functional characteristics and the patterns of their environmental interactions *while maintaining* coherent organization and structural-functional unity of the person as a whole. (p. 49, emphasis added)

Each of the emphasized facets of this definition leads to the need to reconceptualize child psychology's socially conventional ways of deriving the data from the phenomena (Kindermann & Valsiner, 1989). First, the *flow* of interactions between person and context leads to the need to utilize time-preserving analytic units in the empirical research. Such units would be characterized by time-based description of *transformation* of the phenomenon under

study in a specifiable direction. Ford and Lerner (1992, pp. 140–142) formulate the notion of *behavior episode schemas* as an example of time-based units of analysis. In repeated everyday-life contexts, persons construct generalized schemas that would guide their actions in similar-looking settings, depending on their goals. The centrality of the goal-oriented nature of action makes such behavior episode schemas possible to detect. A similar use of molar-level time-bound analytic units occurs in the case of analysis of interaction into *didactic sequences* (Coll & Onrubia, 1994).

Second, the emphasis on emerging *diversity* in the phenomena under study requires that the methods preserve the *variability within the phenomena* when data are being derived. This applies both to intraindividual variability (or variability of the same developing system in its relationship with its context over time) and to interindividual variability (i.e., variability between the systems-within-their-environments). In the practice of child psychology, the latter kind of variability is usually given attention (the so-called "study of individual differences"), but that variability is rarely used as the phenomenon under study (Cox, Ornstein, & Valsiner, 1991; Valsiner, 1984).

Third, the maintenance of *coherent organization* requires from data derivation procedures the use of molar-level systemic units of analysis (i.e., refusal to reduce the phenomena to their elements). This entails individual profile analyses of specific phenomena observable in development (Magnusson, 1988; Magnusson & Stattin, this Volume), in ways that demonstrate both the continuity of the system (coherence) and its flexible transformations over time. Microgenetic methodology necessarily becomes central for developmental research (Draguns, 1984; Siegler & Crowley, 1991). However, the distinction between microgenetic and ontogenetic levels of organization creates a formidable difficulty for the uses of microgenetic methods and for making inferences about ontogenetic changes (Saada-Robert, 1994). All of these implications for developmental methodology lead to the question of which models of causality are appropriate to use in conjunction with models of development (Fentress, 1989).

Models of Assumed Causality

Child psychology cannot productively make use of linear models of causality (X causes Y, or X causes Y given Z; Valsiner, 1987, 1989) and is in need of assuming systemic ones (e.g., a system A-B-C leads to Y; or, a system A-B-C, given catalytic conditions P-Q, leads to Y). These systemic versions of causality entail researchers' focus on cyclical systemic processes that lead to "caused outcomes" mostly as by-products of the self-regenerating (maintaining) activity of the causal system. In this respect, causality in development can be taken to be reciprocal or mutual (Ford & Lerner, 1992, pp. 56–58; Lewin, 1943; Weiss, 1969, 1978). Such cyclical models are normal assumptions in the field of biology (e.g., the "Krebs cycle"), but are rare in psychology.

Furthermore, the assumed causal systems can be viewed not only as reverberating in their established cycles, but as autopoietic in their nature (Maturana, 1980). Under certain conditions, the causal systems innovate themselves by constructing a new part to be incorporated into themselves, or by reorganizing the processes that unite the parts within the system. This possibility creates a specific condition for the study of development, because it renders it impossible to infer, from the outcomes of some developmental process, anything about the causal system that produces the outcome. If an outcome X can be detected, it is not possible to infer that the previously proven causal system (A-B-C) has produced it. The causal system might have modified itself since the time when such proof was obtained previously, and it may *maintain* the outcome X currently in a novel way (e.g., the causal system has changed to A-B-C-D). In a similar way, if a change in the outcome (e.g., Y instead of X) is detected, it is not possible to assume that the previously proven causal system (A-B-C) has changed (into A-B-C-D). It is first necessary to prove that this new outcome could not emerge from the functioning of the previous system. The very same outcome in development can be reached (or maintained) via different causal systems (i.e., the equifinality principle, a characteristic of all open systems), and different outcomes can be generated by the same causal system. This theoretical aspect of development has been noted as a complicating issue for empirical research practices (Baltes & Nesselroade, 1973), and has particular repercussions for human development (Bornstein, 1995; Kojima, 1995).

In the case of human development, the open-systemic nature of the developmental processes entails the possibility for flexible reconstruction (and preconstruction) of semiotic mediating devices (see Bornstein, 1995, p. 130) that would lead to personal construction of goal orientations, and would involve pursuing those in ways that transcend the immediate demand characteristics of any environmental or social context (Valsiner, 1994b, 1996a). The notion of the open-systemic nature of development has been well known in developmental biology for many decades (Bertalanffy, 1950, 1960); yet, in psychology, the need to reiterate it seems to recur with some persistence.

Culture in Human Development

By the close of the 20th century, it became understood in psychology that it is not possible to ignore the major characteristic of human psychological phenomena—their socially constructed meaningfulness. The dream-science of Ebbinghaus, based on the use of nonsense materials, has been demonstrated to have been only a bad dream (for science), and the long denial of the semiotic organization of human psychological phenomena is currently over.

The emergence of various kinds of "cultural psychology" in conjunction with issues of developmental psychology (Boesch, 1989, 1991; Cole, 1990, 1995; Obeyesekere, 1990; Shweder, 1991, 1995; Shweder & Sullivan, 1990, 1993; for reviews, see Jahoda, 1993, 1995; Krewer, 1992; Valsiner, 1997d) provides indication of a tendency to break through the traditions of meanings-avoidance that have been the core of the crisis in the discipline (Bühler, 1927/1978; Vygotsky, 1927/1982). It can be argued that human psychological phenomena exist within the *semiosphere*—a sphere of semiotic signs (Lotman, 1992) being constituted and reconstituted by active persons who are involved in processes of acting and reflecting on actions in parallel.

Semiosphere and Research Methods in Psychology

If the semiosphere of human development is included in the models of development, then most of the assumptions about specific methods, and the notion of the "objectivity" of those methods (Danziger, 1990; Daston, 1988, 1992; Porter, 1994), need reformulation. All methods used habitually by psychologists to collect data—observation, experiment, interview, questionnaire/inventory—become domains of *joint construction* of information by the investigator and the subject (e.g., Hermans, 1991, 1995; Santamaria, 1994). If this is the case, it would be an illusion to consider the investigator as having no impact on the data-collection process. Instead, research involves joint negotiation of meaning of the phenomena, as those are transformed into data.

If the process of research becomes viewed as co-construction of knowledge, then the question of parsimony becomes a methodological problem of major scope. The semiotic construction of knowledge includes the danger of creating jointly "consensually validated" knowledge that in reality is either more complex than the original phenomena or simply a misfit with reality. The principle of parsimony—the rule that the simplest explanation, among the many that are possible, is to be preferred—has served psychology well in its efforts to distinguish its explanations from the mystical constructions of laypeople and social institutions.

If we consider psychological phenomena simultaneously being structured at different levels of organization, the old principle of parsimony—which has legitimized atomistic reductionism—becomes problematic. No longer can explanations for psychological phenomena be acceptable in terms of reduction of the complexity to the lower-level functioning of explanatory mechanisms. Rather, the causal system can be constructed in terms of interlevel integration.

Uses of "Morgan's Canon": From Reductionism to Systemic Analysis

The emphasis on the irreversible, constructive, and hierarchically redundant nature of development leads to a basic necessity to set up clear methodological ground rules through which explanation of development is possible. The principle of parsimony ("Morgan's Canon") has served as the constraint that has guided a number of generations of researchers toward creation of nonsystemic, elementaristic, causal explanations. The canonical form of Morgan's Canon has usually been given in the following terms:

> In no case may we interpret an action as the outcome of the exercise of a higher psychical faculty, if it can be interpreted as the outcome of the exercise of one which stands lower in the psychological scale. (Morgan, 1894, p. 53)

Leaving aside the selectivity of psychologists' construction of the principle of parsimony by borrowing this quote out of the context of the rest of Morgan's texture of thought, it can be emphasized that this principle—as stated—effectively blocks the construction of systemic-causal explanations of development (Lerner, 1995). It forces the investigator to overlook the emergence of new regulatory mechanisms that operate *between* adjacent (i.e.,

both "lower" and "next higher") levels of the "psychological scale." Developmentally, the emergence of a new regulatory mechanism (e.g., a higher-level semiotic mediating device, in the intra- or interpsychological spheres) may be initially "fragile" and ill-formed. Development entails such transitional forms between levels—the higher levels are constantly in formation; yet, before they are formed, they cannot be clearly detected. Hence, the canonical interpretation of Morgan's Canon makes it impossible to explain development. Although development entails the emergence of hierarchically complex regulatory mechanisms (i.e., differentiation), research efforts that follow Morgan's Canon guide psychology's methodology to be directedly "blind" to exactly such emerging mechanisms.

This contrast may be used as an example of high-level semiotic constraint of the activities of scientists who are interested in human development. The "blind spot" in developmental psychology's activities is generated through a highly abstract constraint that has operated across the history of the discipline, and over a varied range of specific research topics. However, it is not constructive to merely demonstrate developmental psychology's self-constraints. Existing constraints need to be adjusted to the nature of developmental phenomena. The following reformulation could adjust the principle of parsimony to the systemic-structural conditions of development (see also Valsiner, 1997b):

> If we assume development to be a multilevel probabilistically epigenetic process, in no case may we interpret an observable (i.e., emerged) outcome as being caused by a unitary lower-level process (within the hierarchical network of processes), but always as a result of causal systemic processes that operate between levels. Attribution of causality to a singular-level ("higher," or "lower") causal system is possible *if and only if* we have ruled out any possible regulatory impacts from adjacent levels, especially by a process at the next higher level in the hierarchy.

This reformulation sets up a sequence of investigative activities in ways that at first require examination for a lack of between-levels ties. If such inquiry rules out such ties, the construction of causal explanations (of a systemic kind) within a given level is possible. *If the examination fails to rule out possible ties between levels,* then the construction of explanatory frameworks needs to retain the hierarchical (between-levels) nature of the phenomena under study, at least to the extent of the immediate next levels of the hierarchy. This latter point is important because (see above) the capacity of human development to construct its own new levels of organization (semiotic mediation) is at issue, and unless it is first proven that such levels have not emerged in a given case, would the "traditional" canonical explanation of the lower-level explanation suffice?

Hierarchies, Ideologies, and Methodology

Hierarchies are used by thinkers who construct models of child development that are ill-defined, and who advocate ideologically flavored concepts. The latter ideological connotation seems to be a transfer of societal models (of citizens' equality, in terms of political freedoms) in a Western democratic society. Given this "baggage" of connotations, the use of hierarchy concepts in differentiation models is often tentative because there is an understanding that the usual view of hierarchy—that of a "top-down," strictly controlled process—may be limiting (Ford & Lerner, 1992, p. 114).

However, hierarchies can be of different kinds and can have different stability. Hence, the use of differentiation models need not signify a reduction of the flexibility of the developmental process to some strict scheme. Any hierarchic organization can be viewed as a temporary construction (which vanishes as soon as its control function is no longer necessary). Nor are hierarchies necessarily strict in their logic.

Transitive and Intransitive Hierarchies. Any hierarchical relationship can be of two possible general kinds: (a) *linear hierarchy,* which is based on the logical relation of *transitivity* (i.e., if $A \leftrightarrow\!\!\!\gg B$ and $B \leftrightarrow\!\!\!\gg C$, then $A \leftrightarrow C$, where $\leftrightarrow$ indicates a dominance relation in an otherwise mutual relationship); or (b) *cyclical hierarchy,* which is based on intransitive relations (e.g., $A \leftrightarrow\!\!\!\gg B$ and $B \leftrightarrow\!\!\!\gg C$ *and* $C \leftrightarrow\!\!\!\gg A$). Usually, when the term *hierarchy* is used in psychology, it is the first kind of hierarchy that is being considered. For example, most of the interpretations of Werner's hierarchical integration notion have assumed the linear (transitive) fixation of the emerging differentiation. In contrast, an intransitive hierarchy could result from flexible hierarchical control processes between the levels of integrated structure.

The second kind of hierarchy—the one based on intransitivities—dominates the regulatory processes in the biological and psychological worlds. Most of the biological regulatory processes are based on a cyclical basic structure. In both kinds of hierarchies, plasticity is embedded in the possibility that change in any particular relationships can proliferate to change the whole structure (e.g., Lerner, 1984). Development entails unity of both change and nonchange, and its study requires methodological sophistication that differs from that of nondevelopmental orientations in psychology.

Implications for the Construction of Methods. The possibility that developmental phenomena are organized into intransitivity-based hierarchies, or cycles, sets up strict restrictions for the construction of specific methods, both for data derivation (Kindermann & Valsiner, 1989) and for further analyses of derived data. The assumption of independence of different data points—parts of the cycles or intransitive hierarchies—need not apply. Yet, the traditions of quantification of psychological data rely heavily on that assumption. In developmental research, this assumption is further questionable because of the basic developmental assumption of *inter*dependence of phenomena in time. If all development is viewed in terms of transformation of structures (however defined) from one state into another in irreversible time, then it becomes impossible to assume that temporally adjacent structures are independent of one another. Furthermore, the "old" (yet ever new) gestalt-psychological notion of irreducibility of the structure into its elements stands firm in developmental methodology. If development entails emergence of structures of variable complexity, it is not possible to study that development via strategies that reduce these complex forms to their elementary constituents.

Given these three general assumptions—(a) cyclicity of regulatory processes, (b) interdependence of developmental phenomena in time, and (c) emergence of structural complexity—the methodological question facing a developmental scientist becomes complicated. What kind of data are to be derived from the phenomena, given the nature of those phenomena, and the goal to make sense of development? Following the historically constructed methodological rules of nondevelopmental psychology, child psychologists usually assume that the data must be quantitative entities. They then proceed with some tactic of quantification of the phenomena as those are turned into data (Valsiner, 1995b). However, making quantification into a habit may be counterproductive when we claim to study development (see above; also Hornstein, 1988). Rather, at first, a choice—based on theoretical considerations and assumptions of the nature of the phenomena—may be necessary: Is quantification appropriate in the given case at all? In some cases, it may be. Yet, many developmental phenomena are structural entities that undergo transformation in the direction of increasing structural complexity. Reduction of the structure of such phenomena to quantified elementaristic representations may lead to the data's becoming false representations of the phenomena. If that is the case, then the whole elaborate enterprise of data analysis that follows quantification is a futile exercise, because the elementaristic (yet accumulated) data fail to represent the complexity of the developmental phenomena from which they were derived. Borrowing methodological practices from nondevelopmental psychology can easily lead child psychology into research practices that result in elimination of access to the processes of development from the outset of an empirical study.

Thus, quantification in the process of data derivation (from the phenomena) is a sensitive operation by the researcher and cannot be accepted axiomatically; it must be proven as to its adequacy in each concrete case. Voices against excessive quantification in data construction, or even quantification in total, have been quite loud in developmental psychology. But those voices have usually been ignored—a result that fits the co-constructionist notion of scientific practices. Among others, James Mark Baldwin, by the end of his life, was explicit about the reasons why quantification is a problem for developmental psychology. He proclaimed:

> The . . . quantitative method, brought over into psychology from the exact sciences, physics and chemistry, must be discarded; for its ideal consisted in reducing the more complex to the more simple, the whole into its parts, the later-evolved to the earlier-existent, thus denying or *eliminating just the factor which constituted or revealed what was truly genetic.* Newer modes of manifestation cannot be stated in atomic terms *without doing violence to the more synthetic modes* which observation reveals. (Baldwin, 1930, p. 7, emphasis added)

Baldwin's claim fits with the notion of development as a systemic transformation process in which novelty is constantly created. This can be captured by construction of different formal "logics" of development (Baldwin, 1930,

himself attempted to construct a system of "genetic logic"). In any case, the kinds of formal models that developmental psychology may find fitting may belong to the realm of qualitative branches of mathematics (Valsiner, 1987, chapter 5).

Given its usual practices of data derivation, developmental psychology has often been at risk for losing track of the phenomena under study (Cairns, 1986), and it is exactly the qualitative (structural) holistic (yet temporary) organization that needs to be retained in data derivation (e.g., Basov's structural and transitional forms; Basov, 1931, 1991). Developmental researchers are closer to researchers in chemistry (who are interested in structural transformations between substances) than to public accountants. However, the latter professional group's models of gaining knowledge (rather than those of classical physicists) have dominated much of the social sciences in their recent history (Porter, 1992).

Implications for Methods of Data Analysis. In the realm of data-analytic strategies, the possibility for intransitivity hierarchies leads to the need to utilize nonlinear formal models. The assumption of linearity is often used at the level of data analysis; the adequacy of the General Linear Model underlies the uses of most statistical data-analytic techniques. For example, the axiom of summativity of variance may be unwarranted when we study development. The data we have derived and must analyze have to retain the crucial property of developmental phenomena—construction of novelty. The latter entails transcending the state of phenomena as those presently exist; yet, decomposing the variance into components attributable to separated causes, and assuming that the decomposed variance components sum to unity, makes the novelty-construction process remain without representation in the data. If such a novelty-constructing component were to be introduced, the analysis-of-variance axiomatics might have to assume that the sum of all components of the variance is at least 1; but if novelty is constructed, it would be bigger than 1. This would entail the application of the old gestalt psychological founding principle (i.e., the gestalt is always greater than the sum of its parts, as there exists unity at the systemic level that cannot be decomposed into a sum of its components). In other terms—the summativity-of-variance axiom of the analysis of variance, and the open-systemic theoretical foundation of development (as it exists in different areas of developmental psychology; e.g., the definition of development by Ford and Lerner, given above)—do not fit with each other. Analysis-of-variance kinds of models are, in principle, not applicable to data analysis in developmental psychology, if the latter uses an open-systemic or a dynamic systems perspective in its axiomatic basis.

Alternative thought models for developmental systems have been available in different areas of mathematics, yet child psychologists have infrequently taken advantage of them. For instance, the open-systemic nature of development—posited axiomatically—leads to the use of some symbolic-logic models (e.g., Herbst, 1995; Valsiner, 1995a). Traditions of dynamic systems theory, and efforts to apply catastrophic–theoretic formalizations (Thom, 1973, 1975) to the study of development, constitute steps in the direction of creating, for the study of development, formal data-analytic systems that take the emergent complexity into account.

Relationships between the Researcher and the Researchee. The notion of researcher–subject co-construction of the phenomena is certainly a new understanding for psychology. It is rooted in the methodological premises of Vygotsky's "method of double stimulation." In Vygotsky's sense of the method, the researcher can never be "in full control" over the data derivation process. There is no guaranteed researcher → subject linear-hierarchical relationship of roles. Instead, a flexible intransitive relation is the rule; given an action by the researcher, the subject may assume a dominant-role relationship over and above that of the researcher. For instance, the act of noncooperation by the subject can emerge as a result of the researcher's previous step, and can lead to subversive response tactics by the subject. As a result, the subject provides the researcher with "inaccurate evidence." In the usual research practice, such evidence—if detected—is not taken into account. However, all evidence obtained in the research process with human subjects is in some form co-constructed. It is a joint result of the interaction of the researcher and the researchee. The adequacy of the evidence depends on the convergence of the goal orientations of the researcher and the subject, which can change at any time in the course of the study process. Thus, the seemingly dominant role of the researcher is in fact at any moment under the control of the subject's decision as to whether to accept the subdominant (controlled) role and cooperate in the data derivation process, or to reverse the control relationship so that the researcher becomes the subject, and the subject becomes a researcher (for purposes other than the originally stated research goals).

IMPLICATIONS FOR FUTURE MODELS

The present analysis of the concept of development—through outlining three kinds of models implemented to explain it—leads to a recognition that the study of child development has been adopted by a metatheoretically distant foster parent: nondevelopmental psychology. The latter has been trying to demonstrate its "objectivity" through emulating the measurement ideals of physics (of the past century), and we can often observe a loss of focus in investigations in child psychology. The myriad of standardized and conveniently labeled "measures" or "variables" may create an illusion that our empirical enterprise of child study has led—or is at least about to lead—to a grand breakthrough in our understanding of children and their development.

When approached from the standpoint of existing theoretical models of development, and after examining their recent history (of about 100 years!), the story has a different ending. The types of models examined—differentiation, equilibration, and teaching/learning systems—are neither new nor vastly improved in their formulation (or methodological implications) over their ancient predecessors. This evaluation may reflect the impasse into which psychology's following of the "hard sciences" has led the discipline. A different foster parent among the hard sciences—chemistry rather than physics—might have provided these models with a more persistent intellectual focus within the discipline, and thereby furthered their elaboration. Thus, the focus on structure and its conditional transformation would be far better aligned with the conceptual sphere of chemistry than with the physics of psychology's construction.

In this respect, it is not uninteresting that the emphasis on *psychological* synthesis—dialectical or otherwise—that was present in the thinking of Wundt, Vygotsky, and others, was modeled after *chemical* synthesis. The widespread argument in favor of systemic units since the turn of the 20th century—that of the irreducibility of water molecules into components of H and O—is likewise a chemical metaphor. Last but not least, the symmetry-breaking structural innovation processes have been demonstrated in the area of physical chemistry (Prigogine, 1973, 1987). Furthermore, modern biological sciences—genetics in particular—are oriented toward providing systemic-regulatory accounts of the biological processes, rather than mere demonstrations of the "fit" of one or another ad hoc formalized model with some percentage of variance in outcome-based data (Crick, 1988).

The advancement of person-centered (as opposed to variable-centered) research orientations in developmental psychology fits with the notion of an irreversible life-course nature of phenomena (Magnusson, 1988; Magnusson & Stattin, this Volume). The traditions of dominance of the statistical inference in the research practices of child psychologists are unlikely to survive the test of both the reality of complex psychological phenomena, and the development of new formal models that advance the notions of differentiation, equilibration, and unity of person–environment structures in mutual teaching–learning processes. Understanding of development itself develops through construction of theoretical models, careful analysis of their nature, proper fit with the phenomena, and retention of those models that maintain the relevant facets of the phenomena of development as abstract generalizations. The three kinds of models—differentiation, equilibration, and teaching–learning—have successfully survived for more than a century, and will enter the new millenium with promises for improving our understanding. However, these promises depend on the construction of a formal abstract framework of theoretical developmental psychology. James Mark Baldwin's call for a "genetic logic" at the beginning of the 20th century is still far from being constructed in general—and even farther from reaching our research practices.

ACKNOWLEDGMENTS

Editorial comments by Richard Lerner were helpful in bringing this chapter to its final form. The author thanks Angela U. Branco, Gilbert Gottlieb, and Jeanette A. Lawrence for their critical comments on earlier drafts of the manuscript.

REFERENCES

Allen, P. (1981). The evolutionary paradigm of dissipative structures. In E. Jantsch (Ed.), *The evolutionary vision: Toward a unifying paradigm of physical, biological, and sociocultural evolution* (pp. 25–72). Boulder, CO: Westview Press.

Allport, G. W. (1937). The personalistic psychology of William Stern. *Character & Personality, 5,* 231–246.

Altman, I. (1993). Dialectics, physical environments, and personal relationships. *Communication Monographs, 60,* 26–34.

Alvarez, A. (1994). Child's everyday life. An ecological approach to the study of activity systems. In A. Alvarez & P. Del Rio (Eds.), *Explorations in socio-cultural studies: Vol. 4. Education as culture construction* (pp. 23–38). Madrid: Fundación Infancia y Aprendizaje.

Amann-Gainotti, M. (1992). Jean Piaget, student of Pierre Janet (Paris 1919–1921). *Perceptual & Motor Skills, 74,* 1011–1015.

Amann-Gainotti, M., & Ducret, J -J. (1992). Jean Piaget élève de Pierre Janet: L'influence de la psychologie des conduites et les rapports avel la psychanalyse. *L'Information Psychiatrique, 6,* 598–606.

Bakhtin, M. M. (1981). *The dialogic imagination.* Austin: University of Texas Press.

Baldwin, J. M. (1894). Personality-suggestion. *Psychological Review, 1,* 274–279.

Baldwin, J. M. (1895). *Mental development in the child and the race.* New York: Macmillan.

Baldwin, J. M. (1897). *Social and ethical interpretations in mental development.* New York: Macmillan.

Baldwin, J. M. (1898). On selective thinking. *Psychological Review, 5*(1), 1–24.

Baldwin, J. M. (1906). *Thought and things: A study of the development and meaning of thought, or genetic logic: Vol. 1. Functional logic, or genetic theory of knowledge.* London: Swan Sonnenschein.

Baldwin, J. M. (1908). Knowledge and imagination. *Psychological Review, 15,* 181–196.

Baldwin, J. M. (1911). *Thought and things: A study of the development and meaning of thought, or genetic logic: Vol 3. Interest and art being real logic.* London: Swan Sonnenschein.

Baldwin, J. M. (1915). *Genetic theory of reality.* New York: Putnam.

Baldwin, J. M. (1930). James Mark Baldwin. In C. Murchison (Ed.), *A history of psychology in autobiography* (Vol. 1, pp. 1–30). New York: Russell & Russell.

Baltes, P. B., & Nesselroade, J. R. (1973). The developmental analysis of individual differences on multiple measures. In J. R. Nesselroade & H. W. Reese (Eds.), *Life-span developmental psychology* (pp. 219–251). New York: Academic Press.

Basov, M. (1929). Structural analysis in psychology from the standpoint of behavior. *Journal of Genetic Psychology, 36,* 267–290.

Basov, M. (1931). *Obshchie osnovy pedologii.* Moscow-Leningrad: Gosudarstvennoe Izdatel'stvo.

Basov, M. (1991). The organization of processes of behavior. In J. Valsiner & R. Van der Veer (Eds.), Structuring of conduct in activity settings: The forgotten contributions of Mikhail Basov: Part 1. *Soviet Psychology, 29*(5), 14–83.

Bekhterev, V. M. (1994). *Collective reflexology.* Commack: NOVA.

Benigni, L., & Valsiner, J. (1985). Developmental psychology without the study of processes of development? *Newsletter of the International Society for the Study of Behavioral Development, 1,* 1–3.

Bergson, H. (1911). *Creative evolution.* New York: Henry Holt.

Bergson, H. (1945). *L'Evolution créatrice.* Genève: Éditions Albert Skira. (Original work published 1907)

Bertalanffy, L. von (1950). The theory of open systems in physics and biology. *Science, 111,* 23–29.

Bertalanffy, L. von (1960). Principles and theory of growth. In W. Nowinski (Ed.), *Fundamental aspects of normal and malignant growth* (pp. 137–259). Amsterdam, The Netherlands: Elsevier.

Boesch, E. E. (1983). *Das Magische und das Schöne: Zur Symbolik von Objekten und Handlungen.* Stuttgart: Frommann.

Boesch, E. E. (1989). Cultural psychology in action-theoretical perspective. In Ç. Kagitçibasi (Ed.), *Growth and progress in cross-cultural psychology* (pp. 41–51). Lisse: Swets & Zeitlinger.

Boesch, E. E. (1991). *Symbolic action theory and cultural psychology.* New York: Springer.

Bornstein, M. H. (1995). Form and function: Implications for studies of culture and human development. *Culture & Psychology, 1*(1), 123–137.

Bourdieu, P. (1973). Cultural reproduction and social reproduction. In R. Brown (Ed.), *Knowledge, education, and cultural change* (pp. 71–112). London: Tavistock.

Bourdieu, P. (1985). The social space and the genesis of groups. *Social Science Information, 24*(2), 195–220.

Branco, A. U. (1996). The "ecological approach": When labels suggest similarities beyond shared basic concepts in psychology. In J. Tudge, M. Shanahan, & J. Valsiner (Eds.), *Comparative approaches in developmental science.* New York: Cambridge University Press.

Branco, A. U., & Valsiner, J. (1992, July 20). *Development of convergence and divergence in joint actions of preschool children within structured social contexts.* Poster presented at the 25th International Congress of Psychology, Brussels.

Branco, A. U., & Valsiner, J. (1997). Changing methodologies: A co-constructivist study of goal orientations in social interactions. In G. Misra (Ed.), *Psychology in developing countries.* New Delhi: Sage.

Brent, S. (1978). Motivation, steady state, and structural development: A general model of psychological homeostasis. *Motivation & Emotion, 2,* 299–332.

Brent, S. (1984). *Psychological and social structures.* Hillsdale, NJ: Erlbaum.

Bronfenbrenner, U. (1979). *The ecology of human development.* Cambridge, MA: Harvard University Press.

Bronfenbrenner, U. (1989). Ecological systems theory. In R. Vasta (Ed.), *Annals of child development.* Greenwich, CT: JAI Press.

Bronfenbrenner, U. (1993). The ecology of cognitive development. In R. Wozniak & K. Fischer (Eds.), *Development in context* (pp. 3–46). Hillsdale, NJ: Erlbaum.

Bronfenbrenner, U., & Crouter, A. C. (1983). The evolution of environmental models in developmental research. In W. Kesson (Ed.), *Handbook of child psychology: Vol. 1. History, theory, and methods* (pp. 357–414). New York: Wiley.

Bühler, K. (1978). *Die Krise der Psychologie.* Frankfurt-am-Main: Ullstein. (Original work published 1927)

Cairns, R. B. (1986). Phenomena lost: Issues in the study of development. In J. Valsiner (Ed.), *The individual subject and scientific psychology* (pp. 97–111). New York: Plenum Press.

Cairns, R. B. (1992). The making of a developmental science: The contributions and intellectual heritage of James Mark Baldwin. *Developmental Psychology, 28*(1), 17–24.

Calil, E. (1994). The construction of the zone of proximal development in a pedagogical context. In N. Mercer & C. Coll (Eds.), *Explorations in socio-cultural studies: Vol. 3. Teaching, learning, and interaction* (pp. 93–98). Madrid: Fundación Infancia y Aprendizaje.

Case, R. (1985). *Intellectual development: Birth to adulthood.* Orlando, FL: Academic Press.

Case, R. (1991). Stages in the development of the young child's first sense of self. *Developmental Review, 11,* 210–230.

Case, R., Hayward, S., Lewis, M., & Hurst, P. (1988). Toward a neo-Piagetian theory of cognitive and emotional development. *Developmental Review, 8,* 1–51.

Cassirer, E. (1923–1929). *Philosophie der symbolischen Formen* (Vols. 1–3). Berlin: Bruno Cassirer Verlag.

Chapman, M. (1988). *Constructive evolution.* Cambridge, England: Cambridge University Press.

Chapman, M. (1992). Equilibration and the dialectics of organization. In H. Beilin & P. Pufall (Eds.), *Piaget's theory: Prospects and possibilities* (pp. 39–59). Hillsdale, NJ: Erlbaum.

Cole, M. (1985). The zone of proximal development: Where culture and cognition create each other. In J. V. Wertsch (Ed.), *Culture, communication, and cognition: Vygotskian perspectives* (pp. 146–161). Cambridge, England: Cambridge University Press.

Cole, M. (1990). Cultural psychology: A once and future discipline? In J. Berman (Ed.), *Nebraska Symposium on Motivation* (Vol. 37, pp. 279–336). Lincoln: University of Nebraska Press.

Cole, M. (1992). Context, modularity and the cultural constitution of development. In L. T. Winegar & J. Valsiner (Eds.), *Children's development within social context: Vol 2. Research and methodology* (pp. 5–31). Hillsdale, NJ: Erlbaum.

Cole, M. (1995). Culture and cognitive development: From cross-cultural research to creating systems of cultural mediation. *Culture & Psychology, 1*(1), 25–54.

Coll, C. (1990). *Aprendizaje escolar y construcción de conhecimento.* Barcelona: Paidós.

Coll, C., Colomina, R., Onrubia, J., & Rochera, M. J. (1992). Actividad conjunta y habla: Una aproximación al estudio de los mecanismos de influencia educativa. *Infancia y Aprendizaje, 59–60,* 189–232.

Coll, C., & Onrubia, J. (1994). Temporal dimension and interactive processes in teaching/learning activities: A theoretical and methodological challenge. In N. Mercer & C. Coll (Eds.), *Explorations in socio-cultural studies: Vol. 3. Teaching, learning, and interaction* (pp. 107–122). Madrid: Fundación Infancia y Aprendizaje.

Colomina, R. M., & Rochera, M. J. (1992, September 6–9). *The negotiation of the situational context: A preliminary task for an adult-child joint activity that is not clearly defined?* Paper presented at the 5th European Conference on Developmental Psychology, Seville.

Cook, G. (1993). *George Herbert Mead: The making of a social pragmatist.* Urbana: University of Illinois Press.

Cox, B. D. (1989). *Development of memory strategies.* Unpublished doctoral dissertation, University of North Carolina at Chapel Hill.

Cox, B. D., Ornstein, P. A., & Valsiner, J. (1991). The role of internalization in the transfer of mnemonic strategies. In L. Oppenheimer & J. Valsiner (Eds.), *The origins of action: International perspectives* (pp. 101–131). New York: Springer.

Crick, F. (1988). *What mad pursuit: A personal view of scientific discovery.* London: Penguin Books.

Danziger, K. (1990). *Constructing the subject.* Cambridge, England: Cambridge University Press.

Daston, L. (1988). *Classical probability in the enlightenment.* Princeton, NJ: Princeton University Press.

Daston, L. (1992). Objectivity and the escape from perspective. *Social Studies of Science, 22,* 597–618.

De Gispert, I., & Colomina, R. (1994). Shared meaning and teaching/learning activities: Is a distal approach useful? In A. Alvarez & P. Del Rio (Eds.), *Explorations in socio-cultural studies: Vol. 4. Education as culture construction* (pp. 183–198). Madrid: Fundación Infancia y Aprendizaje.

Del Rio, P. (1990). La Zona Desarollo Próximo y la Zona Sincrética de Representación: El espacio instrumental de la acción social. *Infancia y Aprendizaje, 51–52,* 191–244.

Del Rio, P. (1994). Extra-cortical connections: The sociocultural systems for conscious living. In J. Wertsch & J. D. Ramirez (Eds.), *Explorations in socio-cultural studies: Vol. 2. Literacy and other forms of mediated action* (pp. 19–31). Madrid: Fundación Infancia y Aprendizaje.

Del Rio, P., & Alvarez, A. (1992). Tres pies al gato: Significado, sentido y cultura cotidiana en la educación. *Infancia y Aprendizaje, 59–60.*

Del Rio, P., & Alvarez, A. (1995). Directivity: The cultural and educational construction of morality and agency. *Anthropology & Education Quarterly, 26*(4), 384–409.

Dewey, J. (1894). The theory of emotion: 1. Emotional attitudes. *Psychological Review, 1*(6), 553–569.

Dewey, J. (1895). The theory of emotion: 2. The significance of emotions. *Psychological Review, 2*(1), 13–32.

Dewey, J. (1896). The reflex arc concept in psychology. *Psychological Review, 3*(3), 357–370.

Dodds, A., Lawrence, J. A., & Valsiner, J. (in press). The personal and the social: Mead's theory of the "generalized other." *Theory & Psychology.*

Draguns, J. (1984). Microgenesis by any other name . . . In W. D. Froelich, G. Smith, J. Draguns, & U. Hentschel (Eds.), *Psychological processes in cognition and personality* (pp. 3–17). Washington, DC: Hemisphere.

Duncker, K. (1945). On problem-solving. *Psychological Monographs, 58*(5), 1–112.

Eckensberger, L. H. (1995). Activity or action: Two different roads towards an integration of culture into psychology? *Culture & Psychology, 1*(1), 67–80.

Edwards, D., & Mercer, N. (1989). *Common knowledge: The development of understanding in the classroom.* London: Routledge & Kegan Paul.

Engeström, Y. (1990). *Learning, working, and imagining.* Hensinki: Orienta-Konsultit Oy.

Engler, R. (1968). *Ferdinand de Saussure Cours de linguistique générale: Édition critique.* Wiesbaden: Otto Harrassowitz.

Eyferth, K. (1976). The contribution of William and Clara Stern to the onset of developmental psychology. In K. F. Riegel & J. A. Meacham (Eds.), *The developing individual in a changing world* (Vol. 1, pp. 9–15). The Hague: Mouton.

Fabricius, W. V. (1983). Piaget's theory of knowledge: Its philosophical context. *Human Development, 26,* 325–334.

Fentress, J. C. (1989). Developmental roots of behavioral order: Systemic approaches to the examination of core developmental issues. In M. Gunnar & E. Thelen (Eds.), *Minnesota symposia of child psychology* (Vol. 22, pp. 35–76). Hillsdale, NJ: Erlbaum.

Fischer, K. W. (1980). A theory of cognitive development: The control and construction of hierarchies of skill. *Psychological Review, 87,* 477–531.

Fischer, K. W., Bullock, D. H., Rotenberg, E. J., & Raya, P. (1993). The dynamics of competence: How context contributes directly to skill. In R. H. Wozniak & K. W. Fischer (Eds.), *Development in context* (pp. 93–117). Hillsdale, NJ: Erlbaum.

Fischer, K. W., & Ferrar, M. J. (1987). Generalizations about generalization: How a theory of skill development explains both generality and specificity. *International Journal of Psychology, 22,* 643–677.

Fischer, K. W., & Ferrar, M. J. (1992). Generalizations about generalizations: How a theory of skill development explains both generality and specificity. In A. Demetriou, M. Shayer, & A. Efklides (Eds.), *Neo-Piagetian theories of cognitive development* (pp. 137–172). London: Routledge & Kegan Paul.

Fogel, A. (1993). *Developing through relationships.* Chicago: University of Chicago Press.

Fogel, A., & Branco, A. U. (1997). Meta-communication as a source of indeterminism in relationships. In A. Fogel, M. Lyra, & J. Valsiner (Eds.), *Dynamics and indeterminism in developmental and social processes.* Hillsdale, NJ: Erlbaum.

Folds-Bennett, T. (1994). Replication: What's the angle? In R. van der Veer, M. H. van IJzendoorn, & J. Valsiner (Eds.), *Reconstructing the mind: Replicability in research on human development* (pp. 207–231). Norwood, NJ: ABLEX.

Ford, D. H., & Lerner, R. M. (1992). *Developmental systems theory.* Newbury Park, CA: Sage.

Fuhrer, U. (1993). Living in our own footprints—and those of others: Cultivation as transaction. *Schweizerische Zeitschrift für Psychologie, 52*(2), 130–137.

Fuhrer, U., Kaiser, F. G., & Hangartner, U. (1995). Wie Kinder und Jugendliche ihr Selbstkonzept kultivieren: Die Bedeutung von Dingen, Orten, und Personen. *Psychologie im Erziehung und Unterricht, 42,* 57–64.

Gigerenzer, G. (1993). The Superego, the Ego, and the Id in statistical reasoning. In G. Keren & C. Lewis (Eds.), *A handbook for data analysis in the behavioral sciences: Methodological issues* (pp. 311–339). Hillsdale, NJ: Erlbaum.

Gigerenzer, G., Swijtink, Z., Porter, T., Daston, L., Beatty, J., & Krüger, L. (1989). *The empire of chance.* Cambridge, England: Cambridge University Press.

Glickman, S. E. (1985). Some thoughts on the evolution of comparative psychology. In S. Koch & D. E. Leary (Eds.), *A century of psychology as science* (pp. 738–782). New York: McGraw-Hill.

Góes, M. C. R. (1994). The modes of participation of others in the functioning of the subject. In N. Mercer & C. Coll (Eds.), *Explorations in socio-cultural studies: Vol. 3. Teaching, learning, and interaction* (pp. 123–128). Madrid: Fundación Infancia y Aprendizaje.

Goldstein, K. (1933). L'analyse de l'aphasie et l'etude de l'essence du langage. *Journal de Psychologie, 30,* 430–496.

Goldstein, K. (1971). Concerning the concept of "primitivity." In A. Gurwitsch, E. M. Goldstein-Haudek, & W. Haudek (Eds.), *Selected papers of Kurt Goldstein* (pp. 485–503). The Hague: Martinus Nijhoff.

Gottlieb, G. (1992). *Individual development & evolution: The genesis of novel behavior.* New York: Oxford University Press.

Groeben, N. (1986). *Handeln, Tun, Verhalten als Einheiten einer verstehend-erklärenden Psychologie.* Tübingen: Francke.

Grossmann, K. E. (1986). From idiographic approaches to nomothetic hypotheses: Stern, Allport, and the biology of knowledge, exemplified by an exploration of sibling relationships. In J. Valsiner (Ed.), *The individual subject and scientific psychology* (pp. 37–70). New York: Plenum Press.

Gupta, S., & Valsiner, J. (1995). *Structural growth in the ontogeny of action and speech.* Unpublished manuscript.

Hardesty, F. P. (1976). Louis William Stern: A new view of the Hamburg years. *Annals of the New York Academy of Sciences, 270,* 31–44.

Herbst, D. (1995). What happens when we make a distinction: An elementary introduction to co-genetic logic. In T. Kindermann & J. Valsiner (Eds.), *Development of person-context relations.* Hillsdale, NJ:Erlbaum.

Hermans, H. J. M. (1991). The person as co-investigator in self-research: Valuation theory. *European Journal of Personality, 5,* 217–234.

Hermans, H. J. M. (1995). The limitations of logic in defining the self. *Theory & Psychology, 5*(3), 375–382.

Hermans, H. J. M., & Bonarius, H. (1991a). The person as co-investigator in personality research. *European Journal of Personality, 5,* 199–216.

Hermans, H. J. M., & Bonarius, H. (1991b). Static laws in a dynamic psychology? *European Journal of Personality, 5,* 245–247.

Hermans, H. J. M., & Kempen, H. J. G. (1995). Body, mind, and culture: Dialogical nature of mediated action. *Culture & Psychology, 1*(1), 104–114

Hooker, C. A. (1994). Regulatory constructivism: On the relation between evolutionary epistemology and Piaget's genetic epistemology. *Biology & Philosophy, 9,* 197–244.

Hornstein, G. A. (1988). Quantifying psychological phenomena: Debates, dilemmas, and implications. In J. G. Morawski (Ed.), *The rise of experimentation in American psychology* (pp. 1–34). New Haven, CT: Yale University Press.

Ignjatovic-Savic, N., Kovac-Cerovac, T., Plut, D., & Pesikan, A. (1988). Social interaction in early childhood and its development. In J. Valsiner (Ed.), *Child development within culturally structured environments: Vol. 1. Parental cognition and adult-child interaction* (pp. 89–153). Norwood, NJ: ABLEX.

Inhelder, B., Cellérier, C., Ackermann, E., Blanchet, A., Boder, A., De Caprona, D., Ducret, J., & Saada-Robert, M. (1992). *Les cheminements de la d'couvert de l'enfant.* Neuchâtel: Delachaux et Niestlé.

Irons, D. (1895a). Prof. James' theory of emotion. *Mind, 3,* 77–97.

Irons, D. (1895b). Recent developments in theory of emotion. *Psychological Review, 2,* 279–284.

Jahoda, G. (1993). *Crossroads between culture and mind.* Cambridge, MA: Harvard University Press.

Jahoda, G. (1995). The ancestry of a model. *Culture & Psychology, 1*(1), 11–24.

James, W. (1884). What is an emotion. *Mind, 9,* 188–205.

James, W. (1890). *Principles of psychology.* New York: Holt.

James, W. (1894). The physical basis of emotion. *Psychological Review, 1,* 516–529.

Janet, P. (1889). *L'automatisme psychologique: Essai de psychologie expérimentale sur les formes inférieures de l'activité humaine.* Paris: Félix Alcan.

Janet, P. (1921). The fear of action. *Journal of Abnormal Psychology and Social Psychology, 16,*(2/3), 150–160.

Janet, P. (1925). *Psychological healing* (Vol. 1). New York: Macmillan.

Janet, P. (1926). *De l'angoisse a l'extase: Un délire religieux la croyance* (Vol. 1). Paris: Félix Alcan.

Janet, P. (1928). *De l'angoisse a l'extase: Un délire religieux la croyance: Vol. 2. Les sentiments fondamentaux.* Paris: Félix Alcan.

Janet, P. (1930). L'analyse psychologique. In C. Murchison (Ed.), *Psychologies of 1930* (pp. 369–373). Worcester, MA: Clark University Press.

Jantsch, E. (1980). *The self-organizing universe.* Oxford, England: Pergamon Press.

Joas, H. (1985). *G. H. Mead: A contemporary reexamination of his thought.* Cambridge, MA: MIT Press.

Junefelt, K. (1994). Blindness and voicing. In J. Wertsch & J. D. Ramirez (Eds.), *Explorations in socio-cultural studies: Vol. 2. Literacy and other forms of mediated action* (pp. 103–114). Madrid: Fundación Infancia y Aprendizaje.

Kaplan, B. (1983). A trio of trails. In R. Lerner (Ed.), *Developmental psychology: Historical and philosophical perspectives* (pp. 29–54). Hillsdale, NJ: Erlbaum.

Kelly, G. (1955). *The psychology of personal constructs* (Vols. 1–2). New York: Norton.

Kindermann, T., & Valsiner, J. (1989). Research strategies in culture-inclusive developmental psychology. In J. Valsiner (Ed.), *Child development in cultural context* (pp. 13–50). Toronto: Hogrefe & Huber.

Kojima, H. (1995). Forms and functions as categories of comparison. *Culture & Psychology, 1*(1), 139–145

Kreppner, K. (1992a). William L. Stern, 1871–1938: A neglected founder of developmental psychology. *Developmental Psychology, 28*(4), 539–547.

Kreppner, K. (1992b, September). *William L. Stern and his concept of individual-environment exchange: Transactional thoughts in the 1910s and 1920s.* Paper presented at the First Conference on Socio-Cultural Studies, Madrid.

Krewer, B. (1992). *Kulturelle Identität und menschliche Selbsterforschung.* Saarbrücken: Breitenbach.

Laboratory of Comparative Human Cognition. (1983). Culture and cognitive development. In W. Kessen (Ed.), *Handbook of child psychology: Vol. 1. History, theory & methods* (pp. 295–356). New York: Wiley.

Lamiell, J. T. (1991, August). *Great psychologists resurrected: William Stern.* Paper presented at the 99th annual convention of the American Psychological Association, San Francisco.

Langer, J. (1970). Werner's comparative organismic theory. In P. H. Mussen (Ed.), *Carmichael's handbook of child psychology* (3rd ed., pp. 733–771). New York: Wiley.

Langer, J. (1980). *The origin of logic: Six to twelve months.* New York: Academic Press.

Langer, J. (1982). From prerepresentational to representational cognition. In G. Forman (Ed.), *Action and thought.* New York: Academic Press.

Langer, J. (1983). Concept and symbol formation by infants. In S. Wapner & B. Kaplan (Eds.), *Toward a holistic developmental psychology* (pp. 221–234). Hillsdale, NJ: Erlbaum.

Langer, J. (1986). *The origins of logic: One to two years.* New York: Academic Press.

Langer, J. (1990). Early cognitive development: Basic functions. In C. -A. Hauert (Ed.), *Developmental psychology: Cognitive, perceptuo-motor, and neuropsychological perspectives* (pp. 19–42). Amsterdam, The Netherlands: North-Holland.

Leontiev, A. N. (1975). *Deiatel'nost', soznanie, lichnost'.* Moscow: Izdatelstvo Politicheskoi Literatury.

Leontiev, A. N. (1981). The problem of activity in psychology. In J. V. Wertsch (Ed.), *The concept of activity in Soviet psychology* (pp. 37–71). Armonk, NY: Sharpe.

Lerner, R. M. (1978). Nature, nurture, and dynamic interactionism. *Human Development, 21,* 1–20.

Lerner, R. M. (1979). A dynamic interactional concept of individual and social relationship development. In R. L. Burgess & T. L. Huston (Eds.), *Social exchange in developing relationships* (pp. 271–305). New York: Academic Press.

Lerner, R. M. (1984). *On the nature of human plasticity.* Cambridge, England: Cambridge University Press.

Lerner, R. M. (1986). *Concepts and theories of human development* (2nd ed.). New York: Random House.

Lerner, R. M. (1990). Plasticity: Person-context relations, and cognitive training in the aged years: A developmental contextual perspective. *Developmental Psychology, 26*(6), 911–915.

Lerner, R. M. (1991). Changing organism-context relations as the basic process of development. *Developmental Psychology, 27,* 27–32.

Lerner, R. M. (1995). The place of learning within the human development system: A developmental contextual perspective. *Human Development, 38,* 361–366.

Lewin, K. (1917). Kriegslandschaft. *Zeitschrift für angewandte Psychologie, 12,* 440–447.

Lewin, K. (1927). Gesetz und Experiment in der Psychologie. *Symposion, 1,* 375–421.

Lewin, K. (1931). The conflict between Aristotelian and Galileian modes of thought in contemporary psychology. *Journal of General Psychology, 5,* 141–177.

Lewin, K. (1933). Environmental forces. In C. Murchison (Ed.), *A handbook of child psychology* (2nd ed., pp. 590–625). Worcester, MA: Clark University Press.

Lewin, K. (1935). Psycho-sociological problems of a minority group. *Character & Personality, 3,* 175–187.

Lewin, K. (1936a). *Principles of topological psychology.* New York: McGraw-Hill.

Lewin, K. (1936b). Some social-psychological differences between the United States and Germany. *Character & Personality, 4,* 265–293.

Lewin, K. (1938). *The conceptual representation and the measurement of psychological forces.* Durham, NC: Duke University Press.

Lewin, K. (1939). Field theory and experiment in social psychology: Concepts and methods. *American Journal of Sociology, 44,* 868–896.

Lewin, K. (1942). Field theory and learning. In N. B. Henry (Ed.), *The forty-first yearbook of the National Society for the Study of Education: Part 2. The psychology of learning* (pp. 215–242). Bloomington, IN: Public School.

Lewin, K. (1943). Defining the field at a given time. *Psychological Review, 50,* 292–310.

Lipps, T. (1903). Einfühlung, inner Nachahmung, und Organempfindungen. *Archiv für die gesamte Psychologie, 2,* 185–204.

Lipps, T. (1923). *Aesthetik.* Leipzig: Barth.

Lotman, J. M. (1992). O semiosfere. In J. M. Lotman (Ed.), *Izbrannye stat'i: Vol. 1. Stat'i po semiotike i tipologii kul'tury* (pp. 11–24). Tallinn: Aleksandra.

Löwy, I. (1992). The strength of loose concepts—boundary concepts, federative experimental strategies and disciplinary growth: The case of immunology. *History of Science, 30*(1, Pt. 4), 376–396.

Lyra, M. C. (1989). *First steps of differentiation and construction of a baby's vocal production in mother-infant dyad.* Paper presented at the tenth biennial meetings of the ISSBD, Jyväskyla.

Lyra, M. C., Pantoja, A. P., & Cabral, E. A. (1991). *A diferenciação da produção vocal do bebê nas interações "mãe-objeto-bebê."* Paper presented at the 43rd meeting of the Sociedade Brasileira para o Progresso da Ciência, Rio de Janeiro.

Lyra, M. C., & Rossetti-Ferreira, M. C. (1995). Transformation and construction in social interaction: A new perspective of analysis of the mother-infant dyad. In J. Valsiner (Ed.), *Child development in culturally structured environments: Vol. 3. Comparative-cultural and constructivist perspectives* (pp. 51–87). Norwood, NJ: ABLEX.

Lyra, M. C., & Winegar, L. T. (1996). Processual dynamics of interaction through time: Adult-child interactions and process of development. In A. Fogel, M. Lyra, & J. Valsiner (Eds.), *Dynamics and indeterminism in developmental and social processes.* Hillsdale, NJ: Erlbaum.

Madinier, G. (1967). *Conscience et mouvement.* Louvain: Editions Nauwaelaerts.

Magalhaes, M. C. C. (1994). An understanding of classroom interaction for literacy development. In N. Mercer & C. Coll (Eds.), *Explorations in socio-cultural studies: Vol. 3. Teaching, learning, and interaction* (pp. 99–106). Madrid: Fundación Infancia y Aprendizaje.

Magnusson, D. (1988). *Individual development from an interactional perspective.* Hillsdale, NJ: Erlbaum.

Maturana, H. (1980). Autopoiesis: Reproduction, heredity and evolution. In M. Zeleny (Ed.), *Autopoiesis, dissipative structures, and spontaneous social orders* (pp. 45–79). Boulder, CO: Westview Press.

Mead, G. H. (1913). The social self. *Journal of Philosophy, 10,* 374–380.

Mead, G. H. (1932). *The philosophy of the present.* Chicago: Open Court.

Mercado, R. (1994). Saberes and social voices in teaching. In A. Alvarez & P. Del Rio (Eds.), *Explorations in socio-cultural studies: Vol. 4. Education as culture construction* (pp. 60–70). Madrid: Fundación Infancia y Aprendizaje.

Meyerson, I. (1947). Pierre Janet et la théorie des tendances. *Journal de Psychologie, 40,* 5–19.

Moessinger, P. (1978). Piaget on equilibration. *Human Development, 21,* 255–267.

Moll, L. C. (1990). Vygotski's zone of proximal development: Rethinking its instructional applications. *Infancia y Aprendizaje, 51–52,* 157–168.

Moll, L. C. (Ed.). (1992). *Vygotsky and education.* Cambridge, England: Cambridge University Press.

Morgan, C. L. (1892). The law of psychogenesis. *Mind, 1,* 72–93.

Morgan, C. L. (1894). *An introduction to comparative psychology.* London: Walter Scott.

Muchow, M. (1931). Zur Frage einer lebensraum-und epochaltypologischen Entwicklungspsychologie des Kindes und Jugendlichen. *Beihefte zur Zeitschrift für angewandte Psychologie, 59,* 185–202.

Muchow, M., & Muchow, H. (1935). *Der Lebensraum des Großstadtkindes.* Hamburg: Riegel.

Newman, D., Griffin, P., & Cole, M. (1989). *The construction zone: Working for cognitive change in school.* Cambridge, England: Cambridge University Press.

Obeyesekere, G. (1990). *The work of culture.* Chicago: University of Chicago Press.

Oliveira, Z. M. R. (1997). The concept of "role" and the discussion of the internalization process. In B. Cox & C. Lightfoot (Eds.), *Sociogenetic perspectives on internalization.* Hillsdale, NJ: Erlbaum.

Oliveira, Z. M. R., & Rossetti-Ferreira, M. C. (1996). Understanding the co-constructive nature of human development. In J. Valsiner & H. -G. Voss (Eds.), *The structure of learning processes* (pp. 177–204). Norwood, NJ: ABLEX.

Oliveira, Z. M. R., & Valsiner, J. (1997). Play and imagination: The psychological construction of novelty. In A. Fogel, M. Lyra, & J. Valsiner (Eds.), *Dynamics and indeterminism in developmental and social processes.* Hillsdale, NJ: Erlbaum.

Onrubia, J., & Mayordomo, R. M. (1994). The construction of shared meanings in the classroom: Is there a role for practice? In A. Alvarez & P. Del Rio (Eds.), *Explorations in sociocultural studies: Vol. 4. Education as culture construction* (pp. 209–226). Madrid: Fundación Infancia y Aprendizaje.

Oyama, S. (1985) *The ontogeny of information.* Cambridge, England: Cambridge University Press.

Pascual-Leone, J. (1976). A view of cognition from a formalist perspective. In K. Riegel & J. Meacham (Eds.), *The developing individual in a changing world* (pp. 89–100). The Hague: Mouton.

Peirce, C. S. (1892). Man's glassy essence. *The Monist, 2,* 1–22.

Peirce, C. S. (1935). *Collected papers of Charles Sanders Peirce.* Cambridge, MA: Harvard University Press.

Penuel, W., & Wertsch, J. (1995a). Dynamics of negation in the identity politics of cultural other and cultural self. *Culture & Psychology, 1*(3), 343–359.

Penuel, W., & Wertsch, J. (1995b). Vygotsky and identity formation: A sociocultural approach. *Educational Psychologist, 30*(2), 83–92.

Piaget, J. (1952). Jean Piaget. In E. G. Boring, H. Werner, H. S. Langfeld, & R. M. Yerkes (Eds.), *A history of psychology in autobiography* (Vol. 4, pp. 237–256). Worcester, MA: Clark University Press.

Piaget, J. (1965). Psychology and philosophy. In B. B. Wolman & E. Nagel (Eds.), *Scientific psychology: Principles and approaches* (pp. 28–43). New York: Basic Books.

Piaget, J. (1970a). *Epistémologie des sciences de l'homme.* Paris: Gallimard.

Piaget, J. (1970b). Piaget's theory. In P. Mussen (Ed.), *Carmichael's handbook of child psychology* (pp. 703–732). New York: Wiley.

Piaget, J. (1970c). *Structuralism.* New York: Basic Books.

Piaget, J. (1971a). *Biology and knowledge.* Chicago: University of Chicago Press.

Piaget, J. (1971b). *Insights and illusions of philosophy.* London: Routledge & Kegan Paul.

Piaget, J. (1972). *The principles of genetic epistemology.* New York: Basic Books.

Piaget, J. (1977). *The development of thought: Equilibration of cognitive structures.* New York: Viking.

Piaget, J. (1980). The psychogenesis of knowledge and its epistemological significance. In M. Piatelli-Palmarini (Ed.), *Language and learning: The debate between Jean Piaget and Noam Chomsky* (pp. 23–34). Cambridge, MA: Harvard University Press.

Piaget, J. (1986). Essay on necessity. *Human Development, 29,* 301–314.

Piaget, J. (1995). *Sociological studies.* London: Routledge & Kegan Paul.

Piaget, J., & Voyat, G. (1979). The possible, the impossible, and the necessary. In F. B. Murray (Ed.), *The impact of Piagetian theory on education, philosophy, psychiatry, and psychology* (pp. 65–85). Baltimore: University Park Press.

Pino, A. (1994). Public and private categories in an analysis of internalization. In J. Wertsch & J. D. Ramirez (Eds.), *Explorations in socio-cultural studies: Vol. 2. Literacy and other forms of mediated action* (pp. 33–42). Madrid: Fundación Infancia y Aprendizaje.

Porter, T. M. (1992). Quantification and the accounting ideal in science. *Social Studies of Science, 22,* 633–652.

Porter, T. M. (1994). Objectivity as standardization: The rhetoric of impersonality in measurement, statistics, and cost-benefit analysis. In A. Megill (Ed.), *Rethinking objectivity* (pp. 197–237). Durham, NC: Duke University Press.

Portes, P. R., Smith, T., & Cuentas, T. E. (1994). Crosscultural parent-child interactions in relation to concept of development: Structure and processes in the ZPD. In A. Alvarez & P. Del Rio (Eds.), *Explorations in socio-cultural studies: Vol. 4. Education as culture construction* (pp. 97–108). Madrid: Fundación Infancia y Aprendizaje.

Prigogine, I. (1973). Irreversibility as a symmetry-breaking process. *Nature, 246,* 67–71.

Prigogine, I. (1976). Order through fluctuation: Self-organization and social system. In E. Jantsch & C. Waddington (Eds.), *Evolution and consciousness: Human systems in transition.* Reading, MA: Addison-Wesley.

Prigogine, I. (1978). Time, structure, and fluctuations. *Science, 201*(4358), 777–785.

Prigogine, I. (1980). *From being to becoming: Time and complexity in the physical sciences.* New York: Freeman.

Prigogine, I. (1982). Dialogue avec Piaget sur l'irréversible. *Archives de Psychologie, 50,* 7–16.

Prigogine, I. (1983). Probing into time. In M. Balaban (Ed.), *Biological foundations and human nature* (pp. 47–80). New York: Academic Press.

Prigogine, I. (1987). Exploring complexity. *European Journal of Operational Research, 30,* 97–103.

Ratner, C. (1991). *Vygotsky's sociohistorical psychology and its contemporary applications.* New York: Plenum Press.

Reed, E. S. (1993). The intention to use a specific affordance: A conceptual framework for psychology. In R. H. Wozniak & K. W. Fischer (Eds.), *Development in context* (pp. 45–76). Hillsdale, NJ: Erlbaum.

Reed, E. S. (1995). The ecological approach to language development: A radical solution to Chomsky's and Quine's problems. *Language & Communication, 15*(1), 1–29.

Riegel, K. (1975). Toward a dialectical theory of development. *Human Development, 18,* 50–64.

Riegel, K. (1976). The dialectics of human development. *American Psychologist, 31,* 689–700.

Rogoff, B. (1990). *Apprenticeship in thinking.* New York: Oxford University Press.

Rogoff, B. (1992). Three ways of relating person and culture: Thoughts sparked by Valsiner. *Human Development, 35*(5), 316–320.

Rogoff, B. (1993). Children's guided participation and participatory appropriation in sociocultural activity. In R. H. Wozniak & K. W. Fischer (Eds.), *Development in context* (pp. 121–153). Hillsdale, NJ: Erlbaum.

Rogoff, B., & Lave, J. (Eds.). (1984). *Everyday cognition.* Cambridge, MA: Harvard University Press.

Rojas-Drummond, S., & Rico, J. A. (1994). The development of independent problem solving in pre-school children. In N. Mercer & C. Coll (Eds.), *Explorations in socio-cultural studies: Vol. 3. Teaching, learning, and interaction* (pp. 161–175). Madrid: Fundación Infancia y Aprendizaje.

Romanes, G. J. (1888). *Mental evolution in man: Origin of human faculty.* London: Kegan Paul, Trench.

Rosa, A. (1993). *Frederick Charles Bartlett: Descripcion de su obra y analisis de su primera postura respecto de las relaciones entre psicologia y antropologia.* Unpublished manuscript, Universidad Autonoma de Madrid.

Rowell, J. A. (1983). Equilibration: Developing the hard core of the Piagetian research program. *Human Development, 26,* 61–71.

Saada-Robert, M. (1994). Microgenesis and situated cognitive representations. In N. Mercer & C. Coll (Eds.), *Explorations in socio-cultural studies: Vol. 3. Teaching, learning, and interaction* (pp. 55–64). Madrid: Fundación Infancia y Aprendizaje.

Santamaria, A. (1994). The experimental situation as a communicative situation. In N. Mercer & C. Coll (Eds.), *Explorations in socio-cultural studies: Vol. 3. Teaching, learning, and interaction* (pp. 65–71). Madrid: Fundación Infancia y Aprendizaje.

Schneider, W., & Hasselhorn, M. (1994). Situational context features and early memory development: Insights from replications of Istomina experiment. In R. van der Veer, M. H. van IJzendoorn, & J. Valsiner (Eds.), *Reconstructing the mind: Replicability in research on human development* (pp. 183–205). Norwood, NJ: ABLEX.

Schütz, A. (1982). *Life forms and meaning structures.* London: Routledge & Kegan Paul.

Schütz, A., & Luckmann, T. (1973). *The structures of the life-world.* Evanston, IL: Northwestern University Press.

Scribner, S., & Cole, M. (1981). *The psychology of literacy.* Cambridge, MA: Harvard University Press.

Segués, M. T., & Onrubia, J. (1992, September 6–9). *The negotiation of a situational context: Is it a preliminary task for children in an ambiguously defined dyadic situation.* Paper presented at the 5th European Conference on Developmental Psychology, Seville.

Sewertzoff, A. (1929). Direction of evolution. *Acta Zoologica, 10,* 59–141.

Shanahan, M., Valsiner, J., & Gottlieb, G. (1997). The conceptual structure of developmental theories. In J. Tudge, M. Shanahan, & J. Valsiner (Eds.), *Comparative approaches in developmental science.* New York: Cambridge University Press.

Shweder, R. A. (1991). *Thinking through cultures.* Cambridge, MA: Harvard University Press.

Shweder, R. A. (1995). The confessions of a methodological individualist. *Culture & Psychology, 1*(1), 115–122.

Shweder, R. A., & Sullivan, M. A. (1990). The semiotic subject of cultural psychology. In L. Pervin (Ed.), *Handbook of personality* (pp. 399–416). New York: Guilford Press.

Shweder, R. A., & Sullivan, M. A. (1993). Cultural psychology: Who needs it? *Annual Review of Psychology, 44,* 497–523.

Siegfried, J. (1994). Common sense language and the limits of theory construction in psychology. In J. Siegfried (Ed.), *The status of common sense in psychology* (pp. 3–34). Norwood, NJ: ABLEX.

Siegler, R., & Crowley, K. (1991). The microgenetic method: A direct means for studying cognitive development. *American Psychologist, 46,* 606–620.

Simmel, G. (1906). The sociology of secrecy and of secret societies. *American Journal of Sociology, 11*(4), 441–498.

Simmel, G. (1908). Vom Wesen der Kultur. *Österreichische Rundschau, 15,* 36–42.

Sjövall, B. (1967). *Psychology of tension.* Nordstets: Svenska Bokförlaget.

Smedslund, J. (1994). What kind of propositions are set forth in developmental research? Five case studies. *Human Development, 37,* 280–292.

Smedslund, J. (1995). Psychologic: Common sense and the pseudoempirical. In J. A. Smith, R. Harré, & L. van Langenhove (Eds.), *Rethinking psychology* (pp. 196–206). London: Sage.

Smolka, A. L. B. (1990, October). *School interactions: An analysis of speech events in a Brazilian public school setting.* Paper presented at the Boston University Conference on Language Development, Boston.

Smolka, A. L. B. (1994). Discourse practices and the issue of internalization. In A. Rosa & J. Valsiner (Eds.), *Explorations in socio-cultural studies: Vol. 1. Historical and theoretical discourse* (pp. 75–83). Madrid: Fundación Infancia y Aprendizaje.

Smolka, A. L. B., Fontana, R., & Laplane, A. (1994). The collective process of knowledge construction: Voices within voices. In A. Rosa & J. Valsiner (Eds.), *Explorations in socio-cultural studies: Vol. 1. Historical and theoretical discourse* (pp. 109–118). Madrid: Fundación Infancia y Aprendizaje.

Smolka, A. L. B., Góes, M. C., & Pino, A. (1995). The constitution of the subject: A persistent question. In J. Wertsch & B. Rogoff (Eds.), *Sociocultural studies of the mind.* Cambridge, England: Cambridge University Press.

Smolka, A. L. B., Góes, M. C., & Pino, A. (1996). (In)determinacy and semiotic constitution of subjectivity. In A. Fogel, M. Lyra, & J. Valsiner (Eds.), *Dynamics and indeterminism in developmental and social processes.* Hillsdale, NJ: Erlbaum.

Sovran, T. (1992). Between similarity and sameness. *Journal of Pragmatics, 18,* 329–344.

Spencer, H. (1864). *First principles.* London.

Sperber, H. (1923). *Einführung in der Bedeutungslehre.* Bonn: Schröder.

Stern, W. (1906). *Person und Sache: System der philosophischen Weltanschauung.* Leipzig: Barth.

Stern, W. (1911). *Differentielle Psychologie.* Leipzig: Barth.

Stern, W. (1918). *Grundgedanken der personalistische Philosophie.* Berlin: Reuther & Reichard.

Stern, W. (1919). *Die menschliche Persönlichkeit* (2nd ed.). Leipzig: Barth.

Stern, W. (1930). William Stern. In C. Murchison (Ed.), *A history of psychology in autobiography* (Vol. 1, pp. 335–388). Worcester, MA: Clark University Press.

Stern, W. (1935). *Allgemeine Psychologie auf personalistischer Grundlage.* Haag: Martinus Nijhoff.

Stern, W. (1938). *General psychology from the personalist standpoint.* New York: Macmillan.

Thom, R. (1973). A global dynamical scheme for vertebrate embryology. *Lectures on Mathematics in the Life Sciences, 5,* 3–45.

Thom, R. (1975). *Structural stability and morphogenesis.* Reading, MA: Benjamin.

Tudge, J., & Winterhoff, P. (1993). Vygotsky, Piaget, and Bandura: Perspectives on the relations between the social world and cognitive development. *Human Development, 36,* 61–81.

Vaihinger, H. (1920). *Die Philosophie des als ob: System der theoretischen, praktischen und religiösen Fiktionen der Menschheit* (4th ed.). Leipzig: Felix Meiner.

Valsiner, J. (1984). Two alternative epistemological frameworks in psychology: The typological and variational modes of thinking. *Journal of Mind and Behavior, 5*(4), 449–470.

Valsiner, J. (Ed.). (1986). *The individual subject and scientific psychology.* New York: Plenum Press.

Valsiner, J. (1987). *Culture and the development of children's action.* Chichester, England: Wiley.

Valsiner, J. (1988). *Developmental psychology in the Soviet Union.* Brighton, England: Harvester.

Valsiner, J. (1989a). Collective coordination of progressive empowerment. In L. T. Winegar (Ed.), *Social interaction and the development of children's understanding* (pp. 7–20). Norwood, NJ: ABLEX.

Valsiner, J. (1989b). *Human development and culture.* Lexington, MA: Heath.

Valsiner, J. (1991a). Construction of the mental: From the 'cognitive revolution' to the study of development. *Theory & Psychology, 1*(2), 477–494.

Valsiner, J. (1991b). Integration of theory and methodology in psychology: The legacy of Joachim Wohlwill. In L. Mos & P. van Geert (Eds.), *Annals of theoretical psychology* (Vol. 7, pp. 161–175). New York: Plenum Press.

Valsiner, J. (1993). Making of the future: Temporality and the constructive nature of human development. In G. Turkewitz & D. Devenney (Eds.), *Timing as initial condition of development* (pp. 13–40). Hillsdale, NJ: Erlbaum.

Valsiner, J. (1994a). James Mark Baldwin and his impact: Social development of cognitive functions. In A. Rosa & J. Valsiner (Eds.), *Explorations in socio-cultural studies: Vol. 1. Historical and theoretical discourse* (pp. 187–204). Madrid: Fundación Infancia y Aprendizaje.

Valsiner, J. (1994b). Culture and human development: A co-constructionist perspective. In P. van Geert, L. P. Mos, & W. J. Baker (Eds.), *Annals of theoretical psychology* (Vol. 10, pp. 247–298). New York: Plenum Press.

Valsiner, J. (1994c). Replicability in context: The problem of generalization. In R. van der Veer, M. H. van IJzendoorn, & J. Valsiner (Eds.), *Reconstructing the mind: Replicability in research on human development* (pp. 173–181). Norwood, NJ: ABLEX.

Valsiner, J. (1995a). Processes of development, and search for their logic: An introduction to Herbst's co-genetic logic. In T. Kindermann & J. Valsiner (Eds.), *Development of person-context relations.* Hillsdale, NJ: Erlbaum.

Valsiner, J. (1995b, September 27). *Meanings of "the data" in contemporary developmental psychology: Constructions and implications.* Gastvorträg am 12. Tagung der Fachgruppe Entwicklungspsychologie der Deutschen Gesellschaft für Psychologie, Leipzig.

Valsiner, J. (1997a). *The guided mind: A sociogenetic approach to personality.* Cambridge, MA: Harvard University Press.

Valsiner, J. (1997b). Constructing the personal through the cultural: Redundant organization of psychological development. In K. A. Renninger & E. Amsel (Eds.), *Construction in development.* Hillsdale, NJ: Erlbaum.

Valsiner, J. (1997c). *Culture and the development of children's action* (2nd ed.). New York: Wiley.

Valsiner, J. (1997d). The cultural psychology of Ernst E. Boesch [Special issue]. *Culture & Psychology, 3,* 3.

Valsiner, J., & Cairns, R. B. (1992). Theoretical perspectives on conflict and development. In C. U. Shantz & W. W. Hartup (Eds.), *Conflict in child and adolescent development* (pp. 15–35). Cambridge, England: Cambridge University Press.

Valsiner, J., & Van der Veer, R. (1993). The encoding of distance: The concept of the zone of proximal development and its interpretations. In R. R. Cocking & K. A. Renninger (Eds.), *The development and meaning of psychological distance* (pp. 35–62). Hillsdale, NJ: Erlbaum.

Valsiner, J., & Van der Veer, R. (1997). *The social mind.* New York: Cambridge University Press. Manuscript in preparation.

Van der Veer, R., & Valsiner, J. (1988). Lev Vygotsky and Pierre Janet: On the origin of the concept of sociogensis. *Developmental Review, 8,* 52–65.

Van der Veer, R., & Valsiner, J. (1991). *Understanding Vygotsky: A quest for synthesis.* Oxford, England: Basil Blackwell.

Van der Veer, R., & Valsiner, J. (1994). *Vygotsky reader.* Oxford, England: Basil Blackwell.

Van der Veer, R., Van IJzendoorn, M. H., & Valsiner, J. (Eds.). (1994). *Reconstructing the mind: Replicability in research on human development.* Norwood, NJ: ABLEX.

Van Geert, P. (Ed.). (1986). *Theory building in developmental psychology.* Amsterdam, The Netherlands: North-Holland.

Van Geert, P. (1988). The concept of transition in developmental theories. In Wm. J. Baker, L. P. Mos, H. V. Rappard, & H. J. Stam (Eds.), *Recent trends in theoretical psychology* (pp. 225–235). New York: Springer.

Van Geert, P. (1991). A dynamic systems model of cognitive and language growth. *Psychological Review, 98,* 3–35.

Van Geert, P. (1994). Vygotskian dynamics of development. *Human Development, 37,* 346–365.

Van Hoorn, W., & Verhave, T. (1980). Wundt's changing conceptions of a general and theoretical psychology. In W. G. Bringmann & R. D. Tweney (Eds.), *Wundt studies* (pp. 71–113). Toronto: Hogrefe.

Van Oers, B. (1996). The dynamics of school learning. In J. Valsiner & H. -G. Voss (Eds.), *Structure of learning processes* (pp. 205–228). Norwood, NJ: ABLEX.

Vegetti, M. S. (1994). Activity theory and historical cultural psychology: A comparative explanation of learning. In A. Alvarez & P. Del Rio (Eds.), *Explorations in socio-cultural studies: Vol. 4. Education as culture construction* (pp. 168–180). Madrid: Fundación Infancia y Aprendizaje.

von Baer, K. (1828). *Über Entwicklungsgeschichte der Thiere: Beobactung und reflexion.* Königsberg: Bornträger.

von Humboldt, W. (1836). *Ueber die Verschiedenheit des menschlichen Sprachbauses und ihren Einfluß auf die geistige Entwicklung des Menschengeschlechtes.* Berlin.

von Uexküll, J. J. (1928). *Theoretische biologie.* Berlin: Julius Springer.

von Uexküll, J. J. (1957). A stroll through the worlds of animals and men. In C. H. Schiller & K. Lashley (Eds.), *Instinctive behavior* (pp. 5–80). New York: International Universities Press.

von Uexküll, J. J. (1980). The theory of meaning. *Semiotica, 42*(1), 25–82. (Original *Bedeutungslehre* from 1940)

Voss, H. -G. (1996). Learning, development, and synergetics. In J. Valsiner & H. -G. Voss (Eds.), *Structure of learning processes* (pp. 17–44). Norwood, NJ: ABLEX.

Voss, H. -G., & Valsiner, J. (1996). Epilogue: The structure of learning—phylogenesis, ontogenesis, and microgenesis. In J. Valsiner & H. -G. Voss (Eds.), *Structure of learning processes* (pp. 329–333). Norwood, NJ: ABLEX.

Vuyk, R. (1981). *Overview and critique of Piaget's genetic epistemology, 1965–1980* (Vols. 1–2). London: Academic Press.

Vygotsky, L. S. (1931). *Paedology of the adolescent.* Moscow-Leningrad: Gosudarstvennoie uchebno-pedagogicheskoe izdatel'stvo.

Vygotsky, L. S. (1934). *Thinking and speech.* Moscow-Leningrad: Gosudarstvennoe Sotsialno-eknomicheskoe Izdatel'stvo. (in Russian)

Vygotsky, L. S. (1933/1966). Play and its role in the mental development of the child. *Voprosy psikhologii, 12*(6), 62–76. [English translation: In J. Bruner, A. Jolly, & K. Sylva (Eds.), *Play* (pp. 537–554). Harmondsworth: Penguin.]

Vygotsky, L. S. (1971). *Psychology of art.* Cambridge, MA: MIT Press. (Original work published 1925)

Vygotsky, L. S. (1982). Istoricheskii smysl krizisa v psikhologii. In *Sobranie sochinenii* (Vol. 1). Moscow: Pedagogika. (Original work published 1927)

Vygotsky, L. S., & Luria, A. R. (1994). Tool and symbol in child development. In R. van der Veer & J. Valsiner (Eds.), *The Vygotsky reader* (pp. 99–174). Oxford, England: Basil Blackwell. (Original work published 1930)

Waddington, C. (1966). Fields and gradients. In M. Locke (Ed.), *Major problems in developmental biology* (pp. 105–124). New York: Academic Press.

Waddington, C. (1970). Concepts and theories of growth, development, differentiation and morphogenesis. In C. Waddington (Ed.), *Towards theoretical biology* (Vol. 1, pp. 1–41). Chicago: Aldine.

Wahlsten, D., & Gottlieb, G. (1997). The invalid separation of effects of nature and nurture: Lessons from animal experimentation. In R. J. Sternberg & E. Grigorenko (Eds.), *Intelligence, heredity, and environment* (pp. 163–192). New York: Cambridge University Press.

Wallon, H. (1942). *De l'act à la pensée.* Paris: Armand Colin.

Wallon, H. (1945). *Les Origines de la pensée chez l'enfant.* Paris: P. U. F.

Weiss, P. (1969). The living system: Determinism stratified. In A. Koestler & J. Smythies (Eds.), *Beyond reductionism: New perspectives in the life sciences* (pp. 3–55). London: Hutchinson.

Weiss, P. (1978). Causality: Linear or systemic. In G. Miller & E. Lenneberg (Eds.), *Psychology and biology of language and thought*. New York: Academic Press.

Werner, C. M., & Altman, I. (1996). A Dialectic-transactional framework of social relations: Implications for children and adolescents. In D. Görlitz, H. J. Harloff, G. Mey, & J. Valsiner (Eds.), *Children, cities, and psychological theories: Developing relationships*. Berlin: Walter de Gruyter.

Werner, H. (1919). *Die Ursprünge der Metaphor*. Leipzig: Barth.

Werner, H. (1926). Über Mikromelodik und Mikroharmonik. *Zeitschrift für Psychologie, 98*, 74–89.

Werner, H. (1930). Die Rolle der Sprachempfindung im Prozess der Gestaltung ausdrückmässig erlebter Wörter. *Zeitschrift für Psychologie, 117*, 230–254.

Werner, H. (1931). Das Prinzip der Gestaltschichtung und seine Bedeutung im kunstwerklichen Aufbau. *Zeitschrift für angewandte Psychologie, Beiheft, 59*, 241–256.

Werner, H. (1937). Process and achievement—A basic problem of education and developmental psychology. *Harvard Educational Review, 7*, 358–368.

Werner, H. (1938). William Stern's personalistics and psychology of personality. *Character & Personality, 7*, 109–125.

Werner, H. (1940a). *Comparative psychology of mental development*. New York: Harper & Brothers.

Werner, H. (1940b). Musical "micro-scales" and "micromelodies." *Journal of Psychology, 10*, 149–156.

Werner, H. (1948). *Comparative psychology of mental development*. New York: International University Press.

Werner, H. (1954). Change of meaning: A study of semantic processes through the experimental method. *Journal of General Psychology, 50*, 181–208.

Werner, H. (1956). Microgenesis and aphasia. *Journal of Abnormal & Social Psychology, 52*, 347–353.

Werner, H. (1957). The concept of development from a comparative and organismic point of view. In D. B. Harris (Ed.), *The concept of development* (pp. 125–147). Minneapolis: University of Minnesota Press.

Werner, H., & Kaplan, B. (1956). The developmental approach to cognition: Its relevance to the psychological interpretation of anthropological and ethnolinguistic data. *American Anthropologist, 58*, 866–880.

Werner, H., & Kaplan, B. (1963). *Symbol formation*. New York: Wiley.

Wertsch, J. V. (1979). From social interaction to higher psychological processes: A clarification and application of Vygotsky's theory. *Human Development, 22*, 1–22.

Wertsch, J. V. (1981). The concept of activity in Soviet psychology: An introduction. In J. V. Wertsch (Ed.), *The concept of activity in Soviet psychology* (pp. 3–36). Armonk, NY: Sharpe.

Wertsch, J. V. (1983). The role of semiosis in L. S. Vygotsky's theory of human cognition. In B. Bain (Ed.), *The sociogenesis of language and human conduct* (pp. 17–31). New York: Plenum Press.

Wertsch, J. V. (1984). The zone of proximal development: Some conceptual issues. In B. Rogoff & J. V. Wertsch (Eds.), *Children's learning in the "zone of proximal development": Vol. 23. New directions for child development* (pp. 7–17). San Francisco: Jossey-Bass.

Wertsch, J. V. (1985). *Vygotsky and the social formation of mind*. Cambridge, MA: Harvard University Press.

Wertsch, J. V. (1990). The voice of rationality in a sociocultural approach to mind. In L. C. Moll (Ed.), *Vygotsky and education* (pp. 111–126). Cambridge, England: Cambridge University Press.

Wertsch, J. V. (1991). *Voices in the mind*. Cambridge, MA: Harvard University Press.

Wertsch, J. V. (1995). Sociocultural research in the copyright age. *Culture & Psychology, 1*(1), 81–102.

Wertsch, J. V., Minick, N., & Arns, F. J. (1984). The creation of context in joint problem-solving. In B. Rogoff & J. Lave (Eds.), *Everyday cognition: Its development in social context* (pp. 151–171). Cambridge, MA: Harvard University Press.

Wertsch, J. V., & Smolka, A. L. B. (1993). Continuing the dialogue: Vygotsky, Bakhtin and Lotman. In H. Daniels (Ed.), *Charting the agenda: Educational activity after Vygotsky* (pp. 69–92). London: Routledge & Kegan Paul.

Wertsch, J. V., & Stone, C. A. (1985). The concept of internalization in Vygotsky's account of the genesis of higher mental functions. In J. V. Wertsch (Ed.), *Culture, communication, and cognition: Vygotskian perspectives* (pp. 162–179). Cambridge, England: Cambridge University Press.

Winegar, L. T. (1988). Children's emerging understanding of social events: Co-construction and social process. In J. Valsiner (Ed.), *Child development within culturally structured environments: Vol. 2. Social co-construction and environmental guidance of development* (pp. 3–27). Norwood, NJ: ABLEX.

Winegar, L. T., Renninger, K. A., & Valsiner, J. (1989). Dependent–independence in adult-child relationships. In D. A. Kramer & M. J. Bopp (Eds.), *Transformation in clinical and developmental psychology* (pp. 157–168). New York: Springer.

Winegar, L. T., & Valsiner, J. (1992). Re-contextualizing context: Analysis of metadata and some further elaborations. In L. T. Winegar & J. Valsiner (Eds.), *Children's development within social context: Vol 2. Research and methodology* (pp. 249–266). Hillsdale, NJ: Erlbaum.

Wispé, L. (1987). History of the concept of empathy. In N. Eisenberg & J. Strayer (Eds.), *Empathy and its development* (pp. 17–37). Cambridge, England: Cambridge University Press.

Witasek, S. (1901). Zur psychologischen Analyse der ästhetischen Einfühlung. *Zeitschrift für Psychologie und Physiologie der Sinnesorgane, 25,* 1–49.

Wohlwill, J. F. (1985). Marta Muchow, 1892–1933: Her life, work, and contribution to developmental and ecological psychology. *Human Development, 28,* 198–209.

Worcester, W. L. (1893). Observations on some points in James' psychology: 2. Emotions. *The Monist, 3*(2), 285–298.

Wozniak, R. (1986). Notes toward a coconstructive theory of the emotion-cognition relationship. In D. J. Bearison & H. Zimiles (Eds.), *Thought and emotion: Developmental perspectives* (pp. 39–64). Hillsdale, NJ: Erlbaum.

Wozniak, R. (1993). Coconstructive metatheory for psychology. In R. Wozniak & K. Fischer (Eds.), *Development in context* (pp. 77–92). Hillsdale, NJ: Erlbaum.

Wundt, W. (1973). *The language of gestures.* The Hague: Mouton.

Youniss, J. (1987). Social construction and moral development: Update and expansion of an idea. In W. M. Kurtines & J. L. Gewirtz (Eds.), *Moral development through social interaction* (pp. 131–148). New York: Wiley.

Zeigarnik, B. (1927). Das Behalten erledigter und unerledigter Handlungen. *Psychologische Forschung, 9,* 1–85.

Zeigarnik, B. (1981). *Teoria lichnosti Kurta Levina.* Moscow: Moscow University Press.

CHAPTER 5

The Significance of Biology for Human Development:
A Developmental Psychobiological Systems View

GILBERT GOTTLIEB, DOUGLAS WAHLSTEN, and ROBERT LICKLITER

This chapter describes the history and current status of a psychobiological systems view of development, its implications for a developmentally oriented conception of behavior genetics, its application to a research area such as intersensory development, and the broader implications of a developmental psychobiological systems view of human development. A brief evaluation of current thinking in biology, developmental neuroscience, developmental psychology, and sociology is included.

Authorship of the chapter's five text sections is as follows: "A Developmental Psychobiological Systems View . . ." (G. G.); "Developmental Behavior Genetics . . ." (D. W.); "Application . . . Intersensory Development" (R. L.); "Broader Implications . . ." (G. G.); "Summary and Conclusion" (G. G.). The historical trends in the first section, leading to the current developmental systems view, are also reviewed in Gottlieb (1996). G. G.'s research and scholarly pursuits are supported in part by NIMH Grant MH-52429. D. W.'s support comes from MT-11728, from the Medical Research Council of Canada, and OGP-45825, from the Natural Sciences and Engineering Research Council of Canada. R. L.'s research is supported in part by NIMH Grant MH-48949.

A DEVELOPMENTAL PSYCHOBIOLOGICAL SYSTEMS VIEW: HISTORY AND CURRENT STATUS[1]

The current definition of *epigenesis* holds that individual development is characterized by an increase in novelty and

[1] This first section heading introduces "A" systems view, not "The" systems view. For a partial illustration of the variety of developmental systems views in the behavioral sciences, interested

complexity of organization over time—that is, the sequential emergence of new structural and functional properties and competencies—at all levels of analysis as a consequence of horizontal and vertical coactions among its parts, including organism–environment coactions (Gottlieb, 1991a). Our present understanding of the various defining features of epigenesis has been laboriously worked out over the past 200 years. This chapter begins with a brief recounting of that intellectual history.

The Triumph of Epigenesis over Preformation

The triumph of epigenesis over the concept of preformation ushered in the era of truly developmental thinking. Namely, to understand the origin of any phenotype, it is necessary to study its development in the individual. This insight has been with us since at least the beginning of the 1800s, when Étienne Geoffroy Saint-Hilaire (1825) advanced his hypothesis that the originating event of evolutionary change was an anomaly of embryonic or fetal development. The origin or initiation of evolutionary change was thus seen as a change in the very early development of an atypical individual. Although not a believer in evolution (in the sense that a species could become so modified as to give rise to a new species), Karl Ernst von Baer (1828) used the description of individual development as a basis for classifying the relationships among species: Those that shared the most developmental features were classified together, while those that shared the fewest features were given a remote classification. Von Baer noticed that vertebrate species are much more alike in their early developmental stages than in their later stages. This was such a ubiquitous observation that von Baer formulated a law to the effect that development in various vertebrate species could be universally characterized as progressing from the homogeneous to the heterogeneous. As individuals in each species reached the later stages of their development, they began to

---

readers are referred to Ford and Lerner's (1992) description of their version of a systems view of human development and, at an even more abstract level, Oyama's (1985) depiction of her ideas about developmental systems and evolution. Figure 5.6 gives the essence of Gottlieb's notion of a developmental psychobiological systems approach as it has been worked out, beginning with the central concepts of bidirectionality and probabilistic epigenesis in 1970.

differentiate more and more away from each other, so there was less and less resemblance as each species reached adulthood. Figure 5.1 is a reproduction of von Baer's classification of various classes of vertebrate species, based on his developmental observations.

The Birth of Experimental Embryology

Von Baer's emphasis on the importance of developmental description represented a great leap forward in understanding the question of "What?" but it did not come to grips with the problem of "How." He and his predecessors evinced no interest in the mechanisms or means by which each developmental stage is brought about—it simply was not a question for them. It remained for the self-designated *experimental* embryologists of the late 1800s to ask that developmental question: Wilhelm His, Wilhelm Roux, and Hans Driesch. His (1888) wrote, in reference to von Baer's observations:

> By comparison of [the development of] different organisms, and by finding their similarities, we throw light upon their probable genealogical relations, but we give no direct explanation of their growth and formation. A direct explanation can only come from the immediate study of the different phases of individual development. Every stage of development must be looked at as the physiological consequence of some preceding stage, and ultimately as the consequence of the acts of impregnation and segmentation of the egg.... (p. 295)

It remained for Roux, in 1888, to plunge a hot needle into one of the two existing cells after the first cleavage in a frog's egg, thereby initiating a truly *experimental* study of embryology.

The arduously reached conclusion that we hold today—that individual development is most appropriately viewed as a hierarchically organized system—began with Hans Driesch's being dumbfounded by the results of his replication of Roux's experiment. Roux found that killing one cell and allowing the second cleavage cell to survive resulted in a half-embryo in frogs; Driesch (reviewed in 1908) found that disarticulating the first two cells in a sea urchin resulted in two fully formed sea urchins, albeit diminished in size. [When the disarticulation procedure was later used in amphibians, two fully formed embryos resulted, as in

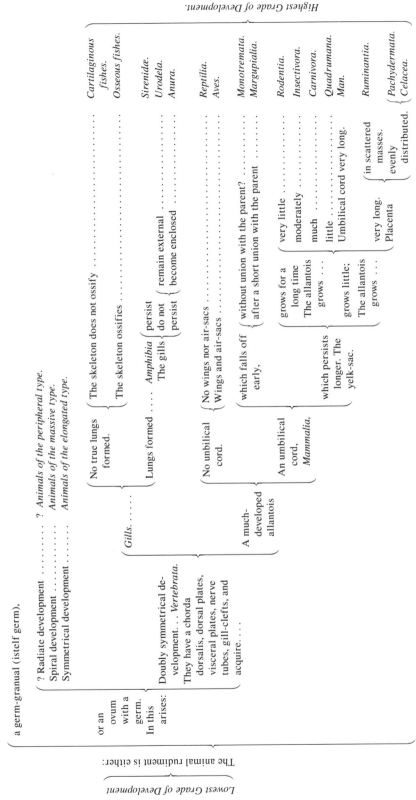

Figure 5.1 Von Baer's scheme of the progress of development. Von Baer's developmental classification of various classes of vertebrate animals (fish, amphibians, reptiles, birds, and mammals [*Monotremata* through *Cetacea*]) appears along the right vertical axis. His three other "types" of bodily organization are briefly designated in the upper left portion of figure. Von Baer's scheme is not evolutionary in the conventional sense of ancestors giving rise to descendants. Rather, he sees an increasing complexity of prenatal structural organization going from the top to the bottom of the figure. For von Baer, the most complex prenatal structural organizations reflect the highest grade of ontogenetic development. Grades of development proceed from lowest (beginning on the left side of the figure) to highest (right side of the figure), whereas structural organizational complexity goes from the lowest (top) to the highest (bottom) on the right vertical axis. From von Baer, 1828. Translated by A. Henfry & T. H. Huxley, "Scientific Memoirs, Selected from the Transactions of Foreign Academies of Sciences, and from Foreign Journals," *Natural History*, 1853. London: Taylor and Francis.

235

Driesch's experiment with sea urchins (Mangold & Seidel, 1927).] Driesch came to believe that some nonmaterial vitalistic influence (an "entelechy") is at work in the formation of the embryo, one that will forever elude our best experimental efforts, so he eventually gave up embryology in favor of the presumably more manageable problems of psychology.

Because Driesch had found that a single cell could lead to the creation of a fully formed individual, he gathered, quite correctly, that each cell must have the same prospective potency, as he called it, and could, in principle, become any part of the body. He thought of these cells as *harmonious-equipotential systems.* For Driesch, the vitalistic feature of these harmonious-equipotential systems is their ability to reach the same outcome or endpoint by different routes, a process that he labeled *equifinality.* Thus, in the usual case, two attached cleavage cells give rise to an embryo; and in the unusual case of two separated cleavage cells, each gives rise to an embryo. To Driesch, these experimental observations provided the most elementary or "easy" proofs of vitalism; for those still laboring in the field of embryology today, they continue to provide a provocative challenge for experimental resolution and discovery.

For the present purposes, it is important to note that, if each cell of an organism is a harmonious-equipotential system, then it follows that the organism itself must be such a system. Driesch's notion of equifinality—that developing organisms of the same species can reach the same endpoint via different developmental pathways—has become an axiom of developmental systems theory.[2] In a systems view of developmental psychobiology, equifinality means that (a) developing organisms that have different early or "initial" conditions can reach the same endpoint, and (b) organisms that share the same initial condition can reach the same endpoint by different routes or pathways (cf. Ford & Lerner, 1992). Both of these outcomes have been empirically demonstrated by the behavioral research of D. B. Miller (Miller, Hicinbothom, & Blaich, 1990) and R. Lickliter (Banker & Lickliter, 1993) in birds, and by Nöel

(1989) and Carlier, Roubertoux, Kottler, and Degrelle (1989), among others, in mammals. The uniquely important developmental principle of equifinality is rarely explicitly invoked in theoretical views of developmental psychology, so it may seem unfamiliar to many readers. K. W. Fischer's (1980) theory of skill development in infancy and early childhood is one of the rare exceptions in that it explicitly incorporates the notion of equifinality: "[D]ifferent individuals will follow different developmental paths in the same skill domain. . . . The developmental transformation rules predict a large number of different possible paths in any single domain" (p. 513).

Microgenetic studies of human development are most likely to reveal equifinality because, under these conditions, the response of individuals to the same challenge is closely monitored and described for shorter or longer periods (e.g., Kuhn, 1995). In one such study, Bellugi, Wang, and Jernigan (1994) monitored the attempted solutions of Williams syndrome and Down syndrome children, aged 10 to 18 years, to the block design subtest on the WISC-R. The children in both groups performed equally poorly, but the attempted solutions by the Down syndrome individuals approximated in a global way the designs they were trying to copy, whereas the Williams group uniquely failed to reproduce the correct global configuration of the blocks. As shown in Figure 5.2, the children in both groups got the same low scores, but they achieved them in very different ways (by different pathways).

Another example involved a study of language development in young hearing and deaf preschool children. Each group devised an arbitrary system of signs to refer to events and objects, but the hearing children achieved the outcome by using the language of their adult caretakers as their model, whereas the deaf preschool children, being born to hearing parents who did not know sign language, developed their own arbitrary set of gestures to communicate meaningfully with peers and adults (Goldin-Meadow, 1997).

As a final example, in lines of mice selectively bred for high and low aggression, individuals in the low line become as aggressive as the high line if they are tested four times from day 28 to day 235 of life (Figure 5.3) (Cairns, MacCombie, & Hood, 1983). Once again, the developmental pathways to the same endpoint are different.

However, in these mouse experiments, equifinality does not mean there is a genetic pathway in the high line and an

---

[2] Egon Brunswik, in his infrequently cited monograph for the International Encyclopedia of Unified Science, *The Conceptual Framework of Psychology* (1952), was the first to call attention to equifinality as an important principle of psychological development.

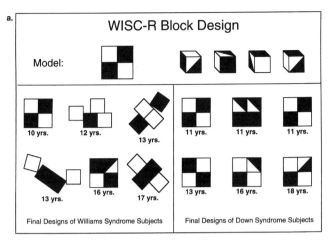

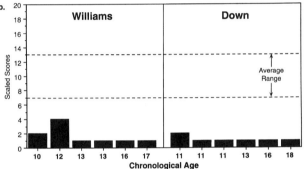

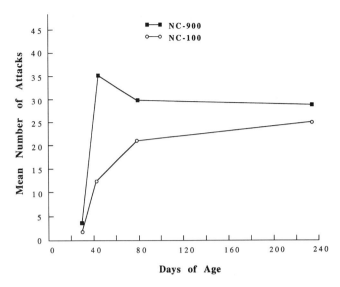

Figure 5.2 Contrasting block design performance in Williams syndrome (WS) and Down syndrome (DS) children. (a) Both WS and DS designs reveal striking differences in their errors. WS subjects uniquely fail to reproduce the correct global configuration of the blocks. (b) The differences in the errors are not reflected in the quantitative scores, which are comparably low. From Bellugi, Wang, & Jernigan, 1994, p. 38. Copyright © 1994 by Dr. U. Bellugi, The Salk Institute, La Jolla, California. Reprinted with permission.

Figure 5.3 Mean number of 5-sec blocks in which subjects of the high-aggressive (NC-900) and low-aggressive (NC-100) lines attacked their test partners. (The same subjects were repeatedly tested at days 28, 42, 72, and 235.) Modified from "A Developmental-Genetic Analysis of Aggressive Behavior in Mice: I. Behavioral Outcomes," by R. B. Cairns, D. J. MacCombie, & K. E. Hood, 1983, *Journal of Comparative Psychology, 97,* pp. 69–89.

Systems versus Mechanico-Reductive and Vitalistic-Constructive Viewpoints

As our overview of the precursors to our present concept of the systems nature of development moves from the late 1800s to the 1930s, we encounter the insights of the systems or organismic embryologists, Paul Weiss and Ludwig von Bertalanffy, and the physiological geneticist Sewall Wright.

In his wonderfully lucid and historically complete opus on the topic of development, *Modern Theories of Development: An Introduction to Theoretical Biology* (originally published in German), von Bertalanffy (1933/1962) introduced the system theory, as he called it, as a way of avoiding the pitfalls of machine theory, on the one hand, and vitalism, on the other. The error of the machine theory of development, as von Bertalanffy saw it, was its attempt to analyze the various aspects of the development process in terms of their individual component parts or mechanisms, conceived of as proceeding independently of one another. Von Bertalanffy believed that the fundamental error of the classical concept of mechanism, which was adopted

experiential pathway in the low line—the expression of aggression is genetically and experientially mediated in both lines. The crucial experience in the developmental pathway to high aggression in the high line is rearing in social isolation between days 21 and 45, whereas the crucial experience in the developmental pathway to high aggression in the low line is repeated testing from days 45 to 235. This latter finding raises a highly significant question: Would the usual line difference in aggression at day 45 be erased if the low line were repeatedly tested before day 45 rather than after day 45?

wholesale from physics, lay in its application of an additive point of view to the interpretation of living organisms.

> Vitalism, on the other hand, while being at one with the machine theory in analyzing the vital processes into occurrences running along their separate lines, believed these to be co-ordinated by an immaterial, transcendent entelechy. Neither of these views is justified by the facts. We believe now that the solution of this antithesis in biology is to be sought in an *organismic* or *system theory* of the organism which, on the one hand, in opposition to machine theory, sees the essence of the organism in the harmony and co-ordination of the processes among one another, but, on the other hand, does not interpret this co-ordination as vitalism does, by means of a mystical entelechy, but through the forces immanent in the living system itself. (von Bertalanffy, 1962, pp. 177–178)

Nowadays, we make von Bertalanffy's point by distinguishing between theoretical and methodological reductionism. Theoretical reductionism seeks to explain the behavior of the whole organism by reference to its component parts— a derivative of the older, additive, physical concept of mechanism. Methodological reductionism holds that not only is a description of the various hierarchically organized levels of analysis of the whole organism necessary, but a depiction of the bidirectional traffic between levels is crucial to a developmental understanding of the individual.[3] For purposes of recognizing historical precedent, it is appropriate here to present the diagrams of Paul Weiss and Sewall Wright, which exemplify the strictly methodological reductionism of the hierarchically organized systems view of development. (We use what we hope is not an annoying plural form of system because the various levels of organismic functioning constitute, within themselves, systems of analysis: the organism–environment ecological system, the nervous system, the genomic system, and others. Von Bertalanffy himself later (1950) came to use the plural form in his conception of General Systems Theory.)

In Paul Weiss's (1959) diagram of the hierarchy of reciprocal influences (Figure 5.4), there are seven levels of analysis. The *gene* (DNA) is the ultimately reduced unit in an ever-expanding analytic pathway that moves from gene to *chromosome*—where genes can influence each other— from cell *nucleus* to cell *cytoplasm,* from cell to *tissue* (organized arrangements of cells that form organ systems such as the nervous system, circulatory system, musculoskeletal system, etc.), all of which make up the *organism* that interacts with the external *environment.* The entire schema represents a hierarchically organized system of increasing size, differentiation, and complexity, in which each component affects, and is affected by, all the other components, not only at its own level but at lower and higher levels as well. Thus, the arrows in Figure 5.4 not only go upward from the gene, eventually reaching all the way to the external environment through the activities of the whole organism, but the arrows of influence return from the external environment through the various levels of the organism back to the genes.

While the feed-forward or feed-upward nature of the genes has always been appreciated, the feed-backward or feed-downward influences have usually been thought to stop at the cell membrane. The newer conception is one of a totally interrelated, fully coactional system in which the

---

[3] Systems thinking is catching on in neuroscience. As a tribute to his long and productive career in neuroembryology, the *International Journal of Developmental Neuroscience* publishes an Annual Viktor Hamburger Award Review. In 1993, the award went to Ira B. Black, who published a review on "Environmental Regulation of Brain Trophic Interactions," which detailed the influence of neural activity on multiple trophic (growth) factors during development, further attesting to the feasibility of working out the bidirectional relations depicted in Figure 5.6. Black himself raised that optimistic question at the conclusion of his review: "Are we now in a position to move from environmental stimulus to impulse activity, trophic regulation, mental function and behavior . . . ?" (p. 409). The most recent Viktor Hamburger Award Review (1994) continued that theme with Carla Shatz's "Role for Spontaneous Neural Activity in the Patterning of Connections between Retina and LGN during Visual System Development," which is also in keeping with the first author's broad definition of the term *experience* ("spontaneous or evoked functional activity")

in this chapter and earlier (Gottlieb, 1976). Even when an organism's experience arises out of an interaction with the external environment, there is an essential internal (cellular) correlate to that activity, so that is the rationale for including endogenous activity as part of the experiential process. Perhaps, for some readers, it would be more appropriate to drop the term *experience* and use the term *functional activity* at both the neural and behavioral levels of analysis. To the first author's way of thinking, experience and functional activity are synonymous.

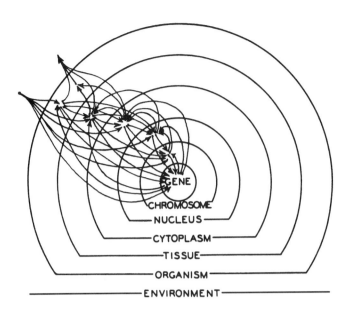

Figure 5.4 Embryologist Paul Weiss's hierarchy of reciprocal influences from the lowest level of organization (gene) to the highest level (external environment). From "Cellular Dynamics," by P. Weiss, 1959, *Reviews of Modern Physics, 31,* pp. 11–20. Copyright © 1959 by Reviews of Modern Physics. Reprinted with permission.

activity of the genes themselves can be affected through the cytoplasm of the cell by events originating at any other level in the system, including the external environment. It is known, for example, that external environmental factors such as social interactions, changing day length, and so on, can cause hormones to be secreted (review by Cheng, 1979), and the hormones, in turn, result in the activation of DNA transcription inside the nucleus of the cell (i.e., "turning genes on"). There are now many empirical examples of external sensory and internal neural events that excite and inhibit gene expression (e.g., Anokhin, Milevsnic, Shamakina, & Rose, 1991; Calamandrei & Keverne, 1994; Mauro, Wood, Krushel, Crossin, & Edelman, 1994; Rustak, Robertson, Wisden, & Hunt, 1990), thereby supporting the *bidirectionality* of influences among the various levels of analysis from gene to environment (to be discussed further below).

Weiss was an experimental embryologist, so it was probably merely an oversight that he did not explicitly include a developmental dimension in his figure. Another schematic

of a systems view, also not explicitly developmental, was put forward by Sewall Wright in 1968. As shown in Wright's schema (Figure 5.5), once again, the traffic between levels is bidirectional and the activity of the genes is placed firmly inside a completely coactional system of influences. It is a small but important step to apply this way of thinking to the process of development (see Figure 5.6, in a later section).

Influence of Sensory Stimulation on Genetic Activity

Some behavioral scientists, including developmental psychologists, seem to be unaware of the fact that the activation of the genes (DNA) themselves is subject to influences from higher levels during the course of development. Therefore, it is useful to stress that contingency as a part of the *normal* process of development. For example, one category of genetic activity, called "immediate early gene expression," is specifically responsive to sensory stimulation. A higher number of neurons is found in the brains of animals that have been appropriately stimulated, and a deficiency in the number of cortical neurons appears in animals that have been deprived of such normal sensory stimulation (e.g., Rosen, McCormack, Villa-Komaroff, & Mower, 1992, and references therein). Not so long ago, neuroscientists of very high repute, including at least one eventual Nobel prize winner, were writing in a vein that seemed to make sensory-stimulated immediate early gene expression an impossibility rather than an important feature of normal neurobehavioral development. For example, Roger Sperry wrote, in 1951: "[T]he bulk of the nervous system must be patterned without the aid of functional adjustment" or, "Development in many instances . . . is remarkably independent of function, even in . . . [the] sense . . . [of] . . . function as a general condition necessary to healthy growth" (p. 271). Twenty years later, Sperry (1971) continued to observe: "In general outline at least, one could now see how it could be entirely possible for behavioral nerve circuits of extreme intricacy and precision to be inherited and organized prefunctionally solely by the mechanisms of embryonic growth and differentiation" (p. 32). Sperry was not alone in expressing a genetically predeterministic conception of neural and behavioral epigenesis. Viktor Hamburger, perhaps the foremost student of Nobel laureate Hans Spemann, echoed Sperry's

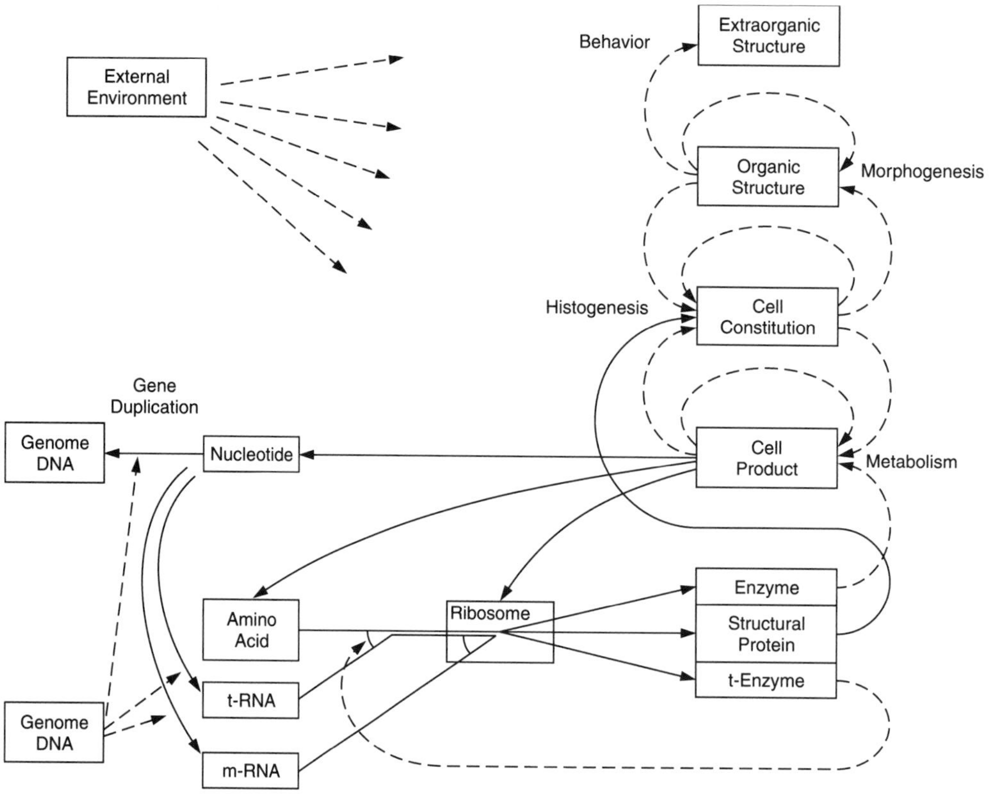

Figure 5.5 The fully coactive or interactional organismic system, as presented by Sewall Wright, a physiologically oriented population geneticist. Modified from *Evolution and the Genetics of Populations: Vol. 1. Genetic and Biometric Foundations,* by S. Wright, 1968. Chicago: University of Chicago Press.

beliefs on several occasions which, to his credit, he later ameliorated:

> The architecture of the nervous system, and the concomitant behavior patterns result from self-generating growth and maturation processes that are determined entirely by inherited, intrinsic factors, to the exclusion of functional adjustment, exercise, or anything else akin to learning. (Hamburger, 1957, p. 56; reiterated *in toto* in 1964, p. 21)

With noted authorities on the development of the nervous system making such statements in books and articles apt to be read by biologically oriented psychologists, it is not surprising that a genetically predeterministic view entered into psychology, especially when psychology was trying to recover its balance from accusations of the other error—environmentalism. One of the values of a systems view of development is its explicit utilization of both genetic and experiential influences, not merely a nervous (and often empty) lip service averring that both are surely necessary.

The Triumph of Probabilistic Epigenesis over Predetermined Epigenesis

In 1970, Gottlieb described an extant dichotomy in conceptualizing individual development as the predetermined and probabilistic epigenesis of behavior. The former saw a genetically inspired structural maturation as bringing about function in an essentially unidirectional fashion, whereas the latter envisaged bidirectional influences between structure and function. The range of application of the probabilistic conception did not seem very broad at the time. In

1976, Gottlieb explicitly added the genetic level to the scheme so that the unidirectional predetermined conception was pictured as

$$\text{Genetic activity} \rightarrow \text{Structure} \rightarrow \text{Function}$$

in a nonreciprocal pathway, whereas the probabilistic notion was fully bidirectional:

$$\text{Genetic activity} \leftrightarrow \text{Structure} \leftrightarrow \text{Function}$$

Now that spontaneous neural activity as well as behavioral and environmental stimulation are accepted as playing roles in normal neural development, and that sensory and hormonal influences can trigger genetic activity, the correctness and broad applicability of the probabilistic notion are undeniable and widely confirmed. In this sense, the probabilistic conception of epigenesis has triumphed over the predetermined view.

Building on the probabilistic notion, Gottlieb (1991a, 1992) has more recently presented a simplified scheme of a systems view of psychobiological development that incorporates the major points of von Bertalanffy's, Weiss's, and Wright's thinking on the subject, and adds some detail on the organism–environment level that is necessary for a thoroughgoing behavioral and psychobiological analysis. Any merit that this way of thinking about development may have must certainly be traced to the pioneering efforts of psychobiological theoreticians such as Z.-Y. Kuo (summarized in 1976), T. C. Schneirla (1960), and D. S. Lehrman (1970). At present, the probabilistic, bidirectional conception is being used both implicitly and explicitly by a number of more recent psychobiologically oriented theorists (e.g., Cairns, Gariépy, & Hood, 1990; Edelman, 1988; Ford & Lerner, 1992; Griffiths & Gray, 1994; Hinde, 1990; Johnston & Hyatt, 1994; Magnusson & Törestad, 1993; Oyama, 1985).

As shown in Figure 5.6, Gottlieb has reduced the levels of analysis to three functional organismic levels (genetic activity, neural activity, and behavior) and has subdivided the environmental level into physical, social, and cultural components.[4] Those of us who work with nonhuman animal

---

[4]Gariépy (1995) has correctly pointed out that psychological functioning as such is not included in the four levels of Gottlieb's

BIDIRECTIONAL INFLUENCES

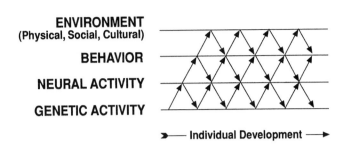

Figure 5.6   A systems view of psychobiological development. From *Individual Development and Evolution: The Genesis of Novel Behavior,* by Gilbert Gottlieb, 1992. New York: Oxford University Press. Copyright © 1992 by Oxford University Press, Inc. Reprinted with permission.

models stress the influence of the physical and social aspects of the environment; those who work with humans prominently include cultural aspects as well. The criticism that one hears most, regarding this admittedly simple-minded scheme, is not that it is overly simple but, rather, that it is too complex: There are too many influences, running in too many directions. In short, a developmental systems approach is alleged to be unmanageable and just not useful for analytic purposes. What we hope to show in the remainder of this chapter is that such a scheme is not only useful but represents individual development at a suitable level of complexity that does justice to the actualities of developmental influences.[5]

---

systems diagram (Figure 5.6). The reason for that omission is that psychological functioning or mediation (perception, thinking, attitudes, love, hate, etc.) must be inferred from analysis at the overt level of behavior and the environment, as made clear by the notion of methodological behaviorism introduced by E. C. Tolman in 1932. In this sense, all psychologists are methodological (not theoretical) behaviorists (cf. Brunswik, 1952).

[5]At the conclusion of their review of genotype and maternal environment, Roubertoux, Nosten-Bertrand, and Carlier (1990) observe: "The effects constitute a very complex network, which is probably discouraging for those who still hope to establish a simple relation between the different levels of biological organization, and particularly the molecular and the behavioral. The picture is indeed more complicated" (p. 239).

Experience Defined as Functional Activity

Before turning to a review of developmental behavior genetics and intersensory influences in an effort to link all four levels of analysis in Figure 5.6, it is necessary to offer a definition of the term *experience* that will allow us to discuss experiential events occurring at each level of analysis, not just at the organism–environment level. Experience is synonymous with function or activity, and is construed very broadly to include the electrical activity of nerve cells and their processes; impulse conduction; neurochemical and hormonal secretion; the use and exercise of muscles and sense organs (whether interoceptive, proprioceptive, or exteroceptive); and, of course, the behavior of the organism itself. Thus, the term *experience,* as used here, is not synonymous with *environment,* but rather stresses functional *activity* at the neural and behavioral levels of analysis. The contribution of such functions to development can take any of three forms: (a) *inductive,* channeling development in one direction rather than another; (b) *facilitative* (temporal or quantitative), influencing thresholds or the rate at which structural and physiological maturation, or behavioral development, occurs; or (c) *maintenance,* serving to sustain the integrity of already induced neural or behavioral systems. The various courses these three experiential influences can take during development are shown in Figure 5.7.

Summary of the Features of a Developmental Psychobiological Systems View

In its finished form, the developmental psychobiological systems approach involves a temporal description of activity at the genetic, neural, behavioral, and environmental levels of analysis, and the bidirectional effects of such activity among the four levels. When the related notions of bidirectionality and probabilistic epigenesis were first put forth (Gottlieb, 1970), they were largely intuitive. They seem now to be established facts in many, if not all, quarters. Given the experimental–embryological heritage of all systems views, two further assumptions or propositions are warranted:

1. Because of the early equipotentiality of cells and the fact that only a small part of the genome is expressed in any individual (Gottlieb, 1992), what is actually realized during the course of individual psychological and behavioral development represents only a fraction of

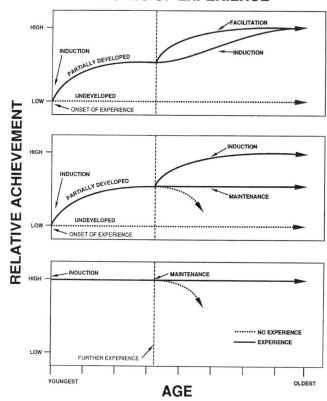

Figure 5.7 The various roles of experience (functional activity) during the course of development at the neural and behavioral levels of analysis. From *Individual Development and Evolution: The Genesis of Novel Behavior,* by Gilbert Gottlieb, 1992. New York: Oxford University Press. Copyright © 1992 by Oxford University Press, Inc. Reprinted with permission.

many other possibilities (also see Kuo, 1976, on this point).

2. A developmental systems view entails the notion of equifinality, i.e., the possibility of variation in pathways to common developmental endpoints. (A more detailed review of the early history and current status of this systems view can be found in Gottlieb, 1997.)

In the next two sections of this chapter, this developmental psychobiological systems view will be further elaborated with reference to developmental behavior genetics and intersensory influences on neural and psychological functioning in the prenatal and postnatal period.

DEVELOPMENTAL BEHAVIOR GENETICS: HEREDITY, ENVIRONMENT, AND DEVELOPMENT

A deeper understanding of developmental systems theory may be achieved by contrasting it with alternative approaches to the nature–nurture question and applying its precepts in designing and interpreting experiments. The theory emerged from failures of earlier attempts to explain development from a solely reductionistic perspective. It has become a general framework of current ideas about development (Ford & Lerner, 1992; Gottlieb, 1991a, 1992), but does not in itself provide answers to specific questions about specific phenotypes of a specific organism. Although the difficult task of filling in the bidirectional details will always require extensive experimentation (e.g., Smith & Thelen, 1993), we maintain that experiments will reveal more of the secrets of development when they are guided by the systems approach.

The neuroembryologist Viktor Hamburger once recommended to students that they pay little attention to the systems view of Paul Weiss (Figure 5.4), advising them instead: "Do not build grand theories, just do experiments" (Hamburger, 1985). However, no scientist can interrogate nature with a completely neutral mind; everyone proceeds at least with implicit theories and all too often with outright prejudices. We believe it is better to be fully aware of alternative modes of explanation, even if one is not committed to a unitary truth.

Two Questions about Development

Research on development usually addresses one of two broad questions and employs the methods appropriate to each question. This approach has often led to misunderstanding, especially on the realm of developmental behavior genetics, when results from one methodology have been invoked to answer a question that requires a different methodology. The two questions concern (a) the development of the individual and (b) individual differences in the population, when the latter is studied by the statistical procedures of quantitative behavior genetics.

The first question concerns the causes of the average or typical course of development from the fertilized ovum to the elaborated adult. This question occupied the earliest embryologists and remains one of the foremost intellectual challenges of modern science. Large differences between species are often examined in this context; the less dramatic variations within a species are of minor interest. Many of the most important advances in understanding average or species-typical development have involved the experimental method (altering the course of individual development via surgical operations, altered sensory experience, or chemical treatments; Jacobson, 1991; Slack, 1991).

This approach (development of the individual) is exemplified in studies of the origin of the nervous system, using tracer molecules such as horseradish peroxidase (HRP). When injected into one cell of a 16-cell frog embryo, the HRP is then transmitted to all cells that are derived from that one by mitosis, and staining the differentiated embryo for HRP several days later reveals the developmental fate of the one cell (Moody, 1987). Although one cell may give rise to a particular kind of neuron in the central nervous system under normal circumstances, when the specific cell is destroyed in the 16-cell embryo, the fate of an adjacent cell is then altered to produce the required neuron (Jacobson, 1981). This kind of experiment reveals the crucial role of interactions between cells for the differentiation of the embryo into a system of organs. However, it manipulates neither the heredity nor the environment of the embryo but instead explores the internal processes of individual development.

The second major question (the population approach) asks about the origins of individual differences within a species. Historically, this has been the focus of psychologists concerned with testing human mental abilities (F. Galton, C. Burt) as well as geneticists interested in crop yields and evolution (R. A. Fisher, S. Wright). In contemporary developmental psychology, this question is sometimes limited to the range of human differences that are commonly found in a country; the relevance of exceptionally large deviations from the mean, or of dramatic experimental manipulations, is explicitly denied (Scarr, 1992, 1993). What sometimes passes for developmental behavior genetic research on human children typically employs correlational methods of statistical analysis and proceeds in virtual isolation from experimental neuroembryology (e.g., Plomin, 1986; also see critique by Gottlieb, 1995).

In its earliest stages, the science of genetics was nondevelopmental. Embryology progressed along a separate course, with little concern for genetics (Allen, 1985).

Mendel believed that his "constant differentiating characters" of garden peas were themselves inherited. His was a mosaic theory of heredity wherein each characteristic of the individual—height, color, or shape—was determined by a separate unit of heredity. This notion was adopted by those who rediscovered Mendel's laws and termed the units *genes,* and from the outset of genetics in the 20th century, a gene was named for its most salient phenotypic effect (e.g., "white eye" in fruit flies and "varitint waddler" in mice), implying that the mutant reveals a gene's true function.

Integrating the Two Approaches

Pursuit of answers to the two major questions need not involve minds inhabiting two solitudes. Darwin integrated knowledge of embryology and individual variation in a masterful way to bolster his conclusions about evolution, and more recent theorists have also highlighted the importance of organismic development for natural selection and evolution (Gould, 1977; McKinney & McNamara, 1991). Indeed, developmental systems theory offers unique insights into the relations among embryogenesis, individual differences, and evolution (Gottlieb, 1992; Johnston & Gottlieb, 1990). Generally speaking, a theory that emphasizes the bidirectional nature of interaction between hierarchical levels of a living system (Figure 5.6) also encourages synergistic relations between allied scientific disciplines. In contrast, the strongly reductionistic approach of quantitative behavior genetics has devoted little attention to the levels between gene and behavior, thereby isolating psychology from comparative embryology and developmental genetics.

From our perspective, experimental analysis of average development can be enhanced by the study of individual variation because a small genetic difference between two individuals can alter the course of development in uniquely noninvasive ways. For example, the embryos of certain strains of mice lack a small bridge of tissue that normally allows axons from the cerebral cortex of mammals to cross between the hemispheres, and this minor deficit leads to a massive structural abnormality in the adult brain: the absence of the corpus callosum (Ozaki & Wahlsten, 1993). Brain surgery on a normal mouse embryo can also create an absent corpus callosum but is more difficult to interpret because several other structures are also damaged, and bleeding occurs from a severed artery (Silver, Lorenz, Wahlsten, & Coughlin, 1982).

Likewise, an adequate understanding of individual variations in the adult is not possible without knowing about processes of individual development. Everyone acknowledges that cellular and neural development intercedes between genes and behavior. However, the purely statistical approach of quantitative behavior genetics presupposes that the genetic composition of a population can be inferred from patterns of correlations among phenotypes of relatives. From this perspective, development is something to be explored *after* genetic effects are documented, and the implicit model of development is a sequential chain of instructions leading upward from gene to behavior in a unidirectional manner. The standard model that justifies heritability analysis presumes that genetic effects occur separately from environmental effects, and vice versa (Wahlsten, 1994a). On the other hand, a bidirectional developmental systems view sees genetic and environmental effects as being interdependent, which means that, in principle, genetic effects leading to individual differences cannot be understood apart from development occurring in a specific environmental context.

Limitations of the Statistical (Population) Approach

Today, it is certain that the study of individual differences cannot provide a comprehensive account of organismic development, for the simple reason that most of the genes we possess are effectively the same in almost all members of a population. A gene is a segment of a long DNA (deoxyribonucleic acid) molecule that occurs at a particular place or locus in a chromosome or a mitochondrion. The gene may be defined as the stretch of DNA that codes for a specific kind of protein molecule. During development, the DNA is transcribed into an intermediary molecule, messenger ribonucleic acid (mRNA), that is subsequently translated into a protein molecule. The DNA is a double helix consisting of two long chains of the nucleotide bases adenine, cytosine, thymine, and guanine (A, C, T, G), in a linear sequence that provides a code for the linear sequence of amino acids in a protein. At this molecular level, it is reasonably accurate to say that the gene *codes* or *programs* the structure of the protein (Stent, 1981). What the consequences of this protein may be for a cellular, neural, or behavioral phenotype depends strongly on the other genes possessed by the individual and the sequence of environments encountered. A specific gene sometimes occurs in two or more forms (alleles) that differ in one or more nucleotide bases in a population of individuals. If these different alleles code for slightly different amino acid sequences in the protein, and if the less common allele occurs with a frequency of at least 1% in the population, the locus is said to cause protein polymorphism. If not, the locus is said to be fixed in the population and does not give rise to noteworthy phenotypic differences among individuals.

Molecular techniques can reveal how many and which kinds of proteins, or even mRNA molecules, are expressed in the brain. By comparing the patterns of expression in different individuals, it is then possible to assess what proportion of the expressed genes are polymorphic. Invariably, this fraction is small in mammals. Among 10 inbred strains of mice, only 12 of 200 proteins measured in the cerebellum were polymorphic (Goldman et al., 1985), and a study of proteins in the mitochondria of the brain found that only 2 of 488 differed between 2 inbred strains (Jungblut & Klose, 1985). It seems likely that fewer than 5% of all genes in mammals give rise to protein polymorphism and individual differences at the phenotypic level. Hence, *the statistical or population approach to behavior genetics is insensitive to the actions of the vast majority of genes.*

The Importance of Animal Models

The numerous fixed loci that are of great importance for proper development can be examined in three ways:

1. The action of a specific gene can be detected by antibody molecules that bind to its expressed protein product or complementary DNA probes that bind to the mRNA transcript; these techniques can be used to ascertain where and when the gene acts in the organism (Wille, Cremer, Barthels, & Goldowitz, 1992) or even to alter its effects in a highly specific way.

2. The gene itself can be altered by inserting a fragment of foreign DNA into it so that the gene cannot be transcribed and is effectively "knocked out" (e.g., Korach, 1994).

3. An entire gene from one species can be injected into an early embryo from another species and then incorporated permanently into its genome (Julien, Tretjakoff, Beaudet, & Peterson, 1987), which may alter the course of development in informative ways (Shea, Hammer, & Brinster, 1987).

Thus, heredity can be modified and controlled experimentally, just as is done with environment, and a great deal can be learned about the average course of development even when all the subjects of the research enter the laboratory with the same genotype.

The elegant and even fantastic experiments that can be done with embryos are of course not available for research on human behavior. Although a detailed description of the usual sequence of events in early human prenatal development has been compiled, and similarities with other mammalian species are apparent (O'Rahilly & Müller, 1987), our most reliable information about mammalian embryogenesis comes from laboratory animals. Ethical considerations rightfully restrict what can be done to the human neonate in the name of science, and here too we must rely on animals to teach us about many biological processes.

In this regard, it is important to recognize the substantial degree of common origin or homology of humans and other animals at the molecular level. Most of the genes found in humans also occur in mice (Copeland et al., 1993). Many genes in the lowly fruit fly also occur in both mice and humans (Merriam, Ashburner, Hartl, & Kafatos, 1991). As a general principle, developmental processes viewed at the molecular level tend to be broadly applicable across a wide range of species, whereas higher-level functions involving behavior or cognition are more apt to be species-specific. Consequently, a psychology of language development in children may find little benefit in attempting to converse with mice and fruit flies, whereas genetic analysis of human characteristics can be illuminated by well-controlled studies of animal development. If a principle such as heredity–environment interaction or the norm of reaction is valid for numerous species, it is not reasonable to hold humans exempt, as is effectively done in quantitative genetic analysis of human behavior (see critiques in Gottlieb, 1995; Wahlsten, 1994a).

Separating the Effects of Heredity and Environment

From its inception, developmental psychology has been keenly interested in the role(s) of heredity (H) and environment (E). Numerous methods have been devised to separate their effects both experimentally and statistically. At the same time, many theorists regard these two entities as fundamentally inseparable. The naturalist John Muir

(1911) expressed the holistic doctrine admirably when he taught: "Whenever we try to pick out a thing by itself, we find it hitched to everything in the universe." Developmental systems theory also emphasizes relationships between things, and it attributes the properties of a living system to the dynamic interactions among its parts and between different levels (Figure 5.6; Ford & Lerner, 1992; Gottlieb, 1992; Oyama, 1985).

However, this systems perspective is by no means a barrier to experimentation. On the contrary, experimentation provides the best possible confirmation of the interconnectedness of heredity and environment. We have learned that changing one gene is likely to have effects on many phenotypes (pleiotropy) and to be contingent on other parts of the genome (epistasis) as well as the environment ($H \times E$ interaction). The best evidence of the inseparability of H and E comes from serious attempts to separate them experimentally.

If we seek to separate heredity and environment, we must define H and E. For a reductionistic theory, this is a rather easy task because the parts of a system are held to possess inherent and intransigent properties that can be added up to characterize the whole organism (the whole equals the sum of its parts). For developmental systems theory, on the other hand, the boundaries drawn for convenience at one moment are expected to become somewhat fuzzy and transient as development proceeds.

At conception of a one-cell embryo, a clear distinction between H and E can be perceived (Figure 5.8). Heredity is everything transmitted from the parents. Every speck of matter in the embryo, the entire organism, is inherited; the chromosomes in the nucleus, the mitochondria and the endoplasmic reticulum and other organelles in the cytoplasm, and even the cell membrane are integral parts of heredity (Ho, 1984). Environment is then the exterior, those aspects of the surroundings that impinge on the embryo but are not part of it. This definition of H and E provides an unambiguous, exhaustive partition of everything in the vicinity of the new organism. For developmental theory, it is more satisfying than the assertion that heredity consists only of DNA molecules, because this dogma leaves most of the embryo out of the picture or classifies the cytoplasm inside the embryo as part of the environment.

Even this definition of H and E at conception entails difficulties. All of the one-cell embryo is transmitted, but not all of it is in turn transmissible to the next generation, and

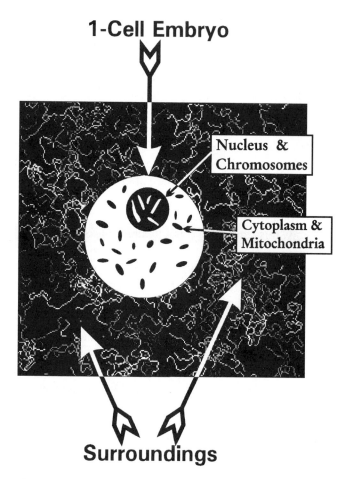

Figure 5.8   Diagram of one-cell embryo in its surroundings after conception. All parts of the embryo are inherited from its parents, including the chromosomes in the nucleus and the mitochondria and other organelles in the cytoplasm.

some of what is obtained from the parents was not possessed by them as heredity. Consider cases where a human embryo has an extra chromosome, such as trisomy 21 (Down syndrome) or the XYY male. These arise *de novo* during germ cell formation; they do not afflict the parent, and they are rarely passed on to the next generation. Thus, there can be a defect of the substance of heredity that is not itself hereditary. Such phenomena reveal the rich diversity of living things and the frailty of our attempts to impose rigid definitions on reality.

Given a competent embryo in an adequate environment, the organism will differentiate and grow. The question of whether H or E is more important for its development is nonsensical because both are absolutely essential. An embryo without an environment is inconceivable. The meaningful question asks about specific features of H and E that are particularly important for average development and individual differences.

The logic of the scientific method provides a general outline of how to answer these questions. To demonstrate the importance of some aspect of heredity for development, one must raise organisms with different heredities in the same environment. Similarly, the role of environment can best be revealed by raising organisms with the same heredity in different environments. It is sometimes argued (see, e.g., Lorenz, 1981), that depriving a bird of the opportunity to hear the song of a conspecific can prove the song is encoded in the genes if the bird sings well despite the lack of a skilled tutor. Notwithstanding the Nobel prize conferred on Lorenz, his logic was flawed (Johnston, 1987, 1988; Lehrman, 1970; Lerner, 1992). The sensory deprivation experiment tests the importance of only one specific feature of the environment that involves learning by observation, and it reveals absolutely nothing about any gene. Likewise, some psychologists argue that monozygotic (one-egg or MZ) twins reared apart can reveal the importance of genes for mental development (Bouchard, Lykken, McGue, Segal, & Tellegen, 1990). This logic is also flawed. MZ twins having the same heredity provide a good opportunity for evaluating differences in environment; a difference between two cotwins could not originate in their different heredities, but concordance of the two reflects identical H, highly similar E, or both.

Studying a Difference in Heredity

There is no way to show the importance of heredity as a whole for development in general, but elegant experiments can prove that a difference in heredity leads to a difference in development. Perhaps the clearest demonstrations are provided by inbred strains of mice that have become genetically pure by over 100 generations of mating brother and sister. At every genetic locus on all chromosomes, each animal is homozygous for the same allele. This extraordinary purity allows the researcher to produce hundreds or even thousands of mice with the same genotype. However, the purity is ephemeral because a spontaneous mutation can transform one allele into a new version of the gene that does not function very well and may even lead to a gross malformation of the brain or a bizarre kind of behavior. The mutant animal can be compared with normal siblings,

and any significant difference in phenotype is attributable to a difference in a single gene. These *coisogenic* mice will be the same at every other genetic locus. Furthermore, they are conceived in the same mother at the same time and nurtured by the same parents in the same laboratory cage.

The *diabetes* gene *(db)* in mice originally occurred as a mutation in the strain named C57BL/6Ks. It is recessive; an animal will exhibit the diabetic and obesity phenotype only if it inherits two copies of the mutation, one from each parent, and has genotype *db/db*. The nondiabetic littermates could have two copies of the "wild type" allele (+), the normal form of the diabetes gene, or they could carry one *db* gene but not express it. That is, the + allele is dominant, and the two genotypes +/+ and +/db are correlated with the same developmental outcome. The design of this experiment then consists of groups that differ only at the *db* locus, and the 25-g difference in their body weights seems to be attributable to the genetic difference. The commercial availability of these mutant mice from the Jackson Laboratory (Bar Harbor, Maine) has greatly facilitated research. Much has been learned about their appetite and metabolism, including the fact that restricting the available food to prevent overeating can prevent the appearance of symptoms of clinical diabetes in "diabetic" mutant mice (Lee & Bressler, 1981). The mutant mice are actually more sensitive to variations in their environment than their normal siblings.

There is no human equivalent to coisogenic mice. When different alleles of a specific gene can be detected from their protein product or from the DNA itself, it is possible to compare two groups of individuals who definitely differ at a single locus, but they will not be identical at other genetic loci or in their upbringing. This heterogeneity creates a danger that the allelic difference in one gene will be correlated with some other difference that is the effective cause of a difference in behavior. Apparently, this happened recently when alcoholism was found to be associated with a particular allele of the dopamine type 2 receptor (DRD2) gene. The frequency of the allele also differs greatly between ethnic groups that differ as well in the rate of alcoholism, creating the possibility of a spurious correlation. When ethnically homogeneous groups were studied, the association of alcoholism with the DRD2 allele vanished (Lander & Schork, 1994). A stronger association has been reported between two alleles of the gene coding for red opsin in the retina and a subtle variation in color vision

(Winderickx et al., 1992). The claim of causation specifically by the red opsin gene was strengthened by direct measurements of the sensitivity of the two different forms of red opsin to various colors of light (Merbs & Nathans, 1992).

Another fascinating example involves the circadian rhythm of activity in mice, which are usually afield during the dark hours and in the nest during daylight. If normal mice are housed for several weeks in a room where 12 hours of darkness are alternated with 12 hours of light, and then the room lights are turned off completely to create constant darkness, the 24-hour rhythm of activity persists. Although the rhythm was intially entrained by sensory stimulation, it becomes endogenous once the internal pacemaker in the brain is set. When a mutation of a gene named *Clock* on chromosome 5 was induced chemically, inbred C57BL/6J mouse individuals inheriting one copy of this mutant gene expressed a slightly longer (24.8 hours) endogenous rhythm (Vitaterna et al., 1994). However, mice inheriting two mutant alleles appear normal during the entrainment phase but completely lose the rhythm under constant darkness; because of a defect in a single gene, they are totally dependent on external stimuli to maintain the beat. Several mutations affecting circadian rhythmicity have also been created in fruit flies (reviewed by Takahashi, 1995).

Documenting the Norm of Reaction

With an inbred strain, dozens of animals having the same genotype can be randomly assigned to different rearing conditions. The C57BL/6J strain is not usually obese, but rearing them on a diet high in fat can cause obesity and physiological diabetes, as indicated by greatly elevated blood glucose and insulin (Surwit, Kuhn, Cochrane, McCubbin, & Feinglos, 1988). Although insulin levels are strongly modified by diet in C57BL/6J mice, other strains are far less sensitive to dietary fat. C57BL/6J mice are usually not vulnerable to seizures induced by a loud noise, but when they are exposed to a priming noise at one of 15 different ages, it is found that exposure on any day, from 14 to 20 days of age, leads to severe sound-induced seizures at 28 days of age (Henry & Bowman, 1970) whereas DBA/2J mice tend to seize without priming (an example of equifinality). When many different environmental conditions are examined, a *norm of reaction* can be documented (see Gottlieb, 1995; Wahlsten & Gottlieb, 1997).

Replicated genotypes are essential for documenting a genotype-specific norm of reaction. An elaborate environmental experiment of this kind is not feasible with most organisms that have not been highly inbred, but a norm of reaction can sometimes be defined as an average across different individuals, provided random assignment to condition is employed (Gupta & Lewontin, 1982). For example, wild alligator eggs taken from the same clutch and incubated in a laboratory at six different temperatures revealed that above 32°C all become male, and below 32°C all become female (Ferguson & Joanen, 1982). Temperature dependent sex determination is widespread in reptiles and different species have different critical temperatures for switching to the male or female pathway (reviews in Bull, 1983; van der Weele, 1995). Random assignment of human volunteers to different conditions, as is often practiced in the laboratory in short-term studies, could potentially reveal an averaged norm of reaction, because random assignment insures that group differences are not correlated with genetic differences. That is, good research on mild environmental effects can be done without genetic homogeneity among the subjects. In this case, however, the variability within conditions may very well reflect genetic differences among individuals, and the profile of group average scores may be thought of as an average of numerous individual norms of reactions.

Can We Separate the Inseparable?

The logic of the simple two-group experiment with coisogenic mice is inscrutable. Because all else seems to be equated, must not the precise numerical magnitude of the difference in group mean scores be attributed solely to the genetic difference? In reality, this inference will be valid only in one situation: when the effects of H and E are strictly additive. If the value of the phenotype is indeed the arithmetic *sum* of components attributable to H and E, then the difference between the group mean phenotypes equals the difference between the group values of H, irrespective of the value of E, as the logic of the experiment implies. If the two factors are not additive and are multiplicative instead (a form of interaction), the group difference in mean phenotypes depends on the difference in H values as well as the specific value of E (Wahlsten, 1990, 1994a). Thus, although the magnitude of the difference in heredities is certainly of critical importance under either situation, when H and E are not additive the observed group difference depends just as much on the one environment chosen for the study as it does on the two genotypes, and the observed group difference is then specific to the environment common to all subjects in the study.

A simple two-group experiment cannot reveal whether H and E are additive or not. Some kind of factorial design is required to test for the existence of interaction or interdependence of H and E. The crucial point is that nonadditivity of H and E will have major consequences for the numerical results of the two-group experiment, even though the interaction effect cannot be perceived in the data when only one factor is manipulated. The seemingly elegant study of coisogenic mice reared in the same laboratory environment is an excellent method for demonstrating the importance of a difference in heredity, but, in principle, it cannot truly separate the effects of heredity and environment quantitatively if they are not separable developmentally.

The same considerations apply to any study of environment with a single inbred strain; the results may illustrate a genotype-specific norm of reaction, but there is no guarantee at all that its shape will be the same for other strains. When there is heredity–environment interaction, the degree of apparent heritability of some characteristic depends on the specific rearing environment, and the environmental plasticity depends on the organism's heredity, whether or not the experimental design is capable of revealing this.

Numerous factorial experiments involving genetically different strains reared under different conditions have been done with fruit flies, rats, and mice. After a thorough review of the available literature on mice, Erlenmeyer-Kimling (1972) concluded that "gene–environment interactions are numerous and . . . treatment effects are frequently reversed in direction for different genotypes" (p. 201). Since then, many other dramatic demonstrations of nonadditivity have been published. Consider the results of Hood and Cairns (1989), who reared two strains of mice (selected for either high or low frequency of fighting) either in isolation or in social groups (see Figure 5.9). The strain difference was very large with isolated mice, which typically are much more feisty, but disappeared when the animals were reared socially in groups. Thus, there is no *general* sense in which one can say that one of the strains is more aggressive than the other.

When there is H × E interaction, the strain-specific norms of reaction will differ. However, it does not follow that the norm of reaction is itself genetically encoded. The

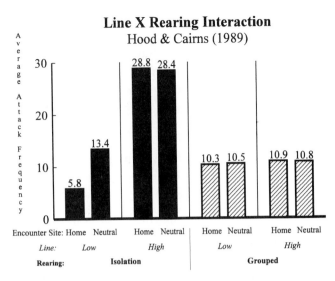

Figure 5.9 Average attack frequency by male mice in two lines that had been selectively bred for either high or low attack frequency. The original selection experiment was done with males that had been reared in isolation prior to testing. In this experiment, half of the males were reared in isolation and the others were grouped, which greatly decreased attacks by the high strain. During the test itself, the mice met in either the home cage, where the mouse being tested confronted an intruder, or in a neutral cage. Clearly, the test situation was of little importance, but the social rearing condition brought about a major reduction in the aggressive behavior of the high strain. Based on data from "A Developmental-Genetic Analysis of Aggressive Behavior in Mice: IV. Genotype–Environment Interaction," by K. E. Hood & R. B. Cairns, 1989, *Aggressive Behavior, 15*, pp. 361–380.

most we can claim is that a *difference* in the two norms of reaction results from a *difference* in heredity when the strains are reared in the same environment until the time in life when the experiment with different environments begins. The norm of reaction, which is characteristic of an entire organism carrying thousands of genes through a multifaceted environment, can itself be modified by the environment. For example, when the ovaries of an inbred BALB donor mouse are grafted into either a BALB or an F_1 hybrid female and then the host female is mated with a BALB male, embryos and later neonates that are all genetically BALB can be observed in two maternal environments (Bulman-Fleming & Wahlsten, 1988). Adult brain size depends on litter size prior to weaning; mice from larger litters have smaller average brain size, but the slope of this norm of reaction is steeper in the inbred than in the hybrid maternal environment.

The typical heritability analysis that is so familiar in quantitative behavior genetic studies of human traits attempts to assess the percentage of phenotypic variance in a population that is attributable to genetic variance. This kind of analysis assumes that there are many genes with small effects, scattered widely across the chromosomes, and that they combine additively with each other (no gene-gene interaction) and with the environment (no H × E interaction) to determine the phenotype of an individual. However, these assumptions are not consistent with current knowledge from molecular and developmental biology (Wahlsten, 1994a). Furthermore, the presence of H × E interaction can markedly alter the estimation of parameters in a multiple regression model (e.g., Tiret, Abel, & Rakotovao, 1993).

It has been claimed that tests of H × E interaction pertinent to human psychological characteristics have been tried but consistently fail to find any such effects (Detterman, 1990; Plomin, 1986). There are two difficulties with this defense of heritability analysis. First, because there are no sources of humans with identical genotypes that can be assigned to different environments, the presence or absence of H × E interaction in studies of human mental abilities is unverifiable. Second, the usual two-way analysis of variance methodology that is used to test for interaction is markedly insensitive to several kinds of real interaction that would be of interest to psychologists (Wahlsten, 1990). The sample sizes required to search for interaction effects with adequate power are usually far greater than those employed to assess main effects in factorial designs (Wahlsten, 1991, 1993).

Separating H and E in Humans

The basic ideas of the norm of reaction and heredity–environment interaction apply to any species—protozoa, insects, vertebrates, and even plants. Human beings have no special properties that render heredity and environment additive. Nonetheless, it is often claimed by behavior geneticists that twin and adoption studies can separate the effects of H and E. The assertion that the adoption method can effectively separate H and E presumes that the prenatal environment is of no account for individual differences or that the uterine environment of all women is virtually the same. This is not at all realistic (Lerner, 1995, p. 152). The state of the mother's health and nutrition during pregnancy has a major impact on the brain development of the fetus, and every mode of sensory experience except vision is active in the fetus during the last trimester of human pregnancy (e.g., Busnel, Granier-Deferre, & Lecanuet, 1992; DeCasper & Spence, 1986; Gottlieb, 1971). Precisely how significant each of these effects may be in the context of an adoption study cannot be determined when rigorous control of conditions is lacking. Prior to being separated from its biological parent(s), the fetus and then the child lives in an environment provided by its genetic benefactors. Consequently, the adoption method cannot conclusively separate the effects of H and E.

In some situations, adoption provides an excellent means to study differences in the postadoption environment. For example, Schiff, Duyme, Dumaret, and Tomkiewicz (1982) compared school performance and IQ test scores of French siblings who had the same poverty-stricken mother; one or two children were adopted into a high socioeconomic status (SES) home, while another child remained with the mother. The mean IQ of the adoptees was elevated by 16 points. The two groups had substantially different postadoption environments but were matched for many factors acting prior to adoption. Capron and Duyme (1989) employed the same approach to conduct a 2 × 2 factorial study of pre- and postadoption SES in relation to later IQ. Contrary to the opinion that their study effectively separated H and E (McGue, 1989), the authors explicitly recognized that preadoption H and E were confounded.

Outstanding control of the H factor can be achieved in humans with genetically identical monozygotic (MZ) twins, but separation of the effects of H and E is not possible because MZ twins share a common prenatal and early postnatal environment. When MZ twins are reared in different homes, there may be an opportunity to assess the plasticity of behavior, provided the environments are sufficiently dissimilar to make the test reasonably powerful. Unfortunately for research, the environments of "separated" MZ twins are often quite similar because they are reared in branches of the same family, in the same neighborhood, or in similar SES homes in the same culture (Farber, 1981; Taylor, 1980). Comparison of MZ twins reared apart clearly points to the importance of nongenetic factors when the twins are substantially different; but when they show a close phenotypic resemblance, it is usually not possible to know why. A high correlation of test scores of MZ twins reared apart provides support for the hypothesis of a strong genetic influence on behavior but cannot prove it true.

Comparing MZ versus dizygotic (two-egg, or DZ) twins reared in the same home involves a similar confounding of H and E. The heredities of MZ twins are surely more similar than those of DZ twins, and so are their environments. Consequently, the elevated phenotypic correlations of MZ twins very likely reflect their common experiences to some unknown extent (Hoffman, 1991). Precisely what fraction of an observed correlation is attributable to nongenetic similarity cannot be determined unless psychologists provide a good measure of the environments that are specifically pertinent to the development of the behavior being studied.

The twin method does offer a very good, albeit underutilized, way to assess environmental cohort effects in families where there is a pair of DZ twins and two or more nontwin siblings. Twins are conceived and born at the same time, whereas nontwin siblings are no more similar or different genetically than DZ twins but come into this world in different years.

Thus, the adoption and twin methods provide useful and well-controlled situations for studying environmental effects on development, even though they cannot cleave precisely the effects of heredity and environment. Adoption and twin studies can provide evidence suggestive of genetic effects on behavior, but the only conclusive way to prove a genetic effect on human behavior is through linkage analysis, whereby behavioral variation in a family is highly correlated with alleles at a marker locus occurring at a specific location in the DNA of a chromosome. Numerous genes with a major impact on human mental development have been mapped to specific chromosomal loci, and these are typically quite rare in the population because their effects are often devastating. Those hypothetical loci with more subtle effects in the normal range of human behavioral variation remain elusive, despite much searching by intrepid gene hunters. Over 4000 neutral marker loci are now available for linkage analysis with humans (Cooperative Human Linkage Center, 1994), so there is no longer any scientific barrier to the discovery of genes correlated with normal behavior. These new molecular DNA marker techniques render adoption and twin studies uninteresting to the geneticist.

An Operational Definition of Heredity

Defining heredity at conception appears to be straightforward, but, as development progresses, the distinction between H and E becomes less apparent. This can be appreciated by examining some of the standard methods used to manipulate and preserve variations in heredity in animals. An inbred strain is created by breeding within a family for dozens of generations. Two inbred strains maintained in the same laboratory environment differ mainly because of their ancestries, the specific parents that served as founders of the strains about 80 years ago. Likewise, selective breeding entails matings of a male and female that both score high or both score low on some test. After only several generations of selective mating *and* rearing in the same laboratory, the high and low lines usually diverge substantially, thereby revealing that at least part of the original phenotypic variation in the foundation population may reflect hereditary differences.

Consider an easily measured phenotype, the size or weight of the adult brain. Inbred strains differ considerably, ranging from 410 mg for DBA/2J to 520 for BALB/cJ (Storer, 1967). Fuller (1979) created two brain-weight selection lines differing by 100 mg by breeding for high or low brain weight relative to body size. Brain size is an outcome of development; it is not encoded in the DNA and it is strongly influenced by nutrition. If the DBA/2J and BALB/cJ strains differ in brain size by about 100 mg, it may seem reasonable to attribute this phenotypic difference to their different heredities if they are reared in the same environment. What, then, is meant by heredity in this context?

The term *heredity* is used in two ways in the scientific literature. One invokes the dogma that all heredity consists of genes or DNA molecules, which requires that any phenotypic difference between strains be deemed genetic. The other invokes an operational definition; if the strain difference reflects a difference in heredity, then heredity in the particular experiment includes *everything that actually differs between the strains*—everything except the laboratory environment they share in common. This latter approach is very much a developmental one because it takes into account all of the factors that could reasonably influence the development of the brain.

Nongenetic Heredity

The DNA molecules in the chromosomes (both the autosomes and sex chromosomes), as well as those in the mitochondria of the cytoplasm, are important components of heredity. The autosomes in the cell nucleus are transmitted via the laws of Mendelian inheritance, whereas the genes resident in the mitochondria are transmitted solely via the female (Grun, 1976). Neurological disorders from defective mitochondrial DNA can affect both the male and female offspring but cannot be transmitted via the male (e.g., Wallace et al., 1988). Another kind of inheritance from parent to offspring involves DNA or RNA of viral origin. Mouse leukemia virus is passed to the embryo via the ovum, and mouse mammary tumor virus is bequeathed to the neonate postnatally through the milk (Grun, 1976). Many strain-specific cancers in mice are transmitted "vertically" from parent to offspring rather than "horizontally" between nonrelatives. Unless special experiments are done, the strain-specific viruses endure for many generations and appear as an integral part of heredity. These non-Mendelian hereditary factors also interact with the host genome; they more readily infect, proliferate, and transmit to offspring in some strains than in others.

The embryo of a certain inbred mouse strain develops in a uterine environment of that strain, and this can contribute to apparently hereditary differences between strains. After birth, the neonate drinks the milk and lives in a nest provided by a female of the same strain. All its social interactions from an early age are with mice of the same strain. Although these features are undoubtedly environmental, they differ substantially between inbred strains and can cause strain differences in the brain or behavior. Viewing the maternal environment as a part of heredity may seem like an unfortunate confusing of two distinct concepts. Nevertheless, comparisons of inbred strains and selectively bred lines that we ordinarily regard as demonstrating effects of heredity do entail differences in maternal environment. Either the maternal milieu is part of heredity in these simple experiments, or strain comparisons cannot by themselves prove the importance of a difference in heredity, let alone a genetic influence. It may be argued that *ultimately* the maternal environment itself depends on strain-specific

genetic activity. Undoubtedly, the mother's uterine environment depends in many ways on her genotype as well as her own environment, and her environment in turn has depended on the grandmother's genotype and maternal environment. From the standpoint of individual development, however, the mother's influences on embryonic development via the genes passed to the new organism and via the uterine environment are quite distinct. The genetic part of heredity exists in the embryo's interior; the maternal environment impinges on its exterior. Because of the confounding of the embryo's genotype, its cytoplasm, and its prenatal environment, most of the commonly employed research designs with standard strains or lines of laboratory animals cannot prove that a strain difference in phenotype arises from a difference in genes acting inside the embryo. A difference between strains does not necessarily reflect a genetic difference.

Dissecting Heredity

Whether a particular component of heredity is important for a specific phenotypic difference between strains can only be ascertained with experimentation. Reciprocal F_1 hybrid crosses, F_2 hybrid crosses, and backcrosses can demonstrate the contributions of autosomes, sex chromosomes, cytoplasmic organelles, and maternal environment (Sokolowski, 1992; Wahlsten, 1979). Using this method, it has been shown that F_2 hybrid mice develop faster than inbred mice partly because they benefit from a superior hybrid maternal environment (Wahlsten & Wainwright, 1977), and that BALB/c mice have large brains partly because of the BALB/c maternal environment (Wahlsten, 1983). The importance of the prenatal maternal environment can be assessed by grafting the ovaries of either of two inbred strains into an F_1 hybrid female, then fostering to a surrogate mother at birth (see Bulman-Fleming, Wahlsten, & Lassalle, 1991; Carlier, Nosten-Bertrand, & Michard-Vanhée, 1992). Carlier, Roubertoux, and Pastoret (1991) combined the reciprocal crossing and ovarian grafting methods and found that the reciprocal hybrid crosses developed differently in inbred and F_1 hybrid maternal environments. Thus, there can be interactions between different components of heredity, and it is not meaningful to state that a certain percentage of a strain difference is attributable to each component of heredity.

Relatively few experiments have attempted to dissect heredity with respect to characteristics of interest to developmental psychologists. Many studies of differences between laboratory strains support but cannot prove the importance of differences in the organisms' genotype, just as adoption and twin studies can support but not prove the importance of similarities and differences in genotype for human behavior. The principal difference between laboratory animals and humans in this respect is that research designs are available in the laboratory that can very effectively analyze the components of heredity and prove the effect of a genetic difference.

A Third Source of Individual Differences

Although it is usually presumed that all differences between individuals emanate from H, E, or a combination of the two, there are now good reasons to believe that a third source may exist that is neither hereditary nor environmental (Baunack, Gärtner, & Schneider, 1986). Instead, interesting differences may emerge from within the developing organisms but not be transmitted to the next generation (Lupski, Garcia, Zoghbi, Hoffman, & Fenwick, 1991). This phenomenon is sometimes termed developmental "noise" or "randomness," to convey the idea that it does not show the regularities typical of genetic effects (Lewontin, 1991). The concept may be invoked in situations where genetically identical individuals are reared in unusually uniform environments but nonetheless differ markedly in phenotypic outcomes (Spudich & Koshland, 1976). This possibility of a third source of variation is inherent in Schneirla's (1957) concept of "circular relationships of self-stimulation in the organism" (p. 86) whereby the organism is "interactive with itself."

An earlier section (p. 247) discusses ways of proving that a difference in heredity *is* important; here, we must prove that a phenotypic difference is *not* hereditary. The methods are similar; for example, mice usually have a consistent asymmetry in the internal organs, but among those homozygous for the *situs inversus (iv/iv)* mutation, about half have reversed asymmetry. When *iv/iv* mice are mated with each other, the frequency of reversed asymmetry in their offspring does not depend on the parental phenotypes (Layton, 1976). As discussed by Collins (1985) with reference to paw preferences in mice, selective breeding has no effect when the phenotype is not hereditary within a strain. If a developmental variant in inbred mice is not hereditary, there will be no correlation between the characteristics of the parents and their offspring.

Negative evidence concerning possible environmental causes of variation within an inbred strain can be obtained in two ways. First, heroic efforts have been made to achieve a uniform environment in the laboratory, yet large individual differences persist (Gärtner, 1990). Second, a large number of measures of the early environment can be gathered and examined for correlations with the phenotypic variant, and combinations of measures can also be evaluated (Bulman-Fleming & Wahlsten, 1991). If large samples are employed, an absence of significant multiple correlations supports the notion that variation is not environmental, although this is not conclusive proof.

It is always possible that the crucial feature of the environment was not measured. If there are unknown aspects of the uterine environment that are important for embryonic brain development, then the observed spatial location of defective and normal embryos within a litter of mice, for example, should exhibit a nonrandom pattern. The actual pattern can be compared with the kind of distribution expected when the occurrence of phenotypic variants is randomized using computer algorithms (Bulman-Fleming & Wahlsten, 1991).

All three of these tests have been applied to the case of absent corpus callosum in BALB/c mice, wherein 20% to 50% of the animals in a genetically uniform strain are clearly defective but the other littermates are normal (Wahlsten, 1994b); the evidence unequivocally supports the idea of a third source of individual differences. The argument is greatly strengthened by detailed studies of the growth of axons in the embryo cerebral cortex (Ozaki & Wahlsten, 1993), where a distinct *threshold* for the formation of the corpus callosum occurs because of the relative timing of two processes: (a) growth of axons toward the middle of the brain and (b) formation of a tissue bridge leading to the opposite hemisphere. Small differences in the timing can move an individual to one side of the threshold or the other.

The third, internal source of individual variation interacts with both H and E. It appears in especially dramatic form only in certain strains of animals, and the variance can be increased by the laboratory breeding regimen (Wahlsten, 1982). Thus, it will generally not be possible to assign a percentage of variance to each of the three causes. Heredity is a complex affair wherein several components interact—with each other and with various aspects of the surroundings and the internal milieu—to create the nervous system of the behaving organism. The components can be defined and dissected, but many experiments reveal that the properties of the organism result from interactions among these components, and the boundaries of the components themselves are indistinct. As will be discussed in the next section, the environment also consists of numerous parts that interact in ways that cast doubt on the strictly additive, reductionistic approach to human development that is standard fare in quantitative behavior genetics.

APPLICATION OF A DEVELOPMENTAL PSYCHOBIOLOGICAL SYSTEMS VIEW: THE CASE OF INTERSENSORY DEVELOPMENT

As the two previous sections of this chapter have made clear, there is a growing appreciation of the value of grounding the study of human development in a system of multiple influences, rather than continuing to utilize simpleminded explanatory dichotomies such as genes or environment, instinct or learning, maturation or experience, structure or function. It seems to us that an emphasis on the various ontogenetic processes involved in the emergence of phenotypic outcomes effectively eliminates these explanatorily empty dichotomies. In their place, a developmental psychobiological systems approach provides a more comprehensive view of development—a view that attempts to integrate genetic, neural, behavioral, social, and cultural levels of analysis (see Figure 5.6). This integrative effort is in keeping with the vision of the pioneering developmentalist Z.-Y. Kuo (1967), who wrote three decades ago: *"The study of behavior is a synthetic science.* It includes comparative anatomy, comparative embryology, comparative physiology, experimental morphology, and qualitative and quantitative analysis of the dynamic relationship between the organism and the external physical and social environment" (p. 25).

Kuo's interdisciplinary, multilevel vision for the developmental analysis of behavior is gradually being incorporated into developmental science. This is seen in the increasing shift away from simple cause-and-effect models of development that rely on predeterminism, linearity, or reductionism, and the move toward more dynamic, hierarchical, systems-oriented approaches to development. This developmental systems approach has become increasingly evident in several subareas within developmental psychol-

ogy in recent years, including the study of motor development (Thelen, Kelso, & Fogel, 1987; Thelen & Ulrich, 1991), cognitive development (Bjorklund, 1995), language development (Dent, 1990; Locke, 1993; Zukow-Goldring, 1990), personality development (Lerner, 1988) and social development (Cairns, Gariépy, & Hood, 1990; Fogel, 1993), to cite but a few examples.

The conceptual and methodological shift to a more systems-oriented approach is also increasingly evident in the study of perceptual development (Gottlieb, 1991a, 1997), and, especially, the study of early intersensory capabilities. How the individual sensory modalities relate to one another and how their functions are integrated in the brain has been of growing concern to a variety of investigators working in developmental psychology (Lewkowicz & Lickliter, 1994a; Rose & Ruff, 1987; Spelke, 1984; Turkewitz & Kenny, 1982), developmental biology (Edelman, 1987, 1992), cognitive science (Damasio, 1989; Smith & Katz, 1996), and the neurosciences (Ettlinger & Wilson, 1990; Merzenich & Kaas, 1980; Stein & Meredith, 1993). Recent empirical and conceptual advances in these related fields have served to guide a growing number of investigators away from simple, single-cause explanations and toward an increasing appreciation of the multiple influences, at various levels of analysis, that contribute to the emergence of intersensory integration.

What follows here is not intended as a comprehensive review of these burgeoning areas of research; rather, it is a brief examination of traditional and emerging conceptual and operational frameworks associated with this area of investigation. The principal goal is to explore how the application of a biologically plausible developmental systems perspective can provide students of perceptual development with a framework that both acknowledges the complex and dynamic nature of development and attempts to integrate developmental data from genetics, neuroscience, and psychology into a coherent and complementary account of how young organisms come to integrate distinct sensory inputs in a coordinated way that allows for a unitary perception of objects and events. Intersensory integration is a fundamental characteristic of normal perception, and to successfully answer the question of "how" it is achieved over the course of development requires an interdisciplinary, multilevel, comparative approach to developmental analysis, as advocated by Kuo (1967) and, more recently, by Gottlieb (1991a, 1996, 1997).

Traditional Approaches to Intersensory Development

Over the past several decades, there has been substantial research on the intermodal capabilities of human infants (Aslin & Smith, 1988; Haith & Campos, 1983; Lewkowicz & Lickliter, 1994b; McKenzie & Day, 1987; Meltzoff, 1990; Rose & Ruff, 1987; Spelke, 1984). In a general sense, this research has been largely descriptive in nature and has been directed at establishing the timing of the emergence of various perceptual competencies over the course of the first year following birth. This work has successfully documented that young infants display a large and diverse repertoire of intersensory abilities, including the ability to match faces and voices on the basis of voice–lip synchrony (Dodd, 1979), speech sounds (Kuhl & Meltzoff, 1984), affective expressions (Walker-Andrews, 1986), and gender of the speaker (Walker-Andrews, Bahrick, Raglioni, & Diaz, 1991). Infants have also been shown to be sensitive to a number of temporal parameters unifying auditory and visual stimulation, including synchrony (Bahrick, 1987, 1988; Lewkowicz, 1986, 1992; Spelke, 1981), rate (Lewkowicz, 1985; Spelke, 1979), rhythm (Allen, Walker, Symonds, & Marcell, 1977; Mendelson & Ferland, 1982), and duration (Lewkowicz, 1986). Related work has also demonstrated impressive haptic–visual connections present over the course of the first year, including tactile discrimination and crossmodal transfer abilities within the first months of postnatal life (Bushnell, 1982; Clifton, Rochat, Robin, & Berthier, 1994; Meltzoff & Borton, 1979; Rochat & Senders, 1991; Rose, 1994; Streri & Pecheux, 1986).

Despite these varied and impressive demonstrations of infants' intersensory capabilities, there has been surprisingly limited concern in this body of work for the various possible contributions of prior prenatal and postnatal experience (see Figure 5.7), and even less concern with the specific processes and mechanisms whereby intersensory functioning is achieved during early development. This state of affairs is no doubt due in large part to the inherent experimental limitations of working with human infants. Experiential manipulations of human fetuses and neonates are necessarily limited in scope and duration, and traditional experimental techniques such as sensory deprivation or sensory augmentation are prohibited. Experimental limitations aside, we believe the general lack of focus on the processes and mechanisms associated with human intersensory development is also the result of the types of questions that have typically been pursued in this area of research.

Perhaps the most prominent question guiding research in the area of infant intersensory development over the past 30 years is a question concerned with direction: Does intersensory development proceed (a) from initially separate senses to coordinated multimodal experience or (b) from an initial unity of the senses to differentiated modalities? The pursuit of answers to this question has resulted in two prevailing (and opposing) theoretical views, known respectively as the "integration view" and the "differentiation view" of intersensory development (see Bahrick & Pickens, 1994; Lewkowicz, 1994; Stein & Meredith, 1993 for brief reviews).

In a general sense, the integration view holds that the different sensory modalities function as separate sensory systems during the initial stages of postnatal development and become integrated and coordinated during development through the infant's activity and resulting repeated experience with concurrent information provided by the different modalities (Birch & Lefford, 1963, 1967; Friedes, 1974; Helmholtz, 1884/1968; Piaget, 1952). For example, Piaget (1952) argued that as infants manipulate objects in their environment, they have multiple opportunities to experience the tactile, auditory, visual, and gustatory properties of these objects. It is hypothesized that, through these repeated experiences, infants gradually come to successfully associate their various multimodal sensations. In contrast, the differentiation view of intersensory development holds that the different senses form a primitive unity early in development, and, as the infant develops, information arising from the different sensory modalities is differentiated (Bower, 1974; E. J. Gibson, 1969; J. J. Gibson, 1966; Marks, 1978; von Hornbostel, 1938). Thus, E. J. Gibson (1969, 1988) has argued that infants possess some intersensory capabilities at birth and are innately able to perceive properties of objects or events that are amodal or invariant across sense modalities (e.g., intensity, duration, rhythm, shape). From this perspective, infants are thought to differentiate finer and more complex multimodal relations through their experience over the course of development. Detection of intermodal invariants is central to this view, and the differentiation and extraction of progressively finer levels of invariant structure is considered to be the main developmental task of the infant (Bahrick, 1988).

Assumptions Underlying Traditional Approaches

The enduring debate between the integration and differentiation views has certainly provided a heuristic for directing much of the empirical work concerned with early intersensory functioning in human infants over the past several decades. Both perspectives have, however, relied on several common underlying assumptions that are now questionable in light of our increasing knowledge of neuroembryology and developmental psychobiology. In particular, several of the usually implicit assumptions common to both integration and differentiation theories fail to adequately recognize the complex and dynamic processes of organization and reorganization occurring within (Freeman, 1991) and between (Radell & Gottlieb, 1992; Symons & Tees, 1990) sensory systems over the course of both prenatal and postnatal development. This has tended to result in an overly simplistic and essentially nondevelopmental characterization of the sensory modalities and their emerging sensitivities on the part of both the integration and the differentiation views. For example, an implicit assumption of both viewpoints has been that the sensory systems start out on an essentially equal basis (Tees & Buhrmann, 1989). This assumption is in contrast to what is known about the neuroembryological development of the sensory systems. The various sensory modalities of birds and mammals (including humans) do not become functional at the same time in development (Alberts, 1984; Bradley & Mistretta, 1975; Gottlieb, 1971); as a result, the various sensory modalities have different developmental histories during the prenatal and postnatal periods. These experiential differences can significantly affect the ability of a particular modality to process a given type of sensory input at a given point in early development (Gottlieb, 1971; Lickliter, 1993; Lickliter & Banker, 1994; Turkewitz & Kenny, 1982).

As a case in point, in humans (and many precocial birds and mammals), the auditory modality becomes functional at some time during the late stages of the prenatal period, whereas the visual modality has its functional onset at birth. A number of recent studies utilizing avian and mammalian embryos and infants have demonstrated that the sequential heterochronic emergence of function in the various sensory systems can have an important influence in determining the nature and modification of intersensory relationships during early development (Foreman & Altaha, 1991; Gottlieb, Tomlinson, & Radell, 1989; Kenny &

Turkewitz, 1986; Lickliter, 1990a, 1990b; Lickliter & Stoumbos, 1991; Symons & Tees, 1990). For example, the auditory modality has been shown to have functional priority over the later developing visual system during the early stages of the postnatal period in several precocial animal infants (Gottlieb & Simner, 1969; Johnston & Gottlieb, 1981; Lickliter & Virkar, 1989; Shillito, 1975). This early sensory dominance hierarchy is due in part to the fact that, at the time of birth, these two sensory systems have had different amounts of prenatal experience (Lickliter, 1994). Neither the integration view nor the differentiation view has typically considered the possible influences of such timing or asynchronicity issues in their accounts of intersensory capacity (but see Mellon, Kraemer, & Spear, 1991; Spear, Kraemer, Molina, & Smoller, 1988). The result has been a general lack of appreciation of the role of functional constraints or limitations in the realization of early patterns of perceptual organization (but see Turkewitz & Kenny, 1982, 1985; Turkewitz & Mellon, 1989).

The integration and differentiation views have also tended to ignore or downplay the fact that the sensory modalities are somewhat specialized for the processing of different kinds of perceptual information. For instance, the auditory modality is known to be relatively more effective at processing temporal rather than spatial changes; in contrast, the visual modality is relatively more effective at processing spatial rather than temporal changes (Kubovy, 1988; Welch & Warren, 1986). In other words, the different senses are not simply equivalent ways of perceiving objects or events; they can differ in both the precision and rapidity of their responsiveness to different perceptual information (Bushnell & Boudreau, 1993). Differential salience rankings inherent in specific kinds of perceptual information can result in some object or event properties (e.g., temperature, texture, size, weight, temporal frequency, spatial motion) being apprehended more quickly or appropriately in one sensory modality than in others. These salience rankings of various stimulus properties are not likely to be the same in any two modalities (Bushnell, 1994), nor are they likely to change within or across modalities in uniform or equivalent ways over the course of development. For example, Lewkowicz (1988, 1992) has shown that, in human infants, the relative dominance of concurrent auditory and visual inputs can be reversed. Thus, the common assumption that responses to amodal properties can be assessed or discussed without reference to the particular properties included, and their relative salience within and across modalities, is overly simplistic. The infant's ability to integrate or differentiate information across the various sensory modalities is likely influenced by the relative salience ranking of different sensory inputs (Bushnell, Shaw, & Strauss, 1985; see also Spear & Molina, 1987).

How such salience factors and their influences are realized and how they change over early development remain poorly understood and have rarely been considered by either integration or differentiation views. This has contributed to an enduring underappreciation of the task-specific and context-sensitive nature of developing intersensory capabilities, in much of the work derived from these opposing views.

Finally, and perhaps most importantly, integration and differentiation theories of intersensory development have generally assumed that intersensory functioning is a unitary phenomenon that can be characterized by a single developmental pathway. However, as noted by Ryan as long ago as 1940, and as echoed more recently by Turkewitz and his colleagues (Botuck & Turkewitz, 1990; Turkewitz & McGuire, 1978; Turkewitz & Mellon, 1989), there are a number of different types or categories of intersensory functioning, including intersensory inhibition and facilitation, association of multimodal characteristics (multimodal coordination), and abstraction of common information (intersensory equivalence). There is no reason to necessarily assume that these different instances of intersensory functioning share common developmental mechanisms or pathways. Indeed, each distinct type of intersensory functioning may have its own developmental trajectory and be influenced by different neural, physiological, psychological, and social mechanisms. In this light, Turkewitz and Mellon (1989) argue:

> It is therefore possible for intersensory equivalence to be both present and absent at birth, for the senses to be simultaneously unified and separate, and for development to proceed by both differentiation and integration. That is, development may be characterized not by the presence or absence of intersensory functioning at various stages, but by the prevalence or conspicuousness of different types of intersensory functioning at different stages of development. (p. 289)

The insight that intersensory perception is not a unitary process (Bahrick, 1992; Turkewitz, 1994; Walker-Andrews,

1994) is not yet widely appreciated, despite growing evidence to indicate that diverse intraorganismic and extraorganismic factors can interact probabilistically to determine whether information to the different sensory modalities will or will not be integrated. Besides the factors briefly reviewed above (i.e., the changing functional properties of the sensory systems, the differential salience hierarchies of the various modalities, and the processes of differentiation and integration), nonspecific stimulus characteristics such as the relative intensity or amount of stimulation presented to the various modalities (Lewkowicz & Turkewitz, 1980; Lickliter & Lewkowicz, 1995; Radell & Gottlieb, 1992; Turkewitz, Lewkowicz, & Gardner, 1983), and specific organismic characteristics such as the state of arousal of the infant (Gardner & Karmel, 1984; Gottlieb, 1993; Karmel, Gardner, & Magnano, 1991) have been shown to contribute to the infant's emerging capacity for specific intersensory functions.

Thus, individual intersensory functioning is multidetermined, with diverse internal and external variables interacting, often in a nonlinear fashion. As recently pointed out by Thelen and Smith (1994), moving and perceiving provides infants with varied, multimodal "takes" on how the world looks, feels, sounds, tastes, and smells. These experiences of hearing and seeing and touching and moving are all time-locked and are known to change together as the infant's activity, state, and actions change (Weiss & Zelazo, 1991). What is needed to more fully unpack and assess these varied factors and their interactions is a developmental systems view that approaches the study of intersensory development at a suitable level of complexity that does justice to these varied influences and provides a biologically plausible, yet conceptually nonreductionistic, account of the development of intersensory functioning. First steps are being made in this direction.

Emerging Systems Approaches to Intersensory Development

Recently, there has been increasing appreciation of the need to move beyond descriptive studies and toward the experimental examination of the various sensory and nonsensory factors that contribute to the emergence of infants' intersensory functioning (Lewkowicz & Lickliter, 1994b; but see Turkewitz, 1994 for an alternative view). As suggested earlier, this shift in focus from "what" and "when" questions to "how" questions is requiring investigators to reconsider and even revamp several of the traditional conceptual and methodological approaches that have been employed in the study of early perceptual organization. The larger goal of this reorientation is to understand and explain individual functioning and its organization without denying the complexity of the phenomena to be understood.

In our view, such a change in focus will best be served by adopting research strategies that are explicitly interdisciplinary in nature and that place strong emphasis on comparative developmental studies. In other words, an empirical concern with the complexity of the processes and mechanisms underlying intersensory development will profit from information obtained from a variety of analytical levels and drawn from a variety of animal species. Given that the development of any specific behavioral capacity is the product of dynamic, bidirectional interaction among multiple, hierarchically organized levels (see Figure 5.6), we believe that the utilization of interdisciplinary, comparative, and convergent research strategies is essential to discovering and defining the various conditions, experiences, and events (both internal and external to the organism) necessary and sufficient to understand normal perceptual development.

As discussed earlier, Gottlieb (1991a, 1992) has distinguished three functional organismic levels (genetic, neural, and behavioral) and three environmental levels (physical, social, and cultural) of analysis central to a developmental psychobiological systems approach (Figure 5.6). The complex network of interdependent bidirectional relationships among gene action, neuroanatomy and physiology, behavior, and social influences clearly poses a challenge for those who still hope to identify simple unidirectional linkages between levels of organization. This complexity also poses a challenge for researchers committed to unraveling the intricate web of nested influences involved in early development, but for different reasons. Such a complex network requires the discovery of dynamic, bidirectional relationships rather than single antecedent–consequent linkages. Despite this challenge, some initial progress is being made in this regard. Although the genetic and cultural levels of Gottlieb's psychobiological systems framework remain unexplored in the study of early intersensory capabilities, several researchers have taken first steps toward attempting to integrate neural and behavioral levels of analysis (e.g., Knudsen & Brainard, 1991; Knudsen &

Knudsen, 1989; Stein, Huneycutt, & Meredith, 1988; Stein & Meredith, 1990; Stein, Meredith, Huneycutt, & McDade, 1989; Tees, 1994), and the physical and social levels of analysis (Gottlieb, 1991c, 1993; Lickliter & Gottlieb, 1985, 1988; Lickliter & Hellewell, 1992; McBride & Lickliter, 1993). These initial efforts at multilevel analysis are all comparative studies and have employed a variety of avian and mammalian subjects.

Operationally, these varied experiments have manipulated the sensory experiences of developing animals and produced systematic changes in neural and/or behavioral responsiveness to multimodal information. For example, Knudsen (1983) raised developing barn owls with one ear plugged, changing the relative timing and intensity of inputs to the two ears and altering the relative weights of the binaural cues used to construct the bird's auditory receptive fields (e.g., auditory map) in the optic tectum, the brain region involved in the localization of sensory events. Despite the fact that these ear-occluded birds had to learn to function on the basis of abnormal binaural cues, they nonetheless developed an auditory map in surprisingly good register with their visual map (Knudsen, 1983). However, when the ear plug was removed after the owls became adults, the input from the previously deprived ear was far stronger than it was when the auditory map was first formed, resulting in misaligned auditory and visual spatiotopic maps. Correction of this misalignment induced by the onset of normal auditory experience was found to be dependent on the availability and use of visual spatial cues. If no visual information was provided (i.e., the owl was reared in the dark), no corrective reorganization was observed (Knudsen, 1985).

King, Hutchings, Moore, and Blackmore (1988) found similar activity-dependent neural and developmental processes in young ferrets. These mammals had either one ear occluded or one eye deviated during early development. In both cases, a shift in the animal's auditory receptive fields was found to be a result of the experimental sensory modification. This functional shift or compensation ensured the successful alignment of the ferret's auditory and visual inputs, despite ongoing experimental modification of either auditory or visual input. Such findings also illustrate how one sensory system's receptive fields or map (the visual) can exert critical developmental influences on the induction and maintenance of another modality's (the auditory) spatiotopic neural map. Presumably, under normally occurring conditions, map alignment reflects on-going experience with auditory and visual stimuli that are concurrently produced by the same object or event and are thus linked in time and space (Stein & Meredith, 1993). The similarity of the results obtained with owls and ferrets demonstrates how altered sensory experience can drive neural change and how neural change can, in turn, drive behavioral change. These two processes work in a reciprocal, interdependent fashion, again illustrating the bidirectional theme promoted throughout this chapter.

Working at the physical and social levels of analysis, several related studies utilizing precocial birds have demonstrated that social interaction with conspecifics can facilitate the often rapid perceptual reorganization required during early development (see Lickliter, Dyer, & McBride, 1993, for a review).

In addition to providing nurturance and protection to the developing organism, the social environment provides an array of perceptual experience, including thermal, tactile, olfactory, auditory, and visual stimulation. Conspecifics can thus be viewed as experiential resources to the developing individual and have been found to play a significant role in the development of species-typical perceptual organization. For example, Lickliter and Gottlieb (1985) found that young ducklings require physically interactive social experience with siblings to exhibit a species-specific visual preference for a familiar maternal hen over an unfamiliar hen of another species. Young birds that were able to see siblings but were denied physical contact with those siblings in the period following hatching failed to show species-typical visual preferences (Lickliter & Virkar, 1989; McBride & Lickliter, 1993).

The importance of tactile contact with siblings to duck-lings' display of auditory preferences for familiar or unfamiliar maternal vocalizations was also demonstrated by Gottlieb (1991c, 1993), who found that physical interaction with siblings enhanced young ducklings' learning of non-conspecific maternal calls. More recently, Lickliter and Lewkowicz (1995) showed the importance of prenatal tactile and vestibular stimulation from broodmates for the successful emergence of species-typical auditory and visual responsiveness in bobwhite quail chicks. Taken together, these studies of precocial birds (a) provide varied examples of the often nonobvious and multilevel influences contributing to the emergence of normal perceptual organization, (b) remind investigators of the need to be open-minded when attempting to identify the experiences that influence a given perceptual capability, and (c) underscore the often critical role of social processes to psychobiological development. This insight is often overlooked, in that the contribution of the social experiences of human infants has been disregarded in most laboratory studies of intersensory integration.

Systems Characteristics of Intersensory Development

A synthesis of the findings of various comparative studies from the neural, behavioral, and social levels of analysis suggests several interrelated defining characteristics of intersensory development. Intersensory development is:

1. *Multidimensional*—no level, component, or subsystem (including those internal to the infant) necessarily has causal priority in the developmental system.
2. *Nonlinear*—the intricacy of developmental causal networks is not always obvious or straightforward; to be identified, the networks require repeated probes at more than one level of analysis.
3. *Activity-dependent*—intersensory abilities emerge from the infant's ongoing activities and encounters with the world.
4. *Context-sensitive*—emerging intersensory capacities can be strongly influenced or modified by specific features of the infant's immediate surroundings.
5. *Task-specific*—local variability can facilitate or interfere with the infant's intersensory performance.

Several of these related characteristics of intersensory development have begun to be acknowledged in work with human infants (in particular, with respect to context-sensitive and task-specific properties; see Lewkowicz, 1994; Morrongiello, 1994; Streri & Molina, 1994). Few investigators, however, have attempted to combine the cross-disciplinary connections and comparative perspectives that would highlight the social, multidimensional, and nonlinear nature of intersensory development. It is unfortunate that insights from a comparative approach to intersensory functioning continue to be largely ignored in much of contemporary developmental psychology. Non-human animal findings can provide potentially useful and productive guidelines for directing the "how" questions about human development. For example, experiential modification studies employing sensory deprivation or sensory augmentation, either prenatally or postnatally, have recently yielded important information regarding the experiential conditions necessary for the normal development of intersensory organization in both altricial and precocial neonates (Banker & Lickliter, 1993; Foreman & Altaha, 1991; Gottlieb, 1971; Gottlieb, Tomlinson, & Radell, 1989; Kenny & Turkewitz, 1986; Lickliter & Hellewell, 1992; Tees & Symons, 1987). However, these findings have rarely been utilized in directing investigations of human functioning (but see Eilers et al., 1993; Lewkowicz, 1988, 1994; Wilmington, Gray, & Jahrsdoerfer, 1994).

Structured Organisms and Structured Environments

The continued resistance to incorporating results from the comparative approach into mainstream developmental psychology, and the resulting underappreciation of the principles of multidimensionality and nonlinearity, perpetuate a radically reductionistic view of the underlying causes of behavior. Many students of human development continue to take for granted that behavior is somehow based on or determined by more "fundamental" or "primary" processes that occur at the genetic and/or neurophysiological level. This linear, unidirectional, bottom-up view of the "biological bases" of behavior—and the privileged status it typically credits to genetic and neurophysiological components of human functioning—is conceptually flawed, despite its widespread use. Specifically, this bottom-up view of development overlooks the fact that genetic or neural factors are always part-and-parcel of the individual organism's entire developmental system (Johnston & Gottlieb, 1990; Lickliter & Berry, 1990; Oyama, 1985). No single element or level in the system necessarily has causal primacy or privilege, and the functional significance of genes, neural structures, or any other influence on phenotypic development can be understood only in relation to the developmental system of which they are a part (see Figure 5.6). At each level of the developmental system, the effect of any level of influence is dependent on the rest of the system, making all factors potentially interdependent and mutually constraining (Gottlieb, 1991a; Oyama, 1993).

Although this relational emphasis makes for complexity, such complexity is not hopeless and can be experimentally unraveled at all four levels of analysis depicted in Figure 5.6 (see review by Gottlieb, 1996).

The important idea that control for any developmental outcome resides in the structure and nature of the relationships within and between internal and external variables (rather than in any individual factor) is not yet widely appreciated in developmental psychology. Nonetheless, we believe this insight from the developmental psychobiological systems approach has important implications for the study of behavioral development. In particular, the notions of diffuse control and reciprocal interaction highlight the need for an explicit empirical concern with the dynamic relationship between the developing organism and its structured environment. From this perspective, it is no longer plausible to attempt to reduce this complex, dynamic relationship to strictly or solely genetic or neurophysiological levels of analysis. The minimum unit for developmental analysis must be the developmental system, comprised of both the organism and the set of physical, biological, and social factors with which it interacts over the course of development.

Recognition of the need for an empirical concern with the relationship between the organism and its environment has, of course, been evident in the work of several prominent students of perception over the past 50 years (e.g., Brunswik, 1952, 1956; E. J. Gibson, 1969). These authors argued that, to construct psychological theories at an adequate level of complexity, it would be necessary to study representative samples of both subjects and their situations. In other words, the relation between the organism and its environment, rather than the nature of the organism itself, was viewed as the appropriate object of study for psychology. For example, J. J. Gibson (1966, 1979) advocated an ecological approach to the study of perception in which the researcher would be explicitly concerned with the structure of the environment, how the organism moves about in it, and what sorts of perceptual information the environment provides to the perceiving organism. From this approach, perception depends on the kinds of experiences that come from having a body with various sensory and motor capacities that are themselves embedded in a more encompassing physical, biological, psychological, and social context (Varela, Thompson, & Rosch, 1991). Developmentalists are thus faced with the challenge of determining both how the environment of the fetus or infant contributes to and constrains the perceptual information available to the young organism *and* how these contributions and constraints are themselves specified by the changing sensorimotor structure and capacities of the developing organism (see Adolph, Eppler, & Gibson, 1993; Lickliter, 1995; Ronca, Lamkin, & Alberts, 1993). This bidirectional view stresses the fundamental connectedness of the organism to its surroundings and recognizes that empirical investigation beyond the boundaries of the organism is essential to a full understanding of the organism and its behavior.

Ironically, this approach is sometimes viewed as being "environmentalist" in orientation and thus in opposition to a "biological" approach to the study of human development. This dichotomous view derives from an implicit developmental dualism, common in developmental psychology, that attempts to delineate between the relative causal power of internal versus external factors thought to be associated with any given behavioral trait or ability. This widespread dualism and its excessive reductionism are explicitly rejected by the developmental psychobiological systems view advocated in this chapter. We believe that a hard-line distinction between genetic and environmental causation, between internal and external sources of control, between nature and nurture, is no longer tenable in developmental science. As a case in point, the multilevel, nonlinear, and activity-dependent processes revealed in comparative work on intersensory development are not adequately captured by the traditional dichotomy of internal versus external causation that is still common in much of developmental psychology. What is needed is an approach to intersensory development in which factors within and outside the organism are studied in explicitly relational terms.

The need for this relational approach is perhaps best illustrated by the notion of "effective" stimulation, an idea originally put forth by the comparative psychologist T. C. Schneirla (1959, 1965). In brief, the idea of effective stimulation holds that the effectiveness of a particular stimulus depends not only on its specific quantitative (physical) value, but also on the properties of the organism's receptors, the organism's general state of arousal, the organism's experiential history, and its developmental condition. In support of Schneirla's insight, there is now a substantial body of evidence showing that an infant's responsiveness to external sensory stimulation is not determined simply by the physical nature of the sensory input provided; rather, the same stimulus can have markedly different effects on the neonate, depending on the amount of concurrent stimulation to which the infant is exposed and on the neonate's current level of arousal (see Gardner, Lewkowicz, Karmel, & Rose, 1986; Karmel, Gardner, & Magnano, 1991; Lewkowicz & Turkewitz, 1981; Lickliter & Lewkowicz, 1995; Radell & Gottlieb, 1992, for examples from both animal and human infants). Quantitative variations in stimulation in one modality can produce systematic changes in responsiveness in another modality, and it is possible to modify the attentional "value" of a given stimulus by altering either the infant's internal state or the amount of external sensory stimulation provided.

This principle of reciprocal determination underscores the insight that early intersensory relationships depend on variables associated with the organism, the nature and history of sensory stimulation provided or denied, and the larger physical, social, and temporal context in which development occurs. In other words, context *and* specific stimulus features both become dominant behavioral determinants, and a depiction of the bidirectional traffic between levels is crucial to a developmental understanding of individual functioning.

BROADER IMPLICATIONS OF A DEVELOPMENTAL PSYCHOBIOLOGICAL SYSTEMS VIEW

In this chapter, we have applied the systems view of psychobiological development only to developmental behavior genetics and to intersensory integration in the infant; therefore, we wish to close our account by calling attention to the wider applicability of the systems concept to human development.

Although there is considerable evidence for vertical as well as horizontal bidirectionality of influences among the four levels of analysis depicted in Figure 5.6 (environment, behavior, neural activity, genetic expression), the top-down flow has not yet been widely understood and appreciated in developmental psychology. Waddington's (1957, p. 36, Figure 5.5) unidirectional understanding of genetic canalization has been the predominant approach for many years and is still promoted in some quarters of developmental psychology (Fishbein, 1976; Kovach & Wilson,

1988; Lumsden & Wilson, 1980; Parker & Gibson, 1979; Scarr, 1993; Scarr-Salapatek, 1976; Sperry, 1951, 1971).

Because the influence of environmental factors on genetic expression is presently being pursued in a number of neuroscience and neurogenetic laboratories, there is now considerable evidence to document that genetic activity is responsive to the developing organism's external environment (Gottlieb, 1992, 1996). In an early example, Ho (1984) induced a second set of wings on fruit flies by exposing them to ether during a certain period of embryonic development; the ether altered the cytoplasm of the cells and thus the protein produced by the DNA-RNA-cytoplasm coactional relationship. This particular influence has the potential for a nontraditional evolutionary pathway in that it continues to operate transgenerationally, as do the effects of many drugs and other substances (Campbell & Perkins, 1988). Because there are now so many empirical demonstrations of external sensory and internal neural events that both excite and inhibit gene expression, the phenomenon has been labeled "immediate early gene expression" (e.g., Anokhin, Milevsnic, Shamakina, & Rose, 1991; Calamdrei & Keverne, 1994; Mack & Mack, 1992; Rusak, Robertson, Wisden, & Hunt, 1990).

In contrast to the (usually) unidirectional bottom-up flow still prominent in developmental psychology, at the behavior–environment level of analysis, bidirectionality was prominently recognized as early as J. M. Baldwin's (1906) "circular reaction," Vygotsky's (van der Veer & Valsiner, 1991) emphasis on persons' coactions with their cultural worlds, and William Stern's (1938) personology or person–*Umwelt* relatedness, among many other more recent examples (Fischer, Bullock, Rotenberg, & Raya, 1993; Ford & Lerner, 1992).

In a recent comparison of the recognition of bidirectional influences in theoretical accounts of biology, psychology, and sociology, although psychological theory recognizes vertical bidirectionality at the environment–behavior level and micro to macro unidirectional flow at the gene to neural level, sociological theory predominantly sees unidirectional vertical influences at the environment–behavior level and a consequent lack of persons affecting their social and cultural worlds (Shanahan, Valsiner, & Gottlieb, 1997). Indeed, Shanahan et al. concluded that, although examples of bidirectionality can be found across disciplines, unidirectional thinking is still quite common. Only recently have biologists found the

macro to micro flow empirically justified, and this top-down influence has not yet taken hold in biology and psychology as a whole (for an exception in developmental psychopathology, see Cicchetti & Tucker, 1994). Sociologists, on the other hand, have not yet widely embraced the micro to macro flow of influences at the behavior–environment level.

Probabilistic Epigenesis

The probable nature of epigenetic development is rooted in the reciprocal coactions that take place in complex systems, as shown in Figures 5.6 and 5.7.

Since the overthrow of biological preformation in favor of epigenesis in the 19th century, it has been recognized that development takes place sequentially and is therefore an emergent phenomenon. And since the advent of experimental embryology in the late 19th century, it is an accepted fact that cellular and organismic development occurs as a consequence of coactions at all levels from the genes to the developing organism itself. With the gradual realization that influences in developmental systems are fully bidirectional and that genes do not, in and of themselves, produce finished (i.e., mature) traits, the predetermined concept of epigenesis has receded from all but a few viewpoints in biology and psychology (cf. Scarr, 1993). Epigenesis is now defined as increased complexity of organization: the emergence of new structural and functional properties and competencies as a consequence of horizontal and vertical coactions among the system's parts, including organism–environment coactions (Gottlieb, 1991a). As noted in the first part of this chapter on a developmental psychobiological systems view, the emergent nature of development is represented well in the concept of equifinality.

As concluded by Shanahan et al. (1997), probabilistic epigenesis is in accord with Baldwin's (1906) understanding of developmental phenomena. The stochastic nature of developmental phenomena ultimately derives from the range of responses at any given level. Thus, responses to tension can vary within levels; and given that responses to stress occur in highly related sets of behavior (i.e., they are organized), there will be variability in the overall patterns between levels. London's (1949) argument for the "behavioral spectrum" exemplifies the concern for a range of responses. From this perspective, developmental phenomena cannot be represented so as to imply subsequent derivations, though they can suggest classes of outcomes. This notion is captured well by Fischer; in his theory of cognition, he adopts the principles of adaptive resonance theory to explain the generation of multiple cognitive forms in ontogeny (Fischer, Bullock, Rotenberg, & Raya, 1993).

Thus, the hallmarks of probabilistic epigenesis—bidirectionality and indeterminacy—are being ever more widely used in developmental psychology, even if they are not yet majority opinions among psychological theorists who are not steeped in our own history of conceptualizing behavior–environment relations, or who have yet to grasp the recent empirical breakthroughs in our understanding of biological development.

SUMMARY AND CONCLUSION

Developmental thinking began in the early 1800s, coincident with the triumph of epigenesis over the concept of preformation. Though practiced only at the descriptive level in this early period, it led to the insight that to understand the origin of any phenotype, it is necessary to study its development in the individual. Late in the 1800s, developmental description was superceded by an experimental approach in embryology—one explicitly addressed to a theoretical understanding and explanation of developmental outcomes. A field or systems view was born when the results of Hans Driesch's experiments made it necessary to conceptualize embryonic cells as harmonious-equipotential systems. Steering a careful path between mechanical–reductive and vitalistic–constructive viewpoints, in the 1930s, Ludwig von Bertalanffy formalized an organismic systems view for experimental embryology, which was later worked out in more formal detail by the embryologist Paul Weiss and the physiologically oriented population geneticist, Sewall Wright.[6] At present, a systems view of psychobiological development has begun to take hold in developmental psychology, developmental neurobiology, and behavior genetics. Thus, although there are dissenters, a psychobiological systems view seems workable and useful in understanding human as well as nonhuman animal psychological development.

A systems view of psychobiological development is a useful framework to guide experiment and theory. It is quite rewarding to those who work with nonhuman animals to note that Ford and Lerner (1992) explicitly advocate the utility of a systems concept for developmental psychologists who work with human beings. As noted earlier, similar points of view have been put forward by psychobiologically oriented developmentalists such as Cairns, Gariépy, and Hood (1990), Edelman (1988), Griffiths and Gray (1994), Hinde (1990), Johnston and Hyatt (1994), Magnusson and Törestad (1993), and Oyama (1985), and this represents a realization of the pioneering theoretical efforts of Z.-Y. Kuo, T. C. Schneirla, and D. S. Lehrman. Because a developmental systems view dates back as far as Hans Driesch's theorizing about his embryological experiments in the 1890s, one cannot call it a "paradigm shift," but certainly it is something relatively new in the field of developmental psychology.

ACKNOWLEDGMENTS

The authors thank Timothy D. Johnston for his comments on a previous draft of this chapter.

REFERENCES

Adolph, K. E., Eppler, M. A., & Gibson, E. J. (1993). Development of perception of affordances. In C. Rovee-Collier & L. P. Lipsitt (Eds.), *Advances in infancy research* (Vol. 8, pp. 51–98). Norwood, NJ: ABLEX.

Alberts, J. R. (1984). Sensory-perceptual development in the Norway rat: A view toward comparative studies. In R. Kail & N. S. Spear (Eds.), *Comparative perspectives on memory development* (pp. 65–101). Hillsdale, NJ: Erlbaum.

Allen, G. E. (1985). Heredity under an embryological paradigm: The case of genetics and embryology. *Biological Bulletin, 168,* 107–121.

Allen, T. W., Walker, K., Symonds, L., & Marcell, M. (1977). Intrasensory and intersensory perception of temporal sequences during infancy. *Developmental Psychology, 13,* 225–229.

Anokhin, K. V., Milevsnic, R., Shamakina, I. Y., & Rose, S. (1991). Effects of early experience on c-fos gene expression in the chick forebrain. *Brain Research, 544,* 101–107.

Aslin, R., & Smith, L. B. (1988). Perceptual development. *Annual Review of Psychology, 39,* 435–473.

---

[6] Some observers note that, with the advent of molecular biology, systems or organismic thinking has taken a back seat to genetic determinism in the field of biology (Strohman, 1997).

Bahrick, L. E. (1987). Infants' intermodal perception of two levels of temporal structure in natural events. *Infant Behavior and Development, 10,* 387–416.

Bahrick, L. E. (1988). Intermodal learning in infancy: Learning on the basis of two kinds of invariant relations in audible and visible events. *Child Development, 59,* 197–209.

Bahrick, L. E. (1992). Infants' perceptual differentiation of amodal and modality–specific audio-visual relations. *Journal of Experimental Child Psychology, 53,* 180–199.

Bahrick, L. E., & Pickens, J. (1994). Amodal relations: The basis for intermodal perception and learning in infancy. In D. J. Lewkowicz & R. Lickliter (Eds.), *The development of intersensory perception: Comparative perspectives* (pp. 205–234). Hillsdale, NJ: Erlbaum.

Baldwin, J. M. (1906). *Thought and things: A study of the development and meaning of thought, or genetic logic: Vol. 1. Functional logic or genetic theory of knowledge.* London: Swan Sonnenschein.

Banker, H., & Lickliter, R. (1993). Effects of early and delayed visual experience on intersensory development in bobwhite quail chicks. *Developmental Psychobiology, 26,* 155–170.

Baunack, E., Gärtner, K., & Schneider, B. (1986). Is the 'environmental' component of the phenotypic variability in inbred mice influenced by the cytoplasm of the egg? *Journal of Veterinary Medicine A, 33,* 641–646.

Bellugi, U., Wang, P. P., & Jernigan, T. L. (1994). Williams Syndrome: An unusual neuropsychological profile. In S. H. Broman & J. Grafman (Eds.), *Atypical cognitive deficits in developmental disorders: Implications for brain functions* (pp. 23–56). Hillsdale, NJ: Erlbaum.

Birch, H., & Lefford, A. (1963). Intersensory development in children. *Monographs of the Society for Research in Child Development, 28*(5, Serial No. 89).

Birch, H., & Lefford, A. (1967). Visual differentiation, intersensory integration, and voluntary motor control. *Monographs of the Society for Research in Child Development, 32*(1-2, Serial No. 110).

Bjorklund, D. (1995). *Children's thinking: Developmental function and individual differences.* New York: Brooks/Cole.

Black, I. B. (1993). Environmental regulation of brain trophic interactions. *International Journal of Developmental Neuroscience, 11,* 403–410.

Blau, H. M., Pavlath, G. K., Hardeman, E. C., Choy-Pik, C., Silberstein, L., Webster, S. G., Miller, S. C., & Webster, C. (1985). Plasticity of the differentiated state. *Science, 230,* 758–766.

Botuck, S., & Turkewitz, G. (1990). Intersensory functioning: Auditory-visual pattern equivalence in younger and older children. *Developmental Psychology, 26,* 115–120.

Bouchard, T. J., Lykken, D. T., McGue, M., Segal, N. L., & Tellegen, A. (1990). Sources of human psychological differences: The Minnesota study of twins reared apart. *Science, 250,* 223–228.

Bower, T. G. R. (1974). *Development in infancy.* San Francisco: Freeman.

Bradley, R. M., & Mistretta, C. A. (1975). Fetal sensory receptors. *Physiological Reviews, 55,* 352–382.

Brunswik, E. (1952). *The conceptual framework of psychology.* Chicago: University of Chicago Press.

Brunswik, E. (1956). *Perception and the representative design of experiments in psychology.* Berkeley: University of California Press.

Bull, J. J. (1983). *Evolution of sex determining mechanisms.* Menlo Park, CA: Benjamin/Cummings.

Bulman-Fleming, B., & Wahlsten, D. (1988). Effects of a hybrid maternal environment on brain growth and corpus callosum defects of inbred BALB/c mice: A study using ovarian grafting. *Experimental Neurology, 99,* 636–646.

Bulman-Fleming, B., & Wahlsten, D. (1991). The effects of intrauterine position on the degree of corpus callosum deficiency in two substrains of BALB/c mice. *Developmental Psychobiology, 24,* 395–412.

Bulman-Fleming, B, Wahlsten, D., & Lassalle, J. M. (1991). Hybrid vigour and maternal environment in mice: 1. Body and brain growth. *Behavioral Processes, 23,* 21–33.

Bushnell, E. W. (1982). Visual-tactual knowledge in 8-, 9½-, and 11-month old infants. *Infant Behavior and Development, 5,* 65–75.

Bushnell, E. W. (1994). A dual-processing approach to crossmodal matching: Implications for development. In D. J. Lewkowicz & R. Lickliter (Eds.), *The development of intersensory perception: Comparative perspectives* (pp. 19–38). Hillsdale, NJ: Erlbaum.

Bushnell, E. W., & Boudreau, J. P. (1993). Motor development in the mind: The potential role of motor abilities as a determinant of aspects of perceptual development. *Child Development, 64,* 1005–1021.

Bushnell, E. W., Shaw, L., & Strauss, D. (1985). The relationship between visual and tactual exploration by 6-month olds. *Developmental Psychology, 21,* 591–600.

Busnel, M. C., Granier-Deferre, C., & Lecanuet, J. P. (1992). Fetal audition. *Annals of the New York Academy of Sciences, 662,* 118–134.

Cairns, R. B., Gariépy, J.-L., & Hood, K. E. (1990). Development, microevolution, and social behavior. *Psychological Review, 97,* 49–65.

Cairns, R. B., MacCombie, D. J., & Hood, K. E. (1983). A developmental-genetic analysis of aggressive behavior in mice: 1. Behavioral outcomes. *Journal of Comparative Psychology, 97,* 69–89.

Calamandrei, G., & Keverne, E. B. (1994). Differential expression of Fos protein in the brain of female mice is dependent on pup sensory cues and maternal experience. *Behavioral Neuroscience, 108,* 113–120.

Campbell, J. H., & Perkins, P. (1988). Transgenerational effects of drug and hormone treatments in mammals. *Progress in Brain Research, 75,* 535–553.

Capron, C., & Duyme, M. (1989). Assessment of effects of socioeconomic status on IQ in a full cross-fostering study. *Nature, 340,* 552–553.

Carlier, M., Nosten-Bertrand, M., & Michard-Vanhée, C. (1992). Separating genetic effects from maternal environmental effects. In D. Goldowitz, D. Wahlsten, & R. E. Wimer (Eds.), *Techniques for the genetic analysis of brain and behavior* (pp. 111–126). Amsterdam, The Netherlands: Elsevier.

Carlier, M., Roubertoux, P., Kottler, M. L., & Degrelle, H. (1989). Y chromosome and aggression in strains of laboratory mice. *Behavior Genetics, 20,* 137–156.

Carlier, M., Roubertoux, P. L., & Pastoret, C. (1991). The *Y* chromosome effect on intermale aggression in mice depends on the maternal environment. *Genetics, 129,* 231–236.

Cheng, M.-F. (1979). Progress and prospects in ring dove: A personal view. *Advances in the Study of Behavior, 9,* 97–129.

Cicchetti, D. V., & Tucker, D. (1994). Development and self-regulatory structures of the mind. *Development and Psychopathology, 6,* 533–549.

Clifton, R. K., Rochat, P., Robin, D. J., & Berthier, W. E. (1994). Multimodal perception in the control of infant reaching. *Journal of Experimental Psychology: Human Perception and Performance, 20,* 876–886.

Collins, R. L. (1985). On the inheritance of direction and degree of asymmetry. In S. D. Glick (Ed.), *Cerebral lateralization in nonhuman species* (pp. 41–71). New York: Academic Press.

Cooperative Human Linkage Center (CHLC). (1994). A comprehensive human linkage map with centimorgan density. *Science, 265,* 2049–2054.

Copeland, N. G., Jenkins, N. A., Gilbert, D. J., Eppig, J. T., Maltais, L. J., Miller, J. C., Dietrich, W. F., Weaver, A., Lincoln, S. E., Steen, R. G., Stein, L. D., Nadeau, J. H., & Lander, E. S. (1993). A genetic linkage map of the mouse: Current applications and future prospects. *Science, 262,* 57–66.

Damasio, A. R. (1989). Time-locked multiregional retroactivation: A systems-level proposal for the neural substrates of recall and recognition. *Cognition, 33,* 25–62.

DeCasper, A. J., & Spence, M. J. (1986). Prenatal maternal speech influences newborns' perception of speech sounds. *Infant Behavior and Development, 9,* 133–150.

Dent, C. H. (1990). An ecological approach to language development: An alternative to functionalism. *Developmental Psychobiology, 23,* 679–703.

Detterman, D. K. (1990). Don't kill the ANOVA messenger for bearing bad interaction news. *Behavioral and Brain Sciences, 13,* 131–132.

Dodd, B. (1979). Lip reading in infants: Attention to speech presented in-and-out of synchrony. *Cognitive Psychology, 11,* 478–484.

Driesch, H. (1929). *The science and philosophy of the organism.* London: A. & C. Black. (Original manuscript published 1908)

Edelman, G. (1987). *Neural Darwinism.* New York: Basic Books.

Edelman, G. (1988). *Topobiology.* New York: Basic Books.

Edelman, G. (1992). *Bright air, brilliant fire: On the matter of mind.* New York: Basic Books.

Eilers, R., Oller, D. K., Levine, S., Basinger, O., Lynch, M., & Urbano, R. (1993). The role of prematurity and socioeconomic status in the onset of canonical babbling in infants. *Infant Behavior and Development, 16,* 297–316.

Erlenmeyer-Kimling, L. (1972). Genotype-environment interactions and the variability of behavior. In L. Ehrman, G. S. Omenn, & E. Caspari (Eds.), *Genetics, environment and behavior* (pp. 181–208). New York: Academic Press.

Ettlinger, G., & Wilson, W. A. (1990). Cross-modal performance: Behavioral processes, phylogenetic considerations and neural mechanisms. *Behavioral Brain Research, 40,* 169–192.

Farber, S. L. (1981). *Identical twins reared apart: A reanalysis.* New York: Basic Books.

Ferguson, M. W. J., & Joanen, T. (1982). Temperature of egg incubation determines sex in Alligator mississippiensis. *Nature, 296,* 850–853.

Fischer, K. W. (1980). A theory of cognitive development: The control and construction of hierarchies of skill. *Psychological Review, 87,* 477–531.

Fischer, K. W., Bullock, D. H., Rotenberg, E. J., & Raya, P. (1993). The dynamics of competence: How context contributes directly to skill. In R. H. Wozniak & K. W. Fischer (Eds.), *Development in context* (pp. 93–120). Hillsdale, NJ: Erlbaum.

Fishbein, H. D. (1976). *Evolution, development, and children's learning.* Pacific Palisades, CA: Goodyear.

Fogel, A. (1993). *Developing through relationships: Origins of communication, self, and culture.* New York: Harvester Wheatsheaf.

Ford, D. H., & Lerner, R. M. (1992). *Developmental systems theory: An integrative approach.* Newbury Park, CA: Sage.

Foreman, N., & Altaha, M. (1991). The development of explorations and spontaneous alteration in hooded rat pups: Effects of unusually early eyelid opening. *Developmental Psychobiology, 24,* 521–537.

Freeman, N. J. (1991). The physiology of perception. *Scientific American,* 78–85.

Friedes, D. (1974). Human information processing and sensory modality: Cross-modal functions, information complexity, memory, and deficit. *Psychological Bulletin, 81,* 284–310.

Fuller, J. L. (1979). Fuller BWS lines: History and results. In M. E. Hahn, C. Jensen, & B. C. Dudek (Eds.), *Development and evolution of brain size: Behavioral implications* (pp. 187–204). New York: Academic Press.

Gardner, J. M., & Karmel, B. Z. (1984). Arousal effects on visual preferences in neonates. *Developmental Psychology, 20,* 374–377.

Gardner, J. M., Lewkowicz, D. J., Karmel, B. Z., & Rose, S. A. (1986). Effects of visual and auditory stimulation on subsequent visual preferences in neonates. *International Journal of Behavioral Development, 9,* 251–263.

Gariépy, J.-L. (1995). The making of a developmental science: Historical and contemporary trends in animal behavior research. *Annals of Child Development, 11,* 167–224.

Gärtner, K. (1990). A third component causing random variability beside environment and genotype. A reason for the limited success of a 30-year-long effort to standardize laboratory animals? *Laboratory Animals, 24,* 71–77.

Gibson, E. J. (1969). *Principles of perceptual learning and development.* Englewood Cliffs, NJ: Prentice-Hall.

Gibson, E. J. (1988). Exploratory behavior in the development of perceiving, acting, and the acquiring of knowledge. *Annual Review of Psychology, 39,* 1–44.

Gibson, J. J. (1966). *The senses considered as perceptual systems.* Boston: Houghton-Mifflin.

Gibson, J. J. (1979). *The ecological approach to visual perception.* Boston: Houghton-Mifflin.

Goldin-Meadow, S. (1997). The resilience of language in humans. In C. T. Snowden & M. Hausberger (Eds.), *Social influences on vocal development* (pp. 293–311). New York: Cambridge University Press.

Goldman, D., Nelson, R., Deitrich, R. A., Baker, R. C., Spuhler, K., Markley, H., Ebert, M., & Merril, C. R. (1985). Genetic brain polypeptide variants in inbred mice and in mouse strains with high and low sensitivity to alcohol. *Brain Research, 341,* 130–138.

Gottlieb, G. (1970). Conceptions of prenatal behavior. In L. R. Aronson, E. Tobach, D. S. Lehrman, & J. S. Rosenblatt (Eds.), *Development and evolution of behavior* (pp. 111–137). San Francisco: Freeman.

Gottlieb, G. (1971). Ontogenesis of sensory function in birds and mammals. In E. Tobach, L. R. Aronson, & E. Shaw (Eds.), *The biopsychology of development* (pp. 67–128). New York: Academic Press.

Gottlieb, G. (1976). Conceptions of prenatal development: Behavioral embryology. *Psychological Review, 83,* 215–234.

Gottlieb, G. (1991a). Experiential canalization of behavioral development: Theory. *Developmental Psychology, 27,* 4–13.

Gottlieb, G. (1991b). Experiential canalization of behavioral development: Results. *Developmental Psychology, 27,* 39–42.

Gottlieb, G. (1991c). Social induction of malleability in ducklings. *Animal Behaviour, 41,* 953–962.

Gottlieb, G. (1992). *Individual development and evolution. The genesis of novel behavior.* New York: Oxford University Press.

Gottlieb, G. (1993). Social induction of malleability in ducklings: Sensory basis and psychological mechanism. *Animal Behaviour, 45,* 707–719.

Gottlieb, G. (1995). Some conceptual deficiencies in 'developmental' behavior genetics. *Human Development, 38,* 131–141.

Gottlieb, G. (1996). A systems view of psychobiological development. In D. Magnusson (Ed.), *Individual development over the life-span: Biological and psychosocial perspectives* (pp. 76–103). New York: Cambridge University Press.

Gottlieb, G. (1997). *Synthesizing nature–nurture: Prenatal roots of instinctive behavior.* Mahwah, NJ: Erlbaum.

Gottlieb, G., & Simner, M. L. (1969). Auditory versus visual flicker in directing the approach response of domestic chicks. *Journal of Comparative and Physiological Psychology, 67,* 58–63.

Gottlieb, G., Tomlinson, W. T., & Radell, P. L. (1989). Developmental intersensory interference: Premature visual experience suppresses auditory learning in ducklings. *Infant Behavior and Development, 12,* 1–12.

Gould, S. J. (1977). *Ontogeny and phylogeny.* Cambridge, MA: Harvard University Press.

Griffiths, P. E., & Gray, R. D. (1994). Developmental systems and evolutionary explanation. *Journal of Philosophy, 91,* 277–304.

Grun, P. (1976). *Cytoplasmic genetics and evolution*. New York: Columbia University Press.

Gupta, A. P., & Lewontin, R. C. (1982). A study of reaction norms in natural populations of *Drosophila pseudoobscura. Evolution, 36*, 934–948.

Haith, M., & Campos, J. L. (Eds.). (1983). *Handbook of child psychology: Vol. 2. Infancy and developmental psychobiology* (4th ed.). New York: Wiley.

Hamburger, V. (1957). The concept of "development" in biology. In D. H. Harris (Ed.), *The concept of development* (pp. 49–58). Minneapolis: University of Minnesota.

Hamburger, V. (1964). Ontogeny of behaviour and its structural basis. In D. Richter (Ed.), *Comparative neurochemistry* (pp. 21–34). Oxford, England: Pergamon Press.

Hamburger, V. (1985, October 24). *Past, present, and future.* Presented at the annual meeting of the Society for Neuroscience, Dallas, TX.

Henfry, A., & Huxley, T. H. (1853). *Scientific memoirs, selected from the transactions of foreign academies of science, and from foreign journals. Natural history.* London: Taylor & Francis.

Henry, K. R., & Bowman, R. E. (1970). Behavior-genetic analysis of the ontogeny of acoustically primed audiogenic seizures in mice. *Journal of Comparative and Physiological Psychology, 70*, 235–241.

Hinde, R. A. (1990). The interdependence of the behavioural sciences. *Philosophical Transactions of the Royal Society, London, B, 329*, 217–227.

His, W. (1888). On the principles of animal morphology. *Proceedings of the Royal Society of Edinburgh, 15*, 287–298.

Ho, M.-W. (1984). Environment and heredity in development and evolution. In M.-W. Ho & P. T. Saunders (Eds.), *Beyond neo-Darwinism: An introduction to the new evolutionary paradigm* (pp. 267–289). San Diego, CA: Academic Press.

Hoffman, L. W. (1991). The influence of the family environment on personality: Accounting for sibling differences. *Psychological Bulletin, 110*, 187–203.

Hood, K. E., & Cairns, R. B. (1989). A developmental-genetic analysis of aggressive behavior in mice: 4. Genotype-environment interaction. *Aggressive Behavior, 15*, 361–380.

Jacobson, M. (1981). Rohon-Beard neurons arise from a substitute ancestral cell after removal of the cell from which they normally arise in the 16-cell frog embryo. *Journal of Neuroscience, 1*, 923–927.

Jacobson, M. (1991). *Developmental neurobiology* (3rd ed.). New York: Plenum Press.

Johnston, T. D. (1987). The persistence of dichotomies in the study of behavioral development. *Developmental Review, 7*, 149–182.

Johnston, T. D. (1988). Developmental explanation and the ontogeny of birdsong: Nature/nurture redux. *Behavioral and Brain Sciences, 11*, 617–663.

Johnston, T. D., & Gottlieb, G. (1981). Development of visual species identification in ducklings: What is the role of imprinting? *Animal Behaviour, 29*, 1082–1099.

Johnston, T. D., & Gottlieb, G. (1990). Neophenogenesis: A developmental theory of phenotypic evolution. *Journal of Theoretical Biology, 147*, 471–495.

Johnston, T. D., & Hyatt, L. E. (1994). *Genes, interactions, and the development of behavior.* Unpublished manuscript.

Julien, J.-P., Tretjakoff, I., Beaudet, L., & Peterson, A. (1987). Expression and assembly of a human neurofilament protein in transgenic mice provide a novel neuronal marking system. *Genes and Development, 1*, 1085–1095.

Jungblut, P., & Klose, J. (1985). Genetic variability of proteins from mitochondria and mitochondrial fractions of mouse organs. *Biochemical Genetics, 23*, 227–245.

Karmel, B. Z., Gardner, J. M., & Magnano, C. L. (1991). Attention and arousal in early infancy. In M. J. S. Weiss & P. R. Zelazo (Eds.), *Newborn attention: Biological constraints and the influence of experience* (pp. 339–376). Norwood, NJ: ABLEX.

Kenny, P., & Turkewitz, G. (1986). Effects of unusually early visual stimulation on the development of homing behavior in the rat pup. *Developmental Psychobiology, 19*, 57–66.

King, A. J., Hutchings, M. E., Moore, D. R., & Blackmore, C. (1988). Developmental plasticity in the visual and auditory representations in the mammalian superior colliculus. *Nature, 332*, 73–76.

Knudsen, E. I. (1983). Early auditory experience aligns the auditory map of space in the optic tectum of the barn owl. *Science, 222*, 939–942.

Knudsen, E. I. (1985). Experience alters the spatial tuning of auditory units in the optic tectum during a sensitive period in the barn owl. *Journal of Neuroscience, 5*, 3094–3109.

Knudsen, E. I., & Brainard, M. S. (1991). Visual instruction of the neural map of auditory space in the developing optic tectum. *Science, 253*, 85–87.

Knudsen, E. I., & Knudsen, P. F. (1989). Vision calibrates sound localization in developing barn owls. *Journal of Neuroscience, 9*, 3306–3313.

Korach, K. S. (1994). Insights from the study of animals lacking functional estrogen receptor. *Science, 266*, 1524–1527.

Kovach, J. K., & Wilson, G. (1988). Genetics of color preferences in quail chicks: Major genes and variable buffering by background genotype. *Behavior Genetics, 18,* 645–661.

Kubovy, M. (1988). Should we resist the seductiveness of the spacetime-vision-auditory analogy? *Journal of Experimental Psychology: Human Perception and Performance, 14,* 318–320.

Kuhl, P. K., & Meltzoff, A. N. (1984). The intermodal representation of speech in infants. *Infant Behavior and Development, 7,* 361–381.

Kuhn, D. (1995). Microgenetic study of change: What has it told us? *Psychological Science, 3,* 133–139.

Kuo, Z.-Y. (1967). *The dynamics of behavior development.* New York: Random House.

Kuo, Z.-Y. (1976). *The dynamics of behavior development* (Enl. ed.). New York: Plenum Press.

Lander, E. S., & Schork, N. J. (1994). Genetic dissection of complex traits. *Science, 265,* 2037–2048.

Layton, W. M., Jr. (1976). Random determination of a developmental process. Reversal of normal visceral asymmetry in the mouse. *Journal of Heredity, 67,* 336–338.

Lee, S. M., & Bressler, R. (1981). Prevention of diabetic nephropathy by diet control in the *db/db* mouse. *Diabetes, 30,* 106–111.

Lehrman, D. S. (1970). Semantic and conceptual issues in the nature–nurture problem. In L. R. Aronson, D. S. Lehrman, E. Tobach, & J. S. Rosenblatt (Eds.), *Development and evolution of behavior* (pp. 17–52). San Francisco, CA: Freeman.

Lerner, R. M. (1988). Personality development: A life-span perspective. In E. M. Hetherington, R. M. Lerner, & M. Perlmutter (Eds.), *Child development in life-span perspective* (pp. 21–46). Hillsdale, NJ: Erlbaum.

Lerner, R. M. (1992). *Final solutions. Biology, prejudice, and genocide.* University Park: Pennsylvania State University Press.

Lerner, R. M. (1995). The limits of biological influence: Behavioral genetics as the emperor's new clothes. *Psychological Inquiry, 6,* 145–156.

Lewkowicz, D. J. (1985). Developmental changes in infants' response to temporal frequency. *Developmental Psychology, 21,* 850–865.

Lewkowicz, D. J. (1986). Developmental changes in infants' bisensory response to synchronous duration. *Infant Behavior and Development, 9,* 335–353.

Lewkowicz, D. J. (1988). Sensory dominance in infants: 1. Six-month-old infants' response to auditory–visual compounds. *Developmental Psychology, 24,* 155–171.

Lewkowicz, D. J. (1992). Responsiveness to auditory and visual components of a sounding/moving compound stimulus in human infants. *Perception and Psychophysics, 52,* 519–528.

Lewkowicz, D. J. (1994). Development of intersensory perception in human infants. In D. J. Lewkowicz & R. Lickliter (Eds.), *The development of intersensory perception: Comparative perspectives* (pp. 165–204). Hillsdale, NJ: Erlbaum.

Lewkowicz, D. J., & Lickliter, R. (Eds.). (1994a). *The development of intersensory perception: Comparative perspectives.* Hillsdale, NJ: Erlbaum.

Lewkowicz, D. J., & Lickliter, R. (1994b). Insights into mechanisms of intersensory development: The value of a comparative, convergent-operations approach. In D. J. Lewkowicz & R. Lickliter (Eds.), *The development of intersensory perception: Comparative perspectives* (pp. 403–414). Hillsdale, NJ: Erlbaum.

Lewkowicz, D. J., & Turkewitz, G. (1980). Cross-modal equivalence in early infancy: Auditory-visual intensity matching. *Developmental Psychology, 16,* 597–607.

Lewkowicz, D. J., & Turkewitz, G. (1981). Intersensory interaction in newborns: Modification of visual preferences following exposure to sound. *Child Development, 52,* 827–832.

Lewontin, R. C. (1991). *Biology as ideology.* Concord, Ontario: House of Anansi Press.

Lickliter, R. (1990a). Premature visual stimulation accelerates intersensory functioning in bobwhite quail neonates. *Developmental Psychobiology, 23,* 15–27.

Lickliter, R. (1990b). Premature visual experience facilitates visual responsiveness in bobwhite quail neonates. *Infant Behavior and Development, 13,* 487–496.

Lickliter, R. (1993). Timing and the development of perinatal perceptual organization. In G. Turkewitz & D. A. Devenny (Eds.), *Developmental time and timing* (pp. 105–124). Hillsdale, NJ: Erlbaum.

Lickliter, R. (1994). Prenatal visual experience alters postnatal sensory dominance hierarchy in bobwhite quail chicks. *Infant Behavior and Development, 17,* 185–193.

Lickliter, R. (1995). Embryonic sensory experience and intersensory development in precocial birds. In J. P. Lecanuet, W. P. Fifer, N. A. Krasnegor, & W. P. Smotherman (Eds.), *Fetal development: A psychobiological perspective* (pp. 281–294). Hillsdale, NJ: Erlbaum.

Lickliter, R., & Banker, H. (1994). Prenatal components of intersensory development in precocial birds. In D. J. Lewkowicz & R. Lickliter (Eds.), *Development of intersensory perception: Comparative aspects* (pp. 59–80). Hillsdale, NJ: Erlbaum.

Lickliter, R., & Berry, T. D. (1990). The phylogeny fallacy: Developmental psychology's misapplication of evolutionary theory. *Developmental Review, 10,* 322–338.

Lickliter, R., Dyer, A. B., & McBride, T. (1993). Perceptual consequences of early social interaction in precocial birds. *Behavioural Processes, 30,* 185–200.

Lickliter, R., & Gottlieb, G. (1985). Social interaction with siblings is necessary for visual imprinting of species-specific maternal preferences in ducklings *(Anas platyrhynchos). Journal of Comparative Psychology, 99,* 371–379.

Lickliter, R., & Gottlieb, G. (1988). Social specificity: Interaction with own species is necessary to foster species-specific maternal preference in ducklings. *Developmental Psychobiology, 21,* 311–321.

Lickliter, R., & Hellewell, T. (1992). Contextual determinants of auditory learning in bobwhite quail embryos and hatchlings. *Developmental Psychobiology, 25,* 17–24.

Lickliter, R., & Lewkowicz, D. J. (1995). Intersensory experience and early perceptual development: Attenuated prenatal sensory stimulation affects postnatal auditory and visual responsiveness in bobwhite quail chicks. *Developmental Psychology, 31,* 609–618.

Lickliter, R., & Stoumbos, J. (1991). Enhanced prenatal auditory experience facilitates postnatal visual responsiveness in bobwhite quail chicks. *Journal of Comparative Psychology, 105,* 89–94.

Lickliter, R., & Virkar, P. (1989). Intersensory functioning in bobwhite quail chicks: Early sensory dominance. *Developmental Psychobiology, 22,* 651–667.

Locke, J. L. (1993). *The child's path to spoken language.* Cambridge, MA: Harvard University Press.

London, I. D. (1949). The concept of the behavioral spectrum. *Journal of Genetic Psychology, 24,* 177–184.

Lorenz, K. Z. (1981). *The foundations of ethology.* New York: Simon & Schuster.

Lumsden, C. J., & Wilson, E. O. (1980). Translation of epigenetic rules of individual behavior into ethnographic patterns. *Proceeding of the National Academy of Sciences USA, 77,* 4382–4386.

Lupski, J. R., Garcia, C. A., Zoghbi, H. Y., Hoffman, E. P., & Fenwick, R. G. (1991). Discordance of muscular dystrophy in monozygotic female twins: Evidence supporting asymmetric splitting of the inner cell mass in a manifesting carrier of Duchenne dystrophy. *American Journal of Medical Genetics, 40,* 354–364.

Mack, K. J., & Mack, P. A. (1992). Induction of transcription factors in somatosensory cortex after tactile stimulation. *Molecular Brain Research, 12,* 141–147.

Magnusson, D., & Törestad, B. (1993). A holistic view of personality: A model revisited. *Annual Review of Psychology, 44,* 427–452.

Mangold, O., & Seidel, F. (1927). Homoplastische und heteroplastische Verschmelzung ganzer Tritonkeime. Roux's *Archiv für Entwicklungsmechanik der Organismen, 111,* 593–665.

Marks, L. E. (1978). *The unity of the senses: Interrelations among the modalities.* New York: Academic Press.

Mauro, V. P., Wood, I. C., Krushel, L., Crossin, K. L., & Edelman, G. M. (1994). Cell adhesion alters gene transcription in chicken embryo brain cells and mouse embryonal carcinoma cells. *Proceedings of the National Academy of Sciences USA, 91,* 2868–2872.

McBride, T., & Lickliter, R. (1993). Visual experience with siblings fosters species-specific responsiveness to maternal visual cues in bobwhite quail chicks. *Journal of Comparative Psychology, 107,* 310–327.

McGue, M. (1989). Nature–nurture and intelligence. *Nature, 340,* 507–508.

McKenzie, B. G., & Day, R. H. (1987). *Perceptual development in early infancy.* Hillsdale, NJ: Erlbaum.

McKinney, M. L., & McNamara, K. J. (1991). *Heterochrony: The evolution of ontogeny.* New York: Plenum Press.

Mellon, R., Kraemer, P., & Spear, N. (1991). Development of intersensory function: Age related differences in stimulus selection of multimodal compounds in rats as revealed by Pavlovian conditioning. *Journal of Experimental Psychology: Animal Behavior Processes, 17,* 448–464.

Meltzoff, A. N. (1990). Towards a developmental cognitive science: The implications of cross-modal matching and imitation for the development and representation and memory in infancy. In A. Diamond (Ed.), The development and neural bases of higher cognitive functions. *Annals of the New York Academy of Sciences, 608,* 1–31.

Meltzoff, A. N., & Borton, R. N. (1979). Intermodal matching by human neonates. *Nature, 282,* 403–404.

Mendelson, M. J., & Ferland, M. B. (1982). Auditory–visual transfer in four-month-old infants. *Child Development, 53,* 1022–1027.

Merbs, S. L., & Nathans, J. (1992). Absorption spectra of human cone pigments. *Nature, 356,* 433–435.

Merriam, J., Ashburner, M., Hartl, D. L., & Kafatos, F. C. (1991). Toward cloning and mapping the genome of *Drosophila. Science, 254,* 221–225.

Merzenich, M. M., & Kaas, J. H. (1980). Principles of organization of sensory-perceptual systems in mammals. *Progress in Psychobiology and Physiological Psychology, 9,* 1–42.

Miller, D. B., Hicinbothom, G., & Blaich, C. F. (1990). Alarm call responsivity of mallard ducklings: Multiple pathways in behavioural development. *Animal Behaviour, 39,* 1207–1212.

Moody, S. A. (1987). Fates of the blastomeres of the 16-cell stage *Xenopus* embryo. *Developmental Biology, 119,* 560–578.

Morrongiello, B. A. (1994). Effects of colocation on auditory-visual interactions and cross-modal perception in infants. In D. J. Lewkowicz & R. Lickliter (Eds.), *The development of intersensory perception: Comparative perspectives* (pp. 235–264). Hillsdale, NJ: Erlbaum.

Muir, J. (1967). My first summer in the Sierra. In D. Brower (Ed.), *Gentle wilderness: The Sierra Nevada.* San Francisco: Sierra Club. (Original manuscript published 1911)

Nöel, M. (1989). Early development in mice: 5. Sensorimotor development of four coisogenic mutant strains. *Physiology and Behavior, 45,* 21–26.

O'Rahilly, R., & Müller, F. (1987). *Developmental stages in human embryos.* Washington, DC: Carnegie Institute.

Oyama, S. (1985). *The ontogeny of information. Developmental systems and evolution.* Cambridge, England: Cambridge University Press.

Oyama, S. (1993). Constraints and development. *Netherlands Journal of Zoology, 43,* 6–16.

Ozaki, H. S., & Wahlsten, D. (1993). Cortical axon trajectories and growth cone morphologies in fetuses of acallosal mouse strains. *Journal of Comparative Neurology, 336,* 595–604.

Parker, S. T., & Gibson, K. R. (1979). A developmental model for the evolution of language and intelligence in early hominids. *Behavioral and Brain Sciences, 2,* 367–408.

Piaget, J. (1952). *The origins of intelligence.* New York: Norton.

Plomin, R. (1986). *Development, genetics and psychology.* Hillsdale, NJ: Erlbaum.

Radell, P. L., & Gottlieb, G. (1992). Developmental intersensory interference: Augmented prenatal sensory experience interferes with auditory learning in duck embryos. *Developmental Psychology, 28,* 795–803.

Rochat, P., & Senders, S. J. (1991). Active touch in infancy: Action systems in development. In M. J. Weiss & P. R. Zelazo (Eds.), *Infant attention: Biological constraints and the influence of experience* (pp. 412–442). Norwood, NJ: ABLEX.

Ronca, A. E., Lamkin, C. A., & Alberts, J. A. (1993). Maternal contributions to sensory experience in the fetal and newborn rat. *Journal of Comparative Psychology, 107,* 1–14.

Rose, S. (1994). From hand to eye: Findings and issues in infant cross-modal transfer. In D. J. Lewkowicz & R. Lickliter (Eds.), *The development of intersensory perception: Comparative perspectives* (pp. 265–284). Hillsdale, NJ: Erlbaum.

Rose, S. A., & Ruff, H. A. (1987). Cross-modal abilities in human infants. In J. D. Osofsky (Ed.), *Handbook of infant development* (pp. 318–362). New York: Wiley.

Rosen, K. M., McCormack, M. A., Villa-Komaroff, L., & Mower, G. D. (1992). Brief visual experience induces immediate early gene expression in the cat visual cortex. *Proceedings of the National Academy of Sciences USA, 89,* 5437–5441.

Roubertoux, P. L., Nosten-Bertrand, M., & Carlier, M. (1990). Additive and interactive effects of genotype and maternal environment. *Advances in the Study of Behavior, 19,* 205–247.

Roux, W. (1974). Contributions to the developmental mechanics of the embryo. In B. H. Willier & J. M. Oppenheimer (Eds.), *Foundations of experimental embryology* (pp. 2–37). New York: Hafner. (Original manuscript published in German, 1888)

Rusak, B., Robertson, H. A., Wisden, W., & Hunt, S. P. (1990). Light pulses that shift rhythms induce gene expression in the suprachiasmatic nucleus. *Science, 248,* 1237–1240.

Saint-Hilaire, E. G. (1825). Sur les déviations organiques provoquées et observées dans un éstablissement des incubations artificielles. *Mémoires. Museum National d'Histoire Naturelle (Paris), 13,* 289–296.

Salthe, S. N. (1993). *Development and evolution: Complexity and change in biology.* Cambridge, MA: MIT Press.

Scarr, S. (1992). Developmental theories for the 1990s: Development and individual differences. *Child Development, 63,* 1–19.

Scarr, S. (1993). Biological and cultural diversity: The legacy of Darwin for development. *Child Development, 64,* 1333–1353.

Scarr-Salapatek, S. (1976). Genetic determinants of infant development: An overstated case. In L. Lipsitt (Ed.), *Developmental psychobiology: The significance of the infant* (pp. 59–79). Hillsdale, NJ: Erlbaum.

Schiff, M., Duyme, M., Dumaret, A., & Tomkiewicz, S. (1982). How much *could* we boost scholastic achievement and IQ scores? A direct answer from a French adoption study. *Cognition, 12,* 165–196.

Schneirla, T. C. (1957). The concept of development in comparative psychology. In D. B. Harris (Ed.), *The concept of development* (pp. 78–108). Minneapolis: University of Minnesota Press.

Schneirla, T. C. (1959). An evolutionary and developmental theory of biphasic processes underlying approach/withdrawal. In M. Jones (Ed.), *Nebraska Symposium on Motivation* (Vol. 7, pp. 1–42). Lincoln: University of Nebraska Press.

Schneirla, T. C. (1960). Instinctive behavior, maturation—experience and development. In B. Kaplan & S. Wapner (Eds.), *Perspectives in psychological theory—Essays in honor of Heinz Werner* (pp. 303–334). New York: International Universities Press.

Schneirla, T. C. (1965). Aspects of stimulation and organization in approach/withdrawal processes underlying vertebrate behavioral development. In D. S. Lehrman, R. Hinde, & E. Shaw (Eds.), *Advances in the study of behavior* (Vol. 1, pp. 2–74). New York: Academic Press.

Shanahan, M. J., Valsiner, J., & Gottlieb, G. (1997). Developmental concepts across disciplines. In J. Tudge, M. J. Shanahan, & J. Valsiner (Eds.), *Comparative approaches to developmental science* (pp. 34–71). New York: Cambridge University Press.

Shatz, C. (1994). Role for spontaneous neural activity in the patterning of connections between retina and LGN during visual system development. *International Journal of Developmental Neuroscience, 12,* 531–546.

Shea, B. T., Hammer, R. E., & Brinster, R. L. (1987). Growth allometry of the organs in giant transgenic mice. *Endocrinology, 121,* 1924–1930.

Shillito, E. (1975). A comparison of the role of vision and hearing in lambs finding their own dams. *Applied Animal Ethology, 1,* 369–377.

Silver, J., Lorenz, S. E., Wahlsten, D., & Coughlin, J. (1982). Axonal guidance during development of the great cerebral commissures: Descriptive and experimental studies, in vivo, on the role of preformed glial pathways. *Journal of Comparative Neurology, 210,* 10–29.

Slack, J. M. W. (1991). *From egg to embryo.* Cambridge, England: Cambridge University Press.

Smith, L. B., & Katz, D. B. (1996). Activity-dependent processes in perceptual and cognitive development. In R. Gelman & T. K.-F. Au (Eds.), *Perceptual and cognitive development: Handbook of perception and cognition* (2nd ed., pp. 413–445). San Diego, CA: Academic Press.

Smith, L. B., & Thelen, E. (Eds.). (1993). *A dynamic systems approach to development: Applications.* Cambridge, MA: MIT Press.

Sokolowski, M. B. (1992). Genetic analysis of behavior in the fruit fly, *Drosophila melanogaster.* In D. Goldowitz, D. Wahlsten, & R. E. Wimer (Eds.), *Techniques for the genetic analysis of brain and behavior* (pp. 497–512). Amsterdam, The Netherlands: Elsevier.

Spear, N. E., Kraemer, P. J., Molina, J. C., & Smoller, D. (1988). Developmental change in learning and memory: Infantile disposition for "unitization." In J. Delacour & J. C. Levy (Eds.), *Systems with learning and memory abilities.* Amsterdam, The Netherlands: Elsevier/North-Holland.

Spear, N. E., & Molina, J. C. (1987). The role of sensory modality in the ontogeny of stimulus selection. In E. M. Blass, M. A. Hofer, & W. M. Smotherman (Eds.), *Perinatal development: A psychobiological perspective* (pp. 85–110). Orlando, FL: Academic Press.

Spelke, E. S. (1979). Perceiving bimodally specified events in infancy. *Developmental Psychology, 15,* 626–636.

Spelke, E. S. (1981). The infant's acquisition of knowledge of bimodally specified events. *Journal of Experimental Child Psychology, 31,* 279–299.

Spelke, E. S. (1984). The development of intermodal perception. In P. Salapatek & L. B. Cohen (Eds.), *Handbook of infant perception* (pp. 233–273). New York: Academic Press.

Sperry, R. W. (1951). Mechanisms of neural maturation. In S. S. Stevens (Ed.), *Handbook of experimental psychology* (pp. 236–280). New York: Wiley.

Sperry, R. W. (1971). How a developing brain gets itself properly wired for adaptive function. In E. Tobach, L. R. Aronson, & E. Shaw (Eds.), *The biopsychology of development* (pp. 28–34). New York: Academic Press.

Spudich, J. L., & Koshland, D. E., Jr. (1976). Nongenetic individuality: Chance in the single cell. *Nature, 262,* 467–471.

Stein, B. E., Huneycutt, W. S., & Meredith, M. A. (1988). Neurons and behavior: The same rules of multisensory integration apply. *Brain Research, 448,* 355–358.

Stein, B. E., & Meredith, M. A. (1990). Multisensory integration: Neural and behavioral solutions for dealing with stimuli from different sensory modalities. *Annals of the New York Academy of Sciences, 608,* 51–70.

Stein, B. E., & Meredith, M. A. (1993). *The merging of the senses.* Cambridge, MA: MIT Press.

Stein, B. E., Meredith, M. A., Huneycutt, W. S., & McDade, L. (1989). Behavioral indices of multisensory integration: Orientation to visual cues is affected by auditory stimuli. *Journal of Cognitive Neuroscience, 1,* 12–24.

Stent, G. S. (1981). Strength and weakness of the genetic approach to the development of the nervous system. *Annual Review of Neuroscience, 4,* 163–194.

Stern, W. (1938). *General psychology from the personalistic standpoint.* New York: Macmillan.

Storer, J. B. (1967). Relation between life-span to brain weight, body weight, and metabolic rate among inbred mouse strains. *Experimental Gerontology, 2,* 173–182.

Streri, A., & Molina, M. (1994). Constraints on intermodal transfer between touch and vision in infancy. In D. J. Lewkowicz & R. Lickliter (Eds.), *The development of intersensory perception: Comparative perspectives* (pp. 285–308). Hillsdale, NJ: Erlbaum.

Streri, A., & Pecheux, M. G. (1986). Vision to touch and touch to vision transfer of form in 5-month-old infants. *British Journal of Developmental Psychology, 4,* 161–167.

Strohman, R. C. (1997). The coming Kuhnian revolution in biology. *Nature Biotechnology, 15,* 194–200.

Surwit, R. S., Kuhn, C. M., Cochrane, C., McCubbin, J. A., & Feinglos, M. N. (1988). Diet-induced type II diabetes in C57BL/6J mice. *Diabetes, 37,* 1163–1167.

Symons, L. A., & Tees, R. L. (1990). An examination of the intramodal and intermodal behavioral consequences of long-term vibrissae removal in the rat. *Developmental Psychobiology, 23,* 849–867.

Takahashi, J. S. (1995). Molecular neurobiology and genetics of circadian rhythms in mammals. *Annual Review of Neuroscience, 18,* 531–553.

Taylor, H. F. (1980). *The IQ game: A methodological inquiry into the heredity-environment controversy.* New Brunswick, NJ: Rutgers University Press.

Tees, R. C., & Symons, L. A. (1987). Intersensory coordination and the effects of early sensory deprivation. *Developmental Psychobiology, 20,* 497–508.

Tees, R. L. (1994). Early stimulation history, the cortex, and intersensory functioning in infrahumans: Space and time. In D. J. Lewkowicz & R. Lickliter (Eds.), *The development of intersensory perception: Comparative perspectives* (pp. 107–132). Hillsdale, NJ: Erlbaum.

Tees, R. L., & Buhrmann, K. (1989). Parallel perceptual/cognitive functions in humans and rats: Space and time. *Canadian Journal of Psychology, 43,* 266–285.

Thelen, E., Kelso, J. A. S., & Fogel, A. (1987). Self-organizing systems and infant motor development. *Developmental Review, 7,* 39–65.

Thelen, E., & Smith, L. B. (1994). *A dynamic systems approach to the development of cognition and action.* Cambridge, MA: MIT Press.

Thelen, E., & Ulrich, B. O. (1991). Hidden skills: A dynamic systems analysis of treadmill stepping during the first year.

Monographs of the Society for Research in Child Development, 56 (Serial No. 223).

Tiret, L., Abel, L., & Rakotovao, R. (1993). Effect of ignoring genotype-environment interaction on segregation analysis of quantitative traits. *Genetic Epidemiology, 10,* 581–586.

Tolman, E. C. (1932). *Purposive behavior in animals and man.* New York: Century.

Turkewitz, G. (1994). Sources of order for intersensory functioning. In D. J. Lewkowicz & R. Lickliter (Eds.), *The development of intersensory perception: Comparative perspectives* (pp. 3–18). Hillsdale, NJ: Erlbaum.

Turkewitz, G., & Kenny, P. (1982). Limitations on input as a basis for neural organization and perceptual development: A preliminary theoretical statement. *Developmental Psychobiology, 15,* 357–368.

Turkewitz, G., & Kenny, P. (1985). The role of developmental limitation of sensory input on sensory/perceptual organization. *Journal of Developmental and Behavioral Pediatrics, 6,* 302–306.

Turkewitz, G., Lewkowicz, D. J., & Gardner, J. M. (1983). Determinants of infant perception. In J. Rosenblatt, C. Beer, R. Hinde, & M. Busnel (Eds.), *Advances in the study of behavior* (pp. 39–62). New York: Academic Press.

Turkewitz, G., & McGuire, I. (1978). Intersensory functioning during early development. *International Journal of Mental Health, 7,* 165–182.

Turkewitz, G., & Mellon, R. C. (1989). Dynamic organization of intersensory function. *Canadian Journal of Psychology, 43,* 286–307.

van der Veer, R., & Valsiner, J. (1991). *Understanding Vygotsky: A quest for synthesis.* Oxford, England: Blackwell.

van der Weele, C. (1995). *Images of development: Environmental causes in ontogeny.* Unpublished doctoral dissertation, Veije University, Amsterdam, The Netherlands.

Varela, F. J., Thompson, E., & Rosch, E. (1991). *The embodied mind: Cognitive science and human experience.* Cambridge, MA: MIT Press.

Vitaterna, M. H., King, D. P., Chang, A.-M., Kornhauser, J. M., Lowrey, P. L., McDonald, J. D., Dove, W. F., Pinto, L. H., Turek, F. W., & Takahashi, J. S. (1994). Mutagenesis and mapping of a mouse gene, *Clock,* essential for circadian behavior. *Science, 264,* 719–725.

von Baer, K. E. (1828). *Über Entwickelungsgeschichte der Thiere: Beobachtung und Reflexion.* Part one. Königsberg: Bornträger. (Reprinted 1966 by Johnson Reprint Corporation) von Bertalanffy, L. (1950). *A systems view of man.* Boulder, CO: Western Press.

von Bertalanffy, L. (1962). *Modern theories of development: An introduction to theoretical biology.* New York: Harper. (Originally published in German in 1933)

von Helmholtz, H. (1968). The origin of the correct interpretation of our sensory impressions. In R. M. Warren & R. P. Warren (Eds.), *Helmholtz on perception: Its physiology and development* (pp. 17–25). New York: Wiley.

von Hornbostel, E. M. (1938). The unity of the senses. In W. O. Ellis (Ed.), *A sourcebook of Gestalt psychology* (pp. 211–216). New York: Harcourt Brace.

Waddington, C. H. (1957). *The strategy of the genes.* London: Allen & Unwin.

Wahlsten, D. (1979). A critique of the concepts of heritability and heredity in behavioral genetics. In J. R. Royce & L. Mos (Eds.), *Theoretical advances in behavior genetics* (pp. 425–470). Germantown, MD: Sijthoff & Noordhoff.

Wahlsten, D. (1982). Mice in utero while their mother is lactating suffer increased frequency of absent corpus callosum. *Developmental Brain Research, 5,* 354–357.

Wahlsten, D. (1983). Maternal effects on mouse brain weight. *Developmental Brain Research, 9,* 215–221.

Wahlsten, D. (1990). Insensitivity of the analysis of variance to heredity-environment interaction. *Behavioral and Brain Sciences, 13,* 109–161.

Wahlsten, D. (1991). Sample size to detect a planned contrast and a one degree-of-freedom interaction effect. *Psychological Bulletin, 110,* 587–595.

Wahlsten, D. (1993). Sample size requirements for the Capron and Duyme balanced fostering study of IQ. *International Journal of Psychology, 28,* 509–516.

Wahlsten, D. (1994a). The intelligence of heritability. *Canadian Psychology, 35,* 244–260.

Wahlsten, D. (1994b). Probability and the understanding of individual differences. In J. Brzeziński (Ed.), *Probability in theory-building* (pp. 47–60). Amsterdam, The Netherlands: RODOPI.

Wahlsten, D., & Gottlieb, G. (1997). The invalid separation of effects of nature and nurture: Lessons from animal experimentation. In R. J. Sternberg & E. L. Grigorenko (Eds.), *Intelligence: Heredity and environment* (pp. 163–192). New York: Cambridge University Press.

Wahlsten, D., & Wainwright, P. (1977). Application of a morphological time scale to hereditary differences in prenatal

mouse development. *Journal of Embryology and Experimental Morphology, 74,* 133–149.

Walker-Andrews, A. S. (1986). Intermodal perception of expressive behaviors: Relation of eye and voice? *Developmental Psychology, 22,* 373–377.

Walker-Andrews, A. S. (1994). Taxonomy for intermodal relations. In D. J. Lewkowicz & R. Lickliter (Eds.), *The development of intersensory perception: Comparative perspectives* (pp. 39–56). Hillsdale, NJ: Erlbaum.

Walker-Andrews, A. S., Bahrick, L. E., Raglioni, S. S., & Diaz, I. (1991). Infants' bimodal perception of gender. *Ecological Psychology, 3,* 55–75.

Wallace, D. C., Singh, G., Lott, M. T., Hodge, J. A., Schurr, T. G., Lezza, A. M. S., Elsas, L. J., II, & Nikoskelainen, E. K. (1988). Mitochondrial DNA mutation associated with Leber's hereditary optic neuropathy. *Science, 242,* 1427–1430.

Weiss, M. J. S., & Zelazo, P. R. (1991). *Newborn attention: Biological constraints and the influence of experience.* Norwood, NJ: ABLEX.

Weiss, P. (1959). Cellular dynamics. *Review of Modern Physics, 31,* 11–20.

Welch, R. B., & Warren, D. H. (1986). Intersensory interactions. In K. R. Boff, L. Kaufman, & J. P. Thomas (Eds.), *Handbook of perception and human performance* (pp. 1–36). New York: Wiley.

Wille, W., Cremer, H., Barthels, D., & Goldowitz, D. (1992). Hybridization analyses of nervous system gene expression. In D. Goldowitz, D. Wahlsten, & R. E. Wimer (Eds.), *Techniques for the genetic analysis of brain and behavior* (pp. 291–315). Amsterdam, The Netherlands: Elsevier Biomedical.

Wilmington, D., Gray, L., & Jahrsdoerfer, R. (1994). Binaural processing after corrected congenital unilateral conductive hearing loss. *Hearing Research, 74,* 99–114.

Winderickx, J., Lindsey, D. T., Sanocki, E., Teller, D. Y., Motulsky, A. G., & Deeb, S. S. (1992). Polymorphism in red photopigment underlies variation in colour matching. *Nature, 356,* 431–433.

Wright, S. (1968). *Evolution and the genetics of populations: Vol. 1. Genetic and biometric foundations.* Chicago: University of Chicago Press.

Zukow-Goldring, P. G. (1990). Socio-perceptual bases for the emergence of language: An alternative to innatist approaches. *Developmental Psychobiology, 23,* 705–726.

CHAPTER 6

Nativism, Empiricism, and the Development of Knowledge

ELIZABETH S. SPELKE and ELISSA L. NEWPORT

Which of our concepts are inherent in our minds, and which are abstracted from our experience of the world around us? What aspects of human knowledge are present at the beginning of life, and what aspects emerge thereafter? What knowledge is constant over development from its emergence to its highest elaboration, and what changes with growth and experience? What knowledge is common to all mature human beings in all cultures, and what varies among people with different interests, experiences, and backgrounds? Can all conceptions be changed if one works hard enough to change them, or are some conceptions a permanent part of people's mental lives?

The writing of this chapter was supported in part by NIH grant HD23103 to E. Spelke and by NIH grant DC00167 to E. Newport.

As many writers have pointed out, these are different questions (see Block, 1979; Oyama, 1985): Knowledge that is inherent in the mind might emerge either early or late in development and be either invariant or subject to change, and abilities abstracted from experience might be either universal or variable across cultures. Nevertheless, these questions have certain points in common. First, they have sparked intense interest for at least 2,000 years, because they all bear on our picture of what it is to be a human thinker and knower. Second, the questions are empirical and have been subject to particularly intense and productive study over recent decades. Third, the questions are central to a dialogue that has pervaded the study of human nature since that study began: the dialogue between nativism and empiricism.

THE NATIVIST–EMPIRICIST DIALOGUE

Nativist and empiricist proposals can be traced back at least to classical Greece and the writings of Plato (1961) and Aristotle (1941). The dialogue between those whose proposals emphasize innate structure and those whose proposals emphasize learning can be followed through the writings of Augustine (389/1876) to those of Descartes (1637/1971a), Locke (1690/1975), Leibniz (1705/1981), and Berkeley (1710/1975), among others. Moving forward, the dialogue rings through the writings of Hume (1748) and Kant (1781/1964) and into the 19th-century reformulations and replies of scientists such as Muller (1837/1842) and Helmholtz (1867/1962). In the 20th century, the dialogue has continued to be enriched by such thinkers as Hebb (1949), Tinbergen (1951), Quine (1960), and Chomsky (1975). Indeed, it is hard to find a thinker of depth who has pondered human nature and human knowledge without asking these central questions.

As any study of the above writings makes clear, questions at the heart of the nativist–empiricist dialogue have been raised for a variety of reasons (see Hatfield, 1990, for illuminating discussion). They speak not only to familiar contemporary questions about how psychological processes work, but also to concerns about human nature, the truth of one's ideas, and the state of the world. For most of the thinkers cited above, these questions were largely empirical in principle, but few practical methods existed for addressing them. In part for this reason, traditional answers to these questions have tended to rest on questionable assumptions and indirect evidence.

Today, the study of cognitive development is in a strange state of richness but disarray. On one hand, developmental psychologists and cognitive scientists now have a wealth of means to address the central questions of the nativist–empiricist dialogue. On the other hand, science and the larger intellectual culture are now dominated by the attitude that questions about the nature and sources of human knowledge are misguided or incoherent. The issues raised by our intellectual predecessors therefore are routinely dismissed as outdated, oversimplified, or logically flawed.

The primary goal of this chapter is to argue that the 2,000-year-long dialogue between nativists and empiricists was on the right track: At its heart are meaningful questions that can be addressed by experiments. Where such experiments have been conducted, their findings have shed light on cognitive development, human knowledge,

and human nature, just as thinkers through the centuries have believed. We focus on human development in four domains—action, perception, language, and reasoning—showing in each case how research has succeeded in teasing apart the constant from the changing, the rigid from the flexible, the universal from the variable, and the inborn from the acquired. This research, we suggest, sheds light on larger questions about the nature of human capacities to act, perceive, talk, and think.

When the nativist–empiricist dialogue has not been dismissed as incoherent, it has usually been declared to be settled on the empiricist side. This is especially true today, owing to the rise of connectionist modeling of human cognition, using systems instantiating associationist learning principles (see Churchland, 1995; Elman, Bates, Johnson, Karmiloff-Smith, Parisi, & Plunkett, 1996; McClelland, 1994). Curiously, those who declare the controversy settled in favor of empiricism rarely appeal to evidence that the emergence of any given cognitive ability depends on learning. Rather, the decision in favor of empiricism usually hinges on considerations of parsimony, burden-of-proof arguments, or analogies to machine learning. We return later to these arguments but note now that they are no substitute for research. Because we want to encourage research addressing the central questions of the nativist–empiricist dialogue, the second goal of this chapter is to illustrate, by example, how experiments undertaken by contributors to both sides of the dialogue have fostered understanding of development. Given the paucity of proponents of nativist theories of cognitive development, we emphasize some of the insights that have come from the nativist side. Our central point, however, is that investigations springing from the dialogue illuminate cognitive development.

We hope this chapter will convince readers that questions about what is innate and what is learned are as meaningful as our ancestors thought they were; that research addressing these questions has already begun to shed light on the origins and development of knowledge; and that future research pursuing these questions holds the highest promise. If it succeeds, we must consider why the field of cognitive development has turned away from the nativist–empiricist dialogue. Why is this dialogue often seen as incoherent? When its questions are not dismissed, moreover, why is any answer short of extreme empiricism viewed as incorrect or even pernicious? Could research returning nativist answers to the traditional questions raised by this dialogue cause harm to the study of human cognition, to society's treatment of children, or to people's views of one another? Our third and last goal is to examine a spectrum of such possibilities. We will conclude, contrary to much current opinion, that both science and society have nothing to lose and a great deal to gain from research that teases apart the roots of human knowledge in human nature and human experience.

In this chapter, we develop four theses:

1. Questions about the sources of knowledge can be addressed by research. Where experiments have been conducted, both innate structure and experience in a structured environment are found to influence the development of knowledge in intricate ways.

2. Empirical studies of the origins of knowledge mesh fruitfully with investigations in both of the major areas of biology: the evolutionary and ecological study of animal behavior, and the mechanistic study of its underpinnings. In particular, these studies reveal both commonalities and differences between the cognitive capacities of humans and of other animals; and illuminate the physical foundations of those capacities.

3. The findings of this research have shed light not only on cognitive development but on human cognition more generally. In conjunction with research in related disciplines within the cognitive sciences, such studies promise to illuminate the nature of knowledge and the mechanisms by which it arises and is used.

4. Experimental studies of the contributions of innate structure and of learning to psychological development begin to suggest a portrait of human nature that is at variance with many popularly held beliefs. This portrait has profound and positive implications for how people view one another and conduct their affairs.

We have chosen to develop these theses by reviewing research on our example domains (action, perception, language, and reasoning) because each of these examples illustrates both remarkable triumphs of empirical research and a set of important themes and issues. Because the example domains are somewhat different in the issues they raise, we will not attempt to review them with a uniform list of themes for all. Rather, we will use each domain in turn to exemplify the particular issues most pointedly addressed within that domain. In our concluding section, we will attempt to assemble and integrate these various issues across the four domains in terms of their import for our views of nativism, empiricism, and the development of knowledge.

We begin with the development of action. Recent study has profoundly altered our understanding of how developmental continuity, as opposed to maturation or learning, can underlie what appear to be the most radical changes in action capacities.

KNOWING HOW TO ACT

The study of coordinated action provides fertile ground for students of development. A casual look at any human society reveals that adults are capable of coordinated, purposive actions of exquisite effectiveness and astonishing diversity, from lassoing a reindeer in flight to skiing down a mountain to performing surgery under a microscope. The most searching look at human newborns suggests that nothing approaching these skilled actions is present at the start of life. Beyond suckling and crying and (to our wonderment) occasionally looking around, newborn infants do not appear to do much. How, then, do mature action capacities arise?

In general, the development of action might be explained in three different ways. Developmental changes could depend on (a) learning processes that shape the child's actions in accord with environmental constraints; (b) the maturation of action systems whose structure is determined by intrinsic developmental processes; or (c) action capacities that are constant over development, but whose expression is first masked and then revealed by changing extrinsic factors.

The magnitude of the change from the novice newborn to the expert hunter or surgeon appears to cast doubt on the third view and to suggest that the study of action development is only the study of change. Moreover, the great variety in skilled performance in different domains appears to cast doubt on the second view and to suggest that the processes that bring about these changes are infinitely variable, such that skilled members of different professions or different cultures have little or no common ground. We will see that these appearances are deceptive. Studies of the development of action reveal both constancy and change over childhood, and both uniformity and variation across cultures. We emphasize invariants and universals because their discovery has been so surprising, so at odds with prevalent views of action development, and such a triumph of recent research. We focus in particular on the development of an activity where change is most pronounced: locomotion.

Locomotion

One of the most dramatic changes in human development occurs between about 9 and 16 months of age, when children become capable of independent, upright locomotion. It is clear to any parent that the transition from crawling to walking reflects a genuine change in ability and not just a change in motivation or preferences. For months before they begin to walk, most children seem to "want" to walk: They struggle into a standing position, inch around furniture while supporting themselves with their arms, and yet cannot manage to walk on their own. The one-year-old child who succeeds at this task undoubtedly has gained the ability to do something new.

The emergence of walking also heralds a development that separates humans from other animals. Whereas the crawling infant engages in locomotor patterns that resemble those of many other terrestrial species, only human children and adults engage in the distinctive pattern of obligatory, upright, bipedal locomotion that frees two limbs for other tasks. What is more, walking emerges far later in development than the locomotion of other mammals: No other animal must wait as long as the human before becoming capable of its own species-specific form of independent movement (Thelen, 1984). When human children begin to walk, therefore, they appear to take a large step away from capacities shared with other animals and into the realm of the distinctively human.

All these features of human locomotion and locomotor development would seem to make this phenomenon a poor place to look for continuity over development. Indeed, earlier treatments of the development of locomotion have linked this change either to the postnatal maturation of higher centers in the human brain (e.g., McGraw, 1940) or to forms of learning, social interaction, or cognitive growth (e.g., Zelazo, 1983). Research over the past two decades nevertheless offers a very different perspective on human locomotor development. Underneath the dramatic changes in the child's locomotor behavior are inborn, foundational action capacities that persist over development and are common across a great range of animal species. These

foundational capacities provide the core of humans' ability to locomote, even though extrinsic factors such as muscle strength and weight distribution limit their expression at early ages. These capacities also serve as fundamental building blocks for the development of the skills that distinguish members of one culture, profession, or avocational group from another.

Both the elegant research and the radical rethinking of locomotor development that we review are the work of Esther Thelen. Although Thelen herself has embraced a very different approach to these phenomena (see Thelen & Smith, 1994, and this Volume), we believe that the nativist and empiricist principles outlined here provide an illuminating perspective on the developmental patterns of invariance and change that her work reveals. Conversely, we believe her research provides an excellent example of how experiments that probe both for continuity and for change, and that tease apart the variable from the invariant, illuminate the nature of human action capacities and their development. The fruits of this research directly counter the view that continuity and change are conceptually inseparable.

The Emergence of Coordination: Kicking

Coordinated actions often are viewed as achievements resulting from practice and exercise (e.g., Piaget, 1952; Thorndike, 1911). The building blocks of this process are reflexes—innate packages of activity that are limited in function and are triggered rigidly by specific external stimulation. Flexibility is achieved, according to such views, as reflexes are exercised in the ways that the child's environment allows: "The child-rearing practices of the particular culture that the infant is born into determine the specific responses from the numerous behaviors in his or her repertoire that are to be encouraged through parental expectation, permission, and practice. With use, those behaviors fostered by the infant's family and culture appear to develop from reflexive to instrumental . . ." (Zelazo, 1983, p. 102).

At first glance, the development of walking appears to accord well with this perspective, and it is the phenomenon on which Zelazo chose to focus. Although newborn infants who are held upright on a surface display a "stepping reflex," moving their legs in an alternating pattern that resembles locomotion, this behavior pattern disappears after a few months unless it is practiced. With practice, however, it is maintained, and its maintenance is associated with an acceleration in the development of walking (Zelazo, 1983). Walking therefore has been proposed to be an instrumental behavior that is built on initially purposeless and reflexive actions, in accord with the experiences afforded by a particular culture.

Is this view correct? A first step toward evaluating it is provided by naturalistic, observational study of the development of patterns of behavior over the first year of life. One such study focused on behaviors in which infants engage repeatedly and rhythmically, such as kicking the legs, waving the arms, and rocking the torso (Thelen, 1979). If coordinated movement emerges through practice and exercise, one would expect these behaviors to show increasing flexibility and coordination as the infant grows; if only reflexive behavior occurs at the start of development, then one should not observe spontaneously generated, rhythmically repeated actions in the youngest infants.

Thelen described 47 different behavior patterns in which infants from 1 to 12 months engaged repetitively and rhythmically. Even in the youngest infants, the patterns appeared to be internally generated and structured, not triggered by external stimuli. Moreover, the patterns resembled actions observed in other species. These observations suggested that coordination does not result from the shaping of rigid reflexes by external environmental circumstances but rather results from endogenous processes: "Rhythmical stereotypes, from their form-specific appearance and from comparisons with stereotyped behaviors in other primate populations, appear to be behaviors under strong central control" (Thelen, 1979, p. 712).

One prominent rhythmical behavior is kicking. Thelen found that kicking was most prominent from 3 to 7 months of age, when infants lay on their back in a state of arousal. At older ages, kicking was observed less frequently, probably because aroused infants were no longer inclined to remain in a prone position; in infants younger than 3 months, it was less frequent as well. Nevertheless, kicking was observed at every age studied, from 4 weeks onward. In later work, it was observed at even younger ages (Thelen & Fisher, 1983a).

How does kicking change qualitatively over development? Do movements of the hip, knee, and ankle begin as random and independent and become coordinated with practice? Thelen addressed this question through detailed measurements of the displacements of the joints and actions of the muscles. Her studies revealed that changes in the flexion or extension of the hip, knee, and ankle are tightly coordinated in the first month of life. Because these joints move together, the state of one joint can be reliably predicted from the state of the others (Thelen & Fisher, 1983a). "These detailed observations of spontaneous leg movement in newborn infants challenge the traditional assumptions that movement in the newborn is random and without structure" (p. 373). Instead, these observations suggest that "early movements are a well-orchestrated ensemble of joint changes with defined temporal parameters and recognizable patterns of EMG [i.e., activity in the muscles]" (p. 380).

Kicking evidently reveals an intrinsic coordination that is present in humans at an early age, but what is its function? To begin to address this question, Thelen viewed this behavior from a comparative and ethological perspective. The coordinated rotations of hip, knee, and ankle in the human infant resembled the movements of a wide range of vertebrates during behavior whose function is clear: locomotion. Could infants' kicking also function as a core coordinative capacity underlying human walking? To approach this question, Thelen, Bradshaw, and Ward (1981) looked in more detail at the form and temporal structure of kicking in 1-month-old infants, and they found striking correspondences between early kicking and mature locomotion in humans and other animals. For example, the leg movements of locomoting humans and other animals can be divided into a stance phase (when the foot is on the ground and supporting weight) and a swing phase (when the foot is off the ground and moving forward). Walking speed is increased primarily by shortening the stance phase while leaving the swing duration nearly constant. Similarly, 1-month-old infants increased the rate at which they kicked by decreasing the length of the interval between kicks (analogous to the stance phase), leaving the duration of the kick itself nearly constant. These and other findings led Thelen and her collaborations to suggest that "human locomotion, like that of other species, is controlled by a central program . . . manifest in human infants long before actual walking matures" (p. 45).

Let us pause to consider this suggestion, which can be broken into two parts. First, human upright, bipedal locomotion looks quite different from the locomotion of other animals such as cats and cockroaches, but it depends on a core coordinative capacity that humans share with other species. Such claims of homology often are greeted with extreme skepticism or are dismissed as errors of "anthropomorphism." Second, 1-month-old infants will display no ability to locomote for another 12 months, on average, but they already possess the core coordinative capacity that will underlie their later success. Again, great skepticism often greets the claim that young infants possess, but do not express, abilities found in adults; this claim often is taken to reflect the false attribution of adult capacities to children.

Is the suggestion of Thelen et al. (1981) prey to these errors? At first glance, it certainly seems to present problems. If human locomotion depends on the same central motor program as locomotion in other species, then why does it take humans a full year to begin walking, whereas goats and cockroaches locomote at birth? If the 1-month-old infant's kicking reveals a coordinated pattern that exists continuously over development and that underlies the older child's walking, why does human locomotion itself undergo radical developmental change? Two developmental changes, in particular, require explanation: (a) the disappearance of the "stepping reflex" at about 2 months and (b) the emergence of independent upright locomotion at about 1 year. Can Thelen's analysis explain these phenomena?

Distinguishing Competence from Performance: Stepping

Thelen's approach to the stepping reflex began with the observation that the 1-month-old infant's stepping and kicking appeared to be very similar actions. Detailed studies of the movements of infants' limbs and the tension in their muscles strongly supported this impression: During stepping and kicking, newborn infants' joints showed the same coordinated displacements, and their muscles showed the same temporal patterns of contraction (Thelen & Fisher, 1982). Thelen and Fisher also discovered that newborn stepping could be converted into kicking, and the reverse, by changing the infant's posture in midstream. These findings suggest that stepping is not a reflex at all; it is a coordinated action pattern expressed under conditions in which babies are appropriately supported, either upright or supine.

Why then does stepping disappear at 2 months? Here, the investigators had a major insight: Perhaps the motor *competence* underlying stepping remains present and functional, but the *performance* of the action is masked by other developmental changes. In particular, stepping competence

may be obscured as the infant gains weight, increasing the mass of the legs to the point where the leg muscles lack the strength to lift them when the infants is in an upright posture.

The distinction between competence and performance is central to this hypothesis. Because this distinction allows developmental psychologists to attribute abilities to children, rather than simply describing changes with age in what children happen to do in particular circumstances, it allows scientists to move from a description of behavior to an account of the underlying neural or mental states that make behavior possible (see Chomsky, 1965; Fodor, 1968). For obvious reasons, the competence–performance distinction was anathema to much of psychology during the reign of behaviorism. Curiously, it is often attacked today as well, even by those who have used it to great advantage: "The distinction between competence and performance does not make sense if cognition is determined by highly interactive systems always in contact with each other and the external world . . ." (Thelen & Smith, 1994, p. 27; see also Oyama, 1985). Rejection of the competence–performance distinction usually is based on the argument that claims of competence are not testable, for how can one ever test whether some competence exists when performance fails to reveal it (e.g., Thelen & Smith, 1994, p. 27)? Should one not be content to describe what infants do, leaving discussion of their mysterious competencies to novelists, philosophers, or mystics?

Contrary to these suggestions, Thelen's research shows that the competence–performance distinction is a source of testable hypotheses providing critical insight into the actions one observes in young infants, the factors that limit those actions, and the factors that bring about developmental change. In a simple and elegant way, Thelen, Fisher, and Ridley-Johnson (1984) tested the hypothesis that infants who no longer step in an upright posture maintained the underlying competence to do so: They plunged the infants' legs under water, reducing the force needed to lift them. Under these circumstances, stepping reemerged! This experiment and others (notably, the complementary experiment in which stepping was abolished in infants who had maintained the pattern, by attaching weights to the legs) showed that the thesis of hidden stepping competence, and the underlying distinction between stepping competence and stepping performance, was not empty talk. Instead,

Thelen's thesis has led to a major insight into the stepping reflex and its developmental vicissitudes. This behavioral pattern disappears not because of disruption of the underlying coordination on which it depends, but because of disproportionate weight gains relative to muscle strength.

The Emergence of New Actions: *Walking*

The thesis of unchanging competence that fails, at some times in development, to be revealed in performance has shed light on one developmental change: the disappearance of early stepping. Further research by Thelen reveals that this thesis also sheds light on the emergence of a new ability: the appearance of independent walking. Upright locomotion depends not on the molding of new coordinations but on the use of the same preexisting coordinative patterns that underlie stepping and kicking. Her rich and intricate evidence for this claim is a triumph of developmental studies. Here, we consider just one aspect of the developing coordinative capacity underlying walking: the use of alternating movements of the two legs to maintain a stable center of gravity as one moves forward.

To walk without losing one's balance, any terrestrial animal must move its limbs in symmetrical or alternating patterns. Precocial animals who walk at birth engage in the appropriate symmetrical or alternating limb movements as soon as they begin to move, in the absence of any trial-and-error learning. Humans, in contrast, do not walk until 1 year of age, and most engage in crawling and other forms of supported locomotion for months before. Does the experience of crawling or "cruising" allow human infants to learn how to step alternately without falling, by trial and error? Or does the appropriate coordinative structure already exist in infants, as it exists in other animals, prior to the time at which it is first used for locomotion?

Studies of supine kicking do not provide a clear answer to this question, because prelocomotor infants do not consistently kick the two legs in alternation. In one study of infants from 2 to 26 weeks of age (Thelen, Ridley-Johnson, & Fisher, 1983), about 70% of kicks involved leg alternation at the youngest ages, and this percentage tended to decline thereafter. Infants' naturally occurring kicking therefore showed little evidence for a clear coordinative pattern of alternation. From these patterns alone, it is not possible to say whether the capacity for coordinated, alternating stepping exists prior to walking.

Thelen (1986) therefore found a new situation in which to study the leg movements of upright but supported infants: on a treadmill. In one study, 7-month-old infants' leg movements were observed when they were supine and also when they were held under the shoulders in an upright posture on a stationary or moving treadmill. In the prone and upright stationary positions, about half the movements involved alternating legs. When the treadmill moved, in contrast, the rate of alternating stepping rose to 85%. Even though the treadmill pulled both legs backward symmetrically, infants responded to its motion with asymmetric, alternating steps. Crucially, *alternating motions occurred in these infants, even though the infants had never supported their own weight during upright locomotion and were not doing so during the experiment.* Although the pattern of alternating stepping functions to enable an upright locomotor to maintain balance, this pattern is present before it is needed for that purpose. It is a competence that does not normally express itself in behavior, but that can be elicited under appropriate supporting conditions.

Further observations reveal additional richness and structure in this initial competence. We have already noted that adults modulate the speed of forward locomotion primarily by varying the duration of the stance phase of the step cycle, when the foot is on the ground. Seven-month-old infants showed the same pattern on the treadmill: They stepped more rapidly when the treadmill moved faster, and they increased their step rate primarily by shortening their stance phase. When children begin to locomote independently, they evidently do not need to learn to alternate their leg movements so as not to fall, or to decrease their stance phase so as to move forward more quickly.

In the above study, infants' two legs stood on a single treadmill and therefore were pulled backward at the same speed. Further research reveals that the coordinative competence underlying alternating gait is robust enough to maintain itself despite perturbations designed to challenge the symmetry of this pattern (Thelen, Ulrich, & Niles, 1987). Having observed that children stepped at a faster rate at the faster treadmill speed, these investigators tested infants on a split treadmill, where the legs were pulled backward at different speeds. In principle, each leg could have moved at the same rate as in the first study, because alternating motions were not needed to maintain support. Instead, the legs moved at rates intermediate between the two step rates observed in the first study, and maintained an alternating gait.

Infants' treadmill walking appears remarkable because of its close relation to the independent, upright locomotion of adults and children. Nevertheless, the coordinative competence revealed on the treadmill is observed in a wide variety of animals, even in the absence of a functional higher nervous system (see Thelen et al., 1987, for review and discussion). These findings suggest that our distinctively human form of upright locomotion depends on a basic coordinative competence that we share with other animals. This competence is used at birth in those animals who begin life with the capacity for independent locomotion. Although it is not used at birth by humans, it nevertheless exists long before it is needed, and its existence is revealed by elegant experiments that remove the extrinsic barriers to its expression. This competence appears to be the product of an evolutionary process, for it is adapted to the demands of locomotion but is not shaped by the process of locomoting. Alternating leg movements serve to maintain support while moving forward, but they are observed in human infants not yet capable of autonomous forward motion.

If young infants possess the basic coordinations that are the building blocks of upright locomotion, why do they not walk until the beginning of the second year? Although Thelen cautions against the search for single-factor answers to this question, her research suggests that physical growth and changing muscle strength contribute prominently to this development. To maintain balance in an upright posture, the child's body proportions need to change so as to lower the center of gravity; to move forward on two legs, the muscles of each leg must increase in strength so that a single leg can support all the child's weight. These factors may limit the emergence of locomotion at least as much as developmental changes in coordinative competence (Thelen, 1984).

Effects of Experience on the Development of Locomotion

With an increased sensitivity to what is constant over development comes an increased understanding of what changes with experience and varies over differing circumstances. Developmental research has revealed a number of sources of variability in locomotor development. For example, very young infants who are held in an upright posture over a flat surface on a regular basis, and therefore are given opportunities to exercise their stepping reflex, tend to maintain the reflex longer and to begin to locomote at a younger age (Zelazo, Zelazo, & Kolb, 1972). Effects of practice may account, to some degree, for cultural variation in the ages at which children begin to walk (Super, 1976). It is likely that these practice effects depend on increases in the strength of the leg musculature that stepping exercise brings (Thelen & Cooke, 1987).

Other effects of locomotor experience have been observed as well. The experience with supported locomotion that young infants receive in a "walker," which supports them in an upright posture while they move around by pressing their feet against the floor, affects their attention to the environment and their memory for the spatial locations of objects (Bai & Bertenthal, 1992; Bertenthal, Campos, & Barrett, 1984). It is likely that locomotor experience also plays a great role in transforming the hesitant and shaky steps of the newly mobile toddler into the confident and graceful strides of the older child, although the contributions of various endogenous and exogenous factors to these changes remain largely to be teased apart. Experience is essential to the transformation from novice to expert in culture-specific forms of locomotion such as skating or mountain climbing. These effects of experience become amenable to more fruitful and focused study as psychologists better appreciate the coordinative competencies that are invariant over locomotor development. To illustrate this point, we turn briefly from locomotor development to the development of much more arbitrary and variable skills.

Learning Arbitrary Actions

Humans are capable of learning all sorts of action patterns, from swimming and climbing trees to hitting golf balls. Moreover, we have a strong penchant for learning from one another—observing how others act in particular circumstances and then perfecting those observed actions ourselves (Tomasello, Kruger, & Ratner, 1993). Even infants engage in such learning (Meltzoff, 1988). Indeed, humans' propensity to learn from the actions of others may explain why tool use has developed so much more in all human cultures than in any societies of nonhuman primates (Tomasello et al., 1993; see also K. Gibson & Ingold, 1993). Does the open-endedness of human motor learning challenge theories that emphasize continuity across species and over development, or can such theories explain how humans learn arbitrary, culture-specific actions?

An important experiment by Thelen and Fisher (1983b) suggests that the basic coordinative structures that underlie universal actions like locomotion also underlie the most prototypic examples of culture-specific learned actions. Their experiment focused on a situation intensively studied by Rovee-Collier (e.g., Rovee-Collier & Gekoski, 1979), in which an infant's leg is tied to a string attached to a mobile. Although we may safely assume that this state of affairs did not prevail during the time period when the basic mechanisms for moving the legs evolved, the infants learned quite readily to move the mobile by moving their own bodies. Thelen and Fisher asked what infants learned to do in this situation: What movements did they learn to make? In principle, infants could have activated the mobile in a variety of ways; a simple rotation of the hip, for example, would have sufficed. In fact, infants moved the mobile by engaging in the same coordinative activity that underlies stepping, kicking, and later walking: They rotated hip, knee, and ankle. Detailed observations of the temporal characteristics of these movements revealed that infants accelerated their kicking, increasing the motion of the mobile, in the same way that adults and other animals accelerate their locomotion: Infants reduced the duration of the interval between kicks while leaving the duration of the kick itself nearly invariant. The learning of this apparently arbitrary skill was not assembled from arbitrary components but from the same core coordinative capacities that underlie universal and species-typical actions.

This study suggests that early-developing core action capacities provide humans not only with the means to accomplish universal, biologically significant tasks like locomotion, but also with building blocks for solving the seemingly arbitrary tasks that humans confront as members of specific cultures. The most open-ended learning may be found, on closer scrutiny, to use these building blocks, providing a universal vocabulary from which culture-specific skills are assembled (see Jensen, Thelen, & Ulrich, 1989, for discussion). Insofar as this thesis is correct, an appreciation of what is given in development will be essential to understanding all the skills that humans achieve, including those attained only by a handful of experts.

The Development of Action: Themes and Prospects

This excursion through the development of locomotion suggests themes that will recur when we turn from the study of action to the study of perception, language, and higher cognition. In our view, the central ideas emerging from this research are that core capacities exist which (a) emerge in anticipation of their function, (b) are constant over development, (c) reflect evolutionary adaptations providing for phylogenetic continuity, and (d) serve as building blocks for the development of culture-specific actions. Each theme has implications for the future study of action development, which we outline in the following subsections.

Core Structure Anticipating Function

If actions were shaped over ontogenesis by environmental demands, then coordinations should emerge after the need for them arises, as children progressively tailor their acts to fit environmental circumstances. Contrary to this expectation, we have seen that action capacities can arise before they are needed. Before children walk, they engage in the alternate leg movements required for upright locomotion. This example and others suggests that many developing capacities do not emerge by trial-and-error learning but in accord with an intrinsically paced schedule. Experience serves to fine-tune these capacities and to coordinate them with one another in the performance of real, complex actions.

The recognition of coordinative structures that exist in the child before they are used commits one to a thesis central to nativism and to a conceptual and empirical possibility central to the nativist–empiricist dialogue: Competence can emerge prior to its manifestation in overt performance and therefore prior to any shaping by the demands of performance. Although this thesis has been criticized as mystical, research on early locomotor competence shows that the criticism is without force. Claims of hidden competence are testable hypotheses, for what is hidden in natural circumstances can be revealed by astute experiments.

Although we have focused on the development of stepping, studies of other aspects of developing locomotion reveal further competences that emerge in anticipation of their function. We cite two examples. First, forward locomotion depends on vestibular and visual mechanisms for maintaining upright posture and reestablishing balance when it has been perturbed; mechanisms accomplishing this task exist in newborn infants (Jouen, 1990; see Bertenthal, in press, for a review). Human children's developing ability to maintain their balance during locomotion does not depend on the development of these mechanisms but on changes in body size and proportion that allow the mechanisms to operate effectively (Thelen, 1984). Second, forward locomotion depends on distal (typically, visual) perception of a supporting surface and on a coordination between perception and action fostering locomotion only on surfaces perceived to afford support. In the next section, we will see that such coordinations exist at birth in precocial animals and are functional in humans before walking begins. In these cases and others, an understanding of foundational capacities has depended on the design of experiments that minimize or circumvent limitations on children's performance in order to reveal their competence.

Core Capacities Constant over Development

Few developmental changes are as dramatic as the emergence of independent walking. The locomoting 1-year-old child faces a new world of possibilities and challenges (see Bertenthal & Campos, 1990). Underlying this change, however, is a set of core competences that the youngest infants share with adults. This set provides continuity over human development.

Theories that recognize continuity over development sometimes are criticized as "antidevelopmental," as if they deny change. Research on locomotor development defeats this criticism by showing how the discovery of developmental continuity allows investigators to pose specific and tractable questions about the nature of developmental change. Thelen's studies of hidden locomotor competence suggest new explanations for developmental changes in locomotion. Two-month-old infants stop stepping when held upright because their legs become too heavy for their weak muscles to lift them; 13-month-old toddlers begin walking because their center of gravity descends to the point where they can remain upright in a state of balance. More generally, this research encourages students of development to focus both on invariance and on change, because discoveries of constant and changing competences elucidate one another. This is the heart of the experimental approach to development that animates the dialogue between nativism and empiricism.

Core Capacities Common across Species

Human locomotion is unique. Only people walk while maintaining an obligatory, bipedal, upright stance, and only people require a full postnatal year to develop their species-typical locomotor pattern. Despite these differences, research on human locomotion reveals strong commonalities with the locomotor capacities of other animals. Vertebrate locomotion appears to depend in large part on a shared set of structures.

This conclusion illustrates a more general point: The human body shows extensive similarities to the bodies of other animals. All animals are composed of the same basic structures at the molecular and cellular levels, and many species share structures at the levels of organs and organ systems. Turning to mind and action, however, it is often assumed that humans are profoundly different from other animals, such that only humans reason, have conscious experience, represent the world, or act intentionally. This assumption follows a peculiar logic: In the absence of evidence concerning whether an animal of a given species can do something that humans can do, it is assumed that the animal differs from humans. This logic has been elevated to a canon (Morgan, 1895) and held as a model of prudent thinking, but it is hardly unassailable. Why not propose the opposite canon and assume, in the absence of evidence for species differences, that an animal with the same molecules, cells, and organs as humans has the same mental and behavioral capacities as well? Contrary both to Morgan's canon and to its opposite, we suggest that questions concerning species commonalities or differences be settled by evidence, not default assumptions. Evidence from the study of locomotion now supports the conclusion that common coordinative structures exist in animals with superficially quite different modes of locomotion, including lamprey, precocial quadrupeds such as goats, and humans. This commonality, in turn, suggests that human action capacities have a strong biological basis (see Thelen, 1984, for eloquent discussion of this point).

Core Capacities as Building Blocks for Later-Developing Skills

Does the discovery of early-developing action capacities that exist in other species and are universal across humans hinder attempts to understand later-developing action capacities that are unique to humans and vary across cultures? The last lesson to be drawn from studies of action development directly counters this concern. As scientists come to understand the core action capacities of humans and the commonalities between humans and other species, this understanding provides special insight into action capacities that are unique to humans and that arise only in specific physical and cultural environments.

In particular, Thelen and Fisher's (1983) study of children learning to activate a mobile suggests that arbitrary actions on objects may be assembled from universal core capacities. Although these capacities exist in other animals, the propensity to assemble them in novel ways may be distinctively human and may underlie phenomena, such as tool use, that are central to human culture (Tomasello et al., 1993). Research on human development combines fruitfully with research in comparative psychology and ethology to shed light on these distinctive action capacities. The same synthesis has led to insights in the second domain on which we focus: perceptual development. Although the development of perceptual knowledge raises new themes, it, too, reveals distinctively human achievements that arise, over development, from structures that humans share with other animals.

PERCEPTUAL KNOWLEDGE

A glance at any natural scene reveals a world that is stable, organized, and meaningful—a world of familiar objects in sensible configurations. Perception of a scene allows for adaptive actions such as reaching for objects and navigating through the layout. Perception of a scene also brings knowledge. One learns, on looking out the window, that it snowed last night or that the neighbors have returned to town. Because perception is so central to the growth of knowledge, questions about the development of perception have always figured prominently in the nativist–empiricist dialogue. To what extent does perception of the world depend on the nature of the perceptual systems with which humans are endowed? In what ways does perception result from the shaping effects of experiences gained by observing the world and acting on it?

Research addressing these questions has made major strides during the past half-century. Experiments on inexperienced animals and on human infants have answered many questions about the origins and development of perception that were outstanding for thousands of years. These answers, in turn, raise further questions for the next generation of scientists. In this section, we first discuss the development of visual perception of the three-dimensional spatial layout, once the most hotly debated issue in

the nativist–empiricist dialogue. Next, we discuss the development of visual perception of objects, an important ability not only for perceiving and acting on scenes but also for talking and thinking about them. Discussion of these two abilities paints a contrasting picture of the progress of the field. In the case of depth perception, we suggest, the central questions of the nativist–empiricist dialogue have been answered. In the case of object perception, some central questions are still outstanding, but insights have been gained over the course of attempts to answer them.

Visual Perception of the Three-Dimensional Layout

What leads humans to experience the world as three-dimensional? Over the centuries, this question has appeared most pressing in the study of vision, where all perception begins with changing patterns of stimulation on a pair of two-dimensional retinal surfaces. Is this changing stimulation automatically transformed by the visual system into representations of a stable layout of surfaces varying in depth and standing at specific distances?[1] Alternatively, do perceivers learn such transformations by acting on a three-dimensional world? If the former (nativist) alternative were correct, then the three-dimensionality of perceptual experience would arise independently of the nature of the visual environment. If the latter (empiricist) alternative were correct, then the three-dimensionality of perceptual experience would stem instead from an ability to learn to induce the spatial structure that the visual environment presents.

Berkeley (1709/1975b) famously articulated an empiricist account of space perception, focusing his discussion on the perception of depth from the cues of accommodation and convergence. The cue of accommodation is based on the geometrical relation among the shape of the lens, the distance of the lens from the retinal surface on which an image is projected (a constant for the human eye at any given point in development), and the distance of the object on which one focuses. For any given distance between the lens and

---

[1] Throughout this section, we use *depth perception* to refer to an observer's apprehension of the relative distances of different parts of a scene, and *distance perception* to refer to the observer's apprehension of the absolute distance of a given part of the scene from the point of observation.

the retina, the lens must be thickened in order to maintain focus on an object as the object's distance decreases. The cue of convergence is based on the geometrical relation among the relative angles of regard of the two eyes, the distance between the eyes (again, a constant for human perceivers of any given age), and the distance of the object at which one is looking. With interocular distance constant, the convergence angle of the two eyes increases as the distance of the viewed object decreases. Berkeley proposed that children learn to see depth from convergence and accommodation by associating the depthless sensations arising from the ocular musculature that controls lens shape and binocular convergence with the sensations evoked by reaching and touching an object or by locomoting toward it. Helmholtz (1867/1962) developed these suggestions, proposing that perceivers learn to apprehend a stable, three-dimensional world from all the cues to depth (some of which are discussed briefly below), by moving through the layout and observing the changing visual sensations that movements produce.

In opposition to these suggestions, nativist thinkers including Descartes (1637/1971b), Kant (1781/1964), and Hering (1920/1964) have argued that spatial learning is possible only for a perceiver who already interprets experience within a spatial framework. Thus, depth perception results not from the formation of associations between visual experiences and motor activity but from prestructured mechanisms that derive information for depth from patterns of visual and muscular stimulation "as it were by a natural geometry" (Descartes, 1637/1971b, p. 250; see Hatfield, 1990, for discussion).

In principle, these contrasting proposals are straightforward to test. One investigates whether a person or animal with no visual experience perceives the same depth and distance relations that experienced people do. In practice, such tests have been difficult to devise, because people or animals with no visual experience have few means to indicate what they see. By the middle of the 20th century, nevertheless, experiments were beginning to bear on the contrasting claims offered by proponents of the two sides of the nativist–empiricist dialogue.

Depth Perception and Locomotion

The first major advance came in the 1950s, when Eleanor J. Gibson and Richard Walk devised a brilliant test for depth perception that can be used with many animals at a wide range of ages. In their studies of the "visual cliff" (Gibson & Walk, 1960; Walk & Gibson, 1961), a young animal or human was placed on a platform between two visible surfaces, one directly below the platform and one considerably farther away. Both surfaces appeared below a sheet of transparent plastic that protected the subject from falling and that removed any nonvisual information that might otherwise distinguish them. If subjects perceived the difference in depth between the two surfaces, Gibson and Walk reasoned that they would avoid crawling onto the deep side of the apparatus and would move preferentially to the shallow side.

Tests performed on a variety of animal species revealed an elegant regularity. As soon as an animal was old enough to locomote independently, the animal avoided the cliff and moved across to the shallow side. In animals that begin to locomote at birth, such as goats, appropriate cliff avoidance was observed when the animals first opened their eyes and began to move. In animals that begin to locomote later, such as rats, cliff avoidance could not be tested at birth. Further experiments with rats revealed, however, that cliff avoidance was independent of visual experience in this species as well. Rats reared in darkness until they were old enough to locomote avoided the cliff on their first exposure to the light, like their normally reared counterparts (Walk, Gibson, & Tighe, 1957).

The most interesting studies of dark-reared animals may be those performed with kittens (see E. Gibson, 1991, for discussion). The visual system of the kitten is very immature at birth, and visual experience serves to fine-tune it. When kittens were reared in darkness until reaching the age at which visually guided locomotion normally appears, they showed no avoidance of the deep side of the cliff on first exposure to the light. This finding suggested that visual experience is necessary for the development of cliff avoidance in this species, but it did not clarify the role that experience plays. Must kittens learn that visually distant surfaces are dangerous? To investigate this possibility, Gibson, Walk, and Tighe (described in Gibson, 1991) allowed a group of dark-reared kittens to locomote with vision for six days, *on the plastic-covered cliff apparatus.* This experience gave the kittens an opportunity to adjust to the light but not to learn that the visible cliff was dangerous. Instead, the kittens' experience was designed to suggest that the cliff was safe. After two days, the kittens, like the young of other species, began to avoid the deep side of the cliff. Further, concordant findings come from the experiments of Held and Hein (1963), who found that cliff avoidance in cats depends on experience with active locomotion but is observed even by kittens whose locomotion takes place entirely within a harness preventing falls. Visuomotor experience evidently fine-tunes a kitten's visual system, allowing the expression of an innate propensity to avoid visible drop-offs.

These experiments provide evidence that a wide variety of animals are endowed with mechanisms for perceiving the distance of surfaces and for using perceived surface distance as a guide to locomotion. "One is struck . . . with the preparedness to engage in perceptually guided behavior when an action system, such as locomotion, has matured to readiness in a normal environment. . . . Normally maturing vision is essential for the proper outcome, but no learning of specific S–R bonds is involved" (E. Gibson, 1991, p. 142).

Do human infants share these mechanisms? Studies of the behavior of infants on the visual cliff apparatus suggest a complex answer to this question. On one hand, human infants avoid the cliff at about the time when crawling begins: at age 7 to 8 months (Campos, Hiatt, Ramsay, Henderson, & Svejda, 1978; Gibson & Walk, 1960; Rader, Bausano, & Richards, 1980). In addition, younger infants who are lowered toward the cliff apparatus show an appropriate "placing response" (lifting their arms in anticipation of contact with a surface) when they approach the shallow but not the deep side of the display, providing evidence that they perceive the relative distances of the two visible surfaces (Campos, Bertenthal, & Kermoian, 1992; Walters, 1981). Nevertheless, two further sets of findings suggest limits to prelocomotor infants' perception of a drop-off. First, if such infants learn to use a walker, which allows them to locomote independently before they can crawl, they do not show cliff avoidance in the walker (Rader et al., 1980). Even infants who have begun to crawl are apt to cross the cliff when placed in a walker. Infants' propensity to cross the cliff in a walker may explain the high rates of accidents reported when infants use walkers in the home. Second, young infants who are placed directly on the deep side of the cliff react with interest, not fear or wariness (Campos et al., 1978, 1992).

These findings suggest that infants use visual information for distance to guide their visual placing and their locomotion before they understand that locomotion off a cliff is dangerous. Infants may show no fear when placed on a cliff because they fail to realize that their propensity to avoid crawling off drop-offs functions to protect them from danger. Additionally, infants may fail to understand that a walker will support them only if it stands on a supporting surface. They may falsely assume that support by a walker, like support in a parent's arms, is possible when one is far from the floor. On either of these accounts, human infants' understanding of visual support appears to be limited—a finding corroborated by research using other methods (e.g., Baillargeon & Hanko-Summers, 1990; Kim & Spelke, 1992).

The dissociation between systems for perceiving drop-offs and systems for reasoning about support, falling, and danger can be found in adults as well. Adults who look down through the floor-to-ceiling glass windows at the top of New York's World Trade Center may understand that they are safely supported while perceiving, with trembling, a dangerous precipice. Conversely, adults may perceive safe surface support while locomoting over terrain that they understand to be unsound. Inhabitants of earthquake zones are possibly in this category. The research reviewed above suggests that this dissociation is first observed early in life. Whereas perception of a precipice develops early, and independently of specific experience, understanding of cliffs, danger, and injury appears to develop later. The latter development may depend in part on experience with falls, for locomotor history has been shown to influence reactions of fear or wariness on the deep side of the cliff apparatus. Compared to age-matched noncrawlers, infants who have begun to crawl independently show greater wariness when placed on the deep side of the cliff. Moreover, prelocomotor infants who are given experience moving in a walker show greater wariness than infants with no such experience (Campos et al., 1992).

Depth Perception and Perceptual Constancies

Although the visual cliff is an excellent tool for probing the emergence of depth perception in nonhuman animals, it cannot be used with very young infants because of their locomotor immaturity. Fortunately, other methods exist for studying younger infants, including studies of visually guided reaching, of defensive reactions to approaching objects, and of linkages between perception of depth and perception of other properties of the spatial layout. All these studies provide evidence that infants perceive depth long before they begin to locomote. Because this research has been reviewed extensively elsewhere (e.g., Kellman & Arterberry, in press; Yonas & Granrud, 1985), we focus only on selected research using the last category of methods.

A hallmark of mature perception of a stable, three-dimensional layout is that objects in the layout appear to maintain constant sizes and positions as perceivers move around them, even though motion of the perceiver brings changes in the sizes and positions of the images objects project in the visual field (see J. Gibson, 1950; Marr, 1982). For geometrical reasons, perception of the constant size and position of an object is possible if a moving perceiver detects information for the object's distance, because the image of an object changes in size and direction in strict relation to its changing distance from the point of observation.[2] One way to investigate whether infants perceive distance, therefore, is to ask whether they perceive objects to maintain constant sizes and positions as the infants' relation to the objects changes.

Kellman, Condry, O'Halloran, Van de Walle, and von Hofsten (described in Kellman, 1993) investigated whether moving infants perceive the constant positions of stationary objects. Infants observed two objects while sitting in a seat that was undergoing lateral translatory motion. One of the objects moved with the infant, producing no subject–relative displacement; the other object was stationary. The experiment was based on prior findings that infants prefer to look at moving objects rather than stationary ones. If infants were capable of position constancy, Kellman and his collaborators reasoned that they would look longer at the moving object. If infants were not capable of position constancy, they would look longer at the stationary object, because only that object projected a moving image as the infant's chair swept past it. Preference for the moving object was observed under all conditions

tested at 4 months of age (see also Kellman, Gleitman, & Spelke, 1987), and it was observed under some conditions at 2 months. Both 2- and 4-month-old infants evidently perceived the constant position and distance of the stationary object.

Evidence for distance perception at 2 months of age rules out a spectrum of empiricist theories of how perceivers come to experience a three-dimensional world. Contrary to Berkeley and Helmholtz, people do not learn to perceive object distances by manipulating objects or crawling toward them, because the young infants in Kellman's experiments (as well as those in studies using other methods; see Yonas & Granrud, 1985) had engaged in neither of those activities. Nevertheless, the youngest infants in Kellman's studies had the benefit of 2 months of visual experience, and active visual experience in itself might serve to calibrate certain perceptual constancies (Banks, 1988; Helmholtz, 1867/1962). Do human infants learn to perceive depth and object constancies over the first 2 months of life?

Two independent experiments addressed this question through studies of newborn infants (Granrud, 1987; Slater, Mattock, & Brown, 1990). In both studies, capacities for perceiving depth were inferred from assessments of size constancy. The experiments were based on a second looking pattern observed throughout infancy: If infants are presented with one object or event repeatedly and then are given a choice between looking at that display and looking at a different display, infants will tend to look preferentially at the novel display. Slater, Mattock, et al. (1990) therefore presented newborn infants with a single object on a succession of trials. On different trials, the object appeared at different distances and therefore subtended images of different sizes in the visual field. The infants then were tested with the same object and with an object of a different real size, presented at new distances that equated the sizes of their images in the visual field. If infants perceived the constant real size of the familiar object over changes in its distance, they were expected to look longer at the new object. The newborn infants indeed showed this preference, providing evidence that they perceived both the objects' distances and their constant sizes. Perception of distance evidently arises independently of visual experience in humans, as it does in other animals.

---

[2] It does not follow from the geometrical analysis that a perceiver must first perceive an object's distance and then infer its size and position. Gibson (1966) and Rock (1983) provide very different reasons why size and position constancy might not depend on an explicit inference of this kind. On all theories of the constancies, however, perceptions of the size, position, and distance of an object are inextricably linked. A perceiver who apprehends an object's constant size and position therefore may be presumed to apprehend its distance as well.

Developing Sensitivity to Information for Depth and Distance

The above experiments resolve one question that has long been central to the nativist–empiricist dialogue: Neither humans nor other animals need to learn to perceive a stable, three-dimensional world. These findings do not imply, however, that depth perception is impervious to visual experience. On the contrary, depth perception is known to undergo changes when adults must perceive the spatial layout under altered conditions of viewing, such as when they adjust to new glasses or look through water (see Helmholtz, 1867/1962; Wallach, 1985). It is nearly certain that children's depth perception also changes with experience, because the developing visual system must adapt to considerable changes in the size of the eyes and in interocular distance—factors that alter the geometrical relations underlying most depth cues (Banks, 1988; Helmholtz, 1867/1962). Finally, adults are known to perceive depth from multiple sources of visual information (see Cutting & Vishton, 1995). Research with infants reveals a series of developmental changes in sensitivity to different cues to depth, which we briefly review (see Yonas & Granrud, 1984, for further discussion).

Although newborn infants' sensitivity to different depth cues has not been tested systematically, it is likely that such infants are most sensitive to the cues of convergence and accommodation, which provide information for the absolute distances of nearby objects from variations in the state of the musculature controlling lens thickness and convergence angle (see Kellman & Arterberry, in press, for discussion of the reasoning behind this conjecture). Research with newborns therefore appears to bear quite directly on the dialogue between Descartes and Berkeley over the origins of sensitivity to this distance information.

Studies manipulating the availability of different sources of distance and depth information provide evidence for an interesting developmental progression after the newborn period. By 4 months at the latest, infants appear to perceive depth by analyzing patterns of visual motion and change. In particular, such infants perceive certain patterns of relative motion as the rigid displacements of three-dimensional surfaces (e.g., Kellman, 1984; see Kellman, 1993, for review), and they perceive certain patterns of accretion and deletion of visual texture as the occlusion of one opaque surface by

another (e.g., Granrud et al., 1984). At 4 to 5 months, infants begin to perceive depth from stereopsis, interpreting small differences in the retinal projections of the images of edges at the two eyes as information for the relative distances of the edges (Fox, Aslin, Shea, & Dumais, 1980; Held, Birch, & Gwiazda, 1980). Careful longitudinal studies reveal that sensitivity to this source of depth information develops very rapidly in the fifth month (Held et al., 1980). Finally, at about 5 to 6 months, infants become sensitive to a variety of static, monocular cues to depth, such as linear perspective (which European painters since the Renaissance have used to convey impressions of depth) and interposition (in which terminating edges give rise to the perception of partly occluded surfaces ordered in depth) (Yonas & Granrud, 1984).

It is not clear from this developmental timetable whether changes in sensitivity to different depth cues depend on maturation of the visual system, visual experience, or an interplay between these factors. In the case of stereopsis, infants who are unable to direct the two eyes to the same object in the visual field show little or no sensitivity to binocular disparity if they are tested immediately after their convergence is optically corrected (Held, 1985; see also Banks, Aslin, & Letson, 1975). This finding provides evidence that visual experience can modulate the development of binocular functioning in humans, but it does not reveal whether visual experience is necessary for its initial development. Nevertheless, studies of the neural basis of binocular vision in cats, monkeys, and other mammals suggest that binocular development results from an exquisite interplay of endogenous processes of neural maturation and experience. This research, a triumph of developmental neurobiology, deserves a brief discussion.

Development of the Neural Mechanisms of Binocular Vision

As noted, stereopsis depends on the detection of small differences in the locations of the projections of surface features at the perceiver's two eyes. Critical inputs to this process are provided by neurons in V1 (the first visual area in the cerebral cortex), each of which responds to stimulation from a small area within the visual field. Classic studies of cats and monkeys by Hubel and Wiesel (e.g., 1962) have revealed that the input layer of neurons in V1 is organized into bands of cells whose primary inputs derive from the left eye, alternating with bands whose inputs derive from the right eye: the "ocular dominance columns." These neurons, in turn, derive their inputs from neurons in a region of the thalamus, the lateral geniculate nucleus (LGN), that is organized into distinct layers of cells receiving inputs from retinal ganglion cells in each of the two eyes.

How do these banded and layered patterns develop, and what role does experience play in their development? Studies of fetal development reveal that cells in the LGN and in the input layer of V1 initially receive inputs from both eyes; later, these inputs are pruned to give rise to the layered and striped patterns (see Shatz, 1992). Because both the layered pattern in the LGN of cats and monkeys and the ocular dominance columns of monkeys are discernible at birth, visual experience is not necessary for their initial emergence (Rakic, 1977; Shatz, 1992). Moreover, studies of cats and monkeys reared in the dark after birth reveal mature patterns of ocular dominance that are indistinguishable from those of animals reared with normal vision, providing evidence that visual experience is not necessary for the later development of these connectivity patterns (LeVay, Wiesel, & Hubel, 1980; Sherk & Stryker, 1976). Nevertheless, famous experiments showed that when a cat or monkey is raised with one eye covered, the banded pattern is detectable but the relative width of the two bands is much changed. Bands of cells receiving input from the occluded eye are narrower than in normally reared animals, and bands receiving inputs from the active eye are correspondingly wider (e.g., LeVay et al., 1980). These findings provide evidence that the basic pattern of neural connectivity that gives rise to ocular dominance columns can be altered in response to experience that is strongly biased.

The findings from studies of monocularly deprived animals have generated a wealth of experiments investigating the mechanisms by which visual experience affects neural connectivity. Although the mechanisms are not fully understood, many neurobiologists believe that neural connections are modified in accord with empiricist principles articulated by Hebb (1949). Hebb suggested that synaptic connections are strengthened when the firing of the presynaptic neuron is immediately followed by the firing of the postsynaptic neuron. Because the latter neuron is more likely to fire when many of its input neurons fire in concert, Hebb's principle implies that connections from a group of neurons onto a common target will be strengthened when the neurons fire in synchrony. In a monocularly

deprived animal, synchronous activity in the visual pathway from the deprived eye may diminish, increasing the strength of connections from the active eye.

Further experiments have investigated how neurons establish appropriate connections in the absence of biasing experience. The primary focus producing these connections obviously cannot be visual experience, because dark-reared and normally reared animals develop the same patterns of connections. The patterns also cannot be genetically coded in detail, for two reasons. First, simple calculations show that animals do not have enough genes to specify where each neuron should grow and form synapses. Second, ocular dominance columns can be induced experimentally in animals that do not normally have them. In particular, frogs have widely spaced eyes that show little overlap in their projections to the optic tectum (a brain structure that plays an important role in amphibian vision). When frog embryos are implanted with a third eye in proximity to one of the two normal eyes, the two proximal eyes project to overlapping regions of the tectum, and they come to do so in a banded pattern of ocular dominance columns (see Constantine-Paton, Cline, & Debski, 1990). Because frogs do not plausibly have genes directing the growth of projections from a third eye, ocular dominance columns evidently develop in the absence of genetic specification.

If neither genetic specification nor visual learning produces these patterns of connectivity, what is their source? Experiments suggest that the same activity-dependent processes that shape neural connectivity in response to visual experience also play a central role in the development of connections in the absence of visual experience. In the eyes of a fetal cat or ferret, retinal ganglion cells are active spontaneously before birth, even before the development of the visual receptors. Elegant experiments by Shatz (1992; Feller, Wellis, Stellwagen, Werblin, & Shatz, 1996) reveal that this activity travels over the retinal ganglion neurons in waves, producing correlated firing patterns among neurons with adjacent cell bodies. The waves, in turn, produce correlated firing patterns among neurons in the LGN receiving input from adjacent locations in a single eye. If these waves of activity modify synaptic connections in the ways Hebb described, by strengthening connections among neurons that fire together and weakening connections among neurons whose firing is uncorrelated, they could produce both the layered organization in the LGN and the retinotopic and banded organization in V1, in the absence of any visual experience. Consonant with this possibility, chemicals that block the spontaneous activity of the ganglion cells were found to prevent the normal development of the connectivity pattern (Shatz & Stryker, 1988).

The research of Shatz and Stryker shows that nativist explanations do not imply genetic determination (also see Block, 1979, 1995). In classical discussions of nativism in visual perception, the concept of innateness did not, of course, refer to genetic specification, but rather to the existence of structured developmental outcomes that arise in the absence of experience of a visible environment. In this sense, the banded pattern of monocularly driven cells in V1 is innate—it arises in the absence of any visual experience—yet it is not encoded in the genes. Rather, it results from a chain of processes that produce spontaneous waves of neural activity. The existence of innate perceptual mechanisms that are not genetically specified undermines recent arguments that perceptual abilities cannot be innate because the human genome does not contain enough information to specify the connections on which those abilities depend (e.g., Edelman, 1987; Thelen & Smith, 1994). Direct genetic specification is not the only process that can produce visual mechanisms that operate prior to one's first encounters with the visual world. Indeed, the central accomplishments of recent research in developmental neurobiology are to reveal a host of epigenetic processes through which neural structures develop in accord with a species-typical, intrinsic plan, without either shaping by the environment external to the organism or detailed genetic instructions. These epigenetic processes may contribute not only to the development of depth perception but also to the development of object perception, our next topic.

Object Perception

Most natural visual scenes are composed of three-dimensional bodies that are stable over time and motion. Nevertheless, these scenes typically are cluttered, such that distinct objects stand side by side and partly occlude one another. When adults view scenes containing multiple adjacent and overlapping objects, they usually perceive each object's unity, boundaries, complete shape, and stability. If an object moves from view, it usually is perceived to persist and to maintain its identity over successive encounters. Because objects have stable and persisting properties, adults also can categorize and recognize objects by analyzing those properties, perceiving a body in a scene as a chair or as one's favorite pen. To what extent are these perceptions shaped by a history of looking at objects, walking around them, manipulating them, and communicating about them? To what extent, in contrast, does object perception depend on mechanisms that develop independently of visual experience?

In the early part of the 20th century, answers to these questions were dominated by the empiricist theories of Helmholtz and his descendants and by the nativist theories of the Gestalt psychologists (e.g., Koffka, 1935; Kohler, 1947; Wertheimer, 1923/1958; see Hochberg, in press, for discussion). As in the case of depth perception, Helmholtz proposed that children learn to perceive objects by handling and moving around them, observing the changing perspectives that active movements reveal. In contrast, investigators in the Gestalt tradition proposed that object perception results primarily from the inherent propensity of the nervous system to assume states of maximal equilibrium, a propensity giving rise to perceptual organizations that are stable and regular.

Discussion of the origins of object perception subsequently was enriched by a number of new ideas. Piaget (1954) proposed that object perception results from the child's progressive coordination among activities such as reaching, grasping, sucking, manipulating, and visual following. Quine (1960) proposed that object perception results from the acquisition of language, particularly from linguistic devices for distinguishing one object from another and for distinguishing bounded objects from unbounded stuff (see Carey, in press, for discussion). Wiggins (1980) and others have proposed that object perception results from the acquisition of systematic knowledge of object kinds, such as *chair, pot, tree,* and *dog.* Although none of these thinkers viewed their contributions within the classic terms of the nativist–empiricist dialogue, all attributed a large role to experience in the development of object perception: sensorimotor experience, experience with language, or experiences giving rise to commonsense understanding of natural kinds and artifacts.

Research addressing these theories has begun to accelerate over the past decade. Experiments with nonhuman animals provide evidence that capacities for perceiving and representing objects emerge after minimal visual experience. Experiments with human infants have shed light on the processes by which infants organize visual scenes, and their findings have narrowed the space of tenable nativist and empiricist theories of object perception. Nevertheless, no experiment yet reveals whether visual experience is necessary for the development of object perception in humans.

Perception of Objects in Nonhuman Animals

Insights into the development of object perception have come from recent studies of imprinting, a striking capacity for object perception and representation in newborn chicks. In nature, chicks imprint to their mother and siblings based on visual exposure to these objects in the first days of life. In field and laboratory experiments, chicks raised without conspecifics have been found to imprint to a variety of visible objects, including simple geometrical solids if the objects are presented in motion (see M. Johnson & Morton, 1991, for review). Imprinting is revealed in laboratory tests in which the imprinted object and a second object are placed at opposite ends of an unfamiliar cage. Chicks spend most of their time near the imprinted object. This phenomenon has permitted the systematic study of young chicks' representations of visually presented objects.

In one series of experiments (Regolin & Vallortigara, 1995), chicks were raised in a closed, homogeneous box with a single yellow triangle dangling from its center. Because no other objects (animate or inanimate) were present in this environment, the object was never occluded by other objects. After two days' exposure to the moving object, the chicks became imprinted to it. On the third day, the chicks were placed in a test cage with a center-occluded triangle on one side and a fragmented triangle with a gap at the location of the first triangle's occluder on the other side. Although both test stimuli corresponded to the imprinted stimulus equally well with respect to the visible areas of the triangle, human adults who are shown these displays perceive only the center-occluded triangle as continuing behind the occluder (Michotte, 1954). The chicks' perception of the relative similarity of the two test stimuli to the original stimulus was inferred from the relative lengths of time that they spent in proximity to each test stimulus. The subjects spent substantially more time in the vicinity of the partly occluded triangle, providing evidence that they, like human adults, perceived this stimulus as more similar to the complete object (see Regolin & Vallortigara, 1995, for further evidence for this interpretation).

In a second series of experiments, chicks were found to represent an imprinted object, and to search for the object, even when it was fully hidden. After one day of imprinting to an inanimate object in a homogeneous environment, 2-day-old chicks watched as the object was moved fully out of view behind one of two screens. Although the chicks had never before witnessed the occlusion of an object, they reliably searched for the hidden object by moving around its occluder (Regolin, Vallortigara, & Zanforlin, 1995a). Successful search was reported even under conditions that required the chick to turn away from the object in order to reach it (Regolin, Vallortigara, & Zanforlin, 1995b). These findings provide evidence that chicks who view a fully occluded object for the first time represent its continued existence over occlusion (see Regolin et al., 1995a, 1995b, for further findings and discussion).

Human Infants' Perception of Objects

Experiments provide evidence that human infants aged 3 months and beyond also perceive objects under certain conditions. Infants perceive the boundaries, unity, persistence, and identity of objects when these properties are specified by the arrangements and motions of surfaces in the visible layout.

Let us begin with infants' perception of the boundaries that separate objects within a single visible scene. Perception of object boundaries has been studied with preferential looking methods, investigating whether familiarization with a given configuration of two objects leads to longer looking at a new display in which the boundaries of the objects are changed, relative to a new display presenting the same or greater changes in the arrangement of visible surfaces but no change in object boundaries. All these studies reveal that young infants perceive the boundaries between two objects if the objects are separated by a gap in three-dimensional space or if they are adjacent to one another but undergo separate motions, as when one object slides across the top of the other (e.g., Kestenbaum, Termine, & Spelke, 1987; Needham & Baillargeon, in press; Spelke, Hofsten, & Kestenbaum, 1989; Xu & Carey, 1994; see also Hofsten & Spelke, 1985, and Spelke et al., 1989, for converging evidence from studies using a reaching method). In contrast, infants sometimes fail to perceive the boundary between two objects that are adjacent and stationary, even if the objects differ in color, texture, and shape and belong to different, familiar kinds such as commonplace toys (Hofsten

& Spelke, 1985; Kestenbaum et al., 1987; Needham & Baillargeon, in press; Spelke, Breinlinger, Jacobson, & Phillips, 1993; Spelke et al., 1989; Xu & Carey, 1994; cf. Needham, Baillargeon, & Kaufman, in press).

When one object is partly occluded such that its ends are visible but its center is hidden, can infants perceive the object as a connected unit that continues behind the occluder? Perception of the connectedness of such objects has been investigated through preferential looking experiments in which infants are familiarized with a center-occluded object and then are tested for novelty reactions (as reflected in longer looking) to displays consisting either of the complete object or of the two previously visible parts of the object separated by a gap. These experiments provide evidence that 4-month-old infants perceive the connectedness of a center-occluded object if the ends of the object undergo a common, rigid translation in three-dimensional space (S. Johnson & Aslin, 1996; S. Johnson & Nanez, 1995; Kellman & Spelke, 1983; Kellman, Spelke, & Short, 1986; Slater, Morison, et al., 1990). In contrast, 4-month-old infants typically fail to perceive the connectedness of a center-occluded object that is stationary (Kellman & Spelke, 1983; although cf., Needham, 1994). Infants who view a center-occluded object while they themselves are in motion perceive the unity of the object if it moves conjointly with them, undergoing no subject-relative displacement, and they fail to perceive the unity of the object if it is stationary, undergoing substantial subject-relative displacement (Kellman et al., 1987). This finding provides evidence that real surface motion, not displacement in the visual field, is informative for infants. It converges with the evidence, reviewed in the previous section, that infants distinguish real object motions from image displacements caused by their own motion (see Kellman, 1993).

Further preferential looking experiments have investigated infants' representations of an object that moves completely out of view. Infants as young as 3 months have been found to represent the continuing existence, position, size, and shape of a fully occluded object (e.g., Baillargeon & Devos, 1991; Craton & Yonas, 1990; Hespos & Rochat, 1996; Wilcox, Rosser, & Nadel, 1994; Wynn, 1992). If part of the object appears behind one side of a central occluder, and then the object completely disappears and a different part of the object emerges from behind the other side under spatiotemporal conditions that specify one continuous motion, 5-month-old infants perceive the two parts to lie on

one connected object (Van de Walle & Spelke, in press). Finally, when a fully visible object moves out of view behind an occluder at one location and then a featurally identical object moves into view at a different location, infants as young as 2.5 months have been found to perceive a single, persisting object over these encounters if they can trace a spatiotemporally connected path of object motion, and they perceive two distinct objects if no such connected path exists (Aguiar & Baillargeon, 1996; see also Spelke, Kestenbaum, Simons, & Wein, 1995; Wynn, 1992; Xu & Carey, 1996). Spelke and Van de Walle (1993) have summarized these findings by proposing that 3- to 5-month-old infants perceive objects in accord with three principles capturing spatiotemporal constraints on object motion: the principles of cohesion, continuity, and contact. These principles dictate that moving objects maintain their connectedness and their boundaries, follow paths that are connected and unobstructed, and influence one another's motion just in case they come into contact.

Spelke (e.g., 1990) further proposed that young infants fail to perceive objects in accord with other visual relationships that specify object unity, boundaries, and identity for adults, such as alignment of surfaces and edges; sameness of surface color, texture, and shape; and goodness of overall object form. Although some more recent findings are consistent with this suggestion (e.g., Needham & Baillargeon, in press; Simon, Hespos, & Rochat, 1995; Xu & Carey, 1996), other findings suggest that this negative conclusion was too strong. In experiments by S. Johnson and Aslin (1996), and by Smith, Johnson, Spelke, & Aslin, 1996), 4-month-old infants' perception of the unity of a center-occluded object was affected by edge alignment. Infants perceived a rigidly moving, center-occluded figure with strongly misaligned edges as two separate objects when the display was two-dimensional, and as indeterminate when the display was three-dimensional. In experiments by Needham (1994), a conjunction of figural goodness and color and texture similarity served to specify the boundary between two stationary adjacent objects for 4.5-month-old infants, although such infants do not use these properties as reliably as do adults and 8-month-old infants (Needham & Baillargeon, in press). Infants therefore show some sensitivity to a variety of sources of information for object unity and boundaries, although they are most sensitive to information provided by motion.

Two further limitations of infants' abilities to perceive and represent objects deserve mention. First, infants under about 8 months of age do not appear to use representations of an occluded object to guide a variety of actions aimed at retrieving the object, including detour reaching (Diamond, 1990), removing the object's occluder (Piaget, 1954), or even pressing a button to bring the object forward (Munakata, McClelland, Johnson, & Siegler, in press). Because monkeys solve object search tasks by 4 months of age (Antinucci, 1989; Hauser & Carey, in press) and chicks solve such tasks at 2 days of age (Regolin et al., 1995a, 1995b), the development of these abilities may depend more on maturation than on experience (see Diamond, 1990, for discussion).

Second, infants under about 11 months of age do not appear to be able to use information about the category membership of an object in perceiving its boundaries or continuing existence over occlusion. This failure has been shown most clearly in a series of studies by Xu and Carey (1994, 1996). By 9 months of age, and possibly much younger, infants have been shown to be sensitive to the categorical differences between toy animals and toy vehicles, both when these objects are presented for active manipulation and when they are presented for visual inspection (Eimas, 1994; Mandler & McDonough, 1993; Van de Walle & Hoerger, 1996). Accordingly, Xu and Carey (1994) investigated 10- and 12-month-old infants' perception of a stationary toy animal that stood on top of a stationary toy vehicle. Surprisingly, 10-month-old infants gave no evidence of perceiving two separate, bounded objects in this situation. In further experiments, 10- and 12-month-old infants viewed a toy vehicle and a toy animal that disappeared and reappeared in succession from behind a single occluder. Although adults perceive two distinct objects in this situation, the 10-month-old infants' perception was indeterminate between events involving one versus two objects (Xu & Carey, 1996). At 12 months, in contrast, infants used the categorical difference between the animal and the vehicle to perceive both the boundary between the two adjacent objects and the distinctness of the two successively visible objects (Xu & Carey, 1994, 1996).

In all of Xu and Carey's experiments, the 10-month-old infants who failed to perceive object boundaries and object identity in accord with information about object categories successfully perceived object boundaries and identity by using the spatiotemporal information discussed in the previous section. They perceived two adjacent objects as distinct if one moved relative to the other, and they perceived two successively visible objects as distinct if no connected path united them. These findings and others (e.g., Simon et al., 1995) provide evidence that a basic process for perceiving objects as spatiotemporally connected and continuous bodies exists prior to the development of abilities to perceive objects by categorizing them as particular kinds, at the level of "vehicle" or "animal," "car" or "duck."

The Role of Experience in the Early Development of Object Perception

All the above studies provide evidence that abilities to organize visual arrays in accord with the basic spatiotemporal properties of objects are present and functional by 3 to 4 months of age in human infants. How do these abilities develop, and what roles do maturation and experience play in their development? Research on infants' perception of objects indicates that certain kinds of experience are *not* necessary for the development of object perception. In particular, this research provides evidence against both the empiricist proposal of Helmholtz and the constructivist proposal of Piaget, according to which object perception results from the child's actions of manipulating objects and moving around them. Because 3-month-old infants have not yet begun to reach for, manipulate, and locomote around objects, early-developing abilities to perceive objects evidently do not depend on these experiences. This research also provides evidence against Quine's proposal that object perception results from the mastery of natural language syntax, because infants divide the perceptual world into objects long before they learn the relevant aspects of language. Indeed, processes for perceiving object boundaries and object identity appear to guide language learning, rather than the reverse (e.g., Bloom, 1995; Markman, 1990; Markman & Wachtel, 1988; Soja, Carey, & Spelke, 1990; although see Imai & Gertner, in press). Finally, this research provides evidence against the thesis that perception of object unity and identity depends on processes for categorizing objects as members of particular kinds such as "chair" and "dog" (Wiggins, 1980), because abilities to represent objects as members of kinds develop considerably later than abilities to perceive and represent objects in accord with spatiotemporal constraints (Xu & Carey, 1996).

Although existing research limits the class of tenable theories of the development of object perception in humans, studies of human infants below 3 months of age present a tantalizingly inconclusive picture of the origins of this ability. Slater, Morison, et al. (1990) conducted a modified version of Kellman and Spelke's (1983) experiment with newborn infants, and found that infants who were familiarized with a moving, center-occluded object looked longer at a complete than at a broken object. This pattern, which is opposite to that observed with older infants and newborn chicks, suggests that the newborn infants did not perceive the center-occluded object as connected behind the occluder. Research by S. Johnson and Nanez (1995) used a similar method to investigate perception of a moving, center-occluded object by 2-month-old infants. After familiarization with the occlusion display, these infants looked equally at a complete and at a broken object, suggesting that 2-month-old infants still fail to perceive a moving object as connected behind a central occluder.

The studies of Slater, Morison, et al. (1990) and of S. Johnson and Nanez (1995) provide evidence for a developmental change over the first 4 months, but what is the nature of this change? On one hand, it is possible that newborn human infants, in contrast to newborn chicks, lack the ability to perceive unitary, partly occluded objects. Abilities to perceive objects may develop between birth and 4 months through maturation, effects of experience, or a combination of these factors. Alternatively, newborn infants may have the competence to perceive object unity from motion information and yet fail to exercise this competence with the displays used successfully in research with 4-month-olds, because their limited sensory capacities preclude their detection of the relevant spatial and kinetic information. In particular, newborn infants may fail to detect that the central occluder stands in front of the moving object and therefore partly hides it, or they may fail to perceive that the visible ends of the center-occluded object undergo a common, rigid motion.

As in studies of motor development, the distinction between perceptual competence and perceptual performance yields testable predictions, and experiments have begun to test them. Slater, Johnson, Kellman, and Spelke (1995) presented newborn infants with an occlusion display in which the distance relations among the infant, the occluder, and the moving object were enhanced. Infants in this experiment showed the same preference for the complete object as did those in Slater's original experiments, suggesting that limits on depth sensitivity do not account for newborn infants' failure to perceive object unity over occlusion. S. Johnson and Aslin (1995) next presented 2-month-old infants with a variety of occlusion displays that reduced the spatial distance between the motions of the visible parts of a center-occluded object. In their experiments, infants looked longer at the test display in which the visible object surfaces were separated by a gap, providing evidence that they perceived the unity of the center-occluded object. These findings suggest that limitations on young infants' sensitivity to common motion across distant regions of the visual field account for some of young infants' failures to perceive object unity over occlusion.

To date, there is no evidence indicating whether the competence revealed by Johnson and Aslin (1995) at 2 months exists at birth as well. It is possible that this competence is absent, in which case experiments presenting occlusion displays with motion relations that are detectable by newborn infants should continue to provide evidence that the infants respond only to the visible surfaces in a display. As a second alternative, it is possible that this competence is present and functional in limited contexts, in which case experiments with center-occluded objects undergoing detectable common motion should yield the same findings with newborn infants as with older subjects. Finally, it is possible that the experimental approach pursued by Slater, Johnson, and Aslin will break down with newborn infants, for there may be no situations in which the common motions of the separated parts of a center-occluded object are detectable. As Banks and Shannon (1993) have suggested in a different context, limits on a newborn infant's visual sensitivity may be so great that no ordinary visual environment will reveal some of the perceptual competences that are present and waiting to be exercised. If that is the case, then the study of the origins of object perception must await the emergence of an investigator with Thelen's genius—someone who can devise situations that circumvent the sensory limitations preventing newborn infants' inherent perceptual capacities from functioning in natural contexts.

Computational Approaches to the Development of Object Perception

In the absence of direct evidence concerning the roles of visual experience and endogenously developing visual mechanisms in the emergence of object perception in humans, theorizing may be sharpened by attempts to model the developmental process with connectionist learning systems (see McClelland, 1994, and Elman et al., 1996, for a discussion of these tools and their potential applications for studies of cognitive development). Although a detailed review of these efforts is beyond the bounds of this chapter, we will try to give a taste of this enterprise by discussing two recent attempts to model the early development of object perception.

Munakata, McClelland, Johnson, and Siegler (in press) focused on the development of the ability to represent the continued existence of an object that moves from view. They designed a network consisting of "input units" that were directly activated by visual scenes and responded only to objects that were visible, "hidden units" that were activated by the input units, and "output units" whose activity constituted the network's prediction of the state of the visible layout at the next moment in time. Critically, the activity of the hidden units persisted briefly after the signal they received from the input units was removed: a property of network architecture called *hysteresis*. At the start of learning, input, hidden, and output units were randomly connected, and so the hidden units activated by a visible object quickly returned to quiescence when the object moved from view. The system therefore did not represent hidden objects over any but the shortest time spans, and it could not track objects over occlusion.

In their simulations, Munakata et al. (in press) presented this system with a simplified visual world in which a single stationary object was occluded and then revealed by a screen that moved at constant velocity. At each time interval, the system predicted the state of the visual scene at the next time interval, representing this prediction as a pattern of activations on the output units. When the next interval arrived, the system detected discrepancies between the scene it predicted and the scene it encountered (i.e., discrepancies between the pattern of activations on the input and the output units), and it modified its connections to reduce those discrepancies. After many time intervals, this system learned to predict successfully when the occluded object would reappear. Most important, the hidden units began to show patterns of activation that were specific to the existence and location of the object while it was occluded.

The simulation by Munakata et al. (in press) is potentially of great interest because their network learned to represent hidden objects purely by visual observation, without

any input from systems for acting on objects or communicating about them. In its current form, however, the system learns to represent hidden objects only when it is trained on a single, exactly repeating event and then is tested with the same event (Marcus, 1996). For example, the system shows no generalization from displays with a stationary object and moving occluder to displays with a moving object and stationary occluder. In addition, this simulation obviously cannot account for the development of object representations in chicks, who represent the existence and location of fully occluded objects without any prior exposure to occlusion events (Regolin et al., 1995a).

A second connectionist project, by O'Reilly and Johnson (1994), approaches the problem of object perception in a somewhat different way. The authors' immediate task was to model imprinting in the chick. They sought to devise a system for learning to recognize a specific object from visual exposure to that object in motion. Their system was a connectionist network whose input units responded to features of objects at particular visible locations, connected to hidden units whose activation again showed hysteresis, connected in turn to a third set of units that may be considered as the system's output. Initially, the connections between the units in these three layers were random. With this architecture, neural connections were modified in accord with the Hebbian principles discussed earlier, by strengthening connections between units which fired in immediate succession. After exposure to a simplified visual environment in which an object with a given set of continuously visible features appeared in continuous motion, some of the hidden units in the system came to be activated reliably by that object. Most important, the three layers of the network developed a regular pattern of connections. Input units that responded to features at nearby locations activated many of the same hidden units, whereas input units that responded to features at distant locations activated different hidden units. Let us call this connectivity pattern "spatiotopic fanning."

Although this system was devised as a model of the learning process that might underlie imprinting in chicks, it is interesting to consider its architecture in light of research on object perception in human infants. Because of spatiotopic fanning, the trained system was more sensitive to simultaneous activation at adjacent regions of the visual field than to simultaneous activation at distant regions of the field. Fanning therefore increased the system's sensitivity to internally connected objects (like a ball) over spatially scattered ones (like a mobile without detectable wires). Because of the combined effects of spatiotopic fanning and hysteresis, the system also was more sensitive to continuous than to discontinuous object motion. Only when an object moved continuously would the persisting activation of units at one location along the object's path combine with the activation of units at its next location. Finally, the combination of spatiotopic fanning and hysteresis increased the system's sensitivity to objects that moved cohesively and to interactions between objects that occurred on contact, because input units activated by cohesive objects or interactions on contact sent their activation along to hidden units within the same fan of connections. O'Reilly and Johnson's connectionist system therefore was structured, partly by its innate architecture and partly by learning about fully visible objects, in accord with the principles of cohesion, continuity, and contact. It represented objects that obeyed these constraints, as do young human infants (see also Mareschal, Plunkett, & Harris, 1995, for a description of a connectionist model of object representation that embodies these principles in a different way).

The systems created by Munakata et al. (in press) and by O'Reilly and Johnson (1994) are simplified models of object perception. In their present forms, neither could cope with the three-dimensional, cluttered, and changing environments that infants routinely encounter. Nevertheless, the efforts of these investigators provide food for thought. First, the simulations of Munakata and her collaborators suggest that the purely visual experience available to young human infants could, in principle, produce important changes in object representation, allowing infants who begin with weak object representations to develop stronger ones. Second, the simulations of O'Reilly and Johnson suggest that visual experience with objects could produce patterns of connectivity that predispose infants to perceive objects in accord with the spatiotemporal principles derived from research with infants: cohesion, continuity, and contact. These modeling efforts therefore lend plausibility to empiricist accounts of the development of object perception. The assertion that empiricist theories cannot be devised to account for the findings of studies of infants (Spelke, Breinlinger, Macomber, & Jacobson, 1992) now seems too pessimistic.

As Munakata et al. (in press) and O'Reilly and Johnson (1994) acknowledge, however, the fact that certain capacities for object perception and object representation *could be learned* from visual experience does not imply that these

capacities *are learned* from such experience. On the contrary, research in developmental neurobiology suggests that much of the structure that is learned in O'Reilly and Johnson's (1994) simulation is innate in mammals and develops prior to their first encounters with the visible environment. In particular, spatiotopic fanning develops in advance of visual experience, even in mammals whose spontaneous visual activity has been blocked (Constantine-Paton et al., 1990). Moreover, spatiotopic projections are a natural consequence of the activity-dependent changes in synaptic connections that occur as a result of the prenatal waves of retinal activity discussed earlier in this section (Shatz, 1992). As waves of activity move across the retinal ganglion neurons (the analog of Johnson and O'Reilly's input units) of fetal animals, connections of adjacent cells to their targets (analogous to Johnson and O'Reilly's hidden units) will tend to be strengthened, whereas connections of distant retinal receptors onto common targets will tend to be weakened. Thus, processes operating in the absence of visual experience may lead to the development of connections that predispose newborn infants to perceive objects in accord with the principles of cohesion, contact, and continuity. The assertion that objects could not be perceived in accord with innate principles because there is no biologically plausible mechanisms for embodying such principles (e.g., Thelen & Smith, 1994) now seems overly pessimistic as well.

Research in computational modeling suggests that the questions at the center of the nativist–empiricist dialogue cannot be settled by a priori considerations of plausibility or parsimony. Theories that seem unparsimonious or implausible under one set of assumptions may appear simple and plausible when background assumptions change. In recent connectionist modeling, we see the germs of new empiricist and nativist theories of the emergence of object perception in infants. Research by neurobiologists and developmental psychologists now can begin to test these theories and their background assumptions.

Object Recognition: Developmental Change and Cultural Variation

However object perception originates, it is clear that a basic process for perceiving spatiotemporally connected and continuous objects arises early in development, without significant tutoring. This process is likely to be universal across human cultures, leading all people to perceive, act on, and talk about the same spatiotemporal bodies.

Consistent with this expectation, all the languages and cultures of the world appear to carve perceptual experience into cohesive and continuous bodies (see Bowerman & Levinson, in press, for evidence and discussion).

Despite these universal spatiotemporal principles, important changes in object perception may occur when children begin to categorize parts of visual scenes as objects of specific kinds, such as "dogs" and "cars." If this developmental change is influenced by the child's social and cultural environment, then it may lead people in different cultures to perceive visual scenes quite differently.

Research in cognitive linguistics, cognitive anthropology, and cross-cultural psychology, focusing on cultural variation in people's linguistic and conceptual categories, suggests some possible differences. For example, children and adults in Western industrialized societies tend to call objects by the same name if the objects have similar shapes, even if they differ greatly in size and material composition. A comb is a comb regardless of whether it fits in the hand of a doll or a giant, and regardless of whether it is made of wood, plastic, or gold (see Landau, Smith, & Jones, 1988). Shape, in turn, appears to be represented as an arrangement of geometrical solids (e.g., Biederman, 1987). In contrast, adults in many traditional societies give common names to objects with a common material composition. A pot is not a pot if it is not made of clay; a roof is not a roof if it is not thatch (Lucy, 1992). When shape does influence descriptions in these languages, moreover, it appears to depend on a parsing of objects into parts that are quite different from the geometrical solids that comprise most factory-made artifacts (see Brown & Levinson, 1993; Levinson, 1994). These differences in language may be accompanied by differences in how people sort objects into categories (Imai & Gertner, in press; Lucy, 1992; although cf. Markman, 1989). Nevertheless, cultural differences in object representations and recognition processes have not been investigated directly.

The Development of Perception: Themes and Lessons

Studies of the early development of perception echo the themes that emerged from studies of the early development of action. Depth perception and object perception both begin to emerge in anticipation of their functions. Infants perceive a three-dimensional surface layout before they use depth and distance information to guide reaching or loco-

motion, and they organize the surface layout into cohesive, separately moving bodies before they use such information to guide their grasping or manipulation. Like action systems, perceptual systems show continuity over phylogeny and over ontogeny. Infants' perception of depth and objects depends on mechanisms that are shared in part with other animals and that persist over the later course of human development.

In addition to these now familiar themes, the study of perceptual development helps to clarify what it means for an ability to be innate. As Block (1979, 1995) has argued, using very different examples, the claim that an ability is innate in no way implies either that the ability depends on structures coded in the genes or that the ability is impervious to experience. Gallistel (1990) has argued that even in the case of cognitive abilities that appear to be hallmarks of human intelligence (e.g., knowledge of number), claims of innateness do not imply that highly elaborate, special-purpose neural machinery is preformed in the newborn's brain. Studies of perceptual development provide clear and concrete illustrations of these points.

In the development of binocular vision, studies of animals reared in darkness reveal that the basic pattern of neural connectivity underlying binocular functioning arises in the absence of visual experience. In the classic language of the nativist–empiricist dialogue, the pattern is innate (LeVay et al., 1980). Nevertheless, studies in developmental neurobiology reveal that the neural connections underlying binocular functioning arise in animals not by genetic specification but by patterns of endogenously generated activity. Moreover, the same activity-dependent processes that shape the brain in the absence of visual experience also shape the brain in response to visual experience. Binocular functioning therefore provides an example of how a pattern of neural connectivity, and the visual functioning to which it gives rise, can be innate without being either genetically coded or impervious to later experience.

Although the neural basis of object perception is less well understood, studies in connectionist modeling provide a concrete example of how a system for perceiving objects in accord with basic spatiotemporal constraints on object motion might follow from simple and general principles of neural architecture, such as hysteresis and spatiotopic fanning projections. Findings that very young infants perceive objects in accord with these principles need not imply that infants are endowed with highly elaborate and specific systems of rules.[3]

More generally, studies in developmental neurobiology and in computational modeling suggest that questions concerning the nature of the brain systems underlying any given perceptual ability are empirical questions that are best addressed through vigorous interdisciplinary research. In particular, it would be a mistake to dismiss the findings of any given study in neurobiology or computational modeling on the grounds that it is based on principles too simple to account for human cognition. It would be equally mistaken to dismiss the findings of any given study of infant perception or cognition on the grounds that it requires neural machinery too elaborate to exist in a young human brain (see Chomsky, 1994, pp. 78–92, for further discussion). Only concerted, interdisciplinary research can reveal what inexperienced humans perceive and the neural computations that underlie their perceptions.

A final lesson from studies of perceptual development comes from very recent research on developmental changes in object perception at the end of the first year of life and on object representation in different human cultures. This research converges to suggest that perception has both universal and culturally specific properties, and that these sets of processes can be distinguished, in detail, through concerted experiments in anthropology and developmental psychology. Humans have an early-developing system of object representation, based on processes for analyzing objects' spatiotemporal properties, that gives rise to the same perceptual organization in all cultures. Humans also have a later-developing system of object representation, based on processes for analyzing other object properties and forming object categories, that may be sensitive to variations in experience and thus may vary from one culture to another.

---

[3] As this chapter was going to press, Elman et al. (1996) published a useful discussion of these issues. They, too, proposed that an ability be considered "innate" if it develops independently of the external environment, regardless of the epigenetic processes involved (pp. 20–23). They further propose that organisms be granted "representations" when the cerebral cortex displays fine-grained connectivity patterns (e.g., p. 25). By these definitions, the findings of Shatz, Rakic, and others reviewed above provide evidence for innate representations, contrary to a central thesis of their book.

Further understanding of perceptual development, therefore, may come from coordinated studies in cognitive anthropology and cognitive development, undertaken with the common goal of teasing apart the constant from the changing and the universal from the variable (see Bowerman & Levinson, in press, and Hirschfeld & Gelman, 1994, for a start).

LEARNING HOW TO TALK

On the face of it, language acquisition would appear to provide the clearest evidence for the purely empiricist side to development. First, languages vary, and children learn the languages they are exposed to. Second, there is developmental change rather than continuity, extending over a lengthy period of early development (measured in years rather than months), and consisting of behavioral output ordered from simple to more complex, as though a great deal of learning were occurring. Nonetheless, some of the most widely known and compelling evidence for nativist approaches to development comes from the study of the acquisition of language. In this section, therefore, we emphasize the evidence for nativism, using the literature on language acquisition to illustrate the issues about nativist views of development that arise in the examination of a system that clearly undergoes learning and developmental change. The themes we wish to emphasize are tightly related to, but slightly different from, those found in the development of action or perception. The evidence for innate factors in language development is extremely strong, but major controversies in the field center around the nature of what is innate: whether there is innate knowledge of language in particular, or whether the innateness derives from perceptual and memorial biases in more general pattern learning, which indirectly predispose the learner toward acquiring languages of certain types. This field therefore illustrates especially well the ways in which empirical enterprises can clarify the ancient nativist–empiricist dialogue.

The basic and most obvious facts about language learning set the stage for these questions. First, every known human culture has a language, each of which is a combinatorial system mapping form and meaning through patterned rule systems that are radically different from any found in nonhuman communication. This dramatic and uncontroversial fact thus demands from the outset a theoretical account involving evolutionarily specialized developmental mechanisms of some type. At the same time, there are thousands of *different* human languages around the world, and this fact requires that human infants be capable of learning any of them. Although the best studied of these are spoken languages, recent research reveals that thousands more are signed languages, which readily arise in every culture in which there is even temporary functional deafness or muteness (Kendon, 1988). The acquisition of language must therefore be subserved by mechanisms involving *both* innateness and learning, and operating equally well on stimuli from multiple modalities.

Two subparts of the literature illustrate particularly well the types of empirical discoveries and theoretical questions on which we focus: the acquisition of phonetic systems, which has been studied largely in spoken languages, and the acquisition of grammatical systems, which has been studied most revealingly in signed as well as spoken languages.

The Acquisition of Phonetic Systems: Reshaping Auditory Sensitivities into Linguistic Representations

The study of the acquisition of phonetic systems, with which we begin, illustrates several important aspects of the issues raised in language development. First, it is often argued that calling a behavior "innate" may lead investigators to believe they have an explanation, and therefore can deter empirical research into how the capacity is acquired. The history of research on phonetic acquisition, however, shows that, even after an ability has been identified as innate, new findings can radically alter our understanding of the character of what is innate, and one type of nativist theory can readily supplant another. Such a shift of consensus has undoubtedly occurred elsewhere, but this field provides a very striking example.

Second, as we have seen in the development of locomotion, behavioral domains unique to humans may arise from foundational roots common to other species. Phonetic acquisition presents a somewhat different case. Here, a system which in early development is like that of other species gradually changes through exposure into one unique to humans. Its study therefore offers an unusual opportunity for understanding how species-specific plasticity might arise.

The Nature of Adult Phonetic Categories

Listening to one's native language, one has the impression that the speech stream consists of distinct words, each composed of sequences of sounds roughly like the corresponding letters of the alphabet. If one listens to a foreign language, however, this impression is quickly dispelled. The sounds run together and are remarkably indistinct; recurring units are difficult to isolate or identify. This latter impression is in fact closer to the physical array. Even repeated tokens of the same syllable vary acoustically from one another, and tokens of the same individual sound (for example, /b/ or /p/) are acoustically quite different when followed by a different vowel.

This discrepancy between the acoustics of human speech and the way we perceive it has been demonstrated in the literature on adult speech perception, and forms the background to an understanding of the developmental process. Beginning in the 1950s, research on speech perception revealed, surprisingly, that adults perceive speech syllables (for example, "ba" or "pa") as categories in their native language (see Liberman, Cooper, Shankweiler, & Studdert-Kennedy, 1967; Lisker & Abramson, 1970, for reviews). Acoustically distinct stimuli varying in the timing of the onset of vocal cord vibration, for example, were perceived either as "ba" (if the voicing began within 30 msec of the onset of the syllable) or "pa" (if the voicing began more than 30 msec after the onset of the syllable); but finer distinctions of voicing onset time, which were not distinctive in the listener's native language, could not be discriminated from one another even in a purely auditory, nonlinguistic discrimination task (Liberman et al., 1967). This phenomenon of *categorical perception* contrasted sharply with the typical ability of perceivers to discriminate many more stimulus contrasts than they could categorize, which appears for both auditory and nonauditory stimuli outside of speech.

The Development of Phonetic Categories

One important question, then, is how this perceptual categorization develops. An obvious possibility is that it is learned, perhaps through some type of feedback about what the language treats as a category. However, this is not what the literature has demonstrated. In a remarkable study published in *Science,* Eimas, Siqueland, Jusczyk, and

Vigorito (1971) used a technique adapted from studies of infant visual perception to ask how infants perceived and discriminated speech sounds. The technique subsequently changed our ability to study foundational capacities in virtually every perceptual domain. Utilizing one of the few expert behaviors of young infants (sucking), they presented a single repeated token of the syllable "ba," contingent on continued sucking, and waited until the infants no longer found this stimulus worthy of their exertion. They could then ask a simple question that was related to the question asked of adult listeners in the categorical perception paradigm: Which other stimuli sound enough like this one that they, like the original "ba," are also unworthy of continued sucking? And, in contrast, which other stimuli, equally physically distant from the original "ba," sound new and distinctive? Remarkably, the infants' answer was like the adults': A new "ba" was boring, while a "pa" was perceptually different, even though the new stimuli differed from the original "ba" by equal physical magnitudes. These findings showed that even 1- and 4-month-old infants perceived speech categorically, long before speech production (and any external feedback for it) was available, and therefore suggested that categorical perception of speech sounds might be innate. More recent research with much younger infants has continued to support this view (for an overview of the relevant findings, see Ch. 4 by Aslin, Jusczyk, & Pisoni, in Volume 2).

The further question occupying subsequent researchers has concerned the nature of the innate abilities. Do infants innately perceive speech in terms of the *linguistic* categories used by languages of the world? This same early research suggested that this was the case: Acoustic stimuli containing the critical onset timing portions of speech stimuli, but which did not themselves sound like speech, were not perceived in this fashion either by adults or by infants (Eimas et al., 1971; Liberman et al., 1967). It therefore appeared that infants entered the acquisition process already equipped with knowledge of the categories of speech sounds that human languages would use.

However, several crucial subsequent studies importantly altered this view. In one of these studies, Kuhl and Miller (1978) showed that chinchillas (which have an auditory system much like that of humans, though, of course, they would not be expected to have particular human linguistic abilities) also perceive speech in the same categories as human adults and infants. Trained to press a bar discriminatively for individual tokens of "ba" and "pa," chinchillas spontaneously generalized their bar presses to the same range of acoustic stimuli that humans heard as "ba" and "pa." Although researchers were unable to determine any simple physical basis for these phonetic categories, the behavior of chinchillas suggested that it must be present and that its perception was not necessarily based on a specific linguistic capacity. By inference, one could argue that human infants begin the speech perception process with this same *auditory* categorization, which could subserve the categorization of speech sounds but was not itself yet particular to language.

In accord with this work, Pisoni (1977) and Jusczyk, Pisoni, Walley, and Murray (1980) showed more directly that human adults and infants perceive nonlinguistic stimuli in the same categories found for speech stimuli. Eimas et al. (1971) had not been able to demonstrate this for the 35-msec onset portions of "ba" and "pa." But Pisoni, Jusczyk, and their colleagues synthesized longer (and therefore more perceptible) stimuli, each composed of two tones whose onsets were either simultaneous (like the voicing aspects of "ba") or different by 10 to 60 msec (like the various tokens of "ba" to "pa"). When presented to adult and infant listeners in the same standard paradigms used for "ba" and "pa," these stimuli varying in "tone onset time" were perceived categorically, just like "ba" and "pa," and even shared a category boundary with them at about a 30-msec delay. Together, these findings suggest that the phenomenon of categorical perception occurs for many classes of auditory stimuli, in humans as well as nonhumans, and is a property of mammalian auditory systems that precedes language.

On this revised view, how does the perception of speech in particular develop? It begins with a perceptual system that is innately built with certain regions of relative sensitivity and other regions of relative insensitivity. These biases in auditory sensitivity thus form the scaffolding for human speech systems. Languages take as their phonetic categories those regions in auditory space that are relatively perceptible (and within which finer distinctions are difficult to discriminate). Regions that are extremely perceptible (for example, the approximately simultaneous onset of voicing and other aspects of syllable onset, as compared with a 30-msec lag between these acoustic events) form phonetic categories in most or all languages of the world; those regions that are moderately perceptible form phonetic categories in some languages; and those regions that are extremely difficult to perceive form phonetic categories in no languages. Although this revised account is still a nativist one (that is, it hypothesizes that there are innate perceptual categories underlying the processing of speech), it is not one that invokes specifically linguistic innate knowledge, and it is therefore not seen as objectionable or mysterious (or even nativist) to an antinativist theoretician.

Superimposed on this innate scaffolding, however, is the effect of linguistic experience—an effect which, to date, has been demonstrated only in human perceptual systems. The perceptual categories shown by very young infants (and presumably by chinchillas, though this has not been tested directly) are those underlying the phonetic systems of all the world's languages. Infants younger than 6 months of age discriminate not only "ba" and "pa" (a contrast used in virtually every language), but also "mba" and "ba" (a contrast used in Hindi, but not in English or in many other languages). At some time between 6 and 12 months of age, however, the ability to discriminate categories that are not contrastive in the surrounding language is lost (Werker & Lalonde, 1988; Werker & Tees, 1984). Older children and adults show categorical perception not for the full range of acoustic/phonetic contrasts, but only for those of their particular native language. In addition, the precise boundaries between these categories (for example, at 30-msec voice onset time in English, but at 25-msec onset in Spanish) have been adjusted to those of the native language. Perception of contrasts not used in the native language can, to some degree, be retrained through feedback in the laboratory, but do not persist in the untrained perception of adults (Pisoni, Aslin, Perey, & Hennessey, 1982; for discussion of the details of these findings, see Aslin, Jusczyk, & Pisoni, Ch. 4, Volume 2). These findings thus suggest that the initial perceptual abilities of infant listeners are adjusted and altered through exposure to surrounding speech, and thereby change from the biases of the general mammalian auditory system into the phonetic systems of particular languages. Moreover, the changes take the form of a loss, not a gain, in perceptual categorization. To a first approximation, American infants hear the categories of both English and Hindi. With growth and experience, American children and adults lose

this perceptual ability for Hindi but retain the categories of English.

We are just beginning to understand the mechanisms by which this perceptual adjustment takes place. Do infant perceptual systems respond to the fact that certain sets of sounds signal contrasts of meaning? Or do they respond more fundamentally to the fact that certain sets of sounds occur more frequently, or with greater correlations to others? Exploration of the details of the adjustment from auditory to linguistic perceptual abilities has only recently begun, but the stage for answering these questions has been set by investigators' continued fascination with issues of nature and nurture, and with the search for how our most unique abilities have arisen evolutionarily. The picture we have obtained thus far has important similarities to the development of specialized abilities in other animals, in which the innate tendencies of systems common to many species become adapted in species-specific ways, through evolution or through evolved abilities to learn from particular aspects of external experience.

In the next section, we review these issues in perhaps their most dramatic form: the acquisition of grammatical systems. Of all the behaviors we study in human infants, the acquisition of grammatical capabilities presents the arena in which questions about what is innate and what is learned have been the most explicit and central.

The Acquisition of Grammar

Undoubtedly, the most well-known discussion of nativism in the acquisition of grammar has been provided by the work of Noam Chomsky (1965, 1975, 1988). Chomsky has framed this discussion in terms of both a formal linguistic theory and a logical argument about development. His linguistic work over the past three decades has centered on providing evidence that, although the languages of the world appear to vary widely in their grammatical properties, they are in fact quite similar to one another, and they share a large set of universal principles of grammatical structure. The enterprise of modern linguistics, as framed by him, is to formalize these principles precisely. Chomsky's accompanying contribution to development has taken the form of a logical argument: Given the existence of universal principles across unrelated languages, and also the great distance between these principles and their instantiation in the physical signals from which a language must be acquired, it could not be the case that languages are in any serious sense "learned." Rather, the universal principles underlying languages must be innate, and most of language development must reflect the emergence of these principles in some articulatory form. On this view, the linguistic environment serves the function of triggering and, in limited ways, of setting some detailed parameters on the instantiation of these principles in a specific language.

This set of arguments is, in some ways, breathtakingly at odds with the obvious facts. As already noted, languages appear to differ fairly wildly—enough so that Chomsky's predecessors used their very differences to argue the opposite of Chomsky's view: "Walking, then, is a general human activity that varies only within circumscribed limits as we pass from individual to individual. . . . Speech is a human activity that varies without assignable limit as we pass from social group to social group, because it is purely a historical heritage of the group, the product of long-continued social usage. . . . Walking is an organic, instinctive function . . . speech is a non-instinctive, acquired, 'cultural' function" (Sapir, 1921, p. 4). Under Chomsky's guidance, however, the field has amassed quite a large number of surprising principles of uniformity, which underlie and structure the apparent diversities.

Still, language development certainly appears to involve what any reasonable person would identify as "learning": a lengthy period of gradual mastery, some rather protracted and different-looking stages along the way, and usually some rather striking resemblances between what the child comes eventually to do (e.g., speak English) and what the child's environment presents (e.g., English). But close empirical examination of these phenomena has supported, at least in general outline, some version of Chomsky's claim. The acquisition of language is heavily shaped by innate tendencies of the learner to acquire languages of particular types, in particular ways.

As we have seen in earlier sections, the question of whether there is some innate component to a developmental process is logically distinct from identifying what precisely is innate, how the innate propensities are enacted in the course of development, and to what degree these propensities are specialized to a particular behavioral domain. In the field of grammatical acquisition, however, this distinction has sometimes been overlooked, and evidence for a nativist approach to the acquisition of syntax is often misinterpreted as evidence in favor of Chomsky's particular nativist theory. In the present review of the literature, we attempt to separate the evidence into two parts: (a) research suggesting that there is an innate component to the acquisition process, and (b) research investigating the nature of the underlying mechanisms of acquisition.

Evidence for Innateness in Learning

Along with Chomsky's formal work on languages and their acquisition, much of the strongest evidence for innateness in the acquisition of grammar comes from comparative studies of children and adults learning languages around the world, under varying circumstances of input and maturational state. As we will see, these studies show that children learn their apparently differing languages in remarkably similar ways, suggesting that they are guided in this process by some type of internal predispositions.

Uniformity in the Course of Acquisition.   Lenneberg (1967) was the first to note that language acquisition proceeded through a reasonably fixed set of stages, or milestones, whose nature and timing were stable even when the linguistic environments were varied. As Lenneberg reported, children universally pass through cooing, babbling, first words, two-word sentences, and then more complex syntax, with each milestone appearing at ages roughly as predictable as those of getting teeth or developing motor abilities. Since the publication of his book on this topic, we have learned that there is a similar course of development for exotic as well as familiar spoken languages (Slobin, 1985, 1992), and even for signed languages (Newport & Meier, 1985; Petitto & Marentette, 1991). Perhaps most surprisingly, deaf children who are not effectively exposed to *any* conventional language devise words and sentences from gesture, and pass through at least the early stages of "acquisition" on their own (Feldman, Goldin-Meadow, & Gleitman, 1978; Goldin-Meadow & Mylander, 1984). Such regularity of development despite varying environments suggests that internal maturational factors heavily dictate the course of acquisition.

Not All Learners Look the Same.   Young human children look remarkably similar to one another as they learn languages, but not every organism exposed to the same linguistic environments displays the same behaviors in response. Dogs and cats produce neither spoken nor signed sentences and understand, at most, a few simple words, even when they are addressed for years with the most loving and tailored forms of speech (Hirsch-Pasek & Treiman, 1982). Devoted caretakers of chimps and gorillas, our nearest evolutionary relatives, have noted in them, at most, some simple elements of human language (Premack, 1976, Savage-Rumbaugh, 1991; although cf., Savage-Rumbaugh et al., 1993). But perhaps the clearest evidence that learning language requires a particular native endowment comes from studies of human adult language learners.

In the same book that noted the regularities of human children's acquisition of language, Lenneberg (1967) suggested that this process, like the development of many other species-typical behaviors (for example, imprinting in birds and ducks, or the acquisition of song in sparrows), might be limited to a maturationally bounded critical period, early in life. It has, however, required several subsequent decades for investigators to determine how to put his hypothesis to empirical test. Lenneberg himself provided a review of the neuropsychological literature, suggesting that reacquisition of language, after damage to the left hemisphere, was successful only in childhood. But this evidence showed only a possible critical period for the acquisition of language by the right hemisphere, and did not address the learning capacities of the intact brain over maturation.

The well-known study of Genie, conducted by Susan Curtiss and her colleagues (Curtiss, 1977), examined the acquisition of English by a girl who was deprived of linguistic exposure (and many other aspects of a normal human environment) until after puberty. In accord with Lenneberg's hypothesis, Genie did not acquire English syntax and morphology normally, even though she did succeed in learning a vocabulary.

Several studies have recently been conducted on deaf adults who were first exposed to American Sign Language (ASL) as their native language at ages ranging from birth to well past puberty (Emmorey, 1991; Mayberry & Fischer, 1989; Newport, 1990). Each of these studies has shown a decline in the ability to learn and process ASL syntax and morphology as the age of first exposure increases.

Finally, several studies have examined the acquisition of English as a second language by adults who were first exposed to it, through immersion in the United States, at ages ranging from 3 to 40 years (Johnson & Newport, 1989, 1991; Johnson, Shenkman, Newport, & Medin, 1996;

Krashen, Long, & Scarcella, 1982; Long, 1990; Oyama, 1978; Patkowski, 1980; Slavoff & Johnson, 1995). Again, each of these studies has shown a decline in the ability to control various aspects of English syntax and morphology as the age of first exposure increases.

These studies thus confirm Lenneberg's hypothesis of a critical period for learning language. In certain details, their results are different from those anticipated by Lenneberg. Human adult language learners do not totally fail to learn new languages. In fact, as any second-language learner knows, human adults are capable of learning quite a bit about a language late in life, and some adults are particularly talented at late-learned languages (Birdsong, 1992; Coppieters, 1987). It is thus perhaps more accurate to say that human language learning shows a sensitive, rather than a critical, period (although virtually every behavior displaying maturational changes in plasticity also shows them in a less-than-absolute form, so such a distinction may not be worth making). Nonetheless, these changes in the ability to learn languages over age are perfectly adequate for making the present point: Not every learning device acquires human languages; only some, with particular internal characteristics we cannot yet specify, are capable of learning languages as children do.

Learners Do Not Always Learn Their Input. Some of the best evidence for innate tendencies in human language learners comes from cases where the learners do not acquire the language to which they are exposed, but rather acquire a system that is structured more like a natural human language. Only tiny fragments of such a phenomenon appear in most language learning; in the ordinary case, children are exposed to a language governed by rules and patterns of the universal sort, and they acquire one that is pretty well indistinguishable from the one to which they were exposed. Under these circumstances, native instincts are hard to discern; a mechanism that had principles of its own, and one that more slavishly followed its input, would both arrive at the same outcome. Only rare but interesting childish errors (for example, the overproduction of rules like adding -ed to form the past tense of irregular verbs) give hint of the tendencies of learners to impose patterns of a particular type.

The more crucial cases for examining the innate tendencies of learners arise in circumstances where the input is not an ordinary human language. Suppose, in the extreme, that a human learner were exposed to well-formed Martian. That is, suppose that the input language did not observe or illustrate the principles universal to human languages. Under these circumstances, a learner natively endowed with tendencies to observe these principles should acquire a language with the properties universal to human languages nonetheless. Such an outcome would provide especially strong evidence for the existence of such innate tendencies, and might even help to articulate what these tendencies are.

Surprisingly, several phenomena with similarities to this scenario have come under empirical study in recent years. One such phenomenon has been claimed to occur in language *creolization* (Bickerton, 1981, 1984; Sankoff & Laberge, 1973). In cases where adult speakers regularly interact across mutually unintelligible languages, they may develop a simple pidgin, which borrows a limited vocabulary from one of the surrounding languages and forms sentences using a few word-order rules, or the differing rules of each of the surrounding languages. Pidgins are, by definition, no one's native language, and they do not display either the consistency or the grammatical complexity of any ordinary natural language. In a small number of cases, pidgin speakers marry, and the pidgin becomes the primary language to which their young children are exposed. Under these circumstances, the language acquired by the first generation of children is called a *creole;* the new term is coined because, it has been claimed, the language of this new generation is strikingly different in structure from the one from which it was formed. Unlike their antecedent pidgins, creole languages are both more consistent and more complex in grammar, and, over subsequent generations, may take on all the properties of ordinary natural languages. Bickerton (1984) and certain other creolists have suggested that these changes arise from the innate predispositions of child language learners. Unfortunately, however, the process of creolization has almost never been observed in progress (though see Sankoff & Laberge, 1973) and is typically reconstructed from the differences in speech among speakers of different ages many years later. Because both the pidgin and the creole arise in regions where large numbers of other languages are spoken, it is difficult to separate language innovation from language borrowing, and creolists often disagree about which of

these is most responsible for the structures that appear in the creole (see the commentary attached to Bickerton, 1984). Nonetheless, creolization studies provide exciting opportunities for empirical research on extraordinarily important cases of language acquisition.

Fortunately for researchers, phenomena like creolization (but without some of the complicating factors) have been found to arise much more commonly in individual deaf children learning signed languages, and even in large deaf communities. Most congenital deafness occurs within otherwise hearing families, where signed languages are typically not used by adult models; in these circumstances, deaf children may develop simple family "home sign" systems, which have some of the grammatical characteristics of early languages (see the earlier subsection, "Uniformity in the Course of Acquisition"). It is believed that full signed languages—for example, ASL (now used by deaf people throughout the United States)—developed spontaneously from these roots, when many deaf children were brought together by the establishment of schools and other organizations that created communities of signers (Fischer, 1978; Woodward, 1978). This process has occurred only recently in Nicaragua, where the creolization of Nicaraguan Sign Language has been observed and recorded by linguists and psycholinguists interested in language acquisition and linguistic structure (Kegl, Senghas, & Coppola, in press; Senghas, 1995). Senghas's landmark dissertation has shown that young deaf children entering this community over a period of 10 to 15 years have gradually added more complex linguistic structure to the community language, even though the input they received was much less grammaticized. Unlike spoken-language creoles, Nicaraguan Sign Language could not have borrowed its linguistic devices from surrounding languages. Because its users were isolated from oral Spanish by their deafness and illiteracy, the language could only have derived its linguistic complexity from the internal tendencies of its users themselves.

Singleton and Newport (1994; Newport, in press; Singleton, 1989) have also documented the acquisition and grammaticization of a signed language by a single child, whose input models they recorded and closely analyzed. The child they studied had deaf parents who used ASL, but who themselves had been exposed to ASL only during adulthood. Because they were late learners of ASL, the parents used only the simpler structures of the language, and used even these with great irregularity. No one else who knew ASL was available to provide additional input to the child. Despite this reduced and inconsistent input, their child acquired a more complex and highly structured form of ASL. Again, this creole-like phenomenon could only have occurred because of the tendency of children to learn languages of particular types.

Taken together, these occurrences of creolization and its relatives, in spoken and signed language communities around the world, provide striking evidence that children are highly biased learners. The acquisition of language is not a slavish reproduction of environmental forms; rather, it is the systematization and reorganization of these forms into patterns, according to the native tendencies of learners.

The Nature of an Innate Mechanism for Learning Languages

The various studies we have reviewed provide empirically detailed and theoretically powerful evidence for Part One of a nativist view of language development: There is indeed a significant contribution of innate factors to the acquisition of language. Because of these studies, some version of Chomsky's hypotheses about language and its acquisition has been accepted, at least in general outline, by most researchers in the field. Probably every student of language acknowledges that there are surprising commonalities among unrelated languages of the world, and that language acquisition takes place in humans, at least in part, because of innate predispositions. But there is, nonetheless, widespread disagreement on Part Two of the nativist question: *What* is innate, and *how* does innately guided learning occur?

The current state of the art provides surprisingly little evidence about the nature of what is innate in the acquisition of language. Because we know that children are capable of learning any language, as long as it conforms to human language principles, it cannot be the case that children innately know any particular language, or even any particular linguistic constructions. Rather, they must be prepared innately to learn languages of the proper kind. Chomsky has suggested that this is accomplished by the child's innately knowing what is universal about languages, and also knowing the dimensions along which languages may vary. But no empirical evidence has been provided that this is the best or only way to construe a nativist account of acquisition, and it is certainly not the only way biology

builds innately guided systems. Feasible (though relatively unarticulated) possibilities include learning mechanisms that do not "know" anything about linguistic universals and variation, but rather perceive, remember, or analyze linguistic input in ways that bias certain outcomes indirectly. As we have argued throughout this chapter, the business of nativist approaches to development is articulating and testing these alternatives.

Theories of Innately Guided Learning

What types of mechanisms are capable of accounting for these phenomena? Two important issues arise in moving toward a model of language acquisition. First, how does one account for the obvious and protracted changes in linguistic behavior over age? Are they an artifact of changing performance abilities, with an underlying continuity of fundamental capacities (as in the development of locomotion), or is there a genuine change, through maturation or learning, in the nature of linguistic capacities? Second, how does one reconcile the evidence for innate factors in the development of language with the obvious evidence for experiential sensitivity? What types of developmental mechanisms might a theorist invoke to account for both innate and experiential aspects of acquisition?

Continuity, Maturation, and Learning

If important innate factors account for the acquisition of language, why does the learner change so dramatically over a period of 4 to 5 years? Until recently, this question received little direct attention in the field. However, in the past few years, several positions have been offered on this issue.

One possibility, termed by Pinker (1984) the "continuity hypothesis," is that both the principles underlying linguistic knowledge and the mechanisms for learning particular languages are unchanging over development, and they constitute a continuous set of core or fundamental capacities that pertain throughout development. On this view, the changing appearance of linguistic behavior must arise from the content of what is learned over time. What is not entirely clear in this position is why the learning process should take so long or should show the recurrent stages that appear; presumably, these arise in large part because of the complexity of the linguistic details to be mastered, and the inherent grading of complexity across constructions.

(Other reasons might include developmental changes in the planning or production of speech itself; see Gerken, 1994, for discussion.) It is of interest to note that the continuity hypothesis is often adopted by researchers whose own view of language acquisition makes the learning of language-particular constructions a fairly trivial part of the acquisition process (see, for example, Hyams, 1986); but the protracted appearance of language in the young child would instead suggest that this learning process is quite significant, and therefore worthy of more attention in the research literature than it has received.

A second possibility is that there is substantial maturational change in some or all parts of the acquisition mechanism, analogous to the (partly) endogenous maturation of other aspects of biological growth. This could involve either maturation within a specific linguistic mechanism (Borer & Wexler, 1987; Chomsky, 1988), or the maturation of nonlinguistic abilities that alter the learning process as development progresses (Newport, 1990). The evidence cited above for a sensitive or critical period in language acquisition suggests that there is indeed a maturational decline, throughout the learning period (see as early as ages 4 to 6), in the ability to acquire a new language; whether there is maturational change during this time (or earlier) that affects the ongoing acquisition of a language encountered from birth remains to be investigated empirically.

Proposals for Integrating Nativism with Experiential Sensitivity

The major theoretical issue that pervades the literature on language acquisition, but has been the subject of surprisingly little empirical research, concerns the character of mechanisms for acquiring language that show both innate propensities and experiential sensitivity.

The best-known proposal on this topic is that of Chomsky (1965, 1981, 1988), who suggests that these two aspects of acquisition correspond to two (or perhaps three) underlying separate mechanisms. The innate restrictions in Chomsky's theory arise from an innate and domain-specific knowledge of the universal properties of linguistic systems. Human children are thought to know innately the primitives out of which languages are built (for example, such concepts as *noun, verb, subject, object*), and the principles by which they may combine to form sentences (for example, that word classes much combine in limited ways to form certain types of phrases; that phrases are always

structured with their major elements in either the first or last position; and that sentences are always comprised of the same phrase types). The experiential sensitivity in this proposal is provided by two other mechanisms: one that knows certain very limited parameters on which the innate principles may show variation (for example, whether the major elements of phrases are in the first or last position) and acquires the appropriate value from "triggering" linguistic input; and one, not described in this theory, that somehow acquires from input the much more variable aspects of languages (such as the particular words). Little research has been conducted on children's acquisition of languages to determine whether this type of proposal is an empirically correct description of development; rather, the main supporting research consists of extensive linguistic analyses of languages of the world (suggesting that they do indeed vary in parametric ways), and studies of acquisition that assume the theory as a framework and then investigate its application to particular languages.

As an alternative, a less well-developed literature suggests that language acquisition may be performed, at least in part, by more domain-general learning mechanisms. The difficulty for this approach lies in accounting for the particular and apparently innate characteristics of languages and their learning, which are stipulated as specific knowledge in the Chomskian proposal. A potential direction of this alternative literature, however, is that the innate characteristics of language learning may result from indirect biases inherent in the nature of children's learning. This literature thus raises an issue we have seen in our earlier discussion of perception: the possibility that nativist approaches can encompass not only genetically determined outcomes (which are in some ways like the Chomskian approach to language acquisition), but also outcomes that result from more indirect, but still innate, predispositions. Below, we review this literature in two parts, focusing first on models of statistical learning, and subsequently on potential sources from which predispositions, or biases, in such learning might be derived.

Connectionist Models and Statistical Learning. In recent literature, an approach to language acquisition called "statistical language learning" has arisen independently in many of the subfields studying natural language, including not only language acquisition, but also sentence processing and computational linguistics. The common influence for these developments is the prominence of connectionist models of language, and most especially the widely discussed connectionist model of the acquisition of the morpheme *-ed* (Rumelhart & McClelland, 1986) and its equally widely discussed critiques (Lachter & Bever, 1988; Pinker & Prince, 1988).

Rumelhart and McClelland's model of the acquisition of -ed took as its focus the question of whether a connectionist device, composed of interconnected units that stored in a superimposed fashion the thousands of tokens of past-tense forms of verbs in English, could succeed in acquiring a simulation of the "Add -ed" rule without explicitly acquiring a "rule." Their model argued (somewhat implicitly; this wording is ours) that the superimposed frequency of forms that end in -ed, distributed widely over verbs of English whose stems were quite variable, could form the basis for the learning of an apparent rule, and even for its overgeneralization during early stages of acquisition. Pinker and Prince (1988) subsequently argued convincingly that this simulation was accomplished incorrectly. It exploited a distribution of tokens that changed over the course of learning and contained at critical moments a frequency distribution uncharacteristic of actual language learners. In addition, Pinker and Prince (1988) and Lachter and Bever (1988) showed that the connectionist device in question contained within it architectural features that mimicked linguistic rule-learning mechanisms, and, where it did not, that it could not acquire the correct properties of natural languages. Rebuttals of these critiques, and rebuttals of the rebuttals, continue (Daugherty & Seidenberg, 1992; MacWhinney & Leinbach, 1991; Marcus et al., 1992; Marcus et al., 1995; Pinker, 1991; Plunkett & Marchman, 1991, 1993).

However one views the outcome of this interchange, it has provided important stimulation for rethinking the role of statistical information (including the frequency of word forms as well as more complex statistics, such as their co-occurrence or conditional probabilities) in the acquisition process. This is in fact an old issue; statistical descriptions of natural language structure (called "distributional analysis") formed the core of linguistics and psycholinguistics in the 1930s to the 1950s (Bloomfield, 1933; Harris, 1955; Miller, 1951), and critiques of this approach were the topic of Chomsky's earliest linguistic work (Chomsky, 1955, 1957). In the enthusiastic embracing of Chomsky's important critiques, however, the potential contributions of statistical information to the learning of languages have until recently been neglected. Recent studies of linguistic input taken from the CHILDES database (MacWhinney & Snow, 1990) have shown that the statistical features of input corpora may provide potentially rich information for the induction of grammatical categories and other linguistic structures (Brent, 1996; Finch & Chater, 1992; Mintz, 1996; Mintz, Newport, & Bever, 1995; Morgan, Shi, & Allopenna, 1995; Redington, Chater, & Finch, 1993; all of these studies follow up on important suggestions made by Maratsos & Chalkley, 1980). In addition, recent empirical studies of infants' and children's learning from input structured solely in terms of statistical information have shown that they are surprisingly adept at acquiring such information (Goodsitt, Morgan, & Kuhl, 1993; Morgan & Saffran, 1995; Saffran, Aslin, & Newport, 1996; Saffran, Newport, Aslin, Tunick, & Barrueco, 1997).

The problem for statistical approaches to language acquisition, noted by Chomsky (1955, 1957, 1988) and others from the 1950s to the present, concerns what might be called "the richness of the stimulus" (Gleitman & Newport, 1995; "the poverty of the stimulus problem," mentioned in earlier sections, is in some sense another way of stating the same difficulty). There is an infinite number of statistical computations that learners might in principle calculate over a body of environmental input. How do real learners hone in on just the right ones? Extant models of acquisition in a connectionist or statistical framework, when they work, are thus far built by hand-tailoring into the model just those computations that solve the problem under study; in this regard, they could be argued to instantiate domain-specific knowledge of linguistic principles (the position on acquisition they attempt to eschew). In the long run, a successful mechanism will need to incorporate just those procedures or architectures that are assumed to be involved in learning (and no others), and to make explicit claims about the nature of these limitations.

Moreover, how can we account for creolization and similar phenomena reviewed in earlier sections, which show that language learners often build a structure that is not represented in the input corpora from which they learn? Again, models either will have to stipulate innate linguistic constraints to solve such problems, or they will have to provide an account of the architectural features of a general learning device that produce the right outcomes.

In the next section, we consider some tentative directions in the search for limitations, biases, or architectural constraints that might provide solutions to these problems.

Inherent Biases in Learning.   Several proposals have suggested that the tendencies of language learners to develop universal features of linguistic systems may arise, at least in part, from inherent biases in the way young children learn seriated, patterned information, rather than from direct knowledge of the way languages must be organized. For example, Bever (1970) and Slobin (1973) suggested that learners may be subject to perceptual or memorial constraints on the encoding of sequential auditory information (for example, a greater ability to notice or remember the ends of units rather than their beginnings). Such constraints might result in the appearance, in languages of the world, of grammatical structures that accord with these constraints (for example, a more widespread appearance of suffixes than of prefixes in word formation rules). Newport (1988, 1990) and Elman (1993) have suggested that the processing limitations of young children in working memory may change the data to which they have access in language learning, and therefore may shape the character of the structures that can be acquired. Surprisingly, both investigators have shown that certain types of complex linguistic structures are learnable only when learners begin their acquisition processes in such limited states (Elman, 1993; Goldowsky & Newport, 1993). Newport has called this the "Less is More" hypothesis. More generally, Turkewitz and Kenny (1982) have hypothesized that many aspects of development may be shaped by the fact that altricial organisms begin learning during a period in which their capacities are particularly limited, and that the slow maturation of these capacities may provide a series of changing opportunities to be affected by selected aspects of experience.

Each of these proposals only hints at the possibility that innate constraints on language learning may arise from forces other than direct knowledge of linguistic principles; none is well enough articulated to account for the detailed structures and constraints that appear in linguistic theories. Nonetheless, the proposals may remind investigators of how little attention has been devoted to the range of ways in which innate factors may direct development, and may suggest directions in which further theorizing and empirical research should be pursued.

The Development of Language: Themes and Questions

The acquisition of language provides a somewhat different type of example for the discussion of nativist–empiricist issues than those we have seen thus far. For each of the other topics we discuss—the development of locomotion, depth and object perception, and spatial knowledge—there has been extensive empirical controversy about whether there is innate knowledge, what form it takes, and how it interacts with experience. Because in each of these arenas the core behaviors are in some clear and obvious ways uniform over members of our species, however, it is possible, at least in principle, to imagine how innate knowledge might organize the developmental process. In the domain of language, the clearest and most obvious fact is that there is diversity, and therefore that development in this arena must involve learning. Children exposed to French learn French, children exposed to Hindi learn Hindi, and children exposed to American Sign Language learn ASL, a communicative system that employs input and output media that are entirely different from those of French or Hindi. If there is a nativist account of the acquisition of language, it must involve a natively based *learning* mechanism, one that operates with equal ease on highly different types of environmental input. Our review of this literature has focused on illustrating the particular types of questions and issues that arise in considering nativist concerns in such a case.

Like the development of action, perception, and spatial knowledge, certain core abilities of humans for the perception of language appear to be shared with other species, and are evident as early in development as researchers have discovered how to test for them. Infants begin their acquisition of the sound systems of natural languages with auditory categories like those of other mammals. But unlike development in these other domains, language development is primarily about the enormous changes that occur from this initial state. With linguistic exposure, infants gradually diverge from nonhuman mammals, and acquire phonetic and grammatical systems that no other species displays. Nonetheless, the character of this experiential sensitivity suggests that innate factors are involved. Children acquire only certain types of languages, sometimes even when their environmental input is highly degraded. Language development thus exemplifies the fact that continuity is not the only form that behavioral domains influenced by innate factors might display; maturation and constrained learning—what

Marler (1991) calls an "instinct to learn"—can also be developmental courses that reveal nativist components.

The study of language acquisition also clearly demonstrates that nature–nurture questions have at least two distinct parts: First, is there a significant contribution of innate factors to the development of the capacity? Second, what is the character of the innate factors? Are the initial abilities that organize the domain particular to language, or are they more general? Is there innate "knowledge" of the structures of languages, or are there instead innate biases in the way the learning mechanism acquires whatever structures it is exposed to? Perhaps most important, how might one empirically distinguish these closely related alternatives from one another? These two parts to the nature–nurture question have not always been clearly distinguished, particularly in grammatical acquisition, where research has focused almost entirely on the first question and has sometimes confused an answer to this question with an answer to the second. In the long run, however, empirical answers are needed for both of these sets of questions.

We believe a further point is illustrated by this field. In our discussion of perceptual development, we noted that innateness is not the same as genetic determinism, and we described cases in which neural circuitry might arise from indirect (though still innate) internal mechanisms, rather than from direct genetic specification. A related issue runs through the literature on language acquisition. As we have described, nativist accounts in this field take either of two forms. One hypothesizes that there is direct stipulation of the possible languages that children can learn, and the other hypothesizes that there may be constraints on learning and these constraints more indirectly lead to these outcomes. These alternatives exemplify two different ways that biology may build developing systems. Our best current understanding of development in other species and for other domains is that the ways in which organisms acquire their species-typical behaviors varies. In some cases, particular developmental outcomes are prespecified in some detail and in terms of representations specific to the domain. One well-known example is the acquisition of song in sparrows. Sparrows are thought to enter the learning environment with an innate template of their species song, and to use this template both to select the stimuli from which they learn and to organize the aspects of these stimuli which are acquired (Marler, 1970, 1991). In contrast, in other cases, particular outcomes are achieved through combining more general perceptual biases or tendencies with dependable species-typical experiences from which the biased organism will learn. An example of this type of alternative appears in accounts of imprinting (Bateson, 1979; Hess, 1973). Ducks and birds begin their learning with an innate propensity to follow moving objects, a set of preferences for the stimuli they will follow (e.g., a sphere is preferred to other shapes), and maturational limits both on when they start to locomote (which begins the critical period) and when they begin to fear novel objects (which ends the critical period). In a natural environment, these biases and tendencies will result in early imprinting to species members, without an initial innate representation of the species. Given these two different types of innately guided development in other organisms, it is sensible to expect that either of these two methods might underlie the development of biologically significant behaviors in humans as well, and that empirical debate between comparable alternatives in the acquisition of language is the sign of healthy science in progress.

Perhaps most important, recent findings in language acquisition suggest at least the beginnings of answers to these questions. It is often argued that nativist accounts are nonexplanatory, and that, by labeling a phenomenon "innate," they serve only to deter empirical investigations into how the capacity is acquired. (The other half of this argument is, of course, that empiricist accounts are therefore preferable, even if the truth is not yet known.) The study of language development, however, provides particularly instructive examples of how empirical findings may inform nativist accounts. Over the past 25 years, new findings have led one type of nativist explanation to be modified into another that is equally nativist but quite different. In the case of speech perception, claims of an innate, species-specific sensitivity to the sounds of language have been replaced by claims of an innate, species-general sensitivity to certain kinds of auditory patterns. In the case of syntax, claims of innate knowledge of grammatical principles now vie with claims of innate predispositions to discover or impose certain kinds of patterns on input data. Rather than bringing empirical investigation to a halt, nativist arguments in language acquisition have provided inspiration to a remarkable range of empirical enterprises, and have given us a new understanding of both the plasticity and the inflexibility of the human capacity to learn. What remains for future work is to clarify the types of mechanisms that might underlie this capacity, and to provide further empirical evidence indicating which of these mechanisms has evolved in human infants to subserve the acquisition of communicative systems.

ABSTRACT KNOWLEDGE: SPACE

Conceptual knowledge is a vast topic, comprising knowledge of categories of objects such as animals or artifacts, events and routines such as school days or picnics, the material world and its behavior, people and their actions, and abstract entities and relations such as number or ownership. We discuss just one content domain within the last category: spatial knowledge. We focus on this example because spatial knowledge has been studied at many levels, from tacit knowledge of the environmental layout to explicit knowledge of formal geometry, and because the development of this knowledge has been a central topic within the nativist–empiricist dialogue from classical times to the present day.

Geometrical knowledge presents a challenge to any naturalist. The objects of Euclidean geometry—dimensionless points, lines of infinite extent and no thickness—cannot be perceived by any biological system. At the base of Euclidean geometry, moreover, are propositions whose truth cannot be verified by experience or deduced from other verifiable propositions. Principles such as Euclid's fifth ("parallel") postulate cannot be proven true, and yet people who think about geometrical relations typically find them intuitively correct.

What are the sources of these intuitions? Socrates suggested that geometrical knowledge is innate in humans and is evoked through a process akin to recollection. He probed this process by conducting what may have been the first study of the development of geometrical knowledge. Plato (1961) recounts his famous interview of a young slave, which elicited geometrical knowledge (for example, knowledge that the area of a square quadruples when the length of a side doubles) purely by posing questions. Because the youth had never studied geometry, Socrates concluded that the knowledge revealed by his questioning was already present in the youth's mind.

Arguments for the innateness of geometric principles were extended as the nativist–empiricist dialogue progressed. Descartes (1641/1971c) considered how one comes to know that the three angles of any triangle together equal two right angles. Because such truths extend beyond concrete experience with any particular figures, Descartes concluded, "My mind is assuredly so constituted that I cannot but assent to them . . ." (p. 102). Kant (1781/1964) considered the origins of spatial knowledge by asking what kinds of creatures humans must be in order to gain such knowledge. Pure creatures of sensation, for whom the world evokes no ideas of space, time, or causality, could never come to conceive of a world with these properties, he reasoned. Experience, moreover, may bring knowledge of how the world *is* but not of how it *must necessarily be;* experience therefore cannot account for the intuition (e.g.) that the three inner angles of a triangle necessarily sum to 180°. Because humans do have knowledge of a spatially extended world, and because some of this knowledge has necessary force, some geometrical knowledge must be a priori.

Empiricist replies to these arguments resound through the dialogue. Arguments for the innateness of geometrical knowledge were challenged by Berkeley (1710/1975a), who denied that humans truly have such knowledge. When one talks of triangles, he suggested, the abstractness of this concept derives from the abstractness of the words used to describe experience. For Berkeley, the acquisition of human language therefore is central to the growth of ideas about space.

Helmholtz later challenged Kant's argument that humans have a priori knowledge of Euclidean geometry by appealing to developments in mathematics and physics that began shortly after Kant's writing (see Hatfield, 1990). The discovery of a family of non-Euclidean geometries, based on a denial of Euclid's fifth postulate, showed that humans can construct systems of spatial representation in which this axiom does not hold. The later discovery that the universe is non-Euclidean showed that humans can even learn that their most basic geometrical intuitions are false. If it is possible to learn that the world is non-Euclidean, Helmholtz argued, then human "knowledge" of Euclidean geometry cannot be a priori. Why not suppose that humans initially learn to perceive and represent space in ways that give rise to Euclidean intuitions?

Like Socrates, Helmholtz viewed this last possibility as an empirical hypothesis: If one could find a way to raise a child in a strongly non-Euclidean environment, one could test whether the child developed geometrical intuitions in accord with Euclid's fifth postulate. Although this experiment is neither practically nor ethically possible, studies of animals and children reared in natural environments have shed considerable light on the normal development of spatial knowledge. We begin with the development of the basic representations underlying navigation and object localization. Then we consider the development of abilities to represent space through two symbolic systems: language and maps. Finally, we discuss the development of the explicit geometrical intuitions whose sources have so intrigued contributors to the nativist–empiricist dialogue.

Spatial Representations for Navigation

Any animal with a stable home must find its way homeward after venturing out to locate food, secure a mate, or defend its territory. Species as diverse as ants, geese, rats, and humans solve this problem, in part, by representing the direction and extent of their locomotion and computing their changing position relative to home. This process of "path integration" (Mittelstaedt & Mittelstaedt, 1980; Muller & Wehner, 1988) or "dead reckoning" (Gallistel, 1990; McNaughton, Knierim, & Wilson, 1995) allows an animal to return home directly from any point in its travels, in the absence of visible landmarks. Dead-reckoning is subject to errors that accumulate over time, however, and require correction through some other process. Most animals correct these errors and reorient themselves by drawing on representations of the environment. We consider each of these processes in turn.

Dead Reckoning

Dead-reckoning abilities testify to perhaps the most basic of spatial representations and computations: the representation of where one is and how one's position changes as one moves. Both the existence and the nature of this representation have been investigated in desert ants, who search for food by traveling from the nest on tortuous paths and then return home directly from a distance of 100 meters or more (Wehner & Srinivasan, 1981). Displacement experiments in which the ants are taken from the nest and released at different points within their territory indicate that they cannot reliably find the nest by perceptual cues, for they wander at random when released further than about 2 meters away (Wehner & Flatt, 1972). Foraging ants therefore must rely on an internal representation of the nest's distance and direction, and so further experiments

tested the precision of this representation. In one series of studies, ants walked freely from the nest to a food source and then were carried to new terrain before beginning their homeward march. The ants moved on a straight path of nearly the same distance and direction as the path that would have led them home had they not been displaced, testifying to a strikingly accurate representation of the nest's location (Wehner & Srinivasan, 1981; see also Muller & Wehner, 1988).

Desert ants are remarkable because their navigation depends on dead reckoning almost exclusively. As we will see in later sections, birds and mammals are more influenced by perceptible landmarks when they navigate and search for objects. Nevertheless, all mobile animals appear to be capable of dead reckoning (see Gallistel, 1990, chapter 4, for a sweeping review of the relevant evidence). For example, rodents have been shown to navigate by dead reckoning in the dark, when perceptible cues to the nest's location are minimized (Etienne, 1987; Mittelstaedt & Mittelstaedt, 1980). Indeed, dead reckoning sometimes overrides immediate perceptual information for the nest location. If a female rodent's nest is moved, she will go to its reckoned position even if her young nestlings plainly can be heard at the new location (Mittelstaedt & Mittelstaedt, 1980).

How does the dead reckoning system develop? Do animals learn, by trial and error, the relation among their current position, current velocity, and resulting position? As far as we know, this question has been addressed experimentally only in avian species, who appear to develop dead-reckoning abilities after minimal locomotor experience. St. Paul (1982) led young alpine geese, who had never left the vicinity of their nest, to a location on the far side of a mountain, where she released them. Most of the goslings took off in the direction of home, on a path that deviated considerably from the circuitous path by which they had arrived. Further experiments involving invisible displacements of the geese (similar in logic to Wehner's displacement experiments with ants) showed that they were not guided by perceptible landmarks in choosing their homeward direction but rather by an internal representation of the home direction that they, like ants, updated as they moved through the layout. Because this representation was computed by goslings who had never previously left the home area, we may conclude that geese do not learn to dead reckon by trial and error. Laboratory studies of 2-day-old chicks, who show appropriate navigation toward an unseen object on the very first trial of a detour experiment, support the same conclusion (Regolin et al., 1995b).[4]

The dead-reckoning abilities of insects and birds are surprising from the perspective of human cognition, for human adults often have trouble determining their position in the larger spatial layout, and nautical navigators spend many years learning to make such calculations explicitly (see Gallistel, 1990, Chapter 3; and Gladwin, 1970). From a different perspective, however, the existence of an early-developing system for dead reckoning should be expected, because such a system is essential for the survival of any animal that forages beyond the bounds of the environment that is immediately perceptible from home. If animals had to learn to dead reckon by trial-and-error wanderings, it is unlikely that many would survive their first journey. Mechanisms for representing one's current position relative to home, and for updating this representation over motion, are an ecological necessity.

Does a system for dead reckoning exist in humans at the time children begin to locomote? The limited research directed to this question suggests that it does. In a study that resembled experiments with ants (Muller & Wehner, 1988), adults and children (aged 2.5 to 3.5 years) were blindfolded and then were walked on linear paths between a starting position and three other locations. Then they were walked from the starting position to one of the other positions and were encouraged to walk to a third position (Landau, Gleitman, & Spelke, 1981). Both the children and the adults performed this task with above-chance accuracy. Indeed, children were no less accurate on the new paths than on the paths on which they had been trained, suggesting that their errors stemmed from limitations on locomotor performance, not from errors in the dead-reckoning computation itself. Nevertheless, children's and adults' accuracy was not as high as that of ants, and further studies have revealed that errors in dead reckoning can be considerable (Loomis

et al., 1993; Newcombe, Huttenlocher, Drummey, & Wiley, 1997).[5] Dead reckoning by adults is quite accurate, however, under certain conditions (e.g., Fukusima, Loomis, & Da Silva, in press).

Repeated testing of a congenitally blind child between the ages of 2.5 and 4 years revealed the same abilities found in sighted children and in other animals. After walking away from a single location on two linear paths, the child returned to that location on a more direct path. As in the case of ants, displacement experiments indicated that the child wandered helplessly and randomly when she was passively lifted and placed at a given location in the room (Landau, Spelke, & Gleitman, 1984). This finding provides evidence that the child's active navigation was not guided by detectable landmarks in the room, contrary to the suggestions of some investigators (Liben, 1988; Millar, 1994). Like sighted children and other animals, the child evidently represented the changing egocentric distances and directions of locations in the room as she locomoted actively. Human children's dead reckoning therefore can survive certain forms of perceptual deprivation. Nevertheless, not all blind people adeptly use this system of spatial representation (see Thinus-Blanc & Gaunet, 1997, for review). Because 2.5-year-old children have walked independently for well over a year, Landau's experiments were consistent with the possibility that locomotor experience underlies the development of dead reckoning.

Further research with younger children has addressed this possibility (Bremner, Knowles, & Andreasen, 1994; Keating, McKenzie, & Day, 1986; Lepecq & Lafaite, 1989; Rieser, 1979). Lepecq and Lafaite (1989) investigated the dead-reckoning abilities of 7- to 19-month old infants during

---

[4] Although the dead-reckoning system appears to develop without trial-and-error learning during large-scale navigation, it remains possible that it is calibrated by experience gained during small-scale travels around the nest area (see McNaughton et al., 1994). In addition, perceptual experience may serve to calibrate the perceptual systems that give input to the dead-reckoning system, at least in some species. In humans, for example, perception of the distance and direction of one's locomotion can be altered through adaptation experiments in which the normal relation between forward locomotion and optical flow is changed (Rieser, 1990).

[5] The experiments of Landau et al. (1981) and of Loomis et al. (1993) differed from that of Muller and Wehner (1988) in certain respects. In particular, Landau tested children's dead reckoning among four locations rather than three, in a situation in which no single location had the priority that the nest may be presumed to have for an ant. In addition, human subjects were tested in a situation lacking any clear perceptual cues to direction; ants rely heavily on directional information from the sun or wind in computing changes in direction and holding a course while returning home. Either of these differences may account for the lower accuracy of human performance. In particular, the absence of a perceptible directional signal may explain why children's paths in Landau et al.'s (1981) experiments were not straight (cf. Millar, 1988).

a continuous, passive rotation in a featureless, cylindrical environment. Children's ability to keep track of their displacement in this environment was inferred from their ability to turn their heads in the direction in which a visible and audible event had previously appeared. Beginning at 11 months, infants showed reliable head orientation in the appropriate direction, providing evidence that they were able to keep track of their own facing position despite the passive turning. Although younger infants failed this task, they have succeeded at similar tasks in more structured environments (e.g., McKenzie, Day, & Ihsen, 1984).

The findings described above have met with considerable skepticism among developmental psychologists, for they make no sense if one believes that spatial knowledge is wholly constructed as the child locomotes (Liben, 1988; Millar, 1994). From a comparative perspective, however, the conclusion that children represent their own position in space at the beginning of locomotion, and that they update this representation as they move around, is not improbable but expected. In the hunter–gatherer societies that existed throughout most of human evolution, our ancestors were central-place foragers, like ants and rodents, and could ill afford to become lost during their long travels from home in search of food. Comparative studies and evolutionary considerations therefore converge with developmental studies to suggest that humans are biologically predisposed to represent their changing position in the layout. This representational capacity emerges early in development, either synchronous with or in anticipation of the development of the navigation performance that it subserves.

As with all the other developmental phenomena that we have considered, the existence of an early-developing dead-reckoning system does not imply that this system is impervious to later experience. Indeed, studies in cognitive anthropology suggest that experience has considerable effect on the extent to which people rely on dead reckoning. Many adults in industrialized societies appear to maintain little or no sense of orientation as they travel, finding their way through the environment by memorizing routes or landmarks. In contrast, people who live in societies lacking maps, street signs, or extensive means of passive transport often rely strongly on dead reckoning to maintain their sense of where they are in relation to distant, significant locations, even when they travel in novel or relatively featureless environments (e.g., Gladwin, 1970; Levinson, in press; Lewis, 1976). Although a dead-reckoning system appears to be present in all people, the extent to which this

system is used may vary greatly, depending on one's culture and experience.

Reorienting

As we noted, dead reckoning is subject to cumulative errors. Birds and mammals correct errors in their reckoned position by drawing on representations of the environmental layout. Evidence both for dead reckoning and for reorientation in accord with the perceptible environment has been provided by research with hamsters (Etienne, 1987), which learned to find food by traveling from a home nest at the edge of a circular arena to the center of the arena, from which they carried the food back to the nest. On a series of test trials, the arena and nest were rotated after the animal's outward journey, so that the direction of home specified by dead reckoning conflicted with its direction within the environmental layout. When these test trials were given in darkness, the animals carried food in the direction specified by their own path of travel, guided by dead reckoning. When the rotation occurred in a lighted environment with a wealth of visual information for the nest's geocentric direction, the animals carried food in the direction specified by the visible environment. This finding suggests that visual information for the environmental layout served to recalibrate the animal's dead-reckoning.

Further experiments have revealed that rats reorient themselves in accord with the shape of the surrounding layout but not with its nongeometric properties (Cheng, 1986; Margules & Gallistel, 1988). If a rat is disoriented in a rectangular room with distinctive odors and patterns at each corner, it uses the shape of the room to reorient up to a 180° ambiguity, but it does not use smells or patterns in the room to resolve this ambiguity. Reorientation in accord with the shape of the environment is highly effective in natural settings, because this information is least likely to change over time. Although the locations of odors and the colors and textures of the terrain often are variable, the shape of the spatial layout—its hills, valleys, and ravines—remains constant through an animal's lifetime. A predisposition to reorient by geometry therefore may maximize the chance that animals will determine their position reliably.

Rats also reorient preferentially in accord with stable features of the environment. In experiments by Biegler and Morris (1993; see also Etienne, Lambert, Reverdin, & Teroni, 1993; Knierim, Kudrimoti, & McNaughton, 1995), rats searched for food that was buried in a chamber in a constant geometric relation to two landmarks. In different conditions, the landmarks either occupied constant locations in the room or they moved together from trial to trial. Rats learned to find the food in the condition with stable landmarks. In the condition with movable landmarks, however, they learned to search near the landmarks but not at the correct location. Reorientation in accord with stable, geometric information also occurs in 12-day-old chicks, although chicks do not rely on geometric information as exclusively as do rats (Vallortigara, Zanforlin, & Pasti, 1990).

In light of these findings, we may ask whether humans also possess a system for reorienting in accord with the most stable, geometric information, and if so, how this system develops. Although considerations of evolution and ecology suggest that the system found in birds and rats might exist in humans, the experiences of many adults suggest otherwise. Adults in Western industrialized societies who are disoriented in a known environment (for example, upon emerging from a subway in a familiar city) may reorient by drawing on nongeometric information that no rat could use, such as the pattern on a building or the name on a street sign. Human adults therefore may reorient quite differently from adult birds and rats.

Studies of the development of reorientation in human children offer a resolution to these conflicting suggestions (Hermer & Spelke, 1994, 1996). Hermer investigated the reorientation processes of 18- to 24-month-old children in a situation much like that used with rats. The children watched a favored object being hidden in a corner of a rectangular room, then were disoriented by being lifted and turned with eyes covered, and finally were allowed to reorient and find the object. Children searched with high and equal frequency at the object's location and at the geometrically equivalent opposite location, despite the presence of nongeometric landmarks that distinguished these locations. Like rats, young children appear to possess a basic system for reorienting in accord with the shape of the environmental layout.

Although rats and children fail to reorient in accord with nongeometric information, experiments have shown that both rats and children detect, remember, and use nongeometric information for other purposes. For example, young children use the distinctive coloring and patterning of a container to locate a hidden object when the container moves, but they do not use the same properties to reorient themselves when the container is stable (Hermer & Spelke, 1996). These contrasting findings suggest that reorientation depends on a system that is task-specific (that is, it

functions only to guide reorientation) and informationally encapsulated (that is, it operates on a subset of the information that the child detects and remembers). Because task specificity and informational encapsulation are central features of modular systems (Fodor, 1983), these findings support Cheng and Gallistel's suggestion that reorientation depends on a "geometric module" (Cheng, 1986; Gallistel, 1990).

To date, research has not probed the developmental processes underlying the emergence of reorientation abilities in children or in other animals. Because the laboratory animals and American children in these studies have not spent their lives in outdoor environments where hills and valleys uniquely specify object positions, but rather in rectangular environments where many symmetries make geometry-based reorientation prone to error, it is likely that this process has been shaped more by evolutionary history than by learning. Nevertheless, such plausibility arguments are no substitute for research. Studies of precocial animals or dark-reared rats, parallel to Gibson and Walk's studies of the visual cliff, may shed significant light on this question.

Unlike rats and young children, human adults can use a nongeometric landmark to locate a hidden object in Hermer's tasks. Their superior performance suggests that some of the limitations of the child's reorientation system are overcome during development. Nevertheless, adults continue to reorient by geometric information, and their ability to do so may depend on a more basic, robust process than their ability to reorient by nongeometric information. Hermer, Spelke, and Nadel (1995) tested adults in a reorientation task while they engaged in a simultaneous interference task in which they attended continuously to a spoken text and repeated what they heard. These participants, like children and rats, reoriented in accord with the shape of the layout but not its nongeometric properties. A basic process for representing one's own position in relation to the stable shape of the layout appears to emerge by the age of 18 months, if not earlier, and to persist throughout human life. With development, however, children may overcome the central limitations of their encapsulated reorientation system.

Representing Object Locations

In addition to representing their own position in the environment, humans and other animals represent the positions of objects. Representations of object positions relative to the self ("egocentric" representations) guide actions such as reaching, and representations of object positions relative to other objects or to the larger layout ("allocentric" representations) guide navigation and object localization from novel points of observation.

A large variety of birds and mammals use allocentric representations in preference to egocentric representations when they attempt to locate hidden objects. Perhaps the most striking demonstrations of allocentric representations come from studies of food-storing birds (see Krebs, Hilton, & Healy, 1990, for review). Observations and experiments reveal that such birds retrieve food that they previously buried in thousands of caches by drawing on memories of the locations of the caches relative to a geometric configuration of landmarks—a classic example of an allocentric representation (e.g., Vander Wall, 1982). In rats, the priority of allocentric over egocentric representations has been demonstrated in experiments that compared the animals' ability to learn to find a hidden object whose location was specified either allocentrically or egocentrically. One experiment (Sutherland & Dyck, 1984) was based on the finding that rats submerged in a cylindrical tank of water containing a hidden platform will seek to escape from the water by climbing on the platform (Morris, 1981). In different conditions of the experiment, the platform was hidden either at a constant allocentric position within the tank or at a constant egocentric position. Although rats quickly learned to find the platform when its allocentric position was stable, they were slower to learn to locate the egocentrically specified platform and never learned to swim to it directly. In this situation and others (e.g., Montgomery, 1952; Olton & Samuelson, 1976; Tolman, 1948), adult rats appear predisposed to represent object locations in allocentric coordinates.

Developmental experiments reveal that the ability to represent the allocentric position of a hidden object emerges at about the same time that rats begin actively to explore environments, at about 3 to 4 weeks of age. Exploration emerges quite abruptly at this time, suggesting that its emergence depends in part on a maturational change in the animals, possibly timed to the onset of weaning (Nadel, 1990).

Like rats, human infants represent both the egocentric and the allocentric positions of objects (e.g., Keating et al., 1986; McKenzie et al., 1984; Rieser, 1979). In experiments by McKenzie et al. (1984), for example, 6- and 8-month-old children learned to look toward a given allocentric location from two different facing positions. When they were subsequently rotated to a novel facing position, the infants turned in a novel egocentric direction so as to look for the event at a constant allocentric position. When infants are trained to localize an object from just one starting position, however, their performance contrasts with that of rats and shows no preference for allocentric representations. For example, Acredolo (1978) trained 6-, 11-, and 16-month-old infants to anticipate, on hearing a bell, that a person would appear in a particular spatial location. When the children were turned to face in the opposite direction and the bell sounded, nearly all the youngest children looked in the familiar egocentric direction to a new allocentric position. Egocentric responding continued to occur at the older ages, although its frequency declined with age. This research suggests a developmental shift, over the first 2 years, from preferential reliance on egocentric spatial representations to preferential reliance on allocentric representations.

Numerous experiments have investigated the factors that influence young children's choice of reference systems (see Acredolo, 1990, for review and discussion). Egocentric behavior increases when children perform the same response repeatedly (Bremner & Bryant, 1977), move passively from one location to another (e.g., Acredolo, Adams, & Goodwin, 1984), or are tested in a symmetrical environment (Keating et al., 1986). A developmental increase in reliance on allocentric representations coincides with the onset of independent walking (Acredolo, 1990; Bertenthal, Campos, & Barrett, 1984) and is enhanced by experience in a walker (Bertenthal & Campos, 1990). Because prelocomotor infants already have the ability to form allocentric representations, however, this ability evidently does not depend wholly on the experiences children gain by moving actively through the layout.

Spatial Language

Language gives children the means to talk about space. Terms such as "left of" and "north of" capture the spatial relationship between two objects in egocentric and allocentric coordinates, respectively, and terms such as "in" and "on" capture such relationships in object-centered coordinates. It has been suggested that spatial language has universal properties, including a restricted vocabulary capturing qualitative relationships between the major axes of objects but ignoring spatial details of the objects or metric properties of the spatial relation. For example, English has terms such as "across" and "near," but no language appears to have terms that might be translated as "across a cylindrical object" or "less than one inch away from an object" (Talmy, 1983; see also Bloom, Peterson, Nadel, & Garrett, 1996; Landau & Jackendoff, 1993). Despite these universals, languages also differ in the ways they capture certain spatial relationships, and some investigators have suggested that these differences influence a speaker's nonverbal spatial representations (Choi & Bowerman, 1991; Levinson, 1996). The latter claim resonates with empiricist theses, suggesting that spatial representations are changed by the experience of learning a language and therefore can differ across different cultures. Here, we focus on research supporting the empiricist perspective.

Consider first how languages represent the spatial relationship between two horizontally separated objects. In languages such as English, this relationship of one object to the other is described most often by the egocentric terms "left," "right," "front," and "back" (e.g., "The ball is in front of the tree"). In a number of languages indigenous to Australia, Central America, and Asia, in contrast, horizontal configurations of objects are described most often by geocentric terms similar to "north" and "east" (e.g., "The rock is south of the tree"; Levinson, 1996). As Levinson has pointed out, each of these systems has advantages and disadvantages. A compass-point system has the virtue of assigning invariant spatial terms to any objects whose positions do not change, irrespective of the viewpoints of speakers and listeners, and a left–right system has the virtue of assigning invariant terms to anything that moves with the reference object (e.g., "my left arm") (see Levelt, 1989, for further discussion).

Recent research by Levinson and his collaborators has shown that these differences affect how people remember and act on spatial relationships. When speakers of a compass-point language gesture, for example, their gestures tend to preserve geocentric directions of motion, whereas the gestures of speakers of left–right languages tend to preserve egocentric relations (Haviland, 1992). Speakers of the two kinds of languages also perform in systematically different ways when they must reproduce the positions of objects from novel viewpoints. Speakers of compass-point languages tend to perform such tasks by preserving compass-point relations, whereas speakers of egocentric languages like English tend to preserve egocentric directions (see Levinson,

1996, for review). Finally, speakers of a compass-point language may rely on dead reckoning more than speakers of a left–right language, maintaining their orientation in the absence of focused attention or strong perceptual support (Levinson, in press). Nevertheless, Levinson notes that speakers of both kinds of languages understand both sets of geometric relations. This observation suggests that the same representational abilities are present in all people, and that language highlights a subset of these representations.

A more radical effect of language on spatial representation has been suggested by Hermer (1994; see also Spelke & Tsivkin, in press), based on her studies of reorientation. Recall that young children reorient themselves only in accord with the stable, geometric properties of their surroundings, whereas adults rely on a wealth of nongeometric information. Hermer suggested that adults' more flexible performance may depend on the acquisition of spatial language, which provides a medium of representation in which information from distinct, encapsulated systems can be combined. When a child learns expressions such as "left of" by mapping words to a set of spatial representations, and terms such as "truck" by mapping words to a set of object representations, the child may gain the ability to conjoin these terms to create representations such as "left of the truck." These new representations, in turn, may guide the disoriented adult's search for objects. If Hermer's hypothesis is correct, then there may be a grain of truth to Berkeley's proposal that geometrical knowledge depends on language. The acquisition of a specific language may permit the development of certain new representations that conjoin information from initially modular systems. To date, however, no evidence bears directly on this hypothesis.

Although research on language and spatial representation has hardly begun, the above studies suggest a picture of the nature and development of spatial representation and of its universal and variable features across cultures (see especially Bloom et al., 1996; Bowerman & Levinson, in press). All people appear to be born with the same propensities to develop a set of representations of space: task-specific egocentric and allocentric representations that capture specific properties of the environment and that serve to locate the self or other objects. Spatial language has universal properties, both because of the universal properties of language itself and because children only learn words for spatial relationships that they can represent (Landau & Jackendoff, 1993; Talmy, 1983). Despite these universals, each language captures only a subset of the spatial relationships that are represented by preverbal children. Where different languages capture different subsets of relations, speakers of those languages may differ in the prominence they assign to different spatial relations and in their abilities to represent conjunctions of spatial and nonspatial information. Communication between speakers of different languages initially may go awry as each interprets the behavior of the other in terms of the relations privileged by his or her own language. At bottom, however, all speakers build their representations of the environment from the same set of core systems.

Making and Understanding Maps and Models

The human species is unique not only in its ability to use language to represent space but also in its ability to construct and use maps and models of the environment. Like spatial language, children's use of maps develops gradually, well after they begin to navigate and represent the positions of themselves and of objects. Here, we discuss only one part of the large literature on the developing use of maps and other spatial representations; we focus on children's emerging understanding of these representations (see Liben, 1988, for a more complete review).

Experiments by DeLoache provide evidence for a striking developmental change in young children's understanding of scale models (see DeLoache & Burns, 1993, for review). Beginning at about 3 years of age, children are able to locate an object that is hidden in a room after viewing the corresponding location of a miniature replica of the object in a scale model of the room. Younger children do not benefit from a scale model in searching for an object. After watching the hiding of a miniature object in a scale model of a room, for example, young children find it much easier to find the miniature object hidden in the model than to find the real object hidden in the room (DeLoache, 1987).

Why do scale models pose difficulties for young children? One possibility is that geometric transformations, such as the change in size from a large room to a smaller-scale model, are problematic for children: Children may fail to detect the spatial relations that are invariant over these changes. A different possibility is that children detect the relevant geometric invariants but fail to understand that a model is a representation that provides information about the environment.

An ingenious study by DeLoache, Miller, Rosengren, and Bogart (1993; see also DeLoache, 1995) tested these two possibilities by presenting young children with a task whose solution required the detection of the same geometric invariants as in the scale model task but required no understanding of models as representations. Children were introduced to a machine that was said to make things smaller, and the shrinking machine's abilities were demonstrated on a toy. Then the children were shown a full-size room in which the toy was hidden, they were told that the machine would shrink the room and toy, and finally they were shown the scale model, which was described as the shrunken room. In these circumstances, children readily found the hidden object in the model. Because this task preserved the geometric component of the original task but removed the symbolic component (i.e., children were led to view the model as a transformation rather than a representation of the room), children's success suggests that their difficulty with models stems from limits on their understanding of representations, not limits on their sensitivity to geometric invariants.

DeLoache's experiment illustrates how studies addressing focused versions of the questions central to the nativist–empiricist dialogue, probing both the capacities that emerge as children begin to use maps successfully and the capacities that exist prior to this development, shed light on the nature of the processes by which children develop an understanding of spatial representations. Her research suggests that an understanding of representations undergoes developmental change in early childhood, but that an understanding of certain geometric transformations (similarity transformations in this case) predates this change. This finding opens the way to further study of the sources of older children's changing understanding and use of representations—a central ability that appears to separate humans from other animals.

Explicit Knowledge of Geometry

At the pinnacle of human spatial knowledge is explicit, statable knowledge of formal geometry. For most Western adults, this knowledge includes all the axioms and some of the theorems of three-dimensional Euclidean geometry, as well as some theorem-proving procedures from elementary logic. For some adults, knowledge extends to certain non-Euclidean geometries and higher-dimensional spaces. What are the sources of this knowledge: Does the 6-year-old child, who is unable to prove the simplest theorem of Euclidean geometry, nevertheless have the intuition that certain theorems are true? How do students extend their geometrical intuitions over the development of formal geometrical reasoning, and what causes these changes?

The experiment by Socrates can be viewed as an attempt to answer these questions. Socrates' experiment was limited in scope, however, and few investigators have followed in his path (although see Piaget, Inhelder, & Szeminska, 1960). Here, we consider one recent extension of Socrates' experiment: an interview study of the geometrical intuitions of 6- and 7-year-old children who, like the young slave, had received no training in geometry (Silberstein & Spelke, 1995).

Children were asked a series of questions designed to elicit their intuitions about points and lines. First, they were shown a rough sketch of a line segment with one dot on it and one dot off to the side, and they were asked to imagine that the segment represented a small part of a straight line that went on and on without turning and that was so thin it had no thickness. Children also were asked to imagine that the dots on the paper represented points so small that they too had no thickness. Children younger than 6 years did not appear to understand these requests and interpreted the questions as pertaining to physical markings on paper.[6] In contrast, 6- and 7-year-old children appeared to understand the requests and served as subjects in the full experiment.

Children first were asked a series of yes/no questions probing their intuitions about some of the central relations captured by Euclid's first four postulates. In accord with those postulates, children judged with near unanimity that two points could always be joined by a straight line, that three points sometimes could not, that many different straight lines could pass through a single point, and that only one line could pass through two distinct points. Children often paused and reflected before responding, but they answered with no prompting, no experimentation with objects or drawings, and no correction.

Because of the significance of Euclid's fifth postulate within the nativist–empiricist dialogue, further questions probed children's intuitions about parallel lines. Children were shown a sketch of two short, nonparallel, nonintersecting line segments, were told that each segment represented a

small part of a straight line of indefinite extent and no thickness, and were asked a series of questions about the extensions of these and other lines. Almost without exception, children judged that the two segments represented lines that would cross on the side where they were closer together, that some pairs of straight lines would never cross, and that no pairs of straight lines would cross more than once. Most children reported that if two lines never crossed and a third line crossed one of them, then it would cross the other line. Again, children typically reflected before answering these questions but then answered, with no prompting or further material aids, in accord with Euclid's fifth postulate.

In an additional part of the interview, children were asked questions about the behavior of lines on one type of non-Euclidean surface: a sphere. They were shown a ball on which a point and a line segment were roughly marked and were asked to imagine a line that continued on the spherical surface without turning. Then the children were asked the same questions about points and lines as for the line on the plane. (Note that in spherical geometry, many answers are different; in particular, all pairs of straight lines intersect twice.) About half the children were able to answer questions about lines on the sphere correctly, but they invariably manipulated the sphere and sometimes drew additional lines before answering. As Helmholtz would predict, children were able to gain knowledge of non-Euclidean spatial relationships by active manipulation of the sphere.[7] In line with the expectations of nativists from Socrates to Kant, however, this knowledge did not arise as readily as knowledge of the behavior of lines on the Euclidean plane.

The findings of these studies support Socrates' conclusion that some geometric intuitions can be attained by children without instruction. At the time when children first begin to communicate about geometric objects such as points and lines, they already share a number of the intuitions that are at the core of Euclidean geometry. Contrary to Socrates' radical suggestion that all geometric knowledge inheres in the human mind, however, the studies suggest that only a subset of our culturally sanctioned geometric knowledge is present prior to the onset of formal training in mathematics. Interestingly, this subset appears

---

[6] Young children's failure may stem from their inability to distinguish material from immaterial entities (see Carey, 1991; Keil, 1979; Smith, Carey, and Wiser, 1985).

[7] This conclusion is not certain, however, for children may have considered the marks on the sphere as circles in three-dimensional Euclidean space, rather than as straight lines in two-dimensional spherical space.

to include all of the axioms and some of the key theorems of Euclidean geometry as it was first formalized.

Silberstein's studies raise many questions about the origins and development of formal geometric knowledge. For example, where do the earliest intuitions about points and lines come from: Do they arise from experience perceiving and imagining and spatial layout, from navigation, or from some other source? What changes occurring at about 6 years of age allow children to talk about abstract geometric objects for the first time, and what later changes allow them to develop ways of extending and testing their geometrical knowledge by proving theorems? How do children develop new conceptions about the properties of points and lines, such as the properties of lines on a sphere? Finally, how do children or adults go beyond their Euclidean intuitions and come to understand that these are not inevitably true? As in the case of locomotion, depth perception, and language, the discovery of initial knowledge within a given cognitive domain does not close off inquiry into developmental change but rather focuses such questions and raises new ones.

Developing Knowledge of Space: Themes and Suggestions

The varied phenomena comprising the development of spatial knowledge illustrate each of the principal themes that emerged from earlier sections of this chapter: Like action and perception, spatial representation depends in part on abilities that emerge in anticipation of their function, that are constant over human development, and that are shared by other species. Like the development of perception and language, the development of spatial cognition appears to depend partly on maturational processes and partly on experience. In addition, studies suggest that initial spatial knowledge is the product of a set of relatively separable cognitive systems, and that developmental processes allow children to transcend the limits of these systems. We focus here on two of these themes—phylogenetic continuity and cognitive modularity—because they run counter to prevalent conceptions of human cognition and cognitive development.

Phylogenetic Continuity and Ecological Adaptedness

Studies of the development of spatially oriented behaviors such as navigation, reorientation, and object localization suggest striking commonalities between the representational capacities of humans and other animals. Although only humans make maps, talk about space, or codify their knowledge

into axiomatic systems, spatial knowledge appears to build in part on cognitive systems that other animals share. Uniquely human forms of spatial representation may arise not from some basic system possessed only by humans but from the distinctive ways in which humans elaborate on the systems of representation that they share with other animals.

We believe that evidence for common representational systems in humans and other animals should not be surprising, for two reasons. First, during human evolution, systems for representing the environment appear to have been subject to many of the same ecological demands as in other animals. Like ants, geese, and rats, for example, humans foraged by venturing from a persisting home, to which they needed to return. Second, human action systems and perceptual systems show deep homologies at all levels with those of other animals. In light of these homologies, it would be surprising if human and animal cognition should turn out to be built from radically different foundations.

Insofar as common representational systems exist in humans and other animals, studies of those systems can proceed in two directions. First, investigators can probe the cognitive capacities common to humans and other animals by bringing to bear a powerful array of converging tools—not only the tools of the cognitive psychologist and cognitive developmentalist, but also those of the behavioral ecologist and the neuroscientist. This convergence has led to striking progress in understanding of action and perception, and it is beginning to advance understanding of spatial cognition (see Gallistel, 1990; Krebs et al., 1990; McNaughton et al., 1995; O'Keefe & Nadel, 1978). Second, investigators can probe in more focused ways those aspects of spatial cognition that are unique to humans, by viewing our distinctive cognitive performance against a background of shared, phylogenetically older abilities. Like studies of locomotion and perception, studies of the representational capacities that are common to humans and other animals will allow investigators to define with greater clarity the ways in which human cognition goes beyond those capacities, yielding unique forms of reasoning.

Cognitive Modularity

Research on the development of spatial representation suggests that some early-developing systems of representation are task-specific and informationally encapsulated. The representations by which children reorient themselves, in particular, do not serve to relocate movable objects, and they capture only a subset of the information about the environmental layout that children perceive and remember. Early in development, human cognition does not appear to depend on a single, general-purpose system for intelligent learning but rather on a collection of more special-purpose cognitive systems. This collection of systems may provide the building blocks for human intelligence and cognitive development (see also Cosmides & Tooby, 1994).

If human knowledge of space begins with a set of separable, task-specific, and encapsulated cognitive systems, the later development of spatial knowledge shows an openness and flexibility that modular systems lack. The discovery by mathematicians and physicists of the non-Euclidean structure of the universe testifies most dramatically to humans' cognitive flexibility, but all humans show this flexibility in mundane ways by reorienting in accord with nongeometric information, talking about space, and drawing maps. Human children and adults evidently move "beyond modularity" in spatial reasoning, and transcend the limits to initial systems of knowledge (Karmiloff-Smith, 1992).

At the time of this writing, research supports only the most tentative suggestions concerning the processes that underlie these developmental changes. (See Carey & Spelke, 1994; Karmiloff-Smith, 1992; Rozin, 1976; and Spelke & Tsivkin, in press, for examples.) Nevertheless, studies of the ways in which children overcome the limits on their initial systems of knowledge may hold a key to understanding the highest, uniquely human forms of cognition. The most distinctive aspects of human cognition may not lie in the core systems of knowledge with which we are endowed, but rather in the processes by which we extend these knowledge systems beyond their initial bounds. The human penchant for extending knowledge by combining distinct cognitive systems may distinguish humans from other primates most clearly (see Gibson & Ingold, 1993), and it even may be responsible for the rapid and multifaceted changes in human cultures that evidently occurred over the past 50,000 years (Mithen, 1996). As others have suggested (Gopnik & Meltzoff, in press; Karmiloff-Smith, 1992), research on cognitive development in children, grounded in an understanding of children's initial systems of knowledge, may provide insights into the nature of these processes.

PERSPECTIVES ON THE DIALOGUE

In each of the domains we have examined, research arising from the nativist–empiricist dialogue provided insights into the sources of human knowledge. The outcomes of these inquiries are not always the same and indeed, we have selected these examples precisely because they shed somewhat different light on the questions of nativism and empiricism. Here, we briefly underline both the recurring and the unique points that we believe these examples offer.

Our current understanding of the development of action, perception, and spatial reasoning reveals several themes. In each of these arenas, human development appears to stem from a set of core capacities that emerge independently of experience and are constant over age and across species. In many cases, these early capacities appear to form the building blocks for later, more culturally specific skills. Although cognitive performance may change considerably over development in each of these domains, the striking continuity of the core abilities that underlie these changes suggests that biology plays a strong role in the growth of knowledge.

The development of language offers a somewhat different perspective on the same issues. Here, capacities are largely neither constant over age nor common across species; human communication systems are enormously different from those of other species and are acquired gradually, over a relatively lengthy period of human development. Nevertheless, the character of this species-specific and protracted acquisition process suggests additional ways in which innate propensities may emerge: through maturational processes, as well as through natively directed learning from experience. Innate capacities do not always appear in earliest development; as in the case of language acquisition, they may be revealed in remarkable capacities to learn, or even in the diminishing ability to learn over age. In this case, the relative independence of acquisition from striking variations in environmental input, the selectivity of what is learned, and the restriction of this learning to a maturationally significant period in development together provide evidence for an innate component to the developmental process.

Finally, research on perceptual development and language development offers particularly interesting examples of what the concept of innateness might mean. Shatz's (1992) elegant work on the development of neural connectivity in the visual system provides a case in which activity, and not genetic determination, shapes the course of development. The activity in question, however, is provided by processes internal to the organism, not by exposure to the visual world. This example demonstrates that nativism does not reduce to the more limited concept of genetic specification of a developmental product, but rather includes a variety of internal mechanisms that predispose development in certain directions, independently of external experience. Similarly, the effects of spatiotopic fanning and hysteresis in models of object perception, Turkewitz and Kenny's (1982) hypothesis of the developmental consequences of early perceptual limitations, and Newport's expansion of this proposal in the "Less is more" hypothesis for language learning all provide examples illustrating that innate predispositions may include a wide range of possibilities—both direct stipulative mechanisms and indirect ones.

Taken together, we believe that recent research in these four domains, as well as many others, presents a rich and complex picture of what can be learned by pursuing questions of innateness and learning. Rather than stifling investigation into the nature of development, the nativist–empiricist dialogue has provided engrossing topics for the scientific study of human knowledge and its acquisition. In light of this progress, one might expect treatments of this dialogue to figure prominently in current discussions of human development. Contrary to this expectation, the nativist–empiricist dialogue has become nearly anathema in contemporary psychology.

Arguments against Nativism

In this section, we explore some of the reasons that are offered for rejecting this dialogue. Because most arguments against the dialogue have been directed against the nativist side, our discussion begins with arguments against nativism. We discuss six widely cited reasons for rejecting nativist claims in developmental psychology. According to these arguments, nativism is (a) conceptually incoherent, (b) empty, (c) unparsimonious, (d) false, (e) denying of human flexibility and potential, or (f) socially and politically dangerous. After examining these arguments and finding none of them compelling, we turn to positive reasons for pursuing research that is guided by the assumption that ground the nativist–empiricist dialogue.

Nativism Is Incoherent

It is commonly argued that both nativist and empiricist claims are incoherent, because all phenotypic characteristics, including the mechanisms underlying behavior, are products of genes and environment. There is no such thing as a genetically determined characteristic or behavior, be-

cause the genome is inert in the absence of an appropriate biochemical environment to activate particular genes in particular spatiotemporal patterns. All biological characteristics therefore depend on indissociable interactions between genes and their surroundings (see Elman et al., 1996; Lehrman, 1970; Oyama, 1985; Thelen & Smith, 1994).

Contrary to this argument, research on gene–environment interactions is irrelevant to the nativist–empiricist dialogue on one reading of the neurobiological findings, and it is supportive of the dialogue on a second reading. Gene–environment interactions are irrelevant to the questions at issue in the nativist–empiricist dialogue, because the dialogue is not about the role of genes in development but about the ways in which both intrinsic structure and a structured, external world shape mind and action. In asking whether knowledge of Euclidean geometry was present in the mind of an untutored youth, for example, Socrates was not asking whether such knowledge is encoded in the human genome but whether it arises in human beings without any shaping by their external environments—in particular, without instruction in geometry. In asking whether abilities to perceive depth, organize scenes into objects, or represent allocentric positions are innate, one is not asking whether these accomplishments depend on neural connections specified directly in the genes, but whether they are independent of learning that the external world is in fact a three-dimensional layout of solid, material bodies at enduring locations. Would a human infant with a normal course of fetal development, but born into a world with a different geometrical and causal structure, perceive and reason about objects and space in the ways that infants born into our world do? These questions are not undermined by studies of epigenetic interactions in morphological development.

Research on the development of ocular dominance columns provides a clear example of the separability of questions of genetic determination from those of innateness and learning. Neurobiological experiments suggest that central features of the organization of the visual cortex in newborn animals depend on spontaneously generated, spatiotemporal patterns of activity in the fetal visual system. Although the patterns of neural connections that result from this activity are not coded directly by the genes, they form without any shaping by the visual world. Insofar as these patterns of connectivity give rise to perception of depth and objects, this research suggests a neurobiological mechanism that could create perceptual abilities that are innate but not genetically determined.

Although the nativist–empiricist dialogue is not about the nature and limits of genetic determination, studies of the processes by which genes and gene products interact in development are relevant to the dialogue at a different level, and they suggest that the dialogue is a rich source of empirical hypotheses. Developmental neurobiologists have created exquisite techniques for teasing apart contributions of genes and their environment to development, from embryonic transplants (e.g., Constantine-Paton et al., 1990) to neural rewiring (e.g., Roe, Pallas, Kwon, & Sur, 1992). As these experiments unravel the epigenetic interactions giving rise to the development of particular phenotypic features, they return ever more precise answers to the question of how organisms of exquisite complexity come to be. Psychologists might well be heartened by the progress of this field and encouraged to probe, in our own distinctive ways, the contributions of intrinsic structure and environment to the development of cognition.

Nativism Is Empty

Perhaps the most common criticism of nativist theories by developmental psychologists is that such theories are not explanatory. The reasoning behind this dismissal can be illustrated by example. Suppose one wanted to understand how high school students come to appreciate that points on a line are infinitely dense: a geometric relationship that young children do not appear to grasp in their verbal reasoning (Piaget, Inhelder, Szeminska, 1960). A nativist would propose that this knowledge is wholly innate. The evidence for this proposal might be provided by studying young babies, devising ever more sensitive tests for their capacities, and finding that babies can answer every question about the infinite density of points on a line that successful high school students answer. In this scenario, however, the psychologist's work has not explained what knowledge of point density is or how students become able to answer questions about it.

This argument can be joined by a parallel argument that empiricist claims are not explanatory. Concerning the development of knowledge of point density, an empiricist might propose that this knowledge is wholly learned. Evidence for this proposal would be provided by devising ever more sensitive tests for learning in children, and finding that all the knowledge manifested by children of all ages results from the same set of learning processes. Again, the psychologist's work would not explain what knowledge of point density is or how it arises. The pure nativist and the pure empiricist can give names to a mystery—knowledge

of point density is a collection of "innate ideas" or "associations," and it arises through "evolution" or "learning"—but neither theorist can describe what students know, predict what further questions students will and will not answer, or explain how students came to have these particular conceptions and not others.

The problem with this argument is that it misconstrues the nativist–empiricist dialogue. The dialogue rests on the thesis that human knowledge is rooted partly in biology and partly in experience, and on the promise that successful explanations of the development of knowledge will come from attempts to tease these influences apart. Return for the last time to students of geometry and to the imaginary career of a third psychologist, working in the tradition of the nativist–empiricist dialogue. This psychologist attempts to disentangle the knowledge that students bring to the learning task from the knowledge they take from it. Studies of infants may reveal an innate system for representing approximate numerosity and exact small numbers (but not large ones), an innate system for representing lines and perceptibly separate points on those lines (but not the infinite density of such points), and a collection of propensities that allow children to learn language and other culture-specific symbolic systems. Further developmental studies may reveal that, as children learn counting, they come to bring some of the machinery in their language system to bear on their knowledge of numbers, generating representations of large numbers and the intuition that the natural numbers have no upper bound (Bloom, 1994; Spelke & Tsivkin, in press; Wynn, 1990). As children learn to represent points and lines with marks on paper or on a blackboard, the latter representations may become linked to the number system through the device of the number line, facilitating developing knowledge of fractions (Gelman, 1991). Finally, children's developing understanding of the density of fractions on a number line may give rise to an understanding of the density of points on the line (Carey & Spelke, 1994).

This speculative account roots knowledge of the infinite density of points on a line in a specific set of innate systems of knowledge, each of which constitutes a small part of mature knowledge of geometry, number, language, and symbols. The account proposes that these separate systems come to grow and change, giving rise to new knowledge, as they interact in specific ways. The account surely is false in detail, and it may be altogether wrong. Our point, however, is that it offers an explanation of the development of knowledge of point density which, if true, would reveal something about what this knowledge is and how it arises. Accounts of development rooted in the nativist–empiricist dialogue both explain development and yield insight into the nature of developing knowledge.

Nativism Is Unparsimonious

Many developmental psychologists have suggested that the most parsimonious theories are those that provide the simplest account of the initial state of development (e.g., Fischer & Bidell, 1991; Thelen & Smith, 1994). Theories with a nativist component are unparsimonious, in this view, because the claim that the newborn infant is a blank slate will always be the most parsimonious claim *about the newborn infant.* Let us call this parsimony principle the "blank-slate assumption."

The blank-slate assumption does not reflect the traditional conception of parsimony in science. Parsimony is a measure that applies to theories as wholes, and the most parsimonious developmental theory provides the simplest account of the *development* of some capacity, not the simplest account of its initial state. A theory attributing minimal capacities to the newborn may not be more parsimonious than a theory attributing greater initial capacities, because all developmental theories need to arrive at same end state—mature knowledge. Indeed, theories offering more parsimonious accounts of the initial state of development may offer less parsimonious accounts of developmental change.

The last consideration suggests a different parsimony principle: If several theories account equally well for the same developmental phenomena, the more parsimonious theory is the one that posits the least amount of developmental change from infant to adult. As we noted, Pinker (1984) advanced this "continuity assumption" in the case of syntactic development, arguing that one should prefer characterizations of children's speech that accord with the grammatical categories of adults' speech in the absence of evidence to the contrary. The continuity assumption also has been urged by Banks and Shannon (1993), writing of the development of sensory processes such as mechanisms for coding color and spatial pattern. These authors consider the evidence for trichromacy in infant color vision, noting that infants' spatial acuity is too low for activity of one of the color channels to be detected by ordinary psychophysical methods. In the absence of evidence for this channel, they suggest, it is most plausible to assume that the channel is present in infants, because it is known to be present at older ages. For these authors, the burden of proof in developmental theories falls on those who propose change. Insofar as the complexity of initial state descriptions and the complexity of descriptions of developmental change are inversely related, different researchers adhering to these two different parsimony principles will arrive at opposite conclusions from the same data.

We are wary of both the blank-slate and the continuity assumptions, and indeed of any conclusions about development based on burden-of-proof arguments. In a field as young as cognitive development, theories should stand on evidence, not on methodological arguments. This is especially true today, because developmental psychologists now have a wealth of tools for collecting such evidence. Once knowledge of specific developmental phenomena is rich and detailed, psychologists may need to confront questions of parsimony in distinguishing rival theories. At that time, serious work will be needed to develop simplicity metrics for developmental theories, weaving an appropriate course between the blank-slate and the continuity assumptions so as to assess the parsimony of theories as wholes, not just their nativist or empiricist components.

Nativism Is False

Many accounts of research in cognitive development offered by textbooks and review chapters give the impression that experience has rich and manifold effects on development. Against a detailed portrait of the learning child, one is told about a few slender threads of evidence for initial knowledge and developmental continuity. Conclusions based on the latter evidence may be treated as uncertain (as they and all other conclusions are), as indicative of earlier learning processes (as they may be), or as local exceptions to the general principle that development is change driven by learning. According to this portrait, nativism is wholly or almost wholly false.

This portrait does not capture the current state of knowledge about development. The impression that developmental studies provide rich evidence for learning and meager evidence for initial knowledge stems, we believe, from two fundamental errors of interpretation of developmental data. The first error is based on a logical fallacy that pervades the study of development: In the absence of evidence for a capacity, investigators are apt to conclude that the capacity is absent. The second error is based on an unwarranted conclusion about developmental change: Learning often is claimed to produce developmental changes, and to underlie the emergence of new abilities, in situations where the only relevant data concern the fact that a change has occurred. When these errors are corrected, we believe a more accurate portrait of the current state of knowledge about cognitive development reveals evidence for innate and learned capacities in approximately equal measure, as well as vast areas where less is known than the standard portrait suggests.

In the history of developmental psychology, examples of the first error abound. The failure to observe visually guided reaching in infants below about 4 months of age, for example, was routinely taken as evidence that younger infants could not use vision to guide their reaching, until the experiments of Hofsten (1982) and Amiel-Tison (1985) showed otherwise. Similarly, the failure to observe differential responses by newborns to stimuli at different distances was taken as evidence that newborns failed to perceive depth, until evidence bearing on newborns' depth perception was collected (e.g., Slater, Morison, et al., 1990). As a last example, the failure to observe search for hidden objects in the spontaneous activities of infants below 8 or 9 months was taken as evidence that younger infants were incapable of acting on representations of objects, until infants' reaching was observed in the dark (e.g., Hood & Willats, 1986).

The fallacy of interpreting an *absence of evidence for a capacity* as *evidence for the absence of the capacity* can be seen in current discussions of the development of explicit memory. In the past 10 years, cognitive psychologists and neuroscientists have developed tools for probing explicit and implicit memory processes in normal and neurologically impaired adults. Although investigators disagree about the nature of the memory systems these tools reveal, there is growing evidence for some distinction between explicit, conscious memory on one hand and implicit, unconscious memory on the other (see Mandler, Ch. 6, Volume 2, for further discussion). Turning to the infant, memory capacities have been documented at early ages by a number of methods. Unfortunately, no one has yet found a way to adapt for infants the tasks that reveal explicit memory in adults (but see McKee & Squire, 1993, and McDonough, Mandler, McKee, & Squire, 1995, for an approach to these questions). Given this situation, one might expect accounts of the early development of memory to conclude that researchers do not know whether young infants are capable of explicit memory. Contrary to this expectation,

one frequently reads that young infants' performance reflects only implicit memory and knowledge.

The second error has been equally frequent. For example, the discovery of developmental changes in patterns of search for hidden objects was routinely interpreted as evidence for effects of experience on search skills, until studies of the development of object search in other vertebrates pointed to the importance of maturational factors (Diamond, 1990; Regolin et al., 1995b). Faced with evidence that sensitivity to a variety of Gestalt relations emerges late in infancy, Spelke (1990) concluded that sensitivity to these relations is learned as well, a conclusion that newer studies all but demolish (Johnson & Aslin, 1996; Regolin & Vallortigara, 1995).

These examples do not show that learning does not take place or cannot be studied. Before one interprets a developmental change as evidence for learning, however, one must tease apart effects of maturational change, exercise, motivation, and other factors on performance. Thelen's studies of stepping, kicking, and walking provide a model of how to do this and a background for studying diverse effects of experience on action. A second kind of evidence for learning comes from studies relating systematic variability in children's or adults' knowledge to systematic differences in their experiences. Studies of children learning different languages, of cultural differences in spatial memory, and of patterns of attention and spatial representation in children with different locomotor competence provide examples. A third kind of evidence comes from experiments in which the environment of a child or animal is systematically altered and the effects of the alteration are assessed or analyzed. Examples include studies of dark-reared cats on the visual cliff, or of students in accelerated science education programs.

If one accepts nativist or empiricist claims only on the basis of evidence, rejecting claims based on default assumptions, faulty logic, or experiments with inadequate controls for alternative explanations, how should one assess the current state of knowledge about cognitive development? We suggest that the development of knowledge does not appear to be sharply skewed toward either pole of the nativist–empiricist dialogue. Some evidence supports nativist claims, documenting capacities that emerge before they are needed under conditions in which alternative explanations of their development can be rejected. Some evidence supports empiricist claims, documenting capacities that differ as a function of specific prior experiences, in ways that cannot be explained as effects of exercise, motivation, or other ancillary factors. Development is both constancy and change, invariance and variability, nature and nurture.

Nativism Denies Flexibility

It has been popular for some time to gloss nativist claims as claims about "constraints on learning" (e.g., Gelman, 1990; Keil, 1981; Spelke, 1990). The claim that children have innate knowledge of language is rephrased as the claim that they are constrained to learn as a primary language only a subset of the logically possible systems of symbolic communication. Similarly, the claim that children have innate knowledge of objects is rephrased as the claim that they are constrained to represent only certain kinds of entities behaving in certain ways.

These rephrasings tend to obscure two related features of human cognition. First, knowledge is always extendable. There appear to be no practical limits to the number of motor skills an athlete can command, the size of the vocabulary a speaker can attain, the number of faces or objects a perceiver can recognize, or the number of scientific theories a thinker can devise. Second, cognitive scientists posit innate cognitive structures in an effort to understand how humans come to know the things they do. The goal of explanation within the nativist–empiricist dialogue is to account for the development of human knowledge. The finding that certain logically possible actions, perceptions, or languages are not readily attained by humans is of interest only insofar as it sheds light on the actions, perceptions, and languages humans do attain. Nativist and empiricist claims are not denials or assertions of flexibility but ways of characterizing and accounting for the distinctive qualities of flexible human thought.

Research grounded in the nativist–empiricist dialogue, probing both the constant and the changing features of human cognition, helps to delineate the circumstances that will maximize flexibility and enhance development. That is why questions at the heart of the nativist–empiricist dialogue have long been considered, with justice, to be central to the development of effective programs of education (for example, see Carey, 1985; Gelman, 1991). Answers to the questions at issue between nativists and empiricists serve as signposts to educators, guiding the design of curricula that build on children's core cognitive capacities and use their existing knowledge to extend that knowledge.

Nativism Is Dangerous

"There are . . . social reasons to be wary about simple innatist interpretations. Scientific claims about the genetic origins of human intelligence and culture have often been misused to justify discriminatory social policies (Lewontin, Rose, & Kamin, 1984). Scientists therefore have a responsibility to proceed with great caution in developing and disseminating theories of this kind" (Fischer & Bidell, 1991, p. 202).

We are tempted by two responses to this argument. The first response is that the job of science is to discover what is true (Scarr, 1993). Science can serve society by providing information, not propaganda. Providing information, in turn, requires that scientists pose questions openly, without prejudice. Political concerns should not affect a scientist's evaluation of theories or evidence.

We are tempted, however, by a different response. Although investigators may aspire to provide information impartially, scientists cannot eliminate social and political considerations from their choice of questions to ask. The considerable energy and resources currently directed to understanding how children learn mathematics, or how children's thinking grows in different social environments, can be justified not only by the inherent interest of these questions but by the likely social benefits that their answers will provide. The renewed interest in measuring racial differences in IQ can be criticized not only because this research has no clear theoretical importance but also because it is unlikely to provide information of any social value to any pluralistic, nonracist society. If the study of constancy and change in cognitive development were devoid of social benefits and plagued by potential ill consequences, perhaps psychologists should stop asking these ancient questions.

A further reason for considering the larger social and political implications of research guided by the nativist–empiricist dialogue is that these considerations always have been prominent in the minds of the participants in the dialogue, and they explain in large part why scientists and laypeople alike find questions of nature and nurture so important. How different would our children and grandchildren be if we changed the society in which we and they lived? How different are people from one another, and how different are the thoughts and values of the members of different cultures, religions, or social groups? Stripping these questions from the nativist–empiricist dialogue impoverishes that dialogue and deprives it of much of its interest. To accept these questions, however, is to accept the possibility that research addressed to the nativist–empiricist dialogue could have consequences beyond the community of scientists. What are those consequences?

First, we must be clear about one consequence that this research does *not* have: The findings of research on the nature and nurture of human knowledge have no implications for accounts of individual differences in knowledge or cognitive abilities. The claim that some body of knowledge is innate in the human species does not entail, or even suggest, that *differences* in knowledge and cognitive performance between different members of the species are innate as well. Individual differences in knowledge and cognitive processes may depend wholly on differences in the opportunities available to different people to elaborate on their common, biologically given knowledge systems. (This is close to our view of the matter.) Similarly, the claim that some body of knowledge is learned in the species is consistent with the thesis that individual differences in the extent of this learning stem from biologically based differences in learning capacities. (This seems to be the view of many modern investigators who argue for innate individual differences in intelligence.) For better or for worse, research such as that described in this chapter does not speak to debates over the sources of individual differences in cognitive performance.[8]

Nevertheless, research in the tradition of the nativist–empiricist dialogue does foster understanding of individual differences in intelligence in two indirect ways. First, insofar as basic research in cognitive development supports theories with a strong nativist component, providing evidence for elaborate systems of knowledge that are common to all people and constant over development, this research suggests that the differences between people detected by instruments such as IQ tests or college entrance examinations are unimportant. If all normally functioning people are endowed with the same rich and intricate systems of knowledge, then individual differences in cognitive performance likely reflect only minor variations in the ways these knowledge systems are elaborated or put to use (see Pinker, 1994). Second, as research in cognitive development in-

creasingly sheds light on the origins and growth of human knowledge, it allows educators and social planners to act more effectively to enhance people's abilities to deploy and extend their knowledge. In this way, studies in the nativist–empiricist tradition indirectly can change the very database of individual variation whose sources are being debated (see Block, 1979).

If evidence for innately coordinated actions, innate perceptions of depth, innate syntax, or innate knowledge of points and lines does not bear on claims about the genetic basis of human differences, does it have any implications for how one views human nature? In the final section of this chapter, we consider a possible implication of such research for how people view themselves and members of other cultures.

The Nativist–Empiricist Dialogue in a Multicultural World

How different are two people from different cultures, with different languages, religions, and social practices? Critics of the nativist–empiricist dialogue, as well as many other modern thinkers, conclude that this is a meaningless question. The universal and the variable can never be disentangled, and so one can never know how similar or unfathomably different the members of different cultures are. In this intellectual vacuum, many people have considered the obvious differences in the appearances and behavior of people in different cultures and concluded that the gulfs separating human beings are immense. Thus, a person of one religion may justify indifference toward those of a different religion because "They don't think of human life the way we do." Or, students may request a university living center open only to members of their culture "so that we can live with people who share our concepts and values." When we asked the authors of these statements to describe the differences in thoughts and values that separated them from others, their responses included a large measure of bewilderment, as if the differences were too great to express or understand.

In the best of times, the belief that the thoughts and values of the members of other religions, races, or cultures differ immeasurably from the thought and values of one's own ethnic group may lead to a patchwork of isolated, homogeneous societies—not a very interesting world. More often, this picture of human difference is more pernicious; always, it is a barrier to understanding others and oneself.

---

[8] Block (1995) discusses further reasons why the genetics-of-IQ debate is logically independent of the nativist–empiricist dialogue, centering on the distinction between nativist explanations and genetic explanations.

Research in the tradition of the nativist–empiricist dialogue suggests that the commonsense assumptions embodied in the above quotations and enshrined in the postmodern and multicultural intellectual movements are false. People from different cultures are not immeasurably, unfathomably different. Rather, people differ in specific, understandable ways. Beneath these differences, the knowledge, beliefs, and values of all people build on a common foundation.

There is no mystery to why the commonsense thinking of 20th-century humans favors the view that people of different cultures differ immeasurably, just as there is no mystery to why the commonsense thinking of 10th-century humans favored the view that the heavens rotate around a stationary earth. People from different cultures act differently on the surface. They utter different sounds so as to produce mutually incomprehensible languages. They eat different food, wear different clothing, and (at least until recently) listen to different music. They also go to different churches, marry different numbers of people under different sorts of arrangements, hold and transfer property differently, and abide by different and sometimes mutually incompatible conventions. Appearances favor the view that people differ profoundly, just as the appearance of the sky favors the view that the sun circles the earth.

Appearances can be misleading, however, and research once again has revealed that they are. People differ from one another in some ways and are the same in other ways. The universal foundations of human cognition provide a common ground on which the differences between people can be described, understood, and bridged.

Where nativist claims have been shown to be true, they illuminate the cognitive abilities that all humans share. By finding and clarifying this cognitive common ground, research in the nativist–empiricist tradition points the way to a set of bonds that unite people across cultures and give each person knowledge of all others. Because the abilities shared by all humans form much of the foundation for the abilities that distinguish us, the most divergent practices of people in different cultures are built largely on a common foundation. Culturally specific practices therefore reveal capacities that are to some degree latent in all humans, and an understanding of the practices of any group of people sheds light on the capacities of everyone. Linguists have appreciated this point for some time, for their research on languages such as Mandarin or Walpiri has served to reveal

previously obscure features of languages such as English. The same point applies to other cognitive abilities. For example, the Australian who travels great distances without map or compass, maintaining with exquisite accuracy a sense of his own changing position, exhibits a capacity for dead reckoning that all humans possess, although many of us make little explicit use of it. In the context of the nativist–empiricist dialogue, human universals and human differences are mutually illuminating, and contact with people from different cultures sheds light on one's own culture and cognition.

Where empiricist claims have been shown to be true, we have reason to believe that people in different cultures could genuinely differ. Research in the tradition of the nativist–empiricist dialogue enables us to discover what those differences are, what has produced them, and what, in principle, would change the conceptions that flourish in one's own culture into conceptions that flourish elsewhere. Despite Americans' predilection for "left" and "right," for example, Americans can understand what Mayan villagers mean when they speak of "the house to the north of the village" and can even understand the advantages of the Mayan terms. The differences between members of different cultures are not unfathomable but rather are describable and explainable in terms of differing experiences of quite specific kinds. These differences can be bridged—always in principle and sometimes in practice—because the members of a different culture are oneself as one would have been, had one's parents made the sound contrasts of their language, or described object positions with respect to the compass points. Describing and demystifying cultural differences do not deny or deprecate those differences. It does become harder to argue, however, that the differences are worth killing and dying for.

Because this is a landmark handbook, appearing on the cusp of the third millennium and calling on its authors to attempt, in a necessarily myopic way, to chart a course for future research, we close by indulging our imaginations and offering a vision for the study of human development. We envisage a developmental psychology that acknowledges, with respect and humility, an intellectual tradition that extends back to the beginning of recorded human inquiry. In this field, questions about the inherent and the acquired, the inevitable and the coincidental, the constant and the changeable, the universal and the variable, are asked openly and are answered not by prejudice or preconception but by evidence. We envisage a flowering of that evidence, as developmental psychologists use the tools already at their disposal to address the questions raised by the nativist–empiricist dialogue, and as the answers they receive open the way to new and better methods for pursuing the next generation of questions. In our vision, advances in developmental psychology will occur in concert with advances in the allied disciplines of biology, cognitive science, and anthropology, so that a panoply of methods and perspectives can shed converging light on human nature and human knowledge. Finally, we envisage a developmental psychology whose findings lead future generations of people to look back on the conceptions that have fueled the ethnic, cultural, and religious conflicts that are closing the second millennium and to say what we now say about the conceptions of the heavens that closed the first: These ideas seemed reasonable at the time, but science has shown that they are wrong, and so has opened new worlds of progress.

ACKNOWLEDGMENTS

We are grateful to Richard Lerner, Yuko Munakata, Randall O'Reilly, and Ted Supalla for helpful comments on an earlier draft.

REFERENCES

Acredolo, L. P. (1978). The development of spatial orientation in infancy. *Developmental Psychology, 14,* 224–234.

Acredolo, L. P. (1990). Behavioral approaches to spatial orientation in infancy. In A. Diamond (Ed.), The development and neural bases of higher cognitive functions. *Annals of the New York Academy of Sciences, 608,* 596–607.

Acredolo, L. P., Adams, A., & Goodwin, S. W. (1984). The role of self-produced movement and visual tracking in infant spatial orientation. *Journal of Experimental Child Psychology, 38,* 312–327.

Adolph, K. E., Eppler, M. A., & Gibson, E. J. (1993). Crawling versus walking infants' perception of affordances for locomotion over sloping surfaces. *Child Development, 64,* 1158–1174.

Aguiar, A., & Baillargeon, R. (1996). 2.5-month-old's reasoning about occlusion events [Abstract]. *Infant Behavior and Development, 19,* 293.

Amiel-Tison, C. (1985). Pediatric contribution to the present knowledge on the neurobehavioral status of infants at birth. In J. Mehler & R. Fox (Eds.), *Neonate cognition.* Hillsdale, NJ: Erlbaum.

Antinucci, F. (1989). *Cognitive structure and development in nonhuman primates.* Hillsdale, NJ: Erlbaum.

Aristotle. (1941). Metaphysics (R. D. Ross, Trans.). In R. McKeon (Ed.), *The basic works of Aristotle.* New York: Random House.

Atran S. (1990). *Cognitive foundations of natural history: Towards an anthropology of science.* Cambridge, England: Cambridge University Press.

Augustine. (389/1876). *The confessions* (J. G. P. Pilkington, Trans.). Cleveland, OH: Fine Editions Press.

Bai, D. L., & Bertenthal, B. I. (1992). Locomotor status and the development of spatial search skills. *Child Development, 63,* 215–226.

Baillargeon, R., & DeVos, J. (1991). Object permanence in young infants: Further evidence. *Child Development, 62,* 1227–1246.

Baillargeon, R., & Hanko-Summers, S. (1990). Is the top object adequately supported by the bottom object? Young infants' understanding of support relations. *Cognitive Development, 5,* 29–53.

Banks, M. S. (1988). Visual recalibration and the development of contrast and optical flow perception. In A. Yonas (Ed.), *Perceptual development in infancy: The Minnesota Symposia on Child Psychology.* New York: Wiley.

Banks, M. S., Aslin, R. N., & Letson, R. D. (1975). Sensitive period for the development of human binocular vision. *Science, 190,* 675–677.

Banks, M. S., & Shannon, E. (1993). Spatial and chromatic visual efficiency in human neonates. In C. E. Granrud (Ed.), *Visual perception and cognition in infancy.* Hillsdale, NJ: Erlbaum.

Bateson, P. (1979). How do sensitive periods arise and what are they for? *Animal Behavior, 27,* 470–486.

Berkeley, G. (1975a). Treatise concerning the principles of human knowledge. In M. R. Ayers (Ed.), *Philosophical works.* London: Dent. (Original work published 1710)

Berkeley, G. (1975b). An essay toward a new theory of vision. In M. R. Ayers (Ed.), *Philosophical works.* London: Dent. (Original work published 1709)

Bertenthal, B. I. (1993). Perception of biomechanical motions by infants: Intrinsic image and knowledge-based constraints. In C. Granrud (Ed.), *Visual perception and cognition in infancy* (pp. 175–214). Hillsdale, NJ: Erlbaum.

Bertenthal, B. I. (in press). Origins and early development of perception, action, and representation. *Annual Review of Psychology.*

Bertenthal, B. I., & Campos, J. J. (1990). A systems approach to the organizing effects of self-produced locomotion during infancy. In C. Rovee-Collier & L. P. Lipsitt (Eds.), *Advances in infancy research* (Vol. 6, pp. 1–60). Norwood, NJ: ABLEX.

Bertenthal, B. I., Campos, J. J., & Barrett, K. (1984). Self-produced locomotion: An organizer of emotional, cognitive, and social development in infancy. In R. Emde & R. Harmon (Eds.), *Continuities and discontinuities in development.* New York: Plenum Press.

Bever, T. G. (1970). The cognitive basis for linguistic structures. In J. R. Hayes (Ed.), *Cognition and language learning.* New York: Wiley.

Bickerton, D. (1981). *The roots of language.* Ann Arbor, MI: Karoma Press.

Bickerton, D. (1984). The language bioprogram hypothesis. *Behavioral and Brain Sciences, 7,* 173–221.

Biederman, I. (1987). Recognition by components: A theory of human image understanding. *Psychological Review, 94,* 115–147.

Biederman, I. (1995). Visual object recognition. In S. M. Kosslyn & D. N. Osherson (Eds.), *An invitation to cognitive science: Vol. 2. Visual cognition.* Cambridge, MA: Bradford/MIT Press.

Biegler, R., & Morris, R. G. M. (1993). Landmark stability is a prerequisite for spatial but not discrimination learning. *Nature, 361,* 631–633.

Birdsong, D. (1992). Ultimate attainment in second language acquisition. *Language, 68,* 706–755.

Block, N. (1979). A confusion about innateness. *Behavioral and Brain Sciences, 2,* 27–29.

Block, N. (1995). How heritability misleads about race. *Cognition, 56,* 99–128.

Bloom, P. (1994). Generativity within language and other cognitive domains. *Cognition, 51,* 177–189.

Bloom, P. (1995). Theories of word learning: Rationalist alternatives to associationism. In T. K. Bhatia & W. C. Ritchie (Eds.), *Handbook of language acquisition.* New York: Academic Press.

Bloom, P., Peterson, M., Nadel, L., & Garrett, M. (1996). *Language and space.* Cambridge, MA: MIT Press.

Bloomfield, L. (1933). *Language.* New York: Holt, Rinehart and Winston.

Borer, H., & Wexler, K. (1987). The maturation of syntax. In T. Roeper & E. Williams (Eds.), *Parameter setting.* Dordrecht, The Netherlands: Reidel.

Bowerman, M., & Levinson, S. (in press). *Language acquisition and conceptual development.* Cambridge, England: Cambridge University Press.

Bremner, J. G., & Bryant, P. E. (1977). Place versus response as the basis of spatial errors made by young infants. *Journal of Experimental Child Psychology, 23,* 162–171.

Bremner, J. G., Knowles, L., & Andreasen, G. (1994). Processes underlying young children's spatial orientation during movement. *Journal of Experimental Child Psychology, 57,* 355–376.

Brent, M. (1996). Computational approaches to language acquisition. *Cognition, 61,* 1–194.

Brown, P., & Levinson, S. (1993). *Linguistic and nonlinguistic coding of spatial arrays: Explorations in Mayan cognition.* Working paper no. 24, Cognitive Anthropology Research Group, Nijmegen.

Campos, J. J., Bertenthal, B. I., & Kermoian, R. (1992). Early experience and emotional development: The emergence of wariness of heights. *Psychological Science, 3,* 61–64.

Campos, J. J., Hiatt, S., Ramsay, D., Henderson, C., & Svejda, M. (1978). The emergence of fear of heights. In M. Lewis & L. Rosenblum (Eds.), *The development of affect* (pp. 149–182). New York: Plenum Press.

Carey, S. (1985). *Conceptual change in childhood.* Cambridge, MA: Bradford/MIT Press.

Carey, S. (1991). Knowledge acquisition: Enrichment or conceptual change? In S. Carey & R. Gelman (Eds.), *The epigenesis of mind: Essays on biology and cognition* (pp. 257–291). Hillsdale, NJ: Erlbaum.

Carey, S. (in press). Mass/count quantification and basic level sortal terms: Evidence from infant studies. In M. Bowerman & S. Levinson (Eds.), *Language acquisition and conceptual development.* Cambridge, England: Cambridge University Press.

Carey, S., & Spelke, E. S. (1994). Domain-specific knowledge and conceptual change. In L. A. Hirschfeld & S. A. Gelman (Eds.), *Mapping the mind: Domain specificity in cognition and culture.* Cambridge, England: Cambridge University Press.

Cheng, K. (1986): A purely geometric module in the rat's spatial representation. *Cognition, 23,* 149–178.

Choi, S., & Bowerman, M. (1991). Learning to express motion events in English and Korean: The influence of language-specific lexicalization patterns. *Cognition, 41,* 83–121.

Chomsky, N. (1957). *Syntactic structures.* The Hague: Mouton.

Chomsky, N. (1965). *Aspects of the theory of syntax.* Cambridge, MA: MIT Press.

Chomsky, N. (1975a) *The logical structure of linguistic theory.* New York: Plenum Press. (Original work published 1955)

Chomsky, N. (1975b). *Reflections on language.* New York: Pantheon Books.

Chomsky, N. (1981). *Lectures on government and binding*. Dordrecht, The Netherlands: Foris.

Chomsky, N. (1988). *Language and problems of knowledge: The Managua lectures*. Cambridge, MA: MIT Press.

Chomsky, N. (1994). *Language and thought*. Wakefield, RI: Boyer Bell.

Churchland, R. (1995). *The engine of reason, the seat of the soul*. Cambridge, MA: Bradford/MIT Press.

Constantine-Paton, M., Cline, H. T., & Debski, E. (1990). Patterned activity, synaptic convergence, and the NMDA receptor in developing visual pathways. *Annual Review of Neuroscience, 13,* 129–154.

Coppieters, R. (1987). Competence differences between native and near-native speakers. *Language, 63,* 544–573.

Cosmides, L. & Tooby, J. (1994). Origins of domain-specificity: The evolution of functional organization. In L. A. Hirschfeld & S. A. Gelman (Eds.), *Mapping the mind: Domain specificity in cognition and culture.* Cambridge, England: Cambridge University Press.

Craton, L. G., & Yonas, A. (1990). The role of motion in infant perception of occlusion. In J. T. Enns (Ed.), *The development of attention: Research and theory.* New York: Elsevier/North-Holland.

Curtiss, S. (1977). *Genie: A psycholinguistic study of a modern day "wild child."* New York: Academic Press.

Cutting, J. E., & Vishton, P. M. (1995). Perceiving layout and knowing distances: The integration, relative potency, and contextual use of different information about depth. In W. Epstein & S. Rogers (Eds.), *Handbook of perception and cognition: Vol. 5. Perception of space and motion* (pp. 69–117). New York: Academic Press.

Daugherty, K., & Seidenberg, M. (1992). Rules or connections? The past tense revisited. *Proceedings of the 14th Annual Conference of the Cognitive Science Society.* Bloomington: Indiana University.

DeLoache, J. S. (1987). Rapid change in the symbolic functioning of very young children. *Science, 238,* 1556–1557.

DeLoache, J. S. (1995). Early symbol understanding and use. In D. Medin (Ed.), *The psychology of learning and motivation* (Vol. 33). New York: Academic Press.

DeLoache, J. S., & Burns, N. M. (1993). Symbolic development in young children: Understanding models and pictures. In C. Pratt & A. F. Garton (Eds.), *Systems of representation in children: Development and use.* New York: Wiley.

Descartes, R. (1971a). *Discourse on the method.* In E. Anscombe & P. T. Geach (Eds. & Trans.), *Philosophical writings.* Indianapolis: Bobbs-Merrill. (Original work published 1637)

Descartes, R. (1971b). Dioptrics. In E. Anscombe & P. T. Geach (Eds. & Trans.), *Philosophical writings.* Indianapolis: Bobbs-Merrill. (Original work published 1637)

Descartes, R. (1971c). Meditations. In E. Anscombe & P. T. Geach (Eds. & Trans.), *Philosophical writings.* Indianapolis: Bobbs-Merrill. (Original work published 1641)

Diamond, A. (1990). The development and neural bases of memory functions as indexed by the AB and delayed response tasks in human infants and infant monkeys. In A. Diamond (Ed.), The development and neural bases of higher cognitive functions. *Annals of the New York Academy of Sciences, 608,* 517–536.

Duhem, P. (1949). *The aim and structure of physical theory.* Princeton, NJ: Princeton University Press.

Edelman, G. (1987). *Neural Darwinism.* New York: Basic Books.

Eimas, P. D. (1994). Categorization in early infancy and the continuity of development. *Cognition, 50,* 83–93.

Eimas, P. D., Siqueland, E., Jusczyk, P., & Vigorito, J. (1971). Speech perception in infants. *Science, 171,* 303–306.

Elman, J. (1993). Learning and development in neural networks: The importance of starting small. *Cognition, 48,* 71–99.

Elman, J., Bates, E., Johnson, M., Karmiloff-Smith, A., Parisi, D., & Plunkett, K. (1996). *Rethinking innateness.* Cambridge, MA: MIT Press.

Emmorey, K. (1991). Repetition priming with aspect and agreement morphology in American Sign Language. *Journal of Psycholinguistic Research, 20,* 365–388.

Etienne, A. S. (1987). The control of short distance homing in the golden hamster. In P. Ellen & C. Thinus-Blanc (Eds.), *Cognitive processes and spatial orientation in animal and man* (pp. 233–251). Dordrecht, The Netherlands: Martinus Nijhoff.

Etienne, A. S., Lambert, S. J., Reverdin, B., & Teroni, E. (1993). Learning to recalibrate the role of dead reckoning and visual cues in spatial navigation. *Animal Learning and Behavior, 21,* 266–280.

Farah, M. J. (1995). Dissociable systems for recognition: A cognitive neuropsychology approach. In S. M. Kosslyn & D. N. Osherson (Eds.), *Visual cognition.* Cambridge, MA: MIT Press.

Feldman, H., Goldin-Meadow, S., & Gleitman, L. (1978). Beyond Herodotus: The creation of language by linguistically deprived deaf children. In A. Lock (Ed.), *Action, symbol, and gesture.* New York: Academic Press.

Feller, M. B., Wellis, D. P., Stellwagen, D., Werblin, F. S., & Shatz, C. J. (1996). Requirement for cholinergic synaptic transmission in the propagation of spontaneous retinal waves. *Science, 272,* 1182–1187.

Finch, S., & Chater, N. (1992). *Bootstrapping syntactic categories.* Proceedings of the 14th Annual Conference of the Cognitive Science Society, Indiana University, Bloomington.

Fischer, K. W., & Bidell, T. (1991). Constraining nativist inferences about cognitive capacities. In S. Carey & R. Gelman (Eds.), *The epigenesis of mind: Essays on biology and cognition.* Hillsdale, NJ: Erlbaum.

Fischer, S. (1978). Sign language and creoles. In P. Siple (Ed.), *Understanding language through sign language research.* New York: Academic Press.

Fodor, J. A. (1968). *Psychological explanation.* New York: Random House.

Fodor, J. A. (1983). *The modularity of mind.* Cambridge, MA: Bradford/MIT Press.

Fox, R., Aslin, R., Shea, S., & Dumais, S. (1980). Stereopsis in human infants. *Science, 207,* 323–324.

Fukusima, S. S., Loomis, J. M., & Da Silva, J. A. (in press). Visual perception of egocentric distance as assessed by triangulation. *Journal of Experimental Psychology: Human Perception and Performance.*

Gallistel, C. R. (1990). *The organization of learning.* Cambridge, MA: MIT Press.

Gallistel, C. R., & Gelman, R. (1992). Preverbal and verbal counting and computation. *Cognition, 44,* 43–74.

Gelman, R. (1990). Structural constraints on cognitive development: Introduction. *Cognitive Science, 14,* 3–9.

Gelman, R. (1991). Epigenetic foundations of knowledge structures: Initial and transcendent constructions. In S. Carey & R. Gelman (Eds.), *The epigenesis of mind: Essays on biology and cognition.* Hillsdale, NJ: Erlbaum.

Gentner, D. (1989). The mechanisms of analogical learning. In S. Vosniadou & A. Ortony (Eds.), *Similarity and analogical reasoning* (pp. 200–241). Cambridge, England: Cambridge University Press.

Gerken, L. (1994). Sentential processes in early child language: Evidence from the perception and production of function morphemes. In H. Nusbaum & J. Goodman (Eds.), *The transition from speech sounds to spoken words.* Cambridge, MA: MIT Press.

Gibson, E. J. (1991). *An odyssey in perception and learning.* Cambridge, MA: MIT Press.

Gibson, E. J., & Walk, R. D. (1960). The "visual cliff." *Scientific American, 202,* 64–71.

Gibson, J. J. (1950). *Perception of the visual world.* Boston: Houghton Mifflin.

Gibson, K. R., & Ingold, T. (1993). *Tools, language, and cognition in human evolution.* Cambridge, England: Cambridge University Press.

Gladwin, T. (1970). *East is a big bird.* Cambridge, MA: Harvard University Press.

Gleitman, L., & Newport, E. (1995). The invention of language by children: Environmental and biological influences on the acquisition of language. In L. Gleitman & M. Liberman (Eds.), *An invitation to cognitive science: Vol. 1. Language* (2nd ed.). Cambridge, MA: MIT Press.

Goldin-Meadow, S., & Mylander, C. (1984). Gestural communication in deaf children: The non-effects of parental input on early language development. *Monographs of the Society for Research on Child Development, 49*(3/4, Serial No. 207).

Goldowsky, B., & Newport, E. (1993). Modeling the effects of processing limitations on the acquisition of morphology: The less is more hypothesis. In E. Clark (Ed.), *The Proceedings of the 24th Annual Child Language Research Forum.* Stanford, CA: CSLI.

Goodale, M. A. (1995). The cortical organization of visual perception and visuomotor control. In S. M. Kosslyn & D. N. Osherson (Eds.), *Visual cognition.* Cambridge, MA: MIT Press.

Goodsitt, J., Morgan, J., & Kuhl, P. (1993). Perceptual strategies in prelingual speech segmentation. *Journal of Child Language, 20,* 229–252.

Gopnik, A., & Meltzoff, A. N. (in press). *Words, thoughts, and theories.* Cambridge, MA: Bradford/MIT Press.

Granrud, C. E. (1987). Size constancy in newborn human infants. *Investigative Ophthalmology and Visual Science, 28,* 5.

Granrud, C. E., Yonas, A., Smith, I. M., Arterberry, M. E., Glicksman, M. L., & Sorknes, A. (1984). Infants' sensitivity to accretion and deletion of texture as information for depth at an edge. *Child Development, 55,* 1630–1636.

Harris, Z. (1955). From phoneme to morpheme. *Language, 31,* 190–222.

Hatfield, G. (1990). *The natural and the normative: Theories of spatial perception from Kant to Helmholtz.* Cambridge, MA: MIT Press.

Hauser, M. D., & Carey, S. (in press). Building a cognitive creature from a set of primitives: Evolutionary and developmental insights. In C. Allen & D. Cummins (Eds.), *The evolution of mind.* Oxford, England: Oxford University Press.

Hauser, M. D., MacNeilage, P., & Ware, M. (1996). Numerical representations in primates. *Proceedings of the National Academy of Sciences, 93,* 1514–1517.

Haviland, J. (1992). Anchoring, iconicity, and orientation in Gu-ugu Yimithirr pointing gestures. *Journal of Linguistic Anthropology, 3,* 3–45.

Hebb, D. O. (1949). *The organization of behavior.* New York: Wiley.

Held, R. (1985). Binocular vision: Behavioral and neural development. In J. Mehler & R. Fox (Eds.), *Neonate cognition.* Hillsdale, NJ: Erlbaum.

Held, R., Birch, E. E., & Gwiazda, J. (1980). Stereoacuity of human infants. *Proceedings of the National Academy of Sciences (USA), 77,* 5572–5574.

Held, R., & Hein, A. (1963). Movement produced stimulation in the development of visually guided behavior. *Journal of Comparative and Physiological Psychology, 56,* 872–876.

Helmholtz, H. von (1962). *Treatise on physiological optics* (J. P. C. Southall, Trans.). New York: Dover. (Original work published 1867)

Hering, E. (1964). In L. M. Hurwich & D. Jameson (Eds. & Trans.), *Outlines of a theory of the light sense.* Cambridge, MA: Harvard University Press. (Original work published 1874–1920)

Hermer, L. (1994, March). *Increasing flexibility for spatial reorientation in humans linked to emerging language abilities.* Poster presented at the 1st annual meeting of the Cognitive Neuroscience Society, San Francisco.

Hermer, L., & Spelke, E. S. (1994). A geometric process for spatial reorientation in young children. *Nature, 370,* 57–59.

Hermer, L., & Spelke, E. S. (1996). Modularity and development: The case of spatial reorientation. *Cognition, 61,* 195–232.

Hermer, L., Spelke, E. S., & Nadel, L. (1995, November). *Conservation of a process for spatial representation and reorientation based on environmental shape across human adults, children and adult rats.* Paper presented at the 26th Society for Neuroscience meeting, San Diego.

Hespos, S. J., & Rochat, P. (1996). Tracking invisible spatial transformations by 4- and 6-month-old infants [Abstract]. *Infant Behavior and Development, 19,* 504.

Hess, E. (1973). *Imprinting.* New York: Van Nostrand-Reinhold.

Hirschfeld, L. A., & Gelman, S. A. (1994). *Mapping the mind: Domain specificity in cognition and culture.* Cambridge, England: Cambridge University Press.

Hirsch-Pasek, K., & Treiman, R. (1982). Doggerel: Motherese in a new context. *Journal of Child Language, 9,* 229–237.

Hochberg, J. (in press). Objects and events: Legacies of Gestalt theory. In J. Hochberg & J. E. Cutting (Eds.), *Handbook of perception and cognition: Vol. 1. Perception and cognition at century's end.* New York: Academic Press.

Hofsten, C. von (1982). Eye-hand coordination in the newborn. *Developmental Psychology, 18,* 450–461.

Hofsten, C. von, & Spelke, E. S. (1985). Object perception and object-directed reaching in infancy. *Journal of Experimental Psychology: General, 114,* 198–212.

Hood, B., & Willats, P. (1986). Reaching in the dark to an object's remembered position: Evidence for object permanence in 5-month-old infants. *British Journal of Developmental Psychology, 4,* 57–65.

Hubel, D. H., & Wiesel, T. N. (1962). Receptive fields, binocular interaction and functional architecture in the cat's visual cortex. *Journal of Physiology, 160,* 106–154.

Hubel, D. H., Wiesel, T. N., & LeVay, S. (1977). Plasticity of the ocular dominance columns in monkey striate cortex. *Philosophical Transactions of the Royal Society of London, 278,* 377–409.

Hyams, N. (1986). *Language acquisition and the theory of parameters.* Dordrecht, The Netherlands: Reidel.

Imai, M., & Gertner, D. (in press). A cross-linguistic study of early word meaning: Universal ontology and linguistic influence. *Cognition.*

Jensen, J. L., Thelen, E., & Ulrich, B. D. (1989). Constraints on multi-joint movements: From the spontaneity of infancy to the skill of adults. *Human Movement Science, 8,* 393–402.

Johnson, J., & Newport, E. (1989). Critical period effects in second language learning: The influence of maturational state on the acquisition of English as a second language. *Cognitive Psychology, 21,* 60–99.

Johnson, J., & Newport, E. (1991). Critical period effects on universal properties of language: The status of subjacency in the acquisition of a second language. *Cognition, 39,* 215–258.

Johnson, J., Shenkman, K., Newport, E., & Medin, D. (1996). Indeterminacy in the grammar of adult language learners. *Journal of Memory and Language, 35,* 335–352.

Johnson, M. H., & Morton, J. (1991). *Biology and cognitive development: The case of face recognition.* Oxford, England: Blackwell.

Johnson, S. P., & Aslin, R. N. (1995). Perception of object unity in 2-month-old infants. *Developmental Psychology, 31,* 739–745.

Johnson, S. P., & Aslin, R. N. (1996). Perception of object unity in young infants: The roles of motion, depth, and orientation. *Cognitive Development, 11,* 161–180.

Johnson, S. P., & Nanez, J. E., Sr. (1995). Young infants' perception of object unity in two-dimensional displays. *Infant Behavior and Development, 18,* 133–143.

Jouen, F. (1990). Early visual-vestibular interactions and postural development. In H. Bloch & B. I. Bertenthal (Eds.),

Sensory-motor organization and development in infancy and early childhood (pp. 199–216). Dordrecht, The Netherlands: Kluwer.

Jusczyk, P. W., Pisoni, D. B., Walley, A. C., & Murray, J. (1980). Discrimination of the relative onset of two-component tones by infants. *Journal of the Acoustical Society of America, 67,* 262–270.

Kant, I. (1964). *Critique of pure reason* (N. Kemp Smith, Trans.). New York: St. Martin's. (Original work published 1781)

Karmiloff-Smith, A. (1992). *Beyond modularity: A developmental perspective on cognitive science.* Cambridge, MA: MIT Press.

Keating, M. B., McKenzie, B. E., & Day, R. H. (1986). Spatial localization in infancy: Position constancy in a square and circular room with and without a landmark. *Child Development, 57,* 115–124.

Kegl, J., Senghas, A., & Coppola, M. (in press). Creation through contact: Sign language emergence and sign language change in Nicaragua. In M. Degraff (Ed.), *Creolization, diachrony, and language acquisition.* Cambridge, MA: MIT Press.

Keil, F. C. (1979). *Semantic and conceptual development.* Cambridge, MA: Harvard University Press.

Keil, F. C. (1981). Constraints on knowledge and cognitive development. *Psychological Review, 88,* 197–227.

Kellman, P. J. (1993). Kinematic foundations of visual perception. In C. E. Granrud (Ed.), *Visual perception and cognition in infancy.* Hillsdale, NJ: Erlbaum.

Kellman, P. J. (1984). Perception of three-dimensional form by human infants. *Perception and Psychophysics, 36,* 353–358.

Kellman, P. J., & Arterberry, M. (in press). *The cradle of knowledge: Development of perception in infancy.* Cambridge, MA: MIT Press.

Kellman, P. J., Gleitman, H., & Spelke, E. S. (1987). Object and observer motion in the perception of objects by infants. *Journal of Experimental Psychology: Human Perception and Performance, 13,* 586–593.

Kellman, P. J., & Spelke, E. S. (1983). Perception of partly occluded objects in infancy. *Cognitive Psychology, 15,* 483–524.

Kellman, P. J., Spelke, E. S., & Short, K. R. (1986). Infant perception of object unity from translatory motion in depth and vertical translation. *Child Development, 57,* 72–86.

Kendon, A. (1988). *Sign languages of aboriginal Australia: Cultural, semiotic and communicative perspectives.* Cambridge, England: Cambridge University Press.

Kestenbaum, R., Termine, N., & Spelke, E. S. (1987). Perception of objects and object boundaries by three-month-old infants. *British Journal of Developmental Psychology, 5,* 367–383.

Kim, I. K., & Spelke, E. S. (1992). Infants' sensitivity to effects of gravity on visible object motion. *Journal of Experimental Psychology: Human Perception and Performance, 18,* 385–393.

Knierim, J., Kudrimoti, H., & McNaughton, B. (1995). Hippocampal place fields, the internal compass, and the learning of landmark stability. *Journal of Neuroscience, 15,* 1648–1659.

Koffka, K. (1935). *Principles of Gestalt psychology.* New York: Harcourt, Brace, & World.

Kohler, W. (1947). *Gestalt psychology.* New York: Liveright.

Krashen, S., Long, M., & Scarcella, R. (1982). Age, rate, and eventual attainment in second language acquisition. In S. Krashen, R. Scarcella, & M. Long (Eds.), *Child-adult differences in second language acquisition.* Rowley, MA: Newbury House.

Krebs, J., Hilton, S. C., & Healy, S. D. (1990). Memory in food-storing birds: Adaptive specialization in brain and behavior? In G. M. Edelman, W. E. Gall, & W. M. Cowan (Eds.), *Signal and sense: Local and global order in perceptual maps* (pp. 475–498). New York: Wiley.

Kuhl, P., & Miller, J. (1978). Speech perception by the chinchilla: Identification functions for synthetic VOT stimuli. *Journal of the Acoustical Society of America, 63,* 905–917.

Lachter, J., & Bever, T. (1988). The relation between linguistic structure and associative theories of language learning—A constructive critique of some connectionist learning models. *Cognition, 28,* 195–247.

Landau, B., Gleitman, H., & Spelke, E. S. (1981). Spatial knowledge and geometric representation in a child blind from birth. *Science, 213,* 1275–1278.

Landau, B., & Jackendoff, R. (1993). "What" and "where" in spatial language and spatial cognition. *Behavioural and Brain Sciences, 16,* 217–265.

Landau, B., Smith, L. B., & Jones, S. S. (1988). The importance of shape in early lexical learning. *Cognitive Development, 3,* 299–321.

Landau, B., Spelke, E., & Gleitman, H. (1984). Spatial knowledge in a young blind child. *Cognition, 16,* 225–260.

Lehrman, D. S. (1970). Semantic and conceptual issues in the nature–nurture problem. In L. B. Aronson, E. Tobach, D. S. Lehrman, & J. S. Rosenblatt (Eds.), *Development and the evolution of behavior.* San Francisco: Freeman.

Leibniz, G. W. (1981). *New essays on human understanding* (P. Remnant & J. Bennett, Trans.). Cambridge, England: Cambridge University Press. (Original work published 1705)

Lenneberg, E. (1967). *Biological foundations of language*. New York: Wiley.

Lepecq, J. C., & Lafaite, M. (1989). The early development of position constancy in a no-landmark environment. *British Journal of Developmental Psychology, 7*, 289–306.

LeVay, S., Wiesel, T. N., & Hubel, D. H. (1980). The development of ocular dominance columns in normal and visually deprived monkeys. *Journal of Comparative Neurology, 191*, 1–51.

Levelt, W. (1989). *Speaking: From intention to articulation*. Cambridge, MA: MIT Press.

Levinson, S. (1992). *Language and cognition: The cognitive consequences of spatial description in Guugu Yimithirr*. Cognitive Anthropology Research Group, Max Planck Institute for Psycholinguistics, Working paper No. 13.

Levinson, S. (1994). Vision, shape, and linguistic description: Tzeltal body-part terminology and object description. *Linguistics, 32*, 791–855.

Levinson, S. (1996). Frames of reference and Molyneux's question: Cross-linguistic evidence. In P. Bloom, M. Peterson, L. Nadel, & M. Garrett (Eds.), *Language and space*. Cambridge, MA: MIT Press.

Levinson, S. (in press). The role of language in everyday human navigation. In M. Bowerman & S. Levinson (Eds.), *Language acquisition and conceptual development*. Cambridge, England: Cambridge University Press.

Lewis, D. (1976). Route finding by desert aborigines in Australia. *Journal of Navigation, 29*, 21–38.

Liben, L. S. (1988). Conceptual issues in the development of spatial cognition. In J. Stiles-Davis, M. Krichevsky, & U. Bellugi (Eds.), *Spatial cognition: Brain bases and development*. Hillsdale, NJ: Erlbaum.

Liberman, A., Cooper, F., Shankweiler, D., & Studdert-Kennedy, M. (1967). Perception of the speech code. *Psychological Review, 74*, 431–461.

Lisker, L., & Abramson, A. (1970). The voicing dimension: Some experiments in comparative phonetics. *Proceedings of the Sixth International Congress of Phonetic Sciences*. Prague: Academia.

Locke, J. (1975). In P. Nidditch (Ed.), *Essay concerning human understanding*. Oxford, England: Oxford University Press. (Original work published 1690)

Long, M. (1990). Maturational constraints on language development. *Studies in Second Language Acquisition, 12*, 251–285.

Loomis, J. M., Klatzky, R. L., Golledge, R. G., Cicinelli, J. G., Pellegrino, J. W., & Fry, P. A. (1993). Nonvisual navigation by blind and sighted: Assessment of path integration ability. *Journal of Experimental Psychology: General, 122*, 73–91.

Lucy, J. (1992). *Language diversity and thought*. Cambridge, England: Cambridge University Press.

MacWhinney, B., & Leinbach, J. (1991). Implementations are not conceptualizations: Revising the verb learning model. *Cognition, 40*, 121–157.

MacWhinney, B., & Snow, C. (1990). The child language data exchange system: An update. *Journal of Child Language, 17*, 457–472.

Mandler, J. M., & McDonough, L. (1993). Concept formation in infancy. *Cognitive Development, 8*, 291–318.

Maratsos, M., & Chalkley, M. A. (1980). The internal language of children's syntax: The ontogenesis and representation of syntactic categories. In K. Nelson (Ed.), *Children's language* (Vol. 2). New York: Gardner Press.

Marcus, G. (1996). *Can object permanence be learned?* Unpublished manuscript, University of Massachusetts.

Marcus, G., Brinkmann, U., Clahsen, H., Wiese, R., Woest, A., & Pinker, S. (1995). German inflection: The exception that proves the rule. *Cognitive Psychology, 29*, 186–256.

Marcus, G., Pinker, S., Ullman, M., Hollander, M., Rosen, T., & Xu, F. (1992). Overregularization in language acquisition. *Monographs of the Society for Research in Child Development, 57*(Serial No. 228).

Mareschal, D., Plunkett, K., & Harris, P. (1995). Developing object permanence: A connectionist model. In J. Moore & J. Lehman (Eds.), *Proceedings of the 17th Annual Conference of the Cognitive Science Society*. Hillsdale, NJ: Erlbaum.

Margules, J., & Gallistel, C. R. (1988). Heading in the rat: Determination by environmental shape. *Animal Learning and Behavior, 16*, 404–410.

Markman, E. M. (1989). *Categorization and naming in children*. Cambridge, MA: Bradford/MIT Press.

Markman, E. M. (1990). Constraints children place on word meanings. *Cognitive Science, 14*, 57–77.

Markman, E. M., & Wachtel, G. F. (1988). Children's use of mutual exclusivity to constrain the meaning of words. *Cognitive Psychology, 20*, 121–157.

Marler, P. (1970). A comparative approach to vocal learning: Song development in white-crowned sparrows. *Journal of Comparative and Physiological Psychology, 71*, 1–25.

Marler, P. (1991). The instinct to learn. In S. Carey & R. Gelman (Eds.), *The epigenesis of mind: Essays on biology and cognition*. Hillsdale, NJ: Erlbaum.

Marr, D. (1982). *Vision*. San Francisco: Freeman.

Mayberry, R., & Fischer, S. (1989). Looking through phonological shape to lexical meaning: The bottleneck of non-native sign language processing. *Memory and Cognition, 17*, 740–754.

McClelland, J. (1994). The interaction of nature and nurture in development: A parallel distributed processing approach. In P. Bertelson, P. Eelen, & G. D'Ydewalle (Eds.), *Current advances in psychological science: Ongoing research.* Hillsdale, NJ: Erlbaum.

McDonough, L., Mandler, J. M., McKee, R. D., & Squire, L. R. (1995). The deferred imitation task as a nonverbal measure of declarative memory. *Proceedings of the National Academy of Sciences, 92,* 7580–7584.

McGraw, M. B. (1940). Neuromuscular development of the human infant as exemplified in the achievement of erect locomotion. *Journal of Pediatrics, 17,* 747–771.

McKee, R., & Squire, L. R., (1993). On the development of declarative memory. *Journal of Experimental Psychology: Learning, Memory, and Cognition, 19*(2), 397–404.

McKenzie, B. E., Day, R. H., & Ihsen, E. (1984). Localization of events in space: Young infants are not always egocentric. *British Journal of Developmental Psychology, 2,* 1–9.

McNaughton, B. L., Knierim, J. J., & Wilson, M. A. (1995). Vector encoding and the vestibular foundations of spatial cognition: Neurophysiological and computational mechanisms. In M. S. Gazzaniga (Ed.), *The cognitive neurosciences.* Cambridge, MA: Bradford/MIT Press.

Meltzoff, A. N. (1988). Infant imitation after a one-week delay: Long-term memory for novel acts and multiple stimuli. *Developmental Psychology, 24,* 470–476.

Michotte, A. (1954). *Les complements amodaux des structures perceptives.* Louvain: Presses Universitaires de Louvain.

Millar, S. (1994). *Understanding and representing space: Theory and evidence from studies with blind and sighted children.* Oxford, England: Clarendon.

Miller, G. (1951). *Language and communication.* New York: McGraw-Hill.

Mintz, T. (1996). *The roles of linguistic input and innate mechanisms in children's acquisition of grammatical categories.* Unpublished doctoral dissertation, Department of Brain and Cognitive Sciences, University of Rochester, New York.

Mintz, T., Newport, E., & Bever, T. (1995). Distributional regularities of form class in speech to young children. In J. Beckman (Ed.), *Proceedings of the North East Linguistics Society* (Vol. 25). Amherst: University of Massachusetts.

Mithen, S. (1996). *The prehistory of the mind.* London: Thames & Hudson.

Mittelstaedt, M. L., & Mittelstaedt, H. (1980). Homing by path integration in a mammal. *Naturwissenschaften, 67,* 566–567.

Montgomery, K. (1952). A test of two explanations of spontaneous alternation. *Journal of Comparative and Physiological Psychology, 45,* 287–293.

Morgan, C. L. (1895). *An introduction to comparative psychology.* London: Walter Scott.

Morgan, J., & Saffran, J. (1995). Emerging integration of sequential and suprasegmental information in preverbal speech segmentation. *Child Development, 66,* 911–936.

Morgan, J., Shi, R., & Allopenna, P. (1995). Perceptual bases of rudimentary grammatical categories: Toward a broader conceptualization of bootstrapping. In J. Morgan & K. Demuth (Eds.), *Signal to syntax: Bootstrapping from speech to grammar in early acquisition.* Hillsdale, NJ: Erlbaum.

Morris, R. G. M. (1981). Spatial localization does not require the presence of local cues. *Learning and Motivation, 12,* 239–260.

Muller, J. (1842). *Elements of physiology* (W. Baly, Trans.). London: Taylor and Walton. (Original work published 1837)

Muller, M., & Wehner, R. (1988). Path integration in desert ants, Cataglyphis fortis. *Proceedings of the National Academy of Sciences USA, 85,* 5287–5290.

Munakata, Y. (in press). Task-dependency in infant behavior: Toward an understanding of the processes underlying cognitive development. In F. Lacerta, C. von Hofsten, & J. Heimann (Eds.), *Transitions in perception, cognition, and action in early infancy.*

Munakata, Y., McClelland, J. L., Johnson, M. H., & Siegler, R. S. (in press). Principles, processes, and infant knowledge: Rethinking successes and failures in object permanence tasks. *Psychological Review.*

Nadel, L. (1990). Varieties of spatial cognition: Psychobiological considerations. In A. Diamond (Ed.), The development and neural bases of higher cognitive functions. *Annals of the New York Academy of Sciences, 608,* 613–626.

Needham, A. (1994). *Infants' use of perceptual similarity when segregating partly occluded objects during the fourth month of life.* Paper presented at the International Conference on Infant Studies, Paris.

Needham, A., & Baillargeon, R. (1996). *Object segregation in 8-month-old infants.* Unpublished manuscript.

Needham, A., & Baillargeon, R. (in press). Effects of prior experience on 4.5-month-old infants' object segregation. *Infant Behavior and Development.*

Needham, A., Baillargeon, R., & Kaufman, L. (in press). Object segregation in infancy. In L. Lipsitt & C. Rovee-Collier (Eds.), *Advances in infancy research.*

Newcombe, N., Huttenlocher, J., Drummey, A. B., & Wiley, J. G. (1997). *The development of spatial location coding: Place learning and dead reckoning in the second and third years.* Unpublished manuscript.

Newport, E. (1988). Constraints on learning and their role in language acquisition: Studies of the acquisition of American Sign Language. *Language Sciences, 10,* 147–172.

Newport, E. (1990). Maturational constraints on language learning. *Cognitive Science, 14,* 11–28.

Newport, E. (in press). Reduced input in the acquisition of signed languages: Contributions to the study of creolization. In M. Degraff (Ed.), *Creolization, diachrony, and language acquisition.* Cambridge, MA: MIT Press.

Newport, E., & Meier, R. (1985). The acquisition of American Sign Language. In D. Slobin (Ed.), *Crosslinguistic study of language acquisition: Vol. 1. The data.* Hillsdale, NJ: Erlbaum.

O'Keefe, J. O., & Nadel, L. (1978): *The hippocampus as a cognitive map.* Oxford, England: Oxford University Press.

Olton, D. S., & Samuelson, R. J. (1976). Remembrance of places passed: Spatial memory in rats. *Journal of Experimental Psychology: Animal Behavior Processes, 2,* 97–116.

O'Reilly, R. C., & Johnson, M. H. (1994). Object recognition and sensitive periods: A computational analysis of visual imprinting. *Neural Computation, 6,* 357–389.

Oyama, S. (1978). The sensitive period and comprehension of speech. *Working Papers on Bilingualism, 16,* 1–17.

Oyama, S. (1985). *The ontogeny of information: Developmental systems and evolution.* Cambridge, England: Cambridge University Press.

Patkowski, M. (1980). The sensitive period for the acquisition of syntax in a second language. *Language Learning, 30,* 449–472.

Petitto, L., & Marentette, P. (1991). Babbling in the manual mode: Evidence for the ontogeny of language. *Science, 251,* 1493–1496.

Piaget, J. (1952). *The origins of intelligence in childhood.* New York: International Universities Press.

Piaget, J. (1954). *The construction of reality in the child.* New York: Basic Books.

Piaget, J., Inhelder, B., & Szeminska, A. (1960). *The child's conception of geometry.* New York: Basic Books.

Pinker, S. (1984). *Language learnability and language learning.* Cambridge, MA: Harvard University Press.

Pinker, S. (1989). *Learnability and cognition: The acquisition of argument structure.* Cambridge, MA: Bradford/MIT Press.

Pinker, S. (1991). Rules of language. *Science, 253,* 530–535.

Pinker, S. (1994). *The language instinct.* New York: Morrow.

Pinker, S., & Prince, A. (1988). On language and connectionism: Analysis of a parallel distributed processing model of language acquisition. *Cognition, 28,* 73–193.

Pisoni, D. (1977). Identification and discrimination of relative onset time of two component tones: Implications for voicing perception in stops. *Journal of the Acoustical Society of America, 61,* 1352–1361.

Pisoni, D., Aslin, R., Perey, A., & Hennessey, B. (1982). Some effects of laboratory training on identification and discrimination of voicing contrasts in stop consonants. *Journal of Experimental Psychology: Human Perception and Performance, 8,* 297–314.

Plato. (1961). Meno (W. K. C. Guthrie, Trans.). In E. Hamilton & H. Cairns (Eds.), *The collected dialogues.* New York: Pantheon Books.

Plunkett, K., & Marchman, V. (1991). U-shaped learning and frequency effects in a multi-layered perception: Implications for child language acquisition. *Cognition, 38,* 43–102.

Plunkett, K., & Marchman, V. (1993). From rote learning to system building: Acquiring verb morphology in children and connectionist nets. *Cognition, 48,* 21–69.

Premack, D. (1976). *Intelligence in ape and man.* Hillsdale, NJ: Erlbaum.

Quine, W. V. O. (1960). *Word and object.* Cambridge, MA: MIT Press.

Rader, N., Bausano, M., & Richards, J. E. (1980). On the nature of the visual-cliff avoidance response in human infants. *Child Development, 51,* 61–68.

Rakic, P. (1977). Prenatal development of the visual system in rhesus monkey. *Philosophical transactions of the Royal Society of London, Series B, 278,* 245–260.

Redington, F., Chater, N., & Finch, S. (1993). Distributional information and the acquisition of linguistic categories: A statistical approach. *Proceedings of the 15th Annual Conference of the Cognitive Science Society.* Hillsdale, NJ: Erlbaum.

Regolin, L., & Vallortigara, G. (1995). Perception of partly occluded objects by young chicks. *Perception and Psychophysics, 57,* 971–976.

Regolin, L., Vallortigara, G., & Zanforlin, M. (1995a). Detour behavior in the domestic chick: Searching for a disappearing prey or a disappearing social partner. *Animal Behavior, 50,* 203–211.

Regolin, L., Vallortigara, G., & Zanforlin, M. (1995b). Object and spatial representations in detour problems by chicks. *Animal Behavior, 49,* 195–199.

Rieser, J. J. (1979). Spatial orientation of six-month-olds. *Child Development, 50,* 1079–1087.

Rieser, J. J. (1990). Development of perceptual-motor control while walking without vision: The calibration of perception and action. In H. Bloch & B. I. Bertenthal (Eds.), *Sensory-*

motor organization and development in infancy and early childhood (pp. 379–408). Amsterdam, The Netherlands: Kluwer.

Rock, I. (1983). *The logic of perception.* Cambridge, MA: Bradford/MIT Press.

Roe, A. W., Pallas, S. L., Kwon, Y. H., & Sur, M. (1992). Visual projections routed to the auditory pathway in ferrets: Receptive fields of visual neurons in primary auditory cortex. *Journal of Neuroscience, 12,* 3651–3664.

Rovee-Collier, C. K., & Gekoski, M. J. (1979). The economics of infancy: A review of conjugate reinforcement. *Advances in Child Development and Behavior, 13,* 195–255.

Rozin, P. (1976). The evolution of intelligence and access to the cognitive unconscious. In J. M. Sprague & A. A. Epstein (Eds.), *Progress in psycho-biology and psysiological psychology* (Vol. 6). New York: Academic Press.

Rumelhart, D., & McClelland, J. (1986). On learning the past tenses of English verbs. In J. McClelland & D. Rumelhart (Eds.), *Parallel distributed processing: Explorations in the microstructure of cognition: Vol. 2. Psychological and biological models.* Cambridge, MA: MIT Press.

Saffran, J., Aslin, R., & Newport, E. (1996). Statistical learning by 8-month-old infants. *Science, 274,* 1926–1928.

Saffran, J., Newport, E., Aslin, R., Tunick, R., & Barrueco, S. (1997). Incidental language learning: Listening (and learning) out of the corner of your ear. *Psychological Science, 8,* 101–105.

St. Paul, U. von (1982). Do geese use path integration for walking home? In F. Papi & H. G. Wallraff (Eds.), *Avian navigation* (pp. 298–307). New York: Springer.

Sankoff, G., & Laberge, S. (1973). On the acquisition of native speakers by a language. *Kivung, 6,* 32–47.

Sapir, E. (1921). *Language: An introduction to the study of speech.* New York: Harcourt Brace.

Savage-Rumbaugh, E. (1991). Language learning in the bonobo: How and why they learn. In N. Krasnegor, D. Rumbaugh, R. Schiefelbusch, & M. Studdert-Kennedy (Eds.), *Biological and behavioral determinants of language development.* Hillsdale, NJ: Erlbaum.

Savage-Rumbaugh, E., Murphy, J., Sevcik, R., Brakke, K., Williams, S., & Rumbaugh, D. (1993). Language comprehension in ape and child. *Monographs of the Society for Research in Child Development, 58*(Serial No. 233).

Scarr, S. (1993). Biological and cultural diversity: The legacy of Darwin for development. *Child Development, 64,* 1333–1353.

Senghas, A. (1995). *Children's contribution to the birth of Nicaraguan sign language.* Unpublished doctoral disserta-

tion, Department of Brain and Cognitive Sciences, MIT, Cambridge, MA.

Shatz, C. J. (1992). The developing brain. *Scientific American, 267,* 60–67.

Shatz, C. J., & Stryker, M. P. (1988). Prenatal tetrodotoxin blocks segregation of retinogeniculate afferents. *Science, 242,* 87–89.

Sherk, H., & Stryker, M. P. (1976). Quantitative study of cortical orientation selectivity in visually inexperienced kitten. *Journal of Neurophysiology, 39,* 63–70.

Silberstein, C. S., & Spelke, E. S. (1995). *Explicit vs. implicit processes in spatial cognition.* Poster presented at the meeting of the Society for Research in Child Development, Indianapolis, IN.

Simon, T., Hespos, S., & Rochat, P. (1995). Do infants understand simple arithmetic? A replication of Wynn. *Cognitive Development, 10,* 253–269.

Singleton, J. (1989). *Restructuring of language from impoverished input: Evidence for linguistic compensation.* Doctoral dissertation, University of Illinois.

Singleton, J., & Newport, E. (1994). *When learners surpass their models: The acquisition of American Sign Language from impoverished input.* Unpublished manuscript, University of Illinois.

Slater, A., Johnson, S. P., Kellman, P. J., & Spelke, E. S. (1995). The role of three-dimensional depth cues in infants' perception of partly occluded objects. *Early Development and Parenting, 3,* 187–191.

Slater, A., Mattock, A., & Brown, E. (1990). Size constancy at birth: Newborn infants' responses to retinal and real size. *Journal of Experimental Child Psychology, 49,* 314–322.

Slater, A., Morison, V., Somers, M., Mattock, A., Brown, E., & Taylor, D. (1990). Newborn and older infants' perception of partly occluded objects. *Infant Behavior and Development, 13,* 33–49.

Slavoff, G., & Johnson, J. (1995). The effects of age on the rate of learning a second language. *Studies in Second Language Acquisition, 17,* 1–16.

Slobin, D. (1973). Cognitive prerequisites for the development of grammar. In C. A. Ferguson & D. J. Slobin (Eds.), *Studies in child language development.* New York: Holt, Rinehart and Winston.

Slobin, D. (Ed.). (1985). *Crosslinguistic study of language acquisition* (Vols. 1 & 2). Hillsdale, NJ: Erlbaum.

Slobin, D. (Ed.). (1992). *Crosslinguistic study of language acquisition* (Vol. 3). Hillsdale, NJ: Erlbaum.

Smith, C., Carey, S., & Wiser, M. (1985). On differentiation: A case study of the development of concepts of size, weight, and density. *Cognition, 21,* 177–237.

Smith, C., Johnson, S., Spelke, E. S., & Aslin, R. N. (1996). Edge sensitivity and temporal integration in young infants' perception of object unity. *Infant Behavior and Development, 19,* 749.

Soja, N., Carey, S., & Spelke, E. S. (1990). Ontological categories guide young children's inductions of word meaning: Object terms and substance terms. *Cognition, 38,* 179–211.

Spelke, E. S. (1990). Principles of object perception. *Cognitive Science, 14,* 29–56.

Spelke, E. S., Breinlinger, K., Jacobson, K., & Phillips, A. (1993). Gestalt relations and object perception: A developmental study. *Perception, 22,* 1483–1501.

Spelke, E. S., Breinlinger, K., Macomber, J., & Jacobson, K. (1992). Origins of knowledge. *Psychological Review, 99,* 605–632.

Spelke, E. S., Hofsten, C. von, & Kestenbaum, R. (1989). Object perception and object-directed reaching in infancy: Interaction of spatial and kinetic information for object boundaries. *Developmental Psychology, 25,* 185–196.

Spelke, E. S., Kestenbaum, R., Simons, D., & Wein, D. (1995). Spatio-temporal continuity, smoothness of motion, and object identity in infancy. *British Journal of Developmental Psychology, 13,* 113–142.

Spelke, E. S., & Tsivkin, S. (in press). Initial knowledge and conceptual change: Space and number. In M. Bowerman & S. Levinson (Eds.), *Language acquisition and conceptual development.* Cambridge, England: Cambridge University Press.

Spelke, E. S., & Van de Walle, G. A. (1993). Perceiving and reasoning about objects: Insights from infants. In N. Eilan, W. Brewer, & R. McCarthy (Eds.), *Spatial representation.* Oxford, England: Basil Blackwell.

Spelke, E. S., Vishton, P., & von Hofsten, C. (1995). Object perception, object-directed action, and physical knowledge in infancy. In M. S. Gazzaniga (Ed.), *The cognitive neurosciences.* Cambridge, MA: MIT Press.

Super, C. (1976). Environmental effects on motor development: The case of African infant precocity. *Developmental Medicine and Child Neurology, 18,* 561–567.

Sutherland, R., & Dyck, R. (1984). Place navigation by rats in a swimming pool. *Canadian Journal of Psychology, 38,* 322–347.

Talmy, L. (1983). How language structures space. In H. Pick & L. Acredolo (Eds.), *Spatial orientation: Theory, research and application* (pp. 225–282). New York: Plenum Press.

Thelen, E. (1979). Rhythmical stereotypies in normal human infants. *Animal Behavior, 27,* 699–715.

Thelen, E. (1984). Learning to walk: Ecological demands and hylogenetic constraints. In L. P. Lipsitt & C. Rovee-Collier (Eds.), *Advances in infancy research* (Vol. 3). New York: ABLEX.

Thelen, E. (1986). Treadmill-elicited stepping in seven-month-old infants. *Child Development, 57,* 1498–1506.

Thelen, E., Bradshaw, G., & Ward, J. A. (1981). Spontaneous kicking in month-old infants: Manifestation of a human central locomotor program. *Behavioral and Neural Biology, 32,* 45–53.

Thelen, E., & Cooke, D. W. (1987). Relationship between newborn stepping and later walking: A new interpretation. *Developmental Medicine and Child Neurology, 29,* 380–393.

Thelen, E., & Fisher, D. M. (1982). Newborn stepping: An explanation for a "disappearing" reflex. *Developmental Psychology, 18,* 760–775.

Thelen, E., & Fisher, D. M. (1983a). The organization of spontaneous leg movements in newborn infants. *Journal of Motor Behavior, 15,* 353–377.

Thelen, E., & Fisher, D. M. (1983b). From spontaneous to instrumental behavior: Kinematic analysis of movement changes during very early learning. *Child Development, 54,* 129–140.

Thelen, E., Fisher, D. M., & Ridley-Johnson, R. (1984). The relationship between physical growth and a newborn reflex. *Infant Behavior and Development, 7,* 479–493.

Thelen, E., Ridley-Johnson, R., & Fisher, D. M. (1983). Shifting patterns of bilateral coordination and later dominance in the leg movements of young infants. *Developmental Psychobiology, 16,* 29–46.

Thelen, E., & Smith L. B. (1994). *A dynamical systems approach to the development of cognition and action.* Cambridge, MA: Bradford/MIT Press.

Thelen, E., Ulrich, B. D., & Niles, D. (1987). Bilateral coordination in human infants: Stepping on a split-belt treadmill. *Journal of Experimental Psychology: Human Perception and Performance, 13,* 405–410.

Thinus-Blanc, C., & Gaunet, F. (1997). Representation of space in blind persons: Vision as a spatial sense? *Psychological Bulletin, 121,* 20–42.

Thorndike, E. L. (1911). *Animal intelligence: Experimental studies.* New York: Macmillan.

Tinbergen, N. (1951). *The study of instinct.* Oxford, England: Clarendon.

Tolman, E. C. (1948). Cognitive maps in rats and men. *Psychological Review, 55,* 189–208.

Tomasello, M., Kruger, A. C., & Ratner, H. H. (1993). Cultural learning. *Behavioral and Brain Sciences, 16,* 495–552.

Turkewitz, G., & Kenny, P. (1982). Limitations on input as a basis for neural organization and perceptual development: A preliminary theoretical statement. *Developmental Psychobiology, 15,* 257–368.

Vallortigara, G., Zanforlin, M., & Pasti, G. (1990). Geometric modules in animals' spatial representations: A test with chicks (Gallus gallus domesticus). *Journal of Comparative Psychology, 104,* 248–254.

Vander Wall, S. B. (1982). An experimental analysis of seed recovery in Clark's nutcracker. *Animal Behavior, 30,* 84–94.

Van de Walle, G. A., & Hoerger, M. (1996). The perceptual foundations of categorization in infancy [Abstract]. *Infant Behavior and Development, 19,* 794.

Van de Walle, G. A., & Spelke E. S. (in press). Spatiotemporal integration and object perception in infancy: Perceiving unity vs. form. *Child Development.*

Walk, R. D., & Gibson, E. J. (1961). A comparative and analytical study of visual depth perception. *Psychological Monographs, 75*(Whole No. 5).

Walk, R. D., Gibson, E. J., & Tighe, T. J. (1957). Behavior of light- and dark-reared rats on the visual cliff. *Science, 126,* 80–81.

Wallach, H. (1985). Learned stimulation in space and motion perception. *American Psychologist, 40,* 399–404.

Walters, C. (1981). Development of the visual placing response in the human infant. *Journal of Experimental Child Psychology, 32,* 313–329.

Wehner, R., & Flatt, I. (1972). The visual orientation of desert ants, Cataglyphis bicolor, by means of territorial cues. In R. Wehner (Ed.), *Information processing in the visual system of arthropods* (pp. 295–302). New York: Springer.

Wehner, R., & Srinivasan, M. V. (1981). Searching behavior of desert ants, genus Cataglyphis. *Journal of Comparative Physiology, 142,* 315–338.

Werker, J., & Lalonde, C. (1988). Cross-language speech perception: Initial capabilities and developmental change. *Developmental Psychology, 24,* 672–683.

Werker, J., & Tees, R. (1984). Cross-language speech perception: Evidence for perceptual reorganization during the first year of life. *Infant Behavior and Development, 7,* 49–63.

Wertheimer, M. (1958). Principles of perceptual organization. In D. C. Beardslee & M. Wertheimer (Eds.), *Readings in perception.* New York: Van Nostrand. (Original work published 1923)

Wiggins, D. (1980). *Sameness and substance.* Oxford, England: Basil Blackwell.

Wilcox, T., Rosser, R., & Nadel, L. (1994). Representation of object location in 6.5-month-old infants. *Cognitive Development, 9,* 193–210.

Woodward, J. (1978). Historical bases of American Sign Language. In P. Siple (Ed.), *Understanding language through sign language research.* New York: Academic Press.

Wynn, K. (1990). Children's understanding of counting. *Cognition, 36,* 155–193.

Wynn, K. (1992). Addition and subtraction in infants. *Nature, 358,* 749–750.

Xu, F., & Carey, S. (1994, June). *Infants' ability to individuate and trace identity of objects.* Paper presented at the International Conference on Infant Studies, Paris.

Xu, F., & Carey, S. (1996). Infants' metaphysics: The case of numerical identity. *Cognitive Psychology, 30,* 111–153.

Yonas, A., & Granrud, C. (1984). The development of sensitivity to kinetic, binocular, and pictorial depth information in human infants. In D. Ingle, D. Lee, & M. Jeannerod (Eds.), *Brain mechanisms and spatial vision* (pp. 113–145). Dordrecht, The Netherlands: Martines Nijoff Press.

Yonas, A., & Granrud, C. (1985). Development of visual space perception in young infants. In J. Mehler & R. Fox (Eds.), *Neonate cognition: Beyond the blooming, buzzing confusion.* Hillsdale, NJ: Erlbaum.

Zelazo, P. R. (1983). The development of walking: New findings and old assumptions. *Journal of Motor Behavior, 15,* 99–137.

Zelazo, P. R., Zelazo, N. A., & Kolb, S. (1972). Walking in the newborn. *Science, 176,* 314–315.

CHAPTER 7

Cognitive Science and the Origins of Thought and Knowledge

FRANK C. KEIL

We can loosely describe cognitive science as the study of how mental representations come to guide our thoughts and actions. This chapter will develop a fuller characterization by discussing the historical roots of cognitive science and, even more importantly, by showing how six questions about the mind require a cognitive science approach for adequate answers. The primary purpose of this discussion, however, is to show how cognitive science in all areas assumes and

relies on issues concerning the origins of thought and knowledge. In doing so, cognitive science makes possible questions and answers about cognitive development that were not normally considered in traditional developmental psychology. At the same time, developmental issues and perspectives are shaping cognitive science in ways that may change its very nature. To illustrate this interdependency, the chapter concludes with a discussion of some new ways of looking at cognitive development that arise largely from a cognitive science perspective.

Cognitive science might appear to be a creature of the past two decades. Nurtured by key funding decisions in the

Preparation of this paper and some of the research described therein was supported by NIH Grant R01-HD23922.

early 1970s, it arose from a surge of theoretical and empirical interactions across several traditional disciplines. The fruits of this surge occupy much of this chapter; but even the most casual appreciation of cognitive science and its relation to developmental psychology must recognize a much longer historical tradition—a tradition that laid the groundwork for the recent, more widely apparent revolution. Looking at cognitive science in a broad historical context also serves the primary mission of this chapter, which is to highlight a long-standing set of connections to issues that have been central to the traditional discipline of developmental psychology. In the past, the integration of developmental issues with other fundamental questions about the mind and human nature was extensive and well-motivated. Presently, such links are often attempted through appeals to "applied" issues or to the political and social consequences of developmental questions.

It is folly to attempt here a comprehensive account of the roots of cognitive science in such a diverse array of disciplines as philosophy, psychology, linguistics, and computer science. Other lengthy treatments of cognitive science that extensively examine its historical roots are invariably highly selective (e.g., Bechtel, 1988a, 1988b; Flanagan, 1984; Livingston, in preparation; Stilling et al., 1995). The goals of this historical discussion are simpler: (a) to show how developmental issues traditionally could not stand in isolation and were inseparable from other questions concerning the mind and human nature; and (b) to illustrate how, for centuries, discussions concerning the nature of the mind and the acquisition of knowledge have been intrinsically multidisciplinary, in the true spirit of cognitive science. Only in this century have discussions tended to be much more provincial in nature. A few historical examples from philosophy, psychology, linguistics, and computer science are sufficient to illustrate these two goals.

COGNITIVE SCIENCE BEFORE ITS TIME: THE MULTIDISCIPLINARY NATURE OF EARLY QUESTIONS ABOUT THE MIND AND ITS DEVELOPMENT

The earliest proposals about the nature of the mind occurred in classical philosophy. Aristotle (1907), for example, especially in *De Anima,* discussed the mind in ways that carried both explicit and implicit proposals about

psychological mechanisms and the acquisition of knowledge. Aristotle was an unrepenting materialist who viewed cognition as another facet of the physiological functioning of the body. He had a highly physical mechanistic theory of mind wherein psychological states were assumed to have direct physiologically and physically specifiable correlates that fully individuated them. If one became sad, a clear physical event occurred in the body (for Aristotle, it occurred in the blood). If one perceived a color, a physical change that directly corresponded to that color occurred in the body. Indeed, each of the sense organs has unique physical correlates of its respective inputs. Each is tuned for particular sets of physical properties, such as eyes for color and ears for sounds.

In discussing these perceptual systems in detail in *De Anima,* Aristotle realized that the sensory transducers posed a special problem. They were biologically tailored for different kinds of inputs, and this specialization forced a series of questions concerning what must happen next in the course of perception and cognition. How were these distinct sources of sensory information integrated to give rise to knowledge and phenomenal experience? Aristotle's solution, which endures in much of cognitive science today, was that the transducers are tailored to yield relatively few and highly simple informational primitives, and a higher general faculty, translated as commonsense, integrates across the modalities. Commonsense also constructs higher-order correlations of these inputs, such as would be necessary for perceiving perceptual patterns such as faces. One of the best known translators of *De Anima,* R. D. Hicks, put it this way in his notes accompanying *De Anima:*

> There could be no sense and no sense organ outside the five he has described, and no one of these five apprehends . . . [Greek word for "movement"]. This is the first step towards developing his doctrine of *sensus communis* . . . in which the five special senses are merged and coalesce. (Aristotle, 1907, pp. 425–426)

What emerges here is a strong forerunner to both 17th-century and current empiricist approaches to cognition and the origins of knowledge. The only biological specializations for distinct kinds of information occur at the sensory periphery. That information is integrated in a common vehicle of thought and knowledge acquisition as it flows inward. Aristotle anticipated the need to look at both physiological and psychological mechanisms, and he made many more proposals about the architecture of each than later philosophers were willing to venture.

Unfettered by disciplinary boundaries that did not even exist at his time, Aristotle demonstrated, in vivid ways, many current reasons for the existence of cognitive science. As he considered fundamental questions about human action, perception, and cognition, and other questions about the nature of knowledge and categorization, he incorporated ideas, models, and observations that drew from what we today think of as the disciplines of biology, psychology, linguistics, and, of course, philosophy. It seemed natural and appropriate to make such integrations. Aristotle was no means unique in making them early on, but his integrations are among the most comprehensive and explicit. Such a feeling of naturalness is only starting to become more widespread today.

A Knowledge Acquisition Device

Aristotle's views, although clearly presaging many issues in current cognitive science, were less explicit about the acquisition of knowledge. The empiricist assumptions are clear, but he was less concerned with directly explaining the many problems of knowledge acquisition and cognitive development. By contrast, in the 17th century, developmental issues dominated discussions of the mind, especially in the writings of Renée Descartes (1977). Descartes's ideas heavily influenced how we think about the mental machinery responsible for the acquisition and representation of knowledge (see also Overton, Ch. 3, this Volume).

Descartes's best known work on the mind deals with the mind–body problem and his commitment to a dualism in which the mind is completely different from the physical world, including the brain. But Descartes's impact on cognitive science extends far beyond the mind–body problem. The majority of contemporary cognitive scientists seem to have rejected dualism in its strong form, and, in doing so, many assume that Descartes is of only modest historical relevance. But one can interpret Descartes's dualist position as the more modern idea that principles of mind are fundamentally different from those of the body, including the brain. (See Fischer & Bidell, Ch. 9, this Volume, for the contrasting view that the principles governing mind and body are essentially the same.) Our mental actions might

well be grounded in a physical base, but attempts to reduce models of cognition to statements regarding physical entities are both misguided and, in principle, uninformative (e.g., Fodor, 1975).

The debates between various forms of reductionism and the extreme of eliminativism continue hotly today, and Descartes's sense of a fundamental mind–body distinction remains a strong and viable view. It also has developmental implications for how the mind and the brain might be related from birth onward. What inferences is one licensed to make about cognitive states and changes based on alterations in underlying physical systems? Is there a level of physical description (say, in terms of functional architecture) that is much more closely linked to the cognitive level than to the real physical substrate? Is there a level where developmental links between mind and brain changes might be most evident?

Descartes also advocated a strong form of nativism; infants come into the world with powerful structures that provide much of the organization of the more obvious and explicit knowledge that we all share. The innate structures, however, had considerably more complexity and subtlety than might appear in some of the cruder characterizations of Descartes. Descartes did maintain, in *Meditations,* that we all come into the world with a mind that is fully ready to understand some principles of logic; geometric figures and principles; and, most importantly for Descartes, God. But this ability to know such components of thought did not mean that full-fledged ideas were present in the newborn. For Descartes, there was an important difference between being natively endowed with a set of concrete and fully articulated ideas and having a set of specific predispositions to acquire those ideas with only very modest experience. He favored a view in which humans have a "natural power" to come to know particular ideas rather than having the ideas themselves. This is a subtler and more interesting view of nativism than is often attributed to Descartes, and it has inspired numerous current scholars in cognitive science (e.g., Chomsky, 1966). Many researchers today are focusing extensively on the challenge of specifying how a specific predisposition to learn a form of knowledge exists without that knowledge itself being present.

Descartes's notions about how innate tendencies come to yield specific sets of ideas are among the best known in pre-20th-century philosophy, but they hardly stand alone. Plato's discussion, in the *Meno,* of how Socrates guided a slave boy to come to recognize certain mathematical and geometrical principles by exploring his own knowledge, is one of the earliest recorded examples of such tendencies, although, for Plato at least, the tendencies were apt to be more circumscribed by the boundaries of mathematics, geometry, and logic. In addition, Plato's views lack the more sophisticated speculations about the nature of the learning process itself that are seen in later treatments, such as those by Descartes and by Leibniz (Leibniz, 1896). Nonetheless, as seen below, even Plato's suggestion that one might uncover formal principles through internal analyses of one's own thoughts is once again being seriously considered in cognitive science.

Linking Elements in the Mind

The 17th and 18th centuries brought the emergence of the British empiricists—most notably, Locke, Berkeley, and Hume—who posited a view of mind much closer to Aristotle's view than to Plato's (Berkeley, 1709/1901; Hume, 1951; Locke, 1690/1964). It was obvious to them that the sensory receptors were designed for particular kinds of information. However, like Aristotle, they argued that shortly after the most basic senses and percepts have been registered, information is acquired through a general learning device—in their view, an associationist one. But to remember these philosophers in this simple way underestimates how much they anticipated a cognitive science approach to the study of mind. Locke, for example, did not blindly promote associationism as the primary mechanism of knowledge acquisition and restructuring. He seemed to foresee the need for two distinct aspects to learning: (a) a simple associative mechanism and (b) a mechanism that involved a more elaborate set of principled connections among ideas. Indeed, he regarded an excessive capture by mere associationist processes as to leading to all sorts of accidental connections that impair rather than help thought (Alexander, 1985).

Locke was also much taken with the chemist Robert Boyle's corpuscular model of matter in which all matter is reducible to tiny corpuscles that have only a small number of primitive qualities. Locke felt that the mind was similarly composed of constituents with only a small number of qualities. This assumption led to an interest in associationism as a way of combining those primitives, but Locke could never escape the view that a different way of combining ideas and primitives was also needed. These issues and

the tensions they create are very much in the current cognitive science literature. Across all areas, researchers are wrestling with the apparent need for hybrid representations that are a mix of associationist-like components and more rule-like, or propositional, ones (Neisser, 1963; Sloman, 1996). These debates are also infused with questions about the appropriate sorts of primitives, such as whether they should be subsymbolic in the connectionist sense or more truly symbolic, again echoing Locke's concerns about the kinds of primitives and their qualities.

The implications of Locke's writings for cognitive science go much further. His writings have clear implications for theories of sense and reference, for the acquisition of word meaning, and for claims of naïve essentialism in adult and child concepts. There are also many implications to be drawn from Berkeley and Hume beyond the general associationist and empiricist views. Berkeley, for example, in true cognitive science fashion, and in addition to extensive discussion of relatively abstract issues such as how knowledge might be acquired through perception, proposed a highly specific psychological and physiological model of how the ability to perceive objects in depth develops in infancy (Berkeley, 1709/1901). The model was meant both as an existence proof of how the more abstract conjectures could work and as an explicit proposal for a mechanism. As objects move closer to the head, the eyes converge more to track the objects; and sensations of increasing convergence, when paired with real distance, provide the data pairs for an associative build-up of an ability to see objects in depth. Infants pair particular sensations of convergence with such things as the amount of reach needed to touch an object. With enough sets of distinct pairs, the angle of convergence can then indicate the distance to the objects. This model was so well worked out and appealing that it continues to be studied in research on infants' perception (Aslin, 1986). It no longer is held to be the primary method through which infants come to see objects in depth, but it does seem to be part of the story.

Berkeley also employed several strong assumptions about the reaching behaviors of infants and the links of such behaviors to an understanding of where objects are in space—again, an area of very active inquiry (Vishton, 1996; Von Hofsten & Fazel-Zandy, 1984). Similar demonstrations can show the relevance to current cognitive science of David Hume's discussions of empiricism and impressions of causality (see, e.g., Cohen & Oakes, 1993; Leslie, 1982; Leslie & Keeble, 1987). As described later in this chapter, there continue to be vigorous debates about the extent to which the emergence of causal understanding can be reduced to tabulations of experienced correlations (e.g., Cheng & Lien, 1995; Glymour, 1987).

Not everyone was convinced that all links between mental elements were products solely of environmental contingencies. Kant was one of the strong opponents. He rejected empiricist views of learning, endorsed a view of the mind as actively constructing knowledge, and advocated a method of inferring, through transcendental deduction, the invisible nature of the mind from inferences about observables, such as behavior (Flanagan, 1984). Kant saw us all as endowed with uniquely human ways of structuring our impressions of the physical and social worlds without necessarily having highly concrete expectations of what is out there. As argued later in this chapter, this is one way of thinking about an abstract-to-concrete shift in cognitive development.

There was, therefore, no consensus in the late 19th century about how thought and knowledge might be structured and how those structures might arise. The debate, however, was wonderfully sophisticated and drew on ideas and models from many diverse fields of inquiry. It was very much in the spirit of modern cognitive science. Questions about the origins of thought and knowledge were often central and seemed to foster the inclusion of ideas from many areas. Consider, for example, how C. S. Peirce, struggling in the late 19th century with questions about the origins of reasoning and logic, turned to the recent ideas of Darwin. Peirce saw reasoning as composed of deduction, induction, and abduction (a special ability to uncover patterns in the real world at much greater than chance levels). Abduction worked because natural selection had endowed us with certain "aptitudes for guessing right" (Peirce, 1960–1966).

In the 20th century, following psychology's splitting off from philosophy, philosophy itself began to be more encapsulated. William James stands out as a notable exception who seamlessly blended a host of philosophical, psychological, and physiological themes in his attempts to understand the mind, but many who followed him turned away from any consideration of the mind at all. The rise of behaviorism in America had a strong influence on philosophical thought. In behaviorism's uneasy alliance with logical positivism, with its own peculiar "anticognitive" take on language, several decades ensued with few contributions for cognitive science (Smith, 1986). Exceptions appeared in the writings of Wittgenstein, Russell, and others, but

central cognitive issues were surprisingly sparse until the mid-1960s, when, in conjunction with several other disciplines, modern cognitive science started to emerge. The recent history of philosophy's role in cognitive science is touched on in later sections of this chapter, but one observation is relevant here. Classic philosophical approaches to the mind, compared to many current approaches, saw developmental issues as much more central. Discussions in an earlier era often asked how a child could come to understand and act upon the world; today, such questions are often pushed to the background, and debates center instead around such issues as the modularity of cognition, the nature of mental representations, and the relations between mind and language. These current issues are of fundamental importance, but, to be rendered fully sensible, even they may require more attention to knowledge acquisition issues, just as questions on knowledge acquisition in psychology require much clearer commitments to philosophical queries concerning modularity, mental representations, and thought and language.

These examples from a few Western philosophers show how easily and naturally their questions about the mind would today be considered in the interdisciplinary spirit of cognitive science. Without the tunnel vision imposed by the disciplines that had not yet emerged, the earlier philosophers naturally connected themes across today's disciplines of philosophy, biology, mathematics, psychology, and linguistics. Although they did not use today's vocabularies of mental representations and processing models, they clearly touched on these issues in rich and comprehensive ways. Indeed, it is difficult not to read the works of any of the great Western philosophers without soon coming across ideas and proposals that are relevant to modern cognitive science. And in those classical accounts, the issue of how we all come to know the world is so completely interwoven with other cognitive science issues that its separation as a distinct question becomes impossible. One suspects that a much broader survey of philosophical traditions across many different cultures would unearth the same multidisciplinary flavor coupled with a recurrent fascination with the developmental origins of understanding.

Mechanisms of Mind

One does not have to go nearly as far back in time to examine the distinctly psychological roots of cognitive science. For the most part, psychology's emergence as a separate discipline, distinct from philosophy, occurred in the last half of the 19th century (Boring, 1957). Several 19th-century scholars played a vital role in the birth of psychology as a new field, and those most emphasized reflect current views of psychology as much as the historical record: Helmholtz (1925), for his contributions to a theory of vision; Wundt (1897), for his development of the first experimental laboratory of psychology; Spencer (1864/1907), for his situating psychology in a broader context of biology and addressing issues of development; Galton (1883), for focusing on individual differences in mental functioning; Broca (1861), for linking specific brain regions to specific cognitive functions; James (1891/1950), for reasons discussed above; and Darwin (1872/1975, 1877), for putting human behavior in more of a comparative and evolutionary context.

All of these pioneers of the new discipline had breadth and vision that went far beyond the more parochial approaches that the mature discipline of psychology seems to demand of its current practitioners. To the extent that these thinkers started to integrate across such topics as linguistic phenomena, psychological processes, and conceptual analyses, they were acting more like cognitive scientists and less like psychologists. Wundt was a superb example. Having worked as an assistant to Helmholtz, he was exposed early on to a powerful mind that drew on topics across many of the sciences. For Wundt, it was only the beginning of an interdisciplinary perspective; he became renowned for his extraordinary polymathic knowledge, which ranged from physiology to anatomy, to psychology, to anthropology, and to linguistics. He is considered the founder not only of experimental psychology but also of psycholinguistics (Blumenthal, 1970, 1975), and, in many ways, he anticipated the need for a cognitive science approach to the mind.

It is easy to find other cases of such higher-level integrations, whether in some of the computational biases shown by Helmholtz, or in the clear blending of philosophy and psychology shown by James. Many of the same people who showed this kind of interdisciplinary vigor also turned strongly to questions of cognitive and perceptual development—Darwin's studies of his own children's development, Spencer's views on education and learning, Galton's raising of nature–nurture questions of development. It is therefore relatively easy to find cognitive science and development themes in the writings of these and

other early psychologists. It is more surprising to find the same pattern in another enormous figure of this period, Sigmund Freud (1905/1976, 1965, 1966), who is most often associated with the origins of personality theory and psychoanalysis.

Freud's legacy for cognitive science is surprisingly strong (Kitcher, 1992). He was completely committed to an interdisciplinary approach to the construction of a theory of mind, and he felt that neglect of this approach would result in impoverished insights. He argued that one must draw on concepts and findings in neuroanatomy, biology, evolutionary theory, psychology, and what we would today consider anthropology and linguistics. Freud tried to develop theories with highly specific ties to empirical findings in such fields as biology and physiology, and to use these findings to guide and constrain theory construction.

Unfortunately, Freud's dream of an integrated science failed in two key respects: (a) he became too wedded to and dependent on preliminary findings in other disciplines, such as biology; and when these changed dramatically, the coherence of his enterprise began to fall apart; and (b) he failed to appreciate the complexities of integrating across disciplines and fell prey to the fallacies of excessively reductionist links between psychology and physiology (Kitcher, 1992). He put together the interdisciplinary integration in an unfortunate way that "made his theories hostage to unfavorable developments in other fields" (p. 63). He was thus correct in seeing the need for an interdisciplinary approach to the study of the mind, but failed to understand how to make that approach work. It is not clear that current cognitive science fully grasps how best to use the interdisciplinary method, but, perhaps only serendipitously, it is succeeding far better than Freud. It is Kitcher's hope that we understand better the collapse of Freud's dream as a guide for our own activities.

Freud was intensely interested in developmental issues in all the relevant disciplines, and his writings illustrate how often the broader cross-disciplinary considerations of mind seem to inevitably bring in developmental considerations. More than almost any other theorist in the history of psychology, Freud created models of adult thinking and behavior that are impossible to understand without a simultaneous account of the developmental histories of those adults. Everything forms a coherent whole that makes little sense when segmented according to arbitrary ages. Given that Freud's approach had so much of a cognitive science flavor, it is all the more intriguing that developmental issues seemed so central and inseparable from other issues. A better understanding of the reasons for the centrality of developmental issues in such cases is one of the main goals of this chapter.

Stages of Mental Development: A Necessary Scaffold for Adult Cognitive Science?

Piaget's name has become synonymous with the systematic study of cognitive development, but, in many other respects, he follows more closely the earlier philosophical and psychological traditions that have such relevance for cognitive science. Piaget's multidisciplinary background is well known, ranging from his precocious publication (at 11 years of age) of a paper on the sighting of an albino sparrow, to a series of papers on mollusks that resulted in an offer of a curatorship at a museum of natural history (Flavell, 1963). These roots in biology were conscious touchstones for Piaget for a great many years thereafter. As his career in psychology developed, he began to draw on materials in disciplines such as philosophy, several branches of mathematics, anthropology, and linguistics.

Piaget could no more be bounded by traditional disciplinary lines than could Freud, and his syntheses across so many areas of inquiry led to much of the genius and creativity in his ideas and experiments. Yet his approach also had serious limitations as an ideal model for cognitive science. He often embraced work in other areas, such as biology or philosophy, more as a loose metaphor for justifying his own ideas in psychology and less as a constraining principle. Moreover, he sometimes misunderstood some basic principles in other fields, such as formal logic and topology, with devastating consequences for the internal coherence of his own theories of cognitive development (Gelman & Baillargeon, 1983; Osherson, 1975; Parsons, 1960). In a sense, he committed errors opposite those of Freud. He adopted ideas so loosely, and sometimes so incorrectly, that they tore away at the theoretical structures he was trying to build. The fault was not so much that these ideas later turned out to be false, but rather that they were not incorporated with sufficient care and critique.

Piaget's influences on current cognitive science are many. He is, of course, best known for a model of cognitive development that consists of a series of qualitatively distinct stages of computational and representational capacities.

These were bold and dramatic proposals based on a huge array of assumptions about the representational nature of the mind, about learning, and about the kinds of mental computations humans can perform. Through his many papers and books, these assumptions gradually became incorporated into the current discourse on both children and adults. Bypassing the behaviorist revolution in America, Piaget kept alive and greatly elaborated a very different view of mind, one in which growth of elaborate mental representations was of a logical and propositional sort, and empirical research was explicitly devoted to answering questions about the manner of representation and computation. The vast majority of Piaget's work preceded the rise of computer science and artificial intelligence, but his ideas laid important groundwork for symbolic and propositional attempts to model the mind (Papert, 1993).

Although few researchers today embrace Piaget's particular stages of cognitive development and his corresponding proposals about underlying mental structures, his ideas remain a constant source of discussion not only in psychology, but in areas of linguistics, philosophy, and computer science. Current attempts to build on a Piagetian approach to cognitive development often preserve this interdisciplinary flavor by referring to principles across several disciplines, ranging from biology to computer science (e.g., Case, 1978; Case, Okamoto, Henderson, & McKeough, 1993; Halford, 1993, 1995). If one looks across all of psychology in the first half of the 20th century, it appears that Piaget's work in cognitive development touched more on cognitive science issues and methods than did any other area of psychology. Indeed, as will be seen below in the discussions of content areas, Piaget employed this kind of approach in an extraordinary range of topics.

Piaget also put forth a theory that assumed a particular philosophy of mind, one that is fascinating and is rarely considered explicitly. He was clearly an empiricist yet was also antiassociationist—an intriguing combination. He strongly rejected nativist views of mind (Piatelli-Palmarini, 1994), yet embraced a universal and rich architecture of mind that yielded, through experience, the inevitable structures and logical forms of his stages. This empiricist approach to learning, blended with knowledge acquisition, fit well with the domain-general nature of Piaget's stages of cognitive development (Keil, 1981). Most intriguing, however, is the attendant notion that the culturally universal logical mental structures of concrete and formal operations were built out of a much simpler set of domain-general primitives in the sensorimotor period of infancy. This form of empiricism would not seem to resonate with the form implicit in most current connectionist models of mind (although see Halford, 1992, 1993, 1995, for proposals that can be seen as interpreting Piaget in a connectionist manner).

Piaget's ideas deserve vastly more space than this chapter allows; fortunately, they are discussed at length throughout much of this *Handbook* (e.g., see Overton, Ch. 3, this Volume; Fischer & Bidell, Ch. 9, this Volume; and Valsiner, Ch. 4, this Volume). It suffices here to note that many of his intuitions about how to study the mind resonate strongly with those in current cognitive science. Moreover, some of the skeletal frameworks he proposed for how to go about asking empirical questions in cognitive science fit with current practice; it was in the details that a smooth transition to cognitive science failed to occur.

From a different perspective and academic background, Vygotsky also anticipated cognitive science by attempting syntheses that did not simply try to account for higher levels of cognitive capacities in terms of physiological primitives. He argued that sophisticated cognitive functions, such as language and symbol use, could be studied experimentally and scientifically by basing experimental studies specifically on psychological constructs that involved mental representations (see Overton, Ch. 3, this Volume; Valsiner, Ch. 4, this Volume). A. R. Luria, the great Russian psychologist, once argued that Vygotsky was perhaps the first to embrace the true scientific study of psychological constructs in their own right, without the ultimate goal of reducing them to physiological correlates (Luria, 1987). Indeed, Vygotsky courageously opposed the views of Pavlov, the most influential and revered member of his psychological community, on the grounds that Pavlov neglected the study of higher-level mental functions in their own right. Such a scientific program comes close to the heart of cognitive science, especially when one considers how Vygotsky drew on ideas not just within psychology, but also in comparative ethology, art, cultural analyses, language, and neuropsychology (Vygotsky, 1962, 1978). Again, it is striking that Vygotsky is perhaps best known for how all these ideas coalesced to form his theory of cognitive development. The developmental perspective was perhaps not even his primary goal at first as much as one

that inevitably unfolded as he looked ever more closely at problems concerning how we all come to understand the world and convey our understandings to others.

Like Piaget, Vygotsky was a stage theorist who embraced broad-sweeping domain-general reorganizations of mind. These stagelike restructurings occurred in a dramatically different way from those of Piaget, and they looked to language as a powerful vehicle of restructuring. But Vygotsky shared with Piaget the notion of global changes in the manner of thinking and, ultimately, seemed to share the empiricist bias as well. He also shared a perspective that drew on many constituent disciplines of cognitive science, but he drew differently than Piaget, more with stress on such areas as language and culture. More importantly, he was never trapped into the paradigms of one discipline, and he realized the value of looking at problems from several different disciplinary viewpoints that converged on a common set of phenomena.

The work of a great many other historical figures in psychology extended the traditional boundaries of the discipline in ways that anticipated some of the spirit of the cognitive sciences: Warren McCulloch (1965), who blended neurophysiology, the fledgling field of cybernetics/computer science, and philosophy in the study of vision and action; A. R. Luria, who blended work in linguistics, neuropsychology, and cognition in his studies of the effects of war wounds on higher-level functioning; and Herbert Simon (1962), who blended formal issues of computation with heuristics and other issues of human problem solving. But the vast majority of psychologists, for more than half of the 20th century, did not engage in research that paved the way for cognitive science. The rise of behaviorism meant the suppression of most experimental studies of cognition, especially from a cognitive science perspective where the study of mental representations themselves is so absolutely central.

Even work that continued in the areas of cognition and perception became increasingly compartmentalized and distinct from other disciplines. As a number of journals emerged reporting on experimental work, research was propelled more by the experimental paradigms and less by basic ideas and questions free from disciplinary boundaries. Most sciences, as they mature, must confront this problem, and psychology was no exception. The rebirth of cognitive psychology in the 1960s did not really break this compartmentalization. For years thereafter, it strongly constrained the methods of research in ways that were far narrower than the questions and phenomena they were ultimately meant to address.

One interesting exception to the general trend of psychological isolation from other disciplines was the work of E. J. Gibson (1969, 1991; Gibson & Spelke, 1983; Gibson & Walk, 1960) and J. J. Gibson (1950, 1955, 1961, 1966, 1972, 1977, 1979). Few would consider either researcher as setting up the psychological groundwork for cognitive science because each had great discomfort with talk of mental representations and internal computational states; yet their approach departed from much of psychology in ways that reflect the spirit of some of the most exciting recent developments in cognitive science. J. J. Gibson's long and distinguished career in perception underwent a profound change during World War II, when he undertook the study of perception from the viewpoint of an airline pilot (Gibson, 1955). Consideration of the problems of perception in a dynamic environment with flowfields led Gibson to examine more closely how the information in the world resonated with our perceptual systems. He discovered many subtle invariants in the dynamic visual array that could be profoundly useful in guiding perception and action.

This focus on patterns in the light led to increasingly formal analyses of visual information and to comparative considerations of how species in different ecological niches might be tuned to different sorts of patterns. It seemed inevitable that this line of thinking should turn to developmental questions as well, and E. J. Gibson developed a major research program devoted to answering fundamental questions about perceptual development. Her work embraced the idea of invariants and also focused on the structure that existed in the world and how it afforded potential for perceptually guided action. The famous visual cliff experiments grew out of such considerations (Walk & Gibson, 1961). In addition, E. J. Gibson (1969) developed a theory of perceptual learning, differentiation, which was a model of how an infant or child might come to see much more in the visual world and learn from experience without focusing on internal representational states and computational procedures.

The Gibsonian approach to perception and perceptual development was not an early version of cognitive science. Its aversion to descriptions of mental representations and computations places it outside of the central discourse of cognitive science today. But, in other ways, it shares important sympathies. It calls for much more detailed structural descriptions of the visual world, descriptions that require not the traditional skills of psychology, but more those of mathematics and physical optics. It suggests comparative analyses of the ecological niches in which different organisms function and develop, and it asks how ecological analyses might be combined with the study of the information used to guide perception and action. It asks fundamental philosophical questions about how the mind might be studied and about the potential pitfalls of realist versus idealist philosophies of mind and nature. Finally, E. J. Gibson's later work on reading took an increasing interest in the structure of linguistic information and how it might be used to guide reading (Gibson & Levin, 1975). In short, the recognition of a need to use methods and theories from such diverse fields as psychology, mathematics, physics, biology, and linguistics, and of the central role of developmental issues, made the Gibsonian approach much like other more obvious precursors of cognitive science.

Perhaps the single most important unifying theme across the work of both Gibsons was an emphasis on function. What was the point of a perceptual system? The focus on function motivated ecological considerations, more formal analyses of environmental conditions, and the importance of considering the real content of behavior.

In all, although some took theoretical and methodological positions that anticipated important aspects of cognitive science, most psychologists in the 20th century did not. Interestingly, those whose work most fully anticipated cognitive science usually included developmental perspectives in their work as one critical facet of addressing some question about the mind. In time, cognitive psychology and developmental psychology drifted apart; the study of cognitive development seemed to become a separate discipline within developmental psychology and largely distinct from the study of cognition in adults. The emergence of cognitive science in the past few decades has changed that pattern dramatically. Surprisingly, one of the most powerful driving forces behind a new cognitive science view of developmental psychology did not emerge from psychology at all. Instead, it came from a different line of study focusing on attempts to formally specify those intangible mental structures that led to the human capacity for language.

Creating and Understanding Intangible Structures: Knowledge of a Natural Language

Although many of the earlier discussions of mind revolved around how we come to apprehend the physical world, an enormous part of our mental lives involves apprehending and creating nonphysical structures. Nowhere is this more evident than in our ability to produce and understand natural language. The history of linguistic inquiry and its relation to cognitive science revolves around one individual more than any other: Noam Chomsky. When his review of Skinner's *Verbal Behavior* appeared in 1959, Chomsky's general approach to linguistics and its relation to other disciplines, such as psychology, suddenly became well known to a huge community of scholars. Previously, it had been largely confined to a much smaller, specialized audience.

The study of grammar is nothing new; indeed, there have been attempts to develop grammars of natural languages since the beginning of written history. For most of that period, however, grammars depicted each language differently, according to its surface appearance. Chomsky had a radically different vision: There might be a highly structured set of core principles that describe the structure not only of all present and past languages, but also of any possible human languages. Chomsky's new approach to grammar offered theoretical advances and a formal power that allowed one to see, for the first time, commonalities across languages that, superficially, seemed different: for example, Turkish, English, Japanese, and Navaho.

There had been some anticipations of Chomsky's ideas, but nowhere on the same scale and scope. Chomsky's mentor, Zellig S. Harris (1981), had first developed the idea of sentences being related to each other through patterns of transformations, and Roman Jakobson (1941/1968) had sensed that there were important universals in some aspects of language, and that these would be related to brain function. But none of these predecessors synthesized an approach to language that could also be so central to cognitive science. In Chomsky's approach, issues of language acquisition were also at the very core of the whole account.

Chomsky's work first appeared in the late 1950s and has continued to develop to this day. Thus, he is part of the historical background that helped spawn cognitive science and is also a major force in its continuing evolution. This discussion focuses on how his earlier ideas helped create and frame the new science of the mind.

Chomsky's central contribution to cognitive science did not lie in his development of a more formal and penetrating approach to grammar. Instead, it came from how he saw a theory of grammar informing basic questions about the nature of the mind and the acquisition of knowledge. The creation of a means for discovering universal structural properties of language led immediately to asking how this sort of knowledge might come about. Chomsky saw linguistic theory as having to satisfy three increasingly stringent criteria of adequacy—criteria that make clear the central problem of acquisition. The first and weakest level of adequacy of a theory of grammar is that it must enumerate all (and only) the natural sentences of a language. The second level, descriptive adequacy, requires that the theory provide the appropriate structural descriptions at all levels that correspond to natural sentences; that is, not just the surface string, but all the underlying structures that predict linguistic intuitions about that string. At the level of linguistic theory, a descriptively adequate theory provides such an account for all natural languages.

The final level of adequacy, explanatory adequacy, was the ultimate standard of whether a theory of language was fully sufficient. It was notably different in focus and especially relevant to understanding relations between cognition and development in a cognitive science perspective:

> To facilitate the clear formulation of deeper questions, it is useful to consider the abstract problem of constructing an "acquisition model" for language, that is, a theory of language learning or grammar construction . . . we can say that the child has developed and internally represented a generative grammar. . . . To learn a language, then, the child must have a method for devising an appropriate grammar, given primary linguistic data. As a precondition for language learning, he must possess, first, a linguistic theory that specifies the form of the grammar of a possible human language, and, second, a strategy for selecting a grammar of the appropriate form that is compatible with primary linguistic data. . . . To the extent that a linguistic theory succeeds in selecting a descriptively adequate grammar on the basis of primary linguistic data, we can say that it meets the condition of explanatory adequacy. That is, to this extent, it offers an explanation for the intuition of the native speaker on the basis of an empirical hypothesis concerning the innate predispositions of the child to develop a certain kind of theory to deal with the evidence presented to him. (Chomsky, 1965, pp. 24–26)

A fully adequate theory of language must therefore show how it is possible for children to acquire all possible natural languages and only those languages, not other non-natural ones of equivalent formal complexity. For Chomsky, if this problem was solved, all other problems of explaining universals, more local grammatical patterns, and levels of representation, would fall out naturally. Otherwise, the account would be incomplete. Interestingly, integrations of formal linguistic theory with the study of language acquisition have been far easier to achieve than those between linguistic theory and models of adult language use (see Chapters 4, 7, 8, and 9, in Volume 2 of this *Handbook*).

Chomsky's linkage of the formal description of a body of knowledge with its patterns of acquisition has rarely extended beyond language to other areas of cognition. This failure to extend such an approach is surprising and disappointing. After all, the levels of adequacy could apply equally well to theories of number, spatial knowledge, and theory of mind. Precise formal descriptions of what it means for knowledge to be natural should be useful in many other domains and should have powerful ties to questions of knowledge acquisition. Yet the general Chomskyean approach is only beginning to be employed elsewhere. Where it has been used, the new insights can be dramatic and sweeping. (Examples will be offered in subsequent discussions of six basic questions for cognitive science.)

Chomsky's ideas have had other important implications for cognitive science and problems of knowledge acquisition. By focusing on the nature of a language acquisition device, he raised the question of the domain specificity of knowledge and of the systems that acquire that knowledge. This question underlies many current debates in cognitive science and is critical to understanding nativist/empiricist debates. Chomsky (1980) developed increasingly subtle and sophisticated views of how a child might be prepared to acquire knowledge, such as invoking the idea of constraints on induction, and considering learning as a function that maps sets of environments onto sets of mental representations. He saw the poverty of the input as demanding sophisticated *a priori* learning structures tailored for language, a view that has galvanized legions of researchers on both sides of the issue and has helped to launch a new area of work focusing on the formal "learnability" of types of knowledge structures (Osherson, Stob, & Weinstein, 1985).

Finally, the competence–performance distinction has become a fundamental issue to consider in study after study across cognitive science; it has also become a valuable way of explaining inconsistencies in research in cognitive development (Gelman, 1978). Chomsky's work naturally blends issues in linguistics with those in philosophy, mathematics, and psychology.

There were false starts in integrating linguistic theory with other disciplines. The most dramatic failure involved early claims of the psychological reality of linguistic theory. It was tempting to assume that the rules and sequences of rule applications of the early generative grammars might have a close correspondence with real-time information-processing sequences. It was, therefore, a heady time when early support for the psychological reality of formal grammars seemed to come from experimental studies on processing speed. Time to verify and process sentences appeared to be a consequence of the derivational complexity of a sentence as predicted by grammatical theory (e.g., Clifton & Odom, 1966; Miller & Isard, 1963; Miller & McKean, 1964). But these early successes soon led to great complexities and the realization that other variables were responsible for predicting speed and difficulty of processing (see Fodor, Bever, & Garrett, 1974, for a review).

Unfortunately, the failures of these early models of the psychological reality of grammar led some to infer that the grammars of linguistic theory could have no relation to psychological issues. This inference was far too strong. There may be no simple linkage between the steps of real-time processing and the steps represented in sets of formal linguistic rules, nor any simple mapping between metrics of structural complexity in linguistic theory and psychological processing complexity; but other potent links with psychological questions remain. A theory of universal grammar might still be able to specify what sorts of linguistic constructions would be cognitively natural in all languages, where cognitive naturalness would help predict judgments about the grammaticality of sentences as well as the ease of learning new structures. Indeed, those interested in adult models of language processing still wrestle mightily with how to link linguistic theory with models of cognitive processing, but a great many researchers, studying the acquisition of both first and second languages, see huge and highly fertile areas of cross-communication between linguistic theory and empirical studies on language acquisition (e.g., Lust, Suner, & Whitman, 1994).

In the end, the cognitive science contributions of linguistic theory seem more closely linked to phenomena of development than any other area of cognitive science (see also Pinker, 1993). One reason for such a connection may be the inadequacy of adult processing models as testing grounds for linguistic theory, and the contrast of those limitations with the powerful successes that occurred when linguistic theory was combined with questions of acquisition.

One of the reasons for the difficulties with adult processing models of language arises from a much larger problem with formulating processing models of the mind in general. There have been tremendous debates about the nature of representation and processing in human cognition—debates that reveal the critical importance of developing more precise chararacterizations of the computational nature of thought. From yet another constitutive discipline, such characterizations have emerged.

The Computational Mind

A critical part of current cognitive science is the notion of the mind as a computational device. That idea has been largely articulated through the perspective of computer science. Computer science, and its constituent discipline of artificial intelligence (AI), is the youngest of the fields comprising cognitive science and, consequently, it is more difficult to look at its own historical precursors to the cognitive science movement. Nonetheless, some of the early themes in this field have interesting links to later developments in cognitive science. Although inevitable speculation about whether computational devices might ever approach the intelligence of humans went on as early as the first part of the 19th century, when Babbage began making computational machines, there was little beyond speculation until the 1960s. More formal and logical theories of computation and recursive functions preceded real electronic computers, and some of the early giants in the field, such as Alan Turing, wondered how one might assess intelligence in a machine, leading to his famous Turing Test, in which a machine could "pass" for a human in an extended discourse exchange (Turing, 1950).

The most powerful contributions to the emerging field of cognitive science from computer science, however, did not come from the high levels of performance of AI programs. Rather, the real insights came from the mere existence of devices that could perform operations that seemed analogous to aspects of human cognition. Just as tape recorders, records, motion picture cameras, and even writing slates had been powerful metaphors for earlier generations of psychologists and philosophers, the computer offered new metaphors both for possible architectures of the mind and for kinds of procedures (Neisser, 1966). Those systems also showed how it is often fundamentally difficult to distinguish between structure and process, a distinction that might seem obvious until one considers the ambiguities raised by complex programs (Newell, 1972). Notions of buffer memories, flow bottlenecks, push-down stacks, and recursive loops had profound effects on those trying to develop computational models of cognition. In a similar way, more recent computational schemes working on massive parallel processing have had comparable effects in triggering new ideas concerning models of cognition. It is also true, however, that just as with earlier devices that suggested metaphors, the potential to be misled by irrelevant aspects of the device also exists for computer models of the mind.

In addition to offering ideas about process, computer models help researchers think more clearly about what representations might be, and how they might work in a machine, without raising the homunculus problem in which some internal mental agent must examine the representation. The whole meaning of representation has gradually shifted, at least in part because of the presence of physical computational devices (Gallistel, 1989; Stalnaker, 1984).

One of the earliest and most visionary descriptions of how symbolic computational architectures might inform the study of the mind came in the form of a monograph by Simon (1962), who compared the child's mind to a computer program. This led to a very different account of cognitive development. As Klahr (1992) puts it:

> Simon's suggestion contained two ideas that departed radically from the then-prevailing views in developmental psychology. The first idea was that theories about thinking could be stated as computer programs. These "computational models of thought," as they came to be called, have one important property that distinguishes them from all other types of theoretical statements: They independently execute the mental processes they represent. . . . The second idea in Simon's suggestion followed from the first: If different states of cognitive development could be described as programs, then the developmental process itself could also be described as a

program that took the earlier program and transformed it into a later one. (p. 276)

Computational models have been used in hard- and soft-core senses, which, in the aggregate, have become an extremely pervasive part of thinking about cognitive development (Klahr, 1992). In the soft-core sense, a great many researchers assume that children's thinking involves the manipulation of symbols according to regular rules. They further assume that this system of rules, representations, and psychological processing constraints is self-modifying and that developmental change consists of such alterations. The hard-core approaches go much further, attempting to implement these general themes in terms of specific computational models that can be tested via simulation on computers. Klahr suggests that a greater use of these hard-core models would considerably enhance the study of cognitive development; but the values of a computational perspective have extended far beyond those who construct and test detailed simulations. Asking more general questions about the nature of information processing and how the mind might learn about and handle that information in discrete ways has proved to be an extremely helpful approach to researchers across much of cognitive science. Even without precise simulations, one can develop plausibility arguments about the computational intractibility of a certain approach, or about how different kinds of information processing must all be present and interact in specific ways if an organism is to solve a given problem.

Although this survey has touched on only a few historical threads that contributed to the emergence of modern cognitive science, it has more than adequately supported the two points it was meant to address: (a) The study of the mind cannot be divorced from the study of how the mind develops, and (b) for centuries, questions about the mind, especially in the context of development, have been intrinsically interdisciplinary in nature. If one considers the broader historical tradition, it is clear that, first, developmental considerations were fully intermingled with other questions concerning the mind, in ways that naturally complemented each other. Second, for early scholars, who were unconstrained by today's disciplines, there were two possible routes in thinking about the mind. They might have chosen to be even more parochial and more narrowly focused on a very specific problem in isolation, or they might have looked to all possible sources of relevant ideas

and information. It is clear that many took the latter route and, in doing so, showed more of the virtues of a cognitive science approach than occurred in much of this century.

Disciplines such as computer science, linguistics, philosophy, and psychology have continued to grow as cognitive science has flowered in the past two decades. Not surprisingly, this disciplinary growth has continued to shape cognitive science which, in turn, has had profound influence on each of these fields. But such events cannot possibly even be surveyed here. Such a survey would require a recounting of the significant disciplinary changes in the past two decades in each field, and then an analysis of how those changes interacted with the emergence of cognitive science. One could easily devote a large set of volumes to such an enterprise and still be incomplete—and that would be before turning to issues of development. The strategy here is to convey some of those events and their important morals in the following discussions of content domains. In those discussions, some connectionist models are also examined, but, given the enormous surge of that perspective in the past decade, it is helpful to relate it briefly to the broader historical context.

From a radically different perspective than that of older symbolic approaches, researchers studying massively parallel systems, or connectionist models, frequently try to build their systems through a learning process rather than by simply implementing the mature form. The learning process often seems to result in "emergent properties" that are unanticipated by their creators. Such systems can achieve striking success at simulating aspects of human cognitive development by capturing apparent instances of structural change as well as stagelike discontinuities (McClelland, McNaughton, & O'Reilly, 1995). Thus, simulations of the knowledge acquisition process itself have become a kind of tool for discovering unanticipated properties of a system. This approach is a wonderful example of how very old themes become elaborated in powerful new ways. There is no question that modern connectionist approaches owe an enormous heritage to the associationists (Clark, 1993). They all share the strong conviction that a primary route to forming knowledge is through mental mechanisms that closely track the environmental contingencies. Co-occurrence patterns between environmental features—often, features that are far more primitive than those of traditional qualia (such as an impression of wetness)—are seen as having far-reaching implications as the building blocks of complex knowledge. This is the ideal empiricist account: A general learning engine with no content-sensitive biases about the world is able to assemble all of knowledge through proper tabulations of environmental contingencies.

Modern connectionism has gone far beyond the ideas of the British empiricists (Clark, 1994; Cummins, 1996). It has developed highly explicit models of how features become associated, and has tried to link such models to properties of some neural circuits. It has been implemented in computers in ways that have produced powerful simulations of an enormous array of phenomena in cognition and perception. It is able to model discontinuities in change and patterns of inferencing that would have never been possible in a simple associative model. But, through all those improvements, it shares the central focus on problems of learning and development. It is virtually meaningless without some notion of constant learning. As argued shortly, connectionism may also offer the most powerful insights on cognition just when it abandons the strong empiricist approach and becomes linked with other approaches to cognition (Clark & Karmiloff-Smith, 1993; Elman et al., 1996). I will suggest that connectionist models can even be central to some nativists' models of the mind and, indeed, that may be where they are most useful and important. To that end, it is now time to turn to more of the real substance of cognitive science and how it helps us understand some of the most basic questions about the mind.

CHARACTERIZING COGNITIVE SCIENCE TODAY—COGNITIVE SCIENCE APPROACHES TO SIX PROBLEMS

It can be painfully difficult to define even the most seemingly straightforward terms. Thus, terms for highly concrete, easy-to-identify things, like tigers, gold, and water, can be notoriously hard to characterize in simple analytic ways (e.g., Lakoff, 1987; Putnam, 1975). The concept of cognitive science has a similar quality. Most people know what cognitive science is when they see it; they have far more difficulty providing a strict definition that goes much beyond the very general sort of description that begins this chapter. Although certain topics repeatedly occur—representation, computation, and knowledge acquisition, for example—these alone are not in themselves defining of the field. For over two millennia, literature has suggested that the minds of others are governed by

principles that determine how they perceive, think, understand, and communicate. In Shakespeare, for example, there are a great many places where a model of some aspect of mind is made apparent. Hamlet talks of having images of his father in his "mind's eye" that no one else could see. Prospero, in *The Tempest,* assumes that Miranda could not have had a memory from when she was 3 years old, thereby stating the notion of infantile amnesia. (Miranda says the memory, however, is only "rather like a dream than assurance.") Finally, Macbeth wonders whether, with a medicine, a doctor might be able to "pluck from the memory a rooted sorrow," and is assured by a doctor that memories cannot be so changed and that "Therein the patient must minister to himself." Indeed, Bloom (1994) goes so far as to argue that Shakespeare completely anticipated all of Freud's most interesting conjectures about the nature of the mind.

These views of the mind were not just those of psychology or linguistics. To be adequately addressed, they seemed to need a much more sweeping scope of inquiry. The same is true today, when one considers what constitutes a full and adequate answer to some of the most basic questions about the mind. For that reason, the easiest and most compelling way to more fully characterize cognitive science, as well as how it has emerged in the past two decades, is to show how we have made progress in answering questions about some of the most basic properties of any mental organism. The six questions listed below are not meant to be exhaustive, or even to be the best possible ones; rather, they simply illustrate the kind of range of issues that point out the merits of a cognitive science perspective over one that limits itself strictly to the confines of one of the older disciplines. The six questions are:

1. How do we recognize and track individuals over time and space?
2. How do we find our way about?
3. How do we communicate messages?
4. How do we quantify entities and perform computations on them?
5. How do we categorize our physical and social worlds?
6. How do we grasp the causal structures of our physical and social worlds?

Each of these questions will show the need for an active interdisciplinary approach, if there is to be any reasonable chance of finding complete answers. In addition, they will all demonstrate that content matters and that it is essential to characterize the real world in which these questions are couched. They are phrased in ways that are not neutral with respect to content; they do not ask "How do we remember information?" or "How do we allocate attentional resources?" or "What associative principles govern how learning one bit of information interferes or facilitates another?" These more information-neutral questions are interesting in their own right, but they are different in two ways: (a) they focus on domain-general properties of cognition that should apply equally to all content; and (b) they embody a kind of solipsism in that they do not ask about functional relations between the organism and its social and physical worlds; rather, the intrinsic properties of the information-processing system are considered largely as a closed system, or at least one for which inputs are arbitrary.

For the questions posed here, the inputs are anything but arbitrary. These questions ask about how our minds connect with the structure of the world, and, in doing so, they highlight the virtues and necessities of a cognitive science perspective.

How Do We Recognize and Track Individuals over Time and Space?

A great many organisms need to know that an entity they are encountering now is the same entity that they encountered at a different point in time and/or space. Whether it is knowing that the animate figure is still one's parent, or that a particular morsel of food is one's own and not another's, identity tracking is so common and presupposed that we can overlook its presence in almost every waking moment. With humans, the demands may be especially intense because the number of things to be tracked in our natural and man-made worlds can be enormous. Moreover, the possible temporal and spatial displacements may be vast as they become mediated by technology and communication. In addition, in a world of artifacts, things that appear to be exactly the same can frequently belong to different individuals and must be kept distinct, an especially difficult challenge not encountered as recently as a few thousand years ago. My preschooler's toy from a fast-food restaurant may appear physically identical to his friend's, but it is his, and he goes to enormous lengths to track its identity and to assure himself and others that the one sitting next to his bed at night is in fact his and not his friend's.

We therefore see two ways to track individuals: (a) we assume the individual has unique perceivable features, or (b) where such features don't exist, we invoke other principles. In a more technical sense, any statable difference, including a spatiotemporal difference, between two instances can be called a feature. Here, features are meant to be those properties of objects that do not refer to temporal and spatial displacements. When unique features are present, the identity-preserving strategy may seem simple enough: Store the unique features and compare them to all new instances. But even then, making a decision about which features or feature configurations are likely to be unique for all future cases can be an extremely complex judgment. Should the dirt on the object be weighed heavily, or at all? Should its predominant external color be important? This is not a good choice for people. The color of clothing would be a very poor feature to use to track a person's identity. Using unique feature configurations to track individuals may require a rich set of expectations about what sorts of features are stable over time and space for particular kinds of things, because features that are stable for one kind may be highly unstable for another. Take color, for example, and temporal displacements of more than 24 hours. Because they change clothes daily, many humans have different colors over 90% of their external surface each day. The sun can change its apparent color quite dramatically through the course of a day, especially when atmospheric moisture or pollution is in the line of sight. A wide variety of objects, when cooked, undergo dramatic color changes. The same kinds of problems with feature stability and variation exist for the shape, size, texture, smell, or other properties of objects. One would seem to need a complex and well-articulated model of properties, property types, and their interactions with kinds of individuals to be able to use properties in any competent way to track identity. It is far too simple to state that one merely stores unique features and compares them to new instances.

The unique-features approach to tracking individuals therefore quickly becomes a complex problem; but matters seem to get even worse where appearances are identical. To distinguish between identical appearing objects, one must appeal to principles governing spatial and temporal displacements and allowable classes of reversible and irreversible transformations. If one takes a bowling ball, melts it down into a puddle of plastic, and then reforms it into a ball that is physically identical with the original, adults can powerfully disagree on whether it is the same object or a new one. Yet, when a transporter on the science fiction series *Star Trek* decomposes a person into an energy/molecule stream and reassembles that stream instantaneously in a geographically distant location, the mechanism is compelling and plausible as one that preserves the identity of the person. What makes one case so much more clear-cut than the other?

Such examples abound and quickly reveal the complexities inherent in tracking identity. Moreover, in many cases, feature clusters are of little use in everyday life. One frequently encounters conditions where the visual information is sufficiently degraded that one is limited to views of ill-defined solids on various trajectories in space. When one stumbles about a strange place on a moonless night, similar conditions prevail. They also hold in a blizzard, or a fog, or when looking through a frosted windowpane. Even when the visual scene is crystal clear and well lit, one's own psychological state may produce the same effects. If situational factors have forced one's attention into one arena, unique features may be largely ignored, especially in peripheral vision, leaving the spatial and temporal patternings as the only recourse for interpreting the identities of objects outside the spotlight of attention (Neisser, 1976).

The time frame over which identity is tracked may also make an enormous difference with respect to the principles that are invoked. Keeping track of individuals from moment to moment as they are briefly occluded or disappear during visual saccades appears to be a very different task from knowing that a pen left on one's nightstand before retiring is the same pen when seen the next morning. The kind of information that is relied on for identity over brief occlusions is almost certainly not the same as that used over much longer time intervals. If a car rushes by me on the street at night, disappears behind a double-parked truck, and then reappears a second later, much of my confidence about its being the same car may spring from its observed velocity before and after the occlusion, and from the duration of the occlusion. By contrast, if I am walking to my office in the morning and see a car that is backing into a parking space, and then notice a similar car pulling out of that space at the end of that day, the car's velocities on those two occasions are largely irrelevant to my judgments of the car's identity. Similarly, I may walk by a large building at night and notice little more than its looming bulk and its location in space. If I become lost during a

walk on the next night and wonder whether I am in the same place as the night before, I'll discount that thought if the large bulk occupies a different location in space relative to the other large buildings. I don't need to have noticed a single local feature of the building, and velocity is certainly not a factor. Instead, I know that large buildings are not capable of moving through space relative to other buildings over the course of a day. Thus, unique feature clusters, velocity information, location in a layout, and very general properties of a superordinate class of objects can all be used selectively to track identity, depending on what the situation requires.

A cognitive science of identity has started to emerge in the past decade and is offering the promise of new insights not apparent from more traditional approaches in psychology and philosophy. Traditional approaches, such as those in developmental psychology, often ignored the preservation of the identity of entities, and focused instead on identity of kinds. Judging whether a dog is the same individual after some properties have been changed is very different from judging whether it is still the same kind of animal (i.e., a dog). Some transformations can destroy individual identity while maintaining kind identity (e.g., tearing apart a vertical bookcase and rebuilding it as a horizontal one), whereas others can do the opposite (e.g., the butterfly that arises from the caterpillar). Identity issues become even more confused as identities of qualities and quantities, such as size or weight, are explored in the same context as identities of objects and kinds. Thus, Piaget's many conservation studies are often linked to basic questions about identity, when the links are in fact indirect and complex.

Consider how discussions of identity start to change as integration occurs across the disciplines of psychology, philosophy, linguistics, and computer science. Identity theory in philosophy is figuring in the rationale and experimental design of studies with humans of all ages. Wiggins's (1980) work on sortals and how one tracks identity has led to proposals about how certain categorical distinctions allow one to solve individual identity problems (Gutheil & Rosengren, in press; Gutheil, Spelke, & Hayes, in preparation). Using the ideas of Hirsch (1982), Quine (1960), and Wiggins (1980), Xu and Carey (1996) were led to the radical proposal that young infants may track individuals by using only spatiotemporal continuity cues, and perhaps some concepts of number, but do not use any cues involving stable feature clusters. This work in turn intersects with a large set of other studies concerning infants' apparent beliefs about physical objects (Baillargeon, 1987, 1995; Baillargeon, Kotovsky, & Needham, 1995; Leslie, 1993; Rochat, 1989; Spelke, in press; Spelke, Breinlinger, Macomber, & Jacobson, 1992; Spelke, Kestenbaum, Simons, & Wein, 1995). If younger infants are unable to individuate kinds in terms of stable properties. they must phenomenally experience objects in a way that is radically different from that of older infants and adults. Instead of seeing a red ball, they would experience something more like "a single bounded object at location x with accompanying sensations of redness and ballness." They notice the redness and ballness but don't assume that those properties are essential to determining identity.

The stage is now set for still further integration with other areas of work in philosophy and computer science. In philosophy, it would seem that work on properties and property theory is critically relevant. If much of identity tracking relies on decisions about what sorts of properties are stable and reliable over certain time intervals, one needs a theory of how to divide properties into different types. One also needs an account of how those properties are related to temporal and spatial displacements as well as to the kinds of objects in which they inhere. Issues of this sort have not been seriously addressed in psychology, but they have received considerable attention in philosophy. Some properties do not work at all for inductions (Goodman, 1955; Shoemaker, 1980, 1984), including many inductions about identity. Some properties can be predicated only for some classes of things (Sommers, 1963), and some are more intrinsically relational than others (Gentner, 1983). These issues have not been easy for philosophers to solve, but several intriguing distinctions have been offered that suggest experimental tests with humans. Equally important, the experimental data are of growing interest to the philosophers.

In computer science, there has been a surge of interest in developing systems that can track objects in both three-dimensional space and two-dimensional representations of space (e.g., videotapes). There are huge incentives for automatically being able to scan the mass of video information that is now digitally accessible throughout the world (Zabih, Woodfill, & Withgott, 1993). Systems are being built and modified with the goal of tracking the same individual across many successive frames and instances of occlusion. One approach works on metrics of distance between two object instances over successive frames, or before and after an occlusion. A variety of mathematical models of distance are being tested with some success. For example, a measure known as the "Hausdorff measure" calculates the closeness of one point set to another point set, by using the fraction of points in one set that are near points in the other. This method avoids having to pair points across successive images and, instead, looks at properties of the point clusters. It has been strikingly successful at tracking individuals in a variety of naturalistic situations (Huttenlocher & Rucklidge, 1992). Such formal models of distance can inform attempts to understand how humans and other species use properties, velocities, and trajectories to make inferences about identity. Indeed, one needs such formalisms even to be able to specify what are cognitively natural integrations across scenes.

The study of identity is also being informed by work in linguistics. Languages take great pains to keep track of individuals through use of determiners, proper nouns, anaphoric relations, and other devices (Lyons, 1977). There are strong links here with logic and the philosophy of language as questions arise concerning how to semantically interpret complex statements about individuals (Chierchia & McConnell-Ginet, 1990). Similarly, patterns of predication in language are linked to theories of property types and kinds. These issues in linguistics should all tie into experimental studies in powerful ways, but, in the short term, linguistic theory has been most useful in providing a tool for exploring identity intuitions, especially in children.

Consider a pattern discovered recently in young children. Two-year-olds will use syntactic information, such as the presence or absence of a determiner (give me Zav versus give me a Zav), in order to decide the linguistic form or class of a novel word as either a count noun or a proper name. However, these children will not attribute proper names to artifacts, regardless of the presence or absence of a determiner. Thus, deciding whether the discourse is asking one to track an individual requires an understanding of the kind of thing being discussed. Preschoolers are also quite willing to state that the identity of an animal remains the same even if its proper name changes (Gutheil & Rosengren, in press). Thus, both syntactic cues and category knowledge guide identity judgments across development (see also Bloom, in press, and Hall, 1996, for more extensive discussions of the relations among concepts of individuals, word meanings, and syntactic structure).

A different line of work examines identity issues in much briefer time slices. How do we acquire our compelling sense of continuous phenomenal experiences of the outside world, even though the input is necessarily discontinuous as our eyes move about and objects become occluded? We are solving thousands of identity problems every few minutes as we walk through a richly cluttered real-world environment; yet the question of what is retained over successive glimpses is beginning to yield answers that are surprisingly counterintuitive (Irwin, 1991; Simons, 1996). People seem to usually forget almost all featural information across saccades and occlusions, retaining instead a representation of overall layout, the contour of solids in a three-dimensional space. People don't think they experience the world in this way, and yet, in most situations, they are remarkably poor at retaining featural information. Only when we strongly verbally encode objects in our environments are feature clusters more likely to be remembered as well (Simons, 1996).

These recent psychological findings regarding what is retained across brief glimpses of the environment are not yet fully understood or smoothly integrated with older studies on what can be remembered from scenes (Nickerson, 1965; Shepard, 1967). It seems likely that a resolution will be greatly aided by work being developed in other disciplines. In computer science, it may well turn out that there are different classes of algorithms and heuristics for tracking individuals over different time scales. Thus, tracking overall layouts of solids might be more computationally tractable under brief time intervals than tracking feature clusters. In addition, it is now feasible to engage in neuroscience explorations of the sorts of information that seem to be encoded at different time intervals. The existence of so called "what" and "where" systems in the visual cortex suggests how one might examine the time courses of encoding of the two kinds of information (Goodale & Milner, 1992; Mishkin, Ungerleider, & Macko, 1983). A cognitive science approach to these issues seems likely to be the most fruitful route to answers.

Research on identity is just at the beginning of interdisciplinary integration across cognitive science. But even at this early point, a cognitive science perspective is allowing us to frame the important questions in powerful and penetrating ways that lead to much more focused research programs. In addition, some of the most impressive experimental findings on identity have emerged in the developmental arena.

The suggestion that young infants might rarely (if ever) use feature clusters to track identity was powerfully influenced by philosophical discussions concerning the nature of objects, kinds, and identity. That work, in turn, now seems to be related to adult performance during brief time intervals. Similarly, distinctions between individual and kind identity, although often ignored in the psychological literature, have been clarified by philosophical discussions.

Why might developmental analyses be so central to understanding identity in general? One answer revolves around the recurrent theme that immature systems often highlight the most fundamental components or allow different functional components to be seen more distinctly. If one thinks that object properties are the primary means for tracking identity, then looking at individuals who notice different sets of properties (and perhaps an extremely limited number) offers one of the most powerful ways of understanding how features might be involved. If use of principles of physical objects and their mechanical interactions is deemed central, then, again, individuals who have much simpler, skeletal sets of principles might well allow much cleaner explorations of how those principles influence notions of identity. If language and labeling are thought to have a critical influence on judgments of individual and kind identity, then preverbal humans should make very different patterns of judgments than are predicted by the theory. A developmental perspective therefore helps to bring into focus some of the most central questions about identity at all ages.

It is also apparent that questions about identity cannot be encapsulated and unrelated to other fundamental questions about the mind. Indeed, all five of the other questions raised earlier both inform and refer to identity issues. Notions of individuals and groups are almost incoherent without some ideas of number. Language relies on identity relations and highlights certain ones that are of interest. The kinds of things, or the categories constructed, will influence the properties and the spatiotemporal information that are used to make decisions about identity. The causal interactions among entities are also critically dependent on which entities retain their identities over time and space, but perhaps the strongest links are to representations of space. Understanding where one is in a layout is not even a coherent question without a simultaneous understanding that there are unique locations in space that are dependent on the presence of unique individuals who help to define that space. For those reasons, it is especially appropriate to now turn to the question of how all animate things keep track of where they are.

How Do We Find Our Way About?

All but a very small handful of animal species move about at some point in their lives, and, in doing so, they immediately confront similar problems in navigating their worlds. They must keep track of where they have gone relative to their starting point, especially if that starting point is their home or a food cache. They must know how to anticipate obstacles without being harmed, how such patterns of avoidance influence where they are, how to get to a goal destination, and how to return to their place of origin. Leaving aside here the important questions of how obstacles are perceived as such and avoided (see Gibson, 1979, for more discussion of this), the focus here is on how we develop representations of spatial layouts. In addition, a critical question revolves around situations where an animal loses track of its recent movement history, either because of a major distraction (e.g., a predator), or a changed state of awareness, such as sleeping. Historically referred to as the use of "cognitive maps," these topics have been an active area of research in psychology for much of the 20th century (Tolman, 1948). Despite this long history, revolutionary changes in understanding such representations have occurred only in the past five years or so. An interdisciplinary convergence across the fields that make up cognitive science appears to have been the catalyst.

One major impetus for this convergence came from Gallistel's (1989) examination of neuropsychological and neuroethological work on animal navigation in the context of formal mathematical analyses of the geometry of space. Gallistel, noting that sets of geometric spaces are equivalent under certain classes of mathematical transformations, asked whether the different groups of geometric equivalences might have distinct representational and computational consequences. His arguments required a synthesis across several disciplines that normally had little commerce: areas of mathematics, including geometry and topology; classical ethological studies on species ranging from desert ants to Clark's nuthatch; and neurophysiological studies of midbrain processing of spatial information. It was only through such a synthesis that a novel set of psychological studies in rats and humans started to emerge.

Many years earlier, Piaget and Inhelder (1956) had used concepts in topology to formulate a theory of the child's developing concepts of space; but, in that early work, a full sampling of relevant literature across all disciplines was not undertaken—an oversight that eventually contributed to undermining the proposal. Piaget and Inhelder described young children as being unable to distinguish topologically equivalent representations (i.e., those that preserve the number of holes on an infinitely elastic surface); for example, they lacked the ability to discriminate shapes that were topologically equivalent. Only later in development were they supposedly able to use Euclidean bases for discriminating shapes. This was a dramatic proposal that intersected with some failures observed in young children, but, in the end, met insurmountable problems as infant researchers began to more carefully show that infants and young children could easily discriminate topologically equivalent shapes. This sequence illustrates that a successful cognitive science approach to such problems requires more than highly selective samplings of one or two constructs in another discipline.

A different set of proposals by Piaget, concerning children's ability to locate themselves in space, has survived to the present day as an important part of the discussion of spatial knowledge. The young child was characterized as encoding spatial relations solely in an egocentric manner. Layout could only be encoded relevant to the child's own point of view and not in terms of an observer-independent representation (Piaget, 1952, 1954). That proposal has turned out to be only partially correct and, for years, inconsistencies between findings favoring an egocentric account and findings favoring viewer-independent representations seemed mysterious and difficult to reconcile. The insights from converging perspectives such as Gallistel's started to suggest a coherent and sensible overall model (see also Koenig, Reiss, & Kosslyn, 1990; Moscovitch, Kapur, Köhler, & Houle, 1995; Pick, 1983).

Part of the problem stems from a need to characterize all the possible forms of information that could help specify spatial relations, as well as the different ways in which such information might be used to address an organism's goals. If one considers the ways in which organisms navigate and act on their real-world environments, one starts to see that all spatial knowledge may not be the same. Knowledge of the layout in which one moves about may be different in large- and small-scale environments (Acredelo,

1981), and both may be different from knowledge of how an object is oriented relative to one's grasp. Different again may be the ability to see spatial relations in maps, pictures, and scale models, and to translate them into the real world (DeLoache, 1987, 1989; DeLoache & Burns, 1994). Finally, all of these lines of work have links to the tracking of individuals. As described earlier, layout information may be far more effectively maintained across distinct visual samplings of the world than object-specific property information (Simons, 1996).

Even if one constrains the discussion to knowing the location of self and other objects with respect to environments of the same scale, the kinds of available information are still extensive, which should be obvious from the sources of information used by marine navigators over the centuries (Dutton, 1978). One can keep track of one's own position by inertial guidance, much as ships used to do—that is, by tracking every physical displacement in terms of accelerations and decelerations that are recorded in the semicircular canals (or from accelerations inferred from visual flow fields). One can keep track of the results of one's motor movements in a manner analogous to "dead reckoning" (the computation of where one is, solely on the basis of internally generated information concerning the speed, direction, and duration of one's movement). Without a map on which to superimpose this kind of information, one can only return to prior locations by reversing the acceleration vectors or the vector outputs of one's motor movements. If one starts with, or builds, a map of the layout, one can use that information to constantly update one's position on a cognitive map, much as a pilot updates positions on a chart.

Location can also be determined through use of landmarks. The crudest method is simply to note proximity to a landmark. When the proximity exceeds a certain threshold, one infers that the current location is specified by that landmark's place on a map. More sophisticated use of landmarks involves noting asymmetric properties of a landmark (or bearings as supplied by a compass). One can then determine the direction in which the landmark is located relative to self, and use its apparent height to calculate distance. Or, one can use multiple landmarks (three will suffice) to compute a unique set of geometric relations that specify one's position in space.

Finally, to locate oneself in space, there is a method that was rarely used in any explicit manner by marine navigators.

(I understand, however, that it may be one of the most reliable methods now used by cruise missiles.) It involves constructing a representation of the overall layout, independent of local landmarks. One forms a representation of the contours of the environment in a manner that uses the outer perimeters of the perceivable area. The perimeter forms a Euclidean planar surface, and one occupies a position on that surface (three-dimensional versions are also possible, but this additional complexity has been explored much less experimentally). This contour computation is an extremely reliable way of knowing where one is, and, in most natural environments, gives a unique solution that is robust over many dramatic changes in more local features (Gallistel, 1989). Only in carefully constructed artificial environments with special symmetries do such representations fail to give unique solutions. Using contour information in a perfectly rectangular enclosure, one can only know a position relative to the long and short walls—information that specifies two points, not just one. For example, if one remembers that desired food is located at a point just before a long wall on one's left converges with a short wall on one's right, that memory alone specifies two locations in the rectangular enclosure, not just one. This method of locating oneself, and its failure in special symmetrical environments, becomes much more apparent when one considers mathematical transformations of space that treat them as equivalent (ibid).

As researchers start to consider problems of knowing one's location in space from the vantage points of many different disciplines and research paradigms, the diversity of approaches makes much clearer the different sorts of information that specify spatial relations, as well as the different uses of that information. Whether the problem is: getting a small robot to keep track of its location; trying to show how a neural circuit could represent location in space and update it (McNaughton, Knierim, & Wilson, 1995; O'Keefe & Nadel, 1978); asking how different human cultures develop models of space and use them for navigation (Gladwin, 1970); asking whether language helps mold the character of spatial representations (Bowerman, 1989; Levinson, 1994; Talmy, 1983); or conceptually analyzing the cognitive and philosophical consequences of different models of space (Hatfield, 1990), interactions among these different traditions are essential. As researchers realize the relevance of all these different lines of work to their own, they start to see ways in which all the diverse forms of information and spatially relevant tasks might fit together. Moreover, they begin to see how each traditional discipline, on its own, is inadequate to fully explain the phenomena. It is not possible here to describe how substantive insights in each discipline have begun to inform each other in ever increasingly fertile ways; indeed, the interaction is so immense at present that any such account would be soon outdated. It suffices here to provide an example, or a case study.

One example of how these different threads start to come together can be seen in a series of recent studies that have started to untangle the apparent contradictions concerning how a child's spatial knowledge might develop (Hermer & Spelke, 1994, 1996). The key question concerned apparent inconsistencies between (a) older human infant and child studies suggesting egocentric representations of space and (b) more recent human studies, and many years of comparative ones, suggesting allocentric representations. Piaget's proposals had gained considerable support over the years, and it was easy to set up experiments in which infants and young children seemed only to know where objects were relative to their own bodies and not the embedding environment (e.g., Acredelo, 1987). Yet, sometimes young children seem to construct allocentric representations, as do members of several other species (Morris, 1981).

An analysis of the research paradigms used across disciplines revealed that they were not strictly the same and might be pulling on different forms of information. Especially relevant were studies showing that rats were so heavily biased, in terms of the sorts of information they used to find concealed objects, that they could be led astray in striking ways (Cheng, 1986). They relied so strongly on the overall contour information that, when disoriented in special symmetrical environments, they would go to the correct location only 50% of the time, even when landmark and other local cues were exceedingly salient and infallible indicators of the location of a hidden object. If young children could be shown to make the same mistakes, it would start to suggest that multiple systems might be at work in the development of spatial representations, and that different tasks might draw on these systems in different ways, thereby creating apparent inconsistencies.

In fact, young children do have several distinct systems for computing and representing spatial relations, and these systems are used in different ways over the course of development. Young preschoolers, in symmetrical environments, react surprisingly like the rats that attend only to general contour information—a response that is at odds with traditional egocentric uses of space. The children are disoriented and then use the environment's shape to figure out the location of the desired object. When the environment is symmetrical, the children will make the same mistakes as the rats, ignoring highly salient and fully disambiguating landmarks (Spelke & Hermer, 1996).

Whether this is strictly allocentric can be complex and depends on finer-grained definitions of egocentric and allocentric responding. A child might think that an object is in a certain location only when the long wall is on the left and the short wall is on the right—a kind of egocentric referencing; but because that child will reorient his or her body until that position is achieved, and uses the environment's shape to do so, he or she is more fundamentally showing allocentric awareness. The full story remains to be told, but it is clearly linked to such things as the child's level of self-locomotion, the degree to which the child becomes disoriented, and the perceived and understood stability of objects in the environment, among other factors. Moreover, in true cognitive science tradition, the developmental work has now informed adult models of spatial representation. Adults can be shown to make astonishing mistakes by overrelying on contour information even in the face of much more unambiguous and starkly salient landmark and property information (Spelke & Hermer, 1996).

Further collaborations across mathematics, computer science, neuroscience, psychology, anthropology, philosophy, and linguistics will greatly enhance our understanding of the nature and use of spatial knowledge. Recent findings that different languages may cause their users to orient themselves in specific ways are now offering the possibility of yet another way of understanding how these different systems that support spatial knowledge might be structured and might function together (Bowerman, 1989; Levinson, 1994; Talmy, 1983, 1995). When an organism solves a cognitive problem by using several distinct functional systems, it can be extremely difficult, from the perspective of one discipline, to uncover all these systems and how they interrelate. From a cognitive science perspective, each discipline offers a different approach and tends to highlight particular systems or parts of those systems. As the points of view across disciplines accumulate, the full set of systems and their interrelations becomes much clearer. This is what is beginning to happen with spatial knowledge.

Even now, in the early stages of cross-disciplinary fertilization, it is possible to see how a cognitive science perspective allows one to pose a new group of questions that were, until now, hardly in the realm of discourse. Consider the following examples: What are the formally possible ways of indicating the locations of objects in space? Of these ways, which ones are cognitively natural and learnable? Why are they natural and in what tasks and contexts are they learnable? If language influences the nature of spatial cognition, what format must the spatial representations have, to be able to interact with language in the ways that they do? As spaces become larger and more cluttered, what sorts of information specifying layout become exponentially more complex and beyond human abilities to track in a cognitively reasonable manner? How is information about space gathered from such diverse modal inputs as locomotion, audition, vision, and touch, to form an integrated sense of layout? How is knowledge of space, as constructed from active movement, different from the same knowledge as constructed from passive movement, and how is it different from not moving at all? Are there neural systems that correspond to the above distinctions? Do both the connectionist and the more symbolic forms of representation of space have specific roles? Are the roles complementary? How might the two roles interact in reading maps of layout?

Some of the most important recent advances in the study of spatial knowledge have occurred because the research was pluralistic—not approached from just one perspective. Insights from mathematics, neuroscience, cognitive psychology, and other fields were all brought to bear in ways that illuminated important new distinctions that could be explored empirically. In turn, that convergence led to questions of the sort just listed, which in turn can lead to new research insights. This is the sort of cycle that makes cognitive science work. Gallistel's (1989) book is a superb example of this process; he moves smoothly across work in a huge array of disciplines and develops a coherent account of how spatial knowledge is used and acquired. Issues of learning and development are absolutely central to that account. Often, and impressively, developmental issues seem to organize both the debate and the direction of research.

Spatial knowledge is a form of knowledge shared with virtually all other animals. The ability to move about

brings with it the need to know where one is, where one has come from, and where one is going. Moreover, this kind of knowledge seems to be largely implicit and nonverbal. Indeed, we have seen that some forms of layout information are relatively impervious to verbal interference. Let us now contrast spatial knowledge with a kind of knowledge that is much less common across species and is arguably unique to humans: the ability to frame our beliefs in such a way that they can be communicated to others through symbols. The human faculty for natural language involves communicable explicit beliefs as well as intricate implicit knowledge about the structure of language itself. That combination has led to richly detailed and often novel models of learning and development. Later in this chapter, questions arise as to whether common development themes exist across these seemingly very different forms of knowledge.

How Do We Communicate Messages?

Humans engage in one behavior that is extremely salient and clear-cut: They utter sounds that are meant to convey messages, and those messages are understood by others. The messages communicated contain an unbounded array of content—one's political philosophy, a recipe for corn bread, the latest theory of natural language grammar, and so on.

The reasons for successful communication are many: the motivations and attentional states of the communicators; their prior knowledge bases; the pragmatic assumptions they have concerning the communicative act; and their abilities to produce and understand language. In the past two decades, research concerning how we communicate has surged ahead, and research on the development of communication abilities has been one of the most dominant activities throughout this period. The enormous progress has been a function of the multidisciplinary approach to this problem, which began after the traditional psychological models of learning and associative memory turned out to be wholly inadequate. A more fully developed and precise characterization of languages was needed, and it was not available in the psychological literature. Traditional linguistics, which had become too limited by surface descriptions of specific languages, became liberated by Chomsky's more formal characterizations, which drew on methods and arguments taken from logic, mathematics, and automata theory (Chomsky, 1957, 1965, 1973).

Through the interactions between newly emerging linguistic theory and research on the psychology of language, a new kind of research on language acquisition began. Today, researchers in language acquisition blend together issues in linguistic theory (e.g., the appropriate formal representation of a competence) with issues in psychological theory (e.g., the nature of particular models of learning and memory) (Gleitman & Warner, 1982; Grimshaw, 1981; Lust et al., 1994; MacWhinney, 1987). Language acquisition researchers in general did not concern themselves with chronometric attempts to verify some aspect of linguistic theory (e.g., using reaction time patterns to try to support a particular theory of grammar); rather, they used linguistic theory as a tool for making precise statements about different kinds of linguistic structures and then exploring proposals of how those structures might be acquired.

Research in this area continues to exemplify a cognitive science approach. Philosophy of language is now essential to a fully developed linguistic theory, whether it involves characterizations of the semantics of a formal language (Chierchia & McConnell-Ginet, 1990) or accounts of the representational consequences of a linguistic system linked to beliefs (Crimmins, 1992). Formal grammar can be no more isolated from questions arising from epistemology and metaphysics than it can from questions about learning, mental representation, and computation.

Neuroscience has also become more relevant as researchers have integrated older neuropsychology models based on brain damage (Geschwind, 1965; Goldstein, 1948; Luria, 1966) with new models based on imaging and Event Related Potentials (ERP) studies of healthy brains (Damasio, 1990; Neville, 1994, in press; Neville, Coffey, Holcomb, & Tallal, 1993; Peterson, 1993). Functional distinctions suggested by linguistic theory and language acquisition data have led to much more focused questions in brain imaging studies, and these studies, in turn, have led to important discoveries about language organization and brain function over the course of development. For example, Neville (1994, 1995, in press) has recently shown converging support from both functional MRI scans and ERP data for a distinct language-processing architecture that is active in comparable ways when both native English and American Sign Language (ASL) learners use their native languages as adults. Thus, areas analogous to the classic Broca's region and Wernicke's region are highly active in the left hemispheres of both English and native ASL learners. Native ASL learners also show roughly equivalent levels of right-sided activation whereas native English learners do not, and the ASL learners seem to have an additional right-sided activation of parietal regions. This neuropsychological work now suggests a wide array of language acquisition studies with deaf and hearing children, to look for common and distinctive processes that are involved in the acquisition of different languages. A common functional core, operating in the left hemisphere for all natural languages, is then supplemented with the aspects of the right hemisphere when the languages also involve signing.

A different tradition concerning the broader social context of utterances has linked ideas in philosophy, psychology, and comparative work across species. For example, joint attention between speakers and listeners on the object of discourse is now considered a critical part of understanding how communication succeeds. Moreover, the development of joint attention has fueled interest in this area as well as in the same topic in adults and across species (Baldwin, 1995; Bruner, 1977, 1983, 1991; Tomasello, 1990; Tomasello, Kruger, & Ratner, 1991). This new area of research requires a blend of speech-act theory in philosophy (see Rommetveit, 1974, for earlier contributions), grammatical theory in linguistics, and perspective-taking skills in psychology.

Computational issues have also become more central to questions about how language works as a communicative system, and, often most importantly, in the study of how language could be learned. Consider, for example, how a formal theory of computing has been combined with linguistic theory in ways that give mutual reinforcement. A parameter-setting model of language acquisition, as formulated by Chomsky (1981), can now be plausibly rendered in a model that fits with formal learning theory, issues of computational plausibility, and psycholinguistic data (Kapur, 1994). This is not to say that the parameter-setting approach has been proven correct, but the convergence is now pushing research in that area ahead with new questions that would not even have been apparent prior to such an integration.

The relations between computational systems and language have been complicated by the rise of connectionism in cognitive science. The heat generated by recent discussions of language and computation has sometimes obliterated all light, but important new collaborations have begun between those interested in formal linguistic theory and those modeling knowledge in terms of massively parallel computational systems. The growth of that new collaboration, and its subsequent insights, is worth looking at a bit more closely. Among other reasons, it showcases the centrality of developmental issues to successful interdisciplinary approaches to the study of language.

The emergence of connectionism was first greeted by some as tolling the end of linguistic theory and perhaps even the end of more traditional psychological models of the acquisition of language. Had that been so, some cognitive science perspectives themselves might have faced dismantling. If, for example, no level of representation allowed for symbols and symbol manipulation, many models of language processing and acquisition would be obsolete. But, as the connectionist systems became more elaborated and better understood, the relevance to linguistic theory and the potential compatibility with more nativist views of language became evident (Kirsh, 1992; Seidenberg, 1992). Indeed, some seem to regard connectionism as the best hope of nativist theories of language acquisition because of its powerful ability to offer a workable learning system within a network of innate constraints. This optimistic viewpoint describes a version of connectionism that is very different from the earliest views:

> . . . when linguists talk about innate capacities for language they have in mind something more specific than a tendency for certain brain areas to be recruited for certain tasks. The inventory of hypothesized innate capacities includes language-specific knowledge structures, tendencies to analyze linguistic input in specific ways, and constraints on the range of hypotheses that are formed, among others. Connectionism is equally compatible with these ideas. Moreover, it provides a basis for exploring exactly how innate capacities of various sorts would affect the course of acquisition. . . . These observations merely establish the simple point that connectionism is compatible with nativism. More important, however, I think that rather than being merely compatible with the nativist view, connectionism is likely to provide what is needed in order to establish the essential correctness of this view with regard to language. (Seidenberg, 1992, pp. 86–87)

More recent work is reinforcing the interdisciplinary relations and is showing in detail how a connectionist architecture might be integrated with both linguistic theory and psychological models, helping each to inform the other. Consider, for example, Prince and Smolensky's (1997) "optimality" approach to grammar. In their attempts to model the use and acquisition of natural language, they found that constraints quite similar to those proposed in formal linguistic theory could be combined with a connectionist learning system in ways that both supported the reality of such constraints and allowed the connectionist architecture to succeed. Moreover, the notion of the constraints themselves changed in this implementation from a set of strictly ordered invariant restrictions to a more complex interactive set of constraints governed by new principles of constraint competition and domination that can rerank constraints. Thus, the synthesis of radically different approaches from linguistic theory, psychology, and computer science led to new views of the constructs in each of these disciplines, such as what constraints on language are and how they might work. In all of this effort, learning—and, by implication, development—was a central theme.

Any talk about what sorts of knowledge connectionist systems "in general" can easily acquire is becoming increasingly incoherent. As the different kinds of connectionist models proliferate and become increasingly integrated within contrasting sets of well-specified constraints on inputs, timing, weighting, and feedback, there is no longer just one kind of knowledge for which they seem to be especially suited. When those additional constraints are included, those systems often become computational hybrids that are no longer purely based on connectionist systems (Clark, 1994). The dogma from all sides seems to be retreating as a more truly interdisciplinary approach is adopted.

In more traditional approaches to the acquisition of language, a series of fixed, and usually a priori, ordered sets of constraints on possible language structures has been posited as guiding language acquisition across all cultures (Chomsky, 1980, 1986). This model of constraints proved extraordinarily valuable in suggesting new lines of research and led to many discoveries about language acquisition across diverse cultures. But it seemed to run into conflict with the emerging field of connectionism, which wanted learning to be more sensitive to statistical information about the linguistic input (Seidenberg, 1997). Indeed, in many connectionist accounts, the child came to the language-learning situation with no a priori constraints that were tailored specifically for language learning. All subsequent patterns of language learning were caused by weights in a network—weights whose values were ultimately caused by sampling statistical patterns in the language input. Often, complex and even surprising interactions among elements in the connectionist nets could lead to developmental discontinuities, U-shaped developmental trends, and other intricate patterns; but all of these were fully the consequences of input patterns in combination with the activities of the connectionist net, which, in its initial state, embodied no expectations whatsoever about the nature of language (Pinker & Prince, 1988).

A stalemate seemed to be emerging. Linguists and language acquisition researchers felt it was impossible to learn a language without prior constraints, and connectionists pointed out the powerful ways in which linguistic knowledge could grow and change as a result of the statistics of language inputs (Plunkett & Marchman, 1993). But this tension created a new series of models that has modified both the views of constraints and the ways in which connectionist networks might get started in a learning cycle. Instead of constraints being seen as "hard" constraints that are necessary, inviolate, and perhaps even rigidly ordered in application, they were recast as a priori biases that are "soft." Their strength and range of application and their interactions with other constraints are all modifiable through linguistic experience in a connectionist system in ways that attend to statistical properties of inputs. The connectionist system's initial state includes those constraints and then allows them to respond sensitively to new statistical patterns when they are encountered (Prince & Smolensky, 1997).

The model developed here with grammar has implications for many other domains of cognition. Parallel distributed processing (PDP) approaches do not need to be set up in opposition to systems with domain-specific biases for acquiring particular kinds of information. They can coexist in ways that would seem to powerfully complement each other. The details of that relationship need to be worked out formally and explored empirically. Can the initial constraints be obliterated completely by appropriate statistical patterns of linguistic input, or are they simply shifted in terms of their weights, range of application, and relative domination relations? How quickly can the constraints be shifted? How would one model such constraints in a bilingual child who is learning two starkly different languages with many local grammatical contrasts? These sorts of questions extend far beyond

language—indeed, they encompass many different approaches to development (e.g., Bronfenbrenner & Morris, Ch. 17, this Volume).

Finally, computational approaches have made a different kind of contribution to the study of language because of a spectacular failure. No artificial systems to date are even close to being able to mimic the real-time language competency of a 3-year-old. Despite the enormous economic incentives to come up with computer systems that could paraphrase, translate, and, in general, "understand" natural language, real progress in this area has been minimal. This failure, in marked contrast to the successes of chess-playing programs and some expert systems, has had a powerful impact on how the language competency is viewed in comparison to other cognitive capacities. Why is language so difficult to implement on a computer when chess, numerical computation, and project planning are relatively easy? Like language, the game of chess would seem to require an ability to interpret and produce an essentially unbounded number of configurations. Why can programs on low-end personal computers so easily exceed all but a tiny percentage of humans in levels of performance? In the early years of digital computers, optimism about computational modeling of language was easily as high as that for chess, but that hope was clearly wrong, and that failure has had a profound influence on how we think about the human capacity for language. This realization could never have occurred without the presence of computer simulations, because many people's intuition seemed to predict the opposite pattern.

Computers themselves, as well as computational theory, have therefore come to have a wide range of influence on how psychologists, philosophers, and linguists think about language. Thus, consideration of the problems of language use and acquisition in the framework of a nonhuman artificial system sheds new light on old problems. A very different illumination was cast by consideration of such problems from the perspective of a nonhuman natural system, namely primates. Failures to obtain sophisticated sign language in even the most intelligent nonhuman primates suggested that humans have a special language-specific endowment that is not the same as general computational and cognitive power (Seidenberg, 1986). This suggestion was reinforced by later data gathered from special groups of humans who were highly sophisticated users of language but who were heavily impaired cognitively. In one such group were people afflicted with Williams syndrome (Bellugi, Birhle, Neville, Jernigan, & Doherty, 1993).

The study of the human ability to use language as a communicative system may be more centrally situated in cognitive science than in any other area of research. It has seemed obvious for some time that no single discipline could answer all of the most basic questions about language, especially questions concerning how language might be acquired. In the study of language acquisition, linguists and psychologists have developed a rich network of fruitful collaborations that offer important potential insights into the nature of adults' language comprehension and use. The constraints discussed by Prince and Smolensky (1997), for example, guide a system's acquisition of language; but those constraints remain in place in adults and might well be vital to an explanation of how language is produced and understood in normal use. As acquisition studies provide evidence for particular forms of these constraints, they also reveal new details about how those constraints might guide language comprehension and production.

At present, four themes are suggested by the body of work on language that emerges from a cognitive science perspective. They can be summarized briefly:

1. Humans' ability for language and communication is not merely a reflection of general cognitive skills or capacities. Comparative data suggest that humans have a special cognitive endowment tailored to facilitate this kind of task. This is one sense in which the ability to acquire and use language is domain-specific.

2. All languages throughout the world do share universal properties, although they are often discoverable only through formal and abstract specifications of linguistic knowledge. These specifications are often not immediately apparent from mere surface impressions of a language.

3. Communication of messages in particular, as opposed to emotional or physiological states, strongly biases a need for a system with properties similar to those of human natural languages; thus, analogies to other sorts of communication seen in various species are indirect and often only weakly analogical.

4. Each of the prior three points suggests a particular pattern of language acquisition. Indeed, during the past decade, major advances in discussions of language and communication have almost invariably brought in questions of acquisition. Children come to the language-learning situation with a set of abstract expectations about the nature of the language to be learned long before they have been taught many of the concrete details of the specific language that will become their mother tongue. The learnability results, the patterns of language universals, and the tendencies of children throughout the world to create new creolized languages in essentially the same ways (Bickerton, 1981, 1995), all point toward children's "knowing" something about the abstract structural properties of natural languages before they master the concrete details. That structural knowledge acts as a kind of skeletal framework within which the details become elaborated. There is only one alternative: Children come to the language-learning situation with no expectations about language, but are able to extract abstract patterns immediately from concrete tokens, and to use those abstractions to guide further learning. Such a proposal is not yet workable and has the additional problem of accounting for the universal properties of natural languages.

These four themes are not universally accepted, but they set up a series of debates that can be addressed by both theoretical and empirical analyses. Their truth matters less here than the fact that it would have been difficult even to pose them and have them be part of the current debate, if they had not developed within a cognitive science perspective.

How Do We Quantify Entities and Perform Computations on Them?

Knowledge of language is knowledge of a nonphysical system with infinite combinatorial possibilities. Our abilities to represent and use such a system seem dramatically different from those we use to represent aspects of the physical world. How different they really are can be better understood by looking at humans' knowledge and universal use of a different nonphysical system: numbers. A great deal of the cognitive power that we bring to bear in our everyday activities involves our ability to, at least temporarily, equate and count a set of entities, whether they are one's children, cars in traffic, or minutes until a dreaded appointment. We are also able to perform computations on our initial quantifications; we add and subtract automatically many times throughout a day, and occasionally we perform more complex mathematical operations such as multiplication and division (controversy surrounds just how complex are the operations that we all intuitively perform, especially when we reason probabilistically) (Gigerenzer & Hoffrage, 1995; Gigerenzer & Hug, 1992).

In these respects, we appear to be no match for computers. Because they can perform computations of all sorts at speeds far superior to those of humans, it is often assumed that humans are weakly endowed with a natural capacity for numerical thought. This view of human numerical competence may be excessively modest, in two respects. First, much of the work involved in quantifying the world lies not in the computations per se, but in knowing what to quantify—that is, what makes a reasonable set of things to count. Computers do not have a clue here; those assumptions must be made for them. Second, in more qualitative terms, humans still far outperform even the most sophisticated computers in making complex assessments of multiple interacting variables. Not even our largest supercomputers are capable, in real time, of tracking and responding to a patient's state while under anesthesia. Anesthesiologists succeed by using qualitative reasoning that deals with inequalities between relative quantities as well as with probability estimates (Gaba, Howard, & Small, 1995). A kind of mathematical thinking is going on in such cases, but not of the sort that computers can simulate very successfully (Forbus, 1985).

To fully understand the human ability to quantify and compute, one needs to engage in several different forms of analyses. One such analysis involves asking what numbers are and what they are used for—questions that sit squarely in mathematics and the philosophy of mathematics. Other questions, normally arising in computer science, ask about the relative complexities of different patterns of computations. Still other questions ask about the processing limitations and compensating strategies used by the human mind. These questions and many others have been pursued vigorously in recent years from a refreshing cognitive science viewpoint that has integrated across perspectives, and, in doing so, has motivated new questions, methods, and research paradigms.

A small sampling of this recent research is offered here, to illustrate the flavor of the cognitive science approach and the insights it is suggesting about the nature of

mathematical knowledge and how it might be acquired. As with other domains of thought, the most profound insights into the nature of mathematical knowledge in recent years appear to have come primarily from a perspective that asks how this knowledge is acquired and how it might have evolved. The vast majority of mature humans show a wide repertoire of mathematical competences, so rich and varied as to defy easy exploration of the fundamental properties of that knowledge. By contrast, developmental and comparative studies and, to a lesser extent, cross-cultural studies, highlight more vividly the underlying structure that makes this knowledge possible.

As adults, we seem to embed our mathematical insights so heavily in language that they may seem impossible without it. This involvement of language has helped motivate a line of research devoted to exploring mathematical knowledge in organisms that have no obvious language within which to couch the mathematics. The subjects here are preverbal humans (infants) and animals. With both types of subjects, the research results have been dramatic and often surprising. Preverbal infants not only seem to understand the basic numerosity of a display of objects independent of concrete properties (Starkey, 1992), but also appear to be able to perform subtraction and addition on those extracted numbers (Simon, Hespos, & Rochat, 1995; Wynn, 1992). To do these tasks, they also must be making assumptions about equivalence classes (for the purposes of counting) and about what properties constitute distinct individuals. (For some alternative views of infants' numerical capacities, see Cohen, 1991; Cohen, Diehl, Oakes, & Loehlin, 1992; and discussions in Fischer & Bidell, Ch. 9; Thelen & Smith, Ch. 10; and Overton, Ch. 3, this Volume).

Animals have sophisticated numerical abilities as well. Counting occurs ubiquitously in other species (Gallistel, 1990; Meck & Church, 1983). Numerical calculations, including those that correspond to addition, subtraction, and rate change calculations, also seem to be present (Gallistel, 1989; Gallistel & Gelman, 1992). The numerical competence of such nonlinguistic minds has prompted a closer look at what sort of representational system might be responsible and, as seen shortly, quite detailed models have been proposed (Meck & Church, 1983).

For older humans, counting behaviors are signs of sophisticated knowledge about how numbers can be used to quantify entities and relations in the world. For that reason, the early emergence of verbal counting behaviors has been presumed to offer important insights into the development of numerical knowledge. Indeed, it is possible to construe early counting behavior in young preschoolers as evidence for knowledge of a highly structured set of abstract principles concerning number, such as objects being counted in a fixed yet arbitrary order (Gelman & Gallistel, 1979). Because animals do not engage in verbal counting, their knowledge of number may be very different, raising the possibility of a special, qualitatively different human capacity for numerical reasoning. These issues have become considerably more complex in recent years (Gallistel & Gelman, 1992; Wynn, 1990). The early ability to count may be more like that seen in other species and may not reflect a full awareness of the numerical properties of the terms used in counting. That awareness may take several additional years to develop and may be a result of an emerging ability to represent numerical relations in a natural language. A better understanding of this process will require a much closer analysis of how numerical relations and concepts are represented in language and how such representations, in turn, might change the character of mathematical knowledge. Thus, the study of numerical knowledge must turn to foundational work in linguistic theory about such issues as semantic relations and logical form.

A different way of thinking about numerical competences might ask about the cognitively natural ways of learning about using numbers. In a manner analogous to the study of natural language, one can ask whether humans are biased to construct numerical knowledge in certain ways and to perform certain classes of computations over others. Several different approaches have been taken in recent years to ask adults these kinds of questions. One might ask about the kinds of numerical systems and mathematical procedures that are seen across all cultures. When such cross-cultural comparisons are made, it is immediately obvious that virtually everyone uses math a great deal in daily life. We all count, and we know how to add and subtract quantities (Bryant, 1995; Saxe, 1983; Zaslavsky, 1973). Given the ubiquity of some forms of mathematical knowledge, a question then arises: Might there be universal properties of this knowledge that exist above and beyond the many patterns of variation? Such universals start to indicate what might be cognitively natural ways of thinking about and using numerical relations. Some patterns appear to be universal—for example, those governing counting (Gelman & Gallistel, 1979) and transitive reasoning about

quantities. But the search for universal, humanly natural ways of representing and using mathematical knowledge is still in the early stages. Consider some speculative ways in which other universals might be present.

One set of universals might be involved in governing mathematical intuitions about such concepts as infinity, parallelism, and recursion. Following Plato's suggestion about how a slave boy might come to discover geometric truths through introspection, researchers now wonder whether a number of principles might have to be part of our natural endowment simply because no set of real-world experiences could ever suggest them. Real-world experience cannot show infinities, nor can it show parallelism and its consequences, or the true concepts of points, lines, and planes that occupy no volumes in space. Could aspects of these ideas be universal? Could such universals be part of early intuitions about number and also provide a foothold for later mathematical growth? This is an area where only a few explorations have been made, but where the research potential seems very large indeed (Silberstein, 1995).

We might also learn more about natural mathematical knowledge by looking at the intuitive physics of everyday life. In especially contrived circumstances, spectacular failures in predictions concerning simple mechanics can be found (McCloskey, 1983). These errors are often interpreted as arising from the use of erroneous causal theories, such as Aristotelian impetus theory, but they might also reveal constraints on mathematical thought. One class of constraints seems to be revealed when people have to grasp certain disparate kinds of mathematical formalisms governing physical bodies (Gilden, 1991; Proffitt & Gilden, 1989). They seem to develop distinct clusters of heuristics, such as for angle relations and speed relations, but are unable to combine them. For example, everyone (including physicists) has problems predicting the movements and forces for such things as spinning tops. These difficulties would seem to be part of the realm of mathematical knowledge because they involve reasoning about quantities. Heuristics, many of which may have strong qualitative reasoning components, are clearly involved; but the difficulties seem to be primarily with combining different kinds of mathematical relationships. The nature of the difficulty could be greatly clarified by looking at formally equivalent problems outside the realm of physical mechanics. In that way, one could tell whether there was a general cognitive difficulty in combining different systems of quantitative reasoning, or whether these difficulties were confined to intuitive physics. Studies of the developmental origins of such biases would also help greatly in determining whether they were arising primarily from the domain of mathematics or of physics.

This brief survey of a few different ways of exploring mathematical knowledge has revealed how insights can arise from many disciplines and approaches. It is especially compelling to show how many of these ideas can be integrated in a single research program to yield powerful new insights. One example is a recent model of the origins of mathematical knowledge put forth by Wynn (1995). Building on her demonstrations that infants as young as 5 months of age were capable of addition and subtraction of simple displays, she began to ask how they might be mentally representing quantities and acting on them. Because 5-month-olds clearly were not using language, models of numerical competences in other species seemed relevant. This relevance was especially vivid when rhesus monkeys performed addition and subtraction in tasks derived from Wynn's work (Hauser, MacNeilage, & Ware, 1996). Wynn turned to a model, sometimes known as the accumulator model, that was initially developed to explain animals' abilities to establish both number and duration (Gallistel & Gelman, 1992; Meck & Church, 1983). When the organism confronts a thing to be counted, the accumulator is filled up to a fixed amount. As each new countable thing is met, the accumulator fills up further by the same amount. When the full set of things has been counted, the number is represented by the end-state level of the accumulator. In the model, an animal has a large array of accumulators that can operate in parallel. All fullness values can be compared to past memory values for the accumulators, thereby enabling the animal to tell whether a number has increased, decreased, or stayed the same.

This model has several important components. The accumulators must be linked to an implicit categorization mechanism for countable things. For comparisons to be meaningful, each set of countable things must be kept distinct and its identity has to be tracked. In addition, the accumulator model predicts that accuracy in discriminating nearby numbers should decrease as the numbers increase (the noise level surrounding any accumulator's level increases as the number increases). This prediction has been confirmed in animals and in humans of all ages (Chi &

Klahr, 1975; Starkey & Cooper, 1980), suggesting that a common mechanism is shared across many species.

The accumulator model, in combination with a well-specified set of operations on the accumulators, can engage in subtraction and addition, but Wynn points out three limitations. First, as other mathematical operations such as multiplication and division are considered, the class of operations on the accumulators becomes much more complex—and, correspondingly, less plausible—as the only way of computing such results. Second, mathematical processes in accumulators are completely bound to the physical tokens that occasion the accumulations. Yet, adult humans freely manipulate formal numerical symbols in their own right and embed them in a system of logical relations. Third, concepts such as infinity and fractions are impossible to represent or learn in a system of accumulators, yet they seem to be important parts of our adult systems of mathematical thought. To try to understand whether these limitations suggested two different components to mathematical thought, Wynn turned to the history of mathematical thought (e.g., Kline, 1972). The historical analyses pointed in two directions: (a) computations easily performed on accumulators, and (b) computations that arose through other means, possibly language.

Wynn suggested that the emergence of verbal counting might provide a means for going beyond the limitations of the accumulator model. She argued, however, that mapping the linguistic counting system onto the kinds of information available in accumulators is a long and complex process that takes years for the child to fully master. But the complexity of such a developmental process is difficult to assess without a more explicit analysis of how language encodes numbers and their mathematical and logical relations. Thus, controversies about the extent to which early counting indicates numerical knowledge (Gallistel & Gelman, 1992) depend critically on more sophisticated linguistic analyses, a point readily acknowledged by Wynn. If linguistic representations provide the crucial vehicle for transforming mathematical thought from an accumulator-based system to a more flexible, abstract system, any account of how that transformation happens will have to give a full description of those linguistic representations.

Wynn's proposal concerning the origins of numerical knowledge shows how cognitive science has transformed the nature of research on number. Her account builds on ideas in psychology, animal behavior, philosophy, linguistics, and, of course, mathematics. Gelman and Gallistel (1979) pioneered this type of approach to number, and it has clearly grown and flourished in the context of modern cognitive science. Other links are also being built—computer simulations of accumulators and other numerical systems, or neuropsychological studies suggesting different systems (McCloskey, 1994). It now seems completely natural to integrate across all these points of view.

Across all studies on mathematical thought, some patterns do seem to emerge. First, there seems to be evidence both for principled sorts of knowledge, which one most easily states in propositional/symbolic form, and for non-symbolic forms, whether in the form of accumulators or associative nets. Repetition and frequency effects abound in mathematical thought; one important line of research focuses on how strategy choices might be influenced by such effects (Siegler, 1995). Equally pronounced is the presence of abstract principles that govern more complex operations—aspects of counting, and concepts such as infinity and fractions. There seems to be a need for knowledge structures that are intrinsically hybrid in nature—that is, they contain both rule-like principles and a means of adjusting such principles by accessing information about frequency of use and exposure.

In the second pattern, some principles may provide a skeletal framework that dictates natural mathematical patterns of thought for the entire life span. And it is here that the developmental work often shows the principles in stark relief before they are clouded over by the massive amount of learning of concrete particulars.

A third pattern involves distinctions that are reminiscent of Chomsky's competence/performance distinction. In one version of this view, Greeno, Riley, and Gelman (1984) talk about conceptual competence (roughly knowing the abstract principles), procedural competence (knowing how to generate specific behaviors that fit with those principles), and utilization competence (knowing what a particular task is asking for in terms of competence). Greeno et al. argue that principles come first but their implementation must be supported by the other two competences, which are more likely to be influenced by general performance factors such as memory and attentional limitations. For example, the general counting principles are not difficult to keep in mind even when there are severe limits on memory and attention, but the specific counting procedures, and

monitoring when they are needed, place much higher demands on these two capacities.

One of the most impressive aspects of numerical knowledge concerns the ability to develop appropriate categories of countable things. The importance of categorization in all domains of thought cannot be overstated. We now turn to that issue.

How Do We Categorize Our Physical and Social Worlds?

It is not hard to see why humans and so many other species engage in categorization behavior. Treating a group of entities as equivalent in some respect is perhaps the most widely recognized method of achieving cognitive economy (Markman, 1989; Simon, 1969; Smith & Medin, 1981). We cannot possibly store every piece of information that we encounter in conjunction with each individual entity. Instead, we frequently assume that an entity (Spot) is a member of a category (dogs), and we store dog-relevant properties at that level. Thus, simply knowing one property (Spot is a dog) allows us to access a great deal of other information about Spot without having to store it repeatedly for Spot, Rover, and Fido. Some version of this strategy is assumed by everyone who studies categorization; yet, there are dramatic differences of opinion on the details. Moreover, some acts of categorization seem much simpler than those that achieve such cognitive economies. It is useful to first consider those simpler forms and their relations to a cognitive science perspective. Indeed, a comparative analysis seems essential to understanding how categorization occurs, and to what extent categorization behavior entitles one to make inferences about such mental entities as concepts. Questions concerning the relations among language, concepts, and categories might be informed by examining categorization in nonhumans. Some researchers argue that the entire notion of animal "concepts" has been rather incoherent and is therefore of minimal relevance to the study of human concepts (Chater & Heyes, 1994; for a contrasting view, see Thompson, 1995). But such claims clarify the need for understanding the different kinds of categorization behaviors and how they might be related to mental representations. Comparative work has helped to reveal far more kinds than might have come to mind in studying humans alone.

When one considers categorization across all species, a sequence of levels is suggested. Herrnstein (1990) proposed five such levels of "stimulus control":

1. Discrimination.
2. Categorization by rote.
3. Open-ended categories.
4. Concepts.
5. Abstract relations.

Discrimination is the degenerate case of categorization, when an organism's ability to tell things apart results in the nondiscriminable items being put into behavioral equivalence classes. Categorization by rote refers to cases where each entity in a category is associated with the same sort of response, but the entities do not have any internal relations. Open-ended categories allow categorization of new instances by gradients of similarity to representations of known instances; the similarity metrics are seen as local penumbras around each instance. The concept level involves a richer interaction among representations of past instances; new instances are categorized according to dimensions arising from comparison across instances. Herrnstein (1990) had in mind here a prototype abstraction of the sort described by Rosch and Mervis (1975). Finally, at the abstract relations level, relations among concepts guide categorization. This level is not discussed to any great extent by Herrnstein.

These different levels illustrate a critical point. Not all forms of categorization behavior are equivalent in terms of the computational and representational demands they impose on the categorizer. Although the details of Herrnstein's specific levels may well be wrong, the general point holds, and it is the reason why papers in the categorization literature often talk past each other. The problem is much more acute when one realizes that Herrnstein's five levels are, by his own admission, only the beginning of a potentially much longer progression of levels in humans. In particular, the level of abstract relations seems to be a catchall level for the other possible forms of categorization. I will argue that, in the end, a close look at the possibilities within this fifth level, including striking data from preverbal children, not only shows more intricacies to categorization, but raises the strong possibility that animals are not as

trapped in the lower levels as they might initially seem (see also Thompson, 1995).

Research on categorization started largely within experimental psychology, but, as it started to broaden to other disciplines, major new insights occurred and a more truly cognitive science perspective evolved. Categorization behavior in humans is usually explained on the assumption that people possess "concepts" as mental representations that enable them to identify instances of categories. Concepts were initially seen as consisting of sets of singly necessary and jointly sufficient features that allowed their owners to pick out all (and only) members of a given category. This hypothesis was no doubt influenced by prior trends in analytic philosophy and logic; but it was also affected heavily by the nature of early experimental stimuli. In such tasks, categorization was usually a meaningless arbitrary concatenation of features. For example, participants might have been asked to learn the category "blik," which stood for large, blue, rectangular shapes with stripes.

This arbitrary character was considered a great benefit because it followed in the tradition of the nonsense syllable, developed in the late 19th century as a tool for exploring the mind without having stimuli contaminated by prior experience (Ebbinghaus, 1885/1964). For such nonsensical, arbitrary categories, the simple singly-necessary-and-jointly-sufficient-features rule often worked very well; its problems were not really apparent until research coming from broader multidisciplinary perspectives started to explore categorization. The first major shift came with Rosch, Mervis, Gray, Johnson, and Boyes-Braem's (1976) pioneering studies on family resemblance categories and the basic level.

When categorization is considered from an anthropological as well as a psychological perspective, methods and questions shift in ways that make natural categories and concepts much more central than artificial and arbitrary ones. Indeed, in many cultures, the artificial categories are regarded as so bizarre and silly that people refuse to take them seriously in cognitive tasks (Cole & Means, 1981). Rosch's earlier work on color terms was part of the impetus for her family resemblance view of categories in general (Heider & Olivier, 1972). In addition, Wittgenstein's philosophical writings on a family resemblance view of concepts were cited as an important influence on her work

(Rosch, 1978; Rosch & Mervis, 1975; see also Hampton, 1976). Taken together, these two additional perspectives helped foster a series of studies showing that the "classical" view of concepts was apparently mistaken. Participants did not see all members of categories as equally good members (a robin seemed a "better" bird than a chicken). They also reported many indeterminate boundary cases (a stereo system might be a marginal member/nonmember of the category of furniture).

The focus on natural categories also led to the discovery that, for some sorts of hierarchies of categories, there was a distinctive level that seemed to be especially psychologically important (Rosch et al., 1976). This basic level of categorization, uncovered for such categories as furniture, vehicles, clothing, and animals, seemed to be at a level where the correlational structure of features and the mental representations of those correlations were different from both superordinate and subordinate levels. Basic-level categories were bristling with featural information that provided much more vivid and psychologically compelling categories.

These developments in categorization research and theory soon had a huge impact on other fields in cognitive science and brought them into the discussion. Researchers in artificial intelligence attempted to model the family resemblance view of concepts and categories; some even adopted new formalisms, such as fuzzy logic, in an attempt to better account for this new view of concepts (Zadeh, 1965). Similarly, the new view of category structure had a powerful effect in linguistics, in views of the lexicon, of metaphor, and of other semantic and thematic roles (Lakoff, 1973, 1987). Equally salient was the emergence of developmental questions in the debate. Even in her early papers, Rosch often referred to developmental findings as one of the most compelling pieces of support for the basic level (e.g., Rosch et al., 1976). It appeared to be the first level of categorization acquired by children. Research on the acquisition of word meaning shifted from chronicles of vocabulary growth to studies of how concepts were initially represented and how those representations became linked to lexical items (Clark, 1983; Keil, 1979; see also Woodward & Markman in Volume 2 of this *Handbook*).

From a cognitive science perspective, research on categorization became increasingly difficult to disentangle from questions about concepts themselves and how they were represented. As research progressed, more doubts were raised about whether the concepts themselves could simply be modeled in a family resemblance format, or indeed in any other format that was basically a consequence of tabulations of feature frequencies and correlations (Armstrong, Gleitman, & Gleitman, 1983; Murphy & Medin, 1985). The debate was intensified by the realization that categorization behavior was not the only way in which concepts might have psychological roles or be assessed; indeed, it began to seem that excessive study of just categorization might lead to distortions of what concepts really were (Rey, 1983). In the end, closer looks both at categorization and at other uses of concepts suggested yet another theory of what concepts were and how they might be linked to categorization, but that new theory dealt more with explanation and causal understanding than with categorization, and is more properly the subject of the next section.

Finally, the development of connectionist attempts to model categorization suggested a radically different underlying mechanism (McClelland & Rummelhart, 1986). In many connectionist systems, categorization is intrinsically a developmental process in that the nature of a mature categorization can only be understood from looking at how the relevant networks get set up through exposure to the appropriate property clusters. In such accounts, it is normally assumed that categorization ability develops as a consequence of increasingly elaborated tabulations of environmental correlations and frequencies. Thus, the ability to correctly categorize dogs arises from frequently experiencing instances of dogs and nondogs, and receiving the appropriate feedback for both kinds of instances.

It is hardly controversial to suggest that the ability to categorize a class of things is related to experience with exemplars. More interesting are claims that connectionist systems can easily model the probabilistic nature of categorization and that the mental substrates for such categorization may not be at the grain of intuitive features such as "has hair," "barks," or "has four legs." Instead, some suggest that "microfeatures," far more fine-grained than those that spring to the conscious mind, are the true basis for building up categorization ability (Rumelhart, 1992).

This microfeatural alternative has potentially dramatic consequences. It suggests that a wide variety of methods that attempt to model categorization in ways that tap into people's conscious awareness of relevant features may be misguided. In addition, it suggests far more continuity with animal models of categorization, and indeed may serve to undermine, or at least make more continuous, the levels of categorization proposed by Herrnstein (1990). Finally, an even stronger discounting of such featural components arises in more recent arguments that the activation levels of single units, even when hidden, may have no featural or microfeatural analogs at all. Only the activation of a full complex of units has any psychological reality, and that activation pattern may correspond to a full-fledged concept such as DOG, and not smaller units (Elman, 1989).

It might seem that connectionist approaches to concept and categorization are straightforward empiricism and simply a high-tech version of what the British empiricists were advocating all along. At first, this may have been largely accurate in systems where the initial configuration of weights was neutral between systems that acquired grammar, concepts, and the ability to see curves. In such systems, the associative relations between input features, in conjunction with very general principles of connectionist learning, completely determined the eventual concept structure. It was not surprising that, early in the connectionist movement, it was seen by many as straightforward associationism (Pinker, 1990). But as the field has developed, many argue that some kinds of connectionist systems can be neutral with respect to nativist–empiricist debates (Clark, 1993; Ramsey, 1992). For example, the classical empiricists certainly wanted the building block features of concepts to be at the level of conscious perceptual features such as color, shape, and texture. They might have acceded to a reformulation in terms of microfeatures, but would have had a great deal more difficulty with networks in which concepts gained meaning only from the network as a whole, and had no psychologically meaningful composite features. By undercutting the building block or atomic primitives metaphor, such a network comes closer to meeting nativist views of concepts (Fodor, 1981), but does not fully meet them because it says nothing about how the network's configuration came into being. A connectionist system could be more squarely nativist if, in a fashion analogous to the current attempts to model natural language grammars, it specified a starting configuration that embodied powerful constraints on classes of concepts. Such approaches are only now being contemplated in a serious manner. It is clear already, however, that this line of work will powerfully shape how we think about the relations between concepts and categorization.

The ubiquitous nature of categorization and its obvious importance to cognitive efficiency have led to considerable research from several diverse perspectives. As studies have moved more to the study of natural categories normally used by humans in everyday life, research traditions from psychology, anthropology, and computer science have become ever more intertwined. At the same time, these research traditions have made increasing appeals to theoretical work in both philosophy and linguistics, and nowhere have those appeals been more obvious or fruitful than with the question of how categorization and the acquisition of word meaning relate. From the start, the developmental question has seemed more relevant to interdisciplinary discussion than the question of how mature lexicons relate to mature categorization.

One of the most dramatic and far-reaching discussions concerning the relations between the lexicon and categorization was put forth in Quine's (1960) *Word and Object*. Quine stated in stark and eloquent terms a formidable problem that involved categorization in the context of communication. The task of discovering what category of things a novel word denoted became vastly more difficult than it first appeared. It might seem that learning the meaning of a novel word consisted simply of noticing correlations between the use of that word and the presence of instances of a specific category. Over repeated trials, a unique category would become evident—"dog" would be learned to correspond to dogs, "gold" to gold, and so on. The problem, however, lay in a fundamental indeterminacy that no amount of experience could rectify, if the learner was assumed to enter the word-learning situation with a completely neutral learning architecture. Consider an oft-cited passage in which one is confronted with the problem of translating a single-word utterance from a member of a completely unknown culture, an utterance that appears to refer to a rabbit being pointed to in a clearing. Quine notes that the simple act of pointing in the direction of a rabbit while uttering a novel word ("gavagai") in no way guarantees success of linking the category of rabbits with that word; indeed, such a specific linkage is highly unlikely for many types of possible learners:

Consider "gavagai." Who knows but what the objects to which this term applies are not rabbits at all, but mere stages, or brief temporal segments, of rabbits? In either event the stimulus situations that prompt assent to "Gavagai" would be the same as for "Rabbit." Or perhaps the objects to which "gavagai" applies are all and sundry undetached parts of rabbits; again the stimulus meaning would register no difference. When from the sameness of stimulus meaning of "Gavagai" and "Rabbit" the linguist leaps to the conclusion that a gavagai is a whole enduring rabbit, he is just taking for granted that the native is enough like us to have a brief general term for rabbits and no brief general term for rabbit stages or parts. . . . Does it seem that the imagined indecision between rabbits, stages of rabbits, integral parts of rabbits, the rabbit fusion, and rabbithood must be due merely to some special fault in our formulation of stimulus meaning, and that it should be resoluble by a little supplementary pointing and questioning? Consider, then, how. Point to a rabbit and you have pointed to a stage of a rabbit, to an integral part of a rabbit, to the rabbit fusion, and to where rabbithood is manifested. Point to an integral part of a rabbit and you have pointed again to the remaining four sorts of things; and so on around. Nothing not distinguished in stimulus meaning itself is to be distinguished by pointing, unless the pointing is accompanied by questions of identity and diversity. (Quine, 1960)

This indeterminacy-of-translation problem helps set up the even more acute acquisition problem. A child not only faces all the standard translation problems, but has additional ones having to do with a highly underdeveloped core language and potentially different ways of categorizing and thinking about the world than is the case with adult users. There are two levels of thinking about Quine's concerns: (a) pragmatic and (b) principled. In pragmatic terms, it is highly implausible that a typical child would have enough experiences of the right type to be able to disambiguate critical alternative meanings of a word like "gavagai." Suppose, for example, that gavagai meant rabbit heads, or rabbit ears. The number of occasions in which a child might encounter a disembodied rabbit head or isolated rabbit ears are, in most cases, zero. Hence, in principle, disambiguation could occur, but most children are unlikely to ever have that experience.

Quine's concern runs much deeper than pragmatic concerns. Perhaps the subtleties of experience are vastly underestimated, and such events as pointing to parts on pictorial representations might provide information that whole rabbits versus rabbit parts are involved. The real force in Quine's example lies in those cases where no amount of experience could ever serve to distinguish between some sets

of possible meanings such as undetached rabbit parts or a temporal slice of rabbits. These meanings have exactly identical "stimulus synonymies," and no amount of experience could ever distinguish between the two. These different meanings, however, are based on different concepts and refer to different sorts of categories, even if they are always extensionally equivalent. "Trilaterals" and "triangles" are different concepts even if they always pick out the same sets of things. Thus, even though the category members are the same, the mental components of those two categorizations are different.

The Quinean dilemma has led to a number of highly specific proposals about how a learner might succeed, and most of these proposals have involved building into the learner certain biases to form some categories over others and/or to link only certain kinds of categories with word meanings. Quine himself proposed that the child must be endowed with perceptual and conceptual "quality spaces"—innate frameworks for guaranteeing that all humans were biased to carve up the world in essentially the same way. The same sorts of categories—categories like whole enduring objects—would therefore spring to mind out of phenomenal experience. The act of linguistic labeling might then further highlight certain categories, such as whole enduring objects and those that were mutually exclusive of each other (Clark, 1987; Markman, 1989; Woodward & Markman in Volume 2 of this *Handbook*).

Under this new perspective, prompted by Quine's original writings in philosophy, links to problems of individual identity became clearer. Thus, principles concerning how infants perceive objects and their behaviors became essential, as did questions about whether infants could even think of stable categories of individuals in terms of their properties (Xu & Carey, 1996). Other ideas from different subfields of linguistics, such as syntactic and semantic theory and pragmatics, were all brought to bear in trying to understand ways in which the number of possible categories for a specific word might be reduced (Markman, 1989; Waxman & Kosowski, 1990). Philosophical and linguistic considerations have demanded that the child come to the word-learning arena equipped with a rich array of biases that enable word/category matches at phenomenal rates. In some cases, these fast mappings seem to approach rates of one new match every waking hour (Carey, 1978; Dromi, 1987). These ways of viewing the problem were not really in the domain of discourse until questions of categorization were adopted from a cognitive science perspective. It is also now apparent how Quine's speculations about early perceptual and conceptual quality spaces might provide a way for connectionist systems to think about the initial configurations of network weights, thus bringing those two lines of thought together as well.

Questions about how words, concepts, and categories are interrelated were also strongly shaped by a different line of work in philosophy and linguistics. In thinking about how adults talk about naturally occurring classes of things, or what are normally called "natural kinds," two different philosophers uncovered, at about the same time, striking phenomena that ultimately demanded dramatically new ways of thinking about categorization and its relations to language. Saul Kripke (1972) and Hillary Putnam (1975) developed what has come to be known as the "causal theory of reference," in which the situations where labeling occurs, and the causal sequences that ensue, are absolutely central to an understanding of categorization and naming. The features of categorized things and the mental states of the users who label those categories were no longer sufficient. The problem is so profound and unsettling of traditional doctrine that it has caused several revolutions in thought about meaning and reference (e.g., Fodor, 1994; Millikan, in press). The dust arising from the debate is far from settled, but the debate itself has spawned an interdisciplinary flurry of research that would not have been even contemplated when viewed from one of the traditional disciplines that intersect with cognitive science.

Putnam and Kripke pointed out that word meaning is not easily characterized by a mental representation that "picks out" a category of things, an assumption that dominated most discussions up to that point and is still the favored default option. The problem is most obvious when one considers how people in the real world attach labels to classes of things and then maintain use of those labels over time—a process that is particularly evident in studies of how scientists conduct their trade and use scientific terms. The most powerful examples arise from thought "experiments" involving (a) uses of a term over long periods of historical change or (b) two different worlds that are phenomenally identical but differ in other critical respects.

Consider, for example how one might learn to attach the word "tiger" to the category of tigers. We all attend to certain typical features of tigers, such as their stripes and predatory behaviors, and, subject to the sorts of constraints

motivated by Quine's arguments, we decide that "tiger" refers to a class of whole enduring objects that typically have an array of features that might be mentally represented in a manner similar to that proposed by Rosch (1978). But what if there was another world that seemed identical to ours in every way except that certain unobservable molecular properties of what its inhabitants called tigers were dramatically different—say, their tiger DNA had twice as many genes and entirely different chromosomal configurations? Putnam argues that, prior to modern molecular biology—say, in the late 19th century—the mental states of matched pairs of people across these two worlds would be identical. Atom for atom, the same things would occur in their minds when they categorized tigers and labeled members of that category. And yet, despite this extremely strong equivalence, Fred on Earth and Fred* on Earth* would have to mean different things when they said "tiger" or thought about tigers.

This difference in meaning is obvious when one considers what happens as science progresses and the two Freds encounter each other in the context of modern molecular biology. Each would insist that what he had meant by "tiger" all along was the sort of animal that existed only in his world. Even though the two Freds might have mistakenly called things in the other world tigers, it is clear from modern science that each Fred meant only those in his own world. The reason appears to revolve around belief in a underlying unknown essence that is the object of the original reference and retains that link through time. The essence might not be known for centuries or indeed ever known (Locke thought that most real essences were, in principle, unknowable), but it is still fully understood as the ultimate arbiter of meaning.

Related cases can be constructed involving historical changes in stereotypical features as contrasted to essence. One might, for example, first encounter a tiger under highly unusual lighting and obscuring vegetation such that one thinks a tiger is green, checkerboard patterned, and docile. For centuries, "tiger" might be used with those particular features in mind as being highly typical of tigers; and yet, if confronted with the true circumstances of the original naming, there is a strong tendency to assume that "tiger" means not the green, checkerboarded, docile animals everyone has talked about for centuries, but the tawny-and-black-striped predator. The causal link back to the original occasion of naming (what Putnam, 1975, calls the "baptism") is critical in understanding meaning even centuries later.

The ultimate impact of the causal theory of reference on cognitive science approaches to categorization is far from clear. So far, however, it has spawned several new research initiatives that have greatly changed how we think about categorization. The emphasis on essence, for example, has led to several studies on whether adults and children have certain essential biases that they bring to bear on categorization (Gelman, Coley, & Gottfried, 1994; Gelman & Medin, 1993; Keil, 1992; Medin & Ortony, 1988). The role of essences in influencing reference and categorization of natural kinds has led to questions about differences between categorization of natural kinds and other sorts of things such as human artifacts (Gelman, 1988; Hatano & Inagaki, 1996; Keil, 1987, 1989; Kemler-Nelson, 1995; Malt & Johnson, 1992). Finally, a focus on the broader situation of term use in the society of communicators has been emphasized (Levy & Nelson, 1994).

In the end, linguistic and philosophical views of concepts, word meanings, and categorization will force a clearer statement of the different levels and kinds of categorization. The vast majority of nonhuman animals do not normally use categories to communicate, and problems such as the indeterminacy of translation or the causal theory of reference seem irrelevant. Yet, labeling is one of the most salient ways in which all of us use our categories, and it can have dramatic influences both on how we form our categories and on what we keep in mind as we integrate across successive glimpses of the natural world. Other influences arise from neuroscience studies of category-specific impairments (Caramazza, 1992; Damasio, 1990; Funnell & Sheridan, 1992; Warrington & Shallice, 1984; Warrington & McCarthy, 1987). That body of work is only just now becoming integrated with psychological and philosophical issues. Consequently, its relevance to questions of concept representation and learning is not well worked out; similar patterns of data are being claimed as support for both nativist and empiricist views of concepts (Farah, 1994; Mauri, Daum, Sartori, & Riesch, 1994; Sartori, Miozzo, & Job, 1993). There is no question that these different lines of work will benefit enormously from a common ground of discourse.

Finally, the problem of knowledge acquisition seems to be the strongest single organizing issue in cognitive science approaches to categorization. In relation to the problem of how categories are initially formed and become linked to labels, the need for interdisciplinary, integrative approaches becomes most obvious and necessary. Problems of acquisition, whether couched in connectionist terms or in those of a language of thought, make quickly apparent the need for better specifying the constraints on natural concepts and the relations between concepts and categorization. Such problems also strongly suggest that one simple model of categorization may not handle all phenomena. In particular, the development of categorization seems to be governed by a cognitive component that is largely compatible with traditional associationism and another component that appeals to principles, rules, and abstract relations; and these components interact heavily in development. Indeed, they may be critical to understanding apparently dramatic patterns of changes in categorization such as seeming characteristic-to-defining shifts in categorization (Keil, 1989; Keil & Batterman, 1984).

The richness and enormous potential of current interactions can be illustrated in several ongoing research programs. Consider, as one example, recent work on categorization in preverbal children (Mandler & Bauer, 1988; Mandler, Bauer, & McDonough, 1991; Mandler & McDonough, 1993). Although earlier work had suggested that young preschoolers, and certainly infants, would be strongly biased toward the basic level of categorization, there were reasons for suspecting an alternative developmental account. The basic level of analysis is compelling for some categories, such as furniture, vehicles, clothing, and some animals, but not for all categories, including many that are apparently very much in the minds of young children. These might include the categories for toys, friends, and pets, among many others.

Mandler and her colleagues devised a series of experiments that argue for categorization abilities far above the basic level, including such categories as vehicles and animals. More importantly, these categories often seem to be more salient and more easily used than basic-level ones. This pattern of findings immediately suggests a host of interrelated questions from a cognitive science perspective—questions that are largely hidden when considered from a more traditional developmental psychology viewpoint: What sort of representational system could be mediating these children's behavior? Because the children do not have any obvious language capacities, are these findings evidence for sophisticated, abstract-relations categorization without language? If so, then Herrnstein's (1990) suggestion that language is the basis for such categorization is undercut, leaving open the real possibility of its existence in other species. Alternatively, perhaps the preverbal children are only able to form such categories because they are using a language of thought that is closely related to their soon-to-be-emerging spoken language. A closer examination of the categories they can and cannot form might help one decide.

Mandler (1992) suggests an interesting middle ground of conceptual primitives in which a relatively small set of "image-schemas" is seen as being sufficiently abstract and relational in character so as to both enable superordinate categorizations in preschoolers and provide a basis for the growth and insertion of such categories into a linguistic system. To buttress her point of view, she turns to current attempts in linguistics to use similar schemas to explain aspects of grammar (Talmy, 1988). In the current cognitive science context, Mandler's research program therefore immediately triggers questions and suggests potential studies across a huge array of methods and perspectives.

It is impressive how issues concerning the development of categorization behavior, when viewed from a cognitive science perspective, become intimately linked to so many other developmental questions that have been discussed here. We cannot fully understand the development of categorization until we also understand the development of identity, number, and language. The most important link, however, is to the development of causal understanding.

How Do We Grasp the Causal Structures of Our Physical and Social Worlds?

In the 1970s, research on categorization started to consider causal understanding from an interdisciplinary perspective. The impetus came largely from two sources: (a) models of categories that were based solely on feature frequencies and correlations (Hampton, 1995; Murphy & Medin, 1985), and (b) discussions of conceptual change and the nature of natural kinds in philosophy. Probabilistic models of categories cannot adequately account for conceptual combinations from constituents (Smith & Osherson, 1984), illusory correlations (Chapman & Chapman, 1969;

Murphy & Medin, 1985), the essentialist bias (discussed earlier), the structures of ad hoc concepts (Barsalou, 1987), and the pattern of conceptual change in childhood (Carey, 1985; Keil, 1987). People seem to know much more about members of categories than about how often features occur or have co-occurred among instances (Murphy & Medin, 1985). Our understanding of the concept of bird, for example, seems to depend on more than just the frequency of co-occurrence of wings, feathers, and flight; it encompasses beliefs about causal relations among such bird properties. Our concepts depend on a model of how those properties are causally interrelated—say, to support flight. Loosely speaking, concepts appear to be embedded in theories; hence the "concepts-in-theories" label for this relatively new view of concepts.

The concepts-in-theories view resonates strongly with issues in the philosophy of science. For many years, philosophers have argued that scientific concepts are interconnected in a large web of beliefs that is full of causal/explanatory constructs. Kuhn's (1970) *Structure of Scientific Revolutions* launched a series of discussions about the extent to which concepts that were embedded in one system of explanation could be made commensurate with those embedded in another. Subsequent studies in cognitive development (Carey, 1985; Keil, 1989; Smith, Carey, & Wiser, 1985; Wellman & Gelman in Volume 2 of this *Handbook*) and in the history and philosophy of science (Kitcher, 1989; Neressian, 1992) relied heavily on the idea that concepts could not be understood without looking at how they were embedded in larger systems of theorylike beliefs.

Philosophers of science have argued that successful advances in scientific understanding of the structure of the world require a causal/functional form of explanation (Salmon, 1989). Science is rarely advanced by simple categorization. Rather, progress depends on an understanding of not just structures, but the forces giving rise to those structures, maintaining them and governing changes in them over time. In the 19th century, C. S. Peirce (1931–1935) argued that induction about the natural world could not succeed without "animal instincts for guessing right." Somehow, the human mind can grasp enough about the causal structure of the world to allow us to guess well. It has been recognized that pure induction is not a viable way of advancing our understanding of the real world (Peirce,

1960–1966). Goodman's (1955) "new riddle of induction" emphasized the need for constraints on induction. Goodman showed that inducing the color of an emerald is logically impossible without some biases to think about colors and physical objects in certain ways. One powerful theme that emerged from such discussions was that humans, and probably many other species, had evolved biases that enabled them to grasp aspects of the causal structure of the world (Cosmides & Tooby, 1987, 1994).

Such biases were normally assumed to reflect distinct and separable ways of thinking about different facets of the world. There was, therefore, a corollary assumption that the kinds of causal patternings that existed in the real world were not all the same. Different sorts of things have distinct causal "signatures" associated with them. Such a view runs counter to some traditional attempts to reduce all of the sciences to the level of core physics, but it fits well with most current thinking in the philosophy of science. While acknowledging ways in which principles at one level of explanation might be stated in terms of another level, current views also maintain that the different sciences have their own patterns of explanation that provide unique and important insights (Salmon, 1989). Biology involves kinds of causal patternings seen nowhere else, and perhaps even unique kinds of cause (Hull, 1974; Ruse, 1989; Sober, 1994; Wright, 1976), and similar arguments are made for other natural and social sciences (Trout, 1991; Von Eckardt, 1993). Thus, one can think of our physical and social worlds as organized into distinct domains of explanation; there is cross-talk across domains, but each domain has its own unique explanatory style.

Our ability to develop distinct sciences of biology, physics, chemistry, and cognition does not mean that each one of these grows from an innate skeletal core system of explanation that is prepared for each mature science. Such an idea seems ludicrous if we consider computer science as another science or, in turn, molecular genetics. Because of such newly emergent sciences, some have argued that causal reasoning might be bootstrapped out of sophisticated ways of detecting not only first-order correlations but also correlations among correlations and other higher order patterns of covariation (Cheng, in press; Glymour, 1987, in press; Spirtes, Glymour, & Scheines, 1993); but such views remain only provocative speculations without detailed supporting simulations. Moreover, older attempts to simulate scientific discovery through a general all-purpose learning system often seem to beg the most interesting questions by quietly building all explanatory principles into how the input information was structured (Langley, Simon, Bradshaw, & Zytkow, 1987).

One intriguing possibility, however, is that a system of covariation detection procedures must interact with a framework of expectations about causal patterns. Thus, notions of "cause" may not be created out of covariation patterns. Instead, different, already present, modes of causal construal are brought to the foreground and sharpened by different patterns of covariation.

Current views on causal understanding are most easily distinguished in terms of how they propose that knowledge came about—the developmental story—and the alternatives echo themes seen elsewhere: a powerful general learner with no initial domain-specific biases; a very small number of "seed domains of explanation" that produce all others; and a greater initial pluralism that still manages, in the end, to account for the much vaster diversity of kinds of explanation. The domain/general learning views have been embraced by researchers from otherwise dramatically different points of view, ranging from connectionist and associationist models to proposition-based AI learning systems. Despite their differences, however, all of these positions inherit a common problem: how to explain how notions of cause and explanation emerge from brute-force tabulations of features and correlations. Every undergraduate with some modest exposure to the social or natural sciences learns that correlation does not mean causation, and that simple fact makes enormous difficulty for models that attempt to build causal understanding out of correlational patterns.

One alternative is to posit some general notion of cause as a conceptual primitive that then gets elaborated into causal theories of different sorts in different domains through means of a more general-purpose learning device. The idea that at least one notion of cause might be a conceptual primitive has gained increasing credence over the years. Infant intuitions about object behaviors are remarkably easy to state if one assumes they have the idea of "cause" (and remarkably difficult otherwise). This idea was suggested by Michotte's (1963) pioneering studies on the perception of causality, and careful follow-up studies have shown that even young infants seem to clearly distinguish between various patterns of contingency and covariation, and those of true causation (Leslie, 1982; Leslie &

Keeble, 1987). Not all infant researchers agree on the evidence for causal cognition in younger infants (e.g., Cohen & Oakes, 1993), but even the harshest critics now acknowledge the presence of causal cognition well before the first year of life.

An emphasis on a generic causal operator that applies across all domains would fit with a number of empiricist proposals for the acquisition of systems of explanation. If one grants to the infant a kind of learning system that is couched in terms of causal predicates and not a much lower subsymbolic format, the problem of getting cause out of correlation is partly finessed. It may not be fully handled, however, because one still has to know which patterns of covariation are good "triggers" for the causal operator and which ones should leave it dormant. This second problem leads many to suspect innate biases specific to particular patterns of causation.

Traditional work in developmental psychology seems to approach the acquisition of causal reasoning largely from an empiricist perspective. Piaget, for example, argued that the young child had not really mastered the basic aspects of the causal operator; the child did not understand, for example, that causes preceded effects in time. The child was a captive of simple primitive notions of spatial and temporal contiguity and did not really have notions of mechanism (Piaget, 1930, 1974). These views fell apart, however, when specific cognitive competences were examined more closely. Very young children could understand the principles that seemed to distinguish cause from covariation (Bullock & Gelman, 1979; Bullock, Gelman, & Baillargeon, 1982; Keil, 1979) and did not seem to gradually discover the principles of causation out of patterns of covariation. In addition, they had well-developed notions of reasonable versus unreasonable causes (Brown, 1989; Bullock, 1979; Goswami & Brown, 1989). This is not to say that subtler aspects of causal understanding did not elude them or that some of the more sophisticated ways of using covariation information to infer cause took no time to develop (e.g., Kuhn, Schauble, & Garcia-Mila, 1992), but the idea of toddlers as completely bereft of causal reasoning collapsed. Moreover, as new research paradigms emerged for studying the young child's understandings of events (Fivush, in press) and of other minds (Dunn & Brown, 1993; Wellman, 1990), it became nearly impossible to talk about their understandings without reference to some kinds of causal knowledge.

The new emphasis on causal understanding in infants and young children roughly coincided with increasing attention to how other disciplines talked about causal thinking and explanation. It also became more common to ask whether young children had separate domains of explanation for different domains of things. The burgeoning work on infant cognition started to suggest sophisticated causal expectations about physical object mechanics (Baillargeon, 1995; Spelke, 1994), and, equally important, a separate and distinct set of expectations about social entities (Leslie, 1995; Spelke, Philips, & Woodward, 1995). These new lines of work have reinvigorated debates about the extent to which infants are continuous with older children and adults in the extent to which they are able to grasp the causal structures of their physical and social worlds (for other aspects of the debate, see Fischer & Bidell, Ch. 9, this Volume). In addition, models of conceptual change started to posit that the child might be initially endowed with two distinct modes of explanation (present from early infancy onward) that came to shape most explanations in the preschool years (Carey, 1985).

Carey (1985) proposed that an intuitive psychology and physical mechanics were used early on to frame explanations for all natural phenomena, and that, through mechanisms of conceptual change, these two primal modes of explanation spawned all others. This proposal addressed several concerns. Cause did not have to be induced out of covariation nor even triggered by it. Instead, much larger relational patterns would trigger either social or physical forms of explanation. There were apparent dramatic cases of conceptual change, and the presence of only two domains early on allowed for dramatic changes as new domains, such as a distinct mode of biological thought, emerged from them. Moreover, these arguments were closely linked to patterns of the development of explanation in the history of science, such as the spawning of distinct notions of heat and temperature out of a precursor, single conceptual structure (Wiser, 1988). Thus, the motivation for the proposal of two primal domains from the start gained impetus from other disciplines outside of psychology.

The final view, advocating more pluralism in initial forms of explanation, also was motivated by discussions across the disciplines. Consider, for example, the domain of biological thought. Anthropological studies of biological explanation throughout the world started to suggest powerful universals in how living kinds were understood, including such things as taxonomic organization of kinds, the presence of a special kind of essence, and the possibility of a special form of teleological/teleonomic causal explanation (Atran, 1996). Thus, as Atran puts it:

> Humans everywhere, it appears, have similar folk biological schema composed of essence-based species and ranked ordering of species into lower-order and higher-order groups. These groups within groups represent the routine products of innate "habits of mind," naturally selected to grasp relevant and recurrent "habits of the world." They are not as arbitrary, and hence not as variable across cultures as, say, the gathering of stars in constellations. (p. 146)

Comparable studies of the history of biological thought suggested powerful cognitive biases that both aided and hindered the growth of biological science. Among these were the essentialist and teleological biases (Hull, 1965; Mayr, 1982, 1988). Indeed, Hull argues that essentialist biases, clearly present as far back as Aristotle's writings, greatly impeded the emergence of evolutionary thought and resulted in "2000 years of stasis."

These developments raised the possibility that the very young child might already have the ability to use multiple modes of explanation, and not just two. Not all adult theories would be present, however. No one wishes to attribute to the toddler even the most skeletal knowledge of a specific molecular biology, or string theory, or quantum mechanics. But perhaps those modes of explanation that are more universal could be present early on, including some that seem to have parallels in other species. Current research on the growth of causal understanding is wrestling with the possibility that even infants may have biases to prefer certain explanatory systems with such things as living kinds, social/intentional agents, simple mechanical bodies, and fluids. These systems, and perhaps a handful more, might be part of the very young child's conceptual armament. But in those younger children, they seem inappropriate to be thought of as full theories. This concern has launched a new line of inquiry that now asks what it means to have causal understanding and explanation, and how important such classic factors as prediction might be.

One way of thinking about such an issue is in terms of "modes of construal" and "causal powers." The young child, like the novice adult in many domains, may not have anything remotely like the deductive-nomological theory that was traditionally thought to be the basis of a mature science (more recently, the deductive–nomological approach has been under concerted attack as being largely irrelevant to how even professional scientists actually go about their business; Salmon, 1989). There is a difference between being able to tell a good explanation from a fishy one without knowing it in advance. There is a difference between being able to know what sorts of properties and relations are likely to matter in an explanation and knowing the precise mechanism that links everything together. In fact, current philosophy of science wonders how often anyone goes much beyond such "causal powers" notions in everyday science. Our notions of clear-cut mechanisms are often just a tiny slice of the whole body of explanation, which is elsewhere cast in much more general terms concerning types of relevant properties and relations (Harre & Madden, 1975).

In all of this, the idea of many early modes of construal still allows for a major empiricist and nativist version. The nativist argues that humans are endowed with a handful of modes of construal that have come to be useful through evolution, even if they were not originally selected for (Gould & Lewontin, 1978). They allow humans to make better sense of a world governed by distinct domains of causal patternings. The world is heterogeneous in causal patterns, and so should be the mind's sensitivity to those patterns (see also Cosmides & Tooby, 1994, for a related argument concerning domain specificity in general). The empiricist posits an extraordinarily sensitive learning device that abstracts away multiple and distinct clusters of causal patterns right from the start in early infancy and uses them to constrain all later learning. Thus, a particular version of empiricism is needed that does not embrace the more traditional notion of a lengthy sequential building up of constituents from smaller and smaller primitives. From the start of learning, higher-order causal patternings are being detected and used to constrain further learning. In theories of perceptual development, the notion of picking up on higher-order relational patterns from the start is hardly new (Gibson, 1969, 1973; Gibson, Owsley, & Johnston, 1978), but in the realm of cognition it is less common.

The nativist version requires much more flexibility and learning than would be allowed by a doctrine stating that all ideas and knowledge structures are innate and preformed. Such an extreme doctrine faces extraordinary challenges when confronted with the constant stream of apparently novel ideas (cellular phone) and theories (string theory) that we encounter in the real world. Instead, the infant is viewed as coming into the world with sets of biases or "modes of construal" that are loosely tailored to resonate with different sorts of causal patternings in the world. A complex matrix of clues might bias a child to infer that the phenomena observed are driven by, say, social agents, and should be inferred in that manner. Thus, the increased temporal lags of social interactions, the apparent cases of action at a distance, the rhythmic flow of reciprocal interactions, and many basic perceptual properties of animate beings might all trigger a system that is prepared to think about and understand patterns of social causation.

That a handful of such biases might be part of initial cognitive structure seems more plausible when some special populations, such as autistic children, are considered. One increasingly supported way of understanding a number of autistic children is that they are much less well prepared to understand patterns of social causation. This lack of preparation is more a consequence of having different sorts of brains and patterns of biological maturation than of having different social experiences (although the two can never be strictly divorced) (Baron-Cohen, 1995; Happe, 1995; Leslie & Thaiss, 1992).

The nativist "modes of construal" claim still has to account for profound developmental change, and it can do so in several ways, many of which are inspired by analogous accounts in the history and philosophy of science. One theme is that the basic modes of construal that we all share are far more influential and prevalent throughout the life span than is normally assumed. Thus, they undergird the vast majority of all later systems of explanation. A basic mechanics of physical bodies is used to understand not only simple bodies; it might also provide a framework for a partial understanding of an earthquake or a camera, and a basic theory of fluids might provide frameworks for weather, electronic circuits, and even aspects of personality. Development might consist far less of developing totally new frameworks of understanding than of deciding which one set of skeletal modes of construal is most relevant, and then filling out that skeleton in each case. This possibility has been informed considerably from philosophical discussions of natural kinds, where it has been realized that the same class of real-world entities might simultaneously be members of several different natural kinds. People can be thought of alternatively as sentient kinds, biological kinds, and simple physical kinds (Dupré, 1981; Keil, 1995). Cases of apparently radical conceptual change may not be so much the development of a wholly new way of understanding as the recognition of the relevance of a different skeletal mode of construal.

There are enormous gaps in our current knowledge about causal understanding; perhaps the most serious gap is that there is nothing close to a consensus toward specifying the format of how causal understanding is mentally represented. There is a strong sentiment that causal understanding entails a kind of mental representation that is different from that which merely represents correlation and contingency. Ever since Michotte's (1946/1963) pioneering studies in which causal relations are immediately perceived, it has seemed powerfully clear that there is something distinctive about the psychological representation of cause. Moreover, the further elaboration of cause into possibly different types of cause, and into a kind of relational structure that constitutes the mental representation of an intuitive theory, is also far from settled. Researchers have begun to posit some essential parts to intuitive theories (Gopnik & Meltzoff, 1997; Gopnik & Wellman, 1994; Wellman, 1990), and these proposals have again benefited greatly from examination of the issue across several disciplines; but at present we are barely at the point of recognizing the nature of the proper questions. Only because of an emerging cognitive science approach to these issues have even the proper questions come into focus.

It is not hard to see why the search for fully comprehensive and meaningful answers to our six questions serves as a testimony to the importance of cognitive science as an approach to the mind and the acquisition of knowledge. Even though each question draws on the various constituent disciplines in different ways and to differing extents, there are some common issues. All of these questions require a precise specification of the kind of information that is involved. In every case, except possibly in regard to number, this means a description of some aspect of the environment. To be able to make such descriptions precise and clear, there are enormous benefits from considering attempts in philosophy, logic, and mathematics, where there are long traditions of careful work in describing what sorts of things there are. The six questions also ask how the organism interacts with the information and how that interaction is related to the structure of the environment. Such subquestions require analyses of what sorts of information the organism could be sensitive to, given its sensory, perceptual, and cognitive systems, and the questions naturally lead to comparative analyses of how different organisms in particular environmental niches might have evolved specialized ways of resonating with certain patterns of information. All of the questions also ask about how the information types might be represented and the kinds of computational loads they might impose. These issues bring in computer science and more traditional cognitive psychology. The questions also raise issues about how information might be brought into explicit awareness, reasoned about consciously, and communicated to others. Such issues naturally involve aspects of language and linguistic theory.

There are many more such commonalities, but these make the point clearly enough. One cannot hope to really understand some of the most fundamental questions about the mind if one asks them solely from the vantage point of one discipline. Scholars cannot be experts at everything, but they do need to recognize the multiple approaches and use them to help frame their own questions.

SOME EMERGENT THEMES LINKING COGNITIVE SCIENCE AND DEVELOPMENT

Characterizing cognitive science as the most natural source of answers to fundamental questions about the mind has repeatedly brought up issues of development. The questions illustrate how the study of the mind from a cognitive science perspective is more often linked to developmental questions than when approached from more traditional disciplines. In addition, the ensuing discussions have begun to highlight some emergent themes concerning the acquisition of knowledge. The following themes seem most dramatic:

1. Development is intrinsic to the study of cognitive systems.
2. The nativist–empiricist controversy is a vital part of cognitive science.
3. Different cognitive fluxes converge to reveal cognitive invariants.
4. Hybrid/computational systems are essential to developmental accounts.
5. Conceptual change has many forms and may often be illusory.

6. Cognitive development is not a progression from concrete to abstract thought.
7. Explanation may be more central to cognitive development than prediction.

Each of these themes, among others, could be explored at extraordinary length; indeed, some aspects of them are the topics of whole chapters in this *Handbook*. Here, they are developed just enough to illustrate how they are changing the thinking about cognitive development and how those changes are linked to a cognitive science perspective.

Development Is Intrinsic to the Study of Cognitive Systems

The field of developmental psychology has often proceeded as a nearly autonomous subdiscipline of psychology. In large academic departments, developmental psychology may have its own administrative, educational, and research units. Among some good reasons for such a division, there is one negative consequence: The study of cognition in children becomes relatively divorced from the study of cognition in adults. Cognitive science has merged the two levels of study. It has repeatedly shown how the study of development is essential to understanding the mature person, and how a careful characterization of adult capacities is critical to posing, and answering, the right developmental questions.

In the biological sciences, it is common to talk about systems in ways that unify developmental and mature functioning. When a particular organ system or physiological function is described, a model of how that system develops is often automatically included because it is assumed to be an essential part of the overall story. For example, most medical texts on organ systems and anatomical structures include extensive descriptions of the development of those systems and structures and frequently refer to those developmental patterns in explaining mature function or malfunction. Some of the most interesting cases arise when a mature structure has a structural ambiguity that makes it difficult to understand what elements constitute the primary framework and what has been built on top of that framework. Patterns of development can often provide the answer. One classic example involves the question of whether a zebra is a white animal with black stripes, or the reverse (Gould, 1983). Inspection of the adult animal is inconclusive; black and white stripes are present in apparently equivalent ways. A look at the origins of the zebra's structural pattern, however, both in development and evolution, makes it clear that a zebra is black with white stripes.

The insights offered by developmental and evolutionary histories can be relevant for many other examples in biology, ranging from functional/architectural ambiguities of the kidney, to questions about the relations among the components of the immune system. Ambiguities in adult cognitive architecture can be similarly informed by developmental data. Some examples arise from the six questions considered in the preceding section. With respect to spatial knowledge, for example, landmark navigation might seem to be the simplest mode, the core ability around which geometric layout is a peripheral add-on skill. This idea would be buttressed by the notion that it seems much easier to design a robotics system that can navigate by using simple landmarks rather than by developing abstractions of the geometric layout and then recognizing this layout from new vantage points and acting on it. Yet, developmental studies suggest that knowledge of spatial layout may be very basic. As discussed earlier, overall layout seems to be developmentally primitive and helps guide aspects of the development of the landmark system. Moreover, it appears that several aspects of adult environmental navigation are better understood by reference to this developmental sequence. Thus, under appropriate environmental distractions, adults can be shown to fall back on the geometric layout system even when other cues might be more valuable (Hermer & Spelke, 1996).

Controversies concerning how human concepts are mentally represented offer a different example of how development can help solve an adult structural ambiguity. The earlier discussions of categorization and causal understanding have revealed that adult concepts appear to be mixes of associative information and more theorylike/explanation-based forms of information. Yet, that mix alone does not help one to understand the relative roles of each. It has often been assumed that the associative structure is a kind of conceptual bedrock that does most of the important work in categorization and other cases of concept use. The explanation-based component is then seen as a kind of optional accessory that further enriches concepts. A corollary assumption was that most concepts in early childhood are primarily or even exclusively associative in

nature. But recent research does not support such a claim; the explanation/theory component seems to be present in some form even in concepts in infancy (Gelman, in press; Keil, Smith, Simons, & Levin, in press; Mandler, in press).

It seems, therefore, that, as with biology, the study of cognition in the mature organism cannot be successfully divorced from the study of how those cognitive capacities and structures develop. Questions about complexly interwoven structures of the adult form are often greatly informed—and in some cases, perhaps *only* informed—by knowledge of how they came to be through development. But an equally strong message runs in the opposite direction: The study of cognitive development is often hampered greatly by downplaying or ignoring attempts to accurately describe the adult competencies (see also Csiksentmihalyi & Rothunde, Ch. 11, this Volume, for an amplification of this point of view). This is especially true in a cognitive science approach, where the relevant specifications of adult competencies may come from a different discipline—not the one in which acquisition and development are initially studied.

Consider the case of language. If one tries to study the acquisition of language solely from a developmental psychological viewpoint, one would focus exclusively on the words children hear and how they develop a language ability out of incorporating those inputs. In doing so, one would be missing a host developmental hypothesis suggested by models in theoretical linguistics that represent the properties of all adult languages. For example, the parameter-setting model of adult linguistics competency has led to extremely focused questions about how exposure to some aspects of a language in development might help set specific parameters that then have a cascading effect on how other inputs are perceived (Reinhardt, 1986; Valian, 1994). Having in mind the best possible accounts of adult cognition invariably makes the developmental research much clearer. One has an idea of where the development is proceeding and what critical distinctions are likely to be learned. One does not know when they will be learned, but it is clear that they should be a focus of intensive examination.

As a second example, consider attempts to study how a child comes to understand biology without a characterization of adult intuitive biologies. It is exceedingly hard to know which aspects of biological knowledge to even explore in children, given the vastness of the topic, unless one has some ideas about the key principles undergirding adult knowledge. Does one simply ask children what it means for something to be alive, or which things are living? Such strategies can yield some surprising results at first, but do not work well as a long-term strategy toward learning more about the origins of biological thought (Huang, 1943; Laurendeau & Pinard, 1962; Piaget, 1929). By contrast, if one looks at anthropological and philosophical discussions concerning what is distinctive about biological thought versus other kinds of thought, several possible principles come to mind, such as a teleological form of causal understanding (Wright, 1976) and a bias to infer rich taxonomic structure for biological kinds (Atran, 1990, 1996). Similarly, an examination of disgust and contamination beliefs among adults, as well as comparative animal literature on taste aversion, has led to novel and informative developmental studies on these aspects of biological thought (Fallon, Rozin, & Pliner, 1984; Rozin, Fallon, & Augustoni-Ziskind, 1985).

The intermingling of development and mature cognition in a cognitive science perspective therefore requires mutual cooperation. Many puzzles about mature cognitive structure are greatly enhanced by looking at origins, but even the most initial characterizations of adult structure, with all its inherent ambiguities, are needed to help pose the most interesting and profitable developmental questions. An iterative positive feedback loop of mutual facilitation results. A preliminary mature model suggests more informed developmental questions, answers to which, in turn, help clarify the mature model. As the model is modified, new developmental questions are raised, and so on. This cyclic symbiosis seems clearly the right way to go about asking questions about cognition in general, and it suggests that a separation of cognition and cognitive development into distinct and semiautonomous research programs is a risky move. Cognitive science may have recognized this unity more wholly just because it so often asks questions that cut across disciplines. In trying to find a common ground across the disciplines, developmental questions often seem to clarify the critical issues. This effect was especially evident in looking at the much older historical precedents to cognitive science, and it is reemerging again today.

It might seem from this discussion that developmental psychology will no longer exist as cognitive science grows and flourishes. Indeed, in a recent book on psychology in the 21st century, Mandler (1995) entitles a chapter "The Death of Developmental Psychology." But, as seen in that chapter, such a fate is largely a matter of how one frames the question. Put differently, all of cognitive science becomes part of developmental psychology, as developmental issues become ever more central to debates in every area. In addition, there are virtues in keeping a distinct field of developmental psychology alive, providing that its practitioners recognize the essential links to cognitive science. Those virtues arise from some of the special viewpoints and insights that emerge from thinking of developmental processes in general, as will be discussed shortly.

The Nativist–Empiricist Controversy Is a Vital Part of Cognitive Science

Versions of the nativist–empiricist controversy have been around as long as recorded history, and probably well before. One of the most popular historical examples is Herodotus's account of how the kings of Egypt and Phrygia, seeking to find out whether Egyptian or Phrygian was the truly innate language, reared children in isolation and observed which language spontaneously emerged first (Feldman, Goldin-Meadow, & Gleitman, 1978). Phrygian supposedly was the first language uttered. Today, and probably among thoughtful courtiers back then, such a version of the nativist hypothesis seems ludicrous. However, when considered more closely, the ways in which it is absurd help illustrate how clarifications of the controversy have made it an important and central theme of cognitive science. Spelke and Newport provide an extensive treatment of this issue in Chapter 6 of this *Handbook*. Here, the purpose is more limited: to show how cognitive science has helped suggest a variant of the nativist–empiricist controversy that is vibrant and extremely relevant to current research. Indeed, it is still a source of many important research ideas. It is often misunderstood, however, and is sometimes a cause of confusion and fruitless debates.

To return briefly to the Herodotus narrative, there seems to be at least one major reason why the experiment seems ludicrous. Virtually no one, even among the strongest proponents of the idea that human language is innate, thinks that any particular language in all its details is prepackaged within the infant and waiting to spring forth. Something more abstract than a particular language would have to be innate. Not just members of the cognitive science community, but almost anyone with a nativist bias would also have intuitive conceptions that some general properties of all languages, not particular properties of a specific language, were innate.

This silly version of nativism, however, has one clear virtue: It has some relevance to other behaviors in other species, such as some "fixed action patterns" and aggression. In these areas, ideas of prepackaged fully detailed structures have indeed been proposed (Lorenz, 1966). Unlike many other cases, this is a truly nativist position (even if an untenable one). By contrast, the following experiment, which has often been proposed and sometimes half-conducted, in itself tells us nothing about nativist versus empiricist alternatives:

> Take a child and the brightest nonhuman known (say, a chimpanzee) and rear them in what seem to be identical environments. If, after a reasonable amount of time, the child learns a language (say, a sign language that is easily within the chimp's manual dexterity) and the chimp does not, then clearly part of language is innate in the child and not in the chimp.

Based on those details alone, such a conclusion is completely unwarranted, and it is important to see why from a cognitive science point of view.

It does not contribute much to the nativist–empiricist debate to show that one organism can acquire a body of knowledge or a behavior that another one cannot. In the extreme, if a child acquires a language and a pet turtle in the same environment does not, no one is surprised. Failure to learn arises for different reasons. General cognitive capacities are necessary for learning something as complex as a language, and an organism below a certain level of neural complexity simply cannot do it. An analogous case occurs repeatedly with computers. Two computers might have identical computational architectures in terms of how they perform arithmetic computations, deal with floating-point decimals, draw lines on the screen, and so on; but one may have 4 megabytes of random access memory (RAM) and another may have 16. Only the 16-megabyte machine may be able to run certain programs or acquire certain kinds of information through those programs, not because it has some special predisposition for using the programs, but merely because it has more capacity for memory. In a similar vein, some computers have faster clock speeds, more hard-disk storage space, or better databases. In the same way, perhaps a primate cannot learn language simply because it has less overall cognitive capacity—it fails to meet some critical threshold. Simply put, it is not smart enough in the "g" sense of intelligence (Spearman, 1927).

There is, however, a way in which differences in learning *ability* between two organisms might emerge. A nonhuman primate with high capability in many cognitive tasks might fail at language acquisition because it lacks innate capacities that are specifically tuned to the learning of linguistic structure. Its failure has nothing to do with its general cognitive capacity; it fails because it did not "know" enough beforehand about some specific properties in the domain of natural language. It can easily learn other complex things, but not language. In the computer metaphor, one personal computer might differ from another, not in terms of raw computational capacity or amount of RAM, but in the absence of specialized processors that are available for graphics displays, complex sounds, or complicated mathematical operations. A computer that lacks these processors cannot acquire some kinds of information at all, or may acquire those information types, but much more slowly and imperfectly. The built-in capacity need not be thought of as simply extra hardware; it could be a kind of read-only program as well.

These two different patterns of acquisition begin to reveal an issue that is at the heart of current cognitive science approaches to the acquisition of knowledge: domain specificity (Fodor, 1983; Hirschfeld & Gelman, 1994; Keil, 1981). Nativists and empiricists disagree, but not on the premise that one organism has something built in that enables acquisition of a behavior or of knowledge while another does not. That very weak version is uninteresting, as the above examples show. Since the British empiricists, and in many respects, ever since Aristotle, the real debate is whether one organism achieves greater learning successes than another organism because its mind is generally more cognitively capable or because it has specialized structures tuned to learn a specific kind of knowledge. This question of domain specificity has become a pivotal issue in cognitive science today.

Domain specificity versus domain generality, however, is not enough to fully explain the nativist–empiricist controversy and how it motivates research. A second contrast is also needed, as can be seen in explicit discussions by the British empiricists, and more implicitly, in discussions long before them. The British empiricists were well aware that humans and all other organisms had sensory specializations that could pick up only certain kinds of information. Sensory transducers such as the eye, the ear, and the nose optimally pick up certain kinds of information, such as light, sound, and chemical gradients. This was not controversial; no one doubted that the eye responded to different kinds of inputs than the ear. (A Gibsonian point of view might argue that the same invariants can be picked up across sensory modalities, and that one can thereby perceive the same information, but this important point seems to rely on different meanings of information. No one doubts that photons are uniquely picked up by the retina and not by the eardrum.) Moreover, many empiricists allowed for built-in information-specific gathering systems above the first line of sensory transducers. Thus, the ability to see primitive features in a visual display might also be a consequence of pretuned mental and neural units.

Empiricists and nativists disagree on how far "upstream" the domain-specific specializations must be for knowledge acquisition to proceed successfully. If there is nothing but general laws of association beyond the sense organs, then we have a very strong empiricist view. If specialized systems are tuned to building up representations for abstract aspects of specific domains, such as social interactions, or moral beliefs, or language, that is a strong nativist position. All of this needs much further clarification, some of which is still ongoing as part of the research program in cognitive science (see also Elman et al., 1996). Some clarifications, however, can be stated. The notion of "upstream" depends greatly on one's views of the mind and of how information is picked up and/or processed. A direct-perception view of our daily lives eschews the idea of successive levels of information processing (Gibson, 1972). Similarly, connectionist approaches certainly do not promote an extensive chain of serial processing. But even within both those perspectives, there are important distinctions that correspond loosely to the upstream notion.

In particular, one can envision a difference between having a system that is tuned to expect certain patterns in a specific modality, such as the eye's expectations concerning reflected light patterns, and a system that has expectations that transcend modalities, such as that two physical bodies cannot interpenetrate. The second expectation can be borne out tactilely, visually, and possibly even auditorily. Notice that this expectation is still domain-specific in

that it applies only to bounded physical objects and not to fluids, gases, or aggregates. Systems that are tuned to patterns that transcend modalities would therefore be more likely to fit with a nativist stance. Even here, however, one can imagine levels of intermodal integrations. A system that integrates tactile and visual information to assess the rigidity of a support surface seems to operate at a different level than one that integrates auditory and visual information to induce rules of a language.

From a connectionist point of view, one can imagine a system that has preset weights that seem to optimize learning for only certain kinds of information. If that information has to do with line continuity patterns in vision, it might be considered a bias that empiricists are willing to acknowledge as part of the elementary feature set. If however, that information seems to be tailored for learning about the interactions among intentional agents and nothing else, and is in a sequestered network that becomes active only when learning about intentional behavior, those weights might well conform to a nativist position (Seidenberg, 1992).

In short, although there may be disagreements about how to distinguish levels, there can be little question that they should be distinguished or that, in concert with domain specificity, nativists and empiricists primarily disagree on the extent to which biases for specific domains of information go beyond those in effect at the levels of sensory transducers. The sense of domain also shifts; domains at the sensory levels are such things as light or sound waves, and domains at higher levels are such things as bounded physical objects, intentional agents, number, or spatial layout. All of these latter domains are clearly amodal and are much more cognitive than perceptual.

Other biases on high-level cognition that work in domain-general ways have a more ambiguous status with respect to nativism and empiricism and will depend on the particular versions of each. Thus, something like the base rate fallacy (Kahneman, Slovic, & Tversky, 1982) would seem to apply to any kind of experienced information, regardless of its domain. As such, it would seem to be like a further modification of general laws of learning, such as those on association—all of which fits with empiricism. If, however, this bias is only observed in conscious propositional thought and never in perceptual tabulations of statistical regularities in vision, it seems that the bias works only with objects of higher-level cognition. This second case still strikes me as a form of empiricism, but there is more room for disagreement here.

Two other issues need clarification regarding the rebirth of nativism–empiricism in the cognitive science approach to development. One concerns a new emphasis on the actual course and manner of learning, and the second concerns the need to capture the intrinsically interactional nature of development, which has been a central issue ever since Lehrman (1953) attacked simplistic versions of nativism (see also Lerner, 1984). With respect to the course and manner of learning, it takes only a little reflection to realize that nativists and empiricists often do not disagree on whether something can be learned, but on how it is learned. A classic example concerns the naturalness of teaching a dog to walk on its hind legs, as inspired by Samuel Johnson's remark that "It is not done well; but you are surprised to find it done at all" (Boswell, 1848). No one doubts that some dogs can be taught to walk primarily, and perhaps even exclusively, on their hind legs; but it is equally obvious that they have no native predisposition to do so and are radically different from humans in that respect. Simply coming to show a behavior is not enough evidence when engaging in comparative studies. One also has to look at how the behavior emerges. Consider the ape/language controversy that occupied so much academic effort some years ago (e.g., Terrace, Petitto, Sanders, & Bever, 1979). One of the strangest parts of the debate was that some primates would achieve their limited successes only after intensive tutoring totally unlike that experienced by the normal human child. In light of such differences in learning and teaching, as well as in the end result, what is one entitled to conclude? Perhaps, like the hapless dancing dog, the signing primate has no native ability to acquire language; or perhaps there is nothing importantly different between such primates and humans. A final answer requires more detailed theories of learning and of how to evaluate the end results. Such efforts are now much more likely to be underway from a cognitive science perspective.

A second issue concerns confusion between specifying particular behaviors or pieces of knowledge as innate, as opposed to specifying the learning function itself and the cognitive biases it engenders. Chomsky (1980) offered a clear statement of this difference when he discussed the idea of mapping functions from sets of environments onto sets of mental representations. Such a formulation allows for some "environments" (e.g., brain surgery, or total deprivation, or sensory overload) in which radically different mental representations may occur that have none of the supposedly universal properties of that domain. The function specifies a range of normal environments, experienced by the vast majority of learners of that species, under which there may be strong guidance (or biases) to learn some classes of mental representations over others. Because those classes can be infinite, no specific mental representation may be predicted. If the biases are not absolutely inviolate, they may only predispose the learner, all other things being equal, and not demand a certain representational outcome.

This way of looking at nativism in terms of a learning function—an intrinsically interactional process between organism and environment—helps avoid the confusion about specific pieces of knowledge being "built in." Lehrman's (1953) well-known arguments against innate fixed behavioral routines or perceptual templates do not apply to statements about built-in forms of functional architecture. Contrasts between domain-specific and domain-general functional architectures for learning and how they might be tuned toward the acquisition and representation of certain kinds of information can also be described for machines that learn, or acquire, store, and perform computations on bodies of information. Such machines help us sharpen the precision of our descriptions for humans and other animals. With both machines and animals, however, if several sequentially ordered learning functions are defined over shorter time intervals (e.g., monthly intervals after birth), they can be seen as changing over successive time intervals as a result of prior experience as well as any endogenous factors. The point here is that, over broader time intervals, learning functions can be specified as intrinsic properties of both machines and organisms.

It is easy to compare alternative computational architectures that solve similar problems either through means of a single domain-general learning and computation system or through a collection of specific processors, each of which is geared to distinct kinds of information. Those systems that have domain-specific sets of processors can then be distinguished in terms of the extent to which that domain specificity is achieved by initial transducers that interface with the world or by more "central" systems that operate on information types integrated across various transducers. That final form of architecture is most analogous to a nativist version of AI architecture. [Even here, things get more complicated. Brooks's (1991) approach to robotics is achieved through a set of domain-specific kluges, but it seems to be an empiricist program because there is no interesting central cognitive architecture.] The notion of centrality helps capture the sort of domain specificity that bears on nativism.

In summary, the nativist–empiricist controversy has been reborn largely through cognitive science approaches to development. These approaches provide sufficiently detailed models of learning, representation, and domain structure so as to enable one to talk about domain specificity, learning, and knowledge. True nativist–empiricist controversies that were partially in the ken of even the oldest philosophers can now be understood as important and critically relevant to current debates in the field. Indeed, it can be argued that an enormous amount of controversy in cognitive science and constituent disciplines revolves around these more sophisticated versions of the nativist–empiricist debate, and that an acknowledgment of that underlying issue can offer important insights.

Different Cognitive Fluxes Converge to Reveal Cognitive Invariants

The cognitive science approach has made much clearer the value of looking at the different kinds of situations that offer large variations. In such patterns of variation, certain invariants patterns come into relief; and to the extent that the same invariant emerges across different kinds of variation, such as historical change versus developmental change, a great deal can be discovered about likely paths of learning and cognitive development.

One of the great insights offered by the study of developing cognitive systems is that developmental changes in those systems allow one to see much more clearly those aspects of cognitive architecture that remain fixed. The fixed parts stand out in relief against the patterns of change. If some aspects of mental structure and function remain constant from early childhood into maturity, they are likely to have a special status as a kind of framework or a set of guiding principles that help move that knowledge development along a given trajectory. This sort of inference has been made in the child's spatial knowledge, mathematical knowledge, grammatical knowledge, or biological knowledge, as was seen in the examples discussed earlier. In all

cases, that aspect of knowledge structure that remained invariant over time was seen as providing a framework on which the developing child could build and elaborate the knowledge gained.

For such insights to emerge, a sufficiently detailed and accurate structural description of some cognitive capacity is needed. Simple performance measures on a task are inadequate unless they can be used to reliably infer the underlying mental states that caused them. Moreover, the structural descriptions are unlikely to be useful if they are excessively bound to highly specific instances of knowledge. Thus, if one describes children's spatial knowledge in terms of the particular familiar layouts that are frequently encountered, such as day care centers for preschoolers, playgrounds and classrooms for elementary school children, and classrooms and shopping malls for adolescents, too much attention to those differing contents might suggest massive developmental changes with nothing in common across ages. A more formal description of those spatial representations might reveal essentially the same means of representing spatial layouts at all ages, regardless of how widely different and developmentally sensitive specific sets of environments might be.

But the search for invariants solely on the basis of development has potential hazards as well. Invariants might appear for spurious reasons that have nothing to do with the intrinsic properties of how human minds acquire bodies of information. In addition, real invariants might be masked or invisible because of other aspects of developmental change. Both of these hazards are easily illustrated. In the first case, suppose that the environments studied are strikingly similar at all ages in a particular study, and the invariants in knowledge simply reflect a very restricted sampling of possible environments. If one studied only the acquisition of grammar in Romance languages, for example, one might infer a host of invariants or principles that guided language acquisition, which were in fact only resulting from constancies in a restricted range of input languages.

The contrasting hazard of missing real invariants could happen for several reasons, ranging from competence/performance deficits to differing effects of pragmatics. Children may seem to have radically different sorts of knowledge and/or methods of computation because other developmental factors obscure their real competence. This was the message of the intensive reevaluation of Piaget's work that occurred in the 1970s and 1980s (Gelman & Baillargeon, 1983).

These hazards are greatly moderated (although not avoided completely) by looking at other types of change as well. Each framework in which there is considerable obvious variation in the nature of knowledge has it own pitfalls, but across several different kinds of change, no one flaw or pitfall is supported; hence, collectively, they make clear the presence and nature of invariant cognitive structures. Any one pattern of change is likely to offer a distorted view of underlying principles whereas, across several different kinds of change, one can start to factor out the distortions.

A different kind of variation is seen across cultures. Cross-cultural research in the cognitive sciences is a vast topic containing many profound, complex, and controversial issues, and a serious discussion of the enterprise is far beyond the scope of this chapter. (See Chapters 5, 15, and 19 of this Volume, and Chapters 8 and 14 of Volume 2 of this *Handbook* for more discussion of cross-cultural issues in developmental research.) The goal here is simply to illustrate how cross-cultural comparisons can be united with developmental ones to greatly enhance research questions in cognitive science.

As one example, consider the case of biological knowledge. Every known group of humans throughout the world recognizes the distinct class of living things as well as the subclasses of plants and animals. It might seem at first glance that the details concerning beliefs about living things can vary dramatically from culture to culture—some being vitalists, other being mechanists; some seeing spirits and reincarnation as the driving forces in animals, or in animals and plants, and so on. These patterns of variation would seem to suggest little in common. Similarly, beliefs about disease can vary from discussions that invoke a germ theory, the evil eye, or ghosts (Berlin & Berlin, in press; Keil, Levin, Richman, & Gutheil, in press; Maffi, in press). If such patterns of variation were the main patterns across cultures, with only the highest categories of animals, plants, and living things being in common, there would be strong developmental implications.

First, one would assume that the only possible invariant in development would be an appreciation of the same high-level categories. There are many developmental arguments as to why the categories might be the same at all ages, but

such a constancy is at least feasible in terms of developmental comparisons. It would also raise more concerted questions about whether the apparently similar categories across all cultures are really so similar. Boundary cases would be studied more intensively, such as plants that seem to move and eat (Venus flytraps), and animals that never move (such as coral). The interlinking of developmental and cross-cultural issues would make a host of questions salient concerning these high-level categories.

If a closer and more systematic look at cross-cultural universals suggests more richness and complexity than is first apparent, the developmental questions become even more structured and focused. A particular contribution of the cognitive science perspective is that the cross-cultural universals are often suggested by disciplines that are different from those looking at developmental issues. Most often, work in anthropology and linguistics might raise issues that then bear on psychological models of knowledge acquisition in children. Instances of such converging insights can be found in many of the areas of inquiry summarized above (cognitive maps, categorization, and number), as well as in many other areas. With biological thought, for example, recent work in anthropology suggests universals far beyond the high-level categories, including the tendencies to form rich hierarchically structured taxonomies, to assume underlying essences, and to adopt a teleological/functional mode of explanation (Atran, 1990, 1996). All of these discoveries in anthropological work, as well as related ones in anthropological linguistics (e.g., Berlin, 1992), have led to new developmental questions. Conversely, new developmental suggestions of invariants in biological thought from toddlerhood to adolescence have motivated cross-cultural researchers to look for subtler constancies and invariants (Atran, 1996; Carey, 1991; Hatano, Siegler, Inagaki, Stavy, & Wax, 1993; Inagaki, 1990; Keil, 1989, 1995; Springer, 1995). It is increasingly clear that the most fruitful work requires a constant dialogue across these disciplines—one that compares invariants discovered through developmental and cross-cultural comparisons. Methods from the perspective of any one pattern of variation or any one discipline will glean far fewer insights.

Cross-cultural and developmental universals do not always indicate something invariant about the mind; they simply might reflect invariants in the environments experienced by all people of all ages in all cultures. Further demonstration that such environmental invariants have corresponding cognitive invariants tailored to apprehend them is one of the most enduring challenges in cognitive science, one that is greatly aided by comparing different patterns of variation. One form of argument that helps support the presence of cognitive universals is documentation of equally prevalent sets of environmental regularities, where only some of them appear to be cognitively salient and understood in the same way and others are either not apprehended by many people or are apprehended in widely disparate ways. Examples here might include differences between views of object solidity (invariant and the same) and views on the nature of gravity (widely varying), even though both sets of regularities seem equally prevalent in the environment (for further discussion of this contrast, see Kim & Spelke, 1992).

A different issue arises in linking cross-cultural and developmental comparisons—one that is surprisingly neglected, given its potential for changing how we might view the acquisition and use of a body of knowledge. Some universals in the representation and use of knowledge may be apparent only early in cognitive development, and may come to be obscured or even overwritten during later development. A trivial version of this view would say that all infants share the same representations through a common ignorance; they have, for example, only a largely unweighted associative net. A more interesting version suggests that much more elaborated sets of beliefs might be present early and shared across cultures, and that they become seemingly more and more disparate with further development.

Margaret Mead (1932) was one of the first to emphasize the disappearance of cognitive universals in childhood as a consequence of overlaid divergent cultural beliefs in adults. She noted, in a research report on animism, that religion and other cultural constructions can sometimes serve to add complexity and variance to a more robust and straightforward set of underlying beliefs. Mead found that animism and other forms of magical thinking were much less common in children than in the adults of traditional cultures. Whereas a child might explain a collapsing bridge in terms of weak and rotting supports, an adult might invoke an elaborate account involving supernatural agents with intricate agendas. A great deal of cultural instruction, as well as certain rites of passage, may be required to be able to tell such supernatural narratives (see also Atran, 1996; Boyer, 1994; Walker, 1992 for related discussions). Sometimes, the heights of a culture's achievements are meant to deliberately contrast with the most widespread and most firmly entrenched daily beliefs. Thus, the Walipiri have a highly advanced manner of talking about everything in terms of opposites, which is considered a ceremonial and intellectually challenging achievement (Hale, 1971). In other cultures, diverse adult accounts about spirits, and other nonphysical forces, may coexist with beliefs about mechanisms shared by all. Many Western practitioners of medicine at some of the most technologically advanced hospitals believe in some version of Judeo/Christian theology that acknowledges a spatially discontinuous and even atemporal intentional agent as ultimately responsible for illness and healing. Yet these same individuals, in their daily practices, rely on highly functional/physical notions of mechanism in their attempts to cure illnesses.

Cross-cultural and developmental change, although the most often studied in cognitive science, are not the only sources of important information concerning variation and invariant structure. A different source comes from historical changes in cognitive structures through successive generations of adults in a particular culture. Such historical patterns of change share interesting properties with both developmental and cross-cultural patterns of variation. With developmental variation, they share the problems of explaining how one form of knowledge specifically leads to another either through continuous and gradual change or through precipitating some sort of conceptual revolution. The dynamics of change are a central theme. With cross-cultural variation, historical changes share the problems of explaining how a different set of beliefs in the larger community influences the beliefs of any one person. For although historical change is usually studied in the context of a single culture, over the centuries, that culture itself can change radically and the study can take on properties of cross-cultural comparisons.

On the flip side, historical change is importantly different from other forms of variation. It differs from developmental change in that the minds under investigation are usually all fully mature, and thus are not influenced by other factors that might make a child's cognitions different (see Elder, Ch. 16, this Volume, for more discussion of these issues, including historical analyses of children and of adults). Even the most radical development-equals-learning views would not equate a 14th-century adult with a later-century child, simply because a great deal about the natural world takes time to learn in any century, and because those of earlier ages had much to learn in that period that is no longer learned now (e.g., methods of keeping warm in winter, storing food, and so on). Describing cognitive change passed from one mature mind to another, often through written or other public forums, is profoundly different from describing developmental change within one and the same child. Historical change differs from cross-cultural variation because there are expectations of strong structural links between sets of comparisons. Earlier historical periods are thought to be causally responsible for later ones in ways that few cross-cultural comparisons ever suggest.

Given the unique and potentially powerful insights that can be offered by such historical analyses, it may seem surprising that so few have entered the domain of discourse of cognitive science. A few cases have done so, however, and have been highly influential. The most studied area has been historical linguistics, wherein at least the written record of a language allows comparisons over time; however, such written records have limitations that are not always apparent. The spoken language and the written language put down on paper by a few learned people can be quite different from one another, and using the written form to make inferences about the historical change of the naturally spoken language is not easy. Moreover, even in contemporary language, the written form results in subtle structural differences from the spoken form. Cognitive limitations imposed by real-time speech are loosened, and other stylistic constraints are added. Despite these limitations, historical linguistics has documented a number of patterns of change in syntactic, morphological, semantic, and phonological structure that have illustrated specific routes through which change can occur and have highlighted invariants across that change (see, for example, Bever & Langendoen, 1971; Traugott & Smith, 1993). Such invariants across cultures and across development and converging sources of support have been found in many cases. In other cases, developmental and historical issues have been blended as the change in a language over time is related to how each new generation of children learns the existing form and builds in new structures. This is especially evident in the process of creolization, wherein a prelanguage pidgin becomes elaborated into a full form by the children, who insert more structure, much of it apparently honoring universal properties of linguistic structure (Bickerton, 1995, 1981).

Other work on historical change has largely been done in the history of science—often in ways that are not connected to cognitive science, at least partly because of the use of different vocabularies and methods. But here, two convergences have become increasingly common and informative. Kuhn's (1970) landmark essay on the structure of scientific revolutions, for example, has had a huge effect on recent thought about the nature of conceptual change and cognitive development in childhood (e.g., Carey, 1985). Initially, the drama of the change itself overshadowed any possibility of invariants of cognitive structure across that change, but later work by Kuhn (1982) and others (Boyd, 1991; Kitcher, 1993), allowed for the possibility of more invariant frameworks surrounding patterns of change. These connections became richer as members of the cognitive science community began to engage in more historical analyses themselves (Gruber, 1981; Tweney, 1991; Wiser, 1988).

These examples illustrate the power of historical analyses for highlighting possible types of conceptual change (see also Siegler & Modell, 1993). Although it was not a major focus of these studies, they also show the potential, as seen in historical linguistics, for uncovering invariants. There are complex challenges and much to be learned in how to link the different kinds of variation, and it is clearly an oversimplification to look at the historical development of a concept in successive generations of adults and compare it directly to how it develops in the modern-day child. Yet, the complexity and subtlety of such comparisons do not detract from the enormous insights they can offer.

Computer science and artificial intelligence have also introduced efforts to understand conceptual change both in an individual and in terms of historical discovery. These efforts range from Langley et al.'s (1987) attempt to rediscover Boyle's gas laws through a program known as BACON (named after its relations to Baconian induction) to explanation-based attempts to mimic such learning (Goel, in press). These attempts still need to be more closely linked to other areas of cognitive science, but in the past few years such attempts have been emerging. One example is evident in a 1997 issue of the *Journal of Learning Sciences,* in which researchers across all disciplines of cognitive science approach the topic of conceptual change.

Other patterns of variation, beyond the cross-cultural, developmental and historical, can offer insights, but they are insights of a different sort and suggest different research strategies. Consider two prominent cases: (a) the study of individual differences among members of a common group and (b) the cross-species comparative analysis of what seem to be similar cognitive capacities. In both of these cases, but especially in (b), the patterns of variation are much less likely to highlight invariants or bring them into relief, at least under any cognitive science perspective that embraces even a modest degree of nativism. Only the staunchest empiricist—someone who holds that all learning and manner of representation is of fundamentally the same sort across all species and individuals—would assume the same invariants would obtain in all cases. If, for example, some simple laws of association explained all of cognition and cognitive development, the species studied would simply be a matter of convenience and pragmatics. If rats or pigeons, for example, were the most economical and efficient subjects, any laws of learning and cognition so obtained would apply to all other species as well, perhaps just with simple scaling factors and variables (Skinner, 1950). Moreover, one does not have to hold a simple associationist view to believe in such an approach. A very sophisticated connectionist approach could also maintain the same position, arguing that the only interesting differences between humans and rats, for example, lie in the numbers of units that can occur at various levels and in the differences coming in from the sensory transducers.

Few cognitive science researchers, however, seem to embrace such a strong view. Instead, most researchers suspect that interesting qualitative differences in cognition and learning will appear as comparisons are made across species. In other cases, it is suspected that there may be only a very limited number of solutions to certain problems concerning pickup and representation of kinds of environmental information, and that most species will be constrained to exploit the same class of solutions. Finally, some degree of cognitive continuity across phylogenetically related species is suspected because this is the case for anatomical structures and physiological organs and processes. In short, no one pattern is likely to emerge from cross-species comparisons of cognition; rather, we can look for a rich array of possibilities that are presumably linked in a systematic way to the kind of cognitive problem confronted and the organism's own capacities

and ecological niche. Presumably, increasingly precise predictions will be possible across different patterns of variation. For example, if a particular way of representing spatial layout seems to have been used by a very wide range of species, one might be more confident about its being universal across human cultures and exhibiting a strong constant framework across development.

Individual differences in cognitive capacities would seem to fly in the face of searches for universals; however, in many ways, the study of individual differences can be complementary (Lerner, 1986). One can focus on special populations of people who are suspected to have specific differences in brain functional architecture that would lead to specific forms of deficits. These might include autistic individuals, those with Williams syndrome, or various groups of aphasic persons. A different approach looks at milder ranges of variation of talents and at what appear to be more domain-general capacities, such as general intelligence. In the context of the other patterns of variation discussed earlier, individual differences can often point out the same invariants across other strong ranges of cognitive capacities. For example, the nature and style of natural language syntax development may not vary much over huge variations in what appear to be general intellectual capacities, suggesting that part of the language acquisition ability is not dependent on the general information-processing capacity of the learner (Bellugi et al., 1993).

In the end, there is no simple recipe prescribing how the study of different patterns of cognitive variation should be linked together to yield insights about the nature of cognition and cognitive development. But case after case illustrates how fruitful and productive such comparisons can be, especially when done from a cognitive science perspective that freely crosses traditional disciplinary boundaries.

Hybrid/Computational Systems Are Essential to Developmental Accounts

As the development of thought and knowledge in different domains is examined more closely, it is striking how often it becomes apparent that at least two very different kinds of knowledge systems are at work. This has been the conclusion of researchers from such diverse domains as number, natural language syntax, spatial knowledge, and many domains of natural kind concepts. Development is one of the most impressive ways in which this hybrid structure is revealed, because distinct aspects of thought and knowledge can be shown to have different sorts of functional roles and patterns of change over time. The precise nature of the hybrid itself is still hotly contested, but the strength of evidence across a wide range of domains of thought and research paradigms suggests not only a need for hybrid models in accounts of the development of thought and knowledge but also some general aspects of what the hybrid must look like. A thread of this idea has been around since the early days of the emergence of cognitive psychology, when Neisser (1963) suggested that there were two very different aspects to cognition and thought and they corresponded roughly to an associative component and a rulelike component. In the context of cognitive science, this idea is now being revived in more powerful terms (Sloman, 1996).

For centuries—indeed, even implicit in Aristotle's writings—there have been suggestions that some aspects of thought involve relatively automatic tabulations of environmental regularities, whereas other aspects involve understanding more rulelike principles concerning information in the physical and social worlds. Most often, the tabulation component is seen as some variant of associationism in that the frequencies of elements and their intercorrelations are monitored and stored by a domain-general associative ability. This proposal became highly explicit in the works of the British empiricists, who often detailed examples of how co-occurrences of instances and properties could provide data for the gradual buildup of knowledge and understanding from simple perceptually recovered features and properties. Thus, one's understanding of dogs developed by noticing more and more about features that co-occurred in dogs and by experiencing whole dogs themselves. Simple laws of association were assumed to be able to predict how this information was noticed, stored, and acted on later.

The British empiricists were normally characterized as believing that such associative mechanisms were the sole means for the growth of knowledge and understanding; but, as indicated earlier, there was, in some of their writings, far more subtlety and often a sensitivity to the need for something quite different that also guided the acquisition and use of knowledge. More recently, the need for hybrid systems requiring both associative and more principled, rule-governed, or explanation-based components, can be seen in all areas of cognitive science and in all subdisciplines. There have been indications of such hybrids in all of the domains discussed earlier, whether they involved

space, number, grammatical forms, or concepts, and researchers in all disciplines of cognitive science are acknowledging a need to use hybrids (e.g., Clark & Karmiloff-Smith, 1993). Equally important is the insight that the hybrids often are present throughout the developmental period—that is, each component needs the other.

Several key questions arise here. Are hybrid mixes required in all natural domains of knowledge? Does the relative mix of the two components show a shift in the course of cognitive development? Is a simple dichotomy really adequate, or are tripartite or even more complex divisions needed? Is the associative part of the hybrid relatively invariant and universal? Are the other parts highly variable as a function of domains? Are qualitative changes in knowledge structure over time occurring predominantly in the nonassociative component? Do the two components normally have different functional roles, such as serving identification heuristics versus making decisions about borderline cases? These questions are only visible because of the hybrid idea itself (Keil, Smith, Simons, & Levin, in press).

Conceptual Change Has Many Forms and May Often Be Illusory

Discussion of conceptual change has become common throughout much of cognitive science. We have seen examples in the history and philosophy of science, in psychological work dating back at least to Piaget (1930) and Vygotsky (1934), in linguistic analysis both of language change over history and of semantic and lexical development in the child, and in increasing references in computer science and artificial intelligence (Ram, 1996). One less obvious consequence of this increasing discussion of conceptual change has been a proliferation of different senses of what conceptual change might mean. Understanding these distinctions serves far more than a classificatory role, because these different senses have very different developmental consequences. Many discussions of whether conceptual change is occurring in a domain are made meaningless because different parties to such discussions have radically different understandings of what counts as a real instance of conceptual change.

At one extreme, any change of knowledge, such as the gradual accretion of facts about phone numbers of classmates, has been called conceptual change. At the other extreme are cases where a particular new concept seems to emerge in development through a sacrificial synthesis of prior ones. There is an urgent need to better clarify these extremes and the intermediate cases. The richest diversity of types of conceptual change arises from considering concepts within the concepts-in-theories perspective summarized earlier in this chapter. In that perspective, concepts are not seen as completely isolated mental units unlinked to other concepts or to larger belief structures that include explanations and theories.

The kinds of cognitive change that end up actually being called instances of "conceptual change" may matter little, and discussions easily may deteriorate into pointless and arbitrary naming decisions. The important task is to lay out principled contrasts that have different consequences for how knowledge might be acquired and used. The following set of candidates offers a kind of continuum from what appear to be the most minimal sorts of change to the most massive. Along this continuum, where one chooses to call the change conceptual may be largely a matter of convention.

A. *Feature or property changes and value changes on dimensions.* With increasing knowledge, different clusters of features might come to be weighted more heavily in a concept; but in their simplest forms, such changes alone would not seem to count as conceptual change. One may, at a greater point of understanding, come to think that a particular feature, *x,* is more critical to understanding a group of things than another feature, but one does so without any major restructuring of the understanding of the group. For example, a young child might think that the most important feature of cats is their meowing, but, somewhat later, may come to weight purring as more critical. Unaccompanied by other changes in beliefs about such things as the causal roles of purring and meowing in cat behavior, this developmental change in ranking a feature's importance may not signify anything more than a changing distribution of encounters with cats or the relative perceptual salience of the isolated features at different ages. Even if an older child were to disagree with a younger one on identifying some marginal cats, that disagreement alone may not amount to an important form of conceptual change. Adults can disagree on marginal instances of many fuzzy categories without believing that their concepts of the relevant kinds are importantly different. What matters are the bases for the disagreement, which can range from profoundly different

beliefs to different certainties about features. I might disagree with a friend over whether Ithaca, New York, is really a city or a town, because one of us weights municipal government structure a little more strongly than certain social services; but that difference in weighting alone might never lead to anything more than a modest shrug to signify a difference of opinion and our mutual belief that it is trivial and unimportant.

The same phenomenon can be seen with value changes on specific dimensions. A child might gradually, with increasing age, come to weight more heavily the larger end of the size dimension in classifying an animal as a horse versus a pony, or a rise of a mountain versus a hill, without having much else change in conceptual structure. There is a difference, to be sure, in the horse concepts that the child possesses with increasing age, but nothing that seems frankly interesting is changing if all that has occurred is a sliding of a size threshold marker further along a dimension. If that shifting weight is connected to beliefs about many other properties of the entity involved, more interesting forms of change might be occurring, but they need not be occurring and often do not occur.

Changes in feature weightings and dimensional value shifts are ubiquitous in cognitive science studies of concepts. They are seen at all ages ranging from studies of infant categorization to adult novice-to-expert shifts. Any time that some bit of information is incrementally added to a knowledge base and results in a different feature weighting, such a change can be seen to have occurred. The important questions arise as to the extent to which such changes have other consequences for how knowledge in a domain is represented. I have argued here that they often do not have such consequences, and that simple changes of this sort should not be seen as inevitably spawning larger-scale structural conceptual changes.

B. *Shifting use of different sorts of properties and relations.* Almost since the beginning of serious thought about the nature of cognitive development, one common idea has been that different feature types are used at different ages. Any proposal that an older child thinks in qualitatively different ways from a younger one has a strong potential to rely on the idea that children at different ages use different sorts of properties and relations in their mental representations and computations.

Perhaps the infant or young child can use only perceptual and not conceptual features to represent classes of things, or perceptual and not functional features, or concrete rather than abstract ones. In more current versions, it might be claimed that young children can use only one-place predicates and not higher-order relational ones (Gentner & Toupin, 1988), or that shape-based features dominate in some contexts (Smith & Jones, 1993; Smith, Jones, & Landau, 1996).

A large range of possible forms of conceptual change can be captured by accounts in which the change is produced by a shift in which features are used or are available for representing some aspect of the world. Despite a wide range of proposals in this area, however, most have always been controversial. To date, there is no consensus on any developmental change in the sorts of properties and/or relations that are available at different ages. This is not to deny a constant stream of new proposals, many echoing older ones and some seeming genuinely novel; but it suggests that they remain difficult to confirm.

Part of the reason they are so difficult to confirm may rest with the need for a better theory of property and relation types. It would naturally be difficult to make claims about such things as perceptual-to-conceptual shifts, or perceptual-to-functional shifts, if one had an unclear account of perceptual versus conceptual features. For that reason, claims of such changes need to tie more closely into more formal philosophical analyses of properties and relations, and those philosophical analyses need to attend more to some of the empirical facts. Without such analyses, it is relatively easy to make trouble for most proposals by showing just how many difficult and indeterminate cases arise.

C. *Changes in computations performed on features.* Even when property types stay constant across development in terms of their presence, dramatic conceptual changes are possible when one considers the sorts of computations performed on those features. In several of the examples considered so far in this chapter, putative shifts in computational manner have been proposed. For example, we have seen claims of shifts from theoretical tabulations of features based on frequency and correlational information to more rulelike organizations of the same features. In other cases, there have been claims of changes from prelogical to quasilogical computations over features (Inhelder & Piaget, 1964); or changes from integral to separable operations on features and dimensions (Kemler & Smith, 1978); or changes from feature frequency tabulations to feature correlation tabulations.

Many other claims have been made along the same lines, where the features and relations encoded remain the same, but the computations performed on those features are different. Such a dichotomy may not be so easy to enforce in practice, however. Changes in the ability to make computations over features might change the meanings of those features or make some features salient that would otherwise be uninteresting and essentially invisible without the computations to highlight their importance. These problems aside, however, such cases are genuine instances of conceptual change insofar as the concepts seem to undergo dramatic change in how they are represented and used.

Two important points must be made about these kinds of change. First, although the proposed models tend to be domain-general, across-the-board changes, they need not be. It is possible that transition from novice to expert knowledge in a well-circumscribed domain results in different sorts of computations being performed on the same feature sets, even as there is no global developmental change in computational ability (Chi, 1992). Second, these models do not require that concepts be interrelated in a larger structure. They are neutral in that respect, and thus they allow each concept to change on its own. In practice, this is highly implausible and may in the end render such models inadequate because they fail to make stronger claims about links among concepts.

There are special cases of this type of change and the one described immediately above, where there is no absolute change in feature or computational type, but rather a strong change in the ratio of the two types. Thus, a younger child may have true conceptual or functional features but may have ten times as many perceptual ones in his or her concepts, whereas an older child may have the opposite ratio. Similarly, a younger child may perform logical computations on feature sets, but may do so much more rarely and may more frequently resort to simpler probabilistic tabulations. This difference is important because it offers a very different characterization of the younger child in terms of basic competencies. Younger children are not incapable of representing certain feature types or engaging in certain computations; rather, they do so much less often, perhaps as a function of being more novice in so many domains (see Keil, 1989, for more discussion of this possible pattern).

D. *Three kinds of cases where theories spawn others and thereby create new sets of concepts.* The most dramatic kinds of conceptual change, and those that invite considerable discussion in cognitive science as well as in the history and philosophy of science, are those that view concepts as embedded in larger explanatory structures, usually known as theories (see the earlier discussions on concepts and theories). In that framework, three types of change are normally described: (a) the birth of new theories and concepts through the death of older ones (Gopnik & Wellman, 1994); (b) the gradual evolution of new theories and concepts out of old ones in a manner that eventually leaves no traces of the earlier ones (usually not a discontinuous revolutionary kind of change but a very gradual one); and (c) the birth of new theories and attendant concepts while leaving the old ones intact (this is one version of Carey, 1985). All of these forms of change may occur and may be associated with specific kinds of knowledge. One key issue in choosing among these kinds of change is the extent to which concepts of one type are not commensurable with, or contradict, those of another type. A related issue asks to what extent contradictions in an older theory demand a radical and quick change of the first sort. It is not possible here to enter into the complex debate about which kinds of conceptual change occur where; rather, I suggest that researchers in cognitive science must take special pains to distinguish among these different forms, for each might have dramatically different consequences for models of cognitive development.

E. *Shifting relevances: illusory conceptual change?* The final kind of change does not reflect the emergence of new theories or the restructuring of concepts; yet, it may often underlie what appear to be the most dramatic cases of conceptual change. It is often much harder to see at first, but as studies accumulate in domain after domain, it repeatedly appears to be the real basis for observed change.

Children often come to dramatic new insights not because of an underlying conceptual revolution or a birth of a new way of thinking, but rather because they realize the preferred status of an already present explanatory system or its relevance to a new set of phenomena. Because the realization can be sudden and the extension to new phenomena quite sweeping, it can have all the hallmarks of profound conceptual change. It is, however, a markedly different sort of change. Children can often have several distinct theories available to them throughout an extensive developmental period, but might differ dramatically from adults in where they think those theories are most relevant. They might not differ at all in their possession of the theories. Those shifts in relevance can masquerade as conceptual changes of the sort that occur where new theories are

spawned, but in reality are not. These kinds of relevance shifts, combined with theory elaboration in each domain, may be far more common than cases where new theories arise out of old ones.

In some cases, relevance shifts reflect an expansion of a theory to a new but related class of objects. An example is the extension of a biological mode of explanation from mammals to insects. In other cases, the extension may be to a more radically different set, such as extending a psychological mode of explanation from humans to computers. In the more extreme cases, the nature of the change may be more difficult to determine. It may exploit analogy (Gentner, 1983; Goswami, 1996; Holyoak & Thagard, 1995), and may require so many new tokens to instantiate variables in the theory, that it starts to take on a new look and perhaps to become a truly different mode of explanation.

Some shifts simply reflect differing default biases that are triggered by such simple pragmatic considerations as the perceived demands of a task. Thus, a child may use a biological mode of explanation spontaneously some of the time, and a psychological mode at other times, even for the same class of things. What may change with development is the relevant class of relations for explaining those entities. In other cases, the spontaneous use may be initially linked more tightly to distinct domains and may then broaden to others as well. Early restriction followed by broadening is one version of the increasing-access idea proposed by Rozin (1976). Rozin suggested that many cases of developmental change that appear to be the dramatic emergence of a new competence are, in fact, cases of increasing access to some body of knowledge or some ability that has previously been circumscribed. For many reasons, an ability, a domain of knowledge, or a method of explanation might be heavily circumscribed early on and then broadened greatly (e.g., Karmiloff-Smith, 1992), and this issue alone is one that could occupy researchers from many parts of cognitive science.

It should be obvious by now that the topic of conceptual change is immense and that a full treatment is far beyond the scope of this chapter. My purpose here is to illustrate how many distinct senses of conceptual change there are, and how important it is to keep them apart. To fail to see these distinctions is to doom many to misguided disagreements only because they are talking past each other and are discussing, unwittingly, fundamentally different developmental phenomena. The increasing awareness of these different kinds of change is very recent and is greatly fostered by a cognitive science perspective. For, as issues cross the disciplines, they get treated in different ways, and different kinds of conceptual change stand out as most prominent.

Cognitive Development Is Not a Progression from Concrete to Abstract Thought

There is a widespread assumption that cognitive development must proceed from the concrete to the abstract. The direction of development can seem to take on an air of logical inevitability when knowledge acquisition is seen as starting from exemplars built up out of sensory primitives. Suppose all knowledge were built up through a serial chain of processing. Sensory processing yields sets of properties that are then processed to yield images of specific objects. Property patterns over instances are then tabulated. These tabulations in turn are processed to yield concepts and other forms of higher-order knowledge. In such a sequence, knowledge would seem to have to start with building a storehouse of concrete knowledge, out of which the child gradually is able to abstract higher-order rules and patterns that govern those primitives.

Despite debates and varying viewpoints on precisely what the terms *concrete* and *abstract* mean, there has been a consistent theme, for a great many years, that the young child and/or infant initially constructs an interpretation of reality only in concrete, instance-bound terms, and then gradually is able to be freed from such a limiting lens on the world. This theme echoes in different ways through the writings of Vygotsky, who saw the internalization of language as freeing the child from concrete thought; of Werner (Werner & Kaplan, 1963), who saw the transition as more of an endogenous sequence; of Piaget, who saw the use of increasingly powerful logical operations as allowing more abstract knowledge; and in contemporary approaches ranging from the connectionist (Elman, 1991) to the symbolic (Gentner & Toupin, 1988).

The research patterns summarized earlier in this chapter suggest that, whatever the formulation of abstract and concrete, a concrete-to-abstract shift is not likely to be the dominant mode of cognitive development. For the purposes of discussion, concrete cognition can be characterized as focusing on information and building representations that correspond to properties of instances. Abstract cognition refers to more formal, principled characterizations of information. Thus, a concrete representation of spatial layout might be a list of landmarks that includes salient features for each landmark, with navigation being driven by an associative model in which activations are stronger when in closer proximity. An abstract characterization is one that relies on some set of geometric principles to construct a map of the layout that ignores many concrete details. The landmark system has no developmental priority. Indeed, in every domain that we have considered, it seems impossible to predict developmental patterns with any reasonable model of a concrete-to-abstract shift.

The entire abstract–concrete dichotomy may be suspect. But if it is to be salvaged in some form, it may be that the clearest cases are of the opposite form: abstract-to-concrete shifts (Simons & Keil, 1995). Consider, for example, a model of grammar acquisition that sees the child as knowing, or immediately extracting, a large set of abstract principles which it then uses to learn the concrete particulars of language. Similarly, a child who represents space in terms of overall geometric contour while ignoring local concrete landmarks even when they are necessary to disambiguate location, seems to be moving from abstract to more concrete representations.

In the end, one has to ask why the idea of a concrete-to-abstract shift is so pervasive when the data seem to be so equivocal. There seem to be two reasons. First, it may have to do with what aspects of phenomena are easiest to talk about explicitly in a natural language. It is often relatively simple to talk about physical properties and harder to talk about nonphysical ones and relations. That ease may give rise to the erroneous impression that such features are cognitively simpler and emerge earlier in development. This intuition, however, loses support when one considers the many complex relational patterns that are immediately available to cognition and perception but are very difficult to talk about. It is also undetermined when other species use comparable sorts of information.

The second reason that a concrete-to-abstract transition may seem the developmental norm may arise from a confusion between abstract and concrete tasks and abstract and concrete cognition. Very often, younger children perform poorly on tasks with arbitrary meaningless stimuli that seem to be disconnected from any natural context. There are hundreds, perhaps thousands, of studies showing that younger children are unable to perform well on tasks that do not make sense to them. They do not classify nonsense categories well, they fail to see hierarchical and taxonomic relations with meaningless stimuli, and they miss causal relations with some schematic illustrations of a mechanical system—among many others. One might then be tempted to see these failures as evidence for a concrete-to-abstract shift because the more difficult stimuli are more "abstract." But such a claim misrepresents the real difficulty, uses a very different sense of abstract and concrete, and indeed is largely irrelevant to the nature of the *representations* that the children are using to solve such tasks.

Consider cases where a younger child fails with stimuli that are governed by a formally simple rule but have no connection to the child's natural world. This was, in fact, the dominant mode of research in cognitive development for many research groups across the years, largely because concerns of stimulus control overrode any concerns about relevance and ecological validity. But failure might have nothing to do with any weakness in abstract thought. If, with more natural stimuli, a set of formal principles is needed for success, and children do succeed, failures on the meaningless stimuli are largely irrelevant.

Explanation May Be More Central to Cognitive Development Than Prediction

It would seem that all of us possess knowledge primarily for the purpose of better predicting future events. Such an assumption has certainly undergirded much of the psychological research on cognition about both physical and social entities. Indeed, it appears to be a necessary assumption. Our mental representations allow us to build up expectancies about aspects of environments so that we can know at greater-than-chance levels what is going to happen next. To a certain extent, this is a logical truism. The only possible utilitarian effect of any state of an organism is on its future states; thus, prediction offers the only way in which an organism can capitalize on experience. But despite this truism, in reality, we may rarely predict future events in any normal sense; instead, we may devote most of our cognitive energy to explaining and understanding events that have already happened. My purpose here is to show some evidence for this pattern across domains, and then to argue as to why it is a very reasonable strategy for all of us, but especially for young children, to engage in.

Perhaps surprisingly, the view that theoretical knowledge enables explanation more than prediction has already gained strong support in disciplines outside of cognitive science. Such a development has been particularly pronounced in economics. There are still many efforts to engage in economic forecasting, but there is an increasingly strong position that explanation and understanding of the full range of possible economic outcomes may be a much more useful way to further economics as a science (Holden, Peel, & Thompson, 1990). There seem to be two reasons for favoring explanation over prediction, among some groups of economists: (a) a conviction that the nonlinear nature of dynamic economic systems makes it impossible to engage in any sort of accurate predictions; and (b) a great deal can be gained by generating patterns of explanations for prior sets of economic events, because such events allow one to posit the structure of underlying forces that drive the particular economy that is under analysis. An understanding of that structure will not allow one to know what economic conditions will be present, say, in a year, but they might allow one to understand and respond more quickly to new economic situations when they do suddenly emerge. In many systems, it can be far easier to accurately and correctly explain a pattern after the fact than to predict it. This is not simply because after-the-fact explanations have the trivial ad hoc advantages of "20–20 hindsight;" rather, it is because fully determinate causal paths can often be uncovered in a system where prior prediction was not possible.

A bit closer to home, the explanation-over-prediction model is the only conceivable model in many areas of perceptual–motor performance. Consider the action of a white-tailed deer running through the Adirondack Mountains in late November with hunters' gunshots echoing on all sides. One might predict that the deer would be more agitated and mobile than normal, and more vigilant. But it would be hopeless to predict particular paths it would take through the woods, or the particular muscle pattern timings as it leaps over each log, or steps carefully through each bog or leaf-filled depression. Thousands of split-second perceptual and motor alterations occur, and no one seriously would consider predicting them for futures beyond 100 milliseconds. There is no magic here; one assumes a fully determinate system with fully specifiable causal chains, but precise predictions of perceptual/motor sequences of more than the shortest time intervals seem foolhardy, even if one has a fully exhaustive specification of the physical environment and the deer's internal states. (For related discussions of these themes, see Fischer & Bidell, Ch. 9; Gottlieb et al., Ch. 5; Smith & Thelen, Ch. 10; and Wapner & Demick, Ch. 13, this Volume.)

So many of our human perceptual/motor skills have this character that we simply assume its presence. Most athletes acquire skills not at making extensive predictions, but at how to rapidly interpret situations and react as quickly as possible. There are local predictions, of course, but again they are driven by a rich and rapid understanding of a situation that then suggests a course of action. A skilled center on an ice hockey team has no idea where he will be in the next five minutes but, wherever he is, his skill enables him to immediately extract meaning and explanation from a configuration of players and use that as a basis for action. His skill derives from developing a vast store of situations linked together by an underlying set of explanations, which then inform action.

Similarly, a chess master never knows what the board will look like after 20 moves, but a master has the ability to instantly interpret whatever configuration is at hand, and to understand the range of possible outcomes that it affords. In many cases, the master may not be able to predict which of several radically different actions the opponent will engage in, but will be far more prepared than most to understand each of these actions immediately and to know how best to respond.

The examples continue into the social realm. Consider a family reunion that occurs over a holiday. Relatives from many places converge on a household and interact, often very intensely, for several days. In most families, the participants in such a gathering arrive with strong expectations about the personalities of each of their relatives. For example, suppose an uncle from Pittsburgh is seen as a moody, brooding man who vacillates from great sentimentality about his profession to defensiveness about the collapse of his career. One might feel that a simple construct about his failed career and its impact on his mood easily explains both states. But one might have enormous difficulty predicting the state he will be in at any point when he is asked about his profession. From an understanding of the underlying dynamics, one gains a better ability to interpret his actions quickly and to know how to better respond to

them. It helps, for example, to know how personally one should take a verbal attack and how one should respond to a similar outburst in the future. One does not know when that outburst will occur, but when it does, one knows why and how to respond. This clearly is not prediction, in any normal sense, because one cannot state, more than seconds in advance, which of several radically divergent social interactions is likely to occur.

Thus, although a sense of prediction is preserved in these examples, it is vital to understand its limitations. Any account of our possessing intuitive theories so as to make accurate long-term predictions needs revision. Much more often, we devote most of our cognitive energies to analyzing what has happened so as to better understand the key underlying principles and causal forces. Those understandings then enable us to encounter new situations with much more effective ways of picking up information rather than of exactly predicting it. Bem (1992) argues strongly for the development of different cultural and subcultural lenses that provide very different perspectives on such things as gender roles. These lenses, however, for all their cognitive complexity and their ability to bring certain issues into sharp focus, would never be characterized as simple predictive devices, any more than would a set of real eyeglass lenses.

Children, even more than adults, appear to use systems of explanation less to make precise future predictions and more to understand what has happened. They do so to develop a more versatile and dependable interpretive system for whatever happens in the future. The disparity between the ability to predict outcomes and the ability to explain them after the fact often is much larger in young children than in older children or adults, and this pattern repeats itself in domain after domain. Moreover, the developmental message could well be taken to heart in all of adult cognitive science as well. Consider the now huge "theory of mind" literature, or what we might more properly call the development of a folk psychology. Many of the most striking early results in this new literature sprang from dramatic failures by young children to predict protagonist behaviors in certain false-belief tasks. It is much less clear whether the same children might not be competent, somewhat earlier, in explaining such behaviors after the fact (Bartsen & Wellman, 1989; Knight, 1989; Robinson & Mitchell, 1995).

It is not immediately obvious why the prediction–explanation gap should be so much larger for younger children. My point is that we are unlikely to understand much about cognitive development if we assume that children are spending most of their time using their cognitive systems to make predictions. Instead, most of their time, perhaps far more than adults, is spent trying to explain things after the fact. Those explanations, in turn, may be critical to making local predictions, but we should ask whether all that cognitive work is often better thought of as providing lenses or real-time interpretive frameworks for future events.

CONCLUSION—THE FULLY INTEGRATIVE NATURE OF DEVELOPMENT IN COGNITIVE SCIENCE

Cognitive science is an important new way of approaching the study of mind, and the values of this approach are now well demonstrated. What has been less obvious perhaps is the extent to which developmental questions have been an integral part of cognitive science from the start, much as they are in most areas of biology. That is the primary message of this chapter. It is important to end, however, with the realization that although cognitive science has changed the nature of developmental psychology, developmental psychology has changed cognitive science in equal if not more profound ways.

Cognitive science has had at least three influences on the study of psychological development. First, it has made a range of disciplines much more relevant to developmental problems. No longer do psychologists narrowly consider problems from their own perspective. We have seen that they incorporate and rely on ideas from disciplines ranging from philosophy to computer science. Second, cognitive science has illustrated how some of the most central questions about the mind have intrinsically developmental components that cannot be divorced, implying that developmental psychologists must have a clear grasp on the mature states as well. Finally, cognitive science provides a vastly larger set of converging forms of support for models and theories. It is now possible to take a shaky idea from the viewpoint of one perspective and make it rock-solid using other forms of support from different disciplines.

Developmental psychology's influence on cognitive science may be a little less obvious, but it is extremely impor-

tant as well. First, it has been the primary force in bringing evolutionary and comparative issues into cognitive science. Its long history of looking across species is only now being understood as essential to cognitive science as a whole. Second, it has made much clearer the issue of ecological validity and why it is important to study how our minds are cognitively adapted to particular environmental niches. More than any other approach, developmental approaches tune us to this issue. Developmental studies force us to be more ecologically honest and to pay more homage to the structure of the environment and the information to be learned, because, without such analyses, young children and infants simply will not engage in the tasks. Finally, developmental studies have made clear the mutual interdependence of social and physical cognition in any reasonable cognitive science. Social and nonsocial cognitions are routinely compared in developmental studies, such as those on autism; and developmental researchers have been far more in the vanguard in such comparisons than those studying only adults. These developmental studies illustrate why it is dangerous to make claims, for example, about adult counterfactual reasoning and not to systematically compare counterfactual reasoning across social and nonsocial domains.

Developmental psychology will surely continue to flourish as a worthy endeavor in its own right. But now, it will clearly be seen in the larger context of cognitive science, just as cognitive science will be seen as having an inseparable developmental component.

ACKNOWLEDGMENTS

The author thanks Andy Clark, Bill Damon, Grant Gutheil, Giyoo Hatano, Richard Lerner, Dan Levin, Helen Neville, Bethany Richman, Dan Simons, Carter Smith, and Doug Thompson for comments on drafts or parts thereof.

REFERENCES

Acredelo, L. P. (1978). Development of spatial orientation in infancy. *Developmental Psychology, 14,* 224–234.

Acredelo, L. P. (1981). Small and large scale spatial concepts in infancy and childhood. In L. Liben, A. Patterson, & N. Newcombe (Eds.), *Spatial representation and behavior across the life span: Theory and applications.* New York: Academic Press.

Acredelo, L. P. (1987). Early development and spatial orientation in humans. In P. Ellen & C. Thinus-Blanc (Eds.), *Cognitive processes of spatial orientation in animal and man: Vol. 2. Neurophysiology and developmental aspects.* Dordrecht, The Netherlands: Martinus Nijhoff.

Alexander, P. (1985). *Ideas, qualities and corpuscles.* Cambridge, England: Cambridge University Press.

Aristotle. (1907). *De anima: With translation, introduction and notes* (R. D. Hicks, Trans.). Cambridge, England: Cambridge University Press.

Aristotle. (1910). *The works of Aristotle.* Oxford, England: Clarendon Press.

Armstrong, S., Gleitman, L., & Gleitman, H. (1983). What some concepts might not be. *Cognition, 13,* 263–308.

Aslin, R. N. (1986). Dark vergence in human infants: Implications for the development of binocular vision. *Acta Psychologica, 63,* 309–322.

Atran, S. (1990). *Cognitive foundations of natural history: Towards an anthropology of science.* Cambridge, England: Cambridge University Press.

Atran, S. (1995). Knowledge of living kinds. In D. Sperber, D. Premack, & A. Premack (Eds.), *Causal cognition: A multidisciplinary debate* (pp. 205–233). Oxford, England: Oxford University Press.

Atran, S. (1996). From folk biology to scientific biology. In D. R. Olson & N. Torrance (Eds.), *Handbook of education and human development: New models of learning, teaching, and schooling.* Cambridge, England: Blackwell.

Baillargeon, R. (1987). Young infants' reasoning about the physical and spatial characteristics of a hidden object. *Cognitive Development, 2,* 179–200.

Baillargeon, R. (1995). Physical reasoning in infancy. In M. S. Gazzaniga (Ed.), *The cognitive neurosciences.* Cambridge, MA: Bradford/MIT Press.

Baillargeon, R., Kotovsky, L., & Needham, A. (1995). The acquisition of physical knowledge in infancy. In D. Sperber, D. Premack, & A. Premack (Eds.), *Causal cognition: A multidisciplinary debate* (pp. 79–116). Oxford, England: Oxford University Press.

Baldwin, D. A. (1995). Understanding the link between joint attention and language. In C. Moore & P. Dunham (Eds.), *Joint attention: Its origins and role in development* (pp. 131–158). Hillsdale, NJ: Erlbaum.

Baron-Cohen, S. (1995). *Mindblindness: An essay on autism and theory of mind.* Cambridge, MA: MIT Press.

Barsalou, L. W. (1987). The instability of graded structure: Implications for the nature of concepts. In U. Neisser (Ed.), *Concepts and conceptual development: Ecological and intellectual factors in categorization.* Cambridge, England: Cambridge University Press.

Bechtel, W. (1988a). *Philosophy of mind: An overview for cognitive science.* Hillsdale, NJ: Erlbaum.

Bechtel, W. (1988b). *Philosophy of science: An overview for cognitive science.* Hillsdale, NJ: Erlbaum.

Bellugi, U., Birhle, A., Neville, H., Jernigan, T., & Doherty, S. (1993). Language, cognition, and brain organization in a neurodevelopmental disorder. In M. Gunnar & C. Nelson (Eds.), *Developmental behavioral neuroscience.* Hillsdale, NJ: Erlbaum.

Bem, S. L. (1993). *The lenses of gender: Transforming the debate on sexual inequality.* New Haven, CT: Yale University Press.

Berkeley, G. (1901). *An essay towards a new theory of vision.* Oxford, England: Clarendon Press. (Original work published 1709)

Berlin, B. (1992). *Ethnobiological classification: Principles of categorization of plants and animals in traditional societies.* Princeton, NJ: Princeton University Press.

Berlin, B., & Berlin, E. A. (in press). *Medical ethnobiology of the highland Maya: The gastrointestinal conditions.* Princeton, NJ: Princeton University Press.

Bever, T. G., & Langendoen, D. T. (1971). A dynamic model of the evolution of language. *Linguistic Inquiry, 2,* 433–463.

Bickerton, D. (1981). *The roots of language.* Ann Arbor, MI: Karoma.

Bickerton, D. (1995). *Language and human behavior.* Seattle: University of Washington Press.

Bloom, H. (1994). *The Western canon: The books and school of the ages.* New York: Harcourt Brace.

Bloom, P. (in press). Theories of word learning: Rationalist alternatives to associationism. In T. K. Bhatia & W. C. Ritchie (Eds.), *Handbook of language acquisition.* New York: Academic Press.

Bloom, P., Peterson, M., & Nadel, L. (1995). *Language and space.* Cambridge, MA: MIT Press.

Blumenthal, A. L. (1970). *Language and psychology: Historical aspects of psycholinguistics.* New York: Wiley.

Blumenthal, A. L. (1975). A reappraisal of Wilhelm Wundt. *American Psychologist, 30,* 1081–1088.

Boring, E. G. (1957). *A history of experimental psychology* (2nd ed.). New York: Appleton-Century-Crofts.

Boswell, J. (1848). In Rt. Hon. John Wilson Croker (Ed.), *Life of Johnson: Including the tour to the Hebrides.* London: J. Murray.

Bowerman, M. (1989). Learning a semantic system: What role do cognitive predispositions play? In M. Rice & R. Schiefelbusch (Eds.), *The teachability of language.* Baltimore: Brookes.

Boyd, R. (1991). On the current status of scientific realism. In R. Boyd, P. Gaspar, & J. D. Trout (Eds.), *The philosophy of science* (pp. 195–222). Cambridge, MA: MIT Press.

Boyer, P. (1994). Cognitive constraints on cultural representations: Natural ontologies and religious ideas. In L. A. Hirschfeld & S. A. Gelman (Eds.), *Mapping the mind: Domain specificity in cognition and culture* (pp. 391–411). Cambridge, England: Cambridge University Press.

Broca, P. (1861). Remarques sur le siege de la faculte du langage articule, suive d'une observation d'aphemie. *Bulletin de la Societe de Anatomie de Paris, 330–357.*

Brooks, R. A. (1991). New approaches to robotics. *Science, 253*(5025), 1227–1232.

Brown, A. (1989). Analogical learning and transfer: What develops? In S. V. A. Ortony (Ed.), *Similarity and analogical reasoning* (pp. 369–412). Cambridge, England: Cambridge University Press.

Bruner, J. S. (1977). Early social interaction and language acquisition. In H. R. Schaffer (Ed.), *Studies in mother-infant interaction* (pp. 271–289). London: Academic Press.

Bruner, J. S. (1983). *Child's talk.* New York: Norton.

Bruner, J. S. (1991). *Acts of meaning.* Cambridge, MA: Harvard University Press.

Bryant, P. (1995). Children and arithmetic. *Journal of Child Psychology and Psychiatry and Allied Disciplines, 36,* 3–32.

Bullock, M. (1979). *Aspects of the young child's theory of causation.* Unpublished doctoral dissertation, University of Pennsylvania, Philadelphia.

Bullock, M., & Gelman, R. (1979). Preschool children's assumptions about cause and effect. *Child Development, 50,* 89–96.

Bullock, M., Gelman, R., & Baillargeon, R. (1982). The development of causal reasoning. In W. Friedman (Ed.), *The developmental psychology of time* (pp. 209–254). New York: Academic Press.

Caramazza, A. (1992). Is cognitive neuropsychology possible? *Journal of Cognitive Neuroscience, 4*(1), 80–95.

Carey, S. (1978). The child as a word learner. In M. Halle, J. Bresnan, & G. Miller (Eds.), *Linguistic theory and psychological reality.* Cambridge, MA: MIT Press.

Carey, S. (1985). *Conceptual change in childhood.* Cambridge, MA: MIT Press.

Carey, S. (1991). Knowledge acquisition: Enrichment or conceptual change? In S. C. R. Gelman (Ed.), *The epigenisis of mind: Essays on biology and cognition* (pp. 257–291). Hillsdale, NJ: Erlbaum.

Case, R. (1978). Intellectual development from birth to adulthood: A neo-Piagetian interpretation. In R. Siegler (Ed.), *Children's thinking: What develops?* (pp. 37–72). Hillsdale, NJ: Erlbaum.

Case, R., Okamoto, Y., Henderson, B., & McKeough, A. (1993). Individual variability and consistency in cognitive development: New evidence for the existence of central conceptual structures. In R. Case & W. Edelstein (Eds.), *The new structuralism in cognitive development. Theory and research on individual pathways* (Vol. 23, pp. 71–100). Basel: Karger.

Chapman, L. J., & Chapman, J. P. (1969). Illusory correlation as an obstacle to the use of valid psychodiagnostic signs. *Journal of Abnormal Psychology, 74,* 272–280.

Chater, N., & Heyes, C. (1994). Animal concepts: Content and discontent. *Mind and Language, 9,* 209–246.

Cheng, K. (1986). A purely geometric module in the rat's spatial representation. *Cognition, 23,* 149–178.

Cheng, P. (in press). From covariation to causation. *Psychological Review.*

Cheng, P. W., & Lien, Y. (1995). The role of coherence in differentiating genuine from spurious causes. In D. Sperber, D. Premack, & A. Premack (Eds.), *Causal cognition: A multidisciplinary debate* (pp. 463–490). Oxford, England: Oxford University Press.

Chi, M. T. H. (1992). Conceptual change within and across ontological categories: Examples from learning and discovery in science. In R. Giere (Ed.), *Cognitive models of science: Minnesota studies in the philosophy of science.* Minneapolis: University of Minnesota Press.

Chi, M. T. H., & Klahr, D. (1975). Span and rate of apprehension in children and adults. *Journal of Experimental Child Psychology, 19,* 434–439.

Chierchia, G., & McConnell-Ginet, S. (1990). *Meaning and grammar: An introduction to semantics.* Cambridge, MA: MIT Press.

Chomsky, N. (1957). *Syntactic structures.* The Hague: Mouton.

Chomsky, N. (1959). A review of B. F. Skinner's verbal behavior. *Language, 35,* 26–58.

Chomsky, N. (1965). *Aspects of the theory of syntax.* Cambridge, MA: MIT Press.

Chomsky, N. (1966). *Cartesian linguistics.* New York: Harper & Row.

Chomsky, N. (1973). Conditions on transformations. In S. Anderson & P. Kiparsky (Eds.), *Festschrift for Morris Halle.* New York: Holt, Rinehart and Winston.

Chomsky, N. (1980). *Rules and representations.* New York: Columbia University Press.

Chomsky, N. (1981). *Lectures on government and binding.* Dordrecht, The Netherlands: Foris.

Chomsky, N. (1986). *Knowledge of language.* New York: Fontana/Collins.

Clark, A. (1993). *Associative engines: Connectionism, concepts and representational change.* Cambridge, MA: MIT Press.

Clark, A. (1994). Representational trajectories in connectionist learning. *Mind and Machines, 4,* 317–332.

Clark, A., & Karmiloff-Smith, A. (1993). The cognizer's innards: A psychological and philosophical perspective on the development of thought. *Mind and Language, 9,* 487–519.

Clark, E. V. (1983). Meanings and concepts. In P. H. Mussen (Ed.), *Handbook of child psychology* (Vol. 3, pp. 787–840). New York: Wiley.

Clark, E. V. (1987). The principle of contrast: A constraint on language acquisition. In B. MacWhinney (Ed.), *Mechanisms of language acquisition* (pp. 1–33). Hillsdale, NJ: Erlbaum.

Clifton, C. J., & Odom, P. (1966). Similarity relations among certain English sentence constructions. *Psychological Monographs, 80,* 1–35.

Cohen, L. B. (1991). Infant attention: An information processing approach. In M. J. Weiss & P. R. Zalazo (Eds.), *Newborn attention: Biological constraints and the influence of experience* (pp. 1–21). Norwood, NJ: ABLEX.

Cohen, L. B., Diehl, R. L., Oakes, L. M., & Loehlin, J. C. (1992). Infant perception of /aba/ versus /apa/: Building a quantitative model of infant categorical discrimination. *Developmental Psychology, 28,* 261–272.

Cohen, L. B., & Oakes, L. M. (1993). How infants perceive a simple causal event. *Developmental Psychology, 29,* 421–433.

Cole, M., & Means, B. (1981). *Comparative studies of how people think.* Cambridge, MA: Harvard University Press.

Cosmides, L., & Tooby, J. (1987). From evolution to behavior: Evolutionary psychology as the missing link. In J. Dupre (Ed.), *The latest on the best* (pp. 277–306). Cambridge, MA: MIT Press.

Cosmides, L., & Tooby, J. (1994). The evolution of Domain specificity: The evolution of functional organization. In L. A. Hirschfeld & S. A. Gelman (Eds.), *Mapping the mind:*

Domain specificity in cognition and culture (pp. 85–116). Cambridge, England: Cambridge University Press.

Cosmides, L., & Tooby, J. (1996). Are humans good intuitive statisticians after all? Rethinking some conclusions from the literature on judgement under uncertainty, *Cognition, 58*(1), 1–73.

Crimmins, M. (1992). *Talk about beliefs.* Cambridge, MA: MIT Press.

Cummins, R. (1996). *Representations, targets, and attitudes.* Cambridge, MA: MIT Press.

Damasio, A. R. (1990). Category-related recognition defects as a clue to the neural substrates of knowledge. *Trends in Neurosciences, 13*(3), 95–98.

Darwin, C. R. (1877). A biographical sketch of an infant. *Mind, 2,* 286–294.

Darwin, C. R. (1975). *The expression of the emotions in man and animals.* Chicago: University of Chicago Press. (Original work published 1872)

DeLoache, J. (1987). Rapid change in the symbolic ability of very young children. *Science, 238,* 1556–1557.

DeLoache, J. (1989). Young children's understanding of the correspondence between a scale model and a larger space. *Cognitive Development, 4,* 121–139.

DeLoache, J. S., & Burns, N. M. (1994). Early understanding of the representational function of pictures. *Cognition, 52*(2), 83–110.

Descartes, R. (1977). *Rene Descartes: The essential writings.* New York: Harper & Row.

Dromi, E. (1987). *Early lexical development.* Cambridge, England: Cambridge University Press.

Dunn, J., & Brown, J. (1993). Early conversations about causality: Content, pragmatics, and developmental change. *British Journal of Developmental Psychology, 11,* 107–123.

Dupré, J. (1981). Biological taxa as natural kinds. *Philosophical Review, 90,* 66–90.

Dutton, B. (1978). *Dutton's navigation and piloting.* Annapolis, MD: Naval Institution Press.

Ebbinghaus, H. (1964). *Memory: A contribution to experimental psychology.* New York: Dover. (Original work published 1885)

Elman, G. (1989). (CRL Tech. Rep. No. 8901). San Diego: University of California.

Elman, G. (1990). Finding structure in time. *Cognitive Science, 14,* 179–211.

Elman, J. L. (1993). Learning and development in neural networks: The importance of starting small. *Cognition, 48,* 71–99.

Elman, J. L., Bates, E. A., Johnson, M. H., Karmiloff-Smith, A., Parisi, D., & Plunkett, K. (1996). *Rethinking innateness.* Cambridge, MA: MIT Press.

Fallon, A. E., Rozin, P., & Pliner, P. (1984). The child's conception of food: The development of food rejections with special reference to disgust and contamination sensitivity. *Child Development, 55*(2), 566–575.

Farah, M. J. (1994). Neuropsychological inference with an interactive brain: A critique of the locality assumption. *Behavioral and Brain Sciences, 17,* 43–104.

Farah, M. J., Hammond, K. M., Mehta, Z., & Ratcliff, G. (1989). Category-specificity and modality-specificity in semantic memory. *Neuropsychologia, 27*(2), 193–200.

Feldman, H., Goldin-Meadow, S., & Gleitman, L. (1978). Beyond Herodtous: The creation of language by linguistically deprived deaf children. In A. Lock (Ed.), *Action, gesture, and symbol: The emergence of language* (pp. 351–414). London: Academic Press.

Fivush, R. (in press). Event memory in early childhood. In N. Cowan (Ed.), *The development of memory.* London: University College London Press.

Flanagan, O. J., Jr. (1984). *The science of mind.* Cambridge, MA: MIT Press.

Flavell, J. (1963). *The developmental psychology of Jean Piaget.* Princeton, NJ: Van Nostrand.

Fodor, J. A. (1975). *The language of thought.* New York: Crowell.

Fodor, J. A. (1981). *The current status of the innateness controversy representations: Philosophical essays on the foundations of cognitive science.* Cambridge, MA: MIT Press.

Fodor, J. A. (1983). *Modularity of mind.* Cambridge, MA: MIT Press.

Fodor, J. A. (1994). Concepts: A potboiler. *Cognition, 50,* 95–113.

Fodor, J. A., Bever, T. G., & Garrett, M. F. (1974). *The psychology of language: An introduction to psycholinguistics and generative grammar.* New York: McGraw-Hill.

Forbus, K. D. (1985). Qualitative process theory. In D. G. Bobrow (Ed.), *Qualitative reasoning about physical systems* (pp. 85–168). Cambridge, MA: MIT Press.

Freud, A. (1946). *The ego and the mechanisms of defense.* New York: International Universities Press.

Freud, S. (1965). *The interpretation of dreams* (J. Strachey, Trans.). New York: Avon Books.

Freud, S. (1966). *New Introductory lectures on psychoanalysis* (J. Strachey, Trans.). New York: Norton.

Freud, S. (1976). Three essays on the theory of sexuality. In J. Strachey (Ed.), *The complete psychological works* (Vol. 7). New York: Norton. (Original work published 1905)

Funnell, E., & Sheridan, J. (1992). Categories of knowledge? Unfamiliar aspects of living and nonliving things. *Cognitive Neuropsychology, 9*(2), 135–153.

Gaba, D. M., Howard, S. K., & Small, S. D. (1995). Situation awareness in anesthesiology. Situation awareness [Special issue]. *Human Factors, 37,* 20–31.

Gallistel, C. R. (1989). *The organization of learning.* Cambridge, MA: MIT Press.

Gallistel, C. R., & Gelman, R. (1992). Preverbal and verbal counting and computation. *Cognition, 44,* 43–74.

Galton, R. (1883). *Inquiries into human faculty and its development.* London: Macmillan.

Gelman, R. (1978). Cognitive development. *Annual Review of Psychology, 29,* 297–332.

Gelman, R. (in press). Domain specificity in cognitive development: Universals and non-universals. *International Journal of Psychology.*

Gelman, R., & Baillargeon, R. (1983). A review of some Piagetian concepts. In J. H. Flavell & E. M. Markman (Eds.), *Handbook of child psychology* (Vol. 3, pp. 167–230). New York: Wiley.

Gelman, R., & Gallistel, C. R. (1979). *The child's understanding of number.* Cambridge, MA: Harvard University Press.

Gelman, S. A. (1988). The development of induction within natural kind and artifact categories. *Cognitive Psychology, 20*(1), 65–95.

Gelman, S. A., Colely, J. D., & Gottfried, G. M. (1994). Essentialist beliefs in children: The acquisition of concepts and theories. In L. A. Hirschfeld & S. A. Gelman (Eds.), *Mapping the mind: Domain specificity in cognition and culture* (pp. 341–365). Cambridge, England: Cambridge University Press.

Gelman, S. A., & Medin, D. L. (1993). What's so essential about essentialism? A different perspective on the interaction of perception, language, and conceptual knowledge. *Cognitive Development, 8,* 157–167.

Gelman, S. A., & O'Reilly, A. W. (1988). Children's inductive inferences within superordinate categories: The role of language and category structure. *Child Development, 59,* 876–887.

Gelman, S. A., & Wellman, H. M. (1991). Insides and essences: Early understandings of the non-obvious. *Cognition, 38,* 213–244.

Gentner, D. (1983). Structure-mapping: A theoretical framework for analogy. *Cognitive Science, 7,* 155–170.

Gentner, D., & Toupin, C. (1988). Systematicity and surface similarity in the development of analogy. *Cognitive Science, 10,* 277–300.

Geschwind, N. (1965). Disconnexion syndromes in animals and man. *Brain, 88,* 237–294, 585–644.

Gibson, E. J. (1969). *Principles of perpetual and cognitive development.* New York: Appleton-Century-Crofts.

Gibson, E. J. (1991). *An odyssey in learning and perception.* Cambridge, MA: MIT Press.

Gibson, E. J., & Levin, H. (1975). *The psychology of reading.* Cambridge, MA: MIT Press.

Gibson, E. J., Owsley, C. J., & Johnston, J. (1978). Perception of invariants by five-month-old infants: Differentiation of two types of motion. *Developmental Psychology, 14,* 407–415.

Gibson, E. J., & Spelke, E. S. (1983). The development of perception. In J. H. Flavell & E. M. Markman (Eds.), *Handbook of child psychology: Vol. 3. Cognitive development* (4th ed., pp. 1–76). New York: Wiley.

Gibson, E. J., & Walk, R. D. (1960). The "visual cliff." *Scientific American, 202,* 64–71.

Gibson, J. J. (1950). *The perception of the visual world.* Boston: Houghton Mifflin.

Gibson, J. J. (1955). The optical expansion-pattern in aerial locomotion. *American Journal of Psychology, 68,* 480–484.

Gibson, J. J. (1961). Ecological optics. *Vision Research, 1,* 253–262.

Gibson, J. J. (1966). *The senses considered as perceptual systems.* Boston: Houghton Mifflin.

Gibson, J. J. (1972). A theory of direct visual perception. In J. Royce & W. Rozenboom (Eds.), *Psychology of knowing* (pp. 215–240). New York: Gordon and Breach.

Gibson, J. J. (1973). On the concept of "formless invariants" in visual perception. *Leonardo, 6,* 43–45.

Gibson, J. J. (1977). The theory of affordances. In R. E. Shaw & J. Bransford (Eds.), *Perceiving, acting, and knowing* (pp. 67–82). Hillsdale, NJ: Erlbaum.

Gibson, J. J. (1979). *The ecological approach to visual perception.* Boston: Houghton Mifflin.

Gigerenzer, G., & Hoffrage, U. (1995). How to improve Bayesian reasoning without instruction: Frequency formats. *Psychological Review, 102,* 684–704.

Gigerenzer, G., & Hug, K. (1992). Domain-specific reasoning: Social contracts, cheating, and perspective change. *Cognition, 43,* 127–171.

Gigerenzer, G., Swijtink, Z., Porter, T., Daston, L., Beatty, J., & Krüger, L. (1989). *The empire of chance: How probability changed science and everyday life.* Cambridge, England: Cambridge University Press.

Gilden, D. L. (1991). On the origins of dynamical awareness. *Psychological Review, 98*(4), 554–568.

Gladwin, T. (1970). *East is a big bird.* Cambridge, MA: Harvard University Press.

Gleitman, L. R., & Warner, E. (1982). Language acquisition: The state of the state of the art. In E. Wanner & L. R. Gleitman (Eds.), *Language acquisition: The state of the art.* New York: Cambridge University Press.

Glymour, C. (1987). *Discovering causal structure: Artificial intelligence, philosophy of science, and statistical modeling.* Orlando, FL: Academic Press.

Glymour, C. (in press). Learning causes. *Minds and Machines.*

Goel, A. (in press). Creative conceptual change. *Journal of the Learning Sciences.*

Goldstein, K. (1948). *Language and language disturbances.* New York: Grune and Stratton.

Goodale, M. A., & Milner, A. D. (1992). Separate visual pathways for perception and action. *Trends in Neurosciences, 15,* 20–24.

Goodman, N. (1955). *Fact, fiction and forecast.* Indianapolis, IN: Bobbs-Merrill.

Gopnik, A., & Meltzoff, A. N. (1997). *Words, thoughts, and theories.* Cambridge, MA: MIT Press.

Gopnik, A., & Wellman, H. M. (1994). The theory theory. In L. A. Hirschfeld & S. A. Gelman (Eds.), *Mapping the mind: Domain specificity in cognition and culture* (pp. 257–293). Cambridge, England: Cambridge University Press.

Goswami, U. (1996). *Analogical reasoning and cognitive development. Advances in Child Development and Behavior* (Vol. 26, pp. 91–138). San Diego, CA: Academic Press.

Goswami, U. B., & Brown, A. (1989). Melting chocolate and melting snowmen: Analogical reasoning and causal relations. *Cognition, 35,* 69–95.

Gould, S. J. (1983). *Hen's teeth and horse's toes: Further reflections in natural history.* New York: Norton.

Gould, S. J., & Lewontin, R. C. (1978). The spandrels of San Marco and the Panglossian paradigm. *Proceedings of the Royal Society, London, 205,* 581–598.

Greeno, J. G., Riley, M. S., & Gelman, R. (1984). Conceptual competence and children's counting. *Cognitive Psychology, 16*(1), 94–143.

Grimshaw, J. (1981). Form, function, and the language acquisition device. In C. L. McCarthy (Ed.), *The logical problem of language acquisition.* Cambridge, MA: MIT Press.

Gruber, H. E. (1981). *Darwin on man.* Chicago: University of Chicago Press.

Gutheil, G., & Rosengren, K. S. (in press). A rose by any other name: Preschoolers' understanding of individual identity across name and appearance changes. *British Journal of Developmental Psychology.*

Gutheil, G., Spelke, E. S., & Hayes, A. F. (in preparation). *Revisiting the ship of Theseus: Common sense understanding of object identity.* Manuscript submitted.

Hale, K. (1971). A note on the Walbiri tradition of antonymy. In D. D. Steinberg & L. A. Jakobovits (Eds.), *Semantics: An interdisciplinary reader in philosophy, linguistics, and psychology* (pp. 472–482). Cambridge, England: Cambridge University Press.

Halford, G. S. (1980). Toward a redefinition of cognitive developmental stages. In J. Kirby & J. B. Biggs (Eds.), *Cognition, development and instruction* (pp. 39–64). New York: Academic Press.

Halford, G. S. (1992). Analogical reasoning and conceptual complexity in cognitive development. *Human Development, 35,* 193–217.

Halford, G. S. (1993, March). *Experience and processing capacity in cognitive development: A PDP approach.* Paper presented at the meeting of the Society for Research in Child Development, New Orleans, LA.

Halford, G. S. (1995). Learning processes in cognitive development: A reassessment with some unexpected implications. Development and learning: Reconceptualizing the intersection [Special issue]. *Human Development, 38,* 295–301.

Hall, D. G. (1991). Acquiring proper names for familiar and unfamiliar objects: Two-year-olds word learning biases. *Child Development, 62,* 873–878.

Hall, D. G. (1996). Preschoolers' default assumptions about word meaning: Proper names designate unique individuals. *Developmental Psychology, 32*(1), 177–186.

Hampton, J. A. (1976). *An experimental study of concepts in language.* Unpublished doctoral dissertation, University of London.

Hampton, J. A. (1995). Testing the prototype theory of concepts. *Journal of Memory and Language, 34,* 686–708.

Happe, F. (1995). *Autism: An introduction to psychological theory.* Cambridge, MA: Harvard University Press.

Harre, R., & Madden, E. H. (1975). *Causal powers: A theory of natural necessity.* Totowa, NJ: Rowman & Littlefield.

Harris, Z. (Ed.). (1981). *Papers on syntax.* Dordrecht, The Netherlands: Reidel.

Hatano, G., & Inagaki, K. (1996). Cognitive and cultural factors in the acquisition of intuitive biology. In D. R. Olson & N. Torrance (Eds.), *Handbook of education and human development: New models of learning, teaching, and schooling.* Cambridge, England: Blackwell.

Hatano, G., Siegler, R. S., Inagaki, K., Stavy, R., & Wax, N. (1993). The development of biological knowledge: A multinational study. *Cognitive Development, 8,* 47–62.

Hatfield, G. (1990). *The natural and the normative: Theories of spatial perception from Kant to Helmholtz.* Cambridge, MA: MIT Press.

Hauser, M. D., MacNeilage, P., & Ware, M. (1996). Numerical representations in primates. *Proceedings of the National Academy of Sciences, 93,* 1514–1517.

Heider, E. R., & Olivier, D. C. (1972). The structure of color space in naming and memory for two languages. *Cognitive Psychology, 3,* 337–354.

Helmholtz, H. V. (1925). *Treatise on psysiological optics* (J. P. C. Southall, Trans.) (Vol. 3, pp. 1–36). Rochester, NY: The Optical Society of America.

Hermer, L., & Spelke, E. S. (1994). A geometric process for spatial reorientation in young children. *Nature, 370,* 57–59.

Hermer, L., & Spelke, E. S. (1996). Modularity and development: The case of spatial reorientation. *Cognition, 61*(3), 195–232.

Herrnstein, R. (1990). Levels of stimulus control: A functional approach. *Cognition, 37,* 133–166.

Hinton, G. E. (1989). Connectionist learning procedures. *Artificial Intelligence, 40,* 185–234.

Hirsch, E. (1982). *The concept of identity.* New York: Oxford University Press.

Holden, K., Peel, D. A., & Thompson, J. L. (1990). *Economic forecasting: An introduction.* Cambridge, England: Cambridge University Press.

Holyoak, K. J., & Thagard, P. (1995). *Mental leaps: Analogy in creative thought.* Cambridge, MA: MIT Press.

Huang, I. (1943). Child's conception of physical causality: A critical summary. *Journal of Genetic Psychology, 63,* 71–121.

Hull, D. (1965). The effect of essentialism on taxonomy: 2000 years of stasis. *British Journal for the Philosophy of Science, 15,* 314–326.

Hull, D. L. (1974). *Philosophy of biological science.* Englewood Cliffs, NJ: Prentice-Hall.

Hume, D. (1951). *Theory of knowledge. Containing the enquiry concerning understanding, the abstract and selected passages from book I of a treatise on human nature.* New York: Nelson.

Huttenlocher, D. P., & Rucklidge, W. J. (1992). *A multi-resolution technique for comparing images using the Hausdorff distance* (Tech. Rep. 92-1321). Ithaca, NY: Cornell University, Computer Science.

Inagaki, K. (1990). Young children's use of knowledge in everyday biology. *British Journal of Developmental Psychology, 8,* 281–288.

Inagaki, K., & Hatano, G. (1993). Young children's understanding of the mind-body distinction. *Child Development, 64,* 1534–1549.

Inhelder, B., & Piaget, J. (1964). *The early growth of logic in the child.* New York: Norton.

Irwin, D. E. (1991). Information integration across saccadic eye movements. *Cognitive Psychology, 23,* 420–456.

Jakobson, R. (1968). *Child language, aphasia and phonological universals.* New York: Humanities Press. (Original work published 1941)

James, W. (1950). *The principles of psychology* (Vol. 1). New York: Dover. (Original work published 1891)

Kahneman, D., Slovic, P., & Tversky, A. (1982). *Judgement under uncertainty: Heuristics and biases.* New York: Cambridge University Press.

Kapur, S. (1992). *Computational learning of languages.* Doctoral dissertation, Cornell University, Ithaca, NY.

Kapur, S. (1994). Some applications of formal learning theory results to natural language acquisition. In B. Lust, M. Suner, & H. Whitman (Eds.), *Syntactic theory and first language acquisition: Cross-linguistic perspectives* (Vol. 2, pp. 491–508). Hillsdale, NJ: Erlbaum.

Karmiloff-Smith, A. (1992). *Beyond modularity: A developmental perspective on cognitive science.* Cambridge, MA: MIT Press.

Karmiloff-Smith, A., Grant, J., & Berthoud, I. (1993, March). *Within-domain dissociations in Williams syndrome: A window on the normal mind.* Paper presented at the meeting of the Society for Research in Child Development, New Orleans, LA.

Keil, F. C. (1979). *Semantic and conceptual development: An ontological perspective.* Cambridge, MA: Harvard University Press.

Keil, F. C. (1981). Constraints on knowledge and cognitive development. *Psychological Review, 88,* 197–227.

Keil, F. C. (1987). Conceptual development and category structure. In U. Neisser (Ed.), *Concepts and conceptual development: Ecological and intellectual factors in categorization.* Cambridge, England: Cambridge University Press.

Keil, F. C. (1989). *Concepts, kinds and cognitive development.* Cambridge, MA: Bradford Books/MIT Press.

Keil, F. C. (1992). The origins of an autonomous biology. In M. R. Gunnar & M. Maratsos (Eds.), *Modularity and constraints in language and cognition: Minnesota Symposium on Child Psychology* (Vol. 25, pp. 103–138). Hillsdale, NJ: Erlbaum.

Keil, F. C. (1995). The growth of causal understandings of natural kinds. In D. Sperber, D. Premack, & A. Premack (Eds.), *Causal cognition: A multidisciplinary debate* (pp. 235–262). Oxford, England: Oxford University Press.

Keil, F. C., & Batterman, N. (1984). A characteristic-to-defining shift in the development of word meaning. *Journal of Verbal Learning and Verbal Behavior, 23,* 221–236.

Keil, F. C., Levin, D. T., Richman, B. A., & Gutheil, G. (in press). Mechanism and explanation in the development of biological thought: The case of disease. In D. Medin & S. Atran (Eds.), *Folkbiology.* Cambridge, MA: MIT Press.

Keil, F. C., Smith, C., Simons, D., & Levin, D. (in press). Two dogmas of conceptual empiricism. *Cognition.*

Kemler, D. G., & Smith, L. B. (1978). Is there a developmental trend from integrality to separability in perception? *Journal of Experimental Child Psychology, 26,* 498–507.

Kemler-Nelson, D. K. (1995). Principle-based inferences in young children's categorization: Revisiting the impact of function on the naming of artifacts. *Cognitive Development, 10,* 347–380.

Kirsh, D. (1992). PDP learnability and innate knowledge of language. In S. Davis (Ed.), *Connectionism: Theory and practice.* Oxford, England: Oxford University Press.

Kitcher, P. (1992). *Freud's dream.* Cambridge, MA: Bradford Books/MIT Press.

Kitcher, P. (1993). *The advancement of science: Science without legend, objectivity without illusions.* New York: Oxford University Press.

Klahr, D. (1992). Information-processing approaches to cognitive development. In M. H. Bornstein & M. E. Lamb (Eds.), *Developmental psychology: An advanced textbook* (2nd ed.). Hillsdale, NJ: Erlbaum.

Kline, M, (1972). *Mathematical thought from ancient to modern times.* New York: Oxford University Press.

Koenig, O., Reiss, L. P., & Kosslyn, S. M. (1990). The development of spatial relation representations: Evidence from studies of cerebral lateralization. *Journal of Experimental Child Psychology, 50,* 119–130.

Kripke, S. (1972). Naming and necessity. In D. Davidson & G. Harman (Eds.), *Semantics of natural language.* Dordrecht, The Netherlands: Reidel.

Kuhn, D., Schauble, L., & Garcia-Mila, M. (1992). Cross-domain development of scientific reasoning. *Cognition and Instruction, 9*(4), 285–327.

Kuhn, T. S. (1970). *The structure of scientific revolutions.* Chicago: University of Chicago Press.

Kuhn, T. S. (1982). Commensurability, comparability, and communicability. *PSA, 2.*

Lakoff, G. (1973). Hedges: A study in meaning criteria and the logic of fuzzy concepts. *Journal of Philosophical Logic, 2,* 458–508.

Lakoff, G. (1987). *Women, fire, and dangerous things: What categories reveal about the mind.* Chicago: University of Chicago Press.

Langley, P., Simon, H. A., Bradshaw, G. L., & Zytkow, J. M. (1987). *Scientific discovery.* Cambridge, MA: MIT Press.

Laurendeau, M., & Pinard, A. (1962). *Causal thinking in the child: A genetic and experimental approach.* New York: International Universities Press.

Lehrman, D. (1953). A critique of Konrad Lorenz's theory of instinctive behavior. *Quarterly Review of Biology, 28,* 337–363.

Leibniz, W. G. (1896). *New essays concerning human understanding* (A. G. Langley, Trans.). New York: Macmillan.

Lerner, R. M. (1984). *On the nature of human plasticity.* New York: Cambridge University Press.

Lerner, R. M. (1986). *Concepts and theories of human development* (2nd ed.). New York: Random House.

Leslie, A. M. (1982). The perception of causality in infants. *Perception, 11,* 173–186.

Leslie, A. M. (1993). A theory of agency. In D. Sperber, D. Premack, & A. Premack (Eds.), *Causal cognition: A multi-disciplinary debate* (pp. 121–141). Oxford, England: Oxford University Press.

Leslie, A. M. (1995). A theory of agency. In A. M. Leslie (Ed.), *Causal cognition: A multi-disciplinary debate* (pp. 121–141). New York: Oxford University Press.

Leslie, A. M., & Keeble, S. (1987). Do six-month-olds perceive causality? *Cognition, 25,* 265–288.

Leslie, A. M., & Thaiss, L. (1992). Domain specificity in conceptual development: Neuropsychological evidence from autism. *Cognition, 9,* 397–424.

Levinson, S. C. (1994). Vision, shape, and linguistic description: Tzeltal body-part terminology and object description. Spatial conceptualization in Mayan languages [Special issue]. *32*(4/5), 791–855.

Levinson, S. C. (1995). Frames of reference and Molyneux's question: Cross-linguistic evidence. In P. Bloom, M. Peterson, L. Nadel, & M. Garrett (Eds.), *Language and space.* Cambridge, MA: MIT Press.

Levy, E., & Nelson, K. (1994). Words in discourse: A dialectical approach to the acquisition of meaning and use. *Journal of Child Language, 21,* 367–389.

Locke, J. (1964). In A. D. Woozley (Ed.), *An essay concerning human understanding.* New York: Meridian. (Original work published 1690)

Lorenz, K. (1966). *On aggression.* London: Methuen.

Luria, A. R. (1966). *Higher cortical functions in man.* New York: Basic Books.

Luria, A. R. (1987). Vygotsky. In R. Gregory (Ed.), *Oxford companion to the mind* (pp. 805–806). Oxford, England: Oxford University Press.

Lust, B., Suner, M., & Whitman, J. (Ed.). (1994). *Syntactic theory and first language acquisition: Cross-linguistic perspectives.* Hillsdale, NJ: Erlbaum.

Lyons, J. (1977). *Semantics* (Vols. 1 & 2). Cambridge, England: Cambridge University Press.

MacWhinney, B. (Ed.). (1987). *Mechanisms of language acquisition.* Hillsdale, NJ: Erlbaum.

Maffi, L. (in press). *"The Blisters": Smallpox and an early case of Mayan self-help.* Paper presented at the proceedings of the 4th International Congress of Ethnobiology, Lucknow, India.

Malt, B. C., & Johnson, E. C. (1992). Do artifact concepts have cores? *Journal of Memory and Language, 31,* 195–217.

Mandler, J. M. (1988). The development of spatial cognition on topological and Euclidean representation. In J. S. Davis, M. Kritchevsky, & U. Bellugi (Eds.), *Spatial cognition: Brain bases and development* (pp. 423–432). Hillsdale, NJ: Erlbaum.

Mandler, J. M. (1992). How to build a baby: II. Conceptual primitives. *Psychological Review, 99,* 587–604.

Mandler, J. M. (1995). The death of developmental psychology. In R. L. Solso & D. W. Massaro (Eds.), *The science of the mind: 2001 and beyond* (pp. 70–89). Oxford, England: Oxford University Press.

Mandler, J. M. (in press). Perceptual and conceptual processes in infancy. *Cognition.*

Mandler, J. M., & Bauer, P. J. (1988). The cradle of categorization: Is the basic level basic? *Cognitive Development, 3,* 247–264.

Mandler, J. M., Bauer, P. J., & McDonough, L. (1991). Separating the sheep from the goats: Differentiating global categories. *Cognitive Psychology, 23,* 263–298.

Mandler, J. M., & McDonough, L. (1993). Concept formation in infancy. *Cognitive Development, 8,* 291–318.

Markman, E. (1989). *Categorization and naming in children: Problems of induction.* Cambridge, MA: Bradford Books/MIT Press.

Mauri, A., Daum, I., Sartori, G., & Riesch, G. (1994). Category-specific semantic impairment in Alzheimer's disease and temporal lobe dysfunction: A comparative study. *Journal of Clinical and Experimental Neuropsychology, 16,* 689–701.

Mayr, E. (1982). *The growth of biological thought.* Cambridge, MA: Harvard University Press.

Mayr, E. (1988). *Toward a new philosophy of biology: Observations of an evolutionist.* Cambridge, MA: Harvard University Press.

McClelland, J. L., McNaughton, B. L., & O'Reilly, R. C. (1995). Why there are complementary learning systems in the hippocampus and neocortex: Insights from the successes and failures of connectionist models of learning and memory. *Psychological Review, 102*(3), 419–437.

McClelland, J. L., Rumelhart, D. E., & The PDP Research Group. (Eds.). (1986). *Parallel distributed processing: Explorations in the microstructure of cognition: Vol. 1. Foundations.* Cambridge, MA: Bradford Books/MIT Press.

McCloskey, M. (1983). Naive theories of motion. In D. Gentner & A. L. Stevens (Eds.), *Mental models* (pp. 299–324). Hillsdale, NJ: Erlbaum.

McCloskey, M. (1994). Architecture of cognitive numerical processing mechanisms: Contrasting perspectives on theory development and evaluation. The neuropsychology of cognitive arithmetic [Special issue]. *Current Psychology of Cognition, 13*(3), 275–295.

McCulloch, W. (1965). *Embodiments of mind.* Cambridge, MA: MIT Press.

McNaughton, B. L., Knierim, J. J., & Wilson, M. A. (1995). Vector encoding and the vestibular foundations of spatial cognition: Neurophysiological and computational mechanisms. In M. S. Gazzaniga (Ed.), *The cognitive neurosciences.* Cambridge, MA: Bradford Books/MIT Press.

Mead, M. (1932). An investigation of the thought of primitive children with special reference to animism. *Journal of the Royal Anthropological Institute, 62,* 173–190.

Meck, W. H., & Church, R. M. (1983). A mode control model of counting and timing processes. *Journal of Experimental Psychology: Animal Behavior Process, 9,* 320–334.

Medin, D. L., & Ortony, A. (1988). Psychological essentialism. In S. Vosniadou & A. Ortony (Eds.), *Similarity and analogical reasoning* (pp. 179–196). New York: Cambridge University Press.

Michotte, A. (1963). *The perception of causality* (T. R. Miles & E. Miles, Trans.). London: Methuen.

Miller, G. A., & Isard, S. (1963). Some perceptual consequences of linguistic rules. *Journal of Verbal Learning and Verbal Behavior, 2,* 217–228.

Miller, G. A., & McKean, K. O. (1964). A chronometric study of some relations between sentences. *Quarterly Journal of Experimental Psychology, 16,* 297–308.

Millikan, R. G. (in press). A common structure for concepts of individuals, stuffs, and real kinds: More mama, more milk and more mouse. *Behavioral and Brain Sciences.*

Mishkin, M., Ungerleider, L. G., & Macko, K. A. (1983). Object vision and spatial vision: Two cortical pathways. *Trends in Neuroscience, 6,* 414–417.

Morris, R. G. M. (1981). Spatial localization does not require the presence of local cues. *Learning and Motivation, 12,* 239–260.

Moscovitch, M., Kapur, S., Köhler, S., & Houle, S. (1995). Distinct neural correlates of visual long-term memory for spatial location and object identity: A positron emission tomography study in humans. *Proceedings of the National Academy of Science, 92,* 3721–3725.

Munakata, Y., McClelland, J. L., Johnson, M. H., & Siegler, R. S. (in press). Rethinking infant knowledge: Toward an adaptive process account of successes and failures in object permanence. *Psychological Review.*

Murphy, G. L., & Medin, D. (1985). The role of theories in conceptual coherence. *Psychological Review, 92,* 289–316.

Neisser, U. (1963). The multiplicity of thought. *British Journal of Psychology, 54,* 1–14.

Neisser, U. (1966). Computers as tools and as metaphors. In C. R. Dechert (Ed.), *The social impact of cybernetics* (pp. 71–94). Notre Dame, IN: University of Notre Dame Press.

Neisser, U. (1976). *Cognition and reality.* San Francisco: Freeman.

Nelson, K. (1985). *Making sense: The acquisition of shared meaning.* Orlando, FL: Academic Press.

Neressian, N. J. (1992). How do scientists think? Capturing the dynamics of conceptual change in science. In R. D. Giere (Ed.), *Cognitive models of science. Minnesota studies in the philosophy of science* (Vol. 15, pp. 344–372). Minneapolis: University of Minnesota Press.

Neville, H. (in press). Neural systems mediating american sign language: Effects of sensory experience and age of acquisition. *Brain and Language.*

Neville, H. (1994–1995). *Biological constraints and effects of experience on cerebral organization for language.* Paper presented at the meetings of the Neuroscience Society and Human Brain Mapping.

Neville, H. J., Coffey, S. A., Holcomb, P. J., & Tallal, P. (1993). The neurobiology of sensory and language processing in language-impaired children. *Journal of Cognitive Neuroscience, 5,* 235–253.

Newell, A. (1972). A note on process/structure distinctions in developmental psychology. In S. Farnham-Diggory (Ed.), *Information processing in children*. New York: Academic Press.

Nickerson, R. S. (1965). Short-term memory for complex meaningful visual configurations: A demonstration of capacity. *Canadian Journal of Psychology, 19*(2), 155–160.

O'Keefe, J. O., & Nadel, L. (1978). *The hippocampus as a cognitive map*. Oxford, England: Oxford University Press.

Osherson, D. N. (1975). *Logical abilities in children: Vol. 30. Reasoning in adolescence: Deductive inference*. Hillsdale, NJ: Erlbaum.

Osherson, D. N., Stob, M., & Weinstein, S. (1985). *Systems that learn*. Cambridge, MA: MIT Press.

Papert, S. (1993). *Mindstorms: Children, computers, and powerful ideas*. New York: Basic Books.

Parsons, C. (1960). Inhelder and Piaget's the growth of logical thinking. *British Journal of Psychology, 51*, 75–84.

Peirce, C. S. (1931–1935). *Collected papers of Charles Sanders Pierce*. Cambridge, MA: Harvard University Press.

Peirce, C. S. (1960–1966). *Collected papers*. Cambridge: Belknap Press/Harvard University Press.

Peterson, S. E. (1993). The processing of single words studied with positron emission tomography. *Annual Review of Neuroscience, 16*, 509–530.

Piaget, J. (1929). *The child's conception of the world*. London: Routledge & Kegan Paul.

Piaget, J. (1930). *The child's conception of physical causality*. London: Routledge & Kegan Paul.

Piaget, J. (1952). *The origins of intelligence in children*. New York: Norton.

Piaget, J. (1954). *The construction of reality in the child*. New York: Basic Books.

Piaget, J. (1974). *Understanding causality*. New York: Norton.

Piaget, J., & Inhelder, B. (1956). *The child's conception of space*. New York: Norton.

Piatelli-Palmarini, M. (1994). Ever since language and learning: Afterthoughts on the Piaget-Chomsky debate. *Cognition, 50*, 315–346.

Pick, H. L. J. (1983). Comparative and developmental approaches to spatial cognition. In H. Pick & L. Acredolo (Eds.), *Spatial orientation: Theory, research, and application* (pp. 73–76). New York: Plenum Press.

Pinker, S. (1994). *The language instinct*. New York: Morrow.

Pinker, S., & Prince, A. (1988). On language and connectionism: Analysis of a parallel distributed processing model of language acquisition. *Cognition, 28*, 73–193.

Plunkett, K., & Marchman, V. A. (1993). From rote learning to system building: Acquiring verb morphology in children and connectionist nets. *Cognition, 48* 21–69.

Prince, A., & Smolensky, P. (1997). Optimality: From neural networks to universal grammar. *Science, 275*, 1604–1610.

Proffitt, D. R., & Gilden, D. L. (1989). Understanding natural dynamics. *Journal of Experimental Psychology: Human Perception and Performance, 15*(2), 384–393.

Putnam, H. (1975). The meaning of meaning. In H. Putnam (Ed.), *Mind, language and reality* (Vol. 2). Cambridge, England: Cambridge University Press.

Quine, W. V. O. (1960). *Word and object*. Cambridge, MA: MIT Press.

Ram, A. (1996). [Special issue]. *Journal of the Learning Sciences*.

Ramsey, W. (1992). Connectionism and the philosophy of mental representation. In S. Davis (Ed.), *Connectionism: Theory and practice* (pp. 247–276). Oxford, England: Oxford University Press.

Reinhardt, T. (1986). Center and periphery in the grammar of anaphora. In B. Lust (Ed.), *Studies in the acquisition of anaphora* (pp. 123–150). Dordrecht, The Netherlands: Reidel.

Rey, G. (1983). Concepts and stereotypes. *Cognition, 15*, 237–262.

Rochat, P. (1989). Object manipulation and exploration in 2- to 5-month-old infants. *Developmental Psychology, 25*, 871–884.

Rommetveit, R. (1974). *On message structure: A framework for the study of language and communication*. London & New York: Wiley.

Rosch, E. (1978). Principles of categorization. In E. Rosch & B. B. Lloyd (Eds.), *Cognition and categorization* (pp. 27–48). Hillsdale, NJ: Erlbaum.

Rosch, E., & Mervis, C. B. (1975). Family resemblances: Studies in the internal structure of categories. *Cognitive Psychology, 7*, 573–605.

Rosch, E., Mervis, C. B., Gray, W. D., Johnson, D., & Boyes-Braem, P. (1976). Basic objects in natural categories. *Cognitive Psychology, 8*, 382–439.

Rozin, P. (1976). The evolution of intelligence and access to the cognitive unconscious. In J. M. Sprague & A. A. Epstein (Eds.), *Progress in psychobiology and physiological psychology*. New York: Academic Press.

Rozin, P., Fallon, A., & Augustoni-Ziskind, M. (1985). The child's conception of food: The development of contamination sensitivity to "disgusting" substances. *Developmental Psychology, 21*(6), 1075–1079.

Rumelhart, D. E. (1992). Towards a microstructural account of human reasoning. In S. Davis (Ed.), *Connectionism: Theory and practice* (pp. 69–83). Oxford, England: Oxford University Press.

Ruse, M. (Ed.). (1989). *What the philosophy of biology is: Essays dedicated to David Hull.* Boston: Dordrecht.

Salmon, W. C. (1989). *Four decades of scientific explanation.* Minneapolis: University of Minnesota Press.

Sartori, G., Miozzo, M., & Job, R. (1993). Category-specific naming impairments? Yes. *Quarterly Journal of Experimental Psychology: Human Experimental Psychology, 46A,* 489–504.

Saxe, G. B. (1983). Culture, counting and number conservation. *International Journal of Psychology, 18,* 313–318.

Seidenberg, M. S. (1986). Evidence from great apes concerning the biological bases of language. In W. Damon & A. Marras (Eds.), *Language learning and concept acquisition* (pp. 29–53). Norwood, NJ: ABLEX.

Seidenberg, M. S. (1992). Connectionism without tears. In S. Davis (Ed.), *Connectionism: Theory and practice* (pp. 84–122). Oxford, England: Oxford University Press.

Seidenberg, M. S. (1992). Language acquisition and use: Learning and applying probabilistic constraints. *Science, 275,* 1599–1603.

Shepard, R. N. (1967). Recognition memory for words, sentences, and pictures. *Journal of Verbal Learning and Verbal Behavior, 6,* 156–163.

Shoemaker, S. (1980). Causality and properties. In P. van Inwagen (Ed.), *Time and cause* (pp. 109–135). Dordrecht, The Netherlands: Reidel.

Shoemaker, S. (1984). *Identity, cause, and mind: Philosophical essays.* Cambridge, England: Cambridge University Press, 1984.

Siegler, R., & Modell, J. (1993). Child development and human diversity. In G. H. Elder, J. Modell, & R. D. Parke (Eds.), *Children in time and place: Developmental and historical insights* (pp. 73–105). Cambridge, England: Cambridge University Press.

Siegler, R. S. (1995). How does change occur: A microgenetic study of number conservation. *Cognitive Psychology, 28,* 225–273.

Silberstein, C. (1995, Fall). Talk given at Cornell University.

Simon, H. A. (1962). An information processing theory of intellectual development. *Monographs of the Society for Research in Child Development, 27*(3), 150–162.

Simon, H. A. (1969). *Sciences of the artificial.* Cambridge, MA: MIT Press.

Simon, T. J., Hespos, S. J., & Rochat, P. (1995). Do infants understand simple arithmetic? A replication of Wynn. *Cognitive Development, 10,* 253–270.

Simons, D. S. (1996). In sight, out of mind: When object representations fail. *Psychological Science, 7,* 301–305.

Simons, D. S., & Keil, F. C. (1995). An abstract to concrete shift in cognitive development: The insides story. *Cognition, 56,* 129–163.

Skinner, B. F. (1950). Are theories of learning necessary? *Psychological Review, 57,* 211–220.

Sloman, S. A. (1996). The empirical case for two systems of reasoning. *Psychological Bulletin, 119*(1), 3–22.

Smith, C., Carey, S., & Wiser, M. (1985). On differentiation: A case study of the development of the concepts of size, weight, and density. *Cognition, 21,* 177–237.

Smith, E. E., & Medin, D. L. (1981). *Categorization and concepts.* Cambridge, MA: Harvard University Press.

Smith, E. E., & Osherson, D. N. (1984). Conceptual combination with prototype concepts. *Cognitive Science, 8,* 337–361.

Smith, L. B., & Jones, S. S. (1993). Cognition without concepts. *Cognitive Development, 8,* 181–188.

Smith, L. B., Jones, S. S., Landau, B. (1996). Naming in young children: A dumb attentional mechanism? *Cognition, 60*(2), 143–171.

Smith, L. D. (1986). *Behaviorism and logical positivism.* Stanford, CA: Stanford University Press.

Sober, E. (1994). *From a biological point of view: Essays in evolutionary philosophy.* Cambridge, England: Cambridge University Press.

Sommers, F. (1963). Types and ontology. *Philosophical Review, 72,* 327–363.

Spearman, C. (1927). *The abilities of man.* New York: Macmillan.

Spelke, E. S. (1994). Initial knowledge: Six suggestions. *Cognition, 50,* 431–445.

Spelke, E. S. (in press). Perceptual knowledge of objects in infancy. In J. Mehler (Ed.), *Perspectives in cognitive psychology.*

Spelke, E. S., Breinlinger, K., Macomber, J., & Jacobson, K. (1992). Origins of knowledge. *Psychological Review, 94,* 605–632.

Spelke, E. S., & Hermer, L. (1996). *Early cognitive development.* In R. Gelman & T. Au (Eds.), *Perceptual and cognitive development* (pp. 72–110). New York: Academic Press.

Spelke, E. S., Kestenbaum, R., Simons, D. J., & Wein, D. (1995). Spatiotemporal continuity, smoothness of motion and object identity in infancy. *British Journal of Developmental Psychology, 13,* 113–142.

Spelke, E. S., Phillips, A., & Woodward, A. L. (1995). Infants' knowledge of object motion and animate action. In D. Sperber, D. Premack, & A. Premack (Eds.), *Causal cognition: A multi-disciplinary debate* (pp. 44–78). New York: Oxford University Press.

Spencer, H. (1907). *First principles* (6th ed.). New York: Appleton. (Original work published 1864)

Spirtes, P., Glymour, C., & Scheines, R. (1993). *Causation, prediction, and search.* New York: Springer.

Springer, K. (1995). Acquiring a naive theory of kinship through inference. *Child Development, 66,* 547–558.

Stalnaker, R. (1984). *Inquiry.* Cambridge, MA: MIT Press.

Starkey, P. (1992). The early development of numerical reasoning. *Cognition, 43,* 93–126.

Starkey, P., & Cooper, R. G. (1980). Perception of numbers by human infants. *Science, 210,* 1033–1035.

Stilling, N. A., Weisler, S. E., Chase, C. H., Feinstein, M. H., Garfield, J. L., & Rissland, E. L. (1995). *Cognitive science: An introduction* (2nd ed.). Cambridge, MA: MIT Press.

Talmy, L. (1983). How language structures space. In H. Pick & L. Acredolo (Eds.), *Spatial orientation: Theory, research, and application* (pp. 225–282). New York: Plenum Press.

Talmy, L. (1988). Force dynamics in language and cognition. *Cognitive Science, 12,* 49–100.

Talmy, L. (1995). Fictive motion in language and "ception." In P. Bloom, M. Peterson, & L. Nadel (Eds.), *Language and space* (pp. 211–276). Cambridge, MA: MIT Press.

Terrace, H., Petitto, L. A., Sanders, R. J., & Bever, T. G. (1979). Can an ape create a sentence? *Science, 206,* 891–902.

Thompson, K. R. (1995). Natural and relational concepts in animals. In H. L. Roitblat & J. Meyer (Eds.), *Comparative approaches to cognitive science.* Cambridge, MA: MIT Press.

Tolman, E. C. (1948). Cognitive maps in rats and men. *Psychological Review, 55,* 189–208.

Tomasello, M. (1990). Cultural transmission in the tool use and communicatory signaling of chimpanzees. In S. Parker & K. Gibson (Eds.), *Language and intelligence in monkeys and apes: Comparative developmental perspectives.* Cambridge, England: Cambridge University Press.

Tomasello, M., Kruger, A. C., & Ratner, H. H. (1991). *Cultural learning* (21). Emory Cognition Project, Atlanta, GA.

Traugott, E. C., & Smith, H. (1993). Arguments from language change. *Journal of Linguistics, 29,* 431–447.

Trout, J. D. (1991). The philosophy of physics. In R. Boyd, P. Gasper, & J. D. Trout (Eds.), *The philosophy of science* (pp. 463–472). Cambridge, MA: MIT Press.

Turing, A. M. (1950). Computing machinery and intelligence. *Mind, 59,* 433–460.

Tweney, R. D. (1991). Informal reasoning in science. In J. F. Voss, D. N. Perkins, & J. W. Segal (Eds.), *Informal reasoning and education* (pp. 3–16). Hillsdale, NJ: Erlbaum.

Valian, V. (1994). Children's postulation of null subjects: Parameter settings and language acquisition. In B. Lust, M. Suner, & H. Whitman (Eds.), *Syntactic theory and first language acquisition: Cross-linguistic perspectives* (Vol. 2, pp. 216–253). Hillsdale, NJ: Erlbaum.

Vishton, P. M. (1996). *Action controls perception just as perception controls action: Evidence from studies of adult driving, infant predictive reaching, and adult manual prehension.* Unpublished doctoral dissertation, Cornell University, Ithaca, NY.

Von Eckardt, B. (1993). *What is cognitive science?* Cambridge, MA: MIT Press.

Von Hofsten, C., & Fazel-Zandy, S. (1984). Development of visually guided hand orientation in reaching. *Journal of Experimental Child Psychology, 38,* 208–219.

Vygotsky, L. S. (1962). *Thought and language* (E. Hanfmann & G. Vakar, Trans.). Cambridge, MA: MIT Press. (Original work published 1934)

Vygotsky, L. S. (1978). *Mind in society: The development of higher psychological processes.* Cambridge, MA: Harvard University Press.

Walk, R. D., & Gibson, E. J. (1961). A comparative and analytic study of visual depth perception. *Psychological Monographs, 75,* 15.

Walker, S. (1992). Supernatural beliefs, natural kinds, and conceptual structure. *Memory and Cognition, 20,* 655–662.

Warrington, E. K., & McCarthy, R. A. (1987). Categories of knowledge: Further fractionations and an attempted integration. *Brain, 110,* 1273–1296.

Warrington, E. K., & Shallice, T. (1984). Category specific semantic impairments. *Brain, 107,* 829–853.

Waxman, S. R., & Kosowski, T. D. (1990). Nouns mark category relations: Toddlers' and preschoolers' word-learning biases. *Child Development, 61,* 1461–1473.

Waxman, S. R., & Markow, D. B. (1995). Words as invitations to form categories: Evidence from 12- to 13-month-old infants. *Cognitive Psychology, 29,* 257–302.

Wellman, H. (1990). *The child's theory of mind.* Cambridge, MA: Bradford Books/MIT Press.

Werner, H., & Kaplan, B. (1963). *Symbol formation: An organismic-developmental approach to language and the expression of thought.* New York: Wiley.

Wiggins, D. (1980). *Sameness and substance.* Oxford, England: Basil Blackwell.

Wiser, M. (1988). The differentiation of heat and temperature: History of science and novice-expert shift. In S. Strauss (Ed.), *Ontogeny, phylogeny, and historical development* (pp. 28–48). Norwood, NJ: ABLEX.

Wright, L. (1976). *Teleological explanations: An etiological analysis of goals and functions.* Berkeley: University of California Press.

Wundt, W. M. (1897). *Outlines of psychology* (C. H. Judd, Trans.). New York: Stechert.

Wynn, K. (1990). Children's understanding of counting. *Cognition, 36,* 155–193.

Wynn, K. (1992). Addition and subtraction in infants. *Nature, 358,* 749–750.

Wynn, K. (1995). Origins of numerical knowledge. *Mathematical Cognition, 1,* 35–60.

Xu, F., & Carey, S. (1996). Infants' metaphysics: The case of numerical identity. *Cognitive Psychology, 30*(2), 111–153.

Zabih, R., Woodfill, J., & Withgott, M. (1993, October). *A realtime system for annotating unstructured image sequences.* Presented at the IEEE Systems, Man, and Cybernetics Conference, Le Touquet, France.

Zadeh, L. (1965). Fuzzy sets. *Information and Control, 8,* 338–353.

Zaslavsky, C. (1973). *Africa counts.* Boston: Prindle, Weber, and Schmidt.

CHAPTER 8

Extraordinary Cognitive Achievements (ECA): A Symbol Systems Approach

HOWARD E. GARDNER

I. THE PHENOMENA OF EXTRAORDINARY COGNITIVE ACHIEVEMENTS (ECA)

Mention the phrase "cognitive development" and a psychologist immediately thinks of certain phenomena and particular research traditions. The phenomena encompass such general capacities as problem solving, classification, and metacognition, as well as more specific forms of understanding such as object permanence, theory of mind, or the appreciation of probability; the traditions include information processing along with the Piagetian, Vygotskian, and various other post-Piagetian traditions. Stated or not, the assumption reigns: The science of cognitive development depicts what one can expect of nearly every individual who lives in a reasonably supportive environment.

Perhaps surprisingly, the study of cognitive development has rarely been construed to extend to phenomena (or research traditions) that reflect unusual accomplishments on the part of individuals. Even though the contributions of exceptional achievers occupy much of our interest as historians or as observers of the contemporary scene, such accomplishments are either ignored altogether or are seen as the concern of a small, quite separate group of investigators. Consider, in this vein, the following instances of exceptional accomplishment:

- In contemporary China, a 4-year-old artist named Wang Yani produced over 4,000 paintings, many of them of monkeys. By preadolescence, she had toured the world as an innovative practitioner of ink-and-brush painting (Goldsmith & Feldman, 1989; Ho, 1989).

- In Japan originally, and then in other countries, millions of youngsters have learned to play the violin in an expert fashion, thanks to the educational regimen developed over the past 40 years by an ingenious pedagogue named Shinichi Suzuki (Gardner, 1993a; Suzuki, 1969).

- In England, a young autistic girl named Nadia depicts animals with the flair of a Renaissance artist. Nadia can neither communicate with others nor solve the simplest classification and conceptual tasks (Selfe, 1977).

- American Michael Kearney was reading within the first year of his life, completed college before the age of 10, and attempted to become a television game show host at age 11 (Winner, 1996).

- Most of the males enrolled in Lewis Terman's study of high-IQ youngsters born in California early in the century went on to lead highly successful lives. Few gained fame in the arts or achieved world-class prominence in politics or science. The sample contained virtually no Asians (Feldman,1986; Friedman, Tucker, Schwartz, & Tomlinson-Keasey, 1995; Terman, 1925; Terman & Oden, 1959).

- The average person can remember approximately seven randomly ordered numbers when their serial digits have been recited for his or her audition. Students trained at Carnegie-Mellon University can learn to recall up to a hundred such numbers (Ericsson, Krampe, & Tesch-Romer, 1993).

- Most of the greatest creators in Western history were not prodigies. Mozart and Picasso, who performed at adult levels as children, proved the exceptions rather than the rule (Gardner, 1993b). Conversely, most of the outstanding prodigies in mathematics and music do not lead their domains as adults. Those who, as adults, gain high ranking in scientific research, the arts, or sports rarely stood out as prodigious children (Bloom, 1985).

- Several of the leading scientists and mathematicians of the 20th century, including John von Neumann, Leo Szilard, and Edward Teller, attended the same high school in Budapest (Rhodes, 1986).

- Highly ranked musical performers are distinguished from their lower-ranked peers chiefly in terms of the number of hours that they have devoted to goal-directed, effortful, "deliberate practice" (Ericsson et al., 1993).

Human achievements of this degree of distinction are familiar to individuals who attend to the media—or, indeed, to readers of boxes and sidebars in psychology textbooks. Rarely, however, have attempts been made in the mainstream cognitive literature to explain the nature of these achievements or to develop a framework by which one can consider their relationship to one another. Faced with such a state of affairs, the student of cognitive development has a number of options:

1. Ignore these phenomena, perhaps suggesting that either they are aberrations or they fall outside the "normal science" of the domain.

2. Treat these occurrences as residual phenomena, to be touched on briefly after the lines of mainstream development have been identified and elucidated.

3. Launch a separate line of study, focusing particularly on the explanation of one or more forms of extraordinary cognitive achievement.

4. Develop a new cognitive framework that is broad enough to account both for ordinary cognitive achievements and for various extraordinary forms, of the sort outlined earlier in this section.

In this chapter, I develop such a new framework, which I have designated as the *symbol systems approach*. To place this approach in perspective, I begin with a targeted review of earlier work in the "parent discipline" of cognitive development.

II. THE FOUNDERS OF COGNITIVE DEVELOPMENT

Each of the major 19th-century students of human nature passed on a legacy to 20th-century students of cognitive development. Charles Darwin (1874) proposed that the human mind represented a culmination of the same evolutionary processes that characterize species evolution more generally; he and his followers—George Romanes (1883) and L. T. Hobhouse (1926), for example—speculated on the relation between primitive and more advanced forms of mentation. Karl Marx (1872/1974), himself an admirer of Darwin, identified the powerful role played by economic and other material conditions in shaping human social life; at the same time, he acknowledged that human beings make their own history. From his vantage point at the close of the 19th century, Sigmund Freud (1900/1938) identified the powerful forces that constitute the human unconscious, giving rise to personality configurations and motivational structures, some of which distinguish among human beings, while others are shared by the entire species.

None of these founders would have considered himself a researcher on human cognitive or intellectual development, but, collectively, their theories and discoveries soon stimulated the founding of the discipline. Figures like G. Stanley Hall (1904/1969) and James Mark Baldwin (1897) in the United States, James Sully (1895) in Great Britain, Edouard Claparede (1912) in France, Wilhelm Preyer (1892) and Wilhelm Stern (1926) in Germany, and Charlotte Buehler (1928) in Austria can lay legitimate claim to parenting in this regard. It is generally agreed that the discipline came into its own through the efforts of a cohort of scholars born during the final decade of the 19th century, chief among them being Jean Piaget (1896–1980), Lev Vygotsky (1896–1934), and Heinz Werner (1890–1964).

Although the many differences among these theorists are well known, it is apt to note a number of features on which these founders of the discipline of cognitive development were in essential agreement (J. Langer, 1969; P. Miller, 1993). These features are probably grasped most clearly in the work of Piaget, who was the most prolific of the founders and the author most consciously identified with the domain of intellectual development.

As a group, Piaget, Vygotsky, Werner, and their scientific contemporaries were, broadly speaking, evolutionists; they saw human beings as privileged in relation to other species, in that mature human adults became more advanced than young children. These researchers took care to root their analyses in biology, on the one hand, and to take into account cultural influences, on the other. They delineated *end-states* of development, in which the rational problem solver (who bore a strong resemblance to the Western-trained scientist) was deemed the apogee of cognitive growth. They were sympathetic to the notion of a series of stages, each having its own coherence, and to across-the-board movement from a more primitive to a more advanced stage—or, more rarely, to regression to a less advanced stage. Unlike Freud, they did not concern themselves in a major way with emotions, motivation, or personality; nor, in contrast to empirically oriented American researchers, were they focused primarily on issues of training and education. Perhaps above all, as heirs to the Kantian tradition, they sought to identify *the universal*—those traits, stages, and structures that characterize all human beings, rather than those that distinguish one person or group of persons from another.

By the time of Werner's death in 1964, the enterprise of a few pioneering individuals had flowered into a discipline with hundreds of researchers drawn from all over the world. Among the other major researchers in the tradition were Bärbel Inhelder (Inhelder, Sinclair, & Bovet, 1974), Jerome Bruner (1965), Lawrence Kohlberg (1969), and Bernard Kaplan (1967), just to mention a few who were closely identified with the founders. It would involve undue stretching to attempt to characterize their work jointly, let alone the work of individuals who subscribed to the goals of the founders but differed about methods and conclusions. Nonetheless, an examination of publications of the era, or even a survey of the third (1970) edition of this *Handbook,* suggests considerable consensus among cognitivists about most of the features of the above characterization.

III. MAJOR AREAS IN NEED OF EXPLORATION, CIRCA 1970

Within the field of cognitive development, various issues were just beginning to be joined at the time of the 1970 *Handbook*. The assumptions involved in speaking of stages were being seriously questioned for the first time (Kessen, 1966; Osterrieth, 1956). The nature of the structures that were hypothesized to underlie stages was also ripe for critical analysis (Bruner, 1959). Piaget's notion of *décalage*—the factor that acknowledged the lack of temporal coincidence among putatively related milestones—stood in need of discussion. It was generally assumed that, absent frank pathology, performances would improve steadily with age and experience; the existence of domains in which performance remained steady, actually declined, or assumed some other form, such as a U-shape, had not been adequately considered.

Looking beyond the field of cognitive development, as it was perceived at the time (Kessen & Kuhlman, 1962), a number of other omissions or minimizations can be identified. Many researchers felt uncomfortable about the gap between the analysis of cognition, on the one hand, and personality, motivation, and affect on the other (R. Gardner, 1959; Piaget, 1954; Wolff, 1960). Lip service was always paid to the interaction of biological and cultural factors, but few had probed this issue in depth, particularly in light of new findings from genetics, evolutionary theory, neurobiology, anthropology, and cultural studies.

The domain that was generally considered as cognitive also merited reanalysis. Piaget and others had thought of the scientist as the end-state *par excellence* of cognition and had not considered alternative possibilities: (a) that other domains could be deemed cognitive; and (b) that domains valued in one culture might not be valued—or even recognized—in others. A reexamination of the domains and end-states of cognition was called for. Relatedly, the role of training, schooling, and other kinds of formal and informal tuition had not been considered a central aspect of the study of cognitive development.

Among other areas of neglect, most scholars of cognitive development focused on processes spanning childhood; the possibility of significant intellectual development beyond adolescence had not been investigated (however, see Baltes, 1983). Cognition took place primarily in school or in the laboratory; a consideration of the workplace, or of ordinary cognition at home or in the streets, was rarely undertaken (Barker, 1968; Lave & Wenger, 1991). In similar fashion, although high levels of performance were of some interest, the use of intellect for original, creative, or other noncanonical purposes was not a subject for study. It hardly needs to be said that religion, spirituality, and other apparently nonrational or even mystical phenomena were not considered relevant by these rationalistically oriented heirs of Darwin, Freud, and Marx (cf. Baldwin, 1897).

Individual differences has long been recognized as a legitimate area of study but, for reasons that are not clear, it generally fell outside of the purview of researchers in cognitive development. No one denied that some individuals "develop cognitively" more rapidly than others, but the possibility that individuals might develop in different ways, or toward different end-states, was not countenanced (Bidell & Fischer, 1992; Kagan, 1984). There were two scientific traditions in psychology, and the tradition that probed *universal processes* was seen as largely unconnected to the tradition that studied *individual differences*.

In the dispensation of 1970, the classical topic of "individual variation in cognitive processes" constituted the focus of this chapter's ancestor (see Kagan & Kogan, 1970). Readers will note, however, that this phrase appears neither in the title nor in the text of the present chapter. Rather, in defiance of earlier practice, I argue here that it is possible—indeed, important—to attempt to link these two traditions. A study of cognitive development that ignores important individual differences is limited, and attempts to explain individual differences ought to grow out of a comprehensive approach to cognitive development, rather than out of a subsidiary, secondary, or independent line of analysis.

Plan for the Chapter

To this point, I have sketched the background of work in cognitive development and argued that this work has unfolded with little concern for the phenomena of exceptional cognitive achievements. I have proposed that investigators attempt to link these two lines of work and nominated the symbol systems approach as one means of achieving such a rapprochement. The intellectual background for, and the main claims of, this approach are outlined in Section IV.

In Section V, I revisit the major phenomena of cognitive development, as seen from a symbol systems perspective. The language of the street and the language of scholarship have jointly produced a rich lexicon to denote extraordinary cognitive accomplishments. In speaking of extraordinary children, we refer to gifted or talented youngsters, intelligent children, creative children, and, in exceptional cases, prodigies, or savants. Extending beyond childhood, these adolescents and adults may be spoken of as intelligent, brilliant, creative, original, expert, and, on rare occasions, genius. Part of an enterprise in the area of ECA should be the development of a terminology, a set of definitions, and, to the extent possible, operationalizations for key terms. (Gardner, 1995c, 1997). I initiate such an enterprise in Section VI, which, along with Section VII, is devoted to a consideration of the way in which the phenomena of extraordinary cognitive achievements might be accounted for in terms of a symbol systems approach.

I conclude by considering the relation of this perspective to other approaches in the areas of cognition and individual differences. I specify major questions that need to be resolved, and I indicate how current views of cognitive development, and of development more generally, might be revised in light of the considerations discussed here.

IV. THE SYMBOL SYSTEMS APPROACH (SSA)

At certain historical moments, new sets of ideas become prominent across academic disciplines. Michel Foucault (1971) has documented the widespread preoccupation, in the 17th century, with issues of classification across such widely separate terrains as economics, linguistics, and biology. Notions of evolution were rampant across the disciplines in the 19th and early 20th centuries (Barzun, 1941; Degler, 1991; Hofstadter, 1945). In the past 100 years, there has been a similar, if less widely appreciated, convergence of interest in the notion of symbols and symbol systems as a key organizing idea, especially in the human sciences and the humanities.

One of the many contributions of the American philosopher Charles Sanders Peirce (1932) was his recognition of the importance of symbolic phenomena. He is credited with giving this concern an early name: "semiotic studies." Probing language and philosophy, Peirce noted that signs of various sorts played an important role in communication and cognition. The central idea in his *semiotic*—which has remained central in succeeding studies in the area—is that, within any community, various entities are accepted as standing for, or referring to, specific concepts and experiences. In his own initial scheme, Peirce distinguished among the sign (or mark), the object (or referent), and the interpretant (the representation created in the mind of the user of the sign). Launching another enduring line of analysis, he arrayed signs in terms of their arbitrariness: The index was the most direct mark of its creator (the footprint of a dog), the icon bore a morphological similarity to its referent (such as a picture of a dog or the sound of barking), and the symbol was a relatively arbitrary indication, such as the phonological pockets of *"chien," "Hund,"* or "dog."

Peirce was neither the first nor the last person who attempted to classify and categorize the various vehicles of meaning. This enterprise was a major concern of scholastics in the Middle Ages; and it spawned an entire academic industry, called semiotics, in the 20th century (Deely, 1990; Eco, 1976; Sebeok, 1989, 1991). Even within developmental psychology, there has been terminological confusion: Piaget (1962), for example, uses the word *signe* to denote an arbitrary mark, while using the term *symbole,* in contradistinction to others, to denote a mark that is motivated (in the manner of Peirce's icon).

The most convincing account of this growing preoccupation with symbolic phenomena is contained in Susanne Langer's classic essay *Philosophy in a New Key,* originally published in 1942. Langer indicates how philosophers had become newly focused on various kinds of symbols and symbolic vehicles. Interest in language and propositions, on the part of Frege (1980) and Wittgenstein (1921/1961), was merged with the concerns for logical and mathematical symbolization, in the tradition of Whitehead and Russell (1910–1913) and their followers in the Viennese logical-positivist tradition.

A separate intellectual tradition, dating back to the writings of the Neapolitan savant Giambattista Vico (1774/1984), explored what Langer termed "nondiscursive symbols"—those involved in myth, religion, ritual, and the arts. Following her own teacher, Ernst Cassirer (1953–1957), as well as some of the interests of Whitehead (1929, 1958), Langer devoted her efforts to an elucidation of the nature and function of *presentational* (nondiscursive) symbols—symbols that did not lend themselves to syntactical analysis and had an impact that was achieved and apprehended holistically.

Langer's somewhat impressionistic work has been followed by more systematic investigation of the nature of different kinds of symbols and symbol systems. The line that has probably most influenced psychology is that undertaken by Nelson Goodman, particularly in *Languages of Art* (1968/1976) and *Ways of Worldmaking* (1978). Goodman stipulates specific syntactic and semantic criteria for distinguishing among two orders of symbolic systems. They are, technically speaking, *notational* (clear distinction among marks and clear relations between particular marks and particular referents); and *nonnotational* or, in Langer's terms, *presentational* (blurry distinctions among marks, multiple overlapping relations between marks and referents).

Although Langer's concerns were directed at the interests of her philosophical antecedents, and her own field of esthetics, an analogous concern with issues of symbolization has been discernible in other, neighboring disciplines. As part of the research program of semiotics, the pioneering linguist Ferdinand de Saussure (1983) launched a study of forms of symbolization. This effort has been carried forward by Roman Jakobson (1963/1971) and now, more broadly, by the various strands of contemporary semiotics (Sebeok, 1991). Those influenced by the contemporary linguist Noam Chomsky (1980) have challenged the notion of a single amalgamated semiotics; they have put forth arguments for why language ought to be construed differently from other semiotic systems (Fodor, 1975, 1983; Sperber, 1975). Much the same controversy has been ongoing in the clinically oriented fields of neurology and neuropsychology: One school underscores the essential connectedness of all forms of symbolization (Bay, 1964; Head, 1920/1963; Lenneberg, 1967); an opposing camp focuses on the neurological and psychological dissociability (and hence, the independence) of different symbolic realms (Geschwind, 1974; Hécaen & Albert, 1978; Luria, 1966).

The field of artificial intelligence grew out of logical-mathematical analysis in the Whitehead–Russell tradition (Gardner, 1985; McCorduck, 1979). Among its bedrock assumptions are the claims that computational systems traffic in the manipulation of strings of symbols, and that electronic circuits can be configured to replicate the elementary relations of logic (McCulloch & Pitts, 1943). Originally designed as "number crunchers," computers now operate on strings of symbols that can denote diverse forms of information. Pioneering investigators Herbert Simon (1985) and Allen Newell (1980) have gone so far as to argue that the computer ought to be considered as a physical symbol system. Recently, a computational approach opposed to the von Neumann serial digital stance has developed; according to proponents of the parallel-distributed-processes (PDP)–connectionist camp, computation can be carried out in the absence of the assumptions and paraphernalia of a symbol systems approach (Rumelhart & McClelland, 1986). There are also attempts abroad to configure computational systems that involve symbolic as well as nonsymbolic computation (Hofstadter, 1995; Kosslyn, 1994; Smolensky, 1988).

Finally, moving to territory likely to be familiar to readers of this *Handbook*, an interest in symbolization has been central in psychology and in neighboring social sciences such as anthropology and sociology. Early psychologists carried out studies that explored the processes and content of language, imagery, and other symbolic realms (Blumenthal, 1970). Researchers in the behaviorist era challenged the legitimacy of these lines of investigation, but the themes were never abandoned completely and were especially recognizable in the work of gestalt psychologists (Wertheimer, 1945). The rise of the cognitive approach at mid-century signaled a renewed interest in vehicles of symbolic activity, in the works of authors such as Jerome Bruner (Bruner, Goodnow, & Austin, 1956), George Miller (1956), Allan Paivio (1971), and Roger Shepard (1978). Looking beyond the cognitive and perceptual spheres, one finds rich interest in symbolic activity among those who endorsed a psychodynamic approach (Freud, 1952; Jung, 1958) and among their followers who engaged in empirical and experimental work (Murray, 1938).

Key Distinctions

In contemplating this rich lode of inquiry, it is helpful to keep in mind a few key distinctions and issues that recur in the remainder of this chapter.

External Symbols versus Internal Symbols

Most researchers in philosophy and linguistics are interested primarily in those symbols that are produced externally and can be observed publicly: written marks, notations, works of art, or behaviors that can be codified into externally manifest forms such as spoken language, dance, or ritual. While sharing this interest, researchers from psychology, and particularly from cognitive psychology, focus their attention on internal symbols—the putative *mental representations* of information that may or may not be realized in external symbols (for example, the steps involved in arithmetical problem solving).

Consider a concrete example. There is little controversy that written language is an external, tangible symbolic form, and most scholars would agree that spoken language can be converted into such forms, even if, as oral communication, it is not itself considered an external form. But just which psychological mechanisms are involved in the use of language, more broadly, is a separate issue. Some scholars posit a mental form of representation—often called mentalese—which is, in many ways, isomorphic to natural language and ought to be considered the basic form of symbolization (Fodor, 1975). Various linguistic tokens are reflections of this underlying language type. Other scholars contend that language is best thought of as represented mentally in *some* kind of symbolic form, but that form need not bear any isomorphism to the natural languages that we encounter externally (Bates, Benigni, Bretheron,

Camaioni, & Volterra, 1979; Neisser, 1976; Putnam, 1980). Still others—dating back to the behaviorists, on the one hand, and reaching forward to PDP advocates, on the other—question the need for positing any kind of internal symbolic language (Shanon, 1993; Shaw & Bransford, 1977). Behaviorists question the utility of any talk of mental representations. Some computer scientists believe that it is proper to speak of representation—after all, knowledge must be represented somewhere, perhaps in connections of various degrees of strength—but these parsimonious theorists claim that it is not necessary to think of representation as occurring in any kind of symbolic medium (e.g., Rumelhart & McClelland, 1986).

Unified versus Modular View of Symbol Systems

One tradition, dating back at least to de Saussure (1916/1983) in linguistics and to Jackson (1932) and Head (1920/1963) in neuropsychology, and given visibility in the writings of Cassirer (1953–1957), stresses the underlying affinity among different kinds of symbol systems. In this view, language, dance, mathematics, and ritual are all seen as manifestations of the same underlying semiotic function. To the extent that this is true, there should be similar developmental progressions for different symbolic systems; relatedly, semiotic functions should be subserved by a single neurological network.

A contrasting point of view holds that, except for casual purposes, it is risky and perhaps misleading to lump together varieties of symbolic forms. Positions range here. Chomsky (1980) and his followers are fundamentally uncomfortable with any discussion of a semiotic capacity, at least if it is to include natural language. Peirce (1932) and the ensuing philosophical tradition (e.g., Goodman, 1968/1976) recognize certain similarities as well as certain differences across a range of symbol systems. A more empirically oriented group entertains the possibility that certain symbol systems may indeed be variants of one another, but maintains that the matter is best resolved through detailed studies of the development, operations, and dissolution of the ensemble of symbolic capacities (e.g., Olson, 1974).

Throughout this Section IV, I indicate my sympathy for the modular view of semiotics, as well as my particular interest in the external approach to symbols. It is important to note at this point that one can adopt a symbol systems perspective even though one may not adhere to a specific perspective on a particular issue. Indeed, part of the power of the symbol systems perspective is that it allows, or encompasses, consideration of these rival perspectives.

Features of a Symbol Systems Approach

Central to the symbol systems approach are the following core assumptions:

1. Human beings are organisms for whom the use of symbols is wholly natural, important from an early age, crucial for survival, and indispensable in educational, occupational, and cultural institutions.

2. Human beings are prepared biologically—through genes and through the organization of the human brain—to use and master symbol systems. Whatever intimations of symbolic activity may exist in other species (Savage-Rumbaugh, 1986; Sebeok, 1972; Tomasello, 1992), symbolization is more important for human beings by several orders of magnitude.

3. Human beings all use certain external symbols, such as natural language and the gestures accompanying speech; other symbol systems may be particular to certain cultures (written language) or subcultures (calculus).

4. The skills involved in the use of symbols are cognitive. (Symbol use also has emotional facets, of course.) One must learn to "read" and "write" symbols. At least some training may be necessary for the acquisition of more complex symbolic and notational systems. Experts in various symbol systems have developed methods for describing and training the skills and competences involved in their mastery.

5. How external symbols are represented internally (mentally) is an important scientific question, but the symbol systems approach can be pursued independent of the ultimate resolution of that issue.

6. Important aspects of cultural survival are involved in the creation and transmission of different forms of symbols. Educators traffic formally in the use of symbols; parents and other elders in the community transmit symbolic competence in less formal ways.

7. Human intellectual proclivities tend to coalesce in the creation and deployment of symbolic and notational systems. Thus, the human linguistic, mathematical, and musical potentials have given rise over the centuries to many kinds of symbol systems across diverse cultures.

8. Symbol systems tend to be organized in given ways. A symbolic system typically exhibits syntax (grammar), semantics (meaning), and pragmatics (function). In those cases where one aspect is apparently muted—e.g., syntax in painting, semantics in music, pragmatics in dreaming—other functions are correlatively highlighted.

9. The symbol systems approach involves the consideration of at least four different levels of analysis and the interactions among them. In the following subsection, I outline these levels and indicate how they are relevant to a performance in the domain of music.

Levels of Analysis

The Biological Level

This approach—admittedly, still in its infancy—begins with a search for information from genetics that may be relevant to skills and performances—for example, evidence with respect to the incidence, distribution, and heritability of that competence within a given population in a given context. Equally important is evidence about the neurological substrate of abilities, in terms of both the structures that subserve performances and the actual in vivo brain processes involved in some kind of performance. Such information can now be obtained from a variety of imaging sources, such as CAT scans, brain scans, MRI, and other emerging technologies.

Applying a biological approach within the area of music, the investigator searches for evidence that specific musical capacities (e.g., perfect pitch) or more general musical capacities (e.g., memory for unfamilar melodies) appear to be under the control of particular gene configurations within a given population. Behavioral genetic evidence, and particularly evidence from identical twins reared apart, can be informative here. A biologically oriented investigator looks as well for evidence of structures—for example, in the right temporal lobes—that may be important for musical capacities (like singing on pitch or recognizing melodies), as well as evidence of possible differences in the preferred mode of neural processing between those who are expert and those who are not. In this case, it is important to confirm recent evidence that, in the processing of music, experts rely relatively more than do novices on the left hemisphere structures (Bever & Chiarello, 1974; Raichle, 1991, 1994; Sergent, 1993).

The Psychological Level (Cognition and Beyond)

Most work in human symbolic functioning—as regards both universal aspects and individual differences—has understandably been carried out in the cognitive and/or developmental traditions outlined above. Other psychological facets should be considered as well, however. It is necessary to determine the role, in symbol use, of personality, motivation, emotion, and social components, as well as elements of desire, fear, and willpower. Moreover, one must note contributions made singularly by these factors and their interactions with one another and with cognitive features.

Pursuing the example of music, a psychological investigator focuses on the mental structures and representations that subserve musical competence in general, and that characterize putative stages or phases of musical development (Bamberger, 1991; Davidson & Scripp, 1988; Dowling & Harwood, 1986; Jusczyk & Krumhansl, 1993; Shuter-Dyson, 1982). Certain populations, such as prodigies or savants, may turn out to be particularly informative, for example, revealing the connections among (or independence of) facets of musical competence or the extent to which training or experience is necessary or sufficient. A psychological perspective also considers other factors that contribute to the inclination and the capacity to participate in musical life—issues of temperament, cultural values, group practices, and individual aspirations—and the various patterns of interaction among these factors (Blacking, 1995; Bloom, 1985; Hargreaves, 1989; Sloboda, 1985, 1988).

The Epistemological Level (The Domain)

In all likelihood, pursuit of any cognitive consequence involves the organization of an area of knowledge. Such an organization is most evident in academic disciplines; their knowledge base is regularly investigated and contributed to by scholars, and their constantly evolving condition is reflected in succeeding generations of textbooks and encyclopedias. However, a knowledge base is also apparent in every craft, art, or practice, though here the knowledge base is more likely to exist in a set of practices rather than in a set of propositions (Dreyfus, 1986). Most areas that have any degree of complexity encapsulate both kinds of knowledge—a propositional framework and a set of practices.

Following the discussion of Feldman (1980, 1986), I use the term *domain* to cover the epistemological component of a cognitive area. Typically, a domain features a characteristic symbol system (or set of symbol systems) as well as operations performed with these symbols. The domain of music is composed of the theory and analysis of different kinds of music (classical, popular, jazz, and the traditional musical corpus of various cultures and subcultures) as well as the established practices of performance, composition, and analysis within and across these different realms of music. Formally, the study of the domain is the concern of musicologists and music theorists; but at a more routine level, any individual involved in performing or listening to music must partake of the knowledge base of that domain. Some of this involvement can be explicit and conscious, but much of the knowledge—for example, expectations about patterns or styles of performance—will be apprehended at a tacit level (Scripp, 1995; Shanon, 1993; Sloboda, 1996; Torff, 1995).

The Sociological Level (The Field)

At least at an analytical level, the domain can be considered apart from specific human practitioners. One can read about the domain of music in a textbook or discern a set of practices from a manual. However, disciplines and crafts are always carried out within the context of a community—the individuals who teach; the individuals who listen to performances; and, above all, the individuals—generally, highly trained—who make consequential judgments about the quality of performances.

Following the discussion of Csikszentmihalyi (1988, 1996), I use the term *field* to refer to the social envelope within which any human performance must occur. The field includes teachers and audience members, but the central figures in the field are the individuals of influence who render judgments about quality. In the field of music, these individuals are impresarios, judges of competitions, executives of recording companies, critics, those who commission compositions or performances, and those who confer prizes such as Grawemeyers, Obies, Oscars, or Pulitzers.

The four levels described above must be considered on their own terms as well as in the light of the various interactions among them. As Csikszentmihalyi (1988) has emphasized, creativity is not a property of a single level, such as that represented by the talented individual, the skilled teacher, or the influential critic. Rather, creativity can best be apprehended as a dialectic among three components or nodes: (a) the individual, with his or her talents or inclinations; (b) the domain, with its own rules and expectations; and (c) the field, which renders judgment about what should be attended to, valued, rewarded, ignored, or scuttled.

Reverting again to the musical example, any society that values music will harbor a number of highly talented musical performers. These individuals will each master the domain, as a result of study under the guidance of individual practitioners and mastery of a body of accumulated knowledge. The performances will be audited by knowledgeable individuals who act as gatekeepers: Of the many individuals "at promise," a few will eventually stand out and become the leading figures of the domain. As for creativity, a very small number of individuals will succeed in devising performances that are sufficiently novel that they change the nature and course of the domain. A succeeding generation of talents will then study a domain that has been altered, courtesy of the creations of selected individuals whose talent has ultimately been identified and rewarded (Gardner, 1993b, 1997).

Further Applications of a Symbol Systems Approach

The analysis applied to music can be duplicated across a range of domains, from academic subjects (like physics or mathematics or history) to artistic activities (like painting or dance) to athletics, games, or crafts. In each case, one should be able to identify a necessary biological substrate; a set of psychological competences and factors; an independently characterizable set of knowledge structures and practices; and a knowledgeable set of individuals who instruct, audit, and/or judge.

From every indication, these levels of analysis assume characteristic forms for the realms to which they apply. Turning first to the biological perspective, some abilities (e.g., spatial skill) may turn out to have high heritability within a population and may even be ultimately linked to a single gene or set of genes; others (e.g., leadership) are likely to emerge as far less heritable, having perhaps a complex genetic basis (Lykken, McGue, Tellegen, & Bouchard, 1992) or no discernible genetic basis at all. Some abilities (perhaps language) will be related to quite specific neural sites and systems; others (perhaps musical or social skills) will allow a variety of neural representations or will involve a large set of neural structures and processes (Damasio, 1994; Sergent, Zuck, Terriah, & MacDonald, 1992).

Similar variability can be anticipated with respect to the remaining levels of analysis. Certain domains may have a readily determinable mental representation and a discrete set of stages of competence (e.g., mathematics); others (e.g., skill at diplomacy) may involve a larger set of structures and far less readily identifiable phases of competence. Other psychological factors—e.g., temperament, social influence, motivation—may play out quite differently with respect to a domain that requires rigorous practice in isolation (e.g., musical performance) in contrast to one that is social in nature (e.g., theatrical improvisation) (cf. Csikszentmihalyi, Rathunde, & Whalen, with contributions by Wong, 1993).

Some domains may feature a structure that is highly and specifically delineated—Chinese painting and Western ballet have been designated as prototypical "vertical domains" (Li & Gardner, 1993). "Horizontal domains"—such as modern Western painting or book reviewing—prove much looser, more flexible, and more permeable to outside influences.

There may also be underlying affinities across areas that appear on the surface to be incomparable. For example, it might appear that contemporary painting is especially susceptible to the arbitrary influence of the field. In the absence of specifiable "objective" standards in this exceedingly horizontal domain, judgments by critics, gallery owners, and purchasers may appear (paradoxically) to be both chimerical and all-important. Mathematics might appear to be totally different, inasmuch as it seems to be a highly structured vertical domain that has clear standards and is hence far more objective. Yet, even here, the field proves crucial. For example, the claim that Fermat's last theorem has been proved can only be confirmed through a gradual consensus among the most knowledgeable members of the field, some of whom may well disagree with one another for a significant period of time. And by coincidence, the medal awarded by the community every four years to the outstanding mathematician under 40 years of age is called the Field Medal.

Advantages and Costs of a Symbol Systems Approach

At this point it is appropriate to ask: What are the benefits—as well as the possible costs—of an approach to cognition in terms of symbol systems? The most evident benefit is the comprehensiveness of the approach. It takes into account a whole range of factors that may possibly contribute to the identification and expression of human cognitive capacities. The correlative cost is that such an approach involves the development of, or coordination of, expertise in several disciplines. It is not always possible to combine these types of expertise in one laboratory, let alone one person; and even when expertise in several fields exists, it is not self-evident how (or even under which circumstances) it should be combined. Thus, a biological approach sometimes sits quite uncomfortably alongside a sociological approach because, for example, the two approaches differ in fundamental assumptions, appear irrelevant to one another, or speak past one another. The coordination of these approaches, while perhaps crucial for a full understanding of a phenomenon, turns out to be a demanding undertaking.

The comprehensiveness of the symbol systems approach permits an analyst to span a number of antinomies that are often ignored or considered irreconcilable. In terms of the issues raised above, a symbol systems approach enables one to consider the nature of, and the relationship between, internal and external symbol systems. In the case of music, for example, one can study the ways in which individuals come to master different kinds of formal notational systems; one can then carry out studies of the psychological processing, and even the underlying neural substrate, of the ability to master and memorize a score with its musical, linguistic, and other graphical symbols. It might be possible to determine, for example, the extent to which skill at sight reading of standard Western notation (as contrasted to, say, skill at formal composition or skill at improvisation) relies on the specifiable psychological and neurobiological structures and mechanisms. It is not evident how such a line of inquiry could be pursued in the absence of an approach grounded in symbol systems—for example, a traditional behaviorist approach or a developmental approach that ignored cultural or educational considerations.

The classic issue of hereditary versus environmental contributions to behavioral competence lends itself to a symbol systems analysis. By argument, at least some of the competences involved in the mastery of a domain will turn out to be explicable in terms of traits or capacities that have a significant heritable component within a population. Yet, the ways in which these practices are realized, taught, and evaluated often differ enormously across cultures and subcultures; and the ultimate types and levels of attainments are always mediated by cultural factors.

The adoption of a symbol systems approach allows one to consider the underlying components of musical memory, for example, and then to probe the way in which musical memory is exploited and enhanced in various cultures. Various notations or other mnemonics can be tremendous aids to musical memory, assuming that they capture crucial aspects of a desired performance and are transmitted effectively to students; in such instances, individual differences in "raw" mnemonic capacities may prove of little relevance. On the other hand, in the absence of such elaborated culturally supported mnemonics, or faced with new forms of music that have not yet been effectively encoded, the apparent heritability of such musical competence may emerge as much greater.

The cost of this flexibility in the symbol systems approach comes in considerations of parsimony. It may be appealing to an analyst to be able to invoke a primary set of factors (e.g., *the* gene complex for musical competence, *the* optimal training regimen for musical mastery) and to pronounce a single conclusion (musical competence reflects the number of hours of deliberate practice on an instrument). The symbol systems approach entails consideration of many factors and their often quite complex interaction.

A final intriguing advantage of the symbol systems approach is its potential to serve as a kind of analytic *tertium quid* among scholars of human behavior and human nature. Among scholars, there is little debate about the need for two modes of analysis: a natural sciences mode, grounded in biological, chemical, or physical studies, on the one hand; and a humanistic, interpretive mode, exemplified by historical, literary, or philosophical studies on the other (Popper, 1976, 1990).

Analytically, these two spheres are too remote from one another, however. The gap between a study of the genes or the brain, on the one hand, and texts or cultural practices on the other, is virtually unbridgeable. Among the potential links, the symbol systems approach suggests a fertile reconciliation of these stances. It is possible to think about symbolic systems and structures in terms of their neurobiological substrate, but also to conceive of these semiotic entities in terms of the ways in which they can be learned, transformed, interpreted, and the like, within a culture.

Thus, a symbol systems approach smooths the way to a more unified approach to the construction of human knowledge.

This disciplinary link can be conveyed as follows. The material genes and the tangible nerve cells in the human body cannot "know" about religions, or sciences, or works of art. The gap is too great. By the same token, the bearers of cultures—parents, teachers, religious leaders—cannot (at least yet) be in a position to evaluate the status of brains or genes.

An analysis in terms of symbol systems can effect a connection here. The human brain and nervous system have evolved to be able to apprehend symbolic material—as argued above, human beings are symbolic creatures *par excellence.* By the same token, the agents of culture monitor their effectiveness by examining cultural products—the stories that children learn and recite, the religious practices that they master, the works of art that they cherish, perform, and create. Thus, if one may express it anthropomorphically, both the genes and the gods are able to make use of human symbolic products as they seek to carry out their respective tasks.

One criticism of this point of view questions its underlying "thema" (Holton, 1988). Perhaps it is not necessary—or indeed it may be wrongheaded—to try to join disciplines of knowledge. On this view, science and scholarship progress through a "divide-and-conquer" strategy. There is no way to resolve the tensions among themata analytically; one simply has to see which "story" proves more convincing to the community of scientists (Gardner, 1993b, 1995a; Kuhn, 1970). The present effort clearly endorses the rival thema—that there are dividends in seeking to link biological, epistemological, psychological, and cultural perspectives on knowledge, particularly when one is seeking to explain extraordinary cognitive achievements.

V. SYMBOLIC DEVELOPMENT— THE GENERAL PICTURE

In this section, I present a sketch of human cognitive development as seen from a symbol systems perspective. The picture laid out here represents my effort to be consensual: I record the ways in which generally acknowledged milestones and processes can be described from a semiotic point of view. This generic description then serves as background for the ensuing discussion (in Section VI) of extraordinary and idiosyncratic cognitive performances.

While seeking to be ecumenical, I should indicate that this portrait is not one that grows directly out of the consensual view, circa 1970. Rather, it has been particularly influenced by the "constraints perspective"—a view that I consider to be the chief new influence on developmental studies in the past 30 years (Carey & Gelman, 1991; Hirschfield & Gelman, 1994; Karmiloff-Smith, 1992; Gardner, 1991).

The constraints perspective builds most fundamentally on Noam Chomsky's work on language (1957, 1965, 1980, 1988; see also Pinker, 1994). Himself influenced by ethological and other biological lines of analysis, Chomsky has argued that the way in which linguistic competence develops in the human species is highly constrained. That is, rather than simply constructing language from scratch or imitating its production from models in the vicinity, the infant is already programmed to make assumptions about the nature of the input, the ways in which that input should be processed and transformed, and the manner in which it should be interpreted.

The specific claims put forth by Chomsky may well be excessive (e.g., his use of the provocative term *innate ideas*) and, if the past few decades serve as any indication, will themselves continue to be transformed in the years to come (Gardner, 1995b). In any event, I offer no brief here for the claims put forth in specific Chomskian texts. Rather, the contribution that Chomsky has made to broader social-scientific inquiry grows out of a key set of demonstrations. Every domain of knowledge is structured; human beings have evolved over thousands of years to make certain initial assumptions about the structure of input and models that they are likely to encounter in their physical and cultural environments, and these assumptions constrain in useful ways the task of learning and the mastery of cultural knowledge. One should take seriously the notion that at least some facets of development may involve the maturation (or "triggering") of certain prepotent structures and processes, rather than their acquisition in a more formal instructional or truly interactional sense.

Chomsky and his colleagues have taken as their task the detailing of the initial structures of "innate" linguistic knowledge; the set of parametric choices to be made, depending on the language(s) that happen to be spoken around the individual, and the means by which those parameters are "set"; and the stages or phases through which the organism passes during its transition from an initial state of knowledge/performance to an adult end-state. They have proposed that language differs in specifiable ways from other domains of knowledge, but have at the same time suggested that a similar line of inquiry ought to be undertaken with respect to other putative domains, ranging from spatial cognition to object knowledge and to facial recognition or music. This perspective, which has influenced many recent workers in the area of cognitive development (Brown, 1990; Carey & Gelman, 1991; Case, 1993; Gardner, 1991; Hirschfield & Gelman, 1994; Karmiloff-Smith, 1992; Keil, 1981; Resnick, 1987), helps set the stage for the picture of cognitive-symbolic development introduced here.

Phase I: Presymbolic and Protosymbolic Phase (The First Year of Life)

Fodor (1975) has argued forcefully that an organism cannot learn from and interact with the world in the absence of some kind of mental representation. In this sense, some form of internal representation or symbolization must be available from the moment of birth [see Bickhard and colleagues (e.g., Bickhard & Richie, 1983) for a critique and alternative perspective]. Indeed, evidence that the newborn is able to recognize the voice of its mother, notice facelike configurations, respond to deviations from already familiar auditory or visual patterns, and/or effect cross-modal matches (Bower, 1982; Mehler & Fox, 1985; Meltzoff, 1990) can all be taken as signs that some kind of "mentalese" is at work.

I demur at the suggestion that one should characterize such competences in the newborn—impressive though they may be—in terms of symbolic capacities. Were one to take this step, then virtually any behavior of any organism along the phylogenetic scale that involved some kind of recognition or transformation would be called symbolic, and the utility of the term would be lost. Here lurk the risks of "originology"—the longing to identify ever-earlier forms of a capacity. Moreover, I do not see at work any kind of representation here: The organism is noticing and reacting, but not referring, not symbolizing.

Still, the preponderance of findings from the past 30 years of research with infants demonstrates that it is not possible to delineate a particular moment or particular behavior at which symbolic activity commences. Rather, the infant possesses a rich repertoire of behaviors and a rapidly increasing set of concepts and distinctions among concepts (Baillargeon, 1987; Spelke, 1991; Strauss, 1979), and on these foundational capacities, more conventional forms of symbolic behavior come to be realized within the first year or two of life.

Consider these examples. The full-blown object concept probed by Piaget does not coalesce until age 18 months. Yet infants of 4 months of age already have clear expectations that objects will endure despite temporary disappearances and will undergo some kinds of changes and deformations but not others (Carey & Spelke, 1994; J. K. Gardner, 1971); such an incipient object sense indicates that objects can be referred to and can themselves serve as referents. The emerging sense of number can now be identified in youngsters of a similar age: 4- and 5-month-olds are able to distinguish among small quantities and can notice when an item has been added to, or deleted from, an array (Wynn, 1992). An appreciation of number, and of numerical symbol systems, is based on these early pattern-recognizing capacities. Studies of social interaction between infant and caretaker (typically, mother) reveal an extensive set of signals that are exchanged, with definite expectations, routines, deviations, and rhythmic cycles (Bates et al., 1979; Brazelton, 1990; Bruner, 1983; Trevarthen; 1977). These elementary patterns of social exchange form the bedrock for later dynamic routines involving language, gesture, and other forms of playful bantering.

Rather than simply constructing sensorimotor knowledge, as the founding generation of cognitivists held, the infant in the first year is already evincing incipient theories about the world of physical objects, and is instituting rich kinds of interchanges with social objects. Early forms of knowledge about numerical patterns, as well as recognition of specific visual and musical patterns (Jusczyk & Krumhansl, 1993; Kagan, Kearsley, & Zelazo, 1980; Papousek, Bornstein, Nozzo, & Papousek, 1990; Papousek, Papousek, & Symmes, 1991; Zentner & Kagan, 1996), can already be discerned. Studies of categorization reveal that, by the end of infancy, the child can not only recognize instances of categories (animals, household objects, kinds of colors) but also can understand the process of category construction (e.g., around prototypical instances, with the potential for subordinate and superordinate classifications as well) (Rosch, Mervis, Gray, Johnson, & Boyes-Braem, 1976; M. Strauss, 1979). Such

emerging categorical competence plays a crucial role in the determination of referents of symbols.

Finally, during infancy, the child is beginning to gain familiarity with the elements that themselves constitute symbols and symbol systems. The infant hears and begins to produce the signs of language (L. Bloom, 1970); gestures meaningfully and apprehends the gestures of others, particularly in highly contextualized situations (Bates, 1976; Bates et al., 1979); is exposed to and recognizes graphic and three-dimensional depictions of common objects and events (Hochberg & Brooks, 1962); and begins to appreciate the syntactic structure of other systems of symbols, such as those involved in the musical languages of the culture (Jusczyk & Krumhansl, 1993; Kessen, Levine & Wendrich, 1978; Papousek et al., 1990, 1991).

If one were to construct a tally sheet, with presymbolic elements/behaviors on one side and legitimately symbolic/ behavioral elements opposed, one would come up with a picture something like this: At the age of 6 months, most of the child's behaviors, reactions, and recognitions are properly construed as presymbolic—independent of involvement in a symbolic community that conveys meanings through structured symbolic systems.

By the age of 12 months, the situation has already changed decidedly. The child is capable of what might be called *mundane* symbolization: recognizing the referent of a single linguistic, pictorial, or gestural symbol, and, at least to a limited extent, producing single instances of symbols in one or more systems. Moreover, delineation of the sets of concepts and categories to which the first generation of symbols will apply has already occurred to a significant degree. In addition, the child has begun to develop clear schemas for effective communicational exchanges, not only those occurring directly through observation of the faces of others but also through the "counters" of words, pointing gestures, pictures, and musical patterns.

Depending on the child's abilities and the demands/opportunities of the culture, the balance of the symbolic ledger will have shifted almost entirely by the age of 2 years. By this age, the number of activities and understandings that are independent of symbolic competence has already declined precipitously. In contrast, nearly all of the child's behaviors are now part of a meaningful situation that involves the creation, observation, or communication of symbols or symbol systems of one or another sort. And in the absence of severe pathology, the individual will remain forever a symbol-using and symbol-creating creature.

Phase II: The Emergence of First-Order Symbolic Competence (The Ages of 2 to 5 Years)

Whether a wholly new level of competence emerges around the age of 2 years is an issue that remains controversial among developmentalists (cf. Fischer, 1980; Leslie, 1987; Olson, 1989; Perner, 1991). Piaget heralded the beginning of the semiotic era at around the age of 18 months, and linked it particularly to the ability to conceive of absent objects. In his account, play, dreams, and imitation (all manifestations of the semiotic function) involved a single underlying capacity to conjure up, and to internally mimic, an earlier evolved understanding or performance. From a quite different epistemological position, Allan Leslie (1987) proposes that the child at this age becomes capable of metarepresentational activity. Rather than simply recognizing/representing an object as itself, the child can adopt a stance toward that recognition or representation. This newly emerging ability allows the child to pretend: to treat an object as if it were something else, to imagine the existence (or nonexistence) of some entity, and to appreciate when someone else is assuming a propositional attitude (e.g., pretense, desire) toward some state of affairs. It has been argued that neural structures evolving at this time make possible the higher form of cognition (Fischer & Rose, 1994; Kagan, 1984) entailed in representational thought.

Alternative points of view have been put forth from several quarters. Some see symbolic activity present at birth (Fodor, 1975); some see a far more gradual, less qualitative change (Bates et al., 1979; Mandler, 1983); still others emphasize the rote imitation involved in early forms of pretense and propose a much more rigorous criterion for genuine symbolic behavior (Bialystok, 1992; Huttenlocher & Higgins, 1978). A decision about the nature and extent of a discrete, stagelike emergence of symbolic behavior clearly rests on the definitions employed and the criteria imposed. It is probably the case, as in much developmental analysis, that what appears as a qualitative change, when viewed from sufficient distance, becomes more fine-grained and quantitative when behavioral change is monitored continually and "from close up." Still, the collection of activities and understandings that we take for granted in

2- and 3-year-olds is remote from that observed in any other animal, and the 1-year-old child remains in many respects a somewhat laggard primate.

The task of symbolic development in the first or second year of life is to establish—or to allow to coalesce—a basic competence in the use of symbols; the task during the remaining preschool years is to establish proficiency in the use of those symbol systems that are highlighted in one's culture. The world over, in the area of language, this attainment occurs rapidly and with surprising similarity across children. Adult modeling is clearly supportive, but any significant exposure to samples of linguistic behavior in context suffices to yield 5-year-olds who are competent in the language(s) spoken in their society (Pinker, 1994).

Each culture features certain genres and usages above others, and these exert a major influence on the ways in which youngsters come to use natural language. Accordingly, where differences in linguistic performances emerge across children and/or across cultures, they occur primarily with reference to the size and content of vocabulary, the major uses to which language is put (descriptive, expressive), and the kinds of linguistic exchanges that are favored (storytelling, tall tales, argument, requesting; cf. Heath, 1983; Olson, 1994; Wells, 1984, 1987; D. Wolf, 1994).

For evident reasons, a significant amount of the research about early symbolization concerns the acquisition and mastery of natural language. The same biases that obtained in earlier times with respect to the scholarly studies of symbolization have carried over into the developmental realm. However, in recent years, there have been analogous efforts to study the phases of development in the use of other common symbol systems. Included have been studies of the development of pretend play (Fein, 1979; Leslie, 1987; Rubin, Fein, & Vandenburg, 1983), graphic symbolization (M. Cox, 1993; Davis, in press; Freeman, 1980; Gardner, 1980; Golomb, 1992), three-dimensional representation (De Loache, 1987; Forman, 1975), skill in vocal musical expression (Davidson & Scripp, 1988; Papousek et al., 1990; Shuter-Dyson, 1982), numerical understanding (Gelman & Gallistel, 1978; Siegler & Jenkins, 1989), gestural competence (Kaplan, 1968), and other nonuniversal symbol systems such as sign language (Klima & Bellugi, 1979; Shotwell, 1979).

Given sufficient exposure to and practice in the use of such symbol systems, children demonstrate characteristic trajectories in each domain. Moreover, although this topic has been insufficiently researched, it appears that the continuities across cultures are strong. With the exception of the study of natural language, the most research has been carried out in the area of graphic symbolization (see Gardner, 1980; Golomb, 1992; Winner, 1982, for reviews). Widespread consensus obtains that a period of graphic exploration and mastery of key graphic gestures and geometric forms precedes the often seemingly abrupt appearance of full-fledged symbolic representations of individual objects; that scribbles are often attempts at symbolization, though the scribbler may attempt to symbolize through action rather than graphic representations; that certain familiar objects are usually depicted first (the human form, the sun, birds, and flowers); that these forms are initially presented in highly schematized forms; that youngsters gradually learn to capture the idiosyncratic contours of objects, to depict a set of objects, and to compose a scene, usually organized against some kind of horizontal baseline.

Certain surprising features are widely reported in studies of graphic symbolization: the tendency to depict the human torso and head with a single circular form (tadpole person); the simultaneous depiction of internal and external features (X-ray drawings); and the initial favoring of forms that feature maximum geometric distancing of the parts (the arms represented as a cross perpendicular to the torso). Experimental interventions suggest the reasons underlying such graphic solutions to representational drawings—for example, the desire to depict what is known rather than what is actually seen, and the need to differentiate features from one another as much as possible (Goodnow, 1977; Karmiloff-Smith, 1992).

Analogous developmental progressions can be obtained in other realms, although the database is more modest and cross-cultural studies are less common. Pretend play has been widely studied in the West, for example, but less evidence exists about the incidence and form of this method of representation in nonliterate cultures. Numerical mastery follows a common pathway, but reflects the nature of the counting system and the primary uses of enumeration within a culture (Griffin, Case, & Siegler, 1994; Saxe, 1981; Stevenson & Stigler, 1992). Youngsters may not increase their numerical competence in the absence of supportive mechanisms; for instance, children do not create number lines (proceeding by steps from zero to large numbers) in lieu of modeling and scaffolding by adults (Griffin, Case, & Siegler, 1994).

Highly ordered progressions have been reported in the area of musical development. Children begin by singing small intervals (minor thirds) and gradually increase the size of the interval, filling in the intervening notes in a regular fashion (Davidson, 1985; Davidson & Scripp, 1988). Early musical development features many invented and spontaneous songs. In the reproduction of melodies, youngsters first present contour schemes, which honor the upward or downward trajectory, and only gradually come to master precise scalar relations. In general, words are mastered before rhythms, and rhythms before exact pitch relations. Children develop characteristic forms of notation that differ in revealing ways from standardized Western notation; for example, an underlying musical pulse is rarely captured (Bamberger, 1991). In the absence of tutelage, there appears to be little natural development in the realm of music beyond the age of 7 or thereabouts (Scripp, 1995; Sloboda, 1991). Sufficient studies have been carried out to reveal the broad line of symbolization across various specific domains and crafts. Two issues of theoretical interest loom against this background: (a) individual differences and (b) a possible unity of symbolic competences.

Individual Differences

Regarding the first issue: To what extent do meaningful differences in symbolic growth obtain across youngsters growing up in the same community? It appears that children indeed differ from one another in a number of respects. Some children show a bias toward the linguistic and pretend-play symbolic systems; these youngsters have been termed "dramatizers." Other children, who show a comparable bias toward graphic and (often) numerical symbolic systems, have been termed "patterners" (Shotwell, Wolf, & Gardner, 1979). [In earlier work, Gardner, Wolf, and Smith (1975) referred to these groups as "verbalizers" and "visualizers."] Within particular symbol systems, there also appear to be revealing differences. In early language use, some children emphasize referential purposes; others stress the use of language for expressive purposes (Nelson, 1981). Later on, some favor a more reportorial or analytic use of language, and others use language in more dramatic or expressive ways (Heath, 1983; Wolf, 1994).

Analogous differences have been reported with respect to other symbol systems. In the mastery of drawing, for example, some youngsters exhibit a predilection toward the copying of contours, showing little concern for the identity of the entities being copied. Others are biased toward the use of readily repeated canonical schemas; they focus particularly on the labeling of the object being depicted, showing little interest in the formal geometric properties per se (Gardner & Wolf, 1983; Golomb, 1992, 1995; Selfe, 1977). By the same token, in the area of music, some youngsters demonstrate an early mastery of pitch relations; others seem insensitive to this dimension but are able to handle lyrical or metrical aspects of music with ease. Children differ in their approaches to counting and adding; some memorize answers, others adopt or adapt strategies, or create their own sequences (Siegler & Jenkins, 1989; Siegler & Randi, 1994). Some of these early differences in symbolic approaches may signal a later capacity and/or inclination to achieve extraordinary performances.

There have been few empirical attempts to determine the extent to which individuals exhibit distinctive profiles of symbolic development. Those attempts that have been made provide modest support for the proposition that children may be differentially skilled (or unskilled) in certain symbolic domains, as compared to others. Working with preschool children, Krechevsky and her associates (Adams, 1992; Chen, 1993; Krechevsky, 1991) have shown that youngsters differ in their symbolic profiles, with most children exhibiting distinctive areas of strength or weakness. Working with young schoolchildren, Ives, Silverman, and Gardner (1981), and Demetriou, Efklikes, and Platsidou (1993) report similarly differentiated profiles.

Possible Unity of Symbolic Competences

The second major issue raised by the data pertains to the extent to which early symbolic development can legitimately be thought of "as a piece." The original *semiotic* position laid out by Piaget (1962) points to a strong tie among various symbolic competences; taken to its logical conclusion, this position suggests that all facets of symbolic development reflect the operation of a single underlying semiotic function, much as all dimensions of sensorimotor intelligence are said to be undergirded by a central structure and associated processing mechanisms.

The rival *modular* position, following from the Chomskian analysis sketched above, posits no necessary links among the trajectories of various so-called semiotic competences. Just as language is seen as separate from other communicative or symbolic competences, it is inferred that each symbolic domain has its own structure and trajectory,

and that the relations that obtain among them would be modest, accidental, and unrevealing.

In a large-scale study of this issue, conducted in the late 1970s and early 1980s, Gardner and Wolf (1983) discovered a pattern that was more complex than either of these polemical positions would predict. When the structural or syntactic properties of each symbol system were examined, few revealing parallels were observed across symbol systems. Specifically, the phases that children pass through when they master the formal aspects of graphic symbolization (creating geometric forms, attempting to follow contours, representing individual elements) appear to be quite unrelated to the phases the children pass through when they master vocal production (figuring out scalar relations, mastering the differences between various kinds of meter) or when they are creating narratives (devising settings, introducing characters, creating dialogue, honoring the moves of genres). Because of the apparent independence of these trajectories, Gardner and Wolf speak of autonomous "streams of development."

Other aspects of semiotic development—in particular, those having to do with semantic or meaning relations—are not equally insular. Indeed, although these semantic milestones may well occur initially with reference to a particular symbol system, they display a tendency to be applied as well in other symbolic domains. Because of this "spillover" tendency, Gardner and Wolf labeled these "waves of development."

The researchers identified four waves that begin at the end of infancy and emerge at approximately year-long intervals during the preschool period. At around the age of 18 to 24 months, the wave of "event/role structuring" emerges. The child at this age is able to appreciate the skeletal elements of an event—an agent is carrying out an action with some goal in mind. Normally, the wave of event structuring emerges simultaneously in the domains of language (brief narratives) and pretend play (brief enactments of events). But, reflecting the nature of waves, aspects of event structuring can be observed in other domains. Thus, for example, when children are engaged in graphic symbolization or block building, they are prone to convert the tools of those domains into agents of narrative. When attempting (usually unsuccessfully) to depict a truck, the child will abruptly transform the marker into an ersatz truck and scratch it across the page, accompanied by the vocalization "Vroom, vroom" (cf. Werner & Kaplan, 1963).

Around the age of 3 years, the wave of "topological/analogical mapping" emerges. The originating locus for this wave is found in graphic symbolization where, for the first time, the child is able without help to create a two-dimensional depiction of an event in the world. As DeLoache (1987; see also Pick, 1988, 1993) has demonstrated, children at about this time are also able to "read" a diagram or model that depicts a larger-scale or life-size version of the same array. Rather than operating in streamlike isolation, however, the topological wave can be observed in other areas. In descriptive language, there is an explosion of metaphoric usage; in narratives, stories tend to feature two opposing characters or forces; in music, complex songs are simplified so that they either proceed in one tonal direction or at one pace, or shift to a sharply distinctive direction or pace (Davidson, 1985; Fischer, 1980; Winner, 1982).

A finer-grained and more precise wave, called "digital mapping," occurs about a year later. The core of this wave involves an appreciation of the basic numerical system and its application in the enumeration of objects in a set (Case, 1993). Wavelike, this capacity is reflected in other forms of symbolization as well. The number of characters in a story is now maintained, just as the number of elements in a drawing is rendered with precision—sometimes, indeed, with inappropriate obsessiveness. Musical renderings are done with accurate rhythm and, increasingly, with reference to pitch relations as well.

Inasmuch as digital mapping may seem an advance over topological mapping—permitting quantitative as well as qualitative understandings—it should be noted that a digital approach does not always prove appropriate in symbolic use. Sometimes a more general connotative relation (larger than, louder than, more numerous than) conveys meanings more effectively than a literally precise one [two more (or less) than]. This situation is especially true in the arts, where presentational symbols express meanings differently from discursive symbols. The shift from topological mapping sometimes signals the beginning of a period when more expressive or allusive communication may be lost (Gardner & Winner, 1982).

A final wave of early symbolization has been termed "notational" or "second-order" symbolization. With mastery of the first-order (or direct) symbolization largely completed, children are in a position to create second-order symbol systems or notations. Children can now devise marks that *themselves* denote first-order systems—written marks to stand for oral language, for direct numerical competence, for musical symbolization, for landmarks in a town, and the like.

At the same time that these symbolic understandings are evolving, another crucial form of understanding is falling into place. Between the ages of 2 and 5 years, children come to understand crucial points about the existence and functioning of the human mind—their own minds, and those of other individuals. Two-year-olds show little understanding of the psychological domain; 3-year-olds are aware of beliefs and desires on their part and on the part of other individuals (Flavell, 1988). As has been shown in an elegant series of experiments, children below the age of 4 years do not readily appreciate that others can hold beliefs different from their own; after the age of 4 years, they are able to ascribe false beliefs to other individuals (Astington, 1993; Perner, 1991; Wellman, 1990). Only after the age of 5 years do youngsters have a sense that individuals may say things in order to deceive one another or to make some kind of an expressive point, as in a joke or metaphor (Winner, 1988).

This understanding of the mind makes an important contribution to the child's symbolic sophistication. To the extent that individuals wish their symbolic products to communicate certain meanings, they must be able to place themselves inside the skin and the senses of a listener or observer, who may not be privy to the same information as they are. By the same token, if an individual is to appreciate the meanings conveyed by other persons, that individual must be able to determine the knowledge base of the communicators and to elicit additional information, as necessary. Symbolic communications are exchanges between human minds; thus, an understanding of the pragmatics of the human mind is a necessary handmaiden of all symbolic communication. Autistic children, who characteristically lack such a theory of mind, are barred from communicating with subtlety (Happé, 1995).

Mastery of notational systems usually occurs only when children enter schools—in fact, one can view schools as institutions that were in part created to teach notational sophistication to children. However, schools could not exist if youngsters were not ready to achieve this form of "second-order" symbolic competence. At least in Western literate culture, children begin to evince the desire to create notational or other second-order systems even before formal instruction begins (Bamberger, 1991; Karmiloff-Smith, 1992; Vygotsky, 1978). Children may find it easier to master the syntactic aspects of such notations than to use them effectively for communicative purposes (Bialystok, 1992). A special genius of the human species is that its development need not end merely with second-order systems; human beings can proceed to create ever more abstract and arcane systems, which themselves refer to earlier, less abstract systems. Western mathematics is the most completely elaborated instance of this process, but it can be discerned as well in the creation of more abstract public or personal systems in any domain in which there has been a lengthy tradition of learning and achievement.

Children's mastery of basic symbol systems allows them to articulate their apprehension of major domains or realms of experience. As has been well documented by many investigators in recent years, youngsters develop, during their preschool years, quite elaborate theories about the world in which they live (Astington, 1993; Carey & Gelman, 1991; Gardner, 1991; Hatano & Inagaki, 1987; Hirschfield & Gelman, 1994; Keil, 1989; Piaget, 1929). To the above-mentioned "theory of mind," one can add categories of "theories of matter" (what is known and believed about the behavior of objects in the physical world) and "theories of life" (what is known and believed about living entities) (Gardner, 1991).

These theories certainly reflect the influences and messages of the ambient cultures, but they are in no sense simple imitations of the theories held by others. Indeed, in many ways, they directly oppose the notions of the adult community—as when children assume that being alive is simply a function of whether a given entity can move, or when children assume that everyone who lives in their neighborhood holds the same views. It seems likely that children arrive at these theories as a result of constraints that encourage them to focus on certain properties of the world (whether something moves) and to use certain prototypical examples as anchoring points (for young children, human beings prove to be the prototypical instances of living creatures; Carey, 1985).

Whether such "emergence of theories" should be collapsed into the language and framework of a symbol systems approach is worthy of brief comment. It could be argued that these theories represent an inference from experiences and do not, as such, depend on the existence and use of symbols. Indeed, as Karmiloff-Smith (1992) has

shown, these theories are often tacit and cannot be articulated by children, unless they have been pressed to contrive an answer in an experimental situation.

To take this position, however, is to adopt too narrow a view of symbol systems. One need only think of what it would mean for a 4-year-old to live in an environment that was not permeated with symbols, or to have failed to develop competence in any symbol system, in order to realize that the child has, by this age, become an entirely symbolic creature. Children's theories are inconceivable in the absence of the symbol systems and codifications devised in their culture. The real issue is not whether these theories require symbolic competence; rather, the issue is *which* symbols and symbol systems, *which* waves and streams and channels, participate in the creation, promulgation, and undermining of various theories.

And so, in attempting to understand the origins of the child's theory of life, one needs to attend to the words and propositions used around the child, the representations encountered in children's books or through the mass media, the kinds of discussions that take place between parent and child or among children, the pretenses in which the child has been involved from an early age. Or, to take another example, in attempting to understand why preschool children divide the world into "good guys" and "bad guys," one needs to take into account the examples of such labeling (e.g., in the media and in games) as well as the reasons why more complex characterizations tend to be reduced and remembered in stereotypical polarized form. Such analyses should help to reveal the sources of children's intuitive theories and, where relevant, to indicate why some youngsters subscribe to different theories than do other children, and why some children hold on with special tenacity to the theories that they have constructed (Gardner, 1991).

From my perspective, there is no mind more fascinating or more enigmatic than that of a 5-year-old child. On the one hand, the child is at the peak of his or her promise. A variety of symbol systems have been mastered and can be used with ease and appropriateness. The child also is expert in seeing connections among realms and in creating powerful metaphors that capture these links. Works of art of this period often exhibit an originality, nuance, expressiveness, and flavorfulness that disappear from most later work. And, of course, the child is poised to be able to master the realms of school and the disciplines of the culture in the coming years (Vygotsky, 1978; S. White, 1970).

Yet, in some ways, the mind of the 5-year-old is distinctly limited. The theories, models, and explanations of the child may be serviceable in various ways, but they are often erroneous, misleading, or just plain wrong. Five-year-olds believe that the world comes in black and white, and they do not appreciate shades of gray; they provide animistic or magical explanations for phenomena that actually reflect the operation of invisible but scientifically demonstrable material entities and forces; they associate right with size and power rather than with reasons and legitimacy. They remain largely egocentric with respect to the perspectives of others. And, not yet immersed in discipline-based notational schemes, they are unable to access much of the knowledge and understanding that have been constructed by their culture (Gardner & Boix-Mansilla, 1994).

Phase III: Mastery of Formal Symbol Systems

Rather than instigating changes that otherwise would never occur, the institution of school exploits changes that are already taking place in children around the world between the ages of 5 and 7 years. In contrast to the preschool child, who still struggles to master symbol systems, the child of this age is now symbolically fluent. In contrast to the child who saw the world largely from his or her perspective, the child of this age is assuming a lively interest in the views and visions of others. Most broadly, children the world over now want to partake as completely as possible of the world of adults, the world constructed by their culture. Modern secular schools offer one avenue, bush schools another, apprenticeships a third—but whatever the institution, the burden of the years of middle childhood is to produce individuals who have sufficiently mastered the agenda of their culture so that they will be in a position to participate in the adult world. In this respect, humans differ fundamentally from other primates, whose cognitive development has essentially terminated after the first quinquennium of life.

In the Western literate societies, as already noted, a chief challenge of the years following early childhood is to master the formal notational or symbol systems of the culture. Schools have evolved in order to help individuals read, write, compute, and master certain other privileged symbol systems, such as those involved in the sciences and in technology. With respect to each of these symbol systems, there exists a great range of competences. The ability to read and write well enough to deal with the demands of life in the early 1900s, for example, is widely considered insufficient for dealing with the demands of today (Marshall & Tucker, 1992; Reich, 1991; Resnick, 1987). Nowadays, there is much technical reading and writing; individuals should be able to operate in complex work environments, which share little in common with the farms and factories of an earlier era.

In addition to the generic abilities to master the three Rs, individuals attending Western schools are also expected to attain a certain degree of mastery in a range of academic disciplines, including ones drawn from the sciences (physics, chemistry, biology), social studies (including history and geography), and the humanities (literature, the arts). Each of these disciplinary areas features its own ensemble of symbol systems—some of them quite arcane, some of them changing quite rapidly. Individuals are expected to be able to combine strands of knowledge as they undertake interdisciplinary work.

Such are the not inconsiderable "symbol-using" demands that are now placed on schools. Individuals living in a Western society are also expected to master the use of various media (including computers) that themselves entail different forms of symbolic reference. These media often serve as purveyors of popular culture, but the ability to use these media purposively (rather than to risk being "used" by them) also entails at least intensive exposure and, quite possibly, formal instruction as well.

The need to master formal symbol systems may seem less pressing in a nonliterate culture, but sophisticated forms of symbol use may be equally pervasive. Often, symbol use is entailed in the mastery of myth, religion, ritual, and cognate spiritual realms. The attainment of sufficient levels of skill at the workplace—be it a hunting, an agricultural, or a crafts society—may also presuppose appreciable symbolic sophistication. Studies of such societal forms as navigation (Gladwin, 1970) or disputation (Hutchins, 1991) in South Sea societies reveal considerable cognitive demands and quite complex forms of symbolic reasoning, often implicit in character. And optimal levels of arts and crafts, while not requiring formal symbol systems, often demand a degree of finesse and versatility that could only be captured in highly sophisticated symbolic expressions (e.g., African tribal music, weaving patterns, Liberian tailoring, and so on; see Blacking, 1995; Lave, 1988; Lord, 1960).

Schools may have appeared to achieve their goals more effectively than traditional apprenticeships, but recent studies call this conclusion into question. Much that is taught in schools is acquired in what might be termed a *narrow scholastic way;* that is, students can repeat or slightly change the propositions and procedures learned in school, but they find themselves quite unable to utilize these skills or understandings appropriately in new situations (see Gardner, 1991, and works reviewed therein). I apportion responsibility for this state of affairs to two primary areas: (a) the failure of teachers to instruct individuals so that they can apply knowledge and skills readily in new areas (admittedly, not an easy task); and (b) the unsuspected strength of early-emerging theories, due to the power of the "unschooled mind" (Gardner, 1991).

An instance drawn from each of the principal disciplinary areas should help to make this point, which has been reinforced by dozens of empirical studies. In the physical sciences, even students who have studied mechanics at the college level continue to offer Aristotelian (or childlike) explanations when asked to explain the trajectory of a tossed coin or to predict the future course of a launched missile. Successful performance in formal class settings does not predict one's ability to apply this knowledge appropriately outside of the scholastic setting. Students of mathematics are able to solve a problem when some indication is given about the particular formalism that is appropriate to the case or data at hand. However, if the students have to select the formalism, or to vary its factors in some unspecified way, most students prove unable to do this; they can only apply algorithms in a rigid way.

Finally, in the humanities and the arts, students can offer complex explanations for historical or artistic phenomena, provided that these explanations have been modeled for them with respect to specific instances. When, however, the students are asked to explicate current events, or to interpret new works of art, not only are they unable to draw on comparably complex (and appropriate) explanatory mechanisms; they instead revert to the same simplistic stereotypes and scripts that a 5-year-old's mind embraces.

Across the curriculum, then, we see that the symbolic competences that have emerged in the absence of formal tuition often exhibit surprising power and tenacity. Even the routines of formal schooling prove unsuccessful at dislodging these views, except perhaps in narrow settings or with unusually apt students. One may infer that theories that have arisen naturally, possibly because of evolutionary considerations, are much more deeply immersed in the neurological and cognitive systems than theories that have been arrived at recently (evolutionarily speaking) in the species, and for which modes of training prove still relatively ad hoc (cf. Cosmides & Tooby, 1994; Pinker, 1994). There is no guarantor, of course, that apprenticeships are superior to schooling on any particular pedagogical dimension. However, apprenticeships do have a track record that reaches back much further than does schooling and that may well draw on mechanisms of observation, practice, and feedback that have proved effective with most human beings across most settings (Hamilton, 1990; Rogoff, 1990). Moreover, apprenticeships tend to be one-on-one and to operate in settings that are similar to those in which knowledge needs to be applied; the master knows how to vary practices so that they are crafted to a given situation. In contrast, most students—and perhaps many teachers—do not readily recognize the ties that obtain between lessons learned in the classroom, on the one hand, and skills that can be readily and appropriately applied to unforeseen problems in the wider world.

This discussion has so far underscored the difficulty of obtaining sophisticated symbolic understanding. The pockets of success should be delineated as well. Even ordinary schools do succeed in making most individuals reasonably literate; and good schools, situated in cultures that value education, succeed in producing a highly literate population (Stevenson & Stigler, 1992). Cognitive changes that occur in the years following early childhood do aid individuals in achieving sophistication in the disciplines; the 10- or 15-year-old is far more capable than the 5-year-old of thinking about abstract matters, of taking a metacognitive approach, and of assuming multiple, less egocentric stances. Moreover, at least some evidence suggests that schools themselves aid youngsters in thinking in more abstract, metacognitive, and pluralistic ways (Cole & Scribner, 1974; Fiske, 1991; Perkins, 1992, 1995; Sizer, 1992). Some students, however, have great difficulty in acquiring the scholastic skills (though they may exhibit nonscholastic forms of intelligence), even as others are able to learn to think abstractly even in the absence of much schooling. (Carraher, Carraher, & Schliemann, 1985; Galaburda, 1989).

Phase IV: Mastery of Societally Valued Symbolic Competences

The search for signs of success in these later phases of symbolic growth points to a number of important, if predictable, points. Mastery of symbolic competences to the level required by the culture is most likely among persons who have had: immersion in a domain for several years; work with masters who are themselves expert and who can convey this expertise; opportunities to practice acquired skills in new situations; and life in a society that values expertise and displays high standards. Absence of some or all of these factors, of course, lowers the possibility that genuine forms of expertise will ever be achieved (Ericsson et al., 1993; Gardner, 1993b; Hayes, 1981; Reich, 1991; Resnick, 1987; Simon, 1985).

Paradoxically, even in societies where schooling is required and valued, there is frequently a reversion to apprenticeship methods when one seeks to inculcate the highest levels of competence. Young lawyers work as clerks to judges; beginning doctors serve as interns and residents to experienced practitioners; graduates of colleges are treated as recruits when they begin to work for a company; and graduate students as well as postdoctoral fellows work directly with advisers who are experts in a particular discipline.

Closing Points

Expert practitioners in professional or skilled domains require a high level of symbolic and notational competence. Worth noting, however, is the fact that the most expert individuals *appear* to work as if they are no longer dependent on formal symbol systems. The knowledge embedded in these symbol systems has been so deeply mastered and internalized that the expert no longer needs to consult them directly: He or she can proceed directly from the setting of a task or a problem to the segment of the repertoire that is most appropriate for the situation at hand. Thus, the medical diagnostician can recognize a disorder directly, rather than reasoning backward or testing hypotheses against the charts; and a proficient performer can improvise on a musical theme without studying the score or planning the transpositions (Patel, Kaufman, & Magder, 1996). One may go so far as to argue that the mastery of symbol systems and notational systems is a

necessary step en route to expertise but is less essential—or, more likely, less necessary to be overt—once one has reached the level of the expert (Chi, Glaser, & Farr, 1988; Dreyfus, 1986; Lave, 1988).

Two points that have remained tacit in this discussion deserve to be made explicit. First, mastery of domains valued by the culture is a task that features many representatives of the social envelope that I have termed (following Csikszentmihalyi, 1988) *the field.* The writers of texts, the creators of lessons, the teachers and masters, are all representatives of the field. As the student/learner proceeds further, he or she is increasingly subjected to the judgments made by more remote representatives of the field—those who determine admission to select programs, conduct performance evaluations within those programs, grant access to jobs, award prizes, and confer the recognition due to an individual who has accomplished at an extraordinary level within the domain. Here (conceptually) is where the transition occurs between ordinary cognitive development and the achievements that are attained by only a select few.

Second, it is important to bear in mind that the individual differences noted with respect to young children scarcely disappear once one has entered school or has begun more direct professional or craft training. On the contrary, differences among individuals color the choices that youngsters (and instructors) make concerning concentration of efforts; the rate and degree of progress made; the ways in which one approaches and understands a domain; and, with little doubt, the ultimate achievements (Bloom, 1985; Ceci, 1991; Winner, 1996).

The system of instruction in a culture can stimulate high levels of performance in targeted domains, even when one pays little attention to individual differences. Naturally, such an accomplishment will not reveal the different approaches that may be used or the different psychic costs that are entailed. This state of affairs has prompted some authorities to emphasize the importance of training per se, and to minimize differences in individual promise or learning style (Ericsson et al., 1993; Stevenson & Stigler, 1992). In any culture where choice is permitted, however, it appears unlikely that individuals and domains will sort themselves randomly. Rather, individuals express different sets of interests and proclivities, even as instructors select certain individuals for admission and for concentration of resources. A huge step has been realized when individuals undergo "crystallizing experiences"—when they make connections to a domain or to an instructor who seems to fit their own predilections (Walters & Gardner, 1986). Conversely, an insistence that an individual persist in a domain, even when he or she shows neither promise nor inclination, is unlikely to yield a productive worker, let alone a master.

Yet to be undertaken is the fine-grained study of the interactions among the various factors described here: an individual's initial talents or inclinations, the early theories that he or she constructs, the requirements of particular symbolic systems, the pedagogical approaches used by masters and teachers inside or outside of school, and the processes of skill acquisition at the microgenetic level. In my view, intensive case studies of these factors ought to be undertaken before systematic experimental work is implemented. Already, however, it is clear that the costs of mismatches among individual, domain, and pedagogy are great; the unschooled mind is very powerful and the road to genuine symbolic mastery is paved with many obstacles, only some of which have been identified.

Before one despairs, however, it is important to recognize that these potential mismatches and obstacles may harbor promise within them. New discoveries and breakthroughs often come about *precisely* because an individual is unable to master or understand in the usual or canonical way, and thus is stimulated to invent new means (Albert & Runco, 1986; Gardner & C. Wolf, 1988; Goertzel & Goertzel, 1962; Simonton, 1994). If Einstein had been as fluent in language as he was in logical and spatial thinking, he might never have made the discoveries that he did. Indeed, as I shall note later, excessively ready mastery, or seamless compliance with the requirements of formal training, may ultimately preclude innovative breakthroughs. In the power of apparently unproductive modes of thinking is, at least on occasion, the seed of a remarkable breakthrough, one that might even facilitate mastery for subsequent workers in a domain.

VI. SYMBOL SYSTEMS AND EXTRAORDINARY COGNITIVE ACHIEVEMENTS: TERMINOLOGICAL CONSIDERATIONS

The foregoing portrait of symbolic development was explicitly formulated to apply to the broad range of individuals growing up within a culture. In this respect, it is faithful to the core precepts of the cognitive development approach, both in its 1970 incarnation and in the light of major lines of development in the post-Piagetian period. To the extent that individual differences were alluded to, they were attributed principally to differences in cultural opportunities—whether as a result of inequitable distribution of resources within a culture or different values across cultures.

I now turn to consideration of more profound individual differences—the kinds that lead us to deem some individuals, such as those cited in the opening pages of this chapter, as extraordinary in one or another respect. I begin by defining, and indicating common operationalizations for, six different forms of extraordinary cognitive accomplishment. Then, in the later sections, I suggest how these forms have been approached in the past and how they can be further illuminated through an application of the symbol systems approach.

1. *Intelligence.* Particularly in Western cultures, some individuals stand out from others because of their superior ability to reason, solve problems, and perform other valued cognitive activities, particularly those at a premium in schools and in certain elite professions. It has become customary to label these individuals as intelligent—or, more pointedly, as highly intelligent. The lay use of the term *intelligent* has been supplanted within psychology by a report of results on certain conveniently administered psychometric instruments; superior performance on these tests denotes an individual as highly intelligent.

Neither the standard definition of intelligence nor the customary means for measuring it has gone unchallenged. What sorts of abilities merit the term *intelligence,* and whether in fact more than one variety of intelligence should be posited, are issues that have been debated throughout the history of intelligence theory and intelligence testing (Block & Dworkin, 1976; Fraser, 1995; Gardner, Kornhaber, & Wake, 1996; Jacoby & Glauberman, 1995; Sternberg, 1985). But however these debates are ultimately resolved, there is little disagreement that certain individuals are distinguished by their ability to perform at a high level on whichever tests or tasks are considered measures of intelligence in their culture.

2. *Creativity.* The history of the conceptualization and study of creativity has to some extent mirrored that of intelligence. Just as some individuals are distinguished in terms of their ability to solve problems rapidly and accurately, other individuals stand out by virtue of their abilities to solve problems, create products, or pose questions in a way that is different (novel, divergent) from the approaches used by most other individuals (Guilford, 1967; Sternberg, 1985). In recent years, the application of the term *creative* has also been extended to individuals who are able to fashion new problems and then come up with solutions to those problems (Arlin, 1975; Getzels & Csikszentmihalyi, 1976).

Initially, it was thought that creativity and intelligence were highly related, but research has suggested enduring differences between these traits (Wallach, 1971; Wallach & Kogan, 1965). The intelligent individual is distinguished by an ability to excel at convergent thinking—a capacity to arrive at a single correct answer to a problem defined by someone else; the creative individual is thought to excel at divergent thinking—a capacity to come up with a number of novel and yet acceptable solutions to problems. Operationalizations indicate that one may be intelligent without being creative, or one may excel in creativity without distinguishing oneself in intelligence. Studies of highly creative individuals indicate that they tend to be above average in intelligence, but, above an I.Q. level of 120 (1.33 standard deviations above the norm), greater psychometric intelligence does not predict greater psychometric creativity (or creativity assessed by other—for example, consensual—means) (Simonton, 1994; Sternberg, 1988; Torrance, 1988).

Intelligence tests are surrounded by controversy, but they continue to be used widely, especially for certain targeted educational and clinical purposes. Routine testing of the intelligence of schoolchildren is no longer done, but intelligence tests are often used in making decisions about the deployment of resources for gifted children or for children with learning disabilities. Creativity tests, patterned after intelligence tests, have not enjoyed the same popularity. This lack of acclaim is probably due in part to a lower level of societal interest in creativity (particularly during the school years), as well as a lack of consensus on whether tests of creativity are actually tapping the forms of originality or inventiveness most valued by a society. Technically, the tests are reliable, but their validity has not been established to the satisfaction of many observers.

3. *Giftedness/Talent.* The terms *intelligent* and *creative* are age-neutral; they can be applied equally to young children and to venerable adults. In most cases, the term *gifted* is restricted to individuals of school age. Indeed, in many school districts, the descriptive gifted translates directly into performance on intelligence tests; youngsters who score above a certain level (e.g., 130, or two standard deviations above the norm) are considered gifted and are thus eligible for special programs and resources. The term *talented* is usually reserved for individuals who display a special strength in a domain removed from straight academic performance (Marland, 1972; Winner, 1996). Children who perform well above the norm in athletics, arts, leadership, and/or other socially valued domains will be labeled as talented.

In recent years, the terms gifted and talented have come to be linked for pedagogical purposes (e.g., in so-called "G and T" programs). Cultures differ on the values placed on these two kinds of performance, and on the allocation of resources, but it is generally recognized that both forms of extraordinariness merit identification and support (Heller, Monks, & Passow, 1993).

4. *Prodigiousness.* In many societies, special notice is taken of youngsters who are truly outstanding, whose score is several standard deviations above the norm. A child may be prodigious in the academic realm (as were John Stuart Mill, Norbert Wiener, William James Sidis, and, more recently, the 10-year-old college graduate, Michael Kearney), or in areas of talent. Consider the musical prodigies (Mozart, Jascha Heifetz, Midori), the chess prodigies (Samuel Reshevsky, the Polgar sisters, Bobby Fischer, Josh Waitzkin), the drawing prodigies (Pablo Picasso, John Millais, Wang Yani), or the gymnastic prodigy, Nadia Komenichi. There is no consensual definition of a prodigy, or of where the line should be drawn between giftedness and prodigiousness. Feldman (1986) makes the useful suggestion that the term *prodigy* should be reserved for a child under 10 years of age who performs at the level of a competent adult in a particular domain or set of domains.

5. *Expertise.* Just as the terms gifted and prodigy are generally applied to young children, the term *expert* is usually restricted to older individuals—adolescents and adults. An expert is an individual who performs at a high level within a domain, without necessarily standing out in terms of general intelligence, creativity, or talent.

Studies of expertise have been carried out chiefly from the information-processing tradition (Klahr & Wallace, 1976; Newell & Simon, 1972; Siegler, 1983). Researchers have demonstrated that expertise is only achieved when an individual has applied effort and practice to tasks in a particular domain over a long period of time. Nearly all experts have worked in a domain for close to 10 years, and most of them have spent many thousands of hours learning to play chess, perform on instruments, or solve math problems (Ericsson et al., 1993; Hayes, 1981).

Although they do not necessarily deny the existence of individual differences in talent or proclivity, researchers in this tradition believe, by and large, that degree of expertise is a direct consequence of amount of practice (Ericsson, 1996). It is generally recognized that an individual who achieves expertise will represent data mentally in ways that are demonstrably different from those of novices. Thus, when recognizing dinosaurs, solving physics problems, remembering meaningful (as opposed to meaningless) positions on a chess board, or learning long strings of digits, experts approach these tasks in characteristic ways, even as they remember and access information in ways that differ from those resorted to by novices or ordinary learners. Briefly, experts perceive meaningful arrays where novices perceive random noise; experts classify instances according to deep and generative principles whereas others would classify those same instances in terms of superficial properties (Chi et al., 1988).

6. *Genius.* The term *genius* has little scientific standing, but it continues to be used widely in the lay literature and in common parlance. Individuals with high IQs, youngsters who perform superlatively in a domain, and individuals who make creative discoveries are all considered geniuses. It would perhaps be advisable to drop the term, particularly since the proposed distinctions among terms may well capture most of the phenomena of genius in less grandiose or less confusing ways. However, it is also possible to give *genius* a more precise meaning.

I propose that the word be restricted to description of those individuals and those products that are so outstanding that they ultimately change a domain wherever it is practiced—or change an ensemble of domains (Gardner, 1997). Thus, although two talented poets may each affect the practice of poetry in a culture or a community, the poet of genius (like Dante or Shakespeare) affects the way poetry is understood and written throughout the world. A scientific genius, like Darwin or Newton, discovers one or more principles that apply across a wide set of domains. By this definition, a genius is an extremely rare phenomenon, perhaps found only once or twice in a generation; and it is

virtually impossible for a child to warrant description as a genius.

VII. SYMBOL SYSTEMS AND EXTRAORDINARY COGNITIVE ACHIEVEMENTS: METHODS AND FINDINGS

Traditional Research

Until recently, nearly all of the studies of extraordinary cognitive achievements have focused on persons of high intelligence, usually as determined by psychometric means. Dating back to the time of Galton (1869, 1883), scholars have isolated those individuals who stand out in terms of intellectual potential or achievement and have sought to identify their chief characteristics. In his own studies, Galton determined that eminence tended to run in families, and he showed little hesitation in attributing these accomplishments to the fact that family members were related biologically. Galton also documented certain intellectual properties of outstanding scientists—for example, the fact that they did not stand out from others in terms of sensory capacities and were actually deficient in mental imagery.

By far the most extensive studies have been carried out on individuals who are recorded as having high psychometric intelligence. The classic study featured the 1,500 youngsters selected by Lewis Terman in the early part of the 20th century on the basis of, first, teacher recommendations, and second, high scores on intelligence tests (usually 140 or higher on the Stanford-Binet). Terman demonstrated at the time that these high-scoring youngsters were not awkward, maladjusted "nerds": They were at least as healthy, athletic, and popular as their less intellectually gifted agemates—and, Terman believed, usually more so (Terman, 1925; Terman & Oden, 1959; Tomlinson-Keasey & Smith-Winberry, 1983).

The Terman study is unique because it has proved possible to follow the subjects over the ensuing decades (the survivors are now in their 80s). As indicated above, these studies reveal a group that is highly successful according to American standards; perhaps the chief discrepant tone is the fact that women in the sample led less happy and fulfilling lives than the men.

Precisely because of the importance of the Terman study, the assumptions and conclusions that were published have been carefully scrutinized. It is worth noting that the population is singularly homogeneous. Very few non-Anglo-Nordic individuals are in the sample, despite the fact that California already had a heterogeneous population. The fact that students were initially nominated by teachers accounts for some of the characteristics of the population. No doubt the profile of his sample emboldened Terman to voice his views (now discredited) about the relation among race, ethnicity, and intelligence. It is also worth noting that the achievements of the Terman group, while impressive, might have been predictable on the basis of social class, inasmuch as most of the subjects came from comfortable middle-class achievement-oriented homes (Ceci, 1991). Finally, the sample is marked by the absence of truly outstanding accomplishment in the creative domain, and by the perhaps surprising absences of President Richard M. Nixon and Nobel laureate William Shockley from the sample (cf. Subotnik & Arnold, 1993).

Subsequent studies of highly intelligent youngsters have not contradicted most of the basic findings of the Terman study. Most noteworthy is the study by Leta Hollingworth of students who had especially high (above 180) IQs (Hollingworth, 1942). The achievements of these students were also impressive; they were often precocious in the domain of moral judgment or interests in philosophical or religious matters, and they showed considerable imaginative powers. But a number of them suffered as a consequence of being so superior intellectually to their peers. Hollingworth describes individuals with neuroses, social isolation, and general unhappiness, sometimes caused by their feelings of alienation in school (cf. Chambers & Dusseault, 1972; Mason & Blood, 1966; Trollinger, 1983).

Stimulated by such findings, Julian Stanley and his associates have devoted themselves to the identification of young students who are academically talented and to the provision of special programs for them (Benbow & Stanley, 1983; Stanley, 1997). Middle-school students with high performances on the SAT are placed in programs for the mathematically gifted, or in analogous programs for humanistically talented students. These programs have been well received and have often prepared youngsters to attend college at an earlier age. Reflecting the social needs of the intellectually gifted, the youngsters themselves report pleasure at being able to associate with others who share their precocity, understand their interests, and exchange ideas as peers.

Studies of such highly intelligent students yield two intriguing findings. First, having an IQ score that is too distant from the population may be socially maladaptive. It is better for one's mental health to be one or two standard deviations above the norm, rather than three of four. Second, youngsters with very high intelligence or intellectual accomplishment benefit from opportunities to interact with others who share their talents; this result should not be construed, however, as implying that there are no problems or social costs involved in the practice of "tracking" students according to abilities (Hopfenberg & Levin, 1993; Oakes, 1985; Wheelock, 1992).

It is appropriate to ask about the particular competences exhibited by individuals with high intelligence. This is an area of great controversy. Many authorities believe that intelligence is a general capacity, perhaps reflecting the basic conduction efficiency of the nervous system (Kinsbourne, 1993). On this analysis, bright students should be good at just about everything that is academic or intellectual. Other scholars—and I place myself in their ranks—believe that academic excellence is simply one of a number of cognitive competences, though admittedly one of great importance in school and in certain occupations.

Whichever position is taken on this issue, it is clear that individuals who excel in psychometric measures of intelligence are skilled in language, verbal memory, logical analysis, and mathematical problem solving. From a symbol systems point of view, they are experts in working with notations and in handling linguistic and logical mathematical symbol systems fluently. They may also be precocious in philosophical or metaphysical discourse and in metacognitive abilities (Alexander, Carr, & Schwanenflugel, 1995; Silverman, 1994). Indeed, there may be some truth to the stereotypical description—that these individuals are often better at manipulating symbols than at dealing with real-world problems. One finds little correlation with the social, artistic, and/or mechanical challenges that are often important at home or on the streets but are essentially irrelevant in the schools (cf. Hollingworth, 1942; Sternberg & Wagner, 1986).

Idiographic and Nomothetic Research

When one compares the study of general cognitive development to the study of extraordinary cognitive achievements, one methodological consideration stands out. By virtue of their unusual or even unique status, there are fewer extraordinary cases; accordingly, it is riskier to lump the extraordinary individuals together. In standard experimental psychology, few researchers object when all 6-year-olds or all 10-year-olds are treated as members of an experimental group and are compared with an equivalent "control" pool; moreover, the populations can be disaggregated (all left-handed Caucasian females between ages 6 years and 6 years, 10 months) and the procedure still seems valid.

Such moves are suspect when applied to extraordinary populations. If one lumps together creative individuals (or prodigies or geniuses), it is far from clear that this aggregation is being accomplished on the basis of the appropriate indicators. Should one lump together creative individuals on the basis of their scores on a creativity test, the sheer novelty of their creations, the acceptance of their creations by peers, or the judgment of some group? If the latter, *which* group—peers, parents, teachers, outside experts, members of the same or of a different culture?

Applying the logic that has been put forth by neuropsychologists (Caramazza, 1988), one could argue that (a) extraordinary individuals should not be classed together at all, and (b) the science should advance strictly by the accumulation of carefully studied individual cases. After all, if there exists no independent way in which to determine that members of a so-called creative group actually share the crucial variable (or that those who share a particular variable necessarily merit a particular label), then one risks drawing erroneous conclusions from such group studies.

I take the position that no research methods ought to be ruled out of court simply because one is dealing with individuals who are extraordinary in some respect (Shallice, 1988; Zurif, Gardner & Brownell, 1989). So long as there is a publicly enunciated criterion—be it a test score or the judgment of experts (Amabile, 1983)—it is proper to treat members as one would treat the members of any independently defined group. Indeed, were the Caramazza strictures to be applied rigidly, some of the most valuable studies in the literature would have to be discarded. Nonetheless, it is well to be cautious about studies of extraordinary cognitive accomplishment that are devoid of reflections about the criteria used in constituting and analyzing groups.

A distinction introduced many years ago in the social sciences is useful for the study of extraordinary cognitive accomplishments (Allport, 1937). *Idiographic* work focuses on the details of individual cases, and the goal is to learn as much as one can about the specifics of a particular person engaged in a particular form of work. In the area of creativity research, for example, Howard Gruber and his students have proceeded largely through idiographic work (Gruber, 1981; Wallace & Gruber, 1990), just as Hollingworth (1942) proceeded with high-IQ children and Feldman (1986) proceeded with prodigies in various domains (see also Holmes, 1985; A. Miller, 1986).

The contrasting *nomothetic* tradition searches for laws or principles that operate within a domain. Such laws are unlikely to be identified and verified in the absence of the accumulation of many instances and the application of appropriate statistical tests. Building on the earlier historiometric work of Kroeber (1944) and Sorokin (1949, 1957), contemporary researchers like Simonton (1994) and Martindale (1992) have used large samples of individuals or works in order to tease out laws that operate in creativity, giftedness, and similar areas. Specimen areas for nomothetic study include the age of peak performance across different domains, or telltale early markers in the lives of individuals who ultimately achieve eminence.

Although these research traditions are generally carried out independently of one another, it should prove possible to combine them. If one accumulates series of individual cases with respect to crucial variables, it may be possible to ferret out laws that are operating. For instance, the appearance of "metaphors of wide scope" in the writings of some scientists but not others might inspire researchers in the Gruber tradition to formulate and to test a law that predicts occurrence or nonoccurrence of such metaphors (based, say, on the extent to which the science in question features spatial thinking). Perhaps more likely, an accumulation of case studies may inspire the nomothetic investigation of such a hypothesis in a more traditional way—perhaps counting metaphors through a content analytic procedure or through configural frequency analysis. It is also possible to use quantitative intraindividual methods (e.g., P-technique factor analysis); the results of these individual factor-analytic studies can then be compared using various factor-comparative methods (Lerner, 1995).

By the same token, nomothetic inquiries may help to explain why an apparently deviant case actually represents the operation of a law that has been discovered in another context. For example, the fact that male scientists often have lost their father, while female scientists usually come from intact families, may reflect a more general principle: Future scientists can usually survive—and may even be strengthened by—one serious trauma but are overwhelmed if they have to overcome too many obstacles (Simonton, 1994).

To make the more general point: Insights about extraordinary cognitive accomplishments can be gained through an assemblage of methods available to the cognitive developmentalist—cross-sectional and longitudinal studies, experimental and observational studies, information-processing or psychodynamic or Piagetian approaches, quantitative and qualitative analyses. But the rarity and elusiveness of the six kinds of extraordinary performances dictate care in the selection of methods as well as caution in the interpretation of results.

How, then, does one apply the symbol systems approach to the study of extraordinary accomplishment? As suggested above, the framework is sufficiently robust that it may well prove applicable to the spectrum of studies in the cognitive–developmental tradition. In the rest of this Section VII, I focus especially on intensive case studies of individuals of extraordinary achievement. This survey is in no sense intended to indicate that the applicability of the symbol systems approach is limited to such cases.

Case Study: The Domain of Music

To introduce a symbol systems approach to extraordinary achievement, I return to the domain of music. Consider four examples of extraordinary accomplishment:

1. A prodigy like Mozart, who was already composing by the age of 5 years and composed works of superb quality during his adolescence.
2. A performing prodigy like Midori, who began performing on the violin at age 4 years and was touring internationally by the age of 11.
3. A highly performing population such as the students enrolled in the Suzuki tradition of violin playing, who begin to work with their mothers while still toddlers and can perform concerti by the time they enter school.
4. A blind autistic child who can perform pieces of music flawlessly on the piano after one or two hearings (L. Miller, 1989).

Turning first to definitional considerations, all of these individuals merit the term gifted, because they stand out from a control population in terms of their musical performances. Mozart and Midori can be considered prodigies because they performed and composed in ways that are indistinguishable from those of adults. The other youngsters were not prodigies. Not even Mozart qualifies as a genius while still a youngster, though few would deny him this appellation once he had become an adult artist.

Other terms may be less applicable. Quite possibly, Mozart and Midori would have performed well on an intelligence test, but high musical performance is not dependent on such scholastic acumen. Not only the autistic child described earlier, but many other musically talented youngsters are not distinguished intellectually from their peers. Interestingly, in her retrospective decisions about the childhood intelligence of eminent individuals, C. Cox (1926) awarded relatively low scores to composers like Mozart and Beethoven.

The term creative proves even less relevant to this small collection. Except for Mozart, none of the other individuals stands out in terms of creativity; indeed, the potentials for creativity are quite modest in the performing realm, as contrasted to the realm of musical composition.

On a literal basis, all of the children have attained some expertise. However, for reasons noted above, the term expert is more likely to be applied to adults than to children. The term fits perhaps most comfortably with the Suzuki youngsters, who are learning to perform well on the basis of an instructional method that has been deliberately designed to elevate the performance of a whole group, rather than, say, a pedagogy suited to a prodigy like Midori, a genius like Mozart, or a musical savant who cannot participate in most other forms of human experience (Suzuki, 1969).

Moving beyond terminology, how should we conceptualize these individuals in terms of the four levels of analysis introduced in Section IV? In truth, no reliable evidence yet exists on the genetics or the neurobiology of these individuals, although it would be possible nowadays to accrue some information on both biological dimensions. One may speculate, nonetheless, that Mozart and Midori were both "prepared" neurologically and genetically to master music very readily; to use the term introduced by William Fowler (1962), they were "at promise" for musical accomplishment. On the basis of scattered neurological evidence, I would speculate that Midori's or Mozart's hypothetical identical twins would also have the potential to be great musicians and that their nervous systems would emerge as different from those of a control population—if not in the early years of their lives, certainly by the time they were young adults (Diamond, 1985; Scheibel, 1985; Sergent, 1993).

Regarding a diagnosis of autism, one stands on firmer ground by assuming some kind of biological substratum, although whether there are genetic components to autism is not yet known (Rimland, 1964; Rutter & Schopler, 1978). The neurobiological substratum is more likely to denote pathology, however, than to denote special talents or resources. Yet some have raised the intriguing possibility of a "pathology of superiority" (Geschwind & Galaburda, 1987); it may be the case that the very fact of neural pathology, as a result of either genetic or early epigenetic factors (e.g., intrauterine stress), may produce an unusual cognitive profile, featuring both special strengths and special weaknesses.

Finally, in the case of the students, there is no reason to conclude that either predisposing genetic or neurobiological factors distinguish a group of gifted 7-year-old "Suzuki violinists" from a control group. Indeed, in certain populations, most children receive an instructive regimen analogous to the Suzuki "method" (e.g., visual arts in contemporary China—cf. Gardner, 1989). Given the absence of contributing biological factors, one must look to other lines of evidence for an explanation of extraordinary performance. Or, to put it differently, the Suzuki method builds on biological proclivities that are universal in normal youngsters.

Proceeding to the psychological level, it is once again necessary to think differently about each of the four examples. In the case of Midori, one has a child of high musical intelligence, combined with exceptional parental support and motivation, and an outstanding teacher—the noted violin pedagogue Dorothy DeLay. Because of her unique status, DeLay encounters a significant percentage of all violin prodigies, and she is able to bring them to extremely high levels of performance. But Midori was already playing the violin at an expert level at the age of 6 years, and this result is unlikely to have been achieved in the absence of a "prepared" musculature, ear, and analytic skill, and a sustained program of steady practice.

Mozart was at least as well prepared as Midori, with one crucial difference. From an early age, indeed at age 5 or 6 years, he was already composing as well as performing. It should be noted that the line between performance and composition was much less sharply drawn in Mozart's day

than in our own, and that Mozart's father was himself a teacher and composer of some repute. Nonetheless, a sharp difference obtains between involvement in music chiefly as an interpreter of the works of others, and involvement as one who creates and notates new works. Mozart composed nearly every day in his youth and so, by the age of 15, he was already an expert in composition. Like Picasso, who had an analogous career, he had available the rest of his (lamentably brief) life for fashioning original creations. But why he wanted to compose, why he devoted his life to it, often in the face of severe criticism and the most adverse of circumstances, and why his music has survived the ages and traversed the globe, are all issues raised by this unique case (Gardner, 1995c, 1997; Hildesheimer, 1983; Morris, 1995; Solomon, 1995).

An individual like Mozart is so surrounded by mythology that it is difficult to determine exactly what his childhood was like. Yet, reports of his feats are so often corroborated by contemporary observers (and we lack similar myths about Bach, Beethoven, or Haydn) that one can attribute at least a certain plausibility to the historical/mythical record. Historical and biographical narratives indicate that Mozart had an incredible ear, memory, and compositional gift. He could identify any pitch, remember and perform even complex pieces after one or two hearings, and compose new, increasingly original pieces at a rapid rate. We do not know how he accomplished these feats, but, absent divine intervention, they need to be explained by the methods and concepts of cognitive science. It would be possible to carry out experimental studies of the techniques and mental representations employed by extraordinary young artists like Midori.

Mozart and Midori serve as excellent examples of what Feldman calls "coincidence"—the powerful convergence of a number of contributing factors (Feldman, 1986). Mozart and Midori achieved so much in so brief a period because they were blessed with coinciding biology, stamina, excellent teachers, a supportive family, and an intense motivation to achieve. Just where this motivation comes from is not clear, although it is evident that, in each case, the parents have been prepared to devote all of their energies to the career of the child. No doubt the child's spectacular achievements while still young encourage such investment on the part of parents (and a feeling of satisfaction on the part of the child). But it is likely that the child contributes obsessive motivation (Feldman, 1986; Greenacre, 1956;

Winner, 1996). The child's life comes to center on music, and if the opportunity to make music is lacking, the child becomes correspondingly frustrated.

If the term *obsession* can be applied to prodigies, it is certainly appropriate in the case of autistic children. Whenever such children have a favored domain, they attend to it for hours at a time and prove extremely difficult to tear away from their pursuit. One has the feeling that the domain is in control of the child, rather than vice versa (Miller, 1989). It is not evident that one should use the term *motivation* here, for perhaps the child has little or no control over what he or she is doing.

Again, the young Suzuki masters stand out from the other youngsters on the psychological dimension. To be sure, effort and motivation are needed, but much of the children's talent is constructed by a well-scaffolded, brilliantly orchestrated environment (Vygotsky, 1978). Founder Suzuki is a master at understanding the competences and the motivation of the average young violin student. Building on this knowledge, Suzuki has devised a regimen that begins shortly after birth and involves such features as the initial teaching of—and by—the mother; use of melodies that are easy to play and enjoyable to hear; joint playing, by mother and child, in a kind of love relation; audition of melodies long before they have to be played; and performance in front of youngsters who are more advanced, as well as in the view of youngsters who are less accomplished. In capable hands, mastery of the violin proves a surprisingly smooth process for any caretaker-and-child duo willing to devote the necessary time to it. No special cognitive or biological contributions are necessary; regular practice and motivation of the child to be with, and to please, the parent prove central to the achievement.

It should be noted, once again, that authorities like Ericsson (Ericsson & Charness, 1994), Sloboda (1991), and Howe (1990) are loathe to attribute special inborn talent to any youngsters; they might deem Mozart or Midori as little different from the average student in the Suzuki class, except in terms of the hours spent in deliberate practice. The most powerful evidence in support of this "training position" is the fact that the most successful music students seem to differ from others chiefly in the amount of practice that they report. However, there is no way of controlling who takes lessons in the first place and who continues to practice faithfully for many years. It seems far more likely that those who are motivated to study for thousands of

hours are individuals who begin with talent (however defined and assessed) and are rewarded for their ready progress than that these individuals represent a random sampling of some population (Winner, 1996).

One line of evidence in support of the special status of gifted young musicians comes from the work of Bamberger (1991). This investigator found such youngsters capable of forming what she terms "multiple representations" of music—the ability to conceptualize a piece simultaneously in terms of its score, the physical gestures involved in performance, the sound of one's own performance and that of others in the ensemble—and says that, in fact, these representations work together in a seamless way. Such seamless synergy tends to break down during adolescence, and the result may well be a cessation of efforts during a musical "midlife" crisis. No doubt rapid mastery of music contributes to the achievement of seamlessness at a time when critical faculties have not yet matured. Intriguingly, from the perspective of the symbol systems approach, gifted youngsters sometimes become frustrated when they are expected to take a more critical approach to the information contained in the musical score, rather than simply treating it as a transparent guide to desired performance.

Continuing this survey of the levels of analysis, I shift attention to the *domain* of music. Each of the various groups considered is involved primarily in the Western classical music tradition. It should be noted that Western music has caught on all over the world, but it is scarcely the only significant musical tradition—it remains to be determined whether musical development occurs differently in Asian or African cultures (Blacking, 1995; Davidson, 1989; McPhee, 1976) where the "musics" are quite different in terms of preferred structure, status of rhythm, kinds of timbre, permissible scales, and other variables.

Even within the world of Western music, however, the domain is not identical for all youngsters. Mozart, of course, lived during the rise of the "classical" tradition and himself contributed to its perfection—and, perhaps inadvertently, to its conclusion. Contemporary youngsters are exposed to many more idioms, and these can be seen at work in the performances of each of the other youngsters in our contemporary "sample." So, for example, the domain of Suzuki music has been rigorously structured so as to maximize ease of learning and performance; autistic performers, for their part, are likely to reproduce passages from the variety of traditions that they happen to hear. The domain of music extends beyond performance of some finite repertoire. As noted, Mozart was actively involved in composition, and some savants engage as well in improvisation, though it may be compulsive in character. Also available for study and mastery are other aspects of music such as history, theory, musicology, and cognate disciplines. Each of these realms embodies its own knowledge structures and practices, and these may be pursued by teachers and students for various reasons.

The final level to be surveyed is the sociological level—that of the field. In the case of the Suzuki violin, there is a well-entrenched field, and the gatekeepers consist of teachers, master teachers, leaders of the various societies, and on up to the nonagenarian Father of the Movement and his formidable wife. Individual children need not become involved in this entire superstructure; the gatekeepers survey the terrain and intervene when it is deemed necessary. In sharp contrast, autistic youngsters are essentially immune from the field. They cannot make contact with others, and while others may exploit them for their own purposes, such exploitation is unlikely to exert significant effect on the autistic children themselves.

In considering prodigies, one sees at work the field in all its complexity. The very notion of a prodigy makes little sense in the absence of a community interested in cultivating and then showcasing talented youngsters. Undoubtedly, there were prodigies before Mozart, but he clearly helped to define the genre for future generations, with his year-long swings through the courts of Europe, his fabled musical demonstrations, his ultimate wizardry, and, not least, his tragic end. The heights and depths of Mozart's career can be characterized in significant measure in terms of the responses that he did (and did not) elicit from relevant facets of the field—ranging from critics to rivals to those in a position to commission (or decommission) his music.

Midori arrived on the scene at a time when prodigies evoked international interest. She and her family were willing to bear this attention—if, indeed, they did not welcome it. The selection of DeLay as a teacher—and DeLay's selection of Midori as a student—involved an endorsement of a certain approach to training, publicity, concerts, reviews, year-long schedules, and the like. Midori's course is not unusual for that of a prodigy, but it is certainly possible for a gifted young child to lead a childhood that is much more cut off from outside publicity. Such sheltering seems to have occurred with the children of classical performing artists of international stature—for example, Pamela Frank, Peter Serkin, and Nina Perlmann.

In our four examplary cases, a different set of interactions is at work among the components and levels of the symbol systems approach. Mozart's case highlights the variables that stimulate a person to compose and then evoke a range of responses from the field over a period of time. Midori's case raises questions about the way in which one can negotiate one's career in the face of tremendous interest on the part of, but also pressures from, the field.

In the case of the autistic musician, attention shifts to other parts of the dynamic: the biological substrate, which is likely to be implicated in the student's particular profile of strengths and weaknesses; and the operation of the field, which has relatively little direct effect on an individual whose communicative capacities are so limited, but may indirectly affect his opportunities (Cameron, 1995). Finally, the case of the Suzuki musician illustrates that high levels of performance can be obtained even from relatively unselected individuals, and it calls attention to a very specific delineation of the domain and field, as initially constructed by one brilliant pedagogue.

The kind of analysis that has been put forth can be applied as well to children who realize unusual accomplishments in other domains. The analysis is perhaps easiest to carry out with respect to relatively *vertical* domains (Li & Gardner, 1993)—domains where the levels of achievement have been carefully delineated; where consensus obtains on what qualifies as good performance; and where, as a result, prodigies are most readily identified. Each of the four kinds of individuals can be identified in the domains of chess playing, mathematics, and graphic artistry (according to strict rules, of the sort that regulate Chinese ink-and-brush painting).

Specifics differ across domains. A pursuit that is inherently a competitive game, like chess, differs from a pursuit that is essentially an isolated activity, like painting. A pursuit that is central in school, like mathematics, proceeds differently from one that is clearly perceived as nonscholastic, such as an art form or a game. Some activities (like musical or gymnastic performance) are mastered chiefly through an intensive relationship to a master; others can be pursued in terms of one's own solitary explorations, such as the solution of mathematical puzzles (Bloom, 1985; Csik-szentmihalyi, 1996; Feldman, Csikszentmihalyi, & Gardner, 1994).

The nature of specific symbol systems is also crucial. In music, some competence can be gained simply by observation and imitation of more proficient musicians, but the mastery of written music is essential for anyone who wants to pursue a career in classical music. The ability to deal competently with the score, *qua* score, is a component that sometimes causes difficulty for youngsters who are otherwise prodigiously gifted (Bamberger, 1982). Youngsters who do not readily acquire such notational skill must either devise substitute methods or devote extra hours to the mastery of decoding routines. Notational systems are also crucial in mathematics, in chess, and in similar areas, if one is to read and master the accounts of earlier work in the domain. However, in other performance domains—for example, gymnastics or graphic artistry—no analogous notational sophistication is required.

So far, discussion has focused largely on the achievement of expertise in the domain—in the sense of the youngster's being able to perform at a high level, either while still a child (a prodigy) or early in adulthood (a youthful master). However, especially in our culture, a premium is placed on individuals who can go beyond expertise—those who can create a product that is unusual and that may, in time, actually affect future work in the domain.

There is no question that youngsters differ from one another in their performance on measures of creativity; moreover, these differences seem to have at least some longitudinal stability (Torrance, 1988), and they relate to other variables such as a desire for solitude (Helson, 1966, 1971), a tendency toward playfulness (Barnett & Fiscella, 1985), and a propensity for a certain form of primary process functioning (Dudek & Verreault, 1989). As for individuals who achieve highly creative outcomes as adults, we have little empirical data on their childhood; yet, much suggestive information can be gleaned from careful case studies (Gardner, 1993b, 1997; Holmes, 1985; A. Miller, 1986; Wallace & Gruber, 1990).

Case studies of highly creative individuals in our century indicate the following state of affairs. By and large, these individuals were not youthful prodigies: Of a sample of seven whom I studied carefully, only Picasso qualified as a prodigy. The childhood years of these individuals were characterized more by the emergence of an ability to work systematically and with discipline in some set of activities than by prodigiousness in their ultimate domain of performance—although they did display relevant talents from an early age (cf. Bloom, 1985).

At least some direction can be seen in these future creators by the end of their teenage years. And shortly thereafter, they selected a domain of expertise, from a constrained set of choices. Yet what emerges strikingly in these case studies is the impression that these individuals do not seem to differ cognitively from many other peers who also are highly competent in the domain. Individuals such as Einstein, Freud, Picasso, Stravinsky, Eliot, Gandhi, and Graham differ most markedly from their peers in the potency of their ambition, the singlemindedness of their involvement in the domain, and their willingness to take risks and to commit again and again, even (perhaps especially) when initial efforts are not successful. Briefly put, the creator seems distinguished more in terms of personality characteristics, motivation, and persistence than in terms of sheer cognitive strength.

Two cognitive features may be important, however. First, each of these creators eventually selected a domain and stuck to it. There may well have been an affinity from an early age between Stravinsky and music, or Einstein and physics. These individuals may well have been able to think naturally in terms of the symbols and notational systems of their respectively chosen domains—the way that most individuals think naturally in words and in visual images. Thus, they differ both from individuals who prove equally strong at a number of pursuits and from individuals who locate a distinct area of strength but find themselves unable to stick to that area.

Second, the highly creative individuals whom I have studied generally exhibit at least two distinct cognitive strengths, and the combination of strengths was unusual for the domain in question. (Thus, Eliot was a scholar as well as a poet, and Freud excelled both in language and in his understanding of other people.) There may also have been telltale weaknesses: Eliot displayed little talent or interest in science or mathematics, and Freud berated his own mathematical and spatial limitations.

As noted, Feldman (1986) has emphasized the importance in prodigies of *coincidence*—the virtually seamless coming together of many factors, allowing youngsters to perform at a dazzling level from a very young age. Creators must follow a different path. If everything goes swimmingly, they are unlikely to find themselves in a position to effect something new. One finds in the lives of creative individuals many examples of asynchronies—what I have elsewhere termed "fruitful asynchronies" (Gardner & Wolf, 1988). Individuals who are stimulated when things do not go well—when they cannot solve a problem, or when they encounter a new and discrepant element—are "at promise" for a creative achievement. Conversely, those who do not detect anomalies, or who find such discrepancies frightening or discombobulating, are unlikely ever to exhibit the pertinacity to formulate a contribution that may alter their chosen domain.

The symbol systems approach seems particularly well honed to deal with these instances of success and failure. If one is to venture beyond weak generalizations, it is essential to enter into the world of particular individuals—noting their strengths and weaknesses, the status of and trends within the domain in which they are working, the operation of the various fields with which they will come into contact. This perspective proves particularly valuable when one focuses on critical moments—the times when an innovation emerges and is recognized in a traditional or novel symbol system. The candidate innovation, recognized as such, becomes the basis for concentrated efforts, and, if one is fortunate, there results a product or problem that proves compelling to knowledgeable others (Gardner & Nemirovsky, 1991).

Other Case and Group Studies

1. *Prodigies.* In recent years, a number of investigators have turned their attention to specific groups of extraordinary achievers. The major study of prodigies has been carried out by Feldman (1986). In this investigation, the prodigy is identified not by a score on a test but by precocious performance in a domain. Feldman and Goldsmith studied youngsters who were precocious in music, mathematics, chess, and language. They found that these students were not necessarily accelerated in their academics more generally, nor were they precocious on Piagetian tests of operational sophistication. Rather, they stood out because of their early interest in, and ability to advance with great rapidity through, a domain that happened to be valued in their milieu (Shore & Kanevsky, 1993). Parents deny that

they initially pushed their youngsters; rather, they describe being faced with a phenomenal talent that cried out, with virtually a spiritual intensity, for nourishment and support. And indeed, much family effort had to be devoted to finding appropriate instruction to buoy and guide this talent. Ultimately, these prodigies are characterized by a coincidence of factors, all of which converge to yield a level of performance that sometimes seems to border on the unbelievable.

These youngsters are also skilled symbolically, but there is no claim that they exhibit any general notational facility. A child can be excellent in music without necessarily displaying any strength in school—or vice versa. Some musical prodigies even have difficulty in reading musical notations; and doubtless the same trends would be found with selected chess or athletics prodigies. What is important is that the child has the potential to gain skill with *some* relevant symbol and notational systems of the domain—musical listening and performance if working in an aural "practice" tradition, musical reading and writing if involved in the performance and/or composition of Western classical music.

Most individuals (including me) who examine prodigies invoke a biological factor or disposition as a contribution to the outstanding performance (cf. Stanley, 1997). However, in recent years, this traditional line of explanation has been opposed by two lines of research, both of which emphasize the importance of practice rather than inborn gifts.

Bloom (1985) performed a retrospective study of individuals who performed at world-class levels in six domains, ranging from swimming to research neurology. They report that these youngsters appear not to have differed from their peers at the earliest point, but that they gradually came to be distinguished because of the quality of their practice and education. Anders Ericsson and his associates (Ericsson, 1996; Ericsson et al., 1993) have studied the attainment of high levels of performance in young musicians, and have compared these profiles with students in areas such as athletics. On their account, the single factor that most clearly differentiates the highest achiever from performers at the second rank is the amount of time invested in deliberate practice.

Occasional studies have been centered on other kinds of extraordinary achievement. Studies of autistic and/or retarded individuals who exhibit an island of strong performance reveal that these domains of talent have emerged at an early age (L. Miller, 1989; O'Connor & Hermelin, 1991; Sacks, 1995; Selfe, 1977). A young child may become involved in drawing, playing an instrument, learning multiplication tables, or memorizing dates, and may then spend hours each day on this pursuit, in a seemingly obsessive way. For some youngsters, the performance can be reduced to the mastery of a simple algorithm. However, other students can go well beyond sheer memorization or rigid application of a single rule—for example, drawing objects in an expressive manner, or improvising new pieces on the piano. At least in these latter cases, it seems clear that the children have preserved the analytic mechanisms that allow productive work within a domain (Geschwind & Galaburda, 1987).

2. *Creators.* Two approaches have been used in the study of creativity. One has examined the correlates of high performance on standard tests of creativity. Studies have indicated that children who excel in divergent thinking tend to come from homes where art and other forms of expression are encouraged; often, these children also exhibit an unusual personality profile, perhaps being loners or undergoing a high degree of anxiety or stress (Stein, 1990). It has not been demonstrated that these early performances predict high creativity in later life, although there is a correlation with involvement in pursuits generally deemed creative, such as the arts (Albert & Runco, 1986; Getzels & Jackson, 1962; Torrance, 1988; Wallach & Kogan, 1965).

The other line of study has examined the childhood years of highly creative individuals, both from the idiographic and the nomothetic traditions (Gardner, 1993b; Goertzel & Goertzel, 1962; Ochse, 1990; Radford, 1990; Simonton, 1994). Individuals who go on to become highly creative adults often come from homes that were reasonably comfortable and that instilled habits of hard work, though not necessarily in the domain where the children will ultimately make a mark. Not infrequently, there is a report of a loss of a parent, or of severe childhood illness, each of which produces a period of stress in childhood (Goertzel & Goertzel, 1962; Simonton, 1994); future creators may benefit from a modicum of stress but are unlikely to be able to cope with an excess of early stress. Indeed, in their study of talented teens, Csikszentmihalyi and colleagues (1993) discern two dimensions that figure in determining the achievement level of a youngster: (a) the amount of support the child receives at home, and (b) the amount of stimulation the child is experiencing. Many creative individuals

are firstborn children, and a higher than expected percentage of iconoclastic individuals are later-born siblings (Sulloway, 1995). In later-born youngsters, a personality develops that is prepared to take risks and to deal with failure without collapsing (Barron, 1969).

The adult creator forms an interesting contrast to the prodigy. The prodigy has mastered a domain at an early age and has brought it to a high level of achievement. However, to go beyond the tradition, the prodigy must eventually become iconoclastic, and this shift typically involves a rejection of the parents and/or the hitherto most valued teachers. In contrast, the creative adult first becomes a certain kind of person—hard-driving, ambitious, thick-skinned, willing to take risks. He or she then selects a domain for creativity, but does so from among constrained options (Gardner, 1993b; Rank, 1932). Eliot might have become a novelist or perhaps a philosopher, but never a musician or physical scientist. Einstein might have become an engineer or mathematician but never a historian or a painter.

3. *Leaders.* In the final group of high achievers are the leaders, particularly those in the political or military ranks (Gardner, 1995a). In contrast to adult creators, future leaders tend not to stand out in particular domains as children; rather, they are often relatively talented across a range of areas and, in most cases, not notably scholarly. The two areas in which they are most likely to excel entail their skills at oral expression and their capacities to understand and—when necessary—to manipulate other individuals. Particularly those who go on to become national leaders often exhibit a vexed relationship with their father; a large number of individuals who become political leaders have lost their father at an early age (Berrington, 1974).

Interesting markers of future leaders include the capacity, at an early age, to conceive of themselves as the equals of individuals who are in leadership roles, and an often surprising willingness to challenge those in authority. These markers may seem tautological, but they are not. Rather, the markers indicate that the future leaders can discern in themselves the capacity to recognize problems, to analyze them, and to make recommendations that (they believe) are at least as worthwhile as those put forth by individuals in the leadership position. A desire, or at least a willingness, to engage in high-stake negotiations or machinations for power is another prerequisite for leadership.

VIII. KEY ISSUES

I have now introduced the three principal elements in this survey:

1. The symbol systems approach, as applied to issues of cognitive development.
2. Representative phenomena of extraordinary cognitive achievements.
3. Selected findings obtained in case studies and group studies.

I have sought to bring out the links among these three vantage points. In this and the following sections of this chapter, I turn my attention to two important concerns: (a) key issues that arise in the particular perspective adopted here; and (b) a comparison of the symbol systems approach with other current perspectives in the domain of cognitive development.

Translating Findings about Extraordinary Achievements into the Symbol Systems Approach

In an effort to reflect the traditions that have been carried out in prior research on extraordinary behavior, I have executed the above summary of findings with only limited explicit reference to the symbol systems approach. A reconciliation of such findings with the symbol systems approach requires three major elements:

1. A consideration of four levels of analysis that participate in the achievement of such high-level performance.
2. A focus on the nature of the domain in which accomplishment takes place, and, in particular, on the various symbol using and notational capacities that are at a premium in domain accomplishment.
3. Examination of the particular symbol-using competences involved in carrying out first-rate work and, where apposite, original work, in a domain (Gardner & Nemirovsky, 1991).

The above discussion of musical competence begins to suggest how such a reconciliation could be carried out in various domains. Thus, whether one is considering composition, performance, or musicological analysis, the psychological analyst must first locate a pattern (or a set of patterns) that describes the acquisition of competence, the continuum ranging from novice to expert. This pattern must be considered in terms of (a) the symbolic or notational systems that are at a premium in these various competences, and (b) the particular skills and abilities that students need in order to negotiate their way to successive levels of competence. In those cases where a step or competence cannot be readily negotiated, it is necessary to examine closely the strategies and approaches that *are* devised, either by the student alone, or with the support of knowledgeable teachers or scaffolders.

Finally, once one has reached the point of generally accepted competence or expertise, it becomes necessary to move beyond general principles: one must ferret out the particular symbolic representations that are valued by the individual(s) in a given setting and investigate the ways in which a move toward virtuosic, original, or even genius-level work is accomplished. In the terms of the Viennese composer Arnold Schoenberg (1950), one must distinguish between the *style* (an idiom that characterizes the typical work of an era) and the *idea* (the unique motif that identifies a particular work). Generalizations at this grain size prove of little use; the important work lies in an analysis of just what was done by a Darwin, a Beethoven, a Virginia Woolf; why they did what they did; and how it was apprehended (and misapprehended) by others (Gardner & Nemirovsky, 1991; Gruber, 1981).

Qualitative versus Quantitative Differences between Ordinary and Extraordinary Achievers

Until this point in the science of extraordinary accomplishments, it has not been possible to determine with any confidence the answer to the most enigmatic issue in the field: To what extent, and in which ways, do putatively extraordinary individuals differ from the rest of us (as my students put it, how do "Big C" creators differ from "little c" creators)? One venerable tradition considers the achievers as a species apart: blessed by the gods; possessed by a spirit; the subject of incredible love, luck, or fate. And there are intimations of this view even in contemporary writings—for example, those of Feldman (1986).

Not surprisingly, there is a rival, robust, "debunking" tradition. Some authorities are uncomfortable with *any* discussion of special talents or gifts (Ericsson et al., 1993; Howe, 1990; Weisberg, 1986). And many others, while recognizing that some individuals ultimately stand out from the pack, are loathe to posit any special processes or traits (Langley, Simon, Bradshaw, & Zytkow, 1987; Perkins, 1981; Simon, 1985). In this conservative view, intelligent, creative, or even prodigious individuals are basically like the rest of us: They simply work harder or advance more rapidly through the same stages, making use of the same mechanisms and strategies.

I disagree with this perspective. Whether because of genetic/biological factors, the conditions of early rearing, the value system of those closest to the individual, or some other factor or combinations of factors, I believe that at least some extraordinary individuals are qualitatively different, a group apart. They do not function just like the rest of us, and we cannot readily extend findings about ordinary individuals in order to explain those who are (or turn out to be) extraordinary. Nonetheless, I believe equally that the symbol system approach is capacious enough to cast light on the extraordinary as well as the ordinary.

Even if this position is basically correct, it needs to be unpacked. Perhaps some individuals have available special information-processing capacities (e.g., the ability to compute numbers without counting them or to translate visually perceived configurations effortlessly into motor movement), or perhaps they develop these special capacities through unusual early practices. Extraordinary individuals might not possess any individual mechanisms that are lacking in all others, but, instead, they may exhibit a combination of such mechanisms, or a procedure of timing or spacing, that is not available to others. Such speculations need to be grounded in careful observations, and, to the extent possible, in experimental data drawn from biological or psychological studies.

Let me indicate some of the bases on which I put forth this audacious view. Although most youngsters show curiosity about a range of realms, certain youngsters are not similarly curious. Instead, they are obsessed with a particular kind of material, and their obsession suggests a preexisting fit between a certain mind/brain state and a material present in the environment. Moreover, going beyond an initial attraction, these youngsters are able to advance, to figure out important aspects of the domain with relatively little support (indeed, in the case of autistic

individuals, they may not even be able to benefit from help). Whereas ordinary individuals may need to rely on general problem-solving mechanisms (or "g"), youngsters gifted in a domain seem able to use strategies that are particularly fitted to the informational patterns of that domain. And they are positively reinforced when they follow their own lights during such explorations (Winner, 1996).

It is possible to posit some of the special-purpose mechanisms on which selected individuals may rely. (Studies of autistic children or idiot savants are particularly helpful in identifying candidate core mechanisms.) In the area of music, certain youngsters may have perfect pitch or extremely good relative pitch; this skill allows them to hear or achieve certain results in ways not available to others. In the area of the visual arts, some youngsters may be able to remember scenes with eidetic fidelity and to translate these into lines on paper; others may be able to extract the contour from a display, and to replicate that contour, rather than operating from simplified geometric schemes. In athletics or dance, some individuals may have bodies and/or sensory systems that allow them to achieve certain feats (moving their bodies in certain ways or directions; being able to notice patterns that cannot be discerned by others) and may be able to remember and replicate bodily configurations to which they have been only briefly exposed. In language, some children may be able to read without instruction or to acquire additional languages with only minimal exposure (Jackson, 1988); and in mathematics, some children may be able to figure out computational procedures, regularities in data, and even higher levels of mathematics (like algebra or plane geometry) just by playing with configurations, numbers, and numerical relations.

It is conceivable that the individuals who appear to be using special mechanisms may actually be making use of the same capacities that nonextraordinary individuals possess but, for whatever reasons, choose not to exercise. (Suzuki teachers and many other pedagogues operate on this assumption.) Even if this is the case, the extraordinary individual may eventually acquire a position where he or she differs qualitatively from a comparison group. If—for whatever reason—a child becomes a precocious reader or performer or calculator, the child will be able to execute projects that are not possible for peers. Moreover, the child will be doing so at an age when he or she has a different conceptual understanding of the world than do older individuals, and is subjected to different social, emotional, and motivational opportunities and pressures. As sample instances, the precocious chess player or musical performer has a very different relation to an audience than does the nonprecocious (and generally older) one. The child may be less concerned about what the audience thinks, and the audience may be more in awe of what the child has accomplished.

In short, what may have begun as a pattern that is only a sped-up version of the norm ultimately yields a configuration that others will never be in a position to duplicate. Moreover, the early achiever benefits from attention (or is harmed by it) in ways that are unavailable to others, and the pattern of cumulative advantage (or, less happily, cumulative disadvantage) again propels the child into a different league.

For all these reasons, it seems to me more reasonable than not to conclude that extraordinary young achievers are not simply exhibiting exaggerated instances of performances that nearly all of us could achieve if we just tried harder. Careful analyses in terms of symbol systems mastered and then reinvigorated should enable us to understand better just what these youngsters are accomplishing and whether (and, if so, in which respects) they indeed represent a different order of individual.

Cultural Considerations

As in many areas of developmental psychology, most of our findings about extraordinary cognitive achievements are derived from studies in the developed West (mostly middle-class United States and, to a lesser extent, Western Europe, with rare data from other industrialized countries such as Japan). It therefore remains unclear whether the terminology, patterns, and findings reported here are truly universal, or whether they reflect the conditions, and possibly the prejudices, of one influential cultural center.

Even the limited cross-cultural evidence available indicates that the realm of extraordinariness is not parsed identically across cultures. In many non-Western cultures, both literate and not, the realm of excellence is considered to span skills and morality. There is, in other words, a belief that a child who excels must do so in terms of the morality,

the ethical tone of his or her behavior. An indvidual who is considered morally callous could not be considered outstanding, even if he or she might be considered highly intelligent or creative in a Western context.

One possibly representative taxonomy is found among the Keres Indians of Pueblo in the American Southwest. According to Romero (1992), who conducted interviews and observations, this population has no direct translation of "gift" or "intelligence." However, they distinguish among four domains of competence: (a) language and communication skills; (b) motor and creative (craft) skills; (c) an amalgam of affective and altruistic behaviors; and (d) the possession of cultural knowlege and lore. An individual who exhibits all four of these traits is considered blessed, and that blessed state designates an obligation, or responsibility, to help others. Honorific words are restricted to such individuals.

In Confucian societies, there is a bias against assuming that any individual is born with special talents. Rather, achievement is presumed to relate to effort and to a certain moral commitment. All can become skilled poets, musicians, archers, calligraphers, and gentlefolk. Even when individuals may stand out, it is expected that they will not show off their skills and talents but will wait to be acknowledged by others and will then respond to such praise with modest disclaimers (Gardner, 1989; Hatano, 1995).

In some preliterate cultures, certain activities are restricted to only a designated proportion of the population. Occasionally, the individuals selected are those who exhibit an early promise at tasks like sailing or storytelling (or, in the case of the future Dalai Lama, signs of spirituality); more commonly, practice is limited to those who come from particular families (Gladwin, 1970; Lord, 1960). In the latter case, the question of whether such prescriptive status actually reflects greater talent cannot be determined; even if superior talent could be demonstrated, the sources of that talent would remain unknown.

No doubt additional "configurations of extraordinary accomplishment" could be gleaned from the anthropological literature, and such an effort is well worth undertaking. By the same token, it is extremely pertinent to study programs for gifted children that use criteria other than psychometric intelligence and that sample from populations that are traditionally underserved (Gallagher, 1993). I believe that such retrospective and contemporary studies would add appreciably to our understanding of the nature of unusual talent, freeing it from possible ethnocentric bias and revealing whether the symbol systems approach could also illuminate the questions of quantitative or qualitative differences introduced above.

IX. A COMPARISON WITH OTHER APPROACHES TO COGNITIVE DEVELOPMENT

The symbol systems approach has a centerpiece—analysis of the nature and representation of various symbol systems—and a designated scope—consideration of four levels of analysis, ranging from the biological to the sociological. In many ways, it can be considered complementary to, or more comprehensive than, other approaches, rather than directly contradictory to them. In any event, it is timely to situate the current work with reference to other more familiar approaches to cognition—in both its ordinary and its extra-ordinary guises.

I begin this charting endeavor by mentioning four approaches that are *least* consistent with a symbol systems approach.

1. *A psychologically isolated approach.* Some analysts believe that psychological phenomena should be accounted for only in psychological terms. Perhaps fearing reductionism or disciplinary imperialism, they are reluctant to consider phenomena from other disciplinary perspectives, such as the biological, the epistemological, or the sociological. Such a stance is inconsistent with the studied ecumenicism that is advocated here.

2. *Behaviorist and learning-theoretical approaches.* For 50 years, American psychology focused almost completely on the analysis of overt behaviors and those principles that were thought to underlie all of learning (Skinner, 1953; Watson, 1919). The behaviorist learning tradition is now generally considered to have been misguided, though its legacy endures in various ways (some more productive than others). An important component of that approach was an unwillingness to countenance the status of such entities as symbols, symbol systems, and other representational vehicles, except perhaps in their pure signaling (Pavlovian) sense. The analysis of syntax, phonology, and systems of meaning undertaken here is not in the spirit of the

Okhamite exercise recommended by the practitioners of classical behavior and learning theory.

3. *Approaches that deny any special status to individuals who attain extraordinary accomplishments.* There is an understandable desire on the part of scientists to attempt to explain as many phenomena as possible in terms of the same basic set of underlying factors and processes (Ericsson, 1996; Ericsson et al., 1993; Howe, 1990; Newell & Simon, 1972; Perkins, 1981; Weisberg, 1986). Much of the effort in this chapter is consistent with that sentiment. However, it is possible to go too far and to question the need for a coherent account of what makes Mozart or Nadia or Michael Kearney different from other children (or other adults). An acceptable psychological theory needs to account for these apparent exceptions, as well as for those individuals who conform to normative expectations.

4. *Approaches that fail to bridge the gap between ordinary and extraordinary achievement.* The opposing sin to denial is divorce. Too many traditions of studying human beings proceed in splendid isolation from one another, with separate researchers and laboratories devoted to gifted children, autistic children, retarded children, those with learning disabilities, and the like. There may be reasonable practical motivations for setting up "special interest groups" focused on these populations, but research scientists ought to construct, insofar as possible, methods and theories that can cut across these various human populations.

Let me now indicate the major ways in which the symbol systems approach relates to several lines of work in the cognitive-development and "individual differences" traditions.

1. *Psychometric approach.* The goal of the psychometric approach is to devise measures for ascertaining the distribution of a population of children (and adults) on variables of interest such as intelligence, creativity, or expertise. By and large, the measures are paper-and-pencil instruments that involve short-answer items; but, in principle, the psychometric approach can be adapted for other kinds of measures, using other kinds of technology. The psychometric approach is not heavily theoretical, although assumptions are built into the notion that there exist traits of intelligence, and so on, that can be measured in relative isolation and without context. The chief considerations of most psychometricians are methodological: Are the measures reliable? Are they valid? Are they biased in some ways? How can they be improved in terms of relevant criteria?

On the basis of psychometric methods, it is possible not only to identify certain populations—the highly intelligent, the minimally creative—but also to trace the links among variables. It is possible to determine, then, the extent to which highly intelligent individuals are also more creative—or more neurotic, or better skilled at mechanical tasks—than an appropriate control group.

The psychometric approach proves most useful in allowing identification of individuals in a reliable manner, and in securing legitimate answers to the relationships among pertinent factors. Its relatively atheoretical stance makes it available for diverse investigators, ranging from those searching for the biological bases of intelligence to those interested in the traits that differentiate the leading lights of the field. In principle, the psychometric approach can be employed to look at all kinds of symbol-using capacities; in practice, however, for reasons of convenience and demand, it has been used chiefly to investigate verbal and logical symbolic behavior. Thus, it has contributed to the relative overrepresentation of these forms of knowledge in the research literature.

2. *Historiometric approach.* The historiometric approach is closely related to the psychometric approach and relies significantly on it. The goal of the historiometric approach is to identify laws that are operating in the realm of ordinary and extraordinary performance. The laws are identified by determining which quantitative data are relevant to a particular question and then arraying and analyzing the data so as to shed light on the motivating question (Martindale, 1992; Simonton, 1994).

Like the psychometric approach, the historiometric approach is not laden with theoretical baggage and it can be utilized by practitioners of diverse theoretical stripes. In many instances, there exists a wealth of information relevant to an issue, and the historiometric method can provide a confident answer to a question of import (e.g., Lehman, 1953). However, as in any statistically driven approach, the quality of the data and the lines of reasoning invoked in their usage prove crucial. So, for example, if one is attempting to determine the relationship between the size of the community in which one poet grew up and the quality of poetry that is ultimately produced by a cohort of poet-residents, the determination of the size of the community is straightforward but the assessment of the quality of the poetry is a more vexing issue. When more different measures can be invoked, then more diverse studies can be carried out, and it becomes less likely that a putative law will turn out to be the accident of a particular set of data, at risk of being undermined by the next historiometric study, with its own possibly idiosyncratic data-base.

The historiometric approach has definite limitations for those engaged in the study of children and development. Whereas the psychometric approach can be used with children from an early age, the historiometric approach is generally restricted to archival material, which rarely exists on young children. The historiometrician is then reduced to inferences about childhood or to questions that make use of data on adult lives.

3. *Biological and contextual approaches.* For the purposes of many analyses, biological and contextual approaches would be opposed to one another. The biologically oriented researcher seeks, as much as possible, to ascertain the genetic, neurobiological, evolutionary, and physiological factors that are underlying competences and behaviors (Crick, 1994; Wilson, 1975). The culturally or contextually oriented researcher, conversely, is ever alert to the particular "field" influences: The society (with its norms), parents, peers, siblings, and teachers, plus the specifics of learning environments, pedagogical opportunities, and direct and indirect messages exchanged between a child and those involved in his or her mastery of domains or procedures, are valued by the culture (Bronfenbrenner, 1979; Rogoff, 1990).

Biologists and contextualists differ within their own ranks on the extent to which they are imperialists or exclusivists (Degler, 1991). Some are uninterested in, or perhaps even ideologically opposed to, the alternative perspective; for a while, students in linguistics at MIT wielded pencils bearing the legend "Context sucks," and many individuals who favor a biological approach have been hounded or even attacked physically by those who fear accounts of human behavior that are rooted in biology. Other researchers are quite interested in the alternative perspective and in ways in which biological and contextual approaches might speak to each other (see, for example, the writings of Gould, 1981; Lewontin, Rose, & Kamin, 1984).

Those who assume this more ecumenical stance will be at ease with a symbol systems approach. After all, the symbol systems approach attempts to incorporate biological evidence at the initial level, and contextual influence at each of the remaining three levels. However, it is possible that others of a biological or contextual disposition will be uncomfortable with a symbol systems approach.

Such discomfort can arise for one of two reasons: (a) the practitioner may be so devoted to a particular stance that he or she may have little patience for explanations that draw on other causal factors, or (b) his or her particular view of the preferred stance may leave little room for a consideration of other semiotic factors.

From the biological perspective, it is possible to assume that a symbolic analysis is only a holding action. Once we understand the nature of language from a biological or genetic perspective, so the argument goes, it will not be necessary to invoke considerations of representations, let alone complex analyses of syntax, grammar, and the like (cf., Rowe, 1994).

Among cultural/contextual analysts, opposition to the symbol systems approach takes a different form. One variety of cultural analyst subscribes to the position that all knowledge is situated and needs to be so analyzed (Lave & Wenger, 1991). Regarding this analysis, it is not valid to speak of competence or mastery of a symbol system in some kind of isolated and decontextualized form. One's knowledge is only expressed, and therefore only needs to be taken into account, at those moments when it has been activated by situational factors: Otherwise, it is essentially nonexistent. Other contextualists would undermine—or at least challenge—the need for an analysis of symbol systems (Gibson, 1966; Shanon, 1993; Shaw & Bransford, 1977), either because human behavior is thought to emerge from dynamic environmental interactions or because human skills are tied to certain practices in certain contexts.

4. *Standard Cognitive Views, Circa 1970.* As indicated earlier in this chapter, the present work grows out of, and to some extent builds on, the consensual views that were articulated earlier in the century by Vygotsky, Werner, Bruner, Piaget, Inhelder, and their associates and followers. A focus on symbol systems is wholly consistent with the kinds of analyses put forth by these pioneers.

The present position goes beyond the founding generation by attempting to incorporate biological, sociological, and epistemological considerations, and by recognizing findings (e.g., from behavioral genetics and neurobiology) and phenomena (e.g., recently reported savants) that could not have been known at the time. The focus on individual differences would seem alien—or at least would represent a "stretch"—to these universally oriented scientists. Probably the line of research that is most discrepant is the focus on the possibly deep differences among symbolic competences and symbolic domains; with certain exceptions, earlier workers were more sympathetic to the notion of a general underlying "semiotic" factor.

Major Cognitive Views at the End of the Century

Most of the major researchers on cognitive development are represented elsewhere in this *Handbook,* where they offer their respective accounts of where the field has been and where it might most appropriately advance (see, among others, the chapters by Brown, Carey, Case, Fischer, Flavell, Gelman, Karmiloff-Smith, Keil, Siegler, and Sternberg). It is not possible here to describe their positions individually or to represent commonalities and divergences (see, for example, Sternberg, 1984), but a few general remarks may be suggestive.

1. *Neo-Piagetian.* Nearly all post-Piagetians concur that Piaget himself paid insufficient attention to the nature of, and possible differences among, domains of competence. Few go so far as Feldman and the present author in highlighting the differences in various domains; but some focus on the constraints that may differ across domains (Brown, 1990; Gelman, 1991; Karmiloff-Smith, 1992; Keil, 1981), and others emphasize the demands of particular tasks and skills (Case, 1985, 1993; Fischer, 1980; Siegler & Jenkins, 1989).

A major point of discussion is whether it still is valid to speak of general developmental stages that obtain across domains; earlier, Case (1985) and Fischer (1980) were sympathetic to this position, but, in more recent writings, they have acknowledged greater task-specificity. Case's (1993) "central conceptual structures" may represent an intermediate position that acknowledges both the generality and the specificity found in cognitive development. Demetriou and associates (1993) have also delineated five different categories of knowledge that can be analyzed in stage-structural terms.

2. *Information processing.* A major line of work that had barely surfaced in the 1960s is the information-processing approach (Klahr & Wallace, 1976; Siegler,

1983). Growing out of computational and cognitive scientific work, this perspective stresses the detailed analysis of individual tasks, and their modeling in computer programs. In the early years, information processors were strongly influenced by the symbol systems approach of Newell and Simon (1972; see also, Klahr & Wallace, 1976); this emphasis is of course congenial with the present one. More recently, other computational accounts have gained in persuasiveness, and these latter approaches are not necessarily congruent—but neither are they necessarily *in*congruent—with a symbol systems approach (Karmiloff-Smith, 1992; Rumelhart & McClelland, 1986; Smolensky, 1988).

The information-processing approach with children has generally devoted little attention to individual differences; when these have been noted, they have been regarded as background noise or normal variation. An important exception in this regard is Siegler (1983), who has called attention to the rise and persistence of different kinds of information-processing strategies in the arithmetical behaviors of young children, and who has insisted that the sources and factors of these distinctive patterns need to be explained (Siegler & Jenkins, 1989). Those concerned with adult differences in competence have generally attributed such differences to expertise and have not searched for qualitatively distinctive patterns.

3. *Constraints.* Probably closest to the position developed here is the constraints perspective, with its origins in linguistic analysis and its more recent application in such domains as physical, biological, and ontological knowledge (see Carey & Gelman, 1991; Hirschfield & Gelman, 1994; and other references cited above in Section V). While not typically employing the language of symbol systems and symbolic structures, the considerations that are brought to bear are similar to those described in this chapter. The theories, structures, and processes probed by constraints researchers are readily parsed in terms of the symbol systems and symbol-using processes that are utilized as children come to know domains like language or music, and as they come to engage in behaviors like naming, classifying, or theory-building. Probably the major contrast with the position detailed here is the focus of constraints researchers on universal (some would say innate) constraints and a correlative ignoring of individual dfferences and differences that reflect the values and practices of a particular culture.

4. *Educational researchers.* In the past few decades, a sizable number of trained developmentalists have become involved in education, often working actively in schools on issues of curriculum and instruction and, sometimes, on broader issues of school reform (Brown & Campione, 1994; Bruer, 1993; Gardner, 1991, 1993c; McGilly, 1994; Perkins, 1992, 1995). This new focus of energies has resulted in much greater interest in a variety of learning contexts (such as schools, museums, and apprenticeships) and in the kinds of areas covered in school—nonuniversal disciplines rather than universal Kantian competences (Brown & Campione, 1994; Feldman et al., 1994; Gardner & Boix-Mansilla, 1994). The educational focus is entirely compatible with the symbol systems approach, except perhaps for uneasiness with biological factors that might (erroneously) be construed as undermining possibilities for learning.

X. CONCLUSIONS

Most of the authors in this *Handbook* have examined well-established disciplines or subdisciplines, though they have put forth their own particular construction of the areas that they have surveyed. In that company, this chapter is unusual. Earlier editions of the *Handbook* have not, except incidentally, examined instances of extraordinary achievement; and the various chapters and handbooks that do focus on extraordinary accomplishment have not "stretched" to encompass the mainstream "universal" patterns of human cognitive growth (Colangelo & Davis, 1997; Heller et al., 1993). Disciplinary lines have traditionally been drawn quite sharply, and the processes by which disciplinary delineations are altered are not well understood. In the present instance, I have sought to influence the discipline of developmental psychology in three ways:

1. The inclusion in this *Handbook* of a chapter on extraordinary achievement represents one incursion on earlier practices.
2. The symbol systems approach presents a new perspective (one might say, a fresh contender) within the family of cognitive-developmental frameworks.
3. The chapter puts forth an apparently paradoxical perspective. On the one hand, I argue that extraordinary individuals may well be qualitatively different from the norm; on the other hand, I argue that extraordinary achievements can—indeed, must—be explicable in the

same terms and concepts that we use in accounting for universal forms of behavior and understanding.

In the best of worlds, this three-pronged attack will work effectively and the connections among the prongs will become manifest. Less happily, my effort may come to be seen as misguided or premature. Even in the latter event, I hope that some readers—students perhaps even more so than their teachers—will become sufficiently intrigued by the Nadias, the Mozarts, and the Suzuki students so as to devote their own investigative efforts to illuminating these fascinating phenomena. Significant scientific progress may depend, in the last analysis, on unusual minds: But intriguing phenomena can stimulate the most ordinary among us to unexpected heights of conceptualization and productivity.

ACKNOWLEDGMENTS

I thank William Damon, Richard Lerner, and Ellen Winner for comments on earlier drafts. Lisa Bromer and Melissa Brand were extremely helpful in securing research materials. Work on this essay was carried out at the Center for Advanced Study in the Behavioral Sciences, Stanford, CA. I thank the MacArthur Foundation, the Rockefeller Foundation, and the Spencer Foundation for supporting my research.

REFERENCES

Adams, M. (1992). An empirical investigation of domain-specific theories of preschool children's cognitive abilities. Unpublished doctoral dissertation. Tufts University, Medford, MA.

Albert, R., & Runco, M. (1986). The achievement of eminence: A model of exceptional boys and their parents. In R. J. Sternberg & J. E. Davidson (Eds.), *Conceptions of giftedness* (pp. 332–357). New York: Cambridge University Press.

Alexander, J. M., Carr, M., & Schwanenflugel, P. J. (1995). Development of metacognition in gifted children: Directions for future research. *Developmental Review, 15*(1), 1–37.

Allport, G. (1937). *Personality: A psychological interpretation.* New York: Holt.

Amabile, T. (1983). *The social psychology of creativity.* New York: Springer-Verlag.

Arlin, P. (1975). Cognitive development in adulthood: A fifth stage? *Developmental Psychology, 23,* 602–606.

Astington, J. (1993). *The child's discovery of mind.* Cambridge, MA: Harvard University Press.

Baillargeon, R. (1987). Object permanence in 3.5- and 4.5-month-old infants. *Developmental Psychology, 23,* 655–664.

Baldwin, J. M. (1897). *Mental development in the child and the race.* New York: Macmillan.

Baltes, P. (1983). Life-span developmental psychology: Observations on history and theory revisited. In R. M. Lerner (Ed.), *Developmental psychology: Historical and philosophical perspectives* (pp. 79–111). Hillsdale, NJ: Erlbaum.

Bamberger, J. (1982). Growing up prodigies: The mid-life crisis. In D. H. Feldman (Ed.), *Developmental approaches to giftedness* (pp. 61–78). San Francisco: Jossey-Bass.

Bamberger, J. (1991). *The mind behind the musical ear.* Cambridge, MA: Harvard University Press.

Barker, R. (1968). *Ecological psychology: Concepts and methods for studying the environment of human behavior.* Stanford, CA: Stanford University Press.

Barnett, L. A., & Fiscella, J. (1985, Spring). A child by any other name . . . a comparison of the playfulness of gifted and nongifted children. *Gifted Child Quarterly, 29*(2), 61–66.

Barron, F. (1969). *Creative person and creative process.* New York: Holt, Rinehart and Winston.

Barzun, J. (1941). *Darwin, Marx, Wagner: Critique of a heritage.* Boston: Little, Brown.

Bates, E. (1976). *Language on context.* New York: Academic Press.

Bates, E. (with Benigni, L., Bretheron, I., Camaioni, L., & Volterra, V.). (1979). *The emergence of symbols: Cognition and communication in infancy.* New York: Academic Press.

Bay, E. (1964). Present concepts of aphasia. *Geriatrics, 19,* 319–331.

Benbow, C. P. (1988). Sex differences in mathematical reasoning ability in intellectually talented preadolescents: Their nature, effects, and possible cures. *Behavioral and Brain Sciences, 11,* 169–232.

Benbow, C. P., & Stanley, J. (1983). *Academic precocity: Aspects of its development.* Baltimore: Johns Hopkins University Press.

Berrington, H. (1974). [Review of the book *The fiery chariot: A study of British Prime Ministers and the search for love*]. *British Journal of Political Science, 4,* 345–369.

Bever, T., & Chiarello, R. (1974). Cerebral dominance in musicians and nonmusicians. *Science, 185,* 537–539.

Bialystok, E. (1992). The emergence of symbolic thought: Introduction. *Cognitive Development, 7,* 269–272.

Bickhard, M., & Richie, D. M. (1983). *On the nature of representation: A case study of James Gibson's theory of perception.* New York: Praeger.

Bidell, T. R., & Fischer, K. W. (1992). Beyond the stage debate: Action, structure, and variability in Piagetian theory and research. In R. J. Sternberg & C. A. Berg (Eds.), *Intellectual development* (pp. 100–140). New York: Cambridge University Press.

Binet, A., & Simon, T. (1909). The intelligence of the feeble-minded. *L'année psychologique, 15,* 1–147.

Blacking, J. (1995). *Music, culture, experience: Selected papers of John Blacking* (R. Byron, Ed.). Chicago: University of Chicago.

Block, N., & Dworkin, G. (1976). *The IQ controversy.* New York: Pantheon Press.

Bloom, B. (with Sosniak, L.). (1985). *Developing talent in young children.* New York: Ballantine Books.

Bloom, L. (1970). *Language development: Form and function in emerging grammar.* Cambridge, MA: MIT Press.

Blumenthal, A. (1970). *Language and psychology: Historical aspects of psycholinguistics.* New York: Wiley.

Bouchard, T., & Propping, P. (1993). *Twins as a tool of behavioral genetics.* Chichester, England: Wiley.

Bower, T. G. R. (1982). *Development in human infancy.* New York: Freeman.

Brazelton, T. B. (1990). *The earliest relationship: Parents, infants, and the drama of early attachment.* Reading, MA: Addison-Wesley.

Bronfenbrenner, U. (1979). *The ecology of human development: Experiments by nature and design.* Cambridge, MA: Harvard University Press.

Brown, A. (1990). Domain-specific principles affect learning and transfer in children. *Cognitive Science, 14,* 107–133.

Brown, A., & Campione, J. (1994). Guided discovery in a community of learners. In K. McGilly (Ed.), *Classroom lessons: Integrating cognitive theory and classroom practice* (pp. 229–270). Cambridge, MA: MIT Press.

Bruer, J. (1993). *Schools for thought.* Cambridge, MA: MIT Press.

Bruner, J. S. (1959). [Review of the book *The growth of logical thinking*]. *British Journal of Psychology, 50,* 363–370.

Bruner, J. S. (1983). *Child talk.* New York: Norton.

Bruner, J. S. (1990). *Acts of meaning.* Cambridge, MA: Harvard University Press.

Bruner, J. S., Goodnow, J., & Austin, G. (1956). *A study of thinking.* New York: Wiley.

Buehler, C. (1928). *Kindheit und jugend.* Leipzig: Hirzel.

Cameron, L. (1995, March 5). Finding his voice in music. *New York Times, 2,* 25–28.

Caramazza, A. (1988). The case for single-patient studies [Special issue]. *Cognitive Neuroscience, 5*(5), 517–527.

Carey, S. (1985). *Conceptual change in childhood.* Cambridge, MA: MIT Press.

Carey, S., & Gelman, R. (Eds.). (1991). *The epigenesis of mind: Essays on biology and cognition.* Hillsdale, NJ: Erlbaum.

Carey, S., & Spelke, E. (1994). Domain-specific knowledge and conceptual change. In L. Hirschfield & S. A. Gelman (Eds.), *Mapping the mind* (pp. 169–200). New York: Cambridge University Press.

Carraher, T., Carraher, D., & Schliemann, A. (1985). Mathematics in the streets and schools. *British Journal of Developmental Psychology, 2,* 21–29.

Case, R. (1985). *Intellectual development: Birth to adulthood.* New York: Academic Press.

Case, R. (1993). *The mind's staircase.* Hillsdale, NJ : Erlbaum.

Case, W., & Simon, H. A. (1973). The mind's eye in chess. In W. G. Chase (Ed.), *Visual information processing* (pp. 215–281). New York: Academic Press.

Cassirer, E. (1953–1957). *The philosophy of symbolic forms.* New Haven, CT: Yale University Press.

Ceci, S. (1991). *On intelligence . . . more or less.* Englewood Cliffs, NJ: Prentice-Hall.

Chambers, J., & Dusseault, G. (1972). Characteristics of college-age gifted. *American Psychological Association: Proceedings of the 80th Annual Convention,* 527–528.

Chen, J. (1993). *Building on children's strengths: Project Spectrum intervention program for children at risk for school failure.* Paper presented at the biennial conference of Society for Research in Child Development, New Orleans.

Chi, M., Glaser, R., & Farr, M. (Eds.). (1988). *The nature of expertise.* Hillsdale, NJ: Erlbaum.

Chi, M., Glaser, R., & Rees, E. (1982). Expertise in problem solving. In R. J. Sternberg (Ed.), *Advances in the psychology of human intelligence* (Vol. 1, pp. 1–75). Hillsdale, NJ: Erlbaum.

Childs, C. P., & Greenfield, P. M. (1980). Informal modes of learning and teaching: The case of Zinacenteco learning. In N. Warren (Ed.), *Studies in cross-cultural psychology* (Vol. 2, pp. 270–316). New York: Academic Press.

Chomsky, N. (1957). *Syntactic structures.* The Hague: Mouton.

Chomsky, N. (1965). *Aspects of a theory of syntax.* Cambridge, MA: MIT Press.

Chomsky, N. (1980). *Rules and representations.* New York: Columbia University Press.

Chomsky, N. (1988). *Language and problems of knowledge: The Managua lectures.* Cambridge, MA: MIT Press.

Claparède, E. (1912). *Experimental pedagogy and the psychology of the child.* New York: Longmans Green.

Colangelo, N., & Davis, G. (Eds.). (1997). *The handbook of gifted education.* Boston: Allyn & Bacon.

Cole, M., & Scribner, S. (1974). *Culture and thought.* New York: Wiley.

Cosmides, L., & Tooby, J. (1994). Origins of domain specificity: The evolution of functional organization. In L. Hirschfield & S. Gelman (Eds.), *Mapping the mind* (pp. 85–116). New York: Cambridge University Press.

Cox, C. (1926). *Genetic studies of genius: Vol. 2. The early mental traits of three hundred geniuses.* Stanford, CA: Stanford University Press.

Cox, M. V. (1993). *Children's drawing of the human figure.* Hillsdale, NJ: Erlbaum.

Crick, F. (1994). *The astonishing hypothesis. The scientific search for the soul.* New York: Scribner's.

Csikszentmihalyi, M. (1988). Society, culture and person: A systems view of creativity. In R. J. Sternberg (Ed.), *The nature of creativity* (pp. 325–339). New York: Cambridge University Press.

Csikszentmihalyi, M. (1996). *Creativity.* New York: Harper-Collins.

Csikszentmihalyi, M., Rathunde, K., & Whalen, S. (with contributions by Wong, M.). (1993). *Talented teenagers: The roots of success and failure.* Cambridge, England: Cambridge University Press.

Damasio, A. (1994). *Descartes' error.* New York: Grosset/Putnams.

Darwin, C. (1874). *The descent of man and selection in relation to sex.* New York: Hurst and Co.

Davidson, L. (1985). Tonal structures of children's early songs. *Music Perception, 2*(3), 361–374.

Davidson, L. (1989, Spring). Observing a *yang chin* lesson: Learning by modeling and metaphor. *Journal of Aesthetic Behavior, 23*(1), 85–100.

Davidson, L., & Scripp, L. (1988). Young children's musical representations. In J. Sloboda (Ed.), *Generative processes in music* (pp. 195–230). Oxford, England: Oxford University Press.

Davis, J. (in press). U-shaped development in graphic symbolization: Cultural implications of the what and the whether. *Human Development.*

Dawson, G., & Fischer, K. (1993). *Human behavior and the developing brain.* New York: Garland Press.

Deely, J. (1990). *Basics of semiotics.* Bloomington: Indiana University Press.

Degler, C. (1991). *In search of human nature.* New York: Oxford University Press.

DeLoache, J. (1987). Rapid change in the symbolic functioning of very young children. *Science, 238,* 1556–1557.

Demetriou, A., Efklides, A., & Platsidou, M. (1993). Meta-Piagetian solutions to epistemological problems. *Monographs of the Society for Research in Child Development, 58,* 192–202.

Diamond, M. C. (1985). On the brain of a scientist: Albert Einstein. *Experimental Neurology, 88,* 198–206.

Dowling, W., & Harwood, D. (1986). *Music cognition.* New York: Academic Press.

Dreyfus, H. L. (1986). *Mind over machine: The power of human intuition and expertise in the era of the computer.* New York: Free Press.

Dudek, S., & Verreault, R. (1989). The creative thinking and ego functioning of children. *Creativity Research Journal, 29*(1/2), 64–86.

Eco, U. (1976). *A theory of semiotics.* Bloomington: Indiana University Press.

Ericsson, K. A. (1996). *The road to excellent: The acquisition of expert performance in the arts and sciences, sports, and games.* Mahwah, NJ: Erlbaum.

Ericsson, K. A., & Charness, N. (1994, August). Expert performance: Its structure and acquisition. *American Psychologist, 49*(8), 725–747.

Ericsson, K. A., Krampe, R. T., & Tesch-Romer, C. (1993, May 5). The role of deliberate practice in the acquisition of expert performance. *Psychological Review, 100*(3), 363–406.

Erikson, E. H. (1963). *Childhood and society* (2nd ed.). New York: Norton.

Erikson, K. (1994). Expert performance: Its structure and acquisition. *American Psychologist, 49*(8), 725–747.

Fein, G. (1979). Play with action and object. In B. Sutton-Smith (Ed.), *Play with learning* (pp. 19–82). New York: Gardner Press.

Feldman, D. H. (1980). *Beyond universals in cognitive development.* Norwood, NJ: ABLEX.

Feldman, D. H. (with Goldsmith, L.). (1986). *Nature's gambit.* New York: Basic Books.

Feldman, D. H., Csikszentmihalyi, M., & Gardner, H. (1994). *Changing the world.* Westport, CT: Greenwood/Praeger.

Fischer, K. (1980). A theory of cognitive development: The control and construction of hierarchies of skills. *Psychological Review, 87*(6), 477–531.

Fischer, K., & Ayoub, C. (1994). Affective splitting and dissociation in normal and maltreated children: Developmental pathways for self in relationships. In D. Cicchetti & S. Toth (Eds.), *Rochester Symposium on Developmental Psychopathology: Vol. 5. The self and its disorders* (pp. 149–222). Rochester, NY: University of Rochester Press.

Fischer, K., & Rose, S. (1994). Dynamic development of coordination of components in brain and behavior: A framework for theory and research. In G. Dawson & K. Fischer (Eds.), *Human behavior and the developing brain* (pp. 3–66). New York: Guilford Press.

Fiske, E. (1991). *Smart schools, smart kids.* New York: Simon & Schuster.

Flavell, J. H. (1988). The development of children's knowledge about the mind: From cognitive connections to mental representations. In J. Astington, P. Harris, & D. Olson (Eds.), *Developing theories of mind* (pp. 244–267). New York: Cambridge University Press.

Fodor, J. A. (1975). *The language of thought.* New York: Crowell.

Fodor, J. A. (1983). *The modularity of mind.* Cambridge, MA: MIT Press.

Forman, G. (1975). *Transformations in the manipulations and productions performed with geometric objects: An early system of logic in young children.* Final report for National Institute of Education Grant, Washington, DC.

Foucault, M. (1971). *The order of things.* New York: Pantheon Press.

Fowler, W. (1962). Cognitive learning in infancy and early childhood. *Psychological Bulletin, 59,* 116–153.

Fraser, S. (1995). *The bell curve wars: Race, intelligence, and the future of America.* New York: Basic Books.

Freeman, N. (1980). *Strategies of representation in young children: Analysis of spatial skills and drawing processes.* London: Academic Press.

Frege, G. (1980). *The foundations of arithmetic: A logico-mathematical inquiry into the concept of number* (J. L. Austin, Trans.). Evanston, IL: Northwestern University Press.

Freud, S. (1938). *The interpretation of dreams.* New York: Modern Library. (Original work published 1900)

Freud, S. (1952). *A general introduction to psychoanalysis.* New York: Washington Square Press.

Friedman, H., Tucker, J., Schwartz, J., & Tomlinson-Keasey, C. (1995). Psychosocial and behavioral predictors of longevity: The aging and death of the "Termites." *American Psychologist, 50*(2), 69–78.

Frith, U. (1991). *Autism: Explaining the enigma.* Oxford, England: Blackwell.

Galaburda, A. (1989). *From reading to neurons.* Cambridge, MA: MIT Press.

Gallagher, J. J. (1993). Current status of gifted education in the United States. In K. Heller, F. Monks, & A. H. Passow (Eds.), *International handbook of research and development of giftedness and talent* (pp. 755–770). Oxford, England: Pergamon Press.

Galton, F. (1869). *Hereditary genius: An inquiry into its laws and consequences.* London: Macmillan.

Galton, F. (1883). *Inquiries into human faculty and its development.* New York: Dutton.

Gardner, H. (1979). Developmental psychology after Piaget: An approach in terms of symbolization. *Human Development, 22,* 73–88.

Gardner, H. (1980). *Artful scribbles: The significance of children's drawings.* New York: Basic Books.

Gardner, H. (1985). *The mind's new science: A history of the cognitive revolution.* New York: Basic Books.

Gardner, H. (1986). The development of symbolic literacy. In M. Wrolstad & D. Fisher (Eds.), *Toward a greater understanding of literacy* (pp. 39–56). New York: Praeger.

Gardner, H. (1989). *To open minds: Chinese clues to the dilemma of contemporary education.* New York: Basic Books.

Gardner, H. (1991). *The unschooled mind: How children think, how schools should teach.* New York: Basic Books.

Gardner, H. (1992, February). *The "giftedness matrix" from a multiple intelligences perspective.* Paper presented at the Symposium on Giftedness, University of Kansas, Lawrence, KS.

Gardner, H. (1993a). *Frames of mind: The theory of multiple intelligences.* New York: Basic Books.

Gardner, H. (1993b). *Creating minds: An anatomy of creativity as seen through the lives of Freud, Einstein, Picasso, Stravinsky, Eliot, Graham, and Gandhi.* New York: Basic Books.

Gardner, H. (1993c). *Multiple intelligences: The theory in practice.* New York: Basic Books.

Gardner, H. (1995a). *Leading minds: An anatomy of leadership.* New York: Basic Books.

Gardner, H. (1995b, March 23). Green ideas sleeping furiously. *The New York Review of Books,* 32–38.

Gardner, H. (1995c). How extraordinary was Mozart? In J. Morris (Ed.), *On Mozart.* Washington, DC: Woodrow Wilson Center Press.

Gardner, H. (1997). *Extraordinary minds: Portraits of exceptional individuals and an examination of our extraordinariness.* New York: Basic Books.

Gardner, H., & Boix-Mansilla, V. (1994, Winter). Teaching for understanding within and across the disciplines. *Educational Leadership, 51*(5), 14–18.

Gardner, H., Kornhaber, M., & Wake, W. (1996). *Intelligence: Multiple perspectives*. Fort Worth, TX: Harcourt Brace.

Gardner, H., & Nemirovsky, R. (1991). From private intuitions to public symbol systems: An examination of creative process in G. Cantor and S. Freud. *Creativity Research Journal, 4*(1), 1–21.

Gardner, H., & Winner, E. (1982). First intimations of artistry. In S. Strauss (Ed.), *U shaped behavioral growth* (pp. 147–168). New York: Academic Press.

Gardner, H., & Wolf, C. (1988). The fruits of asynchrony: Creativity from a psychological point of view. *Adolescent Psychiatry, 15,* 106–123.

Gardner, H., & Wolf, D. (1983). Waves and streams of symbolization: Notes on the development of symbolic capacities in young children. In D. R. Rogers & J. A. Sloboda (Eds.), *The acquisition of symbolic skills* (pp. 19–42). London: Plenum Press.

Gardner, H., Wolf, D. P., & Smith, A. (1975). Artistic symbols in early childhood. *New York University Education Quarterly, 6,* 13–21.

Gardner, J. K. (1971). *The development of object identity in infancy.* Unpublished doctoral dissertation, Harvard University.

Gardner, R. (1959). *Cognitive control: A study of individual consistencies in cognitive behavior.* New York: International Universities Press.

Gelman, R. (1991). Epigenetic foundations of knowledge structures: Initial and transcendent constructions. In S. Carey & R. Gelman (Eds.), *The epigenesis of mind: Essays on biology and cognition* (pp. 213–322). Hillsdale, NJ: Erlbaum.

Gelman, R., & Gallistel, C. R. (1978). *The child's understanding of number.* Cambridge, MA: Harvard University Press.

Geschwind, N. (1974). *Selected papers on language and the brain.* Dodrecht–Boston: Reidel.

Geschwind, N., & Galaburda, A. (1987). *Cerebral lateralizations.* Cambridge, MA: Harvard University Press.

Getzels, J., & Csikszentmihalyi, M. (1976). *The creative vision.* New York: Wiley.

Getzels, J., & Jackson, P. (1962). *Creativity and intelligence: Explorations with gifted children.* New York: Wiley.

Gibson, J. J. (1966). *The senses considered as a perceptual system.* Boston: Houghton Mifflin.

Gladwin, T. (1970). *East is a big bird: Navigation and logic on Puluwat Atoll.* Cambridge, MA: Harvard University Press.

Goertzel, V., & Goertzel, M. (1962). *Cradles of eminence.* Boston: Little, Brown.

Goldsmith, L., & Feldman, D. (1989). Wang Yani: Gifts well given. In W. -C. Ho (Ed.), *Yani: The brush of innocence* (pp. 51–64). New York: Hudson Hills Press.

Golomb, C. (1992). *The child's creation of a pictorial world.* Berkeley: University of California Press.

Golomb, C. (Ed). (1995). *The development of gifted child artists: Selected case studies.* Hillsdale, NJ: Erlbaum.

Goodman, N. (1976). *Languages of art: An approach to a theory of symbols.* Indianapolis, IN: Hackett.

Goodman, N. (1978). *Ways of world making.* Indianapolis, IN: Hackett.

Goodnow, J. (1977). *Children drawing.* Cambridge, MA: Harvard University Press.

Gordon, A. (1987, Spring). Childhood works of artists. *The Israel Museum Journal, 6.*

Gould, S. J. (1981). *The mismeasure of man.* New York: Norton.

Gould, S. J. (1989). *Wonderful life.* New York: Norton.

Greenacre, P. (1956). Experiences of awe in childhood. *Psychoanalytic Study of the Child, 11,* 9–80.

Greeno, J. (1991). Number sense as situated knowing in a conceptual domain. *Journal for Research in Mathematics Education, 22*(3), 170–218.

Griffin, S., Case, R., & Siegler, R. S. (1994). Rightstart: Providing the central conceptual prerequisites for first formal learning of arithmetic to students at risk for school failure. In K. McGilly (Ed.), *Classroom lessons: Integrating cognitive theory and classroom practice* (pp. 25–50). Cambridge, MA: MIT Press.

Gruber, H. (1981). *Darwin on man.* Chicago: University of Chicago Press.

Gruber, H., & Davis, S. N. (1988). Inching our way up Mount Olympus: The evolving systems approach to creative thinking. In R. J. Sternberg (Ed.), *The nature of creativity* (pp. 243–270). New York: Cambridge University Press.

Grybek, D. D. (1995). The lords of fly: Finding teen-age black and hispanic gifted students. *Gifted Education Press Quarterly, 9,* 2–9.

Guilford, J. P. (1967). *The nature of intelligence.* New York: McGraw-Hill.

Hall, G. S. (1969). *Adolescence.* New York: Arno. (Original work published 1904)

Hamilton, S. (1990). *Apprenticeship for adulthood: Preparing youth for the future.* New York: Free Press.

Happé, F. (1995). *Autism: An introductory theory.* Cambridge, MA: Harvard University Press.

Hargreaves, D. (1985). *The developmental psychology of music.* New York: Cambridge University Press.

Hargreaves, D. (1989). *Children and the arts.* Philadelphia: Open University Press.

Hatano, G., & Inagaki, K. (1987, October). Everyday biology and school biology: How do they interact? *The Quarterly Newsletter of the Laboratory of Comparative Human Cognition, 9*(3), 120–128.

Hayes, J. (1981). *The complete problem-solver.* Philadelphia: Franklin Institute Press.

Head, H. (1963). *Aphasia and kindred disorders of speech.* New York: Hafner. (Original work published 1920)

Heath, S. B. (1983). *Ways with words: Language, life, and work in communities and classrooms.* New York: Cambridge University Press.

Hécaen, H., & Albert, M. (1978). *Human neuropsychology.* New York: Wiley.

Heller, K. A., Monks, F. J., & Passow, A. H. (Eds.). (1993). *International handbook of research on giftedness and talent* (pp. 131–145). Oxford, England: Pergamon.

Helson, R. (1966). Personality of women with imaginative and artistic interests; the role of masculinity, originality, and other characteristics in their creativity. *Journal of Personality, 34,* 1–25.

Helson, R. (1971). Women mathematicians and the creative personality. *Journal of Consulting and Clinical Psychology, 36,* 210–220.

Herrnstein, R. J., & Murray, C. (1994). *The bell curve.* New York: Free Press.

Hildesheimer, W. (1983). *Mozart* (M. Faber, Trans.). New York: Vintage Books. (Original work published 1977)

Hirschfield, L., & Gelman, S. (1994). *Mapping the mind.* New York: Cambridge University Press.

Ho, W.-C. (1989). *Yani: The brush of innocence.* New York: Hudson Hills Press.

Hobhouse, L. T. (1926). *Mind in evolution* (3rd ed.). London: Macmillan. (Original work published 1901)

Hochberg, J., & Brooks, V. (1962). Pictorial recognition as an unlearned ability: A study of one child's performance. *American Journal of Psychology, 74,* 624–628.

Hofstadter, D. R. (1995). *Fluid concepts and creative analogies: Computer models of the fundamental mechanisms of thought.* New York: Basic Books.

Hofstadter, R. (1945). *Social Darwinism in American thought: 1860–1915.* Philadelphia: University of Pennsylvania Press.

Hollingworth, L. (1942). *Children above 180 IQ: Their nature and nurture.* Yonkers, NY: World Book.

Holmes, F. L. (1985). *Lavoisier and the chemistry of life: An exploration of scientific creativity.* Madison: University of Wisconsin Press.

Holton, G. (1988). *Thematic origins of scientific thought* (2nd ed.). Cambridge, MA: Harvard University Press.

Hopfenberg, W. S., & Levin, H. (1993). *The accelerated schools resource guide.* San Francisco: Jossey-Bass.

Howe, M. (1990). *The origins of exceptional abilities.* Oxford, England: Blackwell.

Hutchins, E. (1991). The social organization of distributed cognition. In L. B. Resnick, J. M. Levine, & S. D. Teasley (Eds.), *Perspectives in socially shared cognition* (pp. 283–307). Washington, DC: American Psychological Association.

Huttenlocher, J., & Higgins, E. T. (1978). Issues in the study of symbolic development. In W. A. Collins (Ed.), *Minnesota Symposia on Child Psychology* (Vol. 12, pp. 98–140). Hillsdale, NJ: Erlbaum.

Inhelder, B., & Piaget, J. (1958). *The growth of logical thinking from childhood to adolescence.* New York: Basic Books.

Inhelder, B., Sinclair, H. L., & Bovet, M. (1974). *Learning and the development of cognition.* Cambridge, MA: Harvard University Press.

Isakson, S. G., Stein, M. I., Hills, D. A., & Gryskiewicz, S. S. (1984). Proposed model for the formulation of creativity research. *Journal of Creative Behavior, 8*(1), 67–75.

Ives, W., Silverman, J., & Gardner, H. (1981). Artistic development in the early school years: A cross-media study of storytelling, drawing, and clay modelling. *Journal of Research and Development in Education, 14*(3), 91–105.

Jackson, J. H. (1932). *Selected writings.* London: Houghton and Stodder.

Jackson, N. E. (1988). Precocious reading ability: What does it mean? *Gifted Child Quarterly, 32*(1), 200–204.

Jacoby, R., & Glauberman, N. (Eds.). (1995). *The bell curve debate: History, documents, opinions.* New York: Times Books.

Jakobson, R. (1963). *Essais de linguistique générale.* Paris: Editions de Minuit.

Jakobson, R. (1971). *Selected writings* (Vol. 2). The Hague: Mouton.

John-Steiner, V. (1985). *Notebooks of the mind.* Albuquerque: University of New Mexico Press.

Jung, C. G. (1958). *Psyche and symbol: A selection from the writings of C. G. Jung.* V. S. de Laszlo (Ed.). Garden City, NY: Doubleday Anchor.

Jusczyk, P., & Krumhansl, C. (1993). Pitch and rhythmic patterns affecting infants' sensitivity to musical phrase structure. *Journal of Experimental Psychology: Human Perception and Performance, 19*(3), 627–640.

Kagan, J. (1984). *The nature of the child.* New York: Basic Books.

Kagan J. (1994). *Galen's prophecy.* New York: Basic Books.

Kagan, J., Kearsley, R., & Zelazo, P. R. (with Minton, C.). (1980). *Infancy, its place in human development.* Cambridge, MA: Harvard University Press.

Kagan, J., & Kogan, N. (1970). Individual variation in cognitive processes. In P. Mussen (Ed.), *Carmichael's manual of child psychology.* New York: Wiley.

Kaplan, B. (1967). Meditations on genesis. *Human Development, 10,* 65–87.

Kaplan, E. (1968). *Gestural representation of implement usage: An organismic-developmental study.* Unpublished doctoral dissertation, Clark University, Worcester, MA.

Karmiloff-Smith, A. (1992). *Beyond modularity: A developmental perspective on cognitive science.* Cambridge, MA: MIT Press.

Keil, F. (1981). Constraints on knowledge and cognitive development. *Psychological Review, 88*(3), 197–227.

Keil, F. (1989). *Concepts, kinds, and cognitive development.* Cambridge, MA: Harvard University Press.

Keil, F. (1991). The emergence of theoretical beliefs as constraints on concepts. In S. Carey & R. Gelman (Eds.), *The epigenesis of mind: Essays on biology and cognition.* Hillsdale, NJ: Erlbaum.

Kessen, W. (1966). Questions for a theory of cognitive development. *Monographs of the Society for Research in Child Development, 31,* 55–70.

Kessen, W., & Kuhlman, C. (Eds.). (1962). Thought in the young child: Report with particular attention to the work of Jean Piaget. *Monographs of the Society for Research in Child Development, 27*(2, Serial No. 83).

Kessen, W., Levine, J., & Wendrich, K. A. (1978). The imitation of pitch in infants. *Infant Behavior and Development, 2,* 93–99.

Kinsbourne, M. (1993). In T. J. Bouchard & P. Propping (Eds.), *Twins as a tool of behavioral genetics: Report of the Dahlem Workshop on what are the mechanisms mediating the genetic and environmental determinants of behavior?* Chichester, England: Wiley.

Klahr, D. (1984). Transition processes in quantitative development. In R. J. Sternberg (Ed.), *Mechanisms of cognitive development.* New York: Freeman.

Klahr, D., & Wallace, J. G. (1976). *Cognitive development: An information-processing view* (pp. 101–139). Hillside, NJ: Erlbaum.

Klima, E. S., & Bellugi, U. (with Battison, R.). (1979). *The signs of language.* Cambridge, MA: Harvard University Press.

Kohlberg, L. (1969). Stage and sequence: The cognitive-developmental approach to socialization. In D. A. Goslin (Ed.), *Handbook of socialization theory and research.* New York: Rand McNally.

Kosslyn, S. (1994). *Image and brain: The resolution of the imagery debate.* Cambridge, MA: MIT Press.

Krechevsky, M. (1991). Project spectrum: An innovative assessment alternative. *Educational Leadership, 48*(5), 43–49.

Kroeber, A. (1944). *Configurations of cultural growth.* Berkeley: University of California Press.

Krutetski, V. A. (1976). *The psychology of mathematical abilities in schoolchildren.* Chicago: University of Chicago Press.

Kuhn, T. (1970). *The structure of scientific revolutions* (2nd ed.). Chicago: University of Chicago Press.

Landau, B. (1986). Early map use as an unlearned ability. *Cognition, 22,* 201–223.

Langer, J. (1969). *Theories of development.* New York: Holt, Rinehart and Winston.

Langer, S. (1942). *Philosophy in a new key.* Cambridge, MA: Harvard University Press.

Langley, P., Simon, H., Bradshaw, L., & Zytkow, J. M. (1987). *Scientific discovery.* Cambridge, MA: MIT Press.

Larkin, J. (1985). Understanding, problem representation and skill in physics. In S. F. Chipman, J. W. Segal, & R. Glaser (Eds.), *Thinking and learning skills: Vol. 2. Research and open questions.* Hillsdale, NJ: Erlbaum.

Lave, J. (1988). *Cognition in practice: Mind, mathematics, and culture in everyday life.* New York: Cambridge University Press.

Lave, J., & Wenger, E. (1991). *Situated learning: Legitimate peripheral participation.* Cambridge, England: Cambridge University Press.

Lehman, H. (1953). *Age and achievement.* Princeton, NJ: Princeton University Press.

Lenneberg, E. (1967). *Biological foundations of language.* New York: Wiley.

Leslie, A. (1987). Pretense and representation. The origins of "theory of mind." *Psychological Review, 94,* 412–426.

Lewontin, R. C., Rose, S., & Kamin, L. (1984). *Not in our genes: Biology, ideology and human nature.* New York: Cambridge University Press.

Li, J., & Gardner, H. (1993). How domains constrain creativity: The case of traditional Chinese and Western painting. *American Behavioral Scientist, 37*(11), 94–101.

Liben, L. S., & Downs, R. M. (1989). Understanding maps as symbols: The development of map concepts in children. In H. W. Reese (Ed.), *Advances in child development* (Vol. 22). New York: Academic Press.

Lochhead, J., & Mestre, J. (1988). From words to algebra: Mending misconceptions. In A. Coxford & A. Schulte (Eds.), *The ideas of algebra K–12* (pp. 127–135). Reston, VA: National Council of Teachers of Mathematics.

Lord, A. B. (1960). *The singer of tales.* Cambridge, MA: Harvard University Press.

Luria, A. R. (1966). *The higher cortical functions in man.* New York: Basic Books.

Lykken, D., McGue, M., Tellegen, A., & Bouchard, T. J. (1992). Emergenesis: Genetic traits that may not run in families. *American Psychologist, 47*(12), 1565–1577.

Mandler, J. (1983). Representation. In P. Mussen (Ed.), *Handbook of child psychology* (Vol. 3, pp. 420–494). New York: Wiley.

Mandler, J. (1984). *Stories, scripts, and scenes: Aspects of schema theory.* Hillsdale, NJ: Erlbaum.

Marland, S. (1972). *Education of the gifted and talented: Report to the Congress of the United States by the U.S. Commissioner of Education.* Washington, DC: U.S. Government Printing Office.

Marshall, R., & Tucker, M. (1992). *Thinking for a living: Education and the wealth of nations.* New York: Basic Books.

Martindale, C. (1992). *The clockwork muse.* New York: Basic Books.

Marx, K., & Engels, F. (1974). *Capital* (S. Moore & E. Aveling, Trans.). London: Lawrence and Wishart. (Original work published 1872)

Mason, E. P., & Blood, D. F. (1966). Cross-validation study of personality characteristics of gifted college freshmen. *American Psychologist, 21,* 653–654.

McCorduck, P. (1979). *Machines who think: A personal inquiry into the history and prospects of artificial intelligence.* San Francisco: Freeman.

McCulloch, W., & Pitts, W. (1943). A logical calculus of the ideas immanent in nervous activity. *Bulletin of Mathematical Biophysics, 5,* 115–33.

McGilly, K. (1994). *Classroom lessons.* Cambridge, MA: MIT Press.

McPhee, C. (1976). *Music in Bali: A study of form and instrumental organization in Balinese orchestral music.* New York: Da Capo Press.

Mehler, J., & Fox, R. (Eds.). (1985). *Neonate cognition: Beyond the blooming, buzzing confusion.* Hillsdale, NJ: Erlbaum.

Meltzoff, A. (1990). Towards a developmental cognitive science: The implications of cross-modal matching and imitation for the development of memory in infancy. *Annals of the New York Academy of Sciences, 608,* 1–37.

Meltzoff, A., & Moore, K. (1977). Imitation of facial and manual gestures by human neonates. *Science, 198,* 75–78.

Miller, A. (1986). *Imagery in scientific thought.* Cambridge, MA: MIT Press.

Miller, G. (1956). The magical number seven, plus or minus two: Some limits on our capacity for processing information. *Psychological Review, 63,* 81–96.

Miller, L. K. (1989). *Musical savants: Exceptional skill in the mentally retarded.* Hillsdale, NJ: Erlbaum.

Miller, P. (1993). *Theories of developmental psychology* (3rd ed.). New York: Freeman. (Original work published 1983)

Morris, J. (1995). *On Mozart.* Washington, DC: Woodrow Wilson Center Press.

Murray, H. (1938). *Explorations in personality.* New York: Oxford University Press.

Neisser, U. (1967). *Cognitive psychology.* New York: Appleton-Century-Crofts.

Neisser, U. (1976). *Cognition and reality.* San Francisco: Freeman.

Nelson, K. (1981). Individual differences in language development: Implications for development and language. *Developmental Psychology, 17,* 170–187.

Nelson, K. (1986). *Event knowledge: Structure and function in development.* Hillsdale, NJ: Erlbaum.

Newell, A. (1980). Physical symbol systems. *Cognitive Science, 4,* 117–133.

Newell, A., & Simon, H. (1972). *Human problem-solving.* Englewood Cliffs, NJ: Prentice-Hall.

Oakes, J. (with Ormseth, T., Bell, R., & Camp, B.). (1985). *Multiplying inequalities: The effects of race, social class, and tracking on opportunities to learn mathematics and science.* Santa Monica, CA: RAND.

Ochse, R. (1990). *Before the gates of excellence: The determinants of creative genius.* New York: Cambridge University Press.

O'Connor, N., & Hermelin, B. (1991). Talents and preoccupations in idiot savants. *Psychological Medicine, 21,* 959–964.

Oden, M. H. (1968). The fulfillment of promise: 40-year follow-up of the Terman gifted group. *Genetic Psychology Monographs, 77,* 3–93.

Olson, D. (1970). *Cognitive development: The child's acquisition of diagonality.* New York: Academic Press.

Olson, D. (Ed.). (1974). *Media and symbols.* Chicago: University of Chicago Press.

Olson, D. (1989). Making up your mind. *Canadian Psychology, 30,* 617–627.

Olson, D. (1994). *The world on paper.* New York: Cambridge University Press.

Osterrieth, P. (1956). Les problèmes des stades en psychologie de l'enfant; symposium de l'Association de Psychologie Scientifique de Langue Française. In *Bibliothèque Scientifique Internationale, Science Humaines, Section Psychologie*. Paris: Presses Universitaires de France.

Paivio, A. (1971). *Imagery and visual perception.* New York: Holt, Rinehart and Winston.

Papousek, M., Bornstein, M. H., Nozzo, C., & Papousek, H. (1990, October–December). Infant responses to prototypical melodic contours in parental speech. *Infant Behavior & Development, 13*(4), 539–545.

Papousek, M., Papousek, H., & Symmes, D. (1991, October–December). The meanings of melodies in motherese in tone and stress languages. *Infant Behavior & Development, 14*(4), 415–440.

Pariser, D. (1991). Normal and unusual aspects of juvenile artistic development in Klee, Lautrec, and Picasso. *Creativity Research Journal, 4,* 51–65.

Patel, V. L., Kaufman, D. R., & Magder, S. A. (1996). The acquistion of medical expertise in complex dynamic environments. In K. A. Ericsson (Ed.), *The road to excellent: The acquisition of expert performance in the arts and sciences, sports, and games* (pp. 127–166). Mahwah, NJ: Erlbaum.

Pea, R. D. (1990, April). *Distributed intelligence and education.* Paper presented at the annual meeting of the American Educational Research Association, Boston, MA.

Peirce, C. S. (1932). *Collected papers.* (C. Harshore & P. Weiss, Ed.). Cambridge, MA: Harvard University Press.

Perkins, D. N. (1981). *The mind's best work.* Cambridge, MA: Harvard University Press.

Perkins, D. N. (1992). *Smart schools.* New York: Free Press.

Perkins, D. N. (1995). *Outsmarting IQ.* New York: Free Press.

Perner, J. (1991). *Understanding the representational mind.* Cambridge, MA: MIT Press.

Piaget, J. (1929). *The child's conception of the world.* London: Routledge. (Totowa, NJ: Littlefield, 1965.)

Piaget, J. (1954). *Les relations entre l'affectivité et l'intelligence dans le developpement mental de l'enfant.* Paris: Centre de documentation universitaire.

Piaget, J. (1962). *Play, dreams, and imitation.* New York: Norton.

Piaget, J. (1983). Piaget's theory. In P. Mussen (Ed.), *Handbook of child psychology* (Vol. 1). New York: Wiley.

Piattelli-Palmarini, M. (Ed.). (1980). *Language and learning: The debate between Jean Piaget and Noam Chomsky.* Cambridge, MA: Harvard University Press.

Pick, H. L., Jr. (1988). Perceptual aspects of spatial cognitive development. In J. Stiles-Davis, M. Kritchevsky, & U. Bellugi (Eds.), *Spatial cognition: Brain bases and development* (pp. 145–156). Hillsdale, NJ: Erlbaum.

Pick, H. L., Jr. (1993). Organization of spatial knowledge in children. In N. Eilan, R. A. McCarthy, & B. Brewer (Eds.), *Spatial representation: Problems in philosophy and psychology* (pp. 31–42). Oxford, England: Blackwell.

Pinker, S. (1994). *The language instinct: How the mind creates language.* New York: Morrow.

Popper, K. (1976). *Unended quest: An intellectual autobiography.* London: Fontana/Collins.

Popper, K. (1990). *A world of propensities.* Bristol, England: Thoemmes.

Preyer, W. (1892). *The mind of the child.* New York: Appleton.

Putnam, H. (1980). Comments. In M. Piattelli-Palmarini (Ed.), *Language and learning* (pp. 335–340). Cambridge, MA: Harvard University Press.

Radford, J. (1990). *Child prodigies and exceptional early achievement.* London: Harvester.

Raichle, M. (1991). Modular organization of information processing in the normal human brain: Studies with positron emission tomography. In L. R. Squire, N. M. Weinberger, G. Lynch, & J. L. McHaugh (Eds.), *Memory: Organization and locus of change* (pp. 86–94). New York: Oxford University Press.

Raichle, M. (1994, May). Images of the human mind. 19th Collegium Internationale Neuro-Psychopharmacologicum Congress. *Neuropsychopharmacology, 10*(3, Suppl. Pt. 1), 28s–33s.

Rank, O. (1932). *Art and artist.* New York: Knopf.

Reich, R. (1991). *The work of nations: Preparing ourselves for 21st century capitalism.* New York: Knopf.

Resnick, D. P., & Resnick, L. (1985). Standards, curriculum, and performance: A historical and comparative perspective. *Educational Researcher, 14,* 5–20.

Resnick, L. B. (1987). Learning in school and out. *Educational Researcher, 16*(9), 13–20.

Rhodes, R. (1986). *The making of the atomic bomb.* New York: Simon & Schuster.

Rimland, B. (1964). *Infantile autism.* New York: Appleton-Century-Crofts.

Rogoff, B. (1990). *Apprenticeship in thinking: Cognitive development in social context.* New York: Oxford University Press.

Rogoff, B., & Lave, J. (Eds.). (1984). *Everyday cognition.* Cambridge, MA: Harvard University Press.

Romanes, G. (1883). *Animal intelligence.* New York: Appleton.

Romero, M. (1992). *The Keres Study. Identifying giftedness among Keresan Pueblo Indians.* [Technical report] Santa Fe, NM: Santa Fe University.

Rosch, E. (1978). Principles of categorization. In E. Rosch & B. Lloyd (Eds.), *Cognition and categorization*. Hillsdale, NJ: Erlbaum.

Rosch, E., Mervis, C. B., Gray, W. D., Johnson, D. M., & Boyes-Braem, P. (1976). Basic objects in natural categories. *Cognitive Psychology, 8,* 382–439.

Rowe, D. (1994). *The limits of family influence: Genes, experience, and behavior.* New York: Guilford Press.

Rubin, K. H., Fein, G. G., & Vandenberg, B. (1983). Play. In E. M. Hetherington (Ed.), *Handbook of child psychology* (4th ed.) (Vol. 14, pp. 693–774). New York: Wiley.

Rumelhart, D., & McClelland, J. (1986). *Parallel distributed processing: Exploration in the microstructure of cognition: Vol. l. Foundations.* Cambridge, MA: MIT Press.

Rutter, M., & Schopler, E. (Eds.). (1978). *Autism: A reappraisal of concepts and treatment.* New York: Plenum Press.

Sacks, O. (1995). *An anthropologist on Mars.* New York: Knopf.

Saussure, F., de (1983). *Course in general linguistics.* London: Duckworth. (Original work published 1916)

Savage-Rumbaugh, S. (1986). *Ape language: From conditioned responses to symbols.* New York: Columbia University Press.

Saxe, G. (1981). Body parts as numerals: A developmental analysis of numeration among remote Oksapmin village populations in Papua, New Guinea. *Child Development, 52,* 306–316.

Saxe, G., Guberman, S. R., & Gearhart, M. (1987). Social processes in early number development. *Monographs of the Society for Research in Child Development, 216*(2), 25.

Scheibel, A. (1985, April). *Toward cortical substrates of higher brain function.* Paper presented at the Conference on Neurobiology of Extraordinary Giftedness, New York.

Scheibel, A. (1988). Dendritic correlates of human cortical function. *Cortical Function Archives, 126*(4), 347–357.

Schoenberg, A. (1950). *Style and idea.* New York: Philosophical Library.

Scripp, L. (1995). *The development of skill in reading music.* Doctoral dissertation, Harvard Graduate School of Education, Harvard University.

Sebeok, T. (1972). *Perspectives on zoo semiotics.* The Hague: Mouton.

Sebeok, T. (1989). *The sign and its masters.* Lanham, MD: University Press of America.

Sebeok, T. (1991). *Recent developments in theory and history: The semiotic web.* New York: Mouton de Gruyter.

Selfe, L. (1977). *Nadia: A case of extraordinary drawing ability in an autistic child.* New York: Academic Press.

Sergent, J. (1993). Mapping the musician brain. *Human Brain Mapping, 1,* 20–38.

Sergent, J., Zuck, E., Terriah, S., & MacDonald, B. (1992, July). Distributed neural network underlying musical sight-reading and keyboard performance. *Science, 257,* 106–109.

Shallice, T. (1988). *From neuropsychology to mental structure.* New York: Cambridge University Press.

Shanon, B. (1993). *The representational and the presentational: An essay on cognition and the study of mind.* London: Harvester/Wheatsheaf.

Shaw, R., & Bransford, J. (1977). Introduction: Psychological approaches to the problem of knowledge. In R. Shaw & J. Bransford (Eds.), *Perceiving, acting and knowing: Toward an ecological psychology* (pp. 1–39). Hillsdale, NJ: Erlbaum.

Shepard, R. (1978). The mental image. *American Psychologist, 33,* 125–137.

Shore, B. M., & Kanevsky, L. S. (1993). Thinking processes: Being and becoming gifted. In K. A. Heller, F. J. Monks, & A. H. Passow (Eds.), *International handbook of research on giftedness and talent* (pp. 133–148). Oxford, England: Pergamon.

Shotwell, J. (1979). Counting steps. In H. Gardner & D. P. Wolf (Eds.), *Early symbolization. New Directions for Child Development, 3,* 84–96.

Shotwell, J., Wolf, D., & Gardner, H. (1979). Styles of achievement in early symbolization. In M. Foster & S. Brandes (Eds.), *Symbol as sense: New approaches to the analysis of meaning* (pp. 175–199). New York: Academic Press.

Shuter-Dyson, R. (1982). Musical ability. In D. Deutsch (Ed.), *The psychology of music.* San Diego, CA: Academic Press.

Siegler, R. (1983). Information processing approaches to development. In P. Mussen (Ed.), *Handbook of child psychology* (Vol. l). New York: Wiley.

Siegler, R., & Jenkins, E. (1989). *How children discover new strategies.* Hillsdale, NJ: Erlbaum.

Silverman, L. (1994, Winter). The moral sensitivity of gifted children and the evolution of society. *Roeper Review, 17*(2), 110–116.

Simon, H. A. (1985). *Schools of thought.* New Haven, CT: Yale University Press.

Simonton, D. K. (1990). *Historiometrics.* New York: Cambridge University Press.

Simonton, D. K. (1994). *Greatness: Who makes history and why.* New York: Guilford Press.

Sizer, T. (1992). *Horace's compromise.* Boston: Houghton Mifflin.

Skinner, B. F. (1953). *The behavior of organisms.* New York: Macmillan.

Sloboda, J. (1985). *The musical mind: The cognitive psychology of music.* New York: Oxford University Press.

Sloboda, J. (1988). *Generative processes in music.* Oxford, England: Oxford University Press.

Sloboda, J. (1991). Musical expertise. In K. A. Ericsson & J. Smith (Eds.), *Toward a general theory of expertise: Prospects and limits* (pp. 153–171). New York: Cambridge University Press.

Sloboda, J. (1996). The acquisition of musical performance expertise. In K. A. Ericsson (Ed.), *The road to excellent: The acquisition of expert performance in the arts and sciences, sports, and games* (pp. 107–126). Mahwah, NJ: Erlbaum.

Sloboda, J., Hermelin, B., & O'Connor, N. (1985). An exceptional musical memory. *Music Perception, 3,* 155–170.

Smith, N., & Franklin, M. B. (1979). *Symbolic functioning in childhood.* Hillsdale, NJ: Erlbaum.

Smolensky, P. (1988). On the proper treatment of connectionism. *The Behavioral and Brain Sciences, 11,* 1–74.

Solomon, M. (1995). *Mozart: A life.* New York: HarperCollins.

Sorokin, P. A. (1949). *The pattern of the past: Can we determine it?* Boston: Beacon Press.

Sorokin, P. A. (1957). *Social and cultural dynamics: A study of change in major systems of art, truth, ethics, law and social relationships.* Boston: P. Sargent.

Sorokin, P. A. (1962). *Society, culture, and personality: Their structure and dynamics: A system of general sociology.* New York: Cooper Square.

Spearman, C. (1927). *The abilities of man.* New York: Macmillan.

Spelke, E. (1982). Perceptual knowledge of objects in infancy. In J. Mehler, E. Walker, & M. Garrett (Eds.), *Perspectives on mental representation* (pp. 409–430). Hillsdale, NJ: Erlbaum.

Spelke, E. (1991). Physical knowledge in infancy: Reflections on Piaget's theory. In S. Carey & R. Gelman (Eds.), *The epigenesis of mind: Essays on biology and cognition.* Hillsdale, NJ: Erlbaum.

Sperber, D. (1975). *Rethinking symbolism.* Cambridge, England: Cambridge University Press.

Stanley, J. (1997). Varieties of giftedness. *Journal of Creative Behavior, 31*(2), 93–119.

Stanley, J., & Benbow, C. P. (1986). Youths who reason exceptionally well in mathematics. In R. J. Sternberg & J. E. Davidson (Eds.), *Conceptions of giftedness* (pp. 361–387). New York: Cambridge University Press.

Starkey, P., Spelke, E. S., & Gelman, R. (1990). Numerical abstraction by human infants. *Cognition, 36,* 97–127.

Stein, M. (1990). Anabolic and catabolic factors in the creative process: Creativity and health [Special issue]. *Creativity Research Journal, 3*(2), 134–145.

Stern, W. (1926). *The psychology of early childhood up to the age of six.* New York: Holt.

Sternberg, R. J. (1984). *Mechanisms of cognitive development.* New York: Freeman.

Sternberg, R. J. (1985). *Beyond IQ: A triarchic theory of human intelligence.* New York: Cambridge University Press.

Sternberg, R. J. (Ed.). (1988). *The nature of creativity.* New York: Cambridge University Press.

Sternberg, R. J., & Wagner, R. (1986). *Practical intelligence.* New .York: Cambridge University Press.

Stevenson, H., & Stigler, J. (1992). *The learning gap: Why our schools are failing and what we can learn from Japanese and Chinese education.* New York: Touchstone Books.

Strauss, M. (1979). Abstraction of prototypical information by adults and ten-month-old infants. *Journal of Experimental Psychology: Human Learning and Memory, 5,* 618–632.

Subotnik, R., & Arnold, K. (Eds.). (1993). *Beyond Terman: Longitudinal studies in contemporary gifted education.* Norwood, NJ: ABLEX.

Sulloway, F. (1995). Birth order and evolutionary psychology: A meta-analytic overview. *Psychological Inquiry, 6*(1), 75–80.

Sully, J. (1895). *Studies of childhood.* New York: Longmans Green.

Suzuki, S. (1969). *Nurtured by love.* New York: Exposition Press.

Terman, L. M. (1925). *Genetic studies of genius: Vol. 2. Mental and physical traits of a thousand gifted children.* Stanford, CA: Stanford University Press.

Terman, L. M. (1995). In C. K. Holahan & R. R. Sears (Eds.), *The gifted group in later years* (Vol. 6). Stanford, CA: Stanford University Press.

Terman, L. M., & Oden, M. H. (1959). *Genetic studies of genius.* Stanford, CA: Stanford University Press.

Thurstone, L. L. (1938). *Primary mental abilities.* Chicago: University of Chicago Press.

Tomasello, M. (1990). Cultural transmission in the tool use and communicatory signaling of chimpanzees. In S. T. Parker & K. R. Gibson (Eds.), *"Language" and intelligence in monkeys and apes: Comparative developmental perspectives* (pp. 274–311). New York: Cambridge University Press.

Tomasello, M. (1992, March). The social bases of language acquisition. *Social Development, 1*(1), 67–87.

Tomlinson-Keasey, C., & Smith-Winberry, C. (1983). Educational strategies and personality outcomes of gifted and nongifted college students. *Gifted Child Quarterly, 27*(1), 35–41.

Tooby, J., & Cosmides, L. (1990). On the universality of human nature and the uniqueness of the individual: The role of genetics and adaptation. *Journal of Personality, 58,* 17–67.

Torff, B. (1995). *Contextual constraints on implicit learning.* Doctoral dissertation, Harvard Graduate School of Education, Harvard University.

Torrance, E. P. (1988). The nature of creativity as manifest in its testing. In R. J. Sternberg (Ed.), *The nature of creativity* (pp. 43–75). New York: Cambridge University Press.

Trevarthen, C. (1977). Descriptive analyses of infant communicative behavior. In H. R. Schaffer (Ed.), *Studies in mother–child interaction.* New York: Academic Press.

Trollinger, L. M. (1983, Spring). Interests, activities and hobbies of high and low creative women musicians during childhood, adolescent and college years. *Gifted Child Quarterly, 27*(2), 94–97

Vico, G. (1984). *The new science of Giambattista Vico* (B. Goddard & M. H. Fisch, Trans.). Unabridged 3rd ed. (1774). Ithaca: Cornell University Press.

Vygotsky, L. (1962). *Thought and language.* Cambridge, MA: MIT Press.

Vygotsky, L. (1978). *Mind in society: The development of higher psychological processes.* Cambridge, MA: Harvard University Press.

Wallace, D., & Gruber, H. (1990). *Creative people at work.* New York: Oxford University Press.

Wallach, M. (1971). *The intelligence–creativity distinction.* Morristown, NJ: General Learning Corporation.

Wallach, M., & Kogan, N. (1965). *Modes of thinking in young children.* New York: Holt, Rinehart and Winston.

Walters, J., & Gardner, H. (1986). Crystallizing experiences. In R. J. Sternberg & J. Davidson (Eds.), *Conceptions of giftedness* (pp. 306–331). New York: Cambridge University Press.

Watson, J. B. (1919). *Psychology from the standpoint of a behaviorist.* Philadelphia: Lippincott.

Weisberg, R. (1986). *Creativity, genius, and other myths.* New York: Freeman.

Wellman, H. (1990). *The child's theory of mind.* Cambridge, MA: MIT Press.

Wells, G. (1984, Summer). Learning to talk and talking to learn. *Theory into Practice, 23*(3), 190–197.

Wells, G. (1987). The learning of literacy. In C. N. Hedley & E. C. DiMartino (Eds.), *Home and school: Early language and reading.* Norwood, NJ: ABLEX.

Werner, H. (1948). *Comparative psychology of mental development.* New York: Wiley.

Werner, H., & Kaplan, B. (1963). *Symbol formation.* New York: Wiley.

Wertheimer, M. (1945). *Productive thinking.* New York: Harper.

Wheelock, A. (1992). *Crossing the tracks: How "untracking" can save America's schools.* New York: New Press.

White, S. (1965). Evidence for a hierarchical arrangement of learning processes. In L. P. Lipsitt & C. C. Spiker (Eds.), *Advances in child development and behavior* (Vol. 2). New York: Academic Press.

White, S. H. (1970). Some general outlines of the matrix of developmental changes between five and seven years. *Bulletin of the Orton Society, 20,* 41–57.

Whitehead, A. N. (1958). *Modes of thought: Six lectures delivered in Wellesley College, Massachusetts, and two lectures in the University of Chicago.* New York: Capricorn Books.

Whitehead, A. N. (1978). In D. R. Griffin & D. W. Sherburne (Eds.), *Process and reality: An essay in cosmology.* New York: Free Press. (Original work published 1929)

Whitehead, A. N., & Russell, B. (1910–1913). *Principia mathematica.* Cambridge, England: Cambridge University Press.

Wilson, E. (1941). *The wound and the bow: Seven studies in literature.* Boston: Houghton Mifflin.

Wilson, E. O. (1975). *Sociobiology.* Cambridge, MA: Harvard University Press.

Winner, E. (1982). *Invented worlds.* Cambridge, MA: Harvard University Press.

Winner, E. (1988). *The point of words.* Cambridge, MA: Harvard University Press.

Winner, E. (1996). *Gifted children: Myths and realities.* New York: Basic Books.

Wittgenstein, L. (1953). *Philosophical investigations.* Oxford, England: Blackwell.

Wittgenstein, L. (1961). *Tractatus logico-philosophicus* (D. F. Pears & B. F. McGuinnesss, Trans.). London: Routledge & Kegan Paul. (Original work published 1921)

Wolf, D. P. (1994). Children's acquisition of different kinds of narrative discourse: Genres and lines of talk. In J. L. Sokolov & C. E. Snow (Eds.), *Handbook of research in language development using CHILDES.* Hillsdale, NJ: Erlbaum.

Wolff, P. (1960). The developmental psychologies of Jean Piaget and psychoanalysis. *Psychological Issues, 2,* 1–181.

Wynn, K. (1992). Addition and subtraction by human infants. *Nature, 358,* 479.

Zentner, M. R., & Kagan, J. (1996, September 5). Perception of music by infants. *Nature, 383,* 29.

Zurif, E., Gardner, H., & Brownell, H. (1989). The case against the case against group studies. *Brain and Cognition, 10,* 237–255.

CHAPTER 9

Dynamic Development of Psychological Structures in Action and Thought

KURT W. FISCHER and THOMAS R. BIDELL

Human activity is organized. People's activities form coherent patterns, and analysis of those patterns is essential for understanding the activities. Although the variability of activities is enormous and their complexity is vast, systematic analysis of structures or organizations—patterns

of components—gives scientists the tools for finding the order in the variation. This set of assumptions provides the starting point for dynamic structural analysis of the development of human action and thought.

The complexity of human behavior creates special problems for social scientists and often leads to distorting simplifications presented as explanations. Every person has so many different parts—sometimes cooperating; sometimes conflicting and even contradicting; often independent. The result is many ways of acting, thinking, and feeling that are

---

Preparation of this chapter was supported by grants from Mr. and Mrs. Frederick P. Rose, the Spencer Foundation, Harvard University, and Boston College.

467

affected by a wide array of influences in context, culture, and biology. This complexity is a characteristic of many animals (Goodwin, 1994; von Frisch, 1967; Wrangham, McGrew, deWaal, & Heltne, 1994), but it is especially true of human beings with their powerful nervous systems and rich cultures.

Dazzled by all this complexity, scientists often retreat into oversimplification and stereotyping. Most approaches to explaining human activity start with one limited aspect, such as stage of development, logical thought, innate ideas, reinforcement contingency, emotional distortion, competitive advantage, or cultural role. They then attempt to analyze all human complexity in terms of that one aspect. Although these simplifications have their usefulness, they lead to views of human behavior and development that are one-dimensional.

Analysis of the dynamic structures of human behavior provides a way of simplifying without discarding complexity. Contrary to common stereotypes of classic structuralism, modern dynamic structuralism starts with the pervasive variability of human activity and analyzes the patterns of stability and order within the variation (Bidell & Fischer, 1992a; Case & Edelstein, 1993; de Ribaupierre, 1989b, 1993; Fischer & Granott, 1995; Siegler, 1994; Thelen & Smith, 1994, Ch. 10, this Volume; van Geert, 1994). Structure is analyzed into diverse patterns of activity (not static states of consciousness, idealized logical concepts, or other fixed forms), and as in the study of ecology, the analysis begins *in medias res,* in the middle of things. Starting in the middle of things means that people's activities are embodied, contextualized, and socially situated—understood in terms of their ecology (Bronfenbrenner, 1993, and Ch. 17, this Volume; Cairns, 1979; Gibson, 1979) as well as their structure. People act and understand through their bodies, not through a disembodied mind or brain. The brain and nervous system always function through a person's body and through specific contexts composed of particular people, objects, and events, which afford and support the actions (Luria, 1979). People act jointly with other people. People act within culturally defined social situations, in which activities are given meaning through cultural frames for interpretation (Geertz, 1973; LeVine, 1977). Action in context is the center of who people are and how they develop (Bidell & Fischer, 1996; Lerner & Busch-Rossnagel, 1981; see Brandstädter, Ch. 14, this Volume).

Starting in the middle of things with embodied, contextualized, socially situated individual and joint activity necessitates a dynamic, multicomponent approach. A large number of factors contribute to any given activity, and activities vary widely in complexity and content. Using this dynamic approach requires two major steps: (a) to describe basic structures or organizations in activities in context, and (b) to characterize how those structures vary as a function of changes in key dimensions of person, body, task, context, and culture. Whether the focus is on knowledge, action, emotion, social interaction, brain functioning, or some combination, the dynamic structural approach puts the person in the middle of things and frames the person's activity in terms of multiple components working together.

The maturity or complexity of people's behavior varies widely and systematically from moment to moment and across contexts, states, and interpretations or meanings. Each individual person shows such variations, in addition to the wide variations that occur across ages, cultures, and social groups. Consider, for example, the wide variation documented for children's stories about positive and negative social interactions (Buchsbaum, Toth, Clyman, Cicchetti, & Emde, 1992; Fischer & Ayoub, 1994; Hencke, 1996; Raya, 1996): The developmental level, content, and emotional valence of a child's stories vary dramatically as a function of priming and immediate social support, emotional state, and sociocultural factors, including ethnicity and race. Five-year-old Susan watches her counselor act out a pretend story with dolls: A child doll named Mary makes a drawing of her family and gives it to her father, who is playing with her. "Daddy, here's a present for you. I love you." Then the Daddy doll hugs the girl doll and says, "I love you too, and thanks for the pretty picture." He gives her a toy and says, "Here's a present for you too, Mary." The girl promptly acts out a similar story of positive social reciprocity, making Daddy be nice to Mary because Mary was nice to him.

Ten minutes later, the counselor asks the girl to show the best story she can about people being nice to each other, like the one she did before. Instead of producing the complex story she did earlier, she acts out a much simpler story, making the Daddy doll simply give lots of presents to the child doll, with no reciprocal interaction between them. There is no social reciprocity in the story but only a simple social category of nice action.

A few minutes after that, when the girl has spontaneously shifted to playing at fighting, the counselor shows her another nice story about father and child. This time, when the girl acts out her story, she switches the content from positive to negative, with substantial aggression. The girl doll hits the father doll, and then he yells at her, "Don't you hit me," slaps her in the face, and pushes her across the room, showing the kind of violence that often appears in the stories of maltreated children. The girl doll cries and says she is scared. Note that despite the shift to negative affect, Susan sustains a story involving social reciprocity.

Then Susan becomes agitated; yelling, she runs around the room and throws toys. When the counselor asks her to do another story, she makes the dolls hit and push each other, with no clear reciprocity and no explanation of what is happening. With her distress and disorganization, she no longer acts out a complex aggression story but is limited to stories of repeated hitting, even when she is asked to produce the best story she can. She uses a simple social category of mean action.

What is the "real" story for the child? Does she represent relationships between fathers and daughters as positive or negative? Is she capable of representing reciprocity, or is she not? These are the kinds of questions that are often asked in child development, but these questions assume a kind of opposition that makes no sense. Susan plainly shows four different "competences"—for positive reciprocity, positive social category, negative reciprocity, and negative social category. Depending on the immediate situation, her emotional state, and the social support from her counselor, she demonstrates each of these four different "abilities."

Different contexts for assessment routinely produce such radical variations, although developmental theories and methods do not generally deal with these phenomena. Children (and adults) show distinct levels of competence under different conditions, even for a single domain such as stories about nice and mean social interactions between peers (Brown & Reeve, 1987; Fischer & Ayoub, 1994; Fischer, Bullock, Rotenberg, & Raya, 1993). Figure 9.1 shows the best performances of eight 7-year-old children who were acting in (a) several contexts in which an interviewer provided high social support for complex stories, such as prompting the gist of the plot, and (b) several contexts providing no such support. As the context shifted, the children's competence for representing mean, nice, or

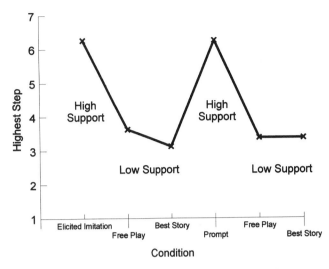

Figure 9.1 Variation in competence for stories as a function of social-contextual support. In the high-support assessments the interviewer either modeled a story to a child (Elicited Imitation) or described the gist of a story as well as some content cues (Prompt), and then the child acted out or told a similar story. In the low-support assessments the interviewer provided no such support but either asked for the best story the child could produce (Best Story) or let the child make up a number of stories in free play with the most complex story determining the child's "competence" for this context (Free Play). Note that children had performed similar stories several times before the assessments graphed here (Fischer et al., 1993).

nice-and-mean social interactions shifted dramatically and systematically. Every individual child showed a similar pattern of shifting across conditions—competence at step 6 or 7 for high-support conditions, and competence at step 2, 3, or 4 for low-support conditions. This variation is an example of *developmental range,* the spread between competence with high support and competence with little support. With both positive and negative stories, Susan demonstrated a developmental range varying from interactions with social reciprocity to interactions based on a single, nonreciprocal category. For example, she showed higher competence when the interviewer first demonstrated a story of nice reciprocity for her and lower competence when she later made up a story without the interviewer's demonstration.

Depending on their emotional state, children also show different emotional valences in their representations, just as Susan did in her shift to negative stories. Maltreated children often shift the content of stories from positive to negative, and when they become agitated, the sophistication of their negative stories deteriorates and remains low until they become calmer (Buchsbaum et al., 1992; Raya, 1996).

These kinds of variations need to be placed at center stage and made the focus of developmental analysis. Only by including these variations as a function of context, culture, state, and other key contributors to behavior can scholars build an effective framework for explaining the many shapes of human development. Dynamic structuralism provides concepts and tools for founding developmental explanation and description on these kinds of variations, and it encourages the building of theory and method that capture the rich complexity that is the legacy of the human species.

ACTIVITY AND THE NEW STRUCTURALISM: STABILITY WITHIN VARIATION

Contemporary developmental theory has reached a point of crisis. At the heart of this crisis is the problem of how to account for the tremendous variability in developmental phenomena, which during the past 15 to 20 years, has increasingly moved from the background to the foreground of developmental research and theory (Damon, 1989). The static notion of stage structure, which dominated theories of cognitive development from its inception as a field of study through the early 1980s, has proven incapable of accounting for the massive and growing evidence of both variation and consistency: wide-ranging variability within and across individuals in the age of acquisition of logical concepts across domains and contexts, systematic sequences in the order of acquisition of many of these concepts and their components, and high synchrony in development of some concepts under some conditions. Wherever stage theory had predicted stability and consistency, research has uncovered variability in general and consistency under some circumstances. By the mid-1980s, the inability of stage theory to account for this combination of variability and consistency had led to a virtual abandonment of stage theory as a framework for research and interpretation.

Because documenting and accounting for systematic variability are central tasks of science, the demise of stage theory might have brought a rush of new theories and models competing to explain the newly discovered patterns of variability and consistency that had eluded stage theory. Yet in the intervening period, no direct explanations of de-

velopmental variability and consistency have emerged but only patchwork "models" to deal with variation in one narrow context or domain. Instead of dealing with variability straightforwardly, scholars either have ignored it, relegating it to the background of research and theory, or have focused selectively on one kind of variability without attempting to explain systematic patterns of variation and consistency.

For example, one approach that focuses on variability is the contemporary consensus around domain specificity—the idea that cognitive abilities are more stable and consistent within a domain than across domains (Carey, 1985; Feldman, 1980; Gardner, 1983; Horn & Hofer, 1992; Keil, 1986; Turiel & Davidson, 1986). The view is an important recognition of the extent of variability, but it does little to explain why particular patterns of variability exist. Instead, it assumes that they exist and describes some of the static characteristics within a domain. Similarly, the movement toward nativist accounts of early cognitive abilities has selectively focused on one consequence of variability—the downward variation in age of onset for concepts like conservation or object permanence that can be achieved with modified methods or simplified tasks (Carey & Gelman, 1991; Chomsky, 1986; Fischer & Bidell, 1991). Scholars in this movement have focused only on the downward variation in age, without considering the complementary, widely observed pattern of increase in age of onset for many tasks and assessment conditions (Kitchener & King, 1990; Pinard, 1981; Zhang & Norman, 1994).

Why have there been so few efforts to account for systematic variability in developmental patterns? We believe that the lack of attention to variability is symptomatic of a wider crisis in psychology and the social and biological sciences—a crisis brought on by fundamental fallacies in our conceptions of both the mind and methods for studying it (Bidell & Fischer, 1996; Goodwin, 1994; Kauffman, 1993; Rotman, 1993). Specifically, there is a widespread tendency toward reductionism, a view of mind and science that seeks to explain action and thought entirely in terms of lower-level processes such as genes, neural activity, and biochemical processes, extracting them out of their natural contexts and isolating them as if they were not interrelated (see Overton, Ch. 3, this Volume). Conceiving of development in terms of genetically unfolding brain structures, or similar reductionist explanations, has led to the erroneous but deeply rooted view of cognitive structures as static forms. The idea of stage structures was only one instantiation of this static view of cognitive structure. Until contemporary models of behavioral structure move beyond static conceptions of form to include variability, the crisis in psychology and related social sciences will continue.

Fortunately, a new view of cognitive structure as a property of *dynamic systems* instead of static forms is beginning to emerge from a growing number of research and theoretical efforts across the field. This interest in dynamic systems is part of a wider movement in contemporary science: away from traditional static, abstract models of reality toward viewpoints that capture the deep complexity, relationship, and dynamism inherent in behavioral, mental, and social phenomena. Dynamic systems approaches have sometimes been referred to as theories of "chaos" and "catastrophe," because they attempt to model and explain processes that seem chaotic or catastrophic when viewed from more simplistic, static models (Kauffman, 1993; Kelso, Ding, & Schöner, 1993; Port & van Gelder, 1995; Prigogine & Stengers, 1984; van Geert, 1994). However, far from modeling randomness or disorder, dynamic systems theories aim to understand the underlying relations among complex processes that give rise to orderly patterns of variability—stabilities within the variations. (See Thelen and Smith, Ch. 10, this Volume, for a review of various dynamic concepts.)

Dynamic systems theory should be distinguished from the older framework of general systems theory (Sameroff & Chandler, 1975; von Bertalanffy, 1968). The two approaches have important commonalities and are linked by historical continuities, but dynamic systems theory constitutes an independent scientific tradition and represents an emerging direction in science in the 20th century. General systems theory has remained a highly abstract and generalized framework for thinking about systems properties; it was mostly applied to analyzing functions of relatively stable systems. Although the dynamics of "open" or living systems were addressed by von Bertalanffy and others, the specific dynamic properties of changing systems remained largely an afterthought, so that growth and development were not a central focus. In contrast, dynamic systems theories focus directly on explaining and modeling processes of change in complex systems. As such, they directly provide a framework for the kinds of dynamic relationships that are involved in developmental processes.

Our aim in this chapter is to show how principles of dynamic systems can be used to further theory and research in development, helping scholars to study and explain heretofore unexplained patterns of variability and thus helping to move the field beyond its current crisis. This purpose would be ill served by simply importing terms and concepts from dynamic systems models in other disciplines on an ad hoc basis. Instead, dynamic systems principles must be rethought and rearticulated within both historical and contemporary contexts of the study of development. For this reason, the present chapter avoids much of the jargon associated with popular accounts of dynamic systems theory and focuses instead on a conceptual and historical account of how the field of development has reached its present juncture and how dynamic systems principles will help to move it forward. In so doing, we use the theory and research of the past two decades to explicate specific theoretical and methodological tools for studying, explaining, and modeling the dynamics of structure and variation in development. Besides theory and methodology, we emphasize cognition and emotion, social foundations of development, microdevelopment as well as macrodevelopment (change over longer periods), and relations between the human brain and behavior.

CONCEPTIONS AND MISCONCEPTIONS OF PSYCHOLOGICAL STRUCTURE

What is psychological structure? Why is it important in explanations of development? The answers to these questions depend on assumptions about the nature of the mind and its relationship to other biological, psychological, and social phenomena. In this section, we define psychological structure as the organizational property of dynamic systems of activity, and we show how this viewpoint has assumptions that are fundamentally different from the traditional view of structure as static form. The concept of stage structure equated form with structure and thus foundered on the "discovery" of variability in development (as do most other traditional psychological concepts). The continued dominance of the structure-as-form paradigm in theoretical movements since stage theory has prevented an adequate resolution of the crisis of variability in developmental theory. We will illustrate how a dynamic structural framework deals with variability and stability simultaneously and thus introduces powerful explanations in cognitive, emotional, and brain development.

Dynamic Structure in Living Systems

All living systems—whether biological, psychological, or social—must be organized to function. A living organism that becomes sufficiently disorganized dies. A disorganized society collapses. A disorganized mind leaves a person helpless in the face of everyday problems. This organizational aspect of living systems is what we call *structure,* a dynamic patterning and relating of components that sustain the organized activities that define life and living things.

To say that a system is structured or organized implies that specific relations exist among its parts, subsystems, or processes. In the human body, for example, the respiratory, circulatory, digestive, metabolic, and nervous systems must all function in very specific relationships to maintain the overall functioning and health of the organism. Similarly in a complex society, the economic system, judicial system, political/electoral system, and governing bodies must maintain specific relationships to sustain the society. In this way, dynamic structure exists only where relationship exists, and structures comprise sets of intrinsic relations among the parts of a system that provide its specific type of organization. These relations include part and whole, such as the relation between a person and his or her respiratory system.

In order to flourish, living systems must be more than just organized. They must be dynamic. Systems must constantly move and change if they are to carry out their functions and maintain their integrity. A system that becomes static—unable to change and adapt to varying conditions—will quickly perish. Social, psychological, or biological systems must be able to stretch the limits of their current patterns of organization, and even to actively guide and reorganize the relations that constitute their structure. An organism or society that becomes inflexible and incapable of adaptive response to variations in its environment will die as surely as one that becomes disorganized. Thus, structure must be distinguished not only from disorganization but also from static form, which really is the antithesis of structure. Structure is fundamentally dynamic because it is a property of living, changing, adapting systems.

For living systems, the dynamic is self-organization. Living systems are agentic or self-moving; they change and adapt as a result of self-regulation and self-organization

(Bullock, Grossberg, & Guenther, 1993; Gottlieb, 1992; Kauffman, 1993). A living system is involved in multiple relations with other living and nonliving systems, and they are part of its dynamics. Their influence functions through the living system's self-regulation and self-organization.

This agency and dynamism lead naturally to variability in systems. If systems were static, they would be unchanging; but because they move and change, they give rise to patterns of variability. The more complex a system, the more relations are entailed by its structure and the greater the variability it is likely to display. This variability can easily elude overly simple theoretical or mathematical models that fail to take into account the dynamic complexity and interrelationships of living systems.

Dynamic Structure in Psychological Systems: *In Medias Res*

The human mind is a specialized living system that participates in and with other bodily as well as social and cultural systems. The specialized function of the human mind is to guide and interpret human activity in relation to the world of people and objects. The activity takes places *in medias res,* in the middle of things, not in the person alone or in the brain. The objects and people in the physical and social world of the actor are actually part of the activity.

Because the human mind is a type of living system, it can be understood in terms of the principles of living systems, including structure, relationship, agency, and dynamics. From this perspective, psychological structure is defined as the organizational property of dynamic systems of activity, both mental and physical. Systems of activity, like other living systems, must be organized to function properly, to maintain themselves and adapt to variation in useful ways. This organization involves relationships among the biological, psychological, and social systems that contribute to any given activity. In agency, people set goals (and regulate their own activities in terms of those goals) with respect to the many systems relationships in which they are embedded. The result of all this complexity is a self-regulated dynamic system of activities in which psychological organization varies widely while at the same time showing important kinds of order and stability within the variation.

As an example of a dynamic system of activity, consider producing a narrative, which is a fundamental human activity. To produce a specific type of narrative such as a story, activities must be organized in a scriptlike way, following specific patterns of sequencing of events (Nelson, 1986; Schank & Abelson, 1977). This organization helps impart meaning to the story, as with 5-year-old Susan's stories about interaction between a girl and her father. Without this script organization, the story becomes a meaningless jumble. It becomes unclear, for example, who is being nice to whom and why, or who is hurting whom and why. Yet the organization of the storytelling activity must also be flexible, so that a storyteller can create new versions for changing people and situations, thereby communicating different ideas and feelings, as Susan changed her stories in relation to her emotional state and to the contextual cuing and support she received from the adult interviewer.

During the course of childhood, people gradually construct narrative skills, in settings where organizing a coherent story in a particular cultural style is key to social participation (Daiute & Griffin, 1993; Fivush & Hudson, 1990; Ninio & Snow, 1996; Snow, Perlmann, & Nathan, 1989). The construction of narrative skills is strongly driven by meaning (Bruner, 1990; Hicks, 1995). Children build new kinds of narratives in order to extend their communicative skills within a discourse community. In this constructive process, children are scaffolded by adults and older children. The children's level of narrative organization is raised so they can better participate with others, until they reorganize their narrative skills at the level needed for independent participation. Note that the constructive process involves a child acting in a dyad or small group, an *ensemble* coparticipating in an activity, not acting alone.

Like other skills, the structural organization of narrative skills varies tremendously as a result of the dynamics of the constructive activity that produces them and the complexity of their relations with other systems, including biological and sociocultural systems such as emotional state and social-contextual support in an ensemble. A child who with scaffolding by an adult is able to actively organize a given type of story—providing, for example, a setting, action, reaction, and resolution—is unable to reproduce it the next moment under less supportive conditions (as Susan showed). Or a child who independently organizes this type of narrative while in a good mood cannot do so minutes later under conditions of emotional stress or fatigue. Additionally, the form of narrative organization varies across cultural groupings and discourse communities as individuals construct different types of narrative skills to participate in different

types of culturally patterned communicative activity. In short, psychological structure is highly variable because it is the organizational property of real, dynamic, self-organizing systems of human activity that are integrally related to the biological and sociocultural systems that support them.

Traditional static conceptions of psychological structure are closely related to a widespread cultural metaphor for development—a ladder. Development is conceived as a simple linear process of moving from one formal structure to the next, like climbing the fixed steps of a ladder. It matters little whether the steps of the ladder are conceived as cross-domain stages, levels of a domain-specific competence, or points on a psychometrically based scale. In each case, the beginning point, sequence of steps, and end point of the developmental process are all linear and relatively fixed, forming a single ladder. With such a deterministic, reductionist metaphor, it is difficult to represent the role of constructive activity or differential contextual support because there appears to be no choice of where to go from each step. The richness of children's development of narrative skills, including the variability in their skills across contexts, is simply lost with the ladder metaphor. Development means just moving to the next step.

An alternative metaphor for development that includes variability as well as stability in development, is the constructive web (Bidell & Fischer, 1992a; Fischer, Knight, & Van Parys, 1993). The metaphor of a web is useful for dynamic models because it supports thinking about active skill construction in a variety of contexts as well as types of variability. Unlike the steps in a ladder, the strands in a web are not fixed in a determined order but are the *joint product* of the web builder's constructive activity and the supportive context in which it is built (like branches, leaves, or the corner of a wall, for a spider web). The activity of an agent in constructing a web is particularly clear. For example, a given strand may be tenuous at first, dependent on surrounding strands for external support, and like the spider, the person can reconstruct it until it becomes a stable part of the web. Also, unlike most spider webs, human developmental webs are constructed jointly by multiple agents, not by an individual alone, although most psychological research examines individuals isolated from their social networks. We will show how people often join together to construct parts of their developmental webs.

The separate strands in a web represent the various pathways along which a person develops. The strands in a web can start in a number of places, take a variety of directions, and come out at a range of end points, all determined by active construction in specific contexts. The several strands composing one line may be constructed in a different sequential order from the strands composing another line in a different section of the web. At the same time, there is order in the web, including similar orderings of spatial positions for some strands, separations and junctions of strands, and related starting and ending points for some strands. Using the constructive web as a metaphor for devising models of development facilitates the unpacking of variability relating to constructive activity and context, which are conflated in the image of a linear ladder of static structures.

Figure 9.2 depicts an idealized constructive web. The lines or strands represent potential skill domains. The connections between strands represent possible relations among skill domains, and the differing directions of the strands indicate possible variations in developmental pathways and outcomes as skills are constructed for participation in diverse contexts. Within each strand, people's activities also vary, demonstrating a developmental range (like Susan's) varying between high competence with contextual support and lower competence without it (Fischer, Bullock, et al., 1993; Fischer & Granott, 1995). In the discussion that follows, the web metaphor will be articulated to facilitate analysis of variability in the development of dynamic skills.

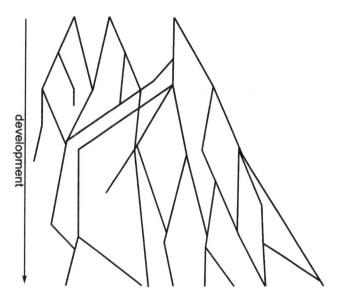

Figure 9.2 Developmental web of constructive generalizations.

The dynamic, activity-based definition of psychological structure is based on concepts that were central to the cognitive revolution of the late 1950s and 1960s (Bruner, 1973a; Gardner, 1985; Schank & Abelson, 1977), the ecological revolution of the 1960s and 1970s (Bronfenbrenner, 1993, and Ch. 17, this Volume; Gibson, 1979; Luria, 1979), and the emotive revolution of the 1970s and 1980s (Barrett & Campos, 1987; Frijda, 1986; Lazarus, 1991). These revolutions have emphasized, for example, the importance of goals, self-regulation, goal orientation, organism-environment interaction, and the social foundations of activity. Piaget (1947/1950, 1968/1970) and Vygotsky (1962, 1978) insisted on activity as the basis of cognitive structure, and they defined structures generally as systems of relations among activities. Most contemporary developmentalists agree that development involves some sort of active construction, and contemporary research increasingly supports a view of developmental processes as being dynamic and variable (Bidell & Fischer, 1996; Brown & Campione, 1990; Damon, 1989; Lautrey, 1993; Lewis, 1994; Siegler, 1994; van Geert, 1994).

The Structure-as-Form Paradigm

In contrast, however, the conceptions of structure operationalized in most developmental research have continued to treat the organization of psychological activity in terms of static form. Most commonly, activities are assumed to take universal forms that somehow exist separately from everyday contexts and impose preexisting organizations on activities.

It is no easy matter to move beyond the static metaphors for structure—metaphors that people typically use unaware. A dramatic, pervasive example is the conduit metaphor for communication (Lakoff & Johnson, 1980; Reddy, 1979). In ordinary discourse about communication of knowledge, people use this metaphor, talking as if the mind is a container for knowledge and as if things that they know are discrete objects. They treat communication as the transfer of the objects from one person to another, as if static objects are being sent through a conduit such as a pipe or telephone line. In both communication and education, this metaphor often leads people to believe that telling someone an item of information (giving them an object) is sufficient to communicate it and even to teach it. If a course or a chapter "covers" a concept, for example, then the student or reader is assumed to have been given that object. If they fail to demonstrate the knowledge specified by that object, they are taken to be ineffective learners (stupid, inattentive, or lazy). In this static metaphor (and others as well) the constructive nature of learning, knowing, and understanding is omitted from the assumed structure of communication and education, and their social nature is minimized, too.

The conceptualization of structure as form treats structure as a static property of knowing and activities that can be separated from the activities themselves, just as the conduit metaphor separates objects of knowledge from activities of knowing. Imagine trying to remove the structure from the Golden Gate Bridge, gather it up somehow, and ship it off to someone else, who would add it to a pile of steel, which would quickly arise to form a replica of the San Francisco landmark. Even more absurd would be trying to extract the structure from the tightly coordinated, self-organizing, physicochemical processes of a living cell and then to apply it to a blob of inert chemical components in hope of generating a new cell. Structure is an inseparable quality of real dynamic systems. In reality structure cannot be separated from its role as the organizational property of dynamic systems.

The absurdity of these images derives from two related fallacies in thinking about structure: reduction and reification. Reductionism is the mental habit of extracting component processes or properties from the context of their actual relationships in real natural or social systems and examining them in isolation. In reduction, structure is treated as a characteristic of individual elements—like the pieces of steel in the bridge—and the dynamic relations among the parts that constitute the real organization of the system are ignored. Reductionism as a scientific method is associated with the classical tradition of Baconian and Cartesian science, but it has roots that extend back at least to Plato. The reductionist approach can be highly efficient for restricted scientific purposes, such as isolating a particular strain of bacteria that causes a human disease. However, it is notoriously ineffective in studying any complex phenomenon involving relations among elements and systems, such as the problem of how some bacteria evolve more virulent strains in the modern context of changing natural and social ecology, growing poverty and hopelessness in many locales, and overuse of antibiotics. Reductionism ignores the relations among systems that give rise to complex dynamics and patterns of change.

Reification is the tendency to treat an abstraction about reality as an object in itself. In reification, structure is treated as a thing or a substance that exists apart from the organization of real objects or organisms, having an independent effect on reality. Once reductionist analysis has removed the complex relations among systems, a quality or process seems to be a static entity that has sprung from nowhere. The reification of the dynamic structure of real systems as static forms is a clear example. When a dynamic system is approached reductionistically, its organization is abstracted as form, a constellation that seems to exist separately from the system and its parts. With no account of the changing relations that brought the system into this constellation, the dynamic organization of the system is confounded with the reified abstraction of a static formal pattern, which seems to have an existence of its own. In Western culture this tendency to use form as a basis for thinking about structure has a long history (Pepper, 1942) extending back at least to Plato's (1941) doctrine of ideal "forms" that exist independently of the imperfect material world and toward which the material world evolves.

Reductionism and reification have been the rule rather than the exception in conceptions of psychological structure. The prominence of these modes of thought in the Western intellectual tradition has encouraged the confounding of dynamic structure with static form. Accordingly, the structure-as-form model has tended to serve as a base metaphor (Pepper, 1942) or paradigm (Kuhn, 1970) for scientific accounts of the organizational properties of natural and social systems, especially in psychology (see Valsiner, Ch. 4, and Overton, Ch. 3, this Volume).

In the study of development, three static conceptions of psychological structure have predominated, all of which have used static forms to "explain" dynamic structures. In many developmental theories, including Piaget's stage theory (Piaget, 1957, 1983), activities take the form of abstract logical structures. In many linguistic and cognitive theories, activities take the form of preformed quasilogical rules, typified by Chomsky's (1965, 1986) theory of innate linguistic competences and its corollary psychological theories of innate cognitive competences (Carey & Gelman, 1991; Fodor, 1983; Spelke, 1991). In many theories in the tradition of Anglo-American empirical psychology, activities take the form of linear input-output rules, as typified by linear models in statistics, information processing, and behavior genetics (Atkinson & Shiffrin, 1968;

Gottlieb, 1995; Horn & Hofer, 1992; Lerner, 1995a; Plomin & McClearn, 1993; Wahlsten, 1990).

These static notions of structure have proven inadequate in explaining the dynamic organization of behavior because they focus research attention on the stability of forms of activity and neglect the pervasive variability. Piagetian stage theory places all human cognitive activities into a sequence of abstract logical forms, but it has proved incapable of explaining the vast array of deviations from stage predictions (Bidell & Fischer, 1992a; Flavell, 1971; Gelman & Baillargeon, 1983). Chomskian linguistic competence theory tries to account for human linguistic behavior on the basis of a few innate rules. It has been notoriously unable, however, to account for either the variations of human languages (Chinese is different from English!) or the highly variable everyday communication skills that individuals develop within and across diverse settings (Cook-Gumperz & Gumperz, 1982; Moerck, 1985; Ninio & Snow, 1996; Snow et al., 1989). Similarly, cognitive competence/performance theories based on the Piagetian and Chomskian models portray cognitive structures as fixed rule sets that specify behaviors but are somehow impervious to or independent of the contexts in which the behaviors occur (de Ribaupierre, 1989a; Flavell & Wohlwill, 1969; Gelman & Gallistel, 1978; Klahr & Wallace, 1976; Overton & Newman, 1982; Pascual-Leone, 1970). These models dismiss variability in cognitive performance either in terms of differential expression of fixed competence or—not unlike Piaget's concept of *décalage*— as an unanalyzed result of environmental "resistance" to the expression of the competence. The linear models of psychometrics, experimental psychology, and behavior genetics treat all behaviors as arising from linear combinations of inputs, tasks, prior conditions, or heredity and environment (Fischer & Bullock, 1984; Thelen & Smith, 1994). Person and environment are partitioned into separate groups of factors instead of being treated as dynamic collaborators in producing activities.

Despite well-publicized disagreements between Piagetian stage theorists and Chomskian innate competence theorists (Carey & Gelman, 1991; Fodor, 1983; Piatelli-Palmarini, 1980; Wozniak & Fischer, 1993), these two frameworks derive their core assumptions from the structure-as-form paradigm, portraying psychological structure in terms of abstract forms existing separately from real self-organizing human activities (Bidell & Fischer, 1992a; Fischer, Bullock, et al., 1993; Rogoff, 1982).

In stage theory, psychological structure was seen as a universal abstract logic imposing itself on the developmental trajectories of every person. Despite Piaget's constructivist philosophy, the base metaphor for his stage theory projected the organization of cognition as successive stages of logic that determine specific cognitive performances across contexts and domains of knowledge, yet are relatively unaffected by the contexts of those performances. Similarly, nativist competence theories project a universal preformed code, blueprint, or set of instructions that somehow exists separately from the activities that it will someday engender. Like Platonic forms, these blueprints lurk among the genes, awaiting the right moment to impose order on behavior.

The experimental/psychometric framework also bases its core assumptions on structure as form, but there the structure is hidden behind standard methods and paradigms for explanation. The assumed linear combinatorial structures of dichotomies—person and environment, input and output, heredity and experience—are embedded in research designs, statistical techniques, and theoretical concepts, but their implicit assumptions about structure are seldom acknowledged (Bronfenbrenner, 1979; Fischer & Bullock, 1984; Wahlsten, 1990; Wittgenstein, 1953). Modern biology has assumed similar reductionist, reifying notions of structure as form (Goodwin, 1994; Gottlieb, 1992; Kauffman, 1993; Weiss, 1970).

The dominance of the structure-as-form paradigm in cognitive developmental theory has forced scholars to choose among these three inadequate notions of structure, which has led to endless debates that bear little fruit. An example is the debate over whether cognitive structure is real. Some scholars, recognizing that conceptions of structure as form are simply reified abstractions, have argued that cognitive structure is only a convenient fiction in the minds of psychologists. Others, recognizing that cognitive systems must be organized to function, have argued that formal abstractions such as stage structure or an innate language acquisition device are real. Rethinking this debate within a dynamic systems framework suggests a straightforward solution to this debate. Psychological structure is real; it exists as a real organizational property of dynamic systems, just as the structure of the human skeletal system is real and can be used to distinguish human remains from those of other primates. But to say that structure is real does not imply that it has an existence separate from the self-organizing systems that create it. Psychological structure is the real dynamic organization exhibited by self-organizing systems of mental and physical activity—not a free-floating ghost that dictates behavior to its human machine.

To build successful models of dynamic psychological structure, it is essential to understand how dynamic structure differs from static form. An essential first step is to focus simultaneously on variability and stability. Indeed, the neglect of variability helps ensure that models remain static—missing the sources of order in the variation, and treating structures as static forms. Any adequate account of psychological structure must explain not only the stability that allows systems to function and maintain themselves over time and space but also the wide variability that arises from the dynamics of self-organizing systems. Models of psychological structure must specify mechanisms by which activities are organized dynamically in relation to multiple influences that are biological, psychological, and social.

DYNAMIC STRUCTURE: ITS NATURE AND ROLE IN COGNITIVE AND EMOTIONAL DEVELOPMENT

To explain both variability and stability in developmental processes, static conceptions of psychological structure must be replaced with dynamic ones, and reified notions of structures existing separately from human activity must give way to a new understanding of structure as the dynamic organization inherent in the activity itself. An alternative framework is needed to replace the structure-as-form paradigm as a basis for research and interpretation. Such a framework seems to be emerging in the contemporary movement toward dynamic systems models across a variety of fields and among a growing number of developmental researchers. (See chapters in this Volume by Brandstädter, Gottlieb et al., Thelen & Smith, Wapner & Demick.)

Common to many dynamic systems models across disciplines is a shift from thinking about order and variation dichotomously to thinking of these two characteristics as intrinsically related (Garcia, 1992; Goodwin, 1994; Oyama, 1985; Port & van Gelder, 1995; Thelen & Smith, 1994; van der Maas & Molenaar, 1992; van Geert, 1994). Phenomena that were once viewed as random or chaotic are now seen as organized in complex ways that lead to specific patterns of variation. Describing and modeling the complex organization provides tools for understanding the relation between organization and variability in specific

phenomena. For instance, the jagged patterns of sea-coasts—seemingly erratic jumbles of random erosions—can be closely modeled with fractal geometry, revealing an intrinsic organization to a geologic process of erosion and sedimentation once thought of as chaotic. Note that the fractal model is not the same as the dynamic structure, which is inherent in the organization of the geologic process itself. By recognizing that organization is related to variability, geologists and mathematicians have been able to create models of the dynamic organization of the process that can predict and explain the variability observed in the eroding coastline (Gleick, 1987). Similarly, biologists are modeling the structures of evolution of living organisms (Kauffman, 1993).

Contemporary advances in human development research form a basis for a dynamic understanding of cognition and emotion. In the present section, we draw on this contemporary body of research in psychological dynamics to outline a framework for analyzing psychological structure. A substantial amount of new research and theory is based specifically on dynamics systems concepts (Fogel, 1993; Goldfield, 1995; Kelso et al., 1993; Lewis, 1994; Thelen & Smith, 1994; van der Maas & Molenaar, 1992, 1995; van Geert, 1991). Even more work relating to dynamics is based in a neo-Piagetian or Vygotskian approach focusing on variations in developmental phenomena such as planning, problem solving, mathematical reasoning, social understanding, and emotional splitting (Case et al., 1996; de Ribaupierre, 1993; Fischer et al., 1993a; Rogoff, 1993; Siegler, 1994).

Full realization of the potential of dynamic systems analysis requires not only applying the broad metaphor of nonlinear dynamic systems to psychological processes but also building explicit dynamic models of those processes. Global concepts can be powerful and useful, but ultimately they must be tested out as models with explicitly defined properties. Only with such models can researchers determine whether the processes they hypothesize in fact produce the dynamic patterns of development and variation that they expect (van der Maas, 1995; van Geert, 1996). Happily, computer-based tools are now available that greatly facilitate both building explicit dynamic models and testing them against empirical data on variation and development (Fischer & Kennedy, 1997; van der Maas & Molenaar, 1995; van Geert, 1994).

From a dynamic systems viewpoint, psychological structure is simply the actual organization of dynamic systems of activity. Instead of a separately existing entity, such as a logical stage dictating behavior, or a preformed capacity awaiting actualization, psychological structure is one of many qualities or properties of human activity systems. Because real systems of activity are dynamic—constantly moving, adapting, and reorganizing—they must be dynamically structured. Variability is a natural consequence of system dynamics, and because systems are organized, the variability is not random but patterned. These patterns of variability provide the key to understanding and modeling the dynamic structure of psychological systems because they reflect not only the potential for mobility and change but also the limits on change inherent in each system's organization. Just as geologists have modeled the structures of coastal evolution and biologists have modeled the structures of evolution of living species, developmental psychologists can analyze the intrinsic connection between structure and variation in order to build models that reflect the true complexity and dynamics of developmental processes.

To move beyond a general call to dynamic structural analysis and model the dynamics of development successfully, scholars need specific psychological constructs that permit the general principles of structural dynamics to be operationalized in particular research problems. There is not one correct construct for a dynamic approach to psychological structure. A number of contemporary constructs are useful for this purpose because they have been developed specifically to facilitate analysis of variation and organization of activities in context. The concept of script, for example, focuses on the organization of everyday activities in terms of narratives, storytelling, goals, and recall for scripted activities in specific contexts (Nelson, 1986; Schank & Abelson, 1977). The concept of strategy has a long history of illuminating variations in the organization of problem-solving activity (Bruner, Goodnow, & Austin, 1956; Kuhn, Garcia-Mila, Zohar, & Andersen, 1995; Siegler & Jenkins, 1989). Concepts such as apprenticeship (Rogoff, 1990), environmental niche (Gauvain, 1995), and setting (Whiting & Edwards, 1988) help analysis of the dynamic social organization of activities across sociocultural contexts.

A construct that we find especially useful for facilitating a dynamic approach to psychological structure is *dynamic skill*. It provides a useful way of integrating many of the necessary characteristics of dynamic psychological structure into a single, familiar idea (Bidell & Fischer, 1992b; Fischer, 1980; Fischer & Ayoub, 1994). In the following discussion, we explicate the construct of dynamic skill, using it to articulate essential characteristics of dynamic psychological structures. We show how the dynamic analysis of structure can both predict and explain specific patterns of developmental variability, focusing on three key types of variability frequently observed in developmental research: (a) range, (b) synchrony, and (c) sequence. In subsequent sections, we show how these dynamic characteristics differ from those in static views of structure, and we develop some implications of dynamic structuralism for the key issues of research methodology for studying change, microdevelopment in learning and problem solving, development of emotion, and the role of brain functioning in development of cognition and emotion.

Psychological Structure as Dynamic Skill

In ordinary English usage, the term *skill* both denotes and connotes many of the characteristics of the dynamic organization of human activities that need to be included in models of development (Bruner, 1973b; Ericsson & Charness, 1994; Saltzman, 1995; Welford, 1968). A skill is a capacity to act in an organized way in a specific context. Skills are thus both action-based and context-specific. People don't have abstract, general skills. Instead, skills are always skills *for* some specific context of activity: a skill for riding a bicycle, a skill for tennis, or a skill for interpersonal negotiation. Skills do not spring up fully grown from preformed rules or logical structures; they are built up gradually through the practice of real activities in real contexts, and are then gradually extended to new contexts through this same constructive process (Fischer & Farrar, 1987; Fischer & Granott, 1995).

The concept of skill is also helpful in conceptualizing the relations among various psychological, organismic, and sociocultural processes because skills draw on and integrate all of these components. It helps to cut through artificial dichotomies between mind and action, memory and planning, or person and context. A skill—say, for storytelling—draws on and unites systems for emotion, memory, planning, communication, cultural scripts, speech, gesture, and so forth. Each of these systems must work in concert with the others for an individual to tell an organized story to specific other people in a particular context, in a way that it will be understood and appreciated. In place of concepts of isolated processes or modules that obscure relations among cooperating systems, the concept of dynamic skill facilitates the study of relations among collaborating systems and the patterns of variation they produce. To see how, let's consider some of the characteristics of skills.

Integration and Interparticipation

Skills are not composed atomistically but are necessarily integrated with other skills. The skill of playing tennis demands that many other skills, such as running, jumping, and visual-motor coordination, all be integrated to function in a coordinated way. Integrated skills are not simply interdependent but *interparticipatory*. True integration means that the systems participate in one another's functioning. Atomistic models allow for simple interdependence: The stones in an arch, the trusses in a bridge, the modules in a serial computer comprise atomistic systems in which parts are interdependent but do not obviously participate in each other's functioning.

In contrast, the components of living systems not only depend on one another but participate in one another. Although at first this concept may seem counterintuitive, there are many obvious examples in familiar processes such as human cellular or organ systems. Any system in the human body is composed of multiple subsystems whose boundaries defy definition. The cardiovascular system, for example, participates in the functioning of every organ system, because every organ depends on receiving oxygenated blood. At the same time, the cardiovascular system includes components from the nervous system, the muscular system, and so forth, so that these other systems in turn participate in it. It makes little sense to think of any of these systems as functioning outside the context of the other systems: Living systems die when cut off from the other systems with which they interparticipate. For living systems, conceptions of structure must reflect the interparticipation of one system in another. Systems of activities are central parts of living systems, especially complex systems such as human beings.

Context Specificity and Culture

Skills are context-specific and are culturally defined. Real systems of mental and physical activities are organized to perform specific functions in particular settings. The precise way a given system is organized—its structure—is essential to its proper functioning, as well as specific to that system at any moment. Good basketball players do not automatically make good baseball players; good storytellers in one culture do not automatically have their stories understood and appreciated in other cultures.

The context specificity of skills is related to the characteristics of integration and interparticipation because people build skills to participate with other people directly in specific contexts for particular sociocultural systems. In turn, people internalize (Wertsch, 1979) or appropriate (Rogoff, 1993) the skills through the process of building them for participating in these contexts, and as a result, the skills take on cultural patterning. Similarly, component systems such as memory, perception, emotion, and even physiological regulation all participate in the culturally patterned skills. The context specificity of skills thus implies more than simply a fit with an environment. Context specificity involves the interparticipation of many levels of biological, cognitive-behavioral, and sociocultural systems in unified and organized activities. Even systems like perception or memory, which are often thought of as being isolated from sociocultural systems, are in fact linked to them through the skills in which they participate.

Self-Organization and Mutual Regulation

Skills are self-organizing. Part of the natural functioning of skills is that they organize and reorganize themselves. Unlike mechanical systems that must be built and maintained artificially through an external agency, the agency that creates and maintains living systems resides in their own functional activities, whether the skills are controlled by an individual or a social ensemble. Maintenance is accomplished not only through self-regulation, but also through mutual regulation, because components interparticipate. To take an obvious example from human biology, as people's level of activity increases, their increased use of energy and oxygen is compensated by increases in rates of breathing and metabolism. No outside agency is involved in adjusting the controls for this interparticipation of motor systems with respiratory and metabolic systems. The living system actively adjusts itself to maintain its own integrity.

The self-organizing properties of living systems also go beyond maintenance to include self-organization and mutual regulation in the growth of new, more complex systems. As organisms and social groups develop, new kinds of systems arise as systems that were previously relatively independent organize themselves into newly integrated wholes, becoming new subsystems (Goodwin, 1994; Gottlieb, 1992). Weiss (1970) has characterized this integrative activity as a process of *coordination*. Through the process of coordination, living systems organize themselves into qualitatively new integrated systems. Emotions play a central role in this regulation process; they modulate and direct it in terms of a person's goals and concerns (Barrett & Campos, 1987; Frijda, 1986; Lazarus, 1991).

Coordination of Hierarchical Levels

Skills are organized in multilevel hierarchies. As skills grow, they are constructed through a process of coordination, as when 5-year-old Susan built stories about affectively loaded social interactions that coordinated multiple actions into social categories and then in turn coordinated social categories into reciprocal activities. In this way, she formed a hierarchy in which individual pretend actions were embedded in social categories, which were in turn embedded in socially reciprocal activities. Existing component skills, controlling activities in specific contexts, are then intercoordinated to create new skills that control a more differentiated range of activities within the context or across previously unrelated contexts. In the newly integrated skills, the component skills still function as subsystems; they support the function of the new skill as a whole.

As skills and other living systems become integrated, subsystems subordinate themselves, of necessity, to new forms of organization and mutual regulation. The newly formed systems represent higher levels of organization in the specific sense that the component systems must conform to the regulatory demands and maintenance needs of the larger entity if the system as a whole is to survive. Thus, the very process of creating new systems through self-organizing coordination leads to a multileveled hierarchical structuring of living systems. Note also that if systems were not integrative—that is, if they were not intrinsically related and interparticipatory—they would not need to be hierarchically arranged. Indeed, "hierarchy" in this sense has a special meaning. Computer programs can be arranged hierarchically in the sense that lower-level outputs feed higher-level procedures, but this organization does not typically involve interparticipation.

Generalization through Construction

The process of skill construction through coordination is closely related to skill generalization. Generalization of

mental and physical activity is a concrete process driven by the goal-oriented activity of an individual or social ensemble, not a predetermined outcome waiting for development to catch up with it. Dynamic systems in general develop via a process of active coordination of component systems. In the case of cognitive-behavioral systems, when a system's functioning in one context is extended to a new context, active coordination of two or more systems is required to form a new, integrated system capable of functioning in an extended context. Several mechanisms of generalization of dynamic skills through coordination, differentiation, and bridging from simple to complex have been specified with some precision (Fischer & Farrar, 1987; Fischer & Granott, 1995). Studying microdevelopment is an especially powerful way of analyzing processes of dynamic generalization, as we will describe in a later section.

The Constructive Web: A Metaphor of Dynamic Skill Construction

The constructive web provides a metaphor for the construction of skills that facilitates reconceptualizing psychological structure in dynamic terms, as shown in Figure 9.2. Unlike the traditional ladder of development, the web highlights integration, specificity, multiple pathways, active construction, and other central properties of skill development (Bidell & Fischer, 1992a; Fischer, Knight, et al., 1993). Building a web is a self-organizing process in which various activities must be coordinated and differentiated. The strands in a web are the joint product of the person's constructive activity and the contexts in which skills are built, including the other people that coparticipate in building them.

Web for Positive and Negative Social Interaction

One example of a developmental web that has been studied and described in some detail is the development of stories about positive and negative social interactions in middle-class Anglo-American children. Children commonly act both nice and mean to each other while playing, and like 5-year-old Susan, they readily act out and tell stories about positive and negative interactions. Research mapping out the developmental pathways for these stories shows the web in Figure 9.3, which has three distinct strands organized by domain (Fischer & Ayoub, 1994; Hencke, Hand, & Fischer, 1996; Raya, 1996). Children told stories about two or three boys or girls playing together, acting either nice or mean or

NICE   NICE & MEAN   MEAN

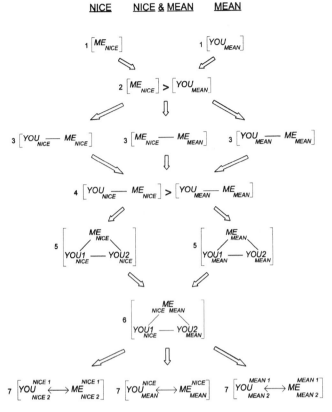

$$[YOU_{NICE} \quad\rule{1cm}{0.4pt}\quad ME_{NICE}]$$ (Formula 1)

represents reciprocity: If you are nice to me, I will be nice to you. Arrows between specific story structures in Figure 9.3 indicate developmental sequencing for those stories, as when step 5 follows step 4 in development along the strand for nice. Step 5 involves the coordination of a step 3 skill with a step 1 skill (one doll acting nice or mean) to construct a three-way reciprocity in which all dolls respond reciprocally in kind as a function of the other dolls' actions.

Thus, each step in Figure 9.3 represents a different level of skill at conceptualizing relations among social interactions. Children's stories develop along strands for each of the content domains of nice, mean, and the nice-and-mean combination. When stories are parallel from left to right, they emerge at approximately the same time in development. Their development also shows many connections among the strands.

In accord with the general tendency for researchers to neglect within-person variation and emphasize between-person variation, people sometimes misunderstand this developmental web, interpreting it to mean that different children are developing along each strand. To the contrary, each child develops simultaneously along each of the strands in the web in Figure 9.3. That is, each child is simultaneously developing understandings about positive valence (how nice interactions occur), negative valence (how mean interactions occur), and combined valence (how nice and mean can be combined in an interaction). When the three strands are all closely parallel, with no clear bias toward one or the other, then the web looks like Figure 9.3, with complexity as the primary determinant of developmental ordering. Steps of the same complexity are parallel in the web, independent of valence.

One characteristic of emotions, however, is that people typically show biases in their actions and thoughts. Biases toward certain action tendencies are one of the defining characteristics of emotions, as will be discussed in a later section on emotional development. Emotional biases often have strong effects on a developmental web; they shift relations between strands, and they change developmental orderings. For the nice-and-mean web, one far-reaching emotional bias is a general favoring over time of one pole of evaluation—toward positive (nice) or negative (mean). One of the most strongly established findings in social psychology is that most people show positivity biases in their activities and evaluations, especially with regard to

Figure 9.3 Developmental web for nice and mean social interactions. The numbers to the left of each set of brackets indicate the complexity ordering of the skill structures. The words inside each set of brackets indicate a skill structure.

a combination of nice and mean. One character usually represented the child telling the story, and the others represented his or her friends or siblings; in some studies, the characters were unknown children. With a separate assessment, children also told similar stories about parent-child interactions.

Skill level for nice and mean stories was measured on a multistep scale, to capture modal development between about 2 and 9 years of age for this population. Later steps generally involve more inclusive skills, constructed by the coordination and differentiation of lower-level component skills. For example, in step 3, the story involves a mapping (reciprocity) between two instances of niceness (or meanness), similar to the stories of 5-year-old Susan: One doll acted mean (or nice) to a second doll who because of the first doll's action, acted mean (or nice) in return. In Figure 9.3, each diagram of YOU or ME acting NICE or MEAN represents a story of a certain structure. The structure attributions about themselves (Greenwald, 1980; Shaver, Schwartz, Kirson, & O'Connor, 1987). Figure 9.4 shows a global bias toward the positive for the nice-and-mean web.

Although positivity biases are pervasive, there are also many instances of negativity biases. Powerful biases toward the negative can be produced by trauma, such as child abuse (Calverley, Fischer, & Ayoub, 1994; Harter & Marold, 1994; Herman, 1992; Raya, 1996; Westen, 1994). When children show a strong and persistent bias toward the negative and against the positive, their entire developmental web is shifted (biased) in the opposite direction from that in Figure 9.4—toward the negative pole. That is, mean interactions are understood earlier than nice ones, and the combination of nice and mean is delayed as well. Besides the long-term effects of experience, there are short-term

within-person effects as a function of context, mood, and similar factors, as when being in a negative mood leads to a bias toward negative stories. In this way, developmental webs can be useful for representing variations in developmental pathways not only between people but also within a person over time.

Modeling Nonlinear Dynamic Growth in a Web

Besides the representations of weblike relations between steps and strands like those in Figures 9.3 and 9.4, various kinds of tools can be useful for analyzing different properties of development. One example that can be particularly powerful is mathematical modeling of growth functions (Willett, 1994; Willett, Ayoub, & Robinson, 1991). Each strand in a web can be described in terms of its growth function, which in this case is represented by a nonlinear dynamic growth model (Fischer & Kennedy, 1997; van Geert, 1991, 1994). Figure 9.5 shows an example of growth curves produced by the model for each of the three strands.

The growth model includes a global positive bias like that in Figure 9.4, and under certain conditions, it also produces stagelike jumps in development. Complexity scaling provides the metric for quantifying growth of the strands, with scaling tools provided by dynamic skill theory (Fischer, 1980). The graph clearly represents the bias toward positive valence and away from negative and combined valences, emphasizing the quantitative advantage of

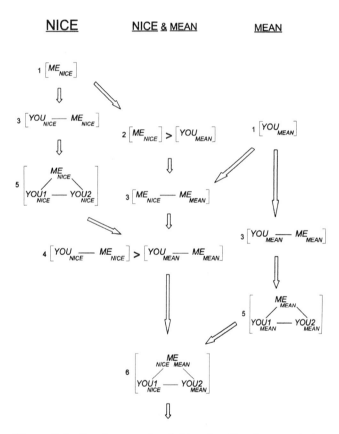

Figure 9.4 Developmental web biased uniformly toward nice interactions. This web includes only the first two thirds of the skills from the web in Figure 9.3. The numbers to the left of each set of brackets indicate the complexity ordering of the skill structures. The words inside each set of brackets indicate a skill structure.

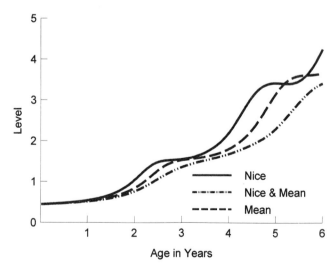

Figure 9.5 Growth functions showing a uniform bias toward nice interactions.

the nice strand over the others. It also highlights the fits and starts in growth and the relations between them—something that is not evident in the web diagram. On the other hand, this quantitative graphing deemphasizes the ordering relations among specific story structures, which are clearly marked in Figures 9.3 and 9.4. Different tools for analysis of developing activity structures will capture different properties of the structures, and no single tool will capture all important aspects.

How Dynamic Skills Explain Variability in Development

The characteristics of skills, including the weblike process of skill construction, can help both to explain and to predict patterns of variability that have eluded traditional static accounts of psychological structure. In this section we show how three basic forms of systematic developmental variability—(a) skill level, (b) sequence, and (c) synchrony—can each be explained in terms of the characteristics of dynamic skills. In a subsequent section, we will consider issues of methodology and measurement used in the precise description and prediction of variability in development.

Developmental Range: Optimal and Functional Levels

A fundamental error stemming from static conceptions of psychological structure is that each individual is treated as "possessing" one fixed level of structure, either across domains or within a domain, as if cognition were a sealed bottle with a fixed level of liquid in it. From this point of view, an individual's behavior is expected to be homogeneously consistent with the fixed level of cognition. Deviations from this fixed level then seem mysterious and appear to call for complicated explanations. More generally, these deviations are ignored; researchers use methods that sum across individuals, activities, and contexts and treat true variations in level as errors of measurement (Estes, 1955; Fischer, Bullock, et al., 1993; Skinner, 1938; Wohlwill, 1973).

A person carrying out activities does not possess one fixed level of organization. The types and complexities of organizations found in dynamic skills are always changing because (a) people constantly vary their activity systems as they adjust to varying conditions and coparticipants, and (b) people are commonly in the process of reorganizing their skills to deal with new situations, people, and problems. For instance, a tennis player will play at top level one day—after a good night's rest, on an asphalt court, against a well-known opponent. The same player will play at a much lower level the next day, with a bad night's sleep, on a clay court, against a new adversary. This reduction in the player's skill level is a real change in the organization of activity. It is not an illusory departure from some "more real" underlying stage or competence. There is a change in the actual relationships among the participating systems of perception, motor anticipation, motor execution, memory (of, for instance, the other player's strengths), and so on. These relations constitute the true dynamic structure of skill. The level of organization of tennis skills varies because coordination among the systems is different on the two days. It is not necessary to posit any additional layers of abstract competence or stage structure to explain this variation. It is accounted for by the dynamic properties of real activity systems.

Comparable variations in skill level occur in most kinds of skills, from playing tennis to interacting socially, planning activities, and reasoning about scientific or literary questions. Vygotsky (1978) suggested one type of order in these variations. He called the variation between performances, with and without scaffolding by an expert, the zone of proximal development (ZPD). Our research has documented one component of this zone—the developmental range introduced earlier, the interval between a person's highest performances with and without social contextual support in some domain. Five-year-old Susan showed a developmental range in her construction of stories about nice and mean interactions between a girl and her father. In a study of nice and mean stories, 7-year-old children telling stories under conditions of high and low social-contextual support showed a consistent developmental range, repeatedly changing to a high level with support and a lower level without it, as shown in Figure 9.1. A typical 7-year-old produced a highest story of step 3 under low-support conditions but achieved step 6 under high-support conditions.

The interval between these two developmental levels, which constitutes a child's developmental range for this domain, is indicated in Table 9.1. The highest skill level when functioning independently (under low support) for a given domain is referred to as the functional level. The highest level with high-support conditions is the optimal level. The interval between optimal and functional levels in Table 9.1 is the same as the difference between high- and low-support conditions in Figure 9.1.

TABLE 9.1   Developmental Range of a 7-Year-Old Telling a Story under Varying Social Support Conditions

Step	Performance Level	Social Support
1		
2		
3	Functional level	None
4		
5		
6	Optimal level	Priming through Modeling, etc.
7		
8	Scaffolded level	Direct participation by adult
9		

The interval of variation for a given skill can extend even further, as suggested in Table 9.1. Social support often goes beyond prompting or modeling to actual coparticipation in a task, where for example an adult takes on acting out the role of one of the dolls in a story with a child. With such scaffolding, the level of task performance can be extended several steps upward because psychological control of the activity is shared with an expert. In contrast, circumstances such as emotional stress, fatigue, distraction, or interference by a coparticipant can lead a person's skill level to fall below what would ordinarily be his or her functional level.

The developmental range seems to extend across most tasks, ages, and cultures, and it grows larger with age, at least through the late 20s (Bullock & Ziegler, 1994; Fischer, Bullock, et al., 1993; Kitchener, Lynch, Fischer, & Wood, 1993; Watson & Fischer, 1980). Most people experience the developmental range directly when they learn something new with a teacher or mentor. With the prompting of the teacher, they understand a new concept or control a new skill at a relatively high level. Without the prompting, their level of skill drops precipitously, such as when they leave the classroom and try to explain the new concept to a friend who knows nothing about it.

A study of Korean adolescents' conceptions of themselves in relationships illustrates the striking gap that commonly occurs between optimal levels and functional levels, as shown in Figure 9.6 (Fischer & Kennedy, 1997; Kennedy, 1994). In this study, adolescents participated in the Self-in-Relationships Interview, which assessed developmental level under two conditions. For the optimal-level condition, high support involved the construction by each adolescent of a detailed diagram of his or her own descriptions of self in several different relationships, such as with

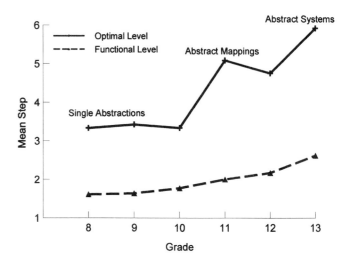

Figure 9.6   Range of developmental levels for Self-in-Relationships Interview in Korean adolescents.

mother, father, sibling, best friend, and teacher. For the functional-level condition, low support involved a relatively open-ended interview that was similar to most traditional self-assessments for adolescents, in which they were simply asked to describe what they were like in each relationship and how their descriptions related to each other.

The variability in developmental level is illuminated further by portraying it in terms of the constructive web. Figure 9.7 represents a developmental web for an individual's conceptions of self in two important relationships, such as with mother and best friend; the relationships are represented as a series of strands being built in a web. The heavy solid line indicates a well established, highly automatized skill for a given context. An individual's performance would be unlikely to drop to this level except in cases of unusual stress, fatigue, or interference. The thinner solid strand represents the functional level of independent control under normal conditions for this context. This level of skill organization is also well established although less automatic. The optimal-level skills indicated by the dashed lines are still under construction, but the individual has achieved a high enough degree of coordination among component skills that modest support such as modeling or prompting is sufficient to allow him or her to hold the skill together. Finally, the dotted lines indicate a skill level that the individual has recently begun to construct. The component skills can only be held in an integrated

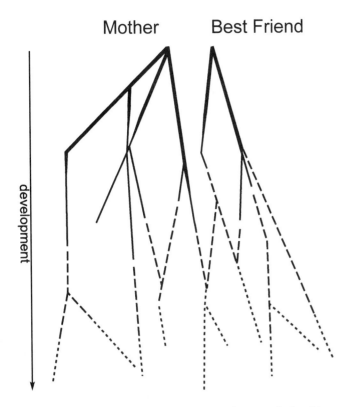

Figure 9.7 Developmental range of a web for two relationships.

structure if there is direct coparticipation of a more capable partner.

From this perspective, it is easy to see why skill levels vary over a wide range. The variation is a direct consequence of the active, constructive, and context-embedded nature of human activity. As Figures 9.6 and 9.7 suggest, adolescents' conceptions of themselves in relationships are not fixed capacities but multilevel structures of dynamic skills under construction. Skills constructed early in a particular developmental sequence are better integrated and more stable across time and conditions than skills more recently constructed or just starting to be constructed. Variability in the organization of a person's skill at holding in mind and organizing the events and characteristics of a social relationship are a natural consequence of these constructive dynamics. There is no need to invoke explanations in terms of formal stage structures or hidden competences hovering over and guiding activities. Variability is explained by constructive dynamics. The task is to build theoretical models that describe these dynamics.

Besides explaining sources of variability in level, the concept of dynamic skill also provides a framework for facilitating the analysis of processes of change in constructive dynamics. Specifying the kinds of conditions that lead to variability, as in developmental range, allows the control of these conditions and the use of them to analyze patterns of change. We have used this control of conditions to illuminate a classic argument about processes of change, the stage debate. Traditionally the dialogue about stage has not always been informative, amounting to assertion without accommodation:

> Stage proponent: "There are stages of cognitive development."
> Nonstage proponent: "No, there are no stages."
> Stage proponent: "Yes, there are."
> Nonstage proponent: "No, there aren't."

Instead of arguing about whether stages exist or not, dynamic skill analysis has provided tools for specifying the conditions for stagelike change and those for continuous, non-stagelike change.

In the study of Korean adolescents, dynamic skill theory was used to predict the conditions and age intervals when growth will show discontinuous jumps in level and those when it will show smooth change. For the age range studied, high-support conditions were predicted to produce two discontinuities marking the emergence of two new levels of coordination of abstractions. Figure 9.7 shows exactly this difference in growth functions: Optimal-level growth spurted twice, at grades 11 and 13, which are comparable to the ages of optimal-level spurts found in research with American samples (Fischer & Kennedy, 1997; Harter & Monsour, 1992). Researchers using the skill theory framework have observed similar patterns in other types of skills, in age groups ranging from preschool to adulthood (Corrigan, 1983; Fischer & Hogan, 1989; Fischer & Kenny, 1986; Fischer, Pipp, & Bullock, 1984; Kitchener et al., 1993; Lamborn, Fischer, & Pipp, 1994; Watson & Fischer, 1980). In each case, the developmental spurt is associated with a major transition in skill level, such as the transitions to abstract mappings and abstract systems in Figure 9.7. In each case, the spurt appears when assessment conditions evoke optimal levels. When optimal and functional levels are lumped together, this discontinuity is masked because the developmental function produced is effectively an average of two different developmental functions, a process that inevitably masks the true growth functions (Estes, 1955; Wohlwill, 1973).

As this and many other possible examples demonstrate, the developmental level of behavior varies with assessment context, coparticipant, state of arousal, emotional state, and goal, just to name a few of the most obvious sources of variation. Some researchers have argued that these variations demonstrate an absence of developmental stages (Brainerd, 1978; Flavell, 1982; Thelen & Smith, 1994), but these arguments are flawed because they overlook the order in the variability. The organization of behavior develops systematically, and it also varies from moment to moment. These facts are contradictory only for overly simple concepts of stage and variation. Real behaviors—and real neural networks as well—function not at a single level but in a range or zone (Brown & Reeve, 1987; Bullock, Grossberg, & Guenther, 1993; Fischer, Bullock, et al., 1993; Fischer & Rose, 1994; Grossberg, 1987; Valsiner, 1987). Research to test for stagelike change must take account of this range and discover which parts of the variation show stagelike characteristics and which do not. Only then will the field move beyond endless arguments in which protagonists focus on only part of the variation and thus draw half-baked conclusions.

The separation of optimal and functional is one example of the way a dynamic skills framework permits the prediction and explanation of patterns of variability that have typically been ignored or explained away by theories relying on static stage or competence models of psychological structure. Although researchers may differ with the specific interpretation given to a phenomenon like the discontinuities in optimal level, the constructive-dynamic framework described here makes it possible to debate the issue empirically, by providing a basis for research methodologies that control and manipulate relevant types of variation in the developmental process. (These research methodologies are further described in a later section.)

Variation in Developmental Synchrony

Another important dimension of development in which variation occurs is developmental synchrony. Stage theories predict high stability across contexts in the level of performance an individual will display. The idea of a "hard stage," an underlying logical system pervading the mind at a given stage (Kohlberg, 1984; Piaget, 1957), implies that a given person should perform logically equivalent tasks— say, conservation of liquid and classification matrices—at the same time, regardless of state or context. It is as if Piaget touched children's heads on their seventh birthday, and instantly they were transformed into concrete operational thinkers. This kind of strong "point synchrony," simultaneous development of new levels across domains, is seldom empirically supported (Fischer & Bullock, 1981). Instead, the research literature shows a high degree of variability in skill level across tasks and contexts, even with tasks that are logically similar. Children who understand conservation of number tasks frequently fail conservation of liquid tasks in which the procedures and questions are nearly identical.

On the other hand, there is evidence of real developmental synchrony as well. As with the stage concept, dynamic structural analysis can move debate beyond dichotomies to explanations of how and when synchrony does and does not occur. The acquisition of equivalent concepts does not show random variation, nor does it vary mainly as a function of experience or rewards. Instead, equivalent concepts show what is sometimes called "interval synchrony," appearing not at the same time but within a relatively short time interval. Moreover, this interval is much smaller for concepts about closely related topics measured in similar tasks, especially when there is a clearly defined conceptual structure that is ecologically valid. The disparity in intervals between concepts grows with differences in content, context, and concept. Case and his colleagues (1996) have even shown that, with a well-defined central conceptual structure, teaching the structure increases the degree of synchrony across domains to the point that the structure accounts for approximately 50% of the variability, which is a remarkably large effect. Kitchener and King (1990) found that four different dilemmas about the basis of knowledge produced nearly identical stages of reflective judgment in most American students (see also Pirttilä-Backman, 1993). Lamborn and her colleagues demonstrated that development of understanding of specific moral concepts such as honesty and kindness related closely to relevant social problem-solving skills but not to other kinds of problem-solving skills (Lamborn et al., 1994).

The systematic variability in developmental synchrony is hard to explain with static concepts of psychological structure such as stage or competence. Piaget and other hard-stage theorists initially waved away evidence by arguing that different tasks posed different forms of resistance to logical structures. The resulting *décalages* (time gaps) were said to result from different resistances, but the processes by which resistance functioned were never explained (Kohlberg 1969; Piaget, 1971).

A straightforward alternative explanation for patterns of variation in developmental synchrony can be derived from the principles of constructive dynamics. Three of these principles are particularly relevant:

1. Skills are constructed hierarchically, by integrating earlier types of skills into a more inclusive whole.

2. Skills are context-embedded in the sense that they are constructed for participation in specific contexts.

3. Skills are not at a single level but at multiple levels for each individual, as reflected by the developmental range.

Even in the simple diagram of two domains in Figure 9.7, it is obvious that among the functional, optimal, and scaffolded levels of a skill, some will be the same across domains, and others will be different for the domains. Taken together, these principles help explain not only why interval synchrony occurs but also why intervals are a function of the relative similarity between contexts and the nature of the assessment procedure.

Note that this account is not the same as a traditional learning theory model (Estes, 1955; Skinner, 1969) because children's concept acquisition varies as a function not only of experience but also of constructive activity in different environments. Moreover, similarity can be judged on a scale of developmental levels, showing greater or lesser synchrony rather than all or none. For many related skills, levels do not show complete asynchrony but are relatively close even when they differ. The growth functions for nice and for mean in Figure 9.5 illustrate how the same growth curves can simultaneously show similarities and differences in the ages of change. Stepping back to look at the broad sweep of change makes the synchronies evident; stepping close to look at the details of change highlights the disparities. Each new skill at a higher level is built from

similar lower-level skills: Each extension of a skill to a new level is a constructive generalization constrained by the component skills available. There is no need to invoke pervasive logical structures or innately determined formal constraints to account for interval synchrony in development. The dynamics of the construction of skills in context provide a direct explanation for both the variability and the relative stability found in patterns of variation in interval synchrony. The modeling of dynamic processes also allows prediction and explanation of these variations, as we shall see.

Variability in Sequence of Acquisitions

Another form of variation involves the sequence in which skills for a given task or context are constructed. Once again, stage and competence theories are hard pressed to account for observed patterns of variability and stability. On the one hand, evidence of variation in specific developmental sequences has been taken as evidence against the notion of hierarchically constructed stages (Brainerd, 1978; Gelman & Baillargeon, 1983). On the other hand, a large number of studies have supported general predictions of long-term Piagetian stage sequences (Biggs & Collis, 1982; Case, 1985; Fischer, 1980; Flavell, 1982; Halford, 1989; Lourenço & Machado, 1996) as well as specific stagelike characteristics of change (Brainerd, 1993; Fischer & Silvern, 1985; Thomas & Lohaus, 1993).

An examination of the evidence shows a familiar pattern: There is high variability in developmental sequences, but this variability is neither random nor absolute. The number and order of steps in developmental sequences tend to vary as a function of factors like learning history, cultural background, content domain, context, coparticipants, and emotional state. In addition, the variability in steps appears to be contingent on the level of analysis at which the sequence is examined.

Developmental sequences tend to appear mainly at two levels of analysis: (a) large-scale, broad sequences covering several years between steps, relatively independent of domain, and (b) small-scale, detailed sequences found within particular domains. Large-scale sequences appear to be relatively invariant. Children do not, for instance, exhibit concrete operational performances across a wide range of tasks, and then years later begin to exhibit preoperational performance on related tasks. On the other hand, small-scale sequences have often been found to vary dramatically (Dodwell, 1960; Lunzer, 1965; Wohlwill & Lowe, 1962).

Typically, variation in small-scale sequences is associated with variation in task, context, coparticipant, or assessment condition. For instance, Kofsky (1966) constructed an eleven-step developmental sequence for classification based on Inhelder and Piaget's (1959/1964) research on concrete-operational thinking and used scalogram analysis to test the sequence. Her predicted sequence followed a logical progression, but it drew on an assortment of different tasks and materials to evaluate each step. The results showed weak scalability with several nonstandard minisequences.

Other sources of variation in small-scale sequences include cultural background, learning history, learning style, and emotion. Price-Williams, Gordon, and Ramirez (1969), for instance, examined the order of acquisition of conservation of number and substance in two Mexican villages. The villages were comparable in most ways except that in one village the children participated in pottery making from an early age. Children of the pottery-making families tended to acquire conservation of substance (tested with clay) before conservation of number, while non-pottery-making children showed the opposite tendency. Affective state can also powerfully affect developmental sequences (Fischer & Ayoub, 1994). For example, inhibited and outgoing children show different sequences in representing positive and negative social interactions, especially those involving the self. Extreme emotional experiences such as child abuse often lead to highly distinctive developmental sequences for representing self and others in relationships.

Furthermore, apparent failures to support developmental sequences can arise from undetected variations in sequence resulting from factors such as learning style, disability, or cultural difference (Fischer, Knight, et al., 1993). That is, task sequences that seem to scale poorly can sometimes be resolved into alternative sequences that scale well. For example, a sequence of six tasks related to reading single words scaled badly when tested on a sample of good and poor readers in first to third grades (Knight & Fischer, 1992). In each task, a child dealt with an individual word, reading it directly (Reading Production), reading it through matching it with a picture (Reading Recognition), producing a word that rhymes with it (Rhyme Production), recognizing a word that rhymes with it (Rhyme Recognition), naming the letters seen in the word (Letter Identification), or describing what the word means (Word Definition). Use of a scaling technique for detecting alternative sequences showed the existence of three different well-ordered sequences in the sample. Subsamples of poor readers showed sequences that reflected their specific kinds of reading difficulties.

The constructive web framework provides a tool for rethinking these patterns of variation in terms of the constructive dynamics of skill development. Alternative developmental pathways can often be traced for different groups of children, such as the three pathways for good and poor readers. When the standard metaphor of the developmental ladder is used, children are compared only in terms of relative progress or delay on a single progression from low to high performance on a single sequence. As long as only a single pathway is considered, there seems only one remedial choice: to work to speed up the apparently delayed group.

Figure 9.8 shows the three pathways using the constructive web metaphor. Instead of comparing each group in terms of achievement on a single, ladderlike sequence, the groups are compared in terms of the web-like pathways they take through a series of tasks. For each group, the order of acquisition for the six reading tasks was tested using *partially ordering scaling,* a statistical technique that is based on the logic of Guttman scaling (Hofmann, 1996; Krus, 1977; Tatsuoka, 1986). In the figure, tasks acquired first are shown at the top of each sequence, and later acquisitions are shown below them. A line between two tasks means that the ordering is statistically reliable, and tasks that are parallel and have no lines between them are acquired at about the same time.

A comparison of the three developmental pathways shows that the poor readers are not simply delayed with respect to a universal sequence of acquisitions, but actually follow *different* pathways in acquiring these skills (Knight & Fischer, 1992). Normal readers all showed one main pathway, but poor readers showed two other pathways different from the normal one. This map of alternative pathways suggests a different remedial educational strategy. Instead of attempting to speed up development in poor readers, teachers can think in terms of helping to channel children following divergent pathways into alternatives that converge on the goal of skilled reading (Fink, 1995; Wolf, in press). By providing environmental support, teachers can channel development, building bridges from the known to the unknown instead of providing frustrating repetitive

(a) Pathway 1: Normative developmental pathway for reading single words.

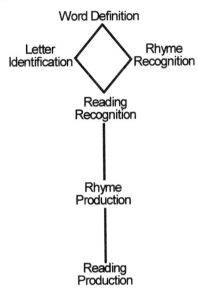

(b) Pathway 2: Independence of reading and rhyming.

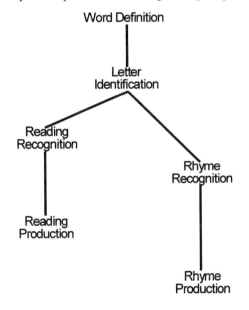

(c) Pathway 3: Independence of reading, letter identification, and rhyming.

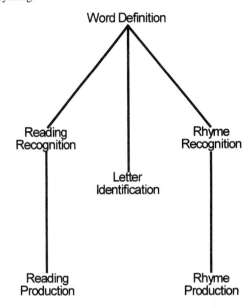

Figure 9.8 Developmental pathways of good and poor readers. The normative pathway for most good readers is shown in (a), whereas the two less integrated pathways followed by poor readers are shown in (b) and (c) (Knight & Fischer, 1992).

encounters with the unknown (Duckworth, 1979; Rogoff, 1990).

From this perspective, the tool of mapping alternative developmental pathways is especially important for the study of development among children from the working class; children of different culture, ethnicity, or race; and children who have disabilities or psychological disorders. Against the backdrop of a developmental ladder based on white, middle-class norms, children from these social groups are frequently seen as exhibiting deficits in development. Within the web metaphor, developmental differences can be analyzed as alternative pathways instead of deficits, and curricula, interventions, or therapies can be created based on these alternative pathways (Fischer & Ayoub, 1994; see Ch. 19, this Volume, Fisher, Jackson, & Villarruce).

Research methods should allow detection of alternative sequences instead of forcing all children to either fit or not fit one sequence. Even research on synchrony benefits from more careful description and differentiation of sequences: A study of the development of perspective taking used standard assessment conditions and comparable definitions of skill structures across diverse tasks and found that careful assessment of sequences showed much more synchrony across perspective-taking domains than had been found in previous research (Rose, 1990).

Remarkably, most research on development has not treated sequences as variable phenomena to be explained. The bulk of work influenced by Piaget continues to treat sequences as if they are fixed ladders instead of webs that vary in ordering and number of steps as well as in branching. In the early 1970s, Flavell (1971) and Wohlwill (1973) called for more research on variation in sequences, but their call has been mostly unheeded. Most neo-Piagetian developmental theories and most domain theories still differentiate only gross stages, ignoring completely the smaller steps in sequences and the variations among steps. Dynamic structural analysis provides tools for dealing with this important pattern of variation, as well as variations in levels and patterns of synchrony.

CRISES OVER VARIABILITY IN COGNITIVE DEVELOPMENTAL THEORIES

In contrast to dynamic structural analysis, traditional cognitive developmental theories have been mostly unable to account for these patterns of variability. Considering the inadequacy of the three dominant concepts of psychological structure, it should not be surprising that none of them has succeeded in what Piaget (1936/1952) and Vygotsky (1978) had at least hoped to achieve: an empirical account of the actual dynamics by which human beings constructively organize their own systems of meaning and activity, creating new types of structures adapted to participate in real-world contexts. The contemporary challenge for the science of development is to devise constructs and methods that will permit us to understand the dynamics of self-organization in real human activity systems.

The most glaring failure of stage and competence models has been their inability to account for patterns of variability in cognitive development. This failure is nowhere as obvious as in the body of research inspired by Piagetian stage theory. In this section, we review in more detail the empirical debate surrounding the concept of stage structure, showing how this debate led to the discovery of variability in level, synchrony, and sequence, and why the formal view of structure was unable to predict or explain this variability. We then argue that three major theoretical movements since stage theory—(a) domain specificity theory, (b) innate competence theory, and (c) competence/performance theory—have also proved inadequate in accounting for variability in structural development because they, too, have failed to move beyond the structure-as-form paradigm. In the subsequent section, we describe a set of methods for moving beyond these approaches to do research that deals with variability more powerfully within a dynamic structural framework, including an outline of how to turn theories about developmental process into specific mathematical models that can be tested against growth patterns of individual children and adults.

The Stage Debate and the Discovery of Variability in Cognitive Development

The strength of the stage structure concept, as with all structure-as-form models, was its account of stability in development. Skills exhibit patterns of stability both in the ways they function and the ways they develop. What would account for such stable patterns in the functioning and development of cognition? Piaget's conception of formal logical stages addressed this question with what seemed to be a powerful and reasonable explanation (Inhelder & Piaget, 1955/1958; Piaget, 1936/1952, 1957): Individuals construct logical structures that preserve the organization of their interpretive or behavioral activities to be applied again at later times or in different situations. The existence of these structures accounts for the ability to apply the same concept or skill across many situations. Similarly, the emergence of concepts in specific sequences was accounted for by the fact that the logical structures underlying the concepts are constructed gradually, so that a partially complete logic would give rise to one concept (e.g., one-to-one correspondence) and the later completion of the logical structure would give rise to a more extensive and logically complete concept (e.g., conservation of number).

However, the strength of the stage structure concept was also its greatest weakness: Whereas universal logical structures accounted elegantly for stability, they offered hardly any explanation for variability in the functioning and development of cognition. Because the stage concept equated psychological structure (the organization of dynamic mental activity) with static form (formal logic), it provided no model of the real psychological mechanisms that might lead to variability and change in development. The idea of a rigid logical structure underlying all of a child's conceptions at a given stage seems to explain observed consistencies in the form of children's thinking, but it predicts much more consistency than children show, and it has proven incapable of explaining departures from the predicted consistency.

Departures from the consistency predicted by stage theory soon proved to be more the norm than the exception as proliferating replication studies introduced a myriad of variations on Piaget's original tasks and procedures. On the one hand, opponents of Piaget's theory, doubting the reality or usefulness of formal stage structures, focused their research on identifying conditions in which stage theory predictions failed. Supporters of Piaget's constructivist view tried to validate the purported products of development—stage sequences, timing, and universality. These researchers focused a great deal of attention on demonstrating conditions in which stage predictions were empirically supported. Today, many researchers still continue along these independent paths, mostly ignoring or dismissing findings of people from the other camp.

The outcome of this protracted and often heated empirical debate has been the discovery of remarkable variability in every aspect of cognitive development studied. As researchers implemented variations in the nature of task materials, complexity of tasks, type of procedures, degree of modeling, degree of training, and methods of scoring across a multitude of replication studies, a consistent pattern of variation emerged (Bidell & Fischer, 1992a; Case, 1985; Fischer, 1980; Halford, 1989; Lourenço & Machado, 1996). To the extent that studies closely approximated the assessment conditions used by Piaget, the findings were similar to those he had reported. When tasks and procedures varied greatly from Piaget's, the findings also varied greatly within certain limits.

A classic example of this pattern of variation is found in research on number conservation. In Piaget's theory, number conservation (the ability to conceptually maintain the equality of two sets even when one set is transformed to look much larger than the other) was seen as a product of an underlying stage of concrete operational logic. In the original number conservation studies, Piaget and Szeminska (1941/1952) had used sets of 8 or 10 objects each and had identified 6 to 7 years as the typical age of acquisition for this concept. In one group of replication studies, Gelman (1972) showed that the age of acquisition for number conservation could be pushed downward from Piaget's norms if the task complexity was simplified by (a) reducing the size of the sets children had to compare and (b) eliminating the requirement for verbal justification of conservation judgments. Under these conditions, Gelman reported that children as young as 3 to 4 years of age could answer conservation questions

correctly. In a further group of studies, however, Halford (1989; Halford & Boyle, 1985) showed that by reintroducing larger comparison sets and requiring justification of children's answers, Piaget's original age norms could be replicated, even with tasks that varied in major ways from his original format.

As replication studies proliferated, this seesaw debate over age of acquisition of logical concepts was extended to other dimensions of cognitive structure where researchers produced similar patterns of variability as a function of assessment conditions. These included variability in the three central characteristics we have described (developmental level, synchrony in level across domains or contexts, and sequence of development in a domain or context) (Bidell & Fischer, 1992a; Gelman & Baillargeon, 1983).

The growing empirical documentation of variability in development posed severe problems for the concept of formal stage structures. If concepts such as conservation of number are supported by underlying logical structures, then why wouldn't the logical structure manifest itself in all situations? Why would a child show logical thinking one moment and, in the next moment, appear to have lost it? If cognitive development consists of the emergence of successive forms of underlying logic, why wouldn't developmental sequences remain the same across domains, contexts, and cultures? The formal concept of stage structure could offer no specific explanation for this pattern of variability.

In one sense, victory in the stage debate went to the skeptical. By the mid-1980s, the inability to account for the dramatic departures from stage theory's predictions of cross-domain, cross-individual, and cross-cultural consistency had resulted in a general flight from stage theory as an explanatory framework (Beilin, 1983). In a more important sense, however, there was no winner because neither side had offered a workable explanation of the patterns of variation the debate uncovered. What concept of psychological structure would explain the fact that cognitive performance varies so greatly with changing conditions and yet also exhibits great consistency under other conditions?

Explaining Variability versus Explaining It Away

From the perspective of the history of science, one might think that the discovery of new patterns of variability in a field of study would be met with excitement and theoretical advance. After all, a central task of science is to discover and account for variability. Theories are constructed and reconstructed to interpret the range of variation observed and to search for patterns of order within it. Indeed, an essential criterion of sound scientific theories is that they account for the full range of variability observed in a phenomenon of interest.

However, change in scientific theories is rarely that simple. Evidence that threatens a prevailing worldview or paradigm can lead to attempts to assimilate the discrepant findings into the current paradigm, either by denying their relevance or by advancing alternative explanations within the dominant paradigm (Hanson, 1961; Kuhn, 1970). Responses to the discovery of variability in development have followed this pattern. Instead of attempting to fully describe the range of variability and explain the reasons for the observed patterns, initial theoretical responses tried to explain away variability through a variety of theoretical maneuvers that included ignoring variability, accepting variability without explaining it, and focusing on selected effects of variability to support existing theory. Each of these theoretical responses to variability has served to preserve some version of the structure-as-form paradigm in the face of the new evidence, but none has succeeded in explaining the evidence.

Reasserting Stage Theory

Piaget (1971), Kohlberg (1969), and other stage theorists at first mostly ignored variability, treating it basically as a nuisance or as error. Differences across domains, tasks, contexts, and coparticipants in phenomena such as age of acquisition, individual level, and developmental sequence were said to represent varying forms of "resistance" to the operation of underlying logical structures. Although Piaget later acknowledged the inadequacy of this position and experimented with alternative constructs from areas such as the logic of meaning (Piaget, 1975, 1981–1983/1987; Piaget & Garcia, 1991), he never succeeded in proposing any alternative concept of structure or specific psychological mechanisms that would predict when and how performance varies, or would explain why observed variations occur.

Several scholars have emphasized that Piaget did indeed believe in the importance of *décalage* and other forms of variation (Beilin, 1983, 1992; Chapman, 1988; de Ribaupierre, 1993; Lourenço & Machado, 1996) and have once again tried to reassert stage theory. Indeed, Piaget did continue to struggle with explaining these phenomena until the

end of his life (Piaget, 1981–1983/1987; Piaget & Garcia, 1991). Yet recognizing that phenomena need to be explained is not the same as explaining them. Piaget and other stage theorists have not specified the processes by which cognitive stage structures and environmental resistances interact to make one kind of task develop later than another in general. They have dealt even less adequately with variations across individuals, in the order and timing of acquisition; or variations within an individual, related to tasks, context, social support, and experience. In short, stage theory has provided no explanation for most observed patterns of variation in developmental level, synchrony, and sequence.

Domain Specificity Theory

As evidence of variability grew and the inadequacy of the classic stage concept became clear, the theoretical crisis deepened. With stage theory losing its potential to generate interesting and credible research and with no clear alternative model of psychological structure available, some framework was needed as a basis for the continued empirical study of development. Domain specificity theory emerged as a way of freeing the field from its dependence on stage theory without demanding a new commitment to any particular model of psychological structure. According to domain specificity theory, psychological processes are not organized in universal structures, but within limited domains that can include content areas such as spatial, linguistic, or mathematical reasoning, or groups of similar tasks such as problem solving or analogical reasoning tasks (Demetriou, Efklides, & Platsidou, 1993; Feldman, 1980; Gardner, 1983; Keil, 1986; Turiel & Davidson, 1986). The domain specificity concept escapes the problem of having to explain patterns of variability—for example, the differences in age of acquisition across different logical concepts—*by simply asserting that they do not have to be explained,* because cognition is organized locally and should not be expected to show cross-domain consistency.

Consequently, the concept of domain specificity in itself does not provide a model of psychological structure. It simply acknowledges the fact of variability while sidestepping a systematic account of its origins. In some ways, this acknowledgment has represented an advance for a field once dominated by stage theory. However, to the extent that domain specificity theory creates the illusion of having solved the problem of variation, it may represent a theoretical detour. Simply to acknowledge that variability across domains exists does not provide explanations for particular patterns of variability. For instance, what concept of psychological structure would explain why clusters of equivalent concepts emerge in different domains around the same time, showing interval synchrony (Case, 1991b; Fischer & Rose, 1994; Fischer & Silvern, 1985)? Or what concept of structure would explain why an individual, working within a single domain and task setting, would exhibit one level of skill organization when working alone, but a much higher level when working with the support of a helpful adult? Although domain specificity theory provides important recognition of developmental variability, it offers no conception of structure to explain the variability across domains.

Neo-Nativism

Another theoretical response to the discovery of variability has been the neo-nativist movement (Carey & Gelman, 1991; Fodor, 1983; Gelman & Gallistel, 1978), which has come to represent a major theoretical alternative to stage theory within the structure-as-form paradigm. With the elimination of the concept of structure as stages of formal logic, the other predominant concept of structure—innate formal rules—seems to be the only remaining alternative, so long as one remains within the structure-as-form paradigm. Unfortunately, the concept of innate formal rules has the same fundamental limitation as its sister concept of formal logic: As a static conception of structure, it cannot adequately account for the variability that arises from dynamic human activity (Bidell & Fischer, 1996; Fischer & Bidell, 1991). Perhaps as a result of this limitation, neo-nativist researchers have focused on selected effects of cognitive variability that seem to support the existence of innate competences. For the most part, they have not attempted to deal with the extensive variability found in performance. Indeed, the modern father of this movement, Noam Chomsky (1965, 1986), specifically rejects the evidence of variability in language, asserting that it is illusory and that the "real" truth is that all people speak the same fundamental language.

During the debate over stage theory, many studies have followed the pattern illustrated in Gelman's (1972) number conservation research. Researchers introduced techniques for simplifying Piagetian task materials and procedures, and provided modeling, training, and other forms of support to children. They thus demonstrated severe violations of Piaget's age norms for logical concepts such as classification and spatial reasoning (Donaldson, 1978) and seriation (Bryant & Trabasso, 1971), in addition to conservation. The manipulations typically had the effect of driving the age of acquisition downward from Piaget's findings. Neo-nativist researchers overlooked the fact that it is equally possible to introduce more complex, less supportive conditions to drive the age of acquisition upward beyond Piaget's norms (Bidell & Fischer, 1992a; Halford, 1989).

A good example of the focus on selected effects instead of variation is the extensive research on the age of acquisition of so-called "object permanence" in early infancy. Researchers used the procedure of dishabituation, which is designed to assess preferences for stimuli without requiring much behavior from the young infant. Infants are shown a stimulus until they are used to it (habituated) and then shown an altered stimulus. If they show increased attention to the new stimulus (dishabituation), the researcher concludes that they have noticed the difference. By combining dishabituation with assessment conditions designed to produce the lowest possible age of acquisition, neo-nativist researchers have demonstrated striking downward variations on Piaget's age norms. These downward variations have then been used selectively to argue for innate determination of object concepts, with no attempt to analyze or understand the full range of variation for age of acquisition.

One of the best known examples is Baillargeon's research on infants' knowledge of object permanence—the ability to understand that an object's existence is conserved despite disappearance or displacement (Baillargeon, 1987; Baillargeon, Spelke, & Wasserman, 1985). To appreciate the problems with focusing on only selective aspects of variability, it is useful to place this study in the context of Piaget's (1936/1952, 1937/1954) original findings and interpretations regarding infant object permanence. Piaget had described a six-stage sequence in infants' construction of object permanence, which subsequent research confirmed with some revision and clarification (Fischer & Hogan, 1989; McCall, Eichorn, & Hogarty, 1977; Uzgiris & Hunt, 1975).

Piaget offered a constructivist interpretation of his observations—a simple, material mechanism to explain transitions from one stage to another. By *coordinating* early sensorimotor activities on objects to form new, more comprehensive action systems, infants gradually constructed more inclusive understandings of what they could do with objects and therefore how objects can behave. For instance, by coordinating the sensorimotor actions for looking at and grasping objects at Stage 2, infants move to a new Stage 3 structure for dealing with objects—visually guided reaching. Because infants who have constructed visually guided reaching can simultaneously hold and observe an object, their knowledge about the object is qualitatively more inclusive than it was before. Piaget described a key transition at Stage 4, when infants of about 8 months of age coordinate different kinds of visually guided reaching skills into a system for searching out objects that have been displaced or hidden. For instance, infants coordinate two schemes: reaching for a rattle to grasp it, and reaching for a cloth that is covering the rattle to remove it. With this stage 4 coordination, they can begin to understand how objects come to be hidden by other objects and why hidden objects remain available to be retrieved. Later stages in this understanding extend to the end of the second year of life, when infants become able to search exhaustively for hidden objects in many possible hiding places.

In contrast to Piaget's model of gradual construction of object permanence, Baillargeon focused on the extreme lower end of the age range in which this concept is acquired (Baillargeon, 1987; Baillargeon et al., 1985). Infants from 3 to 5 months of age were habituated to the sight of a small door that rotated upwardly from a flat position in front of them, tracing a 180° arc away from them to lie flat again on a solid surface. They were then shown two scenes with objects inserted behind the rotating door. In the possible event, the door swung up but stopped at the object. In the impossible event, the object was surreptitiously removed and the door was seen to swing right through the space the object had occupied, as if it moved through the object. Infants as young as 3½ to 4½ months dishabituated to the impossible event significantly more than they did to the possible, and Baillargeon took this behavior as evidence of object permanence. She concluded that infants acquire object permanence 4 to 5 months earlier than Piaget had reported.

Based on findings such as these, neo-nativist researchers have advanced what Fischer and Bidell (1991) have referred to as the *argument from precocity*. The argument runs like this: If behaviors that are sometimes associated with a concept like object permanence can be made to appear much younger than in earlier research, then the concept in question must be present innately. This

argument has led to claims of innate determination for a growing list of concepts, including conceptions of gravity and inertia (Spelke, 1991), Euclidian geometry (Landau, Spelke, & Gleitman, 1984) and numerical abstraction (Starkey, 1992). However, the argument from precocity contains important logical flaws, all related to the failure to consider the full range of variability involved in developmental phenomena.

The argument from precocity takes advantage of the selective focus on downward variation in the age of acquisition. Baillargeon's task and procedures were dramatically different from the more complex method of assessment used by Piaget. In place of independent problem solving in which the infant must actively search for an object hidden in several successive places, Baillargeon substituted a simple look toward one of two stimulus arrays. These conditions simplify the task so greatly that it shifts from a conceptual task to one of perceptual anticipation. Indeed, Mareschal and his colleagues (1995) showed that a neural-network model of the situation could solve a similar task with only such a simple perceptual strategy.

The net effect of such simplification is to drive the age of acquisition downward by several months to its lowest limit and ignore the gradual epigenetic construction that is involved in all conceptual development. The research thus creates the impression that an object concept appears very early, although the more complex behaviors described by Piaget still develop at the usual later ages. The selective focus on one early age for one behavior obscures the constructive mechanisms and makes it seem that the concept of object permanence has suddenly leaped up, fully formed, at 3½ months of age. How could such early development arise except through innate concepts?

Unfortunately, this neo-nativist perspective does little to further the understanding of development. To preserve a static model of psychological structures as innate rule systems, it gives up the widely accepted principle of self-organization in the construction of knowledge, and it makes no attempt to deal with the pervasive evidence of variation of many kinds. Development disappears as innate "concepts" emerge abruptly in the first few months of life.

Competence/Performance Models

Competence/performance models are closely related to innate competence models. The modern version of the competence/performance distinction was proposed by Chomsky

(1965) in an effort to explain why his theory of innate linguistic rules could not predict the wide range of variability observed in actual language usage. Chomsky argued that innate language rules existed separately from the performance of specific acts of communication. The rules governed what communication practices are possible but not which ones will actually take place in a given situation. Many psychologists, faced with the similar problem of explaining why formal conceptions of psychological structure do not predict observed patterns of variability in performance, adopted this distinction (deRibaupierre, 1989a; Flavell & Wohlwill, 1969; Gelman & Gallistel, 1978; Overton & Newman, 1982; Pascual-Leone, 1970).

According to this view, an individual's specific activities in a situation are essentially divorced from the structures that govern them. These structures exist somewhere in the background and serve a limiting function: They determine the upper limit on the range of actions possible at a given time, but they leave open the specific action that will take place. Competence/performance theories are somewhat broader than innate competence theories because they do not necessarily require that psychological structures exist innately—only that they exist separately from the actions that instantiate them. The dynamics of construction of activities leading to wide variation are completely lost.

Greeno, Riley, and Gelman (1984) provide an example of a competence/performance model in the area of children's counting. They observed that 5-year-old children counting a set of 5 objects arranged in a straight line could also count starting in the middle, with, say, the second or fourth object. They view these activities as reflecting a separate competence or "principle" determining the type of performance structures that can be "derived" from the basic concept of number.

> We use Chomsky's (e.g., 1965) theoretical method of analyzing competence with formal derivations that connect postulated competence with properties of performance. Our analysis differs from Chomsky's and other linguistic analyses in the objects that are derived. In linguistic analyses, the derived objects are sentences, corresponding to sequences of behavior. [Instead of sentences,] we derive cognitive procedures, which are capable of producing sequences of behavior . . . . In our analysis, the relation between competence and performance structures has the form of derivations in which performance structures are *consequences* of competence

> structures, derived by a planning system. (Greeno et al., 1984, p. 104, emphasis added)

The formal competence structure stands outside the contextualized counting activity, the structure of which it determines through the mediating agency of yet another structure, also standing outside of the real activity. Because the constructive nature of behavioral development is mystified in such models, innate determination becomes an increasingly attractive explanation. For this reason, competence/performance models must come to rely on innate determination of psychological structures sooner or later. Such conceptions of disembodied structure seem not too distant from the humorous notion of bottling up the structure of the Golden Gate Bridge.

One might well ask what this cumbersome model contributes to explanation. From the perspective of explaining variability, the answer would seem to be *very little*. Like the concept of a logical stage, the concept of a formal competence dictating behavior posits a static structure to explain consistency in behavior across variations in task and context, and it says little or nothing about variations in the organization of counting activities. For example, why does a 5-year-old use a sophisticated counting strategy when assessed in a supportive context, yet show only primitive counting a moment later, when support is withdrawn? Why is it necessary to posit separate levels of structure, existing somewhere (it is unclear where) outside the real activity in question? Why not model the organization of the actual mental and physical activity as it exists in its everyday contexts?

In short, domain specificity, innate competence, and competence/performance models share the same fatal limitations as the logical stage models they were meant to replace. Although the newer models do not make the cross-domain claims that stage models did, they nevertheless retain a conception of psychological structure as some kind of static form existing separately from the behavior it organizes. Whether such static forms are seen as universal logics or domain-specific modules, they offer accounts only of stability in the organization of behavior while ignoring or marginalizing variability. The challenge for contemporary developmental psychology is not to explain away evidence of variability in performance. Instead, researchers need to build models of psychological structure, such as the concepts of skill and the developmental web that we have advanced, that provide methods and concepts to explain both the variability and the stability in the organization of dynamic human activity.

METHODOLOGY OF DYNAMIC STRUCTURAL ANALYSIS

To overcome the limitations of conceptions of structure as static form, we need not only to articulate a framework for dynamic development of structures but also to coordinate that framework with a set of methods that embody the dynamic concepts. Classical research methods embody static notions, indicating the age when a competence emerges (really, the mean or modal age for one context and one group), forcing growth into linear models, or partitioning analysis of activities into dichotomies such as heredity and environment or input and output (Atkinson & Shiffrin, 1968; Gottlieb, 1995; Horn & Hofer, 1992; Lerner, 1995a; Plomin & McClearn, 1993; Wahlsten, 1990; Wohlwill, 1973). Most importantly, effective research needs to be designed so that it can detect variability and, in turn, use the variability to uncover sources of order or regularity in development.

Effective research should be built with designs, measures, analytic methods, and models that can detect variations in growth patterns. Research on development must be designed to take account of these issues of variability, or it is doomed to fail. The examples that are the primary focus of this chapter involve coordination of lower-order components into higher-order control systems—which encompasses many of the behaviors of interest to developmental and educational researchers (Thelen & Smith, 1994; van Geert, 1994). The components of these control systems range from neural networks to parts of the body, immediate contexts (including objects and other people), and sociocultural frameworks for action. Moment by moment, people construct and modify control systems, and the context and goal of the moment have dramatic effects on the nature and complexity of the systems. Often, people do the construction jointly with others. To be effective, research on development must deal directly with these facts of variation. Research must be designed to deal with the wide range of shapes of development that occur for different characteristics of action and thought in diverse contexts and conditions.

Developmental regularities can be found at several levels of analysis, from brain activities to simple actions, complex activities, and collaborations in dyads or larger groups. In analyzing these developmental regularities, it is important to avoid a common mistake. No one regularity applies to all characteristics of developing activity or all levels of analysis. The same developmental regularities will not be found everywhere.

Development has many different shapes! Some behaviors and brain characteristics show one set of developmental regularities, such as continuous growth; others show another set of developmental regularities, such as clusters of discontinuities; and still others show diverse other sets, such as oscillation or growth followed by decay (Fischer & Kennedy, 1997; Tabor & Kendler, 1981; Thatcher, 1994; van Geert, 1994). Ages of development likewise vary dynamically, even for the same child measured in the same domain: Assessment condition, task, emotional state, and many other factors cause ages to vary dramatically.

It is remarkable how pervasively researchers ignore or even deny the variations in shape and age. Developmental scholars committed to a continuous view of development often deny that there are spurts and drops in many developmental functions, insisting that development is smooth and continuous despite major evidence to the contrary (Diamond, 1991; Klahr & Wallace, 1976; Shultz, Schmidt, Buckingham, & Mareschal, 1995). For example, the growth of memory for hidden objects in infancy is commonly described as linear based on the findings of Diamond (1985), even though replications by Bell and Fox (1992, 1994) show nonlinear, S-shaped growth with the same tasks and measures, and many other sets of data show powerfully nonlinear growth in infancy (Corrigan, 1983; Fischer & Hogan, 1989; McCall et al., 1977; Reznick & Goldfield, 1992).

In a similar manner, at the other pole of argument, scholars committed to stage theory often ignore the evidence for continuous growth, even in their own data. For example, Colby, Kohlberg, Gibbs, and Lieberman (1983) asserted that their longitudinal data on moral development showed stages in growth even in the face of clear evidence that growth was gradual and continuous (Fischer, 1983). In the same way for age, scholars routinely talk as if there are developmental "milestones" at specific ages, despite the massive evidence of variability in age of development with variations in conditions of assessment (Case, 1985; Kagan, 1982). Common claims, for example, are that object permanence develops at 8 months of age and conservation at 7 years, although neither statement is tenable without more specification. Even research on early infant reflexes demonstrates the variability in the ages at which they emerge and disappear (Touwen, 1976).

Starting *In Medias Res:* Implications for Design

To study development *in medias res,* research designs need to be broadened so that they capture the range of variation and diversity of human activities in the middle of life. If development is assessed with an instrument that places all behavior on a single linear scale, for example, then nothing but that linear change can be detected. The limitations of most classical developmental and structural research arise from assumptions that restrict observation and theory to one-dimensional analysis. When those assumptions are changed, research opens up to encompass the full range of human activity. By limiting developmental observation and explanation to one-dimensional processes, the problematic assumptions have stymied investigation of the richly textured dynamic variations of development. To do research that facilitates multidimensional-process explanation requires building research designs that go beyond one-dimensional assumptions to provide for the detection of the dynamics of variability (Fischer & Granott, 1995; Lautrey, 1993; Lerner, 1991, 1995b; Thelen & Smith, 1994; van Geert, 1994).

Here are four important one-dimensional assumptions that can be tested (and typically rejected) through the use of designs that assess variability and diversity.

1. *Single-level, single-competence assumption.* At any one moment, a person functions at a single cognitive stage or a single level of complexity and possesses a single competence. Contrary to this one-level, one-pathway assumption, people function at multiple developmental levels concurrently, even within the same situation (Fischer & Ayoub, 1994; Goldin-Meadow, Nusbaum, Garber, & Church, 1993b; Marcel, 1983; Siegler, 1994). In development, a person moves through a web of connected pathways composed of multiple strands (domains or tasks), each involving different developmental levels, as illustrated in the webs in Figures 9.2 and 9.7. Assessments must include multiple pathways and multiple conditions so that the full range of levels and competences can be detected.

2. *Single-shape assumption.* Each developmental pathway shows essentially similar linear or monotonic shapes. Contrary to this linearity assumption, developmental pathways or strands take many different shapes, which frequently include reversals in direction—not only increases but also decreases, as illustrated in Figure 9.9. For real people, growth often occurs in fits and starts, showing oscillations that are intrinsic to the processes of development, for physical as well as psychological growth (Lampl & Emde, 1983; Thatcher, 1994). In development, these fits and starts seem to be especially prevalent and systematic when people are functioning at optimum or when they are building a new skill in microdevelopment (Cooney & Troyer, 1994; Fischer & Rose, 1994; Howe & Rabinowitz, 1994; Thelen & Smith, 1994). Developmental pathways or strands for individual activities move through nonlinear dynamic patterns of change, seldom showing straight lines. In macrodevelopment there are periodic movements to a lower level (regressions), especially after developmental spurts (Bever, 1982; Fischer & Kennedy, 1997; Strauss & Stavy, 1982). In microdevelopment, backward movement to a low-level skill is common before construction of a new skill (Duncker, 1945; Granott, 1993a; Karmiloff-Smith & Inhelder, 1974; Kuhn & Phelps, 1982; Miller & Aloise-Young, in press).

3. *Single-person assumption.* People develop and learn individually, and they sometimes interact and affect each

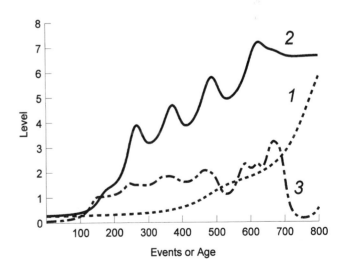

Figure 9.9 Three different growth functions based on the same mathematical growth model (Fischer & Kennedy, 1997).

other. Contrary to this individualist assumption, people do not usually function solo, but instead from birth they act in a fundamentally social way, working together in ensembles that distribute a task across several collaborating partners (Allport, 1961; Bronfenbrenner, 1993; Vygotsky, 1978). Studying development socially is not only more realistic, but it can also make the processes of development more transparent. When people work together, communicating about what they are doing, the internal processes of learning and thinking become externalized, and the processes of social collaboration and interference become evident (Fischer & Granott, 1995; Granott, 1993b; Westerman, 1990).

4. *Single context assumption.* The most effective research typically focuses on one task and variations on it, or one context for assessment. Contrary to this uniformity assumption, research needs to combine multiple tasks and assessment contexts so that it can capture the range of levels and competences, pathways, and social interactions that characterize development (Bronfenbrenner, 1993; Campbell & Stanley, 1963; Fischer, Knight, et al., 1993). If research is to accurately describe people's developing activities, it must be designed with an array of assessment conditions and an array of tasks within conditions.

Guidelines for Developmental Research

To analyze and understand the natural variations in development as well as the consistencies across variations, researchers need to move beyond these limiting assumptions. They need to recognize that people (a) develop along multiple concurrent pathways in a developmental web and (b) function at a range of different levels and competences. They need to describe the full range of shapes of development, including the complex nonlinear fits and starts in many growth curves. They need to include social ensembles in their analysis, to reflect the fundamentally social nature of children's development. They need to investigate a range of tasks and conditions in order to detect the full range of variability in action and thought. Only through analyzing the natural variability in development can researchers come to understand the consistencies inside the variation.

A few straightforward guidelines in designing research and analyzing observations will facilitate uncovering the variation and diversity of development. Investigators

should focus on (a) using well-designed clocks and rulers to measure change and variation, (b) studying several tasks and domains to determine the generality and variation in pathways, (c) varying assessment conditions to uncover the range of variability in level and content, and (d) investigating diverse sociocultural contexts to discover the effects of different cultural groups on development. No one study can investigate all sources of variation at once, but investigators can make sure that several sources are evaluated in each study. Also, to interpret their studies appropriately, researchers need to situate their findings within a conceptual map of the multiple sources of dynamic development, avoiding the pitfall of describing their findings in a reductionist way, as if their study captured all important sources of variation.

Clocks, Rulers, and Repeated Measures

Detection of variations in developmental shapes requires both good clocks and good rulers to measure change. To capture fits and starts in growth, a study must include a clock that can detect the scope and speed of change. Ages or events need to be sampled frequently enough to provide several assessments for each period of increase and decrease. Also, estimates of changes in item or response distributions with age require that ages of assessment must be evenly distributed, so that there are no distortions from biased age distributions. Otherwise, the shape of growth cannot be detected. Much research uses clustered ages, for example with 2- and 4-year-olds clustered tightly around the mean ages of 2 and 4. That kind of design provides a bad clock, because it represents only a few of the many points along the time scale from 2 to 4 years. For example, if major reorganizations of activity are hypothesized to occur approximately every six months in the early preschool years (Case, 1985), then assessments must be made at least every three months to reliably detect the periods of reorganization, and the distribution of ages across three-month intervals needs to be relatively uniform, not clustered at the mean age.

Capturing the shapes of development requires a good ruler as well, one that provides a scale sensitive enough to detect the ups and downs of growth. The best assessments provide a relatively continuous developmental scale of increasing complexity, such as the Uzgiris and Hunt (1975) scales to assess infant development, and the scales for nice and mean social interaction in childhood (Fischer & Ayoub,

1994; Hencke, Hand, & Fischer 1996). It is crucial to avoid scales that combine items in a way that forces growth into a particular function, as when intelligence tests force scales to show continuous linear increases.

A single task seldom makes a good ruler; it provides only a limited sample of behavior (Wohlwill, 1973). Better is a series of tasks or a grouping of tasks that forms coherent developmental scales (Fischer et al., 1984; Rasch, 1966). A series of tasks can be used to assess either (a) a Guttman-type developmental scale (Guttman, 1944) measuring one linear pathway in a developmental web, like the Uzgiris and Hunt scales, or (b) branching pathways like the tasks for nice and mean interactions and those for reading single words (Fischer, Knight, et al., 1993; Hofmann, 1996; Krus, 1977; Tatsuoka, 1986). Through analysis of profiles across tasks, a good ruler can be created for either type of pathway. Alternative methods such as Rasch scaling can also produce useful developmental rulers (Bond, 1995).

Table 9.2 shows a set of profiles for defining the simplest developmental pathway in the development of reading words shown in Figure 9.8—the pathway for normal readers, which includes only one simple branch (Knight & Fischer, 1992). The sequence is determined by the ordering patterns for every pair of tasks. For most profiles in this simple sequence, every task is passed up to a certain point in the table from left to right, and then all tasks are failed thereafter, which is characteristic of a Guttman scale. Branching is indicated by profiles that show variations in this simple pattern, such as step 2b in Table 9.2, where there is a failed task in the middle of a string of passes. Based on profile analysis, each child can be assigned a profile in Table 9.2, and therefore a step in the pathway, even

when assessment is at a single time rather than longitudinal. Also, multistep scales can be used, not just pass/fail; then for each profile, any task earlier in a linear sequence must have a score higher than tasks later in the sequence.

Profile analysis can detect webs as simple as the one for normal readers in Figure 9.8a, or as complex as the one for nice and mean social interactions in Figure 9.3. The logic of analysis is the same for branched webs as for linear Guttman scales, and sequencing is determined by the ordering patterns of all pairs of tasks. Indeed, the same set of tasks can define different webs for different children. For example, different sets of profiles for the tasks in Table 9.2 define the unintegrated webs for poor readers in Figure 9.8, such as the web in which the three domains of identifying letters, reading words, and rhyming words are all independent.

Building effective Guttman-type rulers requires careful attention to similarities and differences among tasks. The most straightforward procedure for building a sequence is to keep tasks similar except for changes in complexity. Indeed, when researchers have attempted to build developmental scales using distinctive tasks to assess different steps, they have typically found that powerful task differences wiped out scaling of steps (Kofsky, 1966; Wohlwill & Lowe, 1962). A good Guttman-type ruler uses tasks that include only variations in complexity or difficulty, with minimal differences in content or procedure. Differences between distinctive tasks are captured by having separate Guttman rulers for each one.

Another kind of ruler uses groupings of similar tasks to provide a scale. For example, in early language development, words can be grouped into classes based on children's usage, to form a sensitive developmental scale. Using this

TABLE 9.2   Task Profiles for Developmental Sequence for Reading Words

Step	Word Definition	Letter Identification	Rhyme Recognition	Reading Recognition	Rhyme Production	Reading Production
0	−	−	−	−	−	−
1	+	−	−	−	−	−
2a	+	+	−	−	−	−
2b	+	−	+	−	−	−
3	+	+	+	−	−	−
4	+	+	+	+	−	−
5	+	+	+	+	+	−
6	+	+	+	+	+	+

Note: Pass = +; fail = −

From Knight and Fischer (1992).

kind of scale with Dutch children, Ruhland and van Geert (1997) grouped pronouns into a class and found a large spurt in the growth of pronouns late in the second year, as shown in Figure 9.10. Other studies have grouped sets of arithmetic problems of similar complexity (Fischer et al., 1984) or sets of answers for a specified stage of explicating dilemmas about the bases of knowledge (Kitchener et al., 1993). Scales based on such groupings of similar tasks can be used to specify the shapes of development in various domains and to compare relations among developments across domains or levels in individual subjects or groups. Like scalogram analysis, they provide a way of testing developmental functions with cross-sectional designs. For example, this method can test for both spurts and bimodal distributions upon emergence of a new developmental level.

The two techniques for combining tasks to form developmental scales (Guttman scales and groupings of similar tasks) provide a repeated-measures assessment that has many of the desirable characteristics of longitudinal assessment, even when there is only a single session. Through analysis of task profiles or task distributions, each subject can be tested to determine whether he or she follows a particular developmental pathway or growth function. Contrary to the conventional wisdom that development can only be effectively assessed longitudinally, these kinds of

repeated-measures assessment can provide powerful tools for describing and testing developmental pathways and growth functions. When they are combined with longitudinal designs, they provide particularly powerful tools for assessing patterns of development (Fischer et al., 1984).

Generalization across Multiple Tasks and Domains

Task differences are typically controlled for and systematically manipulated in the construction of developmental scales. However, task differences are important in their own right. Task is one of the most powerful sources of variability in behavior, as documented by thousands of psychometric and experimental studies across many decades (Fleishman, 1975; Mischel, 1968). An accurate portrait of development requires assessment of different tasks and domains to capture patterns of variation in developmental pathways and growth functions.

For example, assessment of the development of a general concept of number requires the use of an array of tasks, all of which require the use of that number concept. Case and his colleagues (1996) have constructed exactly such an array of tasks for the elementary concept of number as quantitative variation along a dimension (a number line). With those tasks, they have shown convincingly that from approximately 4 to 8 years, children build a central conceptual structure for number. Tasks like reading the time on a clock, counting gifts at a birthday party, and doing simple arithmetic problems in school all share the same structure, as well as having idiosyncratic structures of their own (Lewis, 1994). When the central conceptual structure for number has been explicitly taught, the common variance among the tasks increases dramatically to half or more. Without the array of tasks, the researchers could not have shown the development of a *general* conceptual structure for number. Note also that along with the common variance, there were still large task effects and considerable developmental variation in level. Substantial *décalage* or variability still needs to be explained.

This demonstration of systematic generality in a conceptual structure is relatively rare in the research literature, where careful tests of generalization are infrequent. Many "abilities" that have been described as general competences do not seem to be coherent abilities at all but instead are primarily summary variables for several domain-specific competences that are at most weakly correlated. For exam-

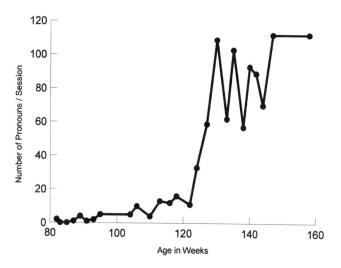

Figure 9.10 Development of pronoun use in the Dutch boy Tomas (Ruhland & van Geert, 1997).

ple, ego-resiliency is a broad characteristic of effective people that has been posited by a number of personality theorists and psychotherapists and subjected to extensive longitudinal study by Block and Block (1980; Block, 1971, 1993). Research on this general competence in 7- to 12-year-old Dutch children indicates that domain-specific competences such as school achievement and social preference contribute directly to the general competence of ego resiliency, but there is not an effect from the general competence back to the specific ones (van Aken, 1992). One might say that ego resiliency may be a useful social construct, but unlike Case's number structure, it does not seem to be a central psychological structure that organizes a number of domain-specific structures in development, at least during childhood.

In the behavioral sciences, researchers commonly wish to generalize from their data to the development of a general domain. The two standard ways of generalizing involve reductionist strategies that prevent understanding of the dynamics of generalization. In one method, which is commonly used in psychometric research such as intelligence testing, many tasks are used to assess abilities or characteristics. The tasks are then summed, and only the summary scores are examined. Most of the variation in individual performances of the tasks is ignored. In the second method, commonly used in experimental psychology and neuroscience, one task is analyzed in several different variations, and the average differences across the task variations are taken to indicate a general effect. Variations among diverse performances are ignored because only one task has been examined.

The psychometric strategy is evident in ability theories, where researchers study some hypothesized general ability such as spatial intelligence or verbal intelligence (Demetriou, Efklides, & Platsidou, 1993; Gardner, 1983; Horn, 1982). The evidence for the coherence of these supposedly modular abilities is not strong in comparison to Case's evidence for a central conceptual structure for number. Most tasks or items that measure each type of ability or intelligence have only minimal variance in common, with correlations among pairs of items typically accounting for approximately 5% of the variance.

Educational researchers have regularly thrown up their hands in dismay that they have found so little transfer of concepts to tasks that are different from those taught (Perkins & Solomon, 1988). For example, when instructors teach concepts such as working memory or optimal level to university students, they commonly find that even intelligent students cannot easily use the concept in tasks different from those explicitly taught in class. This kind of far generalization (use of knowledge in tasks far from the original object of learning) is difficult because generalization is a constructive process that requires time and effort (Fischer & Farrar, 1987). Learning is not a simple transfer of information through a conduit from one person to another.

Generalization is not perfect when one is dealing with a true central conceptual structure. One should not expect generalization when dealing with items that are related only in terms of a weak "structure" such as spatial intelligence or ego resiliency, which has been defined in terms of weak correlations in research that has explicitly ignored the major sources of variability in relevant activities. It is not surprising when this research shows little or no generalization across tasks.

Researchers using the second strategy, experimental manipulation of a task, typically restrict their investigations to one task and variations on it. Their intent is to control for so-called "extraneous" sources of variability, such as task effects, but at the same time, they wish to generalize about broad abilities or concepts, such as object permanence (Baillargeon, 1987; Spelke, 1991), the concept of number (Gelman, 1972; Gelman & Gallistel, 1978), or working memory (Diamond, 1985; Goldman-Rakic, 1987). Unfortunately, the cost of restriction to a single task (or even two) is an absence of generalizability of results beyond that task.

The use of different tasks to assess a domain typically produces very different portraits of development for each task. Indeed, many of the central debates in the study of development center on issues of task difference (Fischer & Bidell, 1991). When do children "really" understand object permanence? When do children control the syntax of their native language? When can people think logically? Such questions cannot be answered without examination of many distinct tasks that index the domain of interest. These endless debates can be resolved only by designing studies to include tasks that differ in important ways even though they are hypothesized to belong to the same domain. Analysis of the dynamics of variability then becomes possible. One summary variable, or performance on one task, can never represent the development of an entire domain.

Multiple Assessment Conditions and Social Support: Developmental Range

Even for a single task performed by a single individual, researchers cannot assume that only one level or type of activity occurs. The phenomenon of developmental range demonstrates baldly that one individual can show vastly different "competence" for a single task or domain as a function of variations in social-contextual support. Other powerful sources of variation for an individual person in a single task include affective state, coparticipant, and microdevelopment or learning. To capture these sources of variation, research should include multiple conditions designed to evoke different levels of performance in each person. It is illegitimate to ignore these variations and claim generalizability of a developmental analysis based on one assessment condition.

Recall the study of Korean adolescents' conceptions of self-in-relationships, which documented the power of variation in developmental range—the contrast between conditions of unassisted performance (low support) and those that provide priming of the gist of a task (high support) (Bullock & Ziegler, 1994; Fischer & Kennedy, 1997; Kennedy, 1994). The upper limit on individual performance under these two kinds of conditions changes powerfully, as shown in Figure 9.6. The gap is robust and cannot be removed by simply increasing training, practice, or motivation. The developmental range illustrated in Figure 9.1 documents this robustness. Performance on stories about nice and mean interactions shifted repeatedly up to optimal level with high social-contextual support and down to functional level with low support, with no lessening of the gap despite practice, instruction, and motivational manipulations (Fischer, Bullock, et al., 1993).

For a high-support assessment to be effective and produce optimal-level performance, the entire procedure must be designed to support high-level performance and minimize interference with it. Tasks should be straightforward and well defined, procedures should be familiar to participants, and there should be no emotional interference. Most important, the context should prime high-level functioning; social priming by a more knowledgeable person is often especially effective. Successful priming procedures have included demonstrating a task and asking people to imitate

it, explaining the gist of a task, and providing a prototype of an effective solution to a task.

The Self-in-Relationships (SIR) Interview illustrates an effective, flexible high-support procedure. Priming was accomplished by having participants build their own tool for priming themselves—a visual representation of themselves in relationships. That representation, in combination with a structured interview, was used to prime high-level functioning, so that the individual performance was socially supported as well. First, participants were asked to describe several characteristics of themselves in relation to each of a series of designated people (shown in Figure 9.11) as well as in the "real me." They wrote each description on a stick-on strip of paper and indicated whether it was positive, negative, or of mixed valence. They then arranged the descriptions on an 18-inch circular self-diagram, placing each self-description within one of three concentric circles that ranged from most important (inner circle) to least important (outer circle). Each student grouped descriptions together

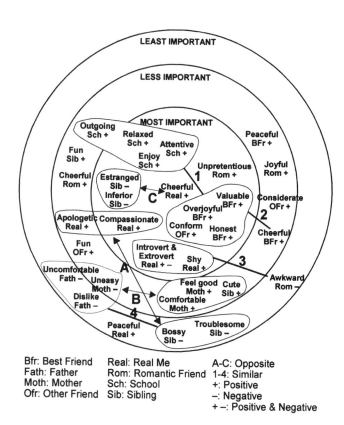

Bfr: Best Friend   Real: Real Me   A-C: Opposite
Fath: Father   Rom: Romantic Friend   1-4: Similar
Moth: Mother   Sch: School   +: Positive
Ofr: Other Friend   Sib: Sibling   –: Negative
                                           + –: Positive & Negative

Figure 9.11 Self-in-Relationships diagram constructed by a 15-year-old Korean girl.

on the diagram and indicated relations between groups or individual descriptions. Once the diagram was created, the interviewer asked specific questions to assess four distinct developmental levels specified by skill theory. For example, the level of abstract mapping of self-understanding was assessed by asking each student to relate (map) two salient abstract self-descriptions to each other, such as attentive and overjoyful in Figure 9.11.

The SIR was designed to assess functional as well as optimal levels of self-understanding. Given at the start of a session, the low-support condition assessed a participant's functional level through the traditional "spontaneous" procedure described by McGuire and McGuire (1982). Participants were asked simply to describe what they were like with each of the designated people and as the real me. After describing themselves in these relationships, students were asked to think about any characteristics that seemed to go together, as well as any that were opposites. Then they moved on to the high-support condition.

Scholars have often claimed that as a result of the collectivist nature of Far Eastern cultures, the people who have been raised there have no clear self-concept comparable to that of people in the West (Markus & Kitayama, 1991; Triandis, 1989; Wallbott & Scherer, 1995). Research with traditional Western low-support assessments has seemed to show that the self-descriptions of people in Far Eastern countries are primitive and simple, like those of children. There has also been little evidence of development of an abstract concept of self during adolescence and early adulthood.

This claim illustrates the limitations of one-condition assessments, which ignore the effects of contextual support on the variability of levels of self-complexity. Because Eastern cultures typically frown on a focus on self in conversation, people in these cultures are likely to show low levels of self-description unless they are given strong social-contextual support for focusing on and elaborating their views of themselves. That explains why the difference between optimal and functional levels was so dramatic in the Korean study (see Figure 9.6). Under low-support conditions, Korean adolescents did indeed show simple, primitive self descriptions, which they presumably also show in much of their spontaneous conversation. High-support conditions, on the other hand, produced complex self-descriptions, comparable in developmental level to those of American adolescents, although emerging about a year later (Kennedy, 1994). Indeed, the gap between optimal and functional levels appears to be larger in Korean youths than in their American counterparts, because of the Korean devaluation of focusing on self.

Sociocultural Variation and Frames of Meaning

A powerful source of variability in developmental pathways is sociocultural context, as reflected by differences across nations, ethnic and racial groups, and social classes (Bronfenbrenner, 1993; Bruner, 1990; Valsiner, 1987; Whiting & Edwards, 1988). To capture the range of variation in human development, researchers need to assess developmental pathways in distinct cultural groups. Doing research in a different culture usually requires working with a native of that culture to ensure that the research engages the meaning systems of the culture instead of misrepresenting them (LeVine, 1989).

Behavioral scientists commonly wish to generalize their findings to all human beings, and developmental scientists are no exception. Nevertheless, making such generalizations requires assessing development in different cultures. Diverse social groups value different activities, teach different contents, prescribe different roles and norms, and practice different child-rearing practices. A method of raising children that is common in one culture (e.g., Western parents' placing their infants in a separate bedroom to sleep) may be more than unusual in other cultures (the Gusii of Kenya consider Western sleeping arrangements abusive) (LeVine, Miller, & West, 1988). Cognitive and emotional development also show powerful differences as well as similarities. The emotion of shame is considered fundamental in Chinese and other Asian cultures; it develops early in children's speech and pervades adults' discourse and emotional concepts. That same emotion is treated as much less important in the United States and Great Britain, where it develops late in children's speech and is minimized in the emotional concepts of most middle-class adults (Kitayama & Markus, 1995; Miyake & Yamazaki, 1995; Shaver et al., 1987; Shaver, Wu, & Schwartz, 1992; Wang, 1994).

In their research, developmental scholars need to explain the diversity and variability of development by examining major sources of variation, such as task, assessment condition, emotional state, and culture. To characterize these variations effectively, they also need to relate those findings explicitly to theories and concepts about development.

Traditionally, theories of development and learning have been replete with complex conceptions of change processes, but there has been no way adequately to test those process claims, to determine whether the processes specified actually produce the growth patterns predicted.

Building and Testing Models of Growth and Development[1]

Developmental theories require complex, sophisticated tools for analysis, tools that go beyond the models of linear main effects that have dominated modeling and statistical analysis in the behavioral sciences. Methods based on nonlinear dynamics as well as neural network simulations provide powerful ways of representing and analyzing change that go beyond the classical linear models. These dynamic methods mesh naturally with developmental theories to allow developmental scholars to begin to capture the complexities of human development.

With these new tools for building operational models of change, the claims of virtually any theory can be explicitly tested in what Paul van Geert (1994) calls "experimental theoretical psychology." Developmental processes can be represented in growth or learning equations, and computers can test out the equations to see whether the growth functions and pathways that they produce fit the claims of the theorists as well as the empirical findings. A model of growth defines a basic growth function or set of functions for each specified component, which is called a "grower" (van Geert, 1994). These growth models can simulate not only quantitative growth, such as complexity level, frequency of an activity, or preference, but also qualitative developments, such as emergence of a new stage, coordination of two strands into one, or splitting of a strand into branches (Fischer & Kennedy, 1997; Mareschal, Plunkett, & Harris, 1995; Shultz et al., 1995; van der Maas, Verschure, & Molenaar, 1990).

Tools for modeling growth and development are generally divided into two kinds, although there are important relations between them: (a) neural network models and (b) nonlinear dynamic models. Neural network models, such as the various parallel distributed processing algorithms,

have been used extensively to model processes of learning and adaptation that involve coordinating or differentiating activities at one or two levels of complexity (Grossberg, 1988; Rumelhart & McClelland, 1988). For example, word inputs are compared to infer how to make a past tense verb in English (Rumelhart & McClelland, 1986). Visual scanning and object characteristics are integrated to infer how an infant looks for objects of a particular type following a specific path (Mareschal et al., 1995). Or visual input and arm-hand control are integrated to produce visually guided reaching (Bullock & Grossberg, 1988).

Nonlinear dynamic models have focused less on the mechanisms of learning and more on how different factors function jointly to produce complex behavior or development (Port & van Gelder, 1995; Thelen & Smith, 1994; van Geert, 1994). They have emphasized the many processes of growth and development other than learning itself, such as competition between components, and support of one component by another. The line between neural networks and nonlinear dynamics is by no means rigid, however. For example, some neural network models have nonlinear properties (van der Maas et al., 1990). The distinction between modeling learning mechanisms and modeling other processes of connection of components captures most of the differences in practice to date.

A difference that is important in evaluating both types of models is whether they reflect the real architecture of the activities they are designed to model. Many models use global, generalized programs to analyze the development or learning of an activity. Although these generalized approaches make models easier to design, they provide blueprints that typically do not closely match the architecture of the real activities. Models that have been constructed specifically to fit the real architecture of the behavior, social interaction, or nervous-system network being modeled have been much more successful. For example, in neural network modeling, adaptive resonance theory has been used to construct models of phenomena by carefully including the architecture of the nervous system, the body, and the senses so far as they are known (Grossberg, 1987, 1988). A model of eye-hand coordination is based closely on how eye, hand, and related cortical networks are actually built (Bullock & Grossberg, 1988). Many neural network models based on other approaches have paid much less attention to the specific architecture of the activity being modeled. A question to ask, then, in evaluating a

---

[1] The arguments in this section are adapted from Fischer and Kennedy (1997).

neural network model or a nonlinear dynamic model is: Is the blueprint a plausible reflection of the architecture of the activity of interest?

Nonlinear Dynamic Models of Growth and Development

Systems theory and nonlinear dynamics have been popular for decades as broad theoretical interpretations of development (Sameroff & Chandler, 1975; von Bertalanffy, 1968), but the tools needed for precise developmental analysis have been missing. As a result, classic work based on systems concepts included few specific tools for analyzing data or modeling theories. Gradually, some investigators did find ways to address a few psychological problems, especially those involving motor coordination (Bullock & Grossberg, 1988; Saltzman, 1995; Thelen & Smith, 1994). More recently, especially with the availability of computer programs for nonlinear modeling, there has been an explosion of systems tools and models for analyzing development, as well as behavior and brain functioning more generally (Case et al., 1996; Fischer & Kennedy, 1997; Port & van Gelder, 1995; Thatcher, 1994; van der Maas & Molenaar, 1995; Wright & Liley, 1996). The newly available methods that we will focus on integrate growth analysis with concepts from nonlinear dynamical theory, popularly known as the theory of catastrophe and chaos. Basic growth processes are defined for various growers, and then they are connected in ways specified by a theory of developmental process. These tools are based primarily on the work of Paul van Geert (1991, 1994).

An important consequence of these new tools is that they lead to more powerful and precise definitions of growth and development. Instead of being defined restrictively as systematic or directional changes (usually, linear increases) in some measure of behavior or bodily state (Rasch, 1966; Willett et al., 1991; Wohlwill, 1973), growth and development are defined through specific models of change processes. Growth is any kind of systematic change, including not only linear increase and decrease but also complex patterns such as increase occurring in successive jumps and dips, or oscillation between limits. The systematic nature of the growth is described by equations that specify growth processes, and the equations predict a family of growth curves, often of many different shapes. Whereas *growth* refers to any systematic change defined by a process model, *development* refers to change that has a clear directionality, although there can be decreases or

fluctuations as well. More important than the precise definitions is the point that growth and development are defined by precise descriptions of change processes, not by the shape of any one particular curve. There is no need for restrictive definitions such as monotonic increase.

Logistic Growth

The basic growth model most commonly assumed is logistic growth. In the three different examples presented in Figure 9.12, the three growers are all produced by the same simple logistic growth equation, which generates the S-shaped curve that typifies much simple growth, characterized by smooth upward movement throughout its trajectory. (Note that even this simplest curve is not linear.) The model is called logistic because the equation includes log values (squares or higher powers of the grower's level).

Many basic growth processes involve this form of growth, where the change at a given time is derived from three parameters: (a) the prior level of the grower, (b) the growth rate of the system, and (c) a limit on the system's level, called the *carrying capacity*. The term "level" refers to some quantity that a grower has reached, potentially involving a wide array of different characteristics, such as developmental level, frequency of response, or amount of activity. In the examples that we use, level *(L)* refers to the complexity of a behavior along a developmental scale defined by Fischer and Kennedy's (1997) analysis of development of self-in-relationships, where the unit intervals mark

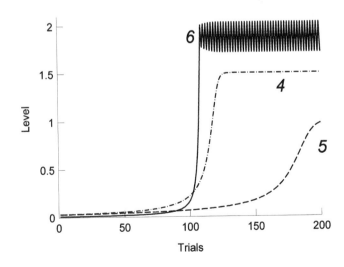

Figure 9.12   Three forms of simple logistic growth.

successive skill levels. Models have also been built for other kinds of development, such as Kitchener and King's (1990) reflective judgment, which develops through seven stages that show growth curves similar to those for self-in-relationships (Kitchener & Fischer, 1990; Kitchener et al., 1993).

By itself, without connection to other growers, the growth equation produces mostly S-shaped growth, as with Growers 4 and 5 in Figure 9.12. Even without connection, however, there is significant variation in the growth curve, as illustrated by the turbulence in Grower 6 as it nears its carrying capacity. The three growth curves in Figure 9.12 all derive from an identical equation, and only the growth parameters differ.

There are several forms of the logistic growth equation. The form of logistic growth that produced these three growth curves, which is the model van Geert (1994) recommends as the best starting point for hierarchical growth, is specified by the following equation for Grower B:

$$L_{B_{t+1}} = L_{B_t} + R_B \frac{L_{B_t}^2}{K_B} - R_B \frac{L_{B_t}^3}{K_B} \tag{1}$$

where $L_{B_{t+1}}$ is the level of Grower B, with subscript t indicating the previous trial, and $t + 1$ indicating the current trial; R_B is the rate of growth of Grower B, specifying the amount of change that occurs in each trial; and K_B is the carrying capacity of Grower B, which is the limit on growth that is characteristic of this particular system in this situation.

The level in the current trial derives from three terms. The level in the previous trial is the starting point for the current trial. Next is the growth term—the growth rate times the square of the level in the previous trial, divided by the carrying capacity. With modest growth rates, this factor produces an increase on each trial. Level is divided by carrying capacity in order to base growth on a *ratio* of the system's capacity instead of its absolute value, because of an assumption that the level operates as a function of the system's capacity. In addition, growth from such ratios is often more stable than that from absolute values.

The growth term in this logistic equation squares the ratio of level to carrying capacity, in contrast to a simpler form of the equation, which uses the ratio without squaring. The current equation seems to represent psychological

growth processes more accurately, in that growth depends on the person's prior level in two ways simultaneously: (a) because current understanding is built on earlier understanding and (b) because level affects the probability of encountering situations that promote growth. Van Geert (1994) elaborates this argument and also shows that this form of the growth equation can fit individual growth curves better than the squared equation (Ruhland & van Geert, 1997). The growth curve for pronoun use by the Dutch child Tomas in Figure 9.10 fits this version of the equation well, but not the simpler version (Fischer & Kennedy, 1997).

The third term provides a form of regulation based on the limits of the system. Without some limit, the level will eventually explode to ever larger quantities. The regulation term subtracts out an amount to limit the system based on its carrying capacity and keep it from exploding. The amount subtracted is the product of the growth term multiplied by the ratio of the level to the carrying capacity. The result is the cubing of level, which leads to this equation's being called the *cubic* logistic equation. (The simpler equation is called the squared version.) When the current level is low in relation to carrying capacity, little is subtracted; but when the current level rises, the amount subtracted becomes larger. As the level approaches the carrying capacity, the amount subtracted becomes large enough to cancel out growth. In this way, the level approaches the carrying capacity as a limit. This growth process does not always produce smooth S-shaped growth, however. When the growth rate is high, the level can show turbulent fluctuations as the level approaches the carrying capacity. Grower 6 in Figure 9.12 shows an example of this turbulence in the model. Note, in Figure 9.10, that Tomas's development of pronoun use also evidenced this kind of turbulence as his pronoun use grew rapidly to a high level.

Growth can be characterized in other kinds of equations—most obviously by equations using differential calculus, instead of difference equations such as Equation 1. Differential equations assume that feedback for change is continuous in time, whereas difference equations assume that feedback occurs between discrete events, such as social encounters or learning situations. The assumption of discrete events seems appropriate for most psychological development. Also, differential equations are mathematically complex and difficult to work with (van der Maas & Molenaar, 1992), whereas difference equations can be used easily in any computer spreadsheet program that allows recurrent trials, such as those for mortgage payments. Van Geert (1994) provides step-by-step guidelines on how to use a spreadsheet program to build a dynamic model.

Connections among Growers

Any single activity is affected by many different components and influences coming together. In a growth model, each component or influence (each grower) is represented by a growth function, and all growers can be connected within the set of growth functions. Each grower starts with a basic growth function like the one shown in Equation 1, and connections are built on that function. The connections range from strong to weak to nonexistent, and the ways that they affect growth take many different forms. Connections between growers can be within a person, or they can be between people, as in a social ensemble (van Geert, 1994).

Different combinations of components can produce different growth curves. With dynamic systems, however, even the same combinations can produce a wide range of growth functions, as illustrated in Figure 9.9. Shapes as diverse as monotonic growth, successive stagelike change, and chaotic fluctuation can all arise from the same set of equations. Growers **1, 2,** and **3** all arise from exactly the same nonlinear hierarchical model of five related tasks, each with five distinct levels. Despite the differences in their shapes, only the values of the parameters in the equations differ. The same growth processes produce virtually monotonic growth (Grower **1**), growth with stagelike spurts and drops (Grower **2**), and fluctuating change (Grower **3**). The model was built to reflect the development of self-in-relationships, with five different relationships and five developmental levels (Fischer & Kennedy, 1997).

The strongest form of connection among growers is hierarchical integration, where each successive step within a strand in the developmental web builds on the previous step. In one example of such integration, two strands come together to form a new single strand, such as when an adolescent girl compares herself in two relationships. The 15-year-old Korean girl represented by the diagram in Figure 9.11 compared what she was like at school (being attentive, enjoying school) with what she was like with her best friend (feeling valuable, being overjoyful); she built a mapping for those characteristics of the two relationships. In the growth model, the strand for each relationship is composed of a series of five growers built successively on

each other—Growers A, B, C, D, and E. A grower later in the sequence starts only after the level of the immediately prior, prerequisite grower has become sufficiently strong and frequent for a person to begin to build on it.

In this kind of prerequisite connection, the prior grower must reach some specified level p before the later grower can begin to change:

$$L_{B_{t+1}} = L_{B_t} + P_{B_t}\left[R_B \frac{L_{B_t}^2}{K_B^2} - R_B \frac{L_{B_t}^3}{K_B^3} \right] \qquad (2)$$

P_{B_t} is the *precursor function* for Grower B at time t:

$$\text{If } L_{A_t} < p, \, P_{B_t} = 0; \text{ If } L_{A_t} > p, \, P_{B_t} = 1 \qquad (3)$$

Before the prerequisite Grower A has reached some level p at time t, such as .2, precursor P_B is 0, and Grower B does not grow. When Grower A reaches .2, precursor P_B becomes 1 and Grower B starts to grow. Specification of the precursor function can be more complex than simply one trial at .2. For example, Grower A might need to stay at .2 for some number of events or trials before Grower B starts to grow, or two different Growers, A_1 and A_2, might both have to reach a prerequisite level.

In addition to strong hierarchical connections among growers, there are also weaker connections, both within and between strands. These weak connections can be difficult to detect at any one moment, such as a single time of assessment, but in growth models they often cumulate, either from repeated action over many occasions or from multiple connections working together at the same time. These "weak" connections then become powerful determinants of the shapes of growth.

One common kind of weak connection is competition, in which growth in one component or strand interferes with growth in another. For example, trying to relate two opposing characteristics of the self, such as feeling comfortable and feeling uneasy, may interfere with earlier understandings of the characteristics themselves. Another common connection is support, in which growth in one component or strand promotes growth in another (understanding how the real me is shy can facilitate understanding of why I am awkward with a boyfriend). Connections of competition and support occur both between successive growers (levels within a strand) and between domains (relationships or strands). We will use within-strand between-level connections to illustrate the processes. Fuller explications are available from van Geert (1994) and Fischer and Kennedy (1997).

The competition of Grower C with Grower B is the product of a competition parameter times the change in Grower C, on the two prior trials, divided by the level of C on the prior trial. This term is subtracted from the growth equation for Grower B:

$$-Cb_{C \to B} \frac{L_{C_t} - L_{C_{t-1}}}{L_{C_t}} \qquad (4)$$

where $Cb_{C \to B}$ is the parameter specifying the strength of the competitive effect of Grower C on Grower B. The competition parameter specifies the strength of the competition effect. Large values of parameters of competition and support can cause major perturbations in growth, including crashes and explosions. The values are usually small, to reflect the weakness of these kinds of connections.

The competition is a function of the change in the level of Grower C relative to its prior level, not of the level by itself. The rationale for this form of competition is that the amount of change involved in growth is posited as the major source of competition, not the level of skill. For example, when an adolescent is working to construct an abstract mapping for comparing her feelings of being comfortable with her mother with her feelings of being uneasy, her new understanding is likely to disrupt her prior understandings temporarily until she can reequilibrate. In addition, the time and effort she spends on building that understanding cannot be used to improve her skill at the prior level. That is why Grower C competes with Grower B as a function of the change in level, not the absolute level itself.

Support of Grower B by Grower C is the product of a support parameter times the level of Grower C, divided by the carrying capacity of C. This term is added to the growth equation for Grower B:

$$+Sb_{C \to B} \frac{L_{C_t}}{K_C} \qquad (5)$$

where $+Sb_{C \to B}$ is the parameter specifying the strength of the supportive effect of Grower C on Grower B. For example, when an adolescent relates her understanding of how her real me is shy with her understanding of how she is awkward with a boyfriend, the relating of the two characteristics can facilitate the separate lower-level understandings of the shyness and the awkwardness. This kind of support from higher growers turns out to be important in producing developmental spurts in growth curves. For many parameter values, it promotes the occurrence of growth patterns like the succession of spurts seen in Figures 9.6 and 9.9 and thus helps explain empirical findings of successive spurts in growth curves like that for the self-in-relationships study.

Addition of the between-level support and competition processes to equation 2 provides this connected growth model for Grower B:

$$L_{B_{t+1}} = L_{B_t} + P_{B_t} \left[R_B \frac{L_{B_t}^2}{K_B^2} - R_B \frac{L_{B_t}^3}{K_B^3} + Sb_{C \to B} \frac{L_{C_t}}{K_C} \right.$$
$$\left. - Cb_{C \to B} \frac{L_{C_t} - L_{C_{t-1}}}{L_{C_t}} \right] \qquad (6)$$

Each successive level in the hierarchy involves a similar growth equation, and together, the equations for the five levels constitute a growth model for one strand in self-in-relationships. The complete model includes five separate relationships (strands), and they have connections of support and competition among them as well. The nature of between-strand competition and support is defined somewhat differently from within-level, especially for support (Fischer & Kennedy, 1997).

These various connections among growers have powerful dynamic effects on the shapes of growth and development. Most neural network models of development, such as parallel distributed processing networks (Mareschal et al., 1995; Rumelhart & McClelland, 1988; Shultz et al., 1995) and adaptive resonance theory (Grossberg, 1988), have dealt primarily with hierarchical combination and competition, while neglecting other types of connections. They have seldom dealt with connections between disparate domains or connections of support between hierarchical levels. The confluence of multiple types of connections turns out to be important for determining the many shapes of development.

Equilibration, Disturbance, and the Shapes of Development

In the model of growth of self-in-relationships, skills for five relationships grow through five hierarchical levels, as shown in Figure 9.13 (Levels Rp3 to Ab4 in dynamic skill

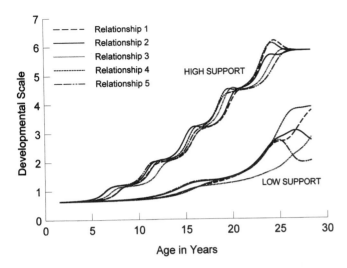

Figure 9.13 Model for development of Self-in-Relationships: Optimal and functional levels for five relationships and five hierarchical levels.

theory, shown later in Table 9.6). If the model is correct, then it should produce growth curves like those obtained in the self-in-relationships study for optimal and functional levels, as well as a number of other kinds of growth curves of interest. Processes such as equilibration, disturbance, regression, and turbulence can also be explored with the model.

The results for development of self-in-relationships include a striking difference between optimal and functional levels, as shown in Figure 9.6, where the measure is the highest level obtained for the entire interview. (It was not possible to score each relationship independently, because there were not independent assessments of level for all relationships.) Under optimal conditions, students showed relatively rapid growth as well as two successive spurts in understanding. Under functional conditions, they underwent slow, monotonic growth.

The model produced growth patterns similar to the empirical ones, with major differences between the levels and shapes for high- and low-support assessments. Figure 9.13 presents growth curves generated by the model for five relationships under high- and low-support conditions. All parameter values are the same, except that high-support growers have a high growth rate and low-support growers have a low growth rate. With differences in rate alone and no other differences among the equations, the shapes shift from strongly stagelike hierarchical growth to more monotonic and variable growth. All the high-support curves

approximate the empirical curve for self-in-relationships under high support. The low-support curves for Relationship 3, which has the slowest growth rate, approximates the empirical curve for low support. Included in the variability of some of the low-support curves is a jump or drop, which presumably represents likely growth patterns when the growth rate is a little higher than it was in the Korean sample. In general, slow growth rates frequently produce relatively monotonic growth, and high rates usually produce a series of discontinuities (spurts and drops).

This change from growth through a series of discontinuities to growth that is variably monotonic defines a broad set of the growth patterns for the model. For example, recall that the growth curves in Figure 9.9 were also generated by this model, and Growers **1** and **2** there represent the same range of variation. Grower **3** represents a more turbulent pattern, which is common when the growth curves are less stable or equilibrated.

Piaget (1957, 1967/1971, 1975) used the concept of equilibration to describe how the person's activity led to regulation of multiple influences in development, producing a series of successive equilibria for new stages in the developmental hierarchy. Spurt-and-plateau growth patterns like the one for high-support growers in Figure 9.13 seem to show such an equilibration process, in that the growers for different domains tend to seek the same levels. This kind of level seeking is often referred to as *attraction* in nonlinear dynamics, because there seems to be an attractor pulling the curves toward a common place. For example, when a grower moves higher than the others, which can be construed as a disturbance from equilibrium, it tends to return toward the common level. On the other hand, the growers for functional level do not show any clear tendency to seek the same level.

Grower 2 in Figure 9.9 shows this effect in an especially dramatic way; there is strong U-shaped growth, with decreases after each spurt. In the history of child development, scholars have often puzzled about the nature and existence of U-shaped growth (Bever, 1982; Strauss & Stavy, 1982; Werner, 1948). In these dynamic growth models as well as in empirical research on optimal levels of hierarchical growth, peaks of growth are often followed by drops (Fischer & Kennedy, 1997; Fischer & Rose, 1994).

Orderly equilibration may be a quality of one class of hierarchical growth curves, but there are many forms that show no such order. Besides curves like those for low support in Figure 9.13, many growth functions spread disturbances throughout a system of growers. Sometimes, these disturbances lead to growth patterns like the one shown in Figure 9.14, which we call the Piaget effect. When Piaget (1935/1970, 1947/1950) criticized efforts to speed up children's early development, he suggested that pushing children beyond their natural levels was like training animals to do circus tricks. Instead of contributing to their normal growth, it could lead to stunted long-term development. The model and growth parameters in Figure 9.14 are the same as those for optimal levels in Figure 9.13, except that Domain 2 was given a special one-time boost to its growth rate at the second level, analogous to special training to produce precocity. The boost caused Domain 2 to immediately grow to higher levels than the other domains, but during later growth, Domain 2 grew less than the others, ending up at a much lower level. Also, the five domains stopped showing equilibration and instead spread out across a wide range of equilibrium levels. In this way, a short-term boost in one grower disturbed the entire system, changing the growth patterns of all the growers it was connected with.

The Piaget effect is still an orderly pattern. Sometimes, the growers in this and related hierarchical models show much wilder disturbances, including crashes, explosions, and turbulent vacillations, analogous to the turbulence produced by the simple logistic growth formula with Grower 6 in Figure 9.12. The same basic hierarchical growth processes produce a full range of shapes of development from monotonic growth to stagelike, equilibrated growth to disturbed growth and turbulent variation. Some of the growth functions of these hierarchical growth patterns even seem to fit the properties of catastrophe and chaos (van Geert, 1994). These are truly nonlinear dynamic systems, and they provide a powerful tool for facilitating description and analysis of the many shapes of human development.

Testing Data for Nonlinear Dynamic Properties

With dynamic models that seem to fit growth data so well, it would be desirable to have statistical techniques for testing data against them. Unfortunately, no statistical techniques are currently available to test convincingly whether data fit nonlinear models. Various investigators are working to try to create such techniques (Fischer & Kennedy, 1997; van Geert, 1994; Willett, 1994).

One procedure that is useful is to compare the fits of different models to a set of data. When the fit between data and one of the models is close, no inferential statistics are required to confirm the usefulness of the model that fits closely. A researcher can simply present the model and the data and ask colleagues to behold the match. The findings of Ruhland and van Geert (1997) on acquisition of pronouns by Dutch toddlers, for example, show a remarkably close match between the empirical growth curve and the cubic version, in contrast to the squared version, of the logistic growth equation, as shown in Figure 9.15.

In the meantime, van der Maas and Molenaar (1992, 1995) have pioneered a technique based on catastrophe theory. Prototypic catastrophe models show periods of rapid discontinuity that have powerful properties beyond mere sudden increase or decrease; that is why they are called catastrophes. The authors have suggested that stage changes are marked by catastrophic discontinuities in performance, which can be represented by the type of catastrophe called a cusp. Figure 9.16 shows two successive cusp catastrophes representing two successive developmental levels. Optimal-level jumps occur when performance is on the upper part of the diagram, where the cusp occurs; more continuous functional-level changes occur on the lower part.

Van der Maas and Molenaar specify eight properties that mark such cusplike changes, which they call catastrophe flags. Researchers can examine their growth data to determine how many of these flags fit the data. The flags

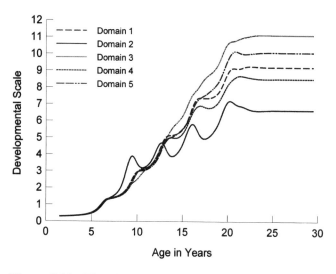

Figure 9.14 The Piaget effect: Disturbance of development caused by early speeding up of growth.

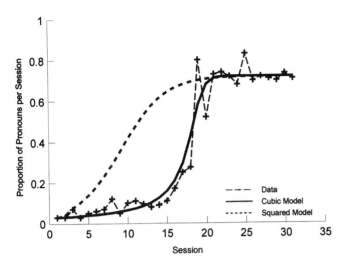

Figure 9.15   Fit between models and data for pronoun use by four Dutch children. Data are from Ruhland and van Geert (1997).

include sudden jumps or drops, bimodal distributions of scores, and anomalous variance. One of the most telling is hysteresis, in which movement through the cusp (period of catastrophe) changes, depending on whether it is approached from the right or the left in the diagram (based on variations in a control parameter). For example, the temperature at which water freezes when heat is removed differs a few degrees from the temperature at which ice melts when heat is added. If such hysteresis were to be

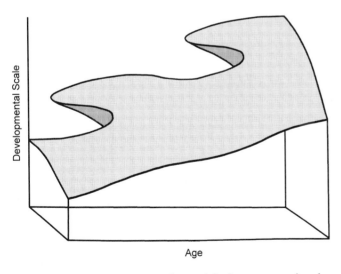

Figure 9.16   A cusp-catastrophe model of two successive developmental levels.

documented in psychological development, it would provide strong evidence that a developmental change was indeed a catastrophe.

These are just a few of the nonlinear dynamic tools for tying down developmental processes and analyzing change. A wide array of such tools is available; many of them were devised in biology to deal with the ecology of species interactions and the dynamics of long-term evolution (Goodwin, 1994; Holland, 1992; Kauffman, 1993). A few scholars have even begun to apply nonlinear concepts to social phenomena, such as how people work together to construct their own development (Fogel, 1993; Vallacher & Nowak, 1994; van Geert, 1994). A particularly promising area for advancing methods and theories of development is the study of transition mechanisms in microdevelopment of both individuals and social ensembles.

BUILDING STRUCTURES: TRANSITION MECHANISMS AND MICRODEVELOPMENT

Because the study of development is the study of change, any adequate account of the development of psychological structures must provide credible explanations of the transition mechanisms by which structures at a given level develop into more complex and inclusive structures through the activities of a constructive agent or ensemble. The vagueness of traditional structuralist developmental theories on transition mechanisms has been a major factor in eroding confidence in structural interpretations and delaying advances in understanding how development is constructed. Recent advances in methods for task analysis in general and microdevelopmental analysis in particular have placed the field in a position to move beyond these obstacles. The outlines of a constructivist model of task- and context-specific developmental transitions are emerging.

The study of transition mechanisms is closely associated with the concept of microdevelopment or microgenesis. Microdevelopment is typically defined as the study of developmental change over short time periods, such as single problem-solving trials, or repeated trials spanning minutes or hours. By studying processes of change over short periods, researchers can analyze changes in activities in real time, producing fine-grained data to follow the course of transitions as they occur (Fischer & Granott, 1995; Granott, 1993a; Kuhn & Phelps, 1982; Siegler & Crowley,

1991). This kind of description is not possible with the widely spaced observations of traditional cross-sectional and longitudinal developmental studies.

However, simply increasing the density of observations is little help without a theoretical framework to guide analysis of the observations, especially a way of relating short-term and long-term change. Past approaches have been less than successful because they have been reductionist—either reducing one type of change to the other or reducing both types to separate and unrelated processes. They have been caught in the problematic unidimensional assumptions about developmental methods and concepts that we outlined earlier. An alternative approach, based on the different assumptions of dynamic structural analysis, provides a solution that specifies the contributions of both micro- and macrodevelopment to transitions in terms of the constructive web.

Rethinking Relations between Micro- and Macrodevelopment

There have been three traditional approaches to relations between short- and long-term change: (a) learning theory, (b) gestalt psychology, and (c) Piagetian theory. All three have muddied analysis of the relations between micro- and macrodevelopment, by either conflating them or treating them as completely separate. What is needed instead is an approach that treats short- and long-term change as two dimensions of the developmental process, each playing a distinct but intrinsically related role.

The simplest traditional approach was classic learning theory, which assumed that all developmental change was reducible to a gradual accretion of learned behaviors (Hull, 1952; Kendler & Kendler, 1962; Skinner, 1969). By reducing development to learned behavior, learning theory excluded *a priori* any distinctive account of long-term developmental processes and how learning processes might contribute to them.

For another form of conflation, associated with the gestalt school, short-term change or microdevelopment (microgenesis) was thought of as simply a speeded-up version of long-term change (ontogenesis) (Köhler, 1970; Werner, 1948). Developmental processes, whether microgenetic or ontogenetic, were seen as following the same linear sequence of unfolding stages from global to differentiated. Although Heinz Werner (1948) was one of the first

to call for multilevel description of developmental processes, he did not specify explicit relations between microgenesis and ontogenesis. Microgenetic research was viewed mainly as a way of manipulating long-term developmental processes so that they could be accelerated and thus observed over short time periods in the laboratory. Developmental processes simply unfolded, either slowly or quickly, with the developing person standing by to witness the results. In one classic example, gestalt researchers fitted individuals with lenses that inverted the perceptual field (Kohler, 1962). The processes of habituation and subsequent dishabituation to these perceptual distortions were treated as a laboratory stand-in for the much longer process of perceptual development from birth to adulthood.

In the third traditional approach, embodied in Piaget's work, short- and long-term changes were viewed as mostly separate and unrelated (Inhelder, Sinclair, & Bovet, 1974; Piaget, 1947/1950). In this view, long-term change was equated with development, and short-term change was equated with learning. The role of long-term developmental processes was to create psychological structures, such as Piaget's logical categories of time, space, motion, and speed. The role of short-term learning processes was to fill those structures with information. Once again, no mechanism was specified for short-term interactions (microdevelopment) to influence long-term change (macrodevelopment) (Bidell & Fischer, 1992b). An outcome of this strong separation was that, ultimately, macrodevelopment was reduced to maturation and microdevelopment to associative learning. If psychological structures unfold independently of experience, and adaptive interactions with the environment lead only to learning, how can the development of structures be constructive or self-regulatory? How can interactions with the environment powerfully influence the course of development, as we now know that they do?

An alternative approach that preserves both constructive and contextual dimensions of development is to treat short- and long-term change as distinct but interrelated dimensions of the developmental process (Bidell & Fischer, 1994, 1996). In this view, microdevelopment is the short-term process by which new skills are first constructed for participation locally in specific contexts; in Vygotsky's (1978) terms, these are called *proximal processes*. Macrodevelopment describes the larger-scale process in which many local constructive activities in different contexts and domains are gradually consolidated, generalized, and related through continual microlevel constructive processes on many fronts. For this approach to be successful, one must use methods and concepts that tie down the meanings of micro- and macrodevelopment and specify the ways they are related.

This approach to micro- and macrodevelopment can be illustrated with the image of the developmental web from Figure 9.7. The microdevelopmental process by which specific skills are constructed for specific contexts is represented by the strands of the web shown under construction (dashed and dotted lines). Note that at any given time a number of strands are under construction, and these strands follow different developmental pathways as people construct skills for participation in different contexts and with different coparticipants. The strands under construction begin at different developmental levels, and each strand spans several levels in the developmental range for that skill, as shown in Table 9.1.

Stepping back a bit, one can scan across the developmental web shown in Figure 9.17 and see a broader picture representing macrodevelopment. Whereas each strand represents a specific microdevelopmental process, the collection of processes involved in constructing the web as a

whole is macrodevelopment. Macrodevelopment is not simply an atomistic heap of many microlevel processes; it is the overall developmental process in which all the microlevel processes participate. In this sense, micro- and macrolevel processes are intrinsically related and interdependent in a way that is analogous to the Newtonian and quantum worlds of physics or the molecular and subatomic worlds of chemistry (Allport, 1961; Hanson, 1961). Neither can exist without the other, but neither can be reduced to the other. At the macrodevelopmental level of analysis, we find phenomena that do not appear at the microlevel, and vice versa.

An example of a macrodevelopmental phenomenon is developmental clustering, the stagelike consistency that can be observed across skills in different domains. This is the phenomenon that allows people experienced with children to predict accurately, before they have ever met a child, most of the kinds of skills the child will be able to use. As indicated by the boxes in Figure 9.17, discontinuities in certain clusters of skills occur in a common time interval marking the formation of a new developmental level. This relative consistency in emergence is not due to any mysterious underlying stage structure. On the contrary, each strand is an individual skill that has its own structure and is constructed for action in a specific context. The consistency arises from the fact that skills are not created *ex nihilo* but are built up through the integration of earlier component skills in a gradual process with constraints. The constraints include sociocultural limitations on the child's activity contexts (Whiting & Edwards, 1988), biological changes to establish sufficient neurological support for developing skills (Fischer & Rose, 1994; Thatcher, 1994), and the limits that available time places on the speed and scope of skill construction.

Developmental clustering is a macrodevelopmental phenomenon that does not appear at the microdevelopmental level of skill construction. Yet it arises from the overall process of microdevelopment in many contexts and domains, which lead gradually to clusters of discontinuities for each in a series of developmental levels. In turn, microdevelopmental processes at any given time are limited by macrodevelopmental constraints because new constructions must be based on the clusters of skills built up over time and must respect the limits of a person's processing systems, such as their optimal levels. To fully understand developmental transitions, we must study not only the

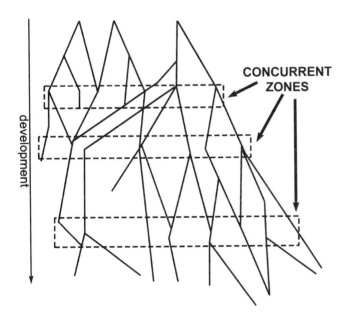

Figure 9.17 Developmental web with concurrent discontinuities across strands. The boxes show three zones of concurrent discontinuities; additional zones occur earlier and later in the web.

micro- and macrodevelopmental processes involved but also the relations between them.

Task Analysis and Construction Processes in Microdevelopment of Activities

A major obstacle to studying the relations between micro- and macrodevelopment has been an absence of research methodologies for including both levels of analysis in the same study. Conceptual frameworks and research methodologies for the study of short- and long-term change have grown up quite independently. On the one hand, macrodevelopment has been studied mainly in terms of the broad structural models of Piaget (1936/1952, 1983), Werner (1948), and the input-output experimental/psychometric approach (Horn, 1982; Sternberg, 1985). Typically, research uses standard cross-sectional or longitudinal methods to describe the successive forms of mental structure or psychometrically scaled performance at widely spaced points over the life span. Such approaches make no reference to the everyday short-term functional adaptations that lead to such changes.

On the other hand, microdevelopment has been studied in functional terms, as a process of relatively immediate adaptation to specific environments. Whether such adaptations are conceived as individual learning (Bandura, 1977; Skinner, 1969) or as internalization of between-person control (Rogoff, 1993; Valsiner, 1987; Vygotsky, 1962, 1978; Wertsch & Stone, 1978), functional approaches have made little reference to long-term structural reorganization.

Contemporary task-analytic methods make it possible to overcome this methodological divide and study the ways that short-term adaptations relate to both short- and long-term reorganization (Case, 1991b; Goldin-Meadow, Nusbaum, et al., 1993; Granott, 1993a; Kuhn et al., 1995; Miller & Aloise-Young, in press; Siegler & Crowley, 1991). Task-analytic theories describe psychological organization in terms of executive control structures for specific tasks, contexts, and coparticipants. By analyzing the structural demands of tasks that have previously been studied in functional terms, it is possible to study the relations between functional adaptation and hierarchical reorganization in the same task. Changes in children's functional performance on a task, such as shifts in problem-solving efficiency, procedures, strategies, and errors, can be directly related to changes in the hierarchical organization of control structures governing such performance.

This research has recently led to advances in our understanding of (a) the mechanism of co-occurrence or shift of focus in transitional states, (b) the microdevelopmental coordination processes producing hierarchical integration, (c) the gradual construction of new psychological structures through restructuring, repetition, and generalization—a process that is especially evident in problem solving by dyads working together, and (d) the process of bridging by which people bootstrap themselves to higher-level skills.

Shift of Focus in Transitional States

One important area of advance is the study of transitional states in development. Researchers who have replaced abstract stage theory formulations with task-specific methods have shown one of the mechanisms by which hierarchical integration occurs: co-occurrence, which is called shift of focus in the terms of dynamic skills theory (Fischer, 1980). Research across dozens of different tasks has used microanalytic methods to converge on a common phenomenon: Just as individuals are beginning to develop a new type of skill, they shift between two different representations or two different strategies, each of which is only partly adequate to the task (Bidell & Fischer, 1994; Goldin-Meadow, Alibali, & Church, 1993; Goldin-Meadow, Nusbaum, et al., 1993). For example, just before solving the task for conservation of liquid in containers of different shapes, children often represent the height of the liquid verbally while simultaneously representing the width in gesture (Perry, Church, & Goldin-Meadow, 1988). A short period later, they have integrated the two dimensions to form a skill for conservation. Goldin-Meadow, Alibali, et al. (1993) have shown that such shifting or dual representations are dependable indicators that an individual is in a transitional state in the development of skills such as conservation and mathematical equivalence. This transition process occurs in emotional development as well, where opposites such as nice and mean routinely co-occur in children's activities when they are working on integrating the opposites (Fischer & Ayoub, 1994).

Many transitions involve such construction of new skills from co-occurring components, although some transitions also involve a simple change in the mixture of skills or strategies applied to a task (Siegler & Jenkins, 1989). The diverse studies of co-occurrence provide a new before-and-after picture of transitions: A person uses less adequate skills for a given task concurrently or in shifts of focus, and that facilitates the integration of the skills to form a new hierarchically inclusive skill that is more adequate to the task.

Mechanisms of Hierarchical Integration

The next question is how the less adequate skills are coordinated to form a new skill. In one recent approach, Bidell (1990; Bidell & Fischer, 1994) has shown how the task-analytic tools of dynamic skills theory can be combined with microdevelopmental methodology to address this question. Skill theory provides a framework for generating task-specific hypotheses about integration processes that can be assessed through microdevelopmental observations of children's activities on a task, as well as through macro-developmental observations. Component and outcome skills are defined in terms of the sources of variation that must be cognitively controlled in a given task, producing specifics that define each skill. The formulas are similar to $[YOU_{NICE} \text{———} ME_{NICE}]$ (Formula 1) and to the activity structures in Figure 9.3 for the stories about nice and mean interactions.

Bidell studied children's construction of new planning skills for the classic Tower of Hanoi task (three-disk version). Children were asked to move a stack of three graduated perforated disks from one wooden post (Start) to a second post (Goal), using a third post (Rest) as a temporary storage place, as shown in Figure 9.18. They had to follow certain rules in moving the disks: They could move only one disk at a time, and they could not place larger disks on top of smaller ones. The key to solving this task lies in planning how to transfer the large disk to the Goal so that the smaller disks can be stacked on it. Planning this transfer demands that the child construct a skill for simultaneously representing (holding in working memory) the specific relations among the four moves leading to this transfer, as illustrated in Figure 9.18. Some other stacking objects embody the rules in the objects (Zhang & Norman, 1994), such as nested cans, with which a large can will not fit inside a small can. For Bidell's task, however, children had to explicitly control the rules in their representations.

To understand what is involved in this construction, the component skills must be analyzed, beginning with the

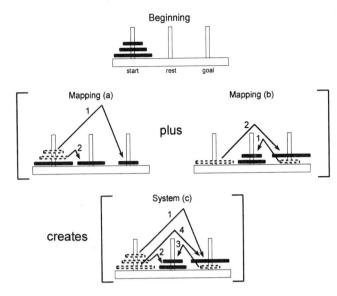

Figure 9.18 Moves that must be integrated to solve the Tower of Hanoi problem. The Beginning shows the layout of the Tower of Hanoi at the start of the problem-solving effort. Parts (a) and (b) show movement patterns fitting representational mappings, and part (c) shows a movement pattern integrating the two mappings to form a representational system. Dotted disks indicate initial positions before moves, and solid disks indicate final positions after moves. Arrows mark moves, with the order of moves designated by numerals.

simplest—the skill for representing or planning the transfer of a single disk from one post to another,

$$\left[\begin{matrix} \textbf{MOVE A} \\ {\scriptstyle S \rightarrow G} \end{matrix} \right] \qquad \text{(Formula 2)}$$

This single-representation skill indicates a plan to move disk A from the Start post (S) to the Goal post (G).

For children to know the exact order in which to execute each of the four required moves of the disks, they must hold in mind not only single moves but specific relations between moves. The next level in building such relations involves a representational mapping, in which two single representations are coordinated so that the individual can relate how one move depends on another. Figure 9.18(a) and 9.18(b) depicts activities controlled by representational mappings, including the mapping for planning to move disk A (the smallest) from S to G in order to move disk B (medium size) from S to the Rest post (R).

$$\left[\underset{S \to G}{\textbf{MOVE A}} \; - \; \underset{S \to R}{\textbf{MOVE B}} \right]$$ (Formula 3)

This mapping involves a child's understanding that the small disk must be transferred first because the transfer of the medium disk depends on it. In another mapping, the child must understand that the medium disk must be moved in order to move the large disk.

To fully understand the necessary sequence of the four moves shown in Figure 9.18(c), children must build a more inclusive skill that integrates mappings to form a representational system capturing the interdependence of four moves. For instance, a child who understands that the small disk must be removed to make way for the next disk does not yet understand that the small disk must be moved to a specific location—the Goal post—on the first move. This only becomes apparent when the child holds in mind this mapping and mentally coordinates it with the mapping for removing the medium disk to the Rest post to free the large disk to move to the Goal:

$$\left[\begin{array}{cc} A_{S \to G} & B_{S \to R} \\ \textbf{MOVE} \leftrightarrow \textbf{MOVE} \\ A_{G \to R} & C_{S \to G} \end{array} \right]$$ (Formula 4)

When these relations are mentally integrated, the child can anticipate that the small disk *must* be transferred to the Goal so that it can subsequently be transferred to the Rest post when the medium disk has arrived there, clearing the Goal post for the transfer of the large disk. The remaining moves to complete the task require simpler mappings and single representations, which are easy for children who have built the complex system in Formula 4. From a skill theory perspective, this complex integration of two mapping skills to form a system is the primary cognitive challenge to children attempting this version of the Tower of Hanoi. They can construct this skill only when their optimal level has reached representational systems.

To learn about how children achieve this integration, Bidell studied 25 children, ages 6 to 12 years, as they solved the Tower of Hanoi (Bidell, 1990; Bidell & Fischer, 1994). After familiarization with a two-disk version of the task, the children were presented with the three-disk task and were videotaped as they solved it. Their behavior was coded on a move-by-move basis as they worked their way to the solution. In Figure 9.19 the durations and latencies for the moves of one child are plotted as they occurred in

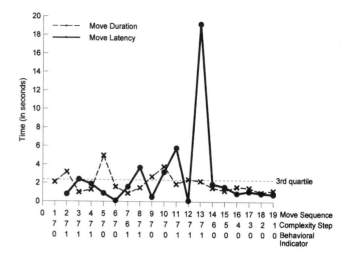

Figure 9.19 One child's moves in solving the Tower of Hanoi. Pauses in problem solving were defined as durations or latencies larger than the 3rd quartile for the whole sample of children, which is marked by the dotted line above the x-axis. The line just below the x-axis gives the sequential number of the move. The second line below the x-axis shows the step of structural complexity required for success at each move attempt. The third line shows the presence or absence of behavioral indicators of presumed reflectivity such as finger tapping, verbalizations such as "hmm . . . ," and pointing from one disk to another.

sequence during the session. The most efficient solution to the task requires seven moves, and the complexity of the task can be coded in terms of these moves, as shown below the move sequence at the bottom of Figure 9.19. Where the problem facing the child demanded a representational system, a 7 is indicated. Complexities of 3 to 6 required types of representational mappings; complexities of 1 to 2 required types of single representations. An efficient move reduced the task complexity by one; an inefficient move maintained or increased the task complexity (for details, see Bidell & Fischer, 1994).

With the exception of a few older children who immediately applied the correct solution, the data showed a pattern of exploration followed by a sudden transition, as exemplified in Figure 9.19. During the first part of her problem-solving session, this girl paused frequently, showed frequent behaviors indicating reflection, and made only inefficient moves (failing to advance toward the goal). Then, suddenly, she switched to completely efficient problem solving, with no behavioral indicators or pauses, systematically reducing the complexity of the task with each move until she had solved it. This kind of sudden switch was common among the children.

Analysis of children's errors during the initial, inefficient phase of problem solving revealed plans based on mapping skills. For instance, a typical error was to lift the small disk off the Goal post and hold it in hand while transferring the large disk to the Goal. This violates the prohibition against moving two disks at once, but it is consistent with a mapping that relates lifting the small disk to transferring the large disk.

These converging sources of evidence provide us with a picture of the relation between functional adaptation and hierarchical integration on this task. Most children seemed to be guided initially by mapping-level plans, leading to inefficient problem solving and signs of reflectivity as they searched for alternative move sequences. In the search for alternative plans, children considered different mapping skills, but no mappings could produce a solution. At a certain point, children were able to simultaneously bring together two of the appropriate mappings and coordinate them into a hierarchically more inclusive system. That was when they often showed a long pause and substantial reflection just before moving to rapid solution. In this way, the activity of problem solving led to a newly constructed skill, which involved an advance in children's developmental level for this task.

Generalization and Consolidation in Social Interaction

Although these kinds of microdevelopment data move beyond static snapshots of developmental processes, they still provide only very short movie clips, capturing a key but brief moment in the transition process. An accurate picture of transitions requires placing such findings in a broader framework of developmental analysis (Bidell & Fischer, 1994; Siegler & Crowley, 1991). Taken alone, the Tower of Hanoi findings may seem to suggest an invariant transition process in which children build a new skill and then have that skill in place. Yet increasing evidence suggests that often transitions are lengthy and involve wide variations in skill until a new skill is consolidated (Fischer & Granott, 1995; Siegler & Jenkins, 1989). Indeed, when given the three-disk Tower of Hanoi a second time in Bidell's study, some of the children who had just solved it were unable to solve it again immediately. They had to go through the microdevelopmental process of problem solving once more.

Their new skill was not yet consolidated at a functional level.

Granott (1993a) used innovative microdevelopmental methodology to analyze the progress of skill construction, generalization, and consolidation. Adult dyads were given a task of determining how a small Lego™ robot functioned. The robot, which was the size of a toy truck and was called a wuggle, was programmed to respond to changes in light, sound, or touch by changing its movement. The dyads were videotaped as they worked together, manipulating, experimenting, and discussing the robot's behavior. The use of dyads helped illuminate the processes of problem-solving being used, because the participants talked to each other about the task and thus exposed their problem-solving activities to observation. In prior microdevelopmental research, it had been difficult to follow the steps in problem solving because people working alone typically do not show overtly how they are moving toward a solution, and afterwards, they typically do not give fully accurate reports of what they have done. Most human learning and problem solving are done socially, not by isolated individuals (Granott, 1993b). The study of individuals learning alone seems to come from the assumptions of an individualistic psychology, which misrepresents people's typical ways of learning.

Granott divided each dyad's interactions into natural episodes, called "interchanges," on which coders readily agreed. Each interchange was scored for the level of skill complexity revealed in the joint behavior of the dyad. For example, when the dyad evidenced understanding of a simple relation between two events—such as that when they shined a light on the robot, it changed its movement—a mapping of actions would be scored.

The dyad Ann and Donald began their initial encounter with a wuggle with substantial confusion about how it operated, and their level of understanding progressed systematically upward during 64 interchanges spanning 10 minutes, as graphed in the bottom, solid line in Figure 9.20. Initially, they began with a low-level understanding, where they confused the effects of their own actions with those of the robot. Gradually, they built up a more complex understanding, slowly discovering how the wuggle moved and how light changed its movement.

In this way, Ann and Donald appeared to have achieved an understanding of the wuggle, but what happened next showed the severe limits of their understanding. They

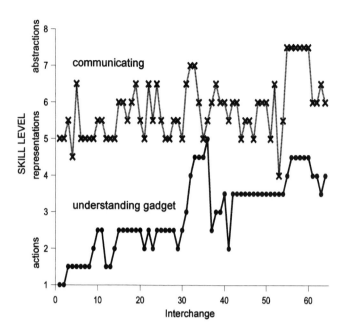

Figure 9.20   Two different threads in Ann and Donald's first problem-solving sequence with a wuggle (Fischer & Granott, 1995).

removed one of the robot's wires from its socket and accidentally placed it into a different socket. With this modified robot, their level of understanding plummeted immediately, and they had to start over, rebuilding their understanding again. However, achieving an understanding a second time still did not produce a stable level of understanding. Two more times, when the situation changed, Ann and Donald lost their understanding—when they tried to explain their knowledge of the robot to another person, and when they changed a wire once more and thereby changed the robot's operation again.

Thus, each time they changed the robot's functioning (moving a wire) or their approach (analyzing its operation versus describing it to someone else), they moved backward to a lower-level skill and reconstructed their understanding again. In each instance, they moved systematically from a low level of egocentric confusion to a more sophisticated understanding of the robot. Such backward movement or regression seems to be a common beginning to construction of a new higher-level skill (Brown & Reeve, 1987; Duncker, 1945; Granott, 1993a; Karmiloff-Smith & Inhelder, 1974; Kuhn & Phelps, 1982; Miller & Aloise-Young, in press).

These regressions and progressions demonstrate the dynamic variations that occur as skills are gradually generalized and consolidated. When people have solved a problem once, they do not then "possess" a skill for understanding it. The skill must be reworked and generalized a number of times with variations before the person can use it routinely without having to rework it again.

Detecting such microdevelopmental progressions is no easy matter. It requires sophisticated task analysis that differentiates several aspects of people's activities, often involving different levels of functioning for the same people. If the different aspects are not differentiated, it becomes impossible to observe the microdevelopment of understanding. Traditional methodologies have assumed that people function at only one level at a time, and they have therefore interfered with detection of microdevelopmental patterns of variation.

The dyads working with the wuggles were scored not only for the level of their conception of the robot's functioning, but also for their level of communication about the wuggle. These two scorings involved exactly the same activities, and exactly the same skill-theoretical definitions of complexity were used. However, different aspects of the activities were analyzed—what Fischer and Granott (1995) call different "threads" within the strand for understanding wuggles in a dyad's developmental web. In contrast to the microdevelopmental progression in understanding the wuggle, communication began at a relatively high skill level and varied, up and down, around that level with little or no evident progression in complexity, as shown in the dotted line in Figure 9.20.

Detecting microdevelopment requires (a) finding the threads that are growing and (b) not confusing them with the threads that are merely varying without growing. Only methods that recognize the multiple levels of functioning in an activity can distinguish these different threads and thus detect microdevelopment. With such methods, it becomes possible to see how people build skills from low levels and how they rebuild them repeatedly in order to generalize and consolidate them.

Bridging: A Process of Building New Knowledge

One of the mysteries of learning has been that people somehow build knowledge that is **new** for them. The origins of new knowledge have puzzled philosophers for centuries (Hume, 1955; Kant, 1958; Plato, 1941) and continue to puzzle 20th-century scholars (Chomsky, 1959; Fodor, 1975). How can we build new knowledge out of nothing? When it appears that people have no knowledge of, say, a wuggle's functioning, how can they build new knowledge of the wuggle?

The reason for this dilemma lies (again) in the limitations of the paradigm of structure-as-form. People do not build new knowledge from nothing! It only seems that way because scholars assume that people function at only one level of knowledge. In fact, people function at multiple levels, and so they can use one level of functioning to direct their activities at another level. They can build up new knowledge by using old knowledge from other contexts to bootstrap themselves.

One important way that people do such bootstrapping to build knowledge is the process of bridging, which has only recently been uncovered and articulated (Granott, Fischer, & Parziale, 1997; but see Case, 1991a). In bridging, people direct the construction of their own knowledge by functioning at two levels simultaneously: They establish a target level of skill or understanding, which lies unconstructed beyond their current level of functioning, and they use it as a shell for constructing understanding. In this process of self-scaffolding, the target shells that people build are partial and fuzzy, but they provide a framework that directs the search for new knowledge. People then use their activities to gradually fill in components of the shell until they have moved themselves to a higher level of understanding for the new task in context.

An example from another dyad working with a wuggle illustrates how bridging works. Kevin and Marvin's wuggle responded to sound, although they did not yet know that. When they began their explorations of the robot, they played with it for a few minutes, exploring what happened with the robot. After some exploration, they showed their first case of bridging—a vague reference to undefined cause and effect that provided an outline around which to build a skill. Marvin placed his hand around the robot in different positions, and Kevin said: *"Looks like we got a re-action there."*

The term "reaction" suggested cause and effect, action and re-action, but Kevin gave no specifics, because he did not yet know anything about the specifics. It was not clear what in Marvin's action (or in something else) was the cause nor how the robot's movement changed in reaction. The two men did not know even that the robot responded to sound, and they did not yet detect relevant patterns in the robot's movements. Still, the term "reaction" did plainly imply a causal connection, except that the content of the connection was unknown. Through the idea of reaction, Kevin and Marvin were setting up a bridging shell that effectively posited two unknown variables, **X** and **Y,** related to each other:

$$\left[\overset{\text{reaction}}{\underset{\text{SHELL}}{(\mathbf{X}) \text{——} (\mathbf{Y})}} \right] \qquad \text{(Formula 5)}$$

Parentheses around the letters in the formula indicate that the components were unknown for Marvin and Kevin. This shell linked action **X** with response **Y** as a reaction to **X.** The shell was still devoid of content, but it marked an existing unknown causal relation. Bridging follows the basic structures of skill development except that some components of the shell start out unknown or partially known. The number and nature of unknown components differ with developmental level.

Through construction of a shell, bridging operates in a manner analogous to the pillars on an overhead highway that is under construction. The pillars have been put in place, but they do not yet carry the roadway that will eventually be built on top of them. Just as the horizontal beams and the concrete between the pillars are still missing, the content—the specific cause and effect—in Kevin's brief statement is missing. Like the empty pillars, the bridging shell traces the target causal mapping and prepares a frame for building it. Although the bridging shell is currently hollow or empty, Kevin and Marvin will organize new experiences in terms of the shell and thus introduce meaning to it.

After Kevin and Marvin introduced the "reaction" shell, they continued to play with the wuggle and observe how it reacted. A few minutes later, they built a causal relation, saying: *"When it comes over here and as soon as it gets underneath part of the shadow there, it starts changing its behavior."*

This statement specified an elementary causal connection between the robot's coming under the shadow and its change in behavior. It thus filled in the first instances of **X** and **Y** in the skill shell:

$$\left[\overset{\text{reaction}}{\begin{array}{cc} \text{UNDER} & \text{CHANGES} \\ \text{SHADOW} & \text{BEHAVIOR} \end{array}} \right] \qquad \text{(Formula 6)}$$

The bridging shell defined by the term "reaction" guided Kevin and Marvin to formulate a first causal relation or hypothesis indicating that a shadow produces a change in the wuggle's behavior. This was only the beginning of their exploration of the reaction shell. After this first bridging, Kevin and Marvin elaborated this shell and used additional shells to grapple their way up to what eventually became a sophisticated understanding of the wuggle. This first use of a shell suffices, however, to illustrate how people set up shells at higher levels than their understanding and use those shells as bridges to build new knowledge.

Bridging can be viewed as a self-scaffolding mechanism that is used by individuals or collaborating dyads to bootstrap themselves to new knowledge. A person or dyad creates a target-level shell as a goal of learning or development. The skills of the target shell have not been constructed yet, but the shell outlines them and thus creates a scaffold within which the skills can develop. The shell or scaffold functions like a grappling hook for mountain climbers, pulling activities up toward the target level. Indeed, bridging has much in common with scaffolding and guided participation in parent-child and teacher-student learning situations, where adult experts try to use the known to create bridges to understanding the new (Brown & Campione, 1990; Newman, Griffin, & Cole, 1989; Rogoff, 1990; Vygotsky, 1978).

Work on developmental transitions and microdevelopment is clearly in its infancy. However, with the advent of task-analytic methodologies, the field is moving past the era in which transitions represented the black box of developmental theory. These powerful new methodologies provide us with tools for prying open the black box and revealing the mechanisms that drive development. Using such methods, researchers can begin to demystify transition processes and replace abstract speculation about factors such as stage equilibration or genetic determination of concepts with concrete knowledge about the mechanisms by which new skills are actually constructed.

The outlines of some of the processes are becoming evident. When people construct skills at new levels of complexity for a given task or situation, these more complex skills are not either present or absent, but they are initially tenuous and only gradually become relatively stable. Working socially as well as individually in transitions, people juxtapose or shift between relevant component skills, and they move gradually through processes of coordinating these components to form higher-level skills. To facilitate their own skill construction, they build shells at higher levels to bridge or bootstrap themselves to new knowledge. Over time, they build and rebuild each skill again and again with each small change in task and context until they consolidate their performance to form a functional skill of some generality. Once new skills are consolidated, people can use them as bases for further constructive activity, including generalizing to new situations and building additional coordinations. Even when skills are consolidated, of course, they are not uniformly available at will. They remain subject to the many dynamically interacting factors that make up human activity.

Microdevelopmental analysis of learning and problem solving makes especially evident the great variability in the structures of human activity from moment to moment. Another traditional domain in which variability is prominent is emotional development. Traditionally, emotion has been seen as separated from cognition (another instance of reductionist distortion). Emotion and cognition are not in fact separate; they are two sides of the same coin. Emotions are a full part of both macro- and microdevelopment. Indeed, microdevelopment and emotion are two of the primary domains in which researchers are having success at moving beyond the structure-as-form paradigm to create the new dynamic structuralism.

EMOTIONS AND THE DYNAMIC ORGANIZATION OF ACTIVITY AND DEVELOPMENT

Emotions provide an especially appropriate illustration of how dynamic structural analysis illuminates human activity and its development. In the past two decades, emotions have reclaimed center stage in the study of human action and thought, after decades of neglect in the mid-20th century, during the eras of behaviorism and cognitivism (Fischer & Tangney, 1995; Frijda, 1986; Lazarus, 1991; Scherer, 1984; Shaver et al., 1987). Scholars have constructed a new framework for understanding emotion that fits in the center of the new dynamic structuralism, combining traditional concerns about both structure and function in a single analytic system. The general framework is typically referred to as the functional approach because of its emphasis on the adaptive (functional) role of emotions in human activity, but this functional focus is combined with structural analysis. A more appropriate label for this approach would therefore be the functional-structural or functional-organizational approach to emotions (Sroufe, 1984). Emotions are analyzed as central influences on human activity, and understanding their influence requires examination of the functioning of interrelated types of structures. We illustrate the use of several kinds of structures to analyze emotional functioning, including information flow, script, categorical hierarchy, dimensional split, developmental level, developmental web, and dynamic growth curve. No single kind of structural analysis by itself can capture all the important aspects of the organization and functioning of emotions.

Emotion and Cognition Together: Emotion Process

Contrary to common cultural assumptions, emotion and cognition operate together, not in contradiction to each other. Indeed, the official journal of the International Society for Research on Emotion is entitled *Cognition and Emotion* to reflect this view. Cognition generally refers to the processing and appraising of information, and emotion refers to the biasing or constraining effects of certain action tendencies that arise from appraisals of what is beneficial or threatening to a person (Frijda, 1986; Lazarus, 1991). Thus, cognition and emotion are two sides of the same coin as characteristics of control systems for human activity. Emotion is together with cognition at the center of mind.

Analysis of emotions highlights the role of the body and social world. Minds are not merely brains that happen to be in bodies. People's minds are parts of their bodies, and their mind-bodies act, think, and feel in a world of objects and other people. This ecological assumption is fundamental to the dynamic structural framework; it applies to analysis of all human activity. Emotions are one of the most important organizing influences on people's contextualized mind-bodies. Emotions are biological processes that shape action and thought. Contrary to common parlance and much classic research, emotions are not merely feelings or inner experiences of individuals but integral parts of human activity, shaping action and thought and founded in social interactions.

In the history of psychology, a distinction has often been made between emotion and affect, with emotion referring to biologically driven reactions and affect emphasizing individual experience and meaning (Brown, 1994). By these definitions, modern functional/structural analyses should be labeled "affectivity" rather than "emotion," but recent researchers' emphasis on biological factors has led to general preference for the term "emotion." In this modern meaning, emotion is used in a broad sense to include the classical meaning of affect. We will use emotion and affect interchangeably to refer to the broad ways in which activities are organized by action tendencies arising from people's appraisals.

Adaptation and appraisal are two fundamental concepts in the functional-structural approach to emotions. They are captured in the basic definition of the processes of emotion: People act in contexts where their activities are embedded in events *(in medias res)*. Emotions arise from appraisals of the events in terms of each person's many specific concerns (goals, needs). An emotion is an action tendency (constraint, bias) that arises from an appraisal and molds or structures a person's activities to shift the state of affairs toward his or her goals and needs. The central process in emotion is the action tendency, the way that an emotion organizes activity. Actions, thoughts, experience, physiological reactions, and expressions of body and voice are all organized by the action tendency of an emotion.

When people feel ashamed, for example, they want to be evaluated positively in some context, but instead someone judges them negatively for something they did or said, or for some characteristic of theirs, especially something that indicates a serious flaw (Barrett, 1995; Tangney, 1995; Wallbott & Scherer, 1995). They typically lower their eyes, conceal their face, blush, and stay quiet. They try to escape or hide, and they may try to blame others for the event or characteristic. Subjectively, people feel uncovered, small, or heavy, and they focus on their shameful flaw. Emotion refers to this entire process, including appraisal, social context, physical reactions, activities, and subjective experiences, but especially the action tendency that organizes the shame reaction.

The processes of emotion are diagrammed in Figure 9.21, which presents a schema for the information processes that many emotion theorists propose (Fischer, Shaver, & Carnochan, 1990; Frijda, 1986; Lazarus, 1991; Scherer, 1984; Shaver et al., 1987). For the situation in which people are acting, they detect a "notable change," involving some difference in the situation or some violation of expectations. For a case of shame, people may notice that they have acted

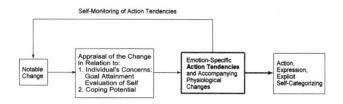

Self-Monitoring of Action Tendencies

Figure 9.21   The processes of emotion.

poorly or broken some rule, or they may observe someone expressing contempt or disgust toward them.

They then appraise the situation for its affective meaning—its significance in terms of their own specific concerns. Despite the cognitive, conscious, deliberate connotations of the word *appraisal,* this process typically occurs unconsciously and quickly. One result of the appraisal is a general positive or negative evaluation of whether the situation promotes or hinders goal attainment or wish fulfillment (promoting accomplishments or preventing troubles, according to Higgins, 1996; Higgins, Roney, Crowe, & Hymes, 1994). Situations that compromise people's concerns produce negative emotions, such as shame, fear, sadness, and anger; those that promote people's concerns produce positive emotions, such as pride, joy, and love or affection.

A person also appraises the situation for coping potential, how well he or she can deal with or change the emotion-producing aspects of the situation. When circumstances are desirable, a person may try to sustain or further them, or may simply enjoy them. When circumstances compromise a goal or need, a person assesses what can be done to change the situation—undoing, altering, or escaping from the negative circumstance. An appraisal that a negative situation can be undone or altered leads to emotions such as anger or guilt; an appraisal that it cannot be undone or changed leads to sadness or shame; and an appraisal that it can be escaped leads to fear or shame.

Each appraisal produces an action tendency, a pattern of activity based on evaluation and coping potential that is effectively a plan of action with regard to the situation. Each emotion has a prototypic, often preemptive, action tendency, which takes over control of activity. People tend to act in a certain way and to perceive and interpret events according to specific biases, and their bodies change physiologically to prepare for the planned actions.

Beyond early infancy, people also engage in self-control efforts, in which they try to alter their own perceptions and actions. To cope with shame, action tendencies include trying to hide or escape from observation, lowering the head or covering the face, feeling small and exposed, and becoming preoccupied with the negative action or characteristic. Self-control efforts include trying to: change the negative action or characteristic, deny or disguise it, or blame someone else for it.

The boxes in Figure 9.21 suggest an approximate order for these emotion processes, although they cannot be separated as fully as the boxes may imply. (The implications of separateness and sequentiality are a limitation of information-flow analysis. In fact, the processes usually occur together in parallel.) After an emotion has fully developed, the processes become seamless and automatic. Emotions appear to occur unconsciously, washing over us autonomously, despite the fact that the processes are complex and derive from a long period of development. The heart of the emotion is the action tendency, which is indicated with darkened lines in Figure 9.21. In addition to the sequence of processes from left to right, there is a feedback loop, in which older children and adults appraise their own affective reactions and move back through the entire set of emotion processes, reacting emotionally to their own emotion and exerting efforts at self-control. This loop thus can result in an emotion about an emotion, as when a person becomes angry about feeling ashamed or becomes afraid about feeling love or affection.

Organizing Effects of Emotions

The ways that emotions organize activities are powerful and pervasive. Among the structural descriptions used to characterize these organizing influences are: (a) scripts for prototypical organizations for particular emotions, (b) categorical hierarchies, and (c) dimensions for relating different emotions to one another.

These empirically derived descriptions of the organizing effects of emotions illustrate especially well how biology and experience work together in human development. Nativist approaches to development emphasize the constraints or biases that genetics places on human action and thought (Carey & Gelman, 1991; Spelke & Newport, Ch. 6, this Volume). At the extreme, nativist researchers look for the early or "first" emergence of some piece of knowledge or emotion, and then claim that this early development shows that the knowledge or emotion is innately present from an early age. Such an approach neglects the developing organization of human activity, reducing analysis to description of a few innate elements (Bidell & Fischer, 1996; Fischer & Bidell, 1991; Gottlieb, 1992). Emotions and emotional development show powerfully how biological constraints dynamically affect the developing organization of activities even while they are constructed through experience and culture. Emotions are a paradigm case of how the dynamics of development can produce simultaneously both "basic" categories and complex behavioral organizations (Camras, 1992).

Scripts

A useful way of describing the organization of emotions is with what Shaver and his colleagues (1987) call prototypical emotion scripts—descriptions of the prototype or best case of the sequence of antecedent events and reactions involved in a common emotion, such as anger, fear, love, or shame. These kinds of scripts have been used extensively in cognitive psychology to describe a standard sequence of events that many people share—the prototype or best instance of a certain category (Nelson, 1986; Schank & Abelson, 1977). A number of scholars have analyzed stories that people tell about emotions, characteristics that people attribute to emotions, and reactions that people

show in affect-inducing situations, and from these data they have inferred prototypic emotion scripts (de Rivera, 1981; Fehr & Russell, 1984; Lazarus, 1991; Scherer, Wallbott, & Summerfield, 1986; Tangney, 1995).

In Shaver's format of describing prototypic scripts, antecedents describe the notable change in the situation that evokes an emotion, responses describe the action tendencies that the emotion produces, and self-control procedures describe the ways that people attempt to change or limit the emotion. Tables 9.3 and 9.4 present prototypes for the positive affect of love and the negative affect of shame. The main organizing influences (action tendencies) for shame are to hide, escape, feel exposed, and become preoccupied with the cause of the shame. The main organizing influences for love are to feel happy and secure, to want to be close to the loved one, and to think about the loved one. Control procedures are typically important for negative emotions such as shame but minimal or nonexistent for positive emotions such as love, because in the prototypic situation, there is no desire to avoid or eliminate the positive emotion. Real-life occurrences of emotions are inevitably more complex than simple prototypes, and control procedures do occur with positive affects as well, depending on the variable circumstances of the specific occurrence.

TABLE 9.3   Prototypical Script for Adult Shame

Antecedents: Flaw, Dishonorable or Deplorable Action, Statement, or Characteristic of a Person

A person acts in a dishonorable way, says something deplorable, or evidences a characteristic that is disgraceful or flawed.

Someone witnesses this action, statement, or characteristic and judges it negatively.

Responses: Hiding, Escaping, Sense of Shrinking, Feeling Worthless

The person tries to hide or escape from observation or judgment, feels small, exposed, worthless, powerless.

The person lowers his or her head, covers the face or eyes, or turns away from other people. Sometimes he or she strikes out at the person observing the flaw.

He or she is preoccupied with the negative action, statement, or characteristic, as well as with negative evaluation of self more generally.

Self-Control Procedures: Undoing and Redefinition

The person may try to change the negative action, statement, or characteristic, or deny its existence, or disguise it.

From Fischer and Tangney (1995).

TABLE 9.4   Prototypical Script for Adult Love

Antecedents: Other Person's Attractiveness, Meeting of One's Needs, Good Communication, Sharing of Time and Special Experiences

The individual finds another person attractive, physically and/or psychologically.

The other person meets some of the individual's important needs.

The two communicate well, which fosters openness and trust; they have spent much time together and shared special experiences.

Responses: Feeling Happy and Secure, Wanting to be Close, Thinking about the Other Person

The individual feels warm and happy and tends to smile.

The individual thinks about the other person, wants to be with him or her, to spend time together (not be separated), to make eye contact, to hold, kiss, and be intimate (psychologically and/or sexually), and to express positive feelings and love to the other.

The individual feels more secure and self-confident, and accentuates the positive side of events.

Self-Control Procedures: Not a Salient Issue

(Suppression of love is possible in the interest of decorum or the avoidance of embarrassment, guilt, or rejection, but such self-control efforts are not prototypical.)

Based on Shaver, Schwartz, Kirson, and O'Connor (1987).

*Families of Emotions, Dimensions, and
Cultural Variations*

Human beings experience many different emotions, and scholars have sought to find an organization underlying all these variations, relying on facial expressions, personality types, words, and various other data to infer relations among emotion types or categories. In general, most categories function through prototypes, forming family resemblances related in terms of similarities to best instances (prototypes). The study of knowledge has been revolutionized in the late 20th century by the realization that most categories function in terms not of exclusive logical definitions but of overlapping prototypes, which organize categories into basic families (Lakoff, 1987; Rosch, 1978). Emotions fit this organization just like most other categories.

One of the striking findings about emotion categories has been the similarity of basic families for emotion words with those for emotional expressions in face, voice, and action (Ekman et al., 1987; Shaver et al., 1987). The convergence across these components of human activity is remarkable, as illustrated by the prototypic families for emotion words in English and Chinese shown in Figure 9.22. The six emotion families of anger, sadness, fear,

shame, love, and happiness also appear in many analyses of facial expressions for basic emotions, along with a few additional emotion categories such as disgust and surprise (which in the hierarchy in Figure 9.22 are not basic families but subordinate items of one of the families).

Besides the basic categories of emotion families, there are higher degrees of abstraction in which families and emotions are related through superordinate categories or dimensions, such as positive-negative evaluation. There are also lower degrees of abstraction, in which families divide into subordinate categories, and then the subordinate categories subdivide further into lower-level categories and eventually specific emotion words. For example, in Figure 9.22 clusters of Chinese emotion words form the subordinate categories of sorrowful love and unrequited love in the Sad Love family and the subordinate categories of guilt/regret and shame in the Shame family. A few of the largest subordinate categories for the Chinese words are shown.

At higher degrees of abstraction, emotion categories fall along several dimensions defining an emotion space. The most prominent dimension is usually evaluation of positive-negative or promotion-prevention; that is why it is included in the emotion process model in Figure 9.21, in which people's first appraisal is whether an event is good or bad for them. This superordinate dimension represents one of the three dimensions that have been found in many different types of research going back to the beginnings of experimental psychology in the 19th century, long before the framework for prototype analysis was devised (Kitayama & Markus, 1995; Lazarus, 1991; Osgood, Suci, & Tannenbaum, 1957; Schlosberg, 1954; Wundt, 1905/1907). The classic three dimensions have been replicated with similar findings across many different methods, data sets, and cultures, although there are some important variations in the exact nature of the dimensions. The general dimensions are (a) evaluation of positive-negative or promotion-prevention (Davidson, 1992; Higgins, 1996), which usually accounts for approximately half the variance and is shown in Figure 9.22, (b) activity or active-passive, and (c) engagement or self-other. Although dimensions (b) and (c) are not shown in Figure 9.22, they are nevertheless present in the hierarchy as additional superordinate categories; however, it is not possible to show all three dimensions in the diagram.

The basic emotion families and the dimensions of emotions are similar across cultures, probably because they

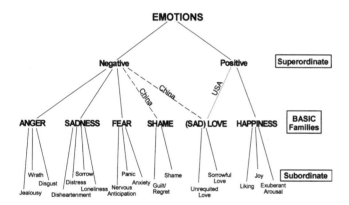

Figure 9.22 Hierarchy of emotion categories in Chinese and English. This hierarchy represents the organization of emotion families in Chinese based on the findings of Shaver and his colleagues (Agnoli, Kirson, Wu, & Shaver, 1989; Shaver et al., 1992). English language results for the United States are also represented. For subordinate categories, the diagram lists only the largest categories from the Chinese sample. Dashed lines indicate findings that held for only the Chinese sample; dotted lines those for only the U.S. sample. Adapted from Fischer & Tangney (1995).

reflect fundamental characteristics of the human species. In this sense, nativist arguments are correct: Emotion categories have an important species-general (hereditary) component (Ekman et al., 1987; Izard, 1977). In the studies that produced the hierarchy in Figure 9.22, Shaver, Wu, Schwartz, and their colleagues began with a standard dictionary in both the United States and China, asking informants to pick words that involved emotions (Shaver et al., 1987; Shaver et al., 1992). Then they used the selected words with another set of informants, who sorted the words into categories. Hierarchical cluster analysis of the sortings produced the dimensions, basic families, and subordinate families shown in Figure 9.22. Chinese and American English showed five common emotion families: (a) anger, (b) sadness, (c) fear, (d) love, and (e) joy—as well as the usual affective dimensions. Other researchers examining different cultures have found groupings of emotions into similar families and dimensions (Heider, 1991; Scherer et al., 1986; Wallbott & Scherer, 1995). Claims that emotions differ fundamentally across cultures (Averill, 1980; Harré, 1986) do not take these broad family groupings into account. In fact, the oft-cited data of Catherine Lutz (1988), which are typically used to counter claims that there are basic emotions, appear to fit the framework of the hierarchy and thus not to violate the basic family model, according to Shaver, Wu, and Schwartz (1992).

Alongside cultural similarities, however, cultural differences are strong and important. The hierarchies for China and the United States illustrate those differences. First, the Chinese organization of love was substantially different from the American one. In the American sample, love was categorized as a fundamentally positive emotion; in the Chinese sample, love was sad and negative. The two main Chinese subordinate categories were sorrowful love and unrequited love, as shown in Figure 9.22. In contrast, the American subordinate categories were primarily positive, including words such as fondness and infatuation. The Chinese and American constructions of the basic family of love are clearly different.

An even greater difference was that the Chinese showed a sixth emotion family, shame, which existed in the U.S. study as only a small subordinate cluster in the sadness family, not as a separate basic family. This finding demonstrates a powerful cultural difference—an entirely different emotion family, presumably reflecting important cultural experiences (Benedict, 1946; Kitayama & Markus,

1995; Miyake & Yamazaki, 1995). Shame is much less salient in America (and in many other Western cultures) than it is in many Eastern cultures.

Wang (1994) followed up this finding by analyzing the categorical organization of the shame family in Chinese, using a method similar to that of Shaver, Wu, and Schwartz (1992). Their study had contained only a handful of shame words, but Wang worked with Mandarin speakers from mainland China to identify 113 words clearly involving shame. Hierarchical cluster analysis of subjects' sortings of these words produced the hierarchy outlined in Figure 9.23. The primary superordinate dimension was self/other (one of the three common dimensions of emotion), and there were six families of shame words, with several subordinate categories for most of the families. The English names for each family and subordinate category were chosen carefully to portray the Chinese meanings, but it is difficult to capture in English the connotations of many of these Chinese emotion concepts. Interestingly, one of the families that seems familiar to American culture is guilt, but it was the least differentiated shame family in Chinese, showing no clear discrimination of subordinate categories despite including an ample number of words (thirteen).

Generally speaking, the organization of emotion concepts seems to have broad similarities across cultures; yet cultural experiences lead to powerful differences in specific emotion concepts and important variations in basic emotion families. Emotion concepts—and emotions more

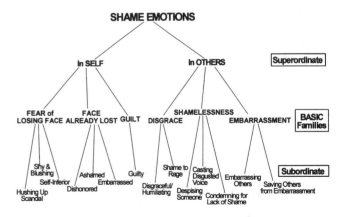

Figure 9.23 Hierarchy of shame categories in Chinese. This hierarchy shows the organization of shame categories in Chinese based on the findings of Wang (1994). For subordinate categories, only the first degree of categories is shown.

broadly—are not simply innate nor entirely variable as a function of vastly different cultures and experiences. Emotion organization is constrained by broad species characteristics at the same time that it is constructed to produce very different structures across cultures and individuals. Techniques that focus on the variations in emotion facilitate not only description of individual variability and cultural diversity but also detection of shared characteristics of emotions across individuals and cultures.

Affectively Organized Development

The action tendencies produced by affects shape activity not only at the moment they occur but also in the longer perspective of development. A general hypothesis is that frequent affective experience of a given type shapes development of a person or ensemble along a particular pathway. Repeated affective experiences such as recurring feelings of shame or recurring abuse lead people to develop along a globally different pathway shaped by these affective organizations. The development of a distinct sixth family for shame illustrates one form of such global effects of emotion, with cultural shame experiences leading to development of an additional major branch in a person's or ensemble's developmental web for emotions. Functional-structural tools facilitate the analysis of a variety of ways that emotions shape development.

One-Dimensional Emotional Effects on the Shapes of Development

Affective experiences have powerful effects on the shapes of development, whether they are governed by cultural norms or more idiosyncratic life events such as trauma. Research on emotional development commonly focuses on these kinds of overarching effects of emotional experiences. Broad, one-dimensional effects can involve creation of a different branch on the developmental web or a broad shifting or biasing in the web.

In one type of broad one-dimensional effect, people develop a branch that would have been minor or nonexistent without the emotional experiences. In China and in many other Asian cultures, for example, children experience shame and shaming repeatedly as a normal part of their socialization (Heider, 1991; Miyake & Yamazaki, 1995; Shaver et al., 1992). As a result, shame words are included in their early vocabulary, children develop well differentiated

scripts and categories for shame, and shame becomes an essential part of their everyday affective experience: $ME_{ASHAMED}$ and $YOU_{ASHAMED}$. In American culture, on the other hand, many children seldom experience shaming, although they do have other kinds of negative experiences as part of their socialization. As a result, most American children do not use shame words in their early vocabulary (Bretherton & Beeghly, 1982), nor do they develop well-differentiated scripts and categories for shame. Instead, they develop other kinds of negative affective scripts and categories such as ones for anger and aggression, or sadness and depression (Barriga & Gibbs, in press; Noam, Paget, Valiant, Borst, & Bartok, 1994; Selman & Schultz, 1990).

In terms of the web metaphor for the structure of development, the American experience with shame involves minimal growth of one large branch of affective development. The shame family develops minimally, at least for concepts and conscious experiences of shame. (Scheff and Retzinger [1991] argue that in America, shame continues to shape activity and experience, operating unconsciously.) The Chinese experience with shame, on the other hand, produces rich growth of the shame branch of affective development, with differentiation of many subsidiary branches, as illustrated in the hierarchy in Figure 9.23.

In the literature on development, the most popular hypotheses about how emotions shape pathways involve a general emotional bias causing one domain to develop globally ahead of others across developmental epochs. The general positivity bias illustrated in Figure 9.4 is one example. Another is the hypothesis that child abuse and neglect can reverse this bias through recurring emotional experiences to produce a developmental web that is biased globally toward the negative, as shown in Figure 9.24. Children who are abused are hypothesized to be biased in general toward negative attributions about social interactions, self, and others. The bias also leads to more differentiated development of the branches on the biased side of the web (Buchsbaum et al., 1992; Calverley et al., 1994; Harter, 1995; Herman, 1992).

Besides affective dimensions, there are biases toward and away from particular emotions. For example, many adults seem to have one or two dominant emotions, such as anger in one person and joy and sadness in another (Plutchik, 1980). In Malatesta's (1988) research, adults were found to have a predominant emotion or two in their facial expressions, even when they tried to pose emotions

NICE NICE & MEAN **MEAN**

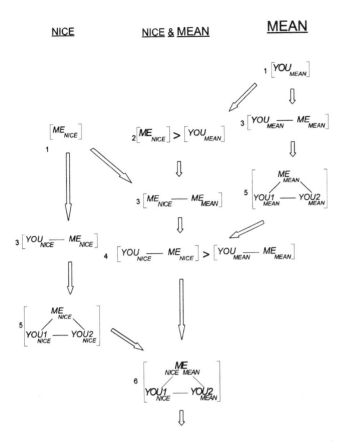

Figure 9.24 Developmental web biased uniformly toward mean interactions because of abuse. This web includes only the first two thirds of the skills from the web in Figure 9.3. The numbers to the left of each set of brackets indicate the complexity ordering of the skill structures. The words inside each set of brackets indicate a skill structure.

other than their dominant one(s). A woman with anger as her dominant emotion, for example, often showed anger on her face even when she was trying to express some other emotion.

Luborsky and Crits-Christoph (1990), as well as others (Horowitz, 1987; Noam, 1990; Selman & Schultz, 1990), have shown that psychotherapy patients typically build upon dominant emotions to form an unconscious script about relationships, which is called a *core conflictual relationship theme.* These scripts involve key wishes or concerns, typical responses by others to those wishes, and one's own actions in response to the others. For example, depressed patients often wish "to be close and accepted . . . loved and understood," but they see others as rejecting and opposing them more often than loving and accepting them. Their response

to the rejection is to feel depressed and helpless (a dominant emotion of sadness), as shown in the script for depression in Table 9.5. A common positive core relationship theme is to wish to be loved and understood, to have one's family treat one in a manner that is loving, helpful, and supportive, and to act confidently (Ainsworth, Blehar, Waters, & Wall, 1978; Shaver & Clark, 1996).

A key question for research is how dominant emotions and relationship themes develop. Luborsky et al. (1996) used their method to analyze pretend stories created by 3- and 5-year-old middle-class Anglo-American children in response to story stems about emotionally loaded situations with family or friends. The basic wishes and expected responses depicted by the children showed patterns similar to those found in adults, although less complex. In this privileged sample, the dominant core relationship theme was positive, not negative: A child wished to be loved and understood or to feel good and comfortable. The other people in the children's stories understood the child and were helpful when help was needed. The child responded confidently and was, in turn, helpful and constructive.

Most of the research illustrating emotional biases in development has treated the emotions as mostly secondary, focusing instead on issues of psychopathology, delinquency, or therapy. Research and theory directly focused on characterizing how emotions shape development have been surprisingly sparse. The two domains where emotional-development research has been extensive are attachment and temperament, both of which are dominant-emotion models. According to attachment theory, children's and adults' relationships, curiosity, and general

TABLE 9.5 Core Conflictual Relationship Script/Theme for Depression

Wish or Concern

A person wishes to be accepted, loved, and understood in a close relationship.

Other's Response

Someone else who potentially could be in a close relationship with the person rejects or opposes him or her even while intermittently showing some love and acceptance.

Self's Response

The person reacts with depression, disappointment, and a sense of helplessness. The dominant emotion is sadness, accompanied by various members of the sadness family.

Derived from findings by Luborsky and Crits-Christoph (1990).

emotional security depend on the nature of their early close relationships with caregivers, usually mothers and fathers. According to traditional temperament theory, babies are born with emotional constitutions that pervasively affect their development and tend to remain similar through to adulthood.

Attachment theory characterizes three major developmental pathways based on babies' affective experience in close relationships: secure (type B), insecure avoidant (type A), and insecure anxious/ambivalent (type C) (Ainsworth et al., 1978). A fourth pathway is sometimes added—disorganized or avoidant/anxious (type D), which is associated with abuse and trauma (Cicchetti, 1990; Crittenden, 1994; Lyons-Ruth, Alpern, & Repacholi, 1993; Main & Hesse, 1990). For each pathway, children develop a working model of close relationships founded on their early experiences with their mothers or other caregivers (Bretherton, 1996; Stern, 1985; Toth & Cicchetti, in press). Each child's internal working model follows a straightforward emotion script for interactions in a close relationship, with one or two emotions dominant in the script (Case, 1996; Shaver & Clark, 1996; Sroufe, 1984).

The working model pervades children's later development, especially in close relationships but also in many other aspects of life. Babies who grow up in a secure relationship build their working models primarily around the emotion of love, trusting that their mothers will be present to take care of them when needed and will allow them independence to explore and learn about the world. Babies who grow up with an avoidant attachment build their working models primarily around a combination of love and fear of rejection, learning that although their mothers usually take care of them, they often reject their babies' affection or closeness. Babies who grow up with an ambivalent attachment build their working models primarily around a combination of love and anger, learning that although their mothers usually take care of them, they often restrict their actions severely or behave inconsistently, making their infants hypervigilant about attachment and angry at restriction. Babies who grow up with a disorganized or avoidant/anxious attachment respond inconsistently with their caregivers or show generally disorganized attachment behavior, not organized consistently around one or two dominant emotions.

Several longitudinal studies have supported the hypothesized stability in attachment pathways, showing moderate correlations in attachment type over several years, espe-

cially in early development (Ainsworth et al., 1978; Bretherton, 1996; Greenberg, Cicchetti, & Cummings, 1990; Lyons-Ruth et al., 1993; Main & Hesse, 1990; Sroufe & Egeland, 1985). At the same time, there is controversy about whether the stability arises from attachment experience, infant affective temperament, or both (Fox, Kimmerly, & Schafer, 1991; Kagan, 1989; Miyake, Chen, & Campos, 1985).

Research on temperament indicates modest substantial long-term stability from the school years through adulthood in several dimensions of temperament, especially introversion/inhibition and anxiety/neuroticism (Digman, 1990; Emde et al., 1992; Kagan, 1989; McCrae & Costa, 1990; Plomin & McClearn, 1993). The most extensive research involves introversion/inhibition, in which a person is wary of novel situations, especially involving other people. This dimension shows moderate stability from infancy through early childhood and substantial stability during adulthood.

Attachment and temperament are primarily one-dimensional explanations, hypothesizing a powerful shaping of development along one affective dimension, although there have been a few efforts to characterize more complex emotional effects (Campos, Barrett, Lamb, Goldsmith, & Stenberg, 1983; Lerner, 1991, 1995b; Sroufe, Egelund, & Kreutzer, 1990; Thomas & Chess, 1980). Structural analysis provides powerful tools for capturing these one-dimensional effects, as illustrated in Figures 9.3, 9.4, 9.5, and 9.24.

Shifting Emotional Biases in Developmental Webs

One of the strengths of the tools for dynamic structural analysis is that they facilitate moving beyond one-dimensional analyses to more differentiated, textured depictions of the organizing effects of emotions on development. Emotional development is not just one-dimensional. Emotional biases shift at different points in development based on, for example, children's changing understandings of themselves and their social world as well as the changing values and expectations of their families and communities and their shifting life situations. Jack and Jeanne Block have argued for several decades that analysis of personality development requires a rich, individualized approach that includes shifts in the meanings of emotions and social categories (Block, 1971, 1993; Block & Block, 1980; van Aken, 1992).

The pervasive positivity bias in development illustrates well the possibilities of a more dynamic, multidimensional analysis of affective biases. Despite the pervasiveness of the positivity bias documented by so much psychological research, positive and negative emotions still act dynamically in development, pulling this way and that—not always in the same direction. In research on development of emotions in self-concepts and social relationships, for example, children have shown developmental shifts in their orientations toward positive and negative (Fischer & Ayoub, 1994; Hand, 1982). In one longitudinal study, 3-, 4-, and 5-year-olds told stories about themselves and other children in nice and mean social interactions: Most 3-year-olds showed a clear negativity bias, both understanding mean stories better and preferring them, but within a few years the children's bias had shifted strongly toward the positive (Hencke, 1996). At age 3 ME_{MEAN} was understood better than ME_{NICE} and preferred. As one 3-year-old said, "Can we do more of these mean stories? They're more fun!" Over the next few years, this negativity bias disappeared and was replaced by a positivity bias that gradually became stronger, as shown in the model for growth functions in Figure 9.25.

Although the modal developmental pathway involved a shift from a mean bias to a nice one, many children did not show this shift. The combination of longitudinal design with Guttman-scale profile analysis provided methods for tracing affective biases in individual children. At 3 years of age, most children who were inhibited or shy (Kagan,

1989) showed a bias toward nice instead of mean, and this pattern was especially strong for inhibited girls.

Undoubtedly, such shifting affective biases are pervasive in development. A general developmental principle seems to be that each new developmental level brings with it specific emotional reactions and distortions, and many of these emotions will change as children develop to higher levels. For example, the research literature illustrates a number of cases of transient emotional defensiveness in early development, based on children's developing (mis)understanding of themselves and their social roles. For the behavioral role of baby, ME_{BABY}, preschoolers show early skill at acting out the baby role in pretend play, even before the role of mother, ME_{MOTHER} (Pipp, Fischer, & Jennings, 1987). As they reach the age of 3 years or so, however, many of them seem to lose the ability to act out the baby role, even though they are now capable of acting out many other simple roles, such as mother, child, doctor, and patient (Watson, 1984). Other cases of emotional defensiveness affecting "cognitive" performance in 3-year-olds include African American children categorizing themselves as white even though they can accurately categorize other people as black or white (Fischer, Knight, et al., 1993; Van Parys, 1981; see also, Clark & Clark, 1939, 1947; Spencer, Brookins, & Allen, 1985), and young boys categorizing themselves as large (old) even though they can accurately categorize other children as small or large (Edwards, 1984).

Generally, children participate in the social relationships and roles that they experience in their lives, and various emotional implications of those relationships and roles become salient to them depending on their developmental levels and the meanings that they ascribe. A classic example of the development of such emotion effects is the Oedipus conflict, which Freud (1909/1955) originally described but which has been the subject of little systematic developmental research except for global cultural comparisons (Levi-Strauss, 1969; Spiro, 1993). According to Freud, preschool children develop a desire to replace their same-sex parent in order to assume a romantic relationship with their opposite-sex parent. Freud builds a large theoretical edifice around this emotional conflict in the nuclear family.

Watson and Getz (1991), who studied the Oedipal phenomena empirically in middle-class white American families, found that indeed children did show a surge of Oedipus-type emotionally organized behaviors at 4 years of age, as shown in Figure 9.26. For example, one girl said

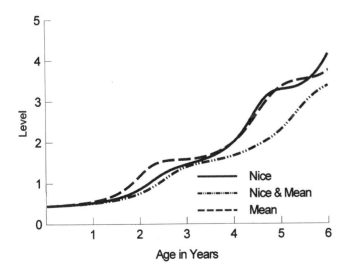

Figure 9.25 Growth functions showing a shifting bias from initial negative toward later positive interactions.

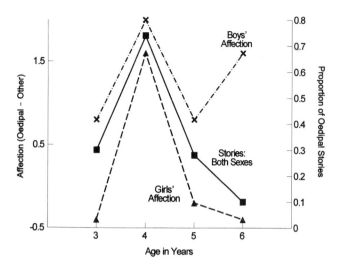

Figure 9.26 Development of Oedipal behaviors in 3- to 6-year-olds. Affection was based on daily parental reports of their children's activities and is shown separately for boys and girls. Oedipal themes were measured in pretend stories that the children told in a laboratory assessment, and boys' and girls' scores are combined in this graph (Watson & Getz, 1991).

to her father, "Daddy, kiss me a hundred times more than you kiss Mommy."

The researchers explained this emergence and decline of Oedipal activities not in terms of castration anxiety and similar violent fantasies that Freud attributed to young children, but in terms of developing understanding of family roles. The first understanding of the special love *relationship* defined by husband and wife roles leads children to want to assume the role with their opposite-sex parent. As a girl named Johanna comes to understand her parents special roles as partners,

$$\begin{bmatrix} JANE \underline{\quad\quad} WALTER \\ {\scriptstyle MOTHER} \quad\quad {\scriptstyle FATHER} \end{bmatrix} \qquad \text{(Formula 7)}$$

she wants to take on the role of her mother so that she can have the special love relationship with her father:

$$\begin{bmatrix} JOHANNA \underline{\quad\quad} WALTER \\ {\scriptstyle MOTHER} \quad\quad\quad {\scriptstyle FATHER} \end{bmatrix} \qquad \text{(Formula 8)}$$

That is why she says things like, "Daddy, kiss me a hundred times more than you kiss Mommy."

This understanding globs together or condenses parental and spousal roles, treating the mother role as including the wife role and the father role as including the husband role. When the roles are separated, children can see that they cannot assume the parental role for themselves (becoming their own father or mother), and they can see other limitations as well, such as that they are too old to marry their parent and that people are not supposed to marry other family members. This emerging, more complete understanding of role relationships in the family leads the child mostly to lose the wish to replace the same-sex parent, unless there are role confusions in the family, such as incest (Fischer & Watson, 1981). She comes to understand the intersection of spousal and parental roles in practice in the family:

$$\begin{bmatrix} {\scriptstyle WIFE} \quad\quad {\scriptstyle HUSBAND} \\ JANE \leftrightarrow WALTER \\ {\scriptstyle MOTHER} \quad\quad {\scriptstyle FATHER} \end{bmatrix} \qquad \text{(Formula 9)}$$

Although many emotional biases come and go with development, others become consistently stronger or weaker over long periods. For example, boys and girls show similar development of understanding social roles for gender and age (girl, boy, woman, man), but the meaning of those roles is markedly different for the two sexes, showing different emotional biases. In two studies of the relation between understanding these roles and using them in self-identification, Van Parys (1981) found that, for white preschool children in Denver, better understanding led to greater gender identification for boys, but not for girls. The girls identified with age roles (child and adult) more as they understood gender and age roles better (Fischer, Knight, et al., 1993). In her study of black and white preschoolers, Van Parys also found that the opposite relation held for black children. Black girls seemed to identify with gender more as they grew older, whereas black boys did not. This racial difference presumably reflects the affective meaning of the gender roles in European American and African American cultures. White Americans typically value the male role more than the female, but for black Americans the female role seems to be more central (Gilligan, 1982; Ogbu, 1978, 1991; Weston & Mednick, 1970).

Webs of Development of Emotional Splitting and Dissociation

One of the most pervasive effects of emotions on developmental pathways is emotional splitting, which involves the basic affective dimension of positive-negative evaluation (Fischer & Ayoub, 1994; Harter & Buddin, 1987). People routinely split positive and negative into separate elements even when they should be combined. The positively biased web for development of nice and mean in Figure 9.4 illustrates one case of this splitting: 2-year-old children commonly represent themselves as nice and other people as mean, and they have difficulty putting the two opposite representations together to see that they themselves can be both nice and mean, as can other people. With time, people develop from splitting toward integration in particular domains, and they construct specific coordinations in each domain. By the grade school years, most children become able to coordinate affects across the positive-negative split in many social situations, as when they represent themselves and other people as simultaneously nice and mean in the stories at steps 6 and 7 in Figures 9.3 and 9.4. For example, in one story, Jason comes up to Seth on the playground, hits him on the arm, and says, "I want to be your friend. Let's play" (a combination of mean and nice actions). Seth responds with appropriate reciprocal nice and mean actions: "I would like to be your friend, but I don't play with kids who hit me." Younger children who are asked to act out or explain stories of this kind commonly split them into two separate stories, one about being nice and a second one about being mean. The middle column (Nice and Mean) in the webs all involve various steps in integration across the positive-negative split.

Splitting is a special case of the more general category of dissociation, in which activities are separated even though they should be coordinated by some external criterion. Emotional splitting involves separation along the positive-negative dimension, or more generally, between opposites. Dissociation typically refers to a stronger separation of elements along dimension(s) besides positive-negative evaluation. The mind is naturally fractionated, as represented by the separate strands in developmental webs. Consequently, splitting and dissociation are pervasive in human activity.

The terms *dissociation* and *splitting* are often used narrowly to refer to the motivated separation that is involved in psychopathology, such as dissociating the self into multiple personalities, or splitting family and friends into good and bad people (Breuer & Freud, 1895/1955; Kernberg, 1976; Noam, Powers, Kilkenny, & Beedy, 1990; Putnam, 1991). Yet splitting and dissociation occur normally and routinely as a result of lack of coordination of skills or experiences that are naturally separate (Chandler, 1994; Feffer, 1982). There need be no pathology. People normally split their world into good and bad, smart and dumb, we and they. In many instances, they strongly dissociate themselves from people, beliefs, and feelings that they disapprove of. Experimental research has established that various forms of active dissociation occur normally, especially during dreaming, hypnosis, and extreme religious experiences, and not only in pathology (Erdelyi, 1985; Foulkes, 1982; Hilgard, 1977; Mischel & Mischel, 1958; Orne, 1959). Splitting and dissociation are normal parts of human development.

Tools for dynamic analysis of development provide new insights into both normal and pathological splitting and dissociation (Fischer & Ayoub, 1994; Fischer & Pipp, 1984). The development of nice and mean shows natural positive-negative splitting, and follows several normal pathways, as we have illustrated. In cases of severe emotional trauma, splitting and dissociation are magnified, and their adaptive value becomes evident. Children subject to severe abuse frequently cultivate skills of dissociation to adapt to the horrendous situations of abuse (Cole & Putnam, 1992; Famularo, Fenton, Kinscherff, Ayoub, & Barnum, 1994; McCann & Pearlman, 1992; Terr, 1991; van der Kolk, 1987). For example, 8-year-old Shirley used dissociation to cope with her father's abuse of her (Canadian Broadcasting Corporation, 1990). Shirley's father repeatedly raped her in her bed in the basement of their home, and he beat her up if she ever resisted his advances. To cope during the rape, she concentrated on a small hole in the wall above her bed, dissociating from her body and feeling that she put herself into the hole. Inside the hole, she could get through the trauma without major distress and without angering her violent father. One day, her father raped her upstairs in the main house instead of in the basement. Without the hole in the wall to support her dissociation, she began screaming and fighting her father. He lost his temper, knocked her unconscious, and then continued with the rape. (Although the father was never arrested for his crimes, Shirley did eventually find help, and she became a competent adult crusading to stop child abuse.)

In a situation like Shirley's, dissociation is a developmental "accomplishment," in which she created a coordination in order to actively dissociate, building skills to keep herself from experiencing the full pain of the trauma. By 4 to 6 years of age, children first demonstrate active dissociation of a few components from one another, as when Shirley put herself in the hole in the wall:

$$\left[\underset{\text{IN HOLE}}{ME\text{-}SHIRLEY} \underline{} \underset{\text{RAPED}}{SHE\text{-}SHIRLEY} \right] \quad \text{(Formula 10)}$$

The block on the line relating the two Shirley roles denotes that the coordination is dissociative. With development, people can construct more complex, sophisticated types of dissociative coordination, actively separating multiple components (Block, 1971; Block & Block, 1980; Freud, 1936/1966; Haan, 1977; Noam et al., 1990; Vaillant, 1977).

Although research is only beginning on the developmental pathways of abused children, data are available to guide an initial sketch of the pathways produced by abuse, including documentation of the pattern of disorganized attachment described earlier (Crittenden, 1994; Fagan & McMahon, 1984; Lyons-Ruth et al., 1993; Main & Hesse, 1990; Raya, 1996; Toth & Cicchetti, 1996; Westen, 1994). In severely abused or neglected children, the organization of development along the positive-negative dimension is powerfully affected. For many children, the normal positivity bias in representations disappears at a young age to be replaced by the opposite—a negativity bias, as shown earlier in Figure 9.24. Instead of focusing their representations of self and important relationships toward the positive, as most children do, many maltreated children characterize the self in pervasively negative terms, endlessly acting out and talking about negative events and interactions.

The findings from one study demonstrate how powerful this reversal can be. A group of adolescent girls hospitalized for depression and conduct disorder (acting out) described themselves in the Self-in-Relationships Interview (Figure 9.11), which was designed to produce rich self-descriptions (Calverley, 1995; Calverley et al., 1994; Fischer, Ayoub, Singh, Noam, & Maraganore, 1997). In one part of the interview, they indicated the importance of various self-characterizations, and in another part they indicated the positivity or negativity of the self-characterizations. Instead of the usual positivity bias shown by adolescents in this interview (Harter & Monsour, 1992; Kennedy, 1994), the girls who had experienced severe and prolonged sexual abuse showed a pervasive negativity bias, as diagrammed in Figure 9.27. Depressed girls in

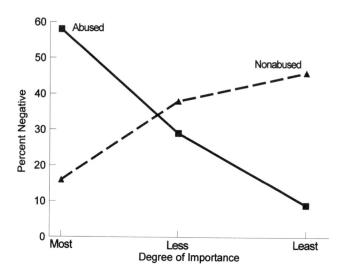

Figure 9.27 Importance of negative self-representations in abused and nonabused depressed adolescent girls (Calverley et al., 1994).

the same hospital who had not been sexually abused showed no negativity bias but a clear positivity bias instead. Contrary to many clinical claims the abused girls did not function at low developmental levels in their self-representations; they produced levels comparable to those of the nonabused girls and to adolescents of similar ages in other populations. The abused girls were developing along a distinctive pathway, not failing to develop.

These kinds of traumatic environments produce distinct developmental pathways that are powerfully affected by the affective experience of abuse and trauma. Children growing up in such environments often produce remarkably sophisticated kinds of dissociation, which, like Shirley's dissociation from being raped, demonstrate great developmental complexity. Figure 9.28 describes an early developmental pathway for a boy named John, who was growing up in hidden family violence, where there is a rigid, socially maintained dissociation between public and private worlds. In private, his father treated him tyrannically, abusing him physically whenever he disobeyed. In public, his father treated him as a good child whom he was proud of. In general, the parents maintained a consistent public image as good citizens and neighbors, and model members of the community, but at home they were violent and abusive.

As John developed working models of close relationships, he constructed his own version of the private-public dissociation that his family maintained. He built increasingly

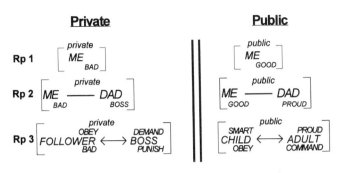

Figure 9.28   Development of dissociated representations (Rp) of private and public relationships in hidden family violence.

complex and generalized representations of tyrant-victim relationships in private and model-family relationships in public (Fischer & Ayoub, 1996). Figure 9.28 illustrates three major levels in this development, between 2 and 7 years of age, for the first three levels of the representational tier (Rp1 to Rp3). At the first level, John represented himself in his private and public roles with his father, but did not maintain a firm dissociation between the two (as indicated by the permeable line dividing the domains). At the second level, he built role relationships, connecting his own and his father's roles and dissociating public and private more firmly. The third level brought a clear generalization of those roles beyond his relationship with his father—relationships with other adults and children.

These results do *not* mean that only abused or traumatized children show emotional splitting and dissociation. Splitting and dissociation are normal processes that everyone shows under many circumstances. Abuse produces different developmental pathways in which the person's working models of relationships are organized powerfully by the abuse, yielding characteristics such as a negativity bias and a sharp dissociation between public good and private violent relationships. Tools for dynamic analyses of development provide ways of detecting these distinctive pathways and avoiding the common error of characterizing complex forms of dissociation and splitting as developmentally primitive.

In summary, emotions act as biasing forces that shape development along particular pathways, including normative pathways such as emotional splitting of positive and negative in representations of self and others. When children have severe emotional experiences such as abuse, their emotional reactions contribute to shaping their development

along unusual pathways that are built on their abusive relationships. Developing understandings affect emotional reactions through changing appraisals, which lead to consequences at certain points in development, such as emotional reactions similar to those that Freud attributed to the Oedipus conflict. In this way, emotions constitute a prime example of the usefulness of dynamic structural concepts and methods for analyzing how different components work jointly to produce development. Emotion and cognition work together, affecting each other's development so extensively that they are difficult to separate. In the big picture of macrodevelopment, many of the large reorganizations seem to occur concurrently for emotion and cognition. Through dynamic structural analysis, it has become possible to build the first detailed models of how these changes in emotion and cognition may relate to brain development.

GROWTH CYCLES OF PSYCHOLOGICAL AND BRAIN ACTIVITY: THE BIG PICTURE OF DEVELOPMENT BETWEEN NATURE AND NURTURE[2]

The dynamic structural framework provides powerful tools for detecting regularities in development. Without these tools, regularities are often swamped by the variability of human activity. The use of dynamic analysis to deal with variability has proven to be especially helpful in the search for relations between behavior and brain development. Dynamic analysis has produced the first specific models of relations between brain and behavior in development—hypothesized growth cycles linking developmental levels of cognition and emotion with growth of cortical activity (Fischer & Rose, 1994, 1996; Thatcher, 1994). Using dynamic analysis, researchers have uncovered rich new findings and built the first detailed models of relations between brain and psychological development. The findings and models provide a powerful illustration of the effectiveness of dynamic structural analysis in facilitating research and theory on development. The analysis of growth cycles also highlights important points about the dynamic structural

---

[2] The arguments in this section are adapted from Fischer and Rose (1994, 1996).

framework, especially the big picture for development from infancy through early adulthood.

Most developmental research fails to deal with the facts of variability, but neglecting those facts is especially perilous for research on relations between brain and behavior development. Development has many different shapes! Some behaviors and brain functions show continuous growth; others show various kinds of discontinuities. Research on relations between brain and behavior needs to start with a developmental framework that encompasses different kinds of growth patterns, providing concepts and methods for determining where to find relations amid all the variability in growth functions. Research should be designed in terms of the wide array of shapes of development for different characteristics of brain and behavior under different assessment conditions. Otherwise, the research is doomed to become swamped by the combined variability in brain and behavior development.

Epigenesis of Psychological and Brain Activity

Today, scientists assume that growth of the brain relates closely to growth of action, thought, and emotion; yet the empirical basis for this belief remains limited. In a few narrow domains, research on neural systems has uncovered close relations between particular brain components and developing behaviors, especially for the visual system (e.g., Hubel & Wiesel, 1977; Movshon & Van Sluyters, 1981) and for some aspects of language (Lieberman, 1984; Neville, 1991). Clear evidence is missing, however, for connections between brain changes and development of action, thought, and emotion more generally.

Happily, recent research provides the possibility of changing this situation. The surge of new knowledge about development of both the nervous system and behavior brings the opportunity for new empirically based epigenetic analyses of the dynamics of brain-behavior development. In both arenas, research shows complex patterns of nonlinear, dynamic growth instead of monotonic growth (Fischer & Rose, 1994, 1996; Lampl & Emde, 1983; Lampl, Veldhuis, & Johnson, 1992; Rakic, Bourgeois, Eckenhoff, Zecevic, & Goldman-Rakic, 1986; Thatcher, 1994; Thelen & Smith, 1994). The new tools for analysis of dynamic growth patterns open opportunities for analyzing these data and using them to build epigenetic models of brain-behavior development

(Fischer & Kennedy, 1997; Grossberg, 1987; van der Maas & Molenaar, 1992; van Geert, 1994).

Between behavior and brain, there are important commonalities that can facilitate the search for regularities. One commonality is the coordination of components into higher-order control systems, which include both neural networks and behaviors (activities). Brain and behavior naturally function together. The control systems also include the body and the immediate context, both of which participate directly in the control systems. Context includes not only objects and events but coparticipants in social ensembles. Brains function to produce an activity in a context, with diverse activities and contexts organizing brain functioning differently (Damasio, 1994; LeDoux, 1989; Luria, 1979). Where brain, action, emotion, and context come together is in the purposes and skills that a person or ensemble constructs. Moment by moment people construct, modify, and elaborate control systems, with concomitant changes in their neurological states and their behaviors. The context and goal of the moment alter the nature and complexity of people's control systems.

Development of both brain and behavior involves epigenesis, movement through qualitative changes like those from egg and sperm to fertilized cell, embryo, newborn infant, and eventually, adult human being. After the classical debate about the nature of embryological development was settled in favor of epigenesis, as opposed to quantitative growth of a preformed human being, the epigenetic conception was extended not only to brain development but also to cognitive and emotional development (Erikson, 1963; Gesell, 1946; Hall, 1904; Piaget, 1947/1950; Werner, 1948).

The study of relations between brain and behavior in development naturally builds on the epigenetic framework (Bidell & Fischer, 1996). From a dynamic perspective, each structure or behavior in epigenesis emerges as a result of the self-organizing activity of previously developed systems through coordination of component processes. In general, the coordination of processes or subsystems is central to the nature of epigenesis (Gottlieb, 1992; Gottlieb et al., Ch. 5, this Volume; Lerner, 1991; Luria, 1979; Oyama, 1985; Thelen & Smith, 1994). Weiss (1970) has demonstrated that such systems are hierarchically organized, with the component systems not only fulfilling more or less separate functions but also functioning together as part of the larger system in which they take part. The emergence of a new system thus requires the active coordination of components to form an integrated whole that goes beyond the component parts by themselves.

Development of brain and behavior involves a long sequence of such epigenetic coordinations, extending from before birth well into adulthood. Processes of coordination are central to development in both domains, so that analysis of coordination processes will provide insights into relations between brain and behavior (Case, 1992; Fischer & Rose, 1994, 1996; Thatcher, 1994). Cognitive and emotional development combines with brain development in a collaboration involving strong relations of neural networks with actions and thoughts. There is no separation of nature and nurture, of biology and environment, or of brain and behavior; there is only a collaborative coordination between them. "Between nature and nurture stands the human agent whose unique integrative capacities drive the epigenesis of intelligence and organize biological and environmental contributions to the process" (Bidell & Fischer, 1996, p. 236).

Principles for Understanding Growth Patterns of Brain and Behavior

Analyzed in terms of nonlinear dynamics of discontinuities in growth, developmental curves for many characteristics of brain and behavior show remarkable similarities, suggesting common epigenetic processes shared by neural networks and optimal levels in behavior. Investigation of these common growth patterns begins with a framework for interpreting patterns of development of brain and behavior, including the wide variability in growth functions. Based on this framework, Fischer and Rose (1994, 1996) examined the empirical findings for patterns of development in both psychological and brain activity and found evidence for two recurring growth cycles. We will first explicate five principles described by Fischer and Rose to characterize the framework, and then we will describe the growth cycles. This analysis was strongly influenced by the work of Thatcher (1991, 1992, 1994) and van Geert (1991, 1994).

Both brain activity and optimal cognitive functioning show nonlinear dynamic growth, often developing in fits and starts. Growth speeds up and then slows down, demonstrating spurts, plateaus, drops, and other kinds of discontinuous shifts in growth patterns. For some types of growth, the fits and starts are systematic; and for others, they are disorderly, showing the variability that is typical of dynamic systems that are affected by many different factors, illustrated in Figure 9.9. For certain properties of brain activity and for the optimal levels of cognition and emotion, the fits and starts are highly systematic, forming clusters of discontinuities at particular age intervals. Understanding the systematicity, however, requires analysis of important kinds of variability in growth. The principles for the dynamic structural framework range from clusters of discontinuities to processes of variability and regularity in growth functions.

Principle 1: Clusters of Discontinuities in Growth of Brain and Behavior. Development of brain activity and development of psychological activity move through a series of clusters of discontinuities (spurts, drops, and other forms of abrupt change) indicating levels of reorganization of control systems for action, thought, and feeling. An important focus for analyzing discontinuities is the leading edge of change, such as the onset of a spurt.

A broad array of evidence indicates a sequence of clusters of discontinuities in brain and behavior development marking a succession of developmental levels and reflecting basic growth processes of brain and behavior. The growth patterns for different variables are not identical but variable, showing the normal diversity of dynamic systems. On the other hand, the regulatory processes of development (what Piaget [1957, 1975] called equilibration) produce important regularities across growth curves, as shown by the dynamic model for weakly linked growers illustrated in Figure 9.13.

Principle 2: Concurrence of Independent Growers. Developing behaviors and brain activities that are mostly independent (belonging to different domains or strands and localized in different brain regions) commonly show discontinuities that are approximately concurrent. The dynamics of the person's growing control systems produce concurrent changes across a number of independent psychological and brain activities.

In the web for multiple developing domains, discontinuities occur in concurrent clusters across domains, as marked by the boxes in Figure 9.17 and the clusters for optimal level in Figure 9.13. Note, however, that the same growth curves also show the relative independence of growers. When small portions of the curves are viewed up close, as in Figure 9.29, the same growers that show clustering in Figure 9.13 are evidently independent, because the short-term concurrence across growers is not strong. Most developmental research takes this up-close, short-term view instead of the distanced, long-term perspective. Clusters of discontinuities coexist with relatively independent growth in dynamic systems, with the (weak) linkages among growers often evident only in the long-term perspective.

A frequent error in the study of development is to assume that growth clusters reflect a single coherent mechanism, such as growth in a memory module that controls all the growers in common. Many cognitive theories posit such a single mechanism of working memory or short-term memory, which acts as a bottleneck limiting development in all domains (Case, 1985; Halford, 1982; Pascual-Leone, 1970). Such single-process explanations do not fit the evidence. Growers that cluster can be independent of each other, with the clusters produced by dynamic regulatory growth processes (Bidell & Fischer, 1992a; Fischer, 1980, 1994; Flavell, 1982). For example, synaptic densities in diverse cortical regions in infant rhesus monkeys develop through approximately concurrent spurts and drops, even though the regions are clearly separate and mostly independent (Bourgeois, Goldman-Rakic, & Rakic, 1994; Bourgeois & Rakic, 1993; Rakic et al., 1986).

Because of the many ways that a dynamic system can produce concurrent discontinuities, analysis of the processes underlying concurrence requires the dynamic research designs that we described earlier. Growth must be investigated under diverse conditions that incorporate assessment of variability, and growth processes must be modeled carefully with procedures such as those of van Geert (1991) or van der Maas and Molenaar (1992). Guidelines for designing studies to disentangle alternative explanations of developmental concurrence have been outlined in several methodological reviews (Fischer, 1987; Fischer & Farrar, 1987; Fischer, Knight, et al., 1993; McCall, 1983; Wohlwill, 1973). For investigations of relations between brain and behavior, these designs should include analyses of domain specificity of behavior and localization of brain function. Contrary to common assumptions, concurrence does not at all contradict domain specificity or localization.

Principle 3: Domain Specificity of Activities and Localization of Brain Functions. Relations between growers that involve different domains or different brain regions can be understood only through analysis of the contributions of domain and localization to the shapes of growth functions. In addition, research on these contributions must focus on growth of individuals, examining each child's growth functions and the nature of their concurrence.

Consider several kinds of activities that exhibit concurrent spurts at 8 months of age but belong to distinct domains and involve different brain regions: (a) spatial skills such as search and locomotion, (b) verbal skills such as using intonation and speaking words and sentences, and (c) socioemotional skills such as recognizing familiar caregivers and striving to stay near them (which are shown by, for example, separation distress and stranger distress). At approximately 8 months, infants typically show spurts in spatial skills, including Piaget's (1937/1954) object-permanence tasks (Campos & Bertenthal, 1987). In the same age range, they demonstrate spurts in skills for vocal imitation (McCall et al., 1977; Petitto & Marentette, 1991;

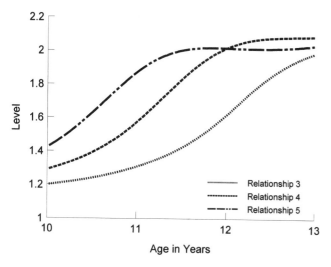

Figure 9.29 Close-up view of three growers in model of self-in-relationships.

Uzgiris, 1976), and for separation and stranger distress (Ainsworth et al., 1978; Campos et al., 1983; Emde, Gaensbauer, & Harmon, 1976; Kagan, 1982). Many infants start to search effectively for toys or cookies hidden successively under different covers; they begin to imitate simple intonation contours and syllables that they hear spoken by their caregivers; and they start to show consistent distress at their mothers' departing and at strangers' appearing. Search for objects, imitation of vocal sounds, and distress at strangers and separation belong to distinct domains, and involve distinct cortical networks.

Growth functions for object search and vocal imitation have been compared to growth functions for cortical activity, as measured by the electroencephalogram (EEG). Researchers have compared the growth functions for the behaviors with those for the cortical activity (Bell & Fox, 1992, 1994). Individual infants showed strongly overlapping concurrence for some domains and regions, but only loose and imprecise concurrence for others. The infants who demonstrated a spurt in search skills between 8 and 12 months produced a concurrent spurt in EEG activity (power) in the frontal cortex, but not elsewhere; and they also showed growing connections between frontal and occipital/parietal cortex, as measured by EEG coherence. In contrast, infants who did not demonstrate clear spurts in search similarly produced no growth spurts for frontal activity.

By analyzing the dynamic variations in growth functions, researchers can move beyond the difficulties of comparison across domains and regions. They can use similarities in growth functions to analyze development of brain-behavior relations, detecting when concurrent discontinuities mesh across behaviors and cortical activities, and when they do not mesh. Clusters of discontinuities seem to reflect emergence of new organizations of brain and behavior, new action control systems linked to neural networks. Discontinuities in EEG activity, cortical connectivity, and psychological activity demonstrate concurrence and reflect the emergence of new control systems and neural networks.

Principle 4: Emergence of Neural Networks and Action Control Systems. With each developmental level, a new kind of control system for action emerges, supported by growth of a new type of neural network linking several brain regions and built upon lower-level skills. Across different brain regions and skill domains, similar (independent) networks and control systems emerge concurrently. They produce clusters of discontinuities in certain characteristics of cortical activity and optimal level. Careful analysis of growth functions allows detection of correspondences beyond global concurrence between cortical regions and skills.

After emergence, the new systems undergo a lengthy period of consolidation, during which they are tuned gradually to form efficient behavioral-neural control systems. Eventually, another new type of control system starts to grow, and another developmental level and cluster of discontinuities begins.

Principle 5: Cycles of Discontinuities Forming Levels and Tiers. In development, simpler networks and control systems are coordinated successively to form a series of increasingly complex networks and control systems. Emergence of these control systems is reflected in a series of clusters of discontinuities. The clusters form cycles that have some of the characteristics of stages, although they arise from dynamic systems and so are variable, not static. One cycle of discontinuities forms a developmental level, and a series of these levels groups into a tier, which comprises a higher-order recurring cycle of growth—a cycle of cycles.

The cycles comprise a cascade of changes in growth that move through brain areas and psychological domains systematically and cyclically (Fischer & Rose, 1994, 1996; Thatcher, 1994). There are no all-or-none changes, occurring everywhere at once as suggested by classical conceptions of stage. The cycles may involve a number of different neural processes, such as synaptic growth and pruning across cortical regions during early development (Huttenlocher, 1994; Rakic et al., 1986), the formation of myelin to insulate neurons and thus produce faster neural impulses and improved coordination (Benes, 1994; Case, 1992; Yakovlev & Lecours, 1967), and diverse other processes that improve communication among brain regions.

Cycles of Reorganization in Development

Psychological activity and brain activity seem to develop through 13 successive levels between birth and 30 years of age, as shown in Table 9.6 using the framework of dynamic skill theory (Fischer, 1980; Fischer & Rose, 1994). These levels are supported by an array of evidence of discontinuities and growth cycles for both behavior (action, thought, and feeling) and brain (physical growth and cortical activity). Various neo-Piagetian theorists have posited stages as well, and many of their stages match some of the 13 levels (Biggs & Collis, 1982; Case, 1985; Halford, 1982; McLaughlin, 1963; Siegler, 1981). However, these alternatives have not been based on clear criteria for what constitutes a stage or level, and what does not; and a number of the stages posited by neo-Piagetians are not supported by empirical evidence for discontinuities (Fischer & Silvern, 1985). Typically, these investigators have merely described a sequence of what they think are important cognitive reorganizations without specifying empirical criteria for stages, except for loosely defined "qualitative change" and an approximate developmental sequence.

The ages for appearance of each level are highly variable, except under optimal assessment conditions. Table 9.6 presents the ages of emergence under optimal conditions, based on criteria of discontinuity, sequence, and qualitative reorganization. At the age of emergence most people can first control several skills at that level of complexity, and by hypothesis, they are growing a new kind of neural network in diverse brain regions, evidenced by clusters of discontinuities in neural activity. Even under optimal conditions, however, exact age of emergence varies across individuals and domains.

Development takes place in three different grains of detail—step, level, and tier. At the finest grain at which developmental ordering can be detected, skills form a sequence of microdevelopmental *steps*. These steps can be separated by relatively short time intervals and small differences in complexity. In dynamic skill theory, the steps are predicted and explained by a set of rules for transforming skills via coordination and differentiation. Most steps are simply points along a strand in a developmental web of skill construction and do not involve discontinuities, and so they are not shown in Table 9.6.

The intermediate grain is developmental *level,* with each level emerging at certain steps in a strand. Levels produce clusters of discontinuities in behavior and brain activity, marking emergence of a new kind of control system and network, and therefore a capacity to construct a new kind of skill. Although many developmental researchers have

not tried to assess fine-grained steps, measurement of steps greatly facilitates detection of levels by providing rulers and clocks for amount and speed of change. Fine-grained rulers and clocks are required for detection of discontinuities, as described in the section on Methodology.

At the broadest grain, levels form cycles of reorganization called *tiers,* defined by a series of four increasingly complex levels, as shown in Table 9.6. With the start of a tier, skills are simplified by being reorganized into a new unit of activity: (a) reflexes, (b) actions, (c) representations, or (d) abstractions, respectively. Skills within a tier grow through four levels, from single units to mappings to systems and finally to systems of systems. The level of systems of systems produces the new type of unit, which initiates the next tier. Development of a new tier brings an unusually strong form of discontinuity, producing radical alterations in brain and psychological activity. For example, late in the second year, children move into the representational tier, beginning to show complex language, independent agency (as in representing ME_{NICE} and YOU_{MEAN}), and a plethora of other radical behavioral changes, as well as major spurts in frontal and occipital-parietal activity. Likewise, at 10 to 12 years, children combine multiple concrete representations to form the first abstractions and begin another new tier.

A new tier requires melding together complex systems to forge a new kind of unit—an achievement that necessitates neural glue to cement the components together. Fischer and Rose (1994, 1996) hypothesize that the frontal cortex provides much of this glue, in consonance with the general functions of frontal cortex (Damasio, 1994; Goldman-Rakic, 1986; Pennington, 1994).

Hypothesis 1: Role of Frontal Cortex in Developmental Cycles. The frontal cortex facilitates cementing skills together to form a new unit at the start of a tier, holding components on line so that they can be joined. Moreover, the frontal cortex plays a significant role in the emergence of each new developmental level within a tier as well, since each level requires coordination of skills from the prior level.

The frontal cortex's role in starting a new tier is evident in a strong surge in EEG relative power in the frontal area at the time of emergence of a new tier. Relative power is an index of the amount of activity in a cortical region, measured by dividing the total power in the EEG by the power in a particular frequency band reflecting cortical activity

TABLE 9.6   Levels of Development of Psychological and Cortical Activity

Level	TIER				Age[1]
	Reflex	Sensorimotor	Representational	Abstract	
Rf1: Single Reflexes	$[A]\ \text{or}\ [B]$				3-4 wk
Rf2: Reflex Mappings	$[A \longrightarrow B]$				7-8
Rf3: Reflex Systems	$\left[A_F^E \longleftrightarrow B_F^E\right]$				10-11
Rf4/Sm1: Single Sensorimotor Actions	$\begin{bmatrix} A_F^E \longleftrightarrow B_F^E \\ \Updownarrow \\ C_H^G \longleftrightarrow D_H^G \end{bmatrix} \equiv [\mathbf{I}]$				15-17
Sm2: Sensorimotor Mappings		$[\mathbf{I} \longrightarrow \mathbf{J}]$			7-8 mo
Sm3: Sensorimotor Systems		$\left[\mathbf{I}_N^M \longleftrightarrow \mathbf{J}_N^M\right]$			11-13
Sm4/Rp1: Single Representations		$\begin{bmatrix} \mathbf{I}_N^M \longleftrightarrow \mathbf{J}_N^M \\ \Updownarrow \\ \mathbf{K}_P^O \longleftrightarrow \mathbf{L}_P^O \end{bmatrix} \equiv [Q]$			18-24
Rp2: Representational Mappings			$[Q \longrightarrow R]$		3.5- 4.5 yr
Rp3: Representational Systems			$\left[Q_V^U \longleftrightarrow R_V^U\right]$		6-7
Rp4/Ab1: Single Abstractions			$\begin{bmatrix} Q_V^U \longleftrightarrow R_V^U \\ \Updownarrow \\ S_X^W \longleftrightarrow T_X^W \end{bmatrix} \equiv [\mathscr{Y}]$		10-12
Ab2: Abstract Mappings				$[\mathscr{Y} \longrightarrow \mathscr{Z}]$	14-16
Ab3: Abstract Systems				$\left[\mathscr{Y}_\mathscr{D}^\mathscr{C} \longleftrightarrow \mathscr{Z}_\mathscr{D}^\mathscr{C}\right]$	18-20
Ab4: Principles				$\begin{bmatrix} \mathscr{Y}_\mathscr{D}^\mathscr{C} \longleftrightarrow \mathscr{Z}_\mathscr{D}^\mathscr{C} \\ \Updownarrow \\ \mathscr{A}_\mathscr{D}^\mathscr{C} \longleftrightarrow \mathscr{B}_\mathscr{D}^\mathscr{C} \end{bmatrix}$	23-25

[1] Ages given are modal ages at which a level first emerges according to research with middle-class American or European children. They may well differ across social groups.

Note: In skill structures, each letter denotes a skill component. Each large letter = a main component (set), and each subscript or superscript = a subset of the main component. Plain letters = components that are reflexes, in the sense of innate action-components. Bold letters = sensorimotor actions; italic letters = representations; and script letters = abstractions. Lines connecting sets = relations forming a mapping, single-line arrows = relations forming a system, and double-line arrows = relations forming a system of systems.

(Fischer & Rose, 1994; Hudspeth & Pribram, 1992). Power is measured by the amount of energy in the wave, which is calculated as the area under the curve for the wave.

The frontal cortex also contributes centrally to the emergence of each developmental level within a tier, as evidenced by discontinuities in measures of cortical connections between frontal and other cortical areas. Connections are measured by EEG coherence (the cross-correlation between wave forms in two cortical regions), which is high if the two regions are connected (Nunez, 1982). Most of the coherence measures that show systematic growth from birth to early adulthood involve the frontal cortex linking with other cortical areas, usually within a hemisphere (Thatcher, 1991, 1992, 1994). For example, Bell and Fox (in press) found a spurt in coherence between the frontal and occipital areas when 8-month-old infants began to crawl, followed by a drop after they had been crawling for a few months. This spurt suggests that during the spurt, the frontal area holds spatial information on line from the occipital area to facilitate the infants' new coordination of information about movement through space. According to Thatcher (1994), the frontal cortex leads or directs the formation of most new cortical network connections for major developmental reorganizations, such as levels and tiers.

A central function of the frontal cortex is maintaining, over time, information about some activity, in the face of the occurrence of other activities (Case, 1992; Goldman-Rakic, 1986; Luria, 1966, 1973; Pennington, 1994). Coordinating two activities requires exactly this function: A person must change the activities from (a) separateness and independence to (b) co-occurrence (being held in mind at the same time or nearly the same time, as in shift of focus) and finally to (c) coordination. This progression toward coordination is the basic mechanism for building skills at a new level from simpler skills at the previous level.

Before explaining the rest of the model of how psychological levels and tiers relate to cycles of brain change, it will be helpful to review briefly the extensive evidence for levels in both psychological and brain development.

Evidence for Psychological Development

The evidence is substantial for discontinuities in development of action, thought, and emotion for most of the 13 levels in Table 9.6. A number of scholars have reviewed the evidence for various age periods (Corrigan, 1983; Fischer

& Hogan, 1989; Fischer & Kenny, 1986; Fischer & Silvern, 1985; Kagan, 1982; Kitchener et al., 1993; McCall, 1983). It is remarkable that many scholars committed to a continuity position have persistently ignored this extensive evidence (Diamond, 1991; Shultz et al., 1995). The precise ages and forms of growth vary dynamically with a plethora of factors contributing to development.

For the first levels, which occur during the initial months after birth, the evidence is supportive, but not extensive. A number of findings seem to show discontinuities during the first months of life at approximately the ages listed in Table 9.6 (e.g., Haith, Bergman, & Moore, 1977; Mounoud, 1976; Papousek & Papousek, 1979; Touwen, 1976; von Hofsten, 1984).

The evidence is powerful for the fourth through twelfth levels, Sm1 through Ab3, because of the prevalence of research focusing on psychological development between 3 months and 20 years. For example, discontinuities at three ages in infancy are evident in Figure 9.30 from an analysis of the longitudinal Berkeley Growth Study by McCall, Eichorn, and Hogarty (1977). Infant test performance showed sharp drops in stability at approximately 8, 13, and 21 months of age, and there was also a rise from low stability at 4 months, which the authors interpreted as evidence for an early discontinuity. Drops in stability of global measures such as infant tests are common during a time of discontinuities in growth (Fischer et al., 1984). A number

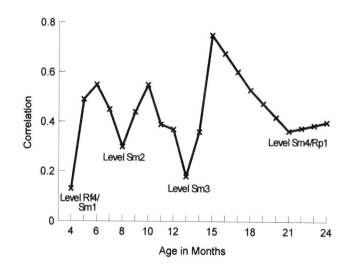

Figure 9.30   Changes in stabilities of infant behavior scores for girls in the Berkeley Growth Study (McCall et al., 1977).

of additional studies have shown spurts in performance and/or drops in stability at these approximate ages in infancy (Bell & Fox, 1994, in press; Corrigan, 1983; Lewis & Ash, 1992; Pipp et al., 1987; Reznick & Goldfield, 1992; Ruhland & van Geert, 1997; Uzgiris, 1976).

The findings for reflective judgment in Figure 9.31 illustrate the patterns of discontinuities for levels in childhood and adolescence (Kitchener et al., 1993). The Reflective Judgment Interview tests the sophistication of arguments about the bases for knowledge in complex dilemmas such as news reports that give conflicting information. In an optimal-level assessment, students showed general increases in level between 14 and 28 years, with spurts centered at approximately 16, 20, and 25 years of age. Other findings cited earlier, such as the evidence for discontinuities in the development of self-in-relationships for Korean adolescents in Figure 9.6 (Fischer & Kennedy, 1997), have manifested similar patterns for optimal conditions. Likewise, many other studies have demonstrated discontinuities in various domains at the age intervals shown in Table 9.6 (e.g., Goodman, Quas, Batterman-Faunce, Riddlesberger, & Kuhn, 1994; Harter & Monsour, 1992; Lamborn et al., 1994; Martarano, 1977; Moshman & Franks, 1986; O'Brien & Overton, 1982; Pillemer, Picariello, & Pruett, 1994; van der Maas & Molenaar, 1995).

It is important to remember that many activities do not exhibit discontinuities at these ages. Discontinuities occur consistently only in activities that reflect the emerging levels—at a minimum, activities that (a) increase in complexity with development, and (b) are assessed under conditions that support optimal performance (the person's optimal level).

Evidence for Brain Development

The evidence is also substantial for a series of discontinuities in brain growth, although it is less extensive than for psychological development. Many of the data have been reviewed by Fischer and Rose (1994) and Thatcher (1994), especially for cortical activity, synaptic density, and head growth. They find that the majority of studies provide globally supportive evidence, but are limited by age sampling that is too infrequent to provide precise estimates of growth functions. The studies with more frequent sampling of age show clear, strong cyclicity of brain growth, with a series of discontinuities at specific age periods.

There is sufficient evidence to test for discontinuities for each of the first twelve levels, although there do not seem to be any data available to test for the thirteenth level in cortical activity. Most body organs grow in fits and starts, and the brain is no exception (Lampl & Emde, 1983; Lampl et al., 1992; Thatcher, 1994; Yakovlev & Lecours, 1967). The brain shows many discontinuities in growth, and in general, many of them cluster at ages that match the developmental levels in Table 9.6. There are important individual differences in the shapes of these growth functions and the ages of discontinuities, as well as differences for various brain regions and diverse brain characteristics. As with psychological development, we will present a few prototypical examples of findings for brain growth.

For the first few months of infancy, there are only a few studies that provide relevant evidence (Dreyfuys-Brisac, 1979; Emde et al., 1976). For instance, head circumference of American infants was measured during visits to a clinic for routine check-ups. Infants showed spurts in head circumference during four successive age periods—at approximately 3–4, 7–8, 10–11 weeks, and 15–18 weeks of age (Fischer & Rose, 1994). (These data were collected by Bonnie Camp of the University of Colorado Health Sciences Center, who kindly shared them with us.) Head circumference has limitations as a measure of brain growth, because it is so indirect and because growth changes are small relative to the error of measurement.

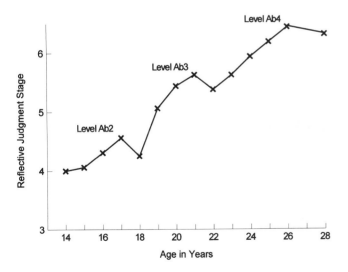

Figure 9.31 Development of optimal level for reflective judgment (Kitchener et al., 1993).

However, the measurement problems are less serious for early infancy, because the amount of growth is large.

For later infancy, evidence is more extensive, with findings of discontinuities at ages similar to those for psychological development—approximately 3–4, 6–8, 11–13 months, and 2 years (Bell & Fox, 1994, in press; Chugani & Phelps, 1986; Hagne, Persson, Magnusson, & Petersén, 1973; Ohtahara, 1981). For example, a study of relative power for occipital EEG in Japanese infants found spurts at approximately 4, 8, and 12 months, as shown in Figure 9.32 (Mizuno et al., 1970).

Evidence of discontinuities during childhood and adolescence cluster at approximately 2, 4, 7, 11, 15, and 20 years (Chugani, Phelps, & Mazziotta, 1987; Dustman & Beck, 1969; Hartley & Thomas, 1993; Mills, Coffey-Corina, & Neville, 1994; Somsen, van Klooster, van der Molen, van Leeuwen, & Licht, in press; Stauder, Molenaar, & van der Molen, 1993; see also Huttenlocher, 1994). Figure 9.33 demonstrates development of relative power in the EEG from a classic Swedish study, with spurts at approximately 2, 4, 8, 12, 15, and 19 years (Hudspeth & Pribram, 1992; Matousek & Petersén, 1973).

Thatcher's (1994) massive study of development of EEG coherence illustrates not only the existence of discontinuities

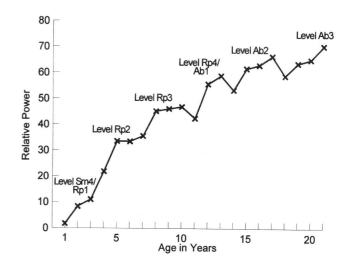

Figure 9.33 Development of relative power in alpha EEG in occipital-parietal (O-P) area in Swedish children and adolescents. Relative power is the amplitude in microvolts of absolute energy in the alpha band divided by the sum of amplitudes in all bands (John, 1977; Matousek & Petersén, 1973).

at appropriate age regions, but also forms of discontinuity more complex than simple spurts or drops. With development, coherence for any pair of EEG sites typically oscillates up and down, and these oscillations show growth cycles, moving through cortical regions in a regular pattern. In addition, the oscillations show strong discontinuities that relate to developmental levels—what Thatcher refers to as cusp catastrophes (as illustrated in Figure 9.16). At approximately 4½, 6, and 10 years, the period of oscillation shifts dramatically, and the relations of patterns of oscillation across brain regions shift from in-phase to out-of-phase, or vice versa. These patterns provide powerful clues for analyzing development of brain-behavior relations.

The extensive evidence for discontinuities in psychological and brain development suggests not only a series of discontinuities but a pair of nested growth cycles linked to tiers and levels. Growth of brain activity and growth of connectivity seem to cycle through specific brain regions in repetitive patterns, as described in Hypotheses 2 and 3 (Fischer & Rose, 1994, 1996; Thatcher, 1994). These patterns are much more specific than the broad-grained surge in frontal EEG activity that marks the start of a tier, which was described in Hypothesis 1.

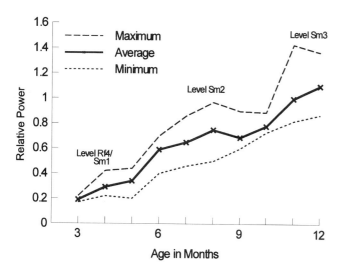

Figure 9.32 Development of relative power in occipital EEG in Japanese infants. Relative power is the ratio of power for the band from 7.17 to 10.3 Hz to power for the band from 2.4 to 3.46 Hz (Mizuno et al., 1970).

Hypothesis 2: Cycle of EEG Activity for Each Tier. Not only is the beginning of each tier marked by a spurt in frontal EEG power, but then the leading edge of growth moves from occipital-parietal, to temporal, to central, and then returns to frontal (generally from back to front). Multiple cortical regions show spurts at each level, but one region leads the others. Each developmental level is associated with a part of this cycle, as diagramed in Figure 9.34.

In the cycle, maximal spurts in EEG activity move systematically across cortical regions. A frontal surge marks the onset of a tier, a maximal spurt in the occipital-parietal region marks the first level, one in the temporal region marks the second level, one in the central region marks the third level, and then, another surge in the frontal region marks the onset of the next tier. The hypothesized cycle is derived from the findings of a classic Swedish study (Matousek & Petersén, 1973) as reanalyzed by Hudspeth and

Pribram (1992). They calculated a single growth index for each cortical region by combining data for the four EEG frequency bands. These data support the cycle of changes hypothesized for the representational and abstract tiers, and we predict similar patterns for the reflex and sensorimotor tiers as well, where the first signs of a new tier are expected at approximately 3–4 weeks and 3–4 months, respectively.

In general, the cycle seems to reflect the movement of development within a tier from more global skills to more differentiated ones. Early in a tier, coordination and integration are prominent, as reflected by the strong involvement of the frontal and occipital regions, especially in the right hemisphere, we hypothesize (Luria, 1973; Thatcher, 1994). Later in a tier, detailed differentiation becomes more prominent, as reflected by the strong involvement of the temporal and central regions, especially in the left hemisphere, we hypothesize. The Swedish data do not allow the fine grain of description that is required to capture the full scope of the cycle because only a few cortical sites were measured, data were combined for the two hemispheres, and subjects' gender was ignored.

The cycle is probably more differentiated than shown in Figure 9.34, possibly involving, for example, more right frontal and left occipital-parietal growth at the start of a tier (Segalowitz, 1994) and more temporal activity across hemispheres at the second level in a tier (Greenfield, 1991). Probably, each tier also has specific characteristics that are not shared with other tiers, and individuals demonstrate important differences in the cycle (Bell & Fox, 1994). In addition, we hypothesize that the cycle involves changes in connectivity similar to those evident in the cycle in Hypothesis 3, which involves a pattern of growth in cortical connections and activity corresponding to each developmental level.

Hypothesis 3: Nested Cycle of EEG Activity and Connectivity for Each Level. At a finer grain, each level comprises a growth cycle nested in the cycle for a tier. In EEG coherence and perhaps EEG activity, the leading edge of growth moves in a systematic pattern around the cortex, showing one full cycle for each level, as diagramed in Figure 9.35.

The connections are typically led by the frontal cortex, beginning with long-distance connections between frontal and occipital regions for both hemispheres. Then the leading edge of growth moves systematically around the cortex,

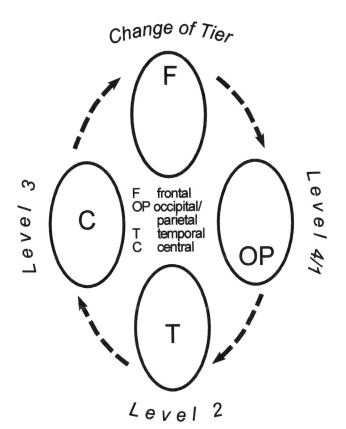

Figure 9.34 A cycle of growth in relative energy of EEG for each tier of skill development (Fischer & Rose, 1994, 1996).

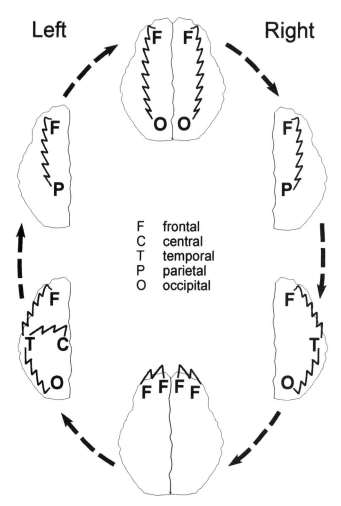

Figure 9.35 A cycle of growth of cortical connections for each level of skill development. Jagged-line connections diagrammed mark the leading edge of growth of coherence. Growth continues for each connection at other times as well. Note that connections between the middle and back of the left hemisphere are more prevalent than similar connections for the right hemisphere, and the temporal-central connection for the left hemisphere is shown as an example of that difference (Fischer & Rose, 1994, 1996; Thatcher, 1994).

extending through the right hemisphere and then through the left. For the right hemisphere, growth begins with long-distance, global connections and contracts toward more local ones. In the left hemisphere, growth begins with more local connections and expands toward more distant ones. In this way, growth moves systematically through cortical areas until it encompasses networks everywhere in the cortex. The cycle thus explains how independent networks

manifest concurrent growth spurts in a general age period, while also predicting fine-grained age differences between networks for each level.

Thatcher (1991, 1992, 1994) first sketched a similar cycle, based on his study of development of coherence. He suggested that the right hemisphere growth process moves from integration to differentiation, while the left hemisphere process moves from differentiation to integration. Hypothesis 3 builds on his proposed cycle, linking it to developmental levels of skill and introducing a few modifications to fit our reading of the data. For the ages included in Thatcher's empirical analyses, the timing of cycles approximates what is predicted by the levels in Table 9.6 (Fischer & Rose, 1994, 1996). A few other findings also support the model, such as Bell and Fox's (in press) study of coherence and crawling, where they found a spurt in frontal-occipital coherence at the age of onset of Level Sm2 in Table 9.6.

The cycles for tiers and levels show intriguing similarities, suggesting that they may be parallel in various ways. They both begin with the front and the back of the cortex, move toward the middle and then return to the front and back. We hypothesize strong parallels between them, with similar movement of the leading edge of growth in both activity and connection of cortical areas.

There is much exciting research to be done to test out these hypotheses about brain-behavior relations in development. It is important to remember, however, that they are dynamic systems, and that they are based on limited data. Developmental functions for psychological and brain activity seem to exhibit major parallels that suggest growth cycles marked by discontinuities. However, they will not take the simple forms suggested in Table 9.6 and Figures 9.30 to 9.35 because they will show important variations across individuals and environmental conditions. We expect future research to show how localization of cortical function and domain specificity of behavior work *with* the growth cycles for levels and tiers, not in opposition to them.

Existing data to test the models are insufficient in two important ways. First, the data are not extensive and allow tests of only a few limited parts of the hypothesized cycles. Second, the studies involve mostly cross-sectional designs for groups of subjects. Individual growth curves will undoubtedly show substantial variability reflecting the nonlinear dynamic properties of brain and psychological activity. Indeed, the few existing longitudinal studies allowing estimation of growth functions for individual children document exactly such variability (Bell & Fox, 1994; Corrigan, 1983; Reznick & Goldfield, 1992; Ruhland & van Geert, 1997).

CONCLUSION: EXPLAINING THE DYNAMICS OF STABILITY AND VARIABILITY IN DEVELOPMENT

A proper focus for understanding human action, thought, and feeling is the organization of human activities and their many variable shapes. Activities form coherent patterns—dynamically varying structures that people actively construct at every moment, using not only their brains but also their bodies, the objects and people around them, and the roles, norms, and values of their culture. The classic frameworks for analyzing structures have not acknowledged either their dynamics or their self-organizing properties, but instead have relied on a static conception of structure as form, seeking simple "main effects" and "stabilities" instead of appreciating the power of analyzing variation. This static conception has reduced structures to one-dimensional forms with most of their components missing. It has reified psychological structures by placing them in logic, innate ideas, or sociocultural systems instead of directly in the activities themselves.

Dynamic structuralism analyzes human activities in all their complexity, moving beyond static, one-dimensional structures by using new concepts and tools from nonlinear dynamics, cognitive science, ecology, and skill theory. Explanation starts with people *in medias res,* and the structures of action, thought, and feeling are analyzed in the activities themselves, not in static logic, innate ideas, or internalized experiences. Although the complexity of activities is great and their variability ranges widely, researchers can use powerful tools from dynamic systems and skill analysis to investigate the structures or organizations (patterns of components) and find the order in the variation.

Using the methodological tools and concepts for analyzing the dynamic structures of human activities requires moving to a different set of assumptions about research and theory. As part of their basic organization, activities include not only people's brains but also their bodies, the objects that participate in the activities, other people who coparticipate, and the cultural roles, norms, and values in which the activities are embedded. When a person acts, he

or she functions on multiple developmental levels simultaneously, not just on a single level. As a person grows, his or her activities develop in many different shapes, not according to one or two basic patterns, as in linear change. Nonlinear dynamics provides powerful tools for analyzing and relating these shapes.

Doing research to understand the variability of human activities turns out to help illuminate the order within the variation. That is, making research appropriately complex leads to new insights about the stabilities inside the variabilities. When development is analyzed as a constructive web instead of a linear ladder, clearly distinct pathways become evident for different people. For example, poor readers are not simply low on the ladder for development of reading, but they are developing their reading skills along more branched, less integrated pathways than normal readers. Abused children are not simply immature on the ladder for emotional stability and social reciprocity, but they have created distinct branched (often dissociated) pathways to cope with their abuse.

When multiple levels of skill are analyzed in each person, the debate about the existence of stages disappears. Under optimal, highly supported conditions, people show jumps in performance that act much like stages; but under ordinary, low-support conditions, the same people show no systematic stages, often progressing in smooth, monotonic growth. The complex shapes of growth curves under these various conditions provide important tools for analyzing relations among different components of human activity, because the shapes can serve as clues for discovering such relations. Analysis of these shapes suggests relations between development of brain electrical activity and behavior, leading to new models of cycles of growth that relate brain activity and connectivity to levels of skill development.

Recognition that individuals function at multiple simultaneous levels also allows the detection of strong microdevelopmental progressions reflecting people's construction of new skills. It illuminates previously unrecognized mechanisms of transition, such as co-occurrence of alternative strategies for approaching a task, and construction of empty shells at high levels to guide one's learning and problem-solving and facilitate building of more complex skills.

When the collaborative nature of most activities is recognized and analyzed (instead of isolating people and studying activities as originating from separate "individuals"), important aspects of development become clarified. Processes of construction of skills can be straightforward detected in many situations, because people interact with each other about their common activities with a task or problem. Many patterns of emotional development become clear because so much emotion arises from people's social relationships. Emotions such as shame and love are obviously social, but even emotions such as fear, anger, and joy grow up in relationships and are defined by social scripts.

Scholars and researchers now have many new tools and concepts for analyzing the richness of human development, moving beyond prior paradigms that presented dynamic organization as static form. Many examples are already in hand of how dynamic structural analysis helps illuminate phenomena that have been perplexing or that have gone undetected in prior paradigms. Finally, developmental scientists have the possibility of capturing human nature in all its richness and variation instead of reducing people to one-dimensional stereotypes.

ACKNOWLEDGMENTS

The authors thank Catherine Ayoub, Daniel Bullock, Bonnie Camp, Robbie Case, Anik de Ribaupierre, Nira Granott, Jane Haltiwanger, Rebecca Hencke, Catherine Knight, Erma Larson, Peter Molenaar, Eagle Moon, Gil Noam, Pamela Raya, Samuel Rose, Phillip Shaver, Robert Thatcher, Han van der Maas, Paul van Geert, and John Willett for their contributions to our development of the arguments and evidence presented herein. This chapter is dedicated to the memory of the late Samuel Priest Rose.

REFERENCES

Agnoli, F., Kirson, D., Wu, S., & Shaver, P. (1989). *Hierarchical analysis of the emotion lexicon in English, Italian, and Chinese.* Paper presented at the annual conference of the International Society for Research on Emotion. Paris, France.

Ainsworth, M. D., Blehar, M., Waters, E., & Wall, S. (1978). *Patterns of attachment: A psychological study of the Strange Situation.* Hillsdale, NJ: Erlbaum.

Allport, F. H. (1961). The contemporary appraisal of an old problem. *Contemporary Psychology, 6,* 195–197.

Atkinson, R. C., & Shiffrin, R. M. (1968). Human memory: A proposed system and its control processes. In K. W. Spence & J. T. Spence (Eds.), *The psychology of learning and motivation: Advances in research and theory* (Vol. 2, pp. 90–195). New York: Academic Press.

Averill, J. R. (1980). A constructivist view of emotion. In R. Plutchik & H. Kellerman (Eds.), *Emotion: Theory, research, and experience* (Vol. 1, pp. 305–340). New York: Academic Press.

Baillargeon, R. (1987). Object permanence in 3½- and 4½-month-old infants. *Developmental Psychology, 23,* 655–664.

Baillargeon, R., Spelke, E. S., & Wasserman, S. (1985). Object permanence in five-month-old infants. *Cognition, 20,* 191–208.

Bandura, A. (1977). *Social learning theory.* Englewood Cliffs, NJ: Prentice-Hall.

Barrett, K. C. (1995). A functionalist approach to shame and guilt. In J. P. Tangney & K. W. Fischer (Eds.), *Self-conscious emotions: The psychology of shame, guilt, embarrassment, and pride* (pp. 25–63). New York: Guilford Press.

Barrett, K. C., & Campos, J. J. (1987). Perspectives on emotional development: II. A functionalist approach to emotions. In J. Osofsky (Ed.), *Handbook of infant development* (2nd ed., pp. 555–578). New York: Wiley.

Barriga, A. Q., & Gibbs, J. C. (in press). Measuring cognitive distortion in antisocial youth: Development and preliminary validation of the How I Think questionnaire. *Aggressive Behavior, 22.*

Beilin, H. (1983). The new functionalism and Piaget's program. In E. K. Scholnick (Ed.), *New trends in conceptual representation: Challenges to Piaget's theory?* (pp. 3–40). Hillsdale, NJ: Erlbaum.

Beilin, H. (1992). Piaget's new theory. In H. Beilin & P. Pufall (Eds.), *Piaget's theory: Prospects and possibilities* (pp. 1–17). Hillsdale, NJ: Erlbaum.

Bell, M. A., & Fox, N. A. (1992). The relations between frontal brain electrical activity and cognitive development during infancy. *Child Development, 63,* 1142–1163.

Bell, M. A., & Fox, N. A. (1994). Brain development over the first year of life: Relations between EEG frequency and coherence and cognitive and affective behaviors. In G. Dawson & K. W. Fischer (Eds.), *Human behavior and the developing brain* (pp. 314–345). New York: Guilford Press.

Bell, M. A., & Fox, N. A. (in press). Crawling experience is related to changes in cortical organization during infancy: Evidence from EEG coherence. *Developmental Psychology.*

Benedict, R. (1946). *The chrysanthemum and the sword.* Boston: Houghton Mifflin.

Benes, F. (1994). Development of the corticolimbic system. In G. Dawson & K. W. Fischer (Eds.), *Human behavior and the developing brain* (pp. 176–206). New York: Guilford Press.

Bever, T. G. (Ed.). (1982). *Regressions in mental development: Basic phenomena and theories.* Hillsdale, NJ: Erlbaum.

Bidell, T. R. (1990). *Mechanisms of cognitive development in problem solving: A structural integration approach.* Unpublished doctoral dissertation, Harvard University, Cambridge, MA.

Bidell, T. R., & Fischer, K. W. (1992a). Beyond the stage debate: Action, structure, and variability in Piagetian theory and research. In R. Sternberg & C. Berg (Eds.), *Intellectual development* (pp. 100–140). New York: Cambridge University Press.

Bidell, T. R., & Fischer, K. W. (1992b). Cognitive development in educational contexts: Implications of skill theory. In A. Demetriou, M. Shayer, & A. Efklides (Eds.), *Neo-Piagetian theories of cognitive development: Implications and applications for education* (pp. 9–30). London: Routledge & Kegan Paul.

Bidell, T. R., & Fischer, K. W. (1994). Developmental transitions in children's early on-line planning. In M. M. Haith, J. B. Benson, R. J. Roberts, Jr., & B. F. Pennington (Eds.), *The development of future-oriented processes* (pp. 141–176). Chicago: University of Chicago Press.

Bidell, T. R., & Fischer, K. W. (1996). Between nature and nurture: The role of human agency in the epigenesis of intelligence. In R. Sternberg & E. Grigorenko (Eds.), *Intelligence: Heredity and environment* (pp. 193–242). Cambridge, England: Cambridge University Press.

Biggs, J., & Collis, K. (1982). *Evaluating the quality of learning: The SOLO taxonomy (structure of the observed learning outcome).* New York: Academic Press.

Block, J. (1971). *Lives through time.* Berkeley, CA: Bancroft Books.

Block, J. (1993). Studying personality the long way. In D. C. Funder, R. D. Parke, C. Tomlinson-Keasey, & K. Widaman (Eds.), *Studying lives through time: Personality and development* (pp. 9–41). Washington, DC: American Psychological Association.

Block, J. H., & Block, J. (1980). The role of ego-control and ego-resiliency in the organization of behavior. In W. A. Collins (Ed.), *Minnesota Symposium on Child Psychology* (Vol. 13, pp. 39–101). Hillsdale, NJ: Erlbaum.

Bond, T. (1995). Piaget and measurement: I. The twain really do meet. *Archives de Psychologie, 63,* 71–87.

Bourgeois, J.-P., Goldman-Rakic, P. S., & Rakic, P. (1994). Synaptogenesis in the prefrontal cortex of rhesus monkeys. *Cerebral Cortex, 4,* 78–96.

Bourgeois, J.-P., & Rakic, P. (1993). Changes of synaptic density in the primary visual cortex of the macaque monkey from fetal to adult stage. *Journal of Neuroscience, 13,* 2801–2820.

Brainerd, C. J. (1978). The stage question in cognitive-developmental theory. *Behavioral and Brain Sciences, 1,* 173–182.

Brainerd, C. J. (1993). Cognitive development is abrupt (but not stage-like). In H. Thomas & A. Lohaus (Eds.), Modeling growth and individual differences in spatial tasks. *Monographs of the Society for Research in Child Development, 58*(9, Serial No. 237), 170–190.

Bretherton, I. (1996). Internal working models of attachment relationships as related to resilient coping. In G. G. Noam & K. W. Fischer (Eds.), *Development and vulnerability in close relationships* (pp. 3–27). Hillsdale, NJ: Erlbaum.

Bretherton, I., & Beeghly, M. (1982). Talking about internal states: The acquisition of an explicit theory of mind. *Developmental Psychology, 18,* 906–912.

Breuer, J., & Freud, S. (1955). *Studies on hysteria* (A. Strachey & J. Strachey, Trans.) (Vol. 2). London: Hogarth Press. (Original work published 1895)

Bronfenbrenner, U. (1979). *The ecology of human development: Experiments by nature and design.* Cambridge, MA: Harvard University Press.

Bronfenbrenner, U. (1993). The ecology of cognitive development: Research models and fugitive findings. In R. H. Wozniak & K. W. Fischer (Eds.), *Development in context: Acting and thinking in specific environments* (pp. 3–44). Hillsdale, NJ: Erlbaum.

Brown, A. L., & Campione, J. C. (1990). Communities of learning and thinking, or a context by any other name. In D. Kuhn (Ed.), Developmental perspectives on teaching and learning thinking skills. *Contributions to Human Development, 21*(4), 108–126.

Brown, A. L., & Reeve, R. (1987). Bandwidths of competence: The role of supportive contexts in learning and development. In L. S. Liben (Ed.), *Development and learning: Conflict or congruence?* (pp. 173–223). Hillsdale, NJ: Erlbaum.

Brown, T. (1994). Affective dimensions of meaning. In W. T. Overton & D. S. Palermo (Eds.), *The nature and ontogenesis of meaning* (pp. 167–190). Hillsdale, NJ: Erlbaum.

Bruner, J. S. (1973a). *Beyond the information given: Studies in the psychology of knowing.* New York: Norton.

Bruner, J. S. (1973b). Organization of early skilled action. *Child Development, 44,* 1–11.

Bruner, J. S. (1990). *Acts of meaning.* Cambridge, MA: Harvard University Press.

Bruner, J. S., Goodnow, J. J., & Austin, G. (1956). *A study of thinking.* New York: Wiley.

Bryant, P. E., & Trabasso, T. (1971). Transitive inferences and memory in young children. *Nature, 232,* 78–96.

Buchsbaum, H. K., Toth, S. L., Clyman, R. B., Cicchetti, D., & Emde, R. N. (1992). The use of a narrative story stem technique with maltreated children: Implications for theory and practice. *Development and Psychopathology, 4,* 603–625.

Bullock, D., & Grossberg, S. (1988). Neural dynamics of planned arm movements: Emergent invariants and speed-accuracy properties during trajectory formation. *Psychological Review, 95,* 49–90.

Bullock, D., Grossberg, S., & Guenther, F. H. (1993). A self-organizing neural model of motor equivalent reaching and tool use by a multijoint arm. *Journal of Cognitive Neuroscience, 5,* 408–435.

Bullock, M., & Ziegler, A. (1994). *Scientific reasoning* (Research Report). Munich: Max Planck Institute for Psychological Research.

Cairns, R. B. (1979). *Social development: The origins and plasticity of interchanges.* San Francisco: Freeman.

Calverley, R. (1995). *Self-representation and self-understanding in sexually abused adolescent girls.* Unpublished doctoral dissertation, Harvard University, Cambridge, MA

Calverley, R., Fischer, K. W., & Ayoub, C. (1994). Complex splitting of self-representations in sexually abused adolescent girls. *Development and Psychopathology, 6,* 195–213.

Campbell, D. T., & Stanley, J. C. (1963). *Experimental and quasi-experimental designs for research.* Chicago: Rand McNally.

Campos, J. J., Barrett, K. C., Lamb, M. E., Goldsmith, H. H., & Stenberg, C. (1983). Socioemotional development. In P. H. Mussen (Series Ed.) & M. M. Haith & J. J. Campos (Vol. Eds.), *Handbook of child psychology: Vol. 2. Infancy and developmental psychobiology* (pp. 783–915). New York: Wiley.

Campos, J. J., & Bertenthal, B. I. (1987). Locomotion and psychological development in infancy. In F. Morrison, K. Lord, & D. Keating (Eds.), *Advances in applied developmental psychology* (Vol. 2, pp. 11–42). New York: Academic Press.

Camras, L. A. (1992). Expressive development and basic emotions. *Cognition and Emotion, 6,* 269–284.

Canadian Broadcasting Corporation. (1990). *To a safer place.*

Carey, S. (1985). *Conceptual change in childhood.* Cambridge, MA: MIT Press.

Carey, S., & Gelman, R. (Eds.). (1991). *The epigenesis of mind: Essays on biology and knowledge.* Hillsdale, NJ: Erlbaum.

Case, R. (1985). *Intellectual development: Birth to adulthood.* New York: Academic Press.

Case, R. (1991a). A developmental approach to the design of remedial instruction. In A. McKeough & J. Lupert (Eds.), *Toward the practice of theory-based instruction* (pp. 117–147). Hillsdale, NJ: Erlbaum.

Case, R. (Ed.). (1991b). *The mind's staircase: Exploring the conceptual underpinnings of children's thought and knowledge.* Hillsdale, NJ: Erlbaum.

Case, R. (1992). The role of the frontal lobes in the regulation of human development. *Brain and Cognition, 20,* 51–73.

Case, R. (1996). The role of psychological defenses in the representation and regulation of close personal relationships across the lifespan. In G. G. Noam & K. W. Fischer (Eds.), *Development and vulnerability in close relationships* (pp. 59–88). Hillsdale, NJ: Erlbaum.

Case, R., & Edelstein, W. (Eds.). (1993). The new structuralism in cognitive development: Theory and research on individual pathways. *Contributions to Human Development, 23.*

Case, R., & Okamoto, Y. (with Griffin, S., McKeough, A., Bleiker, C., Henderson, B., & Stephenson, K. M.). (1996). The role of central conceptual structures in the development of children's thought. *Monographs of the Society for Research in Child Development, 60*(5/6, Serial No. 246).

Chandler, M. (1994). Adolescent suicide and the loss of personal continuity. In D. Cicchetti & S. L. Toth (Eds.), *Disorders and dysfunctions of the self* (Vol. 5, pp. 371–390). Rochester, NY: University of Rochester.

Chapman, M. (1988). *Constructive evolution.* New York: Cambridge University Press.

Chomsky, N. (1959). [Review of the book *Verbal behavior* by B. F. Skinner]. *Language, 35,* 26–58.

Chomsky, N. (1965). *Aspects of the theory of syntax.* Cambridge, MA: MIT Press.

Chomsky, N. (1986). *Knowledge of language: Its nature, origin, and use.* Westport, CT: Praeger.

Chugani, H. T., & Phelps, M. E. (1986). Maturational changes in cerebral function in infants determined by ^{18}FDG Positron Emission Tomography. *Science, 231,* 840–843.

Chugani, H. T., Phelps, M. E., & Mazziotta, J. C. (1987). Positron emission tomography study of human brain functional development. *Annals of Neurology, 22,* 487–497.

Cicchetti, D. (1990). The organization and coherence of socioemotional, cognitive, and representational development: Illustrations through a developmental psychopathology perspective on Down syndrome and child maltreatment. In R. Thompson & R. A. Dienstbier (Eds.), *Nebraska Symposium on Motivation: Vol. 36. Socioemotional development* (pp. 259–366). Lincoln: University of Nebraska Press.

Clark, K. B., & Clark, M. K. (1939). The development of consciousness of self and the emergence of racial identification in Negro preschool children. *Journal of Social Psychology, 10,* 591–599.

Clark, K. B., & Clark, M. K. (1958). Racial identification and preference in Negro children. In E. E. Maccoby, T. M. Newcomb, & E. L. Hartley (Eds.), *Readings in social psychology* (3rd ed., pp. 602–611). New York: Holt.

Colby, A., Kohlberg, L., Gibbs, J., & Lieberman, M. (1983). A longitudinal study of moral judgement. *Monographs of the Society for Research in Child Development, 48*(1, Serial No. 200).

Cole, P. M., & Putnam, F. W. (1992). Effect of incest on self and social functioning: A developmental psychopathology perspective. *Journal of Consulting and Clinical Psychology, 60,* 174–184.

Cook-Gumperz, J., & Gumperz, J. (1982). Communicative competence in educational perspective. In L. C. Wilkinson (Ed.), *Communicating in the classroom.* New York: Academic Press.

Cooney, J. B., & Troyer, R. (1994). A dynamic model of reaction time in a short-term memory task. *Journal of Experimental Child Psychology, 58,* 200–226.

Corrigan, R. (1983). The development of representational skills. In K. W. Fischer (Ed.), *Levels and transitions in children's development. New Directions for Child Development* (Vol. 21, pp. 51–64). San Francisco: Jossey-Bass.

Crittenden, P. M. (1994). Peering into the black box: An exploratory treatise on the development of self in young children. In D. Cicchetti & S. L. Toth (Eds.), *Rochester Symposium on Development and Psychopathology: Vol. 5. Disorders and dysfunctions of the self* (pp. 79–148). Rochester, NY: University of Rochester Press.

Daiute, C., & Griffin, T. (1993). The social construction of written narratives. In C. Daiute (Ed.), *The development of literacy through social interaction. New Directions for Child Development* (Vol. 61, pp. 97–120). San Francisco: Jossey-Bass.

Damasio, A. R. (1994). *Descartes' error.* New York: Grosset/ Putnam.

Damon, W. (1989). Introduction: Advances in developmental research. In W. Damon (Ed.), *Child development today and tomorrow* (pp. 1–13). San Francisco: Jossey-Bass.

Davidson, R. J. (1992). Prologomena to the structure of emotion: Gleanings from neuropsychology. *Cognition and Emotion, 6,* 245–268.

Demetriou, A., Efklides, A., & Platsidou, M. (1993). The architecture and dynamics of developing mind: Experiential structuralism as a frame for unifying cognitive developmental theories. *Monographs of the Society for Research in Child Development, 58*(6, Serial No. 234).

de Ribaupierre, A. (1989a). Operational development and cognitive style: A review of French literature and a neo-Piagetian interpretation. In T. Globerson & T. Zelniker (Eds.), *Cognitive style and cognitive development* (pp. 86–115). Norwood, NJ: ABLEX.

de Ribaupierre, A. (Ed.). (1989b). *Transition mechanisms in child development.* New York: Cambridge University Press.

de Ribaupierre, A. (1993). Structural invariants and individual differences: On the difficulty of dissociating developmental and differential processes. In W. Edelstein & R. Case (Eds.), Constructivist approaches to development. *Contributions to Human Development, 23,* 11–32.

de Rivera, J. (1981). The structure of anger. In J. de Rivera (Ed.), *Conceptual encounter: A method for the exploration of human experience* (pp. 35–81). Washington, DC: University Press of America.

Diamond, A. (1985). Development of the ability to use recall to guide action, as indicated by infants' performance on AB. *Child Development, 56,* 868–883.

Diamond, A. (1991). Neuropsychological insights into the meaning of object concept development. In S. Carey & R. Gelman (Eds.), *The epigenesis of mind* (pp. 67–110). Hillsdale, NJ: Erlbaum.

Digman, J. M. (1990). Personality structure: Emergence of the five-factor model. *Annual Review of Psychology, 41,* 417–440.

Dodwell, P. C. (1960). Children's understanding of number and related concepts. *Canadian Journal of Psychology, 14,* 191–205.

Donaldson, M. (1978). *Children's minds.* New York: Norton.

Dreyfus-Brisac, C. (1979). Ontogenesis of brain bioelectrical activity and sleep organization in neonates and infants. In F. Falkner & J. M. Tanner (Eds.), *Human growth: Vol. 3. Neurobiology and nutrition* (pp. 157–182). New York: Plenum Press.

Duckworth, E. (1979). Either we're too early and they can't learn it, or we're too late and they know it already: The dilemma of "applying Piaget." *Harvard Educational Review, 49,* 297–312.

Duncker, K. (1945). On problem solving. *Psychological Monographs, 58*(Whole No. 270).

Dustman, R. E., & Beck, E. C. (1969). The effects of maturation and aging on the waveform of visually evoked potentials. *Electroencephalography and Clinical Neurophysiology, 265,* 2–11.

Edwards, C. P. (1984). The age group labels and categories of preschool children. *Child Development, 55,* 440–452.

Ekman, P., Friesen, W. V., O'Sullivan, M., Chan, A., Diacoyanni-Tarlatis, I., Heider, K., Krause, R., LeCompte, W. A., Pitcairn, T., Ricci-Bitti, P. E., Scherer, K., Tomita, M., & Tzavaras, A. (1987). Universals and cultural differences in the judgments of facial expressions of emotion. *Journal of Personality and Social Psychology, 53,* 712–717.

Emde, R., Gaensbauer, T., & Harmon, R. (1976). Emotional expression in infancy: A biobehavioral study. *Psychological Issues, 10*(37).

Emde, R., Plomin, R., Robinson, J., Corley, R., DeFries, J., Fulker, D. W., Reznick, J. S., Campos, J., Kagan, J., & Zahn-Waxler, C. (1992). Temperament, emotion, and cognition at fourteen months: The MacArthur Longitudinal Twin Study. *Child Development, 63,* 1437–1455.

Erdelyi, M. H. (1985). *Psychoanalysis: Freud's cognitive psychology.* New York: Freeman.

Ericsson, K. A., & Charness, N. (1994). Expert performance: Its structure and acquisition. *American Psychologist, 49,* 725–747.

Erikson, E. (1963). *Childhood and society* (2nd ed.). New York: Norton.

Estes, W. K. (1955). Statistical theory of spontaneous recovery and regression. *Psychological Review, 62,* 145–154.

Fagan, J., & McMahon, P. P. (1984). Incipient multiple personality in children: Four cases. *Journal of Nervous and Mental Disease, 172,* 26–36.

Famularo, R., Fenton, T., Kinscherff, R., Ayoub, C., & Barnum, R. (1994). Maternal and child posttraumatic stress disorder in cases of child maltreatment. *Child Abuse and Neglect, 18,* 27–36.

Feffer, M. (1982). *The structure of Freudian thought.* New York: International Universities Press.

Fehr, B., & Russell, J. A. (1984). Concept of emotion viewed from a prototype perspective. *Journal of Experimental Psychology: General, 113,* 464–486.

Feldman, D. H. (1980). *Beyond universals in cognitive development.* Norwood, NJ: ABLEX.

Fink, R. (1995). Successful dyslexics: A constructivist study of passionate interest reading. *Journal of Adolescent and Adult Literacy, 39,* 268–280.

Fischer, K. W. (1980). A theory of cognitive development: The control and construction of hierarchies of skills. *Psychological Review, 87,* 477–531.

Fischer, K. W. (1983). Illuminating the processes of moral development: A commentary. In A. Colby, L. Kohlberg, J. Gibbs, & M. Lieberman (Eds.), A longitudinal study of moral judgment.

Monographs of the Society for Research in Child Development, 48(1, Serial No. 200), 97–107.

Fischer, K. W. (1987). Relations between brain and cognitive development. *Child Development, 57,* 623–632.

Fischer, K. W., & Ayoub, C. (1994). Affective splitting and dissociation in normal and maltreated children: Developmental pathways for self in relationships. In D. Cicchetti & S. L. Toth (Eds.), *Rochester Symposium on Development and Psychopathology: Vol. 5. Disorders and dysfunctions of the self* (pp. 149–222). Rochester, NY: University of Rochester Press.

Fischer, K. W., & Ayoub, C. (1996). Analyzing development of working models of close relationships: Illustration with a case of vulnerability and violence. In G. G. Noam & K. W. Fischer (Eds.), *Development and vulnerability in close relationships* (pp. 173–199). Hillsdale, NJ: Erlbaum.

Fischer, K. W., Ayoub, C. C., Singh, I., Noam, G. G., & Maraganore, N. (in press). Psychopathology as adaptive development along distinctive pathways. *Development and Psychopathology.*

Fischer, K. W., & Bidell, T. R. (1991). Constraining nativist inferences about cognitive capacities. In S. Carey & R. Gelman (Eds.), *The epigenesis of mind: Essays on biology and knowledge* (pp. 199–235). Hillsdale, NJ: Erlbaum.

Fischer, K. W., & Bullock, D. (1981). Patterns of data: Sequence, synchrony, and constraint in cognitive development. In K. W. Fischer (Ed.), *Cognitive development. New Directions for Child Development* (Vol. 12, pp. 69–78). San Francisco: Jossey-Bass.

Fischer, K. W., & Bullock, D. (1984). Cognitive development in school-age children: Conclusions and new directions. In W. A. Collins (Ed.), *Development during middle childhood: The years from six to twelve* (pp. 70–146). Washington, DC: National Academy Press.

Fischer, K. W., Bullock, D., Rotenberg, E. J., & Raya, P. (1993). The dynamics of competence: How context contributes directly to skill. In R. H. Wozniak & K. W. Fischer (Eds.), *Development in context: Acting and thinking in specific environments* (pp. 93–117). Hillsdale, NJ: Erlbaum.

Fischer, K. W., & Farrar, M. J. (1987). Generalizations about generalization: How a theory of skill development explains both generality and specificity. *International Journal of Psychology, 22,* 643–677.

Fischer, K. W., & Granott, N. (1995). Beyond one-dimensional change: Parallel, concurrent, socially distributed processes in learning and development. *Human Development, 38,* 302–314.

Fischer, K. W., & Hogan, A. (1989). The big picture for infant development: Levels and variations. In J. Lockman &

N. Hazen (Eds.), *Action in social context: Perspectives on early development* (pp. 275–305). New York: Plenum Press.

Fischer, K. W., & Kennedy, B. (1997). Tools for analyzing the many shapes of development: The case of self-in-relationships in Korea. In K. A. Renninger & E. Amsel (Eds.), *Processes of development* (pp. 117–152). Mahwah, NJ: Erlbaum.

Fischer, K. W., & Kenny, S. L. (1986). The environmental conditions for discontinuities in the development of abstractions. In R. Mines & K. Kitchener (Eds.), *Adult cognitive development: Methods and models* (pp. 57–75). New York: Praeger.

Fischer, K. W., Knight, C. C., & Van Parys, M. (1993). Analyzing diversity in developmental pathways: Methods and concepts. In W. Edelstein & R. Case (Eds.), Constructivist approaches to development. *Contributions to Human Development, 23*, 33–56.

Fischer, K. W., & Pipp, S. L. (1984). Development of the structures of unconscious thought. In K. Bowers & D. Meichenbaum (Eds.), *The unconscious reconsidered* (pp. 88–148). New York: Wiley.

Fischer, K. W., Pipp, S. L., & Bullock, D. (1984). Detecting discontinuities in development: Method and measurement. In R. Emde & R. Harmon (Eds.), *Continuities and discontinuities in development* (pp. 95–121). New York: Plenum Press.

Fischer, K. W., & Rose, S. P. (1994). Dynamic development of coordination of components in brain and behavior: A framework for theory and research. In G. Dawson & K. W. Fischer (Eds.), *Human behavior and the developing brain* (pp. 3–66). New York: Guilford Press.

Fischer, K. W., & Rose, S. P. (1996). Dynamic growth cycles of brain and cognitive development. In R. Thatcher, G. R. Lyon, J. Rumsey, & N. Krasnegor (Eds.), *Developmental neuroimaging: Mapping the development of brain and behavior.* New York: Academic Press.

Fischer, K. W., Shaver, P., & Carnochan, P. G. (1990). How emotions develop and how they organize development. *Cognition and Emotion, 4*, 81–127.

Fischer, K. W., & Silvern, L. (1985). Stages and individual differences in cognitive development. *Annual Review of Psychology, 36*, 613–648.

Fischer, K. W., & Tangney, J. P. (1995). Self-conscious emotions and the affect revolution: Framework and overview. In J. P. Tangney & K. W. Fischer (Eds.), *Self-conscious emotions: The psychology of shame, guilt, embarrassment, and pride* (pp. 3–22). New York: Guilford Press.

Fischer, K. W., & Watson, M. W. (1981). Explaining the Oedipus conflict. In K. W. Fischer (Ed.), *Cognitive development. New Directions for Child Development* (Vol. 12, pp. 79–92). San Francisco: Jossey-Bass.

Fivush, R., & Hudson, J. (Eds.). (1990). *Knowing and remembering in young children.* Cambridge, England: Cambridge University Press.

Flavell, J. H. (1971). Stage-related properties of cognitive development. *Cognitive Psychology, 2*, 421–453.

Flavell, J. H. (1982). On cognitive development. *Child Development, 53*, 1–10.

Flavell, J. H., & Wohlwill, J. F. (1969). Formal and functional aspects of cognitive development. In D. Elkind & J. H. Flavell (Eds.), *Studies in cognitive development* (pp. 67–120). London: Oxford University Press.

Fleishman, E. A. (1975). Toward a taxonomy of human performance. *American Psychologist, 30*, 1127–1149.

Fodor, J. A. (1975). *The language of thought.* New York: Crowell.

Fodor, J. A. (1983). *The modularity of mind: An essay on faculty psychology.* Cambridge, MA: MIT Press.

Fogel, A. (1993). *Developing through relationships: Origins of communication, self, and culture.* Chicago: University of Chicago Press.

Foulkes, D. (1982). *Children's dreams: Longitudinal studies.* New York: Wiley.

Fox, N. A., Kimmerly, N., & Schafer, W. (1991). Attachment to mother/attachment to father: A meta-analysis. *Child Development, 62*, 210–225.

Freud, A. (1966). *The ego and the mechanisms of defense* (C. Baines, Trans.). New York: International Universities Press. (Original work published 1936)

Freud, S. (1955). *Analysis of a phobia in a five-year-old boy* (J. A. Strachey, Trans.). In *Standard edition of the complete psychological works of Sigmund Freud* (Vol. 10, pp. 3–152). London: Hogarth Press. (Original work published 1909)

Frijda, N. H. (1986). *The emotions.* Cambridge, England: Cambridge University Press.

Garcia, R. (1992). The structure of knowledge and the knowledge of structure. In H. Beilin & P. B. Pufall (Eds.), *Piaget's theory: Prospects and possibilities* (pp. 21–38). Hillsdale, NJ: Erlbaum.

Gardner, H. (1983). *Frames of mind: The theory of multiple intelligences.* New York: Basic Books.

Gardner, H. (1985). *The mind's new science: A history of the cognitive revolution.* New York: Basic Books.

Gauvain, M. (1995). Thinking in niches: Sociocultural influences on cognitive development. *Human Development, 38*, 25–45.

Geertz, C. (1973). *The interpretation of cultures.* New York: Basic Books.

Gelman, R. (1972). Logical capacity of very young children: Number invariance rules. *Child Development, 43,* 75–90.

Gelman, R., & Baillargeon, R. (1983). A review of some Piagetian concepts. In P. H. Mussen (Series Ed.) & J. H. Flavell & E. M. Markman (Eds.), *Handbook of child psychology: Vol. 3. Cognitive development* (pp. 167–230). New York: Wiley.

Gelman, R., & Gallistel, C. R. (1978). *The child's understanding of number.* Cambridge, MA: Harvard University Press.

Gesell, A. (1946). The ontogenesis of infant behavior. In L. Carmichael (Ed.), *Manual of child psychology.* New York: Wiley.

Gibson, J. J. (1979). *The ecological approach to visual perception.* Boston: Houghton Mifflin.

Gilligan, C. (1982). *In a different voice: Psychological theory and women's development.* Cambridge, MA: Harvard University Press.

Gleick, J. (1987). *Chaos: Making a new science.* New York: Penguin Books.

Goldfield, E. C. (1995). *Emergent forms: Origins and early development of human action and perception.* Oxford, England: Oxford University Press.

Goldin-Meadow, S., Alibali, M., & Church, R. B. (1993). Transitions in concept acquisition: Using the hand to read the mind. *Psychological Review, 100,* 279–297.

Goldin-Meadow, S., Nusbaum, H., Garber, P., & Church, R. B. (1993). Transitions in learning: Evidence for simultaneously activated rules. *Journal of Experimental Psychology: Human Perception and Performance, 19,* 92–107.

Goldman-Rakic, P. S. (1986). Circuitry of the prefrontal cortex and the regulation of behavior by representational knowledge. In F. Plum & V. Mountcastle (Eds.), *Handbook of physiology* (pp. 373–417). Bethesda, MD: American Physiological Society.

Goldman-Rakic, P. S. (1987). Connectionist theory and the biological basis of cognitive development. *Child Development, 58,* 601–622.

Goodman, G. S., Quas, J. A., Batterman-Faunce, J. M., Riddlesberger, M. M., & Kuhn, J. (1994). Predictors of accurate and inaccurate memories of traumatic events experienced in childhood. *Consciousness and Cognition, 3,* 269–294.

Goodwin, B. (1994). *How the leopard changed its spots: The evolution of complexity.* New York: Charles Scribner's Sons.

Gottlieb, G. (1992). *Individual development and evolution: The genesis of novel behavior.* New York: Oxford University Press.

Gottlieb, G. (1995). Some conceptual deficiencies in "developmental" behavior genetics. *Human Development, 38,* 131–141.

Granott, N. (1993a). *Microdevelopment of coconstruction of knowledge during problem-solving: Puzzled minds, weird creatures, and wuggles.* Unpublished doctoral dissertation, MIT, Cambridge, MA.

Granott, N. (1993b). Patterns of interaction in the coconstruction of knowledge: Separate minds, joint effort, and weird creatures. In R. H. Wozniak & K. W. Fischer (Eds.), *Development in context: Acting and thinking in specific environments* (pp. 183–207). Hillsdale, NJ: Erlbaum.

Granott, N., Fischer, K. W., & Parziale, J. (1997). *Bridging to the unknown: A fundamental transition mechanism in learning and problem-solving* (Cognitive Development Laboratory Research Report). Cambridge, MA: Harvard University.

Greenberg, M., Cicchetti, D., & Cummings, E. M. (Eds.). (1990). *Attachment in the preschool years: Theory, research, and intervention.* Chicago: University of Chicago Press.

Greenfield, P. M. (1991). Language, tools, and brain: The ontogeny and phylogeny of hierarchically organized sequential behavior. *Behavioral and Brain Sciences, 14,* 531–551.

Greeno, J. G., Riley, M. S., & Gelman, R. (1984). Conceptual competence and children's counting. *Cognitive Psychology, 16,* 94–143.

Greenwald, A. G. (1980). The totalitarian ego: Fabrication and revision of personal history. *American Psychologist, 35,* 603–618.

Grossberg, S. (1987). Competitive learning: From interactive activation to adaptive resonance. *Cognitive Science, 11,* 23–63.

Grossberg, S. (1988). Nonlinear neural networks: Principles, mechanisms, and architectures. *Neural Networks, 1,* 17–61.

Guttman, L. (1944). A basis for scaling qualitative data. *American Sociological Review, 9,* 139–150.

Haan, N. (1977). *Coping and defending.* New York: Academic Press.

Hagne, I., Persson, J., Magnusson, R., & Petersén, I. (1973). Spectral analysis via fast Fourier transform of waking EEG in normal infants. In P. Kellaway & I. Petersén (Eds.), *Automation of clinical electroencephalography* (pp. 103–143). New York: Raven Press.

Haith, M. M., Bergman, T., & Moore, M. J. (1977). Eye contact and face scanning in early infancy. *Science, 198,* 853–855.

Halford, G. S. (1982). *The development of thought.* Hillsdale, NJ: Erlbaum.

Halford, G. S. (1989). Reflections on 25 years of Piagetian cognitive developmental psychology, 1963–1988. *Human Development, 32,* 325–357.

Halford, G. S., & Boyle, F. M. (1985). Do young children understand conservation of number? *Child Development, 56,* 165–176.

Hall, G. S. (1904). *Adolescence: Its psychology and its relations to physiology, anthropology, sociology, sex, crime, religion, and education* (2 vols.). New York: Appleton.

Hand, H. H. (1982). The development of concepts of social interaction: Children's understanding of nice and mean. *Dissertation Abstracts International, 42*(11), 4578B.

Hanson, N. R. (1961). *Patterns of discovery.* Cambridge, England: Cambridge University Press.

Harré, R. (Ed.) (1986). *The social construction of emotions.* Oxford, England: Basil Blackwell.

Harter, S. (1995). The effects of child abuse on the self-system. In B. B. R. Rossman & M. S. Rosenberg (Eds.), *Multiple victimization of children: Conceptual, developmental, research, and treatment issues.* New York: Haworth Press.

Harter, S., & Buddin, B. (1987). Children's understanding of the simultaneity of two emotions: A five-stage developmental sequence. *Developmental Psychology, 23,* 388–399.

Harter, S., & Marold, D. B. (1994). The directionality of the link between self-esteem and affect: Beyond causal modeling. In D. Cicchetti & S. L. Toth (Eds.), *Rochester Symposium on Development and Psychopathology: Vol. 5. Disorders and dysfunctions of the self* (pp. 333–370). Rochester, NY: University of Rochester.

Harter, S., & Monsour, A. (1992). Developmental analysis of conflict caused by opposing attributes in the adolescent self-portrait. *Developmental Psychology, 28,* 251–260.

Hartley, D., & Thomas, D. G. (1993). *Brain electrical activity changes and cognitive development.* Paper presented at the meetings of the Society for Research in Child Development, New Orleans, LA.

Heider, K. (1991). *Landscapes of emotion: Mapping three cultures of emotion in Indonesia.* New York: Cambridge University Press.

Hencke, R. W. (1996). *Self stories: Effects of children's emotional styles on their appropriation of self-schemata.* Unpublished doctoral dissertation, Harvard University, Cambridge, MA.

Herman, J. (1992). *Trauma and recovery.* New York: Basic Books.

Hicks, D. (1995). Discourse, learning, and teaching. *Review of Research in Education, 21,* 49–95.

Higgins, E. T. (1996). Knowledge activation: Accessibility, applicability, and salience. In E. T. Higgins & A. W. Kruglanski (Eds.), *Social psychology: Handbook of basic principles* (pp. 133–168). New York: Guilford Press.

Higgins, E. T., Roney, C., Crowe, E., & Hymes, C. (1994). Ideal versus ought predilections for approach and avoidance: Distinct self-regulatory systems. *Journal of Personality and Social Psychology, 66,* 276–286.

Hilgard, E. R. (1977). *Divided consciousness.* New York: Wiley.

Hofmann, R. (1996). *A Guttman scale with branching.* Paper presented at the Symposium of the Jean Piaget Society: Society for the Study of Knowledge and Development, Chicago.

Holland, J. H. (1992). Genetic algorithms. *Scientific American, 266*(7), 44–50.

Horn, J. L. (1982). The theory of fluid and crystallized intelligence in relation to concepts of cognitive psychology and aging in adulthood. In F. I. M. Craik & S. E. Trehub (Eds.), *Aging and cognitive processes* (pp. 237–278). New York: Plenum Press.

Horn, J. L., & Hofer, S. M. (1992). Major abilities and development in the adult period. In R. J. Sternberg & C. A. Berg (Eds.), *Intellectual development* (pp. 44–99). Cambridge, England: Cambridge University Press.

Horowitz, M. J. (1987). *States of mind: Analysis of change in psychotherapy* (2nd ed.). New York: Plenum Press.

Howe, M. L., & Rabinowitz, F. M. (1994). Dynamic modeling, chaos, and cognitive development. *Journal of Experimental Child Psychology, 58,* 184–199.

Hubel, D. H., & Wiesel, T. N. (1977). Functional architecture of macaque monkey visual cortex. *Proceedings of the Royal Society, London, Series B, 193,* 1–59.

Hudspeth, W. J., & Pribram, K. H. (1992). Psychophysiological indices of cerebral maturation. *International Journal of Psychophysiology, 12,* 19–29.

Hull, C. L. (1952). *A behavior system.* New Haven, CT: Yale University Press.

Hume, D. (1955). *An inquiry concerning human understanding.* New York: Liberal Arts Press.

Huttenlocher, P. (1994). Synaptogenesis in human cerebral cortex. In G. Dawson & K. W. Fischer (Eds.), *Human behavior and the developing brain* (pp. 137–152). New York: Guilford Press.

Inhelder, B., & Piaget, J. (1958). *The growth of logical thinking from childhood to adolescence* (A. Parsons & S. Seagrim, Trans.). New York: Basic Books. (Original work published 1955)

Inhelder, B., & Piaget, J. (1964). *The early growth of logic in the child* (G. A. Lunzer & D. Papert, Trans.). New York: Harper & Row. (Original work published 1959)

Inhelder, B., Sinclair, H., & Bovet, M. (1974). *Learning and the development of cognition.* Cambridge, MA: Harvard University Press.

Izard, C. E. (1977). *Human emotions.* New York: Plenum Press.

John, E. R. (1977). *Functional neuroscience. Vol. 2: Neurometrics.* Hillsdale, NJ: Erlbaum.

Kagan, J. (1982). *Psychological research on the human infant: An evaluative summary.* New York: W. T. Grant Foundation.

Kagan, J. (1989). Temperamental contributions to social behavior. *American Psychologist, 44,* 668–674.

Kant, I. (1958). *Critique of pure reason* (N. K. Smith, Trans.). New York: Random House Modern Library.

Karmiloff-Smith, A., & Inhelder, B. (1974). If you want to get ahead, get a theory. *Cognition, 3,* 195–212.

Kauffman, S. A. (1993). *The origins of order: Self-organization and selection in evolution.* Oxford, England: Oxford University Press.

Keil, F. C. (1986). On the structure-dependent nature of stages of cognitive development. In I. Levin (Ed.), *Stage and structure: Reopening the debate* (pp. 144–163). Norwood, NJ: ABLEX.

Kelso, J. A. S., Ding, M., & Schöner, G. (1993). Dynamic pattern formation: A primer. In L. B. Smith & E. Thelen (Eds.), *A dynamic systems approach to development* (pp. 13–50). Cambridge, MA: MIT Press.

Kendler, H. H., & Kendler, T. S. (1962). Vertical and horizontal processes in problem solving. *Psychological Review, 69,* 1–16.

Kennedy, B. (1994). *The development of self-understanding in adolescents in Korea.* Unpublished doctoral dissertation, Harvard University, Cambridge, MA.

Kernberg, O. (1976). *Object relations theory and psychoanalysis.* New York: Aronson.

Kitayama, S., & Markus, H. R. (1995). Culture, self, and emotion: A cultural perspective on "self-conscious" emotions. In J. Tangney & K. W. Fischer (Eds.), *Self-conscious emotions: The psychology of shame, guilt, embarrassment, and pride* (pp. 439–464). New York: Guilford Press.

Kitchener, K. S., & Fischer, K. W. (1990). A skill approach to the development of reflective thinking. In D. Kuhn (Ed.), *Developmental perspectives on teaching and learning thinking skills. Contributions to Human Development, 21*(4), 48–62.

Kitchener, K. S., & King, P. M. (1990). The reflective judgment model: Ten years of research. In M. L. Commons, C. Armon, L. Kohlberg, F. A. Richards, T. A. Grotzer, & J. D. Sinnott (Eds.), *Adult development: 3. Models and methods in the study of adolescent and adult thought* (pp. 62–78). New York: Praeger.

Kitchener, K. S., Lynch, C. L., Fischer, K. W., & Wood, P. K. (1993). Developmental range of reflective judgment: The effect of contextual support and practice on developmental stage. *Developmental Psychology, 29,* 893–906.

Klahr, D., & Wallace, J. G. (1976). *Cognitive development: An information-processing view.* Hillsdale, NJ: Erlbaum.

Knight, C. C., & Fischer, K. W. (1992). Learning to read words: Individual differences in developmental sequences. *Journal of Applied Developmental Psychology, 13,* 377–404.

Kofsky, E. (1966). A scalogram study of classificatory development. *Child Development, 37,* 191–204.

Kohlberg, L. (1969). Stage and sequence: The cognitive developmental approach to socialization. In D. A. Goslin (Ed.), *Handbook of socialization theory and research* (pp. 347–480). Chicago: Rand McNally.

Kohlberg, L. (1984). Moral stages and moralization: The cognitive-developmental approach. In L. Kohlberg (Ed.), *The psychology of moral development: The nature and validity of moral stages* (pp. 170–205). San Francisco: Harper & Row.

Kohler, I. (1962, May). Experiments with goggles. *Scientific American, 206,* 62–86.

Köhler, W. (1970). *Gestalt psychology.* New York: Liveright.

Krus, D. J. (1977). Order analysis: An inferential model of dimensional analysis and scaling. *Educational and Psychological Measurement, 37,* 587–601.

Kuhn, D., Garcia-Mila, M., Zohar, A., & Andersen, C. (1995). Strategies of knowledge acquisition. *Monographs of the Society for Research in Child Development, 60*(4, Serial No. 245).

Kuhn, D., & Phelps, E. (1982). The development of problem-solving strategies. In H. W. Reese (Ed.), *Advances in child development and behavior* (Vol. 17, pp. 2–44). New York: Academic Press.

Kuhn, T. (1970). *The structure of scientific revolutions* (2nd ed.). Chicago: University of Chicago.

Lakoff, G. (1987). *Women, fire, and dangerous things: What categories reveal about the mind.* Chicago: University of Chicago Press.

Lakoff, G., & Johnson, M. (1980). *Metaphors we live by.* Chicago: University of Chicago Press.

Lamborn, S. D., Fischer, K. W., & Pipp, S. L. (1994). Constructive criticism and social lies: A developmental sequence for understanding honesty and kindness in social interactions. *Developmental Psychology, 30,* 495–508.

Lampl, M., & Emde, R. N. (1983). Episodic growth in infancy: A preliminary report on length, head circumference, and behavior. In K. W. Fischer (Ed.), *Levels and transitions in children's development. New Directions for Child Development* (Vol. 21, pp. 21–36). San Francisco: Jossey-Bass.

Lampl, M., Veldhuis, J. D., & Johnson, M. L. (1992). Saltation and stasis: A model of human growth. *Science, 258,* 801–803.

Landau, B., Spelke, E. S., & Gleitman, H. (1984). Spatial knowledge in a young blind child. *Cognition, 16,* 225–260.

Lautrey, J. (1993). Structure and variability: A plea for a pluralistic approach to cognitive development. In W. Edelstein & R. Case (Eds.), Constructivist approaches to development. *Contributions to Human Development, 23,* 101–114.

Lazarus, R. S. (1991). *Emotion and adaptation.* New York: Oxford University Press.

LeDoux, J. E. (1989). Cognitive-emotional interactions in the brain. *Cognition and Emotion, 3,* 267–289.

Lerner, R. M. (1991). Changing organism-context relations as the basic process of development: A developmental contextual perspective. *Developmental Psychology, 27,* 27–32.

Lerner, R. M. (1995a). The limits of biological influence: Behavioral genetics as the emperor's new clothes. *Psychological Inquiry, 6,* 145–156.

Lerner, R. M. (1995b). The place of learning within the human development system: A developmental contextual perspective. *Human Development, 38,* 361–366.

Lerner, R. M., & Busch-Rossnagel, N. A. (1981). Individuals as producers of their own development: Conceptual and empirical bases. In R. M. Lerner & N. A. Busch-Rossnagel (Eds.), *Individuals as producers of their own development: A life-span perspective* (pp. 1–36). New York: Academic Press.

LeVine, R. A. (1977). Childrearing as cultural adaptation. In P. H. Leiderman, S. H. Tulkin, & A. Rosenfeld (Eds.), *Culture and infancy.* New York: Academic Press.

LeVine, R. A. (1989). Cultural environments in child development. In W. Damon (Ed.), *Child development today and tomorrow* (pp. 52–68). San Francisco: Jossey-Bass.

LeVine, R. A., Miller, P. M., & West, M. M. (Eds.). (1988). *Parental behavior in diverse societies. New Directions for Child Development* (Vol. 40). San Francisco: Jossey-Bass.

Levi-Strauss, C. (1969). *The raw and the cooked* (J. D. Weightman, Trans.). New York: Harper & Row.

Lewis, M. D. (1994). Reconciling stage and specificity in neo-Piagetian theory: Self-organizing conceptual structures. *Human Development, 37,* 143–169.

Lewis, M. D., & Ash, A. J. (1992). Evidence for a neo-Piagetian stage transition in early cognitive development. *International Journal of Behavioral Development, 15,* 337–358.

Lieberman, P. (1984). *The biology and evolution of language.* Cambridge, MA: Harvard University Press.

Lourenço, O., & Machado, A. (1996). In defense of Piaget's theory: A reply to 10 common criticisms. *Psychological Review, 103,* 143–164.

Luborsky, L., & Crits-Christoph, P. (1990). *Understanding transference: The CCRT method.* New York: Basic Books.

Luborsky, L., Luborsky, E., Diguer, L., Schmidt, K., Dengler, D., Schaffler, P., Faude, J., Morris, M., Buchsbaum, H., & Emde, R. (1996). Is there a core relationship pattern at age 3 and does it remain at age 5? In G. G. Noam & K. W. Fischer (Eds.), *Development and vulnerability in close relationships* (pp. 287–308). Hillsdale, NJ: Erlbaum.

Lunzer, E. A. (1965). Problems of formal reasoning in test situations. In P. H. Mussen (Ed.), European research in cognitive development. *Monographs of the Society for Research in Child Development, 30*(2, Serial No. 100).

Luria, A. R. (1966). *Higher cortical functions in man.* New York: Basic Books.

Luria, A. R. (1973). *The working brain.* New York: Basic Books.

Luria, A. R. (1979). *The making of mind: A personal account of Soviet psychology.* Cambridge, MA: Harvard University Press.

Lutz, C. A. (1988). *Unnatural emotions: Everyday sentiments on a Micronesian atoll and their challenge to Western theory.* Chicago: University of Chicago Press.

Lyons-Ruth, K., Alpern, L., & Repacholi, B. (1993). Disorganized infant attachment classification and maternal psychosocial problems as predictors of hostile-aggressive behavior in the preschool classroom. *Child Development, 64,* 572–585.

Main, M., & Hesse, E. (1990). Parents' unresolved traumatic experiences are related to infant disorganized attachment status: Is frightened and/or frightening parental behavior the linking mechanism? In M. T. Greenberg, D. Cicchetti, & E. M. Cummings (Eds.), *Attachment in the preschool years* (pp. 161–182). Chicago: University of Chicago Press.

Malatesta, C. Z. (1988). The role of emotions in the development and organization of personality. In R. A. Thompson & R. A. Dienstbier (Ed.), *Socioemotional development. Nebraska Symposium on Motivation* (Vol. 36). Lincoln: University of Nebraska Press.

Marcel, A. J. (1983). Conscious and unconscious perception: Experiments on visual masking and word recognition. *Cognitive Psychology, 15,* 197–237.

Mareschal, D., Plunkett, K., & Harris, P. (1995). Developing object permanence: A connectionist model. In J. D. Moore & J. F. Lehman (Eds.), *Proceedings of the seventeenth annual conference of the Cognitive Science Society* (pp. 1–6). Mahwah, NJ: Erlbaum.

Markus, H. R., & Kitayama, S. (1991). Culture and the self: Implications for cognition, emotion, and motivation. *Psychological Review, 98,* 225–253.

Martarano, S. C. (1977). A developmental analysis of performance on Piaget's formal operations tasks. *Developmental Psychology, 13,* 666–672.

Matousek, M., & Petersén, I. (1973). Frequency analysis of the EEG in normal children and adolescents. In P. Kellaway & I. Petersén (Eds.), *Automation of clinical electroencephalography* (pp. 75–102). New York: Raven Press.

McCall, R. B. (1983). Exploring developmental transitions in mental performance. In K. W. Fischer (Ed.), *Levels and transitions in children's development. New Directions for Child Development* (Vol. 21, pp. 65–80). San Francisco: Jossey-Bass.

McCall, R. B., Eichorn, D. H., & Hogarty, P. S. (1977). Transitions in early mental development. *Monographs of the Society for Research in Child Development, 42*(3, Serial No. 171).

McCann, L., & Pearlman, L. A. (1992). Constructivist self-development theory: A theoretical model of psychological adaptation to severe trauma. In D. Sakheim & S. Devine (Eds.), *Out of darkness* (pp. 185–206). Lexington, MA: Lexington Books.

McCrae, R. R., & Costa, P. T., Jr. (1990). *Personality in adulthood.* New York: Guilford Press.

McGuire, W. J., & McGuire, C. V. (1982). Significant others in the self-space: Sex differences and developmental trends in the social self. In J. Suls (Ed.), *Psychological perspectives of the self.* Hillsdale, NJ: Erlbaum.

McLaughlin, G. H. (1963). Psychologic: A possible alternative to Piaget's formulation. *British Journal of Educational Psychology, 33,* 61–67.

Miller, P. H., & Aloise-Young, P. A. (in press). Preschoolers' strategic behavior and performance on a same-different task. *Journal of Experimental Child Psychology.*

Mills, D. L., Coffey-Corina, S. A., & Neville, H. J. (1994). Variability in cerebral organization during primary language acquisition. In G. Dawson & K. W. Fischer (Eds.), *Human behavior and the developing brain* (pp. 427–455). New York: Guilford Press.

Mischel, W. (1968). *Personality and assessment.* New York: Wiley.

Mischel, W., & Mischel, F. (1958). Psychological aspects of spirit possession. *American Anthropologist, 60,* 249–260.

Miyake, K., Chen, S.-J., & Campos, J. J. (1985). Infant temperament, mothers' mode of interaction, and attachment in Japan. In I. Bretherton & E. Waters (Eds.), Growing points of attachment theory and research. *Monographs of the Society for Research in Child Development, 50*(1/2, Serial No. 209), 276–297.

Miyake, K., & Yamazaki, K. (1995). Self-conscious emotions, child rearing, and child psychopathology in Japanese culture. In J. P. Tangney & K. W. Fischer (Eds.), *Self-conscious emotions: The psychology of shame, guilt, embarrassment, and pride* (pp. 488–504). New York: Guilford Press.

Mizuno, T., Yamauchi, N., Watanabe, A., Komatsushiro, M., Takagi, T., Iinuma, K., & Arakawa, T. (1970). Maturation of patterns of EEG: Basic waves of healthy infants under 12 months of age. *Tohoku Journal of Experimental Medicine, 102,* 91–98.

Moerck, E. L. (1985). Analytic, synthetic, abstracting, and word-class defining aspects of verbal mother-child interactions. *Journal of Psycholinguistic Research, 14,* 263–287.

Moshman, D., & Franks, B. A. (1986). Development of the concept of inferential validity. *Child Development, 57,* 153–165.

Mounoud, P. (1976). Les révolutions psychologiques de l'enfant. *Archives de Psychologie, 44,* 103–114.

Movshon, J. A., & Van Sluyters, R. C. (1981). Visual neural development. *Annual Review of Psychology, 32,* 477–522.

Nelson, K. (1986). *Event knowledge: Structure and function in development.* Hillsdale, NJ: Erlbaum.

Neville, H. J. (1991). Neurobiology of cognitive and language processing: Effects of early experience. In K. R. Gibson & A. C. Petersen (Eds.), *Brain maturation and cognitive development: Comparative and cross-cultural perspectives* (pp. 355–380). New York: Aldine de Gruyter.

Newman, D., Griffin, P., & Cole, M. (1989). *The construction zone: Working for change in school.* Cambridge, England: Cambridge University Press.

Ninio, A., & Snow, C. (1996). *Pragmatic development.* Boulder, CO: Westview.

Noam, G. G. (1990). Beyond Freud and Piaget: Biographical worlds—Interpersonal self. In T. E. Wren (Ed.), *The moral domain* (pp. 360–399). Cambridge, MA: MIT Press.

Noam, G. G., Paget, K., Valiant, G., Borst, S., & Bartok, J. (1994). Conduct and affective disorders in developmental perspective: A systematic study of adolescent psychopathology. *Development and Psychopathology, 6,* 519–523.

Noam, G. G., Powers, S. J., Kilkenny, R., & Beedy, J. (1990). The interpersonal self in life-span developmental perspective: Theory, measurement, and longitudinal case analyses. In P. B. Baltes, D. L. Featherman, & R. M. Lerner (Eds.), *Lifespan development and behavior* (Vol. 10, pp. 59–104). Hillsdale, NJ: Erlbaum.

Nunez, P. (1981). *Electric fields of the brain: The neurophysics of EEG.* New York: Oxford University Press.

O'Brien, D. P., & Overton, W. F. (1982). Conditional reasoning and the competence-performance issue: A developmental analysis of a training task. *Journal of Experimental Child Psychology, 34,* 274–290.

Ogbu, J. U. (1978). *Minority education and caste: The American system in cross-cultural perspective.* New York: Academic Press.

Ogbu, J. U. (1991). Immigrant and involuntary minorities in comparative perspective. In M. Gibson & J. Ogbu (Eds.), *Minority status and schooling*. New York: Garland.

Ohtahara, S. (1981). Neurophysiological development during infancy and childhood. In N. Yamaguchi & K. Fujiwasa (Eds.), *Recent advances in EEG and EMG data processing* (pp. 369–375). Amsterdam, The Netherlands: Elsevier/North Holland.

Orne, M. T. (1959). The nature of hypnosis: Artifact and essence. *Journal of Abnormal and Social Psychology, 58,* 277–299.

Osgood, C. E., Suci, G. J., & Tannenbaum, P. (1957). *The measurement of meaning*. Urbana: University of Illinois Press.

Overton, W. F., & Newman, J. L. (1982). Cognitive development: A competence-activation/utilization approach. In T. M. Field, A. Huston, H. C. Quay, L. Troll, & G. E. Finley (Eds.), *Review of human development* (pp. 217–241). New York: Wiley.

Oyama, S. (1985). *The ontogeny of information: Developmental systems and evolution*. Cambridge, England: Cambridge University Press.

Papousek, H., & Papousek, M. (1979). The infant's fundamental adaptive response system in social interaction. In E. B. Thoman (Ed.), *Origins of the infant's social responsiveness*. Hillsdale, NJ: Erlbaum.

Pascual-Leone, J. (1970). A mathematical model for the transition rule in Piaget's developmental stages. *Acta Psychologica, 32,* 301–345.

Pennington, B. F. (1994). The working memory function of the prefrontal cortices: Implications for developmental and individual differences in cognition. In M. M. Haith, J. B. Benson, R. J. Roberts, Jr., & B. F. Pennington (Eds.), *Development of future-oriented processes* (pp. 243–289). Chicago: University of Chicago Press.

Pepper, S. C. (1942). *World hypotheses*. Berkeley: University of California.

Perkins, D. N., & Salomon, G. (1988). Teaching for transfer. *Educational Leadership, 46*(1), 22–32.

Perry, M., Church, R. B., & Goldin-Meadow, S. (1988). Transitional knowledge in the acquisition of concepts. *Cognitive Development, 3,* 359–400.

Petitto, L. A., & Marentette, P. F. (1991). Babbling in the manual mode: Evidence for the ontogeny of language. *Science, 251,* 1493–1496.

Piaget, J. (1950). *The psychology of intelligence* (M. Piercy & D. E. Berlyne, Trans.). New York: Harcourt Brace. (Original work published 1947)

Piaget, J. (1952). *The origins of intelligence in children* (M. Cook, Trans.). New York: International Universities Press. (Original work published 1936)

Piaget, J. (1954). *The construction of reality in the child* (M. Cook, Trans.). New York: Basic Books. (Original work published 1937)

Piaget, J. (1957). Logique et équilibre dans les comportements du sujet. *Études d'Épistémologie Génétique, 2,* 27–118.

Piaget, J. (1970). *Science of education and the psychology of the child* (D. Coltman, Trans.). New York: Grossman Press. (Original work published 1935)

Piaget, J. (1970). *Structuralism* (C. Maschler, Trans.). New York: Basic Books. (Original work published 1968)

Piaget, J. (1971). *Biology and knowledge: An essay on the relations between organic regulations and cognitive processes* (B. Walsh, Trans.). Chicago: University of Chicago Press. (Original work published 1967)

Piaget, J. (1971). The theory of stages in cognitive development. In D. R. Green, M. P. Ford, & G. B. Flamer (Eds.), *Measurement and Piaget* (pp. 1–11). New York: McGraw-Hill.

Piaget, J. (1975). L'équilibration des structures cognitives: Problème central du développement. *Études d'Épistémologie Génétique, 33.*

Piaget, J. (1983). Piaget's theory. In P. H. Mussen (Series Ed.) & W. Kessen (Vol. Ed.), *Handbook of child psychology: Vol. 1. History, theory, and methods* (pp. 103–126). New York: Wiley.

Piaget, J. (1987). *Possibility and necessity* (H. Feider, Trans.). Minneapolis: University of Minnesota Press. (Original work published 1981–1983)

Piaget, J., & Garcia, R. (1991). *Toward a logic of meanings*. Hillsdale, NJ: Erlbaum.

Piaget, J., & Szeminska, A. (1952). *The child's conception of number* (C. Gattegno & F. M. Hodgson, Trans.). London: Routledge & Kegan Paul. (Original work published 1941)

Piatelli-Palmarini, M. (Ed.). (1980). *Language and learning: The debate between Jean Piaget and Noam Chomsky*. Cambridge, MA: Harvard University Press.

Pillemer, D. B., Picariello, M. L., & Pruett, J. C. (1994). Very long-term memories of a salient preschool event. *Applied Cognitive Psychology, 8,* 95–106.

Pinard, A. (1981). *The concept of conservation*. Chicago: University of Chicago Press.

Pipp, S. L., Fischer, K. W., & Jennings, S. L. (1987). The acquisition of self and mother knowledge in infancy. *Developmental Psychology, 22,* 86–96.

Pirttilä-Backman, A.-M. (1993). *The social psychology of knowledge reassessed: Toward a new delineation of the field with empirical substantiation*. Doctoral dissertation, University of Helsinki, Helsinki.

Plato. (1941). *The republic* (F. M. Cornford, Trans.). London: Oxford University Press.

Plomin, R., & McClearn, G. E. (Eds.). (1993). *Nature, nurture, and psychology.* Washington, DC: American Psychological Association.

Plutchik, R. (1980). *Emotion: A psychoeveolutionary synthesis.* New York: Harper & Row.

Port, R. F., & van Gelder, T. (Eds.). (1995). *Mind as motion: Explorations in the dynamics of cognition.* Cambridge, MA: Bradford Books/MIT Press.

Price-Williams, D., Gordon, W., & Ramirez, M., III. (1969). Skill and conservation: A study of pottery making children. *Developmental Psychology, 1,* 769.

Prigogine, I., & Stengers, I. (1984). *Order out of chaos: Man's new dialogue with nature.* New York: Bantam Books.

Putnam, F. (1991). *Multiple personality disorder.* Cambridge, MA: Harvard University Press.

Rakic, P., Bourgeois, J.-P., Eckenhoff, M. F., Zecevic, N., & Goldman-Rakic, P. (1986). Concurrent overproduction of synapses in diverse regions of the primate cerebral cortex. *Science, 232,* 232–235.

Rasch, G. (1966). An item analysis which takes individual differences into account. *British Journal of Mathematical and Statistical Psychology, 19,* 49–57.

Raya, P. (1996). *Development of emotions in maltreated preschoolers in pair-play therapy.* Unpublished doctoral dissertation, Harvard University, Cambridge, MA.

Reddy, M. (1979). The conduit metaphor. In A. Ortony (Ed.), *Metaphor and thought* (pp. 284–324). Cambridge, England: Cambridge University Press.

Reznick, J. S., & Goldfield, B. A. (1992). Rapid change in lexical development in comprehension and production. *Developmental Psychology, 28,* 406–413.

Rogoff, B. (1982). Integrating context and cognitive development. In M. E. Lamb & A. L. Brown (Eds.), *Advances in developmental psychology* (Vol. 2, pp. 125–170). Hillsdale, NJ: Erlbaum.

Rogoff, B. (1990). *Apprenticeship in thinking: Cognitive development in social context.* New York: Oxford University Press.

Rogoff, B. (1993). Children's guided participation and participatory appropriation in sociocultural activity. In R. Wozniak & K. W. Fischer (Eds.), *Development in context: Acting and thinking in specific environments* (pp. 121–154). Hillsdale, NJ: Erlbaum.

Rosch, E. (1978). Principles of categorization. In E. Rosch & B. B. Lloyd (Eds.), *Cognition and categorization* (pp. 27–48). Hillsdale, NJ: Erlbaum.

Rose, S. P. (1990). *Levels and variations in measures of perspective-taking.* Unpublished doctoral dissertation, University of Denver, Denver, CO.

Rotman, B. (1993). *Ad infinitum—The ghost in Turing's machine: Taking God out of mathematics and putting the body back in.* Stanford, CA: Stanford University Press.

Ruhland, R., & van Geert, P. (1997). *Jumping into syntax: Transitions in the development of closed class words.* Manuscript submitted for publication. Groningen, Netherlands: University of Groningen.

Rumelhart, D. E., & McClelland, J. L. (1986). On learning the past tenses of English verbs. In D. E. Rumelhart & J. L. McClelland (Eds.), *Parallel distributed processing* (Vol. 2, pp. 216–271). Cambridge, MA: MIT Press.

Rumelhart, D. E., & McClelland, J. L. (1988). *Explorations in parallel distributed processing: A handbook of models, programs, and exercises.* Cambridge, MA: MIT Press.

Saltzman, E. L. (1995). Dynamics and coordinate systems in skilled sensorimotor activity. In R. F. Port & T. van Gelder (Eds.), *Mind as motion: Explorations in the dynamics of cognition* (pp. 149–173). Cambridge, MA: MIT Press.

Sameroff, A. J., & Chandler, M. (1975). Reproductive risk and the continuum of caretaking casualty. In F. D. Horowitz (Ed.), *Review of child development research* (Vol. 4, pp. 187–244). Chicago: University of Chicago Press.

Schank, R. C., & Abelson, R. P. (1977). *Scripts, plans, goals, and understanding.* Hillsdale, NJ: Erlbaum.

Scheff, T. J., & Retzinger, S. (1991). *Emotions and violence.* Lexington, MA: Lexington Books.

Scherer, K. R. (1984). On the nature and function of emotion: A component process approach. In K. R. Scherer & P. Ekman (Eds.), *Approaches to emotion* (pp. 293–317). Hillsdale, NJ: Erlbaum.

Scherer, K. R., Wallbott, H. G., & Summerfield, A. B. (Eds.). (1986). *Experiencing emotions: A cross-cultural study.* Cambridge, England: Cambridge University Press.

Schlosberg, H. (1954). Three dimensions of emotion. *Psychological Review, 61,* 81–88.

Segalowitz, S. J. (1994). Developmental psychology and brain development: A historical perspective. In G. Dawson & K. W. Fischer (Eds.), *Human behavior and the developing brain* (pp. 67–92). New York: Guilford Press.

Selman, R. L., & Schultz, L. H. (1990). *Making a friend in youth.* Chicago: University of Chicago Press.

Shaver, P. R., & Clark, C. L. (1996). Forms of adult romantic attachment and their cognitive and emotional underpinnings. In G. G. Noam & K. W. Fischer (Eds.), *Development and vulnerability in close relationships* (pp. 29–58). Hillsdale, NJ: Erlbaum.

Shaver, P. R., Schwartz, J., Kirson, D., & O'Connor, C. (1987). Emotion knowledge: Further exploration of a prototype approach. *Journal of Personality and Social Psychology, 52,* 1061–1086.

Shaver, P. R., Wu, S., & Schwartz, J. C. (1992). Cross-cultural similarities and differences in emotion and its representation: A prototype approach. In M. S. Clark (Ed.), *Review of personality and social psychology* (Vol. 13, pp. 175–212). Newbury Park, CA: Sage.

Shultz, T. R., Schmidt, W. C., Buckingham, D., & Mareschal, D. (1995). Modeling cognitive development with a generative connectionist algorithm. In G. S. Halford (Ed.), *Developing cognitive competence* (pp. 205–261). Mahwah, NJ: Erlbaum.

Siegler, R. S. (1981). Developmental sequences within and between concepts. *Monographs of the Society for Research in Child Development, 46*(2, Serial No. 189).

Siegler, R. S. (1994). Cognitive variability: A key to understanding cognitive development. *Current Directions in Psychological Science, 3,* 1–5.

Siegler, R. S., & Crowley, K. (1991). The microgenetic method: A direct means for studying cognitive development. *American Psychologist, 46,* 606–620.

Siegler, R. S., & Jenkins, E. (1989). *How children discover new strategies.* Hillsdale, NJ: Erlbaum.

Skinner, B. F. (1938). *The behavior of organisms.* New York: Appleton-Century-Crofts.

Skinner, B. F. (1969). *Contingencies of reinforcement: A theoretical analysis.* New York: Appleton-Century-Crofts.

Snow, C. E., Perlmann, R., & Nathan, D. (1989). Why routines are different: Toward a multiple-factors model of the relation between input and language acquisition. In K. Nelson & A. van Kleeck (Eds.), *Children's language* (Vol. 6, pp. 65–97). Hillsdale, NJ: Erlbaum.

Somsen, R. J. M., van Klooster, B. J., van der Molen, M. W., van Leeuwen, H. M. P., & Licht, R. (in press). Growth spurts in brain maturation during middle childhood as indexed by EEG power spectra. *Biological Psychology.*

Spelke, E. S. (1991). Physical knowledge in infancy: Reflections on Piaget's theory. In S. Carey & R. Gelman (Eds.), *The epigenesis of mind: Essays on biology and cognition* (pp. 133–170). Hillsdale, NJ: Erlbaum.

Spencer, M. B., Brookins, G. K., & Allen, W. R. (Eds.). (1985). *Beginnings: The social and affective development of black children.* Hillsdale, NJ: Erlbaum.

Spiro, M. E. (1993). *Oedipus in the Trobriands.* New Brunswick, NJ: Transaction.

Sroufe, L. A. (1984). The organization of emotional development. In K. R. Scherer & P. Ekman (Eds.), *Approaches to emotion* (pp. 109–128). Hillsdale, NJ: Erlbaum.

Sroufe, L. A., & Egeland, B. (1985). The relationship between quality of attachment and behavior problems in preschool in a high-risk sample. In I. Bretherton & E. Waters (Eds.), Growing points of attachment theory and research. *Monographs of the Society for Research in Child Development, 50*(1/2, Serial No. 209), 147–166.

Sroufe, L. A., Egeland, B., & Kreutzer, T. (1990). The fate of early experience following developmental change: Longitudinal approaches to individual adaptation in childhood. *Child Development, 61,* 1363–1373.

Starkey, P. (1992). The early development of numerical reasoning. *Cognition, 43,* 93–126.

Stauder, J. E. A., Molenaar, P. C. M., & van der Molen, M. W. (1993). Scalp topography of event-related brain potentials and cognitive transition during childhood. *Child Development, 64,* 768–788.

Stern, D. N. (1985). *The interpersonal world of the infant: A view from psychoanalysis and developmental psychology.* New York: Basic Books.

Sternberg, R. (1985). *Beyond IQ: A triarchic theory of intelligence.* New York: Cambridge University Press.

Strauss, S., & Stavy, R. (Eds.). (1982). *U-shaped behavioral growth.* New York: Academic Press.

Tabor, L. E., & Kendler, T. S. (1981). Testing for developmental continuity or discontinuity: Class inclusion and reversal shifts. *Developmental Review, 1,* 330–343.

Tangney, J. P. (1995). Shame and guilt in interpersonal relationships. In J. P. Tangney & K. W. Fischer (Eds.), *Self-conscious emotions: The psychology of shame, guilt, embarrassment, and pride* (pp. 114–139). New York: Guilford Press.

Tatsuoka, M. M. (1986). Graph theory and its applications in educational research: A review and integration. *Review of Educational Research, 56,* 291–329.

Terr, L. C. (1991). Childhood traumas: An outline and overview. *American Journal of Psychiatry, 148*(1), 10–20.

Thatcher, R. W. (1991). Maturation of the human frontal lobes: Physiological evidence for staging. *Developmental Neuropsychology, 7,* 397–419.

Thatcher, R. W. (1992). Cyclic cortical reorganization during early childhood development. *Brain and Cognition, 20,* 24–50.

Thatcher, R. W. (1994). Cyclic cortical reorganization: Origins of human cognitive development. In G. Dawson & K. W.

Fischer (Eds.), *Human behavior and the developing brain* (pp. 232–266). New York: Guilford Press.

Thelen, E., & Smith, L. B. (1994). *A dynamic systems approach to the development of cognition and action.* Cambridge, MA: MIT Press.

Thomas, A., & Chess, S. (1980). *The dynamics of psychological development.* New York: Brunner/Mazel.

Thomas, H., & Lohaus, A. (1993). Modeling growth and individual differences in spatial tasks. *Monographs of the Society for Research in Child Development, 58*(9, Serial No. 237).

Toth, S. L., & Cicchetti, D. (in press). The impact of relatedness with mother on school functioning in maltreated children. *Journal of School Psychology.*

Touwen, B. C. L. (1976). *Neurological development in infancy. Clinics in developmental medicine* (Vol. 58). London: Spastics Society.

Triandis, H. C. (1989). The self and social behavior in differing cultural contexts. *Psychological Review, 96,* 506–520.

Turiel, E., & Davidson, P. (1986). Heterogeneity, inconsistency, and asynchrony in the development of cognitive structures. In I. Levin (Ed.), *Stage and structure: Reopening the debate.* Norwood, NJ: ABLEX.

Uzgiris, I. C. (1976). Organization of sensorimotor intelligence. In M. Lewis (Ed.), *Origins of intelligence: Infancy and early childhood* (pp. 123–163). New York: Plenum Press.

Uzgiris, I. C., & Hunt, J. M. V. (1975). *Assessment in infancy: Ordinal scales of psychological development.* Urbana: University of Illinois Press.

Vaillant, G. E. (1977). *Adaptation to life.* Boston: Little, Brown.

Vallacher, R., & Nowak, A. (1994). *Dynamical systems in social psychology.* New York: Academic Press.

Valsiner, J. (1987). *Culture and the development of children's action.* Chichester, England: Wiley.

van Aken, M. A. G. (1992). The development of general competence and domain-specific competencies. *European Journal of Personality, 6,* 267–282.

van der Kolk, B. A. (1987). *Psychological trauma.* Washington, DC: American Psychiatric Press.

van der Maas, H. (1995). Beyond the metaphor? *Cognitive Development, 10,* 631–642.

van der Maas, H., & Molenaar, P. (1992). A catastrophe-theoretical approach to cognitive development. *Psychological Review, 99,* 395–417.

van der Maas, H., & Molenaar, P. (1995). Catastrophe analysis of discontinuous development. In A. A. von Eye & C. C. Clogg (Eds.), *Categorical variables in developmental research: Methods of analysis* (pp. 77–105). New York: Academic Press.

van der Maas, H., Verschure, P. F. M. J., & Molenaar, P. C. M. (1990). A note on chaotic behavior in simple neural networks. *Neural Networks, 3,* 119–122.

van Geert, P. (1991). A dynamic systems model of cognitive and language growth. *Psychological Review, 98,* 3–53.

van Geert, P. (1994). *Dynamic systems of development: Change between complexity and chaos.* London: Harvester Wheatsheaf.

van Geert, P. (1996). The dynamics of Father Brown [Review of book *A dynamic systems approach to the development of action and thought* by E. Thelen & B. Smith]. *Human Development, 39,* 57–66.

Van Parys, M. M. (1981). *Preschoolers in society: Use of the social roles of sex, age, and race for self and others by black and white children.* Unpublished master's thesis, University of Denver, Denver, CO.

von Bertalanffy, L. (1968). *General systems theory.* New York: Braziller.

von Frisch, K. (1967). *The dance language and orientation of bees* (L. E. Chadwick, Trans.). Cambridge, MA: Harvard University Press.

von Hofsten, C. (1984). Developmental changes in the organization of prereaching movements. *Developmental Psychology, 20,* 378–388.

Vygotsky, L. S. (1962). *Thought and language* (E. Hanfmann & G. Vakar, Trans.). Cambridge, MA: MIT Press.

Vygotsky, L. S. (1978). *Mind in society: The development of higher psychological processes* (M. Cole, V. John-Steiner, S. Scribner, & E. Souberman, Trans.). Cambridge MA: Harvard University Press.

Wahlsten, D. (1990). Insensitivity of the analysis of variance to heredity-environment interaction. *Behavioral and Brain Sciences, 13,* 1–27.

Wallbott, H. G., & Scherer, K. R. (1995). Cultural determinants in experiencing shame and guilt. In J. P. Tangney & K. W. Fischer (Eds.), *Self-conscious emotions: The psychology of shame, guilt, embarrassment, and pride* (pp. 466–488). New York: Guilford Press.

Wang, L. (1994). *Analysis of Chinese shame structure.* Unpublished qualifying paper, Harvard University, Cambridge, MA.

Watson, M. W. (1984). Development of social role understanding. *Developmental Review, 4,* 192–213.

Watson, M. W., & Fischer, K. W. (1980). Development of social roles in elicited and spontaneous behavior during the preschool years. *Developmental Psychology, 16,* 484–494.

Watson, M. W., & Getz, K. (1991). The relationship between Oedipal behaviors and children's family role concepts. *Merrill-Palmer Quarterly, 36,* 487–505.

Weiss, P. A. (1970). The living system: Determinism stratified. In A. Koestler & J. Smythies (Eds.), *Beyond reductionism: New perspectives in the life sciences* (pp. 3–55). New York: Macmillan.

Welford, A. T. (1968). *Fundamentals of skill.* London: Methuen.

Werner, H. (1948). *Comparative psychology of mental development.* New York: Science Editions.

Wertsch, J. V. (1979). From social interaction to higher psychological processes: A clarification and application of Vygotsky's theory. *Human Development, 22,* 1–22.

Wertsch, J. V., & Stone, A. (1978). Microgenesis as a tool for developmental analysis. *Quarterly Newsletter of the Laboratory of Comparative Human Cognition, 1*(1), 8–10.

Westen, D. (1994). The impact of sexual abuse on self structure. In D. Cicchetti & S. L. Toth (Eds.), *Rochester Symposium on Development and Psychopathology: Vol. 5. Disorders and dysfunctions of the self* (pp. 223–250). Rochester, NY: University of Rochester.

Westerman, M. A. (1990). Coordination of maternal directives with preschoolers' behavior in compliance problem and healthy dyads. *Developmental Psychology, 26,* 621–630.

Weston, P., & Mednick, M. T. (1970). Race, social class, and the motive to avoid success in women. *Journal of Cross-Cultural Psychology, 1,* 284–291.

Whiting, B. B., & Edwards, C. P. (1988). *Children of different worlds: The formation of social behavior.* Cambridge, MA: Harvard University Press.

Willett, J. B. (1994). Measuring change more effectively by modeling individual growth over time. In T. Husen & T. N. Postlethwaite (Eds.), *International encyclopedia of education* (2nd ed.). Oxford, England: Pergamon Press.

Willett, J. B., Ayoub, C., & Robinson, D. (1991). Using growth modeling to examine systematic differences in growth: An example of change in the function of families at risk of maladaptive parenting, child abuse, or neglect. *Journal of Counseling and Clinical Psychology, 59,* 38–47.

Wittgenstein, L. (1953). *Philosophical Investigations* (G. E. M. Anscombe, Trans.). Oxford, England: Oxford University Press.

Wohlwill, J. F. (1973). *The study of behavioral development.* New York: Academic Press.

Wohlwill, J. F., & Lowe, R. C. (1962). An experimental analysis of the development of conservation of number. *Child Development, 33,* 153–167.

Wolf, M. (in press). A provisional, integrative account of phonological and naming-speed deficits in dyslexia: Implications for diagnosis and intervention. In B. Blachman (Ed.), *Cognitive and linguistic foundations of reading acquisition: Implications for intervention research.* Mahwah, NJ: Erlbaum.

Wozniak, R., & Fischer, K. W. (1993). Development in context: An introduction. In R. Wozniak & K. W. Fischer (Eds.), *Development in context: Acting and thinking in specific environments* (pp. xi–xvi). Hillsdale, NJ: Erlbaum.

Wrangham, R. W., McGrew, W. C., deWaal, F. B. M., & Heltne, P. G. (Eds.). (1994). *Chimpanzee cultures.* Cambridge, MA: Harvard University Press.

Wright, J. J., & Liley, D. T. J. (1996). Dynamics of the brain at global and microscopic scales: Neural networks and the EEG. *Behavioral and Brain Sciences, 19,* 285–320.

Wundt, W. (1907). *Outlines of psychology* (C. H. Judd, Trans.). New York: Stechert. (Original work published 1905)

Yakovlev, P. I., & Lecours, A. R. (1967). The myelogenetic cycles of regional maturation of the brain. In A. Minkowsky (Ed.), *Regional development of the brain in early life* (pp. 3–70). Oxford, England: Blackwell.

Zhang, J., & Norman, D. A. (1994). Representations in distributed cognitive tasks. *Cognitive Science, 18,* 87–122.

CHAPTER 10

Dynamic Systems Theories

ESTHER THELEN and LINDA B. SMITH

Dynamic systems is a recent theoretical approach to the study of development. In its contemporary formulation, the theory grows directly from advances in understanding complex and nonlinear systems in physics and mathematics, but it also follows a long and rich tradition of systems thinking in biology and psychology. The term *dynamic systems*, in its most generic form, means simply systems of elements that change over time. The more technical use, *dynamical systems,* refers to a class of mathematical equations that describe time-based systems with particular properties.

The writing of this chapter was supported in part by NIH RO1 HD22830 and a Research Scientist Award from the NIMH to Esther Thelen and by NIH HD28675 to Linda B. Smith.

In this chapter, we present a theory of development based on very general and content-independent principles that describe the behavior of complex physical and biological systems. Two themes will occur and recur:

1. Development can only be understood as the multiple, mutual, and continuous interaction of all the levels of the developing system, from the molecular to the cultural.

2. Development can only be understood as nested processes that unfold over many time scales, from milliseconds to years.

Dynamic systems provides theoretical principles for conceptualizing, operationalizing, and formalizing these complex interrelations of time, substance, and process. It is a metatheory in the sense that it may be (and has been) applied to different species, ages, domains, and grains of analysis. But it is also a specific theory of how humans gain knowledge from their everyday actions (e.g., Thelen & Smith, 1994).

BACKGROUND: SYSTEMS THEORIES IN DEVELOPMENT

> . . . the induction of novel behavioral forms may be the single most important unresolved problem for all the developmental sciences. (Wolff, 1987, p. 240)

What do we mean when we say that an organism "develops"? Usually, we see that it gets bigger, but always we mean that it gets more complex. Indeed, the defining property of development is the creation of new forms. A single cell and then a mass of identical cells are starting points for legs and livers and brains and hands. The 3-month-old infant who stops tracking a moving object when it goes out of sight becomes the 1-year-old baby who can search systematically in many locations for a hidden object. The 1-year-old baby becomes an 8-year-old child who can read a map and understand symbolically represented locations, and, later, an 18-year-old student who can understand and even create formal theories of space and geometry. Each of these transitions involves the emergence of new patterns of behavior from precursors that themselves do not contain those patterns. Where does this novelty come from? How can developing systems create something from nothing?

Understanding the origins of this increasing complexity is at the heart of our enterprise as developmental scientists. Traditionally, developmentalists have looked for the sources of new forms either in the organism or in the environment. In the first case, complex structures and functions emerge because the complexity exists within the organism in the form of a neural or genetic code. Development, then, consists of waiting until these stored instructions tell the organism what to do. Alternatively, the organism gains new form by absorbing the structure and patterning of its physical or social environment through interactions with that environment. In the more commonly accepted version, the two processes both contribute: organisms become complex through a combination of nature and nurture. For instance, the guiding assumption of the field of developmental behavior genetics is

that the sources of complexity can be partitioned into those that are inherent, and inherited, and those that are absorbed from the environment. But whether development is viewed as driven by innate structures, environmental input, or a combination of the two, the fundamental premise in the traditional view is that "information can preexist the processes that give rise to it" (Oyama, 1985, p. 13).

But if the instructions to develop are in the genes, who turns on the genes? If the complexity exists in the environment, who decides what the organism should absorb and retain? The only way to answer these questions is to invoke yet another causal agent who evaluates the information, whether genetic or environmental, and makes decisions. Some clever homunculus must be orchestrating a developmental score while knowing how it must all turn out in the end. This is a logically indefensible position, however; it says that novelty really does not develop, it is there all along. Postulating an interaction of genes and environment does not remove this logical impasse. It merely assigns the preexisting plans to two sources instead of one.

In this chapter, we follow a different tradition. We agree with Wolff (1987) that the question of novel forms is the great unanswered question. And we also concur that the traditional solutions—nature, nurture, or interaction—are insufficient. The tradition we follow, that of *systems theories of biological organization,* explains the formation of new forms by processes of *self-organization.* By self-organization we mean that *pattern and order emerge from the interactions of the components of a complex system without explicit instructions,* either in the organism itself or from the environment. Self-organization—processes that by their own activities change themselves—is a fundamental property of living things. Form is constructed in developmental process (Gottlieb, Wahlsten, & Lickliter, Ch. 5, this Volume; Oyama, 1985).

Dynamic systems offers general principles for formalizing ideas of biological self-organization in ways that are extraordinarily useful for understanding developmental process and for conducting experimental research. In this chapter and in other writing, we apply these principles most specifically to perceptual, motor, and cognitive development in infants and early childhood (e.g., Jones & Smith, 1993; Thelen, 1989; Thelen & Smith, 1994; Thelen & Ulrich, 1991). But the theme of the developing organism as a holistic, self-organizing system has appeared many times before in biology and psychology. Before we describe and apply dynamic principles, we situate our systems theory in the wider perspective of systems thinking in development. Toward this goal, our review is selective and thematic, rather than exhaustive. Readers are referred to excellent reviews by Ford and Lerner (1992), Gottlieb (1992), Gottlieb et al., Ch. 5, this Volume); Oyama (1985), and Sameroff (1983).

FORM FROM THE FORMLESS EGG: SELF-ORGANIZATION IN EMBRYOGENESIS

A baby's first step or first word is a dramatic example of new behavioral form. But no example of developmental novelty is as compelling as the emergence of an embryo from the initial state of a seemingly homogeneous and formless single cell, the fertilized egg. And no other aspect of development seems so completely "genetic" in the strict unfolding of species-typical structure.

For well over a century, biologists have studied this transformation of a single sphere into an intricate, three-dimensional organism with beautifully formed organs and well-differentiated tissue types. Within the past few decades, however, researchers have made significant advances toward understanding the "impenetrable black box" (Marx, 1984a, p. 425) of this developmental process.

What is now abundantly clear is that embryonic development is an intricate dance between events in the nucleus—the turning off and on of particular gene products—and what one writer has deemed "mundane" biophysical principles in the cell body and surface (Marx, 1984b, p. 1406). Consider how animals get their basic body plans—the specific parts and organs that emerge in orderly time and space dimensions in the first days and weeks of life. Formation of the body pattern occurs when the fertilized egg has divided to about 10,000 cells. By this time, although the cells look like an undifferentiated heap, they are already marked in positions that predict distinct body locations. They have become a kind of founder group of cells.

It is now well established that what appeared to be a homogeneous founder cell or group of cells actually contains various and subtle gradients of substances, which form a very general "prepattern" of the structure that will emerge (Wolpert, 1971). These gradients and patterns, in turn, often arise from the "mundane" effects of gravity, the mechanical effects of molecular structure in the cell and at its surface (the pushing and pulling of particular molecules and crystals), or the regulated amplification of small local fluctuations in physiology or metabolism (Cooke, 1988; Gierer, 1981). Even more remarkable, is that once some initial prepattern is formed, the regulating genes in the nucleus are themselves switched on and off by these changing physical and mechanical events outside of the nucleus. Thus, once the initial generalized body fates are determined, the course of more refined tissue and organ differentiation is equally bidirectional between nuclear processes and other cellular events.

During embryogenesis, cells divide, change character, move, and organize themselves into larger collectives of tissues, organs, and organ systems. The process is highly dynamic; that is, the cell and tissue movements themselves are sources of order and complexity. As groups of cells arising from different local gradients move and come into contact, their new positions further change their character, a process known as *induction*. What is especially relevant to our account here is that no single cell itself gives the signal that this region will become neural tube or limb bud. Rather, it is the group of cells, acting as a collective and within a particular position in the larger collective, that determines their ultimate fate. No one cell is critical, but the history and spatial and temporal dimensions of the collective are. Development is constructed through process:

> The pathways of induction and determination involve a historical series of milieu-dependent gene expressions that are coupled to those mechanical and mechanochemical events that actually govern the achievement of form and pattern. At any one time, there is an interplay between the place, scale, and size of bordering collectives, and various inductive molecular signals not only maintain the pattern so far established but also transform it into a new pattern. (Edelman, 1988, p. 26)

This picture is much different from one that casts the genes as the puppeteer, pulling the right strings at the right time to control the ensuing events in the cells. In a dynamic view, we consider the marionette and the puppeteer as affecting each other equally. Or, more accurately, we do away with the puppeteer and the marionette altogether: *What is important is the relationships among the strings as they pull and then become slack.*

Embryologists have been among the pioneers in using dynamic systems both formally and metaphorically to model developmental processes. Most notable was the preeminent developmental biologist C. H. Waddington. Waddington's primary interest was the genetic influence on tissue differentiation in the embryo, the emergence of sharply distinctive tissue types—bones, muscles, lungs, and so on—from a single cell. Although a geneticist, he was also a thoroughgoing systems theorist. Waddington couched developmental process in explicitly dynamic terms: "We can still consider development in terms of the solutions of a system of simultaneous differential equations," he wrote in 1954 (Waddington, p. 238). Especially in his later writings, Waddington described embryonic change in the language of attractors, bifurcations, open systems, stability, catastrophes, and chaos (Waddington, 1977). Figure 10.1 is one of his depictions, in three dimensions, of the "multidimensional space,

subdivided into a number of regions, such that trajectories starting anywhere within one region converge to one certain end point, while those starting in other regions converge elsewhere" (Waddington, 1957, p. 28). The figure shows how the gradients established in the egg, through time-dependent processes, become stable, differentiated tissue types. Waddington was especially intrigued by the self-stabilizing nature of development, depicted on his now classic "epigenetic landscape" (Figure 10.2). The landscape represents a developing system, where time runs toward the reader, and where the depth of the valleys is an indication of stability (the ball, once in a valley, is hard to dislodge). From an initial undifferentiated state (the ball could be anywhere on the landscape), development creates hillocks and valleys of increasing complexity. As development proceeds, the tissue types become separated by higher hills, signifying the irreversible nature of development. However, the pathways down the landscape also show buffering; that is, development proceeds in globally similar ways despite somewhat different initial conditions, and despite minor perturbations or fluctuations along the way. In his last book, published posthumously in 1977, Waddington called the epigenetic landscape an "attractor landscape"

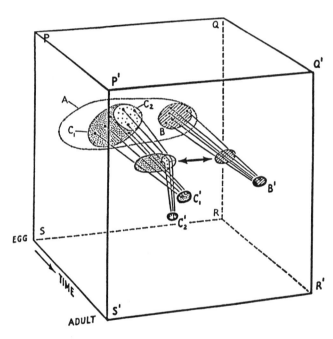

Figure 10.1 Waddington's phase-space diagram of development. Time runs along the z axis, from plane PQRS at the time of fertilization to P'Q'R'S' which is adulthood. The other two dimensions represent the composition of the system. The diagram shows how the egg, which has continuous composition gradients becomes differentiated into specific tissues. Some areas in the state space act as attractors, pulling in nearby trajectories. From *The Strategy of the Genes: A Discussion of Some Aspects of Theoretical Biology,* by C. H. Waddington, p. 28. Copyright © 1957 by Allen & Unwin. Reprinted with permission of Mrs. M. J. Waddington.

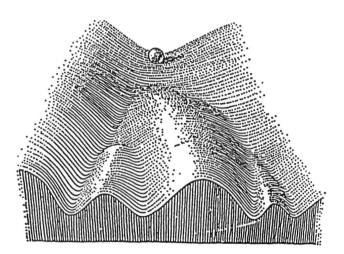

Figure 10.2 Waddington's classic epigenetic landscape. The path of the ball is the developmental history of part of the egg, showing the increasing stability of the developing tissue types. From *The Strategy of the Genes: A Discussion of Some Aspects of Theoretical Biology,* by C. H. Waddington, p. 29. Copyright © 1957 by Allen & Unwin. Reprinted with permission of Mrs. M. J. Waddington.

(p. 105). He asked, "How do we find out the shape of the landscape?" He suggested: "So what we should try to do is to alter it, slightly, in as many ways as possible and observe its reactions. We will find that the system resists some types of changes more than others, or restores itself more quickly after changes in some directions than in others" (Waddington, 1977, p. 113). Similarly, in our version of a dynamic systems account, probing the system's stability is also a critical step.

Since Waddington, theorists and mathematicians have offered numerous dynamic models of morphogenesis, the emergence of form (see, e.g., Gierer, 1981; Goodwin & Cohen, 1969; Meakin, 1986; Tapaswi & Saha, 1986; Thom, 1983; Yates & Pate, 1989, among others). The common features of these models are initial conditions consisting of very shallow gradients, differential mechanical factors such as pressures or adhesions in the cells, or both. The gradient or force fields are represented by one of several classes of differential equations, which express change as a function of time. Some sets of equations involve lateral inhibition, which allows a small local activation to become enhanced and form the node of a pattern. When the equations are solved for a variety of parameters, complex spatial patterns are generated, which may consist of cycles, multiple peaks and valleys, and even fractals (complex scale-independent patterns). Combining two or more gradients with different rates of change and coupling their interactions can lead to highly complex patterns, including stripes, columns, and so on: "[V]ery complex real patterns may arise on the basis of elementary field-forming mechanisms and their combinations" (Gierer, 1981, p. 15).

One of the most delightful and fanciful of these models of pattern formation is that of the mathematician J. D. Murray, who provides an elegant model of the ontogeny of mammalian coat patterns: "how the leopard got its spots" (Murray, 1988, 1993). Think about your last visit to the zoo and the remarkable range of coat markings you saw: the complex spots and stripes of zebras, leopards, and giraffes; the simpler stripes of skunks and badgers; and the softly shaded patterns of some ungulates. Murray shows how a *single* mechanism, modeled by a simple nonlinear equation of the developmental process, can account for all the variations in coat markings. The equation is of the reaction-diffusion type, where an initial gradient of some chemical (the morphogen) can take on particular rates of reaction combined with varying rates of diffusion in a closed surface. The interactions between the chemical reaction and its rate of diffusion are highly nonlinear, meaning that sometimes the reaction proceeds in a stable manner, but, at other values, the reaction is unstable and no pigment is formed. This nonlinearity leads to either a smooth or a patchlike pattern of reaction products on the surface. Critical factors are: the reaction rates and when the process is started, presumably under genetic control, and then, only the geometry and scale of the surface over which the gradients work. For coat color, the initial gradient is believed to be some substance that activates melanin (pigment) production in melanocyte cells in the skin surface during early embryogenesis.

The power of Murray's simple model is illustrated in Figure 10.3, which shows the results of the simulations of the equation with set parameters, changing only the scale of surface of the body over which the chemical dynamics occur. As the body is scaled up over 50,000 times (presumably, from a mouse to an elephant), a regular series of patterns emerges: the solid color of very small animals, the simple bifurcations and the more elaborate spottings, and,

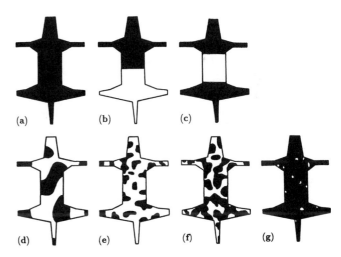

Figure 10.3 The effect of body surface scale on the patterns formed by a reaction diffusion mechanisms for mammalian coat coloration. A single mechanism can account for diverse coat patterns, depending on the parameter values in the equations. From J. D. Murray, 1993, *Mathematical Biology*, (p. 445, 2nd ed.) Berlin: Springer-Verlag. Copyright © 1993 by Springer-Verlag. Reprinted with permission.

again, the nearly uniform coat. (Indeed, very small and very large mammals are more likely to have solid coats.) In real animals, small random variations in the initial gradient would lead to the noticeable individual variations in coat pattern. The important fact for our account is that the dynamics of the reactions create the pattern.

DEVELOPMENTAL PSYCHOLOGY: REEXAMINING THE ROOT METAPHOR

Embryologists and theoreticians of morphogenesis have shown us how, during development, extraordinarily complex structural patterns can arise from very simple initial conditions in dynamic systems. The patterns that result are not specifically coded in the genes. Although all leopards are spotted and all raccoons have striped tails, there is no dedicated gene for spots on the leopard or striped tails for raccoons. Structural complexity is constructed during development because living systems with particular chemical and metabolic constraints spontaneously organize themselves into patterns. In such systems, the issue of "what causes what to happen" is particularly thorny. When all parts of the system cooperate, when a group of cells only takes on a particular fate in the context of its position among other cells, it is simply not feasible to ask whether this structure or this behavior is "caused" by genes or by environment. Through experimentation and modeling, the efforts of embryologists are directed toward a deep and detailed understanding of process.

Although the issues for understanding the development of human behavior and the human mind are the same as those addressed by embryologists, contemporary developmental psychologists have not devoted similar attention to processes of change. Rather, much study has been directed toward discovering invariants—programs, stages, structures, representations, devices, schemas, modules—that underlie performance at different ages. A good part of this search is directed toward which invariants are "innate" (present at birth) and which are "genetic" (hard-wired into the system by natural selection). Thus, especially in the study of cognitive and language development, the focus is on what is stable and universal, rather than on the processes that engender change. For example, some programs of research seek "core" abilities by discovering how early in life infants display elements of knowledge about

mathematics (Gelman & Gallistel, 1978), about the properties of objects (Spelke, Breinlinger, Macomber, & Jacobson, 1992), or about faces (Johnson & Morton, 1991). Alternatively, it is popular to look for systemwide constraints on ability, in the guise of skill levels or processing capacity that may or may not be implemented with specific experiences (e.g., Case, 1985; Kail, 1986; Keil, 1986; van der Maas & Molenaar, 1992).

We suggest here that the fundamental difference between the epigenetic view epitomized by embryology and the theoretical stance of these just-noted themes within contemporary developmental psychology is in the root metaphor that guides the science. In particular, human developmentalists have been strongly influenced by a machine or computational view of human behavior. Cognition works like the operations of a machine, especially a computer. In the traditional machine metaphor, information is "processed" through a serial set of stages from input to output. The real work is done by the devices or structures that encode the rules, like the program in the computer. These formal structures are timeless and represent the person's real "competence." The competence may or may not be displayed in performance, just as the full range of a program's power may not be revealed in each operation. Nonetheless, the rules are abstracted from and are above the performance details. Thus, in developmental studies associated with this tradition, much effort is directed toward extracting these essential rules or constraints from the real-life and messy interruptions of performance.

The classic example is Chomsky's (1986) well-known language device. According to Chomsky, language universals are an abstract knowledge set determined by human evolution. This structure is independent of the vagaries of real-time language use, memory, attention, and other factors that influence what people actually say. Knowledge is like the unchanging "innards" of the machine, and performance subserves the more permanent structure. Much study of cognitive development has been directed toward characterizing these competence structures and their change.

The mind-as-computer metaphor is very deep and powerful. People do have hardware (brains), and they do process information. But computers are static entities whose order comes from the people who build them. The metaphor is not a good one for development, where there is no program and the issue of the origins of order is paramount.

A DIFFERENT METAPHOR

We now introduce a different mind-picture—a mountain stream—to wean ourselves away from the machine metaphor. Consider the patterns in a fast-moving mountain stream. At some places, the water flows smoothly in small ripples. Nearby may be a small whirlpool or a large turbulent eddy. Still other places may show waves or spray. These patterns persist hour after hour and even day after day, but after a storm or a long dry spell, new patterns may appear. Where do they come from? Why do they persist and why do they change?

No one would assign any geological plan or grand hydraulic design to the patterns in a mountain stream. Rather, the regularities patently emerge from multiple factors: the rate of flow of the water downstream, the configuration of the stream bed, the current weather conditions that determine evaporation rate and rainfall, and the important quality of water molecules under particular constraints to self-organize into different patterns of flow. But what we see in the here-and-now is just part of the picture. The particular patterns evident are also produced by unseen constraints, acting over many different scales of time. The geological history of the mountains determined the incline of the stream bed and the erosion of the rocks. The long-range climate of the region led to particular vegetation on the mountain and the consequent patterns of water absorption and runoff. The climate within the past year or two affected the snow on the mountain and the rate of melting. The configuration of the mountain just upstream influenced the flow rate downstream. And so on. Moreover, we can see the relative importance of these constraints in maintaining a stable pattern. If a small rock falls into a pool, nothing may change. As falling rocks get larger and larger, at some point, the stream may split into two, or create a new, faster channel. What endures and what changes?

We liken behavior patterns and mental activity to the eddies and ripples of a mountain stream. They exist in the here-and-now, and they may be very stable or easily changed. Behavior is the product of multiple, contributing influences, each of which itself has a history. But just as we cannot really disentangle the geologic history of the mountain from the current configuration of the stream bed, we also cannot draw a line between the real-time behavior and the lifetime processes that contribute to it. Likewise, there is no separation of the patterns themselves from some abstraction of those patterns.

The mountain stream metaphor depicts behavioral development as an *epigenetic process,* that is, truly constructed by its own history and systemwide activity. In this chapter, we propose that the more general and formal principles of dynamic systems theory are a robust characterization of such systems. With or without the formal language of dynamics, developmentalists have been proposing epigenetic and systems accounts for many years. It is important, therefore, to review the rich history of systems thinking about development.

EMERGENT BEHAVIOR: EPIGENESIS IN DEVELOPMENTAL PSYCHOBIOLOGY

No one understood a systems approach more deeply than a group of developmental psychobiologists working largely in the 1940s, 1950s, and 1960s, especially T. C. Schneirla, Daniel Lehrman, and Zing-Yang Kuo, whose tradition is carried on today most eloquently by Gilbert Gottlieb (Gottlieb et al., this Volume). These biologists used the word *epigenesis* to describe the process of behavioral ontogeny (see Kitchener, 1978, for discussion of the various meanings of the term *epigenesis*). Their vision is best understood as a contrast with the prevailing scientific thought about behavior and its change, and, in particular, the recurrent issue of nature versus nurture.

In those decades, North American psychology was dominated by learning theorists. As is well known, the goal of these experimental psychologists was to elucidate the general laws of behavior as animals are shaped by experience. Behaviorists used a variety of experimental animals such as rats and pigeons, but they believed that the principles of training and reinforcement applied to all species, including humans. Development, according to behaviorist theories, consists of the animal's reinforcement history. The radical environmentalism of behaviorists is captured in a statement from a critical essay by Lehrman (1971):

> Also basic to what I here call the "behaviorist orientation" is the idea that scientific explanations of, and statements of scientific insights into, behavior, *consist* of statements about how the experimenter gains control over the behavior, or about how the actions of the subject can be predicted by the actions of the experimenter. (p. 462)

Although learning continues to be an important aspect of developmental accounts, especially in explaining the socialization of children (Bandura, 1977), learning theories per se have lost favor as general developmental theories. In part, this is due to their inabilities to explain species differences and to provide satisfactory accounts of cognitive and language development. Equally troubling is that learning alone does not tell us how novelty arises.

In the 1950s and 1960s, a view of behavior became popular that strongly opposed pure learning theories. *Ethological theories* came from the European school associated with Konrad Lorenz and his students. Lorenz's work was seminal in reorienting psychologists to the role of species-typical behavior and animals' adaptations to their environments. And although ethologists such as Lorenz considered learning to be important, learning always was placed alongside behavior deemed innate or instinctive. According to Lorenz (1965), this distinction between innate and learned was of primary importance in understanding behavior and its development. Indeed, Lorenz believed that behavior could be broken up into elements that were wholly innate and elements that were learned, although the focus of ethologists' studies was most often on the innate parts. The form of a behavior—for example, particular courtship calls or displays, or, in humans, facial expressions—were believed to be "hard-wired" and not acquired. Lorenz called this class of movements "fixed action patterns" because they were believed to emerge without specific experience. The object and orientation of these displays may be learned, however, during ontogeny. Geese, for instance, instinctively follow objects to which they become imprinted during the first few days, but they could learn to follow Lorenz instead, if he substituted himself for the mother goose at the appropriate time.

The epigeneticists, in contrast to both learning theorists and ethologists, campaigned to eliminate altogether the question of learned versus acquired. They were especially critical of what they considered the vague and ill-defined meaning of such terms as *innate* or *instinctive*. Lehrman's statement in 1953 is as eloquent and relevant today as then:

> The "instinct" is obviously not present in the zygote. Just as obviously, it is present in the behavior of the animal after the appropriate age. The problem for the investigator is: How did this behavior come about? The use of "explanatory" categories such as "innate" and "genetically fixed" obscures the necessity of investigating developmental *processes* in order to gain insight into actual mechanisms of behavior and their interrelations. The problem of development is the problem of the development of new *structures* and activity *patterns* from the resolution of the interaction of existing ones within the organism and its internal environment, and between the organism and its outer environment. (Lehrman, 1953)

In his book, *The Dynamics of Behavior Development: An Epigenetic View,* Kuo (1967) presented a particularly clear statement of developmental process from a systems view. Kuo emphasized that behavior is complex and variable and takes place in a continually changing internal and external environment. The behavior we observe is an integral part of the total response of the animal to the environment, but there are differentiations—or patterned gradients—of response among different parts of the body. He wrote:

> Ontogenesis of behavior is a process of modification, transformation, or reorganization of the existing patterns of behavior gradients in response to the impact of new environmental stimulation; and in consequence a new spatial and/or serial pattern of behavior gradients is formed, permanently or temporarily ("learning") which oftentimes adds to the inventory of the existing patterns of behavior gradients previously accumulated during the animal's developmental history. (Kuo, 1970, p. 189).

During the life span, new patterns are selected from among the range of potential patterns.

> Thus, in every stage of ontogenesis, every response is determined not only by the stimuli or stimulating objects, but also by the total environmental context, the status of anatomical structures and their functional capacities, the physiological (biochemical and biophysical) condition, and the developmental history up to that stage. (Kuo, 1970, p. 189)

In his call for an integrated developmental science, Kuo exhorted scientists to study "every event that takes place under and outside the skin" (1970, p. 190) as part of the behavior gradient, and not to look just at global measures of organism or environment: "[W]e must take quantitative measures of stimulative effects of every sensory modality, and make qualitative analyses of the interactions of the component parts of the environmental context or complex." Kuo's extraordinary vision, fashioned from his work as both an embryologist and a comparative psychologist, did not have a direct influence on the mainstream of child psychology, which became enraptured with Piaget (1952) at that time, and later with Bowlby (1969) and attachment theory. Nonetheless, a broad systems view has continued with a group of comparative developmental psychobiologists who have conducted exquisite and detailed studies of the intricate interrelated mechanisms of offspring, parents, and environment in early life. These include Gilbert Gottlieb, Jay Rosenblatt, Lester Aronson, Ethel Tobach, Howard Moltz, William Hall, Jeffrey Alberts, Patrick Bateson, Meredith West, and others. Gerald Turkewitz has been a pioneer in continuing the Schneirla–Kuo tradition in human infancy studies.

One hallmark of this comparative work is minute and detailed understanding of the experiential context of the developing organism, including factors that are not necessarily the apparent and obvious precursors to a particular behavior, but may indeed be critical contributors. "Experience may contribute to ontogeny in subtle ways," wrote Schneirla (1957, p. 90) and also in ways that are nonspecific. Small effects of temperature, light, and gravity, at critical times, for instance, can cascade into large developmental differences. Nonobvious and nonspecific factors are important considerations in a dynamic systems view as well.

A beautiful example of developmental analysis in the systems tradition of Schneirla and Kuo is the work of Meredith West and Andrew King on the ontogeny of bird song. West and King's studies on song learning in the cowbird, a brood parasite, have uncovered subtleties and variations in the developmental process that raise questions about the more simplistic earlier views: that song learning was either directed by an innate template, or learned by imitation of other singing males. First, they found an overwhelming effect of context on both the learning and the performing of songs—for example, males' being housed with females during rearing affected their song content. Even though females do not sing, they exert social influences on males that are strong enough to override any specific sensory template (King & West, 1988). The mechanism appears to be females' selective responses (by brief wing-flicking movements) during the time when males are learning song. The female cowbird helps shape the male song by her response. Furthermore, experience with cowbird females is essential for appropriate male mating behavior. When male cowbirds were raised with canaries,

they sang to and pursued canaries rather than females of their own species. But this preference was not a rigid imprinting, as the old ethologists would have maintained. When these canary-housed cowbird males were housed with cowbird females in their second season, they reversed their preference.

From this and other evidence, West and King conclude that song development is highly multiply determined and dynamic in the sense of being continually constructed in time and space. An animal's species-typical environment of rearing and its own actions within that environment are as "inevitable [a] source of influence as are an animal's genes" (West & King, 1996). And because these dynamic processes are so interactive and nonlinear, fundamental properties disappear when they are disrupted. For example, experimental perturbations to the expected rearing conditions, such as placing animals in isolation or injecting them with hormones, may have both dramatic and subtle cascading effects. Such manipulations often illuminate the interactions in the system, but they must be interpreted with great care. In a later section, we also raise cautions about interpretations of experiments with infants and children because the interaction between the experimental manipulation and the normal, everyday experiences of the subjects are often unknown. A dynamic systems approach suggests that these contextual factors and their time-functions are the critical aspects of performance.

FORM IN CONTEXT: CONTEXTUAL AND ECOLOGICAL THEORISTS

The tradition of the embryologists and the epigeneticists emphasized self-organization from multiple processes both within the organism and between the organism and its environment. The focus is on relationships among components as the origins of change, rather than a set of instructions. Such a view naturally turns our attention to the physical and social settings in which infants and children are raised, and it requires as detailed an understanding of the context as of the organism situated within that context. Existing developmental theories can be placed on a continuum as to whether they are more concerned with what is in the child's head or with the specific and changing details of the environment. Piagetian, cognitivist, and information-processing accounts of development, for instance, pay little attention to the particular nature of the physical and social worlds of children. The goal of these approaches is to understand general qualities of mind and how they develop. Because the processes are assumed to be universal adaptations to the world by human brains, it is immaterial, for instance, whether a child learns transitive inference from playing with sticks on the ground, or in a structured school, or by observing groups of people talking and acting. The focus is on the individual as the basic unit of analysis, in the sense that individuals all have common structures and processes above and beyond their differing experiences.

For theorists at the other end of the continuum, a person's experiences in context and culture are not just supportive of development, but are the very stuff of development itself. At this end of the continuum, we group developmentalists who are working in the tradition of James Mark Baldwin, John Dewey, Kurt Lewin, and, more recently, A. R. Luria and L. S. Vygotsky, and who, today, are labeled as *ecological, contextual,* or *cross-cultural* theorists. Some versions of *lifespan* perspectives (e.g., Baltes, 1987) also have strong epigenetic and systems assumptions. These views are well represented in this Volume in the chapters by Overton; Valsiner; Gottlieb et al.; Czikszentmihalyi and Rathunde; Magnusson and Stattin; Wapner and Demick; Brandtstäder; Shweder et al.; Elder; Bronfenbrenner and Morris; and Baltes, Lindenberger, and Staudinger. Although there are many versions of contextualism (see reviews by Dixon & Lerner, 1988; Ford & Lerner, 1992), they share certain assumptions about development, and these assumptions overlap with many features of a dynamic systems approach. First and foremost is the quest to eliminate the duality between individual and environment, just as the epigeneticists endeavored to erase the boundaries between structure and function.

All developmental theorists would acknowledge that humans and other living beings can be described over many levels of organization from the molecular and cellular, through the complex level of neural activity and behavior, and extending to nested relationships with the social and physical environments (e.g., Bronfenbrenner, 1979). And all developmental theories also view these levels as interacting with one another. The deep difference between contextualism and more individual-centered approaches is that the levels are conceptualized as *more* than just interacting; instead, they are seen as integrally fused together. Behavior and its development are melded as ever-changing sets of

relationships and the history of those relationships over time. Thus, as mentioned in an earlier section, we must discard our notions of simple linear causality: that event A or structure X *caused* behavior B to appear. Rather, causality is multiply determined over levels and continually changing over time.

Systems ideas have radical implications for the study of mind. For example, the idea that knowledge is emergent and that human behavior is socially constructed in task and history is beautifully illustrated in Hutchins's (1995) recent study of navigation. Navigation in modern navies is achieved via a complex system of interactions among a large number of people and measuring devices. These interactions are shaped and maintained historically by the culture of military practice and language, but also by the geography of large ships, by the measuring devices, by the psychology of individuals, and by the encountered tasks. No one element alone does the navigation. Hutchins's analysis, based on both participant observation and computer simulation, shows how all these elements matter—how the smartness of navigation teams emerges, depends on, and is constrained by the physical components, traditional roles, and culture. Navigation teams *are* smart. Their activity is event-driven and goal-directed. The navigation team must keep pace with the movement of the ship and must maintain progress. When things go wrong, there is no option to quit and start over; the right decision must be made at the moment. Hutchins's work shows how these decisions are distributed over the interactions of individuals—none of whom knows all there is to know about the problem. Nor is the optimal system one in which the problem has been logically divided up into mutually exclusive parts and assigned to individuals in a perfect division of labor. Rather, navigation teams are characterized by partially redundant and sometimes rapidly changing patterns of interactions and information flow. The intelligence sits in the patterns of interactions in the whole and has properties quite unlike those of the individuals who comprise that whole.

At the end of his book, Hutchins reflects on the meaning of culture and socially distributed cognition for cognitive science:

> The early researchers in cognitive science placed a bet that the modularity of human cognition would be such that culture, context, and history could be safely ignored at the outset and then integrated in later. The bet did not pay off.

These things are fundamental aspects of human cognition and cannot be comfortably integrated into a perspective that privileges abstract properties of isolated individual minds. (Hutchins, 1995, p. 354)

It is our contention here that the only framework that is appropriate to characterizing relationships and their changes over all these levels of organization is that of dynamics.

DEVELOPMENT AS A DYNAMIC SYSTEM

We have described theoretical approaches to development at different levels of organization, from embryological to societal. These approaches are based on common assumptions about systems' complexity and the multiple interrelated causes of change. However, the characteristics of developing organisms emphasized in these views—self-organization, nonlinearity, openness, stability, and change—are not confined to biological systems. They are also found in complex physical systems such as chemical reactions, global weather changes, mountain streams, clouds, dripping faucets—wherever many components form a coherent pattern and change over time. The principles of dynamic systems formulated by physicists and mathematicians to describe the behavior of such complex physical systems may also be the best way to study and understand developing organisms. But we are not the first to make this connection.

Kurt Lewin and Dynamic Force Fields

One of the earliest explicitly dynamic formulations of development was Kurt Lewin's (1936, 1946) topological *field theory* of personality development. Lewin was unabashedly antireductionist. How, he asked, can psychology present all the richness of human behavior as the novelist, but "with scientific instead of poetic means" (Lewin, 1946, p. 792)? Referencing Einstein's theoretical physics, Lewin proposed:

> The method should be analytical in that the different factors which influence behavior have to be specifically distinguished. In science, these data have also to be represented in their particular setting within the specific situation. A totality of coexisting facts which are conceived of as mutually interdependent is called a *field*. (1946, p. 792)

According to Lewin, a given physical setting has meaning only as a function of the state of the individual in that setting. Conversely, individual traits do not exist outside of the setting in which they are displayed. Lewin called these fields of interactions *life spaces*—fields of forces with varying strengths. People move dynamically through this force field, depending on their location in the space, their needs, and previous history. Forces may compete, conflict, overlap, or sum, depending on the person's disposition and the environment. Learning—and development—consist of finding a pathway or discovering a new niche in the life space. And as children carve new pathways, they actually create yet new parts of the space to explore, a process of self-organization.

Lewin depicted this developmental dynamic as shown in Figure 10.4. Life spaces at different points in development are represented by layered force fields, with different zones for varying degrees of "attraction" to those fields. The parameters of the life space have several dimensions: size of the space, degree of specificity, separation between reality and "irreality" or fantasy, and the influence of psychological processes across time. The life space of a younger child is more limited and less differentiated, and it

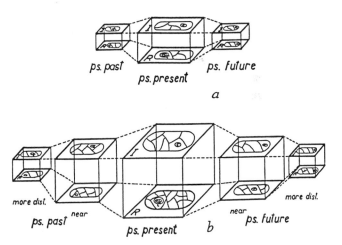

Figure 10.4   Lewin's psychological space (ps.) landscapes, depicted as layered systems of force fields with R = "reality" and I = "Irreality," and showing the connection between the motivational forces in the past, present, and future. The top panel depicts a life space of a young child; the bottom, that of an older child. From "Behavior and development as a function of the total situation," by K. Lewin, 1946, in L. Carmichael (Ed.), *Manual of Child Psychology*, p. 798. New York: John Wiley & Sons. Copyright © 1946 by John Wiley & Sons. Reprinted with permission.

is influenced more by the immediate past and projects more into the immediate future than the more expansive space of the older child. Waddington's 1977 illustration of a phase-space diagram of development, shown in Figure 10.1, is remarkably similar to Lewin's in identifying preferred regions and depicting development as progressive drift through this space.

Systems Theory as Metaphor

Kurt Lewin's dynamic concepts were rich, but vague and difficult to operationalize. His ideas were poorly matched to either the mechanistic flavor of North American experimental psychology during the 1950s and 1960s, or to the mentalistic assumptions of Piagetian developmental psychology, and his impact on child psychology was little felt during those decades. Systems thinking about development underwent a small renaissance in the late 1970s and early 1980s, however, and these versions were much more explicitly tied to the new sciences of complexity in physics, math, and biology. Two authors, Ludwig van Bertalanffy, a biologist, and Ilya Prigogine, a chemist, were especially influential in this renewal.

Ludwig van Bertalanffy (1968) has usually been credited with originating "General Systems Theory." Since the 1930s, he had heralded an antireductionist view of biological systems (Bertalanffy, 1933). The dominant trend in all the sciences, from chemistry to psychology, was to isolate smaller and smaller elements of the system, but Bertalanffy felt that understanding would come, not from these separate parts, but from the relationships among them. So, while animals are made of tissues and cells, and cells are built from complex molecules, knowing the structure of the molecules even in the greatest detail cannot inform us about the behavior of the animal. Something happens when complex and heterogeneous parts come together to form a whole that is more than the parts. The system properties need a new level of description—one that cannot be derived from the behavior of the components alone. These systems principles, in turn, are so universal that they apply to widely diverse beings and entities:

> We can ask for principles applying to systems in general, irrespective of whether they are of physical, biological, or sociological nature. If we pose this question and conveniently define the concept of system, we find that models, principles,

and laws exist which apply to generalized systems irrespective of their particular kind, elements, and "forces" involved. (Bertalanffy, 1968, p. 33)

Bertalanffy provided dynamic equations to illustrate these principles: wholeness, or self-organization; openness; equifinality (self-stabilization); and hierarchical organization. In his discussion of systems applications to psychology, Bertalanffy was especially critical of "homeostasis" models of mental functioning, especially the Freudian assumption that organisms are always seeking to reduce tensions and seek a state of equilibrium. Rather, organisms are also *active;* as open systems, they live in a kind of disequilibrium (what we will call dynamic stability) and actively seek stimulation. This disequilibrium allows change and flexibility; the idea that too much stability is inimicable to change recurs in many developmental accounts (e.g., Piaget, Werner) and is an assumption we also find essential for understanding development.

The Nobel chemist Ilya Prigogine was the second principal contributor to systems theory and an eloquent popularizer as well (see, e.g., Prigogine, 1978; Prigogine & Stengers, 1984). Prigogine was primarily interested in the physics of systems that were far from thermodynamic equilibrium. Recall that, in Newtonian thermodynamics, all systems run to disorder. The energy of the universe dissipates over time. The universe increases in *entropy,* and, as Prigogine puts it, the "arrow of time" runs in only one direction—toward disorganization. But many systems, and all biological systems, live in thermodynamic nonequilibrium. They are thermodynamically open: They take in energy from their environment and increase their order—the arrow of time is at least temporarily reversed. Development is a premier example of a progressive *increase* in complexity and organization. Such systems take on special properties, including the ability to self-organize into patterns and nonlinearity or sensitivity to initial conditions. Again, it is critical that such systems are inherently "noisy," for order arises from such fluctuations. In equilibrium systems, the noise is damped out and the system as a whole remains in equilibrium. In nonequilibrium systems, in contrast, fluctuations can become amplified and overtake the organization of the whole system, shifting it to a new order of organization.

A number of developmentalists immediately recognized the relevance of these explicit systems principles for age-old, yet still critical issues in developmental psychology. Sandor Brent (1978), for instance, saw in Prigogine's formulations of self-organization potential solutions for the questions of the origins of complexity and shifts from one developmental stage to more advanced levels. Moreover, Brent believed that ideas of nonlinearity could explain the seemingly "autocatalytic" aspects of development, where one small transformation acts as the catalyst for subsequent, accelerating changes.

Brent's discussion is strictly theoretical. Arnold Sameroff (1983) tied the new systems ideas more concretely to developmental phenomena. Sameroff has long been interested in developmental outcomes of children at risk, particularly in the failure of linear models to predict pathology from antecedent conditions. In an important and influential paper, Sameroff and Chandler (1975) documented the persistently puzzling finding that some children with very serious risk factors around birth, including anoxia, prematurity, delivery complications, and poor social environments, suffered no or little long-term consequences, while others sustained serious effects. Simple cause-and-effect or medical models of disease must be supplanted with a thoroughgoing organismic model, according to Sameroff, where "Emphasis on a wholistic, actively functioning entity that constructs itself out of transactions with the environment is derived from the properties of biological development" (1983, pp. 253–254).

Adoption of such a systems model, with its assumptions of wholeness, self-stabilization, self-organization, and hierarchical organization, has implications for every aspect of developmental psychology, according to Sameroff. For instance, theories of socialization must become thoroughly contextual, because the notion of open systems means that the individual is always in transaction with the environment. Biological vulnerability or risk, in this case, does not exist in a vacuum, but within the rich network of a more or less supportive family and community culture. Outcome is a joint product of the child and the cultural agenda of the society, and the total system has self-organizing and self-stabilizing characteristics.

Likewise, the issue of *change* motivates the *developmental system theory* of Ford and Lerner (1992). In reasoning that closely parallels our own, Ford and Lerner begin with a view of humans as "multilevel, contextual organizations of structures and functions" (p. 47) who exhibit varying kinds of stability and variability and who can change both within and between levels. Individual development, according to these theorists:

> . . . *involves incremental and transformational processes that, through a flow of interactions among current characteristics of the person and his or her current contexts, produces a succession of relatively enduring changes that elaborate or increase the diversity of the person's structural and functional characteristics and the patterns of their environmental interactions while maintaining coherent organization and structural-functional unity of the person as a whole.* (p. 49, italics in original)

The definition, they maintain, implies a lifelong possibility of change, multiple (although not infinite) and nonlinear developmental pathways, discontinuities, and the emergence of new forms. Furthermore, the definition specifies that development is never a function of person or context alone, but indeed results as a function of their dynamic interaction. Figure 10.5 is Ford and Lerner's model of developmental change as a series of probabilistic states, where control systems interact within the person (the horseshoe shapes) and between the person and the environment. States are thus the current configuration of the system, based both on current status and on the system's immediate and long-term history. We will repeat these themes throughout the remainder of this chapter.

Ford and Lerner's treatise is ambitious in scope; it ties biological and social development into a single developmental systems theory. Their intellectual debt is directly to the "organismic" and contextual school of developmental theory, and less so to physical and mathematical dynamical systems. Likewise, they are not primarily concerned with operational verification of a systems approach, nor do they connect directly with the experimental and observational studies of individual child development. In contrast to Ford and Lerner, other theorists have used explicit mathematical models to address issues of individual cognitive change.

Mathematical Dynamic Models of Cognitive Development

As we mentioned at the outset, *dynamical systems* are a class of mathematical equations that describe time-based systems with particular properties, especially complex, nonlinear behavior over time. The appeal for developmentalists is that

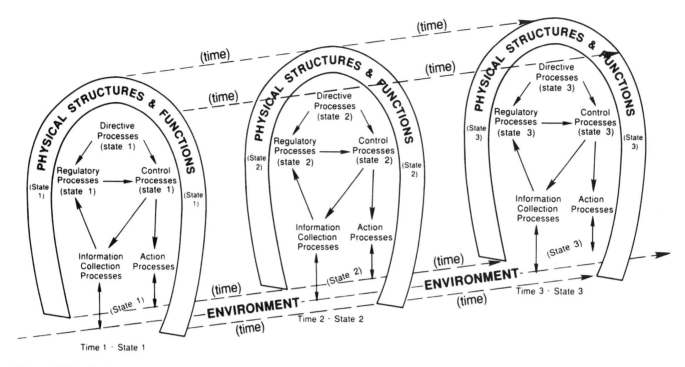

Figure 10.5 Ford and Lerner's model of developmental change as a series of probabalistic states.

real developing organisms behave in many ways like those described by the sets of equations. In recent years, several Dutch theorists have used the formal mathematical properties of dynamic systems to model developmental phenomena. It is instructive to compare these models, first, because they are based on somewhat different assumptions, and second, because they illustrate two different classes of mathematical descriptions.

Catastrophe Models

Peter Molenaar (1986) is a Piagetian stage-theorist who has invoked a particular kind of dynamic model, catastrophe theory, both to confirm the logical possibility of new stages and to provide empirical criteria to recognize stages and changes in stages. Molenaar, like many others, recognized that principles of self-organization must be the only solution to the critical developmental issue of the origins of new forms. In this case, he was responding to a well-known claim of Fodor (1983) that concepts must be innate—that more powerful logical structures cannot be learned from pairings of existing structures. Piaget's position was, of course, that mental structures *could* be constructed through dynamic processes, and Molenaar refers to contemporary

dynamic models to support the Piagetian position. (Earlier versions of Piagetian dynamic modeling were developed by Saari, 1977, and Preece, 1980). In later work, van der Maas and Molenaar proposed that Piagetian stages could be more formally predicted using a version of catastrophe theory, the dynamics of systems that show sudden jumps in behavior. These sudden jumps are analogous to shifts between stable stages, such as between Piagetian nonconservers and conservers.

The basic assumption of the van der Maas and Molenaar model is that children will jump from being nonconservers to conservers when the two strategies are highly activated and compete. This activation causes instability (the system lives on the "cusp" of a bifurcation) so that the system moves to more stable regions of the state space. The transition is signaled by "catastrophe flags," which include high variance, bimodality (children shifting from one strategy to another), slow recovery after perturbation, and hysteresis (the lingering effects of one strategy choice on the choice following). Some of these flags have already been suggested in the voluminous literature on Piagetian conservation, for example, that children at a transition may exhibit both earlier and more mature stages (e.g., Turiel &

Davidson, 1986). The more elaborated van der Maas and Molenaar cusp model, however, has not yet been tested with a real data set.

Van der Maas and Molenaar accept Piagetian structuralism as a starting point and view the changes in mental structures as the data to be modeled by catastrophe theory. Their dynamic approach is compatible with Piaget's process account, where equilibration, or the search for a stable solution through interaction of organism and environment, is the primary driving force in development. But, in a fundamental way, the Dutch authors' structuralism is incompatible with a thoroughly dynamic approach (Thelen & Smith, 1994; van Geert, 1993). This is because the construct of mental structures implies that behind the orderly transition from one stage to a more advanced one is a hidden order, that is, instructions that live and exist outside of the performance of the act itself and therefore direct it. Children fail to conserve volume, according to this view, because they lack the conservation structure or stage. Equilibration (or catastrophe) leads to a new structure, that of conservation of volume, and children behave accordingly. The use of dynamic language does not obviate the old developmental issue of the homunculus: Who or what is orchestrating behavior and its changes?

The catastrophe model assumes that the cognitive system acts as a single uniform structure undergoing transformations. But research in the past two decades has consistently undermined this traditional view. Tasks once believed to directly index their underlying structure—volume conservation, for instance—have proved fickle. When children are tested in different environments, or when the materials or task instructions vary slightly, behaviors believed to be wired-in actually shift and fade. What is the reality of a stage when behavior is in flux?

The Biotope Metaphor and Dynamic Models of Cognitive Growth

Paul van Geert (1991, 1993, 1994) has introduced an important set of dynamic models that begin with entirely different assumptions. Rather than viewing cognitive development as a single ordered sequence of logical structures, van Geert adopts the metaphor of an ecological system consisting of many different growing species. An individual's cognitive development, he argues, can be likened to an island with many plants and animals, each growing, but with changing and complex relations to one another. Just as the island's evolving "biotope" is not instructed (there is no recipe for the changing mix of species) but grows out of the relations among them, so cognitive growth is also a product of the participating subsystems. The metaphor is also apt because islands change both from within and by colonization from other places. Cognitive growth, likewise, is a function of both the individual's subsystem "growers" and the addition of cultural and social forms from the environment.

The core assumption of development as a relational process from multiple components has allowed van Geert to use a simple but extremely powerful mathematical model employed originally to describe changes in complex natural ecosystems. The model asks how such an ecosystem grows (say, from an empty island to one with a mature mix of species). The basic form of the model, called the *logistic difference equation for growth*, says that a level of growth at any time (T_{+1}) depends on the initial growth level (T), the rate of growth, and the relationship between the rate of growth and the "carrying capacity" of the system, because resources are not infinite. A growth curve can then be generated by substituting T_{+1} for T (and so on) and solving the equation again and again for different time samples. Because, in natural systems, species cannot grow indefinitely (they will run out of food!), growth rate slows as the population increases. But as growth rate slows and the population declines, the difference between growth rate and carrying capacity also changes, allowing for the growth level to recover. Thus, the relationship among the variables in growth equations is complex and not linear. (Think of the natural cycles of population change in a predator–prey system, for instance.) Although the form of the logistic equation is simple, very interesting and complex solutions arise when the parameters of the variables involved are changed. Changing the growth rate alone leads to some solutions that oscillate, others that reach stable asymptotes, and still others that jump about in a seemingly random fashion but indeed are deterministically *chaotic,* a term we will define more precisely later.

Van Geert has used the logistic growth equation principally to model a particular aspect of cognitive change, the growth of the lexicon. The dynamic modeling begins by identifying a number of variables that act as the component "growers" (like species) in the biotope. These might include observables such as the number of words acquired, the number of different syntactic rules, the mean length of

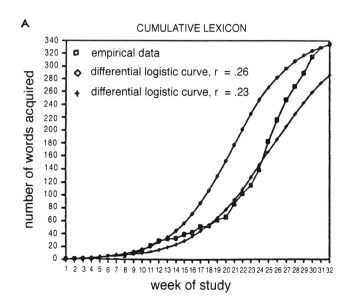

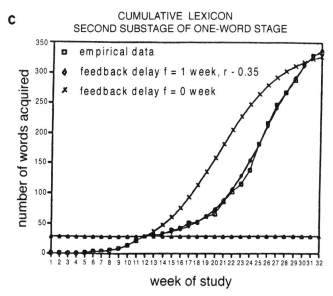

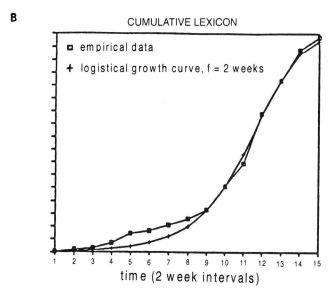

Figure 10.6   Fitting a logistic equation to the growth of the lexicon in a single child. Graph A uses the differential form of the equation with the feedback delay set as zero, and the curve does not fit well. In graph B, the author substituted the difference form with a feedback delay of 2 weeks. Graph C is the best fit by changing the rate of growth and using a feedback delay of 1 week. From "A Dynamic Systems Model of Cognitive Growth: Competition and Support under Limited Resource Conditions," by P. van Geert, 1993, in L. B. Smith & E. Thelen (Eds.), *A Dynamic Systems Approach to Development: Applications,* pp. 296–297. Cambridge, MA: MIT Press. Copyright © 1993 by MIT Press. Reprinted with permission.

sentences, and so on. The second step in the modeling is to postulate some set of interactions among the variables. For instance, some minimal number of words may be needed before syntax is acquired. Or, there might be a form of competition between syntactic and lexical growth, or between phonologic growth and lexical growth. Thirdly, these relations are expressed in equations, which formalize the hypothesized dynamics of the individual growers. Finally, the modeler assigns plausible parameters to the equations.

When the model is fitted with a set of parameters—for instance, the rate of growth of new words—it generates a

trajectory of the variable in a *state space* or a space representing possible values of the parameters. The modeler then compares this theoretical trajectory to real, observed data. If the theoretical curve is close to the observed one, then the dynamic rules that underlie the model are assumed to describe the data of the real subject. If the theoretical trajectory does not match, then the modeler changes the parameters or the basic equations to make a better fit.

An example of this curve fitting is shown in Figure 10.6 (van Geert, 1993), where the growth of a single subject's lexicon is modeled with different versions of the growth equation and different parameters. Here, the parameters changed are the growth rate and the feedback delay. (The feedback delay is added because the influence of, say, the number of words known at T to the words known at T_{+1} may itself be a function of time; the influence may not all pop out at once, but increase over the sampling interval.)

Graph A shows the dynamic model with two different growth rates, .26 and .23; graph B has one feedback delay of 2 weeks. The best fit to the real data is obtained in graph C, with a combination of a growth rate of .35 and a feedback delay of 1 week.

In his work, van Geert convincingly shows the power of these and other dynamic models to generate an impressive variety of trajectories that simulate those we measure in infants and children, including those with oscillations, dips, stagelike transitions, competitive growth patterns, bootstrapping effects, and so on. They provide the very real contribution of demonstration proof: Development could work like this. However, the models are theory-rich and data-poor; that is, the identification of the processes and components and their relations is largely hypothetical. Because it is theoretically possible to find a best fit to a curve by tweaking the equations or the parameters of the model to fit a single growth curve, is there a value to such dynamic models beyond their mathematical elegance? We think yes, but with a caution. The modeling process forces experimenters to understand their systems in a very precise way:

1. Collect data that are amenable to dynamic models.
2. Identify the contributing components and represent their dynamics in a formal way.
3. Think seriously what parameter changes may be influencing the system.

The power of models goes beyond the generation of a curve match, however; it generates new observable properties in the system that can be subjected to empirical test. Thus, although the process of model fitting can be instructive, it remains a hypothetical exercise until the models are continually tested and improved with empirical data. Van Geert has made a wonderful start. We expect that in the future these models will generate further insights as they become increasingly tied to and tested by data.

CONNECTIONISM AND THE STUDY OF CHANGE

Another kind of dynamic systems theory that has been applied to development is connectionism. Connectionist modeling is sometimes characterized as "brain-style" or "neural" network modeling (Rumelhart, 1989) because the connectionist network is made up of many units that, like neurons, only fire or do not fire and have individually no intrinsic meaning. Rather, knowledge and meaning are distributed across units—in patterns of activation. Connectionist networks are also like brains in that they modify themselves. They do so in response to their interaction with the environment in which they are placed. The potential of connectionism for developmental theory and its relation to dynamic systems theories more generally is clarified by considering the basics of how connectionist models work and several applications of such models to developmental problems. (See Munakata, McClelland, Johnson, & Seigler, 1997, for a more complete review of applications of connectionist theorizing to developmental phenomena.)

The simplest connectionist network, a peceptron, consists of two layers of units, as shown in Figure 10.7. The bottom layer of units is the input layer and the top layer is the output layer. Each unit in the input layer is connected to every unit in the output layer, a pattern called complete connectivity. This sample network is also a feedforward network. Activity on the input layer causes activity on the output layer but not vice versa; in other words, the connections are unidirectional. Two more aspects of the connections between the two layers are critical to understanding how these networks work: (a) the strength of each individual connection; and (b) the function that combines all the inputs that converge on a single output unit. The typical approach is to assume that the total input to any one unit on the output layer is simply the weighted sum of the separate inputs to that unit. In other words, each input is multiplied by a weight and summed to get the total input to a unit. Multilayered networks (three or more layers) can be

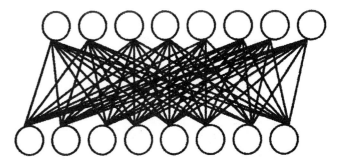

Figure 10.7 A two-layer perceptron.

organized similarly with complete connectivity between successive layers.

What do such patterns of connectivity accomplish? The network in Figure 10.7 is a categorizer; it maps patterns of activation in the input layer to patterns of activation in the output layer. And it does so by using a *single set* of input units and output units for all the objects it categorizes. In so doing, the network capitalizes on and captures the statistical regularities among the input objects and the output responses. The power of statistical regularities *is* the big idea behind connectionism. As Kelly and Martin (1994, p. 107) put it, "The world is awash with stuff best described as 'tendencies,' 'maybes,' 'estimates,' and 'generally speakings.' The central claim of connectionist theories is that much knowledge is an embodiment of the statistical regularities in the input."

Connectionist networks learn these statistical regularities. This learning is based on the Hebbian learning rule (Hebb, 1949): If a unit (u_i) receives input from another unit (u_j) and both of them are highly active, the strength or weight of the connection between the two (w_{ij}) is increased. The connection weights between layers—the response of the network to a specific input—thus depend on the statistical regularities in the network's *history* of experiences.

Many typical connectionist models make use of a variant on this learning scheme in which there is a teaching function. The pattern of activation on the output layer for a given input is compared to a specified target pattern for that input, and an error term that reflects their difference is calculated. Connection weights between inputs and outputs are then changed (according to a predetermined algorithm) to reduce the error. In connectionist networks with multiple layers, an algorithm is used to "back-propagate" the error reduction down successive layers from the output to the input layer (Rumelhart, 1989).

The idea of a target pattern or teaching function has received considerable criticism because, in many developmental tasks, there is no obvious teacher to provide relevant feedback (Pinker & Mehler, 1988). However, the target pattern can be thought of (and realized) either as externally or internally driven. In so-called *supervised* learning, the target pattern is an externally specified right answer and thus an external teacher is posited by the model.

This kind of model is appropriate for some developmental tasks. For example, parents explicitly teach their children names for things. They provide targets (the names of the objects) and they correct children when they misname the objects. Networks can also be constructed that change through *unsupervised* learning. Here, the target pattern for one layer of units is provided by the pattern of activation over another layer of units in the network (e.g., Churchland & Sejnowski, 1992). These networks thus teach themselves through their own activity. This kind of learning would seem appropriate for many developmental tasks.

CONNECTIONIST MODELS OF DEVELOPMENT

Acquisition of the Past Tense

The most well-worked and controversial application of connectionist ideas to a developmental problem concerns children's acquisition of irregular and regular forms of past-tense morphology in English. Classic descriptions of the acquisition of the past tense (e.g., Clark & Clark, 1977) suggested three stages: (a) children first used both regular (e.g., "jumped") and irregular (e.g., "went") forms correctly; (b) they went through a period in which they overregularized the past tense, using such forms as "goed" and "doed"; and (c) they maturely used both regular and irregular forms. For a long time, the overregularizations of the middle period were taken as incontestable proof that children acquired rules. The idea was that children memorized specific irregular and regular forms in the course of early language learning but then induced from the regular forms a general rule that was initially applied too broadly.

Connectionist theory was powerfully introduced to psychology when Rumelhart and McClelland (1986) demonstrated that a connectionist model could learn both irregular and regular forms and, at one point in learning, could overregularize the irregular forms. Thus, the network exhibited rulelike behavior without internally represented rules. Much has happened since that initial demonstration. Rumelhart and McClelland's original two-layer net was criticized on many grounds (e.g., Pinker & Prince, 1988). At present, there are several more complex networks that, with varying degrees of success, acquire and generalize regular and irregular forms and exhibit a period in learning in which irregular forms are regularized (Cottrell & Plunkett, 1991; Gasser & Lee, 1991; Plunkett & Marchman, 1991, 1993).

Critically, this last demonstration, the regularization of irregular forms, may not be as important as it once seemed.

The contentious and concentrated study of the acquisition of the past tense led to the discovery that the original phenomenon did not, in fact, exist. The accepted "fact" of a period of overregularization was based on anecdotal reports from a few observations. With the growing controversy over what these overregularizations meant, Marcus et al. (1992) analyzed 11,521 past-tense utterances from the spontaneous speech of 83 children. They discovered that there is no stage in which children frequently replace correct irregular forms with regularized ones. Instead, children overregularize the regular form in only about 4% of their opportunities. Thus, the phenomenon thought to powerfully show that children learn rules—the same phenomenon that was so dramatically shown *not* to require represented rules at all—does not even exist.

Our intuitions, as scientists, as to what data mean, or what the data even are, are clearly not to be trusted. This is why simulation models, even if in the end they are poor demonstration proofs and inaccurate psychological models, play a critical role in theory development.

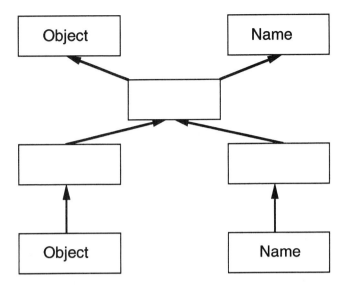

Figure 10.8 An auto-associative network. Redrawn from "Symbol grounding or the emergence of symbols? Vocabulary growth in children and a connectionist net," by K. Plunkett et al., 1992, *Connection Science, 4,* pp. 293–303.

Learning Categories and Words

Several connectionist models have been developed to mimic global properties of the developmental trajectory in category and word learning (Plunkett, 1993; Schyns, 1991; Smith, 1993, 1995). Plunkett (1993) and Plunkett, Sinha, Moller, and Strandsby (1992) focused on the growth of the lexicon. The results (like those of van Geert) show how phenomena such as a vocabulary spurt and the lag between word comprehension and word production may be emergent properties of the dynamics of learning.

The network used by Plunkett et al. (1992) is illustrated in Figure 10.8. As is conventional, each box in the figure represents a set of individual units, and the large arrows between boxes represent the complete connectivity of the units in one layer to the units in the successive one. The network's task is *auto-association:* to reproduce, at the output layers, the inputs it receives. On each trial, the network receives two kinds of inputs: (a) a perceived object and (b) the name for the object. The network responds with two kinds of outputs: (a) an image of an object and (b) the object's name. Learning is thus unsupervised; the target for the output layer is simply the input.

Although the task seems simple (just reproducing what has been put in), it is nontrivial in its psychological

plausibility, in the learning engendered, and in what is required of the network. The nontriviality emerges from the complete connectivity between layers. The object and its name are not simply passed from the input layer to the middle (so-called "hidden") layer. Rather, the input object and name are thoroughly blended at the middle level and must be recovered as separate patterns in the connection weights from the middle layer to the output layers. With learning, this happens. The pattern of activity on an output layer in response to an input becomes more like the pattern at input.

This learning teaches the network to thoroughly associate names and objects so that, given only a name or given only an object, the network can respond with the missing part. Thus, after training, Plunkett et al. (1992) found that given just an object name as input, the network "comprehended" by responding with the correct image of the object as well as the name. And, after training, given just the object as input, the network "produced" the correct name as well as the image of the object. Moreover, Plunkett et al. found the network succeeded on the comprehension task for a given object–name pair before succeeding on the production task. And, also like children, the network's learning was slow at first and then accelerated, showing what might be called a vocabulary spurt.

These findings are in many ways remarkable. Plunkett et al.'s (1992) network uses only the most basic processes of associative learning. These simple associative processes are surely at least a part of the child's psychology, and the simulation results suggest that, by themselves, they are sufficient to produce the macrostructure of the developmental trajectory in early word learning.

Selective Attention and Dimensional Terms

Modeling more complicated details about development requires more complicated networks. Gasser and Smith (1991, 1996) and Smith (1993; Smith, Gasser, & Sandhofer, 1997) built a network made up of two overlapping "subnetworks" to model asynchronies in children's knowledge of dimension words and in their ability to selectively attend to one dimension at a time. Considerable evidence indicates that young children acquire dimensional adjectives (such as *big, red,* or *wet*) with considerable difficulty, at least relative to learning nominal terms (e.g., *bottle, car,* and *dog;* see Gasser & Smith, 1996, for a review). Preschool children also have difficulty in selectively attending—making judgments about sameness of objects on one dimension (e.g., color) while ignoring samenesses and differences along other dimensions (e.g., size or shape; for reviews of this literature, see Aslin & Smith, 1988; Smith, 1993). The problem is that the achievements in the two areas emerge in a seemingly wrong order. Young children learn dimensional terms *before* they successfully compare objects on one dimension at a time. This is problematic because knowing the word *red* would seem to require selective attending to color.

The main idea behind Gasser and Smith's model is that using dimension words and making dimensional sameness judgments involve *some* but not all of the same processes. And critically, because they involve some of the same processes, the developmental trajectories are distinct but overlapping. Learning in one task educates the other.

The network used to model these ideas is illustrated in Figure 10.9. The layers relevant to learning-dimension words are indicated by shading. Again, each box denotes a layer of units, and the arrows between the boxes indicate the complete connectivity of all units in the lower layer to those in the higher layer. The input consists of the sensory input specifying an object paired with a linguistic input. The object is specified in terms of its attributes on the sensory dimensions of color, size, shape, and texture, and the

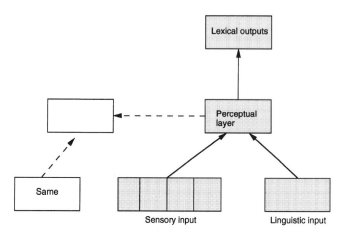

Figure 10.9   The connectionist network used by Gasser and Smith to model the learning of nouns and adjectives.

linguistic input consists of a question about the object, for example, "What color is it?" "What size is it?" The outputs are dimension words (e.g., "red" or "big"). Learning is driven by an externally presented target (the right answer to the question asked).

Gasser and Smith conceptualized the middle layer, the perceptual layer, as corresponding to the contents of subjective experience. Thus, if the network selectively attended to color, the activation on this layer should correspond only to the color of the input object. This must be learned, because the complete connectivity thoroughly blends together the sensory dimensions specifying the object (and the linguistic question).

In their initial simulations, Gasser and Smith asked this part of the network to learn to answer just one question: "What color is it?" The network learned this easily—too easily to be a viable model of children's protracted learning of dimension words. However, children are not asked to learn *just* color words but also size words, texture words, shape words, and more. When the network was presented with this more difficult task, it also learned slowly and made the same kinds of errors children do.

Just like children, the network did ultimately learn to produce the correct dimension words for the questions asked. At this point, Gasser and Smith did something that can be done with models but cannot be done with children. They peeked inside the network's "head" (so to speak) and examined the nature of the solution it had found. Had the network, they asked, learned to selectively attend by learning to label the attributes of objects? Had the network learned to recover at the perceptual layer the information specifying the color of a thing in response to the question: "What color is it?" The answer was a resounding No. Counter to common intuition, the internal isolation of "redness" is not necessary for a device to correctly label all red objects *red*. Again, structure of behavior on the outside is an imperfect guide to the structure of the mechanisms that produce that behavior.

Gasser and Smith used some of these same layers, plus others, to model the development of dimensional sameness judgments. The task here is to judge the sameness of two objects on a specified dimension: to say Yes when presented with two objects of the same color and asked "Same color?" and to also learn to answer the corresponding questions: "Same size?" "Same shape?" and "Same texture?" The network built to model this task used three layers that were also used in the word learning task—(a) the visual input, (b) the perceptual layer, and (c) the linguistic input—plus a second perceptual layer (with which to represent the second object), a similarity layer that measures the similarity of these representations by subtracting them, and a "same" output layer that makes a discrete judgment of whether the two objects are or are not the "same."

Gasser and Smith began by attempting to train the network in just this task of dimensional comparison when the relevant dimension for comparison switched from trial to trial. They found that, by itself, this is *unlearnable*. Dimensional comparison could be learned only if the network was also simultaneously learning dimension words—that is, if the other part of the network was also being trained on its task. Moreover, when the network learned the two tasks together, it followed the same course of learning as children (first words, then dimensional comparison), and it learned to selectively attend *in both tasks*.

These results show how development may emerge out of the complex interplay of the structure of the system, the history of learning in specific tasks, *and* the specific collection of tasks that the system must simultaneously solve.

Multiple Time Scales

The three connectionist models reviewed thus far, although insightful on many grounds, are impoverished models of the dynamics of behavior. Each is a simple feedforward network that models change at one time scale—the time scale of learning and development. Recurrent networks in which information flows in multiple directions and at different rates make more complete models of the dynamics of behavior over the multiple time scales. We review here two noteworthy achievements in developmental theory that used recurrent networks.

Representing Hidden Objects

Munakata, McClelland, Johnson, and Siegler (1997) asked how infants' "out of sight, out of mind" reactions to hidden objects turned to robust representations maintained over long durations. In answering this question, they provide an account of one of the most perplexing developmental *décalages* in contemporary cognitive development.

The original idea that "out of sight" is "out of mind" derives from Piaget's (1954) observations that 6- to 8-month-old infants do not search for objects that go out of sight. Piaget proposed that infants' failures to search reflected an initial understanding of objects that was tightly tied to the "here and now" of perceiving. This conclusion has been challenged by recent work that has used looking rather than searching as a measure of internal representations. Looking studies are based on the fact that infants look longer at unexpected, that is, surprising events. Such studies consistently show that infants (as young as 3½ months) are surprised when an object hidden behind an occluder is subsequently shown not to be where it was put. How, Munakata et al. asked, can infants internally represent hidden objects in looking tasks but not know to reach for hidden objects in search tasks?

They answered this question with a network in which the generation of expectations about objects' locations requires fewer components than reaching for a hidden object. Figure 10.10 shows the two layers of the network involved in both looking and reaching: a percept layer and

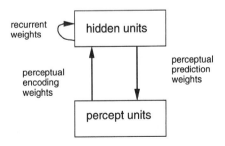

Figure 10.10   A redrawing of Munakata et al.'s (1997) network for learning to represent hidden objects.

an internal representation layer. In this recurrent network, there is connectivity in multiple directions: from the units in the percept layer to the units in the internal representation layer; from the units in the internal representation layer to the units in the percept layer; and from the units in the internal representation layer back to those same units. This pattern of connectivity creates patterns of activity over time that are continuous and are shaped by the activity of the network at just previous moments in time. Specifically, what the network perceives at some moment is a function of both the input at that moment and the internal representation of the just previous moment. The internal representation—what the network is "thinking"—is a function both of the perceptual input and of what the network was just thinking a moment before. In the network, then, there is continuity from one moment to the next; what the network thinks at one moment grows out of and incorporates what the network was thinking at the moment just before.

This network's task is simply to predict what will happen next. Learning is driven by discrepancies between the prediction that the network makes, at each time step, for what it will see next, and the input that it then receives at that next time step. Thus, performance at any moment is created by dynamics operating on two time scales: (a) the dynamics of the task, and (b) the dynamics of the network's history.

Munakata et al. (1997) tracked the network's ability to represent a hidden object as a function of the network's experience at seeing objects appear and reappear. Figure 10.11 represents the series of events shown to the network. What the network "sees" is a barrier with a ball to one side. The ball moves behind the barrier, then the ball comes out. Munakata et al. tracked the changing pattern of activity in the internal representation layer over trials as the network "watched" this event. Initially, activity in the hidden layer tracked the input events. When both the ball and the barrier were in view, there were patterns of activation corresponding to both the barrier and the ball. When the ball disappeared, the pattern of activation on the internal representation layer shifted, signaling that the ball was no longer present. When the ball returned, the pattern of

activation shifted back to that corresponding to the presence of both objects. However, after "watching" this event over and over, the pattern of activation on the internal representation layer maintained a representation of the ball even when it was out of view. The network remembered the ball and expected it to return.

This simulation models the representations that generate surprise in looking experiments—if the remembered ball does not do what is expected at some point. This simulation also generates the internal representation that could underlie a reach for a hidden object while it is still hidden. But reaching requires more than just expecting an object to be in a particular location. The reach and the expectation must be coordinated. Munakata et al. (1997) modeled search tasks by adding a reaching component to the basic two-layer net. Figure 10.12 shows the resulting three-layer network. The input to the reaching component is the internal representation layer, and the training of the connection weights between these layers is driven by an externally specified target for activation on the reaching layer, a target that can be conceptualized as successfully finding the object. By this account, then, representing and predicting the return of the hidden object at the internal representation layer is not enough by itself to generate a successful reach.

The success of this network in modeling expectations and the developmental *décalage* between looking and reaching studies of the object concept emerges in the interactions of processes operating over multiple time scales—the dynamics of predicting from one moment to the next,

Figure 10.11   The repeating series of covering and uncovering an object used to teach the network in Figure 10.10.

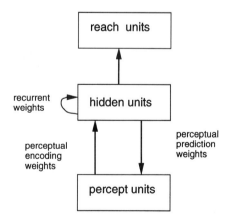

Figure 10.12   A redrawing of Munakata et al.'s (1997) network for looking and reaching.

and the dynamics of learning. In these processes, we see once again how knowing may not be a matter of "having" or "not having" some concept, but rather may be emergent over time in the activity of a system in a particular task.

Interactions between Nature and Nurture

Perhaps the most sophisticated applications of connectionist models to development are Johnson and Morton's (1991) model of the development of face recognition and O'Reilly and Johnson's (1994) model of imprinting in water fowl. Both of these models build explicitly on what is known about the recurrent networks that make up the visual system in the brain. We briefly summarize the key ideas in O'Reilly and Johnson's model of imprinting to illustrate the advance in developmental thinking that these kinds of theories represent.

The central idea of O'Reilly and Johnson's model is that invariant object recognition may grow out of a particular environmental regularity, namely, the fact that objects tend to persist. O'Reilly and Johnson note that objects sometimes move relative to the observer and sometimes disappear, but, more often than not, objects persist over time and space. They use this external regularity, the persistence of things—along with Hebbian learning, recurrent excitatory connections, and laterally inhibiting connections—to create a system of object recognition and preference that, as in precocial birds, imprints on the first conspicuous object seen. Moreover, like birds, the network exhibits a sensitive period for this learning.

This is a milestone theoretical achievement. The very idea of connectionist theories is sometimes criticized on the grounds that they show "catastrophic" learning, that new experiences will supplant and erase earlier learning. This is, of course, the opposite of what happens in imprinting, in which the first object learned has permanent consequences. The fact of sensitive periods has also been viewed as problematic for learning accounts. Sensitive periods seem to suggest a hard-wired maturational process that directs and terminates learning (Lorenz, 1965; Seligman & Hager, 1972; but see Bateson, 1966; Sluckin & Salzen, 1961). O'Reilly and Johnson's model shows how self-terminating sensitive periods, and imprinting on the first conspicuous object, may be created in the hysteresis of recurrent nets and Hebbian learning.

The architecture of their model is illustrated in Figure 10.13. It is explicitly based on what is known about

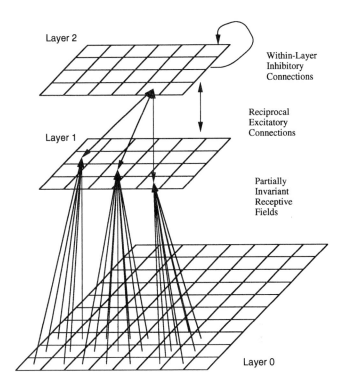

Figure 10.13 Architecture of O'Reilly and Johnson's model of imprinting. Redrawn from "Object recognition in sensitive periods: A computational analysis of visual imprinting," by R. C. O'Reilly and M. H. Johnson, 1994, *Neural Computation, 6,* pp. 357–389.

the patterns of connectivity in the intermediate and medial hyperstriatum ventrale (IMHV) of the chick brain. The model consists of three layers of units, represented by the individual rectangles in the grids. Units in the input layer (Layer 0) connect to the units in Layer 1 (of the modeled IMHV) such that spatially close units on Layer 0 connect to the same unit on Layer 1. The connection weights between these units are malleable; thus, units on Layer 1 have partially invariant receptive fields. The units on Layer 1 project in a predetermined and invariant fashion to those on Layer 2. These connections from layer to layer, unlike the complete connectivity between layers in the previous models reviewed, embody built-in structure in the system. Lateral inhibition is present in each layer of the model in the form of relatively large negative weights among all units in Layer 0. Reciprocal (bidirectional) excitatory connections exist between Layers 1 and 2. The network is trained by giving it repeated presentations of individual objects, one at a time, for extended durations. The outcome of these experiences is preferential recognition of the first object seen. Moreover, the network exhibits a self-terminating sensitivity period that is dependent on experience. If early experience consists of an object that persists for sufficient duration, the strength of that bias cannot be overcome. It effectively maintains itself. If, in contrast, early experience consists of sufficiently many different nonpersisting objects, no preference emerges and the possibility of developing such a preference is lost.

The intricacies of how and why this model learns as it does deserve more attention than we can give them here. The model is a breakthrough achievement on many grounds. It mimics many of the fine details of the empirical phenomena, it is built on known facts about relevant brain systems, and, most importantly to our minds, it presents a clear example of the promise of systems approaches. We see in this model how the directedness of development need not be predetermined but instead may emerge in the activity of complex systems and in the regularities inherent in the external world. We see how structural constraints on the system—the architecture of the network and some "hard-wired" connections—set the stage for development but do not contain the outcome. We see how special-purpose learning, prepared learning, may be built out of the most general processes in the nervous system—Hebbian learning, recurrent connections, and lateral inhibition. Yet, these connections do not make a template for "mother." These, we believe, are the general lessons of dynamic systems.

CONNECTIONISM AND DYNAMIC SYSTEMS THEORIES

Networks are dynamic systems. They may have more or less complex dynamics and they may or may not be accurate models of developmental processes. Often, when networks are as complex as the one proposed by O'Reilly and Johnson, they yield complex patterns of change and, depending on the specifics of experience, large sets of possible developmental trajectories. Network theorists often turn to the formalisms of dynamic systems theory, to the language of attractors and bifurcations and chaos, to understand the properties of change in their model systems. We turn now to these ideas. They comprise a metatheory for

studying change and the creation of novel forms that is applicable to all systems that change: complex networks on computers or in the brain; streams and land formations; the weather; chemical reactions; and development in living organisms.

A DYNAMIC SYSTEMS APPROACH TO DEVELOPMENT

As our overview indicates, systems approaches to development have had an enduring appeal. As developmentalists, we are continually faced with the richness and complexity of the organisms we study and the elaborate causal web between active individuals and their continually changing environments. The metaphor of dynamic systems, whether in words or as mathematical formalisms, allows us to express complexity, wholeness, emergence of new forms, and self-organization. It is a metaphor of change, and a metaphor that can remove teleology from the system. Pattern can arise without design: Developing organisms do not know ahead of time where they will end up. Form is a product of process.

But despite a long tradition of systems thinking in development, from embryology to the study of culture and society, these formulations have remained more of an abstraction than a coherent guide to investigation or a means for synthesis of existing data. In other words, developmentalists may acknowledge that systems matter, but they rarely design and carry out empirical research based on a core of systems principles. In the remainder of this chapter, we set forth a set of dynamic principles applicable to human development and then show how research can be inspired, conducted, and interpreted from a dynamic perspective. We base our account heavily on the brand of dynamics set forth by Haken (1977) and called *synergetics*. Note that other formal systems of dynamics have been applied to development, such as van Geert's logistic growth model, the van der Maas and Molenaar's catastrophe theory that we discussed in an earlier section (and in the network dynamics we illustrated at length previously). Still other examples can be found in Smith and Thelen (1993).

The Behavior of Dynamical Systems

Nature is inhabited by patterns in time. The seasons change in ordered measure, clouds assemble and disperse, trees grow to certain shape and size, snowflakes form and melt, minute plants and animals pass through elaborate life cycles that are invisible to us, social groups come together and disband. Science has revealed many of nature's secrets, but the processes by which these complex systems form patterns—an organized relationship among the parts—remain largely a mystery. In the past decade or so, however, physicists, mathematicians, chemists, biologists, and social and behavioral scientists have become increasingly interested in such complexity, or in how systems with many, often diverse, parts cooperate to produce ordered patterns. The scientific promise is that a common set of principles and mathematical formalisms may describe patterns that evolve over time, irrespective of their material substrates.

Order from Complexity

The key feature of such dynamic systems is that they are composed of very many individual, often heterogeneous parts: molecules, cells, individuals, species. The parts are theoretically free to combine in nearly infinite ways. The *degrees of freedom* of the system are thus very large. Yet, when these parts come together, they cohere to form patterns that live in time and space. Not all possible combinations are seen; the original degrees of freedom are compressed. But the patterns formed are not simple or static. The elaborate shapes or forms that emerge can undergo changes in time and space, including multiple stable patterns, discontinuities, rapid shifts of form, and seemingly random, but actually deterministic changes. The hallmark of such systems is that this sequence of *complexity to simplicity to complexity* emerges without prespecification; the patterns organize themselves. Our mountain stream shows shape and form and dynamic changes over time, but there is no program in the water molecules or in the stream bed or in the changes of climate over geological time that encodes the ripples and eddies.

Developing humans are likewise composed of a huge number of dissimilar parts and processes at different levels of organization, from the molecular components of the cells, to the diversity of tissue types and organ systems, to the functionally defined subsystems used in respiration, digestion, movement, cognition, and so on. But behavior is supremely *coherent* and supremely *complex,* again showing complexity from simplicity from complexity. The self-organization of mountain streams is manifest; we argue

here that the patterns seen in developing humans are also a product of the relations among multiple parts.

Both mountain streams and developing humans create order from dissimilar parts because they fall into a class called *open systems,* or systems that live *far from thermodynamic equilibrium.* A system is at thermodynamic equilibrium when the energy and momentum of the system are uniformly distributed and there is no flow from one region to another. For instance, when we add alcohol to water or dissolve salt in water, the molecules or ions mix or react completely. Unless we heat the system or add an electric current, the system is stable. Nothing new can emerge; the system is *closed.* Systems such as moving stream beds or biological systems evolve and change because they are continually infused with or transfer energy, as the potential energy of water at the top of the mountain is converted to the kinetic energy of the moving water. Biological systems are maintained because plants and animals absorb or ingest energy, and this energy is used to maintain their organizational complexity. Although the second law of thermodynamics holds that systems should run down to equilibrium, this is only globally true. Locally, some systems draw on energy and increase their order.

Open systems, where many components are free to relate to each other in nonlinear ways, are capable of remarkable properties. When sufficient energy is pumped into these systems, new ordered structures may spontaneously appear that were not formerly apparent. What started out as an aggregation of molecules or individual parts with no particular or privileged relations may suddenly produce patterns in space and regularities in time. The system may behave in highly complex, although ordered ways, shifting from one pattern to another, clocking time, resisting perturbations, and generating elaborate structures. These emergent organizations are totally different from the elements that constitute the system, and the patterns cannot be predicted solely from the characteristics of the individual elements. The behavior of open systems gives truth to the old adage, "The whole is more than the sum of the parts."

The condensation of the degrees of freedom of a complex system and the emergence of ordered pattern allows the system to be described with fewer variables than the number needed to describe the behavior of the original components. We call these macroscopic variables the *collective variables* (also called *order parameters*). Consider human walking, a multidetermined behavior. At the microscopic level of all the individual components—muscles, tendons, neural pathways, metabolic processes, and so on—the system behaves in a highly complex way. But when these parts cooperate, we can define a collective variable that describes this cooperation at a much simpler level—for instance, the alternating cycles of swing and stance of the feet. This cyclic alternation is a collective variable, but it is not the only one. We might also look at patterns of muscle firing, or forces generated at the joints. The choice of a collective variable is a critical step in characterizing a dynamic system, but it is not always easy to accomplish, and it may depend considerably on the level of analysis to be undertaken.

Attractors and Dynamic Stability

A critical property of self-organizing, open systems is that, although an enormous range of patterns is theoretically possible, the system actually displays only one or a very limited subset of them, indexed by the behavior of the collective variable. The system "settles into" or "prefers" only a few modes of behavior. In dynamic terminology, this behavioral mode is an *attractor* state, because the system—under certain conditions—has an affinity for that state. Again in dynamic terms, the system prefers a certain location in its *state,* or *phase space,* and when displaced from that place, it tends to return there.

The state space of a dynamic system is an abstract construct of a space of any number of dimensions whose coordinates define the possible states of the collective variable. For example, the behavior of a simple mechanical system such as a pendulum can be described completely in a two-dimensional state space where the coordinates are position and velocity (Figure 10.14). As the pendulum swings back and forth, its motion can be plotted on this plane. The motion of an ideal, frictionless pendulum prescribes an orbit or path through the state space that tracks its regular changes of position and velocity. If we add friction to the pendulum, it will eventually come to rest, and its orbit will look like a spiral.

The circular orbit of the frictionless pendulum and the resting point of the pendulum with friction are the attractors of this system. When friction is present, the attractor is a *point attractor* because all the trajectories on the space converge on that resting point, regardless of the system's starting point or initial conditions. Although the pendulum has only one fixed point, biological systems commonly

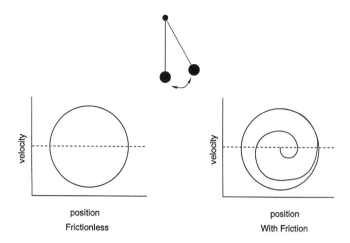

Figure 10.14   A Simple pendulum as a dynamic system. Without friction, the pendulum will exhibit a *limit cycle attractor.* With friction, the pendulum will settle into a single, *point attractor.*

have more than one point attractor; the system may reach one of the several possible equilibrium points, depending on the initial conditions. All the initial conditions leading to a particular fixed point attractor are called *basins of attraction.*

In the pendulum example, without friction, the attractor is of the *limit cycle* or *periodic* type; it will continually repeat its oscillations. When the pendulum is slightly perturbed, it returns, in time, to its periodic behavior. Once the pendulum is given its squirt of energy, these time and space patterns capture all other possible trajectories on the state space, and they represent stable collective variables for the pendulum system. In biological organisms, periodic behavior is often the collective result of the *coordination* of components each with its own preferred pattern (Kugler & Turvey, 1987; Schöner & Kelso, 1988). Consider human locomotion. The cyclic alternation of the legs during normal walking reflects the coupling of two legs 180 degrees out-of-phase. Such coordination dynamics can be represented on a phase space consisting of all the possible phase relationships between the two legs. In dynamic terms, there is a strong attractor at 180 degrees out-of-phase. Given ordinary conditions, people prefer to locomote by using their legs in alternation. However, there are also periodic attractors at 0 degrees (jumping) or 90 degrees (galloping), but they are far less stable under normal circumstances, and thus are rarely seen (at least in adults!).

Finally, a special type of attractor, the *chaotic* attractor, has received much attention in popular accounts of nonlinear dynamics. *Chaos* has a particular technical meaning in dynamics. Chaos describes systems whose behaviors look random at close glance, but, when plotted over a long time on a state space, are not random, but display extremely complex geometric structure. There is growing evidence that many biological systems are chaotic—for example, heart rate fluctuations (Goldberger & Rigney, 1988), electrical activity in the olfactory bulb (Freeman, 1987), and patterns of movements in human fetuses (Robertson, 1989).

For developmentalists, the most important dimension of a behavioral pattern preference or attractor is its *relative stability*. The concept of dynamic stability is best represented by a *potential landscape*. Imagine a landscape of hills and valleys, with a ball rolling among them depicting the state of the collective variable (Figure 10.15). A ball on

the top of a *hill* (A) has a lot of stored potential energy; with just a very small push, it will roll down the hill. Thus, the state of the system, represented by the ball, is very unstable. Any nudge will dislodge it. A ball in a deep valley (B), in contrast, has very little potential energy and needs a large external boost to change its position. The latter is a very stable attractor; the former is called a repellor because the system does not want to sit on the hill. A ball in a shallow well (C) is moderately stable, but will respond to a sufficient boost by moving into the neighboring well (while not dwelling very long on the hillock in between). Over a long enough time, all the balls in the landscape will end up in the deepest valley, although neighboring valleys may be deep enough that escape from them is very unlikely. Figure 10.15D also shows such a *multistable* attractor, with three point attractors and two repellors between them.

The stability of a system can be measured in several ways. First, stability is indexed by the statistical likelihood that the system will be in a particular state rather than other potential configurations. Second is its response to perturbation. If a small perturbation applied to the system drives it away from its stationary state, after some time the system will settle back to its original equilibrium position. As seen in Figure 10.15, when the potential valley is deep and the walls are steep, the ball will return quickly to the bottom. In contrast, the same perturbation applied to a ball in a shallow potential well will take longer to return to equilibrium because the restoring force is less. If the ball is pushed away from a hilltop, however, it will never return. Thus, one indication of system stability is this *local relaxation time* after a small perturbation.

A third measure of stability is related to the system's response to natural fluctuations within the system. Recall that complex systems exhibiting patterns are composed of many subsystems. Each of these subsystems has noise associated with it, and these intrinsic noises act as stochastic forces on the stability of the collective variable. This is another way of saying that complex systems, even apparently stable ones, are nonetheless dynamic. If the system resides in a steep and deep well, these random forces will have little effect and the ball will not fluctuate very much around the mean attractor pattern. In the shallow well, however, these small forces are more effective and the ball should roll around more. The size of the deviations from the attractor state can be measured, for example, by the variance or standard deviation of the collective variable around the

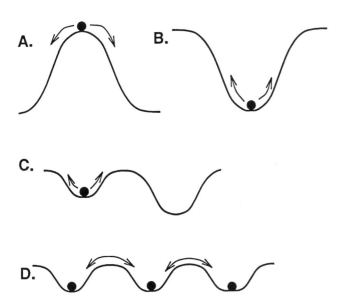

Figure 10.15 Stable and unstable attractors. The stability of the attractor depicted as potential wells. The ball on the top of the hill (A) has a lot of potential energy, and even a very small push will dislodge it; it is a repellor. The ball at the bottom of the step hill (B) requires a large energy boost to send it over the top. If perturbed, it will quickly return to the bottom. It is a stable attractor. The ball in the shallow well (C) is in a less stable situation. Relatively small perturbations will push the ball around, although, given enough time, it will probably end up in the deeper well because of its own stochastic noise. A behavioral system (D) may have multistabiliy.

attractor state. The more stable the attractor, the smaller the standard deviation around the attractor.

Behavior as "Softly Assembled"

As Figure 10.15 indicates, calling a pattern an attractor is a statistical statement about where the system prefers to reside, and how resistant it is to internal and external forces. Although some attractor states are so unstable as to almost never be observed, other attractor states are so stable that they look like they are inevitable. Because these behavioral states are so reliably seen under certain circumstances, it is easy to believe that they are generated by hard-wired structures or programs within the system. Very stable attractors take very large pushes to move them from their preferred positions, but they are dynamic and changeable nonetheless. This is one way of saying that the system is "softly assembled" (Kugler & Turvey, 1987) rather than hardwired or programmed. The components can assemble in many ways, although only one or several of them are stable enough to be seen. We will argue here that, in action and cognition, and in development, many configurations that act like programs, stages, or structures are stable attractors whose stability limits may indeed be shifted under appropriate circumstances. That is to say, many mental constructs and movement configurations—object permanence and walking, for example—are attractors of such strength and stability that only the most severe perturbations can disrupt them. They look as though they are wired-in. Other abilities—transitive inference, visual illusions, and many sport skills, for example—have attractors whose stability is easily upset by contextual manipulations or lack of practice, or by not paying attention.

A good developmental example of a softly assembled system is the infant locomotor pattern of creeping on hands and knees. This pattern has traditionally been described as a "stage" in the ontogeny of human locomotion: Nearly all human infants crawl before they walk. It is tempting to think of crawling as a necessary precursor to upright locomotion; indeed, some physical therapists believe infants must go through this stage for successful sensorimotor integration. In dynamic terms, however, we can see creeping as a temporary attractor, a pattern that the system prefers, given the current status of the infant's neuromuscular system and the infant's desire to get something attractive across the room. When babies do not have the strength or balance to walk upright, creeping is a self-assembled

solution to independent mobility—a statistical probability, but not an inevitable solution. In fact, some infants use anomalous patterns such as crawling on their bellies or scooting on their bottoms, and some infants never crawl at all. The typical crawling pattern then is a preferred attractor, but not a hard-wired stage.

Soft assembly is the core assumption of a dynamic view of development. It banishes forever the vocabulary of programs, structures, modules, and schemas and supplants these constructs with concepts of complexity, stability, and change. Stability defines the collective states of the system, assessed by its resistance to change. Fluctuations around stable states are the inevitable accompaniment of complex systems. These fluctuations—the evidence that a system is dynamically active—are the source of new forms in behavior and development.

How Systems Change; Fluctuations and Transitions

We have defined behavioral patterns as variously stable, softly assembled attractor states. How, then, do patterns change, as they do in development or in learning? Here we invoke the notion of nonlinearity, a hallmark of dynamic systems. A pattern in a dynamic system is coherent because of the cooperation of the components. This coherence is maintained despite the internal fluctuations of the system and despite small external pushes on it. Thus, because walking is a very stable attractor for human locomotion, we can walk across the room in high-heeled shoes, on varied surfaces, and even while we are talking or chewing gum. But as the system parameters or the external boundary conditions change, there comes a point where the old pattern is no longer coherent and stable, and the system finds a qualitatively new pattern. For example, we can walk up hills of various inclines, but when the steepness of the hill reaches some critical value, we must shift our locomotion to some type of quadrupedal gait—climbing on all fours. This is an example of a *nonlinear phase shift* or *phase transition,* highly characteristic of nonequilibrium systems.

In the case of our locomotor patterns, the parameter change was simply the steepness of the hill to climb. Gradual changes in this parameter engendered gradual changes in our walking until a small change in the slope caused a large change in our pattern. In dynamic terminology, the slope changes acted as a *control parameter* on our gait style. The control parameter does not really "control" the system in traditional terms. Rather, it is a parameter to which the collective behavior of the system is sensitive and that thus moves the system through collective states. In biological systems, any number of organismic variables or relevant boundary conditions can act as control parameters. The control parameters can be relatively nonspecific, and often may be changes in temperature, light, speed of movement, and so on.

For example, Thelen and Fisher (1982) discovered that body weight and composition may act as a control parameter for the well-known "disappearance" of the newborn stepping response. Newborn infants commonly make stepping movements when they are held upright, but after a few months, the response can no longer be elicited. Although the traditional explanation has been inhibition of the reflex by higher brain centers, Thelen and Fisher noticed that movements similar to steps did not disappear when infants were supine instead of upright. This made a central nervous system explanation unlikely. Rather, they noticed that infants gained weight, and especially body fat, at a rapid rate during the period when stepping was suppressed. They reasoned that as their legs got heavier without a concomitant increase in muscle mass, the infants had increasing difficulty lifting their legs in the biomechanically demanding upright posture. Body fat deposition is a growth change that is not specific to leg movements, yet it affected the system such that a qualitative shift in behavior resulted.

Change may thus be engendered by components of the system that are non-obvious, but, in other cases, the control parameter may be specific to the system in question. For example, practice or experience with a specific skill may be the critical factor. For instance, 8- to 10-month-old infants do not reach around a transparent barrier to retrieve a toy (Diamond, 1990). Normally, infants have little experience with transparent barriers. However, when Titzer, Thelen, and Smith (1997) gave infants transparent boxes for several months, the babies learned to shift their usual response of reaching in the direct line of sight in favor of reaching into the opening of the box. In this case, infants' learning the perceptual properties of transparent boxes through exploration was the control parameter engendering the new form of knowledge.

As we discussed earlier, not all changes in a system are phase shifts. At some values of a control parameter, the system may respond in a linear and continuous manner. Nonlinearity is a threshold effect; a small change in the control parameter at a critical value results in a qualitative

shift. Control parameters, whether they are nonspecific organic or environmental parameters, or specific experiences, lead to phase shifts by threatening the stability of the current attractor. Recall that all complex systems carry in them inherent fluctuations. When the system is coherent and patterns are stable, these fluctuations are damped down. However, at critical values of the control parameter, the system loses its coherence, and the noise acts as perturbations on the collective variable. At some point, this noise overcomes the stability of cooperative pattern, and the system may show no pattern, or increased variability. Then, as the control parameter passes the critical value, the system may settle into a new and different coordinative mode.

The most elegant demonstration of behavioral phase transitions comes from the work of Kelso and his colleagues in a long series of studies and models of human bimanual coordination (see the extensive discussion in Kelso, 1995). The basic experiment is as follows: participants are asked to move their index fingers, beginning with flexions and extensions either in-phase (both fingers flexed and extended together) or antiphase (one finger flexed while the other is extended). Then they are told to increase the pace of the cyclic movements. Participants who begin in the antiphase condition usually switch to in-phase at some critical frequency, but those who begin in-phase just speed up with no switch in patterns. Thus, both patterns are stable at low frequencies, but only in-phase is stable at higher frequencies. In dynamic terms, the collective variable of *relative phase* is sensitive to the control parameter, frequency.

Using this simple movement, Kelso and his colleagues showed definitively that the phase shift from anti- to in-phase movements was accompanied by a loss of system stability. The standard deviations around a mean relative phase remained small until just before each participant's transition, when the deviations increased dramatically. Then, as the participant settled into the in-phase pattern after the shift, deviations were again small. Likewise, when Scholz, Kelso, and Schöner (1987) perturbed the movements with a small tug during the various frequencies, they observed that recovery to the desired frequency was more difficult as participants approach the anti- to in-phase transition. Disintegration of the system coherence was reflected in diminishing strength of the antiphase attractor to pull in the trajectories from various regions of the state space.

Development as an Attractor Landscape

We have thus far described self-organizing systems as patterns of behavior "softly assembled" from multiple, heterogeneous components exhibiting various degrees of stability and change. According to a dynamic systems view, then, development can be envisioned as a series of patterns evolving and dissolving over time, and, at any point in time, possessing particular degrees of stability. Expanding on the potential landscape representation we introduced earlier, we can depict these changes, in an abstract way, in Figure 10.16. Our depiction closely parallels Waddington's famous epigenetic landscape (Figure 10.2) in both its early (1957) and later (1977) incarnations.

The first dimension in Figure 10.16 is time (Muchisky, Gershkoff-Stowe, Cole, & Thelen, 1996). The landscape

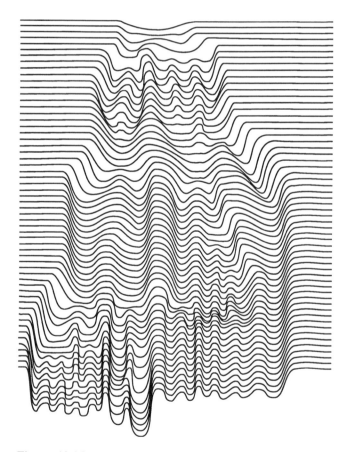

Figure 10.16 An adaptation of Waddington's epigentic landscape (Figure 10.2). This version depicts behavioral development as a series of evolving and dissolving attractors of different stability.

progresses irreversibly from past to present, from background to foreground. The second dimension—the surface—is that of the collective variable, or a measure of the cooperative state of the system. Each of the lines forming the landscape represents a particular moment in time. These lines depict the range of possibilities of the system at that point in time. The configuration of each line is a result of the history of the system up to that point, plus the factors acting to parameterize the system at the time—factors such as the social and physical context, the motivational and attentional state of the child, and so on. The third dimension of the landscape is related to the depth of the variations of the collective variable lines, the various dips and valleys. The depth represents the stability of the system at that point in time and in that particular combination of constraining factors, and thus captures the probabilistic rather than rigidly fixed nature of behavioral and cognitive states.

Nested Time Scales

The landscape represents a critical property of developing dynamic systems: the nesting of changes on multiple time scales. The contexts and conditions that determine the stability of a system at any point in time (t) constitute the initial conditions for the state of the system at the next instant of time, (t + 1). Likewise, the properties of the system at (t + 1) determine its state at (t + 2), and so on. The system is thus *reiterative;* each state is dependent on the previous state.

Most importantly, this reiterative process occurs at all time scales. Thus, a landscape of evolving and dissolving stabilities just as easily depicts the dynamics of a real-time process, such as reaching for an object or producing a sentence or solving an addition problem as it represents changes in those abilities over minutes, hours, days, weeks, or months. In dynamic terms, the time scales may be *fractal* (Grebogi, Ott, & Yorke, 1987), or having a self-similarity at many levels of observation. For example, coastlines are typically fractal—the geometry of the coastline depends entirely on the scale by which it is measured. Represented on a scale of kilometers, the coast may be described as a simple curve, but that simplicity disappears when the measuring scale is meters or centimeters. Nonetheless, the simple curve *is* the collection of small coves and irregularities apparent to the person walking on the beach as well as to the small sand crab inhabiting a different geometric scale. Likewise, we argue, while perceiving, acting, and thinking occur in their own times of seconds and fractions of seconds, these accumulated actions constitute the larger coastline of developmental change.

In a dynamic view, each behavioral act occurs *over time,* showing a course of activation, peak, and decay, and with various levels of stability associated with each point in time, but every act changes the overall system and builds a history of acts over time. Thus, repeating the same behavior within seconds or minutes can lead to habituation or to learning, as the activity of one instant becomes the starting point for the activity of the next. We can thus envision a small-scale landscape evolving in the domain of *real time* (Figure 10.17). In our illustration, for example, consider behavioral act A with a sharp rise time of activation and a very slow decay. With repetition, the threshold for activating A is diminished, because the activity has been primed by previous activations. The behavior becomes more stable, more easily elicited, and less disruptible—the person has learned something. An equally plausible account is that activating A might raise the threshold for a repetition of the same act, as happens in adaptation, habituation, or boredom.

Because the history of acting in real time counts, the real-time dynamics of actions may display this important property of *hysteresis* (e.g., Hock, Kelso, & Schöner, 1993), when the same conditions lead to different behavioral outcomes, depending on the immediate previous history of the system. Behavioral acts therefore carry with them not only the dynamics of their immediate performance, but a kind of *momentum* (e.g., Freyd, 1983, 1992), so that the system is always impacted by every act of perceiving, moving, and thinking, albeit to various degrees. Just as minute-by-minute activities carry with them a history, and build momentum, so also do these accumulated histories constitute the stuff of learning and developmental change. Each line in our landscape depicting the probability of the system's states contains its own fractal time scale. Thinking and acting are functions of the history of thinking and acting at the same time that development is also that history. Habituation, memory, learning, adaptation, and development form one seamless web built on process over time—activities in the real world.

Such a view of nested time scales radically changes our views of what is "represented" in the brain. Typically, in studies of cognitive development, researchers present infants and children with tasks designed to assess what the children really "know." Thus, experiments showing infants possible versus impossible physical events purport to reveal whether they know that objects are solid, or cannot occupy the same space as another object, or obey the laws of gravity and momentum, and so on (e.g., Baillargeon, Spelke, & Wasserman, 1985; but also see Cohen & Oakes, 1993). Or, on the basis of their performance with a series of colored rods, children are assumed to "have" the ability to make transitive inferences—to infer a third relation from two others. ("If the blue rod is longer than the green rod and the green rod is longer than the yellow rod, is the blue rod longer than the yellow rod?") If children fail on these tests, they do not "have" the knowledge of physical properties of objects or the ability to think about two things at the same time.

The core assumption here is that knowledge or abilities are stored "things" that are timeless and exist outside their here-and-now performance. An experimental task is good, then, only as it reflects a "true" reading of the underlying mental structure. This common viewpoint has run into serious difficulties, however, both empirically and theoretically. First, literally thousands of studies have demonstrated that children's knowledge or their ability to use certain procedures is extremely fluid and highly dependent on the entire context of the experimental situation, including the place of the experiment, the instructions and clues, their motivation and attention, and very subtle variations in the task (Thelen & Smith, 1994). For example, based on the colored rod task, Piaget concluded that preschoolers could not make transitive inferences.

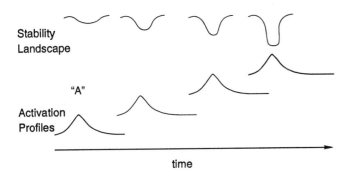

Figure 10.17 Effect of repeating behavior over time. Each activation may act to prime or to lower the threshold for the next repetition. A lowered threshold may make behavior more stable, acting as a local attractor.

However, when Bryant and Trabasso (1971) drilled preschoolers in the premise information until they learned and remembered that "the blue rod is longer than the green one," the preschoolers *could* make these inferences. Similarly, the failure of 6-month-old infants to search for hidden objects led Piaget to believe that infants cannot mentally represent objects when they are out of sight (Piaget, 1954). Yet, at the same age, infants act surprised when they *watch* objects disappear from expected locations.

To explain these strange results—how children can know things in one situation, but not another—developmentalists have proposed that the child has the "real" competence all along, but the failure lies in some performance ability. In the case of transitive inference, Bryant and Trabasso (1971) reasoned that the failure was not in lacking the mental structure, but in remembering the premises. When they trained memory, the competence was revealed. Likewise, 6-month-old infants do know that objects persist, but they are deficient in searching—actually reaching out, removing a cover, and retrieving the object. Changing the task to remove the search component revealed the essential knowledge of object permanence. Very young children may thus possess considerable cognitive competence, but the competence is hidden because of immature memory, motor skills, language, or attention.

This distinction between competence and performance has been a major force in developmental thinking for the past 20 years (Gelman, 1969). In domain after domain, researchers have followed this train of logic: Define the *essence* of some knowledge structure, do a thorough task analysis, strip away the supporting process and performance variables, and see whether children possess the "essential" knowledge. By these procedures, researchers have unmasked cognitive competences at earlier and earlier ages, certainly beyond those proposed by Piaget and his followers. In addition, the competence/performance distinction seems to help explain Piagetian *décalage:* why the same child may perform at one cognitive level in one task and at another level in tasks believed to tap into a similar structure. Again, the difficulty lies in the ability of the task to actually reveal the hidden structure.

Why, then, does a dynamic account render the competence/performance distinction as theoretically insufficient? Because behavior is always assembled *in time*. There is no logical way of deconstructing what is the "essential,"

timeless, and permanent core, and what is only performance and of the moment. Because mental activity has developed in time from fundamentals in perception and action, and because mental activity is always tied in real time to an internal and external context, there is no logical way to draw a line between these continuous processes. The essence of knowledge is not different from the memory, attention, strategies, and motivation that constitute knowing. In addition, seeking a core competence often reduces to an exercise in task analysis. Does watching objects disappear constitute the true measure of object permanence? How many clues are allowed in the experiment, or how many familiarization trials are sufficient to peel away the superfluous performance impedances? Does not being able to retrieve a hidden object mean that the child really "knows," or is knowing separate in this case from knowing in order to act? One danger of such accounts, then, is that, in the quagmire of definitions and task analysis, developmental process itself is lost. How does it happen that this child behaves as she does at this moment in this context? What in the child's history, or in the history of children in general, leads to these patterns in time?

Nested and Layered Processes

The landscape in Figure 10.16 captures a critically important property of a dynamic systems approach to development: the changing stability of patterns over many scales of time. Each line on the landscape represents the states of a behavioral pattern expressed as the collective variable—that is, the condensation of the multiple components into a simpler behavioral expression. Knowing the behavior of the collective variable is an essential first step in discovering the processes of change. But a more complete understanding also requires that we know about the behavior of the components that constitute the cooperative ensemble. This is especially important in developmental studies, because the contributions and weights of the contributing elements may themselves change over time and in different contexts. For example, leg mass and fat-to-muscle ratio may be potent contributors to behavioral expression of stepping at 2 months, but changes in these anatomical parameters may be far less important in the transition to independent walking at 12 months. At the later age, although infants need sufficient leg mass and strength to support their weight, the ability to maintain balance using vision and proprioception may be the critical component. Likewise, although focused attention may determine success in early stages of learning any new skill, as skills become more automatic, the relative contribution of attention is diminished.

Because the components themselves have a developmental history, and because the relationships among the components are continually altered, a fuller representation of our dynamic landscape would look like Figure 10.18. That depiction shows three landscapes layered on top of one another, indicating that the components of the dynamic system themselves have a dynamic. The arrows connecting the layers show that the coupling between the components is complex and contingent, and may change over time. This means that the coupling is always multidirectional, and that

effects of the subsystems on one another may cascade over time. To continue our infant stepping example, increasing leg muscle strength through activity in the first months of life facilitates standing, crawling, and walking. Independent locomotion induces changes in spatial cognition, probably because as infants move around they pay more attention to their spatial landmarks (Acredolo, 1990; Bertenthal & Campos, 1990). But changes in cognition also feed back to locomotor behavior as more skilled infants explore and exploit more and different aspects of their spatial environment, change their motor planning, and are able to make rapid adjustments to unexpected events.

DYNAMICS OF NEURAL ORGANIZATION AND DEVELOPMENT

At the heart of understanding development as a dynamic system, therefore, are processes both nested in time and coupled in levels of organization. There are important implications of this conceptualization:

1. There are no discontinuities between what we conventionally term *action* and what we know as learning and development. Processes meld seamlessly into one another.
2. There are no discontinuities in levels of organization. Behavior is the condensation of all the contributing components, both those within the skin and those in the supporting environment. At the same time, no component or level of organization is causally privileged.

This means that as we search for the mechanisms of change during development, we may define these mechanisms at different levels of organization. For example, by discovering that the deposition of body fat acts as a control parameter in the disappearance of newborn stepping, we have supplied a mechanism of change. A physiologist, in turn, might ask about the metabolic processes that accelerate the deposition of fat in the postnatal period, and that could also constitute a process-based explanation of change. But the metabolic explanation should not be construed as any more basic and more real than one at any other level. Indeed, because levels and processes are mutually interactive, it is impossible to assign one level as the ultimate causation. Descriptions of change of many

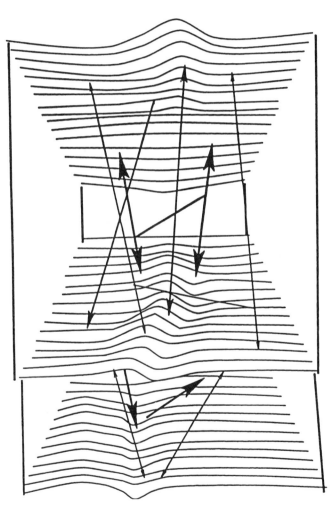

Figure 10.18 The epigenetic landscape as a multilayered system where the components mutually influence each other in changing ways.

components are needed so that multilevel processes and their mutual interactions can be fully integrated.

Moreover, explanations at every level must be consistent and ultimately reconcilable. This is especially important when considering the neural basis of behavior. Since the time of Myrtle McGraw (1932), there has been a tradition in human developmental studies to seek explanation at the neural level, that is, to look for some observed change in behavior *as caused by* a preceding and determining change in the brain. For example, Goldman-Rakic (1987) and others have suggested that massive reorganization of synaptic connections in the prefrontal cortex are the reason why 8- to 12-month-old infants show improvements in spatial cognition, inhibition of prepotent response tendencies, and even the onset of language. Thatcher and others seek to explain Piagetian stages as a result of stagelike changes in brain activity (Thatcher, 1991, 1992).

From a dynamic point of view, we are less concerned with establishing causal links from structure to function than with making our behavioral accounts fully coherent with what is known about the *processes* of neural organization and its development. What is especially exciting is that contemporary work in the neurosciences suggests that common dynamic principles of self-organization govern both behavioral and neural events. In particular, several related discoveries in neuroscience support a dynamic systems account of behavioral development. We discuss these in turn.

The Brain as a Dynamic Collective

In the past decade, there has been a perceptible shift of focus in the neurosciences away from membranes, molecules, single neurons, or tracts to more large-scale and systems views of brain function (e. g. Churchland & Sejnowski, 1992; Crick, 1994; Damasio, 1994; Edelman, 1987; Kelso, 1995; Koch & Davis, 1994). A common theme in this new focus is that the brain works, not like a point-to-point wired switchboard, but in a holistic, plastic, self-organizing fashion, where structural boundaries are less fixed than previously thought, and where collectives of neurons exhibit many dynamic properties, including phase entrainment and chaos.

The foundational insight is that information in the brain is the function of widespread *populations* or groups of neurons that are fluid and are linked by function rather than by strict anatomy. To show this effect of cooperative

populations of neurons, scientists had to develop techniques to record many cells over a distributed area in the brain and to analyze these multiple channels for patterns of group activity.

A remarkable picture of the dynamic functioning of the brain comes from Walter Freeman and his colleagues (Freeman, 1991; Freeman & Skarda, 1985), who have asked how the olfactory system of the rabbit comes to know and recognize different smells. What Freeman discovered was that smells are "represented" in the olfactory bulb of the rabbit not in single, labeled neurons, but in an overall pattern of excitation exhibited by the thousands of neurons sampled by multiple EEG recording electrodes. When rabbits sniff familiar smells, coherent patterns of activity emerge from the background activity of the olfactory neurons. The perceptual information was mapped in terms of waves of amplitude changes over the entire olfactory bulb, much like a topographic contour map. Although the individual participating neurons changed from sniff to sniff, the same smell, under similar conditions, produced a similar overall pattern.

Olfactory perception in the rabbit acts like a dynamic system in several important ways. First, the spatial map that emerges with each familiar sniff self-organizes not just in response to the odor itself, but in a complex context that includes the rabbit's training and arousal state. The amplitude maps, for example, change strikingly with the reinforcement associated with that scent and, even more dramatically, with the rabbit's reinforcement history with other smells as well. For example, rabbits were conditioned to associate the scent of sawdust with a particular reinforcement, and they produced a characteristic sawdust contour map. When, however, they were taught to recognize the odor of banana, a new sawdust plot emerged along with a characteristic banana map.

This can only happen if sawdust is represented in the bulb, not as a fixed structure or schema, but as a dynamic assembly that is always a function of global activity. This means that neurons that participate in sawdust are also affected by the history of neurons encoding banana, and that this history has preeminence over a static representation of the stimulus. Freeman (1987) postulated that groups of mutually excited neurons, which he called the *nerve cell assembly,* participate in the global pattern and form a repository of past association. (Freeman's nerve cell assemblies are similar but not identical to Edelman's neuronal groups, also discussed below.) Nerve cell assemblies are groups of interconnected neurons whose synapses become mutually and simultaneously strengthened by input neurons during learning (so-called Hebbian synapses). In this way, experience sets a certain pattern of cell connections, selectively strengthened for a particular odorant. But because the connections are widely distributed, when any subset of neurons receives familiar input, the entire assembly rapidly responds. Also, because the neurons of the olfactory system are richly interconnected, other sources of input, in addition to the odor itself, impact on the response.

A second elegant example of distributed control in real-time brain dynamics comes from a large body of work from the laboratory of Apostolos Georgopolous and his colleagues (reviewed in Georgopolous, 1986, 1988, 1990), who studied how the motor cortex directs the arm to move in different directions. These researchers recorded from multiple sites in the motor and premotor cortex of awake and behaving monkeys trained to reach in various spatial locations. They found that individual cortical neurons were broadly "tuned," that is, they responded to a range of directions, but showed higher activity when monkeys reached in a particular direction. At the same time, within any recording area, individual cells responded maximally to specific directions.

The question was, therefore, how a particular and unique direction of movement could be generated from these populations of differently tuned cells. Georgopolous and colleagues discovered that the neurons acted as a collective; they worked in concert to generate a motor command by each cell contributing to a population vector that determined the direction of movement. It was as if each cell "voted" in its tuned direction by changing the overall activity by a certain amount. The final movement direction emerged only from the ensemble product of many individual contributing neurons. This population coding was evident in motor and premotor cortex and in many cortical layers.

Two aspects of this work are especially relevant for our dynamic account of development. First, the population vectors detected in the motor cortex could be used to predict the direction of movement some 160 msec before monkeys actually began moving their arms, but after they saw the target direction (Figure 10.19). This means that the *plan* for the movement, not just its execution, was dynamically emergent in the cooperative activity of the groups of cells. Second, the population vectors have a distinctive, real-time dynamic, or pattern of rise and fall over time. As we will

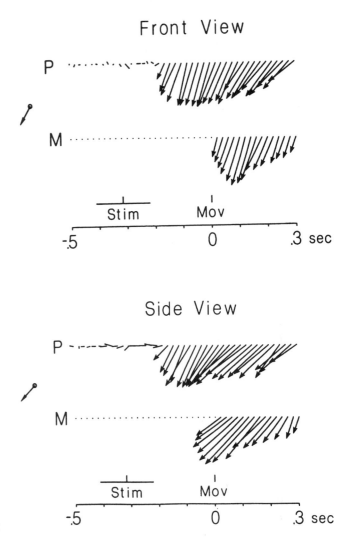

Figure 10.19 Predicting the direction of reaching by the population vectors of directionally specific cortical neurons in monkeys. Front and side views of time series of population (P) and movement (M) vectors are shown. Note that at the onset of the target light (Stim), the population vectors point in the direction of the movement 160 msec before the onset of movement. From "Prime Motor Cortex and Free Arm Movements to Visual Targets in Three-Dimensional Space. II. Coding of the Direction of Movement by a Neuronal Population,"... by A. P. Georgopoulos et al., 1988, *The Journal of Neuroscience, 8(8)*, p. 2932. Copyright © 1988 by The Society for Neuroscience. Reprinted with permission.

discuss later in this chapter, considering behavior and mental events as having these real-time activation dynamics can change how we view the interaction of immediate performance and the history of the system (repeated performance). This is a critical issue, as we defined at the outset:

How do we understand the continuity between everyday, real-time activities and developmental change? The evidence from neuroscience suggests that we consider these activation patterns as they are dynamically iterated many times as children perceive and act in various situations. With experience and over time, the strength and time course of such patterns, and their stability, will change. As we illustrate in our discussion of the A-not-B error in a later section, explanations at the behavioral level can be meaningfully informed by considering the likely nature of underlying neural processes, although we do not, of course, have direct access to those processes in human children.

Temporal Mechanisms of Ensemble Coherence

How do neurons, spatially distributed over relatively large distances within and between brain areas, come to cooperate as an ensemble? There is growing evidence that cells form a dynamically assembled neural collective on the basis of temporally synchronous activity. In a series of important studies, Singer and his colleagues discovered functionally related time-correlated activity in spatially distributed visual cortex neurons (König & Engel, 1995; Singer, 1994). It has been known for many years that individual cells in the cat visual cortex respond preferentially to simple stimuli—for example, light bars of different orientation and direction of movement. What is new is that these stimuli elicit correlated firing—with a zero phase lag—in cells that are not adjacent to one another, but are separated by a considerable distance. Traditionally, when cells fired together, neuroscientists assumed that they were wired together to respond to a common input. But in the visual system, the correlated activity was not obligatory, as would result from hard-wiring. Rather, the degree of correlated activity was entirely stimulus-dependent, and even changed with behavioral state. Function, not anatomy, determined the emergent patterns (König & Engel, 1995).

These results can only be explained in dynamic terms: Assemblies of neurons arise as a function of the task at hand, in networks that are densely interconnected in parallel within a cortical area as well as between areas. The synchrony is self-organizing in the sense that cells mutually entrain, and this entrainment is extremely rapid, yet highly flexible. Indeed, the emergence of synchronized states in cortical and subcortical structures is frequently associated with epochs of oscillatory firing patterns. (In dynamical systems, it is well known that oscillating systems easily entrain or couple to one another.)

This rapid but highly context-dependent neural assembly synchronization suggests a mechanism by which various stimulus features come to be "bound" together. Recall that individual neurons are preferentially tuned to simple stimulus features, but real-life stimuli are composed of complex and changing configurations. A long-debated issue in psychology and neuroscience is how these separate aspects of the world become integrated into a single percept. Search for the "grandfather" neuron that "reads" the input of isolated feature detectors has proved fruitless (Damasio, 1994). But the binding problem may not be a problem after all: Because cells and brain areas are densely and mutually interconnected with one another, a single scene will activate many overlapping assemblies of neurons. The integration of features is thus accomplished at all processing levels in a dynamic and self-organizing fashion. No homunculus is necessary to give meaning to the scene.

This dense web of interconnections means that the nervous system has what Edelman (1987) called *degeneracy*. Degeneracy means that any single function can be carried out by more than one configuration of neuronal signals; no one neuron (or even a group of neurons) is critical because function is distributed in the relations. At the same time, any one cell or neural collective can participate in a number of functional relations. Additionally, because neural groups are both shared and distinct, degeneracy implies that each behavioral act has unique and emergent properties at the same time that it may have common characteristics with similar acts in similar circumstances.

Multimodal Integration

The discovery that populations of neurons in the visual system synchronize as a result of complex and highly nonlinear network dynamics explains how diverse features of a visual scene are perceived in an integrated manner. But there is also increasing evidence that a similar dynamic mechanism unites perception *between* sensory modalities, as well as between sensory and motor areas. Response synchronization in densely interconnected multimodal nets may be a general property of nervous system organization (König & Engel, 1995).

As before, a traditional view of intersensory integration was that the separate sensory modalities (sight, audition, proprioception, and so on) are processed separately and that the experience of linked sight and sound, for example, is a function of higher association areas in the brain. Indeed, according to Piaget (1952), infants must construct unified percepts from these separate perceptual streams, presumably embodied in the later-maturing association areas of the frontal cortex.

Recent neurophysiological studies, however, have raised serious doubts about this account. Neuroscientists have discovered that, along with the separate processing channels for sensory information, are previously unimagined networks of interconnections both within and among anatomically distinct areas. Arbors of individual neurons can branch over whole areas of the brain or spinal cord, ensuring that the output of a single cell is widely distributed to a network of other neurons. When these branches are multiplied by millions of neurons, the result is a vast network of connections. These connections are not just between cells in a single sensory or motor channel; they are widely interspersed across modalities. Thus, information originating from the eyes, for example, is not just projected "downstream" to higher and higher levels of the visual processing system, but "upstream" to earlier areas, and "crosstown" to other modalities and processing levels. These multiple, parallel, and converging streams never really terminate at some final point because there is always reciprocal transmission both forward and backward (Damasio, 1994; Edelman, 1987). Thus, in the cat superior colliculus, a midbrain structure intimately involved in visual processing, a large proportion of the cells respond not just to visual input, but to auditory and somatosensory input as well (Stein & Meredith, 1993). In adult cats, sensations from vision, hearing, and body surface all share the same topographic map, a kind of "multisensory space." In addition, Stein and Meredith suggest that motor responses are similarly integrated into the map. This means that at the same time that visual inputs are processed, "a core of multisensory-multi-motor neurons initiates movements via a common circuit" (Stein & Meredith, 1993, p. 116).

Detailed studies of nervous system functional anatomy have changed views of the brain from a series of modules and processing way stations to one of vastly more distributed processes, with connections within sensory modalities, among different modalities, and between perception and movement. Integration in such a distributed system occurs through common function and mutual excitation of these overlapping circuits. This view of the brain has profound implications for a theory of development. Before we can integrate these new systems theories of brain function with a developmental account, however, one more body of evidence is necessary: experience-dependent plasticity.

Experience-Dependent Plasticity

Neuroscientists have known for nearly half a century that the surface of the cerebral cortex contains maps of the sensory input and movements of various parts of the body, arranged in roughly topographic order. The prevailing assumption was that these neatly ordered representations were established in early life by the maturation of the neural anatomy and remained static thereafter. These old truths have been discarded. In the past decade, it has been discovered that, in monkeys, these maps are established and maintained by function, and, indeed, the adult brain has heretofore unimagined plasticity. Brain plasticity has now been found not just in the somatosensory cortex, but also in somatic senses in subcortical areas and in the visual, auditory, and motor cortices in monkeys and in other mammals (Kaas, 1991). These demonstrations of adult plasticity are very important for understanding development because (a) they demonstrate that brain representations, even those that can be "geographically" located, are dynamic processes, and (b) they provide clues to the very processes by which development may take place.

The now classic experiments were performed by Merzenich and his colleagues on New World monkeys, which have relatively unfissured brains with a clear somatotopic representation of their sensitive hands. A painstaking mapping of the sensation on the finger and hand areas to electrophysiological responses on the cortical surface revealed detailed maps of adjacent areas that were similar, but not identical, in individual monkeys (Jenkins, Merzenich, & Recanzone, 1990). That these areas are plastic, not anatomically rigid, was demonstrated in several ways. First, when the experimenters amputated digits, the maps reorganized so that adjacent areas enlarged to fill in the finger spaces where input was eliminated. Second, when the Merzenich group fused fingers of adult monkeys together, so that the animals used two fingers as one, the monkeys' brains eliminated the boundaries between the digits, and the receptive fields overlapped. When the skin-fusion was surgically corrected, distinctive digit areas returned. Enhanced function of a single finger through training enlarged its cortical representation, which again could be reversed when training ceased. Finally, even when no experimental manipulations were imposed, borders of digit representations changed somewhat over time, presumably reflecting the immediate use-history of the finger. These and other experiments revealed, in the words of Merzenich, Allard, and

Jenkins (1990) that *"the specific details of cortical 'representations'—of the distributed, selective responses of cortical neurons—are established and are continually remodelled BY OUR EXPERIENCES throughout life"* (p. 195) [emphasis and capitals in original].

DEVELOPMENT AS SELECTION

In an earlier section, we proposed very general principles of dynamic systems as a way of conceptualizing developmental change: patterns assembled for task-specific purposes whose form and stability depended on both the immediate and more distant history of the system. We emphasized that a dynamic view meant that there must be continuity among the components of the system, both internal and external, and among the time scales over which the system lives. Contemporary discoveries of brain organization and function are highly consistent with these dynamic principles; indeed, they provide insights into the precise mechanisms of change.

That the brain is a dynamic collective, with self-organizing and dynamic properties; that it is designed to extract coherence from multiple, time-locked input; and that its organization is maintained by function—these properties all point to development as a *selective* process. In the following account, we rely heavily on Gerald Edelman's (1987) *theory of neuronal group selection* (TNGS) as the neural mechanism instantiating dynamic behavioral development.

Several additional assumptions are critical. First, it is assumed that genetic and epigenetic processes during neural embryology produce the global architecture of the brain (see Edelman, 1987, 1988). Within that primary architecture, however, there is enormous variability in both the number of individual neurons and their connectivity. Second, connections between neurons and groups of neurons arise through use. And third, there is an overabundance of neurons and possible connections among them, and thus specificity arises through competition.

Imagine, then, a newborn infant whose first experiences in the world include nursing at the breast. Associated with the perceptions of the baby's own movements of lips, jaws, tongue, and throat are the taste of the milk, the sight and smell of the mother's skin and the sound of her voice, and the whole body tactile experience of contact and warmth.

Because of the degenerate and reentrant web of connections, these perceptions activate time-correlated groups of neurons meshed together, linking the patterns detected by the originally separate sensory systems. It is also highly likely that these perceptions are associated with neural nets from emotional and motivational centers that signal pleasurable feelings (Damasio, 1994; Edelman, 1987). With each suck and swallow, and with each repeated nursing episode, overlapping, but not identical groups of neurons also become activated. Common assemblies become strengthened; less-used pathways become less stable. Because the structure is reentrant, common perceptual elements are extracted from these overlapping inputs that are marked by their correlations in real-world time. This mapping over heterogeneous input is the critical process; new relationships are excited and strengthened because they occur together.

With repetition, such a process of selection by function allows the newborn infant to recognize a constellation of features as a higher-order category: "Time to eat." But it is a dynamic category, invoked now by only partial and incomplete features—the nursing position, for example, or the sight and smell of mother, or the act of sucking itself—and it is continually updated as experience accumulates. When feeding is supplemented by a bottle, for instance, the category "time to eat" may be enlarged to include the perceptual qualities of the bottle and an adjustment in the sucking movements to accommodate changes in the nipple. Higher-order "knowledge" about feeding, about object properties, and about the behavior of other humans is thus built by selection through everyday activities—looking, moving, hearing, and touching.

Development as the Dynamic Selection of Categories

We follow Edelman (1987) in believing that these early perception–action categories are the cornerstone of development. In particular, the emergence of categories is a specific case of dynamic pattern formation. The task facing newborn infants is to reduce the degrees of freedom at many levels: the external world—the potentially indeterminate nature of the stimuli—by forming perceptual categories; and the internal world—the equally indeterminate nature of the multiple joints and muscles—by seeking patterns of motor coordination and control. At the same time, and most importantly, they must match their internal dynamics to those of the world around them; that is, they must make their perceptual categories and their action categories congruent to function in flexible, adaptive ways. In our dynamic approach, perception, action, and cognition are not disjointed; they are part of a singular process.

Thus, we believe that whether we choose the term *pattern formation,* or *coordination,* or *category acquisition,* we are referring to the same dynamic processes whereby complex heterogeneous elements self-organize to produce coherence in time and space. Dynamic patterns can be fleeting or very stable, but, most importantly, they are *time-dependent* and seamless. By time-dependent, we mean that each event in the brain and body has a here-and-now, a history, and an effect on the future. By seamless, we mean that these time domains are themselves without interruption. The stuff of development is the dynamics of perception, action, and cognition in real time. What the infant sees, thinks, and does in the present provides the aliment for what the child is in the future, just as what the child did in the past is the substrate for how he or she sees, thinks, and acts right now. Thus, we can envision the neuronal processes postulated by TNGS as a specific form of dynamic pattern formation, with the patterns being the categories of perception and action that form the developmental core of higher mental functions and the patterns of thought that become increasingly complex and generalized throughout infancy and childhood.

In our discussion thus far, we have reviewed the history of systems thinking in development, and we have suggested that developing organisms are a class of nonlinear, complex dynamic systems. We proposed that dynamic principles are equally suitable for understanding behavior and its neural substrate, and that, indeed, these levels of organization are completely integrated and harmonious. However, our goal from the outset was to go beyond abstractions to apply systems principles to the design and conduct of developmental research, and to the interpretation of developmental data.

FROM THEORY TO PRACTICE: A DYNAMIC SYSTEMS APPROACH TO RESEARCH

The strength of a dynamic approach is its great generality and thus its potential application across many domains and levels of analysis. This means, for instance, that a dynamic approach to development is more a way of thinking about development than a specific theory of, say, personality or the acquisition of formal reasoning. However, a dynamic approach does suggest a powerful research strategy for investigating particular domains. First, we summarize the principle steps in a dynamic strategy. Then we follow with an illustration of the application of this approach to the development of a fundamental motor skill.

Recall that the essential issues are the stability of the system, as indexed by the behavior of some collective measure of the multiple components, and the changes in stability over time. According to dynamic principles, transitions to new forms involve the loss of stability, so that systems can seek new, self-organized patterns (Wapner & Demick, this Volume). At transitions, systems may reveal which of their components may be a control parameter, or a critical element in change. Thelen and Smith (1994) outlined a series of explicit steps for research design, which are detailed in the following subsections.

Identify the Collective Variable of Interest

In a dynamic system, one or two variables can be identified that capture the degrees of freedom of a multidimensional system. In a development study, the goal is to describe the changes in this collective variable over time. It is not easy to find a collective variable in a nonlinear, changing system. Performance measures at one age may not have the same meaning at a later age, because the components of the system, and the relations between them, change. But this is a problem of studies over time, whatever the theoretical motivation!

One important criterion of a collective variable is that it should be a well-defined and observable variable, not a derived construct. Whereas "number of words in the lexicon" is operationally specific, "language processing capability" is not, because it cannot be defined outside of some other concrete behavioral measures. In some behavioral studies, the appropriate collective variable may be a *relationship*—for example, the timing between a stimulus and a response, or between movements of different parts of the body, or of mutual turn-taking during a social dialogue.

Characterize the Behavioral Attractor States

Before beginning a study of change, it is important to understand the preferred states of the collective variable at different points in time and over different conditions. Here is where cross-sectional studies can be very useful. Sometimes, it is most helpful to know how skilled adults or children perform the tasks under varying conditions such as differing speed, accuracy, or spatial demands. It is also critical to sample the stability of the system at different ages, in order to pick appropriate time scales in a developmental study. If there are big differences between 8 and 12 months, for instance, and very little change after 12 months, intensive study would be directed toward the time of rapid transition.

As we mentioned earlier, the stability of a behavioral attractor is indexed by its variability around an average value: how easily it is perturbed, and how quickly the system returns to a stable configuration after perturbation. Performance that varies greatly within the same individual and is easily thrown off course indicates that the attractor state is weak. Conversely, when performance converges on a stable value, especially from different initial conditions and in the presence of distractors and other perturbations, the attractor well is deep.

Describe the Dynamic Trajectory of the Collective Variable

The heart of a dynamic analysis is a map of the stability of the collective variable. A crucial assumption in a dynamic strategy is that the individual (or the family unit) and his or her behavioral changes over time are the fundamental unit of study. It is common in developmental studies to compare groups of children at different ages and infer development from age-related differences in average group performance. Such cross-sectional studies are important for delimiting the boundaries of change, but they cannot inform about the processes that engender change. The essential nonlinear nature of dynamic systems means that attractors "pull in" trajectories from a variety of initial positions. This means that children may end up with similar behavior from very different starting points. At the same time, even very small differences in initial conditions can lead to widely disparate outcomes (Figure 10.15). Group averages cannot disambiguate these pathways; the underlying developmental mechanisms may be profoundly different (or remarkably similar).

Thus, understanding developmental trajectories requires longitudinal study of individuals at appropriately dense sampling intervals to capture the time scale of relevant change. In infancy, for instance, when new behaviors appear almost daily, even weekly observations may miss the critical transitions. Later in life, however, transitions may

be relatively prolonged and much less frequent measures are needed.

Longitudinal studies are designed to probe the stability of systems over time. However, we are really testing systems over two related time scales. The obvious one is change over age, or developmental time. Less explicit is the real time of the experimental task. By assessing performance over various trials and conditions within the single experimental session, we ask about the minute-to-minute dynamics. Thus, the history of the system *within the experimental session* may be very important. Effects of the number of trials and their order are also indexes of the system's stability. Does performance change after many repetitions, or is it stable whatever the preceding tasks?

Probing these two time scales is important because they must be inextricably interwoven in real life; that is, when we observe infants and children at any point in time, their behavior reflects *both* their long-term developmental history *and* their immediate history within the task session. Likewise, developmental changes reflect children's repeated everyday experiences, which themselves modulate performance dynamics. It is useful therefore to consider the participants' *intrinsic dynamics,* or history, as the background on which the experimental tasks are imposed. The intrinsic dynamics are the preferred stability landscapes, given previous history and organic conditions.

Identify Points of Transition

Transitions can be qualitative shifts to new forms, such as the first word spoken or the ability to do a transitive inference task, or they can be quantitative changes in the collective variable, such as a shift in speed or the accuracy of a task. Transitions are critical because when a system is in transition, its mechanisms of change can be identified and manipulated. Stable systems do not change; only when the coherence of the components is weakened are the components able to reorganize into a more stable form.

The branch of dynamics known as *catastrophe theory* is particularly concerned with sudden shifts from one form to another. These sudden jumps are associated with a number of "catastrophe flags," or indicators of shifts without intermediate forms. As discussed earlier, van der Maas and Molenaar (1992) have applied catastrophe theory to Piagetian conservation tasks to ask whether the shift from nonconservation to conservation can be explained by a catastrophe model. Although they did not find strong evidence for a number of the flags, the flags are useful indexes of systems in transition. The flags are:

1. *Bimodal score distribution.* Performance is either "on" or "off," without intermediate forms.

2. *Inaccessibility.* Related to bimodality; intermediate states are not accessible, they are unstable and rarely seen.

3. *Sudden jumps.* People switch from one form to another rapidly, again without intermediate states.

4. *Hysteresis.* The dependence of performance on the immediately past performance. For example, responses might be different when the task is speeded up through a range of speeds as compared to when it is slowed down through the same range.

5. *Divergence.* The system may respond differently to changes in different control variables.

6. *Divergence of linear response.* Nonlinearity, as before, suggests that a small change in a control variable or perturbation can lead to a large effect.

7. *Delayed recovery of equilibrium.* In our earlier terminology, a slow relaxation time after a perturbation.

8. *Anomalous variance.* Another property we discussed in an earlier section.

Identify Potential Control Parameters

The purpose of mapping the dynamics of the collective variable is to discover when systems change. The next step is to find out how and why they change. What are the organic, behavioral, or environmental factors that engender developmental shifts?

Thoughtful experimental design is needed to identify potential control parameters. In some cases, the possible agents of change are fairly obvious; for example, practice facilitates learning to ride a bicycle or doing arithmetic. But, in many instances of developmental change, the critical processes and events are nonobvious and may indeed be in components that seem at first only incidental, or so general or commonplace as to be overlooked. West and King's (1996) study of songbird learning, described in an earlier section, is a good example: Female cowbirds' subtle wing flicks are critical determinants of male song development. Another example is Thelen and Ulrich's (1991) description of treadmill stepping in infants, where improvements in treadmill stepping were related to overall changes in dominant muscle tone.

One way to help discover relevant control variables—in addition to informed guesses—is to actually measure changes in a number of system variables along with the collective variable. Thus, if the behavior of interest is, say, object retrieval in infants, a collective variable might be correct retrievals of a hidden object. But because retrieval performance is a collective of many other processes that may contribute to change, independent, concomitant measures of visual attention or of memory, for instance, may reveal correlated jumps and plateaus.

Instability in the collective variable, in turn, reveals points of transition. Thus, Gershkoff-Stowe and Smith (1996) mapped children's word retrieval errors as a function of the rapid vocabulary growth characteristic of the period between 15 and 24 months. During this time, individual children's retrieval of known object names showed a brief (3- to 6-week) period of disruption. Children would point to a well-known object (say, *cat*) that they had named correctly many times in the past and misname it (for example, *duck*). This transient disruption in lexical access was temporally related in individual children to an increased rate of new word productions, suggesting that the rate of new words being added to the lexicon is the control parameter for these word retrieval processes, and thus, the driver of developmental change in lexical access processes.

Manipulate Putative Control Parameters to Experimentally Generate Transitions

Mapping the dynamics of the collective variable and other components only provides suggestive and correlational evidence for possible control parameters. More convincing is to generate developmental transitions on a real-time or a developmental-time scale by manipulating the suggested control parameters. These simulations of developmental change work at points of transition because the system is not stable and thus is amenable to being affected by interventions.

It is of both theoretical and practical importance to know when interventions are effective in a developing system and when established behavior is so firmly entrenched that intervention is difficult. The Head Start program, for example, was targeted to the early preschool years because researchers discovered that enrichment was less potent with older children whose educational habits were already formed. Once a sensitive period is determined, developmental control parameters can be tested by providing specific interventions that may engender long-range behavioral change. For ethical reasons, these interventions are usually enrichments.

In the example discussed earlier, Titzer, Thelen, and Smith (1997) accelerated infants' abilities to retrieve objects from transparent containers by providing them with a variety of plexiglass boxes to play with at home. Normally, 10-month-old infants have difficulty with the seemingly simple task of retrieving a toy from a plexiglass box when the opening of the box is on the side. Although the toy is in full view, infants reach in their direct line of sight—smack into the plexiglass—and not into the box opening. Titzer et al. reasoned that, because infants lacked experience with the properties of transparency, they relied on their usual pattern of reaching straight to what they see. Here, the control parameter for developmental change was the repeated handling of transparent containers and, thus, learning about objects that could be seen through but not reached through. The experimenters provided 8-month-old infants with varied transparent containers and told the parents to allow their children to play with the containers for 10 minutes twice a day, with no other specific instructions. By 9 months of age, infants in the experimental group were more facile in retrieving toys than a control group of 10-month-olds who did not have enriched experience. Enriched experience, then, pushed the system into new forms.

In a similar vein, Gershkoff-Stowe and Smith (1996) used training to investigate the disruption observed in word retrieval errors, which we described above. These authors reasoned that the disruption in word retrieval with accelerated vocabulary growth was the product of a lexicon crowded with many new and unstable additions. If the retrieval of words in a newly crowded lexicon is easily disrupted because word retrieval is relatively unpracticed, then naming errors during this period should decrease with practice at word retrieval. Here, the control parameter for developmental change was the repeated seeing and naming of objects by the child. These experimenters provided 17-month-olds with extra practice in producing one set of object names. When these children's rate of productive vocabulary began to accelerate, the researchers observed increased word retrieval errors for many known words but not for the words that had received extra training. This training study thus demonstrates how seeing and naming

objects may be the cause of more stable and less perturbable lexical retrieval, and how the activity of the system itself may be the cause of developmental change.

Equally as informative as long-term interventions for testing control parameters are what Vygotsky (1962) called *microgenesis* experiments (e.g., Kuhn & Phelps, 1982; Siegler & Jenkins, 1989). The experimenters try to push children into more mature performance by manipulating possible control parameters over a shorter time period, sometimes within an experimental session. For example, Thelen, Fisher, and Ridley-Johnson (1984) tested their hypothesis that the control parameter for the "disappearance" of the well-known newborn stepping response was the rapid deposition of subcutaneous fat, making the baby's legs relatively heavy. If, they reasoned, the weight of the legs was critical for whether babies stepped or not, changing leg weight should mimic developmental changes, and indeed it did. Decreasing the mechanical load on the legs by submerging the legs in water increased stepping, and adding weights decreased the response.

We emphasize again that many developmental studies manipulate potential control parameters. Those that provide training, enrichment, or increased parental support hope to show more advanced performance; those that increase attentional or processing demands, or offer ambiguous stimuli or distractions, will demonstrate less skilled actions. What is different about a dynamic systems approach is the situating of these experiments in the larger context of the overall collective dynamics so that principled decisions can be made on when to manipulate what, in experimental sessions. In the examples above, the interventions worked because the experimenters knew from other data that the children were in periods of rapid change.

In the following section, we report on a developmental study designed and conducted using these explicit dynamic systems principles. We demonstrate that a dynamic perspective revealed change processes that were not discovered from conventional approaches.

A DYNAMIC SYSTEMS APPROACH TO LEARNING TO REACH

Reaching for and grasping objects is a foundational perceptual–motor skill that is critical for normal human functioning. Normal infants first reach out and grab things they see when they are around $3\frac{1}{2}$ to 4 months old. At first, their coordination and control are poor; they often miss their targets, and their movements are jerky and indirect. Within a few months, they become much more skilled, and by the end of the first year, they can grab things off the supermarket shelves as they are wheeled by in shopping carts.

The pioneering work of Halverson (1931, 1933) and especially of Hofsten (1991) has documented that, within those first months of reaching onset, infants' reaches become more accurate, straighter, and smoother. But the developmental processes involved in the emergence of the skill and its improvement have remained little understood. Reaching is a function of many component structures and processes, including the physiological, metabolic, and biomechanical properties of the muscles and joints, the state of the central nervous system, vision and visual attention, motivation, and so on. All of these elements are changing during the first year of life—some, at a rather rapid rate. What are the control parameters that move the system into new states?

To begin to understand these processes, Thelen and her colleagues designed a study of the emergence of reaching using explicit dynamic systems principles. The focus was on reaching as an emergent perceptual-motor pattern acquired throughout the soft assembly of mutually interacting, multiple components within a context. All of the components are essential for the skill to emerge and improve, but one or more components may act as control parameters at different points during development. The overall design was to measure behavior repeatedly and intensively in a small number of children at multiple levels (from behavioral to patterns of muscle activation) and at multiple time scales (real time and developmental time).

The study involved four infants, Nathan, Gabriel, Justin, and Hannah, whose reaching and nonreaching arm movements were observed weekly from 3 weeks until 30 weeks, and in alternating weeks thereafter. The study tracked *multiple components* in looking at reaching performance: the kinematics (time–space parameters) of the movement trajectories, the coordination between the arms, the underlying torque or force patterns moving the joints, the patterns of muscle activation that generate the forces, and the everyday postural and motor states of the baby. In addition, the study addressed *multiple time scales*. Each week, the experimenters presented the infants with attractive objects in such a way that the reach was embedded within a longer

session, and motor variables were recorded so that the transition from nonreaching movements to reaching could be captured. Thus, they recorded transitions on two time scales: (a) the real time of the trial where the toy was presented, and (b) the developmental time scale, where patterns of stability may evolve and dissolve.

Collective Variable Dynamics

The first step in a dynamic systems approach is to define a reasonable collective variable or variables—measures that capture the state of the system and its developmental changes. Previous descriptions (e.g., Fetters & Todd, 1987; Hofsten, 1991; Mathew & Cook, 1990) suggested that improvement in reaching could be described by two measures of the path of the hand to the offered toy: its straightness and its smoothness. A straight hand path takes the shortest distance from the start of the movement to the target: Adults' hands move in a very nearly straight path for direct reaches. Smoothness is a measure of how often the movement starts and stops or slows down and speeds up. Infants' jerky movements have many "speed bumps" characterized by accelerations and decelerations. In contrast, adults' movements toward a direct target show only one acceleration and one deceleration.

The developmental dynamics of these two collective variables for the four infants are depicted in Figure 10.20 (Thelen, Corbetta, & Spencer, 1996). Overall, the infants clearly became better reachers; they converged on relatively straight and smooth hand paths by the end of the first year. These performance results are consistent with previous reports showing improvement with age (Hofsten, 1991). But the picture revealed by this dense longitudinal study is much richer, and more surprising, than that painted by previous work.

Most notably, the dynamics of reaching performance over the first year were highly nonlinear (in contrast to the seemingly linear improvement revealed by less dense and group data). First, infants differed dramatically in the age of the first transition (from no reaching to reaching). Whereas Nathan reached first at 12 weeks, Hannah and Justin did not attain this milestone until 20 weeks of age. Second, the infants showed periods of rapid change, plateaus, and even regressions in performance. All infants were poor reachers at first. But three of the four infants—Nathan, Hannah, and Gabriel—also showed an epoch where straightness and smoothness appeared to get worse after some improvement

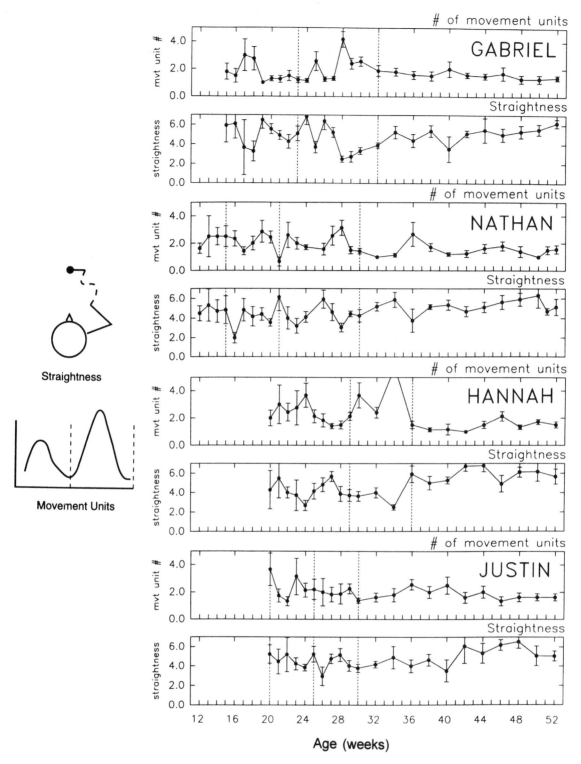

Figure 10.20 Changes in the straightness and smoothness of reach trajectories of four infants followed longitudinally over the first year. The collective variables are number of movement units (fewer = a smoother reach) and straightness index, where a value of 1 = perfectly straight from start to target. From "The development of reaching during the first year: the role of movement speed," by E. Thelen et al., 1996, *Journal of Experimental Psychology: Human Perception and Performance*. Copyright © 1996 by the American Psychological Association. Reprinted with permission.

606

(labeled as "A" in Figure 10.21) Finally, there was in Nathan, Justin, and Hannah a rather discontinuous shift to better, less variable performance (indicated by "T" in Figure 10.21). Gabriel's transition to stability was more gradual, but clearly nonlinear overall. These phase shifts to different states were confirmed statistically.

The developmental course of reaching looks very different when the individual trajectories of change are plotted using dense sampling. Although all four infants converged on remarkably similar values by one year, they did not get there by identical means. Can these collective variable dynamics provide insight to the processes underlying the

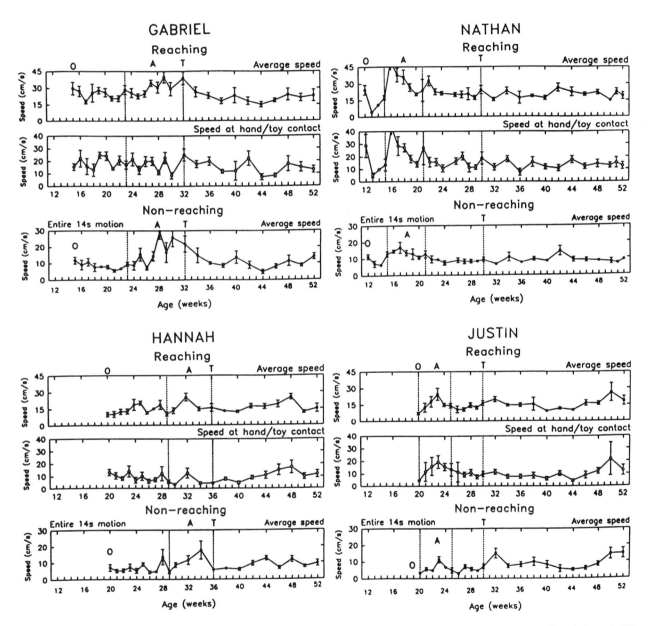

Figure 10.21   Average speed of reaching, speed at toy contact, and speed of nonreaching movements for the four infants in Figure 10.20. From "The development of reaching during the first year: the role of movement speed," by E. Thelen et al., 1996, *Journal of Experimental Psychology: Human Perception and Performance.* Copyright © 1996 by the American Psychological Association. Reprinted with permission.

onset and improvement of reaching? Are there control variables that are common to all four infants? What accounts for their individual differences?

The First Transition: The Onset of Reaching

The longitudinal design allowed Thelen and colleagues to pinpoint with some accuracy the first phase shift, the appearance of successful reaching for and contacting the offered toy. (Note that these weeks of onset were confirmed by the more naturalistic observations of these babies.) Having identified a developmental transition, the next step in a dynamic approach was to look for potential control parameters. Recall that we make strong assumptions of continuity across levels and time scales; discontinuities must arise from, and be part of, these continuous dynamics.

What is continuous for young infants is that they are always moving their limbs, from birth and even before. Reaching, the new form, must emerge from the continuous processes of moving and perceiving that occur before infants perform the first goal-directed reach—and that continue as nonreaching arm movements even after this new behavior appears. Thelen et al. (1993) looked at the transition to first reaching as a process of infants' "discovering" a reach from among many and varied nonreaching movements.

These authors found that the preferred states of infants' motor systems in nonreaching movements—their individual intrinsic dynamics—profoundly influenced the nature of the transition to reaching. In particular, the four infants differed in the amplitude, and especially in the vigor, of their spontaneous arm movements in the months previous to reach onset. Two infants, Gabriel and Nathan, had large and vigorous movements; the other two were quieter and generated fewer and slower, less forceful movements. The task for all the babies was the same: to get their hands in the vicinities of the desired objects. But they had different problems to solve to do this: Gabriel and Nathan had to damp down their forceful movements to gain control; Hannah and Justin had to produce more muscle force to extend their arms forward in space and hold them stiffly against gravity. Examination of the actual torques used to move the arm segments showed that Gabriel and Nathan were using their muscles primarily to counteract the passive inertial forces generated by the rapid movements of their arms, while Hannah and Justin were using their muscles to counteract gravity.

Many components are necessary for infants to begin to reach. They must be able to see the toy (or other target) and locate it in space. And they must want to get it. The visual and motivational aspects of reaching are probably not the control parameters, however, because other evidence suggests that infants can locate objects in 3-D space rather well, if not perfectly, by age 3 months, and that they grasp and mouth objects and show interest in them. More likely, selecting the correct muscle patterns and scaling the activation appropriately allow infants to fashion their first reaches from their undirected movements.

Indeed, analysis of infants' muscle synergies from electromygraphic (EMG) recordings revealed that reaching onset was associated with changes in functional muscle use. Spencer and Thelen (1995), comparing EMG patterns in reaching and nonreaching movements before and after reach onset, discovered that, when reaching, infants frequently recruited their anterior deltoid muscle, alone and in combination with other muscles. This shoulder muscle raises the upper arm. Before reaching, infants sometimes also raised their arms, but they used other combinations of muscles to do this. The ability to selectively activate and control this muscle group was associated with goal-directed movements.

Thelen and colleagues speculated that infants learn specific functional muscle patterns through experience in moving during the weeks and months before reaching actually emerges. Infants' real-time activities of moving—sensing the "feel" of their limb dynamics, and perceiving the consequences of their movements—are time-locked input to the degenerate and reentrant neural nets we described in an earlier section. As a consequence, categories of limb parameters emerge from all the possible combinations that are appropriate to the spatial location of the toy.

Changes in other system components may facilitate this discovery. For example, Thelen and colleagues found that infants did not reach until they could also stabilize their heads in a midline position. Possibly, strength and control of neck and head muscles are necessary before the arm can be lifted independently. Stable head and eyes also facilitates accurate localization of the to-be-reached object in space.

Shifts in Control during the First Year

Recall that in three infants, the collective variable dynamics had a striking nonlinear course over the first year (Figure 10.20), with a distinct period of seeming instability followed by a period of stability. Recall also that the individual infants had very different intrinsic movement dynamics, especially in relation to characteristic speeds. Studies of adult reaching have repeatedly shown that the speed of movements—reflecting the amount of energy delivered to the limbs—is a critical parameter in many aspects of motor control. Faster movements are generally less accurate, probably because there is less time to make fine adjustments (Fitts, 1954). Reach trajectories may require different strategies of control and different patterns of muscle activation, depending on whether they are performed slowly or rapidly (Flanders & Herrmann, 1992; Gottlieb, Corcos, & Agarwal, 1989). Similarly, very fast movements produce much greater motion-related passive forces than slow ones do, and thus pose different problems for neural control (Latash & Gottlieb, 1991; Schneider, Zernicke, Schmidt, & Hart, 1989). Could movement speed be acting as a control parameter in these developmental shifts?

Figure 10.21 illustrates the four infants' characteristic speed of movements over their first year. Plots show average and peak speed of the reach itself, as well as speed at the start and termination of the movement. In addition, Thelen et al. (1996) reported infants' speed of *nonreaching* movements, that is, all the movements infants produced during the 14-second sampling trials when they were not reaching. This analysis revealed several remarkable results. First, infants converged on more or less similar "good" movement and contact speed; it was not functional to grab the toy either too slowly or too rapidly. Second, within this common speed solution, individual speed "personalities" or intrinsic dynamics remained; on average, Gabriel was a faster mover than Hannah. Third, there is close correspondence between characteristic movement speed in reaching and in nonreaching movements. The reaches were not isolated from the ongoing preferences and habits of the babies, but were molded from those dynamics. Finally, periods of faster movements were associated with instability in the collective variables, indicating poor control.

Although the factors that led the infants to move more quickly or more slowly at any point in time are as yet unknown, this overall speed variable clearly acts as a control parameter on the straightness and smoothness of the reach trajectory. Again, individual acts of reaching are fashioned at the moment and carry with them the state of the system at that moment, which, in turn, is determined by the system's history.

Bimanual Coordination

This interplay between task and intrinsic dynamics is equally well illustrated by another aspect of infants' reaching: whether they reach with one or two hands. Gesell (1939; Gesell & Ames, 1947) first noted that the bilateral symmetry and preference of infants was very unstable and frequently shifted from unimanual limb use to bimanual, and from strongly lateralized preference to symmetry. The four infants in the Thelen et al. (1996) study amply demonstrated these shifts. Figure 10.22 (Corbetta & Thelen, 1996) shows individual frequencies of one- or two-handed reaching. Note that, in this situation, toys could always be grasped by one hand, so two-handed reaching was not obligatory for function. Not only did individual infants have mixed preferences, but no two infants were alike in their developmental course.

As in the single-arm trajectory, Corbetta and Thelen (1996) discovered that bimanual coordination was also influenced by infants' intrinsic dynamics—in this case, whether their limbs moved in a coupled fashion in nonreaching movements as well. When infants reached with two hands, the two arms tended to speed up and slow down together in all movements; limbs were symmetrically coupled. In contrast, no such coupling was noted at times when infants preferred to use only one hand to grab the toy. Furthermore, epochs of bimanual symmetry in reaching and nonreaching were associated with *periods of higher speed movements*. Gabriel, for instance, used two hands and had coupled movements almost throughout the year, and he was the most energetic baby. Hannah, in contrast, was largely unimanual and uncoupled (and moved slowly), except for the period in the middle of the year when her movement speed increased and her movement symmetry did as well. Movement speed was clearly a control parameter for both the efficiency of the movement and the strength of bilateral coupling.

Although the infants had an obvious task goal in reaching out to grab a toy, this dynamic act emerged from a background of ongoing movement. The state of the infants' systems was emergent from their body architecture, metabolism, and motivation, and from how they had been moving in the months before. In such a view, no one part of the system is privileged—there is no dedicated reaching code in the brain. Reaching is a pattern that self-organizes from multiple components over several time scales: the

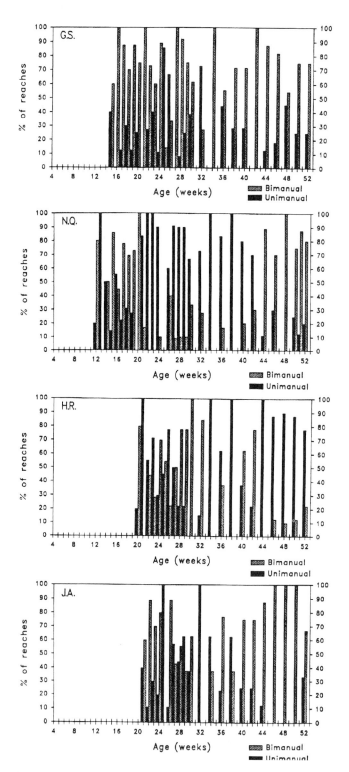

Figure 10.22   Percentages of uni- and bimanual reaches for the four infants in Figure 10.20.

here-and-now dynamics of the task and goal, and the longer-term dynamics of the infants' history of moving and reaching.

A MODEL OF LEVELS OF CONTROL

A dynamic view of the development of reaching revealed stagelike changes in the collective variables at the same time that reaching was embedded in the infants' continuous and ongoing intrinsic dynamics. In this section, we present a dynamic model of emergent control that reconciles these multiple levels and multiple time scales by proposing that they are dynamically *coupled*.

What Is Skill?

It is useful here to digress briefly and ask: What is involved in controlling the arm (or any body part) for successful and adaptive movement?

According to Bernstein (Bernstein, in Latash & Turvey, 1996), one of the hallmarks of skilled activity is the ability to flexibly adapt movements to current and future conditions. What constitutes skilled performance is not just a repeatable and stable pattern, but the ability to accomplish some high-level goal with rapid and graceful, but flexible solutions that can be recruited online or in anticipation of future circumstances. Consider, for example, a skilled equestrian whose goal is to stay on the horse and maintain a graceful posture, while leading the horse through an intended course. Skill in this case means making minute, online adjustments in response to the horse's movements while anticipating changes in the terrain.

Indeed, in movement, as well as in cognitive or social activities, we can define skill as being able to rapidly recruit appropriate strategies that meet the changing demands of the social, task, or physical environment. For reaching, good control means being able to efficiently reach, in all directions, for moving or stationary objects, when the light is bright or dim, from any posture, while our attention is focused or distracted, and so on. Upon further analysis, we can identify the sources of potential disruption as affecting one of three levels of control of the reach. As depicted in the cartoon (Figure 10.23), reaching must be stabilized first against transient mechanical perturbations—that is, various forms of external forces acting on the moving limb in a way that would tend to push the

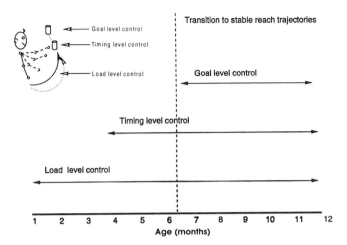

Figure 10.23 A simple model of increasing control over reaching. After Schöner (1994), we have defined control as protecting that level from perturbations from the other levels. The load level involves the internal and external forces acting on the limbs and the associated stretch reflexes. The timing level involves the generation of a trajectory and the timing of the joints and muscles to execute the trajectory. The goal level is the spatial target. Infants only gradually gain control of these levels.

intended trajectory off course. (We know that adults are very good at maintaining their movement trajectory in the face of little bumps against the limb, e.g., Hogan, Bizzi, Mussa-Ivaldi, & Flash, 1987.) Second, reaching must be stabilized in the face of different task demands of the timing of the movement, such as setting the coordination pattern of the various joints and muscles, and producing the time–space trajectory of the arm. (Again, we know that adults can maintain timing very well.) Finally, reaches must be stabilized even when the global goal parameters change—for example, when the target is unexpectedly displaced (adults make these kinds of adjustments quickly and smoothly; Jeannerod, 1988). Using Gregor Schöner's (1994) terminology, we can define these levels of control as the *load, timing,* and *goal* levels.

In ordinary adult skilled actions, these levels are not separable; that is, people perceive, think, and act as one unit within the physical world. Levels of control are revealed only through extraordinary experimental manipulations, for example, when experimenters tell participants to hold a limb position constant when they apply an external load, or to reach to a target that is suddenly displaced. Adults are able, intentionally, therefore, to isolate, protect,

or control their activities at several behavioral levels. This means that, in skilled adults, the levels of control are not tightly coupled; the goal level is not a slave of the arm's biomechanics, although the load level contributes to the movement. Again, we must emphasize that these levels are strictly a function of the imposed task demands. They do not exist anatomically or functionally in the absence of the tasks.

Development of Levels of Control

Infants, in contrast, do not start out with this ability to protect one aspect of the task against perturbations—that is, to control their actions against unanticipated (and even anticipated) bumps from the environment. Indeed, what we want to argue here is that the initial state is highly syncretic; infants' movements are initially tightly coupled to lower-level dynamics, and only through experience and organic changes does a fully protected higher-level goal dynamic emerge.

We can see very clear examples of this in early spontaneous movements of the arms and legs. As we have argued previously, when young infants inject sufficient energy into their limbs, the resulting patterns suggest the dynamics of coupled oscillators with a periodic forcing function. Such dynamics must be the collective result of simple neural patterns in combination with the springlike properties of the joints and muscles and the effects of gravity—the load level dynamics.

In the first months of life, infants are largely the captives of these dynamics. They cannot control well, or at all, the positions of their limbs in space, or the timing of the segments during movement. Thus, the first problem that infants have to solve is control of these load level dynamics; they must begin to weaken the obligatory coupling between the load level and the higher levels of control.

By the time infants first reach and grasp, at age 3 or 4 months, they must have begun, through their repeated movements, to generate a trajectory in time and space to attain something they see. But their reaches are still not fully controllable independent of the load level dynamics. Infants often reach too fast or too slowly; they overshoot, or inject energy bursts in stops and starts, leading to the patterns of acceleration and deceleration so characteristic of early reaching. This model predicts, then, that without good control of the arm, the reach trajectory would degrade when movements are fast. This happens because fast movements create inertial forces between the segments of the arm, which require precise control—something skilled movers have continually. And indeed, this is what happened in the four infant reachers described earlier: When movement speed increased, reach trajectories became more jerky and less straight (Figure 10.21).

The dramatic transition to smoother and straighter reaching that we saw at around age 7 months is, we suggest, the system's discovery of a stable trajectory solution—that is, the isolation and protection of the time–space parameters of getting the felt hand to the seen toy. Thus, by this age, reaches were no longer buffeted by load level dynamics. Infants could reach smoothly and in a relatively straight manner, and they could control the segments against their own inertial forces.

Although 8- to 12-month-old infants, under ordinary and everyday conditions, look like pretty good reachers, we can create conditions that reveal that they have not yet mastered the highest level of skill—the ability to protect the goal from the lower-level dynamics. In the following section, we report on studies where the goal level—the location and nature of the object to be reached—was perturbed. These experiments revealed that, in this unstable period, infants were not flexible; they were held captive, so to speak, by the arm pathways they had previously produced. Their trajectory formation was good but not flexible; they were "stuck" in the habits of previous reaches. We focus on classic object retrieval experiments—Piaget's "A-not-B error." A dynamic systems account challenges the traditional explanations that object retrieval tasks tap into enduring knowledge about objects. Rather, we suggest that infants show traces of obligatory coupling between the goal and timing levels of trajectory control.

THE TASK DYNAMICS OF THE A-NOT-B ERROR

One of the primary tasks of infancy is to learn about the properties of objects in order to act upon them, think about them, and, eventually, talk about them. Literally thousands of papers have been written about the nature of object representation: when and how babies come to understand the spatial and temporal permanence of objects. One signature task that has been used to measure infants' understanding of objects asks infants to retrieve a hidden object. Odd patterns of search errors and dramatic developmental changes

characterize performance between the ages of 6 and 12 months. We review here our dynamic systems account of one of these search errors, the classic Piagetian A-not-B error (Smith, Thelen, Titzer, & McLin, 1997; Thelen & Smith, 1994).

The A-Not-B Error

The error emerges in the following task: The experimenter hides a desired object in location A—for example, under a lid—while the infant watches. After a several-second delay, the infant is allowed to search and finds the object at A. This A trial is then repeated several times with the infant successfully retrieving the hidden object from the A location. The experimenter then hides the object under a second lid, at location B. Although the infant saw the object disappear at B, the infant reaches back to the original and incorrect A location—the place the object was last found.

The A-not-B error has attracted much attention, and with good cause. It is counterintuitive, dramatic, and robust. Piaget attributed this error to infants' immature object concept. He suggested that infants were unable to represent the hidden object as independent of their own action. This provocative proposal and the counterintuitive error itself have generated literally thousands of empirical studies. Just as did Piaget, most of these researchers have worried about what the error means for what children know about the hidden object. Do they remember it? Do they understand that it continues to exist? Do they really believe that an object hidden at B can be found at A?

A dynamic systems approach challenges the fundamental assumptions that motivate these questions. Knowledge may not be a matter of having (or not having) some enduring concept; rather, through the dynamic interaction of many component processes, each of which has its own developmental history, knowing is "softly assembled" within the particular task context. The very character of the A-not-B error suggests the viability of this approach. Although the error is a highly robust phenomenon, it is also empirically confined. First, it is developmentally transitory; infants younger than 7 months do not make the error because they do not search for hidden objects, and infants older than 12 months search correctly and do not typically make the error. Second, the error is contextually determined. It depends, for example, on the delay between the hiding of the object and the release of the infant to search;

on whether the two hiding locations are similar or different in appearance; on whether the locations are far apart or near; or on whether there are just two potential hiding locations or many (Bremner, 1985; Harris, 1987; Wellman, Cross, & Bartsch, 1987).

Using a conventional depiction of dynamics of change, the developmental trajectory looks like the one illustrated in Figure 10.24. Early in development, there is one deep attractor; infants do not reach for completely hidden objects and cannot be induced to do so. At the other end, there is another very deep attractor; older infants always search at B, the location at which they saw the object disappear. In the developmental landscape, the A-not-B error belongs to the bumpy terrain between the two valleys. In our view, the question typically asked about the error—*What does it say about what infants know or do not know about objects?*—is the wrong question. What needs to be explained are the processes that make the developmental landscape look as it does—the processes that make the error emerge at this time, in those certain contexts—and then change so that the error no longer occurs in those same contexts. We provide an explanation in our dynamic systems account, and in so doing we offer a radical reconceptualization of what it means to *know*. In what follows, we first consider our account of the processes that make the error occur. We then reconsider our account in relation to (a) Piaget's theory about the infants' construction of an object concept, (b) recent proposals, from looking studies, that quite young infants "have" an object concept (e.g., Baillargeon & Graber,

1988), and (c) Munakata et al.'s (1997) connectionist model of the graded development of an object concept.

It's about Goal-Directed Reaching

Our account begins not with a focus on object permanence, but with a focus on the behavioral act itself. At the behavior level, the error is an error in reaching; the infant reaches to the wrong location. We propose that the error is a product of the dynamics of goal-directed reaching in unskilled reachers when placed in a task that requires them to repeatedly reach to one location and then reach to another. We expand these ideas below.

The Temporal Reality of the Processes That Create Real Behavioral Acts

The activity that underlies behavior is temporally real, extended in time with real rise times and real decay times. This means that the activity, at any moment, depends on and emerges out of preceding activity. Thus, the cascading processes that comprise the goal, timing, and load levels of a reach all endure. Thus, a reach at one moment will be shaped by the just previous activity at each level. This is a key idea in our account: The A-not-B error is like a tongue twister. The difficulty in saying "Peter Piper picked a peck of pickled peppers" lies not in saying "pickled" but in saying "pickled" *after* "peck"; the infants' difficulty lies in reaching to B after reaching to A.

Everything that is known about the motor control of reaching supports this idea. Especially pertinent is the work of Georgopoulos and colleagues (1988), which we described in an earlier section. These investigators showed how the direction of a reaching is coded by the transient activity of populations of neurons in the motor cortex (reviewed in Georgopoulos, 1986, 1988, 1990). Their major finding was that, in both motor and premotor cortex, the activity of single cells changed in an orderly manner with the direction of the movement in space. Thus, for any given cell, activity was highest in a preferred direction and decreased when the arm moved away from the preferred direction. Note that the cells responded to *actual* direction of movement of the arm, not the direction of the target.

Georgopoulos and colleagues found that, with the recorded area, different cells exhibited different preferred directions, distributed around the three-dimensional space of the possible target directions, but the final movement direction was coded by the overall population vector; that

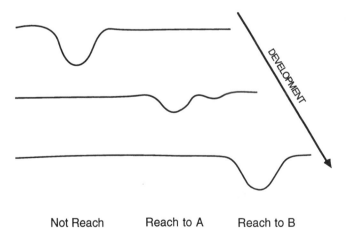

Figure 10.24 Changing attractors in the A-not-B task with development.

is, each cell, broadly tuned to prefer a certain direction, "voted" by changing activity a certain amount. The monkey moves in a direction determined by the vector sum. Critically for our account of the A-not-B error, this population vector of activity can be detected before actual movement begins, and it has a specific rise and decay function. We, of course, do not know the shape and time course of this mental function in infants who have just learned to reach it, but it may well be a different, more globally tuned, direction, and a more sluggish function than that of well-practiced adults. Whatever the precise timing, the fact that the coding for a goal-directed movement persists after that movement means the pattern coding for a reach at one moment will be *laid on top of*—influenced—by the direction of the preceding reach.

In Figure 10.25, we illustrate what this means for the A-not-B error. On the left is a description of the events in the task, and on the right is the hypothesized population vector in the motor cortex. The strength and direction of the vector are represented, respectively, by the length and the direction of the arrow. On the first A trial, as the experimenter directs attention to the toy at location A, the

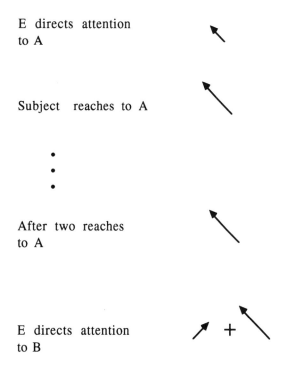

E directs attention
to A

Subject   reaches to A

.
.
.

After two reaches
to A

E directs attention
to B

Figure 10.25 Hypothesized changes in the vector coding the direction of reach as a function of the events in the A-not-B task.

infant's intended movement toward A will be signaled by increased activation in the A direction. The infant's reach to A might be expected to strengthen this pattern of activity. The hiding and reach to location A on the second A trial will be laid on this preceding activity. Thus, the infant's reach to A may actually strengthen and tune this pattern, so that, after several reaches, the coded direction is tightly specified and perhaps somewhat enduring. Now, what will happen when the experimenter hides the toy at B? The experimenter's action at B should pull the intended direction of movement toward B. But that pull must be laid on the remaining activation from previous trials, which is in the direction of A. As a result, the infant may reach to A rather than B.

The Tight Coupling of Levels in Unskilled Reachers

The second dynamic attribute of a real-time act pertinent to our account is stability. As we reviewed in the section on the development of reaching, a *well-controlled* act is one that is flexible, one that preserves the goal under changing circumstances. Using Schöner's terminology, success in the A-not-B task requires the infant to stabilize a reach in the face of changes at both the goal and motor timing levels. Success when the target is displaced from the A to the B location requires coordinated change in the goal and timing levels. We propose that novice reachers have difficulty in coordinating these changes, and that they do so in part because the goal and timing levels are both tightly coupled and easily perturbed. We specifically map the goal level to the visually perceived location of the target and propose that the coded direction of movement and the direction of visual attention are tightly coupled.

A tight coupling of visual attention and the direction of a coded reach makes sense when one thinks about how we typically reach to objects in the world. We look in order to act. We first look at the object, and we move our hand to where we are looking. By our account, this tight coupling (perhaps too-tight coupling in novice reachers) is a key ingredient in creating the error and the cause of its context-specificity. In the world, reachers (including novice reachers) commonly reach for objects that stand out from their background and are perceptually distinct from nearby objects. The distinctiveness of the target object (its contrast with the ground) enables the reacher to look to and maintain attention at one narrowly defined location in visual space. We specifically propose that a narrow, spatially circumscribed spotlight of visual attention pulls and narrowly defines the movement coding in the motor cortex in that direction.

The task in which the A-not-B error emerges, however, is not like the typical situation in which infants reach for objects. Instead, infants are presented with two identical hiding locations (for example, two identical lids or two identical cloths) that are close in space and often indistinct from the background surface. By our account, the static visual properties of the A location and the B location do not provide a very tight pull in any direction. If the direction of visual attention helps sharpen and tune the motor coding of reach, then, in this context, without such a guide, infants will be even more at the mercy of the transient influences from preceding activity. This idea is strongly supported by one widely replicated empirical fact about the error: At no age do infants consistently make the A-not-B error when the two hiding locations are visually distinct (e.g., differently colored or shaped; see Wellman, et al. [1987] for a review and analysis of these data).

Smith, Thelen, et al. (1997) tested the following three predictions derived from this account.

Prediction 1: The Hidden Object Does Not Matter

The first prediction is that the error emerges in the dynamics of successive reaches to two locations; that it does not, in fact, have anything to do with the hidden object or the infants' memory for that object. Smith, Thelen, et al. (1997) tested this hypothesis by presenting two groups of infants with two A-not-B tasks that were identical in every way except (a) in one task, the standard task, an object was hidden, and (b) in the second task, the reaching task, there was no object and no hiding.

The general experimental context for both conditions is as follows. An experimenter sits at one side of the table, and the infant and mother sit at the other side. The experimenter performs some action on the experimental box. This box is a uniform brown color. It has two 8-cm wells whose centers are 10 cm apart. These wells are covered with two identical brown wooden lids. After the experimenter performs the action, there is a variable delay. The box is pushed along a track to arrive within the infant's reach. In the standard condition, the action the experimenter performs is hiding a toy, first for several trials under the A lid and then under the B lid. In the reaching condition, the action is simply lifting a lid, waving it at the infant, and returning it to its place over the well. Following the same format as the standard condition, the experimenter first waves and replaces the A lid, waits for the delay, then pushes the box to the infant. On the critical B trial, the experimenter lifts the B lid instead, waves it, replaces it, and then pushes the box forward to the infant.

The key result was that the pattern of performances by 8- and 10-month-old infants was identical in the two conditions. They consistently reached for the A lid on A trials, both when searching for an object and when reaching to the lid just waved by the experimenter. And, they continued to reach to the A lid on the B trials, even though the experimenter had shifted the action to the B lid. We have here the A-not-B error—but with no hidden object. These results suggest that the hidden object in the standard task is not at all essential to the appearance of this error; that it is, instead, about the dynamics of reaching first to one location and then to another.

Prediction 2: The Strength of the Pull to A Depends on the Number of Prior Reaches

This experiment examined spontaneous reaching. There was no hidden object, just the two lids on the standard brown box. We simply took the box, did not touch or direct attention to one lid or the other, pushed it forward, and verbally encouraged 8- and 10-month-old infants to reach. We repeated this act several times, recording which lid the infant spontaneously reached to. Our account made two straightforward predictions about what should happen. First, each reach in one direction should bias the infant to continue to reach in that direction. Second, the more reaches the infant has made in one direction, the harder it should be to pull the infant's reach in the other direction. Accordingly, we let infants spontaneously reach. Then, after one, three, or five spontaneous reaches, we directed their attention (by lifting the lid and waving) to the lid opposite to the one to which they first reached. We then pushed the box to within the infant's reach.

The results were straightforward. First, unless perturbed, infants continued to reach in one direction. Second, the success of pulling their reach to the other lid by directing visual attention to it depended on the number of prior reaches in one direction. When the experimenter picked up the opposite lid just prior to the second reach, 55% of the infants switched and reached in that direction on the second trial. When the experimenter picked up the opposite lid just prior to the third trial, 50% of the infants switched and reached in that direction. But when the experimenter picked up the opposite lid just prior to the sixth trial—after the infant had made five reaches in the other direction—only 16% of the infants switched and reached toward the lid the experimenter had lifted.

In brief, the recent history of reaches matters. These results strongly support the idea that each reach emerges out of preceding activity. Unless there is a strong counterforce, a reach will be pulled in the direction of that preceding activity.

Prediction 3: Looking and Reaching Are Coupled

In skilled reaching, the strong counterforce to repeating previous activity is a goal level that can be stably isolated from other levels and from the dynamics of the reach itself. For unskilled reachers (e.g., 8- to 10-month-old infants), we propose that the usual strong counterforce to the pull of previous activity is the direction of visual attention. Thus, we predict that infants should look where they reach.

This prediction contradicts Diamond's (1990) claim that, on B trials in particular, infants sometimes reach to A but look to B. This idea is widespread; it has even found its way into introductory textbooks. But, in fact, there have been only anecdotal reports of the observations. Accordingly, we counted all looks and reaches that were in opposite directions in the standard version of the A-not-B task described under Prediction 1 above. Across 80 reaches to A, there was none in which looking and reaching were in opposite directions; across 80 reaches to B, there was only one.

A final experiment provided stronger support that looking and reaching are strongly coupled systems in 8- to 10-month-olds. This experiment employed a standard A-not-B task. However, at various points in the course of the experiment, we perturbed the direction of infants' attention *just prior to the reach*. We did this by tapping a marker on the far A side or the far B side of the infant. The results provide powerful evidence of the coupling of looking and reaching in infants. On both A trials and B trials, wherever we pulled visual attention, we pulled the reach.

Altogether, the empirical results provide strong evidence that the A-not-B error is not about hiding objects and not about hidden objects. Rather, these findings strongly suggest that the A-not-B error is the consequence of the real-time dynamics of goal-directed reaching. The results show that the error emerges because of a tight coupling between where one looks and where one reaches, and because behavior—a reach—emerges from the context of ongoing activity.

Why Does the Error Disappear with Development?

Infants under 7 months of age do not make the error because they do not reach for completely hidden objects. Infants older than 12 months do not make the error because they reach to the location where they last saw the object disappear. The A-not-B error belongs to the time between these two types of behavior, and it represents, in our view, the increasing development of skilled reaching as a result of practice at reaching and practice at maintaining goals in the face of unexpected disturbances. One element of this developmental change is likely to be a flexible decoupling of looking and reaching; adults are not so likely to be pulled in the direction that they look. Another element may be the finer coding and recording of visual space. Given a brown box with two brown lids, 8-month-old infants may coarsely and variably code direction in space; 12-month-old infants, in contrast, may more tightly code location, perhaps because they notice and can attend to the finer visual details that distinguish one lid from another.

These ideas fit well with one of the strongest predictors of success in the A-not-B task in 8- to 12-month-old infants: self-locomotion (Bertenthal & Campos, 1990). Thelen and Smith (1994) suggested that self-locomotion acts as a control parameter for the A-not-B task because the infant's own activity engenders changes in the coupling of looking and reaching: To move about in space, one must maintain the goal level (where one is going) independent of momentary glances in various directions and independent of the specific coordination of joints and muscles required by the terrain and obstacles. Practice at self-locomotion may thus make goal-directed action more controlled. The task of self-locomotion may also foster perceptual learning—the use of smaller details and finer coding of directions in visual space.

One of the core assumptions of the dynamic systems account is that the activity of the system changes the system. The activity of repeated goal-directed reaches makes reaching skilled, and that makes the A-not-B error disappear. This proposal might seem directly counter to the evidence of Diamond (1990), who has proposed that the increased ability of infants to search correctly on B trials is directly due to the maturation of the dorsolateral prefrontal cortex. The involvement of the prefrontal cortex in the error is empirically without question. Lesions specifically in the prefrontal cortex of adult monkeys cause the monkeys to make the error (Diamond & Goldman-Rakic, 1989; Diamond, Zola-Morgan, & Squire, 1989). What we question, however, is the idea that *maturation* of the prefrontal cortex independent of experience causes development. As we reviewed earlier, everything we know about biological development—from gene expression to embryology, and on to neural and behavioral development—indicates that there is no such thing as a *nonexperiential component* to development. We propose that the relevant system for understanding the A-not-B error and the relevant activity for changing that system are both goal-directed reaching.

What Is Knowing?

What does all this mean for Piaget's original conclusions from watching his own children search for objects in the "wrong places"? What does all this mean for the results of Baillargeon and Graber (1988) and others who have found that infants seem to know that objects stay where they are put, in tasks in which they only watch but do not act? How does this dynamic systems account fit with Munakata et al.'s (1997) connectionist account, in which internal representations of objects reside in one set of layers that deliver input to a separate system that acts?

One possible answer to these questions is that the A-not-B error is simply about reaching—not about the object and not about *knowing*. According to this answer, infants in the A-not-B task represent objects *independently from their actions* right from the beginning, although those representations may not, as Munakata et al. (1997) suggest, be strong enough to support goal-directed manual action. This answer divorces knowing from acting; the infants knows where the object is when it is hidden in B, but just cannot control the reach.

We believe this answer is wrong. Knowing is the process of dynamic assembly across multileveled systems in the service of a task. We do not need to invoke represented constructs such as "object" or "extended in space and time" outside the moment of knowing. Knowing, just like action, in this view, is the momentary *product* of a dynamic system, not a dissociable cause of action. This same point has been made by others who also see cognition as a piece with action. Churchland (1986), for example, remarks:

[B]rains are not in the business of pattern recognition for its own sake, and the nature of pattern recognition, as accomplished by brains, must be understood in the context of its role in how brains achieve motor control. Evolution being what it is, pattern recognition is there to subserve motor coordination. . . . if we ignore motor control as the context within which we understand pattern recognition, we run the risk of generating biologically irrelevant solutions. (pp. 473–474)

We think in order to act. Thus, knowing may begin as and always be an inherently sensorimotor act. Our dynamic systems account thus stands on common ground with Piaget in the origins of thought in sensorimotor activity but on common ground with Johnson (1987), Varela, Thompson, and Rosch (1991), Churchland (1986), and Edelman (1987) in the idea that cognition emerges in the recurrent sensorimotor patterns that enable action to be perceptually guided.

THE TEMPORAL REALITY OF COGNITION

In the previous section, we argued that knowledge may not be a matter of having (or not having) some enduring concept, but rather may be "softly assembled" within the particular task context through the interaction of dynamic processes operating over multiple time scales. This idea challenges fundamental assumptions not just about the A-not-B error but about all of cognitive development. We begin this extension of dynamic systems to cognition with a review of textbook facts about perceiving and remembering. A hundred years of research in experimental psychology shows perceiving and remembering processes nested in time and coupled across levels of organization (see Smith & Samuelson, 1996, for a more complete review).

Fact 1. *Perceiving and remembering are tied to the immediate context.* Figure 10.26 illustrates classic examples from perception. Panel A shows how the perceived size of an object depends on surrounding objects: An object looks smaller than it really is when surrounded by objects that are much larger, and it looks larger than it really is when surrounded by objects just slightly larger than itself. Panels B and C show how the perceived similarity of two objects depends on other perceptually present objects. In Panel B, the perceived similarity of objects 1 and 2 is low but the perceived similarity of these same two objects in Panel C is

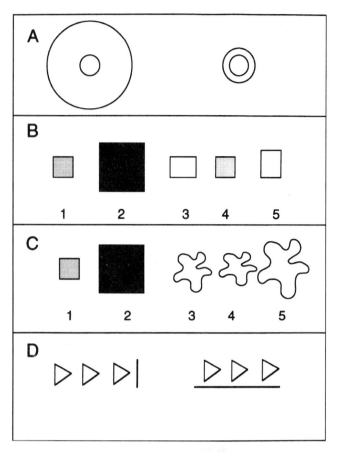

Figure 10.26 Illustrations of context effects in perception. A. Perceived size of center circle depends on size of surrounding circle. B. and C. Perceived similarity of objects 1 and 2 depends on other objects in the comparison set. D. Perceived shape and orientation of triangles depends on the perceived frame.

high (for more relevant data on the context-dependency of perceived similarity, see Goldstone, Medin, & Gentner, 1991). Panel D shows how the addition of a constant line, a small change in context, radically transforms shape and perceived similarity (Palmer, 1989).

The contextual malleability of general cognitive processes is also seen in many memory phenomena. Light and Carter-Sobel's (1970) classic demonstration of encoding specificity provides one good example. They showed that the word *jam* encountered in the context of *traffic* does not lead to the same memory as the word *jam* encountered in the context of *strawberry*. Further, the to-be-remembered word, *jam*, is better recognized in the context that matches the original learning (the word *traffic*) than in a context

that is different. The importance of context for remembering goes far beyond this paradigm (Tulving & Thomson, 1973). Evidence from a variety of memory tasks indicates that what is remembered depends critically on a holistic match between the quite general context of the original event and the context of the moment. Godden and Baddely (1980) found that scuba divers who learned lists of words underwater remembered them better when tested underwater than when tested on land. Similarly, Butler and Rovee-Collier (1989) found that babies who had learned to kick to make a mobile bounce, in a crib with a particularly patterned crib sheet and bumper, remembered what they had learned days later when the crib sheet and bumper were the same as during training, but not when they were different. Other evidence shows that the particular room, the particular voice of a speaker, and even the mood of the participants are factors in what is remembered (Eich, 1985; Palmeri, Goldinger, & Pisoni, 1993; Smith, 1986). In sum, what we remember depends broadly on the moment of learning and the moment of retrieval. The critical point is this: What we think and know is always dependent on and made in the here-and-now.

Fact 2. *Perceiving and remembering are temporally extended; activity at any moment depends on and emerges out of preceding activity.* Because the information-bearing events that comprise perceiving and remembering take time and endure, cognition, just like reaching, will at every point in time be a mixed result of immediate input and just-past activity. This fact, which creates both tongue twisters and the perseverative pull of the A location in the A-not-B error, also makes the phenomena of "priming" ubiquitous. Within a narrow time frame, the perception of a prior word (or object) facilitates the perception of subsequent words (or objects) that are similar in some way. Thus, perceiving the word *doctor* facilitates perceiving *nurse*. Phenomena of "priming" are widespread in lexical processes, picture perception, object recognition, and motor behavior (see, e.g., Harris & Coltheart, 1986; Klatzky, 1980; Rosenbaum, 1991), and they show without a doubt that the thoughts we have at one moment grow out of those just before.

The temporal reality of cognitive processes, the shaping of the present by the just-previous past, is also everywhere evident in adaptation effects. The repeated presentation of an event alters the perception of subsequent events. Adaptation effects characterize the primitive sensations of color, loudness, and pitch (e.g., Anstis & Saida, 1985; Marks,

1993) and the more complicated perceptions of musical chords (e.g., Zatorre & Halpern, 1979), shapes (e.g., Halpern & Warm, 1980), speech sounds (e.g., Remez, Cutting, & Studdert-Kennedy, 1980), and faces (O'Leary & McMahon, 1991). They, like the pervasive priming and context effects, mean that there is a pull for coherence from one thought to the next one, for the meaning of an event to depend on its place in a stream of events.

Fact 3. *Cognitive processes change as a direct consequence of their own activity.* The third textbook fact about processes of perceiving and remembering is that they change themselves. An act of perceiving or remembering causes not only transient changes but also longer lasting, nearly permanent changes. We know that long lasting changes must happen or we would have no memories of the individual events of our own lives and no connectedness with our own past. Empirical evidence suggests further that the power of a single processing event to alter subsequent knowing can be quite remarkable. We mention two such examples, one from studies of adult cognition and one from studies of children.

The example from the adult literature is provided by Jacoby, Kelley, Brown, and Jasechko's (1989) ability to make people famous overnight. They had subjects read a list of names that included all nonfamous people, names like *Samuel Weisdorf.* Twenty-four hours later, they gave subjects a list of famous and nonfamous names and asked subjects to pick out the famous people. Subjects picked out *Samuel Weisdorf* along with *Minnie Pearl* and *Christopher Wren.* Having read the name *once* was sufficient to create a lasting degree of familiarity—one sufficient for a categorization of the name as "famous."

The example from the developmental literature is provided by Perris, Myers, and Clifton's (1990) equally dramatic demonstration of toddlers' memory of a single experimental session that occurred in their infancy. The original experimental event was designed to test infants' use of visual cues to control reaching. Six-month-old children were taught to reach in the dark for different sized objects. The different sizes were signaled by different sounds (e.g., bells for big objects, squeaks for little ones). One to two years after the original experiment, Perris et al. brought these children back to the laboratory. At this point, the children were between 18 and 30 months of age. At this test session, the lights were turned off, the sounds were played, and the children's behavior was observed.

The children who had been in the experiment as babies reached in the dark for the sounding objects; control children who had not participated in the infant study did not. Thus, the one-time experience at age 6 months permanently changed these children, altering the likelihood of behaviors 1 and 2 years later.

There are many more such demonstrations of long lasting facilitatory effects in the experimental literature, of the benefits of a single prior processing experience (with units as small as single words) that have effects days, weeks, or years later (e.g., Brooks, 1987; Jacoby, 1983; Rovee-Collier, Griesler, & Earley, 1985; Salasoo, Shiffrin, & Feustel, 1985). These results indicate that each act of perceiving and remembering changes us.

The accrual of these long-term changes provides a source of stability in a continually changing system. If there are statistical regularities, or *patterns,* in our experiences that recur over and over again, then as each moment of knowing is laid on the preceding moments, weak tendencies to behave and to think in certain ways will become strong tendencies—sometimes so strong that they will not be easily perturbed and thus might *seem* fixed.

How These Facts May Make Categories

The extensive evidence on the contextual nature of perceiving and memory, the temporal groundedness of cognition in preceding activity, and its sensitivity to the history of its own activity speak to the very heart of cognition. Knowing, at any given moment, will be a combination of the immediate input in its full complexity, one's just-preceding cognitive activity, and one's lifetime history of activity. The compression of all these sources of information in a single act means that what we know at a moment is an adaptive mix of the same stable regularities that also form other moments of knowing and the idiosyncrasies of this moment.

We can see these ideas at work in three recent studies of how adults' categories adapt themselves online. In one study, Goldstone (1995) asked participants to judge the hue of objects by adjusting the color of one object (the target) until it matched precisely another (the standard). The individual objects were letters and numbers, presented in a random order. Unbeknownst to the subjects, Goldstone had arranged for the colors and objects to be correlated across trials, as shown in Figure 10.27. Specifically, the letters tended to be redder than the numbers. This fact strongly influenced subjects' judgments. They judged presented

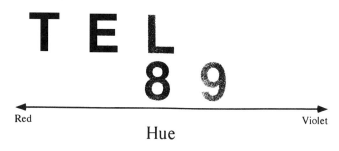

Figure 10.27 Illustration of the correlations instantiated in Goldstone's (1995) experiment on color perception.

letters (e.g., the "L" in Figure 10.27) to be redder than numbers of the exact same hue (e.g., the "8" in Figure 10.27). Apparently, subjects' lifetime history of experience with letters and numbers caused same-category members to influence each other in the here-and-now. Long-term category knowledge combined with the transient effects of seeing letters redder than numbers and with the sensory information presented by the single to-be-judged object. Processes operating over different time scales combined in a single moment of knowing and made an individual letter *look* a particular degree of red.

The semantic congruity effect provides a second example of how knowing in a moment occurs through the combination of long-term changes, transient in-task effects, and the immediate input. The semantic congruity effect refers to the finding that, in comparative judgments, people more readily compare objects on a quantitative dimension when the direction of comparison is congruent with the location of the stimuli on the continuum. For example, when asked to make judgments about the size of animals, subjects more quickly choose the larger of two relatively large animals (e.g., elephant versus hippopotamus) rather than the larger of two relatively small animals (e.g., hamster versus gerbil). Conversely, subjects more quickly choose the smaller of two small animals rather than the smaller of two relatively large animals (Banks & Flora, 1977). This general and robust effect clearly depends on people's long-term and stable knowledge about the sizes of things. Banks and Flora originally suggested that people represent "elephant" as "very big" and therefore can answer questions about bigness directly. By this account, judging that an elephant is small (in comparison to, say, a whale) is difficult because it requires one to override the represented attribute "very big."

This account, however, cannot be the whole story. Our long-term knowledge about the sizes of things is not all that matters in the semantic congruity effect. For example, Cech and Shoben (1985) showed that the direction of the semantic congruity for a pair consisting of a rabbit and a beaver changes, depending on the other pairs being judged in the task. In the context of other pairs of animals varying widely in size (from elephants to mice), "smaller than" judgments were made faster than "larger than" judgments for the rabbit–beaver pair. However, when this same pair was judged in an experiment in which rabbits and beavers were the biggest animals judged, the reverse semantic congruity was found: Subjects were faster at judging which member of the rabbit–beaver pair was larger rather than smaller. Subsequent experiments have shown that the direction of semantic congruity for a given pair will *shift* in the course of an experiment as the sizes of the objects judged prior to the pair shift in one direction or another (Cech, Shoben, & Love, 1990). Thus, the semantic congruity effect is not dependent solely on the absolute value of a given item, nor on our long-term knowledge of the sizes of things. Rather, how fast one answers the question "Is this bigger than that?" depends on long-term knowledge, the preceding items just judged, and the immediate question asked.

The creation of transient "concepts" that meld the information from immediate input, from just previous activity, and from a lifetime of activity seems fundamental to intelligence. One final example that makes this point is Sanocki's (1991, 1992; see also, McGraw & Rehling, 1994) research on people's ease of recognizing letters in quite different fonts. The traditional approach to letter recognition (as we saw in the traditional approach to category recognition generally) is to try to specify the features of a particular letter—the strokes and curves, for example, that enable recognition of all the various forms of "y" in Figure 10.28. Sanocki's results suggest, however, that a single set of represented and abstract features is not what enables us to recognize the letters of distinct fonts. The evidence against such an idea is that people more quickly recognize letters in familiar fonts rather than in novel fonts, and letters that are consistent with the fonts of just previously seen or surrounding letters—even when the fonts are very well known. Altogether, the results suggest that people adjust their definition of features online to fit the font they are reading; for example, a specific "y" that is difficult to recognize in one

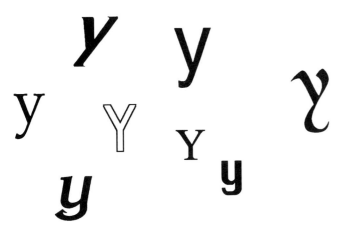

Figure 10.28   The letter "y" in various fonts.

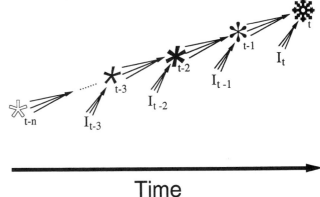

Figure 10.29   Illustrations of how individual moments of knowing (represented by various asterisks) combine immediate input (I), just Previous Activity, and the History of the Activity.

context is easy in another. Again, what we perceive when presented with a particular letter depends *all at once* on the immediate character of that letter, the character of the just previously perceived letters, and one's long-term experience of perceiving particular fonts.

We believe that these three examples—(a) the influence of category knowledge on color perception, (b) the semantic congruity effect, and (c) the perception of letter categories—show that knowing, as well as sensorimotor activity, is dynamically created and exists only as a product of mental activity. This activity occurs in individual mental events with real-time durations that are themselves the product of their own lifetime of activity, the just-previous activity, and the immediate input.

Smith and Samuelson (1996) used the diagram in Figure 10.29 to depict this dynamic sense of what knowing is. The activity of many heterogeneous and interacting subsystems that comprise a moment of knowing is represented by $*_t$. The material causes of the activity at a single moment of knowing are the immediate input, the just-previous activity, and the nature of the cognitive system itself. The immediate input to the system at a particular moment in time is represented by I_t. The multiple processes of perceiving and remembering are indicated by arrows between the input and the individual moment of knowing, and between one moment of knowing and the next. Importantly, because the activity at $*_t$ is in part determined by the activity at $*_{t-1}$, it is also partly determined by the activity at $*_{t-2}$, $*_{t-3}$, ... $*_{t-n}$. Each moment of knowing thus brings with it the history of its own past activity. Further, because each act of knowing permanently changes processes of perceiving

and remembering, the accrued activity changes the cognitive system itself. It will not be the same at t as it was at t_{n-1}. Notice that real time and developmental time are unified here; the very processes that make knowing in the moment also make development.

TOWARD A DYNAMIC SYSTEMS ACCOUNT OF WORD LEARNING

In this final section, we show how the ideas illustrated in Figure 10.29 both fit and are supported by data on children's early word learning. Most contemporary accounts of word learning are based on the idea that word learning is a mapping problem, and that the child's task is figuring out which words map to which concepts. In this framework, words, concepts, and maps are knowledge structures that children either do or do not "have." In presenting our alternative view, we focus specifically on young children's initial generalization of a novel noun to new instances in artificial word learning tasks.

The central finding in artificial word-learning studies is that, after hearing a single object named once, children systematically generalize the novel word to new instances. For example, in one study, Landau, Smith, and Jones (1988) presented 2- and 3-year-old children with a small, blue, wooden, inverted U-shaped object. They told the children that the exemplar object was a "dax." They then asked the children whether any of the other objects was also a "dax." (Figure 10.30 depicts the exemplar and the test objects.) Given these stimuli, the children systematically generalized the name only to test objects that were the same shape as the exemplar—as if they already knew that objects of this shape (but not necessarily a particular color or material) were the same kind of thing. This result has now been replicated many times in many laboratories. Importantly, however, in these tasks, children *do not* just form categories organized by shape. The nature of the categories children form depends on the dynamics of perceiving and remembering, across multiple time scales, the immediate context, the just-previous events, and the child's history of naming things.

Task-Dependent Categories

The first critical fact is that the categories children form depend on the task. Thus, although children's novel word generalizations suggest well-organized categories, their similarity judgments do not. For example, given the objects

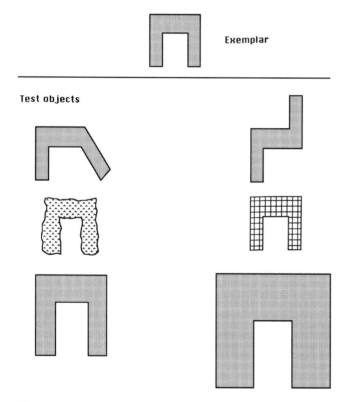

Figure 10.30 Illustrations of the stimuli used by Smith, Jones and Landau (1988). Three-dimensional objects that varied in shape, size, and material (wood, sponge, and wire mesh).

in Figure 10.30, 2- and 3-year-olds do not categorize by shape when asked to make similarity judgments (Landau, Smith, & Jones, 1988). Instead, they form categories based on holistic similarity or changing criteria. In a further study, Landau, Smith, and Jones (in press) showed that children also classify differently when asked the names of things versus when asked to make judgments about function. For example, in one experiment, they used stimuli shaped like those in Figure 10.30, except now the exemplar and some of the test objects were made of sponge. The exemplar was named ("This is a dax") and then the experimenter spilled water on the table and wiped it up with the spongy exemplar. The children systematically generalized that name to same-shape objects, but when asked about function, these same children selected objects made of sponge when asked to wipe up water. The finding that young children form different categories in naming tasks versus similarity judgment versus in making inferences about properties has been replicated a number of times in several laboratories (e.g., Imai, Gentner, & Uchida, 1994; Smith, Jones, & Landau, 1992; Soja, 1992). These findings suggest that children do not have just one fixed concept of a thing but have malleable concepts—concepts that are adjustable to fit the task at hand.

Other studies have shown that children's category judgments and their interpretation of novel words are also organized by more idiosyncratic context effects. For example, Smith, Jones, and Landau (1992, 1996) showed that children's generalizations of a word shifted dramatically (a) from shape to color when the room's lighting was changed to make the colors sparkle and glow, or (b) from global shape to parts when the parts were made larger and more colorful. These findings show that children's categories and novel-word interpretations do not reflect preformed concepts. Instead, they are inventive and are adapted to fit the peculiarities of here-and-now.

Continuity with the Just Previous Past

A growing literature indicates that young children's interpretations of novel words are also strongly influenced by the events occurring just prior to hearing the novel object named (e.g., Baldwin, 1991; Baldwin & Markman, 1989; Olguin & Tomasello, 1993; Tomasello & Kruger, 1992; Tomasello, Strosberg, & Akhtar, in press). In one series of experiments, Akhtar, Carpenter, and Tomasello (1996) created a naturalistic novel, word-learning situation that consisted of a sequence of events. First, the child (age 24 months), along with three adults, was introduced to three novel objects. The objects were played with successively, until the child was highly familiar with each of them; however, *none of these objects was ever named.* Second, the three now-familiar objects were placed in a transparent box along with a novel fourth object, the target object. The adults looked generally at the transparent container (but not at any individual object) and said, "Look it's a modi. A modi." During the third event, the children and adults played successively with each of the four objects, but the adults did not name any of them. The fourth event was the test: the four objects were placed on a table and the child was asked to indicate the "modi." Although all four objects had been present when the novel name was supplied, the children had no trouble determining the referent. The children chose the target object (the most novel of the four when the name was first supplied) when asked to get the "modi." This result fits the idea that, in the moment of hearing a novel name, children link that name to the object that most demands attention. The object most demanding of attention at a particular moment, in turn, depends on its novelty, which depends on prior events.

A second experiment by Akhtar et al. demonstrated the role of context in the sequence of events organizing attention. First, the child and three adults played successively with three novel objects, thus making all these objects familiar to the child. Second, two of the adults left the room and a novel fourth object, the target object, was introduced. The child and the remaining adult played with this novel toy *but the remaining adult never named the object.* By one description—one that centers only on the object and not on the context—the target object was at this point equivalent to the other three in familiarity for the child. Third, the three original toys and the target object were placed together in the transparent box, and the two other adults returned. While looking generally at the transparent box, the two returning adults said, "Look, a gazzer. It's a gazzer." Fourth, all participants played with the four objects. Fifth, on the test trial, the four objects were presented and the child was asked to indicate the "gazzer." The child chose the target object.

These results fit what we know about the context nature of memories; what is remembered depends on the holistic match between the general context of the original event and the context of the moment. This fact suggests the following description of events in Akhtar et al.'s second experiment. In Event 1, three memories are formed. Each consists of the object (O1) and the context of three adults playing and attending (C1). The memories formed thus are O1 + C1, O2 + C1, O3 + C1. Event 2 consists of a different object, the target (OT), and *a different context,* one that does not contain two of the adults. Thus, the memory stored of the second event will be OT + C2. In the critical Event 3, when the novel name is offered, all objects are presented in the transparent box and all three adults are present. This context, C1′, is thus more similar to the original context than is C2. By this analysis, the target object is: the most novel in the context when the name is offered, the one attended to most, and the one most likely to be associated with the novel name.

Many other results in the literature show that the interpretation of a novel name applied to a novel object is a mental event that grows out of and is continuous with just-previous mental activity: Children interpret novel words as referring to novel objects, with the novelty determined by just-preceding events (Markman, 1989; Merriman & Bowman, 1989); children are more likely to map a word to an object and form a well-organized category if the sound of the word has been highlighted by recently hearing other similar words (Merriman & Marazita, 1995; Schwartz, Leonard, Frome-Loeb, & Swanson, 1987); and finally, presenting children with an array of test objects (and thus, variation among potential category members) prior to naming the exemplar alters the formed category (Merriman, Schuster, & Hager, 1991). Children's category formation in the context of interpreting a novel object name is a mental event created in the context of ongoing processes of perceiving and remembering.

A History of Individual Acts of Knowing

Throughout many of these studies of children's novel word interpretations, the task of naming is found to organize performance differently than nonnaming categorization tasks. Smith (1995) proposed that the seemingly special power of the naming task reflects the statistical regularities inherent in languages. By Smith's account, the task of naming acquires its special properties through very general processes of attentional learning. Considerable research in infants, children, adults, and nonhuman animals indicates that the regular association of contextual cues to some property leads to automatic attention to that property in that context.

The language learning task presents the child with many statistical regularities that can guide both attention and language learning. Perhaps associative relations exist between the syntactic frame "This is a _____" and attention to specific object properties. In this view, the categories children form upon hearing a novel object named seem right from an adult point of view because they reflect, at least in part, statistical regularities in how words map to objects.

There is considerable evidence to support Smith's (1995) proposal that the smartness of children's novel word interpretations derives from learned associations among linguistic contexts and the properties of novel objects. The fact that, in many stimulus contexts, children form categories organized by shape similarities makes sense from this point of view. In English, the common nouns that name common concrete objects refer to categories of things of similar shape (Biederman, 1987; Rosch, 1978).

Jones, Smith, and Landau (1996) proposed that children learn to attend to shape as a consequence of learning words that refer to similar things. They reasoned that if attention to shape in the context of naming rigid objects was the product of statistical regularities in the language, then it should emerge only *after* some number of names for rigid things have been learned. They tested the hypothesis in a longitudinal study of children from 15 to 20 months. During this time span, the number of concrete nouns in the children's productive vocabularies increased from an average of 5 to over 150. The children were tested once a month in an artificial word-learning task much like the artificial word-learning task described earlier. The principle result is that the children did not systematically generalize novel nouns to new instances by shape until after they had 50 nouns in their productive vocabulary. This result is consistent with the idea that the shape bias in naming is a product of learning words that refer to objects of similar shape.

The importance of the child's personal history of forming categories is also seen in the growing evidence for cross-linguistic differences (Choi & Bowerman, 1991; Gopnik, Choi, & Baumberger, in press; Imai & Gentner, 1993; Sera, Reittinger, & Pintado, 1991). Several of these cross-linguistic studies focused on the children's naming of objects versus substances. Lucy (1992) predicted cross-linguistic differences in the categorization of these two kinds because languages differ in how they mark countable and noncountable entities—in what kinds of nouns called

"count nouns" take the plural and numerical determiners (e.g., "two dogs") and what kinds called "mass nouns" do not (e.g., "some sugar"). English maps the distinction between count nouns and mass nouns onto the distinction between rigid objects versus substances (Lucy, 1992). The work of Soja, Carey, and Spelke (1991) suggests that very young children learning English generalize names for objects and substances differently—a result that suggests that the object–substance distinction could be universal and independent of language.

However, other languages divide countable and noncountable things differently and in ways that ignore the distinction between rigid things of constant shape and malleable substances of variable shape. For example, in some languages, only categories referring to humans (brother, wife, priest) receive plural marking. In others, the division between kinds of entities that are syntactically marked or not marked for number is between animate things and nonanimate things. Lucy specifically argued that the potency of the contrast between rigidly shaped things and substances might be specific to languages like English which map the count-mass distinction on this contrast; languages that map the distinction on, for example, animates versus inanimates might not direct attention away from the contrast between rigid and nonrigid things.

To test this idea, Lucy (1992) examined the classifications of adult speakers of Yucatec Mayan, a language in which nouns for all inanimate things (rigid objects and nonsolid substances) are treated like English mass nouns and do not take the plural. Consistent with Lucy's prediction, Yucatec-speaking adults, in marked contrast to English-speaking adults, classify rigid objects by material and not by shape. For example, given a cardboard box, a wooden box, and a piece of irregularly shaped cardboard, Yucatec speakers classify the cardboard box with the piece of cardboard; English speakers classify the two boxes together. More recent evidence (Gaskins & Lucy, 1995) suggests that these differences in classification between English-speaking and Yucatec-speaking individuals increase with development—as they should, if they are created by the statistical regularities in a language and the individual's history of category judgments.

Imai and Gentner (1993) provided further evidence for the developmental growth of cross-linguistic differences. Their subjects were English-speaking and Japanese-speaking children. In Japanese, as in Yucatec, inanimate nouns (names for rigid things and nonrigid substances) do not take the plural; all are syntactically like English mass nouns. Imai and Gentner showed that this difference matters for how children generalize novel names to new instances. Specifically, American children formed lexical categories consistent with an object–substance distinction. Japanese children's categorizations were better described by a complex-shape versus simple-shape distinction rather than by rigidity per se. Moreover, these differences were evident at age 2 years but increased dramatically between the ages of 2 and 4 years, and were most marked in adults. These results demonstrate that category formation in the moment—the kind of things children assume to have the same name—is molded by the kinds of categories that children have formed in the past.

Putting It Together

Young children learn names for things rapidly. They are so adept at this learning that they seem to know the category of objects a word refers to from hearing the name of a single object. The evidence reviewed above strongly fits the picture in Figure 10.29. Children's word learning is smart because children create categories online, from their history of experience, the transient effects of preceding activity, and the details of the moment. The wisdom of the past is *fit* to the idiosyncracies of the here-and-now. This is a powerful idea. It means that children can form *novel* categories—think thoughts never thought before—that are adaptive. This can happen because the categories created online will be a unique mix of past and present.

CONCLUSION

Why Dynamics?

We believe that the major contribution of a dynamic approach to development is the potential to bring theoretical coherence to a field that has been beset by dialectics: nature versus nurture, learning versus maturation, continuity versus discontinuity, structure versus process, perceptual versus conceptual, symbolic versus presymbolic, and so on. The danger of such "either–or" thinking is not that good studies have not been done or cannot be done, but that the point of the enterprise, understanding change, can be forgotten. Only the framework and language of dynamics can erase these dualities and shift the focus to *how* the developing system works.

The promise of dynamics is realized through the assumptions of coupling and continuity. Coupling means that all components of the developing system are continually linked and mutually interactive within the individual, and between the individual and the environment. Continuity means that processes are seamless in time and cumulative; mental and physical activity are assembled in the moment, but always as a function of the system's history. Actions done in this moment, in turn, set the stage for behavior in the next second, minute, week, and year. With this formulation, it makes no sense to ask what part of behavior comes from stages, mental structures, symbol systems, knowledge modules, or genes, because these constructs do not exist in timeless, disconnected form. There is no time and no level when the system ceases to be dynamic.

Dynamics is the language of stability and change, and a dynamic approach frames developmental questions in terms of when systems are stable, when they change, and what makes them change. The power of dynamics is that these issues can be posed at many levels and time scales. The system is dynamic all the way down and all the way up! We can ask meaningful developmental questions at the neural level, the physiological level, or the level of individual or social behavior. Because dynamics seeks to be construct-free, there is a real potential for integrating levels of analysis. Likewise, we can probe the system as it changes over the time of a single event, over an experimental session, over more extended training, or over what we consider the "developmental" time scale of weeks or months. We have demonstrated—in our examples of early motor behavior, the A-not-B error, and early word and category learning—that this potential for integration can be realized and that new developmental insights can result.

That dynamics is a framework and a language rather than a specific theory of the development of *something*—language, peer relations, visual perception, adolescent adjustment, and so on—is both a strength and a weakness. The strength is, as we mentioned earlier, the potential for viewing many traditionally separate domains as subsumed under the same dynamic processes. We showed, for instance, how understanding "object permanence" experiments could be informed by knowing about the stability of reaching and looking. The weakness is equally apparent. A dynamic approach per se does little of the real work. It suggests a way of thinking, a strategy for collecting developmental data, and, hopefully, some analysis and modeling techniques that have broad generality. (That's not too bad!) The approach is not a substitute, however, for the hardest part of understanding development: collecting good data and using both descriptive and experimental methods. There are grave pitfalls in collecting data without clear theoretical assumptions, but it is equally dangerous to spin theories, verbal or mathematical, without a constant dialogue with data. Thinking dynamically allowed us to reinterpret the A-not-B error and generate new predictions (Thelen & Smith, 1994), but only trudging back to the laboratory gave substance to the theorizing. These experiments, in turn, hold promise for new theoretical insights, and so forth.

Whither Dynamics?

The dynamic systems view has a long tradition, but it is relatively new in being applied to conventional experimental questions in the development of perception, action, cognition, and social relations (Smith & Thelen, 1993). So, in many ways, the jury is still out. There are real methodological issues. From a dynamic point of view, useful data are time-based and involve collecting time-series data, whether in short or longer time scales. Interventions and experiments may involve intensive training. Data of this nature are difficult and expensive to collect. New tools are needed to identify the relevant variables, and new analyses and modeling methods are necessary to interpret them. There is a serious mismatch at the present time between our ability to collect sufficiently dense data and the assumptions of mathematical dynamics. Most developmentalists are not trained in dynamics and may want to collaborate with scientists who are.

But if such problems can be overcome (and we think they can), there are great benefits as well. Because the point is to understand behavior as it is "softly assembled" in light of developmental history rather than to describe some invariant structure, researchers are free to explore and exploit the natural variability of infants and children as they behave in the world. In a dynamic view, variability is data and not just noise, because high variability may indicate lack of stability, or a multistable system with a number of good enough options. As we described earlier (Thelen & Smith, 1994), adaptive systems live in quasi-stability; reliable enough to make predictions about what is appropriate in a context, but flexible enough to recruit

different solutions if the situation changes. Conversely, immature and nontypical people seem to get stuck in behaviors and thoughts that are rigid and inflexible. (Babies may want to reach for the B lid in the A-not-B task, but they are captives of their previous behaviors.) But this is what we want to know about developing systems: Can they make these adaptive choices?

A second benefit of a new respect for variability is to give theoretical status to individual differences. "Softly assembled" systems whose behavior depends on their histories in nonlinear ways will follow different developmental pathways, even to globally similar outcomes. Understanding the individuality of these pathways tells us about constraints and opportunities. We learned, from Nathan, Gabriel, Hannah, and Justin, that even for seemingly simple motor skills, multiple solutions abound, and these solutions can be discovered by each individual child in relation to his or her own status.

Finally, only a dynamic account captures the richness and complexity of real-life human behavior. The issue is not just how people learn to think in formal, logical, and abstract terms, but how they can do that *and* all the other things people do in this society: use tools, operate sophisticated machinery, find their way around, play sports and games, create art and music, and engage in complex social interactions. These activities require active perception, precisely timed movements, shifting attention, insightful planning, useful remembering, and the ability to smoothly and rapidly *shift* from one activity to another as the occasion demands. They happen in time and they recruit all the elements in the system. The challenge for developmentalists is to understand the developmental origins of this complexity and flexibility. Only dynamics, we believe, is up to the task.

REFERENCES

Acredolo, L. (1990). Behavioral approaches to spatial cognition. In A. Diamond (Ed.), *The development and neural bases of higher cognitive functions* (pp. 596–612). New York: National Academy of Sciences.

Akhtar, N., Carpenter, M., & Tomasello, M. (1996). The role of discourse novelty in early word learning. *Child Development, 67,* 635–645.

Anstis, S. M., & Saida, S. (1985). Adaptation to auditory streaming of frequency-modulated tones. *Journal of*

Experimental Psychology: Human Perception and Performance, 11, 257–271.

Aslin, R. N., & Smith, L. B. (1988). Perceptual development. In M. R. Rosenweig & L. W. Porter (Eds.), *Annual Review of Psychology, 39,* 435–474.

Baillargeon, R., & Graber, M. (1988). Evidence of a location memory in 8-month-old-infants in a non-search AB task. *Developmental Psychology, 24,* 502–511.

Baillargeon, R., Spelke, E. S., & Wasserman, S. (1985). Object permanence in five-month-old infants. *Cognition, 20,* 191–208.

Baldwin, D. (1991). Infants' contribution to the achievement of joint reference. *Child Development, 62,* 791–875.

Baldwin, D. A., & Markman, E. M. (1989). Establishing word-object relations: A first step. *Child Development, 60,* 381–398.

Baltes, P. B. (1987). Theoretical propositions of life-span developmental psychology: On the dynamics between growth and decline. *Developmental Psychology, 23,* 611–626.

Bandura, A. (1977). Self-efficacy: Toward a unifying theory of behavioral change. *Psychological Review, 84,* 191–215.

Banks, W. P., & Flora, J. (1977, May). Semantic and perceptual processes in symbolic comparisons. *Journal of Experimental Psychology: Human Perception and Performance, 3,* 278–290.

Bateson, P. P. G. (1966). The characteristics and context of imprinting. *Biology Review, 41,* 177–220.

Bernstein, N. A. (1996). *Dexterity and its development* (M. L. Latash & M. T. Turvey, Eds. & Trans.). Hillsdale, NJ: Erlbaum.

Bertalanffy, L. von (1933). *Modern theories of development.* London: Oxford University Press.

Bertalanffy, L. von. (1968). *General system theory.* New York: Braziller.

Bertenthal, B. I., & Campos, J. J. (1990). A systems approach to the organizing effects of self-produced locomotion during infancy. In C. Rovee-Collier & L. P. Lipsitt (Eds.), *Advances in infancy research* (Vol. 6, pp. 1–60). Norwood, NJ: ABLEX.

Biederman, I. (1987). Recognition by components: A theory of human image understanding. *Psychological Review, 94,* 115–147.

Bowlby, J. (1969). *Attachment and loss: Vol. 1. Attachment.* New York: Basic Books.

Bremner, J. G. (1985). Object tracking and search in infancy: A review of data and theoretical evaluation. *Developmental Review, 5,* 371–396.

Brent, S. B. (1978). Prigogine's model for self-organization in nonequilibrium systems: Its relevance for developmental psychology. *Human Development, 21,* 374–387.

Bronfenbrenner, U. (1979). *The ecology of human development.* Cambridge, MA: Harvard University Press.

Brooks, L. R. (1987). Decentralized control of categorization: The role of prior processing episodes. In U. Neisser (Ed.), *Concepts and conceptual developments* (pp. 141–174). New York: Cambridge University Press.

Bryant, P. E., & Trabasso, T. R. (1971). Transitive inferences and memory in young children. *Nature, 232,* 456–458.

Butler, J., & Rovee-Collier, C. (1989). Contextual gating of memory retrieval. *Developmental Psychobiology, 22*(6), 533–552.

Case, R. (1985). *Intellectual development: Birth to adulthood.* New York: Academic Press.

Cech, C. G., & Shoben, E. J. (1985). Context effects in symbolic magnitude comparisons. *Journal of Experimental Psychology: Learning, Memory, and Cognition, 11,* 299–315.

Cech, C. G., Shoben, E. J., & Love, M. (1990). Multiple congruity effects in judgments of magnitude. *Journal of Experimental Psychology: Learning, Memory, and Cognition, 16,* 1142–1152.

Choi, S., & Bowerman, M. (1991). Learning to express motion events in English and Korean: The influence of language-specific lexicalization patterns. *Cognition, 41,* 83–121.

Chomsky, N. (1986). *Knowledge of language: Its nature, origins, and use.* New York: Praeger.

Churchland, P. S. (1986). *Neurophilosophy: Toward a unified science of the mind-brain.* Cambridge, MA: MIT Press.

Churchland, P. S., & Sejnowski, T. J. (1992). *The computational brain.* Cambridge, MA: MIT Press.

Clark, H., & Clark, E. (1977). *Psychology and language.* New York: Harcourt Brace Jovanovich.

Cohen, L. B., & Oakes, L. M. (1993). How infants perceive a simple causal event. *Developmental Psychology, 29,* 421–444.

Cooke, J. (1988). The early embryo and the formation of body pattern. *American Scientist, 76,* 35–41.

Corbetta, D., & Thelen, E. (1996). The developmental origins of bimanual coordination: A dynamic perspective. *Journal of Experimental Psychology: Human Perception and Performance, 22,* 502–522.

Cottrell, G. W., & Plunkett, K. (1991). *Learning the past tense in a recurrent network: Acquiring the mapping from meanings to sounds. Proceedings of the thirteenth annual conference of the Cognitive Science Society.* Hillsdale, NJ: Erlbaum.

Crick, F. (1994). *The astonishing hypothesis: The scientific search for the soul.* New York: Charles Scribner's Sons.

Damasio, A. R. (1994). *Descartes' error: Emotion, reason, and the human brain.* New York: Putnam.

Diamond, A. (1990). Development and neural bases of AB and DR. In A. Diamond (Ed.), *The development and neural bases of higher cognitive functions* (pp. 267–317). New York: National Academy of Sciences.

Diamond, A., & Goldman-Rakic, P. S. (1989). Comparison of human infants and rhesus monkeys on Piaget's AB task. Evidence for dependence on dorsolateral prefrontal cortex. *Experimental Brain Research, 74,* 24–40.

Diamond, A. S., Zola-Morgan, S., & Squire, L. (1989). Successful performance by monkeys with lesions of the hippocampal formation on AB and object retrieval, two tasks that mark developmental changes in human infants. *Behavioral Neuroscience, 103,* 526–537.

Dixon, R. A., & Lerner, R. M. (1988). A history of systems in developmental psychology. In M. H. Bornstein & M. E. Lamb (Eds.), *Developmental psychology: An advanced textbook* (2nd ed., pp. 3–50). Hillsdale, NJ: Erlbaum.

Edelman, G. M. (1987). *Neural Darwinism.* New York: Basic Books.

Edelman, G. M. (1988). *Topobiology: An introduction to molecular embryology.* New York: Basic Books.

Eich, E. (1985). Context, memory, and integrated item/context imagery. *Journal of Experimental Psychology: Learning, Memory, and Cognition, 11,* 764–770.

Fetters, L., & Todd, J. (1987). Quantitative assessment of infant reaching movements. *Journal of Motor Behavior, 19,* 147–166.

Fitts, P. M. (1954). The information capacity of the human motor system in controlling the amplitude of movement. *Journal of Experimental Psychology, 47,* 381–391.

Flanders, M., & Herrmann, U. (1992). Two components of muscle activation: Scaling with the speed of arm movement. *Journal of Neurophysiology, 67,* 931–943.

Fodor, J. A. (1983). *The modularity of mind.* Cambridge, MA: MIT Press.

Ford, D. H., & Lerner, R. M. (1992). *Developmental systems theory: An integrative approach.* Newbury Park, CA: Sage.

Freeman, W. J. (1987). Simulation of chaotic EEG patterns with a dynamic model of the olfactory system. *Biological Cybernetics, 56,* 139–150.

Freeman, W. J. (1991). The physiology of perception. *Scientific American,* 78–85.

Freeman, W. J., & Skarda, C. A. (1985). Spatial EEG patterns, nonlinear dynamics and perception: The neo-Sherringtonian view. *Brain Research Reviews, 10,* 147–175.

Freyd, J. (1983). The mental representation of movement when statis stimuli are viewed. *Perception and Psychophysics, 33,* 575–581.

Freyd, J. J. (1992). Five hunches about perceptual processes and dynamic representations. In D. Myer & S. Kornblum (Eds.), *Attention and performance: 14. A silver jubilee.* Hillsdale, NJ: Erlbaum.

Gaskins, S., & Lucy, J. A. (1995). *It's later than you think: The role of language-specific categories in the development of classification behavior.* Paper presented to a conference on Language Acquisition and Conceptual Development, Max Planck Institute for Psycholinguistics, Nijmegen, The Netherlands.

Gasser, M., & Lee, C. D. (1991). A short-term memory architecture for the learning of morphophonemic rules. In R. Lippmann, J. Moody, & D. Touretzky (Eds.), *Advances in neural information processing systems* (Vol. 3). San Mateo, CA: Morgan Kaufmann.

Gasser, M., & Smith, L. B. (1991). *The development of a notion of sameness: A connectionist model.* Proceeding of the 13th Annual Conference of the Cognitive Science Society (pp. 719–723). Hillsdale, NJ: Erlbaum.

Gasser, M., & Smith, L. B. (1996). Learning nouns and adjective meanings: A connectionist account. *Language and Cognitive Processes.*

Gelman, R. (1969). Conservation acquisition: A problem of learning to attend to relevant attributes. *Journal of Experimental Child Psychology, 7,* 167–187.

Gelman, R., & Gallistel, C. R. (1978). *The child's understanding of number.* Cambridge, MA: Harvard University Press.

Georgopoulos, A. P. (1986). On reaching. *Annual Review of Neurosciences, 9,* 147–170.

Georgopoulos, A. P. (1988). Neural integration of movement: Role of motor cortex in reaching. *The FASEB Journal, 2,* 2849–2857.

Georgopoulos, A. P. (1990). Neurophysiology of reaching. In M. Jeannerod (Ed.), *Attention and performance* (Vol. 13, pp. 227–263). Hillsdale, NJ: Erlbaum.

Georgopoulos, A. P., Kettner, R. E., & Schwartz, A. B. (1988). Primate motor cortex and free arm movements to visual targets in three-dimensional space: 2. Coding of the direction of movement by a neuronal population. *Journal of Neuroscience, 8,* 2928–2937.

Gershkoff-Stowe, L., & Smith, L. B. (1996). *A curvilinear trend in naming errors as a function of early vocabulary growth.* Unpublished manuscript.

Gesell, A. (1939). Reciprocal interweaving in neuromotor development. *Journal of Comparative Neurology, 70,* 161–180.

Gesell, A., & Ames, L. B. (1947). The development of handedness. *Journal of Genetic Psychology, 70,* 155–175.

Gibson, E. J. (1991). *An odyssey in learning and perception.* Cambridge, MA: MIT Press.

Gierer, A. (1981). Generation of biological patterns and form: Some physical, mathematical, and logical aspects. *Progress in Biophysics and Molecular Biology, 37,* 1–47.

Godden, D., & Baddeley, A. (1980). When does context influence recognition memory? *British Journal of Psychology, 71,* 99–104.

Goldberger, A. L., & Rigney, D. R. (1988). Sudden death is not chaos. In J. A. S. Kelso, A. J. Mandell, & M. F. Shlesigner (Eds.), *Dynamic patterns in complex systems* (pp. 248–264). Singapore: World Scientific.

Goldman-Rakic, P. S. (1987). Development of control circuitry and cognitive function. *Child Development, 58,* 601–622.

Goldstone, R. L. (1995). Effects of categorization on color perception. *Psychological Science, 6,* 298–304.

Goldstone, R. L., Medin, D. L., & Gentner, D. (1991). Relational similarity and the nonindependence of features in similarity judgements. *Cognitive Psychology, 23,* 222–262.

Goodwin, B. C. (1985). Tip and whorl morphogenesis in *Acetabularia* by calcium-regulated strain fields. *Journal of Theoretical Biology, 117,* 79–106.

Goodwin, B. C., & Cohen, N. H. (1969). A phase-shift model for the spatial and temporal organization of developing systems. *Journal of Theoretical Biology, 25,* 49–107.

Gopnik, A., Choi, S., & Baumberger, T. (in press). Cross-linguistic differences in early semantic and cognitive development. *Cognitive Development.*

Gottlieb, G. (1992). *The genesis of novel behavior: Individual development and evolution.* New York: Oxford University Press.

Gottlieb, G. L., Corcos, D. M., & Agarwal, G. C. (1989). Strategies for the control of voluntary movements with one mechanical degree of freedom. *Behavioral and Brain Sciences, 12,* 189–250.

Grebogi, C., Ott, E., & Yorke, J. A. (1987). Chaos, strange attractors, and fractal basin boundaries in nonlinear dynamics. *Science, 238,* 632–638.

Haken, H. (1977). *Synergetics: An introduction.* Heidelberg: Springer-Verlag.

Halpern, D. F., & Warm, J. S. (1980). The disappearance of real and subjective contours. *Perception and Psychophysics, 28,* 229–235.

Halverson, H. M. (1931). Study of prehension in infants. *Genetic Psychological Monographs, 10,* 107–285.

Halverson, H. M. (1933). The acquisition of skill in infancy. *Journal of Genetic Psychology, 43,* 3–48.

Harris, M., & Coltheart, M. (1986). *Language processing in children and adults: An introduction.* London: Birbeck College, University of London.

Harris, P. L. (1987). The development of search. In P. Salapatek & L. B. Cohen (Eds.), *Handbook of infant perception* (Vol. 2). New York: Academic Press.

Hebb, B. O. (1949). *The organization of behavior.* New York: Wiley.

Hock, H. S., Kelso, J. A. S., & Schöner, G. (1993). Bistability and hysteresis in organization of apparent motion pattern. *Journal of Experimental Psychology: Human Perception and Performance, 19,* 63–80.

Hofsten, C. von (1991). Structuring of early reaching movements: A longitudinal study. *Journal of Motor Behavior, 23,* 280–292.

Hogan, N., Bizzi, E., Mussa-Ivaldi, F. A., & Flash, T. (1987). Controlling multijoint motor behavior. In K. B. Pandolf (Ed.), *Exercise and sport science reviews* (Vol. 15, pp. 153–190). New York: Macmillan.

Hutchins, E. (1995). *Cognition in the wild.* Cambridge, MA: MIT Press.

Imai, M., & Gentner, D. (1993). Linguistic relativity vs. universal ontology: Cross-linguistic studies of the object substance distinction. *Proceedings of the Chicago Linguistic Society,* Chicago, IL.

Imai, M., Gentner, D., & Uchida, N. (1994). Children's theories of word meaning: The role of shape similarity in early acquisition. *Cognitive Development, 9,* 45–76.

Jacoby, L. L. (1983). Perceptual enhancement: Persistent effect of an experience. *Journal of Experimental Psychology: Learning, Memory, and Cognition, 9,* 21–38.

Jacoby, L. L., Kelley, C., Brown, J., & Jasechko, J. (1989). Becoming famous overnight: Limits on the ability to avoid unconscious influences of the past. *Journal of Personality and Social Psychology, 56,* 326–338.

Jeannerod, M. (1988). *The neural and behavioural organization of goal-directed movements.* Oxford, England: Clarendon Press.

Jenkins, W. M., Merzenich, M. M., & Recanzone, G. (1990). Neocortical representational dynamics in adult primates: Implications for neuropsychology. *Neuropsychologia, 28,* 573–584.

Johnson, M. H. (1987). *The body in the mind: The bodily basis of meaning, imagination, and reason.* Chicago: University of Chicago Press.

Johnson, M. H., & Morton, J. (1991). *Biology and cognitive development: The case of face recognition.* Oxford, England: Blackwell.

Jones, S. S., & Smith, L. B. (1993). The place of perceptions in children's concepts. *Cognitive Development, 8,* 113–140.

Jones, S. S., Smith, L. B., & Landau, B. (1996). *The origins of the shape bias.* Manuscript submitted for publication.

Kaas, J. H. (1991). Plasticity of sensory and motor maps in adult mammals. *Annual Review of Neurosciences, 14,* 137–167.

Kail, R. (1986). Sources of age differences in speed of processing. *Child Development, 57,* 969–987.

Keil, F. C. (1986). On the structure-dependent nature of stages of cognitive development. In I. Levin (Ed.), *Stage and structure: Reopening the debate* (pp. 144–163). Norwood, NJ: ABLEX.

Kelly, M. H., & Martin, S. (1994). Domain-general abilities applied to domain-specific tasks: Sensitivity to probabilities in perception, cognition, and language. *Lingua, 92,* 105–140.

Kelso, J. A. S. (1995). *Dynamic patterns: The self-organization of brain and behavior.* Cambridge, MA: MIT Press.

King, A., & West, M. (1988). Searching for the functional origins of cowbird song in eastern brown-headed cowbirds *(Molothrus ater ater). Animal Behavior, 36,* 1575–1588.

Kitchener, R. F. (1978). Epigenesis: The role of biological models in developmental psychology. *Human Development, 21,* 141–160.

Kitchener, R. F. (1982). Holism and the organismic model in developmental psychology. *Human Development, 25,* 233–249.

Klatzky, R. L. (1980). *Human memory: Structures and processes* (2nd ed.). New York: Freeman.

Koch, C., & Davis, J. L. (Eds.). (1994). *Large-scale neuronal theories of the brain.* Cambridge, MA: MIT Press.

König, P., & Engel, A. K. (1995). Correlated firing in sensory-motor systems. *Current Opinion in Neurobiology, 5,* 511–519.

Kugler, P. N., & Turvey, M. T. (1987). *Information, natural law, and the self-assembly of rhythmic movement.* Hillsdale, NJ: Erlbaum.

Kuhn, D., & Phelps, E. (1982). The development of problem-solving strategies. In H. Reese & L. Lipsitt (Eds.), *Advances in child development and behavior* (Vol. 17, pp. 2–44). New York: Academic Press.

Kuo, Z.-Y. (1967). *The dynamics of behavior development: An epigenetic view.* New York: Random House.

Kuo, Z.-Y. (1970). The need for coordinated efforts in developmental studies. In L. R. Aronson, E. Tobach, D. S. Lehrman, & J. S. Rosenblatt (Eds.), *Development and evolution of behavior: Essays in memory of T. C. Schneirla* (pp. 181–193). San Francisco: Freeman.

Landau, B., Smith, L. B., & Jones, S. (1988). The importance of shape in early lexical learning. *Cognitive Development, 3,* 299–321.

Landau, B., Smith, L. B., & Jones, S. (in press). Object shape, object function, and object name. *Memory and Language.*

Latash, M. L., & Gottlieb, G. L. (1991). Reconstruction of joint compliant characteristics during fast and slow movements. *Neuroscience, 43,* 697–712.

Lehrman, D. S. (1953). A critique of Konrad Lorenz's theory of instinctive behavior. *Quarterly Review of Biology, 28,* 337–363.

Lehrman, D. S. (1971). Behavioral science, engineering, and poetry. In E. Tobach, L. R. Aronson, & E. Shaw (Eds.), *The biopsychology of development* (pp. 459–471). New York: Academic Press.

Lewin, K. (1936). *Principles of topological psychology.* New York: McGraw-Hill.

Lewin, K. (1946). Behavior and development as a function of the total situation. In L. Carmichael (Ed.), *Manual of child psychology* (pp. 791–844). New York: Wiley.

Light, L. L., & Carter-Sobel, L. (1970). Effects of changed semantic context on recognition memory. *Journal of Verbal Learning and Verbal Behavior, 9,* 1–11.

Lorenz, K. Z. (1965). *Evolution and modification of behavior.* Chicago: University of Chicago Press.

Lucy, J. A. (1992). *Grammatical categories and cognition: A case study of the linguistic relativity hypothesis.* Cambridge, England: Cambridge University Press.

Marcus, G. F., Pinker, S., Ullman, M., Hollander, M., Rosen, T. J., & Xu, F. (1992). Overregularization in language acquisition. *Monographs of the Society for Research in Child Development, 57*(4, Serial No. 228).

Markman, E. M. (1989). *Categorization and naming in children: Problems of induction.* Cambridge, MA: MIT Press.

Marks, L. E. (1993). Contextual processing of multidimensional and undimensional auditory stimuli. *Journal of Experimental Psychology Human Perception and Performance, 19,* 227–249.

Marx, J. L. (1984a). New clues to developmental timing. *Science, 226,* 425–426.

Marx, J. L. (1984b). The riddle of development. *Science, 226,* 1406–1408.

Mathew, A., & Cook, M. (1990). The control of reaching movements by young infants. *Child Development, 61,* 1238–1258.

McGraw, G., & Rehling, J. (1994). *Roles in letter perception: Human data and computer models.* (CRCC-TR 90)

McGraw, M. G. (1932). From reflex to muscular control in the assumption of an erect posture and ambulation in the human infant. *Child Development, 3,* 291–297.

Meakin, P. (1986). A new model for biological pattern formation. *Journal of Theoretical Biology, 118,* 101–113.

Merriman, W. E., & Bowman, L. L. (1989). The mutual exclusivity bias in children's word learning. *Monographs of the Society for Research in Child Development, 54*(3/4), 130.

Merriman, W. E., & Marazita, J. M. (1995). The effect of hearing similar-sounding words on young 2-year-olds' disambiguation of novel noun reference. *Developmental Psychology, 31,* 973–984.

Merriman, W. E., Schuster, J. M., & Hager, L. (1991). Are names ever mapped onto preexisting categories? *Journal of Experimental Psychology: General, 120,* 288–300.

Merzenich, M. M., Allard, T. T., & Jenkins, W. M. (1990). Neural ontogeny of higher brain function: Implications of some recent neurophysiological findings. In O. Franzn & P. Westman (Eds.), *Information processing in the somatosensory system* (pp. 293–311). London: Macmillan.

Molenaar, P. C. M. (1986). On the impossibility of acquiring more powerful structures: A neglected alternative. *Human Development, 29,* 245–251.

Muchisky, M., Gershkoff-Stowe, L., Cole, E., & Thelen, E. (1996). *The epigenetic landscape revisited: A dynamic interpretation. Advances in infancy research* (Vol. 10, pp. 121–159). Norwood, NJ: ABLEX.

Munakata, Y., McClelland, J. L., Johnson, M. H., & Siegler, R. S. (1997). Rethinking infant knowledge: Toward an adaptive process account of successes and failures in object permanence tasks. *Psychological Review.*

Murray, J. D. (1988). How the leopard gets its spots. *Scientific American, 258*(3), 80–87.

Murray, J. D. (1993). *Mathematical biology* (2nd ed.). Berlin: Springer-Verlag.

O'Leary, A., & McMahon, M. (1991). Adaptation to form distortion of a familiar shape. *Perception and Psychophysics, 49,* 328–332.

Olguin, R., & Tomasello, M. (1993). Twenty-five-month-old children do not have a grammatical category of verb. *Cognitive Development, 8,* 245–272.

O'Reilly, R. C., & Johnson, M. H. (1994). Object recognition and sensitive periods: A computational analysis of visual imprinting. *Neural Computation, 6,* 357–389.

Oyama, S. (1985). *The ontogeny of information: Developmental systems and evolution.* Cambridge, England: Cambridge University Press.

Palmer, S. G. (1989). Reference frames in the perception of shape and attenuation. In B. E. Shepp & S. Ballesteros (Eds.), *Object perception: Structure and process* (pp. 121–164). Hillsdale, NJ: Erlbaum.

Palmeri, T. J., Goldinger, S. D., & Pisoni, D. B. (1993). Episodic encoding of voice attributes and recognition memory for spoken words. *Journal of Experimental Psychology: Learning Memory and Cognition, 19,* 309–328.

Perris, E. E., Myers, N. A., & Clifton, R. K. (1990). Long-term memory for a single infancy experience. *Child Development, 61,* 1796–1807.

Piaget, J. (1952). *The origins of intelligence in children.* New York: International Universities Press.

Piaget, J. (1954). *The construction of reality in the child.* New York: Basic Books.

Pinker, S., & Mehler, J. (1988). *Connections and symbols.* Cambridge, MA: MIT Press.

Pinker, S., & Prince, A. (1988). On language and connectionism: Analysis of a parallel Distributed Processing model of language acquisition. *Cognition, 28,* 193–233.

Plunkett, K. (1993). Lexical segmentation and vocabulary growth in early language acquisition. *Journal of Child Language, 20,* 43–60.

Plunkett, K., & Marchman, V. (1991). U-shaped learning and frequency effects in a multi-layered perception: Implications for language acquisition. *Cognition, 38,* 43–102.

Plunkett, K., & Marchman, V. (1993). From rote learning to system building: Acquiring verb morphology in children and connectionist nets. *Cognition, 48,* 21–69.

Plunkett, K., Sinha, C., Moller, M. F., & Strandsby, O. (1992). Symbol grounding or the emergence of symbols? Vocabulary growth in children and a connectionist net. *Connection Science, 4,* 293–303.

Preece, P. F. W. (1980). A geometric model of Piagetian conservation. *Psychological Reports, 46,* 143–148.

Prigogine, I. (1978). Time, structure, and fluctuations. *Science, 201,* 777–785.

Prigogine, I., & Stengers, I. (1984). *Order out of chaos: Man's new dialogue with nature.* New York: Bantam Books.

Remez, R. E., Cutting, J. E., & Studdert-Kennedy, M. (1980). Cross-series adaptation using song and string. *Perception and Psychophysics, 27,* 524–530.

Robertson, S. S. (1989). Mechanism and function of cyclicity in spontaneous movement. In W. P. Smotherman & S. R. Robinson (Eds.), *Behavior of the fetus* (pp. 77–94). Caldwell, NJ: Telford.

Rogoff, B., Gauvain, M., & Ellis, S. (1984). Development viewed in its cultural context. In M. H. Bornstein & M. E. Lamb (Eds.), *Developmental psychology: An advanced textbook* (pp. 533–571). Hillsdale, NJ: Erlbaum.

Rosch, E. (1978). Principles of categorization. In E. Rosch & B. Lloyd (Eds.), *Cognition and categorization* (pp. 28–46). Hillsdale, NJ: Erlbaum.

Rosenbaum, D. A. (1991). *Human motor control.* San Diego, CA: Academic Press.

Rovee-Collier, C., Griesler, P. C., & Earley, L. A. (1985). Contextual determinants of retrieval in three-month-old infants. *Learning and Motivation, 16,* 139–157.

Rumelhart, D. E. (1989). The architecture of mind: A connectionist approach. In M. I. Posner (Ed.), *Foundations of cognitive science* (pp. 133–160). Cambridge, MA: MIT Press.

Rumelhart, D. E., & McClelland, J. L. (Eds.). (1986). *Parallel distributed processing: Explorations in the microstructure of cognition: Vol. 1. Foundations.* Cambridge, MA: Bradford Books/MIT Press.

Saari, D. G. (1977). A qualitative model for the dynamics of cognitive processes. *Journal of Mathematical Psychology, 15,* 145–168.

Salasoo, A., Shiffrin, R. M., & Feustel, T. C. (1985). Building permanent memory codes: Codification and repetition effects in word identification. *Journal of Experimental Psychology: General, 114,* 50–77.

Sameroff, A. J. (1983). Developmental systems: Contexts and evolution. In P. H. Mussen (Ed.), *Handbook of child psychology* (Vol. 1, pp. 237–294). New York: Wiley.

Sameroff, A. J., & Chandler, M. J. (1975). Reproductive risk and the continuum of caretaking casualty. In F. D. Horowitz, M. Hetherington, S. Scarr-Salapatek, & G. Siegel (Eds.), *Review of child development research* (Vol. 4, pp. 187–244). Chicago: University of Chicago Press.

Sanocki, T. (1991). Intra- and interpattern relations in letter recognition. *Journal of Experimental Psychology: Human Perception and Performance, 17,* 924–941.

Sanocki, T. (1992). Effects of font- and letter-specific experience on the perceptual processing of letters. *American Journal of Psychology, 105,* 435–458.

Schneider, K., Zernicke, R. F., Schmidt, R. A., & Hart, T. J. (1989). Changes in limb dynamics during the practice of rapid arm movements. *Journal of Biomechanics, 22,* 805–817.

Schneirla, T. C. (1957). The concept of development in comparative psychology. In D. B. Harris (Ed.), *The concept of development: An issue in the study of human behavior* (pp. 78–108). Minneapolis: University of Minnesota Press.

Scholz, J. P., Kelso, J. A. S., & Schöner, G. (1987). Nonequilibrium phase transitions in coordinated biological motion: Critical slowing down, and switching time. *Physics Letters, A, 123,* 390–394.

Schöner, G. (1994). Dynamic theory of action perception patterns: The time before contact paradigm. *Human Movement Science, 13,* 415–439.

Schöner, G., & Kelso, J. A. S. (1988). Dynamic pattern generation in behavioral and neural systems. *Science, 239,* 1513–1520.

Schwartz, R. G., Leonard, L. B., Frome-Loeb, D. M., & Swanson, L. A. (1987). Attempted sounds are sometimes not: An expanded view of phonological selection and avoidance. *Journal of Child Language, 14,* 411–418.

Schyns, P. G. (1991). A modular neural network model of concept acquisition. *Cognitive Science, 15,* 461–508.

Seligman, M. E. P., & Hager, J. L. (Eds.). (1972). *Biological boundaries of learning.* New York: Appleton-Century-Crofts.

Sera, M. D., Reittinger, E. L., & Pintado, J. D. C. (1991). Developing definition of objects and events in English and Spanish speakers. *Cognitive Development, 6,* 119–142.

Siegler, R. S., & Jenkins, E. A. (1989). *How children discover new strategies.* Hillsdale, NJ: Erlbaum.

Singer, W. (1994). Putative functions of temporal correlations in neocortical processing. In C. Koch & J. L. Davis (Eds.), *Large-scale neuronal theories of the brain* (pp. 201–237). Cambridge, MA: MIT Press.

Sluckin, W., & Salzen, E. A. (1961). Imprinting and perceptual learning. *Quarterly Journal of Experimental Psychology, 13,* 65–77.

Smith, L. B. (1993). The concept of same. *Advances in Child Development and Behavior, 24,* 216–253.

Smith, L. B. (1995). Self-organizing processes in learning to learn words: Development is not induction. *The Minnesota Symposia on Child Psychology: Vol. 28. Basic and applied perspectives on learning, cognition, and development* (pp. 1–32). Mahwah, NJ: Erlbaum.

Smith, L. B., Gasser, M., & Sandhofer, C. (1997). Learning to talk about the properties of objects: A network model of the development of dimensions. In D. Medin, R. Goldstein, & P. Schyns (Eds.), *The psychology of learning and motivation* (Vol. 36, pp. 358–359). New York: Academic Press.

Smith, L. B., Jones, S. S., & Landau, B. (1992). Count nouns, adjectives, and perceptual properties in children's novel word interpretations. *Developmental Psychology, 28,* 273–286.

Smith, L. B., Jones, S., & Landau, B. (1996). Naming in young children: A dumb attentional mechanism? *Cognition, 60,* 143–171.

Smith, L. B., & Samuelson, L. (1996). Perceiving and remembering: Category stability, variability and development. In K. Lamberts & D. Shanks (Eds.), *Concepts and categories.* Cambridge, England: Cambridge University Press.

Smith, L. B., & Thelen, E. (Eds.). (1993). *A dynamic systems approach to development: Applications.* Cambridge, MA: MIT Press.

Smith, L. B., Thelen, E., Titzer, R., & McLin, D. (1997). *Knowing in the context of acting: The task dynamics of the A not B error.* Manuscript submitted for publication.

Smith, S. M. (1986). Environmental context-dependent recognition memory using a short-term memory task for input. *Memory and Cognition, 14,* 347–354.

Soja, N. (1992). Inferences about the meanings of nouns: The relationship between perception and syntax. *Cognitive Development, 7,* 29–46.

Soja, N., Carey, S., & Spelke, E. (1991). Ontological categories guide young children's inductions of word meanings: Object terms and substance terms. *Cognition, 38,* 179–211.

Spelke, E. S., Breinlinger, K., Macomber, J., & Jacobson, K. (1992). Origins of knowledge. *Psychological Review, 99,* 605–632.

Spencer, J., & Thelen, E. (1995, November). *A new method for detecting muscle pattern changes in unconstrained, multi-joint learning tasks: II. Multi-muscle state activity.* Poster presented at the 25th annual meeting of the Society of Neuroscience, San Diego, CA.

Stein, B. E., & Meredith, M. A. (1993). *The merging of the senses.* Cambridge, MA: MIT Press.

Tapaswi, P. K., & Saha, A. K. (1986). Pattern formation and morphogenesis: A reaction-diffusion model. *Bulletin of Mathematical Biology, 48,* 213–228.

Thatcher, R. W. (1991). Maturation of the human frontal lobes: Physiological evidence for staging. *Developmental Neuropsychology, 7,* 397–419.

Thatcher, R. W. (1992). Cyclic cortical reorganization during early childhood. *Brain and Cognition 20,* 24–50.

Thelen, E. (1989). Self-organization in developmental processes: Can systems approaches work? In M. Gunnar & E. Thelen (Eds.), *Systems and development: The Minnesota Symposia on Child Psychology* (Vol. 22, pp. 77–117). Hillsdale, NJ.: Erlbaum.

Thelen, E., Corbetta, D., Kamm, K., Spencer, J. P., Schneider, K., & Zernicke, R. F. (1993). The transition to reaching: Mapping intention and intrinsic dynamics. *Child Development, 64,* 1058–1098.

Thelen, E., Corbetta, D., & Spencer, J. (1996). The development of reaching during the first year: The role of movement speed. *Journal of Experimental Psychology: Human Perception and Performance, 22,* 1059–1076.

Thelen, E., & Fisher, D. M. (1982). Newborn stepping: An explanation for a "disappearing reflex." *Developmental Psychology, 18,* 760–770.

Thelen, E., Fisher, D. M., & Ridley-Johnson, R. (1984). The relationship between physical growth and a newborn reflex. *Infant Behavior and Development, 7,* 479–493.

Thelen, E., Fisher, D. M., Ridley-Johnson, R., & Griffin, N. (1982). The effects of body build and arousal on newborn infant stepping. *Developmental Psychobiology, 15,* 447–453.

Thelen, E., & Smith, L. B. (1994). *A dynamic systems approach to the development of cognition and action.* Cambridge, MA: Bradford Books/MIT Press.

Thelen, E., & Ulrich, B. D. (1991). Hidden skills: A dynamical systems analysis of treadmill stepping during the first year. *Monographs of the Society for Research in Child Development, 56*(No. 223).

Thom, R. (1983). *Mathematical models of morphogenesis.* New York: Wiley.

Titzer, R., Thelen, E., & Smith, L. B. (1997). *The developmental dynamics of understanding transparency: A new interpretation of the object retrieval task.* Manuscript submitted for publication.

Tomasello, M., & Krueger, A. C. (1992). Joint attention on actions: Acquiring verbs in ostensive and non-ostensive contexts. *Journal of Child Language, 19,* 311–329.

Tomasello, M., Strosberg, R., & Akhtar, N. (in press). Eighteen-month-old children learn words in non-ostensive contexts. *Journal of Child Language.*

Tulving, E., & Thomson, D. M. (1973). Encoding specificity and retrieval processes in episodic memory. *Psychological Review, 80,* 352–373.

Turïel, E., & Davidson, P. (1986). Heterogeneity, inconsistency, and asynchrony in the development of cognitive structures. In I. Levin (Ed.), *Stage and structure: Reopening the debate* (pp. 106–143). Norwood, NJ: ABLEX.

van der Maas, H. L. J., & Molenaar, P. C. M. (1992). Stagewise cognitive development: An application of catastrophe theory. *Psychological Review, 99,* 395–417.

van Geert, P. (1991). A dynamic system model of cognitive and language growth. *Psychological Review, 98,* 3–53.

van Geert, P. (1993). A dynamic systems model of cognitive growth: Competition and support under limited resource conditions. In L. B. Smith & E. Thelen (Eds.), *A dynamic systems approach to development: Applications.* Cambridge, MA: MIT Press.

van Geert, P. (1994). *Dynamic systems of development.* London: Harvester Wheatsheaf.

Varela, F., Thompson, E., & Rosch, E. (1991). *The embodied mind.* Cambridge, MA: MIT Press.

Vygotsky, L. S. (1962). *Thought and language.* Cambridge, MA: MIT Press.

Waddington, C. H. (1954). The integration of gene-controlled processes and its bearing on evolution. *Proceedings of the 9th International Congress of Genetics, 9,* 232–245.

Waddington, C. H. (1957). *The strategy of the genes.* London: Allen & Unwin.

Waddington, C. H. (1977). *Tools for thought.* New York: Basic Books.

Wellman, H. M., Cross, D., & Bartsch, K. (1987). A meta-analysis of research on stage 4 object permanence. The A-not-B error. *Monographs of the Society for Research in Child Development, 5*(3, Serial No. 214).

West, M., & King, A. (1996). Eco-gen-actics: A systems approach to the ontogeny of avian communication. In D. E. Kroodsma & E. H. Miller (Eds.), *The evolution and ecology of acoustic communication in birds* (pp. 20–38). Ithaca, NY: Cornell University Press.

Wolff, P. H. (1987). *The development of behavioral states and the expression of emotions in early infancy: New proposals for investigation.* Chicago: University of Chicago Press.

Wolpert, L. (1971). Positional information and pattern formation. *Current Topics in Developmental Biology, 6,* 183–223.

Yates, K., & Pate, E. (1989). A cascading development model for amphibian embryos. *Bulletin of Mathematical Biology, 31,* 549–578.

Zatorre, R. J., & Halpern, A. R. (1979). Identification, discrimination, and selective adaptation of simultaneous musical intervals. *Perception and Psychophysics, 26,* 384–395.

CHAPTER 11

The Development of the Person: An Experiential Perspective on the Ontogenesis of Psychological Complexity

MIHALY CSIKSZENTMIHALYI and KEVIN RATHUNDE

WHAT IS A PERSON?

The obvious answer to the question "What is a person?" would probably focus on physical characteristics, for example, "An individual member of the human race." Of the 14 major usages of the word listed in the *Oxford Dictionary of the English Language*, most refer to such natural, biological attributes. But it does not take much thought to realize that when we speak of a person, the biological attributes are not the only important ones. The term conveys connotations of dignity, respect, authority, and a great number of other

similar nuances that are equally important to its meaning: for instance, "A man or woman of distinction," or "A human being having rights and duties recognized by the law."

What a person is cannot be defined by relying on objective physical characteristics alone. Or rather, one can do so, but not without trivializing the very concept that needs to be explained. For a person is not a material being, or a natural category, but a sociocultural construction. Each community develops an image of what a person is, what are its defining features, and what constitutes a "good" person. Thus, it is not possible to know what a person is without understanding the qualities that a social group ascribes to a human being that is also a person, and these qualities may change with time and circumstances.

Research reported in this chapter was largely funded by grants from the Spencer Foundation.

For example, the traditional Hindu view is that a person is not an individual, but a position in a network of social relations (Marriott, 1976); a physical specimen of the species *Homo sapiens* is not a person, unless he or she belongs to a group and fulfills the responsibilities thereof. The classical Chinese view and the understanding of the native tribes living along the Amazon River are not that different (Lévi-Strauss, 1967). In most cultures the individual in its physicality is no better than any other animal. It takes the transforming power of culture and society to turn the animal into a person.

Stressing the fact that the concept of person is socially constructed seems to imply a relativistic position. It may suggest that the criteria of personhood are more or less arbitrary, the result of chance historical developments in different places and times. However, we do not believe this to be true. The definition of what a person is may vary a great deal across times and places, yet it seems that certain common core elements appear again and again. These common traits presumably are adaptive and have emerged during the sociocultural evolution of humankind because—relative to alternative definitions—they have been more useful in assisting the biological survival of those who held them and the survival of the culture of which they were a part.

A somewhat crude thought experiment may help illustrate how this evolutionary process might have worked. Suppose somewhere on the globe there existed two neighboring nations, each with its unique culture and language. One of the two, the Agazzi, had developed an image of the person as "someone who is exceptionally good at outsmarting his neighbors." The other group, let's call them the Bambani, defined the person as "someone who fulfills community expectations." Assuming that everything else in the environment of the two groups is the same, and that cooperation is a better survival strategy under environmental pressure, it makes sense to assume that in the face of hardship the Bambani would fare better than the Agazzi and would be less likely to disintegrate.

Of course, real life is much more complex than this simplistic thought experiment suggests. Nevertheless, real societies often approach this level of simplicity in constructing their theoretical model of what a person is. The Yamomamo who live in the jungles of Venezuela assume that human beings are violent and constantly aggressive, and act accordingly (Chagnon, 1979). The Dobuans of Melanesia believed

that all people were deceitful sorcerers, and based their everyday life on constant mutual suspicion (Fortune, 1963). In modern times, the images of Aryan or socialist personhood developed by the Nazis and the Soviets, respectively, made possible the development of policies and institutions that have had profound effects on recent history and justified the murder of tens of millions of individuals who did not fit those images.

Cultures based on naked selfishness and aggression are unlikely to survive long. But even if they do, the point is that the model of personhood a given group adopts is not a neutral choice. It has implications for survival that are in principle no different from what kind of technology the group adopts. If the models adopted by different cultures at different times share important similarities, it is sensible to conclude that those common elements of personhood are important for the survival of any human group, anytime and anywhere.

This image of the person becomes a guiding principle for how the culture deals with human beings: the laws, the institutions, and the behaviors involving people are informed by it. For instance, each culture looks at child rearing and education through the lens of its image of what a person is. If the person is viewed as aggressive and competitive, this belief will inform how children are treated—how adults interpret their behavior, which childhood actions are punished or rewarded. Parents will stress competition, and schools will make sure that each child treats peers as contenders. If the person is viewed as a node in the social network, then child-rearing institutions are more likely to emphasize cooperation and mutual responsibility. In any case, without a concept of personhood, it would be difficult, if not impossible, to sustain social life.

Person and Personality

The word *person* as used in most languages related by common European roots derives from the Latin *per sonare,* "to sound through." This derivation is based on the fact that in ancient Greece and Rome, stage actors wore masks that represented their character (e.g., good or bad), and these masks also served as primitive loudspeakers, helping to amplify the actor's voice. Our concept of personality is influenced by this image of an actor playing his role through a mask that defines and amplifies the script he is following. For this reason, philosophers and social scientists often view personality as something unauthentic, a disguise rather than the expression of the individual's genuine essence.

For example, C. G. Jung (1954, 1959, 1960) borrowed the Latin term *persona* to refer to the social masks we learn to wear to hide, from ourselves and from others, the real desires and possibilities that would be too dangerous or difficult to express. By forming a persona, the individual conforms to a social definition of himself or herself; he or she internalizes the collective ideals of the community (Homans, 1979). The sociologist Erwin Goffman (1959) developed an entire model of selfhood based on such a dramaturgical model. From his perspective, most of what we do in our lives is a stage presentation. People compete for the roles that provide the greatest advantage, and social interaction basically consists in rehearsing, accepting, or rejecting such roles. Both Jung and Goffman saw personality as an artificial, strategic product. A major difference between them is that whereas Jung believed that under the mask of the persona there were deeper and more genuine structures of the self, Goffman seemed to believe that the mask concealed a void.

Personality refers to the differences among individuals wearing different masks, for example, one individual's being more outgoing, or more neurotic, or more introverted than the general norm. In contrast, the term person refers to what is common to all personalities, that is, to what makes all individuals in the same culture able to interact with each other on the same stage. Each person borrows a particular mask from the cultural repertoire so as to represent a given identity that will express and amplify his or her inborn talents. In this process of borrowing and adapting, the individual constructs a personality.

But what is common to all personalities, or, in other words, what is the person? It follows from what we have said so far that the most basic trait must involve the ability to take a role on the cultural stage. This implies the ability to recognize the roles others play, to respond appropriately to cultural cues, to accept one's role in the shared script. It is for this reason that most preliterate societies considered members of other tribes nonpersons, because their languages and habits were not understandable. The Greeks called everyone else "barbarians," because the language they spoke sounded like meaningless *bar-bar* to Greek ears. In many languages, like the Navajo, the term *people* is reserved exclusively for members of one's own tribe. The great world religions that flourished from India to Europe starting about 25 centuries ago began to break down these tribal distinctions and envisioned a common humanity regardless of specific customs and languages.

But personhood still depends on the ability to participate in *some* culture, even if it is not one's own. Thus "feral children" who survive as infants outside the boundaries of society, and grow up without learning a language or a set of norms, are often not considered to be "persons." Nor are generally recognized as persons those unfortunate individuals who, because of genetic defects or some early trauma, live a vegetative life and are unable to interact with anyone else. Crack babies and severely autistic persons are limit cases; whether one considers them persons or not depends on how broad a definition one holds. Some religious people may include them under the category of persons; others may not. The same applies to mass murderers and other psychopaths or sociopaths: they stretch the definition of the concept at the boundaries.

Including and excluding individuals from personhood may seem a cruel act, smacking of prejudice and akin to racism. Yet social groups tend to apply this seal of approval to their members to keep a certain standard, a minimum requirement for being recognized as belonging to the community. A linguistic mark of distinction between those who can and those who cannot take part in normative interaction might be a necessary requirement for maintaining social order. Therefore, the distinguishing traits of personhood depend to a large extent on the priorities that inform a particular culture.

The Construction of Personhood over the Life Span

Because personhood hinges on the ability to interact and function in a sociocultural context, it follows that persons are not born, but are made. Different cultures use different techniques for making sure that children acquire the knowledge, behavior, and emotions that will enable them to function appropriately as adults. This process of socialization is often informal, enforced by the constant pressure of public opinion. But most cultures evolve formal mechanisms of socialization, often reinforced by complex rituals and ceremonies.

India provides some of the clearest examples of this process. The classical Hindu culture has taken great pains to make sure that from infancy to old age its members conform to appropriate ideals of behavior. "The Hindu person is produced consciously and deliberately during a series of collective events. These events are *samskaras,* life cycle rituals that are fundamental and compulsory in the life of a Hindu" (Hart, 1992, p. 1). *Samskaras* help to shape children and adolescents by giving them new "rules of conduct" for each successive step in life (Pandey 1969, p. 32).

As the Indian psychoanalyst Sadhir Kakar (1978) wrote half-facetiously, *samskaras* mean "the right rite at the right time. . . . The conceptualization of the human life cycle unfolding in a series of stages, with each stage having its unique 'tasks' and the need for an orderly progression through the stages, is an established part of traditional Indian thought . . . one of the major thrusts of these rituals is the gradual integration of the child into society, with the *samskaras,* as it were, beating time to a measured movement that takes the child away from the original mother-infant symbiosis into the full-fledged membership of his community" (pp. 204–205).

Rites of passage certify that a child or young adult is ready to enter the next stage of personhood, until he or she grows old and has played every possible role that is available in the community. In some cultures, a man or woman is not considered a full-fledged person until the first grandchild is born. Being a grandparent means, among other things that (a) one is fertile, and therefore endowed with sacred power; (b) one is successful, because only reasonably wealthy parents can find spouses for their children; and (c) one is wise or at least experienced, having lived this long (LeVine, 1979). Only when these qualities are finally achieved is a person finally complete.

In Western societies, transitions to higher levels of personhood are no longer well marked, except in terms of educational progress, where various graduation ceremonies punctuate one's academic career. Religious progress, marked by such ceremonies as the Jewish bar mitzvah and the Catholic sacrament of confirmation, are bare vestiges of the importance that the spiritual formation of personhood had in the Judeo-Christian tradition. But even though in our society we no longer have clearly marked transition points to higher levels of personhood, we do expect different qualities from people at different stages of life.

So, while we lack communal rites to celebrate a person's passage from one stage to another, developmental psychologists recognize the importance of such transitions in their descriptions of the life cycle. For instance, Eric Erikson

(1950) focuses on the sequence of psychosocial tasks we must confront: forming an identity in adolescence, developing intimacy in young adulthood, achieving generativity in middle age, and finally bringing together one's past life into a meaningful narrative at the stage of integrity in old age (see also Vaillant, 1993). Robert Havighurst (1953) shifted the emphasis more on social-role demands, and developed a model of life transitions based on changing expectations related to age: for example, the student, the worker, the parent. Similar models were proposed more recently by Levinson (1980) and Bee (1992). Developmental theories usually do not make the claim that these tasks are always resolved, or even that the person is necessarily aware of them. But unless they are successfully resolved, the person's psychological adaptation is likely to be impaired. Common to these models is the assumption that individuals who deviate from normative developmental stages without good reason run the risk of compromising their chances for full personhood.

And while current social norms allow an astonishing amount of leeway in the kind of behavior and attitudes an individual might display, nevertheless we share a tacit consensus that some ways of being a person are preferable to others, in that they best serve both personal and social growth. We shall focus in particular on these "masks"—or optimal ways of being a person—to identify those adult outcomes that might be most important to recognize and nurture in childhood, when they are still in their embryonic form.

Thus, the purpose of this chapter is to review briefly the most valued traits of personhood recognized in our culture as well as in others. We shall claim that the trait of *psychological complexity* meets the specifications for the central dimension of personhood. Then we shall examine how complexity unfolds through the life cycle, beginning with its manifestations in old age. By starting at the end of the life span and working our way back to childhood, it will be easier to recognize the patterns that are more likely to result in a successful unfolding of the potentialities for personhood. Of course, there is still much disagreement about the nature of continuities throughout the life span, and even about whether any childhood conditions will lawfully relate to adult conditions. We shall not try to address such questions, which are amply dealt with in other sections of this Volume. Suffice it to say that we are in accord, for instance, with the "action-theoretical" perspective developed by Brandstätter in Ch. 14, this Volume, according to which individuals are both the active producers as well as the products of their ontogeny; and with the "modern holistic interactionism" explicated by Magnusson and Stattin (Ch. 12, this Volume), according to which the person develops as an integrated, purposeful, and dynamic component of an individual-environment system. If these perspectives are correct, then knowing the desirable end-points of ontogeny will make it easier for active, intentional individuals to shape their actions early in life so as to make them most likely to achieve optimal developmental outcomes.

Despite differences in content across various cultural contexts, across domains of activity, and across points in the life course, and despite, then, the inevitable differences in what will be recognized as constituting "development" and "optimal functioning," we believe it is possible to say something affirmative about optimal development. One fruitful direction is to look beyond outward appearances and focus on how—within any system—optimal functioning involves the meshing of the needs of the self with those of the other. In addition, from a phenomenological perspective, it is reasonable to believe that a person who succeeds in enjoying the synergy of individual and systemic needs will have achieved that measure of happiness that philosophers have long taught us to be the ultimate goal of existence.

There are compelling reasons to take a position on optimal patterns of development, despite the ambiguity and risk involved. Bruner (1986) has argued that developmental psychologists cannot just describe but must also prescribe optimal ways of developing. If not, they abdicate their role in the construction of the public meanings that societies depend upon for self-regulation. When such metatheories about the "good person" and the "good society" are explicitly delineated, they not only add to the public dialogue, they also provide a selective principle for determining the nature and direction of developmental research. Rogers (1969) said much the same thing in defense of his conception of the optimal person; he challenged others: "If my concept of the fully functioning person is abhorrent to you . . . then give *your* definition of the person . . . and publish it for all to see. We need many such definitions so that there can be a really significant modern dialogue as to what constitutes our optimum, our ideal citizen" (p. 296).

More recently, Wertsch (1991) has argued that the essential task of developmental psychology is to identify and point out the ways individuals learn to enact the roles available in their culture without losing their autonomy in the process.

To accomplish the goals set forth above, we have chosen a somewhat unconventional strategy: to begin at the end of the life cycle and work our way back to infancy. Starting with the fully developed person allows us to draw from a recent study of creativity in later life, in which we describe in detail the mature self-regulation and complexity that *potentially* characterizes later life. Because physical maturational changes culminate in adolescence, and the periods of middle and late adulthood often are marked by declines in some physical and cognitive skills, theorists have struggled to conceptualize whether adults are in fact "developing," declining, or simply changing (Pearlin, 1982). Our perspective on this debate is similar to Baltes and Smith's (1990) "weak" developmental hypothesis about the possibility of adult development culminating in wisdom. This hypothesis states that increasing age does not necessarily result in wisdom, and that on average older adults may not demonstrate more wisdom than younger ones; but because wisdom is conceptualized as an "expertise" that requires cumulative practice, and because increasing age provides for more experience and time for such practice, notable outcomes of wisdom will be disproportionately seen in older adults.

A second reason for starting at the end of the life cycle is that to do so facilitates our search for the beginnings of mature self-regulation and complexity in the periods of infancy and childhood. If one first articulates a clearer picture of desirable adult developmental outcomes, then it is easier to search the literature about earlier developmental periods and, it is hoped, find the connections that link certain patterns in childhood with desirable adult outcomes. We will explore in particular the link between the fully functioning adult and the neotenous development of children that provides opportunities for play and discovery (Gould, 1977).

Ideal Outcomes of Adult Development

What kind of person best represents the goals of human development? At first it might seem that such a question cannot be answered in the abstract, because each culture requires such a different set of roles to be played by a successful adult as to make any generalization impossible. Yet, it could be argued that there is a minimum sets of traits that are valued in every human community, and these could be held up as the ideal outcome that should inform developmental processes from early childhood throughout life. We shall focus here on six conditions for complex adulthood and old age that seem relatively invariant and thus can provide guidelines for optimal development in childhood as well as later in life.

In the first place, older persons who are *healthy* and *fit* can play their role on the cultural stage more effectively and without disrupting the lives of those around them. In earlier historical periods, individuals whose health was dubious rarely survived to old age. In communities that lived on the edge of subsistence, such as the Inuit, the aged who could no longer follow the movements of the tribe in search of game asked to be left behind in an "igloo without doors," to be buried alive, as it were, so as not to jeopardize the survival of their kin by slowing down their progress. In technologically advanced societies, the health costs of the aged—Medicare, nursing homes, and so on—can become a severe financial burden on the younger generations and cause potentially acute social conflicts.

According to current medical opinion, we could live and be healthy much longer than most of us actually manage to do—provided we take adequate care of our physical well-being (Bortz, 1996; Erikson, Erikson, & Kivnick, 1986; Williams, 1995). But it is rarely possible to reverse in the second half of life unhealthy habits acquired in the early years. And while medical advances are constantly adding to our understanding of health and disease, the actual conditions of existence—including environmental factors such as pollution, poor diets, increasing dependence on drugs and on passive entertainment—seem to conspire against developing habits of fitness that will serve us well in later life. For example, the frequency of obesity in childhood and adolescence is increasing in the United States, even while research shows that obese adolescents have a shorter life span and more ailments if they manage to live into old age. An approach to child development that leaves out of reckoning physical criteria of well-being is therefore severely limited.

An emphasis on health should not be construed as implying that only the physically fit can reach a successful adulthood. In fact, many individuals disabled by accidents or congenital illness have lived extremely fulfilling lives and contributed greatly to society. Franklin Delano Roosevelt was not deterred by childhood polio, and Thomas Alva Edison accomplished his extraordinary feats despite a great variety of early health conditions. But it is usually the case that if disabled individuals are not to be a burden to themselves and the community, they have to develop even greater intellectual, affective, and motivational strengths to compensate for a lack of physical performance at levels ordinarily expected from members of the culture.

A second criterion of optimal aging that is unlikely to be contested in any human environment is the ability to *preserve an alert and vital mind*. This is not the place to review the very large literature on cognitive functioning in the later years. The only points relevant to this chapter are that superior intellectual functioning in old age is universally desirable, and that such superior performance is made more likely by the continued exercise of the mind. The tag "Use it or lose it" applies to both physical and mental capacities. The implications of these facts for child development are rather clear, even if not very surprising.

Not so widely understood, however, is the nature of the "exercise" that preserves mental vitality. In our opinion, it is not so much working on the solution of problems that is crucial, as it is to preserve an abiding curiosity and interest in one's surroundings. Adding columns of numbers or solving crossword puzzles is better than not using the mind at all, but the real vital intellect is one that keeps the fresh wonder of childhood into old age. At 76, Jonas Salk, who implemented the vaccine against polio, said "I still feel like a child, an adolescent, as if I still had lots to do," and this perception is quite common among successful older people.[1] The implication for development is not that a child should accumulate facts or knowledge, but rather that he or she should develop habits of intellectual curiosity that lead to genuine lifelong learning.

A third criterion of developmental success is the *continuity of a vocation*. Whether the activity is one the person has pursued throughout the middle years of life, such as a

---

[1] Quotations not otherwise attributed are taken from interviews the authors and other members of the University of Chicago research team collected in the course of a project entitled Creativity in Later Life, sponsored by the Spencer Foundation (see Csikszentmihalyi, 1996).

profession or a family role, or whether it is a new activity that is taken up first in old age, what counts is that the person be committed and involved with a role—or mask—that is valued by the self and preferably by others as well. The role may be an active one or a passive, reflective role, such as that of the Brahmin elder who was expected to withdraw from the cares of the world and meditate after his first grandson came of age. The important issue is that the person continue to remain involved in a meaningful activity.

One of the peculiarities of contemporary cultures is that they have few roles available for older individuals. "In America we no longer value the wisdom of older people," says the novelist Madaleine L'Engle, "whereas in so-called primitive tribes the older people are revered because they have the 'story' of the tribe. And I think as a country, we are in danger of losing our stories. . . . I think chronological isolation is awful and chronological segregation is one of the worst of segregations." The implication of this situation for earlier development is that, for successful aging, a person cannot depend on the assurance that social roles will be available, but must learn to develop skills and interests autonomously. A person who has devoted most of his or her adult life to a business, whether as an assembly-line operator or as a top executive, cannot count on having meaningful opportunities for action after retirement. Unless one is prepared to play a complex role even in the absence of socially structured statuses, it is likely that old age will fail to provide rewarding experiences. It is for this reason, among others, that the cultivation of psychic autonomy all through the life course is such as important part of development (Deci & Flaste, 1995; Deci & Ryan, 1985).

These three prerequisites of successful aging—fitness of body, fitness of mind, and a continuation of active involvement with a meaningful role—are aspects of the continuing differentiation of the person, having to do with the cultivation of individual skills up to the end of life. The next three prerequisites deal with the continuing integration of the person with complex interpersonal systems. To achieve complexity, a person must not only be differentiated as a unique individual, but must be integrated into wider networks of social and cultural relationships.

Successful aging is often defined in terms of *keeping up relationships with family and friends* (Ryff, 1989). In highly technological societies such as ours, geographical mobility tends to weaken social ties, with the result that older persons are often cut off from meaningful contact with other people. It is difficult to keep in touch with one's childhood friends, or even with one's siblings, children, and grandchildren. Yet, older people depend on friendships to maintain the quality of their lives almost as much as teenagers do (Larson, Mannell, & Zuzanek, 1986), so loneliness can become a severe blight in the later years. Conversely, the younger generations also miss the potential contribution of older individuals when society is segregated by age.

What are the implications of this state of affairs for child development? Perhaps the most basic suggestion is that our attitudes toward child rearing have been informed by an excessive emphasis on individuation: we encourage children to value their own freedom, initiative, and personal success at the expense of cultivating a sense of responsibility and belongingness. We should realize that such a one-sided preparation for life is not only destructive of societal cohesion (Bronfenbrenner, 1979; Damon, 1995), but is also a disservice to the individual, who is likely to be unprepared for the parts he or she will have to play in later life. Benjamin Spock, whose *Baby and Child Care* was first published in 1946 and influenced generations of U.S. parents, in a 1991 interview stressed the fact that we have overshot the mark in teaching independence at the expense of interdependence: "men as well as women should re-evaluate what is satisfying, and see that it comes down to human relations. It comes down to love, service, kindliness. And it consists in putting the family in first place . . . and then community relations is second."

In fact, the fifth prerequisite of successful aging is *continued involvement in the community*. This includes not just one-on-one relationships, but taking an active part in the social, political, religious, and cultural affairs of one's environment—whether at the level of the neighborhood or of the nation. Again, the problem is that in our culture there are no ready-made roles for older people to step into. Most meaningful opportunities are reserved for the young. Yet, it is perfectly possible for a person in later life to play a significant role on the social stage, provided he or she prepared for it earlier.

It is important to realize that here, too, what the sociologist Robert Merton has called the "Matthew Principle" applies. The principle refers to a verse in the Gospel of St. Matthew (13.12): "For whosoever hath, to him shall be given . . . but whosoever hath not, from him shall be taken away even what he hath." In other words, a person who has achieved material success can continue in old age to contribute to the community through philanthropy or political influence, and a person who has achieved renown in science or the arts can continue to be active in later life by sitting on boards and commissions or through writings and lectures. Nevertheless, even the average person without much material or cultural capital can find innumerable opportunities for helping the community through volunteer work or more intense forms of personal involvement.

But it is unlikely that a child who has been reared with an exclusive emphasis on personal advancement will be motivated to turn to community action in later life. As Dr. Spock remarks: "I think that our children should be brought up not primarily to get ahead, not primarily to look for prestigious jobs and high income, but with the idea of serving the community and serving the world—even if they get into business." Benjamin Spock's own career serves as a good model of what he preaches: after retirement from teaching medicine at Western Reserve, he worked hard for the National Committee for a Sane Nuclear Policy out of his concern for the effects of nuclear fallout on children; then he ran for the presidency of the United States in an effort to implement the kind of policies he believed would lead to a healthier environment; and in his 80s he is still involved in a variety of activities aimed at improving the quality of life for children and families. Like most persons who show concern for the welfare of the community in later life, Spock absorbed his values in early childhood. "I was brought up by a very moralistic mother," he remembers, "fiercely moralistic, you might say." And although as a young man he rebelled against those strict parental values and was motivated to achieve material success above all else, eventually the seeds planted in the early family environment came to fruition.

The sixth and final part that it is appropriate to play on the cultural stage in the later years of life is that of a *wise person*. Wisdom is a concept with many layers of meaning; here we shall define only some of its more salient attributes. In the first place, wisdom refers to the ability to get at the essence of problems; second, it involves holistic thinking rather than specialized knowledge; third, it refers to virtue or to behavior in line with the common good; and finally, it involves a serene acceptance of one's lot, the joyful performance of the practice of everyday life (Csikszentmihalyi & Rathunde, 1990; Sternberg, 1990). Throughout most of history, and especially during the hundreds of thousands of years before writing was invented and knowledge had to be passed down from the memory of elders to the memory of youth, what we now would call wisdom was a highly prized trait of the old.

This is no longer the case, however. While the production of new information has escalated geometrically in the past few centuries, the knowledge of the older cohorts has become increasingly obsolete. As a result, the younger generation is less likely to take seriously anything their elders say. Teenagers watch with incredulous disdain as their parents fumble with the VCR, cannot find their way through the Internet, and listen with bewildered incomprehension to the latest popular songs—how could these inept oldies have anything worthwhile to say? The sociologist Elijah Anderson (1990) describes how, for instance, the link between the generations has been snapped in most African American neighborhoods in the United States. Young people tended to congregate on street corners around some of the wise elders—or "old heads"—who used to engage them in witty repartee dealing with moral tales of hard work and decency interspersed with practical information about jobs, good manners, and other "tricks of the trade." Nowadays, this essential step in socialization is getting increasingly rare, to the detriment of individual lives and the viability of the community as a whole.

Yet, wisdom does not become obsolete as rapidly as knowledge. We would not take very seriously the scientific ideas or factual information possessed by the ancient Greeks or Romans, whereas the reflections of Socrates or Seneca on the meaning of life are still state-of-the-art. In fact, as knowledge seems to be fragmenting itself in a fair imitation of the biblical Tower of Babel, the need for the qualities of wisdom are becoming more urgent than ever.

It is obvious, however, that wisdom is not simply a matter of age. A scatterbrained youngster will not turn automatically into a wise old person simply because he or she lives many years. What kind of early experiences predispose a person to be wise in old age? There is no systematic information that would answer such a question. But one might expect that a child who is brought up to value decontextualized thinking, specialization, expediency, self-centeredness, immediate gratification, and an exclusive reliance on extrinsic rewards will not be interested in wearing the mask of a wise person in old age. By contrast, if the early environment encourages empathy and a holistic way of thinking, integrity, responsibility, and sensitivity to intrinsic rewards and long-range goals, then interest in wisdom is more likely to develop. And the scant evidence suggests that these attitudes conducive to wisdom are usually learned in the immediate family from one's parents, or, perhaps more typically, from one of the parents.

In addition to these six ways of being a successful older person, it is important to repeat that *how* an individual experiences his or her life is as important as the particular masks he or she wears. A person whose behavior conforms to the highest expectations of the culture but who fails to enjoy the parts he or she plays cannot be considered to have attained an optimal old age. Therefore, one of the essential developmental tasks is to provide young people with the metaskill of turning neutral or adverse everyday situations into enjoyable experiences. In summary, one might say that the ideal of an older person is: *Someone fit of body and mind, who is curious and interested in life, and pursues a vocation with vigor; someone who is close to family and friends, is helpful and involved in the community, and concerned with making sense of the world; and who, in all of these endeavors, finds meaning and enjoyment.*

Given these assumptions about what constitutes optimal aging, it is now time to turn our attention to examining in greater detail what makes it possible to achieve these positive outcomes. We argue that a complex personality supports the ability to play these desirable roles, and then we turn to the childhood antecedents involved in the formation of psychological complexity.

COMPLEXITY AND DEVELOPMENT

We have said that a person is a human being who can speak and be understood, who can relate to other members of a community, and is able to fulfill the roles expected of an individual of a certain age and social position. The concept of the mask was introduced to emphasize that personhood involves playing appropriate roles on a cultural stage.

We have also seen that not all masks are valued equally in society. Therefore, we add here the notion of a *complex mask,* which distinguishes the kind of optimal developmental outcomes that human groups in general tend to consider the most desirable. The complexity of a mask, and thus the complexity of the person, depends upon the quality of the intrapsychic and interpersonal relationships a person is capable of enacting. Starting from a Bakhtinian perspective,

James Wertsch (1991) came to a similar conclusion when he said that the real, unique object of developmental psychology was to study "the processes whereby individuals master voices and patterns of privileging," because only then can we understand how persons can control and shape the forces impinging on them, and achieve a measure of emancipation from the determinism of biology and culture (p. 29). In the terms developed in this chapter, complexity is a measure of how well a person can take on *integrating and differentiating complex relationships,* including, but not exclusively, relationships with other persons. Thus, the concept of complexity makes it possible to construct a unified model of optimal development.

To grasp the function of relationships in the life course, it is helpful to draw upon Levinson's (1986) notion of the life structure. A life structure is the underlying pattern or design of a person's life; to understand development, one needs to understand the evolution of this pattern. In a manner similar to the distinction made earlier between persona and person, Levinson distinguished between personality structure and life structure with two questions: "What kind of person am I?" and "What is my life like now?" The latter question reveals the life structure because it discloses the relationships one has with others, broadly defined as actual persons, imagined figures, social groups or institutions, places, objects, and so on. He comments: "These relationships are the stuff [of which] our lives are made. . . . They are the vehicle by which we . . . participate, for better or worse, in the world around us" (p. 7).

The relationships that constitute the life structure are part of the two systems they connect (i.e., self and environment) and can only be understood as that which creates a link *between* them. The pattern of a life is not only revealed by these relationships, it *is* these relationships. Thus, if we equate the mask with a culturally prescribed role, and the person with the particular voice issuing through the mask, we might say that the essence of personhood is relationship, or more succinctly: persons are relationships. Consequently, as Lerner (1991) has argued, the basic process of development consists in changes in relationships between individuals and their multiple contexts.

What makes one relationship more complex than another? If the goal of personhood is participation in culture while developing unique potentialities, then a complex relationship is one that fosters the integration and differentiation of self and environment and thus allows the fullest and most intense levels of participation. This concept is similar to that of the optimal environment discussed by Magnusson and Stattin (Ch. 12, this Volume), which provides the effective stimulation that allows the individual to differentiate in unique ways (see Gottlieb, Ch. 5, this Volume). But to locate such an answer squarely within classical developmental theory, we shall explore the notion of complexity in terms made familiar by the early developmental literature. We might begin to look at it from a Piagetian perspective.

Piagetian Theory and Complex Relationships

A number of familiar concepts from Piaget's theory are helpful for understanding complexity. For instance, *equilibration* expresses a fundamental insight of Piaget: that development is an evolutionary process that exists "between" subject and object. While some theorists before him explained development from the side of the subject (e.g., through a priori structures, rationalism, or other nativist ideas), and others explained it from the side of the environment (e.g., association, positivism, or other nurture perspectives), Piaget tried to solve the riddle of development with an interactionist, open-systems model. Some may find this statement at odds with the too common interpretation of Piaget as a static stage theorist; this misunderstanding, however, arises from his multiple uses of the term *equilibrium.* For instance, it was sometimes used to refer to moment-to-moment adjustments of assimilation and accommodation, sometimes to the temporary accomplishments of the stages, and sometimes to the ideal endpoint of formal operations. It is at the first level of moment-to-moment interactions that Piaget is most clear that development is an ongoing relationship between self and environment: assimilation and accommodation are in constant search for equilibrium or balance, and acting in the world continually introduces disequilibrium that must be corrected with a dynamic equilibrium.

Despite the fact that maturationists and environmentalists both claim a part of his vision, the theory is more accurately understood as derived from an open-systems model of evolutionary biology: "It [Piaget's theory] does not place an energy system within us so much as it places us in a single energy system of all living things. Its primary attention, then, is not to shifts and changes in an internal equilibrium, but to an equilibrium in the world,

between the progressively individuated self and the bigger life field, an interaction sculpted by both and constitutive of reality itself" (Kegan, 1982, p. 43). Thus, equilibrium describes the state of the open system such that the self and environment are related in a way that is differentiated and integrated; in other words, it describes a state of complexity. Assimilation and accommodation are two facets of a unitary and dynamic evolutionary process and must be understood together: as an organism differentiates, it moves, so to speak, through assimilation toward accommodation (i.e., from structure toward change); this movement calls for a reverse movement through accommodation toward assimilation (i.e., from change to structure) that integrates the organism with the environment in a new way.

By describing development in such general systems terms that focus on the relationship between self and environment, some thorny conceptual dichotomies become less troublesome (e.g., nature/nurture), and the person can be seen less as the *result* of the relational process (i.e., the more traditional interpretation), and more as the *process* of organizing information and creating meaning itself. A new burden, however, is then placed on the theorist, namely, to describe and measure the transitory state of equilibrium. There are at least two basic ways to address this problem: from the "inside," emphasizing how the self experiences the relational process; and from the "outside," looking at practical consequences. Likewise, Levinson (1986) suggested that the relationships of the life structure had an internal and an external reference. To evaluate the satisfactoriness of the life structure one could look at it internally in terms of *suitability,* or how the self can be lived out, passionately invested in, and expressed through the structure; or it could be evaluated in terms of *viability,* or what advantages versus disadvantages for adaptation resulted from the particular life structure.

Kegan (1982) noted that Piaget took the latter course, viewing the process descriptively from the outside, and focused on the successes in problem solving associated with different stages of cognitive development. Consequently, the approach ignored the assimilation/accommodation process from the participatory angle of the self. Presumably, this is one reason why the theory is often faulted for failing to provide a sufficient look at the role of emotion and motivation in development (Sternberg, 1984). In fairness to Piaget, however, there were larger historical reasons that led many psychologists to ignore the internal reference.

Aside from a few existential and phenomenological approaches, these participatory questions have seldom been raised in the field of developmental psychology; when they have, they have often lacked theoretical and methodological rigor to allow intersubjective verification.

In summary, then, Piagetian theory is helpful for linking the notion of complexity to foundational ideas in the developmental literature; but for several reasons it does not suffice for the purposes of this chapter. The theory tells us little about how the relational process between self and environment is *experienced by the self,* thus it tells us little about what—in human terms—motivates development. The notions of assimilation, accommodation, and equilibration, while important for locating the action of development in the relation between self and environment, are notoriously vague as concepts that can be measured and studied; they therefore have limited utility. If, however, a framework of internal reference is adopted, new research opportunities arise. For instance, if equilibrium indicates a complex relationship that is fully involving, then it becomes possible to look at development from a perspective that emphasizes full involvement as a measurable criterion of the self-environment negotiation process. Much can be learned about this process, we believe, by adopting a phenomenological perspective that focuses on the experience of self-environment relations. For instance, what does a complex relationship feel like? How can relationships that are too one-sided—too integrated or too differentiated—be recognized phenomenologically?

Answers to the above questions were alluded to by Piaget in concepts such as *functional pleasure* and in brief references to intrinsic motivation. Unfortunately, he never developed these ideas in much detail. For instance, Piaget observed that infants laughed at their own power, tried to make interesting sights last, and manifested enjoyment (i.e., functional pleasure) when acting competently. Such observations were short-lived and limited to the early sensorimotor stages, however, as he turned his attention to the external manifestations of successful problem solving associated with higher stages of cognitive development. In so doing, a fruitful course of investigation was abandoned, one that might have added significant insights about the search for equilibration, and the enjoyment and intrinsic motivation associated with it.

To say the same thing more directly, the claim here is that complex relationships are experienced by the self as optimally rewarding; to the extent that Piaget was correct in asserting that the search for equilibration energized human development, it is accurate to say that development is also motivated by the search for optimal experience. It is through monitoring such experiences that we can learn to recognize when relationships are complex and when they are too differentiated or too integrated (having overemphasized either assimilation or accommodation). And to the extent that the person is defined less as a static entity and more as a relational process, then a theory of optimal experience becomes an important link to a fuller understanding of the development of the person.

Optimal Experience and Development: Some Previous Perspectives

Before discussing contemporary theories, it is worth mentioning a few of the early proponents of the view that optimal experiences are closely linked with the full development of the person. Although many thinkers could be mentioned here, going as far back as Aristotle (MacIntyre, 1984), we have selected three more recent authors whose insights are relevant: Friedrich Nietzsche, Abraham Maslow, and Carl Rogers. Their views are linked through an idea they shared: *love of fate.* All three believed that love of fate was *the* mark of distinction for the fully developed person, whether that person was called "overman" by Nietzsche, "self-actualizing" by Maslow, or "fully functioning" by Rogers (1969); and all of them depicted the love of fate as a deeply rewarding synchrony between self and environment.

What does it mean to love one's fate? For Nietzsche it meant the affirmation of life through a full acceptance of its circumstances. Despite hardship or obstacle, or perhaps more accurately, because of them, one would not wish for one's life to unfold in any other way. This is so because the process of overcoming obstacles provides the opportunities through which the person is created. *Amor fati,* or love of fate, is a central concept in Nietzsche's philosophy: "My formula for greatness in a human being is amor fati: that one wants nothing to be different, not forward, not backward, not in all eternity. . . . Not merely bear what is necessary . . . but love it" (1968, p. 714). The fully alive person (i.e., the *over* man) is not content with just surviving and adapting, but is intent upon transcending himself or herself. Such experiences of transcendence provided his deepest motivation: "I want to learn more and more to see as beautiful what is necessary in things; then I shall be one of those who make things beautiful" (1974, p. 223).

Maslow's (1971) studies of self-actualization and peak experiences led him to a similar conclusion. The healthy person is not motivated just by deficits, simple endurance in life, or by the survival of self or offspring, but also by growth. Based on his observations and interviews with individuals he considered to be self-actualizing, including creative artists and scientists, he concluded that the processes of growth were often rewarded with fulfilling peak experiences. These experiences coincided with a synchronous relationship between self and environment; he referred to this synchrony as a balance of "inner required-ness" with "outer requiredness," or "I want" with "I must." Especially true of self-actualizing persons, during such experiences "one freely, happily, and wholeheartedly embraces one's determinants. One chooses and wills one's fate" (p. 325).

Rogers (1969) endorsed a very similar perspective. He comments about the fully functioning person: "He wills or chooses to follow the course of action which is the most economical vector in relation to all the internal and external stimuli because it is that behavior which will be the most deeply satisfying" (p. 294). As a result, he continues, "The fully functioning person . . . not only experiences, but utilizes, the most absolute freedom when he spontaneously, freely, and voluntarily chooses and wills that which is absolutely determined" (p. 295). Thus, as with Nietzsche and Maslow, a love of fate corresponds to an inner-outer synchrony that evokes a deeply rewarding experience. And like both of the other thinkers, Rogers (1959) believed that the person was not satisfied with mere survival, but was instead motivated to expand and grow: "The inherent tendency of the organism is to develop all its capacities in ways which serve to maintain or enhance the organism. It involves not only what Maslow terms 'deficiency needs' . . . [but also] expansions in terms of growth. . . . Life processes do not merely tend to preserve life, but transcend the momentary status quo of the organism, expanding itself continually and imposing its autonomous determination upon an ever-increasing realm of events" (p. 196).

Love of fate, then, reveals a complex relationship: a relational synchrony of self with environment; as such, it is the mark of distinction of the developing person. It is deeply

rewarding because it coincides with the most "economical vector" between inner and outer stimuli.[2] Most importantly, it is an experience that confirms, manifests, and accompanies what the organism wants most: to develop and to grow. Such complex relationships maximize being through the differentiation and integration of the person which allows the fullest expression of life and energy. In Piagetian terms, to grow means that a new equilibrium has been attained, one that is "higher" in the sense of being more synchronous with reality (i.e., as formal operations are more attuned to reality than concrete operations). What is added here to that perspective is the internal reference, the interior psychological correlate to moments of growth, or their intrinsically motivating character.

Flow Theory and Complex Relationships

Contemporary theories of intrinsic motivation continue in this tradition of thought. For instance, flow theory (Csik-szentmihalyi, 1975, 1990, 1993) describes a prototypical experience of intrinsic motivation referred to as a *flow experience*. Flow is a deeply involving and enjoyable experience that has been described by a variety of different respondents, in a variety of cultures, in strikingly similar ways (Csikszentmihalyi & Csikszentmihalyi, 1988). Athletes refer to it as being "in the zone," poets as being visited by the muse.

In flow, a person is fully concentrated on the task at hand. There is a feeling that action and awareness merge in a single beam of focused consciousness. In flow, it is very clear what needs to be done from one moment to the next; goals are clearly ordered and sequenced. One also knows immediately how well one is doing: feedback is unambiguous. The tennis player knows whether the ball was hit well, the violinist hears whether the note just played was right or wrong. In flow, a person loses self-consciousness; the

---

[2] It is worth pointing out again that when the person is defined relationally, as in this chapter, it can be misleading to fall into the familiar use of the terms *subject* versus *object, inner* versus *outer,* and so on. This terminology tends to isolate the person from the world, which is not our intention. On the contrary, it is more consistent with our perspective to say that the "location" of the person is neither inner nor outer, or, perhaps better, is both at once.

vulnerable ego disappears. In George Herbert Mead's terms, there is only "I" without a "me" to worry about. The sense of time becomes distorted to fit the experience; hours seem to pass by in minutes. When these dimensions of experience are present, one is willing to do what makes these feelings possible for their own sake, without expecting extrinsic rewards. The poet enjoys the experience of writing, the bond trader enjoys beating the market, and both will continue doing these things because they are enjoyable—even in the absence of the rewards of fame and wealth.

Finally, and most importantly, flow begins to be experienced when there is a fit between the *skills* of the self and the *challenges* afforded by the environment. For example, we cannot enjoy a tennis game if our opponent is either much better or much worse than we are; only a game with a well-matched opponent is likely to be enjoyable. We don't enjoy reading a novel in which plot and characters are too difficult to visualize, nor one that is too obvious and predictable; we enjoy instead the text that fits our imaginative powers. It is this aspect of enjoyment that is most relevant to the relational synchrony that lies at the heart of optimal personhood.

The experience of flow marks an achieved balance of arousal-increasing and arousal-decreasing processes. The flow model describes this balance in terms of the fit between perceived challenges and skills: an activity wherein challenges predominate increases arousal; an activity wherein skills predominate reduces arousal. Thus, a synchrony of challenges and skills permits a state of deep involvement, while the pitfalls of either over- or underarousal (i.e., anxiety or boredom) are avoided. In this sense, flow seems to represent the subjective dimension of that "goodness of fit" between temperament and environment that underlies several developmental perspectives (e.g., Lerner & Lerner, 1987; Thomas & Chess, 1977).

In fact, it could be argued that flow is likely to be experienced when an individual is fully functioning relative to the developmental opportunities that a given stage provides. For instance, in terms of the Eriksonian stages, an infant at the first stage whose only opportunity for action is feeding itself and whose only skill is to suck milk will be in flow when at the nipple. As the opportunities for action in the physical and social environment grow, so must the child's abilities to act increase if the child is to continue to experience enjoyment.

Anxiety and boredom are aversive phenomenological states that result from a disequilibrium in the momentary fit between skills and challenges or self and environment. When challenges are too high relative to skills, the asynchronous relationship leads to anxiety because one feels overwhelmed, out of control, threatened by a loss of integrity and order. In contrast, when skills are too high for the given challenges, the fit between self and environment is too easy and comfortable, resulting in the loss of spontaneity and novelty and therefore a decrease in the sense of focus, urgency, curiosity, adventure, and so on.

The balance of skills and challenges can also be described in Piagetian terms. An assimilative mode of processing indicates the existence of an organized, preexisting structure of information. That structure makes the processing of new information more automatic because it can be organized by the existing structure. The notion of "skills" suggests an analogous process; a skill is a practiced response, one that is habitual and automatic. A skilled pianist, therefore, primarily relies on an assimilative mode when reading an easy piece of music. On the other hand, if the challenge of reading the score is just beyond the skills of the pianist, an accommodative mode predominates. Accommodation is a more effortful response to novelty (Block, 1982). In attentional terms, it uses more controlled, linear processes, rather than automatic and global processes, as does assimilation (Schneider & Shiffrin, 1977). To say, then, that a flow experience is more likely when skills and challenges are in balance, is to say that flow is more likely when assimilation and accommodation are in equilibrium. Other ways to describe the experience are as undivided attention, the combination of controlled and automatic processes, or the joining of effort and habit (Rathunde, 1993).

Piaget (1962, see pp. 147–150) recognized that when assimilation dominates accommodation the fit between self and environment is too rigid and one-sided. In an *overassimilative* mode, the self habitually perceives the environment subject to its own preconceptions, and consequently objectivity is diminished (Kegan, 1982). Overassimilation is equivalent to an imbalance of skills over challenges, and it feels like boredom. When bored, one is too "subjective," too habitual, and closed to new opportunities for action. Conversely, when accommodation dominates assimilation, or when novelty overwhelms the processing capacity of a preexisting structure, the self is placed in a position that is the opposite of embeddedness. In such circumstances, the self is unhinged and oriented outside of itself; it is so decentered toward the uncertainty in the environment that the possibility for feelings of relatedness, connection, and meaning are diminished. *Overaccommodation,* then, is equivalent to the imbalance of challenges over skills, and it is experienced as anxiety. When anxious, one feels at the mercy of environmental circumstances that are beyond one's control, and thus blinded by the excessive stimulation to ways of making sense of the situation.

When skills and challenges are in equilibrium, action is fully centered on the relationship between self and environment. The skilled pianist who performs a challenging score is drawn into a more complex and involving relationship. The automaticity of existing skills provides confidence, structure, integrity, and a foundation from which the new material can be reached; yet the reach is not easy, and the novelty of the score demands careful attention. It is just such a combination that requires full attention—resources brought to bear through habits of "chunking" the information, and resources mustered through effort and step-by-step attention to detail. And this full attention is experienced as a feeling of flow, of being caught up in a single energy system that unites self and environment. Motivation to continue the activity becomes intrinsic—not in the mistaken sense of "in" the self, but rather "in" the self-environment relationship.

Yet another way to look at the full involvement of flow is in terms of the combination of positive affect and heightened concentration. Some activities may evoke positive affect, but will soon be experienced as frivolous if they lack focus and the need for concentration. On the other hand, some activities begin with intense concentration, but are soon experienced as oppressive and alienating because they are devoid of pleasant feelings. Dewey (1913) has called the former experiences "fooling" and the latter "drudgery." In contrast, he described optimal experiences as affectively and cognitively engaging, providing both a sense of playfulness and spontaneity, as well as a corresponding seriousness and focus on goals. For some individuals, work is drudgery because serious concentration is not accompanied by positive emotion, and leisure is fooling because good moods cannot be sustained due to a lack of focus. For other, more fortunate people, work and leisure are both thoroughly enjoyed, and in fact indistinguishable. By splitting positive

affect and heightened concentration, the former individuals experience what may be thought of as "divided" interest; the latter ones, through the synchrony of affect and cognition, experience the fullness of "undivided" interest or *serious play* (see also Rathunde, 1993, 1995).

The implications of an affective-cognitive synchrony for the quality of experience can also be described using the psychoanalytic constructs of *primary* and *secondary process* thinking. These two processes are often dichotomized in an either/or fashion: primary process is identified with the pleasure principle and with dreams, myth, emotional thinking, fantasy, poetic feeling, and so on; secondary process, in contrast, is identified with the reality principle and thus with reason, logic, science, intellect, abstract thought, and so on. A severe split between these two processes is tantamount to pathology. In Freudian terms, relatively uninhibited primary process thought suggests the dominance of the id over and against the ego and superego, whereas the dominance of secondary thought processes is suggestive of the repressive control of the superego over and above the ego and id. A healthy ego, at least to a greater extent than an unhealthy one, is able to synchronize id and superego, primary with secondary process thought, therefore achieving greater self-regulation, freedom, and health. Several psychoanalytic thinkers have also associated such a synchrony with creativity (Jung, 1946; Kris, 1952). The implication here is that healthy ego development is presumably related to negotiating complex relationships and is therefore associated more with optimal experience.

Finally, that optimal experiences synchronize affective and cognitive modes is supported by the descriptions of flow, peak experiences, and the emergent experiences of fully functioning persons. Respondents describe flow as an enjoyable merging of action and awareness in that actions follow each other spontaneously and unselfconsciously, yet there remains an intense and careful monitoring of feedback in relation to one's goals. Maslow (1971) has commented about peak experiences: "We have found that peak experience contains two components—an emotional one of ecstasy and an intellectual one of illumination. Both need to be present simultaneously" (p. 184). Finally, and in a similar vein, Rogers (1969) described the fully functioning person as both a *participant* and an *observer* of an emergent experience: "The sensation is that of floating with a complex stream of experience, with the fascinating possibility of trying to comprehend its everchanging complexity"

(p. 285). Thus, in all of these descriptions there is a component of automatic and controlled attention, a component of primary process thinking that is immediate, and an aspect of secondary process thinking that is monitoring the environment. Such complexity, we believe, like the contrasts of dark and light in a painting, are what makes such experiences interesting and vital.

Flow and Development

Just as we cannot step in the same river twice, we cannot enjoy the same activity with the same intensity more than once. To continue providing optimal experiences, flow activities must constantly be *re-created*. It is this fact that makes the flow model a developmental model. As Piaget also observed, disequilibrium between the processes of assimilation and accommodation is inevitable and needs to be continually addressed. In our phenomenological perspective, disequilibrium is signaled by boredom and anxiety—two inevitable life experiences. In the simplest terms, one escapes boredom by raising challenges and overcomes anxiety by raising skills. It is through this perpetual dialectical process that development proceeds; and it proceeds in the direction of greater complexity because optimal experiences cannot be recaptured through a regression of skills and challenges, but only through their progression (Csikszentmihalyi, 1990; Csikszentmihalyi & Rathunde, 1993).[3]

Figure 11.1 shows how the raising of skills and challenges has been depicted in previous discussions of the flow model. To reenter the "flow channel" from states of boredom or anxiety, challenges and skills must be raised appropriately. In other words, flow can proceed from boredom or from anxiety. Once "inside" the experience, there are common features to flow, but seen in the broader context of before and after, the experiences are quite different. For instance, relief from boredom is a process of *finding* something exciting. Boredom initiates a process of searching for something to do; as interest and curiosity draw the

---

[3] Our focus here remains on immediate subjective experience, but it is possible to adopt other time frames and perceive the same dialectical tension. In other words, one may overcome the anxiety of an entire week, month, or year by finding a way to build new skills. As mentioned earlier, the same is true of the notion of equilibrium; that is, it can refer to immediate experience or stages that characterize larger periods of time.

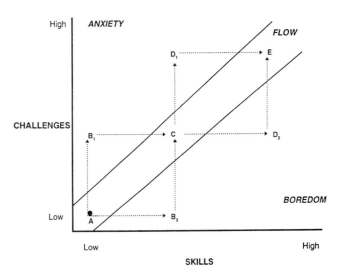

Figure 11.1   The dynamics of flow. A, C, and E are enjoyable states of equilibrium of increasing complexity. B_1 and D_1 are states of anxiety that require learning new skills for a person to return to flow. B_2 and D_2 are states of boredom that require new challenges for a return to flow.

self out of its shell, boredom wanes, and experience becomes more intrinsically rewarding. In contrast, relief from anxiety is more like *solving* a problem. Anxiety initiates a process that tries to resolve a dilemma; with increasing success and a growing sense of resolution, order, or closure, anxiety dissipates, attention becomes more focused, and the quality of experience improves.

Similar to the movement away from boredom, the movement from assimilation toward accommodation involves problem finding in the sense of pushing the limits of an existing information structure. When assimilation is joined by an emergent sense of accommodation, but not overwhelmed by it, experience is optimal. For instance, an individual who has just learned to ski discovers new challenges by testing the limits of his or her skills on new hills; these challenges, if not overwhelming, intensify the skier's experience because they evoke greater concentration and require quicker adjustment. When, however, it becomes clear that a particular challenge is beyond reach, the skier feels out of control and anxiety sets in. In this instance, accommodation that moves toward assimilation is a problem-solving process that rebuilds a new structure. Perhaps the skier needed to learn a more effective way to turn to control the speed of descent; as the first clumsy actions become more practiced and second nature, anxiety lessens, attention is withdrawn from the self-consciousness of "forced" turns, and, at least until the new turns become too automatic, the experience of skiing is again exhilarating.

Apter (1989) has called such changes in the direction of arousal *reversals*. In his reversal theory, he calls the former problem-finding mode *paratelic* and describes it as an arousal-increasing mode wherein attention is focused on the here and now, and more on means as opposed to ends. In contrast, the latter problem-solving mode is referred to as *telic*. In this mode, attention is more focused on the goals of an activity, there is a future-time orientation, and the activity moves toward reducing arousal. In everyday language, the paratelic mode is more spontaneous, fun, and playful; the telic mode is more serious and worklike. The rewards of a paratelic mode are those resulting from the movement from boredom to optimal arousal; in contrast, a telic mode finds optimal rewards by moving from anxiety back to optimal arousal. Consistent with the perspective here, optimal experience is simultaneously paratelic and telic.

Complex Relationships and the Complex Person

What qualities facilitate the kinds of complex relationships, optimal experiences, and trajectories of growth that have been outlined above? Such a question is not intended to change the relational focus in favor of more traditional psychological conceptions of personality traits or characteristics. However, to discuss the person often requires a way of speaking about qualities or characteristics "as if" they were contained in the person. Despite the pitfalls of such language, the qualities discussed can still be thought of in relational terms; and to the extent that they are depicted as relatively stable "traits" of persons, they can also be conceived as stable ways of relating to the environment.

Bronfenbrenner (1992, Ch. 17, this Volume) has recently discussed such personal attributes in terms of their relational potentials and collectively refers to them as *developmentally instigative characteristics*. Such characteristics have two features. The first refers to qualities that encourage or discourage certain reactions from the environment; for instance, a baby acts as a stimulus to others by being either fussy or happy, and calls forth certain corresponding reactions. A more important developmental influence and, according to Bronfenbrenner, one that is much ignored and

in need of study by developmentalists is *developmentally structuring characteristics* that involve an active, selective orientation toward the environment. About such instigative attributes he comments: "When they are manifested over time in particular settings, [they] tend to evoke complementary patterns of continuing developmental feedback, creating more complex developmental trajectories that exhibit continuity through time. The result is a person-specific repertoire of evolving . . . dispositions that continues to be distinguishable over the life course, and hence constitutes what we recognize over the years as the person's individual personality" (1992, pp. 219–220).

There are several examples of developmentally instigative qualities explored in the literature that are relevant to optimal experience. For instance, Block (1982) has discussed how ego resiliency is related to the ability to move through the dialectic of assimilation and accommodation. When novelty overwhelms a particular schema, accommodation is needed to restore psychic equilibrium. However, the movement through assimilation to accommodation may, at first, prolong and intensify an anxious state until progress is made toward reorganizing the structure. If a person is unable to muster the effort needed to push through anxiety, he or she may persist with failed assimilative efforts (i.e., perseveration, fixation, and so on), or might selectively ignore the challenge. An ego-resilient person is better able to keep the two modes in equilibrium and therefore avoid the particular dangers of overassimilation and overaccommodation by being flexible in changing life conditions. Such a person is capable of spontaneity under conditions of overassimilation, and capable of self-direction and organization under conditions of overaccommodation (Block, 1982; Block & Block, 1980).

Bandura's (1977) notion of *self-efficacy* also suggests a relational quality that is relevant for the dialectic of optimal experience. For instance, persons with high self-efficacy *slightly overestimate* their ability to master challenges. This "distortion" has the effect of inducing persons to select challenges that are slightly beyond their current capacities. In other words, it induces the confidence to take a risk. Because the selected challenge is not unrealistic, however, the person is able to master it, thus reinforcing and strengthening the feeling of self-efficacy. The same could be said about the positive feedback loop that coincides with high self-esteem. After experiencing flow, self-esteem increases, and people who experience flow more often (that is, who spend more time in high-challenge, high-skill situations) report higher levels of self-esteem (Adlai-Gail, 1994; Wells, 1988).

Ford and Lerner's (1992) description of the competent person as possessing *flexible* self-regulation is also relevant here: "A competent person can modify effectively his or her own behavior and/or the features of the social situation in which he or she is engaged. . . . People can, for instance, change their topic of conversation if they find they are boring or upsetting others; or if they are bored or upset by what is being said, they can turn the topic of conversation round to more pleasant topics, or terminate it. . . . Such competency—such efficient self-regulation—is an instance of how one may act as a producer of their own development" (p. 85).

Such a competent or flexible person is, of course, not free from the biological and environmental constraints that bind everyone else. We are all limited by particular inherited and learned characteristics, and most settings impose social and physical demands that cannot be ignored. Nevertheless, it is possible to negotiate a *goodness of fit* with the setting. According to Ford and Lerner (1992), flexible persons are better able to (a) evaluate the challenges facing them and their abilities or skills to respond; (b) select and gain access to those contexts where there is a high probability of a good fit, and avoid those contexts where there is not; and, as in the earlier example of a conversation; (c) either change themselves to find a better fit (e.g., change their own pattern of response in a conversation—or accommodate) or try to change the context itself (e.g., try to alter others' topics of conversation—or assimilate). A competency in self-regulation thus allows us to be more active shapers of our development.

Far from reducing an ecological and interactionist perspective to the side of personality, the above remarks reinforce the notion that the self-environment relationship is the primary factor in development. Instigative or structuring qualities, though, set in motion *interaction styles* that are sustained by the accumulation of their own consequences. In other words, results from certain actions instigated by the individual produce a stream of feedback that sustains the trajectory of growth. It is not that the person remains the same in every environment; rather, it is that there is *consistency in the way that a person varies behavior as a function of the environment.* In other words, developmentally instigative characteristics produce a continuity in the way behavior is changed. In this chapter we are especially interested in the continuity of response that directs the person toward self-environment equilibrium and optimal experience.

An example of how such consistency in change might operate is helpful. In overly challenging situations, a person might recognize that arousal reduction and skill building are the appropriate course of action; in times of boredom, the person might seek to increase arousal by seeking higher challenges. Such a person, who at one moment manifests a conservative attitude of perseverance and at another, a confidence aligned with taking risks, might seem to the outside observer to be inconsistent, contradictory, and at the mercy of environmental influences. On the contrary, from the internal reference of subjective experience, such flexibility or complexity of response displays consistency. Only such a person is capable of making choices that move predictably in the direction of optimal experience.

In this chapter, and in previous work (Csikszentmihalyi, 1996; Csikszentmihalyi & Rathunde, 1993), persons that exhibit such active-interactive orientations have been referred to as *complex persons*. A complex person is one who has *the self-regulative capacity to move toward optimal experiences by negotiating a better fit or synchrony of self with environment.* Traditional conceptions of personality that claim a stability of response, regardless of environmental circumstances, have been shown to be lacking (Barker, 1950; Mischel, 1968). We do not dispute the fact that the social and physical demands of different contexts will evoke different behaviors. Traditional conceptions of personality, however, fail to look for *consistency within the change,* or the consistency in the ways that a person varies his or her behavior as a function of the setting (for further discussion of this point, see Cairns & Hood, 1983; Sroufe, 1979).

Physical scientists describing complex systems are also aware of this phenomenon of consistency in change; they call it emergent self-organization (e.g., Prigogine, 1980). Waldrop (1992) comments:

> Self-organizing systems are adaptive, in that they don't just passively respond to events the way a rock might roll around in an earthquake. They actively try to turn whatever happens to their advantage. . . . Complex systems have somehow acquired the ability to bring order and chaos into a special kind of balance. This balance point—often called *the edge of chaos*—is where the components of a system never quite lock

into place, and yet never quite dissolve into turbulence, either. The edge of chaos is where life has enough stability to sustain itself and enough creativity to deserve the name of life. . . . The edge of chaos is the constantly shifting battle zone between stagnation and anarchy, the one place where a complex system can be spontaneous, adaptive, and alive. (pp. 11–12)

Although these words were written to describe the beauty of fractals—the patterned turbulence of rivers, weather, and other natural phenomena—they apply equally to psychological systems. This edge of chaos (and conversely, the "edge of order") has been described here as equilibrium, balance, and synchrony. Optimal development also involves such a predictable unpredictability, and an unpredictable predictability. Note the similarities between the following passage from Roger's (1969) description of the fully functioning person, and the above description of complex physical systems:

> It should therefore be clear that this person will seem to himself to be dependable but not specifically predictable. If he is entering a new situation with an authority figure, for example, he cannot predict what his behavior will be. It is contingent upon the behavior of this authority figure, and his own immediate reactions, desires, etc. He can feel confident that he will behave appropriately, but he has no knowledge in advance of what he will do. . . . It is the maladjusted person whose behavior can be specifically predicted, and some loss of predictability should be evident in every increase in openness to experience and existential living. In the maladjusted person, behavior is predictable because it is rigidly patterned. If such a person has learned a pattern of hostile reaction to authority . . . and if because of this he denies or distorts any experience which should supply contradictory evidence, *then* his behavior is specifically predictable. . . . I am suggesting that as the individual approaches the optimum of complete functioning his behavior, though always lawful and determined, becomes more difficult to predict. (pp. 292–293)

The behavior is lawful, according to Rogers, because the fully functioning person will attempt to select the best path toward growth and the synchrony of inner and outer demands. But this choice, in any given situation, cannot be known in advance, and that is why it is misleading to think of the person in anything but relational terms. Our concept of the complex person tries to avoid static definitions by

viewing the person in terms of the dialectical process of integrating and differentiating self and environment. As Kegan (1982) observes, the person is "an ever progressive motion engaged in giving itself a new form." Here, in contrast to traditional approaches that see the person as a result of this process, the focus is placed not on what a person does, but the doing that a person is. Such an approach distinguishes the notion of person from "self" (i.e., a more psychological, subject-oriented perspective) and from "role" (i.e., a more sociological, object-based perspective). It also, we believe, will facilitate the recognition of similarities in various complex relationships across the life course.

EXAMPLES OF COMPLEXITY IN LATER LIFE

The optimal developmental outcomes described in the previous section are predicated on the achievement of psychological complexity. Complexity describes dialectical polarities in the person that enable him or her to continually negotiate, and renegotiate, an optimally rewarding self-environment fit. On the most general level, these polarities involve structure *breaking* and *building* and problem *finding* and *solving*. A person with such potentialities is presumably better able to "instigate" development by flexibly working at the edges of order and novelty, without letting one or the other dominate.

The dialectical model helps to explain why such polarities are related to the development of optimal personhood. To move from boredom to flow, and from anxiety to flow, structure-breaking and structure-building qualities are needed. In the domain of social relations, agency represents the former and communion the latter (Bakan, 1966; Block, 1973). An enjoyable conversation requires participants to assert differing points of view, but it also requires the coordination of such views for common understandings. The particular qualities that represent complexity depend upon the particular domain of activity, but in general it can be stated that phases of structure breaking require a sense of integrity and order that coincide with the confidence to take risks, test one's limits, be open to new challenges, and seek the edge of chaos. Conversely, structure-building phases require a "foundation" that is ripe with diversity, novelty, and awareness, that coincides with determination, diligence, and patience to seek the edge of order. One goal of this chapter is to summarize the findings from a variety of studies, conducted by the authors and by others, that help to clarify how these abstract notions are translated into the lives of actual persons.

Therefore, we turn now to illustrate more concretely how complexity is manifested by some individuals in later life. While there are a number of dialectical models of adult thinking that are conceptually similar to our notion of complexity, there is still a need for more specificity in regard to how these dialectical thought processes are *actually manifested* by real persons. Recently, we had the opportunity to gather information relevant to this underexplored issue from a pool of interviews collected at the University of Chicago about creativity in later life. The 100 respondents in this study were individuals who had played successfully their part on the cultural stage (13 had been awarded Nobel prizes, and the rest had achieved comparable renown), but their lives can be used as examples of success in a broader sense, as modeling optimal developmental trajectories. In the interviews, they talked about many factors related to their impressive accomplishments, but more important, their words gave excellent descriptions of how complexity is enacted in actual life situations. We draw from these interviews to make more concrete the theoretical ideas that have been presented thus far. These examples of later-life complexity, in turn, set the stage for a discussion of some connections that can be made to current developmental research.

Individuals who have been recognized for their eminent creativity may seem inappropriate for illustrating complexity. Creativity is often identified with one part of the developmental dialectic we have described, namely, the part associated with the escape from accommodation, with breaking structures, finding problems, and so on. It is true that creativity is most often identified with such differentiating responses; but that is probably because many creativity studies have set out to measure creativity in this way. However, creativity sustained over a great length of time and that results in eminent achievement is not something that rests upon divergent thinking alone; convergent, integrative thinking is equally important.

A few perspectives on creativity have recognized a bipolar psychological process that is characterized by an affective immediacy related to divergent thinking, along with convergence achieved through cognitive detachment and objectivity.[4] For instance, Getzels (1975) has commented: "Despite the self-evident need for strenuous effort . . . creative thinking entails, at least in some degree, surrender to freely rising playfulness" (p. 332). Einstein's account of his creative process suggested a similar duality (see Hadamard, 1954, p. 142): a phase of "associative" play and a more "laborious" phase requiring logical coherence. Gardner (1993, Ch. 8, this Volume) has recently suggested that a playful, childlike quality survives alongside the mature intellect of siminal creators (see also Simonton, 1984). Barron (1969) described creativity as a synchrony of immediacy and detachment in a chapter entitled "Cycles of Innocence and Experience." The title is drawn from the poetry of William Blake and contrasts "prelogical" thought that is concrete, spontaneous, and free of abstraction (i.e., innocence) with thought that utilizes "reason" and therefore has a logical structure (i.e., experience).

Why is creativity associated with both immediacy and detachment? Our model suggests that qualities such as curiosity, spontaneity, and divergent thinking move toward the subjective rewards of structure breaking; conversely, qualities that enhance logic, structure, and relatedness move toward the rewards of structure building. Barron's (1969) description of creativity said much the same thing, without the emphasis on subjective experience, "In the creative process there is an incessant dialectic and an essential tension between two seemingly opposed dispositional tendencies: the tendency towards structuring and integration and the tendency towards disruption of structure and diffusion. . . . The task is to avoid sacrificing one possibility to the other. We must be able to use discipline to gain greater freedom . . . tolerate diffusion, and even occasionally invite it, in order to achieve a more complex integration (pp. 177–179).

Seven Dimensions of Complexity

We might summarize the traits involved in optimal development by concentrating on seven polar dimensions. This number is somewhat arbitrary and could be expanded or

---

[4] Although the focus here, as in much of the chapter, is on psychological processes, creativity cannot be reduced to this level.

reduced depending upon the amount of detail we wish to observe.

A central polarity that surfaced in the University of Chicago study was the combination of *agency* and *communion,* that is, the drive toward both independence and interdependence (see Bakan, 1966). This is often seen as an "androgynous" trait, in that it combines elements traditionally associated with both males and females. Why has androgyny been linked to positive developmental outcomes (Baumrind, 1989), as well as to eminent achievement (Spence & Helmreich, 1978)? Our perspective suggests that both characteristics play a role in negotiating optimal experience through structure changing and building; therefore, persons with a predominance of either attribute (i.e., a highly sex-typed individual) are at a disadvantage, at least in domains of activity where these qualities are especially important for competent performance.

One such domain is interpersonal relations or, more concretely, the act of communicating. Skills of communication are essential for playing one's role on the cultural stage, no matter what that role is. It is equally central to business management (Leavitt, Pondy, & Boje, 1989), to the emotional well-being of families (Larson & Richards, 1994), and to political leadership (Gardner, 1995; Kouzes & Posner, 1995).

For instance, students who cannot speak their mind to a teacher (agency) or listen to what that teacher has to say (communion) will not get the most out of the relationship; neither will the teacher. The teacher or student, therefore, who is capable of agency and communion in interpersonal communication—"speaking" as an individual and "listening" in a posture of openness to the other—would presumably be at an advantage for learning from such communication and for experiencing optimal rewards in the process. Charles Cooley (1961), though not discussing androgyny or optimal experience, said much the same thing about the optimally healthy person. After suggesting that males were, in general, less socially impressible and more inclined to an aggressive, solitary frame of mind than females, he commented: "So long as a character is open and capable of growth it retains . . . impressibility, which is not weakness unless it swamps the assimilating and organizing faculty. I know men whose character is proof of stable and aggressive character who have an almost feminine sensitiveness regarding their seeming to others. Indeed, if one sees a man whose attitude towards others is always assertive, never receptive, he may be confident that man will never go far, because he will never learn much. In character, as in every phase of life, health requires a just union of stability with plasticity" (p. 828).

In our interviews with persons who had successfully negotiated adult roles, the combination of agency and communion was often evident. For instance, the path-breaking historian John Hope Franklin told about a memorable teaching experience that involved taking a graduate seminar to North Carolina to study the Reconstruction period. The class was exploring the idea advanced by a book claiming that segregation, and the Jim Crow laws of the 1880–1890s, were relatively new and therefore not "sanctified by age." When asking one of the students how he was progressing, Franklin recalled:

> His eyes were just sparkling. . . . He had found practices, as well as laws, segregating blacks and whites from much earlier. . . . And so he was saying that [the author's] thesis was collapsing. That was an overstatement to be sure. He was overly enthusiastic, but he was excited, and I got excited about a finding like that. . . . of course, [the author] had made some exceptions . . . and this [the student's findings] fell, in part, in the excepted category. But it doesn't detract from the fact that he was excited. And I was excited because he was excited, you see?

In the anecdote, Franklin reveals subtle and complex social skills. He listens to his student with an attitude of acceptance and shared enthusiasm, without, for the moment, judging or correcting his student's overly enthusiastic response. By being unobtrusive, receptive, and patient—in other words, by manifesting some of the key qualities of communion—Franklin was facilitating his student's agency and joyful discovery. Although aware that the student was overly enthusiastic, and somewhat in error about the facts, Franklin decided that the joyful moment was better left alone because the student would need to draw on that excitement to complete the hard work that lay ahead. Franklin continued:

> Those students who will do the long haul are always willing to put the time and attention to the solution that the problem requires; one has to continue to be patient. . . . And that means that the student can't fudge or cheat or stretch his materials. He's got to stick with what the findings are. In my teaching I always give examples of that sort of thing

among reputable historians. Not that I'm trying to debunk or anything like that, but I will point to a passage of widely and highly respected work and indicate to them just the way in which this particular historian misrepresented, and in some instances, prevaricated about the facts. I go back and show them what the facts were. Those are things I think are important.

Thus, the student's excitement stands, for the moment, but it will not stand in the way of the facts. Eventually, through more assertive episodes of instruction, Franklin demands that students coordinate their affectively charged insights with the careful work that distinguishes the scholar. In this way, Franklin balances communion and agency: sometimes he listens to students to support their individuality, but at other times he speaks from a position of authority so that students must adopt a mode of communion and listen to him. Given his complex teaching style, it is not surprising that Franklin said of his over 50 years of teaching that it is "the thing that I like most of all."[5]

A second polarity that emerged from the interviews involved the productive tension in work between *passionate investment* and *detached objectivity*. One of the best examples of this combination emerged from an interview with another leading historian, Natalie Davis. Her awareness of this dialectical tension in her working style was unusually clear:

Well, there're two different things—they overlap. One is this intense interest in finding out what was going on in the past. . . . I like to take mysteries to solve and I'm just very, very intrigued. . . . There is a kind of a rush of affect about it that I think is even more than curiosity. . . . I often say that I

---

[5] We will have more to say later in the chapter about this interpersonal dynamic, and about how qualities such as agency and communion in children may be nurtured in family interaction. For instance, a mother's communion has often acted as a buffer for the father's agency, and vice versa. This traditional, sextyped alliance is but one "solution" for creating a family context that spares children the fate of growing up in a home that overemphasizes one or the other quality and thus forces children into *one pattern of response*. We will return to this observation when considering how early experience within the family may have consequences for attaining complexity in later life. For now, we point out that parents with androgynous parenting styles have reported *more enjoyment in parenting* (Lamb, 1982).

love what I'm doing and I love to write. . . . It's the curiosity part that pushes me to think about ways of finding out about something that I thought, or previous people thought, or people could not find out about, or ways of looking at a subject in ways that had never been looked at before. That's what keeps me running back and forth to the library and just thinking and thinking and thinking.

Equally as important as affect, however, is a mode of *detachment* that allows the person to make sure that the enthusiasm fits reality.

It is very important to find a way to be detached from what you write . . . to let you work out the criticism. You can't be so identified with your work that you can't accept criticism and response. . . . The side of me that is more . . . detached tries to let the situation that I'm writing about, and its complexities . . . just be. The danger of too much affect is not only that the self gets too involved in it where we can't take criticism . . . but also that there's too much restructuring of the people around your own investment.

When asked about how these modes fit together, she elaborated:

It is not as difficult now to be of several minds when I'm writing something: the side that's absolutely carried away, floating along with the project, and the side that's also detached and looking at myself. . . . They fit together. I don't feel it's one phase or the other. . . . It's immense curiosity in the beginning . . . you find all this stuff and then you begin to shape it. . . . The movement between identification, affect on one end, and detachment on the other, it has always got to be. And I feel this is present from the beginning, this kind of vacillation . . . the positioning of myself with different vantage points.

These passages provide a compelling illustration of complexity in action. Davis's passion and curiosity invite differentiation and save her work from tedium and rigidity; her detachment, in contrast, begins the process of criticism and the shaping of the multiple pieces into an organization that is not characterized by premature closure. In Davis's words, moments of synchrony between these two modes achieve a *multiple vision*, or being of "two minds" at once. Having these two vantage points prevents the work from being either conventional or idiosyncratic and allows it to develop and to grow.

A third polarity is related to the previous one, and can be described as the combination of *divergent* and *convergent* thinking. Convergent thinking involves the ability to find commonalities in varied information; it is a rational, problem-solving orientation representative of the kind of intelligence that is often measured by IQ tests. Convergent thinkers have, so to speak, internalized the social mind; their thoughts usually can be predicted from knowing what others have thought. In contrast, divergent thinking is oriented toward individuality and problem finding. In involves fluency, or the ability to generate many ideas, explore multiple perspectives, make unusual associations, and so on (Guilford, 1967; Runco, 1991). This ability has been thought to be synonymous with creative thinking.

Divergent thinking, however, is not much use without convergent thinking as a counterbalance, and vice versa. This point came across in the remarks of another eminent scholar, the historian William McNeill. He described the starting point for his work as a process that led to "finding one's bent." Once an idea appeared in his mind, he found that it would spontaneously "crop up" in many different contexts, including some where he did not expect to find it. At some point in this divergent, differentiating process, however, a more convergent frame of mind was needed to gauge how the idea fit with reality. The later mode helped to bring closure and required more meticulous work, self-criticism, and intellectual integrity. The following quotation discusses this coordination of divergence (openness) and convergence (closure):

> I've looked at myself and my colleagues and thought about what it is that makes some people able to get things done, write books, write articles, complete tasks, and someone else of equal intelligence, perhaps of superior intelligence, never quite gets things done—he wastes time, he throws his time away, deadlines go past and still he isn't done. I think the most important discrimination involves two things. One is the capacity to focus attention—called attention span in small children—which varies enormously. There are people who are always looking for an interruption and run off like that [snaps fingers] given the possible chance. You have to have tunnel vision. . . . The other thing is that you can handle the hypercriticism. . . . I know some of my colleagues who had extremely powerful and original minds, but who looked at what they had written and always said "it's not good enough." That is hypercriticism and they're really frozen by their own critical capacity. There is a nice balance—surely you want to

be critical of what you've done, rewrite it, think it through carefully, not splash it on to a page and say that's it. But too much criticism can be self-destructive, and too much openness can be self-destructive. You have to have a balance, a certain openness up to a certain point, and then get it done, and be willing when it comes time to do it, to say . . . "I'm going to lock on this task now, it's time to do it" . . . . [It is] closing things off at the right time, and not letting your critical faculty get so acute, so sharp that you can't get anything done. Both extremes I've seen act destructively upon . . . achievement. . . . They can be obstructive, perhaps, not destructive, but obstructive. . . . I think if you just study people around you reflecting on those who do and those who don't accomplish things they want to, these are the two pitfalls [too open, or too closed] that I've become aware of, things that obstructed very competent minds from achieving that which they wished to do.

A fourth polarity is again related to the previous two. Similar to the polarities of attachment/detachment and divergent/convergent thinking is the coordination of *playfulness* and *discipline*. The sociologist David Reisman, for instance, succinctly described such a synthesis in his comment that he "wanted at the same time to be irresponsible and responsible." The sculptor Nina Holton articulated in more detail the need for a sense of play and work to permeate the creative process:

> Tell anybody you're a sculptor and they'll say "Oh, how exciting, how wonderful." And I tend to say "What's so wonderful?" I mean, it's like being a mason. Or being a carpenter, half the time. But they don't wish to hear that because they really only imagine the first part, the exciting part. But, as Kruschev once said, that doesn't fry pancakes, you see. That germ of an idea does not make a sculpture which stands up. It just sits there. So, the next stage, of course, is the hard work. Can you really translate it into a piece of sculpture? Or will it be a wild thing which only seemed exciting while you were sitting in the studio alone? Will it look like something? Can you actually do it physically? Can you, personally, do it physically? What do you have by way of materials? So, the second part is a lot of hard work. And sculpture is that, you see. It is the combination of wonderful wild ideas and then a lot of hard work.

A third instance of this polarity was expressed by Jacob Rabinow, one of the most prolific inventors in the world. When working on a project that required more discipline than playful intuition, he would use a mental "trick" to slow himself down:

> Yeah, there's a trick I pull for this. When I have a job to do like that, where you have to do something that takes a lot of effort, slowly, I pretend I'm in jail. Don't laugh. And if I'm in jail, time is of no consequence. In other words, if it takes a week to cut this, it'll take a week. What else have I got to do? I'm going to be here for 20 years. . . . See? This is a kind of mental trick. Because otherwise you say, "My God, it's not working," and then you make mistakes. But the other way, you say time is of absolutely no consequence. People start saying how much will it cost me in time? If I work with somebody else it's 50 bucks an hour, a hundred dollars an hour. Nonsense. You just forget everything except that it's got to be built. And I have no trouble doing this. I work fast, normally. But if something will take a day gluing and then next day I glue the other side—it'll take two days—it doesn't bother me at all.

A fifth polarity that is less obviously related to the preceding ones is the coordination of *extroversion* and *introversion*. It is not uncommon that particular individuals prefer to be either at the center of action or at a spot along the periphery that allows them to observe what is going on. Generally people tend to be either on one or the other side of this dimension; in fact, whether one is extroverted or introverted is held to be one of the basic and most enduring traits of personality (McCrae & Costa, 1984; Costa & McCrae, 1980). Complex persons, on the other hand, seem to enjoy both the company of other people or solitude, depending on the demands of the moment. The physicist and writer Freeman Dyson, for instance, pointed to the door of his office and said:

> Science is a very gregarious business. It is essentially the difference between having this door open and having it shut. When I am doing science I have the door open. I mean, that is kind of symbolic, but it is true. You want to be, all the time, talking with people. Up to a point you welcome being interrupted because it is only by interacting with other people that you get anything interesting done. It is essentially a communal enterprise. . . . There are new things happening all the time and you should keep abreast and you keep yourself aware of what is going on. You must be constantly talking. But, of course, writing is different. When I am writing I have the door shut, and even then too much sound comes through, so, very often when I am writing I go and hide in the library

where nobody knows where I am. It is a solitary game. So, I suppose that is the main difference. But, then, afterwards, of course the feedback is very strong . . . and you get a tremendous enrichment of contacts as a result. Lots and lots of people write me letters simply because I have written books which address a general public, so I get into touch with a much wider circle of friends. So it's broadened my horizons very much. But that is only after the writing is finished and not while it is going on.

In this comment, contact with people—talking, listening—is identified with keeping abreast of new things and different points of view. While interaction is a process of letting in information, closing the door for solitude is a process of limiting information. The door, so to speak, acts as a boundary between self and other much as intellectual detachment creates "distance" from spontaneous action so that feedback can be integrated. Others have noted that social interaction is a dialectical process between forces driving people together and apart, and either excessive openness or closedness has detrimental effects on relationships and personal growth (Altman, 1975; Altman, Vinsel, & Brown, 1981). An excessive orientation toward extroversion or toward introversion reduces our flexibility to negotiate a rewarding self-environment fit; it makes us more predictable, less sensitive to the moment, and therefore less complex in response to the variable needs of the situation. The introvert may forfeit the opportunity to grow because of lack of stimulation, and the extrovert because he or she does not take time out to reflect on experience.

The following quote from Piaget (1952) fits well with Dyson's description of the dialectic of contact and solitude: "It is true that I am sociable and like to teach or to take part in meetings of all kinds, but I feel a compelling need for solitude and contact with nature. After mornings spent with others, I begin each afternoon with a walk during which I quietly collect my thoughts and coordinate them, after which I return to the desk at my home in the country. . . . it is this dissociation between myself as a social being and as a "man of nature" (in whom Dionysian excitement ends in intellectual activity) which has enabled me to surmount a permanent fund of anxiety and transform it into a need for working" (p. 55).

A sixth polarity might be described in terms of the interconnection between periods of *energy* and *quietude*. As one might expect, many of those interviewed for the study worked long hours with great concentration and intensity; however, this did not mean that they were slavishly tied to their work. On the contrary, it was not uncommon to come away from interviews with the impression of persons who were unhurried and at peace with themselves. It is especially startling to hear people with a lifetime of exceptional accomplishments to their credit describe themselves as fundamentally lazy. Only a self-imposed daily discipline, they say, kept them from giving in to the lackadaisical side of their nature.

Several told stories that helped to explain these apparently contradictory traits, stories that portrayed a harmonious interweaving of activity and rest. For instance, the economist Kenneth Boulding described working in beautiful, natural settings by "writing" with a tape recorder while looking at a mountain stream. And there were numerous stories of intense periods of work interspersed with naps, walks, bike rides, gardening, chopping wood, and other diversions that had more than a restorative relation to work. The important theme that emerged linking these diverse anecdotes was that the energy of these persons was not controlled entirely by external schedules. Rather, they instinctively knew when to focus their attention and when to relax it; several commented that they had "mastered their own time." They considered the rhythm of activity and idleness to be important for the success of their work, and they learned such strategies from trial and error. The Canadian novelist Robertson Davies gave the following entertaining example:

> Well, you know, that leads me to something which I think has been very important in my life, and it sounds foolish and rather trivial. But I've always insisted on having a nap after lunch, and I inherited this from my father. One time I said to him, "You know, you've done awfully well in the world. You came to Canada as an immigrant boy without anything and you have done very well. What do you attribute it to?" And he said, "Well, what drove me on to be my own boss was that the thing that I wanted most was to be able to have a nap every day after lunch." And I thought, "What an extraordinary impulse to drive a man on!" But it did, and he always had a twenty-minute sleep after lunch. And I'm the same. And I think it is very important. If you will not permit yourself to be driven and flogged through life, you'll probably enjoy it more.

Finally, complexity was manifested by attitudes toward work that were at once *iconoclastic* and *traditional,* oriented toward blazing new trails while preserving the integrity of their respective domains of action. Contrary to the modern prejudice that holds that old ideas are probably wrong, and that anything new must be better than whatever is old, these individuals understood that ideas and practices that have been passed down through the generations must have had some advantages or they would not have been preserved, whereas novelties have not yet stood the test of time.

Without question, a strong and independent ego characterized many of those we interviewed; yet so did humbleness and a clear awareness that in their work they "stood on the shoulders of giants," and that their achievements were made possible only by the tradition in which they were trained. Confidence often fed into an aggressive, iconoclastic disposition; for instance, the Nobel-prize winning economist George Stigler stated:

> I'd say one of the most common failures of able people is a lack of nerve. And they'll play safe games. They'll take whatever the literature's doing and add a little bit to it. . . . So there's a safe game to play. In innovation, you have to play a less safe game, if it's going to be interesting. It's not predictable that it'll go well.

But innovation for its own sake does not make sense, except in relation to the tradition of thought that provides the background against which novelty can be recognized. The artist Eva Zeisel produces ceramics that have been recognized by the Museum of Modern Art in New York as masterpieces of contemporary design, yet she feels rooted to the artistic folk tradition in which she grew up as a young girl in the early decades of the century. She shows a keen awareness of the interplay between innovation and tradition in the following excerpt:

> This idea to create something different is not my aim, and shouldn't be anybody's aim. Because, first of all, if you are a designer or a playful person in any of these crafts, you have to be able to function a long life, and you can't always try to be different. I mean different from different from different . . . to be different is a negative motive, and no creative thought or created thing grows out of a negative impulse. A negative impulse is always frustrating. And to be different means not like this and not like that. And the "not like"—that's why postmodernism, with the prefix of "post," couldn't work. No negative impulse can work, can produce any happy creation. Only a positive one.

Dialectical Thinking and Optimal Experience

The concepts of agency, passion, divergent thinking, playfulness, extroversion, iconoclasm, and energy share common features, as do communion, detachment, convergent thinking, discipline, introversion, tradition, and quietude. This, of course, is partly due to the selective focus that was brought to bear upon the interviews; in other words, to some extent we found in the interviews what we were looking to find. But there must be more to these polarities; countless related ones have surfaced in many fields of study and in different religions, mythologies, and philosophies in the East and the West. They are present in the Buddhist philosophy associating the optimal experience of Nirvana with the middle path between the so-called yang qualities of the male (e.g., dominance, activity, aggression) and the yin qualities of the female (e.g., passivity, receptivity, yielding) (Kuo, 1976). Notions of dialectical opposition are also woven into the fabric of Western thought from early philosophers such as Anaximander and Heraclitus, through Aristotle and Plato, and continuing through Marx, Hegel, and others (see Adler, 1927; Rychlak, 1976). Such oppositions have also characterized some of the most prominent theories of human development, from Freud's notions of the ego mediating demands from the id and superego to Piaget's dialectical model that we discussed earlier in some detail (see also Lerner, 1976; Riegel, 1973).

The emergence of related dialectical themes from so many different time periods and cultures provides a compelling reason for theorists of human development to continue to puzzle over their meanings. Our interpretation of the polarities culled from the interviews emphasizes the phenomenological perspective that we have tried to develop in this chapter. It looks across all of the complementary pairs and asks: How is each related to the optimal experience associated with structure changing and building, and thus with moving beyond boredom and anxiety? A phenomenological interpretation cannot provide a comprehensive explanation for the existence of these various polarities, but it does provide an often overlooked entry point for theorists and researchers who are interested in exploring dialectical themes.

Table 11.1 summarizes the contrasting traits that were illustrated by the interviews, and it suggests in general terms how they relate to our experiential model. If one of the most important goals of development is a person's

TABLE 11.1   Contrasting Traits Conducive to Optimal Development in Later Life

Qualities Associated with Escaping Boredom through Seeking New Challenges	Qualities Associated with Overcoming Anxiety through Developing New Skills
Agency	Communion
Passion	Detachment
Divergent thinking	Convergent thinking
Playfulness	Discipline
Extroversion	Introversion
Energy	Quietude
Iconoclasm	Tradition

flexibility in adjusting to ever new situations (Kelly, 1955; Lerner, 1984), then the material from the interviews attests to potential for human flexibility in later life. But more important, it helps to explain how experience is optimized by avoiding the boredom of overly integrated states and the anxiety of overly differentiated ones. In other words, the polarities are instructive for understanding the process of finding challenges and building skills, and thus also for understanding the temporary equilibrium of challenges and skills that trigger flow experiences.

Why, for instance, has John Hope Franklin enjoyed teaching so much? How are the qualities of agency and communion related to his enjoyment of teaching? A phenomenological interpretation suggests that his complex teaching style was *self-correcting*, thus allowing him to avoid the negative experiences associated with being too receptive to students or too directive toward them. The former problem plagues those who try to accommodate every encounter with the other; it transforms interaction into an activity that is experienced as overwhelming, lacking in control, and thus inviting anxiety. On the other hand, consistently ignoring the interests and points of view of others, never changing one's behavior in response to the encounter, makes interaction monotonous and boring.

Both extremes are avoided in Franklin's teaching style because he is capable, as the changing situation warrants, of shifting between the qualities of agency and communion. In the example cited earlier, he did not hesitate to be emphatic in response to his student's overly enthusiastic "discovery." He listened attentively to the student, letting him take the lead. Yet based upon knowledge gained through this episode, Franklin will be better able to find the right time to insist that the student check his facts. In this way, his agency as a teacher is supported by insights gained through communion. And the same can be stated in reverse: Franklin's responsiveness to his student was initially set up by taking his class to North Carolina and assigning the study of the Reconstruction period. In this way, the polarity of agency and communion helped to negotiate the most rewarding fit between teacher and student and presumably made this experience of teaching more enjoyable.

A similar reasoning would hold for the other polarities. The process of work (e.g., writing, research, sculpting) was presumably more rewarding for those who described various combinations of playfulness with discipline, passion with detachment, and so on, because of the greater flexibility in forging a self-environment fit. For instance, Davis's notion of observing immediacy (i.e., being of two minds at once) allowed her to recognize problems as they arose in the spontaneous course of working. Curiosity elicited a need for detachment to shape the material generated in this exploratory mode; this feedback from active engagement led to the discovery of problems that needed to be recognized and solved. Borrowing a phrase from the philosopher and theologian Paul Tillich (Gilkey, 1990), it might be said of Davis and others who expressed similar dialectical themes that their *objectivity was based on intense subjectivity*. And the converse of this statement is likewise relevant: *their subjectivity was based on intense objectivity*. In other words, it was through recognizing and solving problems (e.g., through critical revision of written work, "tricking" themselves into more patient modes of work, closing the door for solitude) that they constructed the skills and sense of confidence that, in turn, supported modes of spontaneous exploration.

That subjectivity and objectivity must be coordinated to sustain involvement does not explain how or why this combination facilitates flow experiences. The following analogy is helpful in this regard. Imagine that you are playing a game of bridge or chess. Part of the enjoyment of the game derives from making the best decisions in terms of the rules of the game. In fact, without following the rules scrupulously, one could not even play, let alone enjoy it. Yet if all one had to do was follow a prescribed script, the game would not be enjoyable either. Within the rules there must be space for uncertainty, for individual style, for taking a risk, for expressing one's preferences.

The same is true of interactions in general: one cannot enjoy a conversation unless one pays attention to the other's words and expressions; yet one also has to have an

opportunity to express one's own emotions and ideas. An enjoyable novel has a strong plot and clearly delineated characters that create a concrete, objective world of their own. Yet to be enjoyable, the novel must also leave space for the reader to project his or her imagination between the lines, so that the reading becomes a process of cocreation, rather than the passive decoding of the author's intentions. In each of these instances, enjoyment follows from the dynamic interplay between subjectivity and objectivity, and it is this that leads to higher levels of complexity.

In summary, the polarities described above instigate a person's development while optimizing his or her experiences; each describes, albeit in different ways and in regard to different activities, a flexibility in negotiating a fit between self and environment (for further discussion of goodness-of-fit models see Lerner, 1984; Thomas & Chess, 1977).[6] One extreme of each polarity describes the more aggressive movement of self into environment (i.e., assimilation that moves toward accommodation), and the other half describes the receptive movement of environment into self (i.e., accommodation that moves toward assimilation). A person who is able to enact both processes at the same time can (a) effectively counterbalance the movement toward differentiation with integration, and vice versa; (b) avoid the loss of psychic energy associated with persistent boredom or anxiety; and (c) better direct and invest attention in rewarding and growth-enhancing activities.

Complexity and Wisdom

We have seen earlier that of the roles available in the cultural repertoire for an older person, perhaps the one that best captures the optimal developmental outcome is the notion of *wisdom*. We now return to examine more closely what this concept entails and how it is related to the dynamics of complexity developed in the previous section.

Wisdom as a quality of the long-lived person in a community is a theme that repeatedly occurs in Eastern and Western cultures. Such persons are thought to have a special insight that enables them to make or advise the "best"

---

[6] Lerner (1984), in addition, contains an in-depth, multidisciplinary look at human plasticity, its foundation in evolutionary processes, and the developmental importance of flexible self-regulation.

course of action in a given set of circumstances. The transmission of this idea across countless generations and societies argues for its validity on evolutionary grounds. In other words, just as biological information that helps survival is transmitted from one generation to the next, it is reasonable to believe that the cultural transmission of this concept, with its rich web of meaning, is important for similar reasons (Csikszentmihalyi & Rathunde, 1990).

There are many names by which a wise person is known: mentor, sage, counselor, elder, teacher, and so on. All of them connote one attribute that we believe is central: *an ability to select, or help others select, a course of action that is optimal for survival and growth, based upon insight in regard to the relevant life processes.* The wise person, in the broadest sense, is able to give good counsel about solving fundamental problems of living (Baltes, Ch. 18, this Volume). Such counsel, in both the East and the West, has historically been linked to reflection on life experiences; through reflecting upon the successes and failures in a long life, the wise person develops a *meta-awareness of the process of the self-environment relationship* (Rathunde, in press-c). A wise teacher, for instance, has been described as unobtrusive, discrete, and patient, qualities that facilitate the joyful self-discovery of younger individuals by allowing them to make mistakes that further their growth (Chinen, 1984; Clayton & Birren, 1980). Such decisions of noninterference (or interference) are based upon a superior awareness of complex interpersonal processes, as apparently was the case with the historian John Hope Franklin's interaction with his student.

A central characteristic of wisdom, mentioned earlier, is the ability to transcend narrow, specialized thinking and to see events within their broader contexts. John Reed, CEO of Citicorp and one of the most astute and successful captains of finance, describes his ways of approaching problems:

I have always been a person who had to understand the context within which I operate. Some people are perfectly capable of coming in and saying, "Gee, the cars are going out with bent fenders, what do I have to do to get rid of that?" and they'll just figure out what machine is bending the fender. It'll never interest them who designed the car, who is going to own it, or any of the other externalities. I'm not that way at all. I'll work a problem, but in order for me to identify with it, I have to have a context. So I get curious: Who is going to

drive the car? Why was it designed this way? Does the bending of the fender have to do with the design? That is the pattern of my thought process—I have always tried to put it into a context.

It is important to note that Reed does not claim that his holistic, contextualized approach makes him a more successful businessman; in fact, he provides examples of very effective CEOs whose tunnel vision expresses only convergent thinking. But he claims that personally he enjoys the more complex contextual approach and could not think otherwise. (Of course, to continue in his role, Reed has to satisfy the objective rules expected of a person in his position, and in fact, during the last four years, the value of his company's stock appreciated by over 400%.)

Contemporary research on wisdom suggests useful standards for the process of optimal human development. Sternberg (1990) describes wisdom, in contrast to intelligence and creativity, in the following way: "The wise person seeks to understand the meaning and limitations of this [existing] knowledge. The intelligent person seeks to make optimal use of this knowledge. The creative person, though, wishes to be freed from this knowledge" (p. 153). Using the analogy of three branches of government, Sternberg associates wisdom with a *judicial* function of mental self-government, intelligence with an *executive* function, and creativity with a *legislative* function. Such a tripartite schema is consistent with what has been said thus far about complex systems. A creative/legislative response represents the movement toward differentiation, or the attempt to go beyond what is known and to generate novelty; an intelligent/executive response, in contrast, can be thought of as the movement toward integration, in that it seeks consistency based upon establishing clear and predictable parameters for action. Finally, a wise/judicial response expresses a contextual evaluation of the process of knowing and therefore an understanding of the strengths and limitations of legislative/creative and executive/intelligent responses.

Attaining wisdom, then, allows the person to combine these self-governing functions in a way that is optimal for development. A creative response may generate movement toward change, but for this reason it may not be useful in situations that call for decisive action. An intelligent response may reinforce consistency, but would be inadequate for generating new ideas. A wise response would reflect an awareness of how each function compensated for the limitations of the other: intelligence would be rigid if not informed by creativity, and creativity would lead to chaos if not reined in by the focus of intelligence. In the final analysis, it is wisdom that takes into account specific self-environment circumstances, evaluates them in terms of process, and thus gains oversight as to when creative responses must give way to more intelligent ones, and vice versa. A wise response would therefore reflect what Rogers called the predictable unpredictability of the fully functioning person: whether a particular response (i.e., seeking change or stability) is appropriate may not be known in advance; yet the action that best fits the situation at hand will reliably be chosen, and such actions may reflect either continuity or discontinuity (see also Lerner & Busch-Rossnagel, 1981). Thus, wisdom is yet another way to describe the flexibility of the complex person who finds the best path toward growth and optimal experience (see also Rathunde, 1995).

Recently, a number of researchers investigating adult development and *postformal cognition* have similarly depicted the flexibility and the dialectic performance of so-called wise persons (Brent & Watson, 1980; Clayton & Birren, 1980; Holliday & Chandler, 1986; Kramer, 1983; Labouvie-Vief, 1980, 1982; Pascual-Leone, 1990; Sinnott, 1984). Labouvie-Vief (1990), for instance, notes the dualities described by Piaget (e.g., assimilation and accommodation), by Freud (e.g., primary and secondary processes), by James (e.g., the spontaneous "I" and the conceptual "me"), and even by contemporary neuropsychologists who contrast two different anatomically and chemically based processing systems (see Tucker & Williamson, 1984). She utilizes the historical distinction between *mythos* and *logos* to label these dual modes. Mythos signifies *a close identification of the self with the object of thought* (i.e., a mode of subjectivity where knower and known are indivisible); logos signifies the use of reason, or *the ability of thought to separate subject and object,* to logically analyze a relationship.

Labouvie-Vief (1990) conceives wisdom as *reconnecting* these two important ways of relating to the world. Traditionally, they are often set against each other and dichotomized. Thus, mythos has come to be identified with emotion, the body, subjectivity, and other so-called feminine characteristics; logos, in contrast, because of its correspondence to rational thought, the mind, objectivity, and so on, has been perceived as more masculine.[7] This is also the dichotomy that underlies the gender differentiation of children in our culture (Gilligan, 1982; Gilligan, Lyons, & Hanmer, 1990). If wisdom reconnects these modes by looking beyond their illusory polarization, then such a description comes close to the meaning of complexity.

Others have identified related polarities that are characteristic of wisdom. Meacham (1983) has described a balance of *mature faith* and *cautiousness;* Erikson et al. (1986) discuss the same idea as the blending of *trust* and *skepticism.* Trust and faith allow one to engage activities wholeheartedly and with spontaneity that leads to new ideas and connections; skepticism and caution, in contrast, slow down this movement to integrate the emergent connections in a way that best cuts with the grain of reality. The dissociation of these qualities not only describes a condition that has negative consequences for individuals, it also sheds light on unwise practices in larger social system. For instance, Tillich's project of synthesizing objectivity and subjectivity implied a cultural critique. He suggested that modern science, by overemphasizing the scientist's need to be detached to know the object (i.e., by ignoring the reverse fact that subjectivity provides the basis for objectivity), has primarily identified itself with the objective-detachment pole of the dialectic, resulting in the disassociation of technical knowledge from human concerns and interests. This, in turn, has resulted in the many current problems and dangers associated with the undirected use of technology.

In summary, wisdom is a cultural mask that depicts the fullest expression of what has been described here as complexity. The wise person develops, to a greater extent than most, the capacity to move toward optimal experiences by understanding the dynamic relation of self and environment. This is perhaps why wisdom is often discussed in the context of states of transcendence or ecstasy. The wise person, presumably as the result of reflection on a long and

---

[7] It is worth noting that this alignment of objectivity and subjectivity with masculine and feminine characteristics is best suited to instrumental domains, where it is men who have traditionally had to learn to accommodate to reality demands; this alignment would often be reversed in expressive, social activities, where women have had to assume more objective modes of self-sacrifice.

rich life, understands the twin needs for integration and differentiation: the need to accommodate to avoid anxiety and disorder, and the need to assimilate to avoid boredom and stagnation. Such persons are best prepared to turn any situation to their advantage by consistently moving toward synchrony, but in an unpredictable fashion that depends specifically upon time, place, and context.

Descriptions of the wise person, like descriptions of any complex system, will of necessity be paradoxical, and are best expressed through dialectical notions that emphasize process, opposition, and interaction in specific circumstances. Thus, developmental research aimed at better understanding such instigative characteristics of persons will undoubtedly prove to be difficult. Nevertheless, productive research is already proceeding under the aegis of wisdom as a potential adult outcome (e.g., Baltes, this Volume). A phenomenological interpretation of wisdom may add to this growing body of work. In addition to empirical studies, more hermeneutic studies of wisdom in various cultures and historical periods would also be useful.

Complexity, Ego Control, and Ego Resiliency

Besides theory and research on wisdom there are other connections that might be drawn between the notion of complexity and the literature on adult development. One related perspective focuses on ego control and ego resiliency (Block & Block, 1980). While work in this area does not address the motivational aspects of optimal experience, it does share a conceptual overlap with the ideas presented here in three important ways: (a) a focus on the dynamics of change and process (e.g., assimilation and accommodation); (b) a focus on personal characteristics that identify different capacities for the flexible use of assimilating and accommodating processes for adaptation to environmental circumstances; and, important for our focus on child development later in the chapter, (c) an attention to family dynamics and how socialization impacts a person's flexibility.

Developmental research has often investigated self-control, willpower, postponement of immediate gratification, tolerating frustration, and related processes (e.g., Brandstädter, this Volume). Research in these areas has proceeded in three directions under the intellectual traditions of learning theory, Vygotskian theory, and psychoanalytic theory (see Harter, 1983). Freud linked self-control to ego strength and the person's ability to adhere to the reality principle (Freud, 1922). Work on *ego control* and *resiliency* emerges from this tradition. The former concept describes a person's capacity for self-control. Block and Block (1980) conceptualize ego control on a continuum of undercontrol to overcontrol: undercontrollers have permeable self-other boundaries in the sense that they have an inability to delay gratification, exercise caution, foresee the consequences of their actions, and thus manifest more immediate and direct manifestations of affect; overcontrollers, on the other hand, restrict spontaneous expression of affect, show excessive rigidity, and thus have a much higher threshold of response.

Although neither extreme of ego control is ideal for development, one might think of each as a "positive" characteristic that has been taken too far. For instance, undercontrollers are "open" to the other because of their permeable boundaries, but relatively closed to self-reflection; on the other hand, overcontrollers are "open" to the self because their defensive boundaries allow the self to become an object of reflection, yet they are relatively incapable of spontaneous action. Although originally a description of adult characteristics, the Blocks (1980) suggest that similar traits can be observed in children: undercontrollers are "more active, assertive, aggressive, competitive, outgoing, attention-seeking, extrapunitive, over-reactive to frustration, jealous, exploiting, and less compliant, orderly, yielding, and private than children scoring in the overcontrolled direction" (p. 68).

It is interesting to note the similarities between the characteristics of undercontrollers and overcontrollers and the polarities listed in Table 11.1. The active traits that we identified with moving toward differentiation and finding challenges (e.g., agentic, extroverted, passionate), and those identified with moving toward integration and skill building (e.g., receptive, introverted, detached) are quite similar in meaning to those used to define the two sides of ego control. It is reasonable to see the complex person as someone capable of "loosening" and "tightening" self-other boundaries depending on the particular situation. And this is similar to what the Blocks describe as ego resiliency. The concept of resiliency was derived from Lewin's (1951) notion of elasticity. "Elasticity refers to the capacity of the boundary to change its characteristic level of permeability-impermeability depending upon impinging psychological forces, and return to its original modal level of permeability after the temporary, accommodation-requiring influence is no longer pressing" (Block & Block, 1980, pp. 47–48).

High ego resiliency describes a capacity for flexible adaptation to changing life circumstances, whereas low resiliency results in "ego brittleness." By combining the implications of ego control and resiliency, the Blocks established a fourfold typology: brittle undercontrollers versus resilient undercontrollers, and brittle overcontrollers versus resilient overcontrollers. The brittle ego is subject to the potentially negative consequences of undercontrol (i.e., impulsiveness, restlessness, fidgeting), whereas the resilient ego draws on its strengths (i.e., curiosity, energy, spontaneity). Similarly, the brittle ego suffers the downside of overcontrol (i.e., anxiousness, inhibition), whereas the resilient ego can draw on its advantages (i.e., reflection, calmness, empathy).

Our descriptions of wisdom and the complex person would constitute an additional type: a person who can take advantage of the full range of permeability-impermeability in regard to self-other boundaries to attain optimal experience. Whereas the Blocks' position places a person at one or the other end of the ego control continuum, psychological complexity suggests that both ends can be part of a person's repertoire of masks, to be flexibly used when needed. Our perspective also contrasts with other personality theories that identify major traits thought to be stable during adulthood (e.g., Costa & McCrae, 1980). Such approaches may constrain measurement in ways that identify persons as consistently high or low on one trait (e.g., openness to experience), rather than conditionally high or low depending upon the quality of experience in particular contexts.

Conceptualizing high-level adult thinking in terms of a *flexible repertoire* also provides an alternative to the postmodern practice of identifying a predominant thinking style in different persons and cultures (i.e., masculine versus feminine, individualistic versus communal, and so on), and then presuming that these styles are incompatible (Perkins, 1996). Such differences can be seen as complementary parts of a repertoire. The Japanese, for instance, have a word, *kejime,* to describe the successful ability to shift between spontaneous and disciplined behavior (Bachnik, 1992). Doi (1986) views the Japanese self as organized

by the situational shifting between these two modes, referred to as *ura* (in back) and *omote* (in front), respectively. Other paired terms are used to describe *relationships* between dualities that help a person to locate particular situations on an inner/self or outer/society axis. *Kejime,* or situational shifting, is therefore a crucial social skill for the Japanese and a major pedagogical focus in Japanese education, Bachnik (1992) comments that such a conception calls into question the appropriateness of either/or frames of reference that emphasize self or society: "Shifting would require pluralistic perspectives on the self and social order that could encompass disunity and chaos as well as unity and order" (p. 4).

In this section we have attempted to illustrate more concretely some of the characteristic qualities of complex persons, namely, qualities enabling a harmonious dialectic between differentiation and integration, which lead to the ability to play more meaningful cultural roles while allowing for the development of one's unique individuality. The brief examples of later-life complexity set the stage for discussing two areas of developmental research—wisdom, and ego control and resiliency—that have explored similar themes. These areas of research afford bridges to several ideas in this chapter, and they offer the potential for expanding on them.

Characteristics that make it possible to take an active role in creating one's environment and furthering development comprise only a part, perhaps only a small part, of the vast array of biological and cultural influences on the development of the person. Nevertheless, they comprise the part that is most *human* in human development. The capacity for lifelong learning and the relative lack of "hardwired" responses to the environment are perhaps *the* distinguishing characteristics of humans. Lerner (1984) reached the same conclusion, arguing that what is optimally developed in development is the style or self-regulative capacity to adapt to unforeseen contextual conditions (i.e., changing self to fit context or context to fit self). Although such instigative characteristics are probably related to genetic predispositions (e.g., aspects of temperament may influence modal levels of openness/withdrawal, ability to focus attention, and so on; see Thomas & Chess, 1977), they are also influenced by contexts of socialization, especially the family. Thus, a better understanding of how such characteristics may emerge through child development is a question central to understanding the development of the person.

THE FOUNDATIONS OF COMPLEXITY IN CHILD DEVELOPMENT

Having sketched our ideas about adult complexity in theoretical terms and through examples of desirable outcomes, we turn our attention to examining how the foundations of complexity might be established in child development. Although it is impossible to trace with precision the evolution of the outcomes we have discussed, or support a strong causal position on the link between early experience and these outcomes, the assumption here is that our previous discussion will make it easier to identify processes in the early years that facilitate the full development of the person. Many of the presumed connections that are discussed await further research and verification. To limit the focus of the discussion, we make three additional assumptions:

1. If complex outcomes are manifested by dialectical polarities, then contexts that socialize such outcomes will presumably have a dialectical character.
2. Of the many relationships that are important for child development, one undoubtedly is foundational: *the parent-child relationship.* We therefore limit our discussion to parent-child interaction, starting in adolescence and working our way back to early childhood, and then infancy.
3. If there is a plausible link in the ontogenetic development of complexity from birth to old age, then it is reasonable to assume that human beings are prepared by evolution to (potentially) develop in such a way. Thus, we conclude the chapter by exploring the notion that complexity is a goal of human development rooted in our evolutionary history.

Guided by these limiting assumptions, this section explores the possible relationship between children's socialization and complex outcomes in adulthood. The approach taken is exploratory, with two intentions: to develop further the theoretical perspective in this chapter, and to stimulate future research on these and related issues.

The Importance of Social Context

How is a foundation for later-life complexity established in childhood? We agree with Bronfenbrenner (1992) that mature self-regulation is in large part the legacy of past social

experience: "It is true that individuals often can and do modify, select, reconstruct, and even create their environments. But this capacity emerges only to the extent that the person has been *enabled* to engage in self-directed action as a joint function not only of his biological endowment but also of the environment in which he or she developed. There is no one without the other" (pp. 223–224). As to what type of environment is optimal: "Extremes either of disorganization or rigidity in structure or function represent danger signs for psychological growth, with some intermediate degree of system flexibility constituting the optimal condition for human development" (p. 241).

Following Piaget, most research that has explored the constructive nature of thought has not so valued interpersonal processes. Theoretical work on social cognition, for instance, has focused on how internal constructions—*developed independently of contact with other people*—affect the perception and therefore the dynamics of social interaction (Kahlbaugh, 1993). Many of these theories, in addition, do not incorporate the dialectical insights of Piaget (Kuhn, 1978). Thus, few attempts have been made to theorize how thought, in general, develops out of dialectical interactions between self and other.

In part as a result of the slow assimilation of the Russian perspective on development represented by the work of Luria and Vygotsky, a greater emphasis is currently being placed on how the person develops within a sociocultural context, and how higher mental functions are "internalized" from social interaction (Bruner, 1990; Mead, 1934; Rogoff, 1990; Stern, 1985; Wertsch, 1979, 1985). The time is ripe, then, for approaches that *link dialectical developmental principles to social interaction.* Toward this end, the thought of James Mark Baldwin (1906, 1908, 1911) provides an important historical context (Kalbaugh, 1993) and critical insights for our attempt to link phenomenology to social processes.

An Extension of Baldwin's Views on Development in Context

Baldwin's thought is relevant to the concerns in this chapter for several reasons. His theory of "development" (i.e., progress in constructing "platforms" of organization) is dialectical and rests upon syntheses of dualistic oppositions. Much of what has been said earlier in regard to Piaget also applies to Baldwin: development proceeds through the interplay of a conservative, assimilating function that fits information to preexisting structures and a change-oriented accommodation function that reconstructs the subject due to opposition encountered in environment (see Broughton & Freeman-Moir, 1982).

More important for our purposes are three differences between Baldwin and Piaget. First, Baldwin was more attuned to the importance of subjective rewards associated with successful adaptation; he believed positive experiences induced repetition, and repetition led to the formation of habits. As did his colleagues John Dewey and William James, Baldwin talked at great length about *interest* as the motivating force of attention (1906, see pp. 41–44). Thus, his insights are more in line with our goal of providing a phenomenological rendering of assimilative and accommodative processes.

A second crucial difference is the way Baldwin conceptualized optimal adult development. Piaget emphasized logical thought in his final stage of formal operations and the capacity to formulate rational hypotheses about relationships in the world. In his highest stage, hyperlogic, Baldwin emphasized *an aesthetic appreciation of the world that transcends dualities.* His descriptions of this stage resemble contemporary theories on postformal operations and wisdom (Basseches, 1980; Kramer, 1983), and our earlier comments on complexity in later life: "The intuition of reality reached in aesthetic contemplation preserves all the meaning of fact or truth except its externality to experience, and all that of use or worth except its subjectivity in experience; thus essentially removing from the constitution of the real the opposition of inner and outer, subject and object" (1911, p. 256).

The most important difference between Baldwin's and Piaget's models has to do with the role of social processes. For Piaget, the quality of the social environment could affect the speed with which children develop through various stages, not the quality of the stage itself; and social processes became more important as children developed more mature forms of thought. Social processes were more integral to Baldwin's account of development. He recognized the greater novelty associated with social interaction, and therefore its more important role as a source of resistance that promotes growth: "Persons remain, even after each vital experience with them, still the unreduced; and the individual's mass of surging psychic tendencies and dispositions comes up again and yet again to the task of appropriating them in the molds of habit and recognized

fact" (1906, p. 61). Thus, one reason Baldwin located the development of the person more centrally in social interaction was because the other was more capricious, intrusive, and "self-nucleating," and therefore more of a stimulus to development.

It was through interaction that the assimilating and accommodating functions were stretched to the highest degree, and *these functions were developed from birth in coordination with a primary caretaker.* Through *imitation,* for instance, a child accommodates the other; but imitation is never "pure" in the sense of a replication because actions are infused with private meaning, and what is learned is always in relation to subjective experience. Similarly, when appropriating a word, one makes it one's own by filling it with personal intention (Bakhtin, 1981). In this way, accommodation is "creative" and not passive mimicking. Through a process of *ejecting* the self, on the other hand, the child assimilates the other on its own terms; when contradictions arise, the self is reconstructed. Thus, the dynamics of development are much like Piaget's, but relations with a primary caretaker are seen as essential to the dialectical growth of the self, and social dependency becomes essential for development to occur (see also Tobach, 1981; Tobach & Schneirla, 1968).

Interaction with a more powerful person (in relation to the child) will encourage accommodation; interaction with a less powerful person will favor assimilation. A mother might be thought of as "less powerful" when she is reactive to the wants and desires of the infant; in other words, when *she* accommodates, the child assimilates. A mother is "more powerful" when the child must accommodate, perhaps by imitating actions, reacting to verbal or physical stimulation, adjusting to schedules of feeding, and so on. One can see in this general dynamic how the dialectical growth of the self might proceed in a positive direction through the mutual give and take of mother and child, or how habits of unsuccessful assimilation or accommodation might develop through relations with an overly active or a chronically passive mother.

Stating the same using the commonsense terms *love* and *discipline*[8] to represent parenting behaviors that encourage

---

[8] Too often the word *discipline* is equated with punishment. The word is a derivation of the Latin *discipulus,* meaning pupil. This meaning reflects the idea that discipline is about *training the mind and character through experience.* Insofar as punishment furthers such training or instruction, its meaning is consistent with discipline.

assimilation and accommodation, respectively: When a parent appropriately mixes love with discipline, a child develops successful habits of assimilation and accommodation, thus making the coordination of these modes, and optimal experiences, more likely to occur. Over time, children socialized in homes that balance love with discipline develop a superior capacity to *self-regulate* their attention and respond to the environment in ways that promote optimal experience and growth. In other words, they are more likely to manifest the development-instigating characteristics that are associated with complexity.

There is a variety of ways parents might provide children with a healthy combination of love and discipline. One strategy is what we now think of as the traditional nuclear family. Fathers and mothers have historically created a well-rounded system through a division of labor: fathers play the role of disciplinarian and mothers that of nurturer (Parsons & Bales, 1955). The manifestations of such traditional sex-role divisions are apparent in parental styles of interaction. For instance, fathers, due to their active styles, are more often a source of stimulation, whereas mothers are a source of arousal modulation or comfort (Field, 1985). In general, fathers have been less sensitive to a child's perspective, and thus they have constituted a source of external challenge for the child; mothers have been more willing to subordinate their attention in support of their children's interests.[9] Although contemporary families maintain less rigid boundaries between parental roles, one still can observe strong vestiges of these historical patterns (Larson & Richards, 1994).

The traditional solution, however, is but one of many possible ones. One or both parents, or a single parent, can adopt an *androgynous* role as a nurturer and disciplinarian. Arguably, such a style holds distinct advantages for the well-timed delivery of love and discipline, and thus for achieving a more satisfying parent-child relationship (i.e., a mother would not have to rely on "Wait until your father gets home" to provide discipline, and a father would not have to use the refrain "Go ask your mother" when asked for support). It is not hard to imagine several other ways that love and discipline can be effectively combined. A nurturant family, for instance, may enroll the child in a school that is intellectually and physically rigorous. Or a child with accomplished and demanding parents may be accommodated by an attentive caregiver or by other members of the extended family. The point is not to argue for a particular family organization (although some arrangements may be advantageous); rather, the claim is that *children who develop strong habits of assimilation and accommodation in some proximal context of socialization* are more likely to develop a mature ability to self-regulate as adults.

Parent-Child Interaction and the Growth of Complexity

The above hypotheses about social interaction and dialectical development are used next to explore and integrate various perspectives on parenting over the course of child development. In the following selective review, we attempt to link parental love and discipline, or *support* and *challenge,* to three stages of child development: adolescence, early childhood, and infancy.

Parenting in Adolescence

Does a family still influence adolescent development? Do the qualities of love and discipline still matter, and in the ways discussed above? Even if interactions with parents were related to habits of self-regulation, it could be argued that patterns established in childhood would be relatively "fixed" by the teenage years; in Vygotskian (1978) terms, the "intermental" would have already become the "intramental." Furthermore, adolescents encounter a much wider social circle than young children and fall under the sway of peer influence. They have also wider unsupervised exposure to symbolic media (e.g., television, books, music, and film), as well as the effects of schooling. Despite all of the above influences, however, a great deal of research suggests that parental qualities like love and discipline (referred to by various names in the literature) are still important for adolescent development (Damon, 1983; Irwin, 1987; Maccoby & Martin, 1983).

Diana Baumrind (1987, 1989) has associated the combination of "responsiveness" and "demandingness" (i.e., authoritative parenting) with optimal competence in adolescence, operationally defined as the androgynous combination of *agency* and *communion.* Cooper and her colleagues (Cooper, Grotevant, & Condon, 1983) found

---

[9] If reacting to a "more powerful" father is associated with learning habits of accommodation, then the increasing absence of father involvement in modern homes could help to explain the apparent decline of social integration in many communities.

that the combination of *connection* and *individuality* in family interaction (i.e., listening and coordinating views, and expressing individual options) was related to adolescents' identity achievement and role-taking skills. Both of these outcomes demonstrate effective differentiating and integrating processes: identity achievement requires a period of *crisis* (i.e., the exploration of alternatives) and *commitment* (i.e., firm decisions after considering the alternatives; Marcia, 1966); role taking requires considering others' perspectives, and then integrating one's own (Cooper et al., 1983). Finally, Stuart Hauser's (1991) research has revealed how supportive *(affective enabling)* and challenging *(cognitive enabling)* "moves" in family conversations were related to higher adolescent ego development; it also seems that higher stages of ego development are increasingly dialectical in character (Kegan, 1982; Loevinger, 1966).

Our own research with families and adolescents is consistent with the above findings, although it emphasizes experiential outcome measures. For instance, talented adolescents who perceived their family contexts as supportive and challenging reported more optimal experience and interest in their daily lives, especially while doing school activities; parents perceived by their sons and daughters as supportive and challenging reported more satisfaction in their relationships with their children and in their own lives (Csikszentmihalyi et al., 1993; Rathunde, 1996). A follow-up study of a representative national cross-section of approximately 700 teenagers replicated these findings with a more diverse sample: after adjusting for the adolescents' gender, grade (sixth through twelfth), ethnic background (African American, Asian, Latino, Caucasian), and parental education, adolescents from supportive and challenging families reported more optimal experience and interest in school (Rathunde, in press).

A family environment is challenging when parents expect adolescents to take on more mature responsibilities, learn new age-appropriate skills, take risks that lead toward greater individuation, and so on. Thus, a challenging context is one wherein adolescents acquire the training effect of discipline; they "practice" reorganizing their attention, being more objective, and formulating plans of action that accommodate progressively new expectations and goals. When a parent creates a supportive environment by listening in a nonjudgmental way, allowing the adolescent to explore interests, taking care of everyday necessities that

might be distracting, and so on, an adolescent can engage the world in a way that is less self-conscious, less constrained by the demands of reality, and more attuned to his or her own subjectivity.

A supportive and challenging context thus creates the ideal conditions for assimilating and accommodating and for optimal experiences that emerge when these two modes are in equilibrium. We have found some empirical confirmation for these assertions. Family support was linked specifically to more playful, spontaneous, and affectively charged experiences, and family challenge was linked to more directive, self-conscious, goal-directed states. To the extent that these experiential states are taken to indicate assimilative and accommodative processes, respectively, a supportive and challenging family exercises both aspects of the dialectic, and thus makes it more likely that adolescents can turn boredom and anxiety into flow or interest (see Csikszentmihalyi & Rathunde, 1993; Csikszentmihalyi et al., 1993; Rathunde, 1993, in press).

Parenting in Early Childhood

If adolescent experience is tied to conditions in the home, despite the greater influence of friends, school, and the media, it is likely that the quality of younger children's experience is *even more closely tied to conditions at home.* Barbara Rogoff's (1990) research is especially relevant to this issue. She has studied parents and children in a variety of cultural settings, using a Vygotskian perspective that emphasizes the development of mind through interpersonal interaction. The primary theoretical concept in her approach is the support-challenge combination of *guided participation:* "Guided participation involves adults or children challenging, constraining, and supporting children in the process of posing and solving problems—through material arrangements of children's activities and responsibilities as well as through interpersonal communication, with children observing and participating at a comfortable but slightly challenging level" (1990, p. 18).

The basic processes of guided participation are universal. In all cultural settings, parents and children must *bridge* to a mutual interpretation of a situation that allows *intersubjectivity,* or a common focus of attention and shared presuppositions (Rogoff, Mistry, Goncu, & Mosier, 1993). Thus, all parents use some measure of support and challenge: support to bolster children's attempts to master skills, and challenge to move children toward higher levels of mastery. Support and challenge must be skillfully proportioned by adults to help children avoid situations that are over- or underchallenging. For instance, support might be manifested by simplifying the structure of a task by breaking it down into subgoals, verbally relating new tasks to old ones, carefully following a child's gaze and attention, helping a child avoid frustrating obstacles, and so on. But as a child grows more skilled, the level of challenge could be raised by asking questions that seek more information, releasing some responsibility to the child, *not* intervening when children can be successful on their own, and so on.

A parent must carefully observe a child's cues to effectively guide participation: "Interactional cues—the timing of turns, nonverbal cues, and what each partner says or does not say—are central to the achievement of a challenging and supportive structure for learning that adjusts to the learner's changes in understanding" (Rogoff, 1990, p. 104). A child might explicitly ask for more or less help, or signals could be implicit, involving a look, a gesture, listlessness, or gaze aversion. A number of studies reveal sensitive adjustment in action. For instance, effective tutors hypothesized what was the best level for intervention, and then modified their hypotheses based upon students' reactions (Wood & Middleton, 1975). Mothers assisting 6- and 9-year-old children on a classification task began by giving redundant verbal and nonverbal information; as the session continued, however, their use of redundancy decreased and only reappeared when children showed difficulty or hesitation in solving problems (Rogoff & Gardner, 1984). Finally, similar moment-to-moment dynamics were evident even at the university level when experts tutored students in the fields of chemistry, physics, computer science, and mathematics (Fox, 1988a, 1988b).

The benefits of guided participation emerge from maintaining a child/learner in the *zone of proximal development* (i.e., where the child is challenged slightly beyond his or her skill level, yet is capable of mastering the challenge with the help of a more skilled partner; see Vygotsky, 1978). According to Rogoff, this zone represents a "dynamic region of sensitivity" where development occurs, and the skills of a culture are passed from one generation to the next. From a phenomenological perspective, we would add that a child's subjective experience within this zone is very close to the more optimal, intrinsically rewarding flow experience. In the zone of proximal development, challenges

are slightly higher than skills, and the person experiences the slightly unpleasant state of *arousal,* which will change into flow if the person develops the next level of skills (Csikszentmihalyi & Rathunde, 1993). From a phenomenological perspective, it is the attraction of flow that spurs the child to move out of the zone by acquiring new skills.

A number of studies confirm that guided participation is beneficial for children's development. For instance, it has been linked to infants' and toddlers' communicative competence (Hardy-Brown, Plomin, & DeFries, 1981; Olson, Bates, & Bayles, 1984), to improvement in children's seriation skills (Heber, 1981), and to greater exploration of novel objects by 3- to 7-year-olds (Henderson, 1984a, 1984b). Wood and Middleton (1975) found that when mothers tailored their instruction to their children's needs (i.e., guiding at a slightly challenging level, adjusting their instruction to children's successes, etc.), children performed more effectively on a task of building block pyramids. Interestingly, the number of interventions a mother made did not relate to performance; rather, it was the quality of the interventions that was effective.

While guided participation is a universal process, there are important variations across cultures in terms of the goals that are valued and the means to their attainment: "A major cultural difference may lie to the extent to which adults adjust their activities to children as opposed to the extent to which children are responsible for adjusting to and making sense of the adult world" (Rogoff et al., 1993, p. 9). The former, *child-centered* pattern emphasizes parental accommodation to a child's level by joining the child in play, treating the child as a conversational peer, and so on. Such is the pattern described in the studies cited above, and it is the typical pattern manifested in middle-class families in the United States: "In the middle-class populations that have been studied, the bridge between adults' and children's points of view is often built from children's starting point, with adults building on children's perspectives by focusing on children's direction of attention and adjusting adult concepts to reach children's understanding" (p. 19).

When children are more embedded in the everyday lives and work environments of adults, they are responsible for accommodating to adults through observation and emulation. In this *adult-centered approach,* a child might be expected to speak when spoken to, reply to questions, or simply carry out directions, with adults providing helpful feedback in response to the child's efforts. This pattern has been observed in a variety of non-Western cultures such as in Kaluli New Guinea and Samoa, where children were expected to adapt to normal adult situations (e.g., caregivers modeled unsimplified utterances; Ochs & Schieffelin, 1984). It has also been observed in some African American communities where children were not encouraged to initiate dialogue with their elders and held their parents' attention longer when remaining silent (Ward, 1971), and in Eastern cultures, such as Japan, where parents stressed children's roles as apprentices to more experienced members of the community (Kojima, 1986).

The goal of parenting in Polynesia, according to Martini and Kirkpatrick (1992), is to turn children into 'enana motua, or "parent persons." To achieve this goal, socialization revolves around teaching children how to become competent householders and establish and maintain familiar relations at home, away from home, and in the broader community—while maintaining autonomy in a dense network of binding relationships. This complex balance between group participation and autonomy is further reinforced by the culture, starting with peer interaction among children (Martini, 1994).

Rogoff and her colleagues (1993) argue that people from differing communities could benefit by synthesizing child-centered and adult-centered patterns of socialization. For instance, the child-centered approach in the West is thought to have benefits for developing the "discourse of schooling," whereas the adult-centered approach helps to develop children's observational skills. By encouraging skills of observation, the adult-centered approach might help Euro-American children to better coordinate their actions with others in a group; the child-centered approach, in turn, could help traditional communities, and some minority communities in the West, to access educational opportunities that open doors to Western economic institutions that rely on assertive individuality. Later in the chapter we discuss other benefits that may result from a synthesis of these two patterns.

Parenting in Infancy

A great deal of work on parenting in infancy helps to elaborate the theoretical dynamics under discussion. For instance, Field (1985, 1987) has suggested that whereas infants are born with genetic predispositions that make them differentially responsive to stimulation in the environment (see also Eysenck, 1973; Freedman, 1979; Izard, 1977), mothers who learn their infants' stimulation and arousal modulation needs, *and who match their behavior accordingly,* provide optimal contexts for the development of secure attachment and self-regulation (see also Lewis & Rosenblum, 1974). In other words, a mother modulates her behavior to match her child's need for stimulation or comfort, thus helping the child to maintain an optimal level of arousal. Under normal circumstances, mothers and infants even achieve a synchrony in their behavioral and physiological rhythms (Brazelton, Koslowski, & Main, 1974; Field, 1985; Stern, 1974).

When a mother fails to stimulate or comfort a child in appropriate ways, the child may withdraw from interaction, show gaze aversion, negative affect, elevated heart rate, or other disturbances; such infants, when hospitalized and removed from under- or overstimulating environments, often show improvement (Field, 1987). However, if a mother *consistently* fails to develop a synchronous pattern that fits her child's needs, the child can experience behavioral and psychological disorganization, making him or her vulnerable to a number of later developmental problems. For instance, relationships have been reported between early interaction disturbances and school-age behavioral and emotional problems, including hyperactivity, limited attention span, and disturbed peer interaction (Bakeman & Brown, 1980; Field, 1984; Sigman, Cohen, & Forsythe, 1981).

Some infants (e.g., a preterm or Down syndrome baby) may be "harder to read" in terms of their arousal needs, but parents typically adapt and do a better job than strangers. Interaction coaching studies have also shown that parents can learn to be more sensitive interactive partners. For instance, when asked to mimic their infant's responses, mothers become less active behaviorally and more attentive to their infant's cues; in contrast, when asked to keep their infant's attention, they are less sensitive to infant cues and more active behaviorally (Clark & Seifer, 1983; Field, 1977). The former coaching technique therefore enhances a child-centered approach to parenting, and the latter technique encourages an adult-centered approach.

Intersubjective perspectives are also at the front line of attachment research (Bretherton, 1987). Attachment theory suggests that infants and parents are genetically prepared for mutual negotiation and cooperative action (Bowlby, 1969; for contrasting perspectives see Gottlieb et al., Ch. 5, this Volume; Thelan & Smith, Ch. 10, this

Volume; Trevarthen, 1979), and that even newborn infants are capable of experiencing a sense of emergent self-organization (Stern, 1985). What is particularly useful about attachment research is the abundant empirical and theoretical work that has addressed how early interactions affect later child development. Attachment researchers hypothesize that the quality of the early caregiver-infant interactions affects how children interpret their worlds through the development of a *working model* (see discussion below). In other words, basic styles of relating to the world are thought to be fundamentally connected to the interactive characteristics of early caregiver-infant interactions.

The term *attachment system* refers to a coherent behavioral-motivational system that is organized around a particular figure (or figures). Bowlby (1969) observed that the attachment system was *activated* by perceived danger and *deactivated* by safety. Bretherton (1987) contends that it is more helpful to think of the system as *continually active,* because this clarifies two distinct attachment phenomena: use of the caregiver as a safe base when there is perceived danger, and use of the caregiver as a launching point for exploration. Bretherton's conceptualization allows the attachment system to be seen on a continuum with other optimal arousal models discussed in this chapter. And like the other models discussed, the attachment system combines two "antithetical" human propensities: to seek continuity (comfort) in the face of overwhelming change, and change (stimulation) in the face of numbing continuity.

It is not surprising, then, that a support/challenge combination is also recognized as the most effective way to parent infants. *Secure attachment* is associated with caregiving that is supportive when it needs to be, yet challenging in terms of encouraging exploration and autonomy.[10] Such a balance helps create the synchronous patterns associated with secure attachment (Isabella & Belsky, 1991), such as those observed in feeding situations, face-to-face interactions, responses to crying episodes, and many other types of interactive behaviors (Ainsworth & Bell, 1969; Bell & Ainsworth, 1972). Asynchronous patterns leaning toward over- or understimulation, on the other hand, have been associated with insecure attachment patterns (Isabella & Belsky, 1991).

Because of the dependence of human infants on their caregivers, the latter have enormous influence on the patterning of intersubjective relations during the first year of life. Attachment theory suggests that from these relations children develop an internal working model of how the world works. Such a model serves a functional purpose: it represents reality as it is experienced and therefore allows the utilization of past experience to imagine alternatives and make decisions (Craik, 1943). In an evolutionary perspective, working models provide a survival advantage to the extent that they permit more insightful and adaptive behavior (Johnson-Laird, 1983). The adaptiveness of a model depends upon its correspondence to the actual world (i.e., what is represented has to simulate relevant aspects of the environment); the more complex a working model is, the more flexible are an organism's potential responses.

Based upon interactions with a caregiver, then, a child learns essential information about how self and other are related, and this information becomes a template for future interpretations. Distortions or disturbances in the interactive relationship result in distortions in processing information; because working models become automatic and habitual, these distortions can lead to relatively stable maladaptive patterns of development. Stern (1985) makes the provocative suggestion that when mothers consistently "overattune" or "underattune" to infant cues, they can *undermine infants' ability to evaluate their inner states.* From an experiential perspective, this result would seriously undermine later abilities to evaluate boredom and/or anxiety and respond in ways that promote flow experiences.

Also relevant from an experiential perspective are studies that show attachment patterns have carryover effects that influence children's *style* of engaging activities. For instance, secure attachment at 12 months predicted more adaptive communication in a problem-solving task too difficult for 2-year-olds to perform by themselves. Securely attached infants tried to solve the problem independently, but turned to the mother for help when they got stuck; mothers, in turn, comforted their children and helped them to focus on the task (Matas, Arend, & Sroufe, 1978). Thus, the style of engaging the task reflected the style of interaction in a securely attached dyad (i.e., exploration in a context of support). It is also noteworthy that securely

---

[10] The attachment literature typically describes optimal parenting in terms of a child-centered approach. This is underscored by the fact that most attachment researchers view material insensitivity as a mother's inability to *take the perspective of a child* (see Ainsworth, 1983).

attached toddlers displayed more enthusiasm and task enjoyment.

In summary, several perspectives on parenting in adolescence, childhood, and infancy converge around the idea that parental combinations of support and challenge create optimal contexts for child development. Studies in each area, moreover, inform the phenomenological perspective in this chapter. Combinations of parental support and challenge were associated with adolescents' reports of flow experience in school (Rathunde, 1996, in press); children's engagement in the zone of proximal development (Rogoff, 1990); toddlers' enthusiastic task performance (Matas, Arend, & Sroufe, 1978); and infants' optimal arousal (Field, 1987). Common to all the perspectives reviewed was an emphasis on children's development through intersubjective experience in the family; the historical roots of this perspective can be found in Baldwin (1906), Cooley (1902), Mead (1934), and Vygotsky (1962).

A deeper recognition of continuities across parenting studies is an important step toward more integrative theories of child development. One of the most important areas to explore, we believe, is how child-centered and adult-centered parenting use support and challenge to create optimal learning environments. In the West, it is often taken for granted that a child-centered approach is the best way to socialize children. However, adult-centered approaches are effective in different ways. We elaborate on this distinction next, and offer several hypotheses that we hope will stimulate future research.

Further Thoughts on Child-Centered and Adult-Centered Parenting

Children benefit when they have successful experiences with child-centered and adult-centered parenting approaches. The former, we believe, enhance children's efforts to differentiate the self through mastering *discovered* challenges,[11] and the later facilitates children's efforts to integrate the self through mastering challenges *presented*

by significant others (see Csikszentmihalyi, 1990, on "discovered" and "presented" challenges). In terms of the flow model, matching skills to either type of challenge could lead to flow; however, the lessons learned in terms of self-regulation are very different. Child-centered approaches guide children toward flow, so to speak, from existing skills to higher challenges, or toward equilibration on the path from assimilation toward accommodation. Adult-centered approaches reverse this process, putting challenges ahead of skills and accommodation before assimilation. Thus, successful child-centered approaches are more likely to strengthen children's self-regulative capacities to find enjoyment in an emergent sense of differentiation; successful adult-centered approaches strengthen the ability to seek enjoyment in integration.[12] Children who benefit from success with both types would presumably develop the most complex internal model of the world, one allowing the widest range of options for regulating arousal and instigating development.[13]

The above ideas provide a framework for future research, but we can offer some indirect support for them now. Our study of talented teenagers looked at talent development in the arts (i.e., athletics, music, and visual arts), and the sciences (i.e., math and science; see Csikszentmihalyi et al., 1993). According to the students we interviewed, the former domain was perceived as child-centered: teachers encouraged discovered challenges, student initiative, intrinsic motivation, and so on. In contrast, math and science classes

---

[11] Challenges are "discovered" by children when child-centered parents structure the environment in ways that are sensitive to children's interests and thus more conducive to a discovery orientation.

[12] Perhaps these two general patterns of socialization—one more suited for attempts to differentiate and "break" with tradition, and one more suited for integrative attempts to "build" on tradition—can help to explain the often-cited emphasis on individuality in the West and on social connection in the East. In addition, flow experience in the West is more often a private thing (e.g., in recreation or leisure), whereas flow in strongly adult-centered cultures (e.g., tribal cultures) is often a matter of public ceremony and ritual (see Turner, 1979, on flow and ritual).

[13] To the extent that both parenting approaches characterize one home context, a child presumably benefits. It is also worth noting, however, that a synthesis of sorts might take place when a child gets experience with both patterns as a result of different contexts (e.g., home and school), or perhaps as a result of experience with different age playmates—sometimes having to "follow" and accommodate, and sometimes having to "lead" and organize others' efforts.

were perceived as adult-centered: teachers presented challenges, required student compliance, and instilled extrinsic motivation. Child-centered instruction in the arts apparently created more opportunities for differentiation than integration; students reported feeling good about what they were doing in class, but they did not feel that what they were doing was connected to their future goals. In contrast, the sciences created more opportunities for integration than differentiation; students felt that class activities were related to their goals (e.g., college and jobs) but less often felt personally motivated. Interestingly, those students who went on to develop their talents farthest—*across all of the talent areas*—reported personal enjoyment *and* the feeling that they were working toward important future goals (see also Rathunde, 1993).

While child-centered and adult-centered approaches each build different strengths when effective, they may also lead to different weaknesses when they fail. For instance, a child-centered approach can fail in two ways: parents can overwhelm children with support whenever they show interest in something, or parents can let children select unrealistic challenges. As a result, two kinds of "failure" with assimilation and challenge seeking can occur: the former child will need the help of others to discover challenges (e.g., a child who depends on a parent to combat boredom and needs help in deciding what to do), the latter child will feel frustrated by a pattern of pursuing challenges that always seem out of reach (e.g., a child who deals with anxiety of piano lessons by quitting, selecting another instrument, quitting, and so on). An adult-centered approach can also fail in two ways: parents can prescribe behaviors and then make sure expectations are met through overly close monitoring and guidance, or parents can set expectations too high and fail to provide supportive feedback. These imbalances can lead to two types of failure with accommodation and solving presented challenges: the former child will feel dominated by social circumstances and unable to express individual interests (e.g., a child who passively conforms, following parental expectations blindly), and the latter child will feel frustrated and angry that it is so hard to please others (e.g., a child who rebels or rejects parental wishes).

Although child-centered approaches encourage differentiation and adult-centered approaches encourage integration, the above comments make it clear that *both* approaches can result in outcomes that isolate children from their social

context or embed them too deeply within it. In each case, though, the detachment or enmeshment of children is qualitatively different. Conformity and dependence are both a type of overintegration, and rebellion and disillusionment are both forms of overdifferentiation, but each outcome is unique, and each results from different socialization dynamics. An overly supportive child-centered approach encourages dependence, and an overly supportive adult-centered strategy promotes conformity. Conversely, an overly challenging child-centered approach, by allowing children to "get in over their heads" with unrealistic challenges, encourages disillusionment; an overly challenging adult-centered approach encourages rebellion from adult expectations. Put differently, dependence results when discovered challenges are too easy, and conformity when presented challenges are too easy; both problems are associated with overly "supportive" parents. In contrast, disillusionment results when discovered challenges are too difficult, and rebellion when presented challenges are too difficult; both problems are related to parents who allow children to be challenged beyond their capacities.

In summary, we propose that complexity in adulthood is aided by early social experiences that enhance the differentiation and integration of the self through mastering discovered and presented challenges, respectively. If a person develops through wearing masks on a cultural stage and performance suffers if the role is played mechanically according to script or, on the contrary, unrelated to the script at all, then a person—like a good actor—benefits from following a role from an existing script, but "improvising" on it to make it fit individual traits and interests. Our earlier examples of successful aging indicate how this is possible: complex persons can be traditional or iconoclastic, value continuity or change, be conservative or liberal, depending on what response best fits the situation.

Neoteny and Complexity: The Evolutionary Logic of Unending Childhood

Are the recurring themes in this chapter—the dialectic of assimilation and accommodation, the balancing of skills and challenges, the intersubjective dynamics of support and challenge, and so on—just instances of a selective ordering of information, or do they reflect something intrinsic to human nature? We believe that the connections made thus far between complexity in later life and its foundation in child development have a deeper meaning that can be discerned in an evolutionary framework. In keeping with the strategy of moving from maturity to earlier developmental periods, we take one final step "back," so to speak, to an evolutionary perspective on neoteny.

Neoteny refers to the retardation of development, especially that of the nervous system, such that infants are born relatively immature and must learn what they need to know to survive (Gould, 1977; Lerner, 1984). Compared to other primates, humans are considered neotenous because their rate of development from fetus to adulthood is unusually slow. In fact, adult humans even retain many of the physical traits of the human fetus, such as flat-facedness and minimum body hair (Bolk, 1926). Huxley (1942) and others (see Montagu, 1989) have suggested that neoteny "drives off" of the developmental timescale traits that have been a part of our evolutionary past (e.g., the heavier eyebrow ridges and projecting jaws of adult apes, of Neandertaloids, and so on). More important than the physical characteristics, Lorenz (1971) maintained that the behavioral outcomes of neoteny—the retention of childlike traits such as curiosity, playfulness, and flexibility, to mention just a few—are far more important. He concluded that the defining characteristic of humans was nonspecialization, allowing an *unending state of development* and an ability to change in response to new environments.

In his book *Growing Young,* Ashley Montagu (1989) concurs with this perspective and sums it up in the following ironic phrase: "The goal of life is to die young—as late as possible" (p. 5). He argues that we are biologically prepared by evolution to "grow young," or to emphasize rather than minimize childlike traits as we mature. Although the importance of these ideas are known by a small group of social and natural scientists, Montagu asserts that the enormous ramifications of an *applied understanding of neoteny* have yet to be fully recognized. Such an understanding would explicitly recognize and nurture childlike traits, leading to adjustments in parenting and teaching philosophies; it would also redefine society as a system designed to extend the neotenous traits of humankind.

The universal manifestation of attachment processes provides deeper insight into the evolutionary logic of neoteny. Attachment discloses the fact that heavy parental investments in caregiving have a genetic underpinning (Bowlby, 1969), and that human infants and their parents are biologically prepared for intersubjectivity (Papousek &

Papousek, 1987). In other words, parents and infants come equipped with the necessary skills for dialectic negotiations and joint meaning-making: "Humans are born with a self-regulating strategy for getting knowledge by human negotiation and co-operative action. . . . Thus socialisation is as natural, innate or 'biological' for a human brain as breathing or walking" (Trevarthen, 1988, p. 39).

The concept of neoteny thus provides a unifying link among various parts of this chapter. First, it provides a rationale for the presumed goal of complexity in later life, the defining characteristic of which was unending development due to flexibility (see also Lerner, 1984). The lifelong learners we interviewed can thus be seen as exemplars of the neotenous promise of human evolution. Second, the concept provides a way to link the idea of complexity with our observations about child development in social interaction. The trade-off in having a plastic versus fixed path of development is the enormous dependence that human children have on their parents (Gould, 1977; Lewontin, 1981). This dependence is illustrated by comparisons to other primates; humans give birth at a later age, have fewer young with each gestation, have longer gestation periods, lactate longer, and have fewer children across their lifetime (Altmann, 1989; Johanson & Edey, 1981). The human fetus is also expelled from the womb "early" because the evolution of brain size made premature birth necessary to permit safe passage through the birth canal (Montagu, 1989). This almost total dependence of human infants on caregivers, and the genetic predisposition to form attachments, explain why "individual" development occurs within a social process.

How does this slow and steady "tortoise strategy" lead to adult complexity? And what about this strategy is connected to optimal experiences that we claim are so important for development? These final questions of the chapter are addressed by taking a closer look at the *opportunity for play* afforded by neotenous development. Of the many consequences resulting from this basic human predicament of prolonged dependence, we believe play says the most about human development. Neoteny provides infants with ample time to play in a relatively *unpressured* context; Bruner, Jolly, and Sylva (1976) add that play was favored by evolution as a pressure-free time during which adult skills could be imitated with successful solutions *that lead to pleasure.* The phenomenon of play thus contains the evolutionary logic of neoteny; a closer look at its character will reveal the essential connection among parental protection, optimal experiences, and the growth of complexity.

The Syntelic Character of Play

Baldwin (1906) has analyzed the character of play in a way that links it to the highest levels of human development. He refers to play as *syntelic* to capture its unique confluence of subjective and objective, inner and outer, characteristics:

> Both the inner freedom and the outer semblance must be retained [in play]; the latter gives consistency, pattern, dramatic quality, all that is meant by "semblance"; the former give control, selective character, essential inwardness. (p. 114)

> The play object becomes not the inner or fancy object as such, nor yet the outer present object as such, *but both at once, what we are calling the semblant object,* itself the terminus of a sort of interest which later on develops into that called "syntelic." (p. 116)

Baldwin is suggesting in these comments that play opens up the opportunity for make-believe against a background of reality (i.e., real sense objects); both of these qualities—an essential inwardness and an outer semblance—must be present. If there is no reference in play to the external world, it becomes pure fancy, and it loses its interest and drama. On the other hand, if play is too reality dependent or compulsory, it again loses its interest, but for a totally different reason. Play must retain its character of self-illusion, what Baldwin calls a "don't-have-to feeling," that invests the object with personal meaning, inner determination, and a feeling of self-control; to a certain extent, this quality *tempers* the external control that would otherwise hold. Thus, Baldwin (1906) states, "Play is a mode of reconciliation and merging of two sorts of control. . . . For it provides for the relative isolation of the object and opens the way for its treatment by experimentation" (p. 119).[14]

It is this *syntelic* character of play that makes it crucially important and links it to higher forms of human thought. By allowing the oscillation between subjective and objective modes, Baldwin perceives a developmental link to the emergence of basic human dualisms (e.g., mind/body, self/other, truth/falsity) and the eventual *overcoming* of such dualisms with full development. The legacy of play can thus be seen in the syntelic character of Baldwin's highest form of thought, aesthetic contemplation. As illustrated earlier, his descriptions of aesthetic modes are remarkably close to contemporary perspectives on postformal thought processes, and to our remarks on flow experience: "In aesthetic experience the partial insights of intelligence and feeling are mutually conserved and supplemented" (1911, p. 279). His perspective, though, adds insight to the developmental history of such outcomes; in other words, play is germinal of the highest forms of human thought as its syntelic character is elaborated and reinstated on higher levels of organizations.

The essential benefits of playing, then, lie in the manipulation of information in a pressure-free context that is informed by external and internal determinants, but controlled by neither. Play can retreat from compulsion and the "have-to" state of mind, or escape from the irrelevance of a "don't-have-to" consciousness. Thus, play captures the same self-environment synchrony we described in flow experiences; in addition, the dynamics of both are similar. Berlyne (1960, 1966), for instance, viewed play as serving a stimulus-seeking function when the organism was bored and an arousal-decreasing function when the organism was anxious. Other theorists have emphasized the positives of one or the other function; for instance, Ellis (1973) viewed play as stimulus seeking, and Freud (1959), Vygotsky (1962), and Erikson (1977) thought of play primarily as a safe way to reduce tension by dealing with problems in a symbolic way.

Also like flow, play results in the differentiation and integration of the self. When it is exploratory, it generates novelty (Fagen, 1976); when it is imitative (or repetitive), it builds habits (Piaget, 1966).[15] Vandenberg (1981) likened these differentiating and integrating aspects of play to the functions of genetic mutation and DNA, respectively, in providing for biological diversity and continuity. Play may be no less important in providing for cultural diversity and continuity. A number of theories have drawn

---

[14] Analogously, one can think of the scientific process as syntelic, as an oscillation between theoretical (subjective) and empirical (objective) modes of "control."

[15] An interesting research hypothesis is that child-centered parenting enhances exploratory play, and adult-centered parenting encourages playful imitation.

connections among play and human creativity, achievement, and flexibility (Bruner, 1972; Rubin, Fein, & Vandenberg, 1983; Sutton-Smith, 1976). One of the strongest statements on the importance of play is given by Huizinga (1955), who saw in it the roots of our cultural institutions.

In conclusion, neoteny is connected to play through the establishment of an optimally stimulating context that is free of survival pressure due to parental investments of energy. Groos (1901) notes from an evolutionary perspective that *this period of human immaturity exists precisely for the purpose of play,* and there is a correlation between the length of play and an organism's eventual complexity (see also Gould, 1977; Johanson & Edey, 1981; Lerner, 1984; Lewontin, 1981). When flow experiences are seen on a continuum with play (i.e., as play reinstated on adult levels of organization), Groos's formula can be extended to flow experiences; in other words, *to the extent that adults continue to have flow experiences, their lives reflect a neotenous pattern of unending development.* This observation is consistent with our earlier examples of complexity in later life: these individuals regulated their attention in ways that promoted flow experiences and maintained the ability to "play" in adulthood.[16]

Much can be learned about the development of the person by better understanding the social conditions that take advantage of a neotenous developmental pattern. Important clues about these conditions can be found in the attachment relationship between caregiver and infant. Unless otherwise plagued by problems of their own, parents are prepared by evolution to create a play space through adjustments of support and challenge that helps infants to regulate their arousal. It is not a coincidence, we believe, that optimal developmental outcomes in infancy, childhood, and adolescence are all associated with parental combinations of support and challenge; such combinations—to the extent that they create appropriate conditions for optimal experiences—are consistent with the evolutionary logic of neoteny. Thus, future studies that continue to uncover how families (or other contexts of socialization) facilitate optimal experiences and outcomes will inform the creation of social environments that are more consistent with our biological potentials.

---

[16] In Baldwin's terminology, to "play" in adulthood means having *aesthetic experiences* that allow the reconciliation of the various partial truths (e.g., feeling and intellect, inner and outer).

Another area of research from which much can be learned about unending development is the study of successful aging. The examples of complexity used in this chapter illustrate that it is worthwhile to ask lifelong learners how they were able to stay interested and involved. Much research, however, remains to be done. Do "protective" social conditions still play a role in facilitating optimal experiences in late adulthood? How much of this regulatory function is (or can be) taken over by individuals through the internalization of supportive and challenging conditions they have experienced in their lifetimes? While the focus in this chapter has been on the individual's responsibility for negotiating optimal experience, it is certain that social conditions remain important. For instance, many of those we interviewed had the benefit of tenured or emeritus positions on a faculty; many had extremely devoted spouses; and most seemed free from financial worries. Further studies of successful aging can shed light on how personal instigative qualities, and social conditions, work to maintain the promise of neoteny. To the extent that insights gained are linked to child development, including the earliest moments of parent-child interaction, developmental theory will benefit greatly.

CONCLUSIONS: THE ROLE OF EXPERIENCE IN DEVELOPMENT

Theories of development have tended to look at the individual as an organism propelled along the life course by external forces. From conception to death, individuals were seen as dependent variables who were a function of a host of independent variables: genetic programs, early environments and stimulations, social and cultural contexts. In opposition to such overly deterministic perspectives, recent approaches have emphasized the active, purposeful role of the individual in helping to shape his or her developmental trajectory (e.g., Magnusson & Stattin, Ch. 12, this Volume; Brandtstädter, Ch. 14, this Volume; Bronfenbrenner, Ch. 17, this Volume).

The notion of personhood fits within this latter approach. It brings to the forefront of attention the fact that human beings come into the world exceptionally immature and must depend on a supportive social context to develop their full potentialities. The social context, in turn, expects the growing individual to display certain minimum competencies before he or she can be accepted as a "person." Perhaps the most basic requirements are that the individual be able to communicate with others and be able to play at least the most simple roles available on the cultural stage. In addition, each culture evolves expectations of optimal personhood that serve as the ideal goals of individual development. Some of these ideal traits—wisdom in old age, continued involvement in meaningful goals, the ability to retain control of the body and the mind—seem to be cherished across cultures and historical periods. Psychological complexity, or the ability to develop and use the full range of potentialities open to human beings, is also universally valued.

But why would the individual want to become a complex person? What is the motivation that propels an infant to become a competent child, a productive adult, a wise elder? Developmental theories do not deal with these questions, presumably because they assume them to be trivial. Infants grow into adults because they must, because they have no choice. They develop into complex adults if and when favorable circumstances make it possible. As long as one looks only at *distal* causes for development, neglecting such questions is reasonable. But explanations that only deal with distal causes and ignore *proximal* ones are incomplete. Such proximal explanations must deal with the motivations that prompt individuals to make autonomous choices along the life course. And to understand motivations we must take into account the quality of a person's experience.

A child who is overwhelmed by too many and too difficult opportunities, or who has learned to respond with apathy and indifference to an environment that lacks stimulation, might never learn to enjoy the active shaping of his or her experience. And yet only if one enjoys overcoming obstacles does one acquire *amor fati,* that love of being that lets an individual become a complex person. If one learns to experience flow with other people and also in solitude, through agency as well as through communion, through passion and through detachment, then it is likely that one will continue taking advantage of opportunities for self-discovery and self-organization when these become available.

So the central pragmatic question for development becomes: How do we help children learn to enjoy as many aspects of their lives as possible? How do we create contexts in the family, the schools, the community that will help children enjoy complexity? If we do not approach developmental issues from this perspective, we will miss the fact that to become active agents in their own ontogeny, individuals have to *want* to develop and become more complex. And they will want to do so only if they enjoy it. If they do not, development becomes alienated because the child as well as the adult will learn and grow primarily for extrinsic reasons. The child will study to graduate from school, the adult will work to get a paycheck and be promoted, and both will endure their present conditions listlessly, in anticipation of a more pleasant future. This is not the kind of developmental trajectory that leads to complexity, or to a desirable old age.

By contrast, development is intrinsic if a person feels that every moment of life is worth experiencing for its own sake: if one feels fully engaged, fully present while eating and sleeping, studying, and watching television; if one enjoys being with friends; if one finds exhilarating even being hassled or being involved in conflicts and arguments. And *complex* development is intrinsic if a person learns to enjoy learning, meeting new challenges, overcoming obstacles, unfolding potentialities for being that are not naturally easy to use. When a child can enjoy both quiet and adventure, solitude and gregariousness, discipline and spontaneity, cognitive convergence and divergence, then he or she will *want* to become more complex. Whatever we can do to facilitate that kind of development will benefit the community as well as the child who is about to become a person on its stage.

REFERENCES

Adlai-Gail, W. S. (1994). *Exploring the autotelic personality.* Doctoral dissertation, University of Chicago.

Adler, M. J. (1927). *Dialectic.* New York: Harcourt.

Ainsworth, M. D. S., & Bell, S. M. (1969). Some contemporary patterns in the feeding situation. In A. Ambrose (Ed.), *Stimulation in early infancy.* London: Academic.

Altman, I. (1975). *Environment and social behavior.* Monterey, CA: Brooks/Cole.

Altman, I., Vinsel, A., & Brown, B. (1981). Dialectical conceptions in social psychology: An application to social penetration and privacy regulation. In L. Berkowitz (Ed.), *Advances in experimental social psychology* (Vol. 14, pp. 107–160). New York: Academic Press.

Altmann, J. (1989). Life span aspects of reproduction and parental care in anthropoid primates. In J. Lancaster, J. Altmann, A. Rossi, & L. Sherrod (Eds.), *Parenting across the life span: Biosocial dimensions* (pp. 15–29). New York: Aldine de Gruyter.

Anderson, E. (1990). *Streetwise: Race, class and change in an urban community.* Chicago: University of Chicago Press.

Apter, M. (1989). *Reversal theory.* London: Routledge & Kegan Paul.

Bachnik, J. (1992). The two "faces" of self and society in Japan. *Ethos, 20,* 3–32.

Bakan, D. (1966). *The duality of human existence.* Chicago: Rand McNally.

Bakeman, R., & Brown, J. (1980). Early interactions: Consequences for social and mental development at three years. *Child Development, 51,* 437–447.

Bakhtin, M. M. (1981). M. Holquist (Ed.) & C. Emerson & M. Holquist, Trans., *The dialogical imagination: Four essays by M. M. Bakhtin.* Austin: University of Texas Press.

Baldwin, J. M. (1906). *Thought and things: A study of the development and meaning of thought* (Vol. 1). New York: Macmillan.

Baldwin, J. M. (1908). *Thought and things: A study of the development and meaning of thought* (Vol. 2). New York: Macmillan.

Baldwin, J. M. (1911). *Thought and things: A study of the development and meaning of thought* (Vols. 3–4). New York: Macmillan.

Baltes, P. B., & Smith, J. (1990). Toward a psychology of wisdom and its ontogenesis. In R. J. Sternberg (Ed.), *Wisdom: Its nature, origins, and development* (pp. 87–120). New York: Cambridge University Press.

Bandura, A. (1977). *Social learning theory.* Englewood Cliffs, NJ: Prentice-Hall.

Bandura, A. (1978). The self system in reciprocal determinism. *American Psychologist, 33,* 344–358.

Barker, R. (1950). *Ecological psychology.* Stanford, CA: Stanford University Press.

Barron, F. (1969). *Creative person and creative process.* New York: Holt, Rinehart and Winston.

Basseches, M. A. (1980). Dialectical schemata: A framework for the empirical study of the development of dialectical thinking. *Human Development, 23,* 400–421.

Baumrind, D. (1987). A developmental perspective on adolescent risk taking behavior in contemporary America. In C. E. Irwin (Ed.), *Adolescent social behavior and health* (pp. 93–125). San Francisco: Jossey-Bass.

Baumrind, D. (1989). Rearing competent children. In W. Damon (Ed.), *Child development today and tomorrow* (pp. 349–378). San Francisco: Jossey-Bass.

Bee, H. (1992). *The journey of adulthood.* New York: Macmillan.

Bell, S. M., & Ainsworth, M. D. S. (1972). Infant crying and maternal responsiveness. *Child Development, 43,* 1171–1190.

Berlyne, D. E. (1960). *Conflict, arousal and curiosity.* New York: McGraw-Hill.

Berlyne, D. E. (1966). Curiosity and exploration. *Science, 153,* 25–33.

Block, J. H. (1973). Conceptions of sex-roles: Some cross-cultural and longitudinal perspectives. *American Psychologist, 28,* 512–26.

Block, J. H. (1982). Assimilation, accommodation, and the dynamics of personality development. *Child Development, 53,* 281–295.

Block, J. H., & Block, J. (1980). The role of ego-control and ego-resiliency in the organization of behavior. In W. A. Collins (Ed.), *Development of cognition, affect, and social relations. Minnesota Symposium on Child Psychology* (Vol. 13). Hillsdale, NJ: Erlbaum.

Bolk, L. (1926). *Das Problem der Menschwerdung.* Jena, Germany: Gustav Fischer.

Bortz, W. (1996). *Dare to be 100.* New York: Simon & Schuster.

Bowlby, J. (1969). *Attachment and loss: Vol. 1. Attachment.* New York: Basic Books.

Brazelton, T., Koslowski, B., & Main, M. (1974). The origins of reciprocity: The early mother-infant interaction. In M. Lewis & L. Rosenblum (Eds.), *The effect of the infant on its caregiver* (pp. 49–76). New York: Wiley.

Brent, S. B., & Watson, D. (1980, November). *Aging and wisdom: Individual and collective aspects.* Paper presented at the third annual meeting of the Gerontological Society, San Diego.

Bretherton, I. (1987). New perspectives on attachment relations: Security, communication, and internal working models. In J. Osofsky (Ed.), *Handbook of infant development* (pp. 1061–1100). New York: Wiley.

Bronfenbrenner, U. (1979). *The ecology of human development: Experiments by nature and design.* Cambridge, MA: Harvard University Press.

Bronfenbrenner, U. (1992). Ecological systems theory. In R. Vasta (Ed.), *Six theories of child development* (pp. 187–249). London: Jessica Kingsley.

Broughton, J. M., & Freeman-Moir. (Eds.). (1982). *The cognitive developmental psychology of James Mark Baldwin: Current theory and research in genetic epistemology.* Norwood, NJ: ABLEX.

Bruner, J. S. (1972). The nature and uses of immaturity. *American Psychologist, 27,* 687–708.

Bruner, J. S. (1986). Value presuppositions of developmental theory. In L. Cirillo & S. Wapner (Eds.), *Value presuppositions in theories of human development* (pp. 19–28). Hillsdale, NJ: Erlbaum.

Bruner, J. S. (1990). *Acts of meaning.* Cambridge, MA: Harvard University Press.

Bruner, J. S., Jolly, A., & Sylva, K. (Eds.). (1976). *Play: Its role in development and evolution.* New York: Penguin Books.

Cairns, R. B., & Hood, K. E. (1983). Continuity in social development: A comparative perspective on individual differences prediction. In P. B. Baltes & O. G. Brim (Eds.), *Life-span development and behavior* (Vol. 5, pp. 301–58). New York: Academic Press.

Chagnon, N. (1979). Mate competition favoring close kin, and village fissioning among the Yanomamo Indians. In N. A. Chagnon & W. Irons (Eds.), *Evolutionary biology and human social behavior* (pp. 86–132). North Scituate, MA: Duxbury Press.

Chinen, A. B. (1984). Modal logic: A new paradigm of development and late-life potential. *Human Development, 27,* 42–56.

Clark, G. N., & Seifer, R. (1983). Facilitating mother-infant communication: A treatment model for high-risk and developmentally delayed infants. *Infant Mental Health Journal, 4,* 67–82.

Clayton, V. P., & Birren, J. E. (1980). The development of wisdom across the life span: A reexamination of an ancient topic. In P. B. Baltes & O. R. Brim (Eds.), *Life span development and behavior* (Vol. 3, pp. 103–135). New York: Academic Press.

Cooley, C. H. (1902). *Human nature and the social order.* New York: Scribners.

Cooley, C. H. (1961). The social self. In T. Parsons, E. Shils, K. Naegele, & J. Pitts (Eds.), *Theories of society: Foundations of modern sociological theory* (pp. 822–828). New York: Free Press.

Cooper, C. R., Grotevant, H. D., & Condon, S. M. (1983). Individuality and connectedness in the family as a context for adolescent identity formation and role-taking skill. In H. D. Grotevant & C. R. Cooper (Eds.), *Adolescent development in the family* (pp. 43–59). San Francisco: Jossey-Bass.

Costa, P. T., & McCrae, R. R. (1980). Still stable after all these years: Personality as a key to some issues in adulthood and old age. In P. B. Baltes & J. O. G. Brim (Eds.), *Life-span development and behavior* (pp. 64–103). New York: Academic Press.

Craik, K. (1943). *The nature of explanation.* Cambridge, England: Cambridge University Press.

Csikszentmihalyi, M. (1975). *Beyond boredom and anxiety.* San Francisco: Jossey-Bass.

Csikszentmihalyi, M. (1990). *Flow.* New York: Harper & Row.

Csikszentmihalyi, M. (1993). *The evolving self.* New York: HarperCollins.

Csikszentmihalyi, M. (1996). *Creativity: Flow and the psychology of discovery and invention.* New York: HarperCollins.

Csikszentmihalyi, M., & Csikszentmihalyi, I. S. (Eds.). (1988). *Optimal experience: Psychological studies of flow in consciousness.* New York: Cambridge University Press.

Csikszentmihalyi, M., & Rathunde, K. (1990). The psychology of wisdom: An evolutionary interpretation. In R. J. Sternberg (Ed.), *Wisdom: Its nature, origins, and development* (pp. 25–51). New York: Cambridge University Press.

Csikszentmihalyi, M., & Rathunde, K. (1993). The measurement of flow in everyday life: Towards a theory of emergent motivation. In J. E. Jacobs (Ed.), *Nebraska symposium on motivation: Vol. 40. Developmental perspectives on motivation* (pp. 57–98). Lincoln: University of Nebraska Press.

Csikszentmihalyi, M., Rathunde, K., & Whalen, S. (1993). *Talented teenagers: The roots of success and failure.* New York: Cambridge University Press.

Damon, W. (1983). *Social and personality development.* New York: Norton.

Damon, W. (1995). *Greater expectations: Overcoming the culture of indulgence in America's homes and schools.* New York: Free Press.

Deci, E. L., & Flaste, R. (1995). *Why we do what we do: The dynamics of personal autonomy.* New York: Grosset.

Deci, E. L., & Ryan, R. M. (1985). *Intrinsic motivation and self-determination in human behavior.* New York: Plenum Press.

Dewey, J. (1913). *Interest and effort in education.* Cambridge, MA: Riverside.

Doi, T. (1986). *The anatomy of self.* Tokyo: Kodansha.

Ellis, M. J. (1973). *Why people play.* Englewood Cliffs, NJ: Prentice-Hall.

Erikson, E. H. (1950). *Childhood and society.* New York: Norton.

Erikson, E. H. (1977). *Toys and reasons.* New York: Norton.

Erikson, E. H. (1982). *The life cycle completed.* New York: Norton.

Erikson, E. H., Erikson, J. M., & Kivnick, H. Q. (1986). *Vital involvement in old age: The experience of old age in our time.* New York: Norton.

Eysenck, H. J. (1973). *Eysenck on extroversion.* New York: Wiley.

Fagen, R. M. (1976). Modeling: How and why play works. In J. S. Bruner, A. Jolly, & K. Sylva (Eds.), *Play: Its role in development and evolution* (pp. 96–115). New York: Penguin Books.

Field, T. (1977). Effects of early separation, interactive deficits, and experimental manipulations on infant-mother face-to-face interaction. *Child Development, 48,* 763–771.

Field, T. (1984). Separation stress of young children transferring to new schools. *Developmental Psychology, 20,* 786–792.

Field, T. (1985). Attachment as psychobiological attunement: Being on the same wave length. In M. Reite & T. Field (Eds.), *Psychobiology of attachment* (pp. 415–454). Orlando, FL: Academic Press.

Field, T. (1987). Affective and interactive disturbances in infants. In J. Osofsky (Ed.), *Handbook of infant development* (pp. 972–1005). New York: Wiley.

Ford, D. H., & Lerner, R. M. (1992). *Developmental systems theory: An integrative approach.* Newbury Park, CA: Sage.

Fortune, R. F. (1963). *Sorcerers of Dobu.* New York: Dutton. (Original work published in 1932)

Fox, B. A. (1988a). *Interaction as a diagnostic resource in tutoring* (Tech. Rep. No. 88-3). Boulder: University of Colorado, Institute of Cognitive Science.

Fox, B. A. (1988b). *Cognitive and interactional aspects of correction in tutoring* (Tech. Rep. No. 88-2). Boulder: University of Colorado, Institute of Cognitive Science.

Freedman, D. G. (1979). *Human sociobiology.* New York: Free Press.

Freud, S. (1922). *Beyond the pleasure principle.* London: Hogarth Press.

Freud, S. (1959). Creative writers and daydreaming. In J. S. Strackey (Ed.), *The standard edition of the complete psychological works of Sigmund Freud* (Vol. 9). London: Hogarth Press.

Gardner, H. (1993). *Creating minds.* New York: Basic Books.

Gardner, H. (1995). *Leading minds: An anatomy of leadership.* New York: Basic Books.

Getzels, J. (1975). Creativity: Prospects and issues. In I. Taylor & J. W. Getzels (Eds.), *Perspectives in creativity* (pp. 326–344). Chicago: Aldine.

Gilkey, L. (1990). *Gilkey on Tillich.* New York: Crossroad.

Gilligan, C. (1982). *In a different voice: Women's conception of self and of morality.* Cambridge, MA: Harvard University Press.

Gilligan, C., Lyons, N. P., & Hanmer, T. J. (Eds.). (1990). *Making connections.* Cambridge, MA: Harvard University Press.

Goffman, E. (1959). *The presentation of self in everyday life.* New York: Doubleday Anchor.

Gould, S. (1977). *Ontogeny and phylogeny.* Cambridge, MA: Harvard University Press.

Groos, K. (1901). *The play of man.* New York: Appleton.

Guilford, J. P. (1967). *The nature of human intelligence.* New York: McGraw-Hill.

Hadamard, T. (1954). *The psychology of invention in the mathematical field.* Princeton, NJ: Princeton University Press.

Hardy-Brown, K., Plomin, R., & DeFries, J. C. (1981). Genetic and environmental influences on the rate of communicative development in the first year of life. *Developmental Psychology, 17,* 704–717.

Hart, L. M. (1992, December 2–6). *Ritual art and the production of Hindu selves.* Paper presented at the American Anthropological Association meetings, San Francisco, CA.

Harter, S. (1983). Developmental perspectives on the self-system. In P. H. Mussen (Series Ed.) & E. M. Heatherington (Vol. Ed.), *Handbook of child psychology: Vol. 4. Socialization, personality, and social development* (pp. 275–385). New York: Wiley.

Hauser, S. (1991). *Adolescents and their families.* New York: Free Press.

Havighurst, R. J. (1953). *Human development and education.* New York: Longmans, Green.

Heber, M. (1981). Instruction versus conversation as opportunities for learning. In W. P. Robinson (Ed.), *Communications in development.* London: Academic Press.

Henderson, B. B. (1984a). Parents and exploration: The effect of context on individual differences in exploratory behavior. *Child Development, 55,* 1237–1245.

Henderson, B. B. (1984b). Social support and exploration. *Child Development, 55,* 1246–1251.

Hogan, R. (1987). Personality psychology: Back to basics. In A. J. Aronoff, A. I. Rabin, & R. A. Zucker (Eds.), *The emergence of personality* (pp. 79–104). New York: Springer.

Holliday, S. G., & Chandler, M. J. (1986). *Wisdom: Explorations in adult competence.* Basel, Switzerland: Krager.

Homans, P. (1979). *Jung in context: Modernity and the making of psychology.* Chicago: University of Chicago Press.

Huizinga, J. (1955). *Homo ludens.* Boston: Beacon Press.

Huxley, J. S. (1942). *Evolution: The modern synthesis.* New York: Harper and Brothers.

Irwin, C. E. (Ed.). (1987). *Adolescent social behavior and health.* San Francisco: Jossey-Bass.

Isabella, R. A., & Belsky, J. (1991). Interactional synchrony and the origins of infant-mother attachment: A replication study. *Child Development, 62,* 373–384.

Izard, C. E. (1977). *Human emotions.* New York: Plenum Press.

Johanson, D. C., & Edey, M. A. (1981). *Lucy: The beginnings of humankind.* New York: Simon & Schuster.

Johnson-Laird, P. N. (1983). *Mental models.* Cambridge, MA: Harvard University Press.

Jung, C. G. (1946). *Psychological types.* New York: Harcourt Brace.

Jung, C. G. (1954). The development of personality. In H. Read et al. (Eds.), *Collected works* (Vol. 17). New York: Pantheon Books.

Jung, C. G. (1959). Aion: Researches into the phenomenology of the self. In H. Read et al. (Eds.), *Collected works* (Vol. 9). New York: Pantheon Books.

Jung, C. G. (1960). The structure and dynamics of the psyche. In H. Read et al. (Eds.), *Collected works* (Vol. 8). New York: Pantheon Books.

Jung, C. G. (1961). *The theory of psychoanalysis.* New York: Pantheon Books.

Kahlbaugh, P. (1993). James Mark Baldwin: A bridge between social and cognitive theories of development. *Journal for the Theory of Social Behavior, 23,* 79–103.

Kakar, S. (1978). *The inner world: A psychoanalytic study of childhood and society in India.* New Delhi: Oxford University Press.

Kegan, R. (1982). *The evolving self.* Cambridge, MA: Harvard University Press.

Kelly, G. A. (1955). *The psychology of personal constructs.* New York: Norton.

Kojima, H. (1986). Child rearing concepts as a belief-value system of the society and the individual. In H. Stevenson, H. Azuma, & K. Hakuta (Eds.), *Child development and education in Japan.* New York: Freeman.

Kouzes, J. M., & Posner, B. Z. (1995). *The leadership challenge.* San Francisco: Jossey-Bass.

Kramer, D. A. (1983). Post-formal operations? A need for further conceptualization. *Human Development, 26,* 91–105.

Kris, E. (1952). *Psychoanalytic explorations in art.* New York: International Universities Press.

Kuhn, D. (1978). Mechanisms of cognitive and social development: One psychology or two? *Human Development, 21,* 92–118.

Kuo, Y. (1976). Chinese dialectical thought and character. In J. F. Rychlak (Ed.), *Dialectic: Humanistic rationale for behavior and development* (pp. 72–86). Basel, Switzerland: Karger.

Labouvie-Vief, G. (1980). Beyond formal operations: Uses and limits of pure logic in life span development. *Human Development, 23,* 141–161.

Labouvie-Vief, G. (1982). Dynamic development and mature autonomy. *Human Development, 25,* 161–191.

Labouvie-Vief, G. (1990). Wisdom as integrated thought: Historical and developmental perspectives. In R. J. Sternberg (Ed.), *Wisdom: Its nature, origins, and development* (pp. 52–83). New York: Cambridge University Press.

Lamb, M. (Ed.). (1982). *Nontraditional families: Parenting and child development.* Hillsdale, NJ: Erlbaum.

Larson, R., Mannell, R., & Zuzanek, J. (1986). Daily well-being of older adults with family and friends. *Psychology and Aging, 1*(2), 117–126.

Larson, R., & Richards, M. H. (1994). *Divergent realities: The emotional lives of mothers, fathers, and adolescents.* New York: Basic Books.

Leavitt, H. J., Pondy, L. R., & Boje, D. M. (1989). *Readings in managerial psychology* (4th ed.). Chicago: University of Chicago Press.

Lerner, R. M. (1976). *Concepts and theories of human development.* Reading, MS: Addison-Wesley.

Lerner, R. M. (1984). *On the nature of human plasticity.* New York: Cambridge University Press.

Lerner, R. M. (1991). Changing organism-context relations as the basic process of development: A developmental contextual perspective. *Developmental Psychology, 27,* 27–32.

Lerner, R. M., & Busch-Rossnagel, N. A. (Eds.). (1981). *Individuals as producers of their development: A life-span perspective.* New York: Academic Press.

Lerner, R. M., & Lerner, J. (1987). Children in their contexts: A goodness-of-fit model. In J. Lancaster, J. Altmann, A. Rossi, & L. Sherrod (Eds.), *Parenting across the life span* (pp. 377–404). New York: Aldine de Gruyter.

LeVine, R. (1980). Adulthood among the Gusii. In N. Smelser & E. Erikson (Eds.), *Themes of work and love in adulthood* (pp. 77–104). Cambridge, MA: Harvard University Press.

Levinson, D. J. (1980). Toward a conception of the adult life course. In N. Smelser & E. Erikson (Eds.), *Themes of work and love in adulthood* (pp. 265–90). Cambridge, MA: Harvard University Press.

Levinson, D. J. (1986). A conception of adult development. *American Psychologist, 41,* 3–13.

Lévi-Strauss, C. (1967). *Tristes tropiques.* New York: Atheneum.

Lewin, K. (1951). *Field theory in social science.* New York: Harper.

Lewis, M., & Rosenblum, L. A. (Eds.). (1974). *The effect of the infant on its caregiver.* New York: Wiley.

Lewontin, R. C. (1981). On constraints and adaptation. *Behavioral and Brain Sciences, 4,* 244–245.

Loevinger, J. (1966). The meaning and measurement of ego development. *American Psychologist, 21,* 195–206.

Lorenz, K. (1971). *Studies in animal and human behavior* (Vol. 2). Cambridge, MA: Harvard University Press.

Maccoby, E. E., & Martin, J. A. (1983). Socialization in the context of the family: Parent-child interaction. In P. H. Mussen (Series Ed.) & E. M. Hetherington (Vol. Ed.), *Handbook of child psychology: Vol. 4. Socialization, personality, and social development* (pp. 1–101). New York: Wiley.

MacIntyre, A. (1984). *After virtue: A study in moral theory.* Notre Dame, IN: University of Notre Dame Press.

Marcia, J. E. (1966). Development and validation of ego identity status. *Journal of Personality and Social Psychology, 3,* 551–558.

Marriott, M. (1976). Hindu transactions: Diversity without dualism. In B. Kepferer (Ed.), *Transaction and meaning: Directions in the anthropology of exchange and symbolic behavior.* Philadelphia: ISHI.

Martini, M. (1994). Peer interaction in Polynesia: A view from the Marquesas. In J. L. Roopnarine, J. E. Johnson, & F. H. Hooper (Eds.), *Children's play in diverse cultures* (pp. 73–103). Albany: State University of New York Press.

Martini, M., & Kirkpatrick, J. (1992). Parenting in Polynesia: A view from the Marquesas. In J. L. Roopnarine & D. B. Carter (Eds.), *Annual advances in applied developmental psychology* (Vol. 5, pp. 199–222). Norwood, NJ: ABLEX.

Maslow, A. (1971). *The farther reaches of human nature.* New York: Penguin Books.

Matas, L., Arend, R. A., & Sroufe, L. A. (1978). Continuity and adaption in the second year: The relationship between quality of attachment and later competence. *Child Development, 49,* 547–556.

McCrae, R. R., & Costa, T. (1984). *Emerging lives, enduring dispositions: Personality in adulthood.* Boston: Little, Brown.

Meacham, J. A. (1983). Wisdom and the context of knowledge: Knowing that one doesn't know. In D. Kuhn & J. A. Meacham (Eds.), *On the development of developmental psychology* (pp. 111–134). Basel, Switzerland: Karger.

Meacham, J. A. (1990). The loss of wisdom. In R. J. Sternberg (Ed.), *Wisdom: Its nature, origins, and development* (pp. 181–211). New York: Cambridge University Press.

Mead, G. H. (1934). *Mind, self, and society.* Chicago: University of Chicago Press.

Mischel, W. (1968). *Personality and assessment.* New York: Wiley.

Montagu, A. (1989). *Growing young.* Boston: Bergin & Garvey.

Nietzsche, F. (1968). *The portable Nietzsche* (W. Kaufmann, Trans.) New York: Viking.

Nietzsche, F. (1974). *The gay science* (W. Kaufmann, Trans.) New York: Vintage Books.

Ochs, E., & Schieffelin, B. B. (1984). Language acquisition and socialization: Three developmental stories and their implications. In R. Shweder & R. LeVine (Eds.), *Culture and its acquisition.* Chicago: University of Chicago Press.

Olson, S. L., Bates, J. E., & Bayles, K. (1984). Mother-infant intraction and the development of individual differences in children's cognitive competence. *Developmental Psychology, 20,* 166–179.

Pandey, R. B. (1969). *Hindu samskaras: A sociological study of the Hindu.* New Delhi: Motilal.

Papousek, H., & Papousek, M. (1987). Intuitive parenting: A dialectic counterpart to the infant's integrative competence. In J. Osofsky (Ed.), *Handbook of infant development* (pp. 669–720). New York: Wiley.

Parsons, T., & Bales, R. F. (1955). *Family, socialization and interaction process.* Glencoe, IL: Free Press.

Pascual-Leone, J. (1990). Wisdom: Toward organismic processes. In R. J. Sternberg (Ed.), *Wisdom: Its nature, origins, and development* (pp. 244–278). New York: Cambridge University Press.

Pearlin, L. I. (1982). Discontinuities in the study of aging. In T. K. Hareven & K. J. Adams (Ed.), *Aging and life course perspectives: An interdisciplinary perspective.* New York: Guildford Press.

Perkins, D. (1996, April). *Culture, gender, thinking styles, and intellectual character.* Paper presented at the 1996 annual meeting of the American Educational Research Association, New York.

Piaget, J. (1952). Autobiography. In E. G. Boring et al., (Eds.), *A hitory of psychology in autobiography* (Vol. 4). Worcester, MA: Clark University Press.

Piaget, J. (1962). *Play, dreams, and imitation in childhood.* New York: Norton.

Piaget, J. (1966). Response to Brian Sutton-Smith. *Psychological Review, 73,* 111–112.

Prigogine, I. (1980). *From being to becoming: Time and complexity in the physical sciences.* San Francisco: Freeman.

Rathunde, K. (1993). The experience of interest: A theoretical and empirical look at its role in adolescent talent development.

In P. Pintrich & M. Maehr (Eds.), *Advances in motivation and achievement* (Vol. 8, pp. 59–98), Greenwich, CT: JAI Press.

Rathunde, K. (1995). Wisdom and abiding interest: Interviews with three noted historians in later-life. *Journal of Adult Development, 2,* 159–172.

Rathunde, K. (1996). Family context and talented adolescents' optimal experience in productive activities. *Journal of Research on Adolescence, 6,* 603–626.

Rathunde, K. (in press). Support and challenge in the family: An essential combination for adolescents. In C. Bidwell, M. Csikszentmihalyi, L. Hedges, & B. Schneider (Eds.), *Images and experience of work in American adolescents.*

Rathunde, K., & Csikszentmihalyi, M. (1993). Undivided interest and the growth of talent: A longitudinal study of adolescents. *Journal of Youth and Adolescence, 22,* 1–21.

Renninger, K. A., Hidi, S., & Krapp, A. (Eds.). (1992). *The role of interest in learning and development.* Hillsdale, NJ: Erlbaum.

Riegel, K. F. (1973). Dialectical operations: The final period of cognitive development. *Human Development, 16,* 346–370.

Rogers, C. (1959). A theory of therapy, personality, and interpersonal relationships as developed in the client-centered framework. In S. Koch (Ed.), *Psychology: A study of a science: Vol. 3. Formulations of the person and the social context.* New York: McGraw-Hill.

Rogers, C. (1969). *Freedom to learn.* Columbus, OH: Merrill.

Rogoff, B. (1990). *Apprenticeship in thinking: Cognitive development in social context.* New York: Oxford University Press.

Rogoff, B., & Gardner, W. P. (1984). Adult guidance of cognitive development. In B. Rogoff & J. Lave (Eds.), *Everyday cognition: Its development in social context.* Cambridge, MA: Harvard University Press.

Rogoff, B., Mistry, J., Goncu, A., & Mosier, C. (1993). Guided participation in cultural activity by toddlers and caregivers. *Monographs of the Society for Research in Child Development, 58,* (Serial No. 236).

Rotter, J. B. (1972). *Applications of social learning theory to personality.* New York: Holt.

Rubin, K. H., Fein, G. G., & Vandenberg, B. (1983). Play. In P. H. Mussen (Series Ed.) & E. M. Hetherington (Vol. Ed.), *Handbook of child psychology: Vol. 4. Socialization, personality, and social development* (pp. 693–773). New York: Wiley.

Runco, M. A. (1991). *Divergent thinking.* Norwood, NJ: ABLEX.

Rychlak, J. F. (Ed.). (1976). *Dialectic: Humanistic rationale for behavior and development.* Basel, Switzerland: Karger.

Ryff, C. D. (1989). In the eye of the beholder: Views of psychological well-being among middle-aged and older adults. *Psychology and Aging, 4,* 195–210.

Schneider, W., & Shiffrin, R. M. (1977). Controlled and automatic human information processing: 1. Detection, search, and attention. *Psychological Review, 84,* 1–66.

Shweder, R., & Bourne, E. J. (1984). Does the concept of the person vary cross-culturally? In R. A. Shweder & R. A. LeVine (Eds.), *Culture theory.* New York: Cambridge University Press.

Sigman, M., Cohen, S. E., & Forsythe, A. B. (1981). The relations of early infant mesures to later development. In S. L. Friedman & M. Sigman (Eds.), *Preterm birth and psychological development.* New York: Academic Press.

Simonton, D. K. (1984). *Genius, creativity, and leadership.* Cambridge, MA: Harvard University Press.

Sinnott, J. (1984). Postformal reasoning: The relativistic stage. In M. L. Commons, F. A. Richards, & C. Armons (Eds.), *Beyond formal operations* (pp. 298–325). New York: Praeger.

Spence, J. T., & Helmreich, R. L. (1978). *Masculinity and femininity: Their psychological dimensions, correlates, and antecedents.* Austin: University of Texas Press.

Sroufe, L. A. (1979). The coherence of individual development. *American Psychologist, 34,* 834–841.

Stern, D. M. (1974). Mother and infant at play. In M. Lewis & L. Rosenblum (Eds.), *The effect of the infant on its caregiver.* New York: Wiley.

Stern, D. M. (1985). *The interpersonal world of the infant.* New York: Basic Books.

Sternberg, R. J. (Ed.). (1984). *Mechanisms of cognitive development.* New York: Freeman.

Sternberg, R. J. (1990). Wisdom and its relations to intelligence and creativity. In R. J. Sternberg (Ed.), *Wisdom: Its nature, origins, and development.* New York: Cambridge University Press.

Sutton-Smith, B. (1976). Current research and theory on play, games and sports. In T. Craig (Ed.), *The humanistic and mental health aspects of sports, exercise and recreation.* Chicago: American Medical Association.

Thomas, A., & Chess, S. (1977). *Temperament and development.* New York: Brunner/Mazel.

Tobach, E. (1981). Evolutionary aspects of the activity of the organism and its development. In R. M. Lerner & N. A. Busch-Rossnagel (Eds.), *Individuals as producers of their development: A life-span perspective* (pp. 37–68). New York: Academic Press.

Tobach, E., & Schneirla, T. C. (1968). The biopsychology of social behavior of animals. In R. E. Cooke & S. Levin (Eds.), *Biologic basis of pediatric practice* (pp. 60–82). New York: McGraw-Hill.

Trevarthen, C. (1979). Communication and cooperation in infancy: A description of primary intersubjectivity. In M. Bullowa (Ed.), *Before speech: The beginnings of human communication.* Cambridge, England: Cambridge University Press.

Trevarthen, C. (1988). Universal co-operative motives: How infants begin to know the language and culture of their parents. In G. Jahoda & I. M. Lewis (Eds.), *Acquiring culture: Cross-cultural studies in child development.* London: Croom Helm.

Tucker, D. M., & Williamson, P. A. (1984). Asymmetric neural control systems in human self-regulation. *Psychological Review, 91,* 185–215.

Turner, V. (1979). *Process, performance and pilgrimage.* New Delhi: Concept.

Vaillant, G. (1993). *The wisdom of the ego.* Cambridge, MA: Harvard University Press.

Vandenberg, B. (1981). Play: Dormant issues and new perspectives. *Human Development, 24,* 357–365.

Vygotsky, L. (1962). *Thought and language.* New York: Wiley.

Vygotsky, L. (1978). *Mind in society: The development of higher psychological processes.* Cambridge, MA: Harvard University Press.

Waldrop, M. (1992). *Complexity: The emerging science at the edge of order and chaos.* New York: Simon & Schuster.

Ward, M. C. (1971). *Them children: A study of language learning.* New York: Holt, Rinehart and Winston.

Wells, A. (1988). Self-esteem and optimal experience. In M. Csikszentmihalyi & I. S. Csikszentmihalyi (Eds.), *Optimal experience: Psychological studies of flow in consciousness* (pp. 327–341). New York: Cambridge University Press.

Wertsch, J. V. (1979). From social interaction to higher psychological functions. *Human Development, 22,* 1–22.

Wertsch, J. V. (1985). *Vygotsky and the social formation of mind.* Cambridge, MA: Harvard University Press.

Wertsch, J. V. (1991). A sociocultural approach to mind. In W. Damon (Ed.), *Child development today and tomorrow* (pp. 14–33). San Francisco: Jossey-Bass.

Williams, M. (1995). *Complete guide to aging and health.* San Francisco: Harmony Books.

Wood, D. J., & Middleton, D. (1975). A study of assisted problem-solving. *British Journal of Psychology, 66,* 181–191.

CHAPTER 12

Person–Context Interaction Theories

DAVID MAGNUSSON and HÅKAN STATTIN

The central task for scientific psychology is to understand and explain why individuals think, feel, act, and react as

The work presented here was supported by grants the Swedish Council for Social Research (project 92-0317:3B), and the Swedish Council for Planning and Coordination of Research.

they do in real life. The *individual* is our main concern, but an individual's development and ongoing functioning are not isolated from the environment in which he or she lives. A basic proposition for this chapter's presentation and discussion is that the individual is an active, purposeful part of an integrated, complex, and dynamic person–environment system. Furthermore, within this person–environment system, the individual develops and functions as an integrated, complex, and dynamic totality. Consequently, it is not possible to understand how social systems function without knowledge of individual functioning, and it is not possible to understand individual functioning and development without knowledge of the environment (cf., Coleman, 1990). *The fundamental implication for future psychological research is that we have to change the object of theorizing and empirical research from a context-free individual to a person who functions and develops as an active part of an integrated, complex person–environment system.* In the formulations by Ryff (1987):

> Over 20 years ago, Wrong (1961) faulted contemporary sociology for its oversocialized conception of mankind, arguing that the person is both more and less than an acceptance seeker, a follower of social norms and expectations. Contemporary psychology has likewise suffered from an over-psychologized conception of human nature that sees individuals primarily as cognitive processors operating independently of their ties to the social world, including family, neighborhood, community and culture. These lopsided views must be replaced with conceptions that reveal greater awareness of the complex nature of the individual, the social system, and the ties that bind them together. (p. 1201)

In general, psychological research, including research on development and personality, has three interrelated characteristics. First, psychological problems are formulated in terms of relations among variables. This characteristic has been described as *the variable approach* to psychological research (Block, 1971; Magnusson & Allen, 1983a). Second, the problems are often discussed and investigated in statistical terms. Models and methods for data treatment are frequently presented and discussed with only vague (if any) reference to an explicitly formulated view regarding the nature of the phenomena to which the data refer. Examples occur in discussions of causal models and causal relations (e.g., Hellvik, 1988; von Eye & Clogg, 1994) and of classical test theory (Magnusson, 1967). This tradition has been fostered by the development of sophisticated data-analytic methods. Third, the study of personality has often been defined as the study of individual differences. Study of individual differences at the group level often forms the basis for conclusions about functioning at the individual level.

Our position is that, as a fundamental prerequisite for success, empirical research must start with a careful analysis of the *phenomena* relevant to the specific problem under study. With reference to this proposition, the main part of this chapter is devoted to an attempt to analyze the structures and processes involved in the operation of person–environment systems and the way in which the individual functions and develops within this general type of system. The theoretical approach to the study of individual functioning and development comprises a framework that has been designated *a holistic approach* (Magnusson, 1995). The main thesis emphasizes the close dependency of individual functioning and individual development on the social, cultural, and physical characteristics of the environment. At the end of the chapter, certain methodological and research strategy implications of the theoretical analysis will be presented.

The Goal of Scientific Psychology

The goal of scientific work in general is to formulate the basic principles for how and why various domains of the total space of phenomena function as they do, at varying levels of complexity. This goal is as relevant to the study of human functioning as it is to the study of physics.

The remarkable advances in the physical sciences, and the resulting rapid development of a highly technological society, have resulted in physics becoming the model for other scientific disciplines. That the paradigm of natural sciences applies to all fields of scientific endeavor, including social sciences, was proposed by Pearson (1892) in *The Grammar of Science*. However, other sciences have sometimes adopted the goals and values espoused by physicists, without considering whether the character of the phenomena involved is congruent with the model that physics provides. A central concept supporting the search for precise laws within the framework of the Newtonian mechanistic view of nature is the concept of "prediction." Accurate prediction has been regarded as a main criterion for the validity of a scientific law in psychology since J. B. Watson (1913) defended the status of psychology as a natural science by proposing that "prediction and control of behavior" are the goals of scientific psychology. Fostered by the development and application of technically sophisticated statistical tools, prediction has also become a central goal for research on individual functioning, including research on human ontogeny. The psychological importance of single variables, or composites of variables, in individual development is often estimated by how well they predict later outcomes. The claim that prediction and control are central goals for psychological research continues to be espoused even in areas in which it is not very appropriate. For example, prediction is a central concept in Pervin's (1995) evaluation of a longitudinal research strategy in research on personality development.

Perfect prediction of individual functioning and development as the ultimate goal for psychological research can be questioned on the basis of two interrelated reasons. The first concerns characterizing individual functioning as a dynamic and complex process, and the second concerns the type of laws that direct this process.

One of the fundamental propositions of modern models for dynamic complex processes is that these processes are lawful but unpredictable. Research on human functioning belongs to the "life sciences." Crick, who started his career as a physicist, later worked in molecular biology (and earned the Nobel prize for his research on DNA), and is now doing research on cognition and artificial intelligence, discusses the kinds of laws sought in different disciplines in his book *What Mad Pursuit* (1988). He concludes that the character of the phenomena that are studied in biological systems is such that the same kind of universally valid, strong laws that define physics cannot be found in biology:

> Physics is also different because its results can be expressed in powerful, deep and often counterintuitive general laws. There is really nothing in biology that corresponds to special and general relativity, or quantum electrodynamics, or even such simple conservation laws as those of Newtonian mechanics: the conservation of energy, of momentum, and of angular momentum. Biology has its "laws," such as those of Mendelian genetics, but they are often only rather broad generalizations, with significant exceptions of them. The laws of physics, it is believed, are the same everywhere in the universe. This is unlikely to be true in biology . . . What is found in biology is mechanisms, . . . built with chemical components and . . . often modified by other, later, mechanisms added to the earlier ones. (p. 138)

This discussion is as relevant for research on human functioning from a psychological perspective as it is for research in biology. Given the complex, often nonlinear interplay of mental, biological, and behavioral subsystems within the individual, and the complex interplay between the individual and an environment, operating in a probabilistic, sometimes very uncertain and unpredictable way, it is unrealistic to hope for accurate prediction of individual functioning across environmental contexts of differing character or over the life span. In experimental research, similar initial conditions are regarded as a prerequisite for perfect replication. Psychology, as a science of individual functioning and development, has to consider the fact that conditions of the future are never fully known, in part because humans, more than any other living organism, have purpose, create, and live in a changing biocultural context with novel conditions of life. As people develop, the world around changes as well; and some of these changes may imply novel foci of individual functioning.

In view of this perspective, the final criterion for success in our scientific endeavors is not how well we can predict individual behavior across situations of different character or across the life course, but how well we succeed in explaining and understanding the processes underlying individual functioning and development. The scientific goal is then twofold:

1. To identify the factors operating in human functioning and ontogeny.
2. To identify and understand the mechanisms by which the factors operate.

This formulation directs the main emphasis toward understanding and explaining the lawfulness of the way individuals function in real life (i.e., in the Wundt–James tradition), rather than toward predicting and controlling behavior (as in the Watson tradition).

So far, the overwhelming number of empirical studies have contributed to identifying operating factors, and few have addressed the mechanisms by which such factors work. Two examples from the study of deviant behavior illustrate the point. First, a large number of empirical studies indicate that low sympathetic physiological activity/reactivity is a correlate of various kinds of antisocial behavior. However, we still lack research showing the mechanisms by which this physiological factor operates in the development process leading to criminal activity at adulthood. Second, empirical studies performed mainly in Western countries have identified urbanization as a factor related to crime rate.

What is needed, however, is identification of the mechanisms through which urbanization influences crimes, in order to explain, among other things, why urbanization has this effect in some cultures and not in others (e.g., Japan has a low crime rate and high urbanization).

It should be emphasized that we take issue with complete prediction as an *ultimate goal* for psychological research, not with prediction as a tool in a research design. We argue against using accurate prediction as the *final* criterion for scientific success. Prediction is a useful conceptual and methodological tool in a research design when such a design is appropriate for research on properly analyzed phenomena. The concept of prediction as a tool is also applicable in numerous practical situations to which psychological methods are being applied—for example, in personnel selection or decision making. In such situations, the certainty with which predictions are made—that is, the probability with which certain events may occur—is of basic interest.

Causal Models

Understanding an individual's way of functioning and developing is based principally on assumptions about causal factors. This approach is of special concern when discussing models of the processes by which individuals develop. Understanding causal mechanisms is also a prerequisite for effective intervention.

At a metatheoretical level, it is possible to distinguish three main causal models for individual functioning and development: (a) the mentalistic model, (b) a biological model, and (c) an environmentalistic model (Magnusson, 1990). Few researchers adhere strictly to only one model; the key factor is where the researcher places the center of gravity. The main distinction concerns the focus each approach employs as it interprets the main factors presumed to guide individual functioning and development.

The *mentalistic model* emphasizes mental factors as being central to understanding why individuals function and develop as they do. The focus of interest in theorizing and empirical analyses is on intrapsychic processes of perceptions, thoughts, emotions, values, goals, plans, and conflicts.

In the *biological model,* an individual's thoughts, feelings, actions, and reactions are assumed to be determined basically by his or her biological equipment and its way of

functioning. Primary determining factors are assumed to be found in the physiological system—the brain and the autonomic nervous system. When biological models of individual development are applied, the major determining or guiding factors are genetic and maturational. In its extreme version, this model implies that individual differences in the course of development have their roots in genes, and only a small role is played by environmental and mental factors.

The *environmentalistic model* locates the main causal factors in the environment. This view is reflected in theories and models of individual functioning and development at all levels of generality for environmental factors; macrosocial theories, theories about the role of the "sick family," and S–R models for specific individual variables represent a few examples. In developmental research, the environmentalistic model has been very influential.

A common characteristic of the three general models is their assumption of unidirectional causality; mental factors are the main causes of behavior, and biological factors and environmental factors, respectively, are implicitly assumed to be the basic determinants of mental activities and behavior.

As will be discussed later, modern conceptualizations and applications of these models are more differentiated. In fact, few scholars are likely to identify themselves as representatives of either category. However, we argue that, despite this claim, the models continue to exist and affect what researchers actually do and discuss.

In theoretical and empirical research, each of the metatheoretical approaches to understanding the basic causal mechanisms guiding individual functioning and development has had and still has a strong, sometimes dominating impact. Each has also had far-reaching implications for how societal issues have been discussed and handled, and for psychological application—for example, in discussions of appropriate treatment of mental illnesses. The existence of these approaches reflects a fragmentation of the field into subdisciplines with respect to content, concepts, research strategy, and methodology; that is, their existence has resulted in a diversification of research in specialties, with little or no contact across domains. Nothing is wrong with each of the three explanatory models per se. The problem arises when each of them claims total supremacy, and this has occurred to an extent that has hampered real progress both in research and application. In the end, not unlike

Aristotle's principle of multiple causation, each of the general approaches needs consideration as a given phenomenon is represented in scientific analysis.

Scientific Progress—A Proposition for the Future

A characteristic feature of scientific progress in empirical sciences is increasing specialization. When specialization in a subfield of the natural sciences has reached a certain level, it becomes apparent that further progress lies in integration with what has been achieved in neighboring disciplines. The most important steps forward in the natural sciences have been taken via integration within the interface of what were, earlier, conspicuously different disciplines. This has occurred in the interface of physics and chemistry and recently, in the interface of biology, chemistry, and physics. The earlier unambiguous and clear boundaries between subdisciplines have disappeared.

As noted above, three main causal models for individual functioning and development exist, and specialization takes place in the framework of each of these general models. In some areas, specialization has been very productive and has offered important contributions. There are also tendencies toward integration, for example, between brain research and cognitive psychology, resulting in the presentation of *cognitive neuroscience* as a new scientific discipline (Sarter, Berntson, & Cacioppo, 1996). However, research in the behavioral sciences in general is still characterized more by what Toulmin (1981) once described as "sectorial rivalry" than by real integration. Thus, the following question has to be answered: Why is psychological research, including developmental research, on the whole characterized by specialization with only little integration, when research in the natural sciences is characterized by the iterative process of specialization and integration? Let us offer a possible explanation.

One condition that facilitates the iterative process of specialization and integration in the natural sciences is the existence of a general theoretical framework, *a general model of nature,* for theorizing and empirical inquiry. The fact that psychology lacks a corresponding general theoretical framework for the formulation of problems, for the development of a common conceptual space, and for the development and application of adequate methodologies, is an essential obstacle for further real progress. We need the formulation of *a general model of human beings and society.* The formulations in this chapter attempt to contribute to such a model.

Two Perspectives

An individual's thoughts, feelings, actions and reactions can be the object of study from three perspectives: (a) synchronic, (b) diachronic and (c) evolutionary. This discussion will be restricted to the synchronic and diachronic perspectives. (For a discussion of the evolutionary perspective, the reader is referred to the chapter by Gottlieb et al., Ch. 5, this Volume.)

Research on psychological phenomena in a synchronic perspective is concerned with the processes of thoughts, feelings, actions, and reactions going on within the framework of existing mental, biological, and behavioral structures. In this chapter, this perspective on individual functioning will be referred to as the *current* perspective.

Development is a central concept in the diachronic perspective. In its most general form, development in biology refers to any progressive or regressive change in size, shape, and/or function. Developmental psychology is concerned with this process over the life span, from conception to death. In this definition, two concepts are central: change and time.

Development in psychological research refers to changes in the mental, behavioral, and/or biological structures that are involved in the total process(es) of individual functioning. Change can be studied as absolute, structural, interindividual, or ipsative. In the developmental perspective, the tasks for empirical research are: (a) to identify and describe changes in these domains, (b) to identify principles and mechanisms underlying continuities and changes, and (c) to investigate the implications of changes during the life course.

The definition of development implies that development is not synonymous with time. Although development always has a time dimension, time is not equivalent to development. Consequently, in a strict sense of the definition of the concept, processes that continue within existing mental, behavioral, and/or biological structures do not constitute development. (Elaborated discussions of the concept of development—its theoretical, conceptual, and methodological implications—are presented by Baltes et al., Ch. 18, and Overton, Ch. 3, this Volume.)

The definition of the concept of development implies that two perspectives should be distinguished:

1. Theories and models that discuss individual functioning in a current perspective.
2. Theories and models that address it in a developmental perspective.

Models that are restricted to the current perspective (e.g., some cognitive models) analyze and explain why individuals function, in terms of their contemporaneous mental, behavioral, and biological states, independent of the developmental processes that might have led to the present state of affairs. By contrast, developmental models analyze and explain current functioning in terms of the individual's developmental history. They are concerned with how relevant aspects of the individual and his or her environment have operated in the process leading to the present way of functioning.

Individual development brings successive changes both in the structures and functions of the factors underlying the dynamic processes and in the nature of the processes (Ford & Lerner, 1992). At a certain stage of individual development, the structures of mental, biological, and behavioral systems are the result of maturation and individual experiences—that is, of processes in the frame of restrictions and potentialities given by constitutional factors. The functioning of structures at a certain stage cannot be explained satisfactorily without understanding the processes that have led to such structures. In the perspective that will be argued here, individual development is a matter of how maturation and experiences lead to new structures and patterns, and how new processes emerge in the new structures.

The current and the developmental perspectives on individual functioning are complementary: We need both perspectives. It is possible and scientifically defensible to study individual functioning from a contemporaneous, current perspective, apart from the individual's past developmental history. However, understanding the current functioning of an individual forms the basis for discussing changes in developmental processes. An understanding of an individual's previous experiences contributes substantially to a fuller explanation of his or her present functioning, in the same way that knowledge of a society's history can help make its present conditions more explicable. The above view implies reasons for not maintaining the strict demarcation between personality and developmental research.

The Environment in Psychological Research

A brief summary of the historical background of how the environment has been conceptualized in traditional psychological research may help clarify recent trends, especially the role assigned to environment in contemporary developmental scholarship.

Among researchers in the area of personality, it has long been emphasized at the theoretical level that behavior cannot be understood and explained in isolation from the situational conditions under which it occurs. The importance of the situational conditions for behavior was observed by Reinhardt (1937): "... reliability of predictions as to future behavior ... depends not upon the constancy of individual purpose alone ... but also upon the continuance or occurrence of the same type of situation" (p. 492). The view was strongly emphasized by Brunswik (1952), who suggested that psychology be defined as the science of organism–environment relationships, and it has been held by proponents of very different perspectives: by behaviorists (e.g., Kantor, 1924, 1926), by field theorists (e.g., Lewin, 1931); by purposivists (Tolman, 1949); by personologists (Murray, 1938); by trait psychologists (Allport, 1966; Cattell, 1965; Stagner, 1976); by those advocating a psychodynamic position (e.g., Wachtel, 1977); and by those who define themselves as interactionists (e.g., Sells, 1963a). Of special interest for the theoretical discussion is the fact that Cattell (1965), one of the best known trait theorists, strongly endorsed the importance of considering the situational context in research on personality: "Lack of allowance for the situation is one of the main causes of misjudging personality" (p. 27). The contributions by those referred to above had two characteristics: (a) a focus on *current* behavior of the person, and (b) a focus on *proximal* contexts or situations.

The role of sociocultural factors in the *developmental* process of an individual was discussed by Tetens as early as 1777. A strong proponent of considering environmental factors in individual development was Stern (1927, 1935), who strongly emphasized the role of the environment in terms of the character of the "proximal space." Similarly, the concept of "proximal development" was central in Vygotsky's (1978) theory of cognitive and language development. Barker's (1965) analyses of settings, as well as Bronfenbrenner's (1977, 1979, 1989) analyses of levels of environmental factors, yielded new and substantial content to the discussion of the role of context factors in developmental research. In his discussion of individual development in a life-span perspective, Baltes (1976) emphasized the role of environmental factors, referring to what he designated contextualistic-dialectic paradigms (cf., Riegel, 1976).

Empirical research on the relation between environmental factors as independent variables and person characteristics as outcome variables, adopting a psychometric variable approach, has a long tradition. Good examples in this tradition can be seen in educational research concerned with the role of the home background as it relates to individuals' educational and vocational career. However, until recently, theoretical formulations concerning the role of environmental factors have had relatively little impact on the planning, implementation, and interpretation of empirical research in psychology. Psychology has not developed a language of environments to the same extent that it has developed a language of behavior and personality. This observation is particularly informative in view of the role that environmental theories have played in neighboring disciplines that are concerned with functioning and development of organisms at the individual level. For ethologists, it has always been natural to refer to environmental factors (for example, perceived territories) in explanatory models of animal behavior.

From their various perspectives, anthropologists (Arsenian & Arsenian, 1948; Berger & Luckman, 1966; Chein, 1954; Goffman, 1964; Mead, 1934) and sociologists have also made essential contributions—often overlooked and neglected in psychology—to the theoretical discussion about the role of context factors for human behavior. An early proponent for the role of societal factors in individual development was the father of modern sociology, Durkheim (1897). As early as the 1920s, sociologist William I. Thomas (1927, 1928) discussed many of the issues that are the focus of interest today. He noted the distinction between actual and perceived environments and situations, and explored the problems connected with defining and demarcating a situation. He also stressed the developmental role of the situations an individual encounters, and argued that context conditions must be incorporated into models of actual behavior.

THREE GENERAL CONTEXT MODELS

At a metatheoretical level, three general models for the role of the environmental context for individual functioning and development can be distinguished: (a) *unidirectional causality,* (b) *classical interactionism,* and (c) modern interactionism, here designated *holistic interactionism.* Each has its specific implications for theory building and for implementation and interpretation. A brief summary of the salient characteristics of the three models will be given in this section. The remainder of the chapter will be devoted to description and discussion of a modern holistic interactionistic view, with particular reference to development during childhood and adolescence.

Unidirectional Causality

The traditional view on the role of the environment in development has two essential characteristics: (a) the individual and the environment are regarded, discussed, and treated as two separate entities; and (b) the relation between them is characterized by unidirectional causality.

The unidirectional approach locates the main causal factors for individual functioning in the environment; the individual is the target of contextual influences. The view is reflected in theories and models at all levels of generality, from Marxist models for society to S–R models for very specific aspects of behavior studied in the mainstream of experimental psychology. Classical learning theories basically adhere to this view. It is also manifested in traditional research designs that employ the key concepts of prediction, independent and dependent variables, and predictors and criteria.

A Current Perspective

A unidirectional view on the role of environmental or context factors for current behavior was explicitly formulated by Skinner (1971): "A person does not act upon the world, the world acts upon the individual" (p. 211). (A careful analysis of Skinner's writings, however, shows that his S–O–R model, with its consideration of the operant, is inherently interactive, although operant research is often in violation of this paradigm.) In general terms, this view, which engendered much debate in the 1970s, falls under the rubric of "situationism" in personality research (Forgas & Van Heck, 1992). An overview and an appraisal of the situationist position have been presented by Krahé (1990).

A Developmental Perspective

For a long time, both theory and empirical research on individual development were dominated by a unidirectional view on causality. Theories that are very different adhere basically to this approach. According to classical psychoanalytical theory, the life course of an individual is strongly under the unidirectional influence of the environment, particularly the parents' treatment of the child during infancy. Watson (1930), in his discussion of individual development in a behavioristic perspective, gave the environment a decisive role in the developmental process of an individual: "Give me a dozen healthy infants, well-formed and my own specific world to bring them up and I'll guarantee to take any one at random and train him to become any type of specialist I might select—doctor, lawyer, artist, merchant-chief, and yes, even beggarman, and thief, regardless of his talents, tensions, tendencies, abilities, vocations, and race of his ancestors" (p. 104).

Viewing individuals as primarily the product of the environment, and arguing that complex behaviors are assemblages of simpler behaviors, Simon (1969) expressed a unidirectional view on behavioral development: "A man, viewed as a behavioral system, is quite simple. The apparent complexity of his behavior over time is largely a reflection of the complexity of the environment in which he finds himself" (p. 25). Even in developmental research that did not refer to a behaviorist or psychoanalytic view, the family was most often regarded as influencing the child in a unidirectional way during the socialization process from infancy through adolescence.

An additional line of work that strongly influenced developmental psychology during the 1960s, 1970s, and 1980s is rooted in sociology, where the basic formulations concerning the strong impact of the environment on the life course were formulated by Durkheim (1897). This view is further reflected in the vast amount of research in which individual differences across various aspects of the life course have been interpreted as the result of differences in upbringing environments (cf., Bronfenbrenner & Crouter, 1983, and their discussion of "the new demography"). Research in education offers other illustrations—for example, the classical study of the influence of schooling on IQ by Husén (1951; Husén & Tuijnman, 1991).

Classical Interactionism

The central idea of classical interactionism is expressed in the formula B = f (P, E), that is, behavior equals the individual functioning that results from the interplay of the person and the environmental factors. The formula implies that the focus of interest is the interface of person–environment relations. In contradiction to the traditional unidirectional view on the relation between the individual and the environment, the classical interactionistic formulations emphasize that (a) an individual and his or her environment form a total system in which the individual functions as the active, purposeful agent; and (b) a main characteristic of the causal relations is reciprocity rather than unidirectionality. The process character of the person–environment relation was discussed by Bronfenbrenner (1989) in terms of process–person–context models.

Models for Current Functioning

The main propositions for classical interactionism in a current perspective were summarized by Endler and Magnusson (1976) as follows:

1. Actual behavior is a function of a continuous process of multidirectional interaction (feedback) between the individual and the situation that he or she encounters.
2. The individual is an intentional active agent in this interaction process.
3. On the person side of the interaction, cognitive factors are the essential determinants of behavior, although emotional factors play a role.
4. On the situation side, the psychological meaning of the situation for the individual is the important determining factor.

Theoretical, methodological, and research strategy consequences of these formulations in different subareas were discussed in Magnusson and Endler (1977; cf. also Magnusson, 1976, 1980).

Scholars who have advocated a role of environmental factors, particularly situational ones in a current perspective, in individual behavior have sometimes been described as early interactionists. However, although the readers of the classical theoretical literature will be stimulated by the skillful discussions of the interdependence and accommodation of person and context, holistic principles, objective conceptualizations and subjective representations of stimuli and situations, direct and mediated contextual influences, and distinctions between macro- and microenvironmental impact, they will be equally surprised by the lack of explicit explanation of issues of reciprocity and bidirectional influences. In the B = f (P, E) equation, depending on theoretical preference, P and E were more readily addressed than were the functional relations between them. The term *interaction* was seldom employed in early theoretical works. Moreover, a characteristic feature of much early discussion of the person–situation relation was the focus on *reacting* and *adapting* rather than on *acting,* even when explicitly treating purposive behavior. Even when Sells (1963a, 1963b), for example, described his position as that of an interactionist, and discussed "the principle of interaction," the focus was on the individual's biological and behavioral adaptation to varying contextual conditions.

Classical interactionist formulations for current individual functioning were presented by Pervin (1968), adopting the term "transactional," and by Bandura (1978) using the term "reciprocal determinism." Strelau's (1983) "regulative theory of temperament" also stresses person–environment interaction. Borrowing a term from J. J. Gibson, Eleanor Gibson (1994) used the concept of "affordance" to illustrate organism–situation interaction in animal research in the contemporary perspective.

Particularly during the 1970s and 1980s, the explicit formulations of a classical interactionist model exerted a strong twofold impact on personality research, along with carrying implications for planning, implementing, and interpreting developmental research. First, the issue of cross-situational consistency in individual functioning became a central topic for theoretical debate. Second, this debate led, as a consequence, to an interest in theoretical taxonomies and empirical analyses of contextual characteristics.

Developmental Models

What is here designated as classical interactionism has old roots in developmental psychology. William Stern (1935) was an early, explicit proponent of an interactionistic position. He defined the arena for the reciprocal person–environment interaction as the person's "biosphere" or "personal world" (cf., Kreppner, 1992a). Baldwin explicitly discussed ontogenetic and evolutionary development in such terms in the 1890s. And, as suggested by Cairns and Cairns (1986), there is a direct line from Baldwin to Piaget and Kohlberg, and to others who have influenced various areas of developmental research. A major step forward in the application of an interactionistic view in empirical developmental research was the publication of two articles by Bell (1968, 1971).

During recent decades, the role of person–environment reciprocal interaction for individual development has become accepted theoretically by most developmentalists. Leading researchers in personality and developmental research have used different terms to identify this view, for example, Baltes, Reese, and Lipsitt (1980): "dialectic-contextualistic"; Bronfenbrenner and Crouter (1983): "process–person–context"; Cairns (1979): "developmental synthesis." Lerner and Kauffman (1985) adopted the term "developmental contextualism" for their discussions of an interactionist view of individual development. Oyama (1989) critically discussed what is here designated as classical interactionism, and suggested the term "constructivist interactionism" for her approach—an approach that, in many respects, is similar to the one labeled modern interactionism here.[1]

A primary basis for empirical research on person–environment relations in the development of individuals, in the framework of classical interactionism, has been the "goodness of fit" model (Lerner, 1983), a concept that was already launched by Stern (Kreppner, 1992b). With reference to such a model, Eccles and coworkers (1993) have investigated changes occurring at the time of moving into junior high school.

---

[1] As reported above, different concepts and formulations have been proposed and used for what are here designated "interaction" and "interactionism": "transaction," "reciprocal determinism," "dialectic-contextualistic," "process–person–context," and "developmental contextualism." Our reason for using interaction and interactionism is that, in all other life sciences, these terms are well established as representing a fundamental aspect of the life processes of living organisms. In our view, it can only be harmful and detrimental to scientific progress in our own discipline, which is dependent on collaboration with neighboring sciences for successful scientific progress, if we continuously invent and apply new terms instead of adopting concepts that are already well established in disciplines with which we want to collaborate.

Holistic Interactionism

According to a modern interactionist perspective, here designated *holistic interactionism,* psychological events reflect aspects of two types of interaction processes: (a) the continuously ongoing, bidirectional processes of interaction between the person and his or her environment, and (b) the continuously ongoing processes of reciprocal interaction among mental, biological, and behavioral factors within the individual.

The boundary between classical interactionism and holistic interactionism is not sharp. Transition from one approach to the other in the development of scientific fields is a gradual process. Thus, holistic interactionism builds on and integrates the central formulations of classical interactionism. The extension includes two main elements. Holistic interactionism (a) emphasizes more strongly the holistic, dynamic character of individual functioning and of the total person–environment system, both in a current and in a developmental perspective, and (b) incorporates into the model, in a systematic and explicit way, both biological processes and manifest behavior.

The perspective of holistic interactionism rests on four basic propositions:

1. The individual functions and develops as a total, integrated organism.

2. Individual functioning within existing mental, biological, and behavioral structures, as well as development change, can best be described as complex, dynamic processes.

3. Individual functioning and development are guided by processes of continuously ongoing, reciprocal interaction among mental, behavioral, and biological aspects of individual functioning, and social, cultural, and physical aspects of the environment.

4. The environment, including the individual, functions and changes as a continuously ongoing process of reciprocal interaction among social, economic, and cultural factors.

With some exceptions, the discussion about person–environment relations in the framework of classical interactionism was based on a dualistic view; the environment was a separate element from the organism, which was involved in dynamic interaction with the environment. An essential aspect of a holistic interactionist view is that the individual and his or her environment form an integrated and dynamic system in which the individual and the environment form inseparable elements.

The holistic interactionist view, as summarized in the four propositions above, received new blood from four main sources, the combination of which infused the holistic model with the substantive content that was lacking in the classical approach.

The first main enrichment comes from cognitive sciences. Since the sixties, research on cognitive processes has been one of the most rapidly developing field in psychological theorizing and research. Research on information processing, memory and decision making has made conspicuous progress and has contributed essential knowledge for the understanding and explanation of individual development and functioning.

The second source stems from the rapid development of research in neuropsychology, endocrinology, pharmacology, developmental biology, and other disciplines in the life sciences that are concerned with the internal biological processes of an individual and the interaction of these processes with mental, behavioral, and social factors (Damasio & Damasio, 1996; Hockey, Gaillard, & Coles, 1986; Rose, 1995). Research in these areas will contribute much to our understanding of the ways in which individuals function as totalities. Knowledge from these disciplines has helped to fill the "empty box" in S–R models with substantive content, and has contributed to bridging the gap between contrasting explanations of behavior in terms of mental factors, biological factors, or environmental factors. For example, Kagan (1992) ascribes the strong renewed interest in research on temperament to the extraordinary advances in neuroscience.

The third source lies in modern models for dynamic, complex processes, such as chaos theory (Barton, 1994; Crutchfield, Farmer, Packard, & Shaw, 1986; Gleick, 1987), general systems theory (von Bertalanffy, 1968; Laszlo, 1972; Miller, 1978), and catastrophe theory (Zeeman, 1976; cf., Gottlieb et al., Ch. 5, and Thelen & Smith, Ch. 10, this Volume). These theoretical perspectives, particularly chaos theory, have had an almost revolutionary impact on theory building and empirical research in scientific disciplines that focus on multidetermined stochastic processes, that is, in meteorology, biology, chemistry, ecology, and others (Bothe, Ebeling, Kurzhanski, & Peschel,

1987; Hall, 1991). In psychology, the general systems view has been applied in theoretical analyses more than the chaos theory and the catastrophe theory. A growing number of developmentalists have discussed developmental issues in the framework of systems theory. To an increasing extent, research referring to such a framework is being conducted and reported. For example, Fogel and Thelen (1987) and Lockman and Thelen (1993) have offered examples of the fruitfulness of applying this perspective to research on specific topics: expressive and communicative behavior, and motor development, respectively.

The fourth main source for enrichment of a holistic perspective on individual development lies in the revival of longitudinal research. In tracking individuals over time and context, the inadequacies of the piecemeal or variable oriented approach to the study of developmental issues become obvious, because operating factors necessarily shift over time. It is only the organism that remains distinct and identifiable. Some of the most comprehensive longitudinal programs have been planned and implemented with reference to a holistic view (see, e.g., Cairns & Cairns, 1994; Magnusson, 1988). A manifestation of the recognition of the importance of longitudinal research is the fact that the first scientific network that was established by the European Science Foundation in 1985, had the title Longitudinal Research on Individual Development (Magnusson & Casaer, 1992).

The contributions from cognitive research, from neurosciences, from modern models for dynamic complex processes, and from longitudinal research have enriched the old holistic view of individual functioning and development in a way that makes it a fruitful theoretical framework of empirical research on specific issues. The modern holistic view offers a stable platform for further scientific progress in psychology, enabling us to fall into step with what happens in other scientific disciplines in life sciences.

Models for Current Functioning

Versions of a holistic interactionist view of current individual functioning have been proposed and discussed by Hettema (1989), Kenrick, Montello, and MacFarlane (1985), and Magnusson (1990), among others. An individual continuously encounters new situations, implying new demands, new threats, new opportunities, and so on. In the process of interaction with the environment, the organism must maintain its integrity and the equilibrium of its internal regulations under varying or even extreme conditions. The character of this adaptation process for a certain individual in each specific situation depends on the perceptual-cognitive-emotional (PCE) system (with its goals, motives, plans, and so on), the physiological system, and the behavioral repertoire of the individual, on the one hand, and the situational conditions, on the other.

Figure 12.1 represents the interaction process in which mental, biological, behavioral, and social factors are involved in a current perspective. The figure gives a simplified (but essentially correct) picture of what happens psychologically and biologically in a specific situation with particular features. (It must be emphasized that the figure is only a summarized description of a temporal sequence of events, not a neural network or pathway.)

Suppose, for instance, that an individual encounters a situation that he or she interprets as threatening or demanding. The cognitive act of interpreting the situation

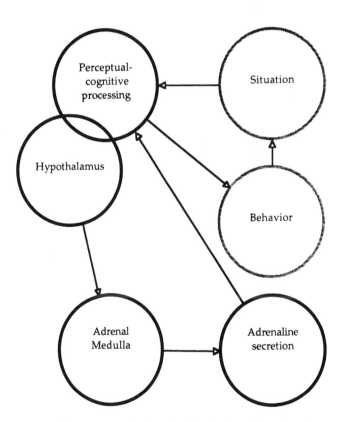

Figure 12.1 A simplified model for the interplay of environmental, mental, biological, and behavioral factors for an individual in a specific situation.

stimulates, via the hypothalamus, the excretion of adrenaline from the adrenal glands, which in turn triggers other physiological processes. The cognitive-physiological interplay is accompanied by emotional states of fear, anxiety, and/or generally experienced arousal. In the next stage of the process, these emotions affect not only the individual's behavior toward and handling of the environment, but also his or her interpretation of the sequences of changes in the situational conditions, and, thereby, his or her physiological reactions during the next stage of the process.

In this view, the PCE system, the biological system, and the behavioral system of an individual are involved in a continuous loop of reciprocal interaction (cf., Hofer, 1981; Weiner, 1977). The way this process functions is contingent on, among other things, the environment as it is perceived and given meaning by the individual. The outcomes of such situation–individual encounters will set the stage for subsequent actions and reactions to psychologically similar situations, as interpreted by the individual in his or her perceptual-cognitive system. An illustration of the application of this perspective is given in the discussion of stress research by Appley and Turnball (1986; cf., Warburton, 1979, discussing physiological aspects of information processing and stress). Over time, in development, this interaction process affects the mental system (for example, in its interpretation of certain types of situations), the behavioral response to such situations, and the physiological system.

The exact nature of this process of current individual functioning on a certain occasion for a certain individual is dependent on the functioning of the PCE system, the biological system, the behavioral system, and the social system. With reference to the formulation of the goal for scientific psychology—to understand and explain why individuals think, feel, act, and react as they do in real life—the crucial role played by the mediating mental system of perceptions, cognition, and emotions in the total interaction process should be emphasized.

For an interactionist model of individual functioning, the essential role played by the individual's interpretation of the environment is of particular interest. The appraisal of external information guides thoughts and actions and evokes physiological systems that, in turn, influence psychological events, thoughts, and emotions. The role of the individual's interpretation and appraisal of stimuli and events in the environment forms an essential element in theorizing and empirical research on coping and adaptation (see, e.g., Smith & Lazarus, 1990; Lazarus & Folkman, 1984).

Developmental Models

Specific elements of a holistic interactionist view of individual development have been presented for some time. Forerunners to this view were Kuo (1967) and Schneirla (1966). Among those who have contributed to the formulations of the modern view are Cairns (1979a, 1983a; 1996), Gottlieb (1991, 1996), Lerner (1984, 1990), Magnusson (1988) and Sameroff (1982, 1983, 1989). The bioecological model presented by Bronfenbrenner and Ceci (1994) is basically in line with the tenets of modern interactionism. An application of the modern interactionistic view in a specific field is Thelen's (1995) presentation of a new synthesis of motor development. Karli's (1996) presentation of an integrated, holistic, biopsychosocial approach to the development of aggressive behavior falls well within the frame of modern interactionism. The same is true for Susman's (1993) discussion of the developmental processes underlying conduct disorder. She concluded that conduct disorder in the developmental perspective must be viewed against the background of an interaction process among psychological, biological, and context factors.

An illustration of the necessity to consider the interplay of mental, biological, behavioral, and social factors in a holistic perspective in order to gain a proper understanding of the developmental process can be drawn from a longitudinal study of Swedish children (Magnusson, Stattin, & Allen, 1985, 1986; Stattin & Magnusson, 1989, 1990). A cohort of all boys and girls in one community in Sweden were followed from the age of 10 years to the age of 30 years. At the age of 14 years, a strong correlation was found between the advent of menarche and (a) different aspects of norm-breaking behavior among girls, (b) school adjustment, and (c) parent and teacher relations. For example, girls who matured very early reported much greater alcohol use than later maturing girls. They also reported more strained parent and teacher relations, and they adjusted less well to school. Interpreted in a cross-sectional perspective, this result indicated that a group of girls at risk for antisocial development had been identified.

However, in the follow-up of the same girls at the age of 26 to 27 years, no systematic relation between the age of menarche and drinking, nor other aspects of socially mal-adapted behavior, was observed. On the other hand, very early biological maturation had far-reaching consequences for education, family, number of children, and job status. The very early maturing girls had married earlier, borne more children, and completed less education relative to average or later maturing girls. These effects could not be attributed to early maturation per se; rather, they were the result of a net of interrelated factors linked to biological maturation during adolescence: self-perception, self-evaluation, and, above all, the social characteristics of close friends. Girls who experienced early biological development perceived themselves in midadolescence as psychologically more mature than agemates, and they associated more with chronologically older peers and with older boyfriends. In brief, they encountered a much more advanced social life, including what is regarded as norm-breaking behavior, than their later maturing agemates. The short-term deviances in norm-breaking behavior and the long-term consequences for family life, education, and job status were observed only among early maturing girls who perceived themselves as more mature than their agemates and who affiliated in early adolescence with older males or with peers who were out of school and working.

The essential point is that the rate of onset of sexual maturity alone does not account for the short- and long-term consequences observed. Early biological maturation provided a predisposing condition for a process in which mental, behavioral, and social factors were involved.

In line with a holistic interactionist view, Stattin and Magnusson (1990) emphasized that the specific short- and long-term consequences of the rate of sexual maturation, among Swedish girls may be different in cultures with other social norms, rules, and role expectations for teenage girls. In a society that promotes contacts between teenagers of various ages, pubertal maturation would have stronger impact than in a society based on age-stratified contacts between adolescents. Caspi and Moffit (1991), replicating the study for a sample of New Zealand girls, found the same early maturation deviance, but only if the girls were enrolled in a coeducational school. Presumably, the opportunities for association with older boys were greater in the coeducational setting than in all-girl schools. Further support for the findings reported by Stattin and Magnusson was presented for youngsters in Germany by Silbereisen and Kracke (in press). It is less clear how very early maturation is linked to norm-breaking behavior among girls in American schools (Cairns & Cairns, 1994; Simmons & Blyth, 1987).

Criticism of an Interactionistic Position

Superficially, the interactionist proposition seems obvious, even trivial. However, if taken seriously, it has far-reaching implications for theory building as well as for planning, implementing, and interpreting empirical research. A modern interactionistic view of individual functioning, as summarized above, is also consistent with progress in related scientific disciplines.

A common skepticism toward an interactionistic approach was summarized by Plomin (1986a), discussing models of the interplay between genetic and environmental factors in developmental processes: "If interactionism were to be believed, it would imply that 'main effects' cannot be found because everything interacts with everything else" (p. 249).

Two comments are pertinent. First, the formulation reflects a surprising misunderstanding of complex and dynamic processes. From the perspective of modern interactionism, everything does not interact with everything else; interaction among operating factors is only one of the basic principles underlying the complex and dynamic processes of individual functioning. Second, operating factors do not interact in a random way. As will be discussed later, the manner in which structures function and processes proceed in a current perspective and change across time is organized and lawful. Nor does the interactive nature of such processes exclude the investigation of main effects in terms of data in empirical investigations. Moreover, personality dispositions (traits) are essential constructs for describing individual functioning and development.

Other, scientifically based, pessimistic views have been expressed by Cronbach (1975) and Gergen (1973), among others, with reference to the complex interactions of factors that we must address in order to understand individual functioning. The comprehensiveness and complexity of the phenomena that should be considered in understanding why individuals think, feel, act, and react as they do in real life make the researcher's task exceedingly difficult. However, the complexity of the phenomena to be analyzed can never be the litmus test of a scientific discipline. Had such a criterion originally been applied in the natural and life sciences, they would not have advanced as they have. The criterion for a scientific discipline cannot reside in the nature of the phenomena under consideration must reside in the way we formulate the problem and plan, implement, and interpret the results of empirical studies. As long as the structures and processes that are our main concern function and proceed in an organized and lawful way, the scientific challenge is to map this lawfulness.

PRINCIPLES IN THE FUNCTIONING OF THE PERSON–ENVIRONMENT SYSTEM

A number of principles are key for understanding individual functioning and development within the total person–environment system: the holistic principle, and the principles of temporality, novelty, dynamic interaction, organization, integration, and amplification of minimal effects.

The Holistic Principle

Psychological research in areas such as perception, cognition, intelligence, personality, and development is dominated by a focus on very specific aspects of the total process(es). These aspects are usually conceptualized and analyzed in terms of variables.

The term *variable* is one of the most misused concepts in psychological research. Misunderstanding is sometimes caused by the fact that the concept is used in two distinctly different senses: as a psychological concept, reflecting a certain aspect of individual functioning—say, intelligence or aggressiveness—and as a statistical concept, referring to the measurement level in terms of data. It might be worth reviewing the original definition of a variable in mathematics: "A quantity that may assume any values or set of values." In psychology, the definition has been extended to mean "a factor, in individuals and/or in the context, which may vary across individuals." One of the misuses of the variable concept is associated with the common tendency to reify psychological phenomena in terms of hypothetical constructs. Hypothetical constructs are basically inferential in nature; they reflect aspects of the total functioning of the individual but *do not exist as separate structural units*. An individual can function in an intelligent, dependent, or helpless way, but intelligence, dependence, and helplessness do not exist per se.

The research strategy focusing on one or a few specific aspects of individual functioning and/or of environments at a time has been designated a *variable approach* (p. 686). Even if this approach is less conspicuous in developmental research than in general psychology, the same tendency is present. Consequently, the nature of the relationship among variables, in terms of R–R relations or S–R relations, becomes a main topic.

The application of a variable approach has its primary theoretical basis in a reductionistic model of humans (see Overton & Reese, 1973; Pepper, 1942). In her discussion of behavioral genetics and developmental research, Scarr (1981) discussed two types of reductionism that are applicable to much of the variable-oriented research: (a) reduction in the level of explanation, "that one appeals to phenomena that are parts or constituents of the phenomena one wants to explain without specifying how other parts are organized into the whole"; and (b) reduction in methods of investigation, "the analysis of phenomenon into bits and pieces that seldom are reassembled in a satisfactory explanation of the original phenomena" (p. 163). These characteristics of the dominating, variable-oriented research strategy should be seen in the perspective of the formulations of modern interactionism.

In summary, in contrast to the traditional variable approach a modern holistic-interactionist view emphasizes an approach to the individual and the person–environment system as organized wholes, functioning as totalities and characterized by the patterning of relevant aspects of structures and processes, in the individual and in the environment. The totality derives its characteristic features and properties from the interaction among the elements involved, not from the effect of each isolated part on the totality. Each aspect of the structures and processes that are operating (perceptions, plans, values, goals, motives, biological factors, conduct, etc.), as well as each aspect of the environment, takes on meaning from the role it plays in the total functioning of the individual.

A single variable does not have the same psychological significance in the developmental process for all individuals, independent of other aspects of individual functioning. In the Stockholm longitudinal study, Magnusson and Bergman (1988, 1990) observed that aggressiveness in childhood was significantly related to adult criminality among males. Further analyses showed that the significant correlation between early aggressiveness and adult criminality was largely found among males who, in their childhood, had shown a combination of aggressiveness, motor restlessness, lack of concentration, poor peer relations, and other problem behaviors. When this multiproblem group of males was removed from the sample, aggressiveness ceased to predict adult criminality. In the same way, parental divorce does not affect children, independent of other aspects of family life and family relations, but is detrimental when it appears together with other risk factors. The same observation held for other experiences during upbringing, such as criminality, alcohol problems, and unemployment in the family.

The whole picture conveys information that extends beyond what is contained in the separate parts. This is "the doctrine of epigenesis": "Behavior, whether social or unsocial, is appropriately viewed in terms of an organized system and its explanation requires a holistic analysis" (Cairns, 1979a, p. 325).

The holistic principle holds for all systems, regardless of the level at which the systems are operating. It holds at the cellular level, at the level of subsystems (e.g., the coronary system, the immune system, the cardiovascular system, the cognitive system, and the behavioral system), and at the level of the individual as a total system. It also holds for the environment and its subsystems (e.g., the peer system among youngsters) as well as for the total person–environment system.

Conceptualizing the individual as the organizing principle in an explanation of individual functioning has roots in the ancient distinction among four basic temperaments. In psychology, the tendency to reduce psychological structures and processes to the smallest possible elements was discussed and criticized by James (1890) and Binet and Henri (1895). Dewey (1896), following James's criticism of the atomistic approach to mental thought processes, warned that the S–R approach could imply a new form of atomism. The general principle—that the whole is more than the sum of the parts—was the fundamental proposition for the gestalt psychologists (see Brunswik, 1929 for a discussion). The proponents of typologies, as well as those arguing for a clinical view on individual functioning, principally adhered to a holistic principle.

In general terms, a holistic approach to individual functioning has been discussed for some time (cf., Allport, 1937; Lewin, 1935; Russel, 1970; Sroufe, 1979). In developmental research, a holistic view has been advocated by Block (1971), Cairns (1979a, 1983a), Ford, (1987), Lerner (1984, 1990), Magnusson (1988, 1995), Sameroff (1982,

1983, 1989), Wapner and Kaplan (1983), and Wolff (1981), among others.

Implications

The holistic interactionist principle has fundamental consequences for the choice and application of appropriate methodologies and research strategies in empirical research on human functioning. An essential implication is that the total process that comprises the focus of interest in a particular study cannot be finally understood by investigating single aspects taken out of the context of other, simultaneously operating factors. If we only think of single cells, we will not understand the functioning of the systems in which they work. Neither the functioning of the individual within current structures, nor developmental changes, can be understood by summing results from studies of single aspects, a point forcefully made by Allport in 1924. As a consequence, the traditional variable-oriented approach needs to be complemented with a *person approach,* which considers a holistic interactionistic framework (cf., Bergman, in press; Magnusson, in press b).

Adoption of a holistic view does not, of course, imply that specific mental, behavioral, and biological aspects of individual functioning cannot or should not be the object of empirical research. The warning by Mayr (1976) with respect to biology is equally applicable to psychology: "The past history of biology has shown that progress is equally inhibited by an anti-intellectual holism and a purely atomistic reductionism" (p. 72). There is no real contradiction between, on the one hand, a holistic approach to theoretical analyses and, on the other, empirical investigations of specific aspects of the structures and processes that are involved, and of specific mechanisms that are operating, in the processes underlying why an individual thinks, feels, acts, and reacts as he or she does (cf., Goodfield, 1974). On the contrary, analyses of such specific aspects provide a necessary foundation for understanding the functioning of the totality. What seems most desirable is a coordinated and mutually enhancing approach to the distinct levels of analysis and the methodological strategies associated with them.

Temporality

One central concept in a holistic interactionist view is the concept of *process.* A process can be characterized as a continuous flow of interrelated, interdependent events.

This definition introduces time as a fundamental element in any model for individual functioning. In modern models of dynamic processes *motion* is a central concept. Key aspects of biological processes are *rhythm* and *periodicity* (Weiner, 1989). In an important article, Faulconer and Williams (1985), drawing on Heidegger, have emphasized the importance of annexing temporality in our endeavors to understand individual functioning. Without the principle of temporality, the fundamental dynamic aspect of the processes of current functioning and development is ignored (cf., Dixon & Lerner, 1988).

The temporal perspective varies with the character of the system under consideration. Processes in systems at a lower level generally are characterized by shorter time perspectives than processes in systems at a higher level. The temporal perspective also implies that the pace at which structures and processes in the individual change as a result of maturation, and experiences varies with the nature of the systems, especially the level of subsystems (see the discussion by Lerner, Skinner, & Sorell, 1980, about "non-equivalent temporal metric"). The anatomical structure of the fetus changes, as a result of cell–environment interaction, at a much faster speed than changes in the individual occur during adolescence.

Because systems at various levels are embedded in each other and are involved in a dynamic and reciprocal interaction, the temporal perspective does not apply to only one subsystem at a time. Rather, the coordination of system components with different time scales is critical. Cairns and Cairns (1986) made a distinction between short-term interactions in the perspective of seconds and minutes, and developmental interactions in the perspective of months and years. They proposed that social learning processes, which are central for short-term, current adaptations, may be reversed or overwhelmed in the long term by slower-acting maturational, biosocial processes (see Riegel, 1975, for a presentation of a dialectical theory of development).

Novelty in Structures and Processes

Some theorizing and empirical research seems to be based on the implicit assumption that individual development is a matter of adding new elements to existing ones in a process of accumulation or, sometimes, acquiring more of the same elements. According to the holistic view espoused here, this assumption is not valid. The characteristic feature of

individual development is that it is a continuous process of restructuring, at the subsystem level and at the whole system level, within the boundaries set by biological and social constraints. "Throughout development, the child or animal refines properties of its expression, combines previously isolated properties together into new packages, and opens up new windows of receptivity to its world while closing other windows on the way to establishing a unique individuality" (Fentress, 1989, p. 35). A change in one aspect affects related parts of the subsystem and, sometimes, the whole organism. At a more general level, the restructuring of structures and processes at the individual level is embedded in and is part of the restructuring of the total person–environment system.[2]

Thus, individual development implies continuous reorganization of existing patterns of structures and processes, and creation of new ones. Sometimes, totally novel behaviors appear. Research from the longitudinal program at Chapel Hill is illustrative (Cairns, Cairns, Neckerman, Fergusson, & Gariépy, 1989). In late childhood, girls develop new techniques of aggressive expression, including the ability to ostracize and ridicule peers in a way that keeps the target unaware of the person attacking him or her. This strategy is employed with increasing frequency by females in late adolescence. The attacks of boys, on the other hand, are characterized by the developmental continuation of confrontational techniques that leave them open to direct and violent reprisals.

One implication of this view is that what seems on the surface to be the same behavior for all individuals at various age levels may have quite different psychological significance for different individuals of the same age and for the same individual over time. This consequence of the principle of novelty in the holistic, integrated developmental process of an individual is often ignored in traditional developmental research in two interrelated ways. The same hypothetical construct is used to represent seemingly identical but qualitatively different behaviors at different age levels. What is designated aggressiveness or intelligence at the age of 5 years is likely to be qualitatively quite different and to play a different role in the

---

[2] In the life-span perspective, novelty implies both growth and decline in structures and processes, as emphasized by Baltes (1987).

total patterning of the child's behavior at the ages of 2, 8, and 15 years. A basic, but incorrect, assumption of the traditional variable approach is that measures that are intended to reflect the same hypothetical construct—say, aggressiveness or intelligence—differ over time only quantitatively, not qualitatively, along a nomothetical dimension.

Dynamic Interaction

Much of the debate on individual functioning in the framework of classical interactionism has been based on empirical studies that investigated person–environment interactions across individuals in statistical terms, using traditional experimental designs (e.g., Hartup & van Lieshout, 1995). In contrast, when we discuss the concept of interaction, it refers to *dynamic interaction* (cf., Lerner, 1978; Magnusson & Endler, 1977). Dynamic interaction is a basic characteristic of (a) the processes going on within the given mental, biological, and behavioral structures of an individual; (b) the processes going on within the environmental system; and (c) the processes of interplay between the individual and proximal and distal environmental factors in the total person–environment system.

Dynamic interaction among operating factors is a fundamental characteristic of the processes of all living organisms *at all levels* (von Bertalanffy, 1968; Miller, 1978). Interaction between elements is also a central aspect of "relational holism" in physics (Zohar, 1990). Components of open systems do not function in isolation, and they usually do not function interdependently in a linear manner. The processes are much more complex, particularly when biological and cognitive systems are involved in mutual operations.

Dynamic interaction is a characteristic of the developmental process of an individual *in the life-span perspective*: from the interaction that takes place between single cells in the early development of the fetus (Edelman, 1989; O'Leary, 1996) to the individual's interplay with his or her environment across the lifespan (Magnusson, 1988). The building stones of all biological organs are the cells. Behind the fact that the individual develops as an organized, functional totality from a single cell is the process of interaction among cells. Each cell develops, functions, and dies as a result of cell–cell interaction, in which information is received from and sent to neighboring cells. By

the application of techniques from molecular biology and biophysics on unicellular model systems—and today, even on transgene organisms—new ways have been opened for understanding the mechanisms that regulate the growth, division, and development of new forms of cells. The essential role of the concept of interaction in the life sciences is reflected in the title of an invited lecture, "Life Is an Interaction" given recently by the cell biologist Uno Lindberg (1992).

In dynamic interaction, two concepts are central: (a) reciprocity and (b) nonlinearity.

Reciprocity

As was pointed out earlier, a strong assumption in traditional psychological research concerns unidirectional causality. Unidirectional relations that influence the functioning of the individual and of the person–environment system obviously exist, mainly in the role played by physical properties of the environment and somatic properties of the individual. For example, the outdoor temperature will affect the individual's choice of clothes and his or her behavior in some respects, in a unidirectional way. Nevertheless, a primary feature of the dynamic complex processes that are our concern here is the *reciprocal* interplay of operating factors.

Reciprocity is a feature of the processes at all levels of individual functioning and of person–environment systems; it is also a feature of the intercellular relationship; of the relationship between cells and their context in the womb during pregnancy; of the way biological and psychological factors operate together within the individual; of the way an individual relates to other individuals in the socialization process; and of the way an individual relates to other aspects of the environment (Bell, 1971; Burgen, 1993; Caspi, 1987). The best illustration of the reciprocity in person–environment interactions can be drawn from person–person interaction, particularly parent–child interaction (see, e.g., Davis & Hathaway, 1982; Hartup, 1978; Murphy, 1983; Parke, 1978; Peterson, 1968, 1979; Sears, 1951). Reciprocity among operating factors contributes to developmental change in the functioning of the total system: "The basic principle underlying reciprocal influences in development arising from parent–offspring interaction is that of a moving bidirectional system in which the responses of each participant serve not only as the stimuli for the other but also change as a result of the stimuli exchanges, leading to the possibility of extended response on the part of the other" (Bell, 1971, p. 822).

Reciprocity in interpersonal relations has been a building block in many theoretical developmental models. Historically, from Bowlby (1952) onward, developmentalists have employed terms that focus on the interdependent, reciprocal character of social interactions. However, although reciprocity is expressed in theory, the reciprocal nature of the concepts used is often lost in actual assessments. When it comes to operationalizations, these concepts have been used as a characteristic either of the person or of his or her surrounding interpersonal context. Is the attachment in the child or in the parents? In the literature, attachment and social support, for example, have been operationalized both as a status of the person and as a characteristic of the interpersonal environment (cf., Lewis & Feiring, 1991; Sarason, Sarason, & Shearin, 1986).

Nonlinearity

As stated previously, psychological research in general is focused on the relations among variables. Most often, the problem is elucidated by investigating the relation across individuals, applying statistical methods. The most frequently used methods assume that (a) the relation among the variables is linear, and (b) the relation obtained *across* individuals holds for the relation among factors operating *within* an individual.

Our concern here is linearity versus nonlinearity in the interrelations among variables operating at the individual level. At this level, nonlinearity, more often than linearity, is a characteristic of most processes. The principle implies, for example, that the effect of hormone A on the dependent hormone B is not necessarily linear; the relation may assume any function. The same holds true for the interplay of a single individual with his or her environment. For example, individuals' psychological and physiological stress reactions to increasing stimulation from the environment are often nonlinear. The inverted U-relation found between on the one hand, performance as well as psychological and physiological stress reactions for individuals, and, on the other, the strength of the demand from the environment, is an obvious example. The nonlinear function for the relation between two operating person-bound factors or the relation between the individual and his or her environment may differ among individuals. Choosing an adequate methodology for studying individual differences—one that takes into

consideration the nonlinear relations among operating factors in the individual—is essential for effective studies of individual phenomena over time.

Causality in Dynamic Interaction

The model for individual functioning that was presented in Figure 12.1 illustrates how perceptual, cognitive-emotional, biological, and behavioral aspects of an individual's functioning, and the perceived and interpreted aspects of the environment, are involved in a continuous loop of reciprocal interaction in a current situation. In the dynamic interaction process, psychological factors may operate as causal factors, and biological factors can influence psychological phenomena. What initiates a specific process and what maintains it over time may vary. A psychological factor may start a biological process, which is then maintained by physiological factors (cf., Gottlieb et al., Ch. 5, this Volume). Similarly, psychological factors can maintain a process that was triggered by biological factors (cf., Krantz, Lundberg, & Frankenhaeuser, 1987). Environmental factors influence an individual's physical and mental well-being, and, at the same time, an individual affects his or her own environment in many different, directly and indirectly ways (see, e.g., Lerner & Busch-Rossnagel, 1981; Magnusson 1981).

The implication of this view is that the concepts of independent and dependent variables, and of predictors and criteria, lose the absolute meaning that they have in traditional research, which assumes unidirectional causality. What may function as a criterion or dependent variable at a certain stage of a process may, at the next stage, serve as a predictor or independent variable.

Organization

A fundamental basis for the scientific analysis of individual functioning and development is the proposition that processes go on in a lawful way within structures that are organized and function as *patterns* of operating factors. Organization is a characteristic of individual structures and processes at all levels; it is a characteristic of mental structures and processes, of behavior, and of biological structures and processes. The lawfulness of the processes, within functionally organized structures, is reflected in the development and functioning of all subsystems as well as in the functioning of the organized totality. Organs and systems of organs constitute functional units of the total organism.

The orderly organization of behavior in a developmental perspective was emphasized and discussed by Fentress (1989). An interesting question is whether the difference between early development and aging is essentially a discontinuity in organizational directionality toward better organization as opposed to toward lesser organization (Baltes & Graf, 1996).

One basic, well-documented principle in the development of biological systems is their ability for self-organization. Self-organization is a characteristic of open systems and refers to a process by which new structures and patterns emerge (Barton, 1994; Eigen, 1971; Hess & Mikhailov, 1994; Kaplan & Kaplan, 1991; Kauffman, 1993; Nicolis & Prigogine, 1977; see also Thelen, 1989, for a discussion of self-organization in developmental processes). From the beginning of the development of the fetus, self-organization is a guiding principle. "Finality in the living world thus originates from the idea of organism, because the parts have to produce each other, because they have to associate to form the whole, because, as Kant said, living beings must be 'self-organized'" (Jacob, 1989).

Within subsystems, the operating components organize themselves to maximize the functioning of each subsystem with respect to its purpose in the total system. At a higher level, subsystems organize themselves in order to fulfill their role in the functioning of the totality. We find this principle in the development and functioning of the brain, the coronary system, and the immune system. "The strength and indeed the very preservation of nascent connections between neurons appear to depend on patterns of neural activity in the developing nervous system and these patterns of activity vary among individuals—at best they are only statistically regular—so that detailed wiring of each individual's brain is distinct" (Stryker, 1994, p. 1244). The principle can also be applied to the development and functioning of the sensory and cognitive systems and to manifest behavior (Carlson, Earls, & Todd, 1988).

Individual Differences

Two aspects of organization are important to the discussion here. First, individuals differ to some extent in the way in which their operational factors are organized and function within subsystems. Individuals also differ in subsystem organization and function. These organizations can be described in terms of patterns of operating factors within subsystems and in terms of patterns of functioning subsystems. Weiner (1989) suggested that even the oscillations produced by the natural pacemakers of the heart, the stomach, and the brain are patterned.

In psychology, the idea of patterning is not new. Galton (1869) concluded that some people are more intelligent than others but each person's pattern of intellectual abilities is unique, and a common type of presentation of analyses of individual differences with respect to intellectual resources is in terms of profiles representing patterns. Based on diaries describing their own children, pioneers of child psychology such as Preyer (1908), Shinn (1900), and Stern (1914) recorded and discussed individual differences in development changes in terms of patterns. Patterning of individual characteristics was also a view reflected in longitudinal research on child development during the period from 1930 to 1950 (Thomae, 1979).

Second, the number of ways in which operating factors in a certain subsystem can be organized in patterns, in order to allow the subsystem to play its functional role in the totality, and the number of ways in which subsystems can be organized to form the total pattern for the total organism, are *restricted* (cf., Gangestad & Snyder, 1985, who argued for the existence of distinct personality types, with reference to shared sources of influence). Only a limited number of states are functional for each subsystem and for the totality (cf., Bergman & Magnusson, 1991; Sapolsky, 1994).

With reference to this analysis, the task for empirical investigations of individual functioning and development in terms of patterns is, in each specific case, twofold: (a) To identify the possible operating factors in the system under consideration, that is, the factors that have to be considered in the particular pattern; and (b) to identify the ways in which these factors are organized, that is, the actual working patterns.

Patterning as a basic characteristic of subsystem functioning can be illustrated by objective data from biological research. Studying cardiovascular responses in a stressful situation, Gramer and Huber (1994) found that the subjects could be classified in three groups on the basis of their distinct *pattern* of values for (a) systolic blood pressure (SBP), (b) diastolic blood pressure (DBP), and (c) heart rate (HR) (see Figure 12.2). A similar study on cardiovascular responses was reported by Mills et al. (1994).

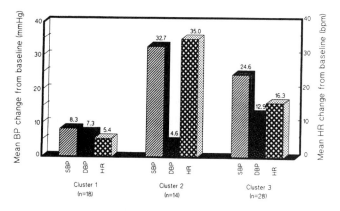

Figure 12.2 Magnitude of SBP, DBP, and HR reactivity in cardiovascular response clusters during speech preparation.

The data presented by Gramer and Huber represent a momentary picture of individual functioning in terms of patterns. How individuals can be grouped on the basis of their distinctly different biological processes has been demonstrated, among others, by Packer, Medina, Yushak, and Meller (1983), who studied the hemodynamic effects of captopril in patients with severe heart problems. Together, these results show a basic principle underlying individual differences in development: At all levels of organization, individual development is manifested in patterns of operating factors. This view leads to the conclusion that individual differences are to be found in the patterning of operating factors within subsystems, and in the patterning of subsystems in the totality—for example, in the way the PCE system, the behavioral system, and the physiological system work together in the total functioning of the individual.

One implication of this perspective is that each subsystem must be analyzed in terms of its context in the total functioning of the individual and the total functioning of the person–environment system, as well as in terms of the manner in which it affects and is affected by other subsystems.

Organization of Environments

Organization is also a fundamental characteristic of the external environment. Both the physical and the social environment are structured and organized. Environmental organization is a prerequisite for the individual to deal with the

external world purposefully and effectively. Two levels of the organization are of interest in this connection.

The first level is the organization, in objective terms, of the physical and the social world. The physical world does not appear in a random fashion; it presents, in many essential respects, a well-structured organization for the individual. The social environment also puts an organized structure at the disposal of an individual in the organization of the school system, the labor market, and so on. The study of the nature of such institutions and of their organization by age, gender, and social class is fundamental to life-course sociology (see Elder, Ch. 16, this Volume).

The second level is the organization of the environment in the eyes of the beholder—how it is perceived and interpreted by the individual. As developing, evolving individuals, we tend to make sense of our world and of ourselves within that world. Particularly salient to the discussion about person–context interactions is the individual's mental organization of the social environments found in families, in peer relations, and in other social networks (Kelvin, 1969). This is a prerequisite for the individual's experience of these networks as meaningful, for the individual's purposeful current functioning, and for the normal development of the individual. The organization of the environment, as it is perceived and interpreted by the individual in terms of organized patterns and structures, is a necessary condition for the individual's ability to deal effectively with and assign meaning to the enormous amount of information that is available at each moment of the person–environment interaction process, and for the individual to use the information for adequate and effective actions. In the developmental process, one of the most important tasks for the caretaker of a child is to act in a way that helps the child to develop valid and effective perceptual-cognitive organizations of the social world (Costanzo, 1991).

Integration of Processes

At all levels of the dynamic holistic processes, the functioning parts are coordinated in their operations so as to serve the goal of the system to which they belong. This principle holds for parts of subsystems at all levels, as well as for the coordination of subsystems in the functioning of the totality. Integration is the principle behind the fact that the total is more than the sum of its parts.

Amplification of Minimal Effects

In chaos theory, the "butterfly effect" refers to the long-term, sometimes potent effects of a seemingly small, negligible event in the long-term development of dynamic, complex processes. A comparable effect in the developmental process of individuals may be the effect Caprara (1992) calls "amplification of minimal effects." It refers to the long-term effects that may result from marginal deviations in the individual's behavior or appearance, as judged against what is regarded as normal. Such deviations may engender reactions from the proximal social environment—reactions that will begin an iterative process of interaction between the individual and the environment. The reactions on both sides become increasingly strong, with long-term detrimental consequences for the individual's developmental process. Say, for example, that a boy, at a certain occasion, involuntarily shows a kind of behavior that is disliked by his parents. They might punish him, become watchful for repetition of this kind of behavior, and look for further indications of a personal disposition that they dislike. In such a situation, some boys will rebel, and increased punishment from a parent, along with undesirable behavior by the boy, may lead to feelings of detachment from the parents and to antisocial behavior (cf., Patterson, 1982).

THE ENVIRONMENT IN THE PERSON–ENVIRONMENT SYSTEM

An individual's way of thinking, feeling, acting, and reacting develops in a process of close interaction with the physical and social environment (Schneider, 1993). Thus, enumeration of certain basic environmental properties that are relevant to understanding the processes involved in individual development is appropriate.

The Concept of Context

In models for individual current functioning and development, a key concept is *context*. The total, integrated, and organized system, of which the individual forms a part, consists of a hierarchical system of elements, from the cellular level of the individual to the macro level of environments (Hinde, 1996; Lerner, 1978; Riegel, 1975; Schneirla, 1957). In actual operation, the role and functioning of each element in the total person–environment system depend on its context *within each level*. The development and functioning of a cell depend on the development and functioning of surrounding cells with which the cell communicates; that is, the cell depends on an influx of information from surrounding cells (Damasio & Damasio, 1996; Edelman, 1987). The development and functioning of the cardiovascular system are dependent on how other bodily systems at the same level—for example, the immune system—develop and function. The development and functioning of an individual depend on the development and functioning of other individuals with which he/she associates. The way a certain element of the Western culture functions is dependent on how other, related elements function.

The total system is hierarchically organized with respect to both structures and processes (Koestler, 1978, used the concept "holarcy" to denote this characteristic feature of a system). Each level of the system is simultaneously a totality seen in relation to lower levels, and a subsystem in relation to higher levels. Systems at *different levels* are mutually interdependent. In the levels-of-understanding model for schizophrenia, it is believed that "the pathology of the disorder can only be understood through a clarification of how its abnormalities at different levels interact with each other" (Mortimer & McKenna, 1994, p. 541). The functioning and development of the social system, of which the individual is a part, depend on the characteristic features of the society and culture (cf., Bateson, 1996; Hinde, 1996).

The following sections on context are restricted to discussion of some aspects of the environment that are external to the individual, that is, to the environment with which the individual must deal and interact. For a fuller conceptual treatment of the environment and of the role of environmental factors in child development the reader is referred to the chapters by Bronfenbrenner and Morris and by Schweder et al., in this Volume.

Conceptual and Empirical Analyses of Environments

A scientific analysis of person–context interaction presupposes dimensionalization and categorization of the environment at different levels (Schneirla, 1957; Sells, 1963b). A first attempt at an analysis of situations and situational conditions was presented by Rotter (1954, 1955), who discussed what he termed "the psychological situation," that is, the situation as it is interpreted and assigned meaning by the individual. The role of the situation as the temporary frame for individual behavior was the focus of the discussion in a volume by Magnusson (1981). In his discussion of context and behavior, Pervin (1978) included an analysis of stimuli, situations, and settings. A recent overview of theory and empirical research on situations was presented by Forgas and Van Heck (1992). Systematic theoretical analyses of the total environment were presented by Bronfenbrenner (1977, 1979, 1989), who introduced a distinction among four levels of what he called the "ecological environment": (a) The microsystem, (b) the mesosystem, (c) the exosystem, and (d) the macrosystem. Barker (1965) used the concepts of "settings" and "behavior settings" for his theoretical and empirical study of individuals in a community in the Midwest.

Perceived and Actual Environments

The environment "as it is" and the environment "as it is perceived," construed, and represented in the minds of individuals is an old distinction. For the environment as it is, Koffka (1935) introduced the term "geographical environment," and Murray (1951) talked about "alpha situations." The perceived environment was referred to by Koffka (1935) as the "behavioral environment," by Lewin (1936) as "life space," by Murray (1951) as "beta situations," by Tolman (1951) as the "immediate behavior space," and by Rotter (1955) as the "psychological situation."

Here, the two aspects will be discussed with reference to the concepts of actual versus perceived environments. Knowledge about the organization and function of the environment in both these perspectives is needed for effective analyses of person–environment interaction processes. It is assumed that the main function of the environment in these processes is the environment as it is perceived and interpreted by the individual. However, individual perceptions and interpretations of the external world are also formed and function with reference to the organization and function of the environment "as it is," the *actual* environment.

The Actual Social Environment

The social environment affects current individual functioning and development at all levels of generalization, from laws and customs at the level of cultures, to the habits, norms, and rules that are specific to, for example, a family or a small group.

For a long time, child research was concerned with contextual aspects of the social environment in rather gross, general terms. However, during recent decades, research has been extended to include more specific aspects of the environment, for example, infant–mother attachment (Ainsworth, 1983), the particular situation for each child in the family setting (Dunn & Plomin, 1990), the family as environment (Maccoby & Jacklin, 1983), and the environment in child-rearing interactions (Radke-Yarrow & Kuczynski, 1983).

Consideration of the character of the social environment is of central concern in clinical work. In this connection, a critique has been raised against the context-free type of classifications of mental disorders that are common in psychiatric practice. Emde (1994), reviewing the discussions about diagnostic classifications in early childhood stated that "current diagnostic classification schemes for this age group were inadequate because of limited coverage and because such schemes did not pay sufficient attention to individuals in context" (p. 72).

The Actual Physical Environment

The importance, for individual functioning and development, of the amount and diversity of physical environmental stimulation has been discussed theoretically and demonstrated empirically. White (1959) emphasized the role of the child's interaction with the inanimate environment in his discussion of competence as an important factor in motivation. Hunt (1961, 1966) underscored the importance of the physical patterning of stimulation when he discussed the development of intelligence and intrinsic motivation. In his analysis of cognitive development, Piaget (1964) stated: "Experience of objects, of physical reality is obviously a basic factor in the development of cognitive structures" (p. 178). The research by Hubel and Wiesel (1970) demonstrated the crucial role of patterned stimulation for the proper development of the perceptual system. The arrangement of the physical environment, as well as the variety of stimulation and information it offers, has implications for the development of sensory perception, as well as for cognitive development.

In early research, the defining of the impact of life events in objective terms was prevalent when the relationship between accumulated stressors and subsequent physical and/or psychological well-being was studied. Stressors were generally defined according to a putatively consensual meaning of their severity (Holmes & Rahe, 1967). In later research, however, the differential impact of life events on human subjects has been recognized in, for example, the Life Experience Survey, in which subjects rate the strength of an event's impact on themselves (Sarason, Johnson, & Siegel, 1978), and in certain interview approaches (e.g., Craig, 1987). However, some researchers (e.g., Headey & Wearing, 1989) continue to use questionnaires (such as the List of Recent Experiences; Henderson, Byrne, & Duncan-Jones, 1981) that assume that the degree of influence on individuals from life events can be objectively defined and can have uniform effects. Both everyday experiences and systematic observations make this assumption only partially true. The impact of environment and situations on human beings is both general and differential. The interpretation of a specific situation by different individuals contains both common and unique variation.

The Environment as a Source of Information and Stimulation

One central principle in an interactionistic view is that the impact of external factors is primarily through individuals' processing of information offered by the environment. The perceptual-cognitive process of selection and interpretation of relevant information from the environment is largely affected by prior experiences, direct or indirect, of similar events in the past, as underscored in modern adaptation-level models (cf., Schneirla's, 1957, discussion of "trace effects"). Prior exposure has formed cognitive schemas, attitudes, and more or less habitual ways of handling, coping with, and securing control of the environment (both behaviorally and cognitive/realistically/illusorily; Thompson, 1981).

Experiences are always interpreted from the current frame of reference. Helson's (1964) adaptation-level theory couches this process in terms of influence from past and repeated experiences of stimuli of a similar kind, present background factors, and residual memories of cognitions, emotions, and actions associated with previously experienced situations that are now recurring. Or, in the words of Nobel laureate Aron Klug: "One doesn't see with one's eyes, one sees with the whole fruit of one's previous experience" (Fensham & Marton, 1991). Krupat (1974) subscribed to similar notions about humans' functioning when he stated that "prior experiences with danger (as well as confidence in one's own ability) act to decrease the subject's sense of vulnerability" (p. 736). In a similar manner, Wheaton (1990) has recently addressed the issue with research indicating that being chronically stress-laden in a specific life domain (e.g., job, marriage) diminishes the impact of supposedly stressful life events, such as loss of a job, or divorce.

Repeated exposure to the same type of environmental event has a variety of effects. It might, for example, lead to a decreased strength of reactivity (Magnusson & Törestad, 1992), to a more positive attitude ("mere exposure effect"; Moreland & Zajonc, 1982), or to substituting, for the original quality of reaction, its opposite "opponent process" (Landy, 1978; Solomon & Corbitt, 1974). Thus, individual differences in the person–environment interaction process leading to the present state, and the functioning of the individuals' PCE systems, lead to individual differences in interpreting the stimuli and events that comprise the objective elements of a current situation. Such individual differences in the interpretation of single situations account for the partly unique way in which individuals cope with situational conditions, that is, responding differently to the same objective situation.

The above discussion is related to the issue of situations or environments as "a source of information" versus "a source of stimulation." A view of the environment as a source of stimulation that elicits individuals' responses has been prevalent in various fields of psychology for decades. This perspective was succinctly formulated by Skinner (1971), as cited on page 691. And it is true that the information conveyed to humans is often subliminally processed with little or no conscious control (Brewin, 1986; Dixon, 1981; Schneider & Shiffrin, 1977; Shiffrin & Schneider, 1977; Zajonc, 1980). However, some researchers (e.g., Mason, 1975) have observed that the impact of physically defined situations (seemingly objectively stressful conditions such as extreme cold) is heavily influenced by persons' own perceptions of them; that is, the effect is mediated by psychological processes. In such cases, the environment must be considered a source of information.

Approaching the environment as a source of stimulation can best be illustrated in experimental psychology and in classical learning theory. An essential feature of the experimental tradition is that the stimulus is defined in objective terms. This tradition incorporates the assumption, often tacit, that the impact of a certain contextual factor is general and has the same meaning and the same stimulus value to all individuals. (See Fechner's reasoning about the objective character of physical stimuli.) The objectively defined environment and its effect, as a source of stimulation, on individual functioning is the main area of study in the rapidly growing field of research generally called environmental psychology, even if the concept of the environment as carrying information is gaining ground (Stokols & Altman, 1987).

Modern learning theories emphasize the role of the environment as a source of information. For example, in Bolles' (1972) specification of laws of learning, two types of information provided by the environment form a basis for learning how to handle the external world effectively. According to this theory, two kinds of contingencies in the surrounding world are learned: (a) children learn to see linkages between certain external conditions and their outcomes (situation–outcome contingencies); and (b) they learn that certain actions they take will lead to predictable outcomes (behavior–outcome contingencies). These two learned contingencies render the environment both predictable and malleable. Seligman's (1975; see also Abramson, Seligman, & Teasdale, 1978) theory of learned helplessness implies that the link between individuals' actions and the information they receive about the impact of these actions on the environment has been seriously distorted, with detrimental consequences for individuals' mental life. If the learned helplessness state is generalized and persistent, individuals will consider the environment impervious to their influence.

Optimal Environments

Related to the discussion of the environment as a source of stimulation is the issue of optimal stimulation (Hebb, 1955), which involves two topics: (a) *preference* (the preferred level of stimulation) and (b) *enhancement* (the developmentally optimal level of stimulation) (Wachs, 1977).

Much of the research on the role of environmental stimulation in individual development seems to imply a monotonic relation between amount of diversity in external stimulation and optimal development (Wohlwill, 1973).

However, there is enough empirical evidence to suggest that there is an optimal level of stimulation with respect to both preference and enhancement. Either too little or too much stimulation will result in less satisfaction and less adequate development than occurs with intermediate stimulation (see Schneirla's, 1959, theory of biphasic approach–withdrawal processes). An example may be drawn from empirical research on stress, in which too-high and too-low demands on activity both lead to the same kind and amount of physiological and psychological stress reactions.

What constitutes optimal environmental conditions varies among individuals, across time and age for a given individual, and between the sexes (Uzguris, 1977; Wachs, 1979). The optimal level of stimulation will vary, depending on each individual's own adaptation level, based on earlier experiences, learning, and maturation.

Optimal conditions can be particularly critical during specific age periods, such as when the organism is prepared for and responsive to stimulation that will not have the same effect at other stages of development (e.g., the concept of readiness). The crucial role of optimal stimulation at a critical period of development is demonstrated in the findings by Hubel and Wiesel (1970), who showed the importance of patterned stimulation during the first period of life for the development of the ocular system in kittens.

For the environment to offer optimal conditions for the current behavior and the developmental processes of a child, two conditions are essential: (a) *consistent patterning* and (b) *influenceability* (Magnusson, 1980; Mineka & Kihlström, 1978). The first requirement is that the environment must be patterned in a consistent way. This is a prerequisite for the individual's assigning meaning to environments, and for his or her forming of valid conceptions about situation–outcome contingencies and behavior–outcome contingencies. Only under such conditions can the individual make valid predictions about the external world. The more the environment is patterned in a way that we can perceive and interpret in a meaningful way, the more it will function optimally both as a source of stimulation and as a source of information.

The second criterion for an optimal environment is that it can be influenced by the individual's action and this can be done in a predictable way; that is, the individual must be able to exert active control within his or her environment. This criterion is a prerequisite for satisfactorily developing self-identity, cognitive and social competence, and feelings of control.

Ordinarily, physical environments are structured, and they function in a consistent manner. The patterning is available to be understood by the child to the extent that he or she has the necessary perceptual-cognitive and intellectual resources and is given the opportunity to observe and deal with it.

In contrast to physical environments, social environments are not patterned in and of themselves. Rather, at an early age, the patterning is created for the child by other people—mostly caregivers. The degree and kind of patterning and consistency in other people's behavior—their demands, the rewards and punishment they deliver—determine whether the social environment can be used for assigning meaning to the environment and for making valid predictions about situation–outcome contingencies and behavior-outcome contingencies in the external world.

The structuring of the social environment in an organized way is particularly important in the early phases of a child's development, when PCE and biological structures are being formed. Structuring is an important prerequisite for developing valid and effective self-perceptions and views of the external world, as well as for developing effective biological systems (pp. 695–696). The role of caregivers in structuring the child's social environment was addressed by Radke-Yarrow and Kuczynski (1983). Olofsson (1973), in a longitudinal study of young criminals, drew the conclusion that the main characteristic of the home environment for the young criminals, compared with that of a group of controls, was the lack of a consistent pattern of simple rules for family life.

Formative and Eliciting Events

Related to the distinction between models for current individual functioning and models for individual development is the difference between *formative* (developmental) and *triggering* (current) events (e.g., Spring & Coons, 1982). This distinction is of particular interest in discussions of antisocial behavior—for example, the occurrence of a criminal act, and its developmental background in the individual—and in discussions of mental disorders—for example, the outbreak of a schizophrenic episode and its developmental background.

Formative life events influence the predisposition for certain kinds of behaviors, including antisocial behaviors and the vulnerability for disorders. Thus, they affect development by increasing or decreasing the probability for later behaviors and disorders (Brown, Harris, & Peto, 1973). On the other hand, triggering events may elicit a certain kind of behavior or a schizophrenic episode without necessarily increasing or decreasing the probability for later behaviors and episodes.

Whereas triggering events clearly are interchangeable because they typically channel their effect through nonspecific routes, like stress in the case of physical and mental disorders, formative events may be more specific and non-interchangeable. From an interactionistic view, formative events would be active in development by shaping individuals' readiness to cope with particular situations. Triggering events, on the other hand, would occur only in the contemporary perspective, and their effects would depend on the developmental history of the individual.

The above distinction between formative and triggering events is close to but not equivalent with the distinction between the "organizational" and "activational" role of hormones in development (Young, 1961), a distinction that is a large issue in developmental psychobiology. The first term has to do with early establishment of tissue structures by hormones; the second has to do with subsequent activation of these structures by hormones (cf., Cairns, 1979).

Significant Events

There are individual differences in both the magnitude and the type of environmental influences that affect the developmental process. Of particular interest is the occurrence of significant single events that may exert a profound impact on the life course of an individual. Although some of these events appear to occur randomly, they are sometimes better seen as a consequence of an individual's readiness for a certain type of action or reaction, such as marriage or a new job, in combination with an opportunity offered by the environment (cf. Bandura's, 1982, discussion of "chance events"). In other cases, a significant event may be the result of deliberate action by the individual or by persons whose actions influence others. Buying a new house in a given area that has specific features in terms of neighbors, job opportunities, schools, and cultural and leisure activities, may have decisive effects on the future life course of all family members. Significant single events may occur across the whole lifespan, and the nature of their effects may depend on the readiness of the individual—mentally and physically—to act and react in relation to the opportunities and restrictions offered by the environment.

Significant events may change the direction of the life course. Sometimes, this effect is not immediately visible but grows slowly and eventually has decisive effects on the individual's life in a manner that is typical of the so-called "butterfly effect" in chaos theory. Originally, attention was drawn to this characteristic of dynamic systems by Poincaré (1946):

> A very small cause, which escapes us, determines a considerable effect we cannot help seeing, and then we say that the effect is due to chance. . . . If we could know exactly the laws of nature and the situation of the universe at the initial instant, we should be able to predict the situation of this same universe at a subsequent instant. . . . But it is not always the case; it may happen that slight differences in the initial conditions produce very great differences in the final phenomena; a slight error in the former would make an enormous error in the latter. Prediction becomes impossible, and we have the fortuitous phenomenon.

Many of the processes that exert decisive effects on the life course of individuals have this characteristic. For example, the choice of spouse or of occupation, both of which have profound implications for the individual, is for many persons the result of a process in which relevant events play a role that was not apparent at the time of these events. In other cases, the effect is more direct and leads to what has been discussed in terms of "turning points" (Pickles & Rutter, 1991). Often, the necessary condition for a significant event to have this dramatic effect is that the individual is in a state of disequilibrium at the time of its occurrence, and the event serves to restore the balance of the total system and give new direction to the life course. Under such conditions, significant events in individual life cycles serve the same function as "bifurcations," addressed by catastrophe theory, in the physical environment.

The existence and role of significant single events in the individual development processes are important for two reasons: (a) they form an important element in the life of an individual, and (b) their existence has methodological and research strategy consequences. The causal role of significant events, and the fact that they occur at different age levels (from very early to very late in life) for different individuals, invalidates the cross-sectional investigation of many aspects of individual development and requires a longitudinal strategy. In such a strategy, significant events form an element of childhood developmental processes that is impossible to handle with traditional statistics, based on data collected across individuals.

Proximal Dynamic Person–Environment Systems

Both for current functioning and for the developmental processes of an individual, the most significant environmental role is played by that part of the environment that an individual confronts directly. Stern (1935), in his discussion of contextual factors, defined this proximal environment "personaler Nahraum" (Kreppner, 1992a, 1992b). Of particular importance is the proximal social setting—the other individuals with whom the child interacts directly. So crucial is this factor that Patterson and Moore (1978) defined interactionism in terms of person-to-person interactions. Peterson (1968) analyzed the role of person-to-person interaction in a developmental perspective, and McClintock (1983) discussed how interactional analyses of social relationships contribute to theoretical and empirical progress.

Proximal social relations with parents, teachers, peers, and others are essential to the establishment, current functioning, and development of an individual's perceptual-cognitive representations and conceptions of the external world (Stern, 1935). In the socialization process through which a child learns and integrates cultural values, norms, roles, and rules into his or her own personality, persons in the proximal social environment play a fundamental role. The extent to which the proximal social environment is structured, and how it functions in a way that is possible for the child to interpret meaningfully, determines the child's adaptation to the society.

A large body of research on socialization is still noncontextual. However, there is increased attention by scholars to interpret, understand, and explain development in terms of reciprocal interactions between characteristics of the socializing environment and characteristics of the individual. Connected with this trend is a growing concern with the role of factors of the sociocultural environment, which form the context for families and peer groups at a higher level. In certain models, emphasis is placed on the commonality among behaviors in diverse contexts (Jessor & Jessor, 1977). Others are more apt to consider the match between impact and opportunities of environments, on the one hand, and the person's need and characteristics, on the other (Eccles et al., 1993; Hunt, 1975; Lerner, 1983, 1984; Lerner & Lerner, 1987); or they entail a systematic study of the patterning of individual functioning in different contexts (Stattin & Magnusson, 1991). Still others are more process-oriented; they examine the moment-to-moment interplay between the socializing agents and the individual person.

In this perspective, two social systems in which a child functions and develops are of particular importance: (a) the family and (b) the peer networks. Both systems are complex and dynamic, and a characteristic feature of both is reciprocity in the person–context relations.

The Family Environment

Primarily, we seek to understand a child's development in the proximal context of the supports and the constraints of the home environment. Socialization research has traditionally focused on the general structure of the home environment, cohesion, parental guidance and rule setting, the ways parents set up a predictive environment for the child, regulations concerning autonomy and responsibility within the family, parental encouragement and support, the parents as role models, family routines and communication, the involvement of children in family decisions, planning and organization, and so on. Decisional autonomy within well-functioning families is considered a developmental task of adolescence. In this context, Baumrind's (1989) differentiation between authoritative and authoritarian disciplinary styles, and the counterpoise of parental control and emotional support, has gained widespread recognition, as has Olson et al.'s (1983) differentiation between cohesion and adaptability in families.

Reciprocity in Relations and Levels of Analysis

The family offers the best illustrations for the inseparability of a person and his or her context. Each member is an active, integrated part of the family system and contributes to form his or her own social context. In her historical overview of the socialization of children, Maccoby (1992) underscored that, apart from increased fragmentation of research, two major changes had occurred in family research over recent decades. The first was a movement from viewing parents as the transmitters of the culture (the top-down view, or a main effects model) to a more interactive view of parent–child processes (cf., Hartup, 1978). The second was a stronger understanding of and preoccupation with the complex mechanisms involved in parenting: moderating and mediating factors, multiple determination, and bidirectional and transactional processes. As summarized and discussed by Kreppner and Lerner (1989), there is also a stronger emphasis on transgenerational issues, orientations toward both psychologization and sociologization of family processes, the start of a more deepened understanding of the role of genetic factors for similarities and differences in socialization of individual children in families, and stronger realization of the close dependence of socialization on the particular historical context.

The realization that parent–child relationship is a bidirectional process, and should be examined from an interactive viewpoint, is perhaps the single most outstanding feature of present day research on family processes (Bell, 1968; Bell & Harper, 1977; Belsky, Lerner, & Spanier, 1984; Kreppner & Lerner, 1989; Sameroff, 1975; Thomas, Chess, Birch, Hertzig, & Korn, 1963). Currently, there is agreement among family researchers that a comprehensive view of family processes must encompass the issue of cooperation, coordination, and coregulation operating between parents and children over time. For example, it has become clear that parental encouragement, participation in the child's school activities, and high educational expectations are related to the child's educational success. Seginer (1983) showed that parents' expectations were strongly linked to academic aspirations and educational outcomes for their children. But outcomes were also dependent on the child's school results. This example reflects the interactive nature of parent–child relations; child behavior is simultaneously influencing and influenced by parental behaviors and attitudes (Lewis, Feiring, & Weintraub, 1981).

This interactionistic conceptualization of socialization implies views of within-family interactions at different levels. Both macro- and microoriented research is needed in order to understand within-family processes more fully. The exchange of behaviors and emotions between parents and children in specific situations, when analyzed on the micro level may not necessarily be reflected in analyses conducted at a more molar level. An illustration is the study, by Dowdney and Pickles (1991), of mothers' and children's expression of negative affect in disciplinary situations. The children were found to respond to the immediate behavior of their mothers in specific situations, whereas the mothers reacted to the children's behaviors maintained over episodes.

In addition to examining relations between family members as dyads, triads, and tetrads (von Eye & Kreppner, 1989), there is a need to define the family system from the viewpoint of each of the family members (Olson et al., 1983), and from the viewpoint of the total family as an object of research. The view of the family as a self-organizing entity and a functional whole has been brought forward in family system models (Belsky, 1981; Hinde, 1992; Minuchin, 1985). However, it is remarkable that, despite the fact that socialization research today has come far in understanding family processes, few attempts have been made to examine family life (attitudes and behaviors) simultaneously from multiple perspectives: from the perspective of the father, the mother, and the children in the family. Family life, according to most studies, primarily consists of the mother and a specific child, as if the father and siblings play only a secondary role (cf., Lamb, 1981).

One of the questions asked lately is what makes siblings so different from each other during upbringing even though they are brought up in the same family environment. The separation of environmental variance into "shared" and "nonshared" components in behavioral genetics has cast doubt on earlier views of a common intrafamilial socialization. In a thought-provoking manner, Plomin (1989) stated that "the single most important finding from the field of human behavioral genetics is the discovery that nearly all environmental influence relevant to behavioral development operates in a 'nonshared' manner . . . siblings are similar; however, their resemblance is due to their hereditary similarity—environmental influences that affect behavioral development make children in the same family different, not similar" (pp. 139–140). Intensive studies of the mechanisms behind the shared and nonshared environmental influences and their impact on the behavior and personality of children are now underway.

Families and the Time Dimension

Issues of parenting, parental attitudes, rules, and disciplinary practices are substantial, but when isolated from other features of the family and from changes in the constellations, structure, and interaction patterns occurring over time in the family, they tend to be handled as static entities or stable characteristics of the parents or the family as a whole. Stability and change are characteristics of parenting. Across the developmental years of the child, parents' behaviors and attitudes change according to the developmental level of the child, and can vary over time among children in the same family.

Notwithstanding substantial changes in socialization practices, parental behaviors and attitudes might at the same time demonstrate high interindividual stability of specific features. This was shown in a birth-to-maturity longitudinal design involving disciplinary practices. The study, by Stattin, Janson, Klackenberg-Larsson, and Magnusson (1995), demonstrates the importance of studying processes through application of a longitudinal design.

From the holistic and system-oriented position on a macro level, it follows that changes on the part of parents, or children, do not occur in isolation from what goes on in the rest of the family. Thus, the overall family process changes over time. For example, Stattin and Klackenberg (1992) examined the relationship between childhood and adolescence for specific patterns of discordant within-family relations (with mother–child, father–child, and mother–father discord as the constituent elements).

An important issue in the discussion of the role of family processes is the transfer of values, norms, habits, and so on, from one generation to the next. This topic was addressed in the Stattin et al. (1995) study, which covered data across two generations. The study was concerned with how parents' punishment practices were reflected in their children's behaviors when the children became parents.

Family in Context

In addition to an increasing emphasis on bidirectionality and complexity, contributed by developmental ecological approaches (Bronfenbrenner, 1979), there is today a stronger articulation of the contextual embeddedness of socialization (Lerner, 1989; Oliveri & Reiss, 1987). The child's functioning and development at day care, at school, and in the peer group are linked to the family context. Among the relevant research are Steinberg's (1987) studies on latchkey children and their peer orientation. Parenting occurs in and is a reflection of: the family itself; the economic situation in the family; the availability and quality of day care, schooling, neighborhood influences; other institutional organizations and social networks; and the wider social and cultural context. How parents react to their children in everyday life is linked with their experiences in other contexts. For example, Greenberger, O'Neil, and Nagel

(1994) reported complex interactions between aspects of the parents' work conditions and their parenting. A strong challenge faces future studies: to reveal the causal relations between home and work influences, and to analyze, in more detail, the aspects of work conditions that are associated with particular aspects of parent–child relations.

Peers

As suggested by an extensive body of literature, peer relations form the context in which much new behavior emerges among children and adolescents. Peer relationships and friendships are particularly important features of the life situation for adolescents (Berndt, 1982; Cairns & Cairns, 1994).

With respect to the role of peers in the social context for development, three themes for research can be distinguished: (a) individual characteristics associated with peer relations; (b) the characteristics and the functioning of the peer group, as they affect individual behavior; and (c) the contextual embeddedness of the peer group.

Individual Behavior as a Function of Peer Association

In this theme, the individual is the object of interest, and the peer group is of interest insofar as it yields information about the individual. During the 1970s and 1980s, hundreds of studies examined individuals' peer status (popular versus unpopular; neglected, controversial, and rejected children) and the associated characteristics: peer interaction; coping and problem solving; social skills and competence; school adjustment and achievement; different aspects of personality; emotions, loneliness, and prosocial and agonistic behavior (e.g., Coie, Dodge, & Coppotelli, 1982; Coie & Kupersmidt, 1983; Dodge, Coie, & Brakke, 1982). In a developmental perspective, social skill problems and low peer status of children and adolescents were related to adjustment problems later in life, such as school dropout, delinquency, and mental health problems (Cowen, Pederson, Babigian, Izzo & Trost, 1973; Kohlberg, LaCross, & Ricks, 1972; Kohn & Clausen, 1955; Roff, 1961; Roff, Sells, & Golden, 1972). This line of research constituted a markedly psychometric and sociometric approach, and reflected mainly a unidirectional view of causality.

Although large numbering, such studies contributed little to the understanding of how the peer climate reinforces individual behavior and how individual behavior develops in the peer group. This fact led some researchers to argue

for attention not only to individuals, but to individuals in a network of relationships (Blyth, 1983; Cairns, 1983b; Hinde, 1992).

Characteristics and Functioning of the Peer Group

The object of interest in the second line of research is the functioning of the peer group and its psychosocial processes. Bronfenbrenner (1943) put forward an essential point that is compatible with the general view of this chapter: "Social development applies not only to the individual but to the social organization of which he is a part. Variations occur not only in the social status of a particular person within the group, but also in the structure of the group itself—that is, in the frequency, strength, pattern, and the basis of the interrelationships which bind the group together and give it distinctive character" (p. 363). In this tradition, the reciprocity in friendships has been examined (Gershman & Hayes, 1983), and similarities between the individual and his or her friends in terms of sociodemographic variables, attitudes, and behaviors have been investigated (Kandel, 1978).

In contrast to the traditional sociometric and psychometric approach that characterized much of the research referred to above, a process-oriented approach has been adopted by Cairns and Cairns (1994) in their longitudinal research program, which has been planned and implemented in the theoretical framework of this chapter. Based on data collected on an individual basis over the whole adolescent period, for a large and almost attrition-free sample, they have been able to study in depth the dynamics of peer relations and the role of these relations for the developmental processes of individuals across the adolescent period (Cairns & Cairns, 1994; Cairns, Leung, Buchanan, & Cairns, 1995; Neckerman, 1992). A program with the same goal (to depict "action in context") is the Berlin Youth Longitudinal Study. Among other things, empirical studies in that program (see Silbereisen & Noack, 1988) have revealed the dual quality of many adolescent behaviors—they comprise momentary or future psychosocial health, and they are tools for satisfying important personal and social goals of the individual (see also Jessor, 1992).

Within the life-course perspective, the question arises: How do characteristics of one's peers affect transitions of behaviors? The study reported by Stattin and Magnusson (1990) demonstrated how social behaviors, in a short-term and in a long-term perspective, are systematically linked with characteristics of peers with whom one associates in early adolescence. Studies from the same program have documented that associations with nonconventional peers, in combination with low educational motivation in adolescence, are important antecedent factors in the determination, among females, of an adult homemaking orientation rather than a career orientation (Gustafson, Stattin, & Magnusson, 1992).

The wealth of studies on peer relations has been more informative about the relationship between peer status and behavior, and the social and personal characterization of the individual relative to the group, than about how the peer climate, over time, reinforces individual behavior; what characterizes the peer group and its stabilization; group processes; and how behavior develops in the peer group context (Hartup, 1996). How do (conventional and delinquent) peer groups react to adverse behavior on the part of individuals? What psychosocial processes in the peer group increase or decrease adverse behavior? The characteristic feature of many deviant social behaviors in adolescence is precisely that they occur in groups. However, even among the best studies, few attempts have been made to examine the group context or group processes in these circles of delinquency-prone teenagers. Various studies include some measures about engaging with delinquent friends, and similarities among peer members have been documented (Jessor & Jessor, 1977; Snyder et al., 1991), but few facts are provided about the nature of these friends. Information is needed about the developmental impact of the delinquent peer group on individual behavior; the role of individual members for directing the activity of the peer group; the factors that, over time, reinforce and weaken the individual's ties to the group; the continuity of such a group; and other aspects that deal with the dynamic network in the group.

In view of the extensive variations in constellations of individual, peer, and setting conditions, one may question whether traditional correlations among individual characteristics, peer characteristics and peer group activities that dominate the empirical research (Hartup, 1996) can illuminate the complex interactions among these factors. What is needed is a more holistic, systems-oriented longitudinal, investigation of the different configurations of these factors, and their developmental significance. The design of the longitudinal program presented by Cairns and Cairns (1994) offers a promising line of research in this direction, as do the experimental studies conducted by

DeRosier, Cillessen, Dodge, and Dodge (1994), aimed at investigating the role of the peer social context for the expression of children's aggressive behavior.

The Contextual Embeddedness of the Peer Group

As has been emphasized earlier, each system at a certain level of the total person–environment system is interacting with and thus dependent on the character and functioning of systems at higher and lower levels. Of particular interest for a discussion of peer relations and peer group functioning is the role of the sociocultural environment as the context for the emergence, structure, and functioning of peer groups. A striking illustration of the role of sociocultural factors can be seen in the formation and functioning of peer groups with respect to the appearance of criminal gangs of youngsters. Emler and McNamara (1996) have argued that the amount of time spent with peers, the extensiveness of one's peer group, and the peer group activities are more strongly tied to the institutional participations of adolescents than is usually assumed in adolescent research. For example, being a student normally offers considerably more opportunities to affiliate with peers, in more varied settings, than being unemployed.

Distal Environments

Family and peers do not constitute the only socialization influences on children and adolescents. The proximal environments are embedded in economic, social, and cultural systems of higher order. The specific nature of distal systems in a certain society decides the opportunities and restrictions for the functioning and development of proximal environments, such as the family and peer groups, as well as the opportunities and restrictions for the functioning and development of individuals. A great deal of research attention lately has been focused on the broader sociocultural influences, as they are represented in the community, the neighborhood, and the school, and in leisure-time settings (e.g., Lerner, 1991).

Social and Economic Conditions

The best-known study of how economic and social distal factors and changes in these respects affect individual behavior is the seminal work by Elder and coworkers, using data from the longitudinal studies gathered at the Institute of Human Development at Berkeley, California (Elder, 1974, 1981, 1995, and Ch. 16, this Volume; Elder, Conger, Forster, & Ardelt, 1992; Elder, Liker, & Cross, 1984; Elder, Van Nguyen, & Caspi, 1985). A series of studies has systematically mapped the impact on family cohesion, parenting, and child behavior of the economic crisis during the Great depression in the early 1930s. Among the findings in these studies is that the "economic press" of severe income loss mainly affected the husbands/fathers in the families (Elder et al., 1985). The increased arbitrary discipline by the fathers, traceable to the income loss, produced problem behavior in the boys in the families. A recent longitudinal study has shown how hard times, economic crisis, and value changes in Albania have affected family relations and child behavior (Kloep, 1995). The psychosocial timetable may be heavily influenced by the broader macro-social conditions and institutions, as was demonstrated by Silbereisen (1995) with respect to vocational choice, when he compared adolescents raised in the former East and West Germany.

Formal and Informal Societal Regulations

To a varying extent, opportunities and restrictions for the functioning and development of individuals and of proximal environments are determined by formal societal rules. Some are age-bound, such as entering and ending compulsory school, joining the army, or retiring. Some are nationally regulated; others may be locally determined. The extent to which legal norms exist varies across countries and societies.

The individual socialization process is also strongly dependent on and influenced by informal societal norms and rules, such as the rules for dating in the traditional U.S. culture, or the rules for female dress in fundamentalist Muslim countries. Informal rules for individual behavior may be general and may even hold across societies; others are more specific and are bound to certain groups (e.g., religious sects) or temporary trends (the hippie movement of the 1960s and 1970s). To some extent, they are normative—for example, they are based on a particular chronological age—and to some extent, they are more individual—for example, they are bound to intellectual competence or membership in a certain social class. The informal societal regulations are not formalized in laws and regulations, but are implicit and sometimes very strong elements of expectations in the sociocultural setting of an

individual and forceful in regulating individual behavior, particularly during puberty and adolescence.

Individual Synchronization

To maintain a developmental perspective, there is a need to understand both the formal and the informal societal influence on behaviors, norms, and roles in child and adolescent development (Ryff, 1987). The infrastructure of formal and informal regulations tends to form a social timetable of demands and opportunities for the individual—a timetable that is sometimes strongly age-graded (Caspi, 1987). Despite the wealth of specific options, the broader institutional infrastructure and the legal system of a country are often similar for the majority, chiseling out normative social roles and standards at different ages. This is not to say that only one route is open to children and adolescents. Multiple paths *are* open. One of the central problems in individual development is the *synchronization* of the individual's mental and behavioral capacities with the demands, opportunities, and restrictions of the proximal and distal environment. The diversity of possible life tracks might create stress and insecurity among young people. What can be considered a favorable pathway toward adulthood in a society depends on the culture's "implicit theory of success" (Klaczynski, 1990; Ogbu, 1981). It also depends on local variations in the ecology. For example, a rural environment typically offers fewer future educational and occupational opportunities, and adolescents' and their parents' educational aspirations tend to be lower than in more urban milieus (Sarigiani, Wilson, Petersen, & Vicary, 1990).

In empirical developmental research, too little attention has been paid to the growing individual's embeddedness in the broader sociocultural timetable. It can be argued that much of young persons' thinking about the future (occupation, education, marriage and family, and material standards) and about themselves is linked in time with formal contextual and age-dependent changes. Rather than being strictly related to cognitive development or to an unfolding of cumulative earlier experiences, thoughts about oneself (identity and self-concept) and one's future (plans, decisions concerning the future, wishes, and fantasies), and the restructuring of these self-views and worldviews, are likely to be determined by the points in time for formal transitions, particularly in education. In Sweden, entering the gymnasium or not—and in the United States, entering college or not—has strong consequences for future work roles (Petersen, 1993). Thus, the unfolding structure of the educational system in a given society can provide much of the incentives for change in adolescence and for decisions that have profound effects on the adult roles of parent, spouse, and worker. Klaczynski (1990) advocated that "as they approach graduation, the social-institutional arrangements of the Western school system may compel students to think more systematically about themselves and to make commitments and form ideologies about their roles in society, religion, and interpersonal relationships" (p. 819). The argument also has been put forward that what may be seen as a general trend—for example, declines in educational motivation in early adolescence—and interpreted as a consequence of characteristics of the developmental period in question, might actually be a reflection of specific changes in the school environment in midadolescence which are unbalanced by individual aspirations (Eccles et al., 1993). With a shared timetable for youngsters in a given society, cross-cultural data are needed to discern the governing role of such social regulation of development (Thelen, 1981).

In genetic research, the concept of "sensitive" periods has been advanced. In these periods, the organism is more open for learning experiences than in other periods (see Gottlieb et al., Ch. 5, this Volume). Analogously, one may delineate the points in time for changes in educational tracks, opportunities to engage in more mature forms of behaviors (such as public dances, movies, etc.), and other environmental changes, as "critical" points in time when contextual influences provoke a restructuring of one's life, both prospectively and contemporaneously.

One aspect of the synchronization process is the timing of the individual's decisions with respect to certain central aspects of social life. Finishing school early is associated with different timetables for future family planning, marriage, occupation, and attainment of material goods than finishing school late (Gustafson & Magnusson, 1991). The same is true of decisions to leave home early or late (Stattin & Magnusson, 1995). Gustafson, Stattin, and Magnusson (1989) showed that girls who started to date boys early tended to display a stronger homemaking rather than career orientation in early adulthood. Overall, these and other examples lend credence to the idea that the timing of social behavior might be critical—and to some extent perhaps more informative for the future life-course development—

than are individual differences measured at a given point in time.

During developmental transitions, self-definitions in relation to formal and informal environmental age-graded developmental norms and expectations may play a central role. Recent studies have convincingly shown that teenagers are quite conscious of whether they are "early," "on time," or "late" with respect to behaviors connected with periods of transition, such as formal age-prescribed behaviors and other less formal behaviors—time to be in after an evening out, bedtime, spending money, choice of clothes, and so on (Brooks-Gunn, & Petersen, 1983). Stattin and Magnusson (1990) found that the definition of oneself as "early" among midadolescent girls tended to be associated with perceiving oneself as popular among boys, having more advanced drinking habits and more norm-breaking behaviors, but also having more school adjustment problems and more psychosomatic and depressive reactions. Studies conducted in Norway and Germany (Alsaker, 1995) also have demonstrated that definitions of oneself as being early or late maturing go hand in hand with engaging in more socially advanced behaviors in adolescence.

In summary, how children and adolescents make use of the contextual opportunities that are in the sociocultural environment, the time at which they make transitions, and how they define themselves in terms of age-graded norms in society, can have profound consequences for their adjustment contemporaneously and for their future life track. To some extent, individual behavior is organized by the broader sociocultural arrangements, but individuals also organize their own development. Thus, through its institutions and age requirements on behavior, society shapes a certain direction and sets the milestones for individual behavior. By their own actions, however, young people select some types of developing environments at the expense of others, and, through these means, they shape their unique development.

Research Implications

Cultural factors affect individual behavior through organizational–institutional arrangements in the proximal settings in everyday life. The question of how the cultural context influences individual behavior is an important central issue in cross-cultural research. In this endeavor, cross-national comparisons can offer important information. Cross-cultural studies conducted in recent decades have successfully documented the existence of similarities and dissimilarities between cultural settings; however, one of the major problems in such research in child development is how to link variations in individual functioning in physical and social settings to the specific cultural elements in each cultural group (Harkness, 1992). Cross-cultural comparisons are particularly needed to examine: whether the setting mechanisms behind behavior are similar across countries; whether the mediators of behavioral, family, and peer processes are similar—or how they differ; and whether the same factors operate as moderating conditions for psychological functioning in the same way across cultures. Ryff (1987), in her discussion of the linking of personality to culture, class, and ethnicity, argued for the complementarity of explanation and description. She stressed the need for both psychologization of empirical research (determine the ways macrosocial variables, such as social class and ethnic membership, influence behavior and social relations on the meso- and microlevels), and sociologization of such research (determine the prevalence of and variations in psychological processes at different ages, in different ethnic groups, and in different social strata).

The Environment as a Changing Stage for Individual Functioning and Development

The environment provides a frame of reference for ongoing individual behavior; it offers a stage on which a wide range of behaviors can be manifested. Changes that are important to individual development therefore take place over time in both the macro- and the microenvironment. Factors in the individual that determine maturation and experiences in the course of individual development are nested within factors in the environment that are changing at the same time.

The developmental timetable with regard to the settings surrounding peer relations offers an illustration of how personal and environmental factors are nested in a reciprocal process of change in both parts. In childhood, peer interaction occurs in the near neighborhood, in nursery school, and, later, at school. In adolescence, leisure activities change from adult-led, organized activities in early adolescence (e.g., sport clubs), and mid-adolescence, to more adultlike, commercial activities (pubs, clubs, and discos) in later adolescence (Hendry, Shucksmith, & Glendinning, 1995). The kind of proximal environments that an individual encounters at a given time in this developmental process is determined by the nature of distal social, economic, and cultural factors and the individual's choices of environments (as long as he or she has options) and actions.

In a long-term perspective, the distal environment is under change. A consequence of such change in the distal environment is the change in the proximal environments of individuals (Elder, in press). Compare, for example, conditions today with conditions only 50 years ago, with respect to travel, communication, exchange of information, and industrial production. Ideological and political movements influence and change educational opportunities and systems, and societal norms, rules, roles, and values. Urbanization, almost all over the world, has not only meant that more people grow up and live in urban areas. The economical, social, and cultural character of urban areas has also changed, sometimes drastically. One implication of these changes is that a person who grows up and stays in the same local environment may die in quite another macroenvironment than the one into which he or she was born. Moreover, different generations are born into and live in different environments with different norms, values, resources, and demands. This change has implications for research strategy in that it is difficult to make valid generalizations about what constitutes the important operating factors from one generation to the next and/or from one culture to another.

THE PERSON IN THE PERSON–ENVIRONMENT SYSTEM

The general framework for the analysis in this chapter is that the individual functions and develops as an active part of an integrated person–environment system. This implies that the central issue for psychological theorizing and empirical research is *not* how the person and the environment interact as two separate parts that are of equal importance. It is how individuals, by their perceptions, thoughts, and feelings, function in relation to an environment that, to some extent, they have purposefully constructed, and how these aspects of individual functioning develop through the course of an ongoing interaction process (Lerner & Busch-Rossnagel, 1981; Magnusson, 1990). This framework motivates a closer look at the individual in the person–environment system.

The Person as an Active Agent in the Person–Environment System

The modern, interactionist view holds that the individual is not a passive receiver of stimulation from the environment. The individual is an active, purposeful agent in the total person–environment interaction process.

The view of the individual as active and purposeful is not new. The dynamic conception of the mind and its mental processes as activities, rather than as an organ receiving and processing information, was advocated by the act psychologists in Europe, such as Brentano (1874/1924) and Stumpf (1883). In the United States, James (1890) was a proponent of the same view. The intentional nature of the individual's way of functioning, which formed a central element in Brentano's view, was also stressed by Tolman (1951) in his focus on purposive behavior. More recently, the individual as an active and purposeful agent has been emphasized in action theory (cf., Brandtstädter, 1993, and Ch. 14, this Volume; Strelau, 1983; see also Pervin, 1990).

The Mediating Mental System

The view of the individual as the active, purposeful agent in the person–environment interaction process carries the implication that a guiding principle in the individual's inner life, and in his or her dealing with the external world in manifest behavior, resides in the functioning of the integrated PCE system, including self-perceptions and world-views, organized in schemas and plans with attached motives, needs, values, and goals. The PCE system forms an element in the dynamic complex processes of an individual, an element that distinguishes these processes from other holistic, dynamic processes for which the general models mentioned earlier—general systems theory, chaos theory, and catastrophe theory—were developed. This emphasis is reflected in the proposals to conceptualize personality as a goal-directed, adaptive, open system (Allport, 1961; Hettema, 1979; Schwartz, 1987).

The PCE system serves as a leading edge for adaptation in individual development, in that it mobilizes neurobiological and physiological modifications. By selecting and interpreting information from the external world and transforming the information into internal and external actions, the mental system permits the organism to shape its effective environment and provides a rapid and reversible strategy whereby organisms can adapt to changing environments (cf., Lerner, 1984, 1990). The strong role of affect in the adaptation process was advocated by Karli (1996), in his discussion of a biopsychosocial model for the development of aggressive behavior.

For the view presented here, the recent development in research on sensory perception and the functioning of the brain in the interpretation of information from the external world is of central interest. In contrast to the mainstream or traditional position, input into sensory processes is regarded as information that is interpreted and integrated by the brain and used in coping with internal and external problems, rather than viewed as stimulation of the sensory organs. The sensory organs function more as sensory systems than as independent sensory structures, and the brain as a whole works as a pattern recognizer rather than as an absolute-magnitude measuring devise. Vision, for example, is an active, not a passive, process of the brain (e.g., Popper & Eccles, 1977; Roland, 1993).

Subconscious Processes

In some psychodynamic models of individual development and the functioning of the mental system, the concept of unconscious processes has played a central role. The debate on this issue has been stimulated during the past few decades through the growing interest in and understanding of the parallel processes of controlled (conscious, attended to, and thus subject to critical analysis) versus automatic (out of attentional focus and awareness) information processing (see, e.g., Bowers, 1981; Brewin, 1986; Greenwald, 1992; Kihlstrom, 1990; Norman & Shallice, 1980). The role of unconscious processing of environmental information in the individual's adaptation to varying environmental conditions was suggested by Sells (1966) in his discussion of feedback mechanisms in the adaptation process. The role of unconscious processes in social cognition was recently discussed by Greenwald and Banaji (1995). It has also been suggested that unrecognized cognitive dysfunctions interfere with the socialization process (Buikhuisen, 1982), inhibit social adaptation, and promote delinquency in juveniles (Buikhuisen, 1987). It is noteworthy that persistent offenders, as a group, have been found to have more central nervous system dysfunctions than do control groups of nonoffenders. Understanding the continuously ongoing processing of out-of-awareness signals impinging on the senses renders new significance to the perceptual-cognitive system; at the same time, it reduces the central role earlier ascribed to conscious functioning.

Values, Norms, Motives, and Goals

A central, sometimes decisive role in the mediating mental processes that guide a person's purposeful dealing with the environment is played by the basic values, norms, goals, and motives that are relevant for the particular issue under consideration (Feather, 1980). The value structure underlies and determines the short-term and the long-term goals that direct an individual's thoughts and actions in current situations (Pervin, 1983). An essential implicit assumption by Max Weber, in his analysis of Protestantism and capitalism, was that the individual's purposive, goal-directed activity is shaped by underlying values and preferences (cf., Coleman, 1990). The history of politics and religion is full of illustrations of the strong impact of values on the functioning of individuals, organizations, and societies. An elaborate model for how personal and social values, through attitudes and subjective norms, affect behavioral intentions and actions in a current perspective, was presented in Fishbein and Ajzen's theory of reasoned action (Ajzen & Fishbein, 1980; Fishbein & Ajzen, 1975). From the perspective of this chapter, it is surprising to note that relatively little developmental research has been devoted to the role of basic values. An important aspect of education in the family and at school is the transfer of social values from one generation to the next. For developmental research the role of values in the socialization process and the role of various agents in the transfer of values and norms to youngsters should be among the most central issues (Costanzo, 1991).

Self-Structures and Self-Perceptions

In the processes of the individual's inner world, as well as in his or her dealing with the environment, self-perceptions and self-evaluations form important aspects of the total mental system. James (1890) devoted a whole chapter to this issue. Epstein (1990), in his cognitive-experiential self-theory, assigned a strong role to the individual's self-perceptions and worldviews in the developmental process.

In a *current* perspective, self-perceptions (manifested in feelings of efficacy, self-esteem, and competence) influence the selection and interpretation of information from the outer world, the individual's conduct in current situations, and the way he or she relates to other people. Self-structures

may purposefully direct individual behavior and associated affects (Markus & Wurf, 1987). Recent studies of how the self directs social cognition and social behavior were reviewed by Banaji and Prentice (1994). The individual can choose to engage in some events rather than others on the basis of feelings of efficacy and motivation. An expanding body of research has demonstrated that how well individuals adjust to and cope with their environment is dependent on their beliefs and their trust in their capacities, and what matters are individuals' internal representations of situation-outcome contingencies and their mental representations of their roles as active participants in exercising control (Bandura, 1977, 1978; Harter, 1990). Children's experiences of handling their environment, of perceived control and predictability, have consequences (a) for their view of themselves as competent or incompetent, as confident or not-confident of their abilities; (b) for their motivation to cope with the demands of particular situations; and (c) for mobilization of their behavioral and emotional resources. The prototype of the child with high self-esteem was described by Harter (1990) as the child who is confident and curious, takes initiatives, and can tolerate frustrations and adjust to environmental changes. The empirical literature on relations between self-esteem and behavior suggests, however, that a lack of high self-esteem is not a necessary characteristic of deviance (Cairns & Cairns, 1994).

The *development* of the individual's self-perception, self-evaluation, and self-respect forms a main element in the process of learning and experience through which he or she gains the ability to exert predictive and active control over the environment (Bandura, 1978; Brandtstädter, 1993; Harter, 1983; Weisz, 1983). Lewis and Brooks-Gunn (1979) stated that the self "is developed from the consistency, regularity and contingency of the infant's action and outcome in the world" (p. 9). The relation of self-identity to personal control over development and future life orientation, and the role of school achievement and school success and of socioeconomic status in the home for these developmental aspects were empirically investigated by Pulkkinen and Rönkä (1994).

The role of the school for the development of self-esteem during adolescence was analyzed by Simmons and Blyth (1987), and the importance of the home atmosphere for the emergence of self-reliant views and for motivation to approach and take initiative in specific situations was demonstrated empirically in the investigation of female life careers reported by Gustafson and Magnusson (1991). On the other hand, Markus and Cross (1990) noted: "Yet despite a growing understanding of the processes and mechanisms of early childhood socialization, the precise ways in which the thoughts, feelings, and behaviors of others are internalized and become significant elements of the self-concept have received little direct empirical attention; their exact role in self-development and in the maintenance of the self-system is only now beginning being closely analyzed" (p. 580). The issue of personality and self in a developmental perspective is dealt with comprehensively by Baltes et al., Ch. 18, this Volume.

Development of the Mediating System

The way an individual's *mediating PCE system* functions at a certain point in time is the result of previous developmental processes of experiences and maturation that take place, within the limits of his or her constitutional dispositions. By assimilating new knowledge and experience into existing structures, and by accommodating old structures and forming new ones, the individual develops a total system of structured contents.

As a result of the person–environment interaction process, the characteristics of the mediating system in a person, and of its way of functioning (the specific cognitive structures that are built up, the specific contents of the structures, the affective tones bound to the structured contents, and the coping strategies), will depend to some extent on the character of the environment that the individual encounters in the developmental process. As was stressed and empirically illustrated by Irvine (1969), the concept of intelligence, as defined in Western cultures, had to be revised in order to use intelligence tests for comparison of mental abilities among different ethnic groups. To the extent that environments in which we are reared are similar, the main features of our world conceptions will share common characteristics. When the environments in which we develop differ markedly—as between cultures, for example—the total mediating system and the resulting differences in the interpretation of the environment, at all levels, will differ. In a series of cross-cultural studies of anxiety-provoking situations, systematic differences were found for children and youngsters in this respect (Törestad, Olah, & Magnusson, 1989). To the extent that our interpretations of the outer world determine our behavior, cross-cultural differences in

actual behavior can be explained even in situations that are similar in an objective sense. In a recent article, Valsiner and Lawrence (1996) analyzed the issue of individual development in cultural context, emphasizing the importance of making interacting person–culture systems the object of analysis.

Even if children are reared in the same family, the physical and social environments are not identical. The proximal environments experienced by early- and late-born children may differ radically, because of the birth order of the children, differences in within-family relations, and changes in family socioeconomic conditions (Dunn & Plomin, 1990). These conditions contribute to interindividual differences in conceptions of the outer world, and thus to differences in the interpretation of single situations, even among children who have grown up in the same general environment.

This view can resolve the dispute between Immanuel Kant's idealistic idea that our consciousness is not shaped by reality but rather that reality is shaped by our consciousness, and Karl Marx's materialistic standpoint that reality is not shaped by our consciousness but our consciousness is shaped by reality. In the view described above, both positions can be substantiated. Over time, consciousness is formed in a continuous process of the individual's interaction with the environment, and thus it is dependent on its characteristic features; at the same time, consciousness defines the reality that forms the basis for the individual's active and purposive dealing with the environment.

However, a caution should be stressed. The foregoing discussion of various facets of the mental system uses a number of terms, some of which reflect hypothetical constructs, such as values, norms, attitudes, and self-perceptions. In using such concepts, it is easy to fall into the trap of reification and forget that these constructs are only abstractions covering different aspects of an organism that functions as an organized whole. In a basic sense, perceptions, cognitions, emotions, values, norms, and attitudes are integrated components of one and the same total process.

Behavior in a Holistic-Interactionistic Perspective

In the unidirectional models of individual functioning, behavior is usually regarded only as an outcome. However, according to an interactionistic model, behavior in all its manifestations, including verbal and motor behavior, plays an essential role in the current person–situation interaction, as well as in the processes of individual development.

As illustrated in Figure 12.1, manifest behavior of an individual is a functional element of the continuously ongoing interaction process. It also serves to change the nature of the total person–environment interaction process in two interrelated respects. First, activities serve an important function for the individual—for example, by changing the situational conditions in order to satisfy personal short-term and long-term needs and to avoid negative cognitive, mental, or biological experiences (Brandstädter, Ch. 14, this Volume; Magnusson, 1981). Second, a child's behavior contributes to his or her own social environment; by adapting to other individuals' behavior, the child develops and maintains effective social relations (Cairns, 1986b).

Biological Factors in the Person–Environment Interaction Process

The incorporation of biological factors into the model for the functioning and development of an individual provides one of the basic new propositions in a modern interactionistic model. For the following discussion, the distinction between "biological" and "inherited" aspects of individual functioning and development must be clear. When a behavior is empirically found to be related to biology, it is too often immediately misinterpreted as being genetically determined. However, biological functioning at a certain stage of development is more than the effect of genes. A developmental analysis is required to determine how constitutional, biochemical, genetic, and experiential factors in the person are interwoven.

In 1883, when Wundt made a plea for psychology as an independent scientific discipline, he emphasized the biological basis of psychological phenomena (Wundt, 1948). In 1899, Angell and Thompson discussed the relation between organic processes and consciousness. Later, in his presentation of functional psychology, Angell (1907) stressed the need for the integration of biological factors in the model of individual functioning. During recent decades, Eysenck (1990; cf., Gray, 1985) has been a strong advocate of the biological bases for personality factors. Lehrman (1970), Schneirla (1957), and Tobach and Schneirla (1968) all discussed the role of biological factors in developmental processes. As emphasized by Lerner

(1983), the interaction process in which an individual is involved with the environment can be described in terms of an active adaptation process. In this adaptation process, biological factors, in constant interaction with the PCE system and behavior, play an important role. For example, the adaptive role of the adrenal cortex, which produces corticosteroids such as cortisol through release of ACTH from the anterior pituitary gland in response to stress, was discussed by Selye (1950). The Swedish psychiatrist Sjöbring, whose work during the first part of the 20th century has been met with renewed interest in recent years, emphasized that many diseases were the outcome of an interplay among hereditary and biological factors, physical and social aspects of the environment, and the individual's experiences in a wide sense (Sjöbring, 1958).

Modern contributions to understanding the significance of biological factors for *current* functioning have been presented by, among others, Hettema (1989), who emphasized the role of biological factors in human adaptation; Strelau (1983), who discussed biological factors and temperament; Zuckerman (1980), who demonstrated a systematic relation between biological factors and sensation-seeking behavior, and later discussed the psychobiology of personality (Zuckerman, 1991); Depue (1995), who analyzed neurobiological factors in personality and depression and proposed mechanism-based treatments that rely on specific neurobiological modifications through systematic use of experience-dependent processes; and Hettema (1995), who included biological factors in his multilevel model for depression and personality. The relation of thoughts, emotions, and behavior to physiological processes has been elucidated in much empirical research (see, e.g., Gunnar, 1986, for a review). Experiments on captive monkeys by McGuire and his coworkers showed how social factors, such as the status of the leader in the group and his interpretation of the behavior of other group members, affect his level of serotonin and 5-HIAA, which are important regulators of individual mood (Raleigh, McGuire, Brammer, & Yuwiler, 1984). In research on free-ranging baboons, Sapolsky (1990) demonstrated how strongly social and biological factors interact and how, for example, the feedback mechanisms of the cortisol system can be blocked in low-status animals.

The role of biological factors in individual *development* was empirically demonstrated and discussed by Kagan (1989, 1994, 1996) in his presentation of a comprehensive program of research on temperament in infants and children. The influence of social factors on biological functions was shown by McClintock (1971), who found that the menstruation cycle in female students who shared dormitory rooms was synchronized within the course of one study year. In many cases, the cycles coincided totally before the end of the school year. The reasons for considering biological factors in research on personality development were summarized by L. Susman (1989) (see also Claridge, 1985; Zuckerman, 1991, 1994), and the role of biological factors in adolescence was discussed by Petersen and Taylor (1980). How concepts from biological theory have been assigned a role in the continuity of social behavior was critically assessed by Cairns and Hood (1983) and recently discussed by Earls and Carlson (1994). Contributions from developmental psychobiology have substantially increased our understanding of the role of biological factors in the individual development processes (Gottlieb, 1991, 1992).

Biology and Antisocial Behavior

Antisocial behavior is an aspect of individual functioning for which a systematic and often replicated relation to physiological activity/reactivity has been demonstrated. In these studies, a negative, sometimes strong correlation between antisocial behavior and low adrenaline excretion has been demonstrated. In a longitudinal study a significant, negative correlation between (a) aggressiveness and hyperactivity and (b) adrenaline excretion in the urine sampled in two independent situations at school (a normal lecture and an examination), was observed for boys at the age of 12 to 13 years (Johansson, Frankenhaeuser, & Magnusson, 1973). Criminal records were obtained for these males through the age of 30. Lower adrenaline production at the age of 12 to 13 years was associated with substantially higher levels of criminal conviction in adolescence and adulthood (Magnusson, af Klinteberg, & Stattin, 1993).

There are at least three possible interpretations of this finding. First, persons with a disposition toward persistent criminal activity may have been born with a constitutional "malfunction" (not necessarily genetic; see Offord, Sullivan, Allen, & Abrams, 1979; Raine & Mednick, 1989) that affects the way their individual system of psychological and physiological factors functions. Second, the psychological and biological reaction pattern among persistent criminals may be learned, as a result of early experiences in an inconsistent social environment. As interpreted here, adrenaline excretion occurs as a result of the individual's interpretation of something in the environment as being threatening or demanding. If reward and punishment in the extreme case are distributed randomly, during the infant socialization process, when biological systems are being established, the mental and physiological system, which regulates adrenaline production, will not learn when and how to react adequately. As a result, the system might become pacified. Recent empirical studies support the assumption of a relation between early social experiences and neuroendocrine adaptation (Earls & Carlson, 1995).

The third possible explanation (and the most probable, in our opinion) is interactionistic. The lower adrenaline excretion in males with a disposition for delinquency may be the result of a combination of an inborn biological vulnerability and lack of consistency in the social environment during the early years, when the functioning of the physiological systems is being established. Thus, a child born with physiological vulnerability may need a more consistent social environment than a child with low vulnerability, who may be able to identify even vague regularities in the social environment and develop adequately.

In spite of the exceptions mentioned above, two characteristics of the biological tradition in psychological research are noteworthy. First, in spite of, for example, Angell's incorporation, at the beginning of the 20th century, of biological factors into what might be seen primarily as a holistic view of individual functioning, biological factors have not been consistently integrated into psychological models. Rather, they have mostly formed an independent line of research that has had little impact on developmental research. Second, to the extent that biological factors have been regarded as important and have been studied empirically, their role in individual functioning has most often been seen as causal; a reductionistic view has dominated. Exceptions can be found in the work of Bronfenbrenner and Crouter (1983), Cairns (1979), and Lerner (1984); and in the presentations by psychobiologists such as Kalverboer and Hopkins (1983) and Levine (1982). More recently, the role of biological factors in the developmental process has been emphasized by Gottlieb (1991, 1992, 1996; Gottlieb et al., Ch. 5, this Volume), among others.

Hereditary and Environmental Factors in Individual Development

One issue of debate since ancient times has concerned the relative role of hereditary and environmental factors in individual functioning, both currently and in a developmental perspective.

Since Galton (1869), it has been taken for granted (and supported by empirical research) that intelligence, as defined in Western cultures, is to a considerable extent inherited. The evidence from family, twin, and adoption studies indicates a genetic contribution to major psychiatric disorders such as schizophrenia and bipolar depression (Gottesman & Shields, 1982; McGue, Gottesman, & Rao, 1986; McGuffin & Katz, 1986; McGuffin, Murray, & Reveley, 1987). Buss and Plomin (1984), and Kagan (1996), have emphasized that individual differences with respect to temperament are determined to some extent by genetic factors. Studies of rodents, dogs, and monkeys have shown that individual differences in aggressive behavior can be strengthened and established by selective breeding (Cairns, MacCombie, & Hood, 1983; Lagerspetz & Lagerspetz, 1971). Using questionnaire data from monozygotic and dizygotic pairs of twins, Rushton, Fulker, Neale, Nias, and Eysenck (1986) drew the conclusion that individual differences in altruism and aggression are substantially inherited. Pedersen (1994) reported figures indicating that 30% to 40% of the variation in personality reflects genetic variation. According to Pedersen, Plomin, Nesselroade, and McClearn (1992), heritability for specific perceptual-cognitive abilities differs, depending on the domain— about 40% for memory, and 50% to 65% for verbal and spatial ability and for perceptual speed. Plomin (1986b) suggested an increasing role of genetic factors up through midlife for most traits. Recent research indicates that there is a decrease in heritability late in life (Finkel, Pedersen, McGue, & McClearn, 1995).

As illustrated above, most research on the effect of hereditary factors on various aspects of individual functioning has been and continues to be concerned with the relative role of hereditary and environmental factors, respectively. The ongoing debate is dominated by references to figures estimating the relative magnitude of group-level variance attributable to these two main sources. This approach to the problem has been criticized from two perspectives.

One criticism was formulated by the Nobel laureate Peter Medawar (1984), who strongly emphasized the meaninglessness of trying to "attach exact percentage figures to the contributions of nature and nurture (Shakespeare's terminology) to differences of intellectual capacities: the reason, which is, admittedly, a difficult one to grasp, is that

the contribution of nature is a function of nurture and nurture a function of nature. The one varying in dependence on the other, so that a statement that might be true in one context of environment and upbringing would not necessarily be true in another" (p. 171).

The other line of criticism follows a proposition by which Anastasi (1958) argued against formulating the problem in terms of "How much?" and suggested instead that the scientifically fruitful formulation should be "How?" This approach has had a number of proponents over the decades. A view along the same line, compatible with the modern interactionist view advocated here, was expressed by Dodge (1990) in his criticism of traditional research on the development of conduct disorder: "Instead of counting and comparing effects of elusive constructs, researchers should focus their efforts on the mechanisms by which conduct-disordered behavioral patterns develop, utilizing the concepts and methods of the emerging field of developmental psychopathology. . . . This research should integrate genetic, acquired biological, and environmental contributions in development rather than pit them against each other. . . . These studies will necessarily focus on transactions, relationships over time, and longitudinal development of behavior in context" (p. 701). The same general view was emphasized by Gottlieb (1996) in his discussion of hereditary factors in normal development. A balanced, insightful analysis of the nature–nurture issue was presented by Cairns (1979). The article in which Bronfenbrenner and Ceci (1994) propose an empirically testable theoretical bioecological model has also contributed to clarifying the issue. (The issue is stressed by Lerner in the introductory chapter of this Volume.)

At a most basic level, the onset and course of certain developmental sequences may be determined genetically to the extent that they are common to all individuals. However, even such developmental sequences as the onset of the menstrual cycle in girls and the regulation of growth in height are somewhat modifiable by environmental factors (Tanner, 1981). The individual phenotype develops within the framework offered by the genotype through reciprocal interaction with the environment, a process that starts at conception and goes on through the life span. On the scene set by inherited factors, many different plays are possible (Waddington, 1962). Within the limits set by inherited factors, there are large potentialities for change, due to the interplay with environmental factors: "To put it more plainly, the science of behavior from the epigenetic point of view is not a 'psychology without heredity,' but a science based on the idea that heredity means merely the fact that the zygote starts to develop with an extremely wide (especially in higher vertebrates), but not unlimited, range of behavior potentials, only a very small fraction of which can be realized during its developmental history" (Kuo, 1967, p. 128). The unidirectional causal model for the role of genetic factors, which he addresses as "neurogenetic determinism," was recently strongly criticized by the developmental biologist Steven Rose (1995), arguing for an interactionist position.

In his analysis of sex dimorphism with reference to the nature–nurture debate, Breedlove (1994) concludes: "This chain of events highlights the futility of trying to separate biological and social influences on sexual differentiation in humans" (p. 413). And Edelman and Tononi (1996), in their discussion of the development of the brain as a complex system, wave aside the idea that either "genetic determinism" or "environmental instructionism" should be enough as explanation. In contrast, they argue that the processes of *epigenesis* and *selection* framed in the context of the global theory of the functioning of the nervous system, the theory of neuronal group selection, are required. "This developmental theory explains regularity at the macro level as a result of epigenetic processes, emphasizes variability at the micro level as a substrate for selection, envisions neural adaptation to short-term regularities of the internal and external environment as resulting from processes of neural selection, and recognizes that there is a continuum between development and experience" (Edelman & Tononi, 1996).

Thus, in most respects, individual development takes place in a process of maturation and experience in interaction with the environment, on the basis of and within the limits set by inherited factors (Plomin, 1989; Scarr, 1981; Scarr & McCartney, 1983). That there is a hereditary predisposition for a certain type of behavior does not mean that it cannot be changed by environmental intervention (Angoff, 1988). Kagan (1992), who argues for a hereditary component in temperament, emphasizes how this influence is modified by the environment. Cairns (1979, 1996), in a 20-year evaluation of the role of heredity and environment in individual differences in aggression, drew the conclusion that the differences in mice obtained by selective breeding over 30 generations show strong environmental specificity. The aggressive behaviors in descendant lines can be modified by

environmental social conditions to such an extent that the inherited differences are eliminated. In well planned longitudinal studies of newborns, Meyer-Probst, Rösler, and Teichmann (1983) demonstrated that favorable social conditions acted as protective factors for later social development among children identified at birth as biologically at risk. Ericsson, Krampe, and Tesch-Römer (1993) emphasized the role of practice in forming individual behavior and argued that this practice diminishes the role of biological factors, which are usually regarded as fixed.

Even in the etiology of major psychoses for which there is a strong heredity component, it is not clear how genes are involved. Neither bipolar disorder nor schizophrenia shows the tidy segregation patterns within families that would suggest a simple Mendelian transmission. The prevailing notion about schizophrenia is a diathesis-stress model (Day, Zubin, & Steinhauer, 1987; Zubin, 1976), which presupposes a genetically transferred and/or early, behaviorally acquired individual vulnerability (among those identified, there exists a lack of ability to process much information simultaneously while in distress) and an environmental stressor (e.g., a family member with an overly emotional, intrusive behavior—so-called expressed emotion) (cf., Leff, 1987).

Figure 12.1 presented a general model for the interplay of the mental, biological, behavioral, and social factors involved in the current functioning of an individual. In this model, interpretation of environmental events leads to activation of the sympathetic nervous system and the excretion of stress hormones such as adrenaline and cortisol. Cannon (1914), in his original model, interpreted the process as the body's preparation for fight or flight under certain contextual conditions. Under normal conditions, the process is an adaptive response, with no detrimental consequences for the individual. However, when persistent stress leads to overproduction of such hormones, they can override genetic regulation during fetal development and early childhood, thus causing a detrimental effect on early development (Kotulak, 1993).

In this perspective, current individual functioning is the result of a life history of a person–environment interaction, in which environmental and inherited factors have participated in a manner that makes it impossible to disentangle their relative role at the individual level. The environment plays a major role in shaping the individuality of a person by shaping the expression of genes. The outcome of the process, at a certain stage of development, depends on the potential resources and limitations of the individual and on the properties of the environment with which the individual interacts during the life course.

Biological Maturation

The rate of maturation is a powerful operating factor influencing a girl's dealing with the environment and the environment's reaction to the girl, as illustrated in the empirical study summarized earlier (p. 697). Effects of the rate of maturation have also been observed in studies of boys (Andersson, Bergman, & Magnusson, 1989).

Traditionally, chronological age has been used as a marker of individual development. This approach implies that the marker of an individual's level of development is the number of times the globe has circled the sun since he or she was born. It seems clear that alternative bases for the study of individual differences in developmental rate ought to be considered (cf., Baltes, 1979; Horn & Donaldson, 1976; Thomae, 1979; Wohlwill, 1973).

Individual differences in growth rate, using chronological age as the marker, occur from the beginning of life throughout the whole life span. Some of these differences already appear during the fetal period, as a result of the interplay between genetic factors and the womb environment (Lagerström, 1991). Later differences occur within the context of the total functioning of the individual, with respect to: somatic and morphological characteristics, PCE and intellectual functioning, physical and mental capacity, and general competence in handling the demands of the total environment. Some features are apparent and important in very early infancy; other features emerge and become essential for individual functioning in adolescence, maturity, and old age.

The rate of biological maturation among individuals of the same chronological age may have profound consequences, not only for individual differences in various aspects of functioning, but also with respect to the way the environment reacts to the individual. Differences in developmental timing thereby are related to individuals' social relations, as well as to their capacity to meet environmental demands and to use environmental opportunities effectively.

The potential existence of strong individual differences in growth rate, as central factors in developmental processes, limits the applicability of a cross-sectional design in studies that control for chronological age (Magnusson,

1985, 1988). These differences may affect research results to an extent that has not always been adequately recognized. Consequently, biological age and what might be designated as *functional age* should be used, in some cases, as markers of individual development. However, to control for biological age instead of for chronological age is a remedy only under certain specified conditions. Biological and chronological factors are nested, because the expression of individual differences in growth rate is sometimes counteracted by societal influences that are bound to chronological age—for example, compulsory school education, compulsory military service (in some countries), and a compulsory age for retirement.[3]

Stability and Change in Individual Functioning— A Matter of Person–Context Interaction

One core issue in the discussion of person–environment relations has been and continues to be what is usually referred to as *personality consistency*.

A Current Perspective

The key issue of cross-situational consistency is the extent to which behavior can be explained in terms of stable dispositions or traits of the individual versus the extent to which behavior is also dependent on specific characteristics of situations. The issue has two dimensions: (a) consistency in terms of manifest behavior and (b) consistency in terms of mediating mental processes (Magnusson, 1976).

The dimension of *consistency of manifest behavior* was raised early and was empirically investigated by Hartshorne and May (1928) and Newcombe (1931). Referring to empirical studies yielding correlation coefficients converging at a level of .30 to .40 for cross-situational consistency, Mischel (1968) expressed strong doubt about the meaningfulness of the concept of traits in investigating individual functioning. However, in spite of the strong formulations

---

[3] "Individual differences in growth rate" should not be interpreted to indicate a single growth pattern. Although this may be generally accurate, it also suggests the possibility of different growth rates of component subsystems relative to each other. Examples would be: cognitive growth, where mental age is different from morphological age; or early sexual maturation, where morphological maturation is different from social maturation.

by many theorists about the role of situational conditions for individual functioning, empirical research on the issues raised by these theories was scarce until the end of the 1960s and the beginning of the 1970s.

In a series of studies using situation-specific data that represented ratings in seminatural situations, this issue was elucidated by applying the design shown in Table 12.1 (Magnusson, Gerzén, & Nyman, 1968; Magnusson & Heffler, 1969). The coefficients are presented for the correlation between ratings of 7-year-old children with respect to three aspects of behavior: (a) ability to follow the rules of the game; (b) endurance and concentration; and (c) reaction toward frustration. The ratings were given by independent observers in two different situations, under variations of group task and group composition in four different conditions: (1) no variation; (2) variation in task; (3) variation in group composition; and (4) variation in both group task and group composition.

The results presented in Table 12.1 demonstrate the need to consider the characteristics of the situational conditions that the individual encounters, in order to understand and explain variation and stability in individual behavior across situations. The results support the interactionist view on the cross-situational consistency issue with respect to manifest behavior. According to this view, manifest behavior is organized in *coherent patterns* that change with changing situational conditions. Because individuals' interpretations differ in a partially idiosyncratic manner, their functioning in various other respects (physiologically and behaviorally) will also vary across situations in a partially specific way. What characterizes an individual is the partially specific way in which that individual deals with and adapts to the situational conditions offered by various

situations, manifested in partially specific cross-situational patterns of behavior. A consequence is that as there is less variation in situational conditions, there is less variation in individual functioning.

The main result of this study was confirmed in a parallel study that employed the same design and used conscripts as subjects and well-trained psychologists as observers (Magnusson, Gerzén, & Nyman, 1968; Magnusson & Heffler, 1969). The theoretical, methodological, and research strategy implications were discussed in Magnusson (1976, 1980).

The individual process of behavioral adaptation to varying situational conditions is guided by the individual PCE system (cf., Magnusson, 1980; Mischel, 1973). Which cognitive, emotional, and other facets of the total *mental system* are brought into action, and to what degree, varies from situation to situation, depending on the nature of the available information and the interpretation made by the individual. As demonstrated in a series of empirical cross-cultural studies of individuals' interpretations of anxiety- and stress-provoking situations, two significant differences that are of direct importance for the issue discussed here have been demonstrated: (a) *individuals* differ with respect to their interpretations of the same situation, and (b) *situations* differ with respect to individuals' interpretation (Magnusson, 1971; Stattin, 1983; Stattin & Magnusson, 1990). The organized pattern of an individual's manifest behavior will vary from one situation to another, as situational conditions are variously interpreted by the same total, flexible operating system. In this perspective, it is noteworthy how little interest traditional cognitive research, with few exceptions (e.g., Shanon, 1993), has shown in the role of varying environmental input in influencing cognitive processes.

To what extent do enduring dispositions—traits—exist and play a role in the cross-situational process? There is no contradiction between traditional trait theories and an interactionistic view on the existence of enduring latent individual dispositions. The argument is about the role of such dispositions in the total functioning of an individual. In an interactionistic model, enduring dispositions of an individual form an essential basis for coherence in the individual's interaction with situations of different character and in the lawful continuity of the individual's interaction with the environment across time. A theoretical contribution to this discussion was presented recently by Mischel and Shoda

Table 12.1   Coefficients for Correlation between Mean Ratings

| | | Task Varied | |
		No	Yes
Group Varied	No	a. 0.514 b. 0.790 c. 0.313	0.205 0.026 0.787
	Yes	a. 0.767 b. 0.595 c. 0.603	0.103 −0.046 0.059

Note: The ratings were given by two observers in one situation and by two different observers in another situation.

(1995), who analyzed traits by processing dispositions with reference to social, cognitive, and biological models. A comprehensive analysis and discussion of the trait concept was recently presented by McCrae and Costa (1995).

Stability and Change in a Developmental Perspective

In the theoretical frame of modern interactionism, a fundamental characteristic of the developmental process of an individual is that the total person–environment system of operating factors, in the individual and in the environment, changes across time. An essential feature of the organismic system is that, when a mental, biological, or behavioral structure has been established during the developmental process, it then becomes resistant to changes into new structures. The transition into new states during the lifetime takes place in a balance between (a) the built-in resistance to change in the subsystems and the total system of an individual, once they have been established, and (b) the sensitivity to individual and environmental factors that press for change.

The total system—and its subsystems of biological, mental, and behavioral structures, which are involved in individual functioning and development—has properties that imply less chaos than is present in the processes studied in meteorology, where the chaos theory was first developed. Each biological system functions and develops in a process in which two forces balance each other: (a) maturation and experiences, which work for change, and (b) the principle of resistance to change. In the face of environmental challenges, physiological systems maintain a dynamic balance. Referring to stability through change in such systems, the concept of *homeostasis* has been replaced by the concept of *allostasis* (Schulkin, McEwen, & Gold, 1994). Each biological system defends itself against inappropriate causes of change that might lead to malfunction or destruction of the system. For example, in the normal functioning and development of the brain, a number of events, which might have led to a detrimental butterfly effect, are ignored, and only those that contribute to effective current functioning and to the development of functional new structures are accepted in normal development.

A special case in this connection is the proposition that a certain class of complex dynamic systems, characterizing individuals, has inherent constraints in terms of states that cannot occur. The recognition of such states is sometimes of importance for understanding functional systems, and

may be even more important than finding typical developmental sequences. What cannot occur sets boundaries to what can occur, and both aspects have to be accounted for in a sound theoretical explanation of some phenomena. This reasoning may be of particular relevance for the study of psychopathology, which is at the boundaries of what can occur when "normal" development gets off track (Bergman & Magnusson, in press).

In development, individuals and environments change and interact as totalities. The individual changes as a result of biological maturation (e.g., growth; myelinization of the brain) and cognitive-emotional experiences gained through interaction with the environment. The environment changes as a consequence of societal changes at different levels, and of the individual's direct and indirect actions in and on it (e.g., choosing a new job or moving to a new environment). As a consequence of simultaneous change in the person and his or her environment, the nature of the interaction processes changes. In the long run, such a change may be radical, partly as a result of the interaction process itself (cf., Lerner, 1991); for example, the nature of the interactive process within a family changes across time. The interaction between a child and its family is different from that same individual's interaction with his or her family in puberty, in middle age, or in retirement. The interaction process per se will thus precipitate development. (See the discussion of novelty as a basic principle in development, on pp. 700–701.)

The Developing Person

One implication of the holistic framework is that developmental changes do not take place in single aspects isolated from the totality. The total individual changes in a lawful way over time; individuals, not variables, develop. At a general level, it is easy to accept this view. However, if taken seriously, the view has far-reaching implications, as will be discussed in a later section.

The developmental process of an individual has its roots in constitutional factors, but, from conception, the developmental process is dependent on contextual characteristics, such as those discussed earlier, and the individual changes as a result of maturation and experience. The course of the developmental process at a certain age depends on constitutional dispositions and on experiences gained during the preceding phases of the life span.

The extent to which individual development is affected by environmental factors varies for different elements. In sexual development, some features, such as gonadal structures and functioning, are strongly regulated by biological factors; yet, other aspects of individual functioning, such as choice of peers and type of sexual relations, may be strongly open to experiential influences (Cairns & Cairns, 1994) and to societal normative factors such as the appropriate time for initiating opposite-sex relations (Maccoby, 1990). One factor influences the extent to which the socialization process of an individual shows high stability from infancy, through childhood and adolescence: the degree of ecological constancy in the upbringing environment (Magnusson & Endler, 1977).

To summarize, all changes during the life span of an individual are assumed to be characterized by *lawful continuity* (Magnusson & Törestad, 1992); the functioning of an individual at any given stage of development is lawfully related to earlier and later stages. Each change in the process of human ontogeny is understandable in the light of the individual's previous life history and the environmental influences operating at the time of the change. *At each phase in the life course of an individual, the present state is the child of the past and the parent of the future.* This tenet holds true even for changes that are so abrupt that they seem to break a stable direction of development. For example, changes that have been characterized as "turning points" sometimes appear as a result of "chance events" or "significant events." In this perspective, the discussion on whether individual development is characterized by *continuity* or *discontinuity* is a matter of developmental processes, not a matter of continuity or discontinuity of specific aspects of individual functioning—the focus that has dominated the debate (cf., Horowitz, 1989). The interesting aspects of this issue are: the character of the significant events that cause abrupt changes in processes, the conditions under which they appear, their possible long-term effects on the life course, and the relation of these aspects to age levels and gender differences.

Lawful continuity as a characteristic of individual functioning and development, which underlie both change and stability, has been claimed for centuries. However, as is the case with many basic propositions that have been accepted and widely endorsed, this proposition has had little impact on empirical research. What is needed now is empirical research taking the theoretical proposition seriously: "What

remains is the formidable task of disentangling causal status among the variables in the developmental sequence, including the transactions that turn genetic chemistry into behavioral individuality and the ways in which social context and social relationships are implicated in both stability and change" (Hartup & van Lieshout, 1995, p. 681). A prerequisite for success in that endeavor is to conduct longitudinal research, following the same individuals across time.

Lawfulness in the individual development process does not imply that changes are necessarily predictable. This circumstance does not preclude a scientific analysis of the process, as demonstrated in the research stimulated by chaos theory. Let us only refer to Scriven (1959), who countered, in his discussion about prediction and explanation in evolutionary theory, the view that high predictability of single events is a prerequisite for real scientific explanation: "Satisfactory explanation of the past is possible even when prediction of the future is impossible" (p. 477; see also Magnusson, 1988).

Homotypic versus Heterotypic Continuity

The distinction between homotypic versus heterotypic development was coined by Kagan and Moss (1962). The issue was then whether, for example, measures of aggression at the age of 7 years, for a sample of boys or girls showed higher correlation, 6 years later, with measures of aggressive than with measures of nonaggressive variables, reflecting homotypic continuity (cf., Olweus, 1979). Alternatively, the measure of early aggression could be most highly correlated with another variable (e.g., motor disturbance) at a later age, resulting in heterotypic continuity (cf., Backteman & Magnusson, 1981).

For a proper evaluation of the homotypic vs. heterotypic continuity issue, one must be keep in mind that they refer to relations among measures of variables in statistical terms (not to the character of the phenomena, in terms of dynamic, lawful processes of individual development). As discussed earlier, novelty is a characteristic of many changes in the development process (see pp. 700–701). This implies, across time, that the total organism undergoes a continuous transformation into new patterns of operating factors, and one needs to consider which factors are operative, their relative roles, and their psychological significance for the functioning of the totality. The individual's biological and mental capacities to deal with external conditions and demands and his or her cognitive-emotional worldviews and views of self, are not the same in childhood and in adolescence. Nor is the physical and social environment, with which the individual interacts, the same for infants and teenagers. This characteristic feature of the individual developmental process limits the application of the statistical concepts of homotypic and heterotypic continuity in developmental research.

ADAPTIVE, MALADAPTIVE, AND PROTECTIVE FACTORS IN THE PERSON–ENVIRONMENT SYSTEM

Making the whole person the object of interest is of particular importance in research on protective factors. Investigation of the development of personal and social maladjustment must attend to both the person and the contextual factors that accentuate the probability of future adversities and promote noninvolvement in such adversities.

Adverse developmental features cannot be isolated from positive personal or environmental characteristics. Yet, much of the research conducted over the years has explained behavioral and interpersonal problems mainly from negative conditions. The example of criminal development is illustrative. As in other psychopathological research, studies of delinquent development have traditionally been oriented toward risk. The theoretical models that exist are much more elaborated with regard to the negative personal and environmental risk conditions involved in delinquent development than they are toward individual opportunities and resources (even where the latter are included). Whereas conceptions of what are negative or undesirable precursors of delinquency are rather similar across criminological models (e.g., Elliot, Huizinga, & Ageton, 1985; Farrington et al., 1990; Hirschi & Gottfredson, 1994; Patterson, DeBaryshe, & Ramsey, 1989; Rutter & Giller, 1983; Wadsworth, 1979), there is less agreement over what constitutes prosocial, desirable social development (i.e., nonparticipation in criminality), how positive factors interact with risk indexes, and what conditions might alter a predicted delinquent course of development. In empirical studies, an overriding objective has been to grasp the factors that increase the probability of later criminality. These studies have provided insights into both the prognostic utility of early risk behaviors and environments (Loeber, 1982; Loeber & Dishion, 1983) and the step-by-step process of

developing delinquency (Loeber & Le Blanc, 1990; Stattin & Magnusson, 1995). However, they have not, to the same extent, illuminated the factors that:

1. Prevent individuals from engaging in delinquent activities in the first place.
2. Reduce the risk for future development of delinquency in individuals characterized by early risk behavior or located in risky environments.
3. Enable individuals to conform after a number of episodes of criminality.
4. Promote a favorable personal and social adjustment of individuals who are chronically delinquent.

A central construct in this discussion is the concept of "protective factors." The term can be used in two ways. It may refer to (a) factors that keep individuals who have come from risky environments (and/or evidence risky behaviors) from turning up with a later maladapted outcome, and (b) factors that contribute to breaking the course of an emerging negative individual development—for example, as manifested in juvenile delinquency—and channeling the development into a positive life course.

Only in recent years has research come to focus on circumstances that may improve the chances for high-risk individuals *not* to develop a delinquent lifestyle (Bliesner & Lösel, 1992; Farrington, 1994a; Farrington, Gallagher, Morley, St. Ledger, & West, 1988; Kolvin, Miller, Fleeting, & Kolvin, 1988; Stouthamer-Loeber et al., 1993; Werner & Smith, 1982). Research in the area of developmental psychopathology has started to focus on individual resources or competencies that might alter or hinder a negative course of development (cf., Rosenbaum, 1988; Rutter, 1974). Inquiries during the past two decades have turned to the adaptive functioning of the individual at different ages, in order to come to terms with factors that might promote positive and healthy development, and might balance or reduce the impact of adversities during upbringing (see Garmezy, 1974; Garmezy, Masten, & Tellegen, 1984; Masterpasqua, 1990; Rutter, 1985, 1990; Werner & Smith, 1982). Concepts such as sense of coherence, hardiness, invulnerability, learned resourcefulness, self-efficacy, stress, and ego resiliency (Antonovsky, 1987; Bandura, 1977; Block & Block, 1980; Kobasa, 1979; Rosenbaum, 1988) have been suggested to aid description of the processes and mechanisms that successfully enable the individual to adapt to and cope with physical and psychosocial stressors, that is, to maintain health in spite of risk conditions and to recover from emotionally threatening circumstances. Contextual and interpersonal factors—school experiences and social relations, friendship formation, association with positive peers, sibling relations, social support and availability of positive adult role models, attachment to socializing agents, parental supervision, and social activities—have received attention in research on protective factors (cf., Farrington et al., 1988; Kolvin et al., 1988; Rutter, 1974; Stouthamer-Loeber et al., 1993). A synthesis of resilience research and life-span developmental psychology has been advanced by Staudinger, Marsiska, and Baltes (1993, 1995).

Overall, there has been a change in emphasis from a risk orientation to an explicit concern with protective factors and mechanisms, along with a concern for both the adaptive and nonadaptive aspects of individual development. What has been termed protective factors is one aspect of the total life situation for the individual, which balance adversities and promote healthy growth. The concept of protective factors is not synonymous with positive factors (Rutter, 1990). Protective factors are studied in relation to risk factors, and they may be both positive and negative; over time, they balance, compete with, compensate for, or reduce the impact of prior risk conditions. However, to demonstrate the risk-reducing impact of a specific protective factor does not automatically explain the issues of how and why; i.e., what mechanisms are involved that can lead to reduced risk for high-risk individuals? Hence, a clear distinction has to be made between protective factors and protective mechanisms (Rutter & Giller, 1983).

The Patterning of Risk and Protective Factors

Most prior research on protective factors has been directed to the search for single factors, in the individual or in his or her environment, that could fulfill the protective role in the development process of an individual. Single potential protective factors have been examined in relation to single risk conditions. However, with reference to a holistic position, protective factors can be set in a broader perspective. In this context, they may refer to *patterns* of individual and environmental conditions.

In its usual definition, a protective factor modifies the risk for a bad outcome associated with a risk factor, so that the risk is smaller when the protective factor is present and larger when the protective factor is absent. When the risk factor is absent, there should be no differential risk according to whether the protective factor is present or absent. Often, single factors have been examined as to their protective function. By applying a person-oriented approach to risk and protective factors, more of the complexities involved in the growth of individuals may be studied. In such analyses, both risk conditions and potential protective factors refer to patterns. Suppose interactions between operating factors are assumed to play a central role in deciding the outcome. One way of taking these interactions into account would be to use an approach where, for instance, two patterns of values for relevant variables are formed for each studied person: (a) the pattern of values in the risk factors, and (b) the pattern of values in the protective factors.

Each pattern is considered as indivisible information characterizing each studied person. A protective pattern would be one that positively modifies the impact of a "bad" risk-factor pattern. Probably, there is not a single protective factor operating, but a pattern of protective factors, which is studied in relation to a pattern of risk factors. Such an enterprise in actual research has not yet been created. However, it is a path well worth pursuing.

Research on factors that promote healthy development and may change a negative developmental tendency, whether for an individual or for his or her environment, is perhaps one of the most important challenges in future research on personal and social maladaptation. Such research is part of the general search for processes and mechanisms that promote personal and social growth and enable growth despite hindrances. Not only should designs of future studies explicitly incorporate personal and contextual factors that promote adaptation and hinder normal functioning, but their simultaneous influence on adjustment should be examined over time. Despite researchers' recent strong interest in issues of risk and vulnerability, and in children and adolescents exposed to stressful settings, many theoretical issues and methodological problems are still unresolved in research on protective factors (Luthar, 1993). Research on the factors that may promote the healthy development of children and adolescents in adverse rearing conditions is still in its introductory phase. Basic research is critical, particularly for the development of sound theories of psychosocial risk. Moreover, as argued by Petersen (1993), consideration of the coexisting influences of positive and negative personal and contextual factors may yield important information to be used in prevention and treatment.

GENDER DIFFERENCES

In both males and females, the rate of biological maturation has been shown to influence individual functioning and long-term outcomes. However, the normative maturation rate is different for boys and girls—another example of the importance of gender differences in planning, implementing, and interpreting results of empirical research. Often, gender differences have been discussed in terms of biological factors. The view advocated here implies that the appropriate final analysis of gender differences refers to differences in the total person–environment system.

Gender differences initially appear in the rate of cell death, an important aspect of the first stages of the development of the nervous system. This difference carries possible consequences for gender differences in temperament, perceptual-motor coordination, and language acquisition (Carlson, Earls, & Todd, 1988). Empirical support for the existence of gender differences has also been reported for a number of other domains that are important to the total process of individual functioning and, thus, to the functioning of the person–environment system: lateralization of the brain (Bryden, 1982; Corballis, 1983; Kinsbourne, 1978); self-awareness (Kagan, 1981); temperament (Earls & Jung, 1987; Kagan, 1994); behavior and social relations (Cairns & Cairns, 1994; Leadbeater, Blatt, & Quinlan, 1995; Maccoby, 1995); relations between adolescent coping and adult adaptation (Feldman, Fisher, Ransom, & Dimicelli, 1995); cognition (af Klinteberg, Levander, & Schalling, 1987); and intellectual functioning (Hedges & Nowell, 1995). The elevated rates of disease and death in males—ranging from higher rates of fetal wastage and infant mortality to accidents, cardiovascular disease, and cancer as major causes of mortality in adult life—reflect gender differences in vulnerability to physical and social stress (Bergman, 1981; Carlson et al., 1988; Frankenhaeuser, Lundberg & Chesney, 1991; Lagerström, 1991). For most psychiatric disorders, including those with a predominantly early onset, such as infantile autism, attention deficit disorder, and conduct disorder, as well as those with a later onset, such as schizophrenia, depression, and anxiety disorders, gender

differences do exist (Earls, 1987; von Knorring, Andersson, & Magnusson, 1987). Gender differences in a contextual perspective were discussed by Clausen (1995).

In an earlier section of this chapter, seven basic principles for the functioning of the person and the person–environment system were summarized (pp. 698–705). These principles are valid for the functioning of both males and females. However, the implication of the existence of gender differences is that the particular developmental processes operate differently for males and females. For example, the biological orchestra playing in the regulation of the menstruation process in females does not have the same composition and does not play the same tune in males. This fact suggests that gender differences exist in the total functioning of females and males, and in the functioning of the person–environment system for males and females. To a large extent, the proximal and distal environments differ between girls and boys from the beginning of life and through socialization.

A methodological consequence of the preceding discussion is the necessity to analyze data for males and females separately. The all-too-common practice of pooling data for males and females can lead to meaningless or even misleading results.

THEORETICAL, METHODOLOGICAL, AND RESEARCH IMPLICATIONS

It is interesting to observe that fundamental propositions can be put forward and widely accepted in psychology, with little impact on empirical research, in spite of their sometimes far-reaching implications. The holistic interactionistic view, advocated in this chapter has decisive research implications. Henceforth, when interactionistic formulations become widely accepted, it is urgent that these consequences are taken seriously. Some of these implications are briefly reviewed here.

Theory

A heavy obstacle to further progress in psychological research, including research on child development, is the fragmentation in separate subareas with respect to concepts, theories, and methods. This fragmentation prohibits planning, implementing, and interpreting results in a common frame of reference and is detrimental to communication among researchers. This has been a concern as far back as Stern's work (1911). The Newtonian view of the physical world has long served the purpose of a general theoretical framework for communication among researchers in the natural sciences. The acceptance of a general model of nature, serving as the common theoretical framework for research in natural sciences, can be regarded as a prerequisite for continuous progress in these fields. The common model has enabled researchers concerned with very different levels of the physical world—for example, nuclear physicists and astrophysicists—to communicate with and understand each other. As suggested in the introduction, a general theoretical framework, *a general model of human beings and society,* serving the same purpose, is sorely needed for further, real progress in psychological research. The holistic, integrated view outlined in this chapter may serve that purpose.

To refute a common misunderstanding and criticism, let us emphasize that a holistic, integrated model for individual functioning and individual development does not imply that the entire system of an individual must be studied in every research endeavor. Acceptance of a common model of nature has never implied that the whole universe should be investigated in every study in natural sciences. The essential function of a general model of homo and society is to enable formulation of specific problems at different levels of the total functioning organism, implementation of empirical studies, and interpretation of the results within a common theoretical framework, with reference to a common space of scientific concepts.

Two interrelated comments are pertinent in this connection. First, there is a growing awareness of the need for a holistic, integrated model among those engaged in developmental psychology. This is documented in the research referred to in earlier sections. Second, the claim for a common theoretical framework for the study of individual development is part of a broader scientific *zeitgeist.* One reflection of this movement is the organization of a Nobel symposium in Stockholm, in 1994, presented in a volume titled *The Life-Span Development of Individuals: Behavioral, Neurobiological and Psychosocial Perspectives* (Magnusson, 1996). Leading specialists in medical and psychological fields, who are concerned with different aspects of individual development, presented the state of the art of their specialties and discussed how knowledge from

these fields could contribute to the understanding and explanation of developmental processes in a holistic and interactionistic perspective. The German research councils, in a joint response to an invitation to comment on the plans for the Fifth Framework Programme of the European Union, refer to this symposium—an indication of the significance of the view presented here.

Toward a Developmental Science

A consequence of the view advocated in this chapter is that, for a full understanding and explanation of the developmental processes of individuals, knowledge from what is traditionally incorporated in developmental psychology is not enough. We need contributions from the interface of a number of traditional scientific disciplines: developmental biology, developmental psychology, physiology, neuropsychology, social psychology, sociology, anthropology, and neighboring disciplines. The total space of phenomena involved in the process of lifelong individual development forms a clearly defined and delimited domain for scientific discovery which involves all these and other disciplines for effective investigation. This domain constitutes a scientific discipline of its own, *developmental science* (Magnusson & Cairns, 1996). Indications of the relevance of this proposition are: the recent establishment of the Center for Developmental Science at the University of North Carolina, Chapel Hill, and a new scientific journal titled *Applied Developmental Science.*

The proposition that research on individual development constitutes a field of research that has special demands of theory, methodology, and research strategy does not mean that it loses its identity as a scientific discipline. Physics, chemistry, and biology did not lose their special merits when new developments created interfaces among them. By contributing essential knowledge to the field of developmental science, psychology strengthens its position as an active partner in the mainstream of scientific progress in life sciences.

Methodological Implications

As a consequence of the formulation of modern interactionism, some methodological issues of developmental research become more conspicuous, and some new issues arise.

Nature of Phenomena–Levels of Analysis

The nature of the processes of individual functioning is dependent on context at various levels of the person–environment system. The nature of the structures and processes involved at different levels varies. It is not possible to collapse one level into another. The problem is one of translation from one level to the other(s).

Thus, a necessary condition for any meaningful interpretation of empirical data as a basis for description and explanation of continuity and lawfulness in individual functioning is that the researcher is aware of and makes explicit the level of complexity of the phenomena at which he or she has located and formulated the problem. The problem may be addressed at the level of the functioning of a specific element within a subsystem (e.g., the role of emotions within the mental system); at the level of the functioning of a subsystem (e.g., the functioning of the immune system); at the level of the functioning of the total individual; or at the level of the interplay between the person and the environment.

The methodological implication of this point is the necessity of specifying the structures and processes involved at the level of the formulation of the problem. Thus, the starting point for planning empirical research on a specific topic is a careful, systematic analysis based on observation of the phenomena at the correct level (Cairns, 1986a; Magnusson, 1992).

Type of Data—Level of Interpretation

The second requirement for effective empirical research is that the data used for analysis must be collected at the appropriate level. If this requirement is not met, even sophisticated analyses of the data will yield meaningless results.

Data aggregated across individuals, variables, situations, and/or time are common in psychological research. The correct use of such data in each specific case presupposes that the aggregated data are relevant for the elucidation of the problem under consideration. Here, attention will be drawn to two aspects of relevance for the interpretation of studies in the person–environment system.

The first aspect is the use and misuse of aggregated data in studying the relative role of person factors, in terms of cross-situationally valid traits, and situational conditions in cross-situational behavior. The trait-oriented model assumes that the characteristic feature of individuals is in

data aggregated across situations. The interactionistic view needs situation-specific data to study cross-situational variation in behavior. The debate becomes meaningless when data aggregated across situations are used as an argument against the existence of person–situation interactions, and when individual differences in cross-situational profiles, based on situation-specific data, are used as an argument against the existence of personality traits.

The second aspect is the interpretation of data from behavior genetics. Usually, the data referred to in the debate about the role of genetic and environmental factors are solid, and the results are well established. However, for a correct interpretation of the results, the properties of the data must be kept in mind. So far, most of the debate has referred to results that describe the role of genetic and environmental factors in terms of the relative contribution of each of these sources to the total variance in a matrix of data gathered across individuals. The goal has been to establish the genetic contribution to the regulation of cognitive and personality dispositions (Loehlin, 1996). Much confusion has been caused by interpreting the numbers as though they referred to individuals. Such data are valuable for discussing the problem at the group level, but they do not say anything about the role of genetic factors, and the mechanisms by which they operate, at the level of the individual's interaction with the environment (Gottlieb, 1996; see also Gottlieb et al., Ch. 5, this Volume).

Methods for Data Collection

Psychological research has been dominated by methodological "monism" or even, in Koch's (1981) terminology, by methodological "fetishism." The experimental method has dominated the scene to the extent that the mainstream of psychology has been referred to as experimental psychology; that is, it is defined with reference to method. In the natural sciences, the experiment has been the classical design for scientific study. It is interesting to note how the relevance of the experimental method in research on dynamic processes is now questioned even in such fields. A debate in *Science,* on the relevance of experiments in ecological research was introduced by the following formulation: "Ecological experiments have become quite good at isolating causes and effects. But there's a debate brewing over whether these results reveal anything about the natural world" (Roush, 1995, p. 313). From the foregoing discussion, it should be clear that the same methodology cannot be applied independent of the level of structures and processes at which a research problem has been formulated. There is no single "scientific" method that can be used for effective research on all types of problems. For example, Binet (Cairns & Ornstein, 1979) made the important point that the most effective techniques for describing outcomes may not be effective for analyzing the processes leading to the outcome.

In psychology, research on individual development is primarily based on quantitative data reflecting individual and environmental functioning at various levels. Discussions on methodological issues and on statistics refer to this tradition. However, our understanding of individual and environmental functioning, and of the functioning of the total person–environment system would gain from extending the arsenal of methods to include qualitative methods, which are frequently and successfully applied in ethnographic research (see Lerner, Ch. 1, this Volume, and Shweder et al., Ch. 15, this Volume). With reference to the holistic interactionistic view on individual development presented here, a complement to the frequently used data-collection techniques is the *narrative approach,* in which individuals' stories of their own lives are analyzed (Sarbin, 1986). An illustration of the fruitfulness of this approach was presented by Manturzewska (1990), in her study of the life-span development of professional musicians. With reference to Tomkins' (1979) "script theory," Carlson (1988) advocated the usefulness of psychobiographical inquiry in several areas of personality research development. The type of interview data collected by Cairns and Cairns (1994) in their longitudinal study of adolescence yields information that cannot be obtained in other ways.

Generalization

The personal and social characteristics of the individual, and the social conditions of the upbringing environment, which we normally associate with transition behaviors and with the timing of developmental events, have been examined largely in the West European countries, in Australia and New Zealand, and in the United States. We have limited knowledge about whether these correlates are similar in countries in the rest of the world. Even where such broader comparisons are made, they have often been done with instruments developed and validated by individuals in Western countries. This state of affairs raises a basic question about the generalization of empirical results (e.g.,

Baltes, Reese, & Nesselroade, 1988): To what degree are results obtained in one context valid in other contexts?

Generalization of results from specific studies is one goal of scientific research. In the tradition of experimental psychology, replicability has been regarded as the main criterion for the validity of results. Unsophisticated use of this rule has sometimes had a wrong consequence: Differences in results from studies on a specific issue in different cultures have been interpreted as errors. This circumstance motivates some comments.

In the introduction to this chapter, two tasks for empirical research on individual functioning were identified: (a) the search for identification of possible operating factors, and (b) the search for principles and mechanisms underlying the simultaneous operation of these factors. In the present context, these tasks have three main implications for the generalization of results:

1. Results concerning possible operating factors in the developmental processes cannot be generalized *across age levels* without giving careful consideration to the character of the phenomena being studied.

2. Results cannot be generalized *from one level of analysis to another,* whether with respect to operating factors or with respect to mechanisms and principles.

3. Results concerning possible factors operating in one *context* cannot be generalized to other contexts without careful consideration and replications. Results concerning the role of specific factors operating in one generation cannot be generalized to another generation, independent of the nature of the structures and processes under study. Nor can results from specific studies obtained in one culture be generalized indiscriminately to other cultures.

A striking example of cross-national differences occurred in a series of studies of German, Russian, and American children's beliefs about their ability to relate to school performance (Little, Oettingen, Stetsenko, & Baltes, 1995; Oettingen, Little, Lindenberg, & Baltes, 1994). In general, few cross-national differences were found with respect to children's views of what factors are important for performance. However, American children systematically reported stronger beliefs that they could influence these factors and, consequently, their performance. Yet, considerably lower belief school grade correlations were obtained for the American children, compared to the European children. Silbereisen and coworkers have compared youngsters raised in the former East Germany with similar groups of young people in West Germany, with respect to correlates and background conditions of transition behaviors. These analyses revealed that many correlates were quite different in the East from those of the West. Results for the youngsters raised in West Germany were often akin to those found in American studies. One illustration is the timing of leaving home to begin an independent life situation (Silbereisen, Meschke, & Schwarz, in press). Two conclusions can be drawn from the comparisons. First (and most obvious), Silbereisen et al.'s findings expose the strong impact of the macrosocial environment on the course of development from childhood into adulthood. Second, the findings show that we often tend to overlook the fact that most studies reported in typical psychological textbooks are based on samples of Western children and adolescents who are raised under similar broad social and cultural conditions. As soon as we address the macrosocial structure that influences upbringing conditions, and make comparisons among individuals raised under quite different cultural, social, and political conditions, other interpretations of transition issues emerge alongside those normally found in the development literature. Typically, we are forced to change our interpretations from an individual-differences perspective on timing of events to a person–environment perspective.

There are, of course, differences among children from various Western countries. For example, the dating system has not existed in Western Europe to the same extent that it has in the United States. Other expectations about young adolescents will obviously follow when they are expected to date at a certain age and are exposed to more informal social regulations. The impact of pubertal development might become radically different in Western Europe, compared to the United States.

This issue was raised in the study by Stattin and Magnusson (1990) on the consequences, for female development, of maturing early or late reported on page 697. As was emphasized by the authors, the specific rate of biological maturation may be due to cultural factors that were typical for Swedish society at the time of the study. In cultures with other norms, the rules and roles for adolescent girls may not be guided by reference to chronological age or to the rate of biological maturation. Another example is sexuality. Sweden is generally recognized as a society with an accepting view of opposite-sex contacts and of sexual behavior among youth, whereas premarital sex is more likely to be considered as a norm violation by parents in the United States. Not unexpectedly, the average age of first sexual intercourse is earlier in Sweden than in the United States.

In some areas, the differences in physical and social environments might be so great between the United States and the Western European countries that it is impracticable to make comparisons between their respective adolescents and young adults. For example, the ecology of some American cities, with their ethnic composition, physical structure, and demographic characteristics, is seldom found in Europe. Because the acts of criminality, the existence of gangs closely tied to certain neighborhoods, and so on, are heavily associated with inner-city ecology, studies of violence and gang criminality in the United States cannot be easily transferred onto the same phenomena in European communities (Shannon, 1988).

These examples demonstrate that what can be generalized about individual current functioning and the individual developmental process from one context to another are not results concerning the role and relative importance of specific operating factors; rather, they are the mechanisms and principles underlying the processes. In this connection, it is worthwhile to recognize that differences in individual functioning and development, related to differences in social and cultural environments, contain important information that is valuable in the search for such principles and mechanisms.

The issue of generalization extends into the areas of intervention and prevention. Preventive strategies that have proved to be effective for American preschool children are not necessarily so when implemented in other countries. Among other things, the preschool infrastructure, the basic content and the organizational structures of activities for children differ markedly among countries.

Statistical Analyses

Statistics are tools that are helpful in analyzing data in order to understand the lawfulness of processes operating within given mental, biological, and behavioral structures, and processes involved in developmental change. Statistics are tools for these purposes in the same way that axes, knives, and razors are tools for cutting (Magnusson, 1992).

Tools are never good or bad in themselves. The only criterion for a good or bad tool is the extent to which it serves its purpose in an appropriate way. The same holds true for statistics as a set of tools for treating data in psychological analyses. Different kinds of statistics answer different questions, and the only relevant criterion for whether they are good or bad is in their application: Do they contribute to answering questions that are formulated with reference to an analysis of the phenomena under investigation? How close is the match between the assumptions underlying the statistical model, on the one hand, and the psychological model, on the other?

A large arsenal of more or less sophisticated statistical models and methods for analyses of quantitative data in developmental psychology is available (e.g., Baltes, Reese & Nesselroade, 1988; Bergman, 1993; Magnusson & Bergman, 1990; Magnusson, Bergman, Rudinger, & Törestad, 1991). It is beyond the scope of this chapter to present a critical evaluation of these methods and to discuss all the theoretical and methodological problems connected with them. Here, two approaches to analysis of data, which have different consequences for planning, implementing, and interpreting developmental research, can be distinguished. The first approach is concerned with the study of relations among variables across individuals. Statistics, in this application, is closely linked to a variable approach to the study of individual functioning and development. The second approach is concerned with statistics for the study of individuals and environments in terms of patterns of operating variables at different levels of the total system.

In sum, the two approaches are complementary. Because the distinction between them concerns both concepts and research strategy, neither can be proven right or wrong by statistical tests. The ultimate criterion of the usefulness of one or the other approach is not its ability to provide strong predictions in statistical analyses, but the extent to which it contributes to understanding the structures and processes being studied. The logic and implications of the two approaches were discussed by Magnusson (in press-a).

Pattern Analysis of Individuals

As discussed in an earlier section of this chapter, the main characteristics of an individual are represented by the *patterning* of structures and the functioning and cooperating of subsystems. This proposition forms the theoretical basis for the operationalization of a problem involving pattern

analyses in the framework of what has been designated a *person approach* (see Bergman & Magnusson, 1983; Block, 1971; Cairns, Cairns, & Neckerman, 1989; Caspi & Bem, 1990; Magnusson, 1985; Magnusson & Allen, 1983a, 1983b; Ozer & Gjerde, 1989; among others). In the area of developmental psychopathology, Cicchetti (1993) formulated his views in a summary of this position: "I contend based on the developmental considerations raised in this paper that progress toward a process level understanding of psychopathology will require research designs and strategies that allow for a simultaneous assessment of multiple domains of variables within and outside each individual. In this regard, I believe that organizational theories will play an important role because they advocate the study of the 'whole person' in context, thereby minimizing fragmentation of individual functioning" (p. 495).

The characteristic feature of a person approach is that the specific problem under consideration is formulated in person terms and is operationalized and studied empirically in terms of patterns of values for variables that are relevant to the problem under consideration. In other scientific disciplines concerned with dynamic complex processes, such as ecology, meteorology, biology, and chemistry, pattern analysis has become an important methodological tool. In developmental psychology, it has been applied in a number of studies (see among others, Andersson, Bergman, & Magnusson, 1989; Asendorpf & van Aken, 1991; Bergman & Magnusson, 1984a, 1984b; 1987, 1991; Bergman & Wångby, in press; Block, 1971; Gustafson & Magnusson, 1991; af Klinteberg, Andersson, Magnusson, & Stattin, 1993; Lienert & zur Oeveste, 1985; Mills et al., 1994; Magnusson, in press-b; Magnusson & Bergman, 1988, 1990; Mumford & Owen, 1984; Pulkkinen & Tremblay, 1992; Stattin & Magnusson, 1990; van Aken & Asendorpf, 1994).

A number of methods for pattern analysis have been presented and applied: Cluster analytical techniques (Bergman, in press; Bock, 1987; Manly, 1994); Q-sort technique (Block, 1971; Ozer, 1993); latent profile analysis (LPA) (Gibson, 1959); configural frequency analysis (CFA) (von Eye, 1990; Krauth & Lienert, 1982); latent transition analysis (LTA) (Collins & Wugalter, 1992); log-linear modeling (Bishop, Feinberg, & Holland, 1975); and multivariate P-technique factor analysis (Cattell, Cattell, & Rhymer, 1947; Nesselroade & Ford, 1987). These methods are applicable for descriptive, cross-sectional analyses of individual functioning in terms of patterns. For the study of developmental issues, the approach has primarily been applied in studies linking patterns observed at one age to patterns observed at another.

However, relatively few attempts have been made to develop and apply methods for the empirical analyses of dynamic, developmental processes in terms of patterns. For further progress in research on human ontogeny, an important challenge lies in the development and application of such methodological tools.

Pattern Analysis of Environments

As argued earlier, both the physical and the social environments are structured and organized. Divorce in the family does not have an independent role in itself, apart from aspects of family life and other social relations. The same holds true for a number of environmental factors that are the subject of empirical research in developmental psychology: unemployment, parental education and income, and criminality and alcoholism among parents, to name a few. The psychological significance of a particular environmental aspect lies in the contribution it makes to a pattern of such factors.

This view leads to the same conclusions for environments as for persons. Studies of single aspects of the environment, taken out of context, do not form the basis for understanding the role of the environment in the processes of individual functioning. Thus, the variable approach must be complemented with an approach in which the structure and functioning of the environment are studied in terms of patterns of factors that are relevant for the problem under consideration. The fruitfulness of such a strategy was demonstrated by Gustafson and Mumford (1995), who investigated the fit between personal style and environmental constraints and opportunities. In a study of female life careers, reported by Gustafson and Magnusson (1991), the females' home background was described in terms of patterns of relevant factors: father's and mother's education; parents' income; parents' evaluation of the girl's capacity for higher education; and parents' evaluation of higher education for the girl.

Pattern Analysis of Person–Environment Systems

Because the individual and his or her environment at the highest level of generalization and analysis function as a total, inseparable, organized system, the appropriate theoretical and empirical analysis at that level should include

analyses in terms of patterns of personal and environmental variables, assessed simultaneously. This analysis can be accomplished by the choice of variables included in the cluster analysis. For instance, Cairns, Cairns, and Neckerman (1989) included both individual variables (e.g., cognition, aggression) and context variables (e.g., socioeconomic status) in constructing developmental patterns related to early school dropout.

Comments

Depending on their specific purpose, methods for linear relations and methods for pattern analysis are useful for the study of individual differences. The measurement task becomes distinctly different in the two approaches. The basic difference is in the psychological significance of a specific datum. The application of linear models for the study of relations among variables, across individuals, is based on the assumption that individuals are positioned on latent dimensions for the relevant factors. The specific datum for a certain individual acquires psychological significance because of its relation to the positions of data for other individuals on the same dimension. Thus, the task is to locate individuals on the dimension(s), and the appropriate measurement technique is the one that discriminates along the whole range of possible individual positions. In contrast, in the pattern analyses, the specific individual datum for a certain variable gets its psychological significance because of the role it plays in the configuration of scores on the relevant dimensions for the same individual. Thus, in the pattern analysis, the task is to assign individuals to categories at the appropriate level, and the measurement problem is to maximize cutting scores on the borders of each category or class.

A consequence of the formulation of theoretical models for complex, dynamic processes in the natural sciences has been the development of adequate methodologies for the study of such processes. One line is the revival of nonlinear mathematics and methods for the study of patterns. For further scientific progress in research on individual functioning, it is important for researchers in our field to take advantage of this development. If adequately applied, the new methodologies for dynamic, complex processes have important implications for theory building and empirical research on the dynamic, complex process of individual development (e.g., Moolenaar, Boomsma, & Dolan, 1991; Wallacher & Nowak, 1994). There is also a growing interest in and application of models and methods in this direction in developmental research. An interesting example is van Geert's (1994) application of a nonlinear dynamic model for the redefinition of Vygotsky's "zone of proximal development" (see also Valsiner, 1994).

However, when these methodologies are considered in psychology, we have to avoid the mistake we made when we took over models and methods from the natural sciences, particularly from physics, at the beginning of the 20th century. Without careful analysis of the phenomena that were the objects of our interest, we applied models and methods from physics in an inappropriate manner. Most researchers now agree that this mistake hampered real scientific progress in psychological research.

It is true that certain similarities exist between the structures and processes studied in the natural sciences and the structures and processes investigated in psychological research. However, essential differences also exist, particularly when our focus is on the functioning of the total organism. At that level, the fundamental characteristics and guiding elements in the dynamic, complex process of individual functioning are *intentionality,* which is linked to emotions and values, and the fact that the individual learns from experience. The latter must be taken into consideration when methods derived from the study of dynamic, complex processes, which do not have these elements, are applied in planning and implementing of empirical research in psychology.

Research Strategy

In connection with various substantive issues in the foregoing sections, a number of implications for effective research strategies—in psychological research in general, and in developmental research in particular—have been outlined. Instead of repeating them here, attention will be drawn to a few consequences that come naturally from the perspective developed in this chapter.

A Multivariate Approach

As long as the interest in a specific study is in the R–R or S–R relation among variables, the study of single variables is appropriate. However, when the interest is in the functioning and development of a system—at the subsystem level, at the level of the total person, or at the level of the person–environment system—the emphasis on multiple causation and the interdependency of operating factors at each level have as a consequence, that the analysis should include a broad range of variables that have been identified, in theoretical and/or empirical analyses, as essential for the understanding of the processes at the appropriate level.

A Longitudinal Design

A consequence of the description and discussion of individual functioning and development in process terms is the application of a longitudinal research strategy. Inherent in the nature of processes is the requirement that they be studied in a temporal context. A major motive for longitudinal research is that it enables the researcher to study causal mechanisms in the developmental processes in a way that is not possible in cross-sectional research. Longitudinal research has a long tradition. The arguments for this approach were formulated forcefully by many developmental researchers (e.g., McCall, 1977), and the merits and pitfalls were also carefully analyzed (see Baltes, Cornelius, & Nesselroade, 1979; Schaie & Baltes, 1975, among others). For different reasons, and for a long time, the merits of longitudinal research were not appreciated to the extent that it resulted in the establishment of strong research programs. During recent decades, however, there has been a growing awareness of the necessity to conduct such research. As manifestation of this trend, the first scientific network established by the European Science Foundation in the mid-1980's was the European Network on Research on Individual Development. In a series of workshops, topics of central interest for the understanding and explanation of individual development were discussed and later published in eight volumes (Baltes & Baltes, 1990; Kalverboer, Hopkins, & Geuze, 1993; Magnusson & Bergman, 1990; Magnusson, Bergman, Rudinger, & Törestad, 1991; Magnusson & Casaer, 1993; de Ribaupierre, 1989; Rutter, 1988; Rutter & Casaer, 1991). An inventory, administered by Schneider and Edelstein (1990) in the framework of the network, identified, in Europe, about 500 ongoing longitudinal research projects concerned with psychosocial development.

The issue of correctly interpreting and generalizing results from longitudinal studies merits some attention. For example, we must avoid confounding age effects and cohort effects, both of which occur as a result of the continuous changes that take place in the environment at all levels (cf., Baltes, Cornelius, & Nesselroade, 1979; Schaie & Baltes, 1975, among others). Bronfenbrenner (1958) studied differences in parenting between lower-class and middle-class families and found that, in some respects, the class differences were reversed between 1930 and the 1950s. The investigation of developmental issues requires that such potential effects must be taken into account in planning and interpreting longitudinal research. Three comments are pertinent here:

1. Differences between cohorts contain valuable information concerning the developmental process of individuals, as demonstrated in the comprehensive studies of generations by Elder and colleagues (Elder, 1979).
2. The extent to which the lawful principles we wish to elucidate are related to cohort properties varies with the kind of problems and the nature of the structures and processes under consideration. For example, it is difficult to see how cohort effects could influence the lawfulness of the interaction among cognitions, neurotransmitters, and emotions in individuals.
3. The issue of the confounding of age, cohort, and time is not restricted to longitudinal studies. It is also important for cross-sectional research, but it is more hidden and is rarely discussed in that context.

Cross-Cultural Research

One implication of the view that individual functioning and development are dependent on the nature and functioning of the environment is a need for systematic cross-cultural research. The role of the environment is not restricted to stimuli and events in the immediate situation. As argued above, each specific situation is embedded in social and cultural systems at different levels, and will be interpreted by the individual in the specific context of these systems. Results of studies of differences in the developmental processes among children and youngsters being raised in different cultures contribute with essential knowledge, with respect to (a) the factors operating in the individual and in the environment, and (b) the principles by which these factors operate. The importance of cross-cultural research is emphasized by Shweder et al., Ch. 15, this Volume.

Multidisciplinary Collaboration

In the perspective argued here, to understand and explain individual functioning and development presupposes knowledge of the role of mental, biological, and behavioral aspects of the individual, and knowledge of environmental factors involved in the person–environment system. As argued above, this implies a need for knowledge gained from research that assumes the interface of a number of disciplines. Such knowledge will come as a result of collaboration, first among researchers in the traditional field of psychology, and then among researchers from psychology and those other disciplines concerned. A prerequisite for such collaboration and communication among researchers is the formulation and consideration of a general, common model of human beings and society. Systematic, well-planned collaboration in the field of developmental science, with reference to such a common model, has strong potentialities.

Prevention, Treatment and Intervention

Research on the mental, biological, behavioral, and social structures and processes operating in individual life courses constitutes a central scientific concern in its own right. However, the societal implications are also important, inasmuch as knowledge about the positive and negative aspects of human development can be used to promote health and prevent harmful development. The holistic interactionistic view has important implications for the kind of knowledge that is needed for effective intervention and treatment in societal policy, manifested in the formation of agencies, programs, and other initiatives.

Empirical research indicates that alcohol and drug abuse, violence and other forms of criminality, mobbing at school and elsewhere, and other negative aspects of the development process of individuals tend to go together (Stattin & Magnusson, in press). More than a matter of, for example, alcohol problems *or* violence, it is a matter of a general process of adjustment problems. The broader range of adjustment problems during adolescence cannot be seen as being isolated from the earlier development process and the social context in which it has taken place. Empirical studies also indicate that single individual problems, and/or the existence of single problems in the social context during childhood and adolescence, have only limited negative influence on the future adjustment of individuals. An increased risk for later maladjustment problems appears in individuals for whom problem behaviors accumulate across time and/or in social contexts characterized by a broad range of risk factors. Adjustment problems of different kinds tend to gravitate toward a limited number of individuals, and this group is responsible for a large portion of adjustment problems manifested in early drug and alcohol abuse, criminality, mobbing, and so on.

In spite of these well-known circumstances, discussions of and research on these types of problems are often focused on a certain variable (e.g., aggressiveness) or a certain problem (e.g., alcohol abuse), while applying a specific perspective (e.g., a sociological, psychological, or criminological perspective). In this situation, intervention programs are often implemented in isolated environments, concentrated on a single problem, and focused on a special age group, with reference to a single perspective. Often, the prophylactic actions and treatment programs are temporary "projects" that have no anchor in an overriding, long-term strategy based on available scientific knowledge and experiences from a broad range of expertise found in those involved in the applied field. Different actors and agencies are active in the same area, often in parallel and sometimes in competition, but they lack both coordination and collaboration.

The holistic interactionistic view on individual functioning and development, as advocated here, implies that, in the development of societal programs for intervention and treatment, the total person–environment system must be considered, not single problems of individual functioning and single risk factors in the social context. Long-term programs and strategies must be worked out based on knowledge from all relevant fields of developmental science, and they must be planned and implemented in close collaboration with professionals who represent different perspectives. Multiple agencies, programs, and initiatives must be integrated if the breadth of the person–context system is to be adequately engaged.

ACKNOWLEDGMENTS

Good colleagues have commented on specific parts of earlier versions of this manuscript. Taking full responsibility for the final version, we thank them all for their valuable comments.

REFERENCES

Abramson, L. Y., Seligman, M. E. P., & Teasdale, J. O. (1978). Learned helplessness in humans: Critique and reformulation. *Journal of Abnormal Psychology, 87,* 49–74.

Ainsworth, M. D. S. (1983). Patterns of infant-mother attachment as related to maternal care: Their early history and their contribution to continuity. In D. Magnusson & V. L. Allen (Eds.), *Human development: An interactional perspective* (pp. 35–53). New York: Academic Press.

Ajzen, I., & Fishbein, M. (1980). *Understanding attitudes and prediction in social behavior.* Englewood Cliffs, NJ: Prentice-Hall.

Allport, G. W. (1924). The study of the undivided personality. *Journal of Abnormal and Social Psychology, 19,* 131–141.

Allport, G. W. (1937). *Personality: A psychological interpretation.* New York: Holt, Rinehart and Winston.

Allport, G. W. (1961). *Pattern and growth in personality.* New York: Holt, Rinehart and Winston.

Allport, G. W. (1966). Traits revisited. *American Psychologist, 21,* 1–10.

Alsaker, F. D. (1995). *Timing of puberty and reactions to pubertal changes.* Unpublished manuscript, University of Berne, Berne.

Anastasi, A. (1958). Heredity, environment and the question "how"? *Psychological Review, 65,* 197–208.

Andersson, T., Bergman, L. R., & Magnusson, D. (1989). Patterns of adjustment problems and alcohol abuse in early childhood: A prospective longitudinal study. *Development and Psychopathology, 1,* 119–131.

Angell, J. R. (1907). The province of functional psychology. *Psychological Review, 65,* 197–208.

Angell, J. R., & Thompson, H. B. (1899). A study of the relations between certain organic processes and consciousness. *Psychological Review, 6,* 32–46.

Angoff, W. H. (1988). The nature–nurture debate, aptitudes, and group differences. *American Psychologist, 43,* 713–720.

Antonovsky, A. (1987). *Unraveling the mystery of health. How people manage stress and stay well.* San Francisco: Jossey-Bass.

Appley, M. H., & Turnball, R. (1986). *Dynamics of stress: Physiological, psychological, and social perspectives.* New York: Plenum Press.

Arsenian, J., & Arsenian, J. M. (1948). Tough and easy cultures: A conceptual analysis. *Psychiatry, 11,* 377–385.

Asendorpf, J. B., & van Aken, M. A. G. (1991). Correlates of the temporal consistency of personality patterns in childhood. *Journal of Personality, 4,* 689–703.

Backteman, G., & Magnusson, D. (1981). Longitudinal stability of personality characteristics. *Journal of Personality, 49,* 148–160.

Baltes, P. B. (1976). In H. W. Reese (Ed.), Symposium on implications of life-span developmental psychology for child development. *Advances in Child Development and Behavior, 11,* 167–265.

Baltes, P. B. (1979). On the potentials and limits of child development: Life-span developmental psychology: Some converging observations on history and theory. In P. B. Baltes & O. G. Brim, Jr. (Eds.), *Life-span development and behavior* (Vol. 2). New York: Academic Press.

Baltes, P. B. (1987). Theoretical propositions of life-span developmental psychology: On the dynamics between growth and decline. *Developmental Psychology, 23,* 611–626.

Baltes, P. B., & Baltes, M. (1990). *Successful aging: Perspectives from the behavioral sciences.* Cambridge, England: Cambridge University Press.

Baltes, P. B., Cornelius, S. W., & Nesselrode, J. R. (1979). Cohort effects in developmental psychology. In J. R. Nesselroade & P. B. Baltes (Eds.), *Longitudinal research in the study of behavior and development* (pp. 61–87). New York: Academic Press.

Baltes, P. B., & Graf, P. (1996). Psychological aspects of aging: Facts and frontiers. In D. Magnusson (Ed.), *The life-span development of individuals: Behavioral, neurobiological and psychosocial perspectives* (pp. 426–460). Cambridge, England: Cambridge University Press.

Baltes, P. B., Reese, H. W., & Lipsitt, L. P. (1980). Life-span developmental psychology. In M. R. Rosenzweig & L. W. Porter (Eds.), *Annual review of psychology* (Vol. 31, pp. 65–110). Palo Alto, CA: Annual Reviews.

Baltes, P. B., Reese, H. W., & Nesselrode, J. R. (1988). *Life-span developmental psychology: Introduction to research methods.* Hillsdale, NJ: Erlbaum.

Banaji, M. R., & Prentice, D. A. (1994). The self in social context. *Annual Review of Psychology, 45,* 297–332.

Bandura, A. (1977). Self-efficacy: Toward a unifying theory of behavior change. *Psychological Review, 84,* 191–215.

Bandura, A. (1978). The self system in reciprocal determinism. *American Psychologist, 33,* 344–358.

Bandura, A. (1982). The psychology of chance encounters and life paths. *American Psychologist, 33,* 344–358.

Barker, R. G. (1965). Exploration in ecological psychology. *American Psychologist, 20,* 1–14.

Barton, S. (1994). Chaos, self-organization, and psychology. *American Psychologist, 49,* 5–14.

Bateson, P. P. G. (1996). Design for a life. In D. Magnusson (Ed.), *The life-span development of individuals: Behavioral, neurobiological and psychosocial perspectives* (pp. 1–20). Cambridge, England: Cambridge University Press.

Baumrind, D. (1989). Rearing competent children. In W. Damon (Ed.), *Child development today and tomorrow* (pp. 349–378). San Francisco: Jossey-Bass.

Bell, R. Q. (1968). Reinterpretation of the direction of effects in studies of socialization. *Psychological Review, 75,* 81–95.

Bell, R. Q. (1971). Stimulus control of parent or caretaker by offspring. *Developmental Psychology, 4,* 63–72.

Bell, R. Q., & Harper, L. V. (1977). *Child effects on adults.* Hillsdale, NJ: Erlbaum.

Belsky, J. (1981). Early human experience: A family perspective. *Developmental Psychology, 17,* 3–23.

Belsky, J., Lerner, R., & Spanier, G. (1984). *The child in the family.* Reading, MA: Addison-Wesley.

Berger, P., & Luckman, T. (1966). *The social construction of reality.* Garden City, NJ: Doubleday.

Bergman, L. R. (1981). Is intellectual development more vulnerable in boys than in girls? *Journal of Genetic Psychology, 138,* 175–181.

Bergman, L. R. (1993). Some methodological issues in longitudinal research: Looking forward. In D. Magnusson & P. Casaer (Eds.), *Longitudinal research on individual development: Present status and future perspectives* (pp. 217–241). Cambridge, England: Cambridge University Press.

Bergman, L. R. (in press). A pattern-oriented approach to studying individual development: Snapshots and processes. In R. B. Cairns, L. R. Bergman, & J. Kagan (Eds.), *The individual as a focus in developmental research.* New York: Sage.

Bergman, L. R., & Magnusson, D. (1983). *The development of patterns of maladjustment* (Report No. 50). University of Stockholm, Individual Development and Adjustment project.

Bergman, L. R., & Magnusson, D. (1984a). *Patterns of adjustment problems at age 10: An empirical and methodological study* (Report No. 615). University of Stockholm, Department of Psychology.

Bergman, L. R., & Magnusson, D. (1984b). *Patterns of adjustment problems at age 13: An empirical and methodological study* (Report No. 620). University of Stockholm, Department of Psychology.

Bergman, L. R., & Magnusson, D. (1987). A person approach to the study of the development of adjustment problems: An empirical example and some research considerations. In D. Magnusson & A. Öhman (Eds.), *Psychopathology: An interactional perspective* (pp. 383–401). New York: Academic Press.

Bergman, L. R., & Magnusson, D. (1991). Stability and change in patterns of extrinsic adjustment problems. In D. Magnusson, L. R. Bergman, G. Rudinger, & B. Törestad (Eds.), *Problems and methods in longitudinal research: Stability and change* (pp. 323–346). Cambridge, England: Cambridge University Press.

Bergman, L. R., & Magnusson, D. (in press). A person-oriented approach in research on developmental psychopathology [Special issue]. *Development and Psychopathology*.

Bergman, L. R., & Wångby, M. (in press). The teenage girl: Syndromes of self-stated adjustment problems and some concomitant factors. *International Journal of Methods in Psychiatric Research*.

Berndt, T. J. (1982). The features and effects of friendships in early adolescence. *Child Development, 53,* 1447–1460.

Binet, A., & Henri, V. (1895). La psychologie individuelle. *L'Annee Psychologique, 2,* 411–465.

Bishop, Y. M. M., Feinberg, S. E., & Holland, P. W. (1975). *Discrete multivariate analysis: Theory and practice.* Cambridge, MA: MIT Press.

Bliesner, T., & Lösel, F. (1992). Resilience in juveniles with high risk of delinquency. In F. Lösel, D. Bender, & T. Bliesner (Eds.), *Psychology and law: International perspectives* (pp. 62–75). Berlin: De Gruyter.

Block, J. (1971). *Lives through time.* Berkeley, CA: Bancroft Books.

Block, J. H., & Block, J. (1980). The role of ego control and ego-resilience in the organization of behavior. In W. A. Collins (Ed.), *Development of cognition, affect and social relations: The Minnesota Symposium on Child Psychology* (Vol. 13, pp. 39–101). Hillsdale, NJ: Erlbaum.

Blyth, D. A. (1983). Surviving and thriving in the social world: A commentary on six new studies of popular, rejected, and neglected children. *Merrill-Palmer Quarterly, 29,* 449–459.

Bock, H. H. (1987). *Classification and related methods of data analysis.* Amsterdam, The Netherlands: North-Holland.

Bolles, C. (1972). Reinforcement, expectancy and learning. *Psychological Review, 79,* 394–409.

Bothe, H. G., Ebeling, W., Kurzhanski, A. B., & Peschel, M. (1987). *Dynamic systems and environmental models.* Berlin: Akademie-Verlag.

Bowers, K. S. (1981). Knowing more than we can say leads to saying more than we can know: On being implicitly informed. In D. Magnusson (Ed.), *Toward a psychology of situations* (pp. 179–194). Hillsdale, NJ: Erlbaum.

Bowlby, J. (1952). *Maternal care and mental health* (2nd ed.). Geneva: World Health Organization.

Brandtstädter, J. (1993). Development, aging and control: Empirical and theoretical issues. In D. Magnusson & P. Casaer (Eds.), *Longitudinal research on individual development: Present status and future perspectives* (pp. 194–216). Cambridge, England: Cambridge University Press.

Breedlove, S. M. (1994). Sexual differentiation of the human nervous system. *Annual Review of Psychology, 45,* 389–418.

Brentano, E. (1924). *Psychologie vom empirischen Standpunkte.* Leipzig: F. Meiner. (Original work published 1874)

Brewin, C. R. (1986). *Cognitive foundations of clinical psychology.* Hillsdale, NJ: Erlbaum.

Bronfenbrenner, U. (1943). A constant frame of reference for sociometric research. *Sociometry, 6,* 363–397.

Bronfenbrenner, U. (1958). Socialization and social class through time and space. In E. E. Maccoby, T. M. Newcombe, & E. L. Hartley (Eds.), *Readings in social psychology* (3rd ed.). New York: Holt, Rinehart and Winston.

Bronfenbrenner, U. (1977). Toward an experimental ecology of human development. *American Psychologist, 32,* 513–531.

Bronfenbrenner, U. (1979). *The ecology of human development: Experiments by nature and design.* Cambridge, MA: Harvard University Press.

Bronfenbrenner, U. (1989). Ecological systems theory. *Annals of Child Development, 6,* 185–246.

Bronfenbrenner, U., & Ceci, S. J. (1994). Nature–nurture reconceptualized in a developmental perspective: A bio-ecological perspective. *Psychological Review, 101,* 568–586.

Bronfenbrenner, U., & Crouter, A. C. (1983). The evolution of environmental models in developmental research. In P. Mussen (Series Ed.) & W. Kessen (Vol. Ed.), *Handbook of child psychology: Vol. 1. History, theories and methods* (4th ed., pp. 357–414). New York: Wiley.

Brooks-Gunn, J., & Petersen, A. C. (1983). *Girls at puberty: Biological and psychosocial perspectives.* New York: Plenum Press.

Brown, G. W., Harris, T. O., & Peto, J. (1973). Life-events and psychiatric disorder: 2. Nature of causal link. *Psychological Medicine, 3,* 159–176.

Brunswik, E. (1929). Prinzipenfragen der Gestalttheorie. In E. Brunswik, Ch. Bühler, H. Hetzer, L. Kardos, E. Köhler, J. Krug, & A. Willwohl (Eds.), *Beiträge zur Problemgeschichte der Psychologie* (pp. 78–149). Jena: Verlag von Gustav Fischer.

Brunswik, E. (1952). *The conceptual framework of psychology.* Chicago: University of Chicago Press.

Bryden, M. P. (1982). *Laterality, functional asymmetry in the intact brain.* New York: Academic Press.

Buikhuisen, W. (1982). Aggressive behavior and cognitive disorders. *International Journal of Law and Psychiatry, 5,* 205–217.

Buikhuisen, W. (1987). Cerebral dysfunctions and juvenile crime. In S. A. Mednick, T. E. Moffitt, & S. A. Stack (Eds.),

The causes at crime. New biological approaches (pp. 168–184). Cambridge, England: Cambridge University Press.

Burgen, A. (1993). Information flow in the nervous system. *European Review, 1,* 31–39.

Buss, A. H., & Plomin, R. (1984). *Temperament: Early developing personality traits.* Hillsdale, NJ: Erlbaum.

Cairns, R. B. (1979). *Social development: The origins and plasticity of interchanges.* San Francisco: Freeman.

Cairns, R. B. (1983a). The emergence of developmental psychology. In P. H. Mussen (Series Ed.) & W. Kessen (Vol. Ed.), *Handbook of child psychology: Vol. 1. History, theories and methods* (4th ed., pp. 41–101). New York: Wiley.

Cairns, R. B. (1983b). Sociometry, psychometry, and social structure: A commentary on six studies of popular, rejected and neglected children. *Merrill-Palmer Quarterly, 29,* 429–444.

Cairns, R. B. (1986a). Phenomena lost: Issues in the study of development. In J. Valsiner (Ed.), *The individual subject and scientific psychology* (pp. 79–112). New York: Plenum Press.

Cairns, R. B. (1986b). A contemporary perspective on social development. In P. S. Strain, M. J. Guralnick, & H. M. Walker (Eds.), *Children's social behavior: Development, assessment, and modification* (pp. 3–47). New York: Academic Press.

Cairns, R. B. (1996). Socialization and sociogenesis. In D. Magnusson (Ed.), *The life-span development of individuals: Behavioral, neurobiological and psychosocial perspectives* (pp. 277–295). Cambridge, England: Cambridge University Press.

Cairns, R. B., & Cairns, B. D. (1986). The developmental-interactional view of social behavior: Four issues of adolescent aggression. In D. Olweus, J. Block, & M. Radke-Yarrow (Eds.), *The development of antisocial and prosocial behavior.* New York: Academic Press.

Cairns, R. B., & Cairns, B. D. (1994). *Lifelines and risks. Pathways of youth in our time.* Hemel Hempstead: Harvester Wheatsheaf.

Cairns, R. B., Cairns, B. D., & Neckerman, H. J. (1989). Early school dropout: Configurations and determinants. *Child Development, 60,* 1437–1452.

Cairns, R. B., Cairns, B. D., Neckerman, H. J., Fergusson, L. L., & Gariépy, J.-L. (1989). Growth and aggression: I. Childhood to early adolescence. *Developmental Psychology, 25,* 320–330.

Cairns, R. B., & Hood, K. E. (1983). Continuity in social development: A comparative perspective on individual difference prediction. In P. B. Baltes & O. G. Brim, Jr. (Eds.), *Life-span development and behavior* (pp. 302–358). New York: Academic Press.

Cairns, R. B., Leung, M.-C., Buchanan, L. D., & Cairns, B. D. (1995). Friendships and social networks in childhood and adolescence: Fluidity, reliability, and interrelations. *Child Development, 66,* 1330–1345.

Cairns, R. B., MacCombie, D. J., & Hood, K. E. (1983). A developmental-genetic analysis of aggressive behavior in mice: I. Behavioral outcomes. *Journal of Comparative Psychology, 97,* 69–89.

Cairns, R. B., & Ornstein, P. A. (1979). Developmental psychology. In E. Hearst (Ed.), *The first century of experimental psychology* (pp. 459–510). Hillsdale, NJ: Erlbaum.

Cannon, W. B. (1914). The emergency function of the adrenal medulla in pain and the major emotions. *American Journal of Physiology, 33,* 356–372.

Caprara, G. V. (1992). Marginal deviations, aggregated effects, disruption of continuity, and deviation amplifying mechanisms. In P. J. Hettema & I. J. Deary (Eds.), *Foundations of personality* (pp. 227–250). Dordrecht, The Netherlands: Kluwer.

Carlson, M., Earls, F., & Todd, R. D. (1988). The importance of regressive changes in the development of the nervous system: Towards a neurobiological theory of child development. *Psychiatric Developments, 1,* 1–22.

Carlson, R. (1988). Exemplary lives: The uses of psychobiography for theory development. *Journal of Personality, 56,* 105–138.

Caspi, A. (1987). Personality in the life course. *Journal of Personality and Social Psychology, 53,* 1203–1213.

Caspi, A., & Bem, D. J. (1990). Personality continuity and change across the life course. In L. A. Pervin (Ed.), *Handbook of personality: Theory and research* (pp. 549–575). New York: Guilford Press.

Caspi, A., & Moffit, T. (1991). Individual differences are accentuated during periods of social change: The sample case of girls at puberty. *Journal of Personality and Social Psychology, 61,* 157–168.

Cattell, R. B. (1965). *The scientific analysis of personality.* Chicago: Aldine.

Cattell, R. B., Catell, A. K. S., & Rhymer, R. M. (1947). P-technique demonstrated in determining psycho-physiological source traits in a normal individual. *Psychometrika, 12,* 267–288.

Chein, I. (1954). The environment as a determinant of behavior. *Journal of Social Psychology, 39,* 115–127.

Cicchetti, D. (1993). Developmental psychopathology: Reactions, reflections, projections. *Developmental Review, 13,* 471–502.

Claridge, G. (1985). *Origins of mental illness: Temperament, deviance and disorder.* Oxford, England: Blackwell.

Clausen, J. A. (1995). Gender, contexts, and turning points in adults' lives. In Ph. Moen, G. Elder, Jr., & K. Luscher (Eds.), *Examining lives in context: Perspectives in the ecology of human development* (pp. 365–389). Washington, DC: American Psychological Association.

Coie, J. D., Dodge, K. A., & Coppotelli, H. (1982). Dimensions and types of social status: A cross-age perspective. *Developmental Psychology, 18,* 557–570.

Coie, J. D., & Kupersmidt, J. B. (1983). A behavioral analysis of emerging social status in boy's groups. *Child Development, 54,* 1400–1416.

Coleman, J. S. (1990). *Foundations of social theory.* Cambridge, MA: Harvard University Press.

Collins, L. M., & Wugalter, S. E. (1992). Latent class models for stage-sequential dynamic latent variables. *Multivariable Behavioral Research, 27,* 131–157.

Corballis, M. C. (1983). *Human laterality.* New York: Academic Press.

Costanzo, P. R. (1991). Morals, mothers, and memories: The social context of developing social cognition. In R. Cohen & A. W. Siegel (Eds.), *Context and development* (pp. 91–134). Hillsdale, NJ: Erlbaum.

Cowen, E. L., Pederson, A., Babigian, H., Izzo, L. D., & Trost, M. A. (1973). Long-term follow-up of early detected vulnerable children. *Journal of Consulting and Clinical Psychology, 41,* 438–446.

Craig, T. K. J. (1987). Stress and contextual meaning: Specific causal effects in psychiatric and physical disorders. In D. Magnusson & A. Öhman (Eds.), *Psychopathology: An interactional perspective* (pp. 289–303). Orlando, FL: Academic Press.

Crick, F. (1988). *What mad pursuit: A personal view of scientific discovery.* New York: Basic Books.

Cronbach, L. J. (1975). Beyond the two disciplines of scientific psychology. *American Psychologist, 30,* 116–127.

Crutchfield, J. P., Farmer, J. D., Packard, N. H., Shaw, R. B. (1986). Chaos. *Scientific American, 252,* 38–49.

Damasio, A. R., & Damasio, H. (1996). Advances in cognitive neuroscience. In D. Magnusson (Ed.), *The life-span development of individuals: Behavioral, neurobiological and psychosocial perspectives* (pp. 265–273). Cambridge, England: Cambridge University Press.

Davis, A. J., & Hathaway, B. K. (1982). Reciprocity in parent-child verbal interactions. *Journal of Genetic Psychology, 140,* 169–183.

Day, R., Zubin, J., & Steinhauer, S. R. (1987). Psychosocial factors in schizophrenia in light of vulnerability theory. In D. Magnusson & A. Öhman (Eds.), *Psychopathology: An interactional perspective* (pp. 25–39). Orlando, FL: Academic Press.

Depue, R. A. (1995). Neurobiological factors in personality and depression. *European Journal of Psychology, 9,* 413–439.

DeRosier, M. E., Cillessen, A. H. N., Dodge, J. D., & Dodge, K. A. (1994). Group social context and children's aggressive behavior. *Child Development, 65,* 1068–1079.

Dewey, J. (1896). The reflex arc concept in psychology. *Psychological Review, 3,* 357–370.

Dixon, N. F. (1981). *Preconscious processes.* Chichester, England: Wiley.

Dixon, R. A., & Lerner, R. M. (1988). A history of systems in developmental psychology. In M. H. Bornstein & M. E. Lamb (Eds.), *Developmental psychology: An advanced textbook* (2nd ed., pp. 3–50). Hillsdale, NJ: Erlbaum.

Dodge, K. A. (1990). Nature versus nurture in childhood conduct disorder: It is time to ask a different question. *Developmental Psychology, 26,* 698–701.

Dodge, K. A., Coie, J. D., & Brakke, N. P. (1982). Behavior patterns of socially rejected and neglected preadolescents: The roles of social approach and aggression. *Journal of Abnormal Child Psychology, 10,* 389–409.

Dowdney, L., & Pickles, A. R. (1991). Expression of negative affect within disciplinary encounters: Is there dyadic reciprocity? *Developmental Psychology, 27,* 606–617.

Dunn, J., & Plomin, R. (1990). *Separate lives. Why siblings are so different.* New York: Basic Books.

Durkheim, E. (1897). *Le suicide: Étude de sociologie* [The suicide: A sociological study]. Paris: Alcan.

Earls, F. (1987). Sex differences in psychiatric disorders: Origins and developmental influences. *Psychiatric Developments, 5,* 1–23.

Earls, F., & Carlson, M. (1994, September 5–9). *Promoting human capability as an alternative to early crime prevention.* Paper presented at the conference Integrating Motivational and Opportunity-Reducing Crime Prevention Strategies, Stockholm.

Earls, F., & Carlson, M. (1995). Promoting human capability as alternative to early crime prevention. In R. V. Clarke, J. McCord, & Wikstrom, (Eds.), *Integrating crime prevention strategies: Propensity and opportunity.* Stockholm: National Council for Crime Prevention.

Earls, F., & Jung, K. (1987). Temperament and home environment characteristics as causal factors in the early development of childhood psychopathology. *Journal of the American Academy of Child Adolescent Psychiatry, 26,* 491–498.

Eccles, J. S., Midgley, C., Wigfield, A., Buchanan, C. M., Reuman, D., Flanagan, C., & MacIver, D. (1993). The impact of stage-environment fit in young adolescents' experiences in schools and families. *American Psychologist, 48,* 90–101.

Edelman, G. (1987). *Neural Darwinism: The theory of neuronal group selection.* New York: Basic.

Edelman, G. E. (1989). Topobiology. *Scientific American, 260,* 44–52.

Edelman, G. M., & Tononi, G. (1996). Selection and development: The brain as a complex system. In D. Magnusson (Ed.), *The life-span development of individuals: Behavioral, neurobiological and psychosocial perspectives* (pp. 179–204). Cambridge, England: Cambridge University Press.

Eigen, M. (1971). Self-organization of matter and the evolution of biological macromolecules. *Die Naturwissenschaften, 58,* 265–523.

Elder, G. H., Jr. (1974). *Children of the Great Depression.* Chicago: University of Chicago Press.

Elder, G. H., Jr. (1979). Historical change in life patterns and personality. In P. B. Baltes (Ed.), *Life-span development and behavior* (Vol. 2). New York: Academic Press.

Elder, G. H., Jr. (1981). Adolescence in historical perspective. In J. Adelson (Ed.), *Handbook of adolescent psychology* (pp. 3–46). New York: Wiley.

Elder, G. H., Jr. (1995). The life course paradigm: Social change and individual development. In Ph. Moen, G. H. Elder, Jr., & K. Luscher (Eds.), *Examining lives in context. Perspectives on the ecology of human development* (pp. 101–139). Washington, DC: American Psychological Association.

Elder, G. H., Jr. (in press). Human lives in changing societies: Life course and developmental insights. In R. B. Cairns, G. H. Elder, Jr., & E. J. Costello (Eds.), *Developmental science.* New York: Cambridge University Press.

Elder, G. H., Jr., Conger, R. D., Foster, E. M., & Ardelt, M. (1992). Families under economic pressure. *Journal of Family Issues, 13,* 5–37.

Elder, G. H., Jr., Liker, J. K., & Cross, C. E. (1984). Parent-child behavior in the great depression: Life course and intergenerational influences. In P. B. Baltes & O. G. Brim, Jr. (Eds.), *Life-span development and behavior: Historical and cohort effect* (Vol. 6, pp. 111–159). New York: Academic Press.

Elder, G. H., Jr., Van Nguyen, T., & Caspi, A. (1985). Linking family hardship to children's lives. *Child Development, 56,* 361–375.

Elliot, D. B., Huizinga, D., & Ageton, S. S. (1985). *Explaining delinquency and drug use.* Newbury Park, CA: Sage.

Emde, R. N. (1994). Individuality, context, and the search for meaning. *Child Development, 65,* 719–737.

Emler, N., & McNamara, S. (1996, May 11–15). *Social structures and interpersonal relationships.* Paper presented at the fifth biennial conference of the European Association for Research on Adolescence, Liège.

Endler, N. S., & Magnusson, D. (1976). Toward an interactional psychology of personality. *Psychological Bulletin, 83,* 956–979.

Epstein, S. (1990). Cognitive-experiential self-theory. In L. A. Pervin (Ed.), *Handbook of personality: Theory and research* (pp. 165–192). New York: Guilford Press.

Ericsson, K. A., Krampe, R. Th., & Tesch-Römer, C. (1993). The role of deliberate practice in the acquisition of expert performance. *Psychological Review, 100,* 363–406.

Eysenck, H. J. (1990). Biological dimensions of personality. In L. Pervin (Ed.), *Handbook of personality: Theory and research* (pp. 244–276). New York: Guilford Press.

Farrington, D. P. (1994, June). *Protective factors in the development of juvenile delinquency and adult crime.* Invited lecture given at the sixth scientific meeting of the Society for Research in Child and Adolescent Psychopathology, London.

Farrington, D. P., Gallagher, B., Morley, L., St. Ledger, R. J., & West, D. J. (1988). Are there any successful men from criminogenic backgrounds? *Psychiatry, 51,* 116–130.

Farrington, D. P., Loeber, R., Elliott, D. S., Hawkins, J. D., Kandel, D. B., Klein, M. W., McCord, J., Rowe, D. C., & Tremblay, R. E. (1990). Advancing knowledge about the onset of delinquency and crime. In B. B. Lahey & A. E. Kazdin (Eds.), *Advances in clinical child psychology* (Vol. 13, pp. 283–342). New York: Plenum Press.

Faulconer, J. E., & Williams, R. N. (1985). Temporality in human action: An alternative to positivism and historicism. *American Journal of Psychology, 40,* 1179–1188.

Feather, N. T. (1980). Values in adolescence. In J. Adelson (Ed.), *Handbook of adolescent psychology* (pp. 247–294). New York: Wiley.

Feldman, S. S., Fisher, L., Ransom, D. C., & Dimiceli, S. (1995). Is "What is good for the goose good for the gender?" Sex differences in relations between adolescent coping and adult adaptation. *Journal of Research on Adolescence, 5,* 333–359.

Fensham, P., & Marton, F. (1991). *High-school teachers' and university chemists' differing conceptualization of the personal activity in constituting knowledge in chemistry.* Department of Education and Educational Research, University of Gothenburg.

Fentress, J. C. (1989). Developmental roots of behavioral order: Systemic approaches to the examination of core developmental issues. In M. R. Gunnar & E. Thelen (Eds.), *Systems and development* (pp. 35–75). Hillsdale, NJ: Erlbaum.

Finkel, D., Pedersen, J. L., McGue, M., & McClearn, G. E. (1995). Heritability of cognitive abilities in adult twins: Comparison of Minnesota and Swedish data. *Behavior Genetics, 25,* 421–431.

Fishbein, M., & Ajzen, I. (1975). *Belief, attitude, intention and behavior: An introduction to theory and research.* Reading, MA: Addison Wesley.

Fogel, A., & Thelen, E. (1987). Development of early expressive and communicative action: Reinterpreting the evidence from a dynamic systems perspective. *Developmental Psychology, 23,* 747–761.

Ford, D. H. (1987). *Humans as self-constructing living systems: A developmental perspective on personality and behavior.* Hillsdale, NJ: Erlbaum.

Ford, D. H., & Lerner, R. M. (1992). *Developmental systems theory: An integrative approach.* Newbury Park, CA: Sage.

Forgas, J. P., & van Heck, G. L. (1992). The psychology of situations. In G. V. Caprara & G. L. van Heck (Eds.), *Modern personality psychology* (pp. 418–455). New York: Harvester.

Frankenhaeuser, M., Lundberg, U., & Chesney, M. (1991). *Women, work, and health.* New York: Plenum Press.

Galton, F. (1869). *Hereditary genius: An inquiry into its laws and consequences.* London: Macmillan.

Gangestad, S., & Snyder, M. (1985). To carve nature at its joints: On the existence of discrete classes in personality. *Psychological Review, 92,* 317–349.

Garmezy, N. (1974). The study of competence in children at risk for severe psychopathology. In E. Anthony & C. Koupernic (Eds.), *The child in his family: Children at psychiatric risk* (pp. 77–97). New York: Wiley.

Garmezy, N., Masten, A. S., & Tellegen, A. (1984). The study of stress and competence in children: A building block for developmental psychopathology. *Child Development, 55,* 97–111.

Gergen, K. J. (1973). Toward generative theory. *Journal of Personality and Social Psychology, 26,* 309–320.

Gershman, E. S., & Hayes, D. S. (1983). Differential stability of reciprocal friendships and unilateral relationships among pre-school children. *Merrill-Palmer Quarterly, 29,* 169–177.

Gibson, E. J. (1994). Has psychology a future? *Psychological Science, 5,* 69–76.

Gibson, W. A. (1959). Three multivariate models: Factor analysis, latent structure analysis and latent profile analysis. *Psychometrica, 24,* 229–252.

Gleick, J. (1987). *Chaos: Making a new science.* New York: Penguin.

Goffman, E. (1964). The neglected situation. *American Anthropologist, 66,* 133–136.

Goodfield, J. (1974). Changing strategies: A comparison of reductionist attitudes in biological and medical research in the nineteenth and twentieth centuries. In F. J. Ayala & T. Dobzhansky (Eds.), *Studies in the philosophy of biology.* Berkeley: University of California.

Gottesman, J. J., & Shields, J. (1982). *Schizophrenia, the epigenetic puzzle.* Cambridge, England: Cambridge University Press.

Gottlieb, G. (1991). Experiential canalization of behavioral development: Theory. *Developmental Psychology, 27,* 4–13.

Gottlieb, G. (1992). *Individual development and evolution: The genesis of novel behavior.* New York: Oxford University Press.

Gottlieb, G. (1996). A systems view of psychobiological development. In D. Magnusson (Ed.), *The life-span development of individuals: Behavioral, neurobiological and psychosocial perspectives* (pp. 76–104). Cambridge, England: Cambridge University Press.

Gramer, M., & Huber, H. P. (1994). Individual variability in task-specific cardiovascular response patterns during psychological challenge. *German Journal of Psychology, 18*(1), 1–17.

Gray, J. A. (1985). Issues in the neuropsychology of anxiety. In A. Hussain Tuma & J. D. Maser (Eds.), *Anxiety and the anxiety disorders* (pp. 5–25). Hillsdale, NJ: Erlbaum.

Greenberger, E., O'Neil, R., & Nagel, S. (1994). Linking workplace and homeplace: Relations between the nature of adults' work and their parenting behaviors. *Developmental Psychology, 30,* 990–1002.

Greenwald, A. G. (1992). Unconscious cognition reclaimed. *American Psychologist, 47*(6), 766–779.

Greenwald, A. G., & Banaji, M. R. (1995). Implicit social cognition: Attitudes, self-esteem, and stereotypes. *Psychological Review, 102,* 4–27.

Gunnar, M. R. (1986). Human developmental psychoendocrinology: A review of research on neuroendocrine responses to challenge and threat in infancy and childhood. In M. E. Lamb, A. L. Brown, & B. Rogoff (Eds.), *Advances in developmental psychology* (Vol. 4, pp. 51–103). Hillsdale, NJ: Erlbaum.

Gustafson, S. B., & Magnusson, D. (1991). Female life careers: A longitudinal person approach to female educational and vocational pathways. In D. Magnusson (Ed.), *Paths through life* (Vol. 3). Hillsdale, NJ: Erlbaum.

Gustafsson, S. B., & Mumford, M. D. (1995). Personal style and person-environment fit: A pattern approach. *Journal of Vocational Behavior, 46,* 163–188.

Gustafson, S. B., Stattin, H., & Magnusson, D. (1989). Aspects of the development of a career versus homemaking orientation among females: The longitudinal influence of educational motivation and peers. *Journal of Research on Adolescence, 2,* 241–259.

Gustafson, S. B., Stattin, H., & Magnusson, D. (1992). Aspects of the development of a career versus homemaking orientation among females: The longitudinal influence of educational motivation and peers. *Journal of Research on Adolescence, 2,* 241–259.

Hall, N. (1991). *The new scientist guide to chaos.* London: Penguin.

Harkness, S. (1992). Cross-cultural research in child development: A sample of the state of the art. *Developmental Psychology, 28,* 622–625.

Harter, S. (1983). Developmental perspectives on the self system. In P. H. Mussen (Series Ed.) & E. M. Hetherington (Vol. Ed.), *Handbook of child psychology: Socialization, personality and social development* (Vol. 4, pp. 275–385). New York: Wiley.

Harter, S. (1990). Causes, correlates, and the functional role of global self-worth: A life-span perspective. In R. J. Sternberg & J. Kolligan, Jr. (Eds.), *Competence considered* (pp. 67–97). New Haven, CT: Yale University Press.

Hartshorne, H., & May, M. A. (1928). *Studies in the nature of character: Studies in deceit* (Vol. 1). New York: Macmillan.

Hartup, W. W. (1978). Perspectives on child and family interaction: Past, present and future. In R. M. Lerner & G. B. Spanier (Eds.), *Child influences on marital and family interaction* (pp. 23–46). New York: Academic Press.

Hartup, W. W. (1996). The company they keep: Friendships and their developmental significance. *Child Development, 67,* 1–13.

Hartup, W. W., & van Lieshout, C. F. M. (1995). Personality development in social context. *Annual Review of Psychology, 46,* 655–687.

Headey, B., & Wearing, A. (1989). Personality, life events, and subjective well-being: Toward a dynamic equilibrium model. *Journal of Personality and Social Psychology, 57,* 731–739.

Hebb, D. D. (1955). The socialization of the child. In E. E. Maccoby, T. M. Newcomb, & E. L. Hartley (Eds.), *Readings in social psychology.* New York: Holt, Rinehart and Winston.

Hedges, L. V., & Nowell, A. (1995). Sex differences in mental scores, variability, and numbers of high-scoring individuals. *Science, 269,* 41–45.

Hellvik, O. (1988). *Introduction to causal analysis. Exploring survey data by crosstabulation.* Oslo: Norwegian University Press.

Helson, H. (1964). *Adaptation level theory.* New York: Harper & Row.

Henderson, A. S., Byrne, D. G., & Duncan-Jones, P. (1981). *Neuroses and the social environment.* New York: Academic Press.

Hendry, L. B., Shucksmith, J., & Glendinning, A. (1995). *Adolescent focal theories: An empirical perspective.* Aberdeen: University of Aberdeen, Department of Education.

Hess, B., & Mikhailov, A. (1944). Self-organization in living cells. *Science, 264,* 223–224.

Hettema, J. (1995). Personality and depression: A multilevel perspective. *European Journal of Personality, 9,* 401–412.

Hettema, P. J. (1979). *Personality and adaptation.* Amsterdam, The Netherlands: North-Holland.

Hettema, P. J. (1989). *Personality and environment: Assessment of human adaptation.* Chichester, England: Wiley.

Hinde, R. A. (1992). Developmental psychology in the context of other behavioral sciences. *Developmental Psychology, 28,* 622–625.

Hinde, R. A. (1996). The interpenetration of biology and culture. In D. Magnusson (Ed.), *The life-span development of individuals: Behavioral, neurobiological and psychosocial perspectives* (pp. 359–375). Cambridge, England: Cambridge University Press.

Hirschi, T., & Gottfredson, M. R. (1994). *The generality of deviance.* New Brunswick, NJ: Transaction.

Hockey, G. R., Gaillard, A. W. K., & Coles, M. G. H. (1986). *Energetic and human information processing.* Dordrecht, The Netherlands: Martin Nijhoff.

Hofer, M. A. (1981). *The roots of human behavior: An introduction to the psychology of early development.* San Francisco: Freeman.

Holmes, T. H., & Rahe, R. M. (1967). The social readjustment scale. *Journal of Psychosomatic Research, 11,* 213–218.

Horn, J. L., & Donaldson, G. (1976). On the myth of intellectual decline in adulthood. *American Psychologist, 31,* 701–709.

Horowitz, F. D. (1989). Commentary: Process and systems. In M. R. Gunnar & E. Thelen (Eds.), *Systems and development* (pp. 35–75). Hillsdale, NJ: Erlbaum.

Hubel, D. H., & Wiesel, T. N. (1970). The period of susceptibility to the physiological effects of unilateral eye closer in kittens. *Journal of Physiology, 206,* 419–436.

Hunt, D. E. (1975). Person-environment interaction: A challenge found wanting before it was tried. *Review of Educational Research, 45,* 209–230.

Hunt, J. McV. (1961). *Intelligence and experience*. New York: Ronald Press.

Hunt, J. McV. (1966). The epigenesis of intrinsic motivation and early cognitive learning. In R. N. Hober (Ed.), *Current research in motivation* (pp. 355–370). New York: Holt, Rinehart and Winston.

Husén, T. (1951). The influence of schooling upon IQ. Theoria. *A Swedish Journal of Philosophy and Psychology, 17*, 61–88.

Husén, T., & Tuijnman, A. (1991). The contribution of formal schooling to the increase in intellectual capital. *Educational Researcher, 20*, 17–25.

Irvine, S. (1969). Culture and mental ability. *New Scientist, 1*, 230–231.

Jacob, F. (1989). *The logic of life: A history of heredity and the possible and the actual*. London: Penguin.

James, W. (1890). *The principles of psychology*. New York: Holt.

Jessor, R. (1992). Risk behavior in adolescence: A psychosocial framework for understanding and action. *Developmental Review, 12*, 374–390.

Jessor, R., & Jessor, S. L. (1977). *Problem behavior and psychosocial development: A longitudinal study of youth*. New York: Academic Press.

Johansson, G., Frankenhaeuser, M., & Magnusson, D. (1973). Catecholamine output in school children as related to performance and adjustment. *Scandinavian Journal of Psychology, 14*, 20–28.

Kagan, J. (1981). *The second year: The emergence of self-awareness*. Cambridge, MA: Harvard University Press.

Kagan, J. (1989). *Unstable ideas: Temperament, cognition, and self*. Cambridge, MA: Harvard University Press.

Kagan, J. (1992). Yesterday's premises, tomorrows promises. *American Psychologist, 28*, 990–997.

Kagan, J. (1994). *Galen's prophecy: Temperament in human nature*. New York: Basic Books.

Kagan, J. (1996). Temperamental contributions to the development of social behavior. In D. Magnusson (Ed.), *The life-span development of individuals: Behavioral, neurobiological and psychosocial perspectives* (pp. 376–393). Cambridge, England: Cambridge University Press.

Kagan, J., & Moss, H. A. (1962). *Birth to maturity*. New York: Wiley.

Kalverboer, A. F., & Hopkins, B. (1983). General introduction: A biopsychological approach to the study of human behavior. *Journal of Child Psychology and Psychiatry, 24*, 9–10.

Kalverboer, A. F., Hopkins, B., & Geuze, R. (1993). *Motor development in early and later childhood: Longitudinal approaches*. Cambridge, England: Cambridge University Press.

Kandel, D. B. (1978). Similarity in real-life friendship pairs. *Journal of Personality and Social Psychology, 36*, 306–312.

Kantor, J. R. (1924). *Principles of psychology* (Vol. 1). Bloomington, IN: Principia Press.

Kantor, J. R. (1926). *Principles of psychology* (Vol. 2). Bloomington, IN: Principia Press.

Kaplan, M. L., & Kaplan, N. R. (1991). The self-organization of human psychological functioning. *Behavioral Science, 36*, 161–179.

Karli, P. (1996). The brain and socialization: A two-way mediation across the life course. In D. Magnusson (Ed.), *The life-span development of individuals: Behavioral, neurobiological and psychosocial perspectives* (pp. 341–356). Cambridge, England: Cambridge University Press.

Kauffmann, S. A. (1993). *The origins of order*. New York: Oxford University Press.

Kelvin, P. (1969). *The bases of social behavior. An approach in terms of order and value*. London: Holt.

Kenrick, D. T., Montello, D. R., & MacFarlane, S. (1985). Personality: Social learning, social cognition, or sociobiology? In R. Hogan & W. H. Jones (Eds.), *Perspectives in personality* (pp. 201–234). Greenwich, CT: JAI Press.

Kihlstrom, J. F. (1990). The psychological unconscious. In L. A. Pervin (Ed.), *Handbook of personality: Theory and research* (pp. 445–468). New York: Guilford Press.

Kinsbourne, M. (1978). *Asymmetrical function of the brain*. New York: Cambridge University Press.

Klaczynski, P. A. (1990). Cultural-developmental tasks and adolescent development: Theoretical and methodological considerations. *Adolescence, 25*, 811–823.

af Klinteberg, B., Andersson, T., Magnusson, D., & Stattin, H. (1993). Hyperactive behavior in childhood as related to subsequent alcohol problems and violent offending: A longitudinal study of male subjects. *Personality and Individual Differences, 15*, 381–388.

af Klinteberg, B., Levander, S. E., & Schalling, D. (1987). Cognitive sex differences: Speed and problem-solving strategies on computerized neuropsychological tasks. *Perceptual and Motor Skills, 65*, 683–697.

Kloep, M. (1995). Concurrent and predictive correlates of girls' depression and antisocial behaviour under conditions of economic crisis and value change: The case of Albania. *Journal of Adolescence, 18*, 445–458.

Kobasa, S. (1979). Stressful life events, personality and health: An inquiry into hardiness. *Journal of Personality and Social Psychology, 37*, 1–11.

Koch, S. (1981). The nature and limits of psychological knowledge: Lessons of a century qua "science." *American Psychologist, 36,* 257–269.

Koestler, A. (1978). *Janus: A summing up.* London: Hutchingson.

Koffka, K. (1935). *Principles of Gestalt psychology.* New York: Harcourt.

Kohlberg, L., LaCross, J., & Ricks, D. (1972). The predictability of adult mental health from childhood behavior. In B. Wolman (Ed.), *Manual of child psychopathology.* New York: McGraw-Hill.

Kohn, M., & Clausen, J. (1955). Social isolation and schizophrenia. *American Sociological Review, 20,* 265–273.

Kolvin, I., Miller, F. J. W., Fleeting, M., & Kolvin, P. A. (1988). Risk/protective factors for offending with particular reference to deprivation. In M. Rutter (Ed.), *Studies of psychosocial risk: The power of longitudinal data* (pp. 77–95). Cambridge, England: Cambridge University Press.

Kotulak, R. (1993, April 11). Unravelling hidden mysteries of the brain. *Chicago Tribune.*

Krahé, B. (1990). *Situation cognition and coherence in personality: An individual centered approach. European Monographs in Social Psychology.* Cambridge, England: Cambridge University Press.

Krantz, D. S., Lundberg, U., & Frankenhaeuser, M. (1987). Stress and Type A behavior. Interactions between environmental and biological factors. In A. Baum & J. E. Singer (Eds.), *Handbook of psychology and health: Stress and coping* (Vol. 5, pp. 203–228). Hillsdale, NJ: Erlbaum.

Krauth, J., & Lienert, G. A. (1982). Fundamentals and modifications of configural frequency analysis (CFA). *Interdisciplinaria, 3,* Issue 1.

Kreppner, K. (1992a). William L. Stern, 1871–1938. A neglected founder of developmental psychology. *Developmental Psychology, 28,* 539–547.

Kreppner, K. (1992b). Development in a developing context: Rethinking the family's role for children's development. In L. C. Vinegar & J. Valsiner (Eds.), *Children's development within social context.* Hillsdale, NJ: Erlbaum.

Kreppner, K., & Lerner, R. M. (1989). Family systems and life-span development: Issues and perspectives. In K. Kreppner & R. M. Lerner (Eds.), *Family systems and life-span development* (pp. 1–13). Hillsdale, NJ: Erlbaum.

Krupat, E. (1974). Context as a determinant of perceived threat: The role of prior experience. *Journal of Personality and Social Psychology, 29,* 731–736.

Kuo, Z.-Y. (1967). *The dynamics of behavior development. An epigenetic view.* New York: Random House.

Lagerspetz, K. M. J., & Lagerspetz, K. Y. H. (1971). Changes in the aggressiveness of mice resulting from selective breeding, learning and social isolation. *Scandinavian Journal of Psychology, 12,* 241–248.

Lagerström, M. (1991). *Pre- and perinatal factors in long-term development.* Doctoral dissertation, Department of Psychology, Stockholm University.

Lamb, M. (1981). *The role of the father in child development* (2nd ed.). New York: Wiley.

Landy, F. J. (1978). An opponent process theory of job satisfaction. *Journal of Applied Psychology, 63,* 533–547.

Laszlo, E. (1972). *The systems view of the world.* New York: Braziller.

Lazarus, R. S., & Folkman, S. (1984). *Stress, appraisal, and coping.* New York: Springer.

Leadbeater, B. J., Blatt, S. J., & Quinlan, D. M. (1995). Gender-linked vulnerabilities to depressive symptom, stress, and problem behaviors in adolescents. *Journal of Research on Adolescence, 5,* 1–29.

Leff, J. (1987). The influence of life events and relatives expressed emotion on the course of schizophrenia. In D. Magnusson & A. Öhman (Eds.), *Psychopathology: An interactional perspective* (pp. 59–76). Orlando, FL: Academic Press.

Lehrman, D. S. (1970). Semantic and conceptual issues in the nature–nurture problem. In L. R. Aronsson, E. Tobach, D. S. Lehrman, & J. S. Rosenblatt (Eds.), *Development and evolution of behavior. Essays in memory of T. C. Schneirla* (pp. 17–52). San Francisco: Freeman.

Lerner, R. M. (1978). Nature, nurture, and dynamic interactionism. *Human Development, 21,* 1–20.

Lerner, R. M. (1983). A "goodness of fit" model of person-context interaction. In D. Magnusson & V. L. Allen (Eds.), *Human development: An interactional perspective* (pp. 279–294). New York: Academic Press.

Lerner, R. M. (1984). *On the nature of human plasticity.* Cambridge, England: Cambridge University Press.

Lerner, R. M. (1989). Individual development and the family system: A life-span perspective. In K. Kreppner & R. M. Lerner (Eds.), *Family systems and life-span development* (pp. 15–31). Hillsdale, NJ: Erlbaum.

Lerner, R. M. (1990). Plasticity, person-context relations, and cognitive training in the aged years: A developmental contextual perspective. *Developmental Psychology, 27,* 911–915.

Lerner, R. M. (1991). Changing organism-context relations as the basic process of development: A developmental contextual perspective. *Developmental Psychology, 27,* 27–32.

Lerner, R. M., & Busch-Rossnagel, N. A. (1981). *Individuals as producers of their development: A life-span perspective.* New York: Academic Press.

Lerner, R. M., & Kauffman, M. B. (1985). The concept of development in contextualism. *Developmental Review, 5,* 309–333.

Lerner, R. M., & Lerner, J. V. (1987). Children in their contexts: A goodness of fit model. In J. B. Lancaster, J. Altmann, A. S. Rossi, & L. R. Sherrod (Eds.), *Parenting across the life span: Biosocial dimensions* (pp. 377–404). Chicago: Aldine.

Lerner, R. M., Skinner, E. A., & Sorell, G. T. (1980). Methodological implications of context/dialectic theories of development. *Human Development, 23,* 225–235.

Levine, S. (1982). Comparative and psychobiological perspectives on development. In W. A. Collins (Ed.), *The concept of development. The Minnesota Symposium on Child Psychology* (Vol. 15). Hillsdale, NJ: Erlbaum.

Lewin, K. (1931). Environmental forces. In C. Murchison (Ed.), *A handbook of child psychology* (pp. 590–625). Worcester, MA: Clark University Press.

Lewin, K. (1935). *A dynamic theory of personality.* New York: McGraw-Hill.

Lewin, K. (1936). *Principles of topological psychology.* New York: McGraw-Hill.

Lewis, M., & Brooks-Gunn, J. (1979). *Social cognition and the acquisition of self.* New York: Plenum Press.

Lewis, M., & Feiring, C. (1991). Attachment as a personal characteristic or a measure of the environment. In J. L. Gewirtz & W. M. Kurtines (Eds.), *Intersections with attachment* (pp. 3–21). Hillsdale, NJ: Erlbaum.

Lewis, M., Feiring, C., & Weintraub, M. (1981). The father as a member of the child's social network. In M. Lamb (Ed.), *The role of the father in child development* (2nd ed.). New York: Wiley.

Lienert, G. A., & zur Oeveste, H. (1985). CFA as a statistical tool for developmental research. *Educational and Psychological Measurement, 45,* 301–307.

Lindberg, U. (1992). *Livet är en interaktion* [Life is an interaction]. Stockholm: Folkuniversitetet.

Little, T. D., Oettingen, G., Stetsenko, A., & Baltes, P. B. (1995). Children's action-control beliefs about school performance: How do American children compare with German and Russian children? *Journal of Personality and Social Psychology, 69,* 686–700.

Lockman, J. J., & Thelen, E. (1993). Developmental biodynamics: Brain, body, behavior connections. *Child Development, 64,* 953–959.

Loeber, R. (1982). The stability of antisocial and delinquent child behavior: A review. *Child Development, 53,* 1431–1446.

Loeber, R., & Dishion, T. J. (1983). Early predictors of male delinquency: A review. *Psychological Bulletin, 94,* 68–99.

Loeber, R., & Le Blanc, M. (1990). Toward a developmental criminology. In M. Tonry & N. Morris (Eds.), *Crime and justice: A review of research* (pp. 375–473). Chicago: University of Chicago Press.

Loehlin, J. C. (1996). Genes and environment. In D. Magnusson (Ed.), *The life-span development of individuals: Behavioral, neurobiological and psychosocial perspectives* (pp. 38–51). Cambridge, England: Cambridge University Press.

Luthar, S. S. (1993). Annotation: Methodological and conceptual issues in research on childhood resilience. *Journal of Child Psychology and Psychiatry, 34,* 441–453.

Maccoby, E. E. (1990). Gender and relationships—a developmental account. *American Psychologist, 46,* 513–520.

Maccoby, E. E. (1992). The role of parents in the socialization of children: An historical overview. *Developmental Psychology, 28,* 1006–1017.

Maccoby, E. E. (1995). The two sexes and their social systems. In P. Moen, G. H. Elder, Jr., & K. Luscher (Eds.), *Examining lives in context. Perspectives on the ecology of human development* (pp. 347–364). Washington, DC: American Psychological Association.

Maccoby, E. E., & Jacklin, C. N. (1983). The "person" characteristics of children and the family as environment. In D. Magnusson & V. L. Allen (Eds.), *Human development: An interactional perspective* (pp. 76–91). New York: Academic Press.

Magnusson, D. (1967). *Test theory.* Reading, MA: Addison-Wesley.

Magnusson, D. (1971). An analysis of situational dimensions. *Perceptual and Motor Skills, 32,* 851–867.

Magnusson, D. (1976). The person and the situation in an interactional model of behavior. *Scandinavian Journal of Psychology, 17,* 253–271.

Magnusson, D. (1980). Personality in an interactional paradigm of research. *Zeitschrift für Differentielle und Diagnostische Psychologie, 1,* 17–34.

Magnusson, D. (1981). *Toward a psychology of situations: An interactional perspective.* Hillsdale, NJ: Erlbaum.

Magnusson, D. (1985). Implications of an interactional paradigm for research on human development. *International Journal of Behavioral Development, 8,* 115–137.

Magnusson, D. (1988). Individual development from an interactional perspective. In D. Magnusson (Ed.), *Paths through life* (Vol. 1). Hillsdale, NJ: Erlbaum.

Magnusson, D. (1990). Personality development from an interactional perspective. In L. Pervin (Ed.), *Handbook of personality* (pp. 193–222). New York: Guilford Press.

Magnusson, D. (1992). Back to the phenomena: Theory, methods and statistics in psychological research. *European Journal of Personality, 6,* 1–14.

Magnusson, D. (1995). Individual development: A holistic integrated model. In P. Moen, G. H. Elder, & K. Luscher (Eds.), *Linking lives and contexts: Perspectives on the ecology of human development* (pp. 19–60). Washington, DC: APA Books.

Magnusson, D. (1996). Towards a developmental science. In D. Magnusson (Ed.), *The life-span development of individuals: Behavioral, neurobiological and psychosocial perspectives* (pp. xv–xvii). Cambridge, England: Cambridge University Press.

Magnusson, D. (in press-a). The logic and implications of a person approach. In R. B. Cairns, L. R. Bergman, & J. Kagan (Eds.), *The individual as a focus in developmental research.* New York: Sage.

Magnusson, D. (in press-b). The patterning of antisocial behavior and autonomic reactivity. In D. M. Stoff & R. B. Cairns (Eds.), *The neurobiology of clinical aggression.* Hillsdale, NJ: Erlbaum.

Magnusson, D., & Allen, V. L. (1983a). Implications and applications of an interactional perspective for human development. In D. Magnusson & V. L. Allen (Eds.), *Human development: An interactional perspective* (pp. 369–387). Orlando, FL: Academic Press.

Magnusson, D., & Allen, V. L. (1983b). An interactional perspective for human development. In D. Magnusson & V. L. Allen (Eds.), *Human development: An interactional perspective* (pp. 3–31). New York: Academic Press.

Magnusson, D., & Bergman, L. R. (1988). Individual and variable-based approaches to longitudinal research on early risk factors. In M. Rutter (Ed.), *Studies of psychosocial risk: The power of longitudinal data* (pp. 45–61). Cambridge, England: Cambridge University Press.

Magnusson, D., & Bergman, L. R. (1990). A pattern approach to the study of pathways from childhood to adulthood. In L. N. Robins & M. Rutter (Eds.), *Straight and devious pathways from childhood to adulthood* (pp. 101–115). Cambridge, England: Cambridge University Press.

Magnusson, D., Bergman, L. R., Rudinger, G., & Törestad, B. (1991). *Problems and methods in longitudinal research: Stability and change.* Cambridge, England: Cambridge University Press.

Magnusson, D., & Cairns, R. B. (1996). Developmental science: Principles and illustrations. In R. B. Cairns, G. H. Elder, Jr.,
& E. J. Costello (Eds.), *Developmental science* (pp. 7–30). New York: Cambridge University Press.

Magnusson, D., & Casaer, P. (1992). *Longitudinal research on individual development: Present status and future perspectives.* Cambridge, England: Cambridge University Press.

Magnusson, D., & Endler, N. S. (1977). Interactional psychology: Present status and future prospects. In D. Magnusson & N. S. Endler (Eds.), *Personality at the crossroads: Current issues in interactional psychology* (pp. 3–31). Hillsdale, NJ: Erlbaum.

Magnusson, D., Gerzén, M., & Nyman, B. (1968). The generality of behavioral data: I. Generalization from observations on one occasion. *Multivariate Behavioral Research, 3,* 295–320.

Magnusson, D., & Heffler, B. (1969). The generality of behavioral data: Generalization potential as a function of the number of observation instances. *Multivariate Behavioral Research, 4,* 29–42.

Magnusson, D., af Klinteberg, B., & Stattin, H. (1993). Autonomic activity/reactivity, behavior, and crime in a longitudinal perspective. In J. McCord (Ed.), *Facts, frameworks, and forecasts* (pp. 287–318). New Brunswick, NJ: Transaction.

Magnusson, D., Stattin, H., & Allen, V. L. (1985). Biological maturation and social development: A longitudinal study of some adjustment processes from mid-adolescence to adulthood. *Journal of Youth and Adolescence, 14,* 267–283.

Magnusson, D., Stattin, H., & Allen, V. L. (1986). Differential maturation among girls and its relation to social adjustment: A longitudinal perspective. In P. Baltes, D. Featherman, & R. M. Lerner (Eds.), *Lifespan development* (Vol. 7, pp. 134–172). New York: Academic Press.

Magnusson, D., & Törestad, B. (1992). The individual as an interactive agent in the environment. In W. B. Walsh, K. Craig, & R. Price (Eds.), *Person-environment psychology: Models and perspectives* (pp. 89–126). Hillsdale, NJ: Erlbaum.

Manly, B. F. (1994). *Multivariate statistical methods. A primer* (2nd ed.). London: Chapman & Hall.

Manturzewska, M. (1990). A biographical study of the life-span development of professional musicians. *Psychology of Music, 18,* 112–139.

Markus, H., & Cross, S. (1990). The interpersonal self. In L. A. Pervin (Ed.), *Handbook of personality: Theory and research* (pp. 576–608). New York: Guilford Press.

Markus, H., & Wurf, E. (1987). The dynamic self-concept: A social psychological perspective. *Annual Review of Psychology, 38,* 299–337.

Mason, J. W. (1975). A historical view of the stress field (in two parts). *Journal of Human Stress, 1,* 6–36.

Masterpasqua, F. (1990). A competence paradigm for psychological practice. *American Psychologist, 44,* 1366–1371.

Mayr, E. (1976). *Evolution and the diversity of life.* Cambridge, MA: Harvard University Press.

McCall, R. B. (1977). Challenges to a science of developmental psychology. *Child Development, 48,* 333–344.

McClintock, E. (1983). Interaction. In H. H. Kelley, E. Berscheid, A. Christensen, J. H. Harvey, T. L. Huston, G. Levinger, E. M. Clintock, L. A. Pepelau, & D. R. Peterson (Eds.), *Close relationships.* New York: Freeman.

McClintock, M. K. (1971). Menstrual synchrony and suppression. *Nature, 229,* 224–225.

McCrae, R. R., & Costa, P. T., Jr. (1995). Trait explanations in personality research. *European Journal of Personality, 9,* 231–252.

McGue, M., Gottesman, J. J., & Rao, D. C. (1986). The analysis of schizophrenic family data. *Behavior Genetics, 16,* 75–87.

McGuffin, P., & Katz, R. (1986). Nature, nurture, and affective disorders. In J. F. W. Deakin (Ed.), *The biology of depression* (pp. 113–129). London: Gaskell Press.

McGuffin, P., Murray, R. M., & Reveley, A. M. (1987). Genetic influences on the functional psychoses. *British Medical Bulletin, 43,* 531–556.

Mead, G. H. (1934). *Mind, self and society.* Chicago: University of Chicago Press.

Medawar, P. (1984). *Plato's republic.* Oxford, England: Oxford University Press.

Meyer-Probst, B., Rösler, H.-D., & Teichmann, H. (1983). Biological and psychosocial risk factors and development during childhood. In D. Magnusson & V. L. Allen (Eds.), *Human development: An interactional perspective* (pp. 344–369). Orlando, FL: Academic Press.

Miller, J. G. (1978). *Living systems.* New York: McGraw Hill.

Mills, P., Dimsdale, J. E., Nelesen, R. A., Jasievicz, J., Ziegler, G., & Kennedy, B. (1994). Patterns of adrenergic receptors and adrenergic agonists underlying cardiovascular responses to a psychological challenge. *Psychological Medicine, 56,* 70–86.

Mineka, S., & Kihlström, J. F. (1978). Unpredictable and uncontrollable events: A new perspective on experimental neurosis. *Journal of Abnormal Psychology, 87,* 256–271.

Minuchin, P. (1985). Families and individual development: Provocations from the field of family therapy. *Child Development, 56,* 289–301.

Mischel, W. (1968). *Personality and assessment.* New York: Wiley.

Mischel, W. (1973). Toward a cognitive social learning reconceptualizing of personality. *Psychological Review, 80,* 252–283.

Mischel, W., & Shoda, Y. (1995). A cognitive-affective system theory of personality: Reconceptualizing situations, dispositions, dynamics, and invariance in personality structure. *Psychological Review, 102,* 246–268.

Moolenaar, P. C. M., Boomsma, D. I., & Dolan, C. V. (1991). Genetic and environmental factors in a developmental perspective. In D. Magnusson, L. R. Bergman, G. Rudinger, & B. Törestad (Eds.), *Problems and methods in longitudinal research: Stability and change* (pp. 250–273). Cambridge, England: Cambridge University Press.

Moreland, R. L., & Zajonc, R. B. (1982). Exposure effects in person perception: Familiarity, similarity and attraction. *Journal of Experimental Social Psychology, 18,* 395–415.

Mortimer, A. M., & McKenna, P. J. (1994). Levels of explanation—symptoms, neuropsychological deficit and morphological abnormalities in schizophrenia. *Psychological Medicine, 24,* 541–545.

Mumford, M. D., & Owen, W. A. (1984). Individuality in a developmental context: Some empirical and theoretical considerations. *Human Development, 27,* 84–108.

Murphy, L. B. (1983). Issues in the development of emotion in infancy. In R. Plutchite & H. Kellerman (Eds.), *Emotion: Theory, research and experience: Vol. 2. Emotions in early development.* New York: Academic Press.

Murray, H. A. (1938). *Explorations in personality.* New York: Oxford University Press.

Murray, H. A. (1951). Toward a classification of interaction. In T. Parsons & E. A. Shils (Eds.), *Toward a general theory of action.* Cambridge, MA: Harvard University Press.

Neckerman, H. J. (1992). *A longitudinal investigation of the stability and fluidity of social networks and peer relationships of children and adolescents.* Doctoral dissertation, University of North Carolina at Chapel Hill.

Nesselroade, J. R., & Ford, D. H. (1987). Methodological considerations in modeling living systems. In M. E. Ford & D. H. Ford (Eds.), *Humans as self-constructing living systems: Putting the framework to work* (pp. 47–79). Hillsdale, NJ: Erlbaum.

Newcombe, N. (1931). An experiment designed to test the validity of a rating technique. *Journal of Educational Psychology, 22,* 279–289.

Nicolis, G., & Prigogine, I. (1977). *Self-organization in nonequilibrium systems.* New York: Wiley.

Norman, D. A., & Shallice, T. (1980). *Attention to action: Willed and automatic control of behavior* (CHIP Report 99). San Diego: University of California.

Oettingen, G., Little, T. D., Lindenberg, U., & Baltes, P. B. (1994). Causality, agency, and control beliefs in East versus West Berlin children: A natural experiment on the role of context. *Journal of Personality and Social Psychology, 66,* 579–595.

Offord, D. R., Sullivan, K., Allen, N., & Abrams, N. (1979). Delinquency and hyperactivity. *Journal of Nervous and Mental Disease, 167,* 734–741.

Ogbu, J. (1981). Origins of human competence: A cultural-ecological perspective. *Child Development, 52,* 413–429.

O'Leary, D. D. M. (1996). Development of the functionally-specialized areas of the mammalian neocortex. In D. Magnusson (Ed.), *The life-span development of individuals: Behavioral, neurobiological and psychosocial perspectives* (pp. 23–37). Cambridge, England: Cambridge University Press.

Oliveri, M. E., & Reiss, D. (1987). Social networks of family members. Distinctive roles of mothers and fathers. *Sex Roles, 17,* 719–736.

Olofsson, B. (1973). *Young delinquents: III. Home upbringing, education and peer relation as reflected in interview and follow-up data* (25). Stockholm: Statens Offentliga Utredningar.

Olson, D. H., McCubin, H. I., Barnes, H., Larsen, A., Muxen, M., & Wilson, M. (1983). *Families: What makes them work.* Los Angeles: Sage.

Olweus, D. (1979). Stability of aggressive reaction patterns in males: A review. *Psychological Bulletin, 86,* 852–857.

Overton, W. F., & Reese, H. W. (1973). Models of development: Methodological implications. In J. R. Nesselroade & H. W. Reese (Eds.), *Life-span developmental psychology: Methodological issues* (pp. 65–86). New York: Academic Press.

Oyama, S. (1989). Ontogeny and the central dogma: Do we need the concept of genetic programming in order to have an evolutionary perspective. In M. R. Gunnar & E. Thelen (Eds.), *Systems and development* (Vol. 22, pp. 1–34). Hillsdale, NJ: Erlbaum.

Ozer, D. J. (1993). The Q-sort method and the study of personality development. In D. C. Funder, R. D. Parke, C. Tomlinson-Keasey, & K. Widaman (Eds.), *Studying lives through time: Personality and development* (pp. 147–168). Washington, DC: American Psychological Association.

Ozer, D. J., & Gjerde, P. F. (1989). Patterns of personality consistency and change from childhood through adolescence. *Journal of Personality, 57,* 483–507.

Packer, M., Medina, N., Yushak, M., & Meller, J. (1983). Hemodynamic patterns of response during long-term captopril therapy for severe chronic heart failure. *Circulation, 68,* 103–112.

Parke, R. D. (1978). Parent-infant interaction: Progress paradigms and problems. In P. B. Sackett (Ed.), *Theory and applications in mental retardation: Observing behavior* (Vol. 1). Baltimore: University Park Press.

Patterson, G. R. (1982). *Coercive family process.* Eugene, OR: Castalia Press.

Patterson, G. R., DeBaryshe, B. D., & Ramsey, E. (1989). A developmental perspective on antisocial behavior. *American Psychologist, 44,* 329–335.

Patterson, G. R., & Moore, D. R. (1978). Interactive patterns of units. In S. J. Suomi, M. E. Lamb, & R. G. Stevenson (Eds.), *The study of social interaction: Methodological issues.* Madison: University of Wisconsin Press.

Pearson, K. P. (1892). *The grammar of science* (2nd ed.). London: Adam and Charles Black.

Pedersen, N. L. (1994). The nature and nurture of personality. In B. de Raad, W. K. B. Hofstee, & G. L. van Heck (Eds.), *Personality psychology in Europe* (Vol. 5, pp. 110–132). Tilburg: Tilburg University Press.

Pedersen, N. L., Plomin, R., Nesselroade, J. R., & McClearn, G. E. (1992). A quantitative genetic analysis of cognitive abilities during the second half of the life span. *Psychological Science, 3,* 346–353.

Pepper, S. C. (1942). *World hypotheses: A study of evidence.* Berkeley: University of California Press.

Pervin, L. A. (1968). Performance and satisfaction as a function of individual environment fit. *Psychological Bulletin, 69,* 56–68.

Pervin, L. A. (1978). Definitions, measurements, and classification of stimuli, situations, and environments. *Human Ecology, 6,* 71–105.

Pervin, L. A. (1983). The stasis and flow of behavior: Toward a theory of goals. In M. M. Page (Ed.), *Nebraska Symposium on Motivation* (pp. 1–53). Lincoln: Nebraska University Press.

Pervin, L. A. (1990). A brief history of modern personality theory. In L. A. Pervin (Ed.), *Handbook of personality: Theory and research* (pp. 3–18). New York: Guilford Press.

Pervin, L. A. (1995). *The science of personality.* New York: Wiley.

Petersen, A. (1993). Presidential address: Creating adolescents: The role of context and process in developmental trajectories. *Journal of Research on Adolescence, 3,* 1–18.

Petersen, A. C., & Taylor, B. (1980). The biological approach to adolescence. Biological change and psychological adaptation. In J. Adelson (Ed.), *Handbook of adolescent psychology.* New York: Wiley.

Peterson, D. R. (1968). *The clinical study of social behavior.* New York: Appleton-Century-Crofts.

Peterson, D. R. (1979). Assessing interpersonal relationships by means of interaction research. *Behavioral Assessment, 1,* 221–276.

Piaget, J. (1964). Development and learning. *Journal of Research in Science Teaching, 2,* 176–186.

Pickles, A., & Rutter, M. (1991). Statistical and conceptual models of "turning points" in developmental processes. In D. Magnusson, L. R. Bergman, G. Rudinger, & B. Törestad (Eds.), *Problems and methods in longitudinal research: Stability and change* (pp. 133–166). Cambridge, England: Cambridge University Press.

Plomin, R. (1986a). Behavioral genetic methods. *Journal of Personality, 54,* 226–261.

Plomin, R. (1986b). *Development, genetics and psychology.* Hillsdale, NJ: Erlbaum.

Plomin, R. (1989). Environment and genes: Determinants of behavior. *American Psychologist, 4,* 105–111.

Poincaré, H. (1946). *The foundations of science.* Lancaster, MI: Science Press.

Popper, K. R., & Eccles, J. C. (1977). *The self and its brain.* Berlin: Springer-Verlag.

Preyer, W. (1908). *The mind of the child.* New York: Appleton-Century.

Pulkkinen, L., & Rönkä, A. (1994). Personal control over development, identity formation, and future orientation as components of life orientation: A developmental approach. *Developmental Psychology, 30,* 260–271.

Pulkkinen, L., & Tremblay, R. (1992). Patterns of boys' social adjustment in two cultures and at different ages: A longitudinal perspective. *International Journal of Behavioural Development, 15,* 527–553.

Radke-Yarrow, M., & Kuczynski, L. (1983). Conceptions of the environment in childrearing interactions. In D. Magnusson & V. L. Allen (Eds.), *Human development: An interactional perspective* (pp. 57–74). New York: Academic Press.

Raine, A., & Mednick, S. A. (1989). Biosocial longitudinal research in antisocial behavior. *Revue of Epidemiology, 37,* 515–524.

Raleigh, M. J., McGuire, M. T., Brammer, G. L., & Yuwiler, J. (1984). Social and environmental influences on blood serotonin concentration in monkeys. *Archives of General Psychiatry, 41,* 405–410.

Reinhardt, J. M. (1937). Personality traits and the situation. *American Journal of Sociology, 2,* 492–500.

Ribaupierre, A. de (1989). *Transition mechanisms in child development: The longitudinal perspective.* Cambridge, England: Cambridge University Press.

Riegel, K. F. (1975). Toward a dialectical theory of development. *Human Development, 18,* 50–64.

Riegel, K. F. (1976). The dialectics of human development. *American Psychologist, 31,* 689–700.

Roff, M. (1961). Childhood social interactions and young adult bad conduct. *Journal of Abnormal and Social Psychology, 63,* 333–337.

Roff, M., Sells, S. B., & Golden, M. M. (1972). *Social adjustment and personality development in children.* Minneapolis: University of Minnesota Press.

Roland, E. (1993). *Brain activation.* New York: Wiley-Liss.

Rose, S. (1995). The rise of neurogenetic determinism. *Nature, 373,* 380–382.

Rosenbaum, M. (1988). Learned resourcefulness, stress and self-regulation. In S. Fisher & J. Reason (Eds.), *Handbook of life stress, cognition and health* (pp. 483–496). New York: Wiley.

Rotter, J. B. (1954). *Social learning and clinical psychology.* Englewood Cliffs, NJ: Prentice-Hall.

Rotter, J. B. (1955). The role of the psychological situation in determining the direction of human behavior. In M. R. Jones (Ed.), *Nebraska Symposium on Motivation* (pp. 245–268). Lincoln: University of Nebraska Press.

Roush, W. (1995). When rigor meets reality. *Science, 269,* 313–315.

Rushton, J. P., Fulker, D. W., Neale, M. C., Nias, D. K. B., & Eysenck, H. J. (1986). Altruism and aggression: Individual differences are substantially heritable. *Journal of Personality and Social Psychology, 50,* 1192–1198.

Russel, R. W. (1970). "Psychology." Noun or adjective. *American Psychologist, 25,* 211–218.

Rutter, M. (1974). Epidemiological strategies and psychiatric concepts in research on the vulnerable child. In E. Anthony & C. Koupernic (Eds.), *The child in his family: Children at psychiatric risk* (pp. 167–179). New York: Wiley.

Rutter, M. (1985). Resilience in the face of adversity: Protective factors and resistance to psychiatric disorder. *British Journal of Psychiatry, 147,* 598–611.

Rutter, M. (1988). *Studies of psychosocial risk. The power of longitudinal data.* Cambridge, England: Cambridge University Press.

Rutter, M. (1990). Psychosocial resilience and protective mechanisms. In J. Rolf, A. Masten, D. Cicchetti, K. H. Nuechterlein, & S. Weintraub (Eds.), *Risk and protective factors in the development of psychopathology* (pp. 181–214). Cambridge, England: Cambridge University Press.

Rutter, M., & Casaer, P. (1991). *Biological risk factors for psychosocial disorders.* Cambridge, England: Cambridge University Press.

Rutter, M., & Giller, H. (1983). *Juvenile delinquency. Trends and perspectives.* Harmondsworth, Middlesex: Penguin Books.

Ryff, C. D. (1987). The place of personality and social structure research in social psychology. *Journal of Personality and Social Psychology, 53,* 1192–1202.

Sameroff, A. J. (1975). Transactional models in early social relations. *Human Development, 18,* 65–79.

Sameroff, A. J. (1982). Development and the dialectic: The need for a systems approach. In W. A. Collins (Ed.), *The concept of development* (pp. 83–103). Hillsdale, NJ: Erlbaum.

Sameroff, A. J. (1983). Developmental systems: Contexts and evolution. In P. H. Mussen (Gen. Ed.) & W. Kessen (Vol. Ed.), *Handbook of child psychology: Vol. 1. History, theory, and methods* (pp. 237–294). New York: Wiley.

Sameroff, A. J. (1989). Commentary: General systems and the regulation of development. In M. R. Gunnar & E. Thelen (Eds.), *Systems and development* (pp. 219–235). Hillsdale, NJ: Erlbaum.

Sapolsky, R. M. (1990). Stress in the wild. *Scientific American, 262,* 106–113.

Sapolsky, R. M. (1994). On human nature. *The Sciences, 34*(6), 14–16.

Sarason, I. G., Johnson, J. H., & Siegel, J. (1978). Assessing the impact of life changes: Development of the life experiences survey. *Journal of Consulting and Clinical Psychology, 46,* 932–946.

Sarason, I. G., Sarason, B. R., & Shearin, E. N. (1986). Social support as an individual difference variable: Its stability, origins, and relational aspects. *Journal of Personality and Social Psychology, 50,* 845–855.

Sarbin, T. R. (1986). The narrative as the root metaphor for psychology. In T. R. Sarbin (Ed.), *Narrative psychology: The storied nature of human conduct* (pp. 3–21). New York: Praeger.

Sarigiani, P. A., Wilson, J. L., Petersen, A. C., & Vicary, J. R. (1990). Self-image and educational plans of adolescents from two contrasting communities. *Journal of Early Adolescence, 10,* 37–55.

Sarter, M., Berntson, G. G., & Cacioppo, J. T. (1996). Brain imaging and cognitive neuroscience. *American Psychologist, 51,* 13–21.

Scarr, S. (1981). Comments on psychology: Behavior genetics and social policy from an anti-reductionist. In R. A. Kasschau & C. N. Cofer (Eds.), *Psychology's second century: Enduring issues* (pp. 147–175). New York: Praeger.

Scarr, S., & McCartney, K. (1983). How people make their own environments: A theory of genotype-environment effects. *Child Development, 54,* 242–435.

Schaie, K. W., & Baltes, P. B. (1975). On sequential strategies in developmental research: Description or explanation? *Human Development, 128,* 384–390.

Schneider, B. H. (1993). *Children's social competence in context: The contributions of family, school and culture. International series in experimental social psychology.* New York: Pergamon Press.

Schneider, W., & Edelstein, W. (1990). *Inventory of European longitudinal studies in the behavioural and medical sciences.* Berlin: Max-Planck-Institute for Human Development and Education.

Schneider, W., & Shiffrin, R. M. (1977). Controlled and automatic human information processing: I. Detection, search, and attention. *Psychological Review, 84,* 1–66.

Schneirla, T. C. (1956). Interrelationships of the innate and the acquired in instinctive behavior. In P. P. Grasse (Ed.), *L'instinct dans le comportement des animaux et de l'homme* (pp. 387–452). Paris: Mason et Cie.

Schneirla, T. C. (1957). The concept of development in comparative psychology. In D. B. Harris (Ed.), *The concept of development* (pp. 78–108). Minneapolis: University of Minnesota Press.

Schneirla, T. C. (1959). An evolutionary and developmental theory of biphasic processes underlying approach and withdrawal. In *Nebraska Symposium on Motivation.* Lincoln: University of Nebraska.

Schneirla, T. C. (1966). Behavioral development and comparative psychology. *Quarterly Review of Biology, 41,* 283–302.

Schulkin, J., McEwen, B. S., & Gold, P. W. (1994). Allostasis, amydala, and anticipatory Angst. *Neuroscientific Biobehavioral Review, 18,* 385–396.

Schwartz, C. (1987). Personality and the unification of psychology and modern physics: A system approach. In J. Aronoff, A. I. Robin, & R. A. Zucker (Eds.), *The emergence of personality* (pp. 217–254). New York: Springer.

Scriven, M. (1959). Explanation and prediction in evolutionary theory. *Science, 130,* 477–482.

Sears, R. R. (1951). A theoretical framework for personality and social behavior. *American Psychologist, 6,* 476–483.

Seginer, R. (1983). Parents' educational expectations and children's academic achievements: A literature review. *Merrill-Palmer Quarterly, 29,* 1–23.

Seligman, M. E. P. (1975). *Helplessness: On depression, development and death.* San Francisco: Freeman.

Sells, S. B. (1963a). An interactionist looks at the environment. *American Psychologist, 18,* 696–702.

Sells, S. B. (1963b). *Stimulus determinants of behavior.* New York: Ronald Press.

Sells, S. B. (1966). Ecology and the science of psychology. *Multivariate Behavioral Research, 1,* 131–144.

Selye, H. (1950). *Stress: The physiology and pathology of exposure to stress.* Montreal: Acta.

Shanon, B. (1993). *The representational and the presentational. An essay on cognition and the study of mind.* New York: Harvester.

Shannon, L. W. (1988). *Criminal career continuity.* New York: Human Sciences Press.

Shiffrin, R. M., & Schneider, W. (1977). Controlled and automatic human information processing: II. Perceptual learning, automatic attending, and a general theory. *Psychological Review, 84,* 127–190.

Shinn, M. W. (1900). *The biography of a baby.* New York: Houghton Mifflin.

Silbereisen, R. K. (1995, May 21–23). *Early adversities and psychosocial development in adolescence: A comparison of the former Germanies.* Paper presented at the Research Colloquium "Growing up in times of social change," Friedrich Schiller University, Jena, Germany.

Silbereisen, R. K., & Kracke, B. (in press). Self-reported maturational timing and adaptation in adolescence. In G. Schulenberg, J. Maggs, & K. Hurrelmann (Eds.), *Health risks and developmental transitions during adolescence.*

Silbereisen, R. K., Meschke, L. L., & Schwarz, B. (in press). Leaving parents' home: Predictors of home leaving age in young adults raised in former East and West Germany. In J. A. Graber & J. S. Dubas (Eds.), *Leaving home: New directions in child development.* San Francisco: Jossey-Bass.

Silbereisen, R. K., & Noack, P. (1988). On the constructive role of problem behaviors in adolescence. In N. Bolgar, A. Caspi, G. Downey, & M. Moorehouse (Eds.), *Persons in context: Developmental processes* (pp. 152–180). Cambridge, England: Cambridge University Press.

Simmons, R. C., & Blyth, D. A. (1987). *Moving into adolescence: The impact of pubertal change and school context.* New York: Aldine.

Simon, H. (1969). *The sciences of the artificial.* Cambridge, MA: MIT Press.

Sjöbring, H. (1958). *Structure and development: A personality theory.* Lund: Gleerups.

Skinner, B. F. (1971). *Beyond freedom and dignity.* New York: Knopf.

Smith, C. A., & Lazarus, R. S. (1990). Emotion and adaptation. In L. Pervin (Ed.), *Handbook of personality* (pp. 609–637). New York: Guilford Press.

Snyder, C. R., Harris, C., Anderson, J. R., Holleran, S. A., Irving, L. M., Sigmon, S. T., Yoshinobu, L., Gibb, J., Langelle, C., & Harney, P. (1991). The will and the ways: Development and validation of an individual-differences measure of hope. *Journal of Personality and Social Psychology, 60,* 570–585.

Solomon, R. L., & Corbit, J. D. (1974). An opponent theory of motivation: I. Temporal dynamics of affect. *Psychological Review, 2,* 119–145.

Spring, B., & Coons, H. (1982). Stress as a precursor of schizophrenia. In R. W. J. Neufeld (Ed.), *Psychological stress and psychopathology.* New York: McGraw-Hill.

Sroufe, L. A. (1979). The coherence of individual development: Early care, attachment and subsequent developmental issues. *American Psychologist, 34,* 834–841.

Stagner, R. (1976). Traits are relevant: Theoretical analysis and empirical evidence. In N. S. Endler & D. Magnusson (Eds.), *Interactional psychology and personality* (pp. 109–124). New York: Wiley.

Stattin, H. (1983). The psychological situation in an interactional perspective of personality: A theoretical background and some empirical studies. Doctoral dissertation, *Reports from the Department of Psychology, University of Stockholm,* Supplement 58.

Stattin, H., Janson, H., Klackenberg-Larsson, I., & Magnusson, D. (1995). Corporal punishment in everyday life: An intergenerational perspective. In J. McCord (Ed.), *Coercion and punishment in long-term perspectives* (pp. 315–347). Cambridge, England: Cambridge University Press.

Stattin, H., & Klackenberg, G. (1992). Family discord in adolescence in the light of family discord in childhood: The maternal perspective. In W. Meeus, M. de Goede, W. Kox, & K. Hurrelman (Eds.), *Adolescence, careers, and cultures* (pp. 143–161). Berlin: De Gruyter.

Stattin, H., & Magnusson, D. (1989). Social transition in adolescence: A biosocial perspective. In A. de Ribaupierrre (Ed.), *Transition mechanisms in child development: The longitudinal perspective* (pp. 147–190). Cambridge, England: Cambridge University Press.

Stattin, H., & Magnusson, D. (1990). Pubertal maturation in female development. In D. Magnusson (Ed.), *Paths through life* (Vol. 2). Hillsdale, NJ: Erlbaum.

Stattin, H., & Magnusson, D. (1991). Stability and change in criminal behaviour up to age 30. *British Journal of Criminology, 31,* 327–346.

Stattin, H., & Magnusson, D. (1995). Onset of official delinquency: Its co-occurrence in time with educational, behavioral and interpersonal problems. *British Journal of Criminology, 35*, 417–449.

Stattin, H., & Magnusson, D. (in press). Antisocial behavior—a holistic perspective [Special issue]. *Development and Psychopathology.*

Staudinger, U. M., Marsiska, M., & Baltes, P. B. (1993). Resilience and levels of reserve capacity in later adulthood: Perspectives from life-span theory. *Development and Psychopathology, 5*, 541–566.

Staudinger, U. M., Marsiska, M., & Baltes, P. B. (1995). Resilience and reserve capacity in later adulthood: Potentials and limits of development across the life span. In D. Cicchetti & D. J. Cohen (Eds.), *Developmental psychopathology: Risk disorder and adaptation* (Vol. 2, pp. 801–847). New York: Wiley.

Steinberg, L. (1987). Latchkey children and susceptibility to peer pressure: An ecological analysis. *Developmental Psychology, 22*, 433–439.

Stern, W. (1911). *Die Differentielle Psychologie in Ihren Metodischen Grundlagen* [Differential psychology in its methodological basis]. Leipzig: Verlag von Johann A. Barth.

Stern, W. (1914). *Psychologie der Frühen Kindheit bis zum sechsten Lebensjahr.* Leipzig: Quelle & Meyer.

Stern, W. (1927). *Psychologie der frühen Kindheit.* Leipzig: Quelle und Meyer.

Stern, W. (1935). *Allgemeine Psychologie auf personalistischer Grundlage.* Den Haag: Nijhoff.

Stokols, D., & Altman, I. (1987). *Handbook of environmental psychology* (Vols. 1 & 2). New York: Wiley.

Stouthamer-Loeber, M., Loeber, R., Farrington, D. P., Zhang, Q., van Kammen, W., & Maguin, E. (1993). The double edge of protective and risk factors for delinquency: Interrelations and developmental patterns. *Development and Psychopathology, 5*, 683–701.

Strelau, J. (1983). *Temperament-personality-activity.* New York: Academic Press.

Stryker, M. P. (1994). Precise development from imprecise rule. *Science, 263*, 1244–1245.

Stumpf, C. (1883). *Tonpsychologie* (Vol. 1). Leipzig: S. Hirzel.

Susman, E. J. (1993). Psychological, contextual, and psychobiological interactions: A developmental perspective on conduct disorder: Toward a developmental perspective on conduct disorder [Special issue]. *Development and Psychopathology, 5*, 181–189.

Susman, L. (1989). Biology—behavior interactions in behavioral development. *ISSBD Newsletter, 15*, 1–3.

Tanner, J. M. (1981). *A history of the study of human growth.* Cambridge, England: Cambridge University Press.

Tetens, J. N. (1777). *Philosophische Versuche über die menschliche Natur und ihre Entwicklung.* Leipzig: Weidmanns Eben und Reich.

Thelen, E. (1981). Kicking, rocking, and waving: Contextual analysis of rhythmical stereotypes in normal human infants. *Animal Behaviour, 29*, 3–11.

Thelen, E. (1989). Self organization in developmental processes: Can systems approaches work? In M. R. Gunnar & E. Thelen (Eds.), *Systems and development* (pp. 77–117). Hillsdale, NJ: Erlbaum.

Thelen, E. (1995). Motor development. A new synthesis. *American Psychologist, 50*, 79–95.

Thomae, H. (1979). The concept of development and life-span developmental psychology. In P. B. Baltes & O. G. Brim, Jr. (Eds.), *Life-span development and behavior* (Vol. 2., pp. 281–312). New York: Academic Press.

Thomas, A., Chess, S., Birch, H. G., Hertzig, M. E., & Korn, S. (1963). *Behavioral individuality in early childhood.* New York: New York University Press.

Thomas, W. I. (1927). The behavior pattern and the situation. Publications of the American Sociological Society. *Papers and Proceedings, 22.*

Thomas, W. I. (1928). *The child in America.* New York: Knopf.

Thompson, S. C. (1981). Will it hurt less if I can control it? A complex answer to a simple question. *Psychological Bulletin, 90*, 89–101.

Tobach, E., & Schneirla, T. C. (1968). The biopsychology of social behavior of animals. In R. E. Cooke & S. Levin (Eds.), *Biological basis of pediatric practice* (pp. 68–82). New York: McGraw-Hill.

Tolman, E. C. (1949). *Purposive behavior and men.* Berkeley: University of California Press.

Tolman, E. C. (1951). A psychological model. In T. Parsons & E. A. Shils (Eds.), *Toward a general theory of action* (pp. 279–364). Cambridge, MA: Harvard University Press.

Tomkins, S. (1979). Script theory: Differential magnification of affects. In H. Howe & R. Dienstbier (Eds.), *Nebraska Symposium on Motivation, 26*, (pp. 201–236). Lincoln: University of Nebraska Press.

Törestad, B., Olah, A., & Magnusson, D. (1989). Individual control, intensity of reactions and frequency of occurrence: An empirical study of cross-culturally invariant relationships. *Perceptual and Motor Skills, 68*, 1339–1350.

Toulmin, S. (1981). Toward reintegration: An agenda for psychology's next century. In R. A. Kasschau & C. N. Cofer (Eds.), *Psychology's next century: Enduring issues* (pp. 264–286). New York: Praeger.

Uzguris, I. C. (1977). Plasticity and structure. The role of experience in infancy. In I. C. Uzgiris & F. Weizmann (Eds.), *The structuring of experience* (pp. 153–178). New York: Plenum Press.

Valsiner, J. (1994). "Vygotskian dynamics of development": Comment. *Journal of Human Development, 37,* 366–369.

Valsiner, J., & Lawrence, J. A. (1996). Human development in culture across the life-span. In J. W. Berry, P. R. Dasen, & T. S. Saraswathi (Eds.), *Handbook of cross-cultural research* (pp. 2–67). New York: Allyn & Bacon.

van Aken, M. A. G., & Asendorpf, J. B. (1994, July 20–23). *A person-oriented approach to development: The temporal consistency of personality and self-concept.* Paper presented at the International Conference on Longitudinal Study on the Genesis of Individual Competencies, Ringberg Castle, Germany.

van Geert, P. (1994). Vygotskian dynamics of development. *Human Development, 37,* 346–345.

von Bertalanffy, L. (1968). *General system theory.* New York: Braziller.

von Eye, A. (1990). *Introduction to configural frequency analysis. The search for types and antitypes in cross-classifications.* New York: Cambridge University Press.

von Eye, A., & Clogg, C. C. (1994). *Latent variables analysis. Applications for developmental research.* London: Sage.

von Eye, A., & Kreppner, K. (1989). Family systems and family development: The selection of analytical units. In K. Kreppner & R. M. Lerner (Eds.), *Family systems and life-span development* (pp. 247–269). Hillsdale, NJ: Erlbaum.

von Knorring, A.-L., Andersson, O., & Magnusson, D. (1987). Psychiatric care and course of psychiatric disorders from childhood to early adulthood in a representative sample. *Journal of Child Psychology and Psychiatry, 28,* 329–341.

Vygotsky, L. (1978). *Mind in society: The development of higher psychological processes.* Cambridge, MA: Harvard University Press.

Wachs, T. D. (1977). The optimal stimulation hypothesis and early development: Anybody got a match? In I. C. Uzgiris & F. Weizmann (Eds.), *The structuring of experiences* (pp. 153–178). New York: Plenum Press.

Wachs, T. D. (1979). Proximal experience and early cognitive-intellectual development: The physical environment. *Merrill-Palmer Quarterly, 25,* 3–41.

Wachtel, P. L. (1977). Interaction cycles, unconscious processes, and the person-situation issue. In D. Magnusson & N. S. Endler (Eds.), *Personality at the crossroads: Current issues in interactional psychology* (pp. 317–332). Hillsdale, NJ: Erlbaum.

Waddington, C. (1962). *New patterns in genetics and development.* New York: Columbia University Press.

Wadsworth, M. (1979). *Roots of delinquency: Infancy, adolescence and crime.* Oxford, England: Robertson.

Wallacher, R. B., & Nowak, A. (1994). *Dynamical systems in social psychology.* San Diego, CA: Academic Press.

Wapner, S., & Kaplan, B. (1983). *Toward a holistic developmental psychology.* Hillsdale, NJ: Erlbaum.

Warburton, D. M. (1979). Physiological aspects of informational processing and stress. In V. Hamilton & D. M. Warburton (Eds.), *Human stress and cognition* (pp. 33–66). Chichester, England: Wiley.

Watson, J. B. (1913). Psychology as the behaviorist views it. *Psychological Review, 20,* 158–177.

Watson, J. B. (1930). *Behaviorism* (2nd ed.). New York: Norton.

Weiner, H. (1977). *Psychology and human disease.* New York: Elsevier.

Weiner, H. (1989). The dynamics of the organism: Implications of recent biological thought for psychosomatic theory and research. *Psychosomatic Medicine, 51,* 608–635.

Weisz, J. R. (1983). Can I control it? The pursuit of veridical answers across the life-span. In P. B. Baltes & O. G. Brim (Eds.), *Life-span development of behavior* (Vol. 5, pp. 233–300). New York: Academic Press.

Werner, E. E., & Smith, R. S. (1982). *Vulnerable but invincible: A longitudinal study of resilient children and youth.* New York: McGraw-Hill.

Wheaton, B. (1990). Life transitions, role histories, and mental health. *American Sociological Review, 55,* 209–223.

White, R. W. (1959). Motivation reconsidered: The concept of competence. *Psychological Review, 66,* 297–333.

Wohlwill, J. F. (1973). *The study of behavioral development.* London: Academic Press.

Wolff, P. H. (1981). Normal variation in human maturation. In K. J. Conolly & H. F. R. Prechtl (Eds.), *Maturation and development: Biological and psychological maturation.* London: Heinemann Medical Books.

Wundt, W. (1948). Principles of physiological psychology. In W. Dennis (Ed.), *Readings in the history of psychology* (pp. 248–250). New York: Appleton-Century-Crofts.

Young, W. C. (1961). The hormones and mating behavior. In C.-W. Young (Ed.), *Sex and internal secretions* (3rd ed.). Baltimore: Williams & Wilkins.

Zajonc, R. B. (1980). Feeling and thinking: Preferences and no inferences. *American Psychologist, 35,* 151–175.

Zeeman, E. C. (1976). Catastrophe theory. *Scientific American, 234,* 65–83.

Zohar, D. (1990). The quantum self: A revolutionary view of human nature and consciousness rooted in the new physics. *Psychological Bulletin, 88,* 187–214.

Zubin, J. (1976). The role of vulnerability in the ethology of schizophrenic disorders. In L. West & D. Flinn (Eds.), *Treatment of schizophrenia: Progress and prospects* (pp. 5–33). Lincoln: University of Nebraska Press.

Zuckerman, M. (1980). Sensation seeking and its biological correlates. *Psychological Bulletin, 88,* 187–214.

Zuckerman, M. (1991). *Psychobiology of personality.* Cambridge, England: Cambridge University Press.

Zuckerman, M. (1994). *Behavioral expressions and biological bases of sensation seeking.* Cambridge, England: Cambridge University Press.

CHAPTER 13

Developmental Analysis: A Holistic, Developmental, Systems-Oriented Perspective

SEYMOUR WAPNER and JACK DEMICK

This chapter describes the origins of the holistic, developmental, systems-oriented perspective (Wapner, 1981, 1987; Wapner & Demick, 1990); its essential features, some selected areas of research in which it has been employed, and its heuristic value in shaping developmental problem areas for study. The perspective to be described is *holistic,* insofar as it assumes that all part processes—biological/physical, psychological (cognitive, affective, valuative), sociocultural—are interrelated; *developmental,* insofar as it assumes, in keeping with the orthogenetic principle (Werner, 1957), that development proceeds from a relative lack of differentiation toward the goal of differentiation and hierarchic integration of organismic functioning; and *systems-oriented,* insofar as the unit of analysis is the *person-in-environment,* where the physical/biological (e.g., health), psychological (e.g., self-esteem), and sociocultural (e.g., role) levels of organization of the *person* are operative and interrelated with the physical (e.g., natural and built environment), interpersonal (e.g., friend, relative), and sociocultural (e.g.,

regulations and rules of society) levels of organization of the *environment.*

It is of interest, indeed of developmental interest, before describing our perspective in detail, to examine its origins. This focus not only throws light on the perspective, but also describes consonant developmental research in perception and language/symbol formation that may be of interest to both those who are and those who are not sympathetic with the theoretical approach and its origins described here.

ORIGINS

Our perspective is an extension (elaborated conceptualization and increased range of empirical study) of some facets of Heinz Werner's (1926; 1940/1957) classic work on *Comparative Psychology of Mental Development;* Werner and Kaplan's (1956, 1963; B. Kaplan, 1966, 1967) characterization of the orthogenetic principle as a formal description of development, the organismic-developmental perspective, and its applicability to the analysis of language and symbol formation (cf., B. Kaplan, 1983); the organismically oriented work on the sensory-tonic field theory of perception (e.g., Wapner, Cirillo, & Baker, 1969, 1971; Werner & Wapner, 1949, 1952); Wapner and Werner's (1957, 1965) work on perceptual development and on body perception; and the extensive collaboration of Werner's, B. Kaplan's, and Wapner's graduate students and colleagues during the past five decades at Clark University (see Barten & Franklin, 1978; Franklin, 1990; Wapner, 1990; Wapner & Demick, 1992; Wapner & Kaplan, 1966, 1983; Werner & Kaplan, 1963; Witkin, 1965).

Ingredient in this variety of contributions was a number of features from the original approach relevant to the holistic, developmental, systems-oriented perspective described here. For example, these features include organismic/holistic functioning; comparative and developmental analyses; self-object differentiation; the role of context in psychological part-processes (e.g., language) and in the broader sociohistorical context of human functioning; analogous processes; the spiral nature of development; form versus content; and an openness to a range of methodologies dependent on the nature of the problem.

Prior to discussing the specific elaboration of our approach, brief synopses of the two major lines of empirical work in relation to their underlying theories (i.e., sensory-tonic field theory and perceptual development, organismic-developmental theory and symbol formation) are presented. This is followed by brief discussions of two more recent theoretical developments (i.e., integration of the sensory-tonic field theory of perception within the broader framework of the organismic-developmental approach, and the systematic introduction of the environmental context) that shaped the holistic, developmental, systems-oriented perspective in its current form.

Sensory-Tonic Field Theory and Perceptual Development

Central to the organismic aspect of the organismic-developmental approach was the programmatic work on perception and its development—characterized as the sensory-tonic field theory of perception (Werner & Wapner,

1949, 1952)—initiated almost five decades ago. The studies on perception were also infused with developmental features, insofar as various analyses devoted to sensory-tonic field theory also included work with a variety of developmentally ordered groups (e.g., exploring ontogenesis, pathogenesis, and the effects of such primitivizing conditions as drugs).

Specifically, in contrast to classical psychophysics that was sensorially oriented, sensory-tonic field theory utilized the notion that perception is a function of the relationship between incoming stimuli from the outside world and the existent state of the organism (neuromuscular, cognitive, affective, valuative). This theory was developed in the context of the so-called new look in perception that focused on subjective as well as autochthonous factors as determinants of perception (see Blake & Ramsey, 1951; Bruner & Klein, 1960; Zener, 1949a, 1949b) and demonstrated, for example, that motivational factors affect size perception (e.g., relative to wealthier children, poorer children perceived a coin as larger; Bruner & Goodman, 1947).

While Bruner and Goodman (1947) and others assumed that sensory and motivational factors simply interact, our focus on a process—rather than an achievement—analysis (Werner, 1937) served to raise the question of how an interaction between so-called objective and subjective factors can be mediated. According to sensory-tonic field theory, the answer was that the two factors were of essentially the same fundamental nature, namely, that no matter how diverse the source of stimulation to the organism (i.e., independent of whether the stimulation came through extero-, proprio-, or intero-ceptors), underlying it was the common feature that all stimulation was sensory-tonic in nature, conceived of as having vectors with direction and magnitude that interacted in those terms. A vectorial correspondence, balance, or harmony of forces between the state of the organism and the stimulation from an object was assumed to define a stable state of the system reflected in a particular percept (e.g., a luminous rod in a darkroom in a given position is perceived as vertical). It is noteworthy that an organism-environment *field* was assumed, with perception reflecting the relation between the state of the organism and the impinging stimulation (here, we see some beginnings that underpin our current formulation that the unit to be analyzed is the person-in-environment system).

The organism-environment relation was also assumed to be regulated by equilibrial processes characterized as stabilization tendencies. Stimuli were differentiated into two classes: *extraneous* stimulation presumed to influence the state of the organism directly and *object* stimulation presumed to involve an interrelationship between the organism and object. Diverse stimuli (those from the state of the organism and those from objects out-there) were said to be *functionally equivalent* insofar as their variation resulted in identical end products. This was readily demonstrated in space perception and, in particular, in aspects of space perception relevant to development (Chandler, 1953; Morant, 1952; Wapner, Werner, & Chandler, 1951; Wapner, Werner, & Morant, 1951; Werner, Wapner, & Chandler, 1951).

Space Perception

Restricting ourselves to aspects of space perception that bear on more general developmental processes, evidence was accumulated that individuals presumed to be less advanced developmentally—young children 6 to 14 years of age; adults over 65 years of age; post-poliomyelitics 9 to 19 years of age; mentally retarded individuals; those under the influence of the primitivizing drug Lysergic acid diethylamide (LSD-25)—perceived the spatial position of a luminous rod in a darkroom more *egocentrically,* that is, as vertical when tilted to the side to which the body was tilted, as compared with normal adults who experienced the rod as vertical when it was tilted to the side opposite body tilt (Blane, 1957; Comalli, Wapner & Werner, 1959; Guyette, Wapner, Werner, & Davidson, 1964; Liebert, Wapner, & Werner, 1957; Wapner, 1968).

A series of formally similar behaviors with respect to other developmental aspects of space perception—that is, the dimensions of up-down, left-right, near-far space—was also demonstrated. For example, for children and schizophrenics, *apparent eye level* (up-down dimension of space) was located above its physical position, whereas in normal adults it was located below (Wapner, 1966; Wapner & Werner, 1965). With respect to the left-right dimension of space, the *apparent straight ahead* shifts in the direction to which a luminous rectangle extended for the younger child, for hemiplegic patients, and for those under a depolarized self-object set (Barton, 1964; Wapner & Werner, 1965).

Finally, with respect to the near-far dimension, evidence (Nair, 1961) was accumulated that the reading skills of emotionally disturbed children were improved when stories read were *psychologically distanced* (e.g., when stories about two young boys having a bloody battle were presented in the past tense and a setting of the Middle Ages) and *physically distanced* (e.g., projected on a screen instead of in a book). Taken together, these studies provided objective evidence of the striking *egocentricity* that occurs in a variety of developmentally less advanced groups (e.g., very young children, older adults, schizophrenics, post-poliomyelitic adolescents, mentally retarded individuals) and conditions (e.g., primitivizing drugs).

Body Perception

It was recognized that the body serves not only as a schema or frame of reference as reflected in egocentricity, but also as a body qua object (e.g., with shape, form, etc.). Accordingly, developmental changes were also expected with respect to the body percept. Such changes were linked to the assumptions that the organism has the capacity to adopt different intentions *(multiple intentionality)* toward the self-world relationship and that these intentions have relevance to two aspects of polar person-environment relations: degree of differentiation or distance between these poles; and pole (self or object) emphasized, salient, or to which the person is directed.

To exemplify the developmental course of the differentiation between these poles, there was evidence, for example, that the disparity between the location of apparent vertical (rod out-there) and body position (self as object) when tilted was *smaller* in younger children compared with adolescents (Wapner, 1968). With respect to directedness toward the body, apparent head width was overestimated in young children, schizophrenics, and retarded adolescents (Guyette et al., 1964; Liebert, Werner, & Wapner, 1958; Wapner, 1978). These and other studies have bearing on the development of the constancy of objects. For example, in an empirical and theoretical analysis, Wapner and Werner (1957) found that lack of thing constancy was manifest in two forms: in *egocentricity* (determination of the object world through self as referent) and *stimulus boundedness* (inordinate responsivity to object stimuli). Object constancy was thought to emerge when these two factors were systematically related to each other (cf. Piaget, 1952).

However, the role of the body (i.e., as a state rather than as an object) is also manifest in complex cognitive operations other than perception, such as learning. For example, Rand and Wapner (1967) found that, relative to incongruent postures (learn erect and relearn supine or vice versa), there were, under congruent postures (learn and relearn erect, learn and relearn supine), significantly greater savings in relearning during the early stages of recall. These and other studies showed that (a) the cognitive operations available to individuals differing in developmental status were linked to different processes even in light of identical achievement; and (b) the means of processing set limits on the nature of the information gleaned from the world of objects.

Two studies illustrated these points effectively. First, Rand and Wapner (1969) found ontogenetic changes in locating a simple figure in a complex configuration. Younger adolescents had greater difficulty in finding the simple figure because the appearance of parts changed as a function of their embeddedness in a strong gestalt, whereas adults possessed hierarchically organized percepts where the parts and the whole existed simultaneously, making for less difficulty in finding the simple figure.

Second, Rand, Wapner, Werner, and McFarland (1963)—in contrast to those who studied performance on the Stroop Color-Word Test using only achievement measures (e.g., time to complete, number of errors)—conducted a detailed qualitative analysis of the processes involved in performance. A number of behavioral categories representing deviations from an ideal performance were uncovered and fell under two sets of processes: *identification* of the appropriate aspect of the stimulus item (e.g., correct color) and *serial organization* (e.g., skipping a stimulus). Overall achievement was dependent on different underlying processes related to age. For example, there was a greater frequency of inappropriate color responses (identification) in the younger age groups. Moreover, whereas inserted linguistic words or phrases decreased with age (serial organization), inserted nonlinguistic utterances increased with age. Thus, what might appear as an error (e.g., providing nonlinguistic utterances coupled with an increase in time to respond) represents a developmentally advanced process.

Accordingly, these studies have clearly pointed to the importance of conducting a process rather than an achievement analysis. Moreover, they throw light on the nature of the development of a significant cognitive process, namely, the capacity to organize serially presented material.

Organismic-Developmental Theory and Symbol Formation

Werner and Kaplan (1963) utilized organismic and developmental assumptions to understand the development of symbolization and language. Unlike most linguistic researchers who typically focus on isolated elements of speech and grammar, they stressed the organismic (holistic) aspect of the living, acting, feeling, and striving organism. In addition, central to the principal roots of the spheres of functioning that were theoretically and empirically examined was the recognition that the orthogenetic principle, albeit an expression of unilinearity of development, "does not conflict with the notion of multilinearity or multiplicity of actual developmental forms" (Werner, 1940/1957, p. 137). While three major lines of cognitive development were delineated—sensorimotor development, perceptual development, and conceptual development—it is to be emphasized that the formation of a more advanced level of functioning does not take the place of an earlier mode of functioning but rather is integrated with it. As noted by Werner (1940/1957), "Though physiognomic experience is a primordial manner of perceiving, it grows, in certain individuals such as artists, to a level not below but on a par with that of 'geometric-technical' perception and logical discourse" (p. 138). Thus, using this multilinear conception of cognitive development, Werner and Kaplan argued that symbolic activities initially emerge out of bodily-organismic (sensorimotor) activities.

For example, they documented that primordial symbol usage included the physical act of (communicative) pointing, motoric imitations (e.g., flickering of eyelids to represent flickering lights), and vocalizations (e.g., cries, calls, expressions of pleasure). They also argued that the early connection between sensorimotor/bodily experience and symbol usage was never completely lost. Using the line schematization technique (representation of concepts through the nonpictorial use of line), Werner and Kaplan (1963) compared linear representation and verbal formulation (e.g., depiction of "rage" with sharp, angular lines and of "loneliness" with curved, rounded lines) as a way of understanding the role of the symbolic medium in forming and expressing meaning. Specifically, they demonstrated that early language (conceptual level of cognitive development) emerges from the convergence of referential intent and depictive ability, both of which first appear at the earlier sensorimotor level of cognitive development.

As part of the overall treatment, Werner and Kaplan's (1963) *Symbol Formation* also expanded the organismic aspect of the theory to include both comparative and developmental aspects. Specifically, it considered the ontogenesis of the representative function in terms of the following operations: "(1) the formation of objects of contemplation; (2) the denotation of objects, that is, reference; and (3) the depiction of objects" (p. 66). The authors further described and evaluated a number of concepts (e.g., primitivity, formal parallelism, polarities, multiple modes of functioning, levels of organization) that bear on a comparative-developmental approach to psychopathology. Given "the assumption that pathology entails some degree of 'primitivization of mentality,' it expects to find, in pathological individuals, a *dedifferentiation* and *disintegration* of functioning" (Kaplan, 1959, p. 665).

B. Kaplan (1959) also offered definitions of symbolization ("representation, in a relatively circumscribed medium, of some organismic experience that would otherwise be ineffable and incogitable," p. 667) and language ("a socially shared instrumentality," p. 667) that are distinguished from speech. Thus, affective, ludic, practical representation and dialectical uses of language were distinguished and symbolization and language usage in both ontogenesis and psychopathology were elaborated.

To illustrate, consider Werner and Kaplan's (1963) analysis of the components that constitute symbol situations: *addressor* (one who uses symbols to communicate), *addressee* (one who is addressed), *referent* (object or event that the addressor calls to the addressee's attention), *context* (situation in which communication takes place), and *medium* (means for representing referents). In general, Werner and Kaplan documented progressive distancing among these components of symbol situations with increase in age (ontogenesis). More specifically, B. Kaplan (1966) has noted that, in schizophrenics (psychopathology), these aspects of the symbol situation are less differentiated and articulated than in normals. For instance, there may be fusion between the person (as addressor) and addressee; fusion and ambivalence with regard to the other; an egocentric-affective posture; relations to objects defined affectively and asocially; obliviousness to the scene; communal symbol system apprehended affectively-mythopoetically; personal meanings penetrating conventional symbols;

transformations of gestures; symbolism-realism; and neologisms (cf., Arieti, 1959).

Considerable empirical research in the Clark University Laboratories, much of which remains unpublished, examined these and related issues. For example, E. Kaplan (1952) found that, relative to speech directed toward others (outer speech), speech directed toward self (inner speech) is more abbreviated, holophrastic, personal, and differentiated with articulated subject matter. Slepian (1959) found that schizophrenics exhibited egocentricity and failure to respond to task demands as evidenced by a lack of differentiation of means (internal versus external speech) appropriate to the required end, namely, object description through communication with self versus with another person. In a task involving interpersonal communication (i.e., subjects had to relate a story to another person who disagreed with their account), Mirin (1955) found that schizophrenics could not adopt a hypothetical attitude, could not maintain a stable orientation to the task, and could not differentiate between speech used for self versus for others. Finally, employing Werner and Kaplan's (1950) Word Context Test (the task is to define the meaning of an artificial word from its use in the context of six sentences), Baker (1953) found that, relative to normals, schizophrenics were less able to differentiate between sound pattern and meaning as well as word and sentence and showed greater concreteness and semantic instability (see Langer, 1970, and Werner & Kaplan, 1963, for additional examples of empirical studies on symbol formation from this approach). Moreover, Bamberg, Budwig, and Kaplan (1991) have more recently attempted to revitalize and extend Werner and Kaplan's orthogenetic principle to functionalist approaches to language usage and acquisition.

Integration of Sensory-Tonic and Organismic-Developmental Theories

Wapner and Werner's (1957) ontogenetic study of perceptual development was guided by both sensory-tonic field theory and comparative developmental theory. An integration began to emerge after Werner and Kaplan (1963) systematized organismic-developmental theory. A significant step was taken when sensory-tonic formulations were integrated within the broader framework of organismic-developmental theory (Wapner & Cirillo, 1973; Wapner, Cirillo, & Baker, 1969, 1971).

Central to this endeavor was the characterization of organisms and their environments as constituting systems with typical structures (involving an integration of parts) maintained by dynamic processes such as equilibration (means-ends relationships). Parallel to the sensory-tonic formulations of "extraneous" and "object" stimulation, "background" and "focal" stimulation, respectively, were conceptualized as processes of equilibration underpinning various aspects of perception and cognition more generally.

Three levels of the system, with a different form of equilibration for each, were distinguished. At the lowest level, *sensorimotor action,* the human being is regarded as "a bilaterally symmetrical organism whose preparedness for action depends upon the maintenance of an erect posture in a physical environment characterized by a gravitational field" (Wapner, Cirillo, & Baker, 1969, p. 498). The state of equilibrium may, for example, be disturbed by asymmetrical stimulation resulting in imbalance. Such stimulation may have differential effects depending on the state of the organism; for example, a person with unilateral cerebral lesions may yield to the stimulus, fall, or counteract the pull (cf., Goldstein, 1942, 1960).

At the second level, *perceptual objectification,* the state of the organism serves as a context (body as background) to which focal stimulation is related. This makes for objectification, that is, a phenomenal object is distanced, stable, and articulated.

The third level is characterized by *experienced relations between percepts* that may take various forms. For example, when the outstretched hand and fingertip are in contact with an object, it may involve the phenomenal experience of "pointing" directed toward a thing viewed as a target, or it may be experienced passively as a force from out-there impinging on the fingertip. These two modes of relationship have significant effects on perceived length of outstretched arm; namely, relative to passive touch, active touch is associated with the experience of longer arm length (Schlater, Baker, & Wapner, 1981).

This theoretical reformulation served to articulate more clearly the differentiation of the organismic system into focal stimulation and context; demonstrate how events on one level holistically influence those on other levels; describe differential linkages among sensorimotor action, perception, and conception; move the theoretical conceptualization toward a transactional systems-oriented emphasis with person-in-environment as unit of analysis; and

provide directions for future developmental studies that "may be found in ontogeny . . . pathological versus normal organisms, or certain drug states under placebo conditions, or low versus optimal levels of arousal, or a variety of other contrasts which remain isolated and conceptually chaotic until approached from a unitary theoretical standpoint" (Wapner, Cirillo, & Baker, 1969, p. 508).

Environmental Psychology

More specific beginnings of the current formulation were evident some two decades ago in a paper bearing on environmental psychology by Wapner, Kaplan, and Cohen (1973) describing "an organismic-developmental perspective for understanding transactions of men and environments," and three years later at a conference at Clark University (see Wapner, Kaplan, & Cohen, 1976) on experiencing the environment, where Kaplan, Wapner, and Cohen (1976) presented a paper on "exploratory applications of the organismic-developmental approach to man-in-environment transactions." Here, the focus was on the physical, interpersonal, and sociocultural aspects of the environment, together with the transactional notion that person-in-environment is the unit of analysis. The methodological implication of this was the need to complement laboratory research with investigations into human functioning in all of its real-life complexity. It is noteworthy that this shift from work in the laboratory to include examination of human functioning in the real world paralleled sociohistorical developments within contemporary society (e.g., the Vietnam War).

Taken together, these four strands of theory and research—on perception, symbol formation, integration of sensory-tonic and organismic-development theories, and environmental psychology—have served to shape our holistic, developmental, systems-oriented perspective, to which we now turn.

THE HOLISTIC, DEVELOPMENTAL, SYSTEMS-ORIENTED PERSPECTIVE

An overall schematic representation of our more recently elaborated approach is presented in Figure 13.1. This complex representation depicts the *organism-in-environment system* as the unit to be analyzed. The organism and

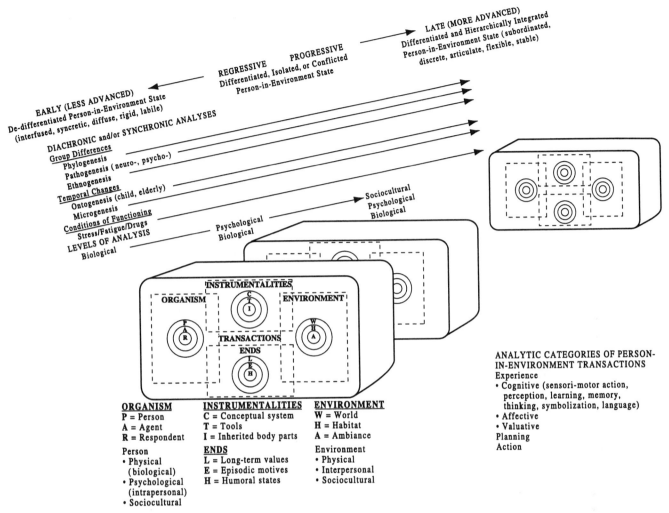

Figure 13.1 A holistic, developmental, systems-oriented approach to person-in-environment functioning (adapted from Wapner, 1986).

environment are linked by *transactions,* which include experience (cognitive, affective, valuative) and action. The organism and environment are the *structural* components of the system. The *dynamic* components are characterized in terms of ends or goals and means or instrumentalities.

The *organism-in-environment system* is characterized in terms of *levels of integration* (Wapner & Demick, 1990; Wapner et al., 1973). Least complex is the *respondent-in-ambience system,* which involves fixed, reflexlike responses of the respondent (R) to ambient (A) stimulation (e.g., optomotor turning of the beetle to the movement of light) and includes such behavior as kineses and taxes (Fraenkel & Gunn, 1961). While biological drives, sensory

systems, and locomotor systems are clearly evident in these respondents, means and ends are more difficult to identify.

At the next level, the organism-in-environment is referred to as an *agent-in-habitat system* (e.g., a chimpanzee reaches for and obtains food behind an obstruction). The agent (A) transacts with the habitat (H) that is comprised of social and nonsocial objects to seek satisfaction of episodic motives (e.g., food, mate). These ends are accomplished through the use of such instrumentalities as tools (e.g., extending reach of the arm with a stick or standing on a stool to reach a banana).

At the most complex level, the organism-in-environment is described as a *person-in-world system.* The person (P;

acculturated human being) transacts with the environment characterized as world (W), which includes sociocultural objects such as a university or political, religious, and kinship rules and regulations. Here, the goals are short- and long-term values and the instrumentalities include the use of conceptual systems (e.g., symbols, mathematics, language) and planning.

Figure 13.1 also includes a list of analytic categories of experience (its cognitive [sensorimotor action, perception, conception], affective, and valuative features), planning, and action. Further, progressive (regressive) development is depicted in terms of the orthogenetic principle (and its polarities), that is, progressive change from relative lack of differentiation to differentiation and hierarchic integration or regressive change as applied to group differences, temporal changes, conditions of functioning, and types of analyses (diachronic and synchronic). Against this backdrop, there follows an elaboration of these features of the perspective and its underlying assumptions.

Finally, although our conceptualization is cast in terms broad enough to apply to organisms-in-environments most generally, we have been primarily interested in, and our research has been almost completely restricted to, the person in his or her world, or to the unit we typically refer to as the *person-in-environment system*.

Theoretical Assumptions and Their Heuristic Potential

Our elaborated perspective is currently comprised of a set of interrelated assumptions about human functioning in the complex everyday life environment. The major assumptions are presented below. What is the status of these assumptions? We regard them as having the heuristic value of guiding both research and the interpretation of empirical findings.

Prior to presenting specific assumptions, it must first be noted that we strongly believe in the related notions of *perspectivism* and of *the interrelations among problem, theory, and method*. Perspectivism—in its simplest, most general form—assumes that any object, event, or phenomenon is always mentally viewed from a particular standpoint, or worldview, which is capable of definition (cf. Lavine, 1950a, 1950b, on interpretationism and below on constructivism). This leads us to assert that inquiry and knowledge are always biased and that there is no process of "neutral"

observation, inquiry, or conclusion in any science (cf. the Heisenberg uncertainty principle in physics for a discussion of the ways in which the observer becomes an integral part of the observation).

We (e.g., Wapner, Demick, Yamamoto, & Takahashi, 1997) also strongly believe in the interrelations among problem, theory, and method in science and maintain that there is considerable value in uncovering the ways in which one's theoretical orientation determines what one studies (problem) and how one studies it (method; cf., Altman, 1997; Overton, Ch. 3, this Volume; Valsiner, Ch. 4, this Volume). Accordingly, following the presentation of each individual assumption inherent in our approach, attempts will be made to demonstrate how each penetrates aspects of our empirical research. The goal of this strategy is to make explicit the heuristic potential of our approach. Examples of research will come primarily from, but are not limited to, the subfield of child development.

Worldview and Philosophical Underpinnings

There is a major difference between the underlying "world view" (Altman & Rogoff, 1987) or "world hypothesis" (Pepper, 1942, 1967) of our approach and many others. Specifically, *our approach adopts elements of both organismic (organicist) and transactional (contextual) worldviews*. The organismic worldview is embodied by an attempt to understand the world through the use of synthesis, that is, by putting its parts together into a unified whole. It stresses the relationship among parts, but the relationships are viewed as part of an integrated process rather than as unidirectional chains of cause-effect relationships (as in mechanistic theories such as behaviorism).

The critical point underlying a transactional worldview is that the person and the environment are conceptualized as parts of a whole; one cannot, so to speak, deal with one aspect of the whole without treating the other (cf., Cantril, 1950; Ittelson, 1973; Lewin, 1935; Sameroff, 1983; Wapner, 1978, 1986, 1987). Specifically, the transactional view treats the "person's behaving, including his most advanced knowings as activities not of himself alone, nor even primarily his, but as processes of the full situation of organism-environment" (Dewey & Bentley, 1949, p. 104). Altman and Rogoff (1987) have more recently characterized transactionalism as follows: "Relations among the aspects of the whole are not conceived of as involving mutual influences of antecedent-consequent causation. Instead, the different aspects of wholes co-exist as intrinsic and inseparable qualities of the whole" (p. 25).

How does this assumption shape our empirical work? Clearly, the philosophical underpinnings of our worldview impact our choice of paradigmatic problems (e.g., critical person-in-environment transitions across the life span) as well as of methods (i.e., methodological flexibility depending on the nature of the problem and multiple methods for a more complete characterization of experience and action). In line with this, we evoke Maslow's (1946) distinction between means-oriented and problem-oriented research: whereas, in the former, the method dictates the range of problems that can be studied, the latter—most consonant with our approach—gives priority to the phenomenon being studied.

Further, in light of the complexity inherent in our conceptualization, we are of the opinion that holistic, ecologically oriented research is a necessary complement to more traditional laboratory work and that it should be conducted through reducing the number of focal individuals (children) studied rather than the number and kind of interrelationships among aspects of the person, of the environment, and of the systems to which they belong. In addition to helping us conceptualize problems that are more in line with the complex character of everyday life, such reframing may also help psychology both to see itself and to be seen by others as a unified science, that is, one concerned not only with the study of isolated aspects of human functioning, but also with the study of problems that cut across various aspects of persons and various aspects of environments (cf. Demick & Wapner, 1988a; Wapner, 1977).

Levels of Integration

This assumption states that *organism-in-environment processes may be categorized in term of levels of integration* (Feibelman, 1954; Herrick, 1949; Novikoff, 1945a, 1945b; Schneirla, 1949), *namely, biological (e.g., breathing), psychological (e.g., thinking), and sociocultural (e.g., living by a moral code)*. Further, while respondent-in-ambience systems function at the biological level, agent-in-habitat systems function at the biological and psychological levels and person-in-world systems function at the biological, psychological, and sociocultural levels. Thus, there is a contingency relationship: functioning at the sociocultural level requires functioning at the psychological and the biological levels, and functioning at the psychological level requires

functioning at the biological level. The levels differ qualitatively, and functioning at one level is not reducible to functioning on the prior, less complex level because we assume that higher-level functioning does not substitute for, but rather integrates and transforms, lower-level functioning (see Wapner & Demick, 1990; Werner, 1940/1957).

This assumption has played a very clear role within our research and highlights two significant driving notions, namely, *rejection of reductionism* and *analogous functions/processes*. Though most theoretical perspectives recognize that various relationships obtain between biological and psychological functioning and between biological and sociocultural functioning, the contingency relationship for defining various levels of integration is interpreted for use in different ways. One alternative that we strongly reject is biological reductionism (see Lerner, Ch. 1, this Volume; Gottlieb et al., Ch. 5, this Volume; Overton, Ch. 3, this Volume), which assumes that functioning is determined completely by the biological structure and state of functioning of the organism. Such a reductionist approach usually means an attempt to understand psychological functioning by translating its principles into those involving only biological terms (e.g., the biological basis of perception is sought, and once that is known, perception is explained). The reductionist views psychological phenomena as epiphenomena or by-products of other phenomena; psychological phenomena are viewed as accompaniments to biological functioning and do not enter into the picture of causality.

In contrast, our approach and the research generated from within it have taken the position that levels of integration must be considered in any analysis of psychological functioning. Focus on a particular level depends on the specific question or issue posed or confronted, together with the recognition that impact on one level affects all other levels of functioning, that is, the functioning of the whole. In general, there is no single way of analyzing or "explaining" experience and action independent of the goals of the analysis. This position permits exploration of the same phenomena that concern both biological and sociocultural determinists without excluding either biology or culture.

For us, an interest in the relationship between biological and psychological functioning would focus on the biological concomitants of any given psychological phenomenon. Just as analogous biological structures (e.g., lungs, gills) may subserve the same general biological function (e.g., respiration), a given function at the psychological level may be subserved by different biological structures or functions. An empirical question, therefore, would involve identifying these biological structures or processes that are in some sense equivalent to given psychological functions. The search for analogous biological structures or processes seems warranted on the basis of studies of "recovery of function" (e.g., Luria, 1972; Stein, 1988). Our nonreductionistic view would also lead us to inquire into the biological consequences of psychological functioning (e.g., dependence of changes in biological structure or functioning on changes in psychological functioning). In all investigations of the relations between biological and psychological functioning, our focus would be on the organization of structures and processes at the two levels rather than on circumscribed or isolated structures and processes. Thus, our approach eschews the search for the biological "loci" of psychological functions, preferring always to view the organism as a functional unit whose parts must be treated within their biological and psychological contexts; moreover, consideration should be given to the sociocultural context.

Issues and problems analogous to those concerning the relations between biological and psychological functioning arise with respect to the relations between psychological and sociocultural functioning. Sociocultural ends may be realized *only* through individual and group actions. Thus, a possible task for our approach would be to describe how each member of society may function to achieve cultural ends. For example, assuming the general sociocultural end of maintaining traditional kinship structures, individuals may function at the psychological level in a variety of ways to achieve this goal (e.g., courting socially sanctioned members of the opposite sex, arranging marriages between children, expressing horror at incest). In all these cases, the same sociocultural end may be discerned even though various functions may subserve this general end. In addition to the search for analogous functions within a given culture, a further empirical problem for our approach would be identification of the various ways that individuals and groups achieve sociocultural ends depending upon the specific culture of which they are members (e.g., see Berry, 1991, on contrasting cognitive styles in hunting-and-gathering vs. agricultural societies). Specifically, societies furnish instrumentalities to their members (acquired gradually during socialization or acculturation), enabling them to interact and perpetuate their culture. These instrumentalities (e.g., gender identity, legal and political systems, implicitly codified language of the community) also determine the psychological functioning of societal members in various ways (e.g., see Lucy, 1992, and Sapir, 1956, on the Sapir-Whorf hypotheses and related issues).

Unit of Analysis

This basic assumption holds that *the person-in-environment system is the unit of analysis with transactional (experience and action) and mutually defining aspects of person and environment.* Treating the person-in-environment as the unit of analysis has the advantages that it corresponds to and represents the complexity of the real-life situation, that it suggests analysis of the individual's behavior and experience in a variety of contexts (thus, environmental context is built into and an essential part of the unit of analysis), and that it is both comprehensive and flexible in uncovering sources of variation underlying behavior. This assumption has figured prominently for some time now in research generated from within our approach. Specifically, it has led to an unwavering commitment to conceptualizing individual (levels of integration), individual-in-group, individual-in-organization, group-in-organization, and organization-in-environment systems. For example, Mayo, Pastor, and Wapner (1995) have employed this conceptualization to delineate new avenues of research linking organizational behavior and environmental psychology.

Holism

The person-in-environment system operates as a unified whole so that a disturbance in one part affects other parts and the totality. This holistic assumption holds not only for functioning among levels of integration (biological, psychological, sociocultural), but also for functioning within a given level. For example, on the psychological level, such part-processes as the cognitive aspects of experience and action (including sensorimotor functioning, perceiving, thinking, learning, imagining, symbolizing) as well as the affective and valuative aspects of experience and action operate contemporaneously and in an integrated fashion in the normal functioning adult (cf., Wapner & Demick, 1990). The person, his or her environment, and the transactions (experience, action) between them involving means and ends are all assumed to be interdependent.

All of our empirical studies to some extent employ holistic conceptualization. For example, our transition studies (see below) have typically included a holistic assessment of the ways the transition impacts self experience (body and self experience), environmental experience (with the physical, interpersonal, and sociocultural aspects of the environment), and self-environment relations, again with respect to the three aspects of environment (e.g., see Demick & Wapner, 1980, on the relocation of a psychiatric therapeutic community). As a second example, Demick and Wapner (1987, 1996) have more recently complemented our earlier experimental work on body perception by augmenting our conceptualization of body experience to include—paralleling our holistic and multilinear view of cognitive development—its sensorimotor (body action), perceptual (body perception), and conceptual (body esteem) aspects (cf., Demick, Ishii, & Inoue, 1997).

Equilibration Tendencies

We assume that the tendency toward equilibration is a basic end that operates at all levels of organization (e.g., homeostatic mechanisms at the biological level, perceptual adaptation at the psychological level, sociocultural adaptation to a new environment following relocation). Thus, *person-in-environment systems are also assumed to operate in a dynamic equilibrium.* Ongoing person-in-environment relations may be disturbed or perturbed by a change in the organism, in the environment, or in both. This may make for dramatic qualitative changes in the relations among system components (organism, environment, transactions, means, ends). Moreover, following perturbation of the organism-in-environment system, the reestablishment of a new dynamic equilibrium or ongoing state directed toward accomplishing goals is assumed to take place.

This process is readily demonstrated in our transition research. For example, to take an extreme case, we have reviewed reports of the course of changes following the impact of a sudden shock to the person-in-environment system (e.g., through tornado, earthquake, atomic bomb) and found that powerful disruptions in system components and the relations between them are followed by a new dynamic equilibrium with new goals being structured and pursued in constructive ways (Wapner, 1987). Similar processes have been found following other person-in-environment transitions, such as the onset of diabetes (Collazo, 1985), psychiatric hospitalization (Demick, Peicott, &

Wapner, 1985), pregnancy and delivery (Coltrera, 1978), and the transition to parenthood (Demick & Wapner, 1992), including the transition to adoptive parenthood (Demick, 1993; Demick & Wapner, 1988b; Silverstein & Demick, 1994).

Aspects of Persons and of Environments

In contrast to many other developmental theories that conceptualize the person in terms of part-processes (e.g., stage of psychosexual development) or as a collection of psychological qualities (e.g., cognitive-developmental status), we define the person with respect to levels of integration and so assume that *the person (here, child) is comprised of mutually defining physical/biological (e.g., health), intrapersonal/psychological (e.g., self-esteem), and sociocultural (e.g., role as child, student, family member) aspects.* Analogous to our conceptualization of person, we assume that *the environment is comprised of mutually defining physical (e.g., natural and built objects), interpersonal (e.g., father, mother, friend),[1] and sociocultural (e.g., rules and mores of the home, school, country, and other cultural contexts) aspects* (cf. Demick & Wapner, 1988a). Again, we do not focus on the person or on the environment per se, but rather consider the person and the environment relationally as parts of one whole (see also Ford & Lerner, 1992).

We have attempted to illustrate at least part of this complexity in much of our empirical work by conducting studies on the interrelations between and among levels of functioning. For example, relevant to the relations between the physical aspect of the environment and the intrapersonal/psychological aspect of the person are a series of studies on the role of cherished possessions in psychological adaptation.

Specifically, Dyl and Wapner (1996) have examined age and gender differences among children concerning the *nature* (types of objects considered special), *meaning* (e.g., person/nonperson, past, present, and future associations), and *function* (e.g., emotional, social, identity development, play) of cherished possessions. They found, for example, that younger children were egocentric in the

---

[1] Included here are dogs, cats, and other animals, who, because they act on, interact with, and develop friendly and other relationships with the focal persons, operate as part of the interpersonal aspect of the environment.

meanings assigned to their cherished possessions, whereas older children held social relationships meaningful; females favored items to be contemplated, and males favored action items; and possessions that were meaningful for the enjoyment they provided decreased after age 6 in females, but persisted in males throughout the ages studied.

Complementing this study is the work of Wapner, Demick, and Redondo (1990), who had nursing home residents respond to questionnaires on cherished possessions and adaptation to the nursing home. They found that (a) relative to those residents without possessions, those with possessions were, for the most part, better adapted to the nursing home; (b) possessions for this group served the major functions of historical continuity, comforter, and sense of belongingness; (c) women were more likely than men to have cherished possessions and were more likely to associate them with self-other relationships; and (d) those residents above the mean on a combined criterion felt more in control, less helpless, more supported by staff, and were judged as more realistic in response to conflict than those below the mean. When these findings are viewed together with the above findings and those that suggest that the presence of cherished possessions aids in the general adaptation of children (Winnicott, 1958, 1971), college students (Schaffer, 1991), and psychiatric patients (Morgan & Cushing, 1966), the psychological importance of the non-human environment, particularly over the course of relocation, is clear.

Structural Aspects of the Person-in-Environment System

From our perspective, *the organism and the environment are viewed as structural components*. Drawing on Werner's (1957) theme of self-world differentiation, our structural, or part-whole, analyses focus on the characteristic structure of person-in-environment systems with an eye toward discerning whether the parts of subsystems (e.g., focal child and mother) are more or less differentiated and/or integrated with one another in specifiable ways (e.g., see Ainsworth & Wittig, 1969, on attachment patterns).

The assumption of structural aspects has permeated our research on environmental transitions (relations among aspects of persons, of environments, and of the person-in-environment system as a whole), as well as on cognitive development across the life span. Since our transition research will be described below in detail, examples here are culled from our work on cognitive development. Based

on Werner's (1940/1957) law of *pars pro toto* (the part has the quality of the whole), Demick, Hoffman, and Wapner (1985) provided an empirical demonstration that feelings about one's immediate environmental context or neighborhood (part) impacts the cognitive organization of and feelings about the larger environment of the city (whole).

In a related vein, Dandonoli, Demick, and Wapner (1990) studied age differences among children (5–7, 8–10, 11–13 years) and adults in the experience and representation of a large-scale space (a university common room) differing in physical arrangement (integrated versus part-quality arrangement). Through verbal recall, drawings, classification, and memory reconstruction, it was found that (a) adults' representations were characterized by an integration of parts into socially relevant, meaningful wholes, whereas children produced representations consisting of groupings of isolated, fragmented parts; (b) on other criteria, 11- to 13-year-olds were more similar to adults, while 8- to 10-year-olds were correspondingly more similar to 5- to 7-year-olds; (c) even when exposed to a part-quality room arrangement, adults experienced and represented the spatial arrangement in terms of socially relevant, meaningful wholes.

These findings on organization culled from a life situation parallel those obtained in a more artificial situation, the perception of inkblots. Relevant here are studies by Friedman (1953), Hemmendinger (1951), and Phillips and Framo (1954), which standardized (using children and psychopathological individuals) a genetic scoring system of the Rorschach based on Werner's (1940/1957) theory. In this system, a distinction is made between genetically low scores (i.e., diffuse or confabulatory percepts deemphasizing relations among parts) and genetically high scores (i.e., precisely formed percepts with differentiated parts and subwholes brought together in an integrated manner). Friedman (1953) and Hemmendinger (1951) found a preponderance of vague, global, diffuse whole responses to inkblots with children and an absence of the highly articulated, well-integrated whole responses characteristic of the normal adult. Our study, in a real-life setting, provides parallel findings insofar as the adults exhibited socially relevant, integrated whole responses in their representation of the environment, whereas the children exhibited responses to parts.

Accordingly, our findings offer added testimony to Piaget's (1952) understanding that "at all levels (viz., that of the living cell, organism, species, society, etc., but also with respect to states of conscience, to concepts, to logical problems, etc.) one finds the same problem of relationship between the parts and the whole" (pp. 241–242). This reinforces the need always to complement traditional content analyses with formal, organizational analyses (focus on form versus content). Further, the study highlights the notion that organizational, part-whole analyses cut across disparate areas of psychology (here, developmental and environmental psychology) and may ultimately serve as an integrative dimension for the field as a whole.

Dynamic Aspects of the Person-in-Environment System

We also assume that *dynamic, or means-ends, analyses* are complementary aspects of a formal description of a person-in-environment system. Focusing on the dynamics of a system entails a determination of the means (e.g., temper tantrums versus child's rational discussion) by which a characteristic structure or goal is achieved or maintained (e.g., ice cream cone). For some time now, we have focused on the cognitive process of planning, that is, the verbalized plotting of a future course of action, as one of a number of means by which the person-in-environment system moves from some initial state of functioning to some end state.

In addition to our research involving the specific cognitive process of planning (e.g., Apter, 1976; Wapner & Cirillo, 1973; Wofsey, Rierdan, & Wapner, 1979), dynamic analyses have also been critical in our work on processes underlying performance on the Stroop Color-Word Test (Stroop, 1935). Here, using both audio- and videotapes, we have empirically demonstrated that multiple means, or in this case cognitive strategies, may lead to successful completion of the task (e.g., on children, see Demick, Salas-Passeri, & Wapner, 1986; Koerber & Demick, 1991; Rand, Wapner, Werner, & McFarland, 1963; Wapner & Rand, 1968; on older adults, Demick & Wapner, 1985, 1991; on Japan versus the United States, see Toshima, Demick, Miyatani, Ishii, & Wapner, 1996; Toshima, Toma, Demick, & Wapner, 1990). This leads directly to consideration of our next assumption.

Process versus Achievement

Like Werner (1937), we assume that the final solution to a problem may be arrived at through diverse processes reflecting different activities of various structures in the central nervous system (cf., Glick, 1992). For example, although two children may obtain the same IQ scores on a standardized intelligence test (e.g., WISC-III), the underlying processes that they have utilized toward obtaining their final answers most probably reflect different patterns of cognitive assets and liabilities. Thus, our approach to *all* psychological tests and measurements, in both research and clinical contexts, has advocated the use of process analyses to complement the more achievement-oriented measures that are customarily employed (e.g., see E. Kaplan, 1983, on a process approach to neuropsychological assessment, and Wapner & Demick, in press, on more general ways that our approach is relevant to the subfield of clinical child psychology).

Teleological Directedness

The inclusion of dynamic components—means and ends—in our conceptualization of the person-in-environment system is consonant with the proposition that *transactions are regarded not simply as random and chaotic but rather as directed and oriented toward both short- and long-term goals.* Here, the approach operates as a framework for describing processes (Werner & Kaplan, 1956) and thereby is comfortable with teleonomy (cf., Ayala, 1970; Campbell, 1974; Hofstadter, 1941; Thompson, 1987).

Constructivism

Our perspective assumes a constructivist view of knowledge. That is, we assume that *the person constructs objects of perception and thought and thereby actively contributes to the cognitive process.* Such an approach rejects all "copy" theories of perception and asserts that reality is relative to the organism's interpretation or construction (see Lavine, 1950a, 1950b). In line with this, human beings are regarded as striving agents capable of creating, constructing, construing, and structuring their environments in various ways and of acting in terms of their own experience. Wapner, Kaplan, and Cohen (1973) have characterized such striving in terms of Kuntz's (1968) notion that the human organism, functioning at the sociocultural level, exhibits a "rage for order." These notions also lead to consideration of the distinction between the *experienced* versus *physical* environment, the first of which has also been referred to as the *behavioral environment* (Koffka, 1935), *umwelt, phenomenal world,* or *self-world* (von Uexkull, 1957), and *psychological environment* (Lewin, 1935).

The constructivist assumption is most readily apparent in the previously cited Dandonoli, Demick, and Wapner (1990) study. In addition to demonstrating the usefulness of part-whole, structural analyses in environmental experience, this study illustrates that the cognitive-developmental status of the individual penetrates and plays a relatively powerful role in the way he or she organizes the environment to which he or she is exposed, insofar as adults experienced and represented part-quality room arrangements (e.g., furniture stacked as in a storeroom) as socially relevant, meaningful wholes (e.g., sitting area, mail area). As a second example from a related perspective, see Bibace and his associates' (e.g., Bibace, Schmidt, & Walsh, 1994) extensive work on children's conceptions of health and illness.

Spatiotemporal Nature of Experience

That the person-in-environment system is in dynamic equilibrium implies that it is always undergoing change. For example, the typical individual in an urban Western cultural setting gets up in the morning, leaves the bedroom, washes in the bathroom, goes to the kitchen, eats breakfast, gets in the automobile, drives to work along the city streets, parks, goes to the office, and so on. In light of this, we assume that, *although this ongoing flow of events is continuous, it is usually structured into a series of discrete units (e.g., having breakfast) that are separated from preceding and subsequent units by temporal boundaries.*

Relatively early on, Wapner and Lebensfeld-Schwartz (1976) demonstrated the power of this assumption in a study of students' experience and memory of a graduate paper conference. Findings indicated that participants generally structured the conference into a series of discrete units. Further, the findings indicated that the abstraction from spatiotemporal change was structured into temporally bounded units independent of space (e.g., the event was described with respect to duration independent of people and/or other objects). Event reconstruction was related to program length (the longer the program, the greater the reference to self), and units referring to self were more highly articulated than those referring to others.

Multiple Intentionality

We also assume that the structuring motive or "rage for order" operates in conjunction with the capacity for multiple intentionality. That is, *a person can adopt different cognitive attitudes or intentions with respect to self-world relations and thereby experience different figure-ground relationships with respect to the person-in-environment*

system of which he or she is a part. The experience of object, or "figure" (versus "ground"), holds not only for the various features of the environment (e.g., size, shape, and form of objects—things and people—"out there"), but also for various features of self (size and shape of body, self-esteem, etc.) and for the relation between self and environment (e.g., feeling comfortable in a location). In line with this, it is further assumed that *the optimal self-world relationship of the person-in-environment system is indicated by the individual's ability to shift back and forth from focusing on the different "objects of experience," namely, on the self, environment, and self-environment relations (microgenetic mobility).*

This assumption has figured prominently in our empirical research because it has suggested a developmental schema for the operationalization of various forms of psychopathology as well as for the assessment of hospitalization outcome. That is, deviations from the optimal self-world relationship (microgenetic mobility) are represented in various psychopathologies. For example, research (Demick & Andreoletti, 1995; Demick & Peicott, 1984; Demick, Peicott, & Wapner, 1985; Demick & Wapner, 1980) has shown—using tasks that have proven fruitful in other experimental studies (e.g., Wapner & Werner's, 1965, apparent head size estimation task; Wapner's, 1977, psychological distance maps for "people" and for "places")—that schizophrenics may be interpreted from an organismic-developmental perspective as exhibiting a lack of differentiation between self and world with an egocentric focusing on self, whereas antisocial personalities, through their characteristic denial, exhibit rigid, differentiated boundaries between self and environment with an overfocusing on environment at the expense of a focus on self. Further, the stress of various environmental relocations exacerbates the symptomatology of developmental regression by creating greater rigidity of the figure-ground relationship typical of the particular psychopathology.

Multiple Worlds

People are assumed to live in different, yet related experiential worlds (Schutz, 1971) or diverse spheres of activity such as the multiple worlds of family, work, school, recreation, community, and others (cf. Werner & Kaplan, 1963, on mythopoetic, ordinary-pragmatic, and scientific-conceptual attitudes and experienced worlds corresponding to these attitudes; also see Bronfenbrenner, Ch. 17, this Volume). Taken more generally, this relationship can be described with respect to a given person's involvement in one or more person-in-environment systems, and the relationship among these worlds may be characterized in structural terms.

Empirical work has clearly demonstrated the heuristic potential of this assumption. For example, Hornstein and Wapner (1984, 1985) and Wapner, Demick, and Damrad (1988) have shown that the structure of an individual's life prior to retirement, defined in terms of the formal relations among experiential worlds, can be used to predict that individual's adaptation following retirement. Individuals with greater integration between work worlds and other experiential worlds (e.g., family, friends, community, recreation) in the preretirement phase of their lives were shown to exhibit more successful adaptation to retirement than those whose structural relationships among their preretirement multiple worlds were characterized as isolated. Similar conceptualization has also been successfully applied to, for example, family transitions such as marriage, parenthood, and grandparenthood (see Demick & Wapner, 1992).

On the most general level, relevant empirical issues concern the relative centrality of these worlds in a person's life, the relation of these worlds to one another, and the manner of movement from one world to another. Are the worlds relatively fused, relatively isolated, in conflict, or integrated with one another? Is there acquisition of a new world (entering nursery school), replacement of one world by another (migration to a new country), or exclusion or deletion of one world (retirement)?

Orthogenetic Principle

Our view of development transcends the boundaries within which the concept of development is ordinarily applied. For most psychologists, development is restricted to child growth, to ontogenesis. We, in contrast, view *development more broadly as a mode of analysis of diverse aspects of person-in-environment functioning* (cf., Glick, 1992; B. Kaplan, 1959, 1967). This mode of analysis encompasses not only ontogenesis, but also microgenesis (e.g., development of an idea or percept), pathogenesis (e.g., development of neuro- and psychopathology), phylogenesis (development of a species), and ethnogenesis (development of a culture).

Components (person, environment), relations among components (e.g., means-ends), and part-processes (e.g., cognition) of person-in-environment systems are assumed to be developmentally orderable in terms of the orthogenetic principle (B. Kaplan, 1959, 1967; Werner, 1940/1957a, 1957b). *The orthogenetic principle defines development in terms of the degree of organization attained by a system.* The more differentiated and hierarchically integrated a system is, in terms of its parts and of its means and ends, the more highly developed it is said to be. Optimal development entails a differentiated and hierarchically integrated person-in-environment system with flexibility, freedom, self-mastery, and the capacity to shift from one mode of person-in-environment relationship to another as required by goals, by demands of the situation, and by the instrumentalities available (B. Kaplan, 1959, 1967; Wapner, 1987; Wapner, Ciottone, Hornstein, McNeil, & Pacheco, 1983; Wapner & Demick, 1990; Wapner, Kaplan, & Ciottone, 1981).

The orthogenetic principle has also been specified with respect to a number of polarities, which at one extreme represent developmentally less advanced and at the other more advanced functioning (cf., B. Kaplan, 1959; Werner, 1940/1957; Werner & Kaplan, 1956). These polarities, using examples relevant to child development, are as follows.

1. *Interfused to subordinated.* In the former, ends or goals are not sharply differentiated; in the latter, functions are differentiated and hierarchized with drives and momentary states subordinated to more long-term goals. For example, for the less developmentally advanced child, watching television is not differentiated from the need to complete a homework assignment (i.e., each is viewed as a short-term goal); in contrast, the more developmentally advanced child differentiates and subordinates the short-term goal (television watching) to the long-term goal (doing well in school).

2. *Syncretic to discrete.* Syncretic refers to the merging of several mental phenomena, whereas discrete refers to functions, acts, and meanings that represent something specific and unambiguous. Syncretic thinking is represented, for example, by the younger (preoperational) child's (as well as the schizophrenic's) lack of differentiation between inner and outer experience (i.e., lack of separation of one's feelings from that of others out-there). In contrast, discrete is exemplified by the older

(concrete operational) child's capacity for accurately distinguishing between one's own feelings and those of others out-there.

3. *Diffuse to articulate.* Diffuse represents a relatively uniform, homogeneous structure with little differentiation of parts, whereas articulate refers to a structure where differentiated parts make up the whole. For example, diffuse is represented by the law of *pars pro toto,* as is the case of the autistic child's displeasure at variation from some routine set of behaviors; articulate is represented by experience where distinguishable parts make up the whole, each contributing to and yet being distinguishable from the whole.

4. *Rigid to flexible.* Rigid refers to behavior that is fixed and not readily changeable; flexible refers to behavior that is readily changeable or plastic. Rigid is exemplified by the compulsive child's perseveration, ceremoniousness, unchangeability, and routine behavior; flexible implies the capacity to change depending on the context and particular arrangements of a given situation.

5. *Labile to stable.* Finally, labile refers to the fluidity and inconsistency that go along with changeability; stable refers to the consistency or unambiguity that occurs with fixed properties. For example, lability is evident in the young child's rapidly changing, fluid, inconsistent behavior, by stimulus-bounded shifts of attention, and by the use of words with many meanings; in contrast, stability is represented by thinking that permits precise definition of terms, ideas, and events.

Based on the notion that "wherever there is life, there is growth and systematic orderly sequence" (Werner, 1940/1957, p. 125), much research within our approach has been concerned with the study of the processes of formation/integration (e.g., development of a cognitive organization of an environment) and of dissolution/disintegration (e.g., developmental changes in experience following onset of a chronic illness such as diabetes) as living organisms attempt to reestablish more optimal relations with their environments. These and related studies will be described below.

Individual Differences

Following from this, there is also a major difference in the concept of individual differences between our approach and many others. That is, several other approaches either interpret individual differences as a source of error or as manifest in different psychopathological states. In contrast, we see *individual differences as contributing to a differential developmental psychology that is complementary to a general developmental psychology* (cf., Wapner & Demick, 1991a, on cognitive style across the life span).

For example, Wapner's (1987) developmental analysis of self-world relations utilizing the orthogenetic principle may be applied to describe individual differences in a broad variety of content areas and modes of coping. For example, least developmentally advanced is the *dedifferentiated person-in-environment system state* (e.g., child immediately, unequivocally, and unquestioningly goes along with parents' wishes). Next are the *differentiated and isolated person-in-environment system state* (e.g., withdrawal and removal of self from desires of parents and others); the *differentiated and in conflict person-in-environment system state* (e.g., the child maintains conflicted relations between his or her own desires and those of parent or teacher); and the *differentiated and hierarchically integrated person-in-environment system state* (e.g., where a distinction is made by the child between short- and long-term goals with the capacity to subordinate the former if requested by the parent). These self-world relationships have also been used successfully to describe the acculturation of adolescent migrants from Puerto Rico into the United States (e.g., Pacheco, Lucca, & Wapner, 1985) and the adaptation of family systems to open versus closed adoption (Demick, 1993; Demick & Wapner, 1988a; Silverstein & Demick, 1994).

Adaptation

We conceptualize *adaptation as consisting of optimal relations between the person (child) and his or her environment.* This stands in marked contrast to those approaches that conceptualize adaptation as either the general adaptation level of the person (Helson, 1948) or adaptation of the individual to a particular sociocultural context such as society or the family (e.g., sociocultural theories).

This assumption has clear heuristic potential. For example, previous research (e.g., Pacheco, Lucca, & Wapner, 1985) has indicated that optimal relations between persons and their environments may be achieved in several ways: the person may conform to the environment (e.g., Puerto Rican migrant adolescents to the United States may adopt the dress and customs of mainland U.S. adolescents); the environment may conform to the person (e.g., mainland U.S. schools may provide lessons in both Spanish and English for Puerto Rican adolescents); or the person and the environment may mutually conform to one another (e.g., attempts may be made both at home and at school to help the child experientially integrate the two cultures).

Problem Formulation and Methodology

In light of the constructivist underpinning of our approach, our research has typically been concerned with *describing the relations both among and within the parts (person, environment) that make up the integrated whole (person-in-environment system) as well as with specifying the conditions that make for changes in the organization of these relations.* Thus, our approach is wedded to the complementarity of explication (description) and causal explanation (conditions under which cause-effect relations occur) rather than being restricted to one or the other.

Assumptions related to problem formulation and methodology impact our choice of paradigmatic problems (e.g., critical person-in-environment transitions induced by perturbations at all levels of integration) as well as our preferred method of research (i.e., flexible drawing from both quantitative and qualitative methodologies depending on the level of integration and nature of the problem under scrutiny). These notions may best be exemplified through consideration of our long-term research program on critical person-in-environment transitions, the topic to which we now turn.

Research Program on Critical Person-in-Environment Transitions across the Life Span

The basis for this research program was laid down more than two decades ago, when Wapner, Kaplan, and Cohen (1973) first sketched an organismic-developmental perspective for understanding transactions of humans and environments. They briefly described a number of studies "designed to investigate structurization (construal and reconstruction) by agents who experience a marked change of social status or a marked change of locale. . . . " These studies were "oriented toward examining human-environment relationships in which the agent either retains the same status (e.g., occupational, marital, social class) or undergoes a marked change in status (e.g., from one occupation to another, single to married, married to divorced,

middle to lower class), and either remains in the same locale or moves (on either a permanent or temporary basis) to a different locale" (p. 280). Though every moment of person-in-environment functioning involves change, our concern has been with those transitions we regard as critical, that is, where a perturbation to any aspect of the person-in-environment system is experienced as so potent that the ongoing modes of transacting with the physical, interpersonal, and sociocultural features of the environment no longer suffice.

The problem is linked to the holistic as well as the developmental aspects of the perspective. This paradigmatic problem was chosen with the holistic assumption that a potent perturbation to any part of the person-in-environment system at any level of organization (e.g., physical/biological, psychological, and sociocultural aspects of the person, of the environment, or of both) would impact the system as a whole. Moreover, with respect to development, we are touching on a set of conditions that has developmental relevance, namely, operations of the person-in-environment system under stressful versus more optimal conditions of functioning. Powerful changes in the person, in the environment, and in the relations between them may make for *developmental regression* in functioning, which may in turn, depending on conditions promoting more optimal functioning, make for *developmental progression* as characterized by the orthogenetic principle. The more or less progressive changes are expected to be manifest in various aspects of the transactions (experience and action) of the person with the environment. Indeed, involvement in a critical person-in-environment transition may serve as a basis for more advanced development, a notion consonant with that of Gesell and Ilg (1943), who suggested that it is sometimes necessary to regress in order to progress.

The research program took more definitive shape when the category system of the elaborated perspective was introduced as a basis for understanding the sites of possible perturbations to the system (Wapner, 1977, 1981, 1987). As shown in Table 13.1, from our perspective, these sites are the three levels of operation of the person (physical/biological, intrapersonal/psychological, sociocultural), the three levels of the environment (physical, interpersonal, sociocultural), and the relations among all of these aspects (e.g., Demick & Wapner, 1988a; Wapner, 1977, 1978, 1981, 1987; Wapner & Craig-Bray, 1992; Wapner & Demick, 1992; Yamamoto & Wapner, 1992).

TABLE 13.1   Sites and Examples of Perturbations to Person-in-Environment System That May Initiate Critical Transitions

Person (× Environment)	Environment (× Person)
<u>Physical (Biological)</u>	<u>Physical</u>
Age (e.g., onset of puberty, menopause, death)	*Objects* (e.g., *acquisition or loss of cherished possessions*)
Pregnancy*	*Disaster* (e.g., *onset of flood, hurricane, earthquake, tornado, volcanic eruption, nuclear war*)
Disability	
Illness	*Relocation* (e.g., *psychiatric community, nursing home, rural,* urban, *transfer to new college, migration*)
–Addiction (e.g., onset and *termination of alcoholism, obesity,* drug addiction)	Urban Change (e.g., decline, *renewal*)
–Chronic (e.g., *onset of diabetes, rheumatoid arthritis*)	Rural Change (e.g., industrialization)
–Acute (e.g., onset and treatment of cancer, *AIDS*)	
<u>Psychological</u>	<u>Interpersonal</u>
Body Experience (e.g., *increase or decrease in size of body,* onset of experience of positive or negative body evaluation, acquisition or loss of cherished possessions)	*Peer Relations* (e.g., *making or dissolving a friendship or social network, falling in or out of love*)
Self-Experience (e.g., self-concept and experience of control, dignity, identity, power, security as in *onset of or recovery from mental illness,* changing role in social network)	Family (e.g., change in extended family, immediate family, parents, relatives)
	Neighbors
	Coworkers
	Roommates
	Teachers
<u>Sociocultural</u>	<u>Sociocultural</u>
Role	Economics (e.g., new technology, job opportunity)
–*Work* (e.g., becoming employed, temporarily employed, *unemployed, retired*)	*Educational* (e.g., *nursery school,* kindergarten, elementary school, *high school, college, sojourn to university abroad,* graduate or *professional school*)
–Financial (e.g., becoming rich as in winning lottery, becoming poor as in stock market crash)	
–Educational (e.g., professor, student, administrator)	*Legal* (e.g., abortion legislation, driving age, *automobile seat belt legislation,* child abuse, retirement legislation, euthanasia)
–*Marital* (e.g., being married, *divorced,* widowed, *parenthood, adoption*)	
–*Religious* (e.g., becoming priest, minister, rabbi, nun, Jesuit, "born again" Christian, conversion)	Mores (e.g., attitude toward sex)
–Political (e.g., becoming a refugee, undercover agent, war veteran, holocaust survivor, survivor of terrorism, elected official)	Political (e.g., social, country, prison, defection)
–Cultural (e.g., becoming a celebrity, member of cult group)	Religious (e.g., oppression, change in policy re family ministers and rabbis, celibacy of priests)
Ethnicity (e.g., becoming aware, proud of, ashamed of background)	*Organizational (Industry) Leadership*
Gender (e.g., changing sexual orientation, from justice to caring orientation)	

* Italicized items indicate published studies or studies in progress.

Table 13.1 also lists examples of studies, some already conducted and others at various stages of planning, that not only contribute to theoretical understanding but also have practical significance for developing more optimal person-in-environment system functioning. As we see it, a developmental analysis ideally involves at the least three tasks: (a) assessment of the developmental status of the focal person made prior to, during, and after the transition; (b) assessment of the context and the contextual conditions or circumstances that might make for change in developmental status, both regressive and progressive; and (c) description of some reasonable interventions that might free transitions from trauma or serve as a basis for facilitating developmentally advanced transactions indicative of optimal person-in-environment functioning (cf., Wapner et al., 1983). Although the studies conducted have not all encompassed these tasks, let us consider some exemplars from each of the categories listed in Table 13.1.

Person (Physical/Biological)

Collazo (1985) initiated a study on the transition from health to illness as exemplified in the onset of diabetes. The focus was on analyzing a number of relations between the focal person (self) and other parts of the person-in-environment system, such as (a) relations between one's psychological and biological self as influenced by changes in the metabolism of sugar; (b) transactions with the physical aspects of the environment (e.g., unwillingness to move beyond the physical area of the home community because of concern for the availability of insulin supplies); (c) relations with the interpersonal aspects of the environment (e.g., fear of getting married, dependence on others); and (d) relations to the sociocultural context (e.g., changes in values and behaviors of the individual related to culturally defined attitudes toward the sick).

Other evidence of the holistic impact of a transition initiated by biological change, involving the onset of juvenile rheumatoid arthritis, comes from a study by Quirk and Young (1990) that was described by Quirk and Wapner (1991) in their paper treating an organismic-developmental, systems-oriented perspective for health education:

Take for example an adolescent who is diagnosed with Juvenile Rhematoid Arthritis (JRA) and a clinical health education specialist working in a medical setting. The clinical health educator who is interested in ensuring anti-inflammatory treatment compliance, as well as more generally helping the adolescent re-establish a new dynamic equilibrium, would need to consider the illness on multiple levels related to the person-in-environment system (Quirk & Young, 1990).

The disruption would impact the person: (1) at the biological/physical level as represented by physical manifestations such as joint swelling, limitations of movement, and pain and tenderness . . . ; (2) at the psychological level as represented by the adolescent's lack of knowledge about the illness, attitude that compliance is not necessary, and by feelings of low self-esteem due to an inability to participate in routine adolescent activities such as sports and recreation . . . ; and (3) at the sociocultural level by viewing self as changed from a healthy to a sick person. . . .

The disruption would impact the adolescent's environment: (1) at the physical level in terms of accessibility; (2) at the interpersonal level as represented by family dysfunction, including feelings of distress and lack of strategies used to cope. . . ; and (3) at the sociocultural level as represented by the bureaucracy of the insurance companies and their insensitivity to incurred costs such as lost time at work for parents, travel to health care facilities, etc. . . .

These repercussions at all levels of person, environment and of the relations between them would be magnified by the critical developmental tasks associated with the child's passage into adolescence (e.g., physical competition, development of self-esteem and independence). (pp. 204–205)

From a developmental point of view, it is noteworthy that "the general aim of health education from our perspective is to foster transactions (experiences and actions) of person-in-environment transitions that achieve optimal functioning of person-in-environment systems. With respect to health, optimal functioning is defined as physical, mental and interpersonal well-being, i.e., freedom from disease, illness and suffering" (Quirk & Wapner, 1991, p. 203).

Studies along the lines of prevention and of following a treatment regimen have been conducted from our perspective in such areas as initiating weight loss, cessation of use of alcohol and tobacco, and prevention of human immunodeficiency virus (HIV). They will be described later when consideration is given to the relation between experience (including intention) and action.

Person (Psychological)

An example is found in a study of 60 adolescents and 45 adults who were patients in an addictions treatment unit of a hospital in Massachusetts with primary diagnosis of alcohol dependence. A variety of tests (e.g., covering rules, regulations, mental illness attitudes—including conceptions of mental illness, perceived attitudes of staff members, expectations about control in the hospital—and expectations concerning length of stay, etc.) were administered on six test occasions (1–2 days after admission; 1, 2, 3, 4, and 5 weeks later, immediately prior to discharge). There was evidence that there were changes in self-world relations: during the stressful transition periods of entering and leaving the hospital setting (with most potent changes occurring immediately following admission and immediately preceding discharge), and, more generally, over the course of hospitalization (in the direction of less denial and thus less rigid differentiation between self and environment). More specifically,

alcoholics, at least prior to treatment, exhibit rigid, differentiated boundaries between self and environment with an overfocusing on the environment at the expense of on self. This supports the general theoretical conceptualization of self-environment differentiation first proposed by Werner (1940/1957). This conceptualization has most commonly been applied to schizophrenia. That is, various investigators (e.g., DesLauriers, 1962) have speculated that the schizophrenic's loss of boundaries (e.g., failure to separate self from environment) is the fundamental defect of this disorder.

. . . it may be assumed that the optimal relationship of the person-in-environment state is indicated by the individual's ability to shift back and forth from focusing on the different objects of experience, viz., on the self, on the environment, and on self-environment relations. Deviations from this optimal condition (i.e., shifts exclusively from a self-focus to an environment-focus or conversely from an environment- to a self-focus) may be considered to represent *regression*. Moving then toward optimal self-world relations may be considered to represent *progression*. (Demick, Peicott, & Wapner, 1985, p. 6)

Person (Sociocultural)

Extensive consideration of the sociocultural aspects of the person with respect to his or her role is readily illustrated in the transition to parenthood, to adoption, and to retirement. Wapner (1993) has presented an analysis of parental development, giving consideration to the question of why people want to become parents, to the so-called stages of parenthood (e.g., Galinsky, 1981), and to some specific issues such as divorce, stepparenthood, parental child abuse, and adoption. The question of why people want to become parents is readily answered by considering factors with respect to the category system of the elaborated perspective.

Under the category of persons, these potential reasons may include:

1. At the *physical/biological* level, age, physical maturity, and fulfillment of biological role

2. At the *psychological* level, for example, fulfillment, expansion, and enhancement of one's self-concept, self-confidence, personal achievement; fulfilling a moral value; stimulation, novelty, fun; ensuring one's contribution to the future; and proving one's maturity

3. At the *sociocultural* level, for example, fulfilling a social role, and validating one's social status

Under the category of environment, these include:

1. At the *physical* level, for example, adding positively to the human population

2. At the *interpersonal* level, for example, enhancing one's marital status, conforming to spousal wishes, creating a family, power and/or influence

3. At the *sociocultural* level, for example, fulfilling a value characteristic of the contemporary society in which one lives, economic feasibility, economic security in old age, fulfilling societal expectations, adhering to one's religious values, and expected lifestyle (Wapner, 1993, pp. 11–12)

Galinsky's (1981) stages of parenthood (image making, nurturing, authority, interpretive, interdependent adolescent, departure), including grandparenthood, may also be analyzed from the holistic, developmental, systems-oriented perspective. This is done by illustrating how some of the general assumptions—person-in-environment as unit of analysis; structural and dynamic analysis of person's transactions (experience and action) with the environment; constructivism; holism; the orthogenetic principle and its five polarities; emphasis on regressive as well as progressive development; concern for underlying process; and modes of coping with transactional conflict—are utilized in analyzing the development of parenthood and grandparenthood.

For example, a number of issues related to parental development are considered. *Divorce,* viewed as a powerful perturbation to parenthood, is expected, in general, to make for regression in the transactions of parents with their children. *Stepparenthood* also represents a critical transition and appears worthy of a similar analysis. *Parental child abuse,* analyzed by Azar (1986, 1989, 1991) from within a social-cognitive framework, has some links to our approach. More specifically:

. . . by treating the relation between characteristics of the parent and child as well as the social context, there is implicit use of the person-in-environment as the unit of analysis; the transactions (experience and action) of the parent with the child are influenced by parental expectations (underpinned by an assumption of intentionality); the child-abusing parent is characterized as lacking control, that is, in keeping with our assumption that his or her behavior is less developmentally advanced, unable to subordinate action to thought processes, diffuse rather than articulate, rigid rather than flexible, and labile rather than stable. As we see it, the child-abusing parent fits strikingly with our person-in-environment system state characterized by differentiation and conflict. (Wapner, 1993, p. 28)

Adoption has been studied extensively by Demick and his associates (Demick, 1993, 1995; Demick, Damrad, & Stern, 1989; Demick & Wapner, 1988a, 1988b; Silverstein & Demick, 1994; Soparker, Demick, Levin, & Wapner, 1988). They approached the problem by exploring differences between two transitions, namely, that of open versus closed adoption (communication versus no communication between biological and adoptive parents). Of particular interest from our perspective is Demick and Wapner's (1988b) analysis of the family patterns generated by the two forms of adoption in terms of the four developmentally ordered self-world categories of our perspective:

. . . adoptive families characterized by a total separation between the adopted child and his or her family of origin—as is usually the case in traditional, closed adoption—may be conceptualized as dedifferentiated (all members of the family consciously or unconsciously deny that the child has been adopted), differentiated and isolated (adoptive parents shelter the adoptee so that he or she will not learn about the biologic parents from others and/or will not have to deal with the stigma of being adopted), or differentiated and in conflict (the adoptee may fantasize that the biologic parents would treat him or her differently and/or may threaten to leave the adoptive family to find the "real parents" when of age). In contrast, the adoptive family characterized by less absolute separation between the adoptee and his or her family of origin (the case in open adoption) may be conceptualized as differentiated and integrated (the adoptee may be able to integrate the various aspects of his or her dual identities, possibly mitigating potential problems with identity and self-esteem; in a similar manner, the adoptive parents may be able to integrate the different aspects of the adoptee's identity so as to avoid blaming "bad blood in the background" for any of their difficulties). (Demick & Wapner, 1988b, pp. 241–242)

Finally, in a culture like ours where social status and self-identity are strongly linked to occupation and where productivity and cultural value depend on one's ability to remain employed, *retirement* is clearly an extremely critical person-in-environment transition in the life cycle. A study utilizing phenomenological methods of inquiry was conducted with the aims of assessing the ways retirement brings about a change in the organization of a person's life and of characterizing the role of the social network in the individual's adaptation to retirement (Hornstein & Wapner, 1984, 1985).

Two groups of individuals participated. Members of the first, so-called *primary group,* were all within one to two months of retirement at the beginning of the study. The second group, *network participants,* was comprised of individuals who were members of the social network of about half of the primary participants. Primary subjects participated in an interview one month prior to retirement and another six to eight months following retirement.

Using a variation of Giorgi's (1971, 1975; see Watkins, 1977) phenomenological method, four types of retirement experience were evident.

Group I Transition to old age. This group experienced retirement as a transition to the last phase of life, old age, involving time to wind down, reduce activity, and settle into a quieter existence.

Group II New beginning. Retirement is experienced as an event of major personal importance, a welcome beginning of a new time in life where one can live in accordance with one's own needs, desires, goals, and so on.

Group III Continuation. For this group, retirement is not an event of major personal importance. There is basic continuity of pre- and postretirement lives, but where valued activities can be continued in a less pressureful way.

Group IV Imposed disruption. Retirement constitutes a loss of a highly valued sphere of activity. Nothing can substitute for the work world. It is as if a part of the person has been removed. He or she is devastated.

These primary groups differed with respect to a number of dimensions, including meaning of retirement, style of making the transition, dominant emotions, attitude toward work, relation to sense of self, orientation toward time, change in life focus, level of activity postretirement, nature of retirement goals and activities, and attitude toward old age. There were also similarities among the four modes: experiencing a slow process of disengagement from one's work organization; developing an internal organization to replace the structure provided by work; and constructing a new sense of identity as a retiree.

Members of the network group differed in their degree of involvement in the retirement transition, in whether there was congruence between the retiree and themselves in how retirement was viewed, and in the degree of impact of retirement on the network member. For these three themes, there were three patterns of relationship: (a) low involvement in planning and support, high congruence, minimal impact on network member's own life; (b) low to moderate involvement in planning and support, moderate incongruence, and some impact, often negative, on network member; and (c) high involvement in planning and strong support to retiree, high degree of congruence, moderate change in network member's life. These findings have implications for preretirement planning and counseling as well as for conditions that may make retirement a period of further development.

Wapner, Demick, and Damrad (1988) conducted a follow-up study eight years later with 17 of the original 24 retirees. The most significant finding was that, for the most part, retirees tended to move toward a state where their lives were very busy; they were filled with working activities including formal employment, rigorous volunteer work, and active involvement in hobbies. That is, regardless of how the retirees were originally categorized, the majority of them sought alternative work or activity postretirement.

Hanson and Wapner (1994) conducted a study on gender differences in retirement using a number of new instruments. Strong evidence was found to support the principle that retirement can be categorized into the four modes of experience noted above. In addition, there were gender differences. For example, relative to men, women had a positive attitude toward work and old age; gave greater importance to informal friendship roles when losing their role as worker; retired at a younger age than men; reported greater financial worry; experienced sense of self as changed with retirement; and reported a greater degree of preretirement planning.

Environment (Physical)

As noted in Table 13.1, a number of critical transitions introduced by a powerful perturbation to the physical environment has been studied. Here we will illustrate by referring to a study initiated by a natural disaster and another study initiated by relocation.

Wapner (1983) has analyzed the problem of living with radical disruptions of person-in-environment systems induced by such *natural disasters* as flood, earthquake, hurricane, tornado, volcanic eruption, and nuclear war. This included an analysis of the disaster cycle including five phases: (a) disastrous event remote (anticipating disaster); (b) disastrous event imminent (warning); (c) impact (system shock); (d) soon after impact; and (e) later on after impact (reconstruction and aftermath).

Where the disastrous event is remote, there exists disbelief despite the evidence that a catastrophic event will occur. When the onset of the event is imminent, there are beginnings of extreme responses, including repression, anxiety, and overactivity. Once the catastrophic event has struck, there are many signs toward less advanced, regressed dedifferentiated person-in-environment states (e.g., panic, disorganization, irrational behavior, disorientation in space and time, and enuresis and night terrors especially in children). During the course of recovery, there may be some positive steps taken, for example, a desire to return to the place where it happened. Independent of the motives for such a concern, from our perspective the "place where it happened" may serve as an anchor point or base of operations on which to build a new cognitive-affective-valuative organization of the person-in-environment system. These may be regarded as conditions that are the basis for a process of developmental progression to take place. Soon after impact, there are the beginnings of coping, of recovery, of reorganization and movement toward more advanced person-in-environment system states. With respect to the atomic bomb, Lifton's (1965) notion of psychic numbing is an example of a coping mechanism formally involving a distancing between self and world or a differentiated and isolated self-world relationship. Suspicion, blame of others (first appearing in the reconstruction phase), and/or negative, hostile feelings toward relief organizations represent an advance to a differentiated and in conflict person-in-environment relationship. With further recovery, there are signs of differentiated and hierarchically integrated relationships where individuals begin to find long-term ways of coping (e.g., trying to prevent the occurrence of a human-made disaster such as nuclear war, finding warning systems) and reducing the impact of natural disasters.

Based on our elaborated approach, a study was conducted on the impact of the 1992 Hurricane Andrew on a Bahamian person-in-environment system. In addition to other findings, for example, on gender differences in couples, there was marked support in the retrospections of the participants for our developmental analysis:

> With Warning of the Disaster persons show evidence conforming to the *dedifferentiated person-in-environment system state* insofar as they exhibit wishful thinking involved in denial of danger (9/58), greater dependence on authority figures and egocentricity (e.g., "it could not happen to me"—15/58). . . .
>
> There were others during Warning of the Disaster who conformed to the *differentiated and isolated person-in-environment system state;* some indicated that they could not do anything about the storm (5/58) and others (2/58) withdrew by action (e.g., locked self in rooms; locked self in church).
>
> Still others (10/58) conformed to the *differentiated and in conflict person-in-environment system state* insofar as they exhibited rebelliousness to authority as evidenced by blaming authorities for not warning properly. . . . There was little evidence at this Warning of the Disaster stage of the differentiated and hierarchically integrated mode of coping, as expressed by one respondent, a youth minister who stated, "I tried to get my situation right. I made sure my house was battened up . . . and then I went out to help some elderly . . . you have to have a plan." (Chea & Wapner, 1995, p. 90)

With impact of the hurricane, the more regressed dedifferentiated mode was in evidence; soon after impact, the differentiated and in conflict person-in-environment state was present. The differentiated and hierarchically integrated state occurred most frequently one year after impact and least frequently in the warning period. In general, the findings are in keeping with the expectation that, with onset of the hurricane, the person's transactions (experience and action) with the environment are regressed and, with time, there appears to be a return to functioning at a more advanced developmental level.

Relocation

Demick and Wapner (1980) examined the transactions (experience and action) of two groups of patients—antisocial personalities and chronic undifferentiated schizophrenics—as well as some members of the staff during the stress induced during relocation of a psychiatric therapeutic community. On the assumption that the individual can actively focus on experiencing the self as object, environment as object, or self-environment relations as object, measures were taken that tapped these three aspects of experience. These measures, collected over a two-month period surrounding the move (3–4 weeks before, 2–3 days before, 2–3 days after, and 3–4 weeks after relocation) showed differential changes over the course of relocation associated with agent status.

1. *Experience of self (body qua object).* Schizophrenics significantly overestimated their apparent head width *more* 2–3 days before and after the move relative to 3–4 weeks before and after the move. In contrast, antisocial personalities overestimated head width *less* on the two occasions immediately surrounding the move. The staff showed a linear decrease with respect to apparent head width (see Wapner & Werner, 1965, for ontogenetic changes). There were no significant effects for the body cathexis and self-cathexis scales (Secord & Jourard, 1953) that assessed evaluation of one's body and self.

2. *Experience of environment.* On approaching relocation, the schizophrenics' descriptions of the *physical* features of the hospital became less accurate and less detailed as evident in their descriptions as well as sketch maps of the setting. Their drawings were vague and lacked detail even after 3–4 weeks in the new setting. In contrast, descriptions made by antisocial personalities showed more detail 3–4 weeks before, a decrease with the approach of relocation, and a marked increase in detail and organization immediately following the move.

3. *Experience of self-environment relations.* Whereas the schizophrenics rated their relationships with others as less "intense" and less "permanent" and the antisocial personalities rated their relationships as more "intense" on the two occasions closest to the move, staff members showed no such differential changes. The differences may be explained by considering the differential response of the two groups to stress. For example, using

Simeons's (1961) terminology, when confronted by a stressful situation, the schizophrenic typically employs a "flight" response and the antisocial personality a "fight" response.

Environment (Interpersonal)

To illustrate the nature of critical transitions with respect to the interpersonal aspect of one's environment, two sets of studies will be briefly described. One is concerned with the development and nature of friendships (Roelke, 1989; Thomason, 1985) and the other with the critical transition involved in the dissolution of a love relationship (King, 1995).

With respect to *friendship,* Thomason (1985) first utilized an in-depth interview with six men and six women at the end of their first year of college and then conducted a follow-up, longitudinal study with 11 men and 26 women using a questionnaire completed two times in the first year, once in the third week and again six weeks later at the end of the semester. Utilizing such dimensions as similarities between self and other, dealing with conflicts and disagreements, and self-disclosure–information shared, it was found that with increasing interdependence, there was, in keeping with the orthogenetic principle, an increase in differentiation and articulation of the parts constituting the friendship relationship, with an *increase of self* to those parts; an increase in the integration of parts within the friendship experience as a whole; and an increase in the flexibility of the friendship experience.

Roelke (1989) collected self-reported experiences from 20 male and 20 female participants in investigating similarities and differences in close as compared with non-close friendship relationships. Descriptions and diagrams representing each friend's involvement in the participant's spheres of activity (e.g., work, recreation) were categorized in keeping with the orthogenetic principle:

(a) Focused friendship experience (undifferentiated insofar as the friend is mainly involved in one sphere); (b) Enmeshed friendship experience (differentiated and overlapping, since the friend is completely involved in all spheres); (c) Segmented friendship experience (differentiated and isolated: The friend is involved in several isolated spheres, some more important in the friendship than others); and (d) Differentiated and integrated friendship experience (the friendship involves a number of interconnected shared spheres, some more important in the relationship than others). As expected, *S*s'

close friendships were categorized at a higher level than their non-close relationships. (Roelke, 1989, p. 1)

Ratings on six social support functions (social integration, contribution to self-esteem, opportunity to give nurturance, assistance, emotional closeness, and stability and reliability) revealed low ratings across all functions for nonclose friendships; for close relationships, emotional closeness, stability, and reliability received significantly higher ratings. More intimate functions (opportunity to give nurturance, emotional closeness, stability and reliability) were rated as particularly important in differentiated and integrated relationships. Thus, the orthogenetic principle operates effectively in developmentally characterizing the nature of friendship and its development.

In a related vein, King (1995) analyzed similarities and differences in experience and action of men and women involved in the *dissolution of a love relationship* with respect to emotional experience, relationship with others, and types of actions used to alleviate the feelings of loss. Thirty female and 22 male undergraduates participated by completing an anonymous questionnaire with open-ended questions and rating scales assessing, retrospectively, their experience (e.g., health, self-esteem, relations with friends and family) and action prior to and following the breakup.

A number of significant findings emerged, including: "actions taken to alleviate feelings of loss, where women desired to talk to others about the situation; yet conversely, also wishing to withdraw and do such activities as listening to music. . . . Women seemed to really invest themselves in the company of others to help them learn about the breakup while the men tended to turn to others to take their mind off the breakup. Concerning the forming of relations with others, both women and men expressed experiencing difficulty in trusting in others; however, women did seem more willing to take the risk to trust again" (King, 1995, pp. 30–31).

A further assessment of the triggers that precipitated the breakup revealed that they fell into three categories inherent within the perspective: psychological experience of the focal person (e.g., not happy, loss of attraction, personal problems, lack of desire); the physical environment (e.g., going away to college, distance); and the interpersonal environment (e.g., argument, unfaithfulness, physical violence, humiliation, change in preference, breaking commitment, incompatibility, unequal effort). While it was expected that the initiators might have a less difficult time than the person who was "dropped," this was not necessarily the case because some initiators sought out ways of punishing themselves to relieve some of their guilt. Noninitiators had a hard time with the breakup because of intense feelings of rejection.

The emotions also appeared to exhibit an interesting sequence, namely, after feelings of sadness and fear diminished, feelings of loneliness were reported especially by women. To help in confirming the transition and distancing themselves from it, many men and women chose to involve themselves in other relationships. The interrelationships of cognitive and affective features of experience are quite apparent and, at the early stages, there is difficulty in subordinating feelings to thought. Most striking is the holistic evidence of interrelations among various aspects of the person-in-environment system, including self-concept, actions taken to alleviate feelings of loss, and the role of friends and family in recovery.

Environment (Sociocultural)

As noted in Table 13.1, critical transitions prior to and following a variety of perturbations have been studied, initiated, or planned for the future. Let us consider a series of studies that range from entering a nursery school to entering and adapting to a professional school, namely, medical school.

The child's transition into a preschool program *(home to nursery school)* typically represents the first separation from home and operates as a process that involves the integration of two worlds, home and nursery school (see Ciottone, Demick, Pacheco, Quirk, & Wapner, 1980; Wapner et al., 1983). Careful examination is required of the nature of the nursery school and the nature of the home environment (e.g., there are differences in goals of mothers of handicapped versus nonhandicapped children; see Quirk et al., 1986; Quirk, Sexton, Ciottone, Minami, & Wapner, 1984). The transition raises such questions as: "How does the child organize or reorganize the cognitive, affective, and valuative experience of the new environment? What impact does the child's experience of the new environment have upon his or her experience of the accustomed surroundings (i.e., the home)? How does the child accomplish the transition over time (viz., develop greater differentiation and integration of the two person-in-environment systems)?" (Ciottone & Quirk, 1985, p. 4).

As noted by Wapner et al. (1983):

> Ideally, the child must operate effectively in two contexts, each with different demands, and must be able to organize his or her transactions at home and at school into differentiated and integrated spheres of activity (multiple worlds).

What are some possible indicators of developmental status at this ideal level of those which fall short of it? When children import behavior as well as objects from one setting to the next indiscriminately, they are exhibiting developmentally less advanced transactions since such behavior implies fusion of the home and school contexts. If with further exposure, their transactions are appropriate to the context—for example, the child states "I am going to *play* school here at home"—then the child is exhibiting actions indicative of more advanced developmental status. Further, means and ends can be ordered developmentally in the context of environmental transition. For example, to what extent does the child behave in ways that reflect a diffuse sense of the means by which to achieve his or her goals (e.g., acting as if blocks and crayons serve the same purpose) as opposed to a differentiation of means-ends transactions with the environment (e.g., tower building with blocks and coloring with crayons)? (pp. 120–121)

Beyond the description of the transactions of the focal person in the transition, there is the further question of the *conditions* under which developmental transformation is arrested, reversed, or advanced. Some of these questions are addressed in the studies that follow.

Some Representative Research: Educational Transitions

Entry into Nursery School: Pilot Study

Ciottone and Quirk (1985) have described an initial investigation involving three parts, namely, retrospective interviews with five mothers of preschool children, taping by three mothers of discussions with their children during the transition, and systematic observation (with videotaping) of one child by the teacher and two research assistants over the course of time following entry into preschool until interpersonal relations are relatively fixed. The use of transitional objects (Winnicott, 1958, 1971) was clearly described in the words of one mother: "When Billy began nursery school, he took a piece of cloth. He had it with him the whole time and the teacher would suggest to him that he could put it in his pocket, but he didn't want it out of his sight. He wanted her to hold it for him so that he could see it. Now he's at a point where he's forgotten it a couple of times and second he does put it in his pocket for much of the day but brings it out when he stays for 'nap time' or when its time to go home and he's real tired" (Ciottone & Quirk, 1985, p. 5).

The use of a transitional object that helps in accomplishing the transition is distinguished from an importation object—such as bringing a book—which presupposes that the child has differentiated one setting from another and which implies ongoing hierarchic integration of those parts. For example, another mother stated: "Benjamin certainly has been willing to share things and bring things from home to nursery school which he did not want to do last year at all. For example, this year he has selected books to bring in for story time which he would never do last year" (Ciottone & Quirk, 1985, p. 6).

Another question explored was the child's choice of anchor points or base of operations. One 2-year-10-month-old child utilized a cash register located in the center of the room, which he encountered on his first visit. He returned frequently to the cash register, even for a few seconds, before moving on to another activity. In contrast to other children, he did not use an interpersonal anchor point (e.g., teacher) and, indeed, never called the teacher by name. The problem of the use of anchor points—physical and interpersonal—requires more systematic study.

Entry into Nursery School: Children's Transactions as a Function of Experience and Age

Ellefsen (1987) investigated children's entry into preschool as a part of the entire process of transition from home to nursery school. Seventeen children (nine 2–3-year-olds entering for the first time and eight 4-year-olds attending since the previous year) participated. Free-play behaviors were videotaped on four occasions: the first two during the first week of entry and the last two during one week two to three months later.

> Differences between the two groups of preschoolers, as well as changes over time, were assessed with respect to the following measures: general salience of physical (i.e., places) and interpersonal (i.e., teachers and peers) anchor points; differential exploration of physical and social aspects of the environment; visits to play areas differing in potential for

social activity; and differential involvement in social activity (including social participation, group and individual play, and interactions with peers). (pp. 56–57)

In keeping with expectation:

> It was found that entering preschoolers, with respect to returning preschoolers, showed greater salience of physical and teacher anchor points, greater exploration of the physical environment, greater degree of contact with teachers, and less involvement in social activity with peers. Returning preschoolers were found to show greater salience of peer anchor points, greater degree of contact with peers, and greater activity involving group play and social interactions with peers. Finally, over time (2–3 months) the entering preschoolers were found to explore the physical environment to a lesser degree, spend more time with peers, and engage in a greater number of interactions with peers. (p. 57)

Transition from Elementary to Junior High School

Yamamoto and Ishii (1995) utilized a microgenetic developmental approach to the transition from elementary school to a big junior high school in Japan. They utilized the psychological distance map (PDM) for people (assessing people important to the subject; see Wapner, 1977) and a rating scale assessing adaptation and anxiety prior to and following the transition. The main findings were that the number of students mentioned on the PDM from the new environment increased and those from the old environment decreased. Moreover, while there was an immediate increase in the number of persons entered on the PDM for students from a large elementary school, the increment was slower for the students from a small elementary school.

Entering College: Physical Environment

Schouela, Steinberg, Leveton, and Wapner (1980) dealt with the process of cognitively organizing the spatial features of a relatively physically circumscribed new environment—a small university—by freshmen over a seven-month period following entry. The study explored the following hypotheses: (a) that the cognitive organization of a large-scale environment unfolds in a manner parallel to the development of more limited percepts such as inkblots (cf. Werner, 1940/1957); thus, with increasing exposure to and/or experience in the new environment, there would be systematic structural changes in the cognitive organization of the physical locale reflected in the form of successively produced sketch-map representations in keeping with the developmental progression defined by the orthogenetic principle; (b) that an anchor point or base of operations is used as the basis for the formation of the cognitive organization of the new environment; thus, elements entered first on sketch-map representations are those that are personally salient in the environmental experience of the person who produced the sketch map; and (c) that such elements will remain invariant in their organizational function as the cognitive spatial organization becomes increasingly differentiated and elaborated over time.

The method involved requesting the participant to draw a sketch map on an 8½-by-11-inch piece of paper, to label or identify the various parts of the drawing, and to place a number next to the parts showing the sequence in which the item was added to the sketch. These sketch maps were drawn 1 to 3 days, and 1 to 3, 7 to 8, 11 to 12, and 24 weeks after arrival on campus (with some individuals missing some test occasions to omit the effect of testing). Some striking findings were as follows: (a) there was gradual (microgenetic) development and elaboration of sketch-map structure; (b) there was consistent use of a particular place as the starting point in each sketch-map representation; (c) all individuals, except one, made mention of the use of a salient anchor point or base of operations in describing the organizational principles they employed; (d) the nature of the anchor point differed (53% drew his or her own dormitory as the first place entered on the sketch map; 17% a major academic building; 8% library; 6% an interesting street; 4% auditorium; 3% bordering street; 1% each an upperclass dorm, tennis courts, and gymnasium); (e) some used the anchor point as a location from which they started moving through the environment, adding parts as they moved through, and others used a more conceptual organization; (f) individuals were highly consistent in employing the same starting point over the entire map series; and (g) there was preliminary evidence that anchor points may also be interpersonal; that is, similar to anchor points for the physical aspects of the environment, anchor-persons played a significant role in the development of social networks upon exposure to the university or other environments (cf., Kaplan, Pemstein, Cohen, & Wapner, 1974; Wapner, 1977; see also Wapner et al., 1981, on the potential for sketch maps to demonstrate both microgenetic and ontogenetic changes). Indeed, as pointed out by Schouela et al. (1980),

the notion of anchor point has very wide application as a fundamental process underpinning the development of any organization, whether it be nonsense syllable learning or more complex phenomena.

Entering College: Interpersonal Environment

Wapner (1978) developed the PDM for people (names of persons in small circles on a piece of paper are placed at varying distances from a small circle at its center labeled "me"; the closer the placement to "me," the greater the importance of that person to the subject; also, a number is placed next to the added circles indicating sequence of entry). The persons entered are characterized as to whether they come from the home or the new environment. It was found that:

> (1) The total number of entries on the PDM for people did not change significantly over the six months of exposure to the university environment. . . . However, the number of entries from the home environment decreased significantly while the number of entries from the university environment increased markedly.

> (2) The proportion of connections of persons between home and university was low. . . . However, the number of subjects reporting at least some home to university connections increased significantly over time. This points to the integration of the home and school worlds from the perspective of the student undergoing the transition. (Wapner, 1978, p. 7)

This general problem was pursued by Minami (1985a, 1985b), who focused on the development of personal networks during the first year of college. A personal network is defined as a total set of relationships between a focal agent and his or her significant others and groups. The central assumption was that "the more highly differentiated and integrated the structural composition and the functional potential of the personal network, the higher the degree of freedom and the supportive resources it provides the agent in his or her transactions with the environment" (Minami, 1985a, p. 40). Development of the personal network was expected to be reflected in development toward (a) increasing differentiation (e.g., wider range and diversity of people; greater focus on shared activities and interests; different supportive functions divided into different clusters based on shared activities, interests, etc.); (b) increasing integration (e.g., more interconnections among subgroups; anchor point agents or centers with connections to others); (c) increasing flexibility (e.g., same support from different members; same member gives different support); and (d) increasing stability (e.g., conflict with one member compensated for by relation with other; balance in give and take of resources).

These expectations were assessed in a year-long project with 35 college freshmen who completed the following tasks during the first month of entry, at the end of the first semester, and at the end of the academic year: PDM for people and a personal network questionnaire (assessing attributes of network members, relations among network members, supportive functions of relationships, etc.). Specifically, Minami (1985b) found:

> The college freshman's network: 1) was dominated by college friends; 2) was composed of stable parts (home) and changing parts (college friends); and 3) was composed of sub-networks which have different structural properties, modes of exchange, type of relationship and locational backgrounds.
>
> The analyses of supportive functions showed that: 1) psychological closeness, continuity and equality in exchange are positively correlated with overall support functions; 2) relationships which involve older people, exhibit multiplexity, show high frequency contact, and provide higher tangible and informational support; 3) relationships based on friendship and work have a wide range of connections and provide higher emotional support and social activities; and 4) freshman gradually shift the source of support from a home network to a college network.
>
> There were two types of tendencies in the formation of and management of old and new relationships. The integrative type assimilates into highly dense, existing networks. The differentiated type, however, tends to keep separating different sub-networks. There was no evidence for higher supportive functions among the integrative type networks compared to differentiated type networks. (p. 2)

Leaving College

A number of years ago, Wapner and colleagues (Wofsey, Rierdan, & Wapner, 1979) raised the question of whether explicit formulation of plans regarding future activity in a new environment would affect the way one construes the base environment in which one is still located. This was assessed by comparing the representations of the Clark University environment by two groups of college seniors: one with clearly articulated plans as to what they would be doing after graduation and the other with no such formulated plans. The two

groups were asked to represent their environment both verbally and pictorially.

There was consonance between the findings for the verbal representations and the drawings. In both cases, the individual with plans tended to represent the university where they were still located in a more impersonal, more objective, and more psychologically distant manner. This is exemplified most strikingly by describing drawings made by different individuals. A participant *lacking articulated plans,* for example, represented the environment as embedded in a drawing with him facing a central university building while in graduation garb, waving to friends he is leaving behind, including details of the building in a three-dimensional perspective. An individual with *articulated plans* for the future showed indications of greater self-world distancing, namely, a maplike representation of the environment from an aerial view with omission of persons or personally relevant details. A participant with *semi-articulated plans* made a maplike aerial view, yet containing a three-dimensional perspective for some of the buildings. An individual with *very highly articulated plans* showed extreme self-world distancing by characterizing Clark University as a dot on the United States in the Western Hemisphere, as if the world were viewed from the moon. The dot represented Worcester and Clark University, and remoteness from the college environment was exaggerated by adding to the drawing the written statement: "Freud spoke here and hated it."

There were analogous findings for the verbal representations. For example, an individual who on the first occasion had articulated plans and exhibited marked psychological distancing in his representations changed by the second test occasion. At that time, his articulated plans fell through, and his present state was coupled with a decrease in psychological distancing on his representations. Thus, participants with well-articulated plans to leave an environment construed the base environment in a manner reflecting greater self-world distancing than did those with less articulated plans.

This problem was pursued by Apter (1976), who studied the relationship between anticipatory planning stages of environmental relocation and transactional conflict. Transactional conflict was defined as the discrepancy between personal expectations of the environment and experienced "environmental actuality," or a transaction where the physical or social environment does not live up to original expectations. Groups of seniors differing in planning (as described in the Wofsey et al., 1979, study) were established. To assess modes of coping with discrepancy between expectation and actuality, participants were asked to recall from their own recent experience incidents involving transactional conflict with the academic, social, administrative, domestic, and physical aspects of the environment.

Plans related to modes of coping as follows. (a) The senior *without plans* is hyperinvested in and identifies with the present environment; he or she copes with transactional conflict by *accommodation*. For example, when a professor did not meet expectations, the student did not withdraw from class but accommodated by accepting it and waiting for things to turn out well. (b) The senior in the *process of actively making plans* is less invested in and more differentiated from the environment; he or she copes with transactional conflict by *nonconstructive ventilation*. For example, when a washing machine did not work, the student kicked the machine and left in disgust. Another typical response by those involved in plans about the future is *disengagement*. For example, when a student's roommate had a compulsion for waxing the floors every week, the student distanced herself from the situation by laughing at it, becoming cynical, or mocking it. (c) The student whose future *plans are securely established* is directed toward a balance between his or her own interests and those of the environment; transactional conflict is handled by such means as *constructive assertion*. This is coping by using planned actions and different alternatives for achieving a goal. For example, when the shower in a university apartment did not work, a student threatened not to pay rent if the shower was not fixed by the next day and the university fixed it right away.

This study, together with the previous one, points to the relation between different stages of planning to leave an environment and construal of that environment in terms of self-world distancing, and transacting in the environment with respect to modes of coping (when there is discrepancy between expectations and actuality). Further, Apter's (1976) analysis served as a basis for describing a more general, formally stated concept of individual differences in coping that is consonant with the orthogenetic principle. For example, *accommodation* represents a dedifferentiated person-in-environment system state; *disengagement* represents a differentiated and isolated person-in-environment system state; *nonconstructive ventilation* represents a differentiated and in conflict person-in-environment system state; and *constructive assertion* represents a differentiated and hierarchically integrated person-in-environment system state. This characterization has been invaluable in characterizing modes of coping in very diverse situations and contexts.

Entering and Adapting to Medical School

Quirk, Ciottone, Letendre, and Wapner (1986, 1987) examined two critical transitions: entering into the first year of medical school, and the shift from preclinical to clinical training that occurs between the second and third years of medical training. Intensive retrospective, introspective, and prospective interviews were used to elicit students' experiences of difficulties and strategies adopted to overcome those difficulties and to achieve their goals (cf. Frey, Demick, & Bibace, 1981).

The student entering medical school has the long-term goals of becoming a physician, having a family, maintaining friendships, keeping physically fit, and so on. The quantity of work and the stressful quality of the experience may make for conflict between short-term goals (e.g., relaxation and enjoyment) and long-term goals that influences modes of coping to achieve these goals. In general, "During the pre-clinical transition there is a significant decline in perceived health, class standing, perceived quality of instruction, and satisfaction with social activities. Concurrently, students experience an increase in the level of felt stress" (Quirk et al., 1987, p. 418). The difficulties included excessive volume of material to be learned experienced as an overwhelming obstacle; the preclinical curriculum interfering with nonacademic activities; and feelings of being forced to learn trivial, uninteresting, and clinically irrelevant information. Strategies included use of support or support systems (e.g., tutors, friends); structuring of time to include activities unrelated to training; and lowering of personal aspirations regarding academic performance.

A parallel set of difficulties and strategies was involved in the transition from nonclinical to clinical training. Difficulties included feeling unprepared; fear of failure to meet patients' needs and of being criticized by peers and professors; difficulty in being separated from one's significant other; and confronting a patient's pain, suffering, and mortality. Strategies to cope included maintaining a balanced diet and exercise; relying on significant others to manage stress; lowering of aspirations to mitigate perceived lack of academic preparation and fear of failing to perform in clinical situations.

From our perspective, we interpret these findings as showing that one out of the following four person-in-environment relations emerges during preclinical and clinical training:

1. A *dedifferentiated self-world relationship* may emerge where the student readily complies with environmental demands (e.g., conforming to the demands of the academic situation, diminishing the role and value of personal goals despite the occurrence of guilt and stress).

2. A *differentiated and isolated relationship* may develop where there is withdrawal from academic aspirations, perseverance with lower aspirations, and/or withdrawal from the system.

3. A *differentiated and in conflict relationship* may emerge where there is a back-and-forth shift between conforming and refusing to conform that may be exacerbated by criticism from peers and faculty.

4. A *differentiated and integrated self-world relationship* may develop "when medical students incorporate strategies (such as seeking social support) which allow them to maintain a feeling of control in the context of the academic environment. This feeling of control is marked by the ability to participate in or reject particular environmental demands . . . " (Quirk et al., 1987, p. 422).

This implies that adaptation is not a one-way process in which the person accommodates. Specifically, this suggests

> that it would be beneficial for faculty and administrators in medical training programs to become aware of the students' expectations, academic and non-academic goals, their feelings such as fear of failure, and strategies including lowering their level of aspiration. . . . It is important to acquire such a breadth and complexity of understanding, so as not to conflate this set of distinguishable emotions, motives, and experiences under the conventional rubric of "stress." This refinement in frame of reference for understanding medical students' experiences is particularly important for the design and implementation of curricular reforms. (p. 422)

Sojourn to a University in a New Culture

Our perspective was recently utilized in analyzing experience (cognitive, affective, valuative) and action of the sojourn of students to a university in a culture different from their own (Wapner, Inoue, Fujimoto, Imamachi, & Toews, 1997). Findings included: Many Japanese students found the United States to be big, inexpensive, ineffective in transportation, dangerous, and free as compared to Japan; U.S. students found Japan to be small, expensive, effective in transportation, safe, and regulated. Both groups experienced an awareness of being a foreigner and language barriers. Japanese students in the United States were more satisfied with academics than their U.S. counterparts in Japan. There was a tendency for the Japanese students to shift in the direction of striving toward multiculturalism (differentiation and hierarchic integration) with a longer stay.

Migration of Adolescents

While the challenges (e.g., adaptation to a change in physical environment, people, and customs) of entering a new environment are evident in migration, this transition is further complicated by a change in another site of the person-in-environment system: the emergence of adolescence (e.g., Lucca-Irizarry, Wapner, & Pacheco, 1981; Pacheco, Lucca, Wapner, 1985; Pacheco, Wapner, & Lucca, 1979).

> A developmental analysis is ingredient in the general goals of migration as indicated by the form of the acculturation adopted by the migrant. For example, there may be assimilation and identification of self with the new culture (e.g., "melting pot"); there may be isolation from and/or conflict with the culture of the host environment (e.g., ethnicity), or there may be flexible maintenance of both values of the culture one enters (e.g., biculturalism . . .). These alternatives formally parallel the self-world relationships implied in the orthogenetic principle as ranging from lesser to more advanced developmental status, that is, from (1) dedifferentiated to (2) differentiated and isolated; or (3) differentiated and in conflict to (4) differentiated and hierarchically integrated. (Wapner et al., 1983, p. 122)

Such a study was carried out with adolescents migrating from Puerto Rico to the United States and then returning to Puerto Rico. How do these adolescents experience the new environment and the return to their home environment?

Lucca-Irizarry, Wapner, and Pacheco (1981) have summarized the findings as follows:

- Relative to younger migrants, older migrant adolescents had a more negative perception and evaluation of the physical environment and reported more difficulties in their relationships with their peers.
- Males tended more often than females to feel uncomfortable with the new residence.
- Participants with higher levels of schooling had more difficulties in dealing with the new environment.
- Migrant adolescents who were born in the U.S. mainland perceived Puerto Rican government employees in more negative terms than Puerto Rican–born return migrants.
- Adolescents who had lived for a longer period in the United States found it harder to relate to peers in Puerto Rico.
- Adolescents from larger families reported more difficulties and tension in their family life following their migration experience.
- Those adolescents who at the time of arrival reported difficulties with the use of the Spanish language showed a more negative evaluation of the physical setting and of the school.
- Those who continued to have language difficulties (until the moment of data collection) showed a negative perception of the physical environment.

Further, in the *self* category, the data showed that:

- Adolescents who had traveled more frequently to and from the U.S. mainland presented the most confused sense of identity; that is, they had serious problems in defining themselves either as Americans or Puerto Ricans as evidenced by their defining their nationality as bilinguals.
- Females more often than males engaged in more constructive actions as a response to problems encountered after migration.
- Return migrant adolescents who were born in the U.S. mainland engaged less frequently in constructive actions than those migrants who were originally born in Puerto Rico.

In the third category, *self and others,* it was found that:

- Adolescents who were less willing to migrate to Puerto Rico experienced a sense of diminished personal freedom following their migration.
- Those who were born in the U.S. mainland considered themselves the object of prejudice and discrimination in Puerto Rico more so than native-born return migrants. (pp. 15–16)

The factors relating to self-identity pervaded the descriptions of the participants. For example, did they identify themselves as American, Puerto Rican, or Nuyorican? Those return migrants identified as Nuyorican by the locals are rejected socially by them. The role of language and adjustment is another prominent theme. For example, in the words of one of the participants, "If I speak Spanish people make fun of me because I don't speak well, and if I speak English people call me *gringa*" (p. 17).

While there is considerable evidence concerning the needs and difficulties of those adolescents involved in migration and return migration from Puerto Rico to the United States, there remains the open, critical problem of how to foster their growth and adaptation in both contexts. In this vein, another study was carried out by Redondo (1983). Specifically, he studied differences between Puerto Rican and Cuban adolescents' experience of migration to the United States. He found differences with respect to attractiveness of the environment (educational opportunities, economic conditions, societal freedom); efficacy of socialistic versus capitalistic upbringing; and prejudice. Of interest for future studies is the suggestion that a counseling program be developed consisting of two parts: (a) transitional peer intervention (assigning each migrant on arrival a peer anchor-person for the first semester, who is equipped to help with personal and academic problems); and (b) group counseling for adolescent migrants, for example, a six-session intervention led by teacher or counselor dealing with such issues as the challenges and vicissitudes of migration in terms of the four migration modes uncovered in the study, namely, irrelevant (move is of no consequence to personal goals), rejection (relevant but of no value for personal goals), partial acceptance (valuable for certain goals but not for others), and total acceptance (valuable for one's personal goals). It is noteworthy that the partial acceptance mode was more prevalent for Puerto Ricans, whereas the total acceptance mode was more frequent among the Cubans. These differences must be taken into account depending on which group is involved in the counseling procedure. Here we are touching on two more general problems: (a) the relations between experience and action; and (b) conditions making for progressive developmental change following a person-in-environment transition. Each will be discussed in turn.

Relations between Experience and Action

Given that transactions with the environment encompass experience (cognitive, affective, and valuative as well as intentional processes) and action, a critical, overarching problem is the relation between these two aspects of human functioning. Here we are concerned with such issues as the translation of experience and intentionality into appropriate behavior (e.g., "Do I, in fact, do what I know I should do or what I want to do?"). There are undoubtedly multiple approaches to this problem that are manifest in numerous areas and levels of human functioning, for example, at the individual level, whether the person changes or does not change his or her own actions in keeping with doctor's orders, his or her own desire to protect self. One can also ask how experience and action at the individual level are related to experience and action at the sociocultural level. Various complexities enter into an analysis designed to answer this question.

For example, the goals and instrumentalities governing action at the sociocultural level differ from the goals and instrumentalities governing action at the individual or interpersonal levels. Instituting a change in policy at the sociocultural level depends on some form of group consensus process, whereas stopping smoking depends on the individual. The relationship between the individual and society (see Demick & Wapner, 1990, on environmental policy) may be *supportive* (e.g., personal opinion and public policy coincide), *antagonistic* (personal experience and public policy are antithetical), or *substitutive/vicarious* (e.g., substituting the good of society for one's own desires; see also Wapner, 1969, for an earlier application of these categories to relations among cognitive processes).

To approach some aspects of the complexity of the relationships between experience and action, we have found it useful to employ Turvey's (1977) musical instrument metaphor, used in understanding neurological mechanisms, in our analysis. This metaphor distinguishes between "tuning" and "activating" inputs. As Gallistel (1980) succinctly stated: "Consider for example a piano or guitar. Turning the tuning pegs to tighten or loosen the strings does not produce music, but it profoundly alters the music that is produced.

The tightness of each string is a parameter of a piano or guitar. Signals that adjust these parameters are called parameter adjusting or tuning inputs to distinguish them from activating inputs like key-strikes and string-plucking" (p. 364).

General Factors and Precipitating Events

More specifically, in our analysis of relations between experience (including intentionality) and action, tuning corresponds to the category of *general factors* preparing the individual for some action (e.g., in our analyses of the usage/nonusage of automobile safety belts, described below, these include knowledge of safety belt effectiveness, anxiety about driving, and prior experience in an accident). *Specific precursors or triggers* for initiating the concrete behavior of "buckling up" in the particular context of the automobile (e.g., imagination of an accident, desire to serve as a role model for children in the car) are analogous to striking a key, which directly leads to the action of automobile safety belt usage. We have found this category system particularly useful.

Our most extensive studies on the problem have been in the health area to promote more optimal functioning of the human being in two ways. First, the use of automobile safety belts, on which extensive work has been done, concerns the problem of taking self-protective action, that is, action that is *preventative* of the dire consequences of an automobile accident that *might* happen. The other body of research also deals with problems of health such as disease prevention and cooperation in adhering to a prescribed treatment regimen for a person with an existing illness.

Automobile Safety Belt Use

In seeking a problem area to study some relations between experience and action, the use of automobile safety belts became focal for two reasons: it is possible to observe action *directly* (this was the case when the studies were conducted; at present, this is not feasible because there are automatic safety belts operative in some automobiles); and there was a change from a lack of legislation to legislation concerning safety belt use in different cultures that provided the possibility of assessing cultural differences in the relation of individual action to the rules and regulations of society.

Experiential Description and Process Analysis.
The first study in this sequence was primarily directed toward obtaining a phenomenologically oriented, structural description of the experience of using automobile safety belts (Rioux & Wapner, 1986). Toward this end, intensive tape-recorded, open-ended interviews were conducted with three groups of people: those who were self-proclaimed as nonusers, variable users, and committed users.

The analysis led to a number of generalizations. (a) *Committed safety belt users* maintained usage through a salient imagination of accident situations, fear of personal injury, memories of accidents involving significant others, perception of potential accidents as dependent on external circumstances, and the desire to be a "responsible citizen" or a good role model for children. (b) *Nonusers,* on the other hand, distanced themselves from the potentially hazardous end-state of an accident and/or injury by perceiving themselves as in control in avoiding potential accidents and by psychologically minimizing the risks involved, particularly the risk of personal injury. (c) *Variable users* were context-oriented. The decision to wear a safety belt depended on such factors as weather conditions, size of car, with whom they were driving, familiarity with the area, and so on; they also exhibited dissonance between perception and action.

Cultural Differences: General. Wapner, Demick, Inoue, Ishii, and Yamamoto (1986) studied experience and action with respect to automobile safety in general in Japan and the United States prior to legislation. Questionnaires given to the three groups of users (described in the previous study) in each sociocultural context revealed differences in: (a) general factors preparing individuals for the action/nonaction of using safety belts (e.g., relative to Americans, the Japanese placed higher value on safety belts); (b) precursors triggering the concrete behavior of "buckling up" in the context of the automobile (e.g., for Americans but not for the Japanese, feelings of preoccupation often caused them to forget to buckle up); and (c) action (e.g., the Japanese wore safety belts on the highway more often than Americans) and experience of this action (e.g., relative to Americans, the Japanese felt "virtuous" but not "confident" when wearing safety belts).

Cultural Differences: Impact of Safety Belt Legislation. Studies were also conducted to assess individuals'

experience and action of safety belt use prior to and following the initiation of mandatory safety belt legislation in Japan (Hiroshima) and the United States (Massachusetts; Demick et al., 1992); some observations were also made in Italy (Bertini & Wapner, 1992). The introduction of the law had a significant effect on increasing use; moreover, all three user groups (nonusers, variable users, and committed users) were found in both cultures. There were, however, differences between the two cultures:

> In the context of the highway, the observed rates are significantly higher in Hiroshima on all occasions—possibly related to stricter enforcement in Hiroshima relative to Massachusetts. However, in the city, the rates are significantly higher in Massachusetts only 2 months after legislation. This may be related to the fact that, on this occasion, safety belt use was enforced on both the highway and in the city in Massachusetts, whereas only on the highway in Hiroshima. However, once safety belt use began to be enforced in the city 1 year later, Hiroshima rates skyrocketed to an astounding 91% in the city and an equally astounding 98% on the highway.
>
> In both sociocultural contexts, there is an increase in drivers' use of safety belts on the highway from the test occasion prior to the passage of the law to the test occasion immediately following legislation. However, although the rates begin to level off and remain constant or further increase in Hiroshima, they continue to decrease steadily in Massachusetts. (Demick et al., 1992, p. 482)

Relevant here are similar and, indeed, more striking findings based on observations in the city of Rome prior to and following introduction of an automobile safety belt law in Italy (G. Bertini & Wapner, 1992). With a sample of 300 individuals on the first four occasions and 200 on the fifth, safety belt usage was as follows: 10.4% prior to legislation (April 26, 1989), 54.8% just after legislation (April 28, 1989), 28.0% six months later (June 11, 1990), and 4.5% three years later (June 6, 1992).

Thus, in Japan, there was a strong adherence to a law requiring safety belt use, whereas in Italy the degree of adherence to the law was almost negligible, and in the United States people in one state voted to repeal the law because it interfered with individual freedom. Hence, in seeking means for advancing use of safety belts that prevent deleterious effects of automobile accidents, it is not only necessary to take into account the individual and his or her characteristics and proclivities, but also the sociocultural context in which he or she lives.

Initiating a Diet Regimen/Cessation of Alcohol and Tobacco Use

In intensive interviews dealing with changes in diet and alcohol and tobacco use, findings were linked to various aspects of the category system of the perspective (Agli, 1992; Raeff, 1990; Tirelli, 1992). Examples follow drawn from these three spheres of activity. For the person, general factors included (a) physical (e.g., "weight is affecting my health"); (b) psychological (e.g., "I hate my body"); and (c) sociocultural aspects (e.g., "did not fit with the image I wanted to project professionally"). For the environment, general factors included (a) physical (e.g., "There wasn't much opportunity to drink"); (b) interpersonal (e.g., "I can remember being consistently harassed by my father to diet"); and (c) sociocultural aspects (e.g., "At the time I lived in the Middle East and everybody smokes there").

Some concrete examples of the precipitating events or triggers reported, again drawn from these three spheres of activity, fall into a number of categories: (a) negative health experience (e.g., "Last summer, I drank a lot and became very sick . . . just made me lose all desire to drink"); (b) eating in an uncontrolled manner (e.g., "I stopped at three ice cream places and again on my way home . . . saw how out of control I was"); (c) interpersonal situation (e.g., "It was the day before my fifteenth birthday. My father came home and was drunk. He threw up all over. I just turned off"); (d) willpower (e.g., "I stopped because I wanted to prove to myself that I could"); (e) medical difficulties (e.g., "I have cirrhosis . . . drinking would be a double hazard"); (f) academic commitment ("I am here as a college student . . . drinking interferes with my main priority"); (g) athletic commitment (e.g., "I stopped drinking because I started the basketball season"); (h) love of life (e.g., "I reached a point where I could not stand it anymore"); (i) reality of drug addiction (e.g., "I realized how dangerous it was for my health and I hated the idea that I couldn't do anything without a cigarette in my hand"); and (j) overwhelmed by reality of actual weight (e.g., "The day after my daughter's wedding, we all sat and looked at the video. I was absolutely stunned . . . freaked out completely . . . got off the plane . . . went to a weight loss program the next day").

Sexual Behavior in Relation to Protection against AIDS

Two interrelated studies concerning AIDS are reviewed here. In the first investigation, Ferguson, Wapner, and Quirk (1993) assessed the relations between experience and action by asking 80 college students (25 men and 55 women) to report on situations where they "did not do what they wanted to do" and situations where they "did do what they wanted to do" regarding protection against sexual transmission of HIV. It was found that, when there was a discrepancy between "wanting and doing," the responses emphasized physical aspects of the environment (e.g., "There were no condoms at my disposal so I didn't use one") and physical condition of self (e.g., "I didn't use condoms because I was drunk"). When there was congruence between "wanting and doing," the responses focused on a combination of the psychological experience of the person (e.g., fear of AIDS) and the physical aspects of the environment (e.g., availability of condoms).

The responses could also be categorized in developmental terms. When participants noted that they "did not do what they wanted to do," their responses were characteristically less advanced, fitting the categories of *differentiated and in conflict* (e.g., "She insisted that I not use a condom so I didn't against my will") and *dedifferentiated* (e.g., "I was so aroused at that point I didn't worry about HIV"). In contrast, when "did what they wanted to do" was the response, the most frequent answers occurred for the developmentally advanced category, *differentiated and hierarchically integrated* (e.g., "I use protection because I am aware of the consequences of unprotected sex . . . protected sex is of utmost importance"). Relatively infrequent was the category *differentiated and isolated* (e.g., "I haven't had sex since my one-night stand without protection"; "I abstain from intercourse; I do everything except that because it decreases my chances of contracting HIV").

Clark (1995) introduced three interventions to change behavior: (a) providing information about the HIV/AIDS disease and how the virus is transmitted; (b) providing information on how HIV/AIDS is transmitted and exposure to the accounts of participants in the previous study (Ferguson, Wapner, & Quirk, 1993) with respect to their reports of actions when they "did not do what they wanted to do" and when they "did what they wanted to do"; and (c) providing information about how HIV/AIDS is transmitted coupled with participation in a tailored imagery exercise where they were asked to imagine the consequences of one of the accounts of reported unsafe behavior from which they were to assume they had contracted HIV. The third group, having the most personalized treatment, which was presumed to *decrease the psychological distance between the subject and the threat of HIV/AIDS,* was expected to report significantly greater frequency of practicing safe sex. This expectation was supported by the findings, and leads us to discuss conditions fostering developmental progression toward more optimal person-in-environment system functioning (see Quirk & Wapner, 1995).

Conditions Facilitating Developmental Change

While the imposition of a perturbation to the person-in-environment system makes for developmental *regression,* it is relevant to ask what conditions and processes—implicit or explicit in the studies reviewed so far—suggest directions for fostering developmental *progression.* A number of these (though not exclusive) may be briefly described here.

Self-World Distancing

Self-world distancing may promote developmental change in two ways. As above, a decrease in self-world distancing between the individual and the consequences of his or her negative actions may lead to safer, more optimal person-in-environment functioning. Conversely, an increase in self-world distancing between the individual and affectively laden material may permit the person to operate more optimally insofar as there is greater separation between cognition and negative affect (Nair, 1961).

Anchor Point

As already noted, both physical (Schouela et al., 1980) and social anchor points (B. Kaplan et al., 1974; Minami, 1985a, 1985b; see also Ainsworth & Wittig, 1969; Winnicott, 1958, 1971) have been shown to play a role in the development of a spatial organization and social network in adapting to a new environment. "Will fostering the child's use of an anchor point (whether an actual or symbolic object) in the new environment help the child move closer to the developmental ideal of integrating the new world of school with the old world of home and in experiencing stability, comfort, and satisfaction in both?" (Wapner et al., 1983, p. 121). "What conditions or circumstances serve to

help the migrant cope with various features of the new environment? Are there key people in the new environment—for example, kin or friends—who will become instrumental in the development of the social network of the migrant and then serve as anchor points or referents for establishing the migrant's social world?" (pp. 123–124).

Reculer Pour Mieux Sauter (Draw Back to Leap)

A negative experience (e.g., loss of self-esteem) may serve the positive function of fostering greater self-insight and providing the formal condition of "dissolution of a prior organization of the self," thereby permitting a creative reorganization of self.

Triggers to Action

There is evidence to suggest that making people aware of the precipitating events or triggers to their own or others' actions leads to a heightened awareness of person-in-environment functioning. This heightened awareness may include consideration of a wider repertoire of triggers for self, which may, in turn, lead to appropriate action and hence more optimal person-in-environment functioning.

Individual Differences in Experiencing Critical Transitions

Various studies from within our approach have suggested that consideration of individual differences may be a route toward fostering developmental progression. For example, consider that retirement means different things to different people. Such differences must then be taken into account in seeing conditions or circumstances that might make for more optimal experience and action during retirement. That is, it is entirely possible that, for people in our fourth group (imposed disruption) who experience retirement as a devastating affair, continued contact with one's fellow workers rather than a sudden break with the work world might make it easier to adapt (e.g., Hornstein & Wapner, 1985).

Moreover, as noted earlier in the medical school context: "it would be beneficial for faculty and administrators in medical training programs to become aware of the students' expectations, academic and non-academic goals, their feelings such as fear of failure, and strategies, including lowering their level of aspiration. . . . [This could be] particularly important for the design and implementation of curricular reforms" (Quirk et al., 1987, p. 422).

Planning

In a related manner, there is also evidence that a simple request for the person to verbalize plans about actions to be taken to advance to a new, more ideal person-in-environment system state may bring the state into effect (cf., Neuhaus, 1988; Shapiro, 1973; Shapiro, Rierdan, & Wapner, 1972; Wapner, 1987).

FUTURE DIRECTIONS

While the perspective described here is embedded in a long history, there remains the potentiality for its further development as well as the manifestation of its heuristic implications for uncovering and shaping significant research problems that have both theoretical and practical value. There are a variety of problem areas worthy of investigation that are suggested by the assumptions, the category system, the pilot and initial studies already analyzed, new problem areas developed through extension of the perspective, and the implications of findings and theory for developmentally advancing the functioning of the individual so that he or she operates at a more optimal level. Let us consider some examples.

Levels of Integration

The notion of levels of integration (biological, psychoogical, sociocultural) is regarded as playing a central role in various aspects of development, including ontogenesis, pathogenesis, and microgenesis. Central to such an analysis is not only the relationship between levels at a given stage of ontogenetic development, but also the significant question of how the relationships between and among the levels of integration change ontogenetically and microgenetically. There are a variety of features of functioning, of course, in which this problem can be analyzed.

Currently, Bertini, Braibante, and Wapner (1996) are involved in analyzing sleep-wake phenomena from our perspective. Specifically, this project is concerned with characterizing sleeping-waking from the fetal stage to old age in a manner that will include a phenomenal description of all stages as well as a characterization of person-in-environment transactions in sleep and wake development. This will involve examination of the underlying processes such as the interaction among the biological (e.g., heart rate, primordial respiratory movement, blood flow), action (e.g., body movement, eye movement), and experiential (e.g., dreaming) levels. Microgenetic, pathological phenomena and ethnological issues will also be considered.

Examination of sleep-wake phenomena represents one among many other areas that could be subjected to such an analysis. For example, within cognitive experience, developmental changes in the relations among sensorimotor, perceptual, and conceptual processes as well as developmental changes (ontogenetic and microgenetic) in the relations among cognition, affect, and valuation are problems that are worthy of careful study (Wapner & Demick, 1987, 1996). In such analyses, it may be productive to raise the question of the nature of the relationships. Are they *supportive* (where one function or process, say cognition, complements and is supportive of another function or process, e.g., emotion)? Are they *antagonistic* (where one function or process is antithetical to another, e.g., operation of a given emotion mitigates the operation of cognition)? Are they *substitutive* (where the operation of one function takes the place of or substitutes for the other, e.g., with introduction of sensorimotor activity there is a diminution of perceived movement)? Are they *correspondent* (where both levels function in the same way)?

This problem of relationships among levels of organization was self-evident in our studies on critical person-in-environment transitions. To illustrate, consider the formulation of a study dealing with the transition from health to illness as obtains in the onset of diabetes, a change at the physical level (Collazo, 1985). There is concern with the relations between one's biological self (e.g., unstable glucose levels) and one's psychological self (e.g., self-esteem); self in relation to physical environment (e.g., because of concern for availability of insulin, one may always remain close to the home community); and transactions related to the sociocultural context (e.g., transactions and values related to sociocultural attitudes toward the sick; see Wapner & Demick, 1990).

Category System: Critical
Person-in-Environment Transitions

The category system used in identifying sites where perturbations may initiate critical person-in-environment transitions represents a treasury of open problems for research. This is evident from a reexamination of Table 13.1, which lists studies already completed and others that are worthy of investigation. Findings obtained from these studies will not only provide an opportunity to revise and advance the theoretical conceptualization, but also provide information that can be used practically.

Planning

Our approach to planning was described by Wapner and Cirillo (1973) as follows: "A plan is a symbolic preparatory action in that the planner conceives of, imagines a method independently of carrying out the concrete actions embodying that method" (p. 13). While there are many possibilities for studying the development of planning both ontogenetically and microgenetically, it is worthy of note that our study of critical person-in-environment transitions provides unique opportunities to study the development of planning.

For example, Wapner (1987) outlined an analysis of planning in connection with the radical disruption of the person-in-environment system by tornado, hurricane, and so on. The analysis proposed includes—at each stage (disastrous event remote, impact/system shock, carrying out plan, and postimpact)—a description of the experience and proposed plans as well as the means (action to be taken, both covert and overt) and ends (projected person-in-environment system state). Such questions may be studied as: Do the changes over the sequence in person-in-environment relations conform to the idealized developmental sequence? Is there evidence that, following system shock, person-in-environment system states become less advanced and that the very operation of planning serves to help move the person-in-environment system state toward the end point postulated by the developmental ideal?

Organizational Psychology

There is growing evidence of the effective applicability of the theoretical perspective to other subfields of psychology such as environmental, social, and clinical as well as developmental (Wapner, 1995). Here, we point to an area that we have not touched on earlier, namely, extension of the person-in-environment unit of analysis so that the role of group and of organization is included. This may be done by examining the individual-in-group (e.g., impact of group composition on the individual's attitudes and behavior), individual-in-organization (e.g., effects of organizational culture on transactions of the individual), group-in-organization (e.g., how intragroup characteristics influence organizations), and organization-in-environment systems (e.g., influence of the organization on the environmental context in which it is located; Mayo et al., 1995).

In a similar manner, Minami and Tanaka (1995) have recently explored the concept of group space (e.g., space use by group members and effect of rules concerning space on transactions of the person in the setting). With such extensions of the conceptualization, the theoretical approach encompasses numerous studies already conducted and operates as a heuristic device that leads to new areas of research. Within such an approach, we see new problems relevant to development. For example, such developmentally oriented research problems become focal as the microgenetic development of an organization, a group, and an individual in different organizational contexts.

There are many other illustrations that can be brought to bear that point to the heuristic value of the approach, such as the study of *individual differences* in experiencing, acting, and coping. However, it is important to add that the perspective serves an important role in counteracting the growing diversity of psychology (see Altman, 1987; Wapner, 1995; Wapner & Demick, 1991b) and, through its formal characterization that applies to numerous content areas, serves to help develop a psychology that is differentiated and hierarchically integrated.

CONCLUSIONS

Inroads have been made in elaborating and extending Werner's (1940/1957) organismic-developmental approach to the analysis of person-in-environment functioning more generally. The elaborated holistic, developmental, systems-oriented approach has been characterized in terms of our broader views of the person, of the environment, and of development. This approach, focusing on formal, organizational characteristics of systems, has broad applicability to diverse content areas of psychology, including but not limited to child development.

As we see it, we strongly disagree with those who might argue that Wernerian theory is a historical relic (see Crain, 1992). As we hope we have illustrated, the original approach and its current elaboration have generated both theoretical and practical research for the past 50 years and will continue to do so for some years to come.

ACKNOWLEDGMENTS

The authors wish to express their deep appreciation to Margery Franklin and Richard M. Lerner for their constructive comments on an early version of this chapter.

REFERENCES

Agli, S. (1992). *General factors and precipitating events involved in the cessation of alcohol consumption among college women.* Honor's thesis, Clark University, Worcester, MA.

Ainsworth, M. D., & Wittig, B. A. (1969). Attachment and exploratory behavior of one-year-old children in a Strange Situation. In B. M. Goss (Ed.), *Determinants of infant behavior* (Vol. 4, pp. 111–136). London: Methuen.

Altman, I. (1987). Centripetal and centrifugal trends in psychology. *American Psychologist, 42,* 1058–1069.

Altman, I. (1997). Environment and behavior studies: A discipline? Not a discipline? Becoming a discipline? In S. Wapner, J. Demick, T. Yamamoto, & T. Takahashi (Eds.), *Handbook of Japan-U.S. environment-behavior research: Toward a transactional approach* (pp. 423–434). New York: Plenum Press.

Altman, I., & Rogoff, B. (1987). World views in psychology: Trait, interactional, organismic and transactional perspectives. In D. Stokols & I. Altman (Eds.), *Handbook of environmental psychology* (pp. 7–40). New York: Wiley.

Apter, D. (1976). *Modes of coping with conflict in the presently inhabited environment as a function of plans to move to a new environment.* Unpublished master's thesis, Clark University, Worcester, MA.

Arieti, S. (Ed.). (1959). *American handbook of psychiatry* (Vol. 3). New York: Basic Books.

Ayala, F. J. (1970). Teleological explanations in evolutionary biology. *Philosophy of Science, 37,* 1–15.

Azar, S. T. (1986). A framework for understanding child maltreatment: An integration of cognitive behavioural and developmental perspectives. *Canadian Journal of Behavioural Science, 18*(4), 340–355.

Azar, S. T. (1989). Training parents of abused children. In C. E. Schaefer & J. M. Briesmeister (Eds.), *Handbook of parent training: Parents as co-therapists for children's behavior problems* (pp. 414–441). New York: Wiley.

Azar, S. T. (1991). *The determinants of "maladaptive" parenting: Validation of a social cognitive model.* Paper presented at the New Direction in Child and Family Research: Shaping Head Start in the Nineties Conference, Arlington, VA.

Baker, R. W. (1953). *The acquisition of verbal concepts in schizophrenia: A developmental approach to the study of disturbed language behavior.* Doctoral dissertation (Microfilm No. 13009), Clark University, Worcester, MA.

Bamberg, M., Budwig, N., & Kaplan, B. (1991). A developmental approach to language acquisition: Two case studies. *First Language, 11,* 121–141.

Barten, S. S., & Franklin, M. B. (Eds.). (1978). *Developmental processes: Heinz Werner's selected writings* (Vols. 1 & 2). New York: International Universities Press.

Barton, M. I. (1964). *Aspects of object and body perception in hemiplegics: An organismic-developmental approach.* Doctoral dissertation (Microfilm No. 64-1360), Clark University, Worcester, MA.

Berry, J. W. (1991). Cultural variations in field dependence-independence. In S. Wapner & J. Demick (Eds.), *Field dependence-independence: Cognitive style across the life span.* Hillsdale, NJ: Erlbaum.

Bertini, G., & Wapner, S. (1992). *Automobile seat belt use in Italy prior to and following legislation.* Unpublished study, Clark University, Worcester, MA.

Bertini, M., Braibanti, P., & Wapner, S. (1996). *Sleep-wake phenomena from a holistic, developmental, systems-oriented perspective.* Manuscript in preparation.

Bibace, R., Schmidt, L. R., & Walsh, M. E. (1994). Children's perceptions of illness. In G. N. Penny, P. Bennett, & M. Herbert (Eds.), *Health psychology: A lifespan perspective* (pp. 13–30). Chur, Switzerland: Harwood Academic.

Blake, R. R., & Ramsey, G. V. (1951). *Perception: An approach to personality.* New York: Ronald Press.

Blane, H. T. (1957). *Space perception among unilaterally paralyzed children and adults.* Doctoral dissertation (Microfilm No. 23893), Clark University, Worcester, MA.

Bruner J. S., & Goodman, C. C. (1947). Value and need as organizing factors in perception. *Journal of Abnormal and Social Psychology, 42,* 33–44.

Bruner, J. S., & Klein, G. (1960). The function of perceiving: New look retrospect. In B. Kaplan & S. Wapner (Eds.), *Perspectives in psychological theory* (pp. 161–177). New York: International Universities Press.

Campbell, D. T. (1974). "Downward causation" in hierarchically organized biological systems. In F. J. Ayala & T. Dobzhansky (Eds.), *Studies in the philosophy of biology.* London: Macmillan.

Cantril, H. (Ed.). (1950). *The why of man's experience.* New York: Macmillan.

Chandler, K. A. (1953). *The effect of moving and non-moving visual stimuli upon head torsion.* Doctoral dissertation (Microfilm No. 5837), Clark University, Worcester, MA.

Chea, W. E., & Wapner, S. (1995). Retrospections of Bahamians concerning the impact of hurricane Andrew. In J. L. Nasar, P. Grannis, & K. Hanyu (Eds.), *Proceedings of the twenty-sixth annual conference of the Environmental Design Research Association* (pp. 87–92). Oklahoma City, OK: Environmental Design Research Association.

Ciottone, R. A., Demick, J., Pacheco, A. P., Quirk, M. E., & Wapner, S. (1980, November 16–20). *Children's transition from home to nursery school: The integration of two cultures.* Paper presented at the American Association of Psychiatric Services for Children (AAPSC), New Orleans, LA.

Ciottone, R. A., & Quirk, M. (1985). *The integration of two worlds: Home and preschool.* Paper presented as part of a symposium on Environmental Psychology: In Search of a Theory at the annual meeting of the Eastern Psychological Association, Boston, MA.

Clark, E. F. (1995). *Women's self-reported experience and action in relation to protection against sexual transmission of HIV: A randomized comparison study of those interventions.* Doctoral dissertation, Clark University, Worcester, MA.

Collazo, J. (1985). *Transition from health to illness: Experiential changes following the onset of diabetes.* Presented as part of a symposium on Environmental Psychology: In Search of a Theory at the annual meeting of the Eastern Psychological Association, Boston, MA.

Coltrera, D. (1978). *Experiential aspects of the transition to parenthood.* Master's thesis proposal, Clark University, Worcester, MA.

Comalli, P. E., Jr., Wapner, S., & Werner, H. (1959). Perception of verticality in middle and old age. *Journal of Psychology, 47,* 259–266.

Crain, W. (1992). *Theories of development: Concepts and applications* (3rd ed.). Englewood Cliffs, NJ: Prentice-Hall.

Dandonoli, P., Demick, J., & Wapner, S. (1990). Physical arrangement and age as determinants of environmental representation. *Children's Environments Quarterly, 7*(1), 26–36.

Demick, J. (1993). Adaptation of marital couples to open versus closed adoption: A preliminary investigation. In J. Demick,

K. Bursik, & R. DiBiase (Eds.), *Parental development* (pp. 175–201). Hillsdale, NJ: Erlbaum.

Demick, J. (1995). *Socioemotional development of adoptees and their parents.* Paper presented at the Symposium on Social and Emotional Development of Children in Adoption: Cross-National Perspectives, Society for Research in Child Development biennial meeting, Indianapolis, IN.

Demick, J., & Andreoletti, C. (1995). Some relations between clinical and environmental psychology. *Environment and Behavior, 27*(1), 56–72.

Demick, J., Damrad, R., & Stern, S. (1989). *Effects of open versus closed adoption: Adoptive couples.* Paper presented at the Eastern Psychological Association annual meeting, Boston, MA.

Demick, J., Hoffman, A., & Wapner, S. (1985). Residential context and environmental change as determinants of urban experience. *Children's Environments Quarterly, 2*(3), 44–54.

Demick, J., Inoue, W., Wapner, S., Ishii, S., Minami, H., Nishiyama, S., & Yamamoto, T. (1992). Cultural differences in impact of governmental legislation: Automobile safety belt usage. *Journal of Cross-Cultural Psychology, 23*(4), 468–487.

Demick, J., Ishii, S., & Inoue, W. (1997). Body and self experience. In S. Wapner, J. Demick, T. Yamamoto, & T. Takahashi (Eds.), *Handbook of Japan-U.S. environment-behavior research: Toward a transactional approach* (pp. 83–99). New York: Plenum Press.

Demick, J., & Peicott, J. (1984). *Temporal changes in hospitalized alcoholics' cognitive organization of space.* Paper presented at the American Psychological Association annual meeting, Toronto, Canada.

Demick, J., Peicott, J., & Wapner, S. (1985). *Temporal changes in hospitalized alcoholic's self-world relationships.* Presented at the American Psychological Association annual convention, Los Angeles, CA.

Demick, J., Salas-Passeri, J., & Wapner, S. (1986). *Age differences among preschoolers in processes underlying sequential activity.* Paper presented at the annual meeting of the Eastern Psychological Association, New York.

Demick, J., & Wapner, S. (1980). Effect of environmental relocation upon members of a psychiatric therapeutic community. *Journal of Abnormal Psychology, 89,* 444–452.

Demick, J., & Wapner, S. (1985). *Age differences in processes underlying sequential activity (Stroop Color-Word Test).* Paper presented at the American Psychological Association annual meeting, Los Angeles, CA.

Demick, J., & Wapner, S. (1987). *A holistic, developmental approach to body experience.* Paper presented at the "Body

Experience and Literature: An Interdisciplinary Conference," SUNY-Buffalo, Buffalo, NY.

Demick, J., & Wapner, S. (1988a). Open and closed adoption: A developmental conceptualization. *Family Process, 27*(2), 229–249.

Demick, J., & Wapner, S. (1988b). Children-in-environments: Physical, interpersonal, and sociocultural aspects. *Children's Environments Quarterly, 5*(3), 54–62.

Demick, J., & Wapner, S. (1990). Role of psychological science in promoting environmental quality. *American Psychologist, 45,* 631–632.

Demick, J., & Wapner, S. (1991). Field dependence-independence in adult development and aging. In S. Wapner & J. Demick (Eds.), *Field dependence-independence: Cognitive style across the life span.* Hillsdale, NJ: Erlbaum.

Demick J., & Wapner, S. (1992). Transition to parenthood: Developmental changes in experience and action. In T. Yamamoto & S. Wapner (Eds.), *Developmental psychology of life transitions* (pp. 243–265). Kyoto, Japan: Kitaohji.

Demick J., & Wapner, S. (1996). *A holistic, developmental, systems-oriented approach to body experience.* Unpublished manuscript, Clark University, Worcester, MA.

DesLauriers, A. (1962). *The experience of reality in childhood schizophrenia.* New York: International Universities Press.

Dewey, J., & Bentley, A. F. (1949). *Knowing and the known.* Boston: Beacon Press.

Dyl, J., & Wapner, S. (1996). Age and gender differences in the nature, meaning, and function of cherished possessions for children and adolescents. *Journal of Experimental Child Psychology, 62,* 340–377.

Ellefsen, K. F. (1987). *Entry into nursery school: Children's transactions as a function of experience and age.* Unpublished master's thesis, Clark University, Worcester, MA.

Feibelman, J. K. (1954). Theory of integrative levels. *British Journal of Philosophy of Science, 5,* 59–66.

Ferguson, E., Wapner, S., & Quirk, M. (1993, April 16–18). *Sexual behavior in relation to protection against transmission of HIV in college students.* Paper presented at the annual meeting of the Eastern Psychological Association, Arlington, VA.

Ford, D. H., & Lerner, R. M. (1992). *Developmental systems theory: An integrative approach.* Newbury Park, CA: Sage.

Fraenkel, G. S., & Gunn, D. L. (1961). *The orientation of animals: Kinesis, taxes, and compass reactions.* New York: Dover. (Original work published 1940)

Franklin, M. B. (1990). Reshaping psychology at Clark: The Werner era. *Journal of the History of the Behavioral Sciences, 26,* 176–189.

Frey, J., Demick, J., & Bibace, R. (1981). Variations in physicians' feelings of control in a family practice residency. *Journal of Medical Education, 56,* 50–56.

Friedman, H. (1953). Perceptual regression in schizophrenia: An hypothesis suggested by the use of the Rorschach test. *Journal of Genetic Psychology, 81,* 63–98.

Galinsky, E. (1981). *Between generations: The six stages of parenthood.* New York: Berkeley Books.

Gallistel, C. R. (1980). *The organization of action: A new synthesis.* Hillsdale, NJ: Erlbaum.

Gesell, A., & Ilg, F. L. (1943). *Infant and child in the culture of today.* New York: Harper.

Giorgi, A. (1970). Towards phenomenologically based research in psychology. *Journal of Phenomenological Psychology, 1,* 75–98.

Giorgi, A. (1971). *Duquesne studies in phenomenological psychology* (Vol. 1). Pittsburgh, PA: Duquesne University Press.

Giorgi, A. (1975). *Duquesne studies in phenomenological psychology* (Vol. 2). Pittsburgh, PA: Duquesne University Press.

Glick, J. (1992). Werner's relevance for contemporary developmental psychology. *Developmental Psychology, 28,* 558–565.

Goldstein, K. (1942). The two ways of adjustment of the organism to cerebral defects. *Journal of Mount Sinai Hospital, 9,* 504–518.

Goldstein, K. (1960). Sensory-tonic theory and the concept of self realization. In B. Kaplan & S. Wapner (Eds.), *Perspectives in psychological theory.* New York: International Universities Press.

Guyette, A., Wapner, S., Werner, H., & Davidson, J. (1964). Some aspects of space perception in mental retardates. *American Journal of Mental Deficiency, 69,* 90–100.

Hanson, K., & Wapner, S. (1994). Transition to retirement: Gender differences. *International Journal of Aging and Human Development, 39*(3), 189–208.

Helson, H. (1948). Adaptation level as basis for a quantitative theory of frame of reference. *Psychological Review, 55,* 297–313.

Hemmendinger, L. (1951). *A genetic study of structural aspects of perception as reflected in Rorschach responses.* Doctoral dissertation (Microfilm No. AAG0274469), Clark University, Worcester, MA.

Herrick, C. J. (1949). A biological survey of integrative levels. In R. W. Sellars, V. J. McGill, & M. Farber (Eds.), *Philosophy for the future* (pp. 222–242). New York: Macmillan.

Hofstadter, A. (1941). Objective teleology. *Journal of Philosophy, 38,* 29–39.

Hornstein, G. A., & Wapner, S. (1984). The experience of the retiree's social network during the transition to retirement.

In C. M. Aanstoos (Ed.), *Exploring the lived world: Readings in phenomenological psychology* (pp. 119–136). Carrollton, GA: Georgia College Press.

Hornstein, G. A., & Wapner, S. (1985). Modes of experiencing and adapting to retirement. *International Journal on Aging and Human Development, 21*(4), 291–315.

Ittelson, W. H. (1973). Environmental perception and contemporary perceptual theory. In W. H. Ittelson (Ed.), *Environment and cognition* (pp. 1–19). New York: Seminar Press.

Kaplan, B. (1959). The study of language in psychiatry. In S. Arieti (Ed.), *American handbook of psychiatry* (Vol. 3, pp. 659–668). New York: Basic Books.

Kaplan, B. (1967). Meditations on genesis. *Human Development, 10*, 65–87.

Kaplan, B. (1983). Genetic dramatism: Old wine in new bottles. In S. Wapner & B. Kaplan (Eds.), *Toward a holistic, developmental psychology* (pp. 53–74). Hillsdale, NJ: Erlbaum.

Kaplan, B., Pemstein, D., Cohen, S. B., & Wapner, S. (1974). *A new methodology for studying the processes underlying the experience of a new environment: Self-observation and group debriefing.* Working notes.

Kaplan, B., Wapner, S., & Cohen, S. B. (1976). Exploratory applications of the organismic-developmental approach to man-in-environment transactions. In S. Wapner, S. B. Cohen, & B. Kaplan (Eds.), *Experiencing the environment* (pp. 207–233). New York: Plenum Press.

Kaplan, E. (1952). *An experimental study on inner speech as contrasted with external speech.* Unpublished master's thesis, Clark University, Worcester, MA.

Kaplan, E. (1983). Process and achievement revisited. In S. Wapner & B. Kaplan (Eds.), *Toward a holistic, developmental psychology.* Hillsdale, NJ: Erlbaum.

King, K. (1995). *Women's experience and action following the dissolution of a love relationship.* Unpublished manuscript, Clark University, Worcester, MA.

Koerber, H., & Demick, J. (1991). *Relations among cognitive styles and reading readiness in preschoolers.* Paper presented at the annual meeting of the Eastern Psychological Association, New York.

Koffka, K. (1935). *Principles of gestalt psychology.* New York: Harcourt Brace.

Kuntz, P. G. (1968). *The concept of order.* Seattle: University of Washington Press.

Langer, J. (1970). Werner's comparative organismic theory. In P. H. Mussen (Ed.), *Carmichael's manual of child psychology* (3rd ed., pp. 733–771). New York: Wiley.

Lavine, T. (1950a). Knowledge as interpretation: An historical survey. *Philosophy and Phenomenological Research, 10*, 526–540.

Lavine, T. (1950b). Knowledge as interpretation: An historical survey. *Philosophy and Phenomenological Research, 11*, 80–103.

Lewin, K. (1935). *A dynamic theory of personality.* New York: McGraw-Hill.

Liebert, R. S., Wapner, S., & Werner, H. (1957). Studies in the effect of lysergic acid diethylamide (LSD-25): Visual perception of verticality in schizophrenic and normal adults. *AMA Archives of Neurology and Psychiatry, 77*, 193–201.

Liebert, R. S., Werner, H., & Wapner, S. (1958). Studies in the effect of lysergic acid diethylamide (LSD-25): Self- and object-size perception in schizophrenic and normal adults. *AMA Archives of Neurology and Psychiatry, 79*, 580–584.

Lifton, R. J. (1965). On death and death symbolism: The Hiroshima disaster. *American Scholar, 34*, 257–272.

Lucca-Irizarry, N., Wapner, S., & Pacheco, A. M. (1981). Adolescent return migration to Puerto Rico: Self-identity and bilingualism. *Agenda: A Journal of Hispanic Issues, 11*, 15–17, 33.

Lucy, J. A. (1992). *Language diversity and thought: A reformulation of the linguistic relativity hypothesis.* New York: Cambridge University Press.

Luria, A. R. (1972). *Man with a shattered world.* New York: Basic Books.

Maslow, A. H. (1946). Problem-centering vs. means-centering in science. *Philosophy of Science, 13*, 326–331.

Mayo, M., Pastor, J. C., & Wapner, S. (1995). Linking organizational behavior and environmental psychology: Relations between environmental psychology and allied fields. *Environment and Behavior, 27*(1), 73–89.

Minami, H. (1985a). *Development of personal networks during the first year of college.* Paper presented as part of a symposium on Environmental Psychology: In Search of a Theory at the annual meeting of the Eastern Psychological Association, Boston, MA.

Minami, H. (1985b). *Establishment and transformation of personal networks during the first year of college: A developmental analysis.* Doctoral dissertation, Clark University, Worcester, MA.

Minami, H., & Tanaka, K. (1995). Social and environmental psychology: Transaction between physical space and group-dynamic processes. *Environment and Behavior, 27*(1), 43–55.

Mirin, B. (1955). A study of the formal aspects of schizophrenic verbal communication. *Genetic Psychology Monographs, 52*(2), 149–190.

Morant, R. B. (1952). *Factors influencing the apparent median plane under conditions of labyrinthian stimulation.* Doctoral dissertation (Microfilm No. AAG0181729), Clark University, Worcester, MA.

Morgan, R., & Cushing, D. (1966). The personal possessions of long stay patients in mental hospitals. *Social Psychiatry, 1*(3), 151–157.

Nair, P. J. (1961). *Distancing: The application of a developmental construct to learning disability.* Doctoral dissertation (Microfilm No. 61/05008), Clark University, Worcester, MA.

Neuhaus, E. C. (1988). *A developmental approach to children's planning.* Doctoral dissertation (Microfilm No. AAG882580), Clark University, Worcester, MA.

Novikoff, A. B. (1945a). The concept of integrative levels and biology. *Science, 101,* 209–215.

Novikoff, A. B. (1945b). Continuity and discontinuity in evolution. *Science, 101,* 405–406.

Pacheco, A. M., Lucca, N., & Wapner, S. (1985). The assessment of interpersonal relations among Puerto Rican migrant adolescents. In R. Riaz-Guerrero (Ed.), *Cross-cultural and national studies in social psychology* (pp. 169–175). Amsterdam, The Netherlands: Elsevier Science.

Pacheco, A. M., Wapner, S., & Lucca, N. (1979). Migration as a critical person-in-environment transition: An organismic-developmental interpretation. *Revista de Ciencias Sociales (Social Sciences Journal), 2l,* 123–157.

Pepper, S. C. (1942). *World hypotheses.* Berkeley: University of California Press.

Pepper, S. C. (1967). *Concept and quality: A world hypothesis.* LaSalle, IL: Open Court.

Phillips, L., & Framo, J. (1954). Developmental theory applied to normal and psychopathological perception. *Journal of Personality, 22,* 464–474.

Piaget, J. (1952). *The origins of intelligence in children.* New York: International Universities Press.

Quirk, M., Ciottone, R., Letendre, D., & Wapner, S. (1986). *Critical person-in-environment transitions in medical education.* Paper presented as part of the symposium Person-in-Environment Transitions Following Change in Person, in Environment, or in Both, at the 21st International Association of Applied Psychology Congress, Jerusalem, Israel.

Quirk, M., Ciottone, R., Letendre, D., & Wapner, S. (1987). Critical person-in-environment transitions in medical education. *Medical Teacher, 9,* 415–423.

Quirk, M., Ciottone, R., Minami, H., Wapner, S., Yamamoto, T., Ishii, S., Lucca-Irizarry, N., & Pacheco, A. (1986). Values mothers hold for handicapped and non-handicapped

pre-school children in Japan, Puerto Rico, and the United States mainland. *International Journal of Psychology, 21,* 463–485.

Quirk, M., Sexton, M., Ciottone, R., Minami, H., & Wapner, S. (1984). Values mothers hold for handicapped and for non-handicapped preschoolers. *Merrill-Palmer Quarterly, 30*(4), 403–418.

Quirk, M., & Wapner, S. (1991). Notes on an organismic-developmental systems perspective for health education. *Health Education Research, 6*(2), 203–210.

Quirk, M., & Wapner, S. (1995). Environmental psychology and health. *Environment and Behavior, 27*(1), 90–99.

Quirk, M., & Young, M. (1990). The impact of JRA on adolescents and their families: Current research and implications for future studies. *Arthritis Care and Research, 3,* 107–114.

Raeff, C. (1990). *General factors and precipitating events influencing action: Initiation of a weight loss regimen.* Master's thesis, Clark University, Worcester, MA.

Rand, G., & Wapner, S. (1967). Postural status as a factor in memory. *Journal of Verbal Learning and Verbal Behavior, 6,* 268–271.

Rand, G., & Wapner, S. (1969). Ontogenetic changes in the identification of simple forms in complex contexts. *Human Development, 12,* 155–169.

Rand, G., Wapner, S., Werner, H., & McFarland, J. H. (1963). Age differences in performance on the Stroop Color-Word Test. *Journal of Personality, 31,* 534–558.

Redondo, J. P. (1983). *Migration as a critical transition: A comparison of the experience of Puerto Rican and Cuban adolescents.* Doctoral dissertation, Clark University, Worcester, MA.

Rioux, S., & Wapner, S. (1986). Commitment to use of automobile seat belts: An experiential analysis. *Journal of Environmental Psychology, 6,* 189–204.

Roelke, D. T. (1989). *A comparison of close and non-close friendships: Shared worlds and contributions to social support.* Doctoral dissertation, Clark University, Worcester, MA.

Sameroff, D. J. (1983). Developmental systems: Contexts and evolution. In P. H. Mussen (Ed.), *Handbook of child psychology* (Vol. 1, pp. 237–294). New York: Wiley.

Sapir, E. (1956). In D. G. Mandelbaum (Ed.), *Culture, language and personality: Selected essays.* Berkeley: University of California Press.

Schaffer, G. (1991). *College students' cherished possessions: Their nature and role in adaptation.* Doctoral dissertation, Clark University, Worcester, MA.

Schlater, J. A., Baker, A. H., & Wapner, S. (1981). Apparent arm length with active versus passive touch. *Bulletin of the Psychonomic Society, 18,* 151–154.

Schneirla, T. C. (1949). Levels in the psychological capacities of animals. In R. W. Sellars, V. J. McGill, & M. Farber (Eds.), *Philosophy for the future.* New York: Macmillan.

Schouela, D. A., Steinberg, L. M., Leveton, L. B., & Wapner, S. (1980). Development of the cognitive organization of an environment. *Canadian Journal of Behavioural Science, 12,* 1–16.

Schutz, A. (1971). In M. Natanson (Ed.), *Collected papers* (Vols. 1–3). The Hague, Netherlands: Nijhoff.

Secord, P., & Jourard, S. (1953). The appraisal of body cathexis: Body cathexis and the self. *Journal of Consulting Psychology, 17,* 343–347.

Shapiro, E. (1973, April). *The effect of verbalization of plans on sequence learning by children and adults.* Paper presented at the University of New Hampshire Psychology Conference, Durham, NH.

Shapiro, E., Rierdan, J., & Wapner, S. (1972). *Effect of articulating plans of how to solve a sequence learning task on the learning of this task by children and adults.* Unpublished manuscript, Clark University, Worcester, MA.

Silverstein, D., & Demick, J. (1994). Toward an organizational-relational model of open adoption. *Family Process, 33*(2), 111–124.

Simeons, A. (1961). *A man's presumptuous brain.* New York: Dutton.

Slepian, H. J. (1959). *A developmental study of inner vs. external speech in normals and schizophrenics.* Doctoral dissertation, (Microfilm No. AAG5906194), Clark University, Worcester, MA.

Soparker, K., Demick, J., Levin, R., & Wapner, S. (1988). *Community attitudes towards open versus closed adoption.* Paper presented at the annual meetings of the Eastern Psychological Association, Buffalo, NY.

Stein, D. G. (1988). *Development and plasticity in the CNS: Organismic and environmental influences.* Worcester, MA: Clark University Press.

Stroop, J. R. (1935). Studies of interference in serial verbal reactions. *Journal of Experimental Psychology, 18,* 643–661.

Thomason, D. L. (1985). *A developmental analysis of friendship.* Master's thesis, Clark University, Worcester, MA.

Thompson, N. S. (1987). Ethology and the birth of comparative telenomy. In R. Compan & R. Zayan (Eds.), *Relevance of models and theories in ethology.* France: Privat I.E.C.

Tirelli, L. (1992). *Resistance from and attempts to stop smoking.* Manuscript on file, Clark University, Worcester, MA.

Toshima, T., Demick, S., Miyatani, M., Ishii, S., & Wapner, S. (1996). Cross-cultural differences in processes underlying sequential cognitive activity. *Journal of Japanese Psychological Research, 38*(2), 90–96.

Toshima, T., Toma, C., Demick, J., & Wapner, S. (1990). Age and cross-cultural differences in processes underlying sequential cognitive activity. In B. Wilpert, H. Motoaki, & J. Misumi (Eds.), *General psychology and environmental psychology. Proceedings of the 22nd International Congress of Applied Psychology* (Vol. 2, p. 189). Hillsdale, NJ: Erlbaum.

Turvey, M. T. (1977). Preliminaries to a theory of action with reference to vision. In R. Shaw & J. Bransford (Eds.), *Perceiving, acting, and knowing.* Hillsdale, NJ: Erlbaum.

Von Uexküll, J. (1957). A stroll through the world of animals and men. In C. H. Schiller (Ed.), *Instinctive behavior.* New York: International Universities Press.

Wapner, S. (1966). An organismic-developmental approach to perceived body-object relations. In N. Jenkin & R. H. Pollack (Eds.), *Proceedings of a conference on perceptual development: Its relation to theories of intelligence and cognition.* Chicago: Institute for Juvenile Research.

Wapner, S. (1968). Age changes in perception of verticality and of the longitudinal body axis under body tilt. *Journal of Experimental Child Psychology, 6,* 543–555.

Wapner, S. (1969). Organismic-developmental theory: Some applications to cognition. In J. Langer, P. Mussen, & N. Covington (Eds.), *Trends and issues in developmental theory* (pp. 35–67). New York: Holt, Rinehart and Winston.

Wapner, S. (1976). Process and context in the conception of cognitive style. In S. Messick (Ed.), *Individuality in learning: Implications of cognitive styles and creativity in human development.* San Francisco: Jossey-Bass.

Wapner, S. (1977). Environmental transition: A research paradigm deriving from the organismic-developmental systems approach. In L. van Ryzin (Ed.), *Wisconsin Conference on Research Methods in Behavior Environment Studies Proceedings* (pp. 1–9). Madison: University of Wisconsin.

Wapner, S. (1978). Some critical person-environment transitions. *Hiroshima Forum for Psychology, 5,* 3–20.

Wapner, S. (1981). Transactions of persons-in-environments: Some critical transitions. *Journal of Environmental Psychology, 1,* 223–239.

Wapner, S. (1983). Living with radical disruptions of person-in-environment systems. *IATSS Review, 9*(2), 133–148.

Wapner, S. (1986). *An organismic-developmental systems approach to the analysis of experience and action.* Paper presented at the conference on Holistic Approaches to the

Analysis of Experience and Action, University of Catania, Sicily, Italy.

Wapner, S. (1987). A holistic, developmental, systems-oriented environmental psychology: Some beginnings. In D. Stokols & I. Altman (Eds.), *Handbook of environmental psychology* (pp. 1433–1465). New York: Wiley.

Wapner, S. (1990). Introduction: Psychology at Clark University. *Journal of the History of the Behavioral Sciences, 26,* 107–113.

Wapner, S. (1993). Parental development: A holistic, developmental systems-oriented perspective. In J. Demick, K. Bursik, & R. DiBiase (Eds.), *Parental development* (pp. 3–37). Hillsdale, NJ: Erlbaum.

Wapner, S. (1995). Toward integration: Environmental psychology in relation to other sub-fields of psychology. *Environment and Behavior, 27,* 9–32.

Wapner, S., Ciottone, R., Hornstein, G., McNeil, O., & Pacheco, A. M. (1983). An examination of studies of critical transitions through the life cycle. In S. Wapner & B. Kaplan (Eds.), *Toward a holistic developmental psychology* (pp. 111–132). Hillsdale, NJ: Erlbaum.

Wapner, S., & Cirillo, L. (1973). *Development of planning* (Public Health Service Grant Application). Worcester, MA: Clark University.

Wapner, S., Cirillo, L., & Baker, A. H. (1969). Sensory-tonic theory: Toward a reformulation. *Archivio di Psicologia Neurologia Psichiatria, 30,* 493–512.

Wapner, S., Cirillo, L., & Baker, A. H. (1971). Some aspects of the development of space perception. In J. P. Hill (Ed.), *Minnesota Symposia on Child Psychology* (Vol. 5, pp. 162–204). Minneapolis: University of Minnesota Press.

Wapner, S., & Craig-Bray, L. (1992). Person-in-environment transition: Theoretical and methodological approaches. *Environment and Behavior, 24,* 161–188.

Wapner, S., & Demick, J. (1987). *Some relations among cognition, emotion and action: A holistic, developmental approach.* Paper presented at the third annual meeting of the International Society for Research on Emotions, Worcester, MA.

Wapner, S., & Demick, J. (1990). Development of experience and action: Levels of integration in human functioning. In G. Greenberg & E. Tobach (Eds.), *Theories of the evolution of knowing. The T. C. Schneirla Conference Series* (Vol. 4, pp. 47–68). Hillsdale, NJ: Erlbaum.

Wapner, S., & Demick, J. (1991a). Some relations between developmental and environmental psychology: An organismic-developmental systems perspective. In R. M. Downs, L. S. Liben, & D. S. Palermo (Eds.), *Visions of aesthetics, the environment and development: The legacy of Joachim Wohlwill* (pp. 181–211). Hillsdale, NJ: Erlbaum.

Wapner, S., & Demick, J. (Eds.). (1991b). *Field dependence-independence: Cognitive style across the life span.* Hillsdale, NJ: Erlbaum.

Wapner, S., & Demick, J. (1992). The organismic-developmental, systems approach to the study of critical person-in-environment transitions through the life span. In T. Yamamoto & S. Wapner (Eds.), *Developmental psychology of life transitions* (pp. 25–49). Kyoto, Japan: Kitaohji.

Wapner, S., & Demick, J. (1996). *Relations between cognition and affect: A holistic developmental, systems-oriented approach.* Unpublished manuscript, Clark University, Worcester, MA.

Wapner, S., & Demick, J. (in press). Developmental theory and clinical child psychology: A holistic, developmental, systems-oriented approach. In W. K. Silverman & T. H. Ollendick (Eds.), *Developmental issues in the clinical treatment of children and adolescents.* Boston: Allyn & Bacon.

Wapner, S., Demick, J., & Damrad, R. (1988). *Transition to retirement: Eight years after.* Paper presented at the annual meetings of Eastern Psychological Association, Buffalo, NY.

Wapner, S., Demick, J., Inoue, W., Ishii, S., & Yamamoto, T. (1986). Relations between experience and action: Automobile seat belt usage in Japan and the United States. In W. H. Ittelson, M. Asai, & M. Carr (Eds.), *Proceedings of the second USA/Japan Seminar on Environment and Behavior* (pp. 279–295). Tucson, AZ: Department of Psychology, University of Arizona.

Wapner, S., Demick, J., & Redondo, J. P. (1990). Cherished possessions and adaptation of older people to nursing homes. *International Journal of Aging and Human Development, 31*(3), 299–315.

Wapner, S., Demick, J., Yamamoto, T., & Takahashi, T. (1997). *Handbook of Japan-US environment-behavior research: Toward a transactional approach.* New York: Plenum Press.

Wapner, S., Inoue, W., Fujimoto, J., Imamachi, T., & Toews, K. (1997). Sojourn in a new culture: Japanese students in American universities and American students in Japanese universities. In S. Wapner, J. Demick, T. Yamamoto, & T. Takahashi (Eds.), *Handbook of Japan-US environment-behavior research: Toward a transactional approach* (pp. 283–312). New York: Plenum Press.

Wapner, S., & Kaplan, B. (Eds.). (1966). *Heinz Werner: 1890–1964.* Worcester, MA: Clark University Press.

Wapner, S., & Kaplan, B. (Eds.). (1983). *Toward a holistic developmental psychology.* Hillsdale, NJ: Erlbaum.

Wapner, S., Kaplan, B., & Ciottone, R. (1981). Self-world relationships in critical environmental transitions: Childhood and beyond. In L. Liben, A. Patterson, & N. Newcombe (Eds.), *Spatial representation and behavior across the life span* (pp. 251–282). New York: Academic Press.

Wapner, S., Kaplan, B., & Cohen, S. B. (1973/1980). An organismic-developmental perspective for understanding transactions of men in environments. In G. Broadbent, R. Bunt, & T. Llorens (Eds.), *Meaning and behavior in the built environment.* New York: Wiley.

Wapner, S., Kaplan, B., & Cohen, S. B. (Eds.). (1976). *Experiencing the environment.* New York: Plenum Press.

Wapner, S., & Lebensfeld-Schwartz, P. (1976). Toward a structural analysis of event experience. *Acta Psychologica, 41,* 308–401.

Wapner, S., & Rand, G. (1968). Ontogenetic differences in the nature of organization underlying serial learning. *Human Development, 11,* 249–259.

Wapner, S., & Werner, H. (1957). *Perceptual development.* Worcester, MA: Clark University Press.

Wapner, S., & Werner, H. (1965). An experimental approach to body perception from the organismic-developmental point of view. In S. Wapner & H. Werner (Eds.), *The body percept.* New York: International Universities Press.

Wapner, S., Werner, H., & Chandler, K. A. (1951). Experiments on sensory-tonic field theory of perception: II. Effect of extraneous stimulation on the visual perception of verticality. *Journal of Experimental Psychology, 42,* 341–345.

Wapner, S., Werner, H., & Morant, R. B. (1951). Experiments on sensory-tonic field theory of perception: IV. Effect of initial position of a rod on apparent verticality. *Journal of Experimental Psychology, 43,* 68–74.

Watkins, M. (1977). *A phenomenological approach to organismic-developmental research.* Unpublished manuscript, Clark University, Worcester, MA.

Werner, H. (1926). *Einführung in die Entwicklungspsychologie.* Leipsig: Barth.

Werner, H. (1937). Process and achievement: A basic problem of education and developmental psychology. *Harvard Educational Review, 7,* 353–368.

Werner, H. (1940/1957). *Comparative psychology of mental development.* New York: International Universities Press. (Originally published in German, 1926 and in English, 1940)

Werner, H. (1957). The concept of development from a comparative and organismic point of view. In D. B. Harris (Ed.), *The concept of development: An issue in the study of human behavior.* Minneapolis: University of Minnesota Press.

Werner, H., & Kaplan, B. (1956). The developmental approach to cognition: Its relevance to the psychological interpretation of anthropological and ethnolinguistic data. *American Anthropologist, 58,* 866–880.

Werner, H., & Kaplan, B. (1963). *Symbol formation.* New York: Wiley.

Werner, H., & Kaplan, E. (1950). Word context test. *British Journal of Psychology, 45,* 134–136.

Werner, H., & Wapner, S. (1949). Sensory-tonic field theory of perception. *Journal of Personality, 18,* 88–107.

Werner, H., & Wapner, S. (1952). Toward a general theory of perception. *Psychological Review, 59,* 324–338.

Werner, H., Wapner, S., & Chandler, K. A. (1951). Experiments on sensory-tonic field theory of perception: III. Effect of body rotation on the visual perception of verticality. *Journal of Experimental Psychology, 42,* 351–357.

Winnicott, D. W. (1958). *Through pediatrics to psychoanalysis.* New York: Basic Books.

Winnicott, D. W. (1971). *Playing and reality.* New York: Basic Books.

Witkin, H. A. (1965). Heinz Werner: 1890–1964. *Child Development, 30,* 308–328.

Wofsey, E., Rierdan, J., & Wapner, S. (1979). Planning to move: Effects on representing the currently inhabited environment. *Environment and Behavior, 11,* 3–32.

Yamamoto, T., & Ishii, S. (1995). Developmental and environmental psychology: A microgenetic developmental approach to transition from a small elementary school to a big junior high school. *Environment and Behavior, 27,* 33–42.

Yamamoto, T., & Wapner S. (1992). Transition to new environments: Some intra- and inter-cultural exemplars. In B. Wilpert, H. Motoaki, & J. Misumi (Eds.), *General psychology and environmental psychology. Proceedings of the Twenty-Second International Congress of Applied Psychology* (Vol. 2, pp. 381–384). Hillsdale, NJ: Erlbaum.

Yamamoto, T., & Wapner, S. (Eds.). (1993). *A developmental psychology of life transitions.* Kyoto, Japan: Kitaoji.

Zener, K. (Ed.). (1949a). Interrelations between perception and personality: A symposium: Part I [Special issue]. *Journal of Personality, 18*(1).

Zener, K. (Ed.). (1949b). Interrelations between perception and personality: A symposium: Part II [Special issue]. *Journal of Personality, 18*(2).

CHAPTER 14

Action Perspectives on Human Development

JOCHEN BRANDTSTÄDTER

THE RISE OF ACTION PERSPECTIVES IN DEVELOPMENTAL PSYCHOLOGY

Developmental psychology has elucidated the conditions and constraints of human ontogeny from a diversity of theoretical perspectives. However, it has not paid a great deal of attention to the developing individual's contribution to the creation of his or her own developmental history over the life span. Through action, and through experiencing the consequences of our actions, we construe representations of ourselves and of our material, social, and symbolic environments, and these representations guide and motivate activities by which we shape and influence our behavior and personal development.

Action thus forms development, and development forms action: The individual is both the active producer and the product of his or her ontogeny. The central tenet of an action-theoretical perspective thus holds that human ontogeny, including adulthood and later life, cannot be understood adequately without paying heed to the self-reflective and self-regulative loops that link developmental changes to the ways in which individuals, in action and mentation, construe their personal development. This should not be read to imply that individuals are the sole or omnipotent producers of their biographies. Like any other type of activity, activities related to personal development are subject to cultural, sociohistorical, and physical constraints. These constraints lie partly or even completely outside of one's span of control, but they decisively structure the range of behavioral and developmental options. Action-theoretical perspectives on development must therefore consider not only the activities through which individuals try to control their development over the life course, but also the nonpersonal or subpersonal forces that canalize such activities.

The idea that human individuals play an active part in shaping their development and aging has never been doubted seriously. Yet, at least until recently, no systematic effort has been made to frame this idea in an elaborated theoretical statement. Actions have been recognized as formative elements of every individual's life history, but they have hardly figured as elements in developmental theories (Dannefer, 1989). Presumably, one reason for this neglect lies in the traditional preoccupation of developmental research with the formative periods from early childhood to adolescence. Activities of self-regulation and intentional self-development are related to personal goals, plans, and identity projects; such orientations typically become more differentiated and concrete in the transition to adulthood, when developmental tasks of independence and autonomy gain importance. It is certainly no mere coincidence that early proponents of action-theoretical perspectives were simultaneously advocates of a life-span perspective in development; Charlotte Bühler (1933) is a prominent example. The neglect of action-theoretical perspectives may also reflect deeper epistemological and methodological reservations. The applicability of causal explanatory schemes to actions is a long-standing and still strongly contested controversy in the philosophy of science, and a final consensus is not in sight (e.g., Brand, 1984; Lenk, 1978; Thalberg, 1977). Moreover, an action perspective that conceives of development as a process that is shaped and canalized by collective and personal action appears to be barely compatible with the search for deterministic laws and universal principles of development. These questions will be discussed at more length later. It should be noted at this juncture, however, that notions of universality, ordered change, and determinism in human development have recently come under attack from various lines (cf. Bruner, 1990a; Gergen, 1980). In the same measure, interest in action-theoretical perspectives has grown over recent decades (e.g., Brandtstädter, 1984a, 1984b; Bruner, 1990b; Chapman, 1984; Dannefer, 1984; Eckensberger & Meacham, 1984; Lerner & Busch-Rossnagel, 1981; Silbereisen, Eyferth, & Rudinger, 1987; Valsiner, 1989).

The actional stance seems to offer a vantage point for integrating developmental and cultural perspectives. In fact, the concepts of development, culture, and action are intrinsically related, as illustrated in Figure 14.1. Development, as the result of personal and collective activity, is essentially a cultural product; this is the core of the arguments advanced in this chapter. Conversely, actions, and self-regulatory activities in particular, are dependent on developmental change; the goals, values, and beliefs that motivate and direct such activities change under the joint influence of ontogenetic and cultural-historical factors. Similar conceptual and functional links also relate the domains of action and culture. Cultures are the collective result of individual actions and decisions, even though the long-term and cumulative dynamics of cultural evolution and change generally are beyond the grasp of any single individual (Hayek, 1979). On the other hand, cultures form action-spaces (Boesch, 1980, 1991) that shape possibilities, outcomes, and meanings of actions; as I shall explain more fully later, certain types of action are intrinsically constituted by cultural institutions. The mentioned relationships also imply a functional interdependence between culture and human ontogeny, which is mediated through constructive and selective action. Individuals shape their developmental ecology and thus regulate their own development; they construct a personal culture (Heidmets, 1985) that becomes a constitutive element of the larger cultural macrosystem. The cultural context, in turn, forms an arrangement of constraints and "affordances"—to use Gibson's (1977) terms—that canalizes and institutionalizes developmental pathways. This canalization is an essential

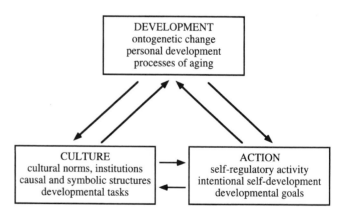

Figure 14.1 Development, culture, and action: interrelated concepts.

requirement for the maintenance and self-perpetuation of the cultural system; conversely, human ontogeny in its physical, social, and psychological aspects is fundamentally dependent on the regulative and protective influences of the cultural context.

The following sections elaborate on these issues; in particular, they focus on the multiple ways in which personal and collective actions, embedded in cultural and historical contexts, form, and are in turn formed by, development over the life span.

Cultural Regulation of Development

The regulation and control of ontogenetic and age-graded change are integral to the processes by which cultures stabilize, reproduce, and reform themselves (e.g., Bourdieu & Passeron, 1977). Every cultural system has at its disposal a broad armamentarium of techniques, institutions, or rules to regulate development, and without such cultural proxies and scaffolds, human development would be virtually impossible. Neonates and young children vitally depend on persons who care for their physical and psychological development and who organize environmental contingencies in ways that enhance growth and fend off harmful influences. The regulation and institutionalization of development becomes increasingly salient in processes of education and socialization that define an arrangement of developmental tasks, affordances, and options across the life cycle. Like development itself, the canalization and control of development is a lifelong process. This process serves to transfer cultural values and problem solutions, and to inculcate attitudes, dispositions, and skills that are, or are considered to be, necessary for existence and coexistence within a cultural-historical context. The ontogenetic necessity of culture, however, is rooted more deeply in the biological constitution and the phylogenetic evolution of *homo sapiens* (see also Tobach, 1981).

Among the evolutionary and biological conditions that make possible, and at the same time enforce, the cultural contextualization of ontogeny are the great plasticity and openness of development. Generally speaking, these features are already implied in the notion of culture, insofar as it connotes the cultivation and perfection of some object or process that is amenable to modification, particularly of life itself. As early as 1777, Johann Nicolas Tetens considered the "perfectibility" of human development as being premised on two basic conditions: (a) the capability for reflexion and self-referential action (*innere Selbsttätigkeit*) and (b) the modifiability of development:

> Among all fellow animate creatures, the human being is by far the most perfectible, the one that, at birth, has the largest potential for development . . . ; the human being is the most flexible and versatile of all creatures, the one that can be modified with the greatest diversity, in accordance with the wide sphere of activity for which it is destined. (Tetens, 1777, p. 40; J. Brandtstädter, Trans.)

The functional relationship between culture and ontogeny is captured even more cogently in the argument that cultural institutions—and the developmental and action potentials necessary for creating culture—compensate for the lack of specialized adaptive automatisms in the human organism. This idea, which can be traced back to the writings of Herder (1772), has been taken up and elaborated in the anthropological system of Gehlen (1955/1988). As Gehlen pointedly states, the human individual is a "deficient being" who is characterized by a lack of physical specialization and of ties to a specific environment, and for this being, culture has thus become a "second nature":

> Man is an acting being. In a narrower sense, he is also "undetermined"—he presents a challenge to himself . . . Actions are the expression of man's need to develop an attitude toward the outside world. To the extent that he presents a problem to himself, he must also develop an attitude toward himself and make something of himself . . . . self-discipline, training, self-correction in order to achieve a certain state of being and maintain it are necessary to the survival of an "undetermined" being. (Gehlen, 1988, pp. 24–25)

According to this stance, culture secures survival and development by providing an artificial arrangement of "outside-the-skin" compensatory means of adaptation. The notion of humans as deficient beings, however, may be misleading as far as it equates lack of specialization with adaptive deficit. In fact, the lack of adaptive automatisms and instinctual regulations is more than offset by the remarkable ability of human agents to cope with adversity through creative and constructive action. In order to respond flexibly to the continuous and fluctuating adaptive challenges posed by a nonstationary environment, behavior must be organized with sufficient latitude for variation and experience-based modification. The excessive growth of the cortical and neocortical areas of the central nervous system lends the requisite openness and variability to the cognitive and motivational control of behavior. Of particular mention here are capacities of abstraction, categorization, and representation, which enhance extraction of order and regularity from the flow of events and allow for a mental simulation of actions and effects. Human adaptive competencies are further boosted by language and communication. Language enables the transmission of knowledge and provides the symbolic means for the social control of behavior, as well as for self-control and self-reinforcement (cf. Luria, 1979; Zivin, 1979). The markedly prolonged period of physiological maturation and growth, the correspondingly long period of protection and care, and the emergence of family and group structures form a complex of mutually supportive evolutionary factors that make for both the vulnerability and the potential of human development (cf. Bruner, 1972; Gould, 1977; Lerner, 1984).

Culture and development thus form a functional synthesis that can be assessed adequately only when the mediating role of actions and self-related activities is considered. Cultures are aggregated systems of problem solutions that have been developed during the process of cultural evolution; they offer solutions to adaptive problems that arise from the biological constitution of the human species, as well as to problems related to the maintenance and further evolution of the cultural system itself; they also offer existential orientations that guide human actors in their search for meaning and purpose. Most importantly, cultures augment action resources and developmental options through compensatory strategies and "prosthetic devices" (Bruner, 1990b), thus enabling the developing subject to transcend constitutional limitations. These compensatory arrangements also comprise "psychological tools" (Vygotsky, 1960/1979), which are embodied in cultural conventions, institutions, and knowledge systems:

> Psychological tools are artificial formations. By their nature they are social, not organic or individual. They are directed toward the mastery or control of behavioral processes . . . . By being included in the process of behavior, the psychological tool alters the entire flow and structure of mental functions . . . just as a technical tool alters the process of a natural adaptation. (Vygotsky, 1960/1979, p. 137)

The common formula that defines development as the joint or interactive product of genetic and environmental influences gives short shrift to the dynamic relationships that mediate development, action, and culture. Environment is "nature organized by organisms" (Lewontin, 1982, p. 160); likewise, developmental ecologies are "intentional worlds" (Shweder, 1990) that constrain and enable intentional self-development.

The semantic and symbolic content that essentially characterizes actions and cultural action spaces cannot be reduced to physical or physiological processes. Although the meaning of actions may be related to, and can partly be extracted from, the physical features of actions, intentional and physical aspects of action are not related in ways that would allow for reductive explanations (Dennett, 1987). This does not mean that an actional stance would necessitate discarding the "natural" bases and constraints of action. Natural and cultural aspects, in fact, influence and pervade each other in the developmental process (Boesch, 1980; Brandtstädter, 1984a, 1984b; Dannefer & Perlmutter, 1990; Gibson, 1977). I have already pointed to the interdependence between the cultural and phylogenetic bases of development. In the field of developmental genetics, increasing recognition is being given to the fact that the genetic regulation of development is, to a considerable extent, mediated by behavioral systems (e.g., Gottlieb, 1992). Individuals choose and create their environments according to preferences and competencies that, as phenotypic dispositions, are linked to genotypic factors; such dispositions also influence the ways in which individuals respond to environmental influences to which they have exposed themselves selectively (cf. the concept of "active genotype–environment covariation"; Scarr & McCartney, 1983; see also Plomin, 1986). Through their actions, individuals form, and continually transform, their phenotype and extend it into their personal culture and developmental history.

Personal Regulation of Developmental Processes

The cultural regulation of human ontogeny is closely intertwined with, and in part mediated by, processes of intentional self-development. The active subject is a constitutive and productive element of the cultural system, which is continually realized, maintained, perpetuated, and reformed through personal action. At the same time, individual action in its physical and symbolic aspects is inherently bound to the action space of a culture; through transaction with the cultural context, individuals construe their prospects of possible and desired developmental courses and acquire the knowledge and means to implement these prospects.

Culture, therefore, is not a system of forces that is intrinsically opposed to self-development, as alienation literature since Rousseau has maintained; rather, cultural contexts both constrain and enable self-regulatory processes. Cultural demands and affordances may be more or less congruent to, and in fact often conflict with, the individual's developmental goals and potentials. The relational pattern of personal and contextual constraints of development is continually redefined and transformed in the course of cultural evolution and individual ontogeny. These changes, which occur in historical as well as in personal-biographical time, permanently induce conflicts and discrepancies in the transaction between the developing individual and the cultural ecology. Developmental tasks, role expectancies, or performance standards may overtax the individual's developmental resources; social opportunity structures may impede realization of personal goals and identity projects; and so on. As dialectic approaches in particular have emphasized (Kesselring, 1981; Riegel, 1976), such discrepancies and conflicts are driving forces in cultural evolution as well as in the individual's development over the life span, because they promote readjustments and new syntheses within the system in which they originate.

Individuals can respond to these kinds of adaptive problems in a variety of ways. They can adapt personal goals and projects to situational constraints and resources, or, conversely, attempt to modify external circumstances to suit personal interests and capabilities; they may try to evade or neutralize normative demands, or accommodate to them. Such adaptive activities generally aim at reducing discrepancies between factual or perceived courses of personal development and the person's normative conception of self and future development; they also serve to stabilize and maintain personal identity, thus displaying the functional characteristics of autopoietic processes through which living systems maintain and perpetuate themselves (cf. Brandtstädter & Greve, 1994; for an explication of the concept of *autopoiesis,* see, e.g., Zélény, 1981).

These considerations support and illustrate the argument that processes of intentional development are integral to human ontogeny over the life span. However, one should be aware that these processes, like any human activity,

involve elements beyond personal control. We organize our life and activities within a sociocultural matrix that structures and constrains personal action and development; our possibilities to alter these contextual constraints are limited. We even have limited influence on the "inner" context of our actions; in particular, we cannot deliberately change our own motives and beliefs (e.g., Gilbert, 1993). Action-theoretical stances here reach limits that have to be carefully fathomed. Finally, one should not discount the influence of accidental, uncontrollable events and "chance encounters" (Bandura, 1982a) in any individual life history, although, even here, some degree of control may be involved, insofar as individuals may deliberately expose themselves to, or actively seek, particular risks or chances.

From the point of view of the acting subject, development over the life span appears as a blend of expected and unexpected, controlled and uncontrollable elements—in other words, as a story of gain and loss, of success and failure (Baltes, 1987; Brandtstädter, 1984a). Efforts to keep this balance favorable are essential aspects of human activity. Individuals differ in the degree to which they feel able to alter the course of personal development, however, and such differences profoundly affect one's emotional attitude toward self and personal future; feeling incapable of achieving desired developmental goals, or of becoming the person one wants to be, is largely coterminous with depression and loss of meaning in life.

Historical Notes

Action approaches to human development have a long history that can be traced back to antiquity. The idea that human beings make themselves was expressed clearly in the philosophical work of Aristotle, who conceived of action as the process by which the person transforms self and life in accordance with ideals of rationality (Müller, 1982). In the Renaissance, notions of self-formation and self-perfection came to flower and even became a dominant form of life. The Renaissance ideal of *uomo universale*—the individual who strives for self-perfection in all areas of development—resounds in the works of Shaftesbury, Herder, Schiller, and Goethe (Spranger, 1914); Tetens's notion concerning the "perfectibility" of human development, which was mentioned above, is still clearly influenced by this ideal. Giambattista Vico (1725/1948) even based his philosophy of history and culture on the argument that we can truly understand only what we ourselves have created (see also Bunge, 1979).

In early German psychology—especially in the philosophically oriented branch of "understanding" psychology (Dilthey, 1924; Spranger, 1914)—human development had always been conceived as a lifelong process of active self-development (Höhn, 1958). In Bühler's conception of development over the life course (Bühler, 1933; Bühler & Marschak, 1969), the theoretical focus was on success and failure in concretizing and realizing life goals, the outlines of which emerge in childhood and adolescence. However, early concepts of intentional self-development were strongly loaded with connotations of freedom and spontaneity, and generally implied an anticausalist methodological stance. Such positions did not find fertile soil in a discipline that identified itself increasingly with the methodological ideals of the natural sciences (cf. Cairns, 1983; Reinert, 1976).

In particular, the rise of behaviorism, with its explicit antimentalist stance, impeded the broader reception and further development of action perspectives. This remains true despite the fact that the behaviorist program promulgated an almost unlimited manipulability and modifiability of developmental processes (Bijou & Baer, 1961; Skinner, 1953; Watson, 1930). Within the behaviorist framework, also, the themes of self-control and self-regulation were first addressed systematically. From the behaviorist point of view, however, self-regulation boils down to a process by which individuals control their own behavior through manipulating stimuli and reinforcement contingencies: "When a man controls himself . . . , he is behaving. He controls himself precisely as he would control the behavior of anyone else—through the manipulation of variables of which behavior is a function" (Skinner, 1953, p. 228). A theoretical stance that rejects mentalistic terms such as personal goals, beliefs, or intentions as explanatory concepts, however, can hardly grasp those very issues that are of central interest to an action perspective; namely, the connection of personal development with the system of meanings, institutions, and norms that constitutes cultural contexts as well as personal activities within cultural settings.

In psychology, interest in these topics has been renewed by the so-called cognitive revolution of the 1950s and 1960s. The philosophical and epistemological critique of methodological behaviorism (e.g., Putnam, 1975) has further contributed to dispelling the skepticism that has surrounded the action concept. Today, action-theoretical approaches figure prominently in many domains of research. There is now widespread agreement that "from a scientific and theoretical point of view, the unsuitability and dispensability of the action model can no longer be supported" (Lenk, 1978, p. 16; J. Brandtstädter, Trans.). Moreover, the traditional dichotomies of explanation versus understanding, freedom versus determinism, or causalism versus intentionalism have lost much of their adversarial fervor; philosophical positions that plea for compatibility or, at least, peaceful coexistence between these stances have been advanced (e.g., Davidson, 1980; Dennett, 1987). The resurgence of cultural perspectives within psychology, and an increased theoretical concern with the cultural bases of behavior and development (Bruner, 1990a, even presages an impending "contextual revolution") finds a natural ally in action-theoretical approaches:

> A cultural psychology, almost by definition, will not be preoccupied with "behavior" but with "action," its intentionally based counterpart, and more specifically, with *situated action*—action as situated in a cultural setting, and in the mutually interacting states of the participants. (Bruner, 1990a, p. 15)

THE CONCEPT OF ACTION

The attempt to explicate the concept of action cannot proceed from a single or unitary theoretical frame of reference. Action-theoretical formulations have been advanced in such diverse fields as psychology, sociology, anthropology, biology, philosophy, and economics; and even within these disciplines, concepts of action come in different shapes.

Within the narrower domain of psychology, we can roughly distinguish among structural, motivational, control-system, and social-constructivist action theories.

Structural Theories of Action

This family of theories centers on the structural analysis of actions. There are different formats of structural analysis, and it is not always possible to separate them clearly. One line of research has focused particularly on the formal structure of actions and of the cognitive operations underlying action; this approach is represented by the work of

Piaget (e.g., 1970b, 1976). Other approaches have centered more strongly on the componential analysis of specific activities and skills (e.g., Fischer, 1980). Yet another variant of the structural approach is instantiated in the analysis of basic syntactic features that constitute different types of actions, such as their actors, instruments, goals, objects, and further contextual elements (e.g., Aebli, 1980; Bruner, 1982; Fillmore, 1968; Schank & Abelson, 1977).

Motivational Theories of Action

Influential action-theoretical formulations have been advanced within motivational psychology; perhaps the most prominent are the expectancy-value models of action originating from the work of Tolman and Lewin (for overviews, see Feather, 1982; Krampen, 1987a). According to the basic explanatory scheme of this approach, actions are explained and predicted as a joint function of (a) personal expectations related to action-outcome contingencies, and (b) the subjective evaluation of expected consequences with regard to personal goals and standards. Different variants and extensions of this basic model have been proposed (e.g., Ajzen, 1988; Atkinson, 1970; Fishbein & Ajzen, 1975; Heckhausen, 1989; Vroom, 1964).

Control-System Theories of Action

In the tradition of Miller, Galanter, and Pribram (1960), this type of action-theoretical approach draws on cybernetic and systems-theoretical concepts. The basic analytic tool is the feedback cycle: Processes related to the transformation of goals into behavior and to the regulation of goal-related activity are described in terms of hierarchically organized levels of discrepancy-reducing feedback loops (e.g., Carver & Scheier, 1981, 1986; Ford, 1987; Powers, 1973).

Social-Constructivist Concepts of Action; Activity Theory

A largely autochthonous strand of action research has emerged in the former USSR from the work of Vygotsky and his pupils (Leont'ev, 1978; Luria, 1979; Vygotsky, 1934/1986). Based on the tenets of dialectical materialism, this approach has a strong sociohistorical orientation. Goal-directed activity is seen as the mediator between external reality and individual consciousness; cognitive structures develop from the individual's interaction with cultural symbols as well as with material objects and tools, which, as objectified ideas and problem solutions, organize

thought and action (see also Cole, 1978; van der Veer & Valsiner, 1991; Wertsch, 1981).

This classification, of course, cannot claim to be exhaustive; there are no sharp boundaries between the theoretical clusters, and there is a broader spectrum of research programs that, to various extents, borrow or integrate elements from the theoretical families described above. Such programs focus, for example, on social-cognitive aspects of action (e.g., Bandura, 1986), on cultural-symbolic perspectives (e.g., Boesch, 1980, 1991; Bruner, 1990a, 1990b), or on processes related to the formation and implementation of actions and action plans (e.g., Frese & Sabini, 1985; Gollwitzer, 1990; Kuhl & Beckmann, 1985; von Cranach, 1982). Influential contributions to action theory have also been advanced in neighboring disciplines, particularly in sociology (e.g., Bourdieu, 1977; Parsons & Shils, 1962; Schütz, 1962) and in anthropology (e.g., Geertz, 1973; Gehlen, 1971; Tyler, 1969). Last but not least, analytical philosophy of action has contributed significantly to elucidating the action concept (for overviews, see, e.g., Brand, 1984; Brand & Walton, 1976; Care & Landesman, 1968; Moya, 1990). Some of the above-mentioned theoretical positions have been cast in a developmental framework from the outset, or are framed as developmental theories; this is particularly true for structuralist and social-constructivist approaches. These approaches contribute important elements to a more comprehensive theoretical perspective of intentional self-development, which shall be outlined in later sections.

These introductory comments should make it clear that the different theories and research programs centering on the concept of action do not form a coherent system. Given the inherently cross-disciplinary nature of the action concept, the vision of a grand unifying action theory seems utopian. This compromises any effort to formulate consensual definitions. To elucidate the concept of action, I shall concentrate, in the following section, on some general and rather uncontroversial elements that seem particularly relevant for conceptualizing the interdependencies between action and development.

Explicating Action: Conceptual Constituents

Is it possible to identify a set of essential and discriminative features that is common to all instances of actions, and that separates actions from other forms of behavior that would not count as actions? When speaking of acts, actions, or actionlike activities, we obviously do not refer indiscriminately to any kind of behavior, but to behaviors that can, and should be, explained and predicted in particular ways. We seem to imply that the observed behavior has been chosen by the individual on the basis of personal beliefs and values, and that it can be interpreted as serving some personal goal or as expressing personal attitudes and values. Accordingly, when accounting for actions, we try to show how they are linked with the actor's values, beliefs, attitudes, or competencies. When interpreting an observed behavior as an action or particular type of act, we suppose that the actor "could have done otherwise" (Chisholm, 1966), and, in particular, that he or she was sufficiently free to refrain from the behavior (even nonbehaving sometimes can be considered as an action). Conversely, behavioral events that are beyond personal control seem not to qualify as actions; physiological reflexes, emotional reactions, and all forms of inadvertent or erroneous behavior (slips of attention, lapses of memory, and so on) are typical examples. These differentiations are also fundamental to moral and ethical evaluations; according to the conceptual rules inherent to moral discourse, standards of justice, rationality, or responsibility apply only to intentional and personally controlled behavior, not to nonintentional behavioral events (Austin, 1956).

There is no one-to-one correspondence between behaviors and actions; a given behavior, taken as an observable physical event, is often only one of several components that constitute an action (Thalberg, 1977). For example, an action of greeting can be instantiated through a multitude of physically different behaviors (e.g., waving the hand, nodding the head, uttering a verbal formula); in turn, a given behavior such as waving the hand may instantiate such different actions as greeting, giving a signal, or chasing away a mosquito, depending on the "inner" context (the individual's intentions, beliefs, and so on) and situational specifics, as well as on the context of symbols, social norms, and conventions according to which certain behaviors in certain situations instantiate a specific action. To categorize a given behavior as an exemplar of a specific type of action thus generally involves an interpretative process that transcends the immediate observable givens; in this sense, actions may be conceived of as interpretative constructs (Lenk, 1981). Occasionally, a distinction is made between actions and acts, in which the latter term is taken to denote the generic category or type of actions to

which a particular action belongs (e.g., Harré & Secord, 1972). Again, the same generic act can be instantiated through different actions, and the same action can instantiate different acts. To count as exemplars of some act or type of action, different actions must bear some structural semblance to one another, that is, they must possess those features that, according to conventions and conceptual rules, are constitutive for the respective act type. Parenthetically, it may be noted that this point is fundamental to the construction of developmental continuity and coherence, which often involves establishing structural or "homotypic" equivalence (Kagan, 1971) between phenomenally different behaviors at different ontogenetic levels.

In a first approximation, we may thus consider criteria such as intentionality, personal control, reflexivity, and (perceived) freedom of choice as defining characteristics of actions (cf., Groeben, 1986; Mischel, 1969). However, none of these criteria is without problems. Considering the criterion of intentionality, it should be noted that intended action outcomes often imply undesired or harmful side effects that are simply tolerated; people may be held morally and legally responsible for such condoned effects even when they did not focally intend them. There are also cases of reduced intentionality, for example, when someone doodles aimlessly on paper while making a phone call. The criterion of personal control has its complications as well. There are many nonintentional behaviors, such as physiological reflexes, that we can control in a technical sense; for example, we can deliberately induce sweating by exposing ourselves to higher temperatures. It does not follow, of course, that such physiological reflexes are actions (although the instrumental activities by which we brought about the response certainly are). On the other hand, it is also true that actions in any phase involve component processes that are not under personal control; we would have no control over our own behavior and development without the help of mediating mechanisms that lie beyond our control. As already intimated, we do not have full command over even the internal context of our actions; thus, we are not at liberty to intend, wish, or believe whatever we want to believe, wish, or intend (e.g., Kunda, 1990; Lanz, 1987).

Within the confines of this chapter, I cannot dwell on the conceptual intricacies surrounding the notion of action (for a more detailed discussion, see, e.g., Greve, 1994;

Moya, 1990). For the present purpose, the considerations above may be condensed in a working definition:

Actions may be conceptualized as behaviors that (a) can be predicted and explained with reference to intentional states (goals, values, beliefs, volitions); (b) are at least partly under personal control, and have been selected from alternative behavioral options; (c) are constituted and constrained by social rules and conventions or by the subject's representation of these contextual constraints; and (d) aim to transform situations in accordance with personal representations of desired future states.

This definition again underscores the intimate relation between action and personal development. Self-referential actions that are intentionally related to personal development, however, have additional properties that will be delineated in later sections. Before addressing these issues, I shall attempt to give a more detailed account of how personal and social factors intertwine in the regulation of action.

Constraints of Action: Constitutive and Regulative Rules

Human action is related to rules in a twofold sense. In a first and familiar sense, actions and personal action spaces are *constrained* by rules; in a second and more fundamental sense, actions, or at least some actions, are *constituted* by rules. Following Searle (1969), one can differentiate between regulative and constitutive rules (the distinction can be traced back to Kant; see also Brandtstädter, 1984b; D'Andrade, 1984; Smith, 1982; Toulmin, 1974).

Regulative Rules

Personal action is regulated by a variety of cultural prescriptions and restrictions, and these can be more or less formal and explicit (laws, norms, customs, social expectations, and so on). Such rules delimit situationally defined zones and margins of action. The limits imposed by regulative rules, however, are not rigid; cultural laws, in contrast to natural laws, can be violated. Regulative rules, however, have "normative force" (Toulmin, 1969); they are linked to subsidiary social forces such as sanctions or mechanisms of reinforcement that tend to increase the frequency and probability of rule-conforming behavior. Regulative rules,

whether they are externally imposed or "internalized" and integrated into the processes of self-regulation, generate regularities in patterns of action and development. For example, the developmental tasks or normative timetables that determine the proper scheduling of biographical events in social contexts (e.g., Chudacoff, 1989; Neugarten & Hagestad, 1976) define systems of regulative rules that institutionalize and synchronize individual life courses and thus impose order and regularity on development.

Constitutive Rules

When one considers acts or action episodes such as marrying, formulating an excuse, promising something, or taking a penalty kick, it is evident that such actions are not simply regulated, but, in a stronger sense, are constituted by rules. Just as one can play chess only within the framework of chess rules, one can marry someone, give a promise, and so forth, only according to specific semantic rules and social conventions that define, at least in outline, the ways and contextual circumstances in which an action has to be performed in order to count as a valid instantiation of the particular act. Describing or understanding an action as an instance of a generic act presupposes familiarity with the corresponding constitutive rules (Winch, 1958). The rules that constitute particular acts are represented individually in scriptlike cognitive structures or schemas (Schank & Abelson, 1977). These scripts or schemas enable us to organize our activities according to socially shared meanings, and to extrapolate, anticipate, and coordinate courses of action in social settings.

Through constitutive rules, certain types of action are linked inseparably to cultural institutions. As D'Andrade (1984) has pointed out, changes in institutional contexts alter the range of possible actions, eventually creating radically new types of action:

One consequence of constitutive rule systems is the enormous expansion of the behavioral repertoire of humans compared with the behavioral repertoire of other animals. For example, without the system of constitutive rules called football, the behaviors of scoring, blocking, passing, and so on would not exist. (p. 94)

The notions of regulative and constitutive rules provide important vantage points for reconstructing developmental regularity and invariance from an action-theoretical point of view. The constitutive rule concept in particular offers a fresh perspective on the traditional theme of developmental universals; as I shall show later, the formal or conceptual rules that determine the structure of particular skills and competencies also impose order on the ontogenetic construction of the corresponding competencies.

The Polyvalence of Actions

The concept of polyvalence is related to the valence concept in Lewinian theory; it refers to the fact that one and the same action can serve different purposes and intentions, and correspondingly can have, and usually does have, multiple meanings at both personal and public levels. For example, the person who quits smoking can do so for health reasons, to avoid social conflicts, for financial reasons, to demonstrate willpower, or for some combination of these reasons. Actions or action tendencies mostly result from a mixture of instrumental, symbolic, expressive, and aesthetic valences, which may sometimes conflict:

> Polyvalent means three things: first, actions, aiming at composite goals, are "overdetermined"; second, they connote different areas of experience; and, third, they draw their justifications not simply from the concrete specific results they (tend to) achieve, but also from the subjective experiences implied, from personal fantasms, cultural rules and values. (Boesch, 1991, p. 363)

From the polyvalent (or polysemous) nature of actions, it follows that one and the same basic action can simultaneously instantiate a multitude of different acts. When Mr. Doe mows the lawn, he is cutting the grass, making noise, and exercising his muscles; by doing this, he is—depending on the given causal, social, and symbolic context—perhaps pleasing his neighbors, evading conflicts with his wife, showing a sense of responsibility, and so forth (Rommetveit, 1980). Some of these effects and implications may be intended; others may be simply tolerated or even remain unnoticed. To capture the multiplicity of levels on which a given action can be described, Goldman (1970) has coined the metaphor of an "act tree" whose branches are generated through causal mechanisms, conventions, or language rules. The ways in which actors construe effects and implications of their own activities, and describe their actions, may differ from the interpretations of external observers.

Such differences may give rise to social conflicts and identity problems, the solution of which often requires negotiation of consensual interpretations. Negotiating meanings is a basic strategy for establishing consensus and coorientation between developing individuals who have to coordinate their actions and developmental goals in, for example, marital relationships or family systems (Berger, 1993; Brandtstädter, Krampen, & Heil, 1986). As is evident from these considerations, the meanings and motivating valences of actions, even of everyday activities, can be, and in fact often are, ultimately rooted in global identity goals and life themes.

Different kinds of knowledge and expertise, and corresponding developmental steps, are required for a differentiated representation of the meanings and effects of action. Knowledge about the causal structure of action spaces is required for gauging possible action-outcome contingencies, whereas the construal of semantic or symbolic implications requires corresponding conceptual knowledge. The polyvalence of actional meanings also implies an emotional polyvalence; when different interpretive schemes can be applied to one's own or to observed actions, mixed emotional evaluations may result. For example, an aggressive action may be coded as an act of self-assertion, an infringement of moral norms, or a lapse of self-control, and may, accordingly, invoke simultaneous feelings of pride, guilt, and shame. The emergence of such mixed feelings appears to be an ontogenetic marker of the individual's developing ability to unfold the causal and semantic implications of observed events and behaviors (Harter, 1986).

Self-control and intentional self-development hinge crucially on the construction and deconstruction of meanings and evaluative standards. A characteristic of human actors is that they can take an evaluative stance with respect to their own intentions, emotions, and actions; for example, we may experience pride or shame with regard to our own feelings. Such metaemotions or second-order evaluations are characteristic of a higher ontogenetic level of action regulation, a level on which moral principles, social norms, and personal representations of "ought selves" (Higgins, 1988) become integrated into the process of intentional self-development. Again, ontogenetic requirements should be noted. The polyvalence of actions reflects the embedding of individual behavior into a hierarchy of contextual levels that—to borrow terms from Bronfenbrenner's (1979) model of developmental ecologies—extends from the encompassing macrosystem of cultural institutions, norms, and symbols through intermediate mesosystems down to the social and physical microsystems that constitute the proximal setting for the individual's activities. The representation of meanings proceeds ontogenetically in a sequence that corresponds to the increasing abstractness and complexity of the contextual levels in which actions are situated. Whereas early in development, the focus for evaluating one's actions is primarily on perceived and anticipated effects within the immediate or proximal environment (e.g., reactions of parents or peers), the evaluative scope widens during subsequent developmental stages so that more complex and abstract system perspectives become progressively influential in self-regulation (Eckensberger & Reinshagen, 1980; Edelstein & Keller, 1982; Harter, 1983; Selman, 1980).

The Context of Action

Psychological action explanations primarily center on the "inner" context of action: the individual expectations, goals, beliefs, and so forth, that determine the intentional structure of action. This explanatory focus, however, provides only a reduced, largely ahistorical and adynamic picture of action that is of limited use for developmental theorizing. To appreciate how an individual's life history relates to the patterning of personal goals, projects, and actions across the life course, external contextual conditions must be taken into account. The particular blending of intended and unintended, expected and surprising outcomes that makes up any biography is essentially determined by the external context of action and its physical, material, and social constraints.

People generally have only limited insight into the contextual conditions of their behavior. The complexity of the causal and symbolic structures that generate meanings and effects of action generally exceeds the representational capacities of the individual actor; unintended and unexpected effects are intrinsic to the reality of action under conditions of "bounded rationality" (Simon, 1983). Although the aspect of unintended consequences has been largely neglected in psychological and philosophical accounts of action (Giddens, 1979), it has profound implications from a developmental point of view. The experience of unintended or unexpected effects provides an impetus for the revision and continuing adjustment of individual goals and beliefs;

surprise induces exploratory activities through which the inner context of an action is modified and accommodated to external constraints. Unintended effects, and the ways in which individuals cope with them, are dramatizing elements in any personal biography (Bruner, 1990a); they shape future action spaces and developmental options, and they provide a corrective for the theories and beliefs that individuals hold about themselves and their environment.

As cultural artifacts, action contexts are, in large part, the result of individual and collective actions. As already emphasized, cultures provide means and prosthetic tools to maximize intended effects of actions and to suppress unintended side effects; they create norms and institutions in order to coordinate the actions of individual actors so that they become mutually compatible. Beyond this, individuals themselves actively control the texture of their action space; actors have an interest in making effects or meanings of their actions converge with their intentions, and they strive to organize the personal action space accordingly. If such efforts fail, individuals may select an ecological niche (Super & Harkness, 1986) that fits better with their intentions or developmental goals. Through selective and constructive activities of this kind, personal action contexts become extensions of the actor's self (cf. Csikszentmihalyi & Rochberg-Halton, 1981; Thomae, 1968).

In general, individuals select and organize contexts and fields of activity according to a principle of "just manageable difficulty" (Brim, 1992). In early childhood, this selection is typically under the control of adult caretakers. Parents structure the activities of the child through restricting its access to certain situations and experiences, as well as through encouraging or supporting particular types of activities; they create "zones of free movement" and "zones of promoted action" (Valsiner, 1987a) that are more or less adjusted to, but at the same time also shape, the "zone of proximal development," that is, the range of developmental tasks or steps that the child has partially mastered already and that can be successfully completed with external support (Vygotsky, 1978; Wertsch, 1984). This structuring of action zones provides a scaffold that organizes and directs developmental progress; examples can be found in the organization of children's action spaces during mealtimes, or of toddlers' climbing activities (Gärling & Valsiner, 1985; Valsiner, 1988a, 1988b).

Harmonizing contextual demands and resources with personal goals and developmental potentials is in itself a fundamental theme of intentional self-development (Kahana, Kahana, & Riley, 1989). Because both external (physical, social, symbolic) contexts and personal resources of action (values, interests, competencies) are involved in historical and ontogenetic change, this mutual accommodation remains a concern over the entire life span, and developmental problems often result from poorness of fit between (or within) these systems of influences at different developmental stages (Brandtstädter, 1985a; Lerner & Lerner, 1983; Thomas & Chess, 1977). Critical events and transitions in the individual's life course involve particularly strong pressures to revise action spaces and developmental goals. In later life, the changes and limitations of action resources, which typically accompany the process of aging, enforce readjustments of personal projects and activities. The importance of such adaptive dynamics for buffering experiences of loss and for preserving a positive view of self and personal development has become a topic in developmental and gerontological research over recent years (e.g., Baltes & Baltes, 1990; Brandtstädter & Renner, 1990). I will address this point in a later section.

The extent to which external contextual constraints fit, or can be made to fit, with personal interests and potentials deeply affects the long-term balance of successes and failures, or of developmental gains and losses, in the individual's life history. Recurring experiences of noncontingency between one's own actions and the context undermine a sense of personal control and self-efficacy and may foster a tendency to avoid tasks and developmental options that involve a risk of failure; yet, precisely these kinds of challenges afford opportunities for further personal development (Bandura, 1981).

DEVELOPMENTAL DIVERSITY AND REGULARITY: ACTION-THEORETICAL RECONSTRUCTIONS

The search for coherence and lawful regularity in human development is a traditional heuristic ideal that has inspired developmental psychology from its very beginnings: "From the colourful play of human changes, we must go back to an invariant order, back as far as possible to the eternal source of phenomenal variation" (Carus, 1823, p. 94; J. Brandtstädter, Trans.). This ideal can be traced back to the philosophical teachings of Parmenides

(540–480 B.C.) and Plato (427–347 B.C.). For Parmenides, the phenomenal world, in all its diversity, was merely the appearance of one immutable substance, whereas Plato considered empirical phenomena to be the reflection or imperfect instantiation of timeless and unchanging ideas (see also Toulmin, 1977).

To what extent are action-theoretical perspectives compatible with this influential epistemic stance? At least at first glance, the rise of action perspectives appears to signal the demise of a Parmenidean or Platonic stance; the arguments that strengthen the case of the latter stance seem to weaken the former, and vice versa. First, a research heuristic aimed primarily at the disclosure of universal ontogenetic principles tends to detract from the institutional, symbolic, subjective-intentional conditions of development—conditions that seem to breed diversity rather than regularity in human ontogeny (Shweder, 1990). Second, the search for universal laws in ontogeny has not been a *succès fou,* to put it mildly; it has generated massive evidence apparently speaking against the assumption of lawful regularities in development. Thus, longitudinal investigations have documented considerable variability and heterogeneity in developmental patterns for many behavioral domains; correspondingly, long-term predictions have evinced a high degree of indeterminacy (Baltes, Reese, & Lipsitt, 1980; Lerner, 1984; Rutter, 1984; Schaie, 1983). Likewise, there is only scarce support for the traditional claim that personality development over the life course is shaped profoundly by early childhood experiences, as has been argued by psychoanalytic theory and partly also by learning theorists (Clarke & Clarke, 1976; Oyama, 1979). Brim and Kagan (1980, p. 13) have aptly described the situation: "... growth is more individualistic than was thought, and it is difficult to find general patterns."

Not surprisingly, these research experiences have strongly encouraged theoretical views that programmatically emphasize the discontinuous, contextualized, and aleatoric (i.e., coincidental or random) character of development over the life span (Baltes & Reese, 1984; Baumrind, 1989; Emde & Harmon, 1984; Gollin, 1981; Lerner, 1984). There even have been claims as to the basic futility of any search for universality and invariance in ontogeny (e.g., Gergen, 1980; Shweder, 1990). However, a note of caution is required here: As long as we cannot rule out that difficulties in extracting structure and lawlike regularity from developmental diversity merely reflect theoretical deficiencies, it would be a weak argument to simply attribute such difficulties to an allegedly unpredictable or inchoate nature of development. Allusions to the fundamental indeterminism of phenomena in quantum physics that recently have become trendy among developmentalists do not seem to be tenable; it may suffice here to note that the uncertainty principle in quantum physics is not a declaration of theoretical ignorance, but a powerful predictive device. In any case, it would be a logical mistake to equate lack of evidence for lawful regularity with evidence for the lack of such qualities. Coherence and universality in development are not observable facts that can be established conclusively; these qualities emerge only by way of theoretical abstraction. In a similar way, plasticity and modifiability are not features that characterize development in an essential or fundamental sense; they have to be conceived as qualities that basically relate to potentials of change and modification within a given cultural and historical frame.

The Construction and Deconstruction of Developmental Coherence

To account for continuity and coherence in developmental patterns, it is usual to invoke causal mechanisms (e.g., Overton & Reese, 1981). A causal or deterministic stance, however, is rendered problematic by the fact that developing organisms have to be conceived as open systems (see also Ford & Lerner, 1992). Only within a system that is closed to external influences can there be causal chains such that subsequent states are linked in a necessary and invariant fashion; the developing organism, however, is functionally coupled to its physical and social environment by the continuous interchange of stimulation and information. Defenders of a determinist stance might argue that such difficulties could be handled simply by expanding the analytic perspective: "If determinism is assumed, alterations in a system which do not appear to occur as the consequence of the presence or operation of antecedent factors or conditions, must be regarded as belonging to a more inclusive system which is deterministic" (Nagel, 1957, p. 17).

If we widen our explanatory scope to include the physical and social ecologies of development, however, it becomes obvious that regularities in human development are not brought about by causal laws alone, but, to a considerable extent, reflect the ways in which institutions, collective

agents, and the developing individuals themselves, purposefully or inadvertently, make use of such laws. In other words, if the notion of causality is taken to refer to invariant sequences of events in which some antecedent condition inevitably generates some consequence (e.g., Bunge, 1979), the regularities that characterize human development as a product of personal and collective action can hardly be described that way. Within cultural contexts, developmental regularities are in large measure patterned and mediated by individual and institutionalized actions, and, by consequence, can also be transformed or suppressed through action. For example, connections between risk factors in early development and unfavorable developmental outcomes generally depend on moderating or mediating variables such as prevailing attitudes in the social environment or the availability of preventive and therapeutic resources (e.g., Busch-Rossnagel, 1981); likewise, age-related decrements in memory, physical stamina, health, and so forth, will be expressed more strongly in contexts (and individuals) in which the motivation, knowledge, or resources to counteract functional loss are lacking (Baltes & Schaie, 1974; Salthouse, 1987). A particularly intriguing example of how a seemingly inevitable causal sequence can be broken up through interventive action is the inherited metabolic disease of phenylketonuria (PKU). Formerly, PKU invariably led to severe mental retardation; today, the metabolic mechanisms involved are sufficiently known, so that it has become possible to suppress insidious developmental consequences by a proper dietary regime. The list of examples obviously could be extended *ad libitum*.

Developmental regularities in actional contexts, thus, essentially arise from personal and institutionalized agentivity. To put it more formally, the tendency within a given social or personal context (C) to produce or forestall a specified developmental outcome or pattern (D) can be conceived as depending on available resources of intervention and the cost of such interventions, as well as on the value (which may be positive or negative) that D has in C (Brandtstädter, 1984c). Accordingly, we would expect that, for developmental domains that are amenable to control, transitions from socially undesirable states to positively valued states should be more frequent or probable than the obverse transitions. Consistent with this assumption, longitudinal observations suggest that, in regard to traits that are socially recognized as positive, the probability that children at lower levels on the trait later come up to a higher level is greater than the reverse case; likewise, socially deviant behaviors seem to show less developmental stability than behavior that conforms to social norms (Kagan & Moss, 1962; Kohlberg, LaCrosse, & Ricks, 1972). Longitudinal findings also hint, for example, that the probability of a delinquent adolescent's exhibiting socially deviant behavior in adulthood is lower than the reverse, retrodictive probability (Rutter, 1984). By the same reasoning, we may infer from the frequent or regular occurrence of a negatively valued developmental pattern or outcome a lack of pertinent preventive knowledge or resources; this argument could, for example, account for the observation that developmental losses in later life are perceived as less controllable when they involve positively valued domains (Heckhausen & Baltes, 1991).

Even biology and developmental genetics no longer provide a safe retreat for deterministic views of invariance and ordered change in development. The genome does not rigidly determine a developmental phenotype; rather, it defines the norm of reaction, that is, the function that, for a given genotype, maps possible environmental influences onto phenotypic outcomes: "genes . . . code for a range of forms under an array of environmental conditions" (Gould, 1981, p. 56; cf. also Gottlieb, 1992). From this point of view, developmental patterns will appear as genetically fixed only as long as relevant epigenetic conditions are held constant or within critical margins. If we define the heritability of a given developmental phenomenon as the portion of phenotypical variance that is accounted for by genetic sources, the obtained estimate is not a natural constant, but depends crucially on the range of variation in critical environmental conditions that is produced or tolerated within a given cultural context. Ethical norms and codes of justice, for example, limit inequalities in the distribution of developmental resources; public health measures restrain detrimental influences; theoretical and technological progress permanently spawns new means of preventive and corrective intervention into human ontogeny. Accordingly, the relative portions of phenotypic developmental variation accounted for by genetic and exogenous influences, respectively, can change over a shorter or longer historical interval; but "change the mix and the answers change" (Plomin, 1986, p. 7). Seen from an action perspective on development, heritability coefficients provide only limited evidence as to the lesser or greater external modifiability of a developmental trait; rather, they reflect propensities and limitations within a given developmental ecology to control critical epigenetic influences (Brandtstädter, 1984b; Lerner & von Eye, 1992; Scarr, 1982).

Developmental Plasticity: Weak and Strong Constraints

The considerations above suggest the following proviso when framing propositions about developmental regularities: No developmental tendency exists that cannot be altered, provided that the individual or collective agents concerned both want to alter it and possess the appropriate means to do so (cf. Watkins, 1957). On closer examination, this proposition turns out to be irrefutable; it is true by virtue of its logical form alone. It does not implicate, however, an unlimited plasticity or modifiability of human ontogeny; neither are all developmental modifications possible, nor are all possible variations desirable or permitted.

We can differentiate between weak and strong constraints on the range of developmental trajectories, that is, between constraints that themselves are, at least in principle, open to change, and those that, for strong reasons, are not. Strong, if also very wide, constraints are imposed on development by the laws of logic (e.g., through logical and mathematical structures); developmental outcomes that involve logical contradictions or combine logically opposed states are *a priori* impossible. Natural laws also constrain the space of possible developmental phenomena in a strong sense. Human beings are both personal actors and, at the same time, organic systems that are subject to physiological, biochemical, and biophysical laws. These laws can eventually be exploited to generate desired developmental outcomes through deliberate manipulation of antecedent conditions, but they cannot be altered, for reasons inherent to the very notion of a natural law. Developmental trajectories necessarily remain within the limits imposed by natural laws, which are narrower than those imposed by logic.

In contrast, the values, technologies, and theories that provide the orienting framework for social and personal regulation of development are not fixed or rigid in a strong sense, but are factually or in principle open to change. The limits of what is possible and desirable in human development are continuously redefined and renegotiated in the process of cultural evolution; it is certainly not by accident that the progressive expansion of cultural resources for developmental intervention and modification coincides with the rise of theoretical paradigms that emphasize the plasticity, multidirectionality, and variability of human ontogeny.

Finally, ontogenetic processes are also constrained by the semantic rules and conceptual structures that are used, in science as well as in everyday contexts, to analyze, and communicate about, development. The semiotic context not only constitutes and constrains spaces of action; it likewise imposes order on developmental sequences. With regard to the distinction between weak and strong limitations, this type of constraint cannot be classified easily. This is an important point that will be discussed more closely when we turn to the issue of developmental universals.

To summarize these considerations, we may picture the different constraints as a hierarchy of inclusive sets (Figure 14.2; see Brandtstädter, 1984c). From the totality of all logically possible states that a developmental system might assume, only a subset of states is compatible with natural laws and with semiotic constraints; from this subset again, only a smaller portion can be realized within the limits of available theoretical and technological means; and finally, only a selection of developmental pathways that could possibly be realized will also be desired or permitted under prevailing normative constraints (here, the reverse is generally also true). The shaded residual area in Figure 14.2 describes the allowable margins of developmental variation within this system of constraints.

Assumptions regarding developmental phases of higher or lower modifiability play an important role in policy decisions concerning the distribution of educational and intervention resources over the life cycle. Often, such

assumptions are based on observed inter- and intraindividual variation in the trait in question. For example, early childhood programs were launched under the premise of a special sensitivity of the early years as compared with later phases in life; this assumption leaned strongly on an analysis of longitudinal variations in the stability of intelligence test scores (cf., Bloom, 1964; Clarke-Stewart & Fein, 1983). The considerations above caution against potential pitfalls of inferring developmental plasticity from observed variability. Because observed variation in a developmental trait depends on the affordances, resources, and constraints realized within a given environmental setting, it obviously can provide only a weak estimate of the potential range of variation. As McCall (1981, p. 9) has put it, "the environments not represented in the sample also have implications for the . . . potential for change." To gauge limits of performance and developmental variation, planned experimental interventions seem to offer a stronger basis; efforts to boost memory performance of elderly subjects through mnemonic training may be considered as an example (Baltes, 1993; Kliegl, Smith, & Baltes, 1989). Even through experimental manipulations, however, limits of potential development cannot be determined in any definitive way, because the results of such interventions always depend on the theoretical and procedural means available in a given cultural and historical situation, and thus are themselves subject to theoretical and technical limitations.

Invariance and Universality in Development: An Action-Theoretical Account

The notorious difficulties in establishing generally valid developmental patterns reflect the general principle that development—as Hegel (1837/1857), in his philosophy of history, once put it—only manifests itself in concrete historical modifications. Thus, one might suspect that theoretical views that consider context, culture, and intentional action as driving forces in human development are likely to end up in a relativism that renders the search for continuity and universality quixotic (Bruner, 1990b; Gergen, 1980). This is a threatening perspective, at least to those developmentalists who still subscribe to the view that the strength of a theoretical framework comes from its ability to encompass differences as well as regularity and invariance in development (Block, 1971; Brandtstädter, 1984c, 1985b; Lerner, 1984; Rosch, 1977). Expanding arguments from the

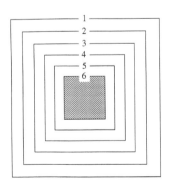

(1) Formal Constraints
   (Logical Structures)

(2) Nomic Constraints
   (Natural Laws)

(3) Semiotic Constraints
   (Language Rules, Semantic Structures)

(4) Epistemic Constraints
   (Knowledge about Development)

(5) Technical Constraints
   (Technical Resources of Control)

(6) Normative Constraints
   (Cultural Norms and Values)

Figure 14.2 Development in action contexts: a system of constraints.

previous section, we will explore here how the traditional issue of developmental universals may be approached from an action perspective. To preview, an action-theoretical account of invariance and universality will differ in some respects from traditional treatments of these issues.

Developmental Universals as Empirical Regularities

As the term is commonly used, *developmental universals* refers to ontogenetic phenomena manifesting themselves in same or similar ways across different social, cultural, or historical contexts. Across all cultures, for example, we observe similar structures and sequences in prenatal development, in the maturation of physiological functions, in early sensorimotor development, in language acquisition, and in cognitive and affective development, as well as in the processes of biological aging (for overviews, see, e.g., Cole & Scribner, 1974; Kagan, 1981b; Warren, 1980). A theoretical emphasis on diversity and multidirectionality in development should certainly not obfuscate the considerable constancy and transcontextual stability in basic patterns and processes of human ontogeny. Cross-cultural research, with its emphasis on documenting cultural specificity, often tends to overlook the conspicuous commonalities in development (Rosch, 1977).

Although developmental commonalities of the mentioned type emerge across a broad range of environmental variation, they necessarily presuppose constancy in those exogenous influences that have an impact on the given ontogenetic functions. As already intimated, genetic mechanisms will generate similar developmental phenotypes only as long as critical epigenetic influences remain sufficiently stable or—in the more interesting case, from an action-theoretical perspective—are actively kept within critical margins. If critical exogenous variations exceed those tolerance margins—for example, as a result of influences that override genetic buffering mechanisms because they occur for the first time in evolutionary history—anomalous developmental patterns emerge; the thalidomide disaster is a dramatic example. The genetic control of ontogenesis thus presupposes mechanisms and structures that regulate and standardize the distribution, intensity, and temporal patterning of critical exogenous variables. The mediating processes that warrant this kind of epigenetic order involve the selective and constructive activities of the developmental organism itself, as well as the "institutionalized operativity" (Warren, 1980, p. 310) of the social and cultural

system. As already stressed, personal and cultural agentivity merge in the regulation of development; both are related to social norms that prescribe and enforce the timing and sequential order of developmental tasks and role transitions across the life span.

An important point that follows from these considerations is that observed regularity of certain ontogenetic forms is not in itself sufficient to establish universality in the strict sense, because observations can always cover only a limited range of situations. Even if an empirical rule has been found valid without exception, this does not warrant its universality across time and space; this is the problem of inductive generalization as classically formulated by Hume. Postulates about universal ontogenetic sequences, as they have been set forth in, for example, stage models of cognitive, sociomoral, or emotional development (e.g., Kohlberg, 1976; Piaget, 1970b; see also Brainerd, 1978), can eventually be refuted, but can never be definitively settled on an empirical base alone.

At this juncture, the above differentiation between weak and strong constraints of development suggests a corresponding distinction between a weak and a strong sense of universality. Traditional notions of developmental universals, as far as they refer to empirical regularities resulting from commonalities in the social and cultural canalization of development, can qualify as universal in, at best, a weak sense (even if no exceptions have ever been observed). By contrast, to claim universality in a strict sense, it has to be demonstrated that falsifying events are logically or conceptually impossible, and thus can be excluded on an *a priori* basis.

Developmental Universals as Structural Implications

As already indicated, the search for universals of human development, or at least for universality in the strict sense, is often deemed to be an obsolete research heuristic, being diametrically opposed to a posture that emphasizes the formative impact of context and culture on human ontogeny. However, it seems that consideration of the formal and conceptual structures that constitute development in action contexts opens a fresh perspective on these issues.

The notion of constitutive rules provides a starting point for elaborating this argument. As introduced above, constitutive rules establish structural criteria that empirical phenomena must satisfy in order to count as an instance of a certain generic category. According to the constitutive rules defining, for example, the concept of altruism, acts of altruism must involve a sacrifice of one's own interests to the advantage of others; this feature serves as a criterion to identify altruistic intentions, and it will therefore be present in all valid exemplars of this type of altruistic act. If there never has been a case of altruistic behavior that did not involve an element of sacrifice, this is not due to some natural law or causal mechanism, but reflects constitutive rules that preclude such an event, quite in the same way as it would be impossible in chess to castle without moving the king two squares toward the rook. In physical theories, we have a similar situation when the measuring of a theoretical variable is based on, or derived from, some theoretical core assumption; here, the gathered data can of course not disconfirm those parts of a theory whose truth is asserted in the very procedure of observation. According to a structuralist view of theories (Balzer & Moulines, 1980; Balzer, Moulines, & Sneed, 1987), this "theoreticity" of measurements should not be viewed as a methodological weakness, but as characteristic of advanced physical theorizing.

Generally, we may assert: When a relationship of the type "If *A*, then *B*" is proposed, and the falsifying event (i.e., the occurrence of *A* without *B*) is excluded for reasons inherent in the formal or conceptual structure—or, as Wittgenstein put it (Waismann, 1979, p. 91), in the "syntax"—of the terms that figure in the proposition, then the proposition becomes a tautology, a statement that is true in all possible worlds. Implications that in this sense structurally preclude the falsifying case may be denoted as *structural implications,* or as propositions involving *implicative structures* (cf. Brandtstädter, 1987; Lenk, 1987). Structural implications in this sense correspond largely with an entailment account of necessary implications as advanced in relevance logic (Anderson & Belnap, 1975). According to relevance logic, the universal validity of necessary implications follows from a relation of entailment in which the meaning of the consequent is nested in the meaning of the antecedent, so that a valid verification of the antecedent condition necessarily involves the verification of the consequent. Interestingly, Piaget, in his late work, espoused a relevance logic point of view to elucidate the notion of necessity and its ontogenetic acquisition (Piaget, 1986, 1987; Piaget & Garcia, 1991; see also Overton, 1990; Ricco, 1993).

Structural implications may easily be confused with empirical hypotheses, at least as long as the structure of the concepts involved is not analyzed sufficiently. There are numerous examples of such confusions in psychological research (cf., Brandtstädter, 1982; Kukla, 1989; Smedslund, 1979, 1984). However, drawing firm distinctions between implicative and empirical relations can be problematic; especially when dealing with "cluster concepts" (Putnam, 1975) that involve a large array of interpretative specifications, the categorial border between meanings that are structurally implied and empirical correlates of the concept may be blurred (Brandtstädter, 1987; Lenk, 1987). Despite such reservations, the notion of implicative structures offers a vantage point for approaching the notion of developmental universals.

The point here is that implicative structures can impose an invariant order on ontogenetic sequences. Some notes of caution are required in advance, to avoid misunderstandings. First, it should be stressed that structural analyses, like empirical ones, are not fail-safe. It is not uncommon, for example, that presumedly "logical" ontogenetic sequences actually do not appear (Fischer, 1980); as Flavell (1972, p. 331) noted, "the path from logical to developmental priority can be an extremely slippery one." Furthermore, structural analyses can never account for a developmental sequence in any empirical detail. For example, scrutinizing the formal or conceptual implications of a developmental task can yield insights as to the steps involved in the acquisition of the pertinent skills or competencies, but may not tell us much about the type of learning experiences or didactic arrangements that might foster this process. By much the same token, structural analyses cannot explain why structurally homologous skills often are acquired at different ages or developmental stages; for example, children develop conservation of substance before conservation of weight, though the tasks have a similar formal structure (cf. Aebli, 1987; Piaget & Inhelder, 1974).

Paying heed to these caveats, the claim that implicative structures impose an invariant order on ontogenetic sequences should be read as follows:

Whenever a developmental state or outcome *D,* by virtue of its (formal, conceptual, material) structure, entails certain constituent elements C_i, then *D* will presuppose C_i also in the ontogenetic sequence. It may be an open empirical question whether C_i will emerge prior to, or simultaneously with, *D;* but to the extent that the occurrence of *D* without C_i can be excluded formally or conceptually, it should be impossible, for the same reasons, for D to precede C_i ontogenetically.

We shall now briefly consider three variants of structural implications that involve different types of structural relationships: (a) formal implications, (b) constructive and conventional implications, and (c) conceptual implications.

Formal Implications

This type of structural implication follows from the formal (logical, mathematical) structure of a given task or competence. As Piaget (e.g., 1970b; Inhelder & Piaget, 1958) has shown for the domain of cognitive development, the formal structure of a task is reflected both in the type of cognitive operations necessary for mastering it, and in the ontogenesis of these operations. For example, seriating objects according to size presupposes an understanding of the transitivity property of asymmetric relations; balance-scale tasks require a grasp of the compensatory relation that holds between the length of levers and the suspended weights; the competencies implicated by these tasks, in turn, presuppose more elementary ones such as detecting and monitoring differences in size or length; and so on. Such developmental sequences can be demonstrated empirically by appropriate methods such as scalogram analysis (Siegler, 1981; Strauss & Ephron-Wertheim, 1986), but they obviously do not reflect simple empirical or causal contingencies. Instead, they follow from the formal characteristics of the particular tasks (see also Smedslund, 1984).

Constructive and Conventional Implications

Actions often involve the competent use of mediating objects; particular skills (e.g., skiing, piano playing) are inherently tied to the competent use of instruments, tools, or other cultural artifacts. Efficient action here presupposes accommodation to the particular constructional features and demands of these mediating means (Kaminski, 1982; Leont'ev, 1978; Oerter, 1991). These structural features often impose strong constraints on the ordering of the steps in the acquisitional sequence (e.g., Resnick, 1973). For example, children will not be able to read the hands of a clock and tell the time unless they have acquired other component skills such as distinguishing between the clock's big and little hands, translating the positions of the hands into particular numerical relations, and so forth. There is no one-to-one relation between the structural features of an object

or instrument and the developmental steps that lead to its competent use (Fischer, 1980); yet, we can safely assume that, in the ontogenetic sequence, a complex skill will not emerge earlier than the constituent skills related to the specific structural features and demands of the objects and instruments involved.

These arguments appear to apply to all kinds of activities that are defined by specific production rules. Actions such as making a promise, dancing a waltz, or cooking Spaghetti Bolognese imply a recurrent configuration of actional and contextual elements, which is encoded in, for example, constitutive rules, prescriptions, or recipes. There may be variants and creative modifications, as well as atypical and less-than-successful realizations of the constitutive rules. In particular cases, categories may be fuzzy; there may even be no criterial feature that would be common to all possible instantiations (Rosch, 1977). In many cases such as the ones mentioned above, however, we can identify structural features that must invariantly be present because they define what counts as a valid instantiation of that type of act. A waltz can only be performed in ¾ time, a promise can only be given by one who understands the concept of obligation, and so forth. By excluding some ontogenetic sequences as structurally impossible, these structural implications also determine ontogenetic invariances.

Conceptual Implications

The meanings of the terms that we use in describing, and communicating about, behavioral or developmental phenomena essentially result from their position in a conceptual network. The semantic relations constituting such a network may be conceived of as a system of rules that determines which terms or attributes are "copredicable" (Keil, 1979), and which are not. The concept of "lie," for example, is semantically related to "truth" and "intention"; when we accuse someone of a lie, we mean that he or she has purposely told an untruth. As Piaget (1932) observed, young children often use the word "lie" in a vague manner to refer to naughty words; during the course of language acquisition, the use of the word gradually becomes restricted to untrue statements made with deceitful intent, thus conforming with established conceptual rules. These rules imply, however, that one cannot possibly identify a "lie" before having grasped the concepts of truth and intention, and that one will not be able to perform an act of lying before being able to discriminate between true and untrue and to act intentionally.

Invariant ontogenetic sequences such as those postulated in cognitive-developmental models of moral judgment can likewise be reconstructed as structural implications. Moral judgments essentially involve ascriptions of guilt and responsibility (Kohlberg, 1976; Turiel & Davidson, 1986); according to conceptual rules that relate responsibility to intentionality, an ascription of responsibility, in turn, implies consideration of the actor's motives, intentions, and constraints. From such analyses, we may derive that competent moral judgment ontogenetically presupposes a capability to assess the motives and intentions of other persons; this also corresponds to theoretical postulates about the "necessity but insufficiency" of social-cognitive competence for competent moral judgment (e.g., Selman & Damon, 1975). It is doubtful, however, that we are dealing here with a proposition that is open to empirical refutation; rather, it seems that the falsifying case (moral competence without social-cognitive competence) is conceptually incoherent and cannot occur—given a conceptually valid assessment of moral competence. Another constitutive feature of moral competence is the ability to evaluate prevalent social norms and institutions with respect to general ethical standards. This assumption is captured in the postulate that principled or postconventional moral judgment presupposes the development of a sociomoral perspective that is system-transcending or "prior to society" (e.g., Kohlberg, 1976). For basic conceptual reasons again, it is difficult to conceive of an ontogenetic pattern that would not conform with this assumption, because ethical principles formally implicate a universal, system-transcendent stance.

These examples give an impression of how ontogenetic forms reflect, and are influenced by, conceptual structures. This formative influence is, of course, particularly obvious in the domain of language acquisition. Through learning and instruction, communicative behavior is gradually made to conform with the established semiotic order. This constructive process is reflected in what Keil and Batterman (1984) have described as the "characteristic-to-defining" shift. When using a concept, children initially focus on salient features that, by way of statistical association, characterize typical instantiations of the concept (from the child's perspective, "uncle" may denote an older adult who sometimes brings a gift when he visits).

As language development proceeds, the child increasingly heeds the structural invariants that define the concept (e.g., "uncle" as defined by a specific kinship relation), and so eventually becomes capable of correctly categorizing atypical exemplars that do not exhibit the expected characteristic features, as well as invalid cases that do so, but lack the defining features.

Conceptual structures do not only shape language development, as the given examples might perhaps suggest. Rather, they impose constraints on ontogenetic patterns wherever developmental phenomena are produced, defined, or assessed with reference to conceptual categories. To briefly illustrate this point, I shall consider some examples from the domain of emotional development. Emotion terms are embedded within, and derive their meaning from, a network of other mental concepts that we use when describing and explaining actions. For instance, "envy" is conceptually related to a process of social comparison; "jealousy" implies the perception of a particular social constellation; "worry" or "fear" implies the anticipation of aversive events, as well as doubts concerning one's ability to avert these events; "pride" points to the perception of a personal success, and so on (Brandtstädter, 1987; Mees, 1991). In the guise of causal hypotheses, relationships of this kind have also been proposed in attributional theories of emotion (e.g., Weiner, 1982). However, for a relationship to qualify as a causal contingency, the effect must be verifiable independently of the cause. Whether the cases considered can meet this formal requirement has to be questioned. If we were to ascribe feelings of, for example, envy to someone, while denying at the same time that he or she experiences the criterial cognitions constituting that emotion, this would not be a conceivable observation, but rather a case of conceptual confusion. Here again, the conceptual structures define a developmental order. If a particular emotion implies a criterial or defining cognition, it will also ontogenetically presuppose the development of the corresponding cognitive competencies. Such structurally implied sequences of emotional development also emerge in empirical studies (cf., Averill, 1980; Brandtstädter, 1987; Frijda, 1986; Reisenzein & Schönpflug, 1992). This does not, however, convert a structural implication into an empirical conjecture; rather, it attests to the conceptual validity of the empirical procedures employed.

It is important to note that, unlike causal structures, semiotic structures or rules have no inherent formative force; their effect on development is mediated by individual and collective action. In fact, the processes of socialization or intentional self-development largely aim at bringing individual behavior and development into a form that justifies the application of certain concepts—concepts, for example, that denote competencies, developmental tasks, or positively valued traits. Furthermore, we should note that implicative structures that (in the mediated way specified above) form development are themselves the product of formative processes (Piaget, 1970b; Wartofsky, 1971). Semiotic structures, unless fixed by terminological dictates, are not invariant; they accommodate to changes in socially shared beliefs and values, so that successive modifications of a concept may eventually be connected only by a loose relationship of family resemblance (Putnam, 1975; Rosch, 1978). The same is true, of course, for norms, institutions, or conventions, and for other structures that generate regular and recurrent developmental forms.

How can we look for invariance and universality on such unstable grounds? To this question, the following comment might be given: Although we can imagine cultures or historical periods in which particular language games and rules simply do not/did not exist, it is likewise true that developmental constructs have no independent existence outside the semiotic and institutional structures that constitute them first and foremost. Developmental patterns that are constructed and defined within given language games will necessarily follow the rules of those games. The games may change, but "When language games change then there is a change in concepts, and with the concepts the meanings of the words change" (Wittgenstein, 1969, p. 65).

To summarize, it appears that an action-theoretical perspective affords an improved understanding of both diversity and invariance in development. In defending this view, we have posited that the range within which developmental processes may vary and be modified is broad, but not unlimited. It is limited by constraints that may change across cultures and epochs (e.g., normative, theoretical, and technological constraints), as well as by constraints that, by definition, are not bound to particular contexts (such as physical laws and logical principles). Constancy and invariance in development often result from commonalities in the ways in which ontogenetic processes are canalized through personal and collective action. We have also tried to show how a stronger concept of developmental universality that

goes beyond mere empirical regularity might be derived from a consideration of the formal, conventional, or material structures that are constitutive of particular developmental phenomena. This puts into perspective any claims that the search for universality is antithetical to an understanding of development and diversity in historical and cultural contexts. An actional perspective on development can apparently encompass both heuristic stances.

INTENTIONAL SELF-DEVELOPMENT AND PERSONAL CONTROL OVER DEVELOPMENT

The individual as a producer of his or her own development—this idea, as presented, is not novel. Interactionist, contextualist, and organismic-structuralist approaches have embraced this notion, and thus have contributed to discrediting lopsided views that portray the developing subject as being only the passive recipient of formative influences (cf. Bronfenbrenner, 1979; Lerner, 1982; Magnusson, 1990; Reese & Overton, 1970; Sameroff, 1975). These approaches, however—and organismic models in particular—have primarily conceived of development as the result of person–environment transactions, rather than as a target area of intentional action; in other words, the relation between action and development has been conceptualized primarily as a functional rather than an intentional one. This focus seems appropriate for early phases of development; the infant certainly does not engage in interactions with the social or material environment with the intention of promoting his or her development. At very early developmental stages, the child's activity may show signs of intentionality, but it is not intentionally directed toward some developmental task or goal. Such intentional orientations generally come into play indirectly through other agents—primarily, through the caregivers who organize and constrain the child's space of action according to an intended developmental agenda, and who thereby shape and canalize the child's further development in co-constructive interaction with the child and with the cultural macrosystem (Goodnow & Collins, 1990; Lerner, 1985; Valsiner, 1988c; Wozniak, 1993).

During the transition to adolescence and early adulthood, the individual's conceptions of self and of personal future become articulated enough to guide intentional activity. External directives and demands originating in the familial and larger social context become increasingly internalized and integrated into processes of self-regulation and self-evaluation; with the progression from a heteronomous, external mode of developmental control to an increasingly intentional and autonomous mode of intentional self-development, a new and higher level in the regulation of ontogeny is reached. This reflexive-intentional mode has been given rather short shrift in developmental research; for an actional perspective, it is of focal interest.

In elaborating this point, it will be necessary to heed the reciprocal character of the action–development relationship. Activities of intentional self-development are themselves developmental outcomes; they change over the life cycle in structure and intentional content. In this section, I shall first try to elucidate the basic processual features of such activities. Based on these analyses, I shall then focus more closely on the ontogeny of self-regulatory activities as well as on modifications and changes in these activities across the life span.

Activities of Intentional Self-Development: Structure and Process

Self-regulative activities in contexts of intentional self-development comprise different functional components. Models of self-regulation differentiate mostly among the following phases or component processes (Bandura, 1986; Carver & Scheier, 1981, 1986; Kanfer & Hagerman, 1981; Karoly, 1993; Schunk, 1991): (a) processes of self-observation and self-evaluation, in which the convergence with an actual and a desired situation or course of events is monitored; (b) predecisional or preparatory processes, which involve the weighing of alternative options, the specification of goals, and the elaboration of plans for goal implementation; (c) executive processes (when goal-directed behavior has to be maintained over longer periods, the executive phase may engage auxiliary processes to buffer implementational intentions against distractive influences and to compensate for the relative absence of external supports); and (d) evaluative processes, in which the efficiency of actions is assessed with respect to intended outcomes, and which also serve to gauge self-views of competence and efficacy. The various phases or levels of action regulation are partly intertwined and often cannot be separated cleanly. In complex, nonroutine tasks, preparatory and executive phases may comprise intermediate action cycles, each of which involves the whole range of processes

distinguished above. It has to be emphasized that the transformation of intention into action is not generally a smooth or automatic process; rather, difficulties may occur in the transition between the different phases or levels of action regulation. Such problems deserve particular attention because they often give rise to feelings of helplessness and depression (Kuhl & Beckmann, 1985).

Figure 14.3 (see also Brandtstädter, 1992) summarizes these considerations, translates them into the realm of development-related action, and serves as an orienting framework for further discussion.

In Figure 14.3, the connection of self-observational and self-corrective phases resembles a feedback loop. In the typical negative feedback loop, observed deviations from a preset standard activate corrective measures designed to counteract the discrepancy (for action-theoretical applications of the feedback loop concept, see Carver & Scheier, 1981; Miller, Galanter, & Pribram, 1960). However, some caveats have to be added. First, it should be clear that activities of intentional self-development may be induced not only by currently perceived but also by anticipated discrepancies from a desired developmental course or outcome. More important yet, activities of intentional self-development may involve not only discrepancy reduction but also discrepancy production, as is the case when persons set themselves new and more ambitious goals. Such self-generated discrepancies are not frustrating, but rather provide positive motivation and a sense of meaning in life (Bandura, 1989, 1991). The positive emotional quality of internally induced (as compared to externally produced) goal discrepancies is presumably related to differences in perceived control; generally, individuals only select new goals that they consider to be attainable. Finally, negative-feedback models of self-regulatory behavior do not provide

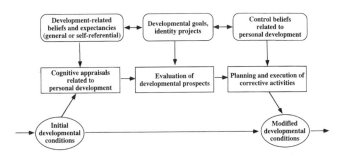

Figure 14.3 Personal control of development: component processes and constraints.

for the important fact that discrepancies between actual and desired situations can be reduced not only by changing the situation in accordance with goals but, conversely, by adjusting goals and conditions to situational circumstances—for example, through rescaling self-evaluative standards or downgrading ambitions (Brandtstädter & Renner, 1990; Elster, 1983; Klinger, 1975, 1987). As I will discuss later in greater detail, this adjustment of preferences is fundamental to understanding changes in themes and goals of intentional development across the life cycle.

Self-Observation and Self-Monitoring in Intentional Self-Development

In self-observation and self-monitoring, bottom-up or data-driven processes are interlinked with top-down or concept-driven processes. To assess, for example, whether some attribute denoting a certain skill or competence applies to oneself, one has to scrutinize behavioral episodes and pertinent representations in episodic memory to ascertain whether they sufficiently match the indicator pattern of the particular attribute. This process is directed and constrained by conceptual rules that are stored in semantic memory and are activated during the process of self-observation (cf., Berzonsky, 1988; Medin & Smith, 1984).

Through elaborating the meaning and implications of observational data, a semantic link or correspondence with self-concept representations is construed, given that goals and self-evaluative standards also are sufficiently elaborated. Self-evaluative processes will not be activated unless such a correspondence is established. To be compared in an evaluative contrast, goals and observations must be represented on a similar level of specification; this hints at a potential trouble spot in self-regulatory processes.

Processes of self-monitoring can differ inter- and intra-individually with respect to their differentiation, thematic focus, and accuracy. These qualities depend on cognitive resources and motivational dispositions, which can change over the life cycle.

Complexity and Differentiation

The more explicit and detailed the monitoring process, the more precise the timing and targeting of corrective interventions can be. For example, one can control one's weight more effectively when changes in weight and related parameters such as calorie intake are monitored closely and

regularly (Bandura, 1982b; Mace, Belfiore, & Shea, 1989; Schunk, 1991). Explicitness and differentiation of self-observation depend on person-specific and situational factors. Of great importance are the complexity and richness of the individual's knowledge base, which itself is dependent on personal and biographical conditions such as cognitive capacity and expertise (Sternberg & Wagner, 1986). The quality of self-observation also depends on personal interests and motivations, insofar as areas of personal importance are generally monitored more intensively and carefully than those of less relevance. In cases where self-referential feedback has threatening or self-depreciating implications, however, defensive processes may be activated that inhibit a careful scrutiny of information (cf. Kruglanski, 1990); we shall discuss this point more closely in later sections.

Attentional Focus

Self-observation involves self-focused attention. The readiness to make oneself (and one's self) the target of attentive observation differs across individuals and situations; dispositional differences are addressed by constructs such as "self-awareness" (Duval & Wicklund, 1972), "self-consciousness" (Fenigstein, Scheier, & Buss, 1975), or "self-monitoring" (Snyder, 1979). A state of self-attentiveness is particularly likely to occur in situations of high personal concern that have implications for the public or private construal of the agent's self, and in which no routinized pattern of action is readily available (Karoly, 1993). Generally, attention is centered on those elements in an action sequence that lack a safe orientational basis, so that additional information has to be gathered or generated to prepare the next steps (Carver & Scheier, 1986, 1990; Parasuraman & Davies, 1984; Vallacher & Wegner, 1987).

The regulation of attention engages automatic as well as strategic-intentional processes (Shiffrin & Dumais, 1981; Shiffrin & Schneider, 1977); as an intentional strategy, self-focused attention may serve purposes of self-cultivation, self-management, or self-presentation, and may enhance a flexible adjustment to changing social situations (Bandura, 1986; Snyder & Campbell, 1982; Tesser, 1986). Within biographical contexts, self-focused attention is intensified when a person is faced with disruptive changes or critical developmental transitions that necessitate a readjustment of personal goals, projects, and behavioral routines. Self-attentive and self-corrective tendencies are generally more pronounced among persons dissatisfied with themselves and their developmental prospects (Brandtstädter, 1989). Self-critical reflection involves a temporary dissociation of the self into a criticizing and a criticized part, a condition that—since Aristotle (Arendt, 1976)—many authors have viewed as pathological or pathogenic (e.g., Ellis, 1976). However, it seems more appropriate to consider self-attention not as the cause, but rather as a symptom of an adaptive problem, or, more precisely, as a functional component in processes of coping and readjustment.

In a broader sense, self-attention may involve all external conditions that are relevant for personal goals and projects. Phases in the life course in which demands from different and potentially conflicting roles and tasks coincide may involve a particularly high attentional load; in everyday contexts, different goals and courses of action are often pursued simultaneously. The strain that results from simultaneously attending to different goals and tasks can be reduced by a decomposition and sequential arrangement of tasks; for example, the diversity of adaptive problems that characterizes physical and social development in adolescence is reduced to a manageable format by addressing the problems sequentially and focusing on only one issue at a time (Coleman, 1980). A decomposition of multiple tasks through sequential focusing is to some extent automatically effected in the process of attention deployment itself (Dörner, 1984). Generally, attention centers on those contents and themes that constitute a person's "current concerns" (Klinger, 1987); with a change in life themes and identity projects, the focus of attention shifts accordingly, even if the individual is not explicitly aware of such changes (Csikszentmihalyi & Beattie, 1979; Erikson, 1959).

Protective and Defensive Mechanisms

Like other perceptual processes, but even more so, the process of representing ourselves is tinged by personal motives, needs, and subjective theories. The processing of self-referential information is subject in particular to constraints that serve to maintain, as far as possible, the integrity and continuity of the self theories that we have devised and consolidated over the course of our lives, and that guide us in organizing our future development (Greenwald, 1980). Observations generally are open to multiple interpretations; from alternative explanatory and interpretative options, those will be preferred most readily that fit best with the person's actual motives and beliefs. Individuals tend to doubt the validity of data that are discrepant to prior beliefs; in extreme cases, a rejection or blatant denial of evidence may occur (Festinger, 1957; Nisbett & Ross, 1980; Wicklund & Brehm, 1976). It is certainly true that the cognitive system is evolutionarily geared to evaluate, rather than preserve, the actor's beliefs. But even if evidence is strong enough to enforce a change in the subject's system of prior beliefs, these changes will obey a principle of conservatism that Quine (1951, p. 41), with regard to the dynamics of scientific theories, has put as follows: "[O]ur natural tendency is to disturb the system as little as possible." A theoretical proposition can, at least in principle, always be defended against discrepant evidence by making adjustments elsewhere in the theoretical system; the same is true for the hypotheses that people hold about themselves.

Apart from consistency effects of the kind mentioned above, established self-referential beliefs are backed by tendencies of self-verification and self-enhancement. Evidence will generally be negotiated in ways that have positive implications for our self-concept and personal view of the world, and self-enhancing interpretations will generally be more readily accessible than self-denigrating ones (Kunda, 1990; Steele, 1988; Swann, 1983). Mechanisms of self-enhancement and cognitive consistency generally merge in the processing of self-referential information (Snyder & Higgins, 1988). In particular cases, however, the tendencies can conflict with one another; for example, self-deprecating or threatening evidence may be so strong that negating it would violate other strong beliefs. There is some evidence that, in such cases, consistency principles dominate over tendencies of self-enhancement (Swann, Griffin, Predmore, & Gaines, 1987).

Concepts such as "self-serving bias," "denial," or "defense" connote a violation of rationality principles; the influence of self-protective mechanisms in information processing seems opposed to a "realistic" self-view, which has been traditionally considered to be a basic requirement of mental health and optimal development. However, even within the limits of rationality, there is generally a broad scope for handling evidence in self-serving ways, so the functionality of such mechanisms must be assessed cautiously (Taylor, 1989). From a developmental perspective, the potential adaptive value of self-protective mechanisms becomes particularly apparent. For example, as people age, the self scheme formed in earlier phases of life is threatened by experiences of loss in various functional and social domains; protective and defensive mechanisms help to preserve self-esteem and personal continuity when individuals confront aversive and irreversible developmental changes. Though they operate largely on a nonintentional level, such mechanisms affect activities of intentional self-development in various ways. By dampening perceptions of loss and identity deficits, protective mechanisms may inhibit self-corrective tendencies, but they also serve to arrange priorities for self-corrective intervention, and to canalize self-regulatory resources into domains that are amenable to change (Brandtstädter & Greve, 1994).

Processes of Self-Evaluation

Self-evaluative reactions mediate between self-observation and self-regulative action. In the process of self-evaluation, the actual self-perceptions are contrasted with representations of desired self-aspects, as manifested in the individual's goals, ambitions, moral orientations, and identity projects (Higgins, Strauman, & Klein, 1986). As mentioned earlier, both self-evaluative standards and observational data have to be represented on an appropriate level of specification for such an evaluative contrast.

During goal implementation, the focus of self-evaluation may shift to temporal, qualitative, or quantitative modalities of goal attainment (to reach a career goal within a certain biographical span; to maintain a given rate of progress toward a goal; and so forth). Such implementational standards are formed in the transition from intention to action, and they are, to some extent, necessary for such a transition to occur. When implementational standards become salient as reference points for self-evaluation, a new level of "metamonitoring" (Carver & Scheier, 1986) is established, which is reflected, for example, in the fact that emotions such as disappointment, pride, or shame are no longer determined by the perceived discrepancy or distance from the goal as such, but rather by the perceived rate, quality, or smoothness of progress toward the goal.

Self-evaluative standards can change over the life cycle; this fact once more highlights the reciprocal influence between action and development. For example, with advancing age, desired features such as health, intellectual efficiency, or professional success may assume partly different meanings, and the corresponding self-evaluative standards may be raised or lowered. Changes in action resources that result from the interaction of age-graded, sociohistorical, and nonnormative factors across the life course (Baltes, Cornelius, & Nesselroade, 1979) may affect the difficulty and, accordingly, the personal costs of realizing certain goals or maintaining certain standards. Shifts in personal goals and standards over the life course may also reflect implicit theories of development and normative age expectations; by defining what expectations persons of a given age should hold for themselves and their future development, normative expectations can either legitimate or discredit personal goals and aspirations. Individuals differ with respect to their flexibility in adjusting goals and standards to changed developmental prospects; as we shall discuss in more depth later, this accommodative flexibility plays an important role in coping with developmental losses and in securing a sense of personal continuity and efficacy over the life span (cf. Atchley, 1989; Brandtstädter & Renner, 1990; Brim, 1992).

Activation and Inhibition of Self-Evaluative Reactions

Self-evaluative reactions depend on how individuals construe the meanings and effects of their actions. It follows that self-evaluative processes, and the ensuing action tendencies, can be enhanced or weakened through destruction or alteration of such meanings and implications. Self-corrective tendencies may be dampened by minimizing or downplaying negative implications of personal conduct or by balancing them against presumed positive effects; the beliefs, theories, or symbol systems that generate negative implications may be doubted or discredited; or, if the individual's behavior or development deviates from social norms, ascriptions of responsibility, self-reproaches, or feelings of guilt may be neutralized, for example, by construing the event as uncontrollable or by portraying it as morally legitimate (Bandura, 1989; Snyder & Higgins, 1988). Self-evaluation is also crucially affected by chosen comparison standards. For example, when evaluating their health or physical capacities, elderly people typically compare themselves to peers rather than to younger persons (or to themselves at a younger age); in this way, the salience of losses or functional impairments is reduced, and a stability of self-description—in the sense of positional stability within a reference group—can be maintained (Brandtstädter & Greve, 1994; Heckhausen & Krueger, 1993).

From an action point of view, however, the self-enhancing effects of "downward" comparisons must be balanced against their potential effect of dampening self-corrective intentions. In contrast, "upward" comparisons (comparisons with admired ideals or competitors of superior competence) may induce a negative self-evaluation, but they can also provide motivating goals for self-development, at least as long as the individual is confident of having the action resources and developmental reserves necessary for realizing these goals (cf., Buunk, Collins, Taylor, VanYperen, & Dakof, 1990; Wills, 1991).

The cognitive and symbolic processes through which self-evaluations are engaged or disengaged are important targets in self-management; for example, mental simulation of positive or aversive outcomes can be an effective means to spur self-corrective tendencies and to maintain a given course of action against obstacles and temptations (Taylor & Schneider, 1989). It would be a mistake, however, to view the above-mentioned processes simply as intentional or strategic behaviors that may be activated at will. Such processes basically hinge on the availability and personal accessibility of pertinent information. For example, biographical experiences determine which episodes are available as reference standards for evaluating actual developmental options, and thus can significantly influence the setting of aspiration levels and the individual's readiness to accept the situation (Strack, Schwarz, Chassein, Kern, & Wagner, 1990). Contrast effects of this nature might possibly account for the well-documented fact that older persons, who mostly have suffered wars and economic crises, seem to be less vulnerable to depression than younger generations (Blazer, 1989; Seligman, 1990). Existential attitudes such as religious beliefs, or a belief in a just world, likewise can influence the accessibility of specific interpretations; for example, in coping with losses, such attitudes may enhance or impede the construction of palliative meanings, depending on responsibility attributions (Montada, 1992).

Developmental ecologies, in general, may differ as to the particular meanings and comparative standards they afford. Cultural and historical influences, as well as factors related to a person's position in the life cycle, shape and constrain the informational and symbolic space in which processes of self-evaluation operate. Social systems institutionalize conceptions of desirable development, and they tend to stabilize such conceptions through contriving legitimating stories and providing arguments and symbols that support them (Dannefer & Perlmutter, 1990). Furthermore, normative expectations and stereotypes about development and aging provide the backdrop against which views are negotiated as to what should be considered as normal, reasonable, or appropriate for individuals of a given age. Such informational and symbolic constraints have a normative and directive influence on processes of intentional self-development.

Emotions in Self-Evaluation

The process of self-evaluation can activate a broad spectrum of positive or aversive emotions. One might look back on one's life course with feelings of pride, anger, or gratitude; future developmental prospects may evoke hope and confidence, or perhaps fear, worry, or despondency. When developmental prospects are ambiguous or polyvalent, a mixture of such feelings often occurs.

Emotions are linked to, and mediate between, cognitions and action tendencies (e.g., Averill, 1980). In contexts of intentional self-development, emotions signaling a mismatch between intended and actual developmental outcomes are of particular interest, because of their inherent potential to enhance corrective action. Affective reactions of guilt, anger, and worry may be considered as examples. As a future-oriented emotion involving the expectation of aversive events, *worry* typically engages preventive tendencies, and it motivates efforts to acquire knowledge and skills that are deemed instrumental for coping with the aversive event. Feelings of *guilt* or *remorse* involve a belief of having violated specific norms, normative expectations, or moral principles; such emotional states may engage tendencies of self-punishment, recompensation, or activities to stabilize threatened self-definitions through "symbolic self-completion" (Wicklund & Gollwitzer, 1982). Feelings of *anger* indicate an obstruction of personal goals; they typically involve a proclivity toward destroying the frustrating obstacles. Reactions of anger are particularly strong when positive contrasts are readily accessible (Kahnemann & Miller, 1986; Miller, Turnbull, & McFarland, 1990). These examples should not be taken to imply that self-referential emotions are important only in self-regulation. Empathetic reactions of pity or sympathy, or feelings of awe or disdain that may be evoked by observing the conduct of other persons, can likewise affect intentional self-development through making salient particular facets of one's own identity and morality (cf., Taylor, 1989).

Through further analysis and cognitive elaboration of a perceived situation, emotional appraisals, as well as the corresponding self-regulatory tendencies, may be modified in intensity and quality (Lazarus & Smith, 1988; Parkinson & Manstead, 1992). Depending on how the person, upon further analysis, appraises the implications of a threatening situation, as well as his or her capabilities of handling them, feelings of anger or worry may be converted into hope or happiness, or into emotional states of hopelessness and despair. When negative events such as developmental losses or impairments are perceived as global and irreversible, feelings of sadness and hopelessness typically result. Such feelings may arise, for example, in later life, when the individual realizes that personally important projects cannot be achieved within the remaining lifetime. Feelings of hopelessness may eventually be transformed into more chronic states of depression if goals and ambitions that have drifted outside the feasible range are maintained tenaciously. Depressive reactions are often characterized by a feeling of not being able to be or become the person that one would like to be; to this extent, such reactions may mark crises as well as turning points in personal development. Often, states of depression can be terminated only by disengaging oneself from barren commitments and turning to new goals; feelings of helplessness may even spur processes of disengagement and reorientation (Brandtstädter, 1989; Carver & Scheier, 1990; Klinger, 1987).

From Goals to Action: Definition and Implementation of Developmental Goals

When different individuals are asked (or the same individuals are asked at different times) to report the goals they pursue for their future, answers will typically differ as to abstractness and globality. The scope of goal perspectives can range from highly abstract ideals (e.g., to actualize personal potentials, to strive for professional competence, to fight for peace and justice) to very concrete tasks and day-to-day projects like visiting a friend or running an errand. Such differences may be related to person-specific factors like value orientations or the range of future perspectives; in later life, the fading of time-yet-to-be-lived may reduce the commitment to long-term projects (cf., Brandtstädter & Wentura, 1994; Kastenbaum, 1982). Goals on different

levels of temporal extension and generality are often pursued simultaneously, so that concrete, short-term projects often serve more long-term or abstract purposes. The hierarchical organization of actions and action plans is reflected in the fact that questions about personal motives or reasons for a given activity ("Why?") typically prompt accounts in terms of higher-level goals, whereas questions concerning the ways in which a particular activity is carried out ("How?") tend to evoke low-level, instrumental goals (Martin & Tesser, 1989). Differences in the "phrasing level" of goals (Little, 1989), however, may also point to the level of regulation in the transition from goal definition to implementation on which the individual's attention is actually centered (cf. Pennebaker, 1989; Vallacher & Wegner, 1987). Attention centers preferably on goals, plans, or steps within an action sequence that pose implementational problems; as intimated above, pondering about basic personal goals and life themes is increased in situations of crisis and conflict. This converges with findings pointing to an association between depression and a predominant concern with high-level strivings (Emmons, 1992).

Developmental research has traditionally addressed life themes and developmental goals from a very global perspective; the emphasis was on establishing a general pattern or sequence of basic motivational concerns over the life cycle. For example, Bühler (1933; see also Bühler & Marschak, 1969) posited five basic life tendencies ("need satisfaction," "adaptive self-limitation," "creative expansion," "establishment of inner order," and "self-fulfillment"), which she assumed to govern behavior and personal development in different phases of the life cycle from early childhood to late adulthood. Elaborating Bühler's model, Erikson (1959) portrayed eight stages of identity development across the life cycle, each with its salient psychosocial crisis and task (e.g., the dominant issues of adolescence and of middle and later adulthood were grouped under the labels of "identity," "generativity," and "ego integrity," respectively). In his model of developmental tasks, Havighurst (1948/1974) defined a basic pattern of priorities for self-development across the life span, which he assumed to reflect the joint influence of biological changes and of age-graded cultural demands. These concepts undoubtedly had a seminal influence in developmental research, but they give short shrift to the variegation of developmental goals in terms of their content, complexity, and abstraction, and to the processes mediating the definition and implementation of goals. Recent approaches within personality and action research provide a more differentiated treatment of these issues; for example, the concepts of "personal strivings" (Emmons, 1986, 1989, 1992), "personal projects" (Little, 1983, 1989), "life themes" (Csikszentmihalyi & Beattie, 1979; Schank & Abelson, 1977), or "life tasks" (Cantor & Fleeson, 1991; Zirkel & Cantor, 1990) are formulated with explicit reference to the regulative role of goals in personal development.

Goals of intentional self-development are reflected in the plans, projects, and courses of action in which the individual invests time and effort. Only rarely, however, are developmental goals represented from the outset in a format that already specifies the means and procedures necessary for goal attainment. Sociocultural developmental tasks (Havighurst, 1948/1974), too, are usually framed with a degree of abstraction that allows the implementation to be tailored to personal and situational circumstances. The implementation of goals basically depends on three types of constraints: (a) how the goal in question is interpreted; (b) the means that are deemed necessary for goal attainment; and (c) whether the relevant means and resources are available on social and personal levels. We shall now take a closer look at the translation of goals into intentions, and of intentions into actions.

Levels of Regulation: Control-System Accounts

According to control-system accounts of action, the process of transforming goals into actions involves a hierarchy of feedback loops; goals on a superordinate level of regulation are converted successively into more specific plans or programs, and then into concrete behavioral sequences (cf., Carver & Scheier, 1986; Powers, 1973). Thus, for example, the abstract principle of "being helpful" may, depending on situational circumstances, activate a specific program such as "helping an elderly person to cross the street," which, in turn, is further specified and translated into behavioral sequences. This top-down process is also constrained by perceptual input to generate situationally appropriate specifications. Within the hierarchy, the progression from lower to higher levels of regulation is mediated by subroutines such as cognitive scripts or production systems; each level sets subgoals or reference values against which activities on the next lower level are monitored.

Activities of intentional self-development may be easily analyzed in similar terms. The most abstract and general life themes and identity projects would then be represented on a superordinate level of regulation, and would be successively specified and transformed on subsequent levels into situationally appropriate plans and behaviors, as outlined above. The heuristic advantages of such hierarchical, top-down concepts of action control are obvious. Perhaps most important, the transition from goals to actions is portrayed as a creative, nondeductive process. For habitualized action patterns, this transition may be partly or fully automatized; in nonroutine situations, however, knowledge structures and heuristic procedures will have to be activated in order to specify and implement goals and intentions. Accordingly, the hierarchic-sequential model also offers vantage points for analyzing disorders in action regulation; obviously, the functional interplay between levels of regulation may be affected in cases in which the actor's knowledge, competencies, or skills do not suffice to link abstract goals with concrete meanings, plans, and procedures.

However, it is necessary to add some reservations to this picture. As already mentioned, any plan or behavior may serve different goals simultaneously. Hierarchic-sequential models have notorious difficulties in accounting for the polyvalence of actions and for the conflicts and compromises that may result from it in the definition and execution of goals. Moreover, we often see only in hindsight how our actions relate to superordinate goals and principles; in the ontogenetic sequence, too, the acquisition of certain action patterns can precede an understanding of their meaning and relevance. The most important objection, however, is that the streamlined format of hierarchic-sequential models gives a biased or inadequate picture of acting and planning in complex situations, in which priorities are often rearranged ad hoc, plans are concretized or revised during implementation, and goals may change in an overtly unsystematic and opportunistic manner. Such "planning in action" (Meyer & Rebok, 1985) is particularly characteristic for global, long-term, or vaguely defined goals. Because of its adaptive flexibility, such "muddling through" may be the most reasonable strategy (if it is one) in situations fraught with uncertainty and complexity (Popper, 1961). Under such conditions, planning activities tend to exhibit an incremental, ad hoc quality rather than a linear, top-down format (Hayes-Roth & Hayes-Roth, 1979); planning about life is perhaps the prototypical case.

These reservations call for a more fine-grained analysis of the processes of goal definition and implementation in intentional self-development. In the following, we shall first address the semantic and procedural specification of goals, and then turn to issues related to the enactment and maintenance of self-regulatory intentions.

Goal Definition: Semantic and Procedural Specification

To serve as guidelines for intentional self-development, goals have to be specified with respect to their semantic implications—that is, as to their meanings and criteria, as well as with respect to procedural implications related to their implementation. It seems important to distinguish carefully between these two dimensions of the goal definition process, because they generally involve different types of knowledge and heuristic procedures. The connection of semantic and procedural specifications of a given goal may be denoted as a *plan* (Friedman, Scholnick, & Cocking, 1987; Nuttin, 1984; Smith, 1996, in press).

Whether we consider professional career goals, goals related to codevelopment in partnerships, or maintenance goals concerning the preservation of physical or mental competencies in later life, the formation of more concrete implementation intentions always requires the unfolding of the semantic implications of the given goal—that is, an explicit representation of criteria or prototypical features that define the intended outcomes. These interpretations may be available already in semantic memory; otherwise, they have to be construed through mediating heuristic activities. Social scripts and institutionalized definitions may aid and direct this interpretative process. Through semantic elaboration, goals are linked with a "recognizer pattern" (Schank & Abelson, 1977) of more explicit indicators, which guides the processing of information in the execution and evaluation of goal-related activities, and which, in particular, facilitates retrieval of relevant procedural knowledge from long-term memory (Taylor & Crocker, 1981).

Semantic specification of goals, however, is not sufficient for regulating goal-related action; representations of intended goal states have to be fleshed out by linking them to representations of the conditions and activities that are relevant for attaining a given intended state. As intimated above, such operative links cannot be formed unless the pertinent procedural information is contextually available and cognitively accessible to the actor. When different and equally effective options for accomplishing a goal are available, actors will generally prefer the one that seems to afford the most favorable balance of desirable and undesirable side effects. For example, in accomplishing some career goal, one will choose an option that appears most compatible with other personal goals and identity projects (such as personal principles of fairness, health-related or family-related interests, and so forth). This highlights the important point that the specification and selection of goals for personal development is subject to optimality principles that take into account the whole system of personal goals and projects, or at least the parts of it that are eventually affected by a given procedure of goal attainment. As a consequence, the procedural specification of goals often involves compromises that may be suboptimal with respect to the given goal but promise a greater utility with respect to the more comprehensive array of personal interests. This more comprehensive perspective may even embrace the needs and interests of other persons. In contexts of marital codevelopment, for example, the life ambitions and developmental goals of partners often have to be mutually adjusted in order to preserve a stable and satisfying relationship (Brandtstädter, Krampen, & Heil, 1986; Ickes, 1985). The degree to which an egocentric stance in the choice and procedural specification of goals is transcended also reflects the actor's sociomoral perspective. Moral and ethical criteria have the essential function of constraining the selection and implementation of personal goals in ways that heed the interests of codeveloping individuals.

Action Paths and Chronic Goals

The procedural specification of goals, and of long-term developmental goals and projects in particular, generally determines a temporal sequence of intermediate steps. The subgoals within a planned action sequence generally encompass a shorter time span than the superordinate or distal goals to which they relate (Carver & Scheier, 1981). The sequential structure of plans is also important from a motivational point of view; reduction of the complexity of a task enhances the perceived control over the actional sequence and affords proximal reinforcements that contribute to the maintenance of intentions over longer periods (Bandura, 1986; Harackiewicz & Sansone, 1991; Pervin, 1991).

Sequences of action steps or subgoals, when they are instrumentally related to a common overarching life theme or goal, form what may be called an "action path" (Raynor, 1981). The individual's self-view and future perspective critically hinge on the temporal extension of, and the progress within, action paths. The initial steps are motivated primarily through anticipation of further achievements within the path; with continuing advancement, retrospection on previous achievements becomes increasingly important as a source of self-evaluation. When paths are terminated by the attainment of a desired final outcome ("closed paths"; Raynor & Entin, 1982, 1983), a loss of meaning and purpose may be experienced (cf. Baumeister, 1986). The emotional quality of personal developmental prospects thus depends crucially on how far the subject succeeds in keeping action paths open or avoiding closure through interlocking paths and creating new and meaningful commitments: "The open path . . . provides a means of understanding the difference between individuals who remain psychologically young through continued becoming and those who become psychologically old through exclusive dependence upon having been . . ." (Raynor, 1982, p. 274). Often, action paths may be extended by a motive to secure, further improve, or embellish what has been achieved (cf. Schank & Abelson, 1977). The sequential arrangement of developmental tasks and normative social expectations across the life cycle may also facilitate a meaningful interlocking of goals and action paths. With advancing age, however, the shrinking of the temporal horizon tends to cut short and finalize action paths; accordingly, reminiscing about biographical achievements becomes increasingly important in later life as a resource of personal continuity and self-respect (Coleman, 1986).

As already mentioned, not all goals can be finally attained through a sequence of instrumental steps. Apart from the trivial fact that goals might be too difficult for the individual to achieve, some goals are chronic or persistent in the sense that, by their very nature, they cannot be reached conclusively. Goals may be rooted in enduring motivational dispositions for which no conclusive consummatory event can be defined—for example, a striving for health, social recognition, or professional success may (perhaps under continual accommodation of standards and criteria) shape and regulate intentional self-development during an entire life. Other goals may function like general maxims or rules of conduct that the person takes into consideration whenever there is a need to act, decide, or make plans. For example, identity goals such as sincerity, fairness, altruism, or wisdom denote qualities of action that are manifested in, rather than achieved by, a particular conduct. In addition, competence goals such as professional expertise or artistic productivity, because of their vagueness and complexity, leave room for permanent renegotiation as to their contents and standards (cf. Atchley, 1989). Chronic or insatiable goals of this kind essentially contribute to keeping action paths and developmental prospects open (Gollwitzer, 1987; Gollwitzer & Moskowitz, 1996; Srull & Wyer, 1986).

Enactment and Maintenance of Self-Regulative Intentions

The enactment of goals can be hampered by a variety of conditions, some of which have been addressed already. Deficits in the semantic and procedural specification of goals are one possible reason why individuals abandon action projects prematurely or fail to initiate them in the first place. Intentions then remain in a rudimentary or degenerated state that may become the source of helplessness and depression (Kuhl & Beckmann, 1985), at least when the goals remain so important that individuals are unable to disengage from them.

The field of internal and external forces that direct and sustain action (motivational states, incentives, resources, constraints of action) is not stationary but typically changes during the implementation of an action or plan. Distractions and enticements may interfere with intentions; unexpected obstacles can alter the subject's balance of costs and benefits; material and physical action resources may become exhausted prematurely. These difficulties arise particularly with long-term projects, and may be aggravated by the lack of concrete, tangible incentives and the considerable delay of gratification that such long-range goals typically involve.

To some extent, intentions are already automatically screened off against competing action tendencies. In predecisional or preparatory stages during which alternative goals and plans are considered, individuals tend to soberly weigh the pros and cons of impending decisions; in contrast, when the die is cast and the person has entered the phase of implementation, cognitions that support maintenance and execution of the plan will become more readily accessible (Gollwitzer, 1990; Heckhausen & Gollwitzer, 1987). Furthermore, difficulties encountered in the execution phase can lead to an increase in the attractiveness of the goal, at least as long as the obstacles appear to be surmountable (cf., Wright & Brehm, 1989); apparently, such reactant increases in goal valence serve to mobilize action resources and to neutralize or counteract inhibiting tendencies. Ambitions of a "just manageable difficulty" (Brim, 1992) often are experienced as more attractive, from the start, than goals requiring low effort, in particular when they are perceived as a challenge and an opportunity to actualize, and to obtain feedback about, personal competencies (see also Locke & Latham, 1990).

On the other hand, a maintaining of intentions can itself become an objective of intentional action (Kuhl & Beckmann, 1994). Terms such as willpower or self-discipline traditionally refer to the capacity to make one's intentions and volitions the target of intentional control. Sometimes, the construct of self-regulation is used to denote just such processes of directional maintenance (cf., Karoly, 1993). Self-regulation, in the given sense, comprises a broad gamut of strategies such as stimulus control and milieu selection (e.g., eliminating distractive influences, selecting facilitative environments), attentional resource allocation (e.g., focusing on intention-enhancing aspects of the situation, disregarding interfering stimuli), or emotion and motivation control (e.g., centering on proximal goals, imagining positive consequences). Basically, all these strategies serve to keep the balance between attractive and aversive valences within margins that are necessary for continuing an intended course of action. To some extent, strategies of self-control are already acquired in early socialization (Harter, 1983; Mischel, 1983; H. Mischel & Mischel, 1983; W. Mischel & Mischel, 1976); the acquisition of such strategies sets the stage for intentional self-development. The processes of self-control are functionally tied to the medium of language; processes of self-encouragement, self-reinforcement, and self-critique presuppose the capacity of symbolically representing oneself, which forms the basis for a conceptual self (cf., Luria, 1979).

PERSONAL CONTROL OVER DEVELOPMENT: EMERGENCE AND DEVELOPMENTAL CHANGE

The question of how the processes of intentional development themselves develop and change over the life span leads into an area that is seriously underresearched. The ontogeny of intentional action generally has not been a focal theme on the agenda of developmental research, although it has drawn increasing attention during the past few years (e.g., Bullock, 1991; Lewis, 1991; Oppenheimer & Valsiner, 1991; Valsiner, 1987a). Even more conspicuous is the lack of research on the genesis and change of those competencies and activities through which individuals shape and organize their own developmental history.

Development-related action, as we have described above, presupposes particular representational capacities. The individual must have formed goals and standards for personal developments, and must be able to evaluate the current situation with regard to these self-guides; furthermore, he or she must have acquired some knowledge about probable and possible courses of future development, and, in particular, about means and strategies for attaining personally and socially desired outcomes. Moreover, specific regulatory competencies are required for enacting self-regulatory intentions and maintaining them over longer intervals. Personal concepts of actual, desired, and possible selves (i.e., representations of how and what one is, should be, could be, and would like to be) provide the motivational basis for such processes (Cantor, Markus, Niedenthal, & Nurius, 1986; Higgins, Klein, & Straumann, 1985). These representations also change, and are socially expected to change in particular ways, over the life cycle.

These preliminary considerations suggest that, in analyzing the ontogeny of intentional self-development, three basic lines of development should be considered: (a) the development of intentional action in general, and of cognitive and representational processes related to intentionality; (b) the formation of beliefs and competencies related to personal control over development; and (c) the development of the self (or self-concept) as a more or less coherent structure of self-referential values, beliefs, and standards that guides and directs self-regulatory processes.

Intentional Action: Developmental Aspects

Intentionality is intrinsically tied to the capacity to recognize regularities in behavior-outcome contingencies and to anticipate the possible effects of one's own behavior (Lütkenhaus & Bullock, 1991). Neonates already show instrumental learning, and thus exhibit some degree of contingency awareness (Olson & Sherman, 1983). An understanding of personal agency, however, presupposes the epistemic separation of self and nonself that gradually evolves from the radically egocentric and syncretic mode of experience that characterizes the primordial phase of cognitive development (Kegan, 1983; Piaget, 1952). This separation is the developmental origin of a conceptually differentiated, categorical self (Butterworth, 1990; Case, 1991; Filipp, 1980; Harter, 1983; Lewis & Brooks-Gunn, 1979).

As hallmarks of emerging intentionality, we may consider early behavioral adaptations that obviously aim at producing or evoking particular consequences (Bell, 1974). In contexts of parent–child interaction, such signs can be observed already in the first months of life—for example, in the instrumental use of vocalizations to influence the parent's behavior:

> How efficiently a 3-month-old infant can control parental behavior is readily observable, for example, in early interactive tickling games, when the child evokes the next repetition by an irresistible squealing . . . . The effectiveness of the contingency experience can be demonstrated easily by temporarily disrupting the child's expectations (e.g., by having the mother briefly close her eyes or turning unresponsively away from her child) . . . . When this happens, even a 2-month-old child will activate a broad repertoire of facial, gestic, or vocal behaviors in an attempt to bring the mother back under his or her control. (Papousek & Papousek, 1989, p. 479; J. Brandtstädter, Trans.)

Recognition of regularities in behavior-effect contingencies is facilitated through the ritualization and mutual coordination of interactive exchanges between parent and child (Brazelton, Koslowski, & Main, 1974; Papousek & Papousek, 1987). The experience of transactional contingencies provides the raw material from which a working model develops that, initially in a rudimentary way, represents causal structures and instrumental relationships. Children in this early phase of development show exuberant emotional reactions when they become aware of their growing ability to produce interesting effects in a regular and reliable manner (Case, 1991; Watson, 1966). As mentioned earlier, caregivers arrange the child's action space in particular ways to promote particular achievements, thus providing a scaffold for further development (Rogoff, 1990; Wood, Bruner, & Ross, 1976). Through affording facilitative means as well as through imposing external barriers and counterforces, the physical and social environment provides feedback concerning actional potentials

and limitations, thereby fostering the progressive differentiation of a conceptual or categorical self (cf., Lewis & Brooks-Gunn, 1979).

As the child comes to separate self from nonself and to see external objects as distinct entities in their own right, he or she also recognizes that actions can generate products that exist, and continue to exist, independently of productive activity, and that possess specific social valences. By the age of 18 months, children attentively monitor the products of their own actions: for example, in playing with building blocks, they pause when they have accomplished their task, and contemplate the result. Around this age, children begin to protest against and actively oppose interference with an intended course of action; this attests to a growing capability of goal-directed planning, and to an emerging sense of personal competence (Geppert & Küster, 1983; Heckhausen, 1984; Trudewind, Unzner, & Schneider, 1989).

A particularly important step in the development of intentionality is the use of intermediary actions for achieving some goal, such as when a 10-month-old child removes an obstacle to recover a toy. Intentionality is manifested even more clearly when different means are employed in order to attain the same goal (Bruner, 1973; Piaget, 1952). The material objects and means that are integrated more and more purposefully into sensorimotor coordinations during the first two years of life are not just "affordances" (Gibson, 1977) that expand the individual's action space; rather, in interaction with such means, experiences of success and failure are first made. The developmental significance of external objects of action has been stressed particularly within activity-theoretical approaches (Leont'ev, 1978; Oerter, 1991; Valsiner, 1987b; Vygotsky, 1978). The use of tools is the paradigm case. For efficient and successful action, the individual's behavior must accommodate to the functions and features of the tool. Being designed for, and in that sense objectifying, a particular type of problem, the mediating means of action—including external objects as well as "psychological tools" as defined above (Vygotsky, 1978)—also implicate particular developmental tasks; achieving such tasks through adjusting to the functional demands of the tools is fostered by an intrinsic motivation for competence and self-agency (Harter, 1978; White, 1959). In early childhood, caregivers support the successful use of objects through structuring zones of activity; in later developmental stages, the guided acquisition of more complicated cultural practices and techniques typically takes the form of learning through apprenticeship (Rogoff, 1990). Thus, object-related and mediated action constitutes the basic process by which the individual comes to recognize the social nature of action, and gradually comes to participate in social networks of knowledge and practice (Lave & Wenger, 1991; Valsiner, 1988a, 1988b; Vygotsky, 1978).

So far, we have addressed some early necessary steps in the genesis of intentional self-development. Further progress is crucially related to the acquisition of language, and to the development of self-related speech in particular. Speech-for-self is a potent means to overcome impediments and unexpected disruptions in an intended course of action and helps to control aversive emotions arising from these experiences (Kopp, 1989; Luria, 1969; Zivin, 1979). In self-referential dialogues, representations of desired and ought selves are actualized and translated into self-directive and self-corrective intentions (Lee, Wertsch, & Stone, 1983). Self-ascription of attributes denoting positively valued personal qualities (e.g., being good, strong, clever, polite) is necessarily tied to the medium of language; thus, emergence of first self-regulative intentions largely coincides, and progresses in stride with, the development of language. The acquisition of symbolic means to describe and evaluate oneself taps a centrally important source of self-regulatory motivation:

> . . . around the world, two- and three-year-olds begin to reflect on the correctness, the competence, and the appropriateness of their actions before, during, and after execution. They compare their behavior, thoughts, and feelings against the standards and try to keep in close accord with the standard, as a space vehicle's program corrects its course in flight. (Kagan, 1984, pp. 129–130)

Development of Control-Related Beliefs and Motivations

Intentions of self-correction and self-development emerge through the contrast of two anticipatory beliefs: expectations of how one's developmental prospects might be ameliorated by corrective intervention are contrasted to the initial or baseline expectation of what would happen without such intervention. Such contrasts between "initial" and "revised" expectations (Valle & Frieze, 1976) become particularly salient in critical transitions and choice points in the life cycle. Generally, the range of feasible developmental options that individuals envisage for themselves depends on the degree of personal control and efficacy that the actor ascribes to himself or herself.

The extent to which one has control over one's life circumstances is jointly determined by personal and situational factors; specifically, it depends on contingencies of the individual's developmental ecology and on his or her potential to act on these contingencies, which, in turn, depends on the availability of pertinent procedural knowledge as well as on the personal accessibility of such knowledge. These diverse aspects or facets are addressed in differentiations of the control construct, such as the distinctions between "contingency judgments" and "competence judgments" (Weisz, 1983; Weisz & Cameron, 1985), between "response–outcome expectancies" and "efficacy expectations" (Bandura, 1977; Heckhausen, 1989), between "strategy beliefs" and "capacity beliefs" (Skinner, 1991, 1995; Skinner, Chapman, & Baltes, 1988), or, with signs reversed, between "universal helplessness" and "personal helplessness" (Abramson, Seligman, & Teasdale, 1978). It should be noted that the formal relation among these facets of perceived control is not symmetrical, in the sense that universal helplessness (the belief that an outcome is generally uncontrollable) implies personal helplessness, but not vice versa. This asymmetry seems important both from a motivational and a developmental point of view, because individuals generally will not form an intention to expand their control capacities unless they recognize that goals that are beyond their actual span of control are not necessarily unattainable in a general or universal sense.

These conceptual distinctions suggest two lines of approach for analyzing the development of control beliefs. First, we may ask how a sense of personal agency grows from the individual's transactions with his or her social and material environment and unfolds into a differentiated system of control beliefs. Second, we should consider how ontogenetic and age-graded changes in physical, temporal, and social resources of action may affect perceived control and efficacy.

Developing a Sense of Control and Personal Agency

The perception of having control over events in one's immediate environment implies a cognitive separation between the acting self and the external objects and effects of action, which we have already mentioned as an essential achievement in early sensorimotor development. The progressive integration of instrumental objects, as well as of other persons, into one's own action sequences promotes an early sense of mediated agency or "proxy control" (Bandura, 1982b), and is thus germinal for the differentiation of means–end or contingency beliefs from efficacy beliefs. During early childhood, control experiences progressively gain an affective valence that not only stems from the pleasure experienced in the process of producing events, but increasingly reflects the valuation of outcomes within the wider social context. In the process of objectifying and instrumentalizing the physical and social environment, the child also comes to recognize his or her own body, and parts of it, as object and instrument; this is a cornerstone for the reflective processes through which the self as a physical and, later, as a psychological entity can become an object of intentional action.

Self-percepts of personal agency and control originate through the experience of behavior–event contingencies. Contextual factors such as the sensitivity and responsiveness of parents or the extent to which task environments or instructional contexts are adapted to the child's skill level and developmental potentials influence contingencies among actions, intentions, and outcomes, and can thus become a source of interindividual differences in perceived control and self-efficacy (Gunnar, 1980; Lamb & Easterbrooks, 1981; Skinner, 1985, 1995). Again, generalization of contingency experiences and integration of them into a conceptual self are tied to language development; between the ages of 2 and 3 years, children begin to grasp the semantic contents and symbolic qualities of their own behavior, and to view themselves in terms of certain distinct qualities and traits. Preschoolers are motivated increasingly by anticipated self-evaluations, and they eagerly seek occasions to test and confirm self-descriptions. Discerning competence and contingency as distinct constituents of personal agency, however, requires further cognitive and conceptual achievements; thus, not until middle childhood, or, in Piagetian terms, until the stage of concrete operations has been reached, do children acquire the distinction between alternative "internal" and "external" causes of performance, such as ability, effort, task difficulty, and luck, and reflect such distinctions in self-evaluative reactions (Nicholls & Miller, 1984, 1985).

Although beginnings of a purposeful coordination of means and ends can be observed by completion of the first year of life, these early coordinations are practical and intuitive only. Attention is centered on immediate, concrete outcomes of actions; not until the emergence of "reflexive abstraction" in later stages of cognitive development (Piaget, 1976, 1978) is attention turned to the action processes themselves as well as to the mechanisms that mediate between actions and outcomes. The representation of personal competencies and contextual contingencies typically attains the form of an implicit theory during preadolescence. The transition toward a hypothetico-deductive or formal-operational mode of thinking is characterized by a growing capacity to hypothetically project alternative courses of future personal development, which is the key cognitive process that guides and motivates life planning and intentional self-development in adolescence and adulthood. However, concrete-operational children already begin to reflect about psychological functions such as memory, attention, or comprehension, and to use metacognitive strategies to control and enhance these functions (e.g., mnemonic strategies, techniques of attention control, comprehension monitoring; cf. Flavell, Speer, Green, & August, 1981; Flavell & Wellmann, 1977; Markman, 1977; Miller & Bigi, 1979). Maintaining or boosting performance through metacognitive strategies remains an important concern of intentional self-development throughout life, and becomes particularly focal in the elderly person's attempts to counteract, and compensate for, functional losses (Baltes & Baltes, 1990; Dixon & Bäckman, 1995).

Action Resources and Perceived Control

The development of action resources over the life span, in many areas at least, tends to follow a curvilinear function; in the earlier segments of the life span, the dominant trend is one of resource expansion, whereas later segments are characterized by maintenance and differential decrease in physical, temporal, social, and material reserves. A similar pattern of growth and decline has generally been expected for the experience of control and agency through life; however, empirical relationships have proved to be considerably more complex (cf. Brandtstädter, Wentura, & Greve, 1993; Heckhausen & Schulz, 1995).

Individual differences in perceived control become manifest by preschool age; in achievement-related contexts, for example, such differences are displayed in risk preferences, in reactions to failure, or in differential persistence on difficult tasks (Heckhausen, 1984). In contrast, the question regarding how the age variable relates to quantitative or qualitative differences in perceived control is far from being settled decisively. Considering the expansion of physical, psychological, and social action resources, as well as the loosening, and progressive internalization, of external directives and regulations, one might expect an increase in internal-autonomous orientations of control from childhood to adolescence; this assumption gains plausibility in view of analogous shifts from heteronomous to autonomous perspectives in moral judgment (Rest, 1982; Selman, 1980). Although some findings seem to converge with this assumption, cross-sectional and longitudinal studies have not borne out a clear-cut and convergent trend (for overviews, see Krampen, 1987b; Skinner & Connell, 1986). We shall not delve here into the methodological difficulties that plague this area of research (see, e.g., Skinner, 1995, for a discussion); obviously, an assessment of internality and externality beliefs poses serious conceptual problems as long as the child has not yet developed a corresponding analytic perspective. Generally, the assumption that perceived control or efficacy is a direct function of available action resources seems too simplistic. A personal sense of control and efficacy should depend primarily on the extent to which available action potentials are sufficient to realize personally important goals and developmental ambitions, or, conversely, reflect the extent to which personal goals and ambitions are adjusted to personal action potentials. We have to note at this juncture that, after an expansion of action resources, goals and aspirations are often calibrated to a larger scale, which may involve new vulnerabilities. By the same token, a shrinking of action resources does not necessarily lead to losses in perceived control when goals are adjusted to changed developmental opportunities (cf., Brandtstädter & Renner, 1990; Brandtstädter & Rothermund, 1994; Heckhausen & Schulz, 1995).

The theoretical significance of this principle becomes particularly evident when we consider later life. As we shall discuss in greater detail below, the accommodation of goals and plans to changed action resources is one of the key processes that helps the elderly person to preserve a sense of personal efficacy and a positive view of self and personal future.

Intentional Self-Development and the Developing Self

Activities of intentional self-development are related to the self in two senses. First, these activities, as well as the processes of self-observation and self-evaluation on which they are based, are reflexive; that is, they are directed back on the acting individuals themselves. Second, and this is a more complicated issue, such activities are also related to the person's self. These two meanings are often confounded; in the present context, they have to be distinguished carefully.

It has become customary to conceive the self—the conceptual or categorical self, or the "me" self as described by James (1890)—as a kind of theory that the individual holds about himself or herself, and that grows out from the social requirement to give consistent and satisfying accounts for oneself and one's behavior (Epstein, 1973; Kihlstrom & Cantor, 1984; Markus, 1977). However, not all perceptions and beliefs that individuals may hold to be true about themselves refer to attributes that characterize and individuate them in essential ways; it therefore appears that the self, in the stronger sense of personal identity, is less, and in some sense more, than the totality of self-referential beliefs. To count as constituents of personal identity, self-descriptive attributes have to satisfy particular criteria (Baumeister, 1986; Brandtstädter & Greve, 1994; McGuire & McGuire, 1981). For one, these attributes must be sufficiently enduring and constant; only attributes that are sufficiently stable (or are construed by the individual as stable self-descriptive features) can warrant self-sameness over time. Furthermore, to be identity-relevant, attributes must also possess some distinctive relevance; that is, they must contribute somehow to establishing the person's individuality. Finally, the attributes must be linked in relevant ways to the person's biography or life course, and must be seen by the person to form an essential particularity of his or her life. Activities of intentional self-development, as far as they serve to realize, stabilize, and maintain personal identity, will reach their full developmental expression when the individual is able to construe a self-schema of personal identity according to such criteria (Norem-Hebeisen, 1981).

The Ontogeny of the Conceptual Self and of Internalized Control

Objects that are seen by the child as belonging to himself or herself (toys, or parts of the body) are the first distinctive markers of individuality (Kopp, 1982; Lewis & Brooks-Gunn, 1979). In early phases of development, identity is often construed in terms of simple discriminative contrasts (child vs. adult, boy vs. girl); concrete, observable attributes are available earlier and more easily for self-description than abstract qualities (such as attitudes, dispositions, traits) that have to be inferred from observations (Broughton, 1978; Selman, 1980). Stable self-categorizations in terms of essential and invariant characteristics emerge in middle childhood in relationship with the comprehension of physical invariances at the level of concrete operational thinking. A central aspect of self-description, which also assumes a pivotal role in the further elaboration of a stable identity, is gender (Guardo & Bohan, 1971; Harter, 1983; Kohlberg, 1966; Marcus & Overton, 1978); particularly in societies with marked sex-role stereotyping, conceptions of an ought self are often introduced in terms of prescriptions of how a girl, or boy, should behave or typically behaves (e.g., rules concerning the public display of emotions; cf., Case, 1991; Stangor & Ruble, 1987, 1989).

Self-regulatory activity is based on self-evaluative standards or "self-guides" (Higgins, 1988) that form the person's desired and ought self. Self-evaluation and self-control originate from early, heteronomous states that are characterized by the external regulation of behavior through directives and physical constraints; with advancing representational capacities, children internalize external directives and apply evaluative and judgmental labels to themselves and their own actions. The emergence of internalized control is certainly one of the most central and significant achievements of early childhood (Diaz, Neal, & Amaya-Williams, 1991; Flavell, 1977; Kopp, 1982, 1987). The notion of internalization of normative orientations may be misleading as far as it connotes the simple transposing of external norms into an "inner" language of control. Rather, internalization should be seen as a constructive process by which external evaluations, standards, and norms are assimilated, interpreted, and realized in a manner corresponding to the child's actual developmental state and potential (Lawrence & Valsiner, 1993).

The emergence of internalized control is marked by the appearance of self-affects such as pride, guilt, or embarrassment, which are typically observed in achievement situations around the age of 3 to 4 years (Heckhausen, 1984). Children at this age vehemently protest against self-discrepant attributions ("I'm not a bad boy!"); such early forms of self-assertion foreshadow processes of self-enhancement and self-verification that later become central aspects of intentional self-development (Kagan,

1981a). Not until middle childhood, however, are self-evaluative concepts or standards represented in episodic and semantic memory with sufficient complexity so that children can explicitly describe situations in which they would be proud or ashamed of themselves (Harter, 1983). Self-evaluative concepts—for example, personal notions of what it means to be good, competent, fair, or responsible—are continuously redefined and endowed with partly new meanings as cognitive and sociomoral development advances; this process does not come to a halt at a particular age, but continues throughout life. The capacity and readiness to step back and critically evaluate oneself, one's actions, and, eventually, one's personal development and contour of life from the perspective of the generalized other and with respect to general ideals, maxims, or principles, characterizes an advanced level of sociocognitive and sociomoral development that presupposes a formal-operational level of thought (Selman, 1980). On this level of cognitive development, individuals first become able to construe a possible self in terms of self-ideals and general ethical principles. Such ideals and principles essentially refer to the relation between the acting subject and his or her social, institutional, and cultural context. As individuals develop a progressively more comprehensive and differentiated view of these relationships, new and broader perspectives become accessible for self-definition and self-evaluation (Damon & Hart, 1982). This change in evaluative perspectives also influences the selection and definition of life goals and identity projects.

Future Selves, Life Plans, and Cultural Scripts

In adolescence and early adulthood, visionary construals of desired possible selves become the key motivational source of intentional self-development. In this transitional phase, constructions of the future self focus mainly on the domains of future occupation and beginning a family and partnership, as well as on developmental tasks and prospects related to these domains (Dreher & Oerter, 1987; Nurmi, 1993; Pulkkinen, 1982). Elementary school children formulate ideas and plans about future roles in life, but these are often vague and fanciful. In adolescence, future goals become more elaborated; they reflect a broader range of realistic options and are linked with concrete procedural intentions and implementation goals (Rosenberg & Rosenberg, 1981; Russell & Smith, 1979).

During adulthood, personal projects and goals for the different segments of the life span eventually merge into a more or less comprehensive and coherent plan of life. Considering the ad hoc, incremental nature of planning about life, Rawls's (1971, p. 93) contention that each individual "has a rational plan of life drawn up subject to the conditions that confront him" has to be taken with some skepticism. Most people, however, have developed at least some ideas concerning the general contour of their life. These ideas are elaborated, adjusted, and reformulated according to actual constraints and affordances that, to some extent, arise in an unpredictable fashion. In shaping and elaborating life plans, parents, partners, and significant others in general play a significant role, both as models and as mentors (Goodnow & Collins, 1990; Levinson, 1978; Smith, 1996; in press). As individuals come to participate in social-role systems of partnership, family, and occupation, it becomes increasingly necessary to coordinate and synchronize personal life plans with those of other individuals; by the process of coordinating life goals, which is particularly important in contexts of marital partnership, personal developmental options are augmented as well as restrained (Brandtstädter, Krampen, & Heil, 1986).

As the individual comes to relate his or her personal development to the norms and role systems of family and occupational cycles, social representations of "normal" or desirable development gain further influence in personal life-planning. Age-graded societies constrain and canalize intentional self-development through prescriptions or normative expectations concerning the proper scheduling of developmental events and transitions; in interaction with biological changes, such norms constitute a cultural script of a life course (Hagestad, 1991; Neugarten & Hagestad, 1976). Deviations from this script arouse attention and a need for explanation or justification; the normative force of cultural scripts of the life course, however, also stems from the fact that deviations from the "normal" pattern have particular symbolic and attributional valences. Divergence from prescribed timetables for developmental transitions may, depending on the particular domain, be taken, for example, as a sign of incompetence, irresponsibility, indifference, or carelessness (Kalicki, 1995); as the individual moves through the life cycle, such symbolic valences gain influence in self-evaluation and intentional self-development.

A sense of personal identity and individuality is, to an essential degree, tied to those elements in the personal life course that deviate from normative or typical patterns; apparently, the cultural standardization of the individual life course tends to reduce its discriminative and individuating value. This problem is somewhat toned down by the fact that developmental tasks and normative expectations about the life course afford some latitude for idiosyncratic interpretation and implementation; thus, it becomes a developmental task of its own to interpret and implement the cultural script of the life course in ways that are compatible with personal goals and identity projects (cf., Dittmann-Kohli, 1986).

The formation of personal identity does not end with a final and stable outcome; it involves continual revisions and readjustments (Gergen & Gergen, 1987). In response to the biological transitions and role changes across adolescence and adulthood, themes of intentional self-development as well as the personal importance of self-descriptive attributes also change (cf., Cantor, Norem, Niedenthal, Langston, & Brower, 1987; Dreher & Oerter, 1986; Nurmi, 1992). The individual's position within educational, occupational, and family cycles influences the personal construal of desired, possible, and ought selves; during positional changes across the life cycle, different standards, rules, and comparative perspectives for self-evaluation become salient (Wells & Stryker, 1988). As individuals travel along the developmental and action paths that form their "thread of life" (Wollheim, 1984), they also tend to shift the temporal focus of self-definition; whereas young adults construe their identity primarily with regard to future possible selves, elderly people derive their self-definitions to an increasing degree from past achievements (Wong & Watt, 1991).

To some extent, however, these developmental adaptations also serve to stabilize and protect core elements of the self system. As with scientific theories, adjustments in some parts of the structure can be necessary to deflect strain from other, more central parts. Generally, change in self-definitions across the life cycle is dampened by an inherent tendency of the self system to preserve personal continuity and integration. Thus, the majority of longitudinal studies give testimony to an impressive stability of self-descriptions across adulthood (Bengtson, Reedy, & Gordon, 1985; Filipp & Klauer, 1985). This stability is particularly impressive in elderly individuals; the aging self appears to have powerful adaptive mechanisms at its disposal that defend the self scheme against experiences of loss and limitation (Atchley, 1989). A comprehensive account of intentional self-development must certainly include some mention of the intentional and nonintentional processes that underlie the adjustment of self-evaluative standards and the negotiation of gains and losses in the transition to later life. My final considerations will address this issue.

Preserving Personal Continuity and Identity: Assimilative and Accommodative Processes

It has become obvious at this point that activities of intentional self-development must be viewed within the larger context of processes that serve to actualize and stabilize personal identity. Over the entire life course, the individual is confronted with events and changes that he or she experiences as gains or losses, and as congruent or dissonant with the self schema consolidated in earlier phases of life. Personal continuity essentially results from the ways in which such changes are negotiated in mentation and action.

The transition to old age brings with it particular threats to self-continuity and integrity. The late phases of life are characterized by an accumulation of uncontrollable changes and irreversible losses. Although there is a considerable amount of interindividual variation in biological, psychological, and social parameters of aging (e.g., Birren & Schaie, 1990; Rowe & Kahn, 1987; Schneider & Rowe, 1991), the reduction of physiological reserve capacities, chronic and disabling health problems, and problems of bereavement and social isolation increasingly take their toll. These adaptive problems are further aggravated by the narrowing of lifetime resources. Becoming aware that important personal goals can no longer be achieved within the remaining time is a particularly aversive experience in later life (Breytspraak, 1984). A picture of a gradual worsening in the subjective balance of developmental gains and losses also emerges from self-reports of elderly people (Brandtstädter, Wentura, & Greve, 1993; Heckhausen, Dixon, & Baltes, 1989). In sum, action resources tend to wane in later life, and questions regarding the projects and goals in which scarce resources should be invested take on increasing significance.

Numerous research programs have centered on the plausible assumption that the experiences of loss, functional limitation, and social marginalization should have a negative impact on self-esteem, personal efficacy, and general well-being in later life. This assumption, however, has found surprisingly little empirical support. There is no general evidence that dissatisfaction, depression, or identity

problems increase in later life, except perhaps in terminal phases in which severely disabling and life-threatening health problems loom large (Blazer, 1989; Newmann, 1989; Stock, Okun, Haring, & Witter, 1983). Likewise, there is no consistent evidence for reduced self-efficacy or perceived control. At every age, perceived control over personal development correlates positively with subjective and objective indicators of well-being, such as health, life satisfaction, and optimism; however, individual differences in perceived control do not appear to be related systematically to the age variable (Abeles, 1991; Heil & Krampen, 1989; Lachman, 1986; Rodin, 1987).

This rather counterintuitive pattern of findings raises questions as to possible methodological artifacts. With regard to the age–depression relationship, it has been argued, for example, that findings might be biased by a reduced motivation of depressed persons to participate in investigations; that relationships might be curvilinear; that elderly people might be more reluctant to report psychological problems; that symptoms of depression in old age often take on a masked or somatized form; or—considering the general predominance of cross-sectional over longitudinal investigations in these areas of research—that the empirical data are liable to confound genuine ontogenetic effects with generational differences (Blazer, 1989; Kessler, Foster, Webster, & House, 1992). We cannot examine these arguments in detail here, but it appears that, in sum, they are not strong enough to explain away the phenomenal stability and integrity of the aging self; in fact, this phenomenon is attracting increasing attention in developmental and gerontological research (Brandtstädter, Wentura, & Greve, 1993; Staudinger, Marsiske, & Baltes, 1995).

Here, the question arises as to what kinds of processes protect and defend the self—in particular, the aging self. From an action-theoretical perspective, two basic adaptive processes—or groups of processes—can be distinguished: On the one hand, individuals may try to alter the situation in an attempt to prevent or avoid undesired or self-discrepant outcomes; on the other hand, evaluative standards, as well as underlying personal goals and ambitions, may be adjusted to situational constraints. For terminological purposes, we can denote the former adaptive mode as assimilative, and the latter one as accommodative. The present use of these concepts (see also Brandtstädter, 1989; Brandtstädter & Renner, 1990) differs from the familiar Piagetian terminology, because we are not referring here to modes of cognitive adaptation, but rather to two complementary processes of achieving congruence between actual and desired situations or states.

Assimilative activities, in the given sense, essentially comprise all forms of intentional and problem-solving action that aim to keep developmental prospects in stride with personal goals and standards, or to alleviate goal discrepancies by actively changing situational conditions (personal life circumstances, behavioral patterns, or attributes). In old age, the preservation of personally valued physical, psychological, and social competencies becomes an important source of self-esteem and a dominant concern of assimilative efforts.

When assimilative actions fail to reduce actual discrepancies and losses, accommodative processes tend to be activated. By facilitating disengagement from barren goals, the accommodative process enhances a reorientation and commitment to new goals and self-evaluative standards, which may then become new reference points for assimilative activities. The theoretical distinction between accommodative and assimilative modes partly converges with other action-theoretical models that also imply a dual-process conception of coping, such as the model of problem-focused versus emotion-focused coping (Folkman, 1984; Lazarus & Launier, 1978), the theory of the incentive-disengagement cycle (Klinger, 1975, 1987), or the model of primary versus secondary control (Heckhausen & Schulz, 1995; Rothbaum, Weisz, & Snyder, 1982). Relationships with these conceptions have been discussed in greater detail elsewhere (Brandtstädter & Renner, 1992).

Here, I shall discuss assimilative and accommodative processes with regard to functional relationships and underlying mechanisms. The discussion focuses on development in late adulthood, but the basic theoretical principles apply to all situations in personal development that involve developmental losses and threats to personal identity.

Preventing or Alleviating Developmental Losses through Assimilative Activity

Preventive or corrective actions that are explicitly and intentionally designed to maintain personally or socially desired performance standards or skills may be considered as prototypical cases of assimilative activities in later life. Depending on subjective means–ends beliefs and competencies, the implementation of such maintenance goals can take many forms—physical exercise, dieting, a careful arrangement of daily routines, using cosmetic or pharmacological tools, and so on. These kinds of self-corrective tendencies generally increase as experiences of functional losses and deficits loom larger; the strength of these relationships generally depends on the degree of perceived control over one's development and aging, and on the personal importance of the domain in question (Brandtstädter, 1989).

Compensatory actions are another variant of assimilative activities that becomes particularly relevant when some functional losses are already irreversible. Compensation as such is a basic category of mediated human action; in a very general sense, any activity that employs auxiliary strategies and means to achieve some goal that otherwise could not be attained involves an element of compensation (Vygotsky, 1979). In later life, acts of compensation specifically aim at maintaining some desired standard of performance in spite of losses in task-relevant functions or skills. Because performance in particular tasks is generally determined by different skill components and external factors, a deterioration of particular components can often be offset by selective use or strengthening of those components that are still functioning well; depending on the functional domain under consideration, compensation may also involve the use of particular metacognitive strategies (e.g., mnemonic aids) or of external prosthetic means (Bäckman & Dixon, 1992; Baltes & Baltes, 1990; Salthouse, 1987). Activities of compensation tend to be most pronounced in areas that have high discriminative and biographical relevance and are of central importance to the person's identity. Like other activities of intentional self-development, compensatory actions depend on the availability of pertinent theoretical and technological knowledge as well as on its personal accessibility.

A further important category of assimilative activity comprises activities of self-verification (Swann, 1983). The self-verification construct refers to a general (but differentially expressed) tendency to preferentially select social or informational contexts that are likely to provide self-congruent feedback on those dimensions of self-description that are central or constitutive to personal identity (Greve, 1990; Rosenberg, 1979; Wicklund & Gollwitzer, 1982). To some extent, self-verification tendencies are already operative on automatic levels; for example, strong self-beliefs have an inherent tendency to reject or discredit discrepant information. This conservative effect may ward off self-discrepant evidence (at least as long as the evidence is not sufficiently strong to override the protective forces), and, in this case, would inhibit assimilative and accommodative responses equally. Only those activities of self-verification that intentionally serve the purpose of reducing the salience of losses or avoiding self-discrepant feedback, however, should be considered as assimilative. For example, elderly people may strategically select social interactions to serve such self-enhancing intentions (cf., Carstensen, 1993; Ward, 1984). People may even change their external appearance (e.g., through cosmetic surgery) in an attempt to elicit feedback from their social environment that conforms with their self-views (Swann, 1983).

A common feature of all assimilative activities is a tenacious adherence to certain goals, ambitions, or standards. The intensity and duration of assimilative activities essentially depend on perceived personal competence and efficacy; if initial control beliefs are strong, difficulties in executing assimilative intentions may incite additional assimilative effort, and even induce a reactant increase of the blocked goal's valence (Klinger, 1975; Wortman & Brehm, 1975; Wright & Brehm, 1989). When the individual is confronted with factually irreversible losses or impairments, however, this tenacity may lead to an inefficient use of resources and may eventually aggravate feelings of helplessness and depression. Here, possible dysfunctional implications of control beliefs become apparent, implications that are gaining increasing attention in clinical and developmental research (Coyne, 1992; Janoff-Bulman & Brickman, 1982; Thompson, Cheek, & Graham, 1988).

As long as assimilative processes dominate, accommodative reactions are inhibited; as long as personal standards or ambitions can be maintained without difficulty, there is no need for revising them. However, when action resources decrease, assimilative activities may become increasingly difficult and taxing. To borrow terms from economics, the "production-possibility frontier" (Samuelson & Nordhaus, 1985) narrows with decreasing production reserves, so that eventually a desired level of production in one domain can be maintained only by lowering levels in other domains. The shrinking of action resources in later life should have analogous effects: to maintain desired standards in some specific domain, the individual may be forced to downgrade standards in other domains. For example, in some fields of athletic activity, older individuals may successfully maintain performance levels through

forced training and sophisticated use of physical reserves (Ericsson, 1990); with advancing age, however, such efforts become increasingly taxing. The psychological problems of aging largely stem from the fact that efforts to compensate for functional losses are subject to a principle of diminishing returns, so that the opportunity costs of maintaining particular standards eventually outweigh the benefits. Under such circumstances, the only way of avoiding or neutralizing feelings of permanent frustration and helplessness is by adjusting goals and ambitions to situational constraints and changed action resources.

Accommodative Processes: Adjusting Goals to Actional Resources

Notions of gain and loss in development involve evaluative elements; whether developmental outcomes or changes are individually experienced as gains or losses depends on how they relate to the person's goals and projects. Accordingly, losses or goal discrepancies may be eliminated not only by changing the actual situation but also by rescaling goals and self-evaluative standards—in other words, by accommodative processes. Such processes, as we shall see, largely operate on nonintentional levels. Thus, the consideration of these mechanisms will take us partly beyond the scope of the paradigm of intentional action; nevertheless, it is of central importance to understand the dynamics of intentional self-development over the life course (see also Skinner, 1995).

Prototypical facets of the accommodative mode involve the devaluation and disengagement of blocked goals, the rescaling of aspirations, and the positive reappraisal of alternative options. Accommodative processes also include interpretative processes that lead to acceptance of an initially aversive situation and thus may facilitate disengagement from barren ambitions. Whereas assimilative activities imply a tenacious adherence to goals and standards, the accommodative process is characterized by the flexible adjustment of goals to situational constraints. Rescaling of standards and aspirations has often been considered to be an inferior form of coping, and has been associated with notions of hopelessness, resignation, or depression. Such connotations are misleading; in fact, feelings of hopelessness and helplessness rather indicate difficulties in letting go of blocked goals, or deficits in accommodative flexibility.

Empirical findings from different lines of research hint at the importance of accommodative processes for neutralizing experiences of loss and stabilizing a positive sense of self in later life. Thus, people tend to devalue developmental goals that have drifted beyond feasible ranges; this tendency appears to be less expressed in depressive subjects (Brandtstädter & Baltes-Götz, 1990). Similarly, persons suffering physical impairments tend to adjust to their handicaps by rearranging goals and ambitions (Schulz & Decker, 1985). Conversely, the difficulty in letting go of barren ambitions appears to be a characteristic of depression (Carver & Scheier, 1990); in later life, continued pursuit of "youthful" goals and self-ideals may thus become a source of continued discontent (Miskimins & Simmons, 1966). Measures of accommodative flexibility have been found to predict coping with problems such as chronic pain, reduced health, or physical handicaps (Brandtstädter, Wentura, & Greve, 1993; Schmitz, Saile, & Nilges, 1996). Moreover, the intriguing stability of generalized control beliefs in later life seems to depend essentially on the accommodation of goals to available resources (Brandtstädter & Rothermund, 1994; Brim, 1992). There is evidence that, with advancing age, preferred modes of coping shift from assimilative-offensive to accommodative forms; in view of the increase of uncontrollable and irreversible losses in later life, this shift is consistent with theoretical expectations.

Readiness or ability to accommodate goals to situational constraints depends on situational and personal conditions. Individuals will find it most difficult to disengage from goals that are central to their identity and for which substitutes or functional equivalents are not easily available. High "self-complexity" (Linville, 1987), that is, a highly diversified and multifocal self-structure, may enhance disengagement from barren life projects and commitment to new goals. A further significant factor that may differ across situations and persons concerns the ability to shift the meanings of aversive states or losses so that these eventually become acceptable. In aversive mood states, accessibility of palliative meanings seems to be lowered by a tendency of the cognitive system to generate mood-congruent cognitions (Blaney, 1986). We should therefore expect that accommodative processes engage mechanisms that override such congruency effects (cf., Taylor, 1991).

As suggested above, such auxiliary mechanisms presumably operate on a subpersonal, automatic level. Accommodation of goals and ambitions needs not to be, and often cannot be, actuated intentionally, although it may have a directive influence on the individual's intentions and decisions. The process of accommodation, however, does not start with, but rather ends with a decision to abandon a goal or dissolve a commitment. Disengagement from barren commitments can be enhanced to some extent by the planful use of self-management and self-instruction techniques, but, like other nonintentional or automatic processes, it can be brought under personal control only in such mediated, technical ways. Just as we cannot accept any beliefs apart from those that seem sufficiently plausible within the context of the beliefs we already hold, so, too, we are unable to discard a goal merely because it seems advantageous to do so (cf., Gilbert, 1993; Kunda, 1990). Action-theoretical research increasingly pays attention to the role that such unintentional or subpersonal automatisms play in the regulation of action (Uleman & Bargh, 1989).

Among the automatisms that support the accommodative process, mechanisms of attentional regulation are of prime importance. As already discussed, attention generally focuses on situational aspects that are relevant with respect to an ongoing course of action; this principle of attention deployment suggests that scarce attentional resources tend to be withdrawn from problems that are perceived to be uncontrollable, or have turned out to be so (Brandtstädter & Renner, 1992). Decentering of attention from uncontrollable problems may be supported by a compensatory tendency to focus on affectively incongruent stimuli (i.e., on stimuli with positive affective valence) after negative feedback (Derryberry, 1993; Tipper & Cranston, 1985). Particular types of problems, however, may continue to bind attention even after repeated futile attempts to solve them; this is particularly true of problems that are personally so important that continued assimilative efforts have a high subjective utility even under very low probability of success. Under such conditions, problem-focused thinking may degenerate into ruminative thinking that cycles around the blocked goal and its implications (Martin & Tesser, 1989); in terms of the dual-process model, such ruminative thought would be symptomatic of difficulties in shifting from assimilative to accommodative modes. However, ruminative thinking may also promote accommodation, because it may enhance the finding of positive meanings, which, because of their palliative effects, should also have a greater chance to be accepted as valid (Brandtstädter & Renner, 1992; Wentura, 1995). Generally, to deconstruct aversive implications of a problem, information has to be generated that invalidates or undermines the aversive conclusions or the underlying premises; this form of focused, preference-driven thinking involves a positivity bias, because the search for further information tends to be stopped after the desired positive result has been reached (Kruglanski, 1990; Kunda, 1990).

The distinction between assimilative and accommodative processes that we have addressed in these final considerations may recall traditional distinctions between active and passive concepts of happiness (Tatarkiewicz, 1976); philosophical notions of wisdom have emphasized the importance of finding the right balance between these two stances. Wisdom, however defined, implies not only knowledge as to which goals are important in life, how these goals may be achieved, and when they are attained, but also involves a sense as to which limitations are unavoidable, and how necessities can be accepted (Kamlah, 1973; Nozick, 1989). Intentional self-development across the life span is based on this interplay between engagement and disengagement, between tenacious goal pursuit and flexible goal adjustment. From the theoretical analysis of these complementary tendencies, we can hope to gain a better understanding of how continuity and change both pervade and enable each other in personal development over the life span.

SUMMARY AND CONCLUSIONS

Cultural systems maintain and perpetuate themselves by regulating and controlling developmental processes over the life span; within the matrix of sociocultural affordances and constraints, the developing person builds, and tries to optimize, his or her personal course of development. Throughout life, individuals are actively engaged in keeping their development in stride with social and personal representations of "successful" development over the life span, and they strive to achieve a favorable balance of developmental gains and losses that conforms with their self-definitions and identity goals. Proceeding on these basic tenets, I have advanced the view that human ontogeny, in theory and research, cannot be understood adequately without taking into account the representational and regulative processes through which individuals control their own and others' development. Goal-directed action is both a driving force and an outcome of personal development over the life

span, and this chapter has made an attempt to integrate both facets.

In contrast to traditional programmatic debates, I hold the view that the merits of any developmental "paradigm" should not be judged on an *a priori* basis, but in light of its heuristic power and with regard to the quality of related research. In this sense, a general strength of action perspectives, which has been stressed throughout this chapter, lies in their potential to integrate cultural, historical, and personalistic aspects of human ontogeny. This integrative power essentially stems from the fact that the concept of action is inherently linked to these different analytical levels. Related to this point, action perspectives on development are distinctive in the way in which they account for phenomena of stability and change, of diversity and universality in human ontogeny. An action perspective suggests that the stability as well as the diversity of developmental patterns are essentially related to the particular arrangement of developmental affordances and constraints prevailing in a given sociohistorical context, and they reflect the ways in which individuals, through constructive and selective activity, make use of and act on these contextual conditions. Thus, the action paradigm provides a framework for integrating theoretical stances that emphasize the malleability and contextual relativity of developmental trajectories. This does not necessarily imply that the traditional issues of continuity, connectedness, and universality would be anathema to an action perspective on development. I have argued to the contrary: The consideration of the different types of constraints that shape and constitute development within cultural and personal contexts of action may help to gain a better understanding of these traditional issues. Though not discarding the notion of causal connectivity in development, an action perspective posits that coherence and continuity in development essentially depend on the way in which, on the cultural and personal level, causal mechanisms are exploited to construct and deconstruct developmental contingencies.

As has become evident throughout this chapter, an action perspective on development cannot be reduced to one single theory in the formal sense. Accordingly, it would be questionable to single out one particular research program as prototypically representative of this stance. The research examples given in the present chapter cover a broad spectrum of themes across the whole life span. With regard to child development, researchers have documented the role that co-constructive interactions between the child and the material and social environment play in the formation of skills and competencies, and in the genesis of self-representations from which activities of intentional self-development originate. In the field of adolescent and adult development, efforts have been made to elucidate how personal goals, values, and control beliefs interact in the processes of life planning and intentional self-development, and how personal and contextual influences shape and modify these orientations as the individual moves through his or her developmental history. With regard to later life, increasing emphasis is given to the activities and processes by which the aging person maintains personal continuity, counteracts developmental losses, and adjusts personal projects to changes in functional reserves. Action-theoretical constructs such as life tasks, personal strivings, self-regulation, future perspectives, self-efficacy, perceived control, life planning, self-verification, or compensation have served as guiding concepts in this research and have become the nuclei of productive theorizing. Although action-theoretical approaches traditionally have an affinity toward hermeneutic or interpretative methods, it is increasingly recognized that a comprehensive analysis of the functional interdependencies among development, culture, and action would be hampered by any methodological parochialism. Current research freely uses, and often strategically combines, a broad gamut of methods ranging from experimental and microprocessual analyses to observational strategies and biographical interviews.

Beyond the theoretical issues on which this chapter has primarily centered, an action perspective on development has particular practical and ethical implications. As long as developmental processes are viewed from a narrow causalist or mechanist stance, they are not amenable to rational or moral evaluation. When the focus is laid on the collective actions that shape and constrain development, however, such evaluations become possible and legitimate. The assumptions, expectations, and theoretical premises that guide goal-directed activities may be evaluated with respect to, for example, their consistency and validity; goals and plans of action may be analyzed with respect to their realizability, intra- and interindividual consistency, and compatibility with ethical standards. This is equally true for activities related to the control of development—all the more so because developmental problems often reflect incompatibilities within the system of goals, values, affor-

dances, and constraints that shapes development on personal and social levels of action. An action perspective on development thus suggests that any effort at "optimizing" development should involve a critical analysis of the beliefs and normative expectations that, tacitly or explicitly, undergird the personal and social regulation of human ontogeny. It also may sensitize developmentalists to the fact that the results of their research and theorizing, when reintroduced into the contexts of socialization and intentional self-development, become part of the antecedent conditions of the processes that they are studying.

ACKNOWLEDGMENTS

The author is grateful to Richard M. Lerner, who provided thoughtful editorial comments on the entire manuscript of this chapter, and to Werner Greve, who gave valuable comments on an earlier draft.

REFERENCES

Abeles, R. P. (1991). Sense of control, quality of life, and frail older people. In J. E. Birren, D. E. Deutchman, J. Lubben, & J. Rowe (Eds.), *The concept and measurement of quality of life in the frail elderly* (pp. 297–314). New York: Academic Press.

Abramson, L. J., Seligman, M. E. P., & Teasdale, E. J. D. (1978). Learned helplessness in humans: Critique and reformulation. *Journal of Abnormal Psychology, 87,* 49–74.

Aebli, H. (1980). *Denken: Das Ordnen des Tuns. Kognitive Aspekte der Handlungstheorie* (Vol. 1). Stuttgart: Klett-Cotta.

Aebli, H. (1987). Mental development: Construction in a cultural context. In B. Inhelder, D. de Caprona, & A. Cornu-Wells (Eds.), *Piaget today* (pp. 217–232). Hillsdale, NJ: Erlbaum.

Ajzen, I. (1988). *Attitudes, personality, and behavior.* Chicago: Dorsey Press.

Anderson, A. R., & Belnap, N. D., Jr. (1975). *Entailment: The logic of relevance and necessity* (Vol. 1). Princeton, NJ: Princeton University Press.

Arendt, H. (1976). *The life of the mind: Vol. 1. Thinking.* London: Secker & Warburg.

Atchley, R. C. (1989). A continuity theory of normal aging. *The Gerontologist, 29,* 183–190.

Atkinson, J. W. (1970). *The dynamics of action.* New York: Wiley.

Austin, J. L. (1956). A plea for excuses. *Proceedings of the Aristotelian Society, 57,* 1–30.

Averill, J. A. (1980). A constructivistic view of emotion. In R. Plutchik & H. Kellerman (Eds.), *Emotion. Theory, research, and experience: Vol. 1. Theories of emotion* (pp. 305–339). New York: Academic Press.

Bäckman, L., & Dixon, R. A. (1992). Psychological compensation: A theoretical framework. *Psychological Bulletin, 112,* 259–283.

Baltes, P. B. (1987). Theoretical propositions of life-span developmental psychology: On the dynamics between growth and decline. *Developmental Psychology, 23,* 611–626.

Baltes, P. B. (1993). The aging mind: Potential and limits. *The Gerontologist, 33,* 580–594.

Baltes, P. B., & Baltes, M. M. (1990). Psychological perspectives on successful aging: The model of selective optimization with compensation. In P. B. Baltes & M. M. Baltes (Eds.), *Successful aging: Perspectives from the behavioral sciences* (pp. 1–34). New York: Cambridge University Press.

Baltes, P. B., Cornelius, S. W., & Nesselroade, J. R. (1979). Cohort effects in developmental psychology. In J. R. Nesselroade & P. B. Baltes (Eds.), *Longitudinal research in the study of behavior and development* (pp. 61–87). New York: Academic Press.

Baltes, P. B., & Reese, H. W. (1984). The life-span perspective in developmental psychology. In M. H. Bornstein & M. E. Lamb (Eds.), *Development psychology: An advanced textbook* (pp. 493–531). Hillsdale, NJ: Erlbaum.

Baltes, P. B., Reese, H. W., & Lipsitt, L. P. (1980). Life-span developmental psychology. *Annual Review of Psychology, 31,* 65–110.

Baltes, P. B., & Schaie, K. W. (1974, March). The myth of the twilight years. *Psychology Today,* 25–40.

Balzer, W., & Moulines, C. U. (1980). On theoreticity. *Synthese, 44,* 467–494.

Balzer, W., Moulines, C. U., & Sneed, J. D. (1987). *An architectonic for science: The structuralist program.* Dordrecht, The Netherlands: Reidel.

Bandura, A. (1977). Self-efficacy: Toward a unifying theory of behavioral change. *Psychological Review, 84,* 191–215.

Bandura, A. (1981). Self-referent thought: A developmental analysis of self-efficacy. In J. H. Flavell & L. Ross (Eds.), *Social cognitive development: Frontiers and possible futures* (pp. 200–239). Cambridge, England: Cambridge University Press.

Bandura, A. (1982a). The psychology of chance encounters and life paths. *American Psychologist, 37,* 747–755.

Bandura, A. (1982b). Self-efficacy mechanisms in human agency. *American Psychologist, 37,* 122–147.

Bandura, A. (1986). *Social foundations of thought and action: A social cognitive theory.* Englewood Cliffs, NJ: Prentice-Hall.

Bandura, A. (1989). Self-regulation of motivation and action through internal standards and goal systems. In L. A. Pervin (Ed.), *Goal concepts in personality and social psychology* (pp. 19–85). Hillsdale, NJ: Erlbaum.

Bandura, A. (1991). Self-regulation of motivation through anticipating and self-regulatory mechanisms. In R. A. Dienstbier (Ed.), *Perspectives on motivation: Nebraska Symposium on Motivation* (Vol. 39, pp. 69–164). Lincoln: University of Nebraska Press.

Baumeister, R. F. (1986). *Identity: Cultural change and the struggle for self.* New York: Oxford University Press.

Baumrind, D. (1989). The permanence of change and the impermanence of stability. *Human Development, 32,* 187–195.

Bell, R. Q. (1974). Contributions of human infants to caregiving and social interaction. In M. Lewis & L. A. Rosenblum (Eds.), *The effect of the infant on its caregiver* (pp. 1–19). New York: Wiley.

Bengtson, V. L., Reedy, M. N., & Gordon, C. (1985). Aging and self-conceptions: Personality processing and social contexts. In J. E. Birren & K. W. Schaie (Eds.), *Handbook of the psychology of aging* (pp. 544–593). New York: Van Nostrand.

Berger, C. R. (1993). Goals, plans, and mutual understanding in relationships. In S. Duck (Ed.), *Individuals in relationships* (pp. 30–59). Newbury Park, NJ: Sage.

Berzonsky, M. (1988). Self-theorists, identity status, and social cognition. In D. K. Lapsley & F. C. Power (Eds.), *Self, ego, and identity* (pp. 243–292). New York: Springer.

Bijou, S. W., & Baer, D. M. (1961). *Child development: Vol. 1. A systematic and empirical theory.* New York: Appleton-Century-Crofts.

Birren, J. E., & Schaie, K. W. (Eds.). (1990). *Handbook of the psychology of aging* (3rd ed.). San Diego, CA: Academic Press.

Blaney, P. H. (1986). Affect and memory. *Psychological Bulletin, 99,* 299–246.

Blazer, D. (1989). Depression in late life: An update. *Annual Review of Gerontology and Geriatrics, 9,* 197–215.

Block, J. (1971). *Lives through time.* Berkeley, CA: Bancroft Books.

Bloom, B. S. (1964). *Stability and change in human characteristics.* New York: Wiley.

Boesch, E. E. (1980). *Kultur und Handlung: Einführung in die Kulturpsychologie.* Bern: Huber.

Boesch, E. E. (1991). *Symbolic action theory in cultural psychology*. Berlin: Springer.

Bourdieu, P. (1977). *Outline of a theory of practice*. Cambridge, England: Cambridge University Press.

Bourdieu, P., & Passeron, J.-C. (1977). *Reproduction in education, society and culture*. Beverly Hills, CA: Sage.

Brainerd, J. (1978). The stage question in cognitive-developmental theory. *The Behavioral and Brain Sciences, 1*, 173–213.

Brand, M. (1984). *Intending and acting: Toward a naturalized action theory*. Cambridge, MA: MIT Press.

Brand, M., & Walton, D. (Eds.). (1976). *The nature of human action*. Dordrecht, The Netherlands: Reidel.

Brandtstädter, J. (1982). Apriorische Elemente in psychologischen Forschungsprogrammen. *Zeitschrift für Sozialpsychologie, 13*, 267–277.

Brandtstädter, J. (1984a). Action development and development through action. *Human Development, 27*, 115–119.

Brandtstädter, J. (1984b). Personal and social control over development: Some implications of an action perspective in life-span developmental psychology. In P. B. Baltes & O. G. Brim, Jr. (Eds.), *Life-span development and behavior* (Vol. 6, pp. 1–32). New York: Academic Press.

Brandtstädter, J. (1984c). Entwicklung in Handlungskontexten: Aussichten für die entwicklungspsychologische Theorienbildung und Anwendung. In H. Lenk (Ed.), *Handlungstheorien interdisziplinär. Vol. 3, II: Wissenschaftliche und psychologische Handlungstheorien* (pp. 848–878). München: Fink.

Brandtstädter, J. (1985a). Entwicklungsberatung unter dem Aspekt der Lebensspanne. Zum Aufbau eines entwicklungspsychologischen Anwendungskonzepts. In J. Brandtstädter & H. Gräser (Ed.), *Entwicklungsberatung unter dem Aspekt der Lebensspanne* (pp. 1–15). Göttingen: Hogrefe.

Brandtstädter, J. (1985b). Individual development in social action contexts: Problems of explanation. In J. R. Nesselroade & A. von Eye (Eds.), *Individual development and social change: Explanatory analysis* (pp. 243–264). New York: Academic Press.

Brandtstädter, J. (1987). On certainty and universality in human development: Developmental psychology between apriorism and empiricism. In M. Chapman & R. A. Dixon (Eds.), *Meaning and the growth of understanding: Wittgenstein's significance for developmental psychology* (pp. 69–84). Berlin: Springer.

Brandtstädter, J. (1989). Personal self-regulation of development: Cross-sequential analyses of development-related control beliefs and emotions. *Developmental Psychology, 25*, 96–108.

Brandtstädter, J. (1992). Personal control over development: Some developmental implications of self-efficacy. In R. Schwarzer (Ed.), *Self-efficacy: Thought control of action* (pp. 127–145). New York: Hemisphere.

Brandtstädter, J., & Baltes-Götz, B. (1990). Personal control over development and quality of life perspectives in adulthood. In P. B. Baltes & M. M. Baltes (Eds.), *Successful aging: Perspectives from the behavioral sciences* (pp. 197–224). New York: Cambridge University Press.

Brandtstädter, J., & Greve, W. (1994). The aging self: Stabilizing and protective processes. *Developmental Review, 14*, 52–80.

Brandtstädter, J., Krampen, G., & Heil, F. E. (1986). Personal control and emotional evaluation of development in partnership relations during adulthood. In M. M. Baltes & P. B. Baltes (Eds.), *The psychology of aging and control* (pp. 265–296). Hillsdale, NJ: Erlbaum.

Brandtstädter, J., & Renner, G. (1990). Tenacious goal pursuit and flexible goal adjustment: Explication and age-related analysis of assimilative and accommodative strategies of coping. *Psychology and Aging, 5*, 58–67.

Brandtstädter, J., & Renner, G. (1992). Coping with discrepancies between aspirations and achievements in adult development: A dual-process model. In L. Montada, S.-H. Filipp, & R. M. Lerner (Eds.), *Life crises and experiences of loss in adulthood* (pp. 301–319). Hillsdale, NJ: Erlbaum.

Brandtstädter, J., & Rothermund, K. (1994). Self-percepts of control in middle and later adulthood: Buffering losses by rescaling goals. *Psychology and Aging, 9*, 265–273.

Brandtstädter, J., & Wentura, D. (1994). Veränderungen der Zeit- und Zukunftsperspektive im Übergang zum höheren Erwachsenenalter: Entwicklungspsychologische und differentielle Aspekte. *Zeitschrift für Entwicklungspsychologie und Pädagogische Psychologie, 26*, 2–21.

Brandtstädter, J., Wentura, D., & Greve, W. (1993). Adaptive resources of the aging self: Outlines of an emergent perspective. *International Journal of Behavioral Development, 16*, 232–349.

Brazelton, T. B., Koslowski, B., & Main, M. (1974). The origins of reciprocity: The early mother-infant interaction. In M. Lewis & L. A. Rosenblum (Eds.), *The effect of the infant on its caregiver* (pp. 45–76). New York: Wiley.

Breytspraak, L. M. (1984). *The development of self in later life*. Boston: Little, Brown.

Brim, G. (1992). *Ambition: How we manage success and failure throughout our lives*. New York: Basic Books.

Brim, O. G., Jr., & Kagan, J. (1980). Constancy and change: A view of the issues. In O. G. Brim, Jr. & J. Kagan (Eds.),

Constancy and change in human development (pp. 1–25). Cambridge, MA: Harvard University Press.

Bronfenbrenner, U. (1979). *The ecology of human development.* Cambridge, MA: Harvard University Press.

Broughton, J. (1978). Development of concepts of self, mind, reality, and knowledge. *New Directions for Child Development, 1,* 75–100.

Bruner, J. S. (1972). The nature and uses of immaturity. *American Psychologist, 27,* 687–708.

Bruner, J. S. (1973). The organization of early skilled action. *Child Development, 44,* 1–11.

Bruner, J. S. (1982). The organization of action and the nature of adult-infant transaction. In M. von Cranach & R. Harré (Eds.), *The analysis of action* (pp. 313–327). Cambridge, England: Cambridge University Press.

Bruner, J. S. (1990a). *Acts of meaning.* Cambridge, MA: Harvard University Press.

Bruner, J. S. (1990b). Culture and human development: A new look. *Human Development, 33,* 344–355.

Bühler, C. (1933). *Der menschliche Lebenslauf als psychologisches Problem.* Leipzig: Hirzel.

Bühler, C., & Marschak, M. (1969). Grundtendenzen des menschlichen Lebens. In C. Bühler & F. Massarik (Eds.), *Lebenslauf und Lebensziele* (pp. 78–88). Stuttgart: Fischer.

Bullock, M. (Ed.). (1991). *The development of intentional action. Cognitive, motivational, and interactive processes: Contributions to human development* (Vol. 22). Basel: Karger.

Bunge, M. (1979). *Causality and modern science* (3rd ed.). New York: Dover.

Busch-Rossnagel, N. A. (1981). Where is the handicap in disability? The contextual impact of physical disability. In R. M. Lerner & M. Busch-Rossnagel (Eds.), *Individuals as producers of their development: A life-span perspective* (pp. 281–312). New York: Academic Press.

Butterworth, G. (1990). Self-perception in infancy. In D. Cicchetti & M. Beeghly (Eds.), *The self in transition. Infancy to childhood* (pp. 119–137). Chicago: University of Chicago Press.

Buunk, P. B., Collins, R. L., Taylor, S. E., VanYperen, N. W., & Dakof, G. A. (1990). The affective consequences of social comparison: Either direction has its ups and downs. *Journal of Personality and Social Psychology, 59,* 1238–1249.

Cairns, R. B. (1983). The emergence of developmental psychology. In W. Kessen (Ed.), *Handbook of child psychology: Vol. 1. History, theory, and methods* (pp. 41–102). New York: Wiley.

Cantor, N., & Fleeson, W. (1991). Life tasks and self-regulatory processes. In M. L. Maehr & P. R. Pintrich (Eds.), *Advances in motivation and achievement* (Vol. 7, pp. 327–369). Greenwich, CT: JAI Press.

Cantor, N., Markus, H., Niedenthal, P., & Nurius, P. (1986). On motivation and the self concept. In R. M. Sorrentino & E. T. Higgins (Eds.), *Handbook of motivation and cognition: Vol. 1. Foundations of social behavior* (pp. 96–121). New York: Guilford Press.

Cantor, N., Norem, J. K., Niedenthal, P. M., Langston, C. A., & Brower, A. M. (1987). Life tasks, self-concept ideals and cognitive strategies in a life transition. *Journal of Personality and Social Psychology, 53,* 1178–1191.

Care, N. S., & Landesman, C. (Eds.). (1968). *Readings in the theory of action.* Bloomington: Indiana University Press.

Carstensen, L. L. (1993). Motivation for social contact across the life span: A theory of socioemotional selectivity. In J. E. Jacobs (Ed.), *Developmental perspectives on motivation: Nebraska Symposium on Motivation* (Vol. 40, pp. 209–254). Lincoln: University of Nebraska Press.

Carus, F. A. (1823). *Psychologie. Erster Band* (2nd ed.). Leipzig: Barth & Kummer.

Carver, C. S., & Scheier, M. F. (1981). *Attention and self-regulation: A control-theory approach to human behavior.* New York: Springer.

Carver, C. S., & Scheier, M. F. (1986). Self and the control of behavior. In L. M. Hartman & K. R. Blankstein (Eds.), *Perception of self in emotional disorder and psychotherapy* (pp. 5–35). New York: Plenum Press.

Carver, C. S., & Scheier, M. F. (1990). Origins and functions of positive and negative affect: A control-process view. *Psychological Review, 97,* 19–35.

Case, R. (1991). Stages in the development of the young child's first sense of self. *Developmental Review, 11,* 210–230.

Chapman, M. (1984). Intentional action as a paradigm for developmental psychology: A Symposium. *Human Development, 27,* 113–114.

Chisholm, R. M. (1966). Freedom and action. In K. Lehrer (Ed.), *Freedom and determinism* (pp. 11–44). New York: Random House.

Chudacoff, H. P. (1989). *How old are you? Age consciousness in American culture.* Princeton, NJ: Princeton University Press.

Clarke, A. M., & Clarke, A. D. B. (Eds.). (1976). *Early experience: Myth and evidence.* New York: Free Press.

Clarke-Stewart, K. A., & Fein, G. G. (1983). Early childhood programs. In M. M. Haith & J. J. Campos (Eds.), *Handbook of child psychology: Vol. 6. Infancy and developmental psychobiology* (pp. 917–999). New York: Wiley.

Cole, M. (Ed.). (1978). *Soviet developmental psychology: An anthology.* White Plains, NY: Sharp.

Cole, M., & Scribner, S. (1974). *Culture and thought: A psychological introduction.* New York: Wiley.

Coleman, J. C. (1980). *The nature of adolescence.* London: Methuen.

Coleman, J. C. (1986). *Aging and reminiscence processes: Social and clinical implications.* New York: Wiley.

Coyne, J. C. (1992). Cognition on depression: A paradigm in crisis. *Psychological Inquiry, 3,* 232–235.

Csikszentmihalyi, M., & Beattie, O. (1979). Life themes: A theoretical and empirical exploration of their origins and effects. *Journal of Humanistic Psychology, 19,* 45–63.

Csikszentmihalyi, M., & Rochberg-Halton, E. (1981). *The meaning of things: Domestic symbols and the self.* Cambridge, England: Cambridge University Press.

Damon, W., & Hart, D. (1982). The development of self-understanding from infancy through adolescence. *Child Development, 53,* 841–864.

D'Andrade, R. G. (1984). Cultural meaning systems. In R. A. Shweder & R. A. Le Vine (Eds.), *Culture theory: Essays on mind, self, and emotion* (pp. 88–119). Cambridge, England: Cambridge University Press.

Dannefer, D. (1984). Adult development and social theory: A paradigmatic reappraisal. *American Sociological Review, 49,* 100–116.

Dannefer, D. (1989). Human action and its place in theories of aging. *Journal of Aging Studies, 3,* 1–20.

Dannefer, D., & Perlmutter, M. (1990). Development as a multidimensional process: Individual and social constituents. *Human Development, 33,* 108–137.

Davidson, D. (1980). *Essays on actions and events.* Oxford, England: Clarendon Press.

Dennett, D. C. (1987). *The intentional stance.* Cambridge, MA: MIT Press.

Derryberry, D. (1993). Attentional consequences of outcome-related motivational states: Congruent, incongruent, and focusing effects. *Motivation and Emotion, 17,* 65–89.

Diaz, R. M., Neal, L. J., & Amaya-Williams, M. (1991). The social origins of self-regulation. In L. Moll (Ed.), *Vygotsky and education* (pp. 127–154). London: Cambridge University Press.

Dilthey, W. (1924). Ideen über eine beschreibende und zergliedernde Psychologie. In B. Groethuysen (Ed.), *Wilhelm Dilthey. Gesammelte Schriften* (Vol. 5, pp. 139–240). Leipzig: Teubner.

Dittmann-Kohli, F. (1986). Problem identification and definition as important aspects of adolescents' coping with normative life-tasks. In R. K. Silbereisen, K. Eyferth, & G. Rudinger (Eds.), *Development as action in context* (pp. 19–38). Berlin: Springer.

Dixon, R. A., & Bäckman, L. (Eds.). (1995). *Compensating for psychological deficits and declines: Managing losses and promoting gains.* Hillsdale, NJ: Erlbaum.

Dörner, O. (1984). Denken und Handeln in Unbestimmtheit und Komplexität. In P. Wapnewski (Ed.), *Wissenschaftskolleg zu Berlin—Jahrbuch 1982/83* (pp. 97–118). Berlin: Siedler.

Dreher, E., & Oerter, R. (1986). Children's and adolescents' conceptions of adulthood: The changing view of a crucial developmental task. In R. K. Silbereisen, K. Eyferth, & G. Rudinger (Eds.), *Development as action in context* (pp. 109–120). Berlin: Springer.

Dreher, M., & Oerter, R. (1987). Action planning competencies during adolescence and early adulthood. In S. L. Friedman, E. K. Scholnick, & R. R. Cocking (Eds.), *Blueprints for thinking: The role of planning in cognitive development* (pp. 321–355). Cambridge, MA: Cambridge University Press.

Duval, S., & Wicklund, R. A. (1972). *A theory of objective self-awareness.* New York: Academic Press.

Eckensberger, L. H., & Meacham, J. A. (1984). The essentials of action theory: A framework for discussion. *Human Development, 27,* 166–172.

Eckensberger, L. H., & Reinshagen, H. (1980). Kohlbergs Strukturtheorie der Entwicklung des moralischen Urteils: Ein Versuch ihrer Reinterpretation in Bezugsräumen handlungstheoretischer Konzepte. In L. H. Eckensberger & R. K. Silbereisen (Eds.), *Entwicklung sozialer Kognitionen* (pp. 65–131). Stuttgart: Klett-Cotta.

Edelstein, W., & Keller, M. (Eds.). (1982). *Perspektivität und Integration. Beiträge zur Entwicklung des sozialen Verstehens.* Frankfurt/M: Suhrkamp.

Ellis, A. (1976). RET abolishes most of the human ego. *Psychotherapy: Theory, Research, and Practice, 13,* 343–348.

Elster, J. (1983). *Sour grapes. Studies in the subversion of rationality.* Cambridge, England: Cambridge University Press.

Emde, R. N., & Harmon, R. J. (Eds.). (1984). *Continuities and discontinuities in development.* New York: Plenum Press.

Emmons, R. A. (1986). Personal strivings: An approach to personality and subjective well-being. *Journal of Personality and Social Psychology, 51,* 1058–1068.

Emmons, R. A. (1989). The personal striving approach to personality. In L. A. Pervin (Ed.), *Goal concepts in personality and social psychology* (pp. 87–126). Hillsdale, NJ: Erlbaum.

Emmons, R. A. (1992). Abstract versus concrete goals: Personal striving level, physical illness, and psychological well-being. *Journal of Personality and Social Psychology, 62,* 292–300.

Epstein, S. (1973). The self-concept revisited or a theory of a theory. *American Psychologist, 28,* 405–416.

Ericsson, K. A. (1990). Peak performance and age: An examination of peak performance in sports. In P. B. Baltes & M. M. Baltes (Eds.), *Successful aging: Perspectives from the behavioral sciences* (pp. 154–196). New York: Cambridge University Press.

Erikson, E. H. (1959). Identity and the life cycle. *Psychological Issues, 1,* 18–164.

Feather, N. T. (Ed.). (1982). Expectations and actions. Expectancy-value models in psychology. Hillsdale, NJ: Erlbaum.

Fenigstein, A., Scheier, M. F., & Buss, A. H. (1975). Public and private self-consciousness: Assessment and theory. *Journal of Consulting and Clinical Psychology, 43,* 522–527.

Festinger, L. (1957). *A theory of cognitive dissonance.* Standford, CA: Standford University Press.

Filipp, S.-H. (1980). Entwicklung von Selbstkonzepten. *Zeitschrift für Entwicklungspsychologie und Pädagogische Psychologie, 12,* 105–125.

Filipp, S.-H., & Klauer, T. (1985). Conceptions of self over the life-span: Reflections on the dialectics of change. In M. M. Baltes & P. B. Baltes (Eds.), *The psychology of aging and control* (pp. 167–205). Hillsdale, NJ: Erlbaum.

Fillmore, C. J. (1968). The case for case. In E. Bach & R. T. Harms (Eds.), *Universals in linguistic theory* (pp. 1–88). New York: Holt, Rinehart and Winston.

Fischer, K. W. (1980). A theory of cognitive development: The control and construction of a hierarchy of skills. *Psychological Review, 87,* 477–531.

Fishbein, M., & Ajzen, I. (1975). *Belief, attitude, intention, and behavior: An introduction to theory and research.* Reading, MA: Addison-Wesley.

Flavell, J. H. (1972). An analysis of cognitive-developmental sequences. *Genetic Psychology Monographs, 86,* 279–350.

Flavell, J. H. (1977). *Cognitive development.* Englewood Cliffs, NJ: Prentice-Hall.

Flavell, J. H., Speer, J. R., Green, F. L., & August, D. L. (1981). The development of comprehension monitoring and knowledge about communication. *Monographs of the Society for Research in Child Development, 46*(Serial No. 192).

Flavell, J. H., & Wellman, H. M. (1977). Metamemory. In R. V. Kail, Jr. & J. W. Hagen (Eds.), *Perspectives on the development of memory and cognition* (pp. 3–33). Hillsdale, NJ: Erlbaum.

Folkman, S. (1984). Personal control and stress and coping processes: A theoretical analysis. *Journal of Personality and Social Psychology, 46,* 839–852.

Ford, D. H. (1987). *Humans as self-constructing living systems: A developmental perspective on personality and behavior.* Hillsdale, NJ: Erlbaum.

Ford, D. H., & Lerner, R. M. (1992). *Developmental systems theory. An integrative approach.* Newbury Park, CA: Sage.

Frese, M., & Sabini, J. (Eds.). (1985). *Goal-directed behavior: Psychological theory and research on action.* Hillsdale, NJ: Erlbaum.

Friedman, S. L., Scholnick, E. K., & Cocking, R. R. (Eds.). (1987). *Blueprints for thinking: The role of planning in cognitive development.* Cambridge, England: Cambridge University Press.

Frijda, N. H. (1986). *The emotions.* Cambridge, England: Cambridge University Press.

Gärling, T., & Valsiner, J. (Eds.). (1985). *Children within environments: Toward a psychology of accident prevention.* New York: Plenum Press.

Geertz, C. (1973). *The interpretation of cultures. Selected essays.* New York: Basic Books.

Gehlen, A. (1971). *Der Mensch. Seine Natur und seine Stellung in der Welt* (9th ed.). Bonn: Bouvier.

Gehlen, A. (1988). *Man, his nature and place in the world.* New York: Columbia University Press. (Original work published in German 1955)

Geppert, U., & Küster, U. (1983). The emergence of "Wanting to do it oneself": A precursor of achievement motivation. *International Journal of Behavioral Development, 6,* 355–369.

Gergen, K. J. (1980). The emerging crisis in life-span developmental theory. In P. B. Baltes & O. G. Brim, Jr. (Eds.), *Lifespan development and behavior* (Vol. 3, pp. 31–63). New York: Academic Press.

Gergen, K. J., & Gergen, M. M. (1987). The self in temporal perspective. In R. P. Abeles (Ed.), *Life-span perspectives and social psychology* (pp. 121–137). Hillsdale, NJ: Erlbaum.

Gibson, J. J. (1977). The theory of affordances. In R. Shaw & F. Bransford (Eds.), *Perceiving, acting, and knowing* (pp. 67–82). Hillsdale, NJ: Erlbaum.

Giddens, A. (1979). *Control problems in social theory. Action, structure and contradiction in social theory.* London: Macmillan.

Gilbert, D. T. (1993). The assent of man: Mental representation and the control of belief. In D. M. Wegner & J. W. Pennebaker (Eds.), *Handbook of mental control* (pp. 57–87). Englewood Cliffs, NJ: Prentice-Hall.

Goldman, A. I. (1970). *A theory of human action*. Englewood Cliffs, NJ: Prentice-Hall.

Gollin, E. S. (1981). Development and plasticity. In E. S. Gollin (Ed.), *Developmental plasticity. Behavioral and biological aspects of variations in development* (pp. 231–251). New York: Academic Press.

Gollwitzer, P. M. (1987). Suchen, Finden und Festigen der eigenen Identität: Unstillbare Zielintentionen. In H. Heckhausen, P. M. Gollwitzer, & F. E. Weinert (Eds.), *Jenseits des Rubikon: Der Wille in den Sozialwissenschaften* (pp. 176–189). Berlin: Springer.

Gollwitzer, P. M. (1990). Action phases and mind-sets. In E. T. Higgins & R. M. Sorrentino (Eds.), *Handbook of motivation and cognition: Foundations of social behavior* (Vol. 2, pp. 53–92). New York: Guilford Press.

Gollwitzer, P. M., & Moskowitz, G. B. (1996). Goal effects on action and cognition. In E. T. Higgings & A. W. Kruglanski (Eds.), *Social psychology: Handbook of basic principles* (pp. 361–399). New York: Guilford Press.

Goodnow, J. J., & Collins, W. A. (1990). *Development according to parents: The nature, sources, and consequences of parents' ideas*. Hillsdale, NJ: Erlbaum.

Gottlieb, G. (1992). *Individual development and evolution: The genesis of novel behavior*. New York: Oxford University Press.

Gould, S. J. (1977). *Ontogeny and phylogeny*. Cambridge, MA: Belknap.

Gould, S. J. (1981). *The mismeasure of man*. New York: Norton.

Greenwald, A. G. (1980). The totalitarian ego: Fabrication and revision of personal history. *American Psychologist, 35,* 603–618.

Greve, W. (1990). Stabilisierung und Modifikation des Selbstkonzeptes im Erwachsenenalter: Strategien der Immunisierung. *Sprache & Kognition, 9,* 218–230.

Greve, W. (1994). *Handlungsklärung*. Göttingen: Hogrefe.

Groeben, N. (1986). *Handeln, Tun, Verhalten als Einheiten einer verstehend-erklärenden Psychologie*. Tübingen: Francke.

Guardo, C. J., & Bohan, J. B. (1971). Development of a sense of self-identification in children. *Child Development, 42,* 1909–1921.

Gunnar, M. R. (1980). Contingent stimulation: A review of its role in early development. In S. Levine & H. Ursin (Eds.), *Coping and health* (pp. 101–119). New York: Plenum Press.

Hagestad, G. O. (1991). Trends and dilemmas in life course research: An international perspective. In W. R. Heinz (Ed.), *Theoretical advances in life course research* (pp. 23–57). Weinheim: Deutscher Studien Verlag.

Harackiewicz, J. M., & Sansone, L. (1991). Goals and intrinsic motivation: You *can* get there from here. In M. L. Maehr &

P. R. Pintrich (Eds.), *Advances in motivation and achievement* (Vol. 7, pp. 21–49). Greenwich, CT: JAI Press.

Harré, R., & Secord, P. F. (1972). *The explanation of social behavior*. Oxford, England: Blackwell.

Harter, S. (1978). Effectance motivation reconsidered: Toward a developmental model. *Human Development, 1,* 34–64.

Harter, S. (1983). Developmental perspectives on the self-system. In E. M. Hetherington (Ed.), *Handbook of child psychology: Vol. 4. Socialization, personality, and social development* (pp. 275–385). New York: Wiley.

Harter, S. (1986). Cognitive-developmental processes in the integration of concepts about emotions and the self. *Social Cognition, 4,* 119–151.

Havighurst, R. J. (1974). *Developmental tasks and education* (3rd ed). New York: McKay. (Original work published 1948)

Hayek, F. A. (1979). *Law, legislation and liberty: Vol. 3. The political order of a free people*. London: Routledge & Kegan Paul.

Hayes-Roth, B., & Hayes-Roth, F. (1979). A cognitive model of planning. *Cognitive Science, 3,* 275–310.

Heckhausen, H. (1984). Emergent achievement behavior: Some early developments. In J. Nicholls (Ed.), *The development of achievement motivation: Advances in motivation and achievement* (Vol. 3, pp. 1–32). Greenwich, CT: JAI Press.

Heckhausen, H. (1989). *Motivation und Handeln* (2nd ed.). Berlin: Springer.

Heckhausen, H., & Gollwitzer, P. M. (1987). Thought contents and cognitive functioning in motivational vs. volitional states of mind. *Motivation and Emotion, 11*(2), 101–120.

Heckhausen, J., & Baltes, P. B. (1991). Perceived controllability of expected psychological change across adulthood and old age. *Journal of Gerontology: Psychological Sciences, 46,* 165–173.

Heckhausen, J., Dixon, R. A., & Baltes, P. B. (1989). Gains and losses in development throughout adulthood as perceived by different adult age groups. *Developmental Psychology, 25,* 109–121.

Heckhausen, J., & Krueger, J. (1993). Developmental expectations for the self and "most other people": Age-grading in three functions of social comparison. *Developmental Psychology, 29,* 539–548.

Heckhausen, J., & Schulz, R. (1995). A life-span theory of control. *Psychological Review, 102,* 284–304.

Hegel, G. W. F. (1857). *Lectures of the philosophy of history.* (J. Sibree, Trans.). London: Bohn. (Original work published in German 1837)

Heidmets, M. (1985). Environment as the mediator of human relationships: Historical and ontogenetic aspects. In T. Gärling

& J. Valsiner (Eds.), *Children within environments. Toward a psychology of accident prevention* (pp. 217–227). New York: Plenum Press.

Heil, F. E., & Krampen, G. (1989). Action theoretical approaches to the development of control orientations in the aged. In P. S. Fry (Ed.), *Psychological perspectives of helplessness and control in the elderly* (pp. 99–118). Amsterdam, The Netherlands: Elsevier.

Herder, J. G. (1772). *Abhandlung über den Ursprung der Sprache.* Berlin: A. Weichert.

Higgins, E. T. (1988). Development of self-regulatory and self-evaluative processes: Costs, benefits, and trade-offs. In M. R. Gunnar & L. A. Sroufe (Eds.), *Self processes in development: Minnesota Symposium on Child Psychology* (Vol. 23, pp. 125–165). Minneapolis: University of Minnesota Press.

Higgins, E. T., Klein, R., & Strauman, T. (1985). Self-concept discrepancy theory: A psychological model for distinguishing among different aspects of depression and anxiety. *Social Cognition, 3,* 51–76.

Higgins, E. T., Strauman, T., & Klein, R. (1986). Standards and the process of self-evaluation. Multiple affects from multiple stages. In R. M. Sorrentino & E. T. Higgins (Eds.), *Handbook of motivation and cognition: Foundations of social behavior* (pp. 23–63). New York: Guilford Press.

Höhn, E. (1958). Entwicklung als aktive Gestaltung. In H. Thomae (Ed.), *Entwicklungspsychologie* (pp. 235–312). Göttingen: Hogrefe.

Ickes, W. (Ed.). (1985). *Compatible and incompatible relationships.* New York: Springer.

Inhelder, B., & Piaget, J. (1958). *The growth of logical thinking from childhood to adolescence.* New York: Basic Books.

James, W. (1890). *The principles of psychology.* New York: Holt.

Janoff-Bulman, R., & Brickman, P. (1982). Expectations and what people learn from failure. In N. T. Feather (Ed.), *Expectations and actions* (pp. 207–237). Hillsdale, NJ: Erlbaum.

Kagan, J. (1971). *Change and continuity in infancy.* New York: Wiley.

Kagan, J. (1981a). *The second year: The emergence of self-awareness.* Cambridge, MA: Harvard University Press.

Kagan, J. (1981b). Universals in human development. In R. H. Munroe, R. L. Munroe, & B. B. Whiting (Eds.), *Handbook of cross-cultural human development* (pp. 53–63). New York: Garland Press.

Kagan, J. (1984). *The nature of the child.* New York: Basic Books.

Kagan, J., & Moss, H. A. (1962). *Birth to maturity.* New York: Wiley.

Kahana, E., Kahana, B., & Riley, K. (1989). Person-environment transactions relevant to control and helplessness in institutional settings. In P. S. Fry (Ed.), *Psychological perspectives of helplessness and control in the elderly* (pp. 121–153). Amsterdam, The Netherlands: Elsevier.

Kahnemann, D., & Miller, D. T. (1986). Norm theory: Comparing reality to its alternatives. *Psychological Review, 93,* 136–153.

Kalicki, B. (1995). *Die Normalbiographie als psychologisches Regulativ. Zum subjektiven Bedeutungsgehalt von Lebensereignissen, die vom normalbiographischen Zeitmuster abweichen.* Unpublished doctoral dissertation, University of Trier, Trier, Germany.

Kaminski, G. (1982). What beginner skiers can teach us about actions. In M. von Cranach & R. Harré (Eds.), *The analysis of action* (pp. 99–114). Cambridge, England: Cambridge University Press.

Kamlah, W. (1973). *Philosophische Anthropologie. Sprachkritische Grundlegung und Ethik.* Mannheim: BI Taschenbücher.

Kanfer, F. H., & Hagerman, S. (1981). The role of self-regulation. In L. P. Rehm (Ed.), *Behavior therapy for depression: Present status and future directions* (pp. 143–180). New York: Academic Press.

Karoly, P. (1993). Mechanisms of self-regulation: A systems view. *Annual Review of Psychology, 44,* 23–52.

Kastenbaum, R. (1982). Time course and time perspective in later life. In C. Eisdorfer (Ed.), *Annual review of geriatrics and gerontology* (pp. 80–101). New York: Springer.

Kegan, R. (1983). A neo-Piagetian approach to object relations. In B. Lec & G. G. Noam (Eds.), *Developmental approaches to the self* (pp. 267–307). New York: Plenum Press.

Keil, F. C. (1979). *Semantic and conceptual development: An ontological perspective.* Cambridge, MA: Harvard University Press.

Keil, F. C., & Batterman, N. (1984). A characteristic-to-defining shift in the development of word meaning. *Journal of Verbal Learning and Verbal Behavior, 23,* 211–236.

Kesselring, F. (1981). *Entwicklung und Widerspruch.* Frankfurt/M: Suhrkamp.

Kessler, R. C., Foster, C., Webster, P. S., & House, J. S. (1992). The relationship between age and depressive symptoms in two national surveys. *Psychology and Aging, 7,* 119–126.

Kihlstrom, J. F., & Cantor, N. (1984). Mental representations of the self. In L. Berkowitz (Ed.), *Advances in experimental social psychology* (Vol. 17, pp. 1–47). New York: Academic Press.

Kliegl, R., Smith, J., & Baltes, P. B. (1989). Testing-the-limits and the study of age differences in cognitive plasticity of a mnemonic skill. *Developmental Psychology, 26,* 894–904.

Klinger, E. (1975). Consequences of commitment to and disengagement from incentives. *Psychological Review, 82,* 1–25.

Klinger, E. (1987). Current concerns and disengagement from incentives. In F. Halisch & J. Kuhl (Eds.), *Motivation, intention, and volition* (pp. 337–347). Berlin: Springer.

Kohlberg, L. (1966). A cognitive-developmental analysis of children's sex-role concepts and attitudes. In E. E. Maccoby (Ed.), *The development of sex differences* (pp. 82–172). Stanford, CA: Stanford University Press.

Kohlberg, L. (1976). Moral stages and moralization. The cognitive developmental approach. In T. Lickona (Ed.), *Moral development and behavior. Theory, research, and social issues* (pp. 31–53). New York: Holt, Rinehart and Winston.

Kohlberg, L., LaCrosse, J., & Ricks, D. (1972). The predictability of adult mental health from childhood behavior. In B. Wolman (Ed.), *Manual of child psychopathology* (pp. 1217–1284). New York: McGraw-Hill.

Kopp, C. B. (1982). Antecedents of self-regulation: A developmental perspective. *Developmental Psychology, 18,* 199–214.

Kopp, C. B. (1987). The growth of self-regulation: Caregivers and children. In N. Eisenberg (Ed.), *Contemporary topics in developmental psychology* (pp. 34–55). New York: Wiley.

Kopp, C. B. (1989). Regulation of distress and negative emotions: A developmental view. *Developmental Psychology, 25,* 343–354.

Krampen, G. (1987a). *Handlungstheoretische Persönlichkeitspsychologie.* Göttingen: Hogrefe.

Krampen, G. (1987b). Entwicklung von Kontrollüberzeugungen: Thesen zu Forschungsstand und Perspektiven. *Zeitschrift für Entwicklungspsychologie und Pädagogische Psychologie, 19,* 195–227.

Kruglanski, A. W. (1990). Lay epistemic theory in social-cognitive psychology. *Psychological Inquiry, 1,* 181–197.

Kuhl, J., & Beckmann, J. (Eds.). (1985). *Action control: From cognition to behavior.* Berlin: Springer.

Kuhl, J., & Beckmann, J. (Eds.). (1994). *Volition and personality.* Göttingen: Hogrefe.

Kukla, A. (1989). Nonempirical issues in psychology. *American Psychologist, 44,* 785–794.

Kunda, Z. (1990). The case for motivated reasoning. *Psychological Bulletin, 108,* 480–498.

Lachman, M. E. (1986). Locus of control in aging research: A case for multidimensional and domain-specific assessment. *Journal of Psychology and Aging, 1,* 34–40.

Lamb, M. E., & Easterbrooks, M. A. (1981). Individual differences in parental sensitivity: Some thoughts about origins, components, and consequences. In M. E. Lamb & R. L. Sher-

rod (Eds.), *Infant social cognition: Empirical and theoretical considerations* (pp. 127–153). Hillsdale, NJ: Erlbaum.

Lanz, P. (1987). *Menschliches Handeln zwischen Kausalität und Rationalität.* Frankfurt/M: Athenäum.

Lave, J., & Wenger, E. (1991). *Situated learning: Legitimate peripheral participation.* New York: Cambridge University Press.

Lawrence, J. A., & Valsiner, J. (1993). Conceptual roots of internalization: From transmission to transformation. *Human Development, 36,* 150–167.

Lazarus, R. S., & Launier, R. (1978). Stress-related transactions between person and environment. In L. A. Pervin & M. Lewis (Eds.), *Perspectives in interactional psychology* (pp. 287–327). New York: Plenum Press.

Lazarus, R. S., & Smith, C. A. (1988). Knowledge and appraisal in the cognition-emotion relationship. *Cognition and Emotion, 2,* 281–300.

Lee, B., Wertsch, J. V., & Stone, A. (1983). Toward a Vygotskyan theory of the self. In B. Lee & G. G. Noam (Eds.), *Developmental approaches to the self* (pp. 309–341). New York: Plenum Press.

Lenk, H. (1978). *Handlungstheorien—interdisziplinär. Vol. II: Handlungserklärungen und philosophische Handlungsinterpretation.* München: Fink.

Lenk, H. (1981). Interpretative action constructs. In J. Agassi & R. S. Cohen (Eds.), *Scientific philosophy today* (pp. 151–157). Dordrecht, The Netherlands: Reidel.

Lenk, H. (1987). Strukturelle und empirische Implikationen: über einige strukturinduzierte Implikationen und deren Umkehrungen in der Soziometrie und Sozialpsychologie. In J. Brandtstädter (Ed.), *Struktur und Erfahrung in der psychologischen Forschung* (pp. 14–34). Berlin: de Gruyter.

Leont'ev, A. N. (1978). *Activity, consciousness, and personality.* Englewood Cliffs, NJ: Prentice-Hall.

Lerner, R. M. (1982). Children and adolescents as producers of their own development. *Developmental Review, 2,* 342–370.

Lerner, R. M. (1984). *On the nature of human plasticity.* Cambridge, England: Cambridge University Press.

Lerner, R. M. (1985). Individual and context in developmental psychology: Conceptual and theoretical issues. In J. R. Nesselroade & A. von Eye (Eds.), *Individual development and social change: Explanatory analysis* (pp. 155–188). New York: Academic Press.

Lerner, R. M., & Busch-Rossnagel, A. (Eds.). (1981). *Individuals as producers of their development: A life-span perspective.* New York: Academic Press.

Lerner, R. M., & Eye, A. von (1992). Sociobiology and human development: Arguments and evidence. *Human Development, 35*, 12–33.

Lerner, R. M., & Lerner, J. V. (1983). Temperament-intelligence reciprocities in early childhood: A contextual model. In M. Lewis (Ed.), *Origins of intelligence: Infancy and early childhood* (2nd ed., pp. 399–421). New York: Plenum Press.

Levinson, D. J. (1978). *The seasons of a man's life.* New York: Alfred Knopf.

Lewis, M. (1991). Ways of knowing: Objective self-awareness or consciousness. *Developmental Review, 11*, 231–243.

Lewis, M., & Brooks-Gunn, J. (1979). *Social cognition and the acquisition of self.* New York: Plenum Press.

Lewontin, R. C. (1982). Organism and environment. In H. C. Plotkin (Ed.), *Learning, development and culture* (pp. 151–170). Chichester, England: Wiley.

Linville, P. W. (1987). Self-complexity as a cognitive buffer against stress-related illness and depression. *Journal of Personality and Social Psychology, 52*, 663–676.

Little, B. R. (1983). Personal projects. A rationale and method for investigation. *Environment and Behavior, 15*, 273–309.

Little, B. R. (1989). Personal projects analyses: Trivial pursuits, magnificent obsessions and the search for coherence. In D. M. Buss & N. Cantor (Eds.), *Personality psychology: Recent trends and emerging directions* (pp. 15–31). New York: Springer.

Locke, E. A., & Latham, G. P. (1990). *A theory of goal setting and task performance.* Englewood Cliffs, NJ: Prentice-Hall.

Luria, A. D. (1979). *The making of mind.* Cambridge, MA: Harvard University Press.

Luria, A. R. (1969). Speech development and the formation of mental processes. In M. Cole & I. Maltzman (Eds.), *A handbook of contemporary Soviet psychology* (pp. 121–162). New York: Basic Books.

Lütkenhaus, P., & Bullock, M. (1991). The development of volitional skills. In M. Bullock (Ed.), *The development of intentional action: Cognitive, motivational, and interactive processes: Contributions to Human Development* (Vol. 22, pp. 14–23). Basel: Karger.

Mace, F. C., Belfiore, P. J., & Shea, M. C. (1989). Operant theory and research on self-regulation. In B. J. Zimmerman & D. H. Schunk (Eds.), *Self-regulated learning and academic achievement: Theory, research, and practice* (pp. 27–50). New York: Springer.

Magnusson, D. (1990). Personality development from an interactional perspective. In L. A. Pervin (Ed.), *Handbook of personality: Theory and research* (pp. 193–222). New York: Guilford Press.

Marcus, D. E., & Overton, W. F. (1978). The development of cognitive gender constancy and sex role preferences. *Child Development, 49*, 434–444.

Markman, E. (1977). Realizing that you don't understand: A preliminary investigation. *Child Development, 48*, 986–992.

Markus, H. (1977). Self-schemata and processing information about the self. *Journal of Personality and Social Psychology, 35*, 63–78.

Martin, L. L., & Tesser, A. (1989). Toward a motivational and structural theory of ruminative thought. In J. S. Uleman & J. A. Bargh (Eds.), *Unintended thought* (pp. 306–326). New York: Guilford Press.

McCall, R. B. (1981). Nature–nurture and the two realms of development: A proposed integration with respect to mental development. *Child Development, 52*, 1–12.

McGuire, W. J., & McGuire, C. U. (1981). The spontaneous self-concept as affected by personal distinctiveness. In M. D. Lynch, A. A. Norem-Hebeisen, & K. J. Gergen (Eds.), *Self-concept. Advances in theory and research* (pp. 147–172). Cambridge, MA: Ballinger.

Medin, D. L., & Smith, E. E. (1984). Concepts and concept formation. *Annual Review of Psychology, 35*, 113–138.

Mees, U. (1991). *Die Struktur der Emotionen.* Göttingen: Hogrefe.

Meyer, J. S., & Rebok, G. W. (1985). Planning-in-action across the life span. In T. M. Schlecter & M. P. Toglia (Eds.), *New directions in cognitive science* (pp. 47–68). Norwood, NJ: ABLEX.

Miller, D. T., Turnbull, W., & McFarland, C. (1990). Counterfactual thinking and social perception: Thinking about what might have been. In M. P. Zanna (Ed.), *Advances in experimental social psychology* (Vol. 23, pp. 305–331). New York: Academic Press.

Miller, G. A., Galanter, E., & Pribram, K. H. (1960). *Plans and the structure of behavior.* New York: Holt, Rinehart and Winston.

Miller, P. H., & Bigi, L. (1979). The development of children's understanding of attention. *Merrill-Palmer Quarterly, 25*, 235–263.

Mischel, H. N., & Mischel, W. (1983). The development of children's knowledge of self-control strategies. *Child Development, 54*, 226–254.

Mischel, T. (1969). Human action: Conceptual and empirical issues. In T. Mischel (Ed.), *Human action: Conceptual and empirical issues* (pp. 261–278). New York: Academic Press.

Mischel, W. (1983). Delay of gratification as process and as person variable in development. In D. Magnusson & U. P. Allen (Eds.), *Human development: An interactional perspective* (pp. 149–165). New York: Academic Press.

Mischel, W., & Mischel, H. N. (1976). A cognitive social-learning approach to morality and self-regulation. In T. Lickona (Ed.), *Moral development and behavior* (pp. 84–107). New York: Holt, Rinehart and Winston.

Miskimins, R. W., & Simmons, W. L. (1966). Goal preference as a variable in involutional psychosis. *Journal of Consulting and Clinical Psychology, 30,* 73–77.

Montada, L. (1992). Attribution of responsibility for losses and perceived injustice. In L. Montada, S.-H. Filipp, & M. Lerner (Eds.), *Life crises and experiences of loss in adulthood* (pp. 133–161). Hillsdale, NJ: Erlbaum.

Moya, C. J. (1990). *The philosophy of action.* Cambridge, MA: Polity Press.

Müller, A. W. (1982). *Praktisches Folgern und Selbstgestaltung nach Aristoteles.* Freiburg: Alber.

Nagel, E. (1957). Determinism and development. In D. B. Harris (Ed.), *The concept of development* (pp. 15–24). Minneapolis: University of Minnesota Press.

Neugarten, B. L., & Hagestad, G. O. (1976). Age and the life course. In R. H. Binstock & E. Shanas (Eds.), *Handbook of aging and the social sciences* (pp. 35–57). New York: Van Nostrand.

Newmann, J. B. (1989). Aging and depression. *Psychology and Aging, 4,* 150–165.

Nicholls, J. G., & Miller, A. T. (1984). Development and its discontents: The differentiation of the concept of ability. In J. G. Nicholls (Ed.), *The development of achievement motivation: Advances in motivation and achievement* (Vol. 3, pp. 185–218). Greenwich, CT: JAI Press.

Nicholls, J. G., & Miller, A. T. (1985). Differentiation of the concepts of luck and skill. *Developmental Psychology, 21,* 76–82.

Nisbett, R., & Ross, L. (1980). *Human inference: Strategies and shortcomings of social judgment.* Englewood Cliffs, NJ: Prentice-Hall.

Norem-Hebeisen, A. A. (1981). A maximization model of self-concept. In M. D. Lynch, A. A. Norem-Hebeisen, & K. J. Gergen (Eds.), *Self-concept: Advances in theory and research* (pp. 133–146). Cambridge, MA: Ballinger.

Nozick, R. (1989). *The examined life. Philosophical meditations.* New York: Simon & Schuster.

Nurmi, J. E. (1992). Age differences in adult life goals, concerns, and their temporal extension: A life course approach to future-oriented motivation. *International Journal of Behavioral Development, 15,* 487–508.

Nurmi, J. E. (1993). Adolescent development in an age-graded context: The role of personal beliefs, goals, and strategies in the tackling of developmental tasks and standards. *International Journal of Behavioral Development, 16,* 169–189.

Nuttin, J. R. (1984). *Motivation, planning, and action: A relational theory of behavior dynamics.* Hillsdale, NJ: Erlbaum.

Oerter, R. (1991). Self-object relation as a basis of human development. In L. Oppenheimer & J. Valsiner (Eds.), *The origins of action: Interdisciplinary and international perspectives* (pp. 65–100). New York: Springer.

Olson, G. M., & Sherman, T. (1983). Attention, learning, and memory in infants. In M. Haith & J. J. Campos (Eds.), *Handbook of child psychology: Vol. 2. Infancy and developmental psychobiology* (pp. 1001–1080). New York: Wiley.

Oppenheimer, L., & Valsiner, J. (Eds.). (1991). *The origins of action. Interdisciplinary and international perspectives.* New York: Springer.

Overton, W. F. (Ed.). (1990). *Reasoning, necessity, and logic: Developmental perspectives.* Hillsdale, NJ: Erlbaum.

Overton, W. F., & Reese, H. W. (1981). Conceptual prerequisites for an understanding of stability-change and continuity-discontinuity. *International Journal of Behavioral Development, 4,* 99–123.

Oyama, S. (1979). The concept of the sensitive period in developmental studies. *Merrill-Palmer Quarterly, 25,* 83–103.

Papousek, H., & Papousek, M. (1987). Intuitive parenting: A dialectic counterpart to the infant's integrative competence. In J. D. Osofsky (Ed.), *Handbook of infant development* (2nd ed., pp. 669–720). New York: Wiley.

Papousek, M., & Papousek, H. (1989). Stimmliche Kommunikation im frühen Säuglingsalter als Wegbereiter der Sprachentwicklung. In H. Keller (Ed.), *Handbuch der Kleinkindforschung* (pp. 465–489). Berlin: Springer.

Parasuraman, R., & Davies, D. R. (1984). *Varieties of attention.* New York: Academic Press.

Parkinson, B., & Manstead, A. S. R. (1992). Appraisal as a cause of emotion. In M. S. Clark (Ed.), *Emotion* (pp. 122–149). Newbury Park, CA: Sage.

Parsons, T., & Shils, E. A. (Eds.). (1962). *Toward a general theory of action* (2nd ed.). New York: Harper & Row.

Pennebaker, J. W. (1989). Stream of consciousness and stress: Levels of thinking. In J. S. Uleman & J. A. Bargh (Eds.), *Unintended thought* (pp. 327–349). New York: Guilford Press.

Pervin, L. A. (1991). Self-regulation and the problem of volition. In M. L. Maehr & P. R. Pintrich (Eds.), *Advances in motivation and achievement* (Vol. 7, pp. 1–20). Greenwich, CT: JAI Press.

Piaget, J. (1932). *The moral judgement of the child.* New York: Harcourt & Brace.

Piaget, J. (1952). *The origins of intelligence in children*. New York: International Universities Press. (Original work published in French, 1936)

Piaget, J. (1970a). *L'epistémologie génétique*. Paris: Presses Universitaires de France.

Piaget, J. (1970b). Piaget's theory. In P. H. Mussen (Ed.), *Carmichael's handbook of child psychology* (Vol. 1, pp. 703–732). New York: Wiley.

Piaget, J. (1976). *The grasp of consciousness: Action and concept in the young child*. Cambridge, MA: Harvard University Press.

Piaget, J. (1978). *Success and understanding*. Cambridge, MA: Harvard University Press.

Piaget, J. (1986). Essay on necessity. *Human Development, 29*, 301–314.

Piaget, J. (1987). *Possibility and necessity: Vol. 2. The role of necessity in cognitive development*. Minneapolis: University of Minnesota Press.

Piaget, J., & Garcia, R. (1991). In P. M. Davidson & J. Easley (Eds.), *Toward a logic of meanings*. Hillsdale, NJ: Erlbaum. (Original work published 1983)

Piaget, J., & Inhelder, B. (1974). *The child's conception of quantities: Conservation and atomism*. London: Routledge & Kegan Paul. (Original work published in French, 1942)

Plomin, R. (1986). *Development, genetics and psychology*. Hillsdale, NJ: Erlbaum.

Popper, K. M. (1961). *The poverty of historicism*. London: Routledge & Kegan Paul.

Powers, W. T. (1973). *Behavior: The control of perception*. Chicago: Aldine.

Pulkkinen, L. (1982). Self control and continuity from childhood to late adolescence. In P. B. Baltes & O. G. Brim, Jr. (Eds.), *Life-span development and behavior* (Vol. 4, pp. 63–105). Hillsdale, NJ: Erlbaum.

Putnam, H. (1975). *Philosophical papers: Vol. 2. Mind, language, and reality*. Cambridge, MA: Cambridge University Press.

Quine, W. V. O. (1951). Two dogmas of empiricism. *Philosophical Review, 60*, 2–43.

Rawls, J. (1971). *A theory of justice*. Cambridge, MA: Cambridge University Press.

Raynor, J. O. (1981). Future orientation and achievement motivation: Toward a theory of personality functioning and change. In G. D'Ydewalle & W. Lens (Eds.), *Cognition in human motivation and learning* (pp. 199–231). Leuven, Belgium: Leuven University Press.

Raynor, J. O. (1982). A theory of personality functioning and change. In J. O. Raynor & E. E. Entin (Eds.), *Motivation, career striving, and aging* (pp. 13–82). Washington, DC: Hemisphere.

Raynor, J. O., & Entin, E. E. (Eds.). (1982). *Motivation, career striving, and aging*. Washington, DC: Hemisphere.

Raynor, J. O., & Entin, E. E. (1983). The function of future orientation as a determinant of human behavior in step-path theory of action. *International Journal of Psychology, 18*, 436–487.

Reese, H. W., & Overton, W. F. (1970). Models of development and theories of development. In L. R. Goulet & P. B. Baltes (Eds.), *Life-span developmental psychology: Research and theory* (pp. 116–149). New York: Academic Press.

Reinert, G. (1976). Grundzüge einer Geschichte der Human-Entwicklungspsychologie. In H. Balmer (Ed.), *Die Psychologie des 20. Jahrhunderts: Bd. 1. Die europäische Tradition. Tendenzen, Schulen, Entwicklungslinien* (pp. 862–896). Zürich: Kindler.

Reisenzein, R., & Schönpflug, U. (1992). Stumpf's cognitive-evaluative theory of emotion. *American Psychologist, 47*, 34–45.

Resnick, L. R. (Ed.). (1973). Hierarchies in children's learning: A symposium. *Instructional Science, 2*, 311–362.

Rest, J. (1982). Morality. In J. H. Flavell & E. M. Markman (Eds.), *Handbook of child psychology: Vol. 3. Cognitive development* (pp. 556–630). New York: Wiley.

Ricco, R. B. (1993). Revising the logic of operations as a relevance logic: From hypothesis testing to explanation. *Human Development, 36*, 125–146.

Riegel, K. F. (1976). The dialectics of human development. *American Psychologist, 31*, 689–700.

Rodin, J. (1987). Personal control through the life course. In R. P. Abeles (Ed.), *Life-span perspective and social psychology* (pp. 103–119). Hillsdale, NJ: Erlbaum.

Rogoff, B. (1990). *Apprenticeship in thinking: Cognitive development in social context*. New York: Oxford University Press.

Rommetveit, R. (1980). On "meanings" of acts and what is meant and made known by what is said in a pluralistic social world. In M. Brenner (Ed.), *The structure of action* (pp. 108–149). Oxford, England: Blackwell.

Rosch, E. (1977). Human categorization. In N. Warren (Ed.), *Studies in cross-cultural psychology* (Vol. 1, pp. 1–49). New York: Academic Press.

Rosch, E. (1978). Principles of categorization. In E. Rosch & B. B. Lloyd (Eds.), *Cognition and categorization* (pp. 27–48). Hillsdale, NJ: Erlbaum.

Rosenberg, M. (1979). *Conceiving the self*. New York: Basic Books.

Rosenberg, M., & Rosenberg, F. (1981). The occupational self: A developmental study. In M. D. Lynch, A. A. Norem-Hebeisen, & K. Gergen (Eds.), *Self-concept: Advances in theory and research* (pp. 173–189). Cambridge, MA: Ballinger.

Rothbaum, F., Weisz, J. R., & Snyder, S. S. (1982). Changing the world and changing the self. A two-process model of perceived control. *Journal of Personality and Social Psychology, 42,* 5–37.

Rowe, J. W., & Kahn, R. L. (1987). Human aging: Usual and successful. *Science, 237,* 143–149.

Russell, G., & Smith, J. (1979). Girls can be doctors, can't they: Sex differences in career aspirations. *Australian Journal of Social Issues, 14,* 91–102.

Rutter, M. (1984). Continuities and discontinuities in socioemotional development: Empirical and conceptual perspectives. In R. N. Emde & R. J. Harmon (Eds.), *Continuities and discontinuities in development* (pp. 41–68). New York: Plenum Press.

Salthouse, T. A. (1987). Age, experience, and compensation. In K. Schooler & K. W. Schaie (Eds.), *Cognitive functioning and social structure over the life course* (pp. 142–150). Norwood, NJ: ABLEX.

Sameroff, A. (1975). Transactional models in early social relations. *Human Development, 18,* 65–79.

Samuelson, P. A., & Nordhaus, W. D. (1985). *Economics* (12th ed.). New York: McGraw-Hill.

Scarr, S. (1982). On quantifying the intended effects of interventions: A proposed theory of the environment. In L. A. Bond & J. M. Joffe (Eds.), *Facilitating infant and early childhood development* (pp. 466–485). Hanover, NH: University Press of New England.

Scarr, S., & McCartney, K. (1983). How people make their own environments: A theory of genotype-environment effects. *Child Development, 54,* 424–435.

Schaie, K. W. (Ed.). (1983). *Longitudinal studies of adult psychological development.* New York: Guilford Press.

Schank, R. C., & Abelson, R. P. (1977). *Scripts, plans, goals and understanding: An inquiry into human knowledge structures.* Hillsdale, NJ: Erlbaum.

Schmitz, U., Saile, H., & Nilges, P. (1996). Coping with chronic pain: Flexible goal adjustment as an interactive buffer against pain-related distress. *Pain, 67,* 41–51.

Schneider, E. L., & Rowe, J. W. (Eds.). (1991). *Handbook of the biology of aging* (3rd ed.). San Diego, CA: Academic Press.

Schulz, R., & Decker, S. (1985). Long-term adjustment to physical disability: The role of social support, perceived control, and self-blame. *Journal of Personality and Social Psychology, 48,* 1162–1172.

Schunk, D. (1991). Goal-setting and self-evaluation: A social-cognitive perspective on self-regulation. In M. L. Maehr & P. R. Pintrich (Eds.), *Advances in motivation and achievement* (Vol. 7, pp. 85–113). Greenwich, CT: JAI Press.

Schütz, A. (1962). *Collected papers* (Vol. 1). The Hague: Nijhoff.

Searle, J. R. (1969). *Speech acts.* London: Cambridge University Press.

Seligman, M. E. P. (1990). Why is there so much depression today? The waxing of the individual and the waning of the commons. In R. E. Ingram (Ed.), *Contemporary psychological approaches to depression* (pp. 1–9). New York: Plenum Press.

Selman, R. (1980). *The growth of interpersonal understanding.* New York: Academic Press.

Selman, R., & Damon, W. (1975). The necessity (but insufficiency) of social perspective taking for conceptions of justice at three early levels. In D. J. DePalma & J. M. Foley (Eds.), *Moral development: Current theory and research* (pp. 57–74). Hillsdale, NJ: Erlbaum.

Shiffrin, R. M., & Dumais, S. T. (1981). The development of automatism. In J. R. Anderson (Ed.), *Cognitive skills and their acquisition* (pp. 111–140). Hillsdale, NJ: Erlbaum.

Shiffrin, R. M., & Schneider, W. (1977). Controlled and automatic human information processing: II. Perceptual learning, automatic attending, and a general theory. *Psychological Review, 84,* 127–190.

Shweder, R. A. (1990). Cultural psychology—what is it? In J. W. Stigler, R. A. Shweder, & G. Herdt (Eds.), *Cultural psychology: Essays on comparative human development* (pp. 1–43). Cambridge, England: Cambridge University Press.

Siegler, R. S. (1981). Developmental sequences within and between concepts. *Monographs of the Society for Research in Child Development, 46*(Serial No. 189).

Silbereisen, R. K., Eyferth, K., & Rudinger, G. (Eds.). (1987). *Development as action in context.* New York: Springer.

Simon, H. A. (1983). *Reason in human affairs.* Oxford, England: Basil Blackwell.

Skinner, B. F. (1953). *Science and human behavior.* New York: Macmillan.

Skinner, E. A. (1985). Action, control judgments, and the structure of control experience. *Psychological Review, 92,* 39–58.

Skinner, E. A. (1991). Development and perceived control: A dynamic model of action in context. In M. Gunnar & L. A. Sroufe (Eds.), *Minnesota Symposium on Child Psychology* (Vol. 22, pp. 167–216). Hillsdale, NJ: Erlbaum.

Skinner, E. A. (1995). *Perceived control, motivation, and coping.* Thousand Oaks, CA: Sage.

Skinner, E. A., Chapman, M., & Baltes, P. B. (1988). Control, means-ends, and agency beliefs: A new conceptualization and its measurement during childhood. *Journal of Personality and Social Psychology, 54,* 117–133.

Skinner, E. A., & Connell, J. P. (1986). Control understanding: Suggestions for a developmental framework. In M. M. Baltes & P. B. Baltes (Eds.), *The psychology of control and aging* (pp. 35–69). Hillsdale, NJ: Erlbaum.

Smedslund, J. (1979). Between the analytic and the arbitrary: A case study of psychological research. *Scandinavian Journal of Psychology, 20,* 129–140.

Smedslund, J. (1984). What is necessarily true in psychology? *Annals of Theoretical Psychology, 2,* 241–272.

Smith, J. (1996). Planning about life: An area in need of social-interactive paradigms? In P. B. Baltes & U. M. Staudinger (Eds.), *Interactive minds: Life-span perspectives on the social foundations of cognition* (pp. 242–275). New York: Cambridge University Press.

Smith, J. (in press). Perspectives on planning a life. In S. Friedman & M. K. Scholnick (Eds.), *Why, how and when do we plan? The developmental psychology of planning.* Hillsdale, NJ: Erlbaum.

Smith, M. J. (1982). *Persuasion and human action. A review and critique of social influence theories.* Belmont, CA: Wadsworth.

Snyder, C. R., & Higgins, R. L. (1988). Excuses: Their effective role in the negotiation of reality. *Psychological Bulletin, 104,* 23–35.

Snyder, M. (1979). Self-monitoring processes. In L. Berkowitz (Ed.), *Advances in experimental social psychology* (Vol. 12, pp. 85–128). New York: Academic Press.

Snyder, M., & Campbell, B. H. (1982). Self-monitoring: The self in action. In J. Suls (Ed.), *Psychological perspectives on the self* (Vol. 1, pp. 185–208). Hillsdale, NJ: Erlbaum.

Spranger, E. (1914). *Lebensformen. Geisteswissenschaftliche Psychologie und Ethik der Persönlichkeit.* Tübingen: Niemeyer.

Srull, T. K., & Wyer, R. S., Jr. (1986). The role of chronic and temporary goals in social information processing. In R. M. Sorrentino & E. T. Higgins (Eds.), *Handbook of motivation and cognition: Foundations of social behavior* (pp. 503–549). New York: Guilford Press.

Stangor, C., & Ruble, D. N. (1987). Development of gender role knowledge and gender constancy. In L. S. Liben & M. L. Signorella (Eds.), *New directions for child development: Vol. 39. Children's gender schemata* (pp. 5–22). San Francisco: Jossey-Bass.

Stangor, C., & Ruble, D. N. (1989). Differential influence of gender schemata and gender constancy on children's information processing and behavior. *Social Cognition, 7,* 353–372.

Staudinger, U. M., Marsiske, M., & Baltes, P. B. (1995). Resilience and reserve capacity in later adulthood: Potentials

and limits of development across the life span. In D. Cicchetti & D. Cohen (Eds.), *Developmental psychopathology: Vol. 2. Risk disorder and adaptation* (pp. 801–847). New York: Wiley.

Steele, C. M. (1988). The psychology of self-affirmation: Sustaining the integrity of the self. In L. Berkowitz (Ed.), *Advances in experimental social psychology: Vol. 21. Social psychological studies of the self: Perspectives and programs* (pp. 261–302). New York: Academic Press.

Sternberg, R. J., & Wagner, R. K. (Eds.). (1986). *Practical intelligence: Nature and origins of competence in the everyday world.* New York: Cambridge University Press.

Stock, W. A., Okun, M. A., Haring, M. J., & Witter, R. A. (1983). Age and subjective well-being: A meta-analysis. In R. J. Light (Ed.), *Evaluation studies: Review annual* (Vol. 8, pp. 279–302). Beverly Hills, CA: Sage.

Strack, F., Schwarz, N., Chassein, B., Kern, D., & Wagner, D. (1990). Salience of comparison standards and the activation of social norms: Consequences for judgments of happiness and their communication. *British Journal of Social Psychology, 29,* 303–314.

Strauss, S., & Ephron-Wertheim, T. (1986). Structure and process: Developmental psychology as looking in the mirror. In I. Levin (Ed.), *Stage and structure: Reopening the debate* (pp. 59–76). Norwood, NJ: ABLEX.

Super, C. M., & Harkness, S. (1986). The developmental niche. *International Journal of Behavioral Development, 9,* 545–570.

Swann, W. B. (1983). Self-verification: Bringing the social reality in harmony with the self. In J. Suls & A. G. Greenwald (Eds.), *Psychological perspectives on the self* (Vol. 2, pp. 33–66). Hillsdale, NJ: Erlbaum.

Swann, W. B., Jr., Griffin, J. J., Jr., Predmore, S. C., & Gaines, B. (1987). The cognitive-affective crossfire: When self-consistency confronts self-enhancement. *Journal of Personality and Social Psychology, 52,* 881–889.

Tatarkiewicz, W. (1976). *Analysis of happiness.* The Hague, The Netherlands: Martinus Nijhoff.

Taylor, C. (1989). *Sources of the self: The making of the modern identity.* Cambridge, MA: Harvard University Press.

Taylor, C., & Schneider, S. K. (1989). Coping and the simulation of events. *Social Cognition, 7,* 174–194.

Taylor, S. E. (1989). *Positive illusions: Creative self-deception and the healthy mind.* New York: Basic Books.

Taylor, S. E. (1991). Asymmetrical effects of positive and negative events: The mobilization-minimization hypothesis. *Psychological Bulletin, 110,* 67–85.

Taylor, S. E., & Crocker, J. (1981). Schematic bases of social information processing. In E. T. Higgins, C. P. Herman, &

M. P. Zanna (Eds.), *Social cognition* (pp. 89–134). Hillsdale, NJ: Erlbaum.

Tesser, A. (1986). Some effects of self evaluation maintenance on cognition and action. In R. M. Sorrentino & E. T. Higgings (Eds.), *Handbook of motivation and cognition: Foundations of social behavior* (pp. 435–464). New York: Guilford Press.

Tetens, J. N. (1777). *Philosophische Versuche über die menschliche Natur und ihre Entwicklung* (Vol. 1). Leipzig: M. G. Weidmanns Erben und Reich.

Thalberg, J. (1977). *Perception, emotion, and action: A component approach.* Oxford, England: Blackwell.

Thomae, H. (1968). *Das Individuum und seine Welt.* Göttingen: Hogrefe.

Thomas, A., & Chess, S. (1977). *Temperament and development.* New York: Brunner/Mazel.

Thompson, S. C., Cheek, P. R., & Graham, M. A. (1988). The other side of perceived control: Disadvantages and negative effects. In S. Spacapan & S. Oskamp (Eds.), *The social psychology of health* (pp. 69–93). Newbury Park, CA: Sage.

Tipper, S. P., & Cranston, M. (1985). Selective attention and priming: Inhibitory and facilitatory effects of ignored primes. *Quarterly Journal of Experimental Psychology, 37A,* 591–611.

Tobach, E. (1981). Evolutionary aspects of the activity of the organism and its development. In R. M. Lerner & N. A. Busch-Rossnagel (Eds.), *Individuals as producers of their development: A life-span perspective* (pp. 37–68). New York: Academic Press.

Toulmin, S. E. (1969). Concepts and the explanation of human behavior. In T. Mischel (Ed.), *Human action. Conceptual and empirical issues* (pp. 71–104). New York: Academic Press.

Toulmin, S. E. (1974). Rules and their relevance for understanding human behavior. In T. Mischel (Ed.), *Understanding other persons* (pp. 185–215). Oxford, England: Blackwell.

Toulmin, S. E. (1977). The end of the Parmenidean era. In Y. Elkana (Ed.), *The interaction between science and philosophy* (pp. 171–193). Atlantic Highlands, NJ: Humanities Press.

Trudewind, C., Unzner, L., & Schneider, K. (1989). Die Entwicklung der Leistungsmotivation. In H. Keller (Ed.), *Handbuch der Kleinkindforschung* (pp. 491–524). Berlin: Springer.

Turiel, E., & Davidson, P. (1986). Heterogenity, inconsistency, and asynchrony in the development of cognitive structures. In I. Levin (Ed.), *Stage and structure: Reopening the debate* (pp. 106–143). Norwood, NJ: ABLEX.

Tyler, S. A. (Ed.). (1969). *Cognitive anthropology.* New York: Holt, Rinehart and Winston.

Uleman, J. S., & Bargh, J. A. (Eds.). (1989). *Unintended thought.* New York: Guilford Press.

Vallacher, R. R., & Wegner, D. M. (1987). What do people think they're doing? Action identification and human behavior. *Psychological Review, 94,* 3–15.

Valle, V. A., & Frieze, I. H. (1976). Stability of causal attributions as a mediator in changing expectations for success. *Journal of Personality and Social Psychology, 33,* 579–587.

Valsiner, J. (1987a). *Culture and the development of children's action.* New York: Wiley.

Valsiner, J. (1987b). *Developmental psychology in USSR.* Brighton: Harvester Press.

Valsiner, J. (Ed.). (1988a). *Child development within culturally structured environments: Vol. 1. Parental cognition and adult-child interaction.* Norwood, NJ: ABLEX.

Valsiner, J. (Ed.). (1988b). *Child development within culturally structured environments: Vol. 2. Social co-construction and environmental guidance in development.* Norwood, NJ: ABLEX.

Valsiner, J. (1988c). Ontogeny of co-construction of culture within socially organized environmental settings. In J. Valsiner (Ed.), *Child development within culturally structured environments: Vol. 2. Social co-construction and environmental guidance in development* (pp. 283–297). Norwood, NJ: ABLEX.

Valsiner, J. (1989). *Human development and culture.* Lexington, MA: Heath.

van der Veer, R., & Valsiner, J. (1991). *Understanding Vygotsky: A quest for synthesis.* Oxford, England: Blackwell.

Vico, G. B. (1948). *The new science of Giambattista Vico* (T. G. Bergin & M. H. Fisch, Trans.). Ithaca, New York: Cornell University Press. (Original work published in Italian, 1725)

von Cranach, M. (1982). The psychological study of goal-directed action: Basic issues. In M. von Cranach & R. Harré (Eds.), *The analysis of action: Recent theoretical and empirical advances* (pp. 35–75). Cambridge, England: Cambridge University Press.

Vroom, V. H. (1964). *Work and motivation.* New York: Wiley.

Vygotsky, L. S. (1978). *Mind in society.* Cambridge, MA: Harvard University Press.

Vygotsky, L. S. (1979). The instrumental method in psychology. In J. V. Wertsch (Ed.), *The concept of activity in Soviet psychology* (pp. 134–143). Armonk, NY: Sharpe. (Original work published in Russian 1960)

Vygotsky, L. S. (1986). *Thought and language* (2nd rev. ed.). Cambridge, MA: MIT Press. (Original work published in Russian, 1934)

Waismann, F. (1979). *Wittgenstein and the Vienna Circle.* New York: Barnes & Noble.

Ward, R. A. (1984). The marginality and salience of being old: When is age relevant? *The Gerontologist, 24,* 227–232.

Warren, N. (1980). Universality and plasticity, ontogeny and phylogeny: The resonance between culture and cognitive development. In J. Sants (Ed.), *Developmental psychology and society* (pp. 290–326). London: Macmillan.

Wartofsky, M. W. (1971). From praxis to logos: Genetic epistemology and physics. In T. Mischel (Ed.), *Cognitive development and epistemology* (pp. 129–147). New York: Academic Press.

Watkins, J. W. N. (1957). Historical explanation in the social sciences. *British Journal for the Philosophy of Science, 8,* 104–117.

Watson, J. B. (1930). *Behaviorism.* New York: Norton.

Watson, J. S. (1966). The development of "contingency awareness" in early infancy: Some hypotheses. *Merrill-Palmer Quarterly, 12,* 123–135.

Weiner, B. (1982). An attributionally based theory of motivation and emotion: Focus, range, and issues. In N. T. Feather (Ed.), *Expectations and actions: Expectancy-value models in psychology* (pp. 163–206). Hillsdale, NJ: Erlbaum.

Weisz, J. R. (1983). Can I control it? The pursuit of veridical answers across the life-span. In P. B. Baltes & O. G. Brim (Eds.), *Life-span development and behavior* (Vol. 5, pp. 233–300). New York: Academic Press.

Weisz, J. R., & Cameron, A. M. (1985). Individual differences in the student's sense of control. In C. Ames & R. E. Ames (Eds.), *Research on motivation and education: The classroom milieu* (Vol. 2, pp. 93–140). New York: Academic Press.

Wells, L. E., & Stryker, S. (1988). Stability and change in self over the life course. In P. B. Baltes, D. L. Featherman, & R. M. Lerner (Eds.), *Life-span development and behavior* (Vol. 8, pp. 191–229). Hillsdale, NJ: Erlbaum.

Wentura, D. (1995). *Verfügbarkeit entlastender Kognitionen. Zur Verarbeitung negativer Lebenssituationen.* Weinheim: Psychologie Verlags Union.

Wertsch, J. V. (Ed.). (1981). *The concept of activity in Soviet psychology.* Armonk, NY: Sharpe.

Wertsch, J. V. (1984). The zone of proximal development: Some conceptual issues. In B. Rogoff & J. V. Wertsch (Eds.), *Children's learning in the zone of proximal development: New directions in child development* (Vol. 23, pp. 7–18). San Francisco: Jossey-Bass.

White, R. W. (1959). Motivation reconsidered: The concept of competence. *Psychological Review, 66,* 297–333.

Wicklund, R. A., & Brehm, J. W. (1976). *Perspectives on cognitive dissonance.* Hillsdale, NJ: Erlbaum.

Wicklund, R. A., & Gollwitzer, P. M. (1982). *Symbolic self-completion.* Hillsdale, NJ: Erlbaum.

Wills, T. A. (1991). Similarity and self-esteem in downward comparison. In J. Suls & T. A. Wills (Eds.), *Social comparison: Contemporary theory and research* (pp. 51–78). Hillsdale, NJ: Erlbaum.

Winch, P. (1958). *The idea of a social science.* London: Routledge & Kegan Paul.

Wittgenstein, L. (1969). In G. E. M Anscombe & G. H. von Wright (Eds.), *Über Gewißheit* [On certainty]. Oxford, England: Blackwell.

Wollheim, R. (1984). *The thread of life.* Cambridge, MA: Harvard University Press.

Wong, P. T. P, & Watt, L. M. (1991). What types of reminiscence are associated with successful aging? *Psychology and Aging, 6,* 272–279.

Wood, D., Bruner, J. S., & Ross, G. (1976). The role of tutoring in problem-solving. *Journal of Child Psychology and Psychiatry, 17,* 89–100.

Wortman, C. B., & Brehm, J. W. (1975). Responses to uncontrollable outcomes: An integration of reactance theory and the learned helplessness model. In L. Berkowitz (Ed.), *Advances in experimental social psychology* (Vol. 8, pp. 278–336). New York: Academic Press.

Wozniak, R. H. (1993). Co-constructive metatheory for psychology: Implications for an analysis of families as specific social contexts for development. In R. H. Wozniak & K. W. Fischer (Eds.), *Development in context. Acting and thinking in specific environments* (pp. 77–92). Hillsdale, NJ: Erlbaum.

Wright, R. A., & Brehm, J. W. (1989). Energization and goal attractiveness. In L. A. Pervin (Ed.), *Goal concepts in personality and social psychology* (pp. 169–210). Hillsdale, NJ: Erlbaum.

Zélény, M. (Ed.). (1981). *Autopoiesis: A theory of living organization.* New York: North-Holland.

Zirkel, S., & Cantor, N. (1990). Personal construal of life tasks: Those who struggle for independence. *Journal of Personality and Social Psychology, 58,* 172–195.

Zivin, G. (Ed.). (1979). *The development of self-regulation through private speech.* New York: Wiley.

CHAPTER 15

The Cultural Psychology of Development: One Mind, Many Mentalities

RICHARD A. SHWEDER, JACQUELINE GOODNOW, GIYOO HATANO, ROBERT A. LeVINE, HAZEL MARKUS, and PEGGY MILLER

The coauthors of this chapter are members of the Social Science Research Council Planning Committee on Culture, Health and Human Development. We were able to develop and undertake this cooperative project, involving an intellectual division of labor and writing, as a result of our colloquies at SSRC. The Planning Committee is supported by grants from the Health Program of the John D. and Catherine T. MacArthur Foundation and the

W. T. Grant Foundation. The Center for Advanced Study in the Behavioral Sciences (where Shweder and Markus were Fellows during the 1995–1996 academic year) and the MacArthur Foundation Research Network on Successful Midlife Development (MIDMAC) provided intellectual and material assistance in the preparation of this review.

Cultural psychology is not a new field. It is more accurately depicted as a re-newed field (Jahoda, 1990, 1992). The cultural psychology approach to the study of mind has deep historical antecedents in the work of such 18th- and 19th-century scholars as Herder, Vico, Dilthey, and Wundt. Herder's premise that "to be a member of a group is to think and act in a certain way, in the light of particular goals, values, pictures of the world; and to think and act so is to belong to a group" (Berlin, 1976, p. 195) is a starting point for the contemporary discipline of cultural psychology. Cultural psychology aims to document historical and cross-cultural diversity in the processes and products of the human mind. It examines the processes of schema activation and social learning associated with becoming a member of a group.

So cultural psychology is not new. What is new, and is news, is that the discipline has experienced a major revival in the 1980s and 1990s, owed in significant measure to developmentalists from several fields (e.g., Bruner, 1990; Cole, 1990, 1996; Goodnow, 1990a; Greenfield, in press; Lave, 1990, LeVine, 1989; Levy, 1973, 1984; Markus & Kitayama, 1991b; J. G. Miller, 1984, 1994b; Miller & Hoogstra, 1992; Much, 1992, 1993; Rogoff, 1990; Rozin & Nemeroff, 1990; Shweder, 1990a, 1991, 1993; Shweder & LeVine, 1984; Stigler, Shweder, & Herdt, 1990; Weisner, 1984, 1987; Wertsch, 1985, 1992). The term cultural psychology has also become increasingly popular among European "activity theorists" (Boesch, 1991; Eckensberger, 1990, 1995; and see Brandtstädter, Ch. 14, this Volume), contextual psychologists of the sociohistorical school (Cole, 1995; Rogoff, 1990; Wertsch, 1991; and see Elder, Ch. 16, this Volume), anthropologists interested in the relationship of symbols and meanings to population-based differences in psychological functioning (D'Andrade, 1995; Howard, 1985; LeVine, 1990a, 1990b; Levy, 1984; Lutz & White, 1986; Shore, 1996; Shweder & LeVine, 1984; White & Kirkpatrick, 1985) and among developmental, social and cognitive psychologists in search of a unit of scientific analysis that is larger rather than smaller than the individual person (Bruner, 1986, 1990; Cole, 1988, 1992; Goodnow, Miller, & Kessel, 1995; Kitayama & Markus, 1994; Medin, 1989; Miller & Hoogstra, 1992; Nisbett & Cohen, 1996; Rogoff, 1990; Yang, in press).

Research in cultural psychology is now featured in several journals, most notably *Culture, Mind and Activity,*

Culture, Medicine and Psychiatry, Culture and Psychology, Ethos: Journal of the Society for Psychological Anthropology, and *Child Development.* Impressive collections of theoretical, methodological and empirical papers have appeared (Goodnow et al., 1995; Holland & Quinn, 1987; Jessor, Colby, & Shweder, 1996; Kitayama & Markus, 1994; Rosenberger, 1992; Schwartz, White, & Lutz, 1992; Shweder, 1991; Shweder & LeVine, 1984; Stigler, Shweder, & Herdt, 1990; White & Kirkpatrick, 1985). Important monographs and empirical studies have been published (D'Andrade, 1995; Fiske, 1991; Kakar, 1982; Kripal, 1995; Levy, 1973; Lucy, 1992a; Lutz, 1988; J. G. Miller, 1984; P. J. Miller, 1982; Parish, 1991). A number of generative proposals have been put forward for comparative research on culture and cognition (Cole, 1990; D'Andrade, 1995; Lave, 1990; Lucy, 1992a, 1992b; Shore 1996), culture and emotion (Kitayama & Markus, 1994; Mesquita & Frijda, 1992; Russell, 1991; Shweder, 1991; Wierzbicka, 1992, 1993), culture and morality (Haidt, Koller, & Diaš, 1993; J. G. Miller, 1994a; Shweder, Mahapatra, & Miller, 1990; Shweder, Much, Mahapatra, & Park, 1997) and culture and the self (Doi, 1981; Herdt, 1981, 1990; Kurtz, 1992; Lebra, 1992; Markus & Kitayama, 1991a, 1991b; J. G. Miller, 1994b; Shweder & Sullivan, 1990). The field has been conceptualized, reconceptualized, and reviewed from many perspectives, in a book length history (Jahoda, 1992), in a book-length program for a cultural psychology rooted in sociohistorical theory (Cole, 1996), in *Handbook* chapters (Greenfield, in press; Markus, Kitayama, & Heiman, in press; J. G. Miller, in press), in the *Annual Review of Psychology* (Shweder, 1993), and in the *Minnesota Symposium on Child Psychology* (Masten, forthcoming).

Moreover, this chapter itself signals a new appreciation of the value and relevance of cultural psychology to developmental studies: this is the first time that the *Handbook of Child Psychology* has included a chapter under the name cultural psychology. It should be acknowledged, however, that this chapter continues a conversation about culture and development that began in previous editions of the *Handbook,* beginning with Margaret Mead's contribution to the first edition, published in 1931. The section of this chapter on the interpersonal worlds of childhood provides an update of Robert LeVine's chapter in the third (1970) edition of the *Handbook.* And, the Laboratory of Comparative Human Cognition's (LCHC) chapter on culture and cognitive development in the fourth (1983) edition of the *Handbook* is an important predecessor to this chapter, especially to the section on cognitive development. We carry forward LCHC's emphasis on the semiotic mediation of experience and on a unit of analysis that does not separate the individual from context.

In this chapter, we selectively discuss the cultural psychology of individual development, with special attention to the way in which culture and psyche "make each other up" in the domains of self-organization, thinking, knowing, feeling, wanting, and valuing. The chapter is organized into five sections: an introduction that lays out major conceptual issues followed by four topical areas—the cultural organization of early experience, language and socialization, self development, and cognitive development. We see these topical areas as paradigmatic in the cultural psychology of development, yet we are also keenly aware that several topics of vital interest receive only passing and scattered attention—gender, morality, play, affect, spirituality, and physical development. Without any pretense of representing all relevant research agendas or conceptions of the field we characterize some of the things cultural psychologists have learned about the interpersonal, ideational, and social communicative dimensions of psychological development. In keeping with cultural psychology's commitment to comparative inquiry within and across cultures, we make a special effort to draw from the empirical record in a way that represents the range of cultural variety in psychological functioning.

The wager of cultural psychology is that relatively few components of the human mental equipment are so inherent, hard wired, or fundamental that their developmental pathway is fixed in advance and cannot be transformed or altered through cultural participation. The bet is that much of human mental functioning is an emergent property that results from symbolically mediated experiences with the behavioral practices and historically accumulated ideas and understandings (meanings) of particular cultural communities. This was the bet of Herder and Vico in the 18th century, of Wundt and Dilthey in the 19th century, and of Ruth Benedict, Margaret Mead, and many other psychological anthropologists in the first half of the 20th century. It is a bet that the renewed discipline of cultural psychology, informed by contemporary research from several disciplines, is still prepared to make today.

CULTURAL PSYCHOLOGY: HOW IT DIFFERS FROM OTHER APPROACHES TO CULTURE AND PSYCHOLOGY

Orienting Definitions

At least since the time of Herder and Vico in the 18th century, "cultural psychology" has been a label for the reciprocal investigation of both the psychological foundations of cultural communities and the cultural foundations of mind. It has been a designation for the study of the way culture, community and psyche make each other up. Alternatively stated, cultural psychology is the study of all the things members of different communities *think* (know, want, feel, value) and *do* by virtue of being the kinds of beings who are the beneficiaries, guardians and active perpetuators of a particular culture.

As a first approximation, we shall define *culture* as a "symbolic and behavioral inheritance" received from out of the historical/ancestral past that provides a community with a framework for other-directed and vicarious learning and for collective deliberations about what is true, beautiful, good and normal. Although it is important to distinguish between the symbolic and the behavioral inheritances of a cultural community (understandings and behaviors are not always fully coordinated from either an acquisitional or developmental point of view and actions do sometimes speak louder than words), given the complexity and richness of culture, any genuine cultural community is always the beneficiary of both types of inheritance, *symbolic* and *behavioral*.

In analyzing the concept of "culture," most definitions extant in the literature have tended to be either purely symbolic in emphasis (culture as "the beliefs and doctrines that make it possible for a people to rationalize and make sense of the life they lead") or purely behavioral in emphasis (culture as "patterns of behavior that are learned and passed on from generation to generation"). In our view, the most useful definitions of culture try to honor both inheritances. Such definitions focus on units of analysis that are simultaneously symbolic and behavioral (e.g., Robert Redfield's 1941 definition of culture as "shared understandings made manifest in act and artifact"). Later in this chapter, we discuss in detail a two-sided unit of analysis for cultural psychology called the "custom complex" (Whiting

& Child, 1953), and we try to acknowledge and honor both the symbolic and behavioral inheritances of any cultural community.

What is the symbolic inheritance of a cultural community? The "symbolic inheritance" of a cultural community consists of its received ideas and understandings, both implicit and explicit, about persons, society, nature and divinity. To illustrate, ideas and understandings that are part of the symbolic inheritance of many enlightened secular folk in the European American cultural region include the understanding that infants are born innocent of any prior sins; the idea that individual wants and preferences matter and should be openly expressed; the belief that the main justification for rules, regulations, and other forms of authority is to promote social justice and enable individuals to pursue their self-interest free of harm and to have the things they want; the conviction that nature is devoid of intentionality and has no will of its own; the doctrine that God and divinity are archaic notions that should be displaced in the contemporary era; and the related idea that the era in which we live should be classified and heralded as the "age of reason."

What is the behavioral inheritance of a cultural community? The "behavioral inheritance" of a cultural community consists of its routine or institutionalized family life and social practices. To illustrate, a few of the routine or institutionalized family life practices that are popular among many rural folk in the South Asian Hindu cultural region include the practice of joint family living, co-sleeping arrangements for parents and children, separate eating arrangements for husband and wife (no family meal), a sexual division of household tasks, prohibitions on premarital dating and sexuality, physical punishment for unruly behavior, and arranged marriage.

Of special import for the cultural psychology of development is that human beings are the kinds of beings who benefit from and carry forward a cultural tradition. They try to promote, promulgate, and share their understandings and practices with their children, their relatives, and their community at large. They are active agents in the perpetuation of their symbolic inheritance, largely because (among other motives) the ideas and understandings that they inherit from the past seem to them to be right-minded, true, or at least worthy of respect.

They are also active agents in the perpetuation of their *behavioral* inheritance. They try to uphold, enforce, and require of each other some degree of compliance with the practices of their community, largely because (among other motives) those practices seem to them to be moral, healthy, natural, rational, or at least "normal."

Thus from the viewpoint of cultural psychology, the most satisfactory definition of culture presupposes the existence of an active mental agent, who not only is the recipient and guardian of a cultural tradition but also participates in some specific way of life. Thus our definition of culture will emphasize both symbols and behavior. Such an approach also means that a major prerequisite for conducting research in cultural psychology is an imaginative capacity to suspend one's disbelief and a willingness to set aside (at least temporarily) one's own negative moral and emotional reactions (e.g., of indignation or disgust) to other people's understandings and practices. To do cultural psychology one must be willing and able to enter into other peoples' conceptions of what is right-minded, normal, beautiful, and true (Shweder, 1996).

Cultural psychology is the study of the mental life of individuals in relation to the symbolic and behavioral inheritances of particular cultural communities. It is the study of the way culture, community, and psyche are mutually instantiating. A cultural tradition dies (it exists only in a canonical text or in an ethnographic book on a library shelf) if there is no community that lives its doctrines, makes manifest its shared understandings, or inhabits its way of life. Similarly, some designated category of persons (e.g., Latinos, non-Hispanic Whites; residents of Pacific Islands; American citizens) is not in and of itself a *cultural* community unless its members actively inhabit, think about, and hold each other accountable to some symbolic and behavioral inheritance from out of some historical/ancestral past that they identify with and claim as their own. Cultural psychology is thus the study of the way culture, community, and psyche become coordinated and make each other possible.

Why Cultural Psychology Is Not Cross-Cultural Psychology

Many proponents of cultural psychology distinguish cultural psychology from "cross-cultural psychology." This is what a few of those authors have to say about the aims of a renewed cultural psychology, and the ways in which it differs from cross-cultural psychology.

Shweder and Sullivan (1993; also Shweder, 1990a) identify the aim of cultural psychology with the study of ethnic and cultural sources of psychological diversity in self-organization, cognitive processing, emotional functioning and moral evaluation. They describe cultural psychology as a "project designed to reassess the uniformitarian principle of psychic unity [which they associate with cross-cultural psychology] and aimed at the development of a credible theory of psychological pluralism." They argue that performance differences and response differentials between populations arise from differences in the normal meaning of stimulus situations and materials across populations (the problem of "partial translation" or "limited commensurability"). They suggest that a special feature of cultural psychology is its recognition that "through the methodical investigation of specific sources of incommensurability in particular stimulus situations (so-called thick description) a culture's distinctive psychology [the way people think and act in the light of particular goals, values and pictures of the world] may be revealed."

A similar point is made by Greenfield (in press) who notes, "It is the human capacity to create shared meaning that produces the distinctive methodological contribution of cultural psychology." She goes on to argue that it is a mistake of modern psychology in general and modern cross-cultural psychology in particular to treat perspective (the shared meanings of a group is a type of perspective) as a form of bias that should be eliminated from research procedures. She contrasts the methodology of cultural psychology with that of modern cross-cultural psychology as follows:

> The methodological ideal of the paradigmatic cross-cultural psychologist is to carry a procedure established in one culture, with known psychometric properties, to one or more other cultures, in order to make a cross-cultural comparison (Berry, Poortinga, Segall, & Dasen, 1992). In contrast, the methodological ideal of the paradigmatic cultural psychologist is to derive procedures for each culture from the lifeways and modes of communication of that culture.

This ideal explains why interpretive methods, especially ethnographic methods, have been so important to many cultural psychologists. Ethnographic approaches were devised originally by cultural anthropologists as a means of understanding other cultures on their own terms—not as projections of the researcher's own ethnocentric assumptions (Malinowski, 1922). The goal is to understand what people say and do from the perspective of insiders to the culture, to render them intelligible within their own collectively shared interpretive frameworks. From this standpoint, comparisons within and across cultures make sense only when they are grounded in descriptions of the local meanings of the people being studied. At the same time, these approaches carry with them the reflexive recognition that researchers too are members of particular communities and cultures and that they may come to see their own local meanings in a new light by way of studying people who construe the world differently. (For further discussion of interpretive and ethnographic methods as applied to the study of children, see Corsaro & Miller, 1992; Erickson, 1986; Gee, Michaels, & O'Connor, 1992; Gilmore & Glatthorn, 1982; Jessor, Colby, & Shweder, 1996.)

To return to Greenfield, one powerful and ironic implication of her analysis would seem to be that the existence of alternative cultural realities is incompatible with the methodological assumptions of cross-cultural psychology. In other words, if your research procedures and instruments travel readily and well (e.g, they are easy to administer and display the same psychometric properties from one test population to another) then you probably have not traveled far enough into a truly different cultural world.

This may explain why fieldwork, language learning, naturalistic observation, and detailed ethnography are central to the study of cultural psychology (yet have played a minimal role in cross-cultural psychology). That may explain why much of the evidence in cross-cultural psychology (yet relatively little of the evidence in cultural psychology) is derived from laboratory, inventory, and test procedures administered to university students in other lands.

The Western institution of the university carries with it many features of an elite cosmopolitan culture wherever it has diffused around the world. University students in Tokyo, Nairobi, Delhi, and New York may be far more like one another (and like the Western researcher) than they are like members of their respective societies whose life ways are embedded in indigenous understandings, institutions and practices. Even if you have traveled 10,000 miles to get there, a university setting in another land may be closer than you think.

Much (1995) drives home this point with the following observation:

It is especially important to be clear about one distinction. Cultural psychology is not the same as "cross-cultural psychology," which is a branch of experimental social, cognitive and personality psychology. The chief distinction is that most of what has been known as "cross-cultural psychology" has presupposed the categories and models that have been available to participate in experiments or even to fill out questionnaires. . . . The argument often assumed to justify the tactic of studying mostly student behavior is based upon a sweeping and gratuitous universalist assumption—since we are all human, we are all fundamentally alike in significant psychological functions and cultural (or social) contexts of diversity do not affect the important "deep" or "hard wired" structures of the mind. There are several problems with this position. One is that there have been few if any satisfactory identifications of deep, hard wired and *invariant* mental structures which operate independently of the context or content of their functioning; the "method variance" problem in experimental psychology is related to this fact. Another problem is that even though there may be certain biologically based psychological foundations . . . this does not necessarily mean (1) that they are invariant across individuals or populations or (2) that culture does not affect their development as psychological structures and functions.

Whereas Greenfield and Much draw methodological contrasts between cultural versus cross-cultural psychology, J. G. Miller (in press) envisions the difference between cultural psychology and cross-cultural psychology in theoretical terms (although a similar theoretical point can be found in Greenfield and Much as well). She suggests, "The dominant stance within cultural psychology is to view culture and psychology as mutually constitutive phenomena which cannot be reduced to each other" and adds that such a stance "contrasts with the tendency in cross-cultural psychology for culture to be conceptualized as an independent variable that impacts on the dependent variable of individual psychology."

Markus, Kitayama, and Heiman (in press) carry forward this point. With an intent to simultaneously study the cultural origins of mind and the mental side of culture, they argue that "culture and psychology, regardless of the level at which they are analyzed, are interdependent and mutually active." Markus et al. suggest:

The communities, societies, and cultural contexts within which people participate provide the interpretive frameworks—including the images, concepts, and narratives, as well as the means, practices and patterns of behavior—by which people make sense (i.e., lend meaning, coherence and structure to their ongoing experience) and organize their actions. Although experienced as such, those organizing frameworks (also called cultural schemas, models, designs for living, modes of being) are not fully private and personal; they are shared.

Markus et al. go on to say:

Importantly, the contention here is that these group-based meanings and practices are not separate from observed behavior. They are not applied as interpretive frameworks after "behavior" has occurred. Instead they are fully active in the constitution of this behavior; they are the means by which people behave and experience, and thus should be taken into account in an analysis of this behavior. The claim is that with respect to the psychological, the individual level often cannot be separated from the cultural level. Many psychological processes are completely interdependent with the meanings and practices of their relevant sociocultural contexts and this will result in systematic diversity in psychological functioning. It follows from this perspective that there may be multiple, diverse psychologies rather than a single psychology.

Multiple, Diverse Psychologies

Perhaps the central claim of cultural psychology (in contrast to other approaches to the study of consciousness and mental life) is that "there may be multiple, diverse psychologies rather than a single psychology," and perhaps the central problematic of the field is to make sense of that provocative claim. Does such a claim entail the denial of universals? If not, what universals of mind are entailed by cultural psychology? How are those universals to be reconciled with the existence of diverse psychologies across human populations without trivializing that diversity or treating it as mere content?

At the moment, there is no single answer to those questions that all cultural psychologists would endorse. One type of answer, with a pedigree stretching back to Vico (Berlin, 1976), suggests that

. . . the nature of [human beings] is not, as has long been supposed, static and unalterable or even unaltered; that it does not so much as contain even a central kernel or essence, which remains identical through change; that the effort of [human beings] to understand the world in which they find themselves and to adapt it to their needs, physical and spiritual, continuously transforms their worlds and themselves. (p. xvi)

A second type of answer to those questions, to be developed in this chapter, starts from the premise that any human nature that we are in a position to understand and render intelligible must have "a central kernel or essence," but that it is rarely a strong constraint. According to this answer, the central kernel or essence of human nature consists of a heterogeneous collection of mutually contradictory structures and inclinations which are differentially and selectively activated, brought "on-line," and substantialized in the course of the historical experience of different cultural communities. "One mind, many mentalities: universalism without the uniformity" is the rallying cry for that type of interpretation of the claim that "there may be multiple, diverse psychologies rather than a single psychology."

The motto "One mind, many mentalities: universalism without the uniformity" advertises a discipline founded on the principle that the abstract potentialities and specific heterogeneous inclinations of the human mind are universal but only gain character, substance, definition, and motivational force (i.e., assume the shape of a functioning mentality) when, and as, they are translated and transformed into, and through, the concrete actualities of some particular practice, activity setting or way of life (Cole, 1990; D'Andrade, 1995; Goodnow et al., 1995; Greenfield, in press; Markus et al., in press; Lave, 1990; Much, 1992; Nisbett & Cohen, 1995; Rogoff, 1990; Shweder, 1991; Shweder & LeVine, 1984). The slogan connects current researchers in cultural psychology with the intellectual ancestors of the field (Vico, Herder, and others) (Berlin, 1976) who, Kant and Hegel-like, believed "Form without content is empty, content without form meaningless."

For at least 200 years, a distinctive tenet of cultural psychology has been the claim that the formal universals of mind and the content-rich particulars of any sustainable mentality or way of life are interdependent, interactive and give each other life. Scholars such as Herder, Vico, and Wundt scoured the historical record for successful (cohesive, shared, stable) fusions of form and content, in which the human imagination has, of necessity, gone beyond the relatively meaning barren constraints of logic and mere perception to construct a picture of the underlying nature

of the world and it values, resulting in a "mentality" (the Homeric mentality, the Hindu mentality) supportive of a "way of life."

They took as their data the great symbolic formations produced by human beings: myths, folk tales, language patterns, naming systems, ethical, social and religious philosophies, and ethnoscientific doctrines. They took as their data the great behavioral formations produced by human beings, including customary practices of various kinds: subsistence activities, games, rituals, food taboos, and marriage rules. They interpreted those symbolic and behavioral formations as alternative substantializations or instantiations of the disparate abstract potentialities of the universal mind, which they believed it was the business of a discipline such as cultural psychology to characterize and to explain.

The Meaning of "Meaning" and a Context for "Context" in Cultural Psychology

Within contemporary cultural psychology, the translation and transformation of one mind into many mentalities is typically conceptualized as a process by which contexts and meanings become essential and active components inside as well as outside the psychological system of individuals. Within cultural psychology, this process is sometimes described as the process by which culture and psyche "make each other up."

This insistence in cultural psychology that contexts and meanings are to be theoretically represented as part and parcel of the psychological system and not simply as influences, factors, or conditions external to the psychological system distinguishes cultural psychology from other forms of psychology which also think of themselves as contextual (or situated). The aim in cultural psychology is *not* first to separate the psychological system from its nonpsychological context and then to invoke some type of external setting effect or outside situational influence on psychological functioning. The aim and the challenge are rather to recast or soften the contrast between person and context (inside vs. outside, subjective perspective vs. external reality) so that the very idea of a context effect will take on new meaning because our theoretical language for psychological description will be contextual from the start. Later in this chapter, we address in some detail this issue of dichotomies that need to be softened or recast (see also Overton, Ch. 3, this Volume).

The distinction between cultural psychology and other contextual approaches in psychology is subtle, important, and easy to overlook because all approaches to psychology that emphasize "context" share much in common, especially their opposition to the idea that the science of psychology is primarily the study of fixed, universal, abstract forms. Thus cultural psychology shares with all forms of contextual psychology the assumption that the mind of human beings (knowing, wanting, feeling, valuing, etc.) can only be realized through some situated or local process of "minding," which is always bounded, conditional or relative to something: shared meanings, goals, stimulus domain, available resources, local artifacts, cognitive assistants, and so on. Beyond that general point of similarity, however, cultural psychology should be understood as a rather special type of contextual approach.

In the conception developed in this chapter, the relevant contexts for the realization of mind are the customs, traditions, practices, and shared meanings and perspectives of some self-monitoring and self-perpetuating group. The primary emphasis is on contexts thought to be relevant for the realization of mind in the sense that such contexts are the means for transforming a universal mind into a distinctively functioning mentality, a distinctive way that "people think and act in the light of particular goals, values and pictures of the world" (Berlin, 1976). In this approach, cultural psychology is not coextensive with contextual psychology (more on this in a moment). More importantly, the contrast between inside and outside, person and context, subjective perspective and external reality is reconceptualized in cultural psychology as a process by which culture and psyche are constantly and continuously making each other up.

THE UNIT OF ANALYSIS PROBLEM

Just as the general field of psychology seems unsure whether its proper subject matter should be the study of behavior or the study of consciousness or the study of the mental life (which is a broader subject than the study of consciousness because it includes states of mind that are not in awareness), so too cultural psychologists do not always seem to agree on their proper unit of analysis. Practitioners of cultural psychology study mentalities, folk models, practices, activity settings, situated cognitions, and ways of life. It is not clear whether these units of analysis mentioned in the literature are different ways of speaking about the same intellectual object or whether it is possible to combine them into a single unit of analysis.

For the sake of clarity in this review, however, we shall adopt a proposal for a common unit of analysis for cultural psychology put forward more than a generation ago (Whiting & Child, 1953) in an exemplary collaboration between an anthropologist and a psychologist. Whiting and Child suggest combining mentalities and practices (the symbolic and behavioral inheritances of a cultural community) into a single unit of analysis called the custom complex, which "consists of a customary practice and of the beliefs, values, sanctions, rules, motives and satisfactions associated with it." If we adopt this proposal, cultural psychology can be defined as "the study of the custom complex."

Although Whiting and Child introduced the idea of a "custom complex" in 1953, its theoretical implications were not widely or fully appreciated at the time. Curiously, the idea was not taken up or carried forward by psychological anthropologists working in the classical tradition of the 1950s. It was not until the 1980s and 1990s with the rebirth of a two-handed cultural psychology focused on the way culture and psyche make each other up, and with the return of an interest in "activity settings" (Cole, 1992, 1995; Weisner, 1984, 1996) and a "practice approach" to developmental studies (Goodnow et al., 1995), that Whiting and Child's conception gained currency and appeal.

According to Whiting and Child (1953, p. 27) a custom complex "consists of a customary practice and of beliefs, values, sanctions, rules, motives and satisfactions associated with it." The idea bears some resemblance to the social psychologist's idea of a personal "life space" (Lewin, 1943), to the sociologist's idea of a societal "habitus" (Bourdieu, 1972, 1990), and to the historian's idea of an epochal "mentality."

Using the custom complex as a unit of analysis makes it possible to conceptualize cultural psychology as the study of the way culture and psyche are socially produced and reproduced, resulting in an intimate association between a mentality and a practice and a partial fusion of person/context, inside/outside, subjective perspective/external reality.

Examples of a custom complex are so commonplace they are easy to overlook. They include the mentalities associated with nursing on demand, co-sleeping in a family bed, enforcing strict "Christian discipline," performing the ritual of "what did you do in school today," or practicing ways to bolster self-esteem.

An Example of a Custom Complex: The Case of Who Sleeps by Whom in the Family

The mentality (what people know, think, feel, want, value and, hence, choose or decide to do) intimately associated with the practice of "who sleeps by whom" in the family provides a paradigmatic example of a custom complex. Who sleeps by whom in a family is a customary practice invested with socially acquired meanings and with implications for one's standing (as moral, as rational, as competent) within some consensus-sensitive and norm-enforcing cultural community.

Research on family life customs in different communities within the United States (Abbott, 1992; Litt, 1981; Lozoff, Wolf, & Davis, 1984; Weisner, Bausano, & Kornfein, 1983) and around the world (Caudill & Plath, 1966; LeVine, 1990a; McKenna et al., 1993; Morelli, Rogoff, Oppenheimer, & Goldsmith, 1992; Shweder, Balle-Jensen, & Goldstein, 1995; Whiting, 1964, 1981) confirms the existence on a worldwide scale of several divergent custom complexes in this domain, each consisting of a network of interwoven and mutually supportive practices, beliefs, values, sanctions, rules, motives and satisfactions. Indeed, on a worldwide scale, the European American who-sleeps-by-whom custom complex is not the one that communities most typically produce, reproduce and enforce with the various formal and informal powers (e.g., legal interventions, gossip destroying your reputation) at their disposal.

The middle-class European American custom complex includes the ritualized isolation of children during the night, the institution of "bedtime," and the protection of the privacy of the "sacred couple" upheld by a cultural norm mandating the exclusive co-sleeping of the husband and wife. This European American custom complex is typically associated with something like the following "propositional attitudes," where knowing, thinking, feeling, wanting and valuing define the set of potential "attitudes," and that which is known, thought about, felt, wanted, or valued is statable in propositional form: I value autonomy and independence; I want my children to become autonomous and independent adults; I know that I can promote autonomy and independence in infants and young children by having them sleep alone; I value sexual intimacy with my spouse; I know that a sleeping space is the most suitable site for sexual intimacy with my spouse; I know that it will not be possible to have sexual intimacy with my spouse if the privacy of the spousal sleeping space

is violated; I know that children have erotic impulses and a sexual fantasy life that should not be aroused or titillated by adults for the sake of the mental health of the child; I feel anxious about touching and having prolonged skin-to-skin contact with a young child; therefore, infants and young children should be trained, encouraged, and if necessary, forced, to sleep alone (Brazelton, 1990).

This custom complex is sanctioned, glorified, rationalized, and enforced in innumerable ways in the European American culture area, although nearly every one of those propositional attitudes is thought to be wrong, bizarre, or beside the point by adults and children in many parts of Asia, Africa, and Central America, where children routinely and habitually co-sleep with one or more of their parents and/or siblings and prefer to do so even when more than ample sleeping space is available for separate sleeping arrangements (Abbott, 1992; Caudill & Plath, 1966; Shweder et al., 1995).

In the early 1960s, Caudill and Plath (1966) discovered that urban Japanese parents felt morally obliged to provide their children with a parental sleeping partner, that husbands and wives were willing to separate from each other to do so, and that approximately 50% of 11- to 15-year-old urban Japanese boys and girls slept in the same room as their mother or father or both. Or, to cite another example, Shweder, Balle-Jensen, and Goldstein (1995) discovered from a record of single-night sleeping arrangements in 160 high-caste households in Orissa, India, that only 12% of the cases matched the European American custom complex in which husband and wife sleep together and separate from their children.

The cluster of propositional attitudes that lend authority to co-sleeping still need to be worked out for the different culture regions of the world (although see Morelli et al., 1992). The Japanese custom complex includes the propositional attitudes "I value and want to promote interdependency and feelings of closeness and solidarity among members of the family" and "I know that co-sleeping will help children overcome feelings of distance and separation from members of the family who are older or of a different sex." The Oriya Hindu custom complex includes the propositional attitudes "I highly value children as members of the family" and "I know that children are fragile, vulnerable, and needy and therefore should not be left alone and unprotected during the night." "Chastity anxiety" and the chaperoning of adolescent females also plays a part in the Oriya custom complex (Shweder et al., 1995).

Examples of the way local "experts" (pediatricians, advice columnists, or social workers) rationalize, uphold and lend authority to the European American custom complex can be found in the responses of "Dear Abby" and "Ann Landers" to the many letters they receive about the perceived problem of parent-child co-sleeping. The following, published May 26, 1994, in the *Chicago Tribune,* is a typical exchange between concerned adults in the European American cultural zone:

Dear Abby: My niece—I'll call her Carol—is a single mother with a 4-year-old son. (I'll call him Johnny.) Carol just turned 40. Since the day Johnny was born, he has slept with his mother in a single bed. They go to bed between 8 and 10 o'clock every night, and always have snacks and drinks in bed. They watch TV and cuddle until Johnny falls asleep in his mother's arms. Abby, this child has never fallen asleep alone. Carol lives with her parents, and there is no shortage of beds in their home. Recently, Carol and Johnny visited me in my country home, and I gave them the bedroom with twin beds. The following morning, I discovered that Carol had pushed the beds together so she and Johnny wouldn't be separated. I think Carol's emotional needs are taking precedence over what is best for her son. He has no father, and his grandparents have no say in his upbringing. I would appreciate your assessment of this situation. No city, please, and sign me, Concerned Aunt.

Dear Concerned: You have good reason to be concerned, You hit the nail on the head—Johnny doesn't need to sleep with his mother nearly as much as she needs to sleep with him. You would be doing Carol an enormous favor if you advised her to get counseling in the rearing of her son. With all her good intentions, she is '(s)mothering' her son. Johnny's pediatrician will be able to recommend the best counselor for Carol and Johnny. It is desperately needed.

In fact, surprisingly little is known about the long-term effects of separation versus co-sleeping in any part of the world, which is a major lacunas in the history of research in cultural psychology.

More on the Custom Complex: The Intimate Association between a Mentality and a Practice Supported by a Cultural Community

The concept of a custom complex presupposes an intimate association between a mentality and a practice that is supported, enforced, defended, and rationalized by members of some cultural community. When such an association is in place it will be the case that other members of one's cultural community will judge the mentality associated with the practice to be normal and reasonable, while any actual participant in the practice will experience the mentality associated with the practice to be "under the skin," "close to the heart," and "self-relevant"; the mentality will have become habitual, automatic, and can be activated without deliberation or conscious calculation. This intimate (some might say "experience-near") connection or partial fusion of a "mentality" and a "practice" does not, however, prohibit us from drawing an analytic distinction between the mentality and the practice that instantiates it. It does not keep us from characterizing the custom complex as two things intimately connected or partially fused.

The study of a custom complex calls for the analysis of a two-sided thing—the intimate connection between a mentality (the symbolic inheritance of a cultural community) and one or more specific practices (the behavioral inheritance of a cultural community). This analysis begins with the systematic identification, through observation and interviews, of the routine or habitual family life and social practices engaged in by members of some self-monitoring and self-regulating group. Some of these practices may surprise, disgust, or enrage an outside observer, although to the jaded eyes of the group members their own practices are likely to seem ordinary, decent and reasonable or at least "normal."

Each of the following practices, for example, is a commonplace way of being, at least for the members of the particular cultural communities that uphold them. In one cultural world, a 2-year-old child gets in bed with his mother, unbuttons her mother's blouse, suckles at her breast, and sleeps by her side throughout the night; whereas in another cultural world, at night each child in the family sleeps in a private sleeping space separated from the sleeping space of all adults. In one cultural world, a woman brings food home from the market and cooks it, and then she and her husband consume the food together; in another cultural world, a man brings food home from the market, his wife cooks it, and then he consumes the food alone and his wife eats separately and later. In one cultural world, children are fostered out by their parents to more prosperous families in their society, who subject these children to ordeals of hardship, physical punishment, and demanding tests of loyalty, and require them to work as family servants until they endure the ordeals and pass the tests (Bledsoe, 1990). Then the children are adopted and supported by those families and patronized and provided for throughout life. In another cultural world, however, parents get upset (even incensed) if another adult touches their child, reprimands or scolds their child, makes strenuous demands of their child, or causes their child to suffer "abuse" in any way.

As noted earlier in the discussion of "who sleeps by whom" in the family, the analysis of a custom complex ends when one is able to spell out as comprehensively as possible the things that the members of some group (tacitly or explicitly, consciously or unconsciously) know, think, feel, want, and value that explain and make intelligible the things that they do. Thus the analysis begins with the identification of practices and it ends with the specification of a distinctive mentality.

This interest in the *distinctive* mentality associated with the practices of a cultural community distinguishes cultural psychology from other approaches to the study of practice domains, in which it is assumed that human activities come in natural domains or universal "kinds" (e.g., religion, economics, family life, schooling, politics) and that members of different cultural communities think and behave more or less alike within the strong constraints of each species of activity, regardless of community. The idea of a custom complex invites a very different approach, in which it is assumed that members of various cultural communities have *distinctive* mentalities associated with each of their practice domains (e.g., a Taiwanese mentality of family life versus a New England mentality of family life), leading members of those cultural communities to engage in divergent patterns of behavior in ostensibly similar domains.

The idea of a custom complex also invites cultural psychologists to address the question whether a particular cultural community has a *characteristic* mentality (for example, the Hindu mentality, the Protestant mentality) which leaves its generalized mark on many domains within that community, thereby making, for example, Protestant economics, Protestant religion and Protestant family life more like each other than like a parallel "natural domain" in another cultural community.

We emphasize, however, that cultural psychology does not presume the existence of global consistency or thematic integration across all practice domains within a culture. Even Ruth Benedict (1934) was quite aware that many cultures are not patterned after some simple mold (Dionysian, Apollonian). She knew, as we know, that the degree to which a small set of core beliefs, goals, or motives can

account for the meaning and behavior of a people across the many domains of their life (family, work, politics) is entirely an open empirical issue.

There is no way to know in advance of years of research in some particular cultural community whether or not their many practice domains all draw on the same mentality. Nevertheless, even if a particular cultural community is not thematically integrated (one small set of core meanings revealed in many practice domains), the custom complex is still a natural theoretical frame of analysis for cultural psychology. The idea defines a parameter space for conceptualizing and modeling the ways that culture and psyche make each other up, resulting, on a worldwide scale, in multiple instances of a relatively stable or equilibrated condition in which a mentality and a practice are mutually sustaining and reciprocally confirmatory. Not all custom complexes are integrated in the same way or cohere to the same degree. Nevertheless, the idea makes it possible for us to ask about the ways and degrees to which a relatively stable equilibrium (the intimate association of a local mentality and a cultural practice) has actually been achieved.

The Classification of Practices

To conduct a relatively complete and systematic empirical study of a community's cultural psychology, it is necessary to identify the members' practices and categorize them into domains. Practices can be categorized in many ways, because any scheme of classification will depend largely on the investigator's theory of human needs (physical, social, psychological, and spiritual) and the research issues at hand.

One of the several ways practices can be classified into domains is from an ontogenetic perspective, with special reference to the development of mastery or expertise in some domain of psychological functioning (knowing, thinking, feeling, wanting or valuing). Thus, practices might be identified and classified by reference to the particular substantive type of competence they promote (e.g., practices promoting social sensitivity, practices promoting moral development, practices promoting cognitive development).

Or a developmentalist might classify practices not so much according to the substantive competence (emotional, moral, cognitive) acquired but rather according to processes of acquisition. Werker (1989; also Gottlieb, 1991), has generated a short list of hypothetical ways that "experience" (read exposure to, or active participation in a cultural practice) can affect the development of any mental skill or ability. She imagines five kinds of processes:

1. Maturation (the practice made no difference; the ability would have developed without it)

2. Facilitation (because of the practice, the ability was attained more quickly than otherwise would have been the case)

3. Induction (without the practice, there would have been no ability at all in this domain)

4. Attunement (because of the practice, a higher level of ability was attained than otherwise would have been the case)

5. Maintenance/loss (the ability was preexisting but would have been lost or deactivated if it had not been kept online through participation in the practice).

At this early stage in the evolution of a cultural psychology of individual development, we can only look forward with excitement to the time when we will have in hand the research designs, methodologies, and systematically collected bodies of evidence that will allow us to classify practices in this way. We look forward to the time when we will be able to distinguish between each of those five interpretations of the effects of participation in a cultural practice on the growth of a mental state or ability.

Cultural psychology is, however, in no way committed to a "blank slate" learning theory and is not equivalent to an induction theory of mental development. Quite the contrary, much of the current research in cultural psychology is quite compatible with (and may even presuppose) either an attunement or a maintenance/loss account of the differential emergence, activation or selective maintenance of particular mental states. Our conception of cultural learning will be discussed later, especially in relationship to innate ideas (see pages 920–922).

In this chapter, we can seldom choose between different interpretations (maturation, attunement, maintenance/loss, etc.) of how participation in a cultural practice affects the activation of a mental state or the emergence of a mental skill. What we can do, however, as an intermediary step in building a full-blown cultural psychology of individual development, is point to some of the research and scholarship in cultural psychology that tries to describe and explain the differential ontogenetic emergence, activation and selective maintenance of what the "I's" in different groups know, think, feel, want, value, and (hence) choose to do, including research on what the "I's" in different groups know, think, feel, want, and value about the "self." Later in this chapter, we examine one important line of cultural psychological research on the development of an "interdependent" (sociocentric, collective) versus "independent" (autonomous, individualistic) self.

There are many other ways to classify practices into domains. From the point of view of personal and social identity, practices might be identified and classified by the existential problems they address. In any society there are many existential questions which must be answered, for the sake of both individual mental health and social coordination. "Self practices" answer the question: "What's me and mine and what's not me and mine?" "Gender practices" answer the question: "What's male and what's female?" "Disciplinary practices" provide an answer to the question "How are norms and rules to be enforced?" "Distributional practices" likewise are a response to the existential question, "How should burdens and benefits be distributed?" (Shweder, 1982). A closely related approach has been proposed by Fiske (1991, 1992), who argues that social life is comprised of four social relationships (communal sharing, authority ranking, equality matching, and market pricing). Fiske's scheme could readily be adapted and used in the classification of practices (practices promoting a sense of commonality, practices promoting a sense of hierarchy, etc.). Some researchers may prefer to identify and classify practices by the institutions in which they are embedded (e.g., family life practices, school life practices). Other researchers with different intellectual aims and inclinations may prefer to classify practices according to the biological needs or physical survival functions they serve (e.g., eating practices, health practices).

Still others may want to proceed emically (Pike, 1967) and let the classification of practice domains go hand in hand with the specification of the mentality of a cultural community, in the anticipation of some counterintuitive and astonishing results. In some cultural communities, for example, among devout Brahmans in India, there is a highly elaborated practice domain that might be labeled "oblations, sacrifices and sacramental offerings." It encompasses the daily preparation and consumption of food and includes in the same general practice domain other activities (e.g., prayer and animal sacrifice) that would never "naturally" go together in the mentality of a Western researcher. Among Brahmanical Hindus in India "food" is not a personal preference system. Given the local culturally elaborated idea that eating is a sacramental offering to a divinity (the "self") residing in a temple (the human body), what you eat, how it has been prepared, and by whom, and the conditions under which you eat it, is a mark of your moral standing in the world.

The Analysis of Mentalities

Mentalities, the other side of the custom complex, can be investigated in the following ways: (a) by analyzing the idea of a mentality into its component parts: knowing, thinking, feeling, wanting, and valuing; (b) by modeling what some ideal or prototypical "I" (subject, agent, individual, self) who might be engaged in this or that practice knows, thinks, feels, wants, and values; (c) by empirically determining the degree of specificity or generality of those components of a mentality for actual agents across practice domains within a cultural community (and perhaps across cultural communities for a particular practice domain); and (d) by pointing to broad patterns of generality for mentalities when and where they exist.

For example, there is good empirical reason to believe that the mentality dubbed "interdependency," "sociocentrism," or "collectivism" supports and maintains a whole array of practices both within and across domains for some populations in Japan, whereas the mentality dubbed "independence," "autonomy," or "individualism" supports and maintains a disparate array of practices both within and across domains for some groups in the United States (Markus & Kitayama, 1991a, 1991b; Triandis, 1989, 1990).

Thus, although cultural psychology is in one major sense the study of the way culture and psyche make each other up, in another closely related sense, it is the study of the origin, structure, function, operation, and social reproduction of that intimate association between a mentality and a practice known as the custom complex.

THE TWO SIDES OF CULTURAL PSYCHOLOGY

Cultural psychology is the study of the way culture and psyche make each other up, resulting in the formation of the custom complex, which is a unit of analysis for characterizing the way "multiple, diverse psychologies" emerge out of the abstract potentialities of a universal mind. Psychological pluralism emerges, at least in part, because peoples think and act in the light of particular goals, values, and pictures of the world, and these factors are rarely the same across cultural communities.

The cultural side of cultural psychology is the study of the mentality-laden practices (including the symbolic forms, communicative exchanges, rituals, mores, folkways, and institutions) developed, promoted, promulgated, enacted, and enforced (and hence judged to be customary, normal, legal, moral, or reasonable) by the "I's" (the subjects, agents, individuals, or selves) of particular groups.

The psychological side of cultural psychology is the study of practice-related mental states, the things that the "I's" (subjects, agents, individuals, selves) of particular groups know, think, feel, want, value, and (hence) choose or decide to do to carry forward the normal practices of their society.

Based on those two sides of cultural psychology, which are fused in the idea of a custom complex, the aim of the discipline is to investigate precisely those cases where the following three conditions hold:

1. A "practice" displays significant variation across groups and differential patterning of within group variations (e.g., there is a far greater probability of children and adults co-sleeping in a family bed in South Asia and Africa than in Europe and the United States and the correlation between social status and co-sleeping is not the same within South Asia and within the United States).

2. The components of a mentality (knowing, thinking, feeling, wanting, and valuing) such as feelings of closeness, pleasure, and serenity versus feelings of anxiety associated with skin-to-skin contact between parent and child, display significant variation across groups and differential patterning of within group variation (e.g., European American males, in comparison to South Asian males, are more likely to feel anxiety associated with skin-to-skin contact between parent and child and feelings of closeness, pleasure and serenity produced by skin-to-skin contact between parent and child may be correlated with gender in the United States but not in South Asia).

3. The distribution of the practice appears to be related to the distribution of the mentality, and vice versa.

Thus, through the idea of a custom complex, cultural psychology joins the study of individual mental states to the study of cultural practices. On the one hand, investigators explore those features of what individuals know, think, feel, want, value, and (hence) choose or decide to do that are primed by, traceable to, or derivable from, participation in the symbolic forms, communicative exchanges, rituals, mores, folkways, and institutions of some consensus-sensitive or norm-enforcing group.

On the other hand, investigators look at the way in which the mentality-laden practices (the custom complexes) of particular groups gain their credibility, reasonableness and motivational force from the very psychological states that they have helped activate and to which they have given life. Cultural psychology is therefore the study of reciprocal connections between culture and psyche and of the various patterns or forms of coherency (custom complexes) that have arisen out of their interactions.

Cultural Psychology's Theory of Mind

On a worldwide scale there is well-documented diversity in the developmentally relevant cultural practices that promote, sustain, and confirm what the "I's" of particular groups know, think, feel, want, value, and (hence) choose or decide to do. Consequently, cultural psychology is concerned not only with the inherent, mandatory, or fundamental aspects of the human mind but also, indeed especially, with those parts of what people know, think, feel, want, value, and (hence) decide to do that are conditional, optional, or discretionary and are primed and activated through participation in the symbolic and behavioral inheritance of particular groups. In effect, cultural psychology is a discipline committed to the study of patterns of psychological difference across groups or subgroups and to the investigation of the emergence (and dissolution) of stable, relatively coherent, and intimate interconnections between cultural practices and individual mental states.

Any study of difference, however, presupposes many commonalities, likenesses, or universals in terms of which attributions of difference become intelligible. A notable feature of our conception of cultural psychology is that it presupposes certain universal truths about what is (and what is not) inherent in human psychological functioning. At a minimum, we are committed to a theory of mind in which everywhere in the world human beings are the kind of beings who have a mental life; who know, think, and use language and other symbolic forms; and who feel, want, and value certain things, which is one way to explain what they do (Donagan, 1987).

Even more deeply, we are committed to the view that psyche consists of certain mental powers. Most notable of these are (a) the representational power to form beliefs about other persons, society, and nature, and about means-ends connections of all sorts; and (b) the intentional power to affect an imagined future state of affairs by means of acts of the "will," which is the human capacity to have a causal influence on the world through acts of decision making and choice.

If the power of representation is an essential feature of the human psyche, then the human psyche can be studied, at least in part, as a knowledge structure. If the power of intentionality is an essential feature of the human psyche, then the human psyche can be studied at least in part, as inherently ends-sensitive, which is, minimally what it means to be agentic.

This view of the inherent powers of the psyche accords reasonably well with William James' (1950) description of the marks of the "mental." According to James:

> The pursuance of future ends and the choice of means for their attainment are thus the mark and criterion of the presence of mentality in a phenomenon. We all use this test to distinguish between an intelligent and a mechanical performance. We impute no mentality to sticks and stones because they never seem to move for the sake of anything, but always when pushed and then indifferently and with no sign of choice. So we unhesitatingly call them senseless. . . . No actions but such as are done for an end, and show a choice of means, can be indubitable expressions of Mind. (p. 1)

The anthropological linguist Anna Wierzbicka (1986, 1991) has shown that the notion of a mental subject or agent ("I") and mental state concepts such as to know, to think, to feel, to want, and to value (as good or bad) are lexicalized in all languages of the world and universally used in folk psychology to explain what people do. And it has been argued by Collingwood (1961, pp. 303, 306; see also Shweder, Much, Mahapatra, & Park, 1997), among many others, that at least one basic sense of the folk psychology concept of a "cause" is the idea of "a free and deliberate act of a conscious and responsible agent" that is best understood in terms of the ends the agent is trying to achieve and the means the agent believes is available for achieving them. With respect to its picture of the component parts of a mentality, folk psychology and cultural psychology presuppose pretty much the same picture of the universal and inherent features of the human psyche. Those marks of the mental include representation, intentionality, knowing, thinking, feeling, wanting, valuing, and (hence) choosing or deciding to do something.

Although cultural psychology is primarily concerned with the emergence and development of psychic pluralism, it makes use of a restricted set of mental state concepts as a universal framework for understanding the organization of psychological differences between the "I's" of different groups. The nature and organization of such differences and the manner of their development are discussed in the following section.

Cultural Psychology's Special Use of Mental State Concepts

In cultural psychology, mental state concepts are used to refer to the causal powers inherent in the mental nature of human beings. Such concepts are not necessarily meant to be descriptions of bits of human consciousness or of deliberative awareness.

One can use a mental state concept to explain what people do without necessarily assuming that the mental events in question are events in consciousness. What a person knows or thinks or wants or values is not always in front of that individual as a piece of awareness, even as it plays a causal role in how the person acts.

This suggests one additional power inherent in the human psyche—the ability to translate or transform a self-conscious deliberative process into a routine, automatic, unconscious, or habitual process. This power to turn a slow calculative process into a rapid response process prepares the individual to respond skillfully, smoothly, and un-self-consciously (indeed almost "mindlessly") in particular ways in particular circumstances. When this translation or transformation is fully accomplished, the associated mentality comes to be "intimate" and implicit in the practice.

As Whiting and Child (1953) pointed out long ago with respect to the beliefs implicit in a practice:

> The performer of a practice does not necessarily consciously rehearse the belief to himself at each performance. [For example, a typical middle-class European American does not

necessarily consciously think to himself "I know that I can promote autonomy and independence in infants and young children by having them sleep alone" every time he goes to bed at night.] If asked, however, he will generally be able to report immediately at least some of the associated beliefs; in this case one may surmise that rehearsal of the belief was not part of the stimulus pattern for the present performance of the custom but rather a significant part of the stimulus pattern earlier in the development of the custom. (p. 28)

This comment by Whiting and Child is important for two reasons. First, it highlights the developmental process of becoming unconscious, whereas most developmental theorists, from Piaget and Vygotsky to Kohlberg, privilege the developmental process of becoming conscious or reflective. Whiting and Child's implication that much of social behavior is habitual and automatic and that social life would not be possible if this were not so accords well with the views of Bourdieu (1972, 1990, 1991), Packer (1987), and others who are concerned with the difference between participating in the world and consciously deliberating about it.

Bourdieu argues that as practices are repeated again and again they come to be seen as part of a natural order, and their original explicit reasons for occurrence may be difficult to resurrect. Packer makes the point that "development" typically involves becoming more fluent at some activity and that this is not necessarily the same as becoming more reflective about that activity (as any serious athlete surely knows) (see also Keil, Ch. 7, this Volume).

The idea of the custom complex and the return of interest to routine or habitual practice is an invitation to rethink some basic and classical ideas about the nature of development (on the intellectual history of the idea of "habit" see Charles Camic [1986]). More needs to be said about the misguided notion that one can define progressive development in terms of some standard formal criterion such as the shift from intuition to reflection or from context-boundedness to context-independence (Kessen, 1990).

One can pile on to the classical image of progressive directional change an indefinitely large series of other dichotomies. Somewhere or other in the vast literature on cognitive development, someone or other has certainly argued that the fully developed mind is complex (vs. simple), complete (vs. incomplete), explicit (vs. tacit), impersonal (vs. personal), taxonomic (vs. associative), elaborated (vs. restricted), concept-driven (vs. percept-driven), detached (vs. affect-laden), consistent (vs. inconsistent), and so on.

As apparent from our discussion of the custom complex and the developmental advantages of tacit understanding, habit, and unreflective but fluent skills, cultural psychology is deeply suspicious of any attempt to define progressive development in terms of decontextualized formal criteria. In some cases, cognitive development is the process of becoming less reflective not more reflective. Again in some cases, the accumulation of tacit understanding is what intellectual growth is all about. It all depends.

The second reason for the importance of Whiting and Child's comment is that it underscores the point that any adequate investigation into the cultural psychology of a person or a people—any description of a custom complex—must characterize the level of consciousness of the mentality that is associated with a particular cultural practice. Are the relevant beliefs, values, motives, and satisfactions active without deliberation, active because of deliberation, reportable reflections, unavailable to reflection, and so on? When it comes to participation in the custom complexes of one's cultural community, to what extent is the course of development from the deliberate to the automatic, or from the self-conscious to the fluent, or from the explicated to the tacitly understood? At the very least, the cultural psychology of development into the customary practices of one's cultural community is likely to be the story of the progressive shift from deliberation and self-consciousness to mindless or intuitive fluency. It is a developmental story that has rarely been acknowledged in child development studies, except perhaps by those interested in the acquisition of such physical skills as walking down stairs, typing a letter, or hitting a golf ball.

SOCIAL DEVELOPMENT WITHIN THE DIVERGENT INTERPERSONAL WORLDS OF CHILDHOOD

Interpersonal Relations during Childhood

From the perspective of cultural psychology, the local world of the child—especially in those dimensions likely to affect behavioral and psychological development—is largely mediated through culture-specific mentalities and practices of child rearing. In documenting variations across populations, cultural psychology considers first of all how the child's experience is routinely organized by responsible caregivers and educators, with special attention to the local

ideas and meanings that support their behavior. If "people think and act in the light of particular goals, values, and pictures of the world" what are the goals, values, and pictures of the world (the mentality) of members of different cultural communities? Are there any generalizations that can be made about how and why differences arise in children's worlds and how they are structured?

As portrayed in the anthropological literature, variations in childhood worlds across human populations can be roughly divided into three categories corresponding to the material, social, and cultural conditions for child development (LeVine, 1989). Material conditions include diet, housing, infant holding devices, and forms of protection against disease and other health risks. Social conditions include the family, peer groups and other aspects of the interpersonal environment. Cultural conditions refer to the local ideational models, combining beliefs and moral norms, that give meaning to all features of the child's world as well as to the child's development.

The focus in this section is on interpersonal aspects of the child's world, as mediated by differing cultures throughout the world. A considerable body of evidence on this subject has accumulated over the past 25 years (since a review of the literature appearing in the third edition of the present work; see LeVine, 1970, and even more since Margaret Mead's review in the *Handbook's* first edition in 1931), permitting some generalizations about the range of variation in children's worlds and their meanings. The interpersonal worlds of children from birth to adolescence in different cultural communities vary widely along dimensions that can be described in quantitative and qualitative terms and that indicate divergent pathways for behavioral and psychological development—particularly when analyzed from the perspectives of interactional theories of development.

We begin by describing how differing organizational settings, caregiving relationships, parental practices, and age-graded participation in activities provide divergent patterns of socially and symbolically mediated experience for children of different cultures. Then we turn to the cultural mentalities that not only rationalize and legitimize these social patterns but also motivate parental behavior. Third, we consider to what extent culturally differentiated social experience during childhood affects the psychological development of individuals—their attachments, skills, competence, preferences, relationships, and emotional experience as adults. Finally, we attempt to generalize about universals and variations in social development and their implications for developmental theory and research.

The Social Organization of Childhood Experience

Organizational Settings

For the first few years of life and often much longer, children in most societies are raised in domestic groups, that is, in the normal residential homes of the adults who care for them. The functions of these groups, and their size, composition, social density, and boundedness—all variable across cultures—influence the quantity and quality of social experience possible for a child in a given society. Many of these features, and the sociospatial arrangement of the family as a domestic group as a whole, are often not matters of personal choice but are standardized in local practice according to the dominant mode of economic production and prevailing ideas of morality.

The Function of Domestic Groups.   In societies with domestic agricultural or craft production, where every family engages in productive work at home, children are raised in local settings designed for economic activities as well as for family residence. In urban-industrial societies like the United States, in which only 2% of adults engage in food production, children are more likely to be raised in home settings specifically designed for child care and segregated from adult economic activity.

This difference between cultural worlds in which work and family have been merged versus cultural worlds in which work and family have been separated (in some cases, as in the upper middle-class European American cultural area, with the family functioning more or less like a Montessori School) makes a great deal of difference for children. Where home is the setting for food or craft production, the attention of mothers is more often divided between child care and other demanding tasks. The family is then more likely to operate as a command hierarchy, with children at the bottom, and children are more likely to be spectators of a wide range of adult activities and to participate in them from an early age (Rogoff, Mistry, Goncu, & Mosier, 1993). A family that functions as an economic production unit, like that of many Third World people today as well as pre-industrial Europe and North America, constitutes a distinctive world of childhood, in which child labor is expected and children's play and education must be accommodated to the workplaces and routines of the home.

The actual amount of children's labor contributions in such families varies from one agricultural people to another (Nag, White, & Peet, 1978). Among those with low-level technology, like the peoples of sub-Saharan Africa, children may have to work a great deal at tasks they can do, such as fetching water, herding animals, caring for babies, and assisting in cultivation. This permits the adults to concentrate on the heavier or more skilled tasks of hoeing, planting, weeding, harvesting, and food-processing. Among peoples with a higher level of agricultural technology including irrigation, draft animals, and plows (e.g., rural villagers of India), the need for domestic labor is less and children may be indulged and have more free time. The actual utility of child labor in a particular setting, however, depends on the specific crops cultivated, their seasonal cycles, the availability of resources such as water, and whether children can be hired outside the family. When new technology is introduced, the situation changes, and children may be freed from labor, unless they are drafted into craft production at home or sent elsewhere as hired hands.

In foraging (i.e., hunting-gathering) and fishing communities and among pastoral nomads, children also participate in productive activities at early ages (by the standards of contemporary industrialized societies), but the degree to which they are confined or free to play in the course of the day and the year varies with the rhythm of the work cycle. As with agricultural communities, domestic economic production largely determines the functional world of children's social lives.

The Size of Domestic Groups.   The number of persons co-residing in domestic units is extremely variable among human societies, and although some of this variation depends on the definition of the unit, it is certain that the nuclear family household of Europe and North America is among the smallest in the world. Anthropologists have reported large domestic groups (up to and more than a hundred) under a single roof or surrounded by a single wall in places as diverse as New Guinea, lowland South America, West Africa, and indigenous North America; and although such groups have internal social boundaries, they certainly provide a child of any age with opportunities for interacting with many and diverse persons most of the time.

This is also true, in a more limited way, of societies with extended or joint family structures in which the domestic unit encompasses two or more nuclear families of two or more generations. Whiting and Whiting (1975) pointed out that when adult women share cooking facilities and yard space, they are more likely to interact with each other's children and cooperate in child care. The joint families of India are an example, as are the large compounds of the Yoruba of southwestern Nigeria and the smaller compounds of the Giriama of coastal Kenya (Wenger, 1989) and the Hausa of northwestern Nigeria (LeVine, LeVine, Iwanaga, & Marvin, 1970; Marvin, VanDevender, Iwanaga, LeVine, & LeVine, 1977). In all these environments, the sheer size of the domestic group guarantees that the child will interact with a large number of women and children from infancy onward.

The Composition of Domestic Groups. In contemporary urban-industrial societies, the domestic group is coterminous with the household, and composition of households with children can usually be classified by whether one or both parents reside there and whether there are other adults such as grandparents. It is more complicated among agrarian and other nonindustrial societies, in which households as physical structures can be situated in larger domestic units usually referred to as *compounds* or *homesteads* by anthropologists.

Among the Gusii of southwestern Kenya, a married woman and her younger children live in a house by themselves, but it is a unit embedded in a homestead owned by her husband or father-in-law, along with the (nearby) houses of her parents-in-law, brothers-in-law, and co-wives. If her husband is a polygynist, he may live in the houses of his other wives all or part of the time or even in a hut of his own separate from all of them, though near enough for children to bring him hot food from their houses.

Furthermore, as the children get older, they leave the mother's house to sleep in the house of an older brother (for boys) or a grandmother (for girls), all within the homestead. The Gusii mother-child household is the elementary unit of family residence, but the homestead is the basic unit of domestic social life from the viewpoint of adults, and its male members form the nucleus of a local patrilineage (LeVine & LeVine, 1966; LeVine et al., 1994). This complex composition of domestic groups is common to many

nonindustrial societies and often means that the child grows up in a more complex residential environment than that of the average American child.

The Social Density of Domestic Groups. The interactive settings in which children spend their early lives—including those of eating, sleeping, work, and play—vary widely in social density across cultures regardless of the size and compositional complexity of domestic groups. Gusii children may grow up in a homestead with as many as 58 inhabitants but spend all their hours in and around their mother's house, interacting only with mother and older siblings during the preschool years.

In contrast, Hausa children, in a much smaller compound, may experience greater social density because the sharing of cooking facilities and yard space among the Hausa women in a walled compound creates more crowded settings for daily interaction involving children. The social density a child experiences, especially during the less mobile early years of life, depends not only on the wealth or resources of the family but on the rules that govern family interaction. It seems hard for Americans and Europeans to believe that people in other cultures may enjoy, indeed prefer, "crowded" settings in which to eat, sleep, work, play and even breast-feed babies (Tronick, Morelli, & Winn, 1987), but such preferences are widespread among the world's peoples, even when they have enough domestic space in which to carry on these activities in isolation.

The Boundedness of Domestic Groups. Interactive patterns in the child's world are constrained by the social boundaries recognized by adults. Boundaries can be physical in form, like the mud walls of a Yoruba or Hausa compound or the cultivated fields that divide the mother-child households of a Gusii homestead from each other. Boundaries can also be invisible or conceptual barriers, as in the local traditions of interhousehold visiting, greeting, and hospitality that limit the interaction of children and adults in many Western and Japanese urban neighborhoods.

In urban India, by contrast, there are middle-class apartment dwellings occupied by kin-related families whose children wander in and out of each other's homes without such restriction. From the children's perspective, the permeability of the household and other domestic units in the immediate environment provides the basis of a cognitive map of their social world.

Care-Giving Relationships

Mothers are the primary caregivers of their children for at least the first 2 years of life in most human societies, but there are significant exceptions, and there is even greater variation in the array of supplementary caregivers who assist mothers and form relationships with young children. The ethnographic record as a whole does not suggest that there is a single system for human child care, but rather a range of parental patterns flexible enough to respond to and enable varying economic, demographic, and technological conditions with diverse care-giving arrangements that affect the interpersonal experience of the growing child.

When women have a heavy workload due to a primary role in food production, then the resultant scarcity of female labor may create a demand for supplementary care-giving arrangements. When children are scarce relative to adult women (due to high rates of infertility, infant and child mortality, or contraception), adult women who are infertile or postmenopausal may be eager to take care of young children born to others. When wet nurses or synthetic milk formulas become available, maternal breast-feeding may decline. Thus variations in caregiving practices and relationships are generated by the differing conditions to which human populations adapt.

There are some human populations in which a *majority* of children under 2 years of age live with and are cared for someone other than their mothers. These fostering and adoption practices have been documented in Micronesia (Carroll, 1970) and West Africa (Bledsoe, 1989). In these cases, young children are distributed among kin, often to mothers and sisters of the women who gave birth to them, after a period of breast-feeding by the mother. There is usually no effort to disguise the original relationship, and children often go back to their mothers after a period of years. Although some mothers do this because they feel obliged to meet the demands of their own mothers or sisters, they usually also feel that the child will benefit from additional sponsorship, as Goody (1982) has described for the fostering of older children among the Gonja of Ghana. All these practices are infused with the assumptions of a kinship ideology in which children are seen as belonging to, and as potential beneficiaries of, a descent group wider than the biological parents. Mothers who do not care for their own children are not viewed as irresponsible or neglectful in these cultural communities.

In a much larger range of societies, children are raised by their mothers, though often with help from others: such as sibling caregivers, grandmothers and other related adult women, and fathers or other men.

Sibling care of infants is widespread not only in sub-Saharan Africa (where it is ubiquitous) but also in Oceania, Okinawa, and parts of Southeast Asia (Weisner, 1982, 1987, 1989a, 1989b; Weisner & Gallimore, 1977). It is more frequent where mothers have extensive responsibility for agriculture.

The practice of sibling caretaking raises the question of whether leaving infants in the care of 5- to 10-year-old children, which would be considered criminal neglect in the United States, harms babies when it has achieved the status of a custom complex and is the routine practice of an entire population.

From the available evidence, the answer to this question is "No, babies are not harmed by this practice," for several reasons: First, 5-year-old children can be, and are, trained to be responsibly protective, if not necessarily sensitive, caregivers, particularly for babies carried on the back. Second, child care is largely conducted in the open air during the day, and neighbors are within earshot in case anything goes wrong. Third, the child nurse is not expected to substitute for the mother in a general sense, but simply to complement her care by protecting and feeding the baby for a few hours at a time. The mother breast-feeds during the day and sleeps with the baby at night, and infants raised under these conditions become attached to their mothers.

Finally, and in light of the foregoing, it seems that the American or European American concern about psychological harm is probably exaggerated. Babies can accommodate comfortably to sibling care, and back-carrying as well as other widespread forms of tactile stimulation promote both physical growth and psychosocial attachment during the first year (LeVine et al., 1994, pp. 257–258).

Furthermore, sibling care can initiate a strong lifelong relationship between an older sister and younger brother, which some cultures selectively promote. Among the Hausa, the marriage of a sister's son to the daughter of the brother she cared for as an infant is a preferred form of cross-cousin marriage. Even in the short run, the relationship of the toddler to his sibling caregiver often introduces the child to a larger group of children who become salient nonparental figures in his life.

Grandmothers and other adult women often play an important supplementary role in infant care, especially where children are raised in large domestic groups. From West Africa to India and China, grandmothers not only are caregivers in the early years but, as the child grows older, often complement the mother's disciplinary role with their unconditional nurturance and emotional support. Children can, and often do, form intense and long-lasting relationships with other resident women in extended family situations.

Fathers and other men are more rarely observed as caregivers for young children, but there is variation across human populations. Hewlett (1992) has provided substantial data from diverse peoples. He distinguishes between the father's *investment* in the child, which may be indirect and consist of providing resources through the mother, and *involvement* with the child, which refers to interaction.

Although paternal interaction with young children is rare relative to that of the mother and other females, and it is unusual cross-culturally for males to be constant and responsible caregivers (as opposed to occasional playmates) for infants or toddlers, the range is quite considerable. Among the Dinka of the Sudan, for example, the exclusion of men from attending the delivery of a child is extended through the early years of a child's life, and the father only interacts with his older children (Deng, 1972). Aka pygmy fathers in Cameroon, however, participate substantially in the care of young children (Hewlett, 1991), and among high-caste Hindu farmers of the Katmandu Valley in Nepal, various men in the extended family take care of infants and toddlers for periods of time during the day (LeVine, n.d.). As Harkness and Super (1992) point out, fathers can be in the presence of young children without interacting with them, and it is only when cultural practices and mentalities favor it, that fathers and other men will assume responsibility for the care of children or engage them in interaction. Infants become attached to their father and other men who interact with them, as they do to their mother, siblings, grandmothers, and other adult women (Ainsworth, 1967).

Parental Practices

An important and culturally variable part of the child's social environment is constituted by the customary activities that parents and others arrange for them. Observational investigators of human and other primate offspring have created a number of dichotomous categories to describe these activities: Child-centered communications versus those that do not include the child, distal (often verbal) versus proximal (usually physical) stimulations, reciprocal or contingent vocalization versus unilateral speech to a child, positive versus negative emotional arousal, soothing versus stimulation, and sensitive versus insensitive response to infant signals.

These dichotomies are behaviorally specified so as to be unequivocally observable in differing contexts of primate behavior, but they nevertheless seem to reflect European American middle-class preferences for child-centered, distal, verbal, reciprocal, emotionally positive, stimulating, and sensitive patterns of parent-child interaction. Studies using these categories cross-culturally usually show that parents in other cultures exhibit some or all of these behaviors less frequently than middle-class European Americans (LeVine et al., 1994; Richman et al., 1988).

However valid these findings of difference in frequencies may be, they are only part of the story, because taking European American custom complexes as the reference point for comparison almost inevitably means overlooking activities and dimensions that are salient only in the other cultures. Without a complementary account of the mentality and point of view of the other culture, this is grossly uninformative, like an African account that might describe the American family as lacking cattle and agriculture.

The findings may indicate that parents in the other culture are not committed to the same custom complex in their observable practices and do not share the European American mentality, but the findings do not describe what custom complex they are committed to and what goals, values, and pictures of the world they are in fact and in practice following. To make sense of observable differences in parents' practices, it is necessary to describe the parents' cultural models of social relations. It is necessary to describe the mentalities that guide and give meaning to their practices and to a child's social participation. Some illustrations will be provided in the next section.

Age-Graded Activities

In all societies, the social interaction of children is altered by their age-related participation in activities at home or school. The institution of schooling creates an extreme form of age-grading. In most schools children, from the ages of 5 to 8 years old onward, tend to be rigidly segregated by age from those older and younger for many of their daytime activities.

The peer groups that result are neither natural nor universal. In societies without schools, children's relationships with each other are formed among siblings or other multiage groups of juveniles (Konner, 1975). In these multiage groups, participants are much more sharply differentiated by authority and knowledge than in school-based peer groups. In such groups, relationships among older and younger children may facilitate the learning of skills by the younger, who observe mature practice performed by someone old enough to be more skilled but close enough in age to be easily imitated (Dunn, 1983).

Sibling relations may also promote interpersonal responsibility, cooperation, and sensitivity to the vulnerability of others on the part of the elder children (Schieffelin, 1990; Weisner, 1982, 1987, 1989a; Whiting & Edwards, 1988). Schools on the other hand may foster interpersonal comparison and competition among peers and, by obstructing the child's observational access to mature practice, make learning more problematic and hence more self-conscious (Lave, 1990; LeVine, 1978; Scribner & Cole, 1973). Cultural variability in age-graded social activities is widened further by specific combinations of siblings, school, and work in the local environments of children, and by culture-specific norms that elaborate or diminish age ranking.

Cultural Mentalities Concerning Childhood Social Relations

Parents do not always try to control the interpersonal environments of their children in detail, particularly after the first two or three years, and when they try to, they are often far from successful. Nevertheless, parents care about and can usually influence the settings in which their children interact with others, their caregivers and companions, and the kinds of interactions that take place (Whiting & Edwards, 1988; Whiting & Whiting, 1975). Thus it matters what parents think and feel about such things, and what they think and feel is framed by the beliefs, values, and pictures of the world of their culture. Parents are culture bearers, and their models of childhood social relations are as variable as their culture's conceptions of the good life and how to live it (Harkness & Super, 1996; LeVine et al., 1994; LeVine, Miller, & West, 1988).

Parental Models and Strategies

Parental behavior is symbolic action in Geertz's (1973b) sense of the term. It reflects a local mentality about what parenthood and child development are and ought to be, as formulated in the symbols of a particular culture. The local cultural mentality gives meaning to the actions of parents and children, and motivates parents to promote certain behaviors and dampen others. A cultural mentality of child care has three components: moral direction, a pragmatic design, and customary scripts for interaction (LeVine et al., 1994).

Moral Direction

Cultural mentalities of child care are goal driven; they are formulated in terms of cultural concepts of virtue toward which a child's behavioral development should move. The vernacular words (e.g., independence, autonomy, and self-reliance in the case of the European American middle class) and the images associated with them that represent virtuous goals of development, help provide parents' rationales for their observable child-care practices.

Research on comparative ethics and development, however, has revealed that the humanly recognizable virtues or moral ends of life can be culturally organized in ways that do not privilege an "ethics of autonomy" (Haidt, Koller, & Dias, 1993; Jensen, 1996; Shweder, 1990; Shweder, Mahapatra, & Miller, 1990; Shweder et al., 1997) and that in some societies an "ethics of community" and/or an "ethics of divinity" leads to an emphasis on alternative virtues and goals of development such as duty, respect, hierarchical interdependency, purity, and sanctity.

Furthermore, each type of ethic highlights a particular view of the self. Shweder et al. (1997) argue that the ethics of autonomy is associated with a conception of the self as an individual preference structure, where the point of moral evaluation is to increase choice and personal liberty; that the ethics of community is associated with a conception of the self as an office holder, in which one's role or station in life is intrinsic to one's identity; and that the ethics of divinity is associated with a conception of the self as a spiritual entity connected to some sacred order of things and as the bearer of a legacy that is elevated and pure. The meaning of child-care practices in any particular community, from disciplinary practices to sleeping arrangements to the practice of circumcision, is often most understandable with reference to the particular moral ends that justify and rationalize those practices in the minds of parents in that local cultural world (on initiation and circumcision see, for example, Kratz, 1994, pp. 341–347).

Pragmatic Design

Cultural mentalities of child care embody strategies not only for facilitating the child's behavioral development in a morally virtuous direction but also for achieving other ends (e.g., survival, health, and economic returns) and for overcoming obstacles to the attainment of all these ends. This is the utilitarian aspect of child-care mentalities that provide them with practical value and that convince parents that they are doing what is necessary as well as what is right.

Customary Scripts for Interaction

The moral and pragmatic aspects of a child-care mentality may or may not be explicitly formulated in general terms, but they are always represented in the social customs that guide the interaction of parents and other caregivers with young and older children. At this level of specificity in social interaction, for example, the script for responding to a baby's cry among the Gusii of Kenya is an immediate soothing response. This response is seen as promoting the calmness and compliance of a young child (the moral direction) as well as the child's health and survival in the early months (part of the pragmatic design); but it is also so customary that allowing a baby to cry more than a few seconds is experienced by Gusii adults as an intolerable breach of caregiving norms.

The Effects of Early Interpersonal Experience

What effects do cultural variations in interpersonal environments and symbolically mediated experience have on the behavioral and psychosocial development of the child? A cultural community or population-level approach provides a clearer picture of the effects of early experience than a focus on the psychology of individual differences (LeVine, 1990b). For example, children who grow up in China obviously learn to speak Chinese, just as those who grow up in Turkey learn Turkish. Less obvious but well established by sociolinguistic investigators of child language is that as young children acquire a first language they also master the communicative practices regulating interpersonal behavior

in their communities (Ochs & Schieffelin, 1984; Schieffelin & Ochs, 1986a, 1986b).

The symbolic mediation of experience and communicative practices will be discussed in the following section of this chapter. The main point of emphasis here is a very simple one: For young children the development of communicative competence reflects their early experience in a particular language environment and constitutes an important part of their early enculturation.

By 3 years of age, children have culture-specific capacities for and expectations of emotionally salient interpersonal behavior, embedded in speech routines and other customs of face-to-face interaction, in the context of specific relationships (Schieffelin, 1990). Their behavioral development has taken a culturally distinctive character and direction, diverging from that of other cultures.

Relatively little research has been done on the behavioral consequences of cultural variations in early social experience, but there is some evidence of measurable effects. Social behaviors shown to differ across culturally varying samples of children include infant-mother attachment (Grossmann & Grossmann, 1981, 1991; Grossmann, Grossmann, Spangler, Suess, & Unzner, 1985); attention-seeking (LeVine et al., 1994; Whiting & Whiting, 1975;); dependence (Caudill & Schooler, 1973); cooperation (Thomas, 1978); and gender orientation (Whiting & Edwards, 1988). In each of these cases, the evidence of behavioral difference has been interpreted by the investigators to reflect the impact of the children's prior experience in divergent cultural environments, although it is probably not possible at this time to choose between different interpretations of this "impact" (e.g., facilitation, attunement, or maintenance/loss, as discussed earlier; Werker, 1989).

An example from infancy research is the Grossmanns' (1981, 1991; Grossmann et al., 1985) study of infant-mother attachment in Bielefeld, North Germany. This German replication of Mary Ainsworth's Baltimore study (Ainsworth, Blehar, Waters, & Wall, 1978) found that the majority of a nonclinical sample of 12-month-olds were classifiable on the basis of the videotaped Strange Situation as "insecurely" attached to their mothers. Forty-nine percent of the sample were classified in the "A" category ("anxious-avoidant"), almost twice as large a proportion as in American samples. The Grossmanns related this departure from American norms to the German mothers' custom complex—their mentality and practices. German mothers, in this region of Germany, prefer a greater physical and interpersonal distance from their infants than Americans, leaving them alone more often and sometimes pushing them away. They would consider American infants rated as "optimal" by attachment researchers to be "spoiled."

According to the Grossmanns' interpretation, the culture-specific preferences of the German mothers was based on a broader cultural mentality, even ideology, emphasizing an ideal of pure independence that is even more exaggerated than the European American ethics of autonomy. For these mothers, this cultural ideology was translated into maternal practices that affected not only their infants' routine expectations for social interaction and comforting but also their response to separation and reunion in the Strange Situation. Their interpretation of their findings implies, though the Grossmanns do not say so, that the profile of attachment ratings of American infants in the Strange Situation can be seen as reflecting the culturally influenced parental practices of European Americans rather than a universal norm for all human populations.

If this is so, then claims of species-typical universality for attachment as observed in the Strange Situation should be considered premature. Infant reactions to reunion with mother after a brief separation at 12 months of age can be reinterpreted as indicators of early enculturation to a cultural standard of interpersonal distance mediated through parental practices of infant care.

The German evidence provides the starting point for a cultural critique of the Bowlby-Ainsworth model of attachment, especially its claims to have discovered the evolutionary origins of human social relationships and the biological basis for judgments of optimality, normality, and pathology in early development. As more detailed and culturally informed evidence on behavioral development in diverse cultures accumulates, a cultural critique of developmental models may serve a useful purpose, particularly if the models themselves continue to ignore cultural variation in early social experience.

At this point, it may not be possible to launch robust generalizations about the psychological effects of early interpersonal experience on the basis of population-level comparisons across cultures. However, as the concepts and techniques for observing and recording infant care and early communicative exchanges involving children have improved, and as comparative evidence has grown, so have the grounds for believing human behavioral development to

be culturally divergent from the early years of childhood onward.

THE SYMBOLIC MEDIATION OF EXPERIENCE: LANGUAGE AND COMMUNICATIVE CUSTOMS IN CULTURAL PSYCHOLOGY

It is a major assumption of cultural psychology that one mind is transformed into many mentalities through the symbolic mediation of experience and that the human conceptual capacities that support culture also support language use, which is the primary means by which the symbolic and behavioral inheritances of a cultural tradition are passed on to the next generation. It is primarily by means of language that human beings negotiate divergent points of view and construct shared cultural realities. In this section, we selectively discuss the role of certain pragmatic forms of linguistic analysis in research on the cultural psychology of development.

As children learn language, they gain entry to existing meaning systems and can access the tools for recreating and transforming those systems. In a wide-ranging review of the literature, Nelson (1996) concludes that language is more than a vehicle of enculturation: to a large extent "language and the surrounding culture take over the human mind" (p. 325), profoundly changing the nature of cognition and communication during the time from 2 and 6 years of age. Language is fundamental not only to meaning construction and socialization but to identity. Through its association with particular contexts, language comes to symbolize and "belong to" particular sociocultural groups. Quite simply, there can be no cultural psychology without language.

This premise is traceable to many intellectual forebears of contemporary cultural psychology. These include the 18th-century European philosophers who laid the groundwork for cultural psychology (Jahoda, 1990); Wilhelm Wundt and other 19th-century proponents of a "second" psychology (Cahan & White, 1992); and Edward Sapir (Mandelbaum, 1951), the anthropological linguist whose works on language in social life and on culture and personality anticipated many topics of current interest to cultural psychologists.

We begin this section of the chapter by discussing the conception of language that is most compatible with the aims of cultural psychology and by identifying resources from allied fields of study that hold promise for deepening our understanding of language in cultural life. We turn next to socialization, one of the fundamental problems of cultural psychology, and review studies that have yielded important insights into the actual process of socialization by examining the forms and functions of everyday discourse. We then single out oral narrative as a paradigm case of everyday discourse, organizing the discussion around issues of diversity.

Although the literature on oral narrative has grown rapidly, relatively few studies have addressed the role of narrative in socialization. Throughout this section, the primary focus is on research with young children. In keeping with the comparative commitment of cultural psychology, examples from the cross-cultural record are included wherever possible.

Language as Practice

The centrality of language to cultural psychology stems not only from historical precedent but from the duality of language: Unlike other domains, language is both a tool of inquiry and an object of inquiry. On the one hand, the use of language as an instrument of inquiry is pervasive; every study of human development depends on verbal communication in one way or another. Children are questioned about the reasons for their moral judgments. Parents are asked to reflect on their child-rearing beliefs. Verbal behaviors are incorporated into observational coding schemes. Experimental tasks have to be explained to participants. On the other hand, language serves as the object of inquiry in many studies that seek to understand the nature and development of the linguistic system itself, including its various subsystems (e.g., syntax, morphology).

This distinction between language as tool and language as object of inquiry serves the interests of cultural psychology by promoting critical examination of the ways in which we as researchers use language in the conduct of our research and by acknowledging the continued importance of understanding the referential dimensions of language. At the same time, this distinction is limiting because it does not readily encompass a third, rapidly growing set of studies of particular interest to cultural psychology.

These studies focus on speech, but they are not concerned with language development per se. They examine what people say to one another in order to understand self-development, family relations, or friendship, but with a focus on how the talk itself contributes to *constituting* the phenomenon under study (Garvey, 1992). These studies take talk seriously as a "substantive, structured, and structuring activity with intrinsic developmental significance" (Packer, 1987, p. 253). Examples are the work by Packer (1987) and Shweder and Much (1987) on moral development; Dunn (1993) on social development; Corsaro (1985) and Corsaro and Rizzo (1988) on peer culture; Bruner (1990), Fivush (1994), and Miller, Potts, Fung, Hoogstra, and Mintz (1990) on self development; Garvey and Kramer (1989) on pretend play; Miller and Sperry (1987) on emotion; and Eisenberg and Garvey (1981) and Garvey and Shantz (1992) on conflict. (See also the collections by Cook-Gumperz, Corsaro, & Streeck, 1986, and Sperry & Smiley, 1995.) Research on language socialization, to be discussed, also falls into this category.

These studies arise from a conception of language that privileges the situated use of language—what is often called simply talk or speech or, more technically, speaking praxis (Bauman & Sherzer, 1989; Hanks, 1996). These terms signal a contrast with the narrowly referential conception of language that holds sway in most research on human development and cross-cultural psychology, which treats language only as a representational system or a repository of knowledge. The view of language that is most compatible with the aims of cultural psychology goes beyond grammatical and lexical meaning to include processes of indexical meaning that anchor utterances to their linguistic and nonlinguistic contexts and most crucially to unspoken background assumptions.

This view of language carries with it the premise that speaking is a form of social action. And like any action, whether verbal or nonverbal, its meaning is never transparent. It is context dependent and implicit and the unsaid must be spelled out in propositional form if it is ever to be understood and rendered intelligible to a nonparticipating audience.

Speaking is intrinsically polysemous when extracted from its context. This does not mean that meaning is free to vary infinitely, but it does mean that speaking requires interpretation. Speaking is treated as a set of practices that are organized beyond the sentence level into dialogues, genres, and multichanneled performances. These larger communicative events and stretches of discourse, while serving as the units of analysis, are themselves multiply embedded in larger sociocultural contexts and networks of cultural practices. The functional inseparability of talk and nonverbal action is thus recognized. In contrast to approaches that take the disembodied word, sentence, or text as the unit of analysis, this approach permits a deeper cultural analysis, for it recognizes that cultural principles are expressed not just in the content of talk but in the way that discourse is organized internally and in relation to larger events and sequences of talk.

Among the many intellectual currents that have fed into practice-centered views of language is sociohistorical theory, with its focus on semiotically mediated activity (Cole, 1990; Wertsch, 1985), and the allied fields of ethnography of communication and language socialization, both of which are situated primarily in anthropology (Bauman & Sherzer, 1989; Schieffelin & Ochs, 1986a). These fields have been centrally concerned with cross-cultural comparisons and hence are especially germane to the comparative mission of cultural psychology. Resting on the assumption that everyday talk is a pervasive, orderly, and culturally organized feature of social life in every culture, they seek to understand the diversity of language use in the conduct and constitution of social life.

These fields provide a rich set of conceptual, methodological, and empirical resources that cultural psychologists should exploit more fully. These include procedures for grounding interpretations of communicative practices in the public cues that participants systematically deploy in interaction (e.g., Duranti & Goodwin, 1992) and critiques of our own social scientific methods as communicative practices whose meaning may not be shared by the people we study (e.g., Briggs, 1986).

Especially provocative for its self-reflective implications is the discovery that some sociocultural groups place a high value on silence (Bauman, 1983; Tannen & Saville-Troike, 1985) and quiet observation (Philips, 1983)—an important reminder to those steeped in academic discourse (see also Rogoff et al., 1993).

In addition, the focus on naturally occurring discursive practices has led to a much more dynamic conception of context and practice than is usually assumed in developmental studies. Contexts and practices are treated not as static givens, dictated by the social and physical environment, but as ongoing accomplishments negotiated by participants. This shift from static to dynamic is signaled by such terms as *contextualization* and *recontextualization*—a move that focuses attention on the process participants themselves use to determine which aspects of the ongoing activity are relevant (Bauman & Briggs, 1990; Duranti & Goodwin, 1992; Ochs, 1990; Schieffelin, 1990). This conceptual innovation offers a holistic conception of individual and context as an interlocking system in which the language practice changes along with the person (see Goodnow et al., 1995, for further discussion of this point; see also Wagner & Demick, Ch. 13, this Volume).

Socialization through Language

The growing literature on language socialization deserves to be singled out for further consideration because it arises from an intellectual project that is basic to cultural psychology. Cultural psychology recognizes that child development is inextricably bound to the process of socialization—of orienting oneself within systems of meaning—and seeks to understand the nature of this process as it is actually enacted by living, experiencing human beings. Cultural psychology is uniquely positioned, by virtue of its interdisciplinary character and commitment to meaning, to claim socialization fully as its own—something that none of the social sciences has succeeded in doing. Because of the way in which human action has been partitioned for study, socialization—known variously as "acquisition of culture," "enculturation," and "development in context"—has remained marginal to the intellectual agenda of any discipline. As a result, it has been extremely difficult to devise an integrated conception of socialization, that slights neither culture nor children.

Research on language socialization provides an important model of how to proceed with this task. Much of this work has been inspired by Edward Sapir's famous words, "Language is a great force of socialization, probably the greatest that exists" (p. 15) (Mandelbaum, 1951). Another touchstone is the Vygotskian idea that sociocultural meanings are created by using language for particular purposes in socially defined activities (Vygotsky, 1934/1987; Wertsch, 1985). If language not only reflects meaning but constitutes meaning, then an adequate theory of socialization must incorporate talk in a principled way.

Such a theory confers three advantages. First, the actual processes of socialization are rendered accessible through analysis of the forms and functions of everyday discourse. Second, in keeping with a basic insight of modern developmental psychology, the child is accorded an active role through a focus on child and caregivers' mutual, negotiated participation in discourse practices (Brandtstädter, Ch. 14, this Volume; Rogoff, 1990). Third, the fact that language practices systematically index social statuses and ideologies helps to explain the varied affective stances—eager acceptance, resistance, playfulness—that children assume as they attempt to invest cultural resources with meaning. Both the nonneutral, ideologically charged nature of the socializing environment and the necessarily evaluative responses of the child-in-context are taken into account (Goodnow, 1990a).

These ideas have been translated into a particular kind of empirical work. In an attempt to discover how cultural communities structure children's entry into meaning, researchers have combined ethnographic description with the meticulous documentation of actual interactions between members and novices as they unfold in particular cultural contexts. The typical study is longitudinal in design and involves extensive fieldwork in the community under study. Although the process of language socialization is assumed to be a lifelong process, most research has focused on the early years. In contrast to many domains of human development, some of the best documented cases of language socialization are non-Western cultures (Kulick, 1992; Ochs, 1988; Schieffelin, 1990; Watson-Gegeo & Gegeo, 1990) and working-class and minority groups in the United States (Heath, 1983; Miller, 1982; Ward, 1971).

What are the chief insights emerging from this work? These and other studies have demonstrated that there is enormous diversity in the cultural organization of caregiving and language learning and that the pattern of sustained dyadic conversation so familiar to many middle-class European Americans is but one variant among many. As noted earlier, groups differ in the physical and social ecology of child care, in folk theories about the nature of children and language learning, in the practices used to encourage mature speech, and in the principles that organize interaction (Fisher, Jackson, & Villarruel, Ch. 19, this Volume).

In the working-class African American community described by Heath (1983), multiparty talk and interaction is the norm and children are almost never alone. Talk *around* the child, rather than talk directly *to* the child is the primary linguistic resource for novice learners. Among the Gusii of Kenya, where family size and maternal workloads are large, women prefer quiet, obedient children. Infants receive relatively little verbal stimulation but are held a great deal (LeVine, 1990a). Direct gaze is discouraged as a

sign of disrespect and an invitation to witchcraft. These are but a few of the examples that could be cited (see Miller & Hoogstra, 1992, and Schieffelin & Ochs, 1986a, for reviews of the literature and Corsaro & Miller, 1992, and Schieffelin & Ochs, 1986b, for collections of studies).

Coexisting with these differences are some important similarities. Across a wide range of cultures, caregivers use explicit instruction to socialize young children into valued ways of acting, feeling, and speaking. This is one of the reasons we could suggest, in our initial discussion of the custom complex, that the course of progressive development is sometimes from the reflective to the unreflective, from the explicit to the tacit.

One of the best examples of explicit parental instruction is "shaping the mind," a symbolically powerful and emotionally intense form of discourse used by Kwara'ae (Solomon Islands) parents to pass on traditional cultural knowledge (Watson-Gegeo & Gegeo, 1990). Marked by a formal discourse register and distinctive prosodic features, "shaping the mind" involves abstract discussion of kinship, religion, land rights, and other domains of knowledge, and provides children with repeated opportunities to practice reasoning and argumentation.

Research on language socialization also has revealed that many of the most powerful socializing messages are implicit and unintended. They are conveyed through tacit routine organizations of time and space, with their associated routines and distributions of social actors, and through contrastive distributions of language forms and functions that index meaning. The implication is that research that begins and ends by simply asking caregivers about their socializing goals is likely to miss the deepest and most subtle dimensions of socialization—those pervasive and fundamental cultural orderings that feel most deeply natural to the native and are least likely to be reflected on.

Research on language socialization also affords insights into cultural patterns of affective experience. Studies from widely varying cultures show that children are able to express affect through customary communicative means from an early age (Schieffelin & Ochs, 1986a, 1986b). By studying emotional events as they unfold in everyday life, researchers have found that to focus only on terms for emotional states, as is common in developmental studies, is to greatly underestimate the communicative resources that children deploy (Miller & Sperry, 1987; Ochs, 1988).

Another focus of research that deserves much more attention concerns the affective consequences of participation in everyday discourse. An excellent example is provided by Schieffelin's (1990) description of how affectively charged relationships between younger Kaluli brothers and older sisters are created through routine participation in a type of interaction in which brothers appeal for help and sisters respond with nurturance. Girls are supposed to "feel sorry" or "have pity" for their brothers, and mothers coach this feeling by using a distinctive voice quality. This kind of work can be seen as an extension of Vygotskian theory into the affective domain.

Vygotsky (1987/1934) proposed that certain kinds of thought (i.e., scientific concepts) develop only in cultural contexts in which children encounter the specialized discourse associated with formal schooling. By analogy, specific affective meanings are constructed through using language routinely for particular purposes in socially defined activities. Among the potential consequences of routine participation in the custom complex of everyday talk is the creation of specific feelings, of emotional bonds with others, and of emotional investment in the discursive practices themselves. These consequences are only now beginning to be recognized as just as important as, and indeed inseparable from, cognitive consequences to be discussed later in this chapter (Goodnow et al., 1995).

Narrative: Getting Those Stories Straight

Narrative, in one form or another, is probably a cultural universal. It is one of the most powerful interpretive tools that human beings possess for organizing experience in time and for interpreting and valuing human action in terms of normative intelligibilities. The literature on narrative is vast and the list of topics relevant to cultural psychology is long. These include the relationship between narrative and memory (Neisser & Fivush, 1994; Wyer, 1995), narrative as a fundamental mode of thinking distinguished from paradigmatic or analytic thinking (Bruner, 1986), the role of narrative in self-construction (Bruner, 1990; Gergen, 1991; Gergen & Gergen, 1983; McAdams, 1993; Nelson, 1989), and narrative as a therapeutic technique in psychotherapy and psychoanalysis (Polkinghorne, 1988; Spence, 1982).

Faced with this embarrassment of riches, we have chosen, inevitably somewhat arbitrarily, to focus on a single issue: the role of oral narrative in socialization. This focus maintains continuity with the previous discussion of socialization through discursive practices while allowing exploration of cultural diversity in greater depth.

Varieties of Oral Narrative

Keith Basso (1984) begins his classic paper on Western Apache oral narratives with an interpretive puzzle. What did Western Apache elders mean when they made the following kinds of statements:

> Our children are losing the land. It doesn't go to work on them anymore. They don't know the stories about what happened at these places. That's why some get into trouble. (p. 21)

> I think of that mountain called 'white rocks lie above in a compact cluster' as if it were my maternal grandmother. I recall stories of how it once was at that mountain. The stories told to me were like arrows. Elsewhere, hearing that mountain's name, I see it. Its name is like a picture. Stories go to work on you like arrows. Stories make you live right. Stories make you replace yourself. (p. 21)

Basso's attempts to understand the significance of these statements within the context of Western Apache culture yielded one of the most comprehensive accounts available of a people's theory of how oral narrative functions in their lives. Working in collaboration with informants whom he had known for many years, Basso discovered that the Western Apache folk theory of storytelling exploited two symbolic resources—land and narrative—for maintaining the moral order.

Western Apache believe that stories about the early history of the group have the power to establish enduring ties between individuals and features of the natural landscape. As a consequence of these bonds, people who have behaved improperly are moved to reflect on and correct their misconduct. At times a member of the community might find it necessary to "aim" a story at an offender. If taken to heart, the story and the place with which it is associated will "stalk" the offender and promote beneficial change.

Basso's study illustrates two issues of plurality that apply to the study of oral narrative as a socializing medium. Most obvious is the issue of narrative diversity across sociocultural groups. Basso (1984) describes a distinctive cultural case that is sufficiently detailed to allow precise comparison and contrast with other cultural cases. Second, although the study focuses primarily on one type of oral narrative—historical tales—it situates them within the full range of native narrative categories. The Western Apache narrative typology also includes myths, sagas, and gossip, each with its own properties and functions. The plurality of types of oral narrative *within* the culture is thus established. Moreover, access to and ownership of narrative genres is socially distributed, introducing another source of intracultural variation. For example, myths are performed only by medicine men and medicine women.

The heterogeneity of speech genres within cultural communities is a theme that resonates strongly with the work of Bakhtin, the Russian literary scholar and philosopher whose vision of language as culturally shaped and socially situated is compatible with the conception of language described earlier (Bakhtin, 1981; Morson & Emerson, 1990; Wertsch, 1991). Bakhtin (1986) stressed that speech is organized into a rich variety of genres associated with particular speech situations. He argued that speech is never free of generic constraints but that speakers can achieve individuality of expression by creatively appropriating and re-accenting existing genres.

Storytelling Begins Early

A question left unanswered by Basso's account is how Western Apache folk theories of narrative intersect with beliefs about children. For example, when do Western Apache begin to aim historical tales at errant children? An exciting trend in recent developmental research is the strong interest in children's early narratives. It is now well established that children from many cultural backgrounds (Mexican, Chinese, European American, African American, working-class, middle-class) begin to recount past experiences in conversation during the second or third years of life (e.g., Eisenberg, 1985; Engel, 1995; Fivush, Gray, & Fromhoff, 1987; Heath, 1983; McCabe & Peterson, 1991; Miller, Fung, & Mintz, 1996; Miller & Sperry, 1988; Nelson, 1989; Snow et al., 1991; Sperry & Sperry, in press). At this surprisingly early age, children are able to step into the narrative practices of family and community, thereby laying claim to a key cultural resource for creating their own socialization (Bruner, 1990).

Only recently, however, have issues of narrative plurality come to the fore in the literature on children's narratives (Haas-Dyson & Genishi, 1994). As researchers begin to apply Bakhtinian constructs to the analysis of children's spoken and written discourse, it is becoming clear that narrative sense-making involves juxtaposing and interweaving multiple texts and orchestrating multiple, even conflicting, voices or ideological perspectives and that every community affords such diversity (e.g., Cazden, 1993; Hicks, 1994; Kamberelis & Scott, 1992; Miller, Hoogstra, Mintz, Fung, & Williams, 1993; Taylor, 1995). From this standpoint, it is important to note that most of the research on young children's narratives has focused thus far on past-time narrations, a focus that is clearly too limiting. Both Nelson (1993) and Taylor (1995) have pointed out the need for studies of children's future-time narrations. In this connection, one promising line of work speaks to intracultural diversity by inquiring into children's narrative repertoires: Which genres do children from a particular cultural community participate in and in what order (Hicks, 1991; Kamberelis, 1993; Preece, 1987)?

In a study of working-class African American children in rural Alabama, Sperry and Sperry (1995) found that fantasy stories flourished early in development and were more elaborated than factual stories of past personal experience. Hypothetical stories were a relatively late development. Boys' efforts to tell fantasy stories received much more support than did girls', a finding that may help to explain how men in this community get to be so good at telling "whoppers."

Interesting gender differences in early narrations have also been reported for middle-class European American children (Fivush, 1993). When asked to elicit stories from their children about specific emotions experienced in the past, mothers co-constructed more elaborate stories about sadness with their daughters than with their sons and encouraged more retaliation when narrating anger stories with their sons than with their daughters. Similar findings emerged when fathers served as co-narrators.

A second line of research (that sometimes occurs in combination with the first) has focused on a particular narrative genre and has asked comparative questions—about the genre's definition, its acquisition, and its role in socialization (e.g., Heath, 1983; Michaels, 1991; Snow et al., 1991). This work is thus oriented to issues of plurality across sociocultural groups.

A narrative genre that is particularly interesting for comparative purposes is personal storytelling. Personal stories are stories—temporally-ordered, evaluated accounts—that people tell in ordinary conversation in which they recreate remembered experiences from their own lives. Personal storytelling is one of the processes by which memories are made collectively and carried forward in time. Because this type of storytelling is explicitly self-referential, it is an especially rich carrier of cultural messages about self, emotion, and morality as well as narrative itself. Unlike literate stories, personal storytelling is a probable cultural universal—and not just for adults. Evidence is accumulating that children from a wide variety of sociocultural groups participate routinely in personal storytelling within their families and communities but that the ways in which personal storytelling is defined and practiced varies a great deal.

For example, Heath (1983) found that members of a working-class European American community in the southeastern United States adhered to a criterion of literal truth when narrating their personal experiences. This contrasted with a nearby working-class African American community for whom a "story" was not a story if it lacked fictional embellishment. These communities also enacted opposing norms toward denigration versus aggrandizement in their portrayals of the self-protagonist.

Another example is provided by comparison of middle-class Chinese families in Taipei, Taiwan, and middle-class European American families in Chicago. Focusing on personal storytelling with 2½-year-olds, Miller, Fung, and Mintz (1996) found that Chinese families were more likely than their European American counterparts to tell stories about the child's past transgressions, to repeatedly invoke moral and social rules, and to structure their stories so as to establish the child's transgression as the point of the story. Discourse analysis revealed that even in those rare instances in which a European American child's past transgression was narrated, a qualitatively different interpretation of the child's experience was constructed, one that acknowledged yet downplayed the child's wrongdoing. These findings suggest that the Chinese families were operating with an explicitly evaluative, overtly self-critical interpretive framework that is compatible with the Confucian emphasis on teaching and strict discipline. By contrast, the European American families seemed to use an implicitly evaluative, overtly self-affirming framework when narrating young children's experience. They went to considerable lengths to portray the child in a favorable light, possibly as a way of protecting or enhancing the child's self-esteem.

The Variability Inherent in Narrative Practices

The point of these examples is that although children and their caregivers routinely participated in personal storytelling in these several communities, they carved out different versions of personal experience for the purposes of storytelling. What is at issue are different definitions of the genre itself, different understandings of how the boundaries should be drawn around personal experience. But there is another equally important and rarely recognized source of variation in personal storytelling, namely variation in the ways in which storytelling is made available to children in the course of their everyday lives (Miller et al., 1990). Note that this kind of variation is discoverable only through observations of how storytelling is actually practiced in families and communities. Although many developmentalists have assumed that young children's social experience of narration takes the form of scaffolded conversations or co-narrations with family members, children's exposure to storytelling is likely to be much wider than this.

Returning to the Chinese and American comparison, for example, Miller, Fung, and Mintz (1996) found that stories of the child's past experiences were told not only *with* the child as co-narrator but *about* the child in the child's presence. Both types of participant structure occurred several times per hour in both cultural cases (also Taylor, 1995). In many communities, stories of other family members' personal experiences are told *around* the child as well. These stories are particularly interesting from the standpoint of socialization and deserve much more research attention. They provide curious children with a constantly updated source of information about the lives of significant others and demonstrate that children participate actively in their own socialization not just by telling stories but by listening.

A focus on narrative practices exposes still another issue of plurality that applies to the study of oral narrative as a socializing medium. When narratives are treated as situated practices, rather than as disembodied texts, it becomes apparent that variability is inherent in storytelling. Stories are embedded in and emerge from the particular circumstances in which they are told. Studies have shown that stories are shaped in systematic ways by the interests of the narrating participants, reflecting, creating, and legitimating asymmetries in power and status (Goodwin, 1990; Ochs & Taylor, 1992; Taylor, 1995). The implication is that narrators are constantly customizing their narrations in relation to here-and-now social contingencies.

The dynamic nature of narrative practices is most apparent, however, when particular stories are told repeatedly. Microlevel analyses of the "natural history" of stories (i.e., of multiple retellings of the "same" story) indicate that the nature and direction of change are systematically related to the larger events and social processes in which the retellings are situated. For example, in a study of an inner-city junior high school, Shuman (1986) found that adolescent girls' stories of minor offenses were structured differently, depending on which phase of the peer dispute process they were embedded in—the beginning of the dispute, the height of the dispute, or after the dispute had been resolved. Wolf and Heath (1992) document children's prolonged engagement with and transformation of particular written stories within the context of ongoing narrative practices in the family. Miller et al. (1993) describe a case in which a 2-year-old child systematically reconfigured the plot of his favorite story and resolved affectively charged conflicts through successive retellings in an interpersonal context in which he was granted considerable latitude as author.

Studies such as these are rare. This is unfortunate for cultural psychology because the process of retelling and revising stories goes to the heart of the socialization process. It is assumed to be transformative in theories ranging from psychoanalysis to the Western Apache model of historical narrative. We need especially to know more about how stories operate over the long term in children's lives.

Again, the Western Apache provide a compelling example. Basso (1984) relates an incident in which an adolescent girl arrived at a ceremonial in hair curlers, a violation of community standards. Some weeks later, when the girl was attending a party at her grandmother's house, the grandmother narrated a historical story about an Apache policeman who suffered dire consequences because he had acted too much like a white man. At the conclusion to the story, the girl left the party. When questioned by Basso, the grandmother explained her granddaughter's sudden departure by saying that she had shot her with an arrow (the story). Two years later, the young woman told Basso that she threw her curlers away after reflecting on her grandmother's story. Referring to the place where the Apache policeman had lived, she said, "I know that place. It stalks me everyday" (p. 40).

The recent literature on oral narrative shows that in many sociocultural groups, people participate with one another in complex and shifting networks of narrative practices characterized by systematic variability and cross-cutting redundancy. Particular frameworks of evaluation and interpretation operate again and again in oral stories, while narrators and listeners respond to and create here-and-now social contingencies. Each co-narrated story, each story aimed at or told around the child provides another opportunity for the child to hear which experiences are reportable and how those experiences should be assessed. Each story provides the child with another opportunity to construct with significant others a culture-specific understanding of his or her experience. In this way, interpretive frameworks get repeatedly instantiated in personally relevant terms. The power of oral narrative stems not only from the narrative form itself, in all its variety, but from the interpenetration of narrative and social life.

Of course, narrative represents only one of the many "families" of discursive practices that will need to be understood if cultural psychology is to realize its promise of revitalizing the study of socialization. Genres of conflict (e.g., arguing, disputing) and play (e.g., joking, pretending), discourses associated with nurturance, instruction, guidance, and healing—these too are enacted differently within and across communities and cultures. As such, they too can be assumed to play a role in transforming one mind into many mentalities. Exciting empirical work is emerging in connection with several of these types of discourse (e.g., Harkness & Super, 1996; Rogoff et al., 1993; Watson-Gegeo & White, 1990). This is a hopeful sign for a cultural psychology that embraces the practice view of language set forth in this section of the chapter.

THE DEVELOPMENT OF SELF

As noted earlier, the psychological side of cultural psychology is the study of the things that the "I's" (the subjects, agents, or selves) of particular cultural communities know, think, feel, want, and value, including what they know, think, feel, want, and value about the self as a mental being capable of subjective experiences and of participation as an agent in a cultural community. A powerful way in which culture and psyche make each other up and come to have an influence on individual behavior, we believe, is through one's way of being a subject or agent in a social world—what is often called "self-functioning."

Indeed, the self can be conceptualized as a primary locus of culture-psyche interaction and of culture-specific being (see Baltes, Lindenberger, & Staudinger, Ch. 18, this Volume). It is where the individual, the biological entity, becomes a meaningful entity—a person, a participant in social worlds (Miller, 1994; Rogoff, Radziszewska, & Masiello, 1995; Weigert, Teitge, & Teitge, 1990). The development of the child's sense of self as a continuous entity and as an agent with intentional powers may appear to arise from highly personal idiosyncratic experiences. It is certainly a defining feature of the European American idea that each self is individualized and distinctive from other selves. Yet studies highlight that although the experience of self and the structures and processes of the self may appear as primarily individual creations, they are in several ways also cultural and historical constructions (Oyserman & Markus, 1993).

Before beginning a full-blown discussion of the cultural psychology of the self, it is important to recognize some of the deep issues and controversies that arise in this area of research. Several trends within philosophy and the social sciences, and within world affairs more broadly, have converged on "self and identity" as popular topics for research.

Perhaps most obviously, as a glance at the headlines of any newspaper will confirm, we are at a period in history when nationalism and a concern for maintaining and asserting ethnic and cultural identity are emerging as a powerful focus in Eastern Europe, the Middle East, Africa, and Asia. In this climate of heightened ethnic identification and conflict, many scholars argue that we can no longer afford to ignore the role of cultural practices and mentalities as sources of personal and social identity or the role of self-management and the management of self-regard in all aspects of social life, particularly in social conflict (e.g., Kakar, 1996).

Perhaps less obviously, certain eternal disputes about the character and causal role of personal identity (one's sense of self) in psychological functioning have resurfaced on the intellectual scene. Several quite disparate currents of thought,

including skeptical postmodernism, connectionist-parallel distributed process models in artificial intelligence and Buddhist philosophical thought (Elster, 1987; Gergen, 1991; Sass, 1992; Varela, Thompson, & Rosch, 1993) have concluded that the self is illusory or epiphenomenal and plays no causal role in mental functioning, whereas other streams of thought have argued that the self is "multiple" or "protean" (Lifton, 1993).

We do not plan to debate here whether the Buddhists have it right that the self is an illusion or whether the Hindus have it right that the self is the real component of pure being. We will simply note that the very existence of human social and moral life seems intimately tied up with the evolution of a species whose central psychological makeup is defined by the existence of a causally active and somewhat unitary self ("One self per customer" is the philosopher Daniel Dennett's phrase; Flanagan, 1992); a self that is free, willful, self-regulating, morally responsible, and conscious; that is the initiator of action, the author of texts, the holder of rights; and that is the subject of evaluation and social scrutiny when questions about rationality, responsibility, normality, and pathology arise.

Once "epiphenomenalism" (the self as unreal) is put to the side, the current choice between "mechanistic" and "vitalistic" approaches to the self does not seem especially inviting (see Kapstein, 1989). Contemporary mechanistic approaches to personal identity argue that one's sense of self (e.g., one's sense of continuity over time) is nothing other than a function of the continuity of one's memory of discrete mental states (perceptions, pleasure, and pain). Contemporary vitalistic approaches to personal identity argue that one's sense of self is a fundamental prewired feature of the human brain. Neither view seems to leave much room for social, interpersonal, or cultural processes in the construction and maintenance of personal identity.

Perhaps there are versions of these approaches that can be made compatible with cultural psychology. From the perspective of cultural psychology, however, the self is not fully reducible to either memory or brain processes. A cultural psychology approach to personal identity examines that part of our sense of self that develops through membership in some local cultural community and through a history of symbolically mediated experiences with the practices of that group. It examines the role and effects of labeling and stereotyping, dialogue and narrative, and moral agency and social practice on self-functions such as self-regard, self-confidence, and self-definition (gender, race, religion). It is concerned with how the self is described, responded to, and evaluated and often regulated by others. Although investigations of cultural psychology acknowledge the crucial principle that the "I" (the subject) is never fully determined by the hegemonic ideologies of one's group or by interpersonal forces alone, their aim is to clarify the way cultural mentalities and practices (including ideologies of the self and symbolic products such as the biographies of exemplary members of one's cultural community) can play a major part in constituting an individual sense of self.

What a cultural psychology perspective can add to knowledge of the development of self is the understanding that particular ways of representing and experiencing a self, both as object and subject of experience, are grounded in the normative understandings and behavioral routines of selfhood in a given sociocultural and historical context (Miller et al., 1996; Oyserman & Kemmelmeier, 1995; Oyserman & Markus, 1993).

From the perspective of cultural psychology, the self can be defined as the mentalities and practices (the custom complex) associated with being an "I" (a subject, a person) in a particular community. Returning to the insights of some of the field's early theorists (e.g., Dewey, 1938; Erikson, 1968), it is evident that culture does not surround or cover the "universal" child. Rather, culture is necessary for development—it completes the child. Culture provides the scripts for "how to be" and for how to participate as a member in good standing in one's cultural community and in particular social contexts. Simultaneously, a cultural psychology perspective recognizes that children are active constituents of their own cultures and that changes in individuals initiate changes in their relations with others and thus in their immediate cultural settings (see Brandtstädter, Ch. 14, this Volume; Csikszentmihalyi & Rathunde, Ch. 11, this Volume).

Defining and Locating the Self

The Self as Dynamic, Multilevel, and Multifaceted

The self can be defined as a multifaceted, dynamic system that regulates and mediates behavior (Banaji & Prentice, 1994; Markus & Wurf, 1986). Neisser (1988, 1991) is quite explicit in constructing the self as a multileveled entity. He

defines five types of self-knowledge: ecological, private, interpersonal, conceptual, and what he labels "extended" (i.e., knowledge of the self over time). Neisser contends that wherever people live or whatever they may believe, people are first of all active, embodied agents in the natural and social environments, and thus will show evidence of ecological and interpersonal selves (Neisser & Jopling, in press).

This multileveled self—in the most general sense, a subject's characteristic way of being a person in the world—is believed to be broadly consequential for individual experience. It provides the framework, the skeleton, and the anchor for the psyche. A subject's way of being a person, whatever cultural form this assumes, affords and constrains what he or she perceives and thinks about, what he or she feels, values, assumes responsibility for, and how he or she organizes, understands, and gives meaning to any experience.

The past decade has been a period of rapidly increasing interest in the nature, functioning, and development of the self and a time of important theoretical activity. A number of themes can be identified that raise challenging questions about what the self is, how to determine who has one, how and when the self comes to be, how it functions, and how it develops.

Many researchers note the need to analyze the self not just as an object of knowledge but also as the subject of experience. This is a need for attention to the embodied self, to the role of intersubjectivity in constructing the self. Other topics requiring further research are the situation, context, or niche within which the self participates, and studies on the self as engaged in meaningful social activity rather than as an isolated and decontextualized entity (Bullock & Lutkenhaus, 1990; Damon & Hart, 1988; Harter, 1983, 1996; Higgins & Parsons, 1983; Stern, 1985; Tomasello, Kruger, & Ratner, 1993). Research from a cultural psychology perspective forcefully underscores the importance of such issues and raises many complementary concerns (e.g., Greenfield & Cocking, 1994; Miller, in press; Neisser & Jopling, in press; Valsiner, 1988).

The Conceptual Self

The self has been variously defined as the "insider's" grasp on the person, as the answer to the "who am I?" question, and as a theory or set of schemas that provides the individual with a sense of continuity. The focus has been on the self as object of knowledge (Allport, 1937;

Eder & Mangelsdorf, in press; Epstein, 1973; Kihlstrom & Cantor, 1984; Sullivan, 1940). Historically, despite many theoretical statements to the contrary, the tendency has been to reify the self and to regard it as a thing, as exemplified in thousands of studies on *the* self-concept, *the* self, or self-esteem.

Research on the development of self has tended to concentrate on what Neisser labels "the conceptual self." And given the general European American tendency to imagine the mind as the source of experience and thus to equate selves with minds, the emphasis on how children think about and represent the self is perhaps obvious. From this theoretical perspective the self becomes an object of knowledge and it becomes natural to imagine that it is the self as represented or the *self-concept* that is the most significant aspect of individual experience.

In research on development of the self-concept, the critical sign of the self has been visual self-recognition as assessed by mirrors and photographs of the self. In summarizing the work in this paradigm, Bullock and Lütkenhaus (1990) conclude that self-recognition begins between the ages of 9 and 16 months and is consolidated by 24 months. By 2 years, most children recognize themselves in the mirror and in photographs. Some (e.g., Lewis, Sullivan, Stanger, & Weiss, 1989) have argued that such self-recognition is a prerequisite for self-awareness. Other studies have focused on speech to find evidence of cognitive representations of self. During the second and third years, children begin to use their name, the terms "I" and "me," and possessively claim objects as belonging to themselves (LeVine, 1983; Van der Meulen, 1986).

The notion that thinking about the self is the key element of self is also underscored by a large collection of studies that have explicitly tied the development of self to advancing cognitive capacities (Leadbeater & Dionne, 1981; Leahy & Shirk, 1985; Montemayor & Eisen, 1977; Rosenberg, 1986). Many studies based on the Piagetian model of cognitive development have shown that as the child advances from preoperational thought to formal operations, the focus of self-definition shifts from concrete, objective, and visible characteristics to abstract, private features of the psychological interior.

A widely cited review by Harter (1983) notes,

> Young children focus on concrete, observable aspects of self such as physical attributes and behaviors, whereas older

children increasingly couch their self-descriptions in terms of trait. With adolescence, there is a further shift toward the use of abstractions and psychological processes such as thoughts, attitudes, and emotions in defining the self. (p. 305)

Still other studies have shown a link between the level of cognitive development and characteristics of the self-concept such as hierarchical organization, integration of opposing conceptions of the self, and the stability of self-conceptions across time and context (see Harter, 1990; Rosenberg, 1986, for reviews).

And indeed from studies with people living in European American contexts, it is evident that the kind of self-concepts of the type described by these studies exists. This type of self-concept includes images and conceptions of the person in the present, but also in the past and in the future—narratives of what could have been and what might be (Higgins, 1990; Markus & Nurius, 1986; Oosterwegel & Oppenheimer, 1993). And this self-concept is functional: It mediates behavior and is implicated in all aspects of behavior from strong academic and athletic performance, to general well-being and life satisfaction. A negative self-concept of this type is related to delinquency, drug use, and depression (see Bracken, 1996, for review).

The Cultural Self

A cultural psychology approach emphasizes the need to expand the analysis of the experience and understanding of self, and to critically examine the cultural presuppositions that are incorporated into much of the research on the development of self. To underscore a point made earlier and to be discussed again in the following section of this chapter, the cultural psychology approach to development is skeptical of most attempts to define progressive development in terms of universal abstract criteria, such as from behavior to traits or from context-dependent to context-free.

In studies of selves in cultural contexts other than the European American, one quickly confronts selves that are not easily characterized in terms of complex mental representation of traits, attributes, preferences, or possessions. It becomes evident that the study of the development of self has proceeded primarily from one cultural point of view and has been rooted in a set of invisible and untested assumptions about the self as an idea or as an objectified and cognitively represented entity.

Comparative research in other cultural communities suggests that selves do not seem to be primarily a matter of relatively stable concepts at all, but rather a set of processes or ways of being. And in some groups, a description of self or others in terms of internal, decontextualized attributes, or qualities simply does not occur (Fajans, 1985; Lillard, in press; Miller, 1984; Ochs, 1988; Rosen, 1995; Shweder & Bourne, 1984).

Hart and Edelstein (1992), in describing a study conducted with adolescents in Iceland, describe one student who struggled mightily to answer the "who am I" question and finally in despair looked up from his blank questionnaire and asked "Are people meant to have kinds of thoughts about themselves?" In many cultural communities, the nature of the self is referenced not to an internal self but instead to a particular social context and characterizing one's self outside that context is unnatural and irrelevant.

Goodnow (1990a, 1990b) has argued that cognitive development involves learning the community's definition of being intelligent. Similarly, developing a self requires incorporating the community's definitions of being a self. And once self-development is considered in cultural context, it is almost immediately apparent that what a self is and what it means to be an "acceptable" or "good" self can vary dramatically from one cultural place to another (Markus & Kitayama, 1991b; Shweder & Bourne, 1984). As Taylor (1989) has argued:

> My self-definition is understood as an answer to the question Who am I. And this question finds its original sense in the interchange of speakers. I define who I am by defining where I speak from, in the family tree, in social space, in the geography of social status and functions. We first learn our languages of moral and spiritual discernment by being brought into an ongoing conversation by those who bring us up. The meanings that the key words first had for me are the meanings they have for us, that, for me and my conversation partners together. So I can only learn what anger, love, anxiety, the aspiration to wholeness, etc. are through my and others' experience for us in some common place. (p. 35)

The Ontological Basis of Self

The Person as an Individual

The study of the self within psychology, as with many aspects of child development, has incorporated the European American definition of being a person. The psychological study of self in Western social science has been firmly rooted in the ontology of individualism (Greenfield & Cocking, 1994; Ho, 1993; Markus & Kitayama, 1994a; Sampson, 1988). And this ontology is extensively incorporated in most child-care practices and in key societal institutions, such as schools.

The Latin word "individual" means indivisible and whole, and the central tenet of individualism is the epistemological priority accorded to the separate, essentially nonsocial, individual. The person is assumed to exist independently and to enter into social relations or sociality on the basis of need and by mutual consent with other individuals. The focus is on the individual rather than on the social unit of which the individual is a part. The person is cast as an entity whose behavior is determined by some amalgam of internal attributes apart from the external situation.

Individualism is typically analyzed as the critical element of Western society (e.g., Baumeister, 1987; Carrithers, Collins, & Lukes, 1987; Guisinger & Blatt, 1994; Sampson, 1985; Triandis, Bontempo, & Villareal, 1988), and many analysts argue that the Enlightenment gave birth to the notion of the Kantian individual and to the importance of individual reason and free will. Others suggest that individualism in its current form shows the stamp of late industrial capitalism. Lebra (1992) further contends that individualism is a function of a Cartesian categorization system that draws a sharp distinction between the self and others.

Within the framework of individualism, it seems natural to assume that selves are objects, that selves should be unified and integrated, that selves should reflect the concerns of others but not be focused on them, and that the central task of the child is to progressively develop the realization that one is separate from others and is autonomous, efficacious, in charge or in control of one's actions. The idea of a bounded individual who is separate from others and who should not be unduly influenced by them also leads to a consistency ethic in which the good or authentic self is the same, relatively unchanging self across different situations. (See Gergen, 1968; Johnson, 1985; Markus & Kitayama, 1994b; Morris, 1994; Shweder & Bourne, 1984, for more elaborate discussion of these ideas.)

The literature on the development of self is also replete with unexamined presuppositions that are the legacy of individualism interwoven with still other cultural and historical assumptions. In this literature, there is a persistent interest in the issue of being a "true" rather than a false self, which probably reflects Victorian concerns with secret or hidden parts of the self (Baumeister, 1987; Harter, 1986). And currently, there is also pervasive attention to raising children who feel good about themselves and who have high self-esteem, issues that derive from societal appropriation of expressing feelings rather than inhibiting them and of actualizing the self and fulfilling one's potential (Maslow, 1954). The literature on self-development also incorporates presuppositions about what type of parenting practices produce these proper or good selves. Thus, the child with high self-esteem is believed to be a product of parenting that is accepting and approving and that highlights a child's successes rather than a child's failures (e.g., Coopersmith, 1967).

The Person as Relational

The individualist model of the self that provides the infrastructure for the field's understanding of the self and of what it means to be or not to be a person is an obvious and natural model for European American researchers. It is a model rooted in a set of Western philosophical positions about human nature and in layers on layers of practice and institutions that give an objective reality to this idea. And it is a powerful and practical model when characterizing selves in European American contexts. It is not, however, the only model of how to be. There are other ontologies and ideologies of human nature that have yet to be reflected in the literature on the development of self. Analyzing the self in cultural context brings these other ontologies and ideologies of the self to light.

Another model of the self stands in significant contrast to individualism, but is generally characteristic of Japan, China, Korea, Southeast Asia, and much of South America and Africa (Triandis, 1989; Triandis et al., 1988). According to this perspective, the self is not and cannot be separate from others and the surrounding social context. The self is experienced as *interdependent* with the surrounding social context. It is the self-in-relation-to-other that is focal in individual experience (Markus & Kitayama, 1991a; Triandis, 1989, 1990). In fact, according to Kondo (1990), from the Japanese perspective the self is fundamentally interdependent with others, and to understand the Japanese sense of self requires dissolving the self/other or

the self/society boundary that is such an obvious starting point in all European American formulations.

An important imperative in this alternative model of the self or way of being is not to become separate and autonomous from others, but instead to fit in with others, to fulfill and create obligation and, in general, to become part of various interpersonal relationships. Individuals are naturally understood as interdependent with others. Sharing, interweaving, or intersubjectivity is the established cultural imperative, and it is not a mystical or magical project (Ames, Dissanayake, & Kasulis, 1994). From this perspective, the individual is an open and communicating center of relationships and thus is intimately connected with other selves. From a Confucian perspective, groups are not separate from individuals. Individuals must work through others—that is their nature. To reveal themselves, they must be parts of groups such as families, communities, and nations (Tu, 1994). And, the sources of action are to be found in a person's pattern of involvements with others rather than in internal mental states or processes.

An interdependent view of self does not, as might be imagined from an European American perspective, result in a merging of self and other, nor does it imply that people do not have a sense of themselves as agents who are the originators of their own actions. According to this view, it takes a high degree of self-control, self-discipline, and agency to effectively adjust oneself to various interpersonal contingencies. Control, however, is directed primarily to personal desires, goals, and emotions that can disturb the harmonious equilibrium of interpersonal transaction.

This can be contrasted with a European American notion of control that implies an assertion of one's desires, goals, and emotions, and a consequent attempt to change features of the social situation. Hamagushi (1985) for example, reports that for Japanese, "The straightforward claim of the naked ego" (p. 303) is experienced as childish. Self-assertion is not viewed as being authentic, but instead as being immature. This point is echoed in M. White and LeVine's (1986) description of the meaning of *sunao*, a term used by Japanese parents to characterize what they value in their children:

> A child that is sunao has not yielded his or her personal autonomy for the sake of cooperation: Cooperation does not suggest giving up the self, as it may in the West: It implies that working with others is the appropriate way of expressing

and enhancing the self. Engagement and harmony with others is, then, a positively valued goal and the bridge—to open-hearted cooperation. (p. 58)

Giving in to others, being receptive to them or influenced by them is not a sign of inconsistency or of false selves at work. Rather it reflects tolerance, self-control, flexibility, and maturity. Within many Asian perspectives, children are assumed to be naturally good and will develop the needed sensitivity to and empathy for others through encouragement and by example. The good child is believed to be a product of parenting practices that are highly responsive and attuned to the child.

Yet good parenting does not ignore a child's failures, shortcomings, or transgressions. In Japan, children are encouraged to engage in self-reflection and self-criticism as necessary steps to self-improvement and mastery (e.g., Lewis, 1995). Similarly, Chinese parents often use an explicitly evaluative, self-critical framework with their children as opposed to an overtly self-affirming framework (Miller et al., 1996). Chinese caretakers claim that shaming as a caretaking practice serves to keep children from falling into disgrace or from losing their all-important connection to others.

Much more could and must be said about these apparently startling differences in ontological assumptions, to which we are alerted by engaging in research in other cultural communities. A comprehensive investigation would not be restricted to a simple contrast between "individualism" and "interdependency," and other ontologies that must also exist on a worldwide scale would be drawn on. Nor does this imply that variability does not exist within Japan, China, or Korea. Our purpose is simply to underscore that comparative research makes us aware that on a worldwide scale divergent views exist of what the self is and should be, and those views are critical underpinnings of self-relevant experiences.

If the self functions as an interpretive, integrative, or orienting framework for individual behavior, then whether one has a self that is shaped by dominant European American ontological traditions or by prevalent Asian ones has the potential to make an enormous difference in individual psychological processing. Comparing behavior that is organized and constructed within a European American frame of individualism to behavior organized and constructed within other cultural frames may be a key to exploring how cultural processes are implicated in the etiology, nature, and functioning of psychological systems. It may help us understand how "multiple, diverse psychologies" arise.

Cultural Diversity in Ways of Being

There is a rapidly expanding literature relevant to any review of cultural variation in the development of self. Much of it does not focus directly or precisely on the nature and functioning of the self system as that psychological system has been defined and operationalized in American and European studies. Nevertheless that comparative literature is relevant to any researcher interested in the origins of culture-specific selves.

In an attempt to focus on the culture-specific nature of selves, Markus, Mullally, and Kitayama (in press) have described the custom complexes associated with being a person. They suggest that cultural and social groups in every historical period are associated with characteristic patterns of sociocultural participation, or more specifically with characteristic ways of being a person in the world. They call these characteristic patterns of participation, *selfways*.

Selfways are patterns or orientations, including ways of thinking, feeling, wanting, and doing, that arise from living one's life in a particular sociocultural context structured by certain meanings, practices, and institutions. People do not live generally or in the abstract. They always live according to some specific and substantive set of cultural understandings (goals, values, and pictures of the world). Selfways thus include key cultural ideas, values, and understandings of what it means to be a self and senses of how to be a good or acceptable self. But selfways are not just matters of belief, doctrine, or ideology. Selfways are also manifest in everyday behavior, in social episodes, both formal and informal, in language practices, in patterns of caretaking, schooling, religion, work, and in the media.

The notion of selfways implies that every sense of self will be grounded in some shared meanings and customary practices and will necessarily bear some important resemblance to similarly grounded selves. From this perspective, to act, live, or function well in a given culture amounts to practicing the underlying cultural views of how to be. Thus, although any two American selves will obviously differ in countless ways, as will any two Japanese selves, cultural participation in either current complex of American or

Japanese practices and institutions will produce some important resemblances.

In broad brushstrokes, and speaking probabilistically and in terms of central tendencies, culturally acceptable European American selves are likely to be (a) separate, bounded, stable, and consistent; (b) attribute-based (e.g., based in traits, preferences, goals); (c) clear, confident, articulated, elaborated; (d) in control; (e) different from others and uniqueness-oriented; (f) particularly sensitive to positive regard, self-enhancing; (g) success-oriented; and (h) expressive and enthusiastic. Culturally acceptable East Asian selves are likely to be (a) connected; (b) context-based; (c) relational, flexible, malleable, responsive to others' expectations, preferences, and feelings; (d) similar to others and concerned with fitting in; (e) particularly sensitive to potential inadequacy, self-critical; (f) improvement and mastery-oriented; (g) open, receptive; and (h) fully engaged.

From the moment of birth (and even earlier in some cultural contexts), individuals are given meaning and engaged as persons. Through this cultural participation, they become selves. An infant's mentality or consciousness or way of being in the world is thus patterned according to the meanings and practices that characterize a given cultural community, and the communities are maintained by these mentalities. There is a continuous cycle of mutual attunement and coordination between psychological tendencies and the social realities on which these tendencies are brought to bear. From our perspective, features of the cultural system such as the characteristic ways in which one is led to focus on and attend to others can become directly incorporated into individual systems of experiencing and organizing the world. They become selfways. Or, as Ingold (1991) characterizes it:

> Like organisms, selves become, and they do so within a matrix of relations with others. The unfolding of these relations in the process of social life is also their enfolding within the selves that are constituted within this process, in their specific structures of awareness and response—structures which are, at the same time, embodiments of personal identity.

In the following section, we will briefly review studies relevant to how selfways develop through cultural participation in the custom complexes characterizing European American and East Asian cultural contexts. Our goal is to highlight the diverse selfways that develop as a consequence of such participation.

Most of the recent research has focused on a contrast between those patterns of cultural participation that emphasize and construct the person as an independent, autonomous entity and those that emphasize and construct the person as an interdependent part of a larger social unit. Some researchers suggest that one or another version of the interdependent pattern is characteristic of about 70% of the world's population (Greenfield & Cocking, 1994; Triandis, 1989).

Selfways in Some European American Contexts

Speaking probabilistically and in broad strokes, the European American middle-class cultural region is characterized by selfways that promote and foster independence of the self. Being a European American person requires the individualizing of experience. The subjectivity of the person is sensed as a more or less integrated whole configured by attributes and values that are contrasted against others or society. (cf., Geertz, 1984). The self is experienced as the meaningful center of the individual and is understood to be rooted in a set of internal attributes such as abilities, talents, personality traits, preferences, subjective feeling states, and attitudes. A major cultural task that is often mutually pursued by caretakers, friends, and teachers is to continually and progressively "individualize" the child. As it becomes increasingly clear that conceptualizing the self as an object and describing one's self in abstract and psychological terms is a culture-specific tendency rather than a consequence of general cognitive development, researchers can begin to investigate those practices that foster and afford this tendency.

Despite an explicit cultural emphasis on the importance of being nice and caring and helpful (Bellah, Madsen, Sullivan, Swidler, & Tipton, 1985; Deci & Ryan, 1990), development in the European American style is almost synonymous with individualizing and decontextualizing the self. Even while they seek out and maintain interdependence with others—social tasks that must be accomplished by people everywhere—they will maintain a sense of boundedness, relatively greater separation from others, and a sense of being "in control." Caring, connecting and relationality are likely to assume a somewhat more individually agentic form. Many of the cultural practices which contribute to a sense of agency are so much a part of everyday, domestic life that they are, for all practical purposes, invisible.

In many English-speaking cultural communities language use itself is a factor in the creation of the decontextualized, agentic "I." Ikegama (1991) notes that English is a language "which focuses on the human being and which gives linguistic prominence to this notion, while Japanese is a language which tends to suppress the notion of the human being, even if such a being is involved in the event" (p. 301). English, in characterizing an event, focuses on the particular person involved whereas Japanese emphasizes the event as a whole, submerging the individual within it. Because the human subject is foregrounded, in English one might say "I have a temperature," whereas in Japanese, one would say roughly "As for me, there is a temperature" or "A temperature goes with me." In English, one might say "John ran out of money," whereas in Japanese, one might say "As for John, money became null."

Along with the foregrounding of the subject (the "I") in English, American English speakers tend to be direct and to assume that it is the speaker who must make himself clear to listeners. This tendency begins early. American mothers compared to Japanese mothers talk more, and more directly, to their children (Azuma, Kashiwagi, & Hess, 1981; Caudill & Weinstein, 1969). In a study of aspects of mother-infant interaction, Morikawa, Shand, and Kosawa (1988) compared the patterns of American and Japanese mothers with their 3-month-old infants. Americans mothers elicited more vocalizations than did their Japanese counterparts and produced more expressions of positive affect. American vocalizations occurred while looking at the baby and when the baby was happy and alert. This pattern is in contrast to those Japanese studied, who were more likely to express negative affect and to do so while the baby was looking away.

Direct and explicit verbal instruction is also a salient feature of teacher-child interactions in the American cultural context (Tobin, Wu, & Davidson, 1989; Wu, 1994). In the course of these direct interactions, the child's distinctive attributes are identified and then they are persistently noted and affirmed. Personal attributes and abilities are assumed to be the defining features of the self—to provide a basis for one's uniqueness and also to be the source of one's current, past, and possible actions.

The explicit goal is the development of individual potential. In an institutional realization of the idea of defining attributes, American children are often grouped and tracked according to the attributes of ability (Stevenson & Stigler, 1992). And when resources permit, the curriculum is often individualized on the assumption that each child has a unique learning style and moves at his or her own pace.

The American schoolchild is objectified, made to feel special, and is praised, encouraged and complimented. In many preschools and schools, each child gets to be a VIP or a star for a week or a day, individual birthdays are celebrated, and children are honored (Markus & Kitayama, 1994a). Writing projects frequently involve autobiographies and descriptions of personal experience, and art projects are focused on self-representation. Many middle-class American children are thus continually encouraged and given the opportunity to express themselves and to present their own ideas in speeches and in writing. A common elementary practice in school is show-and-tell: Children bring items into class that are important in their lives and stand in front of the class and tell a story about their object. All these everyday practices foster an objectification of self and a sense of self as a source of action or of being in control.

Moreover, both individually and collectively, children are encouraged to think about themselves positively as stars, as winners, as "above average," and as the repositories of special qualities. It has become routine in many elementary schools that every child who plays on a soccer or basketball team receives a trophy. This practice may discourage competition and invidious comparison among team members, but it underscores the importance, not of the team or of the group, but of each individual and of each child's special attributes. And even as many current educators worry that they may have used praise too liberally in the past and try to focus on the learning process rather than on the evaluation of the child (Damon, 1995), teachers are persistently urged to find some unique aspects of each child's product.

American children are also encouraged to be independent and autonomous and self-determining (Bellah et al., 1985). In a North American context within the European American middle class, infants are given their own beds and their own rooms to encourage and foster autonomy (Shweder, Balle-Jensen, & Goldstein, 1995). Similarly, most developmental markers center on autonomous activity—rolling over, sitting up, walking, and eating by *one's self.*

American children are also socialized to have distinct preferences. Long before the child is old enough to answer, caretakers pose questions like "Do you want the blue cup or red cup?" With such questions, mothers signal to children that the capacity for independent choice is an important and desirable attribute (Markus & Kitayama, 1994a) and thereby instantiate an "ethics of autonomy" that prevails in certain cultural communities but not others (Haidt et al., 1993; Shweder et al., 1997). And the availability of choice gives rise to the need for preferences by which to make choices. Preschool settings are arranged so that children have a great deal of choice in the activities they pursue. Presumably, these efforts to incorporate self-determination into the school day are designed to safeguard the child's intrinsic motivation. The schedule is often organized so that children can decide for themselves what to do and so that they do not have to conform to the group except during limited parts of the day (Lewis, 1995).

Here then is one way that culture and psyche make each other up. Particular kinds of psychological processes (e.g., the tendency to think about the self as a positive, unique entity) emerge through years of socialization and enculturation as an individual is the recipient and becomes the guardian and perpetuator of the social practices and meanings that are recurrent in his or her cultural community (Kitayama et al., 1997). And these psychological processes, in turn, are integral to reproducing those cultural patterns. So becoming a self (a meaningful cultural participant) in a European American context involves developing and maintaining an autonomous self that is separate from other such selves and from the social context. Those with such independent selves may be motivated to discover and identify positively valued internal attributes of the self, express them in public, and confirm them in private. They are likely to develop processes that enable them to maintain and increase their own self-esteem. And individuals in the European American culture area may be especially tuned to positive characteristics of the self. The data on European American selves indeed support these generalizations.

In a series of studies with young children, Hart and his colleagues (Hart, 1988; Hart & Edelstein, 1992) asked American children to imagine a "person machine." This machine makes the original person (respondent) disappear but at the same time manufactures other people (copies of the original) who receive some, but not all, of the original

person's characteristics. The respondent's task is to judge which new manufactured person—the one with the same physical attributes (looks like respondent), the one with the same social attributes (has the same family and friends), or the one with the same psychological attributes (same thoughts and feelings)—will be most like the original person. By the ninth grade, Hart et al. (1993) have found that most respondents believe the copy with the original's psychological characteristics is most like the original.

Consistent with a number of earlier studies of the development of the self-concept (e.g., Harter, 1983), Stein, Markus, and Moeser (1996) have found that 11- to 14-year-olds, asked to describe themselves, reveal a consensual self which includes the specific attributes of caring, friendly, nice, and worried. And the self-descriptions of the adolescents with high self-esteem matched the consensual self more closely than did those with lower self-esteem. Such findings suggest that the tendency for adolescents to characterize themselves in abstract terms involves incorporating a particular collective idea of "how to be" rather than an increase in cognitive ability. These findings are consistent with those of several other studies on cultural variation in self-categorization (Cousins, 1989; Harter, 1983; Triandis, 1990). Those studies suggest that it is the internal features of the self—the traits, attributes, and attitudes—that are privileged and regarded as critical to self-definition.

Furthermore, in a study comparing the self-efficacy levels of children from Los Angeles, East and West Berlin, and Moscow, Little et al. (1995) found that children from Los Angeles had the most optimistic self-efficacy beliefs whereas children from East Berlin had the most pessimistic beliefs about personal efficacy. The authors argued that the higher self-efficacy ratings of the Los Angeles elementary school students reflect the high levels of individualism and the low power distance between students and teachers.

Oettingen (1995) argues that in individualist cultures, efficacy will depend largely on one's own emotional reactions and evaluations, whereas in collectivist cultures, evaluation by in-group members will be the most important source of efficacy information. In cultures with a large power disparity between members, children will become more inclined to treat parents and teachers as clear superiors. Children of cultures with much less power disparity will have more opportunities to see themselves as "origins" of their own actions. It would be interesting to know how those children of Beilefeld, North Germany, who were reared to be hyperindependent and unspoiled (Grossmann & Grossmann, 1981, 1985, 1991; and see earlier discussion of the culture-specific presupposition of attachment research) would have fared on a self-efficacy index.

As researchers develop methods of assessing the selves of very young children, it is evident that apprehending and experiencing the world in terms of a bounded selfway begins quite early in individualistic cultural communities with a prevailing ethic of autonomy. European American children appear to have some sense of who they are and the attributes that characterize them by 3 years of age (Eder, 1989). Moreover, as early as 4 years of age, European American children show psychological tendencies that suggest a realization of the cultural emphasis on individualization and on separation from others. They describe themselves as better than their peers in all domains. And studies with adults suggest that this type of self-serving bias or sense of false uniqueness is positively correlated with self-esteem (Josephs, Markus, & Tarafodi, 1992). Within a cultural system that is organized to foster and promote the individuality and uniqueness of the self, a general sensitivity to positive self-regard has positive social and psychological consequences.

Selfways in Some East Asian Cultural Contexts

A rapidly expanding literature in psychology, anthropology, and philosophy is now leading to a reasonably nuanced understanding of the cultural form of Japanese, Chinese, and Korean selves. Systematic analyses of Japanese settings (Bachnik, 1994; Lebra, 1993; Peak, 1987; Rosenberger, 1992), reveal a pervasive concern with and attention to the relational side of social life and to one's role or position in the social structure. Markus and Kitayama (1991a, 1991b) suggested that Asian selfways emphasize the fundamental relatedness of individuals to each other. They argue that the relationship rather than the individual may be a functional unit of consciousness. They claim that:

> Experiencing interdependence entails seeing oneself as part of an encompassing social relationship and recognizing that one's behavior is determined by, contingent on, and to a large extent, organized by what the actor perceived to be the thoughts, feelings and actions of others in the relationship. (p. 227)

Lebra (1994) argues that among the Japanese empathy is a psychological mainstay. It is empathy that one must understand if one is to understand almost any aspect of Japanese behavior. Empathy (*omoiyari*) "refers to the ability and willingness to feel what others are feeling, to vicariously experience the pleasure or pain that they are undergoing, and that help them satisfy their wishes" (Lebra, 1976, p. 38). Lebra sees this focus as quite diametrically opposed to the self-focus that is common in many European American practices.

This emphasis on empathy does not imply that Japanese selves should be conceptualized as without individuality or without a separate identity or that autonomy will not be an important issue (Greenfield & Cocking, 1994; Kim, 1987; Oerter, Oerter, Agostiani, Kim, & Wibowo, 1996). It does imply, however, that such empathic ways of being a self that explicitly highlight the state of "being-in-relation" are different from selfways that emphasize and reify the individual. In this particular Japanese mode of being, subjectivity is sensed as interdependence with a larger whole that includes both the person and others and is configured by a constant referencing of the self to the situational setting or context.

Throughout much of the world outside European American contexts, the very task of child rearing is not the European American one of making a dependent baby into an independent adult. The task instead is one of cultivating an unruly asocial baby into a civilized social being (Caudill & Weinstein, 1969). The need to uphold interpersonal obligations and to maintain a connection and a harmony with others is highly elaborated in every sphere of social life. Caudill and Weinstein (1986) find that Japanese mothers hold their 3- to 4-month-old infants more and have more body communication with them than mothers in the United States. Furthermore, as noted earlier, co-sleeping and co-bathings are common. Sleeping babies are rarely left alone in Japan. The close, fully interdependent mother-child dyad is particularly idealized in Japan, and many other relationships in society (e.g., between boss and subordinate) are organized according to this familial model. Greenfield and Cocking (1994) characterize interdependence as a developmental script that stands in sharp contrast to the developmental script of independence. They underscore that although the scripts are intertwined, the two are never balanced. What is a major melody in one society is a minor theme in another.

From an East Asian cultural perspective, a European American style self—distinct, positive, and attribute-based—is not a mature, fully civilized form of human agency. A strongly held, clear sense of self is a sign of childishness because it marks one's failure to take full account of and show sufficient regard for the relationships of which the self is a part. Agency Japanese style results from (a) the sense that the self is afforded and appreciated because of the relationships of which it is a participating part and (b) the sense that the self must flexibly maintain and further the welfare of those relationships.

Such a sense of agency does not mean that the self is passive. It is not the same as just "going with the flow." Inter-individual harmony requires active attention. Mulder (1992) in describing Indonesian harmony (*rukun*) notes, "Rukun does not come as a gift but is the result of the active orientation toward mutual respect and adjustment to each other." From this orientation, it is important to be empathic and flexible so that others are not hurt or embarrassed by one's action. Oerter et al. (1996) in trying to characterize the Japanese perspective on human nature, quotes one of their respondents as claiming that "adulthood" means "good understanding, being flexible and following the general rules set by society. The more you grow as an adult, the smaller your own private fantasy world becomes. . . . You become softer-minded, better fitted to the society, but you also become less sensitive" (p. 41).

Interdependence characterizes many different aspects of Japanese life. As noted previously, the Japanese language minimizes the person as an agent. Self-reference in Japanese is accomplished with an elaborated set of communicative customs based on one's status in the particular relationship. The Japanese word for self (*jibun*) means "my share of the shared space between us." Japanese style interdependence emphasizes the importance of the correct way of living and is continually focused on self-improvement.

Even maternal practices toward infants in Japan seem to involve some communication of correct and expected ways to be. Caudill and Schooler (1973) noted that Japanese mothers produced speech with the apparent intention of directly shaping their infants' physical and emotional states in normative directions. They seem especially concerned not to let infants cry and to calm babies whose serenity has been disturbed (Morikawa et al., 1988). Compared to the reactions of European American mothers, Japanese mothers seem especially alert to infant vocalizations, which

they are prone to interpret as a sign of distress and a distressing sign to which they must respond (Bornstein, Azuma, Tamis-LeMonda, & Ogino, 1990).

American mothers, by contrast, seem to talk more to their infants than Japanese mothers do, and they talk without the intention of directly influencing or altering their infants' behavior. Bornstein et al. give an example of a Japanese mother with a 3-month-old baby saying to the baby who is looking away ("What is wrong with you? and "Don't say _____, say _____ look at me). Japanese mothers were more likely to express negative affect or try to establish mutual gaze or seek information when the infants were gazing away from them than were Americans, apparently in an attempt to reestablish a dyadic connection.

In general, such East Asian parenting and teaching practices appear to encourage interdependence through interaction and mutual engagement. When American mothers and toddlers interact with a new toy, American mothers typically focus on the object and draw the child's attention to it. Japanese mothers use the toy to engage the child in a relational or interactive game and do much less talking, explaining, and questioning (Bornstein et al., 1990; Fernald & Morikawa, 1993). According to Lewis's survey of over 50 preschools, the focus in preschools is on developing children's connections to one another and engaging them in the supposed pleasures and supposed treasures of group life. Instead of celebrating individual success, special events recognize the accomplishments or growth of the whole group. Children routinely produce group pictures or story boards, and no child leaves to go to the playground until all members of the group are ready to leave. Attention to others is among the primary goals of Japanese education, and it is crafted and fostered in many routine practices. Classrooms walls are covered with group goals—"let's cooperate," "let's pool our strength" (Lewis, 1995).

Studies of East Asian child-rearing and schooling practices suggest an emphasis on knowing one's place, role, station, and duties within the social order. This is particularly evident in Chinese cultural contexts which reveal an explicit high regard for self-improvement, order, and hierarchy. In a study of Chinese American and European American mothers' beliefs about what is important for raising children, Chao (1992) found that Chinese American mothers stressed sensitivity to other's expectations and to the demands of the situation, while the European American mothers' responses revealed an orientation aimed at nurturing and building the child's sense of self. The difference here is between parents who are primarily concerned about the hierarchical and interdependent relationship between self and others and the sense of integrity that flows from doing one's duty, versus European American parents, who are primarily concerned with furthering the independence of their children and encourage them to have a strong, positive, even assertive, sense of self-regard.

Chao (1993a, 1993b) found an emphasis on order and respect for hierarchy among Chinese American mothers. They scored higher on scales of parental control, authoritarianism, and what Chao calls "Chinese child rearing ideologies" than their European American counterparts. Thus, Chinese American mothers were more likely than U.S. mothers to endorse items such as "I have strict, well-established rules for my child" and "I do not allow my child to question my decisions," "I make sure I know where my child is and what he is doing at all times" and "I teach my child that in one way or another punishment will find him when he is bad," "Mothers can teach children by pointing [out] good behavior in other children," "When children continue to disobey you, they deserve a spanking," and "Children should be in the constant care of their mothers/family members."

Similarly, Rohner and colleagues found that, in contrast to Americans, Korean adolescents found parental control to be evidence not of hostility and mistrust, but of love and concern (Rohner, 1984; Rohner & Pettengill, 1985). Notably, parental practices that emphasize strict control with the intention of creating a morally dutiful and disciplined sense of agency can also be found within some European American contexts, and they deserve further study.

Differences in selfways are also manifest in play practices. Farver, Kim, and Lee (1995) found in an investigation of free play among European American and Korean American preschoolers that Anglo-American children primarily described their own actions, rejected their partners' suggestions, and used directives (e.g., "I am your king! Do not obey the bad king! I'll save you!"). Korean American children described their partners' actions, used tag questions, semantic ties, statements of agreement, and polite requests (e.g., "He is a king, isn't he? He's the bad guy, isn't he? The good guy caught him, right?").

Overall, in many East Asian contexts, one's sense of well-being is less tied to the realization that one's own goals have been met (the ethics of autonomy) and more tied

to the general understanding that one is doing what is required in a given situation, or that one has done something the right or appropriate way (ethics of community). Already in the first months of preschool, Japanese children are required to perform complicated activities such as arranging their lunch boxes or putting on their clothes for outside activities in the required way (Peak, 1987). As a child, being part of a family or part of a school group often means thinking about the social unit and thinking about one's place within it and doing what is proper for this situation. It involves considerations such as "What do my parents or my peers want me to do?" or "Did I do what they wanted me to do?" Within a Japanese cultural context, a sense of self is developed by being finely attuned to the expectations of others, by not being left out of their sympathy, by making sure you are part of the social process. Perceptually, cognitively, emotionally, and motivationally, it is others, the encompassing social unit, the group and its standards of excellence that are focal or salient. From this perspective the most useful kind of information about the self is information about one's shortcomings, problems, or negative features. Self-criticism is encouraged in all societal settings from the classroom to the boardroom. In general, cultural participation entails discovering what may be missing or lacking in one's behavior and then closing the gap between the actual and the expected behavior (Kitayama et al., 1997; Markus & Kitayama, 1994a, 1994b).

A constant focus on social expectations and whether they are being met appear to go hand-in-hand with a focus on self-improvement in Japan. In a study analyzing the content of essays written by incoming students of a Japanese junior high school, Kitayama and Wakabayashi (1996) found that the vast majority of the essays followed a script of self-improvement. The students discussed their negative aspects (misbehaviors or mistakes) early in the essay and concluded with remarks about how these negative aspects could be corrected or improved in the future. The constant emphasis on self-improvement as a virtue can be seen everywhere in Japanese life. An advertisement urging Japanese workers to stop working and take their vacations exhorted, "Let's become masters at refreshing ourselves" (*New York Times*, May 1995).

The desire for self-improvement has cognitive consequences, for there is a tendency among many Japanese to direct attention to those areas where one needs improvement, while discounting the positive aspects of any performance. That Japanese tendency to discount the positive is often misinterpreted by European American observers, who mislabel it and assimilate it to their own cultural notion of self-depreciation. In Japan, what appears to be self-depreciation from an European American perspective in fact works very well to establish the person as a member in good standing in the community. Perhaps "humility" would be a more accurate label for this culturally valued disposition. In contrast to European Americans for whom self-improvement is equated with individual achievement and who are attuned to the positive features of the self, Japanese respondents are particularly sensitive to the negative features of the self within a given context.

Further, Japanese practices are often framed in terms of *hitonami* (average as a person). As difficult as it may be for European Americans to believe, for many Japanese it is a relief to know that one is average. From a Japanese perspective, being different is to risk being insensitive to the inheritance of one's community and not being part of it. From an interdependent perspective, the self seems best described as a process of self-improvement in which progress means avoiding any disruption of harmony and equipoise and being sensitive to the norms and expectations of others in the group.

Studies of self carried out in Asian contexts all point to self-criticism as a salient component of the self. When answering the Twenty Statements Test Chinese respondents make fewer positive statements about themselves than do their American counterparts (Bond & Cheung, 1983). Ryff, Lee, and Na (1995) also found that Korean respondents were more likely to endorse negative than positive statements about themselves. In contrast, European American respondents showed the opposite pattern.

Stigler, Smith, and Mao (1985) found similar results among Chinese and U.S. elementary school students in their perception of competence. The Chinese students rated their competence lower than did their European American counterparts in the cognitive, physical, and general domains.

The studies of selves in East Asian contexts suggest that being a member in good standing in these cultural places requires not calling attention to the self, deemphasizing the specialness of one's self, and adjusting to the immediate situation of which one is part. Even tasks of individuation, independence and the maintenance of autonomy—social tasks that must be accomplished by people

everywhere—will be grounded in an appreciation and realization of interdependence.

These orientations indicate a cultural mentality deeply at odds with the very practice and methodology of personal self-description and thus with commonly exported social science methods and tasks that require subjects to evaluate and categorize the self (see earlier discussion of the methodological differences between cultural psychology and cross-cultural psychology). Interdependent (or sociocentric) mentalities and practices are distinct from individualistic (or independent or ego-centric) mentalities and practices. When fully considered in their respective cultural contexts, however, these two selfways are equally normal, reasonable, or viable ways of being, although they are associated with patterned or systematic diversity in psychological functioning.

Both types—the individualistic and the interdependent selfways—involve the participation and support of others and are saturated with cultural meanings. The instantiation and realization of individualism is then a type of interdependence and a socially endorsed and constructed cultural practice. As suggested by Vygotsky:

> Every function in the child's development appears twice; first on the social level, and after on the individual level, first between people (interpsychological) and then inside the child (intrapsychological). (Vygotsky, 1987, p. 57)

We have focused on the comparison between European American and East Asian children to highlight divergent selfways. Yet important variations in selfways can also be found within these cultural groups. Harwood and colleagues (Harwood & Miller, 1991; Harwood, Schoelmerich, Ventura-Cook, Schultz, & Wilson, in press) for example, compared Anglo and Puerto Rican mothers living in the United States. They found that both middle- and lower class Anglo mothers, when compared to Puerto Rican mothers, placed significantly greater value on self-confidence and independence and significantly less value on obedience, the capacity for relatedness, and the maintenance of proper demeanor.

Miller and colleagues (1990, 1992a, 1992b) report that the development of autonomy is important in both working-class and middle-class communities in the United States, but that it is fostered differently according to social class. In a study of the co-narration of mothers and toddlers in two communities in the Mid-West they report that middle-class children are accorded speech and author privileges in creating stories about past events. Middle-class mothers are less likely than working-class mothers to challenge the toddlers' versions of reality. Working-class children are also accorded speaker rights—they are, in fact, involved in longer co-narratives than middle-class children, but then they are more often challenged by their mothers and expected to tell the "correct" version of the story rather than their own.

A study by Rogoff et al. (1993) comparing U.S. middle-class and Guatemalan Mayan toddlers finds that autonomy is also important in the socialization of Mayan children and particularly among toddlers who are accorded special privileges and are not expected to conform to the same rules as the older siblings. Older Mayan siblings, however, in contrast to the American children, cooperated interdependently with the toddlers without caregiver intervention, suggesting that development of autonomy among the Mayans is associated with the understanding that one is an interdependent member of the community and is not completely autonomous in the way that infants are allowed to be.

Research from the perspective of cultural psychology challenges some generalizations about self and self-development and significantly strengthens other generalizations. In the next decade, these generalizations likely will result in new paradigms for studying the self. Recent theoretical debates and discussions in the literature from both psychology and anthropology are intended to clarify and specify the general propositions that the self is (a) constituted in interaction with others; (b) collectively constructed through sociocultural participation; and (c) a product of history (see Elder, Ch. 16, this Volume). Each of these propositions reflects an effort to come to terms with a central claim of cultural psychology that in processes of self functioning there is not just a single psychology, but multiple psychologies.

The Self Is Constituted in Interaction with Others

It is an old idea that one cannot be a self by one's self. Although life in the middle-class European American cultural region has highlighted the conceptual self, studies of self in other cultural places underscore the importance of what Neisser (1988, 1991) calls the interpersonal self.

Selves are constituted and develop in interaction with specific others. Individuals become selves within a field of relations with others (Baldwin, 1911; Baldwin & Holmes, 1987; Cooley, 1902; Hallowell, 1955; Ingold, 1991; Rosaldo, 1984; Shweder & LeVine, 1984). Echoing Mead (1934) and reflecting many insights of the early symbolic interactionists, there is a growing appreciation within the self literature of the dynamic, socially constructed nature of the self. An appealing feature of that idea is its potential to bridge the gap between those perspectives that focus primarily on the individual as a cultural learner (Tomasello, Kruger, & Ratner, 1993) and those that focus primarily on the cultural collective of which the individual is an interdependent part (Cole, 1995). It promises to get the person back in the practice and the practice back in the person.

There are focused efforts to understand the mutual constitution of self and other in the development of self, in or just how it is that selves and others make each other up. Once we move out of middle-class European American cultural communities it becomes clear, as noted earlier, that in many parts of the world people prefer crowded living conditions and regard the physical presence of others, especially family members, as absolutely essential for mental health and well-being. Peak (1987), writing about Japan, describes how becoming a person involves learning to appreciate living in human society and learning the pleasures of group life. Similarly, Ochs (1988) reports that Samoans are self-conscious about their need for others to acknowledge them and to sympathize with them. Menon's (1995) detailed interviews with Oriya Hindu women living in extended joint family households make it apparent that in local moral worlds steeped in an ethics of community the idea of living alone and being sane and happy is almost a contradiction in terms (see also Kakar, 1978).

In much European American research on the development of self, others become relevant when selves learn to take the perspectives of these others and get inside their heads (Flavell et al., 1995), or as specific relationships are forged with particular others. It is increasingly evident, however, "others" have a pervasive impact on any person's psychological development in all cultural contexts. Even prior to birth, individuals are immersed in social relations and social activities. From their earliest days, human infants become selves through their engagement in particular, culturally organized settings (Markus et al., in press; Weisner, 1982, 1984, 1987). A growing number of investigators now assume that mutual involvement of self and others is so fundamental to human functioning that others are automatically perceived as relevant to ones sense of self. Gopnik (1993) refers to an innate bridge or intersubjectivity between self and others. Infants seem to be responsive to others' affective expressions, and thus others are immediately expected, implicated, and involved in one's becoming of a self (see also Ingold, 1991).

The Self Develops through Sociocultural Participation

A cultural psychology perspective places considerable emphasis on what Kitayama and colleagues (Kitayama, Markus, Matsumoto, & Norasakkunkit, 1995; Markus et al., in press) have called the collective construction of self. The notion is that selves develop within a dynamic, recursive process in which sociocultural participation in a given cultural system of meanings, practices, and institutions afford characteristic tendencies of the self which further serve to integrate the person into the meanings and practices of a given cultural community (see also Bourdieu, 1972; Giddens, 1984; Martin, Nelson, & Tobach, 1995). This perspective emphasizes that from their earliest moments, selves arise from being a person in particular worlds. From a child's earliest days, partial, incomplete, rudimentary gestures and vocalizations are "infused with specific meanings and significances crucial to enabling the child to become a progressively more competent partner" (Bruner, 1993, p. 532). Children are immediately engaged in the settings of daily life and are subject to the specific normative expectations and the institutional entailments of what Super and Harkness (1986) label a "developmental niche." People always live in culture-specific ways. To live otherwise is impossible.

Super and Harkness's theorizing is yet another example of an attempt to resolve the tension between psychology's excessive view of development as natural growth or an unfolding of abilities in stages and anthropology's excessive view of development as cultural molding or conditioning. Super and Harkness claim that the child's developmental experience is regulated by (a) the settings—physical and social—in which the child lives; (b) the customs of child care and child rearing; and (c) the mentality of the caretakers. These three subsystems are mutually interactive and

function together with other elements of the large culture and environment to constitute a culture-specific child.

The cultural psychology approach to the study of the self does not deny the individuality, idiosyncrasy and uniqueness of self that can be observed within even the most tight-knit and coherent collectives. Children do not become general people, they become particular persons or selves. One of the most significant facts about us, writes Geertz, "may finally be that we all begin with the natural equipment to live a thousand kinds of life but end in the end having lived only one" (1973a, p. 45). Every person participates in combinations of significant cultural settings or niches, which in contemporary American society, could include specific groups such as the family or the workplace, as well as contexts defined by ethnicity, religion, profession, social class, gender, birth cohort, and sexual orientation. Some of the remarkable variation among people results at least in part because people are unlikely to participate in the identical configuration of group memberships. Even those living within similar niches or configurations of cultural contexts will diverge in the specifics of their everyday, symbolically mediated experiences and because prior, innate, received, or temperamental differences in their sense of self, will differentially attend to, seek out, elaborate, and reflect some features of these experiences and not others. Moreover, participation or engagement in the activities of a given cultural setting can assume divergent forms. Cultural participation can be straightforward and unquestioning, resistant, or ironic. Consequently, there is little danger that people of the same sociocultural and historical niches will be clones of one another. Between-group differences do not imply within-group homogeneity.

The Self as a Historical Product

A cultural psychology approach to the development of self has led to a growing appreciation of Bourdieu's idea that the processes of the self are "history turned into nature" (1991, p. 7). Many Western researchers focusing on the self have participated in their discipline long enough now to have noticed that there has been historical change even within the European American cultural zone in the natural and normative self (in the way to be). In the late 1960s and early 1970s, there was a sense of the need to discover one's true, or authentic, self and to get in touch with one's real feelings. In the 1990s there is the need to say "no" not "yes" to experience and to invent or create the proper self. Many current self researchers were themselves raised according to the dictates of Dr. Spock. But as parents they find his prescriptions for producing the good or proper are rigid and inappropriate.

Similarly, American educators note that the requirement that children be happy and feel good about themselves has produced a generation of children with high self-esteem and no basic skills. And programs are currently being developed to raise the educational expectations of American children and to replace an emphasis on positive self-evaluation with an emphasis on building specific skills (Damon, 1995).

General societal imperatives of "the way to be" promulgated by the advertising industry and by the media have a strong effect on practices of nurturing children and on both the lay and scientific conceptions of self. In a comprehensive historical overview of the American self, Cushman (1995, p. 24) argues that to understand the formation of the American self one must understand the interplay between this nation and what it means to be American, between what it means to be an American and what it means to be human, and between the construction of the self and the construction of the country. It is of no small significance to the renewed field of cultural psychology that self researchers are beginning to heed Kessen's claim (1983, pp. 37–38):

> The study of children is not exclusively or even mainly a scientific enterprise in the narrow sense but stretches out toward philosophy and history and demography. If we were to recognize such an expanded definition of child study, we might anticipate a new (science) whose object of study is not the true child or a piece of the true child but the changing diversity of children. (See also Bronfenbrenner, Kessel, Kessen, & White, 1985; Fisher et al., Ch. 19, this Volume; Kessel & Siegel, 1983; Lerner, Ch. 1, this Volume.)

CULTURAL PSYCHOLOGY AND COGNITIVE DEVELOPMENT

To bring out the nature and the implications of a cultural psychological perspective on development, we have been considering some specific topics: interpersonal relations, language and communication, the development of self. We now turn to a fourth and last topic: cognitive development. The general aims remain the same. We wish to continue building a picture of what a cultural psychological perspective involves and how it has been and can be translated into specific research questions. We also wish to bring out the several ways in which a cultural psychological perspective alters our understanding of development (our understanding both of what develops and of the processes by which development takes place).

What does a cultural psychological perspective offer for the analysis of cognitive development? What does its extension to cognitive development add to our general understanding of a cultural psychological approach? To make this double contribution, we begin with some general comments about the nature of cultural psychology, reframing parts of the introduction to this chapter in terms of cognitive studies. We propose that a cultural psychological approach can be defined in terms of a set of distinctive features. We then reexamine a series of dichotomies: thought versus action, mind versus content, head versus heart, persons versus contexts. Various proposals for research emerge. These are related, for instance, to the specific effects of certain kinds of participation in a custom complex or practice, to the connection between the symbolic and behavioral aspects of development, to the significance of "competence" for a sense of self and for membership and identity in a local cultural community, and to ways of making concrete the idea that persons and contexts, cultures and psyches "make each other up."

The final section of the chapter highlights some emerging challenges. How can we take account of the fact that contexts are heterogeneous and historically based? How can a cultural psychological perspective accommodate the increasing emphasis in the cognitive development literature on mind as marked by the presence of innately-given, domain-specific predispositions to make particular distinctions or to draw particular inferences?

Features of a Cultural Psychology Approach

The field of cognitive development has a long history of concern with the significance of social and cultural contexts, a history that is partially captured in this *Handbook* within the chapter by Rogoff and by part of the chapter by Bugental and Goodnow. The field also contains a number of approaches labeled as "cultural psychology."

Valsiner (1994; Ch. 4, this Volume), for example, describes Cole, Shweder and Wertsch as offering three versions of cultural psychology that are especially relevant to the analysis of cognitive development. He also sees his own "co-constructionist" approach as compatible with all three.

What defines a cultural psychological approach? Perhaps the best way to proceed is to define the approach by a set of features, no one of which is sufficient. One cultural psychological approach may differ from another in the degree of emphasis given to each feature and in the ways in which it takes up each feature.

The first feature is really a two-sided goal: the goal of accounting for differences as well as similarities across and within groups. In other words, the search for what is universal, or the assumption of universality, does not dominate the enterprise. Not all forms of diversity and similarity, however, are of equal interest. Those that warrant particular attention by developmentalists are the forms that are used, locally or widely, as markers of maturity, of improvement, of change toward some specifiable end, toward being regarded by others as competent, reasonable, understandable, or a proper male, female, student, child, young person, adult, etc. In effect the forms of diversity and similarity that are of special interest are those that signal development within the norms of particular groups.

A second feature relevant to a cultural psychological approach to cognitive development is a particular assumption about the way development comes about. "Mind" is not seen as evolving from some internally-driven movement toward increasingly sophisticated logical structures or toward greater and greater cognitive capacity. Instead the emphasis falls on a person's involvement in various custom complexes (activities, practices), on the interactions with others that these involve, and on the ways in which custom complexes, activities, and practices contain within themselves the categories, principles, or "mentalities" that are the intellectual resources for becoming a competent member of a group.

The remaining features that define any particular cultural psychological approach have to do with the ways in which those general assumptions are given specific shape. That shape takes first of all the form of re-examining several received dichotomies. The re-examination of dichotomies is a growth industry these days and is far from being unique to analyses of cognitive development or to cultural psychology. A great deal of attention has been given over the past decades to the rethinking of such oppositions as culture/psyche, inside/outside, public/private, male/female, subjective/objective, self/other, and individual/group. The cultural psychology of cognition has given particular attention to some of these dichotomies, those related to thought and action, mind and content, head and heart. Most salient in cultural psychology has been an interest in undoing the overarching contrast between person and context. The aim has been to avoid the common notion of "persons" and "contexts" as separate or independent variables that operate on each other in some one-directional, linear or static X on Y fashion. (Gottlieb, Ch. 5, this Volume; Lerner, Ch. 1, this Volume; Thelen & Smith, Ch. 10, this Volume). The aim instead has been to move toward concepts of interdependence, described in terms of persons and contexts as "creating each other" (Briggs, 1992), as "shaping each other" (Cole, 1990), as "making each other up" (Shweder, 1990), as "co-constructing each other" (Valsiner, 1994; Winegar, 1988; Wozniak, 1993). The specific meanings to those phrases vary and we shall have occasion to examine some of them. The common feature, however, is some representation of the interdependence and mutual influence of person and context.

A fourth feature consists of the proposal to give special attention to some particular forms of interdependence. This consists of concentrating on some particular aspects of practice and some particular aspects of a mentality. To use several phrases from the beginning of this chapter, "the relevant contexts for the realization of 'mind' are the customs, traditions, practices, shared meanings, and perspectives of some self-regulating and self-perpetuating group." These aspects of context, it is proposed, provide "the stuff out of which, by means of which, and in terms of which" there emerge "specific forms of knowing, thinking, feeling, wanting, and doing." The challenge then, as with all concepts of interdependence, is to turn that general concept into specific forms and into researchable questions.

A fifth and last feature to be discussed here involves questions of method. Two general strategies were proposed earlier. One consists of starting from what people do: from common forms of instruction or play, and from common ways of constructing a story or a conversation, solving problems or marking the difference between one social category and another (e.g., the difference between male and female or between bright students and unpromising students). We may then, in ethnographic or experimental fashion, explore the consequences or the correlates of particular modes of participation. Alternately, we may start from some aspect of cognitive functioning (e.g., from a particular understanding of number, biology, or ownership) and ask—again in ethnographic or experimental fashion—what might establish or maintain such forms of mentality. Either approach may involve comparisons not only across cultural groups but also within cultures, with the choice of comparison depending on the questions being asked rather than on the a priori assumption that a contrast between cultures is necessary.

One last general point needs to be made. Earlier, the question was raised as to where a cultural psychological approach fits in relation to other approaches that are also concerned with the interconnections between practices (contexts, activities, settings) and development. We have adopted a definition of cultural psychology based on a particular set of features. We do not, however, see cultural psychology as co-extensive with contextual psychology, if only because the latter covers every feature of context, whereas cultural psychology with its focus on the custom complex is more specialized. We also do not see it as coextensive with cross-cultural psychology, for all the reasons indicated earlier.

That said, we shall nonetheless not ignore what has been offered by cognate approaches to the overall problem of linking contexts and development, and any reader interested in a total picture would do well to read other chapters in this *Handbook* (e.g., chapters by Bugental & Goodnow, Volume 3; by Parke & Buriel, Volume 3; by Rogoff, Volume 2). We will note some of the points emerging from a range of approaches to social or cultural contexts, and then concentrate on what an approach based in cultural psychology adds or could add to these.

Analyzing Cognitive Development and Contexts: Examining Particular Dichotomies

For our current purposes, we single out dichotomies that separate thought from action, from content, from feeling, from values, and from identity, and divide persons (inside) from contexts (outside). We reconceptualize each dichotomy as involving the interconnection of persons and contexts. In the case of each dichotomy, we take up some particular forms of interconnection, with the last section of our discussion reserved for giving specific form to the

general proposal that mentalities and practices make each other up or co-constitute one another.

Thought and Action

The need to examine this dichotomy is a point amply made in an earlier *Handbook* chapter on culture and cognitive development (LCHC, 1983). The term *activity theories* is itself a reminder of the need to regard thought not as some independent director of action but as bound up with action and evolving in its course (Brandstadter, Ch. 14, this Volume). This is the reason for insisting on the custom complex as a central unit of analysis for cultural psychology.

What does a cultural psychological approach add to these earlier analyses? A useful starting point is the proposal that we give special attention to the ways in which individuals participate in the activities or practices of the groups to which they belong. "Participation" refers to the ways in which an individual may take part in a practice: He or she may begin it, end it, join in enthusiastically or reluctantly, pursue it with an active search for help by others or refuse help, work at a self-directed pace or at a pace set by others, leap in at the start with hypotheses or wait until some of the data are in hand, improvise or look first for a "cookbook" procedure, and so on. That type of definition is essentially an expansion of the notion of participation proposed by Lave (1990), and by Rogoff (1990), where the primary reference is to the degree to which an individual operates with guidance or direction from others.

The term practices is used in the sense discussed earlier in connection with the idea of the custom complex: activities that are a repeated, fluent, even habitual part of everyday life (one's own life and the life of others) and that come to be seen as part of a natural or moral order. They are then thought to be right, intelligible, or proper, and are not easily abandoned (cf., Goodnow, 1996; Miller & Goodnow, 1995).

How can we take further the general notion of participation in practices? For that concept to be fully useful, three further steps are called for. First, we need to distinguish among forms of participation, not only because of the need to strengthen the concept but also because of proposals that (a) changes in understanding stem from shifts in the nature of participation (e.g., Fivush, 1993; Lave, 1988; Lave & Wenger, 1991; Miller & Sperry, 1988; Rogoff, 1990, 1995), and (b) one of the many ways practices may be distinguished is in terms of the forms of participation that they invite or allow (e.g., Bourdieu, 1990; Foucault, 1980; Nicolopoulou & Cole, 1993).

An example of the former proposal is the argument that new efforts at understanding are facilitated by sensitively phased guidance that can be reinstated if the new step turns out to be more than can be managed (an argument that Rogoff, 1990, summarizes with the term "guided participation").

An example of the latter proposal is the argument that instructional practices can be distinguished in terms of the kinds of examination that are used for deciding on entry and progression or in terms of the extent to which they allow easy access for all or restrict access to a chosen few (Foucault, 1980). At this point, we note only the need to distinguish among forms of participation. Proposals for meeting the need will emerge as this section proceeds.

Second, we need to recognize that participation in a practice is not a one-person activity. Even on tasks that appear to be carried out in solo fashion (e.g., the apparently solitary struggle with an experimental problem or a school task defined as needing to be done "without help"), the task and the resources provided or denied have been structured by others.

Whenever we start to distinguish forms of participation, then, we are likely to be making relative statements. We usually have in mind, even if implicitly, the extent to which each person contributes, or—a point emphasized by Verdonik and his colleagues—the rights of each person involved to ask the questions or set the pace (Verdonik, Flapan, Schmit, & Weinstock, 1988). Changes in participation mean changes in the way two or more people participate.

In a two-person situation as one person becomes more and more competent, the other can step back. Even if that opportunity is not taken, the knowledge exists on both sides that the possibility is real and *that* reality alters the potential participation of both as well as the relationship. To use Lave's (Lave & Wenger, 1991) phrase, the reference is always to participation within "communities of practice." Changes in what one person does are always related to what others are doing and to the relationship between or among them.

Once pointed out, it is easy to recognize that the participation of one individual is always bound up with the participation of others. To make full use of that proposal, however, research is needed on the ideas people hold about their rights or their obligations to participate in particular ways (Goodnow, 1995; Verdonik et al., 1988). Not everyone has a "voice." Needed also are distinctions among communities of practice (Lave & Wenger, 1991). Participation and ideas about participation, for example, should surely be different in contexts where a shift in competence leads easily to a shift in recognized status, as against contexts where all the competence in the world leaves an individual still subordinate to someone who is less competent than you are but has more seniority.

Third, we need to avoid thinking in terms of one-to-one connections between ideas and forms of participation. Especially when using the research strategy of starting from a practice and from questions about the beliefs, feelings, and values associated with it, it becomes easy to think of these aspects of cognition as linked only to the practices with which we began a particular study. In everyday life, the goals, values, feelings, and pictures of the world we hold are likely to be linked to several practices. Distinctions between males and females, for example, are part of practices related to names, dress, forms of speech, divisions of labor, and space. As noted earlier, it is always an open empirical question whether a mentality generalizes across many practice domains (the Hindu mentality) or is specific to a particular practice domain (the mentality of Hindu sleeping arrangements).

An interesting research question then takes this form: Is there a difference between ideas buttressed by several practices and ideas buttressed by one? That question, together with one possible answer, has in fact already been raised. In investigating why Kwar'ae children, in the Solomon Islands, achieved poorly in school, Watson-Gegeo (1993) came to attribute a large part of the difficulty to the children's perception of school as irrelevant to the significant parts of their lives. That perception, in turn, stemmed from what Watson-Gegeo termed "multilayered" messages. Others in the family who had been to school saw no particular relevance to the Kwar'ae way of life, and warned the child not to expect too much. The curriculum itself, developed for schools in New Zealand, delivered the same message. Anthropomorphic stories about "little red hens" have a certain absurdity for children who, before they begin at school, have been raising chickens for food and have been selling them and other produce in the market. Multilayered messages of any kind, Watson-Gegeo goes on to propose, are especially likely to have particular cognitive consequences. They are likely not only to be attended to but also to be seen as matters of fact with powerful effect, and to be accepted without reflection or question.

Thought and Its Content

Cognitive development has often been thought of in terms of the emergence of some general capacity or of logical structures. These logical structures may then be applied to any content area. Within classical Piagetian theory, the core of what develops consists of logical operations—forms, for example, of logical addition or multiplication—that can eventually be applied with equal facility and skill to any problem regardless of its content. Accompanying that viewpoint has often been the assumption that the natural or proper course of development is toward decontextualization (e.g., Donaldson, 1978). The image of development put forward in classical Piagetian theory is one of directional change in which the mind of the child is said to progress from early intuitive, concrete, undifferentiated, egocentric, context-bound thinking to later self-reflective, abstract, differentiated, decentered (i.e., objective) generalized thinking.

Accompanying the classical Piagetian approach has been a particular view with regard to methods: the notion that one may tap into the "pure core" of cognition by way of abstract tasks or hypothetical vignettes. That view of methods has been justified on the grounds that the content of any task is of minor concern compared to the logical operation it involves and/or that a task of highly familiar content (such as one will find in any "custom complex") may fail to reveal the subject's own logical structures. The methods chosen are then unlikely to include variations deliberately chosen to bring out the impact of cultural salience, familiarity, relevance, or task definition. Moreover, the assumption will usually be made that any mature or right-thinking person will regard two or more tasks as the same if the logical operations called for are the same, regardless of any other aspect of difference. The possibility that tasks might reasonably or legitimately be grouped or framed in any other way then rarely comes to mind (Newman, Griffin, & Cole, 1989).

This type of position has been challenged on several sides. It has been pointed out, for example, that we tend to develop expertise in specific content areas (Chi & Koeske, 1983). It has also been pointed out that we seem biologically predisposed to domain specificity, in the sense that—prior to any experience—we are likely to attend to some events rather than others and to make some inferences

rather than others (Keil, Ch. 7, this Volume; Spelke & Newport, Ch. 6, this Volume). Such cognitive effects have given rise in the minds of some theorists to the notion that we come into life already equipped with a predisposition to acquire naive physics, biology, or psychology (e.g., Carey, 1985; Keil, 1981, Ch. 7, this Volume; Spelke & Newport, Ch. 6, this Volume; Wellman & Gelman, 1992).

From scholars in cultural psychology has come a further proposal with regard to domain specificity. We would do well, the argument runs, to regard ways of thinking, learning, and problem solving as always linked to the specific occasions of their use and/or specific occasions of their acquisition. The strong form of this proposal argues for a critical review of terms such as generalization, transfer, or decontextualization. The strong proposal rejects the assumption that processes of this type are a natural mark of progressive development and calls for the study of change as a process of recontextualization or reframing rather than decontextualization (e.g., Walkerdine, 1988). The less strong forms propose that skills and understandings always develop from the activities in which people engage. Children do not develop a general skill such as "reading" or "arithmetic." Instead they develop the specific reading skills or the specific numerical skills that are appropriate for the occasions when they use reading or make calculations (e.g., Carraher, Carraher, & Schliemann, 1985; Scribner & Cole, 1981). They may be able to draw on these skills in other situations, but the original development is to meet particular demands, and the quality of the understanding or the skill developed is likely to always reflect the occasions of learning.

Both the strong and the less strong versions of the general proposal have been outlined in an earlier *Handbook* chapter (LCHC, 1983). Since the publication of that chapter, there has been added a considerable body of research on the "situated" nature of understanding. Research on one aspect of cognition alone—the use and understanding of number procedures—has yielded an extensive set of studies linking that aspect of development to the specific demands of activities such as cooking, selling candy or lottery tickets on the street, being a bookmaker, becoming a tailor, and learning to navigate (for some summaries and examples, see Ceci, 1993; Chaiklin & Lave, 1993; Nunes, 1995; Saxe, 1991).

What might now be added to this broad discussion? One particular addition has to do with the value of avoiding any sharp dichotomy between situated and generalized knowledge. We would ask instead about the circumstances under which repeated participation in a procedure gives rise to knowledge that is more versus less strongly bound to the original learning situation. A relevant condition now emerging is the extent to which the learner encounters prescriptive procedures ("follow these steps precisely") or the opportunity and the invitation to observe and experiment. That is, the condition emphasized by Inagaki (1990) and Hatano & Inagaki (1992) in an analysis of the extent to which preschool children understand animal biology as a result of two kinds of participation in the practice of raising pets: one in a preschool setting, the other at home. It turns out that the home experience results in greater understanding of questions about the significance of food for animal health or survival, for both the animals raised and other animals, too. The difference in level of understanding can be traced to the greater opportunity at home to vary raising procedures—by design, by accident, or by forgetting—and to observe the consequences. In contrast, the preschool setting emphasized efficiency, a careful repetition of the same procedures, and a nonexperimental attitude.

In effect, a critical condition influencing whether understanding is highly situated may be the nature of participation: the extent to which what one does is specified by others, with little opportunity for spontaneous experimentation and with the implication (nothing ventured, nothing lost) that disaster may follow if one departs from the prescribed ways. Here then is a break from any simple conceptual opposition between understanding as always situated and learning as inevitably moving toward decontextualization. Here also is the pinpointing of a difference in forms of participation that can be linked to a specific difference in the kind of understanding that develops.

Following prescriptive procedures is the usual form of participation in school mathematics within the United States, and pupils come readily to feel that they can succeed (and avoid wild errors) only by following the exact steps provided without attempts at improvisation, shortcuts, or the understanding of principles (Stodolsky, 1988). That they develop this view is not surprising, Stodolsky notes, because teachers have been observed to vary their use of prescriptive procedures when they shift from teaching mathematics to teaching social studies. In the classrooms observed, mathematics was taught with rules that specified exactly how to proceed. In contrast, social studies was taught by projects, with some leeway available for

the problem chosen, the procedures used, and the answer achieved.

Does everything depend then on differences in the overt form of repeated participation? As noted earlier in the discussion of cultural participation and the social formation of the self, even in the face of what may seem to be the same kind of participation, individual differences may emerge. For example, from the repeated experience of cooking (Hatano & Inagaki, 1992), some cooks may emerge with what Hatano and Inagaki (1986) term "routine expertise." The individual displays increasing fluency and skill with the same procedures. Others emerge with "adaptive expertise," with an ability and a readiness to improvise, to depart from "cookbook" procedures. The difference may reflect an original difference in goals or in the identification of oneself as interested in becoming a particular kind of expert: the kind of chef who creates dishes that are a "chef's specialty" or—to take a recently seen menu item—"a la modo mio." The variations in kinds of expertise, however, pinpoint the need to consider more than the overt forms of participation that are provided by particular practices and to keep in mind the contributions of individual skills and individual intentions.

Thought and Feeling

Analyses of cognitive development often leave the impression of thought regarded as an entity in itself, with motives and emotions seen as providing the engine needed to start or sustain thinking (see Shweder, 1992, for a critique). This two-boxes or separate-state notion is now being set against a view of thinking, feeling, and acting as inseparable components. That is found in analyses of attitudes (e.g., Eagley & Chaiken, 1993) and of emotion (e.g., Campos, Campos, & Barrett, 1989; Kitayama & Markus, 1994).

To this general debate and to its implications for development, an approach in terms of cultural psychology adds the need to link cognitive performances to questions both of values and of identity, and to ask how particular linkages arise in the course of various kinds of participation in particular cultural practices.

The Emergence of Cognitive Values

The adult world contains many cognitive values (Goodnow, 1990a, 1990b). Some areas of knowledge, for example, are described as basics whereas others are described as extras or frills. Some problems are labeled as significant, others are relegated to the category of trivial pursuits. Some ways of talking about a problem are privileged (Wertsch, 1991) and are awarded a status that exceeds their effectiveness in solving the problem. The words mystical or religious are often used as epithets. The word science is often used as an honorific label and the "voice of science," for example, with references to statistics or complex hypothetical arguments, is often privileged in discussions that range in content from whether or not nuclear bombs should be banned to how one should answer teachers' requests to describe an object (Wertsch, 1985, 1991).

What kinds of experience or participation encourage the development of particular values or forms of privilege? We know that definitions of value and forms of privilege vary among cultural groups (e.g., Goodnow, 1976; Lucy, 1992a, 1992b). What is less clear, however, is how these aspects of cognition emerge.

The richest set of examples to date comes from Wertsch (1991) in his analysis of the behavior of teachers. Even in periods of show-and-tell, he points out, preference is given by teachers to comments on the abstract properties of an object brought for display. For a piece of lava displayed at show-and-tell, the teacher actively promoted comments on its weight, texture, and physical origin by asking questions and awarding approval as "good" or "interesting." Set aside by the teacher—not responded to—was the child's offering of a more personal history about who gave the lava to the child as a present, how it had been looked after and not lost, and so on. In time, Wertsch (1991) observes, children learn that if they want to participate in ways that will gain attention or praise, they must do so in ways that teachers privilege. In time also, the members of a class come to judge each other's performances in ways that resemble those used by teachers. They will regard as "good" those statements that are heavily laced with scientific terms, even when the argument strikes adults as illogical.

The same type of account is offered by researchers observing the way teachers respond to the stories that children offer during "storytelling time." Only certain kinds of stories are rewarded the accolade of "good." Children accustomed to other forms of story construction, and who enter school already skilled in that form, come to realize that approved participation calls for recognizing and then producing the approved form (Heath, 1983; Michaels, 1991). They may then choose to "convert," to comply on the surface, or to move toward nonparticipation in class.

Linking Forms of Thought to Identity

The importance of considering the link between thought and identity becomes apparent in analyzing forms of participation and of nonparticipation (withdrawal, rebellion). On the one hand, participating in particular activities and in particular ways may be necessary to be regarded as a particular kind of person. Certain ways of approaching arithmetic problems (e.g., by translation into a paper-and-pencil task and following school algorithms or by translation into a familiar practical task) come to be interpreted as signs that one is an "educated" versus a "practical" person. That interpretation is not only made by others. It becomes also a part of a person's self-image and automatically influences the ways in which any new problem is approached, even when alternative approaches are within one's repertoire (Nunes, 1995). In related fashion, the shift from one Japanese orthography to another—from *kana* syllabaries to *kanji-kana* combinations—is largely justified on the grounds that a truly educated person uses the second, more complex system (Hatano, 1995). That particular link to identity is of special interest because the second system confers no obvious functional advantages. Most foreigners, for example, stop with the first system. In addition, Japanese children are skilled readers of *kana* before they make the shift to the second system. The link to identity or the desire to be regarded as intellectually mature, Hatano (1995) proposes, becomes the critical inducement for making the major additional effort. The analysis of Japanese orthography suggests that a useful research strategy consists of turning to occasions where the motive for sustained, effortful participation is a perceived link between performance and personal or social identity.

The opposite approach, but again one that offers useful directions for research, consists of analyzing occasions of nonparticipation. Here again, links to identity stand out. Mathematics, for example, may be avoided by females because it is categorized as a "boys' subject" (Parsons & Kaczala, 1982). Science may be avoided because it is a sign that one has become a "burnout," no longer resisting or rebelling against the pressures of family and school (Eckert, 1991). Effort of any kind in school may be avoided because it indicates that one is no longer one of "the lads" (Willis, 1977). All told, there are good grounds for taking further the general proposal that a great deal of what happens in classrooms or testing situations has as much to do with maintaining or protecting one's identity as it has to do with the acquisition of academic skills (McDermott, Cole, & Hood, 1978).

Up to this point, an approach based in cultural psychology leads to a concern about the link between forms of participation and particular aspects of identity—social identity or personal identity. What else might this approach lead to? Following are three suggestions for future research.

First, the occasions of particular interest may be those where participation threatens identity. A case study of a child with reading difficulties provides an example (Cole & Traupmann, 1981). For this child, a cooking class—where a partner could do the reading while the child could substitute other useful forms of participation—allowed the child to present an image of competence in a cultural community that places high value on personal success and accomplishment is highly valued. In contrast, a spelling bee, where participation required unavoidably and publicly producing a prescribed answer without help, did not sustain that image and was a source of negative feeling for both the child and the class. For any participation, then, it is worthwhile to consider what forms of participation offer particular opportunities or threats for the presentation of oneself as possessing the prized virtues of that cultural community (e.g., competence, deferential behavior and respectful restraint, altruistic sympathy). Worth asking also is the question why are some forms of participation structured in ways that narrow or enlarge those opportunities? Why, for example, to take a large question from Foucault (1980), are examinations structured in some ways rather than others? What goals, values, and pictures of the world are presupposed and implied by that choice?

Second, the occasions of particular interest may be those where people need to manage a double identity. A case in point is the difficult task in some classes of appearing to be one of a "cool" peer group and at the same time impressing the teacher with one's store of information and smartness (Cazden, 1993). A statement such as "La Paz ain't the capital of Peru, Miss," Cazden notes, meets the double aim.

Corsaro (1992) provides some further examples. Preschoolers who wish to appear to be rule-following to their teachers but also to gain the approval of their peers find ways to bend the nursery-school rules. They engage, for example, in no open violation of the rule that toys may not be brought from home to school. Instead, they carry small toys in their pockets and use them to solicit a friend's participation in a shared game. Or, preschoolers may break the rule that certain objects may not be moved from their assigned place. They do so, however, by embedding the movement of the object within a game that teachers, on their own standards, must label as pleasingly imaginative and tolerate for at least a short time. In each such case, Corsaro (1992) observes, preschoolers maintain their image to teachers as reasonable children but gain favor with their peers by their adroit infractions of the teachers' rules.

Also particularly intriguing may be those occasions that lead to innovation. Innovations can be realized with resources that are available in the culture but are not extensively used by a majority of its members, as in the case of an ethnic or local food's gaining popularity. Alternatively, the new knowledge can be produced through nonconventional individual construction based on the database the culture provides, as with the invention of new cuisine by expert chefs (Hatano & Inagaki, 1986). In either case, those possessing a marginal identity may be more likely to initiate changes in practices than those who have fully participated in the consensus-sensitive community of culture of the cultural community. In a sense, some cultures permit or even encourage an individual to hold a marginal identity, so that he or she can generate new knowledge that helps the culture to survive and prosper.

Third, the occasions of particular interest may be those where the identities involved are those of learner or teacher. The identity of pupil or learner, for example, calls for adopting certain forms of participation: learning how and when to ask or answer questions (Mehan, 1979), when and how to place oneself in a position where one may watch without being officially part of the action (e.g., Lave & Wenger, 1991; Rogoff, Mistry, Goncu, & Mosier, 1993).

In any cultural group, children need to learn the proper forms. Mayan children, for example, come to know at an early age that the proper way to learn is by watching. They spend a lot of time observing adults' activities, while drawing little attention to themselves. In contrast, children in the United States come to know at an early age that interruptions are acceptable, especially if one has a good question, and that drawing attention to oneself ("look at what I'm doing") is tolerable, provided that the frequency is within certain limits (Rogoff et al., 1993). Children in European American cultural groups also learn that there are occasions when the best opportunities for learning are by way of unobtrusive eavesdropping or watching. But these seem likely to be occasions of a particular kind; the content area—sex, mortality—seems most often what European American parents think children should not know or not know officially at an early age. Knowledge of those topics, of course, is not withheld from children in all cultural communities. At this point, then, it would be of interest to check directly on the metaknowledge that children in different cultural communities display with regard to tolerated and approved ways of learning in various content areas: ways that are in keeping with the identity of "child" or with the identity of being a good learner.

Persons and Contexts

Studies of development have long included the argument that any complete account of how development takes place will need to consider contributions both from individuals and from the social contexts in which they live. At times, that double need may appear to be forgotten. Sometimes, an emphasis on instruction seems to treat the individual as a blank slate or a sponge that needs only to have information presented in absorbable amounts. There are also times when an emphasis on people as actively making sense of their world, or as selecting their environments, seems to treat the outside world as essentially blank, neutral, or unproblematic, sidelining the questions: What is there to make sense of? What qualities of the database—of the symbolic and behavioral inheritance of the cultural community—influence the nature of any construction?

In general terms, it is necessary to consider the contributions of both individuals and of practices, not only to the development of individuals but also to each other. How can that general proposal be translated into more specific forms? That question, in turn, hinges on the ways in which we define individuals and contexts, and on the feasibility of mapping these definitions on to one another.

One possibility is to begin, for example, with a view of individuals as actively constructing and testing hypotheses about the nature of the world: a view long favored in analyses of cognitive development. What properties of practices might be relevant to this kind of contribution from individuals? Two seem especially relevant. One is the extent to which practices provide "prepackaged" constructions (Shweder, 1982). Many categories have already been constructed by others and are available for use, with the packaging implied either by way of names or by the way objects

are used (e.g., I can convey the notion that something is "fragile" by either method or by combining them). A second property is the extent to which some particular constructions are not only available but are also actively promoted by others. The individual does not operate in a "free-market" world (Goodnow, 1990a, 1990b; Goodnow, Knight, & Cashmore, 1985). Instead, the social world offers constraints and rewards, nudging or channeling constructions in some directions rather than others (Hatano, 1990; Shweder, 1984; Valsiner, 1994).

The interesting research question then becomes: What are the content areas where the individual can operate freely as against those where prepackaging or channeling is more pronounced? People may, for instance, be left to develop their own sense of what objects weigh. They are less likely to be left to develop their own notions of what it means to be "moral," "just," "honest," or "selfish" (Goodnow et al., 1985). The degrees of freedom, to extend some proposals from analyses to actions, seem likely to be least in areas where the cost of error is high, either because a serious social rule is broken (D'Andrade, 1984), because of economic cost (Greenfield & Lave, 1982), or because social harmony and coordination depend on seeing the world in the same terms.

That kind of argument, however, stops at pointing out some interesting aspects of practice that influence our understanding of how individual constructions may proceed. There is as yet no proposal for mutual influence or for anything like an interconnection that could be described as "mutual creation," "co-construction," "co-constitution," or "making each other up." For that step, further proposals are needed.

Suppose, for example, that individuals always transform the packaged messages or categories that they encounter. They inevitably reinterpret. Because their experiences with what appears to be the same situation are never identical, they always give new meanings—new semantic or affective overtones—to the events or the words they encounter. Suppose also that individuals feed these reinterpretations or new shadings back into the groups they belong to, so that they become part of public life, available for use in the interpretations or constructions that other individuals proceed to make. At this point, a spiral of mutual influences may begin. In Valsiner's (1994) terms, we now have a process of co-construction, in which "personal culture" (individual meanings) and "collective culture" (the received interpretations available from the ancestral past) are constantly intertwined.

That proposal still appears to be highly abstract, and an analysis of social categories by the social psychologist Tajfel (1981) can serve to anchor it. Assigned social categories may have negative overtones and be damaging to the individual's sense of personal value. To be categorized as "gay," "queer," "black," "conservative," "a housewife," "a feminist," or a "soft scientist" may—at particular points of history—have negative overtones. For motivational reasons (in Tajfel's account of social and personal identity, everyone seeks to maintain a sense of personal worth), the individual now can choose between two courses of action: to "pass" as a member of a more valued social category, leaving the usual meanings and overtones unchanged, or to redefine the meaning assigned to a particular social category.

It is possible to alter the implications of a term, often by qualifying a label or changing a name so that the overtones are more positive; for example, "gay pride," "gray panthers," or "homemakers." Conservative parties may be renamed "Liberal Parties" or "Progress Parties." We may keep the old name but insist on the right to define its meanings, claiming—as the group most directly involved—the right to use and define such terms as "queer" or "African" any way we want. The impetus behind such moves is more one of identity and self-esteem than of inevitable cognitive transformation. The transformations begin, however, with an individual's reinterpretation of an experienced category and end with that reinterpretation becoming part of what others experience, thereby altering the meanings available for the next round of interpretations.

A second example comes from Kulick's (1992) analysis of how a native language came to disappear from one generation to the next. The language in question was regarded by the adults within a group in New Guinea as a sign of their identity. Nonetheless, for several reasons the children no longer spoke the language. Language socialization was predominantly left to older siblings. The older siblings were now in school, and schools promoted the use of a national language, "pidgin." This much in itself might not have been sufficient to promote the change. Pidgin, however, came to be regarded as the language to be used for important matters, and children perceived the local language as relevant only to domestic or trivial issues. According to Kulick, a group identity remained, but the shared definition across its members, which the older members now had to acknowledge

and use, was more in terms of a place of origin than a local language. The redefinition initiated by one subgroup—the children already in school—altered the definitions available for another (in this case, the children they were teaching to speak), and in time new meanings became available that the whole group began to share.

Although both of these examples come from outside developmental studies, they anchor a concept of interconnection that may otherwise be difficult to pin down. They also provide a base for asking: What new research strategies might then be useful for the analysis of cognitive development? The interesting occasions to watch for, we suggest, are likely to be those where a meaning or a label sits uncomfortably with a sense of value. Interesting occasions also may involve some process of diffusion or changes in meaning over time, either within a peer group or a family, either spontaneously or as the result of a deliberately introduced new meaning. Those occasions may encompass periods of social or political change where, for example, history is reinterpreted. They may also include experience related to the introduction of new terms or new meanings for old terms. In all cases, however, we should look for the ways in which changes of meaning or of practice spread back and forth among individuals within a group.

New Challenges: Shifts in the Definition of Cognitive Development

In keeping with cultural psychology's theory of mind, we have proceeded thus far as if at least some properties of mind were general in nature: the power of representation and intentionality, the power to know, want, feel, value, and decide, and a general interest in active construction, and a general interest in maintaining a sense of personal worth. As is apparent from the earlier discussion of the symbolic mediation of experience many cultural psychologists would add a further general aspect—the interest in being able to communicate with others. This property gives rise to a preference for interpretations of events that enable us to feel comfortable with others or to feel that we are understood by them (e.g., Mugny & Carugati, 1989).

So far, also, we have repeatedly cautioned against proceeding as if practices or contexts were of a single kind. The degree of thematic integration or coherency of a cultural mentality is something to be discovered, not assumed, as has been discovered in research on individualism and the independent versus the interdependent self. Individuals may be members of a group or a culture, but the events to which they are exposed are not always symbolically mediated in a coherent way and in some cases may be quite ambiguous. Again the interpretive power of a symbol system and the degree of coherency of a cultural mentality is something to investigate, not to presume.

Changing Views of Contexts

To complete this section on cognitive development, we consider the question: What happens to the analysis of interconnections as we move toward more complex views of both mentalities and practices (or contexts)? One important reconceptualization consists of the recognition that any context is heterogeneous. As noted earlier in our discussion of the cultural psychology of the self, any society is made up of many social groups, with people belonging to more than one (a point emphasized by Parke & Buriel, Volume 3). That diversity in turn helps enhance the likelihood (present even within a single group) that people will encounter more than one view of events, more than one view of religion, of politics, of children, of achievement, or of schooling. The description of a cultural context then calls for description in terms of the extent to which alternative viewpoints are in competition with one another and of the ways in which particular viewpoints are distributed throughout a population (How far is there consensus? Who holds what view? How much tolerance do the holders of one viewpoint have for those who hold other views?).

This orientation toward the analysis of cultural communities is widespread within anthropology (e.g., D'Andrade & Strauss, 1992; Romney, Weller, & Batchelder, 1986). What are its implications for interconnections between practices and cognitive development? At the least, accounts of development now need to look at the ways in which children become aware of alternatives and come to endorse some but discount others. That process may be actively brought into play by parents as they seek to protect their children from competing viewpoints or prepare them for inevitable encounters with "wrong ideas" and "bad influences" (Goodnow, in press). In addition, children acquire not only general intersubjectivity but also a sense of being most at ease with, and most able to communicate with, some particular others.

Two statuses that exist in any culture—"the old" and "the new"—provide an example of how heterogeneity

within a society may be linked to cognitive change. Analyses of culture contain many statements to the effect that contexts are "historically based" (for a thorough statement of this position, see Tulviste, 1991). Linking history to individual development, however, is a step less often taken. For that step, we take an argument from Wertsch (1991), combining it with some statements from Kristeva (1980) (Bakhtin is an important base for both Kristeva and Wertsch). The argument runs as follows:

1. The past provides a set of "texts," a warehouse of stories or interpretations.

2. In the course of development, we are encouraged to take a particular stance toward the texts of the past that may range from respectful repetition to scorn and parody. We may be encouraged, for example, to regard everything from the past as something to be actively destroyed, as in China's "cultural revolution," or to be looked at with suspicion as the product and the story of "dead white males" or of some despicable bourgeoisie.

3. Each generation may contribute a new text or a new interpretation, drawing from the warehouse and in the process transforming what is withdrawn. Each generation may also rediscover what has been forgotten and change the stance taken toward the past. The classic example of that kind of development is probably the rediscovery of stories told by or about women, and the new awareness of history as containing women. That kind of development—resulting in a change, subtle or radical, in the way one perceives one's self and the social world—can take place at any part of the life span.

Changing Views of Cognitive Development

Recent analyses of cognitive development contain at least three theoretical moves that alter the links perceived between mind and aspects of practice (or context). One is a move toward describing what is "in mind" by reference to the extent to which an idea has been established. This move distinguishes between ideas in the early stages of establishment from those that have been well consolidated.

The second is a move toward dividing cognitive activity in terms of the phase of processing that is most strongly involved (e.g., monitoring, encoding, rehearsing).

The third is a move toward regarding mind as modular or "domain-specific." In essence, this is the proposal that humans are endowed with innate predispositions to attend to specific stimuli or to make specific inferences.

For each of these theoretical shifts, there are some opening hypotheses about the nature of interconnections with social practices. With respect to stages in the establishment of an idea, it has been proposed that information consistent with the idea may be most readily sought or attended to in the early stages. In contrast, information that runs counter to the idea may be of most benefit after consolidation, when the individual can afford to consider alternatives without risking confusion and may welcome the breath of novelty (e.g., Azmitia & Perlmutter, 1989; Phelps & Damon, 1989; Ruble & Seidman, in press).

For information processing, a series of experimental studies with adults has led to the proposal that the current consensus in a group, consensus especially about the affective significance of holding a certain viewpoint, has particular effects on the likelihood that people will continue to monitor events for the extent to which this viewpoint is being respected or questioned (Frijda & Mesquita, 1994). That very alertness on the part of individuals (e.g., alertness to the observance of a rule) may then be seen as feeding back into the nature of a practice, helping to maintain the agreed-on significance of the rule.

The theoretical shift that has perhaps received the most prominence in the literature has to do with domain-specific theories of mind (e.g., Hirschfeld & Gelman, 1994). How are we to connect the cultural psychology emphasis on participation in practice with a view of mind as being inherently predisposed to distinguish between animate and inanimate objects or to make particular inferences about the cause of illness? That kind of question is recognized as pressing and as still very much open (e.g., Cole, 1992; Fischer & Bidell, Ch. 9, this Volume; Hatano, 1993; Overton, Ch. 3, this Volume; Thelen & Smith, Ch. 10, this Volume).

It is worth reiterating that from the viewpoint of cultural psychology, cultural learning is conceptualized as the refashioning of what is inherited, instinctual, prior, built in, or given from the deep past (Shweder & Sullivan, 1993). Issues that remain open, however, are questions such as these: What precisely is given from the deep past and how is it transformed developmentally? Do we come into the world with a plethora or overabundance of specific and contradictory propensities, some of which are selected for cultural elaboration and others suppressed? Do we come into the world with only a few specific propensities (e.g., a sucking reflex), which are then generalized? Or do we come into the world with a few highly general propensities (e.g., a tendency to categorize and treat like cases alike and different cases differently) which are then specified and given character in the course of development? Does development take the form of enriching innate ideas or qualitatively changing them (e.g., Carey & Spelke, 1994)? Or, are those predispositions eventually replaced by acquired knowledge, much of which is cultural in origin and has been learned from other people (D'Andrade, 1981)?

A popular view in this area is the proposal that innate constraints have both restricting as well as facilitating effects. As Karmiloff-Smith (1992) notes, the constraints may "potentiate learning by limiting the hypotheses entertained" (p. 11). They may also place limits on what is readily learnable. What then happens, if what is to be learned is not in line with the ideas with which we start? One possibility is that these innate constraints are so skeletal (Gelman, 1990) that they always have to be complemented by sociocultural constraints. Another possibility is that the innate constraints are hard to violate but only until rich knowledge is acquired through cultural learning.

A further proposal with regard to innately given cognitive states and cultural learning starts from the argument that innate ideas may not be of equal strength. They may be differentiated in terms of the amount of cultural preparation or tutoring needed to take them further or to change them (Geary, 1995; Hatano, 1990). In addition, the ideas with which children start may be instantiated or elaborated in different ways in different cultures. If innately given distinctions between animate and inanimate objects are all that matters, for example, then children in various cultural groups should all make the same distinctions. As it turns out, children in three cultural groups—from Israel, Japan, and the United States—do make many of the same distinctions. Israeli children, however, tend to be underinclusive in their categorization of living species, separating out plants. Japanese children, on the other hand, tend to be overinclusive. The difference, it has been proposed, reflects the presence of different narratives in particular cultures. Japanese culture contains a number of well-rehearsed stories that encourage the perception of many inanimate objects as possessing life. In turn, Israeli culture contains a well-known Biblical passage in which plants are described as created to provide food for animals, birds, and insects (Hatano et al., 1993; Stavy & Wax, 1989).

Innately given categories, the results suggest, serve as a base set for cognitive development but that base can be modified or elaborated by the categories that a culture provides. In future research in communities where the prevailing cultural categories and narratives seem counterintuitive to Western researchers, cultural psychologists are likely to turn up numerous modifications or transformations of other natural kinds (Keil, 1981) now known to be present early in life.

The narrative imagination is a powerful instrument for reframing perceptual categories and rethinking those of our own "natural" inferences that are no longer intuitively obvious in other cultural worlds. In a sense, it is the human imagination and its astonishing yet livable productions that the study of cultural psychology is all about.

CONCLUSION

It is the hope of all those who welcome the return of cultural psychology as a vibrant research enterprise that more and more social scientists from various home disciplines (psychology, anthropology, linguistics, sociology) will become developmental experts on the psychological functioning of members of particular cultural communities around the world. Only then will the many questions raised in this chapter begin to be answered. Only then will the abstract pluralistic idea of "one mind, many mentalities" become substantial and concrete, and thereby come fully to life. It is when another culture's taken-for-granted categories appear to us to be counter-intuitive, or out of line with what we observe as present early in life, that we are most likely to experience the need to rethink our sense of what is "natural."

ACKNOWLEDGMENTS

We are grateful to Diana Colbert of SSRC and Katia Mitova of the University of Chicago who contributed in innumerable and invaluable ways to the completion of this manuscript. We express our heartfelt gratitude to Frank Kessel of SSRC for his substantive and collegial contributions not only to this chapter but to the various activities of the Committee on Culture, Health, and Human Development over the past six years. The skill, balance, and good cheer with which he has shepherded the Committee's activities are deeply appreciated.

REFERENCES

Abbott, S. (1992). Holding on and pushing away: Comparative perspectives on an eastern Kentucky child-rearing practice. *Ethos, 1,* 33–65.

Ainsworth, M. D. S. (1967). *Infancy in Uganda.* Baltimore: Johns Hopkins University Press.

Ainsworth, M. D. S., Blehar, M. C., Waters, E., & Wall, S. (1978). *Patterns of attachment: A psychological study of the Strange Situation.* Hillsdale, NJ: Erlbaum.

Allport, G. W. (1937). *Personality: A psychological interpretation.* New York: Holt.

Ames, R. T., Dissanayake, W., & Kasulis, T. P. (1994). *Self as person in Asian theory and practice.* Albany: State University of New York Press.

Azmitia, M., & Perlmutter, M. (1989). Social influences on children's cognition: State of the art and future directions. In H. Reese (Ed.), *The study of emotional development and emotion regulation.*

Azuma, H., Kashiwagi, K., & Hess, R. D. (1981). *The influence of attitude and behavior upon the child's intellectual development.* Tokyo: University of Tokyo Press.

Bachnik, J. M. (1994). Introduction: Uchi/soto: Challenging our conceptualizations of self, social order, and language. In J. M. Bachnik & C. J. Q. Jr. (Eds.), *Situated meaning.* Princeton, NJ: Princeton University Press.

Bachnik, J. M., & C. J. Q. Jr. (Eds.). (1994). *Situated meaning.* Princeton, NJ: Princeton University Press.

Bakhtin, M. M. (1981). *The dialogic imagination.* Austin: University of Texas Press.

Bakhtin, M. M. (1986). *Speech genres and other late essays.* Austin: University of Texas Press.

Baldwin, J. M. (1911). *The individual and society.* Boston: Boston Press.

Baldwin, M. W., & Holmes, J. G. (1987). Salient private audiences and awareness of the self. *Journal of Personality and Social Psychology, 52,* 1087–1098.

Banaji, M., & Prentice, D. (1994). The self in social contexts. *Annual Review of Psychology, 45,* 297–332.

Basso, K. H. (1984). Stalking with stories: Names, places, and moral narratives among the Western Apache. In E. M. Bruner

& S. Plattner (Eds.), *Text, play and story: The construction and reconstruction of self and society* (pp. 19–55). Washington, DC: American Ethnological Society.

Bauman, R. (1983). *Let your words be few.* Prospect Heights, IL: Waveland Press.

Bauman, R., & Briggs, C. L. (1990). Poetics and performance as critical perspectives on language and social life. *Annual Review of Anthropology, 19,* 59–88.

Bauman, R., & Sherzer, J. (Eds.). (1989). *Explorations in the ethnography of speaking* (2nd ed.). New York: Cambridge University Press.

Baumeister, R. F. (1987). How the self became a problem: A psychological review of historical research. *Journal of Personality and Social Psychology, 52,* 163–176.

Bellah, R. N., Madsen, R., Sullivan, W. M., Swidler, A., & Tipton, S. M. (1985). *Habits of the heart: Individualism and commitment in American life.* New York: Harper & Row.

Benedict, R. (1934). *Patterns of culture.* New York: Houghton Mifflin.

Berlin, I. (1976). *Vico and Herder.* London: Hogarth Press.

Berry, J. W., Poortinga, Y. H., Segall, M. H., & Dasen, P. R. (1992). *Cross-cultural psychology: Research and applications.* Cambridge, England: Cambridge University Press.

Bledsoe, C. (1989). Strategies of child-fosterage among Mende grannies in Sierra Leone. In R. J. Lesthaeghe (Ed.), *Reproduction and social organization in sub-Saharan Africa.* Berkeley: University of California Press.

Bledsoe, C. (1990). No success without struggle: Social mobility and hardship for foster children in Sierra Leone. *Man, 25,* 70–88.

Boesch, E. E. (1991). *Symbolic action theory and cultural psychology.* New York: Springer-Verlag.

Bond, M. H., & Cheung, T. S. (1983). College students' spontaneous self-concept: The effect of culture among respondents in Hong Kong, Japan, and the United States. *Journal of Cross-Cultural Psychology, 14,* 153–171.

Bornstein, M. H., Azuma, H., Tamis-LeMonda, C. S., & Ogino, M. (1990). Mother and infant activity and interaction in Japan and in the United States: I. A comparative macroanalysis of naturalistic exchanges. *International Journal of Behavioral Development, 13*(3), 267–287.

Bourdieu, P. (1972). *Outline of a theory of practice.* Cambridge, England: Cambridge University Press.

Bourdieu, P. (1990). *A logic of practice.* Stanford, CA: Stanford University Press.

Bourdieu, P. (1991). *Language and symbolic power.* Cambridge, MA: Harvard University Press.

Bracken, B. A. (1996). Clinical applications of a context-dependent, multidimensional model of self-concept. In B. Bracken (Ed.), *Handbook of self concept.* New York: Wiley.

Brazelton, T. B. (1990). Parent-infant co-sleeping revisited. *Ab Initio: An International Newsletter for Professionals Working with Infants and Their Families, 1,* 1, 7.

Briggs, C. L. (1986). *Learning how to ask: A sociolinguistic appraisal of the role of the interview in social science research.* New York: Cambridge University Press.

Briggs, J. L. (1992). Mazes of meaning: How a child and a culture create each other. In W. A. Corsaro & P. J. Miller (Eds.), *Interpretive approaches to childhood socialization* (pp. 25–50). San Francisco: Jossey-Bass.

Bronfenbrenner, U. (1979). *The ecology of human development.* Cambridge, MA: Harvard University Press.

Bronfenbrenner, U., Kessel, F., Kessen, W., & White, S. (1985). Toward a critical social history of developmental psychology. *American Psychologist, 41,* 1218–1230.

Bruner, J. (1986). *Actual minds, possible worlds.* Cambridge, MA: Harvard University Press.

Bruner, J. (1990). *Acts of meaning.* Cambridge, MA: Harvard University Press.

Bruner, J. (1993). Do we "acquire" culture or vice versa: Reply to M. Tomasello, A. C. Kruger, & H. H. Ratner, Cultural learning. *Behavioral and Brain Sciences, 163*(3), 515–516.

Bullock, M., & Lütkenhaus, P. (1990). Who am I? Self-understanding in toddlers. *Merrill-Palmer Quarterly, 36*(2), 217–238.

Cahan, E. D., & White, S. H. (1992). Proposals for a second psychology. *American Psychologist, 47,* 224–235.

Camic, C. (1986). The matter of habit. *American Journal of Sociology, 91,* 1039–1087.

Campos, J. J., Campos, R. G., & Barrett, K. C. (1989). Emergent themes in the study of emotional development and emotion regulation. *Developmental Psychology, 25,* 394–402.

Carey, S. (1985). *Conceptual change in childhood.* Cambridge, MA: MIT Press.

Carey, S., & Spelke, E. (1994). Domain-specific knowledge and conceptual change. In L. A. Hirschfeld & S. Gelman (Eds.), *Mapping the mind: Domain specificity in cognition and culture* (pp. 169–200). Hillsdale, NJ: Erlbaum.

Carraher, T. N., Carraher, D. W., & Schliemann, A. D. (1985). Mathematics in the streets and in schools. *British Journal of Developmental Psychology, 3,* 21–29.

Carrithers, M., Collins, S., & Lukes, S. (1987). *The category of the person: Anthropology, philosophy, history.* Cambridge, England: Cambridge University Press.

Carroll, V. (Ed.). (1970). *Adoption in Eastern Oceania.* Honolulu: University of Hawaii Press.

Caudill, W., & Plath, D. W. (1966). "Who sleeps by whom? Parent-child involvement in urban Japanese Families." *Psychiatry, 29,* 344–366.

Caudill, W., & Schooler, C. (1973). Child behavior and child rearing in Japan and the United States: An interim report. *Journal of Nervous and Mental Disease, 157,* 323–338.

Caudill, W., & Weinstein, H. (1969). Maternal care and infant behavior in Japan and America. *Psychiatry, 32,* 12–43.

Caudill, W., & Weinstein, H. (1986). Maternal care and infant behavior in Japan and America. In T. S. Lebra & W. P. Lebra (Eds.), *Japanese culture and behavior: Selected readings* (pp. 201–246). Honolulu: University of Hawaii Press.

Cazden, C. B. (1993). Vygotsky, Hymes, and Bakhtin: From word to utterance and voice. In E. A. Forman, N. Minick, & C. A. Stone (Eds.), *Contexts for learning: Sociocultural dynamics in children's development* (pp. 197–212). New York: Oxford University Press.

Ceci, S. J. (1993). Some contextual trends in cognitive development. *Developmental Review, 13,* 403–435.

Chaiklin, S., & Lave, J. (1993). *Understanding practice: Perspectives on activity and context.* New York: Cambridge University Press.

Chao, R. K. (1992). Immigrant Chinese mothers and European American mothers: Their aims of control and other child-rearing aspects related to school achievement. *Dissertation Abstracts International, 53*(6-A), 1787–1788.

Chao, R. K. (1993a). *Clarification of the authoritarian parenting style and parental control: Cultural concepts of Chinese child rearing.* Paper presented at the meeting of the Society for Research in Child Development, New Orleans, LA.

Chao, R. K. (1993b). *East and West concepts of the self reflecting in mothers' reports of their child rearing.* Los Angeles: University of California.

Chi, M. T., & Koeske, R. (1983). Network representation of a child's dinosaur knowledge. *Developmental Psychology, 19,* 29–39.

Cole, M. (1988). Cross-cultural research in the sociohistorical tradition. *Human Development, 31,* 137–157.

Cole, M. (1990). Cultural psychology: A once and future discipline? In J. J. Berman (Ed.), *Nebraska Symposium on Motivation: Vol. 37. Cross-cultural perspectives.* Lincoln: University of Nebraska Press.

Cole, M. (1992). Context, maturity, and the cultural constitution of development. In L. T. Winegar & J. Valsiner (Eds.),

Children's development within social context: Vol. 2. Research and methodology (pp. 5–31). Hillsdale, NJ: Erlbaum.

Cole, M. (1995). The supra-individual envelope of development: Activity and practice, situation and context. In J. J. Goodnow, P. J. Miller, & F. Kessel (Eds.), *Cultural practices as contexts for development: New directions for child development.* San Francisco: Jossey-Bass.

Cole, M. (1996). *Cultural psychology: A once and future discipline.* Cambridge, MA: Harvard University Press.

Cole, M., & Traupmann, K. (1981). Comparative cognitive research: Learning from learning disabled children. In W. A. Collins (Ed.), *The Minnesota Symposia on Child Psychology: Vol. 14. Aspects of the development of competence* (pp. 125–155). Hillsdale, NJ: Erlbaum.

Collingwood, R. G. (1961). On the so-called idea of causation. In H. Morris (Ed.), *Freedom and responsibility: Readings in philosophy and law.* Stanford, CA: Stanford University Press.

Cook-Gumperz, J., Corsaro, W. A., & Streeck, J. (Eds.). (1986). *Children's worlds and children's language.* Berlin: Mouton de Gruyter.

Cooley, D. H. (1902). *Human nature and the social order.* New York: Scribners.

Coopersmith, S. A. (1967). *The antecedents of self-esteem.* San Francisco: Freeman.

Corsaro, W. A. (1985). *Friendship and peer culture in the early years.* Norwood, NJ: ABLEX.

Corsaro, W. A. (1992). Interpretive reproduction in children's peer culture. *Social Psychology Quarterly, 55,* 160–177.

Corsaro, W. A., & Miller, P. J. (Eds.). (1992). *New directions for child development: Vol. 58. Interpretive approaches to childhood socialization.* San Francisco: Jossey-Bass.

Corsaro, W. A., & Rizzo, T. A. (1988). Discussion and friendship: Socialization processes in the peer culture of Italian nursery school children. *American Sociological Review, 53,* 879–894.

Cousins, S. D. (1989). Culture and self-perception in Japan and the United States. *Journal of Personality and Social Psychology, 56,* 124–131.

Cushman, P. (1995). *Constructing the self, constructing America: A cultural history of psychotherapy.* Boston: Addison-Wesley.

Damon, W. (1984). Peer interaction: The untapped potential. *Journal of Applied Developmental Psychology, 5,* 331–343.

Damon, W. (1995). *Greater expectations: Overcoming the culture of indulgence in America's homes and schools.* New York: Free Press.

Damon, W., & Hart, D. (1988). *Self understanding in childhood and adolescence.* New York: Cambridge University Press.

D'Andrade, R. G. (1981). The cultural part of cognition. *Cognitive Science, 5,* 179–195.

D'Andrade, R. G. (1984). Cultural meaning systems. In R. A. Shweder & R. A. LeVine (Eds.), *Culture theory: Essays on mind, self and emotion.* New York: Cambridge University Press.

D'Andrade, R. G. (1985). A folk model of the mind. In N. Quinn & D. Holland (Eds.), *Cultural models in language and thought.* New York: Cambridge University Press.

D'Andrade, R. G. (1995). *The development of cognitive anthropology.* Cambridge, England: Cambridge University Press.

D'Andrade, R. G., & Strauss, C. (Ed.). (1992). *Human motives and cultural models.* Cambridge, England: Cambridge University Press.

Deci, E. L., & Ryan, R. M. (1990). A motivational approach to self: Integration in personality. In R. A. Dienstbier (Ed.), *Perspectives on motivation: Vol. 38. Nebraska Symposium on Motivation* (pp. 237–288). Lincoln: University of Nebraska Press.

Deng, F. M. (1972). *The Dinka of the Southern Sudan.* New York: Holt, Rinehart and Winston.

Dewey, J. (1938). *Experience and education.* New York: Macmillan.

Doi, T. (1981). *The anatomy of dependence.* Tokyo: Kodansha.

Donagan, A. (1987). *Choice, the essential element in human action.* London: Routledge & Kegan Paul.

Donaldson, M. (1978). *Children's minds.* New York: Norton.

Dunn, J. (1983). Sibling relationships in early childhood. *Child Development, 54,* 787–811.

Dunn, J. (1993). *Young children's close relationships: Beyond attachment.* Newbury Park, CA: Sage.

Duranti, A., & Goodwin, C. (1992). *Rethinking context: Language as an interactive phenomenon.* New York: Cambridge University Press.

Duveen, G., & Lloyd, B. (1990). *Social representations and the development of knowledge.* Cambridge, England: Cambridge University Press.

Eagley, A. H., & Chaiken, S. (1993). *The psychology of attitudes.* New York: Harcourt Brace Jovanovich.

Eckensberger, L. H. (1990). From cross-cultural psychology to cultural psychology. *Quarterly Newsletter of the Laboratory of Human Cognition, 12,* 37–52.

Eckensberger, L. H. (1995). Activity or action: Two different roads towards an integration of culture into psychology. *Culture and Psychology, 1,* 67–80.

Eckert, P. (1991). *Jocks and burnouts: Social categories and identity in the high school.* New York: Teachers College Press.

Eder, R. A., & Mangelsdorf, S. (in press). The emotional basis of early personality development: Implications for the emergent self-concept. In R. Hogan, J. Johnson, & S. Briggs (Eds.), *Handbook of personality psychology.* Orlando, FL: Academic Press.

Eisenberg, A. R. (1985). Learning to describe past experiences in conversation. *Discourse Processes, 8,* 177–204.

Eisenberg, A. R., & Garvey, C. (1981). Children's use of verbal strategies in resolving conflicts. *Discourse Processes, 4,* 149–170.

Elster, J. (1987). *The multiple self.* Cambridge, England: Cambridge University Press.

Engel, S. (1995). *The stories children tell: Making sense of the narratives of childhood.* New York: Freeman.

Epstein, S. (1973). The self-concept revisited or a theory of a theory. *American Psychologist, 28,* 405–416.

Erickson, F. D. (1986). Qualitative methods in research on teaching. In M. C. Wittrock (Ed.), *Handbook of research on teaching* (3rd ed.). New York: Macmillan.

Erikson, E. (1968). *Identity: Youth and crisis.* New York: Norton.

Fajans, J. (1985). The person in social context: The social character of Baining "psychology." In G. M. White & W. J. Kirkpatrick (Eds.), *Person, self, and experience* (pp. 367–400). Berkeley: University of California Press.

Farver, J. M., Kim, Y. K., & Lee, Y. (1995). Cultural differences in Korean- and Anglo-American preschoolers' social interaction and play behaviors. *Child Development, 66*(4), 1088–1099.

Fernald, A., & Morikawa, H. (1993). Common themes and cultural variations in Japanese and American mothers' speech to infants. *Child Development, 64*(3), 637–656.

Fiske, A. P. (1991). *Structures of social life: The four elementary forms of human relations.* New York: Free Press.

Fiske, A. P. (1992). The four elementary forms of sociality: Framework for a unified theory of social relations. *Psychological Review, 99,* 689–723.

Fivush, R. (1993). Emotional content of parent-child conversations about the past. In C. A. Nelson (Ed.), *Memory and affect in development: Minnesota Symposia on Child Psychology* (Vol. 26, pp. 39–77). Hillsdale, NJ: Erlbaum.

Fivush, R. (1994). Constructing narrative, emotion, and self in parent-child conversations about the past. In U. Neisser & R. Fivush (Eds.), *The remembering self: Construction and accuracy in the self-narrative* (pp. 136–157). New York: Cambridge University Press.

Fivush, R., Gray, J. T., & Fromhoff, F. A. (1987). Two-year-olds talk about the past. *Cognitive Development, 2,* 393–410.

Flanagan, O. (1992). *Consciousness reconsidered.* Cambridge, MA: MIT Press.

Flavell, J. H., Green, F. L., & Flavell, E. R. (1995). Young children's knowledge about thinking. *Monographs of the Society for Research in Child Development, 60*(1, Serial No. 243).

Foucault, M. (1980). *Power-knowledge: Selected interviews and other writings.* Brighton: Harvester.

Frijda, N. H., & Mesquita, B. (1994). The social roles and functions of emotions. In S. Kitayama & H. R. Markus (Eds.), *Emotion and culture* (pp. 51–87). Washington, DC: American Psychological Association.

Garvey, C. (1992). Introduction. In C. Garvey (Ed.), Talk in the study of socialization and development [Invitational issue]. *Merrill-Palmer Quarterly, 38*(1), pp. iii–viii.

Garvey, C., & Kramer, T. (1989). The language of social pretend play. *Developmental Review, 9,* 364–382.

Garvey, C., & Shantz, C. V. (1992). Conflict talk: Approaches to adversative discourse. In C. V. Shantz & W. W. Hartup (Eds.), *Conflict in child and adolescent development* (pp. 93–121). New York: Cambridge University Press.

Geary, D. C. (1995). Reflections of evolution and culture in children's cognition: Implications for mathematical development and instruction. *American Psychologist, 50,* 24–37.

Gee, J. P., Michaels, S., & O'Connor, M. C. (1992). Discourse analysis. In J. Preissle (Ed.), *The handbook of qualitative research in education.* San Diego, CA: Academic Press.

Geertz, C. (1973a). The impact of the concept of culture on the concept of man. In C. Geertz (Ed.), *The interpretation of cultures.* New York: Basic Books.

Geertz, C. (Ed.). (1973b). *The interpretation of cultures.* New York: Basic Books.

Geertz, C. (1984). From the natives' point of view. In R. A. Shweder & R. A. LeVine (Eds.), *Culture theory: Essays on mind, self and emotion.* New York: Cambridge University Press.

Gelman, R. (1990). First principles organize attention to and learning about relevant data: Numbers and the animate-inanimate distinction as examples. *Cognitive Science, 14,* 79–106.

Gergen, K. J. (1968). Personal consistency and the presentation of self. In C. Gordon & K. J. Gergen (Eds.), *The self in social interaction* (pp. 299–308). New York: Wiley.

Gergen, K. J. (1991). *The saturated self.* New York: Basic Books.

Gergen, K. J., & Gergen, M. M. (1983). Narratives of the self. In T. R. Sarbin & K. E. Scheibe (Eds.), *Studies in social identity* (pp. 254–273) New York: Praeger.

Giddens, A. (1984). *The constitution of society.* Oxford, England: Polity Press.

Gilmore, P., & Glatthorn, A. A. (Eds.). (1982). *Children in and out of school: Ethnography and education.* Washington, DC: Center for Applied Linguistics.

Goodnow, J. J. (1976). The nature of intelligent behavior: Questions raised by cross-cultural studies. In L. B. Resnick (Ed.), *The nature of intelligence* (pp. 169–188). New York: Erlbaum.

Goodnow, J. J. (1990a). The socialization of cognition: What's involved? In J. W. Stigler, R. A. Shweder, & G. Herdt (Eds.), *Cultural psychology: Essays on comparative human development* (pp. 259–286). New York: Cambridge University Press.

Goodnow, J. J. (1990b). Using sociology to extend psychological accounts of cognitive development. *Human Development, 33,* 81–107.

Goodnow, J. J. (1995). Acceptable disagreement across generations. In J. Smetana (Ed.), *Parents' socio-cognitive models of development: New directions for child development* (pp. 51–64). San Francisco: Jossey-Bass.

Goodnow, J. J. (1996). From household practices to parents' ideas about work and interpersonal relationships. In S. Harkness & C. Super (Eds.), *Parents' cultural belief systems* (pp. 313–344). New York: Guilford Press.

Goodnow, J. J. (in press). Parenting and the "transmission" and the "internalization" of values: From social-cultural perspectives to within-family analyses. In J. Grusec & L. Kuczynski (Eds.), *Parenting strategies and children's internalization of values: A handbook of theoretical and research proposals.* New York: Wiley.

Goodnow, J. J., Knight, R., & Cashmore, J. (1985). Adult social cognition: Implications of parents' ideas for approaches to social development. In M. Perlmutter (Ed.), *The Minnesota Symposia on Child Psychology: Vol. 18. Social cognition* (pp. 287–324). Hillsdale, NJ: Erlbaum.

Goodnow, J. J., Miller, P. J., & Kessel, F. (Eds.). (1995). *New Directions for Child Development: Vol. 67. Cultural practices as contexts for development.* San Francisco: Jossey-Bass.

Goodwin, M. H. (1990). *He-said-she-said: Talk as social organization among black children.* Bloomington: Indiana University Press.

Goody, E. (1982). *Parenthood and social reproduction.* Cambridge, England: Cambridge University Press.

Gopnik, A. (1993). Psychopsychology. *Consciousness and Cognition, 2,* 264–280.

Gottlieb, G. (1991). The experiential canalization of behavioral development. *Developmental Psychology, 27,* 4–13.

Greenfield, P. (in press). Culture as process: Empirical methodology for cultural psychology. In J. W. Berry, Y. H. Poortinga, & J. Pandey (Eds.), *Handbook of cross-cultural psychology: Vol. 1. Theory and method.* Boston: Allyn & Bacon.

Greenfield, P., & Cocking, R. (1994). *Cross-cultural roots of minority child development.* Hillsdale, NJ: Erlbaum.

Greenfield, P., & Lave, J. (1982). Cognitive aspects of informal education. In D. Wagner & H. Stevenson (Eds.), *Cultural perspectives on child development* (pp. 181–207). San Francisco: Freeman.

Grossman, K., & Grossmann, K. E. (1991). Newborn behavior, the quality of early parenting and later toddler-parent relationships in a group of German infants. In J. K. Nugent, B. M. Lester, & T. B. Brazelton (Eds.), *The cultural context of infancy* (Vol. 2). Norwood, NJ: ABLEX.

Grossman, K., Grossmann, K. E., Spangler, G., Suess, G., & Unzner, L. (1985). Maternal sensitivity and newborns' orientation responses as related to quality of attachment in northern Germany. In I. Bretherton & E. Waters, (Eds.), *Growing points of attachment theory and research. Monographs of the Society for Research in Child Development* (Vol. 50, Nos. 1–2). Chicago: University of Chicago Press.

Grossmann, K. E., & Grossman, K. (1981). Parent-infant attachment relationships in Bielefeld. In K. Immelman, G. Barlow, L. Petrovich, & M. Main (Eds.), *Behavioral development: The Bielefeld interdisciplinary project.* New York: Cambridge University Press.

Guisinger, S., & Blatt, S. J. (1994). Individuality and relatedness: Evolution of a fundamental dialect. *American Psychologist, 49,* 104–111.

Haas-Dyson, A., & Genishi, C. (Eds.). (1994). *The need for story: Cultural diversity in classroom and community.* Urbana, IL: National Council of Teachers of English.

Haidt, J., Koller, S., & Dias, M. (1993). Affect, culture, and morality, or is it wrong to eat your dog? *Journal of Personality and Social Psychology, 65,* 613–628.

Hallowell, A. I. (1955). *Culture and experience.* Philadelphia: University of Pennsylvania Press.

Hamagushi, E. (1985). A contextual model of the Japanese: Toward a methodological innovation in Japan studies. *Journal of Japanese Studies, 11,* 289–321.

Hanks, W. F. (1996). *Language and communicative practices.* Boulder, CO: Westview Press.

Harkness, S., & Super, C. M. (1992). The cultural foundations of fathers' roles: Evidence from Kenya and the United States. In B. S. Hewlett (Ed.), *Father-child relations: Cultural and biosocial contexts.* New York: Aldine de Gruyter.

Harkness, S., & Super, C. M. (Eds.). (1996). *Parents' cultural belief systems.* New York: Guilford Press.

Harris, P. L. (1990). The child's theory of mind and its cultural context. In G. Butterworth & P. Bryant (Eds.), *The causes of development* (pp. 215–237). Hillsdale, NJ: Erlbaum.

Hart, D. (1988). The adolescent self-concept in social context. In D. Lapsley & F. Power (Eds.), *Self, ego, and identity: Integrative approaches* (pp. 71–90). New York: Springer-Verlag.

Hart, D., & Edelstein, W. (1992). The relationship of self-understanding in childhood to social class, community type, and teacher-rated intellectual and social competence. *Journal of Cross-Cultural Psychology, 23*(3), 353–365.

Hart, D., Fegley, S., Hung Chan, Y., Mulvey, D., & Fischer, L. (1993). Judgment about personal identity in childhood and adolescence. *Social Development, 2*(1), 66–81.

Harter, S. (1983). Developmental perspectives on the self system. In E. M. Hetherington (Ed.), *Handbook of child psychology: Vol. 4. Socialization, personality, and social development.* New York: Wiley.

Harter, S. (1986). Processes underlying the construction, maintenance and enhancement of self-concept in children. In J. Suls & A. Greenwald (Eds.), *Psychological perspective on the self* (Vol. 3, pp. 136–182). Hillsdale, NJ: Erlbaum.

Harter, S. (1990). Causes, correlates and the functional role of global self-worth: A life span perspective. In R. J. Sternberg & J. J. Kolligian (Eds.), *Competence considered* (pp. 67–97). New Haven, CT: Yale University Press.

Harter, S. (1996). Historical roots of contemporary issues involving self-concept. In B. A. Bracken (Ed.), *Handbook of self-concept.* New York: Wiley.

Harwood, R., & Miller, J. (1991). Perceptions of attachment behavior: A comparison of Anglo and Puerto-Rican mothers. *Merrill-Palmer Quarterly, 3*(4), 583–599.

Harwood, R. L., Schoelmerish, A., Ventura-Cook, E., Schulze, P., & Wilson, S. (in press). Culture and class influences on Anglo and Puerto-Rican mothers: Regarding long-term socialization goals and child behavior. *Child Development.*

Hatano, G. (1990). The nature of everyday science: A brief introduction. *British Journal of Developmental Psychology, 8,* 245–250.

Hatano, G. (1993). A time to merge Vygotskian and constructivist conceptions of knowledge acquisition: A commentary. In E. A. Forman, N. Minick, & C. A. Stone (Eds.), *Context for learning* (pp. 153–166). New York: Oxford University Press.

Hatano, G. (1995). The psychology of Japanese literacy: Expanding "the practice account." In L. Martin, K. Nelson, & E. Tobach (Eds.), *Sociocultural psychology: Theory and practice of doing and knowing* (pp. 250–275). New York: Cambridge University Press.

Hatano, G., & Inagaki, K. (1986). Two courses of expertise. In H. Stevenson, H. Azuma, & K. Hakuta (Eds.), *Child development and education in Japan* (pp. 262–272). San Francisco: Freeman.

Hatano, G., & Inagaki, K. (1992). Desituating cognition through the construction of conceptual knowledge. In P. Light & G. Butterworth (Eds.), *Context and cognition: Ways of learning and knowing* (pp. 115–133). London: Harvester Wheatsheaf.

Hatano, G., Siegler, R. S., Richards, D. D., Inagaki, K., Stavy, R., & Wax, N. (1993). The development of biological knowledge: A multi-national study. *Cognitive Development, 8,* 47–62.

Heath, S. B. (1983). *Ways with words: Language, life and work in communities and classrooms.* New York: Cambridge University Press.

Herdt, G. (1981). *Guardians of the flutes.* New York: McGraw-Hill.

Herdt, G. (1990). Sambia nosebleeding rites and male proximity to women. In J. Stigler, R. A. Shweder, & G. Herdt (Eds.), *Cultural psychology: Essays on comparative human development.* New York: Cambridge University Press.

Hewlett, B. S. (1991). *Intimate fathers: The nature and context of Aka Pygmy Paternal infant care.* Ann Arbor: University of Michigan Press.

Hewlett, B. S. (Ed.). (1992). *Father-child relations: Cultural and biosocial contexts.* New York: Aldine de Gruyter.

Hicks, D. (1991). Kinds of narrative: Genre skills among first graders from two communities. In A. McCabe & C. Peterson (Eds.), *Developing narrative structure* (pp. 55–87). Hillsdale, NJ: Erlbaum.

Hicks, D. A. (1994). Individual and social meanings in the classroom: Narrative discourse as a boundary phenomenon. *Journal of Narrative and Life History, 4,* 215–240.

Higgins, E. T. (1990). Self-state representations: Patterns of interconnected beliefs with specific holistic meanings and importance. *Bulletin of the Psychonomic Society, 28,* 248–253.

Higgins, E. T., & Parsons, J. (1983). Social cognition and the social life of the child: Stages as subcultures. In E. T. Higgins, D. N. Ruble, & W. W. Hartup (Eds.), *Social cognition and social development: A sociocultural perspective* (pp. 15–62). New York: Cambridge University Press.

Hirschfeld, L. A., & Gelman, S. A. (Eds.). (1994). *Mapping the mind: Domain specificity in cognition and culture.* New York: Cambridge University Press.

Ho, D. Y. (1993). Relational orientation in Asian social psychology. In U. Kim & J. W. Berry (Eds.), *Indigenous psychologies:*

Research and experiences in cultural context. Newbury Park, CA: Sage.

Holland, D. C., & Quinn, N. (Eds.). (1987). *Cultural models in language and thought.* New York: Cambridge University Press.

Howard, A. (1985). Ethnopsychology and the prospects for a cultural psychology. In G. M. White & J. Kirkpatrick (Eds.), *Person, self and experience: Exploring specific ethnopsychologies.* Berkeley: University of California Press.

Ikegama, Y. (1991). "DO-language" and "BECOME-language": Two contrasting types of linguistic representation. In Y. Ikegama (Ed.), *The empire of signs: Semiotic essays on Japanese culture* (Vol. 8, pp. 286–327). Philadelphia: John Benjamins.

Inagaki, K. (1990). The effects of raising animals on children's biological knowledge. *British Journal of Developmental Psychology, 8,* 119–129.

Ingold, T. (1986). *Evolution and social life.* New York: Cambridge University Press.

Ingold, T. (1991). Becoming persons: Consciousness and sociality in human evolution. *Cultural Dynamics, 4*(3), 355–378.

Jahoda, G. (1990). Our forgotten ancestors. In J. J. Berman (Ed.), *Cross-cultural perspectives. Nebraska Symposium on Motivation, 1989* (pp. 1–40). Lincoln: University of Nebraska Press.

Jahoda, G. (1992). *Crossroads between culture and mind: Continuities and change in theories of human nature.* London: Harvester Wheatsheaf and Cambridge, MA: Harvard University Press.

James, W. (1950). *The principles of psychology.* New York: Dover.

Jensen, L. A. (1995). Habits of the heart revisited: Autonomy, community and divinity in adult's moral language. *Qualitative Sociology, 18,* 71–86.

Jensen, L. A. (1996). *Different habits, different hearts: Orthodoxy and progressivism in the United States and India.* Unpublished Ph.D. thesis, University of Chicago.

Jessor, R., Colby, A., & Shweder, R. A. (Eds.). (1996). *Ethnography and human development: Context and meaning in social inquiry.* Chicago: University of Chicago Press.

Johnson, F. (1985). The Western concept of self. In A. Marsella, G. DeVos, & F. L. K. Hsu (Eds.), *Culture and self.* London: Tavistock.

Josephs, R. A., Markus, H., & Tarafodi, R. W. (1992). Gender and self-esteem. *Journal of Personality and Social Psychology, 63,* 391–402.

Kakar, S. (1978). *The inner world: A psychoanalytic study of childhood and society in India.* New York: Oxford University Press.

Kakar, S. (1982). *Shamans, mystics and doctors.* Boston: Beacon Press.

Kakar, S. (1996). *The colors of violence: Cultural identities, religion and conflict.* Chicago: University of Chicago Press.

Kamberelis, G. (1993). *Tropes are for kids: Young children's developing understanding of narrative, poetic, and expository written discourse genres.* Unpublished doctoral dissertation, University of Michigan, Ann Arbor.

Kamberelis, G., & Scott, K. D. (1992). Other people's voices: The coarticulation of texts and subjectivities. *Linguistics and Education, 4,* 359–403.

Kapstein, M. (1989). Santaraksita on the fallacies of personalistic vitalism. *Journal of Indian Philosophy, 17,* 43–59.

Karmiloff-Smith, A. (1992). *Beyond modularity.* Cambridge, MA: MIT Press.

Keil, F. C. (1981). Constraints on knowledge and cognitive development. *Psychological Review, 88,* 197–227.

Kessel, F. S., & Siegel, A. W. (Eds.). (1983). *The child and other cultural inventions.* New York: Praeger.

Kessen, W. (1983). The child and other cultural inventions. In F. S. Kessel & A. W. Siegel (Eds.), *The child and other cultural inventions.* New York: Praeger.

Kessen, W. (Ed.). (1990). *The rise and fall of development.* Worcester, MA: Clark University Press.

Kihlstrom, J. F., & Cantor, N. (1984). Mental representations of the self. *Advances in Experimental Social Psychology, 17,* 1–47.

Kim, U. (1987). *The parent-child relationship: The core of Korean collectivism.* Paper presented at the meeting of the International Association for Cross-Cultural Psychology, Newcastle, Australia.

Kitayama, S., & Markus, H. R. (1994). *Emotion and culture: Empirical studies of mutual influences.* Washington, DC: American Psychological Association.

Kitayama, S., Markus, H., Matsumoto, H., & Norasakkunkit, V. (1995). *Individual and collective processes of self-esteem management: Self enhancement in the United States and self-depreciation in Japan.* Kyoto, Japan: Kyoto University.

Kitayama, S., Markus, H. R., Matsumoto, H., & Norasakkunkit, V. (1997). Individual and collective processes in the construction of the self: Self-enhancement in the United States and self-criticism in Japan. *Journal of Personality and Social Psychology.*

Kondo, D. (1990). *Crafting selves: Power, gender, and discourses of identity in a Japanese workplace.* Chicago: University of Chicago Press.

Konner, M. J. (1975). Relations among infants and juveniles in comparative perspective. In M. Lewis & L. Rosenblum (Eds.), *Friendship and peer relations.* New York: Wiley.

Kratz, C. (1994). *Affecting performance: Meaning, movement and experience in Okiek women's initiation.* Washington, DC: Smithsonian Institution Press.

Kripal, J. (1995). *Kali's child: The mystical and the erotic in the life and teachings of Rama Krishna.* Chicago: University of Chicago Press.

Kristeva, J. (1980). *Desire in language: A semiotic approach to literature and art.* New York: Columbia University Press.

Kulick, D. (1992). *Language shifts and cultural reproduction: Socialization, self, and syncretism in a Papua New Guinean village.* New York: Cambridge University Press.

Kurtz, S. N. (1992). *All the mothers are one: Hindu India and the cultural reshaping of psychoanalysis.* New York: Columbia University Press.

Laboratory of Comparative Human Cognition. (1983). Culture and cognitive development. In P. Mussen (Series Ed.) & W. Kessen (Vol. Ed.), *Handbook of child psychology: Vol. 1. History, theory, and methods.* New York: Wiley.

Lave, J. (1990). *Cognition in practice: Mind, mathematics, and culture in everyday life.* Cambridge, England: Cambridge University Press.

Lave, J. (1991). Situating learning in communities of practice. In L. B. Resnick, J. M. Levine, & S. D. Teasley (Eds.), *Perspectives on socially shared cognition* (pp. 63–82). Washington, DC: American Psychological Association.

Lave, J., & Wenger, E. (1991). *Situated learning: Legitimate peripheral participation.* New York: Cambridge University Press.

Leadbeter, B. J., & Dionne, J. P. (1981). The adolescent's use of formal operational thinking in solving problems related to identity resolutions. *Adolescence, 16,* 111–121.

Leahy, R., & Shirk, S. (1985). Social cognition and the development of the self. In R. Leahy (Ed.), *The development of the self.* New York: Academic Press.

Lebra, T. S. (1976). *Japanese patterns of behavior.* Honolulu: University of Hawaii Press.

Lebra, T. S. (1992). *Culture, self, and communication.* Ann Arbor: University of Michigan.

Lebra, T. S. (1993). Culture, self, and communication in Japan and the United States. In W. B. Gudykunst (Ed.), *Communication in Japan and the United States* (pp. 51–87). Albany: State University of New York Press.

Lebra, T. S. (1994). Mother and child in Japanese socialization: A Japan-U.S. comparison. In P. M. Greenfield & R. R.

Cocking (Eds.), *Cross-cultural roots of minority child development* (pp. 259–274). Hillsdale, NJ: Erlbaum.

LeVine, L. E. (1983). Mine: Self-definition in 2-year-old-boys. *Developmental Psychology, 19,* 544–549.

LeVine, R. A. (1970). Cross-cultural study in child psychology. In P. H. Mussen (Ed.), *Carmichael's manual of child psychology* (3rd ed.). New York: Wiley.

LeVine, R. A. (1974). Parental goals: A cross-cultural view. *Teachers College Record, 76,* 226–239.

LeVine, R. A. (1978). Western schools in non-Western societies: Psychosocial impact and cultural response. *Teachers College Record, 79.*

LeVine, R. A. (1989). Cultural environments in child development. In W. Damon (Ed.), *Child development today and tomorrow.* San Francisco: Jossey-Bass.

LeVine, R. A. (1990a). Infant environments in psychoanalysis: A cross-cultural view. In J. W. Stigler, R. A. Shweder, & G. Herdt (Eds.), *Cultural psychology: Essays on comparative human development* (pp. 454–474). New York: Cambridge University Press.

LeVine, R. A. (1990b). Enculturation: A biosocial perspective on the self. In D. Cicchetti & M. Beeghly (Eds.), *The self in transition: Infancy to childhood.* Chicago: University of Chicago Press.

LeVine, R. A., Dixon, S., LeVine, S., Richman, A., Leiderman, P. H., Keefer, C., & Brazelton, T. B. (1994). *Child care and culture: Lessons from Africa.* New York: Cambridge University Press.

LeVine, R. A., & LeVine, B. B. (1966). *Nyansongo: A Gusii community in Kenya.* New York: Wiley.

LeVine, R. A., LeVine, S., Iwanaga, M., & Marvin, R. (1970). *Child care and social attachment in a Nigerian community: A preliminary report.* Paper presented at the American Psychological Association meetings.

LeVine, R. A., Miller, P., & West, M. (Eds.). (1988). *Parental behavior in diverse societies.* San Francisco: Jossey-Bass.

LeVine, S. (n.d.). *Caregiving in Godavari, Nepal, 1990* [Videotape].

Levy, R. I. (1973). *Tahitians: Mind and experience in the Society Islands.* Chicago: University of Chicago Press.

Levy, R. I. (1984). Emotion, knowing and culture. In R. A. Shweder & R. A. LeVine (Eds.), *Culture theory: Essays on mind, self and emotion.* New York: Cambridge University Press.

Lewin, K. (1943). Defining the field at given time. *Psychological Review, 50,* 292–310.

Lewis, C. C. (1995). *Educating hearts and minds.* New York: Cambridge University Press.

Lewis, M., Sullivan, M., Stanger, C., & Weiss, M. (1989). Self-development and self-conscious emotions. *Child Development, 60,* 146–156.

Lifton, R. J. (1993). *The Protean self.* New York: Harper.

Lillard, A. (in press). Body or mind: Children's categorizing of pretense. *Child Development.*

Linde, C. (1993). *Life stories: The creation of coherence.* New York: Oxford University Press.

Litt, C. J. (1981). Children's attachment to transitional objects: A study of two pediatric populations. *American Journal of Orthopsychiatry, 51,* 131–139.

Little, T. O., Oettingen, G., Stetsenko, A., & Baltes, P. B. (1995). *Children's school performance-related beliefs: How do American children compare to German and Russian children.* Berlin: Max Planck Institute for Human Development and Education.

Lozoff, B., Wolf, A. W., & Davis, N. S. (1984). Co-sleeping in urban families with young children in the United States. *Pediatrics, 74,* 171–182.

Lucy, J. A. (1992a). *Grammatical categories and cognition: A case study of the linguistic relativity hypothesis.* New York: Cambridge University Press.

Lucy, J. A. (1992b). *Language diversity and thought: A reformulation of the linguistic relativity hypothesis.* New York: Cambridge University Press.

Lutz, C. (1988). *Unnatural emotions: Everyday sentiments on a Micronesian Atoll and their challenge to Western theory.* Chicago: University of Chicago Press.

Lutz, C., & White, G. (1986). The anthropology of emotions. *Annual Review of Anthropology, 15,* 405–436.

Malinowski, B. (1922). *Argonauts of the Western Pacific.* New York: Dutton.

Mandelbaum, D. G. (Ed.). (1951). *Selected writings of Edward Sapir in language, culture, and personality.* Berkeley: University of California Press.

Markus, H. R., & Kitayama, S. (1991a). Cultural variation in the self-concept. In J. Strauss & G. R. Goethals (Eds.), *The self: Interdisciplinary approaches* (pp. 18–48). New York: Springer-Verlag.

Markus, H. R., & Kitayama, S. (1991b). Culture and the self: Implications for cognition, emotion, and motivation. *Psychological Review, 98,* 224–253.

Markus, H. R., & Kitayama, S. (1994a). The cultural construction of self and emotion: Implications for social behavior. In S. Kitayama & H. R. Markus (Eds.), *Emotion and culture: Empirical studies of mutual influences* (pp. 89–130). Washington, DC: American Psychological Association Press.

Markus, H. R., & Kitayama, S. (1994b). The cultural shaping of emotion: A conceptual framework. In S. Kitayama & H. R.

Markus (Eds.), *Emotion and culture: Empirical studies of mutual influences* (pp. 339–351). Washington, DC: American Psychological Association Press.

Markus, H. R., Kitayama, S., & Heiman, R. J. (in press). Culture and "basic" psychological principles. In E. T. Higgins & A. W. Kruglanski (Eds.), *Social psychology: Handbook of basic principles.* New York: Guilford Press.

Markus, H. R., Mullally, P. R., & Kitayama, S. (in press). Collective self-schemas: The sociocultural grounding of the personal. In U. Neisser & D. Jopling (Eds.), *The conceptual self in context: Culture, experience, self-understanding.* Cambridge, England: Cambridge University Press.

Markus, H. R., & Nurius, P. (1986). Possible selves. *American Psychologist, 41,* 954–969.

Markus, H. R., & Wurf, E. (1986). The dynamic self-concept: A social psychological perspective. *Annual Review of Psychology, 38,* 299–337.

Martin, L., Nelson, D., & Tobach, E. (1995). *Sociocultural psychology: Theory and practice of doing and knowing.* New York: Cambridge University Press.

Marvin, R., VanDevender, T., Iwanaga, M., LeVine, S., & LeVine, R. (1977). Infant-caregiver attachment among the Hausa of Nigeria. In H. McGurk (Ed.), *Ecological factors in human development.* Amsterdam, The Netherlands: North-Holland.

Maslow, A. H. (1954). *Motivation and personality.* New York: Harper.

Masten, A. S. (Forthcoming). Cultural processes of child development. *Minnesota Symposium on Child Development, 29.*

McAdams, D. P. (1993). *Stories we live by: Personal myths and the making of the self.* New York: Morrow.

McCabe, A., & Peterson, A. (1991). *Developing narrative structure.* Hillsdale, NJ: Erlbaum.

McDermott, R. P., Cole, M., & Hood, L. (1978). "Let's try to make it a nice day"—Not so simple ways. *Discourse Processes, 3,* 155–168.

McKenna, J. J., & others. (1993). Infant-parent co-sleeping in an evolutionary perspective: Implications for understanding infant sleep development and the sudden infant death syndrome. *Sleep, 16,* 263–282.

Mead, G. H. (1934). *Mind, self, and society.* Chicago: University of Chicago Press.

Medin, D. L. (1989). Concepts and conceptual structure. *American Psychologist, 89,* 1969–1981.

Mehan, H. (1979). *Learning lessons.* Cambridge, MA: Harvard University Press.

Menon, U. (1995). *Receiving and giving: Distributivity as the source of women's wellbeing.* Unpublished Ph.D. thesis, University of Chicago.

Menon, U., & Shweder, R. (1994). Kali's tongue: Cultural psychology and the power of shame in Orissa, India. In S. Kitayama & H. R. Markus (Eds.), *Emotion and culture: Empirical studies of mutual influence* (pp. 241–284). Washington, DC: American Psychological Association Press.

Mesquita, B., & Frijda, N. H. (1992). Cultural variations in emotions: A review. *Psychological Bulletin, 112,* 179–204.

Michaels, S. (1991). The dismantling of narrative. In A. McCabe & C. Peterson (Eds.), *Developing narrative structure* (pp. 303–351). Hillsdale, NJ: Erlbaum.

Miller, J. G. (1984). Culture and the development of everyday social explanation. *Journal of Personality and Social Psychology, 46,* 961–978.

Miller, J. G. (1994a). Cultural diversity in the morality of caring. *Cross-Cultural Research, 28,* 3–39.

Miller, J. G. (1994b). Cultural psychology: Bridging disciplinary boundaries in understanding the cultural grounding of self. In P. K. Bock (Ed.), *Handbook of psychological anthropology.* Westport, CT: Greenwood Press.

Miller, J. G. (in press). Theoretical issues in cultural psychology and social constructionism. In J. W. Berry, Y. Poortinga, & J. Pandey (Eds.), *Handbook of cross-cultural psychology: Theoretical and methodological perspectives* (Vol. 1). Boston: Allyn & Bacon.

Miller, P. J. (1982). *Amy, Wendy, and Beth: Learning language in South Baltimore.* Austin: University of Texas Press.

Miller, P. J., Fung, H., & Mintz, J. (1996). Self-construction through narrative practices: A Chinese and American comparison of early socialization. *Ethos, 24,* 237–279.

Miller, P. J., & Goodnow, J. J. (1995). Cultural practices: Toward an integration of development and culture. In J. J. Goodnow, P. J. Miller, & F. Kessel (Eds.), *Cultural practices as contexts for development. New directions for child development, Vol. 67* (pp. 5–16). San Francisco: Jossey-Bass.

Miller, P. J., & Hoogstra, L. (1992). Language as tool in the socialization and apprehension of cultural meanings. In T. Schwartz, G. M. White, & G. A. White (Eds.), *New directions in psychological anthropology* (pp. 83–101). New York: Cambridge University Press.

Miller, P. J., Hoogstra, L., Mintz, J., Fung, H., & Williams, K. (1993). Troubles in the garden and how they get resolved: A young child's transformation of his favorite story. In C. A. Nelson (Ed.), *Memory and affect in development: Minnesota Symposia on Child Psychology* (Vol. 26, pp. 87–114). Hillsdale, NJ: Erlbaum.

Miller, P. J., Mintz, J., Fung, H., Hoogstra, L., & Potts, R. (1992). The narrated self: Young children's construction of self in relation to others in conversational stories of personal experience. *Merrill-Palmer Quarterly, 38,* 45–67.

Miller, P. J., Potts, R., Fung, H., Hoogstra, L., & Mintz, J. (1990). Narrative practices and the social construction of self in childhood. *American Ethnologist, 17*(2), 292–311.

Miller, P. J., & Sperry, L. L. (1987). The socialization of anger and aggression. *Merrill-Palmer Quarterly, 33,* 1–31.

Miller, P. J., & Sperry, L. L. (1988). Early talk about the past: The origins of conversational stories of personal experience. *Journal of Child Language, 15,* 193–315.

Montemayor, R., & Eisen, M. (1977). The development of self-conceptions for childhood to adolescence. *Developmental Psychology, 13,* 314–319.

Morelli, G. A., Rogoff, B., Oppenheimer, D., & Goldsmith, D. (1992). Cultural variations in infants' sleeping arrangements: Question of independence. *Developmental Psychology, 28,* 604–613.

Morikawa, H., Shand, N., & Kosawa, Y. (1988). Maternal speech to prelingual infants in Japan and the United States: Relationships among functions, forms and referents. *Journal of Child Language, 15,* 237–256.

Morris, B. (1994). *Anthropology of the self: The concept of the individual in the west.* Boulder, CO: Pluto Press.

Morson, G. S., & Emerson, C. (1990). *Mikhail Bakhtin: Creation of a prosaics.* Stanford, CA: Stanford University Press.

Much, N. C. (1992). The analysis of discourse as methodology for a semiotic psychology. *American Behavioral Scientist, 36,* 52–72.

Much, N. C. (1993). Personal psychology and cultural discourse: Context analysis in the construction of meaning and a women's devotional life in an Indian village. In J. Smith, R. Harre, & L. van Langenhove (Eds.), *Rethinking psychology: Vol. 1. Conceptual foundations.* London: Sage.

Much, N. C. (1995). Cultural psychology. In J. Smith, R. Harre, & L. van Langenhove (Eds.), *Rethinking psychology.* London: Sage.

Much, N. C., & Shweder, R. A. (1978). Speaking of rules: The analysis of culture in breach. In W. Damon (Ed.), *New directions for child development: Moral development.* San Francisco: Jossey-Bass.

Mugny, G., & Carugati, F. (1989). *Social representations of intelligence.* Cambridge, England: Cambridge University Press.

Mulder, N. (1992). *Individual and society in Java: A cultural analysis* (2nd ed.). Yogyakarta: Gayah Mada University Press.

Nag, M., White, B., & Peet, R. C. (1978). An anthropological approach to the study of the economic value of children. *Current Anthropology, 19,* 293–306.

Neisser, U. (1988). Five kinds of self-knowledge. *Philosophical Psychology, 1,* 35–59.

Neisser, U. (1991). Two perceptually given aspects of the self and their development. *Developmental Review, 11*(3), 197–209.

Neisser, U., & Fivush, R. (1994). *The remembering self: Construction and accuracy in the self-narrative.* New York: Cambridge University Press.

Neisser, U., & Jopling, D. (Eds.). (in press). *The conceptual self in context: Culture, experience, self-understanding.* Cambridge, England: Cambridge University Press.

Nelson, K. (Ed.). (1989). *Narratives from the crib.* Cambridge, MA: Harvard University Press.

Nelson, K. (1993). Events, narratives, memory: What develops? In C. A. Nelson (Ed.), *Memory and affect in development: Minnesota Symposia on Child Psychology* (Vol. 26, pp. 1–24). Hillsdale, NJ: Erlbaum.

Nelson, K. (1996). *Language in cognitive development: The emergence of the mediated mind.* New York: Cambridge University Press.

Newman, D., Griffin, P., & Cole, M. (1989). *The construction zone: Working for cognitive change in school.* Cambridge, England: Cambridge University Press.

Nicolopoulou, A., & Cole, M. (1993). The fifth dimension, its play-world, and its institutional contexts: The generation and transmission of shared knowledge in the culture of collaborative learning. In E. A. Forman, N. Minick, & C. A. Stone (Eds.), *Contexts for learning: Socio-cultural dynamics in children's development* (pp. 283–314). New York: Oxford University Press.

Nisbett, R., & Cohen, D. (1995). *The culture of honor: The psychology of violence in the South.* Boulder, CO: Westview Press.

Nunes, T. (1995). Cultural practices and the conception of individual differences: Theoretical and empirical considerations. In J. J. Goodnow, P. J. Miller, & F. Kessel (Eds.), *Cultural practices as contexts for development* (pp. 91–104). San Francisco: Jossey-Bass.

Ochs, E. (1988). *Culture and language development: Language acquisition and language socialization in a Samoan village.* Cambridge, England: Cambridge University Press.

Ochs, E. (1990). Indexicality and socialization. In J. W. Stigler, R. A. Shweder, & G. Herdt (Eds.), *Cultural psychology: Essays on comparative human development* (pp. 287–308). New York: Cambridge University Press.

Ochs, E., & Scheiffelin, B. (1984). Language acquisition and socialization: Three developmental stories. In R. Shweder & R. A. LeVine (Eds.), *Culture theory: Essays on mind, self, and emotion.* New York: Cambridge University Press.

Ochs, E., & Taylor, C. (1992). Family narrative as political activity. *Discourse and Society, 3,* 301–340.

Oerter, R., Oerter, R., Agostiani, H., Kim, H., & Wibowo, S. (1996). The concept of human nature in East Asia: Etic and emic characteristics. *Culture and Psychology, 2*(1), 9–51.

Oettingen, G. (1995). Cross-cultural perspectives on self-efficacy. In A. Bandura (Ed.), *Self-efficacy in changing societies* (pp. 149–176). New York: Cambridge University Press.

Oosterwegel, A., & Oppenheimer, L. (1993). *The self-system: Developmental changes between and within self-concepts.* Hillsdale, NJ: Erlbaum.

Oyserman, D., & Kemmelmeier, M. (1995, June). *Viewing oneself in light of others: Gendered impact of social comparisons in the achievement domain.* Paper presented at the 7th annual convention of the American Psychological Society, New York.

Oyserman, D., & Markus, H. R. (1993). The sociocultural self. In J. Suls (Ed.), *Psychological perspectives on the self* (Vol. 4, pp. 187–220). Hillsdale, NJ: Erlbaum.

Packer, M. J. (1987). Social interaction as practical activity: Implications for the study of social and moral development. In W. Kurtines & J. Gewirtz (Eds.), *Moral development through social interaction* (pp. 245–280). New York: Wiley.

Parish, S. (1991). The sacred mind: Newar cultural representations of mental life and the production of moral consciousness. *Ethos, 19*(3), 313–351.

Parsons, J. F., & Kaczala, C. M. (1982). Socialization of achievement attitudes and beliefs: Parental influences. *Child Development, 53,* 310–321.

Peak, L. (1987). *Learning to go to school in Japan: The transition from home to preschool life.* Berkeley: University of California Press.

Phelps, E., & Damon, W. (1989). Problem-solving with equals: Peer collaboration in a context for learning mathematical and spatial concepts. *Journal of Educational Psychology, 4,* 639–646.

Philips, S. (1983). *The invisible culture: Communication in classroom and community on the Warm Springs Indian reservation.* New York: Longman.

Pike, K. L. (1967). *Language in relation to a unified theory of the structure of human behavior.* The Hague: Mouton.

Polkinghorne, D. E. (1988). *Narrative knowing and the human sciences.* Albany: State University of New York Press.

Preece, A. (1987). The range of narrative forms conversationally produced by young children. *Journal of Child Language, 14,* 353–373.

Redfield, R. (1941). *The folk culture of Yucatan.* Chicago: University of Chicago Press.

Richman, A., LeVine, R. A., New, R. S., Howrigan, G., Welles-Nystrom, B., & LeVine, S. (1988). Maternal behavior to infants in five societies. In R. A. LeVine, P. Miller, & M. M. West (Eds.), *Parental behavior in diverse societies. New Directions for Child Development: Vol. 40.* San Francisco: Jossey-Bass.

Richman, A., Miller, P., & LeVine, R. A. (1992). Cultural and educational variations in maternal responsiveness. *Developmental Psychology, 28,* 614–621.

Rogoff, B. (1990). *Apprenticeship in thinking: Cognitive development in social context.* New York: Oxford University Press.

Rogoff, B. (1995). Development through participation in sociocultural activity. In J. J. Goodnow, P. J. Miller, & F. Kessel (Eds.), *Cultural practices as contexts for development* (pp. 45–66). San Francisco: Jossey-Bass.

Rogoff, B., Mistry, J. J., Goncu, A., & Mosier, C. (1993). Guided participation in cultural activity by toddlers and caregivers. *Monographs of the Society for Research in Child Development, 58*(7, Series No. 236).

Rogoff, B., Radziszewska, B., & Masiello, T. (1995). Analysis of developmental processes in sociocultural activity. In L. M. Nelson & E. Tobach (Eds.), *Sociocultural psychology: Theory and practice of doing and knowing.* New York: Cambridge University Press.

Rohner, R. P. (1984). *Handbook for the study of parental acceptance and rejection* (Rev. ed.). Storrs: University of Connecticut.

Rohner, R. P., & Pettengill, S. (1985). Perceived parental acceptance-rejection and parental control among Korean adolescents. *Child Development, 56,* 524–528.

Romney, A. K., Weller, S. C., & Batchelder, W. H. (1986). Culture as consensus: A theory of culture and informant accuracy. *American Anthropologist, 88,* 313–332.

Rosaldo, M. Z. (1984). Toward an anthropology of self and feeling. In R. A. Shweder & R. A. LeVine (Eds.), *Culture theory: Essays on mind, self, and emotion* (pp. 137–157). New York: Cambridge University Press.

Rosen, L. (1995). *Other intentions.* Santa Fe, NM: School of American Research.

Rosenberg, M. (1986). Self-concept from middle childhood through adolescence. In J. Suls & A. Greenwald (Eds.),

Psychological perspectives on the self (Vol. 3, pp. 107–136). Hillsdale, NJ: Erlbaum.

Rosenberger, N. R. (1992). *Japanese sense of self.* New York: Cambridge University Press.

Rozin, P., & Nemeroff, C. (1990). The law of sympathetic magic. In J. Stigler, R. A. Shweder, & G. Herdt (Eds.), *Cultural psychology: Essays on comparative human development.* New York: Cambridge University Press.

Ruble, D. N., & Seidman, R. (in press). Social transitions: Windows into social psychological precesses. In E. T. Higgins & A. Kruglansky (Eds.), *Handbook of social processes.* New York: Guilford Press.

Russell, J. A. (1991). Culture and the categorization of emotions. *Psychological Bulletin, 110,* 426–450.

Ryff, C., Lee, Y., & Na, K. (1995). *Through the lens of culture: Psychological well-being at midlife.* Unpublished manuscript.

Sampson, E. E. (1985). The decentralization of identity: Toward a revised concept of personal and social order. *American Psychologist, 40,* 1203–1211.

Sampson, E. E. (1988). The debate on individualism: Indigenous psychologies of the individual and their role in personal and societal functioning. *American Psychologist, 43,* 15–22.

Sass, L. A. (1992). The epic of disbelief: The postmodernist turn in contemporary psychoanalysis. In S. Kvale (Ed.), *Psychology and postmodernism* (pp. 166–182). London: Sage.

Saxe, G. B. (1991). *Culture and cognitive development: Studies in mathematical understanding.* Hillsdale, NJ: Erlbaum.

Schieffelin, B. B. (1990). *The give and take of everyday life: Language socialization of Kaluli children.* New York: Cambridge University Press.

Schieffelin, B. B., & Ochs, E. (1986a). Language socialization. In B. Siegel (Ed.), *Annual review of anthropology.* Palo Alto, CA: Annual Reviews.

Schieffelin, B. B., & Ochs, E. (Eds.). (1986b). *Language socialization across cultures.* New York: Cambridge University Press.

Schoneman, T. J. (1981). Reports of the sources of self-knowledge. *Journal of Personality, 49,* 284–294.

Schwartz, T., White, G., & Lutz, C. (1992). *New directions in psychological anthropology.* New York: Cambridge University Press.

Scribner, S., & Cole, M. (1973). The cognitive consequences of formal and informal education. *Science, 182,* 553–559.

Scribner, S., & Cole, M. (1981). *The psychology of literacy.* Cambridge, MA: Harvard University Press.

Shore, B. (1996). *Culture in mind: Cognition, culture and the problem of meaning.* New York: Oxford University Press.

Shuman, A. (1986). *Storytelling rights: The uses of oral and written texts by urban adolescents.* New York: Cambridge University Press.

Shweder, R. A. (1982). Beyond self-constructed knowledge: The study of culture and morality. *Merrill-Palmer Quarterly, 28,* 41–69.

Shweder, R. A. (1984). Anthropology's romantic rebellion against the enlightenment, or, there is more to thinking than reason and evidence. In R. A. Shweder & R. A. LeVine (Eds.), *Culture theory: Essays on mind, self and emotion.* New York: Cambridge University Press.

Shweder, R. A. (1990a). Cultural psychology: What is it? In J. W. Stigler, R. A. Shweder, & G. Herdt (Eds.), *Cultural psychology: Essays on comparative human development.* Cambridge, England: Cambridge University Press.

Shweder, R. A. (1990b). In defense of moral realism. *Child Development, 61,* 2060–2067.

Shweder, R. A. (1991). *Thinking through cultures: Expeditions in cultural psychology.* Cambridge, MA: Harvard University Press.

Shweder, R. A. (1992). Ghost busters in anthropology. In C. Strauss & R. G. D'Andrade (Eds.), *Human motives and cultural models.* New York: Cambridge University Press.

Shweder, R. A. (1993). The cultural psychology of the emotions. In M. Lewis & J. Haviland (Eds.), *Handbook of emotions.* New York: Guilford Press.

Shweder, R. A. (1996). True ethnography: The lore, the law and the lure. In R. Jessor, A. Colby, & R. A. Shweder (Eds.), *Ethnography and human development: Context and meaning in social inquiry.* Chicago: University of Chicago Press.

Shweder, R. A., Balle-Jensen, L., & Goldstein, W. (1995). Who sleeps by whom revisited: A method for extracting the moral goods implicit in praxis. In J. J. Goodnow, P. J. Miller, & F. Kessell (Eds.), *Cultural practices as contexts for development: New directions for child development.* San Francisco: Jossey-Bass.

Shweder, R. A., & Bourne, L. (1984). Does the concept of the person vary cross-culturally? In R. A. Shweder & R. A. LeVine (Eds.), *Culture theory: Essays on mind, self, and emotion* (pp. 158–199). New York: Cambridge University Press.

Shweder, R. A., & LeVine, R. A. (1984). *Culture theory: Essays on mind, self, and emotion.* New York: Cambridge University Press.

Shweder, R. A., Mahapatra, M., & Miller, J. G. (1990). Culture and moral development. In J. Stigler, R. A. Shweder, & G. Herdt (Eds.), *Cultural psychology: Essays on comparative human development.* New York: Cambridge University Press.

Shweder, R. A., & Much, N. C. (1987). Determinants of meaning: Discourse and moral socialization. In W. Kurtines & J. Gewirtz (Eds.), *Moral development through social interaction* (pp. 245–280). New York: Wiley.

Shweder, R. A., Much, N. C., Mahapatra, M., & Park, L. (1997). The big three of morality (autonomy, community, divinity) and the big three explanations of suffering. In A. Brandt & P. Rozin (Eds.), *Morality and health.* New York: Routledge & Kegan Paul.

Shweder, R. A., & Sullivan, M. (1990). The semiotic subject of cultural psychology. In L. Pervin (Ed.), *Handbook of personality: Theory and research* (pp. 399–416). New York: Guilford Press.

Shweder, R. A., & Sullivan, M. (1993). Cultural psychology: Who needs it? *Annual Review of Psychology, 44,* 497–523.

Snow, C. E., De Temple, J. M., Beals, D. E., Dickson, D. K., Smith, M. W., & Tabors, P. O. (1991, April). *The social prerequisites of literacy development.* Symposium presented at the annual meeting of the American Educational Research Association, Chicago.

Spence, D. P. (1982). *Narrative truth and historical truth: Meaning and interpretation in psychoanalysis.* New York: Norton.

Sperry, L. L., & Smiley, P. A. (Eds.). (1995). *Exploring young children's concepts of self and other through conversation. New directions for child development: Vol. 69.* San Francisco: Jossey-Bass.

Sperry, L. L., & Sperry, D. E. (1995). Young children's presentation of self in conversational narration. In L. L. Sperry & P. A. Smiley (Eds.), *Exploring young children's concepts of self and other through conversation. New directions for child development: Vol. 69.* San Francisco: Jossey-Bass.

Sperry, L. L., & Sperry, D. E. (1996). The early development of narrative skills. *Cognitive Development, 11,* 443–465.

Stavy, R., & Wax, N. (1989). Children's conceptions of plants as living things. *Human Development, 32,* 88–94.

Stein, K., Markus, H., & Moeser, R. (1996). *The sociocultural shaping of self-esteem of American adolescent girls and boys.*

Stern, D. (1985). *The interpersonal world of the infant.* New York: Basic Books.

Stevenson, H. W. (1994). Moving away from stereotypes and preconceptions: Students and their education in East Asia and the United States. In P. M. G. R. R. Cocking (Ed.), *Cross-cultural roots of minority child development.* Hillsdale, NJ: Erlbaum.

Stevenson, H. W., & Stigler, J. W. (1992). *The learning gap: Why our schools are failing and what we can learn from Japanese and Chinese education.* New York: Summit Books.

Stigler, J. W., Shweder, R. A., & Herdt, G. (Eds.). (1990). *Cultural psychology: Essays on comparative human development* (pp. 259–286). Cambridge, England: Cambridge University Press.

Stigler, J. W., Smith, S., & Mao, L. (1985). The self-perception of competence by Chinese children. *Child Development, 56,* 1259–1270.

Stodolsky, S. (1988). *The subject matters: Classroom activity in mathematics and social studies.* Chicago: University of Chicago Press.

Sullivan, H. S. (1940). *Conceptions of modern psychiatry.* New York: Wiley.

Super, C., & Harkness, S. (1986). The developmental niche: A conceptualization at the interface of child and culture. *International Journal of Behavioral Development, 9,* 545–569.

Tajfel, H. (1981). *Human groups and social categories.* Cambridge, England: Cambridge University Press.

Takata, T. (1987). Self-deprecative tendencies in self-evaluation through social comparison. *Japanese Journal of Experimental Social Psychology, 27,* 27–36.

Tannen, D., & Saville-Troike, M. (Eds.). (1985). *Perspectives on silence.* Norwood, NJ: ABLEX.

Taylor, C. (1995). *Child as apprentice-narrator: Socializing voice, face, identity, and self-esteem amid the narrative politics of family dinner.* Unpublished doctoral dissertation, University of Southern California, Los Angeles.

Taylor, C. E. (1989). *Sources of the self: The making of modern identities.* Cambridge, MA: Harvard University Press.

Thomas, D. (1978). Cooperation and competition among children in the Pacific Islands and New Zealand: The school as an agent of social change. *Journal of Research and Development in Education, 12,* 88–95.

Tobin, J. J., Wu, D. Y. H., & Davidson, D. H. (1989). *Preschool in three cultures: Japan, China, and the United States.* New Haven, CT: Yale University Press.

Tomasello, M., Kruger, A. C., & Ratner, H. H. (1993). Cultural learning. *Behavioral and Brain Sciences, 16,* 495–552.

Triandis, H. C. (1989). The self and social behavior in differing cultural contexts. *Psychological Review, 93*(3), 506–520.

Triandis, H. C. (1990). Cross-cultural studies of individualism and collectivism. In J. Berman (Ed.), *Nebraska Symposium on Motivation, 1989* (pp. 41–133). Lincoln: University of Nebraska Press.

Triandis, H. C., Bontempo, R., & Villareal, M. (1988). Individualism and collectivism: Cross-cultural perspectives on self-ingroup relationships. *Journal of Personality and Social Psychology, 54,* 323–338.

Tronick, E. Z., Morelli, G., & Ivey, P. K. (1992). The Efe forager infant and toddler's pattern of social relationships: Multiple and simultaneous. *Developmental Psychology, 28,* 568–577.

Tronick, E. Z., Morelli, G., & Winn, S. (1987). Multiple caretaking of Efe (Pygmy) infants. *American Anthropologist, 89,* 96–106.

Tu, W. (1994). Embodying the universe: A note on Confucian self-realization. In R. T. Ames, W. Dissanayake, & T. P. Kasulis (Eds.), *Self as person in Asian theory and practice* (pp. 177–186). Albany: State University of New York Press.

Tulviste, P. (1991). *The cultural-historical development of verbal thinking.* Commack, NY: Nova Science.

Valsiner, J. (1988). *Child development within culturally structured environments: Social co-construction and environmental guidance in development* (Vol. 2). Norwood, NJ: ABLEX.

Valsiner, J. (1994). Co-construction: What is (and what is not) in a name. In P. van Geert & L. Mos (Eds.), *Annals of theoretical psychology* (Vol. 10, pp. 343–368). New York: Plenum Press.

Van der Meulen, M. (1986). Zelfconceptieproblemen bij jonge kinderen: Eenanalyse van spontane, zelfbeschouwende uitspraken. *Nederlands Tijdschrift boor de Psychologie en haar Grensgebieden, 41*(6), 261–267.

Varela, F. J., Thompson, E., & Rosch, E. (1993). *The embodied mind: Cognitive science and human experience.* Cambridge, MA: MIT Press.

Verdonik, F., Flapan, V., Schmit, C., & Weinstock, J. (1988). The role of power relationships in children's cognition: Its significance for research in cognitive development. *Newsletter of Laboratory for Comparative Human Development, 10,* 80–85.

Vygotsky, L. S. (1987). *The collected works of L. S. Vygotsky: Vol. 1. Problems of general psychology.* New York: Plenum Press. (Original work published 1934)

Walkerdine, V. (1988). *The mastery of reason.* London: Routledge & Kegan Paul.

Ward, M. (1971). *Them children.* New York: Holt, Rinehart and Winston.

Watson-Gegeo, K. A. (1993). Thick explanation in the ethnographic study of child socialization: A longitudinal study of the problem of schooling for Kwara'ae (Solomon Island) children. In W. A. Corsaro & P. J. Miller (Eds.), *Interpretive approaches to childhood socialization* (pp. 51–66). San Francisco: Jossey-Bass.

Watson-Gegeo, K. A., & Gegeo, D. W. (1990). Shaping the mind and straightening out conflicts: The discourse of Kwara'ae family counseling. In K. A. Watson-Gegeo & G. M. White (Eds.), *Disentangling: Conflict discourse in Pacific societies* (pp. 161–213). Stanford, CA: Stanford University Press.

Watson-Gegeo, K. A., & White, G. M. (Eds.). (1990). *Disentangling: Conflict discourse in Pacific societies.* Stanford, CA: Stanford University Press.

Weigert, A. J., Teitge, J. S., & Teitge, D. W. (1990). *Society and identity: Towards a sociological psychology.* Cambridge and New York: Cambridge University Press.

Weisner, T. S. (1982). Sibling interdependence and sibling caretaking: A cross-cultural view. In M. Lamb & B. Sutton-Smith (Eds.), *Sibling relationships: Their nature and significance across the lifespan.* Hillsdale, NJ: Erlbaum.

Weisner, T. S. (1984). A cross-cultural perspective: Ecological niches of middle childhood. In A. Collins (Ed.), *The elementary school years: Understanding development during middle childhood* (pp. 335–369). Washington, DC: National Academy.

Weisner, T. S. (1987). Socialization for parenthood in sibling caretaking societies. In J. Lancaster, A. Rossi, & J. Altmann (Eds.), *Parenting across the lifespan.* New York: Aldine.

Weisner, T. S. (1989a). Cultural and universal aspects of social support for children: Evidence from the Alaluyia of Kenya. In D. Belle (Ed.), *Children's social networks and social supports.* New York: Wiley.

Weisner, T. S. (1989b). Comparing sibling relationships across cultures. In P. Zukow (Ed.), *Sibling interaction across cultures.* New York: Springer-Verlag.

Weisner, T. S. (1996). Why ethnography should be the most important method in the study of human development. In R. Jesser, A. Colby, & R. A. Shweder (Eds.), *Ethnography and human development.* Chicago: University of Chicago Press.

Weisner, T. S. (in press). The 5–7 transition as an ecocultural project. In A. Sameroff & M. Haith (Eds.), *Reason and responsibility: The passage through childhood.* Chicago: University of Chicago Press.

Weisner, T. S., Bausano, M., & Kornfein, M. (1983). Putting family ideals into practice. *Ethos, 11,* 278–304.

Weisner, T. S., & Gallimore, R. (1977). My brother's keeper: Child and sibling caretaking. *Current Anthropology, 18,* 169–180.

Wellman, H. M., & Gelman, S. A. (1992). Cognitive development: Foundational theories of core domains. *Annual Review of Psychology, 43,* 337–375.

Wenger, M. (1989). Work, play and social relationships among children in a Giriama community. In D. Belle (Ed.), *Children's social networks and social supports.* New York: Wiley.

Werker, J. (1989). Becoming a native listener. *American Scientist, 77,* 54–59.

Wertsch, J. V. (1985). *Vygotsky and the social formation of mind.* Cambridge, MA: Harvard University Press.

Wertsch, J. V. (1991). *Voices of the mind.* Cambridge, MA: Harvard University Press.

Wertsch, J. V. (1992). Keys to cultural psychology. *Culture, Medicine and Psychiatry, 16*(3), 273–280.

White, G. M., & Kirkpatrick, J. (1985). *Person, self and experience: Exploring Pacific ethnopsychologies.* Berkeley: University of California Press.

White, M. I., & LeVine, R. A. (1986). What is an li ko (good child)? In H. Stevenson, H. Azuma, & K. Hakuta (Eds.), *Child development and education in Japan* (pp. 55–62). New York: Freeman.

Whiting, B. B., & Edwards, C. P. (1988). *Children of different worlds.* Cambridge, MA: Harvard University Press.

Whiting, B. B., & Whiting, J. W. M. (1975). *Children of six cultures.* Cambridge, MA: Harvard University Press.

Whiting, J. W. M. (1964). Effects of climate on certain cultural practices. In W. H. Goodenough (Ed.), *Explorations in cultural anthropology.* New York: McGraw-Hill.

Whiting, J. W. M. (1981). Environmental constraints on infant care practices. In R. H. Munroe, R. L. Munroe, & B. B. Whiting (Eds.), *Handbook of cross-cultural human development.* New York: Garland.

Whiting, J. W. M., & Child, I. (1953). *Child training and personality.* New Haven, CT: Yale University Press.

Wierzbicka, A. (1986). Human emotions: Universal or culture-specific? *American Anthropologist, 88*(3), 584–594.

Wierzbicka, A. (1991). *Cross-cultural pragmatics: The semantics of human interaction.* Berlin: De Gruyter.

Wierzbicka, A. (1992). *Semantics, culture and cognition: Universal human concepts in culture-specific configurations.* New York: Oxford University Press.

Wierzbicka, A. (1993). A conceptual basis for cultural psychology. *Ethos, 21*(2), 205–231.

Willis, P. (1977). *Learning to labor: How working class kids get working class jobs.* New York: Columbia University Press.

Winegar, L. T. (1988). Children's emerging understanding of social events: Co-construction and social process. In J. Valsiner (Ed.), *Child development within culturally structured environments* (Vol. 2, pp. 2–27). New York: ABLEX.

Wolf, S. A., & Heath, S. B. (1992). *The braid of literature: Children's worlds of reading.* Cambridge, MA: Harvard University Press.

Wozniak, R. H. (1993). Co-constructive metatheory for psychology: Implications for an analysis of families as specific social contexts for development. In R. H. Wozniak & K. W. Fischer (Eds.), *Development in context* (pp. 77–91). Hillsdale, NJ: Erlbaum.

Wu, D. Y. H. (1994). Self and collectivity: Socialization in Chinese preschools. In R. T. Ames, W. Dissanayake, & T. P. Kasulis (Eds.), *Self as person in Asian theory and practice.* Albany: State University of New York Press.

Wyer, R. S., Jr. (Ed.). (1995). Knowledge and memory: The real story. *Advances in social cognition* (Vol. 8). Hillsdale, NJ: Erlbaum.

Yang, K.-S. (in press). Indiginizing westernized Chinese psychology. In M. H. Bond (Ed.), *Working at the interface of culture: 20 lives in soial science.* London: Routledge & Kegan Paul.

CHAPTER 16

The Life Course and Human Development

GLEN H. ELDER, JR.

The study of life course and human development has become a flourishing field during the closing decades of the 20th century, extending across substantive and theoretical boundaries of the behavioral sciences. Life course thinking now appears in most disciplines and specialty areas (Featherman, 1983). From this change has come an appreciation for the long way of thinking about personality, development, and life transitions in changing societies. With the dramatic growth of longitudinal studies, we know more now than ever before about behavioral adaptations to the way lives are lived. We are also more aware of individuals as agents of their own lives.

I acknowledge support by the National Institute of Mental Health (MH 41327, MH 43270, and MH 51361), a contract with the U.S. Army Research Institute, research support from the John D. and Catherine T. MacArthur Foundation Program for Successful Adolescent Development among Youth in High-Risk Settings, and a Research Scientist Award (MH 00567).

To grasp the magnitude of this change, consider where we were in the 1960s. C. Wright Mills (1959, p. 149) had just proposed an orienting concept in the behavioral sciences—in his words, "the study of biography, of history, and of the problems of their intersection within social structure." But he had few empirical examples to draw on. Indeed, human lives were an uncommon subject of study, particularly in their social and historical context. The concept of life course had not yet appeared in the scholarly literature and it was not dealt with in the seminars of our leading graduate programs. I left graduate studies without any exposure to, or understanding of, the life course as a theory, field of inquiry, or method.

The unfolding story of life course theory up to the present owes much to a set of pathbreaking studies that were launched more than 60 years ago at the Institute of Child Welfare (now Human Development), University of California—the Oakland Growth Study (birth years, 1920–1921), the Berkeley Growth and Guidance Studies (birth years,

1928–1929). When these studies began, no one could have imagined what they eventually would mean for the field of child development. The investigators did not envision research that would extend into the adult years of their Study members, let alone into the later years of old age. There were many reasons for this limited perspective. Except for support from the Laura Spelman Rockefeller Foundation, substantial funds for longitudinal studies were virtually nonexistent.

In addition, the idea of adult development had not as yet captured the imagination of behavioral scientists. A mature field of adult development and aging was still decades away from becoming a reality, but this did not restrict the studies from continuing into the adult years and middle age. A visitor to the Institute of Human Development (UC-Berkeley) during the early 1960s would have discovered that the Oakland Growth Study members had been contacted for interviews in the early and late 1950s, along with members of the Berkeley Guidance Study under the direction of Jean MacFarlane. Another follow-up, scheduled in 1972–1973, joined the lives of the Study members, their parents, and offspring, within an intergenerational framework. Similar extensions to adulthood were occurring elsewhere, such as the Fels Institute sample in Ohio. Kagan and Moss (1962) completed a study of the Fels sample up to the age of 23, entitled *Birth to Maturity* (1962).

By the 1980s, Jack Block (1971), with the assistance of Norma Haan, had completed a pathbreaking study of personality continuity and change from early adolescence to the middle years in the lives of Study members at the Institute of Human Development, Berkeley. Another study (Elder, 1974) placed the lives of the Oakland Growth participants in the Great Depression and traced the influence of hardship experiences to family life, careers, and health up to mid-life. To cap off this active decade, investigators at the Berkeley Institute of Human Development completed a multifaceted study that revealed patterns of continuity and change in social roles, health, and personality, with a distinctive emphasis on life patterns across the middle years (Eichorn, Clausen, Haan, Honzik, & Mussen, 1981). Both historical cohort comparisons and intergenerational connections were part of this project.

Also during the 1970s, George Vaillant (1977) followed a panel of Harvard men (circa 1940) into the middle years of adulthood, assessing mechanisms of defense and coping. And at Stanford University, a research team headed by Robert Sears was actively following members of the Lewis Terman sample of talented children into their later years. This was the oldest currently active longitudinal study at the time, with birth years extending from 1903 to the 1920s. By the 1990s, the project had assembled 12 waves of data spanning 70 years (Holahan & Sears, 1995); and research had begun to reveal the historical imprint of the times on the Study members' lives (Elder, Pavalko, & Hastings, 1991), from the 1920s to the post-World War II years.

This extension of the early child samples to the adult years gave fresh momentum to the scientific study of adult development and sharpened awareness of the need for a different research paradigm, one that would give attention to *human development beyond childhood and to life trajectories*. What social routes to adulthood favored behavioral continuity or change? Which ones enabled problem children to turn their lives around and become effective adults? Child-based models of development had little to offer since they did not address development and aging in the adult life course. For the most part, studies of continuity and change from childhood to the adult years were limited to evidence of correlational patterns between measures at time 1 and time 2 (Jones, Bayley, Macfarlane, & Honzik, 1971; Kagan & Moss, 1962). The intervening years remained a "black box." Little if anything could be learned about linking events and processes from such analysis.

Kagan and Moss (1962) studied the Fels children from "birth to maturity" by using correlation coefficients to depict behavioral stability across the years, and they did so by ignoring the diverse paths of youth to the young adult years—into work, advanced education, military service. By their 23rd birthday, some would have followed a path of college, full-time employment, and marriage. Others no doubt entered the service or mixed employment and education. Another important feature of the transition to adulthood is the differing timetable for events. Adolescent marriage and parenting are coupled with more social and economic constraints than a normative timetable, whereas late family formation maximizes economic advantages and the disruptive effect of young children.

These limitations posed a number of challenges: first, the need for concepts of human development that applied to the years beyond childhood; second, the necessity for making greater sense of behavioral continuity and change across people's lives, a task that called for thinking about the social organization and dynamics of lives over time; and third, the dramatic social changes of the time called for greater sensitivity to potential historical effects in human development. As a whole, the issues brought to mind a view of human development in context that was advocated many decades earlier by proponents of the early Chicago school of sociology (Abbott, 1997), and especially by William I. Thomas, author of the well-known Thomas Theorem, "If men define situations as real, they are real in their consequences."

During the first decades of the 20th century, a time of massive changes in American society, Thomas made a persuasive case for studying change as "experiments of nature" (to use Bronfenbrenner's term, 1979) in the lives of immigrants and children. Inspired by Thomas and Znaniecki's *The Polish Peasant in Europe and America* (1918–1920), researchers began to use life record data to investigate the impact of social change. Before most of the pioneering longitudinal studies had been launched, Thomas (Volkart, 1951, p. 593) urged in the mid-1920s that priority be given to the "longitudinal approach to life history." He claimed that studies should investigate "many types of individuals with regard to their experiences and various past periods of life in different situations" and follow "groups of individuals in the future, getting a continuous record of experiences as they occur." He also made a case for social interventions that would improve the life situation of problem children through placement in more developmental environments.

The social transformations of the 20th century raised a great many questions about the generalizability of findings. In the classic Middletown studies (Lynd & Lynd, 1929, 1937), findings on families during the 1920s seemed to have little relevance to family life in the Great Depression. Indeed, each of the pioneering longitudinal studies followed different timetables and historical sequences. The Lewis Terman sample, on average, reached the age of majority in the 1930s, the Oakland Growth Study men and women achieved this status during World War II, and the Berkeley Guidance study members became 21 years of age around 1950. Childhood, adolescence, and young adulthood had different meanings for each of these cohorts, a point well documented by Modell (1989) in his study of the emergence of modern adolescence.

Life course theory emerged in partial response to issues of this kind in the 1960s, with particular attention to

people's lives in historical time. In the terminology of this chapter, life course theory represents primarily one form of theory, a theoretical orientation. To borrow from Robert Merton's (1968) distinction, a theoretical orientation establishes a common field of inquiry by defining a framework that guides research in terms of problem identification and formulation, variable selection and rationales, and strategies of design and analysis. Within limits, the chapter also attempts to systematize the literature around empirical generalizations and propositions.

Based in large measure on sociocultural theories of age and social relations (Elder, 1975; Neugarten, 1968; Ryder, 1965), the concept of life course refers to a sequence of socially defined, age-graded events and roles that the individual enacts over time. A sociocultural perspective gives emphasis to the social meanings of age. Birth, puberty, and death are biological facts, but their meanings in the life course are social facts or constructions. Age distinctions are expressed in expectations about the timing and order of a transition, whether early, on-time, or late. This life course can also be placed in history by linking it to specific transitions and to the meanings of cohort status, as obtained from birth records (Riley, Johnson, & Foner, 1972). Birth year locates people in specific birth cohorts and thus according to particular social changes.

I first met such ideas about age and the life course in the 1960s, just after arriving at the Institute of Human Development (U-C Berkeley, 1962) to work with the late sociologist John Clausen on the Oakland Growth Study. The dramatic changefulness of families and individual lives across the 1930s focused my energies on coming up with ways of thinking about the patterning of lives and its relation to a changing socioeconomic system. We needed temporal codes for people's lives instead of the conventional codes for states and times. Age distinctions provided an important step in this direction as I viewed family adaptations as a link between drastic economic decline and the behavioral outcomes of both parents and children. They also provided a way of thinking about the social construction of individual lives, along with ideas from the early Chicago School of Sociology. *Children of the Great Depression* (Elder, 1974) represents the published version of this initial effort to fashion a life course framework.

Over the past 30 years, advances in life course theory and research have come from many quarters across the behavioral and social sciences, identifying key problems and defining approaches. These advances range from sociology (Elder, 1975, 1985; Riley, Johnson, & Foner, 1972) and demography (Ryder, 1965) to history (Hareven, 1978, 1982; Modell, 1989), anthropology (Kertzer & Keith, 1984), and both ecological (Bronfenbrenner, 1979) and life-span developmental psychology (Baltes & Baltes, 1990). They are coupled with:

1. The rapid growth of longitudinal studies and knowledge that link childhood and the adult years, and the latter with late life adaptations (Young, Savola, & Phelps, 1991);

2. The development of life history calendars for the collection of retrospective accounts of life events (Caspi et al., 1996);

3. The development of new statistical techniques for such data, both structural and dynamic models, person- and variable-centered (Magnusson, Bergman, Rudinger, & Törestad, 1991);

4. The construction of cross-disciplinary models of collaboration (Elder, Modell, & Parke, 1993). This chapter draws liberally from these sources in exploring the relevance of contemporary progress for studies of child, adolescent, and adult development.

As will be seen, this relevance centers around the individual life course, its relation to changing social and historical conditions, and its implications for developmental processes. In this respect, life course theory has much in common with interactionist thinking and person-situation models (Magnusson & Allen, 1983), but it also attends to the organization and reorganization of social structures and pathways over the life span. As might be expected, it shares many objectives and concepts with the ecology of human development (Bronfenbrenner, 1979), including its multilevel concept of the environment, from micro to macro. Life course models also share the ambition of life-span developmental psychology in rethinking the nature of human development and aging (Baltes, 1994), but with particular attention to the changing life course.

The chapter begins by viewing the emergence of life course thinking as a response to some of the challenges we have noted, particularly those that stem from following children into the middle- and old-age years. Life-span ideas in developmental psychology were prominent in this conceptual enterprise, as were a life-cycle theory of role sequences, and concepts of the age-graded life course. By the end of the 1970s, a new synthesis, relating theory on relationships, age, and biology had been achieved in the form of a theoretical orientation on the life course.

The basic concepts and distinctions of life course theory are surveyed in the next section, with emphasis on the individual life course, its institutionalized pathways, developmental trajectories, and transitions. Paradigmatic themes of life course theory are identified next and illustrated by research projects. The themes include human agency and choice-making in the construction of lives, the timing of lives, linked or interdependent lives, and human lives in historical time and place. This account concludes with a summary of the distinctive contributions of life course theory to studies of children and adolescents.

The concluding section features the prominence of timing in lives—historical, social, and biological—as expressed in theory and research: ties between history and lives, the process of constructing one's life, and the implications of timing in one person's life for the relations between people and trajectories. Timing in the study of historical influences centers especially on life stage as a contingency. The same historical change has different consequences for people of different ages and developmental stage. By bringing contextual matters to the forefront of human development study, timing distinctions address each of the theoretical challenges that frame this chapter.

THE EMERGENCE OF LIFE COURSE THEORY: A HISTORICAL ACCOUNT

Empirical studies of children into their adult and mid-life years have revealed major limitations in conventional knowledge of human development. Three limitations have played an important role in the emergence of life course theory through their challenges:

1. To replace child-based, growth-oriented accounts of development with models that apply to development and aging over the life course;

2. To think about how human lives are organized and evolve over time;

3. To relate lives to an ever-changing society, with emphasis on the developmental effects of changing circumstances.

Responses to these challenges from the 1960s helped to give shape and scope to the life course as research paradigm and theoretical orientation.

Concepts of Human Development across the Life Span

Proponents of life-span developmental psychology (a field of inquiry first identified by name in 1969) have addressed the first challenge, in particular, by seeking a more satisfying concept of development and aging across the life span that places greater weight on cultural influences and learned experiences or skills in patterns of aging. In theory, historical and cultural variations emerged as particularly influential as sources of adult adaptations and development. The essential behavioral dimensions of these life-span models are still not well-understood, but, as Baltes (1979, p. 265) observed, "it appears that restricting developmental events to those which have the features of a biological growth concept of development is more of a hindrance than a help."

Paul Baltes (1993, 1994) has been a major figure in the conceptual articulation of life-span development since the 1960s. More than most proponents of this perspective, he has interacted with life course ideas and distinctions over the decades. For this reason, it is particularly useful to specify the key dimensions of his view of life-span development as it has evolved with colleagues at his Max Planck research program in Berlin (see his chapter in this Volume). The individual propositions on life-span development are not new in themselves but they add up to a distinctive perspective:

1. Life-span development results from a life-long adaptive process. Some processes are cumulative and continuous, others are discontinuous and innovative, showing little connection to prior events or processes.
2. Ontogenetic development is local, specific, and time-bound; it is never fully adaptive. There is no pure advance or loss in development.
3. Age-graded influences are most important in the dependency years, childhood/adolescence and old age, whereas history-graded and non-normative influences are most consequential across the early and middle years of adulthood.

4. Changes occur in relation to positive and negative events, gains and losses, with the likelihood of expected losses increasing. Biological resources decline over the life span, whereas cultural resources may increase, as in the cultivation of wisdom.
5. Life-span development entails "selection," "optimization," and "compensation." These mechanisms seek to maximize gains and minimize losses or declines. Selective optimization with compensation represents a "life-span model of psychological management that describes how individuals can deal with the dual-faced nature of human aging and the ubiquitous, age-related shift toward a less positive balance of gains and losses" (Baltes, 1993, p. 590).

The way these mechanisms or strategies are put to work in later life is illustrated by Baltes' (1993, p. 590) reference to an interview with the concert pianist Arthur Rubenstein. When asked how he remained a successful pianist in his late years, Rubenstein referred to three strategies: "(1) . . . he performed fewer pieces, (2) he now practiced each more frequently, and (3) he introduced more ritardandos in his playing before fast segments, so that the playing sounded faster than it was." The strategy of selection is illustrated by Rubenstein's concentration on fewer pieces, the more frequent practice of each illustrates the use of optimization, and the greater use of contrast in speed exemplifies a strategy of compensation.

This psychological model of successful aging has relevance for successful development at all ages, including childhood and adolescence. Adaptations in adolescence can be viewed in terms of the guidelines of selective optimization in which gains are maximized and risks, losses, or deprivations are minimized. Youth select activities in which they are competent, whether athletics, academics, or street-life, and optimize benefits through an investment of resources, time, energy, and relationships. Marsiske, Lang, Baltes, and Baltes (1995, pp. 35–36) claim that selective optimization with compensation is best understood as a meta model for life-span development since it applies more broadly to aspects of the "developmental person-context matrix." They provide an excellent source on the theoretical and empirical status of this formulation in the study of life-span development.

Life-span developmentalists, such as Baltes, Warner Schaie, and others, have enriched our thinking about development and aging across the life course, and they have also given some attention to the role of social, cultural, and historical forces in developmental processes. However, concepts of life-span development generally fail to apprehend social structure as a constitutive force in development. The social environment remains little more than a setting that facilitates "maturational unfolding" (Dannefer, 1984, p. 847). This limitation also applies to the field of child development as well, and to all theories of development that view developmental processes from the perspective of the organism. As Hetherington and Baltes (1988, p. 9) point out, "child psychologists are likely to postulate a 'typical' course of ontogeny and to view non-normative and history-graded factors as modifiers, not as fundamental constituents, of development."

The important issue here is to recognize that there is not one "optimum" *point of entry* for studying human development across the life span. Indeed, the multilevel nature of human development invites different points of entry, with their specific research questions, from cultures and social institutions to the human organism. Entry points frequently link or cross levels in the developmental process. Studies commonly employ different points of entry in the same research, though framed by the entry point of its central question. Thus, a project motivated by the impact of rural change on children's social and emotional development should be framed by an initial focus on some aspect of this social process, such as the degree of economic hardship and displacement. Inquiry would explore the process by which this change makes a difference in children's developmental experience. Parts of this study might also investigate the determinants of specific emotional or social outcomes and relevant protective resources within the family, a point of entry that centers on the developmental status of the child. Still other points of entry might begin with the interchange of parents and child or with sibling relationships. Each of these points of entry could become a framing statement for an independent study.

A number of efforts in the psychological sciences were made during the postwar years to link child and adult developmental trajectories to social structure and changes in society, though typically from the perspective of a maturing or aging organism. Research questions did not ask about the implications of environmental change for the developing individual. Erik Erikson's (1950, 1963) theory of psychosocial stages was formulated with an eye to cultural

variations, but he too largely saw the social system and culture from the vantage point of the developing organism. Likewise, Daniel Levinson's (1978) *The Seasons of a Man's Life* outlined a theory of life structure that ignored variations in social structure and culture over historical time. Psychosocial transitions were affixed to age as if immutable to institutional change, such as the mid-life transition between ages 40 and 45.

Within the University of Chicago's Committee on Human Development, postwar studies such as the Kansas City project were more successful than other efforts at the time in linking human development through the adult years to the social structures in which people lived. For example, Bernice Neugarten (Neugarten & Peterson, 1957) observed a relationship between age-linked concepts of self and life stage by socioeconomic position. Working class men and women were older when they entered the self-defined middle years of life, compared to upper status people. Neugarten made a number of important contributions in this early work by connecting socioeconomic careers to adult psychology, role transitions, and the generations. We return to these contributions in the context of age-based perspectives on the life course.

How Lives Are Socially Organized: Roles, Cycles, and Age

An individual's life pattern is structured by multiple role sequences and their transitions. These transitions into and out of social roles across the life span entail changes in status and identity, social and personal (Glaser & Strauss, 1971). In their field studies, anthropologists have referred to a patterned role sequence from birth to death as "a life cycle" (Kertzer & Keith, 1984). Changes in major roles, such as from youth to marriage and parenthood, generally represent changes in social stage across the life cycle.

In concept, the life cycle views life organization in terms of social relationships, particularly kin relationships and generational succession. A dominant concept of the life span, from the early 1900s up to the 1960s, the life cycle generally referred to a sequence of social roles among individuals and families. Erik Erikson, for example, developed his psychosocial theory of ego development around eight stages of a psychological life cycle. Each stage represents a critical period of conflict and possible crisis for the development of an ego quality such as trust and initiative. Ego development unfolds according to an epigenetic ground plan and depends on the interaction between accrued ego strength at each stage and particular role demands. Ego strength at each stage is achieved by integrating "the timetable of the organism with the structure of social institutions" (Erikson, 1950, 1963, p. 246). This achievement depends in part on one's history of ego achievements and failures.

A more precise social meaning of life cycle applies to a sequence of stages in parenting, from the birth of children through their departure from the home to their own childbearing. In this sense, the role sequence refers to a reproductive process that always applies to human populations. Within a life cycle of generational succession, newborns are socialized to maturity, give birth to the next generation, grow old, and die. The "cycle" is repeated from one generation to the next in a human population, but it clearly does not apply to all individuals (O'Rand & Krecker, 1990). Some do not have children and are thus not part of the reproductive process.

Life cycles as reproductive cycles vary greatly in the pace of their revolutions. Early childbearing, shortly after menarche, accelerates the cycle and shortens the distance between the generations (Burton, 1985). When the eldest daughter has a child before the age of 13, her mother may become a grandmother before the age of 30 and a great-grandmother before the age of 50. A sequence of early childbearing across the generations weakens the generational and age basis for family authority and social control. By contrast, late childbearing slows the cycle and minimizes age similarities across adjacent generations. In a rapidly changing world, parents, grandparents, and children share less culture and historical experience.

The life cycle concept incorporates both socialization and social control processes. The predominant roles of a life stage lock people into a set of normative expectations and informal sanctions that provide direction and discipline. Commitments to a line of action arise over time through obligations to significant others. Stable role relationships ensure a measure of personal stability, just as entry into such relationships can stabilize a person's life and minimize involvement in unconventional and dangerous activities. Robins (1966) found that work roles with little supervision and a nurturant spouse increased the chances of adult success for children characterized by sociopathic behavior problems. Likewise, Sampson and Laub (1993)

observed in their sample of men from a low-income urban population that adult bonds to conventional figures and lines of activity defined a route of escape from delinquency for a substantial number of men with a childhood history of delinquency and economic disadvantage.

During the familistic postwar years, the life cycle became well-known as the *family cycle* through the writings of Paul Glick and Reuben Hill; a set of ordered stages of parenthood defined primarily by variations in family composition and size (Elder, 1978). Major transition points included courtship, engagement, marriage, birth of the first and last child, the children's transitions in school, departure of the eldest and youngest child from the home, and marital dissolution through the death of one spouse. Family life in this era provided a better fit to this sequence of roles than it does today. Marriage and parenting have been uncoupled to a considerable extent (Cherlin, 1993). More children than before are born prior to marriage or outside of marriage altogether. The soaring divorce rate has led to multiple families within a person's life and to the likelihood that most children will experience a single-parent household before they enter adulthood.

The life cycle concept and its family cycle version usefully knit together the full array of life stages and generations. They also provide insight into processes of socialization and social control over the life span that link the developing person and his or her career. Having said this, it is important to note that the life cycle's focus on reproduction and parenting has limited its value as a way of viewing the lives and developmental trajectories of children and adults. It is limited because it does not apply to the never-married, to nonparents, and to the multiply-divorced. Its focus on a single career also ignores the realities of multiple careers.

Each person generally occupies multiple roles at the same time, whether spouse and parent or spouse and employee, but these concurrent roles are not part of the life cycle's scope. Consequently, the life or family cycle did not orient research to the management or coordination of multiple roles, such as marriage and work. By the end of the 1960s, a prime era for life cycle research, a survey by Young and Willmott (1973) concluded that studies of work and family had proceeded along separate paths with no significant joint effort to examine their interdependencies. This contrasts rather strikingly to the flourishing study of work and family relations (Crouter & McHale, 1993;

Parcel & Menaghan, 1994), with its emphasis on interlocking trajectories.

In addition, the life cycle is insensitive to temporal location and matters of timing. The concept depicts a sequence of social roles and transitions. Social roles are ordered, but not temporally located within a person's life. In the case of the family cycle, for example, each stage of parenting could be arrayed in a sequence, but it would not be bounded by age, the temporal markers that come with a perspective on the age-graded life course. A life cycle model of a person's life might locate marriage before the first birth, but it would not tell you whether the marriage occurred at 20 or 40 years. Sequence models thus provide only part of the story on life context.

The kinship term of *generation* is part of a life cycle perspective and shares its blindness to temporality. Members of an ancestral generation do not occupy a common historical location relative to events and long-range trends. A parent generation, for example, may have birth years that span up to 30 years, a time frame that could include eras of economic depression, global war, and peace in the 20th century. The greater the time span, the more diverse the historical experience of the generation. With these points in mind, it is apparent that generational role or position cannot offer a precise way of connecting people's lives to the changes in society. Indeed intergenerational studies are generally distinguished by their insensitivity to historical time or location; generations are frequently studied in the timeless realm of the abstract.

Temporal limitations of this kind are generally characteristic of models based on role theory. Ebaugh's recent study of role exits (1988) makes this limitation very clear. Role exit involves a change of identity in terms of the new role and its predecessor, but Ebaugh's makes no explicit reference to timing across the life span or to historical time. Judging from the analysis, one might conclude that it is not consequential whether an illness and death involves a child or a grandparent, whether family separation occurs in one's 20s or 50s, or whether a lay-off occurs at the beginning or the end of one's productive work life. On the contrary, the evidence suggests that timing matters in all of these ways because we are influenced by social timetables, age norms, and age-graded sanctions.

In summary, role sequences and identity change, processes of socialization and social control, the life cycle perspective, and the generations are conceptual elements of a "relationship" view of life patterns and organization that dates back to the 19th century. One of the earliest proponents of this view, sociologist William I. Thomas used life record data to study the emigration of Polish peasants to European and American cities around the turn of the century (Thomas & Znaniecki, 1918–1920). In this pioneering work, the lives of emigrants embodied the discontinuities of the age; they were socialized for a world that had become only a memory. The societies they left and entered presented contrasting "lines of genesis" or primary sequences of social roles for individual adaptation and development. Matters of social and historical time are clearly relevant to this project, and yet Thomas and Znaniecki were largely insensitive to them. They did not locate their Polish peasants in historical time through information on birth year, relate life transitions to particular ages, or consider age at emigration in terms of its adaptive implications.

For many years, the relationship and life cycle perspective offered a valuable way of thinking about the social patterning and interdependence of lives, though limited in a number of respects. During the 1960s, this approach began to converge with newly developing understandings of age to form life course models that combined the virtues of both theoretical traditions; of linked lives across the life span and generations, and of temporality through an age-graded sequence of events and social roles, embedded in a changing world. In addition, these models were informed by life span concepts of human development that underscored the agency of individuals in the social construction of their lives and life courses.

Age and the Life Course

The importance of the 1960s' decade for linking these theoretical traditions on lives had much to do with the appearance of new ways of thinking about age, including an appreciation for its diverse meanings and consequences. These new ways include an emphasis on subjective experiences with the age structures of society and the individual's own construction of a life course, as expressed in the pioneering work of Bernice Neugarten in particular (Neugarten & Datan, 1973). Through the pathbreaking work of Norman Ryder (1965) and Matilda Riley (Riley, Johnson, & Foner, 1972), these new ways also included a more developed articulation of the relation between historical time and lives, as expressed through membership in age cohorts and successive age strata. For the first time, this work joined two relatively independent lines of research on age (Elder, 1975), the sociocultural and cohort-historical.

To highlight these historical developments, I briefly review the early studies of Bernice Neugarten on the social and developmental psychology of age and the life course; discuss the contribution of Matilda Riley to an understanding of age cohorts and grades in patterning the life course; and show the complementarity of relationship and age perspectives in a 1960s study of the life course.

Sociocultural Patterns in Human Experience

The relevance of age for a sociocultural understanding of life organization has evolved over many decades of ethnographic study by anthropologists, as in research on age-grading and age-set societies (Kertzer & Keith, 1984). However, this work generally focused on age structures in particular cultures, whereas the new inquiry explored individual experiences of age and age-grading, giving fresh insights to the social and psychological variability of people's lives.

Contrary to a prevailing modal view of age patterns in cultures (Eisenstadt, 1956; Kertzer & Keith, 1984), studies began to show that people of the same age do not march in concert across major events of the life course; rather, they vary in the pace and sequencing of their transitions and they do so in ways that have real consequences for family pressures, child socialization, and personal well-being. This variation also appears in accounts of differential aging among people who follow different social trajectories.

During the late 1950s and early 1960s, Bernice Neugarten directed a research program that featured a concept of normative timetables and individual deviations from such expectations (Neugarten & Datan, 1973). The timetable of the life course refers to social age, as defined by people's expectations regarding events. In theory, age expectations specify appropriate times for major transitions. There is an appropriate time for entering school, leaving home, getting married, having children, and retiring from the labor force. Neugarten, Moore, and Lowe (1965) observed a high degree of consensus on age norms across some 15 age-related characteristics in samples of middle-class adults. The data reveal general agreement among men and women on the appropriate age for a woman to marry and support the hypothesis that informal sanctions are associated with relatively early and later marriage. Moreover, the women were aware of whether in fact they were on time, late, or early with respect to marriage and other major role transitions.

Though subsequent studies have extended this line of research (Settersten & Mayer, 1997), it is still the case that relatively little is known about age expectations, their boundaries and related sanctions (Marini, 1984); clearly, these topics deserve far more attention than they have received to date. Some notions about the proper phasing of the life course take the form of cognitive descriptions or predictions rather than normative accounts, whether prescriptive or proscriptive. In any case, age expectations are central to socialization and social control, and Feldman's and Rosenthal's (1991) cross-national studies of age expectations on behavioral autonomy suggest some of the possibilities in this line of work. Later expectations of behavioral autonomy are related to monitoring by parents, to a demanding family environment, relatively low levels of autocratic parenting, and the de-emphasis by youth of individualism, outward success, and competence. The process by which age expectations and timetables are constructed, transmitted, and learned remains largely unexplored territory.

For many decades, age grades or categories were inferred as possessing common significance without evidence of their meaning to the individuals involved. At what point do young children take the perspective of a student and when do young adults begin to take an adult standpoint and view themselves accordingly? Is marriage the key transition for an adult perspective or is birth of a child or stable employment? Such questions were of interest in Neugarten's research program and she broke new ground in testing the proposition that life stage is partially a function of one's socioeconomic status and career.

In the mid-1950s, Neugarten found (Neugarten & Peterson, 1957) that men in the lower strata were likely to perceive a more rapid passage through the major age divisions of life than middle-class men; maturity, middle age, and old age come earlier in their life span, owing perhaps to class-linked occupational demands and activities. The man who relies upon mental skills in a sedentary occupation foresees a relatively long period of productivity, while the man who works with his hands expects a relatively short span of productive activity, followed by retirement. This research is one of the earliest contributions to what is now called a "constructionist perspective on the life course" with its emphasis on human agency and choice making.

Other early studies began to fill out available knowledge of age boundaries and the point at which life begins and ends. In a pathbreaking project, Knutson (1967) found large variations among public health professionals in the way they defined and valued a new human life. A sizeable number held judgments that were not consonant with operational definitions in hospital, legal, and medical codes. One-fifth of the professionals assigned full value to the new human life at conception, and approximately two-fifths at birth or shortly thereafter. Most professionals who placed the beginning of a new human life before birth did not assign full value to it until birth or after birth. As might be expected, religion emerged as a principal source of variation in judgments. Compared to the more secular respondents, members of conservative religious groups were more likely to reckon the beginning of a new human life from conception, to assign full value at an earlier developmental time, and to emphasize the importance of "infusion of the soul" in making an organism human.

Age distinctions order social roles, as in the sociocultural perspective of the Neugarten and Knutson studies, but they also order people through age or birth cohorts. Cohorts have long been common to demographic research on marriage, fertility, and divorce. However, these cohort studies were not carried out with an interest in the life course. Spurred perhaps by a new found awareness of the link between life patterns and changes in society (Schaie, 1965), important theoretical work on this link began to appear in the 1960s, featuring Norman Ryder's influential essay on "The Cohort as a Concept in the Study of Social Change." The most comprehensive work was authored by Matilda Riley and her colleagues in *Aging and Society* (Riley et al., 1972).

Age Cohorts in Lives

Riley and her colleagues viewed age as a basis of stratification in historical experience and in role sequences across the life course. "Whereas socioeconomic strata are ranked to form a social hierarchy, age strata are typically ordered by time (hence, are more akin to geological strata," 1972, p. 23). Birth year indicates historical time, and chronological age acquires the meanings of social timing and life

stage. Birth cohorts provide a link between historical change and the life course.

Birth year or date of entry into a system (such as school graduation or marriage) locates the individual according to historical time and related social changes; with age peers in the cohort, this person is exposed to a particular segment of historical experience as he or she moves across the sequence of age-graded roles. To grasp the meaning and implications of birth year and cohort membership, the analyst specifies the distinctive historical events and processes at the time, as well as characteristics of the cohort itself, such as its size and composition. These characteristics are themselves a consequence of historical changes in birth and death rates, immigration, and migration.

Adjacent birth cohorts are most sharply differentiated in the course of rapid change, and represent a vehicle of social change to the extent that cohort differences arise. As successive cohorts encounter the same historical event, they do so at different stages in their life course. This means that different cohorts bring different life experiences to the change. Consequently the impact of the event is contingent on the life stage of the cohort at the point of change.

Ryder (1965) stressed this "life stage principle" in his account of cohort differences in the life course. As each cohort encounters a historical event, whether depression or prosperity, it "is distinctively marked by the career stage it occupies" (1965, p. 846). Examples include the differential age at military entry among American veterans who served in World War II. The age range spanned 20 years; some recruits had just left high school while others were in their mid-30s with family and career. Each age at entry entailed both risks and rewards, but very late entry clearly maximized enduring family and health risks through its disruptive effect (Elder, Shanahan, & Clipp, 1994). These risks were not as great among men who entered the war immediately after high school.

In the Riley model, cohort membership has specific implications for lives when a particular cohort size is paired with available economic opportunities. Richard Easterlin (1980) has pursued this issue in his account of postwar change in the work lives of men. His point of departure is the link between the supply of younger men and their relative economic position; between changing cohort size relative to options and life chances. Other things being equal, the greater the relative supply of young male workers, the weaker their relative economic status and gains. Before 1960, the relatively small birth cohorts of younger men experienced a wide range of advancement opportunities, and their relative economic position (compared with older men) increased significantly. After 1960, the "baby boom" cohorts began entering the young adult category, producing a labor surplus and restricting economic progress.

The behavior of these birth cohorts is symptomatic of the "relative economic squeeze" they encountered. The economic position of young men has deteriorated relative to that of older men, family formation has been delayed by increasing numbers of young adults, and the employment rate of young women has increased more rapidly than that of older women. Among young adult cohorts during this period, we observe an upward trend in the divorce, suicide, and crime rates; and a leveling off of the college-enrollment rate which had climbed steadily since the 1940s.

In this work, as in the age stratification model, theory and research are focused on the aggregate or macro level. The linking mechanisms between lives and changing times are difficult to pin down from this vantage point. Cohorts can be merely "black boxes" with no information on causal dynamics and linkages. Behavioral differences between cohorts do not easily yield an understanding of the social or historical factors that account for them. Speculation frequently takes the place of disciplined explication. The problem has much to do with the varied exposure of people in a birth cohort to environmental changes of one kind or another. Thus, not all grade school children are exposed to the economic stress of a plant closing because some parents work in other places and other families manage to insulate their children from stresses of this kind. In response to this social heterogeneity, more studies are investigating specific types of social change through intracohort analyses.

Before surveying one of these studies, let us sum up the temporality of age by relating three meanings that have special relevance to child development, the ages of life or lifetime, the diverse meanings of social time, and historical time. *Life time* is indexed by chronological age and refers to stage or position in the developmental-aging process. From a developmental standpoint, age alerts the investigator to subgroups that are differentially vulnerable to particular types of social change. The lifetime meaning of age requires specification of the variables it represents. *Social*

time, such as the age-patterned sequence of events, includes "family time" across stages of parenting and the generations. A normative concept of family time indicates an appropriate time for leaving home, for marriage, and for bearing children. Last, *historical time* refers to a person's location in history; membership in a birth cohort indicates this location.

A skeletal life course for a person can be mapped in the three-dimensional space of life, family, and historical time (Figure 16.1). Historical time of birth, coupled with passage through the age structure, define particular life trajectories on the grid of history and age. Persons born in 1920, 1940, and 1960 follow the age gradient, though divergent paths may arise from the variable relation between age and events/roles. Historical events, such as war and economic recession, may alter the correlation between life events and age, or change their temporal arrangements—for example, full-time employment may come after first marriage in the lives of World War II servicemen. Another source of variation is the unstable path of family time. Figure 16.1 lists four generations on the family timetable, but the number and pattern of the generations can vary sharply across a single life span.

Consider a person who was born in the late 1930s and became one of several great-grandchildren of a woman in her nineties. Three higher stations in the generational

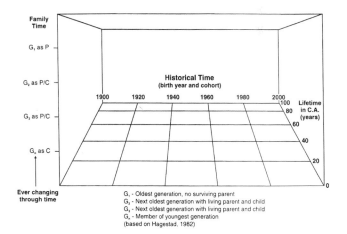

Figure 16.1 Life-course trajectories in three-dimensional space: life, family, and historical time. From *Review of Child Development Research, Vol. 7: The Family: An Interdisciplinary Perspective* (p. 123), edited by R. D. Parke, 1984. Chicago: University of Chicago Press. Reprinted with permission.

series are occupied. This structure continues up to the sixth year of the child when great-grandmother dies. Only three stations remain on the generational ladder. By the time the child enters high school, both grandparents on the maternal and paternal side have died. The structure is now based on two generations, a family cycle of birth, maturation, reproduction, and death. In terms of Figure 16.1, G_1 and G_n make up the generational structure until the 1930s "child" has a child. At this point, she becomes both a parent and a child.

Generational turnover in the structure of family time has implications for change in status and role, self-identity, and behavior (Hagestad, 1982). The parenting behavior of adults varies according to whether they have surviving parents and grandparents. Greater distance seems to occur between parents and offspring when the former move to the last position of the generational line. Identity change is perhaps the most obvious feature of generational turnover; the death of grandparents and parents entails loss of role and of well-established perceptions of self. The schedule of family time and events across the generations brings a uniquely valuable sense of the degree to which a nuclear family and its members are entwined with the fortunes and life course of kin.

Life Cycle and Life Course

In any period of theoretical transition, both old and new models guide research. We see this mix of old and new in the 1960s. Reuben Hill's (1970) three-generation study is a case in point. The grandparent generation married before 1915 and the parent generation between the 1920s and mid-1930s.

Hill made significant contributions to the life cycle model in essays on the family cycle and development, and he launched this multigeneration study to pursue issues of intergenerational continuity and change. However, the dramatic social changes at the time underscored the historical imprecision of generational membership by placing the older and younger members of each generation in different historical epochs. Couples from the parent generation who married in the 1920s had significantly more children than those who married in the depressed 1930s. The two groups were found to be sufficiently different in life course to constitute samples of different populations.

The heterogeneity of generations on historical experience has led some analysts to identify cohorts within each

generation, and Hill used this modification in his work. He investigated strategies of family management which included the timing of marriage and parenthood, the spacing of children, the husband's and wife's entry and reentry into the labor force, and the timing of material acquisitions. Consistent with a life course model, he noted that in periods of rapid change, "each generational cohort encounters at marriage a unique set of historical constraints and incentives which influence the timing of its crucial life decisions, making for marked generational dissimilarities in life cycle career" (Hill, 1970, p. 322). The middle generation in Hill's study clearly followed this pattern of cohort differentiation.

In one sense, the generational dimension of life cycle analysis has helped to contextualize the individual life course by emphasizing the social dynamic of "linked lives"—parents and children, husband and wife, grandparents and grandchildren, siblings and friends. Parents and grandparents are not merely present at a stage in life, but rather appear as lifelong associates. From this vantage point, the life cycle model made adult development especially relevant to an understanding of child development, an important insight that has not been fully realized on studies of children. Any personal or social change in parents has developmental consequences for children (Coyne & Downey, 1991). And change in the behavior of children can alter the behavior and psychology of parents (Bell, 1968). In concept, children had become active agents of their own life course.

This contribution appears in a longitudinal study of Californians from the Oakland Growth sample who were born in the early 1920s, passed through adolescence in the depressed 1930s, and were subject to the manpower needs of World War II (Elder, 1974). The central question concerned the effects of the Great Depression on the lives and development of the Oakland children. An intergenerational framework seemed entirely appropriate for addressing this question, with an emphasis on the process by which economic hardship made a difference in the lives of children by changing family processes and socialization.

But the dramatic changefulness of life experience from the 1920s into the late 1930s raised questions that could not be addressed by the perspective. The effect of change depended on many things, including their exposure to the event and their age or developmental stage, as well as the age of parents. Fast-changing economic and family circumstances called for relating them to the ages of parents and children. These observations made the distinctions of birth cohort and life stage especially relevant:

> At the time of maximum hardship in the early 30s, the Oakland children were well beyond the dependency stage of early childhood, with its consequences for intellectual and emotional development, and they reached the age of majority after opportunities had improved through nationwide mobilization for war. Persons born ten years before the Oakland children would have entered the labor force during the worst phase of the economic collapse, while the welfare of persons in the 1929 cohort would have been entirely dependent on conditions in their families. (Elder, 1974, p. 16)

Family adaptations to economic hardship became a set of linkages between the economic collapse of the 1930s and the developmental experience of children. In place of static concepts of family life, the study turned to notions of the family economy and its multiple actors as a way of thinking about the economic crisis and its implications for children. Through linked relationships and actors, changing economic roles and status shaped the experience of children. Thus, children who acquired paid jobs in the community became more socially independent vis à vis parents than other youth.

An appraisal of growing up in the Great Depression required knowledge of life paths to adulthood, such as education, marriage, work life advancement, and military service. A number of youth might escape hardship through early work and military service. Others might do so through higher education and marriage. But some outcomes have more to do with their timing than with mere occurrence. Marriage is a case in point. Hardship favored early marriage by diminishing the chances of higher education and by making home life unappealing. Likewise, developmental theory suggested that the early work experience of adolescents would accelerate their thinking about work and the timing of their entry into adult work roles.

These and other conceptual issues made theoretical distinctions concerning the age-graded life course especially useful to the study. Consider the sequence of events that link early adolescent work experience and adult work. Family hardship increased the involvement of boys in gainful employment, and through this experience advanced their social independence and sensitivity to matters of vocation. This sensitivity took the form of an early

vocational focus and work commitment that led to work lives which effectively countered any educational handicap of family hardship, even among the sons of working class parents. In the long run, family income losses did not adversely affect the occupational standing of the Oakland men or the status that the Oakland women achieved through marriage.

As noted in this account, *Children of the Great Depression* (Elder, 1974) began with concepts of the life cycle and relationship tradition, such as role sequences and generation; but soon turned to the analytic meanings of age for ways of linking family and individual experience to historical change (especially birth cohort and life stage), and for identifying trajectories across the life course, using a concept of age-graded events and social roles. Both theoretical strands provide essential features of life course theory on matters of time, context, and process. The life course is age-graded through institutions and social structures, and it is embedded in relationships that constrain and support behavior. In addition, people are located in historical settings through birth cohorts and they are also linked across the generations by kinship and friendship.

Contemporary theory on the life course and its social dimensions thus differs from perspectives of an earlier era by joining the life cycle processes of social relationships with the temporality and contextual aspects of age. For examples of this shift, we need only compare Thomas and Znaniecki's *The Polish Peasant in Europe and America* (1918–1920) with its analysis of generations and lineages in a relatively timeless, abstract realm, to the birth cohort, age-graded life course, and intergenerational themes of *Family Time and Industrial Time* (Hareven, 1982)—a study of successive worker cohorts and their families in a large textile mill with declining economic prospects during the 1920s and 1930s. Though explicitly historical, *The Polish Peasant* does not locate the immigrants according to birth year and historical setting, nor does it describe their life stage at the time of their emigration. Hareven's study provides these markers and uses them to assess the implications of industrial change for worker families, parents and children, in the city of Manchester, New Hampshire.

Through the integration of social relationship concepts and age-based distinctions, along with life-span concepts of the person and human organism, the life course became a vital, expanding field of inquiry in the 1970s and 1980s. Both the individual life course and a person's developmental trajectory are interconnected with the lives and development of others. Life course theory thus took issue with life span studies that viewed human development as an unfolding process which was not co-active with social and cultural processes in historical time. The theory has much in common today with Bronfenbrenner's bio-ecological theory (1989), with Lerner's (1991, p. 27) call for more attention to contextual variability, and with an emerging perspective on developmental science (Cairns, Elder, & Costello, 1996; see also Ford & Lerner, 1992; Thelen & Smith, 1994) that extends across system levels and disciplines.

Accordingly, human development in life course theory represents a process of organism-environment transactions over time, in which the organism plays an active role in shaping its own development. The developing individual is viewed as a dynamic whole, not as separate strands, facets, or domains, such as emotion, cognition, and motivation. The course of development is embedded in a dynamic system of social interchanges and interdependencies across and within levels. As noted by Bronfenbrenner (1996), this dynamic in life course theory is illustrated well by the interlocking lives and developmental trajectories of family members who are influenced differentially by their changing world. Last, life course theory is committed to the explication of processes by which social change finds expression in proximal processes (Bronfenbrenner & Ceci, 1994) and child development.

The principal strands of life course theory—social relations, age and temporality, and life span concepts of development—are illustrated in Figure 16.2 by some distinguishing concepts and themes. Under social relations, we include the early work of W. I. Thomas on life histories, G. H. Mead on socialization and the self, Everett Hughes on work and the self, and Kurt Lewin on power-dependence relations, and L. S. Vygotsky on language, the self, and social relationships (Clausen, 1968; Parke, Ornstein, Rieser, & Zahn-Waxler, 1994). The development of social role and self theories belongs within this tradition, and features the writings of sociologist Robert Merton on role sets and reference groups (1968), Morris Rosenberg (1979) on self-esteem, and Urie Bronfenbrenner on socialization (1970). The field of intergenerational relations has expanded from two to three and even four generations, with important contributions to an understanding of three generations from Reuben Hill, Vern Bengtson (both sociologists), James

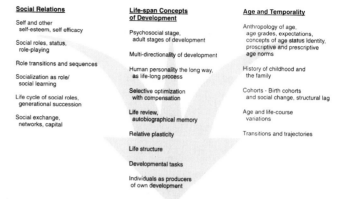

Figure 16.2   The emergence of life course theory (1960s to present): research traditions and their concepts.

Jackson and his three-generation study of African Americans, and Ross Parke (Parke & Ladd, 1992).

Much has been said in this Volume and chapter about contributions to life-span concepts of human development, a second strand, including references to the pioneering work of Erik Erikson on psychosocial stages of development, and Paul Baltes on the process of selective optimization with compensation. The concept of developmental task, first delineated by Robert Havighurst (1949), also represents a way of viewing development across life stages. In his classic writings on personality, Henry Murray (see Shneidman, 1981) argued for a processual view of human development that in broad outline now seems remarkably attune with a contemporary life span model. The entire life-span of a personality represented the unit that "requires formulation." Richard Lerner (1982, 1991) has stressed the relative plasticity and agency of the aging organism (see also Schaie, 1965), the multidirectionality of life span development, and the life-long interaction of person and social context. In Daniel Levinson's writings these interactions form "life structures." Last, the perceived or defined life course can change in the course of aging through successive life reviews in which the past is assessed in light of the present. Staudinger (1989) has focused on the "life review" process as a way of studying intellectual development across the life span.

A number of themes illustrate distinctive contributions to a third strand, the study of age and temporality in lives. The early contributions to age-grading by social and cultural anthropologists and the pioneering analysis of birth cohorts and generation units by Karl Mannheim in the 1920s (Elder, 1975). Bernice Neugarten's work on the social psychology of age has been discussed along with the pathbreaking sociological contributions of Matilda Riley and her collaborators. Demographer Peter Uhlenberg (Hareven, 1978), Dennis Hogan (1981), and John Modell (1989) have produced creative analyses of cohort life patterns and age-grading. In social history, Hareven (1978, 1982) and Modell (1989), among others, have made imaginative contributions to our historical understanding of the life course. As noted, the study of age expectations in child development is illustrated by the work of Shirley Feldman as well as Rainer Silbereisen (Silbereisen & Schmitt-Rodermund, 1995) on timetables for adolescent autonomy.

We turn now to some basic concepts and perspectives that center on the individual life course and developmental processes. These include the elementary concepts of multiple levels—trajectory and transition.

BASIC CONCEPTS AND PERSPECTIVES

The individual life course and its relation to developmental trajectories represent a common meeting ground for life course theory and developmental science, with its "perspective on individual functioning that emphasizes the dynamic interplay among processes that operate across time frames, levels of analysis, and contexts" (Cairns, Elder, & Costello, 1996). Building on advances since the 1960s, life course theory has uniquely forged a conceptual bridge between developmental processes, the life course, and ongoing changes in society, one based on the premise that age places people in the social structure and in particular birth cohorts.

To understand this conceptual bridge, we turn to some elementary concepts, beginning with multiple levels of the life course, ranging from institutionalized pathways to the behavioral routes of individuals and their developmental patterns. In varying degrees, people work out their life course in terms of established or institutionalized pathways. Key temporal concepts, such as trajectory and transition, are taken up next with particular emphasis on the properties of social transitions. Paradigmatic themes of life course theory draw upon these elementary concepts in highlighting distinctive conceptual orientations, such as the relation between changing times and lives.

Social Pathways and the Individual Life Course

Culture, the nation-state, and the social organization of work and residence contribute to the formation of life pathways with specified timetables and sanctions. Institutionalized pathways generally have specified time-boundaries, what Merton (1982) has called "socially expected durations." The legislated ages at maturity for voting and marriage can be viewed as marking off an accepted duration of dependency.

Social pathways are generally age-graded and thus identify relatively early, on-time, and late transitions. Children who are held back in school become aware of their lagging status on the educational ladder (Alexander, Entwisle, & Dauber, 1994), and company managers talk about the relation between age and grade in prospects for promotion to a senior rank (Sofer, 1970, p. 239). By taking established pathways into account, we understand more completely the choices and actions that shape individual life courses and their developmental implications.

According to this perspective, the life course of the individual is worked out over time in terms of the general and more specific dictates of social pathways. For the very young child, these pathways are defined in large measure by the residential and socioeconomic histories of parents. In Israel, the Kibbutzim charted the pathways for some young children through a system of collective child-care (Aviezer, Van IJzendoorn, Sagi, & Schuengel, 1994). In subsequent years, educational institutions, with their tracking systems and levels, acquired prominence in structuring pathways and timetables for performance and activities. Thus, early placement in an elite primary school can ensure in Great Britain what Kerckhoff (1993) calls the "high-road" to the university. A low-status placement ensures the opposite path for students. Across the adult years, large corporations as well as smaller firms establish expectable pathways for their employees.

In the world of work, role sequences become established or institutionalized in the culture through frequent use. Spilerman (1977) has used the term "career lines" to refer to pathways defined by the differentiated and aggregated work trajectories or histories of individuals. In his view, career lines are "shaped by the nature of industry structures (e.g., occupational distribution, mode of recruiting into upper status slots such as promotion from below vs. hiring from outside the firm) and by the institutional demography of the labor market" (p. 552). In an expanding market, these career lines extend across company and industry boundaries. Career lines vary in terms of their receptivity to different times of entry; the trades frequently require early entry through a training program, in contrast to the less age-graded nature of public school teaching and service occupations. The selection and timing of career entry are major determinants of subsequent earnings and work trajectories. A person's work life or career (see Spenner, Otto, & Call, 1982) is one part of the individual's life course which may or may not subscribe to the temporal markers and regulatory pressures of the firm and marketplace.

At the most inclusive macro end of this multilevel system, the terms of the working out process are generally established by government. At lower levels, the terms may be set by institutional sectors (economy, education, etc.), by state government and local communities, and by neighborhoods and schools. Each system level, from macro to micro, socially regulates in part the decision and action processes of the life course, producing areas of coordination as well as discord and contradiction (e.g., the case of marriage, divorce, and adoption laws). At the primary level of the individual actor, some decision pressures and constraints are linked to federal regulation, some to the regulations of an employer, and some to state and community legislation. Following Sameroff's concept of the environtype (Sameroff & Suomi, 1996), regulatory codes on each nested level are suggestive of life course and developmental agenda.

Mayer (1986, pp. 166–167) had the terms of the nation-state in mind when he identified key societal mechanisms "which impose order and constraints on lives." These include the cumulative effects of delayed transitions, institutional careers, the historical circumstances associated with particular cohorts, and state intervention. Growth of the state in social regulation counters the potentially fragmenting effects of social differentiation. At the individual level, the long hand of the state "legalizes, defines and standardizes most points of entry and exit; into and out of employment, into and out of marital status, into and out of sickness and disability, into and out of education. In doing so the state turns these transitions into strongly demarcated

public events and acts as gatekeeper and sorter." These are what Buchmann (1989, p. 28) properly calls events in "the public life course."

Ideally, studies of the developmental consequences of life course change take into account the potential constraints and options associated with particular pathways. However, the realities of research are expressed in a disciplinary division of labor. Historians and sociologists make use of a multilevel view of the life course in their historical and comparative studies. Both attend to issues of contextual variation. As historian E. P. Thompson once put it, "the discipline of history is above all a discipline of context" (cited by Goldthorpe, 1991, p. 212). Developmentalists in psychology may center on the impact of life course change (Noack, Hofer, & Youniss, 1995) or simply ignore it altogether, usually the latter. At least up to the 1990s, the typical longitudinal study of social development among children, as published in *Child Development,* measured the socioeconomic environment only at the beginning of the research (Elder & Pellerin, 1995). And articles still recommend the use of atemporal indicators that provide a snapshot of families and children at a point in time.

Whatever the approach, multiple levels of the life course are clearly evident in the historical contrasts of young people in urban places between the late 19th-century and 20th-century America (Modell, 1989). Mandatory public schooling became an institution across this century. Industrialization during the late 19th century extended a youth's residence in his parental household and in school for the middle class, but urban youth today use far less time in leaving the parental household, in marrying, and in establishing their own household. This conclusion is based in large part on a pioneering investigation of five early life transitions among youth in Philadelphia of 1880 and a 1970 U.S. Census sample—exit from school, labor force entry, departure from the family of origin, marriage, and the establishment of a household (Modell, Furstenberg, & Hershberg, 1976). Across these events, the transition to adulthood has narrowed significantly up to 1970, resulting in a more concentrated sequence of status transitions.

Family transitions are now more often mixed with school completion and work entry. This change reflects a basic change in the family economy, from an era distinguished by marginal economic survival in which households relied upon the earnings of husband and wife, and even children, to a period in which family security is buttressed by the welfare state. The old middle class of entrepreneurs in the United States was supplanted by a new middle class in large-scale bureaucracies. Social regulation of early life transitions had shifted from the family of origin, which permitted a wide latitude of flexibility, to youth themselves and the generalized requirements of formal institutions, such as the workplace in large firms and the credential influences of extended schooling. In the authors' words (Modell, Furstenberg, & Hershberg, 1976, p. 30), "'Timely action' to 19th-century families consisted of helpful responses in times of trouble; in the 20th century, timeliness connotes adherence to a schedule."

Multi-level accounts of the life course are also revealing in cross-national studies of the transition to adulthood, particularly in relation to the social pathways from secondary school to work (Evans & Heinz, 1993; Kerckhoff, 1993). In Great Britain, secondary school-leavers can follow a path to work that consists of technical training programs or schools that provide credentials for a particular craft. With the freedom to make a wide range of choices, students also miss opportunities and desirable job placements. Far more structure is provided working-class German youth in a secondary-level system that joins industrial training and education in an apprenticeship system. Placement in a skilled craft is virtually assured youth who complete their apprenticeships. In Japan, occupational recruitment typically occurs in schools from the secondary-level to higher education, and specific job training is provided by the particular firm, not by schools or craft institutes. American adolescents encounter the least amount of articulation between schooling and workplace. Vocational training in secondary schools is not closely linked to specific industries, their recruitment, and skill needs.

Studies of the life course are taking place on all system levels, with sociologists, historians, and economists focusing on the higher levels and developmental psychologists mainly addressing the functioning and developmental trajectory of individuals. Very little research and theory links both macro and micro levels. The individual life course has been studied in terms of worklife experience, careers, and occupational mobility as well as patterns of marital life and parenting (Rossi & Rossi, 1990), and some of this research examines the process by which changes in work experience make a difference in the quality of parenting by undermining marital support (Conger & Elder, 1994). The link between the changing life course of parents and children's development is under study in a growing number of projects (Parcel & Menaghan, 1994), but the territory remains largely unexplored.

The contemporary challenge is to trace the impact of macro life-course changes across levels to the primary world of families and children. The programmatic study of neighborhood influences on children illustrates how much we have to learn in the cross-level study of child development. Social and economic resources vary significantly by urban neighborhoods, but studies to date suggest that neighborhood effects on child outcomes are surprisingly weak when all factors are considered (Furstenberg & Hughes, in press), including the tendency for families to select their place of residence and even schools for their children. Selection and neighborhood effects must be disentangled to determine genuine contextual effects. More theoretical and empirical efforts are needed through longitudinal studies of people *and* environments in detailing cross-level linkages that have consequences for the life course and children's development.

Trajectory, Transition, and Duration: A Temporal Perspective

Social pathways, the individual life course, and developmental patterns refer to processes that are structured by age norms and other constraints, biological and social. Each concept includes a long and short view of life-course dynamics. *Trajectories* provide a long view by linking social or psychological states over a substantial part of the life span. *Transitions* depict a short view, a change in state or states, such as when children leave home or a mood changes from depressed feelings to happiness. Since transitions are always elements of trajectories, a substantial change in direction during a transition may represent a *turning point* as well.

Trajectories and transitions are elements of established pathways, individual life courses, and developmental patterns. Among individuals, social roles evolve over an extended span of time, as in trajectories of work or family; and they change over a short time span. The latter may be marked by specific events, such as children entering school for the first time, completing the first grade successfully, and graduating from high school. Each transition, combining a role exit and entry, is embedded in a trajectory that gives it specific form and meaning. Thus, work transitions are core elements of a work life trajectory; and births are key markers along a parental trajectory.

Social trajectories and transitions refer to processes that are familiar in the study of work careers and life events. The language of careers has a distinguished history within the field of occupations and the professions, and it still represents one of the rare languages that depict a temporal dimension or process. Work careers have been defined as disorderly and orderly, and achievement is represented as career advancement, whether early or late, rapid or slow (Wilensky, 1960). The term career has also been applied to the trajectories of marriage and parenthood (Hill, 1970). All of these uses fall within the more inclusive definition of a life course trajectory. The term does not prejudge the direction, degree, or rate of change in its course.

The multiple role trajectories of life patterns call for *strategies of coordination or synchronization.* Various demands compete for the individual's or family's scarce resources, time, energy, money. Goode (1960) argues that an individual's set of relationships is both "unique and overdemanding," requiring strategies that minimize demands by scheduling and rescheduling transitions, where possible. To cope with simultaneous, linked trajectories, the scheduling of events and obligations becomes a basic task in managing resources and pressures. The needs of children and financial requirements, for example, play important roles in determining work and leisure options.

The meaning of a transition has much to do with its *timing* in a trajectory. Consider the case of parenthood (Furstenberg, Brooks-Gunn, & Morgan, 1987), for example; the earlier the event, the greater the risk of social and health disadvantages for mother and child. Other temporal features of transitions refer to the order or sequence of changes in state and the time between such changes, called *durations.* The sequence of transitions has particular significance when they are functionally linked, as in skills, and when the order is culturally prescribed. Rindfuss, Swicegood, and Rosenfeld (1987) observed a high level of disarray among transitions in a nationwide sample of young adults and concluded that "understanding the nature and importance of sequence in the life course requires analyzing what the roles themselves mean and how they are causally linked." This task is still largely unfinished.

The concept of *duration* makes reference to the span of time between successive changes in state. The full implications of long and short exposures to a situation depend on the situation itself. Remarkably little is known about experiences in long and short durations, though a lengthy involvement tends to increase behavioral continuity through acquired obligations and investments. The longer the duration of marriage, for example, the greater the chances for marital permanence (Cherlin, 1993). The connection between marital permanence and length of marriage has much to do with material barriers, such as shared material assets (Booth, Johnson, White, & Edwards, 1986). Marital unhappiness has less to do with divorce as shared assets accumulate in long-lived marriages (White & Booth, 1991). Duration of unemployment also increases the risk of permanent unemployment. The latter may involve acquired ties to the unemployed as well as a deskilling process in developing an incapacity to work. To adequately understand these covariations, we need to know more about duration in terms of interpersonal and developmental processes.

This applies to children's exposure to poverty which tends to increase the risk of harsh, erratic punishment (McLoyd, 1989). Although the consequences of poverty duration and its timing are largely unknown, longitudinal studies (Bane & Ellwood, 1986; Duncan et al., 1984) find that family structure and life course transitions are key elements in the transition of children to poverty. The risk of a lengthy exposure is associated with birth in poverty to a single-parent mother of African American status. Bane and Ellwood (1986, p. 21) conclude that "the average poor black child today appears to be in the midst of a poverty spell which will last almost two decades." However, most poverty spells turned out to be very short, owing in large measure to markedly improved earnings. Slightly more than 40% in the Bane and Ellwood analysis ended within a single year. About 70% were over within a period of three years. Only 12% have the character of a chronic state, lasting 10 years or more.

Consider also a study by Alexander, Entwisle, and Dauber (1994; see also Alexander & Entwisle, 1988) of school promotion-retention history of students across the first eight years of school in Baltimore. Though troubled by heavy losses of white students, the study found disorderly promotion histories or trajectories to be the norm for their sample and that retention prospects were foreshadowed by behavior problems prior to entry into the first grade. The children who were held back at the beginning of their school career fared worst over the eight years. In many cases, retention later in the career enabled children to recover a measure of competence, although they did not match the school performance of the never-retained students. The investigators warn that cross-sectional studies need to be aware of the diverse trajectories of students who happen to be in the same grade at a particular time. Evaluations of their behavior should take these histories into account.

A developmental trajectory refers to change and constancy in the same behavior or disposition over time, but consistency of measurement may be difficult to achieve in many cases, especially in the measurement of aggression and dependency (Kagan & Moss, 1962). Nevertheless, it is clear that trajectories of intra-individual change tell a different story from those obtained from cross-section analysis, and that this concept is compatible with widely shared views of development (Rogosa, Brandt, & Zimowski, 1982). Developmental trajectories are also integral to life course theory, especially when they are studied as interdependent with the changing dynamics of social trajectories. In a four-wave study of early adolescents, based on growth curve models, Ge and his colleagues (1994) found that trajectories of depressive symptoms increased sharply among white girls, surpassing the symptom level of boys at age 13; that the increase for girls was linked to their exposure to an increasing level of negative events; and that the initial warmth and supportiveness of mother minimized the subsequent risk of depressed states and negative events among daughters.

The challenge to life course study is to understand the linkages among changing pathways, life patterns, and developmental trajectories. A useful first step in this direction leads to the properties of life transitions and their developmental potential, our next topic under basic concepts and distinctions.

Transitions Link Contexts and Human Agency

The concept of transition links agency and context through its change in states, social and psychological (Clausen, 1972; Glaser & Strauss, 1971). People bring a life history of personal experiences and dispositions to each transition, interpret the new circumstances in terms of this history, and work out lines of adaptation that can fundamentally alter their life course. That is, individual differences interact with the new transition experience to influence behavioral responses and accommodations. Behavioral novelties can arise at this point.

The two faces of a transition—leaving a state and entering a new state—can have different causal explanations, as when divorce is followed by remarriage. Moreover, "leaving a state" is part of the individual's history that shapes the meaning of the new role or situation (Wheaton, 1990). Leaving a conflicted, violent marriage would cast single status as a stress-relieving status. The meaning and developmental implications of a transition also depend on the timing of the change relative to norms and cognitive expectations. Judging from studies conducted to date (McLanahan & Sørensen, 1985; Wortman & Silver, 1990), widowhood is most distressing for young women, a time when the event is least expected or normative. By comparison, job loss during young adulthood is relatively common, and consequentially entails less of an emotional risk when compared to the later years.

The usual contrast between institutionalized transitions along social pathways, and personal, idiosyncratic transition experience can misrepresent reality. In many cases, life transitions are at once an institutionalized status passage in the life course of birth cohorts and a personalized transition for individuals with particular histories and historical times. The latter may represent an individual "working out" of the former. These faces of a transition apply to the normative transitions of life, from birth to school entry, marriage, parenthood, and retirement. Transitions of this kind may seem more predictable and structured than non-normative events, but all transitions can be sorted according to their structuredness or degree of external regulation, duration, timing, predictability, and novelty.

Selection and Transition Effects

In thinking about the behavioral consequences of life transitions, it is essential to distinguish between *selection* and *transition effects* and their statistical interaction. People select themselves into transitions and they are influenced by the social change. Thus, a behavioral effect of a transition may reflect the tendency for individuals to select themselves into self-affirming environments (Lerner, 1982; Scarr & McCartney, 1983). High school students tend to enter college environments that resemble their personal characteristics (Alwin, Cohen, & Newcomb, 1991); assortative processes serve the interests of homophily in forming friendships and heterosexual pairs (Caspi & Herbener, 1990); and risk takers in military service are likely to end up in combat units (Gimbel & Booth, 1996). Transitions of this kind generally accentuate the behavioral effect of the selected dispositions, producing greater individual differences and heterogeniety between groups. Cairns and Cairns (1994, p. 117) observe that social selection and accentuation go together in peer group formation. Once a group is formed in terms of selected attributes (e.g., aggressivity), the selected behaviors are accentuated. This process has obvious social implications when unruly behavior is involved.

Individual differences and their behavioral effects are most likely to be maximized in relatively weak situations, lacking structured, normative control. "Non-normative, less socially regulated, or unexpected transitions permit greater individual heterogeneity, while more highly regulated or normative transitions permit less" (Elder & O'Rand, 1995, p. 463). Caspi and Moffitt (1993, p. 266) arrive at similar conclusions, noting that individual differences are likely to be accentuated by "novelty, ambiguity, and uncertainty." By contrast, transition effects would be maximized in theory by a new situation that resembles a total institution that presses from all angles toward a specific behavioral outcome (pp. 265–266). This category of institution includes the family for preschool children, boarding schools for adolescents, and the military for young adults.

Military induction removes young people from their local environments and their age-graded expectations, basic training defines prior life histories as irrelevant to the larger goal of building fighting units, and the service experience itself tends to broaden knowledge, social perspectives, and skills. For disadvantaged youth, in particular, longitudinal studies (Elder, 1986, 1987; Sampson & Laub, 1996) suggest that the transitions of military mobilization can redirect impaired lives toward greater opportunity and adult advancement. In two samples of youth from the Great Depression era (Elder, 1986, 1987), mobilization into the military established a turning point experience for the disadvantaged.

Early life transitions can have developmental consequences by affecting subsequent transitions, even after many years and decades have passed. They do so through behavioral consequences that set in motion cumulative advantages and disadvantages, with radiating implications for other life domains. One of the simplest versions of this chain of influence is expressed in terms of a history of academic success from childhood into the adult years, followed by strategic placement in a deserved career line, notable career advancement, and mental health (Featherman & Hauser, 1978). Also in a Baltimore study of adolescent mothers who were followed from 1966 to 1984 (Furstenberg, Brooks-Gunn, & Morgan, 1987), variations in personal resources (e.g., IQ) during adolescence affected their economic success by influencing how they timed and ordered early events, from marriage to education and employment. From the vantage point of these studies, the quality of transition experiences early in life may foretell the likelihood of successful and unsuccessful adaptation to later transitions across the life course.

Transitions to parenthood during adolescence in the Baltimore panel study bring up another important general distinction; that life transitions can be thought of as *a succession of mini-transitions or choice-points*. The transition from marriage to divorce is not simply a change in state; the process begins with disenchantment and extends across divorce threats, periods of separation, and the filing of divorce papers. Different causal factors may operate at each phase of the process. The "origin" influences that increase the risk of disenchantment are likely to differ from those that sustain the process toward marital dissolution. In like manner, we can think of the transition to motherhood in adolescence as a *multiphasic process* in which each phase is marked by a choice point, with its options and social constraints.

Young women may choose to engage in premarital sex or not, to use contraception or not, to seek an abortion or not, and to marry the father or not. Only a handful of options lead to an illegitimate birth. At the birth of their child, they face a number of other decisions, such as whether to ask for their own mothers' help in child care or to put the child up for adoption, to marry or remain single, to have more births out of wedlock, to pursue educational and employment possibilities, or to enter the welfare system. The implications of having an illegitimate birth vary according to the options chosen. Some opportunities blend well in favoring positive outcomes; they represent an adaptive strategy, while others do not.

Figure 16.3 presents a series of transitions that can lead to unwed motherhood, as sketched from the Baltimore study. Each choice point occurs at a different state in a young girl's life and thus could involve different life course

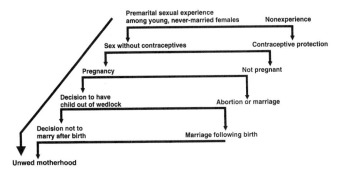

Figure 16.3 The life course of unwed motherhood. As amended from *Family Transitions* (p. 41), edited by P. A. Cowan and M. Hetherington, 1991. Hillsdale, NJ: Erlbaum. Reprinted with permission.

dynamics and explanations. The process of becoming an adolescent mother requires sexual activity, failure to use contraception or to be effective in its use, and, once pregnant, the decision to bear and raise the child. Across these stages of the process, an agency "has several possible points at which to target its interventions; at initiation of sexual activity, at contraception use, or, at the resolution of a pregnancy" (Hofferth, 1987, p. 78). The significance of this formulation becomes apparent when we return to a time when unwed motherhood was viewed simply as one transition, a concept that obscured the strategic points of preventive intervention along the life course.

Linking Mechanisms

I have identified a number of transition properties that specify a way of thinking about social transitions and their psychosocial effects. Another contribution to this perspective comes from *mechanisms* that link transitions and behavior (Elder, 1991, 1996). These include the notion of life stage and its social roles, the social imperatives of new roles or situations, the cycle of losing and regaining control in transition experiences, the connectedness of lives or social interdependence, and the accentuation principle.

According to the *life stage principle,* people of unlike age and those who occupy different roles are differentially exposed to and influenced by particular social transitions. Thus, early adolescents and the young in middle childhood appear to be more vulnerable to divorce than young children (Hetherington & Clingempeel, 1992). Life stage can also matter when certain events or transitions

are not expectable at that time. Loss of a parent, by contrast, entails greater life-long risks for adult mental health when it occurs in childhood rather than in adolescence (McLeod, 1991). The explanatory processes in each case are complex in their extension over time and remain important research foci.

Social imperatives refer to the behavioral demands or requirements of new situations. The more demanding the situation, the more individual behavior is constrained to meet role expectations. In emergency family situations, helpful responses become an imperative for members, what Rachman (1979) has called "required helpfulness." These situations may generate superordinate norms of cooperation among parties that are usually in conflict (Sherif, 1958). In studies of worklives (Kohn & Schooler, 1983), we find that entry into a new set of occupational and workplace imperatives can alter how men and women think and function. Occupational self-direction is the most important imperative, in the sense that workers exposed to it are most likely to become intellectually flexible, open to the thinking and actions of others. Self-directed men seek out work with these qualities and such work reinforces a self-directed life style and personal disposition. Similar processes have been observed among the work experiences of women and the school experiences of children. Kohn's (1977) career-long program of longitudinal research on social class, work experience, and psychological functioning illustrates the potential of life course studies for an understanding of cognitive development.

The concept of *control cycles* is based on the observed loss of personal control that occurs as people enter a social transition which invariably is followed by efforts to restore this control. All social transitions entail disparities between claims and resources, goals and accomplishments. The greater the disparity, the greater the risk of losing control over life outcomes, a state of disequilibrium. The anticipation and experience of such loss tend to prompt personal efforts to regain control, a process well described by W. I. Thomas in his account of control cycles at the turn of the century (see Elder, 1974), and by reactance theory. Feelings of reactance occur whenever one or more freedoms or expectations are eliminated or threatened. Such emotions spur efforts to regain or preserve control. In the Brehms' words (1982, p. 375), "it is the threat to control (which one had) that motivates an attempt to deal with the environment." Once control is achieved, expectations or claims may be raised, thereby setting in motion another round of equilibrating initiatives.

Heavy income loss tends to affect children through family mechanisms of adaptation in the control cycle (Elder & Caspi, 1988). A disparity between claims and resources may occur through increasing claims, declining resources, or a discontinuity between acquired and needed resources. The greater the disparity, the greater the sense of loss. Whether enhanced by personal self-efficacy or not (Bandura, 1997), efforts to restore control involve adjusting claims, resources, or both in terms of their relation. Family expenditures might be cut back, more family members might enter work roles, and living standards could be lowered. Equilibrium is achieved when claims match resources. Alteration of the family life course is likely to occur through new lines of adaptation and their consequences, such as new occupational roles, including self-employment.

The mechanism of *linked lives* assumes that transition effects occur indirectly through the lives of "related" others, such as from the unplanned parenthood of a child to the lives of parents. Personal networks and "convoys" (Kahn & Antonucci, 1980) for the individual across the life course may bring tangible and intangible support, as many studies have shown, but they also may exact a high price (Rook, 1984) through requests for support. A daughter's pregnancy is generally good news to parents when it comes from a married child in adulthood, but may become a burden or tragedy in the life of a teenage child, an event that redefines the mother as a grandmother and involves her in the caregiving task. The social convoys of friends may change in composition for children over time, though continuing their behavioral influence. Cairns and Cairns (1994) found the turnover in friends across the adolescent years to be substantial, although the new people represented the same types in behavioral values. Their study suggests that "relationships are likely to endure when individuals change together and each adopts the goals, values, and behaviors which may be integrated with those of the other person." Caspi and Herbener (1990) report similar empirical findings.

Coleman and Hoffer (1987) use the term "functional community" to refer to a particular system of linked lives, a system in which unrelated people as well as those related by birth and marriage know each other (called "network closure") and accept a common set of values within the community ("value consensus"). Small rural communities are characterized by functional communities of this kind, and so are the parish communities of urban Catholics, according to Coleman and Hoffer. They argue that children who develop within a functional community are exposed to a common culture on appropriate and inappropriate behavior, along with associated sanctions, and are strongly encouraged to behave by family and nonfamily adults. Fletcher, Darling, Steinberg, and Dornbusch (1995) found that such communities are especially effective in the socialization of prosocial behavior. In the inner-city of Philadelphia (Furstenberg, Eccles, Elder, Cook, & Sameroff, in press), African American mothers report that they frequently seek religious communities because they know them to be protective and developmental worlds for their children.

The fifth and last mechanism, known as the *accentuation principle,* relates transition experiences to the individual's life history of past events, acquired dispositions, and meanings. When a transition heightens a prominent attribute that people bring to the new role or situation, we refer to the change as an accentuation effect. Entry into new roles of situations is frequently selective, and thus the accentuation dynamic tends to amplify selection behaviors. In this regard, early transitional experiences become prologues for adult transitions that increase heterogeneity over the life course. We see this development in longitudinal studies of divorce and their increasing attention to the behavioral changes coupled with it (Cherlin et al., 1991). In children as well as adults, the divorce transition appears to accentuate dispositions that were present well before the event itself. Problem boys after the divorce of their own parents were typically engaged in problem behavior before the divorce.

In life course models, efforts to identify the developmental effects of social transitions and relevant mechanisms begin with the transition itself rather than with a particular outcome. What, for example, are the implications of residential change? The residential transition of families out of urban disadvantage turns the focus of attention to the altered well-being of children. Do they profit from the change? This is the question posed by W. I. Thomas (Volkart, 1951) during the mid-1920s when he argued for the study of children across their changing environments. In West's (1982) longitudinal study of boys from inner London, the analyses revealed a decline in delinquency among boys who experienced a family move to outside the metropolis. The change could not be explained in terms of delinquency before the residential change and it was not observed among boys who remained in the inner city. Selection influences are always a question in studies of this kind, but the design does illustrate the potential impact of a total environmental change.

Consider, also, the behavioral effects of a planned residential transition within the city of Chicago. The Gautreaux program began in response to a Supreme Court decision (1976) that favored public housing residents in a lawsuit against the Department of Housing and Urban Development, claiming the practice of racial discrimination in housing policies. The program enabled public housing residents and people on the waiting list to receive housing certificates and subsidies for a residential move to more costly private apartments in mostly White suburbs *or* in the city itself. Between 1976 and the 1990s, over 4,500 families participated in the program, and more than half moved to middle-income, predominantly White suburbs. The program excluded families with more than four children, large debts, or slovenly housekeeping—fewer than 30% of the total applicants.

In the typical move to a middle-class, White suburb, the Black mothers and their children were involved in radically different worlds with higher behavioral imperatives and typically White age-mates. If unemployed before the move, Black mothers who moved to the suburbs were more likely to find jobs and to engage in job searches, when compared to the city movers. In the follow-up, the suburban minority students were more often placed in a college track and were attending a two- or four-year college. If not in college, they were nearly twice as likely as the city movers to be employed full-time with pay greater than the minimum wage and job benefits. The suburban adolescents were also far more likely to be engaged daily in activities with White students, despite racial threats and harassment.

Selection factors are clearly relevant to these findings since the suburban move would appeal to more ambitious mothers and children, despite anticipated costs. Nevertheless, before-after comparisons show that the transition improved life chances. However, the dispositions and life experiences brought to the transition might well be accentuated so that initially ambitious parents and children become even more ambitious upon entering a suburban world in which opportunities are plentiful. Interaction of this kind would also heighten the preferences and dispositions

of families that achieved a new residence within predominantly Black inner-city neighborhoods.

PARADIGMATIC PRINCIPLES AND DISTINCTIVE CONTRIBUTIONS

The emergence of life course theory and its basic concepts reveals central principles that identify distinctive and potential contributions to the field of child development. Central principles in a research paradigm generally guide inquiry on issues of problem identification, model formulation, and research design. They structure a framework of inquiry. Among the principles that come to mind, four qualify as primary (Elder, in press): (1) the interplay of human lives and development with changing times and places; (2) timing of lives; (3) interdependence of human lives, including the relation between social and developmental trajectories; and (4) human agency in choice-making and actions.

The first principle of historical time and place asserts that (1) *the life course of individuals is embedded in and shaped by the historical times and places they experience over their life time.* This principle also reflects the premise that developmental trajectories are changed by changing the life course. The extent to which this occurs depends in part on the nature of the change. The second principle of timing expresses the fundamental bond between age and time; that (2) *the developmental impact of a life transition or event is contingent on when it occurs in a person's life.* Social age, for example, refers to the age at which people enter and leave particular roles. Timing may also be expressed in terms of biological events and transitions, such as puberty, whether relatively early or late.

The third principle on linked lives distinguishes an older "relationship" or role-theoretical view of human lives. It states that (3) *lives are lived interdependently and that social and historical influences are expressed through this network of shared relationships.* Social roles expose individuals to the stresses and strains of others, as well as to the possibility of social support. The fourth principle on human agency reflects an enduring premise of biographical studies on the *constructionist* role of individuals in shaping their life course (Lerner, 1982). It states that (4) *individuals construct their own life course through the choices and actions they take within the constraints and opportunities of history and social circumstances.* The principle expresses the dynamic relation between people and social roles in life course theory. Social roles and situations are selected and shaped by people, but they also constrain behavior, as do internal forces.

Human Lives in Time and Place

The life course became a topic of interest and field of study during an era when the rapidity and discontinuities of social change continually thrust people into new circumstances. The beginnings of life's journey did not ensure a known future. In such times, any behavioral change observed among children could reflect normative development as well as the social changes taking place. A way to distinguish among these explanations locates people in birth cohorts and employs the logic of cohort analysis.

People are assigned to cohorts according to their birth or other times of entry into society, and research compares the life patterns of successive cohorts, prompted by the thesis that people develop and age in different ways according to the nature of social change (Riley, 1988). We have reason to expect cohort effects since differing career stages at the point of change tend to shape the life-course effects of the change. According to the life-stage principle, older and younger children will not experience an economic recession or depression in the same way, owing to their differing roles and resources.

Historical influence takes the form of a *cohort effect* when social change differentiates the life patterns of successive cohorts, such as the older and younger children of the 1920s. Consistent with the life stage principle, the younger children, and especially boys, were most adversely influenced by the economic stresses of the Great Depression (Elder, 1979). Cohort differences may of course take different forms, from a change in the prevalence of a behavior or practice (such as the proportion exposed to war trauma) to a reorganization of the life course and behavior. An example of such change is provided in Hogan's (1981) study of conventional event sequences in the transition to adulthood among cohorts of American men. The conventional sequence of education completion, work entry, and marriage was changed for a large number of young men who served in World War II. In a good many cases, marriage came before the completion of education as veterans returned to college campuses.

The mechanisms of life course and developmental change may also vary across successive birth cohorts. Bronfenbrenner's (1958) discovery of a change in the relation of social class and parental permissiveness (from negative to positive between the 1930s and the 1950s) represents a type of life course change. A changing social mechanism appears in the transition to parenthood across four birth cohorts of White women who settled in Elmira, New York (Forest, Moen, & Dempster-McClain, 1995): 1907–1918, 1919–1923, 1924–1928, and 1929–1933. The first cohort came of age during the Great Depression, the second moved into adulthood during World War II, the third made the transition during the early postwar years, and the fourth became parents during the 1950s. The study found employment before marriage to be a primary source of childbearing delay for women in the first two cohorts. In the two younger cohorts, however, educational advancement played a significant role in the delay of the first birth, far more than premarital work. Advanced education was becoming more important in the lives of women. The trend also applies to women's return to school following marriage and the birth of children (Bradburn, Moen, & Dempster-McClain, 1995). The increase is a function of rising levels of education, divorce, and part-time employment.

In addition to cohort effects, history takes the form of a *period effect* when the influence of a social change is relatively uniform across successive birth cohorts. Rodgers and Thornton (1985, p. 21) conclude that "most of the changes in marriage rates observed during this century are the consequences of period characteristics" rather than of differences between cohorts. They draw the same conclusion about rates of marital dissolution and instability: "... the big picture is one of overwhelming historical effects that influenced all subgroups of the population substantially and surprisingly equally" (Rodgers & Thornton, 1985, p. 29). On divorce, they refer especially to the rising level up to the 1930s, to the decline in the Depression and the rapid recovery from it, to the extraordinary peak in the mid-1940s, and the upward trend of the 1960s and 1970s. The precise factors in these period variations remain to be determined. The explanatory challenge is demanding since any satisfactory explanation must account for the generalized trends across cohorts, family stages, and the life course.

Efforts to disentangle these effects and those associated with maturation or aging have not advanced knowledge on social change in lives. Studies seldom address questions that specify a type of social change or the process that makes a difference. Life span studies frequently assign environmental change to an error term or view cohorts as a test of the generalization boundaries of behavioral outcomes (Baltes, Cornelius, & Nesselroade, 1979). But even when history is substantively important, it may be operationalized as a period or cohort effect that provides no clue as to the precise nature of the process or that serves as proxies for processes that are still unknown.

Theory favors another approach to social change—the comparison of cohort subgroups—that rests on the empirically documented assumption that members of each birth cohort are exposed differentially to trends and events. Not all children who lived through the Great Depression were exposed to severe hardships; and not all veterans of World War II were exposed to heavy combat. In the Great Depression, the economic decline was not uniformly experienced by families, and not all subgroups of children were affected by family hardship in the same way (Elder, 1974). Experiential variations by subgroups within specific birth cohorts represent a significant conceptual distinction. However, a precise focus on exposure to particular change events or processes has more to offer in terms of developmental implications and insights because research is directed to the explication of a specified change process, such as family adaptations to migration.

Historical times are also geographic settings and should be linked to specific places and their properties. Studies of these places would be informed by evidence on community-level processes and institutions, service agencies, informal networks, and modes of social control. In making a compelling case for "dynamic contextualism," Sampson (1993, p. 436) recommends that longitudinal designs follow "not only changes in the structure, composition, and organization of communities, but also in the individuals who reside there. . . ." Consistent with this recommendation, a rural study of family economic distress (Conger & Elder, 1994) has brought evidence of the changing community and its institutions to an understanding of family and child adaptation and health.

Timing and Linked Lives

These two paradigmatic principles address in complementary ways the temporality, process, and context of human lives and development. They also address the role of significant others in regulating life trajectories through networks of informal control (see Hagan, 1991). Through the meanings of age, timing refers: (a) to the way social roles and events are organized across the life course in a concept of age-grading; (b) to a process of life management that schedules transitions in appropriate ways; and (c) to location, both across the life course and history. Linked lives refer to the embeddedness of the life course, intertwined with the lives of others:

> Actors do not behave or decide as atoms outside a social context, nor do they adhere seriously to a script written for them by the particular intersection of social categories that they are happy to occupy. Their attempts at purposive action are instead embedded in concrete, ongoing systems of social relations. (Granovetter, 1985, p. 487)

The interactive nature of relationships represents a lifelong process, linking developmental trajectories, while the temporal arrangement of social roles provides a way of thinking about time as sequence. Through family and intergenerational processes, adult development and life patterns are an integral part of the territory of child development. As Parke and his colleagues observe (1994, p. 35), this has not been a popular view in developmental psychology.

The special relevance of these significant adults can be viewed in terms of a human development triangle (Coleman, 1990). Human capital (such as intelligence, work skills, ambition) is located at the triangle's nodes. These nodes are linked by social capital, the trust, cooperative spirit, and nurturing qualities that foster human development. Social capital is derived from the social relationships and working arrangements that sustain community life. A promotive dynamic for human development requires substantial human capital at the nodes and social capital in the links. Highly conflicted families and single-parent households represent a loss of social capital in the development of children.

The interdependent lives so characteristic of the family world of farm children (Salamon, 1992) ensures a notable measure of social capital, as do the multiple connections between farm households and community institutions, from the church to the school and civic organizations. Within each of these institutions in cohesive rural communities there are many adults who know both parent and child. According to Coleman (1990, p. 593), social capital is found in "closure of a social network involving a child and two (or more) adults. Closure is present only when there is a relation between adults who themselves have a relation to the child. The adults are able to observe the child's actions in different circumstances, talk to each other about the child, compare notes, and establish norms. The closure of the network can provide the child with support and rewards from additional adults that reinforce those received from the first and bring about norms and sanctions that could not be instituted by a single adult alone." Connections of this kind are part of the strategies by which parents maximize the options of children and minimize their risks (Furstenberg et al., in press). These strategies apply to family interactions within the household, as in patterns of praise and encouragement; and to the external world beyond household boundaries, as in the placement of children in community athletic leagues and in special school programs.

Timing distinctions are expressed in the synchronization of linked lives through age-graded pathways, individual life courses, and developmental trajectories; and, therefore, provide an account of their goodness of fit or correspondence. Is the adolescent on course in school, or is he or she off-time relative to school norms and standards? An off-time schedule is coupled with particular kinds of associates as "linked lives." Such issues are typically assessed within a framework linking person and environment. Eccles and Midgley (1989), for example, apply the ideas of person-environment fit to an interpretation of why students who make an early transition to secondary school experience more emotional distress and problem behavior than students who make a later transition, at the eighth grade or so. The latter transition seems to offer a better fit for students. In view of the needs of students,

the environmental changes often associated with the transition to junior high school seem especially harmful in that they disrupt the possibility for close personal relationships between youth and non-familial adults at a time when youth have increased need for this type of social support; they emphasize competition, social comparison, and ability self-assessment at a time of heightened self-focus; they decrease decision-making and choice at a time when the desire for self-control and adult respect is growing; and they disrupt peer social networks at a time when adolescents are especially concerned with peer relationships and social acceptance. (Eccles & Midgley, 1989, p. 9)

Fit interpretations, such as the above, become more complete when they are cast within the framework of life-course theory, with its emphasis on the timing and embeddedness of lives. In the case of school transitions, goodness-of-fit centers on relations among the developmental pattern and status of the student, the individual life course of the student, and the social imperatives of the established school path with its particular features. The issue of match, then, is not between person and environment, but between levels of the life course—the student over time who at any point is located along a general developmental trajectory, the social life course of the student, and the age-graded pathway of the school.

A number of poor matches are suggested by a lack of correspondence across these levels. One example is suggested by the accelerated placement of an adolescent on a school path or track that fails to correspond with the student's own developmental and social status. Eccles and Midgley interpret the sixth to seventh grade transition in this manner. A different kind of mismatch comes about from the disparity between a girl's early physical maturity and her younger age-graded world in school. Both social and psychological disadvantages are coupled with the early physical maturation of girls (Simmons & Blyth, 1987), including poor images of one's physique and low self-esteem. Consistent with Susman's (1993, p. 183) observation, the data seem to suggest that "the timing of contextual influences on development may be as critical as contextual influences per se."

Human Agency in Choice Making and Actions

Concepts of the actor and human agency have always distinguished life history studies, dating back to the 1920s (Thomas & Znaniecki, 1918–1920), and they are equally prominent in contemporary theory. In recent years, a greater appreciation of human agency in selection processes has come from many areas, including work on self-efficacy in social action (Bandura, 1989, 1997), genetic influences (Dunn & Plomin, 1990; Scarr & McCartney, 1983), and the relation between agency and socialization (Baumrind, 1991). Within the constraints of their world, competent people are planful and make choices among alternatives that form and can recast their life course (Clausen, 1993).

Whether leading to action or not, choices have transitional consequences that may entail a turning point, a change in course. The Rutters note (1993, p. 358) that, "what we do, how we behave, and how we relate with other people all serve to select and shape the environments that we experience. However, it is a mistake to see this as just another process. It is often the *lack* of planning that creates the risk and the presence of planful competence that proves protective in the long-term." Hagan and Wheaton (1993) point out that the consequences of inadequate planning are multiplied when parental and educational controls are also lacking in the transition to adulthood.

Choices and options have much to do with "loose coupling" between individual and situation across the life course (Elder & O'Rand, 1995). Loose coupling reflects the agency of people even in constrained situations as well as their accomplishments in rewriting their journeys in the course of aging (Clausen, 1995; Cohler, 1982). The age grades of life and loose coupling exemplify two sides of the life course—its regulatory force in keeping behavior within conventional boundaries and the actor's initiatives and interpretations that press for individuality and deviations from convention. "The policies and processes of social regulation depict a pattern of social order in lives as a social aggregate, while the study of individual lives and actions highlights an element of flux and disorder" (Elder & O'Rand, 1995). The regulatory process operates through the life-long convoys of significant others, local acquaintances, and institutional representatives (e.g., work, school).

Agency in the selection of particular roles or situations represents a mechanism through which life advantages and disadvantages may begin to cumulate according to the Law of Effect in which behavior is sustained or changed by its consequences. Thus, competence in adolescence is rewarded by others, and this behavior is highly predictive of adult competence in the late middle years (Clausen, 1993). One success after another is followed by new opportunities in a process of cumulative advantages. Individual choices may also lead to involvement in a troubled peer group, a relationship that soon becomes a constraint through expectations and commitments. Kandel, Davies, and Baydar (1990, p. 221) observe that "although individual choices are made in part, as a function of the individual's prior attributes, values, and personality characteristics, involvement in the new relationship has further effects and influences on that individual."

One of these effects involves the erection of barriers that prevent troubled youth from leaving an antisocial gang. Youth who begin their antisocial careers at an early age encounter through associates an array of correlated disadvantages that can lock them into a problem career, such as school suspension, drug selling, police arrest, and incarceration. According to Moffitt (1993), life course persistent antisocial behavior typically involves a continuous interaction between neuropsychological deficits and a criminogenic environment, producing a cumulative array of personal and social disadvantages.

Behavioral continuities across the life course are likely to be found in social interactions that are sustained by their consequences *(cumulative)* and by the tendency of these styles to evoke maintaining responses from the environment *(reciprocal—*Caspi, Bem, & Elder, 1989). In *cumulative continuity,* both individual dispositions and family values may favor the choice of compatible environments, and this in turn reinforces and sustains the match. Thus, antisocial youth tend to affiliate with other problem youth, and their interaction generally accentuates their behavior, producing over time what might be described as *cumulative disadvantages* (Cairns & Cairns, 1994; Sampson & Laub, 1997; Simmons, Burgeson, Carlton-Ford, & Blyth, 1987). Among problem youth from inner-city neighborhoods (Furstenberg, Eccles, Elder, Cook, & Sameroff, in press), those who lacked the support of close kin and friends were most negative toward their life chances, did not have a supportive older sib, and were most likely to be involved with deviant friends.

Reciprocal continuity refers to a continuous interchange between person and environment in which action is formed by reaction and then by another cycle of action and reaction. Baldwin (1895) refers to this interchange as "circular functions" in ontogeny. The ill-tempered outburst of an adolescent may provoke a cycle of parental rage and aggression, a widening gulf of irritation, and, finally, parental withdrawal which reinforces the adolescent's initial aggression (Pepler & Rubin, 1991). Over time, the interactional experiences of aggressive children can establish attitudes that lead them to project interpretations onto new social encounters and relationships, thereby ensuring behavior that affirms the expected behavior. Aggressive children generally expect others to be hostile, and thus behave in ways that elicit hostility, confirming their initial suspicions and reinforcing their behavior.

The cycle of *cumulative disadvantage* can be broken by "knifing off" the unwanted past. New life transitions into different environments assist this process by establishing potential turning points for a troubled life course (Laub & Sampson, 1993). A change in schools is one option and military service is another for older youth. Mobilization into World War II broke the cycle of cumulative disadvantage for substantial numbers of youth who grew up amidst poverty and crime. This discontinuity is commonly described by analysts as a *turning point,* a change in life course direction, but a turning point might also depict change in developmental or psychosocial trajectory. Rutter (1996) takes the latter position—turning point effects are enduring changes in psychological functioning that are varied in form and mechanism. Presumably, the two kinds of turning points are correlated.

The concept of turning point also applies to a particular way people view their life—it is a subjective account of lived experience which involves some degree of change in situation, behavior, or meaning. Clausen (1995) has used detailed analyses of life histories to assess the subjective turning points of people who have been part of a longitudinal study for 60 or more years. On the basis of this work, he concludes (p. 371) that "one's life does not have to take a different direction for a person to feel that a turning point has occurred. But one must have a feeling that new meanings have been acquired, whether or not life experiences are much changed."

Contributions to the Study of Child Development

In combination, these four paradigmatic themes of life-course theory identify its core features and its potential contributions to the study of child development. First and foremost is the theory's conceptualization of the maturing individual's changing environment and its developmental relevance. In sociological terms, this changing environment is more than a string of situations or settings. Cultural scripts and social structure play an important role in organizing human lives as life courses, along with human agency and internal forces of self-regulation. Moreover, sociocultural variation and cohort differences in this approach are fundamental to an understanding of the life-course and developmental trajectories.

There are two aspects to this changing environment. One concerns the life course of the individual, the other the broader social and cultural changes (including institutionalized pathways) that affect this life course as historical effects or influences. In theory, these macrochanges influence developmental processes by altering the individual life course through multilevel processes and structures. For children growing up in the Great Depression, hard times shaped their life course by changing their family's experience and trajectory (Elder, 1974). Historical influences were filtered by their cohort membership, middle or working class status in 1929, and actual exposure to severe income loss as expressed in family adaptations.

To capture the developmental relevance of a changing environment, life-course studies use a framing statement in which the research question focuses attention initially on this environment. What are the developmental implications of a sudden income loss in the 1930s or of migration, or even of the departure and addition of family members to the household? For *Children of the Great Depression,* the study derived these implications from an account of how families might respond to an income loss, as change in the household economy or the increased prominence of mother. By posing questions regarding environmental change, a life-course framework differs from customary practice in developmental studies. Here research questions tend to center on the social interchanges or behavior of the individual child, and then lead to the identification of relevant influences (Parke et al., 1994). Differing points of entry into the multilevel developmental system may actually be used in the same study.

Consider *Children of the Great Depression* (Elder, 1974). The framing question for this study concerns the impact of the economic collapse on children, as expressed through family processes. The study traces the implications of drastic income loss for family responses or adaptations, and these adaptations provided a first step toward specifying the plausible effects of income loss on children and their development. At this point, a series of analyses were set up to investigate specific behavioral outcomes, such as emotional distress, regard for parents, and sense of responsibility. These analyses were "nested" in the larger study framework that relates macro change to individual patterns of development. By framing the study around the effects of Depression hardship, the investigation was able to identify *and* assess its potential developmental effects.

Sameroff (1993, p. 8) observes that while literally "thousands of studies have attended to longitudinal continuities in child development, correlating early behavior with later . . . very few studies have examined the consistency of environments over time." And from this, one would conclude that we have not seen adequate tests of his transactional model with its reciprocal influences between child and environment over time. Indeed, very few studies have even measured the socioeconomic environment of the child's family at more than one time, usually at baseline (Elder & Pellerin, 1995). In 1994, *Child Development* (Entwisle & Astone, 1994) published some guidelines for measuring the socioeconomic environment of children that gave details on static indicators and did not review ways of measuring this environment over time. One wonders how behavioral continuities and change among children can be understood without temporal measures of their environment. Issues of this kind were posed more than 30 years ago in the pioneering studies of child development, and they remain even more appropriate today.

Life-course ideas emerged in the 1960s partly in response to the need for a way to think about lives over time and about development within the context of changing lives and times. Consequently, the resulting theory constitutes an advance by offering a way of representing such influences across the life course and linking relevant social actors through people's lives, including family units, schools, workplaces, and communities. It has done so with a multilevel concept of the age-graded life course, from the social pathways of institutions and social organizations to the individual's life course and developmental trajectories. For the life-course analyst in developmental studies, social structure and established pathways are a constitutive force in human development, expressed through the dynamism of lives lived interdependently. Networks of informal social control are sustained by this interdependence. A proximal process of self-development, to use Bronfenbrenner's term (Bronfenbrenner & Ceci, 1994), is an essential part of this dynamism.

Temporal concepts of people's work lives were available in the 1960s, such as disorderly and orderly careers, and they continue to shape thinking about the life course through concepts of trajectory and transition, cumulative advantages and disadvantages, accelerated decline and growth, life review and turning point. This thinking is also reflected in studies of socioeconomic environments and

their impact on the developmental processes of children; an account of interlocking trajectories. Changes in the child's socioeconomic environment are associated with changes in the child's emotional health (Ge et al., 1994; McLeod & Shanahan, 1996). A typical conceptualization of this kind might view the environment as a socioeconomic trajectory that is linked dynamically with the child's trajectory of mental health. Measurement procedures connect SES states as well as mental health states across annual assessments.

This approach provides an opportunity to assess the effects of poverty status at different points in a child's life and its cumulative influence over time. There are compelling theoretical grounds for expecting the impact of poverty to vary across the dependency years in relation to cognitive and emotional processes, including issues of person-environment fit. The mechanisms by which poverty states and transitions make a difference in the functioning of children are also likely to vary across the dependency years.

Life-course theory underscores another angle on this problem, that the child's emotional life is linked to more than simply changing economic circumstances. It is undoubtedly influenced by the social and developmental trajectories of family members and even people outside the household. In longitudinal and cross-section studies, we find that adverse economic change heightens the risk of depressed feelings among parents, thereby promoting marital negativity and non-nurturant parenting (Conger & Elder, 1994; Elder & Caspi, 1988). These depressed feelings may result from a loss of personal efficacy in hard times but also probably magnify the loss over time. In view of such compelling evidence on linked lives in the family, it is troubling that the study of child development has been so typically uninformed by knowledge of the linked trajectories of parents and siblings. Life-course theory makes a strong case for the relevance of adult development in studies of children.

Given these distinctive features, life-course theory is well-suited to any specialty of child development that assigns developmental importance to the changing social, cultural, and physical environments of children. Kohn and Schooler's (1983) pathbreaking studies of tasks and their influences on thinking and emotional health suggest what might be done in studying the family, school, and peer histories of children. Life-course theory makes clear that issues of adult development and aging are fundamental to an understanding of the developmental experience of children. Little is known, for example, about the effect of social and developmental change in new parents and its consequences for the newborn. The acquired wisdom of older adults also has obvious but unexplored relevance for the socialization of their children and grandchildren. New directions for this research are suggested by Baltes and Staudinger (1996) in their provocative book *Interactive Minds.*

Life-course theory has much in common with Bronfenbrenner's ecology of human development, now called a bio-ecological theory (Bronfenbrenner & Ceci, 1994). In *Ecology of Human Development* (1979), Bronfenbrenner proposed a multilevel view of the sociocultural environment that did not elaborate a temporal view of individual development across historical time and changing environments. Some years later, after making a case for the person-process-context model, Bronfenbrenner (1989, p. 201) noted a major lacuna that also applied to "Lewin's original formula—the dimension of time."

The term *ecological transition* had been used in prior writings to refer to environmental change that altered the individual's social situation, but this concept did not attend to developmental change and the proximal processes that occur in organism-environment interactions. Limitations of this kind were corrected by the concept of *chronosystem* and its three interacting elements over time, the developing person, the changing environment, and their proximal processes of interaction. The ecological perspective has been remarkably generative of contextual studies of child development over the past decade (Moen, Elder, & Lüscher, 1995). Hopefully, it will generate more theory and research on social environments over time and on the developmental effects of their pattern of change.

Summary

Life-course theory offers child development studies a fruitful way to think about and investigate the changing environment of the individual and its developmental implications. It does so through an evolving concept of the age-graded life course that is embedded in a matrix of social relationships, an active view of the individual in shaping the life course, and an approach toward understanding historical influences in lives and developmental processes.

Age-linked distinctions of time and timing are central to both contributions. For example, the full negative implications of lengthy dependence on welfare for the education

progress of African American children appears after the third grade (Guo, Brooks-Gunn, & Harris, 1996). Cumulative dependence on welfare markedly increases the risk of grade retention from the third to the ninth grades. The timing and order of events and social roles are as consequential for developmental processes as to whether or not they are experienced. Age and timing distinctions enable the analyst to place people in the historical process and relate their lives to the lives of others and to the behavioral options and demands of multiple settings, family, school, and work.

A concept of the embedded life course has much to do with relationships that are part of the lifetime sequence of social roles, along with markers of historical time and place. Conceived as a sequence of age-graded events and social roles, the life course of individuals cannot be studied in isolation. The multiple roles of work, family, and civic activities link people's lives into an ongoing network of relationships, whether supportive and demanding or disruptive. Another dimension of the embedded life course, the lifelong nature of intergenerational relations, underscores a neglected theme for life-span development, the intergenerational relevance of *all* phases of human development, from infancy through old age. Through intergenerational and cross-age relations, people of all ages are engaged in the life-course process of child development.

Middle-aged parents and their biographical experiences are an integral part of the adolescent experience of their children (Parke, 1988), and the experiences of youth figure prominently in the social world of their parents. Likewise, the significant relationship of grandchildren and grandparents can have much to do with the quality of their own lives and developmental course. For example, wisdom (Baltes, 1994) surely plays an important role in a grandparent's relationship with grandchildren, but it has not been studied in this way. In social meaning or function, parents remain parents for as long as they and their children live. Lives and developmental trajectories are thus embedded in a moving system of intergenerational relationships.

As a final point, we note that history represents an analytical dimension of life-course theory; it is not the background for a research problem nor the setting in which behavior is expressed, as when children in a study reside in a mobilized city during World War II. Rather, the task is to investigate the collective and sequential events and processes by which the life experiences of children were influenced by the war. In a multifaceted program of research along these lines, Cahan, Mechling, Sutton-Smith, and White (1993) pursued ways of linking historical contexts and the practice of childhood across the cultural landscape of 20th-century America; Parke and Stearns (1993) investigated historical change in the practice of fathering; and Schlossman and Cairns (1993) explored change across the 20th century in the meaning of problem conduct among girls.

These efforts take us well beyond historical background and setting, but the journey has only begun in studying child development relative to a changing society. We turn now to some efforts that bear upon core propositions in life-course theory.

THE TIMING OF LIVES: IN THEORY AND RESEARCH

Timing plays a fundamental role in structuring life patterns and developmental experience, from historical to social and biological processes. No distinction offers greater conceptual relevance to life-course theory. To bring out this relevance, we turn to three areas of life-course study where notable timing variations and implications are revealed in theory and empirical work:

1. The relation between social and life history.
2. The process of constructing a life course.
3. The implications of event timing for linked lives and trajectories.

The human implications of historical change vary according to when the event occurs in a person's life; the timing of events determine how people construct their lives through recollection and initiatives; and the timing of events in one person's life has consequences for related others.

The Interplay of History and Lives

Developmental studies with an interest in the effects of macrolevel culture and structure are beginning to view the family unit and its processes as a mediational link to the behavior of children. In Patterson's (1996) coercion theory, for example, the contextual influences of social disadvantage and poverty that increase the risk of children's

antisocial behavior are expressed through the distress of parents, disrupted parental discipline, and ineffective monitoring practices (see also Sampson, 1992). Likewise, studies of neighborhood influences (Furstenberg et al., in press) tend to view family processes and management practices as a mediating bridge to the developmental experience of inner city children.

The same kind of cross-level model has proven useful in efforts to link changing structures and cultures to the life experience of children, especially when the family is represented as a changing environment, adapting to changing circumstances. In the case of children who grew up in the Great Depression (Elder, 1974), the economic decline influenced children by changing their family environment, in terms of family processes and parent behavior. The effect of such change or of any influence on children depended on their age or developmental status (the life-stage principle), especially under conditions of drastic change. This distinction is expressed in the following proposition:

> Human lives are socially embedded in specific historical times and places that shape their content, pattern, and direction. As experiments of nature or design, types of historical change are experienced differentially by people of different ages and roles (life-stage principle). The change itself affects the developmental trajectory of individuals by altering their life course.

Life stage assumes different specifications across children and adults in a family. Consequently, any social change will have differing effects among family members, each shared indirectly through lives lived interdependently. This variation is a potential *major* source of children's non-shared variance on developmental outcomes (Dunn & Plomin, 1990). Consider two sets of children from different families—one born around 1920, the other around 1929. The older children were too young to leave school in the 1930s and face a stagnant labor market, while the younger children were still in a dependent stage relative to the family, a stage that maximized their exposure to economic distress. Presumably, the parents of the older children were older when the economy collapsed, and thus may been less resilient to a job loss. In theory, age and behavioral differences of this kind are important because an economic decline makes a difference in the life experience of children through the lives of parents. The interaction between historical time and lifetime thus represents a function of changes in the life courses of multiple family members.

Life Stage in the Great Depression

Within a life-course framework, a program of research has examined the sociocultural influences experienced by two cohorts of California-born Americans who lived through the Great Depression and World War II (Elder, 1974, 1979, 1981, 1987): the Oakland Growth sample (birthdates 1920–1921) and the Berkeley Guidance sample (birthdates, 1928–1929). With pre-Depression birth dates that differ by about eight years, the two cohorts appear to share historical conditions from the 1920s to the 1940s, but they grew up in different worlds of adolescence, between the depressed 1930s for the Oakland Study members and war-mobilized America (1940–1945) for the Berkeley cohort. Job scarcity and intense financial pressures, crowded living quarters, and emotional stresses were part of a Depression adolescence, while young people during World War II experienced the war-related employment of parents from sun up to sun down, the military service and war trauma of older brothers, and the mobilization of school children for civil defense and the war effort.

The 167 members of the Oakland cohort, approximately half from middle-class homes, were children during the prosperous 1920s, a time of unmatched economic growth in California. Thus, they entered the Great Depression after a relatively secure phase of early development, regardless of socioeconomic level. Later, they missed the damaging experience of joblessness after high school by virtue of wartime mobilization. Nine out of ten Oakland men entered the war by 1945. By contrast, the 214 members of the Berkeley cohort experienced the vulnerable years of early childhood during hard times and the social risks of adolescence during the unsettled through prosperous years of World War II. Over 70% of the Berkeley men eventually entered military service. With all cohort differences in mind, the study expected more adverse effects of Depression hardship among the younger Berkeley Study members, particularly among boys who are at a greater emotional risk of early family disruptions.

The study's central question linked the varying economic loss of families with the life experience of children in the two cohorts. Variation in income loss thus served as a point of departure for assessing the effects of economic change in the two cohorts. In Oakland, two deprivation groups within the middle and working class of 1929 were identified according to income loss (1929–1933) relative to

a decline in cost of living (about 25% over this period). Families suffered losses with some frequency only when the income loss exceeded 40% of 1929 income. Deprived families were thus defined in terms of income losses above 35%; all other families were categorized as nondeprived. A corresponding division proved equally appropriate for the Berkeley cohort.

As noted earlier, heavy income loss prompted three types of changes and adaptations in the Oakland and Berkeley families:

1. Families became more labor intensive, enabling children to play constructive helping roles.
2. Authority and emotional salience shifted in favor of the mother.
3. The level of discord increased.

In both cohorts, loss of income increased the level of indebtedness, the reduction of expenditures, the replacement of funds for service and goods with family labor, and greater use of earnings from mother and children. Adverse changes in family relationships resulted from the father's loss of earnings and withdrawal from family roles. Income loss increased the relative power and emotional status of mother in relation to father among boys as well as girls. Last, income loss heightened the irritability of parents, the likelihood of marital conflict, and heavy drinking.

Young males in the Berkeley cohort were at greatest risk in theory and they turned out to be more adversely influenced by their Depression experience when compared with the younger females and the older cohort as a whole. For illustrative purposes, we focus on this subgroup. Unlike the younger Berkeley males, the Oakland study members were old enough to play important roles in their families. Males from hardpressed families were more likely to be involved in adult-life tasks within the family economy, to aspire to grownup status, and to enter the adult roles of marriage and/or work at an early age. Self-image problems that are common to adolescent development (self-consciousness, emotional vulnerability, desire for social acceptance) were more characteristic of youth from deprived families, but nothing of lasting significance. These men from deprived homes entered adulthood with a more crystallized idea of their occupational future and, despite some handicaps in education, managed to end up at mid-life with a slightly higher occupational rank. The men stressed the value of work, but also were more likely than the nondeprived to consider children the most important aspect of marriage and to favor family activities and the value of dependability in children.

The Berkeley boys encountered the Depression crisis when they were totally dependent on their family and its vicissitudes. Economic scarcity came early in their lives and entailed a more prolonged deprivation experience, from the economic trough of the Depression to the war years and departure from home. As such, the deprived boys were less hopeful, self-directed, and confident about their future than were youth who were spared such hardship. The vulnerability of these boys to family deprivation is in line with findings that show that these conditions are especially pathogenic for males in early childhood (Rutter & Madge, 1976), but why did the Oakland boys fare as well as they did? Part of the explanation centers on their family roles and status at the time. The older Oakland boys were more likely to assume jobs outside the home to aid their financially troubled families. Change of this sort enhanced their social independence and reduced their exposure to family stress. The Oakland girls were more vulnerable to stress of this kind.

What about the later years of the Berkeley boys? Did they carry their early inadequacies into marriage and work? Between their wartime adolescence and the middle years, the Berkeley men from deprived homes followed a different course. As a group, they achieved notable developmental gains in self-adequacy, assertiveness, and emotional health by their 40s, although the gains were not sufficient to erase completely the psychological deficiencies of their early years. In searching for a more satisfactory explanation of this seeming "turnaround," the investigation turned to important transition experiences that placed people on different paths, providing more support and opportunity. These included entry into higher education, the nurturant significance of marriage, and military service. Entry into college opened up social and occupational opportunities, marriage offered the prospect of family stability and support, and military service made all of these changes possible by pulling men out of deprivational circumstances and providing future benefits, such as the G.I. Bill. Of these transitions, military service proved to be the most potent turning point.

Three issues, posed by this project and its findings, warrant particular consideration:

1. The question of generalization to other times and places.
2. The broader usefulness of life stage in understanding the effects of historical change in lives.
3. The timing of family change in a child's life and its consequences.

The boundaries of generalization are uncertain for any study and are only clarified by efforts to test their outer limits. Nevertheless, studies are beginning to identify transhistorical generalizations in this area, as we shall see.

Evidence on the broader usefulness of life stage in studies of historical effects is beginning to emerge from studies of war mobilization in men's lives. The "at risk status" of the younger Berkeley boys raises questions about sensitive developmental times when children are most at risk of adverse family or social changes. Findings on the transition to single-parent status are relevant to this issue.

Findings from the older longitudinal studies are not likely to be replicated by studies in the same historical time, but what about major features of the analytic model? Has the process by which Depression hardship influenced children in the 1930s been documented by more contemporary research? McLoyd's (1989) comprehensive review of the empirical literature on family hardship shows a surprising degree of cumulative knowledge on a process in which economic pressures enhanced the negativity and explosiveness of fathers. For example, the Charlottesville Longitudinal Study (Bolger, Patterson, & Thompson, 1995) found that the impact of economic hardship on Black and White children was mediated in part by such parent behavior.

Even a rural midwest study of families and children in the Farm Crisis (Conger & Elder, 1994), designed to replicate major features of the Oakland-Berkeley studies, reports findings that parallel those obtained from the Depression research. Land values during the early 1980s had fallen by half, pushing many families off the land and most families into greater debt. Leading economic indicators suggest that the decline was more severe than any crisis since the Great Depression. The Iowa Youth and Family Project, with 451 rural families from the north central region of Iowa, includes two parents, a seventh-grade student, and a near sibling. Annual data collections, beginning in 1989, entailed questionnaires and videotaped family sessions. Data were also obtained from local and state statistical records.

Following the general model in *Children of the Great Depression,* the Iowa study assumed that low income, heavy indebtedness, unstable work, and income loss had adverse consequences for the emotional distress and marital relations of the parents by sharply increasing the level of economic pressure—tangible pressures from cutting back on expenditures, running out of money. Marital discord and the individual distress of parents link economic pressure to ineffective parenting (harsh, erratic punishment, etc.) and children's developmental risks, such as academic failure, low self-confidence, and peer rejection.

Using the first wave of data, an analysis of boys found that objective family hardship increased the risk of a depressed mood among mothers and fathers through reported economic pressures (Conger et al., 1992). Depressed feelings heightened the likelihood of conflict in marriage, and consequently increased the risk of disrupted and non-nurturing behavior by both parents. These behaviors, in turn, undermined the boys' self-confidence, peer acceptance, and school performance. Similar results have been reported for the girls (Conger et al., 1993). Empirical tests of this mediational model show results that generally resemble the findings of the Depression studies, with the major exception of mothers. The emotions and behavior of the 1930s mothers were not a strong link between hardship and children's experience, owing perhaps to their more marginal economic role.

Life Stage in Another Context: When War Comes

Entry into military service during wartime provides an opportunity to assess the implications of life stage in a very different historical process from that of an economic crisis, but it is one with major consequences for children through the changing lives of parents (Stolz, 1954). Also, it is different because wars are a prime example of state-initiated change that reduces the scope of individual choice. Historically, military service has been an obligation of mature youth, coming in the midst of the usual transition to adulthood, but extraordinary manpower requirements in wartime have pushed the upper age boundary into the late 30s, as during World War II. For both economic depression and war, life-stage variations indicate something about the life-course fit with the new social regime, and thus specifies potential social and developmental consequences.

When appraised in terms of costs and benefits, military service for Americans has favored the recruit who enters shortly after completing secondary school. As the years pass, the balance tends to shift in favor of costs, especially when military entry occurs in the 30s. An expanding body of empirical research (Clipp & Elder, 1996; Elder, 1986, 1987; Elder et al., 1994; Sampson & Laub, 1993, 1996) has documented the life-course advantages of early mobilization and the disadvantages of relatively late entry, quite apart from the mental health and mortality effects of wartime combat. These disadvantages include family disruption, prolonged father absence, the return of war-damaged fathers and spouses, family discord and divorce (Clipp & Elder, 1996). Before getting into the details of selected studies, consider some basic features of the transition to military service, with reference to the era of World War II, the Korean conflict, and the Vietnam War.

Military mobilization has tended to pull young people from their past, however privileged or unsavory, and in doing so created new beginnings that favored developmental life change among young adults. Training camps defined a recruit's past as irrelevant. This "knifing off" of past experience prompted independence and responsibility, separating recruits from the influence of community and family, and allowing a degree of social autonomy in establishing new ties. Basic training promoted equality and comradeship among unit members, made prior identities irrelevant, required uniform dress and appearance, minimized privacy, and rewarded performance on the basis of group achievement.

A second distinctive feature of military experience is that it generally establishes a clear-cut break from the age-graded career, a time-out in which to sort matters out and make a new beginning. Military duty legitimized a time-out from education, work, and family, and released the recruit from the conventional expectations of an age-graded career, such as expectations regarding progress and life decisions. Presence in the service is unquestioned and so is the lack of discernible career or work progress. As Stouffer and his associates (1949, Vol. 2, p. 572) noted, for many soldiers in World War II, "perhaps for a majority, the break caused by Army service [meant] a chance to evaluate where they had gotten and to reconsider where they were going." This time-out would be far less timely for men and women who were mobilized in the midst of family and career responsibilities.

A third feature of mobilization offered a broadened range of developmental experiences and knowledge, including exposure to in-service skill training and educational programs, as well as exposure to new interactional and cultural experiences through service itineraries that extended across the country and overseas. Out of such experiences came a greater range of interpersonal contacts, social models, and vocational skills. Horizons were broadened and aspirations elevated. A veteran interviewed just after World War II (Havighurst, Baughman, Burgess, & Eaton, 1951, p. 188) commented about the remarkable diversity of his acquaintances in the service and their influence on his views. As he put it, the experience "sort of opens up your horizons . . . . You start thinking in broader terms than you did before." Postwar veteran benefits, particularly the G.I. Bill, gave significant support for these new aspirations.

The creation of new beginnings, a time-out or moratorium to rethink and rework one's future, and a broader range of skills, interpersonal contacts, and cultural experiences do not exhaust key features of military experience for new entrants, but in combination they define, especially for disadvantaged youth, a bridge to greater life opportunity and a potential turning point. As a total institution that presses for compliant behavior from all angles, the military is uniquely suited to recasting life trajectories. Indeed, many years ago, Mattick (1960) found that young men paroled to the Army had a much lower recidivism rate than civil parolees.

Military entry shortly after high school in the United States usually comes before young men are established in families and careers, thereby minimizing life disruption. This entry age is also timely in terms of maximizing the life-course benefits offered by the service, such as vocational education, skill training, and the crystallization of goals and plans. In both the Oakland Growth and Berkeley Guidance samples (Elder, 1986, 1987), with birthdates in the 1920s, young men with disadvantages of one kind or another were likely to join up as soon as they could. Three types of disadvantage were especially consequential: membership in an economically deprived family during the 1930s, poor high school grades, and feelings of inadequacy in adolescence. In combination, these factors predicted early entry into military service and its pathway to personal growth and greater opportunity. Early entrants showed greater life benefits of the service up to the middle years than did later entrants.

Military service opened up the chance for greater life development among the early entrants, and it did so in two ways. One route involved situational changes that made the early entrants relatively more ambitious, assertive, and self-directed by mid-life (Elder, 1986). The second route involved extensive use of the educational and housing benefits of the G.I. Bill which was available for recruits up to the age of 25. The later the entry, the lower the chance for access to the G.I. Bill. The early entrants in both cohorts were more likely to use educational benefits for training and a college education (Elder, 1987). Though initially more disadvantaged, the early entrants at least matched the occupational standing of the nonveterans at midlife, and they displayed greater developmental gains as well. Using Q sort ratings of personality in adolescence and at mid-life (Elder, 1986), the study found that the early entrants showed greater change toward self-direction and confidence than the later entrants. The mental health risks of combat did not alter this effect of life stage and timing in the two cohorts.

Involvement in the military helped to account for why men from hardpressed families in the 1930s have fared well in their adult years, matching if not exceeding the occupational accomplishments of adults from more privileged backgrounds. However, the military experience itself has remained largely a "black box" and a subject of informed speculation. What were the mechanisms of developmental change? Sampson and Laub (1996) provide some answers to this question in a compelling test of the early entry hypothesis. They use life record data on a sample of approximately 1000 men who grew up in poverty areas of Boston (birth years, 1925–1930). More than 70% of the men served in the military. The matched control sample, 500 delinquents and 500 controls, was originally designed for a longitudinal study of delinquency by Sheldon Glueck and Eleanor Glueck (1968).

The delinquent sample of White males, ages 10 to 17, was drawn from a population of youth who were committed to one of two correctional schools in Massachusetts. The matched controls (on age, IQ, race-ethnicity, and neighborhood deprivation) include 500 White males from the Boston public schools, also ages 10 to 17. The two samples are treated in all analyses as independent samples. From 1940 to 1965, the Gluecks collected a rich body of life history information on the study members. With a particular eye to experiences in the military, they assembled unparalleled details on the men's service experience—their in-service training programs, special schools, exposure to the military justice system, and arrests. The life record data on the sample of delinquents have also been coded by Sampson and Laub.

Men in the delinquent and control samples typically entered the service at the age of 18 or 19 years, and most served over two years (more than 60% overseas). Consistent with their history, men from the delinquent sample were far more involved in antisocial conduct during their service time than the controls (official misconduct, number or arrests, dishonorably discharged), and they were less likely to experience in-service training and benefits from the G.I. Bill. Nevertheless, men from the delinquent sample were more likely to benefit from the service over their life course, when compared to the controls, and this was especially true for men who entered the service at an early age.

The findings show that in-service schooling, overseas duty, and use of the G.I. Bill at ages 17 to 25 significantly enhanced subsequent job stability, economic well-being, and occupational status, independent of childhood differences and socioeconomic origins. In particular, benefits of the G.I. Bill were larger for veterans with a delinquent past, particularly when they entered the military at an early age. The significant beneficial effects of the G.I. Bill and overseas duty on social position were observed across the adult years up to age 47.

In combination, these findings provide consistent support for the life-course advantages of early entry into World War II, and one study suggests that it applies as well to the Korean War (Elder, 1986). However, as one might expect, the timing of military service had very different implications in countries that lost World War II, specifically Japan and Germany. German males, born between 1915 and 1925, were drawn very heavily into military action (up to 97% of an age cohort) (Mayer, 1988, p. 234). These veteran cohorts lost as many as nine years of their occupational career in the war. They suffered a high rate of imprisonment during and after the war, and experienced a mortality rate of 25%.

Using data from the Berlin Life History Project, Mayer and Huinink (1990, p. 220) conclude that German children born around 1930 were also hard hit by the war years. The war disrupted their families and education and they entered the labor market in a war-devastated economy. Work placements were often poor, mixed with spells of joblessness, and advancement was unpredictable. Even the economic boom after the deprivational years of recovery did not fully compensate this younger cohort for its wartime losses in occupational advancement. In Japan, these two birth cohorts tell a similar life story (Elder & Meguro, 1987), except that the younger cohort (circa 1930) was mobilized as students for work in the fields and factories. A large number reported bomb-damaged homes and a forced evacuation to the countryside.

An ill-timed entry into World War II brought a great many lifetime disadvantages to men who were widely touted as the best and brightest of a generation, the talented or gifted young men in the Lewis Terman study. Born between the early 1900s and the 1920s, a large number of these men were mobilized into World War II at an age that was too late in life (Elder et al., 1994), beyond the ages of 30 to 32. The men were first surveyed in 1922 and data collections continued every five or so years up to the 1990s. Over 40% of the men entered World War II at an average age of 30. Even the youngest Terman recruits were older at time of entry than early joiners from the Oakland cohort.

Truly late mobilization (age 33 and older) for military duty markedly increased the risk of personal and social disadvantages that endured to late-life. Though better educated than other veterans, these late entrants ranked higher on divorce. They were also more likely to experience a work life of disappointment and a permanent loss of income up to old age, particularly among the professionals. They experienced the risk of an accelerated decline of physical health, mostly after the age of 50, an effect that was not due to their combat history or to individual differences. The late entrants were less likely than other men to remember the service as a beneficial experience in life and to claim that they derived more from their servicetime than they gave to it.

In review, the *life stage* at which people experience drastic social change has much to do with the impact of this social process on their behavioral adaptations, life course, and development. Children who encountered the Great Depression at different life stages were influenced differentially by family misfortune, as seen in the greater impact of family hardship on the developmental course of the younger boys from the Guidance study. Life stage also mattered for the Berkeley and Oakland men who were mobilized into the Armed Forces, but in this case "a timely entry" involved transitions into the service shortly after high school. The social and developmental advantages of military service minimized the long-term adverse effect of growing up in hard times.

The advantages of early mobilization were comparable among men from poverty areas of Boston in the 1930s, especially for the most disadvantaged, and they stand out in relation to the life-course risks of late entry in the Terman sample. However, the meaning of life stage is linked to both historical time and cultural place, as revealed in cohort studies of Japanese and German males. It is also possible that the developmental meaning of family structure varies by historical context. Father absence during the Great Depression had more negative implications for the image of father than the absence of fathers through service in World War II. In a sample of German men, Grundmann (1996) found that father-absence before and after World War II resulted in the postponement of parenthood. This delay did not occur among men who grew up during the war without fathers in the home but with heroic images of them. Historical variations of this kind raise important questions about the generality of findings across time and place, but they also call for empirical study that pushes the outer limits of historical and geographic boundaries.

The relevance of military service, especially in wartime, for children's development has been noted at various points, in the transforming effect of the returning veteran on family life, in the developmental costs of mortality, in the disruption of family life that leads to separation and divorce, and in long-term career setbacks and damaging psychosocial or character changes. The scope of this impact can be appreciated when we realize that over half of all American men over the age of 65 have served in the military.

The Timing of Family Change: Effects on Children

In *America's Children*, Hernandez (1993) explores the implications of what he terms "revolutionary changes" in the family experience of children, with emphasis on the years since 1930. The first change, still in process, involves the movement of men and women out of farming and into nonfarm employment (Figure 16.4). Nearly 70% of all children lived in two-parent farm families in 1830, a figure that has now dropped to less than 5%. Surprisingly, the developmental implications of this historic family transformation are largely unexplored.

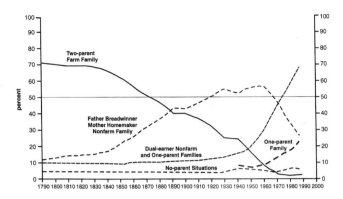

Figure 16.4 Children aged 0–7 in farm families, father as breadwinner families, and dual-earner families: 1790–1989. Estimates for 10-year intervals to 1980, and for 1989. Census PUMS for 1940–1980, CPS for 1980 and 1989, and Appendix 4.1 in *America's Children*. As amended, from *America's Children* (p. 103) by D. J. Hernandez, 1993. New York: Russell Sage. Reprinted with permission.

Nevertheless, one contemporary study has relevance to the issues involved. A midwestern panel study (1980s–1990s) compared the family life of fathers who followed different occupational routes, either staying in farming or moving into nonfarm employment (Elder, King, & Conger, 1996). Most of the 451 families are of German ancestry, and 140 were engaged in farming at the end of the 1980s. The family experience of young adolescents was compared in two types of families, full-time farm and with no relation to farming, including childhood experience. With adjustments for socioeconomic status, children in farm families were more involved in relations with their grandparents, especially on father's side of the family, and their grandparents were more significant in their lives.

These children were also more involved in family labor of one kind or another, and their work was more valued by parents. Farm youth were more engaged in joint activities with parents (both work and recreational activities), and they more strongly endorsed a nonmaterialistic value orientation, when compared with nonfarm youth. In general, farm-based socialization was more adult-sponsored and directed, whereas spontaneous peer culture played a more prominent role in the lives of nonfarm youth. The consistency of these differences is especially noteworthy in view of the shared communities and schools of the two groups, farm and nonfarm, living in eight north central counties of Iowa.

The second revolution identified by Hernandez entailed a profound reduction in the average size of families, a change investigated by Blake's (1989) study of the achievement effects of different size families. Eighty percent of adolescents at the end of the Civil War were living in families with five or more children. This figure dropped to 30% at the end of the 1920s. A third revolution involved a striking educational advancement among both men and women. Smaller families and higher education among women, along with rising consumer needs and stagnant or declining earnings, spurred their involvement in the labor force.

Compared to less than 10% in 1940, a large majority of children in the 1990s have mothers with paid employment, a fourth revolution. This change has focused attention on the dual-career parent and the task of synchronizing work and family needs (Gerson, 1985; Moen, 1992). Questions regarding the effects of maternal employment center on its scheduling and quality (Crouter & McHale, 1993; Parcel & Menaghan, 1994), with some attention on the child's individual differences. The last revolution discussed by Hernandez involves the rising divorce rate and the transition from two-parent to one-parent households. Studies have shifted attention from the effect of divorce on children to the impact of the predivorce family experience and behavior pattern of children (Cherlin et al., 1991). According to Hetherington and Clingempeel (1992), the adverse psychosocial effects of divorce are most acute during the years of middle childhood.

Research is just beginning to investigate the child development implications of these family changes. Consider the long-term effects of divorce based on the British sample of the National Child Development Study, a cohort of children born in 1958. Data were collected at ages 7, 11, 16, and 23. The occurrence of parental divorce was assessed between age 7 and 16. Chase-Lansdale, Cherlin, and Kiernan (1995) found that the event moderately increased the relative risk of serious emotional disorders in adulthood, though only for a small percentage of the individuals with divorced parents. Based on the clinical cut-off of the Malaise Inventory, only 5% of the men and 15% of the women who experienced a parental divorce scored in the serious disorder category. The effect was greater among the better adjusted at age 7, persumably because divorce represented more of a status change for them. Other predivorce factors did not alter the long-term effect of divorce. More needs to be learned about the men and women who were most adversely influenced in

adulthood (age 23) by the divorce of their parents (between ages 7 and 16). Older children at time of divorce were more strongly influenced by the event, compared with younger children, although timing variations were not statistically reliable. The persistent effects of divorce to age 23 occurred in large part through more emotional problems, lower levels of academic achievement, and a diminished economic situation at age 16.

We are still uncertain about how much of a developmental risk is associated with growing up in a single-parent household. Part of the reason has to do with the many contingencies that shape the meaning of this family structure (McLanahan & Sandefur, 1994), from the parent's personal history to socioeconomic conditions. Nevertheless, the likelihood of a child experiencing a single-parent household before maturity has virtually become a majority experience for American children. By the age of 17, approximately one-third of the White children born in the 1960–1964 cohort of the Panel Study of Income Dynamics were not in a first marriage, two-parent family (Hofferth, 1985). This compares to a striking three-fourths of the Black children in the cohort. If these trends continue, the probability for White children in the 1980–1984 cohort will exceed 40%, a figure that is twice as large for Black children.

On average, Black children are more likely than White children to experience a household in which the parent is single, separated, or divorced; they are likely to spend more time in such households up to their eighteenth birthday; and, most surprisingly, they are less apt to be linked to other families through coresidence and financial assistance. It is the single Black parent who is more likely to be isolated, not the single White parent. Little is currently known about the effects of different household structures on children who vary in age or about the social meaning of long and short durations in particular household types.

One of the major unknowns in studies of household structures and income involves the influence of sequences. Does the sequence of household structures matter for children and adults of different ages, and is a particular sequence a determinant of the meaning of specific conditions and their duration? Birth to a single parent may have different consequences depending on what the parent brought to the situation or the sequence the event initiates through marriage, education, or residence with mother.

An important effort to achieve greater understanding of timing issues was launched by Krein and Beller (1988).

They used matched mother-daughter and mother-son samples from the National Longitudinal Surveys, and constructed precise measures of the age and length of time a child lived in a single-parent household. The reports on family structure were retrospective since the mothers were interviewed between the ages of 30 and 44 years, while the young sons and daughters were interviewed when they were 14 to 24 years old. However, such reports are reasonably accurate.

Apart from considerations of income variations, the authors hypothesized that:

1. Duration of residence would diminish the social resources of the family and lessen the educational achievement of offspring.
2. A transition to single-parent status would be most damaging to children's cognitive and educational achievement during the early preschool years, owing to the heavy time demands.
3. Boys would be impaired more than girls, according to modeling processes.

The investigators estimated the effects of residence in a single-parent household by gender and race, and compared results with and without controls on income.

Overall, the study found that the adverse effect of life in a single-parent household increases with the number of years spent in this type of household (duration effect); that the effect was much greater for the preschool versus later years (timing effect in child's life); and that the adverse effect on educational attainment was most negative for boys. Notable variations were also obtained. The strongest and most consistent duration and timing effects were obtained in the subsample of White males, with family income controlled. Black women and men were next in line on effects, followed at some distance by White females. Whether family income was controlled or not, duration of residence in a single-parent household and the timing of its onset in preschool mattered least in the education of these women. The meaning of this result and that of duration in a single-parent household are unknown, though young daughters of single-parent mothers may be protected by maternal support and the model of a self-sufficient woman.

Research should focus more attention on what the historic family transitions entail for child socialization. Leaving the land continues in the last decade of the 20th

century, and thus provides opportunities to assess its implications for family life. Transitions into and out of education and work deserve study in relation to the models and competencies of parents. Across all transitions of this kind, we have learned that their behavioral meaning depends on what people bring to them in life history and dispositions.

Timing issues are also central to the relation between life and social history in choices that construct the life course. Weighing one option versus another invariably includes matters of timing. Some of these options involve stories about one's life, while others entail actions. Both life stories and prospective accounts are key elements of the life course.

Constructing One's Life Course

The choices people make lead to actions that give form and substance to the life course, however constrained. Thus, young adolescents may remain sexually inactive or become sexually involved. If involved, they may use or avoid contraceptives. Each choice point opens up new options and constraints, whether appealing or not, and the decision gives more structure to the adolescent life course. Involvement in deviance and drug use can be viewed in similar terms across a series of choice points.

In addition to lived experience, construction of the life course may take the form of a life story or account. Cohler (1982) describes the process of writing and rewriting the life course as one ages. Rewriting alters the description and explanation of trajectories and transitions, the meaning of a job or residential change, for example. Each transition across the life course calls for an account or story that makes sense to others. The more puzzling the transition to others, the more difficult the task of providing an acceptable account. Puzzles generate questions. Why did you move to this town? Why are you in the fifth instead of the sixth grade?

Mead's theory of the past (Maines, Sugre, & Katovich, 1983) stressed the process by which people make the past meaningful by connecting events and roles in coherent ways. The unexpected event that causes disruptions and discontinuities is diminished in the account. Ross and Buehler (1994) propose, in addition, that accounts of one's past or life course are constructed in terms of the individual's objectives or needs, which may vary according to context and audience. However construed, representations of the life course, both individual and collective, deserve more attention than they have received in studies that investigate the developmental effects of parental lives and life courses for children. A family account of parental lives is no doubt more accessible to children than the actual biography of parents.

The constructionist role of the individual in making a life course should be coupled with recognition that all choices and initiatives are constrained, more or less. The constraints experienced by Chinese young people during the Cultural Revolution represent one extreme (Gold, 1987). They did not have the freedom to move from rural areas to the large cities, and both marital and job choices were ultimately the decisions of work or political units. Within such limits, the Chinese made choices and worked out different life patterns. Sampson and Laub (1997) make the important point that the role of individual differences in shaping choices does not rule out the causal significance of social factors. "Choices generate constraints and opportunities that themselves have effects not solely attributable to individuals" (p. 30). They note that the social disadvantages of decisions pile up most rapidly for the most disadvantaged population of children, while more advantaged youth are better able to escape the constraints of unwise actions.

Individuals construct their own life course through variably constrained choices and behavioral initiatives that are sequenced and linked over time. Not making a choice or not initiating a plan is equivalent to a decision. The process occurs through the selection of social roles and situations with their particular options and constraints; and by telling a narrative story or account of lived experience.

This process is revealed in the lives of Americans who acquired a sense of planful competence during the early years and in the lives of adults with an antisocial record in childhood.

Planful Beginnings

In *American Lives,* Clausen (1993) views men and women from the longitudinal Berkeley studies as people who shaped their lives through the choices they made. The central question was not how social systems or history shaped human lives, but why these Californians made certain choices in particular situations and thereby constructed

their own lives. Clausen focused on the primary causal role of planful competence across the adolescent years. In theory, competent young people who think about the future with a sense of personal efficacy are more effective in making sound choices and in implementing them.

Clausen measured planful competence in terms of three dimensions: self-confidence, dependability, and intellectual investment. A competent adolescent is equipped with the ability to evaluate accurately personal efforts as well as the intentions and actions of others, using an informed knowledge of self, others, and options, and with the self-discipline to pursue chosen goals. Quite apart from IQ and class background, the highly competent males in adolescence were most likely to achieve a successful start through education, occupational careers, and family. And this beginning anticipated accomplishments across the life course, even into the 60s. The planfully competent in adolescence were more likely to have stable marriages and careers, and to find satisfaction and fulfillment during their last decade or so. This social stability is reflected in personality. Men in the top third of planful competence show far more personality stability than men in the bottom third between adolescence and late middle age, Rs of .56 versus .16. The comparable coefficients for women are .40 and .18. Success and failure have self-fulfilling dynamics, consistent with the mechanism of cumulative continuity.

Assortative pairing or mate selection is another mechanism by which planful competence could maximize the chances of marital success and lifelong emotional support. The principle of homogamy, or like selecting like, is well established in studies of social factors, like education, race, and religion. Less is known about selection on the basis of psychological attributes, such as dominance, aggression, and congeniality. However, Caspi and Herbener (1990) show that the Oakland study members who married someone who resembled them on personality (based on the California Q Sort) were most likely to remain the same psychologically over a 10-year period. The lower the psychological match at the beginning, the more unstable the personality. When combined with the Clausen project, this study provides empirical documentation of a process by which the planfully competent maintained their personal continuity across the life course. They married well by selecting a mate who matched them psychologically and who was most apt to provide marital support across the years.

In reviewing the continuity of lives among the most competent members of the Berkeley studies, it is important to appreciate the special circumstances of their early adult lives—the beginning of World War II and an unparalleled era of prosperity. Postwar benefits for veterans encouraged them to obtain a college education. But what if we stepped back a decade or two so that both Depression and global war loomed ahead? Consider, for example, the lives of the Terman men. Lewis Terman began his California study of talented children in the early 1920s, a time when the state's economy seemed to offer unlimited opportunity. Half of the children were born before 1911, the other half by the early 1920s. By selecting only the most able of California's children for the study, Terman focused his attention on great promise and the expected rise of talent to positions of accomplishment and leadership.

Historical change offers another picture of their future (Shanahan, Elder, & Miech, 1996). Consistent with the life stage principle, men of different birth cohorts (older = 1903–1911, younger = 1911–1920) had different life experiences. The older cohort had completed most of its post-high school education by the stock market crash and looked ahead to a stagnant and declining labor market, while the younger men faced the prospects of going to college in the latter years of the Depression decade. Lacking good job prospects, a substantial number of the older men stayed in graduate school, extending their list of degrees. By contrast, the war reduced significantly the educational opportunities of the younger men, while having no impact on the education of the older men who were well past the college years.

As a consequence of these differing historical paths, planful competence in the adolescent years had much greater relevance for the future of the younger men. With the disruption of war to contend with, they had to plan ways of completing their education. The planfulness of these men, as reported by mothers in their adolescence, was highly predictive of their occupational placement and achievement. But this was not true for the older men. Regardless of their planfulness in adolescence, it did not tell anything about the educational level they achieved. In large part, this outcome reflects "warehousing," a process by which the young prolong their stay in school during economically troubled times. School persistence had less to do with personal motivation than with a way of getting out of hardship situations. Consequently, the high level of education

these men achieved bore no relation to their planful competence in adolescence.

A Troubled Life History: The Timing of Onset

The smooth sailing characteristic of the most competent members of Clausen's study contrasts to the troubled life history of youth with behavior disorders or problems of one kind or another. Children with problem behavior in general are at risk of a cumulative process of adverse events across the life course.

Thirty years ago Lee Robins (1966) found that antisocial boys were likely to enter unskilled jobs and experience spells of unemployment, short weeks, and an unstable marriage. More recently, a study of ill-tempered boys in the Berkeley Guidance Study found them to be at risk of the very same kind of disorganized life course (Caspi, Elder, & Bem, 1987). They were not able to maintain social relationships or jobs. Sequences of adverse events are at the core of a cumulative process of life disadvantage. Just how this process unfolds is a subject of much theorizing and research. Patterson (1996) conceptualizes the process in terms of a cascade of secondary problems, such as school failure, depressed mood, and parent rejection. An early history of antisocial behavior is linked to late adolescent conduct through these problem processes.

The chain of events is frequently both complex and loosely coupled. There are few if any direct effects. Quinton, Pickles, Maughan, and Rutter (1993) have charted the process by which conduct-disordered children become antisocial or conventional adults, with emphasis on the bridge or turning point established by a significant other. Conduct disorder is associated with dysfunctional parenting environments. These children were most at risk of deviant friends when they had conflicted, dysfunctional families or homes. A harmonious family sharply reduced this risk. The next step involved selection of a deviant partner, a process that occurred through a deviant peer network. For girls, and especially those not inclined to plan, early pregnancy led to a deviant boyfriend. More planful youth managed to avoid this event and were better able to establish stable relations with nondeviant mates.

Three markers along a disadvantaged life course have been well-established by empirical research—age at first arrest, incarceration or jail time, and unemployment. In combination they underscore the importance of the onset timing of deviant activities. The earlier the age at first arrest, the greater the likelihood of a future criminal career (Farrington et al., 1990). Age at first arrest is a reliable predictor of this future because it sharply increases the likelihood of chronic, violent, and adult offending, as well as the risk of incarceration. More prisons may be a popular response to the crime problem, but the empirical evidence suggests that incarceration is a large part of the problem itself, owing to its role in expanding the disadvantaged population. Using nationwide and local samples, Freeman (cited by Sampson & Laub, 1996) found that in all analyses "having been in jail is the single most important deterrent to employment." This finding held up even with adjustments for individual differences that account for unemployment.

An *early onset* trajectory is defined as a rule by a first arrest before the age of 14. Studies to date link early onset with an earlier onset of an antisocial dynamic (Patterson & Yoerger, in press). Perhaps as early as age 6 or 7, a breakdown in parenting processes increases coercive actions (talking back, explosive behavior, hitting). The resulting interchange leads to fighting, stealing, and truancy. Antisocial actions that are prototypic of delinquent acts, such as stealing from parents and hitting them, increase the risk of delinquency through the medium of deviant friends. The *later onset* of deviant behavior includes more conventional youth who are or might be seen as "transitory delinquents." They are more antisocial than uninvolved youth, but not as antisocial as the early onset youth. Patterson and his colleagues conclude that the most intriguing thing about the late-onset boys is that they tend to be "significantly more socially skilled than are the early-onset boys. We think this is the key to understanding which boys will continue to commit adult crime and which boys will not. Presumably increased social skills will predict greater success in adult work and marital relationships, and this will result in a decreasing risk of adult crime."

The profound life-course implications of early involvement in antisocial behavior will continue to focus empirical work on the dual pathways hypothesis (Farrington & West, 1990; Moffitt, Caspi, Dickson, Silva, & Stanton, 1996; Nagin, Farrington, & Moffitt, 1995). Some studies rely solely upon official record data, while others use information reported by the adolescent. Since the official records always underestimate the prevalence of antisocial behavior, it is not surprising that type of data has much to do with the results—the two types do not produce similar results (Lenox, 1996). Nevertheless, the most important problem

and handicap centers around the assumption that there are two qualitatively different entry points for antisocial behavior relative to antecedents and correlates in all settings. Indeed, the evidence to date suggests that the boundary between early and late onset may vary across different ecologies, even though studies have not been designed to actually assess this variation.

In terms of life-course theory, age at onset of antisocial behavior is most appropriately expressed as a continuous, time-dependent process. From research to date, one would expect causal factors during the early years to feature neurological and social skill deficits as well as impaired family processes and indications of extreme distress. In the later years, other factors would come to the fore, such as deviant peer activities; but when, in fact, they come to prominence may depend on the particular ecology, whether the high-risk environment of the inner-city or the network closure of small rural communities. By employing this analytic model, empirical research and not decisions based on potentially different criteria determine whether and when a break occurs between types of causal influences.

Both planful competence and antisocial dispositions play a role in constructing the life course, typically by guiding the selection of particular environments and associates, but they do not operate in a vacuum. Social constraints, available options, and contingencies collectively shape their expression. Thus, planful competence does not tell us much about educational achievement when schooling becomes a holding operation, a place to wait out better times. And the relevance of conduct disorder or antisocial behavior in childhood for adult functioning depends on both the quality of family nurturance and significant others, such as a marriage partner.

Timing Affects Linked Lives

The connections among lives identify potential sources of emotional and tangible support, as well as obligations and risks. These risks occur through positive and undesirable changes that alter the individual's status and identity. The person involved has little if any control over these changes. Children are subject to the socioeconomic changes of their parents' lives, and the identity of parents has much to do with parental changes in their children's status, the first grandchild. Kessler and McLeod (1984) show that the greater emotional distress of women than men has much to do with their involvement in more extensive networks of personal need or demand.

Asynchronies in the timing of events may occur among age-mates, generating emotional strains, deprivations, and violations of age expectations. A biological transition may prompt such outcomes when it precedes the usual social transition, as in the case of early maturing girls. For example, a Swedish study (Stattin & Magnusson, 1990) found that early maturing girls (reached menarche under the age of 11) were far more involved in misbehavior (getting drunk, taking drugs, staying out late, etc.) than girls who matured at the usual or later age. The social and sexual meanings of advanced physical maturity pulled the early maturers into a world of older girls and their boyfriends. In a New Zealand replication and extension of this project, Caspi, Lynam, Moffitt, and Silva (1993) obtained similar results *only in mixed-sex schools*. In this school environment, the physical signs of early maturation provided ready access to an older mixed-sex group and its norm-breaking behavior.

Early maturation among girls has implications that extend to family as well as school and peers, in part because it challenges age-specific expectations for behavior. The early maturing girl is placed in an accelerated position on age expectations; the presentation of self is older than her actual age. This asynchronous development may be reflected in unusually high levels of emotional distress. A four-year study in rural America (Ge, Conger, & Elder, 1997) found that early maturing girls were more vulnerable to prior psychological problems, to deviant peer pressures, and to the hostile feelings of father, when compared to other youth. Moreover, the emotional distress of the early maturing girls was especially pronounced when they had mixed-sex friends. From the evidence at hand, it is apparent that girls' early maturation redefines their relationships to peers and family in ways that can place them at risk, depending on the social context. However, unsuccessful efforts to replicate these effects of early maturation among girls in the Swedish, New Zealand, and rural America studies (Cairns & Cairns, 1994) underscore their contingent relation to social and historical context.

Asynchrony between lives and trajectories is vividly expressed through off-timed reproductive events. Children are born to "children" in early adolescence and to women over the age of 40, an age spread of more than 25 years. Both of these intergenerational transitions are prominent in contemporary populations; accelerated reproduction among the poor and delayed reproduction among the well-educated. Later childbearing, in the 30s or so, ensures greater resources for the child and the positive qualities of childrearing may increase as the mother's age at birth increases (Vanden Heuval, 1988). A 42-year-old mother would be 62 years old when her child reaches adulthood. Symptoms of aging could turn older women toward themselves and away from the concerns of their children. Rossi (1980) found that older mothers perceived less closeness with children than did younger mothers. With these differences in mind, we state a third proposition on timing:

The temporal relation between lives and trajectories varies according to the timing of transitions. Off-time transitions, whether biological, social, or psychological, produce asynchronies between lives and trajectories that have social and developmental implications.

There are few more consequential events in re-ordering lives than accelerated childbearing. When a 13-year-old has a child, her 28-year-old mother becomes a grandmother, and her grandmother becomes a great-grandmother. Using data on 41 female lineages from urban multigenerational Black families, Burton (1985; Burton & Bengtson, 1985) has creatively explored the "ripple" effects of teenage pregnancy across the generations. The age ranges of respondents in the early lineages were 11 to 18 for the young mothers, 25 to 38 for the grandmothers, and 46 to 57 for the great-grandmothers. The other lineage units were judged "on time" in transitions. The age ranges for mothers, grandmothers, and great-grandmothers were 21 to 26, 42 to 57, and 60 to 73, respectively.

Role transitions that were "on time" were generally welcomed. One 22-year-old mother commented that she had become a mother "at the right time": "I was ready, my husband was ready, my mother was ready, my father was ready, my grandmother couldn't wait." By comparison, the early transitions multiplied social strains and deprivations within the family system, all reflecting the violation of expectations.

With few exceptions, the young mothers expected their own mothers to help care for their child. However, this expectation never materialized in 80% of the cases, in part because the mothers felt they were too young to become a grandmother. As one woman put it, "I can't be a young momma and a grandmomma at the same time. Something seems funny about that, don't you think?" A good many of the mothers resisted the grandparent identity because it conflicted with their availability as dating and sex partners.

The refusal of mothers to become grandmothers, with their normative childcare expectations, led most of the young mothers to shift these duties to their grandmothers, now the baby's great-grandmother. But some of these women felt that the change made their life go by too fast. In the words of a woman beset by too many claims: "I ain't got no time for myself. I takes care of babies, grown children, and old people. I work too. . . . " Some of these newly promoted great-grandmothers felt they had to put their lives on hold until "the older generation died or the three younger generations grew up."

The repercussions of this ill-timed transition across the generations underscore the price of interdependent lives and the support they provide. An ill-timed or unexpected economic event, such as a recession or depression, may also accentuate irritable, unstable tendencies that produce relationship problems. In a four-generation study, Elder, Caspi, and Downey (1986) investigated the proposition that unstable personalities (explosive, volatile) and unstable family relations (marital, parent-child) are mutually reinforcing dynamics across the life course, a dynamic that is energized by family economic hardships, such as occurred in the 1930s.

The intergenerational continuity of unstable, problem behavior was most pronounced among women, and unstable family relationships played an important role in this reproduction. The causal influence flowed from unstable personalities to unstable family relations and then to unstable personalities in the next generation. Relations of hostility and discord linked unstable personalities across successive generations. Similar intergenerational continuities are reported by Whitbeck and his colleagues (1992) in a study of parental rejection and the depressed mood of children. Parental rejection increased the risk of depressed affect among children, and this state enhanced the risk of a rejecting attitude toward offspring in the adult lives of the children. The behavioral continuities are noteworthy, and so is their modest size. Not all children who experience unstable personalities and relationships become unstable or otherwise reproduce such parental behavior.

As surveyed, the timing of lives appears in three differentiated areas of theory and research, but these processes are interwoven in real life. Thus, men who joined the military in World War II often changed the timing of their family and work events in ways that had major consequences for wives. Temporal facts are essential in thinking about the life course and human development, both across time and place. For ecological studies, they provide a way of connecting children and their families across different contexts and institutions.

CONCLUSION

The emergence of life-course theory and its elaboration over the past 30 years can be viewed in terms of prominent challenges to developmental studies that questioned traditional forms of thought and empirical work. They include: (a) the necessity for concepts of development and personality that have relevance beyond childhood and even adolescence; (b) the need for a way of thinking about the social patterning and dynamic of lives over time, as they relate in particular to developmental processes; and (c) the increasing recognition that lives and developmental trajectories may be transformed by a changing society. Each of these challenges were posed by the early longitudinal studies as they continued well into the adult and late life years, and by the mounting realization that much of the story of child development is written across the adult years. In addition, the challenges had much to do with the demographic and political pressures of an aging society.

Social theories of relationships and age converged in the 1960s with emerging concepts of life-span development to produce a theoretical orientation to the life course. More than any other theoretical initiative, life-span developmental psychology has responded to the first challenge by advancing a conceptual orientation on human development and personality across the life span. One result is a concept of ontogenetic development in which social structures and cultures merely establish behavioral settings. By contrast, life-course theory views human development as a coactive process in which sociocultural, biological, and psychological forces interact over time. Social structures and cultures are constituent elements in the developmental process. The individual plays an important role in shaping the life course and development, though choices and initiatives are always constrained by social forces and biological limitations.

In concept, and as discussed in this chapter, the individual life course provides a response to the second challenge, a way of thinking about life patterns or organization. Lives over time do not merely follow a sequence of situations or person-situation interactions. Instead the life course is conceived as an age-graded sequence of socially defined roles and events that are enacted and even recast over time. It consists of multiple, interlocking trajectories, such as work and family, with their transitions or changes in states. People generally work out their life course in relation to established, institutionalized pathways and their regulatory constraints, such as the curricula or tracks of a school, the age-graded expectations of a family, and the work careers of a firm or culture.

The individual life course, developmental trajectories and transitions (as psychobiological continuities and change), and established pathways are key elements in the life-course study of child development. Any change in the life course of individuals has consequences for their developmental trajectory, and historical change may alter both by recasting established pathways. Thus, adultlike expectations for productive work in World War II communities were lowered toward childhood to enable young people to fill needed roles. By placing people in historical locations, life-course theory has oriented research to the third challenge, to understand the process by which societal changes make a difference in the primary worlds and development of children.

This chapter on life-course theory represents the beginning stage of a long journey toward understanding human development in ways that extend across individual lives, the generations, and historical time. Just as major themes of developmental psychology a century ago seem to be regaining prominence in contemporary studies (Parke et al., 1994), from a renewed interest in genetic influences and emotional regulation to the study of hormones, life-course theory can be viewed in terms of renewed priorities (social context and change, life histories) that were once dominant in the past, particularly within the early Chicago School of Sociology. These observed continuities, however, pale in relation to the novel integrations and new directions of contemporary theory. Building upon a wider net of cross-disciplinary scholarship in

developmental science, distinctions of time, context, and process have become central to a life-course theory of child, adolescent, and adult development.

REFERENCES

Abbott, A. (1997). Of time and space: The contemporary relevance of the Chicago School. *Social Forces, 74*(4), 1149–1182.

Alexander, K. L., & Entwisle, D. R. (1988). Achievement in the first two years of school: Patterns and process. *Monographs of the Society for Research in Child Development, 53*(2, Serial No. 218).

Alexander, K. L., Entwisle, D. R., & Dauber, S. L. (1994). *On the success of failure: A reassessment of the effects of retention in the primary grades.* New York: Cambridge University Press.

Alwin, D. F., Cohen, R. L., & Newcomb, T. M. (1991). *Political attitudes over the life span: The Bennington women after fifty years.* Madison: University of Wisconsin Press.

Aviezer, O., Van IJzendoorn, M., Sagi, A., & Schuengel, C. (1994). "Children of the dream" revisited: 70 years of collective early child care in Israeli kibbutzim. *Psychological Bulletin, 116*(1), 99–116.

Baldwin, J. M. (1895). *Mental development in the child and race: Methods and processes.* New York: Macmillan.

Baltes, P. B. (1979). Life-span developmental psychology: Some converging observations on history and theory. In P. B. Baltes & O. G. Brim, Jr. (Eds.), *Life-span development and behavior* (Vol. 2, pp. 256–281). New York: Academic Press.

Baltes, P. B. (1993). The aging mind: Potential and limits. *Gerontologist, 33,* 580–594.

Baltes, P. B. (1994, August). *Life-span developmental psychology: On the overall landscape of human development.* Invited address, Division 7, American Psychological Association, Los Angeles.

Baltes, P. B., & Baltes, M. M. (1990). *Successful aging: Perspectives from the behavioral sciences.* New York: Cambridge University Press.

Baltes, P. B., Cornelius, S. W., & Nesselroade, J. R. (1979). Cohort effects in developmental psychology. In J. R. Nesselroade & P. B. Baltes (Eds.), *Longitudinal research in the study of behavior and development* (pp. 61–87). New York: Academic Press.

Baltes, P. B., & Staudinger, U. M. (Eds.). (1996). *Interactive minds: Life-span perspectives on the social foundation of cognition.* New York: Cambridge University Press.

Bandura, A. (1989). Human agency in social cognitive theory. *American Psychologist, 44*(9), 1175–1184.

Bandura, A. (1997). *Self-efficacy: The exercise of control.* New York: Freeman.

Bane, M. J., & Ellwood, D. T. (1986). Slipping into and out of poverty: The dynamics of spells. *Journal of Human Resources, 21,* 1–23.

Baumrind, D. (1991). Effective parenting during the early adolescent transition. In P. A. Cowan & E. M. Hetherington (Eds.), *Advances in family research: Vol. 2. Family transitions* (pp. 111–163). Hillsdale, NJ: Erlbaum.

Bell, R. Q. (1968). A reinterpretation of the direction of effects in studies of socialization. *Psychological Review, 75,* 81–95.

Blake, J. (1989). *Family size and achievement.* Berkeley: University of California Press.

Block, J. (with Haan, N.). (1971). *Lives through time.* Berkeley, CA: Bancroft Books.

Bolger, K. E., Patterson, C. J., & Thompson, W. W. (1995). Psychosocial adjustment among children experiencing persistent and intermittent family economic hardship. *Child Development, 66*(4), 1107–1129.

Booth, A., Johnson, D. R., White, L. K., & Edwards, J. N. (1986). Divorce and marital instability over the life course. *Journal of Family Issues, 7*(4), 421–442.

Bradburn, E. M., Moen, P., & Dempster-McClain, D. (1995). Women's return to school following the transition to motherhood. *Social Forces, 73*(4), 1517–1551.

Brehm, S. S., & Brehm, J. W. (1982). *Psychological reactance: A theory of freedom and control.* New York: Academic Press.

Bronfenbrenner, U. (1958). Socialization and social class through time and space. In E. E. Maccoby, T. M. Newcomb, & E. L. Hartley (Eds.), *Readings in social psychology* (pp. 400–425). New York: Holt, Rinehart and Winston.

Bronfenbrenner, U. (1970). *Two worlds of childhood: U.S. and U.S.S.R.* New York: Russell Sage.

Bronfenbrenner, U. (1979). *The ecology of human development.* Cambridge, MA: Harvard University Press.

Bronfenbrenner, U. (1989). Ecological systems theory. In R. Vasta (Ed.), *Annals of child development* (Vol. 6, pp. 187–249). Greenwich, CT: JAI Press.

Bronfenbrenner, U. (1996). Foreword. In R. B. Cairns, G. H. Elder, Jr., & E. J. Costello (Eds.), *Developmental science* (pp. ix–xvii). New York: Cambridge University Press.

Bronfenbrenner, U., & Ceci, S. J. (1994). Nature–nurture reconceptualized in developmental perspective: A bioecological model. *Psychological Review, 101*(4), 568–586.

Buchmann, M. (1989). *The script of life in modern society: Entry into adulthood in a changing world.* Chicago: University of Chicago Press.

Burton, L. M. (1985). *Early and on-time grandmotherhood in multigenerational black families.* Unpublished doctoral dissertation, University of Southern California.

Burton, L. M., & Bengtson, V. L. (1985). Black grandmothers: Issues of timing and continuity of roles. In V. L. Bengtson & J. F. Robertson (Eds.), *Grandparenthood* (pp. 61–77). Beverly Hills, CA: Sage.

Cahan, E., Mechling, J., Sutton-Smith, B., & White, S. H. (1993). The elusive historical child: Ways of knowing the child of history and psychology. In G. H. Elder, Jr., J. Modell, & R. D. Parke (Eds.), *Children in time and place* (pp. 192–223). New York: Cambridge University Press.

Cairns, R. B., & Cairns, B. (1994). *Lifelines and risks: Pathways of youth in our time.* New York: Cambridge University Press.

Cairns, R. B., Elder, G. H., Jr., & Costello, E. J. (Eds.). (1996). *Developmental science.* New York: Cambridge University Press.

Caspi, A., Bem, D. J., & Elder, G. H., Jr. (1989). Continuities and consequences of interactional styles across the life course. *Journal of Personality, 57*(2), 375–406.

Caspi, A., Elder, G. H., Jr., & Bem, D. J. (1987). Moving against the world: Life course patterns of explosive children. *Developmental Psychology, 23*(2), 308–313.

Caspi, A., & Herbener, E. (1990). Continuity and change: Assortative marriage and the consistency of personality in adulthood. *Journal of Personality and Social Psychology, 58*(2), 250–258.

Caspi, A., Lynam, D., Moffitt, T. E., & Silva, P. A. (1993). Unraveling girls' delinquency: Biological, dispositional, and contextual contributions to adolescent misbehavior. *Developmental Psychology, 29*(1), 19–30.

Caspi, A., & Moffitt, T. E. (1993). When do individual differences matter? A paradoxical theory of personality coherence. *Psychological Inquiry, 4,* 247–271.

Caspi, A., Moffitt, T. E., Thornton, A., Freedman, D., Amell, J. W., Harrington, H., Smeijers, J., & Silva, P. A. (1996). The life history calendar: A research and clinical assessment method for collecting retrospective event-history data. *International Journal of Methods in Psychiatric Research, 6,* 101–114.

Chase-Lansdale, P. L., Cherlin, A. J., & Kiernan, K. E. (1995). The long-term effects of parental divorce on the mental health of young adults: A developmental perspective. *Child Development, 66*(6), 1614–1634.

Cherlin, A. J. (1993). *Marriage, divorce, and remarriage.* Cambridge, MA: Harvard University Press.

Cherlin, A. J., Furstenberg, F. F., Jr., Chase-Lansdale, P. L., Kiernan, K. E., Robins, P. K., Morrison, D. R., & Teitler, J. O. (1991). Longitudinal studies of effects of divorce on children in Great Britain and the United States. *Science, 252,* 1386–1389.

Clausen, J. A. (Ed.). (1968). *Socialization and society.* Boston: Little, Brown.

Clausen, J. A. (1972). The life course of individuals. In M. W. Riley, M. E. Johnson, & A. Foner (Eds.), *Aging and society: A sociology of age stratification* (pp. 457–574). New York: Russell-Sage Foundation.

Clausen, J. A. (1993). *American lives: Looking back at the children of the Great Depression.* New York: Free Press.

Clausen, J. A. (1995). Gender, contexts, and turning points in adults' lives. In P. Moen, G. H. Elder, Jr., & K. Lüscher (Eds.), *Examining lives in context: Perspectives on the ecology of human development* (pp. 365–389). Washington, DC: American Psychological Association.

Clipp, E. C., & Elder, G. H., Jr. (1996). The aging veteran of World War II: Psychiatric and life course insights. In P. E. Ruskin & J. A. Talbott (Eds.), *Aging and post-traumatic stress disorder* (pp. 19–51). Washington, DC: American Psychiatric Press.

Cohler, B. J. (1982). Personal narrative and life course. In P. B. Baltes & O. G. Brim, Jr. (Eds.), *Life-span development and behavior* (Vol. 4, pp. 205–241). New York: Academic Press.

Coleman, J. S. (1990). *Foundations of social theory.* Cambridge, MA: Harvard University Press.

Coleman, J. S., & Hoffer, T. (1987). *Public and private high schools: The impact of communities.* New York: Basic Books.

Conger, R. D., Conger, K. J., Elder, G. H., Jr., Lorenz, F. O., Simons, R. L., & Whitbeck, L. B. (1992). A family process model of economic hardship and adjustment of early adolescent boys. *Child Development, 63,* 526–541.

Conger, R. D., Conger, K. J., Elder, G. H., Jr., Lorenz, F. O., Simons, R. L., & Whitbeck, L. B. (1993). Family economic stress and adjustment of early adolescent girls. *Developmental Psychology, 29*(2), 206–219.

Conger, R. D., & Elder, G. H., Jr. (1994). *Families in troubled times: Adapting to change in rural America.* Hawthorne, NY: Aldine de Gruyter.

Coyne, J. C., & Downey, G. (1991). Social factors and psychopathology: Stress, social support, and coping processes. In M. R. Rosenzweig & L. W. Porter (Eds.), *Annual review of psychology* (pp. 401–425). Palo Alto, CA: Annual Reviews.

Crouter, A. C., & McHale, S. M. (1993). Temporal rhythms in family life: Seasonal variation in the relation between parental work and family processes. *Developmental Psychology, 29*(2), 198–205.

Dannefer, D. (1984). The role of the social in life-span developmental psychology, past and future: Rejoinder to Baltes and Nesselroade. *American Sociological Review, 49,* 847–850.

Duncan, G. J., Coe, R. D., Corcoran, M., Hill, M., Hoffman, S., & Morgan, J. N. (1984). *Years of poverty, years of plenty: The changing economic fortunes of American workers and families.* Ann Arbor, MI: Institute for Social Research.

Dunn, J., & Plomin, R. (1990). *Separate lives: Why siblings are so different.* New York: Basic Books.

Easterlin, R. A. (1980). *Birth and fortune: The impact of numbers on personal welfare.* New York: Basic Books.

Ebaugh, H. R. F. (1988). *Becoming an ex: The process of role exit.* Chicago: University of Chicago Press.

Eccles, J. S., & Midgley, C. (1989). Stage-environment fit: Developmentally appropriate classrooms for early adolescents. In R. E. Ames & C. Ames (Eds.), *Research on motivation in education* (pp. 139–186). New York: Academic Press.

Eichorn, D. H., Clausen, J. A., Haan, N., Honzik, M., & Mussen, P. H. (Eds.). (1981). *Present and past in middle life.* New York: Academic Press.

Eisenstadt, S. N. (1956). *From generation to generation: Age groups and social structure.* Glencoe, IL: Free Press.

Elder, G. H., Jr. (1974). *Children of the Great Depression: Social change in life experience.* Chicago: University of Chicago Press.

Elder, G. H., Jr. (1975). Age differentiation and the life course. *Annual Review of Sociology, 1,* 165–190.

Elder, G. H., Jr. (1978). Family history and the life course. In T. K. Haraven (Ed.), *Transitions* (pp. 17–64). New York: Academic Press.

Elder, G. H., Jr. (1979). Historical change in life patterns and personality. In P. B. Baltes & O. G. Brim, Jr. (Eds.), *Life-span development and behavior* (Vol. 2, pp. 117–159). New York: Academic Press.

Elder, G. H., Jr. (1981). Social history and life experience. In D. H. Eichorn, J. A. Clausen, J. Haan, M. P. Honzik, & P. H. Mussen (Eds.), *Present and past in middle life* (pp. 3–31). New York: Academic Press.

Elder, G. H., Jr. (1985). Perspectives on the life course. In G. H. Elder, Jr. (Ed.), *Life course dynamics: Trajectories and transitions, 1968–1980* (pp. 23–49). Ithaca, NY: Cornell University Press.

Elder, G. H., Jr. (1986). Military times and turning points in men's lives. *Developmental Psychology, 22*(2), 233–245.

Elder, G. H., Jr. (1987). War mobilization and the life course: A cohort of World War II veterans. *Sociological Forum, 2*(3), 449–472.

Elder, G. H., Jr. (1991). Lives and social change. In W. R. Heinz (Ed.), *Theoretical advances in life course research* (pp. 58–86). Weinheim, Germany: Deutscher Studien Verlag.

Elder, G. H., Jr. (1996). Human lives in changing societies: Life course and developmental insights. In R. B. Cairns, G. H. Elder, Jr., & E. J. Costello (Eds.), *Developmental science* (pp. 31–62). New York: Cambridge University Press.

Elder, G. H., Jr. (in press). The life course as developmental theory. *Child Development.*

Elder, G. H., Jr., & Caspi, A. (1988). Economic stress in lives: Developmental perspectives. *Journal of Social Issues, 44*(4), 25–45.

Elder, G. H., Jr., Caspi, A., & Downey, G. (1986). Problem behavior and family relationships: Life course and intergenerational themes. In A. B. Sorensen, F. E. Weinert, & L. R. Sherrod (Eds.), *Human development and the life course: Multidisciplinary perspectives* (pp. 293–340). Hillsdale, NJ: Erlbaum.

Elder, G. H., Jr., King, V., & Conger, R. D. (1996). Intergenerational continuity and change in rural lives: Historical and developmental insights. *International Journal of Behavioral Development, 19*(2), 433–455.

Elder, G. H., Jr., & Meguro, Y. (1987). Wartime in men's lives: A comparative study of American and Japanese cohorts. *International Journal of Behavioral Development, 10*, 439–466.

Elder, G. H., Jr., Modell, J., & Parke, R. D. (Eds.). (1993). *Children in time and place: Developmental and historical insights.* New York: Cambridge University Press.

Elder, G. H., Jr., & O'Rand, A. M. (1995). Adult lives in a changing society. In K. S. Cook, G. A. Fine, & J. S. House (Eds.), *Sociological perspectives on social psychology* (pp. 452–475). Boston: Allyn & Bacon.

Elder, G. H., Jr., Pavalko, E. K., & Hastings, T. J. (1991, August). Talent, history, and the fulfillment of promise. *Psychiatry, 54*, 215–231.

Elder, G. H., Jr., & Pellerin, L. A. (1995, March). *Social development research in historical perspective, 1965–1989: Is it more longitudinal and contextual today?* Poster presentation at the biennial meeting of the Society for Research in Child Development, Indianapolis, IN.

Elder, G. H., Jr., Shanahan, M. J., & Clipp, E. C. (1994). When war comes to men's lives: Life course patterns in family, work, and health [Special issue]. *Psychology and Aging, 9*(1), 5–16.

Entwisle, D. R., & Astone, N. M. (1994). Some practical guidelines for measuring youth's race/ethnicity and socioeconomic status. *Child Development, 65*, 1521–1540.

Erikson, E. H. (1950). *Childhood and society* (1st ed.). New York: Norton.

Erikson, E. H. (1963). *Childhood and society* (2nd ed.). New York: Norton.

Evans, K., & Heinz, W. (1993). Studying forms of transition: Methodological innovation in a cross-national study of youth transition and labour market entry in England and Germany. *Comparative Education, 29*(2), 145–158.

Farrington, D. P., Loeber, R., Elliott, D. S., Hawkins, D. J., Kandel, D. B., Klein, M., McCord, J., Rowe, D. C., & Tremblay, R. E. (1990). Advancing knowledge about the onset of delinquency and crime. In B. B. Lahey & A. E. Kazdin (Eds.), *Advances in clinical and child psychology* (Vol. 13, pp. 283–342). New York: Plenum Press.

Farrington, D. P., & West, D. J. (1990). The Cambridge study of delinquent development: A long-term follow-up of 411 London males. In H. J. Kerner & G. Kaiser (Eds.), *Kriminalitat: Personlichkeit, lebensgeschichte und verhalten* [Criminology: Personality, behavior and life history] (pp. 115–138). New York: Springer-Verlag.

Featherman, D. L. (1983). The life-span perspectives in social science research. In P. B. Baltes & O. G. Brim, Jr. (Eds.), *Life-span development and behavior* (Vol. 5, pp. 1–57). New York: Academic Press.

Featherman, D. L., & Hauser, R. M. (1978). *Opportunity and change.* New York: Academic Press.

Feldman, S. S., & Rosenthal, D. A. (1991). Age expectations of behavioral autonomy in Hong Kong, Australian and American youth: The influence of family variables and adolescents' values. *International Journal of Psychology, 26*(1), 1–23.

Fletcher, A. C., Darling, N. E., Steinberg, L., & Dornbusch, S. M. (1995). The company they keep: Relation of adolescents' adjustment and behavior to their friends' perceptions of authoritative parenting in the social network. *Developmental Psychology, 31*(2), 300–310.

Ford, D. H., & Lerner, R. M. (1992). *Developmental systems theory: An integrative approach.* Newbury Park, CA: Sage.

Forest, K. B., Moen, P., & Dempster-McClain, D. (1995). Cohort differences in the transition to motherhood: The variable effects of education and employment before marriage. *The Sociological Quarterly, 36*(2), 315–336.

Furstenberg, F. F., Jr., Brooks-Gunn, J., & Morgan, S. P. (1987). *Adolescent mothers in later life.* New York: Cambridge University Press.

Furstenberg, F. F., Jr., Eccles, J., Elder, G. H., Jr., Cook, T., & Sameroff, A. (Eds.). (in press). *Managing to make it: Urban families in high-risk neighborhoods.*

Furstenberg, F. F., Jr., & Hughes, M. E. (in press). The influence of neighborhoods on children's development: A theoretical perspective and a research agenda. In J. Brooks-Gunn, G. Duncan, & J. L. Aber (Eds.), *Neighborhood poverty: Context and consequences for children.* New York: Russell-Sage Foundation.

Ge, X., Conger, R. D., & Elder, G. H., Jr. (1997). Coming of age too early: Pubertal influences on girls' vulnerability to psychological distress. *Child Development, 67*(6), 3386–3400.

Ge, X., Lorenz, F. O., Conger, R. D., Elder, G. H., Jr., & Simons, R. L. (1994). Trajectories of stressful life events and depressive symptoms during adolescence. *Developmental Psychology, 30*(4), 467–483.

Gerson, K. (1985). *Hard choices: How women decide about work, career, and motherhood.* Berkeley: University of California.

Gimbel, C., & Booth, A. (1996). Who fought in Vietnam? *Social Forces, 74*(4), 1137–1157.

Glaser, B. G., & Strauss, A. L. (1971). *Status passage.* Chicago: Aldine.

Glueck, S., & Glueck, E. (1968). *Delinquents and nondelinquents in perspective.* Cambridge, MA: Harvard University Press.

Gold, T. B. (1987, August). *The disrupted life course of China's first communist cohort.* Paper presented at the annual meeting of the American Sociological Association, Chicago.

Goldthorpe, J. H. (1991). The uses of history in sociology: Reflections on some recent tendencies. *British Journal of Sociology, 42*(2), 211–229.

Goode, W. J. (1960). A theory of role strain. *American Sociological Review, 25*(4), 483–496.

Granovetter, M. S. (1985). Economic action and social structure: The problem of embeddedness. *American Journal of Sociology, 91*(3), 481–510.

Grundmann, M. (1996). The historical context of father absence: Some consequences for the family formation of German men. *International Journal of Behavioral Development, 19*(2), 415–431.

Guo, G., Brooks-Gunn, J., & Harris, K. M. (1996). Parental labor-force attachment and grade retention among urban black children. *Sociology of Education, 69,* 217–236.

Hagan, J. (1991). Destiny and drift: Subcultural preferences, status attainments, and the risks and rewards of youth. *American Sociological Review, 56*(5), 567–582.

Hagan, J., & Wheaton, B. (1993). The search for adolescent role exits and the transition to adulthood. *Social Forces, 71*(4), 955–980.

Hagestad, G. O. (1982). Parent and child: Generations in the family. In T. M. Field, A. Huston, H. C. Quay, L. Troll, & G. E. Finley (Eds.), *Review of human development* (pp. 485–499). New York: Wiley.

Hareven, T. K. (1978). *Transitions: The family and the life course in historical perspective.* New York: Academic Press.

Hareven, T. K. (1982). *Family time and industrial time.* New York: Cambridge University Press.

Havighurst, R. J. (1949). *Developmental tasks and education.* Chicago: University of Chicago Press.

Havighurst, R. J., Baughman, J. W., Burgess, E. W., & Eaton, W. H. (1951). *The American veteran back home.* New York: Longmans, Green.

Hernandez, D. J. (1993). *America's children: Resources from family, government, and the economy.* New York: Russell Sage.

Hetherington, E. M., & Baltes, P. B. (1988). Child psychology and life-span development. In E. M. Hetherington, R. M. Lerner, & M. Perlmutter (Eds.), *Child development in life-span perspective* (pp. 1–19). Hillsdale, NJ: Erlbaum.

Hetherington, E. M., & Clingempeel, W. G. (1992). Coping with marital transitions: A family systems perspective. *Monographs of the Society for Research in Child Development, 57*(2/3, Serial No. 227), 1–242.

Hill, R. (1970). *Family development in three generations.* Cambridge, MA: Schenkman.

Hofferth, S. L. (1985). Children's life course: Family structure and living arrangements in cohort perspective. In G. H. Elder, Jr. (Ed.), *Life course dynamics: Trajectories and transitions, 1968–1980* (pp. 75–112). Ithaca, NY: Cornell University Press.

Hofferth, S. L. (1987). Teenage pregnancy and its resolution. In S. L. Hofferth & C. Hayes (Eds.), *Risking the future: Adolescent sexuality, pregnancy, and childbearing* (pp. 78–92). Washington, DC: National Academy Press.

Hogan, D. P. (1981). *Transitions and social change: The early lives of American man.* New York: Academic Press.

Holahan, C. K., & Sears, R. R. (1995). *The gifted group in later maturity.* Stanford, CA: Stanford University Press.

Jones, M. C., Bayley, N., Macfarlane, J. W., & Honzik, M. H. (Eds.). (1971). *The course of human development: Selected papers from the longitudinal studies, Institute of Human Development, the University of California, Berkeley.* Waltham, MA: Xerox College.

Kagan, J., & Moss, H. A. (1962). *Birth to maturity: A study in psychological development.* New York: Wiley.

Kahn, R. L., & Antonucci, T. C. (1980). Convoys of social support: A life-course approach. In S. Kiesler, J. Morgan, & V. Oppenheimer (Eds.), *Aging: Social change* (pp. 383–405). New York: Academic Press.

Kandel, D., Davies, M., & Baydar, M. (1990). The creation of interpersonal contexts: Homophily in dyadic relationships in adolescence and young adulthood. In L. N. Robins & M. Rutter (Eds.), *Straight and devious pathways from childhood to adulthood* (pp. 221–241). New York: Cambridge University Press.

Kerckhoff, A. C. (1993). *Diverging pathways: Social structure and career deflections.* New York: Cambridge University Press.

Kertzer, D. I., & Keith, J. (Eds.). (1984). *Age and anthropological theory.* Ithaca, NY: Cornell University Press.

Kessler, R. C., & McLeod, J. D. (1984). Sex differences in vulnerability to undesirable life events. *American Sociological Review, 49,* 620–631.

Knutson, A. L. (1967). The definition and value of a new human life. *Social Science and Medicine, 1,* 7–29.

Kohn, M. L. (1977). *Class and conformity: A study in values, with a reassessment.* Homewood, IL: Dorsey Press.

Kohn, M. L., & Schooler, C. (1983). *Work and personality: An inquiry into the impact of social stratification.* Norwood, NJ: ABLEX.

Krein, S. F., & Beller, A. H. (1988). Educational attainment of children from single-parent families: Differences by exposure, gender, and race. *Demography, 25*(2), 221–234.

Laub, J. H., & Sampson, R. J. (1993). Turning points in the life course: Why change matters to the study of crime. *Criminology, 31*(3), 301–325.

Lenox, K. F. (1996). *Correlates of police- and self-reported early and late onset offending in a high risk urban sample.* Unpublished dissertation proposal, Department of Psychology, Duke University, Durham, NC.

Lerner, R. M. (1982). Children and adolescents as producers of their own development. *Developmental Review, 2*(4), 342–370.

Lerner, R. M. (1991). Changing organism-context relations as the basic process of development: A developmental contextual perspective. *Developmental Psychology, 27*(1), 27–32.

Levinson, D. J. (1978). *The seasons of a man's life.* New York: Ballantine Books.

Lynd, R. S., & Lynd, H. M. (1929). *Middletown.* New York: Harcourt, Brace.

Lynd, R. S., & Lynd, H. M. (1937). *Middletown in transition: A study in cultural conflicts.* New York: Harcourt, Brace.

Magnusson, D., & Allen, V. L. (1983). In D. Magnusson & V. L. Allen (Eds.), *Human development: An interactional perspective.* New York: Academic Press.

Magnusson, D., Bergman, L. R., Rudinger, G., & Törestad, B. (Eds.). (1991). *Problems and methods in longitudinal research: Stability and change.* New York: Cambridge University Press.

Maines, D. R., Sugre, N. M., & Katovich, M. (1983). The sociological import of G. H. Mead's theory of the past. *American Sociological Review, 48,* 161–173.

Marini, M. M. (1984). Age and sequencing norms in the transition to adulthood. *Social Forces, 63,* 229–244.

Marsiske, M., Lang, F. R., Baltes, P. B., & Baltes, M. M. (1995). Selective optimization with compensation: Life-span perspectives on successful human development. In R. A. Dixon & L. Bäckman (Eds.), *Compensation of psychological deficits and declines: Managing losses and promoting gains* (pp. 35–79). Mahwah, NJ: Erlbaum.

Mattick, H. W. (1960). Parolees in the Army during World War II. *Federal Probation, 24,* 49–55.

Mayer, K. U. (1986). Structural constraints on the life course. *Human Development, 29*(3), 163–170.

Mayer, K. U. (1988). German survivors of World War II: The impact on the life course of the collective experience of birth cohorts. In M. W. Riley (Ed.), *Social change and the life course: Social structures and human lives* (pp. 229–246). Newbury Park, CA: Sage.

Mayer, K. U., & Huinink, J. (1990). Age, period, and cohort in the study of the life course: A comparison of classical A-P-C analysis with event history analysis or farewell to Lexis? In D. Magnusson & L. R. Bergman (Eds.), *Data quality in longitudinal research* (pp. 211–232). Cambridge, MA: Cambridge University Press.

McLanahan, S. S., & Sørensen, A. B. (1985). Life events and psychological well-being over the life course. In G. H. Elder, Jr. (Ed.), *Life course dynamics: Trajectories and transitions, 1968–1980* (pp. 217–238). Ithaca, NY: Cornell University Press.

McLanahan, S. S., & Sandefur, G. (1994). *Growing up with a single parent: What hurts, what helps.* Cambridge, MA: Harvard University Press.

McLeod, J. D. (1991). Childhood parental loss and adult depression. *Journal of Health and Social Behavior, 32*(3), 205–220.

McLeod, J. D., & Shanahan, M. J. (1996). Trajectories of poverty and children's mental health. *Journal of Health and Social Behavior, 37*(3). 207–220.

McLoyd, V. C. (1989). Socialization and development in a changing economy: The effects of paternal job and income loss on children. *American Psychologist, 44*(2), 293–302.

Merton, R. K. (1968). *Social theory and social structure.* New York: Free Press.

Merton, R. K. (1982). *Socially expected durations.* Paper presented at the annual meeting of the American Sociological Association, San Francisco.

Mills, C. W. (1959). *The sociological imagination.* New York: Oxford University Press.

Modell, J. (1989). *Into one's own: From youth to adulthood in the United States 1920–1975.* Berkeley: University of California Press.

Modell, J., Furstenberg, F. F., Jr., & Hershberg, T. (1976). Social change and the transitions to adulthood in historical perspective. *Journal of Family History, 1*(1), 7–32.

Moen, P. (1992). *Women's two roles: A contemporary dilemma.* New York: Auburn House.

Moen, P., Elder, G. H., Jr., & Lüscher, K. (Eds.). (1995). *Examining lives in context: Perspectives on the ecology of human development.* Washington, DC: American Psychological Association.

Moffitt, T. E. (1993). Adolescence-limited and life-course-persistent antisocial behavior: A developmental taxonomy. *Psychological Review, 100*(4), 674–701.

Moffitt, T. E., Caspi, A., Dickson, N., Silva, P., & Stanton, W. (1996). Childhood-onset versus adolescent-onset antisocial conduct problems in males: Natural history from age 3 to 18. *Development and Psychopathology, 8,* 399–424.

Nagin, D. S., Farrington, D. P., & Moffitt, T. E. (1995). Life-course trajectories of different types of offenders. *Criminology, 33*(1), 111–139.

Neugarten, B. L. (1968). *Middle age and aging: A reader in social psychology.* Chicago: University of Chicago Press.

Neugarten, B. L., & Datan, N. (1973). Sociological perspectives on the life cycle. In P. B. Baltes & K. W. Schaie (Eds.), *Life-span developmental psychology: Personality and socialization* (pp. 53–69). New York: Academic Press.

Neugarten, B. L., Moore, J. W., & Lowe, J. C. (1965). Age norms, age constraints, and adult socialization. *American Journal of Sociology, 70*(6), 710–717.

Neugarten, B. L., & Peterson, W. A. (1957). A study of the American age-grade system. *Proceedings of the Fourth Congress of the International Association of Gerontology, 3,* 497–502.

Noack, P., Hofer, M., & Youniss, J. (Eds.). (1995). *Psychological responses to social change: Human development in changing environments.* New York: De Gruyter.

O'Rand, A. M., & Krecker, M. L. (1990). *Concepts of the life cycle: Their history, meanings and uses in the social sciences. Annual review of sociology* (Vol. 16, pp. 241–262). Palo Alto, CA: Annual Reviews.

Parcel, T. L., & Menaghan, E. G. (1994). *Parents' jobs and children's lives.* New York: Aldine de Gruyter.

Parke, R. D. (1988). Families in life-span perspective: A multilevel developmental approach. In E. M. Hetherington, R. M. Lerner, & M. Permutter (Eds.), *Child development in life-span perspective* (pp. 159–190). New York: Wiley.

Parke, R. D., & Ladd, G. W. (Eds.). (1992). *Family-peer relationship: Modes of linkage.* Hillsdale, NJ: Erlbaum.

Parke, R. D., Ornstein, P. A., Rieser, J. J., & Zahn-Waxler, C. (Eds.). (1994). *A century of developmental psychology.* Washington, DC: American Psychological Association.

Parke, R. D., & Stearns, P. N. (1993). Fathers and child rearing. In G. H. Elder, Jr., J. Modell, & R. D. Parke (Eds.), *Children in time and place: Developmental and historical insights* (pp. 147–170). New York: Cambridge University Press.

Patterson, G. R. (1996). Some characteristics of a developmental theory of early-onset delinquency. In M. F. Lenzenweger & J. J. Haugaard (Eds.), *Frontiers of developmental psychopathology* (pp. 81–124). New York: Oxford University Press.

Patterson, G. R., & Yoerger, K. (in press). A developmental model for late-onset delinquency. In D. W. Osgood (Ed.), *Motivation and delinquency.* Lincoln: University of Nebraska Press.

Pepler, D. J., & Rubin, K. H. (Eds.). (1991). *The development and treatment of childhood aggression.* Hillsdale, NJ: Erlbaum.

Quinton, D., Pickles, A., Maughan, B., & Rutter, M. (1993). Partners, peers, and pathways: Assortative pairing and continuities in conduct disorder. *Development and Psychopathology, 5*(4), 763–783.

Rachman, S. (1979). The concept of required helpfulness. *Behavior Research and Therapy, 17*(1), 1–6.

Riley, M. W. (1988). On the significance of age in sociology. In M. W. Riley (Ed.), *Social change and the life course: Social structures and human lives* (pp. 24–46). Newbury Park, CA: Sage.

Riley, M. W., Johnson, M. E., & Foner, A. (Eds.). (1972). *Aging and society: A sociology of age stratification.* New York: Russell-Sage Foundation.

Rindfuss, R. R., Swicegood, C. G., & Rosenfeld, R. A. (1987). Disorder in the life course: How common and does it matter? *American Sociological Review, 52,* 785–801.

Robins, L. (1966). *Deviant children grown up.* Baltimore: Williams & Wilkins.

Rodgers, W. L., & Thornton, A. (1985). Changing patterns of first marriage in the United States. *Demography, 22*(2), 265–279.

Rogosa, D., Brandt, D., & Zimowski, M. (1982). A growth curve approach to the measurement of change. *Psychological Bulletin, 92*(3), 726–748.

Rook, K. S. (1984). The negative side of social interaction: Impact on psychological well-being. *Journal of Personality and Social Psychology, 46*(5), 1097–1108.

Rosenberg, M. (1979). *Conceiving the self.* New York: Basic Books.

Ross, M., & Buehler, R. (1994). Creative remembering. In U. Neisser & R. Fivush (Eds.), *The remembering self* (pp. 205–235). New York: Cambridge University Press.

Rossi, A. S. (1980). Aging and parenthood in the middle years. In P. B. Baltes & O. G. Brim, Jr. (Eds.), *Life-span development and behavior* (Vol. 3, pp. 137–205). New York: Academic Press.

Rossi, A. S., & Rossi, P. H. (1990). *Of human bonding: Parent-child relations across the life course.* New York: Aldine.

Rutter, M. (1996). Transitions and turning points in developmental psychopathology: As applied to the age span between childhood and mid-childhood. *International Journal of Behavioral Development, 19*(3), 603–626.

Rutter, M., & Madge, N. (1976). *Cycles of disadvantage: A review of research.* London: Heinemann.

Rutter, M., & Rutter, M. (1993). *Developing minds: Challenge and continuity across the life span.* New York: Basic Books.

Ryder, N. B. (1965). The cohort as a concept in the study of social change. *American Sociological Review, 30*(6), 843–861.

Salamon, S. (1992). *Prairie patrimony: Family, farming, & community in the midwest.* Chapel Hill: University of North Carolina Press.

Sameroff, A. J. (1993). Models of development and developmental risk. In C. H. Zeanah, Jr. (Ed.), *Handbook of infant mental health* (pp. 3–13). New York: Guilford Press.

Sameroff, A. J., & Suomi, S. J. (1996). Primates and persons: A comparative developmental understanding of social organization. In R. B. Cairns, G. H. Elder, Jr., & E. J. Costello (Eds.), *Developmental science* (pp. 97–120). New York: Cambridge University Press.

Sampson, R. J. (1992). Family management and child development: Insights from social disorganization theory. In J. McCord (Ed.), *Facts, frameworks, and forecasts: Advances in criminological theory* (pp. 1992). New Brunswick, NJ: Transaction Books.

Sampson, R. J. (1993). Linking time and place: Dynamic contextualism and the future of criminological inquiry. *Journal of Research in Crime and Delinquency, 30*(4), 426–444.

Sampson, R. J., & Laub, J. H. (1993). *Crime in the making: Pathways and turning points through life.* Cambridge, MA: Harvard University Press.

Sampson, R. J., & Laub, J. H. (1996). Socioeconomic achievement in the life course of disadvantaged men: Military service as a turning point, Circa 1940–1965. *American Sociological Review, 61*(3), 347–367.

Sampson, R. J., & Laub, J. H.. (1997). A life-course theory of cumulative disadvantage and the stability of delinquency. In T. P. Thornberry (Ed.), *Developmental theories of crime and delinquency: Advances in criminological theory* (Vol. 7, pp. 133–161). New Brunswick, NJ: Transaction.

Scarr, S., & McCartney, K. (1983). How people make their own environments: A theory of genotype—Environment effects. *Child Development, 54,* 424–435.

Schaie, K. W. (1965). A general model for the study of developmental problems. *Psychological Bulletin, 64*(2), 92–107.

Schlossman, S., & Cairns, R. B. (1993). Problem girls: Observations on past and present. In G. H. Elder, Jr., J. Modell, & R. D. Parke (Eds.), *Children in time and place: Developmental and historical insights* (pp. 110–130). New York: Cambridge University Press.

Settersten, R. H., & Mayer, K. U. (1997). The measurement of age, age structuring, and the life course. *Annual Review of Sociology, 23,* 233–261.

Shanahan, M. J., Elder, G. H., Jr., & Miech, R. A. (1997). History and agency in men's lives: Pathways to achievement in cohort perspective. *Sociology of Education, 70*(1), 54–67.

Sherif, M. (1958). Superordinate goals in the reduction of intergroup conflicts. *American Journal of Sociology, 63*(4), 349–356.

Shneidman, E. S. (1981). *Endeavors in psychology: Selections from the personology of Henry A. Murray.* New York: Harper & Row.

Simmons, R. G., & Blyth, D. A. (1987). Moving into adolescence: The impact of pubertal change and school context. New York: Aldine de Gruyter.

Simmons, R. G., Burgeson, R., Carlton-Ford, S., & Blyth, D. (1987). The impact of cumulative change in adolescence. *Child Development, 58*(5), 1220–1234.

Sofer, C. (1970). *Men in mid-career; A study of British managers and technical specialists.* Cambridge, England: Cambridge University Press.

Spenner, K. I., Otto, L. B., & Call, V. R. A. (1982). *Career lines and careers: Entry into career series* (Vol. 3). Lexington, MA: Lexington Books.

Spilerman, S. (1977). Careers, labor market structure, and socioeconomic achievement. *American Journal of Sociology, 83*(3), 551–593.

Stattin, H., & Magnusson, D. (1990). *Pubertal maturation in female development.* Hillsdale, NJ: Erlbaum.

Staudinger, U. M. (1989). *The study of life review: An approach to the investigation of intellectual development across the life span.* Berlin: Edition Sigma.

Stolz, L. M. (1954). *Father relations of war-born children.* Stanford, CA: Stanford University Press.

Stouffer, S. A., Lumsdaine, A. A., Lumsdaine, M. H., Williams, R. M., Jr., Smith, M. B., Janis, I. L., Star, S. A., & Cottrell, L. S., Jr. (1949). *The American soldier: Vol. 2. Combat and its aftermath.* Princeton, NJ: Princeton University Press.

Susman, E. J. (1993). Psychological, contextual, and psychobiological interactions: A developmental perspective on conduct disorder. *Development and Psychopathology, 5*(1/2), 181–189.

Thelen, E., & Smith, L. B. (1994). *A dynamic systems approach to the development of cognition and action.* Cambridge, MA: MIT Press.

Thomas, W. I., & Znaniecki, F. (1918–20). *The Polish peasant in Europe and America* (Vols. 1–2). Urbana: University of Illinois Press.

Vaillant, G. E. (1977). *Adaptation to life.* Boston: Little, Brown.

Vanden Heuvel, A. (1988). The timing of parenthood and intergenerational relations. *Journal of Marriage and the Family, 50*(2), 483–491.

Volkart, E. H. (1951). *Social behavior and personality: Contributions of W. I. Thomas to theory and social research.* New York: Social Science Research Council.

West, D. J. (1982). *Delinquency: Its roots, careers and prospects.* London: Heinemann.

Wheaton, B. (1990, April). Life transitions, role histories, and mental health. *American Sociological Review, 55*, 209–223.

Whitbeck, L. B., Hoyt, D. R., Simons, R. L., Conger, R. D., Elder, G. H., Jr., Lorenz, F. O., & Huck, S. (1992). Intergenerational continuity of parental rejection and depressed affect. *Journal of Personality and Social Psychology, 63*(6), 1036–1045.

White, L. K., & Booth, A. (1991). Divorce over the life course: The role of marital happiness. *Journal of Family Issues, 12*(1), 5–21.

Wilensky, H. L. (1960). Work, careers, and social integration. *International Social Science Journal, 12*(4), 543–560.

Wortman, C. B., & Silver, R. C. (1990). Successful mastery of bereavement and widowhood: A life-course perspective. In P. B. Baltes & M. M. Baltes (Eds.), *Successful aging: Perspectives from the behavioral sciences* (pp. 225–264). New York: Cambridge University Press.

Young, C. H., Savola, K. L., & Phelps, E. (1991). *Inventory of longitudinal studies in the social sciences.* Newbury Park, CA: Sage.

Young, M. D., & Willmott, P. (1973). *The symmetrical family.* New York: Pantheon.

CHAPTER 17

The Ecology of Developmental Processes*

URIE BRONFENBRENNER and PAMELA A. MORRIS

In this chapter, we undertake to bring together and to integrate significant changes in the ecological model of human development that have been introduced since the most recent integrative effort, which was published in the preceding edition of this *Handbook,* now well over a decade ago (Bronfenbrenner & Crouter, 1983). Two considerations dictate the need for a new integration. First, the main focus of that chapter was on the empirical and theoretical roots of a model already in use that centered on the role of the environment in shaping development. By contrast, the present chapter is oriented toward the future, and data from the future are not yet available.

Second, and we hope of greater consequence, the present model introduces major theoretical innovations both in form and content. The new formulation makes no claim as a paradigm shift (if there be such a phenomenon); rather, it represents a marked shift in the center of gravity of the model, in which features of the earlier version are first called into question, but then recombined, along with new elements, into a more complex and more dynamic structure. The dual nature of the shift is telegraphed in the titles of the two chapters—in the 1983 *Handbook:* "The Evolution of *Environmental* Models in Developmental Research"; in the present edition: "The Ecology of Developmental *Processes.*"

* We are grateful to Gerri Jones for her generosity, skill, and resourcefulness at critical stages in the preparation of this chapter and to similar assistance provided by Juleene A. Conner and Heidi E. Godoy. We are also indebted to Dean Francille Firebaugh of the College of Human Ecology at Cornell University for financial support of data analyses.

The emphasized contrast between the two titles is deceptive, for the transition actually took place over an extended period of time [an expression that soon will become all too familiar to the reader]. The distinction was first introduced in the context of Bronfenbrenner's unpublished lectures, colloquium presentations, and contributions to symposia. Not until 1986 did reference to an emergent new model first appear in print (Bronfenbrenner, 1986a). The following extended excerpt conveys both its spirit and intended substance. Because both of these attributes are relevant to the gradual evolution of the model to its present form, we quote from the 1986 statement at some length:

> It is now more than a decade ago that, being somewhat younger, I presumed to challenge the then-prevailing conventions of our field by describing the developmental research of the day as "the study of the strange behavior of children in strange situations for the briefest possible period of time" (Bronfenbrenner, 1974). Instead, I argued (as if it were simply a matter of choice), we should be studying development in its ecological context; that is, in the actual environments in which human beings lived their lives. I then proceeded to outline, in a series of publications, a conceptual framework for analyzing development in context, and to offer concrete examples of how various elements of the schema might be applied both to past studies and to studies yet-to-come. I also emphasized the scientific and practical benefits of a closer linkage, in both directions, between developmental research and public policy (Bronfenbrenner, 1974, 1975; 1977a; 1977b; 1979a; 1979b; 1981).
>
> Now, a dozen years later, one might think that I have good reason to rest content. Studies of children and adults in real-life settings, with real-life implications, are now commonplace in the research literature on human development, both in the United States and, as this Volume testifies, in Europe as well. This scientific development is taking place, I believe, not so much because of my writings, but rather because the notions I have been promulgating are ideas whose time has come. . . .
>
> Clearly, if one regards such scientific developments as desirable, there are grounds for satisfaction. Yet, along with feelings of gratification, I must confess to some discontent. My disquiet derives from two complementary concerns. The first pertains to one of the main roads that contemporary research has taken; the second, to some more promising pathways that are being neglected.
>
> Alas, I may have to accept some responsibility for what I regard as the wayward course. It is an instance of what might be called "the failure of success." For some years, I harangued my colleagues for avoiding the study of development

> in real-life settings. No longer able to complain on that score, I have found a new *bête noir*. In place of too much research on development "out of context," we now have a surfeit of studies on "context without development."
>
> One cannot presume to make so brass an allegation without being prepared to document one's case. I am prepared. (Bronfenbrenner 1986, pp. 286–288)

What then followed was an early version of the newly evolving theoretical framework. The purpose of the present chapter, however, is better served by presenting the model in its current, albeit still-evolving form, now called the *bioecological model*. To orient the reader, here is a preview of what lies ahead.

OVERVIEW

We begin with an exposition of the defining properties of the model, which involves four principal components and the dynamic, interactive relationships among them. As foreshadowed in the title of the chapter, the first of these, which constitutes the core of the model, is *Process*. More specifically, this construct encompasses particular forms of interaction between organism and environment, called *proximal processes,* that operate over time and are posited as the primary mechanisms producing human development. However, the power of such processes to influence development is presumed, and shown, to vary substantially as a function of the characteristics of the developing *Person*, of the immediate and more remote *environmental Contexts*, and the *Time* periods, in which the proximal processes take place.

The sections that follow examine in greater detail each of the three remaining defining properties of the model, beginning with the biopsychological characteristics of the Person. This domain was given sequential priority to fill a recognized gap in earlier prototypes of the ecological model. Thus, at midstage in the development of the present model, Bronfenbrenner criticized its theoretical predecessors, and acknowledged his share of responsibility for failing to deliver on an empirical promise:

> Existing developmental studies subscribing to an ecological model have provided far more knowledge about the nature of developmentally relevant environments, near and far, than about the characteristics of developing individuals, then and now . . . The criticism I just made also applies to my own

writings . . . Nowhere in the 1979 monograph, nor elsewhere until today, does one find a parallel set of structures for conceptualizing the characteristics of the developing person. (Bronfenbrenner, 1989, p. 188)

Three types of Person characteristics are distinguished as most influential in shaping the course of future development through their capacity to affect the direction and power of proximal processes through the life course. The first are *dispositions* that can set proximal processes in motion in a particular developmental domain and continue to sustain their operation. Next are bioecological *resources* of ability, experience, knowledge, and skill required for the effective functioning of proximal processes at a given stage of development. Finally, there are *demand* characteristics that invite or discourage reactions from the social environment of a kind that can foster or disrupt the operation of proximal processes. The differentiation of these three forms leads to their combination in patterns of Person structure that can further account for differences in the direction and power of resultant proximal processes and their developmental effects.

These new formulations of qualities of the person that shape his or her future development have had the unanticipated effect of further differentiating, expanding, and integrating the original 1979 conceptualization of the environment in terms of nested systems ranging from *micro-* to *macro* (Bronfenbrenner, 1979a). For example, the three types of Person characteristics outlined above are also incorporated into the definition of the *microsystem* as characteristics of parents, relatives, close friends, teachers, mentors, coworkers, spouses, or others who participate in the life of the developing person on a fairly regular basis over extended periods of time.

The bioecological model also introduces an even more consequential domain into the structure of the microsystem that emphasizes the distinctive contribution to development of proximal processes involving interaction not with people but with objects and symbols. Even more broadly, concepts and criteria are introduced that differentiate between those features of the environment that foster versus interfere with the development of proximal processes. Particularly significant in the latter sphere is the growing hecticness, instability, and chaos in the principal settings in which human competence and character are shaped—in the family, child-care arrangements, schools, peer groups, and neighborhoods.

The latter theme speaks to the fourth and final defining property of the bioecological model and the one that moves it farthest beyond its predecessor—the dimension of *Time*. The 1979 Volume scarcely mentions the term, whereas in the current formulation, it has a prominent place at three successive levels—micro-, meso-, and macro-. *Microtime* refers to continuity versus discontinuity within ongoing episodes of proximal process. *Mesotime* is the periodicity of theses episodes across broader time intervals, such as days and weeks. Finally, *Macrotime* focuses on the changing expectations and events in the larger society, both within and across generations, as they affect and are affected by, processes and outcomes of human development over the life course. The treatment of this last topic draws on the chapter by Elder in this Volume. Our primary emphasis, however, is on the role of developmental processes and outcomes in producing large-scale changes over time in the state and structure of the broader society over time, and the implications of those changes for the society's future.

Before turning to the task at hand, it is important to make explicit three overarching orientations that define the content and the structure of the chapter as a whole. First, we use the term "development" to refer to *stability and change in the biopsychological characteristics of human beings over the life course and across generations*. There are no restrictive assumptions of change "for the better," nor of continuity in the characteristics of the same person over time. Rather, these are issues to be investigated.

Second, from the perspective of the bioecological model, the forces producing stability and change in characteristics of human beings *across* successive generations are no less important than stability and change in characteristics of the same person over his or her lifetime.

The third orientation is perhaps the most essential, and also the most difficult to achieve. It was Kurt Lewin (cited in Marrow, 1977) who said that there is nothing so practical as a good theory. But to be "good," a theory must also be practical. In science, a good theory is one that can be translated into corresponding research designs that match the defining properties of the theory. In the absence of such research designs—or worse yet, in the application of research designs that fail to match or even violate the defining properties of the theory—science cannot move forward. Hence we have sought, as we proceed through successive stages of theoretical formulation, to specify, and wherever possible to illustrate, the properties of a research design that corresponds with, or at least approximates, the proposed theoretical structure.

DEFINING PROPERTIES OF THE BIOECOLOGICAL MODEL

Before proceeding with formal definitions, it may be useful to point out that traditionally such phenomena as parent-child interaction—or, more generally, the behavior of others toward the developing person—have been treated under the more inclusive category of the environment. In the *bioecological model,* a critical distinction is made between the concepts of "environment" and "process," with the latter not only occupying a central position, but also having a meaning that is quite specific. The construct appears in the first of two Propositions stipulating the defining properties of the model. To place its meaning in context, we cite the second Proposition as well:

Proposition I

Especially in its early phases, but also throughout the life course, human development takes place through processes of progressively more complex reciprocal interaction between an active, evolving biopsychological human organism and the persons, objects, and symbols in its immediate external environment. To be effective, the interaction must occur on a fairly regular basis over extended periods of *time.* Such enduring forms of interaction in the immediate environment are referred to as *proximal processes.* Examples of enduring patterns of proximal process are found in feeding or comforting a baby, playing with a young child, child-child activities, group or solitary play, reading, learning new skills, athletic activities, problem solving, caring for others in distress, making plans, performing complex tasks, and acquiring new knowledge, and know-how.

Proximal processes are posited as the primary engines of development (see Gottlieb, Wahlsten, & Lickliter, Ch. 5, this Volume; Tobach, 1981; Tobach & Schneirla, 1968). A second defining property identifies the fourfold source of these dynamic forces:

Proposition II

The form, power, content, and direction of the proximal processes effecting development vary systematically as a joint function of the characteristics of the *developing person;* of the *environment*—both immediate and more remote—in which the processes are taking place; the nature of the *developmental outcomes* under consideration; and the social continuities and changes occurring over *time* through the life course and the historical period during which the person has lived.

Propositions I and II are theoretically interdependent and subject to empirical test. An operational research design that permits their simultaneous investigation is referred to as a *Process-Person-Context-Time model* (PPCT for short).

Note that characteristics of the person actually appear twice in the bioecological model—first as one of the four elements influencing the "form, power, content, and direction of the proximal process," and then again as "developmental outcomes"; that is, qualities of the developing person that emerge at a later point in time as the result of the joint, interactive, mutually reinforcing effects of the four principal antecedent components of the model. In sum, in the bioecological model, the characteristics of the person function both as an indirect producer and as a product of development (see Lerner, 1982; Lerner & Busch-Rossnagel, 1981).

Finally, because within the bioecological model the concept of proximal process has a specific meaning, it is important that its distinctive properties be made explicit. For present purposes, the following features of the construct are especially noteworthy:

1. For development to occur, the person must engage in an activity.

2. To be effective, the activity must take place "on a fairly regular basis, over an extended period of time." For example, this means that in the case of young children, a weekend of doing things with Mom or Dad does not do the job, nor do activities that are often interrupted.

3. Why not? One reason is that, to be developmentally effective, activities must continue long enough to become "increasingly more complex." Mere repetition does not work.

4. Developmentally effective proximal processes are not unidirectional; there must be influence in both directions. In the case of interpersonal interaction, this means that initiatives do not come from one side only; there must be some degree of reciprocity in the exchange.

5. Proximal processes are not limited to interactions with people; they also can involve interaction with objects

and symbols. In the latter circumstance, for reciprocal interaction to occur, the objects and symbols in the immediate environment must be of a kind that invites attention, exploration, manipulation, elaboration, and imagination.

6. The powerful moderating factors specified in Proposition II produce substantial changes in the content, timing, and effectiveness of proximal processes. In particular:

   a. As children grow older, their developmental capacities increase both in level and range; therefore, to continue to be effective, the corresponding proximal processes must also become more extensive and complex to provide for the future realization of evolving potentials. At the same time, in view of the ongoing developmental advance, the intervals between periods of "progressively more complex" activity can be increasingly longer, although they must still occur on a "fairly regular basis." Otherwise, the pace of development slows, or its course may even reverse direction.

   b. The principal persons with whom young children interact "on a fairly regular basis over extended periods of time" are parents, but especially as children get older, other persons—such as caregivers, relatives, siblings, and peers—also function in this role. These are soon followed by teachers or mentors in other activities, and then by close friends of the same or opposite sex, spouses or their equivalents, and coworkers, superiors and subordinates at work. As the examples indicate, the involvement of persons functioning in this role is not limited to the formative years. Borrowing a term from G.H. Mead (1934), we refer to such persons as "significant others."

The foregoing constitute the principal elements of the emergent theoretical model. If so, the question arises in what sense is the model *bio*ecological? Where and how does biology come into the picture? We present three answers to that question in an order of decreasing certainty about their validity. The first is an unqualified disclaimer. Little in the pages that follow speaks to the operation of biological systems *within* the organism. By contrast, considerable scientific attention is accorded to characteristics of the person generally regarded as *biologically based* that influence proximal processes and their developmental outcomes. Finally, the present model rests on the assumption that biological factors and evolutionary processes not only set limits on human development but also impose imperatives regarding the environmental conditions and experiences required for the realization of human potentials. The position is taken that, to the extent that the necessary conditions and experiences are not provided, such potentials will remain unactualized (Bronfenbrenner & Ceci, 1993, 1994a, 1994b).

It is our hope to persuade the reader that, once applied, the bioecological paradigm will turn out to be scientifically productive. At the present time, however, its most distinguishing characteristic is not its scientific power, but its rarity. To be sure, the rarity is hardly surprising, given the fact that successive revisions of the emerging model began to be published only in the past several years (Bronfenbrenner, 1989, 1990, 1993, 1994, 1995; Bronfenbrenner & Ceci, 1994a). Paradoxically, some concrete examples nevertheless existed much earlier. They were the product of what Bronfenbrenner and Crouter referred to in the 1983 edition of this *Handbook* as "latent paradigms"; that is, theoretical models that were not explicitly stated, but were implicit in the research designs used in analyzing the data (Bronfenbrenner & Crouter, 1983, pp. 373–376). Indeed, a partial precursor of the bioecological model appears in the 1983 *Handbook* chapter under the rubric of a "person-process-context model." In that chapter, however, what is meant by process is never specified, and the overwhelming majority of the examples cited do not include a proximal process component as defined in Proposition I. The same holds true for developmentally relevant characteristics of the Person. Finally, the 1983 chapter makes no reference whatever to Time as a defining property of the theoretical model. In these and other respects to follow, today's bioecological model goes far beyond its predecessors both with respect to basic constructs and their bidirectional, synergistic interrelationships.

FROM THEORY TO RESEARCH DESIGN: OPERATIONALIZING THE BIOECOLOGICAL MODEL

We have come to the point where it is both possible and necessary to examine the requirements imposed by the bioecological model for corresponding research designs. We begin with a concrete example of the latter.

In the 1950s and 1960s, Cecil Mary Drillien (1957, 1964), a physician and Professor of Child Life and Health at the University of Edinburgh, carried out a 7-year longitudinal investigation of psychological development in two groups: 360 children of low birthweight, and a control group selected "by taking the next mature birth from the hospital admission list" (1957, p. 29). In her follow-up assessments, the investigator found that children of low birthweight were more likely to exhibit problems in physical growth, susceptibility to illness, impaired intellectual development, and poorer classroom performance, with all of these tendencies being more pronounced in boys (1964). In a comparison of children's school performance with what would have been expected on the basis of their scores on an intelligence test, Drillien found that those of low birthweight were especially likely to be working below their mental capacity. In relation to this finding, the author comments as follows: "In most cases, failure to attain a standard commensurate with ability was associated with problems of behavior, which were found to increase with decreasing birthweight [and] to be more common in males" (1964, p. 209).

Figure 17.1. depicts the results. The figure does not appear in Drillien's monograph, but was constructed from data presented in tables in that volume. It shows the impact of the quality of mother-infant interaction at age 2 on the number of observed problem behaviors at age 4 as a joint function of social class and three levels of low birthweight—those underweight by a pound or more, not more than one pound, and those of normal birthweight. Measures of maternal responsiveness were based on observations in the home and interviews with the mother. The investigator's measure of social class was a composite index that took into account not only parental income and education, but also the socioeconomic level of the neighborhood in which the family lived. The quality of interaction was assessed in terms of the extent to which the mother was responsive to changes in the state and behavior of the infant. The measure of the developmental outcome was the frequency of reported behavior disturbances, such as hyperactivity, overdependence, timidity, and negativism.

Our primary interest here is not in the research findings per se, but in the extent to which the structure of the research design corresponds with the defining properties of the bioecological theoretical model. The first point to be noted in this regard is that Proposition I defines Proximal Processes as bidirectional. Drillien's measure of process, however, was based only on the mother's responsiveness to changes in the state and behavior of the infant, and no data are reported that would permit calculating a complementary measure of the infant's responsiveness to changes in the state and behavior of the mother. This means that the operational measure available in Drillien's research taps only one side of the theoretical definition of proximal process. For that reason, it appears likely that, to the extent the infant's contribution to reciprocal interaction carries any weight, the obtained results may underestimate the true magnitude of the observed effects.

Nevertheless, as revealed in Figure 17.1, maternal responsiveness across time, a one-sided measure of proximal process, still emerges as the most powerful predictor of developmental outcome. In all instances, responsive maternal treatment reduces substantially the degree of behavioral disturbance exhibited by the child.

Herein lies the main justification for distinguishing between proximal process on the one hand, and, on the other, the environments in which the processes occur; namely, in accord with Proposition I, the former turn out to be the most potent force influencing the developmental outcome (in this case, the frequency of problem behaviors at 4 years of age). Furthermore, as stipulated in Proposition II, the power of the Process varies systematically as a function of

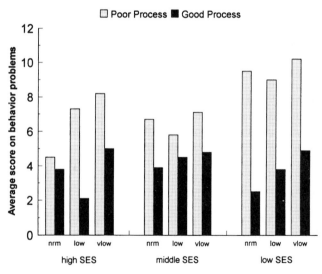

nrm = normal birthweight; low = between normal and 5.5 lbs; vlow = 5.5 lbs or less

Figure 17.1   Effect of mother's responsiveness on problem behavior of child at age 4 by birth weight and social class.

the environmental Context (i.e., social class) and of the characteristics of the Person (i.e., weight at birth). The process appears to have made its greatest impact on young children growing up in the most disadvantaged environment (i.e., the lowest socioeconomic level), but within that environment, it is those who at birth were of normal weight who benefited most. Moreover, it was in this same disadvantaged Context that, under high levels of maternal responsiveness, birthweight showed its most consistent effect, with the number of behavior problems steadily rising as birthweight fell. Finally, across the board, maternal responsiveness had the general result of decreasing or buffering against environmental differences in developmental outcome. Thus, at high levels of mother-child interaction, social class differences in problem behavior became much smaller.

From the perspective of developmental science, what is most noteworthy about these findings is not their specific content but that their simultaneous discovery was made possible by a research design based on a theoretical model that allowed for the emergence of patterns of this form. Not only are the four key components of Process, Person, Context, and Time all represented, but the design also provides for the detection of the kinds of synergistic[1] interdependencies among these components that are posited in the bioecological model as a dynamic theoretical system. Here are two specific examples of such interdependencies revealed in the analysis of Drillien's data:

1. Proposition II stipulates that the developmental effects of proximal processes vary as a joint function of Person and Context; that is, the indirect effects of Person and Context on the relation of Process to outcome are not to be conceived as simply additive. Consistent with this expectation is the finding that proximal processes had their greatest impact in the most disadvantaged environment, but on the healthiest infant. Here the combination of Person and Context exhibit a mutually reinforcing, multiplicative, indirect effect on the power of proximal processes as the "engines of development."

2. In Drillien's research, the frequency of problem behaviors was assessed at two points in time—first when the infants were 2 years old, and then again at 4 years. If one makes the not unreasonable assumption that mothers continued to interact with their children over the intervening period, then the results shown in Figure 17.2 provide evidence for the effect of proximal processes that have taken place "over an extended period of time." Youngsters experiencing low levels of interaction with their mothers exhibited an accelerating increase in the number of problem behaviors from 2 to 4 years of age, whereas those exposed to substantially higher levels of this proximal process showed only a modest rise.

Developmental Science in the Discovery Mode

What about the possibility that the preceding results are chance findings? In fact, some of them are statistically significant. Others could not be tested because the variances needed for calculating error estimates were not reported. But that is not the principal issue at stake. With concrete examples of the relation between theoretical and operational models now before us, we can address what turns out to be a complex and consequential question: What is the function of research design in the bioecological model?

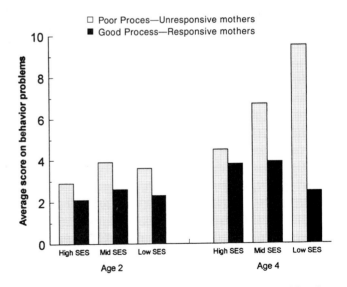

Figure 17.2 Effect of mother's responsiveness on problem behavior of child at ages 2 and 4 by social class.

---

[1] *Synergism* refers to "cooperative action of discrete agencies such that the total effect is greater than the sum of the two or more effects—taken independently" (*Webster's Third New International Dictionary* (Unabridged).

The first point to be made in this regard is that the main function is not the usual one of testing for statistical significance. Rather, the research design must provide for carrying out an equally essential and necessarily prior stage of the scientific process: that of *developing hypotheses of sufficient explanatory power and precision to warrant being subjected to empirical test.* We are dealing with science in the *discovery mode* rather than in the *mode of verification.* In this earlier phase, theory plays an even more critical role. From its very beginnings, the bioecological model, through its successive reformulations, represents a sustained effort to meet this scientific need.

What are the appropriate characteristics of research designs for developmental science in the discovery mode? Finding an answer to this question is complicated by the fact that, compared with the physical and natural sciences, developmental science is admittedly still in an earlier stage of development. Furthermore, because its scope falls between the natural and the social sciences, the discovery process must to some extent be adapted to the requirements of both. Perhaps in part for these reasons, we were unable to find any discussion of the issue in the developmental literature. Under these circumstances, we concluded that the best we could do was to try to make explicit the characteristics of the research designs that had been employed over the past several years to arrive at successively more differentiated formulations of the bioecological model.

These design characteristics depend on the constructs, and the possible relations between them, that are posited in the theoretical model at its present stage of development. Both the constructs, and the possible interrelationships, have been indicated in Propositions I and II, but as yet they appear in a relatively undifferentiated form. For example, the directions of the expected effects of Person and Context on proximal processes for different types of outcomes are not specified. The reason for such lack of specificity is that a more precise formulation could not be deduced either from the theory in its present, still evolving state, or induced from any already available data (at least, to our knowledge). Given these limitations, we concluded that an appropriate design strategy at this point in the discovery process could be one that involves a series of progressively more differentiated formulations and corresponding data analyses, with the results at each successive step setting the stage for the next round. The research designs employed

must be primarily generative rather than confirmatory versus disconfirming.

In this generative process, implications derived from the theoretical model play a more prominent role than those drawn from research findings, but the latter are also critical. Their importance is best conveyed by specifying a key feature of the corresponding research design: It must provide a structured framework for displaying the emergent research findings in a way that reveals more precisely the pattern of the interdependencies that in fact obtain in the data available. Of primary scientific interest are not those aspects of the observed pattern already anticipated in the existing theoretical model, but those features that point to more differentiated and precise theoretical formulations. These can then be evaluated in the light of new evidence, and, if deemed scientifically promising, can be incorporated in the research design for a next step. The proposed strategy for developmental investigations in the discovery mode involves an iterative process of successive confrontations between theory and data leading toward the ultimate goal of being able to formulate hypotheses that both merit and are susceptible to scientific assessment in the verification mode.

In presenting this definition of the discovery mode, we acknowledge that, in actual scientific practice, it is hardly likely to be a "discovery." The process we have described, or something like it, is what scientists have always done. Our primary reason for seeking to make that process explicit was the belief that doing so could further the discovery process. But we also hope that the explication and examples of the discovery mode presented in this chapter will have broader utility in developmental research.

To return to the task at hand, the proposed criteria have more specific implications for the critical role in research design played by statistical analysis. First, in the discovery phase, Type I errors can entail an even greater risk than errors of Type II. To state the issue more broadly, dismissing as invalid a finding that in fact points the way to a fuller and more precise explanation for the phenomenon under investigation may result in a greater loss than that produced by accepting a finding that is highly significant because of as yet undifferentiated and thereby confounded factors producing the phenomenon in question (e.g., the failure to distinguish Process from Context). The greater risk in the discovery process of dismissing findings as Type I errors is further compounded by the phenomenon of "magnification" of early environmental differences over time. Thus, as illustrated by the escalating effects of proximal processes shown in Figure 17.2, changes in outcome associated with a proximal process at Time 1 can be quite small, and nonsignificant statistically. Yet, as shown, they can be powerful predictors of a marked increase in developmental outcome several years later (in the likely event that the process continued to be maintained over the intervening period).

At this point, a methodological note is in order. Statistical models widely used for the purpose of hypothesis testing are often ill-suited as operational models for developmental investigations in the discovery mode. This is particularly true for models that control statistically solely for *linear* relationships among the factors in the research design to obtain an estimate of the independent contribution of each factor in the statistical model to the outcome under investigation. The validity of such analyses rests on what in mathematical statistics is referred to as "the assumption of homogeneity of regression." To illustrate the assumption in its simplest general case: given a dependent variable y and two independent variables x_1 and x_2, then the relation between x_1 and y must be the same at all levels of x_2. This assumption is often not met in developmental data. For example, when applied to the analysis shown in Figure 17.2, it would require that the relation between proximal process and frequency of problem behaviors be the same at every social class level, which is not the case. Nor is this requirement likely to hold with respect to any combination of the four defining properties of the bioecological model. As Bronfenbrenner stated in his 1979 monograph, *"In ecological research, the principal main effects are likely to be interactions"* (p. 38, italics in original).

It follows that any research design based on a bioecological model must allow for the possibility of such interactions. However, it is also essential, especially in the discovery phase, that the particular interactions to be examined be theoretically based, and that—insofar as possible—their anticipated direction and form be specified in advance, so that discrepancies between theoretical expectation and observed reality can be readily recognized and thus provide the basis for a next step in the typically slow, iterative process of seeking more differentiated formulations that merit further exploration both on theoretical and

empirical grounds. In each case, the new formulation should be consistent with the existing theoretical specifications of the bioecological model, but it also must take into account any old or new research findings bearing on the issue.

The foregoing criteria for research in the discovery mode do not imply neglect of the traditional issues of reliability and validity. These are honored in a somewhat different, theoretically guided way. Essentially, the process is one of cross-validation at two levels. First, within a given study, the results at each successive stage of analysis are validated in the next, more differentiated formulation. Second, the generalizations emerging from a given investigation are cross-validated against findings from other studies of theoretically related phenomena but with a specific focus in each case, on the defining components of the bioecological model.

Before we proceed with concrete examples, it is important to emphasize that the criteria we have proposed and applied for conducting developmental science in the discovery mode represent a first attempt to construct a working model. Moreover, the working model is subject to the curious qualification that it is itself the product of the same kind of sequential design that it proposes. The criteria were developed by examining the changes introduced at each successive stage in the evolution of the bioecological model in order to identify the theoretical and operational properties leading to improvement in the model's predictive power. The example that follows illustrates these concurrent processes.

Different Paths to Different Outcomes: Dysfunction versus Competence

In this instance, our exploratory effort took as its point of departure the stipulation in Proposition II that the effects of proximal processes vary systematically depending on the developmental outcome. Once again, rather than taking time to retrace our steps, we begin with where we ended up; namely, with the following initial formulation:

The greater developmental impact of proximal processes on children growing up in disadvantaged or disorganized environments is to be expected to occur mainly for outcomes reflecting developmental *dysfunction*. By contrast, for outcomes indicating developmental *competence,* proximal processes are posited as likely to have greater impact in more advantaged and stable environments.

The term "dysfunction" refers to the recurrent manifestation of difficulties on the part of the developing person in maintaining control and integration of behavior across situations, whereas "competence" is defined as the demonstrated acquisition and further development of knowledge and skills—whether intellectual, physical, socioemotional, or a combination of them (e.g., learning how to care for a young infant involves all three).

The preceding emergent formulation is based on the following considerations. Most parents have the capacity and the motivation to respond to manifestations of physical or psychological distress on the part of their children. In deprived or disorganized environments, such manifestations of dysfunction have been shown to be both more frequent and more severe (e.g., in Drillien's research), thus drawing on more of parents' available time and energy. Accordingly, to the extent that, in disadvantaged settings, parents are able to engage in proximal processes, these are likely to have greater impact in reducing dysfunction rather than in enhancing their children's knowledge about and skill in dealing with the external environment. With respect to problems of dysfunction, in deprived environments there is usually a match between young children's needs and their parents' capacity to meet those needs. This does not mean, however, that children in such environments will end up functioning as well as their agemates growing up in more favorable circumstance, but rather that, over similar periods of time, they will show greater improvement in control over their own problem behaviors as a function of parental responsiveness.

The situation in advantaged and stable environments is rather different. Manifestations of dysfunction are likely to occur less often and to be less intense. Under these circumstances, parents are more apt to be attracted by and respond to the more frequent and more gratifying signs of their children's growing competence, with the result that proximal processes may to be focused mainly in this latter sphere. In addition, parents living in a middle-class world are themselves more apt to possess and exhibit the knowledge and skills they wish their children to acquire. They also have greater access to resources and opportunities outside the family that can provide needed experiences for

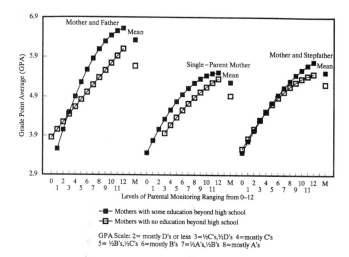

Figure 17.3   Effect of parental monitoring on grades in high school by family structure and mother's level of education. Analyses and graph based on data archives generously provided by Professors Stephen A. Small (University of Wisconsin) and Tom Luster (Michigan State University).

their children. Taken together, the foregoing considerations led to the formulation of the previously stated "proto-hypothesis."

Because Drillien's study of the influence of mother-infant interaction dealt with only one developmental outcome, one has to look elsewhere for evidence that effects of such processes vary depending on the nature of the outcome under consideration. A rich data archive generously made available by Small and Luster (1990) from their statewide studies of youth at risk in Wisconsin met this need.* Figure 17.3 depicts the results from an analysis of the differential effects of parental monitoring on the academic achievement of high school students living in one of the three most common family structures found in the total

* The analyses of data from the Wisconsin archive reported in this chapter were carried out in collaboration with Stephen A. Small (University of Wisconsin) and Tom Luster (Michigan State University). Small and Luster designed and conducted the survey from which the data are drawn. We are deeply indebted to them for the theoretical thinking that underlies the construction of the survey. It is an excellent example of developmental science in the discovery mode. We are also grateful to Regina Cannon (then a graduate student at Cornell University) who carried out the statistical analyses with care and dispatch.

sample of over 2,500 cases.[2] The students were between 14 and 16 years of age. It was also possible to stratify the sample by two levels of mother's education, with completion of high school as the dividing line. Parental monitoring refers to the effort by parents to keep informed about and set limits on their children's activities outside the home. In the present study, it was assessed by a series of items in a questionnaire administered to adolescents in their school classes. All items referred to "parents" in the plural, with no distinction as to whether the mother or the father was doing the monitoring. Levels of parental monitoring, ranging from 0 to 12, are shown on the horizontal axis, and grade point average (GPA) is shown on the vertical. The markers to the right of each curve record the mean GPA for each of the six groups.

Once again, the results reveal that the effects of proximal processes are more powerful than those of the environmental contexts in which they occur. In this instance, however, the impact of the process was greatest in what emerges as the most advantaged ecological niche—families with two biological parents in which the mother had some education beyond high school. Moreover, the developmental effect of the proximal process on school grades—a measure of *competence*—was stronger for families living in more advantaged socioeconomic circumstances. This finding is directly opposite to that revealed by the analysis of Drillien's data, where the outcome was one of psychological dysfunction (i.e., the frequency of problem behaviors). At the same time, the principal finding from both studies documents the powerful effect of proximal processes on human development, a result consistent with the first

defining property of the bioecological model stipulated in Proposition I.

The reader may well ask why the data in each scattergram were fitted to a curve with a declining slope rather than simply with a straight line. In accord with the criteria for research in the discovery mode, the introduction of the quadratic term was based on theoretical considerations. Higher levels of academic performance require mastery of more complex tasks, and hence are more difficult to achieve. As a result, at each successive step, the same degree of active effort would be expected to yield a somewhat smaller result. More specifically, for pupils who are not doing so well in school, parental monitoring can have a substantial effect by ensuring more stability of time and place so that *some* learning can occur. But for superior school achievement, students would require in addition high levels of motivation, focused attention, prior knowledge, and—especially—actually working with the material to be learned. These are all qualities that stability of time and place by itself cannot provide.

As can be seen in Figure 17.3, the relation between parental monitoring and school grades shows a curvilinear trend. Moreover, in accord with criteria for research in the discovery mode (see pp. 999–1001), both in its direction and form the trend corresponds with theoretical expectations in being more pronounced when the mother has some education beyond high school, especially in a two-parent family structure. A test for heterogeneity of regression confirms visual inspection. The differences in slopes between the two educational levels are highly significant ($p \leq .01$), with the quadratic component emerging as reliable only in the higher educational group.[3] Also statistically significant are differences in school achievement by family structure within each level of mother's education, with students growing up in two-parent families getting the highest grades, and those from single-parent families the lowest, a rank order corresponding to the power of the proximal process in each group as measured by the slopes of the associated regression coefficients.

---

[2] The large number of cases in this study should not be taken to imply that the bioecological model can be applied only in samples with a large *N*. As illustrated here, precision in the formulation of the theoretical model and in its translation into a closely corresponding research design can produce reliable findings even when there are relatively few cases in some, or even all, the cells of the model. This comes about because, in effect, the bioecological model requires, in its discovery phase, advance specification primarily not of main effects but of also in the form and direction of their most plausible interactions in the light of both the evolving theoretical model and the then available research evidence. This is especially true for well-designed experiments. For examples, see pp. 1007–1008.

---

[3] The degree of curvilinearity is measured by the corresponding regression coefficients and not by difference in the length of each curve from top to bottom. The latter is determined by empty cells in the scatter plot below or above which entries for *both* monitoring level and GPA were available.

Finally, a result not shown on the graph provides additional evidence pointing to another tentative generalization. The first indication appeared in the analysis of Drillien's data, which, among other findings, revealed that maternal responsiveness had the general effect of decreasing or buffering against environmental differences in developmental outcome. Thus, at high levels of mother-child interaction, social class differences in problem behavior became smaller. A similar pattern emerges for the effects of parental monitoring on school grades. Across the six groups shown in Figure 17.3, stronger parental monitoring was associated not only with a higher mean on school performance, but also with a lower standard deviation. These differences, too, were statistically reliable. Hence the following working hypothesis:

> For outcomes of *competence,* proximal processes not only lead to higher levels of developmental functioning but also serve to reduce and act as a buffer against effects of disadvantaged and disruptive environments.

To turn from substance to method, the foregoing findings also demonstrate that tests of significance have a place in research in the discovery mode, but, as with hypothesis verification, only *after* a specific theoretical expectation has been formulated in advance.

In a discovery context, however, the aim is not to claim empirical validity for a particular theoretical formulation but to indicate its plausibility for inclusion in the research design at subsequent stages of exploratory work. To be sure, doing so may result in a failure of replication. But *not* doing so risks missing potentially important, theoretically guided research opportunities not yet recognized. Garmezy and Rutter (1983), in their landmark studies of stress and coping in children's development, did not differentiate between those protective or disruptive forces emanating from the environment, and those that inhere in the biopsychological characteristics of the person. As evidenced from the analysis of Drillien's data shown in Figure 17.1, these vectors do not always operate in the same direction. Nevertheless, Garmezy and Rutter's formulations and findings played a significant role in the early stages of the process through which the bioecological model reached its present, still-evolving form.

The still-evolving form imposes the obligation to take advantage of existing opportunities for continued exploration.

With respect to the present inquiry, the next step in that process was once again to pose the question about the extent to which the research design meets the defining properties of the bioecological model. At first glance, we appear to be confronted with the same problem that we encountered with Drillien's study. Proposition I defines proximal processes as bidirectional. As previously noted, Small and Luster defined parental monitoring as the effort by parents to keep informed about and set limits on their children's activities outside the home. As stated, such behavior implies influence from one side only—that of the parents. An examination of the actual items used in their questionnaire, however, revealed that they were of two kinds. Some were cast in the language of parental expectation and prescription (e.g., "If I am going to be home late, I am expected to call my parent(s) to let them know"; "When I go out, my parent(s) ask me where I'm going"). By contrast, other items implied that the desired expectations or prescriptions were in fact being met (e.g., "My parent(s) know where I am after school"; "I tell my parent(s) who I'm going to be with before I go out"). Although the first type of item is unidirectional, the second entails some degree of reciprocity to the extent that the adolescent is providing the information desired by the parents. Accordingly, we hypothesized that items of the second type would show stronger relationships to developmental outcomes than those that described only the parents' expectations of how they wished their children to behave.

Separate analyses of scales based on each type of item provided substantial support for our working hypothesis. Although responses to both types of questions showed reliable effects on school performance, the relationships for the "reciprocity" scale were significantly stronger and were much more likely to show curvilinear effects. Accordingly, the latter was the scale used in analyzing the results presented in Figure 17.3.

From the perspective of the biological model, the research design producing the results shown in that figure is missing an important Person component. It is a general finding in educational research that at the high school level female students score higher on measures of academic performance than do males. The question therefore arises: To what extent is this gender difference attributable to variations in proximal process? Figure 17.4 provides a tentative answer to this question for students whose mothers had more than a high school education. Within each family

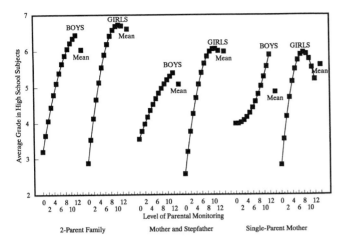

Figure 17.4 Parental monitoring and high school grades by gender: mothers with more than a high school education. Analyses and graph based on data archives generously provided by Professors Stephen A. Small (University of Wisconsin) and Tom Luster (Michigan State University).

structure, parental monitoring exerted a more powerful effect on the school achievement of girls than of boys, a result that is paralleled by corresponding differences in average GPA for the two sexes.[4] In each of the three family structures, girls received higher grades than boys, with the difference being most pronounced in two-parent households and lowest in single-mother families.

As seen in Figure 17.4, however, a distinctive feature of the pattern for girls is a marked flattening of the curve, especially for daughters of single-parent mothers. This result suggests that, in each of the three family structures, mothers may be pushing their already successful daughters to the point where conformity to maternal control no longer brings educational returns, particularly when the mother is the only parent.

An analysis of data on students whose mothers had no more than a high school education showed a similar general pattern, but the effects were less pronounced. The influence of monitoring was appreciably weaker, and its greater benefit to girls was also reduced. Nevertheless, girls with less-educated mothers both in single-parent and

in stepfamilies still had higher GPA scores than boys. This means that some other factor not yet identified must account for this difference.

Although a number of possibilities come to mind regarding this unknown, regrettably the Wisconsin archive does not contain any data on the principal suspects. What is available is information about another trail of discovery that we have already begun to explore. Our successively more differentiated working models, both conceptual and operational, for assessing the effects of parental monitoring on school achievement have provided increasing support for the tentative hypothesis that, for outcomes reflecting developmental *competence,* proximal processes are likely to have greatest impact in the most advantaged environments. But what about the other half of the original formulation: the complementary postulate that the greater developmental impact of proximal processes growing up in poor environments is to be expected to occur mainly for outcomes reflecting developmental *dysfunction?*

Data from Small and Luster's archive also provide the opportunity for cross-validating this provisional claim. In addition to measures of academic achievement, the Wisconsin study also included information on teenagers' sexual activity. The decision to analyze this outcome in the context of a bioecological model was prompted by Small and Luster's (1990) finding that such behavior varied systematically by family structure. Sexual activity was measured by a single question: "Have you ever had sexual relations with another person?"

This documentation of variations in sexual activity by family structure takes on special significance in the light of broader social changes taking place in the lives of children, youth, and families in contemporary American society. Today, the United States has the highest rate of teenage pregnancy of any developed nation, almost twice as high as that of its nearest competitors (Bronfenbrenner et al., 1994, p. 117). Adolescent sexual activity is also one of the prominent elements in the so-called "teenage syndrome," an escalating pattern of co-occurring behaviors including smoking, drinking, early and frequent sexual experience, adolescent pregnancy, a cynical attitude toward education and work, and, in the more extreme cases, drugs, suicide, vandalism, violence, and criminal acts (for references and successive summaries of the evidence, see Bronfenbrenner, 1970, 1975, 1986b, 1989, 1990, 1992; Bronfenbrenner & Neville, 1994; Bronfenbrenner et al., 1996).

---

[4] Within each pair, both means and regression coefficients were statistically significant, the latter confirming reliable differences in slope.

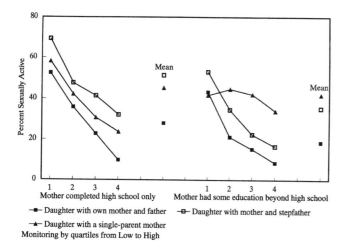

Figure 17.5 Effect of monitoring on girls' sexual activity (high school students between 14 and 16 years of age).

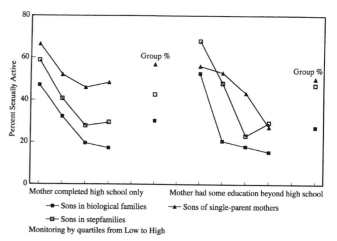

Figure 17.6 Effect of parental monitoring on boys' sexual activity (high school students between 14 and 16 years of age).

In anticipating the effects of parental monitoring on teenagers' sexual activity, we were again confronted with the issue of the possible direction of influence. In relation to sexual activity as an outcome, however, some leverage for the resolution of the issue was provided because each direction could be expected to produce opposite effects. On the one hand, if parental monitoring functions to defer sexual activity, then the more monitoring the less sexual activity. On the other hand, if the parents begin to monitor only after the fact, the association would be reversed, with monitoring occurring in reaction to the adolescent's behavior; hence sexually active adolescents would be monitored more.

The results of the analysis are shown in Figures 17.5 and 17.6.*

The most salient finding for both sexes is that parental monitoring does substantially reduce adolescents' sexual activity. In many other respects, however, the patterns for female and male adolescents are quite different. The results for girls in Figure 17.5 show that the effect of parental monitoring is stronger for daughters of mothers with no education beyond high school—a finding consistent with the

working hypothesis that, for outcomes reflecting lack of control, proximal processes have greater impact in poorer environments. Tests for heterogeneity of regression confirm that this finding holds for each of the three family forms.

Yet, as shown in Figure 17.6, the corresponding analysis of the data for boys reveals the very opposite result. Parental monitoring has a more powerful effect on boys whose mothers have had *more* education rather than less. Once again, the finding holds within each family structure and is confirmed by tests for heterogeneity of regression.

Nor is this the only departure from the expectations generated by the most recent working model. For example, there was not always correspondence between the developmental power of proximal processes in a given family structure and the percentage of sexually active adolescents in that structure. A case in point is stepfamilies in which the mother has only a high school education. Here maternal monitoring of daughters is as high as it is in two-parent families, but the percentage of sexually active girls is even greater than that for single-parent mothers at the same educational level. The finding is consistent with research indicating that living in a family with a stepfather entails a special developmental risk for girls (Hetherington & Clingempeel, 1992).

And so once again we find ourselves engaged in a next stage of the discovery process in which we are seeking to develop a more differentiated formulation that, through a corresponding research design, will be most effective in

---

*We are also indebted to Kristen Jacobson, now a doctoral student at Pennsylvania State University for her ingenuity and accuracy in translating into a common format data archives recorded on different computing systems.

reducing the observed empirical departures from expectations based on the existing working model. The first step is to ask an obvious question: What is most likely to account for such discrepancies? Restating the question from the perspective of the bioecological model, which of the four components is a likely suspect? It has to be somebody who is already on the scene. Parents are already there. Who else is around who could exert some influence on the sexual activity of high school students? The question answers itself—the peer group. And if it is indeed true that proximal processes are at least as powerful determinants of development as either the characteristics of the person or of the environment, what might that process be?

A tentative first nomination is "progressively more intense interaction with peers who are already sexually active." Among other considerations, this suggestion is guided by the possibility that peer pressure to engage in sexual activity and the prestige that such activity brings are likely to be higher for boys from less educated families with the result that parental monitoring is not as effective. With respect to the other components in the model, given the findings just reported, gender would still be a Person characteristic of major importance. The choice of an appropriate environmental Context depends on the precise research question being asked. Family structure would also still be appropriate. But from the perspective of the bioecological model, an option to consider would be the parents' beliefs about the kinds of activities they wanted their adolescent son or daughter to engage in or refrain from, as well as the closeness of the parent-child relationship.

We offer these suggestions not for their relevance to this particular issue but to illustrate two additional emergent corollaries of the bioecological model:

1. The specific components of Process, Person, Context, and Time to be included in a given investigation should be those that, from a theoretical perspective, are maximally relevant to the research question under investigation and complementary to each other in relation to the given developmental outcome.

2. From a theoretical perspective, the power of a PPCT design is most effectively enhanced by including more than one proximal process in the model.

The next section leads to yet another corollary.

The Role of Experiments in the Bioecological Model

The examples considered thus far are essentially "experiments of nature"; that is, they show how development is influenced by variations in the components of the bioecological model occurring in already existing societies. They tell us nothing about whether, to what extent, or how these elements and their combinations can be changed. This limitation applies particularly to the most consequential component of the bioecological model—proximal processes. We know of no research bearing specifically on this question, but some indirect evidence does exist. In research findings already presented, improving the quality of the environment has been shown to increase the developmental power of proximal processes. The indirect evidence comes from experiments in which researchers have systematically introduced conditions into the environment in which people lived that were hypothesized to enhance their psychological functioning beyond existing levels.

Here are two examples at contrasting ages.

Environmental Dynamics in Old Age

The first example is Langer and Rodin's oft-cited experimental intervention conducted with residents of a New Haven nursing home for the aged (Langer & Rodin, 1976; Rodin & Langer, 1977). The contextual manipulation employed in this study is well summarized in the authors' words:

> The hospital administrator gave a talk to residents in the experimental group emphasizing their responsibility for themselves, whereas the communication to a second, comparison group stressed the staff's responsibility for them as patients. To bolster the communication, residents in the experimental group were offered plants to care for, whereas residents in the comparison group were given plants that were watered by the staff. (Rodin & Langer, 1977, p. 897)

Residents were assigned at random to either the experimental or the control group. Data on psychological and health characteristics were collected at three time points: (a) just prior to the introduction of the experiment; (b) three weeks later, when the experiment was formally ended; and (c) in a follow-up study conducted 18 months later.

The substantial effects of intervention found at the end of the experiment (Langer & Rodin, 1976) were still in evidence in the follow-up assessment. To be sure, because the residents were almost a year-and-a-half older, the added age had taken some toll, but, nevertheless, those in the "induced responsibility" group not only significantly surpassed their controls, but were appreciably better off, both psychologically and physically, than they had been months earlier before the intervention had begun. In ratings by observers blind to the experimental conditions, they were judged to be more alert, sociable, and vigorous. The most striking results were seen in the comparison of death rates between the two treatment groups. Taking the 18 months prior to the original intervention as an arbitrary comparison period, in the subsequent 18 months following the intervention, 15% in the "responsibility-induced" group died, compared with 30% in the control group.

Environmental Dynamics in Infancy

A remarkable, independent cross-validation of Langer and Rodin's principal hypothesis appears in the findings of another intervention experiment—this one almost unknown—that was carried out at about the same time with a sample of 100 9-month-old infants and their mothers in the Dutch city of Nijmegen (Riksen-Walraven, 1978). Although this author, Marianne Riksen-Walraven, appears not to have been aware of Langer and Rodin's work conducted during the same period, one of the two intervention strategies she employed with her sample of infants was similar to that used in the New Haven study of elderly patients. Mothers, randomly assigned to what Riksen-Walraven called the "responsiveness" group, were given a "workbook for parents" stressing the idea that "the infant learns most from the effects of its own behavior" (p. 113):

> Caregivers were advised not to direct the child's activities too much, but to give the child opportunity to find out things for himself, to praise him for his efforts, and to respond to his initiations of interaction. (p. 113)

By contrast, mothers of infants in the "stimulation" group received a workbook that emphasized the importance of providing the infant with a great variety of perceptual experiences of all kinds, "to point to and name objects and persons," and "to speak a lot to their infants" (p. 112).

In the follow-up assessment conducted 3 months later, infants of mothers who had been encouraged to be responsive to their babies' initiatives exhibited higher levels of exploratory behavior and were more likely to prefer a novel object to one that was already familiar. The babies also learned more quickly in a learning contingency task.

Neither of the preceding investigations included any systematic assessment of the activities in which the participants in the experiment subsequently engaged, of the balance between unidirectional and bidirectional behavior in the two groups, or of any other specific feature that could provide a measure of the extent to which proximal processes were in fact operating in each of the two contrasting experimental conditions.

In both of the preceding experimental studies, elegant as they are, the keystone of the bioecological model—a measure of proximal process—was not included in the research design. In addition, the demonstration (in Figure 17.3) of the joint, indirect effects of family structure and parents' education on the relation of proximal processes to school grades does only half the job, for it provides no information on whether differences in students' personal characteristics (such as gender) exert a similar indirect effect. Nevertheless, viewed from the theoretical perspective of a bioecological model, all these findings are impressively consistent with expectations derived from the model; the findings illustrate the model's practicability, and—perhaps most promising for the future of developmental science—generate questions that, when answered, provide ways for enhancing the model's scientific power. It is these questions and answers that are addressed in the following sections.

Up to this point, our exposition has given primary attention to the core concept of proximal process and its key position in the bioecological model as a whole. We now proceed to a more detailed examination of each of the other three defining properties of the model—Person, Context, and Time.

HOW DO PERSON CHARACTERISTICS INFLUENCE LATER DEVELOPMENT?

As already indicated, at midstage in the development of the bioecological model, an effort was begun to arrive at some answers to this question, and it has continued up to the present day. As before, rather than describe the successive stages in this emergent reconception, we present it in its most recent, still-evolving form.

Most developmental research treats the cognitive and socioemotional characteristics of the person as dependent variables; that is, as measures of developmental outcomes. Far less often are such characteristics examined as precursors and producers of later development (but see other systems' perspectives in this Volume, e.g., Wagner & Demick; Gottlieb et al.; Thelan & Smith; Brandtstedter; and Lerner). From the perspective of the bioecological model, their effectiveness in the latter role derives from their capacity to influence the emergence and operation of proximal processes.

Accordingly, in an effort to identify such process-relevant Person characteristics, we applied the sequential design strategy described in the preceding section. Beginning with implications derived from the theoretical model, which are then related to existing research findings, successive applications of this strategy have resulted in the conceptualization of three kinds of process-relevant Person characteristics, which, for convenience of brevity, we have labeled as Person *forces, resources,* and *demands.*[5]

Force Characteristics as Shapers of Development

In the bioecological model, the characteristics of the Person most likely to influence future development would be active behavioral dispositions that can set proximal processes in motion and sustain their operation, or—conversely—actively interfere with, retard, or even prevent their occurrence. It is therefore useful to distinguish between these two propensities. We refer to the former as *developmentally generative* characteristics; to the latter as *developmentally disruptive.*

Examples of developmentally disruptive dispositions come more readily to mind. At one pole, they include such characteristics as impulsiveness, explosiveness, distractibility, inability to defer gratification, or, in a more extreme form, ready resort to aggression and violence; in short, difficulties in maintaining control over emotions and behavior. At the opposite pole are such Person attributes as

apathy, inattentiveness, unresponsiveness, lack of interest in one's surroundings, feelings of insecurity, shyness, or a general tendency to avoid or withdraw from activity.[6] Persons exhibiting either of the preceding propensities would find it difficult to engage in proximal processes requiring progressively more complex patterns of reciprocal interaction over extended periods of time.

By contrast, developmentally generative characteristics involve such active orientations as curiosity, tendency to initiate and engage in activity alone or with others, responsiveness to initiatives by others, and readiness to defer immediate gratification to pursue long-term goals.

We have found few investigations that shed light on the developmental effects of either type of dynamic characteristics on proximal processes and their outcomes. A major reason for this shortcoming is the absence of theoretical constructs for conceptualizing their changing nature over the course of development from early infancy, through adolescence, into and beyond early adulthood. The following framework is offered as an initial basis for meeting this requirement beginning in the Person domain in greater need of conceptual definition—that of developmentally generative characteristics. The corresponding structure for developmentally disruptive Person qualities can then be derived as an inverted mirror image of the former.[7]

Developmentally Generative Dispositions in Life Course Perspective

The first and earliest manifestation of generative dispositions takes the form of what we call *selective responsiveness.* It involves differentiated response to, attraction by, and exploration of aspects of the physical and social environment.

The next generative characteristic to evolve goes beyond selective responsiveness to include the tendency to engage and persist in progressively more complex activities; for example, to elaborate, restructure, and even to create new features in one's environment—not only physical and social,

---

[5] As is documented later in this chapter (pp. 1018–1019), the recently renewed, and far stronger, claims by behavior geneticists for the predominant role of genetic factors in determining both individual and group differences in all forms of human characteristics are directly challenged by alternative explanations and research findings derived from the bioecological model.

[6] To be sure, depending on the available alternatives, withdrawal may be the only course left for dealing with an unbearable situation.

[7] The material that follows represents a further development by the present authors of ideas first introduced in Bronfenbrenner (1989).

but also symbolic. We refer to propensities of this kind as *structuring proclivities.*

The transition from one to the other of these dynamic forms of orientation during early childhood is illustrated in successive publications from a longitudinal study of infants being carried out by Leila Beckwith, Sarale Cohen, Claire Kopp, and Arthur Parmelee at UCLA (Beckwith & Cohen, 1984; Beckwith, Rodning & Cohen, 1992; Cohen & Beckwith, 1979; Cohen, Beckwith, & Parmelee, 1978; Cohen & Parmelee, 1983; Cohen, Parmelee, Beckwith, & Sigman, 1986). Their imaginative and careful work reveals a progressive sequence of such environmentally oriented dispositions from birth through 7 years of age. Thus, immediately after birth, infants are especially responsive to vestibular stimulation (being picked up and held in a vertical position close to the body), which has the effect of soothing babies so that they begin to engage in mutual gazing; by 3 months, visual exploration extends beyond proximal objects, and the mother's voice is most likely to elicit responses especially in the form of reciprocal vocalizations.

From about 6 months on, the infant begins actively to manipulate objects spontaneously in a purposeful way and to rearrange the physical environment. By now, both vocalization and gesture are being used to attract the parents' attention and to influence their behavior. In addition, there is a growing readiness, across modalities, to initiate and sustain reciprocal interaction with a widening circle of persons in the child's immediate environment. This is the emergence of what we call structuring proclivities.

A number of other investigations have yielded comparable findings, and have extended them to still other activity domains; for example: individual differences in children's creativity in play and fantasy behavior (Connolly & Doyle, 1984; MacDonald & Parke, 1984); Jean and Jack Block's longitudinal studies of "ego resiliency" and "ego control" (Block & Block, 1980; Block, Block, & Keyes, 1988).

The nature of the third and final class of developmentally generative Person characteristics reflects the increasing capacity and active propensity of children as they grow older to conceptualize their experience. It deals with what we call *directive belief systems* about oneself as an active agent both in relation to the self and to environment, or, for short, *directive beliefs.* The oldest concept of this kind is Rotter's construct and measure of "locus of control" (Rotter, 1966). Subsequently, a more sophisticated formulation of the concept was introduced by Bandura

(1977, 1982) under the rubric of self-efficacy. The principal distinction between these earlier constructs and their counterparts in the bioecological model is that the latter are conceptualized primarily not as characteristics of the person sufficient unto themselves but as directional dispositions interacting synergistically with particular features of the environment to generate successive levels of developmental advance.

The closest approximation to an operationalized bioecological model in which directive beliefs function as Person characteristics appears in a series of findings arising from a doctoral dissertation by Tulkin (1973, 1977; Tulkin & Cohler, 1973; Tulkin & Kagan, 1972). The investigator studied social class differences both in the behaviors and the beliefs of mothers of 10-month-old girls. The research was conducted in the home, employing both interviews and observations. Middle-class mothers were distinguished from their working-class counterparts not only by higher levels of reciprocal interaction with their infants, but also in their views about what a 10-month-old could do, and about their own abilities to influence their baby's development; the more advantaged mothers attributed greater potentials both to their infants and themselves. In addition, the correlations between maternal behavior and attitudes were substantially greater in middle-class than in lower-class families. Several years later, Tulkin and a colleague (Tulkin & Covitz, 1975) reassessed the same youngsters after they had entered school. The children's performance on tests of mental ability and language skill showed significant relationships to the prior measures of reciprocal mother-infant interaction.

Perceptive readers may have detected a sleight of hand in our analysis of Tulkin's research when examined from the perspective of the bioecological model. Within that framework, we have been discussing characteristics of the developing Person that influence proximal processes and their outcomes. In Tulkin's work, the developing Person is the infant. But the directive beliefs we have been discussing are those of the mother. The reason for the substitution is the following. Although, in the line of work stimulated by Rotter and Bandura there are many investigations of the relation between personal beliefs and development, to our knowledge there have been no studies of the effect of personal beliefs on the proximal processes in which the developing person herself or himself becomes engaged. To provide an example, we resorted to a substitution of roles.

The substitution also provides an opportunity to introduce a corollary formulation, the evidence for which appears later in this and subsequent sections of this chapter.

In proximal processes involving interpersonal interaction, the personal characteristics that influence the power of the process and its effects are the same for all parties involved.

To return to the task at hand, we present a second form of Person characteristic posited as affecting future psychological growth—what we have called developmental *resources*.

RESOURCE CHARACTERISTICS OF THE PERSON AS SHAPERS OF DEVELOPMENT

These are Person characteristics that in themselves involve no selective disposition to action, but constitute biopsychological liabilities and assets that influence the capacity of the organism to engage effectively in proximal processes. In the first category are conditions that limit or disrupt the functional integrity of the organism. Some obvious examples include genetic defects, low birthweight, physical handicaps, severe and persistent illness, or damage to brain function through accident or degenerative processes. By contrast, developmental assets take the form of abilities, knowledge, skill, and experience that, as they evolve over most of the life course, extend the domains in which proximal processes can do their constructive work—thereby becoming another source of the "progressively more complex" patterns of interaction constituting a defining property of proximal processes.

The similarity between the definitions for the two types of developmental resources, and for the earlier distinction between developmental outcomes reflecting dysfunction versus competence, derives from the fact already noted that characteristics of the Person appear on both sides of the bioecological equation. Developmental outcomes at Time 1 indirectly influence developmental outcomes at Time 2 through their effect on proximal processes during the intervening period. The difference, therefore, lies not in the concepts themselves but in their place in the bioecological model.

A concrete example of a deficiency in developmental resources has already been documented in the analysis of Drillien's results depicted in Figure 17.1. Proximal processes exerted their most powerful effect on children growing up in the most disadvantaged environment, but within that environment youngsters who at birth were of normal weight benefited most. Weight at birth does not per se imply a directed propensity to engage in or refrain from a particular kind of behavior. What it does represent is variation in the biological resources available to engage in any activity requiring directed activity or response over extended periods of time. Thus, in the present instance, one plausible explanation for the observed asymmetric pattern is that, among families living in stressful environments, infants who are physically healthy from birth are more able to engage in reciprocal interaction than those who are biologically impaired.

This interpretation is called into question, however, by the corresponding results, shown in the same graph, for infants raised under the most favorable socioeconomic circumstances. Here, infants of normal birthweight profited least from interaction with their mothers. How might this paradox be resolved?

Even though the corresponding interaction term is statistically significant, under normal circumstances the preceding result would—and properly should—be called into question as a post hoc finding. But, in the present instance, that is not quite the case. To be sure, there was no a priori hypothesis predicting the precise pattern of the obtained results. The pattern is consistent, however, with several possibilities envisioned for a third Person attribute posited as influencing proximal processes and their developmental effects. And for science in the discovery mode, post hoc findings that are theoretically relevant are not to be lightly dismissed.

DEMAND CHARACTERISTICS OF THE PERSON AS DEVELOPMENTAL INFLUENCES

The distinguishing feature of this last set of Person characteristics affecting development is their capacity to invite or discourage reactions from the social environment of a kind that can disrupt or foster processes of psychological growth; for example, a fussy versus a happy baby; attractive versus unattractive physical appearance; or hyperactivity versus passivity. Half a century ago, Gordon Allport (1937), borrowing a term originally introduced by Mark A. May (1932), spoke of such characteristics as constituting "personality" defined in terms of its "social stimulus value." Rephrasing this concept in terms of its analogue in contemporary theories of perception, we refer to such Person qualities as *demand characteristics*.

A striking example of the developmental effect of such a feature emerges as a major finding in one of the follow-up studies of children of the Great Depression carried out by Elder and his colleagues (Elder, Van Nguyen, & Caspi, 1985). The investigators found that economic hardship adversely influenced the psychosocial well-being of girls (but not boys) through its tendency to increase the rejecting behavior of fathers. The effects of rejection, however, varied inversely as a function of the daughter's physical attractiveness. In the authors' words, "Attractive daughters were not likely to be maltreated by their fathers, no matter how severe the economic pressure. [The results] underscore the importance of viewing economic decline in relation to both the child's characteristics and parenting behavior" (p. 361). Here is a classic instance of the power of a Process-Person-Context-Time model in revealing the complex interactions between organism and environment that drive the process of development.

The concept of demand characteristics also introduces a new perspective for interpreting the contrasting developmental effects of birthweight by social class shown in Figure 17.1. As noted earlier, at the lowest socioeconomic level it was the children of normal birthweight who benefited most from maternal responsiveness. But does that mean they were also the ones who got the most attention from their mothers? Paradoxically, the picture turns out to be just the reverse. Only 14% of these lower-class mothers were judged to be responsive to changes in their infants' state or behavior, whereas the percentage for mothers of low-birthweight babies was more than twice as high (averaging 37%). In short, lower-class mothers were responding mainly to those infants who most needed their attention, albeit with a lower return on their investment.

But what characteristics of these babies were capturing the mothers' attention? It appears likely that in this instance, the mothers were responding mainly to their infants' expressions of distress—behavior less apt to occur among those of normal birthweight. If we look at the corresponding data for families at the highest socioeconomic level, we discover a rather different picture. Here mothers are more responsive to the healthiest infants than to those of lowest birthweight, but as shown in Figure 17.1, they get the

least return for their pains. Once again a key question becomes "What is capturing the mother's attention?" A plausible answer for children of normal birthweight living in the most favored circumstances is that their mothers would be responding primarily not to manifestations of problem behavior, but of growing competence.

The Role of Focus of Attention in Proximal Processes

The preceding considerations, generated by a confrontation of data with theory, call for more differentiated formulations within the existing bioecological model. Here is the first of two tentative responses to the call:

> When a proximal process involves interaction with another person, the power of the bioecological model is substantially enhanced by including in the research design a measure of the other person's *focus of attention on the particular aspects of the behavior of the subject that are presumed, on theoretical and empirical grounds, to be most closely related to the developmental outcome.*

For Drillien's study, the measure of proximal process is the mother's responsiveness, but we do not know to what particular behaviors of her baby she was responding. As already suggested, the aspect most relevant for reducing future problem behaviors might be expressions of distress. If so, a more precise conceptual and operational definition of the proximal process in this study would be the proportion of manifestations of distress that were responded to by successful efforts to reduce that distress.

However, even though in the Drillien study the mothers' focus of attention was not known, the extent of her responsiveness was still a strong predictor of the outcome. In other words, even when the theoretical and operational requirements of the bioecological model are not met in full, the results can still contribute to understanding the forces that shape human development.

A second, complementary tentative formulation derives from the definition of proximal processes as bidirectional. Stated succinctly, it posits that the preceding formulation also holds in reverse. Here it is in expanded form:

> When a proximal process involves interaction with another person, the power of the bioecological model is substantially enhanced by including in the research design a measure of the

developing person's *focus of attention on the particular aspects of the behavior of the other person that are presumed, on theoretical and empirical grounds, to be most closely related to the developmental outcome.*[8]

Proximal Processes in Solo Activities with Objects and Symbols

The foregoing considerations and complexities give added importance to those proximal processes that do not involve interpersonal interaction but instead focus on "progressively more complex reciprocal interaction with objects and symbols." These are activities that can be carried on in the absence of other persons, and therefore the magnitude and effectiveness of the proximal process are not influenced by another participant's behaviors. One would therefore expect that the person's own dispositions and resources would play a far stronger role in affecting the direction and power of the proximal process than in the case of interpersonal interaction. Furthermore, such "solo activities" significantly change the processes involved, their outcomes, and the features of the environment that become most relevant. The contrast in all three domains involves a focus on *human relationships* on the one hand, and *tasks* on the other. To understand the developmental importance of this contrast requires a fuller exposition of the features of the environment that influence proximal processes and their effects.

But before turning to this topic, we must give due recognition to three other Person characteristics that push us in the same direction. They are also so pervasive in affecting future development that their possible influence routinely needs to be considered in relation to the particular phenomenon under investigation (see Fisher, Jackson, & Villarruel, Ch. 19, this Volume). These are the familiar demographic factors of age, gender, and ethnicity. Another reason for this recommendation is that all three of these factors, although based on differing physical characteristics of the Person, also place that person in a particular environmental

niche that defines his or her position and role in society. Recognition of that ambiguity moves us to a change in focus from the developmentally relevant characteristics of the Person to their counterparts in the structure and substance of environmental Contexts as they affect developmental processes and outcomes.

The Microsystem Magnified: Activities, Relationships, and Roles

In addressing this topic, we return to the earliest formulation of the ecological model. Today, as then, "the ecological environment is conceived as a set of nested structures, each inside the other like a set of Russian dolls" (Bronfenbrenner, 1979a, p. 3). The contemporary definition of the innermost of these structures is similar, but contains additional elements that link it to the "center of gravity" of the bioecological paradigm:

> A microsystem is a pattern of activities, social roles, and interpersonal relations experienced by the developing person in a given face-to-face setting with particular physical, social, and symbolic features that invite, permit, or inhibit, engagement in sustained, progressively more complex interaction with, and activity in, the immediate environment. (Bronfenbrenner, 1994, p. 1645)[9]

We begin with consideration of the first feature of the environment introduced in the foregoing definition.

Effects of the Physical Environment on Psychological Development

The pioneering work in this sphere has been done by Theodore Wachs. In 1979, he published a seminal paper in which he showed a consistent pattern of relationships between certain features in the physical environment of infants during the first two years of life and their cognitive development over this same period. To permit examining effects over time, data were grouped into successive 3-month blocks. The results are reported in the form of correlations between characteristics of the environment at an

---

[8] In terms of research design, both of the stated formulations are best assessed through direct observation, but, given the clarity and contrasting nature of the predicted relationship, valid measures can be obtained for older children and adults through well-designed interviews, and even for young children from information provided by parents and other family members.

---

[9] The 1979 definition reads as follows: "A microsystem is a pattern of activities, roles, and interpersonal relationships experienced by the developing person in a given setting with particular physical and material characteristics."

earlier time and the developmental status of the infants at a later time.

From the complex results of the study, we focus on those physical features in the environment that were most frequently and strongly associated with cognitive functioning. These included a physically responsive environment, presence of sheltered areas, "The degree to which the physical set-up of the home permits exploration," low level of noise and confusion, and "the degree of temporal regularity" (Wachs, 1979, p. 30).

Regrettably, few researchers have followed the exciting scientific path that Wachs has been the first to chart. Taken as a whole, his original and subsequent work (Wachs, 1987a, 1987b, 1989, 1990, 1991; Wachs & Chan, 1986) suggests two areas especially worthy of further systematic investigation, in terms of both conceptualization and measurement. The first remains strictly within the realm of the physical environment per se. The second raises the issue of proximal processes as they relate to that environment.

In the first domain, Wachs's findings point to two general aspects of the physical environment that can affect the course of cognitive development—one for better, the other for worse. On the constructive side are objects and areas that invite manipulation and exploration, whereas instability, lack of clear structure, and unpredictability of events undermine the developmental process. From an ecological perspective, the existence of these countervailing forces in the physical environment leads to a new working hypothesis:

> Not only do developmentally generative features of the surroundings have greater impact in more stable settings, but they also function as a buffer against the disruptive influences of disorganizing environments.

The second issue introduces an additional component into the research design. As stipulated in Proposition I, proximal processes involve progressively more complex interactions not only with persons, but also with objects and symbols. The question therefore again arises as to what extent solitary activities involving objects and symbols—such as playing with toys, working at hobbies, reading, or fantasy play—can also foster psychological development? And to what degree does involvement in both produce synergistic developmental effects in each domain? The answers to these questions are as yet unknown, but are readily discoverable through the use of appropriate designs

that differentiate between measures of process and of environmental structure.

However, the most promising terra incognita for research on the role of the physical environment in human development may well lie beyond the realm of childhood in the world of adults. A preview of this promise appears in the successive publications of the sociologist Melvin Kohn and his colleagues (for an integrative summary, see Kohn & Slomczynski, 1990) demonstrating the powerful effect of work environments on intellectual development in adulthood. Of particular importance in this regard turns out to be the complexity of the task that a given job entails.

At the conclusion of the preceding section, we called attention to a contrast that cuts across all four domains of Process, Person, Context and Developmental Outcome. The contrast in all four domains involves a primary focus on *relationships* versus *tasks*. The findings of both Wachs and Kohn fall mainly in the latter category, whereas Drillien's data on mother-infant interaction and infants' problem behavior in lower-class families fall mainly in the former (i.e., an increase in maternal responsiveness functions as a buffer against problems in this sphere of emotional and behavioral control).

But that is not the only effect of rising levels of proximal process.

The Mother-Infant Dyad as a Context of Development

A substantial body of research indicates that such processes also foster the development of a strong emotional attachment between mother and child, which, in turn, increases the quality of future interaction between the two parties (Ainsworth, Blehar, Waters, & Wall, 1978; Bowlby, 1969, 1973). In addition, the more recent work in this sphere strongly suggests that, as a result of continuing reciprocity in the context of a close relationship, the infant begins to develop a definition of self that mirrors the form and content conveyed through the evolving patterns of interchange between mother and child (Sroufe, 1990). Thus, proximal processes become the measurable mechanisms for bringing about what in an earlier era of developmental theory and research was called *internalization*.[10] Moreover, this sequential process does double duty. Though operating

---

[10] A resurgence of theoretical and research interest in this sphere has been stimulated by the elegant studies of Kochanska and her colleagues.

primarily on the relationship side, it also furthers task performance.

According to attachment theory, the emotionally loaded patterns of interchange processes between the infant and the primary caregiver become internalized in the form of "internal working models" (Bowlby, 1969, 1973). Such working models are representations of the infant in relation to others and become the basis for the development of the self (Sroufe, 1990). Through interactions between the infant and the primary caregiver, the infant develops expectations of the caregiver's behavior and complementary beliefs about him- or herself. For example, an infant who has experienced a history of contingent responsiveness from a primary caregiver will develop a model of that caregiver as available, and expect such behavior. That child will also develop a complementary sense of self that he or she is worthy of responsive care. On the other hand, an infant who has experienced unresponsive care will develop a very different model of the relationship, expecting the caregiver to be unavailable. Such an infant is expected to develop a sense of self as unworthy of responsive care.

More generally, these internalized working models are seen as providing a framework for future interactions, resulting in a repetition of the early attachment relationship (Bowlby, 1973; Sroufe, 1990). The child seeks, responds, and interprets events based on the model that he or she has developed during infancy, and that model in turn, is adapted based on new experiences with the environment. A child who has developed a secure attachment relationship is likely to expect positive interactions with teachers, and thus elicit responsive care reminiscent of his/her caregiver's behavior. An insecure child, expecting rejection, will approach relationships with increased hostility, ultimately resulting in further experiences with rejection.

Support for these theoretical expectations comes from a number of studies. For example, the quality of the child's early attachment relationship with the mother has been found to affect the child's later functioning in social interactions with teachers and peers. Thus, early proximal processes produce proximal processes throughout development. Children judged as securely attached in infancy have been shown to approach unfamiliar peers and adults more positively and with greater acceptance (Booth, Rose-Krasnor, McKinnon, & Rubin, 1994; Main & Weston, 1981; Pastor, 1981). Furthermore, they have more positive relationships with peers and teachers in preschool (Sroufe, Fox, & Pancake, 1983; Turner, 1991). Because secure children

have developed a positive internal working model in the context of a secure attachment relationship with a primary caregiver, these children expect and elicit positive interactions with other social partners.

This body of attachment theory and research has important implications for the bioecological model. Its relevance is most succinctly conveyed in operational terms, by assessing quality of attachment in different positions in the research design; for example, as an outcome at Time 2 of proximal processes at Time 1, or, alternatively, in the form of strong versus weak contextual dyads at Time 1 moderating the power of a proximal process to influence developmental outcomes at Time 2. The latter design fits a long-standing proposition derived from the bioecological model, which reads as follows:

> In order to develop—intellectually, emotionally, socially, and morally—a child requires, for all of them, the same thing: participation in progressively more complex reciprocal activity, on a regular basis over extended periods of time with one or more other persons with whom the child develops a strong, mutual, irrational attachment,[11] and who are committed to that child's development, preferably for life. (Bronfenbrenner, 1989b, p. 5)

A second proposition goes a step further:

> The establishment and maintenance of patterns of progressively more complex interaction and emotional attachment between caregiver and child depend in substantial degree on the availability and active involvement of another adult who assists, encourages, spells off, gives status to, and expresses admiration and affection for the person caring for and engaging in joint activity with the child. (Bronfenbrenner, 1989b, p. 11)

Taken together, the foregoing propositions present an important qualifier to the general finding that children growing up in single-parent families are at greater developmental risk than those in two-parent structures. What counts most is the quality of the relationships and activities that take place within the family, and situations can occur in which, from this perspective, quality overrides quantity (Hetherington & Clingempeel, 1992).

---

[11]What is meant by the term "irrational attachment"? One answer: This is the first child you try to save in a fire.

Both propositions take on added importance because their relevance may extend beyond parental ties to close relationships with other caregivers, relatives, peers, teachers, mentors, coworkers, and supervisors. The propositions may also apply beyond childhood and adolescence to relationships in adulthood and old age. So far as we have been able to discover, these possibilities still await systematic investigation in correspondingly appropriate research designs.

BEYOND THE MICROSYSTEM

It is a basic premise of ecological systems theory that development is a function of forces emanating from multiple settings and from the relations among these settings. How can such multiple forces and their interrelations be conceptualized, and what kinds of research designs can be employed to measure their combined effects? The first stage in such an expanded model of the environment involves what in ecological systems theory is called a *mesosystem,* defined as comprising the relationships existing between two or more settings; in short, it is a system of two or more microsystems. Mesosystems and their operationalization in a research design are best conveyed through a concrete example.

Steinberg, Darling, and Fletcher (1995) reported on what they described as "an ecological journey," which was the consequence of a deliberate decision made at the outset of their research. The initial focus of investigation was on the impact of authoritative parenting on adolescents' academic achievement. They had at their disposal a range of data collected from a large multiethnic, multiclass sample encompassing several family structures. Under these circumstances, they concluded:

> [I]t made no sense at all to control for ethnicity, social class, or household composition in an attempt to isolate "pure" process. No process occurs outside of a context. And if we want to understand context, we need to take it into account, not pretend to control it away. (Steinberg et al., 1995, p. 424)

No sooner had the investigators embarked on this unconventional course than they encountered some unexpected findings. The first of these occurred not in the realm of environmental context but of developmental outcome. When they analyzed adolescents' school performance, they found that, in contrast to youth from European family backgrounds, Hispanic, African, or Asian American youth did not benefit from authoritative parenting. A first clue to this puzzle emerged when the investigators identified the values held by the different "peer crowds" (e.g., "jocks, brains, nerds, preppies, or druggies") in the nine high schools included in their sample. Their subsequent analysis revealed that 'European-American youngsters from authoritative homes are more likely to belong to peer crowds that encourage academic achievement" (Steinberg et al., 1995, p. 445).

On the basis of these and related findings, Steinberg and his colleagues formulated the following, new working hypothesis:

> There is a strong but indirect path between parenting practices and adolescent peer group affiliations . . . by fostering certain traits in their children, parents direct a child toward a particular peer group. Thus to the extent that parents can influence characteristics by which adolescents are associated by peers with a crowd, parents can "control" the type of peer group influences to which their child is exposed. . . . In essence, parents have a direct and primary impact on adolescent behavior patterns—prosocial as well as antisocial. Peer groups serve primarily to reinforce established behavior patterns or dispositions. (Steinberg et al., 1995, pp. 446–447)

But when the investigators put their new hypothesis to the test, they were confronted by yet another unexpected result:

> When we attempted to apply this model to youngsters from minority backgrounds, we were in for a shock. We found that among Black and Asian students, there was *no relation* between parenting practices and peer crowd membership.

Once again, the researchers' "multiple context model" paved the way to solving the puzzle:

> Why was there not significant relation between parenting and peer group selection among minority youth? The answer, we discovered, is that models of peer group selection that assume an open system, in which adolescents can select into any number of groups as easily as ordering food off a restaurant menu, fail to take into account the tremendous level of ethnic segregation that characterizes the social structure of most

ethnically mixed high schools in the United States. (Steinberg et al., 1995, pp. 447–448)

The authors' findings with respect to specific minority groups are of considerable interest:

Although [African American] parents score highest on our measure of parental involvement in schooling, [Black adolescents] find it much more difficult to join a peer group that encourages the same goal. (Steinberg et al. 1995, p. 449)

By contrast:

More often then not, Asian American students have no choice but to belong to a peer group that encourages and rewards academic excellence. . . . Asian Americans report the highest level of peer support for academic achievement. Interestingly, and in contrast to popular belief, [their] parents are the *least* involved in their youngsters' schooling. (Steinberg et al., 1995, p. 448)

The Expanding Ecological Universe

As if disappointed at not being confronted with yet another unexpected finding, Steinberg and his colleagues moved on to extend the ecological model to its next higher systems level—that of the *exosystem*. The formal definition of this environmental structure reads as follows:

The exosystem comprises the linkages and processes taking place between two or more settings, at least one of which does not contain the developing person, but in which events occur that indirectly influence processes within the immediate setting in which the developing person lives. (Bronfenbrenner, 1993, p. 24)

The particular exosystem that Steinberg et al. (1995) undertook to investigate was "the network of families that develops through the child's peer relationships," more specifically, "the parenting practices of their peers' parents" (p. 450). The investigators' analyses led to a series of interrelated findings; here are two examples:

Adolescents whose friends' parents are authoritative earn higher grades in school, spend more time on homework . . . have more positive perceptions of their academic competence, and report lower levels of delinquency and substance use.

Adolescents whose parents are already more authoritative appear to benefit more from membership in a peer network with other authoritatively reared youngsters than do adolescents in similar networks, but from less authoritative homes. It appears that adolescents need certain "home advantages" in order to be able to take advantage of the social capital in their social networks. (Steinberg et al., 1995, pp. 452–453)

Presumably even an ecological model can only be taken so far, but Steinberg and his colleagues appear to be trying to push it to its limits—their next analysis moves from the parental network of the adolescent's peers to the neighborhood's level of *social integration*. The measure of integration was based on a series of questions about parents' contact with their children's friends, participation in community and social activities, and ties to other families in the neighborhood. An analysis of the data revealed a "modest" effect of neighborhood integration on adolescent development. However, this finding was qualified in an important way that refocused attention on the key role played by family processes. In the author's words:

When we reran these analyses separately in neighborhoods characterized by a high proportion of effective versus non-effective parents, we find that . . . social integration only benefits adolescents whose families live in neighborhoods characterized by good parenting. Social integration into a neighborhood characterized by a high proportion of bad parents has a harmful effect on adolescents' school performance and behavior. (Steinberg et al., 1995, p. 457)

A subsequent analysis revealed a second, equally critical but not surprising qualifier: "Living in a neighborhood characterized by a high degree of social integration is only beneficial to an individual adolescent if the child's family is also socially integrated" (Steinberg et al., 1995, p. 457).

Steinberg et al.'s final analysis adds psychological substance to social structure. By aggregating information on parenting practices and attitudes within a neighborhood, he and his associates were able to calculate a measure of the degree of consensus among parents in a given neighborhood. Once again, the principal finding emerging from the analysis was conditioned by a psychological reality:

High neighborhood consensus augments the association between parenting and adolescent outcomes only when the consensus is around good parenting. . . . In other words, it is what parents agree about, not merely whether they agree, that makes the difference. (Steinberg et al., 1995, p. 458)

In this particular study, the investigators did not examine the extent to which the biopsychological characteristics of adolescents, or of their parents, influenced developmental processes and outcomes. Today, a growing body of researchers (e.g., Plomin, Reiss, Hetherington, & Howe, 1994) claims strong evidence for the view that individual and group differences in a wide range of developmental outcomes are mainly driven by differences in genetic endowment ("Ability Testing," 1992; Plomin, 1993; Plomin & Bergeman, 1991; Plomin & McClearn, 1993; Scarr, 1992). This claim is called into question, however, by alternative explanations and evidence based on the bioecological model (see also Lerner, 1995).

Nature-Nurture Reconceptualized: A Bioecological Model

The theoretical argument is set forth in a series of hypotheses, each accompanied by a corresponding research design (Bronfenbrenner & Ceci, 1994b).

Hypothesis 1. Proximal processes raise levels of effective developmental functioning, and thereby increase the proportion of individual differences attributable to actualized genetic potential for such outcomes. This means that heritability (h^2) will be higher when proximal processes are strong and lower when such processes are weak.

Hypothesis 2. Proximal processes actualize genetic potentials both for enhancing functional competence and for reducing degrees of dysfunction. Operationally, this means that as the level of proximal process is increased, indexes of competence will rise, those of dysfunction will fall, and the value of h^2 will become greater in both instances.

   1. The power of proximal processes to actualize genetic potentials for developmental competence (as assessed by an increase in h^2) will be greater in advantaged and stable environments than in those that are disadvantaged and disorganized.

   2. The power of proximal processes to buffer genetic potentials for developmental dysfunction will be greater in disadvantaged and disorganized environments than in those that are advantaged and stable.

Hypothesis 3. If persons are exposed over extended periods of time to settings that provide developmental resources and encourage engagement in proximal processes to a degree not experienced in the other settings in their lives, then the power of proximal processes to actualize genetic potentials for developmental competence will be greater for those living in more disadvantaged and disorganized environments.

To test the preceding hypotheses, Bronfenbrenner and Ceci (1994b) reviewed literature on genetic inheritance:

We have been able to find no studies of genetic inheritance in contrasting environments that also contained data on proximal processes and hence would permit a direct test of the above hypotheses. Hence, most of the available evidence is indirect.

An indirect test can be carried out only when estimates of heritability are reported for the same developmental outcome in different environments. It is fortunate that there are several studies that meet this criterion. To begin with, both Scarr-Salapatek (1971) and Fischbein (1980) found support for the prediction that values of h^2 for IQ would be greater in higher than in lower social class groups. Subsequently, a group of Norwegian investigators (Sundet, Tambs, Magnus, & Berg, 1988) undertook to clarify a series of earlier findings regarding secular trends over recent decades in heritability for measures of cognitive functioning. Using IQ scores as outcome data, the investigators found some support for results of a previous study of educational attainment (Heath et al., 1985) that had shown an increase in h^2 for twins born after 1940. The trend for their own mental test data, however was considerably weaker. The authors offered the following interpretation of the observed similarity and contrast:

This is probably due at least partly to the fact that the Norwegian government in the postwar period has offered loans to young people seeking education, thus enabling youngsters with poor parents to attend higher education. Such factors, together with a more positive attitude toward education among poor people, would tend to decrease the effect of familial environments and maximize genetic potential. (Sundet et al., 1988, p. 58)[12]

---

[12] Sundet (personal communication, March 17, 1993) reported that, in response to a preliminary version of the article by Bronfenbrenner and Ceci (1994), he and his colleagues undertook a preliminary analysis that yielded the following results: "For twins with mothers having the least education, the correlation between identical twins is .80, whereas the correlation for fraternal twins is .47. For the twins having mothers with more education, these correlations are .82 and .39, respectively. As you will

There are also a number of investigations that permit an indirect test of the hypothesized reverse pattern when the outcome is one of developmental dysfunction. For example, Jenkins and Smith (1990) found that the positive effect of a good mother-child relationship on children's problem behavior was stronger in a troubled marriage than in a harmonious one. More generally, in a recent review, Rutter and Rutter (1992) concluded that the impact of protective factors in buffering developmental disorders is greater in "circumstances of risk." (p. 56)

So much for Process, Person, and Context as shapers of development. It is time to turn to *Time*.

TIME IN THE BIOECOLOGICAL MODEL: MICRO-, MESO-, AND MACRO-

Time, a defining property of the bioecological paradigm, appears more than once in the model's multidimensional structure. Indeed, its first appearance, in the second sentence of Proposition I, may have well gone unnoticed. Following the definition of proximal processes as involving progressively more complex reciprocal interaction, the Proposition stipulates that to be effective, the interaction must occur on a "fairly regular basis."

Why this proviso? A first indication appears in the findings from Wachs's research (1979) on the features of the environment most frequently and strongly associated with individual differences in cognitive competence. Prominent among them were a physically responsive environment, presence of sheltered areas, instability and unpredictability of events, the "the degree to which the physical set-up of the home permits exploration," low level of noise and confusion, and "the degree of temporal regularity" (p. 30). As noted earlier, it follows from such findings that proximal processes cannot function effectively in environments that are unstable and unpredictable across space and time.

---

see, this yields a heritability estimate of .66 for the first group, whereas it is .86 for the second group. If I understand your [Hypothesis 2] correctly, this is in accordance with your predictions. However, the difference between the two DZ [dizygotic] correlations does not seem to reach statistical significance, although it is quite near."

It also follows that the cumulative effects at this *mesosystem* level are likely seriously to jeopardize the course of human development. One reason for expecting such an escalating effect is that, at this next higher level of environmental structure, similarly disruptive characteristics of interconnected microsystems tend to reinforce each other.

The most informative research evidence bearing on this issue comes from a longitudinal study conducted by the Finnish psychologist, Lea Pulkkinen (1983). Beginning when participating children were 8 years of age, she investigated the effect of environmental stability and change on the development of children through adolescence and young adulthood, The "steadiness" versus "unsteadiness" of family living conditions was measured by the frequency of such events as the following: the number of family moves, changes in day care or school arrangements, extent of family absence, incidence of divorce and remarriage, and altered conditions of maternal employment. Greater instability in the family environment was associated with greater submissiveness, aggressiveness, anxiety, and social problems among children in later childhood and adolescence, leading to higher risks of violence and criminal behavior in early adulthood (Pulkkinen, 1983; Pulkkinen & Saastamoinen, 1986). Moreover, the factor of stability of family living conditions appeared to be a stronger determinant of subsequent development than was the family's socioeconomic status.

Analogous findings for the contemporary American scene were obtained by Moorehouse (1986) in a study of how stability versus change over time in the mother's work status during the child's preschool years affected patterns of mother-child communication, and how these patterns in turn influenced the child's achievement and social behavior in the first year of school. A key analysis involved a comparison between mothers who had maintained the same employment status over the period of the study, and those who had changed in either direction: that is, to working more hours, fewer hours, or none at all. The results revealed that significant effects of work status were pronounced only in the group that had changed their working status. Although the disruptive impact was greatest among those mothers who had moved into full-time employment, it was still present even for those who had reduced their working hours or had left the labor force. Moorehouse concluded that "instability, on the whole, is associated with less favorable school outcomes than stability" (p. 103).

Within the framework of the discovery mode, we are once again at a point where a series of findings from different studies suggests yet another tentative formulation. The corollary follows:

The degree of stability, consistency, and predictability over time in any element of the systems constituting the ecology of human development is critical for the effective operation of the system in question. Extremes either of disorganization or rigidity in structure or function represent danger signs for potential psychological growth, with some intermediate degree of system flexibility constituting the optimal condition for human development. In terms of research design, this proposition points to the importance of assessing the degree of stability versus instability, with respect to characteristics of Process, Person, and Context, at each level of the ecological system.

This formulation also applies at the macrolevel to the dimension of Time, both during the individual's life course, and through the historical period in which the person has lived (see Proposition II). It was this observation that gave rise to the first systematic formulation of what was to become the ecological model of human development. The formulation appeared almost four decades ago in an article entitled "Socialization and Social Class through Time and Space" (Bronfenbrenner, 1958). In that article, Bronfenbrenner reanalyzed what appeared to be contradictory findings on social class differences in patterns and outcomes of child rearing. The analysis reveals that when the obtained results were reorganized in terms of the years in which the data were collected, the contradictory findings disappeared. Instead, there was a systematic gradual change over time over the period just after World War II until the late 1950s, with middle-class parents moving away from originally more authoritarian patterns toward greater permissiveness and lower-class families going in the opposite direction. Changes in patterns of child rearing over historical time and their effects on development have been recurring themes in Bronfenbrenner's work beginning in the late 1950s (1958) and continuing up to the present (Bronfenbrenner, 1970, 1975, 1984, 1990, 1994; Bronfenbrenner & Cranter 1982; Bronfenbrenner et al., 1996); but in terms of theoretical and empirical contributions this work pales in comparison with that of Elder, beginning with his classic study, *Children of the Great Depression* (Elder, 1974; see also Elder, Ch. 16, this Volume).

As Bronfenbrenner has noted, Elder's work on life course development played a significant role in the formulation of the original ecological model (Bronfenbrenner, 1979a, see especially pp. 266–285 and 273–285), and has exerted even greater influence on the model's subsequent evolution within this same domain (Bronfenbrenner, 1986a, 1986b, 1989, 1993, 1995).

Because Elder's contributions deservedly receive extended coverage in Chapter 16 of this Volume, we confine ourselves here to the four defining principles of life course theory as presented in their most recent formulation (Elder, in press),[13] along with implications for corresponding research designs, and examples of relevant research findings.

The first principle is that of *historical time and place,* defined by Elder as follows: *"The life course of individuals is embedded in and shaped by the historical times and events they experience over their life time."*

History is exploited as an experiment of nature. The corresponding research design compares groups similar in other respects who have been exposed, versus not exposed, to a particular historical event; for example, Elder's studies of the Great Depression (Elder, 1974); military service and actual combat in World War II and Korea (Elder, 1986; Elder, Shanahan, & Clipp, 1994); and the Iowa farm crisis (Conger & Elder, 1994; Elder, King, & Conger, 1996); urban inequality (Elder, Eccles, Ardelt, & Lord, 1995); and, Elder's most recent work, research on youth sent to the countryside during China's cultural revolution (Elder, Wu, & Jihui, 1993).

The second principle, called *timing in lives,* states that *"the developmental impact of a succession of life transitions or events is contingent on when they occur in a person's life."*

Here an appropriate research design is one that compares early versus late arrivals at a particular transition with respect to their subsequent life course. For example, Elder, Shanahan, and Clipp (1994) reanalyzed follow-up data on subjects from Terman's 1925 classic *Genetic Studies of Genius* (all subjects with very high IQs) and were able to show marked differences in subsequent adult development depending on early versus late entrance into military service during wartime. Here are some of the costs of late entry:

---

[13] For an earlier, but more comprehensive account, see Elder's Chapter 16 in this Volume.

- A higher risk of divorce and separation.
- A work life of disappointment and loss of lifetime income.
- An accelerated decline of physical health, most notably after the age of 50.

On the opposite side:

- For many men, and especially those who entered at an early age, military service was a recasting experience. It provided a bridge to greater opportunity and an impetus for developmental growth up to the middle years.

One is reminded of Brutus's fateful choice in response to Cassius's urgings:

> There is a tide in the affairs of men
> Which, taken at the flood, leads on to fortune;
> Omitted, all the voyage of their life
> Is bound in shallows and in miseries.
>
> —Shakespeare, *Julius Caesar* (IV. iii. 218–221)

The third principle, *linked lives,* asserts that *"lives are lived interdependently and social and historical influences are expressed through this network of shared relationships."* The basic research design corresponding to this principle involves examining the differential impact of historical events and role transitions on different members of the same family experiencing these same events and transitions. In a study of mother-daughter dyads in the broader historical context of the societal changes in gender roles that have taken place since World War II, Moen and Erickson (1995) offered the following concluding comment, on the basis of their statistical analysis of data across two generations:

> Conventional mothers embracing traditional gender roles may find themselves with daughters who are in the vanguard of the women's movement. Some mothers may even push their daughters to achieve what was impossible for themselves. The fact that mothers and daughters experience historical events and social changes from different vantage points means that their lives are differentially touched by them and that their perspectives may well diverge. (p. 180)

Environmental changes across historical time can produce significant developmental changes in either direction.

On the one hand, they can disrupt the timing and duration of normative transitions during the life course, thus interrupting the sequence of learning experiences that are essential for meeting societal expectations as one gets older. On the other hand, they can offer to the person new, at once more stable and more challenging opportunities that enhance psychological growth or even reverse a previously downward course (e.g., Elder's 1974 studies of effects of military enlistment on young men from poverty backgrounds).

FROM RESEARCH TO REALITY

The fourth and last of Elder's principles of life course development he calls *human agency.* It states that *"individuals construct their own life course through choices and actions they take within the opportunities and constraints of history and social circumstances."* A striking example is his finding that the young men most likely to volunteer early for service in World War II were often those who came from the most deprived circumstances, but then benefitted the most from the opportunities of training and experience that the military provided. Nevertheless, he cautions that "Not even great talent and industry can ensure life success over adversity without opportunities." (Elder, 1997).

Finally, to Elder's four principles, we add a fifth, which in effect reverses the direction of his very first principle regarding the importance of historical changes in shaping the course of human development. Simply stated, the fourth principle asserts that changes over time in the four defining properties of the bioecological model are not only products but also *producers* of historical change. To spell out the argument and evidence on which the principle is based: Periodically since the late 1950s, Bronfenbrenner together with colleagues has been publishing articles documenting changes over time in three domains: child-rearing practices; the relation of these practices to child outcomes, and in family demographics reported annually in the U.S. Census and other government publications.

The most recent of these analyses appears in a volume entitled: *The State of Americans: This Generation and the Next* (Bronfenbrenner et al., 1996). The book consists of almost 300 pages and 150 graphs, but, for present purposes, the principal findings can be summarized in ten points shown in Table 17.1. Considered as a whole, the

TABLE 17.1   Summary of Selected Findings from *The State of Americans: This Generation and the Next* Bronfenbrenner et al. (1996). New York: The Free Press.

1. Annual surveys over the past two decades reveal growing cynicism and disillusionment among American youth, reflected in a loss of faith in others, in their government, in the basic institutions of their society, and in themselves.

2. In the United States far greater percentages of youth and women are victims of homicide, with rates more than 10 times as high as those for any other developed country.

3. The young are not only likely to be the victims of murder, they are also more likely to commit it. Youth and young adults (ages 18–25) now account for the majority of those arrested for homicide.

4. The percentage of Americans in prison is four times higher than in other developed countries, and the number is rising rapidly.

5. Despite recent gains made by youth from Black families, American high school students are still far behind those from other developed countries in academic achievement. This includes the top 10% of students in each nation. The trend already threatens our productivity and capacity to compete economically in the future.

6. The United States stands in first place in the percentage of children growing up in single-parent families, which now includes over a quarter of all America's children under 6 years of age.

7. Families with children under 6, particularly single-parent mothers, are those who most seek—and desperately need—a job. But they also have the highest unemployment rates. The proportion of Black mothers working full time is much higher than that for White mothers (in 1994, 76% vs. 29%).

8. The percentage of U.S. children living in poverty today is twice as high as that for any other developed nation.

9. Among developed nations, the incomes of rich versus poor families are farthest apart in the United States. We are rapidly becoming a two-class society.

10. Two-thirds of children in poverty live in families with a working adult. Less than one-third of poor families with a young child rely solely on welfare.

We are indebted to our colleagues who, as coauthors of chapters of the volume *The State of Americans: This Generation and the Next,* provided the findings summarized in Table 17.1. Besides ourselves, they include the following: Steven J. Ceci, Helen Hembrooke, Peter McClelland, Phyllis Moen, Elaine Wethington, and Tara L. White.

findings constitute the basis for our proposed addition to Elder's four principles.

At a more general level, the research findings here presented reveal growing chaos in the lives of families, in child care settings, schools, peer groups, youth programs, neighborhoods, workplaces, and other everyday environments in which human beings live their lives. Such chaos, in turn, interrupts and undermines the formation and stability of relationships and activities that are essential for psychological growth. Moreover, many of the conditions leading to that chaos are the often unforeseen products of policy decisions made both in the private and in the public sector. Today, in both of these arenas, we are considering profound economic and social changes, some of which threaten to raise the degree of chaos to even higher and less psychologically (and biologically) tolerable levels. The most likely and earliest observed consequences of such a rise are still higher levels of youth crime and violence, teenage pregnancy and single parenthood,[14] as well as reduced school achievement, and, ultimately, a decline in the quality of our nation's human capital (Bronfenbrenner et al., 1996).

Thus, we have arrived at a point where the concerns of basic developmental science are converging with the most critical problems we face as a nation. That convergence confronts us, both as scientists and as citizens, with new challenges and opportunities.

THE BIOECOLOGICAL MODEL: A DEVELOPMENTAL ASSESSMENT

In this chapter, we have undertaken two challenging tasks, each an example of science in the discovery mode with developmental science as its subject matter. The first was to describe a next stage in the evolution of an ecological theory of human development, first introduced more than 15 years ago. The second task was unintended, but nevertheless begun, for this chapter also documents early steps in the design of a third-generation model.

As one of those early steps, we found it necessary to spell out the requirements for conducting developmental research in the discovery mode. To our knowledge, this is a first effort to do so systematically, and may therefore receive—and deserve—more criticism than any other section in the chapter. But at least readers will know what criteria we were trying to meet and will have a basis for assessing the validity of the proposed strategy as reflected in the more differentiated theoretical and operational models emerging from the successive confrontations between theory and data.

---

[14] Once again we would emphasize that the relationships and activities in which parent and child are involved can override the influence of purely demographic factors such as mother's age and family structure (p. 1015).

Among the more promising products of this effort is the demonstration of the power of *proximal processes* as the engines of development, and their systematic variation as a function of the characteristics of both *Person* and *Context.* We have also presented evidence that, in accord with specifications of the bioecologicl model, different pathways through space and time lead to different outcomes. In this regard, distinctions between two types of outcome appear especially relevant—the first between outcomes of competence versus dysfunction; the second between activities focusing primarily on interpersonal relationships versus objects and symbols. A third potentially productive contrast speaks to the question of "Who develops and who doesn't?" by identifying dispositional characteristics of the Person that are *developmentally generative* versus *developmentally disruptive.* Two additional Person characteristics deemed consequential for development are also distinguished and illustrated. The first are *resources* in terms of ability and acquired knowledge and skill. The second are *demand* characteristics that attract or encourage progressively more complex interaction. An analogous taxonomy is proposed for the quality of environments, accompanied by illustrations of their corresponding differential effects on proximal processes and outcomes. In each instance, the evolving tentative hypotheses derived from successively more differentiated formulations based on the bioecological model are accompanied by their operational analogues in terms of corresponding research designs and the findings generated by them.

The discovery process points also to the scientific need and benefit of including, in research designs for the same subjects, two different developmental outcomes that complement each other. For theoretical reasons deriving from the bioecological model, likely to be even more productive would be the inclusion in the same research design of two different, but theoretically complementary proximal processes.

Finally, in our view, the most scientifically promising formulation emerging from the discovery process documented in this chapter is easily stated, but it is also one that presents the greatest theoretical challenge:

> The four defining components of the bioecological model should be theoretically related to each other and to the developmental outcomes under investigation. This means that the choice of variables to represent each of the defining

properties should be based on explicit assumptions about their presumed interrelations.

This may seem a disappointing conclusion for so long an exposition. Perhaps even more in developmental science than in other fields, the pathways to discovery are not easy to find. The trails are not marked, there are many dead ends, the journey is far longer than expected, and at the end, little may be there. What counts is what one learns along the way and passes on to future explorers of the uncharted terrain.

ACKNOWLEDGMENTS

In preparing this chapter, we are especially grateful for the thoughtful criticisms of earlier drafts of the manuscript generously provided by the following colleagues: Jay Belsky, Rick Canfield, Nancy Darling, Glen H. Elder, Jr., Steven F. Hamilton, Kurt Lüscher, Melvin L. Kohn, Laurence Steinberg, and Sheldon H. White.

We owe particular thanks to Prof. Susan Crockenberg and her students at the University of Vermont who, in the course of a graduate seminar, carefully reviewed the penultimate draft of this chapter, and made many constructive suggestions. We have done our best to meet the high standards that they commendably set. We are also especially thankful to Phyllis Moen, Director of the Bronfenbrenner Life Course Center; to Donna Dempster McClain, Assistant Director; and to our most severe and most constructive critic, Liese Bronfenbrenner.

Finally, we wish to express gratitude to Richard M. Lerner and William Damon, the editors of this Volume and of the series as a whole, for their wise advice, encouragement, and patience; and to two superb text editors—Nancy M. Land and Charlotte Saikia.

REFERENCES

Ability testing. (1992). [Special section] *Psychological Science, 3,* 266–278.

Ainsworth, M. D., Blehar, M. C., Waters, I., & Wall, S. (1978). *Patterns of attachment: A psychological study of the Strange Situation.* Hillsdale, NJ: Erlbaum.

Allport, G. W. (1937). *Personality: A psychosocial interpretation.* New York: Holt.

Bandura, A. (1977). Self-efficacy: Toward a unifying theory of behavior change. *Psychological Review, 84,* 191–215.

Bandura, A. (1982). Self-efficacy mechanism in human agency. *American Psychologist, 37,* 122–147.

Beckwith, L., & Cohen, S. E. (1984). Home environment and cognitive competence in preterm children during the first five years. In *Home environment and early cognitive development* (pp. 235–271). New York: Academic Press.

Beckwith, L., Cohen, S. E., Kopp, C. B., Parmalee, A. H., & Marcy, T. G. (1976). *Child Development, 47,* 579–587.

Beckwith, L., Rodning, & Cohen, S. (1992). Preterm children at early adolescence and continuity and discontinuity in maternal responsiveness from infancy. *Child Development, 63,* 1198–1208.

Block, J. H., & Block, J. (1980). The role of ego-control and ego-resiliency in the organization of behavior. In W. A. Collins (Ed.), *Minnesota Symposia on Child Psychology, 13,* (pp. 39–101). Hillsdale, NJ: Erlbaum.

Block, J., Block, J. H., & Keyes, S. (1988). Longitudinally foretelling drug usage in adolescence: Early childhood personality and environmental precursors. *Child Development, 59,* 336–355.

Booth, C. L., Rose-Krasnor, L., McKinnon, J., & Rubin, K. H. (1994). Predicting social adjustment in middle childhood: The role of preschool attachment security and maternal style. *Social Development, 3*(3), 189–204.

Bowlby, J. (1969). *Attachment and loss: Vol. 1. Attachment.* New York: Basic Books.

Bowlby, J. (1973). *Attachment and loss: Vol. 2. Separation.* New York: Basic Books.

Bronfenbrenner, U. (1958). Socialization and social class through time and space. In E. E. Maccoby, T. M. Newcomb, & E. L. Hartley (Eds.), *Readings in social psychology* (pp. 400–425). New York: Holt, Rinehart and Winston.

Bronfenbrenner, U. (1970). *Children and parents* (Report of Forum 15, 241–255). Washington, DC: U.S. Government Printing Office.

Bronfenbrenner, U. (1974). Developmental research, public policy, and the ecology of childhood. *Child Development, 45,* 1–5.

Bronfenbrenner, U. (1975). Reality and research in the ecology of human development. *Proceedings of the American Philosophical Society, 119,* 439–469.

Bronfenbrenner, U. (1977a). Toward an experimental ecology of human development. *American Psychologist, 32,* 513–531.

Bronfenbrenner, U. (1977b). Lewian space and ecological substance. *Journal of Social Issues, 33,* 199–212.

Bronfenbrenner, U. (1979a). *The ecology of human development: Experiments by nature and design.* Cambridge, MA: Harvard University Press.

Bronfenbrenner, U. (1979b). Contexts of child rearing. *American Psychologist, 34,* 844–858.

Bronfenbrenner, U. (1981). *Die Oekologie der menschlichen Entwicklung.* Stuttgart, Germany: Klett-Cotta.

Bronfenbrenner, U. (1982). New images of children, families, and America. *Television and Children, 5,* 3–16.

Bronfenbrenner, U. (1986a). Recent advances in research on the ecology of human development. In R. K. Silbereisen, K. Eyferth, & G. Rudinger (Eds.), *Development as action in context: Problem behavior and normal youth development* (pp. 286–309). New York: Springer-Verlag.

Bronfenbrenner, U. (1986b, July 23). *A generation in jeopardy: America's hidden family policy.* Testimony presented to the committee on Rules and Administration, Washington, DC.

Bronfenbrenner, U. (1989a). Ecological systems theory. In R. Vasta (Ed.), *Annals of child development. Six theories of child development: Revised formulations and current issues* (pp. 187–249). London: JAI Press.

Bronfenbrenner, U. (1989b). *Who cares for children?* Paris: UNESCO.

Bronfenbrenner, U. (1989c). The ecology of the family as a context for human development: Research perspectives. *Developmental Psychology, 22,* 723–742.

Bronfenbrenner, U. (1990). Oekologische Sozialisationsforschung. In L. Kurse, C.-F. Graumann, & E.-D. Lantermann (Eds.), *Oekologische Psychologie. Ein Handbuch in Schlusselbegriffen* (pp. 76–79). Munich, Germany: Psychologie Verlags Union.

Bronfenbrenner, U. (1992). Child care in the Anglo-Saxon mode. In M. E. Lamb, K. J. Sternberg, C. P. Hwang, & A. G. Broberg (Eds.), *Child care in context* (pp. 281–291). Hillsdale, NJ: Erlbaum.

Bronfenbrenner, U. (1993). The ecology of cognitive development: Research models and fugitive findings. In R. H. Wozniak & K. Fischer (Eds.), *Scientific environments* (pp. 3–44). Hillsdale, NJ: Erlbaum.

Bronfenbrenner, U. (1994). Ecological models of human development. In T. Husen & T. N. Postlethwaite (Eds.), *International encyclopedia of education* (2nd ed.) (Vol. 3, pp. 1643–1647). Oxford, England: Pergamon Press/Elsevier Science.

Bronfenbrenner, U. (1995). Developmental ecology through space and time: A future perspective. In P. Moen, G. H. Elder, Jr., & K. Lüscher (Eds.), *Examining lives in context: Perspectives on the ecology of human development.* Washington, DC: American Psychological Association.

Bronfenbrenner, U., & Ceci, S. J. (1993). Heredity, environment and the question "How?" A new theoretical perspective for the 1990s. In R. Plomin & G. E. McClearn (Eds.), *Nature, nurture, and psychology* (pp. 313–324). Washington, DC: American Psychological Association.

Bronfenbrenner, U., & Ceci, S. J. (1994a). Nature–nurture reconceptualized: A bioecological model. *Psychological Review, 101,* 568–586.

Bronfenbrenner, U., & Ceci, S. J. (1994b). *"The Bell Curve": Are today's "New Interpreters" espousing yesterday's science?* Unpublished manuscript, Cornell University, Department of Human Development and Family Studies, Ithaca, NY.

Bronfenbrenner, U., & Crouter, A. C. (1982). Work and family through time and space. In S. Kamerman & C. D. Hayes (Eds.), *Children in a changing world* (pp. 39–83). Washington, DC: National Academy Press.

Bronfenbrenner, U., & Crouter, A. C. (1983). The evolution of environmental models in developmental research. In W. Kessen (Series Ed.) & P. H. Mussen (Vol. Ed.), *Handbook of child psychology: Vol. 1. History, theory, and methods* (4th ed., pp. 357–414). New York: Wiley.

Bronfenbrenner, U., McClelland, P., Wethington, E., Moen, P., & Ceci, S. J. (1996). *The state of Americans: This generation and the next.* New York: Free Press.

Bronfenbrenner, U., & Neville, P. R. (1994). America's children and families: An international perspective. In S. L. Kagan & B. Weissbourd (Eds.), *Putting families first* (pp. 3–27). San Francisco: Jossey-Bass.

Cohen, S. E., & Beckwith, L. (1979). Preterm infant interaction with the caregiver in the first year of life and competence at age two. *Child Development, 50,* 767–776.

Cohen, S. E., Beckwith, L., & Parmelee, A. H. (1978). Receptive language development in preterm children as related to caregiver-child interaction. *Pediatrics, 61,* 16–20.

Cohen, S. E., & Parmelee, A. H. (1983). Prediction of five-year Stanford-Binet scores in preterm infants. *Child Development, 54,* 1242–1253.

Cohen, S. E., Parmelee, A. H., Beckwith, L., & Sigman, M. (1986). *Developmental and Behavioral Pediatrics, 7,* 102–110.

Conger, R. D., & Elder, G. H., Jr. (1994). *Families in troubled times: Adapting to change in rural America.* Chicago: Aldine-de Gruyter.

Connolly, J. A., & Doyle, A. (1984). Relation of social fantasy play to social competence in preschoolers. *Developmental Psychology, 20,* 797–806.

Drillien, C. M. (1957). The social and economic factors affecting the incidence of premature birth. *Journal of Obstetrical Gynecology, British Empire, 64,* 161–184.

Drillien, C. M. (1964). *Growth and development of the prematurely born infant.* Edinburgh and London: E. & S. Livingston.

Elder, G. H., Jr. (1974). *Children of the great depression.* Chicago: University of Chicago Press.

Elder, G. H., Jr. (1986). Military times and turning points in men's lives. *Developmental Psychology, 22,* 233–245.

Elder, G. H., Jr. (1997). Life course and development. In W. Damon (Editor-in-Chief) & R. M. Lerner (Vol. Ed.), *Handbook of child psychology: Vol. 1. Theoretical models of human development* (5th ed.). New York: Wiley.

Elder, G. H., Jr. Eccles, J. S., Ardelt, M., & Lord, S. (1995). Inner city parents under economic pressure: Perspectives on the strategies of parenting. *Journal of Marriage and the Family, 57,* 771–784.

Elder, G. H., Jr., King, V., & Conger, R. D. (1996). Intergenerational continuity and changes in rural lives: Historical and developmental insights. *International Journal of Behavioral Development, 10,* 439–466.

Elder, G. H., Jr., Shanahan, M. J., & Clipp, E. C. (1994). When war comes to men's lives: Life course patterns in family, work, and health. *Psychology and Aging, 9,* 5–16.

Elder, G. H., Jr., Van Nguyen, T. V., & Caspi, A. (1985). Linking family hardship to children's lives. *Child Development, 56,* 361–375.

Elder, G. H., Jr., Wu, W., & Jihui, Y. (1993). *State-initiated change and the life course in Shanghai, China* (Unpublished project report). Chapel Hill, NC: Carolina Population Center.

Fischbein, S. (1980). IQ and social class. *Intelligence, 4,* 51–63.

Garmezy, N., & Rutter M. (1983). *Stress, coping, and development in children.* New York: McGraw-Hill.

Gottlieb, G., Wahlsten, D., & Lickliter, R. (1997). In W. Damon (Editor-in-Chief) & R. M. Lerner (Vol. Ed.), *Handbook of child psychology: Vol. 1. Theoretical models of human development* (5th ed.). New York: Wiley.

Heath, A. C., Berg, K., Eaves, L. J., Solaas, M. H., Corey, L. A., Sundet, J., & Nance, W. E. (1985). Educational policy and the heritability of educational attainment. *Nature, 314,* 734–736.

Hembrooke, H., Morris, P. A., & Bronfenbrenner, U. (1996). Poverty and the next generation. In U. Bronfenbrenner, E. Wethington, P. McClelland, S. J. Ceci, & P. Moen (Eds.),

The state of Americans: This generation and the next (pp. 150–188). New York: Free Press.

Hetherington, E. M., & Clingempeel, W. G. (1992). Coping with marital transitions. *Monographs of the Society for Research in Child Development, 57*(2/3).

Jenkins, J. M., & Smith, M. A. (1990). Factors protecting children living in disharmonious homes: Maternal reports. *Journal of the American Academy of Child and Adolescent Psychiatry, 29,* 60–69.

Kochanska, G. (1991). Socialization and temperament in the development of guilt and conscience. *Child Development, 62,* 1379–1392.

Kochanska, G. (1993). Toward a synthesis of parental socialization and child temperament in early development of conscience. *Child Development, 64,* 325–347.

Kochanska, G. (1995). Children's temperament, mother's discipline, and security of attachment: Pathways to emergent internalization. *Child Development, 66,* 597–615.

Kochanska, G., & Aksan, N. (1995). Mother-child mutually positive affect, the quality of child compliance to request and prohibitions, and maternal control as correlates of early internalization. *Child Development, 66,* 236–254.

Kochanska, G., Aksan, N., & Koenig, A. L. (1995). A longitudinal study of the roots of preschoolers' conscience: Committed compliance and emerging internalization. *Child Development, 66,* 1752–1770.

Kochanska, G., Murray, K., Jacques, T. Y., Koenig, A. L., & Vandergeest, K. A. (1996). Inhibitory control in young children and its role in emerging internalization. *Child Development, 67,* 490–507.

Kochanska, G., Padovich, D. L., & Koenig, A. L. (1996). Children's narratives about hypothetical moral dilemmas and objective measures of their conscience: Mutual relations and socialization antecedents. *Child Development, 67,* 1420–1436.

Kohn, M. L., & Slomczynski, K. M. (1990). *Social structure and self-direction: A comparative analysis of the United States and Poland.* Oxford, England: Basil Blackwell.

Langer, E. J., & Rodin, J. (1976). The effects of choice and enhanced personal responsibility for the aged: A field experiment in an institutional setting. *Journal of Personality and Social Psychology, 34,* 191–198.

Lerner, R. M. (1982). Children and adolescents as producers of their own development. *Developmental Review, 2,* 342–370.

Lerner, R. M. (1995). The limits of biological influence: Behavioral genetics as the emperor's new clothes [Review of the book *The limits of family influence*]. *Psychological Inquiry, 6,* 145–156.

Lerner, R. M., & Busch-Rossnagel, N. A. (Eds.). (1981). *Individual as producers of their development: A life-span perspective.* New York: Academic Press.

Lewin, K. (1943). Psychology and the process of group living. *Journal of Social Psychology, 17,* 113–131.

Lewin, K. (1946). Action research and minority problems. *Journal of Social Issues, 2,* 34–46.

MacDonald, K., & Parke, R. D. (1984). Bridging the gap: Parent-child play interaction and peer interactive competence. *Child Development, 55,* 1265–1277.

Main, M., & Weston, D. R. (1981). The quality of the toddler's relationship to mother and to father: Related to conflict behavior and the readiness to establish new relationships. *Child Development, 52,* 932–940.

Marrow, A. J. (1977). *The practical theorist: The life and work of Kurt Lewin.* New York: Teachers College Press.

May, M. A. (1932). The foundations of personality. In P. S. Achilles (Ed.), *Psychology at work.* New York: McGraw-Hill.

Mead, G. H. (1934). *Mind, self, and society.* Chicago: University of Chicago Press.

Moen, P., & Erickson, M. A. (1995). Linked lives: A transgenerational approach to resilience. In P. Moen, G. H. Elder, Jr., & K. Luscher (Eds.), *Examining lives in context: Perspectives on the ecology of human development* (pp. 169–210). Washington, DC: American Psychological Association.

Moorehouse, M. (1986). *The relationships among continuity in maternal employment, parent-child communicative activities, and the child's social competence.* Unpublished doctoral dissertation, Cornell University, Ithaca, NY.

Morris, P. A., Hembrooke, H., Gelbwasser, A. S., & Bronfenbrenner, U. (1996). American families: Today and tomorrow. In U. Bronfenbrenner, P. McClelland, E. Wethington, P. Moen, & S. J. Ceci (Eds.), *The state of Americans: This generation and the next* (pp. 92–149). New York: Free Press.

Pastor, D. L. (1981). The quality of the mother-infant interaction and its relationship to toddlers' initial sociability with peers. *Developmental Psychology, 17*(3), 326–335.

Plomin, R. (1993). Nature and nurture: Perspective and prospect. In R. Plomin & G. E. McClearn (Eds.), *Nature, nurture, and psychology* (pp. 459–486). Washington, DC: American Psychological Association.

Plomin, R., & Bergeman, C. S. (1991). The nature of nurture: Genetic influence on "environmental" measures. *Behavioral and Brain Sciences, 4,* 373–427.

Plomin, R., & McClearn, G. E. (Eds.). (1993). *Nature, nurture, and psychology*. Washington, DC: American Psychological Association.

Plomin, R., Reiss, D., Hetherington, E. M., & Howe, G. W. (1994), Nature and nurture: Genetic contributions to measures of the family environment. *Developmental Psychology, 30,* 32–43.

Pulkkinen, L. (1983). Finland: The search for alternatives to aggression. In A. P. Goldstein & M. Segall (Eds.), *Aggression in global perspective* (pp. 104–144). New York: Pergamon Press.

Pulkkinen, L., & Saastamoinen, M. (1986). Cross-cultural perspectives on youth violence. In S. J. Apter & A. P. Goldstein (Eds.), *Youth violence: Programs and prospects* (pp. 262–281). New York: Pergamon Press.

Riksen-Walraven, J. M. (1978). Effects of caregiver behavior on habituation rate and self-efficacy in infants. *International Journal of Behavioral Development, 1,* 105–130.

Rodin, J., & Langer, E. J. (1977). Long-term effects of a control-relevant intervention with the institutionalized aged. *Journal of Personality and Social Psychology, 35,* 897–902.

Rotter, J. (1966). Generalized expectancies for internal versus external locus of control of reinforcement. *Psychological Monographs: General and Applied, 80,* 1–28.

Rutter, M., & Rutter, M. (1992). *Developing minds: Challenge and continuity across the life span.* New York: Penguin Books.

Scarr, S. (1992). Developmental theories for the 1990s: Development and individual differences. *Child Development, 63,* 1–19.

Scarr-Salapatek, S. (1971). Race, social class, and IQ. *Science, 174,* 1285–1295.

Small, S., & Luster, T. (1990, November 27). *Youth at risk for parenthood.* Paper presented at the Creating Caring Communities Conference, Michigan State University, East Lansing.

Sroufe, L. A. (1990). An organizational perspective on the self. In D. Cicchetti & M. Beeghly (Eds.), *The self in transition: Infancy to childhood.* Chicago: University of Chicago Press.

Sroufe, L. A., Fox, N. E., & Pancake, V. R. (1983). Attachment and dependency in developmental perspective. *Child Development, 54,* 1615–1627.

Steinberg, L., Darling, N. E., & Fletcher, A. C. (1995). Authoritative parenting and adolescent adjustment: An ecological journey. In P. Moen, G. H. Elder, Jr., & K. Luscher (Eds.), *Examining lives in context: Perspectives on the ecology of human development* (pp. 423–466). Washington, DC: American Psychological Association.

Sundet, J. M., Tambs, K., Magnus, P., & Berg, K. (1988). On the question of secular trends in the heritability of intelligence test scores: A study of Norwegian twins. *Intelligence, 12,* 47–59.

Terman, L. M. (1925). *Genetic studies of genius: Vol. 1. Mental and physical traits of a thousand gifted children.* Stanford, CA: Stanford University Press.

Tobach, E. (1981). Evolutionary aspects of the activity of the organism and its development. In R. M. Lerner & N. A. Busch-Rossnagel (Eds.), *Individuals as producers of their development: A life-span perspective* (pp. 37–68). New York: Academic Press.

Tobach, E., & Schneirla, T. C. (1968). The biopsychology of social behavior of animals. In R. E. Cooke & S. Levin (Eds.), *Biologic basis of pediatric practice* (pp. 68–82). New York: McGraw-Hill.

Tulkin, S. R. (1973). Social class differences in infants' reactions to mothers' and stranger's voices. *Developmental Psychology, 8*(1), 137.

Tulkin, S. R. (1977). Social class differences in maternal and infant behavior. In P. H. Leiderman, A. Rosenfeld, & S. R. Tulkin (Eds.), *Culture and infancy* (pp. 495–537). New York: Academic Press.

Tulkin, S. R., & Cohler, B. J. (1973). Child-rearing attitudes and mother-child interaction in the first year of life. *Merrill-Palmer Quarterly, 19,* 95–106.

Tulkin, S. R., & Covitz, F. E. (1975). *Mother-infant interaction and intellectual functioning at age six.* Paper presented at the meeting of the Society for Research in Child Development, Denver.

Tulkin, S. R., & Kagan, J. (1972). Mother-child interaction in the first year of life. *Child Development, 43,* 31–41.

Turner, P. J. (1991). Relations between attachment, gender, and behavior with peers in preschool. *Child Development, 62,* 1475–1488.

Wachs, T. D. (1979). Proximal experience and early cognitive intellectual development: The physical environment. *Merrill-Palmer Quarterly, 25,* 3–42.

Wachs, T. D. (1987a). Specificity of environmental action as manifest in environmental correlates of infant's mastery motivation. *Developmental Psychology, 23,* 782–790.

Wachs, T. D. (1987b). The short-term stability of aggregated and non-aggregated measures of infant behavior. *Child Development, 58,* 796–797.

Wachs, T. D. (1989). The nature of the physical microenvironment: An expanded classification system. *Merrill-Palmer Quarterly, 35,* 399–402.

Wachs, T. D. (1990). Must the physical environment be mediated by the social environment in order to influence development: A further test. *Journal of Applied Developmental Psychology, 11,* 163–170.

Wachs, T. D. (1991). Environmental considerations in studies with non-extreme groups. In T. D. Wachs & R. Plomin (Eds.), *Conceptualization and measurement of organism-environment interaction* (pp. 44–67). Washington, DC: American Psychological Association.

Wachs, T. D., & Chan, A. (1986). Specificity of environmental actions as seen in physical and social environment correlates of three aspects of 12-month infants communication performance. *Child Development, 57,* 1464–1475.

CHAPTER 18

Life-Span Theory in Developmental Psychology

PAUL B. BALTES, ULMAN LINDENBERGER, and URSULA M. STAUDINGER

Life-span developmental psychology deals with the study of individual development (ontogenesis) from conception into old age (P. Baltes & Goulet, 1970; P. Baltes & Reese, 1984; Dixon & Lerner, 1988; Neugarten, 1969). A core assumption of life-span developmental psychology is that development is not completed at adulthood (maturity). Rather, the basic premise of life-span developmental psychology is that ontogenesis extends across the entire life course and that lifelong adaptive processes are involved. A further premise is that the concept of development can be used to organize the evidence about lifelong adaptive processes, although it is necessary to reformulate the traditional concept of development (D. Harris, 1957; Wohlwill, 1973) for this purpose.

Sequencing in the life span gives temporal priority to earlier times and events in life. Aside from this temporal order of any developmental process, however, life-span developmental researchers expect each age period of the life span (e.g., infancy, childhood, adolescence, adulthood, old age) to have its own developmental agenda; and to make some unique contribution to the organization of the past, present, and future in ontogenetic development. Moreover, life-span developmental scholars, if they focus on processes and mechanisms of mind and behavior (such as identity of self or working memory) rather than age, proceed from the assumption that these processes and mechanisms express manifestations of developmental continuity and change across the entire life span.

Psychology deals with the scientific study of mind and behavior, including practical applications that can be derived from such scientific inquiry. Within this substantive territory of psychology, the objective of life-span psychology is: (a) To offer an organized account of the overall structure and sequence of development across the life span; (b) to identify the interconnections between earlier and later developmental events and processes; (c) to delineate the factors and mechanisms which are the foundation of life-span development; and (d) to specify the biological and environmental opportunities and constraints which shape life-span development of individuals. With such information, life-span developmentalists further aspire to determine the range of possible development of individuals, to empower them to live their lives as desirably (and effectively) as possible, and to help them avoid dysfunctional and undesirable behavioral outcomes.

To this end, life-span researchers have focused on searching for models and definitions of successful (effective) development. One general approach to this topic has been to define successful development as the maximization of gains and the minimization of losses (M. Baltes & Carstensen, in press; P. Baltes, 1987; Baltes & Baltes, 1990b; Brandtstädter & Wentura, 1995; Marsiske, Lang, Baltes, & Baltes, 1995). Such an approach is consistent with the postulate that there is no development (ontogenetic change) without a loss, as there is no loss without a gain (P. Baltes, 1987; P. Baltes, Reese, & Lipsitt, 1980; Labouvie-Vief, 1982). What is considered as a gain in ontogenetic change and what is a loss, is a topic of theoretical as well as empirical inquiry. Suffice it at this point to mention that the nature of what is considered a gain and what a loss changes with age, involves objective in addition to subjective criteria, and is conditioned by theoretical predilection, cultural context, as well as historical time.

We offer one more introductory observation on the objectives of life-span developmental psychology which it shares with other developmental specialties. Methodologically speaking, the study of ontogenesis is inherently a matter of general *and* differential psychology (P. Baltes, Reese, & Nesselroade, 1988; Kreppner, 1992; R. Lerner, 1986; Weinert & Perner, 1996). Thus, life-span research and theory is intended to generate knowledge about three components of individual development: (a) Commonalities (regularities) in development; (b) inter-individual differences in development, and; (c) intra-individual plasticity in development (Anastasi, 1970; P. Baltes et al., 1980; R. Lerner, 1984; Nesselroade, 1991a, 1991b). Joint attention to each of these components of individual variability and intra-individual potential, and specification of their age-related interplays, are the conceptual and methodological foundations of the developmental enterprise. Recognizing the methodological significance of the distinction among, and subsequent theoretical integration of, commonalities in development, inter-individual differences in development, and intra-individual plasticity has been a continuing theme in life-span research and theory since its inception (Stern, 1911; Tetens, 1777).

What about the status and location of life-span developmental psychology within the territory of developmental psychology? Is life-span developmental psychology a special developmental psychology, is it the overall integrative developmental conception of ontogenesis, or is it simply one of the many orientations to the study of development (P. Baltes, 1987)? Perhaps most scholars view life-span developmental psychology as one of the specializations in the field of developmental psychology, namely, that specialization which seeks to understand the full age spectrum of ontogenesis. In this case, the lens of life-span developmental psychologists is focused on the entire life course with less consideration for the details of age-related specificities.

Life-span theory, however, can also be seen as the coordinated integration of various age-based developmental specializations into one overarching, cumulative framework of ontogenesis. Using such a life span-coordinating lens, one could argue that, if there is a general theory of ontogenetic development, it needs to be a theory that takes into account that ontogenesis extends from conception into old age. Thus, even if one is primarily interested in the study of infants and infant development, part of one's intellectual agenda requires attention to life-span development (Brim, 1976; Lipsitt, 1982; Thompson, 1988). One example relevant for infancy researchers is the interest in the sequelae of infancy, in the search for its long-term consequences. Another example is the developmental context of infancy, which includes adults as socialization agents who themselves develop. Thus, to understand infant-adult interaction, it is important to recognize that adults are not fixed personages but that they are themselves subject to developmental goals and challenges (Hetherington, Lerner, & Perlmutter, 1988; see also, Elder, this Volume).

What about the organizational frame of life-span theory? On a strategic level, there are two ways to construct life-span theory: *Person-centered (holistic)* or *function-centered.* The holistic approach proceeds from consideration of the person as a system and attempts to generate a knowledge base about life-span development by describing and connecting age periods or states of development into one overall, sequential pattern of lifetime individual development (see also, Magnusson & Stattin, Ch. 12, this Volume; Thelen & Smith, Ch. 10, this Volume). An example would be Erikson's (1959) theory of eight life-span stages. Often, this holistic approach to the life span is identified with *life-course psychology* (Bühler, 1933; see also, Elder, 1994, Ch. 16, this Volume).

The second way to construct life-span theory is to focus on a category of behavior or a function (such as perception, information processing, action control, identity, personality traits, etc.) and to characterize the life-span changes in the mechanisms and processes associated with the category of behaviors selected. An example would be the life-span comparative study of the developmental organization, operation, and transformation of working memory or fluid intelligence (Salthouse, 1991c).

To incorporate both approaches to life-span ontogenesis, the holistic person-centered and the function-centered one, the concept of *life-span developmental psychology* (P. Baltes & Goulet, 1970) was advanced. From our point of view, then, life-course psychology is a special case of life-span developmental psychology. However, this distinction between life-course and life-span developmental psychology should not be seen as categorically exclusive. It's more a matter of pragmatics and scientific history. In the history of the field, scholars closer to the social sciences, the biographical study of lives, and personality psychology have come to use the term life-course development (e.g., Bertaux & Kohli, 1984; Bühler, 1933; Caspi, 1987; Clausen, 1986; Elder, 1994; Mayer, 1986). Scholars closer to psychology, with its traditional interest in mechanisms and processes as well as the decomposition of mind and behavior into its component elements, seem to

prefer life-span developmental psychology, the term chosen when the West Virginia Conference Series on the field was initiated (Goulet & P. Baltes, 1970).

HISTORICAL INTRODUCTION

While this section may seem to speak more about the past than the present, it is important to recognize that present theoretical preferences are in part the direct result of historical contexts of science and cultural scenarios rather than of carefully elaborated theoretical arguments. And some of the current issues surrounding life-span developmental psychology and its location in the larger field of developmental psychology are difficult to appreciate unless they are seen in their historical and societal contexts (R. Lerner, 1983; Reinert, 1979; Riegel, 1973a, 1973b). For instance, how is it that, especially in North America, life-span developmental psychology is a relatively recent advent? Historically speaking, this is surprising because the life-span view of human development is not new at all but can be traced to the very origins of developmental psychology as several reviews have demonstrated (P. Baltes, 1979a, 1983; P. Baltes & Goulet, 1970; Groffmann, 1970; Hofstätter, 1938; Lehr, 1980; Reinert, 1979).

Many German developmental historians, for instance, consider Johann Nikolaus Tetens as the founder of the field of developmental psychology (Müller-Brettel & Dixon, 1990; Reinert, 1979). To Anglo-American developmentalists, however, Tetens is a relatively unknown figure. When Tetens published his two-volume monumental work on human nature and its development *(Menschliche Natur and ihre Entwicklung)* more than 200 years ago, in 1777, the scope of this first major opus covered the entire life span from birth into old age (see also, Carus, 1808, for another early contribution to the field of developmental psychology). The length and intellectual effort which Tetens devoted to all age periods of the life course was about the same. In addition, as elaborated at length by Reinert (1979) and also by P. Baltes (1979a, 1983), the content and theoretical orientation of this historical classic by Tetens included many of the current-day signatures of what has come to be known as the life-span developmental theoretical orientation. For instance, development was not only elaborated as a life-long process by Tetens, but also as a process which entails gains and losses, a process embedded in and constituted by sociocultural conditions, and as a process which is continuously refined and optimized *(vervollkommnet)* by societal change and historical transformations (see Table 18.1).

The second major early work on human development, written some 150 years ago by the Belgian Adolphe Quetelet (1835, translated in 1842 into English), continued in a similar tradition. His treatment of human qualities and abilities was entirely life-span in orientation, and because of his analysis of the dynamics between individual and historical development, Quetelet prefigured major developments in developmental methodology (P. Baltes, 1983). For instance, he anticipated the distinction between cross-sectional and longitudinal study designs as well as the need to conduct successions of age studies in order to disentangle effects of age from those of secular change and historical period (P. Baltes, 1968; Schaie, 1965; Schaie & P. Baltes, 1975).

The 1777 work of Johann Nikolaus Tetens was never translated into English. This is unfortunate because reading Tetens' deep insights into the interplay among individual, contextual, and historical factors is a humbling experience. Equally impressive are his many concrete everyday examples and analyses of phenomena of human development (for instance, in the area of memory functioning), which make clear that ontogenetic development is not simply a matter of growth but the outcome of complex and multilinear processes of adaptive transformation. Because of these consistencies between the early work of Tetens and Quetelet and modern research in life-span development, life-span

researchers like to argue that these are examples of why and how a life-span orientation spawns a particular theoretical and methodological manner of looking at human development (P. Baltes, 1987; P. Baltes et al., 1980).

Indeed, inspecting and comparing the largely forgotten Tetens (or other early heralds of developmental psychology such as F. A. Carus and Quetelet) with modern life-span theory suggests that there is a conceptual orientation toward a science of ontogenesis that emerges when considering the entire life span rather than focusing on its onset, such as on infancy or childhood. As we know from other scholarly endeavors, the point of departure can make a difference in what one finds along the way. As a result, the relative emphasis on particular age periods in the study of development has resulted in variations in theory and research. For example, how the topical and institutional territory of developmental psychology is charted today differs considerably, for instance, between German- and English-speaking countries. In German-speaking countries, developmental psychology is institutionalized in textbooks and scientific organizations as a field that covers the entire life span. Thus, for German-speaking psychologists (P. Baltes, 1983; Bühler, 1933; Grossmann, 1996; Lehr, 1980; Oerter & Montada, 1995; Thomae, 1959, 1979; Weinert, 1994a), developmental psychology never became almost synonymous with child psychology, as seems to be true for many North American developmental psychologists.

There are several reasons why German developmental psychology never lost its integrative concern for ontogenesis as life-long development. It is difficult to trace historical lines and identify major reasons for such country differences, but among them could be the disciplinary foundations from which developmental psychology arose and was nurtured. In German-speaking countries, for instance, philosophy, in addition to biology, was a major springboard. Note that at the time of the publication of Tetens' work in 1777, there was no established field of psychology as an empirical science, nor was there a science of ontogenesis grounded in the field of genetics and evolutionary biology. One dominant approach to human development, at least in continental Europe of that time, was shaped by the humanities and philosophy, and within philosophy by the tradition of the philosophy of idealism. This philosophical tradition included a strong concern for questions of optimality in human development and the role of education *(Bildung)*.

Table 18.1   Table of Contents of Tetens (1777), Vol. 2: *On the Perfectability and Development of Man*

Chapter	Title
1	On the perfectability of human psyche *(Seelennatur)* and its development in general
2	On the development of the human body
3	On the analogy between the development of the psyche (mind) and the development of the body
4	On the differences between men (humans) in their development
5	On the limits of development and the decline of psychological abilities
6	On the progressive development of the human species
7	On the relationship between optimization *(Vervollkommnung)* of man and his life contentment *(Glückseligkeit)*

Because of this close tie to philosophy and the humanities, human development in Germany was widely understood to reflect factors of education and socialization. In addition, there was also a focus on the topic of human development beyond early adulthood (Groffmann, 1970; Reinert, 1979). The widespread knowledge and discussion of essays on old age, such as the ancient texts of Cicero (44 B.C., 1744) or the then contemporary text of Grimm (1860), are examples of this 19th-century interest among German scholars in issues of development beyond early adulthood. According to these traditions, fueled primarily by philosophy and the humanities, a widely held position among German scholars was that it was within the medium of "culture" that individuals "developed." With very little biological science on "maturity" or "growth" at that time, there was no reason to assume that development should be identified with physical growth and, therefore, should stop at adolescence or early adulthood. One could argue that this productive interplay between the humanities and developmental psychology in Germany continues into the present, for instance, regarding such topics as collective-societal memory (J. Assmann, 1992) and wisdom (A. Assmann, 1994).

In contrast, the *Zeitgeist* in North America and also in some other European countries, such as England, was different when developmental psychology emerged as a speciality, around the turn of the century (1900). At that time, the newly developed fields of genetics and biological evolution (such as Darwinism) were in the forefront of ontogenetic thinking. From biology, with its maturation-based concept of growth, may have sprung the dominant American emphasis in developmental psychology on child psychology and child development. In North America, at least until the advent of social-learning and operant psychology-based theory in the 1960s (Bandura & Walters, 1963; Bijou & Baer, 1961; Reese & Lipsitt, 1970), biological conceptions of "growth" and "maturation" (D. Harris, 1957) led the organization and intellectual agenda in ideas about development.

Not surprisingly, therefore, in combination with other political and social forces, children became the primary focus of attention in North American developmental psychology. In fact, in North America the focus on childhood was so pervasive that historical accounts of developmental psychology published in the centennial birth year of American psychology (Parke, Ornstein, Rieser, & Zahn-Waxler,

1991) were entirely devoted to child and adolescent development. No mention was made of the major historical life-span scholars such as Tetens, Charlotte Bühler, or Sidney Pressey. Even Sheldon White, the author of the article on G. Stanley Hall, one of the American founders of developmental psychology who late in his career turned to adulthood and old age to complete his agenda of developmental studies (Hall, 1922), ignored this opportunity to treat ontogenesis as a life-long phenomenon. White (1992) mentioned the fact of Hall's late-life publication, but did not elaborate.

Before the life-span view of ontogenesis entered the field of developmental psychology more forcefully in North-American circles in the 1960s and 1970s (Brim & Wheeler, 1996; Erikson, 1959; Goulet & Baltes, 1970; Havighurst, 1948; Neugarten, 1969), several earlier contributions attempted to broaden developmental psychology toward a consideration of the entire life span (e.g., Hollingworth, 1927; Pressey, Janney, & Kuhlen, 1939; Sanford, 1902). In our view, these early American publications on themes of life-span development resulted not so much in redirecting developmental psychology from child psychology, but in setting the foundation for the emergence of the field of aging (gerontology). Indeed, many of the active life-span psychologists who promoted life-span thinking were closely affiliated with efforts to build a psychological science of aging (Birren, 1959; Birren & Schaie, 1996; Goulet & Baltes, 1970; Havighurst, 1948, 1973; Kuhlen, 1963; Neugarten, 1969; Riegel, 1958; Schaie, 1970; Thomae, 1959, 1979; Welford & Birren, 1965).

As a consequence, in American psychology there evolved a strong bifurcation between child developmentalists and adult developmentalists or gerontologists. One indication of this bifurcation was the creation of two relatively independent divisions concerned with ontogenesis within the American Psychological Association (Division 7: Developmental Psychology; Division 20: Maturity and Old Age, later renamed into Adult Development and Aging). This divide was also reflected in APA publications. Whereas the first developmental journal of the American Psychological Association, *Developmental Psychology,* started in 1969 as a life-span developmental publication, the introduction of *Psychology of Aging* in 1986 marked a departure from such a life-span integrative posture and regenerated separatism. In the interdisciplinary science of ontogenesis, too, age-specific organizations and journals were created, such as the journal of *Child Development* by the Society for Research in Child Development and the *Journal of Gerontology* by the Gerontological Society of America, resulting in further age segmentation.

On the one hand, the creation of a multitude of organizations and journals heralded the arrival of a comprehensive behavioral science of ontogenesis. On the other hand, for life-span developmental scholars, these age-specific creations were unfortunate events because they did not promote an integrative effort at constructing life-span theory. The only institutional exception to this trend was the formation of the *International Society for the Study of Behavioral Development* in 1969, which defined as its substantive territory the study of development at all stages of the life span. The German Hans Thomae was the leader in creating this society.

That a life-span approach became more prominent during the recent decades was dependent on several other factors and historical trends. A major factor was a concurrent concern with issues of life-span development in neighboring social-science disciplines, especially sociology. In sociology, *life-course sociology* took hold as a powerful intellectual force (Brim & Wheeler, 1966; Clausen, 1986; Elder, 1985, 1994; Featherman, 1983; Kohli, 1978; Neugarten, 1969; Riley, 1987; Riley, Johnson, & Foner, 1972; Sorenson, Weinert, & Sherrod, 1986).

Within psychology, three conditions nurtured the burgeoning of interest in life-span development (P. Baltes, 1987). First, demographically speaking, there was the fact that the population as a whole was "aging." In order to be responsive to issues of social policy and modernity, developmental psychologists were challenged to generate knowledge relevant to the lives of the fastest growing segment of the population, the group of older adults (Eisdorfer & Lawton, 1973). Meanwhile, this historical change in the demographic context of human development has been fully reflected in the organization of the American Psychological Association. Perhaps surprising to child developmentalists, the Division (20) devoted to adult development and aging has grown larger than Division 7, called developmental psychology but which, when using the focus of the work of the scholars elected to its presidency, or the scope of its primary journal as indicators, is more or less entirely devoted to the topic of development from infancy through adolescence.

The second related historical event of life-span work in the study of ontogenesis was the concurrent emergence of gerontology (aging research) as a field of specialization, with its search for the life-long precursors of aging (Birren, 1959; Birren & Schaie, 1996; Cowdry, 1939). The Gerontological Society of America, for instance, is larger than its counterpart organization, the Society for Research in Child Development. In fact, linking the study of gerontology to the study of life-span development is a critical task of current developmental theory. Are theories of development the same as theories of aging? Do we need different conceptions of ontogenesis to characterize development and aging (Welford & Birren, 1965)? For instance, does one approach deal with phenomena of growth, and the other with decline?

A third factor, and a major source of rapprochement between child developmentalists and adult developmentalists, was the "aging" of the participants and of the researchers in the several classical longitudinal studies on child development begun in the 1920s and 1930s (Caspi & Elder, 1988; Grossmann, 1996; Kagan, 1964; Kagan & Moss, 1962; Sears & Barbee, 1977; Thomae, 1959). What are the effects of child development on later life? Which childhood developmental factors are positive or risk-prone for later healthy development? These were questions that were increasingly pursued beginning in the 1970s as the children of the classical longitudinal studies reached early adulthood and midlife (P. Baltes, 1976; Eichorn, Clausen, Haan, Honzik, & Mussen, 1981; Elder, 1974). Some of these studies have even provided a basis for a better understanding of processes in the last phases of life (Block, 1971, 1981, 1993; Elder, 1985, 1986, 1994; Holahan, Sears, & Cronbach, 1995; Sears & Barbee, 1977).

Out of these developments has emerged new territory in developmental scholarship. The need for better collaboration among all age specialities of developmental scholarship, including child development, has become an imperative of current-day research in developmental psychology (Hetherington et al., 1988; Lipsitt, 1982; Rutter & Rutter, 1993; Thompson, 1988). But for good life-span theory to evolve, it takes more than courtship and mutual recognition. It takes a new effort and serious exploration of theory that—in the tradition of Tetens (1777)—has in its *primary* substantive focus the structure, sequence, and dynamics of the entire life course.

TOWARD PSYCHOLOGICAL THEORIES OF LIFE-SPAN DEVELOPMENT: FIVE LEVELS OF ANALYSIS

We will approach psychological theories of life-span development in five sequential but interrelated steps. Each step will bring us closer to specific psychological theories of life-span development. As shown in Table 18.2, we move from the distal and general to the more proximal and specific in our treatment of life-span ontogenesis. This movement also implies a movement from the metatheoretical to the more empirical.

Specifically, we consider five levels of analysis. Level 1, the most distal and general one, makes explicit the cornerstones and "norms of reaction" or "potentialities" (Brent, 1978a, 1978b; R. Lerner, 1986; Schneirla, 1957; see also, Gottlieb, Wahlsten, & Lickliter, this Volume) of life-span ontogenesis. With this approach, which is also consistent with the levels of integration notion of Schneirla, we obtain information on what we can expect about the general scope and shape of life-span development based on evolutionary, historical, and interdisciplinary views dealing with the interplay between biology and culture during ontogenesis (Asendorpf, 1996; P. Baltes & Graf, 1996).

Levels 2 and 3 bring us closer and closer to psychological theories of individual development. On these levels of analysis, while keeping the initial overall framework in mind, we shall describe, using an increasingly more fine-grained level of analysis, specific conceptions of life-span developmental psychology. We begin with a general view on the overall form of gains and losses across the life span (Level 2) followed by the description of a family of metatheoretical perspectives (Level 3). We argue that this family of metatheoretical perspectives is useful when articulating more specific theories of life-span development. On Level 4, we advance one concrete illustration of an overall life-span developmental theory, a theory which is based on the specification and coordinated orchestration of three processes: Selection, optimization, and compensation. On Level 5, we move to more molecular phenomena and functions. Specifically, we characterize life-span theory and research in such areas of psychological functioning as cognition, intelligence, personality, and the self.

We have chosen this approach—of proceeding from a broad level of analysis to more and more specific and micro levels of psychological analysis—because it illustrates one of the central premises of life-span developmental psychology, that development is embedded in a larger historical and cultural context (P. Baltes et al., 1980; Labouvie-Vief, 1982; R. Lerner, 1986; Magnusson, 1996; Riegel, 1973a). Moreover, this strategy permits us to join the early origins of life-span theory (Tetens, 1777) with present theories. Without having a good understanding of either biological evolution or societal functioning, Tetens had communicated a deep belief in the power of the past, present, and future social-cultural context on the "nature" of human development. Similarly, though at a much higher level of precision, current-day psychologists claim to have achieved new insights from studying the evolutionary precursors and cultural-social conditions of human behavior (e.g., Asendorpf, 1996; Barkow, Cosmides, & Tooby, 1992; Bateson, 1987; Cole, 1996; Cosmides & Tooby, 1989; Durham, 1991; Gigerenzer, 1996; Gottlieb, 1991, 1996; Gould, 1984; Grossmann, 1996; Hammerstein, 1996; Klix, 1993; Trevarthen, 1993). In short, there is a strong argument for the conclusion that the form of current-day ontogenesis has powerful determinants in past biological and cultural evolution. Moreover, psychological theories which are blind to evolutionary and cultural perspectives on the nature of human behavior run the risk of ignoring some of the most important sources of human behavior and its ontogeny.

Recognizing the powerful conditioning of human development by biological and cultural evolution and

Table 18.2   Toward Psychological Theories of Life-Span Development: Five Levels of Analysis

Level 1:	Biological and Cultural Evolutionary Perspectives: On the Incomplete Architecture of Human Ontogenesis and the Life-Span Developmental Dynamics between Biology and Culture
Level 2:	Dynamics of Gains and Losses: Life-Span Changes in the Relative Allocation of Resources in Development to Functions of Growth vs. Maintenance (Resilience) vs. Regulation of Loss
Level 3:	A Family of Metatheoretical Propositions about the Nature of Life-Span Development
Level 4:	An Example of a Systemic and Overall Theory of Successful Life-Span Development: Selective Optimization with Compensation
Level 5:	Life-Span Theories in Specific Functions and Domains: Intelligence, Cognition, Personality, Self

co-evolution (P. Baltes, 1991; Durham, 1990, 1991; see also, chapters by Gottlieb et al., Thelen & Smith, Ch. 10, this Volume) emphasizes that the future is not fixed either, but includes features of an open system. In other words, the future is not something we simply enter but also something that we help create and that is dependent on future genetic, environmental, and cultural conditions. Appreciating this potential of the future is especially important as we contemplate the nature of old age. Human aging, gerontologists like to argue, carries a paradoxical feature. Historically and anthropologically speaking, old age is young and, therefore, still rather underdeveloped. Thus, it is in the second half of life where the relative incompleteness of the biology- and culture-based architecture of human development becomes most conspicuous (P. Baltes, 1994, 1996, 1997; Baltes & Baltes, 1992; P. Baltes & Graf, 1996).

The Overall Architecture of Life-Span Development: A First View from the Perspectives of Biological and Cultural Co-Evolution (Level 1)

Let us now turn in our quest for understanding life-span development to the first level of analysis chosen, the overall biological and cultural architecture of life-span development (P. Baltes, 1993, 1996, 1997). The catch-phrases we use for this purpose comes from the changing dynamics between biology and culture across the life span and the associated incompleteness of the architecture of human ontogenesis.

The questions about the how and why of the role of biology (heredity) and culture (environment) have formed one of the main intellectual frames in developmental psychology (Anastasi, 1970; Asendorpf, 1996; R. Lerner, 1986; Plomin, 1994; Plomin & Thompson, 1988; Scarr, 1993). What is the role of cultural and biological factors in ontogenesis, how do they interact and condition each other? What is the "zone of development," the "norm of reaction" (Hirsch, 1970; R. Lerner, 1986; Schneirla, 1957) that we can expect to operate during ontogenesis? Based on genetic and evolution-based factors and on cultural structures, for instance, only certain pathways can be implemented during ontogenesis, and some of these are more likely to be realized than others (P. Baltes, 1987; Cole, 1996; Edelman, 1987; Edelman & Tononi, 1996; Labouvie-Vief, 1982; R. Lerner, 1986; Maciel, Heckhausen, & Baltes, 1994; Marsiske et al., 1995; Staudinger, Marsiske, & Baltes,

1995; Waddington, 1975; see also, chapter by Gottlieb et al., Ch. 5, this Volume). Despite the sizeable plasticity of homo sapiens, not everything is possible in ontogenetic development and development follows principles which make universal growth impossible.

With a view on the future and future societal changes, we need to recognize first that the overall architecture of human development is incomplete (P. Baltes, 1994, 1997; P. Baltes & Graf, 1996): The overall biological and cultural architecture of human development continues to evolve. A second insight is that what is most "undeveloped" in the gene-environment interplay is both the genetic base and the culture of old age (Baltes & Baltes, 1992; P. Baltes & Graf, 1996). While earlier age periods of the life course have a long tradition of biological and cultural co-evolution (Durham, 1991) and fine-tuning, the "anthropological tradition" of biological and cultural co-evolution for later phases of life, historically speaking, is younger. The evolutionary (biological and cultural) incompleteness of the overall architecture of the life span increases, therefore, as we move from childhood to old age.

Figure 18.1 illustrates the main lines of argument (P. Baltes, 1994, 1997). Note first that the specific form (level, shape) of the functions characterizing the overall life-span dynamics between biology and culture across the life span is not critical. What is critical is the overall direction and reciprocal relationship between these functions. Figure 18.1 identifies three such directional principles that regulate the nature of ontogenetic development.

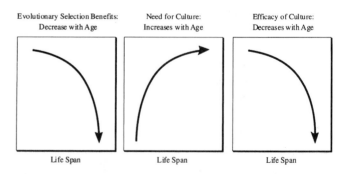

Evolutionary Selection Benefits: Decrease with Age	Need for Culture: Increases with Age	Efficacy of Culture: Decreases with Age
Life Span	Life Span	Life Span

Figure 18.1   Schematic representation of basic facts about the average dynamics between biology and culture across the life span (after Baltes, 1995). There can be much debate about the specific forms of the functions, but less about directionality.

Evolutionary Selection Benefits Decrease with Age

Figure 18.1(a) represents the first part of the argument that derives from an evolutionary perspective on the nature of the genome and its age-correlated changes in expressivity (Finch, 1990, 1996). It shows that the benefits resulting from evolutionary selection display a negative age correlation.

During evolution, the older the organism, the less the genome benefitted from the genetic advantages associated with evolutionary selection. Certainly after maturity, *with age the expressions and mechanisms of the genome lose in functional quality.* This assertion is in line with the idea that evolutionary selection was tied to the process of reproductive fitness and its midlife location in the life course. Reproductive fitness, in other words, related primarily to the context of fertility and parenting behavior, functions that typically extend from conception to adulthood. As a consequence, reproductive fitness-based evolutionary selection—which in the long run resulted in a better and better genome—operated *primarily* during the first half of life. Whatever happened later in the life span benefitted less from the optimizing power of evolutionary selection pressure. This general statement holds true even though there are "indirect" positive evolutionary selection benefits carried into and located in old age, for instance, through processes of grandparenting (Brent, 1978a; Mergler & Goldstein, 1983), coupling, or exaptation (Gould, 1984).

During evolution, this age-associated diminution of evolutionary selection benefits was further enhanced by the fact that in earlier historical times only few people reached old age. Thus, in addition to the negative correlation between age and selection pressure, evolutionary selection could not operate as frequently to begin with when it came to older individuals. Most individuals died before possible negative genetic attributes were activated or possible negative biological effects of earlier developmental events became manifest. Therefore, and quite aside from other factors of the biological processes of aging (Finch, 1990; Martin et al., 1996; Osiewacz, 1995; Yates & Benton, 1995), it has been argued that genes active at later stages of the life course are more often deleterious or dysfunctional genes than those operative at earlier times in the life span. Note in this context that not the entire genome is active in a consequential sense at a given time during ontogenesis, such as at birth, and that

there are genes (such as late-life genes; Finch, 1990) which become operative at later stages during ontogenesis. Such late-life genes can remain relatively silent until advanced age, another reason why they may have been less selected for than genes active at earlier parts of the life span.

One concrete illustration of this aging-based weakening of evolutionary selection benefits is the existence of late-life illnesses such as Alzheimer dementia. This disease typically does not become manifest until age 70. After age 70, however, it increases markedly in frequency such that among 90- to 100-year-olds Alzheimer dementia has a prevalence of about 50% (Helmchen et al., in press). Following the argument outlined in Figure 18.1(a), this disease is at least in part a late-life disease because reproductive fitness-based evolutionary pressure was unable to select against it. Martin et al. (1996) call such an outcome "selection neutrality."

There are other aspects of a biology of aging which imply an age-associated loss in biological functioning. Many of these are associated with the mechanisms of ontogenesis itself. Among the prevalent models of biological aging are wear-and-tear theories, entropy-based conceptions, as well as interpretations related to the sources of age-accumulated increases in mutations. Currently, for instance, age-associated increases in oxidative damage are proffered as a key possibility to account for aging-associated losses in biological efficacy (Martin et al., 1996).

From a life-span theory point of view, each of these conceptions of biological aging reflect a gain-loss dynamic and the costs involved in creating and maintaining life (Danner & Schröder, 1992; Finch, 1990, 1996; Martin et al., 1996; Osiewacz, 1995; Yates & Benton, 1995). Consider bone growth, a critical part of physical maturation during childhood. A long-term negative side effect of bone growth in early life may be atherosclerosis in old age. This logic of long-term negative "side" effects of growth toward maturity is a cornerstone of the so-called counterpart theory of aging (Birren, 1988, 1995; Yates & Benton, 1995). The counterpart theory of aging proffers that aging processes in part are the negative bi-products of the early life process of growth (P. Baltes & Graf, 1996). Related to this view is the genetic mechanism of *antagonist pleiotropy* (Martin et al., 1996).

These various considerations about the role of genetic factors result in a converging conclusion regarding the role of biological factors in life-span development. Where evolutionary selection and the biology of aging are concerned, the ontogenetic life span of humans displays a kind of unfinished architecture; because of this incompleteness of biological ontogenesis, biology-based negative consequences increase with age. These insights may be captured with the sentence: "Biology is not a good friend of old age." Certainly after physical maturity, the biological potential of the human organism declines. With age, the genetic material, associated genetic mechanisms, and genetic expressions become less effective and less able to generate or maintain high levels of functioning.

Age-Related Increase in Need for Culture

What about the role of culture and culture-related factors during ontogenesis? With culture, we mean here the entirety of psychological, social, material, and symbolic (knowledge-based) resources which humans developed over millenia; and which, as they are transmitted across generations, make human development as we know it possible (Cole, 1996; Damon, 1996; D'Andrade, 1995; Durham, 1990, 1991; Klix, 1993; Shweder, 1991; Valsiner & Lawrence, 1996). These cultural resources include cognitive skills, motivational dispositions, socialization strategies, physical structures, the world of economics as well that of medical and physical technology.

Figure 18.1(b) and 18.1(c) summarizes our view of the life-span dynamics associated with culture and culture-based processes. Figure 18.1(b) represents in graphic form the proposition that an age-associated increase in the "need" for cultural resources characterizes the interplay between culture and age across the life span. There are two parts to the argument for an *age-related increase in the "need" for culture.*

The first argument is that for human ontogenesis to have reached higher and higher levels of functioning, whether in physical (e.g., sports) or cultural (e.g., reading and writing) domains, there had to be a conjoint evolutionary increase in the richness and dissemination of culture (Cole, 1996; Durham, 1991; Shweder, 1991; Valsiner & Lawrence, 1996). Thus, human development the way we know it in the modern world is essentially and necessarily tied to the evolution of culture. And the further we expect human ontogenesis to extend itself into adult life and old age, the more it will be necessary for particular cultural factors and resources to emerge to make this possible. A case in point

is the historical evolution of medical knowledge, knowledge about health behavior, and the availability of economic resources to create and use medical technology.

To appreciate the power of the evolution of such culture-based resources consider what happened to average life expectancy during the 20th century in industrialized countries. It was not the genetic make-up of the individual or the population that evinced marked changes during this time. On the contrary, it was economic and technological innovations that produced significant additions to average life expectancy, from an average of about 45 years in 1900 to about 75 years in 1995. Similarly, the dramatic increase in literacy rates over the last centuries in industrialized nations were not the result of a change in the genome (that requisite evolution took place at a much earlier time many millenia ago; e.g., Klix, 1993), but above all a change in environmental contexts, cultural resources, and strategies of teaching.

The trajectory depicted in Figure 18.1(b), however, does not mean that children require little cultural input and support. Early in ontogenetic life, because the human organism is still undeveloped biologically, infants and children need a wide variety of psycho-social-material-cultural support. But in terms of overall resource structure, this support in childhood is focused on basic levels of functioning such as environmental sensory stimulation, nutrition, language, and social contact. Subsequent age stages, however, require increasingly more and more differentiated cultural resources, especially if one considers the high levels of knowledge and technology that adults need to function well in modern societies. Thus, it is primarily through the medium of more advanced levels of culture that individuals have the opportunity to continue to develop across life (Cole, 1996; D'Andrade, 1995; Shweder, 1991).

There is a second argument for the theory that, with age, the need for the supportive role of culture increases. Because of the biological weakening associated with age described in Figure 18.1(a), the "need" for culture increases even further as individuals reach old age. While individuals aspire to maintain their previous levels of functioning as they age, the biological resources available for that purpose are increasingly declining. That is, the older individuals are, the more they are in need of culture-based resources (material, social, economic, psychological) to generate and maintain high levels of functioning.

Age-Related Decrease in Efficiency of Culture

Figure 18.1(c) illustrates a further overall characteristic of the life-span developmental dynamic between culture and age. Here, the focus is on a third cornerstone of the overall architecture of the life course, that is, the efficacy or *efficiency* of cultural factors and resources. During the second half of life, and despite the advantages associated with the developmental acquisition of knowledge-based mental representations (Klix, 1992, 1993), we submit that there is an age-associated reduction in the efficiency of cultural factors. With age, and conditioned primarily by the negative biological trajectory of the life course, the relative power (effectiveness) of psychological, social, material, and cultural interventions becomes smaller and smaller, even though there likely are large inter-individual differences in onset and rate of these decreases in effectiveness (Maddox, 1987; Nelson & Dannefer, 1992; Schaie, 1996).

Take cognitive learning in old age as an example (Bäckman, Mäntylä, & Herlitz, 1990; P. Baltes, 1993; Craik & Salthouse, 1992; Kliegl, Mayr, & Krampe, 1994; Lindenberger & Baltes, 1995a; Salthouse, 1991c). The older the adult, the more time, practice, and more cognitive support it takes to attain the same learning gains. And moreover, at least in some domains of information processing, and when it comes to high levels of performance, older adults may never be able to reach the same levels of functioning as younger adults even after extensive training (Kliegl & Baltes, 1987; Kliegl, Smith, & Baltes, 1990).

We submit that the three conditions and trajectories outlined in Figure 18.1 form a robust fabric (architecture) of the life-span dynamics between biology and culture. We argue that this fabric represents a first tier of life-span theory, though psychologists often prefer more proximal and more domain-specific forms of predictive and causal analysis. However, whatever the specific content and form of a given psychological theory of life-span continuity and change, we maintain that it needs to be consistent with the frame outlined in Figure 18.1.

To illustrate further the general implications of this Level 1 analysis, consider the following examples. During the last decade we have witnessed the advancement of "growth" models of adult development and aging (e.g., Alexander & Langer, 1990; P. Baltes, Smith, & Staudinger, 1992; Commons, Richards, & Armon, 1984; Labouvie-Vief, 1995; Perlmutter, 1988; Ryff, 1984, 1989a). With the

perspectives presented, we argue that the opportunity for positive development in the second half of life would need to rest primarily in culture-based incentives and resources. Furthermore, based on the arguments outlined in Figure 18.1, any theory of life-span development which were to posit "general" positive advances across broad domains of functioning in later adulthood is probably false. On the contrary, because of the overall architecture of life-span development as we deduced it from biological and cultural evolutionary perspectives, a major theme of the second half of life must be the management and regulation of losses in biological functioning and the reduced efficiency of optimizing interventions.

Furthermore, any developmental theory that would maintain that ontogenetic development is inherently and entirely a matter of gain, of a positive change in adaptive capacity, is likely to be false as well. Rather, it is more likely that ontogenesis right from the beginning involves multilinear and multidirectional patterns of change, as shown in the life-span dynamics represented in Figure 18.1. Why? As is true for evolution, in some sense ontogenetic adaptivity and ontogenetic attainments are always local, that is, space- and time (age)-bound As we will describe later, this recognition of development as being time- and space-bound has led life-span researchers to reject any conception of development that is unilinear and based solely on the notion of growth as gain in quantity and quality of functioning (P. Baltes, 1979a, 1987; P. Baltes et al., 1980; Brandtstädter, 1984; Labouvie-Vief, 1980, 1982; Labouvie-Vief & Chandler, 1978; Uttal & Perlmutter, 1989).

The overall landscape of life-span development summarized in Figure 18.1 links life-span theory and research with other important topics in the study of human behavior as well. Take the mind-body problematic as an instance. The scenario characterized in Figure 18.1 is the illustration of what has been identified, by cultural anthropologists and philosophers (Elwert, 1992; Plessner, 1965), as the growing gap (hiatus) between mind and body as ontogenesis extends into old age. In the developmental psychology of intelligence (P. Baltes, 1993; Cattell, 1971; Horn, 1970), the age-related increase in the gap between the fluid mechanics and the crystallized pragmatics is an illustration of this scenario (see below).

The future of old age, therefore, will depend to a large measure on our ability to generate and employ culture and culture-based technology in compensating for the unfinished architecture of biology, for the age-correlated decrease in biological functioning, for the growing gap between mind and body. This age-associated increase in the gap between biological and cultural resources has many consequences. One is life-span changes in the functions of development to which resources are allocated, as discussed in the next section.

Life-Span Changes in the Relative Allocation of Resources to Distinct Functions of Development (Level 2)

Growth versus Resilience versus Regulation of Loss

Having characterized the overall landscape of human development as it has evolved through biological and cultural evolution, we now take the next step toward the specifics of a psychological theory of life-span human development. In doing so, we move toward a level of organization closer to central concepts of developmental psychology. In Table 18.2, this was designated as Level 2.

We take this next step by reflecting about functions (goals) of development. Thus, we ask to what degree the overall architecture of age-related dynamics between biology and culture outlined in Figure 18.1 prefigures pathways of development and the kind of adaptive challenges that individuals face as they move through life. One possibility is to distinguish between two functions of ontogenetic development: growth and resilience (maintenance and recovery) of functioning (Cicchetti, 1993; Garmezy, 1991; Rutter, 1987; Staudinger, Marsiske, & Baltes, 1993, 1995). Life-span researchers have added to these functions that of management or regulation of losses (P. Baltes, 1987; Brandtstädter & Baltes-Götz, 1990; Brandtstädter & Greve, 1994; Brim, 1988; Dixon & Bäckman, 1995; Staudinger et al., 1995).

Figure 18.2 displays our general life-span developmental script about the allocation of available resources for these three major adaptive tasks of growth, maintenance/recovery (resilience), and regulation of loss (P. Baltes, 1997; Staudinger et al., 1993, 1995). With the adaptive tasks of *growth,* we mean behaviors aimed at reaching higher levels of functioning or adaptive capacity. Under the heading of *maintenance* and *resilience,* we group behaviors which are aimed at maintaining levels of functioning in the face of

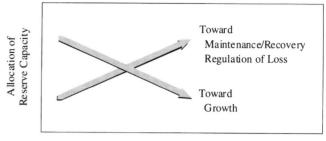

Figure 18.2   Life-span changes in the allocation of resources into distinct functions (objectives) of development: Growth, maintenance and recovery (resilience), and regulation (management) of loss (after Staudinger et al., 1995).

challenge or returning to previous levels after a loss. With the adaptive task of *regulation of loss,* we identify those behaviors which organize adequate functioning at lower levels when maintenance or recovery, for instance because of external-material or biological losses, is no longer possible. Note that for the present purpose, we have grouped together in Figure 18.2 resource allocations for the two functions of maintenance and recovery into one single category (resilience).

We proffer that there is a systematic script to these life-span changes in the relative allocation of resources. In childhood, the primary allocation of resources is directed toward growth; during adulthood, the predominant allocation is toward maintenance and recovery (resilience). In old age, more and more resources are directed toward regulation (management) of loss. In old age, few resources remain available to be allocated to growth. Such a characterization is an oversimplification as individual, domain, and contextual differences need to be taken into account. Thus, the characterization is one about relative probability.

Our general approach in this chapter on life-span theory is to exploit consistencies between levels of analysis. Therefore, note first that the scenario offered is consistent, in principle, with the life-span architecture of the dynamics between biology and culture outlined earlier (Figure 18.1). Growth, maintenance and recovery (resilience), and regulation of loss are important at all stages of the life course. However, their relative saliency and composition changes.

Let us reiterate the chief rationales underlying the life-span dynamic between growth, maintenance, and regulation of losses outlined in Figure 18.2. Four factors are critical:

1. An age-related general reduction in the amount and quality of biology-based resources as individuals move toward old age.
2. The age-correlated increase in the amount and quality of culture needed to generate higher and higher levels of growth.
3. The age-associated biology-based loss in the efficiency with which cultural resources are used.
4. The relative lack of cultural, "old age-friendly" support structures.

As alluded to before, old age is young in the sense that, historically and demographically, the life period of old age is too recent to have permitted the evolution and refinement of an age-friendly biology and culture (Baltes & Baltes, 1992; Riley & Riley, 1989).

In our view (e.g., P. Baltes, 1987; Staudinger et al., 1995; for related arguments, see also, Brandtstädter & Greve, 1994; Brim, 1992; Edelstein & Noam, 1982; Labouvie-Vief, 1982), the life-span shift in the relative allocation of biology- and culture-based resources to the functions of growth, resilience, and the management of loss is a major issue for any theory of life-span development. This is true even for those theories that, on the surface, deal only with growth or positive aging (e.g., Erikson, 1959; Perlmutter, 1988; Ryff, 1984). In Erikson's theory, for instance, the acquisition of generativity and wisdom are the positive developmental goals of adulthood. Despite the growth orientation of these constructs, note that even in Erikson's theory their attainment is inherently tied to recognizing and managing issues of generational turnover as well as of one's finitude and impending death.

In the history of life-span developmental psychology, the relative importance of resilience and the regulation of losses became more and more evident as researchers studied the everyday life context of adult and aging individuals. This was one reason that life-event theory became an early focus of researchers interested in the study of life-span development (Bandura, 1982; Brim & Ryff, 1980; Dohrenwend & Dohrenwend, 1974; Filipp, 1981; Hultsch & Plemons, 1979; Montada, Filipp, & Lerner, 1992). Furthermore, from the beginning efforts to construct a life-span

theory of developmental tasks (Havighurst, 1948, 1973), the adaptive challenges resulting from health-related issues as well as the loss of significant partners due to death in the period of adulthood and old age were highlighted.

The life-span trajectories outlined in Figure 18.2 regarding the functions of growth, resilience, and regulation of loss also emphasize the significance of the dynamics between these functions. Thus, the mastery of life often involves conflicts and competition among the three functions and objectives of human development. And in old age, the dynamic tilts more and more in the direction of management of vulnerability and loss (Baltes & Baltes, 1990b). Not surprisingly, therefore, life-span researchers have explored the notion that the occurrence and effective mastery of crises and conflicts represent not only risks, but also opportunities for new developments. Thus, dialectical conceptions of development were at the core of early work in life-span developmental theory (Datan & Reese, 1977; Riegel, 1976), as were theoretical efforts to identify tradeoffs resulting from development-enhancing and development-challenging conditions (Labouvie-Vief, 1980, 1982).

As to current-day research, one telling example of the dynamics among the functions of growth, resilience, and regulation of loss is the life-span comparative study of the interplay between autonomy and dependency in children and older adults (M. Baltes, 1995, 1996; M. Baltes & Silverberg, 1994; M. Baltes & Wahl, 1992). While the primary focus of the first half of life is the maximization of autonomy, the developmental agenda changes in old age. In old age, to deal effectively with age-based losses and to retain some independence, the productive and creative use of dependency becomes critical. According to Margret Baltes, in order for older adults to maintain autonomy in select domains of functioning, the effective exercise and use of dependent behavior is a compensatory must. By invoking dependency and support, resources are freed up for use in other domains involving personal efficacy and growth.

In sum, we submit that a further step in developing life-span theory is to recognize and specify the nature of the dynamics of resource allocation for growth, maintenance (resilience), and regulation of loss. Of particular importance is the nature of the shift in this systemic interplay and orchestration over the life course. The script changes from a primary concern with growth toward a stronger and stronger concern with maintenance and recovery (resilience) and management of losses.

Deficits as Catalysts for Progress (Growth)

The attention given to the age-related weakening of the biological foundation in Figures 18.1 and 18.2 may have suggested that the consequences of such a loss in biological quality implies also a pervasive age-related loss in behavioral functioning. In other words, that there may be no opportunity for growth at all in the second half of life in those domains where biological factors are important.

To prevent this possible misunderstanding, we describe in the following why this is not necessarily so, why deficits in biological status also can be the foundation for progress, that is, antecedents for positive changes in adaptive capacity (P. Baltes, 1987, 1991; Uttal & Perlmutter, 1989). At least since the publication of *Limits of Growth* by the Club of Rome, there has been increasing public awareness that more is not always better and that progress is possible even in the context of limitations and constraints. Similar perspectives derive from considerations of the adaptive processes in evolution as well as from consideration of the function of compensation during ontogenesis (see also, P. Baltes, 1991; P. Baltes & Graf, 1996; Brandtstädter, this Volume; Brandtstädter & Greve, 1994; Dixon & Bäckman, 1995; Durham, 1990; Elwert, 1992; Gehlen, 1956; Labouvie-Vief, 1982; LeVine, 1968). Because this view that deficits including losses can spell advances is essential to understanding the notion of development advanced by life-span developmental researchers, we present in the following one more general conceptual basis for this argument.

The most radical view of this issue is contained in the notion of *culture as compensation*. The position has been advanced, especially in the cultural sciences, that it is exactly the condition of a limitation or a loss which generates new forms of mastery and innovation. Under the influence of cultural-anthropological traditions (Brandtstädter & Wentura, 1995; Elwert, 1992; Gehlen, 1956; Klix, 1993), some contemporary behavioral scientists maintain that suboptimal biological states or imperfections are catalysts for the evolution of culture and for the advanced states achieved in human ontogeny. In this line of thinking, the human organism is by nature a "being of deficits" (Mängelwesen; Gehlen, 1956) and social culture has developed or emerged in part to deal specifically with biological deficits. Memorization strategies, for instance, were developed in part because human memory is not optimal. To

give another example: The fact that humans are biologically vulnerable regarding outside temperatures (lack of perfect thermo-regulation) is among the reasons for a highly developed body of knowledge, values, and technology about textiles and clothing.

This "deficits-breed-growth view" (P. Baltes, 1991; P. Baltes & Graf, 1996; Brandtstädter & Wentura, 1995; Uttal & Perlmutter, 1989) may account not only for cultural evolution but also play a role in ontogenesis. Thus, it is possible that when individuals reach states of increased vulnerability in old age, they invest more and more heavily in efforts that are explicitly oriented toward regulating and compensating for age-associated biological deficits, thereby generating a broad range of novel behaviors, new bodies of knowledge and values, new environmental features, and as a result, a higher level of adaptive capacity. Research on psychological compensation is a powerful illustration of this idea that deficits can be catalysts for positive changes in adaptive capacity (Bäckman & Dixon, 1992; Baltes & Baltes, 1990b; Dixon & Bäckman, 1995; Klix, 1993; Marsiske et al., 1995).

A Family of Metatheoretical Propositions about Life-Span Developmental Theory (Level 3)

Because of the complexities associated with life-span ontogenetic processes and the challenge involved in the articulation of adequate theoretical concepts, there has been much discussion in life-span work about metatheory of development (e.g., P. Baltes, 1979a, 1983; P. Baltes et al., 1980; Brim & Kagan, 1980; Labouvie-Vief, 1980, 1982; R. Lerner, 1983, 1986, 1991; Nesselroade & Reese, 1973; Overton & Reese, 1973; Reese, 1994; Riegel, 1976). Included in this discussion was a continuing dialogue about the shortcomings of extant conceptions of development as advanced primarily by child developmentalists (e.g., Collins, 1982; D. Harris, 1957). A *family of metatheoretical propositions* intended to characterize the nature of life-span development was one outcome of this extensive discussion (P. Baltes, 1979a, 1987; R. Lerner, 1983).

In the following, we attempt to update this effort at a metatheory of life-span development (Table 18.3). In doing so, we will also point out that similar metatheoretical work exists in other quarters of developmental theory, particularly in conceptual work associated with cultural psychology (Cole, 1996; Valsiner & Lawrence, 1996), evolutionary

Table 18.3   Family of Theoretical Propositions Characteristic of Life-Span Developmental Psychology (updated from P. Baltes, 1987)

Life-Span Development

Ontogenetic development is a lifelong process. No age period holds supremacy in regulating the nature of development.

Life-Span Changes in the Dynamic between Biology and Culture

With age and certainly after adulthood, there is a growing gap between biological potential and individual-cultural goals. This gap is fundamental to ontogenesis as the biological and cultural architecture of life is incomplete and inevitably results in loss of adaptive functioning and eventually death.

Life-Span Changes in Allocation of Resources to Distinct Functions of Development: Growth vs. Maintenance vs. Regulation of Loss

Ontogenetic development on a systemic level involves the coordinated and competitive allocation of resources into distinct functions: Growth, maintenance including recovery (resilience), and regulation of loss. Life-span developmental changes in the profile of functional allocation involve a shift from the allocation of resources to growth (more typical of childhood) toward an increasingly larger and larger share allocated to maintenance and management of loss.

Development as Selection (Specialization) and Selective Optimization in Adaptive Capacity

Development is inherently a process of selection and selective adaptation. Selection is due to biological, psychological, cultural, and environmental factors. Developmental advances are due to processes of optimization. Because development is selective and because of age-associated changes in potential, compensation is also part of the developmental agenda.

Development as Gain/Loss Dynamic

In ontogenetic development, there is no gain without loss, and no loss without gain. Selection and selective adaptation are space-, context-, and time-bound. Thus, selection and selective adaptation imply not only advances in adaptive capacity but also losses in adaptivity for alternative pathways and adaptive challenges. A multidimensional, multidirectional, and multifunctional conception of development results from such a perspective.

Plasticity

Much intraindividual plasticity (within-person variability) is found in psychological development. The key developmental agenda is the search for the range of plasticity and its age-associated changes and constraints.

Ontogenetic and Historical Contextualism as Paradigm

In principle, the biological and cultural architecture of human development is incomplete and subject to continuous change. Thus, ontogenetic development varies markedly by historical-cultural conditions. The mechanisms involved can be characterized in terms of the principles associated with contextualism. As an illustration: Development can be understood as the outcome of the interactions (dialectics) between three systems of biological and environmental influences: Normative age-graded, normative history-graded, and non-normative (idiosyncratic). Each of these sources evinces individual differences and, in addition, is subject to continuous change.

Toward a General and Functionalist Theory of Development: The Effective Coordination of Selection, Optimization and Compensation

On a general and functionalist level of analysis, successful development, defined as the (subjective and objective) maximization of gains and minimization of losses, can be conceived of as resulting from collaborative interplay among three components: Selection, optimization, and compensation. The ontogenetic pressure for this dynamic increases with age, as the relative incompleteness of the biology- and culture-based architecture of human development becomes more and more pronounced.

psychology (e.g., Bateson, 1996; Gottlieb, 1991, 1996), and systems theory (e.g., D. Ford, 1987; Ford & Ford, 1987; D. Ford & Lerner, 1992; Thelen, 1992; Thelen & Smith, 1994; see also, Fischer & Bidell, Gottlieb et al., Thelen & Smith, Wapner & Demick, this Volume). In the present context, however, we will emphasize the uniqueness of the positions advanced by life-span scholars. This focus will also permit us to explicate the consistency of the metatheoretical framework with the other levels of analysis presented; that is, the consistency with the life-span dynamics between biology and culture derived from evolutionary considerations as well as the age-related shift in allocation of resources from functions of predominant growth to maintenance (resilience) and management of loss.

Reformulating the Concept of Development from a Functionalist Perspective: Development as Change in Adaptive Capacity

From a life-span theory point of view, then, it was important to articulate concepts of development that go beyond unidimensional and unidirectional models, which had flourished in conjunction with the traditional biological conceptions of growth or physical maturation (Labouvie-Vief, 1982; R. Lerner, 1983; Sowarka & Baltes, 1986). In these traditional conceptions (D. Harris, 1957; Wohlwill, 1973), attributes such as qualitative change, ordered sequentiality, irreversibility, and the definition of an end-state played a critical role. Primarily by considering ontogenetic development from a functionalist perspective (Dixon & Baltes, 1986), the traditional conception of development was challenged.

Development as Selection and Selective Adaptation (Optimization).

The traditional concept of development emphasizes a *general* and *universal* development of an entity geared toward a higher level of functioning which, in addition, incorporates most if not all previously developed capacities (D. Harris, 1957; R. Lerner, 1983, 1986; Werner, 1948; S. White, 1983; Youniss, 1995). Historically, this view of ontogenetic development has been pictured as the unfolding and emergence of an entity, primarily formed from sources within that entity and by mechanisms of transformation or stage-like progression. Such a general and organismic script figured prominently among structural cognitivists and, intentionally or not, evinced strong connections to physical growth models of developmental biology (Overton & Reese, 1973).

Such a unidirectional, growth-like view of human development appeared contradictory to many findings in lifespan psychology, which included negative transfer from earlier development to later developmental outcomes, differences in rates, age-onsets, and age-offsets of developmental trajectories, multidirectional patterns of age-related change, as well as discontinuities in prediction. Figure 18.3 represents an early representation of this differentiated view of development elicited by life-span thinking and findings, which posed a challenge to traditional conceptions of development as unilinear and holistic growth (see also, Labouvie-Vief, 1980, 1982).

In their ensuing conceptual work, life-span developmentalists attempted to either modulate the traditional definitional approach to development or to offer conceptions highlighting the view that ontogenetic development was not identical with the notion of holistic and unidirectional growth, according to which all aspects of the developing system were geared toward a higher level of integration and functioning. In these efforts, life-span scholars shared the goal of reformulating the concept of development, although they differed in the degree of radicality and in specifics.

Labouvie-Vief (1980, 1982; see also, Edelstein & Noam, 1982; Pascual-Leone, 1983; Riegel, 1976), for instance, introduced new forms (stages) of systemic functioning for the period of adulthood, based on conceptions of development as adaptive transformation and structural reorganization, thereby opening a new vista on Neo-Piagetian

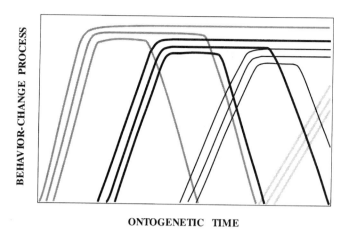

Figure 18.3 Hypothetical examples of life-span developmental processes. Developmental functions (behavior-change processes) differ in terms of onset, duration, termination, and directionality when charted in the framework of the life course. Moreover, developmental change is both quantitative and qualitative, not all developmental change is related to chronological age, and the initial direction is not always incremental (after Baltes et al., 1980).

constructivism. Baltes and his colleagues (e.g., P. Baltes, 1983, 1987; P. Baltes et al., 1980), but also others such as Brandtstädter, Featherman, and Lerner (Brandtstädter, 1984; Featherman & Lerner, 1985; Featherman, Smith, & Peterson, 1990; R. Lerner, 1983), were perhaps more radical in their departure from extant theoretical models of development and attempted to approach the conceptualization of development by a theoretical framework of neofunctionalism (Dixon & Baltes, 1986) and contextualism (R. Lerner, 1991; Magnusson, 1988, 1996). This resulted in an effort to reformulate development as *selective age-related change in adaptive capacity.* Because of the multiple influences on election including the role of individuals as selector agents (R. Lerner & Busch-Rossnagel, 1981), development as selection and selective adaptation displays many attributes. For instance, it can be active or passive, conscious or subconscious, internal or external, and continuous or discontinuous.

In the view of Baltes and his colleagues, such a neofunctionalist approach was the most open to a full consideration of the new facets of ontogenetic change (such as multidirectionality, multifunctionality, adaptive specificities, and predictive discontinuity) that life-span researchers were confronted with. At the same time, however, this conception permitted maintaining traditional growth-like conceptions of development as a special class of developmental phenomena.

This intellectual movement toward a broadly based functionalist conception of ontogenesis entailed a number of features. For instance, to reflect more accurately their understanding of the empirical evidence about life-span changes, and also drawing from alternative conceptions of ontogenesis such as canalization and selective neuronal growth (Edelman, 1987; Waddington, 1975), self-organization (Barton, 1994; Brent, 1978a, 1978b; Lewis, 1995; Maturana & Varela, 1980; Prigogine & Stengers, 1984), as well as expert systems (Chi, Glaser, & Farr, 1991; Chi, Glaser, & Rees, 1982; Ericsson & Smith, 1991; Weinert & Perner, 1996), life-span researchers began to emphasize that any process of development is not foremost the unfolding of an entity. Rather, they focused on development as ontogenetic selection from a pool of more or less constrained potentialities and the subsequent selective optimization of the entered pathways (P. Baltes, 1987, 1997; Labouvie-Vief, 1982; Marsiske et al., 1995; Siegler, 1989, 1994). As a given pathway of ontogenetic development is chosen and optimized, others are ignored or suppressed. In short, some life-span theorists ventured a new start and suggested treating ontogenetic development as a process of selective adaptation reflecting the interaction of biological, cultural, and contextual factors.

Even though life-span researchers increasingly argued for pluralism in conceptions of development, and used concepts such as selection, selective adaptation, and adaptive transformation to characterize ontogenesis, they did not want to communicate that these concepts incorporate all facets and ingredients of development. They did recognize the power of the traditional growthlike concept of development and the attractiveness of enriching this approach by new perspectives (e.g., Labouvie-Vief, 1982). However, in their arguments some life-span researchers were primarily driven by a reaction to the concept of development as indicating universal, cumulative-integrative, and sequentially-ordered movement toward a higher level of functioning and a single endstate. They felt such restricted definitions of development carried major disadvantages, if not fatal flaws, for the articulation of life-span theory; definitions that because of prominent use in child-developmental theory were difficult to overcome. In our view, it is an open question whether these alternative, more functionalist conceptions will offer a viable alternative to enrich and reformulate the traditional concept of development, or whether in the long run, the traditional concept of development will disappear as a theoretical guidepost and thereby permit a radically new approach to the concept of development itself.

Let us return to the effort to redefine development as age-related change in adaptive capacity. Selection and associated changes in adaptive capacity can be based on a variety of processes and sources which need further elaboration. (One example is presented below under the heading of selective optimization with compensation.) Some of the processes involved in selection and selective adaptation are related to genetically-based dispositions, for instance those related to age-graded physical maturation or genetically-based differences in temperament. In this context, theoretical conceptions of self-organization (Barton, 1994; Lewis, 1995; Thelen & Smith, 1994) are important ingredients. Other sources originate in environmentally-based histories of learning and the sequential structures of culture-based life opportunities, such as those associated with school curricula, professional careers, and status passages (Brim & Wheeler, 1966; Clausen, 1986; Featherman, 1983).

In any case, with the focus on selection and selective adaptation, life-span researchers were able to be more open about the pathways of life-long ontogenesis (P. Baltes, 1987; Labouvie-Vief, 1982). For instance, with this neo-functionalist approach (Dixon & Baltes, 1986) it becomes possible to treat the developing system as a multivariate and flexible one, in which differing domains and functions develop in a less than fully integrated (holistic) manner, and where trade-offs between functional advances are the rule rather than the exception.

Furthermore, by using and exploring the functionalist concept of selection, the issue of gains and losses in human development becomes prominent. Whereas the traditional concept of development neglects or even hides issues such as negative transfer, undeveloped pathways, or the long-term costs of growth (such as entropy), the concepts of selection and of selective optimization bring such questions to the foreground and require their explicit treatment. As mentioned already, in this regard life-span theory and research have joined other efforts at articulating new conceptions of development such as dynamic systems theory and theories of self-organization (P. Baltes & Graf, 1996; D. Ford, 1987; Thelen & Smith, 1994).

Development as a Gain-Loss Dynamic. A related change in emphasis advanced in life-span theory and research was on viewing development as *always* being constituted by gains and losses (P. Baltes, 1979a, 1987; P. Baltes et al., 1980; Brandtstädter, 1984; Brim, 1992; Labouvie-Vief, 1980, 1982). Aside from functionalist arguments, there were several empirical findings which gave rise to this focus.

One example important to life-span researchers was the differing life-span trajectories proposed and obtained for the fluid mechanics and crystallized pragmatics of intelligence (P. Baltes, 1993; P. Baltes & Schaie, 1976; Cattell, 1971; Horn, 1970; Horn & Hofer, 1992; Schaie, 1996). Very much in line with the life-span dynamic between biology and culture expressed in Figure 18.1, intellectual abilities that are thought to reflect the neurobiologically-based mechanics of intelligence—like working memory and fluid intelligence—typically showed normative (universal) declines in functioning beginning in middle adulthood. Conversely, intellectual abilities that primarily reflect the culture-based pragmatics of intelligence—such as professional knowledge and wisdom—may show stability or even increases into late adulthood. As to the ontogenesis of intelligence, then, gains and losses were postulated to co-exist (see also, the following section).

There were other arguments for the gain-loss dynamic view. The open systems view of the incomplete biological and cultural architecture of life-span development and the multiple ecologies of life also made it obvious that the postulation of a single endstate to development was inappropriate (P. Baltes et al., 1980; Chapman, 1988b; Labouvie-Vief, 1977, 1980, 1982). Furthermore, when considering the complex and changing nature of the criteria involved in everyday life contexts of adaptation (which, for instance, at any age and across age differ widely in the characteristics of tasks demands; e.g., P. Baltes & Willis, 1977; Berg & Calderone, 1994; Berg & Sternberg, 1985a), the capacity to move *between* levels of knowledge and skills rather than to operate at one specific developmental level of functioning appeared crucial for effective individual development. Finally, there were the issues of individual differentiation, for instance by social class and occupational careers (Dannefer, 1984; Featherman, 1983) and negative transfer associated with the evolution of any form of specialization or expertise (Ericsson & Smith, 1991), which required a departure from a monolithic orientation to development as universal growth.

Thus, as some life-span theorists considered substituting the concept of an age-related selection-based change in adaptive capacity for the concept of development (P. Baltes, 1987; Featherman & Lerner, 1985), one of the topics that motivated their agenda was the importance of viewing as fundamental to any ontogenetic change the notion of simultaneous gains and losses associated with these changes. From a functionalist point of view (Dixon & Baltes, 1986), it is more or less understood that changes in adaptive capacity can be positive or negative, that a given change in developmental capacity may imply different consequences depending on the outcome criteria and the adaptive contexts involved. Thus, the radical view was advanced that, contrary to traditional conceptions of development, there was *no gain in development without loss, and no loss without gain* (P. Baltes, 1987, 1997). Life-span researchers, then, conceive of ontogenetic development not as a monolithic process of progression and growth, but as an ongoing, changing, and interacting system of gains and losses in adaptive capacity. Throughout life, development always consists of the joint occurrence of gains and losses, both within and across domains of functioning. Such an approach does not preclude, of course, that on some level of systemic analysis (that is, considering the entirety of adaptive capacity in a fixed cultural context), ontogenetic development evinces an overall increase in adaptive capacity.

To strengthen the general case for reformulating the concept of development, life-span researchers also suggested applying this multifunctional, multidimensional, and multidirectional view of development to the field of child development (P. Baltes, 1976, 1987; Labouvie-Vief, 1982). Consider as an example the ontogenesis of language recognition and language acquisition in childhood. When one language is acquired as mother tongue, sound recognition and sound production capacity for other languages decreases, especially if such second and third languages are acquired after early childhood (Levelt, 1989).

The study of tasks requiring probability-based imperfect rather than logic-based perfect solutions is another example (P. Baltes, 1987). The more advanced the cognitive status of children (in the sense of capacity for formal-logical reasoning), the less children are able to respond to cognitive problems that are essentially not perfectly solvable and therefore require the use of maximization rather than optimization strategies. Weir (1964) conducted an early critical experiment on this question in the domain of probability-based learning. In probability learning tasks without perfect solutions, there is the seemingly paradoxical finding that very young children outperformed older children and college students. Considering adaptive trade-offs between levels (stages) of cognitive functioning, this finding becomes meaningful. It is likely that the older children and young adults achieved lower performance outcomes because they understood the experimental task as a logical problem-solving task and, therefore, continued to employ task-inappropriate but developmentally more "advanced" cognitive strategies aimed at a "perfect" optimization.

In retrospect, it is perhaps not surprising that the gain-loss dynamic was identified primarily by life-span researchers as a central topic of ontogenetic analysis. On the one hand, life-span researchers, because of their concern for longterm processes, were pushed toward recognizing the varied forms of developmental change associated with cultural evolution (Nisbett, 1980). On the other hand, on a subjective-phenomenological level, the issue of gains and losses becomes more conspicuous as one considers adult development and aging. In this phase of life, declines and losses, especially those due to biological aging, are difficult to ignore. However, as life-span researchers explored this issue more fully and in terms of functionalist conceptions of development, they were persuaded to argue that the gain-loss dynamic is universal and operates in infancy and childhood as well. Meanwhile, and not the least because of the increasing attention in human-development research given to evolutionary principles of selection and adaptation, similar views on the nature of development have become prominent in other quarters of developmental scholarship as well (e.g., Cairns & Cairns, 1994; Lewis, 1995; Magnusson, 1996; Siegler, 1994; Thelen, 1992; Thelen & Smith, 1994).

Recently, in addition to multidimensionality, multidirectionality, and multifunctionality, one additional concept has been advanced to characterize the nature of life-span changes in adaptive capacity. This concept is *equifinality*. Equifinality highlights the fact that the same developmental outcome can be reached by different means and combination of means (Kruglanski, 1996). The role of equifinality (a related notion is the concept of overdetermination) is perhaps most evident when considering the many ways by which individuals reach identical level of subjective well-being (Baltes & Baltes, 1990b; Brandtstädter & Greve, 1994; Staudinger et al., 1995). Other examples come from research on goal attainment conducted in the framework of action psychology (Brandtstädter, this Volume; Gollwitzer & Bargh, 1996). In this approach,

researchers have distinguished between two general categories of equifinality: equifinality associated with contextual (contingency) match and equifinality based on substitutability (Kruglanski, 1996). In life-span research, notions of equifinality are important, for instance, when attempting to speak of "general-purpose" mechanisms and ways to compensate, both in the domains of intelligence and personality (see later sections). The potential for developmental impact is larger if the resources acquired during ontogenesis in the sense of equifinality carry much potential for generalization and use in rather different contexts.

A Focus on Plasticity and Age-Associated Changes in Plasticity

A further development in life-span research was a strong concern with the notion of plasticity. The focus on plasticity highlights the search for the potentialities of development including its boundary conditions. Implied in this idea of plasticity is that any given developmental outcome is but one of numerous possible outcomes, and that the search for the conditions and range of ontogenetic plasticity, including its age-associated changes, is fundamental to the study of development (P. Baltes, 1987; Coper, Jänicke, & Schulze, 1986; Gollin, 1981; R. Lerner, 1984; Magnusson, 1996).

In fact, the notion of plasticity can be taken so far as to challenge the conceptual foundation of any genetically-based fixity in ontogenesis including whether it is useful to consider the existence of such phenomena as "the" norm of reaction (see also, Gottlieb et al., Ch. 5, this Volume). In a later section, we offer our view on the nature of evidence which is provided by behavior-genetic analysis. Suffice it here to state that we subscribe to an interactive and dynamic view of gene-environment relationships in the sense of conceptions of plasticity. At the same time, we believe that the human genome contains most important information regarding the structure and sequence of cultural evolution and human ontogenesis. We owe the structure and potential of human ontogenesis foremost to these genetically-based condition for life. Cultural evolution, nevertheless, involves the continuing, but never successful search to detach itself from these genetic programs and boundaries.

There were several reasons why life-span researchers increasingly moved in the direction of making the study of plasticity a cornerstone of their metatheoretical posture and empirical work. In retrospect, we emphasize two such reasons. First, as many life-span researchers did work in the field of aging, plasticity-related ideas such as modifiability were important to them, to counteract the prevailing negative stereotype of viewing aging as a period of universal decline with no opportunity for positive change (P. Baltes & Labouvie, 1973; P. Baltes & Willis, 1977; Labouvie-Vief, 1977; Neugarten, 1969; Perlmutter, 1988). Thus, when aging researchers demonstrated in intervention-oriented research the enhancement possibility of the aging mind, even in domains such as fluid intelligence and memory where decline was the norm, this was counterintuitive evidence.

Second, the use of the concept of plasticity accentuated the view that life-span development did not follow a highly constrained (fixed) course, especially where culture- and knowledge-based characteristics are concerned. On the contrary, the focus on plasticity brought into the foreground that "humans have a capacity for change across the life span from birth to death . . . (and that) the consequences of the events of early childhood are continually transformed by later experiences, making the course of human development more open than many have believed" (Brim & Kagan, 1980, p. 1).

Such an emphasis on life-long plasticity is consistent with the approach described earlier in this chapter of viewing life-span development as incomplete in biological and social-cultural architecture. The insistence on life-long plasticity in human development is also consistent with the argument advanced most prominently by social scientists that much of what happens in the life course is a direct reflection of the goals, resources, and norms of a given society and that societal contexts differ in the structure, emphases, and sequential ordering of such factors (Brim & Wheeler, 1966; Clausen, 1986; Elder, 1979, 1994; Featherman, 1983; Mayer, 1986, 1990; Riley, 1987; Sorenson et al., 1986). Social scientists also emphasize that these sociocultural differences apply both to within—and between—society characteristics (Dannefer, 1984, 1989).

As a result, the concept of plasticity became a mental script which supported the general idea of development as being more open and pluralistic than traditional views of development. For instance, this metatheoretical proposition was opposed to any characterization of the life course as an inverted U-function of growth, followed by stability, and then by decline. Specifically, the concept of plasticity highlighted the metatheoretical posture *that any course of*

development is but one of a pool of potentialities; that the "nature" of human development is not fixed; and that (aside from the fact of finitude) there is no single endstate to human development. In this search for plasticity, life-span researchers found conceptual and empirical support in the work of others, such as neurobiologically inclined investigators (Cotman, 1985; Edelman, 1987; Gollin, 1981; Rowe & Kahn, 1987), who elevated the exploration of the range and the conditions of behavioral and brain plasticity to the central question of developmental studies.

As life-span psychologists initiated systematic work on plasticity, further differentiation of the concept of plasticity was introduced. One involved the question of general versus domain-specific conceptions of plasticity (Marsiske et al., 1995). Furthermore, emphasis on individual differences and ontogenetic age changes in the extent of plasticity became prominent. Thus, the search for the range of plasticity resulted not only in evidence for malleability and plasticity; it also produced new evidence on individual and age-based constraints in the range (norm of reaction) of possible development (P. Baltes & Lindenberger, 1988; Plomin & Thompson, 1988). In work on cognitive aging, for instance, two faces of plasticity emerged. On the one hand, there was increasing evidence that older individuals continued to possess sizeable plasticity. On the other hand, there also was evidence of robust aging-related losses in plasticity (Kliegl & Baltes, 1987; Kliegl et al., 1990).

Differentiation between *baseline reserve capacity* and *developmental reserve capacity* also emerged. Baseline reserve capacity identifies the current level of plasticity available to individuals. Developmental reserve capacity is aimed at specifying what is possible in principle if optimizing interventions are employed to test future ontogenetic potential. Furthermore, major efforts were made to specify the kind of methodologies, such as developmental simulation, testing-the-limits, and cognitive engineering, that lend themselves to a full exploration of ontogenetic plasticity and its limits (P. Baltes, 1987, 1997; Baltes, Cornelius, & Nesselroade, 1979; Kliegl & Baltes, 1987; Lindenberger & Baltes, 1995b).

Ontogenetic and Historical Contextualism as Paradigm

A further key metatheoretical element of life-span developmental psychology is ontogenetic and historical contextualism. Such a contextualist view, rather than a focus on "mechanist" or "organismic" models of development

(Overton & Reese, 1973; Reese & Overton, 1970), evolved with force in the 1970s (Datan & Reese, 1977; R. Lerner, Skinner, & Sorell, 1980; Riegel, 1976) and continues into the present (P. Baltes & Graf, 1996; Elder, 1994; R. Lerner, 1991; Magnusson, 1996). This approach was similar to the evolution of ecological-contextualist perspectives offered by cultural psychology (Bronfenbrenner, 1977; Bronfenbrenner & Ceci, 1994; Cole, 1990). Related to this metatheoretical orientation of ontogenetic and historical contextualism were other theoretical positions, such as action theory (Bandura, 1982, 1986, 1995; Boesch, 1991; Brandtstädter, 1984; Chapman, 1988a; Heckhausen & Schulz, 1995), which makes equally explicit the importance of both individual action and social-contextual factors in the regulation of development.

According to contextualism and also action theory (Boesch, 1991; see also, Brandtstädter, Ch. 14, this Volume), individuals exist in contexts that create opportunities for and limitations to individual developmental pathways. Delineation of these contexts in terms of macrostructural features, like social class, ethnicity, roles, age-based passages and historical periods, is a major goal for the sociological analysis of the life course (e.g., Brim & Wheeler, 1966; Clausen, 1986; Elder, 1994, Ch. 16, this Volume; Featherman, 1983; Kohli & Meyer, 1986; Mayer, 1986; Riley, 1987; Sorenson et al., 1986).

One model that attempted to integrate sociological and psychological approaches to the structuring of developmental influences was one (P. Baltes et al., 1980) which distinguished among three sources of biological and environmental influences in order to understand the entire fabric of development-producing contexts: *Normative age-graded influences, normative history-graded influences,* and *non-normative* influences. To understand a given life course, and inter-individual differences in life-course trajectories, this model suggests that it is necessary to consider the interaction among these three classes of influences (Figure 18.4). These sources contribute to similarities in development, but also, because they exist in systematic variations, for instance by social class, genetic dispositions, and ethnicity, they also contribute to systematic inter-individual variations and subgroup-specific patterns of life-span development (P. Baltes & Nesselroade, 1984; Dannefer, 1984, 1989).

Age-graded influences are those biological and environmental aspects that, because of their dominant age

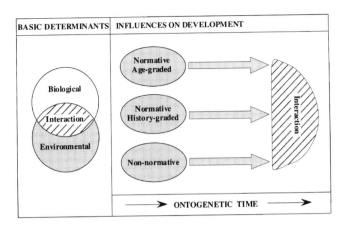

Figure 18.4 Representation of the operation of three major influence systems on life-span development: Normative age-graded, normative history-graded, and non-normative (idiosyncratic) life events. Normative in this content indexes primarily the notion of statistical patterning or generality. These influence systems vary in their interactions for different individuals and for different behaviors and therefore also generate social differentiation. As a whole, the operation of these systems produce commonalities and individual differences in ontogenesis (after Baltes et al., 1980).

correlation, shape individual development in relatively normative ways for all individuals. Consider the temporal and domain structure of life-span developmental tasks (Havighurst, 1948) and the age-based process of physical maturation as examples.

History-graded influences are those biological and environmental aspects that may make ontogenetic development different across historical cohort and periods. Consider the historical evolution of the educational and professional system as an example, or, for a more punctuated period-specific example, the advent of a war. Thus, a given ontogeny proceeds at the same time in the contexts of age-based ontogenetic time as well as historical cohort time. This position has been argued most fervently by Matilda Riley (1987). In developmental psychology, research on birth-cohort effects has made the strongest case for consideration of historical contextualism (P. Baltes, 1968; P. Baltes et al., 1979; Caspi, 1987; Elder, 1974, 1990; Nesselroade & Baltes, 1974; Schaie, 1965, 1996). The topic of historical embeddedness, and the extricating of age-based versus cohort-based differences in ontogenetic development, was also the foundation for the formulation of new developmental methodologies such as cross-sectional and longitudinal sequences (see below).

Non-normative (idiosyncratic) influences on development, finally, reflect the individual-idiosyncratic biological and environmental events that, while not frequent, can have powerful influences on ontogenetic development (Bandura, 1982; Brim & Ryff, 1980; Datan & Ginsburg, 1975; Hultsch & Plemons, 1979). The influence of these non-normative events (such as winning a lottery, losing a leg in an accident) is especially powerful because they generate conditions that are less predictable, less amenable to social control and support, and therefore may represent extreme situations of challenge (approaching testing-of-limits), not unlike the concept of *Grenzsituation* introduced by the philosopher Karl Jaspers (Kruse, 1992; Maercker, 1995).

Individual development, then, proceeds within these closely intertwined contexts of age-graded, history-graded, and non-normative life events. None of these patterns of biologically and environmentally based influences is likely to operate independently from the other. In life-span theory these three sources of influence create the contexts within which individuals act, react, organize their own development, and contribute to the development of others (R. Lerner & Busch-Rossnagel, 1981). Such a focus on contextualism also makes explicit the lack of full predictability of human development as well as the boundedness individuals experience as they engage in the effort to compose and manage their lives (Brandtstädter, 1984; R. Lerner, 1984, 1991). And finally, such a focus on contextualism places individual development in the context of the development of others. It is not surprising, therefore, that life-span researchers have easily embraced concepts such as collaborative development, collaborative cognition, or interactive minds (Baltes & Staudinger, 1996a; Resnick, Levine, & Teasley, 1991; Rogoff, 1990a).

What remains underdeveloped in life-span psychology, however, is the empirical counterpart to this theoretical position. Only recently have we witnessed research efforts to include these contextual- and social-interactive approaches in the study of interactive networks such as communities of learning (Mandl, Gruber, & Renkl, 1996), life-course convoys (Kahn & Antonucci, 1980), mentors (Bloom, 1985), cohort formations (Riley, 1987), kinship relationships (Hammerstein, 1996), cohort-related changes in education and health (Schaie, 1996) as well as the role of neighborhoods. Contextual network conditions formed by history-graded and non-normative life events (for instance,

illness-related social support groups) seem equally understudied in their contribution to the organization and regulation of life-span development (see, however, Elder, 1974, Ch. 16, this Volume).

Methodological Developments

We mentioned already that since the very early origins of life-span developmental psychology (e.g., Quetelet, 1842), the search for methodology adequate for the study of developmental processes was part of the agenda of life-span researchers (P. Baltes, Reese, & Nesselroade, 1988; Cohen & Reese, 1994; Magnusson, Bergman, Rudinger, & Törestad, 1991; Nesselroade & Reese, 1973). In our view, this concern about adequate methodology was so important to life-span researchers because their orientation toward long-term ontogenetic processes and linkages represented an extreme challenge to the goals and methods of developmental analysis. We will briefly illustrate this continuing concern of life-span researchers with issues of methodology with four examples. Each of these examples reflects one or more of the family of metatheoretical principles of life-span developmental psychology outlined in the previous section.

From Cross-Sectional to Longitudinal to Sequential Methodology. A first example is the development of methods appropriate to the study of age-related change, inter-individual differences in age-related change, and the role of historical changes in the contexts of development. Traditionally, the main designs used in developmental psychology were the cross-sectional and the longitudinal method (Nesselroade & Baltes, 1979, for historical review). The focus on the interplay between age-graded, history-graded, and non-normative factors suggested, however, that such methods were insufficient (P. Baltes, 1968; N. Ryder, 1965; Schaie, 1965).

Cross-sectional methods, on the one hand, in which different age groups (say 10-, 20-, 30-, and 40-year-olds) are compared at one historical point in time (such as in 1990), were shown to represent an inherent confound of age and generational membership (cohort). This disadvantage of the cross-sectional method exists in addition to the inability of the cross-sectional method to track trajectories of individual change. The age-cohort confound is present in cross-sectional findings because the comparison age groups "developed" in different historical periods. Longitudinal methods, on the other hand, while capturing change on the individual level directly, are restricted to the ontogenetic development of a single cohort. Thus, if historical change is relevant in the regulation of human development, longitudinal findings cannot be generalized across birth cohorts. In a certain way, and for historically sensitive phenomena, findings from longitudinal research can be "obsolete" as soon as they have been collected.

This challenge to track both historical and individual-ontogenetic change resulted in the formulation of so-called sequential methods (P. Baltes, 1968; Schaie, 1965, 1996). Figure 18.5 depicts the basic arrangement of what Schaie and Baltes (1975) have come to label as *cross-sectional* and *longitudinal sequences*. Cross-sectional sequences consist of successions of cross-sectional studies; longitudinal sequences of successions of longitudinal studies. When applied in combination, the two types of sequential designs produce, on a descriptive level, exhaustive information about age- and cohort-related change as well as about inter-individual differences in change trajectories. The cross-sectional arrangements can also be used to control for retest effects which make the interpretation of simple longitudinal results difficult (P. Baltes, Reese, & Nesselroade,

1988; Schaie, 1965, 1996). The sequential design also permits the identification of punctuated historical effects, so-called period effects. In contrast to cohort effects, which extend over longer time spans of historical change (such as effects associated with mass education or the introduction of computer technology), the concept of period effects is typically applied to more transient historical events and their consequences, such as a natural catastrophe or a war.

There is much research in human development that has demonstrated the important role of historical cohort effects. Schaie (1996), for instance, has compared both in cross-sectional and longitudinal sequences the adult age-development of several birth cohorts from 1956 into the present and reported impressive evidence that, during middle adulthood, cohort effects can be as large as age effects; moreover, Schaie's work has also shown that the directionality of age and cohort gradients can differ (see too, the next section of this chapter). Similarly, Nesselroade and Baltes (1974), in an early application of longitudinal sequences to the study of adolescence, presented evidence that personality development during adolescence in such measures as achievement and independence evinced major cohort differences over time intervals as short as two years. Their interpretation focused on the role of the Vietnam War as the critical modulator variable and its impact on American youth culture.

Meanwhile, through application of sequential methods, there is a large body of evidence on cohort effects available in developmental psychology, but especially in comparative sociology; evidence that makes explicit one of the important ingredients to life-span theory, namely, the interplay between individual development and a changing society (cf., Elder, Ch. 16, this Volume). Also important in this work is the growing recognition of when cohort effects are likely to be relevant and when not. For instance, researchers now distinguish between at least three types of cohort effects requiring different kinds of interpretative efforts (Nesselroade & Baltes, 1979):

1. Cohort as a *theoretical process* denoting historical change which alters something fundamental about the nature of ontogenesis (e.g., changing gender roles).

2. Cohort as a *dimension of quantitative generalization* (e.g., higher levels of cognitive skills due to an increase in education).

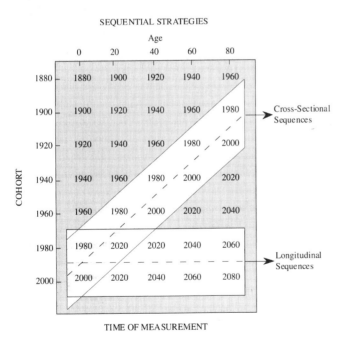

Figure 18.5 Ilustration of cross-sectional and longitudinal sequences (bottom). Modified from Baltes (1968) and Schaie (1965).

3. Cohort as *transitory disturbance* (e.g., fluctuant changes in attitudes due to singular events as often reported in opinion survey research).

Life Events and Event-History Analysis.   A second methodological development spurred on by life-span researchers concerns methods to organize and study the temporal flow, correlates, and consequences of life events. Life-course sociologists, in particular, have made major contributions to the advancement of this methodology. Among the relevant methods, models of event-history analysis and associated methods such as hazard rate analysis are especially important (Blossfeld, Hamerle, & Mayer, 1991; Blossfeld & Rower, 1995; Featherman & Lerner, 1985; Hertzog, 1996; Magnusson et al., 1991; Schaie, 1988; Willett & Singer, 1991).

As summarized in the family of metatheoretical propositions presented in Table 18.3, life-span theory and research requires a concerted effort toward the multivariate and temporal organization of the conditions and events that shape and regulate human development. The focus on historical embeddedness and contextualism is symbolic for this orientation as is the concern with non-normative and more idiosyncratic factors. Event-history analysis is designed to deal with this requirement.

The Experimental Simulation of Development.   A third strategy which was developed primarily by life-span researchers is the explicit use of simulation paradigms in the study of human development. Again, use of such an approach was enhanced by the fact that life-span ontogenetic processes are time-extensive and, therefore, difficult to study without simulation (P. Baltes & Goulet, 1971; Lindenberger & Baltes, 1995).

Table 18.4 summarizes the approach of developmental simulation. In a general sense, the experimental simulation approach is a theory-testing device that arranges for conditions thought to be relevant for the phenomenon of interest. Thus, experimental developmental simulations simulate or mimic variations which are thought to exist in real-time and real-world ontogenesis. As a research strategy, the design of developmental simulation consists of a coordinated sequence of seven steps which, however, do not need to be performed in the sequence specified. A developmental phenomenon is considered to be well understood if knowledge based on all steps is available.

Table 18.4   The Logic of Experimental Simulation in the Study of Development: A Coordinated Sequence of Steps

1. Definition and description of target developmental phenomenon to be studied.
2. Postulation of a causal hypothesis or causal structure about underlying mechanisms and contextual conditions.
3. Experimental manipulation of relevant variables in the laboratory.
4. Test of experimental data against target phenomenon: isomorphism check.
5. Reexamination of causal hypothesis or causal structure (confirmation/rejection/modification) and search for alternative explanations.
6. Evaluation of external validity: descriptive evidence.
7. Evaluation of external validity: interventive evidence.

Modified by Lindenberger and Baltes (1995) after P. Baltes et al. (1988).

In life-span research, such simulations have been used, for instance, to examine the effects of aging-associated changes in sensory input. For this purpose, auditory and visual acuity of adults was reduced to the level of older persons and then tested for cognitive performance (Dickinson & Rabbitt, 1991; Lindenberger & Baltes, 1996). Another example is a research program by Margret Baltes on the many faces of dependency and autonomy in old age (1988, 1996; M. Baltes & Wahl, 1992). In this research program, the key questions were concerned with the conditions and range of autonomy and dependence including their multifunctional characteristics and plasticity.

The opening steps (1–3 in Table 18.4) of this research on autonomy and dependency in old age conducted by Margret Baltes and her colleagues were observations that many older adults display major deficits in autonomy in the domain of self care. In addition to biological aging loss, social-environmental factors, such as negative aging stereotypes and social interactions, were assumed to play a major role in this age-associated emergence of dependent rather than independent behavior. To examine this hypothesis, a series of experimental laboratory studies were conducted to explore the effects of learning conditions (stimulus control, practice, reinforcement schedules) on self-care behavior in older adults. This work demonstrated that many aspects of older adult's dependent behaviors were found to be reversible, supporting the notion that environmental factors (e.g., behavioral contingencies) exert some influence on the aging-associated emergence of dependency or loss of autonomy.

In their research, reflected in steps 4 to 6 in Table 18.4, Margret Baltes and her colleagues observed the social conditions surrounding the occurrence of self-care in the elderly in the natural environment. Indeed, in line with their basic set of hypotheses, they observed the existence of two social-interactive scripts: A *dependency-support* script and an *independence-ignore* script. In other words, social partners of older persons in the context of self-care exhibited a high frequency of behaviors indicative of support of dependence. At the same time, these social partners ignored the occurrence of independent self-care behaviors of older persons and treated those in the same way as they responded to dependent behaviors. Research was also conducted to examine whether the same dependence-support and independence-ignore scripts existed in other settings, for instance, in homes for children or in family settings. The dominant finding was that these scripts were more typical of social interactions with older persons than with other age groups, and that with the elderly, they occurred both in nursing homes and private home contexts.

The ultimate step in this program of research (step 7) was to manipulate the relevant causal variables in the natural environment of older persons. For this purpose, the researchers (see M. Baltes, 1996; M. Baltes, Neumann, & Zank, 1994) intervened in the social environment of older persons in nursing homes. This was done by training nursing home staff to downplay the dependence-support script and move toward an independence-support script. By and large, these changes in the natural environment resulted in the expected outcome. Older persons displayed a higher level of independence in self-care.

Researchers interested in more narrow age spectrums, of course, use similar strategies of experimental simulation of development (Kuhn, 1995). However, we claim that life-span researchers are particularly dependent on the creative use of such arrangements; and, moreover, that life-span researchers are especially aware of the many methodological limitations (such as lack of measurement equivalence, isomorphy, and external validity) associated with such and with other age-comparative research. The explicit use of the term of simulation to denote these limitations underscores this awareness.

Testing-the-Limits. Our fourth example of methodological innovations involves a strategy which life-span researchers have developed to examine the scope and limits

of *plasticity* (P. Baltes, 1987; Kliegl & Baltes, 1987), another key aspect of the family of propositions advanced in life-span theory. This method is similar to efforts in child development to study the zone of proximal development, for instance, through methods of microgenetic analysis or cognitive engineering (Brown, 1982; Kliegl & Baltes, 1987; Kliegl, Smith, & Baltes, 1990; Kuhn, 1995; Siegler & Crowley, 1991).

Again, because of the long time frame of life-span ontogenesis, it is very difficult in life-span research to identify the sources and scope of intra-individual plasticity (malleability) and its age-related changes. At the same time, one key question of life-span researchers is *what is possible in principle* in human development across the life span. One example: Cognitive aging researchers attempted to answer the question of whether what we observe in old age is the reflection of a context that is dysfunctional and not supportive of the optimization of aging. One of the perennial questions of cognitive aging researchers, therefore, was whether aging losses in functions reflect experiential practice deficits rather than effects of biological aging (Baltes & Labouvie, 1973; Denney, 1984; Kausler, 1994; Salthouse, 1991c; Willis & Baltes, 1980). In other words, the central argument was that older persons may display deficits because they have less practice than younger age groups in those tasks and tests which cognitive psychologists typically study.

The resulting method has been labelled the *testing-the-limits paradigm* (Kliegl & Baltes, 1987; Lindenberger & Baltes, 1995; Schmidt, 1971). In testing-the-limits research, the goal is to "compress" time by providing for high density "developmental" experiences; and by doing so to arrange for the best conditions possible and to identify asymptotes of performance potential (plasticity). These asymptotes, obtained under putatively optimal conditions of support, are expected to estimate the upper range of the age-specific developmental potentiality comparable to the traditional notion of the upper limit of the "norm of reaction." The use of testing-the-limits procedures has generated new insights into what is and what is not possible in development. The section in this chapter on intellectual development across the life span summarizes some of the evidence.

Testing-the-limits research, however, is not only relevant for the study of long-term ontogenetic processes. It is equally relevant for other important aspects of developmental research and theory. Two examples follow to illustrate.

A first is the question of sex or gender differences in cognitive functioning. From our point of view, much of the relevant research is not suited to answer the key question: Are there biologically-based differences in various components of cognitive potential? What would be foremost necessary is to depart from simple, non-interventive comparative research and to invest scientific resources into testing-the-limits work. Such research, which admittedly is experiment- and experience-intensive at the individual level of analysis, would be based on the premise that the relevant information is knowledge about differences in asymptotic levels of functioning. Small, carefully selected samples could be used for this purpose (e.g, P. Baltes & Kliegl, 1992; Kliegl & Baltes, 1987; Lindenberger, Kliegl, & Baltes, 1992). The same perspective would hold true for another hotly debated topic; that is, research into genetic differences (R. Lerner, 1995; Plomin, 1994). Rather than investing most of the available resources into largely descriptive behavior-genetics studies, an alternative would be to expose smaller samples of participants to time-compressed experiential interventions and to search for inter-individual differences at the upper or lower levels of functioning (see also, Kruse, Lindenberger, & Baltes, 1993).

An Example of a Systemic and Overall Theory of Life-Span Development: Selective Optimization with Compensation (Level 4)

In the following, we take one further step toward a more psychological level of analysis of the nature of life-span development. For this purpose, we describe a model of development, selective optimization with compensation (SOC), which Margret Baltes, Paul Baltes, and their colleagues have developed over the last decade (M. Baltes, 1987; M. Baltes & Carstensen, in press; P. Baltes, 1987, 1997; Baltes & Baltes, 1980, 1990b; P. Baltes, Dittmann-Kohli, & Dixon, 1984; Marsiske et al., 1995; see also, Featherman et al., 1990). This model offers a systemic view of human development across the life span involving many of the features of life-span development presented in the previous sections. In fact, it is fair to say that the evolution of this model and the articulation of metatheoretical principles of life-span theory proceeded in close contact with each other. A related model was developed by Heckhausen and Schulz (Heckhausen & Schulz, 1995; Schulz & Heckhausen, 1996).

The SOC model has been developed within the context of considerations about the nature of successful development and successful aging (Baltes & Baltes, 1990a). This may not be surprising since historically, the concept of development has always been intimately linked with the search for positive functioning and improvement (S. White, 1983). To this end, presenting any general model of life-span development requires some statement about desirable ends.

In our general approach, successful development is defined as the conjoint maximization of gains (desirable goals or outcomes) and the minimization of losses (avoidance of undesirable goals or outcomes). As alluded to before, the nature of what constitutes gains and losses, and of the dynamic between gains and losses, is conditioned by cultural and personal factors as well as the lifetime of individuals. Thus, a given developmental outcome achieved through SOC can at a later ontogenetic time or in a different context be judged as dysfunctional. Moreover, what constitutes a gain and what a loss is also dependent on whether the methods used to define are subjective or objective (Baltes & Baltes, 1990b).

In our view, the SOC model in its generality is still located at a level of analysis that is distant from specific theory. Thus, as the model is applied to specific domains of psychological functioning (such as autonomy or professional expertise), it requires further specification to be derived from the knowledge base of the domain of functioning selected for application (e.g., Abraham & Hansson, 1995; M. Baltes & Lang, 1996; Featherman et al., 1990; Freund & Baltes, 1996; Marsiske et al., 1995). At the same time, however, because of this generality in formulation, the model of SOC is rather open as to its deployability and domain-specific refinement.

Definition of Selection, Optimization, and Compensation

As mentioned above, we proceed from the assumption that any process of development involves selection and selective changes in adaptive capacity (P. Baltes, 1987; Featherman et al., 1990; Marsiske et al., 1995). Selection from a potential pool of developmental trajectories makes directionality of development possible. We further assume that for selection to result in successful development (maximization of gains while minimizing losses), it needs to work in conjunction with processes of optimization and compensation.

If approached within an action-theoretical framework, the following characterizations of these three components hold:

1. *Selection* involves goals or outcomes.
2. *Optimization* involves goal-related means to achieve success (desired outcomes).
3. *Compensation* involves a response to loss in goal-relevant means in order to maintain success or desired levels of functioning (outcomes).

Figure 18.6 (Baltes & Baltes, 1990b; Marsiske et al., 1995) presents the overall framework of SOC and examples of the kind of events which we classify as selection, optimization, and compensation. An everyday example may help to clarify these distinctions, drawn from the context of aging research that we used in our early efforts at developing the SOC model (P. Baltes, 1984). When the concert pianist Arthur Rubinstein, as an 80-year-old, was asked in a television interview how he managed to maintain such a high level of expert piano playing, he hinted at the coordination of three strategies. First, Rubinstein said that he played fewer pieces (selection); second, he indicated that

he now practiced these pieces more often (optimization); and third, he said that to counteract his loss in mechanical speed he now used a kind of impression management such as introducing slower play before fast segments, so to make the latter appear faster (compensation).

The use of action-theoretical perspectives to illustrate the operationalization of the SOC model might suggest the conclusion that SOC is intended always to be a process with intention and rationality. This is not so. Each of these elements or components can be active or passive, internal or external, conscious or unconscious (Baltes & Baltes, 1996; Marsiske et al., 1995). Moreover, depending on the function of these components in a given behavioral unit, the characterization of a behavioral event can change, for instance, from active to passive. These terms (active vs. passive, internal vs. external, conscious vs. unconscious) are not to be understood in a strict categorical and exclusive sense. They denote a "more or less" quality. In this sense, we side with the Aristotelian principle that all causes (e.g., material, efficient, formal, final) can be simultaneously invoked when trying to understand the totality of a given behavior or action unit. The situation is further complicated by the fact that it is an essential characteristic of the data-theory dynamic in ontogenetic

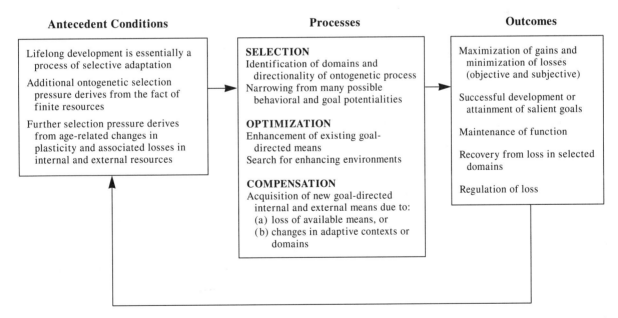

Figure 18.6   The life-span model of selective optimization with compensation. The essentials of the model are proposed to be universal, but specific phenotypic manifestations will vary by domain, individual, sociocultural context, and theoretical perspective (adapted from M. Baltes, 1987; P. Baltes, 1987, 1997; Baltes & Baltes, 1990b; Marsiske et al., 1995).

development (Reese, 1994) that the processes can change, for instance, from conscious to unconscious, as a skill becomes automatic and routinized (Ericsson & Smith, 1991).

Selection. As defined above, *selection involves directionality, goals, and outcomes.* Strictly speaking, selection already begins in embryonic development with features of the sensory system, such as differential sensitivity to light and pattern configurations. Neurophysiological processing of information represents another fundamental example of selection and selection-based specialization (Barkow et al., 1992; Johnson & Karmiloff-Smith, 1992; Karmiloff-Smith, 1992; Klix, 1993; Siegler, 1989).

In our approach to SOC, selection implies a focus of mind and behavior that identifies the domains of behavior and directs behavior and its development. By selection, a given individual (actively or passively) samples from a population of possibilities or opportunities. At the same time, a certain restriction results. Alternative options are not pursued. One concrete illustration of selection in development can be associated with a concept from developmental biology: Selection as the "canalized" (Waddington, 1975) realization of a set of outcomes from the "potentialities of ontogenesis" (plasticity). Another example of selection is the goal system (ranging from skills to attitudes and values), which defines the social and personal frames of desirable development. Selection, of course, can also involve the avoidance of specific outcomes of development such as the undesired self.

In our measurement framework (P. Baltes, Baltes, Freund, & Lang, 1995), we make an effort to distinguish between two kinds of selection: *elective* and *loss-based selection.* Elective selection is assumed to be primarily the result of a prepared module- and motivation-driven selection from a number of possible pathways. Loss-based selection results from the current unavailability of previously existing resources and from the limitations in resources created by an antecedent selection. Table 18.5 (from P. Baltes, Baltes, Freund, & Lang, 1995) contains sample items from a questionnaire to illustrate further this distinction.

Optimization. The focus of *optimization is on goal- or outcome-relevant means or resources.* Thus, while selection is a necessary condition for successful development (defined as the maximization of gains and minimization of losses), selection is not a sufficient condition.

In addition, conditions and procedural mechanisms of goal-attainment, that is, methods of optimization, are required. Optimization, then, involves processes aimed at the generation and refinement of means-ends resources and motivational-goal explication to achieve development-oriented positive outcomes (goals). In general, optimization is not the refinement of a single means. Rather, optimization requires a mutually enhancing coalition of factors, including health, environmental, and psychological conditions (Marsiske et al., 1995; Staudinger et al., 1995).

Table 18.5 Selection, Optimization, and Compensation (SOC) Embedded in an Action-Theoretical Framework (after P. Baltes, M. Baltes, Freud, & Lang, 1995). Note that this specification reflects our specific explication of our general theoretical orientation, that is, from the point of view of action theory.

Selection (Goals/Preferences)	Optimization (Goal-Relevant Means)	Compensation (Means/Resources for Counteracting Loss/Decline in Goal-Relevant Means)
Elective selection	—attentional focus	—substitution of means
—specification of goals	—effort/energy	—neglect of optimizing other means
—evolution of goal system (hierarchy)	—time allocation	—increased effort/energy
—contextualization of goals	—practice of skills	—increased time allocation
—goal-commitment	—acquiring new skills/resources	—activation of unused skills/resources
	—modeling successful others	—acquiring new skills/resources
Loss-based selection	—motivation for self-development	—modeling successful others who compensate
—focusing on most important goal(s)		—use of technical aids
—search for alternate goals		—use of assistance/help/therapy
—reconstruction of goal hierarchy		
—adaptation of standards		

As was true for selection, optimization can be active and passive, conscious and subconscious, internal or external. Moreover, optimization can be domain- and goal-specific as well as domain- and goal-general. The most domain-general notion of optimization is the generation of developmental reserve capacity (P. Baltes, 1987; Kliegl & Baltes, 1987), or plasticity of general-purpose mechanisms (see below).

Compensation. *Compensation involves a functional response to the loss of a goal-relevant means* (see also, Brandtstädter & Wentura, 1995; Dixon & Bäckman, 1995). This definition of compensation is more specific or restricted than the one proposed by Bäckman and Dixon (1992)—that is, it restricts compensation to responses to losses of means (resources) once available for goal attainment. There are two major functional categories of compensation. A first is to enlist new means as strategies of compensation to reach the same goal. The second compensatory strategy is to change goals of development themselves (Baltes & Baltes, 1990b; Brandtstädter & Baltes-Götz, 1990; Brandtstädter & Wentura, 1995; Heckhausen & Schulz, 1995). This second category, a compensatory change in goals, is related to what we earlier called a loss-based selection effect.

Two main causes give rise to a compensatory situation (Marsiske et al., 1995). A first is conditioned by the very fact of selection and optimization. For reasons of limited capacity of time and effort, selection of and optimization toward a given goal can imply the loss of means relevant for the pursuit of other goals. When an athlete aims for a high-level performance in the shot put, it is unlikely that comparable high levels of performance can be achieved in other types of sports such as gymnastics. As discussed above, there is no selection without loss, and where compensation is concerned, this selection-based loss means a reduction of resources that would be necessary to continue to pursue other developmental goals. Negative transfer is a related result of selection and optimization. The acquisition of a targeted expert skill system "A" can result in negative transfer to another skill system "B" (Ericsson & Smith, 1991). This example highlights the more general phenomenon that any process of development is a process of selective adaptation and, therefore, at the same time produces losses in means (resources) relevant for other goals of development.

A second category of causes of compensation stems from environment-associated changes in resources and age-associated changes in behavioral plasticity. Changing from one environment to another may involve a loss in environment-based resources (means) or may make some acquired personal means dysfunctional. Losses due to the biology of aging are perhaps the best known age-associated negative changes in behavioral plasticity. With aging, there is a reduction in the rate and scope of plasticity (P. Baltes, 1987; Cotman, 1985; Woodruff-Pak & Hanson, 1995). Such normative age-associated decline in plasticity can be accelerated further by non-normative events such as accidents or illnesses. In each of these instances, the central issue is a loss in goal-relevant means. As a result, the evolution of compensatory responses is a continuously changing dynamic of development in the second half of life.

Distinguishing between these categories of causes for compensation is not always easy as multicausality and multifunctionality suggest that multiple antecedent and outcome criteria can be involved. Moreover, the categorical status is likely to change, for instance, as the compensatory responses become automatic and can then be used for other functions such as optimization.

Selective Optimization with Compensation: Coordination and Dynamics in Development

We have noted already that, due to changes in the functional and contextual location, one conceptual and methodological difficulty is uncertainty about whether a given event is selection, optimization, or compensation. Indeed, it is central to ontogenetic development (because of multicausality, multifunctionality, equifinality, and age-related changes in these characteristics) that the logical status of selection, optimization, and compensation varies (Marsiske et al., 1995). However, their collaborative function is always to achieve "successful development" as defined above.

For instance, whether a given behavioral event is classified as selection, optimization, and compensation can vary depending on the point of scientific perspective and entry into the stream of observation of a developmental process. Perspectives vary in terms of the definition of units, of outcomes, as well as of the spatial (contextual) and temporal (developmental) location. In other words, whether a given behavior is interpreted as selection, optimization, or compensation is conditioned by such issues as multicausality and multifunctionality in behavior and development. In addition, the specification can vary because there are ontogenetic changes in functionality (their use and consequences) of the processes.

Understanding this changing developmental dynamic is particularly important regarding the conceptual distinctiveness of optimization and compensation (Marsiske et al., 1995). At the point of origin, for instance, some behavior may have been compensatory (such as acquiring nonverbal techniques of communication due to a loss of foreign language proficiency), at later points in ontogeny or in different contexts these same compensation-based behavioral means (nonverbal techniques of communication) can be used as a technique of optimization, such as when improving one's performance as an actor. It is important, therefore, to specify the context and the developmental space in which a given behavioral event is considered when deciding about its category allocation to either selection, optimization, or compensation.

As the model of SOC does not designate the specific content and form of desirable developmental outcomes, it is applicable to a large range of variations in goals and means of development. Thus, without offering prescriptive specifications, the nature of SOC is conditioned upon the personal and social definition of the targets of ontogenesis; that is, of the desired and undesired goals or outcomes. In this sense, then, SOC is at the same time *relativistic* and *universal*. Its relativity lies in the variations of motivational, social, and intellectual resources, as well as in the criteria used to define successful development, which can be multivariate and involve both objective and subjective indicators (Baltes & Baltes, 1990b). Its universalism rests in the argument that any process of development is expected to involve components of selection, optimization, and compensation (Baltes & Baltes, 1990b; Marsiske et al., 1995).

Table 18.6 offers a few examples of SOC-related biographies. As can be seen from the examples given, the assumption of the SOC model is that three elements (selection, optimization, and compensation) constitute the basic component processes for age-related change in selective adaptive capacity (development). It is also assumed that in reality the three components are always intertwined, that they form a cooperative (interactive) system of behavioral action or outcome-oriented functioning.

Table 18.6   Selective Optimization with Compensation: Biographical Examples (after Marsiske et al., 1995)

Source	Selection	Optimization	Compensation
Athlete Michael Jordan (Greene, 1993)	Focused only on basketball in youth, excluding swimming and skating	Daily line drills and upper body training	Reliance on special footwear to deal with chronic foot injury
Scientist Marie Curie (Curie, 1937)	Excluded political and cultural activities from her life	Spent a fixed number of hours daily in isolation in her laboratory	Turned to the advice of specific colleagues when encountering scientific problems that were beyond her expertise
Concert pianist Rubinstein (Baltes & Baltes, 1990b)	Played smaller repertoire of pieces in late life	Practiced these pieces more with age	Slowed performance before fast movements (ritardando) to heighten contrast

Without specifying the substantive goals and outcomes of development, the SOC model is intended to characterize the processes that result in desired outcomes of development while minimizing undesirable ones. Depending upon which level of analysis is chosen (societal, individual, microbehavioral, etc.), selective optimization with compensation requires the use of a different lens for different levels of measurement and specification. For instance, at a biographical level of analysis, the lens might focus on the interplay among educational, family, professional, and leisure careers. But when studying cognitive reserve capacity, for instance by means of dual- or parallel-task processing, the lens might focus on the SOC-related interplay between components of working memory and other attentional resources.

In the following two sections dealing with life-span developmental theory and research in two domains of functioning, we will occasionally return to SOC-related interpretations. However, our intent is not to elevate the SOC-model to the one overarching model of life-span development. This would be inappropriate. In our view, the model of selective optimization with compensation is but one of the theoretical efforts that life-span research and theory have spawned. However, we believe SOC to be a model that displays much consistency across levels of analysis and can be usefully linked to other current theoretical streams in developmental psychology, such as to dynamic systems theory.

INTELLECTUAL FUNCTIONING ACROSS THE LIFE SPAN

As discussed in the previous section, a genuine life-span orientation to developmental change depends critically on articulating the theoretical propositions regarding the macroscopic overall landscape of the entire course of ontogeny with more microscopic research on specific developmental functions, processes, and age periods. Specifically, the knowledge bases generated by researchers interested in different aspects of infancy, childhood, adolescence, adulthood, and late life need to be combined and compared with each other, and organized by the themes and propositions that guide the life-span approach. The resulting life-span integration of perspectives and findings, in turn, is hoped to feed back into the more age- and process-specific developmental specialities, providing for larger interpretative frameworks and provoking the investigation of new or formerly neglected research questions.

Currently, perhaps no other field within developmental psychology is better suited to demonstrate the potential of this dynamic than the field of *intellectual development,* which captured early (Hollingworth, 1927; Sanford, 1902) and thereafter continued attention in life-span developmental psychology. Central themes of intellectual development, such as relative stability (i.e., covariance change over time), directionality (i.e., mean change over time), plasticity (i.e., the malleability of mean and covariance changes), and the role of knowledge-based processes in cognitive development also played a prominent role in life-span theorizing, and are well suited to depict the implications of the life-span approach.

The Biology and Culture of Life-Span Intellectual Development

Our proposed view of the overall landscape of ontogenesis, as it was summarized in Figure 18.1, puts constraints upon the possible form and content of theories about life-span intellectual development. Foremost, any model or theory

on life-span intellectual development needs to recognize that ontogenesis is embedded within two streams of inheritance, the biological and the cultural (Durham, 1990, 1991), and needs to provide a framework for the developmental investigation of these two streams of inheritance in different domains, and at different levels of analysis. Specifically, the model should be consistent with the three-fold characterization of the life-span dynamics between biology and culture: (a) a decrease in the degree of biological orchestration and the quality of genome expression with advancing age; (b) an increase in the need for culture to achieve and maintain adaptive functioning; (c) increased difficulties for culture and individuals to produce adaptive outcomes due to decrements in the quality of the expressed genome.

We posit that this fundamental shift in balance between biology and culture during ontogeny has to occupy a central place in any life-span approach to intellectual development. In addition, models of life-span intellectual development are expected to be consistent with the family of theoretical propositions summarized in Table 18.3. For instance, they need to recognize that development is a life-long process of local (i.e., context-specific and time-bound) selection and adaptation embedded in a changing ontogenetic and sociohistorical context. Moreover, such models (Figure 18.6) need to be prepared to deal with idiosyncratic (non-normative) events which can enter the life course at unexpected times and with possibly powerful consequences.

The Two-Component Model of Life-Span Cognition: Mechanics versus Pragmatics

In the past, one of us (P. Baltes, 1987, 1993, 1994; cf., P. Baltes et al., 1984; P. Baltes & Graf, 1996) has proposed a theoretical framework for the study of intellectual development in which two main categories or components of intellectual functioning are set apart: The *mechanics* and the *pragmatics* of cognition. The model draws on earlier formulations, such as the theory of fluid and crystallized intelligence by Cattell and Horn (Cattell, 1971; Horn, 1982), and the distinction between intellectual power and intellectual products by Hebb (1949). In analogy to computer language, one may refer to these two categories or components as the hardware (cognitive mechanics) and the software (cognitive pragmatics) of the mind. Juxtaposing the two does not imply that they are independent or exclusive. As we will argue in more detail below, the mechanics and pragmatics interact across ontogenetic and microgenetic time in the production of intelligent behavior. For instance, the pragmatics clearly cannot exist without the mechanics.

The two-component model of life-span intellectual development is consistent with our general notions of the dynamic between biology and culture during ontogenesis. In fact, historically, our views on the overall landscape of human development were developed in close connection with the broadening and systematization of the mechanic-pragmatic distinction (P. Baltes, 1987, 1993, 1997). For this reason, the research agenda entailed by the meta-theoretical propositions of the life-span approach are well articulated within this particular domain of functioning. Specifically, we construe the *mechanics* of cognition as an expression of the neurophysiological architecture of the mind as it evolved during biological evolution (cf., Barkow, Cosmides, & Tooby, 1992; Tooby & Cosmides, 1995) and unfolds during ontogenesis (Rakic, 1995). In contrast, the *pragmatics* of cognition are associated with the bodies of knowledge available from and mediated through culture (see upper portion of Figure 18.7).

The Mechanics.   In the mechanics of cognition, biological including neurophysiological brain conditions reign supreme, and the predominant age-graded ontogenetic pattern is one of maturation, stability, and aging-induced decline. Age-based changes in this component early and late in ontogeny are assumed to be strongly influenced by genetic and other brain-status related factors, albeit in fundamentally different ways (P. Baltes, 1994; P. Baltes & Graf, 1996). Early in ontogeny (i.e., during embryogenesis, infancy, and early childhood), age-based changes in the mechanics are assumed to reflect, for the most part, the unfolding and active construction of more or less domain-specific and predisposed processing capabilities (Fischer & Hencke, 1996; Karmiloff-Smith, 1992; Siegler & Crowley, 1994; Wellman & Gelman, 1992). In contrast, negative changes in the mechanics of cognition late in life presumably result from brain-related consequences of less effective phylogenetic selection pressures operating during this period (P. Baltes, 1994, 1997; see the second part of this chapter). In that sense, the life-span trajectory of level changes in the mechanics of cognition can be derived from the life-span changes shown in Figure 18.1(a).

The cognitive mechanics, then, reflect fundamental organizational properties of the central nervous system

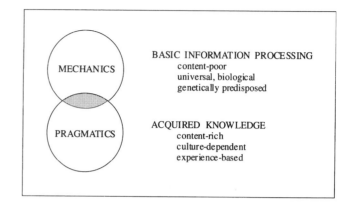

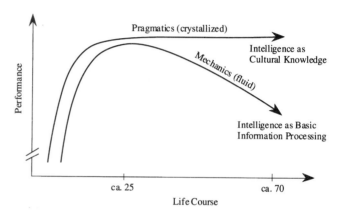

Figure 18.7   Life-span research on two components of cognition, the fluid mechanics, and the crystallized pragmatics. The top section defines the categories, the bottom section illustrates postulated life-span trajectories (after Baltes & Graf, 1996; cf. Cattell, 1971; Hebb, 1949; Horn & Hofer, 1992). The advanced old age, the trajectories evince less and less differentiation (cf. P. B. Baltes & Lindenberger, 1997, see below).

(W. Singer, 1995). In terms of psychological operations, we assume that the cognitive mechanics are indexed by the speed, accuracy, and coordination of elementary processing operations as they can be assessed in tasks measuring the quality of information input, sensory and motor memory, discrimination, categorization, and selective attention, as well as reasoning ability in highly overlearned or novel domains (Craik, 1986; Craik & Jennings, 1992; Craik & Salthouse, 1992; Dawson & Fischer, 1994; Hartley, 1992; Kausler, 1994; Klix, 1992; Moscovitch & Winocur, 1992; Plude, Enns, & Brodeur, 1994; Schieber & Baldwin, 1996).

The Pragmatics.   In contrast to the mechanics, the pragmatics of the mind reveal the power of human agency and culture (Cole, 1996; Lawrence & Valsiner, 1993; Shweder, 1991). Developmental changes in this component reflect the acquisition of culturally transmitted bodies of declarative and procedural knowledge that are made available to individuals in the course of socialization. Some of these socialization events are normative but specific to certain cultures (e.g., formal schooling), others are more universal (e.g., mentoring), and still others are idiosyncratic or person-specific (e.g., specialized ecological and professional knowledge). In any case, the corresponding bodies of knowledge are represented both internally (e.g., semantic networks; cf., Kintsch, 1988) and externally (e.g., books). These knowledge systems are *acquired* during ontogeny but may build on evolutionarily prestructured, domain-specific knowledge (Karmiloff-Smith, 1992). In this way, the pragmatics of cognition direct the attention of life-span developmentalists towards the increasing importance of knowledge-based forms of intelligence during ontogeny (Baltes & Baltes, 1990b; Ericsson & Lehmann, 1996; Ericsson & Smith, 1991; Featherman, 1983; Labouvie-Vief, 1982; Rybash, Hoyer, & Roodin, 1986; Weinert & Perner, 1996). Typical examples include reading and writing skills, educational qualifications, professional skills, and varieties of everyday problem-solving, but also knowledge about the self and the meaning and conduct of life (Berg, 1996; Blanchard-Fields, 1996; Bosman & Charness, 1996; Cornelius & Caspi, 1987; Marsiske et al., 1995; Marsiske & Willis, 1995; Staudinger et al., 1995; Walsh & Hershey, 1993; see the next section of this chapter).

Divergence in Life-Span Trajectories between Mechanics and Pragmatics. The preceding considerations imply specific predictions regarding the shape of ontogenetic trajectories for mechanic and pragmatic aspects of intellectual functioning (see lower portion of Figure 18.7). Specifically, the *level* of performance within these two categories of intellectual functioning is assumed to be governed by two different sources of influence: biological-genetic for the mechanics, and environmental-cultural for the pragmatics. The expected divergence in age trajectories is seen as a consequence of this difference in composition.

Empirical evidence in support of this assumption comes from a great variety of different research traditions (see below). Probably the most longstanding supportive evidence is the difference between maintained and vulnerable intellectual abilities (Denney, 1984; Salthouse, 1991c; cf.,

Jones & Conrad, 1933). Abilities that critically involve the mechanics, such as reasoning, memory, spatial orientation, and perceptual speed, generally show a pattern of monotonic and roughly linear decline during adulthood, with some further acceleration of decline in very old age. In contrast, more pragmatic abilities, such as verbal knowledge and certain facets of numerical ability, remain stable or increase up to the sixth or seventh decade of life, and only start to evince some decline in very old age.

Figure 18.8, which is based on the fifth data collection of the Seattle Longitudinal Study (Schaie, 1996), serves as an illustration (for similar evidence with respect to episodic versus semantic memory, see Nyberg, Bäckman, Erngrund, Olofsson, & Nillson, 1996). It displays cross-sectional adult age gradients based on multiple indicators

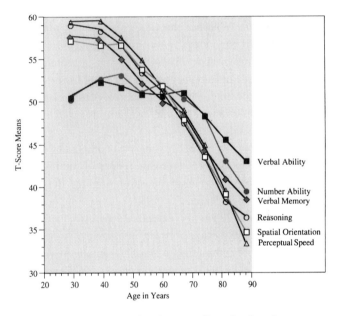

Figure 18.8 Cross-sectional age gradients in six primary mental abilities *(N = 1628)*. Abilities were assessed with 3 to 4 different tests, and are scaled in a T-score metric (i.e., *mean* = 50, *SD* = 10). Verbal ability and number ability peak during middle adulthood, and show little or no age decrements before the age of 74. In contrast, perceptual speed, inductive reasoning, spatial orientation, and verbal memory show steady monotonic decline. This differential pattern of prevailing growth, maintenance, and subsequent loss supports two-component theories of life-span intellectual development, such as the distinction between fluid and crystallized intelligence made by Cattell (1971) and Horn (1982), or the juxtaposition of the mechanics and the pragmatics of cognition proposed by P. Baltes (1987, 1993, 1997) (based on Schaie & Willis, 1993).

for six intellectual abilities (Schaie & Willis, 1993). Verbal ability and number ability peak during middle adulthood and show little or no age decrements before the age of 74, whereas perceptual speed, inductive reasoning, spatial orientation, and verbal memory show steady monotonic decline. Data on longitudinal age gradients provide converging evidence (Salthouse, 1991c; Schaie, 1994, 1996).

The Two-Component Model: Relations to Other Theories

As mentioned already, the closest relative, both conceptually and historically, to the two-component model of life-span intellectual development is the theory of fluid (Gf) and crystallized (Gc) abilities by Cattell (1971) and Horn (1982). One rationale common to both conceptualizations is to provide a theoretical explanation for the different age gradients of psychometrically assessed intellectual abilities. However, the two frameworks differ in scope and research emphasis. Whereas the Gf-Gc distinction remains, empirically and theoretically, within the confines of the psychometric research tradition, the mechanic-pragmatic distinction links developmental findings obtained within the psychometric tradition to perspectives from cognitive psychology, evolutionary psychology, cultural psychology, and developmental biology.

Other approaches related to the two-component model include Sternberg's (1985) triarchic theory of intelligence, especially its developmental interpretation by Berg and Sternberg (1985a), Denney's (1984) distinction between unexercised and optimally exercised cognitive abilities, Hebb's (1949) distinction between intelligence A (i.e., intellectual power) and intelligence B (i.e., intellectual products), Ackerman's (1996) recently proposed PPIK (process, personality, interests, and knowledge) theory, and the encapsulation model of adult intelligence proposed by Rybash, Hoyer, and Roodin (1986; Hoyer, 1987). In addition, Hunt (1993) recently offered an information-processing reinterpretation of the Gf-Gc theory which resonates well with the two-component model (see also, Welford, 1993).

In the following, the two-component model will be further elaborated in three separate sections: Mechanics, pragmatics, and their interrelations. In each section, we first present select concepts and research, and provide empirical examples for prototypical life-span trends. The aim of these three sections is not to be comprehensive, but to further specify the two components of cognition as well as their interaction. More comprehensive discussions of

important topics in life-span research on intellectual development are provided in subsequent sections.

The Fluid Mechanics of Cognition

We start this section with a life-span summary of research on constructs that have been proposed to cause or mediate age-based changes in the mechanics of cognition. We then argue that much of the available evidence about age-based changes in the mechanics derives from measures that are contaminated by pragmatic influence, and we underscore the need to arrive at more valid estimates of individual differences in the upper limits of mechanic functioning. In line with the two-component model, we predict that age differences in the mechanics are magnified under purified measurement conditions; and we provide an empirical example from adulthood in support of this prediction.

The Search for Determinants of Mechanic Development

Despite a large overlap in approaches to the study of intellectual development (cf., Lindenberger & Baltes, 1994a), such as the *psychometric* (Cattell, 1971; Horn & Hofer, 1992; Humphreys & Davey, 1988), *information-processing* (Craik, 1983; Kail, 1991; Salthouse, 1991c), and *expertise* (Chi & Koeske, 1983; Ericsson, Krampe, & Tesch-Römer, 1993; Weinert, Schneider, & Knopf, 1988), there are surprisingly few attempts to pursue the themes of infant and child development into adulthood and old age, or to identify thematic and predictive antecedents of adulthood and old age in childhood.

An important exception in this regard concerns work on age changes in general information-processing constraints on intellectual functioning across the life span, or what we would call research on the *determinants of age-based changes in the mechanics of cognition*. Researchers both in the fields of child development (Bjorklund & Harnishfeger, 1990; Case, 1992; Fischer & Rose, 1994; Kail, 1991; McCall, 1994; Pascual-Leone, 1983; Siegler & Shipley, 1995) and cognitive aging (Birren, 1964; Birren & Fisher, 1995; Cerella, 1990; Craik & Byrd, 1982; Hasher & Zacks, 1988; Salthouse, 1996) have been trying to identify developmental determinants or "developables" (Flavell, 1992) that regulate the rate of age-based changes in cognitive and intellectual functioning. More importantly, some scholars have begun to link these two lines of inquiry, and to provide unified accounts of age-based changes in the structure and/or efficiency of information processing (e.g., Dempster, 1992; Kail & Salthouse, 1994; Mayr, Kliegl, & Krampe, 1996; Pascual-Leone, 1983; Salthouse & Kail, 1983).

In our view, this search for maturational and/or aging-induced general processing constraints may help to identify the processes and mechanisms that underlie positive age gradients in the mechanics of cognition during infancy and childhood, and negative age gradients during late adulthood and old age. So far, three constructs have been studied most extensively: *information processing rate, working memory,* and *inhibition.* Research from all periods of the life span suggests that the functional levels of these three mechanisms follow the inverse U-shape pattern predicted by the two-component model. In principle, then, any combination of these mechanisms could act as a pacemaker of life-span development in the mechanics of cognition. Accordingly, these mechanisms often are defined in resource terminology (e.g., energy, time, or space; cf., Craik, 1983; Spearman, 1927). Moreover, first attempts have been made to relate these mechanisms to age-based changes at a more physiological level (Case, 1992; Dempster, 1992; Fischer & Rose, 1994; Moscovitch & Winocur, 1992).

Information Processing Rate.   Across a wide variety of cognitive and perceptual tasks, speed of responding increases from childhood to early adulthood, and decreases thereafter. Figure 18.9 provides an illustration of this ubiquitous finding. It displays normative data for two tests of perceptual speed of the Woodcock-Johnson Tests of Cognitive Ability (1990). The data are based on a representative sample of over 6,000 US citizens ranging from six to 80 years of age. The observed age differences are expressed in standard deviation units of a reference group of more than 250 18-year-old individuals. Six-year-old individuals performed about five, and 75-year-old individuals more than two standard deviations below the young-adult mean. Thus, the data clearly follow the inverted U-shape pattern.

The longstanding observation of generalized age changes in response latency has led to the processing rate hypothesis of cognitive development and aging. Probably, this hypothesis holds a more central place in cognitive aging research (Birren, 1964; Birren & Fisher, 1995; Cerella, 1990; Salthouse, 1996; Welford, 1984) than in research on child development (Hale, 1990; Kail, 1991). In the case of cognitive aging, the general slowing-down of

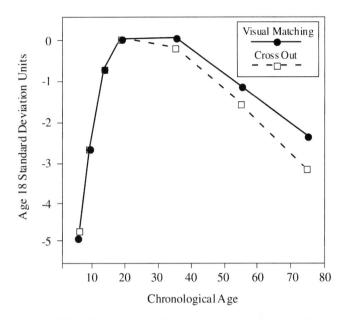

Figure 18.9   Cross-sectional age gradients for two tests of perceptual speed from the Woodcock-Johnson Tests of Cognitive Ability (1990). The figure displays normative data based on over 6,000 individuals between six and 80 years of age. Mean performance levels at different ages are expressed in standard deviations units of 18-year-old individuals (based on Kail & Salthouse, 1994).

cognitive behavior with advancing age is portrayed as the consequence of a general decrement in information processing rate. In agreement with this hypothesis, correlational evidence has supported the prediction that psychometrically assessed perceptual speed accounts for most or all negative adult age differences in other intellectual abilities, even if these other abilities are assessed under time-relaxed or untimed testing conditions (Hertzog, 1989; Lindenberger, Mayr, & Kliegl, 1993; Nettelbeck & Rabbitt, 1992; Salthouse, 1991b).

Additional evidence in support of the processing rate hypothesis has come from meta-analyses of latency data examining the relation between mean latencies for groups of old adults and the mean latencies for groups of young adults (Cerella, 1990; Myerson, Hale, Wagstaff, Poon, & Smith, 1990; but see Perfect, 1994, for methodological problems). Similar analyses of children's versus young adults' reaction time data have led to analogous results (Kail, 1991). Thus, it appears that both children's and old adults' reaction times can be expressed as a function of young adults' reaction times across a relatively wide range of different tasks, a finding that supports the idea of general age-based changes in speed of processing. At the same time, it needs to be acknowledged that processing rate, as an explanatory construct, is perhaps not unitary (Graf & Uttl, 1995) and, so far, has no direct analogue at the biological level (Bashore, 1993; Wickett & Vernon, 1994). Future research needs to intensify attempts to provide more direct links between psychological changes in speed of processing and ontogenetic neuronal changes, such as increasing myelination during childhood or loss of connectivity in old age (cf., Deary, 1996).

Working Memory. Generally, working memory denotes the ability to preserve information in one or more short-term stores while simultaneously transforming the same or some other information (Baddeley, 1986; Just & Carpenter, 1992). Age differences in working memory have been invoked as a possible cause for intellectual growth during childhood (Case, 1985; Chapman & Lindenberger, 1992; Halford, 1993; Pascual-Leone, 1970), and for age-based decrements during adulthood and old age (Craik, 1983; Craik & Byrd, 1982).

With respect to childhood, Neo-Piagetian theorists have argued that changes in working memory are among the primary pacemakers of intellectual child development (Chapman, 1990). In some conceptions, the capacity of working memory stays constant over age but is used in increasingly efficient ways (Case, 1985). In other models, working memory capacity or M-Space is assumed to increase linearly from one unit at the ages of 3 and four to seven units at the age of 15 (cf., Pascual-Leone, 1970; Ribeaupierre & Bailleux, 1994).

One way to study the effect of age differences in working memory on intellectual functioning is to vary the relative importance of temporary storage and processing (i.e., information transformation) demands within or across tasks. Generally, this research has demonstrated that positive age differences during childhood and negative age differences during adulthood are more pronounced when demands on processing are increased (Craik & Jennings, 1992; Mayr, Kliegl, & Krampe, 1996). In other words, age differences are especially pronounced for tasks that put high demands on the simultaneous coordination of incoming and/or stored information. In addition, more specific longitudinal links during childhood between earlier individual differences in

storing and processing phonological information and later individual differences in vocabulary have been observed (Gathercole & Baddeley, 1993). Finally, correlational studies suggest that working memory measures contribute to positive age differences in the fluid-mechanic component of intelligence during childhood (Chapman & Lindenberger, 1989), and to negative age differences in this component during adulthood and old age (Salthouse, 1991b).

Despite this supportive evidence, the explanatory power of the working-memory construct is difficult to judge. For instance, age-based changes in working memory are often explained by alluding to changes in processing efficiency or processing speed (Case, 1985; Salthouse, 1996). By this account, working memory is not the driving force of developmental change, but the indirect expression of a different developmental mechanism. Another problem concerns our limited knowledge about a central function of working memory—*the conscious control of action and thought.* In the most influential working-memory model (Baddeley, 1986), this task is assigned to the central executive. Evidence from developmental psychology (Dempster, 1992; Houdé, 1995), cognitive-experimental psychology (Conway & Engle, 1994), and the cognitive neurosciences (Goldman-Rakic, 1995; Shallice & Burgess, 1991) suggests that the *abilities to inhibit actions and thoughts and/or to avoid interference* are crucial for the efficient functioning of this component, rather than working-memory capacity per se (cf., Brainerd, 1995; Stoltzfus, Hasher, & Zacks, 1996).

Inhibition and Interference. Recently, developmentalists from different traditions and fields of research have intensified their interest in inhibition and interference (Bjorklund & Harnishfeger, 1990, 1995; Harnishfeger, 1995; Hasher & Zacks, 1988; Houdé, 1995; McCall, 1994; McDowd, Oseas-Kreger, & Filion, 1995; Stoltzfus, Hasher, & Zacks, 1996). This interest in inhibition has led to reinterpretations of available evidence and to the collection of new data trying to support the notion that age differences in the efficiency of inhibitory processes are of general relevance for age differences in cognitive functioning.

For instance, Houdé (1995) and others (Bjorklund & Harnishfeger, 1990, 1995) have argued that children's difficulties in solving certain cognitive tasks (e.g., the A-not-B task) are well explained by their inability to inhibit distracting information. Moreover, recent empirical work with the negative-priming paradigm suggests that some variants of inhibition function less effectively in children and older adults than in young adults (May, Kane, & Hasher, 1995), and that older adults show more proactive interference in verbal learning than young adults (Kliegl & Lindenberger, 1993). Finally, curvilinear life-span age gradients that resemble those found for measures of perceptual speed have been obtained with typical tests of interference proneness, such as the Stroop color-word test (Comalli, Wapner, & Werner, 1962; cf., Dempster, 1992). At present, however, it is unclear whether these age gradients reflect genuine curvilinear age gradients in interference proneness, or whether they can be portrayed as an epiphenomenon of age differences in speed of responding (Salthouse & Meinz, 1995) and/or selective attention and discrimination (Engle et al., 1995).

Summary and Prospects. Age-comparative research on information-processing determinants has produced a rich and solid empirical data base about life-span changes in fundamental dimensions of the cognitive mechanics. Specifically, processing rate, working memory, and inhibition all evince a pattern of rapid growth during infancy and childhood followed by aging-induced monotonic decline during later parts of adulthood and old age. In addition, this field has witnessed the formulation of specialized developmental theories that are truly life-span in kind (e.g., Kail & Salthouse, 1994; Pascual-Leone, 1983).

Given the propensity of research in this area, and the interdisciplinary potential of the topic, we expect that current conceptions of life-span changes in the mechanics of cognition will undergo important changes during the next decade. Specifically, the search for life-span determinants of the mechanics of cognition is likely to increasingly profit from the general progress in the cognitive neurosciences (Gazzaniga, 1995). In light of the rapid expansion and refinement of theories and methods in that field, and their growing application to cognitive development (C. Nelson, 1995), it seems likely that the domain-general determinants identified so far will undergo revision, and that new determinants will be identified. For instance, closer contact to the neurosciences may help to decide whether the three different determinants identified so far constitute distinct developmental entities, or whether they are differentiated expressions of a common cause. Moreover, such contact will also enhance our knowledge about the systemic properties of developing brains (Fischer & Rose, 1994;

Johnson & Rybash, 1993; Li, Lindenberger, & Frensch, 1996; van der Maas & Molenaar, 1992). One example in this regard is the potential adaptive value for maturing systems to start small and get larger, or the benefits of immaturity (Bjorklund & Green, 1992; Elman, 1993; Kareev, 1995; Newport, 1990; Turkewitz & Kenny, 1982). Finally, developmentalists need to learn more about the dimensionality of age-based changes in the mechanics, that is, about the degree to which such changes are general or function-specific (e.g., modular; cf., Giambra, 1993; Johnson & Rybash, 1993; Light & LaVoie, 1993; Madden & Plude, 1993; Naito & Komatsu, 1993). In cognitive aging research, this issue has led to productive controversies at the interface between different methodological and theoretical approaches, such as the multivariate-psychometric, cognitive-experimental, and neuropsychological (Anderson, 1992; Cerella, 1990; Hertzog, 1996; Kliegl, Mayr, & Krampe, 1994; Maylor & Rabbitt, 1994; Molenaar & van der Molen, 1994; Perfect, 1994; Rabbitt, 1993; Salthouse, 1994).

Age-Based Differences in the Mechanics of Cognition: The Need for Purification of Measurement

Observed age differences or age changes on intellectual tasks and tests, as obtained in standard cross-sectional and real-time longitudinal research, cannot be regarded as direct and pure reflections of age-based changes in the mechanics of cognition. Rather, in addition to the mechanics, such differences or changes are influenced by a wealth of additional factors, ranging from pragmatic components of cognition (e.g., task-relevant pre-experimental knowledge) to other person characteristics (e.g., test anxiety, arousal; cf., Fisk & Warr, 1996). For this reason, much of our knowledge about the life-span trajectory of the mechanics of cognition is based on relatively imprecise indicators.

A likely indication for this admixture of pragmatic variance to supposedly mechanic measures is the secular rise in performance on typical psychometric marker tests of fluid intelligence (cf., Flynn, 1987). Apparently, performance on these tests is more sensitive to short-term historical trends in schooling and acculturation than originally assumed. Another example concerns the measures of perceptual speed that form the basis of Figure 18.9. One of them, the Visual Matching Test, requires individuals to locate and circle the two identical numbers in a row of six numbers. Proficiency in this task is not a pure function of perceptual speed but also reflects, to some degree, specific experience in dealing with numbers, which most likely introduces a bias against children.

The need for better estimates of individuals' performance potential in the mechanics of cognition is further nurtured by the life-span proposition that epigenesis is probabilistic but not random (P. Baltes, 1987; Gottlieb, 1983, 1996; Gottlieb et al., Ch. 5, this Volume; R. Lerner, 1984; see Table 18.3). In biological terms, an implication of this view is that individuals' cognitive performance as it can be observed under standard testing conditions represents just one possible phenotypic manifestation of their range of performance potential, or "norm of reaction." Therefore, if the goal is to separate the possible from the impossible over age, and to solidify the evidence on age differences in the mechanics of cognition, the context of measurement needs to be moved towards the *upper limits* of the performance potential. This line of reasoning resembles claims made by other research traditions, such as clinical and developmental diagnostics (Carlson, 1994; Guthke & Wiedl, 1996), the differentiation between performance and competence, gestalt and cultural-historical theoretical orientations (Rogoff, 1995; Vygotsky, 1962; H. Werner, 1948; cf., Brown, 1982), and work on age differences in learning (Reese & Lipsitt, 1970). Large differences in epistemology and purpose notwithstanding, all these traditions are inspired by an interest in exploring individuals' upper limits of intellectual performance.

Testing-the-Limits of Age Differences in the Mechanics of Cognition. Within life-span developmental psychology and as alluded to above, the testing-the-limits paradigm has been introduced as a research strategy to uncover age differences in the upper limits of mechanic functioning (P. Baltes, 1987; Kliegl & Baltes, 1987; Kliegl et al., 1990; Lindenberger & Baltes, 1995b). The main focus of this paradigm is to arrange for experimental conditions that produce maximum (i.e., asymptotic) levels of performance. Thus, similar to stress tests in biology and medicine (M. Baltes, Kühl, Gutzmann, & Sowarka, 1995; Fries & Crapo, 1981), testing-the-limits aims at the assessment of age differences in maximum levels of cognitive performance by providing large amounts of practice and/or training combined with systematic variations in task difficulty. Furthermore, and in line with the microgenetic approach to the study of change (Kuhn, 1995; Siegler & Crowley, 1991; Siegler & Jenkins, 1989), testing-the-limits

is based on the assumption that changes occurring on different time scales share essential features (cf., H. Werner, 1948). Therefore, in addition to the more general goal of measurement purification, the detailed analysis of time-compressed developmental change functions is assumed to enhance our understanding of the mechanisms and the range of medium- and long-term developmental changes.

A Prototypical Example: Adult Age Differences in Upper Limits of Short-Term Memory (Serial Word Recall)

Most age-comparative testing-the-limits research has been conducted with adults of different ages, rather than with children of different ages, or with children and adults. Figure 18.10 shows the result of a study involving a total of 38 sessions of training and practice in the Method of Loci, a mnemonic technique for the serial recall of word lists. Two findings from this study are noteworthy. First, adults in both age groups greatly improved their memory performance. This findings confirms earlier work on the continued existence of cognitive plasticity in cognitively healthy (i.e., nondemented) older adults (P. Baltes & Lindenberger, 1988; P. Baltes & Willis, 1982; Denney, 1984; Verhaeghen, Marcoen, & Goossens, 1992).

Second, however, practice and training resulted in a close-to-perfect separation of the two age groups, thereby

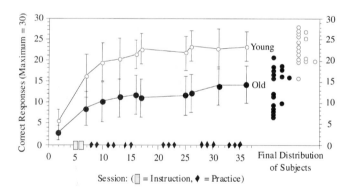

Figure 18.10 Testing-the-limits research, which is aimed at the identification of asymptotes of performance potential, suggests the existence of robust age-related losses in the mechanics of cognition. The example given involves a memory technique, the Method of Loci. After 38 sessions of training, most older adults did not reach the level of performance reached by young adults after only a few sessions. In the final distribution, not a single older person was performing above the mean of the young adults (adapted from P. Baltes & Kliegl, 1992).

demonstrating the existence of sizeable negative age differences at limits of functioning. Even after 38 sessions of training, most older adults did not reach the level of performance that young adults had reached after only a few sessions. Moreover, at the end of the study, not a single older person functioned above the mean of the young-adult group.

The findings obtained with the testing-the-limits paradigm are consistent with our general notion that the mechanics of cognition decrease during adulthood and old age. It appears worthwhile to intensify the use of this paradigm with lower age groups to obtain genuine life-span gradients regarding maximum limits of performance potential in different domains (see Levinson & Reese, 1967, for an early example in this regard). In addition, the focus on age differences in maximum level needs to be complemented by an emphasis on age-differential changes in variances and covariances with practice (P. Baltes, Labouvie, & Frohring, 1973; Rogers, Fisk, & Hertzog, 1994). Given our assumptions regarding life-span changes in adaptive capacity of the mechanics of the mind and the knowledge-contaminated nature of standard assessments, our prediction is that life-span peaks in performance levels are shifted towards younger ages when individuals are given the opportunity to come close to the upper limits of their mechanic potential.

The Crystallized Pragmatics of Cognition

We now direct our attention toward the ontogeny of the cognitive pragmatics, or the cultural and knowledge-rich dimension of intellectual life-span development. First, we discuss the relation between mechanics and pragmatics from an evolutionary perspective. Then, we introduce the distinction between normative and person-specific forms of pragmatic knowledge, and discuss stage- and knowledge-oriented approaches to the issue of intellectual growth after adolescence. To illustrate the knowledge-oriented approach, we end this section with a prototypical example from our own research on expert knowledge about the fundamental pragmatics of life (wisdom).

Mechanics and Pragmatics in Evolutionary Perspective

In recent years, nativist approaches to infant cognitive development have revealed the evolutionary prestructured nature of the human processing system (Mandler, 1992; Spelke & Newport, Ch. 6, this Volume; Spelke, Vishton, & von Hofsten, 1995). Through innovative advances in experimental methodology, it has become increasingly clear that infants and young children cannot be considered a cognitive *tabula rasa,* as extreme versions of constructivist (e.g., Piaget, 1967/1971, but see Piaget, 1980, pp. 11–12) or behaviorist (e.g., Skinner, 1966) theorizing may suggest. Rather, not unlike members of other species, humans begin their extra-uterine lives with a well-orchestrated set of domain-specific constraints and expectations that guide behavior and form the basis for later acquisitions (cf., Karmiloff-Smith, 1995; Smotherman & Robinson, 1996).

We assume that the pragmatics of cognition, or the bodies of knowledge provided by culture (P. Baltes, 1993), build on, extend, and reorganize these prestructured core domains (Perner, 1995; Wellman & Gelman, 1992). Taken together, these processes of extension and transformation eventually give rise to forms of knowledge and behavior that are, in part by virtue of necessity, *compatible* with the biological architecture of the mind, but cannot be characterized as the *direct consequence* of evolutionary selection pressures.

The resulting potential of ontogenesis to create and adapt to the new, or the difference between current functions and evolutionary history, is sometimes referred to as exaptative generalization or *exaptation* (Gould & Vrba, 1982). Exaptation helps to explain why members of the human species are good at doing things that were certainly not directly at the focus of natural selection, such as reading a book or driving a car (cf., Sherry & Schacter, 1987). Put more generally, exaptation may help to characterize the early ontogeny of the link between the pragmatics and the mechanics of cognition. It also reminds us that the evolution of culture must reflect some degree of match with, and reciprocal influence on, evolution-based genetic disposition (cf., Durham, 1991). For instance, pragmatic knowledge may evolve from and/or mimic predisposed knowledge in evolutionarily privileged domains, but come with the advantage of being tuned to the idiosyncratic demands of specific cultures, biographies, and contexts (cf., Siegler & Crowley, 1994).

Normative versus Person-Specific Pragmatic Knowledge

An important, albeit necessarily imperfect, distinction within the pragmatics of cognition concerns normative versus person-specific knowledge. *Normative* bodies of knowledge are of general value to a given culture. Typical examples include verbal ability (e.g., verbal fluency, vocabulary, reading, writing), number proficiency (e.g., subtraction, addition), and basic general knowledge about the world (e.g., Maylor, 1994). Individual differences in these domains are closely linked to years of education and other aspects of social stratification, and are amenable to psychometric testing (Cattell, 1971). In contrast, *person-specific* bodies of knowledge that branch off from the normative knowledge-acquisition path are less closely tied to mandatory socialization events, and result from specific combinations of experiential settings, personality characteristics, motivational constellations, and cognitive abilities or talent (Marsiske et al., 1995). As a consequence, these bodies of knowledge often escape psychometric operationalization, and are more amenable to study within the expertise paradigm (Ericsson & Smith, 1991).

Normative Pragmatic Knowledge.   Due to their general value for a given society, age-based differences in normative pragmatic knowledge are well captured by standard psychometric testing procedures, and are well explained by psychometric theory (Cattell, 1971; Horn, 1982). According to Cattell's (1971) line of reasoning, individuals invest their cognitive potential (e.g., Gf) into culturally valued bodies of knowledge during schooling and later periods of ontogeny. As a consequence of this investment relationship, resulting competencies, referred to as crystallized abilities, are acquired later during ontogeny than the abilities that are invested.

To motivate the idea that crystallized abilities (e.g., the normative pragmatics) are less prone to aging-induced decline than fluid abilities (e.g., the mechanics), Horn and Hofer (1992) invoked the analogy of neuronal overdetermination. Specifically, they argued that the kind of knowledge typical for crystallized abilities is implemented in highly interconnected networks that contain many possible ways to access a given piece of information (e.g., overdetermined information access). It follows that an age-associated loss in brain efficiency (e.g., connectivity) is relatively inconsequential as long as the number of remaining connections remains sufficiently large to activate the relevant information (cf., MacKay & Burke, 1990).

Person-Specific Pragmatic Knowledge.   Psychometric research on crystallized abilities needs to be supplemented by approaches with a more explicit focus on knowledge acquisition and utilization to more fully capture the diversity and specificity of pragmatic knowledge. Whereas normative pragmatic knowledge applies in similar ways to most individuals of a given society, person-specific pragmatic knowledge is seen as a response to idiosyncratic adaptive demands and opportunities (e.g., the work place). Metaphorically speaking, person-specific knowledge systems branch off or diversify from the normative path into individualized pathways.

For the most part (but see Bjorklund, Schneider, & Harnishfeger, 1992; Brown, 1982; Chi & Koeske, 1983; Schneider, Gruber, Gold, & Opwis, 1993; Weinert & Perner, 1996; Wilkening & Anderson, 1990), developmental research on person-specific bodies of knowledge has been undertaken with adults. A typical approach has been to identify the effects of domain-specific knowledge by comparing the performance of experts and novices both inside and outside their domain of expertise. Examples include the classical domains of expertise research such as chess (Charness, 1981) and card games (Bosman & Charness, 1996; Charness, 1983; Knopf, Kolodziej, & Preussler, 1990).

Two main conclusions can be drawn from this research. First, expertise effects, or the consequences of specific bodies of declarative and procedural knowledge, rarely transcend the boundaries of the target domain. Specifically, there is little evidence to suggest that the mechanics of cognition are altered in themselves by domain-specific knowledge (Salthouse, 1991a). Whenever there is evidence for effects of a more general kind, *transfer of pragmatic knowledge* (positive or negative) appears to be a more plausible explanation than the postulation of a basic change in the mechanics.

One example in this regard comes from life-span sociology, and concerns transfer from professional attitudes and behavior to coping with retirement and old age (Featherman et al., 1990). Specifically, Featherman and his colleagues hypothesized that expert engineers with reflective planning orientation are more likely to adapt to life challenges after retirement than expert engineers with a rational problem-solving orientation, because the former are more experienced in dealing with ill-structured tasks than the latter. Another example comes from longitudinal work by Kohn and Schooler (1983) on the relationship between the substantive complexity of work and ideational flexibility. Kohn and Schooler found that work complexity predicts increments in ideational flexibility over a period of 10 years, even after controlling for initial differences in ideational flexibility. It should be noted, however, that the interpretation of findings of this type in terms of experiential factors is rendered difficult through nonrandom placement of individuals into experiential settings (Davies & Sparrow, 1985; Waldman & Avolio, 1986; cf., Scarr & McCartney, 1983).

The second major conclusion concerns the power of pragmatic knowledge to make up for losses in the mechanics *within* the domain of expertise (Bosman & Charness, 1996; Hess & Pullen, 1996; Maylor, 1994; Morrow, Leirer, Fitzsimmons, & Altieri, 1994). Here, the results from several studies suggest that acquired knowledge endows aging individuals with a form of natural and local (e.g., domain-bound) ability to withstand the consequences of aging-induced losses in the mechanics. This finding is of central importance for the issue of successful intellectual aging, and supports the general life-span theory of selective optimization with compensation (P. Baltes, 1993; Staudinger et al., 1995; see the next section). In addition, the idea that knowledge compensates mechanic decline is consistent with the observation that negative adult age differences, compared to standard psychometric or cognitive-experimental assessments, tend to be attenuated in knowledge-rich domains of everyday relevance, such as practical problem solving (Berg, 1996; Heidrich & Denney, 1994; Park, 1992; Sternberg & Wagner, 1986; Sternberg, Wagner, Williams, & Horvath, 1995), social intelligence (Blanchard-Fields, 1996; Cornelius & Caspi, 1987), memory in context (Hess & Pullen, 1996; Perlmutter, Kaplan, & Nyquist, 1990), and interactive-minds cognition (P. Baltes & Staudinger, 1996a, 1996b; Dixon & Gould, 1996; Graf, 1996; Mandl, Gruber, & Renkl, 1996; Staudinger, 1996b; Staudinger & Baltes, 1996).

Intellectual Growth during Adulthood: Stage Conceptions versus Functionalist Approaches

An important debate within life-span intellectual development refers to the question of (a) whether adult intellectual development follows a stage-like logic, and can be described as a movement toward higher forms of reasoning and thought (Basseches, 1984; Labouvie-Vief, 1982); or (b) whether functionalist approaches (P. Baltes & Graf, 1996; Dixon & Baltes, 1986) emphasizing the local nature of developmental adaptations, as they prevail in the study

of knowledge acquisition, selective specialization, and transfer provide a better, or at least more parsimonious and operationalizable, description of adult intellectual growth (Alexander & Langer, 1990; Blanchard-Fields, 1989, 1996; Dixon, Kramer, & Baltes, 1985; Kramer, 1983; Labouvie-Vief, 1982, 1992; Riegel, 1976; Rybash, Hoyer, & Roodin, 1986).

Much of the search for more advanced forms of reasoning and thought in adulthood originates in Piaget's theory of cognitive development (Chapman, 1988a; Labouvie-Vief, 1982; Pascual-Leone, 1983; Piaget, 1970; Riegel, 1976), and posits the possible emergence of one or more post-formal or dialectical stages of cognitive development after the advent of formal operations. The conceptual description of these stages often connects personality development (e.g., generativity in the Eriksonian sense) with logical considerations (e.g., awareness and acceptance of contradiction). As a consequence of this particular linkage, the emergence of such stages is assumed to be accompanied by increments in reflexivity and general awareness for the human condition (cf., Fischer & Bidell, Ch. 9, this Volume; Keil, Ch. 7, this Volume; Spelke & Newport, Ch. 6, this Volume; Thelen & Smith, Ch. 10, this Volume; also see the next section of this chapter). Evidence in support of such stages is scarce, which is not surprising given the difficulties in obtaining reliable indicators of stage-like cognitive change (cf., Molenaar, 1986; van der Maas & Molenaar, 1992).

Despite his constructivist and dialectical epistemology (Chapman, 1988a; Garcia, 1980; Lourenço & Machado, 1996; Piaget, 1980; Piaget & Garcia, 1983), Piaget himself was reluctant to posit any stages beyond formal operations. Instead, he argued on one occasion (Piaget, 1972), that the notion of *horizontal décalage* gives sufficient room to adult intellectual growth within his theory. Specifically, he expected that late adolescents and adults would exhibit formal-operational reasoning within their areas of expertise, but not necessarily across all possible domains of knowledge. This view seems consistent with the two-component model of fluid-crystallized or mechanic-pragmatic intelligence in that the potential for adult intellectual growth is linked to factors operating within rather than across domains (e.g., acquisition of pragmatic knowledge; cf., Flavell, 1970).

Although the debate over the existence of stages in adult intellectual development is far from being settled, it appears to us that a knowledge-based functionalist approach is more amenable to operational definition and empirical investigation. From this perspective, *the structuralist search for higher forms of reasoning can be reframed as the search for bodies of knowledge with a high degree of generality and meaning* (Dörner, 1986). In full agreement with the intent of structuralist theorizing on adult intellectual development, the acquisition of such bodies of knowledge is assumed to counteract the life-span tendency toward fragmentation and specialization induced by less general bodies of knowledge. In this context, *wisdom,* or expertise about the fundamental pragmatics of life, has been proposed as a prototypical example (P. Baltes & Smith, 1990; P. Baltes & Staudinger, 1993; Clayton & Birren, 1980; Sternberg, 1990).

A First Prototypical Example: Expertise in the Fundamental Pragmatics of Life (Wisdom)

Most people, lay persons and researchers alike, regard wisdom as the hallmark of positive intellectual aging (Clayton & Birren, 1980; Sternberg, 1990). Based on the two-component model of intellectual development, P. Baltes and Staudinger (1993; see also, P. Baltes & Smith, 1990) defined wisdom as "an expertise in the fundamental pragmatics of life permitting exceptional insight and judgment involving complex and uncertain matters of the human condition." Accordingly, the fundamental pragmatics of life are defined to embody valuable information about the conduct, interpretation, and meaning of life, including its developmental variability, plasticity, and limitations. Furthermore, wisdom involves the fine-tuned coordination of cognition, motivation, and emotion as it is illustrated in wisdom as the combination of exceptional insight and mature character (P. Baltes & Smith, 1990; P. Baltes & Staudinger, 1993; Staudinger & Baltes, 1994). More specifically, wisdom-related knowledge and judgment have been characterized by a family of five criteria (factual knowledge, procedural knowledge, contextualism, value relativism, and uncertainty).

Thus far, our main methodological strategy in investigating wisdom as an expertise in the fundamental pragmatics of life has been to ask persons to think aloud about difficult life problems. These responses are then evaluated on the five wisdom-related criteria by a trained rater panel. Figure 18.11 displays the results of one of these studies (P. Baltes, Staudinger, Maercker, & Smith, 1995). In

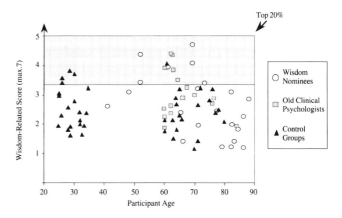

Figure 18.11 Wisdom-related performance of four different groups of individuals averaged across two wisdom-related tasks and five evaluative criteria (factual knowledge, procedural knowledge, contextualism, relativism, and uncertainty). There were no age differences in the age range from 25 to 75 years. In addition, wisdom nominees and clinical psychologists provided significantly more high-level (top 20%) performances than the old control group. Max. = maximum (after P. Baltes, Staudinger, Maercker, & Smith, 1995).

Figure 18.11, an overall wisdom score based on all five criteria is plotted against age for four different groups: Wisdom nominees (i.e., distinguished individuals nominated as being wise in a two-step Delphi technique), clinical psychologists, and two control groups involving adults with comparable advanced levels of education (young and old).

Two findings are noteworthy. First, when comparing adults of about 25 to 75 years of age, there was no indication of a negative age trend in wisdom-related performance. This finding has been replicated in five other studies (cf., Staudinger & Baltes, 1996). Second, older persons with wisdom-facilitative experiences (e.g., older clinical psychologists and wisdom nominees) contributed a disproportionately large share to the top responses (see also, Smith, Staudinger, & Baltes, 1994; Staudinger, Smith, & Baltes, 1992). Both findings stand in clear contrast to the negative age gradients observed for the cognitive mechanics (see Figure 18.10), thereby providing further support for the two-component model.

The findings also demonstrate that living long (age) in itself is not a sufficient condition for the development of wisdom. Rather, as suggested by our working model of the ontogenesis of wisdom (Figure 18.12), it appears that favorable macro-structural contexts (e.g., historical period),

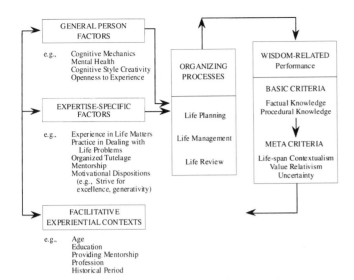

Figure 18.12 A research framework describing antecedent factors and mediating processes for the acquisition and maintenance of wisdom-related knowledge and skills across the life span. The likelihood of attaining expert levels of performance in this prototypical domain of the cognitive pragmatics is assumed to depend upon an effective coalition of life-context, expertise-specific, and general person-related factors (after P. Baltes & Staudinger, 1993; Staudinger & Baltes, 1994).

expertise-specific factors (e.g., experience and training in the fundamental pragmatics of life, strive for excellence, mentorship), and general person factors (e.g., fluid mechanics, cognitive style, openness to experience) need to work in coalition to move people toward wisdom (cf., P. Baltes & Staudinger, 1993). Some of these wisdom-facilitative factors (such as generativity) are age-related; however, there are also wisdom-debilitating influences (such as rigidity, decrease in fluid mechanics) that might come with age. On average, the net result of age-related facilitators and debilitators seems to equal out. Only under favorable conditions, facilitators outweigh debilitators and thus result in an increase of wisdom-related performance with age.

At a more general level of analysis, our research on wisdom serves to highlight the *relative independence of the pragmatics of cognition vis-à-vis the biology-based mechanics*. In fact, within the normal range of adult mechanic functioning, the mechanics' contribution to individual differences on wisdom-related tasks is small, both in absolute terms and relative to other factors such as personality and task-relevant life experience. For instance, in one

adult-developmental study (Staudinger, Maciel, Smith, & Baltes, 1996), the most important contributors to wisdom-related performance were personality characteristics as measured by the NEO as well as wisdom-relevant professional training and experience, rather than psychometrically assessed intelligence or chronological age. However, when it comes to very old age, additional evidence (P. Baltes et al., 1995) suggests that the mechanics of cognition delimit wisdom-related performance if they fall below a critical threshold of functional integrity. Based on our own data, we tentatively suggest that the ninth decade of life may represent such a threshold.

Varieties of Mechanic/Pragmatic Interdependence

The mechanics and pragmatics of life-span intellectual development are intertwined in many ways and at various levels of analysis (cf., Bosman & Charness, 1996). At the phylogenetic level, they are connected in the sense that members of the human species are biologically predisposed to acquire cultural knowledge (cf., Klix, 1993; Plessner, 1965). At the ontogenetic level, the interdependence also runs both ways. For instance, the potential to acquire and use pragmatic knowledge is conditioned by the development of the mechanics. At the same time, the mechanics alone are of little use for problem solving in highly specialized domains of knowledge; in many cases, domain-specific knowledge (Ericsson, Krampe, & Tesch-Römer, 1993; Ericsson & Lehmann, 1996) or common sense (Sternberg et al., 1995) is more critical.

In the following sections, we further elucidate different facets of this interdependence. We then argue, with respect to the overall landscape of life-span development, or the ontogenetic dynamics of gains and losses, that the mechanic-pragmatic interdependence converges upon the notion of a *compensatory relation between mechanic efficiency and pragmatic knowledge*. This compensatory relation increases in importance with advancing age and culminates in old age.

The Mechanic-Pragmatic Interdependence: Evidence at the Cortical Level

One intriguing demonstration for the interdependence between mechanic and pragmatic development concerns the increased cortical representation of the left hand in players of string instruments (Elbert, Pantev, Wienbruch, Rockstroh,

& Taub, 1995). Compared to normal individuals, areas of the somatosensory cortex representing the fingers of the left hand seem to occupy more space in string players. Most likely, this increase in cortical representation has been induced by large amounts of goal-directed and deliberate practice (cf., Ericsson et al., 1993). In this sense, the increase is a representation of pragmatic knowledge (of a procedural kind, in this case).

At the same time, Elbert et al. (1995) provided clear evidence in support of age-graded differences in cortical plasticity (Figure 18.13). Specifically, the brain's physiological aptness to provide more cortical space for the fingers of the left hand was found to depend upon the chronological age at inception of musical practice. As this example illustrates, the ability to acquire pragmatic knowledge (e.g., the potential for developmental change in the pragmatic component) is conditioned by the age-graded status of the mechanics.

The Age of Peak Performance in Complex Skills

The mechanics of cognition not only condition the acquisition, but also the expression of pragmatic knowledge (Bosman & Charness, 1996; Molander & Bäckman, 1993).

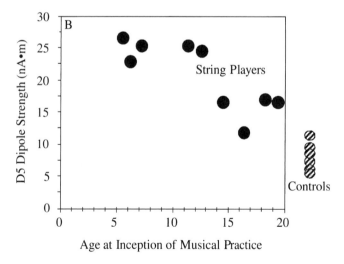

Figure 18.13 The cortical representation of the fingers of the left hand is increased in string players, but the magnitude of the increase depends on the age at inception of musical practice. The findings illustrates how life-span changes in the potential for the acquisition of new pragmatic knowledge are conditioned by age-based changes in the mechanic component (adapted from Elbert et al., 1995).

A good example in this regard is the difference in peak age for tournament versus correspondence chess (Charness & Bosman, 1990). The mean age at which a world championship is first won is about 46 years of age for correspondence chess, but about 30 years of age for tournament chess. In correspondence chess, players are permitted three days to deliberate a move; in tournament chess, deliberation averages three minutes per move. Thus, the difference in peak age between the two activities seems to reflect differences in the relative importance of cognitive/perceptual speed and knowledge.

This example points to a general dilemma governing the relation between the mechanics, the pragmatics, and age/time (cf., Ericsson, 1990). On the one hand, the acquisition of expertise takes time. For instance, Simon and Chase (1973) argued that ten years of deliberate practice are needed to reach excellence in a particular domain of functioning. For this reason alone, experts tend to be older than novices (cf., Lehman, 1953). On the other hand, decrements in certain aspects of the mechanics, such as perceptual speed, can be reliably identified by age 30 (Salthouse, 1991c). Therefore, differences in peak age across domains can be seen as ontogenetic compromises between biology and culture, and are probably good indicators of the relative importance of pragmatic knowledge and mechanic processing efficiency.

To avoid misunderstandings, we hasten to add that an exclusive focus on ages of peak productivity or peak achievement would hide essential and unique features of late-life intellectual growth. For instance, some exceptional individuals seem to escape mechanic decline well into the ninth decade of their lives. If these individuals also happen to be experts in a particular domain, they can produce outstanding works throughout their life. One example might be Sophocles (497–406 B.C.), who won his first prize for the best drama of the year at age 28, wrote over 120 dramas, and developed a new dramatic style in his 80s. Commenting on his own late-life artistic development, Sophocles said that he finally had liberated himself from the artificiality of his earlier style, and had found a language that was the best and the most ethical (Schadewaldt, 1975, p. 75).

Another example pointing to the uniqueness of late-life experts comes from a study on classical composers by Simonton (1988, 1989). Guided by the general notion that artists facing death may feel the need to make optimal use of their limited future, Simonton examined the relationship between closeness to death and a set of criterion variables for a sample of 1,910 works written by 172 classical composers. Last works scored lower in melodic variability and performance duration, but higher in repertoire popularity and aesthetic significance. Based on this evidence, Simonton argued that this tendency towards condensed expression of the essential is a general feature of late-life intellectual productivity.

A Third Prototypical Example: Speed and Knowledge in Aging Typists

The preceding considerations indicate that the degrees of freedom within the pragmatic component of cognition are constrained by age-based changes in the potential and status of the mechanic component. However, in agreement with the notion of culture-biology co-evolution (Durham, 1991), we argue that the interdependence between the mechanics and the pragmatics also runs in the other direction.

First, the pragmatics of cognition provide the *medium* or content for the phenotypic unfolding of the mechanics during ontogeny. A good example is the mapping of Universal Grammar onto the structures of a specific language during first-language acquisition (cf., Pinker, 1994). Second, the pragmatics of cognition serve to *optimize* levels of performance in content-rich and evolutionarily nonprivileged domains of intellectual functioning, as research on expertise has convincingly demonstrated (Ericsson & Lehmann, 1996). Third, pragmatic knowledge helps to *compensate* for age-based losses in the mechanic component. For this reason, the pragmatic component, when compared to the mechanics rather than to itself across ontogeny, actually appears in a more aging-friendly light. In fact, we expect that more and more of an individual's potential for continued growth and maintenance of functioning is shifted away from the mechanic component, and into the continued refinement (e.g., optimization) and use of the pragmatic component.

A good empirical demonstration of the ensuing gain/loss dynamic between the cognitive mechanics and the cognitive pragmatics comes from a study on aging typists using the so-called molar equivalence/molecular decomposition approach (Salthouse, 1984). In this paradigm, adults of different ages are equated in general (e.g., molar) task proficiency to investigate whether equal levels of criterion performance are attained through age-differential profiles

of "molecular" component processes (Charness, 1989). Thus, age differences at the molecular level of analysis are seen as a reflection of age-based changes in the relative contribution of knowledge and basic processing efficiency to criterion performance.

Using this paradigm, Salthouse (1984) studied a total of 74 transcription typists ranging from 19 to 72 years of age. Figure 18.14 displays an interpretation of the main findings of this study in terms of the two-component model. In this sample, age and level of typing skill (i.e., net words per minute) were uncorrelated (e.g., molar equivalence). Age was negatively related to measures of perceptual/motor speed (e.g., tapping speed), but positively related to eye-hand span. In other words, older typists were slower in tapping speed but looked further ahead in the text to-be-typed. These findings are consistent with the interpretation that aging typists extend their eye-hand span to counteract the consequences of aging losses in perceptual/motor speed, and illustrate the compensatory relationship between knowledge and speed.

In fact, to the extent that selective attrition does not play a prominent role, the performance pattern of older typists is, in part, the result of *loss-induced development,* or compensation in the strict sense of the term (Baltes & Baltes, 1990b; Dixon & Bäckman, 1995; Salthouse, 1995). With respect to methods, this example demonstrates how the combination of

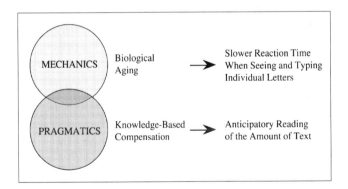

Figure 18.14 Older typists can maintain a high level of functioning by reading farther ahead in the text to be typed, despite a loss in reaction time when typing individual letters. The example illustrates the compensatory relationship between the pragmatics and the mechanics of cognition, and suggests that selective optimization with compensation may play a key role in successfully adapting to aging-induced losses in the mechanics of cognition (based on Salthouse, 1984).

expertise and information-processing approaches may lead to a better understanding of the compensatory relation between acquired bodies of cultural knowledge and basic aspects of information processing efficiency.

Malleability (Plasticity) in Intellectual Functioning across Historical and Ontogenetic Time

As is true for development in general, life-span changes in intellectual functioning represent the overdetermined antecedents, correlates, and outcomes of a large variety of different sources of influence (e.g., mechanics, pragmatics, motivation, personality, societal opportunity structures). Therefore, differences in level of intellectual performance reflect, within the age-graded boundaries provided by the mechanics, variations in physical and sociocultural aspects of environmental conditions (Klix, 1993). In the following section, we report two interrelated lines of research in support of this contention. The first line of research addresses environmental change at a large (i.e., historical) time scale. The second example refers to the malleability of adult-intellectual functioning in the context of cognitive intervention studies.

Cohort Effects, Period Effects, and Environmental Change

As expected on the basis of life-span contextualism, ontogenetic processes unfold in a constantly changing social and cultural environment. As a consequence, age gradients in intellectual abilities are not fixed but reflect history-graded systems of influence, such as enduring differences between individuals born at different points in historical time (cohort effects), specific influences of historical events across chronological age (period effects), or generalized and enduring shifts in the environment affecting individuals of all ages and subsequent cohorts (general environmental change). For methodological reasons, discriminating among these varieties of environmental change is not easy (P. Baltes, 1968; P. Baltes, Cornelius, & Nesselroade, 1979; Lindenberger & Baltes, 1994a; Magnusson et al., 1991; Schaie, 1965, 1994).

A first step to discern effects of large-scale environmental change is to compare the performance of same-aged individuals across historical time (i.e., time-lagged comparisons). With some exceptions (e.g., number ability; cf., Schaie, 1989), the general picture resulting from such comparisons is that higher test scores are obtained at more recent times (Flynn, 1984; Schaie, 1983). Probably, this historical increase in test scores across historical time is not due to changes in the genetic composition of the population or differential sampling bias, but reflects some general change (i.e., improvement) in health- and education-related conditions. The magnitude of these effects can be quite large. For the U.S. population during the 20th century, for instance, they sometimes exceeded a standard deviation within a 30-year range of historical change (Schaie, 1996). It should be cautioned, however, that we do not know whether environmental-change effects of the same order of magnitude would be observed with pure indicators of the mechanics of intelligence. For instance, much of the measures used in the battery of the Seattle Longitudinal Study (Schaie, 1996) have a strong cultural-knowledge component, and are more likely to be affected by historical change and dissipation than other, less knowledge-loaded measures of brain efficiency.

Studies with cohort-sequential (e.g., mixed) designs such as the Seattle Longitudinal Study (Schaie, 1983, 1996) are well suited for three different kinds of comparisons across age: Cross-sectional, longitudinal, and independent-sample same-cohort comparisons (e.g., age comparisons based on independent samples from the same birth cohort). In the case of the Seattle Longitudinal Study, for example, independent-sample same-cohort and cross-sectional comparisons were found to yield practically identical estimates of seven-year change after controlling for the general increase in performance over historical time revealed by time-lagged comparisons (Salthouse, 1991b). In contrast, longitudinal age changes, also corrected for historical change, showed somewhat less of a decrement with age. Given the convergence between cross-sectional and independent-sample same-cohort comparisons, the more positive age gradients found with longitudinal samples may be partly due to practice effects and selective attrition.

Theoretically, the direction and precise magnitude of historical-change effects is generally of little importance. From a history-of-science point of view, however, such effects, and especially their interpretation as culturally-based cohort effects, were instrumental in pointing to the substantial malleability (plasticity) of intellectual performance during all periods of the adult life span (P. Baltes, 1973). The resulting growth in awareness for the existence of life-span plasticity eventually led to advances in life-span theorizing, and to more controlled investigations into the range of intellectual plasticity and its age-based limits (P. Baltes & Kliegl, 1992; P. Baltes & Lindenberger, 1988; P. Baltes & Willis, 1982; Willis, 1987, 1990).

Cognitive Intervention Work: Activation of Learning Potential among Older Adults

Intervention work (P. Baltes & Willis, 1982; Denney, 1984; Willis, 1987, 1990) is a more direct (i.e., experimentally controlled) way to explore the degree of plasticity in intellectual functioning than cohort-comparative research. In the field of adult development and aging, intervention studies were done to examine whether age-based decrements in standard psychometric tests of intellectual functioning are reversible, in full or in part, through training and practice (Schaie & Willis, 1986; Willis & C. Nesselroade, 1990). For the most part, interventions involved older adults only, and focused on tests from the fluid (mechanical) ability domain.

The major results of this cognitive intervention work can be summarized in five points (cf., P. Baltes & Lindenberger, 1988):

1. Training gains in the practiced tests among healthy older adults are substantial (i.e., they roughly correspond to the amount of naturally occurring longitudinal decline between 60 and 80 years of age).

2. Transfer, however, is limited to similar tests of the same ability.

3. Training gains are maintained over lengthy periods of time up to several years (Neely & Bäckman, 1993; Willis & C. Nesselroade, 1990).

4. The factor structure of the ability space is not altered substantially through training (Schaie, Willis, Hertzog, & Schulenberg, 1987).

5. In persons at risk for Alzheimer's disease or afflicted by other forms of brain pathology (Nebes, 1992), training gains have been found to be restricted to experimental conditions of high external support (Bäckman, Josephsson, Herlitz, Stigsdotter, & Viitanen, 1991) or to be nonexistent (M. Baltes, Kühl, & Sowarka, 1992; M. Baltes et al., 1995).

These results indicate that the majority of healthy older adults, including those who display the typical pattern of age-related losses in the mechanics of cognition (e.g., fluid abilities) under untrained conditions, are able to greatly improve their performance after a few sessions of task-related training or practice. Thus, cognitive plasticity in the mechanics of cognition is preserved into old age, and is easily activated through experiential manipulations (cf., Woodruff-Pak, 1993, for relevant neurophysiological evidence). However, there is little evidence to suggest that training gains generalize to related abilities or to everyday functioning. Moreover, the results of testing-the-limits research presented above clearly indicate that the *amount* (scope) of plasticity decreases with advancing age, at least during adulthood. At limits of functioning, older adults definitely display less potential. Finally, it is difficult to counter the rival interpretation, namely that training gains are primarily due to pragmatic rather than mechanic components of performance potential.

Relative Stability in Intellectual Functioning across the Life Span

The issue of continuity and discontinuity, or stability and change, has a long tradition within developmental psychology at large (Kagan, 1980), and life-span intellectual development, in particular (Collins & Horn, 1991; Hertzog & Nesselroade, 1987; McArdle & Epstein, 1987; Nesselroade, 1989, 1991c; Schaie, 1989, 1994). Different forms of stability, such as stability in level, rank order, and profiles, have been set apart (Caspi & Bem, 1990). The main emphasis of the following life-span synopsis of intellectual development is on inter-individual rank order, or on what Kagan (1980) has called relative stability, which denotes the extent to which individual differences during later periods of ontogeny can be predicted on the basis of individual differences observed during earlier periods. In addition to our primary focus on relative stability, we will also address changes in level (e.g., ontogenetic increases and decreases in functional competence), especially with respect to the period of adulthood and old age.

Statistically, stability in rank order and stability in level can vary independently. Empirically, they often seem to covary across ontogeny. For instance, periods in which level stability is high, such as middle adulthood and early old age, also show a high degree of relative stability (rank order of inter-individual differences) per unit of ontogenetic time. Conversely, periods of pronounced change in level, such as early and middle childhood, also tend to show less inter-individual stability. An explanation for this congruence between changes in rank and level is offered below.

In most cases, evidence on the relative stability after infancy is based on undifferentiated measures of general intelligence, or IQ tests. We agree with others that an exclusive focus on these omnibus measures hides essential features of life-span intellectual development and the structure of intelligence (cf., Cattell, 1971; Gardner, Ch. 8, this Volume; Horn, 1989). Specifically, such measures can be seen as mixtures of mechanic and normative-pragmatic components of intellectual functioning which approximate, to varying degrees, the centroid of the intellectual ability factor space (i.e., Spearman's g). With this qualification in mind, we restrict the following discussion, with one exception (i.e., infant development), to undifferentiated or IQ-like measures of intellectual functioning.

Predicting Childhood Intelligence on the Basis of Infant Behavior

Until the end of the first half of this century, it was generally believed that intelligence was an immutable characteristic of the individual, which led to the unchallenged assumption that individuals maintain their rank order on measures of intellectual functioning throughout life. Starting in the 1960s, however, it was found that stability in early mental test performance was low (McCall, 1979). On the basis of this evidence, it was concluded that standardized tests of infant development do not predict later intelligence at useful levels of prediction until after 18 to 24 months of age. The apparent lack of inter-individual temporal stability was attributed to fundamental changes in the nature of intelligence from infancy through childhood to adulthood (Kopp & McCall, 1982). For instance, it was believed that mental development during infancy consists of specific stages of an invariant developmental program, and that individual differences reflect transient and inconsequential fluctuations in the rate at which this program is expressed, rather than enduring inter-individual differences in intellectual functioning.

This majority view of ontogenetic instability of inter-individual differences during infancy was successfully challenged by research using habituation and recognition-memory paradigms (Bornstein & Sigman, 1986). In contrast to standardized infant tests of sensorimotor capacities, these two paradigms were originally based on operant-conditioning and/or information-processing perspectives, and refer to infants' tendency to change their behaviors as a function of prior exposure to a stimulus (e.g., decrements in attention in the case of habituation, or novelty preference in the case of recognition memory). On average, individual differences in habituation and recognition memory performance between 2 and 8 *months* were found to be moderately correlated with standard tests of intelligence such as the Wechsler, Bayley, or Binet administered between 1 and 8 *years* (median correlation, $r = .45$; after attenuation for unreliability, $r = .70$; cf., Bornstein, 1989; McCall & Carriger, 1993). Behavior-genetic research suggests that individual differences in at least some of the measures used for prediction have a genetic component (Benson, Cherny, Haith, & Fulker, 1993; Cardon & Fulker, 1991; DiLalla et al., 1990).

These results show that both change *and* stability are important aspects of life-span intellectual development from its very beginning. According to one interpretation (Bornstein, 1989; Fagan & McGrath, 1981), infants who habituate more efficiently, and who tend to look at the novel object, rather than the old, are better able to inhibit action tendencies associated with already existing representations (cf., McCall, 1994). The hypothesis that inhibition may mediate the predictive link is consistent with neuropsychological investigations of infants' recognition memory (e.g., Diamond, 1988; Johnson, Posner, & Rothbart, 1991). It also supports the more general claim that inhibition ability and novelty preference are central features of intelligence (cf., Berg & Sternberg, 1985b).

Relative Inter-Individual Stability after Infancy

For reasons that are not yet well understood (Cardon & Fulker, 1991; McCall & Carriger, 1993), the magnitude of the correlation between infant measures of habituation (i.e., 2 to 8 months) and childhood measures of intelligence (i.e., 1 to 12 years) is temporally stable or even increasing (Cardon & Fulker, 1991; DiLalla et al., 1990), rather than decreasing over time. In contrast, relative stability after infancy is rather well described on the basis of quasi-simplex assumptions (Humphreys & Davey, 1988; Molenaar, Boomsma, & Dolan, 1991). Thus, adjacent time points in ontogeny tend to be more highly correlated than more distant time points.

In addition, stability coefficients computed over identical lapses of time show a considerable increase in magnitude from childhood to adolescence into middle adulthood and early old age (Gold et al., 1995; Hertzog & Schaie, 1986, 1988; Humphreys & Davey, 1988). For instance, Humphreys and Davey reported a continuous increase in *one-year* stability coefficients of general intelligence, with a value of .76 between the ages of 4 and 5, and a value of .90 for the ages of 8 and 9. With respect to later ages, Hertzog and Schaie (1986) found that *seven-year* stability coefficients for a general ability composite ranged from .89 to .96 in samples with mean ages between 25 and 67 years at first test. These are extraordinarily high levels of inter-individual long-term stability.

In agreement with others (e.g., Humphreys & Davey, 1988; Molenaar, Boomsma, & Dolan, 1993), we propose that these *age-based changes in relative inter-individual stability should be interpreted in connection with age-based changes in level*. According to this line of reasoning, inter-individual differences change more rapidly early in development because the intellectual repertoire is smaller but growing faster than at later points during ontogeny, thereby giving room for larger amounts of new variance per unit time (both environmental and genetic). By the same token, we expect that aging-induced losses not only lead to decrements in level, but also to a reshuffling of individual differences in very old age (Lindenberger & Baltes, 1994a, 1994b). In accord with this prediction, recent longitudinal studies on the oldest old report a decrease in relative stability after age 70 (e.g., Mitrushina & Satz, 1991).

Changes in Heritability across the Life Span

We now turn to the study of age-based changes in the contribution of genetic and environmental sources of inter-individual variability to individual differences in intelligence. We start with a consideration of general and ability-specific effects, and then turn our attention to life-span changes in heritability estimates for general (i.e., undifferentiated) measures of intelligence across the life span.

Before we turn to the evidence on life-span changes in heritability estimates, we will briefly summarize our view of the meaning, strength, and limitations of the behavior-genetics approach (Baltes, Reese, & Nesselroade, 1988). Given the critical debates surrounding the interpretation of behavior-genetic data (cf., Bronfenbrenner & Ceci, 1994; Burgess & Molenaar, 1995; Gottlieb et al., Ch. 5, this Volume; R. Lerner, 1995; Scarr, 1993), such a note may help to avoid possible misunderstandings.

A Note on the Nature of Behavior-Genetic Evidence

A detailed coverage of the full range of behavior-genetic research designs, including their recent links to molecular genetics (Boomsma, 1996; McClearn, Plomin, Gora-Malask, & Crabbe, 1991) and their important role in the study of developmental pathologies (Rutter, 1993, 1997), is beyond the scope of this note. Rather, we restrict our commentary to the interpretation of heritability estimates in normal samples. We will explicate three points that are relevant both for the following section on intellectual functioning as well as on personality and the self.

The first point is intended to show that heritability coefficients in human research (where selective inbreeding and exposure to extreme environments is limited) are statements about the scope of inter-individual differences more so than statements about the processes and mechanisms of genetic expression at the individual and intra-individual level of analysis. The second point highlights the fact that the overall role of environmental forces is not best tested by behavior-genetics models. The power of environmental forces is best tested by environmental variation studies which are designed to generalize *across* inter-individual differences in genetic dispositions. The third point emphasizes that heritability estimates are fixed-level statistics. In other words, heritability estimates are always restricted to what consequences (phenotypic expressions) are produced under a given and specific set of inter-individual differences in genetic and environmental conditions.

As to the first point: Heritability estimates are statements about inter-individual differences more so than statements about the processes and mechanisms of genetic expression at the individual level of analysis. In other words, heritability-based estimates cannot be generalized to the individual level of analysis and within-person (intra-individual) functioning. This critical view of heritability information and its limited value for understanding genetic processes is the predominant position of molecular biologists who work on the level of gene expression (e.g., Gottlieb et al., Ch. 5, this Volume). They claim that the search for gene expression through behavior-genetic work is at best indirect. Population-based behavior genetics can give clues about the existence of heritability of inter-individual differences, but knowledge about heritability in the general population is not an immediate guidepost for identifying the specific locations and the biological-genetic ways of gene expression (see, however, Boomsma,

1996; McClearn, Plomin, Gora-Malask, & Crabbe, 1991; Nilsson et al., 1996, for ways to bridge the gap).

The second point highlights the fact that the overall role of environmental factors or *levels* of performance is best tested, not by heritability estimates, but by studies which examine the role of the impact of environmental factors across the population and across inter-individual differences in genetic make-up. Often, high heritability estimates are interpreted as if they would preclude the operation of environmental factors. This is simply wrong. Consider as a first example the study of expertise (Ericsson & Smith, 1991) where the typical finding is major increases in performance for *all* persons who participate in expertise-inducing interventions. Another example is the historical evolution of cultural skills such as reading or writing in industrialized countries, from a low of a few percent in the middle ages to close to 100% in modern times (Olson, 1995), or the evolution of life expectancy during the 20th century in industrialized countries, from an average of about 45 years to an average of about 75 years (P. Baltes & Graf, 1996). During these times, it was not the genetic make-up of the population or of individuals which changed to permit the acquisition of reading and writing or to live longer. What changed was primarily the set of environmental conditions (such as schooling, medical technology, etc.) which regulated the probability of optimizing the genetic potential available to practically all members of society.

The third point emphasizes that heritability estimates are always fixed-level statistics (P. Baltes, Reese, & Nesselroade, 1988; Plomin & Thompson, 1988). This applies both to the expressed genome as well as to the environment. In the experimental design literature, for instance, a fixed-level statistic means that the "treatment" conditions are not a random sample of the full spectrum of treatment possibilities. On the contrary, fixed-level statistics are specifically instantiated levels of the treatment. Therefore, the results obtained from human behavior-genetic research cannot speak to what genetic and environmental effects exist in principle, but only to the conditions defined by the levels chosen or available. Therefore, in behavior-genetic work, heritability estimates of inter-individual differences reflect only those genetic and environmental conditions that exist at a given point in history and in a given demographic and sociocultural context. If a behavior-genetics study, for instance, is conducted in Sweden, it is the genetic and environmental context of Sweden, and its possible

inter-individual variations, which is under study, and the resulting heritability coefficients reflect that fixed or specific level of "Swedish" environmental modulation of "Swedish" inter-individual differences in genetic make-up. To counterbalance this restriction to generalizability, behavior-genetics research aims at comparative studies in which other and possibly wider or more restricted environmental conditions and genetic samples are observed (e.g., Finkel, Pedersen, McGue, & McClearn, 1995; Pedersen, 1993).

Despite these limitations in interpretation, we suggest that information deriving from behavior-genetics research is important. Findings based on behavior-genetics research, especially if based on longitudinal and cross-cultural comparative data, provide *estimates* of the degree to which, on a population level of analysis, *inter-individual differences in developmental outcomes* are co-determined by inter-individual differences in genetic predispositions and extant environmental variations. Thus, everything else being equal, high heritability estimates of a given behavioral outcome suggest that *inter-individual differences* in this behavioral outcome and in this "life space" (Lewin) are strongly genetically determined, stronger than those *inter-individual differences* in behavioral outcomes with low heritability estimates. Note again, however, that high heritability does not speak to the level (plasticity, malleability) of developmental outcomes (expression) that is available to all members of the population; nor does it imply that inter-individual differences are genetically fixed.

Genetic and Environmental Influence over Ontogenetic Time: Specific and General Effects

Numerous studies have shown that genetic and environmental influences can be operative in the regulation of individual differences at both ability-specific and more general levels (Cardon & Fulker, 1993, 1994; Pedersen, Plomin, & McClearn, 1994). In longitudinal analyses of hierarchically organized intellectual abilities obtained from genetically informative data sets, it is possible to determine the genetic and environmental contributions to stability and change in rank order and mean level both at the level of specific abilities and at the level of a general factor.

An interesting example for the class of findings that can be obtained with this method comes from child cognitive development. In an analysis of data from the Colorado

Adoption Project, Cardon and Fulker (1993, 1994; Fulker, Cherny, & Cardon, 1993) found that strong novel contributions of genetic variance at the general level emerge at the ages of 3 and 7, but are absent at the ages of 4 and 9. This pattern is consistent with the notion of generalized, discontinuous changes in intellectual functioning (e.g., Piaget, 1970). In addition, it suggests that a major portion of inter-individual differences in this transition are genetic in origin.

Estimates of Heritability of Inter-Individual Differences across the Life Span

Similar to life-span changes in stability, heritability (e.g., the amount of inter-individual variance in intellectual functioning attributable to genetic differences) increases from about 40% to 50% during childhood and adolescence to about 80% in early and middle adulthood (cf., McGue, Bouchard, Iacono, & Lykken, 1993b). In contrast, shared environmental influences on inter-individual differences generally do not persist beyond the period of common rearing (McGue et al., 1993b).

It should be kept in mind that these findings are based on samples representing the normal range of environments and genes, and cannot be generalized beyond this normal range (e.g., to extremes of environmental deprivation or reshuffled environments). Within this normal range, however, the life-span increase in heritability of inter-individual differences is consistent with the notion that adolescents and adults have more of a chance to actively select environments that match their genes than infants and children (Scarr & McCartney, 1983). With respect to late-life heritability, recent data from the Swedish Adoption Twin Study of Aging (SATSA) suggest that heritability of inter-individual differences in intellectual functioning may drop to values around 55% after age 70 (Finkel, Pedersen, McGue, & McClearn, 1995).

Based on the preceding summaries, it appears that relative stability and heritability exhibit similar life-span age gradients (cf., Plomin & Thompson, 1988). More behavior-genetic longitudinal evidence is needed to fully understand the covariance dynamics of this life-span parallelism. One possibility would be that individual differences in intellectual functioning around middle adulthood are highly stable because the genetic variance component has stabilized at a high level (e.g., not much new genetic variance is added over time), and because environments (which, in part, have

been selected on the basis of genetic endowment) also tend to be stable during this period of the life span. Similarly, the breakdown of well-orchestrated genome expression in very old age (see above) may cause late-life decrements in level, relative stability, and heritability.

The Mechanics and Pragmatics in Very Old Age

So far, our discussion of life-span intellectual development was organized around topics, rather than age periods. In this last section, we deviate from this practice by giving special attention to the life period of very old age. In our view, this last phase of life merits such attention because it represents a natural boundary condition for the validity of the two-component model of intelligence and cognition. Specifically, we expect that an increasing portion of the very old population eventually attains levels of mechanic functioning that are sufficiently low to impair intellectual functioning in a relatively global manner.

A number of recent empirical observations from the Berlin Aging Study (BASE; cf., Baltes, Mayer, Helmchen, & Steinhagen-Thiessen, 1993) support and qualify this prediction. The first-wave sample of this study consists of 516 individuals between the ages of 70 and 103 stratified by age and gender. Cognitive functioning was assessed with a psychometric test battery comprising multiple indicators of reasoning, perceptual speed, and memory (i.e., short-term acquisition and retrieval) from the fluid-mechanic domain, as well as verbal knowledge and word fluency from the normative-pragmatic domain (cf., Lindenberger, Mayr, & Kliegl, 1993). Three results from this very old sample are most pertinent to the two-component model (cf., P. Baltes & Lindenberger, 1997; Lindenberger & Baltes, 1997).

Covariance Dedifferentiation

First, ability intercorrelations both between and within fluid-mechanic and normative-pragmatic domains were of much higher magnitude in old age than corresponding ability intercorrelations during middle and early adulthood. Based on these data, the amount of covariation among intellectual abilities, or the prominence of g, seems to increase considerably in very old age. The idea that g may vary as a function of age and/or ability level dates back to Spearman (cf., Deary & Pagliari, 1991), and has led to the differentiation/dedifferentiation hypothesis of life-span intelligence (cf., Garrett, 1946; Lienert & Crott, 1964;

Reinert, 1970). Due to methodological difficulties in testing this hypothesis (Nesselroade & Thompson, 1995), the evidence obtained so far is still inconclusive, but generally seems supportive (P. Baltes et al., 1980; Deary et al., 1996; Schaie, Willis, Jay, & Chipuer, 1989).

From the perspective of the two-component model of cognitive development, the decrease of ability intercorrelations during childhood and the increase of intercorrelations in very old age point to age-based changes (i.e., decrements and increments) in the importance of domain-general processing constraints. In fact, there are clear indications from the Berlin Aging Study that dedifferentiation in very old age transcends the cognitive domain, and also affects sensory functioning (e.g., vision and hearing) and sensorimotor functioning (e.g., balance/gait), which gives further credibility to this line of reasoning (P. Baltes & Lindenberger, 1997; Lindenberger & Baltes, 1994b; cf., Schieber & Baldwin, 1996).

Directionality Dedifferentiation

The second finding from the Berlin Aging Study concerns the directionality of the age gradients. In very old age, differences in directionality between mechanic and normative-pragmatic abilities tend to disappear. Instead, we observe gradations of age differences in the negative direction. For instance, fluid-mechanic abilities show somewhat more decline (e.g., $r = .49$ to $.59$) than normative-pragmatic abilities (e.g., $r = .41$ to $.46$). Albeit statistically significant, this difference is relatively small. The tendency towards the unification of age gradients in very old age supports our claim (see Figure 18.1) that biology puts increasingly severe constraints upon intellectual life with advancing age.

Maintenance of Divergence in Explanatory Correlational Patterns

Given the two preceding findings, one may begin to wonder whether the distinction between the mechanics and the pragmatics of cognition loses all of its empirical foundation in very old age. Figure 18.15 suggests that this is not the case, comparing the correlational patterns of perceptual speed, a fluid-mechanic ability, and verbal knowledge, a normative-pragmatic marker, with variables related to individual differences in sociostructural-biographical or biological status.

Without exception, correlations to indicators of biological functioning were more pronounced for perceptual

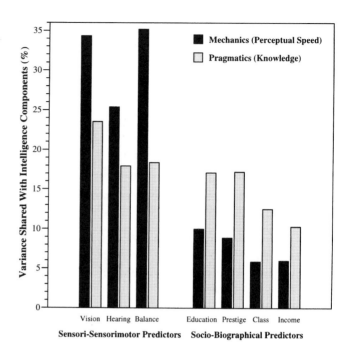

Figure 18.15 The divergent validity regarding explanatory sources of the two-component model of life-span intellectual development continues into very old age. The figure displays differential correlational links of perceptual speed, a marker of the fluid mechanics, and verbal knowledge, a marker of the crystallized pragmatics, to indicators of sociostructural-biographical and biological (e.g., sensory) status. The marker of cognitive mechanics was more highly correlated with biological indicators than verbal knowledge, the marker of cognitive pragmatics, and verbal knowledge was more highly correlated with sociostructural-biographical indicators than perceptual speed. Thus, despite a general tendency towards dedifferentiation due to age-based losses in the mechanics on the descriptive level, the two components of life-span cognition in old age evince the expected divergence regarding its explanatory sources (biological vs. cultural). Data are taken from the Berlin Aging Study ($N = 516$, *age range* = 70—103 years) (after Lindenberger & Baltes, 1997).

speed (e.g., the mechanics) than for verbal knowledge (e.g., the pragmatics). The reverse was also true: Correlations to sociostructural-biographical markers were more pronounced for verbal knowledge than for perceptual speed. Apparently, then, the mechanic-pragmatic distinction does not dissolve completely in very old age, but is maintained in the guise of divergent relations to biological and cultural systems of influence.

Life-Span Intellectual Development: Conclusions

Based on the foregoing (admittedly selective) review of research and theory, we would like to propose the following synopsis of the overall ontogenetic landscape of life-span intellectual development:

1. To capture the life-span dynamics between biology and culture in the domains of intelligence and cognition (P. Baltes, 1987, 1993), we contrasted the mechanics with the pragmatics, and propose a two-component model of intellectual development. This model is inspired by the psychometric theory of fluid and crystallized intelligence (Cattell, 1971; Horn, 1970, 1982). At the same time, it calls for a wider range of conceptualization, including evolutionary-psychological, cognitive-experimental and expertise approaches, to arrive at more valid and comprehensive representations of life-span intellectual development. The two-component model accurately predicts a relatively late life-span peak followed by maintenance and only a late-life decline for the knowledge-saturated cognitive pragmatics, and a much earlier life-span peak followed by monotonic decline for the cognitive mechanics. It also accurately predicts differential ontogenetic sources of explanation. In adulthood and old age, for instance, the mechanics are primarily regulated by biological factors, whereas the cognitive pragmatics evince, in addition, a substantial link to culture-based experiential factors.

2. In terms of mechanisms, age-related changes in information processing rate, working memory capacity, and the inhibition of irrelevant information are the three most prominent candidates for the explanation of life-span changes in the mechanics of cognition. At present, these constructs tend to suffer from a lack of formalization, a lack of direct evidence at the physiological level, and from difficulties in making differential predictions. It is expected that a closer link to the cognitive neurosciences will foster further progress in this area of research.

3. Extant measures of mechanic functioning tend to be contaminated by pragmatic influences. To arrive at more accurate descriptions of life-span gradients in the mechanics of cognition, and to move towards explanation in terms of critical components and mechanisms, measurement needs to be purified through the utilization of methods that are better able to assess individuals' upper limits of functioning. As predicted by theory, the use of such methods (e.g., testing-the-limits) results in cleaner separations of individuals from different ages than the use of standard measures.

4. In contrast to the mechanics, the knowledge- and culture-based pragmatics of cognition offer the potential for positive change during adulthood and old age. Within the pragmatic domain, we proposed the distinction between normative and person-specific bodies of knowledge. Normative bodies of knowledge are acquired in the context of general socialization events, such as basic cultural skills and educational curricula, and in general are well amenable to psychometric testing (e.g., vocabulary tests, aptitude tests). Person-specific knowledge refers to specialized knowledge systems that branch off from the normative (average) path, with professional expertise being the most prominent example studied so far. The content of person-specific bodies of knowledge differs widely across individuals, and is better captured within the expertise paradigm (Ericsson & Smith, 1991).

5. The acquisition of expert levels of knowledge during adulthood may lead to an increasing fragmentation of the intellectual system, but it also may offer the opportunity for acquiring bodies of knowledge with a wide range of applicability, generality, and integration. Wisdom-related knowledge, or knowledge about the meaning and conduct of life, is a prototypical example in this regard. The likelihood of acquiring such domain-general bodies of person-specific knowledge depends upon a special coalition of life-history, expertise-specific, and person-related factors.

6. Throughout ontogeny, the pragmatics and mechanics of cognition are intertwined. In everyday life, intellectual functioning and intellectual products represent joint effects of both. For instance, the emergence of domains of pragmatic knowledge builds on, and presumably extends and modifies, evolutionarily predisposed core domains (Karmiloff-Smith, 1992). The mechanisms of this pruning of cultural knowledge onto species-specific architecture await further study. Another example of pragmatic/mechanic interdependence concerns the acquisition and use of pragmatic knowledge to compensate for mechanic decline. In close agreement with our general conception of the overall landscape of life-span

development, this compensatory function of the pragmatics increases in importance with advancing age but also loses in efficiency. Therefore, in advanced old age, pragmatic performances decline as well.

7. The study of plasticity (malleability) of intellectual functioning has been a cornerstone of life-span research (P. Baltes, 1987). Intellectual performance is malleable throughout life. With some exceptions (e.g., dementia of the Alzheimer type), and within the limits provided by the mechanics, there is room for sizeable plasticity at all ages and for all individuals. Evidence in support of this contention comes both from the study of long-term environmental change and from cognitive intervention studies. At the same time, age-based losses in the mechanics lead to a reduction in the amount of plasticity with advancing age. The resulting bounded openness of life-span intellectual development is consistent with the contextualist framework of life-span developmental psychology.

8. The joint consideration of different strands of research reveals a striking congruence between three different life-span trajectories: Heritability of inter-individual differences, relative stability, and level changes in the normative pragmatics (e.g., crystallized intelligence). In all three cases, there is an increase from childhood to middle and late adulthood, coupled with indications of decline in very old age. This life-span parallelism between the genetic component of inter-individual differences, continuity of inter-individual differences, and general knowledge is consistent with the notion of gene-environment correlations in behavioral genetics (Scarr & McCartney, 1983), and the notion of niche picking in ethology (Dawkins, 1982). Whether one likes it or not, this parallelism testifies to the existence of a powerful life-span synergism between sociostructural and genetic inter-individual differentiation, at least within the range of developmental conditions offered by Western industrialized societies.

FOCI AND FACETS OF LIFE-SPAN DEVELOPMENT IN SELF AND PERSONALITY

We now illustrate what life-span theory has to offer in organizing and instigating research on the development of self and personality. To do so, we will first introduce three

areas and perspectives that in our view currently have a prominent place in theory and research on personality development. The first area can be subsumed under the heading of personality, the second under the heading of self concept and identity, and the third under the notion of self-regulatory processes. These three areas and perspectives are related to different construct clusters, and cross-links are still somewhat rare, especially in the context of life-span development.

In presenting the research and attempting an integrative view on the three areas selected, we will explore how the levels of analysis approach introduced above applies to the field of self and personality. Thus, theory and evidence available in the area of self and personality development will be used to illustrate the biology-culture interface and the differential allocation of resources idea. Furthermore, three of the life-span propositions introduced above that bear special relevance for the life-span development of self and personality are discussed in more detail and at the level involving psychological characteristics and mechanisms. These three issues are stability and change in self and personality development across the life span, opportunities and constraints of personality development, and the adaptive potential or reserve capacity of the self.

Current Research Traditions in the Field of Self and Personality Development

Research and theory building in the field of self and personality have been quite diverse (e.g. Hogan, 1995; Pervin, 1990). For the present purpose, we divide this large and heterogeneous field into three distinct and—at least functionally—interrelated areas:

1. Personality.
2. Self-concept, self-definition, or identity.
3. Self-regulatory processes.

To the expert, each of these areas belongs to a different theoretical frame, employs different methods, and possesses its own and somewhat unique agenda. Nevertheless, we will attempt to emphasize integrative perspectives among these three areas.

Under the heading of *personality*, we subsume efforts to characterize individuals in terms of attributes and behavioral dispositions, a line of research that originated primarily in the psychometric tradition. Research in this area focuses on the identification of the structure of personality, on inter-individual differences, and the extent of longitudinal stability. This agenda is in line with a life-span perspective which is interested in the emergence, maintenance, and transformation of personality structure, and the conditions of constancy and change in inter-individual differences (Brim & Kagan, 1980). Furthermore, a life-span perspective is aimed at discerning the degree to which these personality attributes and behavioral dispositions evince intra-individual change trajectories and intra-individual plasticity (malleability). Such questions are pursued in the exemplary research programs involving scholars such as Block (e.g., 1981, 1995), Costa and MacCrae (1994, 1995), Goldberg (1993), and Nesselroade (e.g., 1989, 1991b).

Under the heading of *self-concept, self-definition,* and *identity,* we subsume lines of work that characterize individuals as multifaceted dynamic structures of a relatively stable array of self-conceptions (e.g., Baumeister, 1992; Greenwald & Pratkanis, 1984; Markus & Wurf, 1987). Self-conceptions are not meant to encompass any self-referent attitude but rather are confined to those beliefs or cognitions that constitute important (fundamental) self components. Work under the heading of identity focuses on the social meaning of such attitudes (e.g., Gergen, 1971; Marcia, 1976; Waterman & Archer, 1990). Different situations or contexts activate different subsets of this composite structure of self-conceptions or self schemata. Markus and Wurf (1987) have called this the working self-concept. This view of the self as both stable and dynamic fits life-span conceptions that emphasize the potential for continuity as well as change as a characteristic feature of transactional adaptation during development. In contrast to personality research that aims at inferring behavioral dispositions "from the outside," research on self-conceptions is often (but not necessarily) related to what Singer (Singer, 1984; Singer & Kolligian, 1987) has called the study of private experience or private personality, and Ryff (1984) has labelled as the study of personality from the inside. Operationally, however, at least as most of the adult research is concerned, both traditions, that is research on personality and on self-conceptions, rely on self-report. Besides the classics such as Erikson (e.g., 1959) or Bühler (e.g., 1933), research programs around scholars such as Loevinger (e.g., 1976), Levinson (e.g., 1986), Ryff (e.g., 1984, 1989b, 1995), Whitbourne (e.g., 1987), Dittmann-Kohli (e.g., 1991), and Markus and Herzog (1991) focus on the life-span development of the self-concept and of its adaptive qualities.

Finally, under the heading of *self-regulatory processes,* we subsume all efforts that are aimed at characterizing the organized abilities and skills a person brings to bear on monitoring behavior and experience. With regard to life-span development it is the regulatory behaviors of reaching, maintaining, and regaining psychological equilibrium—in particular one's sense of coherence, continuity, and purpose under conditions of microgenetic and ontogenetic change—that are of particular interest. A host of constructs discussed in the literature can be subsumed under this heading, such as self-evaluative processes, goal-related processes, coping, control beliefs and self-efficacy, or emotional regulation. The focus of such research is on investigating the self-related adaptive potential and the reserve capacities as well as their limits in the course of life-span development. As this field encompasses many different constructs, the group of scholars engaging in this type of endeavour is quite large and still growing. Thus, we can only mention a few names in order to illustrate the type of work we include under the heading of self-regulatory processes in a life-span perspective, such as Brandtstädter (e.g., Brandtstädter & Greve, 1994; see also, Brandtstädter, Ch. 14, this Volume), Cantor (e.g., Cantor & Fleeson, 1994), Carstensen (e.g., Carstensen, 1993), Filipp (e.g., Filipp & Klauer, 1991), Labouvie-Vief (e.g., 1992), Lachman (e.g., Lachman, 1986), and Blanchard-Fields (e.g., Blanchard-Fields & Norris, 1994). Another example is the effort by Heckhausen and Schulz (1995) to construct a life-span theory of self-based control.

In the following section, we will not only present relevant information, but also attempt to integrate these three areas of research and their related perspectives in a life-span definition of self and personality. As we attempt this integration, a necessary by-product is that we are tempted occasionally to transform the foci that were at the core of the work of the original proponents.

Key Features of a Life-Span Approach to the Development of Self and Personality

Definition and Meta-Theoretical Notes

We define self and personality as denoting *the ways in which human beings behave, experience, believe, and feel with regard to themselves, others, and the material world.*

With regard to the sources and outcomes of human development, self and personality have *multiple functions* (cf., principles of multicausality and multifunctionality). First, self and personality develop, that is, they are the outcome of developmental processes. Second, self and personality also as antecedents influence developmental processes, and co-regulate outcomes. And finally, self and personality are correlates of other developmental processes.

Taking a life-span view implies (a) that we are concerned with the *commonalities* in how self and personality develops. This is reflected in developmental models like the one presented by Erikson (e.g., 1959) but also in theories about the driving forces and the mechanisms of personality development (e.g., Bandura, 1984; R. White, 1959). At the same time, as life-span developmentalists we are also interested in (b) the *inter-individual differences* in the development of self and personality characteristics. For instance, do developmental trajectories become less and less similar as transactions between a given personality make-up and particular environmental conditions accumulate across the life span? R. Lerner (1988) has used the notion of "social genotype" to describe this life-span change. (c) Finally, we want to learn about the *intra-individual variability or plasticity* in the ways an individual behaves, experiences, believes, and feels about him- or herself, others, and the material world. Is it possible, for example, that an extraverted person under certain circumstances behaves more like an introvert? And does this plasticity increase or decrease with age, or does it stay the same?

These three questions of commonalities, inter-individual differences, and of intra-individual plasticity can be pursued within a *structural* and a *process-oriented* approach to the study of self and personality and its development. Under the heading of form or structure, it is primarily the classic personality dispositions and the self-conceptions, schemata, or images that are considered. Under the heading of process research, self-regulatory mechanisms are most prominent. At least five categories can be distinguished within that category: emotional regulation, coping, self-evaluation, goal seeking, and goal restructuring.

Finally, all three facets of structure, process, and function can be approached from a *componential* (multivariate) and a *holistic* (ipsative) view (see also, R. Lerner, 1986). The componential approach is illustrated by evidence on the Big Five personality factors (e.g., Costa & McCrae, 1995; Goldberg, 1993). And Block's ipsative approach to personality assessment (e.g., Block, 1995) is an inspiring example of the holistic approach. We suggest that life-span work on self and personality development profits from integrating both.

The Search for General Purpose Mechanisms in the Area of Self and Personality Development

Throughout this chapter, we have emphasized the significance in life-span work of the search for the conditions of successful development. From the field of cognitive psychology, we have taken the idea of general purpose mechanisms. Thus, we ask whether in the field of self and personality it is possible also to articulate *general purpose mechanisms*. With general purpose mechanisms, we mean (internal and external) resources and capacities that individuals employ to master rather varied developmental challenges. General purpose mechanisms in the field of self and personality might help the individual to organize and coordinate the ways in which he/she behaves, experiences, believes, and feels with regard to him/herself, others, and the material world such that the goal of maximizing gains and of minimizing losses is approached.

There seems to be a foundation of research on which to build when exploring the notion of general purpose mechanisms. Empirical evidence, especially when focusing on longitudinal studies that search for predictors of adaptive developmental outcomes, has identified a number of candidate concepts. Impulse control or ego control, perceived control, delay of gratification and ego resilience/flexibility, for instance, suggest to us that they might possess the characteristics of such general purpose mechanism qualities in the self and personality domain (e.g., Bandura, 1993; Block, 1993; Caspi & Bem, 1990; Kagan & Zentner, 1996; Lachman, Ziff, & Spiro, 1994; Mischel, Shoda, & Rodriguez, 1989; Rutter & Rutter, 1993; Skinner, 1995; E. Werner, 1995). As is true in cognitive psychology, such general purpose mechanisms will not function by themselves. Rather, they are part of a system of personality characteristics and self-regulatory mechanisms that are functional or adaptive only under specific circumstances.

One reason why we chose to explore the power of the notion of general purpose mechanisms is the relative openness and broad contextuality of human development (Maciel et al., 1994). From a life-span point of view, there is no single endpoint and singular context of development of any facet of self and personality. The challenge is to coordinate resources under varying conditions. Thus, there seems to be theoretical and empirical grounds for the assumption that self and personality functioning is efficacious if (a) many different ways of being are available (e.g., being internally as well as externally controlled, being optimistic as well as pessimistic, being introverted as well as extraverted) and if (b) adaptive algorithms that monitor the dialectic between such supposedly antagonistic states are accessible (e.g., Blanchard-Fields & Norris, 1994; Colvin & Block, 1994; Labouvie-Vief, 1982). By means of such algorithms the most functional personality characteristic for a given time, place, and circumstance is exhibited. This restates in different terms what has been characterized as a wise person (e.g., Staudinger & Baltes, 1994; Sternberg, 1990). The approach is also similar to the notion of fluid intelligence in the domain of intellectual functioning (see above). It is a special characteristic of that category of the intellect that in the sense of a general purpose mechanism it can be applied to, invested into, a large variety of cognition problems (Cattell, 1971).

The Executive Function of Self and Personality

Life-span theory further suggests a *systemic view* on psychological phenomena. This systemic view has at least two consequences for the way we think about the self and personality. First, we believe that the different components of self and personality, introduced above, *together* form the self and personality system. Dynamic systems theory postulates that, by means of recursive interactions, such components form the basis of self-organization as well as the emergence and stabilization of new forms (e.g., Ford & Lerner, 1992; Lewis, 1995; Thelen, 1992; see also, Thelen & Smith, Ch. 10, this Volume). Second, the systemic view directs our attention also to the cross-linkages between self and personality and other subsystems of the developing individual, such as physiological and cognitive functioning. As mentioned already, it seems that the self and personality have something like an *orchestrating or executive function* with regard to these other systems and the developmental changes occurring in these systems (e.g., Caprara, 1996; Erikson, 1959; Mischel & Shoda, 1995; Waterman & Archer, 1990). The psychology of action (Brandtstädter, Ch. 14, this Volume; Gollwitzer & Bargh, 1996) has recently been suggested as a unifying framework for the microgenetic study of the interplay of cognition, emotion,

and motivation. Efforts are also made to extend action psychology to issues of life-span development (e.g., Baltes & Baltes, 1990a; Brandtstädter & Greve, 1994; Heckhausen & Schulz, 1995). The question whether and how principles of microgenetic action regulation change when applied to an ontogenetic life-span framework has opened a whole new vista of research.

For example, self and personality develop to serve a self-reflective function. Self and personality reflect and evaluate developmental changes in the other subsystems and try to integrate them. This integrative function of self and personality is also mirrored in the fact that subjective measures of adaptation such as subjective well-being or happiness are often used as measures of self. Empirically, this is not without costs. The problem of circularity of argument and measurement dependency has to be critically examined when relating characteristics of self and personality to self-report measures of adaptivity (e.g., Staudinger & Fleeson, 1996).

Providing Links from Infancy to Old Age

A further issue with regard to a life-span view on the definition and study of self and personality development concerns encompassing the ontogenetic course from *infancy* to *old age*. Empirically and theoretically, this distance may often still appear as a gap. Infancy and childhood research on the one hand and adulthood and old age research on the other typically proceed independently from each other with little overlap in concepts, methodology, and consequently empirical data base.

Search for Continuity in the Face of Transformations. Bridging this gap and achieving interconnectivity indeed is not easy (e.g., Brim & Kagan, 1980). It seems necessary to identify constructs that have been used to describe personality development across the life span or have at least shown predictive relationships. This concerns the question of homotypic and heterotypic continuity, a terminology introduced by Kagan and Moss (1962), or of Block's notion of temporal coherence (e.g., Block, 1981). The notion of heterotypic continuity implies that the phenotypic behavior might change between childhood and adulthood, but that specific behaviors in childhood might still be conceptually consistent with adult behaviors. Phenotypically different but conceptually related responses might be derivatives of earlier behavior (e.g., Livson & Peskin, 1980;

Moss & Susman, 1980). Ryder (1967), for example, found that childhood task persistence was related to adult achievement orientation. Caspi, Bem, and Elder (1989) reported that males who showed dependency in childhood transformed this interactional style into a mature, nurturant style characterized by being calm, warm, giving, and sympathetic, qualities that fit well in intimate relationships and the family world.

There are a number of interesting candidates that could serve as examples of constructs that span a lifetime, such as attachment style, control beliefs, or the self-concept. For its recent surge and relatedness to what we call a general purpose mechanism and to a systemic view, we opted for another sample case, *temperament*. Not only has temperament been shown to provide quite strong predictive links between early infancy and even old age in multiple studies (e.g., Caspi & Bem, 1990; Friedman et al., 1995; Kagan & Snidman, 1991; Lerner & Lerner, 1983; Thomas & Chess, 1977), but temperament also provides the possibility to link a biological level of analysis with a psychological one without implying a reductionistic approach (cf., Zuckerman, 1994, 1995).

The Sample Case of Temperament. From an ontogenetic perspective, temperament might be called the first inter-individual differences indicator of personality, making individuals distinct even in the womb. Temperament can be called an umbrella term. Although various temperamental facets have been identified by different authors, there seems to be consensus that activity, reactivity, emotionality, and sociability are four of the major components of temperament (e.g., Bates, 1994; G. McCall, 1987; Strelau & Augleitner, 1997). Kagan and colleagues (Kagan & Zentner, 1996), for example, have focused on one temperamental facet, that is, behavioral inhibition. Behavioral inhibition is defined as the tendency to be extremely shy and restrained in response to unfamiliar people and situations. From Kagan's approach, it is also clear that temperament carries a general-purpose and a systemic quality. For instance, inhibition as one temperamental facet may at a very microanalytic level of analysis provide a link between personality and cognitive development (e.g., Hasher & Zacks, 1988; Pascual-Leone, 1983).

Quite robust evidence also suggests that inter-individual differences in temperament stay fairly stable throughout the life course (e.g., Bates & Wachs, 1994). In a longitudinal

adoption and twin study, Buss and Plomin (1984) found that temperament had a considerable heritability component. Between 50% and 60% of the inter-individual variability in temperamental measures during infancy and childhood seems to be due to genetic influences. And at least up to early adulthood this heritability component did not seem to be subject to age-related changes.

With regard to spanning the life time, it seems that temperamental differences in aggression or shyness or dependency among children are preserved from infancy through middle and later childhood, adolescence and into adulthood (e.g., heterotypic continuity; Kagan & Moss, 1962). Caspi and colleagues (Caspi, Elder, & Bem, 1987) have shown, using data from the Berkeley Growth and Oakland Guidance Studies, for example, that ill-tempered boys become ill-tempered men. In another study, it was found that temperament as assessed through behavioral ratings at age 3 predicted personality as assessed by the MMPI at age 18 (Caspi & Silva, 1995). In specific, the undercontrolled temperament type related positively to later impulsivity, danger seeking, aggression, and interpersonal alienation. The inhibited temperament type, contrariwise, related negatively to later impulsivity, danger-seeking, aggression, and social potency. In addition, the so-called well-adjusted temperament at age 3 related to a normal personality profile at age 18 (Caspi & Silva, 1995).

These kinds of predictive relationships should not be interpreted as a deterministic argument. The work by Chess and Thomas (1984) as well as Lerner and Lerner (1983) on temperament illustrates this point. They have used the notion of "goodness of fit" between child and context to point to the importance of the interaction between child and context. On the one hand, they found that many children with difficult temperaments became maladjusted adults. In such cases, they were able to show that the parents did not manage to adapt to the temperament of the child. On the other hand, these researchers also demonstrated that difficult children with parents who were better able to deal with the temperament of their child developed into well-adapted adults. Lerner and coworkers have extended the work on the "goodness-of-fit" idea, but focused not only on the match between child and parent but also considered the match between child and peers or child and teacher. In a similar vein, they found that children's fit with their peers' temperamental preferences resulted in higher sociometric ratings and also, through the better quality of their peer relations, indirectly influenced adjustment at a later point in time (East, Lerner, Lerner, & Soni, 1992; J. Lerner, Nitz, Talwar, & Lerner, 1989).

There has been notable progress in identifying some of the mechanisms that might link infant temperament and adult personality and that might enable a joint organization of concepts of temperament and personality (e.g., Eysenck & Eysenck, 1985; Strelau & Angleitner, 1991; Zuckerman, 1995). Zuckerman (1994), for example, has proposed what he calls the turtle model of personality. In this model, personality traits at the top are linked to genetics at the bottom through (from top down) social behavior, conditioning, physiology, biochemistry, and finally neurology. This model is not meant to be reductionistic; it is necessary to study each level of analysis with its own intellectual agenda to gain a complete understanding. As Zuckerman (1995, p. 331) puts it, "We do not inherit temperamental patterns as such. What is inherited are chemical templates that produce and regulate proteins involved in building the structure of nervous systems and the neurotransmitters, enzymes, and hormones that regulate them. . . . We are born with differences in reactivities of brain structure and differences in regulators." Very much in line with our systemic emphasis, it is included in this multiple levels of analysis model of Zuckerman that the type of temperamental pattern, which initially may have a strong genetic component, attains features of contextually-based self-organization. Thus, the temperamental pattern is transformed by context and experience in ways that it becomes an outcome of a multicausal and self-organizing process. In this sense, the developed temperament—if adaptive—might be called a general purpose mechanism and becomes an organizing force as the individual deals with his or her environment and the developmental themes and tasks of later ontogeny.

Of the small number of higher-order factors that have been consistently identified to describe personality (e.g., Goldberg, 1993), two have been of special interest to research on temperament. Those are negative emotionality, which includes variables such as fearfulness, anxiety/tension, inhibition, and dysphoria, and positive emotionality, which includes enthusiasm, excitement, and happiness. Zuckerman (1994) makes a good case for a third dimension, termed impulsive, unsocialized sensation seeking, which appears to be separate from positive and negative emotionality. This impulsivity dimension, the counterpart to

Kagan's behavioral inhibition, seems to be closely related to what Eysenck has called Psychotism, Block's Ego Control, and Costa and McCrae's Conscientiousness. Relationships between this impulsivity dimension and deviant behavior have been found in multiple studies (e.g., Horvath & Zuckerman, 1993; Newcomb & McGee, 1991). Similarly, Caspi and colleagues have demonstrated that childhood temper tantrums predicted delinquency in adolescence (e.g., Caspi, Ch. 6, Volume 3; Caspi, Elder, & Bem, 1987).

We have presented an integrative view on research on the development of personality, self-concepts, and self-regulatory processes. In order to gain an understanding of the life-span development of self and personality, it seems useful to consider structure and processes, as well as functions. A dynamic systems approach to development provides a useful theoretical framework for the integration of the different components of self and personality discussed in the literature. In addition, interest centers on features—such as temperament—that operate across multiple settings and across the life span and, if adaptive, possess attributes of general purpose mechanisms. Based on this conceptualization, we will now apply the level of analysis approach, introduced in the beginning of this chapter, to the field of self and personality.

Illustrations of the Role of Biology and Culture in Self and Personality Development

How does Figure 18.1 apply to the field of self and personality? Working from the assumption that the genome and its expressions, by means of evolution, are not yet optimized with regard to old age, what are the implications for self and personality functioning across the life span? So far the evolutionary base of personality—both in terms of biological and cultural-social forces in the sense of co-evolution—has received less attention than the evolution of cognition (e.g., Asendorpf, 1996; Barkow, Cosmides, & Tooby, 1992; Klix, 1993).

As selection primarily worked through fertility and parenting behavior, most of the evolutionary work in the field of personality (in the widest sense) has focused on gender differences in altruism, cooperative behaviors, sexual competition, or jealousy (e.g., DeKay & Buss, 1992; Hammerstein, 1996). In addition, however, arguments have been raised that the ability for self-deception might have been favoured by evolution because it seems to increase the ability to deceive others (e.g., Gigerenzer, 1996; Lockard & Paulhus, 1988; Trivers, 1985). The evolutionary importance of the ability to deceive others in turn is related to the crucial role of reciprocal relationships for reproductive fitness (e.g., Axelrod, 1984). We would like to suggest that this ability "to deceive oneself," or one could also say "redefine reality," indeed serves an important adaptive function across the life span and probably increasingly so in old age. Thus, the fact that the evolutionary base has been less optimized for the postreproductive phases of life than for younger ages may not be as detrimental for the ontogenesis of self and personality as for biological and cognitive functioning. Perhaps what is relevant here is that the "mechanics of the mind" which evince definite aging losses (see above), either carry little implication for self and personality functioning, or that evolutionary selection in humans provided a different genetic basis for personality and self than for intellectual functioning.

This interpretation of findings from evolutionary psychology, that self and personality are less at a genetic disadvantage than cognition and biological functioning, is supported by findings on the genetic component of inter-individual differences in personality functioning as advanced by behavior-genetic research. Evidence from the cross-sectional as well longitudinal analyses of the genotype and the phenotype of self and personality characteristics seem to point to a different pattern than the one just reported for the domain of intellectual functioning. During the life course, stability or slight *decreases* in heritability coefficients (in the sense they have been introduced in an earlier section) have been found (e.g., Pedersen, 1993). Moreover, at least until the eighth decade of life (Smith & Baltes, 1993, in press-a) there is very little evidence for age-related losses in self and personality functions.

This very general summary statement, however, needs qualification and differentiation. So far, only few behavior-genetic studies of personality based on longitudinal data with extensive age intervals are available. Highly complex statistical methods that allow modelling of the genetic architecture of development (Pedersen, 1991) by simultaneously taking into account mean levels and growth curves (e.g., Hewitt, Eaves, Neale, & Meyer, 1988; McArdle, 1986; Molenaar, Boosma, & Dolan, 1991) have become available. However, due to the lack of appropriate data sets and to the recency of their availability, they have not been widely applied yet. Therefore, authors in the field of behavioral

genetics consider the available evidence as preliminary (e.g., Loehlin, 1993; Pedersen, 1993; Rowe, 1993).

Taking such limitations into account, the following preliminary insights into the developmental behavioral genetics of personality seem to find consensus among behavioral geneticists (e.g., Brody, 1993; Pedersen, 1993). First, results of behavior-genetic analyses of personality assessments are difficult to compare with the equivalent analyses of intelligence assessments because the latter are based on behavioral performance measures, whereas personality measures typically refer to self-reports. Thus, strictly speaking, personality-related analyses refer to the heritability and its life-span changes in how people report about themselves. Second, the extent to which genetic influences account for phenotypic variability in personality measures is smaller than for measures of intelligence, with heritability coefficients between .4 and .6 depending on the personality trait and the age of assessment. Third, the importance of genetic influences on inter-individual differences in personality seems to decrease slightly with increasing age (e.g., McCartney, Harris, & Bernieri, 1990; McGue, Bacon, & Lykken, 1993a; Pedersen, 1993). And fourth, there is initial evidence for a quite high overlap in the genetic effects operating on personality expression at different ages, although at each point in time they account for not more than half of the variance (e.g., McGue et al., 1993a; Pedersen, 1993).

How can we try to understand the two findings that genetic influence at any given age is about half of the inter-individual variance in personality measures, but that at the same time the genetic influence on the stability and change of personality attributes seems to decline? Genes may exert their influence on complex psychological traits through various types of gene-environment interactions (e.g., Scarr & McCartney, 1983). For example, environments react in a certain way to certain persons (evocative type), or certain persons with certain genomes seek out certain environments (proactive type). And indeed there is indication that incidental differences in personality development are primarily, and increasingly with age, influenced by environmental events not shared by individuals reared together (e.g., Plomin, Chipuer, & Loehlin, 1990); whereas shared rearing environments seldom account for more than 10% of the variation in personality late in life (Pedersen et al., 1991). In addition, we suggest that—very much in line with dynamic systems theory (Fischer &

Bidell, Ch. 9, this Volume; Ford & Lerner, 1992; Thelen & Smith, 1994; Thelen & Smith, Ch. 10, this Volume)—individuals strive toward maintaining identity; and that the application of self-regulatory principles are successful in enhancing stability in self organization.

The finding of age-related stability or even a decrease of the longitudinal genetic influence on individual differences in personality across the life span is in contrast with genetic influences in other domains of behavioral functioning, such as cognitive development. The dominant finding there had been one of *increasing* heritability of individual differences (Plomin, Pedersen, Lichtenstein, & McClearn, 1994). Combining this evidence with the finding that no major declines (at least up until the age 75–80) in self-related functioning are observed (see below), can be taken to imply that functioning in the domain of self and personality is to a lesser degree subject to the detrimental effects of the incomplete evolutionary architecture of human ontogenesis (see Figure 18.1(a)). Unless pathological conditions, such as Alzheimer's disease, infect the whole system, no age-related increases of pathological conditions in the personality domain are recorded. Conversely, however, more recent evidence from the Berlin Aging Study (Smith & Baltes, 1993, in press-a, in press-b) points to more discontinuity in functional status of self and personality in *advanced* old age. Indeed, it appears as if the study of the very old (above age 85) may reveal losses in personality and self-functioning as well. At this point, it is unclear whether this increasing instability is primarily due to overriding conditions of morbidity or whether self and personality functioning itself undergoes such changes in very old age.

The Allocation of Resources in the Area of Self and Personality

In an earlier section, we emphasized the life-span developmental script of a reallocation of resources, from a predominant allocation into growth to an increase in relative allocation into maintenance and management of losses (see also, Staudinger et al., 1995). Thus, in contrast to the domain of cognitive functioning where resources in old age are depleted to maintain a certain level of functioning, the resource situation for life-span growth in self and personality might present itself more favorably. Taking a system's view on psychological functioning, we can assume

therefore that the self by virtue of being the self-reflective head of the living system "human being" (a quality emerging during childhood) might be able to continue to deliver its orchestrating or executive function with regard to managing the gains and losses across various domains of functioning (cf., Staudinger et al., 1995).

It is an open question, however, whether self-related resources are available in old age to promote the further development of the self-system itself. In other words, as life reaches old age available self-related resources are invested in managing cognitive, physical, and social declines and losses. Possibly only under very favorable developmental conditions would self-related resources be sufficient to invest in further development of the self itself. Although, in principle, life-span changes in self and personality could include advances, we do not expect them to occur in everyone. Under very favorable conditions, personality growth might even involve such high goals as wisdom (cf., Erikson, 1959; see Table 18.7; see also, P. Baltes, Smith, & Staudinger, 1992).

Further, we assume that the "self" also manages and organizes the extension of internal resources (e.g., cognitive capacity, physical strength, personality characteristics) by referring to others and the physical and institutional context as resources (for overview see Staudinger et al., 1995). Others can help to do things that one's own health or time or ability does not allow. External memory aids can help to compensate for the loss in memory performance. Given this line of thought, one can also conceive of a situation that allows the self to optimize the use of external resources such that enough internal resources are left for further personality development, for example, toward wisdom. An extreme case for such self-based orchestrating of resources aimed at selective optimization is the loss of independent functioning. There the task is to accept dependency in such domains as household management in order to free up resources for other purposes (M. Baltes, 1996).

The notion that self and personality perform an orchestrating or executive function with regard to the management and identification of resources raises the following question: Is it possible to distinguish the mechanisms and characteristics that support the overarching orchestrating or executive functions from those that constitute one of the three domains of psychological functioning, that is intelligence and cognition, self and personality, and social relations, or are both inextricably intertwined? This is a question which is discussed in research on *resilience* (Staudinger et al., 1995). By taking such a research perspective on the origins, maintenance, and consequences of self and personality—ideally in a longitudinal manner—it becomes possible to identify, for instance, whether, or how, the self and personality manage themselves while at the same time manage extraordinary challenges such as losses in cognitive functioning or losses of significant others due to death, or to challenges of one's own finitude. Each process and each characteristic constituting the self and personality can thus be identified as phenomenon in itself but also in its executive and orchestrating function.

The Development of Self and Personality as Life-Long Transactional Adaptation

In the following, we will discuss in more detail three issues of life-span development of self and personality. The first is the question of stability and change across the life span. Aside from questions of stability in individual rank order, this issue can also be phrased as investigating the gains, maintenance, and losses in the area of self and personality. The second issue relates to the opportunities and constraints of self development. And finally, the third issue will illustrate the adaptive self-related potential across the life span, which arguably might present the most comprehensive general purpose mechanism involved in the conduct of life-span development.

It is a core assumption that follows from a life-span perspective that self and personality development occurs from birth until death. "Transactional adaptation" (e.g., R. Lerner, 1984, 1986) or person-environment interaction (e.g., Kindermann & Valsiner, 1995; Magnusson, 1990; Magnusson & Stattin, Ch. 12, this Volume) are considered the central developmental processes. Self and personality do not simply passively unfold as a consequence of pre-wired maturational programs or the mechanistic reaction to environmental stimuli. Self and personality develop out of a constant and active process of the individual's transactions with changing internal and external influences, including changes in historical conditions of society. In this process of transactional adaptation of self and personality, systemic principles of self-organization (e.g., Lewis, 1995) are key ingredients.

We need to take into consideration, however, that not only self and personality develop, but also that internal and external contexts (and their associated risks and resources) as well as the functional consequences (evaluative criteria) change with age. As described earlier, multicausality and multifunctionality are an essential characteristic of life-span development. To give an example, it is not only the self-concept that changes with age but also the social and material contexts of its acquisition and application in everyday life. The research program of Damon and Colby (e.g., Colby & Damon, 1992; Damon, 1996) illustrates this notion for the sample case of moral goals and moral behavior. Furthermore, the criteria according to which the level and form of self-concept development is evaluated undergo age-related changes. We will later argue that in addition to the behavioral level of functioning, the amount of available self-related reserve capacity also changes. Self and personality development is brought about by continuous *and* discontinuous internal and external factors and associated processes. Therefore, in life-span thinking any argument in favor of *either* continuity *or* discontinuity is inherently misplaced. By the very nature of the developmental process, the system of self and personality in a life-span perspective is one of both continuity and change.

We will begin by presenting evidence for continuity and stability in personality development on both the mean-level and with regard to inter-individual differences. This information is captured most precisely by the so-called trait-models of personality development (e.g., Kogan, 1990). At the same time, however, and as persuasively argued by Nesselroade (e.g., 1991a) on both theoretical and empirical grounds, there is also sizable evidence for intra-individual (within-person) variability. Thus, there are two sides to consider: Changing amounts of inter-individual continuity on a group level of analysis as well as changing amounts of intra-individual plasticity (see also, Brim & Kagan, 1980).

Trait Models of Personality: Focus on Stability and Continuity of Personality Development

Trait models of personality approach the question of continuity and discontinuity and stability and instability from the continuity side. Trait-oriented researchers are interested in exploring and possibly arriving at a structure of personality characteristics that captures an individual's experiences and behaviors in a way that is as comprehensive and continuous as possible. Roughly, two major approaches can be distinguished. One is the lexical tradition (e.g., Allport & Odbert, 1936; Cattell, 1943), which selected from the Webster's dictionary such single-word descriptors that allow the comprehensive description of the consistent and stable modes of an individual's adjustment to his or her environment. As Cattell put it, this approach was based on the lexical hypothesis that all aspects of human personality that are or have been of importance, interest, and utility have already become recorded in the substance of language (Cattell, 1943, p. 483). Using adjective-based ratings as the method of personality assessment, this approach has been carried into the present (e.g., Goldberg, 1993; Nesselroade & Bartsch, 1977; Norman, 1963).

The other approach is based on questionnaire items. Through Cattell's work (Sixteen Personality Factor 16PF; Cattell, Eber, & Tatsuoka, 1970) this approach can also be traced back to the lexical tradition, but it is influenced as well by personality theories that were developed independent of the lexical approach, for instance, by Murray's theory of human needs, which is reflected in the Personality Research Form (Jackson, 1984). In this tradition and with much interest in life-span development, Costa and McCrae (e.g., 1995) have worked since the 1970s on identifying the personality dimensions which form the common denominator of available personality questionnaires and to trace their ontogeny across the adult life span.

Both approaches, the lexical and the questionnaire approach, have been statistically related to each other and among a large number of personality researchers there is presently consensus that personality can be reasonably well described by the so-called "Big Five." The Big Five have been identified by means of factor analysis across different instruments and different samples, though labels vary somewhat among authors (cf., John, 1990). We have chosen Costa and McCrae's factor names to convey the information: Extraversion, agreeableness, conscientiousness, neuroticism, and openness to experience.

Recently, there has been heated debate about whether these five superfactors indeed capture all there is to personality (see Block, 1995; Costa & McCrae, 1995; Goldberg & Saucier, 1995). We do not want to elaborate on this discussion; we would only like to alert the reader to the fact that on the one hand, the Big Five structure has been shown to be useful in describing personality and predicting developmental outcomes, but on the other hand, it should not be mistaken to imply that there are no other facets of personality. As most of this work has been informed by a personality-psychology rather than a developmental

perspective, there has been, to our knowledge, no systematic study of the factor structure of the *original* pool of adjectives by age group. The selection work on the original pool of adjectives was done with young adults (for an overview see Block, 1995).

A longitudinal study of adolescent personality by John and others (John, Caspi, Robins, Moffitt, & Stouthamer-Loeber, 1994) is informative in this respect. In this study, using a childhood version of a standard personality assessment instrument (California Adult Q-set; McCrae, Costa, & Busch, 1986) that had been shown to reflect the Big Five (McCrae et al., 1986), two additional factors of activity and irritability were identified. The two additional factors were primarily based on items characterizing specific aspects of adolescent personality that are not included in the adult version. In their careful interpretation of the finding, the authors suggest that indeed activity and irritability cannot be reduced to the adult factors of extraversion and neuroticism but that they might be linked to each other in the sense of heterotypic continuity (Kagan & Moss, 1962). Similar arguments may apply to other stages of the life span.

Growth Models of Personality Development

As mentioned before, stability and continuity are only one side of the coin. However, some stability and continuity most likely is a must for the evolution of personal coherence and adaptive fitness. However, precisely because of life-long ontogenetic challenges and motivation for improvement (White, 1959), self and personality development also involves discontinuities and changes in directionality (gains and losses). The growth models of self and personality development as exemplified in the notions of identity development, ego development, or the concept of developmental tasks capture one aspect of this phenomenon, namely that of a systemic advance in level of self- and personality-based functioning (e.g., Bühler, Erikson, Havighurst, Jung, Loevinger).

We would like to offer a selection of such models without trying to be comprehensive. Rather, we aim at combining developmental models from quite different traditions and with quite different goals in order to show the overarching themes and structures that cut across different theoretical models and different facets of self and personality development. Table 18.7 lists the theoretical models of seven developmentalists. They range from the development

Table 18.7   Overview of Source Life-Span Models with Relevance to Self and Personality Growth

Piaget & Pascual-Leone	Kohlberg	Labouvie-Vief	Loevinger	Erikson	Havighurst
Sensorimotor		Sensorimotor	Presocial	Trust vs. mistrust Hope	Maturation of sensory and motor functions Social attachment Emotional development Sensorimotor intelligence and primitive causality Object permanence
Preoperational	*Preconventional* Punishment -Obedience	Presymbolic	Symbiotic	Autonomy vs. shame Will power	Elaboration of locomotion Self-control Fantasy and play Language development
Concrete Operational		Symbolic	Impulsive	Initiative vs. guilt Purpose	Sex role identification Early moral development Group play Development of self-esteem
Formal Operations	Instrumental- Hedonistic	Intrasystemic	Self-protective	Industry vs. inferiority Competence	Friendship Self-evaluation Concrete operations Skill learning Team play
Late formal	*Conventional* Good boy morality Authority Orientation		Conformist	Identity vs. confusion Fidelity	Physical maturation Emotional development Formal operations Internalized morality Membership in peer groups Heterosexual relationships Autonomy from parents Sex role identity Career choice
Predialectical	*Postconventional* Morality of contract	Intersystemic	Conscientious	Intimacy vs. isolation Love	Marriage Childbearing Work Life style
Dialectical	*Postconventional* Morality of contract	Autonomous- Integrated	Autonomous	Generativity vs. stagnation Care	Nurturing the marital relationship Management of household Child rearing Management of career
Transcendental	Individual principles of conscience		Integrated	Integrity vs. despair Wisdom	Promoting intellectual vigor Redirecting energy towards new roles Accepting one's life Developing a point of view about death Coping with physical changes of aging Developing a psychohistorical perspective Traveling uncharted terrain

of basic cognitive functioning to ego and identity development in the sense of Loevinger and Erikson. These models differ in the degree to which they focus on the development of structure of self-concept, personality, and self-regulatory processes that self and personality serve throughout the life span.

We have chosen to include Labouvie-Vief's (1982) general model of the development of mature thought rather than any of her more specific ones because we believe it is this fundamental developmental structure that then can be applied to such seemingly diverse areas as development of emotional regulation and representation or self representation (Labouvie-Vief, Chiodo, Goguen, Diehl, & Orwoll, 1995; Labouvie-Vief, DeVoe, & Bulka, 1989; Labouvie-Vief, Hakim-Larson, DeVoe, & Schoeber-lein, 1989). In a similar way as, for instance, Pascual-Leone, Labouvie-Vief attempts in her theoretical considerations to integrate the development of cognition, motivation, and emotion.

It may seem surprising that cognitive models such as that of Labouvie-Vief are included in this overview table. However, if one assumes that self-reflexivity and aspects of intersubjectivity and social cognition are important components of self and personality, cognitive development has its natural place in any developmental model of self and personality. Developmental research previously has rarely dealt with the interplay between cognitive and personality development. One important exception was theorizing and empirical research in the Vygotskian tradition (e.g., Overton, Ch. 3, this Volume; Rogoff, 1990a; Valsiner, Ch. 4, this Volume; Wertsch, 1991). Recently, there seems to be a change in this attitude and a renaissance of Vygotskian ideas (e.g., Bornstein & Bruner, 1989; Cohen & Siegel, 1991; Wozniak & Fisher, 1993). Similarly, work stemming from other traditions, such as social intelligence, collaborative cognition, and interactive minds, has moved in this direction (e.g., P. Baltes & Staudinger, 1996a; Resnick, Levine, & Teasley, 1991; Wellman & Gelman, 1992). Dunn's work on the interaction between development of attachment and theory of mind is another interesting example from childhood research (Dunn, 1995). Another recent exception is the application of a dynamic systems perspective to personality development. Lewis (e.g., 1995; see also Caprara, 1996; Mischel & Shoda, 1995), for example, argued that it is through the interactions between cognition and emotion that personality and social development are propelled.

At the heart of most of the selected developmental models lies—according to our reading—aside from the focus on age-graded tasks, the basic idea of the dialectics of development, and in this regard especially the coordinated dialectics between the self and the other (Kramer, 1983; Riegel, 1973b). This implies that in a first developmental step the basic "constitution" (of e.g., emotion, self, morality, world) has to be acquired. In early ontogeny, this happens in an absolutist fashion, which implies that there is one truth about such diverse matters as the world, myself, or my emotions. In the next developmental step, primarily

due to cognitive advances permitting the occurrence of social decentering and intersubjectivity, and the emergence of the sense of a socially differentiated identity, it becomes possible to acknowledge that there are multiple views of the same phenomenon. Cognitively guided models further argue that under favorable conditions, multiple views are subsequently integrated without, however, loosing the flexibility to switch among different ones. In Piagetian terms, a coordinated system of horizontal and vertical décalage of selfhood and selves evolves. A similar developmental progression can also be identified in psychoanalytically informed models such as the one by Erikson (1959) or more recently Vaillant's model of ego development (Vaillant, 1993). Within the framework of a reciprocal developmental relationship between self and other, we would still argue that the developmental organization is described to move from the self as focus to the other and eventually to the integration of both. First, self-related attributes (including receiving relationships with others) such as trust, hope, competence, and identity are acquired, before we become able to turn to others and give, or, in Eriksonian terms, develop love and generativity. Eventually, under ideal conditions, we should become able to integrate our selves and our lives including the contributions by and views of others.

Havighurst's model of developmental tasks (Havighurst, 1948; see Table 18.7) differs from the others in that it focuses on the development of the orchestrating or executive function of the self-society match rather than on the development of self and personality per se. For each life period, the model lists the challenges that are presented by different areas of life such as physical, cognitive, personality, and social functioning. It is interesting to note that with increasing age, Havighurst's tasks become more and more social and biological in nature. On the one hand, this is to a certain degree a reflection of the nature of life-span development and the increasing gap between mind and body (see also, Baltes, Reese, & Lipsitt, 1980, Figure 18.3). But on the other hand, it may also reflect the interdisciplinarity of life-span scholars (Havighurst, 1973) and especially their strong connection to sociology with its focus on age-graded norms, roles, and passages. Therefore, we believe that it might be especially fruitful to combine, for example, Labouvie-Vief's model, which starts out from Piaget's theory of cognitive development and extends and modifies it by a more explicit account of the effects of emotions and social relations on cognitive development, with Havighurst's quite comprehensive listing of age-related social and biological requirements. What is also lacking in the models listed is an explicit concern with historical change (see however, Elder, Ch. 16, this Volume).

A second meta-analytical perspective offered by Table 18.7 refers to the fact that the development of self and personality per se encompass two aspects that are captured by the different models in differing degrees. Recent empirical evidence suggests that there is one aspect of self and personality growth which refers to the internal and more cognitive side of the self, and another which refers to the external or psychosocial side of ego development (e.g., Helson & Wink, 1987; Labouvie-Vief, Hakim-Larson, DeVoe, & Schoeberlein, 1989; Vaillant & McCullough, 1987).

Development of the cognitive internal side of the self is exemplified by the notion of ego development (e.g., Loevinger, 1976), or the notion of post-formal operations as it has been proposed in the Piagetian tradition (e.g., Basseches, 1984; Labouvie-Vief, 1992; Pascual-Leone, 1983; Riegel, 1973b). This cognitive side of ego development focuses on growth in cognitive complexity, tolerance of ambiguity, and objectivity, and is closely linked to cognitive development. The other aspect of self and personality growth refers to the "external" psychosocial maturity and the continued exchange with social norms and expectations. The Erikson model of psychosocial crises (e.g., Erikson, 1959) or Vaillant's model of the development of adjustment (e.g., Vaillant, 1977, 1990) are examples for this aspect of self and personality growth.

Of the models listed, Erikson's is perhaps the best known, although empirically still underdeveloped. In his epigenetic theory of personality development, Erikson (1963) distinguished eight "ages of life" (life tasks) representing critical, age-specific challenges that have to be successfully mastered for the individual to develop optimally. The eight life tasks and associated ego skills characterizing human life-span development are listed in Table 18.7. Erikson links these themes to certain ages. One should keep in mind, however, that although Erikson implied a certain predominance of a given task at a given age, he also suggested that these tasks are present in principle at all ages and represent a life-long continuing template. Achieving each succeeding stage requires, on the one hand, successful mastery of the previous life tasks and, on the other hand, accelerative and supportive conditions associated with the material and social environment.

Psychosocial development for Erikson (1959, 1963) denotes growth and change in the individual as both person and society evolve. At the end of an optimal developmental trajectory, according to Erikson, stands a self characterized by the following ego skills: Hopeful, willful, finding purpose in life, competent, loyal, capable to love, caring, and wise. Such a patterns of attributes represents the cluster of Western Christian values or virtues. It is occasionally argued that this pattern has an elitist and absolutist flavor which is more monopolistic than cultural and personal variations of life-span development suggest. In this sense, Erikson's model may lack the pluralism and flexibility that some life-span researchers have claimed to be essential to a comprehensive model of life-span development (e.g., P. Baltes, 1987, 1997; Chapman, 1988b; Maddox, 1987; Valsiner & Lawrence, 1996).

Self and Personality: Between Stability, Growth, and Decline or between Continuity and Discontinuity

After elaborating on some of the theoretical models that underlie either personality stability or personality growth, we will now turn to an overview of the available evidence with regard to the questions of stability, growth, and decline in self and personality characteristics.

Defining Gains (Growth) and Losses (Decline) with Regard to Personality Development

Using the notions of growth and decline or gain and loss with regard to personality characteristics makes the criterion problem of what is a gain and what a loss even more obvious and pressing than it is with regard to intellectual functioning. In cognitive research, it seems obvious that the more words one can remember, the better; the faster we can complete a problem solving task, the higher the level of performance. But even with regard to intellectual functioning such criteria of adaptive fitness, of what is a gain and what a loss, may need to undergo revision in everyday life. When it comes to self and personality, we are presented with the problem of determining a "best" direction of personality development. What is the desirable end state of personality development? Is there one, or are there many potentially incompatible ends depending on the outcome criteria we examine? To what degree do subjective and objective criteria converge?

For example, let us take extraversion and assume that being extraverted is set as an aspired goal of personality development. We can think of occasions, however, when, on the contrary, introversion turns out to be the more adaptive personality feature. Similarly, it is very important to strike a balance between affiliation and solitude or between autonomy and dependence. Such considerations remind us of the argument presented above about general purpose mechanisms. We argued there that it is the flexibility and the availability of a monitoring algorithm that defines context-dependent optimality with regard to self and personality functioning, rather than one or the other personality characteristic. Similar views can be applied to coping research. There, high domain-specificity with regard to the functionality of coping behaviors has been identified. Furthermore, coping behaviors which are adaptive as immediate responses need not be adaptive in the long run. Thus, even with regard to coping, implications for everyday functioning are not fully known (Filipp & Klauer, 1991).

One possible solution of this dilemma is to invoke subjective assessments, for instance, about the perceived desirability or undesirability of a given self-related attribute to obtain estimates of what is considered a gain. In a series of studies on beliefs and expectations about development, Heckhausen and Baltes found that people have quite clear conceptions about what they consider to be a desirable and what an undesirable developmental outcome and also when it is supposed to occur. For example, only two desirable personality characteristics were thought to continue to grow in old age, that is wisdom and dignity, whereas many other positive characteristics were mentioned for the periods of young and middle adulthood (cf., Heckhausen, Dixon, & Baltes, 1989). It was also found in these studies that people of different ages and socioeconomic backgrounds agree about how personality develops and about what is a desirable and what undesirable personality development, that is, what is a gain or a loss.

In the following section, as we characterize gains and losses in life-span development of self and personality, we use two approaches. A first is based on research on subjective conceptions of the desirability of developmental outcomes. The second is our assessment of which self and personality characteristics are based on growth models of development (e.g., ego maturity, integrity, generativity) or on general conceptions of functionality and dysfunctionality (e.g., neuroticism). We alert the reader to the problem

that these categorizations are preliminary and by no means absolute. They are most likely oversimplifications because of the multidimensionality and multifunctionality of characteristics contributing to adaptive fitness.

Evidence Based on Trait Models of Personality

With regard to the stability and change of personality dispositions, there is wide-ranging consensus that the Big Five, that is neuroticism, extraversion, openness to experience, agreeableness and conscientiousness, show a high degree of stability after age 30 and far into old age (e.g., Conley, 1985; Costa & McCrae, 1994; Kogan, 1990). With regard to the statistical determination of stability, at least four interpretations can be distinguished (e.g., Nesselroade, 1989, 1991b). One refers to the stability of mean levels, the second to the stability of inter-individual differences, the third to the stability of covariances or structural stability, and the fourth one to the stability of one person's personality profile. With regard to the Big Five, the first three facets of stability have been much investigated and the evidence demonstrates a high degree of stability.

Structural Invariance of Personality. Among others, life-span methodologists have convincingly argued (e.g., Nesselroade, 1989) that meaningful comparisons of personality dimensions across the life span require the investigation of the degree of structural invariance of the underlying set of dimensions. The question of structural invariance involves two subtopics. A first is substantive and asks whether the structural properties change with age, for instance, in the number of traits or their interrelationships. The second is methodological and concerns measurement equivalence across age. Thus, when comparing extraversion scores of adolescents to those of old adults, it is important to know whether the same psychometric construct can be assumed to exist in the two age groups.

For the Big Five factorial model of personality, much information on structural stability is available (e.g., Conley, 1985; Costa, McCrae, & Dye, 1991; McCrae & Costa, 1997). It shows that a high degree of structural similarity can be assumed above age 10. Below that age, either observer ratings or information on temperament can be used as precursors of later personality dispositions (see above). Both strategies, however, could not be used to extend information about structural invariance below age 10, which is usually accepted as the lower limit for meaningful administration of personality questionnaires (e.g., Eysenck & Eysenck, 1975).

The evidence on structural invariance across most of the adult life span is restricted, however, by two limiting conditions. A first is the content generality of the traits measured. Would structural invariance be demonstrated if traits were measured context-specific and especially if age-specific contexts (e.g., work vs. retirement contexts) were compared? Furthermore, we know very little about the degree of structural similarity in old age.

Stability and/or Change of Inter-Individual Differences. Costa and McCrae have made it a focus of their work and have invested impressive energy and diligence in collecting and organizing the available longitudinal evidence on personality development across the life span (e.g., Costa & McCrae, 1992, 1994, 1995). Table 18.8 lists their compilation of longitudinal studies using the Big Five framework and varying in measurement intervals from 6 to 30 years.

It seems to be the case that stability coefficients decline with increasing time intervals between measurements, from .83, .82, .83, .63, .79 (6 or 3 years) to .56, .56, .62, .65, .64 (30 years), respectively. In general, it seems that about half of the inter-individual variance is accounted for by stability and half by change. Costa and McCrae do not follow this interpretation because they argue that these stability coefficients need to be corrected for measurement error. When they do so and in addition project the development of coefficients over a 50-year interval from age 30 to 80, they arrive at the conclusion "that three-fifths of the variance in true scores for personality traits is stable over the full life span." (Costa & McCrae, 1994, p. 33). In contrast, other authors using a meta-analytic or multitrait-multimethod approach arrive at the conclusion that a 50% change and 50% stability division is the best description of the available evidence (e.g., Conley, 1984, 1985; McGue et al., 1993a; Pedersen, 1993; Schuerger, Zarella, & Hotz, 1989; Siegler, Zonderman, Barefoot, & Williams, 1990).

We would like to note that when interpreting such longitudinal evidence, it should be taken into account that most of the studies cited worked with highly positively selected samples to start with, and certainly they have sample attrition over a time span of 30 or 50 years. It remains unclear whether positively selected samples might result in more or less stability than more heterogeneous samples. In none

Table 18.8 Stability Coefficients for Selected Personality Scales in Adult Samples

Factor/Scale	Source	Interval	r
Neuroticism			
NEO-PI N	Costa & McCrae, 1988	6	.83
16PF Q4: Tense	Costa & McCrae, 1978	10	.67
ACL Adapted Child	Helson & Moane, 1987	16	.66
Neuroticism	Conley, 1985	18	.46
GZTS Emotional Stability (low)	Costa & McCrae, 1992	24	.62
MMPI Factor	Finn, 1986	30	.56
		Median:	.64
Extraversion			
NEO-PI E	Costa & McCrae, 1988	6	.82
16PF H: Adventurous	Costa & McCrae, 1978	10	.74
ACL Self-Confidence	Helson & Moane, 1987	16	.60
Social Extraversion	Conley, 1985	18	.57
GZTS Sociability	Costa & McCrae, 1992	24	.68
MMPI Factor	Finn, 1986	30	.56
		Median:	.64
Openness		6	.83
NEO-PI O	Costa & McCrae, 1988	10	.54
16PF 1: Tender-Minded	Costa & McCrae, 1978	24	.66
GZTS Thoughtfulness	Costa & McCrae, 1992	30	.62
MMPI Intellectual Interests	Finn, 1986	Median:	.64
Agreeableness		3	.63
NEO-PI A	Costa & McCrae, 1988	18	.46
Agreeableness	Conley, 1985	24	.65
GZTS Friendliness	Costa & McCrae, 1992	30	.65
MMPI Cynicism (low)	Finn, 1986	Median:	.64
Conscientiousness		3	.79
NEO-PI C	Costa & McCrae, 1988	10	.48
16PF G: Conscientious	Costa & McCrae, 1978	16	.67
ACL Endurance	Helson & Moane, 1987	18	.46
Impulse Control	Conley, 1985	24	.64
GZTS Restraint	Costa & McCrae, 1992	Median:	.67

Note: Interval is given in years; all retest correlations are significant at $p < .01$. NEO-PI = NEO Personality Inventory, ACL = Adjective Check List, GZTS = Guilford-Zimmerman Temperament Survey, MMPI = Minnesota Multiphasic Personality Inventory. Taken from Costa, P. T., & McCrae, R. R. (1994).

of the studies have systematic selectivity analyses been conducted either. Consequently, one can only speculate whether the subjects that dropped out would have increased or decreased the stability of inter-individual differences. Moreover, as argued most persuasively by Nesselroade (1989, 1991b), it is important to acknowledge that the pool of items and scales selected for use in this longitudinal work is selected toward stability. Traditionally, psychometric construction favored items which evinced temporal stability.

Stability and/or Change of Mean Levels.   Studying the age-related development of mean-levels of personality dimensions is the next natural step. For example, do we become more or less open to experience as we age or do we stay the same? Again, most of the available evidence on this question is based on cross-sectional studies. The main and replicated finding of those studies (e.g., Costa & McCrae, 1992, 1994) show that across an age range from, for instance, 29 to 93 or 21 to 64 years on average there are relatively small changes. The dominant result is age-related continuity in mean levels. For instance, age correlations are of modest size. Negative age correlations are found for neuroticism ($r = -.15$ or $r = -.12$), openness ($r = -.16$ or $r = -.12$), and extraversion ($r = -.16$ or $r = -.12$). Modest positive age correlations were obtained for agreeableness ($r = .18$ or $r = .17$) and conscientiousness ($r = .05$ or $r = .09$). All correlations were significant but accounted for only about 3% of the variance in any of the scales. So, put in everyday terms, it seems that over the adult life span, the aging population on average becomes less open to new experiences and less outgoing, less neurotic, more easy to deal with, and more reliable. In terms of gains and losses—as indexed by subjective assessments of desirability—this pattern leans somewhat more towards gains. However, cohort effects may overlap with age effects in these cross-sectional studies.

When it comes to longitudinal studies, Costa and McCrae only report one seven-year study in which participant age, however, is averaged across an age span of 20 years (29–49 yrs.; Costa & McCrae, 1992). This design or manner of analyzing the data makes it very hard to follow developmental trajectories and discover potential age-graded changes. It actually works against discovering potential mean-level changes. Using this procedure, Costa and McCrae reported an increase in level of conscientiousness for women of the size of one third of a standard deviation. In addition, individual facets of openness and extraversion decreased by a similar magnitude for men and women alike. In the instance of longitudinal evidence, it seems that the pattern of results leans a little bit more toward neutral than toward gains.

In sum, methodological problems not withstanding, it seems fair to conclude that a major feature of life-span development in personality is sizeable stability of structure, sizeable continuity in inter-individual differences (close to 50%), as well as only moderate changes in mean levels. The latter can be interpreted to constitute a neutral to gain rather than a loss pattern. Recently, it has been suggested, however, that when it comes to *very* old age, the pattern of results seems to change towards a loss pattern (P. Baltes & Mayer, in press; Smith & Baltes, 1993, in press-b). A key task now seems to be the search for the conditions of continuity and especially of shifts in inter-individual differences. We need to learn more about the changing half of the distribution. Equally important is to complete the lifetime connection between childhood and adulthood as well as that between adulthood and old age.

Empirical Evidence Based on Growth Models of Personality Development

A major shortcoming of trait models of personality may be the relatively high level of aggregation of the structural conceptions as well as their psychometric foundation in stability. More open towards the possibility of development-related gains and actually providing theoretical grounds for such gains are what have been called the "growth" models of personality. One of the central historical figures of this school of thought is Erikson (1959, 1963; see also, Levinson, 1980; or Vaillant, 1990), with his theory of eight ego-developmental stages. Erikson's theory, for instance, predicts that in the second half of life, individuals in the post-reproductive phase of life either develop generativity and wisdom or fall into stagnation and despair (see also, Table 18.7; Erikson, Erikson, & Kivnick, 1986).

Traits as Facilitative Constraints for Adaptive Change.   Given the fact that one of the functions of self and personality is to provide a continuous basis to an individual's planning, action, and evaluation, it would be surprising not to find facets of self and personality that serve exactly that purpose and demonstrate continuity (Filipp & Klauer, 1986). Rather than precluding transactional change in self and personality, it is possibly exactly the continuous and coherent personality structure as measured within the psychometric or trait approach to personality that provides the frame for effective transactional adaptations to changing developmental contexts.

In a similar vein, in behavior-genetic research the notion "norm of reaction" has been coined to identify the constraints that the genome places on developmental trajectories. Taking a dynamic view of the notion of norm of reaction, we would argue that depending on their personality trait profile, individuals will show different adaptational changes in self and personality functions. We suggest that it is in this sense that research based in growth models of personality development (see Table 18.7) has identified changes on personality features like generativity or integrity. Thus, personality growth becomes a developmental outcome and personality traits are subsumed as "facilitative constraints" on the antecedent side. By and large the empirical evidence, especially of the longitudinal type, to support these theoretical contentions is still scarce. In addition, measurement instruments used in the tradition of personality growth are less developed with regard to criteria of psychometric quality.

Stability of Inter-Individual Differences.   The Berkeley and Oakland Longitudinal Studies (e.g., Block, 1971; Haan, 1981; Haan, Millsap, & Hartka, 1986) by now cover more than 50 years, from ages of 5 to 60. Personality assessment in these studies was done predominantly by means of the California Q-sort (Block, 1961) and the CPI (Gough, 1957) but only at some measurement points. In the research reported here, the Q-sort data subsequently were clustered using a component analysis (Meredith & Millsap, 1985). Six components were derived: self-confident, assertive, cognitively committed, outgoing, dependable, and warm. Componential analysis according to the authors solves the problem of negative correlations due to ipsative measurement, which characterizes the California Q-sort. The authors report reliabilities of .67, which are somewhat lower than those of trait measures. Although some overlap with CPI scales has been demonstrated, it does not seem to be the case that these six components are just another reflection of the Big Five.

Bridging a time span of 50 years (5 to 60), Haan and others reported stability coefficients (of inter-individual differences) on the six components ranging from .14 to .37. It seems that this data set is telling a somewhat different story than the Costa and McCrae (e.g., 1994) work, when it comes to the stability of inter-individual differences. In order to interpret and compare these findings, however, one needs to take into consideration at least three factors. First of all, there is the difference in measurement instruments including their psychometric qualities. Second, the Oakland and Berkeley Studies started personality assessment in early childhood and extended into late adulthood,

whereas the previously reported studies all started in young adulthood, around age 30, and then extended into old age. Third, there is a methodological problem that deserves consideration. It deals with the fact that the six personality components that were extracted on average explained 61% of the variance in the data. Thus, a considerable reduction in variance was involved. All of these issues might have contributed to the relatively low long-term stability coefficients.

As a consequence, it is difficult to treat these data as strong evidence for the adaptational potential of self and personality. In our theoretical framework, however, we would like to treat such results at least as first indicators of that potential which, as mentioned before, is *not* juxtaposed to the psychometrically very strong evidence for continuity presented above. Rather, it is our goal to convey the notion of a multifaceted self and personality that encompasses components supporting continuity as well as those producing change. Not unlike the fluid-crystallized distinction in work on intellectual functioning, it may be crucial to take such findings as evidence for different interacting components of a larger personality-self system that includes stable dispositions as well as more fluctuant and dynamic features.

Mean-Level Stability.   Also with regard to mean-level stability, the Berkeley and Oakland Studies report more lifetime changes. Costa and McCrae (1992, 1994) do acknowledge these findings and attribute the difference to the longer time span. They agree that up to age 30 more pronounced mean-level changes are to be observed, as this is still the formative stage of personality. Adolescents seem to report higher levels of neuroticism and extraversion and lower levels of agreeableness and conscientiousness when compared to young adults. Men and women in their twenties seem to report intermediate levels located between adolescents and middle-aged adults (e.g., Costa & McCrae, 1994).

Although using a different personality assessment instrument (the California Q-sort involving 6 personality components: Self-confident, assertive, cognitively committed, outgoing, dependable, warm), data from the Haan et al. study (1986) also support this view. Haan and colleagues found the lowest correlation between late adolescence and early adulthood ($r = .33$ vs. $r = .58$, $r = .47$, $r = .61$, $r = .44$, $r = .49$). Dependability increased between age 17 and somewhere in the 30s, which theoretically could be related to the positive age differences in conscientiousness found by Costa and McCrae (1994). Alternatively, the increase identified as "warmth" for females can be seen to parallel, over the same time span, the positive age difference in agreeableness and the negative age differences in neuroticism in the Costa and McCrae research.

In the study of Haan et al. (1986; see also, Jones & Meredith, 1996), however, sizable mean-level changes were also identified *after* age 30. Between the 30s and the 40s, the components self-confident and outgoing showed increases for both genders, and assertive and cognitively committed increased only in females. Between the 40s and 50s the component warmth increased for both males and females. Even Costa and McCrae (1994, p. 145) suggest that, using the language of the Eriksonian tradition, one might call this an increase in maturity (cf., Vaillant, 1977, 1993; Whitbourne & Waterman, 1979). These findings seem also to support the assumption that developmental tasks and themes, as presented in Table 18.7, do provide a useful logic for the description of lifetime personality development, and may be invoked to intertwine findings on various indicators of personality- and self-related functioning.

Studies in the tradition of motives and needs, à la Murray (1938), have also provided evidence for increases, decreases, as well as stability in personality development across the whole life span. In a life-span study assessing two nationally representative samples (21 yrs. and older) at two points in time about 20 years apart, Veroff and others (Veroff, Reumann, & Feld, 1984) found that the affiliation and the achievement motives declined for women starting in their 40s, whereas fear of weakness and hope of power stayed the same. For males, the hope for power was especially high in midlife. Using a very elaborate cross-sequential design and the Edwards Personal Preference Scale, Stevens and Truss (1985) could also demonstrate that when grouping individuals according to their trajectories on the 16 EPPS Scales (age range: 20–48 yrs.), most participants in their adult years demonstrated increases in relative need strength on achievement, autonomy, and dominance, and decreases in affiliation and abasement. No change was found for the majority of individuals on deference, order, exhibition, succorance, and endurance.

Evidence about personality growth as described in Erikson's or Loevinger's model (see Table 18.7) is still scarce and hardly any longitudinal studies are available. With respect to the concept of generativity, for example, there is cross-sectional research suggesting that older adults more than younger adults redirect their ambition toward offspring rather than toward their own achievements (McAdams & St.Aubin, 1992; Ochse & Plug, 1986). Whitbourne and others (Whitbourne, Zuschlag, Elliot, & Waterman, 1992), to our knowledge, conducted the only longitudinal and even cohort-sequential study using measures representing the Eriksonian stages. This study covered the time span between 21 and 43 years of age. Strong increases in industry and strong decreases in integrity across this age range were observed. Only slight age-related changes were discovered on the other Eriksonian measures (trust, initiative/guilt, autonomy, identity, generativity, and intimacy). This study is also of interest because it permits consideration of the historical cohort dimension which life-span theory considers an important ingredient of human ontogeny. Thus, Withbourne and her colleagues based on their cohort-comparative evidence concluded that the decrease in integrity scores cutting across the three cohorts may reflect a more general, societywide crisis of morality and purpose affecting adults of all ages rather than an age-based developmental trend.

One aspect of what Erikson has called ego integrity, and what other developmental theorists have referred to as maturity (e.g., Loevinger, 1976; Vaillant, 1977), can also be conceptualized as a process of gaining perspective and competence in mastering one's own emotional life. Several studies suggest that older adults seem to be better able to manage their emotions and deal with emotional issues (e.g., Blanchard-Fields, 1986; Cornelius & Caspi, 1987; Staudinger, 1989). Labouvie-Vief and her colleagues (Labouvie-Vief et al., 1989), for example, have developed a four-level assessment scheme for the understanding and control of emotional states, such as anger, sadness, fear, and happiness during adulthood. They reported that middle-aged and older participants demonstrated developmentally higher levels of emotional understanding and control than did young adults.

Another major effort at not only articulating a theoretical conception about change (and growth) in self and personality functioning but also at generating a solid body of empirical evidence is that of Ryff and her associates. Their findings (Ryff, 1989a, 1995; Ryff & Keyes, 1995) provide joint evidence for stability, growth, and decline. The dimensions of autonomy and environmental mastery showed positive age difference when comparing young, middle-aged, and old adults. The dimensions "purpose in life" and "personal growth" evinced negative age differences between middle and old age. This last finding is in line with a study on age differences in the level of self-representation. In this study, Labouvie-Vief et al. (1995) found that self-representations demonstrated the highest level of complexity during midlife. In both studies it has be taken into account, however, that effect sizes were moderate to small ($\frac{1}{2}$ to $\frac{2}{3}$ of a standard deviation) and that there is a real need for longitudinal evidence.

Age changes or age differences in themselves, of course, are not the final answer to developmental analysis. Age is not the only developmental organizer. It is also crucial to decompose the sources of influence associated with age. More and more evidence illustrates that variables other than age seem to be relevant when searching for personality growth. Age-comparative studies of wisdom-related knowledge and judgment, for example, have found that experiential contexts such as professional careers and historical events play a central role (P. Baltes et al., 1995; Smith, Staudinger, & Baltes, 1994; Staudinger, Maciel, Smith, & Baltes, in press; Staudinger, Smith, & Baltes, 1992). As far as biological processes are reflected in chronological age, age puts constraints on personality growth in the early years as well as in old age (see Figure 18.1). Only under very favorable conditions can these constraints be overcome and result in personality growth well into old age.

Summary on Stability and Change in Self and Personality across the Life Span

We have witnessed a strong trend toward the study of adult life-span development in self and personality. Although the evidence is far from complete—especially due to a lack of long-term longitudinal and cohort-sequential studies covering the whole life span that concern themselves with the intersection between self and personality—there appears much promise. Most importantly, we argue that it is critical to move beyond antagonism between stability- and change-oriented approaches.

The answer to the question asked at the beginning of this section, does personality change or does it stay the same, is "both." The stable components as assessed in trait models of personality provide the frame within which the transactional adaptation of self and personality can take place. Personality structure seems to exert a function not unlike

the one discussed under the heading of "norm of reaction" in behavior genetics (although in a dynamic sense as introduced earlier in this chapter), which asserts that genetic inheritance contributes to the constraints exerted on self and personality development and thus codetermine the potential for developmental change in transactional-adaptive capacity. In this sense, one might argue that this stable frame, which seems to reflect a person's sense of continuity and coherence, contributes to the *potential* of self and personality processes to master developmental changes and also to flexibly adapt to changing circumstances. Once accepting such a position, the more exciting question becomes how stable and changing components of self and personality can be predicted and how they work in collaboration. This question will be addressed in the next section dealing with the various internal and external opportunities and constraints of self and personality development, and how they interact.

What Are the Intra- and Extrapersonal Conditions That Transact to Produce Continuity or Discontinuity? Opportunities and Constraints of Self and Personality Development

As described above, the life-span perspective defines development—and this includes personality development—as an ongoing process of transactional adaptation. Thus, development is always the simultaneous and complex outcome of forces of nature and nurture, of genes and environment, of intra- and extrapersonal influences. In the beginning of this self and personality section, we discussed the evidence with regard to genetic and environmental contributions to personality and personality development and reported that in young adulthood, about half the variability in personality trait measures is accounted for by genetic influences. Recent evidence suggests this proportion is reduced to about 30% in later adulthood (Pedersen, 1993).

As noted earlier, P. Baltes, Reese, and Lipsitt (1980) have proposed a tripartite model of development of internal and external contextual influences: Normative age-graded influences, normative history-graded influences, and non-normative (idiosyncratic) influences. These three sets of influences may serve important analytic and explanatory functions in understanding both interpersonal and intercultural regularities and differences in developmental trajectories of self and personality characteristics. Table 18.9

Table 18.9 Illustrating the System of Opportunities and Constraints Influencing Self and Personality Development across the Life Span. These Sources also Interact.

The Grading of Opportunities and Constraints by	Opportunities and Constraints of Self-Development	
	Biology	Sociocultural Context

Age	Neuronal Maturation
	Physical Growth
	Puberty
	Pregnancy
	Menopause
	Increasing Morbidity
	Changes in Level
	  of Energy
	Changes in Sensory-
	  Motor Function
		Family of Origin
		Peers
		Teacher and Mentors
		Professional Context
		Financial Context
		Partnership and Family
		Social Network
		Retirement

History	Altered Ecologies
	Nutrition
	Medical System
	Cultural and
	  Biological
	  Co-Evolution
		Value Changes
		Role Changes
		War
		Economic Depression
		Technological Changes

Non-Normative	Specific Physical
	  Strength and
	  Weaknesses
	Genetic Risk
	Premature Birth
	Accidents
	Person-Specific
	  Health Stresses
	Nuclear Catastrophies
		Orphanhood
		Unemployment
		Divorce
		Widowhood
		Win in Lottery
		Crime

illustrates the interplay between the two major developmental influences on the one hand and the three gradings of such influences on the other. The variables mentioned in each cell only serve illustrative purposes and by no means are meant to be exhaustive. The scheme is further complicated by the fact that the three gradings also interact with each other such that, for example, it might depend on the age of an individual as to which effect a certain historical event has (e.g., Elder, 1994). Moreover, these life events differ in management-relevant features such as desirability and controllability (Brim & Ryff, 1980).

What has been called sociocultural context is a system of interlocking frames ordered along a dimension of proximity. A number of scholars have been very diligent in spelling out the different kinds of social contexts influencing development, which range from the day-to-day interactions with our closest social and physical environment to the world of institutions and constitutions (e.g., Bronfenbrenner, 1979; Lawton, 1988; R. Lerner & von Eye, 1992; Magnusson, 1995; Moen, Elder, & Lüscher, 1995). For a long time, the facilitative and debilitative effect of social interaction in the most proximal sense has been an important topic of social psychology (see for review, Staudinger, 1996b). In developmental psychology, it has been prominent in childhood research following the legacy of Vygotsky (e.g., Azmitia, 1996; Cole, 1996; Rogoff & Chavajay, 1995). But recently, research on life-span development has rediscovered the opportunities and constraints for development related to social interaction and interacting minds (e.g., P. Baltes & Staudinger, 1996b). Understanding (a) the conditions that optimize the facilitative effect of social interactions and interacting minds and (b) the ways by which such social transactions give directionality and enhance goal attainment are the major objectives of such efforts.

The interaction between biology and sociocultural contexts with regard to age-graded influences is well recognized by the models of self and personality development such as those of Erikson's or Havighurst's listed in Table 18.7. Historical and idiosyncratic influences of both kinds have been less systematically considered in existing models of self and personality development. But there is extensive research in both areas. With regard to the grading of biological and sociocultural influences through history, for example, certainly the seminal work of Elder and colleagues on the consequences of historical events on development deserve mention and are described elsewhere in this Volume (e.g., Elder, 1980, 1994; see also, Ch. 16, this Volume). One of the very important points to remember from this research is that the historical event by itself does not determine the developmental outcome. Rather, it needs to be taken into account at which age and under which idiosyncratic circumstances the historical event "meets" the individual. In addition, Elder shows that historical effects (such as the Great Depression) on development can be mediated through generational lineages and need not become obvious immediately (e.g., Elder, 1994). More recently, a similar research program on the interplay between individual development and historical change has evolved around the unification of Germany (e.g., Little, Oettingen, Stetsenko, & Baltes, 1995; Mayer et al., 1995; Oettingen, Little, Lindenberger, & Baltes, 1994; Trommsdorff, 1995).

The matrix of opportunities and constraints that shape personality development, of course, needs to be projected into time as well, in order to become a truly developmental approach. The question not only refers to how opportunities and constraints at a given point in time shape self and personality, but also whether, and if so how, opportunities and constraints present at one point in time have relevance for self and personality at a later point in time. One can ask, for instance, whether childhood opportunities and constraints persist in their influence into adolescence and even adulthood. Moreover, one can examine whether such connections follow a "simplex" model, that is, adjacent periods influence each other strongly but with an increasing time interval correlations decrease. An alternative model would be a "sleeper effect" model suggesting that constraints and opportunities exhibit time-delayed consequences. Finally, it can be investigated whether what has been an opportunity at one point in time becomes a constraint later on in personality development and vice versa. This exemplary list of questions demonstrates the complexity of possible nature/nurture by age and ontogenetic time interactions.

The presentation of empirical evidence with regard to the question of whether early personality profiles continue to exert positive or negative effects may serve as an example. A number of recent reviews on this question come to the conclusion that long-term relationships are much weaker than stereotypes of continuity may lead us to expect. It seems that long-term maladaptive outcomes require a combination of at least three, largely independent factors:

1. A particular personality profile or temperament.
2. An environment which amplifies this psychological vulnerability (and this environment needs to be maintained in order to be effective over longer periods of time).
3. Stressors that precipitate the symptoms (Jessor, 1993; Kagan & Zentner, 1996; Rutter & Rutter, 1993; Werner, 1995).

The reviews listed cite a number of biological and environmental constraints such as maternal deprivation, loss of parent, extreme malnutrition, low economic status—all of these constraints seem to be "counterbalanced" at the latest by young adulthood, however, if the just introduced combination of factors is not present. The most robust finding is the one between impulsivity and lack of control during the first four years of age and asocial or delinquent behavior in adolescent males. But again, once those adolescents reach adulthood only a small percentage is still delinquent (e.g., MacFarlane, 1963; Werner, 1995). This finding speaks to the complexity of human behavior and development, but also speaks to the adaptive power of the self and personality during childhood and adolescence.

Does such a nonlinear model of the development of personality disorder find its counterpart in a model for the development of personality growth? Mapping the findings from the realm of developmental psychopathology onto the realm of developmental growth seems not as easy. Easy temperament and a supportive environment over extended periods of time and the absence of stressful events do not ensure growth (e.g., Rutter & Rutter, 1993; Skolnick, 1975). Rather, it seems that too smooth and successful a childhood might even have maladaptive effects because it lacks the challenges and crises that might spur personality development and growth (see also, discussion of the steeling effects of critical life events; Elder, 1994; Filipp & Olbrich, 1986; Magnusson, 1996; Riegel, 1976).

Reserve Capacities of Self and Personality Development

As a further life-span problematic, we have selected the notion of reserve capacity (P. Baltes, 1987) and resilience for further elaboration. This notion gains special importance for a functional perspective on personality development, that is, for perspectives that aim at an analysis of the orchestration of self and personality as a system of adaptive functioning. The topic of reserve capacity and resilience in the domain of self and personality relates to the allocation of resources introduced above but discusses this theme at a more microanalytic level of analysis. What are the self-related mechanisms and characteristics that either show or contribute to reserve capacity?

Traditionally, the central role of reserve capacity, or related concepts such as resilience, is articulated within the province of child development (e.g., Cicchetti & Cohen, 1995). More recently, this view has been extended to include adulthood and old age (e.g., P. Baltes, 1991; Rutter & Rutter, 1993; Staudinger et al., 1995; Staudinger, Freund, Linden, & Maas, in press; Vaillant, 1990, 1993). For the present purpose, we have chosen aging as a forum of illustration. We have opted for this selection for several reasons. One is the relative novelty of this age period for researchers in child development. Another is because presenting research on aging permits us to elaborate more clearly the theme of gains and losses and the dynamic of differential allocation of resources into growth, maintenance, and management of losses.

We have discussed that little or no correlation between age and trait-based personality structure is found. In a similar vein, there is little correlation between age and various self-related indicators of adaptation (e.g., P. Baltes, 1991, 1993; Brandtstädter, Wentura, & Greve, 1993), including self-esteem (e.g., Bengtson, Reedy, & Gordon, 1985), sense of personal control (e.g., Lachman, 1986), or happiness and subjective well-being (e.g., Costa et al., 1987; Ryff, 1989b; Smith, Fleeson, Geiselmann, Settersten & Kunzmann, in press). This also includes 70- to 80-year-olds (Smith & Baltes, 1993). Only in advanced old age, do we seem to observe more salient changes towards a lower level of desirable functioning in traitlike dispositions (Smith & Baltes, in press-b). Thus, on the group level, for the larger part of the adult age spectrum, age does not seem to be a "risk" factor for these aspects of self and personality.

The absence of strong relationships between age and self-related indicators of well-being, despite what we have characterized above as an increase in risks and potential losses with advancing age, but also for certain disadvantaged groups, is theoretically and methodologically important. Indeed, the discrepancy between an increasing number of risks on one hand, and maintenance of adaptive functioning in the self on the other, is perhaps one of the most persuasive indicators of the power of self and personality in dealing with reality (Baltes & Baltes, 1990b; Brandtstädter & Greve, 1994). It is suggested that the self exhibits resilience, or reserve capacity, in the face of age-related risks and primarily health-related losses. In a similar way, it has been argued in childhood research conducted in the field of developmental psychopathology that certain self and environment constellations allow maintenance of adaptive development even in the face of adversity (e.g., Garmezy, Rutter, Werner).

Multiple arguments can be presented to understand this discrepancy between an age-related increase in risks and stability in self-related indicators of well-being (see also, Staudinger & Fleeson, 1996). First, age is only a rough proxy of increasing risks; not everyone of a given age cohort needs to be concerned by them. Therefore, the negative effects need not necessarily show on a group level. Second, as argued above (e.g., Brandtstädter & Greve, 1994; Filipp & Klauer, 1986), the self has a strong interest in continuity and growth. Over a given period of time, the self adapts to even adverse circumstances as if nothing or not much has happened. Thus, for researchers interested in the "self at work," it seems crucial at which point in this adaptational process the assessment takes place. Third, the changes due to increasing risks may be chronic rather than acute and therefore might not affect the self suddenly, but gradually. It may be difficult, therefore, for the self to recognize them and reflect them in self-report measures.

In the following section, we illustrate the reserve capacity of self and personality by citing select findings ordered according to the distinction introduced above between (a) form and structure of self and personality and (b) self-regulatory and self-transformational processes. Except for few studies with objective indicators of adaptivity, such as longevity or professional success, in most of the studies adaptivity is measured by self-report indicators of well-being. First, with regard to form or structure we will highlight information on differences in the adaptive fitness of personality and self profiles. Second, we will select evidence on the adaptive value of self-regulatory processes in three domains for further illustration of life-span developmental changes: (a) Goal seeking and reorganization; (b) self-evaluative comparison processes; and (c) coping.

Evidence for Reserve Capacity in Indicators of Self and Personality Structure

Which Personality Profile Develops More "Successfully"?   The current body of research suggests that personality traits might indeed serve a mediating function between age and indicators of self-related resilience such as subjective well-being (e.g., Costa et al., 1987; Diener, Saudvik, Pavot, & Fujita, 1992). Individuals with certain patterns of personality characteristics are likely to master challenging events better than others. Neuroticism and extraversion have been shown, for example, to evince significant predictive relations to subjective well-being as measured by the Bradburn Affect Balance Scale. Over a period of 10 years during middle adulthood, neuroticism was found to predict the degree of negative affect, and extraversion the level of positive affect (Costa, McCrae, & Norris, 1981). In a study with young adults, Magnus and colleagues (Magnus, Diener, Fujita, & Pavot, 1993) found, for example, that over a period of four years, extraversion predisposed people to experience positive events and neuroticism to experience negative events. Although both sources of variation were not assessed independently of each other, the investigators had tried to differentiate more "objective" from "subjective" events. This finding is consistent with an interpretation that events not only happen to people but that people also seek out events according to their personality (e.g., R. Lerner & Busch-Rossnagel, 1981; Scarr, 1993).

An often used index of successful life-span development is length of life (longevity, mortality). Evidence on the personality predictors of longevity has recently been reported from the longitudinal data set of the Terman study of gifted children, which was started in 1921 when participants were 11 years. The data set by now contains information about seven decades and has an attrition rate of only 10%. Although the gifted people of the Terman study are a positively selected group with regard to intellectual functioning (reduced variability in measures of intelligence) because this was the original purpose of the study, we assume that, as cognitive indicators typically are not highly related to personality functioning, this selective sampling effect is of less relevance for variability in personality variables.

Using survival analysis, it was found that conscientiousness reduced and cheerfulness increased the mortality risk (Friedman et al., 1993). A person in the 75th percentile or above on conscientiousness had only 77% the risk of a person in the 25th percentile of dying in any given year. The same was found for cheerfulness, but quite unexpectedly in the other direction. That is, the more cheerful as a child the greater the later risk for mortality. With regard to effect size, these risk factors for mortality are comparable to biological risk factors such as systolic blood pressure or serum cholesterol.

The risk related to cheerfulness in childhood seems contradictory to findings from short-term longitudinal studies in adulthood (e.g., 10 years), where optimism has been found to be highly protective (e.g., Cohen & Williamson, 1991; Scheier & Carver, 1987; Somervell et al., 1989). The authors acknowledge this contradiction and propose various explanations. Taking a life-span perspective, one of the more persuasive explanations seems to be that it is important to distinguish between short-term and long-term

predictions. The authors suggest that humor and optimism might be very effective coping mechanisms in particular situations rather than lifelong protective temperamental dispositions. Also interesting is that neuroticism, which had often been identified as a risk factor for adaptive outcomes, did not show significant effects. However, this lack of significant effects of neuroticism may also be due to unreliability of measurement and therefore not be very informative.

The protective power of *conscientiousness* obtained in the Friedman et al. (1993) work is in line with findings on other personality constructs such as *ego strength, ego resilience, tough mindedness, cognitive investment,* and *competence.* Such measures have been found to be positively related to various measures of well-being and adaptation, both cross-sectionally and longitudinally (e.g., Ardelt, 1997; Block, 1981; George, 1978; Haan, 1981; Helson & Wink, 1987; Robins et al., 1996). In further studies, Friedman and colleagues investigated possible mediating mechanisms of this protective power (Friedman et al., 1995). They found that neither cause of death nor health behavior seemed to be related to the protective effect of conscientiousness. Rather, the authors concluded that the effect of conscientiousness on longevity might be mediated through psychosocial processes. Conscientious people may be better able to cope with stressful events because they are better prepared psychologically (e.g., anticipation) and pragmatically (e.g., with insurance). Conscientious people are also more dependable and reliable and therefore may have more stable social relationships and better systems of social support, which have been shown to predict health and longevity (e.g., House, Landis, & Umberson, 1988).

When we turn from extraversion, neuroticism, and conscientiousness to *openness to experience,* there is indication that individuals with a greater degree of openness to experience (Costa & McCrae, 1985) are better able to adapt to changes and that this characteristic increases until the middle years and declines afterwards (Haan, 1981). An aging individual who is experientially open, as captured by characteristics such as being emotionally responsive, seeking variety, being intellectually curious and broad-minded, may be more aware of bodily changes, and may also be able to devise innovative strategies to adapt to them. Empirical evidence with regard to the adaptivity of openness to experience is still scarce (Whitbourne, 1987). From research on the personality correlates of wisdom, however, there is a suggestion that individuals who are more open to new experiences and who hold a middle position on the introversion-extraversion dimension also evince higher levels of wisdom-related performance (Staudinger, Lopez, & Baltes, in press; Staudinger, Maciel, Smith, & Baltes, in press). In the same vein, research from the Seattle Longitudinal Study (Schaie, Dutta, & Willis, 1991) has suggested that maintaining "behavioral flexibility" may be an important covariate of late-life adaptation: The progression of intellectual ability from middle to old age was substantially related to a flexible personality style over time. Taken together, these findings imply that in addition to a lack of neuroticism, an intermediate degree of extraversion and a high degree of openness to experience seem to be protective factors when it comes to managing the self-related challenges of old age.

Evidence from the field of *control beliefs* (e.g., Lachman, 1986; Lachman, Weaver, Bandura, Elliott, & Lewkowitz, 1992; Lachman, Ziff, & Spiro, 1994; Skinner, 1995) has demonstrated that, on the one hand, internal control beliefs stay relatively stable across the life span and continue to be adaptive. On the other hand, beliefs about the power of others over one's life increase with age-related changes in contingencies (e.g., Nurmi, Pulliainen & Salmela-Aro, 1992). For older adults it is adaptive to place greater weight on external resources and thereby compensate for decreases in internal resources (see also, M. Baltes, 1996). Thus, if older persons believe in the power of others over one's life this is not synonymous with giving up responsibility over one's life. Rather, it may imply that others are incorporated to become part of one's resources. In sum, internal control beliefs, that is, the belief that one has power over one's life has high adaptive value across the whole life span (M. Baltes & P. Baltes, 1986; Bandura, 1995; Skinner, 1995). With increasing age, the adaptive value of external control beliefs increases due to changes in the availability of internal resources. This increase in external control beliefs, while on the surface characterizable as a loss, may signify, however, an adaptive response (see also, Heckhausen & Schulz, 1995, regarding the dynamics between primary and secondary control or Brandtstädter & Greve, 1994).

The idea of *ego maturity* and its putative benefits for functioning and subsequent development have been discussed in other approaches to the study of personality development such as Loevinger's model of ego development (Loevinger, 1976), Vaillant's model of adult adjustment

(e.g., Vaillant, 1977, 1990), Haan's development of ego structures (Haan, 1977), or concepts of maturity as derived from scales of the California Personality Inventory (CPI; e.g., Helson & Wink, 1987). Ego level as measured according to Loevinger's Sentence Completion Test is reported to display a positive relation with reality-oriented and flexible coping (e.g., Picano, 1989) as well as with tolerance, sensitivity, and responsibility (e.g., M. White, 1985). With regard to its relation to higher levels of adjustment, the empirical evidence is equivocal (e.g., McCrae & Costa, 1983). In a longitudinal study, comparing two conceptions of maturity, Helson and Wink (1987) found that different measures of maturity predicted different aspects of adjustment (e.g., self-related, other-related).

In sum, there is longitudinal and cross-sectional evidence that individual differences in largely stable personality characteristics contribute to the level of adaptation. From a life-span perspective, it is important to note that the adaptive patterns differ somewhat depending on whether short- or long-term predictions are considered. This applies especially to two traits widely assumed to constitute a risk or a protective factor, that is, neuroticism and optimism or cheerfulness. Both have been reported to be a risk or a protective factor respectively when it comes to shorter time spans (up to 10 years). However, when considering predictions across a lifetime, neuroticism becomes neutral and cheerfulness actually turns into a risk factor. Thus, it seems necessary to distinguish between lifelong protective dispositions or general purpose mechanisms and adaptive mechanisms with regard to certain situations or life periods. Very little is known yet about the mediating processes that lead to such differentiation. As very few life-time studies are available, our knowledge about the long-term protective personality profile to date is still limited. Nevertheless, it seems safe to say that across a number of studies, positive expressions of the following personality characteristics have been demonstrated to increase adaptive fitness: Conscientiousness, extraversion, openness to experience, behavioral flexibility, ego resilience, ego level, internal control or agency (efficacy) beliefs, and cognitive investment.

Multiple and Possible Selves. Another strand of research focuses less on trait-based personality characteristics than on the structure and content of self-conceptions. Evidence is accruing that a multifocal and diversified structure of priorities and self-conceptions, or identity projects, makes transactive adaptation to developmental changes easier (e.g., Cross & Markus, 1991; Linville, 1987; Thoits, 1983). Adults who define their "selves" through multiple though interconnected identities that are richly construed, positively evaluated, and anchored in the present, are more successful (as measured by subjective well-being) in their mastery of negative developmental changes associated with their health condition (Freund, 1995). Similarly, a variety of sociologically-oriented studies suggest that a greater number of identities (e.g., family and work) is related to better mental health (Coleman & Antonucci, 1982; Kessler & McRae, 1982). The adaptivity of interconnected multiple selves forming a dynamic self system should not be confused, however, with the pathological category of a multiple personality constituted by structurally unrelated identities.

Along these lines, research by Markus and others (e.g., Cross & Markus, 1991; Markus & Nurius, 1986) is particularly informative. In this work, Markus and her colleagues have demonstrated that, for example in negotiating the changes and transitions of adulthood, "possible selves" (i.e., those identities which are either feared or hoped for in the present, in the past, or in the future) are used as resources to motivate and defend the individual. For instance, an individual currently dissatisfied in the workplace might use the hoped-for possibility of a future promotion as a facilitator for subjective well being for self-esteem, and as a motivator for continued engagement. Such findings point to the possibility that having access to a larger set of well-developed and systemically interrelated possible selves may be a protective factor as we confront and manage growing old. In a study on possible selves and perceived health (Hooker, 1992), the majority of older adults had possible selves in the domain of health, and also they rated the most important possible self as being in the realm of health. In addition, self-regulatory processes (e.g., perceived efficacy, positive outcome expectancy) explained over half of the variance in self-perceived health when it was also listed as the most important hoped-for self component. In other words, older adults felt subjectively healthier if at the same time they reported hopes for their health and believed that they had some control over their health. In the same vein, a study on the effects of community relocation on mental health in old age found that the psychological centrality of certain life domains (e.g.,

family, economics) moderated the resilience-increasing effect of social comparisons and of self-perceptions of activity level (Ryff & Essex, 1992).

Evidence for Reserve Capacity in Self-Regulatory Processes: The Goal System and Self-Evaluation

Selection of Goals and Life Priorities. Life-span theory emphasizes the critical importance of selection of domains and life priorities for effective regulation of developmental processes. In this sense, personality traits as well as possible selves act as motivational sources and are linked to goals that are either strived for or avoided. Content and priorities of life goals and personal life investments are not arbitrary but embedded in subjective conceptions of the life course, as well as reflecting the changing developmental tasks and themes of life (Cantor & Blanton, 1996; Cantor & Fleeson, 1994).

In a cross-sectional survey study of 25- to 103-year-olds, for instance, it was found that the four domains with highest personal investment in terms of time and effort followed the developmental tasks and themes of the respective life period (Staudinger, 1996a; Staudinger & Fleeson, 1996). From 25 to 35 years of age, it was work, friends, family, and independence that were ranked highest with regard to the degree of personal life investment. From 35 to 45 years of age it was family, work, friends, and cognitive fitness. From 55 to 65 the top four ranks of personal life investment were held by family, health, friends, and cognitive fitness. Not much changed in the rank order for the 70- to 85-year-olds: Family, health, cognitive fitness, and friends. Finally, in the age range from 85 to 103 years, health had become the most important investment theme and was followed by family, thinking about life, and cognitive fitness. Such findings are depicted in Table 18.10 and illustrate the kind of life-span developmental scripts and ecologies that regulate the motivational forces of life-span development. Similar findings have been reported for importance ratings of life domains across the life span (Heckhausen, in press).

Similar to findings on cognitive pragmatics of the mind (e.g., expertise research), these results also point to selection into individual life contexts and the importance of internal and external contexts in defining salient features of the self across the life span (see also, Brandtstädter & Rothermund, 1994; Cantor & Fleeson, 1994; Carstensen, 1993, 1995). In socioemotional selectivity

Table 18.10   Patterns of Degree of Personal Life Investment across the Adult Life Span (Listing of top four; after Staudinger, 1996a)

Young Adulthood	Middle Adulthood	Late Adulthood	Later Adulthood	Very Late Adulthood
25–24 Years	35–54 Years	55–65 Years	70–84 Years	85–105 Years
Work	Family	Family	Family	Health
Friends	Work	Health	Health	Family
Family	Friends	Friends	Cognitive fitness	Thinking about life
Independence	Cognitive fitness	Cognitive fitness	Friends	Cognitive fitness

theory, Carstensen, for instance, argues that there are systematic life-span changes in the goals we pursue and the priorities we set in the domain of social relationships. Of the two main social motives, Carstensen (1995) claims that in later adulthood emotional regulation and not information seeking are the driving forces for contacts. Fredrickson and Carstensen (1990) found, for instance, that older people, in contrast to younger adults, reported preferring familiar over novel social partners. Older people—in contrast to younger adults—also reported that they preferred social relationships that are related to anticipated affect rather than information seeking or future contact. When asked why, older people would quite explicitly state that they had no time to waste and had to be careful about their choices. So, it seems that lifetime constraints in the social domain may involve a shift in the criteria used in the selection of social relationships (Carstensen, 1993).

Age-related changes in goal structures that reflected developmental tasks were also found on a meta-level of aggregation. Using a sentence completion technique, Dittmann-Kohli (1991) demonstrated that older adults find meaning in life predominantly by searching for "contentment," whereas younger adults more often reported that they searched for "happiness." In this view, Emmons (1996) has recently provided an overview of research on the adaptivity of goal selection and comes to the conclusion that it is the attainment of *meaningful* goals that seems adaptive rather than the sheer act of attainment. Furthermore, Ryff (1989b) determined that younger people are more likely to assess their subjective well-being in terms of accomplishments and careers, whereas older people are more likely to associate well-being with good health and the ability to accept change. It seems to be highly protective to renounce or

relegate to the periphery of importance those roles and commitments that are no longer serviceable, and to invest in others more "in tune" with current conditions of living (e.g., Brim, 1992; Dittmann-Kohli, 1991; Lazarus & De-Longis, 1983; see Table 18.11). Again, the general line of argument is that selection and resetting of priorities are facilitated if there is a rich variety of self-defining concepts to select from and to rearrange. In this sense, a rich variety of interrelated but well-articulated life priorities is part of a person's developmental reserve capacity (cf., P. Baltes, 1991; Staudinger et al., 1995).

Adjustment of Aspirational Levels through Social Comparisons.   In addition to the change in content and ranking of self-concepts and goals, there is evidence for other self-regulatory processes protecting or putting at risk the self throughout adulthood. For instance, research on the self also suggests that aging individuals modify their aspirational levels within given domains of functioning in order to adapt to decreases in their behavioral competence or negative changes in their health condition. We would like to emphasize again that we expect similar processes to operate at younger ages as well. We focus primarily on old age because we believe that these processes are more easily identified at higher ages than at younger age levels. In some respects, old age is a more powerful "research model" for the investigation of the dynamics involved in the availability and activation of reserve capacity than is childhood.

Adjustment of aspirational levels can occur through a variety of mechanisms. Quite often, it is related to processes of social comparison and other forms of interactive minds (e.g., Baltes & Baltes, 1990b; P. Baltes & Staudinger, 1996a; Festinger, 1954; Schulz & Heckhausen, 1996; Wills, 1981). New reference groups are selected in order to permit a reorganization of personal standards of evaluation. This might be done, for example, by comparing

Table 18.11   Life-Span Differences in Meaning of Life and Determinants of Well-Being

	Meaning of Life and Determinants of Well-Being	
	Young Adulthood	Later Adulthood
Dittmann-Kohli (1991)	Happiness	Contentment
Ryff (1989)	Accomplishment Career success	Good health Ability to accept change

oneself to specific subgroups, such as age, gender, and ethnic-cultural groups, rather than the population at large. Three types of social comparisons, that is downward, lateral, and upward comparisons can be distinguished and serve distinct and age-related, self-regulatory functions. Downward comparisons, in which individuals compare themselves to people who are worse off in a relevant domain of functioning, may become more and more important with age or with increasing levels of maladaptation (Heckhausen & Krueger, 1993; Heidrich & Ryff, 1993; Markus & Cross, 1990; Taylor & Lobel, 1989; Wood, 1989). For example, women with breast cancer rated their postsurgery level of well-being as positive, even as more positive than before they were diagnosed with cancer. The same women reported overwhelmingly that they were doing as well or better than other women in a similar situation (Wood, Taylor, & Lichtman, 1985). Similarly, in a study of the effect of community relocation on subjective well-being, it was demonstrated that endorsement of social comparisons predicted various aspects of well-being (e.g., personal growth, self-acceptance; Ryff & Essex, 1992).

In general, then, the contention is that internal or external selection of appropriate comparison groups is an important protective mechanism that empowers the adult and aging individual to manage the gains and losses of aging. Better functioning groups are selected for comparison, that is upward comparison, if the goal is to maintain and to improve, while more poorly functioning group referents, that is downward comparisons, tend to be selected if the goal is to deal with losses. Note that despite the discussion of these comparison strategies as though they were operating at a conscious level, little is known about the level of consciousness at which such mechanisms operate. And, again, note also that similar comparison processes operate in childhood, adolescence, and young adulthood.

The research evidence is not as clear cut as regards the very intuitively appealing theoretical contention that downward comparisons are protective. Many reasons can account for this. For example, much of the evidence is derived from either laboratory studies or studies with clinical populations and other results stem from correlational survey work. Furthermore, the operationalization of what is called a downward comparison varies markedly between studies and makes the comparative evaluation of different studies very difficult. Some studies, for instance, evaluate spontaneously provided reasons for certain self-evaluations,

which are later coded for which kind of comparison standard was mentioned. Other studies ask for the frequency with which social upward, downward, and lateral comparisons are made and relate this to measures of well-being (e.g., Filipp & Buch-Bartos, 1994; Taylor & Lobel, 1989). Still other studies have participants rate themselves and a generalized other on certain personality dimensions, and then indirectly infer upward or downward comparisons and how this is related to self-related adaptation (e.g., Heckhausen & Krueger, 1993). As suggested above, it seems that the most critical question regarding the adaptiveness of such mechanisms might be the use of the functional comparison at the appropriate time during the transactional adaptation to the situation. Goals shift in any activity during the life span, and those shifts lead to shifts in the selection and weighting of comparative information (Bandura & Cervone, 1983; Frey & Ruble, 1990).

The adaptive value of such attributional patterns has caused lively discussion, centered around the issue of the adaptivity of the discrepancy between reality and attribution. Is it true that *positive illusions* always are more adaptive than veridical views (e.g., Baumeister, Smart, & Boden, 1996; Taylor & Brown, 1988)? Or does this relationship follow an inverted U-shaped function? Baumeister (1989) has introduced the notion of the optimal margin of illusion. With this notion he implies that, if the discrepancy between reality and attribution becomes too large, touch with reality is lost and this attributional style may become maladaptive (e.g., Colvin & Block, 1994; Lopez, Little, Oettingen, & Baltes, 1996).

It seems that general statements such as "positive illusions are adaptive" need qualification in order to adequately reflect the complexity of mechanisms of self-regulation. They need qualification with regard to the circumstances under which they are adaptive (e.g., at which point in the action sequence). It may, for instance, be adaptive to have positive illusions before the action is completed in order to keep up motivation. But it may be dysfunctional to keep up positive illusions when interpreting outcomes, because this may hinder adequate actions to be taken. Along this line of reasoning, Taylor and Gollwitzer (1995) have shown, for example, that people think more realistically when *setting* goals than when *implementing* them. In this context, the notion of mental simulation and its adaptive value has recently attracted much research activity (e.g., Taylor & Pham, 1996). Positive illusions might also need specification with regard to which self-regulatory components are concerned. The work by Oettingen (1996; Oettingen & Wadden, 1991) has shown, for example, that positive behavior outcome *expectations* but negative *fantasies* about the same outcome resulted in the best behavioral outcome.

Evaluative Adjustment through Lifetime (Temporal) Comparisons.   Besides social comparisons, comparisons across one's own lifetime constitute an important resource for the self. Suls and Mullen (1982) have suggested that temporal comparisons, especially retrospective temporal comparisons, provide an additional strategy for effective self-management and self-evaluation in adulthood. Indeed, they have argued that with increasing age, social comparisons become less frequent and lifetime (temporal) comparisons increase in frequency. The evidence to support this hypothesis, however, is still scarce (e.g., Filipp & Buch-Bartos, 1994). Filipp and Buch-Bartos (1994), for instance, found that when older adults were asked to explain certain self evaluations provided earlier in time, they tended to do more prospective than retrospective temporal comparisons. And indeed those prospective comparisons were negatively related to well-being. With regard to retrospective temporal comparisons, Woodruff and Birren (1972) actually retested a sample after 25 years using the CPI and found that participants had a tendency for what one might call "time enhancement." That is, they perceived improvement as compared to their own past, whereas the actual CPI ratings collected at the two occasions did not reveal significant change. Again, it seems that it is not the temporal comparison per se that is protective; rather, depending on the characteristic or the domain selected and on the point in the self-regulatory process, lifetime comparisons can result in either the realization of, or loss in, self-enhancement.

In earlier age-comparative research on beliefs about development across the life span, it has already been demonstrated that such beliefs differ when people are asked to generate expectations about themselves, versus a generalized other, versus a personal ideal, and retrospectively versus prospectively (Ahammer & Baltes, 1972; Harris, 1975; Ryff & Baltes, 1976). This approach of systematic instructional variation (e.g., age referent, social referent) has been explored with regard to the question of age-related change versus stability of subjective well-being. In this vein, it seems that for many older adults shifting the temporal

point of reference may be an effective strategy in maintaining high subjective well-being across the life span. Ryff (1984, 1991) has found that when different age groups are asked to report on their current functioning in different facets of personality (such as autonomy, social relations, personal growth), they do not differ. Age differences become apparent, however, when instructional variations in temporal referent are introduced. Younger adults have a more positive evaluation of their future and a less positive evaluation of their past than older adults. Conversely, it seems that older adults, perhaps due to fewer opportunities to achieve in the present and a richer set of positive experiences in the past, increasingly refer to successes of the past. Indeed, reference to earlier achievements may fortify current levels of optimism and energy for dealing with present challenges. Selectively attending to positive aspects of the self at different points in the lifetime can serve to support a positive sense of self at the present. The endorsement of selective lifetime comparisons may contribute to the finding that in concurrent (present-day) self evaluations, only few age differences emerge.

Beyond the possibility to uncover more change than present self ratings suggest, temporal instructions for the assessment of personality, that is asking individuals not only about their self descriptions at present but also in the past and in the future, gives additional meaning to present ratings of personality. Fleeson and Baltes (1996), for example, collected data which showed that past and future ratings of personality predicted well-being above and beyond present ratings. One result suggested, for instance, that a medium-level of extraversion as assessed under the present instruction, that is combined with a high-level rating by the same person under past instructions, has a different meaning than the same present rating when it is combined with a low-level past rating. These differences in the predictive value for adaptive outcomes cannot be discovered when only present ratings are assessed.

In future work on life-span personality development, therefore, it seems important to introduce a stronger focus on *subjective lifetime comparisons*. Such work would be less aimed at reconstructing or preconstructing ontogenetic reality as it was or will be. Rather, the goal would be to introduce in personality assessment a perceived lifetime dimension of change and continuity: Who was I, who am I, who will I be?

Coping: Further Evidence for Reserve Capacity Related to Self-Regulatory Processes

Stress and coping are concepts that match very well the developmental task perspective on self and personality development that is illustrated by Havighurst's model (see Table 18.7). Each developmental task can be viewed as a stressor with which the individual has to cope one way or the other. With increasing age the stressors, or the developmental tasks, become more and more complex, both in scope and temporal extension. More and more different domains of life are concerned and need to be monitored and managed at the same time. Life complexity is also increased by the history and experiences that characterize certain life domains and certain social relations. The number of people we have to deal with and the number of life domains that are relevant to a given developmental task systematically increases until middle adulthood and decreases thereafter. This is not meant to imply that middle age is the most stressful and difficult life period, because this characterization of complexity does not touch upon the resources that, on average, are also very rich during midlife. Therefore, when taking into consideration both available resources and degree of challenges or stress, it seems fair to speculate that the net demand exerted by different life periods may be comparable. Smith and Baltes (in press-b) suggest, however, that this may not be true for advanced old age, a suggestion that is in line with many other findings about the nature of advanced old age (P. Baltes, 1997; P. Baltes & Mayer, in press). In fact, an alternative speculation would be that the life-span challenge or stress curve follows the life-span mortality curve.

In the 1970s, Pfeiffer (1977) suggested that with increasing age, *regressive* coping tendencies increase. In the same year, however, Vaillant (1977) reported an age-related increase in *mature* coping mechanisms. In his model of adult adjustment, Vaillant (e.g., 1977, 1990) extended psychoanalytic conceptions of defense mechanisms into a developmental framework of more or less mature or adaptive defense mechanisms. Vaillant (e.g., 1983) argued that mature defenses may provide an explanation for some of the "invulnerability" among the disadvantaged. More recently, he provided evidence from long-term longitudinal data for this protective and development-enhancing power of mature defenses in middle and later adulthood (Vaillant, 1990).

In a similar vein, Folkman, Lazarus, Pimley, and Novacek (1987), for example, found that older respondents were less likely to seek social support or use confrontive coping and were more likely to use distancing and positive reappraisal. In fact, more and more of the recent evidence supports this "growth" view of coping in adulthood and old age (e.g., Aldwin, 1991; Diehl, Coyle, & Labouvie-Vief, 1996; Irion & Blanchard-Fields, 1987; Labouvie-Vief, Hakim-Larson, & Hobart, 1987; McCrae, 1989) or at least speaks for stability in coping behavior.

With respect to the developmental stability of coping behavior during adult life, it has been observed, for instance, that individual differences in the endorsement of coping mechanisms are more a function of the type of stressful event than of age (McCrae, 1989). This finding is extended by evidence from the Berlin Aging Study. In that study, based on data from a representative sample of 70- to 105-year-olds, it is suggested that those old individuals who reported selective flexibility in their use of coping strategies also demonstrated the highest level of well-being (Staudinger & Fleeson, 1996). Figure 18.16 illustrates this finding.

Similar findings are reported in research on depression in old age. Rather than any particular form of coping, it seems that self-related resilience as indicated by measures of mental health is related to the availability of a large number of different forms of coping (Forster & Gallagher, 1986). We have argued above that the multiplicity of self definitions has protective value, and it has been demonstrated that, similarly, social relations with multiple functions are a richer resource than other types of relationships (for an overview, see Staudinger et al., 1995). This evidence suggests that access to a wide repertoire in functioning (e.g., coping, self definitions, functions of a relationship) may be a key "general-purpose" resource, as it facilitates the person-situation fit.

Furthermore, older adults seem to be more flexible in adapting their coping response to the characteristics of the situation (e.g., controllability) than younger adults (e.g., Aldwin, 1991). Such evidence is congruent with findings that, in comparison to younger adults, older adults have been found to demonstrate an accommodative coping style in the face of adversity or failure; that is, older adults were more flexible and better able to adjust their strivings to changed circumstances than were young

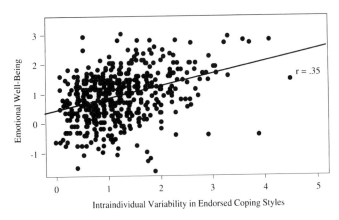

Figure 18.16   The greater the intraindividual variability (plasticity) in endorsed coping styles (i.e., some styles are endorsed strongly and others very little), the higher the level of well-being (adapted after Staudinger & Fleeson, 1996). Each dot represents one person. This is evidence taken from aging research to illustrate the notion of self-related general purpose mechanisms. It seems that the availability of a rich variety of self-regulatory processes including algorithms guiding adaptive application constitute such a general purpose mechanism.

adults (Brandtstädter & Renner, 1990). Conversely, younger adults were more likely to adhere to their once established goals (i.e., assimilative coping), even if they were no longer realizable. With age, Brandtstädter and Renner (1990) have demonstrated that adults favor *accommodative* (goal flexible) over *assimilative* (goal persistent) coping. In a similar vein, Heckhausen and Schulz (1993) have more recently proposed and presented empirical evidence (Heckhausen, in press) that an age-related shift from *primary* to *secondary control* strategies takes place in order to master the tasks of aging.

In our view, such evidence on age-related stability and positive transformations in coping efficiency is significant for two reasons. First, if later adulthood and old age are characterized by an increasing number of varied stressful events, then the findings on coping efficiency seem to suggest the presence of another component of self-related reserve capacity. Second, in contrast to stereotypical conceptions of the elderly as rigid, the evidence suggests that, based on processes of self-representation, self-regulation, and self-enhancement, older adults possess a substantial capacity for adjustment and flexible mastery of demands. We need to acknowledge, however, that this efficacy of

self-related mechanisms may find its limits in extreme situations including the challenges of advanced old age (P. Baltes, 1997).

Summarizing Foci and Facets of Life-Span Development in Self and Personality

In this section, we brought together theory and research from three different areas of research, that is, personality, self-conceptions and identity, and self-regulatory processes. Each of these areas is characterized by its own foci and methodological approaches. We have argued that a life-span perspective on self and personality development, rather than viewing these three approaches as relatively independent from each other or even mutually exclusive, tries to incorporate theoretical and empirical evidence from these fields. Dynamic systems theory and similar theoretical perspectives provide useful theoretical guidance for this endeavor:

1. A central feature of personality development is the emergence of personality and self structures and of an associated system of self-regulatory mechanisms that mediate successful transactional adaptation. Beginning in childhood, we obtain solid evidence for structure, a sense of coherence, and some stable modes of adaptive behavior (e.g., Caspi & Bem, 1990). Such a view is represented in dynamic-system models of development (Lewis, 1995; Magnusson, 1996), where principles of structural emergence and self-organization are critical for successful ontogenesis. Structural organization and coherence of personality, self, and self-regulatory mechanisms are a necessary precondition (constraint) for adaptive fitness and further growth.

2. We have learned from personality research that about 50% (and up to 75%) of the inter-individual variance in major traits such as the Big Five is stable. And it has been reported from evidence based on growth models of personality that personality characteristics are indeed changing as we move through different developmental periods. This seemingly contradictory empirical evidence is congruent with an interpretation that adaptive self and personality functioning is constituted by a dialectic between continuity and change.

From the perspective of dynamic-systems models of development but also dialectical life-span theory (Datan & Reese, 1977), conflict and synergism between continuity and change are important ingredients to adaptive functioning and developmental advances. If researchers such as Costa and McCrae (e.g., 1995), for instance, report a high level of inter-individual stability in personality structure, this should not be taken as counterevidence for ontogenetic development. Rather, such evidence should be taken to indicate that people's self and personality are organized. By no means does such evidence preclude, within this frame of a stable structure or this sense of coherence, individuals from transactively adapting to their developmental contexts and thereby also developing additional characteristics of self and personality. To appreciate the facilitative effects of a stable system, it may be useful in personality development research to apply modes of thinking similar to the concept of constraint in cognitive psychology.

3. We have argued and provided some evidence that within limits, the negative life-span trajectory of biological functioning is less of a debilitating factor to self and personality functioning than it is to cognitive functioning. In dealing with the opportunities and constraints of life-span development, self and personality, therefore, manage to serve a lifelong orchestrating function with regard to the activation and allocation of internal and external resources. Limits to this overall efficacy exist, however, in extreme conditions such as advanced old age and conditions of psychopathology.

4. Self and personality as a dynamic system composed of various components with different properties holds a domain-general potential for the transactional adaptation of the developing organism. We argued and presented evidence that self and personality serve an executive or orchestrating function with regard to the management of gains and losses during ontogeny. Self and personality possess a great ability to negotiate the opportunities and constraints of development that come with age, historical, and idiosyncratic conditions. What we have called general purpose mechanisms play a central role in this adaptational process. Besides a protective self and a coherent personality structure, it is primarily the availability of a rich variety of self-regulatory mechanisms, and of an adaptive algorithm which monitors their application,

that contribute to the adaptational power of self and personality. Table 18.12 summarizes these protective features in more detail. This adaptive potential reaches its limits in very old age when, due to biological processes, the functional losses may for more and more persons reach an overwhelming degree or at earlier ages when other extreme life circumstances result in an imbalance of gains and losses (P. Baltes, 1997; Staudinger et al., 1995).

5. The systemic and overall developmental theory of selective optimization with compensation introduced in the first part of this chapter serves as a useful theoretical tool when analyzing the adaptive potential of the self and personality (Baltes & Baltes, 1990b). When orchestrating the optimization of development by processes such as selection and compensation, the appraisal of resources is of central importance. Questions such as how to evolve a goal structure and the associated goal-relevant means and motivational investment strategies, how to deal with selection-related disengagements from other possible goals, when to accept a loss and reorient one's life, and when to still strive

Table 18.12 Summary of Protective and Optimizing Characteristics of Self and Personality

Self and Personality Components	Protective and Optimizing Characteristics (Examples)
Personality	Conscientious, extraversion, openness to experience, behavioral flexibility, ego resilience, advanced ego level, and cognitive investment
Self-Concept	Interrelated, well-articulated variety of self-conceptions and life priorities Positive agency (efficacy) beliefs
Self-Regulation and Life-Management	
• Self-evaluation	Application of the functional type of comparison (up, down, lateral, temporal) at the appropriate time and context in the adaptational process
• Goal setting and restructuring	Selection and reorganization of life priorities
• Coping styles	Intraindividual plasticity and flexibility in coping styles and compensatory strategies Flexibility in adapting goals to circumstances
• Systemic processes	Selective optimization with compensation

harder because current behavior is not yet employed to its fullest capability becomes crucial in composing life development. Brim has argued, for example, that one criterion for making this decision could be to consider something like a "performance/capacity ratio" (Brim, 1992). According to this rationale, acceptance of a certain loss becomes necessary when the display of the behavior requires a "dysfunctionally" high amount of reserve capacity.

6. For future research, we suggest a stronger focus on constructs that are suitable for the investigation of self and personality development throughout the life span. Second, we would like to suggest that the links between cognitive and personality development need more intensive research efforts. Moreover, future work needs to address the question of the joint operation and interface of structural and dynamic components of self and personality, perhaps not unlike the distinction between fluid and crystallized components in the area of intelligence, where fluid intelligence is considered a general purpose resource. We need to learn more about the modulating effects of personality dispositions as general risk and protective factors for the optimization of one's self-enhancement. And finally, we suggest the use of testing-the-limits paradigms, as proposed in cognitive-developmental work, to gain additional insights into the range and age-associated limits of self and personality functioning.

CONCLUDING COMMENTARY

This chapter presented life-span developmental psychology as a theoretical orientation to the study of human development. Because the dominant theoretical approaches in developmental psychology have been formed primarily by research on infants, children, and adolescents, we made special efforts to highlight the uniqueness in developmental theory that emanates from a life-span developmental framework. An unfortunate by-product of this strategy of presentation may have been the relative inattention paid to important commonalities between age-specialized developmental theories and theoretical efforts in life-span work.

In fact, we believe that there is a larger (and growing) commonality in theoretical approach between more age-specialized developmental theories and life-span developmental theory than might appear to be the case based on the arguments presented in this chapter (e.g., Scarr, 1986). In part, this is true because there are several new sources (only alluded to in this chapter) from which innovative theoretical efforts in various quarters of developmental psychology have emerged and which contain a structure of arguments similar to those put forward in life-span developmental theory. In our view, work in cultural psychology, dynamic systems theory, and on other forms of self-organization in ontogenesis, are examples of this new theoretical treatment of ontogenesis that is beginning to pervade the developmental field as a whole.

As was true for life-span psychology and the benefits it derived from its contact with the biology of aging, these new kinds of theoretical treatments have benefitted much from transdisciplinary dialogue, especially with modern developmental biologists but also anthropologists. Biologists, for instance, have perhaps led the way in moving research away from unilinear, organismic, and deterministic models of ontogenesis to a theoretical framework that highlights the contextual, adaptive, probabilistic, and self-organizational dynamic aspects of ontogenesis (P. Baltes & Graf, 1996; Magnusson, 1996). In a similar vein, cultural psychologists and anthropologists (e.g., Cole, 1996; Durham, 1991; Valsiner & Lawrence, 1996) have succeeded equally in convincingly demonstrating that human ontogenesis is not only strongly conditioned by culture, but that the architecture of human development is essentially incomplete as to the culturally-engineered pathways and possible endpoints (P. Baltes, 1997).

Not the least because of this transdisciplinary dialogue, a new conception has emerged regarding the "nature" (Kagan, 1984) of human development. In the modern context, its nature no longer refers to the fixed-biological (P. Baltes, 1991, 1997; R. Lerner, 1984; Magnusson, 1996). Rather, in modern versions of ontogenesis, its nature is both biological and cultural, and both of these categories are subject to dynamic and interactive changes as well as systemic transformations. Of all developmental specialties, life-span development, because of its intimate connection with long-term processes of individual development, cultural evolution, and generational transmission is perhaps the field most dependent on, and committed to, such views.

The future of life-span developmental theory will depend significantly on the extent to which the metatheoretical perspectives advanced turn out to be useful in the conduct of empirical inquiry. On this score, the 1980s have witnessed impressive growth. In the area of intellectual development, for instance, we now have available a cohort- and age-sequential study that extends over close to 40 years (Schaie, 1996) and demonstrates the varied conditions and outcomes which we can observe when placing adult development into the context of historical change and, in addition, consider processes of individual differentiation. There also have been advances in demonstrating the usefulness of the life-span approach for other specialties such as clinical (Staudinger et al., 1995; Vaillant, 1990) and applied psychology (Abraham & Hansson, 1995; Sterns & Dorsett, 1994). In fact, these intersects of the life-span approach to the study of human development with other psychological specialties need to be identified and nurtured.

Close to 20 years ago, one of us (P. Baltes) wrote (1979b, p. 1): "There can be no strong field of life-span developmental psychology without a solid foundation in and connection to childhood. By the same token, the study of child development does not exist in a vacuum, but is vitally enriched by considering the aftermath of childhood." Since then, there has been much progress in elaborating this reciprocal connection between age-focused developmental specialities and their integration into a life-span view of human development, but at the same time, this challenge continues to be with us.

ACKNOWLEDGMENT

We acknowledge many valuable discussions with our colleagues at the Max Planck Institute for Human Development, Berlin, and in the Research Network on Successful Midlife Development of the MacArthur Foundation (chair: Orville Brim).

REFERENCES

Abraham, J. D., & Hansson, R. O. (1995). Successful aging at work: An applied study of selection, optimization, and compensation through impression management. *Journal of Gerontology: Psychological Sciences, 50B,* 94–103.

Ackerman, P. L. (1996). A theory of adult intellectual development: Process, personality, interests, and knowledge. *Intelligence, 22,* 227–257.

Ahammer, I. M., & Baltes, P. B. (1972). Objective versus perceived age differences in personality: How do adolescents, adults, and older people view themselves and each other? *Journal of Gerontology, 27,* 46–51.

Aldwin, C. M. (1991). Does age affect the stress and coping process? Implications of age differences in perceived control. *Journal of Gerontology: Psychological Sciences, 46,* 174–180.

Alexander, C., & Langer, E. J. (Eds.). (1990). *Beyond formal operations: Alternative endpoints to human development.* New York: Oxford University Press.

Allport, G. W. (1937). *Personality.* New York: Holt.

Allport, G. W., & Odbert, H. S. (1936). Trait names: A psycho-lexical study. *Psychological Monographs, 47*(Whole No. 211).

Anastasi, A. (1970). On the formation of psychological traits. *American Psychologist, 25,* 899–910.

Anderson, M. (1992). *Intelligence and development: A cognitive theory.* Oxford, England: Blackwell.

Ardelt, M. (1997). Wisdom and life satisfaction in old age. *Journal of Gerontology: Psychological Sciences, 52B,* P15–P27.

Asendorpf, J. B. (1996). Die Natur der Persönlichkeit: Eine ko-evolutionäre Perspektive. *Zeitschrift für Psychologie, 204,* 97–115.

Assmann, A. (1994). Wholesome knowledge: Concepts of wisdom in a historical and cross-cultural perspective. In D. L. Featherman, R. M. Lerner, & M. Perlmutter (Eds.), *Life-span development and behavior* (Vol. 12, pp. 187–224). Hillsdale, NJ: Erlbaum.

Assmann, J. (1992). *Das kulturelle Gedächtnis, Schrift, Erinnerung und politische Identität in frühen Hochkulturen.* München: C. H. Beck.

Axelrod, R. (1984). *The evolution of cooperation.* New York: Basic Books.

Azmitia, M. (1996). Peer interactive minds: Development, theoretical, and methodological issues. In P. B. Baltes & U. M. Staudinger (Eds.), *Interactive minds: Life-span perspectives on the social foundation of cognition* (pp. 133–162). New York: Cambridge University Press.

Bäckman, L., & Dixon, R. A. (1992). Psychological compensation: A theoretical framework. *Psychological Bulletin, 112,* 1–25.

Bäckman, L., Josephsson, S., Herlitz, A., Stigsdotter, A., & Viitanen, M. (1991). The generalizability of training gains in dementia: Effects of an imagery-based mnemonic on face-name retention duration. *Psychology and Aging, 6,* 489–492.

Bäckman, L., Mäntylä, T., & Herlitz, A. (1990). The optimization of episodic remembering in old age. In P. B. Baltes & M. M. Baltes (Eds.), *Successful aging: Perspectives from the behavioral sciences* (pp. 118–163). New York: Cambridge University Press.

Baddeley, A. D. (1986). *Working memory.* Oxford, England: Clarendon Press.

Baltes, M. M. (1987). Erfolgreiches Altern als Ausdruck von Verhaltenskompetenz und Umweltqualität. In C. Niemitz (Ed.), *Der Mensch im Zusammenspiel von Anlage und Umwelt* (pp. 353–377). Frankfurt: Suhrkamp.

Baltes, M. M. (1988). The etiology and maintenance of dependency in the elderly: Three phases of operant research. *Behavior Therapy, 19,* 301–319.

Baltes, M. M. (1995). Dependency in old age: Gains and losses. *Current Directions in Psychological Science, 4,* 14–19.

Baltes, M. M. (1996). *The many faces of dependency in old age.* New York: Cambridge University Press.

Baltes, M. M., & Baltes, P. B. (Eds.). (1986). *The psychology of control and aging.* Hillsdale, NJ: Erlbaum.

Baltes, M. M., & Carstensen, L. L. (1996). The process of successful ageing. *Ageing and Society, 16,* 397–422.

Baltes, M. M., Kühl, K.-P., Gutzmann, H., & Sowarka, D. (1995). Potential of cognitive plasticity as a diagnostic instrument: A cross-validation and extension. *Psychology and Aging, 10,* 167–172.

Baltes, M. M., Kühl, K.-P., & Sowarka, D. (1992). Testing the limits of cognitive reserve capacity: A promising strategy for early diagnosis of dementia? *Journal of Gerontology, 47,* 165–167.

Baltes, M. M., & Lang, F. R. (in press). Differences in daily life between successful and unsuccessful agers. *Psychology and Aging.*

Baltes, M. M., Neumann, E.-M., & Zank, S. (1994). Maintenance and rehabilitation of independence in old age: An intervention program for staff. *Psychology and Aging, 9,* 179–188.

Baltes, M. M., & Silverberg, S. B. (1994). The dynamics between dependency and autonomy: Illustrations across the life span. In D. L. Featherman, R. M. Lerner, & M. Perlmutter (Eds.), *Life-span development and behavior* (Vol. 12, pp. 41–90). Hillsdale, NJ: Erlbaum.

Baltes, M. M., & Wahl, H.-W. (1992). The dependency-support script in institutions: Generalization to community settings. *Psychology and Aging, 7,* 409–418.

Baltes, P. B. (1968). Longitudinal and cross-sectional sequences in the study of age and generation effects. *Human Development, 11,* 145–171.

Baltes, P. B. (1973). Life-span models of psychological aging: A white elephant? *Gerontologist, 13,* 457–512.

Baltes, P. B. (Ed.). (1976). Symposium on implications of life-span developmental psychology for child development. *Advances in Child Development and Behavior, 11,* 167–265.

Baltes, P. B. (1979a). Life-span developmental psychology: Some converging observations on history and theory. In P. B. Baltes & O. G. Brim, Jr. (Eds.), *Life-span development and behavior* (Vol. 2, pp. 255–279). New York: Academic Press.

Baltes, P. B. (1979b, Summer). On the potential and limits of child development: Life-span developmental perspectives. *Newsletter of the Society for Research in Child Development,* 1–4.

Baltes, P. B. (1983). Life-span developmental psychology: Observations on history and theory revisited. In R. M. Lerner (Ed.), *Developmental psychology: Historical and philosophical perspectives* (pp. 79–111). Hillsdale, NJ: Erlbaum.

Baltes, P. B. (1984). Intelligenz im Alter. *Spektrum der Wissenschaft, 5,* 46–60.

Baltes, P. B. (1987). Theoretical propositions of life-span developmental psychology: On the dynamics between growth and decline. *Developmental Psychology, 23,* 611–626.

Baltes, P. B. (1991). The many faces of human aging: Toward a psychological culture of old age. *Psychological Medicine, 21,* 837–854.

Baltes, P. B. (1993). The aging mind: Potential and limits. *Gerontologist, 33,* 580–594.

Baltes, P. B. (1994, August 13). *Life-span developmental psychology: On the overall landscape of human development.* Invited address, Division 7, American Psychological Association.

Baltes, P. B. (1996). Über die Zukunft des Alterns: Hoffnung mit Trauerflor. In M. M. Baltes & L. Montada (Eds.), *Produktives Leben im Alter* (pp. 29–68). Frankfurt: Campus.

Baltes, P. B. (1997). On the incomplete architecture of human ontogeny: Selection, optimization, and compensation as foundation of developmental theory. *American Psychologist, 52,* 366–380.

Baltes, P. B., & Baltes, M. M. (1980). Plasticity and variability in psychological aging: Methodological and theoretical issues. In G. E. Gurski (Ed.), *Determining the effects of aging on the central nervous system* (pp. 41–66). Berlin: Schering.

Baltes, P. B., & Baltes, M. M. (Eds.). (1990a). *Successful aging: Perspectives from the behavioral sciences.* New York: Cambridge University Press.

Baltes, P. B., & Baltes, M. M. (1990b). Psychological perspectives on successful aging: The model of selective optimization with compensation. In P. B. Baltes & M. M. Baltes (Eds.), *Successful aging: Perspectives from the behavioral sciences* (pp. 1–34). New York: Cambridge University Press.

Baltes, P. B., & Baltes, M. M. (1992). Gerontologie: Begriff, Herausforderung und Brennpunkte. In P. B. Baltes & J. Mittelstrass (Eds.), *Zukunft des Alterns und gesellschaftliche Entwicklung* (pp. 1–34). Berlin: de Gruyter.

Baltes, P. B., & Baltes, M. M. (1996). *Selective optimization with compensation: Basic definitions.* Unpublished manuscript, Max Planck Institute for Human Development and Education, and Free University, Berlin, Germany.

Baltes, P. B., Baltes, M. M., Freund, A. M., & Lang, F. R. (1995). *Measurement of selective optimization with compensation by questionnaire.* Berlin: Max Planck Institute for Human Development and Education.

Baltes, P. B., Cornelius, S. W., & Nesselroade, J. R. (1979). Cohort effects in developmental psychology. In J. R. Nesselroade & P. B. Baltes (Eds.), *Longitudinal research in the study of behavior and development* (pp. 61–87). New York: Academic Press.

Baltes, P. B., Dittmann-Kohli, F., & Dixon, R. A. (1984). New perspectives on the development of intelligence in adulthood: Toward a dual-process conception and a model of selective optimization with compensation. In P. B. Baltes & O. G. Brim, Jr. (Eds.), *Life-span development and behavior* (Vol. 6, pp. 33–76). New York: Academic Press.

Baltes, P. B., & Goulet, L. R. (1970). Status and issues of a life-span developmental psychology. In L. R. Goulet & P. B. Baltes (Eds.), *Life-span developmental psychology: Research and theory* (pp. 4–21). New York: Academic Press.

Baltes, P. B., & Goulet, L. R. (1971). Exploration of developmental variables by manipulation and simulation of age differences in behavior. *Human Development, 14,* 149–170.

Baltes, P. B., & Graf, P. (1996). Psychological aspects of aging: Facts and frontiers. In D. Magnusson (Ed.), *The life-span development of individuals: Behavioural, neurobiological and psychosocial perspectives* (pp. 427–460). Cambridge, England: Cambridge University Press.

Baltes, P. B., & Kliegl, R. (1992). Further testing of limits of cognitive plasticity: Negative age differences in a mnemonic skill are robust. *Developmental Psychology, 28,* 121–125.

Baltes, P. B., & Labouvie, G. V. (1973). Adult development of intellectual performance: Description, explanation, modification. In C. Eisdorfer & M. P. Lawton (Eds.), *The psychology of adult development and aging* (pp. 157–219). Washington, DC: American Psychological Association.

Baltes, P. B., Labouvie, G. V., & Frohring, W. R. (1973). Changing relations between recall performance and abilities as a function of age of learning and time of recall. *Journal of Educational Psychology, 64,* 191–198.

Baltes, P. B., & Lindenberger, U. (1988). On the range of cognitive plasticity in old age as a function of experience: 15 years of intervention research. *Behavior Therapy, 19,* 283–300.

Baltes, P. B., & Lindenberger, U. (1997). Emergence of a powerful connection between sensory and cognitive functions across the adult life span: A new window to the study of cognitive aging? *Psychology and Aging, 12,* 12–21.

Baltes, P. B., & Mayer, K. U. (Eds.). (in press). *The Berlin Aging Study: From 70 to 100.* New York: Cambridge University Press.

Baltes, P. B., Mayer, K. U., Helmchen, H., & Steinhagen-Thiessen, E. (1993). The Berlin Aging Study (BASE): Overview and design. *Ageing and Society, 13,* 483–515.

Baltes, P. B., & Nesselroade, J. R. (1978). Multivariate antecedents of structural change in adulthood. *Multivariate Behavorial Research, 13,* 127–152.

Baltes, P. B., & Nesselroade, J. R. (1984). Paradigm lost and paradigm regained: Critique of Dannefer's portrayal of life-span developmental psychology. *American Sociological Review, 49,* 841–846.

Baltes, P. B., & Reese, H. W. (1984). The life-span perspective in developmental psychology. In M. H. Bornstein & M. E. Lamb (Eds.), *Developmental psychology: An advanced textbook* (pp. 493–531). Hillsdale, NJ: Erlbaum.

Baltes, P. B., Reese, H. W., & Lipsitt, L. P. (1980). Life-span developmental psychology. *Annual Review of Psychology, 31,* 65–110.

Baltes, P. B., Reese, H. W., & Nesselroade, J. R. (1988). *Life-span developmental psychology: An introduction to research methods.* Hillsdale, NJ: Erlbaum.

Baltes, P. B., & Schaie, K. W. (1976). On the plasticity of intelligence in adulthood and old age: Where Horn and Donaldson fail. *American Psychologist, 31,* 720–725.

Baltes, P. B., & Smith, J. (1990). The psychology of wisdom and its ontogenesis. In R. J. Sternberg (Ed.), *Wisdom: Its nature, origins, and development* (pp. 87–120). New York: Cambridge University Press.

Baltes, P. B., Smith, J., & Staudinger, U. M. (1992). Wisdom and successful aging. In T. Sonderegger (Ed.), *Nebraska Symposium on Motivation* (Vol. 39, pp. 123–167). Lincoln: University of Nebraska Press.

Baltes, P. B., & Staudinger, U. M. (1993). The search for a psychology of wisdom. *Current Directions in Psychological Science, 2,* 1–6.

Baltes, P. B., & Staudinger, U. M. (Eds.). (1996a). *Interactive minds: Life-span perspectives on the social foundation of cognition.* New York: Cambridge University Press.

Baltes, P. B., & Staudinger, U. M. (1996b). Interactive minds in a life-span perspective: Prologue. In P. B. Baltes & U. M. Staudinger (Eds.), *Interactive minds: Life-span perspectives on the social foundation of cognition* (pp. 1–32). New York: Cambridge University Press.

Baltes, P. B., Staudinger, U. M., Maercker, A., & Smith, J. (1995). People nominated as wise. A comparative study of wisdom-related knowledge. *Psychology and Aging, 10,* 155–166.

Baltes, P. B., & Willis, S. W. (1977). Toward psychological theories of aging and development. In J. E. Birren & K. W. Schaie (Eds.), *Handbook of the psychology of aging* (pp. 128–154). New York: Van Nostrand-Reinhold.

Baltes, P. B., & Willis, S. L. (1982). Plasticity and enhancement of intellectual functioning in old age: Penn State's Adult Development and Enrichment Project (ADEPT). In F. I. M. Craik & S. E. Trehub (Eds.), *Aging and cognitive processes* (pp. 353–389). New York: Plenum Press.

Bandura, A. (1982). Self-efficacy mechanism in human agency. *American Psychologist, 37,* 122–147.

Bandura, A. (1984). Representing personal determinants in causal structures. *Psychological Review, 91,* 508–511.

Bandura, A. (1986). *Social foundations of thought and action: A social cognitive theory.* Englewood Cliffs, NJ: Prentice-Hall.

Bandura, A. (1993). Perceived self-efficacy in cognitive development and functioning. *Educational Psychologist, 28,* 117–148.

Bandura, A. (Ed.). (1995). *Self-efficacy in a changing society.* New York: Cambridge University Press.

Bandura, A., & Cervone, D. (1983). Self-evaluative and self-efficacy mechanisms governing the motivational effects of goal systems. *Journal of Personality and Social Psychology, 45,* 1017–1028.

Bandura, A., & Walters, R. H. (1963). *Social learning and personality development.* New York: Holt, Rinehart and Winston.

Barkow, J. H., Cosmides, L., & Tooby, J. (Eds.). (1992). *The adapted mind: Evolutionary psychology and the generation of culture.* New York: Oxford University Press.

Barton, S. (1994). Chaos, self-organization, and psychology. *American Psychologist, 49,* 5–14.

Bashore, T. R. (1993). Differential effects of aging on the neurocognitive functions subserving speeded mental processing. In J. Cerella, J. Rybash, W. Hoyer, & M. L. Commons (Eds.), *Adult information processing: Limits on loss* (pp. 37–76). San Diego, CA: Academic Press.

Basseches, M. (1984). *Dialectical thinking.* Norwood, NJ: ABLEX.

Bates, J. E. (1994). Introduction. In J. E. Bates & T. D. Wachs (Eds.), *Temperament: Individual differences at the interface of biology and behavior* (pp. 1–14). Washington, DC: American Psychological Association.

Bates, J. E., & Wachs, T. D. (Eds.). (1994). *Temperament: Individual differences at the interface of biology and behavior.* Washington, DC: American Psychological Association.

Bateson, P. (1987). Biological approaches to the study of development. *International Journal of Behavioral Development, 10,* 1–22.

Bateson, P. (1996). Design for a life. In D. Magnusson (Ed.), *The life-span development of individuals: Behavioural, neurobiological and psychosocial perspectives* (pp. 1–20). Cambridge, England: Cambridge University Press.

Baumeister, R. F. (1989). The optimal margin of illusion. *Journal of Social and Clinical Psychology, 8,* 176–189.

Baumeister, R. F. (1992). Neglected aspects of self theory: Motivation, interpersonal aspects, culture, escape, and existential value. *Psychological Inquiry, 3,* 21–25.

Baumeister, R. F., Smart, L., & Boden, J. M. (1996). Relation of threatened egotism to violence and aggression: The dark side of high self-esteem. *Psychological Review, 103,* 5–33.

Bengtson, V. L., Reedy, M. N., & Gordon, C. (1985). Aging and self-conceptions: Personality processes and social contexts. In J. E. Birren & K. W. Schaie (Eds.), *Handbook of the psychology of aging* (pp. 544–593). New York: Van Nostrand Reinhold.

Benson, J. B., Cherny, S. S., Haith, M. M., & Fulker, D. W. (1993). Rapid assessment of infant predictors of adult IQ: Midtwin-midparent analyses. *Developmental Psychology, 29,* 434–447.

Berg, C. A. (1996). Practical intelligence and problem solving: Searching for perspectives. In F. Blanchard-Fields & T. M. Hess (Eds.), *Perspectives on cognitive change in adulthood and aging* (pp. 323–357). New York: McGraw-Hill.

Berg, C. A., & Calderone, K. S. (1994). The role of problem interpretations in understanding the development of everyday problem solving. In R. J. Sternberg & R. K. Wagner (Eds.), *Mind in context* (pp. 105–132). New York: Cambridge University Press.

Berg, C. A., & Sternberg, R. J. (1985a). A triarchic theory of intellectual development during adulthood. *Developmental Review, 5,* 334–370.

Berg, C. A., & Sternberg, R. J. (1985b). Response to novelty: Continuity vs. discontinuity in the developmental course of intelligence. In H. W. Reese (Ed.), *Advances in child development and behavior* (pp. 2–47). New York: Academic Press.

Bertaux, D., & Kohli, M. (1984). The life story approach: A continental view. *Annual Review of Sociology, 10,* 215–237.

Bijou, S. W., & Baer, D. M. (1961). *Child development: A systematic and empirical theory* (Vol. 1). New York: Appleton-Century-Crofts.

Birren, J. E. (1959). Principles of research on aging. In J. E. Birren (Ed.), *Handbook of aging and the individual: Psychological and biological aspects* (pp. 3–42). Chicago: University of Chicago Press.

Birren, J. E. (1964). *The psychology of aging.* Englewood Cliffs, NJ: Prentice-Hall.

Birren, J. E. (1988). A contribution to the theory of the psychology of aging: As a counterpart of development. In J. E. Birren & V. L. Bengtson (Eds.), *Emergent theories of aging* (pp. 153–176). New York: Springer.

Birren, J. E. (1995). Editorial: New models of aging: Comment on need and creative efforts. *Canadian Journal on Aging, 14,* 1–7.

Birren, J. E., & Fisher, L. M. (1995). Aging and speed of behavior: Possible consequences for psychological functioning. *Annual Review of Psychology, 46,* 329–353.

Birren, J. E., & Schaie, K. W. (Eds.). (1996). *Handbook of the psychology of aging* (3rd ed.). San Diego, CA: Academic Press.

Bjorklund, D. F., & Green, B. L. (1992). The adaptive nature of immaturity. *American Psychologist, 47,* 46–54.

Bjorklund, D. F., & Harnishfeger, K. K. (1990). The resources construct in cognitive development: Diverse sources of evidence and a theory of inefficient inhibition. *Developmental Review, 10,* 48–71.

Bjorklund, D. F., & Harnishfeger, K. K. (1995). The evolution of inhibition mechanisms and their role in human cognition and behavior. In F. N. Dempster & C. J. Brainerd (Eds.), *Interference and inhibition in cognition* (pp. 141–173). San Diego, CA: Academic Press.

Bjorklund, D. F., Schneider, W., & Harnishfeger, K. K. (1992). The role of IQ, expertise, and motivation in the recall of familiar information. *Contemporary Educational Psychology, 17,* 340–355.

Blanchard-Fields, F. (1986). Reasoning on social dilemmas varying in emotional saliency: An adult developmental perspective. *Psychology and Aging, 1,* 325–332.

Blanchard-Fields, F. (1989). Postformal reasoning in a socioemotional context. In M. L. Commons, J. D. Sinnott, F. A.

Richards, & C. Armon (Eds.), *Adult development: Comparisons and applications of developmental models* (pp. 77–93). New York: Praeger.

Blanchard-Fields, F. (1996). Social cognitive development in adulthood and aging. In F. Blanchard-Fields & T. M. Hess (Eds.), *Perspectives on cognitive change in adulthood and aging* (pp. 454–487). New York: McGraw-Hill.

Blanchard-Fields, F., & Norris, L. (1994). Causal attributions from adolescence through adulthood: Age differences, ego level, and generalized response style. *Aging and Cognition, 1,* 67–86.

Block, J. (1961). *The Q-sort method in personality assessment and psychological research.* Springfield, IL: Thomas.

Block, J. (1971). *Lives through time.* Berkeley, CA: Bancroft Books.

Block, J. (1981). Some enduring and consequential structures of personality. In A. I. Rabin (Ed.), *Further explorations in personality* (pp. 27–43). New York: Wiley.

Block, J. (1993). Studying personality the long way. In D. C. Funder, R. D. Parke, C. Tomlinson-Keasey, & K. Widaman (Eds.), *Studying lives through time: Personality and development* (pp. 9–41). Washington, DC: American Psychological Association.

Block, J. (1995). A contrarian view of the five-factor approach to personality description. *Psychological Bulletin, 117,* 187–215.

Bloom, B. (1985). *Developing talent in young people.* New York: Ballantine Books.

Blossfeld, H.-P., Hamerle, A., & Mayer, K. U. (1991). Event-history models in social mobility research. In D. Magnusson, L. R. Berman, G. Rudinger, & B. Törrestad (Eds.), *Problems and methods in longitudinal research* (pp. 212–235). Cambridge, England: Cambridge University Press.

Blossfeld, H.-P., & Rower, G. (1995). *Techniques of event history modeling: New approaches to causal analysis.* Mahwah, NJ: Erlbaum.

Boesch, E. E. (1991). *Symbolic action theory and cultural psychology.* Heidelberg: Springer.

Boomsma, D. I. (1996). Using multivariate genetic modeling to detect pleiotropic quantitative trait loci. *Behavior Genetics, 26,* 161–166.

Bornstein, M. H. (1989). Stability in early mental development: From attention and information processing in infancy to language and cognition in childhood. In M. H. Bornstein & N. A. Krasnegor (Eds.), *Stability and continuity in mental development* (pp. 147–170). Hillsdale, NJ: Erlbaum.

Bornstein, M. H., & Bruner, J. S. (Eds.). (1989). *Interaction in human development.* Hillsdale, NJ: Erlbaum.

Bornstein, M. H., & Sigman, M. D. (1986). Continuity in mental development from infancy. *Child Development, 57,* 251–274.

Bosman, E. A., & Charness, N. (1996). Age-related differences in skilled performance and skill acquisition. In F. Blanchard-Fields & T. M. Hess (Eds.), *Perspectives on cognitive change in adulthood and aging* (pp. 428–453). New York: McGraw-Hill.

Brainerd, C. J. (1995). Interference processes in memory development: The case of cognitive triage. In F. N. Dempster & C. J. Brainerd (Eds.), *Interference and inhibition in cognition* (pp. 108–139). San Diego, CA: Academic Press.

Brandtstädter, J. (1984). Personal and social control over development: Some implications of an action perspective in life-span developmental psychology. In P. B. Baltes & O. G. Brim, Jr. (Eds.), *Life-span development and behavior* (Vol. 6, pp. 1–32). New York: Academic Press.

Brandtstädter, J., & Baltes-Götz, B. (1990). Personal control over development and quality of life perspectives in adulthood. In P. B. Baltes & M. M. Baltes (Eds.), *Successful aging: Perspectives from the behavioral sciences* (pp. 197–224). New York: Cambridge University Press.

Brandtstädter, J., & Greve, W. (1994). The aging self: Stabilizing and protective processes. *Developmental Review, 14,* 52–80.

Brandtstädter, J., & Renner, G. (1990). Tenacious goal pursuit and flexible goal adjustment: Explication and age-related analysis of assimilative and accommodative models of coping. *Psychology and Aging, 5,* 58–67.

Brandtstädter, J., & Rothermund, K. (1994). Self-perceptions of control in middle and later adulthood: Buffering losses by rescaling goals. *Psychology and Aging, 9,* 265–273.

Brandtstädter, J., & Wentura, D. (1995). Adjustment to shifting possibility frontiers in later life: Complementary adaptive modes. In R. A. Dixon & L. Bäckman (Eds.), *Psychological compensation: Managing losses and promoting gains* (pp. 83–106). Hillsdale, NJ: Erlbaum.

Brandtstädter, J., Wentura, D., & Greve, W. (1993). Adaptive resources of the aging self: Outlines of an emergent perspective. *International Journal of Behavioral Development, 16,* 323–349.

Brent, S. B. (1978a). Prigogine's model for self-organization in nonequilibrium systems: Its relevance for developmental psychology. *Human Development, 21,* 374–387.

Brent, S. B. (1978b). Individual specialization, collective adaptation and rate of environmental change. *Human Development, 21,* 21–23.

Brim, O. G., Jr. (1976). Life-span development of the theory of oneself: Implications for child development. In P. B. Baltes (Ed.), *Advances in Child Development and Behavior, 11,* 242–251.

Brim, O. G., Jr. (1988). Losing and winning: The nature of ambition in everyday life. *Psychology Today, 9,* 48–52.

Brim, O. G., Jr. (1992). *Ambition: How we manage success and failure throughout our lives.* New York: Basic Books.

Brim, O. G., Jr., & Kagan, J. (1980). Constancy and change: A view of the issues. In O. G. Brim, Jr. & J. Kagan (Eds.), *Constancy and change in human development* (pp. 1–25). Cambridge, MA: Harvard University Press.

Brim, O. G., Jr., & Ryff, C. D. (1980). On the properties of life events. In P. B. Baltes & O. G. Brim, Jr. (Eds.), *Life-span development and behavior* (Vol. 3, pp. 367–388). New York: Academic Press.

Brim, O. G., Jr., & Wheeler, S. (1966). *Socialization after childhood: Two essays.* New York: Wiley.

Brody, N. (1993). Intelligence and the behavioral genetics of personality. In R. Plomin & G. E. McClearn (Eds.), *Nature, nurture and psychology* (pp. 161–178). Washington, DC: American Psychological Association.

Bronfenbrenner, U. (1977). Toward an experimental ecology of human development. *American Psychologist, 32,* 513–532.

Bronfenbrenner, U. (1979). *The ecology of human development.* Cambridge, MA: Harvard University Press.

Bronfenbrenner, U., & Ceci, S. J. (1994). Nature–nurture reconceptualized in developmental perspective: A bioecological model. *Psychological Review, 101,* 568–586.

Brown, A. L. (1982). Learning and development: The problem of compatibility, access, and induction. *Human Development, 25,* 89–115.

Bühler, C. (1933). *Der menschliche Lebenslauf als psychologisches Problem.* Göttingen: Hogrefe.

Burgess, R. L., & Molenaar, P. C. M. (1995). Commentary. *Human Development, 38,* 159–164.

Buss, A. H., & Plomin, R. (1984). *A temperament theory of personality development.* New York: Wiley.

Cairns, R. B., & Cairns, B. D. (1994). *Lifelines and risks: Pathways of youth in our time.* Cambridge, England: Cambridge University Press.

Cantor, N., & Blanton, H. (1996). Effortful pursuit of personal goals in daily life. In P. M. Gollwitzer & J. A. Bargh (Eds.), *The psychology of action: Linking cognition and motivation to behavior* (pp. 338–359). New York: Guilford Press.

Cantor, N., & Fleeson, W. (1994). Social intelligence and intelligent goal pursuit: A cognitive slice of motivation. *Nebraska Symposium on Motivation, 41,* 125–179.

Caprara, G. V. (1996). Structures and processes in personality psychology. *European Psychologist, 1,* 14–26.

Cardon, L. R., & Fulker, D. W. (1991). Sources of continuity in infant predictors of later IQ. *Intelligence, 15,* 279–293.

Cardon, L. R., & Fulker, D. W. (1993). Genetics of specific cognitive abilities. In R. Plomin & G. E. McClearn (Eds.),

Nature, nurture, and psychology (pp. 99–120). Washington, DC: American Psychological Association.

Cardon, L. R., & Fulker, D. W. (1994). A model of developmental change in hierarchical phenotypes with application to specific cognitive abilities. *Behavior Genetics, 24,* 1–16.

Carlson, J. S. (1994). Dynamic assessment of mental abilities. In R. J. Sternberg et al. (Eds.), *Encyclopedia of intelligence* (pp. 368–372). New York: Macmillan.

Carroll, J. B. (1993). *Human cognitive abilities.* New York: Cambridge University Press.

Carstensen, L. L. (1992). Social and emotional patterns in adulthood: Support for socioemotional selectivity theory. *Psychology and Aging, 7,* 331–338.

Carstensen, L. L. (1993). Motivation for social contact across the life-span: A theory of socioemotional selectivity. *Nebraska Symposium on Motivation, 40,* 205–254.

Carstensen, L. L. (1995). Evidence for a life-span theory of socioemotional selectivity. *Current Directions in Psychological Science, 4,* 151–156.

Carus, F. A. (1808). *Psychologie. Zweiter Teil: Specialpsychologie* [Psychology: Part Two: Special Psychology]. Leipzig: Barth & Kummer.

Case, R. (1985). *Intellectual development: From birth to adulthood.* New York: Academic Press.

Case, R. (1992). The role of the frontal lobes in the regulation of human development. *Brain and Cognition, 20,* 51–73.

Caspi, A. (1987). Personality in the life course. *Journal of Personality and Social Psychology, 53,* 1203–1213.

Caspi, A., & Bem, D. J. (1990). Personality continuity and change across the life course. In L. A. Pervin (Ed.), *Handbook of personality: Theory and research* (pp. 549–575). New York: Guilford Press.

Caspi, A., Bem, D. J., & Elder, G. H. (1989). Continuities and consequences of interactional styles across the life course. *Journal of Personality, 57,* 375–406.

Caspi, A., & Elder, G. H., Jr. (1988). Childhood precursors of the life course: Early personality and life disorganization. In E. M. Hetherington, R. M. Lerner, & M. Perlmutter (Eds.), *Child development in life-span perspective* (pp. 115–142). Hillsdale, NJ: Erlbaum.

Caspi, A., Elder, G. H., & Bem, D. J. (1987). Moving against the world: Life-course patterns of explosive children. *Developmental Psychology, 23,* 308–313.

Caspi, A., & Silva, P. A. (1995). Temperamental qualities at age three predict personality traits in young adulthood: Longitudinal evidence from a birth cohort. *Child Development, 66,* 486–498.

Cattell, R. B. (1943). The description of personality: I. Foundations of trait measurement. *Psychological Review, 50,* 559–594.

Cattell, R. B. (1971). *Abilities: Their structure, growth, and action.* Boston: Houghton Mifflin.

Cattell, R. B., Eber, H. W., & Tatsuoka, M. M. (1970). *Handbook for the sixteen personality factor questionnaire (16PF).* Champaign, IL: Institute for Personality and Ability Testing.

Cerella, J. (1990). Aging and information processing rate. In J. E. Birren & K. W. Schaie (Eds.), *Handbook of the psychology of aging* (pp. 201–221). San Diego, CA: Academic Press.

Chapman, M. (1988a). *Constructive evolution: Origins and development of Piaget's thought.* New York: Cambridge University Press.

Chapman, M. (1988b). Contextuality and directionality of cognitive development. *Human Development, 31,* 92–106.

Chapman, M. (1990). Cognitive development and the growth of capacity: Issues in NeoPiagetian theory. In J. T. Enns (Ed.), *The development of attention: Research and theory* (pp. 263–287). Amsterdam, The Netherlands: North-Holland.

Chapman, M., & Lindenberger, U. (1989). Concrete operations and attentional capacity. *Journal of Experimental Child Psychology, 47,* 236–258.

Chapman, M., & Lindenberger, U. (1992). Transitivity judgments, memory for premises, and models of children's reasoning. *Developmental Review, 12,* 124–163.

Charlesworth, B. (1994). *Evolution in age-structured populations* (2nd ed.). Cambridge, England: Cambridge University Press.

Charness, N. (1981). Search in chess: Age and skill differences. *Journal of Experimental Psychology: Human Perception and Performance, 7,* 467–476.

Charness, N. (1983). Age, skill, and bridge bidding: A chronometric analysis. *Journal of Verbal Learning and Verbal Behavior, 22,* 406–416.

Charness, N. (1989). Age and expertise: Responding to Talland's challenge. In L. W. Poon (Ed.), *Everyday cognition in adulthood and late life* (pp. 437–456). Cambridge, England: Cambridge University Press.

Charness, N., & Bosman, E. A. (1990). Expertise and aging: Life in the lab. In T. H. Hess (Ed.), *Aging and cognition: Knowledge organization and utilization* (pp. 343–385). Amsterdam, The Netherlands: Elsevier.

Chess, S., & Thomas, A. (1984). *Origins and evolution of behaviour disorders.* New York: Brunner/Mazel.

Chi, M. T. H., Glaser, R., & Farr, M. J. (Eds.). (1991). *Toward a general theory of expertise.* Hillsdale, NJ: Erlbaum.

Chi, M. T. H., Glaser, R., & Rees, E. (1982). Expertise in problem solving. In R. J. Sternberg (Ed.), *Advances in the psychology of human intelligence* (Vol. 1, pp. 7–75). Hillsdale, NJ: Erlbaum.

Chi, M. T., & Koeske, R. D. (1983). Network representation of a child's dinosaur knowledge. *Developmental Psychology, 19,* 29–39.

Cicchetti, D. (1993). Developmental psychopathology: Reactions, reflections, projections. Setting a path for the coming decade: Some goals and challenges [Special issue]. *Developmental Review, 13,* 471–502.

Cicchetti, D., & Cohen, D. J. (Eds.). (1995). *Developmental psychopathology* (Vols. 1 & 2). New York: Wiley.

Cicero, M. T. (44 B.C.). *Cato major—de senectute* (Original work translated by J. Logan, 1744, as *Cato major or his discourse of old age*). Philadelphia, PA: Benjamin Franklin. (Reprinted by Arno Press, 1979)

Clausen, J. A. (1986). *The life course: A sociological perspective.* Englewood Cliffs, NJ: Prentice-Hall.

Clayton, V. P., & Birren, J. E. (1980). The development of wisdom across the life span: A reexamination of an ancient topic. In P. B. Baltes & O. G. Brim, Jr. (Eds.), *Life-span development and behavior* (Vol. 3, pp. 103–135). New York: Academic Press.

Cohen, R., & Siegel, A. W. (Eds.). (1991). *Context and development.* Hillsdale, NJ: Erlbaum.

Cohen, S. H., & Reese, H. W. (Eds.). (1994). *Life-span developmental psychology: Methodological contributions.* Hillsdale, NJ: Erlbaum.

Cohen, S., & Williamson, G. M. (1991). Stress and infectious disease in humans. *Psychological Bulletin, 109,* 5–24.

Colby, A., & Damon, W. (1992). *Some do care: Contemporary lives of moral commitment.* New York: Free Press.

Cole, M. (1990). Cultural psychology: A once and future discipline? *Nebraska Symposium on Motivation, 38,* 279–335.

Cole, M. (1996). Interacting minds in a life-span perspective: A cultural/historical approach to culture and cognitive development. In P. B. Baltes & U. M. Staudinger (Eds.), *Interactive minds: Life-span perspectives on the social foundation of cognition* (pp. 59–87). New York: Cambridge University Press.

Coleman, L. M., & Antonucci, T. C. (1982). Impact of work on women at midlife. *Developmental Psychology, 19,* 290–294.

Collins, L. M., & Horn, J. L. (Eds.). (1991). *Best methods for the analysis of change: Recent advances, unanswered questions, future directions.* Washington, DC: American Psychological Association.

Collins, W. A. (Ed.). (1982). *Minnesota Symposia on Child Psychology: The concept of development* (Vol. 15). Hillsdale, NJ: Erlbaum.

Colvin, C. R., & Block, J. (1994). Do positive illusions foster mental health? An examination of the Taylor and Brown formulation. *Psychological Bulletin, 116,* 3–20.

Comalli, P. E., Wapner, S., & Werner, H. (1962). Interference effects of Stroop color-word test in childhood, adulthood, and aging. *The Journal of Genetic Psychology, 100,* 47–53.

Commons, M. L., Richards, F. A., & Armon, C. (Eds.). (1984). *Beyond formal operations: Late adolescent and adult cognitive development.* New York: Praeger.

Conley, J. J. (1984). Longitudinal consistency of adult personality: Self-reported psychological characteristics across 45 years. *Journal of Personality and Social Psychology, 47,* 1325–1333.

Conley, J. J. (1985). Longitudinal stability of personality traits: A multitrait-multimethod-multioccasion analysis. *Journal of Personality and Social Psychology, 49,* 1266–1282.

Conway, A. R., & Engle, R. W. (1994). Working memory and retrieval: A resource-dependent inhibition model. *Journal of Experimental Psychology: General, 123,* 354–373.

Coper, H., Jänicke, B., & Schulze, G. (1986). Biopsychological research on adaptivity across the life span of animals. In P. B. Baltes, D. L. Featherman, & R. M. Lerner (Eds.), *Life-span development and behavior* (Vol. 7, pp. 207–232). Hillsdale, NJ: Erlbaum.

Cornelius, S. W., & Caspi, A. (1987). Everyday problem solving in adulthood and old age. *Psychology and Aging, 2,* 144–153.

Cosmides, L., & Tooby, J. (1989). Evolutionary psychology and the generation of culture: Part II. Case study: A computational theory of social exchange. *Ethology and Sociobiology, 10,* 51–97.

Costa, P. T., & McCrae, R. R. (1985). *The NEO personality inventory.* Odessa, FL: Psychological Assessment Resources.

Costa, P. T., & McCrae, R. R. (1992). Trait psychology comes of age. In T. B. Sonderegger (Ed.), *Nebraska Symposium on Motivation 1991: Psychology and aging* (Vol. 39, pp. 169–204). Lincoln: University of Nebraska Press.

Costa, P. T., & McCrae, R. R. (1994). Set like plaster? Evidence for the stability of adult personality. In T. F. Heatherton & J. L. Weinberger (Eds.), *Can personality change?* (pp. 21–40). Washington, DC: American Psychological Association.

Costa, P. T., & McCrae, R. R. (1995). Longitudinal stability of adult personality. In R. Hogan, J. A. Johnson, & S. R. Briggs (Eds.), *Handbook of personality psychology.* New York: Academic Press.

Costa, P. T., McCrae, R. R., & Dye, D. A. (1991). Facet scales for agreeableness and conscientiousness: A revision of the NEO Personality Inventory. *Personality and Individual Differences, 12,* 887–898.

Costa, P. T., McCrae, R. R., & Norris, A.-H. (1981). Personal adjustment to aging: Longitudinal prediction from neuroticism and extraversion. *Journal of Gerontology, 36,* 78–85.

Costa, P. T., Zondermann, A. B., McCrae, R. R., Cornoni-Huntley, J., Locke, B. Z., & Barbano, H. E. (1987). Longitudinal analyses of psychological well-being in a national sample: Stability of mean levels. *Journal of Gerontology, 42,* 50–55.

Cotman, C. W. (Ed.). (1985). *Synaptic plasticity.* New York: Guilford Press.

Cowdry, E. V. (1939). *Problems of aging: Biological and medical aspects.* Baltimore: Williams & Wilkins.

Craik, F. I. M. (1983). On the transfer of information from temporary to permanent memory. *Philosophical Transactions of the Royal Society of London, B 302,* 341–359.

Craik, F. I. M. (1986). A functional account of age differences in memory. In F. Klix & H. Hagendorf (Eds.), *Human memory and cognitive capabilities, mechanisms, and performance* (pp. 409–422). Amsterdam, The Netherlands: North-Holland.

Craik, F. I. M., & Byrd, M. (1982). Aging and cognitive deficits: The role of attentional resources. In F. I. M. Craik & S. Trehub (Eds.), *Aging and cognitive processes* (pp. 191–211). New York: Plenum Press.

Craik, F. I. M., & Jennings, J. M. (1992). Human memory. In F. I. M. Craik & T. A. Salthouse (Eds.), *The handbook of aging and cognition* (pp. 51–110). Hillsdale, NJ: Erlbaum.

Craik, F. I. M., & Salthouse, T. A. (Eds.). (1992). *The handbook of aging and cognition.* Hillsdale, NJ: Erlbaum.

Cross, S., & Markus, H. (1991). Possible selves across the life span. *Human Development, 34,* 230–255.

Curie, E. (1937). *Madame Curie.* Vienna: Baumann-Fischer Verlag.

Damon, W. (1996). The lifelong transformation of moral goals through social influence. In P.-B. Baltes & U. M. Staudinger (Eds.), *Interactive minds: Life-span perspectives on the social foundation of cognition* (pp. 198–220). New York: Cambridge University Press.

D'Andrade, R. (1995). *The development of cognitive anthropology.* Cambridge, England: Cambridge University Press.

Dannefer, D. (1984). Adult development and social theory: A paradigmatic reappraisal. *American Sociological Review, 49,* 100–116.

Dannefer, D. (1989). Human action and its place in theories of aging. *Journal of Aging Studies, 3,* 1–20.

Danner, D. B., & Schröder, H. C. (1992). Biologie des Alterns (Ontogenese und Evolution). In P. B. Baltes & J. Mittelstrass

(Eds.), *Zukunft des Alterns und gesellschaftliche Entwicklung* (pp. 95–123). Berlin: de Gruyter.

Datan, N., & Ginsberg, L. H. (Eds.). (1975). *Life-span developmental psychology: Normative life crises.* New York: Academic Press.

Datan, N., & Reese, H. W. (Eds.). (1977). *Life-span developmental psychology: Dialectical perspectives on experimental research.* New York: Academic Press.

Davies, D. R., & Sparrow, P. R. (1985). Age and work behavior. In N. Charness (Ed.), *Aging and human performance* (pp. 293–332). New York: Wiley.

Dawkins, R. (1982). *The extended phenotype: The gene as the unit of selection.* Oxford, England: Oxford University Press.

Dawson, G., & Fischer, K. W. (Eds.). (1994). *Human behavior and the developing brain.* New York: Guilford Press.

Deary, I. J. (1996). Reductionism and intelligence: The case of inspection time. *Journal of Biosocial Science, 28,* 405–423.

Deary, I. J., Egan, V., Gibson, G. J., Austin, E. J., Brand, C. R., & Kellaghan, T. (1996). Intelligence and the differentiation hypothesis. *Intelligence, 23,* 105–132.

Deary, I. J., & Pagliari, C. (1991). The strength of g at different levels of ability: Have Detterman and Daniel rediscovered Spearmans law of diminishing returns? *Intelligence, 15,* 251–255.

DeKay, W. T., & Buss, D. M. (1992). Human nature, individual differences, and the importance of context: Perspectives from evolutionary psychology. *Current Directions in Psychological Science, 1,* 184–189.

Dempster, F. N. (1992). The rise and fall of the inhibitory mechanism: Toward a unified theory of cognitive development and aging. *Developmental Review, 12,* 45–75.

Denney, N. W. (1984). A model of cognitive development across the life span. *Developmental Review, 4,* 171–191.

Diamond, A. (1988). Abilities and neural mechanisms underlying A-B performance. *Child Development, 59,* 523–527.

Dickinson, C. M., & Rabbitt, P. M. A. (1991). Simulated visual impairment: Effects on text comprehension and reading speed. *Clinical Vision Sciences, 6,* 301–308.

Diehl, M., Coyle, N., & Labouvie-Vief, G. (1996). Age and sex differences in strategies of coping and defense across the life span. *Psychology and Aging, 77,* 727–739.

Diener, E., Saudvik, E., Pavot, W., & Fujita, F. (1992). Extraversion and subjective well-being in a U.S. national probability sample. *Journal of Research on Personality, 26,* 205–215.

DiLalla, L. F., Thompson, L. A., Plomin, R., Phillips, K., Fagan, J. F., Haith, M. M., Cyphers, L. H., & Fulker, D. W. (1990). Infant predictors of preschool and adult IQ: A study of infant twins and their parents. *Developmental Psychology, 26,* 759–769.

Dittmann-Kohli, F. (1991). Meaning and personality change from early to late adulthood. *European Journal of Personality, 1,* 98–103.

Dixon, R. A., & Bäckman, L. (Eds.). (1995). *Compensating for psychological deficits and declines: Managing losses and promoting gains.* Mahwah, NJ: Erlbaum.

Dixon, R. A., & Baltes, P. B. (1986). Toward life-span research on the functions and pragmatics of intelligence. In R. J. Sternberg & R. K. Wagner (Eds.), *Practical intelligence: Nature and origins of competence in the everyday world* (pp. 203–234). New York: Cambridge University Press.

Dixon, R. A., & Gould, O. N. (1996). Adults telling and retelling stories collaboratively. In P. B. Baltes & U. M. Staudinger (Eds.), *Interactive minds: Life-span perspective on the social foundation of cognition* (pp. 221–241). New York: Cambridge University Press.

Dixon, R. A., Kramer, D. A., & Baltes, P. B. (1985). Intelligence: A life-span developmental perspective. In B. B. Wolman (Ed.), *Handbook of intelligence: Theories, measurements, and applications* (pp. 301–350). New York: Wiley.

Dixon, R. A., & Lerner, R. M. (1988). A history of systems in developmental psychology. In M. H. Bornstein & M. E. Lamb (Eds.), *Developmental psychology: An advanced textbook* (2nd ed., pp. 3–50). Hillsdale, NJ: Erlbaum.

Dohrenwend, B. S., & Dohrenwend, B. P. (Eds.). (1974). *Stressful life events.* New York: Wiley.

Dörner, D. (1986). Diagnostik der operativen Intelligenz. *Diagnostica, 32,* 290–308.

Dunn, J. (1995). Children as psychologists: The later correlates of individual differences in understanding of emotions and other minds. *Cognition and Emotion, 9,* 187–201.

Dunn, L. L. (1965). *A short history of genetics.* New York: McGraw-Hill.

Durham, W. H. (1990). Advances in evolutionary culture theory. *Annual Review of Anthropology, 19,* 187–210.

Durham, W. H. (1991). *Coevolution: Genes, culture and human diversity.* Stanford, CA: Stanford University Press.

East, P. L., Lerner, R. M., Lerner, J. V., & Soni, R. T. (1992). Early adolescent-peer group fit, peer relations, and psychosocial competence: A short-term longitudinal study. *Journal of Early Adolescence, 12,* 132–152.

Edelman, G. M. (1987). *Neural Darwinism: The theory of neuronal group selection.* New York: Basic Books.

Edelman, G. M., & Tononi, G. (1996). Selection and development: The brain as a complex system. In D. Magnusson (Ed.), *The life-span development of individuals: Behavioural, neurobiological and psychosocial perspectives* (pp. 179–204). Cambridge, England: Cambridge University Press.

Edelstein, W., & Noam, G. (1982). Regulatory structures of the self and "postformal" stages in adulthood. *Human Development, 6,* 407–422.

Eichorn, D. H., Clausen, J. A., Haan, N., Honzik, M. P., & Mussen, P. H. (Eds.). (1981). *Present and past in middle life.* New York: Academic Press.

Eisdorfer, C., & Lawton, G. V. (Eds.). (1973). *The psychology of adult development and aging.* Washington, DC: American Psychological Association.

Elbert, T., Pantev, C., Wienbruch, C., Rockstroh, B., & Taub, E. (1995). Increased cortical representation of the fingers of the left hand in string players. *Science, 270,* 305–307.

Elder, G. H., Jr. (1974). *Children of the great depression.* Chicago: University of Chicago Press.

Elder, G. H., Jr. (1979). Historical change in life patterns and personality. In P. B. Baltes & O. G. Brim, Jr. (Eds.), *Life-span development and behavior* (Vol. 2, pp. 117–159). New York: Academic Press.

Elder, G. H., Jr. (1980). History and the life course. In D. Bertaux (Ed.), *Biography and society* (pp. 77–115). Beverly Hills, CA: Sage.

Elder, G. H., Jr. (Ed.). (1985). *Life course dynamics: Trajectories and transitions 1968–1980.* Ithaca, NY: Cornell University Press.

Elder, G. H., Jr. (1986). Military times and turning points in men's lives. *Developmental Psychology, 22,* 233–245.

Elder, G. H., Jr. (1990). Studying lives in a changing society: Sociological and personological explorations. In A. Rabin, R. Zucker, R. Emmons, & S. Frank (Eds.), *Studying persons and lives* (pp. 201–247). New York: Springer.

Elder, G. H., Jr. (1994). Time, human agency, and social change: Perspectives on the life course. *Social Psychology Quarterly, 57,* 4–15.

Elman, J. L. (1993). Learning and development in neural networks: The importance of starting small. *Cognition, 48,* 71–99.

Elwert, G. (1992). Alter im interkulturellen Vergleich. In P. B. Baltes & J. Mittelstrass (Eds.), *Zukunft des Alterns und gesellschaftliche Entwicklung* (pp. 260–282). Berlin: de Gruyter.

Emmons, R. A. (1996). Striving and feeling: Personal goals and subjective well-being. In P. M. Gollwitzer & J. A. Bargh (Eds.), *The psychology of action: Linking cognition and motivation to behavior* (pp. 313–337). New York: Guilford Press.

Engle, R. W., Conway, A. R. A., Tuholskic, S. W., & Shisler, R. J. (1995). A resource account of inhibition. *Psychological Science, 6,* 122–125.

Ericsson, K. A. (1990). Peak performance and age: An examination of peak performance in sports. In P. B. Baltes & M. M. Baltes (Eds.), *Successful aging: Perspectives from the behavioral sciences* (pp. 164–196). Cambridge, England: Cambridge University Press.

Ericsson, K. A., Krampe, R. T., & Tesch-Römer, C. (1993). The role of deliberate practice in the acquisition of expert performance. *Psychological Review, 100,* 363–406.

Ericsson, K. A., & Lehmann, A. C. (1996). Expert and exceptional performance: Evidence of maximal adaptation to task constraints. *Annual Review of Psychology, 47,* 273–305.

Ericsson, K. A., & Smith, J. (Eds.). (1991). *Towards a general theory of expertise: Prospects and limits.* New York: Cambridge University Press.

Erikson, E. H. (1959). *Identity and the life cycle. Psychological Issues Monograph 1.* New York: International University Press.

Erikson, E. H. (1963). *Childhood and society* (2nd ed.). New York: Norton.

Erikson, E. H., Erikson, J. M., & Kivnick, H. (1986). *Vital involvement in old age: The experience of old age in our time.* London: Norton.

Eysenck, H. J., & Eysenck, M. W. (1985). *Personality and individual differences: A natural science approach.* New York: Plenum Press.

Eysenck, H. J., & Eysenck, S. B. G. (1975). *Manual of the Eysenck Personality Questionnaire.* San Diego, CA: EdITS.

Fagan, J. F., & McGrath, S. K. (1981). Infant recognition memory and later intelligence. *Intelligence, 5,* 121–130.

Featherman, D. L. (1983). The life-span perspective in social science research. In P. B. Baltes & O. G. Brim, Jr. (Eds.), *Life-span development and behavior* (Vol. 5, pp. 1–59). New York: Academic Press.

Featherman, D. L., & Lerner, R. M. (1985). Ontogenesis and sociogenesis: Problematics for theory and research about development and socialization across the life span. *American Sociological Review, 50,* 659–676.

Featherman, D. L., Smith, J., & Peterson, J. G. (1990). Successful aging in a "post-retired" society. In P. B. Baltes & M. M. Baltes (Eds.), *Successful aging: Perspectives from the behavioral sciences* (pp. 50–93). New York: Cambridge University Press.

Festinger, L. (1954). A theory of social comparison processes. *Human Relations, 7,* 117–140.

Filipp, S.-H. (1978). Aufbau und Wandel von Selbstschemata über die Lebensspanne. In R. Oerter (Ed.), *Entwicklung als lebenslanger Prozeß* (pp. 111–135). Hamburg: Hoffmann & Campe.

Filipp, S.-H. (Ed.). (1981). *Kritische Lebensereignisse.* München: Urban & Schwarzenberg.

Filipp, S.-H., & Buch-Bartos, K. (1994). Vergleichsprozesse und Lebenszufriedenheit im Alter: Ergebnisse einer Pilotstudie. *Zeitschrift für Entwicklungspsychologie und Pädagogische Psychologie, 26,* 22–34.

Filipp, S.-H., & Klauer, T. (1986). Conceptions of self over the life-span: Reflections on the dialectics of change. In M. M. Baltes & P. B. Baltes (Eds.), *The psychology of aging and control* (pp. 167–204). Hillsdale, NJ: Erlbaum.

Filipp, S.-H., & Klauer, T. (1991). Subjective well-being in the face of critical life events: The case of successful coping. In F. Strack, M. Argyle, & N. Schwarz (Eds.), *The social psychology of subjective well-being* (Vol. 21, pp. 213–234). Oxford, England: Pergamon Press.

Filipp, S.-H., & Olbrich, E. (1986). Human development across the life-span: Overview and highlights of the psychological perspective. In A. B. Sörensen, F. E. Weinert, & L. R. Sherrod (Eds.), *Human development and the life course: Multidisciplinary perspectives* (pp. 343–375). Hillsdale, NJ: Erlbaum.

Finch, C. E. (1990). *Longevity, senescence, and the genome.* Chicago: University of Chicago Press.

Finch, C. E. (1996). Biological bases for plasticity during aging of individual life histories. In D. Magnusson (Ed.), *The life-span development of individuals: Behavioural, neurobiological and psychosocial perspective* (pp. 488–511). Cambridge, England: Cambridge University Press.

Finkel, D., Pedersen, N. L., McGue, M., & McClearn, G. E. (1995). Heritability of cognitive abilities in adult twins: Comparison of Minnesota and Swedish data. *Behavior Genetics, 25,* 421–431.

Fischer, K. W., & Hencke, R. W. (1996). Infants' construction of actions in context: Piaget's contribution to research on early development. *Psychological Science, 7,* 204–210.

Fischer, K. W., & Rose, S. P. (1994). Dynamic development of coordination of components in brain and behavior: A framework for theory and research. In G. Dawson & K. W. Fischer (Eds.), *Human behavior and the developing brain* (pp. 3–66). New York: Guilford Press.

Fisk, J. E., & Warr, P. (1996). Age-related impairment in associative learning: The role of anxiety, arousal, and learning self-efficacy. *Personality and Individual Differences, 21,* 675–686.

Flavell, J. H. (1970). Cognitive changes in adulthood. In L. R. Goulet & P. B. Baltes (Eds.), *Life-span developmental psychology: Research and theory* (pp. 247–253). New York: Academic Press.

Flavell, J. H. (1992). Cognitive development: Past, present, and future. *Developmental Psychology, 28,* 998–1005.

Flavell, J. H., & Wohlwill, J. F. (1969). Formal and functional aspects of cognitive development. In D. Elkind & J. H. Flavell (Eds.), *Studies in cognitive development: Essays in honor of Jean Piaget* (pp. 67–120). New York: Oxford University Press.

Fleeson, W., & Baltes, P. B. (1996). *The predictive power of perceived lifetime personality.* Berlin: Max Planck Institute for Human Development and Education.

Flynn, J. R. (1984). The mean IQ of Americans: Massive gains 1932 to 1978. *Psychological Bulletin, 95,* 29–51.

Flynn, J. R. (1987). Massive IQ gains in 14 nations: What IQ tests really measure. *Psychological Bulletin, 101,* 171–191.

Folkman, S., Lazarus, R. S., Pimley, S., & Novacek, J. (1987). Age differences in stress and coping processes. *Psychology and Aging, 2,* 171–184.

Ford, D. H. (1987). *Humans as self-constructing living systems: A developmental perspective on behavior and personality.* Hillsdale, NJ: Erlbaum.

Ford, D. H., & Lerner, R. M. (1992). *Developmental systems theory: An integrative approach.* London: Sage.

Ford, M. E., & Ford, D. H. (1987). *Humans as self-constructing living systems: A developmental perspective on behavior and personality.* Hillsdale, NJ: Erlbaum.

Forster, J. M., & Gallagher, D. (1986). An exploratory study comparing depressed and nondepressed elders coping strategies. *Journals of Gerontology, 41,* 91–93.

Fredrickson, B. C., & Carstensen, L. L. (1990). Choosing social partners: How old age and anticipated endings make people more selective. *Psychology and Aging, 5,* 335–347.

Freund, A. M. (1995). *Wer bin ich? Die Selbstdefinition alter Menschen.* Berlin: Sigma.

Freund, A. M., & Baltes, P. B. (1996). *Selective optimization with compensation as a strategy of life-management: Prediction of subjective indicators of successful aging.* Unpublished manuscript, Max Planck Institute for Human Development and Education, Berlin, Germany.

Frey, K. S., & Ruble, D. N. (1990). Strategies for comparative evaluation: Maintaining a sense of competence across the life span. In R. J. Sternberg & J. John Kolligian (Eds.), *Competence considered* (pp. 167–189). New Haven, CT: Yale University Press.

Friedman, H. S., Tucker, J. S., Schwartz, J. E., Tomlinson-Keasey, C., Martin, L. R., Wingard, D. L., & Criqui, M. H. (1995). Psychosocial and behavioral predictors of longevity: The aging and death of the "Termites." *American Psychologist, 50,* 69–78.

Friedman, H. S., Tucker, J. S., Tomlinson-Keasey, C., Schwartz, J. E., Wingard, D. L., & Criqui, M. H. (1993). Does childhood personality predict longevity? *Journal of Personality and Social Psychology, 65,* 176–185.

Fries, J. F., & Crapo, L. M. (1981). *Vitality and aging.* San Francisco: Freeman.

Fulker, D. W., Cherny, S. S., & Cardon, L. R. (1993). Continuity and change in cognitive development. In R. Plomin & G. E. McClearn (Eds.), *Nature, nurture, and psychology* (pp. 77–97). Washington, DC: American Psychological Association.

Garcia, R. (1980). Postface: Dialectique, psychogenèse et histoire des sciences. In J. Piaget (Ed.), *Les formes et les mentaires de la dialectique* (pp. 229–249). Paris: Gallimard.

Garmezy, N. (1991). Resilience in children's adaptation to negative life events and stressed environments. *Pediatric Annals, 20,* 459–466.

Garrett, H. E. (1946). A developmental theory of intelligence. *American Psychologist, 1,* 372–378.

Gathercole, S. E., & Baddeley, A. D. (1993). *Working memory and language.* Hove, England: Erlbaum.

Gazzaniga, M. S. (Ed.). (1995). *The cognitive neurosciences.* Cambridge, MA: MIT Press.

Gehlen, A. (1956). *Urmensch und Spätkultur.* Bonn: Athenäum.

Gelman, R. (1993). A rational-constructivist account of early learning about numbers and objects. In D. Medin (Ed.), *The psychology of learning and motivation* (Vol. 30, pp. 61–96). San Diego, CA: Academic Press.

George, L. K. (1978). The impact of personality and social status factors upon levels of activity and psychological well-being. *Journal of Gerontology, 33,* 840–847.

Gergen, K. J. (1971). *The concept of self.* New York: Holt, Rinehart and Winston.

Giambra, L. M. (1993). Sustained attention in older adults: Performance and processes. In J. Cerella, J. Rybash, W. Hoyer, & M. L. Commons (Eds.), *Adult information processing: Limits on loss* (pp. 259–272). San Diego, CA: Academic Press.

Gigerenzer, G. (1996). Rationality: Why social context matters. In P. B. Baltes & U. M. Staudinger (Eds.), *Interactive minds: Life-span perspectives on the social foundation of cognition* (pp. 317–346). New York: Cambridge University Press.

Gold, D. P., Andres, D., Etezadi, J., Arbuckle, T., Schwartzman, A., & Chaikelson, J. (1995). Structural equation model of intellectual change and continuity and predictors of intelligence in older men. *Psychology and Aging, 10,* 294–303.

Goldberg, L. R. (1993). "The structure of phenotypic personality traits": Author's reactions to the six comments. *American Psychologist, 48,* 1303–1304.

Goldberg, L. R., & Saucier, G. (1995). So what do you propose we use instead? A reply to Block. *Psychological Bulletin, 117,* 221–225.

Goldman-Rakic, P. S. (1995). Toward a circuit model of working memory and the guidance of voluntary motor action. In J. C. Houk, J. L. Davis, & D. G. Beiser (Eds.), *Models of information processing in the basal ganglia: Computational neuroscience* (pp. 131–148). Cambridge, MA: MIT Press.

Gollin, E. S. (1981). Development and plasticity. In E. S. Gollin (Ed.), *Developmental plasticity: Behavioral and biological aspects of variations in development* (pp. 231–251). New York: Academic Press.

Gollwitzer, P. M., & Bargh, J. A. (Eds.). (1996). *The psychology of action: Linking cognition and motivation to action.* New York: Guilford Press.

Gottlieb, G. (1982). *Individual development and evolution: The genesis of novel behavior.* New York: Oxford University Press.

Gottlieb, G. (1983). The psychological approach to developmental issues. In P. H. Mussen (Series Ed.) & M. M. Haith & J. J. Campose (Vol. Eds.), *Handbook of child psychology: Vol. 2. Infancy and biological bases* (4th ed., pp. 1–26). New York: Wiley.

Gottlieb, G. (1991). Experiential canalization of behavioral development: Theory. *Developmental Psychology, 27,* 4–13.

Gottlieb, G. (1996). A systems view of psychobiological development. In D. Magnusson (Ed.), *The life-span development of individuals: Behavioural, neurobiological and psychosocial perspectives* (pp. 76–103). Cambridge, England: Cambridge University Press.

Gough, H. (1957). *Manual for the California Psychological Inventory* (1st ed.). Palo Alto, CA: Consulting Psychologist Press.

Gould, S. J. (1984). Relationship of individual and group change: Ontogeny and phylogeny in biology. *Human Development, 27,* 233–239.

Gould, S. J., & Vrba, E. S. (1982). Exaptation—A missing term in the science of form. *Paleobiology, 8,* 4–15.

Goulet, L. R., & Baltes, P. B. (Eds.). (1970). *Life-span developmental psychology: Research and theory.* New York: Academic Press.

Graf, P. (1996). Interactive minds from a cognitive psychologist's perspective. In P. B. Baltes & U. M. Staudinger (Eds.), *Interactive minds: Life-span perspectives on the social foundation of cognition* (pp. 413–420). Cambridge, MA: Cambridge University Press.

Graf, P., & Uttl, B. (1995). Component processes of memory: Changes across the adult life span. *Swiss Journal of Psychology, 54,* 113–130.

Greene, B. (1993). *Hang time: Days and dreams with Michael Jordan.* New York: St. Martin's Press.

Greenwald, A. G., & Pratkanis, A. R. (1984). The self. In R. S. Wyer & T. K. Srull (Eds.), *Handbook of social cognition* (Vol. 3, pp. 129–178). Hillsdale, NJ: Erlbaum.

Grimm, J. (1860). Rede über das Alter. In *Kleinere Schriften von Jacob Grimm* (Vol. 1, pp. 188–210). Berlin: Harrwitz und Grossmann.

Groffmann, K. I. (1970). Life-span developmental psychology in Europe. In L. R. Goulet & P. B. Baltes (Eds.), *Life-span developmental psychology: Research and theory* (pp. 54–68). New York: Academic Press.

Grossman, K. E. (1996). Ethological perspectives on human development and aging. In C. Magai & S. McFadden (Eds.), *Handbook of emotion, adult development and aging* (pp. 43–66). New York: Academic Press.

Guthke, J., & Wiedl, K. H. (Eds.). (1996). *Dynamisches Testen.* Göttingen: Hogrefe.

Haan, N. (1977). *Coping and defending. Processes of self-environment organization.* New York: Academic Press.

Haan, N. (1981). Common dimensions of personality development: Early adolescence to middle life. In D. H. Eichorn, J. A. Clausen, N. Haan, M. P. Honzik, & P. H. Mussen (Eds.), *Present and past in middle life* (pp. 117–151). New York: Academic Press.

Haan, N., Millsap, R., & Hartka, E. (1986). As time goes by: Change and stability in personality over fifty years. *Psychology and Aging, 1,* 220–232.

Hale, S. (1990). A global developmental trend in cognitive processing speed. *Child Development, 61,* 653–663.

Halford, G. S. (1993). *Children's understanding: The development of mental models.* Hillsdale, NJ: Erlbaum.

Hall, G. S. (1922). *Senescence: The last half of life.* New York: Appleton.

Hamilton, W. D. (1966). The molding of genescence by natural selection. *Journal of Theoretical Biology, 12,* 12–45.

Hammerstein, P. (1996). The evolution of cooperation within and between generations. In P. B. Baltes & U. M. Staudinger (Eds.), *Interactive minds: Life-span perspectives on the social foundation of cognition* (pp. 35–58). New York: Cambridge University Press.

Harnishfeger, K. K. (1995). The development of cognitive inhibition: Theories, definitions, and research evidence. In F. N. Dempster & C. J. Brainerd (Eds.), *Interference and inhibition in cognition* (pp. 176–204). San Diego, CA: Academic Press.

Harris, D. B. (Ed.). (1957). *The concept of development.* Minneapolis: University of Minnesota Press.

Harris, L. (1975). *The myth and reality of aging in America.* Washington, DC: National Council on the Aging.

Hartley, A. A. (1992). Attention. In F. I. M. Craik & T. A. Salthouse (Eds.), *The handbook of aging and cognition* (pp. 3–49). Hillsdale, NJ: Erlbaum.

Hasher, L., & Zacks, R. T. (1988). Working memory, comprehension, and aging: A review and a new view. *The Psychology of Learning and Motivation, 22,* 193–225.

Havighurst, R. J. (1948). *Developmental tasks and education.* New York: Davis McKay.

Havighurst, R. J. (1973). History of developmental psychology: Socialization and personality development through the life span. In P. B. Baltes & K. W. Schaie (Eds.), *Life-span developmental psychology* (pp. 3–24). New York: Academic Press.

Hebb, D. O. (1949). *The organization of behavior.* New York: Wiley.

Heckhausen, J. (in press). *Developmental regulation in adulthood: Age-normative and sociostructural constraints as adaptive challenges.* New York: Cambridge University Press.

Heckhausen, J., Dixon, R. A., & Baltes, P. B. (1989). Gains and losses in development throughout adulthood as perceived by different adult age groups. *Developmental Psychology, 25,* 109–121.

Heckhausen, J., & Krueger, J. (1993). Developmental expectations for the self and most other people: Age-grading in three functions of social comparison. *Developmental Psychology, 29,* 539–548.

Heckhausen, J., & Schulz, R. (1993). Optimization by selection and compensation: Balancing primary and secondary control in life span development. *International Journal of Behavioral Development, 16,* 287–303.

Heckhausen, J., & Schulz, R. (1995). A life-span theory of control. *Psychological Review, 102,* 284–304.

Heidrich, S. M., & Denney, N. W. (1994). Does social problem solving differ from other types of problem solving during the adult years? *Experimental Aging Research, 20,* 105–126.

Heidrich, S. M., & Ryff, C. D. (1993). The role of social comparison processes in the psychological adaptation of the elderly. *Journals of Gerontology: Psychological Sciences, 48,* 127–136.

Helmchen, H., Baltes, M. M., Geiselmann, B., Kanowski, S., Linden, M., Reischies, F., & Wilms, H.-U. (in press). Psychische Erkrankungen im Alter. In K. U. Mayer & P. B. Baltes (Eds.), *Die Berliner Altersstudie.* Berlin: Akademie Verlag.

Helson, R., & Wink, P. (1987). Two conceptions of maturity examined in the findings of a longitudinal study. *Journal of Personality and Social Psychology, 53,* 531–541.

Hertzog, C. (1989). Influences of cognitive slowing on age differences in intelligence. *Developmental Psychology, 25,* 636–651.

Hertzog, C. (1996). Research design in studies of aging and cognition. In J. E. Birren & K. W. Schaie (Eds.), *Handbook of the psychology of aging* (pp. 24–37). San Diego, CA: Academic Press.

Hertzog, C., & Nesselroade, J. R. (1987). Beyond autoregressive models: Some implications of the trait-state distinction for the structural modeling of developmental change. *Child Development, 58,* 93–109.

Hertzog, C., & Schaie, K. W. (1986). Stability and change in adult intelligence: 1. Analysis of longitudinal covariance structures. *Psychology and Aging, 1,* 159–171.

Hertzog, C., & Schaie, K. W. (1987). Beyond autoregressive models: Some implications of the state-trait distinction for the structural modeling of developmental change. *Child Development, 58,* 93–109.

Hertzog, C., & Schaie, K. W. (1988). Stability and change in adult intelligence: 2. Simultaneous analysis of longitudinal means and covariance structures. *Psychology and Aging, 3,* 122–130.

Hess, T. M., & Pullen, S. M. (1996). Memory in context. In F. Blanchard-Fields & T. M. Hess (Eds.), *Perspectives on cognitive change in adulthood and aging* (pp. 387–427). New York: McGraw-Hill.

Hetherington, E. M., Lerner, R. M., & M. Perlmutter (Eds.). (1988). *Child development in life-span perspective.* Hillsdale, NJ: Erlbaum.

Hewitt, J. K., Eaves, L. J., Neale, M. C., & Meyer, J. M. (1988). Resolving causes of developmental continuity or "tracking": I. Longitudinal twin studies during growth. *Behavior Genetics, 18,* 133–151.

Hirsch, J. (1970). Behavior-genetic analysis and its biosocial consequences. *Seminars in Psychiatry, 2,* 89–105.

Hofstätter, P. R. (1938). Tatsachen und Probleme einer Psychologie des Lebenslaufs. *Zeitschrift für angewandte Psychologie und Charakterkunde, 53,* 274–332.

Hogan, R. (Ed.). (1995). *Handbook of personality.* New York: Academic Press.

Holahan, C. K., Sears, R. R., & Cronbach, L. J. (1995). *The gifted group in later maturity.* Stanford, CA: Stanford University Press.

Hollingworth, H. L. (1927). *Mental growth and decline: A survey of developmental psychology.* New York: Appleton.

Hooker, K. (1992). Possible selves and perceived health in older adults and college students. *Journal of Gerontology: Psychological Sciences, 47,* 85–95.

Horn, J. L. (1970). Organization of data on life-span development of human abilities. In L. R. Goulet & P. B. Baltes (Eds.), *Life-span developmental psychology: Research and theory* (pp. 423–466). New York: Academic Press.

Horn, J. L. (1982). The theory of fluid and crystallized intelligence in relation to concepts of cognitive psychology and aging in adulthood. In F. I. M. Craik & S. Trehub (Eds.), *Aging and cognitive processes* (pp. 237–278). New York: Plenum Press.

Horn, J. L. (1989). Model of intelligence. In R. L. Linn (Ed.), *Intelligence: Measurement, theory, and public policy* (pp. 29–73). Urbana: University of Illinois Press.

Horn, J. L., & Hofer, S. M. (1992). Major abilities and development in the adult period. In R. J. Sternberg & C. A. Berg (Eds.), *Intellectual development* (pp. 44–99). New York: Cambridge University Press.

Horvath, P., & Zuckerman, M. (1993). Sensation seeking, risk appraisal, and risky behavior. *Personality and Individual Differences, 14,* 41–52.

Houdé, O. (1995). *Rationalité, développement, et inhibition.* Paris: Presses Universitaires de France.

House, J. S., Landis, K. R., & Umberson, D. (1988). Social relationships and health. *Science, 241,* 540–545.

Hoyer, W. J. (1987). Acquisition of knowledge and the decentralization of g in adult intellectual development. In C. Schooler & K. W. Schaie (Eds.), *Cognitive functioning and social structure over the life course* (pp. 120–141). Norwood, NJ: ABLEX.

Hultsch, D. F., & Plemons, J. K. (1979). Life events and life-span development. In P. B. Baltes & O. G. Brim, Jr. (Eds.), *Life-span development and behavior* (Vol. 2, pp. 1–37). New York: Academic Press.

Humphreys, L. G., & Davey, T. C. (1988). Continuity in intellectual growth from 12 months to 9 years. *Intelligence, 12,* 183–197.

Hunt, E. (1993). What do we need to know about aging? In J. Cerella, J. Rybash, W. Hoyer, & M. L. Commons (Eds.), *Adult information processing: Limits on loss* (pp. 587–598). San Diego, CA: Academic Press.

Irion, J. C., & Blanchard-Fields, F. (1987). A cross-sectional comparison of adaptive coping in adulthood. *Journals of Gerontology, 42,* 502–504.

Jackson, D. N. (1984). *Personality research form manual* (3rd ed.). Port Huron, MI: Research Psychologists Press.

Jessor, R. (1993). Successful adolescent development among youth in high-risk settings. *American Psychologist, 48,* 117–126.

John, O. P. (1990). The "big five" factor taxonomy: Dimensions of personality in the natural language and in questionnaires. In L. A. Pervin (Ed.), *Handbook of personality: Theory and research* (pp. 66–100). New York: Guilford Press.

John, O. P., Caspi, A., Robins, R. W., Moffitt, T. E., & Stouthamer-Loeber, M. (1994). The "little five": Exploring the nomological network of the five-factor model of personality in adolescent boys. *Child Development, 65,* 160–178.

Johnson, M. H., & Karmiloff-Smith, A. (1992). Can neural selectionism be applied to cognitive development and its disorders? *New Ideas in Psychology, 10,* 35–46.

Johnson, M. H., Posner, M. I., & Rothbart, M. K. (1991). Components of visual orienting in early infancy: Contingency learning, anticipatory looking, and disengaging. *Journal of Cognitive Neuroscience, 3,* 335–344.

Johnson, S. H., & Rybash, J. M. (1993). A cognitive neuroscience perspective on age-related slowing: Developmental changes in the functional architecture. In J. Cerella, J. Rybash, W. Hoyer, & M. L. Commons (Eds.), *Adult information processing: Limits on loss* (pp. 143–173). San Diego, CA: Academic Press.

Jones, C. E., & Meredith, W. (1996). Patterns of personality change across the life span. *Psychology and Aging, 11,* 57–65.

Jones, H. E., & Conrad, H. (1933). The growth and decline of intelligence: A study of a homogeneous group between the ages of ten and sixty. *Genetic Psychological Monographs, 13,* 223–298.

Just, M. A., & Carpenter, P. A. (1992). A capacity theory of comprehension: Individual differences in working memory. *Psychological Review, 99,* 122–149.

Kagan, J. (1964). American longitudinal research on psychological development. *Child Development, 35,* 1–32.

Kagan, J. (1980). Perspectives on continuity. In O. G. Brim, Jr. & J. Kagan (Eds.), *Constancy and change in human development* (pp. 26–74). Cambridge, MA: Harvard University Press.

Kagan, J. (1984). *The nature of the child.* New York: Basic Books.

Kagan, J., & Moss, H. (1962). *Birth to maturity.* New York: Wiley.

Kagan, J., & Snidman, N. (1991). Temperamental factors in human development. *American Psychologist, 46,* 856–862.

Kagan, J., & Zentner, M. (1996). Early childhood predictors of adult psychopathology. *Harvard Review of Psychiatry, 3,* 1–10.

Kahn, R. L., & Antonucci, T. C. (1980). Convoys over the life course: Attachment, roles, and social support. In P. B. Baltes & O. G. Brim, Jr. (Eds.), *Life-span development and behavior* (Vol. 3, pp. 253–286). New York: Academic Press.

Kail, R. (1991). Developmental change in speed of processing during childhood and adolescence. *Psychological Bulletin, 109,* 490–501.

Kail, R., & Salthouse, T. A. (1994). Processing speed as a mental capacity. *Acta Psychologica, 86,* 199–225.

Kareev, Y. (1995). Through a narrow window: Working memory capacity and the detection of covariation. *Cognition, 56,* 263–269.

Karmiloff-Smith, A. (1992). *Beyond modularity: A developmental perspective on cognitive science.* Cambridge, MA: MIT Press.

Karmiloff-Smith, A. (1995). The extraordinary cognitive journey from foetus through infancy. *Journal of Child Psychology and Allied Disciplines, 36,* 1293–1313.

Kausler, D. H. (1994). *Learning and memory in normal aging.* San Diego, CA: Academic Press.

Kessler, R. C., & McRae, J. A. (1982). The effects of wives' employment on the mental health of married men and women. *American Sociological Review, 47,* 216–227.

Kindermann, T. A., & Valsiner, J. (Eds.). (1995). *Development of person-context relations.* Hillsdale, NJ: Erlbaum.

Kintsch, W. (1988). The role of knowledge in discourse comprehension: A construction-integration model. *Psychological Review, 9,* 163–182.

Kliegl, R., & Baltes, P. B. (1987). Theory-guided analysis of mechanisms of development and aging mechanisms through testing-the-limits and research on expertise. In C. Schooler & K. W. Schaie (Eds.), *Cognitive functioning and social structure over the life course* (pp. 95–119). Norwood, NJ: ABLEX.

Kliegl, R., & Lindenberger, U. (1993). Modeling intrusions and correct recall in episodic memory: Adult age differences in encoding of list context. *Journal of Experimental Psychology: Learning, Memory, and Cognition, 19,* 617–637.

Kliegl, R., Mayr, U., & Krampe, R. T. (1994). Time-accuracy functions for determining process and person differences: An application to cognitive aging. *Cognitive Psychology, 26,* 134–164.

Kliegl, R., Smith, J., & Baltes, P. B. (1990). On the locus and process of magnification of age differences during mnemonic training. *Developmental Psychology, 26,* 894–904.

Klix, F. (1992). *Die Natur des Verstandes.* Göttingen: Hogrefe.

Klix, F. (1993). *Erwachendes Denken: Geistige Leistungen aus evolutionspsychologischer Sicht.* Heidelberg: Spektrum Akademischer Verlag.

Knopf, M., Kolodziej, P., & Preussler, W. (1990). Der ältere Mensch als Experte: Literaturübersicht über die Rolle von Expertenwissen für die kognitive Leistungsfähigkeit im höheren Alter. *Zeitschrift für Gerontopsychologie und -Psychiatrie, 4,* 233–248.

Kogan, N. (1990). Personality and aging. In J. E. Birren & K. W. Schaie (Eds.), *Handbook of the psychology of aging* (pp. 330–346). New York: Academic Press.

Kohli, M. (Ed.). (1978). *Soziologie des Lebenslaufs.* Darmstadt: Luchterhand.

Kohli, M., & Meyer, J. W. (1986). Social structure and social construction of life stages. *Human Development, 29,* 145–180.

Kohn, M. L., & Schooler, C. (1983). *Work and personality.* Norwood, NJ: ABLEX.

Kopp, C. B., & McCall, R. B. (1982). Predicting later mental performance for normal, at-risk, and handicapped infants. In P. B. Baltes & O. G. Brim, Jr. (Eds.), *Life-span development and behavior* (Vol. 4, pp. 33–61). New York: Academic Press.

Kramer, D. A. (1983). Postformal operations? A need for further conceptualization. *Human Development, 26,* 91–195.

Kreppner, K. (1992). Development in a developing context: Rethinking the family's role for children's development. In L. T. Winegar & J. Valsiner (Eds.), *Children's development within social context* (Vol. 1, pp. 161–182). Hillsdale, NJ: Erlbaum.

Kruglanski, A. W. (1996). Goals as knowledge structures. In P. M. Gollwitzer & J. A. Bargh (Eds.), *The psychology of action: Linking cognition and motivation to behavior* (pp. 599–618). New York: Guilford Press.

Kruse, A. (1992). Alter im Lebenslauf. In P. B. Baltes & J. Mittelstrab (Eds.), *Zukunft des Alterns und gesellschaftliche Entwicklung* (pp. 331–355). Berlin: de Gruyter.

Kruse, A., Lindenberger, U., & Baltes, P. B. (1993). Longitudinal research on human aging: The power of combining real-time, microgenetic, and simulation approaches. In D. Magnusson (Ed.), *Longitudinal research on individual development: Present status and future perspectives* (pp. 153–193). Cambridge, England: Cambridge University Press.

Kuhlen, R. G. (1963). Age and intelligence: The significance of cultural change in longitudinal versus cross-sectional findings. *Vita Humana, 6,* 113–124.

Kuhn, D. (1995). Microgenetic study of change: What has it told us? *Psychological Science, 6,* 133–139.

Labouvie-Vief, G. (1977). Adult cognitive development: In search of alternative interpretations. *Merrill-Palmer Quarterly, 23,* 277–263.

Labouvie-Vief, G. (1980). Beyond formal operations: Uses and limits of pure logic in life-span development. *Human Development, 23,* 141–161.

Labouvie-Vief, G. (1982). Dynamic development and mature autonomy: A theoretical prologue. *Human Development, 25,* 161–191.

Labouvie-Vief, G. (1992). Neo-Piagetian perspective on adult cognitive development. In R. J. Sternberg & C. A. Berg (Eds.), *Intellectual development* (pp. 197–228). Cambridge, England: Cambridge University Press.

Labouvie-Vief, G. (1995). *Psyche and eros: Mind and gender in the life course.* New York: Cambridge University Press.

Labouvie-Vief, G., & Chandler, M. J. (1978). Cognitive development and life-span developmental theory: Idealistic versus contextual perspectives. In P. B. Baltes (Ed.), *Life-span development and behavior* (Vol.1, pp. 182–210). New York: Academic Press.

Labouvie-Vief, G., Chiodo, L. M., Goguen, L. A., Diehl, M., & Orwoll, L. (1995). Representations of self across the life span. *Psychology and Aging, 10,* 404–415.

Labouvie-Vief, G., DeVoe, M., & Bulka, D. (1989). Speaking about feelings: Conceptions of emotion across the life span. *Psychology and Aging, 4,* 425–437.

Labouvie-Vief, G., Hakim-Larson, J., DeVoe, M., & Schoeberlein, S. (1989). Emotions and self-regulation: A life-span view. *Human Development, 32,* 279–299.

Labouvie-Vief, G., Hakim-Larson, J., & Hobart, C. J. (1987). Age, ego level, and the life-span development of coping and defense processes. *Psychology and Aging, 2,* 286–293.

Lachman, M. E. (1986a). Locus of control in aging research: A case for multidimensional and domain-specific assessment. *Psychology and Aging, 1,* 34–40.

Lachman, M. E. (1986b). Personal control in later life: Stability, change, and cognitive correlates. In M. M. Baltes & P. B. Baltes (Eds.), *The psychology of control and aging* (pp. 207–236). Hillsdale, NJ: Erlbaum.

Lachman, M. E. (1991). Perceived control over memory aging: Developmental and intervention perspectives. *Journal of Social Issues, 47,* 159–175.

Lachman, M. E., Weaver, S. L., Bandura, M., Elliott, E., & Lewkowicz, C. (1992). Improving memory and control beliefs through cognitive restructuring and self-generated strategies. *Journals of Gerontology: Psychological Sciences, 47,* 293–299.

Lachman, M. E., Ziff, M., & Spiro, A. (1994). Maintaining a sense of control in later life. In R. Abeles, H. Gift, & M. Ory (Eds.), *Aging and quality of life* (pp. 116–132). New York: Sage.

Lawrence, J. A., & Valsiner, J. (1993). Conceptual roots of internalization: From transmission to transformation. *Human Development, 36,* 150–167.

Lawton, M. P. (1988). Behavior-relevant ecological factors. In K. W. Schaie & C. Schooler (Eds.), *Social structures and aging: Psychological processes* (pp. 57–78). Hillsdale, NJ: Erlbaum.

Lazarus, R. S., & DeLongis, A. (1983). Psychological stress and coping in aging. *American Psychologist, 38,* 245–254.

Lehman, H. C. (1953). *Age and achievement.* Princeton, NJ: Princeton University Press.

Lehr, U. (1980). Die Bedeutung der Lebenslaufpsychologie für die Gerontologie. *Aktuelle Gerontologie, 10,* 257–269.

Lerner, J. V., & Lerner, R. M. (1983). Temperament and adaptation across life: Theoretical and empirical issues. In P. B. Baltes & O. G. Brim, Jr. (Eds.), *Life-span development and behavior* (Vol. 5, pp. 198–231). New York: Academic Press.

Lerner, J. V., Nitz, K., Talwar, R., & Lerner, R. M. (1989). On the functional significance of temperamental individuality: A developmental contextual view of the concept of goodness of fit. In G. A. Kohnstamm, J. E. Bates, & M. K. Rothbart (Eds.), *Temperament in childhood* (pp. 509–522). Chichester, England: Wiley.

Lerner, R. M. (Ed.). (1983). *Developmental psychology: Historical and philosophical perspectives.* Hillsdale, NJ: Erlbaum.

Lerner, R. M. (1984). *On the nature of human plasticity.* New York: Cambridge University Press.

Lerner, R. M. (1986). *Concepts and theories of human development* (2nd ed.). New York: Random House.

Lerner, R. M. (1988). Personality development: A life-span perspective. In E. M. Hetherington, R. M. Lerner, & M. Perlmutter (Eds.), *Child development in life-span perspective* (pp. 21–46). Hillsdale, NJ: Erlbaum.

Lerner, R. M. (1991). Changing organism-context relations as the basic process of development: A developmental contextual perspective. *Developmental Psychology, 27,* 27–32.

Lerner, R. M. (1995). The limits of biological influence: Behavioral genetics as the emperor's new clothes. *Psychological Inquiry, 6,* 145–156.

Lerner, R. M., & Busch-Rossnagel, N. (Eds.). (1981). *Individuals as producers of their development: A life-span perspective.* New York: Academic Press.

Lerner, R. M., & Eye, A. von (1992). Sociobiology and human development: Arguments and evidence. *Human Development, 35,* 12–33.

Lerner, R. M., Skinner, E. A., & Sorrel, G. T. (1980). Methodological implications of contextual/dialectical theories of development. *Human Development, 23,* 225–235.

Levelt, W. J. M. (1989). *Speaking: From intention to articulation.* Cambridge, MA: MIT Press.

LeVine, R. A. (1968). Culture, personality, and socialization: An evolutionary view. In D. A. Goslin (Ed.), *Handbook of socialization theory and research* (pp. 503–541). Chicago: McNally.

Levinson, B., & Reese, H. W. (1967). Patterns of discrimination learning set in preschool children, fifth-graders, college freshmen, and the aged. *Monographs of the Society for Research in Child Development, 32.*

Levinson, D. J. (1980). Toward a conception of the adult life course. In N. J. Smelser & E. H. Erikson (Eds.), *Themes of work and love in adulthood* (pp. 265–290). Cambridge, MA: Harvard University Press.

Levinson, D. J. (1986). A conception of adult development. *American Psychologist, 41,* 3–13.

Lewis, M. D. (1995). Cognition-emotion feedback and the self-organization of developmental paths. *Human Development, 38,* 71–102.

Li, S.-L., Lindenberger, U., & Frensch, P. A. (1996, April). *Interference, reduced processing resources, and cortex: In search of a general computational framework for theories of cognitive aging.* Poster presented at the sixth Cognitive Aging Conference, Atlanta.

Lienert, G. A., & Crott, H. W. (1964). Studies on the factor structure of intelligence in children, adolescents, and adults. *Vita Humana, 7,* 147–163.

Light, L. L., & LaVoie, D. (1993). Direct and indirect measures of memory in old age. In P. Graf & M. E. J. Masson (Eds.), *Implicit memory: New directions in cognition, development, and neuropsychology* (pp. 207–230). Hillsdale, NJ: Erlbaum.

Lindenberger, U., & Baltes, P. B. (1994a). Aging and intelligence. In R. J. Sternberg et al. (Eds.), *Encyclopedia of intelligence* (pp. 52–66). New York: Macmillan.

Lindenberger, U., & Baltes, P. B. (1994b). Sensory functioning and intelligence in old age: A strong connection. *Psychology and Aging, 9,* 339–355.

Lindenberger, U., & Baltes, P. B. (1995). Testing-the-limits and experimental simulation: Two methods to explicate the role of learning in development. *Human Development, 38,* 349–360.

Lindenberger, U., & Baltes, P. B. (1996). *The age-based dynamics between sensory and intellectual functioning: Testing the role of peripheral sensory factors.* Poster presented at the sixth Cognitive Aging Conference, Atlanta.

Lindenberger, U., & Baltes, P. B. (1997). Intellectual functioning in old and very old age: Cross-sectional results from the Berlin Aging Study. *Psychology and Aging, 12.*

Lindenberger, U., Kliegl, R., & Baltes, P. B. (1992). Professional expertise does not eliminate negative age differences in imagery-based memory performance during adulthood. *Psychology and Aging, 7,* 585–593.

Lindenberger, U., Mayr, U., & Kliegl, R. (1993). Speed and intelligence in old age. *Psychology and Aging, 8,* 207–220.

Linn, R. L. (1989). *Intelligence.* Chicago: University of Illinois Press.

Linville, P. W. (1987). Self-complexity as a cognitive buffer against stress-related depression and illness. *Journal of Personality and Social Psychology, 52,* 663–676.

Lipsitt, L. P. (1982). Infant learning. In T. M. Field, A. Huston, H. C. Quay, L. Troll, & G. E. Finley (Eds.), *Review of human development* (pp. 62–78). New York: Wiley.

Little, T. D., Oettingen, G., Stetsenko, A., & Baltes, P. B. (1995). Children's action-control beliefs about school performance: How do American children compare with German and Russian children? *Journal of Personality and Social Psychology, 69,* 686–700.

Livson, N., & Peskin, H. (1980). Perspectives on adolescence from longitudinal research. In J. Adelson (Ed.), *Handbook of adolescent psychology* (pp. 47–98). New York: Wiley.

Lockard, J. S., & Paulhus, D. L. (Eds.). (1988). *Self-deception: An adaptive mechanism?* Englewood Cliffs, NJ: Prentice Hall.

Loehlin, J. C. (1993). What has behavioral genetics told us about the nature of personality? In T. J. Bouchard, Jr. & P. Propping (Eds.), *Twins as a tool of behavioral genetics* (pp. 109–119). Chichester, England: Wiley.

Loevinger, J. (1976). *Ego development: Conception and theory.* San Francisco: Jossey-Bass.

Lopez, D., Little, T., Oettingen, G., & Baltes, P. (1996). *Children's active control beliefs about school performance: Is there an optimal beliefs-performance discrepancy?* Berlin: Max Planck Institute for Human Development and Education.

Lourenço, O., & Machado, A. (1996). In defense of Piaget's theory: A reply to 10 common criticisms. *Psychological Review, 103,* 143–164.

MacFarlane, J. W. (1963). From infancy to adulthood. *Child Education, 39,* 336–342.

Maciel, A. G., Heckhausen, J., & Baltes, P. B. (1994). A life-span perspective on the interface between personality and intelligence. In R. J. Sternberg & P. Ruzgis (Eds.), *Intelligence and personality* (pp. 61–103). New York: Cambridge University Press.

MacKay, D. G., & Burke, D. M. (1990). Cognition and aging: A theory of new learning and the use of old connections. In T. M. Hess (Ed.), *Aging and cognition: Knowledge organization and utilization* (pp. 213–263). Amsterdam, The Netherlands: North-Holland.

Madden, D. J., & Plude, D. J. (1993). Selective preservation of selective attention. In J. Cerella, J. Rybash, W. Hoyer, & M. L. Commons (Eds.), *Adult information processing: Limits on loss* (pp. 273–300). San Diego, CA: Academic Press.

Maddox, G. L. (1987). Aging differently. *Gerontologist, 27,* 557–564.

Maercker, A. (1995). *Existentielle Konfrontation. Eine Untersuchung im Rahmen eines psychologischen Weisheitsparadigmas.* Berlin: Max Planck Institut für Bildungsforschung.

Magnus, K., Diener, E., Fujita, F., & Pavot, W. (1993). Extraversion and neuroticism as predictors for objective life events: A longitudinal analysis. *Journal of Personality and Social Psychology, 65,* 1046–1053.

Magnusson, D. (1988). *Individual development from an interactional perspective: A longitudinal study.* Hillsdale, NJ: Erlbaum.

Magnusson, D. (1990). Personality development from an interactional perspective. In L. A. Pervin (Ed.), *Handbook of personality: Theory and research* (pp. 193–222). New York: Guilford Press.

Magnusson, D. (1995). Individual development: A holistic, integrated model. In P. Moen, G. H. Elder, & K. Lüscher (Eds.), *Examining lives in context* (pp. 19–60). Washington, DC: American Psychological Association.

Magnusson, D. (Ed.). (1996). *The life-span development of individuals: Behavioural, neurobiological and psychosocial perspectives.* Cambridge, England: Cambridge University Press.

Magnusson, D., Bergman, L. R., Rudinger, G., &. Törestad, B. (Eds.). (1991). *Problems and methods in longitudinal research: Stability and change.* Cambridge, England: Cambridge University Press.

Mandl, H., Gruber, H., & Renkl, A. (1996). Communities of practice toward expertise: Social foundation of university instruction. In P. B. Baltes & U. M. Staudinger (Eds.), *Interactive minds: Life-span perspectives on the social foundation of cognition* (pp. 394–411). New York: Cambridge University Press.

Mandler, J. M. (1992). How to build a baby: II. Conceptual primitives. *Psychological Review, 99,* 587–604.

Marcia, J. E. (1976). Identity six years after: A follow-up study. *Journal of Youth and Adolescence, 5,* 145–160.

Markus, H. R., & Cross, S. (1990). The interpersonal self. In L. A. Pervin (Ed.), *Handbook of personality: Theory and research* (pp. 576–608). New York: Guilford Press.

Markus, H. R., & Herzog, A. R. (1991). The role of the self-concept in aging. *Annual Review of Gerontology and Geriatrics, 11,* 111–143.

Markus, H. R., & Nurius, P. (1986). Possible selves. *American Psychologist, 41,* 954–969.

Markus, H. R., & Wurf, E. (1987). The dynamic self-concept: A social psychological perspective. *Annual Review of Psychology, 38,* 299–337.

Marsiske, M., Lang, F. R., Baltes, M. M., & Baltes, P. B. (1995). Selective optimization with compensation: Life-span perspectives on successful human development. In R. A. Dixon & L. Bäckman (Eds.), *Compensation for psychological defects and declines: Managing losses and promoting gains* (pp. 35–79). Hillsdale, NJ: Erlbaum.

Marsiske, M., & Willis, S. L. (1995). Dimensionality of everyday problem solving in older adults. *Psychology and Aging, 10,* 269–283.

Martin, G. M., Austad, S. N., & Johnson, T. E. (1996). Genetic analysis of ageing: Role of oxidative damage and environmental stresses. *Nature Genetics, 13,* 25–34.

Maturana, H., & Varela, F. (1980). *Autopoiesis and cognition: The realization of the living.* Boston: D. Reidel.

May, C. P., Kane, M. J., & Hasher, L. (1995). Determinants of negative priming. *Psychological Bulletin, 118,* 35–54.

Mayer, K. U. (1986). Structural constraints on the life course. *Human Development, 29,* 163–170.

Mayer, K. U. (1990). Lebensverläufe und sozialer Wandel. Anmerkungen zu einem Forschungsprogramm. *Kölner Zeitschrift für Soziologie und Sozialpsychologie, 42*(Sonderheft 31), 7–21.

Mayer, K. U., Huinink, J., Diewald, M., Solga, H., Sørensen, A., & Trappe, H. (1995). *Kollektiv und Eigensinn. Lebensverläufe in der DDR und danach.* Berlin: Akademie-Verlag.

Maylor, E. A. (1994). Ageing and the retrieval of specialized and general knowledge: Performance of masterminds. *British Journal of Psychology, 85,* 105–114.

Maylor, E. A., & Rabbitt, P. M. A. (1994). Applying Brinley plots to individuals: Effects of aging on performance distributions in two speeded tasks. *Psychology and Aging, 7,* 317–323.

Mayr, U., Kliegl, R., & Krampe, R. T. (1996). Sequential and co-ordinative processing dynamics in figural transformations across the life span. *Cognition, 59,* 61–90.

McAdams, D. P., & de St. Aubin, E. (1992). A theory of generativity and its assessment through self-report, behavioral acts, and narrative themes in autobiography. *Journal of Personality and Social Psychology, 62,* 1003–1015.

McArdle, J. J. (1986). Latent-variable growth within behavior genetic models. *Behavior Genetics, 16,* 79–95.

McArdle, J. J., & Epstein, D. (1987). Latent growth curves within developmental structural equation models. *Child Development, 58,* 110–133.

McCall, G. J. (1987). The structure, content, and dynamics of self: Continuities in the study of role-identities. In K. Yardley & T. Honess (Eds.), *Self and identity: Psychosocial perspectives* (pp. 133–145). New York: Wiley.

McCall, R. M. (1979). The development of intellectual functioning in infancy and the prediction of later IQ. In J. D. Osofsky (Ed.), *Handbook of infant development* (pp. 707–740). New York: Wiley.

McCall, R. M. (1994). What process mediates predictions of childhood IQ from infant habituation and recognition memory? Speculations on the roles of inhibition and rate of information processing. *Intelligence, 18,* 107–125.

McCall, R. M., & Carriger, M. S. (1993). A meta-analysis of infant habituation and recognition memory performance as predictors of later IQ. *Child Development, 64,* 57–79.

McCartney, K., Harris, M. J., & Bernieri, F. (1990). Growing up and growing apart: A developmental meta-analysis of twin studies. *Psychological Bulletin, 107,* 226–237.

McClearn, G. E., Plomin, R., Gora-Maslak, G., & Crabbe, J. C. (1991). The gene chase in behavioral science. *Psychological Science, 2,* 222–229.

McCrae, R. R. (1989). Age differences and changes in the use of coping mechanisms. *Journal of Gerontology: Psychological Sciences, 44,* 919–928.

McCrae, R. R., & Costa, P. T. (1983). Psychological maturity and subjective well-being: Toward a new synthesis. *Developmental Psychology, 19,* 243–248.

McCrae, R. R., Costa, P. T., & Busch, C. M. (1986). Evaluating comprehensiveness in personality systems: The California Q-Set and the five-factor model. *Journal of Personality, 54,* 430–446.

McDowd, J. M., Oseas-Kreger, D. M., & Filion, D. L. (1995). Inhibitory processes in cognition and aging. In F. N. Dempster & C. J. Brainerd (Eds.), *Interference and inhibition in cognition* (pp. 363–400). San Diego, CA: Academic Press.

McGue, M., Bacon, S., & Lykken, D. T. (1993). Personality stability and change in early adulthood: A behavioral genetic analysis. *Developmental Psychology, 29,* 96–109.

McGue, M., Bouchard, T. J., Jr., Iacono, W. G., & Lykken, D. T. (1993). Behavioral genetics of cognitive ability: A life-span perspective. In R. Plomin & G. E. McClearn (Eds.), *Nature, nurture, and psychology* (pp. 59–76). Washington, DC: American Psychological Association.

Medawar, P. B. (1946). Old age and natural death. *Modern Quarterly, 1,* 30–56.

Meredith, W., & Millsap, R. E. (1985). On component analyses. *Psychometrika, 50,* 495–507.

Mergler, N. L., & Goldstein, M. D. (1983). Why are there old people? Senescence as biological and cultural preparedness for the transmission of information. *Human Development, 26,* 72–90.

Mischel, W., & Shoda, Y. (1995). A cognitive-affective system theory of personality: Reconceptualizing situations, dispositions, dynamics, and invariance in personality structure. *Psychological Review, 102,* 246–268.

Mischel, W., Shoda, Y., & Rodriguez, M. L. (1989). Delay of gratification in children. *Science, 244,* 933–938.

Mitrushina, M., & Satz, P. (1991). Stability of cognitive functions in young-old versus old-old individuals. *Brain Dysfunction, 4,* 174–181.

Moen, P., Elder, G. H., Jr., & Lüscher, K. (Eds.). (1995). *Examining lives in context: Perspectives on the ecology of human development.* Washington, DC: American Psychological Association.

Molander, B., & Bäckman, L. (1993). Performance of a complex motor skill across the life span: General trends and qualifications. In J. Cerella, J. Rybash, W. Hoyer, & M. L. Commons (Eds.), *Adult information processing: Limits on loss* (pp. 231–257). San Diego, CA: Academic Press.

Molenaar, P. C. M. (1986). On the impossibility of acquiring more powerful structures: A neglected alternative. *Human Development, 29,* 245–251.

Molenaar, P. C. M., Boomsma, D. I., & Dolan, C. V. (1991). Genetic and environmental factors in a developmental perspective. In D. Magnusson, L. R. Bergman, G. Rudinger, & B. Törestad (Eds.), *Problems and methods in longitudinal research: Stability and change* (pp. 250–273). Cambridge, England: Cambridge University Press.

Molenaar, P. C. M., Boomsma, D. I., & Dolan, C. V. (1993). Genetic and environmental factors in a developmental perspective. In D. Magnusson, L. R. Bergman, G. Rudinger, & B. Törestad (Eds.), *Problems and methods in longitudinal* research: *Stability and change* (pp. 250–273). Cambridge, England: Cambridge University Press.

Molenaar, P. C. M., & van der Molen, M. W. (1994). On the discrimination between global and local trend hypotheses of life-span changes in processing speed. *Acta Psychologica, 86,* 273–293.

Montada, L., Filipp, S.-H., & Lerner, M.-J. (Eds.). (1992). *Life crises and experiences of loss in adulthood.* Hillsdale, NJ: Erlbaum.

Morrow, D. G., Leirer, V. O., Fitzsimmons, C., & Altieri, P. A. (1994). When expertise reduces age differences in performance. *Psychology and Aging, 9,* 134–148.

Moscovitch, M., & Winocur, G. (1992). The neuropsychology of memory and aging. In F. I. M. Craik & T. A. Salthouse (Eds.), *The handbook of aging and cognition* (pp. 315–372). Hillsdale, NJ: Erlbaum.

Moss, H. A., & Sussman, E. J. (1980). Longitudinal study of personality development. In O. G. Brim, Jr. & J. Kagan (Eds.), *Constancy and change in human development* (pp. 530–595). Cambridge, MA: Harvard University Press.

Müller-Brettel, M., & Dixon, R. A. (1990). Johann Nicolas Tetens: A forgotten father of developmental psychology? *International Journal of Behavioral Development, 13,* 215–230.

Murray, H. A. (1938). *Explorations in personality.* New York: Oxford University Press.

Myerson, J., Hale, S., Wagstaff, D., Poon, L. W., & Smith, G. A. (1990). The information-loss model: A mathematical theory of age-related cognitive slowing. *Psychological Review, 97,* 475–487.

Naito, M., & Komatsu, S. (1993). Processes involved in childhood development of implicit memory. In P. Graf & M. E. J. Masson (Eds.), *Implicit memory: New directions on cognition, development, and neuropsychology* (pp. 231–260). Hillsdale, NJ: Erlbaum.

Nebes, R. D. (1992). Cognitive dysfunction in Alzheimer's disease. In F. I. M. Craik & T. A. Salthouse (Eds.), *The handbook of aging and cognition* (pp. 373–446). Hillsdale, NJ: Erlbaum.

Neely, A. S., & Bäckman, L. (1993). Long-term maintenance of gains from memory training in older adults: Two 3½-year follow-up studies. *Journal of Gerontology, 48,* 233–237.

Nelson, A. E., & Dannefer, D. (1992). Aged heterogeneity: Fact or fiction? The fate of diversity in gerontological research. *Gerontologist, 32,* 17–23.

Nelson, C. A. (1995). The ontogeny of human memory: A cognitive neuroscience perspective. *Developmental Psychology, 31,* 723–738.

Nesselroade, J. R. (1989). Adult personality development: Issues in addressing constancy and change. In A. I. Rabin, R. A. Zucker, R. A. Emmons, & S. Frank (Eds.), *Studying persons and lives* (pp. 41–85). New York: Springer.

Nesselroade, J. R. (1991a). The warp and the woof of the developmental fabric. In R. M. Downs, L. S. Liben, & D. S. Palermo (Eds.), *Visions of aesthetics, the environment and development: The legacy of Joachim Wohlwill* (pp. 213–240). Hillsdale, NJ: Erlbaum.

Nesselroade, J. R. (1991b). Inter-individual differences in intra-individual change. In L. M. Collins & J. L. Horn (Eds.), *Best methods for the analysis of change* (pp. 92–105). Washington, DC: American Psychological Association.

Nesselroade, J. R., & Baltes, P. B. (1974). Adolescent personality development and historical change: 1970–1972. *Monographs of the Society for Research in Child Development, 39.*

Nesselroade, J. R., & Baltes, P. B. (Eds.). (1979). *Longitudinal research in the study of behavior and development.* New York: Academic Press.

Nesselroade, J. R., & Bartsch, T. W. (1977). Multivariate perspectives on construct validity of the trait-state distinction. In R. B. Cattell & R. M. Dreger (Eds.), *Handbook of modern personality theory.* Washington, DC: Hemisphere.

Nesselroade, J. R., & Reese, H. W. (Eds.). (1973). *Life-span developmental psychology: Methodological issues.* New York: Academic Press.

Nesselroade, J. R., & Thompson, W. W. (1995). Selection and related threats to group comparisons: An example comparing factorial structures of higher and lower ability groups of adult twins. *Psychological Bulletin, 117,* 271–284.

Nettelbeck, T., & Rabbitt, P. M. A. (1992). Aging, cognitive performance, and mental speed. *Intelligence, 16,* 189–205.

Neugarten, B. L. (1969). Continuities and discontinuities of psychological issues into adult life. *Human Development, 12,* 121–130.

Newcomb, M. D., & McGee, L. (1991). Influence of sensation seeking on general deviance and specific problem behaviors from adolescence to young adulthood. *Journal of Personality and Social Psychology, 61,* 614–628.

Newport, E. L. (1990). Maturational constraints on language learning. *Cognitive Science, 14,* 11–28.

Nilsson, L.-G., Sikström, C., Adolfsson, R., Erngrund, K., Nylander, P. O., & Bäckman, L. (1996). Genetic markers associated with high versus low performance on episodic memory task. *Behavior Genetics, 26,* 555–562.

Nisbett, R. E. (1980). *History of the idea of progress.* New York: Basic Books.

Norman, W. T. (1963). Toward an adequate taxonomy of personality attributes: Replicated factor structure in peer nomination personality ratings. *Journal of Abnormal and Social Psychology, 66,* 574–583.

Nurmi, J. E., Pulliainen, H., & Salmela-Aro, K. (1992). Age differences in adults' control beliefs related to life goals and concerns. *Psychology and Aging, 7,* 194–196.

Nyberg, L., Bäckman, L., Erngrund, K., Olofsson, U., & Nilsson, L.-G. (1996). Age differences in episodic memory, semantic memory, and priming: Relationships to demographic, intellectual, and biological factors. *Journal of Gerontology: Psychological Sciences, 51B,* P234–P240.

Ochse, R., & Plug, C. (1986). Cross-cultural investigation of the validity of Erikson's theory of personality development. *Journal of Personality and Social Psychology, 50,* 1240–1252.

Oerter, R., & Montada, L. (1995). *Entwicklungspsychologie: Ein Lehrbuch.* München: Urban & Schwarzenberg.

Oettingen, G. (1996). Positive fantasy and motivation. In P. M. Gollwitzer & J. A. Bargh (Eds.), *The psychology of action: Linking cognition and motivation to action* (pp. 236–259). New York: Guilford Press.

Oettingen, G., Little, T. D., Lindenberger, U., & Baltes, P. B. (1994). Causality, agency, and control beliefs in East versus West Berlin children: A natural experiment on the role of context. *Journal of Personality and Social Psychology, 66,* 579–595.

Oettingen, G., & Wadden, T. A. (1991). Expectation, fantasy, and weight loss: Is the impact of positive thinking always positive? *Cognitive Therapy and Research, 15,* 167–175.

Olson, D. R. (1995). Conceptualizing the written word: An intellectual autobiography. *Written Communication, 12,* 277–297.

Osiewacz, H. D. (1995). Molekulare Mechanismen biologischen Alterns. *Biologie in unserer Zeit, 25,* 336–344.

Overton, W. F., & Newman, J. L. (1982). Cognitive development: A competence-activation/utilization approach. In T. Field, A. Houston, H. Quay, L. Troll, & G. Finlay (Eds.), *Review of human development* (pp. 217–241). New York: Wiley.

Overton, W. F., & Reese, H. W. (1973). Models of development: Methodological implications. In J. R. Nesselroade & H. W. Reese (Eds.), *Life-span developmental psychology: Methodological issues* (pp. 65–86). New York: Academic Press.

Park, D. C. (1992). Applied cognitive aging research. In F. I. M. Craik & T. A. Salthouse (Eds.), *The handbook of aging and cognition* (pp. 449–493). Hillsdale, NJ: Erlbaum.

Parke, R. D., Ornstein, P. A., Rieser, J. J., & Zahn-Waxler, C. (1991). Editors' introduction to the APA Centennial Series. *Developmental Psychology, 28,* 3–4.

Pascual-Leone, J. (1970). A mathematical model for the transition rule in Piaget's developmental stages. *Acta Psychologica, 32,* 301–342.

Pascual-Leone, J. (1983). Growing into human maturity: Toward a metasubjective theory of adulthood stages. In P. B. Baltes & O. G. Brim, Jr. (Eds.), *Life-span development and behavior* (Vol. 5, pp. 117–156). New York: Academic Press.

Pedersen, N. L. (1991). Behavioral genetic concepts in longitudinal analyses. In D. Magnusson, L. R. Bergman, G. Rudinger, & B. Törestad (Eds.), *Problems and methods in longitudinal research: Stability and change* (Vol. 5, pp. 236–249). Cambridge, England: Cambridge University Press.

Pedersen, N. L. (1993). Genetic and environmental continuity and change in personality. In T. J. Bouchard, Jr. & P. Propping (Eds.), *Twins as a tool of behavioral genetics* (pp. 147–162). Chichester, England: Wiley.

Pedersen, N. L., McClearn, G. E., Plomin, R., Nesselroade, J. R., Berg, S., & de Faire, U. (1991). The Swedish Adoption/Twin Study of Aging: An update. *Acta Geneticae Medicae et Gemellologiae Twin Research, 40,* 7–20.

Pedersen, N. L., Plomin, R., & McClearn, G. E. (1994). Is there G beyond g? (Is there genetic influence on specific cognitive abilities independent of genetic influence on general cognitive ability?). *Intelligence, 18,* 133–143.

Perfect, T. J. (1994). What can Brinley plots tell us about cognitive aging? *Journal of Gerontology: Psychological Sciences, 49,* 60–64.

Perlmutter, M. (1988). Cognitive potential throughout life. In J. E. Birren & V. L. Bengtson (Eds.), *Emergent theories of aging* (pp. 247–268). New York: Springer.

Perlmutter, M., Kaplan, M., & Nyquist, L. (1990). Development of adaptive competence in adulthood. *Human Development, 33,* 185–197.

Perner, J. (1995). The many faces of belief: Reflections on Fodor's and the child's theory of mind. *Cognition, 57,* 241–269.

Pervin, L. A. (Ed.). (1990). *Handbook of personality: Theory and research.* New York: Guilford Press.

Pfeiffer, E. (1977). Psychopathology and social pathology. In J. E. Birren & K. W. Schaie (Eds.), *Handbook of the psychology of aging* (pp. 650–671). New York: Van Nostrand Reinhold.

Piaget, J. (1970). Piaget's theory. In P. H. Mussen (Ed.), *Carmichaels manual of child psychology* (pp. 703–732). New York: Wiley.

Piaget, J. (1971). *Biologie et connaissance: Essai sur les relations entre les régulations organiques et les processus cognitifs*

(Biology and knowledge: An essay on the relations between organic regulations and cognitive processes). Chicago: University of Chicago Press. (Original work published 1967)

Piaget, J. (1972). Intellectual evolution from adolescence to adulthood. *Human Development, 15,* 1–12.

Piaget, J. (1980). *Les formes et les mentaires de la dialectique.* Paris: Gallimard.

Piaget, J., & Garcia, R. (1983). *Psychogenèse et histoire des sciences.* Paris: Flammarion.

Picano, J. J. (1989). Development and validation of a life history index of adult adjustment for women. *Journal of Personality Assessment, 53,* 308–318.

Pinker, S. (1994). *The language instinct.* New York: Morrow.

Plessner, H. (1965). *Die Stufen des Organischen und der Mensch: Einleitung in die philosophische Anthropologie.* Berlin: de Gruyter.

Plomin, R. (1994). *Genetics and experience: The interplay between nature and nurture.* Thousand Oaks, CA: Sage.

Plomin, R., Chipuer, H. M., & Loehlin, J. C. (1990). Behavioral genetics and personality. In L. A. Pervin (Ed.), *Handbook of personality: Theory and research* (pp. 225–243). New York: Guilford Press.

Plomin, R., & McClearn, G. E. (1993). *Nature, nurture, and psychology.* Washington, DC: American Psychological Association.

Plomin, R., Pedersen, N. L., Lichtenstein, P., & McClearn, G. E. (1994). Variability and stability in cognitive abilities are largely genetic later in life. *Behavior Genetics, 24,* 207–215.

Plomin, R., & Thompson, L. (1988). Life-span developmental behavioral genetics. In P. B. Baltes, D. L. Featherman, & R. M. Lerner (Eds.), *Life-span development and behavior* (Vol. 8, pp. 1–31). Hillsdale, NJ: Erlbaum.

Plude, D. J., Enns, J. T., & Brodeur, D. (1994). The development of selective attention: A life-span overview. Life span changes in human performance [Special issue]. *Acta Psychologica, 86,* 227–272.

Pressey, S. L., Janney, J. E., & Kuhlen, R. G. (1939). *Life: A psychological survey.* New York: Harper.

Prigogine, I., & Stengers, I. (1984). *Order out of chaos.* New York: Bantam Books.

Quetelet, A. (1842). *A treatise on man and the development of his faculties.* Edinburgh, England: Chambers.

Rabbitt, P. M. A. (1993). Does it all go together when it goes? The Nineteenth Bartlett Memorial Lecture. *Quarterly Journal of Experimental Psychology, 46A,* 385–434.

Rakic, P. (1995). Corticogenesis in human and nonhuman primates. In M. S. Gazzaniga (Ed.), *The cognitive neurosciences* (pp. 127–145). Cambridge, MA: MIT Press.

Reese, H. W. (1994). The data/theory dialectic: The nature of scientific progress. In S. H. Cohen & H. W. Reese (Eds.), *Life-span developmental psychology: Methodological contributions* (pp. 1–27). Hillsdale, NJ: Erlbaum.

Reese, H. W., & Lipsitt, L. P. (1970). *Experimental child psychology.* New York: Academic Press.

Reese, H. W., & Overton, W. F. (1970). Models of development and theories of development. In L. R. Goulet & P. B. Baltes (Eds.), *Life-span developmental psychology: Research and theory* (pp. 115–145). New York: Academic Press.

Reinert, G. (1970). Comparative factor analytic studies of intelligence throughout the life span. In L. R. Goulet & P. B. Baltes (Eds.), *Life-span developmental psychology: Research and theory* (pp. 476–484). New York: Academic Press.

Reinert, G. (1979). Prolegomena to a history of life-span developmental psychology. In P. B. Baltes & O. G. Brim, Jr. (Eds.), *Life-span development and behavior* (Vol. 2, pp. 205–254). New York: Academic Press.

Resnick, L. B., Levine, J. M., & Teasley, S. D. (Eds.). (1991). *Perspectives on socially shared cognition.* Washington, DC: American Psychological Association.

Ribeaupierre, A. de, & Bailleux, C. (1994). Developmental change in a spatial task of attentional capacity: An essay toward an integration of two working memory models. *International Journal of Behavioral Development, 17,* 5–35.

Riegel, K. F. (1958). Ergebnisse und Probleme der psychologischen Alternsforschung. *Vita Humana, 1,* 52–64, 111–127.

Riegel, K. F. (1973a). Developmental psychology and society: Some historical and ethical considerations. In J. R. Nesselroade & H. W. Reese (Eds.), *Life-span developmental psychology: Methodological issues* (pp. 1–23). New York: Academic Press.

Riegel, K. F. (1973b). Dialectic operations: The final period of cognitive development. *Human Development, 16,* 371–381.

Riegel, K. F. (1976). The dialectics of human development. *American Psychologist, 31,* 689–700.

Riley, M. W. (1987). On the significance of age in sociology. *American Sociological Review, 52,* 1–14.

Riley, M. W., Johnson, M., & Foner, A. (Eds.). (1972). *Aging and society: A sociology of age stratification* (Vol. 3). New York: Sage.

Riley, M. W., & Riley, J. W., Jr. (Eds.). (1989). The quality of aging: Strategies for interventions. *Annals of the American*

Academy of Political and Social Sciences (Vol. 503). Newbury Park, CA: Sage.

Robins, R. W., John, O. P., Caspi, A., Moffitt, T. E., & Strouthamer-Loeber, M. (1996). Resilient, overcontrolled, and undercontrolled boys: Three predictable personality types. *Journal of Personality and Social Psychology, 70,* 157–171.

Rogers, W. A., Fisk, A. D., & Hertzog, C. (1994). Do ability-performance relationships differentiate age and practice effects in visual search? *Journal of Experimental Psychology: Learning, Memory, and Cognition, 20,* 710–738.

Rogoff, B. (1990a). *Apprenticeship in thinking: Cognitive development in social context.* New York: Oxford University Press.

Rogoff, B. (1990b). *The child as apprentice: A new metaphor for cognitive development.* New York: Oxford University Press.

Rogoff, B. (1995). Observing sociocultural activity on three planes: Participatory appropriation, guided participation, and apprenticeship. In J. V. Wertsch, P. del Rio, & A. Alvarez (Eds.), *Sociocultural studies of mind* (pp. 139–164). Cambridge, England: Cambridge University Press.

Rogoff, B., & Chavajay, P. (1995). What's become of research on the cultural basis of cognitive development? *American Psychologist, 50,* 859–877.

Rowe, D. C. (1993). Genetic perspectives on personality. In R. Plomin & G. E. McClearn (Eds.), *Nature, nurture & psychology* (pp. 179–195). Washington, DC: American Psychological Association.

Rowe, J. W., & Kahn, R. L. (1987). Human aging: Usual and successful. *Science, 237,* 143–149.

Rutter, M. (1987). Resilience in the face of adversity: Protective factors and resistance to psychiatric disorder. *British Journal of Psychiatry, 147,* 598–611.

Rutter, M. (1997). Nature–nurture integration. *American Psychologist, 52,* 390–398.

Rutter, M., & Rutter, M. (1993). *Developing minds: Challenge and continuity across the life span.* New York: Basic Books.

Rybash, J. M., Hoyer, W. J., & Roodin, P. A. (1986). *Adult cognition and aging: Developmental changes in processing, knowing, and thinking.* New York: Pergamon Press.

Ryder, N. B. (1965). The cohort as a concept in the study of social change. *American Sociological Review, 30,* 843–861.

Ryder, R. G. (1967). Birth to maturity revisited: A canonical re-analysis. *Journal of Personality and Social Psychology, 7,* 168–172.

Ryff, C. D. (1984). Personality development from the inside: The subjective experience of change in adulthood and aging. In P. B. Baltes & O. G. Brim, Jr. (Eds.), *Life-span development*

and behavior (Vol. 6, pp. 249–279). New York: Academic Press.

Ryff, C. D. (1989a). Beyond Ponce de Leon and life satisfaction: New directions in quest of successful aging. *International Journal of Behavioral Development, 12,* 35–55.

Ryff, C. D. (1989b). Happiness is everything, or is it? Explorations on the meaning of psychological well-being. *Journal of Personality and Social Psychology, 57,* 1069–1081.

Ryff, C. D. (1991). Possible selves in adulthood and old age: A tale of shifting horizons. *Psychology and Aging, 6,* 286–295.

Ryff, C. D. (1995). Psychological well-being in adult life. *Current Directions in Psychological Science, 4,* 99–104.

Ryff, C. D., & Baltes, P. B. (1976). Value transition and adult development in women: The instrumentality-terminality sequence hypothesis. *Developmental Psychology, 12,* 567–568.

Ryff, C. D., & Essex, M. J. (1992). The interpretation of life experience and well being: The sample case of relocation. *Psychology and Aging, 7,* 507–517.

Ryff, C. D., & Keyes, C. L. M. (1995). The structure of psychological well-being revisited. *Journal of Personality and Social Psychology, 69,* 719–727.

Salthouse, T. A. (1984). Effects of age and skill in typing. *Journal of Experimental Psychology: General, 113,* 345–371.

Salthouse, T. A. (1991a). Expertise as the circumvention of human processing limitations. In K. A. Ericsson & J. Smith (Eds.), *Towards a general theory of expertise: Prospects and limits* (pp. 286–300). New York: Cambridge University Press.

Salthouse, T. A. (1991b). Mediation of adult age differences in cognition by reductions in working memory and speed of processing. *Psychological Science, 2,* 179–183.

Salthouse, T. A. (1991c). *Theoretical perspectives on cognitive aging.* Hillsdale, NJ: Erlbaum.

Salthouse, T. A. (1994). How many causes are there of aging-related decrements in cognitive functioning? *Developmental Review, 14,* 413–437.

Salthouse, T. A. (1995). Refining the concept of psychological compensation. In R. A. Dixon & L. Bäckman (Eds.), *Compensating for psychological deficits and declines* (pp. 21–34). Mahwah, NJ: Erlbaum.

Salthouse, T. A. (1996). The processing-speed theory of adult age differences in cognition. *Psychological Review, 103,* 403–428.

Salthouse, T. A., & Kail, R. (1983). Memory development throughout the life span: The role of processing rate. In P. B. Baltes (Ed.), *Life-span development and behavior* (Vol. 5, pp. 89–116). New York: Academic Press.

Salthouse, T. A., & Meinz, E. J. (1995). Aging, inhibition, working memory, and speed. *Journal of Gerontology: Psychological Sciences, 50B*, 297–306.

Sanford, E. C. (1902). Mental growth and decay. *American Journal of Psychology, 13*, 426–449.

Scarr, S. (1986). How plastic are we? *Contemporary Psychology, 31*, 565–567.

Scarr, S. (1993). Biological and cultural diversity: The legacy of Darwin for development. *Child Development, 64*, 1333–1353.

Scarr, S., & McCartney, K. (1983). How people make their own environments: A theory of genotype environment effects. *Child Development, 54*, 424–435.

Schadewaldt, W. (1975). *Nachwort zu Elektra (Epilogue to Electra)*. Stuttgart: Reclam.

Schaie, K. W. (1965). A general model for the study of developmental problems. *Psychological Bulletin, 64*, 92–107.

Schaie, K. W. (1970). A reinterpretation of age-related changes in cognitive structure and functioning. In L. R. Goulet & P. B. Baltes (Eds.), *Life-span developmental psychology: Research and theory* (pp. 485–507). New York: Academic Press.

Schaie, K. W. (1983). The Seattle Longitudinal Study: A 21-year exploration of psychometric intelligence in adulthood. In K. W. Schaie (Ed.), *Longitudinal studies of adult psychological development* (pp. 64–135). New York: Guilford Press.

Schaie, K. W. (1988). Variability in cognitive functioning in the elderly: Implications for societal participation. In A. D. Woodhead, M. A. Bender, & R. C. Leonard (Eds.), *Phenotypic variation in populations: Relevance to risk assessment* (pp. 191–212). New York: Plenum Press.

Schaie, K. W. (1989). The hazards of cognitive aging. *Gerontologist, 29*, 484–493.

Schaie, K. W. (1994). The course of adult intellectual development. *American Psychologist, 49*, 304–313.

Schaie, K. W. (1996). *Intellectual development in adulthood: The Seattle Longitudinal Study*. New York: Cambridge University Press.

Schaie, K. W., & Baltes, P. B. (1975). On sequential strategies in developmental research: Description or explanation? *Human Development, 18*, 384–390.

Schaie, K. W., Dutta, R., & Willis, S. L. (1991). Relationship between rigidity-flexibility and cognitive abilities in adulthood. *Psychology and Aging, 6*, 371–383.

Schaie, K. W., & Willis, S. L. (1986). Can decline in adult intellectual functioning be reversed? *Developmental Psychology, 22*, 223–232.

Schaie, K. W., & Willis, S. L. (1993). Age difference patterns of psychometric intelligence in adulthood: Generalizability within and across ability domains. *Psychology and Aging, 8*, 44–55.

Schaie, K. W., Willis, S. L., Hertzog, C., & Schulenberg, J. E. (1987). Effects of cognitive training on primary mental ability structure. *Psychology and Aging, 2*, 233–242.

Schaie, K. W., Willis, S. L., Jay, G., & Chipuer, H. (1989). Structural invariance of cognitive abilities across the adult life span: A cross-sectional study. *Developmental Psychology, 25*, 652–662.

Scheier, M. F., & Carver, C. S. (1987). Dispositional optimism and physical well-being: The influence of generalized outcome expectancies on health. *Journal of Personality, 55*, 169–210.

Schieber, F., & Baldwin, C. L. (1996). Vision, audition, and aging research. In F. Blanchard-Fields & T. M. Hess (Eds.), *Perspectives on cognitive change in adulthood and aging* (pp. 122–162). New York: McGraw-Hill.

Schmidt, L. R. (1971). Testing the limits im Leistungsverhalten: Möglichkeiten und Grenzen. In E. Duhm (Ed.), *Praxis der klinischen Psychologie* (Vol. 2, pp. 9–29). Göttingen: Hogrefe.

Schneider, W., Gruber, H., Gold, A., & Opwis, K. (1993). Chess expertise and memory for chess positions in children and adults. *Journal of Experimental Child Psychology, 56*, 328–349.

Schneirla, T. C. (1957). The concept of development in comparative psychology. In D. B. Harris (Ed.), *The concept of development* (pp. 78–108). Minneapolis: University of Minnesota Press.

Schuerger, J. M., Zarrella, K. L., & Hotz, A. S. (1989). Factors that influence the temporal stability of personality by questionnaire. *Journal of Personality and Social Psychology, 56*, 777–783.

Schulz, R., & Heckhausen, J. (1996). A life-span model of successful aging. *American Psychologist, 51*, 702–714.

Sears, P. S., & Barbee, A. H. (1977). Career and life satisfactions among Terman's gifted women. In J. Stanley, W. George, & C. Solano (Eds.), *The gifted and the creative: A fifty-year perspective* (pp. 28–65). Baltimore: Johns Hopkins University Press.

Shallice, T., & Burgess, P. (1991). Deficits in strategy application following frontal lobe damage in man. *Brain, 114*, 727–742.

Sherry, D. F., & Schacter, D. L. (1987). The evolution of multiple memory systems. *Psychological Review, 94*, 439–454.

Shweder, R. A. (1991). *Thinking through cultures*. Cambridge, MA: Harvard University Press.

Siegler, I. C., Zonderman, A. B., Barefoot, J. C., & Williams, R. B. (1990). Predicting personality in adulthood from college MMPI scores: Implications for follow-up studies in psychosomatic medicine. *Psychosomatic Medicine, 52,* 644–652.

Siegler, R. S. (1989). Mechanisms of cognitive development. *Annual Review of Psychology, 40,* 353–379.

Siegler, R. S. (1994). Cognitive variability: A key to understanding cognitive development. *Current Directions in Psychological Science, 3,* 1–5.

Siegler, R. S., & Crowley, K. (1991). The microgenetic method: A direct means for studying cognitive development. *American Psychologist, 46,* 606–620.

Siegler, R. S., & Crowley, K. (1994). Constraints on learning in nonprivileged domains. *Cognitive Psychology, 27,* 194–226.

Siegler, R. S., & Jenkins, E. (1989). *How children discover new strategies.* Hillsdale, NJ: Erlbaum.

Siegler, R. S., & Shipley, C. (1995). Variation, selection, and cognitive change. In T. Simon & G. Halford (Eds.), *Developing cognitive competence: New approaches to process modeling* (pp. 31–76). Hillsdale, NJ: Erlbaum.

Simon, H. A., & Chase, W. G. (1973). Skill in chess. *American Scientist, 61,* 394–403.

Simonton, D. K. (1988). Age and outstanding achievement: What do we know after a century of research? *Psychological Bulletin, 104,* 251–267.

Simonton, D. K. (1989). The swan-song phenomenon: Last-works effects for 172 classical composers. *Psychology and Aging, 4,* 42–47.

Singer, J. L. (1984). The private personality. *Personality and Social Psychology Bulletin, 10,* 7–30.

Singer, J. L., & Kolligian, J., Jr. (1987). Personality: Developments in the study of private experience. *Annual Review of Psychology, 38,* 533–574.

Singer, W. (1995). Development and plasticity of cortical processing architectures. *Science, 270,* 758–764.

Skinner, B. F. (1966). The phylogeny and ontogeny of behavior. *Science, 153,* 1205–1213.

Skinner, E. A. (1995). *Perceived control, motivation, and coping.* Thousand Oaks, CA: Sage.

Skolnick, A. (1975). The family revisited: Themes in recent social science research. *Journal of International Interdisciplinary History, 5,* 703–719.

Smith, J., & Baltes, P. B. (1993). Differential psychological aging: Profiles of the old and very old. *Ageing and Society, 13,* 551–587.

Smith, J., & Baltes, P. B. (in press-a). A psychological perspective on aging: Trends and profiles in very old age. In P. B. Baltes & K. U. Mayer (Eds.), *The Berlin Aging Study: From 70 to 100.* New York: Cambridge University Press.

Smith, J., & Baltes, P. B. (in press-b). Profiles of psychological functioning in the old and oldest-old. *Psychology and Aging.*

Smith, J., & Fleeson, W., Geiselmann, B., Settersten, R., & Kunzmann, U. (in press). In P. B. Baltes & K. U. Mayer (Eds.), *The Berlin Aging Study: From 70 to 100.* New York: Cambridge University Press.

Smith, J., Staudinger, U. M., & Baltes, P. B. (1994). Occupational settings facilitative of wisdom-related knowledge: The sample case of clinical psychologists. *Journal of Consulting and Clinical Psychology, 62,* 989–1000.

Smotherman, W. P., & Robinson, S. R. (1996). The development of behavior before birth. *Developmental Psychology, 32,* 425–434.

Somervell, P. D., Kaplan, B. H., Heiss, G., Tyroler, H., Kleinbaum, D., & Obrist, P. A. (1989). Psychological distress as a predictor of mortality. *American Journal of Epidemiology, 130,* 1013–1023.

Sorenson, A. B., Weinert, F. E., & Sherrod, L. (Eds.). (1986). *Human development and the life course: Multidisciplinary perspectives.* Hillsdale, NJ: Erlbaum.

Sowarka, D., & Baltes, P. B. (1986). Intelligenzentwicklung. In W. Sarges & R. Fricke (Eds.), *Psychologie für die Erwachsenenbildung-Weiterbildung* (pp. 262–272). Göttingen: Hogrefe.

Spearman, C. E. (1927). *The abilities of man.* New York: Macmillan.

Spelke, E., Vishton, P., & von Hofsten, C. (1995). Object perception, object-directed action, and physical knowledge in infancy. In M. S. Gazzaniga (Ed.), *The cognitive neurosciences* (pp. 165–179). Cambridge, MA: MIT Press.

Staudinger, U. M. (1989). *The study of life review: An approach to the investigation of intellectual development across the life span* (Vol. 47). Berlin: Sigma.

Staudinger, U. M. (1996a). Psychologische Produktivität und Selbstentfaltung im Alter. In M. M. Baltes & L. Montada (Eds.), *Produktives Leben im Alter* (pp. 344–373). Frankfurt: Campus.

Staudinger, U. M. (1996b). Wisdom and the social-interactive foundation of the mind. In P. B. Baltes & U. M. Staudinger (Eds.), *Interactive minds: Life-span perspectives on the social foundation of cognition* (pp. 276–315). New York: Cambridge University Press.

Staudinger, U. M., & Baltes, P. B. (1994). The psychology of wisdom. In R. J. Sternberg et al. (Eds.), *Encyclopedia of intelligence* (pp. 1143–1152). New York: Macmillan.

Staudinger, U. M., & Baltes, P. B. (1996). Weisheit als Gegenstand psychologischer Forschung. *Psychologische Rundschau, 47,* 57–77.

Staudinger, U. M., & Baltes, P. B. (1996). Interactive minds: A facilitative setting for wisdom-related performance? *Journal of Personality and Social Psychology, 71,* 746–762.

Staudinger, U. M., & Fleeson, W. (1996). Resilience of the self in very old age. *Development and Psychopathology, 8,* 867–885.

Staudinger, U. M., Freund, A., Maas, I., & Linden, M. (in press). Self, personality, and life regulation: Facets of psychological resilience in old age. In P. B. Baltes & K. U. Mayer (Eds.), *The Berlin Aging Study: From 70 to 100.* New York: Cambridge University Press.

Staudinger, U. M., Lopez, D. F., & Baltes, P. B. (in press). The psychometric location of wisdom-related performance. *Personality and Social Psychology Bulletin.*

Staudinger, U. M., Maciel, A., Smith, J., & Baltes, P. B. (in press). What predicts wisdom-related knowledge? A first look at the role of personality, intelligence, and training and practice in clinical psychology. *European Journal of Personality.*

Staudinger, U. M., Marsiske, M., & Baltes, P. B. (1993). Resilience and levels of reserve capacity in later adulthood: Perspectives from life-span theory. *Development and Psychopathology, 5,* 541–566.

Staudinger, U. M., Marsiske, M., & Baltes, P. B. (1995). Resilience and reserve capacity in later adulthood: Potentials and limits of development across the life span. In D. Cicchetti & D. Cohen (Eds.), *Developmental psychopathology: Vol. 2. Risk, disorder, and adaptation* (pp. 801–847). New York: Wiley.

Staudinger, U. M., Smith, J., & Baltes, P. B. (1992). Wisdom-related knowledge in a life review task: Age differences and the role of professional specialization. *Psychology and Aging, 7,* 271–281.

Staudinger, U. M., Smith, J., & Baltes, P. B. (1994). *Manual for the assessment of wisdom-related knowledge* (Research Material No. 46). Berlin: Max Planck Institute for Human Development and Education.

Stern, W. (1911). *Die differentielle Psychologie in ihren methodischen Grundlagen.* Leipzig: Barth.

Sternberg, R. J. (1985). *Beyond IQ: A triarchic theory of human intelligence.* New York: Cambridge University Press.

Sternberg, R. J. (1990). Wisdom and its relations to intelligence and creativity. In R. J. Sternberg (Ed.), *Wisdom: Its nature, origins, and development* (pp. 142–149). New York: Cambridge University Press.

Sternberg, R. J., & Wagner, R. K. (Eds.). (1986). *Practical intelligence: Nature and origins of competence in the everyday world.* Cambridge, England: Cambridge University Press.

Sternberg, R. J., Wagner, R. K., Williams, W. M., & Horvath, J. A. (1995). Testing common sense. *American Psychologist, 50,* 912–927.

Sterns, H. L., & Dorsett, J. G. (1994). Career development: A life span issue. *Experimental Aging Research, 20,* 257–264.

Stevens, D. P., & Truss, C. V. (1985). Stability and change in adult personality over 12 and 20 years. *Developmental Psychology, 21,* 568–584.

Stoltzfus, E. R., Hasher, L., & Zacks, R. T. (1996). Working memory and aging: Current status of the inhibitory view. In J. T. E. Richardson (Ed.), *Working memory and human cognition* (pp. 66–88). Cambridge, England: Oxford University Press.

Strelau, J., & Angleitner, A. (Eds.). (1991). *Explorations in temperament: International perspectives on theory and measurement.* New York: Plenum Press.

Suls, J. N., & Mullen, B. (1982). From the cradle to the grave: Comparison and self-evaluation. In J. N. Suls (Ed.), *Psychological perspectives on the self* (Vol. 1, pp. 97–128). Hillsdale, NJ: Erlbaum.

Taylor, S. E., & Brown, J. D. (1988). Illusion and well-being: A social psychological perspective on mental health. *Psychological Bulletin, 103,* 193–210.

Taylor, S. E., & Gollwitzer, P. M. (1995). Effects of mindset on positive illusions. *Journal of Personality and Social Psychology, 69,* 213–226.

Taylor, S. E., & Lobel, M. (1989). Social comparison activity under threat: Downward evaluation and upward contacts. *Psychological Bulletin, 96,* 569–575.

Taylor, S. E., & Pham, L. B. (1996). Mental stimulation, motivation, and action. In P. M. Gollwitzer & J. A. Bargh (Eds.), *The psychology of action: Linking cognition and motivation to behavior* (pp. 219–235). New York: Guilford Press.

Tetens, J. N. (1777). *Philosophische Versuche über die menschliche Natur und ihre Entwicklung.* Leipzig: Weidmanns Erben und Reich.

Thelen, E. (1992). Development as a dynamic system. *Current Directions in Psychological Science, 1,* 189–193.

Thelen, E., & Smith, L. B. (1994). *A dynamic systems approach to the development of cognition and action.* Cambridge, MA: MIT Press.

Thoits, P. A. (1983). Multiple identities and psychological well-being: A reformulation and test of the social isolation hypothesis. *American Sociological Review, 8,* 174–187.

Thomae, H. (1959). *Entwicklungspsychologie.* Göttingen: Hogrefe.

Thomae, H. (Ed.). (1979). The concept of development and life-span developmental psychology. In P. B. Baltes & O. G. Brim, Jr. (Eds.), *Life-span development and behavior* (Vol. 2, pp. 282–312). New York: Academic Press.

Thomas, A., & Chess, S. (1977). *Temperament and development.* New York: Brunner/Mazel.

Thomas, A., & Chess, S. (1984). Genesis and evolution of behavioral disorders: From infancy to early adult life. *American Journal of Psychiatry, 141,* 1–9.

Thompson, R. A. (1988). Early development in life-span perspective. In P. B. Baltes, D. L. Featherman, & R. M. Lerner (Eds.), *Life-span development and behavior* (Vol. 9, pp. 130–172). Hillsdale, NJ: Erlbaum.

Tooby, J., & Cosmides, L. (1995). Mapping the evolved functional organization of mind and brain. In M. S. Gazzaniga (Ed.), *The cognitive neurosciences* (pp. 1185–1197). Cambridge, MA: MIT Press.

Trevarthen, C. (1993). The self born in intersubjectivity: An infant communicating. In U. Neisser (Ed.), *The perceived self: Ecological and interpersonal sources of self-knowledge.* New York: Cambridge University Press.

Trivers, R. L. (1985). *Social evolution.* Menlo Park, LA: Benjamin/Cummings.

Trommsdorff, G. (1995). Person-context relations as developmental conditions for empathy and prosocial action: A cross-cultural analysis. In T. A. Kindermann & J. Valsiner (Eds.), *Development of person-context relations* (pp. 113–146). Hillsdale, NJ: Erlbaum.

Turkewitz, G., & Kenny, P. A. (1982). Limitations on input as a basis for neural organization and perceptual development: A preliminary theoretical statement. *Developmental Psychobiology, 15,* 357–368.

Uttal, D. H., & Perlmutter, M. (1989). Toward a broader conceptualization of development: The role of gains and losses across the life span. *Developmental Review, 9,* 101–132.

Vaillant, G. E. (1977). *Adaptation to life.* Boston: Little, Brown.

Vaillant, G. E. (1983). *The natural history of alcoholism: Causes, patterns and paths to recovery.* Cambridge, MA: Harvard University Press.

Vaillant, G. E. (1990). Avoiding negative life outcomes: Evidence from a forty-five year study. In P. B. Baltes & M. M. Baltes (Eds.), *Successful aging: Perspectives from the behavioral sciences* (pp. 332–355). New York: Cambridge University Press.

Vaillant, G. E. (1993). *The wisdom of the ego.* Cambridge, MA: Harvard University Press.

Vaillant, G. E., & McCullough, L. (1987). The Washington University Sentence Completion Test compared with other measures of adult ego development. *American Journal of Psychiatry, 144,* 1189–1194.

Valsiner, J., & Lawrence, J. A. (1996). Human development in culture across the life span. In J. W. Berry, P. R. Dasen, & T. S. Saraswathi (Eds.), *Handbook of cross-cultural psychology* (Vol. 2). Boston, MA: Allyn & Bacon.

van der Maas, H. L., & Molenaar, P. C. M. (1992). Stagewise cognitive development: An application of catastrophe theory. *Psychological Review, 99,* 395–417.

Verhaeghen, P., Marcoen, A., & Goossens, L. (1992). Improving memory performance in the aged through mnemonic training: A meta-analytic study. *Psychology and Aging, 7,* 242–251.

Veroff, J., Reuman, D., & Feld, S. (1984). Motives in American men and women across the adult life span. *Developmental Psychology, 20,* 1142–1158.

Vygotsky, L. S. (1962). *Thought and language.* Cambridge, MA: MIT Press.

Waddington, C. H. (1975). *The evolution of an evolutionist.* Edinburgh, England: Edinburgh University Press.

Waldman, D. A., & Avolio, B. J. (1986). A meta-analysis of age differences in job performance. *Journal of Applied Psychology, 71,* 33–38.

Walsh, D. A., & Hershey, D. A. (1993). Mental models and the maintenance of complex problem-solving skills in old age. In J. Cerella, J. Rybash, W. Hoyer, & M. L. Commons (Eds.), *Adult information processing: Limits on loss* (pp. 553–584). San Diego, CA: Academic Press.

Waterman, A. S., & Archer, S. L. (1990). A life-span perspective on identity formation: Developments in form, function, and process. In P. B. Baltes, D. L. Featherman, & R. M. Lerner (Eds.), *Life-span development and behavior* (Vol. 10, pp. 29–57). Hillsdale, NJ: Erlbaum.

Weinert, F. E. (1994a). Altern in psychologischer Perspektive. In P. B. Baltes, J. Mittelstrass, & U. M. Staudinger (Eds.), *Alter und Altern: Ein interdisziplinärer Studientext zur Gerontologie* (pp. 180–203). Berlin: de Gruyter.

Weinert, F. E. (1994b, September). *Kognitive Entwicklung im Kindesalter: Universelle Veränderungen oder individueller Kompetenzerwerb?* Paper presented at the 39th Congress of the German Psychological Society, Hamburg, Germany.

Weinert, F. E., & Perner, J. (1996). Cognitive development. In D. Magnusson (Ed.), *The life-span development of individuals: Behavioural, neurobiological and psychosocial perspectives* (pp. 207–222). Cambridge, England: Cambridge University Press.

Weinert, F. E., Schneider, W., & Knopf, M. (1988). Individual differences in memory development across the life span. In P. B. Baltes, D. L. Featherman, & R. M. Lerner (Eds.), *Life-span development and behavior* (Vol. 9, pp. 39–85). Hillsdale, NJ: Erlbaum.

Weir, M. W. (1964). Developmental changes in problem-solving strategies. *Psychological Review, 71,* 473–490.

Welford, A. T. (1984). Between bodily changes and performance: Some possible reasons for slowing with age. *Experimental Aging Research, 10,* 73–88.

Welford, A. T. (1993). The gerontological balance sheet. In J. Cerella, J. Rybash, W. Hoyer, & M. L. Commons (Eds.), *Adult information processing: Limits on loss* (pp. 3–10). San Diego, CA: Academic Press.

Welford, A. T., & Birren, J. E. (Eds.). (1965). *Behavior, aging, and the nervous system.* Springfield, IL: Thomas.

Wellman, H. M., & Gelman, S. A. (1992). Cognitive development: Foundational theories of core domains. *Annual Review of Psychology, 43,* 337–375.

Werner, E. E. (1995). Resilience in development. *Current Directions in Psychological Science, 4,* 81–85.

Werner, H. (1948). *Comparative psychology of mental development.* New York: International Universities Press.

Wertsch, J. V. (1991). *Voices of the mind: A sociocultural approach to mediated action.* Cambridge, MA: Harvard University Press.

Whitbourne, S. K. (1987). Personality development in adulthood and old age: Relationships among identity style, health, and well-being. *Annual Review of Gerontology and Geriatrics, 7,* 189–216.

Whitbourne, S. K., & Waterman, A. S. (1979). Psychosocial development during the adult years: Age and cohort comparisons. *Developmental Psychology, 15,* 373–378.

Whitbourne, S. K., Zuschlag, M. K., Elliot, L. B., & Waterman, A. S. (1992). Psychosocial development in adulthood: A 22-year sequential study. *Journal of Personality and Social Psychology, 63,* 260–271.

White, M. S. (1985). Ego development in adult women. *Journal of Personality, 53,* 561–574.

White, R. W. (1959). Motivation reconsidered: The concept of competence. *Psychological Review, 66,* 297–333.

White, S. H. (1983). The idea of development in developmental psychology. In R. M. Lerner (Ed.), *Developmental psychology: Historical and philosophical perspectives* (pp. 55–78). Hillsdale, NJ: Erlbaum.

White, S. H. (1992). G. Stanley Hall: From philosophy to developmental psychology. *Developmental Psychology, 28,* 25–34.

Wickett, J. C., & Vernon, P. A. (1994). Peripheral nerve conduction velocity, reaction time, and intelligence: An attempt to replicate Vernon and Mori (1992). *Intelligence, 18,* 127–131.

Wilkening, F., & Anderson, N. H. (1990). Representation and diagnosis of knowledge structures in developmental psychology. In N. H. Anderson (Ed.), *Contributions to information integration theory* (pp. 45–80). Hillsdale, NJ: Erlbaum.

Willett, J. B., & Singer, J. D. (1991). Applications of survival analysis to aging research. *Experimental Aging Research, 17,* 243–250.

Willis, S. L. (1987). Cognitive training and everyday competence. In K. W. Schaie (Ed.), *Annual review of gerontology and geriatrics* (Vol. 7, pp. 159–188). New York: Springer.

Willis, S. L. (1990). Contributions of cognitive training research to understanding late life potential. In M. Perlmutter (Ed.), *Late-life potential* (pp. 25–42). Washington, DC: The Gerontological Society of America.

Willis, S. L., & Baltes, P. B. (1980). Intelligence in adulthood and aging: Contemporary issues. In L. W. Poon (Ed.), *Aging in the 1980's: Psychological issues* (pp. 260–272). Washington, DC: American Psychological Association.

Willis, S. L., & Nesselroade, C. S. (1990). Long-term effects of fluid ability training in old-old age. *Developmental Psychology, 26,* 905–910.

Wills, T. A. (1981). Downward comparison principles in social psychology. *Psychological Bulletin, 90,* 245–271.

Wohlwill, J. F. (1973). *The study of behavioral development.* New York: Academic Press.

Wood, J. V. (1989). Theory and research concerning social comparisons of personal attributes. *Psychological Bulletin, 106,* 231–248.

Wood, J. V., Taylor, S. E., & Lichtman, R. R. (1985). Social comparison in adjustment to breast cancer. *Journal of Personality and Social Psychology, 49,* 1169–1183.

Woodcock, R. W., & Johnson, M. G. (1989, 1990). *Woodcock-Johnson Psycho-Educational Battery-Revised.* Allen, TX: DLM Teaching Resources.

Woodruff, D. S., & Birren, J. E. (1972). Age changes and cohort differences in personality. *Developmental Psychology, 6,* 252–259.

Woodruff-Pak, D. S. (1993). Neural plasticity as a substrate for cognitive adaptation in adulthood and aging. In J. Cerella, J. Rybash, W. Hoyer, & M. L. Commons (Eds.), *Adult information processing: Limits on loss* (pp. 13–35). San Diego, CA: Academic Press.

Woodruff-Pak, D. S., & Hanson, C. (1995). Plasticity and compensation in brain memory systems in aging. In R. A. Dixon

& L. Bäckman (Eds.), *Compensating for psychological deficits and declines: Managing losses and promoting gains* (pp. 191–217). Mahwah, NJ: Erlbaum.

Wozniak, R. H., & Fischer, K. W. (Eds.). (1993). *Development in context: Acting and thinking in specific environments.* Hillsdale, NJ: Erlbaum.

Yates, E., & Benton, L. A. (1995). Biological senescence: Loss of integration and resilience. *Canadian Journal on Aging, 14,* 106–120.

Youniss, J. (1995). The still useful classic concept of development. *Human Development, 38,* 373–379.

Zuckerman, M. (1994). Impulsive unsocialized sensation seeking: The biological foundations of a basic dimension of personality. In J. E. Bates & T. D. Wachs (Eds.), *Temperament: Individual differences at the interface of biology and behavior* (pp. 219–255). Washington, DC: American Psychological Association.

Zuckerman, M. (1995). Good and bad humors: Biochemical bases of personality and its disorders. *Psychological Science, 6,* 325–332.

CHAPTER 19

The Study of African American and Latin American Children and Youth

CELIA B. FISHER, JACQUELYNE FAYE JACKSON, and FRANCISCO A. VILLARRUEL

Ethnic, racial, and cultural diversity represent dimensions, of global society that have both built and separated communities. Social and demographic changes, along with evolving political conditions and new economies, reinforce the notion that ethnicity, race, and culture are dynamic concepts representing fluid dimensions of individual and community life. In the United States, immigration and migration, increased mobility, redefinitions of community, technological innovations, and the integration of ethnic and cultural practices into the larger society are challenging the American racial order through conflict and accommodations between the emerging political identities of different ethnic minorities and the country's racial ideologies,

policies, and practices (cf. Chan & Hune, 1995). As the content and importance of ethnic categories in individual lives and sociopolitical spheres continue to evolve, the imagery of the American melting pot is being transformed into an American mosaic. The historical American ideal of cultural flexibility, exemplified in the melting pot metaphor and idealized as the ability to overlook differences in physical appearance, personal beliefs, lifestyles, and values, is giving way to new ideals based on mutual respect for culturally diverse practices. Charter school movements that are based on cultural values and teachings (e.g., Afrocentric Schools, Japanese Suzuki Schools) and the establishment of culturally based community centers emphasize current individual and collective interest in maintaining one's ethnic roots. For those who have sought comfort in ethnocentrism, racism, or other principles of exclusion, it is disturbing to recognize that culturally distinct values and behaviors can persist by choice rather than in reaction to discrimination and prejudice.

As American society strives to adapt to the cultural heterogeneity of its citizenry, researchers, practitioners, and policy makers are engaged in difficult dialogues regarding how an understanding of diversity, plurality, multiculturalism, and multilingualism can best be applied to promote the welfare of children and youth. One dimension of this dialogue focuses on how the scientific observation, description, and explanation of human development can establish an empirical foundation on which service delivery and social policy can evolve for ethnically diverse communities (Fisher, Hatashi-Wong, & Isman, in press). The importance and urgency of developing a deeper understanding of normative, but possibly different, cultural paths of development is underscored by the 1990 census, documenting the significant growth rate among African American and Latin American populations in the United States (U.S. Census Bureau, 1993). Thus, future developmental theory, research designs, and interventions formulated around labeling and conceptualizing members of these ethnic groups as "minorities" will lag behind changes in the demographic landscape. To address the changing demographic needs of communities, research that approximates the new composition and unique developmental trajectories of racial and ethnic minorities is not only warranted, but a prerequisite for creating sound, theoretically based social programs.

One paradox of the increase in African American and Latin American populations is that the focus of research and policy has been on the involvement of these groups in societal "ills" (e.g., teenage pregnancy, juvenile delinquency, and school underachievement) as opposed to the resiliency or unique developmental aspects of their families and communities. Current efforts to ground social programs and policies in a strong foundation of empirically based knowledge are thwarted by the paucity of research on the normative growth and development of ethnic minority children and families. Child development experts are recognizing the need for scientific information that represents a synthesis of research and applications to describe, explain, and promote optimal developmental outcomes in diverse individuals, families, and communities (Fisher et al., 1993; Fisher & Lerner, 1994; Fisher & Murray, 1996). At the core of this concern resides a debate, not only in the scientific community, but also in the general population that reflects one of the objectives of this chapter. Specifically, we must ask ourselves: Is knowledge based on traditional beliefs about development (scientific and otherwise) sufficient to inform social policy and provide a foundation for effective social programs directed toward the core needs of culturally and linguistically diverse communities? Or should we strive to revise our belief systems and social policies to more adequately mirror the distinctive values of various racial and ethnic communities and, thus, generate new knowledge and modes of scientific thinking?

THE SCOPE AND FOCUS OF THIS CHAPTER

This chapter examines these questions by reviewing research conducted by psychologists, anthropologists, and sociologists that has contributed to our knowledge of infant, child, and adolescent development within two ethnic and racial communities in the United States: African American and Latin American. To address issues salient to the study of ethnic minority development, several decisions were made to make this a more manageable task and to permit us to focus on what we defined as the core questions. First, although there is literature on virtually every ethnic minority group in the United States, we have chosen to focus our review predominantly on African American and Latin American issues. The main reason for this decision was the fact that there is a substantial amount of research that has attempted to consider and document how heritage has contributed to the development of a broad arena of behaviors and identity within both of these groups. There are fewer systematic attempts to understand other ethnic groups; although there is exciting research focusing on East Asian and Native American children and youth (see, for example, Chan & Hune, 1995; Joe, 1994; LaFromboise, 1988; Manson, Bechtold, Novins, & Beals, 1997; Ryu & Vann, 1992; Takanishi, 1994; Tharp, 1994).

Second, we needed to address issues of group terminology. Our review of the literature indicated a reliance on panethnic terms to describe research participants (i.e., African American, Black, Hispanic, Latino, Latina) that impedes the ability to understand and identify developmental patterns specific to distinct ethnic and cultural groups (i.e., African, Caribbean, Puerto Rican, Mexican). Moreover, we became more sensitive to the significant challenges faced by investigators in their efforts to define participant ethnic identities, especially when individual participants may not agree with currently used classificatory labels. The debate over which ethnic terms are appropriate or inappropriate to use is beyond the scope of this manuscript, but it is critical to our understanding of how history and culture contribute to our understanding of human development (Sampson, 1993). In the absence of knowledge about the specific ethnic membership of research participants, we have had to report findings in terms of the panethnic terms employed by the original investigators. We have used terms such as Latino and Hispanic and Black and African American interchangeably and whenever possible, information on the specific ethnicity of groups has been noted.

Third, space limitations and the limited knowledge of ethnic factors in some areas of investigation meant that we needed to focus our review on specified theoretical domains. We have, therefore, chosen those theoretical frameworks that have received the most attention from researchers and society at large, that have become popular despite lack of strong empirical evidence, or that hold out the promise of generating information that can both broaden and deepen our understanding of minority development. We regret that this chapter cannot include all the pioneering work on substantive aspects of African American and Latin American children that has appeared within the past decade.

Fourth, we had to confront the potential danger of focusing a significant portion of this chapter on theories associated with developmental risk and problem behaviors. As we approach the end of the 20th century, literature directly addressing minority development remains scant. Consequently, any conclusions regarding differential ethnic patterns of risk and resilience are premature. When African American and Latin American children and adolescents are studied, there is still a tendency to focus solely on risk factors in predominantly inner-city, low-income populations. Relatively little is known about how working and middle-class ethnic minority children and youth develop. In the absence of data on protective factors, middle-class populations, and the conventional behaviors of the majority

of African Americans and Latin Americans, a review of the last decade of theories tied to research on ethnic minority development in the United States runs the risk of perpetuating negative stereotypes. At the same time, ethnic minority children and adolescents are disproportionately at risk for the social problems facing all American families, and to ignore literature on these problems introduces the greater risk of failing to provide data underscoring the need for social policies designed to protect and promote their future.

In the remainder of this introduction, we describe the changing U.S. demographic landscape in terms of shifts in population trends accompanied by changes in socioeconomic patterns, family forms, and student characteristics. We then describe and assess the extent to which developmental science has kept pace with these demographic changes with respect to representation of minority populations in research publications, omitted factors in such research, and the cultural lens through which minority development has and can be conceptualized. In the third section, we analyze how developmental science has responded to the changing U.S. demographic landscape in terms of theoretical paradigms guiding ethnic research, and the use and adequacy of definitions and measurements of race and ethnicity. We then examine the role and assessment of ethnic identity and acculturation as a means of understanding minority development, and the need to conceptualize ethnicity in terms of both ascribed social definitions and personal meaning. The fourth section looks at theories of developmental risk applied to ethnic minority children and youth with an emphasis on theories stressing biological versus ecological influences. We challenge the adequacy of current evolutionary and sociobiological theories that characterize problems faced by lower income, minority families as inevitable and biologically determined. We then review theories that move beyond the investigation of intra-individual, familial, and peer factors into the larger ecological domains of the neighborhood and social institutions, and which suggest that public policies and social institutions aimed at promoting minority development may in fact be propelling African American and Latin American children and youth toward debilitating developmental trajectories. We conclude this chapter by looking at ways in which the investigator's worldview can influence the design and interpretation of ethnic minority research raising a number of ethical, conceptual, and methodological issues that we believe researchers and students of human development should consider in the future.

THE CHANGING U.S. DEMOGRAPHIC LANDSCAPE

According to Rix (1990), approximately one in four U.S. residents is of non-European ancestry. On the basis of the influx of documented and undocumented immigrants from Latin America and the high cumulative fertility among Mexican Americans, it has been predicted that by the year 2020 Latin Americans will constitute the largest minority group in the United States (21%), with African Americans constituting 15%, Asian Americans 10%, and American Indians 1% . The non-Hispanic White population will drop from the present 75% of the population to 53% (U.S. Bureau of the Census, 1991; Vega & Amaro, 1994). Within the next half century, ethnic minority groups will make up almost half of the U.S. population. While proposed policy changes aimed at reducing immigration makes predictions based on previous population patterns tenuous, the drastic changes that have already occurred make it crucial for researchers, practitioners, and policy makers to have a sound understanding of the diverse ethnicities of families they study and serve.

Concern is growing that all is not well for residents of the United States. Fueled by perceived failings of communities, institutions, and policies to provide sufficient resources for quality of life, educational opportunity, and economic and family stability, there is increasing evidence that many of our nation's children are facing profound risks. This is especially true of African American and Latin American children and youth whose development, and even chance of survival, have been compromised by extraordinarily high levels of poverty, family disruption, domestic and community violence, drug and alcohol abuse, and unsafe sexual practices (Center for the Study of Social Policy, 1992; Dryfoos, 1990; Huston, 1991; Padilla, 1991; Tienda, 1989; W. J. Wilson, 1987).

Increases in Family Poverty

Increased levels of poverty have distressed families throughout the United States. In spite of elevated economic growth among the nation's business sector, families and communities have experienced heightened levels of economic hardship. During the 1990s, for example, almost half of America's children and adolescents were considered to be impoverished or living in families experiencing extreme economic hardship (Washington, 1991). Empirical studies indicate that poverty exacerbates developmental risk in infancy, childhood, and adolescence, and is a life-long issue for America's youth, families, and communities (Duncan, Brooks-Gunn, & Klebanov, 1994; Garrett, Ng'andu, & Ferron, 1994; Hashima, & Amato, 1994; Huston, 1991; Huston, McLoyd, & Garcia Coll, 1994; Lerner, 1993). Although government assistance buffers some of the impact of economic stress, the probability of being poor is not the same for all racial and ethnic groups. For example, during 1979–1989, only a slight increase in the proportion of African American families was noted: however, the number of poor African American families increased from 1,484,000 to 2,343,000 (Hill, 1997). The incidence of poverty is most extreme among African American, single-parent families, with over 50% of these families classified as living within economically distressed conditions (Jaynes & Williams, 1989). Despite the fact that the proportion of African American families in poverty appears to have slowed, African American families and youth are still more likely than non-Hispanic Whites to experience economic hardship (Chase-Landsdale, Brooks-Gunn, & Zamsky, 1994; Hill, 1997; McLoyd, 1990; Washington, 1991).

When compared to African American and non-Hispanic White families, the proportional increase in poor Latin American families was dramatic during the 1980s. While increases in youth poverty were noted across all racial and ethnic groups between 1979–1989, youth poverty increased by 9% for European Americans, by 5% for African Americans, and by 25% for Latin Americans (Center for the Study of Social Policy, 1993). By 1992, the Latin American poverty rate (26.2%) was approaching the rate of African American poverty (30.9%), which was significantly higher than the rate of poverty among non-Hispanic Whites (8.9%) (U.S. Bureau of the Census, 1993). In contrast to African American economic patterns, the largest share of the increase in Latin American poverty appeared in married couples—18.5% in 1992, 6 percentage points higher than in 1979 (U.S. Bureau of the Census, 1993).

The Latin American poverty rate, however, should be interpreted with caution, because not all Latin American ethnic groups have been equally impacted by economic hardship. The 1990 rate of child poverty among Puerto Ricans, for example, exceeded 40% whereas the rate of child poverty among Cubans was less than 20% (Aponte, 1991; Miranda, 1991; U.S. Bureau of the Census, 1991, 1993). Similarly, although the rate of poverty among Mexican American families increased by 2% between 1979 and 1989, the rate decreased by 3.8% among Puerto Rican families (Aponte, 1991).

Changes in the economic stability in the latter half of the 20th century, as well as unequal access to and benefits from the growing economy of the United States in the early half of the century, have continuously impacted racial and ethnic minorities, their families, and communities. Throughout the 20th century, African American and Latin American families have been buffeted by severe threats to their economic viability brought on by structural changes in the American economy, and they confront daunting prospects that this will continue into the 21st century. Disappearance of the agricultural economy in the South in the early part of the century led to African American emigration to low paying jobs and tenuous employment opportunities in highly discriminatory labor markets in the industrial Northeast, Midwest, and West (Rifkin, 1995). Once settled in the North after World War II, African Americans found job opportunities fleeting and now confront a job market where work opportunities have disappeared (Wilson, 1996). Throughout the late 1980s and early 1990s, an increase in low-wage agricultural jobs in the Southwest encouraged migrant Mexican, Salvadorian, and Guatemalan migrants to settle in this region (Housing Assistance Council, 1994; Rumbaut, 1994). For many ethnic minority groups, the recent reduction in the size of big businesses and scope of industrial production has eliminated many of the unskilled jobs on which they depended.

The Changing Structure of Families and Communities

During these economic shifts, African Americans (Benin & Keith, 1995; Stack, 1974, Sudarkasa, 1988) and Latin Americans (Keefe, 1984; Vega, Hough, & Romero, 1983) have utilized multigenerational kinship networks to provide for the care and upbringing of children as well as subsistence of network members. A strategic goal pertaining to child rearing has been to support the employment activity of as many able-bodied family members as possible. As a result, not only have mothers been employed at high rates, even when they are welfare recipients (Harris, 1993), but men and women have accepted less desirable work conditions to stay in the workforce (Presser, 1986, 1987) and maintained multiple, concurrent jobs outside the home in both the official (Stinson, 1990) and unofficial work markets (Valentine, 1978). The employment of African American and Latin American women and mothers is not a new phenomenon—what has changed is the fact that many are now holding concurrent employment in both the office and home based work arenas. The cost to women has been reduced family satisfaction (Broman, 1991). To sustain these efforts in families with children, grandmothers (Pearson, Hunter, Ensminger, & Kellam, 1990; Presser, 1989) (and sometimes grandfathers) (Kivett, 1991) have played a key role in child care in both low- and moderate-income minority families, even when they themselves worked.

Among African Americans, community norms include expectations that absent fathers provide family support (Connor, 1986, 1988) and adolescent fathers actually contribute more to their families than they receive (Goldscheider & Goldscheider, 1991). Fathers of African American children with adolescent mothers contribute child care and support even when these fathers do not reside with their children (Danziger & Radin, 1990), just as fathers in two-parent families (Ahmeduzzaman & Roopnarine, 1992). In Latin American families, the cultural value of *familism* encourages adolescent males to contribute economically to family welfare and adolescent females to assist in the caregiving of younger siblings (Fracasso & Busch-Rossnagel, 1992).

In the United States, the intact, never-divorced, two-parent-two-child family stereotype has been replaced by a variety of family forms. At some point in their lives, almost half America's children will experience discontinuities in their family structure and/or economic context (Ahlburg & De Vita, 1992; Featherman, Spenner, & Tsunematsu, 1988; Hernandez, 1993, 1994). Such dynamic changes in context can impact individual growth and development and underscores the importance of careful documentation and examination of race, ethnicity, family structure, and social class in developmental research (Dilworth-Anderson & Burton, 1996). In today's social and economic climate, failure to examine the conditions that facilitate and disrupt the development of ethnic minority children has been viewed by some as ethically indefensible (McLoyd, 1994).

The Changing School Population

Youth and parents living with economic hardship and poverty face increased risk related to individual and family development (Huston, 1991; Lerner, Castellino, Terry, McKinney, & Villarruel, 1995). Empirical work documents that ethnic minority groups, especially African Americans and Latino Americans, are at greater risk for negative consequences of life than most other populations living in the United States. The school population, for example, is rapidly becoming more minority, more heterogeneous, and more financially disadvantaged relative to the current European American, middle-class student majority (Meier & Stewart, 1991; U.S. Department of Education, 1991), and educators are worried. Minorities are a large portion of the lowest achieving 40% of students, and there is some threat that their increasing numbers will mean that the majority of our nation's students will be "at-risk" for poor educational outcomes in the 21st century (e.g., Chapa & Valencia, 1993; Hodgkinson, 1993; Humphrey, 1988).

DEVELOPMENTAL SCIENCE AND THE FUTURE OF ETHNIC MINORITY CHILDREN AND YOUTH

The challenge of constructing research paradigms responsive to ethnic minorities and their communities and of identifying supportive interventions that can benefit diverse individuals is becoming a central focus for many social scientists. The need for effective societal responses to the multifaceted problems faced by our country's children and youth has mobilized developmental scientists to provide ecologically sensitive and valid approaches to understanding the diverse characteristics of different cultural groups (Fisher & Brennan, 1992) and build upon the social capital that exists within ethnically diverse communities and individuals (Bourdieu, 1986; Lerner, 1993; Lerner & Fisher, 1994; Stanton-Salazar & Dornbusch, 1995). As McLoyd (1994) notes, "The economic well-being of the nation will depend even more than at present on its ability to enhance the intellectual and social skills of all its youth, as these will be crucial for maximum productivity in the workplace" (p. 60).

Representation of Minority Populations in Developmental Research

Given the demographic trends in the United States, as well as the increased interest in research that involves ethnic and racial minorities, it would seem logical that developmental scientists would be at the forefront of examining how each ethnic and racial group is impacted by structural changes in the economy and society. The ecological, life-span, transactional, developmental contextual, applied developmental, and relational theoretical perspectives (i.e., Baltes, 1987; Bronfenbrenner, 1979; Bronfenbrenner & Morris, Ch. 17, this Volume; Fisher et al., 1993; Fisher & Tryon, 1990; Lerner, 1986; Overton, Ch. 3, this Volume; Sameroff & Chandler, 1975) are among the conceptual approaches that have the potential to provide guidance. Yet, despite the emergence of these contextually sensitive theoretical frameworks and the magnitude of structural, economic, and demographic changes in the United States, the majority of developmental research is not focused on, and in general does not include, ethnic and racial minorities and diverse families. In fact, the majority of studies published in the leading scientific journals in child and adolescent development have virtually ignored development within non-European, non-middle class children and families (Busch-Rossnagel, 1992; Fisher & Brennan, 1992; Graham, 1992; Hagen, Paul, Gibb, & Wolters, 1990; Loo, Fong, & Iwamasa, 1988).

Graham, for example, conducted a content analysis of six American Psychological Association (APA) journals to document the status of African American research in mainstream psychology journals (including *Developmental Psychology*) covering a 20-year period beginning in 1970. Only about 5.5% of the articles published during 1970–1974 pertained to African Americans, *decreasing* to 1.5% during 1985 and 1989. Perhaps more alarming was the finding that the majority of articles that included African American populations failed to utilize acceptable measures of standard SES indices (e.g., Hollingshead, Warner, and Duncan scales), did not measure SES accurately, or did not consider the variable appropriately in subsequent analyses (e.g., comparing low-SES Blacks with either middle-SES Whites alone or both low- and middle-SES Whites).

In a content analysis of empirical articles published in 1980 and in 1987 in the journals *Child Development, Developmental Psychology,* and the *Journal of Applied Developmental Psychology,* Fisher and Brennan (1992) found they could not accurately assess the actual incidence of ethnic minorities in the developmental research surveyed since over half of the articles did not report the cultural background or ethnicity of their sample. When ethnicity was mentioned, the sampling descriptions often tended toward general descriptors (e.g., "ethnically heterogeneous," "predominantly White children") that prevented both identification of the proportion of participants sampled from different ethnic groups and examination of potential group similarities or differences in response to planned procedures. Moreover, when members of ethnic groups were a focus of study, there was a tendency to sample only those of low socioeconomic status. The authors concluded that research sampling characteristic of articles published in mainstream development journals serve to reinforce the stereotypic view that ethnic families are monolithic (McAdoo, 1990) and generally "different" than the "normative middle-class white families," as well as the unsupported assumption that with educational and occupational mobility, ethnic minorities will become indistinguishable from White middle-class families in their cultural patterns.

Discrimination: An Omitted Factor in Research on U.S. Minorities

While poverty has begun to receive attention as a variable in developmental research with minority subjects, racial discrimination has received, at best, minimal attention at the conceptual or empirical level as a major factor in the ecology of growth, development, and adaptation of African American and Latin American children and families. A small group of scholars have begun to call attention to the psychological impact of racial and ethnic prejudice, oppression, and exploitation on behavior and personality development as well as individual differences in responding to discrimination (Boykin & Toms, 1985; Gaines & Reed, 1995; Phinney, 1996; Sue, 1993).

Job and Housing Discrimination

Race comparative research designs typically omit middle-class African American and Latin American subjects, and compare low-income minorities to low- and middle-income European Americans. The apparent rationale is that social class supersedes race as a determinant of developmental outcomes and ecological niches. Data on the prevalence of job discrimination, suggest that this is an unwarranted

assumption. Even when job discrimination is not interwoven with the issue of low-income status, job discrimination is pervasive for African Americans and Hispanics. A recent government report found under-representation, career ladder truncation, and income disadvantage for African Americans and Hispanics in managerial and professional occupations relative to comparably qualified European American males in every industrial sector of the business economy (Federal Glass Ceiling Commission, 1995).

Analyses of the housing sector not only document the pervasiveness of discrimination, but indicate different patterns of treatment for various racial and ethnic groups. This suggests yet another reason for why theoretical models and research designs need to differentiate between minority groups to conduct ecologically valid studies. National data on home mortgage lending reveal discrimination in lending at all income levels against African Americans and Hispanics relative to European Americans, but no discernable discrimination against Asians in lending for home purchase (Campen, 1994; Canner et al., 1994; Canner & Smith, 1992). Analyses of national data on rental housing show discrimination against African Americans and Latin Americans relative to European Americans (Turner, 1992). Analyses of the housing market for African Americans reveals that housing discrimination plays an important role in employment and earnings disadvantages of African American workers (Kain, 1992). For child and adolescent development, housing discrimination is particularly important because it constricts African American and Hispanic options for school choice and access to growth-enhancing community resources. Available data suggest that Asians suffer discrimination in home improvement financing relative to European Americans (Canner et al., 1994; Canner & Smith, 1992). This may compromise Asians' relative social standing in neighborhoods, but does not limit school choices or access to public community resources. Thus, there are empirical indications that studies in emerging areas of research on minority children and youth, such as homelessness and neighborhood effects on development, would be improved by inclusion of discrimination specific to racial or ethnic group membership as a factor in their conceptual models.

Resegregation in the Schools

School desegregation and compensatory education have been the major educational policies for improving academic achievement of African Americans and Latin Americans in the last 25 years, but the changes they brought are modest at best (Armor, 1992; Conciatore, 1990; Ortiz, 1986; Urban Education, 1991). A frequent explanation for these minimal improvements is the contention that the objectives of desegregation and compensatory education were seriously undermined by the ways in which policies were implemented. Under the guise of desegregation, minority students—African American students, particularly—have been "resegregated." In purportedly desegregated schools, they are now found in low tracks, pull-out tutoring, and remedial special education programs; they are also subjected to harsh discriminatory discipline and suspensions, and otherwise denied the quality education needed for achievement (Arnez, 1978; Epstein, 1985; Eyler, Cook, & Ward, 1983). Over time segregation has increased, in spite of desegregation policy, and Latin Americans as well as African Americans attend highly segregated schools (Rumberger & Willems, 1992).

Some maintain that the minimal effects of compensatory education in the racially concentrated schools that African Americans and Latin Americans attend are attributable to an embedded disincentive to school systems to produce more than marginal improvements in achievement. As a matter of federal policy, schools with high levels of achievement lose funding because they become reclassified as no longer disadvantaged (Jendryka, 1993). Nonetheless, desegregation and compensatory education are critical to the small gains that have been made. Instances where these policies have been retracted have been followed by achievement losses. Elimination of mandatory busing to achieve desegregation in one southeastern city, for example, was followed the next year by marked decline in compensatory education students' achievement (Ikpa, 1993).

Discrimination in the Juvenile Justice System

Discrimination in the criminal justice system pertaining to drug trafficking has direct implications for the development of many African American and Latin American youth. Recent reports have revealed a disproportionately high number of and virtually exclusive focus on ethnic minorities in federal drug trafficking sentencing relative to European Americans who are involved with illegal drugs (U.S. Sentencing Commission, 1995). This finding is mirrored in patterns of African American and Latin American juvenile detention (Wordes, Bynum, & Corley, 1994), and

highlighted by the fact that drug-related involvement with the juvenile justice system is highest for African Americans even though juvenile rates of use of all illegal substances including crack cocaine are markedly lower for them as compared to European American or Latin American youth (Johnston, O'Malley, & Bachman, 1993). Thus, apparent discrimination in the penal system plays a key role in the life trajectories of African American and Latin American youth that is not accounted for in current conceptualizations or studies of their development.

Discrimination that ethnic minorities deal with in their personal and community lives may offer support to the notion that the developmental and ecological dimensions of growth and development may not be universal. As a consequence, contextual dimensions of the macrosystem and exosystem (Bronfenbrenner, 1977) should become more of a focus of empirical investigations that explore the developmental trajectories of ethnic and racial minorities. Failure to focus on discrimination may result in erroneous conclusions as to the significant factors that contribute to parental socialization, peer socialization, and in general, intrapersonal development.

The Cultural Lens of Ethnic Minority Research

Over the last decade, various researchers (e.g., Busch-Rossnagel, Vargas, Knauf, & Planos, 1993; Graham, 1992; Harrison, Serafica, & McAdoo, 1984; Huston, McLoyd, & García Coll, 1994; McAdoo, 1993; McKinney, Abrams, Terry, & Lerner, 1994; McLoyd, 1994; McLoyd & Randolph, 1984; Stanfield & Dennis, 1993) have argued that methodological practices for studying ethnic minority youth and families have not captured the specific contextual and interpersonal dimensions that contribute to and are a part of development. Padilla (1995), for example, has argued that cultural biases within current theoretical and methodological paradigms, lead social scientists to overlook or misinterpret developmental patterns that are normative within ethnic and racial minority communities.

Comparative and Deficit-Oriented Models of Ethnic Minority Development

Historically, studies of African American and Latin American children and youth have utilized comparative or nomethetic approaches in which the developmental patterns of European Americans serve as a standard for the selection of behaviors to be studied and data interpretation (e.g., Adler, 1982; Azibo, 1988; Lerner, 1991; Marín & Marín, 1991; McAdoo, 1990, 1993; Padilla, 1995). These mono-cultural procedures typically indicate lower or "deficit" developmental outcomes for ethnic minorities (Banks, 1993; Graham, 1992; Kohout & Pion, 1990; Sears, 1986), translating "us" versus "them" social prejudices into presumably value-free "adaptive" versus "maladaptive" categories of racial behavior (Takanishi, 1994; Tharp, 1994). The use of comparative and deficit-oriented methodologies have resulted in an erroneous monolithic view of ethnic minority development and a general failure to explore differences within populations that are harmonious with the basic values and characteristics of specific ethnic communities (Graham, 1992; Harrison et al., 1984; Laosa, 1990; McLoyd & Randolph, 1984).

Cultural Models of Ethnic Minority Development

While these deficit-oriented models and comparative studies have dominated research (Graham, 1992; Harrison et al., 1984; McAdoo, 1993; McLoyd & Randolph, 1984), a new paradigm is appearing. This research moves away from the deficit-oriented models and comparative studies and focuses on cross-cultural elements (Greenfield & Cocking, 1994). Frameworks such as the sociocultural paradigm (Laosa, 1989), the cultural-ecological model (Ogbu, 1981), the human ecological model (Bronfenbrenner, 1977, 1979; Bronfenbrenner & Morris, Ch. 17, this Volume), the developmental contextual model (Lerner, 1986, 1991, 1995, in press), the applied developmental science (Fisher et al., 1993), and the ethnocultural approach (Cooper, 1994; Tharp, 1994) assert the common perspective that in order to understand human development, multiple levels of organization are presumed to comprise the nature of life (Tobach & Greenberg, 1984). To understand individual growth and development, the changing relations among biological, psychological, and social contextual levels that comprise the process of developmental change must be examined concurrently (Lerner, 1991, 1995; Overton, Ch. 3, this Volume).

In response to the limitations of the comparative approach, some investigators have grounded their work in qualitative methods and idiographic paradigms that employ conceptual categories and worldviews adopted from traditional indigenous cultures (Burton, 1992; Cooper, 1994; Delgado-Gaitan, 1994; Jarrett, 1994, 1995; Suina & Smolkin, 1994). According to Azibo (1988), for example,

the Afrocentric approach challenges comparative studies that employ theory or methods designed to maintain African American inferiority. Similarly, Marín and Marín (1991), and more recently Padilla (1992) argue that researchers who study Latin American members need to understand fundamental cultural values and practices of the ethnic group under investigation to carry out useful research with this population.

Rogler (1989) has proposed that culturally sensitive research needs to include an open-ended series of substantive and methodological insertions and/or adaptations designed to mesh the process of scientific inquiry with the cultural characteristics of the group being studied. Investigations utilizing noncomparative methodologies stress the careful documentation of demographic parameters (e.g., language, community networks and the role that extended and fictive kin assume in child socialization, and conduct interviews in the participant's language of preference (e.g., Diaz-Soto, 1989). These studies generally shift their lens to document the assets, strengths, and resiliencies that exist not only in families, but also in the environments in which they interact so that the characteristics associated with normative and healthy development can be utilized in the formation of developmental theory, programs, and policies. In the sections that follow, we identify the general perceptions of race and ethnicity that underlie different empirical approaches to understanding ethnic minority development.

CONCEPTUALIZATIONS OF RACE AND ETHNICITY

In contemporary society and social science literature, terms such as *race* and *ethnicity* are used categorically without clear definitions of what these terms mean (Yee, Fairchild, Weizmann, & Wyatt, 1993). Some have argued that racial definitions represent a fluid social phenomenon "negotiated in a pattern of conflict and accommodation between the social movements of a nation's racial minorities and the state's policies and programs" (Chan & Hune, 1995, p. 209). According to this perspective, social, economic, and political forces continuously shape and redefine racial meanings (Chan & Hune, 1995; Omi & Winant, 1986). All too often these meanings, when applied to African American and Latin American populations, carry connotations of lives characterized by lower socioeconomic status and urban dwelling. Use of ethnic and racial labels to categorize individuals in social science research enables investigators to avoid dealing with the complexities of intra-individual differences within racial, ethnic, and cultural groups and the sociological and personal significance of these terms for the individual, the investigator, and the public (Cocking, 1994; Oboler, 1995; Ogbu, 1994; Stanfield, 1993).

A second, and perhaps more serious shortcoming of race-related research is the assumption that race and ethnicity are equivalent. The term race, for example, refers to groups that are socially constructed on the basis of physical similarities assumed to reflect phenotypic expressions of shared genotypes, whereas ethnicity refers to groups that are socially constructed on the basis of assumed cultural, linguistic, religious, and historical similarities (Oboler, 1995; Phinney, 1996; Ragin & Hein, 1993). Based on these definitions, African Americans, for example, can be regarded as a racial and/or ethnic group. Traditional psychology has, however, tended to regard African Americans solely as a race, subsequently ignoring issues of culture (i.e., attitudes, behaviors, beliefs, and values) that contribute to development (Anderson, 1991; Landrine & Klonoff, 1994; McAdoo 1993; Sudarkasa, 1997). The problem is exacerbated by the current fractionalized racial system utilized in the social sciences: each person is supposedly either European American or African American, non-Hispanic White or Latino/Latina. This fractionalization fails to capture the experiences of mixed-race or bicultural persons (Phinney & Alipuria, 1990; Root, 1992) and misses the opportunity to examine the conjoint influence of societal labels, familial attitudes, and social experiences underlying ascribed or chosen racial/ethnic identifications.

Biological versus Cultural Definitions of Race and Ethnicity

Theoretical and operational definitions of race and ethnicity are embedded within the social and political culture. As such, they have tended to ignore potential developmental differences between (a) individuals raised in families with a generational history of oppression in the United States and (b) recent immigrants from different generational circumstances (Oboler, 1992, 1995; Ogbu, 1993, 1994). As a result, the defining characteristics of race, ethnicity, and social class implicitly assumed in any empirical investigation of

African Americans and Latin Americans need to be explicitly described to allow the findings to be evaluated with respect to differences in participants' socioeconomic, educational, and historical experiences with oppression and exploitation and the theoretical, social, and political race-relevant conceptual frameworks that may be driving the research (Gimenéz, 1992).

Phenotypic Definitions

The utilization of racial categories in psychological research is grounded in folk beliefs derived from precolonial era thinking about the inherent superiority and inferiority of populations along phenotypic and genetic lines. This historical attempt to distinguish between self and others has implicitly driven social science constructions of psychologically meaningful racial categories (Essed, 1991). The result of these efforts, as summarized by Stanfield (1991), has been the tendency for descriptions of the "phenotypically different other" that is not only extremely negative, but is also the result of historical cultural traditions attempting to link phenotypic differences with presumptions about moral character, personality, interpersonal behavior, and intelligence. For this reason, current racial categorizations may have little psychological meaning outside of studying reactions to how one is treated by others on the basis of racial characteristics (Phinney, 1996).

The common classification of different populations on the basis of phenotypic and genotypic criteria in social science research has gone virtually unchallenged. Despite the fact that social scientists often lack training in biology and genetics, they frequently attribute, implicitly or explicitly, genetic meaning to differences between ethnic groups or statistics indicating correlations between developmental outcomes and race (e.g., Belsky, Steinberg, & Draper, 1991). Much of this type of comparative work focuses on cross-sectional analyses of diverse individuals and communities that yield static slices of social phenomena and ignore the meaning of actions and the nature of diverse developmental pathways within the historical and ecological circumstances in which they occur (Champagne, 1993).

Phenotypic definitions of race, based on physical characteristics (e.g., skin color, hair texture, facial features) reflect an arbitrary means of constructing groups based on common characteristics that can be traced to geographically similar environments (Jones, 1991). By focusing on the broader construct of race (which some consider as a proxy for genetic similarities) cultural and social variables that undergird behavior, beliefs, and values are often overlooked (Zuckerman, 1990).

Cultural Definitions

The concept of culture can be used broadly to refer to humans in general, a nationality, or a particular group. Culture usually refers to group ways of thinking and living, and includes the shared knowledge, consciousness, skills, values, expressive forms, social institutions, and behaviors that allow individuals to survive in the contexts within which they live (Nobles, 1985). The significance of this definition is that it underscores the notion that individuals possess particular, yet unique ways of interpreting and perceiving reality based on a collectivity of experiences, resulting in cultural knowledge. Thus, according to Spradley (1972), cultural knowledge refers to the learned behaviors, beliefs, and ways of relating to people and the environment that members of a cultural group acquire through normal processes of enculturation.

Weber (1973) defined ethnic groups as human groups, other than kinship groups, that cherish a belief in their common origins of such a kind that it provides a basis for the creation of community (Stone, 1985). In this definition, the fundamental characteristics of the phenomenon of ethnicity center on a set of beliefs and not on any objective features of group membership such as shared language, religion or biological traits associated with the everyday understanding of race. Examples of this approach can be noted in the work of Cross (1991), Nobles (1985), and, more recently, Padilla (1995). From this perspective, ethnic membership per se does not necessarily result in ethnic group formation, but only provides the resources that may, under the right circumstances, be mobilized into a developing person's choice to accept certain values and beliefs as well as the choice of a community to accept an individual. That is, individuals may be excluded from, or choose to exclude themselves from particular communities depending on whether the dimensions of similarity are sufficient to define or bind community members (Dennis, 1993). As such, the focus within a Weberian paradigm is not on the content of ethnicity, but rather, on the process and mechanisms that convert the potential ethnic attributes into full-fledged communities, thus, undergirding and influencing development. This approach leads to questions such as: "What are the distinctive dimensions that yield ethnic group formation?" "What are the distinctive markers that are selected and utilized to determine ethnic group membership?" "How are ethnic markers distinguished and maintained?" "How are these boundaries impacted and altered as a consequence of assimilation into new and different social groupings?"

A related perspective of race and ethnicity has been embedded in the theories of symbolic interactionism (Lal, 1990; Massey & Denton, 1993), which attempt to document the social processes as opposed to the social structures that contribute to individual development through the individual's own understanding of school, community, and governmental influences. Investigations can occur at multiple levels of the ecological system including how parents, teachers, and social institutions (e.g., schools, community centers, healthcare facilities, government institutions) contribute to individual development, as well as how individuals impact these ecologies (Donald & Rattansi, 1992; Rutherford, 1990).

To acknowledge that individuals enculturated within a common group experience share a distinct mode of social thought and a shared body of cultural knowledge implies that individual development is inextricably linked to ecological dimensions of one's environment. This shared cultural knowledge includes the skills, awareness, consciousness, and competence that permit members of ethnic minority groups in the United States to participate meaningfully in their culture as well as in all of its changing socioeconomic and regional variations. Support for this perspective is drawn from various disciplines documenting differences between shared knowledge in African American and European American cultures, including perceptual and value orientations (e.g., Burlew, Banks, McAdoo, & Azibo, 1992; Nobles, 1985; Walker, 1991), language patterns (e.g., Heath, 1989; Shade, 1982; S. W. Williams, 1991), and worldview (e.g., Meyers, 1988, Walker, 1991). According to Moll, Amanti, Neff, and Gonzalez (1992), failure to incorporate these cultural assets into research designs minimizes empirical efforts to document and comprehend development across the life-span from a cultural-historical and a social-cultural perspective.

Race and Ethnicity as Political and Social Constructs

Some have taken the view that racial variation is always created in the context of class differentiation governed by political and social constructs (Miles, 1989). Investigations embedded within this type of Marxist pedagogy, attempt to document the changes in racial and ethnic identity in historically situated events. Thus, some scholars do not focus on asking whether race is an ontologically valid concept, but rather examine what kinds of racialized identities are formed and developed within changing societies (Caldaron, 1992; Goldberg, 1992).

Support for the importance of understanding social and individual development related to historical dimensions of culture is illustrated in the work of Ogbu and his colleagues (e.g., Gibson & Ogbu, 1991; Ogbu, 1978, 1990, 1993; Ogbu & Matute-Bianchi, 1986). According to Ogbu (1990, 1993), one significant dimension that contributes to variable patterns of development of minorities in the United States is related to distinctions between U.S. born and immigrant populations. Ogbu argues that discontinuities in culture, language, and power relations on the one hand, and minorities' disproportionate achievements in a variety of areas (e.g., schooling, employment) on the other hand, may be related to different patterns of adaptation, different historical experiences that lead to different adaptive responses, and finally, to the intergenerational and intracultural support mechanisms that contribute to the development of individuals from culturally, ethnically, and racially diverse backgrounds.

Autonomous, Voluntary, and Involuntary Minorities

According to Ogbu (1991), the social, individual, and familial dimensions of development are significantly influenced by the historical and cultural dimensions of children and their families. These cultural-historic dimensions are defined by the context of individual or familial experiences related to the transition to life in a new society and to the status of an American minority. Autonomous minorities are people who are considered to be minorities primarily in a numerical sense. Examples of autonomous minorities in the United States would include Mormons, the Amish, and people of Jewish or Muslim faith. (See Ogbu, 1978, for an extended discussion of this category.) Immigrant or voluntary minorities are people who have moved, more or less voluntarily into the United States (or any other society) because they desire an enhanced economic well-being, better overall opportunities, and/or greater political freedom. Castelike or involuntary minorities are individuals who were originally brought into the United States or any other society against their will (e.g., through slavery, conquest,

colonization, or forced labor). Involuntary minorities were often relegated to menial positions and denied true assimilation into the mainstream society.

The utility of this framework lies in the fact that it encourages a conceptualization of development in terms of historically based cultural adaptations and collective identity. Voluntary minorities, for example, may be characterized by primary cultural differences (e.g., practices and values rooted in the country of origin, such as language and religion), whereas involuntary minorities may be characterized by secondary cultural differences (e.g., cultural perceptions and values that develop in response to political, social, and economic discrimination). Theoretical and methodological attention to individual and familial immigration histories expand the study of African American and Latin American development to include the nature of interactions with members of other cultural and ethnic backgrounds. It can lead developmental scientists to examine how cognitive, communicative, motivational, and social-emotional competencies may be strengthened or compromised through the assimilative and discriminative histories of individuals, families, and communities.

Accommodation to New Environments

While researchers have generally not focused on the historical aspects of societal integration or assimilation, there has been a significant amount of research in the realm of accommodation to new environments, generally discussed under the rubric of acculturation. Study of the mutual adjustment of person-to-culture and culture-to-person can bring theoretical and empirical clarity to the concept of culture as a dynamic process of person-environment interactions. Although, to date, the study of acculturation has been limited by lack of conceptual and methodological consensus, it has provided some preliminary insight into how cultural contributions to development are influenced by ongoing modifications of cultural practices based on individual, familial, and community accommodations to society at large.

Race and Ethnicity: Ascription versus Self-Identification

Struggles over ethnic labels in social science research is frequently embedded within social and political structures, either by design or by default. Given the ideological basis of racial and ethnic labels, it is not surprising that the inclusion of ethnicity in developmental science has been fraught with methodological and conceptual assumptions that, for the most part, result in findings and interpretations that are of limited significance. Specifically, the emphasis on ethnicity has generally focused on diluted, and fairly meaningless broader groupings, thus minimizing the opportunities that have been available to understand which historical and cultural patterns of that group may contribute to individual development. The majority of research tends to ignore participant definitions of race and ethnicity (Hilliard, 1989) and apply panethnic labels (such as Black or Hispanic) that obscure experiential and cultural differences among various African heritage or Spanish-speaking communities.

Panethnicity: An Attributional Approach to Understanding Race and Ethnicity

According to Gimenéz, (1989), the introduction and acceptance of panethnic terms impedes policy makers and researchers from truly understanding the real and identifiable traits that exist among, and between, ethnic minorities. Gimenéz argues that the panethnic definitions of African American, Asian, Hispanic/Latino, and Native American are not only exceedingly broad, but have the objective effect of "MINORitizing" and obscuring actual social-class and national-origin differences within ethnic minority populations.

For example, panethnic terms such as Latino/Latina and Hispanic most broadly include individuals who trace their cultural heritage back to the Iberian peninsula and whose heritage includes the Spanish language. The terms tend to obscure differences in national origin (e.g., Mexico, the Iberian peninsula, countries in Central and South America, and the three major Caribbean islands with a culture from Spain, Cuba, Puerto Rico, and the Dominican Republic). Any scientific or governmental effort to homogenize immigrants/emigrants or U.S. minorities and their decedents by applying panethnic terms like Hispanic (referring to a Spanish-speaking person) or Latino (referring to those whose origins are in Central and South America) is likely to unleash a heated political debate among those affected (Murguia, 1991).

Although the terms Latino and Hispanic are multinational in scope, in some contexts, they are not used in this manner. On occasion, these terms are used to refer to a single national origin group. The population of South Texas (largely Mexican in origin), the Bronx (largely Puerto Rican in origin) or Miami (largely Cuban in origin), for example, can all be referred to as "Hispanics" or "Latinos," and in these situations, the focus is on specific ethnic issues as opposed to panethnic (e.g., the aggregation of all Latin American) groups and issues. However, confusion results when research findings from these communities are generalized to different "Hispanic" or "Latino" groups in different parts of the country or even different regions of the same city or state.

Similar issues are beginning to be raised by the use of the panethnic term African American to describe individuals with a cultural heritage back to the African continent that may also obscure differences in language and national origin (e.g., colonial North American, South American, African mainland, or English and French speaking islands of the Caribbean). In addition, more general terms, such as "minorities" or "people of color" misconstrue scientific findings when they are used to exclusively refer to a singular panethnic group, that is, African Americans.

The use of panethnic labels should be interpreted with caution, especially when demographic trends are presented (Hayes-Buatesta & Chapa, 1987). First, these terms overlook qualitative differences between U.S. minority groups and newly arrived emigrants/immigrants of the same ethnic background. This leads to the denial of the historically developed identities and cultures of U.S. ethnic and racial minorities and of colonized minorities, emigrants, and immigrants (Nelson & Tienda, 1985). For example, striking differences in illicit drug use have been observed between American born "Hispanics" and those who emigrated to the United States (Amaro, Whitaker, Coffman, & Heeren, 1990; Gil, Vega, & Dimas, 1994). Thus, use of panethnic data to document the prevalence and incidence of indicators of developmental risk may over- or underrepresent true rates, and result in policy efforts that are not equally effective. Panethnic labels also tend to ignore variation in religious practices and differences in ties to the nation's metropolises versus agricultural-rural industries (Rochin & de la Torre, 1992). Finally, the use of panethnic labels may also result in an over/under representation of the true rates on various indices. For example, if one were to analyze Cuban, Puerto Rican, and Mexican origin data as a single Latino group data set, the results would be misleading because of the divergence in regions, demographic characteristics such as age and fertility, and in the socioeconomic standing of each group.

Another set of problems associated with these labels has to do with the meaning that can be attributed to comparisons among populations identified only in racial/ethnic terms (Hayes-Buatesta & Chapa, 1987). What does it mean to compare, for example, White, and Hispanic fertility? Or White and African American crime rates? Or onset of sexual behaviors among Asian, Hispanic, Black, and White youth? Or substance abuse patterns among Native American, Latino, and African American youth? Because the populations included in these labels differ in terms of national origin, social class, and socioeconomic status, such broad comparisons may contribute to the creation or the reinforcement of long-standing stereotypes about White superiority and minority inferiority, lack of self-control, lack of social responsibility, lower intelligence, and other racial myths.

Panethnic terms are also insensitive to issues of stress that may be related to the transition from one's country of origin to the United States, and which may vary at different politically salient points in history. For example, during the 1980s and 1990s, and especially since the passage of Proposition 187 in California, Mexicans as well as many Central and South Americans, are perceived as "uninvited" guests, whereas during times of U.S. economic prosperity or during national need (e.g., World War II), they were generally welcome. Thus, depending on popular views of immigration as contributing to or jeopardizing the American economy, immigrant groups are likely to receive differential treatment from broader sectors of U.S. society, which in turn will have differential impact on individual and family development (Portes & Rumbaut, 1990).

There is a great deal of diversity on various contextual variables such as social class, level of identification with the country and culture of origin, race, and level of assimilation into the mainstream culture of the United States (Muñoz, 1982). And even within specifically defined ethnic groups, individuals are heterogeneous with respect to income, socioeconomic status, immigration status, family structure, and group identification (Zuckerman, 1990). On this basis, some have recommended that to accurately document ethnic categories researchers collect information on race, place of origin, acculturation, age, socioeconomic level, ethnic identification, and other variables (Entwisle & Astone, 1994; Marín & Marín, 1991). Others warn that such within-group variation, makes it unlikely that ethnic membership alone predicts behavior in any psychologically meaningful way (Phinney, 1996).

Individual Meanings of Race and Ethnicity

Even when the problem of panethnic labels is addressed, investigators still need to consider whether ethnic ascriptions are consistent with the meaning of ethnicity to the individuals and communities under study. In traditional investigations, the experimenter ascribes ethnicity for the participants, or the participant is asked to respond to a relatively narrow set of choices. Take for example, the situation of a participant in an investigation who is of Cuban ancestry, living in Miami, and of African descent. An experimenter may erroneously assign this individual to the category of Black race (or more inaccurately, as African American), when the individual considers him- or herself to first be Cuban/Latino, and secondly, of African descent, and least of all, of African American descent. Moreover, the salience of these different aspects of ethnicity to the individual may change at different points in development and across different contexts. Thus, experimenters must reconsider not only the measurement of race and ethnicity, but more importantly, the meaning of race and ethnicity at the individual level.

Consideration of the meaning of ethnicity to individual research participants can challenge the utility of defining race simply in terms of physical characteristics (e.g., skin color, hair texture, facial features), the validity of equating race and ethnicity, and the assumption that ethnicity contributes to individual development in the same manner for all members. As Spencer (1995) notes, ethnicity can be increased or decreased in terms of individual ethnic self-awareness or identity in the physical, social, and cultural markers that become the basis for ethnic differences; in the number of ethnic groups in existence at any time; in the extent to which ethnicity organizes social interaction; and in terms of group (i.e., community) formation. Research on African American and Latin American children and youth can also be guided by the three overlapping aspects of ethnicity suggested by Phinney (1996): (a) cultural values, attitudes and behaviors; (b) subjective sense of ethnic group membership; and (c) experiences associated with minority status (i.e., powerlessness and discrimination).

RACIAL AND ETHNIC IDENTIFICATION

A "social characteristics model" of development suggests that differences between majority and ethnic minority developmental outcomes, especially those related to problem behaviors, can be explained by differences in social characteristics such as income, education, and employment status (Slonim-Nevo, 1992). Such a perspective assumes that intergroup differences disappear when ethnic groups are of similar demographic backgrounds. By contrast, the "subcultural group model," while recognizing the influence of demographic variables on development, emphasizes the independent role of minority group status on developmental risk and protective factors (Slonim-Nevo, 1992). The traditional approach to ethnic minority research associated with the subcultural group model assumed a cross-cultural perspective, where members of an ethnic group were compared to members of other populations (generally European Americans) to determine whether group differences emerged on some dependent behavior (e.g., academic achievement). If differences were noted, an interpretation was generally put forth that offered a "cultural" explanation for the group differences.

During the past decade, scientific investigation of ethnic minority development has shifted to a focus on individual and parental levels of cultural identity as a moderator variable in the normative development of children and youth (Burton, 1990, 1992; Cooper, 1994; Jarrett, 1994, 1995; Phinney & Chavira, 1995). Data from these investigations have demonstrated that universalistic principles of behavior do not always apply in societal conditions where structural and societal inequities (both real and perceived) exist and thus, impact an individual's ability to fully participate and benefit from various societal institutions (Cuellar, Arnold, & Maldonado, 1995). While the research emphasis on cultural identification has resulted in a movement away from comparative "cross-cultural" models to an emphasis on understanding the heterogeneity that underlies intragroup differences, to date the lack of consistency in definitions and measurement of ethnic and cultural identity has limited the extent to which current research findings expand our understanding of the dynamic interaction between development and context.

Racial and Ethnic Socialization

Understanding the early environments in which children first acquire a sense of themselves as racial or ethnic group members, and the contextual factors that influence their adolescent years is critical to an understanding of ethnic minority development. Various socializing agents (e.g., parents, relatives, and teachers) have contributed to the development of individual and group identity, but none as important as the family (Spencer, 1983). Research with African American families suggests that many African American parents socialize their children to be proud of their race and to develop coping styles to deal with racist practices, providing a foundation for the development of positive feelings and self-confidence as individuals of African American culture and heritage (e.g., Spencer, 1983; Thornton, Chatters, Taylor, & Allen, 1990). Harrison, Wilson, Pine, Chan, and Buriel (1990) suggest that in Latin American cultures *familism* is a key adaptive strategy for ethnic minority families, with adaptive strategies defined as cultural patterns that promote the survival and well being of the community, family, and individual members of the group. From this perspective, a positive view of self, family, and history are integral aspects of a child's developing ethnic identity.

Recent research underscores the importance of parental socialization in promoting cultural pride and buffering the impact of negative racial stereotypes (Bowman & Howard, 1985; Demo & Hughes, 1990). Parental messages regarding race can take on various forms (Boykin & Toms, 1985; Burlew & Smith, 1991; Cole, 1970; Jones, 1991). Some parents may view reactions to and compensation for racial oppression as the defining feature of their ethnic identity. Others may take a proactive, stance, celebrating the positive and unique aspects of their culture independent of the discriminatory practices of the larger society. Still other parents may ignore the cultural dimensions of their experiences in American society. Several scholars have begun to examine the impact of race-related parental messages on African American identity development (e.g., Parham & White, 1993; Thornton et al., 1990).

To date, the most extensive instrument development and validation studies has been conducted by Stevenson (1993, 1994, 1995) on the Scale of Racial Socialization for Adolescents (SORS). Drawing upon literature on key areas germane to African American family life Stevenson developed 45 items reflecting six domains:

1. Perception of education as racist and/or important for social advancement;
2. Awareness of racism in society;
3. Appreciation of spirituality and religion as key areas of strength and empowerment for many African Americans;
4. Promotion of Black heritage and culture;

5. Appreciation of extended family involvement; and

6. Acceptance of child rearing as it relates to survival of the family for the future.

Stevenson's program of research provides a model for the improved measurement of racial socialization based on value orientations indigenous to the family culture under investigation.

Racial and Ethnic Identity as a Life Course Process

Ethnic identity is a multidimensional concept that includes ethnic awareness, ethnic self-identification, ethnic attitudes, and ethnic behaviors (Phinney, 1990). The term has also been applied to define class experiences, linguistic styles, and certain values, behaviors, and attitudes that are assumed to be part of one's national origin (Oboler, 1992, 1995). With respect to group processes, ethnic identity has been viewed as an important means of:

1. Maintaining cohesiveness and stimulating ethnic group action;

2. Defining cultural traditions, values, beliefs, and social support networks; and

3. Facilitating the scientific community's effort to understand these dimensions of human development (Royce, 1982; Sampson, 1993).

From the perspective of the individual, ethnic identity, refers to one's sense of belonging to an ethnic group and the part of one's thinking, perceptions, feelings, and behavior that is due to ethnic group membership (Cross, 1991; Rotheram & Phinney, 1987; Spencer, 1988). As part of self-esteem and a child's broader sense of identity, ethnic identity contributes to the more global internalized, self-selected regulatory system that represents an organized and integrated sense of self (e.g., Cross, 1991; Spencer, 1995). Conceptually, identity development is achieved through the interactions of individuals with family, peers, and members of various social groups that individuals are exposed to or with whom they choose to interact. Ethnic identity is best conceptualized as an ongoing process related to developmental changes in experience and the meaning of group membership across the life course (Cross, 1991; Helms, 1990; Phinney, 1990). Ethnic

identity thus has profound implications for the ongoing experiences and psychological well being of African Americans and Latin Americans of all ages (Phinney, 1996; Spencer, 1995; Spencer, Swanson, & Cunningham, 1991).

Concepts and Measures of Racial and Ethnic Identity Development

Spencer and Markstrom-Adams (1990), in their review of identity processes among racial and ethnic minority children in the United States, discuss several methodological problems associated with the measurement of identity. Some of these shortcomings are common across the study of many different psychosocial constructs (e.g., instruments designed for and normed on middle-class Anglo populations). One methodological issue that emerges in the study of ethnic identity development is the possibility that constructs selected for measurement may represent self-attributes that are desirable in the dominant society, but not in the particular ethnic minority cultures. One such value orientation that has drawn increased attention is cultural differences between individualism and collectivism.

Individualism and Collectivism: Implications and Caveats.   Many measures of identity development derived from studies of middle-class children of European ancestry emphasize independence and autonomy as positive developmental outcomes. By contrast, interdependence or collectivism is a dimension of self-identity that is highly valued among some U.S. ethnic minority groups. Collectivism is characterized by an emphasis on interdependence, connectedness, and a general orientation toward the group (Markus & Kitayama, 1991; Triandis, 1989). Individualism and collectivism represent points on a cultural continuum, in which cultural ideals influence the socialization process, the nature of social relations, and the trajectory of individual development (Greenfield, 1994).

Recognition that African American and Latin American families may differ from their European American counterparts with respect to individualistic versus collectivistic value orientations has important implications for: (a) understanding patterns of attachment and reciprocity within nuclear and extended families (White & Parham, 1990); (b) avoiding misdiagnosing ethnic minority children as having psychological disorders associated with separation and individuation (Canino & Guarnaccia,

1997); and, (c) recognizing how mainstream school socialization practices may be discontinuous with interdependent family socialization patterns and children's sense of family responsibility (Fracasso & Busch-Rossnagel, 1992; Marín & Marín, 1991; Vargas & Busch-Rossnagel, in press). However, it would be a mistake to assume that interdependence as an element of ethnic identity takes the same form across and within different ethnic groups. For example, in some communities, valuing collectivism may have less to do with aspects of interpersonal dependency, but rather with the collectivity of family and community members that creates an extended environment of support, socialization, and solidarity that nurtures individual growth and development (Martinez, 1988; Vega, Patterson, Salles, & Nader, 1986). Given the heterogeneity and continual flux of cultural influences on individual development, it would be just as erroneous to assume that interdependence is a value held by all ethnic minority children. For example, the centrality of familial interdependence versus independence for ethnic identity development has been found to be tied to variations in immigration status and intergenerational differences in acculturation to dominant society values (Szapocznik, Scopetta, Aranalde, & Kurtines, 1978; Vega & Rumbaut, 1991). Thus, developmental scientists need to be sensitive to individualism and collectivism as a dimension of personality development and at the same time avoid assuming that the ethnic identity of individual African American or Latin American children is collectively characterized.

Ethnic "Minority" Identity, the Risks of Collectivism, and the Challenge of Duality. Gonzales and Cauce (1995) have raised the intriguing possibility that minority youth of today, especially poor urban youth, may not readily identify themselves with their cultures of origin, but as "ethnic" individuals defined by pervasive negative media portrayals of African American and Latin American youth as aggressive, violent, and nonconforming. As Heath (1995) points out, whereas previous generations of ethnic minority youth were raised in culturally homogeneous ghettos with identifiable enemies such as segregation laws and the KKK, today's lower income African American and Latin American teenagers grow up in culturally heterogeneous enclaves with abstract enemies like economic recession and cutbacks in school funding. For these youth, "ethnic" identification, if it reflects a collectivistic orientation, may be a developmental risk factor if it signifies

affiliating with local gangs for short-term survival, precluding future escape from the cycle of poverty and ethnic isolation (Heath, 1995).

For African American and Latin American children and adolescents, ethnic identity may also be conceptualized as a reactive process against negative social stereotypes (Matute-Bianchi, 1986). A perceived lack of status and economic opportunity may lead to internalized negative self-evaluations or to rejection of mainstream ideals (Gonzales & Cauce, 1995). For some adolescents, this reactive process may be expressed in their choice of an "ethnically oriented reference group" (Rotheram-Borus, 1993) with rigid boundaries and separatist attitudes that contribute to a strong sense of cohesion (Gonzales & Cauce, 1995). For others, reactions against negative societal stereotypes can result in a duality of warring identities (DuBois, 1903/1989) or may place them in what Boykin (1986) described as the "triple quandary" of developing a cohesive identity that incorporates components of their being American, Black [or Hispanic], and a minority. Within this framework, identity development may be conceptualized as lifelong tensions (a) between integrating the norms and values associated with one's culture of origin and with the dominant society, and (b) rejecting those mainstream values that demean one's ethnic origins (Phinney, 1990).

Racial Mistrust. A related and relatively ignored area of ethnic identity development is racial mistrust. Some have suggested that social disadvantage not only operates to increase ethnic "minority" identity, but to compound prejudice toward other groups (Demo & Hughes, 1990). Several investigators have suggested that ethnic minority adolescents learn to distrust Whites through cautionary information provided by parents, personal experience, and exposure to the media (Grier & Cobbs, 1968; Sanchez & Fernandez, 1993; Terrell, Terrell, & Miller, 1993; Thompson, Neville, Weathers, Poston, & Atkinson, 1990). Fordham and Ogbu (1986) in their analysis of Black high school students on the West Coast of the United States, described an "oppositional" identity that emerged in disconnection and alienation from a racist White society. For these adolescents, racial mistrust may be maladaptive if it causes them to withdraw from activities geared toward societal opportunity and reward or motivates them to engage in rebellious behavior deviating from standard norms (Biafora et al., 1993). Utsey and Ponterotto (1996) have recently developed a promising line of research validating the Index of Race-Related Stress (IRRS) to measure the stress experienced by African Americans as a result of their daily encounters with racism and discrimination.

Other scholars propose that it may be adaptive to develop a "healthy cultural paranoia" to deflect feelings of personal threats and assuage negative self images (Grier & Cobbs, 1968; Ramseur, 1989; Thompson et al., 1990). Cross (1995) goes further, proposing that for many minorities, and African Americans in particular, defensive oppositional identity is a bicultural strategy that has historically offered protection against prejudice and injustice while simultaneously enabling minority members to engage in socially constructive behaviors. Terrell and Terrell (1981, 1996) have developed measures of cultural mistrust for Black adults and children which, while still in their pioneering stages, deserve attention in studies designed to understand processes contributing to African American development. Versions adapted for Latin American (see Mena, Padilla, & Maldonado, 1987) and other ethnic minority groups can enable investigators to examine this important and understudied aspect of minority life.

Doll Preference as a Measure of Ethnic Identity. Presenting children with dolls with different racial or ethnic features to elicit their opinions regarding which dolls look like themselves, look nice, or are preferred playmates has and continues to be the classic method of studying ethnic identity in African American children. When doll selection methods are used, young children demonstrate a capacity for recognizing observable racial or ethnic attributes of a person as early as three years of age (Spencer & Markstrom-Adams, 1990). However, when responding to dolls, African American children are inclined to misidentify themselves in terms of race, even though they have emerging cognitive capacities for correct identification (Cross, 1985, 1991; Spencer, 1985, 1988). Some have suggested that this phenomenon reflects the learning of negative values attached to Negroid features communicated through the media and other sources of social knowledge (Semaj, 1980).

Spencer (1982) offers the provocative theses that high self-esteem might foster identification with White features because they are associated with valued traits. Alternatively, children's responses might reflect emerging capacities for employing socially desirable responses in testing situations. This thesis is supported by the finding that African Americans can be trained to prefer dolls with Negroid traits, although this training has only a short-term impact and is most effective if conducted by a member of the high status racial group (i.e., a White person) (Gopaul-McNicol, 1988; Powell-Hopson & Hopson, 1988; Spencer, 1985, 1988). Findings such as these have been viewed by some as points of reference for preschool education programs promoting pride in minority children's own ethnic and racial background to offset the tendency toward overwhelming White preference (Hale-Benson, 1990), although this position is controversial (Frisby & Tucker, 1993; LaBelle & Ward, 1994).

Acculturation

The term *acculturation* generally refers to the transfer of culture from one group to another. Within the social scientific community of the United States, the term has more commonly been used to refer to the adaptation of members from immigrant groups of values held by the majority group's culture (Mena et al., 1987). Within the context of the United States where European Americans constitute the dominant group, those of non-European American backgrounds are said to have become acculturated to the "American" lifestyle when they have acquired the language, customs, values, and other behaviors of the U.S. European American culture (Negy & Woods, 1992).

Rumbaut (1991) asserts that changes in cultural attitudes, behaviors, beliefs, and values at the individual level, while not a linear or orthogonal process, represents the evolution of a new identity of choice for individuals. Assimilation has been used to describe the loss of an original cultural identity and the subsequent acquisition of a new identity (LaFromboise, Hardin, Coleman, & Gerton, 1993). It is generally understood that within the process of assimilation or acculturation, that the individual adopts or adapts his or her behaviors, language, beliefs, practices, and values of the group to which he or she is acculturating, or undergoes what Mendoza and Martinez (1981) refer to as a cultural shift.

Efforts to understand the relationship between development and acculturation have been embedded within two broad frameworks: Centrality (the degree of immersion in a cultural group) and salience (the degree of personal identification with a cultural group). Acculturation, then, loosely refers to the extent, and process through which ethnic or cultural minorities participate in the cultural traditions, values, beliefs, assumptions, and practices of the dominant society, remain immersed in their own cultures, or participate in traditions of their own and of the dominant culture (i.e., the degree to which one can be considered to be bicultural).

The Dynamic and Heterogeneous Nature of Acculturation

The importance of considering stability and change in cultural influences on an individual's development and relationships has been a focus of recent scholarship (Ogbu, 1988; Phinney, 1991, 1992; Phinney & Chavira, 1995; Takanishi, 1994). In the study of culture, much work has been done that compares individuals from differing national or cultural groups on the basis of global qualities, particularly individualism or collectivism (e.g., Markus & Kitayama, 1991). These approaches tend to view cultural qualities as stable and uniformly held among individuals within each ethnic and cultural group. Yet, as developmental scholars have begun to document pressures to change that arise in response to new circumstances such as industrialization or immigration, they are beginning to consider culture to be dynamic (Cooper, 1994), with some cultural values and qualities assuming new forms as a result of interaction with different social ecologies (Kim & Choi, 1994).

Immigration History and Acculturation. Whether voluntary or forced, aspects of the process of acculturation (or lack thereof) can affect the adaptation of individuals to the host culture, impacting development in the domains of language use, cognitive style, personality, identity, attitudes, and stress (Berry, 1980). Furthermore, the acculturation process affects groups of people and systems as well as individuals. Recent research, for example, suggests that to a large extent, parents and other family members mediate children's ability to acculturate to various situations and environments (García Coll & Meyer, 1993; García Coll, Meyer, & Brillion, 1995; Stevenson, 1995), although increased acculturation can decrease the perception of family as cultural referents (Sabogal, Marín, Otero-Sabogal, Marín, & Pérez, 1987). Moreover, while certain behaviors and values may change with increasing acculturation, other cultural values and practices may remain constant (i.e., maintenance of the internal family system and maintenance of the perception of family support). For example, individuals as well as families may chose to acculturate in situations that do not require them to relinquish their traditional cultural values. Thus acculturation may not be linear and in fact, may occur only when individuals believe that the cultural behaviors they are relinquishing do not reflect their own personal values and beliefs (Phinney, 1996; Sabogal et al., 1987).

An important extension of the notion that acculturation may not be uniform across different environments and conditions can be noted in the seminal work of Rumbaut (1991) with Indochinese refugees. Rumbaut proposed that social scientists need to focus more attention on the "1.5" or "one-and-a-half" generation defined as those who were born abroad but who were educated and came of age in the United States. These individuals must cope, he argues, with two crisis-producing and identity-defining transitions: (a) adolescence and the task of managing the transition from childhood to adulthood; and (b) acculturation and the task of managing the transition from one sociocultural environment to another. According to this view, "first" generation ethnic minority members grow up fully identifying with the "old world" and thus face only the latter developmental task. "Second" generation ethnic minorities, born and reared in the United States, grow up to identify with the "new world" and thus need to confront only the former. But members of the "1.5" generation form a distinctive cohort in that in many ways they are marginal to both the old and new worlds, and fully part of neither.

As Portes and his colleagues (Portes & Bach, 1985; Portes & Rumbaut, 1990) have also noted, immigrant groups, especially if the expatriation has been involuntary, pass through three stages in their adaptation to a new homeland. Initially, the immigrant tries to deny the fact of displacement, a stage that has been referred to as substitutive, marked by an effort to create substitutes or copies of the home culture. The second stage, destitution, reflects recognition that there is little, or no opportunity to return to their beloved homeland. At this point, they may feel displaced from their sense of identity previously rooted in their homeland. The third, and final stage, institution, reflects the establishment of a new relation between the person and the place. Slowly, immigrants come to realize that they do have a new homeland, one where they can begin to establish roots.

Biculturalism.   Berry (1980) noted that some individuals develop a bicultural orientation, successfully integrating cultural aspects of both groups and a level of comfort within both communities as well. Biculturalism has been defined as: (a) a process by which an individual knows and understands both majority and minority cultures and alternates between them on a voluntary basis (LaFromboise et al., 1993); (b) a process in which individuals combine or deemphasize culture (Birman, 1994); or, (c) a process in which an individual retains a strong identification with their ethnic culture and a distance from the mainstream group (Berry, 1990). Drawing upon responses from African American and Mexican American adolescents, Phinney and Devich-Navarro (1997) have described these three modes of biculturalism as alternative, blended, and separated respectively. For many ethnic minority children and youth, subcultural values within their communities may be in conflict with norms of the larger American culture. Conflict of cultural values may pose psychosocial risks, especially during adolescence when minority youth learn that values of home are not supported at school (Galan, 1988; Szapocznik & Kurtines, 1980). While, biculturalism is a construct that has not been employed in empirical studies of African American parenting, it fits well with recent research on racial socialization. For example, Billingsley (1992) found that a clear majority of African American adults identified themselves as both Black and American, indicating they subscribed to a bicultural personal identity, which they would presumably pass on to their children. Some have suggested that the development of a bicultural competence skills repertoire serves as an important protective factor against adolescent problem behaviors by allowing youth to blend adaptive roles from both cultures (Bettes, Dusenbury, Kerner, James-Ortiz, & Botrin, 1990; LaFromboise, 1988; LaFromboise & Rowe, 1983; Parke & Buriel, this Volume; Schinke et al., 1988; Szapocznik & Kurtines, 1980).

The antithesis of acculturation and biculturation, as might be expected, is cultural resistance or separation, where the individual resists acceptance of the values and beliefs related to a second culture. Cuellar, Arnold, and Maldonado (1995) highlight a fourth distinctive process of acculturation: marginalization. Specifically, they note that some individuals may choose to abandon their original ethnic/cultural identification for identification with another group, only to be rejected by the group to which they were acculturating. The consequence of this stress between individual and community can leave an individual with little or no attachment to supportive networks.

Acculturation and Developmental Risk

An understanding of acculturation, biculturalism, resistance, and marginalization can guide research on dynamic within group differences in behaviors which promote or compromise development. Findings related to acculturation and negative outcomes have been well documented: Increased rates of alcohol, cigarette, and substance abuse (Caetanno, 1987; Gilbert & Cervantes, 1986; Goldberg & Botvin, 1993; Neff, Hoppe, & Perea, 1987; Sabogal, Otero-Sabogal, Perez-Stable, Marín, & Marín, 1989), increased rates of infant mortality (Becerra, Hogue, Atrash, & Perez, 1991), increased incidence of low birth weight (Guendelman, Gould, Hudes, & Eskenazi, 1990; Mendoza et al., 1991), and increased rates of delinquent behavior and adolescent pregnancy (Vega, Gil, Warheit, Zimmerman, & Apospori, 1993; Ventura & Tappel, 1985). These studies and other recent research with ethnic minority adolescents and adults suggest that adherence to traditional cultural values may serve as a protective factor, or buffer for engagement in risk behaviors while simultaneously enhancing health status. For example, Sommers, Fagan, and Baskin (1993) argue that continued adherence to the Hispanic value of *familism* in low-acculturated youth serves as a buffer against antisocial acts. Cooper (1994) also documents that when stress between parents and children on issues of culture are minimal, resiliency and the ability to cope with stressful situations (e.g., poverty) are enhanced. According to this perspective, adopting the values of the larger society can deprive Latino youth of the protective factors associated with other Latino values such as *respeto* (deference and respect for authority).

Acculturative Stress.   Whereas previous studies of acculturation saw adaptation to mainstream values as promoting psychological development, more recent research has been concerned with its potentially negative impact, "acculturative stress" (Gil, Vega, & Dimas, 1994). Although acculturation measures were traditionally assumed to measure levels of cultural congruity and change, they are increasingly used as proxy indicators of stress vulnerability. It has been proposed that acculturative stress can occur as a result of tensions that accrue for developing persons "choosing" to abandon, accept, or attempt to live between the world of parents and their local community or the "new world" of peers and mainstream society (Cooper, 1994; Gil et al., 1994; Tropp, Erkut, Alarcón, García Coll, & Vásquez, in press). Individuals attempting the transition into a new culture may experience difficulties in the areas of language, perceived discrimination, and, in the commitment or lack of commitment to culturally prescribed protective values such as *familism* and cultural pride (Vega, Zimmerman, Gil, Warheit, & Apospori, 1992). A focus on acculturative stress thus suggests that cultural congruity or conflict may be a mediating factor in an individual's ability to adapt successfully to his or her environment (Miranda & Castro, 1985; Vega et al., 1993; Williams & Berry, 1991). The central premise of these perspectives is that negative outcomes occur when stressors exceed the individual's coping resources, or stress mediators. Acculturative stress has also been used to explain conflict and communication problems between adolescents and their parents (Szapocznik & Kurtines, 1993; Szapocznik, Santisteban, Rio, Perez-Vidal, & Kurtines, 1989).

Measures of Acculturation

The conceptual and methodological issues involved in the study of acculturation have been discussed across a growing range of members of ethnic minority groups in the United States including Latinos (e.g., Garza & Gallegos, 1985; Ortiz de la Garza, Newcomb, & Myers, 1995; Rogler, Cortes, & Malgady, 1991; Rueschenberg & Buriel, 1989; Saldaña, 1995; Triandis, Kashima, Shimada, & Villareal, 1986), Koreans (Kim, 1988), Asian Americans (e.g., Suinn, Richard-Figueroa, Lew, & Vigil, 1987; American Indians (Oetting & Beauvais, 1990–91), and more recently, African Americans (Belgrave et al., 1994; Brookins, 1994; Landrine & Klonoff, 1994; Munford, 1994; Thompson, 1984).

The utilization and development of scales of acculturation have included a variety of approaches, including a focus on predominant language spoken, semantic differential techniques, generational level, family attitudes, and combinations of sociocultural characteristics (e.g., SES, years of education, number of family members, citizen status) as a proxy measure of acculturation (e.g., Griffith, 1983; Lang, Muñoz, Bernal, & Sorensen, 1982; Neff, Hoppe, & Perea, 1987; Negy & Woods, 1992; Padilla, Olmedo, & Loya, 1982; Ramirez, 1969; Taylor, Hurley, & Riley, 1986). For example, Padilla (1980) identified two

factors (cultural heritage and language preference) to measure the broad category of cultural awareness, and two dimensions (attitudes related to ethnic pride and affiliation, and perceptions of discrimination) to assess the attitudinal component of acculturation focusing on ethnic loyalty. Scales of acculturation which have expanded Padilla's work include specific measures of cultural preferences in social/recreational activities and foods, language preference or use, religious attitudes, folk superstitions, and loyalty to or distrust of a particular ethnic group (e.g., Cuellar, Harris, & Jasso, 1980; Hoffman, Dana, & Bolton, 1985; Keefe & Padilla, 1987; Landrine, & Klonoff, 1994; Marín, Sabogal, Marín, Otero-Sabogal, & Perez-Stable, 1987; Montgomery & Orozco, 1984; Suinn et al., 1987; Szapocznik, Scopetta, & Aranalde, 1978; Yao, 1979).

While each of these approaches may have inherent strengths, the apparent lack of agreement on an operational definition and assessment device for acculturation may contribute to the conflicting findings characterizing the literature. In addition, until recently, most scales have relied on a single sum score for an acculturation rating, thereby failing to adequately measure biculturality. Félix-Ortiz, Newcomb, and Myers (1994) have begun to address this latter problem in their multidimensional measure of cultural identity for Latino and Latina adolescents. There is also growing evidence that as with other developmental processes, the transmission of culture across generations and its individual meaning is dynamic. For example, Portes and Rumbaut (1990) suggest that the content and significance of culture changes over time, is flexible, and is based on the multiple-network participation of individuals, familial sociodemographic markers, and common cultural experiences. Thus, new measures of acculturation must include ways of assessing the dynamic and individual meaning of culture for individuals of differing generations, immigration status, and different social milieus.

Defining Racial and Ethnic Identity as the Joint Products of Individual and Social Processes

To be useful, research directed toward identifying determinants of racial and ethnic variation must first reasonably determine the universe of variables that may be expected to afford some degree of theoretical explanation (Bean & Frisbee, 1978). When defining race or ethnicity as an experimental variable, investigators need to operationalize whether they are referring to differences of language, religion, color, ancestry, and/or culture to which social meanings are attributed and around which identity and group formation occurs (Nagel, 1995); keeping in mind that race and ethnicity may be defined through self-identification or ascription. Some have argued that the range of racial and ethnic choices is different for different people. Waters (1990), for example, noted that a wide array of "ethnic options" is available to European Americans (with reference to ancestry), whereas there is a much narrower set of choices available to American minorities. Indeed, while documenting the changing definitions of *Who Is Black in the United States,* Davis (1991) acknowledged the powerful ascriptive character of the Black racial-ethnic label in American Society.

Many factors promote racial and ethnic composition and identification, including choices of community residency and residential segregation (e.g., Massey & Denton, 1993), as well as other social, economic, and political processes (Portes & Manning, 1986; Portes & Rumbaut, 1990; Spencer, 1995). For some Latin American individuals, a major force in the maintenance and expansion of ethnic identification and ties in the United States is immigration. Whether they intend to return to their countries of origin, or are refugees who are temporarily or permanently exiled from their homeland, or immigrants who plan to permanently relocate in the host country, migrants are often seen by the host society as competitors for jobs, housing, social services, and educational opportunities (Belanger, & Pinard, 1991; Portes & Rumbaut, 1990). Ethnic distinctiveness of immigrant communities, and the impact on individual and family development, are enhanced and generally maintained when immigrants cluster together in ethnic neighborhoods or enclaves. Such communities may provide services to immigrants, such as assistance in finding jobs, housing, ethnic foods, foreign-language newspapers, social contacts, cultural events, and nonformal and formal education programs (Portes & Manning, 1986). At the same time, these communities may also serve to induce stress and conflict among members who attempt to acculturate to mainstream values.

Investigators examining racial and ethnic identity development have begun to conceptualize identity formation as an ongoing process formed from an individual's own experiences and the expectations and attitudes conveyed within the family, the community, and society at large.

Longitudinal studies based on culturally relevant aspects of self-awareness and self-esteem as well as community practices that facilitate or impede positive identification with ethnic minority status are needed to further our understanding of the impact of family and community on ethnic identity development and the meaning of racial and ethnic identity in the lives of members of minority groups throughout the life course. From birth through adulthood, members of minority groups are exposed to alternative sources of identification including their own ethnic group and the mainstream or dominant culture (McAdoo, 1990). Growing up in a society where the mainstream culture may differ significantly in values and beliefs from their culture of origin, racial and ethnic minorities face the task of achieving integration and reconciliation of different identities into a single self-identity. As we move into the 21st century, developmental scientists can no longer conceptualize race and ethnicity in terms of stable categories based on biological or traditional cultural values or ignore the impact of discrimination and ethnic prejudice on the socialization practices of African American and Latin American parents and on the social and personality development of ethnic minority children and youth.

THEORIES OF DEVELOPMENTAL RISK APPLIED TO ETHNIC MINORITY CHILDREN AND YOUTH: BIOLOGY AND ECOLOGY

Growing segments of the ethnic minority population in the United States are facing crises in the educational and public health arenas. The economic instability of the 1970s, the decrease in urban industrial jobs, and the fleeing of middle-class families from urban centers has created an ethnic minority underclass characterized by a chronic cycle of poverty, low academic achievement, and lack of employment prospects leading to high rates of crime, drug use, and other health-compromising behaviors (Glick & Moore, 1990; Padilla & Baird, 1991; Sommers et al., 1993; Tienda, 1989; Wilson, 1987).

Public school education and achievement of African American and Latin American children in economically distressed urban areas present a sobering profile. Racial concentration is associated with schools that are more poorly equipped and staffed (Ferguson, 1991; Klingele & Warrick, 1990; So, 1992), have larger class sizes (Tomlinson, 1990), and have more temporary teachers and higher rates of teacher absenteeism (Pitkiff, 1993). Recent research documents continuation of a long-standing trend of increasing achievement discrepancy between minority and European American achievement as students progress through the grades (Caldas, 1993).

Problems related to school achievement have continuously been found to predict later drug use, delinquent behavior, and early initiation of sexual activity (Nettles & Pleck, 1994). Low grades, lowered academic aspirations, and frequent absences from school have been found to be associated with smoking and marijuana use in African Americans and Latin Americans (Botvin et al., 1993; Brunswick & Messeri, 1984; Delgado, 1990; Jessor & Jessor, 1977; Scott-Jones & White, 1990; Smith & Fogg, 1978). Latin American youth who remain in school are also less likely to engage in substance use than European Americans (Chavez & Swaim, 1992; Johnston, O'Malley, & Bachman, 1992). Moreover, relatively lower educational attainment and higher levels of school stress for African American and Latin American adolescent females from all socioeconomic levels has been correlated with younger age of initiation of sexual activity and first conception (DuRant, Pendergrast, & Seymore, 1990; Gibbs, 1986; Gibson & Kempf, 1990; Holmbeck, Waters, & Brookman, 1990; Morrison, 1985; Murry, 1992; Robbins, Kaplan, & Martin, 1985).

Ethnic minority youth are also disproportionately at risk for public health problems. African American adolescents are more likely to die of injuries received from the gun of a friend or acquaintance than any other cause (Christoffel, 1990; Fingerhut, Ingram, & Feldman, 1992; Hammond & Yung, 1993; National Center for Health Statistics [NCHS], 1991), while the incidence of violent death for Latin American youth is three to four times higher than for European Americans (Loya et al., 1986; Smith, Mercy, & Rosenberg, 1987). While surveys consistently indicate lower rates of alcohol, marijuana, and cocaine use for African American teenagers when compared to European American high school students, once they reach adulthood these youth are just as likely as other groups to use "hard" drugs and run a greater risk of alcoholism and related diseases (Benson & Donahue, 1989; Gibbs, 1988; Jaynes & Williams, 1989; Johnston et al., 1992; National Institute on Drug Abuse [NIDA], 1991). Across ethnic groups within the United States, the age of first coitus, the frequency of sexual

activity, and teen pregnancies are highest for African American adolescents (Gibbs, 1986; Hofferth, Kahn, & Baldwin, 1987; Rotheram-Borus & Gwadz, 1993; St. Lawrence & Brasfield, 1991; Sonenstein, Pleck, & Ku, 1991). While Latin American girls have lower rates of sexual activity (Aneshensel, Fielder, & Becerra, 1989; DuRant, Pendergrast, & Seymore, 1990; Torres & Singh, 1986), disproportionate numbers of African American and Latin American adolescents have been diagnosed with acquired immunodeficiency syndrome (AIDS) (Bowler, Sheon, D'Angelo, & Vermund, 1992; Centers for Disease Control [CDC], 1992; Hein, 1989; Menendez et al., 1990).

Family income, parental education, parental involvement, and family structure have repeatedly been viewed as factors determining options available to minority parents and children and influencing development (Comer, 1989; Connell, Spencer, & Aber, 1994; Galambos & Silbereisen, 1987; Huston, 1991; McLoyd, 1989, 1990; Nettles & Pleck, 1994; Slaughter, 1983; Spencer, Cole, DuPree, Glymph, & Pierre, 1993). In some studies of low achievement and problem behavior, ethnic group main effects disappear when socioeconomic status is partialled out (Dodge, Pettit, & Bates, 1994; Hogan & Kitigawa, 1985). In other studies, the influence of socioeconomic factors on minority development is mediated by their impact on parenting variables or moderated by available community resources and family form (e.g., single versus dual parent families) (Barnes, Farrell, & Banerjee, 1995; Taylor & Roberts, 1995; Zimmerman, Salem, & Maton, 1995). Moreover, although high levels of parental support and positive communication often emerge as protective factors in low-income neighborhoods in which minority children and adolescents live, association with peers also serves to deter or promote problem behaviors (Elliot, Huizinga, & Ageton, 1985; Jessor, Van Den Bos, Vanderryn, Costa, & Turbin, 1995; Steinberg, Dornbusch, & Brown, 1992). Research indicates that while parental support and individual characteristics can buffer the effect of negative peer influences (Barnes et al., 1995; Cairns & Cairns, 1995; Gillmore et al., 1990), even with strong family controls, experiences with deviant peer groups (often encountered in disadvantaged schools) can weaken family control over involvement in problem behavior (Sommers et al., 1993; Steinberg et al., 1992). It is thus difficult to tease apart the effects of culture, family form, parental stress, and community resources from the effect of socioeconomic status per se on levels of achievement and developmental risk in ethnic minority children and youth.

In recent years, two distinct explanatory models for the relationship among developmental risk status, parenting practices, and ecological stressors have appeared in the literature—one is based on evolutionary determined adaptations leading to a culturally deficient lifestyle of broken families and welfare dependence, the other is based upon understanding how different ecological constructs within neighborhood and community institutions directly and indirectly influence development. In the next section, we begin with a discussion of the evolution-based model.

Evolution-Based Theories of Parent-Child Relationships and Ethnic Minorities

Evolution-based theories of parent-child relations and family life that are central to the current zeitgeist in developmental science are being used implicitly as explanatory constructs for ethnic minority development in contemporary America. The complex interrelationship between theoretical and sociopolitical trends in the United States requires a critical analysis of current assumptions regarding the environment of early human evolution in general and the economic, social, and physical environment of contemporary minority children and families in particular.

Throughout the 20th century, ethnic minorities have been buffeted by severe threats to their economic viability brought on by structural changes in the American economy, and they confront daunting prospects that this will continue into the 21st century. In recent years, reduction in size of big businesses and scope of industrial production has eliminated many of the unskilled jobs on which ethnic minorities depended (W. J. Wilson, 1996) and has ushered in an era in which many of the less skilled comprise an "underclass" characterized by chronic unemployment of large percentages of men, a radical increase in female headed households attributable to male unemployment, and deplorable social conditions that attend the poverty in which they must live (W. J. Wilson, 1987). Projections are that these trends will continue unless major social policies divert them. Although many believe that federally sponsored social programs developed in response to the civil rights movement of the 1960s countered the chronic, oppressive economic conditions under which ethnic minorities lived historically, a recent analysis (Jewell, 1988) indicates that the social and economic policies of the 1960s and 1970s, as well as those of the 1980s have undermined ethnic minority family development and the potential for academic achievement of ethnic minority children and youth. In this climate, a recurring set of ideas has resurfaced: Public resources should not be allocated to efforts to insure minority-majority equity in school achievement and social opportunity since biologically determined factors render some minorities, especially those present in the largest numbers, incapable of forming stable social attachments or learning on a par with European Americans.

In the domain of school achievement, this perspective is exemplified in the thesis of *The Bell Curve: Intelligence and Class Structure in American Life* (Herrnstein & Murray, 1994), that genetic endowment of African Americans will not support learning on par with European Americans and therefore African Americans are inevitably relegated to the lower class in a societal structure that increasingly demands high cognitive abilities of those in the middle and top tiers. Dunn (1987) maintains that low IQ and low achievement test performance of Hispanics are also attributable to group genetic deficiencies relative to the European American majority that cannot be fully remedied. Psychologists who adhere to this classical definition of IQ as a measure of intellectual potential concur that seeking parity of educational outcomes of African Americans and Latin Americans relative to European Americans is fruitless (Jensen, 1991). Still others maintain that a broad spectrum of adverse developmental outcomes observed in adults are due to genetic determinants (Scarr, 1992). Oddly, these contentions have received widespread attention just as results of extended-term programs of research on cognitive abilities are producing findings leading to contrasting inferences (Anderson, 1992; Baron & Sternberg, 1986; Ceci, 1990; Garber, 1988; Garber, Hodge, Rynders, Dever, & Velu, 1991; Gardner, 1993; Jackson, 1993). Moreover, cogent critics of the basic *Bell Curve* premise put forth by sociologists (e.g., Fischer, Hout, Sanchez Jankowski, Lukas, Sidler, & Voss, 1996) maintain that it is a myth and ruse that distracts scholars from compelling evidence of deleterious social policies and a purposefully created societal hierarchy that confines disparaged minorities to the bottom rung.

Scholars with biological orientations toward social development have taken a more indirect approach in providing deterministic explanations for patterns of family instability observed in some high risk ethnic minority communities. They have superimposed an ethological or sociobiological thesis onto the cultural-deficit models that assume that a maladaptive culture locks inner-city people into poverty (Baca Zinn, 1989). According to the cultural-deficit hypothesis people become poor by developing a set of wrong attitudes (e.g., men with little prospect for employment seek escape from parental responsibility) and by making wrong choices (e.g., women have children out of wedlock to obtain increased welfare benefits) that causes further breakdown of the family (Marks, 1991; C. Murry, 1984). Like the earlier cultural-deficiency approaches, the evolution based models rest on a family-pathology explanation which lays the cause of social risk and reduced employment opportunities to universal biological orientations which result in maladaptive patterns of development for low-income ethnic minorities.

Questionable Assumptions of Attachment Theory

The Bowlby-Ainsworth attachment construct (Ainsworth, Blehar, Waters, & Wall, 1978; Bowlby, 1969/1982, 1973, 1980) assumes an evolved specieswide propensity to form an essentially lifelong emotional bond to a mother figure for which the core affective elements develop in the first few years of life. It also postulates that identifiable varieties of such emerging bonds transcend cultural groups and experiences, are dependent on observable mother figure behaviors reflecting sensitivity to infant needs, are indicative of variations in infant mental health, and prognosticate future mental health (Waters, Vaughn, Posada, & Kondo-Ikemura, 1995). The theory and methods for differentiating types of attachments assume universal applicability even though criteria for classifying secure and insecure attachments and for prediction of attachment classifications based on maternal history were derived from maternal interviews, q-sorts, and observations of healthy, low-risk European American middle-class infants and mothers from two-parent families, and despite empirical challenges to the ubiquity of maternal sensitivity for infant attachment and later social development emerging from studies on these European American families (e.g., Seifer, Schiller, Sameroff, Resnick, & Riordan, 1996). Recent scholarship suggests that relationships among mother-infant attachment, maternal sensitivity, intergenerational attachment history, and an infant's life-long development may not be

rooted in evolutionary-based behavior patterns nor generalizable to ethnic minority mother-infant dyads.

Specieswide Primacy of the Infant-Mother Dyad. Consistent with traditional European and European American family forms, a key assumption of attachment theory is that infants are biologically driven to develop an exclusive secure-base relationship with a major (mother figure) parent who is not only emotionally sensitive, but who, by implication, is physically available for a large portion of the infant's day. This key assumption has specific, and potentially negative, implications for predictions regarding the social development of ethnic minority children in the United States who are often raised in multigenerational, extended, or single-parent-working-mother families. The extended and single-working-parent family forms in which many ethnic minority children grow and develop is inconsistent with the constantly available, exclusive caregiver mother-child relationships serving as the evolutionary-based family prototype for the attachment model. The assumption implied by the Bowlby-Ainsworth construct that the dyadic infant-mother bond served a pivotal adaptive function in the evolutionary history of the species has rarely been questioned.

According to Bowlby (1969/1982) infants were subject to predation in the environment of nomadic hunter-gatherers in which humans evolved. As a consequence, a species propensity for its young to seek protective contact with a specific mother figure when predatory danger arose was naturally selected. Correspondingly, reliability of mother figure responsiveness to infant distress was selected as the main mechanism for promoting an adaptive infant-mother-figure relationship and ultimately infant emotional security became a byproduct of these adaptive relationships. Maternal behaviors judged to be sensitive in contemporary infant-mother-figure social life are considered modern correlates of such mother-figure responsiveness in the environment of evolutionary adaptiveness. Central problems with this explanation are the absence of evidence that infants were subject to detectable predation in evolutionary history, such as attack by carnivorous animals, and the open question of whether a mother figure could have independently provided meaningful protection from such predators if they had been a threat. Actually, substantial information on hominoid evolutionary history suggests other scenarios for infant and child care than those proposed by attachment theory.

Homo sapiens are distinguished as a species by universal manipulation and controlled use of fire of 300,000 years or more (James, 1989). The probable use of fire as a weapon against predation (Goudsblom, 1989) would have provided not only mother figures but other figures in the small 20 to 50 person living groups in which hominoid life evolved with the capacity to ward off predators, and this suggests that infant survival would have been determined by the protective responsiveness of any band member if predatory threat occurred. Actually, authoritative opinion (Meindl, 1992) maintains that predators were undetectable microbes rather than carnivorous animals, and that infectious disease was the primary cause of death among hunter-gatherers. As a consequence, the greatest threat to infant and child survival was death of caregivers due to the ravages of disease; the life expectancy was 20 to 22 years old. Archeological studies of extinct hunter-gatherers as well as ethnographic studies of extant hunter-gatherers, also indicate that hunter-gatherer bands have a much larger percentage of dependent children than any contemporary developing or post-industrial society (Meindl, 1992). From an evolutionary perspective, all of this suggests that infants would develop survival mechanisms that would take into account the high probability that an infant's biological mother would not survive his or her infancy or would at any one point in time be focused on other offspring. Such survival mechanisms would lead to an evolved ability to form multiple and flexible attachment bonds that could facilitate protection by any one of the different members of a hunter-gatherer band.

In support of an evolved, multiple attachment perspective is anthropological evidence suggesting that the human species developed cultural variations in patterns of mating and caregiving during the hunter-gatherer epoch that revolved around the question of who the child caregivers were to be in that specific human group (Dunbar, 1992). In this regard, the multigenerational kinship networks characteristic of both lower income and middle-class African American families (Chatters, Taylor, & Jayakody, 1994; Dilworth-Anderson, 1992; McAdoo, 1980), and possibly other ethnic minority families, are consistent with caregiver patterns that would have been adaptive in the hunter-gatherer epoch and with probable, evolved infant capacities for multiple and flexible attachment bonds. Overall, information on the environment in which humans evolved points to the improbability that one pattern of dyadic infant-mother relations would emerge as an optimal universal determinant of infant survival patterns and, by logical extension, propensity for later emotional attachments.

Pathogenesis of Ethnic Minority Family Forms and Practices.   The majority of information regarding attachment patterns in the United States has emerged indirectly when minorities were included in small percentages in samples of ethnically heterogeneous infants from low-income families tested by the Strange Situation method (e.g., Lyons-Ruth, Connell, Grunebaum, & Botvin, 1990; Pianta, Egeland, & Sroufe, 1990; Shaw & Vondra, 1995). Moreover, even in studies with substantial or exclusively minority samples, ethnicity has been confounded with other variables, such as treatment condition, infant health status, and socioeconomic status (e.g., Anisfeld, Casper, Noyzyce, & Cunningham, 1990; Rodning, Beckwith, & Howard, 1990; Stahlecker & Cohen, 1985). With rare exception, ethnically homogeneous minority samples of substantial size have not been studied, leaving unanswered questions of typical distribution patterns for specific minority groups. Nonetheless, references to studies that actually included only a small proportion of minority families are often mistakenly presumed by others to be based on work with ethnic minorities primarily, apparently because the samples were described as low income and high risk (e.g., Baumrind, 1995; M. N. Wilson, 1986).

A key finding of reviews of studies using Strange Situation methods is a larger proportion of infant-mother figure behaviors classified as indicative of insecure attachment (45%–54%) among low-income infants in comparison to middle-class European American samples (33%; Van IJzendoorn & Kroonenberg, 1988). Typically, the classifications of the minority infants who are among the low-income subjects are assumed to be valid (e.g., Frodi et al., 1984) and the interpretation of this finding is that there are more insecurely attached infants among minorities due to the stressful life experiences commonly associated with their low-income circumstances (e.g., Broussard, 1995).

A few studies of specific minority groups suggest that minority cultural experiences affect Strange Situation classifications and lead to developmental correlates that are not explained by the attachment construct. For example, Fracasso, Busch-Rossnagel, and Fisher (1994) after finding high levels of insecure mother-infant attachments in female, but not male lower income Dominican and Puerto

Rican infants, proposed that the Hispanic cultural value of *machismo*—an emphasis on male independence and assertiveness—may have been operating to promote secure attachments for male infants in spite of environmental stressors. Contrary to expectations based upon observations of non-Hispanic dyads, Fracasso and her colleagues also found that increased use of maternal physical interventions was positively associated with secure attachment classification. The researchers entertained the provocative possibility that sensitive parenting among low-income Hispanics who often live in crowded homes may be reflected in abrupt physical interventions aimed at protecting infants from physical hazards. Harwood's (1992) finding that Puerto Rican mothers place a high value on socializing their infants for appropriate public demeanor (in contrast to European American mothers' concern with infant autonomy) similarly suggests that parental correlates of secure attachments may differ for some Hispanic and European American groups.

Studies with African American mother-infant dyads fail to support current theoretical linkages among attachment classifications, maternal sensitivity, the mother's own working model of attachment, and infant social behavior (e.g., Bakeman & Brown, 1980; Kennedy & Bakeman, 1984). Bakeman has noted that secure African American infants who appeared to avidly explore the environment in the Strange Situation playroom might be erroneously categorized as avoidant in the conventional classification scheme (Kennedy & Bakeman, 1984). In a related study, Jackson (1986, 1993) found that neither the strange situation nor a longer modification of it elicited distress in a majority of African American infants. In interpreting her findings, Jackson (1986, 1993) highlighted the African American cultural premise that infants have the capacity for multiple attachments and diffusion of attachment affect across a number of caregivers (Shimkin, Louie, & Frate, 1978), and suggested that African American attachments from infancy onward are both more flexible and more complex than those described for European American samples.

The Need for Culturally Anchored Conceptions of Attachment. Findings like those reported above are not interpretable within the conventional attachment theoretical framework, thus highlighting the need to reexamine several assumptions of the theory about contemporary and primordial ecological factors that are presumed to impinge on attachment formation capacities. The assumption that maternal sensitivity is a transcultural, socially independent, historically determined factor in attachment formation for individuals in cultural groups with complex family patterns or those in clinical groups with culturally atypical family histories has not been empirically validated. Even though contemporaneous measurement of maternal images of childhood attachments (i.e., representations) predicts infant-mother attachments in the Strange Situation for European American samples (van IJzendoorn, 1995), it does not logically follow that mothers' actual childhood experiences determine such images (Fox, 1995). The possibility that multilinear ontogenetic influences, multilinear concurrent influences, and interactions of these types of influences operate to define cultural as well as individual determinants of maternal sensitivity and intergenerational patterns of attachment is not precluded by the evidence. The incoherence and diversity of research findings on maternal sensitivity and intergenerational attachments for minorities in the United States raises the question of universality of construct validity for these operational concepts. At a minimum, they highlight the need for cultural specificity and clear delineation of the social ecology of infancy in future studies of the attachment construct.

Jackson (1986, 1993) proposed that a culturally anchored conception of infant social experiences needs to be coordinated with attachment theory to derive meaningful understanding of infant social development for specific cultural groups. Jackson's perspective suggests that in extended and multikin ethnic minority families, measurements of maternal sensitivity of individual caregivers might not predict individual attachments in an independent linear manner. For example, individual infants with multiple caregivers might form inequitable attachments to individual caregivers, complicating univariate predictions of secure-base behavior based upon the relationship with the primary caregiver. Alternatively, an infant might have equitable affective investment in several caretakers, but these might produce dissimilar attachment-related responses. Another alternative is that minority infant attachment, especially in extended or multikin networks, is vested in a set of figures such that experiences of security or insecurity would require multiperson presence for activation. Yet another alternative is that all of these possibilities obtain at different times over the course of early and lifelong development. In essence, security of attachment is a culture and context-bond phenomenon.

Evolution, Early Socialization, and Reproduction: Hypothetical Linkages

Belsky, Steinberg, and Draper (1991) proposed that humans have a biological disposition to acquire one of two distinct reproductive strategies: sexual promiscuity or enduring pair bonding. The Type I and Type II divergent pathways toward what Belsky et al. (1991) labeled reproductive "success" closely resemble popular stereotypes of minority, low-income and European American middle-class families, respectively.

In the Type I strategy, parents, who have inadequate financial resources, high stress, and marital discord (or father absence) subject their children to harsh, rejecting, and inconsistent child-rearing environments. As a consequence, children from low-income families form insecure attachments, generalized mistrust, and opportunistic interpersonal orientations manifested in aggressive and noncompliant male behaviors and anxious depressed female behaviors. These factors combine to force premature puberty, early sexual activity, short-term and unstable pair-bonds, and limited parental investment. In contrast, financial security and spousal harmony in Type II families leads to sensitive, supportive, and affectionate parenting producing secure attachment, trust, and a reciprocally rewarding interpersonal orientation. Such parenting results in delayed puberty and sexual activity for offspring, and leads to long-term enduring pair bonds and greater parental investment.

Pubertal Timing: Omitted Roles of Nutrition and Living Conditions. The Belsky et al. (1991) model, while loosely based on correlational data with humans and experimental data with animals, gains little support from each. For example, the authors rely on "unspecified biological mechanisms" to explain the influence of stressful family experiences on accelerated puberty. However, such speculations run counter to evidence that pubertal timing is influenced by genetic factors (Plomin & Fulker, 1987) and socioeconomically linked variations in obesity (Morrison et al., 1994). Moreover, a study designed to directly test the stress-somatic hypothesis found no relationship between internalizing and externalizing problems at age seven and early maturation (Moffit, Caspi, & Belsky, 1990). In fact,

pubertal onset is *inversely* correlated with poor nutrition (Marshall, 1978) and adequacy of living conditions such that earlier puberty is associated with better living conditions for Black African (Cameron & Wright, 1990), Asian (So & Yen, 1992), and Caucasian (Tanner, 1992) groups on a worldwide basis. For Caucasians, a very rapid decrease from age of menarche at approximately 16 years to 13 years occurred during the Industrial Revolution from 1860 to 1960 (Tanner, 1992); a period that produced the adequate financial resources, life expectancies, and long-term marital histories that ostensibly resemble those of the Type II family. Moreover, contemporary native Japanese who live under good environmental conditions undergo menarche a year before their Caucasian counterparts (Tanner, 1992), yet Japan has the lowest rate of single-parent households of all developed countries (Lloyd & Duffy, 1995), and Japanese are noted for particularly attentive mothering practices that provide a distinctive harmonious, minimally stressful childhood social relational experience for children (Lebra, 1994). Belsky et al. (1991) attempt to address the incompatibility of their theory to current empirical findings by suggesting an unspecified curvilinear approach to the relationship between stress and maturation. As Hinde (1991) points out, however, such an approach "makes it possible for almost any general prediction about the effects of stress to be confirmed given the right circumstances" (p. 674).

Primordial and Contemporary Parental Pair Bonding. Another problem is Belsky et al.'s (1991) presumption that an expectation of weak pair bonding leads to an "adaptive, quantitative" approach to reproduction, characterized by multiple births to single mothers. Such a perspective does not take into account the possibility that in an environment with few economic resources, in which females cannot count on males to support them, sexual promiscuity and subsequent increased childbearing can directly threaten the survival of both the mother and other offspring (Maccoby, 1991). As currently articulated, the sociobiological perspective also fails to take into account the equally plausible possibilities that an expectant mother's decision to remain single can represent planful competence rather than interpersonal deviance when the father does not have either the financial or emotional resources to make a positive contribution to the offspring's development (Elder & Ardelt, in press) or that an adolescent's reproductive behavior is influenced by cultural values that involve prospective grandparents' and community standards for accepting adolescence as the period of opportunity for initiating parenthood (Stack & Burton, 1993).

The hypothesis that pair bonding behaviors are a function of childhood experiences is also inconsistent with data on worldwide trends in family structure. Research (e.g., Bruce, Lloyd, Leonard, Engle, & Duffy, 1995) in developing as well as developed countries has shown a rapid, worldwide increase in the rate of single-parent households within the space of 10-year intervals that is greater than individual differences in ontogenetic experiences could produce; researchers judge the trend to be an effect of structural, worldwide economic changes. Similarly, African Americans (W. J. Wilson, 1987), Puerto Ricans, Mexicans, and some Salvadorians living in the United States have experienced a rapid increase in the number of single-parent households in the last three decades that has been attributed to structural economic changes that have displaced them from the workforce. For low-income African Americans and Latin Americans who have lived in the United States throughout the period after World War II, stable pair bonding has been further eroded on a widespread basis for the displaced who rely on public assistance by historical and current public assistance agency policies, such as enforcement of "man-in-the-house" rules prohibiting female recipients from consorting with men (Piven & Cloward, 1993; Richardson, 1995). Thus, many empirically documented social contextual factors beyond the control of individuals explain differences in rates of single-parent families that Belsky, Steinberg, and Draper attribute to predisposition to one of two reproductive strategies.

Parental Investment in Offspring. Gender differences in parental investment are identified as central to the sociobiological perspective in which Type I males are characterized as less involved and nonsupportive of their children. However, the actual behaviors of minority men do not comport with the neglecting father image put forth by the theory. In particular, as noted earlier, recent research indicates that across different socioeconomic levels and family forms African American, Mexican, and Puerto Rican fathers are as inclined or more inclined than European American fathers to provide support for their children, although there are culturally linked differences in the type of support (e.g., financial, in-kind, direct

child-care provided) (Ahmeduzzaman & Roopnarine, 1992; Danziger & Radin, 1990; Roopnarine & Ahmeduzzaman, 1993; Stier & Tienda, 1993; Zimmerman, Salem, & Maton, 1995).

Stier and Tienda (1993) studied fathers in inner city Chicago with a range of economic statuses, but a substantial percentage were low income and separated from their children. Their sample was sufficiently large to differentiate between African American, Mexican, Puerto Rican, and European Americans. They found that minority fathers who did not reside with their children were as inclined or more inclined than European American fathers to provide support for their children, but there were ethnic variations in the form of support. Mexican fathers provided more financial support, less in-kind support, but the least caregiving and child visitation in comparison to the others. African Americans and European Americans were equally inclined to provide financial support, and in-kind support, but African American fathers were distinguished by greater frequency of daily contacts with their children, lowest frequency of no daily contacts with their children, lowest frequency of no contact with their children, and the highest rates of providing direct child care. Puerto Rican fathers occupied a medial position between African Americans and Mexican fathers in frequency of providing different forms of support to their children. Danziger and Radin (1990) studied parent involvement among fathers of children born to minority (primarily African American) and European American adolescent mothers and found the fathers of minority mothers' children were more likely to be involved and that the younger the father of the minority mother's child, the more likely he was to be involved; age of fathers of children of European American mothers had no effect on involvement. Ahmeduzzaman and Roopnarine (1992) studied African American fathers of preschoolers in two-parent families and found that neither paternal age nor income were determinants of extent of support; education and extra-familial supports such as extended family help, however, were positively associated with paternal involvement. For Puerto Rican fathers in two-parent families (Roopnarine & Ahmeduzzaman, 1993), neither income nor education were associated with degree of involvement.

Parental investment alone determines both quantity and quality of child rearing in the Belsky et al. (1991) thesis even though, as discussed earlier, neither hominoid evolutionary history (Dunbar, 1992) nor modern cross-cultural ethnography support such a limited view of who significant child caregivers might be (Murdock, 1962). Related problems with the sociobiological perspective is the indeterminate meaning of "security of attachment" outside of European American middle-class contexts (see above) and the documented contributions of extended family among African Americans (e.g., McAdoo, 1978, 1980; Stack, 1974; Stier & Tienda, 1993) even when economic hardship is a concomitant of such contributions (Minkler & Roe, 1993).

Ethnicity as a Buffer against Maltreatment. Commonplace opinion holds that low-income people are more abusive than higher income people, and life under poverty conditions is associated with a higher incidence of child maltreatment (Baumrind, 1995). However, there are several rarely acknowledged factors that buffer children against maltreatment even under poverty conditions, and minority ethnic background is one of those buffering factors (Garbarino & Ebata, 1983). Although minority children are overrepresented among maltreated children who come to the attention of public agencies, studies such as the one conducted by Zuravin and Greif (1989) comparing African Americans and European Americans find that minorities are as or less likely to have been maltreated by their mothers and suggest that minority parents are less likely to be perpetrators of abuse (National Center on Child Abuse and Neglect, 1988; Zuravin & Greif, 1989). Although some studies find that minority children are overrepresented among the officially neglected (e.g., Giovannoni & Becerra, 1979; Ringwalt & Caye, 1989; Saunders, Nelson, & Landsman, 1993; Wolock & Horowitz, 1979), as distinguished from the abused, this has been attributed to greater material inequity between minority and majority mothers.

Saunders, Nelson, and Landsman (1993) studied African American and European American families for which child neglect had been alleged in a large urban setting. Even though virtually all families were low income, they found that the African American mothers were lower income than their European American counterparts, were lower income than their predominantly African American neighbors, suffered poorer physical health than their European American counterparts, but suffered no more psychological distress on measures of depression and two other mental health

problems and suffered less anxiety than their European American counterparts. National epidemiological surveys of the incidence of child maltreatment have not reported patterns of maltreatment by perpetrator. However, they do report finding a complete absence of association of race or ethnicity with any category of maltreatment as well as no association of race or ethnicity with maltreatment in general (National Center on Child Abuse and Neglect, 1988). As contrary to commonplace opinion of minority child rearing as these findings may be, those on values and attitudes toward potential maltreatment provide even more stunning ethnic and social class contrasts to these assertions.

Giovannoni and Becerra (1979) conducted a large survey of African American, Hispanic, and European American adults representative of households in Los Angeles to examine ethnic differences in philosophy of child rearing and perceptions of social conditions that might forewarn of impending child abuse. Using a large set of vignettes to elicit respondent opinions on severity of abuse or potential abuse, they found that minorities rated the circumstances described as more serious than European Americans and that lower class and less educated respondents rated the vignettes as more serious than higher and more educated respondents. Even though some differences existed between African American and Hispanics in relative ranking of different types of abuse, African American and Spanish-speaking Hispanics gave the highest ratings of seriousness to the descriptions of abuse and potential abuse. Ringwalt and Caye (1989) essentially replicated these findings a decade later in a sample of African American and European American adults in the rural south. They found lower income and lesser educated respondents rated threat of abuse more seriously than higher income and more educated respondents. Their test for racial group differences, with income and education controlled, was marginally significant, indicating African Americans rated maltreatment and prospective maltreatment more serious than European Americans. Thus, the empirical record provides data indicating minority child rearing values are likely to foster adult responsiveness to the needs of children to promote secure attachment formation. It also provides a plausible explanation of the buffering influence of minority status against child maltreatment under the hazardous living conditions that low income imposes in the United States. In sum, a confluence of empirical findings indicate cultural and social class child rearing actualities that countermand the applicability of Belsky, Steinberg, and Draper's (1991) theory for racial and ethnic minorities in the United States.

In the absence of prospective longitudinal research, speculative, universal, deterministic models of adolescent sexual behavior with their societal implications for policies directed at low-income minority youth remain untested. Ecologically based theories of development underscore the need for research on ethnic minority adolescent risk behaviors that examine: (a) variation in the individual, familial, and neighborhood contexts; (b) the reciprocal and continuous interplay between person and environment; (c) factors contributing to the ability of low-income families to provide loving and supportive parenting; (d) subcultural values that serve as protective factors in high stress environments; (e) neighborhood effects that can exert influences above and beyond biological and parental variables; and (f) the potential impact of racism and discrimination on a sense of futility in the future for which behaviors such as early sexual intimacy and childbearing may be seen as providing purpose and life satisfaction.

Neighborhoods and Schools: Ecologies of Risk and Opportunity

There is an emerging literature on high-risk behaviors in ethnic minority youth that moves beyond the investigation of intra-individual, familial, and peer factors into the larger ecological domains of the neighborhood and social institutions (Aber, 1994; Brooks-Gunn, Duncan, Klebanov, & Sealand, 1993; Dornbusch, Ritter, & Steinberg, 1991; Hogan & Kitigawa, 1985). While research on community influences is still scarce, there is a trend toward combining psychological and sociological theory to develop methodologies that can broaden our understanding of how different ecological constructs directly and indirectly influence development (Crane, 1991; Jencks & Mayer, 1990; Sampson & Groves, 1989; Wilson, 1987). The integration of psychological and sociological theory allows investigators to move beyond the study of direct demographic, personalogical, and familial effects to examine how these factors interact with formal institutions and informal community networks to promote or prevent high-risk behaviors (Heitgerd & Bursik, 1987; Kornhauser, 1978). The scholarly pursuit of neighborhood effects has been propelled by the alarming statistics on the significant proportions of

economically disadvantaged minority youth at risk for poor academic achievement, delinquency, substance abuse, and the consequences of early sexual activity, pregnancy, and sexually transmitted diseases. Not surprisingly, therefore, most theory and research in this area has focused on development within lower income "ghetto" neighborhoods.

Social Disorganization Theory

Drawing upon the work of Shaw and McKay (1942/1969), Sampson and Groves (1989) have proposed that deviant child and adolescent behaviors emerge when a community is unable to realize the common values of its residents and to maintain effective social controls. "Social disorganization" within a community is a product of structural barriers (e.g., low economic status, ethnic heterogeneity, and residential mobility) which lead to disruption of community social organization and impedes the development of formal and informal kinship and friendship ties that enable community members to solve common problems (Kornhauser, 1978; Sampson & Groves, 1989).

Low-family income contributes to social disorganization through the lack of money and personal resources available to maintain and participate in community organizations. As a consequence, adolescents may engage in more deviant behavior as a result of decreased opportunity for involvement in community sponsored activities and less institutionalized formal constraints (e.g., effective schools and law enforcement agencies). Ethnic heterogeneity contributes to social disorganization through promoting fear and mistrust among residents from different subcultures. The indirect effect of heterogeneity on deviant behavior comes from a weakening of social structures to control disorderly peer groups. For example, Aber (1994) found that the degree of neighborhood ethnic diversity was positively associated with behavioral symptomatology for African American, inner-city youth. Similarly, residential mobility, characteristic of many low-income neighborhoods, disrupts a community's network of social relations and makes it more difficult for individuals to assimilate into extensive social networks. Weak local friendship networks reduce the ability of community members to recognize strangers and to work together to decrease victimization (Skogan, 1986). Although, given the increased residential mobility of low-income families, caution must be taken not to conclude that concurrent community influences are indicative of antecedents effects.

Community Supervision and Adolescent Employment.   A central feature of the relationship between social disorganization and deviant adolescent behavior is the premise that communities that lack strong formal and informal structures are unable to supervise and control teenage peer groups (McLoyd & Wilson, 1991). From this lack of supervision, spontaneous play groups of childhood can metamorphosize into street corner congregations, which in turn lead to adolescent deviant peer groups and gangs (Skogan, 1986). Communities unable to control street corner teen groups will have higher rates of delinquency, leading to higher rates of adult crime (Sampson & Groves, 1989). Family structure may also decrease informal adolescent supervision at the community level by failing to provide a sufficient network of collective family control. For example, a large proportion of single-parent households reduces the amount of adult supervision available for one's own children and children in the community (Hogan & Kitigawa, 1985; Reiss, 1986; Sampson, 1987).

The impact of work on adolescent involvement in delinquent behaviors has also been a focus of recent study. Some theorists argue that work should reduce delinquency by making it unnecessary to turn to crime to meet survival or status needs, by strengthening bonds to conventional institutions, and by improving future marketability (Cloward & Ohlin, 1960; D'Amico, 1984; Gottfredson, 1985). By contrast, others argue that work might increase delinquency by decreasing parental control, homework time, and school motivation (Greenberger, 1983; Hirschi, 1969; Steinberg et al., 1992). Data from the Office for Juvenile Justice and Delinquency Prevention suggests a more complex picture of interactive and reciprocal effects of gender, cultural background, interpersonal orientation, family attitudes toward work and school, and work status on school attendance and deviant behavior (Gottfredson, 1985).

The Dynamic Nature of Community Ecologies.   A variation of the social disorganization theory proposes that ghettos are communities that have experienced epidemics of social problems (Crane, 1991). These epidemics are characterized by nonlinear neighborhood effects such that, at the bottom of the distribution of neighborhood quality, there is a sharp increase in social problems leading to the catastrophic effects of social disorganization. According to this view, once community social problems reach a critical point, the process spreads creating an epidemic of social deviance and despair. Epidemic theory draws on "contagion theory" (Jencks & Mayer, 1990) in assuming that at some critical point social problems are contagious and spread through peer influence.

Social disorganization can also reduce a neighborhood's "social capital" (Coleman, 1990), the network of social relationships that provide community members access to resources. According to collective socialization theory (Jencks & Mayer, 1990), the percentage of workers in the neighborhood who hold "high status" professional or managerial jobs provide positive role models, and give children incentive to stay in school. In addition, high status community members can use affluence and influence to make services in the neighborhood better and provide better networks to higher paying jobs (Brooks-Gunn et al., 1993; Crane, 1991). The epidemic and collective socialization theories are supported by census tract data indicating higher rates of out-of-wedlock births for African American, Latin American, and European American adolescent females living in communities within the lowest third of the neighborhood quality continuum and with few professional/managerial workers (Brooks-Gunn et al., 1993; Crane, 1991; Hogan, Astone, & Kitigawa, 1985; Hogan & Kitigawa, 1985).

While the preponderance of research focusing on youth violence is conducted in urban communities in which most families are living in poverty conditions, not all youth who live in these communities participate in delinquent behavior. To the contrary, many of the youth who live within these areas seem to overcome the odds, or alternatively, are enrolled in gangs that are not engaged in interpersonal violence or property destruction (Taylor, 1995). Recent research suggests that there is a complex interplay between neighborhood quality and family characteristics on problem behaviors. For example, poor neighborhoods may have particularly detrimental effects for males living in single-parent homes and well-off adolescents via the contagion effect for increased association with deviant peers (Brooks-Gunn et al., 1993; Kupersmidt et al., 1995). Conversely, these children may benefit the most from residences in middle-class neighborhoods with more positive and less negative role models, more educational and career opportunities, and less chance of being recruited by gangs (Johnstone, 1983). On the other hand, when compared to middle-class families, poorer families may not benefit as much from advantaged neighborhoods because their income is too constraining or affluent school mates and institutions set standards that are difficult to attain and discouraging.

The interactive nature of neighborhood effects should lead investigators to critically evaluate the different meanings that community ecologies may have to individuals of different ethnic and socioeconomic status. For example, interpretation of data yielded by recent laudatory efforts to extend the study of achievement and risk factors for ethnic minorities beyond the ghetto and into the lives of individuals living in middle-class neighborhoods (e.g., Steinberg, Dornbusch, & Brown, 1992) must take into account the strong possibility that African American, Latin American, and European American youth who share similar working or middle-class environments are distinguished by dissimilar experiences derived from their ethnic minority versus majority status. As an example, demographic studies of suburbanization and ethnicity (Massey & Denton, 1988) find that African Americans are markedly less likely than European Americans to live in suburbs, but when they do, they are highly segregated in those settings, when compared to other ethnic minorities. Hispanics, on the other hand, while residentially more integrated into suburban neighborhoods represent a markedly subordinate group with respect to socioeconomic status and therefore are often socially marginal in these settings. Consequently, conclusions drawn about ethnic differences found in the relationship among academic achievement, problem behaviors, peer options, and parenting practices in suburban settings may be constrained by the socially marginal and unrepresentative nature of the ethnic minority samples. In summary, evidence of variation in the extent to which ethnic minorities may suffer from residence in low-income neighborhoods or benefit from affluent neighbors points to the need for more research on social competition and person-environment fit models (Braucht, 1979; Jencks & Mayer, 1990) which take into account the probability that neighborhoods may be potent constructive or destructive forces in minority development.

American Schools: Contexts for Developmental Risk

Minority vulnerability resulting from poverty, low educational attainment, limited-English speaking backgrounds, and low achievement have been long-standing issues of concern to those who design interventions for schools (e.g., Williams, 1992). However, in recent years, a new concern

has arisen: that policies designed to increase minority educational achievement may have unintentionally created greater obstacles to academic success and school participation (e.g., Foster, 1994). These concerns have intensified in reaction to surveys indicating a continuing trend of increasing achievement discrepancy between minority and European American achievement as students progress through elementary and high school (Caldas, 1993).

School desegregation and compensatory education have been the major educational policies for improving academic achievement of minority students in the past 25 years, but the results of the changes they brought are modest at best (e.g., Mahard & Crain, 1983; Weinberg, 1983). The war on poverty initiated by the Johnson administration in the 1960s launched many early interventions with the lofty objective of bringing low-income and minority children to functional parity with middle-class children at school entry (Zigler & Valentine, 1979). More than a decade after implementation of these early intervention programs, evaluation findings are not so sanguine (Haskins, 1989). A collaborative evaluation of twelve independent programs (deemed high quality by educators and academicians) found substantial effects soon after interventions ended, but diminishing effects over the course of elementary schooling (Lazar, Darlington, Murray, Royce, & Snipper, 1982).

Recent analyses based on the National Assessment of Educational Progress database present a mixed picture that verifies modest gains for African Americans, but attributes them to improvements in family SES rather than desegregation or compensatory education (Armor, 1992). A recurring finding is small rates of improvement in reading achievement of African Americans and Latin Americans even though they continue to lag behind the European American majority (e.g., Ortiz, 1986), no improvement in writing (e.g., Lapointe, 1986), and confirmation of a marked lag in mathematics such that few are prepared for college level mathematics (e.g., Johnson, 1990). A Government Accounting Office (GAO) analysis of the impact of desegregation, compensatory education, and educational reforms of the 1980s (reforms that instituted more demanding curricula with the intent of raising achievement of all students) found only minimal effects for African American and Latin American students (Conciatore, 1990; Urban Education, 1991). A frequent explanation for these minimal improvements is that the objectives of desegregation and compensatory education were seriously undermined by the ways in which policies were implemented. This has led to an entirely different line of discourse focused on the identification of impediments to African American and Latin American achievement in spite of major educational policies to promote achievement advances.

Admission and Retention Policies for the Transition into Kindergarten. At one time, kindergarten in America was supposed to provide a pleasant bridge between home life and formal learning. In the United States in the 1980s, kindergarten became the antithesis of this in many ways. In a reform climate that emphasized performance excellence, kindergarten was no longer a place to acquire school readiness, but a place to demonstrate it. Meisels (1992) has detailed the ways in which public educational policy on kindergarten frequently dictated early standardized testing and grade retention if child performance did not meet specified standards. This change has produced a four-tiered system of initial public education where: (a) some school systems are promoting older age at entry; (b) many states and cities have implemented mandatory testing at the end of kindergarten and retention for those who do not meet specified standards (i.e., many children "flunk" kindergarten); (c) some school systems assign children who do not meet performance standards to an extra year of kindergarten, which is essentially similar to retention in kindergarten; and (d) some parents hold their children out of school for a year (parents voluntarily forego enrolling children they deem unready for the rigors of kindergarten until the age for mandatory schooling at 6 years old).

Minority children, who are particularly likely to be judged not ready for formal learning, are more frequently retained in kindergarten, while kindergarten holding out is more common in higher income neighborhood schools. Developmentally, the long-term, disproportionately negative consequences of these policies on minorities, and males in particular, are evident in government statistics. In 1985, 44.5% of African American male 13-year-olds were one or more years below age-typical grade level in comparison to 29% of their European American counterparts, and 35% of African American female 13-year-olds were below grade level in comparison to 21% of their European American counterparts (Meisels, 1992). Moreover, recent research suggests detrimental rather than advantageous long-term

consequences of retention (Holmes, 1989), and studies of age at entry into first grade show that achievement advantages in elementary school associated with older entry age disappear by high school age (Langer, Kalk, & Searls, 1984). When comparisons of retained and non-retained students are restricted to low-income, inner-city minority students in under-funded, *de facto* segregated schools, the retained students are not remarkably disadvantaged and, consequently, their circumstance has been characterized as success in spite of failure to be promoted (Alexander, Entwisle, & Dauber, 1994). However, the data supporting this interpretation are equally consistent with a characterization of the situation of both retained and non-retained students as communality in failure over time because of stunted achievement growth and stifled motivation of the non-retained students as well as deficient performance of the retained.

The Effect of Developmentally Inappropriate Kindergarten Curricula. Minority children with preschool and kindergarten experiences that enhance their cognitive (as opposed to social) readiness are better prepared for the demands of formal school learning in first grade, and those without such experience are at heightened risk of beginning an inauspicious developmental trajectory toward achievement failure (Entwisle, Alexander, Cadigan, & Pallas, 1987). There is, however, growing evidence that ethnic minority children may disproportionately receive developmentally "inappropriate" kindergarten curricula characterized by the National Association for the Education of Young Children as an emphasis on workbook/worksheet activities as opposed to self-directed activities and story listening (Burts et al., 1992). Of equal concern is the finding that developmentally inappropriate kindergarten curricula appear to induce stress reactions that vary for ethnic minority and European American children, that in turn can undermine developmental competence and motivation to learn (Burts et al., 1992).

These findings raise important questions concerning the theory that ethnic minority children, and African American children in particular, have a distinctive behavioral style and preference for psychomotor learning and variety of activities, labeled "psychological verve" (Boykin, 1978; Hale-Benson, 1986) which makes them "unsuited" for traditional forms of school instruction. The prevalence of developmentally inappropriate classroom experiences in kindergarten programs attended by African American students and their corresponding stress reactions raises the intriguing possibility that psychological verve is substantially a stress reaction rather than a racial or cultural orientation. Boykin in fact suggested this possibility, remarking that, "perhaps we are simply witnessing the reactions of normal children who are bored, restless, and unstimulated . . ." (Boykin, 1978, p. 353).

Declining Minority Achievement over the Course of Schooling.   Research has documented a continuing trend of teacher-student interactions that convey messages of disapproval and devaluation to ethnic minority children entering elementary school, which in turn leads to alienation from learning experiences and underachievement. More than two decades ago, ethnographic study of a first-grade classroom identified ways in which teachers devalue children from low SES background. Rist (1970) described how first-grade teachers provided better instruction and more attention to African American children who exhibited the personal grooming and language patterns of the middle class. Over 15 years later, another ethnographic analysis of six first-grade desegregated classrooms (Grant, 1984, 1985) found that irrespective of teacher race, compared to European American students, African American children received more equivocal and less positive teacher feedback, were disproportionately relegated to low ability tracks within the first few weeks of school, and (African American males) were reprimanded more than other children. Garcia and Hurtado (1995) have suggested that teacher devaluation of ethnic minority students is a natural outcome of "Americanization" as a primary educational objective of American schools. "Americanization" conceptualizes White, middle-class mainstream culture as essential for economic and academic success, seeks through the educational process to eliminate linguistic and cultural differences deemed inconsistent with mainstream values, and assumes that children who are not part of the mainstream are as a group culturally flawed.

The work of Entwisle and her associates (Alexander & Entwisle, 1988; Entwisle & Hayduk, 1978, 1982) suggest that during the first and second grades, such teacher expectation effects may send low-income minority children on a spiral of decline characterized by an increasing grade and achievement gap and decreasing association between ethnic minority parents' estimates of their children's school success and children's actual performance. Entwisle (1990) argues that the achievement trajectories of minorities with large numbers of underachieving students are set early in their educational careers, well before high school. One theoretical implication of her argument is that differences in the influence of adolescent peer relations and parental styles observed in African American, Latin American, and European American youth (e.g., Steinberg, Mounts, Lamborn, & Dornbusch, 1991) may be reactions to the intractability of an unfavorable position in the achievement hierarchy established at the beginning of formal schooling.

Cultural Inversion and Cultural Identity.   Ogbu and Fordham (Fordham & Ogbu, 1986; Ogbu, 1986) have proposed that African Americans (and some Latin Americans) reject educational achievement as a worthwhile pursuit not only because rewards for their efforts are denied by discriminatory exclusion from the desirable job market, but because they associate most trappings of the learning process with European Americans who are viewed as adversaries. For achieving minority students, these cultural inversion processes (cf. Holt, 1972) within their peer group can lead to ridicule and ostracism and secreting of accomplishments. For underachievers, it can lead to the valuing of behaviors perceived as antithetical to conventional European American norms (Fordham & Ogbu, 1986).

The thesis that cultural inversion is an impediment to achievement striving in ethnic minority youth has generated an exciting new direction in research and has gained partial support in subsequent studies. Overall, research suggests that while perceptions of discrimination and racial distrust are related to attitudes about the value of school and occupational expectations, other factors, such as socioeconomic level, the school context (e.g., Catholic versus public schools), ethnic identity and self-concept, and a pragmatic view of the relationship between educational achievement and later success are more highly related to actual school achievement (Mickelson, 1990; Taylor, Casten, Flickinger, Roberts, & Fulmore, 1994; Terrell et al., 1993). However, recent work by Ford and Harris (1992, 1996) also suggests that while many ethnic minority students may not subscribe to the view that peer pressure or discrimination are impediments to achieving, the interaction of school-designated learning potential and gender may exert an effect on achievement that has potentially negative consequences for males.

Minority children are largely invisible beings in the developmental and educational literature on the schooling process, unless they have problems. We have little information about their perceptions and experiences of normally occurring learning processes. Data is limited to their responses to difficulties and distress, and to a lesser degree their responses to institutional efforts to alleviate distress. To date, empirical tests of the cultural inversion hypothesis have not directly studied the role of ethnic identity, level of development, level of self-awareness, or racial socialization experiences on student achievement. For example, studies are needed to examine what happens when youth with little racial socialization and relatively ambiguous, emerging ethnic identities become aware of the personal implications of discrimination and the American racial job ceiling. Applying a process-oriented approach, Cross, Parham, and Helms (1991) proposed that African American youth identity development evolves from unconsciously internalized versions of the European American culture's pejorative identification of African Americans, through emotionally wrenching rejection of the subordinated identity, through movement toward an initially inchoate African American identity, to an earned independent nondefensive bicultural identity (Stevenson, 1995). Future research on the achievement opportunities and risks faced by minority children entering schools in the United States will benefit from theoretical frameworks which consider process-oriented models of ethnic identity development in dynamic interaction with individual ability and experience, familial resources and practices, and institutional policies and expectations.

CULTURAL BIAS AND CULTURAL SENSITIVITY IN FORMULATING RESEARCH QUESTIONS

For researchers, becoming culturally competent, that is, understanding the unique cultural aspects that influence the theories we generate and the scientific questions we examine, is part of our own life-span growth. As a discipline, we must take the time to reflect on what we have learned, the academic and sociopolitical values that have driven our work, and to discover what we still do not know. The challenge of examining sociopolitical influences on

ethnic minority scholarship and the consequences of social science practices on policies directed toward culturally and linguistically diverse populations in the United States is not a simple task. Scholarly discourse is fraught with emotional and pedagogical issues that must, we assert, be a focal point of any scientific endeavor that seeks to produce valid descriptions of and explanations for how our country's children live and develop.

Race and the Investigator's Worldview

A growing number of scholars are giving voice to a widely held belief in the ethnic minority community that conventional explanations of development have given insufficient attention to understanding why minorities behave the way they do from the point of view of the minorities themselves (Gibson & Ogbu, 1991; Gordon, 1973; Nobels, 1973; P. J. Williams, 1991). They assert that the majority of research to date has not only neglected to include ethnic minority participants (e.g., Graham, 1992), but has failed to adequately address their psychological development by evaluating behaviors exclusively in terms of the dominant group's perceptions of social reality (Daniel, 1994). According to Hilliard (1989), the general perceptions of race that European American researchers bring to empirical investigations may be misinformed, pejorative, and potentially harmful. Such perceptions influence how researchers ask questions, design studies, and interpret results; which in turn can produce research findings that reinforce negative characterizations of the ethnic group studied. For example, early research questions about African American families were formed in terms of the group's perceived dysfunctions, and as a consequence, data generated from such research supported stereotypes of African American families as deviant, pathological/social organizations unable to fulfill the major responsibilities of socializing their members for productive roles in society (Allen, 1978; Moynihan, 1965). Such an approach reflects an ongoing analytic framework that seeks explanations within the character of the individual rather than within features of the social structure (Sampson, 1993), thereby sustaining the sociopolitical interests of the dominant majority at the expense of ethnic community members (Caplan & Nelson, 1973).

Current theoretical explanations for the variability found in minority development has usually been constructed without consideration of the functional significance of specific behaviors to ethnic group members themselves. Some, like Sampson (1993), argue forcefully that failure to give ethnic minority members a voice in a scientific enterprise designed to determine their identity and subjectivity challenge the capability of the social sciences to respond to the full diversity of human nature. To construct a more adequate explanation of individual variability in the development of minorities, it is necessary to incorporate the perceptions and understanding that minorities have of their own social realities, as well as a historical perspective of their life in and immigration to the United States. The need to incorporate minority perspectives into developmental theory and research design raises questions not only concerned with how to capture the views of ethnic minority research participants, but with who in the scientific community has legitimate authority to speak on multi-cultural issues (Parham, 1993).

Racial Suspicion and Mistrust

Counseling psychologists began the 1990s with a sobering dialogue between European American and U.S. ethnic minority researchers that is instructive for developmental scientists. A symposium organized to examine and solicit reactions of noted ethnic-minority researchers on the contributions of European American pioneers in research on U.S. ethnic minorities revealed striking differences between the way European American and ethnic minority counseling psychologists viewed the fruits of their investigatory labor (Casas & San Miguel, 1993; Mio & Iwamasa, 1993). While the European American investigators framed the rationale and outcomes of their work in both ethical and altruistic terms, an overriding conclusion of the ethnic minority commentators was that research by European Americans, having ignored the theoretical and methodological perspectives of minority scholars, often cost minority communities more than it benefited them due to ill-derived conclusions that stigmatized community members.

For example, Helms (1993) pointed out that the issue of White racial identity as a factor in the worldview that European American investigators bring to the study of U.S. ethnic minorities is rarely acknowledged, less frequently analyzed, and is a primary determinant of the types of research that are permitted in the professions through the role of European American scholars as the primary evaluators of journal articles, dissertations, and

other professional development activities that perpetuate constricted research even when researchers are ethnic minorities. Sue (1993) and Parham (1993) attributed the current chasm of worldviews and atmosphere of resentment and mistrust between European American and ethnic minority researchers to several long-standing factors, including: (a) the historic portrayal of minorities as maladjusted, delinquent, and pathological; (b) the denigration of and failure to give credit to the pioneering contributions of ethnic minority researchers to current scholarship on multicultural issues; (c) inequitable standards for review and acceptance of articles submitted for publication; (d) racially discriminatory review and funding of grant proposals (U.S. Government Accounting Office, 1994, June); and (e) denial of tenure and promotion to minority researchers because their work is criticized as too narrowly focused on minorities while European American investigators use ethnic minority research as a vehicle for advancement and are considered innovators. That many European American scholars would be surprised at or in disagreement with these attributions serves to underscore the current chasm between majority and minority worldviews.

When Worldviews Collide: The Youth Violence Initiative

As noted, research on ethnic minority children is often driven by sociopolitical concerns (i.e., academic underachievement, adolescent violence, and pregnancy) rather than grounded in theory. Moreover, these sociopolitical concerns are usually framed within the cultural lens of dominant group political leaders and scholars. Failure to take into account the perspectives of ethnic minority scholars and citizens when designing socially relevant research can have negative consequences for research participants, the communities they represent, and the enterprise of science. These consequences are illustrated by the recent controversy surrounding the National Institutes of Health's (NIH) Violence Initiative: the federal government's response to the sharp escalation in violence among urban African American youth in the 1980s. In a meeting of the National Mental Health Advisory Council in February 1992, Dr. Frederick Goodwin, then director of the National Institute of Mental Health, was quoted as likening the violent behavior of inner-city ghetto males to jungle monkeys (Leavy, 1992). Many African Americans felt that the Violence

Initiative raised the specter of research with genocidal intent similar to how members of their community viewed the Public Health Service supported infamous "Tuskegee study" which for 40 years misled African American men in Alabama who had syphilis to believe they were receiving medical treatment (J. H. Jones, 1993).

A storm of protest ultimately led to the cancellation of a NIH planned conference on genetic factors in crime (Babington, 1992) and appointment by the Secretary of the U.S. Department of Health and Human Services (DHHS) of a blue-ribbon panel of African Americans to determine whether DHHS was sponsoring research attempting to establish that a genetic factor accounted for correlations between race and violent behavior and was planning to target African American males between 5 and 9 years old to administer medications to control their behavior (Wheeler, 1992). Concerned that Attention Deficit Hyperactivity Disorder (ADHD) was a diagnostic classification which risked disproportionate assignment of African Americans to pejorative categories (Randolph, 1991) and cognizant that conduct disorder is frequently considered a comorbid disorder with ADHD, particularly in low-income children (Hinshaw, 1987), some panel members sought a more thorough review of other studies involving invasive drug treatments of children (Bennett, 1993). This request was denied on the basis that DHHS staff viewed federally supported research on ADHD involving medication to be completely distinct from research on aggression, antisocial behavior, and violence (Jenifer, 1993). After a three-year delay and the inclusion of some former critics, the conference on genetics and crime was held in 1995 (Maass, 1995).

Many ethnic minority scholars and community members continue to express the view that government and institutional human subjects review boards have demonstrated incapability of providing assurance of protection from group stigmatization and personal harm to minority participants (J. F. Jackson, M. H. Bennett, H. Dent, H. Fairchild, R. Jones, & P. Rhymer-Todman, personal communication, January 21, 1993). They maintain that researchers seeking to study minority community members, including investigators who are themselves members of the ethnic group(s) to be studied, should routinely seek proposal review and the advice of psychologists who are respected members of the community to be studied. Such steps are implicitly recommended in the APA Ethics Code which requires that "As part of the process of development and implementation of research projects, psychologists consult those with expertise concerning any special population under investigation or most likely to be affected" (APA, 1992, Standard 6.07d). In response to these concerns, social scientists investigating ADHD and other factors placing ethnic minority children at risk, have begun to form community advisory task forces comprised of ethnic minority scholars, practitioners, and community members charged with assisting in the development of culture-fair assessment procedures, fair representation of ethnic minority members as research participants, and adequate informed consent and debriefing procedures (Fisher, Hoagwood, & Jensen, 1996). However, the extent to which group stigmatization should be considered in determining participant risk in research projects is still a pressing issue in need of resolution.

Recalculating the Cost-Benefit Analysis of Ethnic Minority Research

Overall, the views expressed by the minority counseling psychologists and the controversy generated by the Youth Violence Initiative can be construed as posing an overarching ethical question: Should research on ethnic minorities be conducted if ethnic minorities, including professionally trained researchers do not view it as an asset to their community? Ponterotto and Casas (1991), for example, criticizes current ethical guidelines for human subjects research for their emphasis on avoidance of harm rather than promotion of benefit. They argue that this emphasis is derived from fundamentally self-protective motives on the part of social scientists to avoid lawsuits, and is an insufficient ethical justification for conducting research on ethnic minorities. A disciplinary emphasis on harm avoidance does raise questions of scientific responsibility, since it can be interpreted as placing the ethical burden on participants and/or their communities to demonstrate they have been harmed, and away from investigators who need not demonstrate that their research will result in any good.

A related issue is raised by those who have asserted that group stigmatization should be considered in determining risks to participants in behavioral science work (Fisher & Rosendahl, 1990; Mio & Iwamasa, 1993; Parham, 1993; Sarason, 1984; Zuckerman, 1990). Some have argued eloquently about the need to keep societal concerns out of the process of science (Scarr, 1988). According to this view, consideration for the practical consequences of social science research inhibits scientific progress and academic freedom. From this perspective, statements about the limitations of one's work in the final paragraphs of a journal article provide sufficient ethical safety mechanisms and/or alleviate the investigator of further moral responsibility, against society's (mis)use of the products of his or her work. A counterpoint to this view is that all research is value-laden and thus sociopolitical in nature (Harrington, in press; Kurtines, Azmitia, & Gewirtz, 1992), particularly when ethnic minorities and other historically oppressed groups are the focus of study (Sampson, 1993; Zuckerman, 1990). In a society in which minority racial groups have been historically oppressed both through discriminatory laws and discriminatory practices, developmental scientists must recognize that any research on ethnic minority communities can have direct impact on public attitudes and policies directed toward research participants and the communities they represent. That policy makers and nonscientist citizens "are not likely to make the distinction between scientific theory and what seems to be its political implications, or between generalizations based on population statistics and their applications to individual members of a given group" (Zuckerman, 1990, p. 1301), leads to the more persuasive argument for including societal concerns as a part of scientific responsibility.

We hold the view that consideration of the sociopolitical consequences of experimental findings reflects appropriate scientific procedures rather than censorship because it is an essential means of selecting experimental variables that reflect the actual life contexts of individuals studied (Fisher & Rosendahl, 1990). When investigators weigh the importance of a scientific question against the harm it might do in reinforcing negative stereotypes or fostering social policies destructive for ethnic communities, they are forced to identify and critically analyze their own worldviews and the ways in which such views, and the hypotheses and research designs derived from them, are illuminating or obscuring identification of variables critical to our understanding of development within human communities.

Informed Consent, Paternalism, and Racial Mistrust

Racial mistrust is also an overlooked variable in the relationships between developmental scientists and research participants representing minority groups within the United States. The scandals surrounding the Tuskegee syphilis study (Jones, 1993) and the government radiation experiments (Advisory Committee on Human Radiation, 1996) as well as the sociopolitical and ideological forces that continue to propel scholarly debates concerning race differences in IQ, the necessity for academic tracking, and the value of bilingual education have all served to undermine trust in social scientists as guardians of ethical treatment when ethnic minorities are the focus of research.

The ethical consequences of investigators' failure to recognize the suspicion with which their work is regarded by ethnic minority members is no better exemplified than in the current misuse of passive consent (a letter asking parents to respond only if they do *not* want their child to participate in the research) as a means of overcoming perceived barriers to subject recruitment. Difficulties in acquiring guardian consent is not in itself ethical justification for what in practical terms amounts to a waiver of parental consent (Fisher, Hoagwood, & Jensen, 1996; Nolan, 1992; Office for Protection from Research Risks, 1993). The current use of passive consent to solve recruitment challenges for ethnic minority research violates the moral values of respect for self governance and justice since its use implies that children from low-income ethnic minority homes need not receive the protection of active guardian consent afforded White, middle-income children (Fisher, 1993). Child development researchers need to develop (and funding agencies need to support) more efficacious procedures for establishing community liaisons and personal contact with guardians of minority children (Fisher, 1993, in press; Scott-Jones, 1996; Thompson, 1984) to both increase positive responses to requests for participation and insure that these responses are informed and voluntary.

Protecting Participant Rights in Treatment Settings

Developmental scientists often assume that research makes an ultimate if not an immediate constructive contribution to society and that it is at least neutral if not helpful to study participants. As the following case highlights, that assumption may not be justified when minorities are research participants, and when research is conducted in community agencies. Moreover, the assumption may not be shared by minority community members. In 1993, community agencies making up the California Adolescent Family Life Programs (AFLP) were directed by an office within the state Maternal and Child Health branch to administer an assessment instrument to determine the extent of childhood and adolescent sexual abuse experienced by the African American and Latin American adolescent mothers they served. The assessment battery was long and included deeply probing questions about sexual practices, incest, other forms of sexual abuse, and use of illegal substances.

The assessment instrument and procedures were described to local agency staff as an "anonymous" needs assessment, which according to project coordinators did not require either review of a human subjects research panel nor the information typically provided in research related informed consent forms. However, in reality, the "anonymous" survey would become part of the responding clients' files at the agency, information from it would be entered into a statewide database (presumably available on an unrestricted basis for any uses the state offices might determine), and disclosure of abuse would require staff reporting to Child Protective Services based on agency reporting requirements. The one-page consent form attached to individual assessment forms informed prospective respondents that the survey would ask personal information about unwanted sexual experiences and stated that information on abuse would be reported, but it did not state to whom the information would be reported nor what the consequences of reporting might be. Even though participation was to be presented as voluntary, local agency staff were urged to get every client to respond to the survey, including reluctant and hard-to-reach clients, and were encouraged to present the assessment battery during service delivery.

Failing to receive support from the Maternal and Child Health branch (R. Shah, personal communication, 1994), protesting agency staff brought the matter to the attention of the Association of Black Psychologists, which evaluated the assessment program as a threat to the psychological well-being and rights of vulnerable adolescent clients, and offered to refer the project investigators to African American psychologists for expertise and consultation to bolster the cultural, clinical, and research competence of the study design (A. Jackson, personal communication, May 4, 1994). Following an inquiry by the federal Office for the Protection from Research Risks, the California Health and Welfare Agency's Committee for the Protection of Human Subjects (J. D. White, memorandum, August 5, 1994) determined that since regulatory exemptions of committee review of surveys did not apply to minors (who must have parental consent for participation) and because the assess-

ment project involved more than minimal risk to targeted participants, the assessment came under the definition of research and could not be exempted from Human Subjects review. Second, the Committee noted the original consent form was inadequate. In particular it noted as misleading a statement in the form assuring subjects that responses would be kept private when investigators knew that instances of abuse would be reported to Child Protective Services. Third, the Committee ruled that the project was suspended, that no new subjects could be enrolled, and the data that had already been collected would not be used for publication in scientific journals. Unfortunately, by the time of the Committee's evaluation, 34 of the 37 AFLP agencies had surveyed all of their clients.

As with much research on ethnic minority development, the AFLP sexual abuse study was based on perceived societal need, rather than culturally sensitive developmental theory and practice. To many ethnic minority professionals and community members, the AFLP sexual abuse study became a documented case of harm to and oppression of minorities through large scale research. It corroborates the fears of many minorities that the probability, not only the possibility, of genocidal research such as the Tuskegee study, is both real and current. Thus, special efforts are needed to ensure that research is likely to benefit minority participants, and to promote justified confidence that the work of developmental science is beneficial and fair to ethnic minorities. Many of the problems identified in the foregoing study might have been averted if the investigators had consulted with agency and individual professionals representing the minority community affected. Investigators can also enhance developmental research design, ethical procedures, and community trust through solicitation of the views of prospective participants from the ethnic communities that are the target of study (Fisher, in press; Fisher, Higgins-D'Allesandro, Rau, Kuther, & Belanger, 1996).

Grounding Theory in Culture

Challenges to the scientific understanding of human development arise from conventional perspectives which view cultural variation as superfluous to core elements of psychological continuities and discontinuities across the life span (Jackson, 1993). Recent attempts to understand the cultural context of development are also limited by the way race and ethnicity have been treated as "add-ons" to the traditional study of White, European American culture (Winkler, 1992). Such an accommodative approach is not seen to be constitutive of developmental phenomena in general, but simply a way of expanding upon dominant worldviews and in some ways shielding the traditional theoretical frameworks from transformation (see Broughton, 1987; Sampson, 1993).

As we move into the 21st century, development scientists must not only consider the policy ramifications and the cultural (in)appropriateness of past research and current methodological approaches, but we must establish discourse and develop new methodologies that are neither ideologically determined nor derived from previously generated culturally biased knowledge. This requires recognition that various constructs used repeatedly in the social sciences, were derived from culturally insensitive approaches and through conceptually biased lens rooted firmly in historically specific folk notions and socially constructed racial differences that reinforced political, sociological and educational practices of their time (Stanfield, 1993). Accordingly, child development specialists should be cautious in extending to ethnic minorities traditional experimental designs, theoretical frameworks, and empirical findings that may have been innovative when first constructed, but which may not meet goodness-of-fit criteria for newer generations and different cultural communities (Stanfield, 1993).

Imposed and Derived Etics

Cross cultural psychology has long understood the tension between an emic approach which seeks to understand human behavior within a single culture from the point of view of members of that culture and an etic approach which seeks to produce generalizations about human behavior across cultures from a point of view external to the perspectives of individuals studied (Berry, 1969, 1979, 1989). By contrast, developmental psychology in its examination of the psychological trajectories of children and youth growing up in the United States, has failed to understand this tension and has instead relied upon untested universal assumptions about development to compare members of various ethnic subcultural groups. This tendency to apply measures constructed for hypothesis testing in one culture to predict the outcome in another culture achieves only an imposed etic (Berry, 1969, 1989); the illusion that similarities and differences in response to such measures

reflect variation in universally valid constructs for both cultures (see Jackson, 1993).

Berry (1989) and Pike (1967) have identified the importance of considering both the etic and emic approaches. The etic approach provides (a) a perspective within which cultural similarities and differences can be recognized, and (b) techniques and theoretical frameworks that can serve as a point of entry into an analysis of a newly examined culture. The emic approach (a) permits an understanding of how culture is constructed as a "working whole" (Pike, 1967, p. 41), and (b) how individuals understand the biological, psychological, relational, and physical contexts of their lives. By combining these two approaches, investigators can achieve a derived etic (Berry, 1979, 1989)—the identification of similarities and differences based upon assessment instruments known to be valid and meaningful within both cultures.

Berry (1989) has outlined the steps necessary to achieve a derived etic. Following the intracultural (emic) investigation of a question in one culture, the researcher attempts to use the same concept or instrument to study behavior in a second culture (imposed etic). In contrast to traditional subcultural comparative research, identification of discrepancies in responses between the two cultures are not used to conclude that they differ on a universal dimension, but provide the basis for an emic analysis of the second culture. In the final step, the individual emics derived from both cultures are then compared and a derived etic is identified only from those areas in which there is commonalty across the two emics. For example, if shared caregiving roles among extended family members are not common to the concept of parenting for both African American and European American mothers (see Jackson, 1993), then it cannot be a dimension on which the two groups can be compared.

Combining Quantitative and Qualitative Methodologies

To achieve a derived etic and focus future research efforts within a culturally sensitive milieu implies that quantitative and qualitative modalities should no longer be considered separate realms of psychological research. Traditionally, quantitative techniques have relied upon representative samples to test nomethetic hypotheses about how individuals and families develop in general. Quantitative approaches apply these nomethetic typologies to categorize patterns of development as "normative" or "atypical." By contrast, qualitative approaches, have relied upon the examination of perceptions, behaviors, structures, patterns, and strategies unique to the individual being studied to examine idiographic hypotheses about how a single individual or family functions in particular. As such, qualitative approaches attempt to capture the interpretations, and voice of individuals in their context by emphasizing an "insider's view" of the meaning of behaviors (see Freidenberg, Mulvihill, & Caraballo, 1993; Imig, 1993; Imig & Phillips, 1992).

The decision to utilize quantitative or qualitative techniques in ethnic minority research, reflects the investigators worldview concerning the nature of development within and between individuals and families. If the investigator believes that all individuals do not perceive, interpret, and understand similar life phenomena in the same way, than it becomes imperative to draw upon qualitative techniques to gain understanding about cultural and individual differences in the significance and meaning of behaviors and events. Investigators can then build upon qualitatively derived data to create culturally valid instruments to quantify significant aspects of development. Investigations that incorporate both qualitative and quantitative techniques can document in greater depth the common and unshared dimensions of development and ultimately empower individuals in ways that positively maximize their life outcomes (Freidenberg et al., 1993).

Understanding the Cultural Context of Development: A Research Agenda for the 21st Century

Research and theory that focuses on the development of ethnic minority children and youth must begin to include consideration and direct measures of cultural elements if investigators wish to construct a valid knowledge base relevant to behavioral variations within and between individuals from the diverse ethnic groups compromising the population of the United States (Betancourt & López, 1993). As Bronfenbrenner (1977) pointed out over two decades ago, children do not develop in a vacuum; nor is the context of their development limited to parental influences. The behaviors and subjectivity of children and youth are shaped by their unique individual characteristics in dynamic interaction with the nature of their neighborhoods, the quality of their public and private institutions, the values of their cultural community, and the ideologies of their nation. Developmental scientists must also increase sampling of ethnic minority members in general,

and of economically diverse members of ethnic communities in particular. Moreover, future investigators will need to devote additional attention to inter-ethnic as well as intra-ethnic issues related to the increases in biracial, biethnic, and bicultural marriages and families.

While it is important that child developmentalists recognize ethnic diversity and its meaning for the types of challenges and opportunities various ethnic minority families face within the majority culture, we must avoid simplistic, misleading, or inappropriate conclusions about race and ethnicity. To accomplish this, we need to acknowledge that we currently lack and must begin to construct valid definitions of race, ethnicity, and culture. A primary conceptual shortcoming in our definitions of culture is the failure to recognize that an evident aspect about culture is that it is not static. Current research on ethnic minority identity development and acculturation attempt to document the extent to which individuals behave like or identify with either their cultural group or the dominant group. This outcome-oriented emphasis generally ignores the mechanisms, mediating processes, or cultural clashes experienced both structurally and symbolically by minority groups (Phinney, 1996; Spencer et al., 1991). Culture is transitional. Cultural subgroups exert an influence over and are influenced by individuals who are members of those subgroups as well as other cultural groups with which opportunities for socialization and interaction occur. Moreover, the new wave of immigrants, the changing global economy, as well as global societies are dynamic factors affecting communities which need to be integrated into theories of development. In addition to influencing the developing person's perceptions of the meaning of events, culture also contributes to an individual's use of time, energy, space, material, control, affect, meaning, and content (Imig, 1993). Thus, the singular focus on bivariate relationships between certain behavioral outcomes and culture contributes little to our understanding of developmental processes (Heath, 1997; Phinney & Chavira, 1995; Spencer, 1995; Spencer et al., 1991). A fundamental implication of the transitional dimension of culture and ethnicity is that researchers continually assess the evolving nature of cultural categories and how the influence of these evolving cultural components on development change over time.

Continued failure to conduct research that documents the unique, and normative developmental milestones within and between ethnically diverse communities, will only further intensify the information needs of future ethnically diverse communities. Global models of development and research that ignore the unique and normative patterns of development of diverse communities, both within and between them, provides an inadequate base for the construction of valid developmental theories and responsive programs and policies. The lack of research examining the impact of culture on the development of nonminorities exacerbates this problem through its implicit assumption that culture is a single variable that accounts for differences between minorities and nonminorities, but not for the "normative" development of nonminority children. Future developmental research needs to be directed away from comparative approaches which result in prioritizing one ethnicity over another, and toward contextual approaches which decipher the meanings of race, ethnicity and social class as they relate to optimal or compromised development of ethnic minority children and youth.

Cultural borrowing, shock, conflict, biculturalism, assimilation, and adaptation all have different impacts on the development of children and youth from culturally and linguistically diverse groups. Issues of poverty, the underclass, colonialism, racism, and powerlessness further confound the impacts of cultural diversity in the United States. Inaction or avoidance of these factors and of culturally sensitive and competent approaches to understanding human diversity is extremely costly to members of culturally disadvantaged populations. As Laosa (1990) notes, scientific sensitivity to and exploration of differences within populations are needed to insure that efforts to develop policies, services, or institutions aimed at enhancing developmental outcomes are harmonious with the basic values and characteristics of diverse populations. Without such knowledge, policies and programs may be only marginally effective. A research agenda aimed at understanding fully the meaning of race and ethnicity as an intrinsic part of development, and the broader social and political implications of its use in the design and delivery of programs for ethnic minorities, will expand human knowledge to meet society's current and future needs.

REFERENCES

Aber, J. L. (1994). Poverty, violence, and child development: Untangling family and community level effects. In C. A. Nelson (Ed.), *Threats to optimal development: Integrating biological, psychological, and social risk factors. The Minnesota Symposia on Child Psychology* (Vol. 27, pp. 229–272). Hillsdale, NJ: Erlbaum.

Aboud, F. E., & Doyle, A. B. (1993). The early development of ethnic identity and attitudes. In M. E. Bernal & G. P. Knight (Eds.), *Ethnic identity: Formation and transmission among Hispanics and other minorities* (pp. 47–60). Albany, NY: SUNY Press.

Adler, L. L. (1982). Cross-cultural research and theory. In B. Wolman (Ed.), *Handbook of developmental psychology* (pp. 76–90). Englewood Cliffs, NJ: Prentice-Hall.

Advisory Committee on Human Radiation (ACHRE). (1996). *The human radiation experiments: Final report of the president's advisory committee.* New York: Oxford University Press.

Ahlburg, D. A., & De Vita, C. J. (1992). New realities of the American family. *Population Bulletin, 47*(2), 1–44.

Ahmeduzzaman, M., & Roopnarine, J. L. (1992). Sociodemographic factors, functioning style, social support, and fathers' involvement with preschoolers in African-American families. *Journal of Marriage and the Family, 54,* 699–707.

Ainsworth, M. D. S., Blehar, M. C., Waters, E., & Wall, S. (1978). *Patterns of attachment.* Hillsdale, NJ: Erlbaum.

Alexander, K. L., & Entwisle, D. R. (1988). Achievement in the first 2 years of school: Patterns and processes. *Monographs of the Society for Research in Child Development, 53*(2, Serial No. 218).

Alexander, K. L., Entwisle, D. R., & Dauber, S. L. (1994). *On the success of failure: A reassessment of the affects of retention in the primary grades.* New York: Cambridge University Press.

Allen, W. (1978). The search for applicable theories of Black family life. *Journal of Marriage and the Family, 40,* 111–129.

Amaro, H., Whitaker, R., Coffman, J., & Heeren, T. (1990). Acculturation and marijuana and cocaine use: Findings from the HHANES 1982–1984. *American Journal of Public Health, 80,* 54–60.

American Psychological Association. (1992). Ethical principles of psychologists and code of conduct. *American Psychologist, 47,* 1597–1611.

Anderson, L. P. (1991). Acculturative stress: A theory of relevance to Black Americans. *Clinical Psychology Review, 11,* 685–702.

Anderson, M. (1992). *Intelligence and development: A cognitive theory.* Cambridge, MA: Blackwell.

Aneshensel, C. S., Fielder, E. P., & Becerra, R. M. (1989). Fertility and fertility-related behavior among Mexican-American and non-Hispanic White female adolescents. *Journal of Health and Social Behavior, 30,* 56–76.

Anisfeld, E., Casper, V., Noyzyce, M., & Cunningham, N. (1990). Does infant carrying promote attachment? An experimental study of the effects of increased physical contact on the development of attachment. *Child Development, 61*(5), 1617–1627.

Aponte, R. (1991). Urban Hispanic poverty: Desegregation and explanations. *Social Problems, 38,* 516–528.

Armor, D. J. (1992). Why is Black educational achievement rising? *Public Interest, 108,* 65–80.

Arnez, N. L. (1978). Implementation of desegregation as a discriminatory process. *Journal of Negro Education, 46,* 28–34.

Azibo, D. A. (1988). Understanding the proper and improper usage of the comparative research framework. *Journal of Black Psychology, 15,* 81–91.

Babington, C. (1992, September 5). U-Md. cancels conference on genetic link to crime: NIH pulled funds over proposed conference. *The Washington Post,* pp. A1, A14.

Baca Zinn, M. (1989). Family, race, and poverty in the eighties. *Signs: Journal of Women in Culture and Society, 14,* 133–174.

Bachman, J. G., Wallace, J. M., Jr., O'Malley, P. M., Johnston, L. D., Kurth, C. L., & Neighbors, H. W. (1991). Racial/ethnic differences in smoking, drinking, and illicit drug use among American high school seniors. *American Journal of Public Health, 81,* 372–377.

Bakeman, R., & Brown, J. V. (1980). Early interaction: Consequences for social and mental development at three years. *Child Development, 51*(2), 437–447.

Baltes, P. B. (1987). Theoretical propositions of life-span developmental psychology: On the dynamics between growth and decline. *Developmental Psychology, 23,* 611–626.

Banks, J. A. (1993). The canon debate, knowledge construction, and multicultural education. *Educational Researcher, 22,* 4–16.

Barnes, G. M., Farrell, M. P., & Banerjee, S. (1995). Family influences on alcohol abuse and other problem behaviors among black and white adolescents in a general population sample. In G. M. Boyd, J. Howard, & R. A. Zucker (Eds.), *Alcohol problems among adolescents: Current directions in prevention research* (pp. 13–32). Hillsdale, NJ: Erlbaum.

Baron, J. B., & Sternberg, R. S. (Eds.). (1986). *Teaching thinking skills: Theory and practice.* New York: Freeman.

Baumrind, D. (1995). *Optimal caregiving and child maltreatment: Continuities and discontinuities in etiology. Michigan State University series on children, youth, and families* (Vol. 1). New York: Garland.

Bean, F. D., & Frisbee, W. P. (Eds.). (1978). *The demography of racial and ethnic groups.* New York: Academic Press.

Beauvais, F., Oetting, E. R., Wolf, W., & Edwards, R. W. (1989). American Indian youth and drugs, 1976–1987: A continuing problem. *American Journal of Public Health, 79,* 634–636.

Becerra, J., Hogue, C., Atrash, H., & Perez, N. (1991). Infant mortality among Hispanics. *Journal of the American Medical Association, 265,* 217–221.

Belanger, S., & Pinard, M. (1991). Ethnic movements and the competition model: Some missing links. *American Sociological Review, 56,* 446–457.

Belgrave, F. Z., Cherry, V. R., Cunningham, D., Walwyn, S., Latlaka-Rennert, K., & Phillips, F. (1994). The influence of Afrocentric values, self-esteem, and black identity on drug attitudes among African American fifth graders: A preliminary study. *The Journal of Black Psychology, 20,* 143–156.

Belsky, J., Steinberg, L., & Draper, P. (1991). Childhood experience, interpersonal development, and reproductive strategy: An evolutionary theory of socialization. *Child Development, 62,* 647–670.

Benin, M., & Keith, M. (1995). The social support of employed African American and Anglo mothers. *Journal of Family Issues, 16*(3), 275–297.

Bennett, M. H. (1993, February). President's message: Actions on the "Federal Violence Initiative." *Psych Discourse: Association of Black Psychologists' News Journal, 24*(2), 4–8.

Benson, P. L., & Donahue, M. J. (1989). Ten year trends in at risk behaviors: A national study of Black adolescents: Black adolescents [Special issue]. *Journal of Adolescent Research, 4*(2), 125–130.

Bernal, M. E., Knight, G. P., Garza, C. A., Ocampo, K. A., & Cota, M. K. (1990). The development of ethnic identity in Mexican-American children. *Hispanic Journal of Behavioral Sciences, 12*(1), 3–24.

Berry, J. W. (1969). On cross-cultural comparability. *International Journal of Psychology, 4,* 119–128.

Berry, J. W. (1979). Introduction to methodology. In H. C. Triandis & J. W. Berry (Eds.), *Handbook of cross cultural psychology: Vol. 2. Methodology* (pp. 1–28). Boston: Allyn & Bacon.

Berry, J. W. (1980). Acculturative stress: The role of ecology, culture and differentiation. *Journal of Cross-Cultural Psychology, 5,* 382–406.

Berry, J. W. (1989). Imposed etics-emics-derived etics: The operationalization of a compelling idea. *International Journal of Psychology, 24,* 721–735.

Berry, J. W. (1990). Psychology of acculturation. In J. Berman (Ed.), *Cross-cultural perspectives: Nebraska Symposium on Motivation* (pp. 201–234). Lincoln: University of Nebraska Press.

Betancourt, H., & López, S. R. (1993). The study of culture, ethnicity, and race in American psychology. *American Psychologist, 48,* 629–637.

Bettes, B. A., Dusenbury, L., Kerner, J., James-Ortiz, S., & Botvin, G. J. (1990). Ethnicity and psychosocial factors in alcohol and tobacco use in adolescence: Minority children [Special issue]. *Child Development, 61*(2), 557–565.

Biafora, F. A., Jr., Warheit, G. J., Zimmerman, R. S., Gil, A. G., Apospori, E., & Taylor, D. (1993). Racial mistrust and deviant behaviors among ethnically diverse Black adolescent boys. *Journal of Applied Social Psychology, 23,* 891–910.

Billingsley, A. (1992). *Climbing Jacob's ladder: The enduring legacy of African-American families.* New York: Simon & Schuster.

Birman, D. (1984). Acculturation and human diversity in a multicultural society. In E. Trickett, R. Watts, & D. Birman (Eds.), *Human diversity: Perspective on people in context* (pp. 261–284). San Francisco: Jossey-Bass.

Botvin, G. J., Baker, E., Botvin, E. M., Dusenbury, L., Cardwell, J., & Dias, T. (1993). Factors promoting cigarette smoking among Black youth: A causal modeling approach. *Addictive Behaviors, 18,* 397–405.

Bourdieu, P. (1986). Forms of capital. In J. G. Richardson (Ed.), *Handbook of theory and research for the sociology of education* (pp. 241–260). Westport, CT: Greenwood Press.

Bowlby, J. (1973). *Attachment and loss: Vol. 2. Separation, anxiety and anger.* New York: Basic Books.

Bowlby, J. (1980). *Attachment and loss: Vol. 3. Loss, sadness and depression.* New York: Basic Books.

Bowlby, J. (1969/1982). *Attachment and loss: Vol. 1. Attachment* (2nd ed.). New York: Basic Books.

Bowler, S., Sheon, A. R., D'Angelo, L. J., & Vermund, S. H. (1992). HIV and AIDS among adolescents in the United States: Increasing risk in the 1990s. *Journal of Adolescence, 15,* 345–371.

Bowman, P. J. (1990). Coping with provider role strain: Adaptive cultural resources among Black husband-fathers. *Journal of Black Psychology, 16*(2), 1–21.

Bowman, P. J., & Howard, C. (1985). Race related socialization, motivation, and academic achievement: A study of Black youths in three-generation families. *Journal of American Academy of Child Psychiatry, 24,* 134–141.

Boykin, A. W. (1978). Psychological/behavioral verve in academic/task performance: Pre-theoretical considerations. *Journal of Negro Education, 47,* 343–354.

Boykin, A. W. (1986). The triple quandary and the schooling of Afro-American children. In U. Neisser (Ed.), *The school achievement of minority children* (pp. 57–92). Hillsdale, NJ: Erlbaum.

Boykin, A. W., & Toms, F. (1985). Black child socialization: A conceptual framework. In H. McAdoo & J. McAdoo (Eds.), *Black children: Social, educational, and parental environments* (pp. 32–51). Newbury Park, CA: Sage.

Braucht, G. N. (1979). Interactional analysis of suicidal behavior. *Journal of Consulting and Clinical Psychology, 47,* 653–669.

Broman, C. L. (1991). Gender, work-family roles, and psychological well-being of Blacks. *Journal of Marriage and the Family, 53*(2), 509–520.

Bronfenbrenner, U. (1977). Toward an experimental ecology of human development. *American Psychologist, 32,* 513–531.

Bronfenbrenner, U. (1979). *The ecology of human development.* Cambridge, MA: Harvard University Press.

Brookins, C. C. (1994). The relationship between Afrocentric values and racial identity attitudes: Validation of the belief systems analysis scale on African American college students. *The Journal of Black Psychology, 20,* 128–142.

Brooks-Gunn, J., Duncan, G. J., Klebanov, P. K., & Sealand, N. (1993). Do neighborhoods influence child and adolescent development? *American Journal of Sociology, 99,* 353–395.

Broughton, J. M. (1987). An introduction to critical developmental psychology. In J. M. Broughton (Ed.), *Critical theories of psychological development* (pp. 1–30). New York: Plenum Press.

Broussard, E. R. (1995). Infant attachment in a sample of adolescent mothers. *Child Psychiatry and Human Development, 25*(4), 211–219.

Bruce, J., Lloyd, C. B., Leonard, A., Engle, P. L., & Duffy, N. (1995). *Families in focus: New perspectives on mothers, fathers, and children.* New York: Population Council.

Brunswick, A. F., & Messeri, P. (1984). Causal factors in onset of adolescent cigarette smoking: A prospective study of urban Black youth. In H. Shaffer & B. Stimmil (Eds.), *The addictive behaviors.* New York: Haworth Press.

Burlew, A. K., Banks, W. C., McAdoo, H. P., & Azibo, D. A. (Eds.). (1992). *African American psychology: Theory, research and practice.* Newbury Park, CA: Sage.

Burlew, A. K., & Smith, L. R. (1991). Measures of racial identity: An overview and a proposed framework. *Journal of Black Psychology, 17,* 53–71.

Burton, L. M. (1990). Teenage childbearing as an alternative life-course strategy in multigeneration black families. *Human Nature, 1,* 123–143.

Burton, L. M. (1992). Black grandparents rearing children of drug-addicted parents: Stressors, outcomes, and social service needs. *The Gerontologist, 32,* 744–751.

Burts, D. C., Hart, C. H., Charlesworth, R., Fleege, P. O., Mosley, J., & Thomasson, R. H. (1992). Observed activities and stress behaviors of children in developmentally appropriate and inappropriate kindergarten classrooms. *Early Childhood Research Quarterly, 7*, 297–318.

Busch-Rossnagel, N. (1992). Commonalities between test validity and external validity in basic research on Hispanics. In K. F. Geisinger (Ed.), *Psychological testing of Hispanics* (pp. 195–214). Washington, DC: American Psychological Association.

Busch-Rossnagel, N., Vargas, M., Knauf, D. E., & Planos, R. (1993). Mastery motivation in ethnic minority groups: The sample case of Hispanics. In D. Messar (Ed.), *Mastery motivation in early childhood* (pp. 132–148). London: Routledge & Kegan Paul.

Caetanno, R. (1987). Acculturation and drinking patterns among U.S. Hispanics. *British Journal of Addiction, 82*, 789–799.

Cairns, R. B., & Cairns, B. (1995). *Lifelines and risks: Pathways of youth in our time.* London: Paramount.

Caldaron, J. (1992). A Hispanic and a Latino: The viability of categories for panethnic unity. *Latin American Perspectives, 19*, 18–36.

Caldas, S. J. (1993). Reexamination of input and process factor effects on public school achievement. *Journal of Educational Research, 86*(4), 206–214.

Cameron, N., & Wright, C. A. (1990). The start of breast development and age at menarche in South African black females. *South African Medical Journal, 78*(9), 536–539.

Campen, J. (1994, January/February). Lending insights: Hard proof that banks discriminate. *Dollars and Sense, 191*, 16–19, 36–37.

Canino, G., & Guarnaccia, P. (1997). Methodological challenges in the assessment of Hispanic children and adolescents. *Applied Developmental Science, 1*(3), 124–134.

Canner, G. B., Passmore, W., Smith, D. S., Koenig, K., Johnson, C., Phipps, J., & Rhyne, M. (1994). Residential lending to low-income and minority families: Evidence from the 1992 HMDA data. *Federal Reserve Bulletin, 80*(2), 79–108.

Canner, G. B., & Smith, D. S. (1992). Expanded HMDA data on residential lending: One year later. *Federal Reserve Bulletin, 78*(11), 801–824.

Caplan, N., & Nelson, S. D. (1973). On being useful: The nature and consequences of psychological research on social problems. *American Psychologist, 28*, 199–211.

Casas, J. M., & San Miguel, S. (1993). Beyond questions and discussions, there is a need for action: A response to Mio and Iwamasa. *The Counseling Psychologist, 21*(2), 233–239.

Ceci, S. J. (1990). *On intelligence . . . more or less: A bio-ecological treatise on intellectual development.* Englewood Cliffs, NJ: Prentice-Hall.

Center for the Study of Social Policy. (1992/1993). *1992 KIDS COUNT data book: State profiles of child well-being.* Available from the Center for the Study of Social Policy, Suite 503, 1250 Eye Street, NW, Washington, DC 20005.

Centers for Disease Control. (1992, April). *HIV/AIDS surveillance report.* Atlanta, GA: Author.

Champagne, D. (1993). Toward a multidimensional historical comparative methodology: Context, process, and causality. In J. H. Stanfield & R. M. Dennis (Eds.), *Race and ethnicity in research methods* (pp. 233–253). Newbury Park, CA: Sage.

Chan, K. S., & Hune, S. (1995). Racialization and panethnicity: From Asians in America to Asian Americans. In W. D. Hawley & A. W. Jackson (Eds.), *Toward a common destiny: Improving race and ethnic relations in America* (pp. 205–236). San Francisco: Jossey-Bass.

Chapa, J., & Valencia, R. R. (1993). Latino population growth, demographic characteristics, and educational stagnation: An examination of recent trends. *Hispanic Journal of Behavioral Sciences, 15*(2), 165–187.

Chase-Lansdale, P. L., Brooks-Gunn, J., & Zamsky, E. S. (1994). Young African-American multigenerational families in poverty: Quality of mothering and grandmothering. *Child Development, 65*(2), 373–393.

Chatters, L. M., Taylor, R. J., & Jayakody, R. (1994). Fictive kinship relations in Black extended families. *Journal of Comparative Family Studies, 25*(3), 297–312.

Chavez, E. L., & Swaim, R. C. (1992). An epidemiological comparison of Mexican-American and White non-Hispanic 8th and 12th grade students' substance use. *American Journal of Public Health, 82*, 445–447.

Christoffel, K. K. (1990). Violent death and injury in U.S. children and adolescents. *American Journal of Diseases of Childhood, 144*, 697–706.

Cloward, R. A., & Ohlin, L. E. (1960). *Delinquency and opportunity: A theory of delinquent gangs.* New York: Free Press.

Cocking, R. R. (1994). Ecologically valid frameworks of development: Accounting for continuities and discontinuities across contexts. In P. M. Greenfield & R. R. Cocking (Eds.), *Cross-cultural roots of minority child development* (pp. 393–410). Hillsdale, NJ: Erlbaum.

Cole, J. (1970). Negro, Black, and nigger. *Black Scholar, 1*, 40–44.

Coleman, J. S. (1990). *Foundations of social theory.* Cambridge, MA: Harvard University Press.

Comer, J. P. (1989). School power: A model for improving Black student achievement. In W. D. Smith & E. W. Chunn (Eds.), *Black education: A quest for equity and excellence* (pp. 187–200). New Brunswick, NJ: Transaction.

Conciatore, J. (1990). Nation's report card shows little progress: Black students close gap. *Black Issues in Higher Education, 6*(22), 30–31.

Connell, J. P., Spencer, M. B., & Aber, J. L. (1994). Educational risk and resilience in African-American youth: Context, self, action, and outcomes in school. *Child Development, 65*(2), 493–506.

Connor, M. E. (1986). Some parenting attitudes of young black fathers. In R. A. Lewis & R. E. Salt (Eds.), *Men in families* (pp. 159–168). Beverly Hills, CA: Sage.

Connor, M. E. (1988). Teenage fatherhood: Issues confronting young black males. In J. T. Gibbs, A. F. Brunswick, M. E. Connor, R. Dembo, T. E. Larson, R. J. Reed, & B. Solomon (Eds.), *Young, Black, and male in America: An endangered species* (pp. 188–218). Dover, MA: Auburn House.

Cooper, C. R. (1994). Cultural perspectives on continuity and change in adolescents' relationships. In R. Montemayor, G. R. Adams, & T. P. Gullotta (Eds.), *Personal relationships during adolescence* (pp. 78–100). Thousand Oaks, CA: Sage.

Crane, J. (1991). The epidemic theory of ghettos and neighborhood effects on dropping out and teenage childbearing. *American Journal of Sociology, 64*, 32–41.

Cross, W. E. (1985). Black identity: Rediscovering the distinction between personal identity and reference group orientation. In M. B. Spencer, G. K. Brookins, & W. R. Allen (Eds.), *Beginnings: The social and affective development of black children* (pp. 155–172). Hillsdale, NJ: Erlbaum.

Cross, W. E. (1991). *Shades of Black: Diversity in African-American identity.* Philadelphia: Temple University Press.

Cross, W. E. (1995). Oppositional identity and African American youth: Issues and prospects. In W. D. Hawley & A. W. Jackson (Eds.), *Toward a common destiny: Improving race and ethnic relations in America* (pp. 185–204). San Francisco, CA: Jossey-Bass.

Cross, W. E., Parham, T. A., & Helms, J. E. (1991). The stages of Black identity development: Nigrescence models. In R. L. Jones (Ed.), *Black psychology* (3rd ed., pp. 319–338). Berkeley, CA: Cobb & Henry.

Cuellar, I., Arnold, B., & Maldonado, R. (1995). Acculturation rating scale for Mexican Americans: II. A revision of the original ARSMA scale. *Hispanic Journal of Behavioral Sciences, 17*, 274–304.

Cuellar, I., Harris, L. C., & Jasso, R. (1980). An acculturation scale for Mexican-American normal and clinical populations. *Hispanic Journal of Behavioral Sciences, 2*, 199–217.

D'Amico, R. (1984). Does working in high school impair academic progress? *Sociology of Education, 57*, 157–164.

Daniel, J. H. (1994). Exclusion and emphasis reframed as a matter of ethics. *Ethics & Behavior, 4*, 229–235.

Danziger, S. K., & Radin, N. (1990). Absent does not equal uninvolved: Predictors of fathering in teen mother families. *Journal of Marriage and the Family, 52*(3), 636–642.

Davis, J. F. (1991). *Who is Black? One nation's definition.* University Park: Pennsylvania State University.

Delgado, M. (1990). Hispanic adolescents and substance abuse: Implications for research, treatment, and prevention. In A. R. Stiffman & L. E. Davis (Eds.), *Ethnic issues in adolescent mental health.* Newbury Park, CA: Sage.

Delgado-Gaitan, C. (1994). Socializing young children in Mexican-American families: An intergenerational perspective. In P. M. Greenfield & R. R. Cocking (Eds.), *Cross-cultural roots of minority child development* (pp. 55–86). Hillsdale, NJ: Erlbaum.

Demo, D. H., & Hughes, M. (1990). Socialization and racial identity among Black Americans. *Social Psychology Quarterly, 53*, 364–374.

Dennis, R. M. (1993). Studying across difference: Race, class and gender in qualitative research. In J. H. Stanfield, III & R. M. Dennis (Eds.), *Race and ethnicity in research methods* (pp. 53–74). Newbury Park, CA: Sage.

Dilworth-Anderson, P. (1992). Extended kin networks in Black families. *Generations, 16*(3), 29–32.

Dilworth-Anderson, P., & Burton, M. (1996). Rethinking family development: Critical conceptual issues in the study of diverse groups. *Journal of Social and Personal Relationships, 13*, 325–334.

Dodge, K. A., Pettit, G. S., & Bates, J. E. (1994). Socialization mediators of the relation between socioeconomic status and child conduct problems. *Child Development, 65*, 649–665.

Donald, J., & Rattansi, A. (1992). *"Race," culture and difference.* London: Sage.

Dornbusch, S. M., Ritter, P. L., & Steinberg, L. (1991). Community influences on the relation of family statuses to adolescent school performance: Differences between African Americans and non-Hispanic Whites. *American Journal of Education, 99*(4), 543–567.

Dryfoos, J. G. (1990). *Adolescents at risk: Prevalence and prevention.* New York: Oxford University Press.

Dubois, W. E. B. (1989). *The souls of Black folk.* New York: Penguin. (Original work published 1903)

Dunbar, R. (1992). Mating and parental care. In S. Jones, R. Martin, D. Pilbeam, & S. Bunney (Eds.), *Cambridge encyclopedia of human evolution* (pp. 150–154). Cambridge, England: Cambridge University Press.

Duncan, G. J., Brooks-Gunn, J., & Klebanov, P. K. (1994). Economic deprivation and early childhood development. *Child Development, 65,* 296–318.

Dunn, L. (1987). *Bilingual Hispanic children in the U.S. mainland: A review of research on their cognitive, linguistic, and scholastic development.* Minneapolis, MN: American Guidance Service.

DuRant, R. H., Pendergrast, R., & Seymore, C. (1990). Sexual behavior among Hispanic female adolescents in the United States. *Pediatrics, 85,* 1051–1058.

Elder, G. H., Jr., & Ardelt, M. (in press). Family influences and adolescents' lives. In F. F. Furstenberg, Jr., J. Eccles, G. H. Elder, Jr., T. Cook, & A. Sameroff (Eds.), *Managing to make it: Urban families in high risk neighborhoods.* Chicago: University of Chicago Press.

Elliot, D. S., Huizinga, D., & Ageton, S. (1985). *Explaining delinquency and drug use.* Beverly Hills, CA: Sage.

Entwisle, D. R. (1990). Schools and the adolescent. In S. S. Feldman & G. R. Elliott (Eds.), *At the threshold: The developing adolescent* (pp. 197–224). Cambridge, MA: Harvard University Press.

Entwisle, D. R., Alexander, K. L., Cadigan, D., & Pallas, A. M. (1987). Kindergarten experience: Cognitive effects or socialization? *American Educational Research Journal, 24*(3), 337–364.

Entwisle, D. R., & Astone, N. (1994). Some practical guidelines for measuring youth's race/ethnicity and socioeconomic status. *Child Development, 65,* 1521–1540.

Entwisle, D. R., & Hayduk, L. A. (1978). *Too great expectations: The academic outlook of young children.* Baltimore: Johns Hopkins University Press.

Entwisle, D. R., & Hayduk, L. A. (1982). *Early schooling: Cognitive and affective outcomes.* Baltimore: Johns Hopkins University Press.

Epstein, J. (1985). After the bus arrives: Resegregation in desegregated schools. *Journal of Social Issues, 41*(3), 23–43.

Essed, P. J. M. (1991). *Understanding everyday racism.* Newbury Park, CA: Sage.

Eyler, J., Cook, V. F., & Ward, L. E. (1983). Resegregation: Segregation within desegregated schools. In C. H. Rossell & W. D. Hawley (Eds.), *The consequences of school desegregation* (pp. 126–162). Philadelphia: Temple University Press.

Featherman, D. L., Spenner, K. I., & Tsunematsu, N. (1988). Class and the socialization of children: Constancy, change, or irrelevance? In R. M. Lerner, E. M. Hetherington, & M. Perlmutter (Eds.), *Child development in life-span perspective* (pp. 67–90). Hillsdale, NJ: Erlbaum.

Federal Glass Ceiling Commission. (1995). *Good for business: Making full use of the nation's human capital. The environmental scan.* Washington, DC: U.S. Government Printing Office.

Félix-Ortiz, M., Newcomb, M. D., & Myers, H. (1994). A multidimensional measure of cultural identity for Latino and Latina adolescents. *Hispanic Journal of Behavioral Sciences, 16,* 99–115.

Ferguson, R. F. (1991). Racial patterns in how school and teacher quality affect achievement and earnings. *Challenge, 2*(1), 1–35.

Fingerhut, L., Ingram, D., & Feldman, J. (1992). Firearm and nonfirearm homicide among persons 15–19 years of age. *Journal of the American Medical Association, 267,* 3048–3053.

Fischer, C. S., Hout, M., Sanchez Jankowiski, M., Lucas, S. R., Swedler, A., & Voss, K. (1996). *Inequality by design: Cracking the bell curve myth.* Princeton, NJ: Princeton University Press.

Fisher, C. B. (1993). Integrating science and ethics in research with high-risk children and youth. *SRCD Social Policy Report, 7*(4), 1–27.

Fisher, C. B. (in press). A relational perspective on ethics-in-science decision making for research with vulnerable populations. *IRB: Review of Human Subjects Research.*

Fisher, C. B., & Brennan, M. (1992). Applications and ethics in developmental psychology. In R. M. Lerner & M. Perlmutter (Eds.), *Life-span development and behavior* (Vol. 11, pp. 189–219). Hillsdale, NJ: Erlbaum.

Fisher, C. B., Hatashi-Wong, M., & Isman, L. (in press). Ethical and legal issues in clinical child psychology. In W. K. Silverman & T. H. Ollendick (Eds.), *Developmental issues in the clinical treatment of children and adolescent.* New York: Allyn & Bacon.

Fisher, C. B., Higgins-D'Allesandro, A., Rau, J. M. B., Kuther, T. L., & Belanger, S. (1996). Referring and reporting adolescent research participants at risk: A view from urban youth. *Child Development, 67,* 2086–2100.

Fisher, C. B., Hoagwood, K., & Jensen, P. (1996). Casebook on ethical issues in research with children and adolescents with mental disorders. In K. Hoagwood, P. Jensen, & C. B. Fisher (Eds.), *Ethical issues in research with children and adolescents with mental disorders* (pp. 135–238). Hillsdale, NJ: Erlbaum.

Fisher, C. B., & Lerner, R. M. (Eds.). (1994). *Applied developmental psychology.* New York: McGraw-Hill.

Fisher, C. B., & Murray, J. P. (1996). Applied developmental science comes of age. In C. B. Fisher, J. P. Murray, & I. E. Sigel (Eds.), *Applied developmental science: Graduate training for diverse disciplines and educational settings* (pp. 1–22). Norwood, NJ: ABLEX.

Fisher, C. B., Murray, J. P., Dill, J. R., Hagen, J. W., Hogan, M. J., Lerner, R. M., Rebok, G. W., Sigel, I. E., Sostek, A. M., Smyer, M. A., Spencer, M. B., & Wilcox, B. (1993). The National Conference on Graduate Education in the applications of developmental science across the life span. *Journal of Applied Developmental Psychology, 14,* 1–10.

Fisher, C. B., & Rosendahl, S. A. (1990). Psychological risks and remedies of research participation. In C. B. Fisher & W. W. Tryon (Eds.), *Ethics in applied developmental psychology: Emerging issues in an emerging field* (pp. 43–60). Norwood, NJ: ABLEX.

Fisher, C. B., & Tryon, W. W. (Eds.). (1990). *Ethics in applied developmental psychology: Emerging issues in an emerging field.* Norwood, NJ: ABLEX.

Flynn, J. R. (1991). *Asian Americans: Achievement beyond IQ.* Hillsdale, NJ: Erlbaum.

Forbes, J. (1992). The Hispanic spin: Party politics and governmental manipulation of ethnic identity. *Latin American Perspectives, 75,* 59–78.

Ford, D. Y., & Harris, J. J. (1992). The American achievement ideology and achievement differentials among preadolescent gifted and non-gifted African American males and females. *Journal of Negro Education, 61*(1), 45–64.

Ford, D. Y., & Harris, J. J. (1996). Perceptions and attitudes of Black students toward school: School, achievement, and other educational variables. *Child Development, 67*(3), 1144–1152.

Fordham, S., & Ogbu, J. U. (1986). Black students' school success: Coping with the "burden of 'acting White.'" *Urban Review, 18*(3), 176–206.

Foster, M. (1994). The role of community and culture in school reform efforts: Examining the views of African-American teachers. *Educational Foundations, 8*(2), 5–26.

Fox, N. (1995). Of the way we were. Adult memories about attachment experiences and their role in determining infant-parent relationships: A commentary on Van IJzendoorn. *Psychological Bulletin, 117*(3), 404–410.

Fracasso, M. P., & Busch-Rossnagel, N. A. (1992). Parents and children of Hispanic origin. In M. E. Procidano & C. B. Fisher (Eds.), *Contemporary families: A handbook for school professionals* (pp. 83–98). New York: Teachers College Press.

Fracasso, M. P., Busch-Rossnagel, N. A., & Fisher, C. (1994). The relationship of maternal behavior and acculturation to the quality of attachment in Hispanic infants living in New York City. *Hispanic Journal of Behavioral Sciences, 16*(2), 143–154.

Freidenberg, J., Mulvihill, M., & Caraballo, L. R. (1993). From ethnography to survey: Some methodological issues in research on health seeking in East Harlem. *Human Organization, 52,* 151–161.

Frisby, C. L., & Tucker, C. M. (1993). Black children's perception of self: Implications for educators. *Educational Forum, 57*(2), 146–156.

Frodi, A., Keller, B., Foye, H., Liptak, G., Bridges, L., Grolnick, W., Berko, J., McAnarney, E., & Lawrence, R. (1984). Determinants of attachment and mastery motivation in infants born to adolescent mothers. *Infant Mental Health Journal, 5*(1), 15–23.

Gaines, S., Jr., & Reed, E. (1995). Prejudice from Allport to DuBois. *American Psychologist, 50,* 96–103.

Galambos, N., & Silbereisen, R. (1987). Income change, parental outlook, and adolescent expectations for job success. *Journal of Marriage and the Family, 49,* 141–149.

Galan, F. J. (1988). Alcoholism prevention and Hispanic youth. *Journal of Drug Issues, 18,* 49–68.

Garbarino, J., & Ebata, A. (1983). The significance of ethnic and cultural differences in child maltreatment. *Journal of Marriage and the Family, 45*(4), 773–783.

Garber, H. L. (1988). *The Milwaukee project: Preventing mental retardation in children at risk.* Washington, DC: American Association of Mental Retardation.

Garber, H. L., Hodge, J. D., Rynders, J., Dever, R., & Velu, R. (1991). The Milwaukee project: Setting the record straight. *American Journal of Mental Retardation, 95*(5), 493–525.

Garcia, E. E., & Hurtado, A. (1995). Becoming American: A review of current research on the development of racial and ethnic identity in children. In W. D. Hawley & A. W. Jackson (Eds.), *Toward a common destiny: Improving race and ethnic relations in America* (pp. 163–184). San Francisco: Jossey-Bass.

García Coll, C. T., & Meyer, E. C. (1993). The sociocultural context of infant development. In C. H. Zeanah (Ed.), *Handbook of infant mental health* (pp. 56–59). New York: Guilford Press.

García Coll, C. T., Meyer, E. C., & Brillion, L. (1995). Ethnic and minority parenting. In M. H. Bornstein (Ed.), *Handbook of parenting* (Vol. 2, pp. 189–209). NJ: Erlbaum.

Gardner, H. (1993). *Multiple intelligences: The theory in practice.* New York: Basic Books.

Garrett, P., Ng'andu, N., & Ferron, J. (1994). Poverty experiences of young children and the quality of their home environments. *Child Development, 65,* 331–345.

Garza, R. T., & Gallegos, P. I. (1985). Environmental influences and personal choice: A humanistic perspective on acculturation. *Hispanic Journal of Behavioral Sciences, 7,* 365–379.

Gibbs, J. T. (1986). *Psychosocial correlates of sexual attitudes and behaviors in urban early adolescent females: Implications for intervention.* New York: Haworth Press.

Gibbs, J. T. (1988). Conclusions and recommendations. In J. T. Gibbs, A. F. Brunswick, M. E. Conner, R. Dembo, T. E. Larson, R. J. Reed, & B. Solomon (Eds.), *Young, black, and male in America: An endangered species* (pp. 317–363). Dover, MA: Auburn House.

Gibson, J. W., & Kempf, J. (1990). Attitudinal predictors of sexual activity in Hispanic adolescent females. *Journal of Adolescent Research, 5,* 414–430.

Gibson, M. A., & Ogbu, J. U. (1991). *Minority status and schooling: A comparative study of immigrants and involuntary minorities.* New York: Garland.

Gil, A. G., Vega, W. A., & Dimas, J. M. (1994). Acculturative stress and personal adjustment among Hispanic adolescent boys. *Journal of Community Psychology, 22,* 43–54.

Gilbert, M. J., & Cervantes, R. (1986). Patterns and practices of alcohol use among Mexican Americans: A comprehensive review. *Hispanic Journal of Behavioral Sciences, 8,* 1–60.

Gillmore, M. R., Catalano, R. F., Morrison, D. M., Wells, E. A., Iritanim, B., & Hawkins, J. D. (1990). Racial differences in acceptability and availability of drugs and early initiation of substance use. *American Journal of Drug and Alcohol Abuse, 16,* 185–206.

Gimenéz, M. E. (1989). Latino/Hispanic—who needs a name? The case against a standardized terminology. *International Journal of Healthy Services, 19,* 557–571.

Gimenéz, M. E. (1992). U.S. ethnic politics: Implications for Latin Americans. *Latin American Perspectives, 19,* 7–17.

Giovannoni, J., & Becerra, R. M. (1979). *Defining child abuse.* New York: Free Press.

Glick, R., & Moore, J. (1990). *Drugs in Hispanic communities.* New Brunswick, NJ: Rutgers University Press.

Goldberg, C. J., & Botvin, G. J. (1993). Assertiveness in Hispanic adolescents: Relationship to alcohol use and abuse. *Psychological Reports, 73,* 227–238.

Goldberg, D. T. (1992). The semantics of race. *Ethnic and Racial Studies, 15,* 543–569.

Goldscheider, F. K., & Goldscheider, C. (1991). The intergenerational flow of income: Family structure and the status of Black Americans. *Journal of Marriage and the Family, 53*(2), 499–508.

Gonzales, N. A., & Cauce, A. M. (1995). Ethnic identity and multicultural competence: Dilemmas and challenges for minority youth. In W. D. Hawley & A. W. Jackson (Eds.), *Toward a common destiny: Improving race and ethnic relations in America* (pp. 131–162). San Francisco: Jossey-Bass.

Gopaul-McNicol, S. (1988). Racial identification and racial preference of Black preschool children in New York and Trinidad. *Journal of Black Psychology, 14*(2), 65–68.

Gordon, T. (1973). Notes on White and Black psychology. *Journal of Social Issues, 29,* 87–95.

Gottfredson, D. C. (1985). Youth employment, crime, and schooling: A longitudinal study of a national sample. *Developmental Psychology, 21,* 419–432.

Goudsblom, J. (1989). The domestication of fire and the origins of language. In J. Wind, E. G. Pulleyblank, E. de Grolier, & B. H. Bichakjian (Eds.), *Studies in language origins* (Vol. 1, pp. 159–172). Amsterdam, The Netherlands: John Benjamin.

Graham, S. (1992). "Most of the subjects were white and middle class": Trends in published research on African Americans in selected APA journals, 1970–1989. *American Psychologist, 47,* 629–639.

Grant, L. (1984). Black females' "place" in desegregated classrooms. *Sociology of Education, 57,* 98–111.

Grant, L. (1985). Race-gender status, classroom interaction, and children's socialization in elementary school. In L. C. Wilkinson & C. B. Marrett (Eds.), *Gender influences in classroom interaction.* New York: Academic Press.

Greenberg, G., & Tobach, E. (Eds.). (1984). *Behavioral evolution and integrative levels.* Hillsdale, NJ: Erlbaum.

Greenberger, E. (1983). A researcher in the policy arena: The case of child labor. *American Psychologist, 38,* 106–111.

Greenfield, P. M. (1994). Independence and interdependence as developmental scripts: Implications for theory, research, and practice. In P. M. Greenfield & R. R. Cocking (Eds.), *Cross-cultural roots of minority child development* (pp. 1–37). Hillsdale, NJ: Erlbaum.

Greenfield, P. M., & Cocking, R. R. (Eds.). (1994). *Cross-cultural roots of minority child development.* Hillsdale, NJ: Erlbaum.

Grier, W., & Cobbs, P. (1968). *Black rage.* New York: Bantam Books.

Griffith, J. (1983). Relationship between acculturation and psychological impairment in adult Mexican-Americans. *Hispanic Journal of Behavioral Sciences, 5,* 431–459.

Guendelman, S. S., Gould, J., Hudes, M., & Eskenazi, B. (1990). Generational difference in perinatal health among the Mexican American population: Findings from HHANES, 1982–1984. *American Journal of Public Health, 80,* 61–65.

Hagen, J. W., Paul, B., Gibb, S., & Wolters, C. (1990, March). *Trends in research as reflected by publications in Child Development: 1930–1989.* Paper presented at biennial meeting of the Society for Research on Adolescence, Atlanta, GA.

Hale-Benson, J. (1986). *Black children: Their roots, culture, and learning styles* (Rev. ed.). Baltimore: Johns Hopkins University Press.

Hale-Benson, J. (1990). Visions for children: African-American early childhood education program. *Early Childhood Research Quarterly, 5*(2), 199–213.

Hammond, W. R., & Yung, B. (1993). Psychology's role in the public health response to assaultive violence among young African-American men. *American Psychologist, 48,* 142–154.

Harrington, A. (in press). Studying race differences, or the problem of "value-free" science. *Psychologische Beitrage.*

Harris, K. M. (1993). Work and welfare among single mothers in poverty. *American Journal of Sociology, 99*(2), 317–352.

Harrison, A. O., Serafica, F., & McAdoo, H. P. (1984). Ethnic minority families of color. In R. D. Parke (Ed.), *The family: Review of child development research* (Vol. 7, pp. 239–371). Chicago: University of Chicago Press.

Harrison, A. O., Wilson, M. N., Pine, C. J., Chan, S. Q., & Buriel, R. (1990). Family ecologies of ethnic minority children. *Child Development, 61*(2), 347–362.

Harwood, R. L. (1992). The influence of culturally derived values on Anglo and Puerto Rican mothers' perceptions of attachment behavior. *Child Development, 63*(4), 822–839.

Hashima, P. Y., & Amato, P. R. (1994). Poverty, social support, and parental behavior. *Child Development, 65,* 394–403.

Haskins, R. (1989). Beyond metaphor: Efficacy of early childhood education. *American Psychologist, 44*(2), 274–282.

Hayes-Buatesta, D., & Chapa, J. (1987). Latino terminology: Conceptual bases for standardized terminology. *American Journal of Public Health, 77,* 61–68.

Heath, S. B. (1989). Oral and literate traditions among Black Americans living in poverty. *American Psychologist, 44,* 367–373.

Heath, S. B. (1995). Race, ethnicity, and the defiance of categories. In W. D. Hawley & A. W. Jackson (Eds.), *Toward a common destiny: Improving race and ethnic relations in America* (pp. 39–70). San Francisco: Jossey-Bass.

Heath, S. B. (1997). Culture: Contested realm in research on children and youth. *Applied Developmental Science, 1*(3), 113–123.

Hein, K. (1989). Commentary on adolescent acquired immunodeficiency syndrome: The next wave of the human immunodeficiency virus epidemic? *The Journal of Pediatrics, 114,* 144–149.

Heitgerd, J. L., & Bursik, R. J., Jr. (1987). Extracommunity dynamics and the ecology of delinquency. *American Journal of Sociology, 92,* 775–787.

Helms, J. E. (1990). *Black and white racial identity: Theory, research, and practice.* New York: Greenwood Press.

Helms, J. E. (1993). I also said, "White racial identity influences White researcher." *The Counseling Psychologist, 21*(2), 240–243.

Hernandez, D. J. (1993). *America's children: Resources from family, government, and the economy.* New York: Russell-Sage Foundation.

Hernandez, D. J. (1994). Children's changing access to resources: A historical perspective. *Social Policy Report, 8*(1), 1–21.

Herrnstein, R. J., & Murray, C. (1994). *The bell curve: Intelligence and class structure in American life.* New York: Free Press.

Hill, R. B. (1997). Social welfare policies and African American families. In H. P. McAdoo (Ed.), *Black families* (3rd ed., pp. 349–363). Thousand Oaks, CA: Sage.

Hilliard, A. G., III. (1989). Kemetic (Egyptian) historical revision: Implications for cross-cultural evaluation and research in education. *Evaluation Practice, 10,* 7–23.

Hinde, R. A. (1991). When is an evolutionary approach useful? *Child Development, 62,* 671–675.

Hinshaw, S. P. (1987). On the distinction between attentional deficits/hyperactivity and conduct problems/aggression in child psychopathology. *Psychological Bulletin, 101*(3), 443–463.

Hirschi, T. (1969). *Causes of delinquency.* Berkeley: University of California Press.

Hodgkinson, H. (1993). American education: The good, the bad, and the task. *Phi Delta Kappan, 74*(8), 619–623.

Hofferth, S. L., Kahn, J. R., & Baldwin, W. (1987). Premarital sexual activity among U.S. teenage women over the past three decades. *Family Planning Perspective, 19,* 46–53.

Hoffman, T., Dana, R. H., & Bolton, B. (1985). Measured acculturation and the MMPI-168 performance of Native American adults. *Journal of Cross-Cultural Psychology, 16,* 243–256.

Hogan, D., Astone, N. M., & Kitigawa, E. M. (1985). Social and environmental factors influencing contraceptive use among Black adolescents. *Family Planning Perspective, 17,* 165–169.

Hogan, D., & Kitigawa, E. (1985). The impact of social status, family structure, and neighborhood on the fertility of Black adolescents. *American Journal of Sociology, 90,* 825–855.

Holmbeck, G. N., Waters, K. A., & Brookman, R. R. (1990). Psychosocial correlates of sexually transmitted diseases and sexual activity in Black adolescent females. *Journal of Adolescent Research, 5,* 431–448.

Holmes, C. T. (1989). Grade level retention effects: A meta-analysis of research studies. In L. A. Shepard & M. L. Smith (Eds.), *Flunking grades: Research and policies on retention* (pp. 16–33). Philadelphia: Falmer Press.

Holt, G. S. (1972). "Inversion" in black communication. In T. Kochman (Ed.), *Rappin' and stylin' out: Communication in urban Black America* (pp. 152–159). Chicago: University of Illinois Press.

Housing Assistance Council. (1994). *Taking stock of rural poverty and housing for the 1990s.* Washington, DC: Housing Assistance Council.

Humphrey, L. G. (1988). Trends in levels of academic achievement of Blacks and other minorities. *Intelligence, 12*(3), 231–260.

Huston, A. C. (Ed.). (1991). *Children in poverty: Child development and public policy.* Cambridge, England: Cambridge University Press.

Huston, A. C., McLoyd, V. C., & Garcia Coll, C. T. (1994). Children and poverty: Issues in contemporary research. *Child Development, 65,* 275–282.

Ikpa, V. (1993). Gender, race, Chapter I participation: The effects of individual characteristics upon academic performance in the elementary grades. *Educational Research Quarterly, 16*(1), 15–24.

Imig, D. R. (1993). Family stress: Paradigms and perceptions. *Family Science Review, 6,* 125–136.

Imig, D. R., & Phillips, R. G. (1992). Operationalizing paradigmatic family theory: The family regime assessment scale (FRAS). *Family Science Review, 5,* 217–234.

Jackson, J. F. (1986). Characteristics of Black infant attachment. *American Journal of Social Psychiatry, 6*(1), 32–35.

Jackson, J. F. (1993). Human behavioral genetics, Scarr's theory, and her view on interventions: A critical review and commentary on their implications. *Child Development, 64*(5), 1318–1332.

James, S. R. (1989). Hominoid use of fire in the lower and middle Pleistocene. A review of the evidence. *Current Anthropology, 30*(1), 1–26.

Jarrett, R. L. (1994). Living poor: Family life among single parent, African-American women. *Social Problems, 41,* 30–49.

Jarrett, R. L. (1995). Growing up poor: The family experiences of socially mobile youth in low-income African American neighborhoods. *Journal of Adolescent Research, 10,* 111–135.

Jaynes, G. D., & Williams, R. M. (1989). *A common destiny: Blacks and American Society.* Washington, DC: National Academy Press.

Jencks, C. M., & Mayer, S. (1990). The social consequences of growing up in a poor neighborhood: A review. In M. McGreary & L. Lynn (Eds.), *Concentrated urban poverty in America.* Washington, DC: National Academy.

Jendryka, B. (1993). Failing grade for federal aid: Is it time to close the book on Chapter 1? *Policy Review, 66,* 77–81.

Jenifer, F. G. (1993, January 15). *Report of the Secretary's blue ribbon panel on violence prevention.* Washington, DC: Department of Health and Human Services.

Jensen, A. R. (1991). Spearman's g and the problem of educational equality. *Oxford Review of Education, 17*(2), 169–187.

Jessor, R., & Jessor, S. L. (1977). *Problem behavior and psychosocial development—A longitudinal study of youth.* New York: Academic Press.

Jessor, R., Van Den Bos, J., Vanderryn, J., Costa, F. M., & Turbin, M. S. (1995). Protective factors in adolescent problem behavior: Moderator effects and developmental change. *Developmental Psychology, 31,* 923–933.

Jewell, K. S. (1988). *Survival of the Black family: The institutional impact of U.S. social policy.* New York: Praeger.

Joe, J. R. (1994). Revaluing Native-American concepts of development and education. In P. M. Greenfield & R. R. Cocking (Eds.), *Cross-cultural roots of minority child development* (pp. 107–114). Hillsdale, NJ: Erlbaum.

Johnson, J. R. (1990). How prepared are our minority students for college-level mathematics? *New Directions for Institutional Research, No. 65, 17*(1), 83–97.

Johnston, L. D., O'Malley, P. M., & Bachman, J. G. (1992). *Smoking, drinking, and illicit drug use among American high school students, college students, and young adults, 1975–1991* (Vol. 1, NIH Publication No. 93-3481). Washington, DC: U.S. Government Printing Office.

Johnston, L. D., O'Malley, P. M., & Bachman, J. D. (1993). *National results on drug use from Monitoring the Future Study, 1975–1992: Vol. 1. Secondary school students.* Rockville, MD: National Institute on Drug Abuse.

Johnstone, J. W. C. (1983). Recruitment to a youth gang. *Youth and Society, 14,* 281–300.

Jones, A. R. (1991). Psychological models of race: What have they been and what should they be? In J. D. Goodchilds (Ed.), *Psychological perspectives on human diversity in*

America (pp. 5–46). Washington, DC: American Psychological Association.

Jones, J. (1991). The politics of personality: Being Black in America. In R. L. Jones (Ed.), *Black psychology* (pp. 305–318). Hampton, VA: Cobb & Henry.

Jones, J. (1993). *Bad blood: The Tuskegee syphilis experiment* (Rev. ed.). New York: Free Press.

Kain, J. F. (1992). The spatial mismatch hypothesis: Three decades later. *Housing Policy Debate, 3*(2), 371–462.

Keefe, S. E. (1984). Real and ideal extended familism among Mexican Americans and Anglo Americans: On the meaning of "close family ties." *Human Organization, 43,* 65–70.

Keefe, S. E., & Padilla, A. M. (1987). *Chicano ethnicity.* Albuquerque: University of New Mexico Press.

Kennedy, J. H., & Bakeman, R. (1984). The early mother-infant relationship and social competence with peers and adults at three years. *Journal of Psychology, 116,* 23–34.

Kim, U. (1988). *Acculturation of Korean immigrants to Canada: Psychological, demographic, and behavioral profiles of emigrating Koreans, non-emigrating Koreans and Korean-Canadians.* Unpublished doctoral dissertation, Queen's University, Kingston, Ontario, Canada.

Kim, U., & Choi, S. (1994). Individualism, collectivism, and child development: A Korean perspective. In P. M. Greenfield & R. R. Cocking (Eds.), *Cross cultural roots of minority child development* (pp. 227–257). Hillsdale, NJ: Erlbaum.

Kivett, V. R. (1991). Centrality of the grandfather role among older rural Black and White men. *Journals of Gerontology, 46*(5), s250–s258.

Klingele, W. E., & Warrick, B. K. (1990). Influence of cost and demographic factors on reading achievement. *Journal of Educational Research, 83*(5), 279–282.

Kohout, J., & Pion, G. (1990). Participation of ethnic minorities in psychology: Where do we stand? In G. Stricker, E. Davis-Russell, E. Bourg, E. Duran, W. Hammond, J. McHolland, K. Polite, & B. Vaughs (Eds.), *Toward ethnic diversification in psychology education and training* (pp. 153–165). Washington, DC: American Psychological Association.

Kornhauser, R. (1978). *Social sources of delinquency.* Chicago: University of Chicago Press.

Kupersmidt, J. P., Griesler, P. C., DeRosier, M. E., Patterson, C. J., & Davis, P. W. (1995). Childhood aggression and peer relations in the context of family and neighborhood effects. *Child Development, 66*(2), 360–375.

Kurtines, W. M., Azmitia, M., & Gewirtz, J. L. (1992). *The role of values in psychology and human development.* New York: Wiley.

LaBelle, T. J., & Ward, C. R. (1994). *Multiculturalism and education: Diversity and its impact on schools and society.* Albany, New York: SUNY Press.

LaFromboise, T. (1988). American Indian mental health policy. *American Psychologist, 43,* 388–397.

LaFromboise, T., Hardin, L., Coleman, K., & Gerton, J. (1993). Psychological impact of biculturalism: Evidence and theory. *Psychological Bulletin, 114,* 395–412.

LaFromboise, T., & Rowe, W. (1983). Skills training for bicultural competence: Rationale and application. *Journal of Counseling Psychology, 30,* 589–595.

Lal, B. B. (1990). *The romance of culture in an urban civilization: Robert E. Park on race and ethnic relations in cities.* London: Routledge & Kegan Paul.

Landrine, H., & Klonoff, E. A. (1994). The African American acculturation scale: Development, reliability, and validity. *The Journal of Black Psychology, 20,* 104–127.

Lang, J. G., Muñoz, R. F., Bernal, G., & Sorensen, J. L. (1982). Quality of life and psychological well-being in a bicultural Latino community. *Hispanic Journal of Behavioral Sciences, 4,* 433–450.

Langer, P., Kalk, J. M., & Searls, D. T. (1984). Age of admission and trends in achievement: A comparison of Blacks and Caucasians. *American Educational Research Journal, 21*(1), 61–78.

Laosa, L. M. (1989). Social competence in childhood: Toward a developmental, socioculturally relativistic paradigm. *Journal of Applied Developmental Psychology, 19,* 447–468.

Laosa, L. M. (1990). Population generalizability, cultural sensitivity, and ethical dilemmas. In C. B. Fisher & W. W. Tyron (Eds.), *Ethics in applied developmental psychology: Emerging issues in an emerging field* (pp. 227–252). Norwood, NJ: ABLEX.

Lapointe, A. (1986). The state of instruction in reading and writing in U.S. elementary schools. *Phi Delta Kappan, 68*(2), 135–138.

Lazar, I., Darlington, R., Murray, H., Royce, J., & Snipper, A. (1982). Lasting effects of early education: A report from the consortium for longitudinal studies. *Monographs of the Society for Research in Child Development, 47* (2/3, Serial No. 195).

Leadbeater, B. J., & Bishop, S. J. (1994). Predictors of behavior in preschool children of inner-city Afro-Americans and Puerto Rican adolescent mothers: Children and poverty [Special issue]. *Child Development, 65*(2), 638–648.

Leavy, W. E. (1992, March 8). Struggle continues over remark by mental health official. *New York Times,* p. 34.

Lebra, T. S. (1994). Mother and child in Japanese socialization: A Japan-U.S. comparison. In P. M. Greenfield & R. R. Cocking

(Eds.), *Cross-cultural roots of minority child development* (pp. 259–274). Hillsdale, NJ: Erlbaum.

Lerner, R. M. (1986). A life-span developmental view of childhood predictors of later psychotherapy: Commentary. In L. Erlenmeyer-Kimling & N. Miller (Eds.), *Life span research on the prediction of psychopathology* (pp. 169–174). Hillsdale, NJ: Erlbaum.

Lerner, R. M. (1991). Changing organism-context relations as the basic process of development: A developmental-contextual perspective. *Developmental Psychology, 27,* 27–32.

Lerner, R. M. (1992). *Final solutions: Biology, prejudice, and genocide.* University Park: Pennsylvania State University.

Lerner, R. M. (1993). Early adolescence: Towards an agenda for the integration of research, policy, and intervention. In R. M. Lerner (Ed.), *Early adolescence: Perspectives on research, policy, and intervention* (pp. 1–13). Hillsdale, NJ: Erlbaum.

Lerner, R. M. (1995). *America's youth in crisis: Challenges and options for programs and policies.* Thousand Oaks, CA: Sage.

Lerner, R. M. (in press). Diversity and context in research, policy, and programs for children and adolescents: A developmental contextual perspective. In G. K. Brookins & M. B. Spencer (Eds.), *Ethnicity & diversity: Implications for research policies.* Hillsdale, NJ: Erlbaum.

Lerner, R. M., Castellino, D., Terry, P. A., McKinney, M. H., & Villarruel, F. A. (1995). The ecology and parenting: A developmental contextual perspective. In M. H. Bornstein (Ed.), *Handbook of parenting: Vol 2. Ecology and biology of parenting: Part 1. Ecology of parenting* (pp. 285–309). Hillsdale, NJ: Erlbaum.

Lerner, R. M., & Fisher, C. B. (1994). From applied developmental psychology to applied developmental science: Community coalitions and collaborative careers. In C. B. Fisher & R. M. Lerner (Eds.), *Applied developmental psychology* (pp. 503–522). New York: McGraw-Hill.

Lerner, R. M., Villarruel, F. A., & Castellino, D. (in press). Adolescence. In W. K. Silverman & T. H. Ollendick (Eds.), *Developmental issues in the clinical treatment of children and adolescents.* New York: Allyn & Bacon.

Lloyd, C. B., & Duffy, N. (1995). Families in transition. In J. Bruce, C. B. Lloyd, A. Leonard, P. L. Engle, & N. Duffy (Eds.), *Families in focus: New perspectives on mothers, fathers, and children* (pp. 5–23). New York: Population Council.

Loo, C., Fong, K. T., & Iwamasa, G. (1988). Ethnicity and cultural diversity: An analysis of work published in community psychology journals, 1965–1985. *Journal of Community Psychology, 16,* 332–349.

Loya, F., Garcia, P., Sullivan, J., Vargas, L., Mercy, J., & Allen, N. (1986). Conditional risks of homicide among Anglo, Hispanic, Black, and Asian victims in Los Angeles, 1970–1979. In *Report of the Secretary's Task Force on Black and Minority Health* (Vol. 5, pp. 137–144).

Lyons-Ruth, K., Connell, D. B., Grunebaum, H. U., & Botvin, S. (1990). Infants at social risk: Maternal depression and family support services as mediators of infant development and security of attachment. *Child Development, 61*(1), 85–98.

Maass, P. (1995, September 22). Conference on genetics and crime gets second chance. *Washington Post,* p. B01.

Maccoby, E. E. (1991). Different reproductive strategies in males and females. *Child Development, 62,* 676–681.

Mahard, R. E., & Crain, R. L. (1983). Research on minority achievement in desegregated schools. In C. H. Rossell & W. D. Hawley (Eds.), *The consequences of school desegregation* (pp. 103–125). Philadelphia: Temple University Press.

Manson, S. M., Bechtold, D. W., Novins, D. K., & Beals, J. (1997). Assessing psychopathology in American Indian and Alaska Native children and adolescents. *Applied Developmental Science, 1*(3), 135–146.

Marín, G., & Marín, B. (1991). *Research with Hispanic populations.* Newbury Park, CA: Sage.

Marín, G., Sabogal, F., Marín, B., Otero-Sabogal, R., & Pérez-Stable, E. J. (1987). Development of a short acculturation scale for Hispanics. *Hispanic Journal of Behavioral Sciences, 9,* 183–205.

Marks, C. (1991). The urban underclass. *Annual Review of Sociology, 17,* 445–466.

Markus, H. R., & Kitayama, S. (1991). Culture and the self: Implications for cognition, emotion, and motivation. *Psychological Review, 98*(2), 224–253.

Marshall, W. (1978). Puberty. In F. Falkner & J. Tanner (Eds.), *Human growth* (Vol. 2, pp. 212–233). New York: Plenum Press.

Martinez, C., Jr. (1988). Clinical guidelines in cross-cultural mental health. In L. Comas-Diaz & E. E. Griffith (Eds.), *Wiley series in general and clinical psychiatry* (pp. 182–203). New York: Wiley.

Massey, D. S., & Denton, N. A. (1988). Suburbanization and segregation in U.S. metropolitan areas. *American Journal of Sociology, 94*(3), 592–626.

Massey, D. S., & Denton, N. A. (1993). *American apartheid: Segregation and the making of the underclass.* Cambridge, MA: Harvard University Press.

Matute-Bianchi, M. E. (1986). Ethnic identities and patterns of school success: An ecological model of externalizing in African American adolescents: No family is an island. *Journal of Adolescent Research, 4,* 639–655.

McAdoo, H. P. (1978). Factors related to stability in upwardly mobile Black families. *Journal of Marriage and the Family, 40*(4), 761–778.

McAdoo, H. P. (1980). Black mothers and the extended family support network. In L. F. Rodgers-Rose (Ed.), *The Black woman* (pp. 125–144). Beverly Hills, CA: Sage.

McAdoo, H. P. (1990). The ethics of research and intervention with ethnic minority parents and their children. In C. B. Fisher & W. W. Tyron (Eds.), *Ethics in applied developmental psychology: Emerging issues in an emerging field* (pp. 273–284). Norwood, NJ: ABLEX.

McAdoo, H. P. (1993). *Family ethnicity: Strength in diversity.* Newbury Park, CA: Sage.

McKinney, M. H., Abrams, L. A., Terry, P. A., & Lerner, R. M. (1994). Child development research and the poor children of America: A call for a developmental contextual approach to research and outreach. *Family and Consumer Science Research Journal, 23,* 26–42.

McLoyd, V. C. (1989). Socialization and development in a changing economy: The effects of paternal job and income loss on children. *American Psychologist, 44,* 293–302.

McLoyd, V. C. (1990). The impact of economic hardship on black families and children: Psychological distress, parenting, and socioemotional development. *Child Development, 61,* 311–346.

McLoyd, V. C. (1994). Research in the service of poor and ethnic/racial minority children: A moral imperative. *Family and Consumer Science Research Journal, 23,* 56–66.

McLoyd, V. C., & Randolph, S. M. (1984). Secular trends in the study of Afro-American children: A review of Child Development, 1936–1980. *Monographs of the Society for Research in Child Development, 50,* 78–92.

McLoyd, V. C., & Wilson, L. (1991). The strain of living poor: Parenting, social support, and child mental health. In A. C. Huston (Ed.), *Children in poverty: Child development and public policy* (pp. 105–135). New York: Cambridge University Press.

Meier, K. J., & Stewart, J. (1991). *The politics of Hispanic education: Un paso para adelante y dos para atras.* Albany, NY: SUNY Press.

Meindl, R. S. (1992). Human populations before agriculture. In S. Jones, R. Martin, D. Pilbeam, & S. Bunney (Eds.), *Cambridge encyclopedia of human evolution* (pp. 406–410). Cambridge, England: Cambridge University Press.

Meisels, S. J. (1992). Doing harm by doing good: Iatrogenic effects of early childhood enrollment and promotion policies. *Early Childhood Research Quarterly, 7,* 155–174.

Mena, F. J., Padilla, A. M., & Maldonado, M. (1987). Acculturative stress and specific coping strategies among immigrant and later generation college students. *Hispanic Journal of Behavioral Sciences, 9,* 207–225.

Mendoza, F., Ventura, S., Valdez, B., Castillo, R., Saldivar, L., Baisden, K., & Martorell, R. (1991). Selected measures of health status for Mexican-Americans, mainland Puerto Rican, and Cuban American children. *Journal of the American Medical Association, 265,* 227–232.

Mendoza, R. H., & Martinez, J. L. (1981). The measurement of acculturation. In A. Baron (Ed.), *Explorations in Chicano psychology* (pp. 71–82). New York: Praeger.

Menendez, B. S., Drucker, E., Vermund, S. H., Costano, R. R., Perez-Agosto, R. R., Parga, F. J., & Blum, S. (1990). AIDS mortality among Puerto Rican and other Hispanics in New York City, 1981–1987. *Journal of Acquired Immunodeficiency Syndrome, 3,* 644–648.

Meyers, L. J. (1988). *Understanding the Afrocentric world-view.* Dubuque, IA: Kendall/Hunt.

Mickelson, R. A. (1990). The attitude-achievement paradox among Black adolescents. *Sociology of Education, 63*(1), 44–61.

Miles, R. (1989). *Racism.* London: Routledge & Kegan Paul.

Minkler, M., & Roe, K. M. (1993). *Grandmothers as caregivers: Raising children of the crack cocaine epidemic.* Newbury Park, CA: Sage.

Mio, J. S., & Iwamasa, G. (1993). To do, or not to do: That is the question for White cross-cultural researchers. *The Counseling Psychologist, 21*(2), 197–212.

Miranda, L. C. (1991). *Latino child poverty in the United States.* Washington, DC: Children's Defense Fund.

Miranda, M. R., & Castro, F. (1985). A conceptual model for clinical research on stress and mental health status: From theory to assessment. In W. A. Vega & M. R. Miranda (Eds.), *Stress and Hispanic mental health: Relating research to service delivery* (pp. 174–201). Rockville, MD: National Institute of Mental Health.

Moffit, T., Caspi, A., & Belsky, J. (1990, March). *Family context, girls' behavior, and the onset of puberty: A test of a sociobiological model.* Paper presented at the biennial meeting of the Society for Research in Adolescence, Atlanta, GA.

Moll, L. C., Amanti, D., Neff, A. D., & Gonzalez, N. (1992). Funds of knowledge: Using a qualitative approach to connect homes and classrooms. *Theory into Practice, 31,* 132–141.

Moncher, M. S., Holden, G. W., & Trimble, J. E. (1990). Substance abuse among Native-American youth. *Journal Consulting Clinical Psychology, 58,* 408–415.

Montgomery, G. T., & Orozco, S. (1984). Validation of a measure of acculturation for Mexican Americans. *Hispanic Journal of Behavioral Sciences, 6,* 53–63.

Morrison, D. M. (1985). Adolescent contraceptive behavior: A review. *Psychological Bulletin, 98,* 538–568.

Morrison, J. A., Barton, B., Biro, F. M., Sprecher, D. L., Falkner, F., & Obarzanek, E. (1994). Sexual maturation and obesity in 9- and 10-year-old black and white girls: The National Heart, Lung, and Blood Institute growth and health study. *Journal of Pediatrics, 124*(6), 889–895.

Moynihan, D. P. (1965). *The Negro family: The case for national action.* Washington, DC: U.S. Government Printing Office.

Munford, M. B. (1994). Relationship of gender, self-esteem, social class, and racial identity to depression in Blacks. *The Journal of Black Psychology, 20,* 153–174.

Muñoz, R. F. (1982). The Spanish-speaking consumer and community mental health center. In E. E. Jones & S. J. Krochin (Eds.), *Minority mental health.* New York: Praeger.

Murdock, G. P. (1962). Ethnographic atlas. *Ethnology, 1*(1), 113–134.

Murguia, E. (1991). On Latino/Hispanic ethnic identity. *Latino Studies Journal, 2,* 8–17.

Murry, C. (1984). *Losing ground.* New York: Basic Books.

Murry, V. M. (1992). Sexual career paths of Black adolescent females: A study of socioeconomic status and other life experiences. *Journal of Adolescent Research, 7,* 4–27.

Nagel, J. (1995). Resource competition theories. *American Behavioral Scientist, 38,* 442–458.

National Center on Child Abuse and Neglect. (1988). *Study findings. Study of national incidence and prevalence of child abuse and neglect: 1988.* Washington, DC: Author.

National Center for Health Statistics. (1991). *Health, United States, 1990.* Hyattsville, MD: Public Health Service.

National Institute on Drug Abuse. (1991). *National household survey on drug abuse: Main findings.* Rockville, MD.

Neff, J. A., Hoppe, S. K., & Perea, P. (1987). Acculturation and alcohol use: Drinking patterns and problems among Anglo- and Mexican-American male drinkers. *Hispanic Journal of Behavioral Sciences, 9,* 151–181.

Negy, C., & Woods, D. J. (1992). A note on the relationship between acculturation and socioeconomic status. *Hispanic Journal of Behavioral Sciences, 14,* 248–251.

Nelson, C., & Tienda, M. (1985). The structuring of Hispanic ethnicity: Historical and contemporary perspectives. *Ethnic and Racial Studies, 8,* 49–74.

Nettles, S. M., & Pleck, J. H. (1994). Risk, resilience, and development: The multiple ecologies of black adolescents in the United States. In R. J. Haggerty, L. Sherrod, N. Garmezy, & M. Rutter (Eds.), *Stress, risk, and resilience in children and adolescents: Processes, mechanisms, and interventions* (pp. 147–181). New York: Cambridge University Press.

Nobles, W. W. (1973). The effects of African identification versus American identification and cultural message versus economic message exposure on group unity. *Dissertation Abstracts International, 338a,* 4531.

Nobles, W. W. (1985). *Africanicity and the Black family.* Oakland, CA: Black Family Institute.

Nolan, K. (1992, Summer). Assent, consent, and behavioral research with adolescents. *AACAP Child and Adolescent Research Notes,* 7–10.

Oboler, S. (1992). The politics of labeling: Latino/a cultural identities of self and others. *Latin American Perspectives, 19,* 7–17.

Oboler, S. (1995). *Ethnic labels, Latino lives: Identity and the politics of (re)presentation in the United States.* Minneapolis: University of Minnesota Press.

Oetting, E. R., & Beauvais, F. (1990–1991). Orthogonal cultural identification theory: The cultural identification of minority adolescents. *International Journal of the Addictions, 25,* 655–685.

Office for Protection from Research Risks (OPRR), Department of Health and Human Services, National Institutes of Health. (1993). *Protecting human research subjects: Institutional review board guidebook.* Washington, DC: U.S. Government Printing Office.

Ogbu, J. U. (1978). *Minority education and caste: The American system in cross-cultural perspective.* New York: Academic Press.

Ogbu, J. U. (1981). Origins of human competence: A cultural ecological perspective. *Child Development, 52*(2), 413–429.

Ogbu, J. U. (1986). The consequences of the American caste system. In U. Neisser (Ed.), *The school achievement of minority children: New perspectives* (pp. 19–56). Hillsdale, NJ: Erlbaum.

Ogbu, J. U. (1988). Cultural diversity and human development. In D. T. Slaughter (Ed.). *Black children and poverty: A developmental perspective* (pp. 11–27). San Francisco: Jossey-Bass.

Ogbu, J. U. (1990). Minority status and literacy in comparative perspective. *Daedalus, 119,* 141–168.

Ogbu, J. U. (1991). Immigrant and involuntary minorities in comparative perspective. In M. A. Gibson & J. U. Ogbu (Eds.), *Minority status and schooling: A comparative study of immigrant and involuntary minorities* (pp. 3–36). New York: Garland Press.

Ogbu, J. U. (1993). Differences in cultural frame of reference. *International Journal of Behavioral Development, 6,* 485–506.

Ogbu, J. U. (1994). From cultural differences to differences in cultural frame of reference. In P. M. Greenfield & R. R. Cocking (Eds.), *Cross-cultural roots of minority child development* (pp. 365–392). Hillsdale, NJ: Erlbaum.

Ogbu, J. U., & Matute-Bianchi, M. E. (1986). Understanding sociocultural factors in education: Knowledge, identity, and adjustment in schooling. In California State Department of Education, Bilingual Education Office, *Beyond language: Social and cultural factors in schooling language minority students* (pp. 73–142). Sacramento: California State University, Los Angeles, Evaluation, Dissemination, and Assessment Center.

Omi, M., & Winant, H. (1986). *Racial formation in the United States.* New York: Routledge & Kegan Paul.

Ortiz, V. (1986). Reading activities and reading proficiency among Hispanic, Black, and White students. *American Journal of Education, 95*(1), 58–76.

Ortiz de la Garza, M. F., Newcomb, M. D., & Myers, H. F. (1995). A multidimensional measure of cultural identity for Latino and Latina adolescents. In A. M. Padilla (Ed.), *Hispanic psychology: Critical issues in theory and research* (pp. 26–42). Thousand Oaks, CA: Sage.

Padilla, A. M. (1980). The role of cultural awareness and ethnic loyalty in acculturation. In A. M. Padilla (Ed.), *Acculturation: Theory, models and some new findings* (pp. 47–84). Bolder, CO: Westview Press.

Padilla, A. M. (1991). On the English-only movement: Reply to Murray. *American Psychologist, 46*(10), 1091–1092.

Padilla, A. M. (1992). Reflections on testing: Emerging trends and new possibilities. In K. F. Geisinger (Ed.), *Psychological testing of Hispanics* (pp. 272–283). Washington, DC: American Psychological Association.

Padilla, A. M. (1995). *Hispanic psychology: Critical issues in theory and research.* Thousand Oaks, CA: Sage.

Padilla, A. M., & Baird, T. L. (1991). Mexican-American adolescent sexuality and sexual knowledge: An exploratory study. *Hispanic Journal of Behavioral Sciences, 13,* 95–104.

Padilla, E. R., Olmedo, E. L., & Loya, F. (1982). Acculturation and the MMPI performance of Chicano and Anglo college students. *Hispanic Journal of Behavioral Sciences, 4,* 451–466.

Parham, T. A. (1993). White researchers conducting multicultural counselling research: Can their efforts be "mo betta"? *The Counseling Psychologist, 21*(2), 250–256.

Parham, T. A., & White, P. T. (1993). The relationship of demographic and background factors to racial identity attitudes. *Journal of Black Psychology, 19,* 7–24.

Pearson, J. L., Hunter, A. G., Ensminger, M. E., & Kellam, S. G. (1990). Black grandmothers in multigenerational households: Diversity in family structure and parenting involvement in the Woodlawn community. *Child Development, 61*(2), 434–442.

Phinney, J. S. (1990a). Ethnic identity in adolescents and adults: Review of research. *Psychological Bulletin, 108,* 499–514.

Phinney, J. S. (1990b). Stages of ethnic identity development in minority group adolescents. *Journal of Early Adolescence, 9,* 39–49.

Phinney, J. S. (1991). Ethnic identity and self-esteem: A review and integration. *Hispanic Journal of Behavioral Sciences, 13,* 193–208.

Phinney, J. S. (1992). Acculturation attitudes and self-esteem among high school and college students. *Youth and Society, 23,* 299–312.

Phinney, J. S. (1996). When we talk about American ethnic groups, what do we mean? *American Psychologist, 51,* 918–927.

Phinney, J. S., & Alipuria, L. (1990). Ethnic identity in college students from four ethnic groups. *Journal of Adolescence, 13,* 171–183.

Phinney, J. S., & Chavira, V. (1995). Parental ethnic socialization and adolescent coping with problems related to ethnicity. *Journal of Research on Adolescence, 5,* 31–53.

Phinney, J. S., & Devich-Navarro, M. (1997). Variations in bicultural identification among African American and Mexican American adolescents. *Journal of Research on Adolescence, 7,* 3–32.

Pianta, R. C., Egeland, B., & Sroufe, L. A. (1990). Maternal stress and children's development: Prediction of school outcomes and identification of protective factors. In J. Rolf, A. S. Masten, D. Cicchetti, & K. Nuechterlein (Eds.), *Risk and protective factors in the development of psychopathology.* Cambridge, England: Cambridge University Press.

Pike, K. L. (1967). *Language in relation to a unified theory of the structure of human behavior.* The Hague: Mouton.

Pitkiff, E. (1993). Teacher absenteeism: What administrators can do. *National Association of Secondary Schools Principals (NASSP) Bulletin, 77*(551), 39–45.

Piven, F. F., & Cloward, R. A. (1993). *Regulating the poor: The functions of public welfare* (Updated Ed.). New York: Vintage Books.

Plomin, R., & Fulker, D. (1987). Behavioral genetics and development in early adolescence. In R. Lerner & T. Foch (Eds.), *Biosocial-psychosocial interactions in early adolescence* (pp. 63–94). Hillsdale, NJ: Erlbaum.

Ponterotto, J. G., & Casas, J. M. (1991). *Handbook of racial/ethnic minority counseling research.* Springfield, IL: Thomas.

Portes, A., & Bach, R. L. (1985). *Latin journey: Cuban and Mexican immigrants in the United States.* Berkeley: University of California Press.

Portes, A., & Manning, R. (1986). The immigrant enclave: Theory and empirical examples. In S. Olzak & J. Nagel (Eds.), *Competitive ethnic relations* (pp. 47–68). New York: Academic Press.

Portes, A., & Rumbaut, R. G. (1990). *Immigrant America: A portrait.* Berkeley: University of California Press.

Powell-Hopson, D., & Hopson, D. S. (1988). Implications of doll color preferences among Black preschool children and White preschool children. *Journal of Black Psychology, 14*(2), 57–63.

Presser, H. B. (1986). Shift work among American women and child care. *Journal of Marriage and the Family, 48,* 551–563.

Presser, H. B. (1987). Work shifts of full-time dual-earner couples: Patterns and contrasts by sex of spouse. *Demography, 24*(1), 99–112.

Presser, H. B. (1989). Some economic complexities of child care provided by grandmothers. *Journal of Marriage and the Family, 51,*581–591.

Ragin, C. C., & Hein, J. (1993). The comparative study of ethnicity: Methodological and conceptual issues. In J. H. Stanfield, III & R. M. Dennis (Eds.), *Race and ethnicity in research methods* (pp. 254–272). Newbury Park, CA: Sage.

Ramirez, M. (1969). Identification with Mexican-American values and psychological adjustment in Mexican-American adolescents. *International Journal of Social Psychiatry, 15,* 151–156.

Ramseur, H. P. (1989). Psychologically healthy Black adults: A review of theory and research. In R. L. Jones (Ed.), *Black adult development and aging.* Berkeley, CA: Cobb & Henry.

Randolph, S. (1991, March/April). Testimony presented to the Joint Senate and House Committee on Labor and Education: Notes on the mislabeling of African American children. *Psych Discourse: Association of Black Psychologists' Newsletter, 22*(4), 6–8.

Red Horse, J. (1980). Family structure and value orientation in American Indians. *Social Casework, 61,* 462–467.

Reiss, A. J., Jr. (1986). Why are communities important in understanding crime? In A. J. Reiss, Jr. & M. Tonry (Eds.), *Communities and crime* (pp. 1–33). Chicago: University of Chicago Press.

Richardson, L. (1995, August 20). Ethics of state welfare fraud study questioned. *Los Angeles Times,* pp. A1, A34–A35.

Rifkin, J. (1995). *The end of work: The decline of the global labor force and the dawn of the post-market era.* New York: Putnam.

Ringwalt, C., & Caye, J. (1989). The effect of demographic factors on perceptions of child neglect. *Children and Youth Services Review, 11*(2), 133–144.

Rist, R. C. (1970). Student social class and teacher expectations: The self-fulfilling prophecy in ghetto education. *Harvard Educational Review, 40,* 411–451.

Rix, S. E. (1990). *The American women, 1990–1991: A status report.* New York: Norton.

Robbins, C., Kaplan, H. B., & Martin, S. S. (1985). Antecedents of pregnancy among unmarried adolescents. *Journal of Marriage and the Family, 47,* 567–583.

Rochin, R. I., & de la Torre, A. (1992). Rural issues pertaining to the rise of Hispanics in America. In G. Johnson & J. Bonner (Eds.), *Agricultural agendas for the rural and basic social sciences.* East Lansing: Michigan State University Press.

Rodning, C., Beckwith, L., & Howard, J. (1990). Characteristics of attachment organization and play organization in prenatally drug-exposed toddlers. *Development and Psychopathology, 1*(4), 277–289.

Rogler, L. H. (1989). The meaning of culturally sensitive research in mental health. *American Journal of Psychiatry, 146,* 296–303.

Rogler, L. H., Cortes, D. E., & Malgady, R. G. (1991). Acculturation and mental health status among Hispanics: Convergence and new directions for research. *American Psychologist, 46,* 585–597.

Roopnarine, J. L., & Ahmeduzzaman, M. (1993). Puerto Rican fathers' involvement with their preschool-age children. *Hispanic Journal of Behavioral Science, 15*(1), 96–107.

Root, M. (1992). *Racially mixed people in America.* Newbury Park, CA: Sage.

Rotheram, M. J., & Phinney, J. S. (1987). Ethnic behavior patterns as an aspect of identity. In J. Phinney & M. J. Rotheram (Eds.), *Children's ethnic socialization: Pluralism and development* (pp. 201–217). Newbury Park, CA: Sage.

Rotheram-Borus, M. J. (1993). Biculturalism among adolescents. In M. E. Bernal & G. P. Knight (Eds.), *Ethnic identity: Formation and transmission among Hispanic and other minorities* (pp. 81–102). Albany, NY: SUNY Press.

Rotheram-Borus, M. J., & Gwadz, M. (1993). Sexuality among youths at high risk. *Sexual and Gender Identity Disorders, Child and Adolescent Psychiatric Clinics of North America, 2,* 415–430.

Royce, A. (1982). *Ethic identity: Strategies of diversity.* Bloomington: Indiana University Press.

Rueschenberg, E. J., & Buriel, R. (1989). Mexican American family functioning and acculturation: A family systems perspective. *Hispanic Journal of Behavioral Sciences, 11,* 232–242.

Rumbaut, R. (1991). The agony of exile: A study of migration and adaptation of Indochinese refugee adults and children. In F. L. Ahean, Jr. & J. L. Athey (Eds.), *Refugee children: Theory, research, and services.* Baltimore: Johns Hopkins University Press.

Rumbaut, R. (1994). The crucible within: Ethnic identity, self-esteem, and segmented assimilation among children of immigrants. *International Migration Review, 28,* 748–794.

Rumberger, R., & Willems, J. D. (1992). The impact of racial and ethnic segregation on the achievement gap in California high schools. *Educational Evaluation and Policy Analysis, 14*(4), 377–396.

Rutherford, J. (1990). *Identity, community, culture, difference.* London: Lawrence & Wishart.

Ryu, J. P., & Vann, B. H. (1992). Korean families in America. In M. E. Procidano & C. B. Fisher (Eds.), *Contemporary families: A handbook for school professionals* (pp. 117–134). New York: Teachers College Press.

Sabogal, F., Marín, G., Otero-Sabogal, R., Marín, B., & Pérez, E. J. (1987). Hispanic familism and acculturation: What changes and what doesn't. *Hispanic Journal of Behavioral Sciences, 9,* 397–412.

Sabogal, F., Otero-Sabogal, R., Pérez-Stable, E., Marín, B., & Marín, G. (1989). Perceived self-efficacy to avoid cigarette smoking and addiction: Differences between Hispanic and non-Hispanic Whites. *Hispanic Journal of Behavioral Sciences, 11,* 136–147.

St. Lawrence, J. S., & Brasfield, T. L. (1991). *Survey of youth risk behavior in Mississippi: Profile of a generation at risk.* Jackson, MS: State Department of Education.

Saldaña, D. H. (1995). Acculturative stress: Minority status and distress. In A. M. Padilla (Ed.), *Hispanic psychology: Critical issues in theory and research* (pp. 43–56). Thousand Oaks, CA: Sage.

Sameroff, A., & Chandler, M. J. (1975). Reproductive risk and the continuum of caretaking causality. In F. D. Horowitz (Ed.), *Review of child development research* (Vol. 4). Chicago: University of Chicago Press.

Sampson, E. E. (1993). Identity politics: Challenges to psychology's understanding. *American Psychologist, 48,* 1219–1230.

Sampson, R. (1987). Urban violence: The effect of male joblessness and family disruption. *American Journal of Sociology, 93,* 348–405.

Sampson, R. J., & Groves, W. B. (1989). Community structure and crime: Testing social disorganization theory. *American Journal of Sociology, 94,* 774–802.

Sanchez, J. I., & Fernandez, M. (1993). Acculturative stress among Hispanics: A bidimensional model of ethnic identification. *Journal of Applied Social Psychology, 23,* 654–668.

Sarason, S. B. (1984). If it can be studied or developed, should it? *American Psychologist, 39,* 477–485.

Saunders, E. J., Nelson, K., & Landsman, M. J. (1993). Racial inequality and child neglect: Findings in a metropolitan area. *Child Welfare, 72*(4), 341–354.

Scarr, S. (1988). Race and gender as psychological variables: Social and ethical issues. *American Psychologist, 43*(1), 56–59.

Scarr, S. (1992). Developmental theories for the 1990s: Development and individual differences. *Child Development, 63*(1), 1–19.

Schinke, S. P., Botvin, G. J., Trimble, J. E., Orlandi, N. A., Gilchrist, L. D., & Locklear, V. A. (1988). Preventing substance abuse among American-Indian adolescents: A bicultural competence skills approach. *Journal of Counseling Psychology, 35,* 87–90.

Scott-Jones, D. (1996, April). *Parental consent: Ethical and scientific issues.* Paper presented at the symposium on "Recent Developments and Dilemmas in Ethical Issues for Developmental Research," biennial meeting of the Society for Research in Child Development, Washington, DC.

Scott-Jones, D., & White, A. B. (1990). Correlates of sexual activity in early adolescence. *Journal of Early Adolescence, 10,* 221–238.

Sears, D. O. (1986). College sophomores in the laboratory: Influence of a narrow data base on social psychology's view of human nature. *Journal of Personality and Social Psychology, 51,* 515–530.

Seifer, R., Schiller, M., Sameroff, A., Resnick, S., & Riordan, K. (1996). Attachment, maternal sensitivity, and infant temperament during the first year of life. *Developmental Psychology, 32,* 12–25.

Semaj, L. (1980). The development of racial evaluation and preference: A cognitive approach. *Journal of Black Psychology, 6*(2), 59–79.

Shade, B. (1982). Afro-American cognitive style: A variable in school success? *Review of Educational Research, 52,* 219–244.

Shaw, C., & McKay, H. (1942/1969). *Juvenile delinquency and urban areas.* Chicago: University of Chicago Press.

Shaw, D. S., & Vondra, J. I. (1995). Infant attachment security and maternal predictors of early behavior problems: A longitudinal study of low-income families. *Journal of Abnormal Child Psychology, 23*(3), 335–357.

Shimkin, D., Louie, G., & Frate, D. (1978). The Black extended family: A basic rural institution and a mechanism of urban adaptation. In D. Shimkin, G. Louie, & D. Frate (Eds.), *The extended family in black societies* (pp. 25–147). The Hague: Mouton.

Skogan, W. (1986). Fear of crime and neighborhood change. In A. J. Reiss, Jr. & M. Tonry (Eds.), *Communities and crime* (pp. 203–229). Chicago: University of Chicago Press.

Slaughter, D. T. (1983). Early intervention and its effects on maternal and child development. *Monographs of the Society for Research in Child Development, 48,* 1–83.

Slaughter-Defoe, D. T., Nakagawa, K., Takanishi, R., & Johnson, D. (1990). Toward cultural/ecological perspectives on schooling and achievement in African- and Asian-American children. *Child Development, 61*(2), 363–383.

Slonim-Nevo, V. (1992). First premarital intercourse among Mexican American and Anglo American adolescent women: Interpreting ethnic differences. *Journal of Adolescent Research, 7*(3), 332–351.

Smith, G. M., & Fogg, C. P. (1978). Psychological predictors of early use, late use, and nonuse of marijuana among teenage students. In D. B. Kandel (Ed.), *Longitudinal research on drug use: Empirical findings and methodological issues.* Washington, DC: Hemisphere.

Smith, J., Mercy, J., & Rosenberg, M. (1987). Suicide and homicide among Hispanics in the southwest. *Public Health Reports, 101,* 265–270.

So, A. Y. (1992). The Black schools. *Journal of Black Studies, 22*(4), 523–531.

So, L. L., & Yen, P. K. (1992). Secular trend of menarcheal age in southern Chinese girls. *Zeitschrift fur Morphologie und Anthropologie, 79*(1), 21–24.

Sommers, I., Fagan, J., & Baskin, D. (1993). Sociocultural influences on the explanation of delinquency for Puerto Rican Youths. *Hispanic Journal of Behavioral Sciences, 15,* 36–62.

Sonenstein, F. L., Pleck, J. H., & Ku, L. C. (1991). Levels of sexual activity among adolescent males in the Unites States. *Family Planning Perspectives, 23,* 162–167.

Spencer, M. B. (1982). Preschool children's social cognition and cultural cognition: A cognitive developmental interpretation of race dissonance findings. *Journal of Psychology, 112,* 275–286.

Spencer, M. B. (1983). Children's cultural values and parental childrearing strategies. *Developmental Review, 3,* 351–370.

Spencer, M. B. (1985). Cultural cognition and social cognition as identity factors in black children's personal-social growth. In M. B. Spencer, G. K. Brookins, & W. R. Allen (Eds.), *Beginnings: The social and affective development of black children* (pp. 215–230). Hillsdale, NJ: Erlbaum.

Spencer, M. B. (1988). Self-concept development. In D. T. Slaughter (Ed.), *Black children and poverty: A developmental perspective* (pp. 59–74). San Francisco: Jossey-Bass.

Spencer, M. B. (1995). Old issues and new theorizing about African-American youth: A phenomenological variant of ecological systems theory. In R. L. Taylor (Ed.), *Black youth: Perspectives on their status in the United States* (pp. 37–70). Westport, CT: Praeger.

Spencer, M. B., Cole, S. P., DuPree, D., Glymph, A., & Pierre, P. (1993). Self-efficacy among urban African American early adolescents: Exploring issues of risk, vulnerability, and resilience. *Development and Psychopathology, 5,* 719–739.

Spencer, M. B., & Markstrom-Adams, C. (1990). Identity processes among racial and ethnic minority children in America. *Child Development, 61,* 290–310.

Spencer, M. B., Swanson, D. P., & Cunningham, M. (1991). Ethnicity, ethnic identity, and competence formation: Adolescent transition and cultural transformation. *Journal of Negro Education, 60,* 366–387.

Spradley, J. P. (1972). Foundations of cultural knowledge. In J. P. Spradley (Ed.), *Culture and cognition: Rules, maps, and plans* (pp. 3–38). Prospect Heights, IL: Waveland Press.

Stack, C. (1974). *All our kin.* New York: Harper & Row.

Stack, C., & Burton, L. M. (1993). Kinscripts. *Journal of Comparative Family Studies, 24*(2), 157–170.

Stahlecker, J. E., & Cohen, M. C. (1985). Application of the strange situation paradigm to a neurologically impaired population. *Child Development, 56*(2), 502–507.

Stanfield, J. H., II. (1991). Racism in American and other race-centered societies. *International Journal of Comparative Sociology, 32,* 243–260.

Stanfield, J. H. (1993). Epistemological considerations. In J. H. Stanfield & R. M. Dennis (Eds.), *Race and ethnicity in research methods* (pp. 16–36). Newbury Park, CA: Sage.

Stanfield, J. H., & Dennis, R. M. (1993). *Race and ethnicity in research methods.* Newbury Park, CA: Sage.

Stanton-Salazar, R. D., & Dornbusch, S. M. (1995). Social capital and the social reproduction of inequality: Informational networks among Mexican-origin high school students. *Sociology of Education, 68,* 116–135.

Steinberg, L., Dornbusch, S. M., & Brown, B. B. (1992). Ethnic differences in adolescent achievement. *American Psychologist, 47*(6), 723–729.

Steinberg, L., Mounts, N. S., Lamborn, S. D., & Dornbusch, S. M. (1991). Authoritative parenting and adolescent adjustment across varied ecological niches. *Journal of Research on Adolescence, 1*(1), 19–36.

Stevenson, H. C. (1993). Validation of the scale of racial socialization for African American adolescents: A preliminary analysis. *Psych Discourse, 24,* 12.

Stevenson, H. C. (1994). Validation of the scale of racial socialization for African American adolescents: Steps toward multidimensionality. *Journal of Black Psychology, 20,* 445–468.

Stevenson, H. C. (1995). Relationship of adolescent perceptions of racial socialization to racial identity. *Journal of Black Psychology, 21*(1), 49–70.

Stier, H., & Tienda, M. (1993). Are men marginal to the family? Insights from Chicago's inner city. In J. C. Hood (Ed.), *Men, work, and family* (pp. 23–44). Newbury Park, CA: Sage.

Stinson, J. F. (1990). Multiple job-holding up sharply in the 1980s. *Monthly Labor Review, 113*(7), 3–10.

Stone, J. (1985). *Racial conflict in contemporary society.* Cambridge, MA: Harvard University Press.

Sudarkasa, N. (1988). Interpreting the African heritage in Afro-American family organization. In H. P. McAdoo (Ed.), *Black families* (2nd ed., pp. 27–43). Newbury Park, CA: Sage.

Sudarkasa, N. (1997). African American families and family values. In H. P. McAdoo (Ed.), *Black families* (3rd ed., pp. 9–40). Thousand Oaks, CA: Sage.

Sue, D. W. (1993). Confronting ourselves: The White and racial/ethnic-minority researcher. *The Counseling Psychologist, 21*(2), 244–249.

Suina, J. H., & Smolkin, L. B. (1994). From natal culture to school culture to dominant society culture: Supporting transitions for Pueblo Indian students. In P. M. Greenfield & R. R. Cocking (Eds.), *Cross-cultural roots of minority child development* (pp. 115–130). Hillsdale, NJ: Erlbaum.

Suinn, R. M., Richard-Figueroa, K., Lew, S., & Vigil, P. (1987). The Suinn-Lew Asian self-identity acculturation scale: An initial report. *Educational and Psychological Measurement, 47,* 401–407.

Szapocznik, J., & Kurtines, W. M. (1980). Acculturation, biculturalism, and adjustment among Cuban Americans. In A. Padilla (Ed.), *Acculturation: Theory, models, and new findings.* Boulder, CO: Westview Press.

Szapocznik, J., & Kurtines, W. M. (1993). Family, psychology, and cultural diversity: Opportunities for theory, research, and application. *American Psychologist, 48,* 400–407.

Szapocznik, J., Santisteban, D., Rio, A., Perez-Vidal, A., & Kurtines, W. M. (1989). Family effectiveness training: An intervention to prevent drug abuse and problem behaviors in Hispanic adolescents. *Hispanic Journal of Behavioral Sciences, 11,* 4–27.

Szapocznik, J., Scopetta, M. A., & Aranalde, M. (1978). Theory and measurement of acculturation. *Interamerican Journal of Psychology, 12,* 113–130.

Szapocznik, J., Scopetta, M. A., Aranalde, M., & Kurtines, W. M. (1978). Cuban value structure: Treatment implications. *Journal of Consulting and Clinical Psychology, 46,* 961–970.

Takanishi, R. (1994). Continuities and discontinuities in the cognitive socialization of Asian-originated children: The case of Japanese Americans. In P. M. Greenfield & R. R. Cocking (Eds.), *Cross-cultural roots of minority child development* (pp. 351–362). Hillsdale, NJ: Erlbaum.

Tanner, J. M. (1992). Human growth and development. In S. Jones, R. Martin, D. Pilbeam, & S. Bunney (Eds.), *Cambridge encyclopedia of human evolution* (pp. 98–105). Cambridge, England: Cambridge University Press.

Taylor, R. D., Casten, R., Flickinger, S. M., Roberts, D., & Fulmore, C. D. (1994). Explaining the school performance of African-American adolescents. *Journal of Research on Adolescence, 4*(1), 21–44.

Taylor, R. D., & Roberts, D. (1995). Kinship support and maternal and adolescent well-being in economically distressed African American families. *Child Development, 66,* 1585–1597.

Taylor, R. L. (Ed.). (1995). *Black youth: Perspectives on their status in the United States* (pp. 37–70). Westport, CT: Praeger.

Taylor, V. L., Hurley, E. C., & Riley, M. T. (1986). The influence of acculturation upon the adjustment of preschool Mexican-American children of single-parent families. *Family Therapy, 13,* 249–256.

Terrell, F., & Terrell, S. L. (1981). An inventory to measure cultural mistrust among Blacks. *Western Journal of Black Studies, 5,* 180–185.

Terrell, F., & Terrell, S. L. (1996). An inventory of assessing cultural mistrust in Black children. In R. L. Jones (Ed.), *Handbook of tests and measurements for Black populations* (Vol. 1, pp. 245–247). Hampton, VA: Cobb & Henry.

Terrell, F., Terrell, S. L., & Miller, F. (1993). Level of cultural mistrust as a function of educational and occupational expectations among Black students. *Adolescence, 28*(11), 573–578.

Tharp, R. G. (1994). Intergroup differences among Native Americans in socialization and child cognition: An ethnogenetic analysis. In P. M. Greenfield & R. R. Cocking (Eds.), *Cross-cultural roots of minority child development* (pp. 87–105). Hillsdale, NJ: Erlbaum.

Thompson, C., Neville, N., Weathers, P., Poston, C., & Atkinson, D. (1990). Cultural mistrust and racism reaction among

African-American students. *Journal of College Student Development, 31,* 162–168.

Thompson, T. L. (1984). A comparison of methods of increasing parental consent rates in social research. *Public Opinion Quarterly, 48*(4), 779–787.

Thornton, M. C., Chatters, L. M., Taylor, R. J., & Allen, W. R. (1990). Sociodemographic and environmental correlates of racial socialization by Black parents. *Child Development, 61*(2), 401–409.

Tienda, M. (1989). Puerto Ricans and the underclass debate. *The Annals of the American Academy of Political and Social Science, 501,* 105–119.

Tobach, E., & Greenberg, G. (1984). The significance of T. C. Schneirla's contribution to the concept of levels of integration. In G. Greenberg & E. Tobach (Eds.), *Behavioral evolution and integrative levels* (pp. 1–7). Hillsdale, NJ: Erlbaum.

Tomlinson, T. M., (1990). Class size and public policy: The plot thickens. *Contemporary Education, 62*(1), 17–23.

Torres, A., & Singh, S. (1986). Contraceptive practice among Hispanic adolescents. *Family Planning Perspectives, 18*(4), 193–194.

Triandis, H. C. (1989). Cross-cultural studies of individualism and collectivism. *Nebraska Symposium on Motivation, 37,* 41–133.

Triandis, K., Kashima, Y., Shimada, E., & Villareal, M. (1986). Acculturation indices as a means of confirming cultural differences. *International Journal of Psychology, 21,* 43–70.

Tropp, L. R., Erkut, S., Alarcón, O., García Coll, C. T., & Vásquez, H. A. (in press). Measuring psychological acculturation: An expanded approach with U.S. Hispanics. *Hispanic Journal of Behavioral Sciences.*

Turner, M. A. (1992). Discrimination in urban housing markets: Lessons from fair housing audits. *Housing Policy Debate, 3*(2), 185–216.

U.S. Bureau of the Census. (1990). *Household and family characteristics: March 1990 and 1989.* Current Population Reports Series P-20, No. 447. Washington, DC: U.S. Government Printing Office.

U.S. Bureau of the Census. (1991). *Race and Hispanic origin, 1990.* Census Profile, No. 2. Washington, DC: U.S. Government Printing Office.

U.S. Bureau of the Census. (1993). Current population reports, P23-183, *Hispanic Americans Today.* Washington, DC: U.S. Government Printing Office.

U.S. Department of Commerce. (1993). *Poverty in the United States: 1993* (Current Population Reports, Series P- 60, No.1 178). Washington, DC: U.S. Government Printing Office.

U.S. Department of Education. (1991). *The condition of education, 1991: Vol. 1. Elementary and secondary education.* Washington, DC: National Center for Education Statistics.

U.S. Government Accounting Office. (1994, June). Report to the Chairman, Committee on Governmental Affairs, U.S. Senate. *Peer review: Reforms needed to ensure fairness in federal agency grant selection.* Washington, DC: Author.

U.S. Sentencing Commission. (1995). *Special report to the Congress: Cocaine and federal sentencing policy.* Washington, DC: Author.

Urban Education. (1991). The effect of education reform on student achievement: GAO report. *Urban Education, 26*(2), 60–75.

Utsey, S. O., & Ponterotto, J. G. (1996). Development and validation of the Index of Race-Related Stress (IRRS). *Journal of Counseling Psychology, 43,* 49–501.

Valentine, B. (1978). *Hustling and other hard work: Life styles in the ghetto.* New York: Free Press.

Van IJzendoorn, M. H. (1995). Adult attachment representations, parental responsiveness, and infant attachment: A meta-analysis on the predictive validity of the Adult Attachment Interview. *Psychological Bulletin, 117*(3), 387–403.

Van IJzendoorn, M. H., & Kroonenberg, P. M. (1988). Cross-cultural patterns of attachment: A meta analysis of the strange situation. *Child Development, 59,* 147–156.

Vargas, M., & Busch-Rossnagel, N. A. (in press). Authority plus affection: Latino parenting during adolescence. In F. S. Villarruel & M. M. Sieburth (Eds.), *Latino adolescents: Building upon Latino diversity.*

Vega, W. A., & Amaro, H. (1994). Latino outlook: Good health, uncertain prognosis. *Annual Review of Public Health, 15,* 39–67.

Vega, W. A., Gil, A. G., Warheit, G. J., Zimmerman, R. S., & Apospori, E. (1993). Acculturation and delinquent behavior among Cuban American adolescents: Toward an empirical model. *American Journal of Community Psychology, 21,* 113–125.

Vega, W. A., Hough, R., & Romero, A. (1983). Family life patterns of Mexican Americans. In G. J. Powell, J. Yamamotom, A. Romero, & A. Morales (Eds.), *Psychosocial development of minority group children.* New York: Brunner/Mazel.

Vega, W. A., Patterson, T., Salles, J., & Nader, P. (1986). Cohesion and adaptability in Mexican-American and Anglo families. *Journal of Marriage and the Family, 48,* 857–867.

Vega, W. A., & Rumbaut, R. G. (1991). Ethnic minorities and mental health. *Annual Review of Sociology, 17,* 351–383.

Vega, W. A., Zimmerman, R. S., Gil, A. G., Warheit, G. J., & Apospori, E. (1992). Acculturative strain theory: Its application in explaining drug use behavior among Cuban and non-Cuban Hispanic youth. In M. De la Rosa (Ed.), *Drug abuse among minority youth: Advances in research methodology*. Rockville, MD: National Institute of Drug Abuse.

Ventura, S. J., & Tappel, S. M. (1985). Child bearing characteristics of U.S. and foreign born Hispanic mothers. *Public Health Reports, 100,* 647–652.

Villarruel, F. A., Imig, D. R., & Kostelnik, M. J. (1995). The diverse culture of families. In E. E. Garcia & B. M. McLaughlin (Eds.), *Meeting the challenges of linguistic and cultural diversity in early childhood* (pp. 103–124). New York: Teachers College Press.

Villarruel, F. A., & Lerner, R. M. (Eds.). (1994). *Promoting community-based programs for socialization and learning*. San Francisco: Jossey-Bass.

Walker, A. (1991). *Reach wisely: The Black cultural approach to education*. San Francisco: Aspire Books.

Washington, V. (1991). Black adolescents, the impact of federal income assistance policies. In R. M. Lerner, A. C. Peterson, & J. Brooks-Gunn (Eds.), *Encyclopedia of adolescence* (pp. 79–84). New York: Garland.

Waters, E., Vaughn, B. E., Posada, G., & Kondo-Ikemura, K. (1995). Caregiving, cultural, and cognitive perspectives on secure-base behavior and working models: New growing points of attachment theory and research. *Monographs of the Society for Research in Child Development, 60* (144, Nos. 2–3).

Waters, M. (1990). *Ethnic options: Choosing identities in America*. Berkeley: University of California Press.

Weber, M. (1973). Max Weber on race and society (J. Gittleman, Trans.). *Social Research, 38,* 30–41. (Original work published 1910)

Weinberg, M. (1983). Inner city education: Reading the writing on the wall. *Perspectives: The Civil Rights Quarterly, 15*(1/2), 38–43.

Welte, J. W., & Barnes, G. M. (1987). Youthful smoking: Patterns and relationships to alcohol and other drug use. *Journal of Youth and Adolescence, 10,* 327–340.

Whaley, A. L. (1993). Self-esteem, cultural identity, and psychosocial adjustment in African American children. *Journal of Black Psychology, 19*(4), 406–422.

Wheeler, D. L. (1992, November 4). Ambitious federal plan for violence research runs up against fear of its misuses. *The Chronicle of Higher Education*, pp. A7, A9.

White, L., & Parham, T. (1990). *Psychology of Blacks: An African American perspective*. Englewood Cliffs, NJ: Prentice-Hall.

Williams, B. F. (1992). Changing demographics: Challenges for educators. *Intervention in School and Clinic, 27*(3), 157–163.

Williams, C. L., & Berry, J. W. (1991). Primary prevention of acculturative stress among refugees. *American Psychologist, 46,* 632–641.

Williams, P. J. (1991). *The alchemy of race and rights*. Cambridge, MA: Harvard University Press.

Williams, S. W. (1991). Classroom use of African American language: Educational tool or social weapon? In C. E. Sleeter (Ed.), *Empowerment through multicultural education* (pp. 199–216). Albany, NY: SUNY Press.

Wilson, M. N. (1986). Perceived parental activity of mothers, fathers, and grandmothers in three-generational Black families. *Journal of Black Psychology, 12*(2), 43–59.

Wilson, W. J. (1987). *The truly disadvantaged: The innercity, the underclass, and public policy*. Chicago: University of Chicago Press.

Wilson, W. J. (1996). *When work disappears: The world of the new urban poor*. New York: Knopf.

Winkler, K. J. (1992, November 25). Race, class, gender in American studies: "Mantra" or new conception of the field? *The Chronicle of Higher Education*, pp. A6-A7.

Wolock, I., & Horowitz, B. (1979). Child maltreatment and material deprivation among AFDC recipient families. *Social Service Review, 53*(2), 175–194.

Wordes, M., Bynum, T. S., & Corley, C. J. (1994). Locking up youth: The impact of race on detention decisions. *Journal of Research in Crime and Delinquency, 31*(2), 149–165.

Yao, E. L. (1979). The assimilation of contemporary Chinese immigrants. *Journal of Psychology, 101,* 107–113.

Yee, A. H. (1992). Asians as stereotypes and students: Misperceptions that persist. *Educational Psychology Review, 4,* 95–132.

Yee, A. H., Fairchild, H. H., Weizmann, F., & Wyatt, G. E. (1993). Addressing psychology's problem with race. *American Psychologist, 49,* 748–754.

Yinger, M. (1985). Ethnicity. *Annual Review of Sociology, 11,* 151–180.

Zigler, E. F., & Valentine, J. (Eds.). (1979). *Project Head Start: A legacy of the war on poverty*. New York: Free Press.

Zimmerman, M. A., Salem, D. A., & Maton, K. I. (1995). Family structure and psychosocial correlates among urban African American adolescent males. *Child Development, 66,* 1598–1613.

Zuckerman, M. (1990). Some dubious premises in research and theory on racial differences: Scientific, social, and ethical issues. *American Psychologist, 45,* 1297–1303.

Zuravin, S., & Greif, J. L. (1989). Normative and child-maltreating AFDC mothers. *Social Casework, 70*(2), 76–84.

Author Index

Subject Index